# 80th Association for Information Science and Technology Annual Meeting

## Diversity of Engagement: Connecting People and Information in the Physical and Virtual Worlds

Proceedings of the Association for Information Science and Technology Volume 54



Washington, DC, USA
27 October - 1 November 2017

**Editors:**

**Sanda Erdelez** **Naresh Agarwal**

ISBN: 978-1-5108-8443-4

**Printed from e-media with permission by:**

Curran Associates, Inc.
57 Morehouse Lane
Red Hook, NY 12571

**Some format issues inherent in the e-media version may also appear in this print version.**



Printed by Curran Associates, Inc. (2019)



Association for Information Science and Technology (ASIS&T)
8555 16th Street, Suite 850
Silver Spring, Maryland 20910
USA

Phone: 301-495-0900
Fax: 301-495-0810

asist@asist.org

**Additional copies of this publication are available from:**

Curran Associates, Inc.
57 Morehouse Lane
Red Hook, NY 12571 USA
Phone: 845-758-0400
Fax: 845-758-2633
Email: curran@proceedings.com
Web: www.proceedings.com

# Proceedings of the 80th ASIS&T Annual Meeting

## *Diversity of Engagement: Connecting People and Information in the Physical and Virtual Worlds*

Volume 54


**Proceedings Editors**

**Sanda Erdelez**
University of Missouri

**Naresh Agarwal**
Simmons College



Published for the
**Association for Information Science & Technology**

by
John Wiley & Sons, Inc.
Somerset, NJ


asis&t
Association for Information Science and Technology

**e-ISSN (2373-9231**





Association for Information Science and Technology
8555 16th Street, Suite 850, Silver Spring, Maryland 20910

# TABLE OF CONTENTS

# TECHNICAL PROGRAM COMMITTEE MEMBERS

**Conference Co-Chairs & Proceedings Editors:**

**Sanda Erdelez**
University of Missouri, USA

**Naresh Kumar Agarwal**
Simmons College, USA

**Paper Co-Chairs & Proceedings Associate Editors:**

**Samuel K.W. Chu**
The University of Hong Kong, Hong Kong

**Mega Subramaniam**
University of Maryland, USA

**Panel & Workshop Co-Chairs & Proceedings Associate Editors:**

**Dania Bilal**
The Univ. of Tennessee, Knoxville, USA

**Nouf Khashman**
Qatar National Library, Qatar

**Visual Presentation Co-Chairs & Proceedings Associate Editors:**

**Kanwal Ameen**
University of the Punjab, Pakistan

**Kyungwon Koh**
University of Oklahoma, USA

# ASIS&T BOARD OF DIRECTORS, 2016-2017

# REVIEWERS

(236 reviewers completed 892 reviews)

## Top Reviewers (across all submission types)

Cecelia Brown
Charles Cole
Christine Urquhart
Diane Kelly
June Abbas
Lorraine Normore
Melissa Adler
Shawne Miksa
Tamara Heck
Yejun Wu

## Papers (169 reviewers)

June Abbas
Denice Adkins
Melissa Adler
Naresh Kumar Agarwal
Denise E. Agosto
Robert B. Allen
Tatjana Aparac
Diana Ascher
Denise A. D. Bedford
G Benoit
Wade Bishop
Elizabeth Bonsignore
Matt Bouchard
Cecelia Brown
Harry Bruce
George Robert Buchanan
Sarah Buchanan
John Budd
Julia Bullard
Joseph Busch
Mary Cavanagh
Tiffany Chao
Hsin-liang Chen
Samuel K.W. Chu
Charles Cole
Kevin James Comerford
Andrea Copeland
Edward Corrado
Andrew Cox
Mats Dahlström
Keren Dali
Sylvie Davies
Ying Ding
Devan Ray Donaldson
Philip Doty
Thomas Dousa
Tina Du
Sanda Erdelez
Craig Stephen Evans
Ixchel M. Faniel
Katrina Fenlon
Sean Fitzhugh
Rebecca Parks Follman
Eric Forcier
Dominic Forest
Luanne Freund
Jenny Fry
Norbert Fuhr
Rich Gazan
Twyla Gibson
Sarah Ann Gilbert
Devon Greyson
Joachim Griesbaum
Matthew Griffis
Gussun Gunes
Stefanie Haustein
Tamara HeckDonal Hei-
denblad
Hans-Christoph Hobohm
Mary Horman
Lynne Howarth
Ji-Lung Hsieh
Xiao Hu
Mu-hsuan Huang
Hong Huang
Isto Huvila
Aylin Ilhan
Md Anwarul Islam
Jenna Jacobson
Jim Jansen
Boryung Ju
Charles-Antoine Julien
Diane Kelly
Youngseek Kim
Emily Knox
Adam Kriesberg
Barbara Kwasnik
Kathryn La Barre
Jin Ha Lee
Dirk Lewandowski
Ping Li
Ying-Hsang Liu
Christopher Lueg
Lai Ma
Millicent Mabi
Stephann Makri
Thomas Mandl
Zinaida Manžuch
Laura Marcial
Betsy Martens
Konstantina Martzoukou
Matt Mayernik
Philipp Mayr
David McMenemy
David Melero-Fuentes
Eric Matthew Meyers
Shawne Miksa
Karen Miller
Erik Mitchell
Lorri Mon
Joi Moore
Heather Lea Moulaison
Jinfang Niu
Lorraine Normore
Heather O'Brien
Fatih Oguz
Randy Oldham
Shannon Oltmann
Peter Organisciak
Tuulevi Ovaska
Anindita Paul
Heather D. Pfeiffer
Christina Pikas
Devendra Dilip Potnis
Muhammad Asim Qayyum
Edie Rasmussen
Diane Rasmussen Pennington
Casey Rawson
Kathleen Reed
Colin Rhinesmith
Soo Young Rieh
Marc Rittberger
Michelle L. Rogers
Howard Rosenbaum
Alan Rubel
Ellen Rubenstein
Robert Sandusky
Christian Schloegl
Jodi Schneider
Ryan Benjamin Shaw
Laura Skouvig Dagobert
Soergel
Beth St. Jean
Suzanne Stauffer
Wolfgang G. Stock
Emma Stuart
Mega Subramaniam
Shigeo Sugimoto
Sue Yeon Syn
Sanna Talja
Rong Tang

Natalie Greene Taylor
Joseph T. Tennis
Mike Thelwall
Emma Tonkin
Yasar Tonta
Tien-I Tsai
Giannis Tsakonas
Christine Urquhart
Andre Vellino
Sirje Virkus
Nina Wacholder
Nicholas Weber
Rosina Weber
Lynn Westbrook
Rebekah Willson
Christian Wolff
Dietmar Wolfram
Christa Womser-Hacker
Adam Worrall
Yejun Wu
Iris Xie
Erjia Yan
Kwan Yi
Cindy Yu
Ning Yu
Xiajun Yuan
Md Hassan Zamir
Maja Zumer

## Panels & Workshops (64 reviewers)

Denice Adkins
Tatjana Aparac
Shimelis Assefa
Judit Bar-Ilan
Denise A. D. Bedford
Dania Bilal
Jenny Bossaller
Matt Bouchard
Leanne Bowler
Alison Brettle
Cecelia Brown
Sarah Buchanan
George Robert Buchanan
Julia Bullard
Joseph Busch
Tiffany Chao
Hsin-liang Chen
Andrea Copeland
Edward Corrado
Andrew Cox
Mats Dahlström
Keren Dali
Sylvie Davies
Philip Doty
Katrina Fenlon
Sean Fitzhugh
Donald Force
Dominic Forest
Melodie Fox
Rob Fox
Luanne Freund
Henry Gabb
Rich Gazan
Twyla Gibson
Sarah Ann Gilbert
Devon Greyson
Isto Huvila
Aylin Ilhan
Jenna Jacobson
Boryung Ju
Unmil P. Karadkar
Nouf N. Khashman
Kyung-Sun Kim
Ping Li
Kun Lu
Lai Ma
Betsy Martens
Stasa Milojevic
Joi Moore
Jinfang Niu
Fatih OguzPeter Organisciak
Isabella Peters
Heather D. Pfeiffer
Luz Quiroga
Muhammad Rafiq
Edie Rasmussen
Diane Rasmussen Pennington
Colin Rhinesmith
Alan Rubel
Ellen Rubenstein
Robert Sandusky
Christian Schloegl
Ryan Benjamin Shaw
Beth St. Jean
Andre Vellino
Julian Warner
Barbara Wildemuth
Dietmar Wolfram
Yejun Wu

## Visual Presentations (137 reviewers)

Melissa Adler
Denise E. Agosto
Robert B. Allen
Jack Andersen
Tatjana Aparac
Shimelis Assefa
Judit Bar-Ilan
David Bawden
Denise A. D. Bedford
G Benoit
Jenny Bossaller
Matt Bouchard
Leanne Bowler
Cecelia Brown
Harry Bruce
George Robert Buchanan
Sarah Buchanan
Julia Bullard
Simon Burnett
Sean Burns
Joseph Busch
Suzanne Carroll
Mary Cavanagh
Tiffany Chao
Charles Cole
Kevin James Comerford
Colleen Cool
Andrea Copeland
Edward Corrado
Andrew Cox
Keren Dali
Sylvie Davies
Ron Day
Ying Ding
Philip Doty
Jennifer Douglas
Ashlee Edwards
Yuanyuan Feng
Sean Fitzhugh
Schubert Foo Shou Boon
Donald Force
Melodie Fox
Rob Fox
Luanne Freund
Henry Gabb
Rich Gazan
Twyla Gibson
Lisa M. Given
Jane Greenberg
Devon Greyson
Matthew Griffis
Gussun Gunes
Stephanie Haas
Tamara Heck

Donal Heidenblad
Bradley Hemminger
Mary HormanMu-hsuan
Huang
Isto Huvila
Aylin Ilhan
Md Anwarul Islam
Charles-Antoine Julien
Unmil P. Karadkar
Diane Kelly
Kyung-Sun Kim
Youngseek Kim
Emily Knox
Kyungwon Koh
Barbara Kwasnik
Vincent Lariviere
Dirk Lewandowski
Ping Li
Ying-Hsang Liu
Kun Lu
Christopher Lueg
Lai Ma
Millicent Mabi
Laura Marcial
Betsy Martens
Konstantina Martzoukou
Matt Mayernik
David McMenemy
David Melero-Fuentes
Shawne Miksa
Stasa Milojevic
Erik Mitchell
Joi Moore
Heather Lea Moulaison
Jinfang Niu
Lorraine Normore
Fatih Oguz
Randy Oldham
Shannon Oltmann
Peter Organisciak
Anindita Paul
Heather D. Pfeiffer
Sarah Polkinghorne
Anabel Quan-Haase
Luz QuirogaMuhammad Rafiq
Edie Rasmussen
Diane Rasmussen Pennington
Kathleen Reed
Soo Young Rieh
Howard Rosenbaum
Mark Rosso
Alan Rubel
Ellen Rubenstein
Robert Sandusky
Paul Scifleet
Michael Seadle
Ryan Benjamin Shaw
Suzanne Stauffer
Emma Stuart
Natalie Greene Taylor
Yin Leng Theng
Emma Tonkin
Giannis Tsakonas
Christine Urquhart
Olga Vechtomova
Andre Vellino
Nina Wacholder
Peiling Wang
Julian Warner
Nicholas Weber
Lynn Westbrook
Rebekah Willson
Dietmar Wolfram
Christa Womser-Hacker
Shuheng Wu
Yejun Wu
Iris Xie
Erjia Yan
Kwan Yi
Cindy Yu
Xiajun Yuan
Md Hassan Zamir

## Doctoral Colloquium (29 reviewers)

June Abbas
Noa Aharony
Judit Bar-Ilan
Dania Bilal
Gary Burnett
Kathleen Burnett
Brian Butler
Kristin Eschenfelder
Pnina Fichman
Luanne Freund
Noriko Hara
Caroline Haythornthwaite
Michelle Kazmer
Xiaozhong Liu
Eric Meyer
Stasa Milojevic
Javed Mostafa
Lisa P. Nathan
Marie L. Radford
Soo Young Rieh
Howard Rosenbaum
Steve Sawyer
Patrick C. Shih
Katie Shilton
Diane H. Sonnenwald
Besiki Stvilia
Joseph T. Tennis
Mike Thelwall
Christine Urquhart

# PREFACE

It is our pleasure and honor to serve as the co-chairs of the 2017 Annual Meeting (AM17) of the Association for Information Science & Technology (ASIS&T) in the year when our organization celebrates the 80th anniversary of its establishment.

The theme of AM17 -- ***Diversity of Engagement: Connecting People and Information in the Physical and Virtual Worlds***, is focused on the diverse ways in which people from different backgrounds, cultures, and disciplines forge connections with each other, discover and use information, and engage with technology. AM17 addresses the opportunities and challenges of navigating through physical and digital/virtual realm with computers, tablets or smartphones to interact in work and everyday activities. Within this information environment, there are also those who have no access to or knowledge of technology and those who choose to disengage, widening the digital divide.

AM17 provides an interactive platform for exploration of these complex and rapidly changing technological and socio-cultural developments through 51 full papers selected in a rigorous peer-review among 133 submissions (38% acceptance rate). These papers are published in the proceedings as well as 11 peer-reviewed short papers, 24 panels, and 102 visual presentation proposals (58% acceptance rate). The full papers cover the following areas: bibliometrics & altmetrics; big data & information organization; community informatics; digital humanities, archives & libraries; digital youth; diversity & international information; health informatics; human-computer interaction; information behavior; information retrieval; information use; scientific information; serendipity & information encountering; social media; trust & information ethics; and user experience & analytics.

The proceedings are arranged first by submission category (Papers, Panels, and Visual Presentations) and then alphabetically by first author's last name in each category. In the Paper category, full-length papers (up to 10 pages) are listed first, followed up by short papers (up to 4 pages). The panel submissions provide descriptions of the topics presented at the panels and short biographies of the panelists. The visual presentation submissions include short summary descriptions (up to 2 pages) of poster and digital presentations.

Many thanks go to the members of the Annual Meeting 2017 Program Committee, who also serve as Associate Editors for the proceedings: Paper Co-Chairs - Sam Chu, The University of Hong Kong, Hong Kong and Mega Subramaniam, University of Maryland, USA; Panel & Workshop Co-Chairs: Dania Bilal, The University of Tennessee, Knoxville, USA and Nouf Khashman, Qatar National Library, Qatar; and Visual Presentation Co-Chairs: Kanwal Ameen, University of the Punjab, Pakistan and Kyungwon Koh, University of Oklahoma, USA. This international group of researchers and information professionals tirelessly coordinated the review of submissions and prepared the technical program for the AM.

The AM program could not have been completed without the commitment of 236 reviewers who spent countless hours to complete a total of 892 submission reviews (across all submission types, including doctoral colloquium); their names are listed in the introduction of the proceedings.

We are grateful to ASIS&T President Lynn Silipigni Connaway for entrusting us with the responsibility to co-chair this premier event for ASIS&T, as well as our wonderful colleagues at the ASIS&T headquarters, Lydia Middleton, ASIS&T Executive Director, Stephan Addo, Maureen Markey, Carline Haynes, and DeVonne Parks, for their herculean efforts in managing all the AM17 logistics. Thanks also goes to the HQ staff who helped in the early stages of the AM17 preparation. Finally, we and the members of the Program Committee are thankful to our home institutions for supporting our engagement on this important project.

**Proceedings Editors and ASIS&T AM17 Co-Chairs**

**Sanda Erdelez**
*School of Information Science & Learning Technologies, University of Missouri, USA*

**Naresh Agarwal**
*School of Library and Information Science, Simmons College, USA*

# LISTING OF SUBMISSIONS

## Papers

## Short Papers

## Panels

# Visual Presentations

# Tweets May Be Archived: Civic Engagement, Digital Preservation and Obama White House Social Media Data

**Amelia Acker**
*University of Texas at Austin, School of Information, USA.*
*aacker@ischool.utexas.edu*

**Adam Kriesberg**
*University of Maryland, College of Information Studies, USA.*
*akriesbe@umd.edu*

## ABSTRACT

**As part of his presidential transition, the administration of Barack Obama included social media data among the materials transferred to the National Archives and Records Administration (NARA). In addition, this social media collection comprising data from Twitter, Facebook and Vine was distributed to organizations and researchers to explore and investigate. In this paper, we present our initial observations on the first social media presidency through the lens of its data, extracted from their native platforms. While the data speak to the engagement cultivated by the administration in its use of social media, the collection contains as many questions as it does answers. The completeness, metadata and accessibility of these materials remain unclear, potentially limiting the use of the collections in research and beyond. The paper analyzes platform-specific issues and offers potential solutions to address the preservation and access challenges to social media data. We conclude with implications for the digital preservation community and social media researchers to consider when approaching social media data collections.**

## KEYWORDS

digital preservation, social media, data collection, cultural heritage

## INTRODUCTION

In October 2016, the Obama administration's Office of Digital Strategy announced plans for the presidential transition, featuring plans for preserving the digital history of the 44th presidential administration, including its social media data archive. In addition to transferring the social media data to NARA, the White House committed to opening the data to the public and announced an early access pilot program (Schulman, 2016). The authors responded to this call and were granted early access to the Obama administration's Twitter, Facebook, Vine and Instagram data (Miller, 2017).

For many Americans, Barack Obama is considered the first social media president. Known for leveraging social media platforms and mobile phone outreach during the 2008 and 2012 campaigns, the Obama administration was also the first to utilize new social media platform features to engage with citizens – from Facebook live in the Oval Office to broadcasting town hall meetings with citizens on YouTube. The Obama administration not only created accounts on different platforms, but provided citizens the opportunity to engage with President and First Lady Obama in a number of interesting, innovative and sometimes bleeding edge ways. For example, the Digital Strategy office implemented a Facebook messenger bot for citizens to directly engage with the President (known to have personally read and replied to many since it was implemented) (Goldman, 2016); the 2016 State of the Union speech debuted a Snapchat filter (Tarantola, 2016); even First Lady Obama went viral with her #TurnipForWhat Vine video that played on the viral music video single, "Turn Down for What" by DJ Snake and Lil Jon (LaMonica, 2014).

According to the administration's digital transition statement on the social media data archive, "This digital infrastructure is an asset not just for the next president but for all future presidents to build off of. The archive belongs to the American people" (Schulman, 2016). The Obama administration not only used the most popular social media platforms like Facebook and Twitter, but also created accounts on platforms that have since shuttered, retired or pivoted in purpose. For example, the White House still has a MySpace page ("White House (whitehouse) on Myspace," n.d.). Now, mostly used a music platform, the MySpace account features a number of 2009 photo albums from Obama's first year in the White House. The White House created a number of "tips" on the geo-tagging check-in site Foursquare beginning in June 2012 before becoming inactive on the platform in 2014 ("The White House on Foursquare," n.d.). While these inactive accounts still exist in platforms that have plateaued, they remain evidence of the Obama administration's willingness to experiment, test, depart and sometimes abandon social media platforms to engage with American citizens.

## ACCESSING AND PRESERVING SOCIAL MEDIA

Social media data is a new form of evidence of online behavior. For researchers, it not only represents a new object of study, but a new form of instrumentation for collecting data about the behavior of people, networks and contemporary forms of communication. Increasingly we see social media posts as part of the visual landscape of news reporting on the web and television and used as evidence in scholarly publishing as both primary and secondary source material. However,

80th Annual Meeting of the Association for Information Science & Technology, Washington, DC | Oct. 27-Nov. 1, 2017

for those information scholars concerned with digital preservation and the transmission of culture, social media data presents a host of problems that have yet to be tackled and continue to unfold around context, collection and preservation for future access. These problems range from data extraction from platforms themselves, selective access for researchers, limited replicability and ethical and privacy issues, among others.

For starters, social media data are largely found in commercialized platforms that are subject to market forces, weaponization and surveillance, and increasingly fake user accounts and bot spam. A recent study found that up to 15% of Twitter's monthly active user accounts are bots with the ability to target specific platform users (Varol, Ferrara, Davis, Menczer, & Flammini, 2017). Moreover, once data has been extracted or scraped from platforms it is not standardized data and can come in a variety of formats. While *de facto* format standards exist (largely as activity streams and JavaScript Object Notation), understanding these data once they have been extracted from platforms is still a bespoke process that requires the re-construction of context contained within the original platform. Further, many platforms curate the possible data points that can be extracted and do not publish what data is withheld when using platform-specific extraction methods.

While social media data can be extracted using application programming interfaces (APIs) and sometimes scraped from the web, layers of metadata, particularly related to engagement (the very activities that makes social media data "social"), are often stripped, incomplete or subject to terms of service, data management and storage policies that limit researchers from sharing, collecting or using data in secondary use scenarios such as replicating an experiment or comparing posts over time. Further, we lack a common language for understanding key terms and features in these platforms, e.g., what's a heart, fave, friend or follower? How do these features signal strong or weak network ties? Or levels of audience (or perhaps even civic) engagement? And further, how do these activity statuses denote online or networked behavior? Contemporary web archiving techniques focus on scraping text from webpages, however these techniques often neglect the look and feel of the platform layout, rapid updates, and the methods for platform engagement (such as mobile apps, SMS clients or online browsers) make it harder for digital archivists to preserve the layers of context in these networked platforms. In short, social media data activity streams resist traditional forms of web archiving and data collection that social scientists and computer scientists have traditionally employed in studying online behavior and digital media.

In addition to these concerns that information and communication scholars have identified, there is an emerging consensus amongst archivists, librarians and digital preservation professionals that social media data are unlike other kinds of digital records and datasets that they preserve and provide access to because social media data (or "activity streams" or "social feeds" as they are often called) don't have discrete endpoints. Further, these data are at risk of being misconstrued because they are subject to the platform's API and many platforms do not publish information about what data is (and isn't) made available through these methods (Thomson & Kilbride, 2015). More simply, social media continue to unfold and collect layers of context, even after they are collected. Users may delete, unfav or edit their comments after a researcher or developer has used the platform API to scrape and collect data for analysis (Tufekci, 2014).

Moreover, different API client codes oblige researchers and developers who have collected social media posts, such as tweets that have since been deleted or user data from public accounts that have become private, to delete these data and update their collections ("Streaming message types — Twitter Developers," n.d.). Other researchers who are aiming to collect social media related to events as they unfold have come up against API quotas which limit the amount of data that you can scrape at any given time. Still further, the terms of service often discourage researchers from sharing their collected data. For example, Twitter allows data consumers who extract data from APIs to share unique Tweet IDs but not the content of tweets or collections of metadata. To work around this constraint, some innovative researchers have created tools for "rehydrating" Tweet IDs in order to share collections, such as Ed Summers' TWARC tool that allows users to collect and hydrate Tweets (Summers, n.d.). Yet, because of the reasons listed above (and more), there are very few ways to confirm a reliable sampling or to know whether you have the same engagement data as another researcher. In their analysis of Twitter collection processes and APIs, Driscoll and Walker (2014), raise a number of questions about the reliability and reproducibility of data gathered through Twitter's API services, including the variety of rate limits that each API affords users.

The examples above illustrate the complexities of studying these platforms, extracting the data in them, understanding the content they contain within their metadata and, perhaps most importantly, the reliability and repeatability of results generated through analysis of these datasets. Indeed, the platforms themselves do not strive for completeness in the ways they limit developers' ability to scrape and extract data from the platform. Twitter's description of the Search API says it is "focused in relevance and not completeness" and "not all Tweets are indexed" meaning that both user accounts and relevant tweets will be missing from most search results ("Why am I missing from search?," n.d.). The uneven, fractured, incomplete realities of collecting social media has serious implications for how scholars, librarians and archivists can create a reliable cultural and civic digital record and, in turn, transmit this networked cultural memory. Still further, incomplete collections of social media data and access limitations will also influence how our digital history is told and interpreted in the near future.

Given these constraints, this paper discusses some of the common issues that we have confronted as we work specifically with the Obama social media data archive that has now been opened for public use. As a kind of sandbox, the Obama social media data is open for public use and we argue it can act as a kind of premiere testbed for researchers in discovering common problems, diagnosing issues, teaching digital preservation and developing workarounds to work with this rich dataset[1]. First, we discuss related work on politics and digital preservation of social media; then we present our research agenda focused on the preservation of a presidential administration's social media data; followed on by the data collection process, our method and some initial findings based on our analysis and teaching with the data.

Our findings are intended to shed light on the processes of creation, data collection, collection transmission, as well as new platform features of the three kinds of social media found in the open data project. We encourage other readers to download the data and follow along. Or as others have described, open up the black box as we are working in it so that others may understand how we are contending with the rapid rate of change and incomplete record sets (Acker, 2015; Trace, 2011). As we have argued, social media data not only offers scholars new phenomena to analyze and interpret, it offers us new forms of instrumentation to support observation and digital preservation. Our methods and findings move between these two poles as we aim to bring a platform perspective to these new media and preservation infrastructures.

## CONTEXT AND BACKGROUND

### *Politics and Social Media*

On February 10, 2007, when he announced his candidacy for the Democratic party's nomination, many of the most popular social media platforms of 2017 were in their infancy. Twitter was a niche application without widespread popularity. Facebook had opened up its network beyond college students less than a year before. Vine was still more than five years away from launch. Yet, the 2008 presidential election demonstrated the potential for politicians who could make use of these platforms to engage with voters in new ways. Following the campaign, the Pew Center for Research reported that nearly 20% of internet users engaged in political discussion online during the campaign (Smith, 2009).

While not the first to use social media platforms, Barack Obama's presidency incorporated social media and the internet in ways not seen in previous administrations. In the popular press, commentary about the use of social media during the 2008 presidential election sought to compare the number of friends Obama and John McCain had on Facebook and MySpace (e.g., Lardinois, 2008). Following his election, these platforms multiplied and grew alongside President Obama's expanded use.

Since 2007 and the first presidential campaign of Barack Obama, the role of politics on social media has rapidly evolved into an integral part of many major platforms. From the role of Twitter and Facebook in the Arab Spring (Howard et al., 2011) to the connections between use of social networking sites and political engagement in the United States (Gil de Zúñiga, Jung, & Valenzuela, 2012), politics has become entwined with the culture and community of online platforms. Political leaders from India (Pal, Chandra, & Vydiswaran, 2016) to the United States have also adopted social media as a means to engage directly with constituents. The current U.S. president used Twitter as a vital element of his campaign, even using the platform as a means to engage other world leaders (e.g., Paletta, 2017). While social media was a growing but still niche part of the internet in 2007, today it is a core component of the web. In politics, as in every other element of society, social media plays a significant role in influencing the conversation and facilitating a broad degree of interaction among users.

### *Digital Preservation and Social Media*

The preservation of social media has proven to be a difficult challenge for the digital preservation community. While the content of social media platforms is potentially valuable and worthy of long-term preservation, the very nature of social media data resists traditional web archiving techniques (Thomson & Kilbride, 2015). While websites and some digital records exist as discrete units of information, social media data are activity streams ("Activity Streams 2.0," 2017). Concern about capacity to handle social media data is reflected across the preservation community. A 2016 survey conducted by the National Digital Stewardship Alliance found that 70% of respondents were concerned about their institution's ability to manage and preserve social media content (NDSA, 2017).

Among the most prominent efforts to preserve and provide access to social media materials outside of their native environment has been the Library of Congress' Twitter archive project. First announced in 2010, the library planned to acquire the entire collection of historical tweets, develop a method to process new posts on an ongoing basis and build an access system for researchers to query the collection (Raymond, 2010). While the project has been successful by some metrics (Allen, 2013), they have not yet been able to provide a public portal where users can interact with archival Twitter data; the project appears to be on indefinite hold. Michael Zimmer highlighted these challenges, pointing to the volume of data transferred to the library, questions about access and content presented in the collection and ongoing privacy concerns among the reasons the project has not yet achieved its stated goals and access for citizens and researchers (Zimmer, 2015).

The very nature of social media data resists traditional web archiving techniques given social network platforms' functionality, features and layers of engagement. While websites

[1] The Obama White House Social Media Data Archive is in the public domain and can be downloaded from the Internet Archive here: https://archive.org/details/ObamaWhiteHouseSocialMediaArchive

and some digital records exist as discrete units of information, social media data are activity streams that have a number of complex interactive metadata elements (often hidden from the front end). Still further, most platforms are now built for a mobile app experiences with the ability to upload geo-tags and comments and to give feedback in a personalized user "in-app" experience. If you download your personal Twitter archive, it is only a snapshot of your feed at the time of capture. Follower counts, likes, reposts and other features are likely to change, making reproducibility and comparative analysis difficult. This has proven challenging for the web archiving community as well. The Internet Archive's Wayback Machine does not gather much information from dynamic, flash-based webpages (Arora et al., 2016).

Additionally, the data available from social media platforms does not exist in interoperable, open formats such as HTML. Each app and platform has a proprietary data model and organizational vision for its content and different rules for how this is made available to users, third-party developers and others. Twitter's API rules change regularly, Facebook's archive functionality reflects its platform design, and other sites may not even have functionality that supports downloading a user's data. These features of social networking platforms are a direct result of the business models of the companies that create them. Unique features, data types and closed standards set new platforms apart and attract users, allowing parent companies in turn to generate funding via venture capital or other revenue sources (Boyd & Ellison, 2007). Problems for researchers arise when they want to utilize social media data beyond what it was designed for.

## RESEARCH QUESTIONS

Given the landscape of preservation infrastructures and social media data collection and the significance of the presidential social media transition, this project is motivated by the following broad research question: What is the value of preserving the social media data of a U.S. president? Our interest in this area arises from an understanding of the challenges in preserving social media and other dynamic content online. Further, we're interested in how the impact of an administration's use of platforms and new tools to engage with citizens not only represents a new form of communicating with governments and state organizations, but also raises questions of preservation of a new kind of digital cultural heritage – that of networked, platformed and social media records, that for many reasons (social, political, technical and economic) resist being easily archived and preserved for future access. For researchers interested in understanding how changes in social platforms affect the ways in which citizens interact with the government (and each other), it is critical that digital archivists capture and preserve the context, to the extent that it is available from these sites, that is so central to the experience of using social media sites. Our long-term project addresses the research question above, but for this paper we will address these questions: 1) What data exists? 2) What data appears (if at all) to be missing, obscured or unknown? 3) What are some known and pressing issues with preserving these data? We address these questions across three platforms and cover a number of known and documented issues as they relate to digital preservation and access for scholarly inquiry.

## DATA COLLECTION

In this paper, we draw upon data from the social media accounts of the Obama administration, specifically the Vine, Twitter and Facebook data of @POTUS and @Whitehouse accounts. The data was transferred to the research team following their response to a public call by the administration's digital transition team for ideas on how to use and provide access to President Obama's social media data (Schulman, 2016). In addition to analysis, the authors have incorporated these data collections into curriculum and assignments for master's level graduate students enrolled in on metadata and digital curation courses at the University of Texas at Austin's School of Information and the College of Information Studies at the University of Maryland.

The data themselves were transferred from social media firms to the White House for a variety of uses. In addition to deposit with the National Archives, the outgoing transition team used the public solicitation to identify a range of organizations to distribute the data to for further projects (Miller, 2017). The research team comprising the authors of this paper was one of those selected. Other recipients of the Obama social media data included the Internet Archive, which was given copies of these files for preservation purposes, and ArchiveSocial, a business which provides preservation and access to social media data for government and private sector clients, which built a public access portal where users can search posts from Facebook, Twitter, Flickr, Instagram, Google+ and Pinterest (ArchiveSocial, 2017). Additional organizations using this data for projects include Rhizome, which has a number of digital preservation programs that support the preservation and access to new media and netart. Rhizome created a number of online exhibits using WebRecorder ("Our First Social Media President, Through Three Webrecorder Narratives," n.d.). In addition to these creative art projects, a few universities, including MIT and NYU interactive arts and engineering programs, leveraged the data in teaching and student programs in 2017. According to coordination conversations, correspondence and reporting, we believe that the files we received from the White House Digital Transition Team represent what was given to the White House by each respective company. The data presented in this paper is drawn from our analysis of these files, which are the same as those.

## METHOD

Following on Bruns and Weller's (2016) framework for understanding Twitter data as a cultural artifact by drawing concepts from traditional source criticism and applying them to new media, we used infrastructural analysis and digital forensics to reconceptualize the Obama White House social media data from Facebook, Twitter and Vine as historical source material. In their work on Twitter data as historical, primary source material, Bruns and Weller show that most contextual information surrounding collections of tweets (the responses to or engagement data with tweets in particular) is lost by virtue of data extraction sampling, API rate limits, platform functionalities and the viral distribution of outward information to "receivers" (audience, followers, friends) (p. 184). In response to this constant risk of loss as we have outlined above, our agenda specifically focused on the pacing and features of the platforms themselves. We wanted to understand how the Obama social media data archive originated, was developed and matured *through* each platform. We created a timeline of maturity, development and featured rollouts in order to understand the contexts for which this data was created. Then we collected developers' documentation, ranging from API changelogs to descriptions of features, versions, new terms of service updates, client codes, policy statements, even laws – all supporting documents related to the maturity of these social media platforms as information infrastructure. By observing and documenting changes in and around the Obama social media data, these strategies allow us to understand and interpret the evolution of these social media platforms. We suggest, therefore, that these kind of platform studies are not only integral to interpreting the information cultures of this moment in a networked era, but as a result of the long-term cultural significance of these collections (and their vulnerability), essential to providing access to these sources as historical information necessary for telling the history of civic engagement and participation in the early 21st century.

## FINDINGS

The findings and observations listed below will be useful for scholars of digital communication and online behavior, but also those information professionals concerned with the preservation, provenance, authenticity and source material these data represent as records (and by extension records requirements for compliance) in an era of born networked records (Acker, 2014). First, we describe data from the platform Vine, which was recently shuttered and transformed into a camera app for Twitter. Then we describe the Facebook data, which is the largest dataset within the collection, though arguably the most decontextualized. Finally, we discuss the Twitter data from three different accounts, which was found to be the cleanest and most flexible to use.

### *Vine*

Vine is a platform for hosting short videos, founded in 2012 and owned for the majority of its active life by Twitter, which announced that the service would stop the upload of new videos in late 2016. The Obama administration received copies of Vine videos and associated metadata for the account named "The White House."

Public news reports date the first Vine by the White House to April 22, 2013, at the White House Science Fair. This first post saw Bill Nye and LeVar Burton welcoming attendees to the fair (Franchesci-Bicchierai, 2013; Mack, 2013). However, this is not the earliest Vine in the archived collection, which instead dates to May 9, 2013 and shows the President eating at Stubbs BBQ in Austin, Texas (The White House, 2013). This difference highlights some of the questions around provenance and collection-level metadata for this material. How was it extracted from the platform and packaged for transmission to the White House? What metadata might be different between the archive and web-accessible versions of posts? It looks like the Science Fair Vine was posted to another account, named "White House Video," which posted eight Vines, all but one of which were from the 2013 White House Science Fair (White House Video, 2014).

This issue highlights the fragility of social media collections as well as reliability and authenticity issues, given that both user accounts were verified and vetted by Vine's verification feature. In beginning or experimental phases, users may change accounts or engage in other behavior, which makes preservation and stewardship more difficult when a service such as Vine shuts down. The dual accounts of the White House highlight these challenges, reminding archivists, curators and researchers that social media collections may hide their imperfections due to organizational moves such as the shift from WHVideo to The White House user accounts as the official Vine account for President Obama.

As the White House Vine account continued to mature, First Lady Michelle Obama emerged as one of the account's most popular contributors. Her engagement across social media demonstrates her deep understanding of the technologies and cultures surrounding these platforms and an ability to connect with citizens through hashtags such as #askthefirstlady (Opam, 2016). Vines including the First Lady were highly liked and Revined, a feature similar to retweets on Twitter. One post in particular (screenshot in Figure 1 below) generated significant amounts of attention; it featured the first lady saying, "Turnip for what" before nodding her head to the beat of the Lil Jon song "Turn Down for What." This Vine got over 300,000 likes and nearly 200,000 Revines, making it one of the most successful posts on the account. The post received significant amounts of coverage on blogs and digital publications, heralding it as an excellent political Vine post (e.g. Peraudin, 2014; Rose, 2014).

***Figure 1****. Michelle Obama's "Turnip for what" Vine on the White House account*

When Twitter (which owns Vine) announced that Vine would shut down in October 2016, many decried the loss of the app for multiple reasons. As the Vine community expanded and matured, the app became a home for black culture and humor and the elimination of the service meant the end for a unique community of creators of color using the app to generate fascinating six-second videos (e.g., Hughes, 2016; Romano, 2016). While it remained popular throughout its life, some of its core features, unique when it launched, by 2016 had been incorporated into other social media apps including Instagram and Snapchat.

The sunsetting of Vine highlights the questionable longevity of social media platforms, and speaks to the perpetual march mergers and acquisitions and of new features in apps designed to draw traffic from more well-established platforms. Today's killer new feature is tomorrow's commodity, and

Vine embodies this concept (Lorenz, 2016). The use of video on social media platforms is now widespread, allowing less space for single-feature apps with stagnant user bases.

### *Facebook*

The collection of Facebook data from the Obama administration demonstrates the president's prolific use of the world's largest social networking platform. A page for "The White House," initially set up by the George W. Bush administration, became a core element of the social media engagement strategy of President Obama and his team. The posts available through the Obama Social Media Archive show the ways in which Facebook was used by the President to promote legislative achievements, share pictures of meetings with world leaders, send holiday greetings and reveal a less formal side of life in the White House. These posts demonstrate knowledge of how Facebook functions and a willingness to use its structure and strengths in service of communications goals.

During the course of the Obama presidency, Facebook introduced many new features to its platform, some of which were adopted by the administration in surprising ways. The timeline, first unveiled in 2011 (Slater Tow, 2011), allowed users to designate "Life Events" to document graduations, relationship milestones, moves and similar moments (Varol, Ferrara, Davis, Menczer, & Flammini, 2017). On its face, this feature seems like a natural extension of the platform. However, the ways in which Obama used this feature demonstrate the creative and unexpected uses of software that the developers likely could not have predicted.

On May 2, 2011, U.S. Special Forces in Pakistan killed Osama Bin Laden. Hours later, the President addressed the country live on television announcing the success of the raid. This speech marking the event was posted on the President's Facebook timeline but also added as a Life Event.

While the Facebook data from President Obama's administration clearly demonstrates his team's skill utilizing the platform, the contents of the archive make research difficult. For example, it is not easy to search the collection's posts; only browsing by year is enabled through the file structure in the archive package. Furthermore, the photographs, which document the eight years of the Obama presidency, are not searchable and lack basic metadata such as titles, dates, or EXIF information.

### *Twitter*

Twitter is a social networking service that allows users to create, share, read and respond to short posts, which are 140 character messages called "tweets." Registered users of the platform may read and post tweet messages, follow and be followed by other users and engage with networked content (such has hearting another user's post or retweeting another user's post to their followers). Users can access and publish tweets through a browser interface (twitter.com), a number of browser-based dashboards (such as tweetdeck.com), SMS or an app on a number of different mobile operating systems.

The Obama social media data archive consists of three Twitter accounts, including @WhiteHouse, @POTUS and @FLOTUS accounts, which were transferred to the Trump administration on January 20, 2017. Ostensibly, the Obama administration tweets from these three accounts have been archived on the platform itself and usernames have been changed to @ObamaWhiteHouse, @POTUS44, @FLOTUS44. Since January 20, 2017, the National Archives and Records Administration (NARA) now administer each of these archived accounts on Twitter. According to a statement from the Barack Obama Presidential Library, the accounts are considered historical, and most functionalities of the accounts have been turned off "to maintain as much of the original look and feel as possible" (2016).

Twitter began as a text messaging microblogging platform in 2006 but soon transitioned to a web-based networking platform shortly after the company created official support for the user-generated feature of hashtags in 2007. In the last decade, the social networking platform has seen a growth in a variety of different ways for stakeholders in addition to users (or data producers, themselves). As a data intermediary, the Twitter platform provides access to its user data (known as the "firehouse") through APIs, selective sampling, rate limits. Data consumers, such as researchers, activists, policy makers and technologists in private and public sectors have leveraged collected social media data from Twitter to influence disaster response, interpret social movements, influence direct government action, event foment and create democratic participation. It has and remains an important political tool and increasingly, a critical communication infrastructure at the beginning of the 21$^{st}$ century; however, the platform itself creates issues for scholarly research and reliability. The quality, veracity and provenance of data extraction from Twitter remains subject to a number of technical and policy issues concerning deleted or modified contents (made by data producers); data sharing and data storage policies that consumers like researchers and marketers are subject to and ongoing data request policies made by intermediaries and producers based on records compliance laws, police inquiries or government data requests.

We have come to understand that the Twitter data in the collection was requested and compiled by the White House Digital Strategy office in compliance with the Presidential Records Act (National Archives and Records Administration, 2017), and now the accounts are administered by NARA. These data contain original Tweet contents, user retweets, tweet IDs, tweet URLs, time of publication and location; they are formatted in CSV files and summarized in Table 1 below.

| Account Name | Number of Tweets |
|---|---|
| @POTUS | 321 |
| @FLOTUS | 4,029 |
| @WhiteHouse | 27,428 |

***Table 1****. Twitter data overview*

The Twitter data contains little or no engagement data, and while Tweets may be looked up /re-hydrated through tweet IDs this is a time-consuming process. For a President who sought to directly engage with citizens through platforms like Twitter, this data could be valuable to future researchers or others wanting to know about how President Obama used technology platforms to engage the public. Beyond account retweets and likes, the structure of the archived data make it very difficult to view the replies and @messages to the account, which would add an additional layer of meaning and context of reach to the collection.

APIs and data request policies structure what data can be extracted from platforms, and intermediaries themselves govern the technology being used and features that may affect the outcome of the collected data (e.g., formatting, data models, etc.). Recent research uncovered differences in sampling and size of data found in the different Twitter APIs – known as rest, search and stream. As a result, researchers trying to collect data at the same time (or even from the same tools) must adjust the expectation that they will end up with the same data collection (Bruns, 2013).

Overall, we believe that we have all the tweets that were published; however, we have less confidence in the completeness of metadata that may have been lost during extraction and transmission, particularly concerning the number of retweets and likes. The dataset contains tweets with zero likes, which is unusual and not consistent with information available online at the tweet URLs. As these posts and activity feeds represent snapshots in time when they are extracted from their native platforms for archival purposes, it is difficult to determine why the basic engagement data from @POTUS differs significantly from the archived @POTUS44 account information available on the Twitter platform.

A key challenge for future researchers and archivists managing Twitter data such as this will be to locate its provenance, including targeted assessments of the levels of error, veracity and engagement metrics, as these represent among the most meaningful interactions on the platform. Once removed from its native platform, social media data loses important context and becomes a snapshot of a moment in time. Metadata and other features of the data can change due to shifting API rules, platform redesigns and other decisions which are not undertaken with academic research in mind but which nevertheless affect such work. If the accuracy of engagement metadata cannot be trusted, the value of Twitter as a long-term asset for social science research will diminish unless researchers develop a new vocabulary for reckoning with the gaps in these materials.

## DISCUSSION

This paper uses the Barack Obama social media collection as a lens to explore both the first social media presidency and the challenges inherent in the preservation and management of social media data. Despite the challenges inherent in conducting secondary analysis of this data, it nevertheless demonstrates the success of President Obama in engaging with citizens on social media. The administration displayed a savvy understanding of how these platforms work and the ability to generate buzz around their content for serious issues (i.e., the flu or Ebola) and fun (i.e., holiday greetings).

Interoperability and a lack of descriptive standards will continue to impede cross-comparison of social media data without significant data wrangling and standardization efforts – there are no data models for cross-walking or mapping like-with-like across platforms, for example a tweet, a Facebook post and a YouTube video that all link to the same content or event such as a town hall live feed. Many standards engineers and metadata librarians have begun to confront the format issues and metadata that digital media data contain, however posts with layers of engagement data continue to be overlooked.

What would preservation metadata for social media for long-term archival access and secondary use applications look like? Engagement data in particular seems to be lacking in much of what we analyzed in this paper. In fact, most data management policies and terms of service for these platforms do not allow users or consumers to scrape or collect engagement data from accounts. It is very difficult to tell which posts are most popular – viral or 'seeded' other conversations. Based on our work and the research of others on the limits and scoping problems of social media data, there is clear research benefit here in examining small to medium size collections of social media data as a means of forensically examining and documenting the history and development of platform features and the development of records in social media platforms, including their metadata. Until social media activity streams are standardized into exchangeable formats, there remains plenty of work for information scholars and preservation professionals to address, including (but not limited to) re-contextualizing layers of engagement data, verifying metadata and creating data models for ontological, semantic and content descriptions of posts, accounts and stream activity.

## CONCLUSION

This paper represents our first analysis of these data in a long-term study of the value of social media data from presidential administrations. We hope that these findings will benefit those scholars, information professionals and data workers concerned with the long-term preservation, access and secondary use cases of social media collections. As we have demonstrated here, these records of Obama on social media are acknowledged as a public interest collection, but the materials themselves lie within fundamental business systems driven by for-profit models over long-term public trust and accountability.

Social media platforms support active communities where citizens access, create and engage with information, news and contemporary digital culture. Increasingly these platforms are in the public consciousness due in part to their role in political discourse, civic engagement and the proliferation of news, fake or authentic. Further, as next generation mobile networks reach higher wireless internet coverage, these platforms are undergoing tremendous technical and social change. Yet most social media platforms lack long-term preservation and access strategies for citizens, journalists and research institutions that support scholarly inquiry and access to reliable evidence and authentic information. Few social media preservation initiatives address metadata solutions, extraction and preservation techniques *across platforms*. Further, the data structures and formats for each are unique.

Since this paper was authored, peer reviewed, revised and now published a number of ongoing debates and decisions related to social media, digital preservation and the status of presidential and official White House tweets in the United States of America have occurred publicly and bring more layers to our research. In early spring, the National Archives contacted White House officials in the Trump administration to remind them that the Presidential Records Act (PRA) includes preserving tweets that have been edited and deleted from the @POTUS account (Braun, 2017). The COVFEFE Act, introduced by Representative Mike Quigley, explicitly adds "social media" to the PRA and ensures that tweets from President Trump's personal account (@realdonaldtrump) are archived as presidential records (Shaban, 2017). On June 5, the Office of Special Counsel concluded that White House Director of Social Media Dan Scavino, Jr. violated the Hatch Act when he tweeted in his official capacity about political activities in April (Galinda-Marrone, 2017). On June 19, 2017, the Supreme Court unanimously ruled that accessing social media platforms is a constitutional right and that states cannot limit access to social media given that they act as a "modern public square" and that having access to public spaces online is a fundamental First Amendment principle (Packingham v. North Carolinea, 2017).

In light of these events and amongst many others that continue to unfold, we suggest that social media scholars and digital preservationists continue to, as this ongoing research project aims to do, facilitate the growth and sustainability of social media data archives and digital preservation infrastructures by identifying the technical, ethical, policy and community issues that animate landscape of social media collections across platforms. It is incumbent upon us to address urgent gaps in the world's fastest growing digital collections and platforms, with a focus on interpreting the decisions which shape these materials and structure their value and use as research products. This includes current and future training of information professionals concerned with long-term digital collections, organizational transition, metadata transformation, current and forthcoming social media data collections in the public sphere that shape civic life at the beginning of the 21st century.

## ACKNOWLEDGMENTS

We wish to acknowledge and thank the Obama White House Office of Digital Strategy for the inviting us to use this open data collection for social media data research.

## REFERENCES

Acker, A. (2015). Radical appraisal practices and the mobile forensic imaginary" *Archive Journal* 5(1).

Acker, A. (2014). Born networked records: A history of the short message service format. University of California, Los Angeles.

Activity Streams 2.0. (2017, April 13). Retrieved April 14, 2017, from https://www.w3.org/TR/activitystreams-core/

Admin. (2016, December 20). Archived White House websites and social media [Text]. Retrieved from https://www.obamalibrary.gov/research/archived-white-house-websites-and-social-media

Allen, E. (2013, January 4). Update on the Twitter Archive at the Library of Congress | Library of Congress Blog [webpage]. Retrieved from //blogs.loc.gov/loc/2013/ 01/update-on-the-twitter-archive-at-the-library-of-congress/

ArchiveSocial. (2017). The Obama White House - Social Media Archive. Retrieved from http://obamawhitehouse. gov.archivesocial.com/

Braun, S. (2017, April 3). National Archives tells White House to save all of Trump's tweets, even ones deleted or corrected. Retrieved from http://www.pbs.org/ newshour/rundown/national-archives-tells-white-house-save-trumps-tweets-even-ones-deleted-corrected/

Bruns, A. (2013). Faster than the speed of print: Reconciling "big data" social media analysis and academic scholarship. *First Monday*, *18*(10). https://doi.org/10.5210/fm.v18i10.4879

Bruns, A., & Weller, K. (2016). Twitter as a first draft of the present: And the challenges of preserving it for the future. In *Proceedings of the 8th ACM Conference on Web Science* (pp. 183–189). New York, NY, USA: ACM. https://doi.org/10.1145/2908131.2908174

Driscoll, K., & Walker, S. (2014). Big data, big questions| Working within a black box: Transparency in the collection and production of big Twitter data. *International Journal of Communication*, *8*(0), 20.

Franchesci-Bicchierai, L. (2013, April 22). White House publishes first vine. Retrieved from http://mashable.com/2013/04/22/white-house-first-vine/#o7lWSM22jgqz

Galinda-Marrone, A. (2017, June 5). OSC File No. HA-17-2986 [Letter written June 5, 2017 to Adam J. Rappaport].

Gil de Zúñiga, H., Jung, N., & Valenzuela, S. (2012). Social media use for news and individuals' social capital, civic engagement and political participation. *Journal of Computer-Mediated Communication*, *17*(3), 319–336. https://doi.org/10.1111/j.1083-6101.2012.01574.x

Goldman, J. (2016, August 10). Now you can message President Obama on Facebook. Retrieved April 13, 2017, from https://obamawhitehouse.archives.gov/ blog/2016/08/10/now-you-can-message-president-obama-facebook

Howard, P. N., Duffy, A., Freelon, D., Hussain, M. M., Mari, W., & Mazaid, M. (2011). Opening closed regimes: What was the role of social media during the Arab spring? *SSRN Electronic Journal*. https://doi.org/10.2139/ssrn.2595096

Hughes, J. (2016, October 31). Vine dries up. Black humor loses a home. *The New York Times*. Retrieved from https://www.nytimes.com/2016/11/01/arts/vine-jay-versace-black-culture.html?_r=0

LaMonica, G. (2014, October 15). Turnip + Michelle Obama cutting loose=viral Vine. Retrieved April 13, 2017, from http://www.cnn.com/2014/10/15/health/ michelle-obama-turnip-vine/index.html

Lardinois, F. (2008, November 5). Obama's social media advantage. Retrieved from http://readwrite.com/ 2008/11/05/social_media_obama_mccain_comparison/

Lorenz, T. (2016, October 29). Inside the secret meeting that changed the fate of Vine forever. Retrieved from https://mic.com/articles/157977/inside-the-secret-meeting-that-changed-the-fate-of-vine-forever#.x2QylPTYw

Mack, E. (2013, April 22). Bill Nye, LeVar Burton in first White House Vine. Retrieved from https://www.cnet.com/news/bill-nye-levar-burton-in-first-white-house-vine/

Miller, J. (2017, January 5). New lenses on the first social media presidency. Retrieved February 22, 2017, from https://obamawhitehouse.archives.gov/blog/2017/01/05/new-lenses-first-social-media-presidency

National Archives and Records Administration. (2017, February 15). Presidential Records Act (PRA) of 1978. Retrieved from https://www.archives.gov/presidential-libraries/laws/1978-act.html

Opam, K. (2016, March 14). @MichelleObama An exclusive look at how the First Lady mastered social media. Retrieved from http://www.theverge.com/ 2016/3/14/11179572/first-lady-michelle-obama-vr-interview-social-media-pictures

Our First Social Media President, Through Three Webrecorder Narratives. (n.d.). Retrieved April 23, 2017, from http://rhizome.org/editorial/2017/jan/05/the-first-social-media-president/

Packingham v. North Carolina. (2017, June 19). Retrieved from https://www.supremecourt.gov/opinions/16pdf/15-1194_08l1.pdf

Pal, J., Chandra, P., & Vydiswaran, V. V. (2016, February 20). Twitter and the rebranding of Narendra Modi. *Economic and Political Weekly*, *LI*(8), 52–60.

Paletta, D. (2017, January 3). China shrugs off Trump Twitter jab on North Korea. Retrieved from https://www.wsj.com/articles/donald-trump-chides-north-korea-china-on-twitter-1483406717

Perraudin, F. (2014, October 15). Michelle Obama's "turnip for what" is just the latest great political Vine. Retrieved from https://www.theguardian.com/media/2014/oct/15/ michelle-obamas-turnip-for-what-great-political-vine

Raymond, M. (2010, April 14). How tweet it is!: Library acquires entire Twitter archive | Library of Congress blog [webpage]. Retrieved April 23, 2017, from //blogs.loc.gov/loc/2010/04/how-tweet-it-is-library-acquires-entire-twitter-archive/

Romano, A. (2016, October 28). You may not have understood Vine, but its demise is a huge cultural loss. Retrieved from http://www.vox.com/2016/10/28/ 13439450/vine-shutdown-loss-to-black-culture

Rose, R. (2014, October 14). Michelle Obama makes best Vine ever for "turnip for what." Retrieved from http://jezebel.com/michelle-obama-makes-best-vine-ever-for-turnip-for-what-1646473285

Schulman, K. (2016, October 31). The digital transition: How the presidential transition works in the social media age. Retrieved February 22, 2017, from https://obamawhitehouse.archives.gov/blog/2016/10/31/digital-transition-how-presidential-transition-works-social-media-age

Shaban, H. (2017, June 12). The COVFEFE Act would preserve Trump's tweets as presidential records. Retrieved from https://www.washingtonpost.com/news/ the-switch/wp/2017/06/12/the-covfefe-act-would-preserve-donald-trumps-tweets-as-presidential-records/?utmterm=.aaed103129df

Slater Tow, C. (2011, September 22). Tell your story with timeline. Retrieved April 23, 2017, from https://www.facebook.com/note.php?note_id=10150289612087131

Smith, A. (2009). *The Internet's Role in Campaign 2008*. Pew Research Center. Retrieved from http://www.pewinternet.org/2009/04/15/the-internets-role-in-campaign-2008/

Streaming message types — Twitter Developers. (n.d.). Retrieved April 13, 2017, from https://dev.twitter.com/ streaming/overview/messages-types#status_deletion_notices_delete

Summers, E. (n.d.). DocNow/twarc. Retrieved April 23, 2017, from https://github.com/DocNow/twarc

Tarantola, A. (2016, January 11). Go behind the scenes of the State of the Union with Snapchat. Retrieved April 13, 2017, from https://www.engadget.com/2016/01/11/ obamas-final-sotu-snapchat/

The White House. (2013, May 9). Six seconds with POTUS, sitting down for savory BBQ at Stubb's in Austin, TX. Retrieved April 23, 2017, from https://vine.co/v/b23riwn59BO/

The White House on Foursquare. (n.d.). Retrieved March 15, 2017, from https://foursquare.com/p/the-white-house/12485552

Thomson, S. D., & Kilbride, W. (2015). Preserving social media: The problem of access. *New Review of Information Networking*, *20*(1–2), 261–275. https://doi.org/10.1080/13614576.2015.1114842

Trace, C. B. (2011). Beyond the magic to the mechanism: Computers, materiality, and what it means for records to be "born digital." *Archivaria*, *72*(0), 5–27.

Tufekci, Z. (2014). Big questions for social media big data: Representativeness, validity and other methodological pitfalls. In *Proceedings of the 8th International Conference on Weblogs and Social Media, ICWSM 2014* (pp. 505–514). Ann Arbor, MI: The AAAI Press. Retrieved from https://uncch.pure.elsevier.com/en/ publications/big-questions-for-social-media-big-data-representativeness-validi

Varol, O., Ferrara, E., Davis, C. A., Menczer, F., & Flammini, A. (2017). Online human-bot interactions: Detection, estimation, and characterization. *arXiv:1703.03107 [Cs]*. Retrieved from http://arxiv.org/ abs/1703.03107

White House Video. (2014). Vine. Retrieved April 23, 2017, from https://vine.co/WHVideo/

White House (whitehouse) on Myspace. (n.d.). Retrieved February 22, 2017, from https://myspace.com/whitehouse

Why am I missing from search? (n.d.). Retrieved from https://help.twitter.com/articles/66018?lang=en

# Not Reinventing the "Reel:" Adaptation and Evaluation of an Existing Model for Digital Video Information Seeking

**Dan Albertson**
*University at Buffalo, State University of New York, USA. dalbert@buffalo.edu*

**Melissa P. Johnston**
*University of West Georgia, USA. mjohnsto@westga.edu*

## ABSTRACT

**Information seeking research has provided models across different contexts in order to depict the phenomena and processes of users in their search for information. Yet, no recognized model or generalization of the digital video information-seeking process exists. The current study seeks to address this gap. Areas such as image information seeking have been examined, and existing research in these related areas demonstrates potential to support progress in digital video information seeking. In the current study, variables were adapted from an existing image seeking model and incorporated into a survey to measure their representation of video information seeking. The goal of the current analysis is to quantitatively measure and validate the phases of a selected image seeking model as also representing underlying factors of an information seeking process for digital video if adapted accordingly. Further, correlations between extracted factors were also tested in order to measure the interrelationships as part of a larger representation of digital video seeking. Results supported the factors as being representative of digital video information seeking and also produced significant correlations between them. Implications of these findings address the central research problem, in that a generalized representation of digital video information seeking has been examined and supported through the adaptation and evaluation of an existing model.**

## KEYWORDS

information seeking, visual information seeking, digital video, human information behavior

## INTRODUCTION

Information seeking, as an area of research, has a long, rich history. Studies in this area have examined and explained many phenomena that occur before, during and after humans' pursuit of information. Established information seeking studies have produced widely adopted models, which depict phases that span (information) need realization, action, assessment and decision-making. Studies of information seeking have been conducted across many contexts, such as professional and/or academic domains, demographic groups, information retrieval (IR) systems, information tasks and situations, and formats of media or information resources.

Further, the information seeking process for visual information specifically has been previously examined. Visual information seeking, such as for images, is particularly significant to the body of research as individual factors can be differentiated from findings in other areas, such as textual information seeking. Existing image-based research in particular demonstrates potential to support the development, evaluation and validation of a model or representation of information seeking for other contexts that involve visual information, including for digital video.

## RESEARCH PROBLEM AND MOTIVATION

Despite the long history of information seeking research, opportunities remain for further studies that are specific to different information or media types. Momentum in information seeking research never progressed to the point of establishing a model or generalization for all primary types of information. Moreover, among the models that exist today, including those that span different situations, domains, systems/tools and information formats, there is still no recognized model of digital video information seeking. This gap is pertinent; it demonstrates a need for further user-centered foundations applicable specifically to video information. An individualized study should strive to provide a conceptual or generalized depiction of users in a video information seeking process, which is a highly common search context.

The need for further progress in digital video information seeking is self-evident. The fact that there are no established models is both intriguing and motivating. Further, video information seeking studies can be supported by the existing body of research, including areas that are closely aligned and relevant to such a context. Prior studies can offer examples to ground and frame new research. An image seeking model, specifically, can be examined for potential adaptation and application to a video-specific context. Thus, there is potential to frame and evaluate a model for digital video seeking without having to completely recreate the wheel or construct a model from the bottom up.

A generalization of digital video information seeking would be important to the field; video is a resource which comprises text, image, audio and moving image – all of which can be automatically extracted from content – in a time-based format. As a result, video can be a central attribute to a distinct

80th Annual Meeting of the Association for Information Science & Technology, Washington, DC | Oct. 27-Nov. 1, 2017

information context; thus, it would be expected to invoke unique aspects of the information-seeking process as well. Therefore, there is the need to make progress in research that examines digital video information seeking.

## RELATED LITERATURE

The field of information science is replete with studies that examine users' information seeking behaviors. As an area of research, it has examined and explained many phenomena which occur as part of the pursuit of information. Established information seeking studies have provided widely adopted models, which generally speaking, include the phases of a holistic process (e.g., Bates, 1989; Belkin, 1980; Ellis, 1989; Kuhlthau, 1991; Wilson, 1999). Studies have been conducted with various user groups, throughout different domains, and employed a variety of methods (e.g., Catalano, 2013; Davies, 2007; Ellis, Cox, & Hall, 2003; Leckie, Pettigrew, & Sylvain, 1996; Marchionini, 1995; Urquhart, 2011). It is not the intention of the current study to review models of information seeking, which have been comprehensively surveyed, including across different perspectives (e.g., Bates, 2010; Case, 2012; Greifeneder, 2014; Julien, Pecoskie, & Reed, 2011; Vakkari, 2008), but to provide a background for visual information seeking and to identify a gap that exists for digital video information seeking.

## VISUAL INFORMATION SEEKING

Visual information seeking is an area of research that has been of interest since researchers began analyzing how people go about interactively finding and acquiring information. This interest has increased with the advances in technology and the prevalence of online searching for digital images and video (Albertson, 2015; Matusiak, 2017). Visual information seeking can be considered a distinct category of research within the larger body of information-seeking research (Albertson, 2015). There is a body of literature that examines the information needs and interactions from a user-centered approach including how users search, browse and assess items which comprise visual elements, such as images and videos (Albertson, 2015). Prior research has demonstrated that visual information "inherently produces outputs and outcomes that can be differentiated from those of other information seeking processes. Differences among users' needs, tasks, criteria, considerations, and decision-making occur" and the "multidimensional makeup of visual formats [can influence] users' actions, assessment, and selections of items" (Albertson, 2015, p. 1092).

As visual information use has become pervasive in a wide variety of domains and in personal information practices, numerous studies have examined the image searching process in particular across a variety of contexts. In 2015, Albertson presented a thorough review of visual information seeking research guided and organized according to a set of generalized stages or phases from information seeking models, including users' needs, actions and assessments. Additionally, the research methods employed in these empirical studies of visual information seeking were also discussed and shown to span experiments, surveys, systematically collected data and other data collection and analysis techniques (Albertson, 2015).

## VIDEO INFORMATION SEEKING

Included in Albertson's (2015) review is research on video as visual information, yet there is significantly less research that examines video information seeking. Albertson asserts that "video unlike any other information resource, enables the automatic extraction of text, image, moving image, and audio, and, in addition, is a time-based format ... and as a result, video, ... warrants independent analysis and thus separate evaluation frameworks and guidelines, as its structure affects users differently than text, image, and speech do alone" (Albertson, 2013, p. 672). Yet, research specific to video information seeking is very limited with no established models or generalizations to utilize for a foundation (Albertson, 2013; Ju & Albertson, 2015; Yang & Marchionini, 2004).

Various studies have been conducted to examine video interaction and other user-centered phenomena as part of a digital library usage context. Lee and Smeaton (2000) applied information seeking models to frame general user interactions with digital video libraries. Marchionini, Geisler and Brunk (2000) developed the Agileviews Model to represent how people interact with information, inclusive of video, through views. In 2006, Marchionini, Wildemuth and Geisler presented a revised evaluation framework that accounts for the constructs that influence human video interaction. Their framework "embeds tasks in larger life goals and considers the overall interaction of goals, tasks, individual characteristics, video characteristics, and video surrogates as part of an activity flow that requires human effort to achieve outcomes" (p. 1639). Albertson's 2015 review demonstrates the research efforts into understanding how users find digital visual information, but also illuminates the need for a model to serve as a foundation and interpretive tool for research and the practical problems of the users in a video-specific context due to the distinctions as explained above.

## A REVIEW OF THE IMAGE SEEKING MODEL ADAPTED FOR THE CURRENT STUDY

The Image Seeking Process Model developed by Conniss, Ashford and Graham (2000) was selected and utilized for the purposes of the current study because it is the only comprehensive model specific to image seeking and demonstrates potential to adapt for a video seeking context.

The Conniss et al. (2000) model was the result of an exhaustive qualitative study that investigated image seeking behaviors of users throughout a variety of visually oriented domains (e.g., museums, art history, police officers, radiology and others). Conniss et al. (2000) utilized different methods, including questionnaires, informal observation, in-depth interviews and existing documentation, in order to increase understanding of how and why people search for and use visual information as part of their everyday professional tasks. Their study found that the image seeking process is influenced by contextual factors, such as workplace, existing resources, personal experiences and influences, communications and interactions, and access mechanisms. It is considered to be one of the more in-depth and thorough investigations of image information seeking behavior. As part of the study, a model was formed which included the phases of *starting*, *scoping*, *applying*, *selecting*, *iterating*, and *ending*. Each of these phases comprises a series of sub-processes and decisions for the users. These primary phases were used to establish factors and draw out variables for the evaluation of the current study. Each phase is further described here.

### STARTING

The information seeking process begins when the user "defines/refines the need/request in order to develop a set of criteria for assessing image suitability, often incorporating considerations of context of use" (Conniss et al., 2000, p. 101). There can be many criteria for assessing item suitability, including image quality, format, physical size, audience, salient features, visual appearance, copyright restrictions, semantic value, date (i.e., recentness) and others (Conniss et al., 2000). The starting phase can be rapid or develop over a significant amount of time and can be individual or collaborative in nature. Here, "boundaries" of the need are set as well as flexibility which can be revisited throughout the image seeking process.

### SCOPING

The second phase defined in the framework is scoping, where users either implicitly or explicitly decide on the general approach and strategy that will best facilitate their searching. Some will start broadly by using general terms and search criteria in order to receive as many options as possible, while others will be more specific, using more precise search terms, combined with targeted search features. The scoping process, which can occur continually throughout the information seeking process, entails user modifications to the search criteria and queries to either broaden or narrow the search (Conniss et al., 2000).

### APPLYING

In this phase, the user initiates formal interaction(s) with the information resources; therefore, they must decide what to use and in what ways. Their choices are many times influenced by time, expense, existing knowledge and level of experience with finding relevant images. Exploratory search strategies can also be present in this phase in an effort to overcome gaps in knowledge with the subject area, which in turn can provide the user with more information to utilize going forward in the search for visual information (Conniss et al., 2000).

### SELECTING

Following a search, a set of results (e.g., images) is returned to the user. The user will make decisions on what to select from a returned set, which is a process that can occur in a single action or span multiple stages. Once the user chooses to look through a set of search results, they then assess the returned items for potential selection, according to the criteria as established and make relevance judgments (Conniss et al., 2000).

### ITERATING

Searching for visual information rarely involves just one search instance or action, but rather usually involves some sort of modification to the search or corresponding criteria. This process may occur over the course of more than one session, and search modifications can take place throughout an entire process, as the user adapts their search strategies. Users may decide to modify their search in order to find the best possible images or to re-scope the search to either increase or decrease the number of search results to choose from (Conniss et al., 2000).

### ENDING

In the ending phase, the search process is finalized and the user decides to stop searching, whether successful or not. There are different explanations as to why users decide to end a search for visual information. These reasons may include "exhaustive," where users feel they have covered all available searching options and believe they have the best possible match or have found no suitable items; "non-exhaustive," where users search through only a portion of the returned images, but end the search based on time or if they feel as though they have sufficient set of items; and "non-exhaustive – exact match" where users find the precise image that satisfies their need and therefore ends the search without any additional search iterations (Conniss et al., 2000, p. 121-122).

### METHOD

The present study utilized and evaluated the Image Seeking Process Model developed by Conniss et al. (2000) for the purposes of representing video information seeking. The model was chosen due to the overlaps between images (e.g. digital photographs) as an information type and video information. Even though video is time-based and thus contains audio and moving images, certain criteria for images are also applicable to video in an information seeking context, such as resolution, formats, search and browse approaches, visual relevance, among others. The current study utilized the image seeking model to construct and adapt factors containing individual variables for video seeking. A quantitative methodology was utilized for data collection and analysis to establish the phases of the model as factors reliably representative of video information seeking. Variables, as extracted from the individual phases of the Conniss et al. (2000) model, were then specifically adapted and evaluated for video (see Table 1).

### INSTRUMENTATION

A web-based survey was chosen for data collection due to the versatility and ability to get responses from a wide range of targeted participants across different locations in the United States. Considering the variables as examined in the current study are grounded in the literature, a survey method to collect data from users was deemed suitable.

The phases of the Image Seeking Model by Conniss et al. (2000), as reviewed above, was used to formulate the underlying factors of video information seeking to be evaluated. Further, individual factors derived directly from five of the specific phases. The factors (corresponding to the phases of the image seeking model) included:

- starting (STR)
- scoping (SCP)
- applying (APP)
- selecting (SEL) and
- iterating (inclusive of ending) (ITR)

In total, 24 survey statements (i.e., variables) were created to define these five factors (Table 1). Each of the 24 survey statements was prefaced with the directive statement of "When I search for video." Again, these variables as incorporated in the survey derived directly from the observations of Conniss et al. (2000) as part of the phases of the image information seeking process. Where needed, individual survey statements (i.e., variables) were adapted to resemble aspects of video seeking, making the results applicable to video; although, some variables were deemed representative of video seeking as they currently were.

## PARTICIPANTS

The population chosen for the current study included professionals that regularly search for and use digital video to achieve job-related objectives. Currently, this sample includes K-12 educators from across the United States, which represents a domain that regularly uses digital video for applied (e.g., instructional) purposes. In total, 252 K-12 teachers completed the online survey. To measure the suitability of this sample, when asked how often they search for videos, 18.3% (n=46) participants responded "all the time," 36.5% (n=92) responded "often" and 33.7% (n=85) stated that they "sometimes" search for video. Only 8.3% (n=21) responded that they "rarely" search and 2.4% (n=6) reported that they "never" search for video online. If a participant responded that they never searched for video online, the survey was ended for them.

The participants were recruited via postings on national and state K-12 education listservs, as well as national and state school library listservs. Twitter and other social media sites were also used to distribute the survey. The distribution of participants across age ranges included 21-30 (12%, n=30), 31-40 (18%, n=46), 41-50 (27%, n=68), 50-60 (31%, n=78), 61+ (11%, n=29), with 1 participant choosing not to identify. The distribution of the gender of the participants resembled that of the overall teaching population, with 7.5% participants designating themselves as male (n=19) and 92.5% as female (n=233). The years of experience for participants ranged from one year to those with over 30 years of experience. Computer/internet skills were self-reported at 17.9% (n=45) being Experts, 55% (n=139) as Above Average, 24% (n=61) as Average, 2% (n=5) as Below Average, and .8% (n=2) as Beginner.

| DIGITIAL VIDEO INFORMATION SEEKING | | |
|---|---|---|
| **Factor (Factor Identifier)** | **Variable Identifier** | **Variables** |
| **Starting (STR)** | | |
| | STR1 | Knowing what video is needed |
| | STR2 | Knowing why a video is needed |
| | STR3 | Knowing how a video helps achieve goals |
| | STR4 | Knowing the format, quality, and length of a video |
| | STR5 | Knowing the age of a video |
| | STR6 | Knowing the intended audience of a video |
| | STR7 | Knowing the style of a video |
| **Scoping (SCP)** | | |
| | SCP1 | Knowing that I can search broadly |
| | SCP2 | Knowing that I can refine searches |
| | SCP3 | Knowing that searches can be specific |
| | SCP4 | Knowing that searches can be broadened |
| **Applying (APP)** | | |
| | APP1 | Knowing that the search tool will give useful results |
| | APP2 | Knowing that the search tool is intended for a specific audience |
| | APP3 | Knowing that the search tool is geared towards my ability |
| | APP4 | Knowing that the search tool will give up-to-date results |
| | APP5 | Knowing that the search tool contains a large collection to select from |
| | APP6 | Knowing that I can search within a collection |
| **Selecting (SEL)** | | |
| | SEL1 | Having textual descriptions available to me for deciding to select on a video |
| | SEL2 | Having visuals (stills, frames) from the video |
| | SEL3 | The ability to select multiple videos to use |
| **Iterating (ITR) and Ending** | | |
| | ITR1 | Having the ability to perform multiple searches in one session |
| | ITR2 | Having the ability to adjust or revise a search |
| | ITR3 | Being provided with videos from previous searches |
| | ITR4 | Knowing that the search for video has been exhaustive |

**Table 1.** Tested Factors and Variables

## ANALYSIS

The aim of the study's analysis was to quantitatively measure and validate the phases as the underlying factors (or unobserved variables) of the information seeking process for digital video and to test the interrelationships between them. The overarching analysis, as performed, included factor analysis of all individual factors (corresponding to phases of the selected model) followed by correlation tests between each of them. Other tests were performed to determine suitability of factor analysis, including testing the adequacy of the sample and reliability. The steps as performed for this methodology, including the specific statistical tests of each, included:

1. Measure suitability of factor analysis and sample adequacy:
    - Inter-item correlations
    - Kaiser-Meyer-Olkin Measure of Sampling Adequacy
    - Bartlett's Test of Sphericity
    - Diagonals of the anti-image correlation matrix
2. Perform factor analysis to extract significant factors and measure the relationship and variance of each observed variable on the unobserved factors:
    - Factor loadings
    - Communalities
    - Eigenvalues and percentage of variance
    - Rotated factor leadings (where applicable)
3. Measure descriptive statistics of extracted factors and demonstrate reliability of factors:
    - Descriptive analysis
    - Cronbach's alpha
4. Measure correlations between the extracted and reliable factors:
    - Correlation analysis

This approach to data analysis allowed the evaluation of factors as adapted directly from an existing model to determine their level of representation of digital video information seeking.

## RESULT

Results are summarized here according to the conducted tests as listed above.

### Suitability of Factor Analysis and Sample Adequacy

First, inter-item correlations across all individual variables (i.e., survey items) were tested for all five performed factor analyses. All correlation coefficients, with the exception of one (between STR1 and STR4), were shown to be statistically significant at $p<0.01$ (50 out of 51 correlations). The correlation test between STR1 and STR4 produced a level of significance at $p=0.05$, the only $p$ value with a significance statistic higher than 0.01 among all other inter-item variables across the STR, SCP, APP, SEL, and ITR factors (see Table 1 for listing of all individual observed variables among the different factors).

The Kaiser-Meyer-Olkin (KMO) test of adequate sample and Bartlett's Test of Sphericity were both performed as preliminary measures of sampling adequacy (MSA) to ensure appropriateness of all factor analyses as conducted. All KMO and Bartlett's values were well within the acceptable levels. Only one KMO value was less than .7 (SEL produced a value of .649). All Bartlett's Test of Sphericity values for all evaluated factors were significant at $p=.000$.

Results from the anti-image correlation matrices produced diagonal values that further support sampling adequacy and appropriateness of all individual observed variables. All diagonal coefficients–across all factor analyses–exceeded $r=.500$, the sufficient level, with a range between $r=.622$ and $r=.845$.

Therefore, based on adequacy of the sample and significance of the inner-relationships between the observed variables, the suitability for factor analysis as part of the current study is supported, and all individual observed variables were deemed appropriate and thus included in the performed analyses.

### Factor Analysis

Importantly, all factor loadings from each respective analysis were sufficient (Tables 2-6). In the original sets of (un-rotated) factor loadings, all observed variables load sufficiently onto the first extracted factor (for STR, SCP, APP, SEL and ITR). Results show that only the factor analysis of STR extracted more than one factor; two factors were extracted (Table 2). The other factor analyses (i.e., for SCP, APP, SEL and ITR) all extracted exactly one factor. As a result, Table 2 for the factor analysis of STR reports both original and rotated factor loadings, while Tables 3-6 provide only original (un-rotated) loadings due to only one extracted factor for the other analyses. An eigenvalue of 1.0 was the threshold for factor extraction; these values are also presented in Tables 2-6 along with the percentage of variance for each of the extracted factors.

All communalities for the individual survey items (i.e., observed variables), as also found in Tables 2-6, were shown to be suitable across the five factor analyses; all values were above .4, with the majority being over .5. Based on factor loadings and communality values, no observed variables were removed from analysis and interpretation.

| | Factor | | Communalities | Rotation[a] | |
|---|---|---|---|---|---|
| | 1 | 2 | | 1 | 2 |
| STR1 | .561 | .564 | .632 | | .793 |
| STR2 | .680 | .553 | .768 | | .863 |
| STR3 | .726 | .402 | .689 | | .779 |
| STR4 | .650 | | .640 | .797 | |
| STR5 | .600 | | .585 | .764 | |
| STR6 | .770 | | .658 | .750 | |
| STR7 | .753 | | .638 | .745 | |
| Initial Eigenvalues | 3.249 | 1.363 | | | |
| % of Variance | 46.408 | 19.466 | | | |

*Note:* [a]*Varimax Rotation with Kaiser Normalization*

***Table 2.*** *Factor analysis of starting (STR)*

| | Factor | Communalities |
|---|---|---|
| | 1 | |
| SCP1 | .741 | .550 |
| SCP2 | .848 | .718 |
| SCP3 | .865 | .749 |
| SCP4 | .859 | .737 |
| Initial Eigenvalues | 2.754 | |
| % of Variance | 68.849 | |

***Table 3.*** *Factor analysis of scoping (SCP)*

| | Factor | Communalities |
|---|---|---|
| | 1 | |
| APP1 | .639 | .408 |
| APP2 | .645 | .416 |
| APP3 | .650 | .423 |
| APP4 | .703 | .495 |
| APP5 | .713 | .508 |
| APP6 | .677 | .459 |
| Initial Eigenvalues | 2.708 | |
| % of Variance | 45.136 | |

***Table 4.*** *Factor analysis of applying (APP)*

| | Factor | Communalities |
|---|---|---|
| | 1 | |
| SEL1 | .778 | .606 |
| SEL2 | .811 | .657 |
| SEL3 | .733 | .538 |
| Initial Eigenvalues | 1.801 | |
| % of Variance | 60.019 | |

***Table 5.*** *Factor analysis of selecting (SEL)*

| | Factor | Communalities |
|---|---|---|
| | 1 | |
| ITR1 | .803 | .645 |
| ITR2 | .801 | .642 |
| ITR3 | .683 | .467 |
| ITR4 | .783 | .544 |
| Initial Eigenvalues | 2.298 | |
| % of Variance | 57.448 | |

***Table 6.*** *Factor analysis of iterating (ITR)*

### *Descriptive Results and Reliability Among Factors*

After factor extraction, descriptive statistics of each were measured, which are presented in Table 7. Here, means are shown; the scale for all observed variables was based on 1 (very important) to 5 (not at all important). Skewness and kurtosis are provided, with all values showing appropriate distributions. Cronbach alphas, as assessed for each of the multi-variable factors, are also provided in Table 7; all values were above 0.7. STR and SCP as factors measured above 0.80. These data were used to support the reliability of the survey instrument (as further described below).

| Factor | N. of items | Mean | SD | Skewness | Kurtosis | Cronbach's α |
|---|---|---|---|---|---|---|
| Starting (STR) | 7 | 1.501 | .445 | .618 | -.290 | .800 |
| Scoping (SCP) | 4 | 1.707 | .518 | .133 | -.626 | .843 |
| Applying (APP) | 6 | 1.647 | .464 | .330 | -.417 | .750 |
| Selecting (SEL) | 3 | 1.692 | .563 | .456 | -.357 | .765 |
| Iterating (ITR) | 4 | 1.831 | .550 | .211 | -.526 | .741 |

***Table 7.*** *Descriptive and reliability results*

### *Correlation Results Between Factors*

Relationships between the primary extracted factors were also measured. Considering the factors constitute unobserved variables, a subsequent set of correlation tests was conducted between STR, SCP, APP, SEL and ITR to measure the significance of any interrelationships (as opposed to cause and effect). These results are shown in Table 8.

| | STR | SCP | APP | SEL | ITR |
|---|---|---|---|---|---|
| STR | 1.000 | .549** | .529** | .457** | .448** |
| SCP | | 1.000 | .566** | .528** | .582** |
| APP | | | 1.000 | .542** | .613** |
| SEL | | | | 1.000 | .512** |
| ITR | | | | | 1.000 |

*Note. **p<0.01*

***Table 8.*** *Correlation coefficients between factors*

## DISCUSSION

### *Factors of Digital Video Information Seeking*

Factor analysis supported the primary factors as formulated for the research goals of the current study. Furthermore, STR, SCP, APP, SEL and ITR were all extracted based on eigenvalues, and all tests showed the observed variables to sufficiently load onto their respective factor.

Of particular note, the analysis of STR extracted two factors, reducing the number of seven observed variables to two unobserved (see Table 2). In the original set of (un-rotated) factor loadings, all items load sufficiently onto factor 1, demonstrating significance for STR as a phase overall or individually, while only STR1, STR2 and STR3 loaded onto the second extracted factor. The rotated set of factor loadings provides more specificity of the two factors. In the rotated results, STR4, STR5, STR6 and STR7 load sufficiently onto factor 1, while STR1, STR2 and STR3 load together on factor 2.

The extraction and support of two viable factors for the STR phase is significant. Based on the observed variables themselves, the two extracted factors of STR – as a part of the larger digital video information seeking process – can be interpreted to make distinctions between processes of *Need Development* and *Defining Criteria of Video Content*. These sub-processes are defined in Table 9, including the significant variables that load onto each as used for interpretation. This finding lends itself to better understand the starting phase of video information seeking, which can include distinct sub-phases.

| Starting (STR) | |
|---|---|
| **Need Development** (Extracted Factor 1) | **Defining Criteria for Content** (Extracted Factor 2) |
| Observed Variables | Observed Variables |
| STR4. Knowing the format, quality, and length of a video | STR1. Knowing what video is needed |
| STR5. Knowing the age of a video | STR2. Knowing why a video is needed |
| STR6. Knowing the intended audience of a video | STR3. Knowing how a video helps achieve goals |
| STR7. Knowing the style of a video | |

***Table 9.*** *Interpretation of results of starting (STR) factor.*

The other (four) factor analyses (i.e., for SCP, APP, SEL and ITR) each extracted one factor. Therefore, the original factors, as presented in Table 1, are adequately and wholly represented by the observed variables listed for each, with all variables being statistically significant. This finding in particular is also important, because it establishes support for the other evaluated factors as forming significant phases of a holistic video information seeking process. With all factors significant, the adaptation of phases from an existing image seeking model for the purposes of digital video seeking is supported.

### *Interrelationships Between the Supported Factors*

As previously shown, all correlation coefficients between the primary factors (as extracted) were significant at the $p<0.01$ level. Such positive relationships would be expected if each phase was connected and thus contributed positively toward a larger information seeking process. In other information seeking contexts, there is the assumption that all phases of a larger model are all interrelated at a certain level, not necessarily sequential or cause-and-effect. In addition, an information seeking process is typically depicted as being capable of initiating, proceeding, and/or concluding or reiterating at any point of the process or at any stage. Therefore, the nature and level of these sets of interrelationships between the identified factors, as shown quantitatively, is appropriate and supportive to the research goals of the current study. A cause-and-effect or predictive analysis would not be suitable in this case considering the inexact nature of human behavior in an information seeking process.

### *Assessment of the Instrument*

Cronbach's alpha values supported the reliability of the multi-question factors by demonstrating a high level of internal consistency and thus providing confidence in instrument design. Construct validity was supported by the results of the factor analyses, as described, by observing that all factor loadings exceeded the sufficient level across each test. Therefore, construct validity of the different factors, based on their individual sets of observed variables, was sufficiently supported. Providing these results, the instrument of the current study, along with the sets of primary factors and observed variables, are supported by both reliability and validity.

## IMPLICATIONS

The primary implication of the current study is that the problem of not having an information seeking model or other representation for digital video has been explored and addressed. A quantitative methodology was employed to measure the significance of factors and variables, as adapted from an existing image information seeking model, in order to validate their level of representation of information seeking from a digital video context. Not only were the factors supported, but the contributions (i.e., loadings) of the individual observed variables for each factor were all significant as well. Results of the current study also provided additional specificity in understanding the starting (i.e., initiating) stage of the video information seeking process; two individual factors were extracted from the variable set, which can be generalized to represent need development (including intentions for the video) and, secondly, users' defining the criteria of the digital video content itself as part of the need. Furthermore, this finding is a unique to this area of research and also complementary to existing visual information seeking research.

Next, after validating the primary factors, correlation tests were then conducted, which showed all interrelationships to be significant, providing further support to having a holistic generalization in this context.

The bottom line for the current findings is that demonstrable progress toward a more general understanding of video information seeking and a future model has been provided. Not having an established model is significant (and concerning) because of the level of impact and insightfulness information seeking research has had on our understanding of the relationships and processes between humans (users) and information.

The other primary implication for the current study is that the quantitative approach as employed here can serve as an example for future analyses which aim to formulate, analyze and model information experiences through quantitative analyses based on adapted versions of established models. Further, this methodology can serve as a basis for other studies not wanting to completely replicate existing research, but rather employing already available work as having the capability to be adapted for new purposes.

## CONCLUSIONS AND FUTURE WORK

The current study constitutes a first attempt to examine and represent the information seeking process for digital video. Considering that substantial research exists in the general area of information seeking, the feasibility of adapting an existing model to be representative of video information seeking was explored. Video, as an information format, comprises visual qualities; therefore, an image seeking model was deemed to have potential for these research purposes.

While the results of the current study demonstrate progress and understanding in digital video seeking, results are not considered absolute or comprehensive. Further, other variables and even larger factors may exist, which would warrant more in-depth exploration and explanation. Furthermore, the observed variables as examined here constitute one set, derived and adapted from an existing model as developed in a prior study. The image seeking study employed as the basis of the current analysis was comprehensive; however, other in-depth studies of video information seeking, as conducted separately, may extract or expose other pertinent variables and factors for that particular context, which may have not been present in the image study utilized in this examination. This is where future research opportunities remain. Now that significant results have been produced, the justification for having a representation or model specific to digital video seeking is suggested. Therefore, a comprehensive qualitative study may be warranted in the future in order to develop a holistic and conceptual model of video information seeking, specifically.

In the meantime, however, the current findings can still serve as a basis for user-centered studies of digital video. The current study achieved what it set out to accomplish, to provide a valid and generalized representation of the digital video information seeking process by drawing upon the existing relevant knowledge and without having to "reinvent the 'reel.'"

## REFERENCES


Albertson, D. (2015). Visual information seeking. Journal of the Association for Information Science and Technology, 66(6), 1091-1105.

Albertson, D. (2013). An interaction and interface design framework for video digital libraries. Journal of Documentation, 69(5), 667-692.

Bates, M. J. (2010). Information behavior. In M. J. Bates & M. N. Maack (Eds.), *Encyclopedia of library and information sciences* (pp. 2381–2391). New York, NY: CRC Press.

Bates, M. J. (1989). The design of browsing and berrypicking techniques for the online search interface. Online Review, 13(5), 407-424.

Belkin, N. J. (1980). Anomalous state of knowledge for information retrieval. Canadian Journal of Information Science, 5, 133-143.

Case, D. O. (2012). Looking for information: A survey of research on information seeking, needs, and behavior (3rd ed.). Bingley, UK: Emerald Group.

Catalano, A. (2013). Patterns of graduate students' information seeking behavior: A meta-synthesis of the literature. *Journal of Documentation, 69*(2), 243–274.

Conniss, L. R., Ashford, A. J., & Graham, M. E. (2000). Information seeking behaviour in image retrieval: Visor I final report. Newcastle-upon-Tyne: University of Northumbria at Newcastle, Institute for Image Data Research. (Library and Information Commission research report 95)

Davies, K. (2007). The information-seeking behaviour of doctors: A review of the evidence. Health Information and Libraries Journal, *24*(2), 78-94.

Ellis, D. (1989). A behavioral approach to information retrieval design. Journal of Documentation, 45(3), 171-212.

Ellis, D., Cox, D., & Hall, K. (1993). A comparison of the information seeking patterns of researchers in the physical and social sciences. Journal of Documentation, 49(4), 356-369.

Greifeneder, E. (2014). Trends in information behaviour research. Information Research, 19(4). Retrieved from http://InformationR.net/ir/19-4/isic/isic13.html

Ju, B., & Albertson, D. (2015). Examining user-driven factors for intentions to use video digital libraries. In Proceedings of the Annual Meeting of the Association for Information Science and Technology, St. Louis, MO.

Julien, H., Pecoskie, J. L., & Reed, K. (2011). Trends in information behavior research, 1999-2008: A content analysis. Library & Information Science Research, 33(1), 19-34.

Kuhlthau, C. C. (1991). Inside the search process: Information seeking from the user's perspective. Journal of the American Society for Information Science, 42(5), 361-371.

Leckie, G. J., Pettigrew, K. E., & Sylvain, C. (1996). Modeling the information seeking of professionals: A general model derived from research on engineers, health care professionals, and lawyers. Library Quarterly, 66(2), 161-193.

Marchionini, G. (1995). Information seeking in electronic environments. New York, NY: Cambridge University Press.

Marchionini, G., Geisler, G., & Brunk, B. (2000). AgileViews: A human-centered framework for interfaces to information spaces. In Proceedings of the Annual Meeting of the American Society for Information Science. Silver Spring, MD.

Marchionini, G., Wildemuth, B., & Geisler, G. (2006). The Open Video Digital Library: A Mobius strip of research and practice. Journal of the American Society for Information Science & Technology, 57(12), 1629-1643.

Matusiak, K. K. (2017). Studying information behavior of image users: An overview of research methodology in LIS literature, 2004–2015. Library & Information Science Research, 39(1), 53–60.

Urquhart, C. (2011). Meta-synthesis of research on information seeking behavior. Information Research, 16(1). Retrieved from http://www.informationr.net/ ir/16-1/paper455.html

Vakkari, P. (2008). Trends and approaches in information behaviour research. Information Research, 13(4). Retrieved from http://www.informationr.net/ir/13-4/paper361.html

Wilson, T. (1999). Models in information behavior research. Journal of Documentation, 55(3), 249–270.

Yang, M., & Marchionini, G. (2004). Exploring users' video relevance criteria – A pilot study. In Proceedings of the Annual Meeting of the Association for Information Science and Technology, Silver Spring, MD.

# Awareness and Usage of Altmetrics: A User Survey

**Htet Htet Aung**
*Centre for HEalthy and Sustainable CitieS (CHESS), Nanyang Technological University, Singapore. hhaung@ntu.edu.sg*

**Yin-Leng Theng**
*Centre for HEalthy and Sustainable CitieS (CHESS), Nanyang Technological University, Singapore. TYLTheng@ntu.edu.sg*

**Mojisola Erdt**
*Centre for HEalthy and Sustainable CitieS (CHESS), Nanyang Technological University, Singapore. Mojisola.Erdt@ntu.edu.sg*

## ABSTRACT

**As the way of evaluating research outputs has gradually changed, and the dissemination of scholarly materials online has gotten easier, research studies investigating the awareness and usage of social media in academia have also been on the rise. The number of user surveys on the awareness and usage of altmetrics (emerging alternative metrics based on social media) has, however, remained low. This paper presents the findings of an online survey, which are the results of the first phase data collection of a user survey on the awareness and usage of altmetrics in academia. Our findings show that article views and downloads from online digital libraries or repositories are very well-known. The most used altmetrics are mentions and shares on social networks. Mentions in blog posts and topics in a forum are also popular altmetrics. Interestingly, this study reveals a tendency for non-faculty staff to be more aware of altmetrics. Furthermore, we also investigate how the usage of social media correlates with the usage of altmetrics. The findings show medium to large correlations between the usage of social media and the usage of altmetrics, which means academics who use social media often, also tend to use altmetrics often.**

## KEYWORDS

altmetrics, awareness, usage, survey, social media

## INTRODUCTION

In research on the evaluation of scholarly communication, many useful metric tools and impact measures have been proposed and investigated to determine the impact of research outputs, such as academic journals, articles and authors; among such tools are the Journal Impact Factor (JIF), the Immediacy Index, and the EigenFactor. In addition, databases such as Scopus (https://www. scopus.com) and Web of Science (http://wokinfo.com), also provide metrics such as the number of citation counts or the number of publications, with the aim to identify how well an author or article has contributed to or is perceived by the scholarly community (Bar-Ilan et al., 2012).

In earlier investigations, the perception of researchers on peer review of data and publications has been studied (Kratz & Strasser, 2015). The study pointed out that among traditional metrics, citation counts was observed as the most effective tool to measure the impact of a research article. Another international study that measured the attitudes of researchers toward peer review revealed that researchers consider peer review as the most imperative evaluation process in scholarly research (Mulligan, Hall & Raphael, 2013).

However, a few drawbacks of traditional metrics have been pointed out over the decades. For example, Haustein and Siebenlist (2011) and Schloegl and Stock (2004) revealed that citation counts are a bit restrictive in that they capture only the author's perspective. Haustein (2012) also pointed out that traditional citation counts need to consider the non-academic audience. Moreover, another major limitation of citation counts is their slow speed or lack of timeliness, as it can take a few years for a newly published article to be first cited (Sud & Thelwall, 2014).

Over the last decade, with the emergence of Web 2.0 tools and the popularity of electronic journals, the methods of disseminating research articles have changed, and scholarly communication is occurring increasingly on social media (Gu & Widén-Wulff, 2011). To supplement the traditional ways of measuring research outputs, usage metrics, such as article downloads and views, emerged (Bollen, Van De Sompel, Smith & Luce, 2005; Schloegl & Gorraiz, 2011). Alternative metrics, which are new metrics based on social media platforms, are often called *altmetrics* (Priem, Taraborelli, Groth & Neylon, 2010). Altmetrics aim to provide a holistic approach to measuring the impact of research outputs.

As such, the interest and popularity of social media in academia has been growing, with several studies already measuring the usage of social media and altmetrics in academia (Sugimoto, Work, Larivière & Haustein, 2016). It has even been suggested that social media may eventually play a role in academic tenure and promotion (Gruzd, Staves & Wilk, 2011). Although researchers generally tend to view social

80th Annual Meeting of the Association for Information Science & Technology, Washington, DC | Oct. 27-Nov. 1, 2017

media positively, there are still barriers to using social media in academia, as the exact benefits to the researcher are not always clear (Rowlands, Nicholas, Russel, Canty & Watkinson, 2011). Altmetrics however face several challenges such as the inconsistency and lack of normalization of altmetrics, as well as attempts to manipulate the counts (Wouters & Costas, 2012). Another challenge is the heterogeneous nature of altmetric data sources (Haustein, 2016). The definition of altmetrics also remains a challenge and there is still no consensus over the scope of the definition (Glänzel & Gorraiz, 2015). In this paper, we apply a broader definition of altmetrics to include article views and downloads from online digital libraries or repositories.

## RESEARCH QUESTIONS

With the aim to complement these investigations of the usage of social media in academia and contribute to existing research on altmetrics, our study investigates the awareness and usage of altmetrics and the relationship between the usage of social media tools and the usage of altmetrics of *faculty staff* (professors, associate professors, assistant professors, instructors and lecturers) and *non-faculty staff* (research staff, librarians, research students and others). Therefore, the following research questions are addressed in this study:

**RQ1:** To what extent are academics aware of altmetrics? Of those who are aware of altmetrics, how often do they use altmetrics? Are faculty staff more aware of altmetrics than non-faculty staff?

**RQ2:** How does the usage of social media correlate with the usage of altmetrics?

In the following sections, we present related work, the methodology we used in this study and the results that aim to answer the research questions. We then discuss the results, limitations of this study and conclude with future work.

## RELATED WORK

Recently, the state-of-the-art on the usage of social media and altmetrics in academia was analysed in an extensive literature review (Sugimoto, Work, Larivière & Haustein, 2016). The findings show that several large-scale surveys report a high usage of social media platforms (up to 75% to 80% of researchers). The studies, however, investigate very diverse social media tools and report varying results on usage (Sugimoto, Work, Larivière & Haustein, 2016).

A study of 2,414 researchers shows that 63% of researchers actively use collaborative authoring tools, whereby nearly half of them use Google Docs (https://docs.google.com), and more than a third use Wikipedia (https://www.wikipedia.org). Of the 48% of researchers actively using conferencing tools, the majority use Skype (https://www.skype.com). 41% of the researchers say they use scheduling and meeting tools, with quite a few of them using Google Calendar (https://calendar.google.com) and Doodle (http://doodle.com). 27% say they use social networking tools, Facebook (https://www.facebook.com) being the most popular, followed by LinkedIn (https://www.linkedin.com). 23% use image or video sharing, whereby the majority say they use YouTube (https://www.youtube.com), others say they use Slideshare (http://www.slideshare.net), as well as Flickr (https://www.flickr.com). 15% of the researchers claim to be active bloggers, using WordPress (http://wordpress.com) and Blogger (http://blogger.com). Only 9% say they actively use microblogging, whereby most say they use Twitter (https://twitter.com). Social tagging and bookmarking tools such as Delicious (http://delicious.com) or CiteULike (http://citeulike.org) were used by only 9%. Furthermore, the usage of microblogging had a correlation of 0.46 with blogging and 0.42 with social networking (Rowlands, Nicholas, Russel, Canty & Watkinson, 2011).

Another survey of 2,117 researchers across six UK universities finds that most UK academics use at least one or more social media tools. Nearly half of them say they use blogs and read user comments in online articles. More than half of them say they use online videos/ YouTube. About a third of them use podcasts, and fewer use RSS and Twitter feeds. Furthermore, it was found that researchers who use blogs, online videos and podcasts tend to read more books and other publications. Twitter users tend to read more of all scholarly materials. Participants in user comments in online articles read more articles and other publications, but fewer books (Tenopir, Volentine & King, 2013).

Focusing more on social networking tools for researchers, a survey of over 3,000 scientists and engineers shows that the majority are aware of Google Scholar (https://scholar.google.com), ResearchGate (https://www.researchgate.net), LinkedIn, Facebook Google+ (https://plus.google.com) and Twitter. The intensity of usage of these sites was, however, very varied, with slightly over 60% visiting Google Scholar regularly, whereas only slightly more than 10% visit Twitter regularly. Slightly less than half of the respondents were aware of Mendeley (https://www.mendeley.com) and 29% of Academia.edu (https://www.academia.edu). There were multiple reasons for using these sites, for example, to maintain a scholarly profile, to track metrics, to discover jobs, peers and recommended papers, to follow discussions, to actively discuss and comment on research, to post and share links to content, to be contacted and to contact peers or simply for curiosity only (Van Noorden, 2014).

With the rapid rise in the usage of social media among the scholarly community, not only publications, but also diverse research outputs such as datasets, presentation slides, images, patents, etc., have been made available online, and altmetrics play an increasingly important role in measuring these research outputs. Thus, academic communities including both individual researchers and librarians, as well as organizations such as research institutes and funding agencies, have changed their way of evaluating research outputs. For example, in 2013, the U.S. National Science Foundation (NSF) started the practice of including non-traditional research products produced by principal investigator in assessing research grant proposals (Piwowar, 2013).

Since many social media data sources allow researchers to disseminate and share their scholarly content, comment and discuss with each other, they have more opportunities to introduce their work outside of academic boundaries. Some studies report different data sources, for example, Wikipedia (Nielsen, 2007), Twitter (Desai et al., 2012; Priem & Costello, 2010; Shuai, Pepe & Bollen, 2012), F1000, CiteULike, Mendeley, Connotea and BibSonomy (Bar-Ilan et al., 2012; Haustein & Siebenlist, 2011; Li & Thewall, 2012). Moreover, many altmetrics studies have been done to assess and evaluate research impact. Priem and Hemminger (2010) consolidated the list of research assessment tools such as microblogging, reference managers, bookmarking, recommender systems, Wikipedia, etc. Li, Thelwall and Giustini (2011) also discussed Mendeley and CiteULike for evaluation of scholarly impact. The authors also investigated the correlations between readership counts of two reference managers and WoS citation counts and showed significant results.

The focus of altmetrics research in earlier investigations was mostly to determine the correlation between citation counts and altmetrics (Thelwall, Haustein, Larivière & Sugimoto, 2013; Costas, Zahedi & Wouters, 2014). A meta-analysis of altmetrics research found that there is a small to medium correlation between citation counts and most altmetrics (Erdt, Nagarajan, Sin & Theng, 2016). Thelwall, Haustein, Larivière and Sugimoto (2013) compared 11 alternative metrics (*tweets, Facebook wall posts, research highlights, blogs, google+, mainstream media citation count, reddits, forums, Q&A, pinterest and LinkedIn*) with Web of Science citations. The study found out some statistically significant correlations in six of the 11 altmetrics, and authors pointed out the effect of time in article ranking that would affect the relationship between article metrics and citations. The association between early downloads of articles and later citations was also investigated and some correlation found (Brody, Harnad & Carr, 2006; Watson, 2009).

A survey of bibliometricians' points of view on the potential of altmetrics revealed that downloads and views of articles were considered to have the most potential as altmetric indicators (Haustein et al., 2014). Another user survey of 860 Mendeley users revealed the use of bookmarking counts in Mendeley as a possible indicator of readership (Mohammadi, Thelwall & Kousha, 2016). 87% of survey respondents reported using Mendeley as a reference manager and the majority of them across most disciplines also stated that they bookmarked articles in Mendely for later reference and possible citation. As a complement to existing studies on the awareness and usage of social media in academia and other works on altmetric research, in this study we investigated the awareness and usage of altmetrics in academia and the relationship between using social media tools and altmetrics.

## METHODOLOGY

### Study Design

To understand the awareness and usage of altmetrics in academia, the targeted sample for this study was academics. For the study, we categorised faculty as professors, associate professors, assistant professors, instructors and lecturers, while non-faculty comprised research staff, librarians, research students and others. An online survey was distributed by email to both faculty and non-faculty staff employed at universities. Before conducting the actual survey, we conducted a pilot study with six researchers from different disciplines, to assess if the questionnaire was understandable. From the findings of this pilot study, we modified the questionnaire according to the comments and feedback we received during the pilot study. The Research Support Office at Nanyang Technological University approved the ethics proposal for this study in July 2016. This study is the first phase of a user survey investigating the awareness and usage of altmetrics and traditional metrics in academia. The data collection period for this first phase study was a five-month period from August to December 2016. No incentive was given to participants during this data collection period.

### Survey Instruments

Following a thorough literature review and insightful feedback from experienced researchers, a structured questionnaire was designed to investigate the awareness and usage of altmetrics. The demographic information and general research related questions such as career level, years of experience in academia, academic discipline, gender and age were also collected. In this study, "awareness" was assessed as having heard, seen or read about altmetrics in evaluating research articles or researchers (a binary yes or no question). The frequency of usage was measured on a 5-point Likert scale with "1" being never and "5" being always. The question on frequency of usage was asked only if the participants said "yes" to being aware of altmetrics. Furthermore, the social media usage of the participants was also investigated. The list of altmetrics was inspired by the categories of research metrics by Plum Analytics[1] (*usage, captures, mentions, social media and citations*) and list of events on social media tracked by altmetric aggregators (Erdt, Nagarajan, Sin & Theng, 2016).

## RESULTS

In this section, the descriptive statistics of participants in the survey is presented, followed by the results for RQ1 and RQ2. Discussion of results and limitation of this study are discussed thereafter.

### Survey Participants

A total of 85 academics participated in the survey. Most participants were from Asian (38.8%) and European (38.8%) countries. Of the survey participants, 67.1% were male and 32.9% were female. 71.8% of the participants were below 45

[1] http://plumanalytics.com/learn/about-metrics/. Accessed 21 July 2017.

| | | Count | % |
|---|---|---|---|
| **Gender** | Male | 57 | 67.1 |
| | Female | 28 | 32.9 |
| **Age** | 25 years and below | 1 | 1.2 |
| | 26-35 years | 29 | 34.1 |
| | 36-45 years | 31 | 36.5 |
| | 46-55 years | 11 | 12.9 |
| | 56-65 years | 12 | 14.1 |
| | 66 years and above | 1 | 1.2 |
| **Academic Discipline** | Science | 45 | 52.9 |
| | Social Science | 34 | 40.0 |
| | Arts & Humanities | 6 | 7.1 |
| **Career Level** | **Faculty:** | | |
| | Professor | 16 | 18.8 |
| | Associate Professor | 14 | 16.5 |
| | Assistant Professor | 13 | 15.3 |
| | Instructor | 2 | 2.4 |
| | Lecturer | 4 | 4.7 |
| | **Non-faculty:** | | |
| | Research Staff | 21 | 24.7 |
| | Others | 15 | 17.6 |
| **Years of Experience** | Less than 5 years | 32 | 37.6 |
| | 5-10 years | 24 | 28.2 |
| | 11-15 years | 12 | 14.1 |
| | 16 years and above | 17 | 20.0 |
| **Region** | Asia | 33 | 38.8 |
| | Europe | 33 | 38.8 |
| | North America | 11 | 12.9 |
| | Africa | 5 | 5.9 |
| | South America | 2 | 2.4 |
| | Oceania | 1 | 1.2 |

***Table 1.*** *Demographics of survey participants (N=85)*

years of age and slightly more than half (52.9%) were from the sciences discipline, followed by social sciences with 40.0%, and arts and humanities with 7.1%. 62.3% of the participants indicated that they had had more than 5 years of experience in academia. This could be due to most participants being faculty: professors (18.8%), associate professors (16.5%), assistant professors (15.3%), instructors (2.4%) and lecturers (4.7%). The remaining were research staff (24.7%) and others (17.6%). The demographic information of the participants is in Table 1.

Figure 1 shows the usage of social media by the participants. YouTube is the most popular social media channel, followed by Wikipedia, LinkedIn and ResearchGate. Among social media channels, 25.9% of participants always use Wikipedia while 20.0% and 17.6% of participants always use YouTube and Facebook, respectively. In general, more than half of the participants use blogs, SlideShare, Google+, Mendeley, Academia.edu, Twitter and Vimeo. Interestingly, academic social media platforms are also used by most participants, ResearchGate (83.5%), Mendeley (54.1%) and Academia.edu (52.9%). However, more than 90% of the participants have never used F1000 (90.6%), Publons (91.8%), Sina Weibo (94.1%) nor Connotea (97.6%). The purpose of using social media channels was not asked in this question.

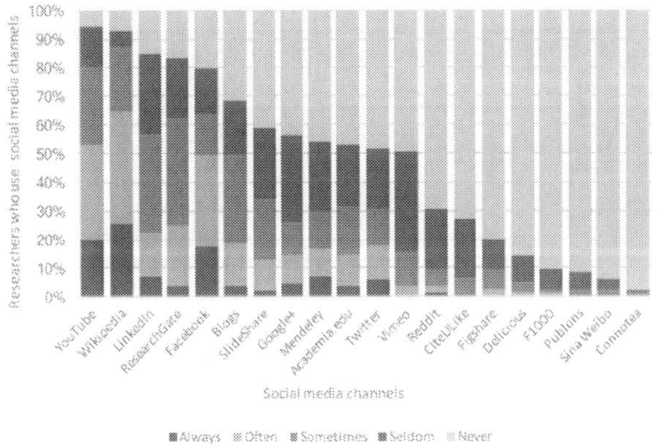


***Figure 1.*** *Social media usage (N=85)*

### *Results of RQ1*

The awareness and usage of altmetrics were investigated in RQ1. Participants who did not answer the question on the awareness of altmetrics were excluded from the analysis, thus a total of 78 participants were analysed. The findings for the awareness of altmetrics are presented in Figure 2. Among the different metrics, participants (78.2%) are most aware of A1 "Number of article views/downloads from online digital libraries/repositories," followed by A2 "Number of readers of articles" (60.3%) and A3 "Number of followers of researchers" (51.3%). More than a quarter of the participants were aware of metrics measured on social networks such as A5 "Number of 'Likes' on social networks" (43.6%), A8 "Number of 'Shares' on social networks" (37.2%), A13 "Number of comments on social networks" (33.3%) and A14 "Number of mentions on social networks" (29.5%).

Furthermore, a chi-square test for independence with Yates' Continuity Correction was applied to investigate if there is any association between the awareness of altmetrics and faculty and non-faculty staff (that is, are faculty more aware of altmetrics than non-faculty staff?). The results are shown in Table 2. Interestingly, the test revealed that non-faculty staff generally have heard more, seen more or read more about altmetrics in evaluating researchers or research outputs than faculty staff. Specifically, non-faculty staff (56.3%) are more likely to be aware of A6 "Number of video plays" than faculty staff (28.3%) with $\chi^2$ (1, N=78) = 5.06, $p$<.05. Non-faculty staff were more aware than faculty staff in several other altmetrics as well, such as A3 "Number of followers of researchers" with $\chi^2$ (1, N=78) = 10.66, $p$<.01, A17 "Number of exports or saves to online digital libraries" with $\chi^2$ (1, N=78) = 4.06, $p$<.05, A18 "Wikipedia mentions/links" with $\chi^2$ (1, N=78) = 5.13, $p$<.05, A15 "Number of recommendations received" with $\chi^2$ (1, N=78) = 4.21, $p$<.05, and A8 "Number of shares on social networks" with $\chi^2$ (1, N=78) = 4.81, $p$<.05.

| | Altmetrics | Academic Staff | Awareness | | Continuity Correction | p |
|---|---|---|---|---|---|---|
| | | | Yes | No | | |
| A1 | Number of article views/downloads from online digital libraries/repositories | Faculty<br>Non-faculty | 35 (76.1%)<br>26 (81.3%) | 11 (23.9%)<br>6 (18.8%) | .07 | .79 |
| A2 | Number of readers of articles | Faculty<br>Non-faculty | 23 (50.0%)<br>24 (75.0%) | 23 (50.0%)<br>8 (25.0%) | 3.94 | .05 |
| A3 | Number of followers of researchers | Faculty<br>Non-faculty | 16 (34.8%)<br>24 (75.0%) | 30 (65.2%)<br>8 (25.0%) | 10.66 | <.01 |
| A4 | Number of subscribers in media sharing sites (e.g., YouTube) | Faculty<br>Non-faculty | 18 (39.1%)<br>16 (50.0%) | 28 (60.9%)<br>16 (50.0%) | .52 | .47 |
| A5 | Number of 'Likes' on social networks | Faculty<br>Non-faculty | 16 (34.8%)<br>18 (56.3%) | 30 (65.2%)<br>14 (43.8%) | 2.72 | .10 |
| A6 | Number of video plays | Faculty<br>Non-faculty | 13 (28.3%)<br>18 (56.3%) | 33 (71.7%)<br>14 (43.8%) | 5.06 | .02 |
| A7 | Number of tweets and re-tweets | Faculty<br>Non-faculty | 15 (32.6%)<br>15 (46.9%) | 31 (67.4%)<br>17 (53.1%) | 1.08 | .30 |
| A8 | Number of 'Shares' on social networks | Faculty<br>Non-faculty | 12 (26.1%)<br>17 (53.1%) | 34 (73.9%)<br>15 (46.9%) | 4.81 | .03 |
| A9 | Number of reviews | Faculty<br>Non-faculty | 14 (30.4%)<br>14 (43.8%) | 32 (69.6%)<br>18 (56.3%) | .93 | .33 |
| A10 | Number of favorites on media sharing sites (e.g., YouTube) | Faculty<br>Non-faculty | 13 (28.3%)<br>14 (43.8%) | 33 (71.7%)<br>18 (56.3%) | 1.38 | .24 |
| A11 | Ratings for articles | Faculty<br>Non-faculty | 12 (26.1%)<br>15 (46.9%) | 34 (73.9%)<br>17 (53.1%) | 2.74 | .10 |
| A12 | Number of bookmarks | Faculty<br>Non-faculty | 11 (23.9%)<br>15 (46.9%) | 35 (76.1%)<br>17 (53.1%) | 3.50 | .06 |
| A13 | Number of comments on social networks | Faculty<br>Non-faculty | 13 (28.3%)<br>13 (40.6%) | 33 (71.7%)<br>19 (59.4%) | .80 | .37 |
| A14 | Number of mentions on social networks | Faculty<br>Non-faculty | 10 (21.7%)<br>13 (40.6%) | 36 (78.3%)<br>19 (59.4%) | 2.39 | .12 |
| A15 | Number of recommendations received | Faculty<br>Non-faculty | 9 (19.6%)<br>14 (43.8%) | 37 (80.4%)<br>18 (56.3%) | 4.21 | .04 |
| A16 | Number of mentions in blog posts | Faculty<br>Non-faculty | 10 (21.7%)<br>12 (37.5%) | 36 (78.3%)<br>20 (62.5%) | 1.60 | .21 |
| A17 | Number of exports or saves to online digital libraries | Faculty<br>Non-faculty | 8 (17.4%)<br>13 (40.6%) | 38 (82.6%)<br>19 (59.4%) | 4.06 | .04 |
| A18 | Wikipedia mentions/links | Faculty<br>Non-faculty | 7 (15.2%)<br>13 (40.6%) | 39 (84.8%)<br>19 (59.4%) | 5.13 | .02 |
| A19 | Number of topics in a forum | Faculty<br>Non-faculty | 5 (10.9%)<br>6 (18.8%) | 41 (89.1%)<br>26 (81.3%) | .43 | .51 |

***Table 2.*** *Chi-Square tests for awareness of altmetrics among faculty and non-faculty staff*

*NFaculty = 46, NNon-faculty = 32*

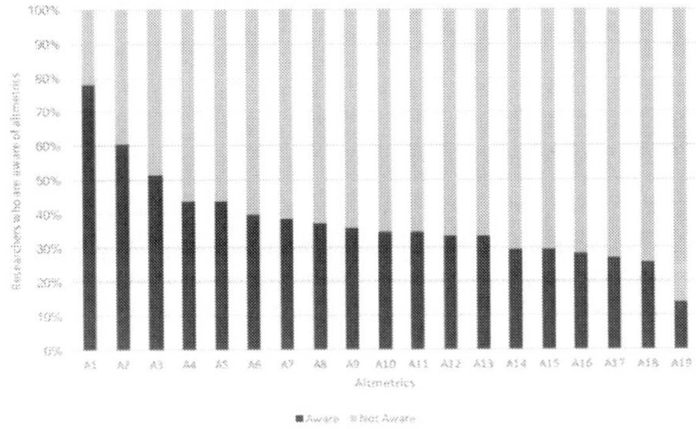


***Figure 2**. Awareness of altmetrics (N=78)*

*A1: Number of article views/ downloads from online digital libraries/ repositories; A2: Number of readers of articles; A3: Number of followers of researchers; A4: Number of subscribers in media sharing sites (e.g., YouTube); A5: Number of 'Likes' on Social Networks; A6: Number of video plays; A7: Number of tweets and re-tweets; A8: Number of 'Shares' on Social Networks; A9: Number of reviews; A10: Number of favorites on media sharing sites (e.g., YouTube); A11: Ratings for articles; A12: Number of bookmarks; A13: Number of comments on Social Networks; A14: Number of mentions on Social Networks; A15: Number of recommendations received; A16: Number of mentions in blog posts; A17: Number of exports or saves to online digital libraries; A18: Wikipedia mentions/ links; A19: Number of topics in a forum.*

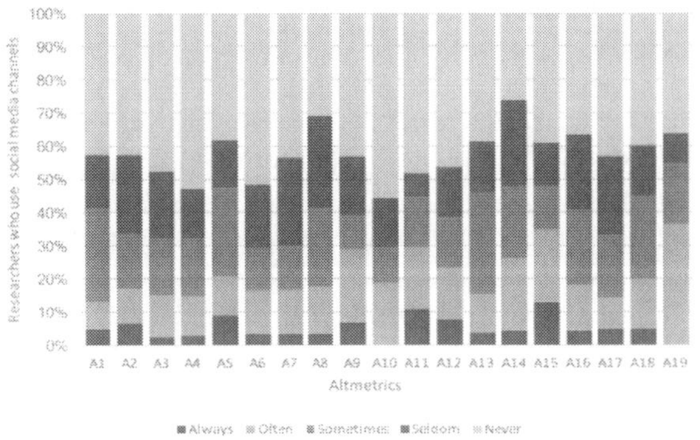


***Figure 3**. Usage of individual altmetrics*

*A1(N=61): Number of article views/ downloads from online digital libraries/ repositories; A2(N=47): Number of readers of articles; A3(N=40): Number of followers of researchers; A4(N=34): Number of subscribers in media sharing sites (e.g., YouTube); A5(N=34): Number of 'Likes' on Social Networks; A6(N=31): Number of video plays; A7(N=30): Number of tweets and re-tweets; A8(N=29): Number of 'Shares' on Social Networks; A9(N=28): Number of reviews; A10(N=27): Number of favorites on media sharing sites (e.g., YouTube); A11(N=27): Ratings for articles; A12(N=26): Number of bookmarks; A13(N=26): Number of comments on Social Networks; A14(N=23): Number of mentions on Social Networks; A15(N=23): Number of recommendations received; A16(N=22): Number of mentions in blog posts; A17(N=21): Number of exports or saves to online digital libraries; A18(N=20): Wikipedia mentions/ links; A19(N=11): Number of topics in a forum.*

Figure 3 shows the results of the usage of altmetrics. The question on the usage of altmetrics is asked only if the respondent is aware of a specific metric (i.e., answered with "yes"). Thus, the number of participants for each metric is based on the number of participants who say they were aware of that metric, and this varies accordingly. The most popular altmetric used by 73.9% of participants is A14 (N=23) "Number of mentions on social networks," followed by 69.0% using A8 (N=29) "Number of 'Shares' on social networks." A16 (N=22) "Number of mentions in blog posts" and A19 (N=11) "Number of topics in a forum" were also used often by 63.6% of participants. A10 (N=27) "Number of favorites on media sharing sites (e.g., YouTube)" was least popular with only 44.4% using this, and no one claiming to use it always.

### Results of RQ2

Spearman correlations between the usage of individual altmetrics and the usage of social media channels were calculated to address RQ2. The interpretation of the correlation results follow the guidelines of Cohen (1988), where the correlation value r=.10 to .29 is considered small, .30 to .49 medium, and .50 to 1.0 large correlations, being either positive or negative. The statistical significance levels are reported at **p<.01 and *p<.05. The results are presented in Table 3.

Participants are most aware of A1 (N=61) "Number of article views/downloads from online digital libraries/ repositories" and shows a medium correlation (r=.35, p<.01) with using social media. The second altmetric participants are most aware of is A2 (N=47) "Number of readers of articles." This also shows a medium correlation (r=.34, p<.05) with social media usage. The most popular altmetric used by most participants is A14 (N=23) "Number of mentions on social networks" and shows a medium correlation (r=.48, p<.05) with social media usage. The second most used altmetric A8 (N=29) "Number of 'Shares' on social networks" shows a large correlation (r=.58, p<.01) with using social media. A16 (N=22) "Number of mentions in blog posts" showed the largest correlation (r=.68, p<.01) with using social media. Followed by A11 (N=27) "Ratings for articles" (r=.66, p<.01), A18 (N=20) "Wikipedia mentions/links" (r=.62, p<.01), and A13 (N=26) "Number of comments on Social Networks" (r=.61, p<.01). A15 (N=23) "Number of recommendations received" (r=.54, p<.01), and A5 (N=34) "Number of 'Likes' on social networks" (r=.51, p<.01) also had large correlations with using social media. Furthermore, medium correlations were observed between using social media and using A7 (N=30) "Number of tweets and re-tweets" (r=.44, p<.05), A17 (N=21) "Number of exports or saves to online digital libraries" (r=.44, p<.05), A4 (N=34) "Number of subscribers in media sharing sites (e.g., YouTube)" (r=.43, p<.05), and A3 (N=40) "Number of followers of researchers" (r=.35, p<.05).

### Discussion of Results

Interestingly, the altmetrics that academics have heard more, seen more or read more about were not the most used altmetrics. Also, rather surprisingly, our findings show that non-faculty staff (comprising research staff and others) are generally more aware of altmetrics, than faculty staff (professors, associate professors, assistant professors, instructors and lecturers). These findings would need to be further investigated with interviews.

The usage of social media, however, does correlate to a large extent with the usage of altmetrics. This means researchers and academics who frequently use social media tend to use altmetrics more often, and those who do not use social media often tend not to use altmetrics often. This could be a strong motivation to encourage the usage of social media in academia. To investigate this further, we also tested the Spearman correlation between the usage of individual altmetrics and the usage of individual social media channels. As expected, the usage of YouTube had a medium correlation (r=.49, p<.01) with the usage of related altmetrics such as A4 (N=34) "Number of subscribers in media sharing sites (e.g., YouTube)", and A10 (N=27) "Number of favorites on media sharing sites (e.g., YouTube) (r=.46, p<.05). Also, medium correlations were found between the usage of Facebook and the usage of A5 (N=34) "Number of 'Likes' on social networks" (r=.47, p<.01), A14 (N=23) "Number of mentions on social networks" (r=.45, p<.05), and A13 (N=26) "Number of comments on social networks" (r=.42, p<.05). Similarly, academics who use Twitter also use altmetrics such as A7 (N=30) "Number of tweets and re-tweets" (r=.55, p<.01) and A3 (N=40) "Number of followers of researchers" (r=.47, p<.01) more often. The usage of academic social media platforms such as Academia.edu and Mendeley also had medium to large correlations with the usage of most of the altmetrics.

| | Altmetrics | N | Spearman Correlation (r) with Social Media Usage |
|---|---|---|---|
| A1 | Number of article views/ downloads from online digital libraries/ repositories | 61 | .35** |
| A2 | Number of readers of articles | 47 | .34* |
| A3 | Number of followers of researchers | 40 | .35* |
| A4 | Number of subscribers in media sharing sites (e.g., YouTube) | 34 | .43* |
| A5 | Number of 'Likes' on social networks | 34 | .51** |
| A6 | Number of video plays | 31 | .03 |
| A7 | Number of tweets and re-tweets | 30 | .44* |
| A8 | Number of 'Shares' on social networks | 29 | .58** |
| A9 | Number of reviews | 28 | .15 |
| A10 | Number of favorites on media sharing sites (e.g., YouTube) | 27 | .26 |
| A11 | Ratings for articles | 27 | .66** |
| A12 | Number of bookmarks | 26 | .32 |
| A13 | Number of comments on social networks | 26 | .61** |
| A14 | Number of mentions on social networks | 23 | .48* |
| A15 | Number of recommendations received | 23 | .54** |
| A16 | Number of mentions in blog posts | 22 | .68** |
| A17 | Number of exports or saves to online digital libraries | 21 | .44* |
| A18 | Wikipedia mentions/links | 20 | .62** |
| A19 | Number of topics in a forum | 11 | .30 |

**p<.01 and *p<.05

***Table 3.** Spearman correlations between usage of individual altmetrics and overall usage of social media.*

Some unexpected results were also found in this analysis; for example, the usage of SlideShare and Reddit had correlations with most of the altmetrics. The correlations were medium to large for SlideShare and small to large for Reddit. Using SlideShare had the largest correlations with using A16 (N=22) "Number of mentions in blog posts" (r=.76, p<.01) and A18 (N=20) "Wikipedia mentions/links" (r=.76, p<.01). Large correlations were also found between the usage of Reddit and the usage of A15 (N=23) "Number of recommendations received" (r=.67, p<.01) and A16 (N=22) "Number of mentions in blog posts" (r=.67, p<.01). However, due to the small sample sizes, these findings must be interpreted with care. Thus, we would like to further investigate and delve deeper into the findings with a larger sample size that we hope will be collected during the second phase of the ongoing user survey.

We also conducted analyses of the awareness and usage of altmetrics considering discipline, age group and years of experience. However, the results were not very insightful as none or very few results were significant. This might be again due to the limited sample size in this study.

### *Limitations*

The responses from the participants in the study were self-reported answers to the questions asked, thus the accuracy of the answers depends on the participants' responses. A sample size of 78 is also rather small, and some of the altmetrics analysed had even smaller sample sizes, such as A19 (N=11) "Number of topics in a forum," thus no insights could be gained for this altmetric in this study. Furthermore, the breakdown by region was biased towards academics in Asia (38.8%) and Europe (38.8%), leaving the other regions (in particular, North America, with only 12.9%) inadequately represented, thus the findings from this study cannot be generalized and cannot be said to be representative of the academic population across all regions.

## CONCLUSION

In this paper, we present the results of a survey on the awareness and usage of altmetrics in academia. Our findings show a tendency for non-faculty staff to be more aware of altmetrics than faculty staff. We also find that views and downloads in digital libraries or repositories are the most well-known altmetric. The most used altmetrics are, however, mentions and shares on social networks. Furthermore, the findings revealed that the usage of social media correlates with the usage of most of the altmetrics, thus hinting that academics who use social media frequently tend to use altmetrics more often. Spearman correlation results showed medium to large significant correlations between the usage of social media and the usage of altmetrics, particularly with metrics based on social networks such as the number of "shares" on social networks and the number of comments on social networks.

We are currently running the second phase of the user survey investigating the awareness and usage of traditional metrics and altmetrics. We hope to attract a larger number of respondents by offering an incentive to participate in the survey. With a larger sample, we would be able to investigate further questions such as the effects of demographics, disciplinary and regional differences, as well as to analyse how researchers promote their research and barriers for not using metrics.

In future work, more in-depth interviews and surveys should be encouraged to gain a deeper insight into how altmetrics are being perceived and used for measuring research outputs. It would be beneficial to conduct a qualitative investigation into the perception on altmetrics, the problems encountered when using altmetrics and the opinions on disseminating research outputs on social media by the academic community (comprising researchers, librarians, funding agencies, etc.) to get a better understanding of how the evaluation of research outputs are perceived and used. Thus, we have started conducting semi-structured interviews with NTU researchers from different disciplines to complement the findings from our ongoing user survey.

## ACKNOWLEDGMENTS

This research is supported by the National Research Foundation, Prime Minister's Office, Singapore under its Science of Research, Innovation and Enterprise programme (SRIE Award No. NRF2014-NRF-SRIE001-019).

## REFERENCES

Bar-Ilan, J., Haustein, S., Peters, I., Priem, J., Shema, H., & Terliesner, J. (2012). Beyond citations: Scholars' visibility on the social web. *Proceedings of 17th International Conference on Science and Technology Indicators*, 52900, 98–109.

Bollen, J., Van De Sompel, H., Smith, J.A., & Luce, R. (2005). Toward alternative metrics of journal impact: A comparison of download and citation data. *Information Processing & Management, 41*(6), 1419– 1440.

Brody, T., Harnad, S., & Carr, L. (2006). Earlier web usage statistics as predictors of later citation impact. *Journal of the Association for Information Science and Technology, 57*(8), 1060-1072.

Cohen, J. (1988). Statistical power analysis for the behavioral sciences (2nd ed.) Hillsdale, New Jersey: Routledge.

Costas, R., Zahedi, Z. & Wouters, P. (2014). Do 'altmetrics' correlate with citations? Extensive comparison of altmetric indicators with citations from a multidisciplinary perspective. *Journal of the Association for Information Science and Technology*.

Desai, T., Shariff, A., Shariff, A., Kats, M., Fang, X., Christiano, C., & Ferris, M. (2012). Tweeting the meeting: An in-depth analysis of Twitter activity at Kidney Week 2011. *PloS one, 7*(7), e40253.

Erdt, M., Nagarajan, A., Sin, S.-C. J., & Theng, Y.-L. (2016). Altmetrics: An analysis of the state-of-the-art in measuring research impact on social media. *Scientometrics, 109*(2), 1117-1166.

Glänzel, W., Gorraiz, J. (2015). Usage metrics versus altmetrics: Confusing terminology? *Scientometrics*, 3(102), 2161-2164.

Gruzd, A., Staves, K., & Wilk, A. (2011). Tenure and promotion in the age of online social media. *Proceedings of the American Society for Information Science and Technology*, 48(1), 1-9.

Gu, F., & Widén-Wulff, G. (2011). Scholarly communication and possible changes in the context of social media: A Finnish case study. *Electronic Library*, 29(6), 762–776.

Haustein, S. (2016). Grand challenges in altmetrics: Heterogeneity, data quality and dependencies. *Scientometrics, 108*(1), 413-423.

Haustein, S. (2012). Multidimensional journal evaluation. Analyzing scientific periodicals beyond the impact factor. Berlin/Boston: De Gruyter Saur.

Haustein, S., & Siebenlist, T. (2011). Applying social bookmarking data to evaluate journal usage. *Journal of Informetrics*, 5(3), 446–457.

Haustein, S., Peters, I., Bar-Ilan, J., Priem, J., Shema, H., & Terliesner, J. (2014). Coverage and adoption of altmetrics sources in the bibliometric community. *Scientometrics, 101*(2), 1145-1163.

Kratz, J. E., & Strasser, C. (2015). Researcher perspectives on publication and peer review of data. *PLoS One, 10*(2), e0117619.

Li, X., & Thelwall, M. (2012). F1000, Mendeley and traditional bibliometric indicators. In *Proceedings of the 17th international conference on science and technology indicators* (Vol. 2, pp. 451-551).

Li, X., Thelwall, M., & Giustini, D. (2011). Validating online reference managers for scholarly impact measurement. *Scientometrics, 91*(2), 461-471.

Mohammadi, E., Thelwall, M., & Kousha, K. (2016). Can Mendeley bookmarks reflect readership? A survey of user motivations. *Journal of the Association for Information Science and Technology, 67*(5), 1198-1209.

Mulligan, A., Hall, L., & Raphael, E. (2013). Peer review in a changing world: An international study measuring the attitudes of researchers. *Journal of the American Society for Information Science and Technology*, 64(1), 132-161.

Nielsen, F. Å. (2007). Scientific citations in Wikipedia. *arXiv preprint arXiv:0705.2106.*

Piwowar, H. (2013). Altmetrics: Value all research products. *Nature, 493*(7431), 159-159.

Priem, J., & Costello, K. L. (2010). How and why scholars cite on Twitter. *Proceedings of the Association for Information Science and Technology, 47*(1), 1-4.

Priem, J., & Hemminger, B. H. (2010). Scientometrics 2.0: New metrics of scholarly impact on the social Web. *First Monday, 15*(7). Retrieved from http://firstmonday.org/ojs/index.php/fm/article/view/2874/2570%3e. Accessed on 18 July 2017.

Priem, J., Taraborelli, D., Groth, P., & Neylon, C. (2010). Altmetrics: A manifesto. Retrieved from http://altmetrics.org/manifesto. Accessed on 15 March 2017.

Rowlands, I., Nicholas, D., Russell, B., Canty, N., & Watkinson, A. (2011). Social media use in the research workflow. *Learned Publishing, 24*(3), 183-195.

Schloegl, C., & Gorraiz, J. (2011). Global usage versus global citation metrics: The case of pharmacology journals. *Journal of the American Society for Information Science and Technology*, *62*(2005), 161–170.

Schloegl, C., & Stock, W. G. (2004). Impact and relevance of LIS journals: A scientometric analysis of international and German-language LIS journals - Citation analysis versus reader survey. *Journal of the American Society for Information Science and Technology*, *55*(13), 1155–1168.

Shuai, X., Pepe, A., & Bollen, J. (2012). How the scientific community reacts to newly submitted preprints: Article downloads, twitter mentions, and citations. *PloS one*, *7*(11), e47523.

Sud, P., & Thelwall, M. (2014). Evaluating altmetrics. *Scientometrics*, *98*(2), 1131–1143.

Sugimoto, C. R., Work, S., Larivière, V., & Haustein, S. (2016). Scholarly use of social media and altmetrics: A review of the literature. *arXiv preprint* arXiv:1608.08112.

Tenopir, C., Volentine, R., & King, D. W. (2013). Social media and scholarly reading. *Online Information Review*, *37*(2), 193-216.

Thelwall, M., Haustein, S., Larivière, V. & Sugimoto, C. R. (2013). Do altmetrics work? Twitter and ten other social web services. *PLOS ONE*, *8*(5), e64841.

Van Noorden, R. (2014). Scientists and the social network. *Nature*, 512(7513), 126-129.

Watson, A. B. (2009). Comparing citations and downloads for individual articles at the Journal of Vision. *Journal of Vision*, *9*(4), i-i.

Wouters, P., & Costas, R. (2012). Users, narcissism and control: Tracking the impact of scholarly publications in the 21st century. *SURFfoundation Utrecht*.

# "It Lives All Around Us": Aspects of Data Literacy in Teen's Lives

**Leanne Bowler**
*University of Pittsburgh, USA. lbowler@pitt.edu*

**Wei Jeng**
*National Taiwan University, Taiwan. wjeng@ntu.edu.tw*

**Amelia Acker**
*University of Texas at Austin, USA. aacker@ischool.utexas.edu*

**Yu Chi**
*University of Pittsburgh, USA. YUC73@pitt.edu*

## ABSTRACT

**In this paper, we examine young people's data literacy in terms of their awareness of data and the rhetoric that surrounds it, as well as their knowledge of data flows. This is the first phase of the Exploring Data Worlds at the Public Library research study research study, a two-year research study that explores the ways that libraries can address data literacy programming by helping teens understand, create and manage the digital traces of their data in meaningful, efficacious, and ethical ways. In this first phase of the study we explored the question *What do young people understand about data* within the context of their everyday lives and in relation to personal data management. We present here the findings from a series of semi-structured interviews with young people, ages 11 to 18, that examined teens' perceptions and general knowledge of data in their lives. Results suggest that the teens in this study had varying interpretations of the nature of data and a broad understanding of the lifecycle of data, but most found it difficult to connect with data at a concrete and personal level, with the notion of a personal data dossier either non-existent or abstract.**

## KEYWORDS

data science education, data awareness, data lifecycle, data literacy, social media, public libraries, user characteristics-adolescents

## INTRODUCTION

Today's young people are growing up in a data driven world, their personal histories and identities captured in the data traces left behind in their medical, educational and financial records and through their use of social media and wireless mobile devices. These data collections begin to accrue before birth, with the first ultrasound. As babies, their parents might monitor their sleep patterns through digital devices. Their toys – a doll perhaps – talk to them through the internet, leaving traces of robot/child interactions. Later, when children start school their learning will be recorded, as initiatives in the educational sector work toward mass data collection and analytics about student learning. Parents and family friends will add to a child's data dossier by publishing photos and information to social media services, and later, children will make their own contributions to their data footprint through social media, text messaging, mobile applications (apps), online games, learning machines and other digital activities. As they grow into adolescence they may acquire a variety of internet connected digital devices – from learning iPads in school to handheld gaming systems to smart phones connected to mobile broadband internet, embedded with powerful cameras, sensors and geolocation tools.

We report on this research by starting from the premise that all people, including youth, have data rights. Young people can therefore play a role in the construction and management of their personal data dossier and those who are aware of their digital subjectivity might nurture it better if they have a stronger sense of their data dispositions, which encompass a variety of ethical, civic and legal issues. We propose that the public library can play a role in helping young people navigate their complex data worlds, helping them to become data literate citizens. To achieve these outcomes, the Exploring Data Worlds at the Public Library research study research study aims to conceptualize and map out how public libraries can help young people, as data subjects, gain a sophisticated understanding of the data lifecycle, including the processes involved in data creation, collection and aggregation with networked devices, platforms and information services. These are all facets of data literacy – the capacity to understand, create and manage data in meaningful, efficacious and ethical ways.

A necessary first step in this process is to reveal what librarians and young people know and believe about data, to discover what preconceptions they bring to any conversation around data. In this paper, we focus specifically on the data awareness of young people (future work will explore the data awareness of teen librarians), excavating their thoughts in relation to the nature of data and the rhetoric associated with it, their knowledge of where data lives and how data flows. What do young people think about digital data? Do they understand how it is created, the purposes to which it is used, where it lives, how it travels, who owns it and who has access to it? Do they have the awareness and necessary agency needed to control their own data?

80th Annual Meeting of the Association for Information Science & Technology, Washington, DC | Oct. 27-Nov. 1, 2017

## BACKGROUND

### *Young People and Data*

Data, like information, is an ambiguous concept. In most discussions about data literacy, the "data" part is accepted to mean "numbers" or "quantified evidence." In the world of academic librarianship, data is often interpreted as the evidence to arise from research studies, frequently digital, often amassed in collections of big data and requiring complex digital curation skills (Koltay, 2015; ACRL, 2012; ACRL, 2014). Fontichiaro and Oehrili (2016), in an article introducing data literacy to K-12 school librarians, begin by associating data with numeric and quantitative information. But despite five centuries of usage, there is no consensus definition of *data* (Borgman, 2015, p. 28). Data is situated, taking its meaning from its context and the perspective of its beholder (Borgman, 2015, p. 18). Even its very classification as data can be contested and, as Ford (2015) notes, "the classification of a particular stimulus as data or information is relative, and depends on a person's perception of a meaningful pattern in the data. Thus, one person's data might be another's information and vice versa" (p. 13). What might be devoid of meaning for some has the potential to inform others. Clouds, to a skilled meteorologist who knows how to read cloud patterns, are highly informative and tell a story. To the rest of us, clouds just tell us if it will rain.

This leads us to ask the following: *In the everyday lives of young people, what might the term* data *mean?* This is an especially critical question, given young people's propensity to mediate much of their lives through digital, networked platforms that have the capacity to capture their every online interaction. These new forms of user-generated digital traces of online interactions with people and information objects, created consciously and unconsciously, collectively make up our virtual, quantified selves and suggest that a different stance on data is needed. Marchionini (2008) calls these new forms of user-created data "proflections of self" – digital data that emerges out of our everyday lives and which tells the world the story of us (p. 172). These are the data traces created with digital, networked platforms, often supported through internet connected digital devices and applications, created by the user or by external entities. Despite this vast enterprise, little is known about the effect of mass data collection on the long-term development of young people. Evidence suggests that there are consequences: From algorithmic biases to filter bubbles created through personalization, young people are encountering a world in which their personal digital data may serve to shape their opportunities and very identities (Friedman & Nissenbaum, 1996; Introna & Nissenbaum, 2000; Pariser, 2012; Sweeney, 2013; Zang, Dummit, Graves, Lisker & Sweeney, 2015).

Messages in popular media often suggest that young people are savvy data creators and consumers. The use of applications and devices that leave traces of data has, for young people, become a form of belonging in our networked society, engagement in the participatory environment of the online world being a necessary entrée to peer culture (Ahn, 2011; Agosto, Abbas & Naughton, 2012; boyd, 2014; Moore, 2016, Livingstone, 2014, Lenhart, 2015). However, research on young people's awareness of data is limited. While many social media researchers have examined what it means to grow up, flirt, make friends and get bullied with networked devices and social media platforms, few scholars have examined young people's understanding of their data worlds *through their data footprints*. We can infer from the research that young people do have a notion of how their digital data, by way of their online behavior, connects to their privacy and autonomy (Marwick & boyd, 2014). Nevertheless, young people need to develop a more nuanced understanding of data so they can participate more actively in the management of their personal data.

### *Data Literacy*

Data literacy is a new construct, its meaning still open to negotiation. Though there is a robust literature about digital youth and information literacy skills, data literacy is under-theorized and continues to be focused on more formal learning contexts. Situating data literacy in the context of personal data management gives young people a meaningful frame to apply as they work toward the development of analytic skills needed to create, collect, manage and curate datasets in their lives.

The skills and knowledge needed by young people to create and manage their own data will impact their interactions with, and access to, the participatory culture of the networked digital world of the 21st century. As part of this data-intensive world, teens (and their educators, families, the public) are increasingly in need of humanistic heuristics for interpreting the contexts of data creation and human activity. Such interpretive skills may include approaches such as "data habits of mind" (Finzer, 2013, p. 5); telling data stories; and on-going curation applications such as collecting, wrangling and cleaning data for future access and re-use. Looking for stories behind data can range from becoming more aware of the privacy issues of using wireless devices to the fragility and maintenance of digital machines.

Deahl (2014), in a master's thesis about youth data literacy (one of the few explorations into youth, data literacy and informal learning), argues that there is a wide disconnect between the data practices of government and corporations and the data skills, knowledge and level of awareness of the general public. Conversations about data literacy, she states, typically refer to college and professional education and rarely include the general public, let alone children and youth. Deahl makes the point that data literacy is a mix of both quantitative and qualitative data and is more than numeracy skills and computation. She defines data literacy for the public as the following: "Data literacy is the ability to understand, find, collect, interpret, visualize, and support arguments using quantitative and qualitative data" (p. 41). While targeting a specific set of data literacy competencies is important, Deahl suggests that simply raising an interest in data is an important outcome of any youth data literacy program.

Within the LIS literature, two approaches to data literacy exist – both situated within the world of academic libraries and higher education. Both approaches are relevant to the study of data subjects, but have yet to be tested among youth. Prado and Marzal's (2013, p. 130-131) map core data literacy competencies to a traditional information literacy framework that includes understanding data, finding and obtaining data, reading, interpreting and evaluating data, managing data and, finally, using data.

Carlson and Johnston (2015) present an alternative approach in their book, *Data Information Literacy: Librarians, Data, and the Education of a New Generation of Researchers*. This model is grounded entirely in the academic environment and, as the authors themselves note, is particular to the STEM disciplines. Their project set out to explore the role of the research library in supporting the data management and curation skills needed by graduate students who work with data. The authors worked directly with faculty and students to identify a set of 12 data information literacy (DIL) competencies that touch on a range of tool-based and theory-based competencies that map to the data lifecycle (discovery and acquisition of data, databases and formats, data conversion and interoperability, data processing and analysis, data visualization and representation, data management and organization, data quality and documentation, meta data and representation, and cultures of practice).

Carlson and Johnston's DIL model is one of the few (if not only) *empirical* models of data literacy that is situated within a library context. It is, however, in need of further elaboration. First of all, although the 12 DIL competencies are mapped to the data lifecycle, the framework has little to say about the actual creation of data. Yet, the evidence based upon youth engagement with digital platforms and ownership rates of mobile and personal computing devices marks this generation as the fastest growing segment of data creators. As researchers interested in how youth are generating and understand data about themselves (Marchionini's (2008) "proflections of self" category of information), this is a gap in the DIL model that needs to be explored further.

We suggest that work in the data literacy field needs to be done in the context of life wide learning beyond the academy. As well, Carlson and Johnston (2015) have argued that research should explore methods for delivering data management and curation instruction "just in time" and in meaningful ways (p. 244). A powerful platform for developing such meaningful experiences with data may be in the interest-driven, non-formal learning that happens in the context of youth libraries. In the world of non-formal learning, public libraries are already providing learning experiences with data through digital media labs and youth hackathons, albeit indirectly and not as a planned outcome (Deahl, 2014, p. 113).

## METHODOLOGY

### Data Collection

The research reported in this paper is part of the Exploring Data Worlds at the Public Library research study, a project investigating youth data literacy in the context of youth services at the public library. Results from the broader study, to be reported in future publications, will provide a preliminary framework to support the training of data literate youth librarians and the design of data literacy programs that are meaningful to young people and do-able within public library contexts. For purposes of this paper, however, we focus specifically on the results from a series of interviews with young people, ages 11 to 18, designed to answer the question, *what do young people understand about data?* Each interview lasted approximately 20 minutes.

The data used for analysis in this study are derived from the transcripts from 13 interviews with 22 young people. The interviews were conducted in three urban library branches at the Carnegie Library of Pittsburgh, in the "The Labs," the technology-based spaces for teens at the Carnegie Library of Pittsburgh, where teens hang out together to work on projects, homework or just play games and socialize. We offered teens the option to be interviewed individually or in groups. In the event, five of the interviews were with individual teens; the remaining eight were group interviews, with two to three teens at one time.

The interviews followed a semi-structured protocol that covered themes related to the meaning and rhetoric of data, data systems and flows, data agency and subjectivity, rights and values, data management skills and, finally, young people's views on the role of public library vis à vis data. These themes fit within a larger conceptual structure driving this project, which envisions data as an interplay between collections and community practices.

### Data Analysis

The interviews were transcribed verbatim and then carefully de-identified (e.g., real identifiers were replaced with pseudonyms). The analysis proceeded through five consecutive phases, each phase designed to gradually reduce the data to essential themes associated with teen data literacy. It is important to recall that the interview protocols, as noted above, had already imposed a thematic structure upon the interviews. As well, this paper focuses specifically on the coding related to awareness of data and data flows and associated metaphors for data. Future publications will investigate in greater detail the themes that circle around data management skills, privacy, agency and values, etc.

| Base Codes | Definition |
|---|---|
| Affective characteristics | Feelings and emotions associated with data. |
| Data lifecycle | Awareness or perception of data flows and the points it touches along the way, from creation to preservation. Includes awareness of data systems and the entities that have access to data. |
| Data representations | Literal representations of data (i.e., numbers, graphs and pie charts). When teens think of data what do they see, in concrete terms? Note: Figurative language expressing metaphor has its own category. |
| Identity | The self as a data subject, as represented in data or shaped by data. The self that is projected through data, whether it is the real self or not. |
| Information technology | Devices, platforms, services, software, apps |
| Locality | Data in relation to a place; a data situation that is related to place; can include virtual/digital spaces. |
| Metaphor | The figurative language that young people use to describe data. A form of analogous thinking that expresses abstract ideas or concepts and is often represented through text, speech or visually. |
| Privacy | Perceptions of personal autonomy, freedom from intrusion, ability to be apart. Or the opposite – a sense of being surveilled, watched over, followed, tracked. |
| Rights | A sense of justice and fairness; self-efficacy and a sense of agency with regard to data; beliefs about the ability to control the forces of data. |
| Skills & Aptitudes | Things that teens can do with data. Their perceptions of their natural abilities with regard to data. May be aligned with data management in the data lifecycle but also includes cross cutting skills and aptitudes (example: knowledge of privacy policy). May be related to specific IT. |
| Temporal | Characteristics related to time; a data situation related to time. |
| Values | Systems for judging the worth, importance or utility of data. Examples: Market values (i.e., commodification of data), social values, dark values, etc. |
| New Code | Open coding. |

***Table 1.*** *Coding framework for interview transcripts*

Before pilot coding, we assembled a list of primary observations to help guide coding. We then interrogated a sample set of two transcripts, allowing for both open coding and the application of a framework determined *a priori*: *What is data? Where is data? When is data? Why is data? Metaphors for data, Data makes me feel,* and *The absence of data awareness*. In the event, the coders found this framework to be too vague in that it didn't capture the essence of the data. On the other hand, open coding generated 215 codes. After debriefing and discussion, our team of four researchers regrouped these new codes to create a set of 12 base codes, but with the continued allowance for new codes to flag anomalous data not mapping to existing base codes. The final coding matrix is provided in Table 1.

Four researchers then divided the 13 interview transcriptions into two groups, such that each interview was analyzed and coded by two researchers. Under each of the base codes, we added a descriptive qualifier if needed. For example, after the base code "Skill," we might add "data visualization." Or after "Metaphor" we might add the word "cloud." While coding we also wrote extensive memos and then, after completing each transcript, wrote a summary note for each transcript. In the final stage of analysis, we reviewed the "base code" coding, the memos and summaries, looking for patterns and insights related to the particular focus of this paper – young peoples' perceptions and general knowledge of data and data flows.

## RESULTS

We present here our preliminary findings about what young people know and believe about data through three thematic lenses: young peoples' concrete understandings of data, the rhetoric that surrounds data as represented through metaphor and the systemic knowledge of data flows.

### What is Data? Young Peoples' Concrete Understandings of Data

When young people think of data, what do they see? Given that a consensus definition of data does not exist and further, data is generally interpreted through a contextual lens, we expected a wide range of responses when we asked young people the question "What is data?" The young people in this study, in fact, presented two distinct views of data.

Eleven of the 22 young people interviewed thought of data as numbers, as a form of evidence, sometimes as the tangible output of scientific inquiry, one teen explaining, "When I think of data, I thought of percentages of things. I thought of grades, like charts. Population, just the amount" (Larry, age 16). Another interviewee explained, "I feel that data is a quantitative measurement… it shows meaningful values and it is referenced a lot in research. I do a lot of science fairs and usually the winning projects have some type of significant data collection. It'll have a very nice table or graph or multiple graphs" (George, age 13).

As with George above, several young people saw data in terms of the structure within which numbers are presented – a graph, a pie chart, an Excel table or a more complex visualization. In other words, data is that which is processed, possibly reduced and ultimately presented in a visual structure rather than a raw, untreated entity that we call "the number." This fine distinction is probably not understood by young people (nor most of us who think of data) and represents a particular stance on what constitutes evidence.

References to science class or a science fair throughout suggest that this quantitative, evidentiary perspective on data is built upon school-based experiences with science. Given that, at least for these young people, the notion of data is inexorably linked to the science lab at school rather than out-of-school social contexts and behavior, one can see how it might be difficult to make a link between data and online behavior.

A second set of young people thought in terms of the internet, the digital traces we leave behind and surveillance. Seven of the 22 interviewees variously referenced big data, wifi, data plans, government and secret services. Adam (age 11) explained that data is "stuff that has been created and it's sent across [the internet] and everyone links to it, pretty much." Later, Adam also compared data to memory, referencing the amount of data available on a mobile device:

**Adam**: "Like on your phone, you have a certain amount of memory, so you can do a certain amount of stuff and it can remember a certain amount of the stuff you did."

Adam eventually cycled back to the idea that data is evidence, saying that he also thinks in terms of "data on the fact that this is wood. So, we have data on the fact that this is a table."

While most young people took one of two stances on data – that it is either a form of quantitative evidence or, a part of our internet activity – some did take an anomalous position. One teen, suggesting a broad-based, more colloquial meaning for data, said, "In the sort of vaguest, most spoken, informal sense, I would think of information and stuff like that" (Dana, age 15).

### Metaphors for Data

The section above described young people's concrete ideas about data. In this section, we explore the rhetoric of data through the metaphors – the figurative language – that young people use about data. Metaphors say one thing is something else in order to reveal the meaning of human experience (Lakoff & Johnson, 1980, Lakoff, 1993). Metaphor is a form of analogous thinking and the basic mechanism through which humans make sense of their world. To reveal the metaphor is to reveal the human mind. A verbal metaphor expresses abstract ideas or concepts that are represented through text or speech. Visual metaphors also express abstraction, but do so through the use of a visual display, such as a drawing, photograph or other form of visual art.

In the field of human information behavior, Cole and Leide (2006) use metaphor to reveal information seekers' cognitive models (p. 172). Hartel and Savolainen (2016) have explored the use of metaphors in understanding how students in information studies programs interpret the meaning of information. Bowler (in press) has used metaphor to expose the metamemory of teens in the context of information re-finding behavior. Following in this tradition of using metaphor to expose conceptual structures, we might then ask the following: What metaphors do young people use to to explain the meaning of data in their lives?

During our interviews, we asked versions of the question, "What are you picturing in your head as we talk about data?" At times, young people provided their own metaphors for data without prompting. Among the 22 teens we interviewed, only 10 were able to share a metaphor for data. These metaphors, however, indeed reveal what data means to young people.

Danny (age 17), Beth (15) and Cara (14) equated data with storage, as something that is located in a specific physical structure or container: "stacks of books," "storage systems for everything," "files and stuff" and "special buildings or something." This view demonstrates that underlying the metaphor is an understanding of the tangibility of data, but also, an idea that data is static and it "lives" in one place, organized like a library.

But others had non-traditional images of data. As Fatima (age 17) explains, "You know those old cartoons where they would go into the computer and then they'd kind of be traveling along in the web? That's what I think of" (One assumes she is talking about the television show, *The Magic School Bus*). Within this visual image of virtual space, there are a set of metaphors for data (cartoons, traveling as if in a vehicle) that are drawn from pop culture – movies and games – that speak to a vision of data that is a systemic but unfixed, changeable.

A movie informed the metaphor that Ginny (age 16) envisioned, clearly linking data to digital contexts. "I think of the Matrix with the green stuff just raining down," referencing the science fiction movie *The Matrix*, a story set within a simulated reality. To Ginny, data is about hacking and secret codes. Similarly, Fatima's (age 17) description of data was from a movie but a story about spies. She associates data with secrecy, encryption and hacking rather than the personal data generated through her own online behaviors:

**Fatima**: "There's this website that… It's like, Code something, and you just type and then… You can type in anything and it comes up in these spy movie codes or whatever. So you can be sitting in Starbucks and be like… And it looks like you're hacking into the government or something. So funny."

Henry (age 17), explaining a particular form of data – that which is created through social media – used the analogy of "the first date with a girl" to explain social media data in relation to privacy and personal information.

**Henry**: "You're on your first date, you're going to ask this girl… You're not going to be talking about personal information like that. You're going to be talking about, you're trying to expose who you are as a person socially, and your personality. Your address and your personal information, your social security card, that has nothing to do with you as a person."

This analogy shows that he sees a difference between his personal information (his real self) and his social-based data (his performed self). Posting data on social media is like a first date. You don't reveal everything about yourself.

As part of the generation most familiar with ubiquitous computing technologies, one might expect young people to have more elaborated understandings of data – at both the concrete and metaphoric levels. We found in general, the young people we interviewed did not hold complex understandings of data and most in fact, had rarely considered it beyond the data they generate in science class or the data plans that dictate their use of mobile apps. Only a small number of teens could think of data in metaphoric terms. Even fewer were those who could think in both metaphoric and concrete terms about data and where it lives (i.e., server banks, cell towers, inside a cell phone, stored by services, etc.). Kevin (age 14) was one teen who could. When asked the question – "Where's the cloud?" – he answered that the cloud lives in server banks. He then elaborated on the pathway that data takes from device to server. We were impressed that this young person had both a metaphoric and literal understanding of the internet – a more complex view of data. Where did he gain this understanding? Did they talk about this at school? In other words, as part of the curriculum. Kevin said no, this wasn't a topic covered at school but his "dad works a lot with data" and perhaps "he teaches me more about it, so I don't know if other people have the same level of understanding that I do."

### *Data Lifecycle: The Systemic Knowledge of Data Flows*

A broad theme from the interviews relates to teens' perceptions of the data lifecycle. Throughout the interviews we asked participants about their understandings of data creation and collection contexts, including how data flows, moves through infrastructure and is managed by companies, data brokers, information institutions (such as the library or high school); and in turn, how teens themselves manage their own data. Interviewers also asked participants about their understandings of their peers' perceptions of data culture and collections to discover some "known unknowns" with which our participants are familiar. Traditional interpretations of the data lifecycle focus on the creation and management of collections, particularly with regard to labeling and metadata for re-use in secondary applications, such as scientific research or scholarly publications. Further, most research on where people are inculcated into the data lifecycle process (like many other information literacy and data literacy programs) focuses on higher education contexts and the training of early-career scientists. Few studies examine teens' awareness of data management skills and the data lifecycle.

In analyzing our interview data, we found that teens had a broad understanding of the lifecycle of data, particularly the beginnings and ends of the cycle, but little knowledge of data flows and infrastructure. By data flows, we mean the ways in which data moves across different contexts, particularly in the ways in which it can be collected and connected from different accounts, platforms and devices. Many teens had strong associations, if less sophisticated, understandings about how the government collects metadata for surveillance and how surveillance programs and policing relates to user data collected as part of terms of service with platforms, such as mobile apps or social media like Snapchat or Twitter. Older teens mentioned how data can or is already collected for secondary use applications by the government, corporations for advertising and for targeting users in search platforms based on their use habits. For example, Kevin (age 14) explained that Amazon tracked shopping habits over time, but also expressed a temporal sense of how data can be collected and used in different contexts as well as over time. He illustrated this idea with an example of coursework:

**Kevin**: "[…] if you get a bad grade, it usually sticks with you for a while, and you can see all your grades and they, like…Colleges look all the way back."

In addition to how data moves across contexts, participants displayed varied, sometimes sophisticated awareness of how wireless devices connected to the internet support the creation of data and its storage in cloud storage services. However, these descriptions of networked technology were often followed by the "I don't know" mantra of novice users (and teens in general). When Isaac (age 17) and Henry (17) were asked to explain how data gets created as a result of networked communication, they describe the intrinsic nature of creating data traces as essential to the technology:

**Isaac**: […] it has to be in some form of technology it has to be in, in order for it to work.

**Henry**: It has to be recorded, created.

While some subjects had a general understanding of how extrinsic data is created as a result of wireless communication and the use of internet-connected platforms, there was a departure in explaining, and oftentimes a basic awareness of, the intrinsic nature of unique data creation and management contexts that are specific to individuals based on their online behavior and user habits. For many of our subjects, there appeared to be a distancing practice between the creation of data and its collection, which points to a lack of perception related to issues of ownership, identity and understanding of control in the creation of data traces in networked platforms. For most teens in our study, the notion of creating unique data dossiers in part or alongside a personal sense of self or subjectivity was an abstraction, brushed off and sometimes disregarded. Throughout their interview, Isaac and Henry claimed they had very little personal information or intrinsic data related to their selves as data subjects:

**Henry**: I don't even know. So how would data reflect me, as an individual? Data about myself. I don't think I can answer that. I know I give data, but…

**Isaac**: I don't have any data of myself, unless it's actual documents of myself, like my birth certificate, stuff like that. I don't have data about myself now.

While many subjects had a strong sense of where data is created (in user accounts, networked platforms, apps and devices), as well as the kinds of traces that data brokers collect about their habits (Amazon, Google Ads, YouTube), there was little understanding of data flows, wireless infrastructure or networked collections over the long term. Further, most teens had limited ideas about the possibilities of personal control over the long-term collections of data, and perhaps most disconcerting to us as researchers, very little expectation of privacy from data brokers and the government. This was evidenced by a number of jokes, illustrations and definitions throughout the interviews of "data collections" being enrolled in government surveillance programs.

Fatima (age 17), Ginny (16) and Hannah (18) expressed concerns that other teens had little understanding that online activities were being tracked and sold to advertising companies in the moment. Several teens throughout interviews expressed nuanced understandings of the commodification and valuation of data – in online market places, college applications and government surveillance contexts. However, a few of the teens expressed confusion about how data is valued and priced, especially with regard to mobile broadband internet access from mobile service providers. Interviewers often had to parse out definitions of data from mobile data plans (which are often referred to "data" or "unlimited data"). For example, when asked about his definition of data, Larry (age 16) says:

**Larry**: "I thought about it, because I often get confused with, like I said, data marketing, phone bills, data. I just get it confused."

Despite the confusion between data creation and data bandwidth, most teens were able to define bandwidth with an economic-based understanding of the pricing of network bandwidth, coming to their data flows definition with a market value understanding of access. This is likely because most American youth who own mobile devices are on shared family plans where data rates and access are throttled after a certain amount of data bandwidth has been consumed through a billing cycle, and it is not uncommon for families use bandwidth at different rates.

Some interviewees (Emma, age 14, Dana, 15, Fatima, 17, Ginny, 16, and Hannah, 18) described limited understandings of the length or liveliness of their digital footprints beyond the initial interaction with social media posts. Moreover, perceptions of control of the long-term data lifecycle were limited to surveillance contexts or departing (quitting) a platform and deleting a user account. A few respondents expressed conservative ideas about having a single online and offline persona. For example, George (age: 13) told an interview that people shouldn't change their views often:

**George**: I don't know, if you believe something… Like, I believe that the invasion of privacy is not such a big deal as long as you don't take severe action and like, the stuff that you say and do and if it's collected in data that you can present… You shouldn't be different things for different people, you know?

**Interviewer**: Okay, so you should be the same kind of person?

**George**: You should have a set opinion and you should know what you want and why you want it and stuff. Not change views very often.

This notion – of being a different person to different audiences – continues to be an area of development on the web as we move from web 2.0 technologies, to mobile computing and social network platforms that rely on users to be less and less anonymous. Other internet and social media researchers have observed this change from anonymous users to single identities as a result of real name policies, whereas, many social theorists have argued that online anonymity and the ability to change identities or amend ideas is one of the true innovations of the internet and social media, and that real name policies and the move away from anonymous browsing and usernames leads to chilling effects.

Perhaps it is no surprise that young adults who are creating their own identities and plans for the future of their lives have a strong sense of the creation beginnings of the lifecycle, but are unsure or wary of what will happen next with their data (I don't know). However, the lack of knowledge, or willingness to intervene into their own data dossiers after the point of creation is striking. A thorough understanding of the whole data lifecycle reveals opportunities for data subjects to craft new sense of self, privacy, agency and identity. A limited understanding and awareness of the data lifecycle, including opportunities for management, curation and preservation is proven out in these interviews, and, further, points to opportunities for young adult librarians to guide and focus programming to the stages of identification, description, curation and preservation.

## DISCUSSION

In this study, we explored what young people understand about data, with the goal of addressing the interpretive aspects of data, particularly with regard to the creation of personal data traces using internet-connected digital devices and platforms. We discovered that, while aware of the security issues related to social media, teens have spent little time thinking more broadly about the digital traces of their data and implications for their future selves.

Notions about data fell into two camps: data as the product of a scholarly enterprise or data as the digital traces of our online behavior. These various views on the nature of data have implications for youth data literacy. While associating data with scientific inquiry, evidence and facts, is a hopeful sign in these times of "fake news" and science skepticism, in terms of data literacy it is a rather narrow view and one which disassociates young people from their quantified selves. Ironically, our interviews do show that young people are well aware of the purposes and uses of social media data (i.e., personalization and marketing). Most simply don't connect these activities with the term *data*.

For the second group of young people who think of data in terms of the digital, networked world, this was sometimes in the context of their own data plans. In order to navigate a digital world without boundaries, young people need have access to data, and so a critical question for them is, *How much data do I have?* This focus on data shows a basic awareness that somewhere, somehow, the digital traces of our data are being measured. But does this concern with access to data translate to a concern for how other entities might interact with it? For some young people, yes. We found a repeated association between data, government, spying and surveillance. Interestingly, the idea that outsiders connect with our data was only rarely linked to entities such as families (parents or caregivers), schools or corporations. But while the teens in this study had a broad understanding of the lifecycle of data and a general concern about government looking at it, most found it difficult to connect with data at a concrete and personal level, with the notion of a personal data dossier either non-existent or abstract. This is a concern. When we are aware of data – when the nature of data is concrete, tangible, locatable – it then becomes something that we are more likely to manage to our own benefit.

Where then can teens learn about data? The role of schools vis à vis data, at least to the participants in this study, seems to be relegated to the arena of research data, not data dossiers. In one instance, a teen spoke of a father who worked with data and, not surprisingly, this young person had a good understanding of data flows and infrastructure. This points to a particular form of inequity – not all young people have parents who work with data or who can provide a basic grounding in data awareness – leading to a gap in support for data literacy. This gap in learning opportunities about data can be addressed through data literacy services for teens (and perhaps the broader public) at the public library.

These preliminary findings suggest that data – what it is, where it lives, who has access to it and how it might be controlled – is not yet part of the thought processes of young people. Our interviews may have been the first time that some thought of their data traces in the networked world in these terms. It was fascinating to watch the blinkers pulled from the eyes of the participants as the interviews progressed, the young people becoming more aware that there is a data world and they have a role to play in it, leading one participant to say that our interview had inspired him to go "deeper into data." Simply raising an interest in, and awareness of, data is an important outcome for any youth data literacy program at the public library.

## CONCLUSION

Data science education programs are moving into the mainstream core curriculum of library and information science (LIS) programs but for the most part, those that are taking up the charge of data are doing so from the perspective of scholarly, research data. There are, however, many roles for the data savvy information professional – data archivist, data journalist, data analyst, data engineer, data steward and, finally, data librarian (Lyon, 2014). The data librarian role in the context of services for youth has yet to be elaborated, and work is needed to build out this aspect of the public library mission. We will be extending this research to look at data literacy through the perspectives of teen librarians.

Using the coding structure developed in this first phase of our project, we also intend to continue our exploration into young peoples' interactions with data, focusing in greater detail on their data management skills, sense of privacy and agency and associated values. Our hope is that this work exploring how teens perceive data in the broader context of their everyday lives, and specifically in relation to the management of their personal digital data, will provide a first step in developing data services for young people at the public library.

## ACKNOWLEDGMENTS

We thank the young people and library staff who participated in this study. Their contributions are invaluable.

This project was made possible by a grant from the Institute of Museum and Library Services. The project's grant number is RE-31-16-0079-16.

## REFERENCES

ACRL, (2012). ACRL research planning and review committee. Top ten trends in academic libraries. A review of the trends and issues affecting academic libraries in higher education. *College & Research Libraries News, 73*(6), 311-320.

ACRL, (2014). ACRL research planning and review committee. Top ten trends in academic libraries. A review of the trends and issues affecting academic libraries in higher education. *College & Research Libraries News, 75*(6), 294-302.

Agosto, D. E., Abbas, J., & Naughton, R. (2012). Relationships and social rules: Teens' social network and other ICT selection practices. *Journal of the American Society for Information Science and Technology, 63*(6), 1108-1124.

Ahn, J. (2011). The effect of social network sites on adolescents' social and academic development: Current theories and controversies. *Journal of the American Society for information Science and Technology, 62*(8), 1435-1445.

boyd, d. (2014). It's complicated: The social lives of networked teens. New Haven, CT: Yale University Press.

Borgman, C. L. (2015). Big data, little data, no data: Scholarship in the networked world. Cambridge, MA: MIT Press.

Calzada Prado, J., & Marzal, M.Á. (2013). Incorporating data literacy into information literacy programs: Core competencies and contents. *Libri, 63*(2), 123-134.

Carlson, J. & Johnston, L. R. (Eds). (2015). Data information literacy: Librarians, data, and the education of a new generation of researchers. (Purdue Information Literacy Handbooks). Ashland, OH: Purdue University Press.

Cole, C. & Leide, J. E. (2006). A cognitive framework for human information behavior: The place of metaphor in human information organizing behavior. In *New directions in human information behavior* (pp. 171-202). Netherland: Spring.

Deahl, E. (2014). Better the data you know: Developing youth data literacy in schools and informal learning environments. Unpublished master thesis, Massachusetts Institute of Technology.

Finzer, W. (2013) The data science education dilemma. *Technology Innovations in Statistics Education, 7*(2), 1-9.

Fontichiaro, K. and Oehrili, J. (2016). Why data literacy matters. *Knowledge Quest, 44*(5), 20-27.

Ford, N. (2015). *Introduction to information behaviour*. London: Facet Publishing.

Friedman, B., & Nissenbaum, H. (1996). Bias in computer systems. *ACM Transactions on Information Systems (TOIS), 14*(3), 330-347.

Introna, L. D., & Nissenbaum, H. (2000). Shaping the web: Why the politics of search engines matters. *The Information Society, 16*(3), 169-185.

Hartel, J. & Savolainen, R. (2016). Pictorial metaphors for information. *Journal of Documentation, 72*(5), 794-812.

Koltay, T. (2015). Data literacy: In search of a name and identity. *Journal of Documentation, 71*(2), 401-415.

Lakoff, G & Johnson, M. (1980). *Metaphors we live by*. Chicago: University of Chicago Press.

Livingstone, S. (2014). Developing social media literacy: How children learn to interpret risky opportunities on social network sites. *Communications, 39*(3), 283-303.

Lyon, L. (2014). Learning about research data management in the lab at the Pitt iSchool. Library Connect. Retrieved from https://libraryconnect.elsevier.com/articles/learning-about-research-data-lab-pitt-ischool.

Marchionini, G. (2008). Human-information interaction research and development. *Library and Information Science Research, 30*(3), 165-174.

Marwick, A. E., & boyd, D. (2014). Networked privacy: How teenagers negotiate context in social media. *New Media & Society, 16*(7), 1051-1067.

Moore, C. L. (2016). A study of social media and its influence on teen information seeking behaviors. *The Serials Librarian, 71*(2), 138-145.

Pariser, E. (2012). The filter bubble: How the new personalized web is changing what we read and how we think. New York, N.Y: Penguin Books/Penguin Press.

Sweeney, L. (2013). Discrimination in online ad delivery. *Communications of the ACM, 56*(5), 44–54.

Zang, J., Dummit, K., Graves, J., Lisker, P., & Sweeney, L. (2015). Who knows what about me? A survey of behind the scenes personal data sharing to third parties by mobile apps. *Technology Science, 30*

# Big Data, Big Metadata and Quantitative Study of Science: A Workflow Model for Big Scientometrics

**Sarah Bratt**
*Syracuse University, USA. sebratt@syr.edu*

**Jeff Hemsley**
*Syracuse University, USA. jjhemsle@syr.edu*

**Jian Qin**
*School of Information Studies, Syracuse University, USA. jqin@syr.edu*

**Mark Costa**
*Newhouse School of Public Communications, Syracuse University, USA. mrcosta@syr.edu*

## ABSTRACT

**Large cyberinfrastructure-enabled data repositories generate massive amounts of metadata, enabling big data analytics to leverage on the intersection of technological and methodological advances in data science for the quantitative study of science. This paper introduces a definition of big metadata in the context of scientific data repositories and discusses the challenges in big metadata analytics due to the messiness, lack of structures suitable for analytics and heterogeneity in such big metadata. A methodological framework is proposed, which contains conceptual and computational workflows intercepting through collaborative documentation. The workflow-based methodological framework promotes transparency and contributes to research reproducibility. The paper also describes the experience and lessons learned from a four-year big metadata project involving all aspects of the workflow-based methodologies. The methodological framework presented in this paper is a timely contribution to the field of scientometrics and the science of science and policy as the potential value of big metadata is drawing more attention from research and policy maker communities.**

## KEYWORDS

big metadata analytics, workflows, methodology, scientometrics

## INTRODUCTION

Research data repositories store massive amounts of data. An example is the GenBank data repository administered by the National Center for Biotechnology Information (NCBI) that stores genetic sequence data and serves "more than 30 terabytes of biomedical data to more than 3.3 million users every day" (NLM, 2015). Every dataset in these repositories includes metadata that documents items such as the intellectual contributors, property rights, knowledge indicators and many other fields. Thus, since each dataset includes its own metadata, we now have not only big scientific data but also *big metadata*. The GenBank data repository hosted at NCBI, for example, contains 1.9 trillion sequences, with an annual increase rate of 36.8% in 2016, where each sequence includes metadata (Benson et al., 2017).

As scientific data is pivotal to modern science, big metadata about scientific data is also pivotal for data discovery, sharing, reuse, crediting authors and research reproducibility. More recently, and with the emergence of data science, such metadata is being used as trace data that offers insight and policy prescriptions about the scientific enterprise. Triangulating these quantitative metadata with social, political and economic events creates unprecedented opportunities for science of science and policy research in the big data era.

While opportunities for doing research with such vast metadata resources are exciting and promising, there are major challenges in using it to conduct research. The large scale means most work requires computational efforts requiring skilled workers and costly resources. Additionally, the metadata are often messy, complex, ambiguous and unstructured. Further, idiosyncratic structures and formats in data repositories vary greatly from discipline to discipline. Together, these factors mean that researchers tend to develop one-off custom solutions to process and prepare the data for analysis. The lack of methodological guidance can leave researchers in a constant exploratory data-processing mode. We contend that most big metadata projects will have to execute similar tasks in roughly the same order. Is there a methodological framework that can guide the data processing and analysis in using big metadata from scientific data repositories as the data source? What would such a methodological framework look like?

This paper attempts to address the above research questions through a project case. We argue that the development of workflow methods is a necessary step to increase transparency and contribute to research reproducibility in scientometric work and data-driven policy development, especially when work is iterative, ad hoc, exploratory, and messy. Such a methodology could also help researchers avoid reinventing the wheel for each project and give researchers a descriptive shortcut by allowing them to indicate workflows by name, instead of describing their isolated parts.

80th Annual Meeting of the Association for Information Science & Technology, Washington, DC | Oct. 27-Nov. 1, 2017

To accomplish these goals, we first provide a definition of the term *big metadata* in the context of science data repositories as well as the challenges in using it. Following this is a brief description of the workflow-based methodological framework, with examples from our four-year-long big metadata analytics project. The description is further illustrated by the GenBank metadata analytics project and lessons learned from our experience. Finally, the paper concludes with a discussion of all aspects of the workflow-based methodologies and future study. The methodological framework presented in this paper is a timely contribution to the field of scientometrics and the science of science and policy as the potential value of big metadata is drawing more attention from research and policy maker communities.

## BIG METADATA AND THE CHALLENGES

Metadata in scientific data repositories are used to document the creators and attributes of data, record associated projects and physical artifacts that have been used to produce the data and link to publication output. Some scientific data repositories were established before the web was invented, such as GenBank, while others are relative newcomers, e.g., Dryad (http://datadryad.org) and the Knowledge Network for Biodiversity (KNB) (https://knb.ecoinformatics.org/). Many of these data repositories are international in scope, that is, data may be submitted by anyone in the research community from anywhere.

As researchers submit science data into the repository, they also submit information about the data (metadata). The quality of this metadata depends on the input tool and underlying supporting technologies. Technologies and "x-informatics," as Jim Gray (Hey, Tansley & Tolle, 2009) famously put it, where x may be substituted by any discipline name (e.g., biomedical and ecological), have supported massive data in physics, astrophysics, biological sciences, ecological systems, geography and many other fields during the last three decades. The x-informatics phenomenon implies that the tools and technologies were developed in consultation with field specialists who are far more interested in the quality of the scientific data than the metadata that describes it. Thus, across the fields, big metadata are often no less massive or complex than the data they represent.

The term *big metadata* can be found in literature as early as 2013, but it was used to refer to the management of metadata for big data (Smith et al., 2014). Broadly speaking, indexing databases, such as the Web of Science, and catalogs such as WorldCat are in the big metadata domain, but they are not the subject of this paper. In the context of this paper, we use the term *big metadata* to refer to the structured, semi-structured or unstructured descriptions of scientific data stored in repositories. Such descriptions usually follow a metadata standard recognized by a research community and are created by researchers. For example, ecosystems data in the KNB repository are described by the Ecological Metadata Language (EML) and the tool Morpho[1] was developed to support the use of this community metadata standard in submitting datasets to the repository.

The metadata in such systems can be treated as trace data that supports research exploring a range of questions about the scientific enterprise. For example, we can examine how collaborations and research networks rise and fall, or how the scale and structure of these networks relate to productivity. Linking to additional data sources opens a vast set of additional questions. We might wish to study the collaborative processes from data generation to the publication of scholarly papers to applying for and securing patents or funding. Alternately, we might analyze the diffusion of knowledge across media or the economic impact of patents and successful grant applications. In other words, these metadata support research in areas with profound social, economic and policy implications.

The promises of big metadata, however, come with equally big, if not greater, challenges. These challenges require both computationally intensive processing and, more importantly, careful research design. One key computational problem is that names and organizations often need to be disambiguated. Figure 1 provides an example of GenBank metadata record. Personal names include the full last name with first and middle name initials. In big metadata, we find that multiple people can have identical last names and first (and middle) initials. Such ambiguities can damage the accuracy of data and cause negative ripple effects, e.g., to affect the validity of analytics. We also find inconsistencies and errors in names; in one record, a person may list a middle initial and in another maybe not. Computationally, such cases will appear to be two different people. Similarly, the same organization may be listed with inconsistent abbreviations, organization units in different orders or the inclusion or exclusion geographic locations across records. In sum, these concerns can jeopardize the quality of the final analysis. Although standard identifier systems that resolve these ambiguities have begun deployment (e.g., Microsoft's Academic Graph (Sinha et al., 2015)), most older scientific data repositories have not implemented similar systems on new data entry, much less for those in the vast legacy metadata in these repositories. Thus, each new research project must disambiguate named entities, a non-trivial task that makes data processing costly in time and effort. It also makes linking data fields on names difficult, both within the same data collection and across different databases.

An assumption of many new big metadata researchers is that the open availability (e.g., accessible to FTP) of the data means it is structured, formatted, complete, accurate, standardized and consistent across sources. For reasons discussed

[1] https://www.dataone.org/software-tools/morpho

above, such assumptions are more illusory than reality. The range of data problems across the numerous systems means that researchers tend to develop their own tools that focus on solving the specific data problems they face. The result is that few general, open source tools exist, placing the burden on other researchers to solve the same, or similar, problems with each new research project. When we note that different researchers have different levels of skills and experience we are led to conclude that knowledge claims in our field could rest on dramatically different levels of data cleaning quality.

```
LOCUS       NC_030982             1051730 bp    DNA     linear   CON 22-SEP-2016
DEFINITION  Saccharomyces eubayanus strain FM1318 chromosome VII, whole genome
            shotgun sequence.
ACCESSION   NC_030982
VERSION     NC_030982.1
DBLINK      BioProject: PRJNA342694
            BioSample: SAMN02716114
            Assembly: GCF_001298625.1
KEYWORDS    WGS; RefSeq.
SOURCE      Saccharomyces eubayanus
  ORGANISM  Saccharomyces eubayanus
            Eukaryota; Fungi; Dikarya; Ascomycota; Saccharomycotina;
            Saccharomycetes; Saccharomycetales; Saccharomycetaceae;
            Saccharomyces.
REFERENCE   1  (bases 1 to 1051730)
  AUTHORS   Baker,E., Wang,B., Bellora,N., Peris,D., Hulfachor,A.B.,
            Koshalek,J.A., Adams,M., Libkind,D. and Hittinger,C.T.
  TITLE     The Genome Sequence of Saccharomyces eubayanus and the
            Domestication of Lager-Brewing Yeasts
  JOURNAL   Mol. Biol. Evol. 32 (11), 2818-2831 (2015)
   PUBMED   26269586
REFERENCE   2  (bases 1 to 1051730)
  CONSRTM   NCBI Genome Project
  TITLE     Direct Submission
  JOURNAL   Submitted (20-SEP-2016) National Center for Biotechnology
            Information, NIH, Bethesda, MD 20894, USA
REFERENCE   3  (bases 1 to 1051730)
  AUTHORS   Wang,B., Baker,E., Libkind,D., Goncalves,P., Sampaio,J.P. and
            Hittinger,C.T.
  TITLE     Direct Submission
  JOURNAL   Submitted (05-MAY-2015) Laboratory of Genetics, University of
            Wisconsin-Madison, 425-G Henry Mall, 2434 Genetics/Biotechnology
            Center, Madison, WI 53706-1580, USA
```

***Figure 1.*** *A sample metadata record for a genetic sequence in GenBank repository (Source: https://www.ncbi.nlm.nih.gov/nuccore/1069890484?report=genbank).*

Clearly, the challenges in using big metadata for analytics can lead to pitfalls and affect the validity and reliability of research. Sound methodological approaches and reporting become critical in mitigating some of these challenges. The following section will discuss the methodological approaches to big metadata analytics from a workflow perspective.

## METHODOLOGIES

As used by industry, *workflow* describes the orchestrated and repeatable patterns of business activities performed in a sequence of operations (BPM Center of Excellence, 2009). With respect to e-science, we can think of workflow orchestration as "the activity of defining the sequence of tasks needed to manage a business or computational science or engineering process. A workflow is a template of such an orchestration" and has a lifecycle that encompasses four broad aspects: composition, mapping, execution and provenance (Deelman et al., 2009, p. 529). The concept of workflow orchestration and its four broad aspects for e-science sets the context in which the workflow in big metadata analytics is defined. Although Deelman et al.'s four broad aspects of workflows are used to assess workflow tools for highly computational science, they provide a framework for discussing the methodology for big metadata analytics.

A workflow in big metadata analytics is composed of a sequence of tasks and activities that are performed iteratively to achieve the goal of the workflow. A collection of interrelated and interdependent workflows, together with methods and the rationale for why and how the methods are used, forms the methodology (or template) for conducting big metadata analytics. An important characteristic of this workflow-based methodology is *iterativity*, that is, the tasks and activities in workflows are often recurrent, overlapping, and repeated. With every iteration, the methodology is refined and enhanced.

### *Workflows in Using Big Metadata*

Big metadata analytics consists of several stages that are iterative and overlapping. Two types of workflows are involved in these stages: conceptual workflows and computational workflows (see Figure 2). Connecting conceptual and computational workflows, and running simultaneously with all stages, is *collaborative documentation*, which is a team-based effort to record goals, rationales, strategies, steps and activities for search, reuse and informational purposes. Conceptual workflows identify goals for both the milestones of the study and activity areas for achieving the milestones. At this conceptual level, the rationale and methods will also be articulated and documented. These may be revised and updated iteratively as the research progresses. Corresponding to the conceptual workflows are the computational workflows that essentially codify what has been defined at the conceptual level for machine execution.

Computational workflows may be divided into interdependent task-level and activity-level workflows. Task-level workflows are generally characterized by inputs, outputs and processes/parameters, where outputs are task specific, e.g., creating code to parse data fields in a table by indicating where to fetch data from, the criteria or conditions used in the parsing, and where the output should be sent to. Task-level workflows tend to be iteratively tested and adjusted, and the successful completion of a task often affects the execution of other task-level workflows. Activity-level workflows have a broader goal than task-level workflows and usually take a group of task-level workflows to accomplish. For example, author name disambiguation is a typical activity in big metadata analytics that requires several steps or processes to complete, depending on the disambiguation strategies employed. Each of the steps or processes involves planning, organizing and executing some task-level workflows. For big metadata analytic projects, these workflows can be described as analytical pipelines that orchestrate tasks and activities for big metadata analytics projects

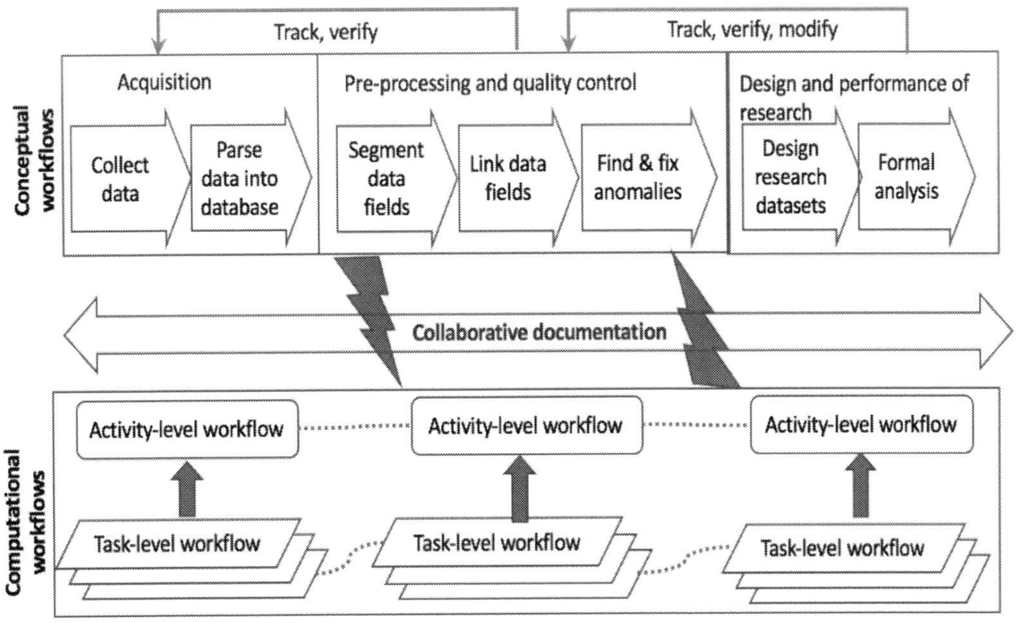


***Figure 2.*** *A workflow-based methodological framework for big metadata analytics. The conceptual workflows define the goals and strategies of activities, whereas computational workflows codify the conceptual workflows for machine execution. Any of the stages in a conceptual workflow may be iterated when processing and/or analytic results need to be tracked and verified and methods need to be modified.*

The workflow stages in Figure 2 approximately correspond to Stanton's model of the data science areas and lifecycle: *architecture*, *acquisition*, *analysis* and *archiving* (Stanton, 2013). For our purposes, these data science areas can be refined and interpreted to better reflect the context of big metadata from scientific repositories (see Table 1). For big metadata, *acquisition* consists of data collection activities, such as extracting metadata from data repositories and any subsequent data additions from other sources. *Pre-processing and quality control* encompasses computational and other types of data processing (e.g., data cleaning or wrangling), including algorithm design and script development. It also includes exploratory analyses such as descriptive statistics and visualization as well as collaborative logical interpretation and synthesis of results of those analyses. *Design and performance of research* refers to the creation of datasets based on research questions and other resultant data products.

| Areas in Big Metadata Analytics | Areas in Data Science |
|---|---|
| Acquisition | Acquisition |
| Pre-processing and quality control | Analysis, Architecture |
| Design and performance of research | Archiving, Analysis, Architecture |
| Collaborative documentation | Archiving, Analysis |

***Table 1.*** *Comparison of areas between big metadata analytics and data science*

### *Stages and Workflows*

#### *Acquire Data*

In this stage, decisions are made about the scope and type of metadata to collect based on the intended research, making data collection a part of the conceptual workflow. However, the nature of scientometric analysis often is characterized by uncertainty about what data will best support the research. For example, are we interested in scientific collaboration as the focus of our research? Do we need the scientific data associated with the metadata because understanding its size and complexity may be related to the amount of work done by the submitting actor in a network? These questions require a careful consideration of human and technical resource constraints and suggest possible task-level methodological and technical solutions. Thus, they play a central role in this very first step of the big metadata workflow. Ideally, during their deliberations, the team should also consider the "downstream" steps of the workflow, e.g., data processing, data analysis and interpretation of results.

In our example, the GenBank FTP server stores semi-structured, compressed genetic sequence data files submitted by researchers from around the world. Most of these compressed files are anywhere from 2MB-80MB. As of 8/16/2012 when we downloaded the data, it contained 1,723 data files and 129 index files, all in the compressed .gz format. The size of the compressed sequence data was approximately 75GB and that of the index files 8GB. Each GenBank record contains both metadata describing the submission as well as the genetic sequencing information. The sequencing information comprises the bulk of the file size (over 90% of the file in many cases) and is not needed for the purposes of our study.

#### *Parse data into database*

The second step of the workflow is parsing the data into the database. This work often involves data exploration efforts aimed at understanding what the data look like. The challenge here is that the metadata is not structured and is often inconsistent. Thus, this step often involves a great deal of data cleaning and checking one's own efforts. Parsing scripts may be developed alongside scripts that test the assumptions of the parsing scripts. We often find that the first pass of the work does not correctly parse all the data and that additional parsing rules need to be incorporated. Sometimes successive rounds resolve increasingly smaller numbers of errors until we have all, or nearly all, problems resolved. The team collectively evaluates the errors and error rates to determine if there is an acceptable error rate. The very process of scripting parsers and resolving errors leads to a deeper understanding of data. We also note that the process is much easier when at least one member of the team has domain knowledge and understands what the data should look like.

The architecture part of this second stage consists of the design and selection of a big metadata analytics infrastructure. Our project's architecture comprises an ecosystem of servers, applications and databases. The data ingestion and storage layer includes a Linux server with a MySQL database. We use Microsoft R Open[1] on an Ubuntu virtual machine for analysis and visualization. R Open includes a refactorization of some base functions to support native parallelization of those functions, meaning that the Microsoft version of R can use the machine's multiple processors and so is suitable for big metadata analytics. Packages that we have found useful include foreach[2], doParallel[3], data.table[4], Matrix[5] and igraph[6]. The server is configured to support data sharing and multiple concurrent users. Other collaboration technologies that orchestrate the team's work include GitHub, Google Drive, Evernote, Email and Dropbox.

#### *Segment data fields*

Segmenting data in certain fields becomes an unescapable step for almost any big metadata analytic project due to the characteristics of big metadata discussed in the previous section. The need for segmentation arises when a field contains multiple values, each of which needs to be stored separately. Typical data fields that have such conditions include author name field, subject and/or keyword field, author affiliation field, among others. Effective analytics requires a fine granularity and structure in the datasets that are designed to address research questions. Breaking down coarsely granular data fields into smallest data atoms is a step to meet this requirement.

This step often requires some analysis, such as whether the record is flat or hierarchical (nested), and the record's general structural complexity. The author name field, for example, often requires several steps to separate individual names into a single name per row. This formatting task may take several iterations to complete because of inconsistently abbreviated names or the inclusion of "and" or "&." Often, specific data cleaning techniques such as author name disambiguation must be employed to ensure clean, accurate data. Like the previous step, segmenting also requires quality checks to verify data assumptions. Thus, we often develop test scripts alongside parsing scripts. As before, working with the data in this way leads to a growing depth of knowledge about the data.

#### *Link data fields*

In this step, segmented data fields need to be meaningfully connected in the database to prepare for queries that generate

---

[1] https://mran.revolutionanalytics.com/open/
[2] https://cran.r-project.org/web/packages/foreach/
[3] https://cran.r-project.org/web/packages/doParallel/
[4] https://cran.r-project.org/web/packages/data.table/
[5] https://cran.r-project.org/web/packages/Matrix/
[6] https://cran.r-project.org/web/packages/igraph/

required datasets. If the original format of the metadata description was designed for human viewing and understanding, then determining relationship rules will require re-modeling to support big metadata analytics, which requires the data to be meaningfully structured in ways that make computational processing and execution possible. While there are many possible linkages between data fields, we remain aware of the existing relationships and stay focused on the ones that can help us address the research questions. These are among the questions that must be asked: What relationships exist in the raw metadata? How might they be reflected in the new database? What new relationships need to be established for addressing the research questions? Linking also requires understanding the data at depth and the nature of the fields to make valid linkages between data tables.

#### *Find and fix data anomalies*

Data anomalies can occur because of human error, irregularities or inconsistencies in formatting, or even as computational processing errors by the research team. That is, anomalies can be produced by human error and machine error. In either case, it is important to explore the root of the problem: whether the anomaly was caused by human error or machine error, the error's location in the data lineage and how it might have happened. Further research may be necessary to track down the originally-collected big metadata and other references to provide clues for solving the anomalies.

At this stage, exploratory data analysis can be useful to discover the shape, structure and inclusivity of the data to make an informed decision of how to ameliorate the anomalies and to determine how they will impact statistical analyses or visualizations (Tukey, 1977). At the task level, descriptive statistics and visualizations can be effective methods for testing assumptions about the distribution and shape of data. It is also useful to draw out subsets of data to test our assumptions and ensure that the segmenting tasks accomplished the tasks they were designed to complete before we apply the code to the whole dataset.

#### *Design datasets based on research questions and hypotheses*

Once the data cleaning and quality verification are done, datasets may be extracted based on criteria driven by research questions and hypotheses. For the study to stand on a solid methodological ground, the design of the datasets requires a team effort. During this stage, incorporating data from other sources may occur depending on the research plan. If the source needed is not in the plan, then the workflow goes back to the drawing board in first stage. Even without additional data, we do many tests and trials before settling down on the final datasets because the reliability and validity of research findings rely on these data. Also, the final datasets will be shared with the research community and undergo the scrutiny of peer review.

#### *Conduct analysis*

Many analytic methods are available for analyzing the datasets: statistical methods, social network analysis, machine learning, visualization and combinations thereof. From a methodological perspective, the key aspect of this step is not the specific methods used but rather that the rationale and procedures are well thought through and documented. The importance of a conceptual workflow becomes evident in that it provides a robust template for a well-justified and supported study.

While the big metadata workflow steps are ordinal in their numbering, the stages are often iterative and often lead to more questions or unexpected results. For example, the collection of data precedes parsing and processing, though later we may later realize we need additional data. Segmenting data fields could also be revisited as more is learned about the data. Thus, the workflow is conceived as an executable flow of stages not because they are in a rigid chronology but because they unfold in a roughly stepwise manner.

In its entirety, the process is about developing a deeper and deeper understanding of the data: what is in it, what its limitations are, what structures and patterns there are in the data, and given its quality, what kinds of questions the data may support answering. The exploratory steps of data verification, question surfacing and examining data structures are central to a workflow of big metadata when a lack of shared standards, documentation and structure make uncertainty a staple of big metadata analytics. A key strength of a named workflow, then, is that it facilitates organization and determination of where to return in the workflow during iteration.

### ***Cross-Stage Components***

#### *Collaborative Documentation*

Documentation occurs, and often is required, at almost every stage of a research lifecycle and throughout both conceptual and computational workflows. Documentation is done for different purposes and with various tools. The most striking characteristic in team projects is the collaboration involved in creating, maintaining and managing such documentation. Collaboration in documentation is guided by the data management plan and orchestrated by clear policy and persistent enforcement within a team.

Collaborative documentation becomes critically important when task-based and activity-based workflows are created by different team members, as well as when there is a change of team member composition. The choreography of the artifacts generated from collaborative documentation serves as the cohesive medium for maintaining coherence between distributed team members' analyses and results. That is, the processes are held together by making sense of graphical results and writing down findings, issues and the logic of the steps they took in analysis. In this stage, the research team produces documents such as memos and notes with tools such as Evernote and cloud storage systems to record and share their work.

#### *Data wrangling*

Data wrangling consists of any transformations needed to support exploratory analysis, quality checks or final analyses.

Aggregations, filtering, sub-setting and sorting are all data wrangling tasks. Sometimes called *data cleaning*, data wrangling happens at multiple points during the workflow and can be, by itself, an iterative operation. Exploratory data analysis (EDA) (Tukey 1977) is a crucial element of this work. We use it to understand how the data is structured before and after any data transformations.

### *Data Quality Checks*

Data quality checks include any efforts to ensure the data appear as expected. Different from finding and fixing anomalies, the focus of quality checks is on verifying the results of script runs and data transformations. For example, once we insert data into the database we run checks to ensure it was inserted correctly. We note here that we embed in the code our assumptions about how it does and should work. However, because our assumptions are not always right, part of a quality check is thinking through assumptions. Team discussions help uncover these hidden assumptions and help identify what should be tested and how to test it.

### *The Case of GenBank*

In this section, we illustrate the use of workflow-based methodology in our big metadata analytics project and demonstrate how the stages and workflows iteratively unfold as research commonly progresses. The goal of this project was to demonstrate the feasibility of using big metadata for studying the impact of cyberinfrastructure-enabled science on the formation, thriving and cooling down of research collaboration networks over time. Collaboration networks that arise from authorship of data and publications may be considered a symbolic representation of scientific capacity of a country or institute. The project went through the workflow stages from data acquisition through to analysis after numerous iterations. The final data collection includes not only the complete metadata records from GenBank made available at the time of downloading from the FTP site, but also the NCBI Taxonomy7 that was incorporated into the database and linked to GenBank metadata records based on the taxon lineage in the records. The incorporation of NCBI Taxonomy makes it possible for big metadata analytics based on taxonomic classes.

In the big metadata collection from the GenBank FTP server, we linked segmented attributes by identifying relationship rules, for instance, 1) a publication metadata record is associated with one or many authors; 2) a data submission is associated with one or many annotations; and 3) an annotation is associated with one or many data submissions. From these rules, it is clear that a many-to-many relationship between the annotations and data submission records requires linking to normalize the fields.

To test a series of workflows for studying a sub-community in the GenBank data repository, we selected metadata records for DNA sequences related to the West Nile Virus because outbreaks in infectious diseases often generate new discoveries of virus genes that result in a concentrated period and a higher frequency of data submissions. In designing the conceptual workflows, the team collected information from the Centers for Disease Control (CDC) to learn about the history and extent of the disease's spread. Studying this research community through big metadata can help identify the hub of researchers and new discoveries of virus strains, and possibly link the basic research to clinical and drug developments.

The first step was to extract data by querying our database. Because the study of the West Nile virus research community required we use a subset of our preprocessed data, certain stages related to data parsing and cleaning were performed only when special needs arose. The subset of data included records of publications, data submissions and patents associated with West Nile virus in our database. In the conceptual workflows, several key areas helped the computational workflows stay on track: 1) we developed a concept map, or copy of the database schema, showing the relationships of the records and indicating which metadata were necessary and sufficient to ensure validity; 2) we leveraged background knowledge in the biological sciences to ascertain that the query was representative of the object intended for extraction; and 3) we checked the internal logic of the algorithm, as well as the meaning of the metadata, to validate that our query was consistent, valid, and thorough.

For example, in executing a query for the West Nile virus records, the analyst must know that a) the default setting of the regular expression matching algorithm is "greedy," and returns both upper and lower-case entries and b) the "title" field includes data submissions. After meeting with a more senior project researcher, the analyst received feedback on her work and found that the grep() algorithm *did not* match the data submission for West Nile; for these records, the analyst must join across database tables to query for the precise taxonomy IDs that corresponds to West Nile virus. As we proceeded with finding and fixing anomalies in this way, we discovered that there were 12 taxonomy IDs describing West Nile virus data submissions, which were best suited for the research questions. Another example arose when we realized that if science policy prioritized West Nile virus *environmental* research during the time we chose, then the data extraction method should include the taxonomy ID that reflects 'ENV' (i.e., environmental sampling) sequences.

The formal research was performed on the extracted subset of data to explore the network patterns, research productivity and knowledge diffusion within the West Nile virus authors, inventors and scientists. Since the patent data in GenBank was a new addition to the whole data collection and the patent

[7] The NCBI Taxonomy database is a curated classification and nomenclature for all the organisms in the public sequence database. https://www.ncbi.nlm.nih.gov/taxonomy

inventors' names were not previously disambiguated, the research team went back to the parsing and preprocessing stages to parse, segment and disambiguate the inventor name by utilizing algorithms and dataset from Li et al. (2011) and Lai et al. (2011). Next, we visualized the network and analyzed network and node-level statistical properties to gain a better sense of the modularity and community structures such as transitivity and clustering coefficients. We also identified node-level properties such as the distribution of centrality scores for individual nodes, with relations defined as co-authorship, co-sequence submission, or co-patent invention (Costa, 2016).

These exploratory and confirmatory analyses were extended as we dug deeper into the West Nile virus metadata to compare it with other infectious disease research communities, such as SARS, H1N1 and Influenza. Sporadic data wrangling and quality checks were conducted along the way as needed. Further, we found that though many members of the team had moved on, their documentation made the reuse of scripts and quality checks easy. An important activity implied but not explicitly entered in the workflows was that, through the process, we met many times a week, communicated via email and shared files in Evernote and Dropbox, and consulted with team members to synthesize results and disseminate significant findings.

### *Lessons learned: Documentation, documentation, and documentation*

The importance of documentation during a research lifecycle cannot be overemphasized. Procedures, workflows, programming code strategies, research ideas and questions alike should be well documented. The nature of our methodologies required sustained scrutiny over data quality. Documentation offers a valuable repertoire for provenance of research information.

Documentation contributes to the transparency and reproducibility of research. Using collaboration tools to collaboratively document methodologies used at different stages, especially where iterations took place, can greatly enhance the completeness and accuracy of such documentation. For this project, our team used the following tools for collaborative documentation, management, versioning and group sharing.

**GitHub:** Processing documentation, documented workflows and code are stored here, which provides history and version tracking.

**Evernote:** On-the-fly naming for each message, with datasets, scripts and other artifacts from analysis are attached in notes.

**RStudio:** A dedicated server on which team members have accounts where formal analysis and collaborative documentation is done.

**Email:** Notes from email discussing technical concerns, such as the connection to the database, memory allocation issues opened and resolved with IT personnel, all these issues are integral to the workflow documentation, and data provenance.

**MySQL Workbench:** Justifying steps in comments and stored procedures and extracting research datasets comprise the use of MySQL. Referencing schema such as the Entity Relationship Diagram (ERD) also helped to inform the researchers' extraction of datasets.

**Dropbox:** Used for file storage and document sharing and as a citation repository before the introduction of a citation manager such as Zotero. Overwriting and co-editing documents presents issues, but it is used for file and R script sharing.

**Google Drive**: Documents such as notes and papers reporting research findings are shared among team members to enable collaborative writing and editing. Files are exchanged here when space constraints in other platforms proved limiting.

**Drupal:** The public face of the project is maintained through the content management system, which serves as the backend of the project website. Dissemination of research papers, data products, and other media are housed on the site which is managed by a subset of team members.

It is worth noting that documenting all steps involved in big metadata analytics is impractical nor necessary. Information critical to methodology justification, reproducibility and continuity must be documented formally by an Evernote entry or a text document; whereas small adjustments of code in computational workflow creation and testing are not needed since GitHub tracks changes and we can comment the work. Automated documentation aids the iterative process of data analysis and reporting immensely; however, this tends to be available only for simple descriptions, such as keyword searching old Evernote documents, email messages, Dropbox files, GitHub commits, R scripts. The search algorithms for each are also different, requiring specialized knowledge for finding old files, notes or data objects. Yet such automated and manual documentation is critical for revisiting analyses over time.

### *Lessons learned: Know Thy Methodology, Know Thy Data*

Big metadata analytics requires careful design of datasets based on research questions. A misstep in data prep may cause a stalled server, never-ending loops or very large datasets being exploded out of proportion. When we initially started working with GenBank data, the massive size of 24 million rows caused server stalls due to excessive memory usage, and none of the team members could access the working environment.

In cases of not-so-huge data, we also encountered cases where data caused issues like disconnection from the network due to inactivity for a long time. The main reason behind this challenge was multiple or never-ending loops. A classic example of one such scenario is when SQL queries require multiple tables to be joined to filter out the required data.

There were also instances where, while merging datasets, data exploded out of proportion due to data matching issues. For example, in GenBank metadata, every patent has multiple references. When trying to merge authors who were involved in research pertaining to a certain organism, we decided to merge it with data from Dataverse repository data. Due to multiple references per column the dataset exploded from some thousand rows to tens of millions of rows.

It is also important that we understand if the metadata adheres to any published content standards or best practices, such as the international data repository bioinformatics standards, publication and submission reference standards, or U.S. Patent and Trademark Office (USPTO) standards, and whether the fields use any known and shared vocabularies. Linking data fields pivots on the extent to which metadata conforms to these employed standards, the formal or informal practices of data entry and vocabularies. For example, in our project we were able to take advantage of the standardized fields and effectively link USPTO data (Li et al., 2014) to NCBI GenBank metadata and NCBI Taxonomy database to create a richer, triangulated big metadata system.

Detecting data anomalies and ameliorating data entry errors generally involves writing code to check the work that has been done. For many analysts, this validity checking is not explicit, but an intuitive part of the data exploration and confirmation process. It can get lost if documentation consists of, e.g., an R script that is not commented at all or contains comments that are specific to the analysis, in language that does not make the thoughts of the analyst transparent.

## DISCUSSION AND CONCLUSION

Big metadata analytics has a great potential for studying the science enterprise at an unprecedented scale. The proliferation of data and metadata in scientific repositories makes linking and triangulating multiple data sources possible, which promotes the reliability, transparency and reproducibility of scientometric research. Based on our project experience, we generalized the challenges in using big metadata as a source of data for scientometric analytics and developed a methodological framework for big metadata analytics. The methodological framework was motivated by our own experience in mining one of the largest scientific data repositories as well as the pitfalls we encountered and mistakes we made. Although the methodological framework is created in the context of big metadata analytics, it is also possible that it be applied to other areas of big data analytics where similar data situations are encountered.

To use big metadata (or, big data for that matter) effectively and meaningfully, it is more important to be able to articulate the research question and the methodology used to address the research question then simply to calculate statistics and create data visualizations. The methodological framework we developed offers guidance on a workflow-based approach to working with big metadata. It adds a novel way of thinking about organizing work to address the problems and challenges of working with big metadata.

While previous studies repeatedly emphasize the need for improved metadata management and provide examples of how their laboratory or company faced and addressed issues in big metadata analytics, solutions are often *ad hoc*, one-off fixes without formalized workflows. The *ad hoc* approaches are neither generalizable nor scalable for big metadata analytics. Big metadata analytics performed on an *ad hoc* basis is more likely to suffer from mistakes made in both conceptual and computational workflows. The research may become costly, or worse, result in methodologically fundamental problems that can undermine the reliability and validity of research. Without explicit workflows, metadata analysis remains opaque, irreproducible, *ad hoc* and inaccessible. To the extent that data-driven science policy relies on accurate, careful, big metadata analysis, our methodological model of workflows fully exploits opportunities offered by the confluence of data repositories and data science. The opportunities highlighted by scientometric researchers are great, yet can are often disparate, one-off analyses. Such work can be guided by data science workflow theory. That is, it can start from the proposed methodological model to better leverage the intersection of technological and methodological advances in data science and the large-scale scientific data repositories that generate massive amounts of metadata.

Future work will explore the applicability of our methodological framework for data analytics outside of the scientific data repository domain. For example, we plan to explore the ways scientific repository big metadata are different from traditionally conceived big data in terms of science of science and policy research. Likewise, we want to examine the features of big metadata science that distinguish it from its corollary big data science, and compare how workflows in analysis might be similar. Overall, the methodological framework presented in this paper is a needed contribution to both the scientometrics and science of science and policy, as data repository metadata will remain central to big science going forward.

**Acknowledgements:** The authors thank the support of NSF SciSIP grant #1561348, the reviewers for their time and insight, and Shrutik Katchhi and Suchitra Deekshitula for their technical assistance.

## REFERENCES

Benson, D. A., Cavanaugh, M., Clark, K., Karsch-Mizrachi, I., Lipman, D. J., Ostell, J., & Sayers, E. W. (2017). GenBank. *Nucleic Acids Research*, *45*(Database Issue), D37–D42. https://doi.org/http://doi.org/10.1093/nar/gkw1070

BPM Center of Excellence. (2009, October 26). Business Process Management Center of Excellence Glossary [Government]. Retrieved from https://www.ftb.ca.gov/aboutFTB/Projects/ITSP/BPM_Glossary.pdf

Costa, M. R. (2016). *The interdependence of scientists in the era of team science: An exploratory study using temporal network analysis.* (Dissertation). Syracuse University, Syracuse, NY. Retrieved from http://surface.syr.edu/etd/425

Deelman, E., Gannon, D., Shields, M., & Taylor, I. (2009). Workflows and e-Science: An overview of workflow system features and capabilities. *Future Generation Computer Systems*, *25*(5), 528–540. https://doi.org/10.1016/j.future.2008.06.012

Galison, P., & Hevly, B. W. (1992). *Big science: The growth of large-scale research*. Stanford University Press. Retrieved from https://books.google.com/books?hl=en&lr=&id=zGmsRqIILx8C&oi=fnd&pg=PR9&dq=Galison,+P.+1992.+Big+Science:+The+Growth+of+Large-Scale+Research.+Stanford,+CA:+Stanford+University+Press&ots=P_gg5wpg7Y&sig=Zpv-uEVQhIvHbT37G8MfnQi2YmE

Greenberg, J., White, H. C., Carrier, S., & Scherle, R. (2009). A metadata best practice for a scientific data repository. *Journal of Library Metadata*, *9*(3-4), 194–212. Retrieved from http://www.tandfonline.com/doi/abs/10.1080/19386380903405090

Hey, tony, Tansley, S., & Tolle, K. T. (2009). Jim Gray on eScience: A transformed scientific method. In *The fourth paradigm: Data intensive scientific discovery* (First Edition, pp. xvii–xxxi). Redmond, WA: Microsoft. Retrieved from http://languagelog.ldc.upenn.edu/myl/JimGrayOnE-Science.pdf

Interactive Crowdsourced Literature Key-Value Annotation Library - iCLiKVAL. (n.d.). Retrieved April 10, 2017, from http://iclikval.riken.jp/

Lai, ronald, D'Amour, A., Yu, A., & Fleming, L. (2011). Disambiguation and Co-authorship Networks of the U.S. Patent Inventor Database (1975 - 2010) [Dataset]. Retrieved from https://dataverse.harvard.edu/dataset.xhtml?persistentId=hdl:1902.1/15705

Li, G.-C., Lai, R., D'Amour, A., Doolin, D. M., Sun, Y., Torvik, V. I., … Fleming, L. (2014). Disambiguation and co-authorship networks of the U.S. patent inventor database (1975–2010). *Research Policy*, *43*(6), 941–955. https://doi.org/http://doi.org/10.1016/j.respol.2014.01.012

Light, R. P., Polley, D. E., & Börner, K. (2014). Open data and open code for big science of science studies. *Scientometrics*, *101*(2), 1535–1551. Retrieved from http://link.springer.com/article/10.1007/s11192-014-1238-2

NLM. (2015). Congressional Justification FY 2015 [Document]. Retrieved from https://www.nlm.nih.gov/about/2015CJ.html

Sinha, A., Shen, Z., Song, Y., Ma, H., Eide, D., Hsu, B. (Paul), & Wang, K. (2015). An overview of Microsoft Academic Service (MAS) and applications. In *Proceedings of the 24th international conference on world wide web*. Florence, Italy: ACM. https://doi.org/10.1145/2740908.2742839

Smith, K., Seligman, L., Rosenthal, A., Kurcz, C., Greer, M., Macheret, C., … Eckstein, A. (2014). "Big metadata": The need for principled metadata management in big data ecosystems. In *Proceedings of workshop on data analytics in the cloud* (pp. 13:1–4). Snowbird, UT, USA: ACM. https://doi.org/10.1145/2627770.2627776

Stanton, J. (2013). *Introduction to Data Science*. (Third Edition, Vols. 1–1). Syracuse, NY: Syracuse University. Retrieved from https://itunes.apple.com/us/book/introduction-to-data-science/id529088127?mt=11

Tukey, J. W. (1977). *Exploratory Data Analysis*. Reading, Mass.: Pearson.

Weingart, S., Guo, H., Börner, K., Boyack, K. W., Linnemeier, M. W., Duhon, R. J., … Biberstine, J. (2010). Science of Science (Sci2) tool user manual. *Cyberinfrastructure for Network Science Center, School of Library and Information Science, Indiana University, Bloomington. Retrieved January 15*, 2011.

Özdemir, V., Kolker, E., Hotez, P. J., Mohin, S., Prainsack, B., Wynne, B., … others. (2014). Ready to put metadata on the post-2015 development agenda? Linking data publications to responsible innovation and science diplomacy. *Omics: A Journal of Integrative Biology*, *18*(1), 1–9. Retrieved from http://online.liebertpub.com/doi/abs/10.1089/omi.2013.0170

# Agreeing to Disagree: Reconciling Conflicting Taxonomic Views Using a Logic-based Approach


**Yi-Yun Cheng**
*School of Information Sciences, University of Illinois at Urbana-Champaign, USA. yiyunyc2@illinois.edu*

**Nico Franz**
*School of Life Sciences, Arizona State University, USA. nico.franz@asu.edu*

**Jodi Schneider**
*School of Information Sciences, University of Illinois at Urbana-Champaign, USA. jodi@illinois.edu*

**Shizhuo Yu**
*Department of Computer Science, University of California at Davis, USA. szyu@ucdavis.edu*

**Thomas Rodenhausen**
*School of Information, University of Arizona, USA. thomas.rodenhausen@gmail.com*

**Bertram Ludäscher**
*School of Information Sciences, University of Illinois at Urbana-Champaign, USA. ludaesch@illinois.edu*



## ABSTRACT

**Taxonomy alignment is a way to integrate two or more taxonomies. Semantic interoperability among datasets, information systems and knowledge bases is facilitated by combining the different input taxonomies into merged taxonomies that reconcile apparent differences or conflicts. We show how alignment problems can be solved with a logic-based region connection calculus (RCC-5) approach, using five base relations to compare concepts: *congruence*, *inclusion*, *inverse inclusion*, *overlap* and *disjointness*. To illustrate this method, we use different geo-taxonomies, which organize the United States into several, apparently conflicting, geospatial hierarchies. For example, we align $T_{CEN}$, a taxonomy derived from the Census Bureau's regions map, with $T_{NDC}$, from the National Diversity Council (NDC), and with $T_{TZ}$, a taxonomy capturing the U.S. time zones. Using these case studies, we show how this logic-based approach can reconcile conflicts between taxonomies. We have implemented these case studies with an open source tool called Euler/X which has been applied primarily for solving complex alignment problems in biological classification. In this paper, we demonstrate the feasibility and broad applicability of this approach to other domains and alignment problems in support of semantic interoperability.**



## KEYWORDS

taxonomy alignment, RCC-5, semantic interoperability


## INTRODUCTION

*[Amy and Tina meet at the water cooler]*

***Tina**: Hey Amy, can you recommend a signature dish from where you live?*

***Amy**: Oh, definitely the half-smokes from the Northeast! They are these tasty half-pork and half-beef sausages.*

***Tina**: What a coincidence! We have half-smokes in the South, too! Where do you live in the Northeast? New York? Boston?*

***Amy**: Wrong guesses! Where do you live in the South?*

*Tina and Amy together: Washington, D.C.*

*[The two of them look at each other, confused.]*

Vocabulary misunderstandings are common in our everyday lives. According to Bowker and Star (2000), "in the face of incompatible information or data structures among users or among those specifying the system, attempts to create unitary knowledge categories are futile. Rather, parallel or multiple representational forms are required" (p.159). In this fictional dialogue, neither Tina nor Amy is wrong. Perhaps Tina viewed Washington D.C. from the National Diversity Council's perspective of the United States, whereas Amy saw the United States according to the Census Regions map (Figure 1). We could attempt to ask the two to agree on one of the two taxonomies, but other human communicators will still have other ways to classify the United States with yet other categories.


80th Annual Meeting of the Association for Information Science & Technology, Washington, DC | Oct. 27-Nov. 1, 2017

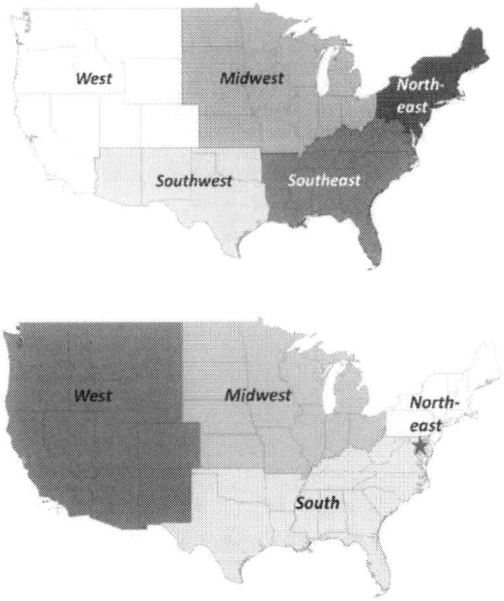


*Figure 1. Different geo-taxonomies of the contiguous United States, i.e., the 48 adjoining states and Washington DC (red star): National Diversity Council map NDC (top) and Census Bureau map CEN (bottom)*

The information sciences community has studied semantic interoperability extensively. For example, equivalence, hierarchical and associative relationships are often used to align multiple knowledge organization systems (KOS). However, these relationships can be defined ambiguously. For instance, equivalency among KOS can mean synonyms or near-synonyms; hierarchy may refer to exceedingly generic is-a relationships; and associative relationships may indicate everything that seems relevant. Such mapping relationships can be especially troublesome in crosswalks because they attempt to create a 'unitary' view of knowledge among different structures that are each internally coherent when used in specific contexts, but which appear to be in conflict when combined indiscriminately. In the end, this may result in data quality problems in the original KOS, such as granularity or meaning loss (de Andrade & Lopes Ginez de Lara, 2016; Chan & Zeng, 2006; Zeng & Chan, 2009).

We draw attention particularly to one type of KOS –taxonomies. Taxonomies, in a broad sense, are hierarchical structures that group similar objects together (Hodge, 2000). *Taxonomy alignment* is the term we use to address the issue of bridging, mapping or aligning two or more taxonomies. Taxonomies can be aligned in reference to a variety of similarity indicators, such as nomenclatural relationships, member composition or diagnostic features of child or parent nodes (Franz et al, 2015, 2016a, 2016b).

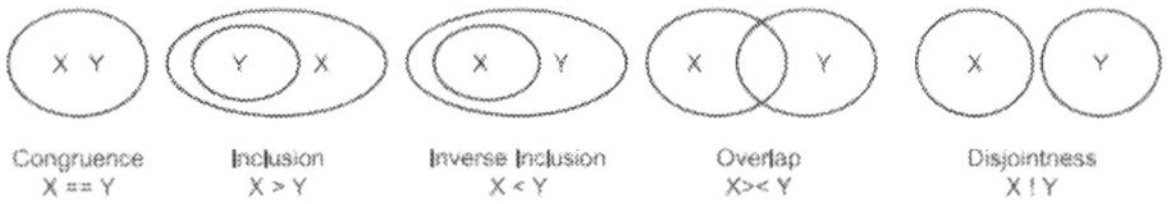


***Figure 2**. The region connection relations used in RCC-5*

Many fields have contributed to taxonomy alignment research, but the key new idea in our line of work (Chen et al., 2014; Franz et al., 2015, 2016a, 2016b; Thau & Ludäscher, 2007) is to compare concepts $X$ and $Y$ via five exhaustive and mutually exclusive relationships – *congruence, inclusion, inverse inclusion, overlap* and *disjointness* (Figure 2) from the region connection calculus RCC-5 (Randell et al., 1992; Cohn & Renz, 2008).

Our objectives for this paper are two-fold: first, we show the feasibility of using a logic-based approach for taxonomy alignment with RCC-5. Second, we illustrate the value of multi-taxonomy alignments in a way that both preserves the internal coherence and context of the input taxonomies $T_1$ and $T_2$, while at the same time providing a reconciled combined view $T_3$. $T_3$ exposes all relations between concepts in $T_1$ and $T_2$, implied by the input articulations $A$. We do this by providing two case studies that use a logic-based tool named Euler/X to align several geo-taxonomies derived from U.S. maps. First, we will align the National Diversity Council (NDC) map with the Census Bureau's Census Regions map (CEN), on the state-level, taking a bottom-up approach. Second, we will align the United States Time Zone (TZ) and CEN, on a regional level, taking a top-down approach.

## RELATED WORK

### *Semantic Interoperability*

Semantic interoperability is the capability for communication ensuring that the *meaning* or semantics of data, information or knowledge across sources is bridged. Semantic interoperability is particularly relevant between different knowledge organization systems (KOS), which are controlled vocabularies used in organizing information. Types of KOS include term lists, classifications (subject headings or taxonomies) and relationship models (Hodge, 2000). If existing KOS are different in structure, domain, language or granularity, it is necessary for the KOS to be transformed, mapped or merged to enable interoperability. Semantic interoperability in taxonomies means that the definitions and relations within different taxonomy systems are well-mapped (Zeng & Chan, 2009).

Three main types of mapping relationships between KOS (especially in the thesauri context) are equivalence, hierarchical and associative relationships. In crosswalks, in fact, equivalent mapping (or exact mapping) is the most prevalent relationship for linking two classification schemes together, and this is termed *absolute crosswalking*. It is usually used when two concepts in two or more KOS are synonyms or near-synonyms; and if there is no equivalent counterpart, absolute crosswalking mapping will not occur.

A less strict crosswalking approach is relative crosswalking, which means that all entities in one KOS will be mapped to at least one entity in the other KOS. However, this mapping process disregards whether or not the two entities are semantically equivalent. As long as there is a relevant entity to be matched with, relative crosswalking will occur.

Each crosswalking approach has its pros and cons. Absolute crosswalking ensures the equivalencies in concepts, but the data values will be empty whenever the mapping did not occur; relative crosswalking can overcome the data conversion problem that will happen with absolute crosswalking, but it will result in data quality problems if we want to trace back and resurrect the original KOS, such as losing granularity or missing meanings in the final integrated mapping work (de Andrade, J., & Lopes Ginez de Lara, 2016; Chan & Zeng, 2006; Zeng & Chan, 2009).

Equivalent mapping further creates problems when the original KOS includes a membership is-a condition. Different KOS differ strongly in granularity, naming systems and modeling styles, regardless of using either manual or automatic matching tools, researchers usually only map the equivalency on the superclass-level. Members in a superclass that were not mapped just automatically inherit the equivalency to the counterpart superclass in the other KOS (Kless, Milton, Kazmierczak & Lindenthal, 2015; Pfeifer & Peukert, 2015).

### The Taxonomy Alignment Problem (TAP)

From the KOS perspective, we have said that taxonomies, in a broad sense, are hierarchical structures that group similar objects together (Hodge, 2000). Taxonomies permit the assembly of multiple alternative, internally coherent hierarchies where all concepts derived from one hierarchy can be connected via parent-child ("is-a") relationships (Thau & Ludäscher, 2007; Thau, Bowers, & Ludäscher, 2008).

In this paper, we focus on *taxonomy alignment problems* (TAP), where the given taxonomies $T_1$, $T_2$ are inter-linked (or "formally crosswalked") via a set of input *articulations* $A$, defined as RCC-5 relations (see below), to yield a "merged" taxonomy $T_3$. Any solution taxonomy $T_3$ of a TAP must satisfy all logic constraints implied by the inputs $T_1$, $T_2$, and $A$ (so $T_3$ must be *sound*) and must reveal all pairwise relationships between concepts in $T_1$ and $T_2$ (so $T_3$ must be *complete*). A TAP with inputs $T_1$, $T_2$, and $A$ may have zero, one or many solutions $T_3$, in which case we call the input TAP, *inconsistent*, *unique* or *ambiguous*, respectively. If a TAP is inconsistent, this means it contains a logical contradiction, and some articulation constraints in $A$ have to be relaxed (e.g., adding a disjunction to allow for multiple options), repaired (choosing a different articulation relationship) or even dropped. Multiple solutions $T_3$ are generated by the Euler/X tool, e.g., in the form of multiple *answer sets* (Gebser, Kaminski, Kaufmann & Schaub, 2012) or *possible worlds* (Denecker, Lierler, Truszczynski & Vennekens, 2012).

Different fields have contributed to taxonomy alignment research. In discussing semantic heterogeneity problems in digital libraries, Jung (2006) computes the similarity in distance between the concepts in different digital libraries and tries to align them. In text mining, Pfeifer and Peukert (2015) proposed a schema-based and instance-based similarity alignment for taxonomies using statistical metrics. We propose to use RCC-5 with its five base relations when aligning taxonomies, and we propose this as a complementary, "high resolution" approach for cross walking and integrating taxonomies.

Though taxonomy alignment problems are applicable in many domains, such as corporate taxonomies, website taxonomies and scientific taxonomies (Souza, Tudhope, & Almeida, 2012), Linnaean taxonomies are probably one of the oldest and most prominent examples. These taxonomies organize (typically) perceived species of living organisms into higher-level classifications (Franz & Thau, 2010). Concepts can be aligned in reference to a variety of similarity indicators, such as nomenclatural relationships, member composition or diagnostic features of child or parent nodes (Franz et al., 2015). Other domains include phonetics and genealogies and taxonomies in comparative sub-disciplines as well as in conservation (Franz et al., 2016b). As described in Franz et al. (2016a), biological classifications evolve in light of new knowledge while re-using existing names under a complex set of rules. Over time, this leads to many-to-many relationships between properly formed taxonomic names and their (former versus current) biological meanings (Remsen, 2016). The temporal evolution of biological classifications can be complex, due to the interaction of new and revised insights with naming rules established in this community. Therefore, if there is a need to integrate biodiversity data across taxonomies, using just taxonomic names and nomenclatural relationships will not be enough to understand and reconcile the different taxonomic perspectives (Franz et al., 2016a).

### Euler/X

Euler/X (https://github.com/EulerProject/) is an open source logic-based tool that uses RCC-5 to align and reconcile taxonomies. Different underlying reasoners can be used by Euler/X, solving TAPs via FO (first-order), ASP (answer set programming) or direct RCC reasoning, i.e., X∈{FO, ASP, RCC}. A detailed system overview of Euler/X can be found in Chen et al. (2014). We have used the current Euler2 prototype of the toolkit in our research. The following are among the terms related to the Euler/X tool:

### Articulations

An articulation is a constraint or rule that defines a relationship (a set constraint) between two concepts from different taxonomies. Each articulation is of the form $X$ o $Y$, where $X$ and $Y$ are concepts from $T_1$ and $T_2$, respectively, and where "o" is a RCC-5 relation. Articulations can come from domain experts (who may link them to the relevant underlying evidence), or may be generated from data directly. Given two taxonomies $T_1$, $T_2$, an example of an articulation is [T1.Cherry_Blossom **equals** T2.Sakura]. Taxonomy $T_1$ has the concept Cherry_Blossom, whereas in $T_2$ its equivalent counterpart concept is named Sakura.

### *Region Connection Calculus (RCC)*

RCC is used for qualitative (often, but not necessarily spatial) representation and reasoning and can be seen as a decidable fragment of first-order predicate logic (Cohn & Renz, 2008). This fragment is also closely related to set constraints and monadic first-order logic (Bachmair, Ganzinger & Waldmann, 1993; Bodirsky & Hils, 2012). RCC-5 is the variant of the RCC family used in Euler/X, consisting of five pairwise disjoint and mutually exclusive relations (Figure 2), i.e., *congruence* (equals or "==" in Euler/X-generated figures), *proper inclusion* (includes or ">" in Euler/X), *inverse proper inclusion* (is_included_in or "<"), *overlap* (overlaps or "><"), and *disjointness* (disjoint or "!") .

### *Possible Worlds*

When encoding and solving TAPs via ASP, the different answer sets represent alternative taxonomy merge solutions or possible worlds (PWs). Each PW satisfies all given TAP constraints and assigns exactly one of the basic five RCC-5 relations to each pair of concepts, removing disjunctive ambiguity. Thus, each PW provides a distinct solution for satisfying all input conditions.

## RESEARCH DESIGN

We use a case study design with two cases. Figure 3 shows how we implemented logic-based mapping using Euler/X. The three main steps to implement this logic-based approach are:

**Step 1.** Supply input taxonomies $T_1$ and $T_2$
**Step 2.** Formulate RCC-5 articulations between $T_1$ and $T_2$
**Step 3.** Iteratively edit articulations in Euler/X

### *Step 1: Supply input taxonomies $T_1$ and $T_2$*

Our two cases use these three maps rendering the contiguous United States in three different ways:

1. The Census Regions Map1 (CEN), consists of four regions: West, Midwest, Northeast and South, i.e., the contiguous 48 states and Washington D.C.
2. The National Diversity Council Map2 (NDC), consists of five regions: West, Southwest, Midwest, Northeast, Southeast, the 48 states and Washington D.C.
3. The Time Zone map3 (TZ), consists of four regions: Pacific, Mountain, Central and Eastern.

To prepare these regions for entry into Euler/X, we transcribe each map into a hierarchical taxonomic structure in plain text format, (**PARENT** CHILD1 CHILD2 ...):

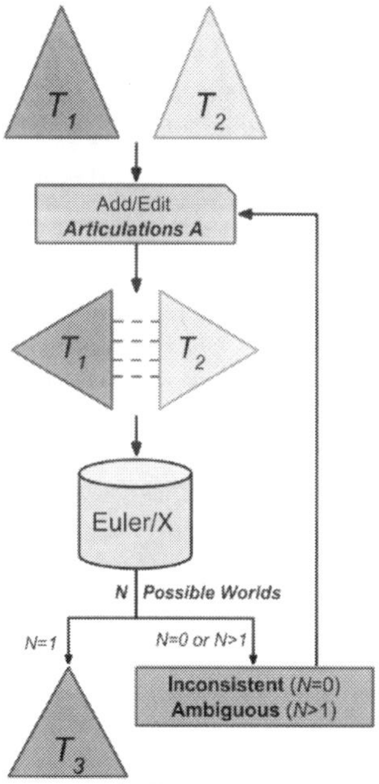


***Figure 3.*** *The process of aligning taxonomies T1 and T2 with Euler/X*

*1.* ***CEN***

For example, in the CEN case, the four regions Northeast, Midwest, South and West are all children of USA:

(**USA** Northeast Midwest South West)

Then, we indicate the states within each region (States abbreviated in 2 letters) in the same parent-child structure:

(**Northeast** CT MA ME NH NJ NY PA RI VT)

(**Midwest** IL IN IA KS MI MN MO NE ND OH SD WI)

(**South** AL AR DE DC FL GA KY LA MD MS NC OK SC TN TX VA WV)

(**West** AZ CA CO ID MT NV NM OR UT WA WY)

*2.* ***NDC***

Analogously, we convert the NDC map into this taxonomic structure:

(**USA** Midwest Northeast Southeast Southwest West)

(**Northeast** CT DC DE MD MA ME NH NJ NY PA RI VT)

(**Midwest** IA IL IN KS MI MN MO ND NE OH SD WI)

(**Southeast** AL AR FL GA KY LA MS NC SC TN VA WV)

(Southwest AZ NM OK TX)

(**West** CA CO ID MT NV OR WA WY UT)

---

[1] CEN: https://www2.census.gov/geo/pdfs/maps-data/maps/reference/us_regdiv.pdf
[2] NDC: http://www.nationaldiversitycouncil.org/wp-content/uploads/2017/12/us_regions.jpg
[3]TZ:https://nationalmap.gov/small_scale/printable/images/pdf/reference/timezones4.pdf

### 3. *TZ*

In the TZ taxonomy, a single state can have counties with different time zones. For example, some parts of Indiana use Central Time while other parts use Eastern Time. This means that there are overlaps between the regional boundaries of times (e.g., Eastern, Central) and those of states (e.g., Indiana). Also, the TZ map itself (Figure 4) does not label the state-level concept names, therefore, we modelled the TZ taxonomy with just one line:

(**USA** Pacific Mountain Central Eastern)

### Step 2: Formulate RCC-5 articulations

In our case studies, we are comparing (1) the CEN taxonomy with the NDC taxonomy and (2) the CEN taxonomy and the TZ taxonomy for the contiguous United States (48 states and D.C.). The comparisons are fairly straightforward from looking at the maps so that users can easily formulate their own articulations. In general, in order to compare taxonomies in a specific domain, we may need a domain expert's input on how to formulate the articulations between taxonomies. Using RCC-5 relationships equals (==), includes (>), is_included_in (<), overlaps (><) and disjoint (!), the following are the articulations we formulated:

(1) **CEN vs. NDC** (49 articulations, all with 'equal' relationships; only 5 shown here):

[CEN.AL equals NDC.AL]
[CEN.AR equals NDC.AR]
[CEN.AZ equals NDC.AZ]
[CEN.CA equals NDC.CA]
[CEN.CO equals NDC.CO]

(2) **CEN vs. TZ** (12 articulations):

[CEN.Midwest disjoint TZ.Pacific]
[CEN.Midwest overlaps TZ.Eastern]
[CEN.Midwest overlaps TZ.Mountain]
[CEN.Northeast is_included_in TZ.Eastern]
[CEN.South disjoint TZ.Pacific]
[CEN.South overlaps TZ.Central]
[CEN.South overlaps TZ.Eastern]
[CEN.South overlaps TZ.Mountain]
[CEN.USA equals TZ.USA]
[CEN.West disjoint TZ.Central]
[CEN.West disjoint TZ.Eastern]
[CEN.West overlaps TZ.Mountain]

To demonstrate how we formulated the (2) CEN-TZ articulations, we compare the Time Zone map (Figure 4) directly with the Census Regions map (Figure 5). We started by looking at one region from TZ first, and came up with all the articulations about that region, then move on to the next. For example, we can start with TZ.Eastern, and it is very obvious that TZ.Eastern cannot geographically relate to CEN.West, therefore we can determine that CEN.West is disjoint with TZ.Eastern. Next, we can also see clearly from the two maps that the area for TZ.Eastern is bigger than that of CEN.Northeast, so we can make the assumption that the whole area of CEN.Northeast is_included_in TZ.Eastern. However, not all TZ.Eastern is an inclusion of CEN.South, only the southern part of TZ.Eastern is included in CEN.South; likewise, only a few parts around the Michigan Lake Area for TZ.Eastern is included in the CEN.Midwest. Thus, we can formulate our articulations such that CEN.South and CEN.Midwest overlaps with TZ.Eastern. In the same manner, we can formulate articulations for the Central, Mountain, and Pacific Time Zone areas.

### Step 3: Iteratively edit articulations within Euler/X

Given taxonomies $T_1$, $T_2$, and articulations $A$, Euler/X infers from these all *possible worlds* $W_1, W_2, \ldots, W_N$. Each world $W_i$ represent a solution taxonomy $T_3$, simultaneously satisfying $T_1$, $T_2$, and $A$. If there are no possible worlds ($N$=0) (Figure 3) then the input TAP is inconsistent (i.e., a contradiction can be derived) and the user must repair, relax, or drop some articulations in $A$. Conversely, if $A$ is underspecified and ambiguous, a large (exponential) number of worlds ($N$>1) may be derived. Usually, the objective is to find a unique world ($N$=1) that includes the input taxonomies, or a small number of worlds that reflect ambiguities that cannot be resolved (Franz et al., 2015).

When formulating articulations, we may overlook some articulations that the reasoning process requires in order to find only one or few suitable alignments. This problem will become more severe as our taxonomy alignment problems become larger. For example, in the CEN versus NDC taxonomy case, it is understandable that when we are writing out articulations, we may lose track and forget one or two states in the articulations. Or, when specifying the input for the CEN versus TZ example, it might not be obvious how to write out all 12 articulations needed to obtain one possible world, and we might only have, e.g., 11 at first. For example, when comparing Figures 4 and 5, it may not be obvious that there is a small area in Texas of TZ.Mountain that happens to be overlapping with CEN.South area. These missing articulations will result in underspecified input TAPs and thus in multiple possible worlds.

Euler/X can identify which sets of articulations are ambiguous and derive articulations that are logically implied, but not part of the given user input. This automatic 'ambiguity check' is not available when we do other types of aligning work such as absolute crosswalking or relative crosswalking. If the user underspecified an element in a relative crosswalking method, there will be no simple means to detect it and make it explicit. By iteratively checking the results Euler/X generated, and fixing the equivocal articulations, we can eventually get to the single solution (possible world) we are seeking.

## RESULTS

The first part of the results is on the CEN-NDC case, while the second part describes the CEN-TZ case. All the files and figures we showed in this study is available in this repository: https://github.com/EulerProject/ASIST17.

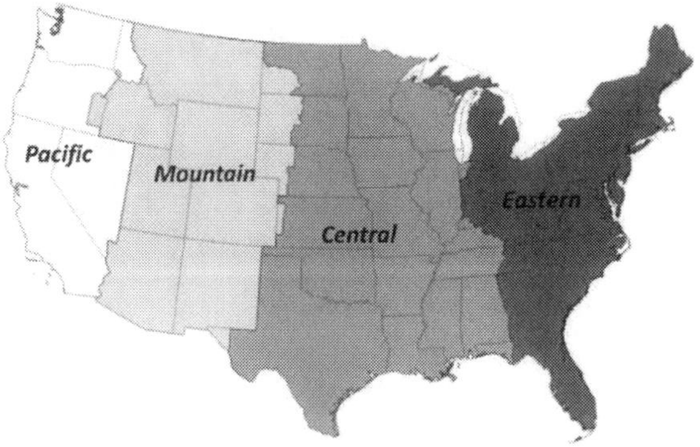

*Figure 4. Time Zone map (TZ) for contiguous U.S*

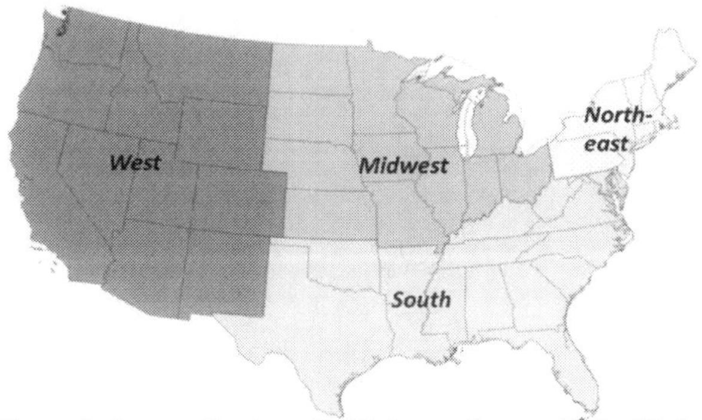

*Figure 5. Census Regions (CEN) for contiguous UnitedStates*

## CASE 1: CEN VERSUS NDC

### *State-level alignments are all congruent*

Case 1 aims to align the National Diversity Council taxonomy with the Census Regions taxonomy. This case serves as an example of the bottom-up approach of resolving taxonomy alignment problems. Corresponding to Figure 2, this use case entails the NDC taxonomy, CEN taxonomy and the 49 articulations that the users formulated as the input file into the Euler/X tool. Euler/X then can produce the input visualization shown in Figure 6 (next page). We can easily see that the 48 states and Washington D.C. from either side of the taxonomy are mapped with 'equal' signs. This is the input articulations that we put in, Euler/X has not yet inferred anything for us in this input visualization.

In Figure 7 (next page), the output is a single possible world, automatically generated and visualized by Euler/X. Euler/X depicts pairs of congruent concepts in the same grey rounded box. We can see that each of the states (and D.C.) from the two taxonomies are all in grey boxes, denoting that these lowest level (the children) alignments are congruent. In other words, both taxonomies agree at the lowest level (children) that the physical boundaries for each state are the same for either NDC or CEN. Interestingly, the two taxonomies also agree completely on the Midwest.

### *Inferred new articulations for regional-level alignments*

On the upper-level classifications, we can see from the input visualization (Figure 6) that the big clusters of the CEN and NDC corresponding parents (CEN.West, South, Northeast, Midwest; NDC.West, Southeast, Southwest, Northeast, Midwest) are slightly off-center and do not align properly with each other like the states did. However, just from the input file we formulated on our own, it is not clear what the relationships between the upper-level classifications are, or what relationships the states have on upper-level concepts. Does NDC.Northeast equal CEN.Northeast? Does CEN.West include NDC.Southwest? The upper-level alignments were underspecified before Euler/X automatically inferred the relationships for us. The newly inferred articulations (Figure 7) made are depicted as red arrows, while the dotted lines tell us which concepts are overlapping.

The inferred articulations about the parents (CEN.West, South, Northeast, Midwest; NDC.West, Southeast, Southwest,Northeast, Midwest) are:

[CEN.USA equals NDC.USA]
[CEN.West includes NDC.West]
[CEN.South includes NDC.Southeast]
[CEN.South overlaps NDC.Southwest]
[CEN.South overlaps NDC.Northeast]
[CEN.Northeast is_included_in NDC.Northeast]
[CEN.Midwest equals NDC.Midwest]

The results explicitly constrain certain parent-level articulations that were not explicitly provided in the user's input articulations. In that sense, the reasoning has newly expressed information that we can now add to the original input to obtain a better-specified new input version.

In this case, we can also see our claim that using a RCC-5 logic-based approach in Euler/X allows us to preserve the original taxonomies in the merged view (Figure 7). This is a unique possible world, where the two taxonomies can both reside in and still maintain their own taxonomic names and hierarchical taxonomy structure.

Revisiting our introductory prompt about Tina and Amy and the half-smokes, the Euler/X-inferred graph (Figure 7) allows us to understand that although our speakers agreed on the lowest (state or city) level that they are congruent in both taxonomies, their disagreement is seen on a higher, regional-level. In Figure 7, marked in orange dotted boxes and bolded arrows, Washington D.C. is actually included in the South region in the CEN taxonomy, whereas in the NDC taxonomy, D.C. is included in the Northeast region.

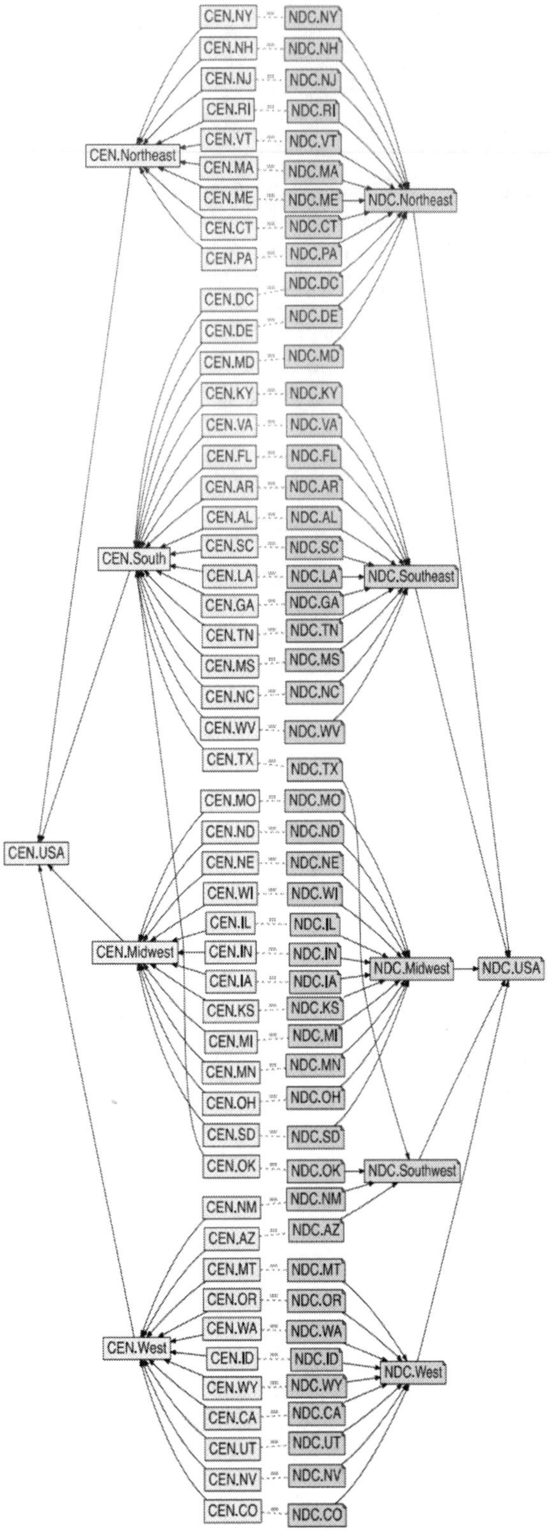


***Figure 6.*** *CEN-NDC taxonomy alignment problem with 49 input articulations between $T_{CEN}$ and $T_{NDC}$*

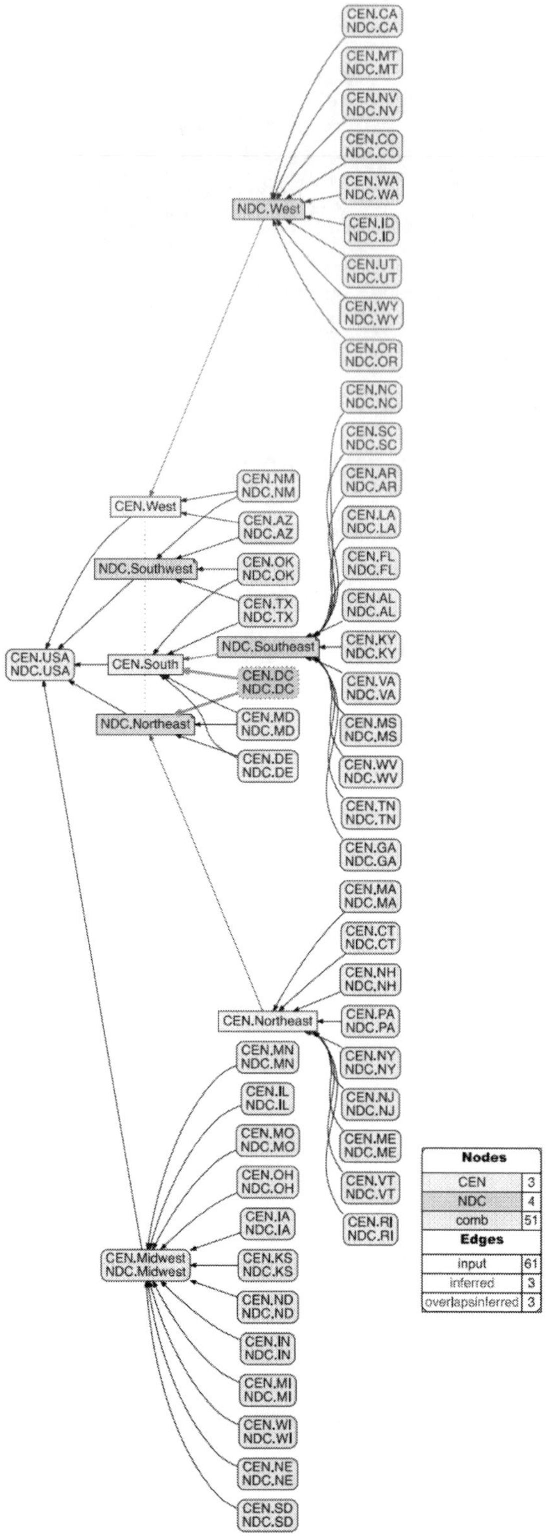


**Figure 7.** The unique possible world (PW) $T_3$ reconciling $T_{CEN}$ and $T_{NDC}$ via inferred relationships

### *Case 2: CEN versus TZ*
### *Top-down regional alignment*

The Census Regions taxonomy versus Time Zone case serves as a top-down example for taxonomy alignments. Since state boundaries are non-congruent with time zone boundaries, it is hard to model the articulations on the state-level alignments like we did with Case 1. For example, in Figure 4 where Mountain Time Zone and Central Time Zone overlap, we may be able to point out that the state on the very top is North Dakota, but we cannot really discern which counties of North Dakota are in the Mountain Time Zone and which other ones are in the Central Time Zone. If we want to model the situation as in Case 1 where all lowest-level alignments are equal, in this case, we may have to be more granular and model county-level articulations. This would work in theory, but it would be an onerous process since the contiguous (i.e., lower 48) US states consist of more than 3000 counties, requiring us to model as many county-level articulations.

An alternative way to represent the non-congruent parent regions is to provide the higher-level regional articulations directly to the Euler/X toolkit as input. The following input shows how we represent the corresponding two taxonomies with just 12 articulations:

**taxonomy CEN Census_Regions**
(**USA** Midwest South West Northeast)
**taxonomy TZ Time_Zone**
(**USA** Pacific Mountain Central Eastern)
**articulations CEN TZ**
[CEN.Midwest disjoint TZ.Pacific]
[CEN.Midwest overlaps TZ.Eastern]
[CEN.Midwest overlaps TZ.Mountain]
[CEN.Northeast is_included_in TZ.Eastern]
[CEN.South disjoint TZ.Pacific]
[CEN.South overlaps TZ.Central]
[CEN.South overlaps TZ.Eastern]
[CEN.South overlaps TZ.Mountain]
[CEN.USA equals TZ.USA]
[CEN.West disjoint TZ.Central]
[CEN.West disjoint TZ.Eastern]
[CEN.West overlaps TZ.Mountain]

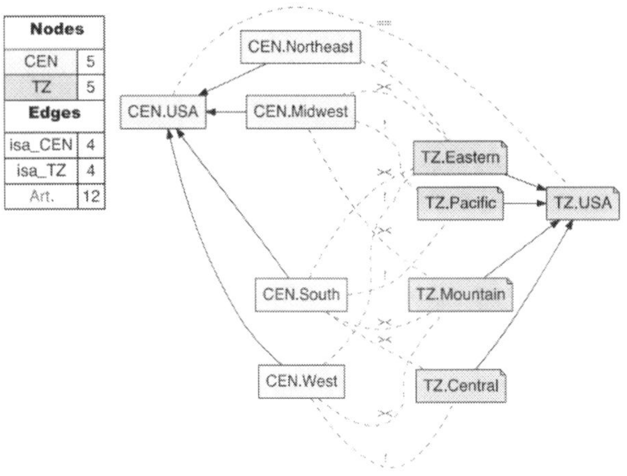


***Figure 8**. Input visualization of the region-level input alignments between $T_{CEN}$ and $T_{TZ}$*

Figure 8 shows the visualization for these input constraints, where none of the input regions show congruent (==) articulations. Every link is either overlapping, disjoint, proper inclusion.

The single possible world Euler/X generated for this alignment can be seen in Figure 9. This gives us a view in which Time Zone regions are aligned with the Census Regions but at the same time the original taxonomies are still preserved. We can see this by looking at the colored boxes in Figure 9: CEN concepts are in yellow boxes, while TZ concepts are in green clipped boxes. Euler/X also infers underspecified articulations in the input file; these are shown in the red arrows and dotted lines in Figure 9. For example, the Pacific Time Zone is properly included in the West Census Region, as shown by the red arrow pointing from TZ.Pacific to CEN.West.

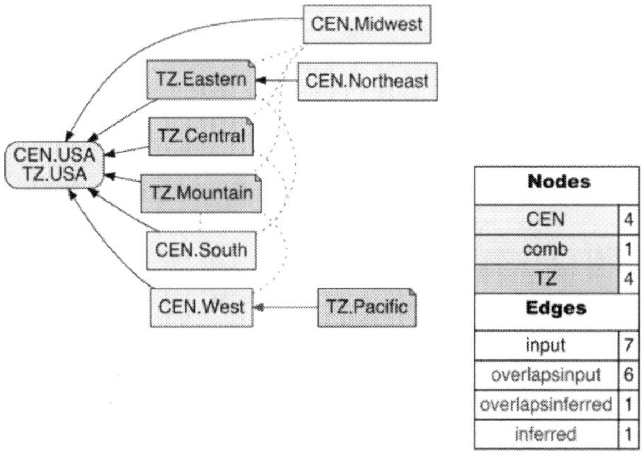


***Figure 9.** The unique PW for the $T_{CEN}$ with $T_{TZ}$ alignment*

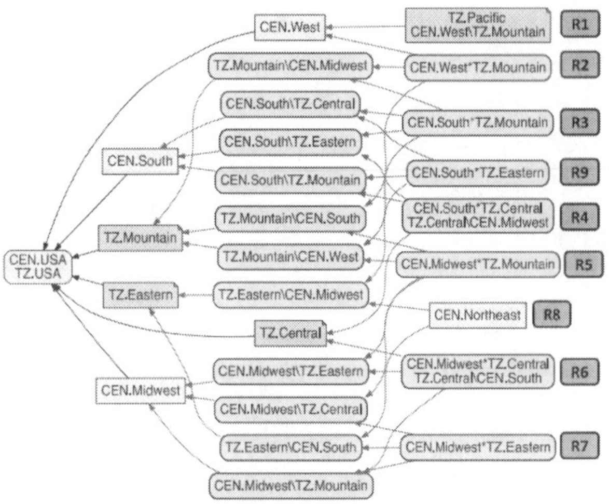


***Figure 10.*** *Combined concepts solution for $T_{CEN}$ and $T_{TZ}$*

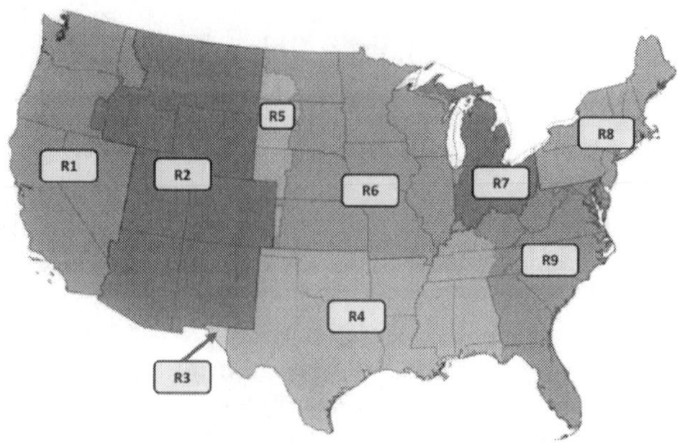


***Figure 11.*** *A GIS overlay of CEN and TZ maps confirms the logically derived solution with 9 new regions*

### *Combined concepts solution for regional-level alignments*

In the $T_{CEN}$ and $T_{TZ}$ case, since there are a lot of overlapping relationships (Figure 9), it seems even more necessary than in Case 1 ($T_{CEN}$ and $T_{NDC}$) to represent which subregions overlap at a granular level. According to Euler/X's combined concepts solution (Figure 10), there are 18 new combined concepts regions (pink round-edges boxes) formed from our case. For instance, we can now tell that only the intersection of Census Regions West and Mountain Time Zone (denoted CEN.West*TZ.Mountain) can be counted as properly included in CEN.West. We can also infer from this graph that the intersection area of TZ.Central and CEN.Midwest (CEN.Midwest*TZ.Central) is congruent with the Central Time Zone area excluding the Census Region's South (TZ.Central \ CEN.South).

### *Comparing Euler solutions with a GIS solution*

When overlaying the four regions in TZ and the five regions in CEN with a geographic information system (GIS), a new map with nine regions is created (Figure 11). These correspond to the nine leaf nodes produced by Euler/X (Figure 10). A total of 18 new concepts are generated by Euler/X to explain all containment and overlaps relationships in the result via concept *intersection* $A*B$ and *difference* $A\backslash B$.

By using only the merged GIS results, we can see what the new nine regions are, but there are no terms to describe each region except by creating new names. In Euler/X, when we resolve the output regions individually using the new labels, it tells us how regions are aligned – at the granular output region level – in order to form the 18 new regions. The Euler combined concept visualization also indicates that not all nine output regions are entirely new. The newly formed ones – those for which there is no adequate input region vocabulary – are the seven leaf-level regions in pink (Figure 10). We also labelled the corresponding nine regions of the GIS view from R1 to R9 in Figure 10.

Using the Euler/X results, we can name the new 18 regions based on our original taxonomies using $A*B$ (again: "*" means *intersection* or AND), and $A\backslash B$ ("\"denotes *set difference* or NOT). For instance, we see that R1 is simply TZ.Pacific; alternatively we can say it is CEN.West without the TZ.Mountain area (CEN.West\TZ.Mountain). Similarly, we can describe R3 as the intersection between TZ.Mountain and CEN.South (TZ.Mountain*CEN.South).

In the special case of spatial taxonomies chosen for our study here, we are able to visualize how two maps relate to each other by overlaying them in a GIS. Here, the GIS merged results serve as a "ground truth" with which to independently assess the validity of the Euler/X results, and the former demonstrate clearly that the Euler/X alignments are an adequate method for taxonomy alignments.

However the more typical cases for taxonomy alignment require articulations between non-spatial taxonomies, i.e., for which no GIS route or direct visual cues about regional extensions are available. In general, the use of RCC-5 as an alignment vocabulary is a suitable approach to perform a wide range of multi-hierarchy reconciliations, whether these are spatial in an immediate sense or in a more abstract sense of aligning the extensions of different conceptual regions.

## DISCUSSION

Based on the findings of this study, we hold that our logic-based taxonomy alignment approach can be used to solve a broad spectrum of crosswalking issues of concern to the information sciences community. If taxonomies are aligned not just based on their names or equivalent crosswalking, but based on the extent of congruence that each concept has with its counterparts, then we will be able to mitigate the membership condition problems that occur in equivalent crosswalking. By logically aligning each concept with its counterpart in another taxonomy, members of a superclass will have a comprehensive set of reasoner-validated relations to other concepts, instead of automatically inheriting the relationship from its superclass. In addition, our logic-based RCC-5 approach preserves the original taxonomies while providing an alignment view. Such alignments can solve data integration problems that happen in the more coarse-grained relative crosswalking, which otherwise is subjected to information loss. If future studies based off of our integrative alignments want to recover each unaltered input taxonomy, the semantics and structures in both taxonomies will be well-preserved and reproducible.

An implication is that our study also underscores the benefits of designing different alignment workflows, e.g., here *bottom-up* versus *top-down*, to match the needs of specific taxonomy alignment problems. The bottom-up approach seems to work well whenever we have non-overlapping relationships at the leaf-level (lowest-level) articulations, and we are not sure how the higher-level concepts should be aligned. The bottom-up alignment can help us to infer the underspecified articulations at the parent level(s). The top-down alignment approach, on the other hand, seems favorable when there is an expectation of certain higher-level articulations in conjunction with under-specified, complex, and often overlapping leaf-level relations. Expert input will frequently be needed to establish such expectations under the top-down approach.

## CONCLUSIONS

In our study, we have explored the feasibility of using logic-based RCC-5 articulations to align different regional classifications of the United States. Our results demonstrate that this approach to taxonomy alignments is feasible and it suggests a promising way to enhance semantic interoperability.

In Case 1, we compared the National Diversity Council map with the Census Regions map in a bottom-up approach, in which 49 tip-level articulations (the 48 states and Washington D.C.) can be congruently asserted, not in the absolute crosswalking sense but using the logic-based RCC-5 relation. We call this case a bottom-up approach because Euler/X can leverage these tip-level articulations to unambiguously infer the higher, region-level articulations (e.g., that CEN.West includes NDC.West).

On the other hand, in Case 2, we aligned the U.S. Time Zone map with the Census Regions map in a top-down manner, realizing that it is laborious to use a bottom-up approach when different subsets of counties of one state participate in multiple time zones. We provided 12 articulations – none of them congruence – that show how each higher-level input region can be spatially reconciled with its respective counterparts. In this case, we were able to also visually represent alignments at the more granular level of the output regions generated by overlapping input regions. By contrasting Euler/X's alignments with the GIS results, we can see that Euler/X is able to identify nine new regions that result from partial input region overlap while at the same time still uses and newly combines the names the input regions to create unique output region labels (e.g. Region 9 is "TZ.Eastern*CEN.South"). This extended or hybrid vocabulary preserves the provenance of input region naming while generating new and more granular label sets needed to characterize each alignment region at the fine-grained level, whereas the GIS results provide no such provenance-aware region-identifying terminology for each output region.

To conclude, we have shown that the logic-based taxonomy alignments in RCC-5 can align distinct taxonomies to facilitate semantic interoperability, while preserving the internal coherence and context of each taxonomy. In future research, we envision investigating more sophisticated alignment cases in information science, such as aligning multiple metadata standards. We also envision that one day, in the face of conflicting views, we will be more willing to agree to disagree, and perhaps even redefine *synthesis* this way.

## ACKNOWLEDGMENTS

Support of the authors' research through the National Science Foundation is kindly acknowledged (DEB-1155984, DBI-1342595, and DBI-1643002). The authors thank Professor Kathryn La Barre for her comments and suggestions. We would also like to thank Dr. Laetitia Navarro and Jeff Terstriep for help with creating map overlays in QGIS.

## REFERENCES

Bachmair, L., Ganzinger, H., & Waldmann, U. (1993). Set constraints are the monadic class. *Logic in Computer Science*, 75–83. doi:10.1109/LICS.1993.287598.

Bodirsky, M., & Hils. (2012). Tractable set constraints. *J. Artif. Int. Res.* 45 (1): 731–759.

Bowker, G. C., & Star, S. L. (2000). Sorting things out: Classification and its consequences. MIT Press.

Chan, L. M. & Zeng, M. L. (2006). Metadata interoperability and standardization–A study of methodology part I. D-*Lib Magazine, 12*(6).

Chen, M., Yu, S., Kianmajd, P., Franz N., Bowers, S., and Ludäscher, B. (2014). *Provenance for explaining taxonomy alignments.* In *Provenance and annotation of data and processes*, 258–60. Springer, Cham. doi:10.1007/978-3-319-16462-5_27.

Cohn, A. G., & Renz, J. (2008). Qualitative spatial representation and reasoning. *Foundations of Artificial Intelligence*, 3, 551-596.

de Andrade, J., & Lopes Ginez de Lara, M. (2016). Interoperability and mapping between knowledge organization systems: Metathesaurus—unified medical language system of the National Library of Medicine. *Knowledge Organization, 43*(2).

Denecker, M., Lierler, Y., Truszczynski, M., & Vennekens, J. (2012). A Tarskian informal semantics for answer set programming. Intl. Conf. on Logic Programming (ICLP), 17:277–289. LIPIcs. Dagstuhl, Germany. doi:10.4230/LIPIcs.ICLP.2012.277.

Franz, N. M., Chen, M., Kianmajd, P., Yu, S., Bowers, S., Weakley, A. S., & Ludäscher, B. (2016a). Names are not good enough: Reasoning over taxonomic change in the Andropogon complex1. *Semantic Web, 7*(6), 645-667.

Franz, N. M., Chen, M., Yu, S., Kianmajd, P., Bowers, S., & Ludäscher, B. (2015). Reasoning over taxonomic change: exploring alignments for the Perelleschus use case. *PloS One, 10(2)*.doi:10.1371/journal.pone.0118247.

Franz, N. M., Pier, N. M., Reeder, D. M., Chen, M., Yu, S., Kianmajd, P. & Ludäscher, B. (2016b). Two influential primate classifications logically aligned. *Systematic Biology, 65*(4), 561-582.

Gebser, M., Kaminski, R., Kaufmann, B., & Schaub, T. (2012). Answer set solving in practice. *Synthesis Lectures on Artificial Intelligence and Machine Learning, 6*(3), 1-238.

Hodge, G. (2000). *Systems of knowledge organization for digital libraries: Beyond traditional authority files.* Washington, D.C.: Digital Library Federation, Council on Library and Information Resources.

Jung, J. J. (2006, November). Taxonomy alignment for interoperability between heterogeneous digital libraries. In International conference on asian digital libraries (p. 274-282). Berlin Heidelberg: Springer.

Kless, D., Milton, S., Kazmierczak, E., & Lindenthal, J. (2015). Thesaurus and ontology structure: Formal and pragmatic differences and similarities. *Journal of the Association for Information Science and Technology, 66*(7), 1348-1366.doi:10.1002/asi.23268.

Pfeifer, K., & Peukert, E. (2013, September). *Integration of text mining taxonomies.* In International joint conference on knowledge discovery, knowledge engineering, and knowledge management (p. 39-55). Berlin Heidelberg: Springer. doi:10.1007/978-3-662-46549-3_3.

Randell, D. A., Cui, Z., & Cohn, A. G. (1992). A spatial logic based on regions and connection. *Knowledge Representation and Reason, 92*, 165-176.

Remsen, D. (2016). The use and limits of scientific names in biological informatics. *ZooKeys*, (550), 207.

Souza, R. R., Tudhope, D., & Almeida, M. B. (2012). Towards a taxonomy of KOS: Dimensions for classifying knowledge organization systems. *Knowledge Organization, 39*(3), 179-192.

Thau, D., & Ludäscher, B. (2007). Reasoning about taxonomies in first-order logic. *Ecological Informatics, 2*(3), 195-209.

Thau, D., Bowers, S., & Ludäscher, B. (2008, October). Merging taxonomies under RCC-5 algebraic articulations. In Proceedings of the 2nd international workshop on ontologies and information systems for the semantic web (p. 47-54). ACM.

Zeng, M. L., & Chan, L. M. (2009). Semantic interoperability. Encyclopedia of Library and Information Sciences, 3rd Edition, 4645–62. CRC Press.

# Before Information Literacy [Or, Who Am I, As a Subject-Of-(Information)-Need?]

**Ronald E. Day**
*Dept. of Information and Library Science. Indiana University-Bloomington, USA. roday@indiana.edu*

## ABSTRACT

In this paper, I discuss an alternative to information literacy and technical fixes for fake news and other such misleading information: the education and self-interrogation of the subject who needs information. Information has many different forms, types of truth claims and criteria for truth. Much of our daily information intake has nothing to do with true or untrue knowledge, but rather, involves tastes and opinions. If we confuse the conditions for public or learned knowledge with these, or even if we do not recognize how such knowledge also has its own institutional senses of taste, we will mislead ourselves based on false assumptions about what it is that different documents can inform us of. The subject-of-(information)-need, or the "user," is the bedrock notion of the subject in information retrieval, but it is constructed by the information environment it finds itself within. If the user cannot judge this environment before using it, then information literacy cannot be of enough help.

## KEYWORDS

subject, information need, users, document, fake news

## INTRODUCTION

There has been much discussion of how the internet and, particularly, social networks, have led to a post-subject world, or at least a world of a new subjectivity. But it may be objected that this is not necessarily true by evoking one simple example: that of so-called *fake news*. Fake news is nothing new, but what is new is how such news is delivered as a product of information technologies. The suggested response to this has been two fixes: first, that of developing better algorithms to sort the true from the false. The second is that of an older tradition, information literacy. We can see from these two sides, however, that we have not left the subject-object, subject-information divide. Here, I would like to insert a third alternative, a certain form of information literacy, but one that takes place before the evaluation of "information." I would like to suggest that a fundamental issue in information seeking is that of, first, the question of what is information on the internet, and with this, the very personal question that the subject must ask him or herself even before searching, namely, what sort of subject-of-(information)-need am I? We will see here that many of the most fundamental issues of human existence and information seeking are the same as they have always been. One problem is how and why this is obscured in the comparatively recent medium. Another issue is the difficulty of obtaining and using knowledge and how this cannot be separated from having and trusting in modern institutions. Knowledge may result in information, but information doesn't necessarily have to come from or result in knowledge. Information can be opinion, instruction and so forth (as Plato recognized).

## INFORMATION AND DOCUMENT

For the first question of what is information on the internet, there is a surprisingly easy answer. As I discussed in my book *Indexing it All: the Subject in the Age of Documentation, Information, and Data* (Day, 2014), if we examine the history of information science during its development in the 1960s through the 1980s and beyond, we see a shift from document retrieval to information retrieval. Before information retrieval in the mid-1960s and beyond, the term *information* largely referred to the retrieval of physical, documentary items (or their photocopied replica). Gradually in the 20$^{th}$ century, starting with Paul Otlet's work at least, a more secondary meaning became primary: the meaning of the text or content of what was within the document (its "aboutness"). This shift from an interest in retrieving documents to retrieving information (this term corresponding to the aboutness of documents) was afforded by the greater emphasis upon the reading of descriptive metadata, not just as a heuristic of finding the document, but as a substitute for the document itself.

Within what we'll call traditional document retrieval, the retrieval of a physical item was gotten through the shelf placement of the document (let us take books as the privileged form here) and the knowledge of the librarian or the owner of the book, or, through bibliographic metadata such as titles, author name, item number and placement (for example, call numbers), and of course, subject or other indexing terms that described the "aboutness" of the book. These devices were not the information of the book, but rather, information about the book. But gradually, not only in modern information retrieval, but also before that in the increasing reliance of readers upon back of the book indexes and in journal abstracts, we see the emergence of a type of information that is representational, rather than hermeneutic in its reading, where the aboutness substitutes for the original text and where the metadata information substitutes for the information or knowledge that the book contains. This is a type of reading that begins, at least, with browsing.

80th Annual Meeting of the Association for Information Science & Technology, Washington, DC | Oct. 27-Nov. 1, 2017

(To be fair, however, we have to recognize that these phenomena are also just extensions of the documentary tradition of the book itself, whereby "knowledge" is seen as contained in a book, where signs within the book substitute for the processes of their inscription, and where libraries, rather than, say, expeditions and laboratories – as per (Latour, 1996) –or lived experience, are the privileged sites for knowledge. This world of *documentation* is one that we are still within, though now the internet often substitutes for the library.)

Through a small collection of representational vocabulary, then, information (like before it bibliographic documentation) becomes born, re-presenting documentary texts, which themselves constitute evidence of the rea. With scholarly communication, this sometimes leads to narrow, but still significant, domains of knowledge, because the original source is itself composed of narrow, professionally controlled, vocabulary. However, on the internet we encounter two differing issues: first, most searches are not for knowledge (at least institutionally mediated knowledge embodied in vetted documents), but rather for objects of taste (i.e., for information that I like or I agree with) and second, what is indexed is not necessarily vetted for knowledge by any institution.

To assess this, we need, again, to historically look back to the history of information retrieval, particularly what is known as "the cognitive turn" and "user studies" in library and information science (LIS) at the end of the last century.

If we look to the work of one of the most canonical and cited authors in information science in this area of research in LIS we can see several suggestions as to what starts any search for "information." In Belkin's theory of ASK (for example, (Belkin, 1977)), we see that information begins with 1) a need and 2) with the fulfillment of that need by searching for the right vocabulary. (Belkin's "anomalous structure of knowledge" or ASK is a condition of not knowing the right term to use for a search). Put in Lacanian language (R. E. Day, and Lau, A.J. , 2010), this is the "subject of need," which begins any search for "information" (R. E. Day, 2014; Thomas, 2012). The acronym "ASK" may be a convenient heuristic for a theory of information seeking in an age when reference desks were still popular, but it somewhat obscures what's going on with information seeking and its search. The subject is not really lacking knowledge in the search, but rather, first, the subject is searching for information (knowledge may or may not be what is sought), and second, he or she is lacking vocabulary for such a search.

Perhaps unlike Belkin's theory, I would position the subject's need not as originating in a subject's cognitive state originally, but rather, as the dialectical product of whatever the forms and collections of information may be (R. E. Day, and Lau, A.J. , 2010). This I ground in the fundamental condition of searching either in a physical or a virtual collection, namely, what is available in the situation of a task. That task can be concisely defined or vague, leisurely or scholarly. We start with a feeling of what we must do and what we must need to do, and we then see what is available in order to do it. The specific information need is a product of what we see as available. It is a product of best fit, rather than exact match (exact match, if it does occur, comes later in time or it earlier occurs in place of a subject search, say in a bibliographic query).

What we still call "the internet" or "the web" today is composed of many different forms of information retrieval and linking, from search engines to social network algorithms. These serve different genres of information, knowledge and communication. And the authority levels of these range from personal to institutional authority, from opinion to knowledge, and from individual to collective social judgments.

Searching on the internet, as well as belonging to specific social networks, requires finding the right vocabulary term for what I need or who I am. Am I looking for photos of Coney Island hotdogs (also known as frankfurters, sold in Coney Island, New York) or am I looking for dogs that are hot and sweating in Coney Island some July day? For this, I rely on the socially privileged websites and terms that Google Search indexes (finding that the frankfurters vastly outrank the sweaty dogs in popularity, and so, ranking results). Likewise, on social networks the issue is vocabulary: am I a Harley-Davidson guy or an anorexic, and where do I find a group that corresponds to this name and the connotations or sociocultural feelings that I attach to that name?

What is unique about new media technologies (i.e., internet technologies) that use user-driven, post-coordinate, indexing and searching is that documents of text are indexed and searched for based on these small, representational units, that represent the document and thus, also, the searcher or user of information. Whereas in the book tradition bibliographic metadata was a heuristic in finding the text to be read, as modernity progresses the bibliographic material is not only representative of the text, but as data, it comes to constitute the text. In the case of social big data analysis, this latest documentary stage also treats the user's behavior as metadata, rather than (as was the case in the blurring of texts and human psychology in 19th and 20th century hermeneutic tradition) positing the human psyche or soul as a text to be read.

Where do these metadata of need and identity then come from? Here again, as throughout the documentary tradition, we must look at the sociotechnical systems involved. Google Search is a link analysis system whose influences were science based bibliometric citation analysis systems and sociometrics (Rieder, 2012). The distance between scholarly bibliometrics and Google Search are significant, however, as peer review documents and domain specific vocabulary are not the totality of what Google indexes and searches, nor are professional communities dominant in social networks. Instead, the internet includes not only vetted knowledge, but also a wide range of opinion, trivia and other information. Indeed, as new media has gradually been remediated by old media, we see the same old media support of popular taste and corporate sponsorship of expression shaping the new media, particularly in online journalism.

In the light of all sorts of fake news, illegitimate knowledge, our addiction to our electronic devices, etc., we need to come to terms with a fundamental fact: knowledge is hard to create and come by. It requires education, methods, institutions, the preservation, organization and access to valid and reliable documents and data (the information domain traditional given to libraries), good faith dialogue and continuous traditions. For the most part, though, we are the same as most creatures and we simply follow each other through forests of information by habit and taste, even sometimes when we are being knowledge producing or rational creatures. Knowledge requiring senses of procedure and rigor of various degrees and types in the production and judgment of signs as being "knowledge." To put it succinctly: knowledge requires institutions and institutional parameters for its production; it is hard, and in all senses of the term, costly work for individuals and for society. Information may or may not want to be free, but knowledge is not. We shouldn't be fooled otherwise.

This fact brings us to a position that sometimes clashes with notions that the internet (earlier, libraries – this was the basis of modern public libraries out of "working men's" libraries, after all) make every man or woman a knowledge holder and knowledge producer. An information seeker and an information user or producer is not necessarily a knowledge seeker and a knowledge user or producer – as can easily be seen with fake news.

This brings us back to what began this article. Information literacy claims that it is the evaluation of documents – internally in terms of their rhetorical composition, and externally in terms of their relation to producers – which gives us knowledge-reliable information or not. This is not totally ungrounded. However, I would suggest that prior to this it is education which gives us a user interested in knowledge or not and able to discern the difference between what he or she or anyone else simply says and what constitutes conditions for seeking and producing knowledge. For a user interested in knowledge, the information of the internet – or any documentary space, however (and this is a much more radical claim, namely one challenging the privilege of libraries as the primary space of knowledge) – cannot be sufficient, in itself. Knowledge is a product of institutions, their methods, their techniques and their means and conditions of judgment. Particularly academic libraries are important institutions in these processes, but they too require educated people to use them. In turn, education requires, too, a politics that supports the creation of educated people and knowledge. The failure to achieve these elements even today is very much in evidence in fake news.

## WHO AM I, AS A SUBJECT-OF-(INFORMATION)-NEED?

The fundamental question that a user has to ask, prior to any search or any judgment of information is, then, What kind of subject of an information need am I? What am I looking for? For knowledge or opinion? For what type of knowledge? What are the conditions by which information in a domain or sources becomes or is presented as knowledge? What are the conditions by which truth claims may be made, and what are the different types and stabilities of truth claims within a domain? And most of all, what am I trying to do with the information? Some of these questions can be handled within the arena of information literacy; some are much broader, lying not only in media literacy, but also in understanding how knowledge is done, and also, an honest assessment of what my relation to such processes are.

Being a subject of the need for knowledge is not easy: it takes patience in reading, education and understanding. It takes trust in institutions and in certain traditions. It requires a political state that supports such institutions, traditions and persons. And, on the other hand, being a subject of need with taste may not be easy either, in another way, as I can be led astray by the brand and by crowd psychology and forget my own bodily limits in the face of desirous, but also disastrous, lifestyles (excess exercise, eating disorders, etc.) or even my own ignorance and prejudices, which find easy company with others on the internet.

The subject of need has to choose what information to use and what information tools to use in order to get different types of information. Am I a gamer, a browser, a scholar with these materials? What type of scholar? How does the information system socially and epistemically position me in not only relationship to certain documentary materials, but also in relationship to my very being and my use of time and my relationships to others? How much is my time spent on information systems, and for what purposes? How does such a mediation create a further subject and subject of need as me, not only in terms of information needs, but in terms of subjects of needs more generally, and even more, of knowledge and information able to serve others' needs? In short, how do varieties of information and information systems – and indeed, documentary and information systems more broadly – shape the agency and person of myself and the world around me? What am I going to do with my time?

As with all information systems – physical libraries, museums, online databases and the internet – the choice of when and how to use them and for what ends shapes the mind and agency of the person using them – i.e., the subject.

Some have proposed that the internet creates a post-subjective political space, because of its collectivity and the collective, emergent, nature of information on it. But, on the one hand, I still retrieve documents that I need. And on the other, through socially mediated algorithms, such documents increasingly appear to me in terms of an "I" whose need is obviously socially constructed.

## CONCLUSION

We are left with the conclusion that information literacy, much less technologically mediated means for finding true information, can only be incomplete responses to fake news and other misleading forms of information. This is because not all information needs involve knowledge and not all information can be knowledge. If we say that information is informative, then the term *information* applies to a vast amount of information that lies outside of those institutions and practices that constitute, at least public, knowledge. An "information age," in this sense, is something closer to an age of attention, on the one hand, and an age of documents on the other. What it isn't necessarily, however, is an age of knowledge.

Since so much of our lives are now mediated by information and communication devices, and so much of that mediation involves information that is not knowledge, the subject must be able to interrogate him or herself about the constitution of self and mind which such ever-present mediation results in. So, too, must education institutions reassess the relatively recent, and sometimes still held, belief that information and communication technologies in education themselves directly result in more knowledgeable people.

The relation of the subject to documentation has changed recently, with greater social mediation of its representation and retrieval. However, the fundamental ethical relation of the subject to the symbolic has not changed, other than now inhabiting a much greater portion of our lives. In the midst of this increased symbolic mediation by the omnipotence of digital technologies in our lives, the interrogation of the self and the need for education becomes even more intense. The subject has not gone away at all, but in fact, has returned with a vengeance in its coming to and going from digital information and communication technologies like the internet. And too, the problem of the time of the subject stands out even more. And last, but not least at all, knowledge remains still a difficult and hard to achieve goal for people and societies – harder still, in some ways, given the proliferation and ubiquity of all sorts of information. We are still very, very far away from a "knowledge society" as the basis for politics. Education for knowledge remains a goal. And we often lose an educated self, as well.

In short, the enlightenment project remains quite unfulfilled, even in the midst of the information explosion, and the ethics of the self remains more pressing than ever. If anything, fake news and the politics and psychology of such should tell us how pressing these issues are. We cannot escape these issues by simply speaking of techniques or new technologies to address fake news. For fake news is part of a phenomenology of information which now awakens the dormant questions of knowledge and the self which its explosion momentarily, once again, hid.

## ACKNOWLEDGEMENTS

I am grateful for discussions had with Niels-Peder Osmundsen Hjørllund during his visit to Indiana University several years ago for emphasizing the concept of the subject-of-need in information systems. I am also grateful to Neal Thomas for his development of the concept of need in new media.

## REFERENCES

Belkin, N. J. (1977). Internal knowledge and external information. In M. de Mey (Ed.) *International workshop on the cognitive viewpoint* (University of Ghent, Ghent, 1977). 187-194.

Day, R. E. (2014). *Indexing it all: The subject in the age of documentation, information, and data*. Cambridge, Mass.: MIT Press.

Day, R. E., and Lau, A.J. (2010). Psychoanalysis: Freud, Lacan, and Deleuze and Guattari. In Lisa M. Given and Gloria J. Leckie (Eds.), *Critical theory in library and information science: Exploring the social from across the disciplines*. Santa Barbara, CA: Libaries Unlimited.

Latour, B. (1996). Ces réseaux que la raison ignore - laboratoires, bibliothèques, collections. *Le pouvoir des bibliothèques. La mémoire des livres dans la culture occidentale.* Paris: Albin Michel. 23-46.

Rieder, B. (2012). What is in PageRank? A historical and conceptual investigation of a recursive status index. *Computational Culture,* (2).

Thomas, N. (2012). *Algorithmic subjectivity and the need to be informed*. First Conference Proceedings of the Technology and Emerging Media Track, Canadian Communication Association conference, Kitchener-Waterloo, Ontario. http://www.tem.fl.ulaval.ca/en/waterloo-2012/

# Fiction as Informative and its Implications for Information Science Theory

**Philip Doty**
*School of Information, University of Texas at Austin, USA.*
*pdoty@ischool.utexas.edu*

**Ramona Broussard**
*School of Information, University of Texas at Austin, USA.*
*ramonab@utexas.edu*

## ABSTRACT

**Reading fiction is a neglected area of study in information behavior research, even as such research has expanded to include investigation of different kinds of behavior by more kinds of people, and an expanded repertoire of research methods and fields. Using data from a small empirical study (n=8) and research from five fields other than information science, the paper reports on participants' reading of fiction and those five fields' study of how reading fiction is informative. Considering fiction informative has two important outcomes: we (1) understand information behavior better and (2) address important problems in information science theory. Such problems include frustrated attempts to define *information*, the (generally hidden) gendered character of information science and information behavior research, the misguided conduit metaphor and an overemphasis on cognition at the expense of practice, documents and materiality.**

## KEYWORDS

information behavior, reading fiction, information science theory, history of information science

## INTRODUCTION

Our research aims, in part, to add to work in information behavior (IB) by exploring other fields' understanding of fiction as informative. It also complements these fields' work with the insight into information behavior provided by the umbrella field of information studies, including information science. There is wide recognition that, "when it comes to studying human behaviour, real life is so complex that multiple views can all be useful" (Ford, 2015, p. 213; Capurro & Hjørland, 2002; Case & Given, 2016).

As illustrated below, several fields demonstrate that reading fiction is one of many ways people learn about values, social norms, empathy and even "facts." Thus, if we wish to understand information behavior as broadly and deeply as possible, it is important for our field to consider fiction beyond limited concepts such as information seeking, decision making and problem solving, no matter how rich those concepts are. Fiction does NOT fit easily into an information-seeking mold, thus there has been little sustained empirical and theoretical attention in the field to fiction as an informative genre. What might we learn about information behavior by focusing on the reading of fiction?

To begin to address that question, we performed an empirical study the major research question of which was, How do readers use young adult (YA) fiction, a form of imaginative writing, as a "roadmap" for lived situations? The eight study participants were women and men, ranging in age from the mid-20s to the mid-50s. The study involved semi-structured individual interviews, two performed face-to-face and six by telephone that lasted 25-45 minutes and were recorded. The sample comprised a convenience sample known to one or both of the researchers, and all eight participants were native speakers of English educated in the United States. Seven attended U.S. high schools, some public, some private, while one informant was home schooled. The semi-structured interview schedule focused on asking the informants about their reading of YA fiction while teenagers, but almost all of them mentioned other forms of imaginative literature as well. These other forms of fiction included classic literature common to adolescents' school reading requirements. The interview protocol was based on R.S. Weiss (1995) on qualitative interviewing and included questions about memorable and liked books read as teens, lending and borrowing books, reading that may have helped change participants' minds, books assigned for reading and forbidden books. We pursued these questions in a semi-structured fashion, and data analysis of responses emphasized thematic sorting (Braun & Clarke, 2006).

## SOME RESULTS FROM THE EMPIRICAL STUDY

In an earlier paper (Broussard & Doty, 2016), we identified five fields whose research into reading fiction is particularly valuable for helping information science and information studies more broadly to appreciate reading fiction as an important information behavior. We also reported data from the first two participants in our study. These five fields comprised philosophy, psychology, education and entertainment studies, and literary studies. While the eight research participants spoke broadly and deeply about many themes of interest to information studies, organizing some of their responses under the five fields reveals important themes related to how fiction is informative.

## PHILOSOPHY/MAKING MEANING

As noted in Broussard & Doty (2016), a particular contribution that philosophers make to our understanding of fiction is how readers use fiction to explore and make values or, as

80th Annual Meeting of the Association for Information Science & Technology, Washington, DC | Oct. 27-Nov. 1, 2017

some put it, make meaning (e.g., Belfiore, 2014; Currie, 1994; Nussbaum, 1992 [many thanks to an anonymous reviewer for this suggestion]; Paskins, 1977). Meaning here does not simply imply the resolution of what the fiction says happened, but rather how fiction helps readers make meaningful lives. In our study, Respondent 5 (R5) explained how reading novels about others from a similar minority cultural and linguistic community affirmed that informant's (minority) cultural heritage. Such affirmation came from everything from the major characters' demographic identities to the recipes, foodways and family mores the novel featured.

R7 spoke explicitly about how her reading of adolescent and adult fiction and poetry in the fantasy genre helped raise and consider spiritual questions. This participant often read these books with a younger sibling and/or other family members, explicitly considering what it means to be religious and to resolve ethical questions. This outcome was especially important because the family was "spiritual but not religious," as R7 expressed it, and together they "plumbed spiritual questions [about the world and our place in it] through fantasy."

As noted briefly in our earlier paper, Respondents 1 and 2 asserted that books they read as adolescents helped them to understand what they termed *human nature* and *model behavior*. More specifically, particular books helped them understand foibles common to people generally, e.g., the tendency to abuse social power, as well as gendered elements of social life, e.g., the importance of strong female characters to emulate and the sexism common in many imaginative works.

In terms of exploring values and learning how to live, R8 offered a particularly nuanced view of death and young people's fiction. It is a truism that seeing fictional characters die or address the death of others "helps" young people understand grief, death and loss. This respondent spoke about how one particular novel that featured mortal danger to characters and death did the opposite: a classmate died at about 11 years old, and R8 learned that death in fiction, no matter how well portrayed, does not give any indication of the extreme difficulty of coping with the loss of someone close. This counterexample serves as a useful tonic to adults' presumptions about the simplicity of children's emotional lives and children's reading and serves to demonstrate the complexity of the learning (the "informing") that reading fiction can provide.

### Psychology/Understanding Others

This section considers a theme common to psychology and literary studies: what psychologists term *theory of mind* and literary scholars more informally refer to as social understanding. For example, Gotschall (2012) specifies how cognitive and evolutionary psychologists regard reading fiction as an evolutionary behavior that uses artistic expression to socialize human beings to each other and their socially significant groups. More specifically, human beings develop a "theory of mind" that allows us to understand, in part, what the world looks like from another person's perspective. Kidd & Castano (2013) and Oatley (2009) are exemplars of research showing that, as we seek to understand other human beings, we develop empathy, even for fictional characters in stories. Fiction expands our understanding of the range of emotions, actions and thoughts possible in the human experience. This research demonstrates that fiction can increase our understanding in multiple ways, i.e., to help us change.

There is a lively conversation in literary studies about the status of empathy and narrative fiction, especially about whether empathy toward some characters in a work of fiction undermines empathy for others (Hammond & Kim, 2014; Keen, 2007; Lindhé, 2016). Other literary theorists (e.g., Boyd, 2009; Meretoja, 2016; Radway, 1991; Zunshine, 2006), in contrast, identify the value of fiction for increasing our social understanding: understanding of ourselves in relation with others and of social norms, whether to support or undermine those norms (see below). Our research participants agreed with this latter group.

For example, study Respondents 3 and 4 explicitly noted that books they read as adolescents notably increased their sympathy for and understanding of children in poverty, those who were homeless, those who suffered in the Holocaust and institutionalized persons.

R8 explained that reading fiction provided a much "broader view of the world around us." R7 struck a similar note by telling us that adolescent fiction helped this informant to "know the world around us" as parents and other family members encouraged each other to "read all things." In addition, Respondents 3 and 7 said that the books they read as adolescents introduced them to and helped them appreciate knowledge of child abuse and the behavior of dysfunctional parents.

### Education and Entertainment Studies/Understanding the World by Understanding Language

The fields of education and entertainment studies have found, unsurprisingly, that fiction helps readers learn about the world despite fiction's "made up" character (e.g., Krashen, 2004; Singhal, 2004; Zillman & Bryant, 1994; noted in our earlier paper). Our respondents particularly emphasized how fiction helped them understand the world and how the world is made in part by language.

Six of our eight informants expressed that one of the most valuable things they learned from reading fiction as adolescents was how authors can create worlds where readers can live vicariously. They especially discussed authors' literary styles and how those styles helped or hindered the "availability" of stories. R5 reiterated how reading fiction featuring characters, events and foods similar to those in the participant's life affirmed the value and shared character of speaking a language other than English at home. Using a linguistic trope to reinforce the earlier theme of expanded empathy and theory of mind, R3 and R5 spoke with feeling about how literature can, as one put it, amplify "voices that came from grief and suffering."

### *Literary Studies/Contesting Social Norms*

Our 2016 paper highlighted some important findings in literary studies related to reading fiction as an information behavior. Bettelheim (1975) discusses how engagement with fiction implicates the formation of important social boundaries and a deepened understanding of those boundaries. Buckingham (1993) and Finders (1997) also assert the deep relationship between social boundaries and reading fictional works. They emphasize, however, that fiction is an arena where readers, alone and together, can both confirm and contest social boundaries.

Respondents 3, 6, and 8 talked about their deliberate use of lists of books and movies "forbidden" by religious organizations, schools, libraries, individual teachers and parents. R6 said that parents and teachers gave great encouragement "to sample everything that was out there," including fiction portraying transgressive behaviors and attitudes. R4 spoke with great emotion, even after 40 years, of finding it "so astounding" to read about girls' first periods and teenagers having sex, topics largely unspoken in family, school and other settings.

Respondent 5, who grew up in a relatively small town, largely socially, culturally and ethnically homogeneous, said that reading fiction as an adolescent was immensely liberatory. This informant remembered thinking, even as a very young adolescent, that "'there's gotta be more out there'" than this home town provided, and fiction suggested some of what that "more" might be. On a less impassioned note, Rs 5 and 6 noted that reading adolescent fiction helped them understand relations among siblings, especially socially approved (loving and considerate) and disapproved (incestuous and violent) kinds of relationships.

This last theme, reading as transgressive, is important not simply in the context of developmentally appropriate identity formation among adolescents, but also more broadly in the reading of fiction by adults. Explorations of this theme include Radway's and others' finding that fiction particularly gives readers a way to make sense of social norms, and, through that understanding, fiction also provides a means of resistance to those norms (1991).

As these excerpts and themes show, readers use fiction to identify and regard the possible, and inform their thinking about the world and their places in it. In a word, fiction is informative for its readers, yet we face a relative paucity of systematic inquiry about fiction in information science.

## INFORMATION SCIENCE AND READING FICTION

Few information science researchers have explored fiction, but those who have include Ross (1999), Rothbauer (2004 and 2013), Ross et al. (2006), Agosto & Hughes-Hassell (2010) and Thelwall & Kousha (2017). Additional information science research exploring fiction include work about information behavior and affect (e.g., the chapters in Nahl & Bilal, 2007, especially McKechnie et al.), so-called confessional methods in information behavior research (e.g., Davenport, 2010), materials challenged in libraries (e.g., Pattee, 2008), and "the pleasurable" and fiction (Kari & Hartel, 2007). There is also a literature on fiction as the particular object of search (e.g., Ooi & Liew, 2011; Anna & Pertti, 2017), on the difficulties of cataloging and intellectual control of more creative works especially novels and other works of fiction (e.g., Cawkell, 1997; Maker, 2008), public libraries and fiction (e.g., Carrier, 1965; Snape, 1995; Williams, 1988), and bibliotherapy (e.g., Brewster, 2008, and Sturm, 2003 [thanks to Michael Buckland for this useful suggestion]).

Our earlier paper identified a number of reasons why information science has not considered fiction as informative, including the privileged financial and political support of scientists' and engineers' information behavior, conceptual and terminological maturity of scientific and technical disciplines, gender biases and a presumed fact-fiction distinction (on this last point, see, e.g., Case & Given, 2016, pp. 66-67). In addition to those reasons there are many others. Three particularly troublesome obstacles to looking beyond a scientific and technical focus for information science spring from information science's birth just before, during and after WWII that especially emphasized the concept of "information." Signal moments, contributors and sources of that concept still hold special meaning in information science:

- Information theory and its genesis in Shannon & Weaver's 1949 *Mathematical Theory of Communication*; on the hegemony of Shannon's information theory in information science see, e.g., Cornelius (2002, pp. 393ff)
- Cybernetics, command and control first expressed in an integrated fashion in Norbert Weiner's 1948 *Cybernetics, or Control of Communication in the Animal and the Machine*
- The fantasy of a universal library of scientific and technical literatures on the desktop as in Vannevar Bush's 1945 "As We May Think" and MEMEX; see Burke (2007, p. 12) on the "'Bush mystique'" in information science as well as Houston & Harmon (2007).

A result of the canonization of these texts and concepts in information science was a conviction that the "singular purpose of the field is to create 'effective retrieval'" (Day, 2005, quoting Jacob and Shaw, 1998). There are additional reasons our field has tended to neglect fiction such as the following:

- Our focus on the utilitarian and workday, not leisure
- Our positing of "information needs" and, thus, focus on how to "satisfy" them
- Our overarching emphasis on information seeking, information retrieval and the concerns thereto
- Our presumption that fiction cannot be informative because of the presumed existence of a fact-fiction distinction.

With regard to this last, Donald Case & Lisa Given (2016) devote Chapter 6 to "Related Concepts," including a section on fiction and similar entertaining media. The section is entitled "Information versus Entertainment" (pp. 127-134), and they begin by calling such a distinction "artificial." They cite Cermak (1996, p. 116) and Zillman & Bryant (1986) that, while information and entertainment are difficult to disentangle, many scholars easily condemn entertainment as escapist and untoward in some way. Case & Given and others, e.g., Radway (1991) and Mendelsohn (1966), argue that there is a "bias against entertainment." Such bias springs, in large part, from a cultural preference, important in information science, to "see people primarily as *thinking* beings," stressing our cognitive abilities (Case & Given, p. 127, emphasis in the original).

As noted above, however, there is a growing body of research, in information science and beyond, that embraces the hedonic, exploring examples such as sports, stock trading, genealogy, watching movies and TV, and other pursuits that are information-intensive but also pleasurable (p. 133). But our field and others tend to focus on decision-making, problem solving, addressing work-related questions and reduction of uncertainty when discussing information behavior. As human beings, however, we know phenomenologically that "utilitarian behavior" and the knowable are only part of how we live and only part of what we are informed about. Fiction, especially the novel, has the ability to underscore how unknowing is also an essential part of human existence. Thus, such works inform us about that which we cannot know, in part by drawing our attention explicitly and self-referentially to the questionable fact-fiction distinction.

Case & Given cite Reeves that, "It is still reasonable to assume that people judge some information as factual, some as lies, and some as fantasy . . . . There is fact in fiction and vice versa" (pp. 130-131). We learn from fiction in many ways. That learning comes in part from how fiction helps us understand possible worlds and the nuanced character of temporality (Meretoja, 2016). Further, much of fiction has a "double quality": "it is not meant to be understood as true and yet is meant to shape our beliefs about the actual world" (Nielsen, Phelan & Walsh, quoted in Meretoja, p. 374). Fiction, especially realist fiction, works in part by immersing us in situations to increase our empathy for characters, especially those *in extremis*. At the same time, however, literary elements such as authors' prefaces to works of fiction and direct authorial commentaries work as paratextual frames to help readers know how to read the fictive work (Dawson, 2016, p. 145).

Our empirical data and research in other fields clearly indicate the depth and breadth of how we learn from fiction. Such learning is especially valuable in understanding others, understanding relationships and anticipating some of life's more complex situations. To grasp some of this complexity, however, it is useful to recall that even novels classified as "realist," such as those written by Jane Austen, Charles Dickens or Edith Wharton are not exact portrayals of reality. Instead they are accurate representations in contrast to more fanciful genres, such as romance or poetry. They make sense of some aspect of reality such as extensive and "profound social change" (Kaplan, 1992). In addition, Penelope Lively in her 2014 memoir and Kurt Vonnegut in the Introduction to *Slaughterhouse-Five* (1969) describe how writing novels aids in this kind of making sense of complex events even if those novels are not considered "realistic" in the sense of works by Dickens or Austen. Such self-consciousness shows us realism's skeptical attitude about itself, reflecting the novel's nature as being but not being at the same time, as Bridget Chalk (2016) writes in her review of Peter Boxall's *The Value of the Novel*. That "not being" includes the mysterious yet mundane character of much of even a reflective life. More particularly, fictional works point us to the "opaque or unknowable" persons all around us and life's sometimes constitutive "inscrutability" (Martin, 2015, p. 177).

The next section of the paper specifies more fully why thinking of fiction as informative gives us a better view of information behavior and useful leverage in addressing important theoretical questions in information science.

## WHY IT MATTERS IF FICTION INFORMS ITS READERS

What do we gain by asserting that fiction can be informative? We might say that we have seen three answers to that question thus far. First, insights from other disciplines' study of fiction deepen our understanding of fiction, its important and multiple roles in people's lives and how it informs them. Second, these other disciplines have identified potential avenues of empirical and historical inquiry for information scholars. Third, such conceptually rich findings from other disciplines suggest ways that information science, and information studies more broadly, can inform those disciplines with the findings, methods and other research tools at our command. But we can go further and deeper into the field of information science by exploring more carefully how fiction is informative.

One important part of that exploration involves the well-known pragmatist (or pragmatic) maxim. While the term has inspired a flurry of commentary, a "classic" expression appears in Peirce's "How to Make Our Ideas Clear" (1878):

Consider what effects, which might conceivably have practical bearings, we conceive the object of our conception to have. Then our conception of those effects is the whole of our conception of the object.

This locution is more than a little gnomic, and Peirce and others have given the idea several subsequent and sometimes conflicting interpretations (Hookway, 2005). A valuable short interpretation of the maxim is, "How does thinking this way help us to see better?" In response, we can say that identifying reading fiction as an information behavior can provide a perspective, a vantage point, on matters that interest us. This section considers how.

Identifying fiction as informative helps address important theoretical problematics in the field of information studies, particularly information science. These problematics are many, but we highlight two: the definitional conundrum of *information* and the often-ignored gendered character of information science. We briefly mention three other theoretical problems in information science that we cannot explore further: the conduit metaphor, the benefits of deemphasizing cognition in information behavior and the benefits of emphasizing information practices, documents and materiality. These problematics have often tied the field in conjectural knots. Thinking about reading fiction as a key information behavior illustrates ways out of what some may term these theoretical dead ends.

### Sidestepping the Definitional Conundrum of Information

Farkas-Conn (1990) shows how the current Association for Information Science and Technology, one of the major professional associations in the field, arose immediately before World War II. Under Watson Davis, the then-American Documentation Institute aimed primarily to provide scientists with information for their research (see Broussard & Doty [2016] for a brief summary of information science's long emphasis on scientists and engineers). When the ADI became the American Society for Information Science (ASIS) in 1968, a major goal of the society was to understand "'the properties and behavior of information'" (Farkas-Conn, p. 199). Especially influential in that effort were Bateson (1972) on information as a difference that makes a difference and Brookes (1980) on the fundamental equation of information science, particularly as our field held to a "faith in the possibility of a science of information" (Burke, 2007, p. 26).

Presuming that we possess a unifying definition of *information* allows us to pretend that information exists as an external phenomenon, that it is a stable thing, and that we all agree about what that stable thing is. As explored below, the embrace of information has also been done for purposes of professional status. Agre (1995, p. 226) reminds us that the locution and ideology of information in discussing various literatures and fields allows information professionals to avoid deep disciplinary rifts such as those about what literatures count, which research initiatives are primary, which origin stories are canonical and so on.

An important element of the locution and ideology of information in information science is the supposed hierarchy from (facts to) data to information to knowledge to wisdom, commonly abbreviated as the DIKW hierarchy (Frické, 2004; Ma, 2010; Rowley, 2006). Persistent questions in information science are elided rather than answered by this presumed hierarchy. For example, are there such things as "raw data" (see, e.g., Gitelman, 2013)? How do data "become" information? How does information "become" knowledge and knowledge wisdom? (Capurro & Hjørland, 2002; Cornelius, 2002; Day, 2005; Frohmann, 2004; *inter alia*). These and other fundamental questions animate a growing number of information and communication scholars on information determinism (e.g., Buckingham, 2008, on youth and identity; Srinivasan et al., 2017, on development).

In the western cultural tradition, there is a long-standing belief in a sharp disjunction between fact and fiction. An example is the widespread acceptance of logician and philosopher of mathematics Gottlob Frege's assertion that "fiction lacks truth value" (Meretoja, 2016, p. 374). Recent work in literary studies and elsewhere asks us to question this easy distinction, e.g.: "There are serious debates about the classification of works as fiction or nonfiction outside philosophy" (Friend, 2008, p. 150). Further, this presumption of a fracture between fiction and fact allows us to focus too closely on information as a means for problem solving, decreasing uncertainty and decision-making rather than directing us to how people are informed in practice.

Further complicating matters, as Agre (1995, p. 225) notes, information is sometimes located (consider metaphors such as "overload," "information poverty"), sometimes abstract ("content," "information transfer"), the latter akin to what Nunberg (1996) calls a purported "morselized" noble substance. Agre, along with Duguid (1996), Frohmann (2004), Blanchette (2011), and many others, offers critiques of the presumed abstract neutrality of information and the reductive conception of information as a resource.

Nigel Ford's recent book on information behavior is indicative that information science's overall context for studying information behavior is "to enhance the effectiveness with which we go about learning, decision making and problem solving" (2015, p. 242 *et passim*). Ron Day points to the field's work to establish "modernist foundations," especially its search for an integrated "sense of theory" and claims of "being *in all aspects*, a 'science'" (2005, pp. 591 and 602; emphasis in the original). In contrast to this scientistic, utilitarian and information-centric view, Capurro & Hjørland assert that our field's focus on information may have "misdirected" us. Quoting Alan F. Chalmers, Capurro & Hjørland ask us to consider the value of *not defining* information, "'It might be that this word is most useful when left without any formal definition'" (2002, pp. 350 and 348). Such an outcome may seem nonsensical to some and even scandalous to others because of its "failure" to identify clearly the focus of the science of information.

What we gain, however, by agnosticism about the question of what information "is" includes an ability to see more clearly what people do and why they behave as they do, and we achieve theoretical clarity about other important concerns. As Cornelius (2002, p. 408) says, research in information studies has burgeoned without a universal embrace of any particular definition of *information* and without a focus on the concept at all: "It is as if we do not really need a theory of information" (p. 420).

### Exploring the Gendered Character of Information Science

As with all human activities and research, information science is gendered. While a comprehensive review of the field's gendered character is not possible here, considering reading fiction as an information behavior helps foreground important gender elements of information science. The most important of those elements are a related triad:

- The field's emphasis on scientific and technical information and advanced digital and other technologies, both generally gendered male, e.g., information retrieval.
- More widely, information science's focus on professional activities. This focus reinforces the mistaken but widely accepted naturalized division of life into "separate spheres" – the masculine public sphere of work and politics and the feminine private sphere of domesticity and familial relations. See, e.g., Rosenberg (1983), Kerber (1988), and McGaw (1989) for substantial critiques of this misguided metaphor.
- Information science's efforts to distinguish itself from the (largely feminized) field of librarianship, especially by emphasizing IT and information (e.g., Capurro & Hjørland, 2002, pp. 383 and 396). There is a well-known witticism from earlier decades that information science is simply librarianship for men. Related are the continuing advantages that men have in leadership positions even in the largely feminized world of libraries and archives, e.g., Christine Williams' metaphor of the glass escalator (1992 and 1995).

Fiction itself is often categorized as female, most especially because of its presumed emphasis on the "confessional," the domestic and relations among characters (see, e.g., Watt, 1965, for a classic discussion). What does it reveal about information science if we largely ignore fiction in people's lives and the ways that it informs them? Doing more research about how reading fiction, in all its various incarnations, informs people can help the field further identify and address its serious masculinist emphases.

There are at least three other problems in information science theory that regarding fiction as informative sheds valuable light on, and we discuss them briefly here. Space precludes their further exploration, but subsequent work will consider them and other themes more discursively.

### *Avoiding the Conduit Metaphor, Undermining the Cognitive Hegemony and Embracing Materiality, Behavior and Documents*

Another conceptual difficulty in information science that a focus on reading fiction allows us to avoid is the conduit metaphor that lies at the heart of Shannon's information theory and many impoverished models of education. First described as such and critiqued by Reddy (1993/1979), this metaphor describes communication in terms of containers, "content," data or information "extraction," transfer of meaning, and an unproblematic identity of the sender and receiver's points of view and use of language. These all characterize many conceptual foundations of research in information science, especially in information retrieval (IR), data mining and what is widely termed information transfer. Questioning the conduit metaphor, of course, problematizes the presumed DIKW hierarchy discussed above and undermines information transfer's hegemony in IR theory and practice (Cornelius, 2002, p. 407). Other critiques of this metaphor have included Lakoff & Johnson (2008/1980) as well as Day (2000) and Cornelius (2002), while other scholars have vigorously defended its use, e.g., Grady (1998) and Eubanks (2001).

Fiction, as other fields' research and our study reveal, informs people in many ways without invoking the conduit metaphor, the DIKW hierarchy or locutions of information extraction. Instead, research about fiction demonstrates alternative ways that fiction informs its readers, about other people, about cultural and social norms, or about oneself.

A second information theory difficulty we can mention only in passing involves the increased focus on cognitivism in information science over the past 40 years, which shows little likelihood of diminishing. The cognitive turn was very valuable in turning attention to people (usually constructed as "users"), rather than only to information systems. As is well known to ASIS&T members, the work of Wilson, Saracevic, Kuhlthau, Ingwersen, Dervin, Belkin and Bates and their students are leading examples. But, as its many critics assert, privileging cognition can atomize and psychologize individuals as well as unproblematized representationalism and the correspondence theory of language. With its emphasis on a "narrative of mental events" (Frohmann, 1992, p. 305), cognitivist research in the field can ignore other constitutive elements of information behavior such as language, the material foundations of behavior, social practices, the uncertainty in communication, social and political power and emotion, especially the role they all play in knowing or not knowing (e.g., Day, 2005; Frohmann, 1992 and 1994; Nahl & Bilal, 2007).

As noted above, concerns about the presumed "nature of information," effective information retrieval and emphasis on people as atomized cognitive actors have largely dominated information science research for decades, as both supporters and detractors of these research streams have indicated. Investigating how fiction is informative helps us address, or avoid, entrenched conflict in the field about such matters. Such research reaffirms the importance of materiality, documents and practice in the lives of people and social relations, turning our focus to what people do, not to what we presume they should do. A further advantage of seeing reading fiction as informative is that it helps us look beyond the concept of affordances and presumed inherent characteristics of objects. We can think instead of how use of informative objects, especially in embodied material, temporalized and power-sensitive circumstances, is behavior that informs people widely.

## CONCLUSION

Given our small study's empirical results and the research of the five fields we briefly discuss above, it seems that fiction helps us understand information behavior better, and it helps us address important questions in information science theory. We conclude that viewing fiction as informative is useful for expanding our view of information behavior to include more than simply "information seeking." We can do so in at least three important ways.

First, such study will enrich our understanding of information behavior by expanding its purview while helping to integrate theoretical insights and continuing empirical research into users' behavior. For example, fiction reaches beyond historical realism, explodes the "realistic illusion," and helps us understand "actual (past and present) worlds" by its intertextuality and other reminders that "the world is mediated by culturally and historically constituted sense-making practices that define a historical world" (Meretoja, 2016, pp. 375, 384ff.).

Second, we can bring our field's understanding of information behavior to the larger research conversation about reading, especially reading fiction, in which many disciplines and researchers participate. This is a unique contribution that our field can make to important ongoing research conversations in psychology, literary theory, education and beyond. These disciplines would benefit greatly from the theoretical and empirical insights information behavior researchers in information science and information studies can provide.

Third, our field's greater use of the research tropes, techniques and findings of other fields' investigations of readings can contribute to our understanding of information behavior broadly and of reading fiction in particular. We believe that even our small study demonstrates that the contributions of philosophy, psychology, literary theory, entertainment studies and education can deepen our understanding of how fiction is an informative genre. They show us some of the ways that reading fiction is a complex, rich and shared information behavior.

In offering an overview of Dervin's (1976) critique of 10 mistaken assumptions about communication and information, Case & Given say that we do not understand "how people inform themselves, how they make connections *over time*, the sense they make of their world between significant events" (emphasis in the original). They make this observation discussing Dervin's challenge of the 10th assumption that "[p]eople make easy, conflict-free connections between external information and their internal reality" (2016, p. 12). As our research findings and other fields' research show, the study of fiction can, in fact, help us better understand how people inform themselves.

Three contrasting views of "information" may show why studying reading fiction as informative is not simple in our field. The first is from Philip Agre (1995, p. 229):

> [A]t best, [information is] a superficial generic term for a broad range of categories whose forms can be described in terms of genres but whose nature can ultimately only be understood within a larger system of structural relationships and ideologies.

Luciano Floridi, the best known and admired philosopher of information, enthusiastically reifies information (2002, p. 141; also see Stonier 1991, and Davies & Gregersen, 2010):

> Information has thus arisen as a concept as fundamental and important as being, knowledge, life, intelligence, meaning, and good and evil – all pivotal concepts with which it is interdependent – and so equally worthy of autonomous investigation.

Day (2005, p. 581) offers another view that "reopening . . . information to something other than representation, fact or 'true belief' constitute[s] a challenge to the metaphysical and epistemological assumptions" of information science.

Can our field live comfortably with these descriptions as well as other understandings of what we are about? Or, better yet, perhaps we can eschew the definition of information and concentrate instead on people's informing practices. Reading in particular holds great promise in this regard, some of it already realized. Day (2005, p. 603) critiques the epistemological and linguistic presumption in information science that reading is just representational or reproducing, that is, just "'literary' in terms of correctness and correspondence." Ford (2015, p. 24) claims that reading is merely decoding and thus of little interest to information behavior research. McKechnie et al., however, remind us that "Reading is more than just a process of making sense, of interpretation, of decoding," and is instead "an experience of overlapping worlds that is made meaningful to readers through reflective responses and processes as they engage textual materials" (2007, p. 193).

Some scholars separate knowing into the literary, scientific and religious (Bruner, 1979, p. 54), recalling Kant's distinction among the aesthetic, ethics and knowledge (Meretoja, 2016, p. 392). Alternatively, Burke (2007, p. 26) reminds us that information science programs range from those that are akin to computer science and engineering, to those that more closely resemble psychology and sociology programs, to those that emphasize the liberal arts and humanities. Information science and information studies more generally are not just computational, not just social scientific, but also humanistic modes of systematic inquiry. The heterogeneity and health of the iSchool movement and widespread creative currents in information studies demonstrate that claim.

As our empirical data and other research show, literary knowing, the kind of knowing that results from reading fiction, is a matter of some interest to information science and to information behavior research. Researchers in our field and beyond are demonstrating the value of such research and likely will continue to do so.

## REFERENCES


Agre, Philip E. (1995). Institutional circuitry: Thinking about the forms and uses of information. *Information, Technology and Libraries, 14*(4), 225-230.

Agosto, Denise E., Hughes-Hassell, & Sandra. (2010). *Urban teens in the library: Research and practice*. Chicago: American Library Association.

Anna, Mikkonen, & Pertti, Vakkari. (2017). Reader characteristics, behavior, and success in fiction book search. *Journal of the Association for Information Science and Technology*.

Bateson, Gregory. (1972). Steps to an ecology of mind: Collected essays in anthropology, psychiatry, evolution, and epistemology. Chicago: University of Chicago Press.

Belfiore, E. S. (2014). *Tragic pleasures: Aristotle on plot and emotion*. Princeton, NJ: Princeton University Press.

Bettelheim, B. (1975). The uses of enchantment: The meaning and importance of fairy tales. New York: Random House.

Blanchette, Jean-François. (2011). A material history of bits. *Journal of the American Society for Information Science and Technology, 62*(6), 1042-1057.

Boyd, B. (2009). *On the origin of stories: Evolution, cognition, and fiction*. Cambridge, MA: Belknap Press of Harvard University Press.

Braun, V., & Clarke, V. (2006). Using thematic analysis in psychology. *Qualitative Research in Psychology, 3*(2), 77-101.

Brewster, Liz. (2008). Medicine for the soul: Bibliotherapy. *Australasian Public Libraries and Information Services, 21*(3), 115-119.

Brookes, Bertram C. (1980). The foundations of information science. Part I: Philosophical aspects. *Journal of Information Science, 2*, 125-133.

Broussard, Ramona, & Doty, Philip. (2016). Toward an understanding of fiction and information behavior. Annual Conference of the Association for Information Science & Technology. Copenhagen, Denmark. (10 pp.)

Bruner, Jerome S. (1979). *On knowing: Essays for the left hand* (Revised ed.). Cambridge, MA: Harvard University Press.

Buckingham, David. (2008). Introducing identity. In David Buckingham (Ed.), *Youth, identity, and digital media* (pp. 1-24). Cambridge, MA: MIT Press.

Burke, Colin. (2007). History of information science. *Annual Review of Information Science and Technology* (Vol. 41, pp. 3-53). Medford, NJ: Information Today.

Capurro, Rafael, & Hjørland, Birger. (2002). The concept of information. *Annual Review of Information Science and Technology* (Vol. 37, pp. 343-412). Medford, NJ: Information Today.

Carrier, E. J. (1965). *Fiction in public libraries, 1876-1900*. Lanham, MD: Scarecrow Press.

Case, Donald O., & Given, Lisa. (2016). Looking for information: A survey of research on information seeking, needs, and behavior (4th ed.). Bingley, UK: Emerald Publishing.

Cawkell, A E. (Ed.). (1997). Special issue: Electronic access to fiction. *Information Services and Use, 17*(2-3).

Chalk, Bridget. (2016). [Review of the book *The Value of the Novel*, by Peter Boxall]. *Studies in the Novel, 38*(3), 384-385.

Cornelius, Ian. (2002). Theorizing information for information science. *Annual Review of Information Science and Technology* (Vol. 36, pp. 393-425). Medford, NJ: Information Today.

Currie, G. (1995). The moral psychology of fiction. *Australasian Journal of Philosophy, 73*(2), 250–259.

Davenport, Elisabeth. (2010). Confessional methods and everyday life information seeking. *Annual Review of Information Science and Technology* (Vol. 44, pp. 533-562). Medford, NJ: Information Today.

Davies, Paul, & Gregersen, Niels Henrik. (2010). *Information and nature: From physics to metaphysics*. Cambridge, UK: Cambridge University Press.

Dawson, Paul. (2016). From digressions to intrusions: Authorial commentary in the novel. *Studies in the Novel, 48*(2), 145-167.

Day, Ronald E. (2005). Poststructuralism and information studies. *Annual Review of Information Science and Technology* (Vol. 39, pp. 575-609). Medford, NJ: Information Today.

Day, Ronald E. (2000). The "conduit metaphor" and the nature and politics of information studies. *Journal of the American Society for Information Science, 51*(9), 805-811.

Dervin, Brenda. (1976). Strategies for dealing with human information needs: Information or communication? *Journal of Broadcasting, 20*(3), 324-351.

Duguid, Paul. (1996). Material matters. In Geoffrey Nunberg (Ed.), *The future of the book* (pp. 63-102). Berkeley, CA: University of California Press.

Eubanks, Philip. (2001). Understanding metaphors for writing: In defense of the conduit metaphor. *College Composition and Communication, 53*(1), 92-118.

Farkas-Conn, Irene S. (1990). From documentation to information science: The beginnings and early development of the American Documentation Institute – American Society for Information Science. New York: Greenwood Press.

Finders, M. J. (1997). *Just girls: Hidden literacies and life in junior high*. New York: Teachers College Press.

Floridi, Luciano. (2002). What is the philosophy of information? *Metaphilosophy, 33*(1/2), 123-145).

Ford, Nigel. (2015). *Introduction to information behaviour*. London: Facet Publishing.

Frické, Martin. (2009). The knowledge pyramid: A critique of the DIKW hierarchy. *Journal of Information Science, 35*(2), 131-142.

Friend, Stacie. (2008). Imagining fact and fiction. In Kathleen Stock & Katherine Thomson-Jones (Eds.), *New waves in aesthetics* (pp. 150-169). Houndmills, Basingstoke, Hampshire, UK: Palgrave Macmillan UK.

Frohmann, Bernd. (2004). Documentation redux: Prolegomenon to (another) philosophy of information. *Library Trends, 52*(3), 387-407.

Frohmann, Bernd. (1994). Discourse analysis as a research method in library and information science. *Library & Information Science Research, 16*(2), 119-138.

Frohmann, Bernd. (1992). The power of images: a discourse analysis of the cognitive viewpoint. *Journal of Documentation*, 48(4), 365-386.

Gitelman, Lisa. (Ed.). (2013). *Raw data is an oxymoron*. Cambridge, MA: MIT Press.

Gottschall, J. (2012). *The storytelling animal: How stories make us human*. New York: Houghton Mifflin Harcourt.

Grady, Joseph. (1998). "The "conduit metaphor" revisited: A reassessment of metaphors for communication. In Jean-Pierre Koenig (Ed.), *Discourse and cognition: Bridging the gap* (pp. 205-218). Stanford, CA: CLSI Publications.

Hammond, Meghan Marie, & Kim, Sue J. (Eds.). (2014). *Rethinking empathy through literature*. New York: Routledge.

Hookway, Christopher. (2005). The pragmatist maxim and the proof of pragmatism. *Cognitio, 6*(1), 25-42.

Houston, Ronald D., & Harmon, Glynn. (2007). Vannevar Bush and Memex. *Annual review of information science and technology* (Vol. 41, pp. 55-92). Medford, NJ: Information Today.

Kaplan, Amy. (1992). *The social construction of American realism*. Chicago: University of Chicago Press.

Kari, Jarkko, & Hartel, Jenna. (2007). Information and higher things in life: Addressing the pleasurable and the profound in information science. *Journal of the American Society for Information Science and Technology, 58*(8), 1131-1147.

Keen, Suzanne. (2007). *Empathy and the novel*. Oxford, UK: Oxford University Press.

Kerber, Linda K. (1988). Separate spheres, female worlds, women's place: The rhetoric of women's history. *The Journal of American History, 75*(1), 9-39.

Kidd, David Comer, & Castano, Emanuele. (2013). Reading literary fiction improves theory of mind. *Science, 342*(6256), 377-380.

Krashen, Stephen D. (2004). *The power of reading: Insights from the research* (2nd ed.). Westport, CT: Libraries Unlimited.

Lakoff, George, & Johnson, Mark Johnson. (2008). *Metaphors we live by*. Chicago: University of Chicago Press. (Original work published 1980.)

Lindhé, Anna. (2016). The paradox of narrative empathy and the form of the novel, or what George Eliot knew. *Studies in the Novel, 48*(1), 19-42.

Lively, Penelope. (2014). *Dancing fish and ammonites: A memoir*. New York: Viking.

Ma, Lai. (2012). Meanings of information: The assumptions and research consequences of three foundational LIS theories. *Journal of the American Society for Information Science and Technology, 63*(4), 716-723.

Maker, R. (2008). Finding what you're looking for: A reader-centered approach to the classification of adult fiction in public libraries. *The Australian Library Journal, 57*(2), 169-177.

Martin, Linda. (2015). Elegy and the unknowable mind in *Jacob's Room*. *Studies in the Novel, 47*(2), 176-192.

McGaw, Judith A. (1989). No passive victims, no separate spheres: A feminist perspective on technology's history. In Stephen Cutcliffe & Robert Post (Eds.), *In context: History and the history of technology* (pp. 172-191). Bethlehem, PA: Lehigh University Press.

McKechnie, Lynne (E.F.), Ross, Catherine Sheldrick, & Rothbauer, Paulette. (2007). Affective dimensions of information seeking in the context of reading. In Diane Nahl & Dania Bilal (Eds.), *Information and emotion: The emergent affective paradigm in information behavior research and theory* (pp. 187-195). Medford, NJ: Information Today.

Mendelsohn, Harold. (1966). *Mass entertainment*. New Haven, CT: College & University Press.

Meretoja, Hanna. (2016). Fiction, history, and the possible: Jonathan Littell's *Les bienveillantes*. *Orbis Litterarum, 71*(5), 371-404.

Nahl, Diane, & Bilal, Dania. (Eds.). (2007). Information and emotion: The emergent affective paradigm in information behavior and theory. Medford, NJ: Information Today.

Nunberg, Geoffrey. (1996). Farewell to the Information Age. In Geoffrey Nunberg (Ed.), *The future of the book* (pp. 103-133). Berkeley, CA: University of California Press.

Nussbaum, Martha C. (1992). *Love's knowledge: Essays on philosophy and literature*. Oxford, UK: Oxford University Press.

Oatley, K. (2011). *Such stuff as dreams: The psychology of fiction*. Oxford, UK: John Wiley & Sons.

Ooi, Kamy, & Li Liew, Chirn. (2011). Selecting fiction as part of everyday life information seeking. *Journal of Documentation, 67*(5), 748-772.

Paskins, B. (1977). On being moved by Anna Karenina and *Anna Karenina*. *Philosophy, 52*(201), 344–347.

Pattee, Amy. (2008). Considering popular fiction and library practices of recommendation: The literary status of "The Clique" and its historical progenitors. *The Library Quarterly, 78*(1), 71–98.

Peirce, Charles Sanders. (1878). How to make our ideas clear. *Popular Science Monthly, 12*, 286-302.

Radway, Janice A. (1991). *Reading the romance: Women, patriarchy, and popular literature*. Chapel Hill, NC: University of North Carolina Press.

Reddy, Michael J. (1993). The conduit metaphor: A case of frame conflict in our language about language. In Andrew Ortony (Ed.), *Metaphor and thought* (2nd ed., pp. 164-201). Cambridge, UK: Cambridge University. (Original work published 1979.)

Rosenberg, Rosalind. (1983). *Beyond separate spheres: Intellectual roots of modern feminism*. New Haven, CT: Yale University Press.

Ross, Catherine Sheldrick. (1999). Finding without seeking: The information encounter in the context of reading for pleasure. *Information Processing & Management, 35*(6), 783-799.

Ross, Catherine Sheldrick, McKechnie, Lynne (E.F.), & Rothbauer, Paulette. (2006). *Reading matters: What the research reveals about reading, libraries, and community*. Westport, CT: Libraries Unlimited.

Rothbauer, P. M. (2013). "People aren't afraid anymore, but it's hard to find books": Reading practices that inform the personal and social identities of self- identified lesbian and queer young women. *Proceedings of the Annual Conference of CAIS/Actes du congrès annuel de l'ACSI*.

Rothbauer, P. (2004). Finding and creating possibility: Reading in the lives of lesbian, bisexual and queer young women. Unpublished dissertation.

Rowley, Jennifer. (2006). The wisdom hierarchy: Representations of the DIKW hierarchy. *Journal of Information Science, 33*(2), 163-180.

Singhal, Arvind. (2004). Entertainment-education and social change: History, research, and practice. Mahwah, NJ: Lawrence Erlbaum Associates.

Snape, Robert. (1995). *Leisure and the rise of the public library*. London: Library Association Publishing.

Srinivasan, Janaki, Finn, Megan, & Ames, Morgan. (2017). Information determinism: The consequences of faith in information. *The Information Society, 33*(1), 13-22.

Stonier, Tom. (1991). Towards a new theory of information. *Journal of Information* Science, 17(5), 257-263.

Sturm, Brian W. (2003). Reader's advisory and bibliotherapy: Helping or healing? *Journal of Educational Media & Library Sciences, 41*(2), 171-179.

Thelwall, M., & Kousha, K. (2017). Goodreads: A social network site for book readers. *Journal of the Association for Information Science and Technology*, *68*(4), 972-983.

Vonnegut, Kurt. (1969). Slaughterhouse-five, or the Children's Crusade: A duty-dance with death. New York: Random House.

Watt, Ian. (1965). The rise of the novel: Studies in Defoe, Richardson and Fielding. Berkeley: University of California Press.

Weiss, R.S. (1995). Learning from strangers: The art and method of qualitative interview studies. New York: Simon and Schuster.

Williams, Christine L. (1995). *Still a man's world: Men who do women's work.* Berkeley, CA: University of California Press.

Williams, Christine L. (1992). The glass escalator: Hidden advantages for men in the "female professions." *Social Problems*, *39*(3), 253-267.

Williams, P. (1988). The American public library and the problem of purpose. New York: Greenwood Press.

Zillman, D., & Bryant, J. (1994). Entertainment as media effect. In J. Bryant and D. Zillman (Eds.), *Media effects: Advances in theory and research* (pp. 437-461). Hillsdale, NJ: Lawrence Erlbaum Associates.

Zunshine, L. (2006). *Why we read fiction: Theory of mind and the novel*. Columbus, OH: Ohio State University Press.

# Healthy Users' Personal Health Information Management from Activity Trackers: The Perspective of Gym-Goers

**Yuanyuan Feng**
*College of Computing & Informatics, Drexel University, USA.*
*yf93@drexel.edu*

**Denise E. Agosto**
*College of Computing & Informatics, Drexel University, USA.*
*dea2@drexel.edu*

**Kai Li**
*College of Computing & Informatics, Drexel University, USA.*
*kl696@drexel.edu*

## ABSTRACT

**This paper examines how healthy activity tracker users, particularly gym-goers, manage personal health information generated by their activity tracking devices. Findings from 117 valid responses to a web survey are presented to provide an overall picture of healthy activity tracker users' health or fitness-related needs, their personal health information management (PHIM) practices and the gaps between their needs and PHIM. Based on the survey findings, we suggest considering future activity tracker design improvements for addressing users' currently unmet needs while recognizing the limitations of current technology. We conclude with a discussion of the necessity for reexamining PHIM in a new era of broader self-tracking activities and needs.**

## KEYWORDS

activity trackers, personal health information management, personal information management, information behavior, human-computer interaction

## INTRODUCTION

Today's commercial mobile and wearable devices are often equipped with activity tracking functions, allowing users to access data about their physical activities (Consolvo et al., 2008; Sun et al., 2010). The data generated by these devices is often presented to users via various health or fitness applications, including computer, mobile and wearable applications that offer a variety of health-related services. To understand how people interact with different aspects of activity tracking technology, activity tracker user research has received attention from many disciplines, including human-computer interaction, information science and health informatics.

An *activity tracker*, also known as a *fitness tracker*, is defined by Oxford Dictionaries (2017) as "a wearable device or a computer application that records a person's daily physical activity, together with other data relating to their fitness or health, such as the number of calories burned, heart rate, etc." In this paper, the term *activity tracker* refers to fitness bands, smartphones and smartwatches that provide physical activity tracking functions. We also focus on health or fitness applications that can be used to access or manage activity tracker-generated information.

Activity trackers have drawn strong interest from consumers. According to a report from the Consumer Technology Association (CTA; 2016, p.130), 143.5 million wearable computing devices were shipped to markets worldwide in 2015, among which 97.6 million were sports, fitness and wellness trackers, and 17.2 million were smartwatches.

However, the increasing popularity among consumers does not match the expected positive outcomes that activity tracker manufacturers promise. A business survey showed that more than half of U.S. consumers who have owned an activity tracker no long use it (Endeavour Partners, 2014). Researchers also found similar results in activity tracker user studies, including low user adoption rates, limited user engagement and short-lived usage (Gouveia, Karapanos & Hassenzahl, 2015; Shih, Han, Poole, Rosson & Carroll, 2015).

To address these issues, activity tracker user research has focused on persuasive technology to increase user adoption and engagement (Consolvo, Klasnja, McDonald & Landay, 2009; Halko & Kientz, 2010; Fritz, Huang, Murphy & Zimmermann, 2014; Gouveia et al., 2015; Shih et al., 2015). However, current research does not provide much data regarding activity tracker users' personal health information management practices. Consistent and appropriate management of personal health information provides users better support to achieve their health or fitness goals, so it is time to examine personal health information management (PHIM) with this new type of information.

A branch of activity tracker user research, particularly in the health informatics, has extensively explored how activity tracking technology can support health interventions for patients with lifestyle-related medical diseases, such as obesity, hypertension and type 2 diabetes (Lewis, Lyons, Jarvis & Baillargeon, 2015; Cadmus-Bertram, Marcus, Patterson, Parker & Morey, 2015; Chiauzzi, Rodarte & DasMahapatra, 2015). However, not much research attention has been paid to healthy populations, who, despite being generally healthy,

80th Annual Meeting of the Association for Information Science & Technology, Washington, DC | Oct. 27-Nov. 1, 2017

tend to have distinct and compelling personal health information management needs. Therefore, we specifically examine the topic of PHIM from the perspective of healthy users.

In this paper, we present a web survey study that examines a less studied research topic (PHIM) and a less focused population (healthy users) in activity tracker user research. Building upon personal information management theories from information science and empirical studies with activity tracking technology from human-computer interaction, this research aims to bring together previously disparate areas of PHIM research and contribute new knowledge to the emerging area of activity tracker user research.

## LITERATURE REVIEW

### *Personal Health Information Management (PHIM)*

#### *PHIM in Information Science*

Personal information management (PIM) is an area of information science research that "refers to both the practice and study of activities a person performs in order to locate, or create, store, organize, maintain, modify, retrieve, use and distribute information in each of its many forms as needed to meet life's many goals and to fulfill life's many roles and responsibilities" (Jones, 2012, p.3). Personal health information management (PHIM) is often considered a sub-area of PIM. In this sense, the theories of PIM also apply to PHIM; thus, we use PIM theories as the conceptual foundation for this study.

#### *PIM/PHIM Theories*

According to Jones (2007 & 2012), a mapping is the connection between information and needs and can serve as a high-level conceptual framework. In the case of PIM, the mapping is everything that connects personal information and personal needs, which is observable as various PIM activities that people engage in.

In PIM, ***needs*** are personal and diverse, which should be differentiated from ***information needs*** in information seeking behavior research. ***Information need*** is a central concept to information behavior research from individual, organizational and societal perspectives. The concept is used to explain the motivations for information seeking behavior, which is fundamental in many influential information behavior models (Wilson, 1999; Naumer & Fisher, 2010). However, PIM includes a wider range of management behavior that people perform with their personal information. Thus, we used the term need in this research to address users' more varied behaviors.

PIM activities are often viewed as an effort to establish, use and maintain the mapping between personal information and various personal needs. Jones (2012) identifies two directions in which the mapping can be traversed: (1) ***Finding*** activities move from need to information. Specifically, in efforts to meet a need, people seek information; (2) ***Keeping*** activities move from information to need. In other words, people also keep information at hand, and then determine what they need to do with this information. There are additional PIM activities that do not exhibit a specific direction in the mapping but encompass the connection between information and needs. These activities are collectively referred to as (3) ***meta-level*** activities by Jones, including maintaining and organizing, managing privacy and the flow of information, measuring and evaluating, and making sense of and using information.

The mapping, needs and PIM activities serve as the conceptual foundation for our research investigation. Despite the relevance, few studies have applied PIM theories to examine personal health information from activity trackers.

#### *PHIM in Health Informatics*

Information science researchers have developed relatively comprehensive PIM/PHIM theories, but there have been few PHIM empirical studies within the information science field, probably because of limited access to users' personal health information. Traditionally, most personal health information is medical and confidential in nature and often resides behind research firewalls in the information systems of healthcare-related institutions (e.g. clinics, hospitals).

Health informatics is the primary discipline that extensively investigates PHIM to improve medical practices and outcomes by utilizing all types of personal health information, with a focus on electronic health records (EHRs) in medical settings (Pratt, Unruh, Civan & Skeels, 2006; Häyrinen, Saranto & Nykänen, 2008; Archer, Fevrier-Thomas, Lokker, McKibbon & Straus, 2011). Since we focus on healthy users, the body of PHIM research in health informatics is outside the scope of our research.

With the increasing popularity of activity tracking technology, activity tracker-generated personal health information has introduced new research opportunities to human-computer interaction. This area of research is discussed in the following section.

### *Activity Tracker User Research*

#### *Self-tracking research*

With the increasing adoption of mobile and wearable technologies in recent years, there is an emerging body of literature in human-computer interaction that is also related to PHIM – self-tracking research. Humans have a long history of self-tracking. For example, people keep personal logs or diaries to track their personal activities and life experiences. It was not until recent decades that people started to employ digital technologies to help with their self-tracking efforts. According to Lupton (2014, p.77), self-tracking refers to "the practice of gathering data about oneself on a regular basis and then recording and analyzing the data to produce statistics and other data (such as images) relating to regular habits, behaviours and feelings." In this paper, we use *self-tracking research* as the umbrella term for several emerging yet similar concepts in human-computer interaction, including life-logging (Gurrin, Smeaton, & Doherty, 2014), quantified self (Choe, Lee, Lee, Pratt, & Kientz, 2014) and personal informatics (Li, Dey, & Forlizzi, 2010).

The self-tracking research tends to embrace various aspects of personal information, including people's physical activities, health data, food intake, mental status and everyday whereabouts. In this study, we examine activity tracker-generated information about people's daily physical activities, which is narrower in scope than the overall self-tracking research.

### *Adoption and engagement*

Many empirical studies in human-computer interaction have examined user adoption or user engagement with activity trackers and respective health or fitness applications, including both research prototypes (Consolvo et al., 2008, Gouveia et al., 2015) and commercial devices (Shih et al, 2015; Asimakopoulos, Asimakopoulos, & Spillers, 2017).

Shih and colleagues (2015) conducted a six-week user study based on Fitbit usage logs and surveys. They found half of the participants stopped using their devices after two weeks, and only nine out of 26 participants ended up in their high usage group. Similarly, Gouveia and colleagues (2015) analyzed the usage data of Habito, a health application developed by the research team, to study users' engagement with their activity trackers. Only 97 out of 256 users used the application longer than a week. Among those who adopted Habito for more than a week, most users only took brief glances to check out their current activity levels without further interaction. These two studies show that the major issues of activity tracker usage include low user adoption rate and limited user engagement.

To understand the underlying factors that cause issues in adoption and engagement, researchers have taken different approaches. Lazar and colleagues (2015) examined why users abandon smart devices. Seventeen participants were given a budget to purchase smart devices toward their self-defined goals, but 80% abandoned their smart devices after two months. The research team specifically analyzed the data from non-adopters and identified reasons for their abandonment, including devices not fitting with participants' self-conceptions, the data collected by devices being perceived as not useful and device maintenance becoming unmanageable.

More recently, Asimakopoulos and colleagues (2017) recruited 34 active fitness tracker users and explored the factors that motivate them to use their devices in the long-run. The research team synthesized seven user experience heuristics for mobile healthcare wearables to promote motivation and user engagement. However, this study only looked at users of two fitness tracker brands (Fitbit and Jawbone) and did not provide a full picture of activity tracker users that uses different devices.

Together these two studies show the importance of examining adopters as well as non-adopters to draw design implications. To gain a comprehensive understanding of healthy activity tracker users' PHIM, our study aims to recruit both adopters and non-adopters from the healthy user population.

### *Persuasive technology*

A major theme of activity tracker user research is persuasive technology that is intentionally designed to change a person's attitudes or behaviors. Many researchers have explored various techniques and mechanisms to optimize persuasive technology for activity trackers, such as goal setting, framing, feedback, rewards, coaching and social factors (Halko & Kientz, 2010; Adams, Costa, Jung & Choudhury, 2015; Mercer, Li, Giangregorio, Burns & Grindrod, 2016). However, findings from these studies were largely inconsistent and uncovered further design challenges for persuasive technology in support of behavior change.

With the increasing adoption of commercial activity trackers, Fritz and colleagues (2014) conducted a qualitative interview study with 30 participants who adopted wearable activity trackers for between 3 and 54 months to examine the effectiveness of persuasive technology in a non-experimental condition. They discovered that it was the *reflective* aspect (the technology helps people reflect on their behavior) rather than the *persuasive* aspect (the technology that pushes people to do something with limited knowledge of their current statuses) of personal informatics technology that provided more long-term motivation to adopters. This study shows that investigating adopters of activity tracker in a naturalistic setting can generate valuable design implications to support long-term engagement with activity trackers.

In current activity tracker user research, persuasive technology is the primary approach to address issues such as low adoption rates and limited user engagement. Many empirical studies have shown evidence that other advanced aspects, such as better visualization and analytics of activity tracker-generated information, should be incorporated into persuasive technology design (Munson, 2012; Bentley et al., 2013; Faisal, Blandford & Potts, 2013; Fritz et al., 2014).

## RESEARCH QUESTIONS

Building upon PIM theories from information science and empirical studies from human-interaction, our study examines healthy activity tracker users' PHIM of the information generated by their devices. To contribute new knowledge to PHIM research and to generate design implications for future activity tracking technology, we address the following three research questions:

**RQ1:** What are healthy activity tracker users' health or fitness-related needs regarding their activity tracker use?

**RQ2:** How do healthy activity tracker users manage personal health information generated by their devices?

**RQ3:** What are the gaps between healthy activity tracker users' needs and their PHIM?

## METHODOLOGY

### The Web Survey Method

We chose the web survey method to shed light on our research questions. Surveys are usually designed to produce statistics about a target population on a specific research topic (Fowler, 2009) and are suitable for gathering general data to draw an overall picture of our target population – healthy activity tracker users. Specifically, we chose the web survey method using computer-assisted, self-administered questionnaires (CSAQ) to collect data from healthy activity tracker users, because of its low cost and ability to reach a relatively large number of potential respondents (Bethlehem & Biffignandi, 2011).

### Questionnaire Design

The web survey questionnaire was designed to address the three research questions. It contained four sets of questions:

- **Background.** This included close-ended multiple choice questions on demographics, gym visits and health or fitness-related goals from gym visits, providing general information about respondents and data for RQ1.
- **Activity trackers and health or fitness applications.** This included questions on respondents' current use of activity trackers and health or fitness applications as well as their predicted future use. Most of the questions were multiple choice questions, except for questions on predicted future use, which were open-ended to allow text input from respondents. This set of questions aimed to provide data for RQ1 and RQ2.
- **Information from activity trackers and PHIM.** This included questions on the types of personal health information generated by activity trackers as well as opinion questions on the information and PHIM of such information. Because PHIM is a complicated information behavior, open-ended questions were included for more details. This set of questions aimed to answer RQ2.
- **Expectations and concerns.** This included several open-ended questions that allow respondents to comment on their expectations and concerns with current activity tracking technology. This set of questions aimed to provide detailed qualitative data to answer RQ3, as well as to supplement RQ1 and RQ2.

The Institutional Review Board-approved questionnaire was imported into Qualtrics web survey software and distributed on the internet.

### Recruitment

Since this research focuses on healthy users, we employed purposive sampling, "a form of nonprobability sampling in which the selection of the sample is based on the judgment of the researcher as to which elements best fit the criteria of the study" (Bethlehem & Biffignandi, 2011, p.32). To reach healthy activity tracker users, we targeted a population who intentionally participate in physical exercise – gym goers. To be eligible to participate the study, individuals needed to meet the following requirements: (1) be over 18 years old; (2) self-identify as healthy; (3) be fluent in speaking and writing English; (4) have/had used at least one activity tracker.

In August 2016, we conducted a small-sized pilot study by inviting one researcher's Facebook friends who were gym goers to complete the web survey questionnaire. After improving the questionnaire based on the pilot study results, we partnered with a large-sized university-affiliated gym located in a large city in the Eastern United States and invited its members to complete the web survey questionnaire via two rounds of email invitations between August and November in 2016. Note that our partner gym not only serves students, faculty and staff of the university but also has a considerable number of paid members from outside the university community.

### Data analysis

A total of 117 valid responses were received. Quantitative data from close-ended questions, including multiple-choice questions and Likert-type scale questions, was analyzed and presented using basic descriptive statistics methods. We used simplified thematic analysis (Braun & Clarke, 2006) to extract themes from the qualitative data from open-ended questions.

## FINDINGS

### Respondents and Their Activity Trackers

In this section, we provide a demographic picture of the respondents and their activity tracker usage, which serves as background for later sections in the Findings.

#### Demographic Information

As we did not have access to personal health records, we chose to use self-identification to define "healthy" users. All respondents identified their physical health levels as either "healthier than average" or "among average" in comparison with people in their age group.

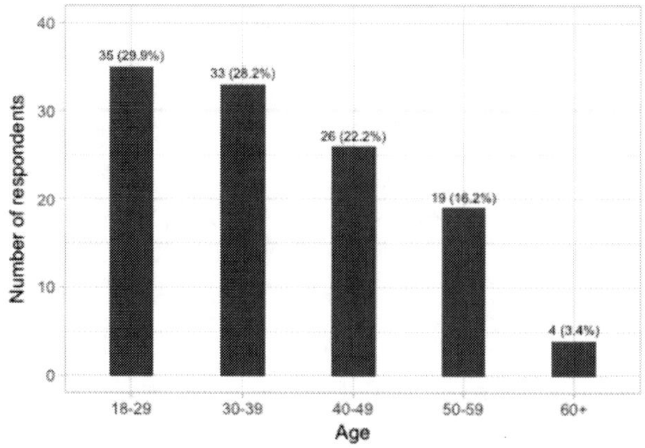


*Figure 1. Respondents' Age Distribution*

Among the 117 respondents, 40 (34.2%) were male, 75 (64.1%) were female, and two (1.7%) identified as "other gender." The gender ratio is slightly imbalanced with more female respondents. Figure 1 and Figure 2 show the age and profession distributions of all respondents. For age distribution, more than half of the respondents were in their 20s (29.9%) and 30s (28.2%), but the sample also has relatively good representation from older age groups. For profession distribution, many respondents work in higher education, with 33 staff (27.4%) and 14 faculty (12.0%), which was to be expected, given the context of the study.

The demographic data indicates that our web surveys reached relatively heterogeneous groups of activity tracker users and that the participant recruitment method was effective in reaching a diversity of healthy users.

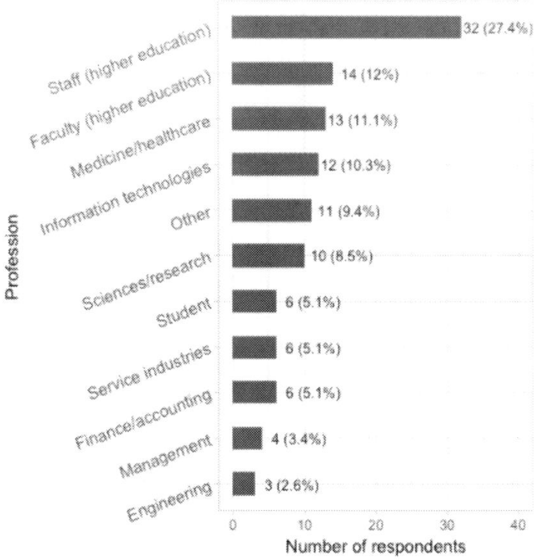


***Figure 2.*** *Respondents' profession distribution*

### *Gym Visits*

Respondents were asked about their gym visit frequency and the types of physical activities (or physical exercise) during their visits. Table 1 shows the reported frequency of gym visits. More than two thirds of the respondents reported that they visit the partner gym or other gyms at least twice a week, indicating a generally high level of planned physical activity within the respondent group.

| Frequency | # of Respondents |
|---|---|
| 4-7 times a week or more | 43 (36.8%) |
| 2-3 times a week | 39 (33.3%) |
| Once a week | 18 (15.4%) |
| Less than once a week | 17 (14.5%) |
| Total | 117 (100%) |

***Table 1.*** *Gym visit frequency*

Other questions addressed the physical activities (or physical exercises) that respondents engage in during their gym visits. They reported participation in a range of physical activities, as shown in Table 2. The most popular activities are walking or running and strength training exercises, both of which were reported by 72 respondents (61.5%). In addition, many respondents also engaged in swimming, cycling or biking, and attending various instructor-led exercise classes. The data on gym visits confirms that the survey reached relatively healthy activity tracker users who engage in diverse physical activities or exercises during gym visits. Their participation in the diversity of activities is likely to influence their health or fitness-related needs regarding their activity tracker use.

| Physical Activity | # of Respondents |
|---|---|
| Running/walking | 72 (61.5%) |
| Weights/Strength training | 72 (61.5%) |
| Group Exercise Classes | 36 (30.8%) |
| Cycling/biking | 35 (29.9%) |
| Swimming | 26 (22.2%) |
| Other | 22 (18.8%) |

***Table 2.*** *Physical activities during gym visits*

### *Activity Trackers Used*

At the time of the study, 71 out of the 117 respondents (60.7%) had used at least two activity trackers at any previous point in time. Six respondents reported having used more than five activity trackers. Conversely, 46 respondents (39.3%) had used only one activity tracker.

For the type of activity trackers used, 84 (48.8%), 65 (37%), and 23 (13.4%) reported that they have used fitness bands, smartphones and smartwatches, respectively. Since many respondents have used more than one activity trackers, there are overlaps among these three types.

We also asked each respondent to identify the primary device among all the activity trackers he or she used. Fitbit is the most popular brand with 51 respondents (43.6%) identifying various Fitbit devices as their primary device, followed by Garmin (16, 13.7%), Apple Watch (9, 7.7%), Android phone (9, 7.7%), Jawbone (6, 5.1%), and iPhone (6, 5.1%).

This data shows that our respondents have used a diversity of activity trackers and many tend to try different devices, which allows this study to generate more comprehensive results than previous studies that focused on one type of activity tracker or a single application (Consolvo et al., 2008; Cadmus-Bertram, et al., 2015; Shih et al., 2015).

### *Current Users and Past Users*

Also at the time of the study, 94 respondents (80.3%) reported still actively using at least one activity tracker. We refer to these users as "current users." Twenty-three respondents (19.7%) reported no longer using an activity tracker. We refer to these respondents as "past users." In later sections, current users' and past users' survey results are analyzed separately.

| Length | Current Users | Past Users |
|---|---|---|
| More than one year | 71 (75.1%) | 5 (21.7%) |
| 4-12 months | 17 (18.1%) | 6 (26.1%) |
| 1-3 months | 5 (5.3%) | 8 (30.8%) |
| 1-4 weeks | 0 (0%) | 2 (8.7%) |
| Less than one week | 1 (1.1%) | 2 (8.7%) |
| Total | 94 (100%) | 23 (100%) |

***Table 3**. Length of activity tracker usage*

Table 3 shows the length of reported activity tracker use. More than two-thirds of current users (75.1%) had been using activity trackers for more than a year. Even most past users (82.6%) had used their activity trackers for at least a month before they ceased use. Our respondents tended to use their activity trackers for relatively long periods of time. Even past users had used their devices longer than many non-adopters, who usually gave up using within two weeks in previous studies (Gouveia et al., 2015; Shih et al, 2015).

### *RQ1: Health or Fitness-related Needs*

#### *Goals from Gym Visits*

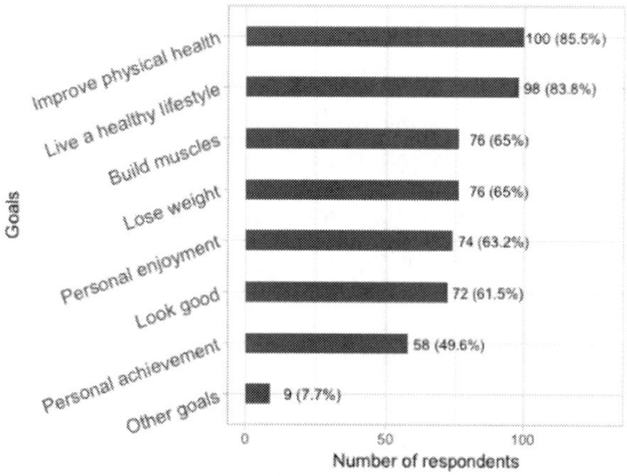


***Figure 3**. Goals from gym visits*

Respondents expressed a combination of goals they expected from their gym visits, as shown in Figure 3. Based on the findings, we identify three major themes of health or fitness-related goals: (1) to stay healthy, such as to improve physical health (100, 85.5%) or to live a healthy lifestyle (98, 83.8%); (2) to stay in shape, such as to look good (72, 61.5%), to lose weight (76, 65%) or to build muscles (76, 65%); and (3) for personal fulfillment, such as for personal enjoyment (74, 63.2%) or personal achievement (58, 49.6%). Nine respondents identified additional goals, including longevity, stress management and social interaction with "other liked-minded people."

#### *Unmet Needs*

The information behavior literature has shown that users may not be able to articulate their needs (Kuhlthau, 1991; Julien & Duggan, 2000). To supplement the results above, we analyzed the respondents' comments from optional open-ended questions and extracted themes about their health or fitness-related needs. Both past and current users expressed high levels of unmet needs.

Ten out of 23 past users had given up using activity trackers due to health or fitness-related needs that their devices could not meet. Similar to Lazer et al.'s (2015) findings, the main reason was that their devices failed to capture information that was important to them, especially the lack of ability to track strength training data (e.g., weights and repetitions). For example, one respondent commented, "*My tracker was unable to capture (without manual input) most of the information that made my activities interesting to me.*"

Another major reason was the mismatch between past users' needs and the motivation design of their devices. Two standout comments were "*I am very internally motivated and felt that I did not need the tracker to keep me on track*" and "*I didn't see the value or impact on my exercise routines.*"

Current users reported more diverse unmet needs than past users. Most unmet needs were technical, such as the need for longer battery life, better water resistance, smaller device size, more accurate heart rate data and more types of information. Current users' needs for persuasive technology design varied more: some expected to have more motivating reminders pushing them to engage in physical activities, but others expected better personalization or customization and minimal invasiveness from health of wellness applications.

#### *Overarching Needs*

Respondents' comments also show that their activity tracker use or non-use often served their overarching health or fitness-related needs. These overarching needs are often relevant to the more general goals from their gym visits, such as "improve physical health" and "live a healthy lifestyle." Nine respondents commented that they also actively track their food intake using applications like My Fitness Pal in addition to what is tracked by their devices. Though food logging is outside the scope of this study, respondents' comments show that their health or fitness-related needs can be all-encompassing, whereas activity tracking technology only partially satisfy their needs.

### *RQ2: PHIM Practices*

#### *Types of Information*

To examine how healthy users manage their personal health information from activity trackers, we first need to know the types of personal health information provided by their devices. Table 4 lists the common types of information provided by respondents' activity trackers in descending order by the number of respondents reporting them.

| Type of Information | # of Respondents |
|---|---|
| Steps | 98 (83.8%) |
| Distance (ran, walked, or biked) | 98 (83.8%) |
| Calories (burnt through physical activities) | 90 (76.9%) |
| Sleep (e.g., time, quality) | 63 (53.8%) |
| Heart rates | 55 (47%) |
| Route (ran, walked, or biked, displayed on a map) | 45 (38.5%) |
| Elevation (e.g., stairs climbed) | 43 (36.8%) |
| Other | 11 (9.4%) |

***Table 4.*** *Information provided by activity trackers*

The range of information provided includes relatively raw data that is directly generated by activity tracker sensors, such as steps, distance, elevation and heart rates, as well as more complex information that is often processed or computed by health or fitness applications, such as a route displayed on a map and calories burnt during a workout. Eleven respondents (9.4%) mentioned other types of information available to them, including active/stationary time and cadence.

Note that more than half of respondents lacked access to heart rates, route and elevation information from their devices. These types of data usually require more costly sensors or computation power that are usually available on high-end activity trackers. Different devices and different types of information available lead to very different user experiences with activity tracking technology, which may eventually influence users' adoption decision.

| |
|---|
| **Statement 1(S1):** The information provided by my activity tracker is/was accurate in recording my daily activity. |
| **Statement 2(S2):** The information provided by my activity is/was consistent over time. |
| **Statement 3(S3):** The information from my activity tracker is/was presented clearly (in charts, tables, timelines, etc.) |
| **Statement 4(S4):** I can/could easily export, manage or store the information. |
| **Statement 5(S5):** I can easily share the information with my friends and family. |

***Table 5.*** *Opinion statements*

### *Opinions on Information and PHIM*

Since respondents use a wide variety of activity trackers that provide various types of information, it is not feasible to investigate their opinions on specific types of personal health information using the survey methods. Therefore, we used five statements listed in Table 5 to collect respondents' overall opinions. Three statements (S1, S2, S3) are about the personal health information provided by their devices and two statements (S4, S5) are about their PHIM experience.

Table 6 presents the means and standard deviations of both current users' and past users' ratings on these five statements using a five-point Likert scale described in the table.

| Statement | **Scale:** 1=strongly disagree; 2=disagree; 3=neither disagree or agree; 4=agree; 5=strongly agree. | | | |
|---|---|---|---|---|
| | **Current Users (N=94)** | | **Past Users (N=23)** | |
| | Mean | SD | Mean | SD |
| **S1** | 4.20 | 0.74 | 3.83 | 0.72 |
| **S2** | 4.35 | 0.67 | 4.04 | 0.64 |
| **S3** | 4.45 | 0.77 | 3.96 | 1.02 |
| **S4** | 3.69 | 1.05 | 3.35 | 0.83 |
| **S5** | 3.64 | 0.96 | 3.57 | 0.73 |

***Table 6.*** *Likert scale rating on five statements*

Overall, both current users and past users positively rated all five statements (mean > 3). Current users had slightly higher rating than past users on all five statements, which may explain why they continued to use their activity trackers.

Comparing the ratings across statements, both current and past users' ratings on statements about personal health information provided by their devices were slightly more positive than their ratings on statements about their PHIM experience, indicating that there is room for improving PHIM functionality in activity tracking technology.

### *Health or Fitness Applications as PHIM Tool*

All respondents reported that health or fitness applications were the primary tool for managing personal health information from activity trackers. These applications had taken over many responsibilities of most finding and keeping activities in PIM (Jones, 2012) to make users' lives easier.

We asked respondents to identify all the health or fitness applications they had used. They reported 31 different applications in total. The range of health or fitness applications included device-based applications that are often the default applications developed by activity tracker manufacturers, such as Fitbit app, Garmin app, Apple Health and S Health by Samsung, as well as other applications that offer more specific or advanced functionality, such as Nike app, My Fitness Pal, Map My Run and Strava.

The most popular application was Fitbit app, which 64 respondents (54.7%) reported using, followed by Apple Health (32, 27.4%), My Fitness Pal (28, 23.9%), Garmin app (21, 17.9%), Map My Run (18, 15.4%), Nike app (16, 13.7%). We also found that 41 respondents (35.0%) had used only one application, while the remaining 76 respondents (65.0%) had tried multiple applications.

When asked about predicted future use of these health or fitness applications in six months, 86 (91.5%) out of 94 current users predicted they would continue to use current applications for reasons such as "low maintenance" and "consistency." For example, one respondent commented "*My use (of applications) is determined by the technology (activity tracker) I get.*" Specifically, 21 in these 86 current users explained that they were open to trying new (and possibly better) applications if they were to become available. For example, one respondent commented, "*I haven't found a really great third-party app that adds anything useful to my Fitbit app, but I'd like to be able to plot data easily.*" The remaining eight (8.5%) out of all 94 current users would discontinue using the current applications, because they intended to upgrade their activity trackers and would switch to the default applications associated with their new devices.

The data on health or fitness applications indicates that most current users tended to continue using the applications that they use now. Also, it shows evidence that the default applications of activity trackers cannot satisfy some users' needs, so they use multiple applications or stay open-minded to try new applications.

#### *Other PHIM Practices*

Besides using various health or fitness applications, 27 out of 94 current users commented that they used other methods for managing personal health information from their activity trackers. Specifically, 18 (19.1%) keep some type of exercise journals on paper, calendars, spreadsheets or web services, and five (5.3%) have exported the raw data recorded by their activity trackers for further personal analysis. These respondents who made extra efforts in PHIM often had advanced health or fitness-related needs, such as training for running races or improving exercise performance, that the applications they were using could not fully support. For example, one respondent commented, "*I copy the information into a paper journal and add notes about what was special about that particular run – if it was a race, or if the weather or my health impacted the run, etc.*" The other PHIM practices were meta-level PIM activities that allowed users to gain insights and added value from their information.

### *RQ3: Gaps Between Needs and PHIM*

By analyzing respondents' comments on expectations and concerns of activity tracking technology, as well as by relating the findings of RQ1 and RQ2, we identified three underlying gaps between healthy activity tracker users' health or fitness-related needs and their PHIM of information from activity trackers.

#### *Unmet Needs vs. Limitations of Technology and Design*

Respondents' unmet needs were often connected to the limitations of current technology and design. For example, one respondent wrote an interesting comment on her expectations –"*My ideal tracker would be waterproof, would have an extensive inventory of food/portions for calorie recording, would have a heart rate monitor and be able to accurately record cycling, would never need to be charged.*" Most of her expectations (waterproof, battery and data accuracy) are bounded by current technology and can only be achieved through the advance of activity tracking technology, but her expectation for improved food logging can be attained by optimizing the design of technology.

#### *Overarching Needs vs. Information Fragmentation*

Despite being healthy, many survey respondents exhibited overarching needs regarding their health or fitness, which require a wider scope of PHIM than that provided by activity tracking technology. Most notably, 28 respondents have used My Fitness Pal, a fitness application that incorporates state-of-art food logging functions to combine different aspects of personal health information in PHIM.

Such overarching needs are compromised by the information fragmentation caused by using multiple health or fitness applications. As one commented "*I'd like to take the best aspects of Jefit for weight training, Endomondo for running, and My Fitness Pal for food logging, and have them altogether in one app.*" There are many business factors and practical difficulties hindering better interoperability among applications, so the gap between overarching needs and information fragmentation is likely to linger.

#### *Personal Control vs. Technology Convenience*

Respondents' expectations and concerns of activity tracking technology brought up another gap between personal control and technology convenience regarding PHIM.

Privacy and security concerns were the primary theme found in the comments. For example, one respondent commented on privacy that "*It is disconcerting that my sleep and exercise information is all known,*" while another commented on security "*When running outdoors alone I'm concerned about others being able to view my location.*" However, respondents felt it was something they had to compromise if they wanted to enjoy the convenience of activity tracking technology. Another recurring theme in the comments was the difficulty exporting data from the default health or fitness applications, which was often restricted by activity tracker manufacturers. Respondents showed the need to take control of their own personal health information but often give in to the technology convenience that they need.

## DISCUSSION AND DESIGN IMPLICATIONS

This web survey study has yielded rich findings on PHIM of activity tracker-generated information from the healthy users' perspective. This section provides further discussion and design implications based on the findings.

### *Addressing Unmet Needs*

One notable finding from the survey was the level of unmet health or fitness-related needs among the participant group. Even among respondents who continued to use their devices there was widespread expression of frustration and disappointment with device functionality. We found that respondents, both past and current users, expressed an array of unmet needs. Still, it is likely that there were additional unexpressed needs, an area for future investigation.

However, some unmet needs could be addressed in a relatively short time through improved designs of PHIM tools. Such unmet needs included request for "visual indication of how far ahead or behind I was in previous runs" and "segment comparisons (during a run)" and "better integration among applications." Still, a portion of healthy activity tracker users expressed very advanced needs for PHIM, such as personalized exercise journals and in-depth data analytics.

### Recognizing the Limitations of Technology

We have identified gaps between healthy activity tracker users' health or fitness-related needs and their PHIM practices, which tells us that some gaps are more challenging, such as fulfilling the range of unmet needs and allowing personal control over personal health information.

The diversity of needs reported from health activity tracker users makes it critical to recognize the limitations of current activity tracking technology and recognize that not all needs can be met through technology in the near future (e.g., privacy concerns). However, as one respondent commented, "*Even with all of the issues with current technology, I love having data that influences what I do for the rest of the day and allows me to compare one day to the other.*" We should also acknowledge what activity tracking technology has accomplished and focus on what we can do now to make it better. Now that we have the capability to collect relevant data about our physical activities, we should focus on making it easier to personalize, organize, store, manipulate and assess such data.

### Supporting Needs through PHIM Tool Design

Though some of the needs expressed may only be solved by future technology advances, we can still address a few needs by improving the design of current activity tracking technology. The findings of this study indicate several design implications for PHIM tools to support healthy users' needs.

#### Supporting Advanced Health or Fitness-related Needs

The findings show a significant portion of healthy activity tracker users exhibit advanced needs, which are often associated with their performance goals such as training for races. These needs require more accurate data, better scientific analysis and freedom for customization. Future PHIM tools should place more emphasis to support healthy activity tracker users' advanced needs.

#### Incorporating Diverse Motivation Mechanisms

The findings also show that some healthy users may not react well to the motivation mechanisms associated with current persuasive technology designs, which mainly aim to get inactive populations to move more, such as daily step goals. We found evidence that healthy activity tracker users, especially gym goers who are physically active, tend to be more self-motivated and such motivation mechanisms have little influence over their physical activity level. Therefore, incorporating diverse motivation mechanisms that address performance and long-term maintenance goals into activity tracker-related PHIM tools may increase adoption and continuous engagement among healthy users who are physically active.

#### Mitigating information fragmentation

The information fragmentation reported by respondents is largely rooted in the commercial nature of activity trackers and their default health or fitness applications. However, better design of PHIM tools still can mitigate this obstacle by improving interoperability, allowing individualization and providing advanced data analyses and visualizations, so that activity tracker users do not have to use multiple applications to tailor their overarching health or fitness-related needs.

### Reexamining PHIM in a New Era

This study extended the understanding of PHIM with a new type of personal health information. With the advance of activity tracking technology, PHIM has entered a new era where people's personal health information can be automatically gathered by mobile and wearable devices in their everyday life. The range of personal health information available to people has extended from medical settings to every life health information.

This also influenced their PIM/PHIM activities, where two basic activities – finding and keeping – are increasingly being automatically completed by technology, and people are moving towards focusing more on meta-level activities that provide insights and added values. These changes urge information science researchers to re-examine PIM/PHIM in new contexts.

## CONCLUSION AND FUTURE WORK

This paper presented a web survey study that depicts an overall picture of healthy activity tracker users' health or fitness-related needs, their PHIM with activity tracker-generated information, and the gaps between their needs and PHIM. The findings contributed new knowledge to both PHIM and activity tracker user research by focusing on a less studied topic and a less identified user segment.

However, practical limitations of the web survey method meant that we could only collect limited qualitative data. We were not able to analyze respondents' deeper underlying motivations for their PHIM practices. The next step in the research process is to invite web survey respondents to participate in an in-depth interview study to reveal more specific PHIM behaviors and underlying motivations of healthy activity tracker users, which could lead to a theoretical contribution to information science and to more deeply developed ideas for design improvements.

## REFERENCES


Adams, A. T., Costa, J., Jung, M. F., & Choudhury, T. (2015). Mindless computing: Designing technologies to subtly influence behavior. In *Proceedings of the 2015 ACM international joint conference on pervasive and ubiquitous computing* (pp. 719-730). ACM.

Archer, N., Fevrier-Thomas, U., Lokker, C., McKibbon, K. A., & Straus, S. E. (2011). Personal health records: A scoping review. *Journal of the American Medical Informatics Association, 18*(4), 515-522.

Asimakopoulos, S., Asimakopoulos, G., & Spillers, F. (2017). Motivation and user engagement in fitness tracking: Heuristics for mobile healthcare wearables. *Informatics 4*(1), 5.

Bentley, F., Tollmar, K., Stephenson, P., Levy, L., Jones, B., Robertson, S., ... & Wilson, J. (2013). Health mashups: Presenting statistical patterns between wellbeing data and context in natural language to promote behavior change. *ACM Transactions on Computer-Human Interaction (TOCHI), 20*(5), 30.

Bethlehem, J., & Biffignandi, S. (2011). The road to web surveys. *Handbook of web surveys* (Vol. 567) (pp. 1-36). Hoboken, NJ: John Wiley & Sons.

Cadmus-Bertram, L. A., Marcus, B. H., Patterson, R. E., Parker, B. A., & Morey, B. L. (2015). Randomized trial of a Fitbit-based physical activity intervention for women. *American Journal of Preventive Medicine, 49*(3), 414-418.

Chiauzzi, E., Rodarte, C., & DasMahapatra, P. (2015). Patient-centered activity monitoring in the self-management of chronic health conditions. *BMC medicine, 13*(1), 77.

Choe, E. K., Lee, N. B., Lee, B., Pratt, W., & Kientz, J. A. (2014). Understanding quantified-selfers' practices in collecting and exploring personal data. In *Proceedings of the 32nd annual ACM conference on human factors in computing systems* (pp. 1143-1152). ACM.

Consolvo, S., McDonald, D. W., Toscos, T., Chen, M. Y., Froehlich, J., Harrison, B., ... & Smith, I. (2008). Activity sensing in the wild: A field trial of ubifit garden. In *Proceedings of the SIGCHI conference on human factors in computing systems* (pp. 1797-1806). ACM. doi: 10.1145/1357054.1357335

Consolvo, S., Klasnja, P., McDonald, D. W., & Landay, J. A. (2009). Goal-setting considerations for persuasive technologies that encourage physical activity. In *Proceedings of the 4th international conference on persuasive technology,* No. 8. ACM.

Consumer Technology Association (2016). Digital America: State of the U.S. consumer technology industry. Retrieved April 17, 2017 from: https://www.cta.tech/CTA/media/News/2016_DigitalAmerica.pdf

Endeavour Partners (2014). Inside wearables. Retrieved April 19, 2017 from: https://endeavourpartners.net/white-papers/inside-wearables/

Fritz, T., Huang, E. M., Murphy, G. C., & Zimmermann, T. (2014). Persuasive technology in the real world: A study of long-term use of activity sensing devices for fitness. In *the Proceedings of the SIGCHI conference on human factors in computing systems*. ACM.

Faisal, S., Blandford, A., & Potts, H. W. (2013). Making sense of personal health information: Challenges for information visualization. *Health Informatics Journal, 19*(3), 198-217.

Fowler, F. J. (2009). Types of error in surveys. In *Applied social research methods: Survey research methods (4th ed.)* (pp. 11-17). Thousand Oaks, CA: SAGE Publications.

Gurrin, C., Smeaton, A. F., & Doherty, A. R. (2014). Lifelogging: Personal big data. *Foundations and Trends® in Information Retrieval, 8*(1), 1-125.

Gouveia, R., Karapanos, E., & Hassenzahl, M. (2015). How do we engage with activity trackers?: A longitudinal study of Habito. Paper presented at *the Proceedings of the 2015 ACM international joint conference on pervasive and ubiquitous computing*.

Halko, S., & Kientz, J. A. (2010). Personality and persuasive technology: An exploratory study on health-promoting mobile applications. In *Proceedings of the 5th international conference on persuasive technology* (pp. 150-161). Springer-Verlag.

Häyrinen, K., Saranto, K., & Nykänen, P. (2008). Definition, structure, content, use and impacts of electronic health records: A review of the research literature. *International Journal of Medical Informatics, 77*(5), 291-304.

Jones, W. (2007). Personal information management. *Annual review of information science and technology, 41*(1), 453-504.

Jones, W. (2012). The future of personal information management, part I: Our information, always and forever. *Synthesis lectures on information concepts, retrieval, and services, 4*(1), 1-125.

Julien, H., & Duggan, L. J. (2000). A longitudinal analysis of the information needs and uses literature. *Library & Information Science Research, 22*(3), 291-309.

Kuhlthau, C. C. (1991). Inside the search process: Information seeking from the user's perspective. *Journal of the American Society for Information Science, 42*(5), 361.

Lazar, A., Koehler, C., Tanenbaum, J., & Nguyen, D. H. (2015). Why we use and abandon smart devices. In *Proceedings of the 2015 ACM international joint conference on pervasive and ubiquitous computing* (pp. 635-646). ACM.

Lewis, Z. H., Lyons, E. J., Jarvis, J. M., & Baillargeon, J. (2015). Using an electronic activity monitor system as an intervention modality: A systematic review. *BMC Public Health, 15*(1), 585.

Li, I., Dey, A., & Forlizzi, J. (2010). A stage-based model of personal informatics systems. In *Proceedings of the SIGCHI conference on human factors in computing systems* (pp. 557-566). ACM.

Lupton, D. (2014). Self-tracking cultures: Towards a sociology of personal informatics. In *Proceedings of the 26th Australian computer-human interaction conference on designing futures* (pp. 77-86). ACM.

Mercer, K., Li, M., Giangregorio, L., Burns, C., & Grindrod, K. (2016). Behavior change techniques present in wearable activity trackers: A critical analysis. *JMIR mHealth and uHealth, 4*(2).

Munson, S.A. (2012). Mindfulness, reflection, and persuasion in personal informatics. In *Extended abstracts of the SIGCHI conference on human factors in computing systems*.

Naumer, C. M., & Fisher, K.E. (2010) Information needs. In *Encyclopedia of library and information sciences*. (3rd ed., Vol.1, pp. 2452–2458). Boca Raton, FL: CRC Press.

Oxford Dictionaries. (2017). Activity tracker. Retrieved April 17, 2017 from: https://en.oxforddictionaries.com/definition/us/activity_tracker

Pratt, W., Unruh, K., Civan, A., & Skeels, M. M. (2006). Personal health information management. *Communications of the ACM, 49*(1), 51-55.

Shih, P. C., Han, K., Poole, E. S., Rosson, M. B., & Carroll, J. M. (2015). Use and adoption challenges of wearable activity trackers. *iConference 2015 proceedings*.

Sun, L., Zhang, D., Li, B., Guo, B., & Li, S. (2010). Activity recognition on an accelerometer embedded mobile phone with varying positions and orientations. In *International conference on ubiquitous intelligence and computing* (pp. 548-562). Springer Berlin Heidelberg. doi: 10.1007/978-3-642-16355-5_42

Wilson, T. D. (1999). Models in information behaviour research. *Journal of Documentation*, 55(3), 249-270.

# Toward a Characterization of Digital Humanities Research Collections: A Contrastive Analysis of Technical Designs

**Katrina Fenlon**
*School of Information Sciences, University of Illinois at Urbana-Champaign, USA. kfenlon2@illinois.edu*

## ABSTRACT

**Scholarship across disciplines is changing in the face of digital methodologies, novel forms of evidence and new communication technologies. In the humanities, scholars are confronting and often pioneering innovative ways of viewing, reading, interacting with, collecting, interpreting, contextualizing and sharing their sources, including digital primary sources and data derivatives. This paper reports on one piece of a multimodal study that aims to help us characterize an important, still evolving genre of digital scholarship: the thematic research collection. Using a close, systematic analysis of collections' data models and infrastructures, this study considers the questions: How do the technical designs of thematic research collections contribute to their purposes, functions and uses? What do variations in their designs teach us about the genre as a whole? An analysis of the purposes and designs of scholar-built collections of humanities evidence has implications for the development of digital collections and aggregations generally and the future shapes of digital scholarship and communication.**

## KEYWORDS

collections, scholarly communication, digital scholarship, digital humanities, data curation

## INTRODUCTION

Across the disciplines, scholarship is changing in the face of digital methodologies, novel forms of digital evidence, and new communication technologies. In the humanities scholars are confronting, and often pioneering, new ways of viewing, reading, interacting with, collecting and sharing their evidence, including digital primary sources and derivatives of those sources, such as humanities data. Following a wave of large-scale digitization efforts for historical and literary resources in the 1990s-2000s, collections were thrown into the spotlight of digital humanities research. Among many others, the *Walt Whitman Archive*, the *Valley of the Shadow*, and the *World of Dante* were early exemplars, and these and contemporary collections are now well known and firmly established platforms for humanities research. Scholars have continued to build collections to facilitate research – both for themselves and others – and these collections increasingly experiment with and adopt new shapes and functions to accomplish their specific research goals. In addition, these collections often serve other purposes, including teaching, facilitating use and reuse of humanities data, acting as hubs for communication among scholars within and across fields of interest and serving as public faces for research.

In the information sciences, collections are familiar constructs. We have long studied collections generally, and digital research collections in the humanities in particular (Palmer, 2004). However, we do not know enough about the emerging shapes of digital scholarship. More specifically, we do not know enough about one still evolving and dynamic genre of digital scholarship in the humanities: the thematic research collection.

This paper reports on one piece of a multimodal study that investigates thematic research collections: what they are, how they work and how to sustain them – both as significant contributions to our intellectual and cultural heritage and as dynamic platforms for new analysis and research.

*Thematic research collections*, often called by other names – *archives*, *digital projects*, etc. – are defined here as collections of primary sources and other materials gathered by scholars to support research on a theme. Such collections abound; together they constitute a highly, perhaps essentially, diverse and vibrant genre. See, for example, *Nineteenth-Century Disability: Cultures and Contexts* (http://www.nineteenthcenturydisability.org/), which gathers evidence and historical narrative about popular conceptions of disability in the 19th century; and *"O Say Can You See": The Early Washington, D.C. Law and Family Project* (http://mith.umd.edu/research/o-say-can-see-early-washington-d-c-law-family-project), which explores early 19th-century D.C.'s multigenerational black and white family networks.

This study addresses the following questions: How do the technical designs of thematic research collections contribute to their goals, functions and uses? What might differences and similarities in their designs teach us about the genre as a whole?

---

80th Annual Meeting of the Association for Information Science & Technology, Washington, DC | Oct. 27-Nov. 1, 2017

This is one part of a larger project that considers more fundamental questions, including these: What are the defining features of thematic research collections as a scholarly genre? What kinds of thematic research collections are there? What are the challenges for libraries and digital humanities centers in supporting the genre, from creation to maintenance and preservation?

I first review the literature on collections and digital humanities projects in order develop a set of potential attributes that is as inclusive and exhaustive as possible. From these attributes, I derive a set of categories through which I analyze the collections. The methods for identifying and refining categories, and the resulting analytic protocol, are discussed under "Analytic protocol," below. I then apply this protocol to analyze and contrast the technical designs of two collections: *The Shelley-Godwin Archive* (http://shelleygodwinarchive.org/) and *The Vault at Pfaff's* (https://pfaffs.web.lehigh.edu/).

## BACKGROUND

Palmer (2004) gives the most detailed account of thematic research collections and their roles in research and communications processes. Palmer anticipated that "scholar-created research collections are likely to increase in number as the work of producing them becomes more widely accepted as legitimate scholarship." In the intervening decade or more since Palmer's account, the genre has indeed grown and diversified. There are hundreds or more thematic collections, usually created by scholars in cooperation with digital humanities centers or digital scholarship units within libraries.

Despite widespread acknowledgement of digital collections as a mode of scholarly production (see for example Price, 2009; Flanders, 2014; Thomas, 2015), we do not know enough about the genre – even conclusively whether it is a single, self-contained genre. We have yet to comprehend the various ways in which collections contribute to humanities discourse or how best to integrate collections into systems of peer review, discovery and long-term maintenance.

The evolution of public-facing humanities discourse, long-term access to collections of evidence and the completeness of the scholarly record depend in part on a more systematic understanding of collections as one among emergent genres of digital scholarship.

The study reported in this paper focuses on the technical underpinnings of collections, which determine a collection's uses and functions and which are driven by the intended purposes and contributions of the project. Technical designs determine how the items in a collection hang together, how they are represented to users and what can be done with the collections in the short and long terms.

By "design analysis" I mean an analysis of how a collection has been designed or constructed. The study relies on the concept of data modeling in the humanities. A data model is "a model of some real (or fictional) world segment" that has been devised to "make some aspects of the data computable and to enable consistency constraints" in order to fulfill user requirements (Flanders & Jannidis, 2015). Data models function to enable and constrain uses of data and to describe the entities and relationships in a conceptual space. Viewed through this frame, collections can be seen to integrate layers of data models, including instantiated descriptive schemas, markup standards, interface elements, interlinking between items and so on (Flanders, 2014; Flanders and Muñoz, 2012).

## ANALYTIC PROTOCOL

The first step of this study was to collect a set of different potential attributes or characteristics of digital collections. This is a step toward answering the overarching research question: what are the defining features of the genre? The set aims to represent, as completely as possible, attributes derived from existing studies and literature on collections, publishing in the humanities, and evaluation and best practices for digital humanities projects.

The second step was to derive from those found attributes a set of categories through which we can analyze collections and how they operate in greater depth. This is a variation on the qualitative content analysis method (Zhang and Wildemuth, 2009), which is generally focused on systematic interpretation of texts. I adapt that process to a systematic study of the multiple media, models and tools that constitute collections. Conventional content analysis begins with the construction of a code book: a set of categories, with definitions and examples, which frame the analysis. The code book is iteratively refined as it is applied to the objects of study. The analytic protocol for this study is analogous to a code book.

The analytic protocol derives from a broad review of existing literature, to ensure analysis reflects the broad range of current thought and practice among experts and practitioners in relevant fields: the humanities, digital scholarship and publishing, and library and information sciences. Because the boundaries between collections and other kinds of digital resources and projects in the humanities are often indistinct, and because the genre continues to evolve and experiment at its own edges, I did not limit my sources to those specific to collections. In casting a wide net for sources, and in liberally identifying any potential aspects of collections that they mention, I sought to ensure that the categories used for analysis represent collections as completely as feasible.

| Cluster | Categories of analysis |
|---|---|
| Context | Theme ; Intended contributions ; Multiplicity of purpose ; Impact ; Creators ; Audience ; Documentation ; Data provenance / custodial history; Related collections ; Related projects and publications ; Review ; Funding ; Developmental stage ; Host or imprint ; Rights; Sustainability and preservation plans ; Method |
| Content | Items ; Diversity ; Size ; Narrativity ; Quality ; Language ; Tone or narrative style ; Exhaustiveness, representativeness, completeness of coverage ; Density ; Spatial coverage ; Temporal coverage ; Composition / interrelatedness / interconnectedness |
| Design | Data models ; Navigation ; Infrastructural components ; Interface design ; Interactivity ; Interoperability ; Openness of components ; Identification and citation ; Modes of access and acquisition ; Accessibility ; Flexibility |

***Table 1.*** *Overview of analytic protocol*

The protocol was derived from 27 sources on the following topics: alternative or multimedia digital publishing (e.g., Ball, 2012); conceptual and empirical literature on digital collections (e.g., Palmer, 2004; Flanders, 2014); collection description schema (DC-CAP); and evaluation guidelines and recommended practices for digital humanities projects (e.g., Bates, et al., 2006; DHCommons[1]; IDE, 2014[2]; MLA Guidelines[3]; Rockwell, 2012; etc.). For a complete list of sources, see the full data set at https://github.com/kfenlon/collections.

From these sources, I identified approximately 150 potential aspects of digital collections, including the types and extents of items they gather, how they may be navigated and searched, their functionality and their underlying data models. There was significant conceptual overlap among attributes discovered across the literature, even if they were named or described differently depending on their authorship or the context of the source. Where overlap was discerned, categories were combined.

For example, while one source asks, "Is there a legible intentionality behind the structure of the data?" (NINES/NEH[4]), another asks the closely related questions, "Is there a clear statement of the standards that have been used and an explanation of their benefits and/or limitations? Have the data been well constructed?" (Bates et al., 2006). These questions, and the collection attributes they imply, were combined with several others under the more generous category of "data models," to be discussed below. This example illustrates another way in which aspects of collections gleaned from the literature were refined into analytical categories: by discarding what is prescriptive or normative in their description and drilling down to characteristics at their cores. The aim of this analysis, after all, is not to evaluate the degree to which collections adhere to evaluation standards or best practices, but to make headway on the more fundamental questions of what these things are and how they work.

Finally, the list of approximately 50 categories was organized into three clusters, indicating thematic relationships between groups of categories: context, content and design. These groupings are intentionally loose. There is essential overlap within and between the clusters, and beyond that there are important relationships of other sorts obtaining between categories in different clusters, including dependencies[5]. The clusters are intended to give the set some organization, for approachability, rather than represent any ontological commitments.

Table 1 gives an overview of the analysis protocol[6].

Categories within the context cluster pertain to a collection's motivations, impacts and other context, including where it came from, how it relates to the landscape of extant scholarly projects and the provenance of its items (or data). The content cluster includes categories about the nature and extent of what a collection contains. The design cluster holds categories pertaining to the technical design of collections. The last

[1] http://dhcommons.org/
[2] http://www.i-d-.de/publikationen/weitereschriften/criteria-version-1-1/
[3] 3https://www.mla.org/About-Us/Governance/Committees/Committee-Listings/Professional-Issues/Committee-on-Information-Technology/Guidelines-for-Evaluating-Work-in-Digital-Humanities-and-Digital-Media
[4] http://institutes.nines.org/docs/2011-documents/recommendations-for-chairs/
[5] These relationships may be worthy of exploration in future research.
[6] The full protocol, which gives definitions and examples for each category, in addition to linking each category to its sources in the literature, is available at https://github.com/kfenlon/collections

category is the focus of this paper, and I apply the design categories to an analysis of two collections in the next section.

Together, these categories represent the potential characteristics of digital research collections in the humanities, as suggested by relevant literature. But how do different collections manifest these characteristics, and to what ends?

## DESIGN ANALYSIS OF COLLECTIONS

This paper systematically analyzes and compares the technical designs of two thematic research collections, by applying the analytic categories falling under the heading of "Design" in the protocol given in Table 1. A complete analysis of even one collection, in terms of every category in the protocol, is beyond the scope of this paper. I focus on technical design because it is woven into every other aspect of collections. From basic architectures and data representations, to enabling different kinds of inquiry and interpretation, technical design is significantly determined by and in turn significantly determines other characteristics of collections and their uses. This paper limits the analysis to the five design aspects that are most revelatory of important differences between the collections: data models, navigation, infrastructural components, interface design and interactivity.

After describing the collections to be studied, the following analysis steps through each of the five selected design categories. For each, the category is defined, and I examine how each of the two collections manifests it, using evidence from the collection or supporting documentation.

### *Collection summaries*

Two collections were chosen from among approximately 100 identified and typed in prior work (see Fenlon, 2017). The collections chosen for in-depth analysis here were selected in part for their similarities – both are literary-historical collections of texts – and in part for their significant and illustrative differences. They each exemplify a different "type" of digital thematic research collection, as described in Fenlon (2017).

#### *The Shelley-Godwin Archive*[7]

This collection offers digitized, transcribed manuscripts from the influential Shelley-Godwin family of 18th- and 19th-century writers, including Percy Bysshe Shelley, Mary Wollstonecraft Shelley, William Godwin and Mary Wollstonecraft. A substantial and still growing body of Shelly-Godwin manuscripts – including major works such as *Frankenstein* (M. W. Shelley) and *Prometheus Unbound* (P. B. Shelley) – appear both as digitized page images and as encoded texts. Manuscripts are supplemented with biographical, bibliographical and other secondary sources. The purposes or intended contributions of this collection to scholarship include the following:

provide unified access to related digital manuscripts that are scattered across a few collections;

- provide high-quality diplomatic transcriptions, with encodings that also highlight different authors' hands on the same manuscript;
- provide flexible views and multimodal access to primary sources; and
- facilitate collaboration and curation.

#### *The Vault at Pfaff's*[8]

This collection gathers primary and secondary sources about the historically significant bohemians of antebellum New York, U.S.A., particularly the large group of people "who were connected to the bohemian scene at Pfaff's,"[9] the historical restaurant and saloon that became an epicenter for a literary movement in the United States. The site makes searchable an annotated bibliography of more than 8,000 texts by and about the "Pfaffians," linking to full-text primary sources both internal and external to the site wherever possible. The site also provides secondary sources, including a map, timelines, biographies and historical accounts. These are among its purposes or intended contributions to scholarship:

facilitate unified search across a group of related people and the works variously associated with them, which are scattered across several digital collections;

provide original, digitized page images of several influential periodicals of the era;

identify relationships among historically significant people and groups and draw connections from people and groups to texts.

### *Data models*

This category is concerned with how items are represented and how data models determine those representations. At one level of representation, items may be understood as the "data" of the collection. How they are modeled, or how abstract data models are applied to represent them, has implications for the use of the collection. As discussed above, data models include things like metadata schemas and encoding or markup schemes. While it is often difficult to unravel data models from other technical aspects of collections, such as navigational features, other infrastructural components and interface design, the distinctions may sometimes be revelatory. In particular, I consider how data models are purposively employed to create coherence between how items are represented and the overarching purposes of the collection.

---

[7] http://shelleygodwinarchive.org/
[8] https://pfaffs.web.lehigh.edu/
[9] https://pfaffs.web.lehigh.edu/

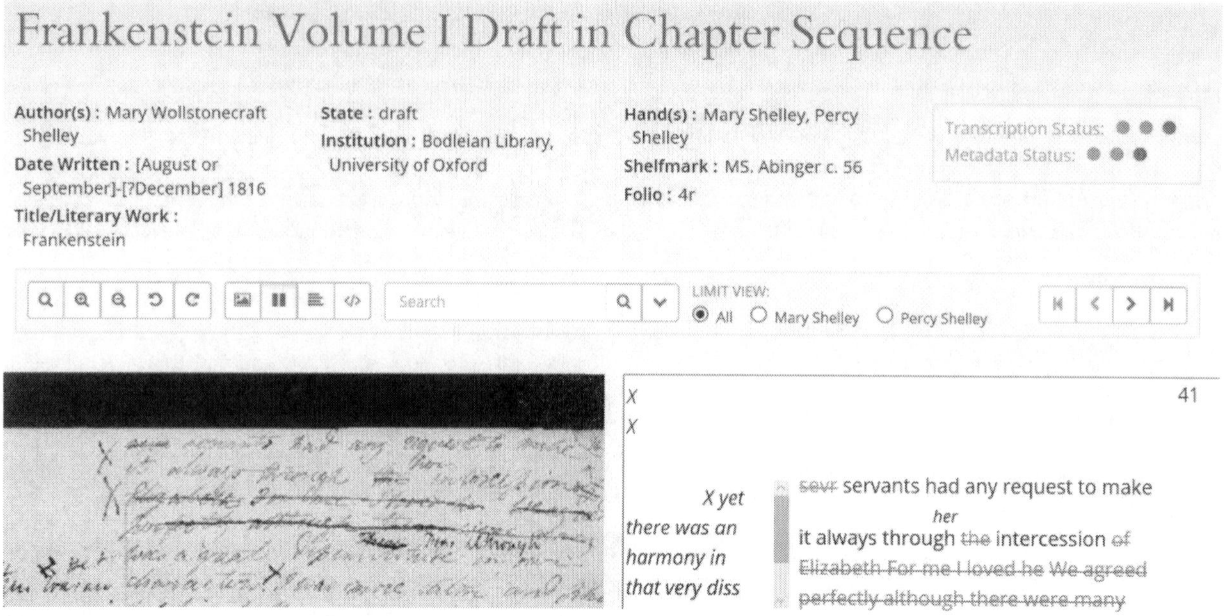

*Figure 5.* Item view in Shelley-Godwin

### Data models: Shelley-Godwin Archive

The Shelley-Godwin Archive (S-GA) primarily relies on two data models to represent manuscripts: the Text Encoding Initiative *Guidelines for Electronic Text Encoding and Interchange* (TEI) and the Shared Canvas data model. TEI is "a markup language for representing the structural, renditional, and conceptual features of texts."[10] Which elements of TEI are employed to encode documents, and how they are applied, are essential representational choices that determine how the documents may be used and interpreted and what functionalities may be built upon them. S-GA employs the TEI "Module for Transcription of Primary Sources,"[11] to represent *diplomatic* transcriptions of manuscript page images. Its encodings are "designed to capture important information about the state of the physical manuscript document,"[12] rather than other elements that could be subject to scholarly interpretation, such as characters, themes, events, etc. Because the manuscript pages retain traces of authors' composition processes, such as strikethroughs and insertions, S-GA encoding captures the visible revision history of the manuscripts. Finally, the encoding aims to capture any variations in the authorship of a text, as distinguishing "interventions by different hands" becomes important "in those manuscripts where Mary and Percy Shelley worked together."[13]

Figure 1 exemplifies a representation of an item (*Frankenstein Volume 1 Draft*) in S-GA. This page gives a comparative view of the digitized manuscript page image (left) with changeable representations of the page's encoding (right). Bibliographic and transcription metadata, which is all embedded in the item's data model (in the TEI header), contextualize the individual pages as part of overarching works or manuscripts. Representation options render visible and invisible different aspects of the TEI encoding, such as "hand" (whether that of Mary or Percy Shelley), and "</>" to show TEI-XML as opposed to presentational format.

S-GA relies on the *page* as the basic unit of representation (as opposed to *work*, for example), because this more granular representation enables one of the collection's important functions: representing primary sources in different orders to reflect different literary-historical views of a text. For example, "The pages of [*Frankenstein* manuscript] c.56 can be accessed in three different sequences: (1) in their current physical sequence below; (2) in their order within a virtually reconstituted Notebook A; and (3) in the linear sequence of the two-volume draft."[14] Figure 2 compares the "Work" landing screen for *Frankenstein*, which gives a hierarchical view of page images by chapter, with that of the Notebook landing screen, showing ordered manuscript page images.

The second data model in play in S-GA is Shared Canvas, which is used to represent pages of texts as abstract "canvases," thereby opening them up according to linked open data principles, making them subject to collaborative annotation, curation and connection to other media and resources[15]. In the next phase of S-GA development, the collection aims to rely on this data model to facilitate more direct interaction,

---

[10] http://www.tei-c.org/Guidelines/
[11] http://www.tei-c.org/release/doc/tei-p5-doc/en/html/PH.html
[12] http://shelleygodwinarchive.org/about/#encodingthesga
[13] http://shelleygodwinarchive.org/about/
[14] http://shelleygodwinarchive.org/contents/ms_abinger_c56
[15] http://shelleygodwinarchive.org/about/#sharedcanvaslinkedopendata

to "enable participatory curation, for engaging scholars, students, and the public."[16]

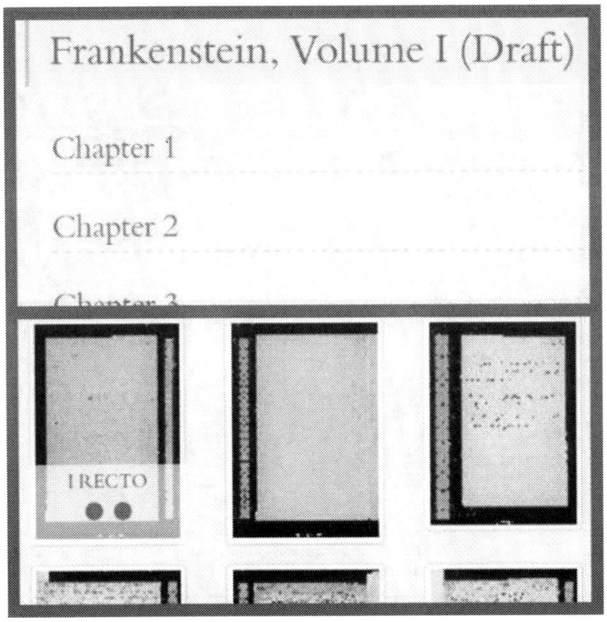


*Figure 2. Work landing page vs Notebook landing page*

### *Data models: Vault at Pfaff's*

While S-GA hosts the items that it gathers, Vault at Pfaff's (VaP) is mostly aggregative: it aggregates metadata about (including links to) many of the items in its collection, which reside in other, external collections, including the Making of America[17], Google Books and certain subscription databases. VaP hosts some of its primary sources in a local instance of CONTENTdm[18], which is a popular content management solution for digital collections. A second fundamental difference is that textual items made available by VaP are not encoded; indeed, they are not transcribed. Of course, linked items in external collections are represented in myriad different ways.

Because of these differences, much of VaP's representation of items relies on bibliographic metadata as a data model. The metadata scheme on which it relies appears to be simple (lacking documentation, I cannot characterize it in full detail). Items are represented using conventional fields including title, creator, publication information, type, genre and abstract. However, VaP surrounds the minimalistic representation of items with heavily hyperlinked contextual information, particularly about people who created or are referenced in the primary source (see Figure 3). The data model underlying these relationships is presumably a database schema, which is not publicly documented. People are represented in much the same way as primary sources in VaP (cf. Figures 3 and 4). In this way, representations of people are given equally high priority as representations of primary sources in VaP's underlying data model and receive more narrative and editorial context.

Figure 3 gives a snippet of a representation of an item in VaP, a newspaper column by Ada Clare[19]. Figure 4 gives a comparative view of Clare's own representation as a person entity in the collection. Note that both representations foreground connections to other entities, including people, relationships and works in the network.

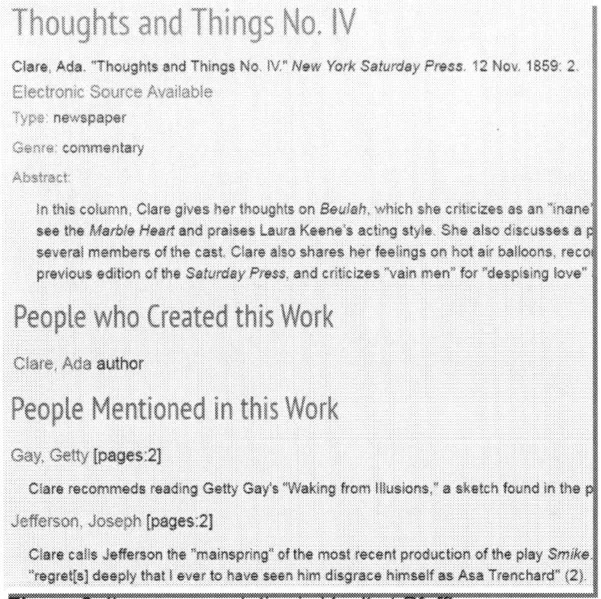


*Figure 3. Item representation in Vault at Pfaff's*

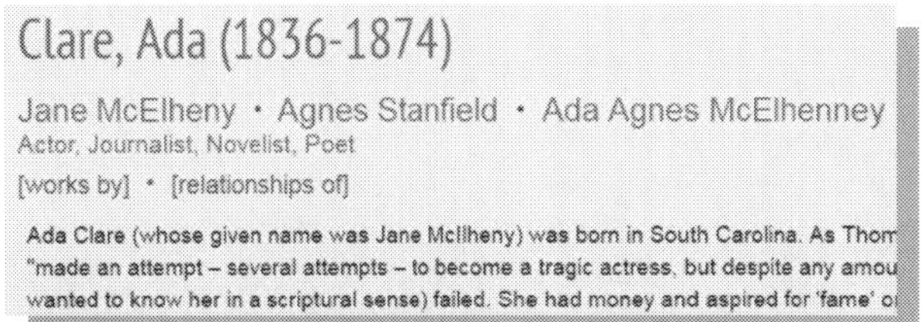


*Figure 4. Person representation in Vault at Pfaff's*

### *Navigation*

This category considers how a collection may be navigated, especially how search and browse are supported and how users may navigate between items and other resources. Included in this category are things like classification or faceting schemes employed to organize search and browse across the collection, what navigational features render visible and most prominent, and how users may move between and among items (and different views and components of items) within the collection.

---

[16] http://shelleygodwinarchive.org/about/
[17] http://quod.lib.umich.edu/m/moagrp/
[18] http://www.oclc.org/en/contentdm.html
[19] http://pfaffs.web.lehigh.edu/node/57815

*Navigation: Shelley-Godwin Archive*
I discussed under "Data models" above that S-GA supports different ways of encountering items by facilitating virtual reordering of texts into works and manuscripts. This is a central feature of S-GA's navigation, and it directly relates to a central purpose of the collection. Encodings support keyword search across the full texts of the collection, including a faceted option to limit results by authorial hand. Faceted search also takes advantage of the Work/Manuscript distinction that is central to the item representations and browse functionality. See Figure 5. In this way, there is a coherence between the major navigational functions of the site and the goals of the collection.

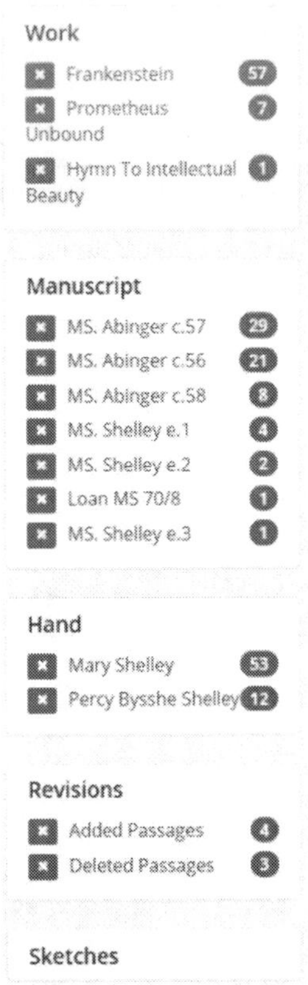


***Figure 5**. Facets in Shelley-Godwin*

*Navigation: Vault at Pfaff's*
Without full texts, VaP's search and browse functions rely bibliographic metadata. Unlike S-GA, and in light of the greater diversity of kinds of primary sources in this more heterogeneous collection, VaP uses controlled vocabularies for types and genres. The most common of the controlled types are foregrounded as browsing options on the homepage, under "Works": Artwork, Books, Periodicals, Theater, and Manuscripts.

In addition, as mentioned under "Data models" above, VaP foregrounds the navigation of different kinds of relationships between various entities, through hyperlinks embedded in item/person descriptions and a dedicated "Relationships" browser. Figure 6 shows how the relationships of Ada Clare are made navigable. Here, too, VaP employs controlled vocabulary for human relationship types, which have been manually asserted by editors of the project. Relationships between people and works are navigable as annotated links on relevant landing screens.

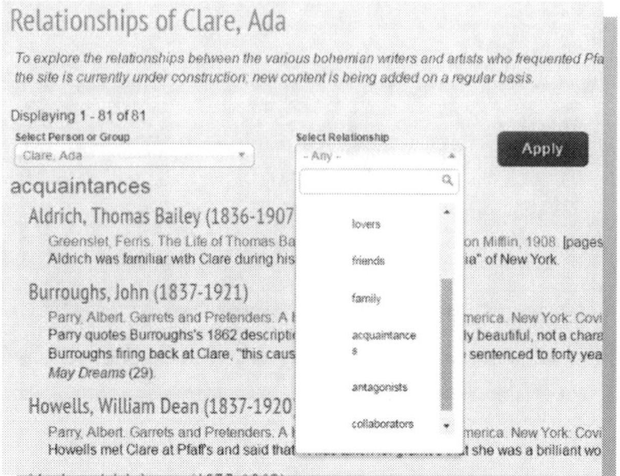


***Figure 6**. Relationship representation in Vault at Pfaff's*

***Infrastructural components***
This category concerns components of the technological infrastructures of collections that (1) are not data models and (2) enable and constrain collections' representations, functions, uses and in short how they are constituted (Flanders, 2014). Though infrastructure may refer to the broader sociotechnical infrastructure upon which projects are built, the category here refers to discrete technological components, ranging from database systems and search algorithms to tools used for data manipulation and to support advanced functionalities. There are different conceivable ways to approach the infrastructure: for example, in terms of the uses it enables or in terms of the assumptions and theories baked into infrastructure. Because infrastructure has implications for understanding the content of a collection and constraining and enabling its use, it may be misleading to fully distinguish infrastructure from content in this analysis, or indeed from any of the other categories.

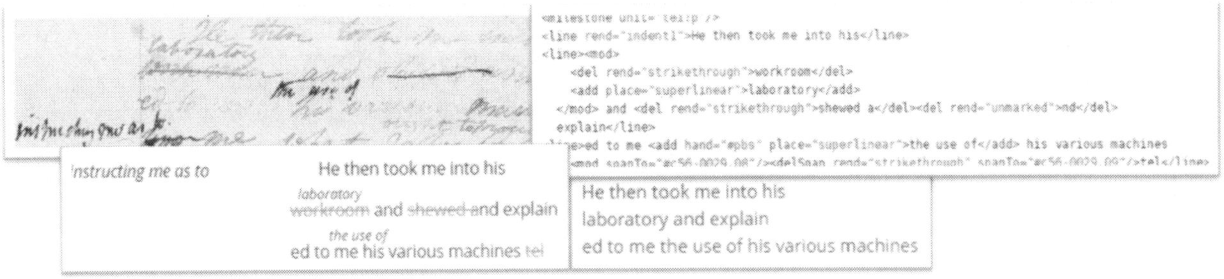


***Figure 7.*** *Comparative views of primary source in Shelley-Godwin*

*Infrastructural components: Shelley-Godwin Archive*

S-GA relies on GitHub as a platform for collaborative development and encoding work, and as a project archive and hub for extensive project and data documentation[20]. Comparative views of different versions of items in the collection, enabled by the encodings, are presented by a homegrown Shared Canvas viewer. Figure 7 shows comparative views of the same snippet of text (clockwise from top left): the page image, the TEI-XML encoding, the fair copy text and the text with markup showing revisions in situ. The collection also relies on a search service that builds in accommodations for aspects of the encodings. And finally, S-GA has employed several processes and one-off scripts for semi-automatic processing of the texts and encodings, all of which bear of the provenance of the underlying data.

*Infrastructural components: Vault at Pfaff's*

Because VaP does not make its technological documentation publicly available, there is less to say about its infrastructure, or how it supports the affordances of the collection. We can presume that VaP relies on an unidentified relational database and an independent, linked CONTENTdm server. Much of the relationship information that constitutes one of the unique contributions of the collection appears to be manually gleaned from reading primary sources and doing editorial and research work, rather than relying on automated manipulations of any sort. It is not clear what tools or processes are applied to the generation and manipulation of metadata.

### *Interface design*

This category covers information about the design of the interface and aesthetic of the site. This study specifically considers two aspects of the interface design of collections: how they organize elements on the screen, and what rhetorical functions the appearance and aesthetic of the collection can be discerned to serve. Because interface design is often the least-documented aspect of the technical design of a digital resource, and to avoid reading too much into design choices, this study focuses on what can be empirically determined about a collection's interface, such as what imagery a collection foregrounds, what elements it makes most and least visible, and how it interrelates elements on the screen.

*Interface: Shelley-Godwin Archive*

Throughout this analysis of S-GA, it has become clear that the collection facilitates multiple modes of reading and encountering works, ranging from heavily mediated by editorial and scholarly effort (e.g., visible TEI encodings or reconstituted virtual orderings of page images) to not (e.g., digitized page images in manuscript order). In this and every aspect of design so far explored, the S-GA has prioritized two things: transparency and multiple ways of encountering and exploring content. This emphasis on transparency and multiple points of access is reiterated by the design of the collection homepage, which places extraordinary emphasis on offering the user multiple forms of guidance and entrance to the collection, in the form of several prominent links and informational elements: "About the archive," "Not sure where to start?," rotating imagery along with "Featured works" to give the user some orientation and easy entrée into the collection, and browsing tabs for "About," "Explore…" and "Using the Archive." This is clearly a user-oriented collection. This aspect homepage design also suggests, however, that the intended use of the collection is highly *facilitated* at present and focused on reading as the primary function of the site. One of the future aspirations of the collection is to support more user-led interaction, curation and annotation. It will be interesting to see whether that phase of development alters S-GA's interface design.

*Interface: Vault at Pfaff's*

Meiman (2015) gives a persuasive account of the rhetorical functions of VaP's interface design. In particular, Meiman argues that the organization of multiple points of access on the collection's homepage serves to foreground its goal of situating people, groups and primary sources in relation to one another: "the new design brings these multiple points of access to the top page, emphasizing the group and its geographic place, as well as promoting other access points to the collection...Similarly, the illustration [on the homepage] reflects the collection's emphasis on the group...visually underscoring the importance of the literary community" (Meiman, 2015, p. 186-187). This, along with the representational and functional choices discussed under "Data models" and "Navigation" above, reaffirm what Meiman terms the collection's "networked approach to literary history."

---

[20] https://github.com/umd-mith/sga/

### *Interactivity*

While every web-based collection can be considered interactive to some degree, this category is particularly concerned with interactions that the collection facilitates or enables between user and collection, beyond searching, browsing and reading/viewing. Some collections create interactivity through built features, which allow different kinds of use of items. Some facilitate interactivity not only with the collection itself, but with other users of the collection, turning the collection into a potential hub for collaboration or discourse, for example by adding links to social media or forums, or adding annotation, commenting or feedback mechanisms. Other collections enable interactivity not by building additional uses or functions into the site, but by removing barriers to unanticipated use of collection contents and code, e.g., by opening their underlying data to use. This is the distinction between facilitated interactivity and enabling potential. Another term used to describe this notion is "extensibility": an extensible collection is amenable to unanticipated uses. This category corresponds closely to the categories of "openness" (discussed below) and "flexibility."

#### *Interactivity: Shelley-Godwin Archive*

Beyond the multiple modes of facilitated interaction with the collection and its items, described in detail above, the S-GA strongly emphasizes the extensibility of the data and code underlying the collection, and in this way the collection encourages users to interact deeply, and in potentially unanticipated ways, with its offerings. S-GA's encodings – the data files that underpin the collection contents – are readily accessible under a CC0 license (which dedicates them to the public domain). Indeed, the reliance on principles and data models of linked open data (discussed under "Data models," above) in the construction of the collection is one way it affords interactivity by design: "By allowing visitors to create connections to secondary scholarship, social media, or even scenes in movies, projects built on Shared Canvas attempt to break down the walls that have traditionally enclosed digital archives and editions.[21]" Data and collection architecture are transparently documented in the collection's GitHub archive, which has been used already to facilitate distributed, collaborative transcription/encoding work. S-GA indicates that this experiment in collaborative encoding will be scaled up in its next phase of the project's development, helping to "move humanities research into the classroom and out to the public." By inviting and facilitating collaboration for the development of the collection, S-GA has fostered meta-level interactivity with the collection as a whole, in addition to interactivity with individual items.

#### *Interactivity: Vault at Pfaff's*

VaP broaches interactivity from a different angle: by building relationships between people and texts both internal and external to the collection. Through hyperlinks and federated search, the collection interacts directly with other collections; and users are encouraged to navigate among them. This is particularly visible in VaP's use of the NINES search box, as Meiman (2015) notes. NINES is a scholarly collective that aggregates primary sources from peer-reviewed research collections pertaining to 19th-century literature and history. Through its participation in NINES, and by featuring the NINES search box prominently on its site (see Figure 8), VaP effectively creates a door between these two collections, which offer different and rich contexts for items.

***Figure 8**. Vault at Pfaff's integrated NINES search box*

## DISCUSSION AND FUTURE WORK

Collections are a familiar construction in library and information sciences; the field has long been concerned with how best to develop, organize, model, present and preserve digital collections of different kinds, ranging from massive digital libraries and cultural heritage aggregations to highly specialized sets of resources designed for intensive study. Though the genre has largely grown up within the humanities, libraries have long played foundational roles in the conception and development of these collections. Beyond this, thematic research collections bear significant implications for librarians, information scientists and technologists.

*First*, any effort toward the collection or aggregation of thematically related content – whether by manual or computational assessments of relevance and relatedness – may learn from how scholars gather and organize resources for their own use, balancing coherence with diversity, and quality content with curated context (Palmer, 2004). This study on thematic collections is related to prior and ongoing work on the creation of *worksets* in computational environments (Fenlon, et al., 2014), and the analysis and identification of topical pools within massive aggregations (Palmer, Zavalina, and Fenlon, 2010). Future work will explore and expand upon these connections.

*Second*, collections have implications for open-access and alternative scholarly communication and publishing. They teach us about the various ways in which purpose may be embodied in design. They confirm the continued tension between, on the one hand, the drive to create innovative expressions of research that are truly and dynamically fit to their purposes and, on the other hand, the complexity of maintaining unique and performative digital works over time. Comparing the technical underpinnings and design aspects of two

[21] http://shelleygodwinarchive.org/about/

thematic research collections has revealed significant differences in what collections aim to do and how collections enact these purposes. The analysis of S-GA reveals how the collection's architecture and design reflect its ambitious goals of providing multimodal access to sources and facilitating collaborative curation. At the heart of VaP's purpose, in contrast, is the notion of connection: VaP exists to forge and document connections among sources, people and groups. By studying how purpose is embodied in technical choices, cast into data models and their implementation, we can apply these models more effectively to the next generation of experimental publication. In addition, the analysis of collections may help us understand how conventions of peer review and evaluation may be most effectively adapted to new digital scholarship. The analytic protocol employed in this study represents one preliminary outcome. By synthesizing relevant literature on digital humanities evaluation, it may represent a step toward more systematic description and understanding of digital humanities projects, generally.

*Third*, thematic research collections constitute an important case study for digital preservation. The heterogeneity we witness in the technical design of collections is partly to blame for the difficulty of systematizing library treatment of this and other genres of open-access digital scholarship. How are libraries to systematically "collect," describe, represent, sustain or preserve digital resources that are by nature experimental, dynamic, flexible and performative? Other factors are social: when should a library assume responsibility for a scholarly work that continues to grow in phases over the course of years, and which may never really be done? If collections have documented their intended purposes and contributions, those may serve as a guide to the curation and preservation processes that will best serve future users of the collections and their items. This is especially true if those purposes correspond to concrete, explicit aspects of the underlying data and infrastructures. I am not sure we have the language for expressing these purposes or how they may be located in collections' architectures; this study aims to contribute toward that end.

*Fourth*, study of these collections suggests new directions toward exploiting the untapped richness of humanities evidence across the web. How do we leverage existing cultural heritage and literary resources, scattered throughout libraries and lingering deep within massive aggregations, into new thematic platforms for research? Indeed, many thematic research collections are oriented toward providing public access to humanities sources, serving to broaden the international impact of humanities research. At some point, widely used collections may be understood to enter the public trust, representing significant pieces of cultural heritage. As the S-GA project documentation notes, one of its development goals is to extend its reach into the classroom and public sphere, "to make students and 'citizen humanists' active, knowledgeable, and critical participants in the great cultural migration now underway of our literary inheritance into digital form."22

Future work aims to extend this analysis in several directions. The full analytic protocol, not just the limited subset applied here, will be brought to bear on these and other collections to yield a richer depiction of how collections are constituted, and to what ends. This empirical study of collections will be augmented with interviews of collection creators to understand more holistically how these resources work and their implications for the evolution of digital scholarship, and the concomitant demands on evolving library practice.

Ongoing study of these collections aims to yield insights about the challenges and opportunities confronting digital scholarship and publication in other disciplines, including the sciences and social sciences. Researchers across disciplines increasingly seek to collect and share evidence in ways that meaningfully and reliably connect data to essential context and interpretation, e.g., through hybrid publications, linked data and complex research objects. This study hopes to lay a foundation for understanding collections as a significant, vibrant, dynamic exemplar of how digital scholarship continues to evolve, with implications for research and communication across disciplines.

## REFERENCES

Ball, C. (2012). Assessing scholarly multimedia: A rhetorical genre studies approach. *Technical Communication Quarterly, 21*(1), 61-77. Retrieved from http://ceball.com/wp-content/uploads/2012/01/TCQ-Ball-publishedversion.pdf

Bates, D., Nelson, J., Roueché, C., Winters, J. & Wright, C. (2006). *Peer review and evaluation of digital resources for the arts and humanities: Final report and recommendations*. University of London: Institute of Historical Research. Retrieved from http://www.history.ac.uk/projects/digital/peer-review

Fenlon, K. (2017). Toward a typology of digital thematic research collections. Presented at the Digital Humanities (DH2017), Montréal, Canada.

Fenlon, K., Senseney, M., Green, H., Bhattacharyya, S., Willis, C. & Downie, J. S. (2014). Scholar-built collections: A study of user requirements for research in large-scale digital libraries. *Proceedings of the American Society for Information Science and Technology, 51*(1), 1–10. https://doi.org/10.1002/meet.2014.14505101047

Flanders, J. (2014). Rethinking collections. In P. L. Arthur & K. Bode (Eds.), *Advancing digital humanities* (pp. 163-174). Palgrave Macmillan UK. Retrieved from http://link.springer.com/chapter/10.1057/9781137337016_11

landers, J., & Jannidis, F. (2015). *Knowledge organization and data modeling in the humanities*. Providence, R. I.: Workshop on Knowledge organization and data modeling in the humanities, Brown University. Retrieved from http://www.wwp.north-

[22] http://mith.umd.edu/shelley-godwin-archive-textual-digital-condition/

eastern.edu/outreach/conference/kodm2012/flanders_jannidis_datamodeling.pdf

Flanders, J., & Muñoz, T. (2012). An introduction to humanities data curation. In *DH Curation: A community resource guide to data curation for the digital humanities*. Champaign, IL. Retrieved from http://guide.dhcuration.org/intro/

Meiman, M. (2015). *Digitizing the nineteenth century: Scholarly editing, interface design, and affordances for public engagement*. University of Delaware. Retrieved from http://udspace.udel.edu/handle/19716/17209

Palmer, C. (2004). Thematic research collections. In *A companion to digital humanities*. Blackwell Publishing.

Palmer, C. L., Zavalina, O. L. & Fenlon, K. (2010). Beyond size and search: Building contextual mass in digital aggregations for scholarly use. *Proceedings of the American Society for Information Science and Technology*, *47*(1), 1-10. https://doi.org/10.1002/meet.14504701213

Price, K. M. (2009). Edition, project, database, archive, thematic research collection: What's in a name? *Digital Humanities Quarterly*, *3*(3). Retrieved from http://www.digitalhumanities.org/dhq/vol/3/3/000053/000053.html

Rockwell, G. (2012, December 19). Short guide to evaluation of digital work. Retrieved April 6, 2016, from http://journalofdigitalhumanities.org/1-4/short-guide-to-evaluation-of-digital-work-by-geoffrey-rockwell/

Thomas, W. G. (2015). The promise of the digital humanities and the contested nature of digital scholarship. In S. Schreibman, R. Siemens, & J. Unsworth (Eds.), *A new companion to digital humanities* (pp. 524-537). John Wiley & Sons, Ltd. Retrieved from http://onlinelibrary.wiley.com/doi/10.1002/9781118680605.ch36/summary

Zhang, Y., & Wildemuth, B. M. (2009). Qualitative analysis of content. In *Applications of social research methods to questions in information and library science* (pp. 308-319). Retrieved from https://www.ischool.utexas.edu/~yanz/Content_analysis.pdf

# Re(a)d Wedding: A Case Study Exploring Everyday Information Behaviors of the Transmedia Fan

**Eric Forcier**
*Faculty of Health, Arts and Design, Swinburne University of Technology, Australia. eforcier@swin.edu.au*

## ABSTRACT

**As practitioners of new forms of consumption and production, fans represent an important area for research. Specifically, fans of "transmedia systems" – media-hopping networks of intertextualities that extend the narrative world of an original production – employ unique tactics for negotiating a complex information space. The study of such tactics provides valuable insights on the everyday information behaviors of modern post-digital readers and media consumers that could benefit literacy and community engagement. Despite this, fans have received little attention in the information behavior literature. Therefore, this paper seeks to contribute new empirical understandings of the transmedia fan to the information behavior domain. The author undertook a pilot case study of the *Game of Thrones* transmedia fandom. Using a grounded theory approach, the qualitative coding of 400 online user comments revealed four types of tactics employed by fans to negotiate the transmedia system: sentimental, reasoned, relational and comic. A discussion of these tactics and the ways in which fans use them results in a preliminary definition and information behavior cycle model for the *transmedia fan*. The study's findings offer key observations about the everyday information behavior of fans and about reading and media consumption practices in general.**

## KEYWORDS

information behavior, transmedia, game of thrones, fans, everyday life

## INTRODUCTION

The study of fans is a field that increasingly influences the everyday information behaviors of contemporary post-digital society. As Price & Robinson (2016) have noted, fans are practitioners of new forms of consumption and production arising from internet technologies and, in particular, social media. Moreover, as fandom – "regular, emotionally involved consumption of a given popular narrative or text" (Sandvoss, 2007, p. 22) – moves away from the subcultural fringes and is observed in the everyday practices of mainstream culture (Booth, 2015), the unique behaviors it represents are normalized. As such, contemporary fans represent an emergent model for the consumer as someone that unselfconsciously moves information among hypermediated, mediated and unmediated modes of experience through their emotional narrative engagement. Understanding the ways in which this activity takes place is of utmost importance to LIS scholars, educators and practitioners; not only does the study of fans reveal trends in cultural consumption relevant to fostering literacy and engagement in communities, but it demonstrates new strategies for negotiating ever-expanding networks of information across the physical and digital realms.

HBO's *Game of Thrones* is a fantasy television series currently spanning six seasons and 60 episodes, with an average global viewership (from its most recent season) of 25.1 million viewers per episode (Shepherd, 2016). It has prompted the production of five video games, a graphic novel adaptation, several companion books, two rap albums, a 28-city orchestral tour, a wide variety of tabletop games, toys, merchandise, musical tributes and mobile apps, and countless podcasts, fanfics and other fan-based creations. The series itself is an adaptation of a book series with a pre-existing fandom (Martin, 1996). The series, the novels it adapts and the variety of productions it has generated are all part of the same *storyworld*: a transmedia system that contains a complex network of texts, paratexts and intertexts that fans enthusiastically negotiate through their engagement.

The purpose of the current pilot case study is to examine the information behavior of *Game of Thrones* fans through the lens of everyday practice, as defined by Michel de Certeau (1984) and elaborated by Paulette Rothbauer (2004; 2010). Through the application of constructivist grounded theory (i.e., Charmaz, 2006), a qualitative coding of online user comments identifies specific behaviors and discursive tactics of fans. A discussion of results explores the role of information and digital technology in media fandom and proposes a preliminary definition and model for the *transmedia fan*.

## LITERATURE REVIEW

### *The Study of Fans in LIS*

In their survey of scholarship on the information behavior of fans, Robinson & Price (2016) observe that there currently exists little interaction between library and information studies (LIS) and fan studies as distinct fields of research. They note that most scholarship emerging from LIS ignores the unique social context of fans, while fan studies (generally considered a sub-domain of cultural studies) rarely and inadequately address information issues. As such, Robinson &

80th Annual Meeting of the Association for Information Science & Technology, Washington, DC | Oct. 27-Nov. 1, 2017

Price's study stands out in its approach to integrating the literatures of these two disparate fields.

When compared to different, broader and nonetheless related categories of information user, such as amateurs, readers and everyday consumers, fans have been largely overlooked in LIS. Hart et al. (1999) suggest the reason for this historical gap in LIS literature is that fans are dismissed as "at best deviant or at worst dangerous" (p. 82). This position reflects popular negative characterizations of "fannish" behavior as obsessive and/or hysterical, deviant and even pathological (Jenson, 1992). Early fan studies scholars refuted these stereotypes by providing evidence of fan communities that developed unique practices as a means of resisting the impositions of dominant social structures (Abercrombie & Longhurst, 1998; Gray, et al., 2007). Despite almost 30 years of fan studies research and a massive shift in the technological landscape that has pushed fandom into a mainstream position, negative stereotypes of the "hyperfan" persist (Booth, 2017). For this reason, perhaps, fans have only been studied in limited and indirect ways in LIS literature.

Indeed, fans under the guise of amateur producers, or "produsers" (Price & Robinson, 2016), have been more frequently covered in the LIS literature. The creation of fanfiction, unauthorized texts that expand upon an existing authorized narrative, have earned the most attention in this regard (e.g., Gursoy, 2015; Peckosie & Hill, 2015). Other forms of fan production have also been explored in recent studies; for example, Rasmussen-Pennington (2016) examines the information behavior and production practices of music fans, while Nyman (2010) studies practices emerging from the role-playing game (RPG) community.

Fans have also been studied in their context as readers. Kofinel (1997) and Serantes (2014) examine the diverse reading experiences of science fiction and comics readers, while Rothbauer explores reading as everyday life practice in the context of lesbian, bisexual and queer and rural youth (e.g., 2004; 2011). All three address readers in their role as "fans" through their emotional narrative engagement. The act of *reading* – broadly defined by Dresang & Koh (2009) to include practices surrounding digital and mobile media – is particularly relevant to the documentation of "invisible" literacies resulting from the "undeniably media-rich and technologically mediated lives" of individuals (Rothbauer, 2011). The affective and interpersonal negotiations inherent in reading are representative of de Certeau's (1984) concept of everyday production ("making do"), while remaining far less visible than the amateur fan productions more commonly studied in fan studies under various terms (e.g., "participatory culture," "produsers" etc.). Rothbauer highlights the need for research to critically examine the appeal of a diverse range of "mass media texts" (2004, p. 128), including digital and internet-based texts (e.g., e-zines, web comics, message boards and social media). More recently, Rothbauer has framed reading as a social practice that is situated: "reading must be thought of partly as realizing an intention, partly as an answer to a text read in context." (2016, p. 4)

### Information Behavior in Fan Studies

While the models and theories established in LIS are rarely – if ever – invoked by fan studies scholars, concepts representing information behavior are consistently referenced using context-specific terminology. For example, Aardse (2014) examines how fans and players of *The Lost Experience* ARG were encouraged to "seek out information, solve complicated covert riddles and clues, and create a semblance of story through their own media sifting and rearranging" (p. 116). Soto (2015) and Henderson (2015) contribute insights into the role fanfiction plays in the development of traditional and digital literacy among young people. Pugh (2005) reveals various active reading and production practices surrounding fanfiction that are recognizably information behaviors (e.g., beta-reading, resource guide writing and Livejournal rec listing). Van Steenhuyse (2013) expands Pugh's conclusions, noting how Jane Austen fans read stories across media and negotiate – internally and with others – a contextual frame (i.e., their own personal understanding of the storyworld). Ganzon (2013) describes how video game fans used digital tools such as YouTube, DeviantArt, Wikipedia, Facebook, Twitter, Tumblr, Fanfiction.net and BSN (BioWare's Social Network) to "compile information, compare readings, make suggestions and voice criticism" (pp. 134-135). These examples provide evidence of many information behaviors specific to fans.

### What is Post-digital?

Cramer (2015) defines *post-digital* as the "state in which the disruption brought upon by digital information technology has already occurred" (p. 20). Floridi (2015) states that, for many people today, it is "no longer sensible" to distinguish between being online or offline (p. 1). The concepts of "onlife" (as opposed to online) and "infosphere" emerge from this observation, referring to the modern-day pervasiveness and inescapability of information and communication technologies (ICTs) and their potentially radical effects on the human condition (Floridi, 2014). Similarly, Jenkins, Ford & Green (2013) describe a "networked culture" in which the same information sharing activities that took place in a "predigital world" now take place at an exponentially greater speed and scope. The concept of "media convergence" (Jenkins, 2006) is likewise associated with the new post-digital paradigm.

The use of the word *post-digital* in the current paper is intended to emphasize a shift in the perception and use of digital media from exclusive to commonplace. Contemporary post-digital society is thus defined as a culture in which digital media have become integral to the practice of everyday life, and yet so commonplace as to be invisible and indistinguishable from non-digital practices.

### Transmedia Systems and Fans

The definition of *transmedia* is the source of some debate among researchers (e.g., Stein & Busse, 2012; Harvey, 2015; Kurtz & Bourdaa, 2016). The current study adopts a broad definition of *transmedia storytelling* as a process whereby elements of a narrative world (i.e., "transtexts") are dispersed across multiple media channels and result in an immersive and unified entertainment experience (Jenkins, 2006; Stein & Busse, 2012; Kurtz & Bourdaa, 2016). This definition includes official narrative articulations (e.g., core and canonical texts, including adaptations), unofficial narrative articulations (e.g., tie-ins), fan productions and paratextual content (e.g., fanfiction, fan films, reviews, blogs, memes, etc.). Therefore, a transmedia system, or *storyworld*, is co-constructed between industry producers, authors and fans.

### *Post-digital Everyday Life Practice*

Rothbauer (2004) defines everyday life practice as the "informal, routine, mundane activities of daily life." (p. 14) Tactics are the underlying structures that form these activities; they represent resistances, but they also signify the "hidden production" of users (de Certeau, 1984, xii-xiii; Rothbauer, 2004). According to de Certeau, "tactics" function in counterbalance to "strategies," which are imposed by institutions and define the boundaries of the system, as a way of "escaping without leaving" and "making do" (Ibid.; Rothbauer, 2010).

In contemporary post-digital society – and particularly within transmedia fandoms – the spaces between "comfortable binaries" (e.g., production/consumption, reading/writing, online/offline) are constantly and often invisibly negotiated (Rothbauer, 2010). These negotiations occur every day: compulsively checking one's Twitter or Facebook feed, tuning in to a favorite podcast, binging on Netflix, searching a wiki or posting in an online forum. Moreover, these negotiations represent tactics for accessing and managing information within a system imposed by the technologies consumers use and, in the case of media fans, the conventions established by the media industry.

## RESEARCH DESIGN

### *Spoiler Alert: Red Wedding in Context*

*Game of Thrones* has been selected for study due its definition as a transmedia blockbuster (Bourdaa, 2014). The world of HBO's *Game of Thrones* is set in the epic fantasy genre. The premise is deceptively simple: Seven kingdoms struggle for control over the Iron Throne. The show aspires to a gritty realism and is intensely violent and sexually graphic. It is adapted from the ongoing book series written by George R.R. Martin, entitled *A Song of Ice and Fire*.

One of the most dramatic and controversial moments in the source material (Martin, 2000; Strang, 2013) was adapted to the screen in the ninth episode of the third season, "The Rains of Castamere" (Benioff & Weiss, 2013). In this episode, Robb Stark, his pregnant wife, Talisa, his mother, Catelyn, and most of his family, retainers and soldiers are murdered in cold blood at the hands of their supposed allies, the Freys and the Boltons. While readers familiar with the novels had long anticipated (and dreaded) the events of the so-called "Red Wedding," fans who had not read the books were presumably unprepared for the ultra-violent outcome of that pivotal episode.

### *Design and Methods*

As a pilot study aimed at defining the *transmedia fan* based on observed everyday information behaviors, the current research undertakes a comparative analysis of publicly posted conversations of *Game of Thrones* fans on the review website *The AV Club*. For the first four seasons of the series, staff writers at *The AV Club* (www.avclub.com) published two reviews for each episode: one for viewers familiar with the books (i.e., "experts", http://www. avclub.com/tvclub/game-of-thrones-experts-the-rains-of-castamere-for-98086) and one for viewers unfamiliar with the books and averse to "spoilers" (i.e., "newbies", http://www.avclub.com/tvclub/game-of-thrones-newbies-the-rains-of-castamere-for-8087). Communities of "expert" and "newbie" fans formed on the website and, once published, each review engendered discussions in which community members enthusiastically participated. The two reviews of "The Rains of Castamere," therefore, document the fans' initial reactions, impressions and interpretations related to the episode: one comment thread where fans/commenters were aware, in general, what the episode had in store and one thread where the fans – if they had successfully avoided spoilers – would have no warning.

The experts thread includes ~2,200 comments while the newbies thread includes ~3,300 comments. In order to reach a saturation of qualitative codes, 200 comments from each thread (i.e., a total of 400 comments) were coded separately for emergent themes. The analysis adopted a constructivist grounded theory approach, as defined by Charmaz (2006), which permits an inductive and recursive development of ideas and theoretical models through the empirical analysis of textual data. A text file of each comments thread was imported into NVivo 11 for analysis. Threads were coded in chronological order. This purposive sampling approach ensured results captured fans' initial reactions and were not weighted toward conversations taking place days or weeks after experiencing the episode. Once complete, the qualitative coding for each comments thread was compared. A set of four overarching forms of negotiation or tactics (Table 1), was compiled specific to the negotiation of a transmedia system (i.e., *Game of Thrones*).

These tactics provide insight into the information behaviors of *Game of Thrones* fans and transmedia fans in general. It is possible that further coding of comments would reveal additional themes; however, this sample was sufficient to capture the initial reactions of "newbies" and "experts." The next section presents results, followed by discussion of findings. In the final section, we propose a preliminary definition and model of the transmedia fan based on findings, as well as address limitations of the study and future research.

## RESULTS

Four forms of negotiation tactics demonstrating how fans made sense of the viewing experience were identified in the

| Tactics | Examples |
|---|---|
| Sentimental negotiation<br>*i.e., sharing feelings* | *(Screams)* – E1<br>*God, it was awful. Maybe the most viscerally awful violence ever on Game of Thrones.* – E35 |
| Reasoned negotiation<br>*i.e., use of logic* | *Guess her character in the books isn't all that important.* – E5 |
| Relational negotiation<br>*i.e., use knowledge of inter/paratextual information* | *Yeah, I actually had to look it up on wiki of fire & ice.* – E51<br>*Just like the gypsy woman said!* – E7 |
| Comic negotiation<br>*i.e., use of humor* | *In this setting, you'd be a fool not to expect something terrible at all the weddings.* – N18 |

***Table 1.*** *Tactics observed in* AV Club *comments from* Game of Thrones *fans*

analysis: sentimental, reasoned, relational and comic (Table 1). In addition, the theme of spoilers emerged as particularly significant in the context of information behavior.

Theoretically, tactics are interpreted as a form of resistance against the media industry, executive producers, writers, the author, the website, etc.; however, the examples studied tended to reflect a process of identity formation rather than resistance. The central question underlying comments is how the commenters identify themselves as a *Game of Thrones* fan—or *if* they (still) identify themselves as such. This process of identification also demonstrates how some commenters perceive themselves in other ways: as newbies or experts, as members of other fandoms, as critics. The episode also forces fans to decide if the violent and unpleasant depictions are justified and to explore how this might impact their continued enjoyment of the storyworld.

As examples are examined in the following sections, a concise definition of each tactic will be provided which conforms to the style set out in de Certeau's (1984) example of *la perruque* ("the wig"): *La perruque* is an everyday practice wherein "the worker's own work is disguised as work for his employer" (pp. 25-26), i.e., using "company time" in the pursuit of personal interests. De Certeau describes this as a minor form of resistance, but it is also the locus for identity formation. Today, fans might snatch a minute or two at work to watch a YouTube video they were told about or check the latest posts on social media. This tactic is a mundane, everyday method of negotiating an information-rich world that incrementally shapes an identity.

Finally, it must be stated that the four tactics are not mutually exclusive. For instance, the example by user E7 in Table 1 may be interpreted as both relational and comic, while user E51's comment may be both relational and reasoned. Since only a sample of comments have been studied, it is possible that other tactics may be identified in future research.

### *Sentimental Negotiation*

Sharing feelings in the form of an outburst of emotion and/or by commiserating with others about their own affective experience is a negotiation tactic that allows fans to deconstruct their own interpretation of the storyworld. This tactic permits the fan to reevaluate the merits of the storyworld and their enjoyment of it.

Fans had strong affective responses to "The Rains of Castamere." Sharing this emotional response may be cathartic or it may be a way for commenters to confirm that they are not alone in feeling the way they do. Regardless, the first posts on both threads were sentimental:

*(Screams)* – E1 (Experts)

> *F**K THIS SHOW! F**K THIS SHOW IN ITS COLD BLACK ABSCESS OF A HEART! At this point, I'm only waiting for our Dragon Overlords to BURN THE ENTIRE F**KING CONTINENT TO THE GROUND!* – N1 (Newbies)

Responses ranged from grief to rage, from awe to confusion. Additionally, there were comments that addressed how the emotional toll of the episode carried on after its conclusion:

> *My wife, who has not read the books looked at me in shocked silence, like she couldn't believe I would read and enjoy something so horrible. So I was like "THAT'S NOT IN THE BOOK, I SWEAR!" and then she started to cry. Thanks a lot HBO. Now I have to deal with a sobbing wife who thinks I'm a monster.* – E22

> *My wife's 9 months pregnant and I was going back and forth whether or not to warn her... no tears for her, but she's a bit shell shocked.* – E53

Despite these accounts, very few fans indicated dissatisfaction or an intent to quit the show. A surprising finding was that the experts demonstrated sentimental negotiation as often as newbies, despite having foreknowledge of the Red Wedding. On the other hand, while the experts thread expressed surprise, disgust and bewilderment regarding the depiction of violence committed against Talisa (different from the character of Robb's bride in the books who avoids a similar fate), the newbies participated in a collective revenge fantasy that visited unprintable tortures on Frey and Bolton, the murderers.

### *Reasoned Negotiation*

Another tactic observed in fans is the logical examination and critique of technical elements in the show and the discussion of potentially significant clues to future events. This tactic fulfills fans' impulse to fill narrative gaps they perceive and to shore up their understanding of the storyworld. It is also closely related to the production practice of fan theories.

Most interestingly, reasoned negotiations were not observed in opposition to emotional responses, but rather as a result of them. For example, the experts' surprise over Talisa's death results in a lengthy exchange comparing the events of the episode to those in the novel; this exchange leads to speculation about what Talisa's death may suggest about Jeyne Westerling – her still-alive novelized analog – in future books. Similarly, shock and disgust at depictions of violence in general in the newbies thread leads to a debate about whether or not it may be "the most violent thing ever shown on television."

### *Relational Negotiation*

In order to make sense of new information, fans will compare it to knowledge they already have that they perceive as related in order to fit it into their contextual frame for the storyworld. This tactic is known as relational negotiation and is observed when fans compare their experience to other similar narrative experiences they have had.

Relational negotiation tended to inform one or more of the other three tactics employed. For instance, fans might compare what they are feeling to a time when they felt the same way:

> *How about Rory dumping Dean for Jess in Gilmore Girls? That's high up there for me.* – N14

Or, it might follow from a reasoned response, as in the newbies' debate mentioned above, where *Spartacus*, *Casino*, *Breaking Bad*, *Twin Peaks* and other media productions were compared for their depictions of violence.

It might also be a reference made for comic effect, as when user E7 writes "Just like the gypsy woman said!" referring to a popular *Archer* meme about doomful prediction (Table 1).

### *Comic Negotiation*

Humor is a powerful tool that is used to diffuse tension, share an opinion, highlight an issue and/or express complex emotions. As a tactic for fans, it is also employed to creatively negotiate meaning through the use of pastiche.

*The AV Club* commenters used humor frequently, even and sometimes especially when discussing controversial themes:

> *Seeing everyone die was harrowing, but her death was particularly gutting.* – E65
>
> *couldn't stomach it, eh?* – S16
>
> *I've had a bellyful of these puns.* – E68

The use of humor was a convention shared in both threads. This takes a variety of forms including sarcasm, puns and pastiche. In some cases, comedy also served as a form of social commentary, or satire, particularly when addressing objectionable depictions in the narrative. Pastiche was used typically in combination with relational negotiation, relying on a reference to another narrative and applied to the current context, which might result in an interesting insight or cognitive dissonance (if *too* incongruous). In one instance, newbie N34 quotes Stephen's (Samuel L. Jackson's) monologue from the film *Django Unchained*, adapted so that the monologue is directed at Walder Frey and updated to reference characters in *Game of Thrones*. The passage is unsettling, particularly as it follows from the collective revenge fantasy that took place in the newbies thread (discussed above).

### *Spoilers: Experts vs. Newbies*

A "spoiler" is when narrative information is shared with a person who intends to fully experience the narrative, and when foreknowledge may negatively impact their experience. While the expert and newbie threads are ostensibly separated to prevent non-reader (i.e., newbie) fans from having their experience spoiled by readers of the source material, there are a significant number of fans that post under both. As such, fans that are particularly opposed to spoilers must remain vigilant, even when participating in the newbies thread. For the most part, the so-called experts that comment in the newbies thread are respectful, and spoilers only tend to slip in by accident or when a non-reader fan has explicitly asked for clarification about character or setting. In a discussion on the thread where non-reader fans share how certain elements of the episode were spoiled for them, one expert implies that readers should not be obligated to spare the feelings of non-readers with spoiler warnings. This fan is roundly criticized for sharing their opinion.

What is it about you ASoIaF fans that makes you think everyone on the planet is obliged to read fantasy novels the moment they come out? – N47

> *[Username]'s attitude is why I wish they'd rename the "experts" thread to something that doesn't have the same gravitas.* – N122

Fewer commenters attempt to defend the fan:

> *I think [username] is talking more about forums OUTSIDE of this one.* – S8

While one commenter debated the issue directly with the fan:

> *Although I disagree, I hear you. The problem is that for the first time in history, all of us--most of the seven billion--have access not only to all the literature man has created ever, but to all the worlds' TV and movies, and so gripes about the entertainment being old enough not to need a spoiler warning are meaningless...* – N46

In these examples, the negotiations of fans play out in the ways they respond to the expert fan's opinion. Is it possible for fans to effectively avoid and/or withhold information that might result in spoilers? This is a question that each fan wrestled with through their engagement with the *Game of Thrones* storyworld.

## DISCUSSION

### *Post-digital Reading*

As everyday practice, the activity investigated in this study falls somewhere between reading (Dresang & Koh, 2009; Rothbauer, 2016) and production (Price & Robinson, 2016;

Jenkins, 2006). Consider the approximate chronology of the experience of the fans in question: they viewed the episode on television or computer screen, in most cases in the Sunday night hour when it first aired. As Van Steenhuyse (2013) has noted, transmedia fans develop their own contextual frame based on their consumption of narrative content. The immersive experience of watching "Rains of Castamere" transformed each fan's contextual frame for the *Game of Thrones* storyworld, providing new information and knowledge that they were required to make sense of. They then visited the *AV Club* website – for many of them, as existing members of the community, this represented part of their regular media fan experience: an everyday practice dictated by habit or impulse or compulsion rather than an articulated information need. Wilson & Walsh's (1996) general model of information behavior accounts for "passive attention" and "passive search" as information-seeking behaviour; Laplante & Downie (2011) provide an example of the application and adaption of this model in their study of music information-seeking in everyday life. The process of seeking paratextual content in the form of a review or of community interaction is similar to the music information-seeking experience, which results in hedonic outcomes (experience of pleasure and engagement). "Hedonic outcomes" are described as a type of information use (Laplante & Downie, 2011). By clicking to one review page or the other, each fan allowed a particular label to be assigned to them, defining them within the fandom as newbie or expert. They may or may not have read the review published by the staff writer, but they certainly scrolled to the bottom of the page, read the comments posted and then added their own. In many cases, posting resulted in exchanges, a dialogue with other fans. This dialogue – the focus of the current project – is but one site where each fan's negotiation of *Game of Thrones* played out. The sensemaking process would have continued for all of them, as they each took something away from their interactions that would shape the storyworld in their own minds. According to Hills (2002), this aspect of negotiating a transmedia system is hyperdiagetic; it is a gap-filling process, where fans are invited to speculate and assign their own affective meanings. This quality may also be applied to post-digital reading practices, as described by Rothbauer (2016): an answer to a text read in context.

### Engagement

The behavior that prompts this study is the fundamentally interactive act of posting (i.e., writing) about *Game of Thrones*. The underlying information behaviors of *Game of Thrones* fans – the characteristic ways in which they post – are what this study ultimately articulates. Besides implications regarding identity formation (discussed below), the four tactics revealed in the analysis are all about *making sense of* new narrative information. Each tactic describes how fans undertake this task, and as such demonstrates information behaviors specific to the negotiation of a transmedia system.

The more slippery – and altogether relevant – question is why they do it. In information behavior (IB) research, practices are often determined based on motivations and needs. Engagement as a theoretical concept has been addressed less commonly in IB studies and usually as a desirable outcome of a user experience. Laplante & Downie (2011) define *engagement* as a quality characterized by challenge, esthetic and sensory appeal, feedback, awareness, motivation, interest, and affect. Engagement is discussed as an *effect* of activity, rather than an *impetus* to act. This may be an aspect of IB that has been previously overlooked, since immersive engagement in the storyworld is what motivates these *Game of Thrones* fans to extend their experience into an interactive forum online. As Rothbauer (2016) notes of reading, this aspect of fan information behavior can be understood as realizing an intention. This finding suggests that further investigation into engagement as a corollary to motivation and information need is required.

By contrast, engagement is a central theme in fan studies literature, and as such its theoretical exploration in that domain represents a valuable resource for IB research. Evans (2016) defines engagement in the context of fans and audiences as a type of behavior. Her analysis finds three main types of engagement discussed by transmedia producers and audiences, which are immersive, interactive and para-active. While all three influence the information behavior of fans, para-active engagement is the most relevant to the current study: it represents the activities that happen *around* the narrative source text. It also represents a form of information seeking, where the fan seeks to fill perceived narrative gaps in the storyworld. Evans includes reading of paratexts, such as wikis and comments threads (i.e., lurking), as a type of para-active engagement. Each of the four tactics explored in the analysis provide evidence of para-active engagement. Other researchers, by comparison, define engagement in terms of production (Stein & Busse, 2012; Jenkins, 2006; Booth, 2015). Citing an influential blog post by a fan, Stein & Busse (2012) and Booth (2015) study fan engagement in terms of affirmational fandom (i.e., sanctioned fan production, e.g., memes, fanfiction, etc. that promotes the authorized source material) and transformational fandom (i.e., non-sanctioned production that seek to fix perceived issues in the source material). Booth (2015) provides a nuanced interpretation that suggests the information behaviors of fans tend to hover somewhere between "affirmational" and "transformational" engagement. The examples discussed in results demonstrate the complex relationship *Game of Thrones* fans have with the show and novels.

The use of digital media to share information and publish fan productions is the most visible outcome of fan engagement (e.g., *SuperWhoLock* Tumblr, as described by Booth, 2015, p. 25). However, a less visible, more mundane form of fan engagement becomes evident in the post-digital reading practices of *Game of Thrones* fans. Finally, Jenkins, through his evolving definition of the concept of participatory culture, has repeatedly addressed the role of digital media in empowering and engaging fans, providing new and improved means of sharing, appropriating, remixing, annotating and archiving texts (Jenkins, 2006; Jenkins, 1992/2013). Arguably, the everyday information behaviors of the fans studied in the current research might be described as participatory culture.

### *Identity Formation*

A key finding that emerges from this study is evidence of how transmedia negotiations shape fan identity. This finding is made clear through an examination of three emergent themes in the analysis of comments: (1) the critical evaluation of graphic depictions, (2) the reaction to and treatment of spoilers, and (3) the use of humor and pastiche.

The show has not been without its share of controversy over its hyperviolent depictions (e.g., Ferreday, 2015; Strang, 2013), and it is likely that fans are aware of these broader cultural debates about the representation of sex and violence in media. Comments are dominated by examples of fans wrestling with the graphic representations in the episode. All four tactics observed contribute to this behavior. As a fictional representation, some fans question if the violence in the episode is justified. Some express their ambivalence by comparing the visual depiction with elements from the novel, while others compare it to violent scenes from other films and television shows. The comments studied demonstrate how each fan's experience of the episode shapes their critical response and continued self-identification as a fan. Once more, this is evidence of the hyperdiagetic nature of transmedia information behavior and post-digital reading (Hills, 2002). But it is also evidence of how everyday life practices contribute to identity formation. Abercrombie and Longhurst (1998) describe a spectacle/performance paradigm (SPP) in which being a member of an audience is closely associated with the construction of the person. Their characterization of SPP is echoed by authors in fan and information studies, such as Floridi (2015), Rothbauer (2004), Gray, et al. (2007) and Booth (2015), observing how people's everyday activities increasingly cast them in the role of audience member; Abercrombie and Longhurst point out that the qualities of being part of an audience, therefore, "leak out" into the wider realms of everyday life. From our present historical position, this effect can be attributed to the increasing pervasiveness of digital technologies.

As Jenkins (2006) has observed, spoilers play an important role in the construction of fandom. In transmedia fan communities, where distributed transtexts and paratexts compete for a fan's attention, spoilers may be even more relevant to community and individual identity formation. The analysis of comments confirms this observation, demonstrating how the treatment of spoilers takes place in a fan community. This observation is consistent with the SPP paradigm (Abercrombie & Longhurst, 1998). Spoilers are representative of information avoidance as opposed to information seeking. Avoiding information in the form of spoilers has been explored in IB literature (e.g., Harviainen and Savolainen, 2014). However, as indicated previously, few IB studies have examined the information behavior of fans specifically. Future research would be needed to more fully explore information avoidance in the context of fans and everyday life practice.

The examples of comic negotiation described above provide evidence of fan pastiche and satirical humor. Fan pastiche is defined as the mimicry or "deliberate imitation of an act or text" (Booth, 2015, p. 2). Booth (2015) characterizes it in opposition to parody, the appropriation and aping of activity with commercial intent. On the surface, then, pastiche represents affirmational fandom. A surprising finding of this study, however, was how fans employed pastiche and the humorous treatment of narrative content in a wide variety of transformative (i.e., critical) and intertextual ways. Just as spoilers influence the formation of communities and individuals, the comedic conventions observed in fan interactions reflect the construction of fan identity.

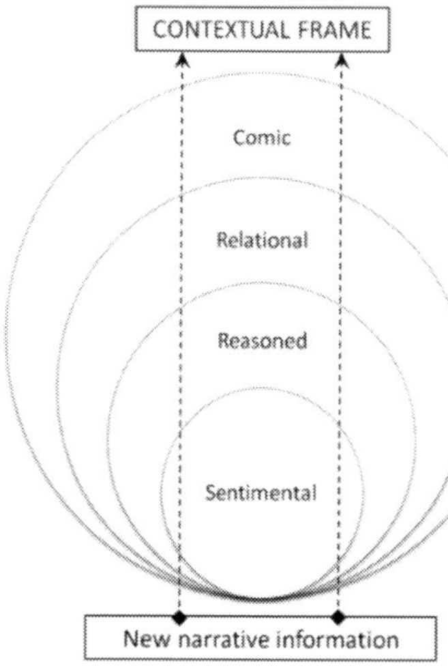


***Figure 1.*** *Everyday Tactics for negotiating narrative information*

## CONCLUSIONS

The above findings support a preliminary definition of the transmedia fan as a post-digital reader that negotiates transmedia systems through sentimental, reasoned, relational and comic tactics. The identity of the transmedia fan is constructed through their everyday negotiation of the transmedia system (i.e., storyworld). A post-digital reader engages with a narrative through a hyperdiagetic sensemaking process. Transmedia fans are further distinguished by para-active engagement in the storyworld, i.e., information-seeking behavior.

Rather than distinct operations, tactics are used in combination. In addition, a causal relationship is observed in the ways tactics are employed. Sentimental negotiation is observed as a fan's initial gut reaction, while reasoned negotiation applies logical evaluation that qualifies and sometimes revises emotionally-driven judgment. Relational and comic tactics for making sense of new narrative information are also employed cumulatively, building upon the fan's ongoing emotional and para-active engagement. This process of negotiation allows for the transmedia fan to fit new narrative information into their contextual frame of the storyworld. Figure 1 provides a visual representation of how tactics occur causally and in combination.

An emergent everyday information behavior cycle model of the transmedia fan demonstrates how tactics are used to negotiate narrative information through para-active engagement, and thus shape the fan's contextual frame of the storyworld (Figure 2). As the transmedia fan is continually exposed to new narrative information, either through active or passive everyday information seeking, this study theorizes that a continual process of negotiation takes place. Future research could determine if this model is is equally applicable in alternative cases of transmedia fandoms, as well as in the broader conception of the post-digital reader and everyday consumer.

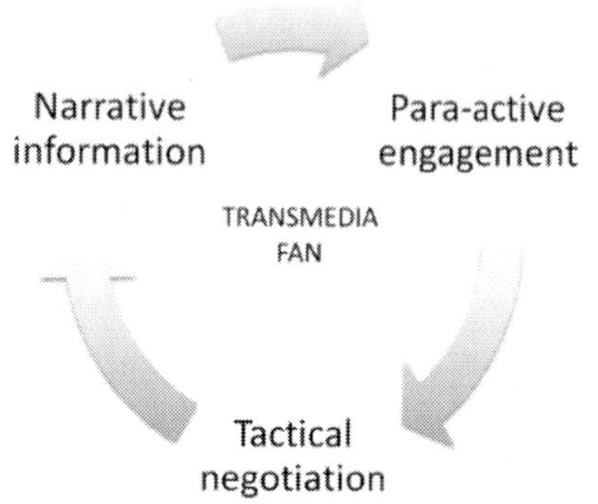


***Figure 2.*** *Everyday information behavior cycle model of the transmedia fan*

As a pilot case study, this research is limited in its scope. Since research is ongoing, findings are considered preliminary. The analysis of a larger sample of comments from the respective datasets may reveal additional themes related to fans' everyday information behavior. Future case studies, as well as qualitative and quantitative research on fan populations, could shed light on the nature of transmedia fandom and the information behavior of transmedia fans. This study has sought to address a gap in LIS research on fans as information users. In doing so, it has also provided a roadmap for bridging everyday information behavior and fan studies scholarship.

Definitions, models and findings on the transmedia fan and on post-digital reading are significant since new understandings of information practices impact library service delivery and literacy in contemporary post-digital society. The everyday tactics observed and theorized in this paper provide valuable insight into how people manage information in a media-rich and technologically-mediated world. What we have characterized as "post-digital" information behavior is increasingly becoming the "new normal," as Floridi (2015) and others have emphasized and must therefore be included in the ongoing study of everyday life.


## ACKNOWLEDGEMENTS

I would like to thank Dr. Lisa Given for her feedback and encouragement in undertaking this project. Institutional support for the study has been provided by Charles Sturt University and Swinburne University of Technology.


## REFERENCES


Aardse, K. (2014). Alternate reality games, narrative disbursement and canon: The lost experience. In K.M. Barton & J. M. Lampley (Eds.), *Fan CULTure: Essays of participatory fandom in the 21st century* (pp. 106-118). Jefferson: McFarland.

Abercrombie, N., & Longhurst, B. (1998). Audiences: A sociological theory of performance and imagination. London: Sage.

Benioff, D. & Weiss, D. B. (Writers), & Nutter, D. (Director). (2013). The Rains of Castamere. In D. Benioff & D. B. Weiss (Producers), *Game of Thrones*. HBO.

Booth, P. (2015). Playing fans: Negotiating fandom and media in the digital age. Iowa City, IA: University of Iowa Press.

Booth, P. (2017). Fandom in the classroom. *Uncanny: A magazine of science fiction and fantasy*. Retrieved April 16, 2017 from http://uncannymagazine.com/article/fandom-in-the-classroom/.

Bourdaa, M. (2014). This is not marketing. This is HBO: Branding HBO with transmedia storytelling. *Networking Knowledge, 7*(1), 18-25. Retrieved April 16, 2017 from http://www.ojs.meccsa.org.uk/index.php/netknow/article/view/328.

de Certeau, M. (1984). *The practice of everyday life*. Trans. Steven Randall. Berkeley: University of California Press.

Charmaz, K. (2006). Constructing grounded theory: A practical guide through qualitative analysis. Thousand Oaks: Sage.

Cramer, F. (2015). What is 'post-digital'? In D. M. Berry & M. Dieter (Eds.), *Postdigital aesthetics: Art, computation and design* (pp. 12-26). London: Palgrave.

Dresang, E.T., & Koh, K. (2009). Radical change theory, Youth information behavior, and school libraries. *Library Trends, 58*(1), 26-50.

Evans, E. (2016). Negotiating "engagement" within transmedia culture. Paper presented at the Summer School in Cultural Studies, University of Jyvaskyla, Finland. Retrieved December 30, 2016 from http://www.academia.edu/26560923/Negotiating_Engagement_within_Transmedia_Culture

Ferreday, D. (2015). Game of Thrones, Rape culture and feminist fandom. *Australian Feminist Studies* 30: 21-36. Retrieved April 16, 2017 from: http://dx.doi.org/10.1080/08164649.2014.998453

Floridi, L. (2014). The fourth revolution: How the infosphere is reshaping human reality. Oxford: Oxford University Press.

Floridi, L. Ed. (2015). The onlife manifesto: Being human in a hyperconnected era. New York: Springer.

Ganzon, S. C. (2014). Control, destroy, merge, refuse, retake: Players, the author function, and the *mass effect* ending controversy. In T. Ravy & E. Forcier (Eds.), *Words, worlds and narratives: Transmedia and immersion* (pp. 126-146). Oxford: Inter-Disciplinary Press.

Gray, J., Sandvoss, C., & Harrington, C. L. (2007). Introduction: Why study fans? In J. Gray, C. Sandvoss, and C. L. Harrington (Eds.), *Fandom: Identities and communities in a mediated world* (pp. 1-16). New York: New York University Press.

Gursoy, A. (2015). Evaluating fan fiction metadata for preservation use. *Proceedings of the 78th ASIS&T Annual Meeting: Information science with impact: Research in and for the community*. St Louis, MO. Retrieved April 16, 2017 from https://www.asist.org/files/meetings/am15/proceedings/submissions/posters/247poster.pdf.

Hart, C., Schoolbred, M., Butcher, D., & Kane, D. (1999). The bibliographic structure of fan information. *Collection Building, 18*(2), 81-89.

Harvey, C. (2015). Fantastic transmedia: Narrative, play and memory across science fiction and fantasy storyworlds. London: Palgrave.

Harviainen, J. T., & Savolainen, R. (2014). Information as capability for action and capital in synthetic worlds. *Proceeds of ISIC: Part 1*. Retrieved April 16, 2017 from http://www.informationr.net/ir/19-4/isic/isic12.html#.WPP8F9IrJaQ.

Henderson, S. (2015). *The Hunger Games fanfiction as a community of practice: forming identities in online communities* (Thesis). University of British Columbia, Canada, 2015. Retrieved April 16, 2017 from https://circle.ubc.ca/handle/2429/54488.

Hills, M. (2002). *Fan cultures*. London: Routledge.

Jenkins, H. (1992/2013). *Textual poachers: Television fans and participatory culture*. Updated Twentieth Anniversary Edition. New York: Routledge.

Jenkins, H. (2006). *Convergence culture: Where old and new media collide*. New York: New York University Press.

Jenkins, H., Ford, S., & Green, J. (2013). *Spreadable media: Creating value and meaning in a networked culture*. New York: New York University Press.

Jenson, J. (1992). Fandom as pathology: The consequences of characterisation. In Lewis, L. (Ed.), *The adoring audience: Fan culture and popular media* (pp. 9-29). London: Routledge.

Kofmel, K. (1997). Solitary act and social interaction: Adults reading science fiction and fantasy. *Canadian Association of Information Studies (CAIS/ACSI)*. Retrieved April 16, 2017 from http://www.cais-acsi.ca/ojs/index.php/cais/article/view/178/353.

Kurtz, B. W. D. L., & Bourdaa, M. (2016). The world is changing… and transtexts are rising. In B. W. D. L. Kurtz & M. Bourdaa (Eds.), *The rise of transtexts: Challenges and opportunities*. New York: Routledge.

Laplante, A., & Downie, J. S. (2011). The utilitarian and hedonic outcomes of music information-seeking in everyday life. *Library & Information Science Research, 33*, 202-210.

Martin, G. R. R. (1996). *A Game of Thrones*. New York: Voyager Books.

Nyman, N. (2010). *Information behaviour in World of Warcraft* (Thesis). Umeå University, Sweden. Retrieved April 16, 2017 from http://umu.diva-portal.org/smash/get/diva2:394752/FULLTEXT01.pdf.

Peckosie J., & Hill H. (2015). Beyond traditional publishing models: An examination of the relationships between authors, readers, and publishers. *Journal of Documentation, 71*(3), pp. 609-626.

Price, L., & Robinson, L. (2016). "Being in a Knowledge Space": Information behaviour of cult media fan communities. *Journal of Information Science*. Retrieved April 16, 2017 from https://doi.org/10.1177/0165551516658821.

Pugh S. (2005). The democratic genre: Fan fiction in a literary context. Bridgend: Seren.

Rasmussen Pennington, D. (2016). "The most passionate cover I've seen": Emotional information in fan-created U2 music videos. *Journal of Documentation, 72*(3), pp. 569-590.

Rothbauer, P. (2004). *Finding and creating possibility: Reading in the lives of lesbian, bisexual and queer young women* (Doc. dissertation). Western University, Canada. Retrieved April 16, 2017 from https://works.bepress.com/paulette_rothbauer/17/.

Rothbauer, P. (2010). Beyond a signpost for resistance: The promise of Michel de Certeau's practices of everyday life for LIS sholarship. In G. J. Leckie, L. M. Given, and J. E. Buschman (Eds.), *Critical theory for library and information science: Exploring the social from across the disciplines* (pp. 53-62). Santa Barbara: ABC-CLIO, LLC.

Rothbauer, P. (2011). Rural teens on the role of reading in their lives. *The Journal of Research on Libraries and Young Adults, 1*(2). Retrieved April 16, 2017 from http://www.yalsa.ala.org/jrlya/2011/02/rural-teens-on-the-role-of-reading-in-their-lives/.

Sandvoss, C. (2007). The death of the reader? Literary theory and the study of texts in popular culture. In J. Gray, C. Sandvoss, and C. L. Harrington (Eds.), *Fandom: Identities and communities in a mediated world* (pp. 19-32). New York: New York University Press.

Serantes, L. C. (2014). Young adults reflect on the experience of reading comics in contemporary society: Overcoming the commonplace and recognizing complexity (Doctoral dissertation). Western University, Canada. Retrieved April 16, 2017 from http://ir.lib.uwo.ca/cgi/viewcontent.cgi?article=3442&context=etd.

Shepherd, J. (2016). Game of Thrones season 6 ratings: Show brought in 25.1 million viewers on average per episode. July 19, 2016. *The Independent*. Retrieved April 16, 2017 from http://www.independent.co.uk/arts-entertainment/tv/news/game-of-thrones-season-6-ratings-show-brought-in-251-million-viewers-on-average-per-episode-a7144261.html.

Rothbauer, P., Skerdingstad, K. I., McKechnie, L. & K. Oterholm, Eds. (2016). *Plotting the reading experience: Theory/practice/politics*. Waterloo: Wilfrid Laurier University Press.

Soto, C. B. (2015). *The role of online reading and writing in the literacy practices of first-year writing students* (Doctoral dissertation). University of Massachusetts-Amherst, USA. Retrieved April 16, 2017 from http://scholarworks.umass.edu/dissertations_2/326/.

Stein, L. E., & Busse, K. (2012). Introduction: The literary, televisual and digital adventures of the beloved detective. In L. E. Stein & K. Busse (Eds.), *Sherlock and transmedia fandom: Essays on the BBC series*. Jefferson: McFarland.

Strang, F. (2013). SPOILER ALERT: Too gory even for Game of Thrones? *Daily Mail Online*. Retrieved April 16, 2017 from http://www.dailymail.co.uk/tvshowbiz/ article-2335087/Game-Thrones-left-fans-left-sickened-bloodshed-touted-gruesome-scenes-TV-history.html.

Van Steenhuyse, V. (2014). Oh, the angst! Emotional immersion in jane austen fan fiction. In T. Ravy & E. Forcier (Eds.), *Words, worlds and narratives: Transmedia and immersion* (pp. 103-125). Oxford: Inter-Disciplinary Press.

Wilson, T. D., & Walsh, C. (1996). Information behaviour: An inter-disciplinary perspective. London: British Library Research & Innovation Centre. Retrieved April 16, 2017 from http://informationr.net/tdw/publ/infbehav/.

# Trust in Qualitative Data Repositories

**Rebecca D. Frank**
*School of Information, University of Michigan, USA.*
*frankrd@umich.edu*

**Kara Suzuka**
*School of Education, University of Michigan, USA.*
*klms@hawaii.edu*

**Zui Chen**
*School of Information, University of Michigan, USA.*
*zuic@umich.edu*

**Elizabeth Yakel**
*University of Michigan School of Information, USA.*
*yakel@umich.edu*

**Erica Crawford**
*School of Education, University of Michigan, USA.*
*zawackie@umich.edu*

## ABSTRACT

**This paper applies Pirson and Malhotra's (2011) framework for organizational trust to data reuse in an educational context. Their framework delineates stakeholders along two axes: depth of the interactions (e.g., shallow or deep) and the locus of the relationship (e.g., internal or external). We analyzed 139 survey responses and 44 in-depth interviews with users of repositories holding video records of practice. We found that factors such as data quality, co-production of data between the repository and data producer, responsiveness of staff, and transparency of curation processes influenced trust, and that responsiveness and transparency were of particular importance for trust development for users with deeper interactions and a more internal loci of relationships to repositories.**

## KEYWORDS

data reuse, digital curation, digital repositories, qualitative data, trust

## INTRODUCTION

Data reuse is a practice that relies on trust among data reusers, data producers, data repositories and the data itself. Trust in this context is a multidimensional concept. Reusers' decisions about data selection and reuse are influenced by the depth of their interactions and positioning of their relationships to the data producer, repository and data (Pirson & Malhotra, 2011). The depth of reuse (extent and intensity) and locus (internal or external) of relationships come into play when considering how trust influences the reuse of video records of practice in education. Video records of practice consist of raw or produced footage of actual teaching and/or learning activities in a classroom. Some document specific events and last a few minutes; others last for hours and document an entire lesson or set of lessons. Video records of practice are a key type of data used in educational research and are also used in pre-service and continuing teacher education (Bass et al., 2002). Because video records of practice are costly, time consuming and can be challenging to produce, researchers and educators increasingly rely on repositories to curate, preserve and provide access to these data. The organizations that provide video records of practice for reuse range from traditional data repositories to diverse education organizations serving the profession, institutions and individuals.

Given the range of organizations involved in curating video records of practice, we were interested in exploring issues of trust in the repositories and the data. Previous studies have focused on more traditional data and repositories and trust (Donaldson & Conway, 2015; Yakel, Faniel, Kriesberg & Yoon, 2013) or research data that is more numerical or textual (Yoon, 2014). In the management information systems literature, trust in institutions is linked to data quality, but this research centers on for-profit organizations (Lee, Strong, Kahn & Wang, 2002).

In this paper, we apply Pirson and Malhotra's (2011) framework for organizational trust to data reuse in an education context. The framework delineates stakeholders along two axes: depth of the interaction with the data and the institution (e.g., shallow or deep) and the locus of the relationship (e.g., internal or external) (2011, p. 1091). In their study, Pirson and Malhotra also identified transparency as a dimension of trust in organizations, in cases where stakeholders have deep, internal relationships to organizations (2011, p. 1097). This framework provides an interesting basis for examining trust in the data reuse process. We defined depth of interaction as the extent or intensity of data reuse and it fell along a continuum from those who engaged in less extensive reuse, such as reusing a single, targeted video to illustrate an approach to teaching fractions, to reusers deeply engaged in highly intense research reuse who utilize multiple videos of particular teachers over time. We analyzed the relationship with the repository dimension along a continuum ranging from reusers who had worked for the repository to those who knew little about the repository and may only have interacted with the website to access digital records of practice.

We extend previous studies by asking whether interactions between data reusers and repository staff influence attitudes about, and trust in, repositories. The notion that repositories can better meet the needs of their users through sustained interactions is consistent with Kelton's argument that "Trust

80th Annual Meeting of the Association for Information Science & Technology, Washington, DC | Oct. 27-Nov. 1, 2017

does not flow from a trustor to a trustee; rather, it emerges from their interaction over time" (Kelton, Fleischmann, & Wallace 2008, p. 364).

Our study is motivated by the following research questions:

- What is the number and range of repositories with which data reusers interact?
- How can we assess the depth of interactions that data reusers have with repositories and repository staff?
- How do data reusers' relationships to repositories along an internal/external continuum influence their behaviors and attitudes toward repositories?
- When and how do depth of interaction and/or relationship with the repository influence data reusers' trust in digital repositories and the data that they provide?

We report on the results of a mixed methods study involving 139 survey responses from users of three repositories and 44 in-depth interviews with reusers of video records of practice. We focused on data reusers' interactions with repository staff, relationships with repositories and how those interactions influenced their attitudes about repositories, including trust in the repository and trust in the data that it curates and makes accessible.

## LITERATURE

### Data Reuse

Researchers engaged in data reuse or secondary use of research data often have different goals than those of the original data producer (Corti, 2000; Karasti & Baker, 2008; Yoon, 2016; Zimmerman, 2008). In the field of education, data reusers have three main goals for their reuse: research, teaching and professional development (e.g., Derry et al., 2010; Gaudin & Chaliès, 2015; Gonzalez, Deal & Skultety, 2016). Therefore, data originally created for research can be used not only to answer different research questions, but also for the entirely different end goal of professional education.

Data reuse depends in part on data sharing, and in order for data to be shareable it must be both searchable and usable (Poole, 2015; Schofield et al., 2009). Data sharing and reuse are challenging even when best practices for data management are followed (Akmon, Zimmerman, Daniels & Hedstrom, 2011; Poole, 2015). Qualitative data in particular presents unique challenges, relating to the need for sufficient contextual information to facilitate the work of data reusers (Corti, 2000; Mauthner & Parry, 2009).

Although many of the unique challenges of providing this contextual information are put upon the data producers, data sharing and reuse are facilitated by the people and technologies that form the data curation infrastructure (e.g., Bishop, 2012; Donnelly & North, 2011; Poole, 2015; Pryor & Donnelly, 2009). Digital repositories, as part of that infrastructure, support data producers and reusers throughout the data lifecycle: from helping data producers develop data management plans at the outset of their research, to supporting data management during a project and encouraging preservation and facilitating data reuse.

### Data Repositories, Data Curation, Repository Staff

In addition to preserving, curating and providing access to data (Corti, 2011; Giarlo, 2013), one of the primary aims of data repositories is "to facilitate communication, collaboration and interactions" among data producers and reusers (Chowdhury, 2010). The responsibility to meet the needs of repository reusers beyond mere access to data (Russell & Day, 2010; Yoon, 2014) may be in conflict with some of the ways that repositories are structured.

For example, Margaryan and Littlejohn (2008) argued that repositories are designed for the capabilities of technology rather than the needs of users. In a study examining the sharing and reuse of digital learning resources, they found that repository managers were focused on long-term preservation and repository-centric data management activities to support those long-term goals, while users focused on short-term outcomes and a wider range of contextual factors to meet their immediate needs. They also found that interoperability issues with repository tools and users' technology was a barrier to repository use (Margaryan & Littlejohn, 2008). Similarly, in a previous study we found that specialized repository tools for working with data were a barrier to reuse of digital records of practice in education (Frank, Suzuka & Yakel, 2016). Russell and Day (2010) have also noted the disconnect between repository goals and user needs. Their findings suggest that increased interaction between repository staff and users can improve user experience and engagement with repositories.

### Trust in Repositories

We use a broad definition of *repository* as "any type of organization that holds documents, including business, institutional, and government archives, manuscript collections, libraries, museums, and historical societies, and in any form, including manuscripts, photographs, moving image and sound materials, and their electronic equivalents . . . where things can be stored and maintained."1 We focus on digital repositories where "contemporary understanding has broadened from an initial focus on software systems to a wider and overall commitment to the stewardship of digital materials; this requires not just software and hardware, but also policies, processes, services, and people, as well as content and metadata."2

We also use the definition of *trust* established by Yoon, "Trust is the data reusers' belief that the data will result in positive outcomes, leading to the reuse of such data in their research. Data reusers' trust judgments can be understood as psychological processes, and whether they accept and use certain data can be seen as an indication of trusting behavior" (2016, p. 2). Researchers can engage in different levels of trust throughout the process of data reuse in response to a va-

[1] http://archivists.org/glossary/terms/r/repository
[2] http://www.dcc.ac.uk/resources/briefing-papers/introduction-curation/digital-repositories

riety of factors, such as data quality, data completeness, curation and data management practices (Yoon, 2016).

The varying nature of the trust relationship has also been explored by Bak (2016), who described trust in the context of digital repositories as both social and contingent, embedded within relationships. This view of trust is pertinent to our study, which examines how interaction with data and the repository staff influences attitudes about, and trust in, digital repositories.

The concept of trustworthiness for digital repositories is based on a perspective that relies on research from both archival science and web credibility (Donaldson & Conway, 2015). Examining trust from these two perspectives provides an understanding from both the perspective of repository staff as well as users. In addition to trust in digital repositories, trust among data producers, repository staff and data reusers is foundational for data sharing and reuse (e.g. Akmon et al., 2011; Faniel & Jacobsen, 2010; Poole, 2015; Yakel et al., 2013). Yakel et al. (2013) found that reuser trust in digital repositories is linked to repository processes. In this paper, we argue that interaction and communication between repository staff and data reusers can help reusers to understand repository processes for curating and managing qualitative data in education.

### *Digital Records of Practice in Education*

Qualitative data in the field of education frequently consists of records of practice. Records of practice are "detailed documentation of teaching and learning" (Bass et al., 2002, p. 79). They generally depict the work of teaching and learning that takes place in a classroom environment and can include video, audio, still images, lesson plans, student work and transcripts. Digital records of practice, such as classroom video, present curation and reuse challenges for repositories as well as data reusers.

We focus here on video records of practice, which have a long history of use in the field of education for research, teaching and professional development (e.g. Burleigh & Peterson, 1967; Shelton, Archambault, Warren, Ahmad & Nevárez, 2016; Stigler, Gallimore & Hiebert, 2000). One important way that video records of practice are used in teacher education and professional development is to help pre-service and in-service teachers develop professional vision and noticing skills (e.g., Penn-Edwards, 2012; Rook & McDonald, 2012; van Es & Sherin, 2002). For research, video records of practice enable multiple researchers to view and re-view classroom events (Hadfield & Haw, 2012).

Despite these benefits and affordances, Pea has argued that "there is a serious and persistent gap between such promise and the usefulness of video records" (Pea, 2006, p. 1325). Some of the issues that persist include problems with capture, storage and sharing of video files (e.g., Zhang, Lundeberg, Koehler, & Eberhardt, 2011).

## RESEARCH METHODS

This paper is part of a larger research project, Qualitative Data Reuse: Records of Practice in Educational Research and Teacher Development (QDR), which examines the reuse of qualitative video data in education through a mixed methods approach utilizing surveys, interviews, web analytics and observations. The results in this paper draw upon the survey and interview results. The Institutional Review Board at the primary author's university reviewed the research design and deemed it exempt.

### *Interviews*

We conducted 44 interviews with educational researchers and both pre-service and in-service teacher educators who reuse digital video. We used a convenience sampling technique to recruit initial interviewees. This included recruiting data reusers who we identified through the research literature, at professional conferences (i.e., those presenting on their work with video records of practice) and by employing a snowball sampling technique that asked interviewees to recommend others. Of the 44 interviewees, 31 identified themselves as university faculty, five as graduate students, two as postdoctoral researchers and six as other types of education professionals.

We focused this analysis on the 21 interviewees who said that they had interacted with repository staff. Of those 21 interviewees, 11 identified as faculty, five as graduate students, one as a postdoctoral researcher and five as other types of education professionals. These interviewees also identified their primary area of data reuse, with 11 reporting their primary reuse for research, eight for pre-service teacher training, one for teacher professional development and one for personal study. Although 17 of the 21 interviewees identified as data producers as well as reusers, only five said that they have deposited their own data in a repository.

We asked the interviewees about their data reuse practices, including questions about interactions with repository staff, issues around trust and attitudes about digital repositories. Each semi-structured interview lasted approximately one hour and was audio-recorded and then transcribed for analysis.

We analyzed the transcripts using NVivo, a qualitative data analysis software. Our code set was based on themes from the literature as well as themes that arose during the coding and analysis (Miles & Huberman, 1994; Saldaña, 2015). After a series of paired coding on the same transcripts, the coders reached a reliability rating of 0.712 (for interviews focused primarily on research) and 0.732 (for those focused on teaching) using Scott's Pi, a statistic that measures inter-rater reliability for coding textual data (Holsti, 1969).

After the first round of coding, we used axial coding to examine the data further, focusing on the following codes: interaction with repository staff, attitudes about repositories and trust in repositories.

### *Survey*

We developed the survey based on preliminary interviews, a review of the literature and cognitive walkthroughs with preliminary versions of the survey itself. The survey is divided into sections focusing on reuse goals (i.e., research, teaching and personal study), as well as questions about general reuse, and participant demographics.

We received 139 responses from the users of three repositories. Our respondents included students, faculty and researchers who reported using digital records of practice for research, teaching and personal study.

We analyzed survey responses using SPSS, a statistical analysis software package. For this article, we focused specifically on questions about interaction with repository staff and participant attitudes about repositories.

## FINDINGS

Our findings are organized into three sections. First, we examine data reuser interaction with repositories, including the types of interaction with repository staff. Second, we discuss data reuser attitudes about repositories. And finally, we explore data reusers' trust in digital repositories.

### *Interaction with Repositories*

Survey respondents were asked to report the repositories they used to find digital records of practice (Table 1). Data reusers were permitted to identify multiple repositories.

| Repository | Type | # of Data Re-users |
|---|---|---|
| Accomplished Teaching, Learning and Schools (ATLAS) | Profes-sional Org. | 27 |
| The Inter-University Consortium for Political and Social Research (ICPSR) | University-based Video Archives | 2 |
| Teaching and Learning Exploratory (TLE) | University-based Video Archives | 33 |
| Teaching Channel | Non-profit Org. | 44 |
| Trends in International Mathematics and Science Study Video (TIMSS) | University-based Video Archives | 22 |
| Virtual Learning Community (VLC) | University-based Video Archive | 20 |
| Not Sure | | 3 |
| Other | | 26 |

*Table 1: Repository usage (n=84)*

Respondents reported interactions with a range of organizations serving as repositories for video records of practice. On average, they used 2.1 repositories. Twenty-two respondents (26.2%) used a single repository, 40 (47.6%) used two repositories, 14 (16.7%) used three repositories and seven (8.3%) used four repositories. One respondent reported using five, the maximum number of repositories named in the survey. Due to the survey design, all respondents to this question reported using at least one repository.

Of the repositories listed in Table 1, one is managed by professional organization, one by a not-for-profit organization, and four are university-based video collections. ATLAS3 is managed by the National Board for Professional Teaching Standards and is meant to illustrate and support the work of board-certified teachers. Teaching Channel4 was established as a grant-funded, non-profit providing an interactive platform where teachers can use video and other records of practice for learning and development. ICPSR5, TLE6, TIMSS7 and VLC8 are all university-based video archives that provide access to videos and other records of practice for research, teaching and professional development.

We found that three respondents were not sure about the source of the videos that they have used, and 26 respondents reported using at least one repository that was not listed in our survey.

We also asked participants how frequently they used digital records of practice. Of the 130 respondents who answered this question, 31 (23.8%) said that they used digital records of practice frequently and that they were a major basis for their research or teaching; 85 respondents (65.4%) used digital records of practice occasionally, for a particular class topic or research purpose; and 14 respondents (10.8%) used digital records of practice rarely.

### *Interaction with Repository Staff*

Findings from both the survey and the interviews indicated that few data reusers interacted with staff from any repository. Those who did interact did so for a variety of reasons, including incidental interaction at professional conferences or workshops, email correspondence requesting help, interaction via colleagues or team members and previous experience working with or for a repository. These types of interactions and relationships with the repository show the range of depth of interaction as well as the closeness of affiliation (internal/external) suggested by Pirson and Malhotra (2011).

We asked our survey respondents if they had interacted with repository staff members when reusing digital records of practice from a repository. Of the 122 respondents who answered this question, a majority (105 respondents, or 86.1%) had not; only 17 respondents (13.9%) reported seeking assistance from repository staff when using digital records of practice. The lack of staff interaction is not surprising. Anecdo-

[3] http://www.nbpts.org/atlas
[4] https://www.teachingchannel.org
[5] https://www.icpsr.umich.edu
[6] https://tle.soe.umich.edu
[7] http://www.timssvideo.com
[8] https://vlc.uchicago.edu

tally, during the cognitive interviews for the survey, one participant expressed surprise that one could even reach out to a staff person through a digital repository.

Though the survey questions did not explicitly quantify participants' reasons for their interactions with repository staff, one question probed for the types of assistance they requested and yielded 12 responses. Nine needed technical assistance or help troubleshooting software applications provided by the repository, and four reported requesting help with navigation and/or questions about the resources themselves. One respondent asked about further development of repository services for increased usability.

The respondents who reported interacting with repository staff were further asked to assess the importance of the assistance that they received. Of the 17 respondents who were given this question, 15 reusers (88.2%) indicated that staff were either "very helpful" or "essential" to their activities. Only two respondents described repository staff as being "somewhat helpful," and none responded that they were unhelpful.

The interviewees provided more in-depth discussions of the nature of repository staff assistance. Two interviewees described readily available support from repositories in using their data; both also noted that the help was invaluable in facilitating their reuse of records of practice. Interviewee 029 described attending a repository workshop about using a particular dataset and emphasized that this intensive, in-person interaction continued to be helpful for years: "I went to the workshop at [repository], maybe almost two years ago at this point, which is really helpful in orienting to that data." Interviewee 029 is interesting because her discussion demonstrates that although her reuse might be shallow in terms of the quantity of videos used, it was critical to her research, so intensity may be another way to measure the depth of the interaction.

Interviewee 037 had been using videos from the same repository for several years, and the help she received eliminated challenges that interfered with her ability to reuse video records of practice, "I've been with them for a couple years now, and any time there's been a challenge, I call them up and say, 'Can you help me fix this?'" She continued, "They're pretty quick at responding, too. I have three points of contact in the office . . . I had a technical problem one time, and I could get on the site but the video wasn't working, and [name of repository] was down. They got working on it, and like two minutes before my class began, they got it back up and running. I call them in an emergency. It's usually last minute."

Interviewees 002, 006, 008, 014, 040 and 041 all explained that they knew the staff in the repositories because they had previously worked with or for those repositories, "I started doing some consulting work for the [organization] on their video archives" (002). These reusers represent a group with both intensive and deep use of the resources and stronger internal ties to the repositories they used. Repository processes were also more transparent to them than to reusers with less experience working in and directly with repositories.

Interaction with repository staff was also facilitated by colleagues. Interviewee 022 said that her research team was working directly with the staff of a repository and that the partnership came about through one of her team members, "And then now that [repository] is up and running, we're actually partnering with them, for a different research study, not the one I just described."

Both survey respondents and interviewees described interactions with repository staff across diverse activities and contexts. These interactions demonstrate both data use and repository relationships of varying depth and breadth. In many cases repository staff provided support or assistance to facilitate the reuse of digital records of practice, and, when this occurred, the interactions were generally described in positive terms by the reusers.

### *Attitudes about Repositories*

We next examined the attitudes about digital repositories, in light of participant interaction with repositories and repository staff. We found that a majority of survey respondents would use data from a repository again. Interviewees who interacted with repository staff had mixed feelings about using a repository again, with positive, negative and ambivalent or uncertain attitudes.

Our survey asked data reusers about their intentions to again reuse digital records of practice: "I would use digital records of practice from third party repositories or organizations for future projects." This was asked of all respondents, regardless of whether they had reported interaction with repository staff or not. Of the 126 respondents who answered this question, 115 (91.3%) answered positively that they would use digital records of practice from a repository again in the future. Of the 17 respondents who reported interacting with repository staff, all (100%) affirmed that they expected to use digital records of practice from repositories in the future.

Survey respondents indicating they would use repository data again in the future were given the option to include their reasoning. Of the 17 respondents who had both requested assistance from repository staff and expect to use digital records of practice in the future, nine (52.9%) provided this additional input. These responses generally emphasized the importance of access to a large variety of videos as well as the relevance of the videos to their work.

Interviewees 005, 009 and 022 were less closely associated to the repositories they used. Each expressed positive views about how digital repositories curated the collections. For example, 005 talked about the usefulness of repositories and the curation work by repository staff, "I think, that as a teacher-educator the ones that are pretty curated are often useful because you often are trying to look for really specific types of things. If I wasn't involved in [repository], I can't really imagine wanting to sit there and watch all of that video to try to find whether or not there were things I could use in my math methods class."

Similarly, 009 noted the added value of highly curated repository collections for teacher-educators using video records of practice for their own professional learning, "if you are just on your own, like me, where you're not in a PD [professional development], you don't have anybody working with you, you don't have anybody facilitating, you don't have anything, that when you find something, what you watch something on [repository], they have all those questions, the scaffolding on the side . . . And also the way they have the documents attached." She also explained that she appreciates the predictability that comes with searching for records of practice in a highly curated repository collection, "because they're all such high quality that happens in a very predictable way, there's always something else good to watch."

Interviewee 022 emphasized the value and importance of repositories making video records of practice available and findable in her field, "There could be amazing video out there, but if I can't find it, then it doesn't help me, you know? So if somebody is making it available and findable, I think that is a huge value add."

In all three cases, interviewees found that the work of repository staff to make collections usable and accessible facilitated added value to their own work with video records of practice. Interviewee 017 framed this value in broad terms, as a service to the field of education, "I think it's a tremendous and important service to the field." When asked if those repositories added value to the records of practice that they curate, she was similarly positive and appreciated the transparency of their actions. "I haven't had tons of experience with it . . . but I do know like the more thoughtfully done it is done, the more useful it is to the field. And so I've had some interaction with folks at [institution]...around the repository that they're trying to develop and have just really appreciated some of the detail of like how they're trying to figure it out and how to make it accessible."

Some interviewees tempered their positive views of repositories with cautionary statements about either the completeness of collections or curation work that appeared to be pushing an agenda. Interviewee 018 explained that in addition to making video records of practice accessible, repositories also "provide some kind of context" which adds value to the records of practice. However, she cautioned that this kind of work is only helpful if repositories are "doing something in a very neutral way . . . but if they have some kind of hidden agenda and they are kind of making things look a certain way" then she thought of the repository as less trustworthy and the work of repository staff less valuable.

Several interviewees were more critical in their views about digital repositories. Interviewee 002 had experience working as a consultant for a repository, which made her skeptical about the availability and/or quality of support that she could expect from repositories generally, "I just was doubtful they would respond if I wrote... It's writing the national government. Like, who's really gonna respond? ...But I know that people reach out when they're trying to use the [repository]. When we were trying to tag in the [repository], there were multiple emails that got sent out. And the most frustrating thing is there was no response and we were working for them." After the conclusion of her work for the repository she reached back out to the staff with questions about using the data, but "there was never ever any follow up and I was just done." In this case, a deep, internal relationship with a repository increased her desire for transparency and responsiveness.

Interviewee 040, who also had previously worked for a repository, was also wary of repositories with an agenda. "It's tough because I think they add value but at the same time for the most part of what I've seen is they're actually marketing tools. It's like, 'Here we'll give you some free lessons and now buy this book of ours.' Or, 'This lesson is ... you can see how a teacher taught this lesson by buying this video of ours or buying this.'" Thus, transparency and knowing about repository actions can also have negative consequences not envisioned by Pirson and Malhotra (2011), particularly if stakeholders disagree with facets of the practices to which they've become privy.

Despite their interactions with repository staff, several of the interviewees were ambivalent or uncertain about the role of repositories with regard to curating, providing access and preserving digital records of practice. Some had given it little thought. For example, when asked if repositories have trustworthy processes for curating and preserving data, 012 responded, "Hopefully, probably. I mean, I think I would imagine so. ... It doesn't cross my mind as a particularly big concern." Interviewee 014 answered with uncertainty, "I don't think I understand enough about how things are saved to really be able to give any intelligent answer to that question." When asked whether she considers the trustworthiness of the repository when selecting data for reuse, 018 responded describing trustworthiness as a tacit consideration, "I suppose that's just something that is, you know, latent in your decision making, so I've never had to explicitly say that that's what I do, but that's definitely the case."

### *Trust in Repositories*

Interview participants described several factors that contributed to their decisions about whether to trust a repository, including data quality, co-production of data between the repository and the data producer, responsiveness of repository staff, and curation practices. Some of these factors align with Pirson and Malhotra's (2011) model of the depth of interaction or the closeness of affiliation.

#### *Data Quality*

Interviewees discussed indicators of trustworthiness, such as data quality, as markers that help them determine whether or not to trust a particular repository. Interviewee 002, who worked as a consultant for a digital repository, said that problems with data such as mislabeling can be indicators of bigger problems, and as a result she does not trust data with those kinds of errors, "If I see problems like that, I have no faith in the data and I won't dig into it." This is similar to what Lee et al. (2002) refer to as representational consistency or the extent to which data are presented in a professional manner, error free and compatible over time. Representational consistency is a major indicator of credibility.

Interviewee 044 discussed the importance of curation processes and data quality in repository trustworthiness, "I think that in order for them to be valuable to teach education they have to have some sort of curation process. It has to be something that says that establishes a baseline of quality and I think we have that. We can't just let it be this wild thing where random videos are posted. It has to be at least a framework which gets us back to the idea that everything is curated with a particular thing in mind."

### *Co-production of Data between the Data Repository and Producer*

Interviewee 008 trusted data from a particular repository because of her experiences working there and her trust in the data producer. "Part of the reason I work there is, I so completely believe in the product and [data producer's] work behind it." She went on to explain that she would be more likely to trust other repositories based on the recommendations or support of other researchers she knows and trusts. "Because I know and trust the validity, the reliability and the work that has been done to even post those resources as valuable. So, it's almost that that's the piece that I look for, is I look for the experts out there to either have created their own or have said, 'Yeah, we really like [data producer's] work, so we're kind of putting a check next to his name and that's a good one.'"

### *Responsiveness of Staff*

Among interviewees who interacted with repository staff, responsiveness emerged as another important trust factor. Previously, we quoted interviewee 037 who described in great detail her experiences working with very responsive repository staff. Interviewee 002 explained that unresponsive repository staff and practices that lacked transparency were a barrier to developing trust with a repository, "Because I need to be able to trust the other decisions and things that they're telling me, and if I see a lot...I'm not looking for a typo and then writing something off, but if I see things that are obviously problematic, then I won't. And I think that the researchers, the original project managers need to be accessible. So, if you shoot off someone an email and you asked them about something... If they are not responsive, that's also a red flag for me."

### *Curation Processes*

As noted in the previous sections, we found that knowledge of data curation processes was an underlying factor that intersected with other dimensions of repository trustworthiness. Interviewees who had experience working for a repository or serving on an advisory board, such as 037, 040 and 008, explained that their understanding of repository processes helped them to trust the repository and its data. "I've been pretty close to their process. I don't know about everything...I trust things that have – I'm not so convinced by [repository] or [repository], whatever it is. I don't know about them. I'm not sure who they're videotaping or why they're videotaping or how they're getting access to classrooms or what they're doing in terms of archiving their data. I think I feel more informed by [repository] or [organization], and so I'm comfortable" (037).

Interviewee 040 said that repositories "should be transparent." However, he also explained that his knowledge of repository processes was the result of participation on advisory boards rather than from information freely available to the general public, "The problem is – luckily we get invited to a lot of advisory boards because of this, because we have this video collection. We're working, we're on the advisory board for some other thing."

When discussing what makes her think that a particular repository is trustworthy, interviewee 026 explained that she believed the repository's processes for curating data were trustworthy because, "I know the people. I think the same thing of [repository], that they have a reputation. They're well-established and they care about things like that." She also trusted that the repository had the necessary permissions and rights to make video records of practice available, "For the [repository], I knew that whatever they put up, they had the right to put it up and make it available."

Interviewee 010 said that she trusts a particular repository because of how well they curated their collections, "one of the reasons I rely on [repository] so much is because I, they often do, they curate their videos, and I often appreciate their curation...I think they do a pretty good job of selecting the things that they put up there." She continued, "there's definitely things that I wouldn't show but in general, I trust most of their videos." Despite her overall trust for this particular repository, she was careful to note that she does not trust the repository's video descriptions, "I often don't trust those because there isn't I don't think, a common vocabulary for talking about teaching. Even if there is sort of kind of summary of what the video is, I don't often believe that that's going to tell me what I need to know. So, I'll often end up watching it anyway."

## DISCUSSION

Pirson and Malhotra's (2011) model posited that stakeholder trust in repositories would align with two dimensions: intensity of data reuse and the closeness of the relationship or affiliation with the repository. We found evidence of both of these dimensions among our survey respondents and interviewees, but found that the closeness of the relationship was a stronger factor with regard to trust in digital qualitative data repositories containing video records of practice.

We found that our survey respondents and interviewees fell across the spectrum that Pirson and Malhotra (2011) described (i.e., depth of interaction and locus of relationship). We had 23.8% of survey respondents saying that they are frequent data reusers, and 13.9% saying they have interacted with repository staff, both indicators of deeper interaction. Among interviewees, those who have worked at or consulted for a repository tended to have had the deepest interactions with repositories.

We also found strong evidence that a relationship or affiliation with a repository influences trust. The interviewees had a variety of types of relationships ranging from knowing a repository's reputation (minimal external relationship) to attending a workshop to interacting with staff to serving on an advisory board, being a consultant or working as staff (intense internal relationship). Interviewees who spoke most strongly about trusting the repository had a stronger affiliation (e.g., interviewees 002, 004, 008, 010, 037, 040, 044). Furthermore, each of these individuals had some type of insider knowledge that gave them insight into the work of the repository and in particular its curation practices.

Factors such as data quality, the co-production of data between the data repository and producer, and staff responsiveness influenced trust in digital repositories. These factors, however, were confounded by curation practices. Knowledge of curation practices was raised alone as well as in conjunction with data quality and data repository/data producer actions. Thus, we identified knowledge of curation processes as the strongest link to repository trust. Our study found that trust in data extended to the metadata and that the quality and care of the curation processes influenced trust in the repository. Previous research also demonstrates that data quality is a signal of trust in the data (Donaldson & Conway, 2015; Faniel & Jacobsen, 2010).

We identified some evidence that interactions between data reusers and repository staff in particular influenced their attitudes about, and trust in, digital repositories. Although reusers who interacted with repository staff were in the minority, these interactions were generally productive and those reusers tended to have positive attitudes toward repositories. No matter where data reusers fell along the shallow/deep encounters and internal/external affiliation with the repository, their interactions with repository staff often indicated areas where they experienced vulnerability. Overall, our interviewees appeared to have positive expectations when they asked questions, assuming that their questions would be answered (Pirson & Malhotra, 2011), indicating some measure of trust. Furthermore, reusers who interacted with repository staff only when they encountered a problem reported positive attitudes about those repositories when staff members were responsive, repository processes transparent, and the result was access to high quality data. This aligns with Pirson and Malhotra's research findings on transparency.

Research on trust in digital preservation suggests that repository users develop trust over time through repeated interactions (e.g., Kelton, Fleischmann & Wallace, 2008; Yoon, 2016), and this is consistent with our findings. We found that data reusers value responsiveness and transparency of curation processes. Problems with data or other repository issues, if handled quickly and clearly, do not necessarily result in negative attitudes about repositories or a loss of trust.

### *Implications for Repositories*

These findings suggest several implications for qualitative data repositories. Depth of interaction with repositories was correlated with trust, and the deep interactions with repositories that our interviewees reported were most frequently through official programs or channels (e.g., workshops and consulting or advisory roles). This suggests that repositories wishing to cultivate relationships with users may want to consider additional ways to create opportunities for formal interactions and/or participation with members of their user communities over an extended period of time. This approach has been discussed more extensively in the archival research regarding participatory archives (e.g., Huvila, 2008). Our findings also suggest that transparency of repository practices, and especially data curation practices, are important for trust. This is consistent with findings from other studies (e.g., Yakel et al., 2013), and suggests that repositories should be transparent about the decisions underlying data curation and repository management practices whenever possible.

## CONCLUSION

For data reusers, trust is essential at the data and the repository levels. By adapting Pirson and Malhotra's (2011) model of depth of interaction with data or staff and closeness of the relationship to digital repositories with research data, we have found evidence demonstrating the importance of closeness of the relationship. The closeness is particularly important when it includes information about curation processes. This adds to our knowledge of trust in data and repositories and provides support for Pirson and Malhotra's (2011) model for assessing that trust.


## ACKNOWLEDGMENTS

This research is funded by the Institute of Museum and Library Services # LG-06-14-0122-14.


## REFERENCES


Akmon, D., Zimmerman, A., Daniels, M., & Hedstrom, M. (2011). The application of archival concepts to a data-intensive environment: Working with scientists to understand data management and preservation needs. *Archival Science*, *11*(3-4), 329-348. https://doi.org/10.1007/s10502-011-9151-4

Bak, G. (2016). Trusted by whom? TDRs, standards culture and the nature of trust. *Archival Science*, *16*(4), 373-402. https://doi.org/10.1007/s10502-015-9257-1

Bass, H., Usiskin, Z., Burrill, G., National Research Council (U.S.), Mathematical Sciences Education Board, & United States National Commission on Mathematics Instruction (Eds.). (2002). *Studying classroom teaching as a medium for professional development proceedings of a U.S.-Japan workshop*. Washington, DC: National Academy Press. Retrieved from http://www.nap.edu/catalog/10289.html

Bishop, L. (2012). Using archived qualitative data for teaching: Practical and ethical considerations. *International Journal of Social Research Methodology*, *15*(4), 341-350. https://doi.org/10.1080/13645579.2012.688335

Burleigh, J. C., & Peterson, H. W. (1967). Videotapes in teacher education. *The Elementary School Journal*, *68*(1), 35–38.

Chowdhury, G. (2010). From digital libraries to digital preservation research: The importance of users and context. *Journal of Documentation*, *66*(2), 207-223. https://doi.org/10.1108/00220411011023625

Corti, L. (2000). Progress and problems of preserving and providing access to qualitative data for social research—The international picture of an emerging culture. *Forum Qualitative Sozialforschung/Forum: Qualitative Social Research*, *1*(3). Retrieved from http://www.qualitative-research.net/index.php/fqs/article/view/1019

Corti, L. (2011). The European landscape of qualitative social research archives: Methodological and practical issues. *Forum Qualitative Sozialforschung/Forum: Qualitative Social Research*, *12*(3). Retrieved from http://www.qualitative-research.net/index.php/fqs/article/view/1746

Derry, S. J., Pea, R. D., Barron, B., Engle, R. A., Erickson, F., Goldman, R., … Sherin, B. L. (2010). Conducting video research in the learning sciences: Guidance on selection, analysis, technology, and ethics. *Journal of the Learning Sciences*, *19*(1), 3-53. https://doi.org/10.1080/10508400903452884

Donaldson, D. R., & Conway, P. (2015). User conceptions of trustworthiness for digital archival documents. *Journal of the Association for Information Science and Technology*, n/a-n/a. https://doi.org/10.1002/asi.23330

Donnelly, M., & North, R. (2011). The milieu and the message: Talking to researchers about data curation issues in a large and diverse e-science project. *International Journal of Digital Curation*, *6*(1), 32–44. https://doi.org/10.2218/ijdc.v6i1.170

Faniel, I., & Jacobsen, T. (2010). Reusing scientific data: How earthquake engineering researchers assess the reusability of colleagues' data. *Computer Supported Cooperative Work (CSCW)*, *19*(3), 355–375. https://doi.org/10.1007/s10606-010-9117-8

Frank, R. D., Suzuka, K., & Yakel, E. (2016). Examining the reuse of qualitative research data: Digital video in education. In *Archiving Conference* (Vol. 2016, pp. 146-151). Washington, DC: Society for Imaging Science and Technology. https://doi.org/10.2352/issn.2168-3204.2016.1.0.146

Gaudin, C., & Chaliès, S. (2015). Video viewing in teacher education and professional development: A literature review. *Educational Research Review*, *16*, 41-67. https://doi.org/10.1016/j.edurev.2015.06.001

Giarlo, M. (2013). Academic libraries as data quality hubs. *Journal of Librarianship and Scholarly Communication*, *1*(3). https://doi.org/10.7710/2162-3309.1059

Gonzalez, G., Deal, J. T., & Skultety, L. (2016). Facilitating teacher learning when using different representations of practice. *Journal of Teacher Education*. https://doi.org/10.1177/0022487116669573

Hadfield, M., & Haw, K. (2012). Video: Modalities and methodologies. *International Journal of Research & Method in Education*, *35*(3), 311-324. https://doi.org/10.1080/1743727X.2012.717434

Holsti, O. R. (1969). *Content analysis for the social sciences and humanities*. Reading, MA: Addison-Wesley Pub. Co.

Huvila, I. (2008). Participatory archive: Towards decentralised curation, radical user orientation, and broader contextualisation of records management. *Archival Science*, *8*(1), 15-36. https://doi.org/10.1007/s10502-008-9071-0

Karasti, H., & Baker, K. (2008). Digital data practices and long term ecological research program growing global. *The International Journal of Digital Curation*, *3*(2), 42–58. https://doi.org/10.2218/ijdc.v3i2.57

Kelton, K., Fleischmann, K. R., & Wallace, W. A. (2008). Trust in digital information. *Journal of the American Society for Information Science and Technology*, *59*(3), 363–374. https://doi.org/10.1002/asi.20722

Lee, Y. W., Strong, D. M., Kahn, B. K., & Wang, R. Y. (2002). AIMQ: A methodology for information quality assessment. *Information & Management*, *40*(2), 133-146. https://doi.org/10.1016/S0378-7206(02)00043-5

Margaryan, A., & Littlejohn, A. (2008). Repositories and communities at cross-purposes: Issues in sharing and reuse of digital learning resources. *Journal of Computer Assisted Learning*, *24*(4), 333-347. https://doi.org/10.1111/j.1365-2729.2007.00267.x

Mauthner, N. S., & Parry, O. (2009). Qualitative data preservation and sharing in the social sciences: On whose philosophical terms? *Australian Journal of Social Issues*, *44*(3), 291–307,238.

Miles, M. B., & Huberman, A. M. (1994). *Qualitative data analysis: An expanded sourcebook*. Thousand Oaks: Sage Publications.

Pea, R. D. (2006). Video-as-data and digital video manipulation techniques for transforming learning sciences research, education, and other cultural practices. In J. Weiss, A. P. J. Nolan, J. Hunsinger, & P. P. Trifonas (Eds.), *The international handbook of virtual learning environments* (pp. 1321-1393). Springer Netherlands. Retrieved from http://link.springer.com/chapter/10.1007/978-1-4020-3803-7_55

Penn-Edwards, S. (2012). Human factors affecting the use of video recording methodology in qualitative research. *International Journal of Multiple Research Approaches*, *6*(2), 150-159. https://doi.org/10.5172/mra.2012.6.2.150

Pirson, M., & Malhotra, D. (2011). Foundations of organizational trust: What matters to different stakeholders? *Organization Science*, *22*(4), 1087-1104. https://doi.org/10.1287/orsc.1100.0581

Poole, A. H. (2015). How has your science data grown? Digital curation and the human factor: a critical literature review. *Archival Science*, *15*(2), 101-139. https://doi.org/10.1007/s10502-014-9236-y

Pryor, G., & Donnelly, M. (2009). Skilling up to do data: Whose role, whose responsibility, whose career? *International Journal of Digital Curation*, *4*(2), 158-170. https://doi.org/10.2218/ijdc.v4i2.105

Rook, M. M., & McDonald, S. P. (2012). Digital records of practice: A literature review of video analysis in teacher practice (Vol. 2012, pp. 1441-1446). Presented at the Society for Information Technology & Teacher Education International Conference. Retrieved from http://www.editlib.org/p/39784/

Russell, R., & Day, M. (2010). Institutional repository interaction with research users: A review of current practice. *New Review of Academic Librarianship*, *16*(sup1), 116-131. https://doi.org/10.1080/13614533.2010.509996

Saldaña, J. (2015). *The coding manual for qualitative researchers* (3rd edition). Thousand Oaks, CA: Sage Publications.

Schofield, P. N., Bubela, T., Weaver, T., Portilla, L., Brown, S. D., Hancock, J. M., … Rosenthal, N. (2009). Post-publication sharing of data and tools. *Nature*, *461*(7261), 171-173. https://doi.org/10.1038/461171a

Shelton, C., Archambault, L., Warren, A., Ahmad, O., & Nevárez, V. (2016). Examining preservice teachers' beliefs, experiences, and expectations regarding the use of video in education. In *Proceedings of Society for Information Technology & Teacher Education international conference 2016* (pp. 465-468). Chesapeake, VA: Association for the Advancement of Computing in Education (AACE). Retrieved from http://www.learntechlib.org/p/171717

Stigler, J. W., Gallimore, R., & Hiebert, J. (2000). Using video surveys to compare classrooms and teaching across cultures: Examples and lessons from the TIMSS video studies. *Educational Psychologist*, *35*(2), 87-100. https://doi.org/10.1207/S15326985EP3502_3

van Es, E., & Sherin, M. (2002). Learning to notice: Scaffolding new teachers' interpretations of classroom interactions. *Journal of Technology and Teacher Education*, *10*(4), 571-596.

Yakel, E., Faniel, I., Kriesberg, A., & Yoon, A. (2013). Trust in digital repositories. *International Journal of Digital Curation*, *8*(1), 143–156. https://doi.org/10.2218/ijdc.v8i1.251

Yoon, A. (2014). End users' trust in data repositories: Definition and influences on trust development. *Archival Science*, *14*(1), 17-34. https://doi.org/10.1007/s10502-013-9207-8

Yoon, A. (2016). Data reusers' trust development. *Journal of the Association for Information Science and Technology*. https://doi.org/10.1002/asi.23730

Zhang, M., Lundeberg, M., Koehler, M. J., & Eberhardt, J. (2011). Understanding affordances and challenges of three types of video for teacher professional development. *Teaching and Teacher Education*, *27*(2), 454-462. https://doi.org/10.1016/j.tate.2010.09.015

Zimmerman, A. S. (2008). New Knowledge from old data: The role of standards in the sharing and reuse of ecological data. *Science, Technology & Human Values*, *33*(5), 631-652. https://doi.org/10.1177/0162243907306704

# Critical Moments in Participatory Design: Engaging NASA Astrobiology Researchers via Scientometric Visualizations

**Rich Gazan**
*University of Hawaii, USA. gazan@hawaii.edu*

## ABSTRACT

**NASA astrobiology researchers from diverse fields often have little sense of how their work relates to one another. Using document analysis and participatory design methods, this paper reports on a scientometric analysis project to distill essential elements of astrobiology documents to identify them across diverse domains. Twelve NASA astrobiology researchers and administrators were presented with scientometric visualizations in a live setting and (i) demonstrated engagement by actively proposing alternative terms they felt best represented their team's research, (ii) confirmed that the effects of 2007-2008 cuts in research funding had been accurately reflected in the document corpus and (iii) identified persistent differential impacts on research output across astrobiology's diverse constituent disciplines. The results suggest that this participatory design method provided a critical boundary space where conversations between diverse researchers took place that would have been unlikely to occur otherwise and illustrates the kind of unique contribution information science researchers and professionals can make to interdisciplinary scientific collaborations.**

## KEYWORDS

interdisciplinary science, scientometrics, document analysis, interdisciplinary collaboration

## INTRODUCTION

While prior research has argued convincingly that system designers and researchers should have a more prominent role in facilitating scientific collaborations, opportunities to engage with interdisciplinary scientists in a group setting for participatory design feedback are scarce. This paper reports on the results of one such critical moment: a project to develop data-driven indicators of the interdisciplinary impact of astrobiology by analyzing research literature across diverse domains and to develop a "signature" of astrobiology-related work. Scientometric visualizations of research publications were presented to researchers in a virtual case study setting as a representation of their work and yielded valuable engagement and feedback for iterative development.

80th Annual Meeting of the Association for Information Science & Technology, Washington, DC | Oct. 27-Nov. 1, 2017



Scientometric analysis has been used to distinguish characteristics of diverse research fields: as disciplines with a core of knowledge, or as inter-disciplines, connecting and contributing to other domains (Blackwell, 2015; DiSalvo et al., 2010; Dörk et al., 2011; Hooper et al., 2013; Kim, 1990, Liu et al., 2014). This paper describes the result of applying similar methods to the NASA Astrobiology Institute (NAI), a research community whose explicit goal is to catalyze interdisciplinary science (NAI, 2017). In the NAI, approximately 800 researchers work within and across multiple institutions and disciplinary boundaries to address the questions of how, where and whether life might exist elsewhere in the universe.

The NAI is an example of a complex sociotechnical information system that takes diverse and discrete multidisciplinary knowledge as input and transforms it into integrated, interdisciplinary knowledge about the nature and extent of life. Astrobiology researchers need tools that support their own science, help them interact productively with colleagues who are working on related problems in different fields and help them understand where their work fits into the bigger picture. Administrators need to coordinate researcher efforts, allocate resources effectively and provide accounting and metrics of how ever-scarcer funds are being translated into measurable research output.

Information science researchers and professionals working in collaborative design projects must bring tangible skills, perspectives and value to these projects, while at the same time being flexible and reflective enough to help make meaningful integration happen amidst the messy realities of actual practice. The skills that are necessary to translate and transport concepts in effective interdisciplinary collaborations are similar to those needed to distill potentially useful practices reported in case studies such as the one presented here and to transport and gauge their effectiveness in other environments.

## BACKGROUND

NASA Ames Research Center, where the NAI is headquartered, has a long history of integrating HCI research into its systems and practices, including participatory design, social computing (Barrientos et al., 2009), open source contribution (Green et al., 2009) and contrasting high- and low-fidelity prototypes (McCurdy et al., 2006).

The NAI's mission explicitly mandates collaboration, catalysis and change (NAI, 2017):

- carry out, support and catalyze collaborative, interdisciplinary research;

- explore new approaches using modern information technology to conduct interdisciplinary and collaborative research amongst widely-distributed investigators.

Idea generation (or ideation) systems can improve performance and engagement in large teams (Chan et al., 2016; Javadi et al., 2013). Tausch et al. (2016) found that groups exposed to visualizations of ideation systems were "more productive, more satisfied and participate in a more balanced way." Studies of distributed groups like software developers (Cleidson et al., 2016), collaborative writing teams (Olson & Olson, 2013; Wang et al., 2015) and video game players (Kim et al., 2016) have suggested important social benefits to allowing members to view individual and group performance (Engel et al., 2015).

Systems supporting interdisciplinary teams must account for differences in goals and practices embedded in the cultures of the participants, which impact system use and evaluation (Harmon & Nersessian, 2008). They can function as boundary objects, spaces or negotiating artifacts (Star & Griesemer, 1989; Lee, 2007) for communication among diverse members (Hendry 2004), but especially in distributed teams, there are few opportunities for group assessment in real time.

Bibliometric and scientometric methods are frequently used to trace the evolution of disciplines and interdisciplines (Chen et al., 2015). Since these methods employ data-driven aggregation and analysis of research artifacts, and employ some of the same quantitative methods as astrobiology's constituent sciences, the bibliometric approach aligns with the practices of the group the system intends to support. However, since analyzing publication and citation patterns is an inherently inexact and probabilistic activity, it requires input from researchers in the field (Rhoten, 2003), both to evaluate the extent of the entire proposed astrobiology publication corpus and to identify how their individual fields are represented within it.

Implementation of participatory design methods, where intended contributors and users have a formal role in the design process, brings with it a set of unique challenges. These include assembling and communicating accurate representations and visualizations of participants' contributions and intended uses, meaning making and member checking, all executed within the constraints of participants' time, attention and shared understanding (Selvin et al., 2010).

When participants from different backgrounds collaborate on complex, large-scale scientific research projects such as astrobiology, challenges multiply. In participatory design sessions, Sawyer (2004, p. 12) describes the balance between prompting participants to address planned questions and staying in dialogue to elicit unexpected insights as a "disciplined improvisation." This proved to be a valuable perspective.

## METHOD

To present NAI researchers with a broad overview of the astrobiology research literature, the set of 1,943 content-bearing terms associated with astrobiology research generated by Miller et al. (2014) were queried across the Web of Science database suite, to generate a broad initial set of publications possibly relevant to astrobiology. The resulting documents were then grouped by Web of Science Subject Category, a list of 250 broad fields associated with the publication in which each paper appears. For example, the term *life* within the Astronomy & Astrophysics Subject Category is likely relevant to astrobiology, while *life* in Biology is likely not. The aim of this step is to generate term/subject pairs associated with research publications in astrobiology and its related fields, toward the larger goal of determining a likely signature of an astrobiology document that might be tested in broader document collections.

Following Gowanlock et al. (2013), the resulting Web of Science Subject Categories associated with astrobiology were conflated into three broad subject groups: Astronomy, Biology and Earth/Planetary Science. We can then conduct a term frequency/inverse document frequency (*tf/idf*) analysis as a rough relevance rank, to determine which terms are common within the subject group, but rare elsewhere. Since we are interested both in astrobiology documents within disciplines and interdisciplines, we conduct the analysis in the three conflated subject groups (A, B, E), and in their areas of intersection (AB, AE, BE, ABE). This allows us to identify, for example, certain terms appearing commonly in both Astronomy and Biology subject categories that are rare elsewhere. The results of this analysis are shown in Figure 1.

To determine how astrobiology-related terms have migrated across disciplines over time, an intentionally broad initial document set was created, encompassing areas outside astrobiology. Web of Science was again searched for the astrobiology-related terms from Miller et al. (2014), and publications containing two or more terms entered the corpus. Filtering these terms by the broad Astronomy, Biology and Earth/Planetary Science categories, then sorting by publication year, provides a high-level snapshot of the evolution of the field. We then normalize for the difference in the overall number of publications added to Web of Science per year.

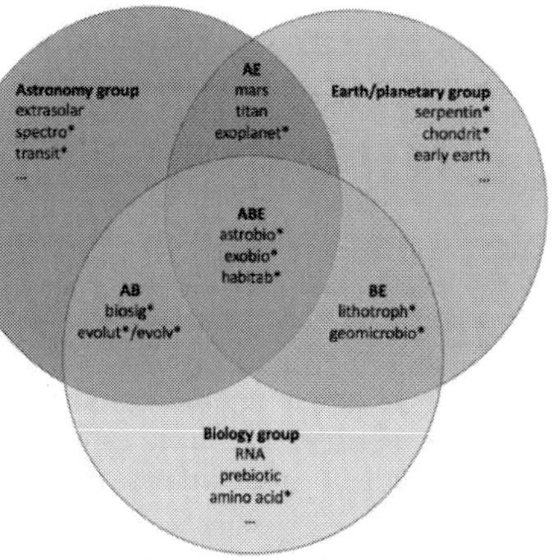


***Figure 1.*** *Term/subject pairs most common within astrobiology research publications, Web of Science 1994-2015. Asterisks indicate truncated/variant forms of the root term.*

The findings were presented in a March 2016 virtual focus group setting to 12 researchers, team leaders and administrators, representing the approximately 800 researchers in the NASA Astrobiology Institute. This group, the NAI Executive Council (NAI, 2017b), consists of the principal investigators of every NAI team, and meets regularly to share ideas in a "workshop without walls" (Arslan et al., 2011), coordinated from NAI Central headquarters at Ames Research Center (Figure 2). The meeting was recorded for later analysis.

Data for each of the subject groups was visualized in both merged and separate forms, to provide researchers a view of their own broad research areas, as well as a combined view where terms from all areas were represented. Raw and normalized data for astrobiology publications in the overall set is presented in Figure 3, followed by the Astronomy subject group (Figure 4), the Biology subject group (Figure 5), and the Earth/Planetary Science subject group (Figure 6). One of the initial data collection goals was to compare the feedback received from the separate and combined visualizations during the focus group session. For example, if researchers and team leads made no contribution or comments outside of their own research area, the visualizations would not have demonstrated effectiveness as interdisciplinary representations.

***Figure 2:** NASA Astrobiology Institute video conference facility at Ames Research Center (Arslan et al., 2011).*

## RESULTS

### *Engagement via term suggestions*

The suggested term/subject pairs most common within astrobiology research publications are presented in Figure 1. This visualization was presented to researchers first, after a brief introductory slide describing the scientometric methodology.

All six NAI researchers and administrators who responded confirmed that these terms described astrobiologically relevant processes (e.g., serpentinization) or analytic methods (e.g., spectroscopy), and that the term within the subject group(s) would be an accurate indicator of an astrobiology research document. They discussed the extent to which truncated term variants might introduce precision errors (e.g., spectro* might return a significant number of irrelevant items), but a recall error was identified as well. Astronomy researchers speculated that allowing a broad range of variants for transit* (the transit method is one way astronomers detect extrasolar planets) into the corpus could reveal potentially relevant literature and create connections with a fast-growing body of research in astronomy that had not yet in their opinion engaged with the astrobiology research literature.

Five of the 12 (two from astronomy, two from earth/planetary science and one from biology) also volunteered alternative terms, and three debated among themselves as to which terms they would expect to be present in the corpus to cover research relevant to their area and team. They reported that an overview visualization such as this would be particularly helpful for postdoctoral researchers and graduate students to help them better understand astrobiology terms within and outside their home discipline.

Researchers were particularly interested in how their work, and that of their teams, was represented and assessed. Three individuals appeared to view the scientometric analysis as a kind of search engine optimization problem and asked which terms they should encourage their teams to use in future publications to best emphasize their perceived interdisciplinary contributions.

One researcher, whose team worked on a diverse set of astrobiology-related questions, appeared to initially interpret the Figure 1 visualization as a map and asked where his team's research would be located. While a representation of common term/subject pairs may be useful in identifying astrobiology-related documents, this researcher emphasized that uncommon term/subject pairs might be a strong indicator of interdisciplinary research and suggested that there should be a way to filter and identify those papers for review.

### *Engagement via data interpretation*

The longitudinal astrobiology publication profile (Figure 3) mapped 7,286 documents across 21 years and merged the three broad subject areas in a single view. This visualization was presented to researchers immediately after the term/subject pairs map in Figure 1 and was planned as a member check to show researchers one view of the growth and extent of the astrobiology research literature for their feedback. However, Figure 3 immediately raised questions from the researchers and administrators about the decline in the number of publications in 2007-2008, an effect seen in both the raw and normalized numbers.

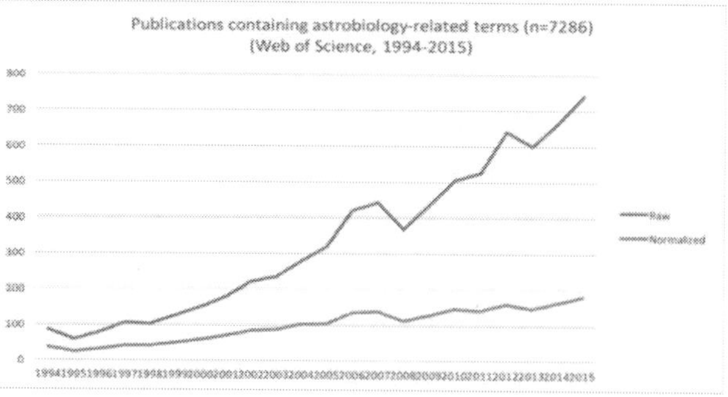


***Figure 3.** Astrobiology research publications, Web of Science 1994-2015. Normalized data expresses astrobiology-related publications as a percentage of the total records added to Web of Science in the corresponding year.*

The Figure 3 visualization served as a boundary negotiating artifact (Lee, 2007), around which NAI researchers and administrators reported that those years had seen severe funding cuts, which they agreed were accurately reflected in the associated decline in publications.

During this part of the session, so many people were contributing ideas that it was difficult to track who had said what. Funding cuts in large-scale science generally have a ripple effect; postdoctoral researchers and graduate students tend to go where funding is available and are often warned by their advisors about entering fields where funding is unreliable.

While the researchers and administrators were generally familiar with the year-to-year trends of NAI research output, they were surprised to see this level of impact across the larger astrobiology research literature, which includes work not funded by the NAI. Those who had been present during the budget cuts speculated that the brief spike in research productivity immediately before the downturn might be related to rumors of impending cuts and a desire to produce as many publications as possible before moving on to other projects.

As an interdisciplinary field without an established network of funding sources, dedicated academic departments and journals, researchers who might otherwise have engaged in astrobiology scholarship were likely forced to withdraw to their home disciplines, and work in the established disciplinary area where they received their degrees.

### *Engagement via cultural exchange*

Breaking down the longitudinal publication profile in Figure 3 by broad subject category illustrated both differential publication patterns and the differential impact of the budget cuts across astrobiology's constituent fields. In Figure 4, the results suggest that astrobiology-related raw and normalized publication numbers in astronomy journals recovered fairly quickly after the 2007-2008 budget cuts.

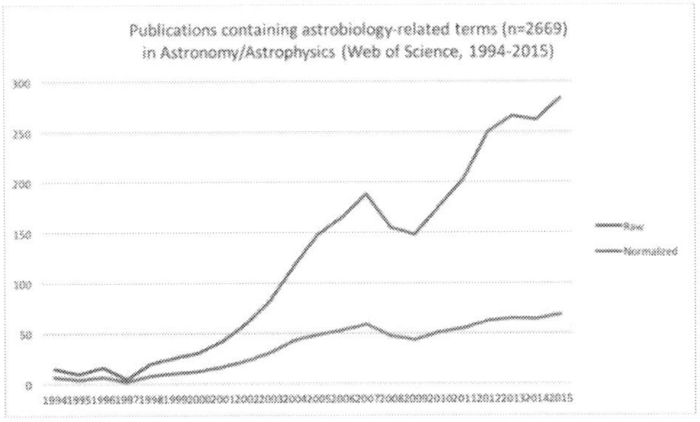


***Figure 4.** Astrobiology research publications in Astronomy subject group, Web of Science 1994-2015.*

As a check on the possibly uneven coverage of astronomy in the Web of Science database suite, a similar search was run in the Astrophysics Data System (NASA/ADS), a database with extensive coverage of the astronomy research literature, and these results were presented to researchers as seen in Figure 4a. A similar profile of year-to-year growth in astronomy-related astrobiology publications can be seen in the NASA/ADS collection as well, with a steep rise beginning in 2000, a significant drop in 2007, then a continued rise in subsequent years.

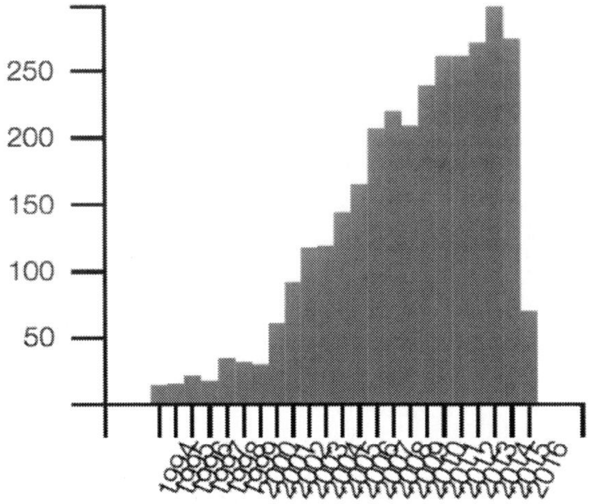


***Figure 4a.** Astrobiology research publications in Astronomy subject group, NASA/ADS 1994-2015.*

Astronomy is generally considered the disciplinary center of astrobiology; in the Web of Science corpus, more documents were published in the Astronomy subject group (2,669) than in Biology and Earth/Planetary Sciences combined (2,171). Researchers accurately predicted that astrobiology-related publications returned to previous levels in astronomy journals more quickly than those in biology and earth/planetary science other fields.

Interdisciplinary impact is a primary concern of NAI, and the results suggest that on a normalized basis, astrobiology publications in Biology (Figure 5) and Earth/Planetary Sciences (Figure 6) have yet to reach their pre-cut maximum levels, even 10 years later.

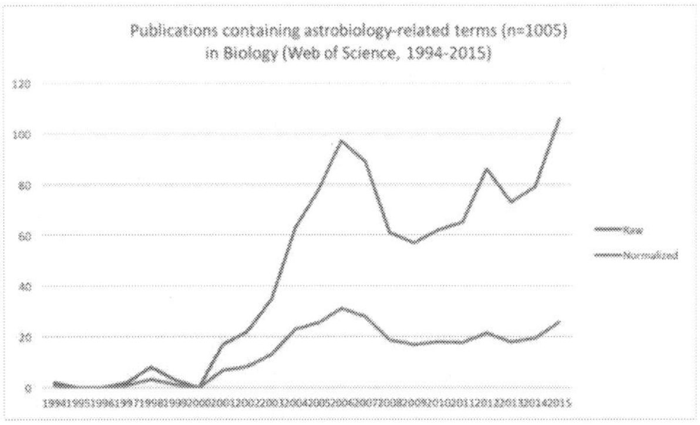


***Figure 5**. Astrobiology research publications in Biology subject group, Web of Science 1994-2015.*

Two of the researchers returned to a metaphor of maps and distances, speculating that since biology and earth/planetary sciences were "further from the core" of astrobiology than astronomy, it might be a greater risk for researchers in those fields to pursue astrobiology research, especially when funding is uncertain. If true, this directly works against one of the core goals of NAI, which is to create a supportive environment where interdisciplinary research can thrive.

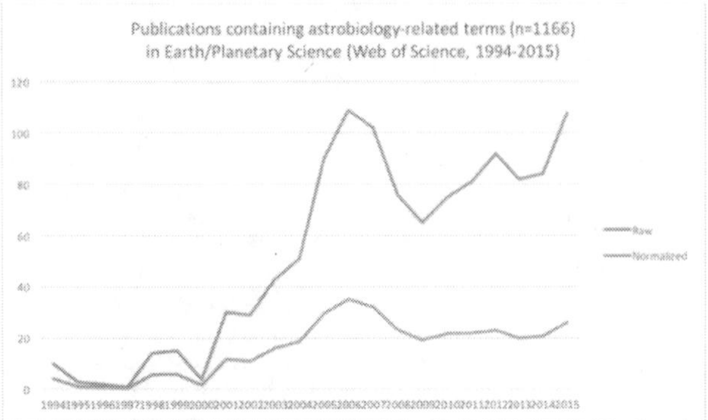


***Figure 6.*** *Astrobiology research publications in Astronomy subject group, Web of Science 1994-2015.*

## DISCUSSION

The scientometric visualizations presented to researchers helped elicit discussions that both usefully addressed and usefully diverged from the initial goal of member checking a developing system designed to support interdisciplinary science. It is important to emphasize that the focus group setting of the presentation and discussion, with researchers and administrators from the entire range of NAI science teams either present or virtually present, was an extremely rare opportunity. For information science researchers and professionals in this or any collaboration, moments when diverse stakeholders come together are critical in the participatory design process and can be where engagement with those stakeholders can be won or lost. The study reported here focused on visualization of research publications and yielded valuable researcher engagement and feedback.

- Presenting merged overviews first, where all members' data is represented in a single visualization, elicited immediate engagement: first, with the "where's my team's data?" question, followed by higher-level conversations and questions about how the visualization was created, both in terms of the software and the data behind it. A merged overview also emphasizes the sense of shared enterprise critical to the success of any collaboration. Even when participants misinterpreted the meaning or intent behind a visualization, it revealed actionable design suggestions for the next iteration.
- Once a shared understanding had been established and scaffolded in the merged visualization, breaking down the publication data into subareas in the subsequent images allowed all participants to see differential impacts of funding decisions and changing conditions over time. The subarea visualizations addressed the previous "where's my data?" question many of the participants raised, keeping them engaged, while simultaneously allowing them to see how researchers in other subareas had been affected. This is an extremely valuable element of interdisciplinary scientific collaborations, but one that is rarely addressed directly: how can participants understand the effect and potential impact each team's work – and funding variability – has on others? In the case of NAI, a common potential domain of collaboration might be how datasets from different researchers or fields support or call into question certain assumptions when integrated with others. If a visualization indicates that less research in specific areas is being carried out and published over time, researchers can use this information to identify potentially endangered datasets that rely on consistent longitudinal studies. Similarly, administrators may wish to use this information to focus discretionary funds (NAI, 2017a) to support targeted areas. On a higher level, the ability to understand the different norms, expectations and pressures researchers from different areas bring to the same collaboration can create deeper understanding of not just the science, but of the people doing the science.
- Making interdisciplinary research metrics transparent, and giving participants a voice in the process by which their work is represented, creates a pathway and incentive for them to actively seek understanding and contribute more substantive feedback. As was the case here, assumptions can be tested, potential inaccuracies identified and new approaches can be suggested. Researchers and administrators both within the focus group and in subsequent conversations expressed a desire to learn more about how their teams' contributions were represented using scientometric methods, and several identified potential weaknesses of the approach, such as neglecting non-textual research contributions like dataset publications and the problems inherent in labeling any research publication with one and only one discipline for analysis. As mentioned previously, researchers sometimes attempted to apply models from other areas such as search engine optimization onto the analysis so they could better understand (or perhaps game) the system.

NAI researchers come from an extremely diverse group of scientific traditions and perspectives, and while there are many potentially productive points of overlap, identifying them is not trivial. However, all researchers understand publication metrics, research assessment and giving career advice to students and junior researchers. As a result of this interaction, several of them concluded the session by discussing advice they would give to early career researchers. They used the publication data as evidence to discuss and exchange cultural practices, for example whether they would advise a strong student in their discipline to embrace or avoid interdisciplinary research.

While it should be emphasized that scientometric approaches describe aggregate trends and require continual updating and refinement, these data-driven methods also demonstrated to

NAI researchers and administrators the beginnings of an astrobiology publication signature based on term/subject pairs, and a longitudinal overview of the publication patterns of the field, both of which they reported as novel, insightful and useful.

NAI is a distributed research organization that prides itself on bringing scientists from diverse fields together to catalyze interdisciplinary science. Both the scientometric visualizations and the ways in which diverse researchers communicated around them contributed to the NAI's mission in a unique way. The common language of scientometric analysis of research publications, the common platform of data visualization and the common space of an interdisciplinary research meeting created a rare confluence point among diverse researchers and is an example of the kind of unique contribution information science researchers and professionals can make to interdisciplinary scientific collaborations. The participatory design methods described here helped structure this critical moment for maximum engagement, feedback and discovery.

## CONCLUSION

Astrobiology is inherently interdisciplinary, but actionable methods to encourage and measure interdisciplinary science are scarce. Allowing researchers to view with more precision where their work fits with others, and to interact in boundary spaces to discuss the story the data tell, creates a more researcher-centered collaborative environment. The results suggest that this participatory design method can help document astrobiology's evolution, engage researchers and catalyze interdisciplinary science.

## ACKNOWLEDGMENTS

I would like to thank the anonymous reviewers for their helpful comments. I am especially grateful to the researchers, administrators and staff of the NASA Astrobiology Institute, led by Carl Pilcher and Ed Goolish, for their enthusiastic support for this project and for all the work they do in the search for life in the universe.

## REFERENCES

Arslan, B.K., Boyd, E.S., Dolci, W.W., Dodson, K.E., Boldt, M.S., & Pilcher, C.B. (2011). Workshops without walls: Broadening access to science around the world. *PLoS Biol 9(8)*: e1001118.

Barrientos, F.A., Foughty, E.A., McIntosh, D.M. & Matthews, B.L. (2009). Bringing web 2.0 to government research: A case study. In *CHI '09 extended abstracts on human factors in computing systems* (CHI EA '09), 2899-2902.

Blackwell, A.F. (2015). HCI as an inter-discipline. In *CHI '15 extended abstracts on human factors in computing systems* (CHI EA '15), 503-516.

Chan, J., Dang, S. & Dow, S. (2016). Comparing different sensemaking approaches for large-scale ideation. In *Proceedings of the 2016 CHI conference on human factors in computing systems* (CHI '16), 2717-2728.

Chen, S., Arsenault, C., Gingras, Y., & Larivière, V. (2015). Exploring the interdisciplinary evolution of a discipline: The case of biochemistry and molecular biology. *Scientometrics 102(2),* 1307-1323.

Cleidson R.B., de Souza, C.R.B., Figueira Filho, F., Miranda, M., Pina Ferreira, R., Treude, C., & Singer, L. (2016). The social side of software platform ecosystems. In *Proceedings of the 2016 CHI conference on human factors in computing systems* (CHI '16), 3204-3214.

DiSalvo, C., Sengers, P., & Brynjarsdóttir, H. (2010). Mapping the landscape of sustainable HCI. In *Proceedings of the SIGCHI conference on human factors in computing systems,* (CHI '10), 1975-1984.

Dörk, M., Carpendale, S. & Williamson, C. (2011). The information flaneur: A fresh look at information seeking. In *Proceedings of the SIGCHI conference on human factors in computing systems* (CHI '11), 1215-1224.

Engel, D., Williams Woolley, A., Aggarwal, I., Chabris, C.F., Takahashi, M., Nemoto, K., Kaiser, C., Kim, Y.J., & Malone, T.W. (2015). Collective intelligence in computer-mediated collaboration emerges in different contexts and cultures. In *Proceedings of the 33rd annual ACM conference on human factors in computing systems* (CHI '15), 3769-3778.

Gowanlock, M.G., & Gazan, R. (2013). Assessing researcher interdisciplinarity: A case study of the University of Hawaii NASA Astrobiology Institute. *Scientometrics 94(1),* 133-161.

Green, C., Tollinger, I., Ratterman, C., Pyrzak, G., Eiser, A., Castro, L. & Vera, A. (2009). Leveraging open-source software in the design and development process. In *CHI '09 extended abstracts on human factors in computing systems* (CHI EA '09), 3061-3074.

Harmon, E., & Nersessian, N.J. (2008). Cognitive partnerships on the bench top: Designing to support scientific researchers. In *Proceedings of the 7th ACM conference on designing interactive systems* (DIS '08). ACM, New York, NY, USA, 119-128.

Hendry, D.G. (2004). Communication functions and the adaptation of design representations in interdisciplinary teams. In *Proceedings of the 5th conference on Designing interactive systems* (DIS '04). ACM, New York, NY, USA, 123-132.

Hooper, C.J., Millard, D., Fantauzzacoffin, J., & Kaye, J. (2013). Science vs. science: The complexities of interdisciplinary research. In *CHI '13 extended abstracts on human factors in computing systems* (CHI EA '13) 2541-2544.

Javadi, E., Mahoney, J., & Gebauer, J. (2013). The impact of user interface design on idea integration in electronic brainstorming: an attention-based view. *Journal of the Association for Information Systems 14(1),* 1–21.

Kim, J., Keegan, B.C., Park, S., & Oh, A. (2016). The proficiency-congruency dilemma: Virtual team design and performance in multiplayer online games. In *Proceedings of the 2016 CHI conference on human factors in computing systems* (CHI '16), 4351-4365.

Kim, S. (1990). Interdisciplinary cooperation. In Brenda Laurel and S. Joy Mountford (Eds.), *The art of human-computer interface design.* Addison-Wesley, 31-44.

Lee, C.P. (2007). Boundary negotiating artifacts: Unbinding the routine of boundary objects and embracing chaos in collaborative work. *Comput. Supported Coop. Work 16(3),* 307-339.

Liu, Y., Goncalves, J., Ferreira, D., Xiao, B., Hosio, S., & Kostakos, V. (2014). CHI 1994-2013: Mapping two decades of intellectual progress through co-word analysis. In *Proceedings of the SIGCHI conference on human factors in computing systems* (CHI '14), 3553-3562.

McCurdy, M., Connors, C., Pyrzak, G., Kanefsky, B., & Vera, A. (2006). Breaking the fidelity barrier: An examination of our current characterization of prototypes and an example of a mixed-fidelity success. In *Proceedings of the SIGCHI conference on human factors in computing systems* (CHI '06), 1233-1242.

Miller, L.J., Gazan, R., & Still, S. (2014). Unsupervised classification and visualization of unstructured text for the support of interdisciplinary collaboration. In *Proceedings of the 17th ACM conference on computer supported cooperative work & social computing* (CSCW '14), 1033-1042.

NASA Astrobiology Institute (2017). Retrieved March 16, 2017 from https://nai.nasa.gov/about/

NASA Astrobiology Institute (2017a). NAI Director's Discretionary Fund. Retrieved April 6, 2017 from https://nai.nasa.gov/funding/nai-directors-discretionary-fund/

NASA Astrobiology Institute (2017b). NAI Executive Council. Retrieved April 6, 2017 from https://nai.nasa.gov/executive-council/

Olson, J.S., & Olson, G.M. (2013). Working together apart: Collaboration over the internet. Springer.

Rhoten, D. (2003). A multi-method analysis of the social and technical conditions for interdisciplinary collaboration. Hybrid Vigor Institute report NSF BCS-0129573. http://www.ncar.ucar.edu/Director/survey/Rhoten_NSF-BCS.FINAL.pdf

Sawyer, K. (2004). Creative teaching: Collaborative discourse as disciplined improvisation. *Educational Researcher 33(2)*, 12–20.

Selvin, A.M., Buckingham Shum, S.J., & Aakhus, M. (2010). The practice level in participatory design rationale: Studying practitioner moves and choices. *Human Technology 6(1)*, 71-105.

Star, S.L., & Griesemer, J.R. (1989). Institutional ecology, 'translations' and boundary objects: Amateurs and professionals in Berkeley's Museum of Vertebrate Zoology, 1907-39. *Social Studies of Science 19(3)*, 387-420.

Tausch, S., Ta, S., & Hussmann, H. (2016). A comparison of cooperative and competitive visualizations for co-located collaboration. In *Proceedings of the 2016 CHI conference on human factors in computing systems* (CHI '16), 5034-5039.

Wang, D., Olson, J.S., Zhang, J., Nguyen, T, & Olson, G.M. (2015). DocuViz: Visualizing collaborative writing. In *Proceedings of the 33rd Annual ACM conference on human factors in computing systems* (CHI '15), 1865-1874.

# Do Games Make a Difference in the Crowdsourcing of Mobile Content?

**Dion Hoe-Lian Goh**
*Wee Kim Wee School of Communication and Information, Nanyang Technological University, Singapore.*
*ashlgoh@ntu.edu.sg*

**Chei Sian Lee**
*Wee Kim Wee School of Communication and Information, Nanyang Technological University, Singapore.*
*leecs@ntu.edu.sg*

**Ei Pa Pa Pe-Than**
*Institute for Software Research, School of Computer Science, Carnegie Mellon University eipa@cmu.edu*

**Alton Y.K. Chua**
*Wee Kim Wee School of Communication and Information, Nanyang Technological University, Singapore.*
*altonchua@ntu.edu.sg*

## ABSTRACT

**The layering of games over crowdsourcing tasks has increasingly become a viable approach to motivate participation in crowdsourcing projects. A crowdsourcing game utilizes entertainment to generate useful outputs as byproducts of gameplay. Since crowdsourcing relies on individuals' participation, understanding actual contribution patterns is an important area of research. However, this phenomenon has yet to be adequately investigated. In this paper, we build on our prior research to attempt to answer the question of whether a non-game-based mobile app for the crowdsourcing of location-based content would yield different types of contributions when compared against a game-based app. Our content analysis of 2,386 contributions in both apps reveals nine categories, divided into (1) those that provide information for navigational purposes or for others to learn about a specific place and (2) those that were meant for personal expressions related to the content creator or those around him/her with the location as a backdrop. The distribution of categories varied between the apps, indicating that the features afforded by the game shaped behavior differently from the non-game-based approach to crowdsourcing. Analysis of the contributions also suggests that the game-based app produced much higher informational content than the non-game-based one.**

## KEYWORDS

crowdsourcing games, mobile content, evaluation, content analysis, human computation.

## INTRODUCTION

Crowdsourcing utilizes online users to address specific problems and makes it possible to mobilize skills and expertise beyond the restrictions of time and space (Doan, Ramakrishnan & Halevy, 2011; Schenk & Guittard, 2011). In the domain of user-generated content, it has been utilized to populate information-rich environments. For example, crowdsourced mobile content, that is, using mobile devices to generate location-based content, include creating posts to describe locations of interest, providing reviews of businesses, as well as generating/verifying maps.

Crowdsourcing projects commonly employ volunteers or paid human experts. For the former, recruitment and retention are challenging since volunteerism is dependent on individuals' willingness to devote their time and effort to crowdsourcing projects (Yuen, Chen & King, 2009). Paying for expertise is thus an alternative and has yielded positive outcomes. However, paying for crowdsourcing work is potentially costly and this approach requires projects to be backed with adequate funding. Further, ascertaining appropriate monetary amounts to incentivize workers (Ipeirotis & Paritosh, 2011) as well as concerns of fraud (Thomsen, 2013) are challenges yet to be addressed adequately. Consequently, other motivational mechanisms to attract participants have been explored.

Here, a viable alternative is to layer computer games over crowdsourcing tasks as a means to recruit participants. Computer games offer some of the most intense, rich and engaging experiences of all interactive products and have seen tremendous growth over the years. Also known as human computation games, or crowdsourcing games, players contribute their time and effort to a given endeavor through enjoyable gameplay (Goh & Lee, 2011). For example, in the domain of crowdsourcing mobile content, players in Geo-zombie (Prandi, Salomoni, Roccetti, Nisi & Nunes, 2016) associate urban elements with categories from a predefined list and create new information, such as descriptions and photos, to earn points. These points are then exchanged for ammunition to shoot zombies that attack the players.

Crowdsourcing games have correspondingly attracted research interest, primarily focusing on game design issues (e.g., Tuite, Snavely, Hsiao, Tabing & Popovic, 2011), with relatively less work done on usage motivations (e.g., Han, Graham, Vassallo & Estrin, 2011) and player perceptions (e.g., Pe-Than, Goh & Lee, 2013). A significant research gap is that there is insufficient work done in investigating actual content creation patterns of crowdsourcing games. Understanding actual usage is essential for verifying the outcomes of design and perceptions research, for identifying challenges

80th Annual Meeting of the Association for Information Science & Technology, Washington, DC | Oct. 27-Nov. 1, 2017

that users face while using these applications as well as for ascertaining the quality of generated outputs. Further, the layering of games over crowdsourcing applications could modify usage behavior because of the entertainment component not found in non-game-based versions.

Of the few examples, Goh, Lee and Low (2012) conducted a content analysis of the contributions made in a mobile crowdsourcing game to uncover motivations for sharing, while Celino et al. (2012) found that the number of contributions in a mobile game for linking urban data was relatively high. However, one shortcoming of prior research is the lack of comparative analysis of contributions against other systems. Thus, would a non-game-based crowdsourcing app yield different types of contributions against a game-based app? Understanding the nature of crowdsourced content and differences across application types would translate into a better understanding of user behavior, leading to better designed applications that would benefit users and foster sustained usage.

We aim to address this research gap by fulfilling two objectives in the present study. First, we develop two crowdsourcing apps for mobile content creation: a game-based version that employs a virtual pet genre where players rescue pets, and a non-game version. Second, we compare both apps to shed light on actual usage patterns, focusing on the types of content created by users.

## RELATED WORK

### *Crowdsourcing Games*

Crowdsourcing games may be considered dual-purpose applications that perform tasks and offer entertainment concurrently. They rely on individuals' desire to be entertained to perform tasks as byproducts. These games are built on the premises of collective intelligence and that humans outperform their computing counterparts in certain tasks (Pe-Than, Goh & Lee, 2013).

The ESP Game (von Ahn & Dabbish, 2004) is a well-known example whose purpose is to label images, an activity that is considered difficult for computers to perform but easy for humans, although potentially tedious. In gameplay, two randomly paired players on the web are shown the same image. The game rule is that a player has to guess the words that might be used by his/her partner to describe a given image, and both players will be rewarded when their terms match. While being entertained, players produce labels as byproducts that can be harnessed to improve image search engine retrieval performance.

Although traditionally developed for web platforms, mobile crowdsourcing games have gained traction in the recent few years given the accessibility of content and services afforded by mobile devices. Such games allow players to perform crowdsourcing tasks anytime, anywhere. Location-based crowdsourcing games are typical examples that collect geospatial content about real-world locations. In Eyespy (Bell, Reeves, Brown, Sherwood, McMillan, Ferguson & Chalmers, 2009), players generate photos and texts of geographic locations to support navigation or creation of tourist maps. Players take pictures of locations and share them with others who then have to determine where these pictures were taken. Points are awarded for producing more recognizable images and for confirming the images of other players. This encourages players to create images of more popular and interesting locations. Tidy City (Wertzel, Blum & Oppermann, 2012) presents riddles that are displayed on a map. The player's task is to determine what real-world locations each riddle describes and verify it physically. Players are rewarded with points for solving riddles, and these solutions become descriptors for the corresponding locations.

Using OpenStreetMap data, Urbanopoly (Celino et al., 2012) challenges players to participate in mini-games in which information creation or verification tasks are embedded so they can conquer the venues and become rich landlords. As a byproduct of gameplay, players contribute geospatial data that is useful for other locative services. SPLASH employs a collaborative pet-based game genre to share location-based content (Pe-Than, Goh & Lee, 2014). In particular, locations are represented by pets, and players "feed" content so that they can evolve. The appearance of pets changes depending on the quality, quantity, recency and sentiment of content fed. The content associated with pets describes the respective locations and is accessible by other players. Finally, in GEMS (Geolocated Embedded Memory System; Procyk & Neustaedter, 2014), players document location-based stories for personal reflection and for future generations to find. Players receive directives from a game character. They can complete these directives by creating a memory record, which includes a combination of text, audio, photographs or video clips, to capture a particular experience and the place of origin. As players create records, they earn points and access tokens that can unlock secret information about the game character.

### *Understanding Usage Patterns*

As highlighted above, there is relatively little work done on understanding usage patterns in crowdsourcing games. UrbanMatch (Celino et al., 2012) is one of the few available. The game's aim is to find the most representative photos related to points of interest (POIs) in Milan. Players are presented with a photo of a POI from a trusted source, and they have to link it to other photos from non-trusted sources. If more players couple an untrusted photo with the trusted one, the former becomes a strong candidate to represent the POI. Based on the contributions of 54 players who tested 2006 links, 99.4% of links between a trusted source and untrusted source were found to be correct. Additionally, Bell et al. (2009) examined the images contributed in Eyespy (described earlier) to uncover nine categories including those relating to shops, signs and buildings. These categories were consistent with the game's purpose of generating content for aiding street navigation. The authors also compared the photos contributed in Eyespy against similar photos in Flickr, and they found that the former were more helpful for navigation.

Procyk and Neustaedter (2014) organized content contributed in GEMS into different axes including writing style (e.g., accounts of specific events or descriptions of a location's significance) and location type (e.g., public places, countries/cities, vehicles). Interviews with participants suggested that the act of creating and accessing stories in GEMS was useful in learning and connecting with the places being described. As well, Massung, Coyle, Cater, Jay and Priest (2013) compared three mobile crowdsourcing apps to collect data on shops for pro-environmental community activities. One app used points and badges as virtual rewards for data collected, another used financial incentives, while another served as a control without any incentives. Results suggest that the quality of the data collected was similar across all apps, but the app with financial incentives yielded the most data, followed by the app that used points and badges and, finally, the control.

An analysis of crowdsourced SPLASH content (Goh, Razikin, Chua, Lee & Tan, 2011) uncovered 15 categories of contributions ranging from food, emotions, places of interest as well as people. Interestingly, nearly 10% of the content was nonsensical in nature. Two possibilities were suggested, with one being that users were new to the game and were testing its functionality with short posts. However, another was that users attempted to "game" the system since contributing content earned points. This was verified by follow-up interviews where some users admitted to wanting to earn as many points as possible to either purchase in-game items and/or rise in rankings. Finally, in work that the present study builds upon, Goh, Pe-Than and Lee (2016) analyzed 3,024 comments created by two crowdsourcing apps for mobile content creation. One was a game-based app that required players to compete for pet ownership through content creation, while another was non-game-based. Ten categories of content were uncovered, with the game-based app producing more than double the number of contributions than the non-game-based version. The distribution of categories varied across the apps, indicating that the features afforded by games shape behavior differently from non-game-based approaches to crowdsourcing. However, this study was limited by its short usage duration of one day per participant. Hence, content categories may not be reflective of actual usage in the field.

## APPLICATIONS DEVELOPED

Two mobile apps for crowdsourcing location-based content were developed: Collabo, a collaborative crowdsourcing game; and Share, a non-game app. The reasons for developing our own apps were that we would have better control over the look-and-feel of the interfaces and easy access to the contributed content.

Both mobile apps share a similar purpose of crowdsourcing location-based content. The content model is based on an earlier crowdsourcing game we developed called SPLASH which is briefly described here. More details about SPLASH may be found in (Goh, Lee, Chua, Razikin & Tan, 2011). Crowdsourced content is referred to as "comments," comprising a title, tags, descriptions, media elements (e.g., photos) and ratings. SPLASH organizes comments on two levels: places and units. Places represent geographic points of interest such as buildings and parks, and each of these can be divided into more specific units, which hold the respective comments. For instance, if a mall is considered a place, a particular store within it will be one of its units containing comments. Both mobile apps offer a map-based interface to facilitate creation of, and access to, comments. Specifically, places are indicated by map markers in the shape of mushroom houses (see Figure 1). Each house has a number of units, and each unit contains the crowdsourced comments.

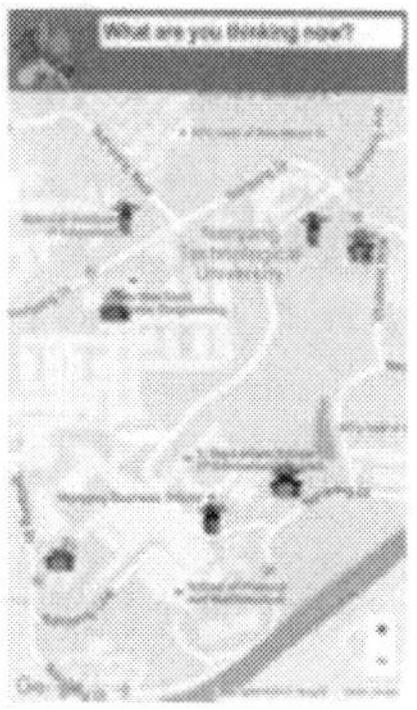

***Figure 1.*** *The map interface*

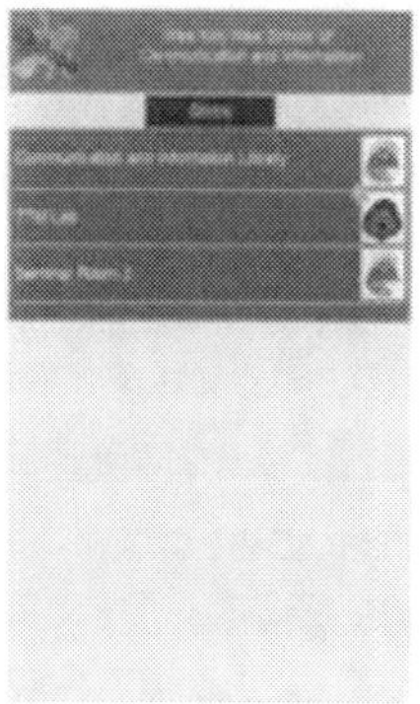

***Figure 2.*** *A list of pets where starving ones are marked with a star*

Returning to the two apps, Collabo is a virtual pet game that asks players to form a team with others to rescue starving pets that live in units within places. Once a place is selected, the game shows a list of pets, where starving ones appear sad and sickly (refer to Figure 2). To rescue a pet, players need to feed it with comments or rate comments created by others on a five-star scale. Pets being rescued are anchored by a star, which signals other players to join the rescue team. Once a pet is rescued, the game allocates an equal amount of points to the team members and displays a winning message (refer to Figure 3). Collabo differs from the original SPLASH in that the latter offers more features such as avatars, virtual chat rooms and mini-games. In the present study, we wanted to have a simpler game to make better comparisons against a non-game variant. This meant focusing only on the feeding of virtual pets and excluding the other game-based features of SPLASH. In doing so, both Collabo and Share (described next) would have one primary task of generating mobile content.

Share is a non-game-based mobile app for crowdsourcing content that serves as a control. It does not have any game elements and offers commonly found features for contributing and accessing mobile content. A user accesses comments by tapping on a mushroom house on the map, after which a list of units is presented. When a unit is selected, a list of comments associated with it is displayed (see Figure 4). Users can view and rate a comment by tapping on it. They can also create new comments by tapping on a button displayed in the top panel of each unit. Players are not awarded with any game points or rewards for their activities. Instead, they can view statistics such as the number of comments and ratings created.

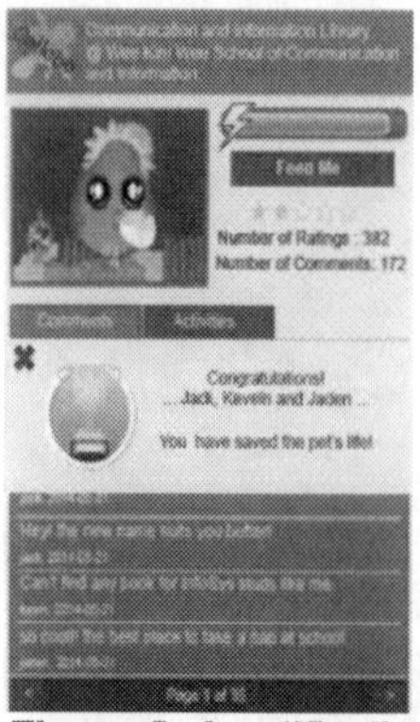

*Figure 3. A notification that a pet has been rescued*

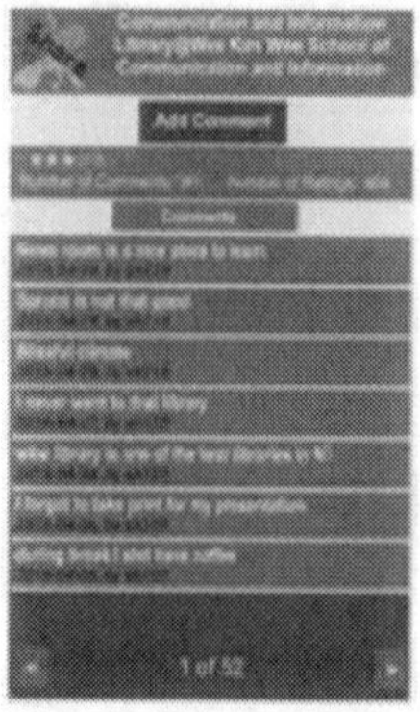

*Figure 4. A comment list in Share*

## METHODOLOGY

### Participants

A total of 46 participants were recruited from universities in Singapore. Of these, 16 were female. Their ages ranged from 21 to 35 years. Participants were from backgrounds such as computer science/information technology (17.39%), engineering (45.65%), while the remainder (36.96%) were from disciplines such as education, business, arts and social sciences.

In the sample, 60.87% used social network applications on their mobile phones while 41.30% used the location check-in features of such applications. The majority of participants (84.78%) stated that they used mobile phones to share multimedia information. Slightly above half of the participants (56.52%) had experience with online games, and 21.74% reported to be regular players.

### Procedure

Participants were divided into two groups, with half using Collabo and the other half using Share. To equalize the profiles, random assignment was used. Participants in each group were not told about the existence of the other group. Before the study began, participants attended a briefing session in which the concepts of crowdsourcing and mobile content sharing were first introduced. For each group, the usage of the respective application was then demonstrated, followed by a short practice session. In particular, to help participants better understand how each application worked, usage scenarios involving working together to rescue pets by feeding them with content (for Collabo), as well as creating, browsing and rating content (for Share) were presented.

The study then commenced, and participants could either use their own mobile phones or borrow ones from the researcher. Participants using their own phones had to ensure these phones met minimum requirements in terms of screen size and processor power to ensure a similar user experience. Within each group (Collabo or Share), participants were told to use their assigned application for seven days. Further, for each of the seven days, they were instructed to use the application at two specific time points for 30 minutes each: one at noon, and another in the evening. Beyond these time points, they were encouraged to use the application for as much as possible. To provide focus to the contributed content, participants were asked to create comments (or feed a starving pet in the context of Collabo) to describe places of interest so that other users could learn about these locations. In other words, contributed comments were to be meaningful, relevant and/or useful for others. In addition, to ensure a sufficient concentration of content and users, there were two prescribed areas where comments were to be created – at a local university or at a nearby shopping area.

### Analysis

At the end of the study, all comments created using the two mobile apps (Collabo and Share) were extracted, analyzed and coded via an iterative procedure common in content analysis (Neuendorf, 2002). The unit of analysis was a comment (i.e., contributed content). First, each comment was classified based on categories derived from related earlier studies (e.g., Goh, Pe-Than & Lee, 2016; Naaman, Boase & Lai, 2010). Next, for those not classifiable into these categories, we inductively constructed new categories by identifying similarities across entries and coding them into logical groupings (Heit, 2000). This addition of new categories required that entries that were previously categorized be reviewed to check if they needed to be reclassified. This process was repeated till all comments could be consistently categorized. Categories and their definitions were recorded in a codebook where they were fully explained to coders.

In the present study, two coders were independently involved in the content analysis procedure, and the intercoder reliability using Cohen's kappa was found to be .89 for Collabo and .83 for Share. These values are above the recommended average (Neuendorf, 2002).

## RESULTS

In total, 2,386 comments were contributed by our participants and analyzed. Of these, 1,477 were created using Collabo and 909 were created using Share. Interestingly, although participants in both groups were given the same set of instructions and tasks, there were significantly more crowdsourced contributions (62.5%) for Collabo than Share. The final set of nine categories derived is presented in Table 1 while their percentage distribution is shown in Figure 5. New categories that were uncovered in this study were "App-related" and "Complaints" and "Compliments." A description of these categories is presented in the following paragraphs, together with excerpts from relevant contributed comments.

| Category | Collabo (N=1477) | Share (N=909) |
|---|---|---|
| App-related | 3 (0.20%) | 20 (2.02%) |
| Complaints | 98 (6.64%) | 96 (10.56%) |
| Compliments | 284 (19.23%) | 192 (21.12%) |
| Humor | 3 (0.20%) | 15 (1.65%) |
| Provide information | 566 (38.32%) | 69 (7.59%) |
| Queries | 30 (2.03%) | 16 (1.76%) |
| Recommendations | 33 (2.23%) | 6 (0.66%) |
| Spam | 25 (1.69%) | 51 (5.61%) |
| Status Updates | 435 (29.45%) | 444 (48.44%) |

***Table 2.** Distribution of categories for contributed comments*

Notably, the category showing the greatest difference between the two apps was "Provide information," that is, comments that described or provided information about a specific location for the benefit of others. These locations were those that participants found interesting, meaningful or useful. A feature of these comments is that the tone was primarily objective or descriptive in nature. Personal opinions or subjective content were absent. In Collabo, it attracted the largest proportion of comments at 38.32%, while in Share, the proportion was only 7.59%. Here, the major types of comments shared included activities and events that are occurring, will occur or have occurred (*"there is a 1 for 1 offer at [café name] now"*, *"the student union is giving away goodie bags at the Canopy!"*) as well as those providing navigational information to a place of interest (*"the cafeteria is on the same level as Lee Wee Nam library"*, *"the nearby bus-stop has red/blue line, also 199"*). Another popular content type was more general and involved describing a particular location such as what could be found there (*"there is a cinema here"*, *"there's a rock climbing wall for all rock climbing enthusiasts"*), what could be done there (*"can buy sandwiches here"*, *"you can apply for supermarket membership here"*) and what was nearby (*"there are ATM machines near to the canteen"*, *"swimming pool nearby"*).

The category that attracted the largest proportion of comments for Share was "Status Updates" (48.44% of all contributions), and it was also the second largest category for Collabo (29.45%). Here participants treated both apps as a social media platform to share their thoughts and activities, much like Twitter and Facebook. A key distinction between this category and "Provide Information" is that comments were subjective and participants injected personal commentaries or opinions in the postings. Specifically, these were among the comments:

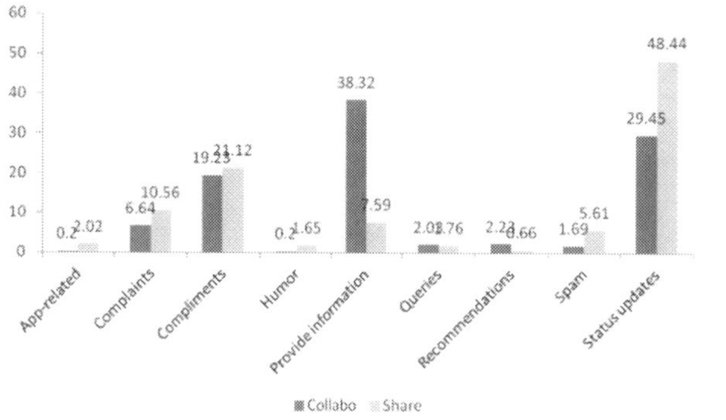


***Figure 5.** Percentage distribution of categories*

- How the participant feels. For example, an international student posted a series of comments while presumably studying in the library: *"I'm feeling sick," "terrible mood," "miss my home too."*
- What the participant is doing, did or will do, such as one who announced, *"I'm working in the library now,"* and another posted of a hairdresser *"may try the perm someday."*
- What the participant thinks, such as *"Wish I have enough money to buy vanilla ice latte :("* and *"cooking with friends so happy."*
- What the participant sees around him/her. For example, *"it's very crowded now as its dinner time"* was posted by a participant at a shopping mall restaurant, while conversely, another remarked about a different cafe *"this place is dead in the afternoons."*

The second largest category for both Collabo and Share was "Compliments," and both apps had similar proportions of comments (19.23% and 21.12%, respectively). This category involved providing positive remarks about a particular place. This may involve its attributes such ambience (*"very peaceful"* – to describe a building with a view), appearance (*"beautiful building construction"* – to describe a unique building in the university) and location (*"convenient place for students"* – to describe a mall's easy access to university students). Praise was also given to what was found at a particular place, such as the amenities and services provided (*"we have an excellent gymnasium"* – in praise of the university's facilities, and *"the staff here a very friendly"* – to describe the service attitude of staff at a cafe).

Comments critical of a particular place were categorized as "Complaints" but these were much fewer in number for both Collabo (6.64% of all contributions) and Share (10.56%). Similar to "Compliments," negative remarks were targeted at a place's ambience (*"the air conditioning needs to be controlled. it's freezing in the classrooms"*), as well as its amenities and services (*"the toilet is kinda dark wet. doesn't look good"* and *"Long queues everywhere so crowded... People hawking for seats"*). It should be noted that while "Compliments" and "Complaints" are commentaries or opinions about places, they are distinguished from "Status Updates" in that the former two categories focus on the place itself, while the latter focuses on the individual within a particular place.

The remaining categories had relatively small numbers of comments, but many were notable for their different contribution patterns. "Spam" was surprisingly one of the smallest categories across both apps, although in terms of percentages, Share (5.61%) had more than three times the number of comments than Collabo (1.69%). This category refers to comments with meaningless irrelevant content. We postulate that these comments were used as a means to make contributions to fulfill the study's requirements with as little effort as possible. Examples include "*done,*" "*I have nothing to say*" and "*I DONRHOW.TO PLOT SOCIAL LEARNING.CURVE.*"

"Queries" (2.03% for Collabo, 1.76% for Share) contained comments in which participants asked questions or requested assistance relevant to various locations. For example, a participant asked if a cafe ("*Spruce*") served lunch options, "*Can I get anything for lunch from spruce?*" while another asked about an additional charge for cold drinks in a supermarket ("*Prime*"), "*why does prime charge 15 cents for cold beverage???*" Interestingly, queries from Collabo participants garnered replies but those from Share did not. In response to the lunch question, one participant offered, "*@cb125... I doubt whether you could get something for lunch there.....maybe you can get a snack.*" As an answer to the query about cold drinks, another participant said, "*@cb128, not just in prime it's common in all supermarkets.*"

Complementing "Queries" is the "Recommendations" category, which comprised comments where users independently offered suggestions relevant to particular places or provided assistance in response to other participants' queries. In Collabo, such contributions constituted 2.03% of the dataset and this was much smaller for Share, at only 0.66% of the dataset. A majority of the suggestions involved what to eat and what to do, with examples such as a comment about a university building ("*Hive*") "*hive can be one of the best photo taking shots for graduation ceremony and wedding pictures!*", another about the use of a sports center "*If you wanna avoid crowds, come in the morning*" and one about a restaurant "*The bibimbap is a must try. its delecious and affordable.*"

Finally, other small categories of comments were "Humor" and "App-related." Jokes or humorous remarks were categorized as "Humor" (0.20% for Collabo, 1.65% for Share) and these were often related to a given location. Examples included "*one guy is burning books in the library, haha*" and "*Gonna buy some alcohol one day! After exams.*" Next, the "App-related" category contained contributions about the software or gameplay. In Collabo only 0.20% of all comments belonged to this category, while in Share, it attracted 2.02% of all comments. The small number of comments for Collabo came as a surprise since the expectation was that participants would post about their gameplay experiences or communicate with each other to discuss strategy. Examples of comments include "*almost forget to submit my comment...*", and "*a great pet APP.*"

## DISCUSSION

The results of our study showed that participants using Collabo created about 62% more comments (1,477) than those using Share (909). Since all participants underwent the same study procedure, were given the same instructions in terms of content creation and were randomly assigned the use the applications, it would indicate that our game-based approach to crowdsourcing mobile content could better motivate contributions than the non-game-based one. This finding is in agreement with prior work demonstrating that the enjoyment derived from gameplay encouraged further usage of crowdsourcing games (Pe-Tan, Goh & Lee, 2014).

Our analysis of the contributions showed that both apps yielded similar content categories, although their proportions differed, suggesting that the features afforded by games influence behavior differently from non-game-based approaches to crowdsourcing. Interestingly, when compared against Share, Collabo participants created more comments that conformed more to the notion of location-based content being utilized as a means to learn about a specific place or for navigational purposes (Yap, Bessho & Sakamura, 2012). This was in line with the instructions given to participants at the beginning of the study. Specifically, this referred to the categories of "Provide Information," "Complaints," "Compliments," "Recommendations" and "Queries." The focus of these categories was about describing various aspects of particular locations, which could be primarily objective, such as "Provide Information" ("*The admission for the exhibition is ticketed. Tickets can be purchased in the counter inside the building to enter the exhibition and museum*") or had elements of subjectivity as in the other categories ("*red line dropped me here. I have to wait for another*" - a comment referring to the same place as the museum exhibition).

Collectively, these categories constituted 68.45% of the total number of comments in Collabo and only 41.69% in Share. That is, participants using the game-based approach to crowdsourcing (Collabo) contributed more than two-thirds of the comments that conformed to the specifications of the study, while less than half of the contributions in the non-game-based approach (Share) did so. Put differently, the information content in Collabo was about 2.6 times that of Share. This would also suggest that game-based approaches to crowdsourcing location-based content seem to be more effective in generating potentially useful contributions in describing various aspects of places of interest.

In contrast, participants using Share contributed more comments that were about themselves or others situated in a location, rather than on the location itself. Put differently, participants treated Share as a mobile social media platform such as Twitter. Here, the focus was more on the individual or other people, and the location was less of an interest but becomes a backdrop for personal expression or sharing. Categories of comments comprised “App-related,” “Humor” and “Status Updates.” These constituted 52.70% for Share and 29.86% for Collabo. Consider for example comments about a café located in the university campus. A Collabo participant shared that the food and drinks were 10% cheaper than same stores off-campus, "*The [café name] drinks and pastry, etc. sold in NTU are considered cheaper than [café name] located outside NTU. The price is catered for the community in NTU with a 10% discount.*" On the other hand, a Share participant posted something more personal about the same café, "*Happiness is having coffee at Starbucks with friends.*"

We offer two plausible and related reasons for the different proportions of contributions between Collabo and Share. One, Collabo was social in nature, requiring participants to work together to achieve the objective of saving pets. Participants may have felt obliged to conform to the instructions of the study so as to either not let other players down or not be conspicuously noncompliant by deviating from the type of content to be posted. Conversely, contributions in Share were primarily a solo activity and participants probably did not feel the need to conform to any normative behavior. Thus, peer influence or the lack of, may have played in a part in the contribution patterns of both apps (Peng & Hsieh, 2012). The social nature of content creation afforded by Collabo is also reflected in the presence of interactions between participants who posted queries and those who responded to them, as noted above. Such interactions were non-existent in Share, and queries (such as "*anyone can share experiences of the game room inside?*") were left unanswered.

Two, the presence of incentives may have played a part as well. Collabo offered entertainment to motivate gameplay, keeping participants engaged in using the app. Beyond this, there was perhaps a sense of reciprocity among participants in that in exchange for such entertainment, they were more likely to adhere to the objectives of the study which was to create location based content for the benefit of others. Share however, did not offer any incentives to contribute content apart from a count of the number of posts made. Consequently, this could have led to a relative lack of engagement when compared with Collabo. This lack of engagement may then have translated into contributions that did not conform to the aims of the study. Instead, Share participants likely looked for an efficient way to complete the study. This came in the form of categories related to personal expression ("App-related," "Humor" and "Status Updates"). Unlike the categories that provided information about locations ("Provide Information," "Complaints," "Compliments," "Recommendations" and "Queries"), content in the former set of categories could be considered as less cognitively demanding since participants could draw from their personal experience, thoughts and feelings. Content in the latter set of categories required more effort to create because participants had to be familiar with what a particular place had to offer (FitzGerald, 2012).

Surprisingly, there was a low occurrence of "Spam"-related contributions in both apps, although Share had relatively more than Collabo (1.69% versus 5.61%). There are possibly two reasons for this. First, novelty effects due to the newness of the apps to participants could have played a role, especially for Collabo. This perhaps made participants less inclined to create spam comments. Second, the specific instructions given in the study about content creation (see above) may have influenced contribution patterns by giving participants a focal point. Even though Share participants generated more personal expressions, they were still centered around specific locations. Third, because of the flexibility in terms of content creation in both apps, there was not much of a need to create spam. Participants instead could use the app to express themselves in various ways, as reflected in the range of content categories uncovered. As highlighted previously, some participants used the apps as an alternative social media platform (Humphreys, Gill, Krishnamurthy & Newbury, 2013) to share whatever came to mind instead of posting meaningless or irrelevant content.

Finally, interesting findings can be gleaned in terms of content quality. Our past research suggested that while games make crowdsourcing tasks more enjoyable, and people prefer to use them over non-game-based applications, the resulting contributions may not be of high quality. For instance, in the case of image tagging (Goh & Lee, 2011), game-based approaches yielded lower quality tags when compared to a non-game-based application. In the case of location-based content creation (Goh, Pe-Than & Lee, 2016), participants using a game generated more contributions with personal expressions than informational ones. They also created significantly more app-related content in an apparent bid to efficiently meet the requirements of the study. In contrast, the present study provides evidence to the contrary, that participants using Collabo generated contributions with higher informational content, which was the expressed intent of the study. This could indicate that more potentially useful content was created than those using Share.

There are a couple of possibilities to account for this difference in contribution patterns. First, past studies were short in duration, lasting for a single session, and for a day or less. In the present study, which lasted for a week, participants were better able to familiarize themselves with their respective apps, gain an understanding of what they could do with them and settle into a more stable content creation rhythm. Thus, we contend that our current results may be more reflective of contribution patterns. Second, the present study provided more focus to participants through specific instructions encouraging them to create informational content, while past studies did not. Although we did not monitor contribution patterns nor inject periodic reminders once participants began the study, the initial instructions appeared sufficient to steer those using Collabo better than Share.

Nevertheless, the categories related to personal expressions may meet other needs beyond those informational categories for navigation and knowledge acquisition (Wiener, Buchner & Holshcer, 2009). Prior research has demonstrated that people use crowdsourcing games to meet various needs apart from information seeking and sharing (Lee, Goh, Chua &

Ang, 2010). This includes the expression of one's thoughts and feelings, influencing how others view oneself, building new and/or maintaining existing social relationships and killing time. Set in this context, the various forms of personal expressions may fulfill needs such as "App-related" content for competitive gameplay or killing time and "Status Updates" and "Humor" for self-expression or self-presentation. This ability by Collabo and Share to meet information as well as other types of needs may bode well for recruiting and sustaining participation for the longer term.

## CONCLUSION

In this paper, we extend work in understanding perceptions and behaviors of crowdsourcing games by analyzing the content created by users of two mobile apps, a collaborative mobile game (Collabo) and a non-game version (Share), for generating mobile content. The following implications may be drawn, arising from our findings.

First, although games may provide enjoyment and encourage participation better than non-game applications, the contributions may not always conform to the intended goal of the crowdsourcing task. Our findings showed that a respectable 68.45% of all contributions conformed to the specifications of the study. However, this meant that about 31% of the contributions did not. Here perhaps, the layering of a game alters users' behaviors as they respond to the excitement and challenge of accomplishing its objectives (Goh & Lee, 2011). Consequently, the actual crowdsourcing objective potentially becomes secondary. Second, people participate in crowdsourcing for many reasons (Brabham, 2012), and some of these motivations may not always align with the objectives of the project. The use of games may introduce or augment unintended motivations, such as self-expression, self-presentation or socializing, as revealed in our study. These could further distract participants from the original crowdsourcing effort. Nevertheless, these motivations may also serve as a means to attract new users and sustain existing ones. Third, games can attract participation in crowdsourcing tasks in a couple of ways: (1) the availability of content that is of higher quantity and quality over non-game-based alternatives as demonstrated in our study and described earlier; and (2) better engagement due to the offering of entertainment in exchange of task completion.

In terms of practical implications, our work suggests that in the quest to implement crowdsourcing games that are enjoyable to attract participation, developers need to be mindful of incorporating mechanisms that facilitate the production of useful contributions. One approach is to incorporate quality control mechanisms (e.g., ratings, reviews and reporting abuse) as well as player reputation systems that emphasize quality of contributions. Another possible way is via concerted messaging that stresses the intended goal of the crowdsourcing game so that players are fully aware of their primary objective during gameplay, which is to produce useful contributions while having fun at the same time. This approach has been reported to be effective in prior work (Kaufman, Flanagan & Punjasthitkul, 2016). A second practical implication is to consider providing support to accommodate players' various motivations beyond content sharing. This includes features for building communities where relationships can be established, categorization of contributions to facilitate future access, as well as customization of player profiles to support self-presentation.

Although this study has yielded useful insights, there are some shortcomings that could limit the generalizability of our findings. The first concerns the profile of our participants, who were recruited from Singapore universities and within a relatively young age range. Outcomes could differ with participants from other backgrounds such as those with different age groups or who are working adults. Additionally, our crowdsourcing game was based on a collaborative virtual pet genre with a particular set of rules and objectives which may have influenced the perceptions and behaviors of our participants. Investigating other game genres would be useful to ascertain if the contribution patterns uncovered in this study are stable. Finally, the present study employed content analysis as the primary research method. Triangulating with other methods such as surveys or interviews with participants would be another fruitful area of future work.

## ACKNOWLEDGEMENTS

This work was supported by MOE/Tier 1 grant RG64/14.

## REFERENCES

Bell, M., Reeves, S., Brown, B., Sherwood, S., McMillan, D., Ferguson, J., & Chalmers, M. (2009). Eyespy: Supporting navigation through play. *Proceedings of the SIGCHI conference on human factors in computing systems*, 123-132.

Brabham, D.C. (2012). Motivations for participation in a crowdsourcing application to improve public engagement in transit planning. *Journal of Applied Communication Research*, 40(3), 307-328.

Celino, I., Cerizza, D., Contessa, S., Corubolo, M., Dell'Aglio, D., Valle, E.D., & Fumeo, S. (2012). Urbanopoly--A social and location-based game with a purpose to crowdsource your urban data. *Proceedings of the 2012 international conference on privacy, security, risk and trust (PASSAT) and social computing (SocialCom)*, 910-913.

Doan, A., Ramakrishnan, R., & Halevy, A.Y. (2011). Crowdsourcing systems on the world-wide web. *Communications of the ACM*, 54(4), 86-96.

FitzGerald, E. (2012). Creating user-generated content for location-based learning: An authoring framework. *Journal of Computer Assisted Learning*, 28(3), 195-207.

Goh, D.H., Lee, C.S., & Low, G.H. (2012). I played games as there was nothing else to do: Understanding motivations for using mobile content sharing games. *Online Information Review*. 36(6), 784-806.

Goh, D.H., Razikin, K., Chua, A.Y.K., Lee, C.S. & Tan, K.T. (2011). Understanding sharing location-based information in a mobile human computation game. *Proceedings of the 2011 international conference on internet of things and 4th international conference on cyber, physical and social computing*, 209-216.

Goh, D.H., Lee, C.S., Chua, A.Y.K, Razikin, K. & Tan, K.T. (2011). SPLASH: Blending gaming and content sharing in a location-based mobile application. *Proceedings of the 3rd international conference on social informatics*, 328-331.

Goh, D.H. & Lee, C.S. (2011). Perceptions, quality and motivational needs in image tagging human computation games. *Journal of Information Science*, 37(5), 515-531.

Goh, D.H., Pe-Than, E.P.P., & Lee, C.S. (2016). Crowdsourcing mobile content through games: An analysis of contribution patterns. *Proceedings of the 79th ASIS&T annual meeting*. Available at: https://www.asist.org/files/meetings/am16/proceedings/submissions/papers/35paper.pdf.

Han, K., Graham, E.A., Vassallo, D., & Estrin, D. (2011). Enhancing motivation in a mobile participatory sensing project through gaming. *Proceedings of the 2011 IEEE 3rd international conference on privacy, security, risk and trust (PASSAT) and social computing (SocialCom)*, 1443-1448.

Heit, E. (2000). Properties of inductive reasoning, *Psychonomic Bulletin and Review*, 7(4), 569-592.

Humphreys, L., Gill, P., Krishnamurthy, B., & Newbury, E. (2013). Historicizing new media: A content analysis of Twitter. *Journal of Communication*, 63(3), 413-431.

Ipeirotis, P.G. & Paritosh, P.K. (2011). Managing crowdsourced human computation: A tutorial. *Proceedings of the 20th international conference companion on world wide web*, 287-288.

Kaufman, G., Flanagan, M., & Punjasthitkul, S. (2016). Investigating the impact of 'emphasis frames' and social loafing on player motivation and performance in a crowdsourcing game. *Proceedings of the 2016 CHI conference on human factors in computing systems*, 4122-4128.

Lee, C.S., Goh, D.H., Chua, A.Y.K., & Ang, R.P. (2010). Indagator: Investigating perceived gratifications of an application that blends mobile content sharing with gameplay. *Journal of the American Society for Information Science and Technology*, 61(6), 1244-1257.

Massung, E., Coyle, D., Cater, K.F., Jay, M., & Preist, C. (2013). Using crowdsourcing to support pro-environmental community activism. *Proceedings of the SIGCHI conference on human factors in computing systems 2013*, 371–380.

Naaman, M., Boase, J., & Lai, C.H. (2010). Is it really about me? Message content in social awareness streams. *Proceedings of the 2010 ACM conference on computer supported cooperative work*, 189-192.

Neuendorf, K. A. 2002. *The content analysis guidebook*, Sage Publications: Thousand Oaks, CA.

Pe-Than, E.P.P., Goh, D.H. & Lee, C.S. (2013). A typology of human computation games: An analysis and a review of current games. *Behavior and Information Technology*, 34(8), 809-824.

Pe-Than, E.P.P., Goh, D.H., & Lee, C.S. (2014). Making work fun: Investigating antecedents of perceived enjoyment in human computation games for information sharing. *Computers in Human Behavior*, 39, 88-99.

Peng, W. & Hsieh, G. (2012). The influence of competition, cooperation, and player relationship in a motor performance centered computer game. *Computers in Human Behavior*, 28, 2100-2116.

Prandi, C., Salomoni, P., Roccetti, M., Nisi, V., & Nunes, N.J. (2016). Walking with Geo-Zombie: A pervasive game to engage people in urban crowdsourcing. *International Conference on Computing, Networking and Communications*, 1–5.

Procyk, J. & Neustaedter, C. (2014). GEMS: The design and evaluation of a location-based storytelling game. *Proceedings of the 17th ACM conference on computer supported cooperative work & social computing*, 1156-1166.

Schenk, E. & Guittard, C. (2011). Towards a characterization of crowdsourcing practices. *Journal of Innovation Economics and Management*, 1(7), 93-107.

Thomsen, D. (2013). Solving wicked problems. In P. Michelucci (Ed.), *Handbook of human computation* (pp. 265-275). New York: Springer.

Tuite, K., Snavely, N., Hsiao, D.-Y., Tabing, N., & Z. Popović. (2011). PhotoCity: Training experts at large-scale image acquisition through a competitive game. *Proceedings of the 2011 SIGCHI conference on human factors in computing systems*, 1383-1392.

von Ahn, L. & Dabbish, L. (2004). Labeling images with a computer game. *Proceedings of the 2004 SIGCHI conference on human factors in computing systems*, 319-326.

Wetzel, R., Blum, L., & Oppermann, L. (2012). Tidy City: A location-based game supported by in-situ and web-based authoring tools to enable user-created content. *Proceedings of the international conference on the foundations of digital games*, 238-241.

Wiener, J.M., Buchner, S.J., & Holscher, C. (2009). Taxonomy of human wayfinding tasks: A knowledge-based approach. *Spatial Cognition and Computation*, 9(2), 152-165.

Yap, L.F., Bessho, M., & Sakamura, K. (2012). User-generated content for location-based services: A review. In A.A. Lazakidou (Ed.) *Virtual communities, social networks and collaboration* (pp. 163-179) New York, NY: Springer.

Yuen, M.-C., Chen, L.-J., & King, I. (2009). A survey of human computation systems. *Proceedings of the 2009 international conference on computational science and engineering*, 723-728.

# Effects of a Visual Representation of Search Engine Results on Performance, User Experience and Effort

**Roberto González-Ibáñez**
*Departamento de Ingeniería Informática, Universidad de Santiago de Chile, Chile. roberto.gonzalez.i @usach.cl*

**Verónica Proaño-Ríos**
*Departamento de Ingeniería Informática, Universidad de Santiago de Chile, Chile & Departamento de Ciencias Exactas, Universidad de las Fuerzas Armadas ESPE, Ecuador. veronica.proano @usach.cl*

**Gary Fuenzalida**
*Departamento de Ingeniería Informática, Universidad de Santiago de Chile, Chile. gary.fuenzalida @usach.cl*

**Gonzalo Martinez-Ramirez**
*Departamento de Ingeniería Informática, Universidad de Santiago de Chile, Chile. gonzalo.martinez@usach.cl*

## ABSTRACT

**Search engine results have been predominantly displayed as a vertical list of textual items. While this presentation approach has proven effective in well-known search engines, there are search tasks where users could benefit from other presentation styles. In this study, we compare two approaches to displaying search engine results. The first corresponds to a traditional one (vertical list) with 10 results per page, whereas the second one consists of a visual representation of 400 results displayed at once. We perform this comparison in the context of a recall-oriented search task where multiple relevance criteria must be satisfied. Our study focuses on the effects of the two representation approaches on performance, user experience and effort. Results from this study suggest that exposing participants to a large number of search results using adequate visual cues helps to reduce visual and physical effort without compromising to a great extent performance and user experience. More importantly, the exposure to a large volume of results does not increase cognitive load, nor worsen affective experience.**

## KEYWORDS

search engine results, visualization, user experience, performance, effort

## INTRODUCTION

For more than half a century the common approach to displaying results from an information retrieval (IR) system has been a vertical list. In the web era, modern search engines have adopted this presentation style in what is known as search engine results page (SERP). A SERP is often characterized by a list of 10 (by default) or more results per page. In this list, each result consists of a page title, URL and a text summary of query terms in context. While other presentation styles have been explored, vertical lists have proven effective in general-purpose search engines.

Despite the effective and predominant usage of vertical lists, this display approach may not be suitable for all kinds of search tasks. For instance, search engines are quite good for factual information search tasks. Indeed, these systems typically respond rather well to users' queries by placing relevant results – according to some ranking algorithm - in the first positions of the list. In some cases, users can even find the answers they look for directly from the document surrogates provided in the list. On the other hand, in more complex tasks, such as exploratory search, users must employ different strategies to find information. In such scenarios, traditional SERPs provide a partial view of the information space, which is often limited to the top $k$ results derived from ranking algorithms. As a result, users typically need to formulate several queries, visit various pages, engage in multiple search sessions and spend extended periods of time before their information needs are met, if they are. To better illustrate this type of search tasks, consider the following three examples: (1) a user looking for a product that has a good reputation, uses state-of-the-art technology and is the cheapest among its kind; (2) a journalist writing a news article about an environmental disaster. He has to find reliable and accurate information (i.e., articles, media, etc.) about the earliest and the most recent events involving the entities taking part in the disaster; and (3) an educator gathering material for students of a particular class. The material must be reliable and accurate, fresh, and it has to match students' reading skills.

Exploratory search is often characterized by high levels of uncertainty. Under this scenario, users may not be able to formulate appropriate queries to express their needs because they may not have a clear understanding of the problem itself. It may also be the case that users have a reasonable understanding of their real need (Mizzaro, 1998), but it could be unfeasible for them to express this need into queries that can be processed by a search engine. In this type of search tasks, users may use a variety of implicit and explicit evaluation criteria to determine whether an information object is useful or relevant to them. Such criteria can be complex (e.g., multidimensional) and search interfaces may not provide adequate tools to help users in the navigation and filtering of a large volume of information.

80th Annual Meeting of the Association for Information Science & Technology, Washington, DC | Oct. 27-Nov. 1, 2017

It has been stated that adequate interfaces could ease users' search processes, especially when query formulation is an obstacle (Fu et al., 1998). Examples include faceted search interfaces (e.g., Yee et al. (2003), Capra, (2007)) and visualization of search results (e.g., Hearst (1995), Spoerri (1993; 2007)). These approaches in some cases have been positively evaluated in terms of usability (Hearst et al., 2002), but not necessarily regarding performance. While the majority of these display approaches often rely on both text and organization strategies, few rely primarily on visual cues. In this regard, to what extent the visualization of search results could help to reduce cognitive, physical and visual effort, improve affective experience and performance and leverage visual intelligence, is an open research problem.

In this study, we propose an approach to displaying search results using a variety of visual cues derived from quantitative measures (i.e., search engine ranking, readability, freshness, reputation) that help in the characterization of information objects. The interface is capable of displaying hundreds of results at once. Furthermore, it is designed for search tasks where multiple relevance criteria must be satisfied. Then, to address the above research problem, we designed an experiment to compare our visual representation of search engine results with a traditional one (text-based vertical list). We performed this comparison in the context of an exploratory search task, specifically during the selection and organization of information. We hypothesize that a visual representation of search results is better than a traditional one regarding performance ($H_1$), user experience ($H_2$) and effort ($H_3$).

Next, we present theoretical aspects and related work. Then we describe methodological aspects of this study. Following, we present our results. Finally, we conclude with a discussion of our findings, its implications and future work.

## BACKGROUND AND RELATED WORK

When users search for information online, search engine results offer a partial view of the whole information space of relevant information. In traditional search interfaces, results are typically presented in vertical lists with individual results expressed as text surrogates. Today, some search engines also use a technique called blended results, which combines text surrogates with images, videos and other sources. More recently, Google also displays semantic associations between results based on its Knowledge Graph.

Document surrogates may be the first approach of users to get a glance of what information might be relevant to them. Even in search tasks such as fact-finding, a surrogate may be enough to satisfy users' needs.

Despite the prevalent use of vertical lists and the effectiveness of text to communicate abstract ideas, the way surrogates are designed and how search results are displayed are active research areas (Koshman, 2006; Hearst, 2011). One challenge in this type of research is how to provide an informative surrogate, achieve good information exposure and not to fall into information overload. In this regard, information visualization appears as a plausible alternative to address this particular challenge. The primary objectives of information visualization are the rapid assimilation of information and the possibility to handle a large volume of data (Card et al., 1998)

In the context of information search and retrieval, Hearst (2011) refers to different types of visualization approaches such as boolean syntax, representation of query terms within retrieved documents and visual representations for text mining. In the mid-1990s various scholars explored visualization techniques to represent search results. For instance, Mann (1999) presents different alternatives to visualize search results in a bi-dimensional space. These representations vary according to the level of complexity of the information being displayed. Likewise, Sebrechts et al. (1999) conducted an evaluation to compare the visualization of search results in two and three dimensions. Results from this study showed that the tridimensional display (a sphere) was useful when exploring a large volume of information. This visualization was also found to be easy to use by users when accessing the different elements and checking the relations among them. Later, Nguyen et al. (2006) presented *WebSearchViz*, an interactive visualization system designed to ease the navigation and exploration process of users using the solar system as an analogy (i.e., query as the Sun and planets as the documents). According to the authors, users performed better with *WebSearchViz* than with a traditional interface. Likewise, Spoerri developed different visualization tools such as *InfoCrystal* (Spoerri, 1993) and *MetaCrystal* (Spoerri, 2006). Some of his results showed that novice users could be benefited by visual cues to determine whether a document is relevant or not. Other contributions in this area include *CubanSea* (Tilsner et al., 2009), VIBE (Koshman, 2005), and Periscope (Cellary et al., 2004).

Besides studies focused on performance and usability, as perceived by the users, some have studied search engine results presentation styles through eye-tracking technology. For example, Joachims et al. (2005) found that users' behavior in Google was influenced by the ranking of results, where users' attention was strongly biased toward the first positions of the results list. However, almost a decade later, Maynes et al. (2014) found that users exhibit different patterns in the interaction with Google's SERPs. This was explained by aspects such as the resources that Google introduced on its search interface over the years and the possibility that such resources can be located in different places on the interface. More recently, Wittek et al. (2016) found, among other aspects, that users do not attend to all results when the task is perceived as difficult.

At a more general level, Rayner (2009) analyzed cognitive processes in complex tasks such as reading and visual search. The authors focused on fixations (time that eyes remain still in a given position) and saccades (rapid eye movements between fixations). According to Rayner, the amount of information processed in each fixation varies according to the type of task. In particular, he found that fixations and saccadic movements are greater in visual scenes than in reading. Additionally, results showed that when tasks become more difficult, fixations become larger, and saccades are shortened.

Finally, in addition to tools and studies conducted for research purposes, different tools and systems for visualizing search results have been developed for commercial and non-commercial purposes (e.g., *Zakta*[1], *oSkope*[2]). For instance, *oSkope* allows users to display search results from services such as Amazon and Flickr through different visualization styles (e.g., grid, pile, stack, etc.). Through *oSkope* one could quickly find a product based on two combined criteria (e.g., price and sales rank).

This sample of studies and developments illustrates various attempts and approaches to visualize search results. Despite their pros and cons, which may depend on the context and the type of information being displayed, ultimately it may also depend on the users themselves. In this sense, it is important to consider that users may have different types of intelligence and in turn different skills and ways to understand the world (Gardner, 1983).

## METHOD

To test our hypotheses, we conducted a controlled experiment to compare the two representations styles (i.e., traditional and visual). This section provides a detailed description of the study design, search task, participants and instrumentation that was devised for this research.

### Study Design

Our user study is based on a crossover experimental design. This design allows the exposure of users to both the traditional and visual representations with alternate orders. Then, within- and between-subjects comparisons can be performed. This design also let us control for some confounding factors (e.g., learning and tiredness). In this study, our independent variable corresponds to the representation style of search results, which has two levels: traditional (T) and visual (V). On the other hand, three groups of dependent variables are studied, namely: performance, user experience and effort.

According to this design, we defined two groups or sequences. In the first group ($T_1$-$V_2$) users performed a search task using first the traditional representation ($T_1$) followed by the visual one ($V_2$). Conversely, users in the second group ($V_1$-$T_2$) began with the visual representation ($V_1$) and finalized with the traditional one ($T_2$). In both groups, users performed the same search task varying the document collection for the first ($et_1$) and second ($et_2$) exposure time.

To encourage participants to perform well in the study, we adopted a competition approach used in previous studies (e.g., Shah et al. (2011)). Specifically, we offered a token of appreciation to the best performing users.

### Evaluation Framework and Instruments

As stated above, we focused our study on the effects of the two representation styles (i.e., traditional and visual) on performance, user experience and effort. Each of these aspects represents a group of dependent variables.

#### Performance

Performance is expressed in terms of precision (Eq.1), recall (Eq.2) and F1-Measure (Eq.3), which are computed from a user's perspective based on their information coverage (Shah et al., 2011).

$$Precision(u) = \frac{RelevantCoverage(u)}{Coverage(u)} \quad \text{(Eq.1)}$$

$$Recall(u) = \frac{RelevantCoverage(u)}{U_r} \quad \text{(Eq.2)}$$

$$F_1(u) = 2 * \frac{Precision(u) * Recall(u)}{Precision(u) + Recall(u)} \quad \text{(Eq.3)}$$

However, unlike Shah's et al. study, the search system used in this study consists of a close environment with known items (more details in the following sections). Therefore, some key measures in these equations are computed differently. First, *Coverage(u)* corresponds to the set of web pages collected and organized by user *u*. Second, *ur* (universe of relevant documents) corresponds to the set of all relevant documents in the document collection. Finally, *RelevantCoverage(u)* is the set of all relevant web pages that user *u* was able to collect and organize correctly.

#### User Experience

We define user experience in terms of four dimensions, namely: usability, engagement, cognitive load and affective experience. We measure each of these dimensions through the following instruments: (1) usability through the Computer Usability Satisfaction Questionnaire (CUSQ) (Lewis, 1995); (2) engagement through the User Engagement Scale (UES) (O'Brien et al., 2013); (3) cognitive load through the NASA Task Load Index (NASA TLX) (Hart et al., 1988); and (4) affective experience through the Self-Assessment Manikin (SAM) (Bradley et al., 1994).

#### Effort

We focused on physical and visual effort. On the one hand, physical effort corresponds to actions performed through the body to interact with search results. We operationalize physical effort as the number of mouse actions, specifically clicks and scrolling. On the other hand, visual effort corresponds to the visual demand that a given representation style requires to locate and process search results. We operationalize visual effort as the number of eye fixations, fixation duration, number of saccadic movements, length of saccades, pupil size and fixations density (Henderson & Hollingworth, 1999) on a particular area of interest (AOI). The latter is computed as the ratio between the number of eye fixations and the AOI expressed in square centimeters (Eq.4).

[1] http://marketing.zakta.com/

[2] http://www.oskope.com/

$$\rho = \frac{\#fixations}{AOI} \qquad \text{(Eq.4)}$$

Data to compute these measures were captured with The Eye Tribe eye tracker. Despite being a low-cost device, with proper calibration and settings, the quality of the data provided by this instrument can be comparable to that of more precise and expensive tools (Ooms et al., 2015). We used this device to track participants' eye movements at 60Hz on a 24" screen with a resolution of 1920x1080 pixels.

### Search Task

Overall, we studied two specific tasks: selection-organization of relevant documents and synthesis; however, this article focuses on the first one. As a topic, we chose the British Petroleum (BP) oil spill that occurred in the Gulf of Mexico in 2010. This topic and subtopics about (1) effects on wildlife, (2) areas affected, (3) mitigation plans and (4) responsibilities, has been used in previous information seeking studies (e.g., Shah et al., 2011).

To make the search scenario more realistic, we contextualized the task in an asynchronous collaborative search process inspired in role-based models like those studied by Pickens et al. (2008) and Shah et al. (2010). Specifically, participants were instructed to select and organize relevant information from a list of documents. These documents were previously obtained by a fictitious collaborator who issued several queries targeting information about the four subtopics listed above. To properly select and organize relevant documents into the four subtopics, participants must apply the following combination of relevance criteria:

1. *Effects on wildlife*: documents with the highest ranking and the highest readability score (easy to read)
2. *Areas affected*: documents with the highest readability score (easy to read) and the highest reputation
3. *Mitigation plans*: oldest documents with the lowest readability score (difficult to read)
4. *Responsibilities*: most recent documents with the highest reputation

### Document Collection

Previous studies using the BP oil spill search task allowed participants to search for information on the open web using any search engine. In our case, we developed our own document collection to use it in a closed search environment. Overall, the collection used in this study consists of 800 documents grouped into four general queries linked to the subtopics mentioned above. The complete set of documents includes both non-relevant and relevant ones, where the latter are classified based on their topical relevance to one or more subtopics (e.g., relevant to subtopic 1 and 3).

To build this collection we used a total of seven queries – related to the four subtopics – on the Google search engine. We also used the Google Chrome extension *MozBar* to obtain the list of results per query and a set of features for each document (e.g., document title, URL, snippet and the number of incoming links). Following, we download full websites from the URLs in the list obtained with *MozBar*. Overall, 1565 webpages were collected, but several were removed after a cleaning procedure.

In addition to the data provided by *MozBar* for each document, we computed their readability score. Note that these features relate to the selection criteria specified for the subtopics in the task. Below we provide a list of the features specified for each result.

- *Ranking* corresponds to the position of a document in a SERP according to the search engine ranking.
- *Publication date* corresponds to the date in which a document was published or most recently updated (freshness). This data was obtained directly from each document.
- *Readability Score* refers to the expected difficulty to read a document. We measured readability through an adaptation of the Flesch Reading Ease (Fernández-Huerta, 1959) for the Spanish language. The higher the score of a text (in a scale of 0-100), the easier to read it.
- *Reputation* is defined as the external perception and reach of an information object. We operationalized the reputation of a document as the number of incoming links from external sources.

We systematically assigned documents to two sets. Each set consists of 400 documents, 100 per subtopic. Note that these two sets relate to the two-exposure time in our study design ($et_1$:$T_1/V_1$; $et_2$:$T_2/V_2$). Finally, from each set, we selected 10 relevant documents per subtopic. This selection considers both topical relevance and the selection criteria specified for the four subtopics. As a result, 10% of the documents in the collection is relevant.

### Participants

We recruited 20 volunteers for this study. Each participant was randomly assigned to sequence $T_1$-$V_2$ or $V_1$-$T_2$ until having 10 users per group. Seven participants were women and 13 were men. One participant was left-handed and the remaining ones were all right-handed. On average, participants were 23.9 (SD=1.83) years old. The majority (90%) of the participants were undergraduate or graduate students from different engineering areas. The remaining 10% were from humanities and other science-related fields. Finally, 80% of the participants declared using Microsoft Windows as their primary operating system and 65% used Google Chrome as default Web browser.

### System

To carry out the study we developed SERVS (Search Engine Results Visualization System). This system is capable of displaying search results in two different ways: a vertical list (traditional approach) and a visual representation. The design of our traditional representation (Figure 1a) mimics the interface of Google, Bing and other general-purpose search engines. The interface follows the standard of listing 10 results per page. However, some differences must be highlighted: (1) the search box is replaced by four tabs with predefined queries (related to the four subtopics); (2) once a result is clicked, the webpage is opened in a new tab in the web browser; (3) webpage surrogates consist of page title, URL, snippet, publication date, ranking, readability score and reputation; (4) a tool for ordering results in ascending or descending order, according to the selection criteria, is provided; and (5) each result in the list has colorized checkboxes on the left side to let users classify relevant documents in each group.

Second, the design of our visual representation (Figure 1b) was the result of an iterative process in which four visualization prototypes were tested. These prototypes used four visualization techniques available in the *D3.js* library, namely, circle packing, bubble chart, collapsible indented tree and treemap. From these four visualization styles, the one that allowed us to best illustrate document features using visual cues, as the primary resource, was bubble chart with a spiral order. In this visual representation, a search result is represented by a plain circle (bubble). Its appearance is modified based on the particular properties of the result (i.e., ranking, publication date, reputation and readability score). From these properties, the only one that is explicitly presented in text format is the reputation value, which is displayed within the circle as a normalized score (0-100). The remaining features are used as follows:

(a)

(b)

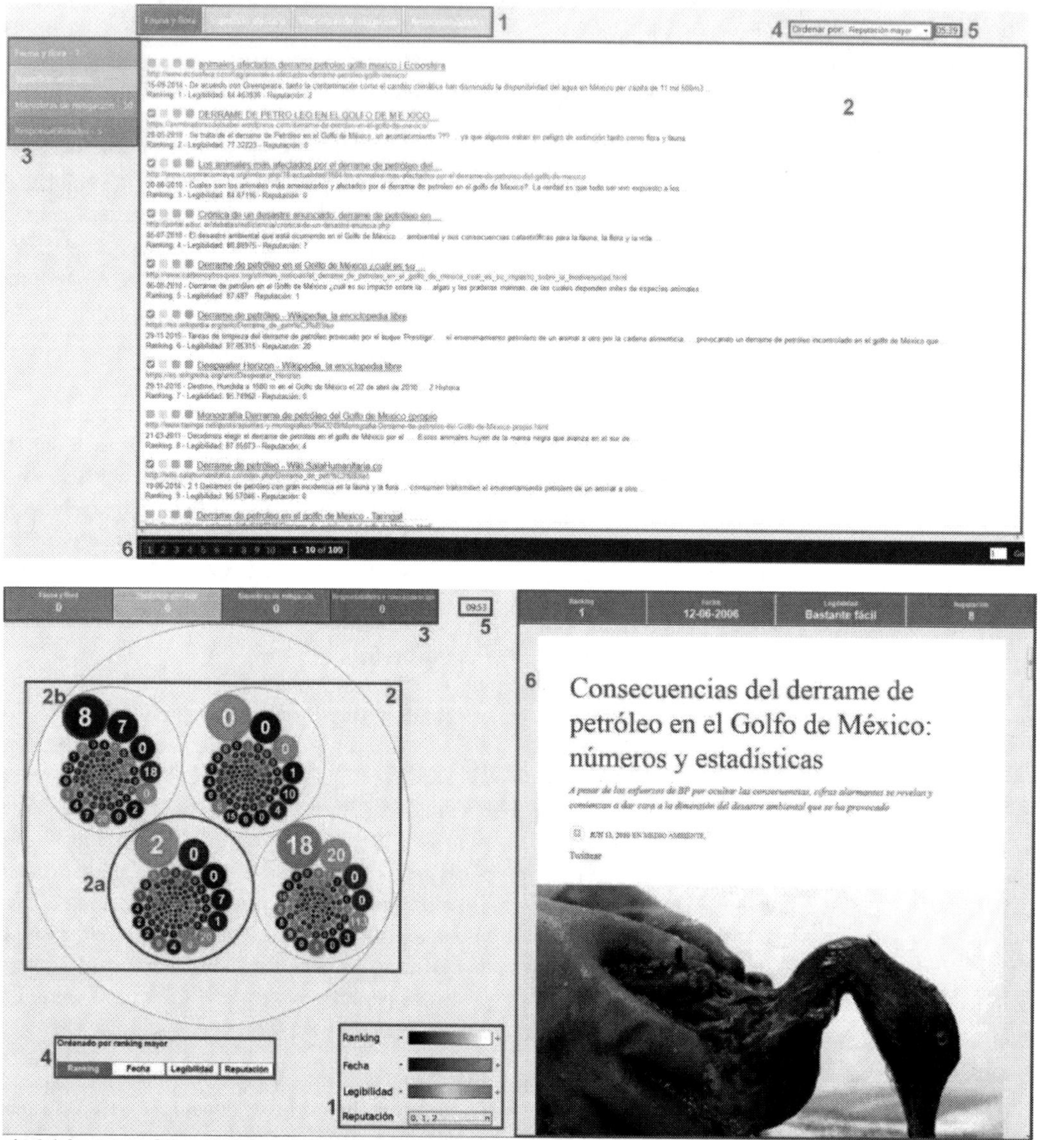


***Figure 1:*** *(a) Layout of the traditional (T) representation interface. (1) Query area, (2) search results area, (3) subtopics with users' selected documents, (4) ordering dropdown list, (5) remaining time, and (6) SERPs navigation bar*
*(b) Layout of the visual (V) representation interface. (1) Interface legend, (2) search results area, (2a) query container, (2b) search result, (3) subtopics with users' selected documents, (4) ordering options, (5) remaining time, and (6) webpage content container with key features on top*

- *Ranking* is used to set the text color property (in a gray scale) of the number in the center of the circle. In this scale, white color represents the highest ranking, whereas black represents the lowest one.
- *Publication date* is used to set the background color property (in a blue scale) of the circle representing a search result. In this scale, light blue represents documents recently published, whereas dark blue represents the old ones.
- *Readability score* is used to set the border-color property (in a green-red scale) of the circle representing a search result. In this scale, green represents documents that are easy to read, whereas red represents documents that are difficult to read.

Besides the manipulation of these visual properties, the size of circles changes according to the ordering options provided to users (AOI 4). Therefore, the size of circles is not tied to a single feature. Instead, it acts as a complement of other visual cues.

Given the little space required to represent a search result, this visualization approach allows displaying hundreds of results at once. The four queries are represented as big circles, each containing 100 results. Furthermore, enough space is left to display a full webpage on the right side of the screen once a result is clicked. Note that based on our task design, users could select a page as relevant according to the combined criteria specified above without having to visit the actual page. Still, additional details of the search result can be obtained by hovering the mouse over a circle.

The visual interface also provides four containers (one per subtopic) where users can drag and drop individual results when selecting a document as relevant. Moreover, like in the traditional interface, users can choose to display search results in ascending or descending order according to the four criteria.

Finally, in addition to the two representation styles, SERVS also implements a session workflow that semi-automatically guides participants through the study, it controls time, and administers electronic versions of the CUSQ, UES, SAM and NASA TLX questionnaires.

### Session Workflow

Overall, sessions consisted of a total of 31 steps in approximately 73 minutes. We now focus on the selection-organization stage and describe key steps for the proper understanding of this study. First, participants were introduced to the study. Second, they proceeded to read and sign a consent form. Third, the eye tracker was calibrated for each participant. Fourth, participants received instructions on how to use the first interface (traditional or visual depending on the interaction sequence) followed by a few minutes to practice on a task. Fifth, they completed pre-task questionnaires (mainly SAM). Sixth, they received a printed copy of the selection-organization task and they were allowed to work on it for 10 minutes. Seventh, post-task questionnaires were responded (i.e. SAM, NASA TLX, CUSQ, and UES). After the first task was completed, the same procedure, starting in the fourth step, was applied in the second interaction (traditional or visual depending on the sequence) was used. At the very end of sessions, participants were briefly interviewed focusing on their experiences and possible issues they found during their sessions.

## RESULTS AND DISCUSSION

This section presents results according to the evaluation framework introduced in the previous section. Our focus is on the effects of the two representations of search results on performance, user experience and effort. For each group of measures, we performed within- and between-subjects comparisons according to our crossover experimental design. Therefore, comparisons were performed either through paired t-test (pt), two-sample t-test (t2), Wilcoxon signed-rank test (ws) and Wilcoxon rank-sum test (wr), depending on the distribution of the data, which was tested with the Shapiro-Wilk test. Table 1 concentrates on the significant results described in the following subsections. Note that results in Table 1 are linked to the hypotheses stated in the Introduction section.

### Performance

To evaluate performance, we computed recall (Eq. 1), precision (Eq. 2) and F1-measure (Eq. 3) for each participant. As shown in Table 1, some differences were found between the visual and traditional representations for these three measures; however, these were not consistent across time. For instance, between-subjects comparisons revealed that recall was significantly higher ($p<.05$) in the traditional representation (Mdn=.25) than in the visual one (Mdn=.08) during $et_2$ ($V_2$ and $T_2$). However, such difference was not observed during $et_1$ ($V_1$ and $T_1$). Likewise, within-subjects comparisons for recall showed significant differences ($p<.05$) between the two representations, being higher for the traditional interface in the $T_1$-$V_2$ sequence. On the other hand, in the opposite sequence (i.e. $V_1$-$T_2$) differences were only marginally significant ($p\sim.05$). Despite the level of significance, one can see that medians and means were consistently higher for the traditional interface in all comparisons. Moreover, if we consider the second exposure time as a stabilization point where all the participants grasped the task, one could state that the traditional representation allowed better performance in terms of recall.

Regarding precision, a significant difference was observed only when contrasting $V_2$ and $T_2$. In this case, results were higher at $p<.05$ in the traditional representation (M=.56) than in the visual one (M=.30). Unlike recall, results for precision, regardless of their significance level, were not always higher for the traditional representation. For instance, during the first exposure time, precision in the visual representation (M=.44) was slightly higher than in the traditional one (M=.42).

Finally, F1-Measure was found to be significantly higher at $p<.05$ in $T_1$ (Mdn=.21) than in $V_2$ (Mdn=.12), which is mainly influenced by recall.

| Group | Measure | Between Subjects: V1 vs T1 | Between Subjects: V2 vs T2 | Within Subjects: V1 vs T2 | Within Subjects: T1 vs V2 | Between Subjects: T1 vs T2 | Between Subjects: V1 vs V2 |
|---|---|---|---|---|---|---|---|
| PERFORMANCE (H1) | Recall | wr=90.00 | **wr=77.00** | *ws=6.00* | **ws=43.50** | wr=91.50 | wr=120.00 |
| | | p=0.27 V1<T1 | **p=0.04** V2<T2** | *p=0.05* V1<T2* | **p=0.01** T1>V2** | p=0.32 T1<T2 | p=0.27 V1>V2 |
| | | $Mdn_{V1}$ = 0.14 (0.12) | **$Mdn_{V2}$ = 0.08 (0.15)** | *$Mdn_{V1}$ = 0.14 (0.12)* | **$Mdn_{T1}$ = 0.19 (0.13)** | $Mdn_{T1}$ = 0.19 (0.13) | $Mdn_{V1}$ = 0.14 (0.12) |
| | | $Mdn_{T1}$ = 0.19 (0.13) | **$Mdn_{T2}$ = 0.25 (0.16)** | *$Mdn_{T2}$ = 0.25 (0.16)* | **$Mdn_{V2}$= 0.08 (0.15)** | $Mdn_{T2}$ = 0.25 (0.16) | $Mdn_{V2}$ = 0.08 (0.15) |
| | Precision | t2=0.19 | **t2=-2.44** | pt=-1.36 | pt=2.05 | t2=-1.29 | t2=1.37 |
| | | p=0.85 V1>T1 | **p=0.03** V2<T2** | p=0.21 V1<T2 | p=0.07 T1>V2 | p=0.21 T1<T2 | p=0.19 V1>V2 |
| | | $M_{V1}$ = 0.44 (0.25) | **$M_{V2}$ = 0.30 (0.20)** | $M_{V1}$ = 0.44 (0.25) | $M_{T1}$ = 0.42 (0.22) | $M_{T1}$ = 0.42 (0.22) | $M_{V1}$ = 0.44 (0.25) |
| | | $M_{T1}$ = 0.42 (0.22) | **$M_{T2}$ = 0.56 (0.28)** | $M_{T2}$ = 0.56 (0.28) | $M_{V2}$ = 0.30 (0.20) | $M_{T2}$ = 0.56 (0.28) | $M_{V2}$ = 0.30 (0.20) |
| CUSQ (H2) | UX | t2=1.02 | wr=118.50 | pt=0.17 | **ws=0.00** | t2=-0.84 | wr=90.00 |
| | | p=0.32 V1>T1 | p=0.33 V2>T2 | p=0.87 V1>T2 | **p=0.00*** T1<V2** | p=0.41 T1<T2 | p=0.27 V1<V2 |
| | | $M_{V1}$ = 4.53 (1.01) | $Mdn_{V2}$ = 5.00 (1.27) | $M_{V1}$ = 4.53 (1.01) | **$Mdn_{T1}$ = 3.84 (1.50)** | $M_{T1}$ = 3.95 (1.50) | $Mdn_{V1}$ = 4.39 (1.01) |
| | | $M_{T1}$ = 3.95 (1.50) | $Mdn_{T2}$ = 4.18 (1.14) | $M_{T2}$ = 4.45 (1.14) | **$Mdn_{V2}$ = 5.00 (1.27)** | $M_{T2}$ = 4.45 (1.14) | $Mdn_{V2}$ = 5.00 (1.27) |
| | USE | t2=1.07 | wr=106.00 | pt=-0.35 | **ws=4.00** | t2=-1.26 | wr=88.00 |
| | | p=0.30 V1>T1 | p=0.97 V2>T2 | p=0.73 V1<T2 | **p=0.02** T1<V2** | p=0.23 T1<T2 | p=0.21 V1<V2 |
| | | $M_{V1}$ = 4.45 (0.98) | $Mdn_{V2}$ = 5.31 (1.54) | $M_{V1}$ = 4.45 (0.98) | **$Mdn_{T1}$ = 3.69 (1.62)** | $M_{T1}$ = 3.81 (1.62) | $Mdn_{V1}$ = 4.31 (0.98) |
| | | $M_{T1}$ = 3.81 (1.62) | $Mdn_{T2}$ = 5.00 (1.54) | $M_{T2}$ = 4.70 (1.54) | **$Mdn_{V2}$ = 5.31 (1.54)** | $M_{T2}$ = 4.70 (1.54) | $Mdn_{V2}$ = 5.31 (1.54) |
| | INFOQUAL | t2=0.73 | wr=116.50 | ws=32.50 | pt=-2.15 | wr=108.00 | t2=-0.16 |
| | | p=0.47 V1>T1 | p=0.40 V2>T2 | p=0.26 V1>T2 | p=0.06* T1<V2 | p=0.85 T1>T2 | p=0.87 V1<V2 |
| | | $M_{V1}$ = 4.59 (1.10) | $Mdn_{V2}$ = 4.86 (1.25) | $Mdn_{V1}$ = 4.43 (1.10) | $M_{T1}$ = 4.17 (1.42) | $Mdn_{T1}$ = 4.21 (1.42) | $M_{V1}$ = 4.59 (1.10) |
| | | $M_{T1}$ = 4.17 (1.42) | $Mdn_{T2}$ = 4.07 (1.35) | $Mdn_{T2}$ = 4.07 (1.35) | $M_{V2}$ = 4.67 (1.25) | $Mdn_{T2}$ = 4.07 (1.35) | $M_{V2}$ = 4.67 (1.25) |
| | INTERQUAL | t2=1.05 | t2=1.16 | pt=-0.11 | **pt=-4.50** | t2=-1.11 | t2=-1.35 |
| | | p=0.31 V1>T1 | p=0.26 V2>T2 | p=0.92 V1<T2 | **p=0.00*** T1<V2** | p=0.28 T1<T2 | p=0.19 V1<V2 |
| | | $M_{V1}$ = 4.43 (1.24) | $M_{V2}$ = 5.17 (1.19) | $M_{V1}$ = 4.43 (1.24) | **$M_{T1}$ = 3.73 (1.71)** | $M_{T1}$ = 3.73 (1.71) | $M_{V1}$ = 4.43 (1.24) |
| | | $M_{T1}$ = 3.73 (1.71) | $M_{T2}$ = 4.50 (1.37) | $M_{T2}$ = 4.50 (1.37) | **$M_{V2}$ = 5.17 (1.19)** | $M_{T2}$ = 4.50 (1.37) | $M_{V2}$ = 5.17 (1.19) |
| ENGAGEMENT (H2) | Focused attention | wr=113.00 | t2=0.33 | ws=37.50 | **pt=2.33** | t2=0.99 | wr=120.00 |
| | | p=0.57 V1>T1 | p=0.74 V2>T2 | p=0.09 V1>T2 | **p=0.04** T1>V2** | p=0.34 T1>T2 | p=0.27 V1>V2 |
| | | $Mdn_{V1}$ = 4.36 (0.98) | $M_{V2}$ = 3.70 (0.72) | $Mdn_{V1}$ = 4.36 (0.98) | **$M_{T1}$ = 3.96 (0.73)** | $M_{T1}$ = 3.96 (0.73) | $Mdn_{V1}$= 4.36 (0.98) |
| | | $Mdn_{T1}$ = 4.14 (0.73) | $M_{T2}$ = 3.57 (0.99) | $Mdn_{T2}$ = 3.71 (0.99) | **$M_{V2}$ = 3.70 (0.72)** | $M_{T2}$ = 3.57 (0.99) | $Mdn_{V2}$ = 4.00 (0.72) |
| | Aesthetics | t2=1.76 | **t2=2.29** | **pt=2.79** | **pt=-2.65** | t2=0.26 | t2=0.13 |
| | | p=0.10 V1>T1 | **p=0.03** V2>T2** | **p=0.02** V1>T2** | **p=0.03** T1<V2** | p=0.80 T1>T2 | p=0.90 V1>V2 |
| | | $M_{V1}$ = 3.84 (1.19) | **$M_{V2}$ = 3.78 (0.88)** | **$M_{V1}$ = 3.84 (1.19)** | **$M_{T1}$ = 2.94 (1.10)** | $M_{T1}$ = 2.94 (1.10) | $M_{V1}$ = 3.84 (1.19) |
| | | $M_{T1}$ = 2.94 (1.10) | **$M_{T2}$ = 2.82 (0.99)** | **$M_{T2}$ = 2.82 (0.99)** | **$M_{V2}$ = 3.78 (0.88)** | $M_{T2}$ = 2.82 (0.99) | $M_{V2}$ = 3.78 (0.88) |
| VISUAL EFFORT (H3) | Fixations Duration | **wr = 1094200** | **wr = 867250** | ws = 19 | ws = 18 | **wr = 768960** | **wr = 1086700** |
| | | **p= 0.00*** V1<T1** | **p= 0.00*** V2<T2** | p=0.432 V1<T2 | p=0.652 T1>V2 | **p=0.00*** T1<T2** | **p=0.00*** V1<V2** |
| | | **$Mdn_{V1}$=249 (647.62)** | **$Mdn_{V2}$ =283 (532.31)** | $Mdn_{V1}$ =249.0(647.62) | $Mdn_{T1}$ =333(511.00) | **$Mdn_{T1}$=333(511.00)** | **$Mdn_{V1}$=249 (647.62)** |
| | | **$Mdn_{T1}$= 333(511.00)** | **$Mdn_{T2}$ =366 (619.67)** | $Mdn_{T2}$ =366 (619.67) | $Mdn_{V2}$ =283 (532.31) | **$Mdn_{T2}$=366(619.67)** | **$Mdn_{V2}$=283 (532.31)** |
| | Saccades length | wr= 953190 | **wr= 1143000** | **ws=48** | ws=7 | **wr= 904700** | **wr= 1081700** |
| | | p=0.051* V1>T1 | **p=0.00*** V2>T2** | **p=0.04** V1>T2** | p=0.074 T1<V2 | **p=0.00*** T1>T2** | **p=0.00*** V1<V2** |
| | | $Mdn_{V1}$=244.27(361.34) | **$Mdn_{V2}$=272.51(340.85)** | **$Mdn_{V1}$=244.27(361.34)** | $Mdn_{T1}$= 239.97(241.02) | **$Mdn_{T1}$=239.97(241.02)** | **$Mdn_{V1}$=244.27(361.34)** |
| | | $Mdn_{T1}$=239.97(241.02) | **$Mdn_{T2}$=210.65(289.01)** | **$Mdn_{T2}$=210.65(289.01)** | $Mdn_{V2}$= 272.51(340.85) | **$Mdn_{T2}$=210.65(289.01)** | **$Mdn_{V2}$=272.51(340.85)** |
| | Pupil size | wr = 1002200 | **wr = 1373300** | **ws = 48** | ws = 10 | wr = 1106500 | wr = 989590 |
| | | p= 0.76 V1<T1 | **p=0.00*** V2>T2** | **p=0.04** V1>T2** | p=0.16 T1<V2 | p= 0.00*** T1>T2 | p= 0.00*** V1<V2 |
| | | $Mdn_{V1}$= 18.28 (5.74) | **$Mdn_{V2}$ = 21.08 (5.10)** | **$Mdn_{V1}$ = 18.28 (5.74)** | $Mdn_{T1}$ = 19.31 (3.91) | $Mdn_{T1}$= 19.31 (3.91) | $Mdn_{V1}$ = 18.28 (5.74) |
| | | $Mdn_{T1}$= 19.31 (3.91) | **$Mdn_{T2}$ = 16.23 (3.76)** | **$Mdn_{T2}$ = 16.23 (3.76)** | $Mdn_{V2}$ = 21.08 (5.10) | $Mdn_{T2}$= 16.23 (3.76) | $Mdn_{V2}$ = 21.08 (5.10) |
| PHYSICAL EFFORT (H3) | Mouse actions | **wr=69.00** | **wr=19.00** | **ws=1.00** | **ws=35.00** | t2=-0.06 | wr=38.50 |
| | | **p=0.009*** V1<T1** | **p=0.03** V2<T2** | **p=0.004*** V1<T2** | **p=0.02** T1>V2** | p=0.96 T1<T2 | p=0.62 V1<V2 |
| | | **$Mdn_{V1}$ = 87 (73.77)** | **$Mdn_{V2}$ = 93 (63.75)** | **$Mdn_{V1}$ = 87 (73.77)** | **$Mdn_{T1}$= 191.5 (150.23)** | $M_{T1}$=243.12(150.23) | $Mdn_{V1}$ = 87 (73.77) |
| | | **$Mdn_{T1}$=191.5(150.23)** | **$Mdn_{T2}$ = 177 (172.16)** | **$Mdn_{T2}$ = 177 (172.16)** | **$Mdn_{V2}$ = 93 (63.75)** | $M_{T2}$=247.40(172.16) | $Mdn_{V2}$ = 93 (63.75) |

***Table 1.*** *Summary of performance results for performance, engagement, visual effort and physical effort. Related hypotheses are indicated in parentheses next to each group of measures in the first column. (M) Mean, and (Mdn) median. Values in parentheses next to M and Mdn correspond to standard deviation. (*) marginally significant result at p~0.05, (**) significant result at p<.05, (***) significant result at p<.01.*

These performance results could be explained by the particular interaction models implemented in the two representations and the familiarity level of the participants with the two representations of search results. For instance, in the traditional representation participants were able to select and organize results using a list of checkboxes next to each result (Figure 1). On the other hand, in the visual representation participants had to drag and drop results (circles) into specific containers representing the four subtopics (AOI 3 in Figure 2). This way one could speculate that interactions in the traditional representation promoted rapid selection and organization of results, whereas in the visual representation interactions were slightly complex and slower. Indeed, on average participants were able to select more documents in the traditional interface (M=20.7) than in the visual one (M=16.75). Yet, medians for the number of selected documents were rather close (13.5 and 12.5 respectively), which relates to values concentrated in a small range in the traditional interface. This particular result could be explained by the participants being more familiar with the traditional interface, which allowed all of them to perform similarly. On the other hand, in the visual interface – which was very unfamiliar to all the participants – some participants might have reached a good understanding of the visual cues and thus succeeded in the task. However, others were not able to properly grasp the interface and its advantages for the particular task they had to solve, hence their results were poor. Overall, these results do not support $H_1$, hence our visual representation of search results does not help to improve performance nor it does not worsen it in a consistent and significant way.

### User Experience

#### Affective Experience

First, the affective dimension was measured at three time points in each interaction (i.e., before reading the task, after reading the task and after completing the task). Therefore, a total of six SAM questionnaires was responded to by each participant. Note that the SAM questionnaire comprises three 9-points scales, namely valence (positive – negative), arousal (activated – calm) and dominance (controlled – in control).

Overall, no differences were found for this particular dimension. More importantly, while the two representations had some effects on the participants' affective experiences when contrasting the second and third application of the test in both interactions, these were rather consistent. As a result, no significant differences were reported.

#### Cognitive Load

Second, the cognitive dimension was measured through the NASA TLX right after completing the task with each interface. The idea was to compare the perceived cognitive demand after performing the task with the two representations of search results. Neither between- nor within-subjects comparisons reported significant differences. Indeed, it was found that the average task load indexes (TLX) for the two representations were rather homogeneous ranging between 56.03 and 62.44.

### Usability

Third, the CUSQ questionnaire was used to measure usability regarding four components: user experience (UX), system use (SYSUSE), information quality (INFOQUAL) and interface quality (INTERQUAL). Results for this dimension are summarized in Table 1. Like NASA TLX, this questionnaire was administrated after completing the task with each interface. In this case, significant differences were reported only at the within-subjects level for the first sequence ($T_1$-$V_2$). In this particular case, UX, SYSUSE and INTERQUAL were found to be better evaluated in the visual interface during the second exposure time. However, no significant differences were found in the $V_1$-$T_2$ sequence.

### Engagement

Finally, engagement was measured through UES. We focused on the three dimensions that O'Brien found to be stable (i.e., perceived usability, aesthetics and focused attention). As shown in Table 1, the only one that showed rather consistent results was aesthetics, which was positively evaluated in the visual representation ($p<.05$). On the other hand, isolated significant differences at $p<.05$ were found for focused attention being greater for $T_1$ than $V_2$.

In summary, it is possible to state that findings do not support $H_2$ consistently. The only aspect that was consistently better across time was aesthetics, which can be explained by the ludic and interactive resources introduced in the visual representation. Another interesting result, though consistent only in the sequence $T_1$-$V_2$, was the positive reception of the visual representation regarding usability (UX, SYSUSE and INTERQUAL). Given that this result was not observed in the opposite sequence ($V_1$-$T_2$), it could be the case that when being exposed to both a new interface and a new task, the interface was evaluated negatively. However, when the task was familiar, as in $V_2$, the unfamiliarity with the interface does not pose a degradation in the participants' perception.

### Effort

#### Physical Effort

To measure physical effort, we focused on mouse actions, specifically clicks and scrolling. We compared these actions in the area where search results are displayed in both interfaces (AOI 2). As reported in Table 1, mouse actions were found to be significantly lower in the visual representation than in the traditional one. Note that such differences were consistently different across time and no differences were observed when contrasting the same interface across time (i.e. $T_1$ vs $T_2$ and $V_1$ vs $V_2$). This finding can be explained by the fact that given that all 400 results were presented at once and that each result was characterized by visual cues, actions such as scrolling and clicking on results in the visual representation were not necessary.

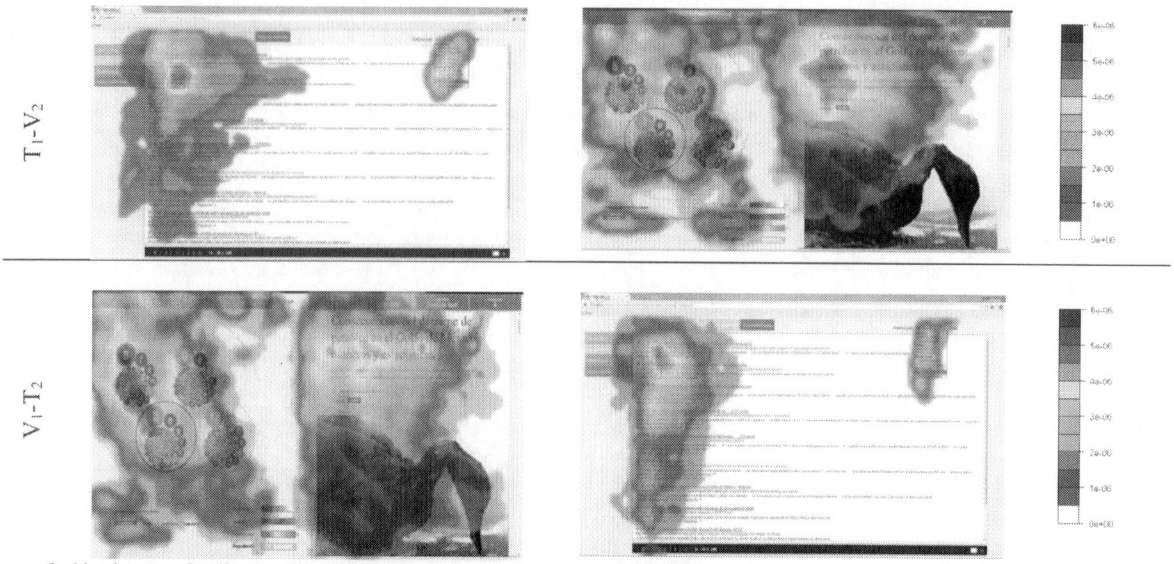


*Figure 3: Heat maps for the traditional interface and the visual interface in $T_1$-$V_2$ and $V_1$-$T_2$*

### *Visual Effort*

Results for visual effort – based on the six measures in our evaluation framework – are summarized in Table 1. First of all, no significant differences were observed regarding the number of fixations. Consistently, no differences were found with respect to the number of saccades.

Surprisingly, unlike previous studies that have shown that fixations last longer in visual tasks than in textual tasks (e.g., Rayner (2009)), our results for between-subject comparisons showed that fixations were significantly shorter at $p<.05$ in the visual representation than in the traditional one.

Using eye fixations, we generated four heat maps as illustrated in Figure 3 to visualize participants' attention on the different AOIs in both interfaces. In the case of the traditional interface, the F-shaped pattern is rather clear and consistent with what has been found in previous studies (Nielsen, 2006). On the other hand, it is interesting to observe that while part of the attention of the participants in the visual interface was in the search results area, they were also distracted by the actual page content that was displayed on the right side of the screen. According to some participants, this was considered a useful feature; however, for this particular task of selection and organization, the content of a page was not necessary to accomplish the task successfully. Indeed, the participant who achieved the highest recall in this study in both the traditional and the visual interface (User 21) was characterized by his attention to the search results with little to no attention to the content of pages. This could mean that this particular user made a proper association between the task selection criteria and the visual cues in our visualization.

As for saccades length, our results support the idea that the visual representation promoted visual inspection and localization rather than reading. As shown in Table 1, between-subject analyses showed that these were significantly longer at $p<.05$ in the visual representation than in the traditional one. On the other hand, within-subject analyses indicate that saccades during the $et_1$ in the visual representation ($V_1$) were significantly longer ($p<.05$) than in the traditional one in $et_2$ ($T_2$). This is explained by the participants looking at the different visual features of the results in the visual representation, compared to short saccadic movements in the traditional representation, which are common in reading tasks (Rayner, 2009).

Regarding pupil size, our results for between-subject analyses indicate that this measure was significantly greater at $p<.01$ in the visual representation than in the traditional one during the second interaction ($V_2$ vs. $T_2$). Within-subject analyses showed that pupil size was significantly greater at $p<.05$ in the visual representation, but only in the sequence $V_1$-$T_2$. No significant differences are observed in the alternate order ($T_1$-$V_2$). Therefore, we attribute pupil dilation in $V_1$ to attention and cognitive processing being divided between understanding the task and understanding an unfamiliar visualization interface.

Finally, our last measure for visual effort corresponds to density. This measure relates to the number of eye fixations per square centimeter on a particular area of interest (AOI). This measure has been related to the importance of the area when contrasted to other AOIs in the same interface (Goldberg et al., 1999). In this study, we compared the density of eye fixations in the area where results are displayed in both types of interfaces (AOI 2). To compute these measures, we first calculated the actual area of the AOIs in both interfaces. In the case of the traditional representation, this AOI corresponds to 761.61 $cm^2$, whereas in the visual representation this AOI corresponds to 521.93 $cm^2$. Surprisingly, in spite of this difference in size and the large number of search results displayed at once in the visual interface (40 times more than in the traditional interface), no differences were observed in terms of density.

Overall, our findings for effort support $H_3$. In this case, it is possible to state that once the task is grasped, visual effort is lower in the visual representation than in the traditional one. Moreover, in spite of the large volume of information condensed in a small area in the visual representation, no differences were observed with the traditional interface in terms of number of fixations, number of saccades and density. On the other hand, our results indicate that our representation required less physical effort – expressed by mouse actions – than the traditional one since users had to perform fewer actions to explore search results.

## CONCLUSION

In this article, we have presented a comparison of a visual and a traditional representation of search results. Our study focused on the effects of these two representations on performance, user experience and effort. To carry out the study we developed SERVS (Search Engine Results Visualization System), which allowed us to compare the two types of representations following a crossover experimental design.

From our three hypotheses, our results only support the one related to effort ($H_3$). More specifically, our findings suggest that exposing participants to a large number of search results using adequate visual cues, help to reduce physical and visual effort without compromising to a great extent performance and user experience. While some performance measures were better in the traditional interface and some user experience measures were better in the visual interface, such differences were not consistent across time. Likewise, no differences were found at the level of affective experience and cognitive load. The latter is quite relevant considering that in the visual interface the participants were exposed to 40 times more results than in the traditional one. This finding suggests that in particular search scenarios, it is possible to expose users to a large number of results using appropriate visualization techniques without causing information overload, higher cognitive load, unpleasant feelings and an increment in visual and physical effort.

We speculate that performance results for our visual interface are somehow related to usability issues. Some of them were discovered during an interview process that was carried out at the very end of each session. From this interview, we learned that some features were missing in the visual interface (e.g., an indicator of which pages were visited, which in a traditional interface is typically highlighted with a different color once a link is clicked). On the other hand, a visual analysis of eye-tracking data revealed that the participants were somehow distracted by the content of the page displayed on the right side of the visual interface.

Another reason that could be related to the rejection of $H_1$ is the possibility that the traditional interface was good enough to allow the participants to find documents according to two combined criteria. Considering that our visual representation provides visual cues for up to four attributes, it may be the case that in tasks requiring three or four selection criteria, the visual interface could outperform the traditional one.

Perhaps one of the strongest reasons behind the rejection of $H_1$ and $H_2$ relates to the adoption process of the visual interface and user expertise (Koshman, 2005). While the participants received some training to use both interfaces and they were allowed to have some practice with them, it is clear that this short period using a new interface was not enough to equate several years of experience with the traditional representation of search results.

Based on these speculations, in our future work we will focus on the following three aspects: (1) addressing usability issues reported during the interviews and also those detected through eye tracking data; (2) improving the adoption process of our visualization approach so that the participants get familiar with it before the actual study; and (3) conducting a study that focuses on the selection and organization of documents using one to four criteria.

## ACKNOWLEDGMENTS

The work presented in this article was partially funded by Proyecto DICYT, Código 061519GI, Vicerrectoría de Investigación, Desarrollo e Innovación, Universidad de Santiago de Chile

## REFERENCES

Bradley, M. M., & Lang, P. J. (1994). Measuring emotion: The self-assessment manikin and the semantic differential. *Journal of Behavior Therapy and Experimental Psychiatry*, 25(1), 49-59.

Capra, R., Marchionini, G., Oh, J. S., Stutzman, F., & Zhang, Y. (2007). Effects of structure and interaction style on distinct search tasks. In *Proc. of the 7th ACM JCDL* (pp. 442-451). ACM.

Card, S. K., Mackinlay, J. D., & Shneiderman, B. (1999). *Readings in information visualization: using vision to think*. Morgan Kaufmann.

Cellary, W., Wiza, W., & Walczak, K. (2004). Visualizing web search results in 3D. *Computer*, 37(5), 87-89.

Fernández-Huerta, J. (1959). Medidas sencillas de lecturabilidad. *Consigna*, 214, 29–32.

Fu, W. T., Kannampallil, T. G., & Kang, R. (2010). Facilitating exploratory search by model-based navigational cues. In *Proc. of the 15th Intl. Conf. on IUI* (pp. 199-208). ACM.

Gardner, H. (2011). Frames of mind: The theory of multiple intelligences. Basic books.

Goldberg, J. H., & Kotval, X. P. (1999). Computer interface evaluation using eye movements: Methods and constructs. *Intl. Journal of Industrial Ergonomics*, 24(6), 631-645.

Hart, S. G., & Staveland, L. E. (1988). Development of NASA-TLX (Task Load Index): Results of empirical and theoretical research. *Advances in Psychology*, 52, 139-183.

Hearst, M. A. (1995). TileBars: Visualization of term distribution information in full text information access. In *Proc of the SIGCHI conference* (pp. 59-66). ACM Press/Addison-Wesley Publishing Co.

Hearst, M., Elliott, A., English, J., Sinha, R., Swearingen, K., & Yee, K. P. (2002). Finding the flow in web site search. *Communications of the ACM*, 45(9), 42-49.

Hearst, M. (2011). User interfaces for search. In R. Baeza-Yates & B. Ribeiro-Neto (Eds.). *Modern information retrieval - the concepts and technology behind search*. (pp. 21-55). Pearson Education.

Henderson, J. M., & Hollingworth, A. (1999). High-level scene perception. *Annual review of psychology*, 50(1), 243-271.

Joachims, T., Granka, L., Pan, B., Hembrooke, H., & Gay, G. (2005). Accurately interpreting clickthrough data as implicit feedback. In *Proc. of the 28th the ACM SIGIR conference* (pp. 154-161). Salvador, Brazil.

Koshman, S. (2005). Testing user interaction with a prototype visualization-based information retrieval system. *Journal of the Association for Information Science and Technology*, 56(8), 824-833.

Koshman, S. (2006). Visualization-based information retrieval on the web. *Library & Information Science Research*, 28(2), 192-207.

Lewis, J. R. (1995). IBM computer usability satisfaction questionnaires: Psychometric evaluation and instructions for use. *Intl. Journal of Human-Computer Interaction*, 7(1), 57-78.

Mann, T. M. (1999). Visualization of WWW-search results. In *Proc. of the 10th intl. workshop on database and expert systems applications* (pp. 264-268). IEEE.

Maynes, R., & Everdell, I. (2014). The evolution of Google search results pages and their effects on user behaviour. *Mediative*.

Mizzaro, S. (1998). How many relevances in information retrieval? *Interacting with Computers*, 10(3), 303-320.

Nguyen, T., & Zhang, J. (2006). A novel visualization model for web search results. *IEEE Transactions on Visualization and Computer Graphics*, 12(5).

Nielsen, J. (2006). F-shaped pattern for reading web content. Alertbox: Current Issues in Web Usability.

O'Brien, H. L., & Toms, E. G. (2013). Examining the generalizability of the User Engagement Scale (UES) in exploratory search. IP&M, 49(5), 1092-1107.

Ooms, K., Dupont, L., Lapon, L., & Popelka, S. (2015). Accuracy and precision of fixation locations recorded with the low-cost Eye Tribe tracker in different experimental setups. *Journal of Eye Movement Research*, 8(1).

Pickens, J., Golovchinsky, G., Shah, C., Qvarfordt, P., & Back, M. (2008). Algorithmic mediation for collaborative exploratory search. In *Proc. of the 31st ACM SIGIR conference* (pp. 315-322), Singapore.

Rayner, K. (2009). Eye movements and attention in reading, scene perception, and visual search. *The Quarterly Journal of Experimental Psychology, 62*(8), 1457-1506.

Sebrechts, M. M., Cugini, J. V., Laskowski, S. J., Vasilakis, J., & Miller, M. S. (1999). Visualization of search results: A comparative evaluation of text, 2D, and 3D interfaces. In *Proc. of the 22nd ACM SIGIR conference* (pp. 3-10). Berkeley, USA.

Shah, C., & González-Ibáñez, R. (2011). Evaluating the synergic effect of collaboration in information seeking. In *Proc. of the 34th ACM SIGIR* (pp. 913-922). Beijing, China.

Spoerri, A. (1993). InfoCrystal: A visual tool for information retrieval & management. In *Proc. of the 2nd CIKM* (pp. 11-20). ACM.

Spoerri, A. (2006). Visualizing meta search results: Evaluating the MetaCrystal toolset. In *Proc. of the 69th ASIS&T*, 43(1), 1-20.

Tilsner, M., Hoeber, O., & Fiech, A. (2009). Cubansea: Cluster-based visualization of search results. In *Proc. of the 2009 IEEE/WIC/ACM*, Vol. 3 (pp. 108-112). IEEE Computer Society.

Wittek, P., Liu, Y. H., Darányi, S., Gedeon, T., & Lim, I. S. (2016). Risk and ambiguity in information seeking: Eye gaze patterns reveal contextual behavior in dealing with uncertainty. *Frontiers in psychology*, 7.

Yee, K. P., Swearingen, K., Li, K., & Hearst, M. (2003). Faceted metadata for image search and browsing. In *Proc. of the SIGCHI conference* (pp. 401-408). ACM.

# Constructing Knowledge and Ignorance in the Social Information Worlds of Young Mothers

**Devon Greyson**
*BC Children's Hospital Research Institute, University of British Columbia, Canada. dgreyson@bcchr.ubc.ca*

**Heather O'Brien**
*School of Library, Archival & Information Studies, University of British Columbia, Canada. h.obrien@ubc.ca*

**Jean Shoveller**
*School of Population & Public Health, University of British Columbia, Canada. jean.shoveller@ubc.ca*

## ABSTRACT

**The socially constructed information worlds within which individuals live, work and play necessarily shape their information practices. One way in which this occurs is through the social construction of knowledge, expertise and ignorance, including which actors are considered to possess authoritative knowledge through administrative authority or lay expertise. Using Adele Clarke's situational mapping techniques, this paper examines the discursive construction of knowledge and ignorance in the information worlds of young mothers in the Greater Vancouver region of Canada. Data was collected via observations at school-based Young Parent Programs and interviews with 37 young mothers over a 15-month time period. Gendered and racialized young parent social worlds discursively constructed the "teen mom" as knowledgeable in matters of sexuality and technology and ignorant in matters of parenting and health. Further, certain forms of experiential expertise common to marginalized groups were sometimes constructed in such information worlds as forms of ignorance. Recognizing the diversity of knowledge and expertise among young mothers rather than perceiving them as unilaterally information poor may lead to improved information and support services for young parents.**

## KEYWORDS

information worlds, knowledge, expertise, situational analysis, youth

## INTRODUCTION

The socially constructed information worlds within which individuals live, work and play necessarily shape their information practices. One way in which this occurs is through the social construction of knowledge, expertise and ignorance, including who is considered to possess authoritative (true or reliable) knowledge, either through administrative authority (e.g., expert status such as that conferred by professional credentials) or lay expertise (e.g., experientially acquired skill). The lived experiences of individuals whose expertise is regularly contested due to their social locations (e.g., ethnicity, age, socioeconomic class markers) are necessarily affected by others' assumptions regarding their knowledge and/or ignorance. This research focuses on one such group: young mothers.

Young mothers in contemporary North America live within a broader social and political climate that casts parents in their teen years and early 20s as knowledge deficient, as well as socially and medically problematic. In efforts to improve outcomes for young mothers and their children, multiple stakeholders provide information to, and collect information from, young mothers. This occurs both formally (e.g., by public health or social welfare) and informally (e.g., by peers and neighbors) in physical and virtual spaces. Such information interventions, as well as young mothers' own information behaviors and practices (analyzed in Greyson, 2016, 2017; see also related work on first-time mothers by Loudon, Buchanan & Ruthvan, 2016) are situated in socially constructed worlds. Within these worlds, information, knowledge and expertise are negotiated in order to determine who needs information, who is knowledgeable and whose knowledge is valued as expertise. This analysis explores the social constructions of knowledge and ignorance in the information worlds of a group of young mothers in the Greater Vancouver region of Canada.

## INFORMATION WORLDS

"Information worlds" is a phrase commonly used for conceptual spaces in which information-related activities, behaviours and practices take place, yet there remains some lack of clarity around what is intended by this metaphor (Yu, 2012). Burnett and Jaeger's (2008; Jaeger & Burnett, 2010) information worlds theory integrates Chatman's (1991) small worlds of marginalized people in localized contexts with Habermas' (1991) conceptualization of the public sphere, resulting in a multi-level theory that asserts that information worlds overlap and interact at levels from the individual (micro) through community (meso) to whole societies (macro). Jaeger & Burnett (2010) focus on five aspects of information worlds: social norms, social types, information value, information behaviour and boundaries at which information worlds come into contact with each other.

80th Annual Meeting of the Association for Information Science & Technology, Washington, DC | Oct. 27-Nov. 1, 2017

According to sociologist Adele Clarke (2005), "Social worlds...generate shared perspectives that then form the basis for collective action..., while individual and collective identities are constituted through commitments to and participation in social worlds and arenas" (p.45). Taking a postmodern, Foucauldian approach, Clarke conceives social worlds as containing structures and actors of various social types. These social worlds engage in struggle with each other over boundaries, social norms and discourses within arenas in a manner similar to that of Burnett and Jaeger's (2010) information worlds. Social norms, actors of various types, constructed values, and negotiations of relationships and boundaries are common elements of both situational analysis and information worlds theory, which may be integrated to focus specifically on the analysis of social information worlds. By using Clarke's situational analysis methods to investigate social information worlds of young parents – a population whose knowledge and expertise is contested – we may elucidate values and norms of and about actors within these worlds, providing insight into the construction of their information behaviours and practices.

## CONSTRUCTIONS OF KNOWLEDGE, IGNORANCE AND EXPERTISE IN SOCIAL INFORMATION WORLDS

The study of social constructions of knowledge, or the ways people construct, act on and institutionalize shared understandings (Berger & Luckmann, 1967), has been a mainstay of sociological inquiry since the mid-20th century. After the postmodern turn, in which many social theorists rejected the notion of universal metanarratives, inquiry into social knowledges became an explicitly multi- and interdisciplinary endeavor, incorporating science and technology studies as well as more traditional sociological and philosophical traditions, and using discourse analysis as a core method for interrogating knowledge constructions and related social practices (see, for example, Camic, Gross & Lamont, 2011). Tuominen and Savolainen (1997) laid the groundwork for discursive inquiry into the social construction of information use, which has been influential to scholars of information behavior and practices (see for example Karlova & Fisher, 2013; McKenzie, 2003).

While a great deal of study has gone into understanding knowledge production, the phenomenon of ignorance and the structures that shape it are a newer area of investigation. Proctor (2008) identifies three types of ignorance, which have been further theorized by intersectional scholars who identify the interconnections between race and epistemologies of ignorance. These are 1) ignorance as naïve state that may be remedied by acquiring knowledge (e.g., white privileged ignorance of racism (Sullivan & Tuana, 2007)); 2) ignorance as lost realm of knowledge forgone (as when English colonists suppressed knowledge of the abortifacient properties of native flora when importing plants to Europe (Schiebinger, 2004)); and 3) ignorance as strategic ploy to maintain doubt (evident in situations such as black slaves in the Americas feigning ignorance for their own safety). Young people are frequently perceived to inhabit a naïve state, requiring knowledge acquisition (often via formal education) in order to properly mature. However, other forms of ignorance may also be re/produced in certain youth contexts. For example, young people may actively construct ignorance in order to perpetuate uncertainty (e.g., to evade responsibility or surveillance) or may possess knowledge that is suppressed or devalued by adults who encourage pursuit of other types of knowledge. Similar to intersectional agnatology, Chatman's information worlds theories for marginalized populations recognize strategic ignorance practices such as secrecy, apathy and disinformation, considering them hallmarks of "information poverty" (Chatman, 1996) and a highly surveillanced "life in the round" (Chatman, 1999).

Actors in social information worlds engage in tensions and negotiations in order to determine who lacks knowledge, who has knowledge and whose knowledge counts as expertise. Within these social worlds, there are individuals and "types" of people who are looked to as authoritative information providers. These people may possess a high level of knowledge-related cultural capital (assets that facilitate social mobility, e.g., education, professional credentials) or they may rely on lay or experiential expertise. Building on Collins and Evans (2007; 2002) taxonomy of "expertises" and Eyal's (2013; Eyal & Buchholz, 2010) distinction between "experts" and "expertise," we may conceptualize knowledge and expertise as belonging both to laypeople with experiential expertise and to formal experts in a field when exploring discourses of knowledge in young parent social worlds. Many information worlds include both "official" or "authoritative" information sources and informal or social information sources, but individuals attribute value and trust to sources in varying ways. Studies of information behaviour have found resonance in theories that acknowledge the general human inclination toward easy access and good-enough information, such as the principle of least effort (Zipf, 1949) and sense-making (Dervin, 1992; Savolainen, 1993). In practice, these theories suggest that, while expert information may be desired, trusted and even actively sought on certain topics and by certain information users, sources that pose the least barriers and are the most congruent with the seeker's life are typically consulted first – be this a quick internet search or asking friends or coworkers for their input. Social groups may have informal information specialists who are the group "knowers" with expertise on particular topics. Social media fora or face-to-face gathering spaces may serve as "information grounds" (Fisher & Naumer, 2006) for peer-to-peer information exchange.

## THE CONTEXT FOR YOUNG MOTHERHOOD

Young pregnancy and parenting have long been constructed as a societal problem in North America (Bonell, 2004; Furstenberg, 1976; Kelly, 2000). Despite a decline in teen pregnancy and childbearing over the past half century (Duncan, 2007; Langille, 2007), an infantilizing discourse persists over the alleged crisis of "children having children" (Fields, 2005). Public health constructs teenage pregnancy as a socially contagious "disease" (Barcelos, 2013; Breheny & Stephens, 2010) that requires preventative and remedial education and surveillance. While socio-medical research historically found an association between young childbearing and poorer outcomes, both social (Basch, 2011; Hanna, 2001; Hoffman & Maynard, 2008), and medical (Dryburgh, 2000; Fraser, Brockert & Ward, 1995; Scholl et al., 1992), recent evidence indicates that such differences are in fact attributable to underlying social determinants rather than maternal age itself (Gold, Kawachi, Kennedy, Lynch & Connell, 2001; Penman-Aguilar, Carter, Snead & Kourtis, 2013). Indeed, for some young mothers, becoming a parent is associated with significant improvements to their health, education and social welfare status, providing a valued social role, inspiring career aspirations and bringing community support (Anwar & Stanistreet, 2015; Seamark & Lings, 2004). Despite growing evidence of the complexity of the effects of early parenthood on the lives of young mothers and their children, public health, social science and medicine interact with media narratives and dominant cultural values to co-construct and reinforce the notion of the "teen mom" (a label commonly applied to young-appearing mothers in their teens and early 20s) as morally problematic (Chabot, Shoveller, Johnson & Prkachin, 2010). In her ignorance, she is either a passive victim or a poor decision-maker (Kelly, 2007), reinforced by racialized and classed social narratives (Barcelos & Gubrium, 2014).

By portraying young mothers as immature and inexperienced, society at large discursively constructs the "teen mom" as ignorant. Young mothers, as well as those tasked with educating them in attempts to remedy their perceived ignorance (lack of knowledge), are situated within and amidst socially-constructed worlds. This analysis centers on the social worlds that host and implement formal and informal information interventions aimed at improving the well-being of young mothers and their children by means of education and/or surveillance. The objective herein is to explicate social worlds within which young mothers seek, use and share information, describe the roles and tensions among the various social worlds at play, and characterize discourses of knowledge and ignorance regarding young mothers, including their intersections with young mothers' social locations.

## METHOD

### Study Setting

This study took place in the third largest metropolitan area in Canada, Greater Vancouver, home to 2.3 million people (Statistics Canada, 2012). Each city within the region hosts a Young Parent Program (YPP), which serves as a hub for secondary education, health, childcare and social support programming to young parents. External to the YPPs are a variety of health and social support services, which often work in collaboration with the YPPs to provide services ranging from food assistance to health education to young parents and their children. The primary locations for this study's fieldwork were two Greater Vancouver YPPs. Additional data collection was conducted at community organizations that serve young parents, including the non-school based setting for a third YPP.

### Data Collection

Data was collected via ethnographic observation at YPPs and individual interviews with young mothers. Data collection began in October 2013 and continued through December 2014. Interview participants were initially purposively recruited from YPPs to select pregnant or parenting youth. As the study progressed, interview participants were purposively and theoretically sampled from YPPs as well as from other community organizations that provided young parent services to provide additional diversity of age and education, to engage youth not in school and to test emerging theories. Semi-structured interviews covered a range of topics spanning health, housing, childcare and parenting, education and career, and information practices. Interviewees were invited to participate in follow-up interviews approximately every four to six months (for a maximum of three interviews within the study timeframe) in order to follow participants' evolving lives and practices.

### Data Analysis

This article presents a situational analysis (Clarke, 2003; 2005) of the social information worlds of young mothers. Situational analysis is a grounded theory-based analytic method that uses visual diagramming methods to analyze social worlds and elucidate the tensions therein, the power relationships among actors and the discourses they construct. In situational analysis, social worlds are "universes of discourse," through which individuals and social groups co-construct each other (Clarke, 2005, p. 55). Situational analysis has only rarely been used within information science research, and typically been applied to conceptualizing library spaces, programming and roles (Batool & Webber, 2016; Grace & Sen, 2013) rather than exploring users' information worlds. For the current analysis, member-checked interview transcripts and observational field notes were first coded and analyzed in accordance with constructivist grounded theory (Charmaz, 2007, 2009), using QSR NVivo 10 software. We then engaged the coded data in a variety of Clarke's situational analytic data mapping exercises in order to interrogate the social information worlds of young mothers. Specifically, we used a) situational mapping to classify and examine relationships among human and non-human actors in the social worlds, b) social worlds/arenas mapping to focus in on the worlds within the young parent arena and c) positional maps to flesh out discourses of ignorance and knowledge regarding study participants. For more detail on these mapping methods, refer to Clarke (2003, 2005).

## RESULTS

Over the course of 15 months of data collection, we conducted 50 days of naturalistic observation at YPPs and interviewed 37 young mothers ages 16-22. All interview participants participated in 90-minute individual intake interviews. Eighteen young mothers completed a second interview of approximately 45-60 minutes four to six months after their intake interview, and three also completed third interviews, which were also 45-60 minutes in length. Over half of the young mothers in this study were visible minorities, 40% of them had at least one parent born outside of Canada and six of the 37 were themselves immigrants. Three identified at one or more interview as bisexual or pansexual and two as questioning or unsure; the remainder identified as straight or heterosexual. One mother identified as gender non-binary and the rest as women.

In analyzing the socially constructed information worlds that made up the young parent arena, three key findings emerged. The first was that while experts from various social worlds aimed to educate young mothers, young mothers also possessed and developed lay expertise. The second was that young mothers were discursively constructed as paradoxically ignorant and knowledgeable. The third was that the relationships among social worlds, as well as the discourses of knowledge and ignorance, were constructed in a gendered and racialized manner.

### *Information Worlds in the Young Parent Arena*

Through situational mapping of coded interview transcripts and observation field notes, a young parent social arena emerged that was centered on the YPPs and contained multiple, overlapping, health-related social information worlds. Chief among these were the worlds of the organizations that participate in the day-to-day administration of the YPPs: the secondary school and the associated child daycare facility. These two social worlds were ones with which student parents in the YPPs interacted every school day. In addition, professionals from public health, nursing and non-governmental organizations (both faith-based and secular) were regularly on site, providing programming and recruiting participants for their own services. Figure 1 contains a social information world map of this young parent arena, centering on the YPPs. Larger ellipses represent worlds that were more prominent in the data and, while it is impossible to depict all interrelationships among worlds in a two-dimensional image, overlap indicates porous boundaries among related social worlds.

For many young mothers, support from their family of origin was instrumental to their ability to attend school while parenting, and family members were key sources of information and support. Some young mothers who did not live with their families received government support, allowing them to live in foster care while parenting or to live independently under legal agreements with the province called Youth Agreements. Family and "the State" were two social worlds that were ever-present even without representatives of those worlds physically setting foot in the YPP. This presence took the form of family and government support for young parent success, as well as family conflict issues, the workings of government surveillance and the related threat of child apprehension. Cultural groups, ranging from religious congregations to refugee settlement services, reflected aspects of students' social arenas and provided social worlds external to the YPPs that played an important role in the experiences and identities of some young mothers. Medical communities of various types were prominent within the young parent arena, for example the overlapping worlds of western medicine, nurses, public health and the perinatal health community. The influence of each of these authoritative health information worlds was strong, as the health information they provided was frequently referred to as *expert* information. There was wide variation in the degree of direct contact between these worlds and the YPP programs, with medicine being the most separate and public health nursing the most intertwined.

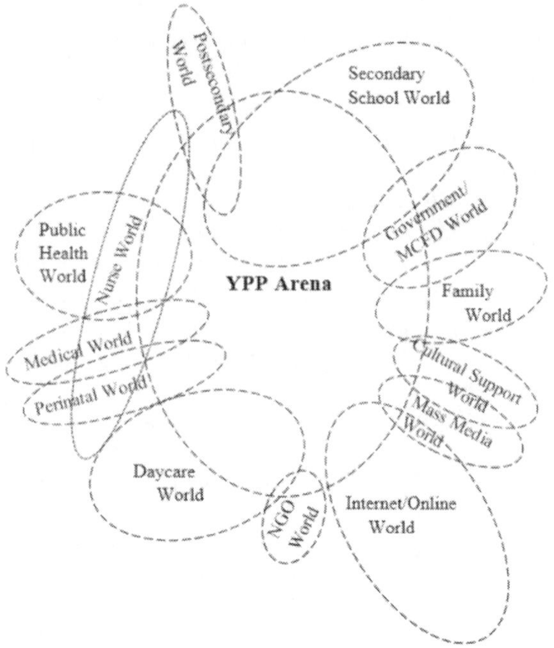


***Figure 1.*** *Social information world map: young parent arena*

The internet was a major social world interacting with the young parent arena, working its way into every significant information issue eventually, whether via smartphone use in the classroom, as a link for relationship maintenance with peers, as a reference source more frequently consulted than any print material or as a topic for regular discussion and concern (e.g., online privacy risks and norms). The internet as used by young mothers in this study was an important virtual social world, which interacted with the mass media – most particularly the genre of reality television shows such as MTV's *16 and Pregnant* and *Teen Mom*.

These multiple social information worlds interacted with each other, sometimes directly (as in the case when a student mother's own parents came to register her for the YPP alternative school) and sometimes indirectly (as when youth workers would help young mothers navigate paperwork to apply for government benefits). While they sometimes worked in concert to reinforce each other's information, they also engaged in conflicts over which health information was current and authoritative, as well as the extent to which young mothers were in need of education and surveillance.

### *Constructions of Expertise in Young Mother Information Worlds*

The social information worlds in this study contained actors representing many positionalities within the young parent arena. Some actors, such as teachers, doctors, parents and public health nurses, were officially tasked with educating young mothers on health-related matters, while others were more arms-length to these information interactions. The degree to which these actors were constructed as experts and non-experts also varied, as vertical (within a social world) and horizontal (across social worlds) hierarchies and power dynamics shaped administrative authority. Expert status was conferred via formal credentialing or by approval of someone with administrative authority. However, expertise could be constructed in multiple, sometimes shifting ways. A person could recognize herself as holding expertise based on extensive experience, while others could construct a position of expertise for someone by deferring to or consulting her in matters on which she was experienced.

Major actors in the core YPP social worlds of secondary education and daycare included teachers, youth workers and daycare staff, all of whom were positioned as credentialed experts (in academics, supportive services and parenting skills) in relation to student-parents. Additionally, the YPPs were sites of frequent visits by outside health educators such as public health nurses, student nurses from local colleges and young parent support workers of various types from local non-governmental organizations, all of whom contributed their expertise to the program by providing various forms of health education. Although not recognized as part of a formal community of experts, young parents acted as information sharers and mediators within the young parent arena in a variety of ways, some of which conferred a form of lay expertise status among peers.

Other young people within a variety of social information worlds – including schools, cultural support groups and the family domain – often viewed young parents as lay experts in matters of reproductive labor, inclusive of childbearing and parenting, but extending to intimate relationships and household management as well. In interviews, young mothers described other youth in their communities approaching them with questions about pregnancy and parenting, often when suspecting or learning that they might themselves be pregnant. Seventeen-year-old young mother Crystal[1] explained, "I've had lots of friends who have had questions about, 'Oh, I think I might be pregnant,' or 'I'm pregnant right now...what should I do? Should I abort? Should I keep it? How was it for you?'" Young mothers also spoke of friends seeking their advice on family issues beyond pregnancy and infant caregiving. Eighteen-year-old Rey described her friends as being very active in information sharing according to their various areas of lay expertise. In addition to checking with each other about health and relationship concerns, she explained that sometimes, "They come with a question like 'What do I do when I don't know how to take care of my daughter' or, you know, financially and stuff like that."

In addition to acting as a peer resource for expertise on matters of reproductive labor, some young mothers were recognized for expertise with childcare and parenting by older community members. This type of situation arose in this study most frequently in indigenous families whose intergenerational parenting practices had been disrupted by structures of colonization, such as residential schools and child welfare apprehension. JBiebs, a 16-year-old expectant mother, had been participating in the care of her younger brother since his infancy. Although JBiebs was pregnant with her first child at the time of our first interview, she was already recognized in her family and community as a reliable parenting expert. When asked if there were people who came to her for information or advice about child caregiving, JBiebs explained,

> *Surprisingly, my mom does. 'Cause I've been raising my brother and my brother loves my mom, he loves her so much, but he acts different around her 'cause he thinks he can get what he wants and stuff [....]I tell my mom..."I don't raise [him] that way."...[S]he has asked me a few times, like, "Oh, [he] is asking for this" or "[He] wants this, should I give it to him?" I'm, like, "Does he deserve it?" Like, I'll bring her through those and she can make the decision herself. [...Also] my friend's mom. I used to babysit her son and her niece at the same time so she always asked me, like, "Oh what do I do, my baby is teething?" And I'm, like, okay, well I just told her, "Give him frozen waffles [to suck on in order to soothe his gums. I know] it helps 'cause that's what I did with my little brother."*

There were also certain topics on which YPP students demonstrated a higher level of proficiency and knowledge than adults formally positioned to educate them. This happened in a variety of knowledge areas ranging from parenting to technology, and most prominently in the area of information and communications technology. During observations, there were myriad small instances of teachers or youth support workers asking students to either search online for an answer to a class question or to explain a new media app or platform to the adults in the room. For example, teacher Roger asked for student help finding online video tutorials the class could watch, and visitors from a community-based young parent support program asked young parents to explain new smartphone apps. While this type of expertise was frequently devalued in young parent social worlds as a natural attribute of contemporary youth who are "digital natives" (Palfrey, 2008; Prensky, 2001), youth were at times positioned as valued guides and instructors whose knowledge was actively sought by adults.

At times, young parents were constructed as local experts within social worlds due to acknowledged work and experi-

[1] All names used to refer to study participants are pseudonyms.

ence on their own behalf. Twenty-year-old Riley, for example, completed secondary school as a young mother via a YPP. After beginning college with a career goal of social work or nursing, Riley noted that she had become a resource for the very workers whose job it had been to support her and other young parents. By drawing on the combination of her experience as a young parent and the new medical information she was learning in college, she noted that, "I'm able to help them out 'cause they're not – a lot of them aren't...health people. They're just for support. So sometimes I'm able to help with them or share with them." Although aware that she had developed scientific knowledge that was out of the support workers' scope, Riley still moderated her explanation of this information mediation, correcting her initial wording to imply that she was "sharing" information with support workers previously positioned as experts to support her, rather than providing help in their area of weakness.

Actors in the various young parent health information worlds were engaged in constant negotiations over the boundaries of knowledge and expertise, such as when teacher Roger asked the young mothers to help him use YouTube or aspiring nurse Riley provided health information to her former support workers. Resulting from these negotiations, in the context of broader societal constructions of young mothers, were discourses that represented and maintained power relations. The following section presents a positional mapping-based exploration of these discourses.

### Discourses of Knowledge and Ignorance Applied to Young Mothers

Actors within multiple social worlds provided health information to young mothers based on the construction of young mothers as information deficient, and a reliance on health behavior models that suggest that receipt of information leads to knowledge and ultimately behavior change to improve health outcomes. However, within the young parent arena and related social worlds, young mothers were discursively constructed as both knowledgeable and ignorant. These discourses were not uniform but rather varied and intermingled across and within given subject areas. Table 1 summarizes a positional map of the basic discursive constructions of knowledge and ignorance by subject areas ranging from the social to the technical.

| | Social/sexual | Practical/ parenting | Technological/ information |
|---|---|---|---|
| Knowledgeable/ Experienced | Promiscuous "baby-mamas" | Experienced caregivers | Digital natives |
| Ignorant/Naïve | Victims of predators | Risky parents | Technology poor |

*Table 1. Discourses of young mother knowledge and ignorance*

#### Social and Sexual Knowledge

Young mothers are subject to a great degree of social stigma, spanning health care (SmithBattle, 2013), education (Kelly, 1997) and public discourse (Kelly, 1996; Yardley, 2008). Nearly every mother in this study described having been stereotyped as "slutty" by the media, other young people and older people in their communities. Most expressed frustration at the unfairness of this assumption that teenage mothers are promiscuous. As 16-year-old Alex pointed out, "Some people have sex once and get pregnant. But it's still perceived as you've slept with this [large] amount of people." The "teen mom" was constructed by actors in most of the young parents' social worlds as sexually experienced, particularly as compared with non-parenting peers. In some cases, these young women were cast as calculating and manipulative (e.g., getting pregnant to "trap" a man), while others were portrayed as naïve girls who had been taken advantage of by older men, removing attribution of agency along with blame. The dominant paradox of sexual experience (scheming promiscuity) yet ignorance (presumed non-use or ineffective use of contraceptives) failed to capture the reality of many young mothers in this study.

#### Practical Parenting Knowledge

In contrast with discourses related to sexual knowledge, the dominant construction of young mothers regarding parenting was that of ignorance. Informally, in families and community spaces, it was common for young mothers to receive unsolicited child caregiving advice from well-intentioned laypeople, or what one participant called "community grandmas." The YPP spaces were explicitly created with the mandate to educate young parents, via both secondary school curricula and parenting-specific interventions and support. In addition to providing academic instruction, YPPs were host to visiting experts who provided parenting instruction, such as formula bottle preparation and child sleep training, in accordance with current public health guidelines. Both lay advice and formal instruction were provided to remedy the perceived information needs of young parents.

In interviews, however, it became clear that it was common for young mothers to have previous child-raising experience and confidence, often through previous experience caring for younger siblings or other family members (e.g., cousins, nieces/nephews). The caregiving experience many young mothers possessed was often not acknowledged or valued by adults in the young mothers' social worlds, especially those adults with expert status and administrative authority. Jessica, a 17-year-old expectant mother who helped care for a younger sister with a chronic illness as well as a baby brother, explained that her child caregiving experience left her feeling confident about the challenges of young parenting. She disagreed with the assessment of herself as needy regarding child caregiving information.

I always had that responsibility of taking care of [my sister] ever since I was two years old, taking care of her, taking care – and then when my baby brother came out, you know taking care of him. I just loved him! I'd just always change his diaper. I would feed him, I would burp him, I would play with him, I would, you know, wake up and see him. I was so close to my baby brother. I just loved him. He was my baby. And I still do now.[...]still to this day I always take care of my little brother and I always take care of my little sister. I take them out, I feed them, I take them out to go out, I just – you know, I'm not like [their] sister. I'm just like, more like a second or third parent to them. So when I found out I was pregnant, I didn't have the problem inside of me where I was just like, "Oh my god, I don't know how to take care of a kid" or "Oh my God it's gonna be terrible. I don't wanna have a kid right now."

Despite the childcare experience of many of the young mothers, they were perceived to be in need of intensive education and surveillance. This construction of young mothers as inexperienced and lacking proper parenting knowledge had multiple elements: lack of life experience (years lived), assumption of social deprivation due to statistics correlating lower socioeconomic status with early childbearing and the notion that early childbearing must be unplanned and due to contraceptive ignorance or lack of self-efficacy.

### *Technological Knowledge*

Although hands-on experience was usually insufficient to qualify young mothers as officially knowledgeable parents, life experience as a digital native was adequate to construct them as fluent in information and communications technologies. However, there was an opposing position on this spectrum applied to the most socially and economically marginalized youth in the study. Although all young parents in the study had access to the internet and smartphones, those with the most transient and marginal lives had the poorest and least reliable access, sometimes losing or having to sell their phones for example, and rarely having a home computer.

Another subset of young mothers in this study had access to technology, but disabilities (sensory, learning, cognitive or medical) limited their full participation in information technology. Seventeen-year-old Courtney, for example, had family members with computer skills and education, but explained that she rarely used computers for schoolwork or social media because she developed migraine headaches whenever she looked at a screen for a prolonged period of time. Given that Courtney came from a middle-class socioeconomic background, neither the polarized discursive construction of the affluent digital native nor that of the marginalized youth without access to technology accurately captured her experience. Such positions that deviated from stereotypes were silenced in two ways, as the minimizing of experiences that did not fit the expected narrative (of digital youth) intersected with the stigma and self-stigma (Ali, Hassiotis, Strydom, & King, 2012) that impact youth with disabilities, often limiting their desire to speak publicly about their technology access or use challenges.

## ***Social Locations in Information Worlds***

The young parent arena and the construction and valuation of young mothers' expertise therein were shaped in part by social constructions of gender and ethnicity. The social locations of individual young mothers – in other words their positionality at the intersection of identity factors including but not limited to ethnicity, socioeconomic class and gender – shaped their experiences and relationships with actors in the social worlds within the young parent arena. In particular, gender and ethnic norms were observed to strongly influence the YPPs and related social worlds, informing information interactions and affecting negotiations over the value of different types of knowledge.

### *Gendered Worlds*

The young parent arena in general, and the YPPs in particular, were highly feminized social worlds. Most information providers, ranging from teachers and youth workers to family and friends, were women. Male staff in these feminized environments assumed the responsibility of role modeling, regularly commenting on gender equity issues and demonstrating "involved fatherhood" or pro-feminist attitudes – for example teacher Roger describing the way he and his wife balanced night time care of their own baby. Despite the presence of these male role models, the participation of young fathers in programs aimed at young parents was low. This absence reflects the intensive focus on young mothers that was evident in the YPPs, as well as more broadly in society, and may also relate to hegemonic gender norms for young fathers (e.g., pressure to drop out of school to work or enter vocational training programs). Historically, most young parent services only accepted mothers, but in recent years many have adopted more unisex names and policies. The YPPs in this study were officially open to young fathers, and they occasionally enrolled (usually along with their female partners).

The YPP staff acknowledged a double bind around father inclusion: while they felt compelled to customize their programs to the participants (primarily young women), they recognized that this might inadvertently make fathers feel unwelcome. When a young father attended a YPP, negotiations often ensued regarding participation in "feminized" activities, for example craft projects or contraceptive education. This focus on young mothers existed in several of the other social information worlds in the arena, ranging from government to the mass media. Official statistics on young fathers were rarely collected, obtaining funding for young father-specific programs was a challenge for community, and there is no "Teen Dad" reality show. The primary discursive construction of young fathers in this study was that of conspicuous silences and absences within the social arena, implying that young fathers are ignorant and unmotivated to learn about parenting due to the intersection of their age and gender.

The interactions and negotiations among social worlds in the young parent arena were also gender-informed. Virtual worlds such as the mass media and internet notwithstanding, information worlds in the young parent arena varied in degree of direct contact with YPPs, and this degree of contact was often gendered in nature. For example, medicine (masculinized world) was quite separate from the YPP, while public health nursing (feminized world) was intimately intertwined, with nurses frequently visiting and sending information to the

YPPs and other programs. Although the physicians that young mothers were seeing on a regular basis – family doctors, obstetrician/gynecologists and pediatricians – were among the most feminized fields of medicine (Canadian Medical Association, 2015), medicine has historically held, and continues to carry a more masculine connotation than nursing (David, 2000; C. Davies, 1996). The influence of both authoritative health information worlds was strong, but in situations in which a young mother's doctor's advice contradicted public health advice, she was likely to place more authority on the information from her doctor – despite, or perhaps because of, this gendered distance.

Paralleling the higher authority placed on the more distant and masculinized information worlds within the young parent arena, higher value was placed by service providers on the more masculinized, technical or scientific forms of knowledge held by young mothers. Discursive positions that attributed expertise to young mothers in technical matters (e.g., "scientific" mothering practices, fluency with information technology) increased their status within many associated social worlds. Experiential expertise in feminized reproductive and domestic matters, while sometimes valued by peers, did not grant expert status and associated cultural capital. Experience that was too "social" in nature (e.g., about relationships or sexuality) held the potential to stigmatize, either regarding taboo female promiscuity or by being too "non-scientific."

### *Ethnic and Cultural Norms*

The young parent social arena in Greater Vancouver was reflective of the broader cultural norms of the region. While the young mothers in this study were a diverse group, bringing to the YPPs and other shared spaces a variety of cultural practices, the construction of certain knowledges as valued and authoritative gave preferential treatment to health and parenting practices that conformed to Eurocentric ideals and a culture of "intensive mothering" – an ideology of motherhood that requires mothers to seek and use scientific information as well as extensive time and financial resources in monitoring and guiding child development (Hays, 1996). Knowledge and practices that were cast as "ethnic" or "native" generally served to lower young mothers' cultural capital and increase their positions as information needy in various worlds within the young parent arena, including the YPPs and daycare, and with government and health care providers. While professionals who interacted with the young mothers undoubtedly intended to be culturally sensitive – and some worked very hard to value and respect the home cultures of immigrant and refugee students in particular – this was sometimes at odds with the overarching mandate of educational interventions to help young mothers comply with approved Canadian mothering practices (i.e., those promoted by medical associations and public health organizations).

Tensions arose around the assimilation of immigrant mothers and suppression of cultural parenting practices that contradicted hegemonic Canadian norms. Young mothers could respond to such pressures by adhering to their traditional practices or by recognizing the differences in context and (at least publicly) changing their actions/language. In one YPP, during an education session on baby feeding, an immigrant student attempted to disengage from a conversation with staff members who were trying to change her baby-feeding habits by saying, "Us [ethnic group] people; we raise babies kind of differently." The teacher responded by telling her, "This is not culture. This is scientific." The student continued to resist the intervention, stating, "I just follow what my mom told me." Another immigrant young mother from the class was then called upon to model her baby feeding practices, which conformed to current public health recommendations. Through interactions such as this one, young mothers who maintained the cultural parenting practices of their families of origin were constructed as more information needy and less knowledgeable than immigrants who were willing to assimilate.

Indigenous mothers' cultural parenting and health expertise were sometimes seen as non-authoritative in a manner similar to those of immigrant mothers. In addition, many of today's young indigenous mothers in Canada are in the position of being the first generation in their families after the closure of residential schools and the "60s scoop" that removed indigenous children from family in the 1960-80s (Johnston, 1983; Sinha et al., 2011). JBiebs, whose own mother consulted her for parenting advice, was one of the young Native mothers who discussed this positionality. JBiebs' mother and grandmother had not had the opportunity to be fully raised by their own parents due to colonial policies of removal and forced assimilation, and she herself was a ward of the state. However, like other indigenous interviewees, she articulated a strong desire to parent her own child in a blend of scientific and traditional practices and was recognized within her family and community as a parenting expert. Elements of this dynamic may also be transferrable to other situations in which cohorts of children were not raised by their own parents, effectively robbing them of the ability to pass down parenting knowledge and skills, altering relationships among social worlds in the young parenting arena.

These tensions between marginalized cultural practices and Western, "scientific," intensive mothering was complicated by the fact that not all of the marginalized practices were "traditional" in terms of being pre-colonial. In some cases they were indeed (e.g., infant co-sleeping), but in others (e.g., feeding soft drinks to very young children) they were unhealthy legacies of Western colonization and oppression. Colonization thus manufactured ignorance by suppressing and delegitimizing traditional parenting and health practices. In such cases, while an individual young mother may be naïve to certain parenting information, this was due to the loss or theft of cultural knowledge over generations.

## DISCUSSION

The young parent arena contained multiple social information worlds, comprising both formal spaces for education and surveillance as well as other spaces that functioned as information grounds. Within these worlds, actors including teachers, health professionals, family members and other youth constructed understandings of expertise and knowledge. Young mothers' experiential expertise was sometimes recognized, but was expected to defer to the knowledge of credentialed experts. Experts such as teachers, youth workers and health care providers were subject to some of the same tensions as were young parents. Such mid-level experts were often highly aware of competing systems of valuing knowledges and the many and varied levels and types of expertise young mothers possessed. However, they worked within programs and organizations with a mandate to educate and inform this population in accordance with Western scientific and intensive mothering ideologies.

This study focused primarily on Proctor's first and simplest form of ignorance, as a naïve state in which young mothers are discursively constructed to be ignorant in ways that may be remedied by applying information. However, both other forms of ignorance – lost/stolen knowledge and obfuscation of knowledge – were evident as well in young mothers' social information worlds. Chatman's construction of information poverty, however, only partially applied to the positionality and practices of the young mothers in the current study, who did manage their own release of personal information in exchange for health and social services, and at times colluded with their portrayal as ignorant, aware that their expertise would not be welcomed or valued by experts. However, at the same time, most of the study population lived up to their youth-related reputation for digital literacy and connectedness and were readily able to access information from beyond the bounds of their immediate social worlds via the internet, decreasing information imbalances between themselves and experts.

### *Limitations and Strengths*

As is common for a qualitative study, this investigation did not aim for generalizability. We cannot state with certainty how representative this sample was of the larger population of young mothers. In particular, it is likely that our recruitment methods may not have reached mothers on both the most- and least-disadvantaged ends of the spectrum, as they would be the least likely to be engaged with young parent services such as YPPs. That said, the use of multiple forms of data collection to triangulate and enrich findings, along with the longitudinal approach over 15 months' time, allowed both establishment of trust relationships with study participants and the opportunity to confirm emerging interpretations of the data with service providers and with young mothers themselves, increasing the credibility and dependability of these findings, as well as their likely transferability to populations beyond the study sample.

### *Implications for Research and Practice*

This study furthers the use of situational analysis as a tool for qualitative investigation in information behavior research, including as a lens through which to analyze information worlds. Findings related to gendered and racialized and age-related discourses of risk underscore much of the extant literature, while contributing to an ongoing discussion of the relationship between agnatology (Proctor, 2008), the study of the cultural production of ignorance, and the theory of information poverty (Chatman, 1996), which includes social practices of disinformation and assessment of situational relevance of information that are largely associated with class. Understanding the social information worlds of young mothers, and in particular the conflicts that may arise between cultural knowledges and western scientific discourses of parenting, can aid in tailoring education programming aimed at supporting the well-being of young mothers and their children. It may be helpful for information providers to consider to what extent stereotypes of young people and young parents may be limiting acknowledgement of lived expertise, even while encouraging pursuit of more formal education that may lead to increased cultural capital across social worlds. Culturally specific parenting and educational interventions (e.g., indigenous parenting programs) are well-equipped to bridge information worlds that promote both traditional parenting practices and the modern Canadian context, recognizing the value of young parents' experiential expertise while providing valuable new information.

## CONCLUSION

This analysis explored the information worlds of young mothers and examined the construction of expertise according to social hierarchies of power therein. It elucidated discourses of knowledge and ignorance applied to young mothers, in which the "teen mom" is portrayed paradoxically as knowledgeable and networked yet ignorant and inexperienced. Despite the fact the many young parents have a great deal of childcare experience, they are (stereo)typically perceived as in need of intensive parenting education by virtue of their age. Social and cultural expertise, while sometimes respected by peers and educators, did not generally increase the cultural capital of young mothers. While many education interventions are built on models that portray information as key to building knowledge and changing behaviours, young mothers may already possess expertise that may conflict with the authoritative information being communicated. Navigating these complexities with nuance, rather than understanding young mothers as unilaterally information needy, may enable more effective interventions to improve the well-being of young mothers and their children.

## ACKNOWLEDGMENTS

The authors would like to thank the young parents and service providers who participated in this study, sharing their many forms of knowledge and expertise. This study was funded by the Canadian Institutes of Health Research grants GIR-127079 and MOP-126032.

## REFERENCES


Anwar, E., & Stanistreet, D. (2015). "It has not ruined my life; it has made my life better": A qualitative investigation of the experiences and future aspirations of young mothers from the North West of England. *Journal of Public Health, 37*(2), 269-76. https://doi.org/10.1093/pubmed/fdu045

Barcelos, C. A. (2013). Producing (potentially) pregnant teen bodies: Biopower and adolescent pregnancy in the USA. *Critical Public Health, 24*(4), 476-488. https://doi.org/10.1080/09581596.2013.853869

Barcelos, C. A., & Gubrium, A. C. (2014). Reproducing stories: Strategic narratives of teen pregnancy and motherhood. *Social Problems, 61*(3), 466-481. https://doi.org/10.1525/sp.2014.12241

Basch, C. E. (2011). Teen pregnancy and the achievement gap among urban minority youth. *The Journal of School Health, 81*(10), 614–618. https://doi.org/10.1111/j.1746-1561.2011.00635.x

Batool, S. H., & Webber, S. (2016). Conceptions of school libraries and the role of school librarians: Findings from case studies of primary schools in Lahore. In *Proceedings of the ninth international conference on conceptions of library and information science, Uppsala, Sweden, June 27-29, 2016* (Vol. 9). Uppsala, Sweden. Retrieved from http://www.informationr.net/ir/22-1/colis/colis1606.html

Berger, P. L., & Luckmann, T. (1967). *The social construction of reality: A treatise in sociology of knowledge*. Garden City, N.Y: Doubleday.

Bonell, C. (2004). Why is teenage pregnancy conceptualized as a social problem? A review of quantitative research from the USA and UK. *Culture, Health & Sexuality, 6*(3), 255-272. https://doi.org/10.1080/1369105031000164302

Breheny, M., & Stephens, C. (2010). Youth or disadvantage? The construction of teenage mothers in medical journals. *Culture, Health & Sexuality, 12*(3), 307-322. https://doi.org/10.1080/13691050903513234

Burnett, G., & Jaeger, P. T. (2008). Small worlds, lifeworlds, and information: The ramifications of the information behaviours of social groups in public policy and the public sphere. *Information Research, 13*(2). Retrieved from http://informationr.net/ir/13-2/paper346.html

Camic, C., Gross, N., & Lamont, M. (2011). *Social knowledge in the making*. University of Chicago Press.

Chabot, C., Shoveller, J. A., Johnson, J. L., & Prkachin, K. (2010). Morally problematic: Young mothers' lives as parables about the dangers of sex. *Sex Education: Sexuality, Society and Learning, 10*(2), 201-215.

Charmaz, K. (2007). *Constructing grounded theory: A practical guide through qualitative analysis*. Thousand Oaks, CA: Sage Publications.

Charmaz, K. (2009). Constructivist grounded theory methods. In J. M. Morse (Ed.), *Developing grounded theory: The second generation* (pp. 127-154). Walnut Creek, CA: Left Coast Press.

Chatman, E. A. (1991). Life in a small world: Applicability of gratification theory to information-seeking behavior. *Journal of the American Society for Information Science, 42*(6), 438–449. https://doi.org/10.1002/(SICI)1097-4571(199107)42:6<438::AID-ASI6>3.0.CO;2-B

Clarke, A. (2005). *Situational analysis: Grounded theory after the postmodern turn*. SAGE.

Clarke, A. E. (2003). Situational analyses: Grounded theory mapping after the postmodern turn. *Symbolic Interaction, 26*(4), 553-576. https://doi.org/10.1525/si.2003.26.4.553

Collins, H., & Evans, R. (2007). *Rethinking expertise*. Chicago, IL: University of Chicago Press.

Collins, H. M., & Evans, R. (2002). The third wave of science studies studies of expertise and experience. *Social Studies of Science, 32*(2), 235-296. https://doi.org/10.1177/0306312702032002003

Dervin, B. (1992). From the mind's eye of the "user": The sense-making qualitative-quantitative methodology. In *Qualitative research in information management* (pp. 61-84). Libraries Unlimited. Retrieved from http://www.ideals.illinois.edu/bitstream/handle/2142/2281/Dervin1992a.htm

Dryburgh, H. (2000). Teenage pregnancy. *Health Reports, 12*(1), 9-19.

Duncan, S. (2007). What's the problem with teenage parents? And what's the problem with policy? *Critical Social Policy, 27*(3), 307-334. https://doi.org/10.1177/0261018307078845

Fields, J. (2005). "Children having children": Race, innocence, and sexuality education. *Social Problems, 52*(4), 549-571. https://doi.org/10.1525/sp.2005.52.4.549

Fisher, K. E., & Naumer, C. M. (2006). Information grounds: Theoretical basis and empirical findings on information flow in social settings. In *New directions in human information behavior* (pp. 93-111).

Fraser, A. M., Brockert, J. E., & Ward, R. H. (1995). Association of young maternal age with adverse reproductive outcomes. *The New England Journal of Medicine, 332*(17), 1113-1117. https://doi.org/10.1056/NEJM199504273321701

Furstenberg, F. F. (1976). The social consequences of teenage parenthood. *Family Planning Perspectives, 8*(4), 148-164. https://doi.org/10.2307/2134201

Gold, R., Kawachi, I., Kennedy, B. P., Lynch, J. W., & Connell, F. A. (2001). Ecological analysis of teen birth rates: Association with community income and income inequality. *Maternal and Child Health Journal, 5*(3), 161-167.

Grace, D., & Sen, B. (2013). Community resilience and the role of the public library. *Library Trends, 61*(3), 513-541.

Greyson, D. (2016). Evolution of information practices over time. *Proceedings of the Association for Information Science and Technology, 53*(1). doi: 10.1002/pra2.2016.14505301052

Greyson, D. (2017). Health information practices of young parents. *Journal of Documentation, 73*(5).

Habermas, J. (1991). *The structural transformation of the public sphere: An inquiry into a category of bourgeois society*. MIT Press.

Hanna, B. (2001). Negotiating motherhood: The struggles of teenage mothers. *Journal of Advanced Nursing*, *34*(4), 456–464.

Hoffman, S. D., & Maynard, R. A. (2008). *Kids having kids: Economic costs & social consequences of teen pregnancy*. Washington, DC: The Urban Institute Press.

Jaeger, P. T., & Burnett, G. (2010). *Information worlds: Social Context, technology, and information behavior in the age of the internet*. London, UK: Routledge.

Karlova, N. A., & Fisher, K. E. (2013). "Plz RT": A social diffusion model of misinformation and disinformation for understanding human information behaviour. *Information Research*, *18*(1), paper 573.

Kelly, D. M. (2000). *Pregnant with meaning: Teen mothers and the politics of inclusive schooling*. New York, NY: Peter Lang.

Kelly, D. M. (2007). Young mothers, agency and collective action: Issues and challenges. *Journal of the Motherhood Initiative for Research and Community Involvement*, *9*(1). Retrieved from http://pi.library.yorku.ca/ojs/index.php/jarm/article/view/5131

Langille, D. B. (2007). Teenage pregnancy: trends, contributing factors and the physician's role. *CMAJ*, *176*(11), 1601-1602. https://doi.org/10.1503/cmaj.070352

Loudon, K., Buchanan, S., & Ruthven, I. (2016). The everyday life information seeking behaviours of first-time mothers. *Journal of Documentation, 72*(1), 24-46. doi: 10.1108/JD-06-2014-0080

McKenzie, P. J. (2003). A model of information practices in accounts of everyday-life information seeking. *Journal of Documentation*, *59*(1), 19-40. https://doi.org/10.1108/00220410310457993

Penman-Aguilar, A., Carter, M., Snead, M. C., & Kourtis, A. P. (2013). Socioeconomic disadvantage as a social determinant of teen childbearing in the U.S. *Public Health Reports (Washington, D.C.: 1974)*, *128 Suppl 1*, 5–22.

Proctor, R. (2008). Agnotology: A missing term to describe the cultural production of ignorance (and its study). In R. Proctor & L. L. Schiebinger (Eds.), *Agnotology: The making and unmaking of ignorance*. Stanford, Calif: Stanford University Press.

Savolainen, R. (1993). The sense-making theory: Reviewing the interests of a user-centered approach to information seeking and use. *Information Processing & Management*, *29*(1), 13-28. https://doi.org/10.1016/0306-4573(93)90020-E

Schiebinger, L. (2004). Feminist history of colonial science. *Hypatia*, *19*(1), 233-254. https://doi.org/10.1111/j.1527-2001.2004.tb01276.x

Scholl, T. O., Hediger, M. L., Huang, J., Johnson, F. E., Smith, W., & Ances, I. G. (1992). Young maternal age and parity. Influences on pregnancy outcome. *Annals of Epidemiology*, *2*(5), 565-575.

Seamark, C. J., & Lings, P. (2004). Positive experiences of teenage motherhood: A qualitative study. *The British Journal of General Practice*, *54*(508), 813-818.

Statistics Canada. (2012). *Population and dwelling counts, for census metropolitan areas, 2011 and 2006 censuses* (2011 Census). Ottawa, Ontario: Government of Canada.

Sullivan, S., & Tuana, N. (Eds.). (2007). *Race and epistemologies of ignorance*. Albany: State University of New York Press.

Tuominen, K., & Savolainen, R. (1997). A social constructionist approach to the study of information use as discursive action. *Information Research, ISIC '96 Proceedings of an international conference on Information seeking in context*, 81–96.

Yu, L. (2012). Towards a reconceptualization of the "information worlds of individuals." *Journal of Librarianship and Information Science*, *44*(1), 3-18. https://doi.org/10.1177/0961000611424586

Zipf, G. K. (1949). *Human behavior and the principle of least effort* (Vol. xi). Oxford, UK: Addison-Wesley Press.

# Understanding and Modeling Behavior Patterns in Cross-Device Web Search

**Shuguang Han***
*University of Pittsburgh, USA. Shh69@pitt.edu*

**Yu Chi**
*University of Pittsburgh, USA. yuc73@pitt.edu*

**Daqing He**
*University of Pittsburgh, USA. dah44@pitt.edu*

## ABSTRACT

**Recent studies have witnessed an increasing popularity of cross-device web search, in which a user resumes a previously started search task from one device to a later session on another. The complexity of this novel search mode, mainly due to the involvement of interruptions and multiple devices, makes users conduct new types of search behaviors and adopt novel search patterns. Though past research has studied this new search mode, there still lacks a sufficient understanding of cross-device search behaviors. To better understand users' behavioral patterns, we adopted hidden Markov model (HMM) to model observed cross-device search behaviors and their underlying search pat- terns under the same framework. HMM is a widely adopted machine learning technique with the main assumption that observations (e.g., observed search behaviors) are driven by hidden variables (e.g., hidden behavioral patterns). Utilizing the data collected from a user study consisting of two types of cross-session search conditions – mobile-to-desktop (M-D) and desktop-to-desktop (D-D) – we demonstrate the validity of using HMM for modeling and identifying hidden behavioral patterns, and based on the identified patterns, we discover that re-finding is a common pattern at the beginning of the continued search session, and querying, exploitation and exploration contribute to the dominated behaviors in later search stages. Our results also show clear device effects on cross-device search (M-D) vs cross-session search (D-D). All these evidences confirm that better support mechanisms are in critical need for a cross-device search and the HMM- based modeling can help.**

## KEYWORDS

cross-device web search, cross-session web search, search pattern analysis, information seeking process

## INTRODUCTION

With the wide adoption of mobile devices (e.g., tablets, smartphones) in web search, researchers have started to analyze users' mobile search behaviors and investigate effective ways of supporting such behaviors (Han et al., 2016; Song et al., 2013). Mobile devices bring both opportunities and challenges for search. On the one hand, mobile devices break the time and location barriers so that people can search for information at any time and place where their information needs are triggered. On the other hand, they also have several physical constraints – small screen and keyboard sizes, constrained mobile data usage and limited cellphone battery – all of which impede the continuity of users' search processes on mobile devices. As a result, search engines have recently observed an increasing trend of cross-device web search (Montanez et al., 2014).

Through analyzing Microsoft Bing's web search logs in 2014, Montanez et al. (2014) found that more than 5% of searchers are now multi-device users, and they are highly active users and take account for about 16% of all search queries. Similarly, using sampled search engine behavior logs from Microsoft Bing in 2012, Wang et al. (2013) discovered that 15% of device switches are accompanied with task continuation. A recent Facebook study also revealed that people are entering a multi-device world and around 40% of online adults have the experience of starting a task on one device but finishing it on another. With several years of development, it is also reasonable to believe that these numbers are further increased at the current moment.

The growing trend of cross-device web search has intrigued several recent studies (Montanez et al., 2014; Wang et al., 2013) to investigate cross-device web search behaviors, such as users' topical, temporal and geo-spatial search processes, as well as ways of automatic detecting web search tasks that will be continued in the near future (Agichtein et al., 2012; Wang et al., 2013). The above studies presented some initial understanding of cross-device web search; however, there remain few analyses regarding the complicated behaviors in this new search format. The complexity of a cross-device web search lies on the fact that it involves multiple sessions and devices and interruptions between sessions. Therefore, traditional research findings based on single session/device cannot truly reflect users' search processes in this search scenario because users often develop new search patterns to cope with the complexity.

To uncover users' behavioral patterns, this paper adopted hidden variable models, in which each hidden variable is assumed to be a search pattern and user behaviors are driven by

---

80th Annual Meeting of the Association for Information Science & Technology, Washington, DC | Oct. 27-Nov. 1, 2017


*Shuguang Han is currently working at Google.

hidden variables. In fact, the hidden variable approach was studied as a promising direction for analyzing behavior patterns in many other search conditions (Han et al., 2013; Luo et al., 2014; Yue et al., 2014).

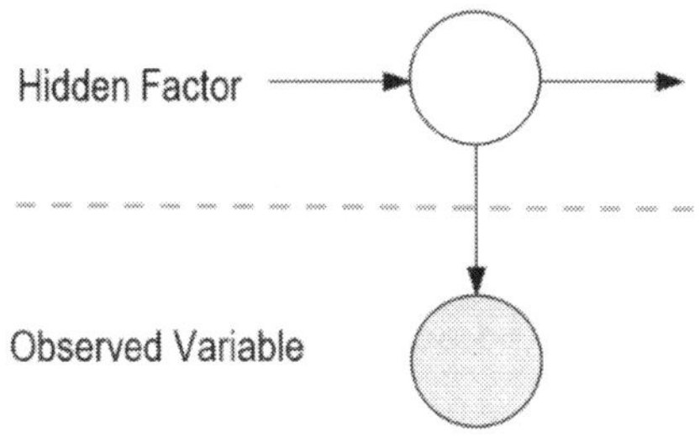


***Figure 1:*** *Hidden variable model for behavior modeling*

To be specific, a search pattern refers to a high-level plan designed by a user to facilitate her search (Bates, 1979). For example, a user, in the continued search session, may sometimes plan to restore her task contexts (because of forgetting) so that she is likely to re-visit previously accessed information. At the other time, she may want to explore in breadth; thus, she searches a general topic and clicks several relevant or marginal relevant documents to cover multiple topics. To automatically discover hidden search patterns, we adopted an unsupervised hidden variable approach proposed by Yue et al. (2014), who employed the standard hidden Markov model (HMM) for automatically bridging search patterns (modeled as the hidden variables in HMM) with observed search actions. It assumes a Markov process on search patterns, and all search actions are generated by them (see Figure 1). The hidden factor may change or update with users continuing searching and exploring the result space.

The major goal of this paper is to uncover hidden search patterns based on the observed search actions. To provide a deeper and more comprehensive understanding of a cross-device search process, we also included a baseline with multiple search sessions all performed on the same device. This was motivated by existing literature, finding that people's search behaviors often change significantly across different devices (Song et al., 2013; Yi et al., 2008). For example, compared to desktop search, mobile device search is less convenient for typing search queries and reading thoroughly on webpages. In terms of the cross-device search conditions, although there are other forms of cross-session or cross-device web search (i.e., M-M and D-M), this paper only focused on mobile-to-desktop (M-D) search and involved desktop-to-desktop (D-D) search as a baseline. This is because studying all four conditions significantly increased the cognitive loads of the participants we recruited to generate the search data.

Additionally, we assume that the cross-session web search we study here only contains two search sessions, one initial session before the interruption and one continued session after the interruption. This follows most of the existing studies on this topic, and both sessions are taken into account when analyzing cross-device search behaviors.

Overall, this paper studies the following two research questions.

**RQ1**: What are the major search patterns in a cross-device web search, and what are the differences between these patterns in the initial search session (first session) and that in the continued session (second session)?

**RQ2**: What are the differences between users' search patterns in cross-device web search and that in the same-device cross-session web search using desktop?

## RELATED WORK

The review of relevant literature focuses on two areas: understanding cross-device web search behaviors and modeling these behaviors. Since the study of cross-device web search remains in a limited number, the following literature review mainly focused on cross-session web search without a further consideration of device difference.

### *Understanding Cross-Session Web Search Behavior*

Users of modern search engines are increasingly engaged in complex and exploratory search tasks, which often trigger them to search for a long period of time, either in one continuous session or across multiple sessions. The latter is called cross-session web search in literature (Agichtein et al., 2012), and when different devices are adopted, it is referred as cross-device web search (Montanez et al., 2014).

Based on a diary study, Sellen et al. (2002) found that 40% of people's information gathering tasks cannot be completed in one single session, mainly due to interruption. Mark et al. (2005) showed that users often require a recovery from an interruption – a process called task resumption. Through a university-based user study, Teevan et al. (2007) identified that people often forgot their original search queries even within a short time interruption like one hour. In order to resume the previously started task in a later session, users in a cross-session search process often issued duplicated queries or revisited the same webpages at the beginning of the continued session. This was studied as information re-finding in the literature (Tyler and Teevan, 2010). According to Morris et al. (2008), many users (63.2%) have to utilize external tools for better assisting their memorization for task resumption; otherwise, they may easily forget information.

In addition to the analysis of user behavior types, many other prior studies found that users' search content also changes across multiple search sessions. Eickhoff et al. (2014) found that with search going on, users tend to issue more complex search queries and explore more diverse content. A possible reason is that the later session is the continuation from the previous one, in which users may have already mastered partial knowledge so that they do not need to search from scratch in the continued search session (Han et al., 2015b).

Most of the previous studies focused on analyzing search behavior for the same-device cross-session web search, whereas the understanding of cross-device search behaviors remains to be quite limited. Song et al. (2013) found that transferring information from search activities on desktop computers could improve the users' search performance on the continued mobile devices such as tablet and smartphone.

### *Modeling Cross-Session Web Search Behavior*

Because of the novelty of cross-device web searches, there are few related studies working on modeling such behaviors. However, there are indeed relevant studies attempting to model user behaviors for similar search conditions such as long-time single-session search.

When modeling search behaviors in a long-term web search process, researchers often went beyond the observed search actions and explored the underlying principles (or patterns) of search behaviors. Based on recorded user behaviors, Hölscher and Strube (2000) examined and compared different search stages and search strategies between internet experts and newbies, Chen and Cooper (2002) identified several usage patterns in a web-based library catalog using a stochastic model. However, these studies simply treated the aggregation of several consecutive system-logged actions as a search stage or a strategy. A recent study by Xie and Joo (2010) raised the importance of using search patterns as a means to examine search behaviors, and they manually categorized 13 different search patterns, including learning, exploring, examining search results, modifying search items, monitoring search progress, preserving relevant information, etc. Since most of these search patterns are manually defined and categorized by domain experts, it has limited scalability and generalizability.

To fix this gap, Han et al. (2013) and Yue et al. (2012, 2014) proposed to employ the hidden Markov model (HMM) for automatic search pattern identification, in which a search pattern was treated as a hidden state and each search action (e.g., query, click, etc.) was thought as being generated by different search patterns. Since HMM is a well-established unsupervised machine learning approach, it can be easily applied to any large-scale dataset. Besides, HMM makes it possible to interpret users' observed actions using the automatically discovered hidden search patterns. Therefore, following previous studies, this paper also applied HMM to model search behaviors across the whole cross-device web search process.

## DATA COLLECTION

To examine the two research questions stated in the introduction, we need data collections in the first step. Although modern search engines can provide large-scale search transaction logs from a massive number of users, an accurate extraction of cross-session web search tasks from these search logs requires significant post-processing effort. To create an ideal cross-device web search environment, researchers often conducted lab-controlled user studies (Han et al., 2015 a, b; Liu et al., 2013), in which they can monitor the whole search process.

In this paper, we directly use the user study data provided by Han et al. (2015b) for two reasons. Firstly, it includes users' web search data for both cross-device and same-device cross-session web searches, which can help us answer RQ1. Secondly, the dataset includes users' web search behavioral logs, which provide us with rich information for follow-up data analysis. In terms of search tasks, the dataset contains six properly-designed cross-session web search tasks, including two people search (PE) tasks, two product search (PD) tasks and two news search (NE) tasks. All of these task topics were surveyed from Mechanical Turk. Two of them are searching for the comparisons between different products (e.g., one of the task topic is to search for iPad mini vs. Android tablets vs. Windows tablets), another two tasks were to explore the biographical information about celebrities (e.g., one of them is to search for research fields, contribution and collaboration about a famous scientist) and the last two were looking for news about the growth/decline of two industries (e.g., the expansion and growth of Facebook). The detailed descriptions of each task can be found in Han et al. (2015b).

We acknowledge that the lab study might introduce artificial factors since the search tasks were pre-assigned instead of being originated from users themselves. However, the task simulation approach has demonstrated to be effective in analyzing and evaluating interactive information retrieval systems (Borlund, 2000; Kelly, 2009).

The dataset contains web search logs from 24 participants, including 16 undergraduate and eight graduate students. All of them are self-rated experienced searchers, and they conduct web searches on a daily basis. The dataset contains 1,419 search queries (794 from the initial session and 625 from the continued one), 3,186 click-through webpages (1,736 from the initial session and 1,450 from the continued one) and 2,108 saved webpages (1,191 from the initial session and 917 from the continued one).

## MODELING SEARCH BEHAVIOR WITH HMM

As mentioned in the Introduction section, hidden Markov model (HMM) is adopted in this paper to model sequential search behaviors and automatically discover hidden patterns. HMM is a commonly adopted machine learning algorithm for modeling the sequential data patterns. It assumes that there is a sequence of hidden states, each of which drives the adoption of an observed action. An illustration of the HMM for this study can be shown in Figure 2, in which users' search behaviors ($A$) such as query and click are observed variables, and they are driven by hidden search patterns ($H$) with different probabilities (i.e., emission probability). The search behavior sequence forms a Markov chain, where each search pattern can transfer to or be transferred from another search pattern with different probabilities (i.e., transition probability). A simpler and more detailed description of the HMM-based behavior modeling can be found in Han et al. (2013).

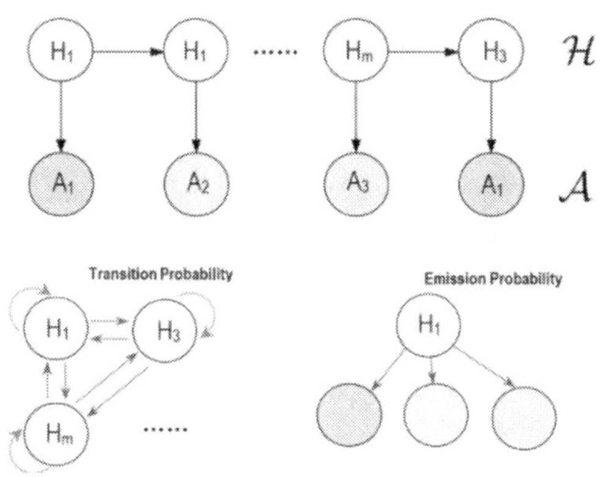


*Figure 2: A Hidden Markov model (HMM) based approach for search process modeling*

### *Defining Observed Search Actions*

*A* denotes a set of observed search actions. Han et al. (2013) and Yue et al. (2014) defined a set of simple search actions such as query, click and save. However, these behaviors are often too coarse-grained and are unable to further distinguish the same action with different intents. For example, clicking a document with a long-dwell time might indicate that a relevant document is found, whereas a short-dwell click often indicates that a document is marginally relevant or irrelevant (Han et al., 2016; Hassan et al., 2013). Because of this, Luo et al. (2014) and Guan et al. (2013) further divided the click actions into the SAT (satisfactory) click (a click with more than 30-second dwell) and regular click.

In this paper, we also use dwell time to distinguish different observed search actions. Dwell time of a clicked document is computed based on the time interval between the click and the next search action. If a click is the last logged search action in a session, the dwell time is labeled as unknown since the time cannot be reasonably inferred. In addition, if a user stays more than three minutes on one webpage, it might indicate that she has left, so we also label it as unknown.

A cross-device web search includes multiple search sessions, in which users often adopt different strategies (Han et al., 2015). Therefore, we define four types of behaviors for the initial session – query (QU), long-dwell click (LD), short-dwell click (SD) and click with unknown time (UN). However, these actions cannot fully cover the more complex search behaviors for the continued sessions. For example, due to the interruption between the initial and the continued session, users in the continued session might want to re-find documents that have clicked in the initial session. Therefore, two clicked documents with the same level of dwell time in the continued session might represent different intentions: a short-dwell click on an already-visited document might be for reminding memory, whereas a short-dwell click on a new document usually indicates that the document is less relevant (Hassan et al., 2013). Therefore, in the continued session, we distinguish whether a click is a repeated click or a new click. Here, we do not model the within-session repeated clicks although we acknowledge that they do exist too.

Consequently, the observed search actions in the continued session have three dimensions, query vs. click, new vs. repeat, and short-dwell vs. long-dwell. Also, as shown in Table 1, we define eight different types of observed search actions in the continued session: the first two (RQU and NQU) are related to query, the next three (RCLD, RCSD, and RCUN) are related to repeated clicks and the last three (NCLD, NCSD, and NCUN) are regarding to new clicks.

| Session | Abbr. | Action | Description |
|---|---|---|---|
| initial | QU | query | issues a query |
| initial | LD | long-dwell click | clicks a document and stays more than 30 seconds |
| initial | SD | short-dwell click | clicks a document and stays less than 30 seconds |
| initial | UN | new query | issues a new query |
| continued | RQU | repeat query | issues a query that was used in the initial search session |
| continued | NQU | new query | issues a query that was not used in the initial session |
| continued | RCLD | long-dwell repeat click | clicks a document accessed in the initial session, and stays more than 30 seconds |
| continued | RCSD | short-dwell repeat click | clicks a document that was accessed in the initial session, and stays less than 30 seconds |
| continued | RCUN | unknown-dwell repeat click | clicks a document that was accessed in the initial search session, and stays with unknown time |
| continued | NCLD | long-dwell new click | clicks a document that was not accessed in the initial session, and stays more than 30 seconds |
| continued | NCSD | short-dwell new click | clicks a document that was not accessed in the initial session, and stays less than 30 seconds |
| continued | NCUN | unknown-dwell new click | clicks a document that was not accessed in the initial session, and stays with unknown time |

*Table 1: A detailed description of the observed search actions in a cross-device cross-session search.*

In this paper, a query $q_j$ is defined as a repeated query if it matches any query $q_i$ from the prior session with more than 80% of similarity (we also tried thresholds like 75% and 85%, the HMM results looked quite similar for both). Here, the similarity is computed with the #overlapped query terms / max (length of $q_i$, length of $q_j$ ).

### *Determining the Number of Hidden States*

*H* represents a set of hidden states (i.e., search patterns) a user employs. In a fully automated algorithm, the number of search patterns *m* is an important parameter to setup, which refers to the model selection problem. A complex model with a larger number of hidden states can describe the model more precisely but has the risk of overfitting. *A* simple model is less likely to be over-fitted, but might be unable to discover proper data patterns. For model selection, we directly adopt a commonly used Bayesian information criterion (BIC). A more detailed explanation about BIC and its usage can be referred to Schwarz (1978). In general, lower BIC values indicate better HMM models.

We used our adopted dataset to setup the model parameters. We constructed separate HMM models for the initial search session and the continued search session since the two sessions show different search patterns. For the HMM of the initial session, the BIC model indicates that three hidden states are optimal, whereas the HMM of the continued session has four hidden states.

## SEARCH BEHAVIORS IN M-D SEARCH

As stated, an HMM consists of three important components – the prior probability (i.e., the likelihood of a state being a starting state), emission probability (i.e., the probability of a hidden state in generating different search actions) and transition probability (i.e., the probability of a hidden state transits to another hidden state). Through them, we can establish connections between a hidden state and the corresponding observed search actions, based on which the name or the meaning of hidden states can be manually assigned. In the following sections, we conduct a simple manual analysis of the search patterns in different conditions.

### Patterns in the Initial Session of M-D Search

Figure 3 shows that the HMM of the initial session of M-D search includes three hidden states. Their labels are manually crafted based on their emission and transition probabilities. According to the model, H1 is associated with query action. Therefore, we label it as *Querying*.

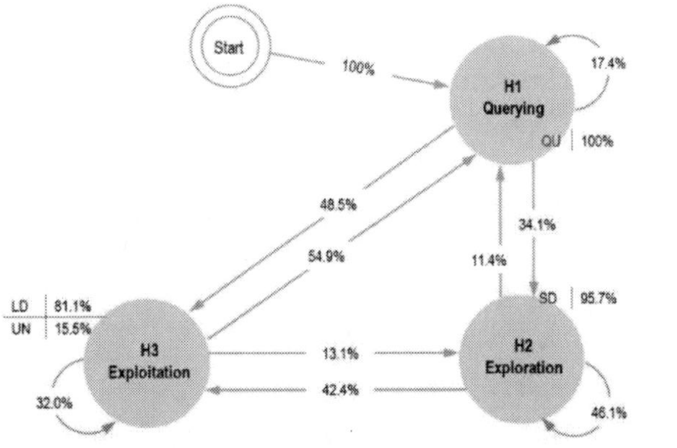


***Figure 3:** HMM patterns for the initial session of M-D. The shaded circles with labels H1 to H3 denote the three hidden states, the double circle with label start indicates the start state and the numbers from this state denote the prior probabilities, a probability table near each hidden state represents the emission probability and arrows among hidden states denote the transition probability. Here, we only report the emission/transition probabilities larger than 5%.*

In H2, almost all actions are connected with clicking a result page but staying a relatively short period of time (SD). We assume that it might be due to that the participant is exploring information and encounters only marginally relevant or non-relevant results. The majority actions of H3 are associated with participants' clicks of SERP results with long-dwell time (LD). This usually means that the participant finds a relevant document.

When labeling hidden states in the HMM model, we stay consistent with existing literatures and adopt the concepts proposed by previous studies unless there are no appropriate names. During their study of hidden states in a single long search session, Luo et al. (2014) defined four states in two dimensions (2-by-2 states): 1) the relevant dimension, describing whether a user finds a *relevant* or *non-relevant* document and 2) the exploration dimension, indicating whether a user is *exploring* a new topic or *exploiting* the current topic. Their results revealed that *exploration* is the dominating state for non-relevant documents, whereas *exploitation* is the dominated state for relevant documents.

Their definitions are consistent with the H2 and H3 hidden states in the HMM results in Figure 3, in which H2 is the exploration state for short-dwell clicks (that usually indicates a non-relevant or marginally relevant document), and H3 is the exploitation state for long-dwell clicks (that often implies a relevant document). As a result, we label H2 and H3 as *Exploration* and *Exploitation* respectively, to highlight their differences.

These three search patterns (H1, H2 and H3) and their transition probabilities indicate that the initial session of M-D search looks similar to Marchionini (1995)'s theoretical discussion of single-session behavioral patterns, in which querying, examining results and extracting information is a set of central sub-processes and the transitions between them are high. Also, our model is consistent with Yue et al. (2014)'s HMM for individual search.

### Patterns in the Continued Session of M-D Search

Figure 4 shows the HMM for the continued session of M-D search. The label for each hidden state is also manually crafted based on the qualitative understanding of emission and transition probabilities. Similar to the HMM for the initial session of M-D search, this model also has three hidden states named as *Querying* (H2), *Exploration* (H3) and *Exploitation* (H4).

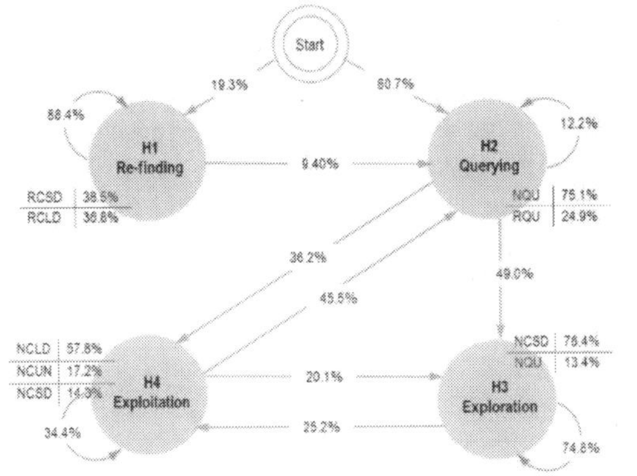


*Figure 4: HMM results for the continued session of M-D Search. Notations and symbols are the same as Figure 3.*

In addition, a new hidden state H1 is presented in this model. H1 is mainly related to the observed search actions RCLD and RCSD. It is likely that H1 stands for re-finding, whose goal is to restore task that often happens at the beginning of the continued session. Thus, we name it *Re-finding*.

To review the temporal distribution of each search pattern over the continued search session, we plotted the percentages of identified hidden states based on their timestamp in the session. As shown in Figure 5, *Re-finding* and *Querying* are more likely to occur at the beginning of the continued session – around 40% to 50% of *Re-finding* (H1) and *Querying* (H2) occurred within the first minute of the continued session. This is consistent with the conclusion from Tyler and Teevan (2010) based on a large-scale analysis of Microsoft Bing's search logs.

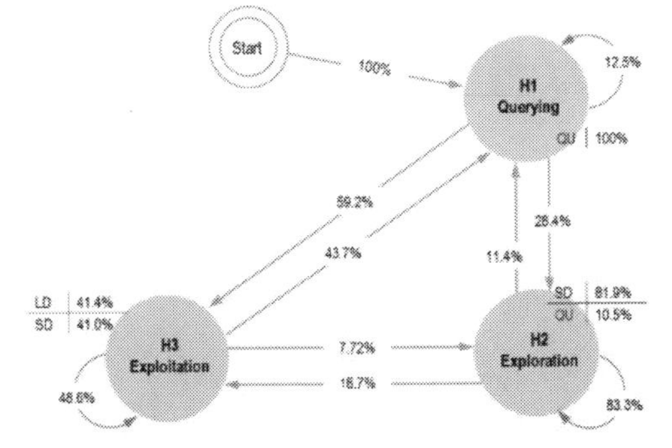


*Figure 5: HMM results for the initial session of the desktop-to-desktop search. Notations and symbols are the same as Figure 3.*

When examining the transition probabilities among different hidden states, it is interesting to see that about 20% of the searches directly started with a re-finding pattern rather than querying (which is around 80%). This is a relatively high proportion and highlights the importance of the re-finding pattern in the continued session. It is also notable that the self-state transition of the *re-finding* state (88.4%) is greatly higher than its transition to the *Querying* (9.4%), which demonstrates that re-finding is employed intensively at the beginning of the initial session.

Comparing the two HMM models in Figures 4 and 5, it is obvious that both models detect querying, exploration and exploitation as three important hidden patterns.

However, the HMM of the continued session (Figure 4) has lower transition probabilities from *Querying* to *Exploitation*, from *Exploration* to *Exploitation*, and they have higher transition probabilities from *Querying* to *Exploration*. This indicates that participants in the continued session tend to be more selective for relevant documents, probably because they have already explored relevant documents in the initial session, making the search for novel and relevant documents more difficult.

## COMPARISON TO D-D SEARCH

For the purpose of comparison, we also obtained two HMM models for the initial session and the continued session of the desktop-to-desktop (D-D) search using the data presented in the data collection. Through running BIC evaluation, we choose three hidden states for the initial session, and four hidden states for the continued session. The proportion of different types of search actions on D-D are also very similar to M-D; thus, we do not plot the details as Figure 6.

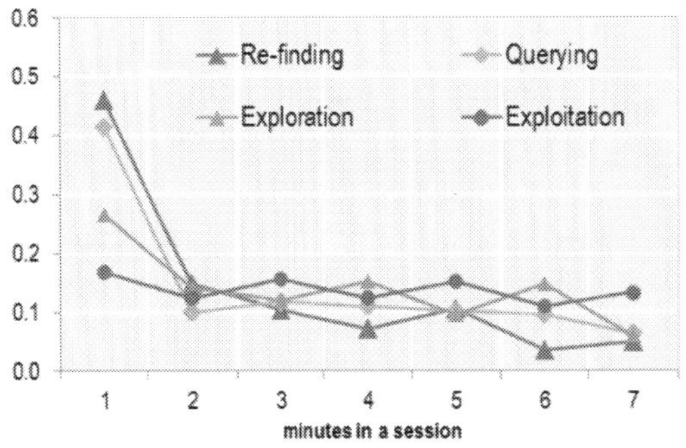


*Figure 6: The temporal distribution of search patterns, i.e., the percentage of certain pattern over different time slots. The X-axis rep- resents the Nth minute for each session, and Y-axis denotes the percentage of such pattern in the whole search session.*

Comparing between the HMM for the initial session of D-D (see Figure 6) and the HMM for the initial session of M-D (see Figure 3), we can see that desktop users performed more transition from *Querying* to *Exploitation* (59.2% vs 48.5%) but fewer *Querying* to *Exploration* (28.4% vs 34.1%) and fewer *Exploration* to *Exploitation* (16.7% vs 42.4%). This implies that users come out of relatively high-quality queries in the initial session of D-D comparing to M-D, thus tend to be more selective and keep exploring till finding high-quality documents. Possible reasons for such difference might be the small screen size and the inconvenience of typing queries on the mobile device.

In contrast, the HMM outputs for the continued session of D-D (see Figure 7) show similar results as that of M-D (see Figure 5). The emission probabilities and the transition probabilities of most hidden states are similar between the two HMMs, except that HMM for D-D has higher transition probability from *Exploitation* to *Querying* (56.0% vs 45.5%) but less from *Exploitation* to *Exploration* (9.25% vs 20.1%). This could be due to the effect of better-performed searches in the initial session of D-D in which users could already explore more comparing to the initial session of M-D.

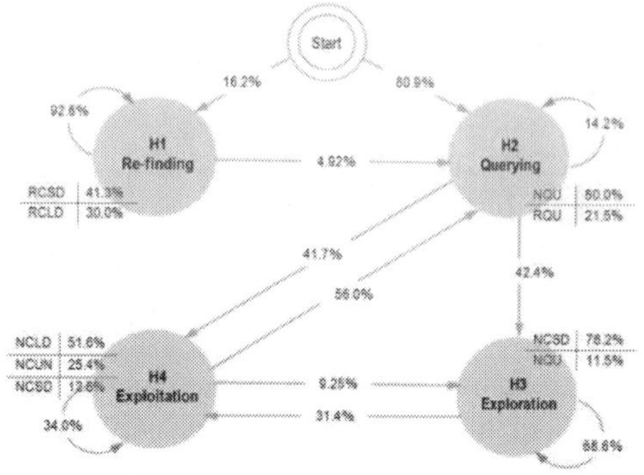


***Figure 7:*** *The HMM results for the search behaviors in the continued session of desktop-to-desktop search. Notations and symbols are the same as Figure 3.*

## PREDICTING RE-FINDING USING HMM OUTPUTS

The above analysis demonstrates that HMM indeed uncovers important search patterns from observed search actions and thus is capable of modeling search behaviors for long-session search with diverse types of search behaviors. However, there still lacks a clear message about whether and how HMM outputs can be applied in the real-world, cross-device search tasks. Given the importance of re-finding behaviors for task resumption, we further attempt to apply the HMM results for locating the re-clicked documents. More specifically, we try to predict the documents from the initial session that are more likely to be re-clicked at the beginning of the continued session. The following section will elaborate the predictions of the re-finding behaviors for both M-D and D-D datasets.

HMM maps each observed search action with a hidden state. When conducting predictions, we assumed that clicks under one particular hidden state (this study used the hidden state *H3: Exploitation* for both M-D and D-D datasets) as the ones that will be re-visited in the future. To understand how good the prediction is, we computed precision, recall and F1.

We also established a set of baselines for comparisons. The baseline forecasts repeat clicks in the future based on dwell time, so we involved two baselines – *short-dwell* and *long-dwell* approaches forecast all short-dwell and long-dwell clicks as repeat clicks. Meanwhile, we also considered a low baseline – *random*, randomly choosing a click as a repeat click based on the average probability of repeat.

Figure 8 demonstrates that the HMM-based approach indeed brings positive results for M-D search: compared to other approaches (random approach, short-dwell approach and long-dwell approach), it improves precision, recall and F1. We also repeated the same experiment on the desktop-to-desktop search condition. As shown in Figure 9, the HMM output can help predict the re-finding information with the highest recall and F1 and does not sacrifice precision.

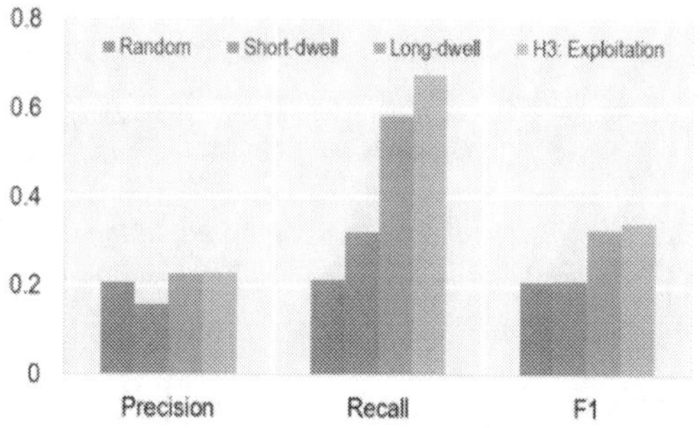


***Figure 8:*** *A comparison of different repeated-click prediction approaches for the continued session of M-D. The Random approach randomly (based on the proportion of repeat clicks over all clicks) chose a click as a repeat one. The Short-dwell (Long-dwell) approach forecast all short-dwell (long-dwell) clicks as repeat clicks. The H3: Exploitation approach predicted all clicks under such state as repeat clicks.*

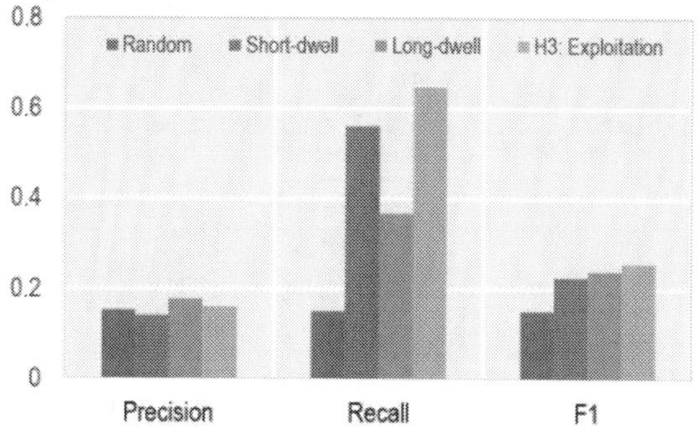


*Figure 9: A comparison of different approaches for predicting repeated clicks for the continued session of D-D. Notations and symbols are the same as Figure 8.*

## DISCUSSION

### *Benefits of Hidden Markov Modeling*

Compared to prior studies that only considered simple counts or coupled search actions (Chen and Cooper, 2002; Xie and Joo, 2010; Zhang et al., 2015), our HMM-based modeling integrates observed user actions with hidden search patterns into one unified framework and further assumes a generative process from hidden search patterns to observed actions. This makes the developed models more interpretative and expandable with further hidden patterns. For example, the current model does not consider the content of search action, which could be important future expansions of the model.

Furthermore, the HMM outputs are validated through the observation of the consistence between the identified hidden search patterns and the findings from previous studies on exploration/exploitation (Luo et al., 2014) and information refinding (Tyler and Teevan, 2010). We would like to include more validations with larger datasets and/or with more human-involved interpretations.

### *Behavior Patterns in Cross-Device Search*

Consistent with the findings of prior studies (Teevan, 2007; Teevan et al., 2007; Tyler and Teevan, 2010), our HMM discovers plenty of information re-finding patterns in the continued session. There is a high chance that a continued session starts with an immediate re-finding pattern in both M-D search and D-D search, indicating a commonly existed phenomenon in multiple-session searches. In addition, re- finding is a pattern that concentrates at the beginning of the continued session. Once users restore their knowledge about the search, they seldom perform re-finding in the rest of the session. This indicates that any support mechanisms for re-finding have to take effect at the beginning of the continued session if not before the start of that session.

Despite re-finding pattern being unique in the continued session, the search process is still dominated by querying, exploration and exploitation (finding for information instead of refinding) and they are all interconnected with each other. HMM outputs clearly show that users in these three patterns tend to look for novel documents. This can be used to guide the development of a better search engine to support cross-session web search.

The difference between finding and re-finding patterns calls for search support algorithms that can automatically identify the pattern behind each user action and thus can customize search results based on different patterns. We acknowledge that the HMM-based approach discussed in this paper cannot be directly applied since it relies on the post-task behavior analysis. However, since time in a session is a strong indicator for differentiating re-finding pattern from the three finding patterns, the time can be used as a simple way to uncover the behavior patterns.

### *Effects of Devices*

Although the HMM models obtained in this paper can be easily applied to any cross-session condition, the direct comparison between M-D and D-D does show the effects of devices. Mobile search interface might constrain users from performing better search patterns. Therefore, users' task progress in M-D search is less advanced than that in D-D search. This is reflected by the fact that D-D users exhibit more selective behaviors in the initial session, while in the continued session, they employ higher transitions from exploitation of relevant documents to querying. In addition, M-D users show more re-finding patterns in the continued session which might because they have not fully completed their search on the mobile device.

## CONCLUSION AND FUTURE WORK

With the goal of understanding and modeling the mobile-to-desktop (M-D) cross-device search patterns, we proposed to use a hidden Markov model (HMM)-based approach. Through assuming that users' search actions are all driven by hidden search patterns, we applied the HMM in both mobile-to-desktop (M-D) and desktop-to-desktop (D-D) conditions.

Our results show the validity of using HMM for modeling purpose, and based on the identified hidden patterns, we found that re-finding is a common pattern at the beginning of a continued session, and the other three patterns (querying, exploitation and exploration) contribute to the dominated behaviors for information finding. Our results also reveal clear device effect between cross-device search (M-D) and the same-device cross-session search (D-D). All demonstrate that the support mechanisms in cross-device search need to be able to automatically identify the finding and re-finding, as well as the timing of supporting users in different patterns.

Our future work includes a more careful investigation of automatic detection of search patterns based on features available up to the current search and also the actual design and implementation of the support in the cross-device search.

## ACKNOWLEDGMENTS

This work was partially supported by National Natural Science Foundation of China project #71673204.

## REFERENCES

Agichtein, E., White, R., Dumais, S. and Bennet, P. (2012). Search, interrupted: Understanding and predicting search task continuation. In *SIGIR*, pages 315-324.

Bates, M. J. (1979). Information search tactics. *Journal of the American Society for information Science*, 30(4):205-214.

Borlund, P. (2000). Experimental components for the evaluation of interactive information retrieval systems. *Journal of Documentation*, 56(1):71-90.

Chen, H.-M. and Cooper, M. D. (2002). Stochastic modeling of usage patterns in a web-based information system. *Journal of the American Society for Information Science and Technology*, 53(7):536-548.

Eickhoff, C., Teevan, J., White, R. and Dumais, S. (2014). Lessons from the journey: A query log analysis of within- session learning. In *WSDM*, pages 223-232.

Guan, D., Zhang, S., and Yang, H. (2013). Utilizing query change for session search. In Proceedings of the 36th international ACM SIGIR conference on research and development in information retrieval, pages 453-462. ACM.

Han, S., He, D., Yue, Z., and Brusilovsky, P. (2015a). Supporting cross-device web search with social navigation-based mobile touch interactions. In *User modeling, adaptation and personalization-23rd international conference*, pages 143-155.

Han, S., Yi, X., Yue, Z., Geng, Z. and Glass, A. (2016). Framing mobile information needs: An investigation of hierarchical query sequence structure. In *Proceedings of the 25th ACM international on conference on information and knowledge management*, pages 2131-2136. ACM.

Han, S., Yue, Z., and He, D. (2013). Automatic detection of search tactic in individual information seeking: A hidden Markov model approach. *arXiv preprint arXiv:1304.1924*.

Han, S., Yue, Z., and He, D. (2015b). Understanding and supporting cross-device web search for exploratory tasks with mobile touch interactions. *ACM Transactions on Information Systems (TOIS)*, 33(4):16.

Hassan, A., Shi, X., Craswell, N., and Ramsey, B. (2013). Beyond clicks: Query reformulation as a predictor of search satisfaction. In *CIKM*, pages 2019-2028.

Holscher, C. and Strube, G. (2000). Web search behavior of internet experts and newbies. *Computer networks*, 33(1):337-346.

Kelly, D. (2009). Methods for evaluating interactive information retrieval systems with users. *Foundations and Trends in Information Retrieval*, 3(1-2):1-224.

Liu, J., Belkin, N. J., Zhang, X., and Yuan, X. (2013). Examining users knowledge change in the task completion process. *Information Processing & Management*, 49(5):1058-1074.

Luo, J., Zhang, S., and Yang, H. (2014). Win-win search: Dual-agent stochastic game in session search. In *Proceedings of the 37th international ACM SIGIR conference on research & development in information retrieval*, pages 587-596. ACM.

Marchionini, G. (1995). *Information seeking in electronic environments*. Number 9. Cambridge University Press.

Mark, G., Gonzalez, V. M., and Harris, J. (2005). No task left behind?: Examining the nature of fragmented work. In *Proceedings of the SIGCHI conference on human factors in computing systems*, pages 321-330. ACM.

Montañez, G. D., White, R. W., and Huang, X. (2014). Cross-device search. In Proceedings of the 23rd ACM international conference on conference on information and knowledge management, pages 1669-1678. ACM.

Morris, D., Ringel Morris, M., and Venolia, G. (2008). Search-bar: A search-centric web history for task resumption and information re-finding. In *Proceedings of the SIGCHI conference on human factors in computing systems*, pages 1207-1216. ACM.

Schwarz, G. (1978). Estimating the dimension of a model. *The annals of statistics*, 6(2), 461-464.

Sellen, A. J., Murphy, R., and Shaw, K. L. (2002). How knowledge workers use the web. In *Proceedings of the SIGCHI conference on human factors in computing systems*, pages 227-234. ACM.

Song, Y., Ma, H., Wang, H., and Wang, K. (2013). Exploring and exploiting user search behavior on mobile and tablet devices to improve search relevance. In *Proceedings of the 22nd international conference on world wide web*, pages 1201-1212. International World Wide Web Conferences Steering Committee.

Teevan, J. (2007). The re:search engine: Simultaneous sup- port for finding and re-finding. In *Proceedings of the 20th annual ACM symposium on user interface software and technology*, pages 23-32. ACM.

Teevan, J., Adar, E., Jones, R., and Potts, M. A. (2007). Information re-retrieval: Repeat queries in Yahoo's logs. In *Proceedings of the 30th annual international ACM SIGIR conference on research and development in information retrieval*, pages 151-158. ACM.

Tyler, S. K. and Teevan, J. (2010). Large scale query log analysis of re-finding. In *Proceedings of the third ACM international conference on web search and data mining*, pages 191-200. ACM.

Wang, Y., Huang, X., and White, R. W. (2013). Characterizing and supporting cross-device search tasks. In *Proceedings of the sixth ACM international conference on web search and data mining*, pages 707-716. ACM.

Xie, I. and Joo, S. (2010). Transitions in search tactics during the web-based search process. *Journal of the American society for information science and technology*, 61(11):2188-2205.

Yi, J., Maghoul, F., and Pedersen, J. (2008). Deciphering mobile search patterns: A study of Yahoo! mobile search queries. In *Proceedings of the 17th international conference on world wide web*, pages 257-266. ACM.

Yue, Z., Han, S., and He, D. (2014). Modeling search processes using hidden states in collaborative exploratory web search. In *Proceedings of the 17th ACM conference on computer supported cooperative work & social computing*, pages 820-830. ACM.

Yue, Z., Han, S., Jiang, J., and He, D. (2012). Search tactics as means of examining search processes in collaborative exploratory web search. In *Proceedings of the 5th Ph.D. workshop on information and knowledge*, pages 59-66. ACM.

Zhang, X., Liu, J., Cole, M., and Belkin, N. (2015). Predicting users' domain knowledge in information retrieval using multiple regression analysis of search behaviors. *Journal of the Association for Information Science and Technology*, 66(5):980-1000.

# On Shapes and Sizes: Measuring Diversity of Technological Engagement Through Digital Visitors and Residents Maps

**William Harvey**
*OCLC Research, USA. harveyw@oclc.org*

**Lynn Silipigni Connaway**
*OCLC Research, USA. connawal@oclc.org*

**Erin M. Hood**
*OCLC Research, USA. hoode@oclc.org*

## ABSTRACT

**The Digital Visitors and Residents (V&R) project developed a mapping exercise to help individuals better understand their engagement with technology and the web. The map creation process and the opportunity for individuals to share their stories in a group setting can be fun, informative and educational. In this paper, we show that collections of V&R maps can be sources of rich and interesting information about similarities and differences in individuals' engagement with technology. Computational methods such as shape analysis and machine learning can be used to distill this information from collections of V&R maps. We present several models, techniques and algorithms for V&R map analysis that may be familiar to many data scientists and software developers, including a shape metric that captures properties of shapes with intuitive meaning and interpretation in the V&R context. Patterns and trends emerging from collections of maps can help a team better understand their similarities and differences in engagement with technology or help inform decisions on the design of information technology or library technology services. We provide examples of these techniques using data collected in various V&R mapping sessions. Finally, we introduce a V&R mapping web application designed for touchscreens that can ease data collection for computational analysis and provide a fun and engaging experience for mapping exercise participants.**

## KEYWORDS

shape analysis, ethnographic methods, technology, visitors, residents, machine learning

## INTRODUCTION

It is important to identify behaviors exhibited by diverse individuals functioning in different contexts and situations to develop systems for discovery and access and ways to engage with individuals to assist with finding information. There are a variety of ways for individuals to get their information. One way of accessing information is by using technology, such as web browsers, mobile phones and apps. To identify how individuals engage with technology and get their information, we must talk to and observe them. The library and information science (LIS) field employs different data collection and analysis methods to investigate user behavior and information-seeking (Chu, 2015; Connaway & Radford, 2017; Luo & McKinney, 2015). There also is a body of literature that links the context and situation of the need and individual characteristics, such as educational level, socio-economic level, demographic information, etc., to how individuals access information (Chatman, 1987; Chatman, 1992; Cool, 2001; Prabha, Connaway, Olszewski, & Jenkins, 2017; Wilson, 1981).

To better understand how individuals from different backgrounds engage with technology and get their information, we previously developed a data collection method using focus group and individual interview data collection methods. Using the Visitors and Residents (V&R) framework, we can collect information about how individuals from diverse backgrounds use and engage with technology to access information in both their everyday lives (personal) and their professional and/or academic lives (institutional) (White, 2008; White & Le Cornu, 2011).

In what follows, we explore several quantitative analysis techniques, including shape analysis, for exploring and investigating the graphical data that we collect during V&R mapping exercises. We propose several techniques for extracting patterns and trends from this data and apply these techniques to real data that were collected during a variety of V&R mapping sessions. The techniques reveal commonalities and differences in the way that we engage with virtual environments and technologies.

## BACKGROUND

### *Visitors and Residents (V&R) Project*

The V&R project began as a collaborative effort between OCLC, the University of Oxford and in partnership with the University of North Carolina, Charlotte, with partial funding from JISC. The project attempts to fill in the gap in user behavior studies identified in the JISC Digital Information Seeker Report (2010). In that report, Connaway and Dickey (2010) call for a longitudinal study "to identify how individuals

80th Annual Meeting of the Association for Information Science & Technology, Washington, DC | Oct. 27-Nov. 1, 2017

engage in both the virtual and physical worlds to get information for different situations" (p. 56). This effort is combined with the V&R premise put forth by White (2008) and White and Le Cornu (2011) in which it is hypothesized that it is not age nor gender that determines one's skill level when it comes to technology and digital spaces. Rather, the V&R project presents a continuum on which an individual's mode of engagement will be more Visitor or Resident depending on their personal motives and the context and situation at the time.

### *V&R Mapping Exercise*

A mapping exercise component was introduced to the V&R project to investigate how U.S. and UK individuals engage with technology and how this engagement may or may not change as the individuals transition through their educational stages (White & Connaway, 2011-2014). The purpose of the mapping session is to identify how and why individuals engage with different technologies and why they do or do not share their thoughts, ideas and actions in this digital environment. The idea is to map the responses of interview and diary participants on a grid depicting visitor and resident engagement in personal and institutional (academic and professional) situations. The mapping exercise helps individuals understand their own engagement with technology. An individual's engagement can be compared with the engagement of others, revealing similarities and differences that stimulate conversation and introspection and help groups to understand their diversity in engagement. Mapping sessions were first conducted in 2013. Initially, mapping was conducted in interactive group settings where project investigators could lead participants through the exercise. Maps were drawn on paper using combinations of pens, pencils, markers and colored pencils. Demographic information also was collected on the mapping sheets to provide more insight into the maps. Photos of the finished maps were taken with camera or tablet so that the maps could be displayed on a projector for discussion. Additionally, the finished maps were collected and analyzed qualitatively (Connaway, 2016a; 2016b; Connaway, Lanclos, & Hood, 2013a).

The basic idea behind a V&R map is as follows. Individuals typically will think of a list of things they do, or websites that they visit, when they use the internet or technology. The user then draws each of those activities as one or more shapes inside of a 2D coordinate system. The horizontal axis of this coordinate system spans from Visitor on the left (the individual does not wish to leave a trace behind, using the technology as if it were a tool in a toolbox) to Resident on the right (the individual wishes to leave traces behind and inhabit a virtual space). The vertical axis spans Personal (friends, family, private life, etc.) and Institutional (work, school, etc.) engagement. The placement of a shape within this coordinate system indicates how an individual typically wishes to interact with the shape's corresponding technology or activity in a given situation.

The V&R mapping differs from information horizons mapping (Sonnenwald, 1999), which requires individuals to describe information-seeking situations. The development of the V&R mapping is to address the technologies used by individuals in specific situations (their personal or institutional/academic) and contexts (dissertation research, 5% of grade for undergraduate class, health and travel, etc.) and to determine if the individuals are consuming and not sharing information (Visitors) using these technologies or both consuming and sharing or sharing (Residents) information using these technologies. The findings from the V&R semi-structured interviews and diaries indicate that individuals can be residents using some technologies and within some situations and contexts, while they are visitors in others. These maps represent an individual's digital footprint.

Since semi-structured interviews are time consuming to plan, conduct and analyze and there was an interest in replicating and testing the V&R framework, the mapping sessions were developed to learn how individuals engage with different technologies in different contexts and situations. Individuals participating in mapping sessions are introduced to the V&R terms, with definitions, and observe the moderator creating a map and explaining the reasons for including the technologies, apps, etc., on the maps.

### *Shape Analysis Overview*

Shape analysis is a research area that spans a variety of different scientific fields, including mathematics, computer vision, image processing, machine vision, geographic information systems and computer graphics. There is a vast body of literature related to statistical shape analysis, and applications of these techniques are seen in a wide array of fields ranging anywhere from medical imaging, optical character recognition and interpretation of hand gestures to bird migration (Srivastava et al. 2011; Belongie, Malik, & Puzicha 2002; Joshi et al. 2016; Pavlovic, Sharma, and Huang 1997; Su et al. 2014). Loncaric (1998) provides a comprehensive review of shape analysis techniques available nearly two decades ago, motivating the exposition in the context of grayscale image processing systems. Dryden and Mardia (2016) provide a more recent resource on statistical shape analysis, outlining many algorithms and mathematical formulations motivating modern approaches.

## METHODOLOGY

In this paper, we explore the use of quantitative methods for analyzing V&R maps. The basic workflow for analyzing collections of V&R maps is as follows:

1. Capture a digital image of each map.
2. Align the map axes within each image to a common coordinate system, optionally performing some image cleanup such as removing image artifacts and shadows.
3. Vectorize (trace) each map using a graphics editing software application.

4. Explore trends related to the activities reported in maps using bag-of-words and set-theoretic models in a traditional setting.
5. Investigate the geometric configuration of maps using combinations of compositing and shape analysis techniques such as the Wasserstein metric.

We provide examples of these techniques applied to data acquired during various mapping exercise sessions.

### Preprocessing and Image Normalization

We assume that each physical map has been captured as a digital image. Such an image may be acquired using, e.g., a digital DSLR camera, a tablet or cellphone camera or a flatbed scanner. For best results, images should be acquired under reasonable conditions: sufficient lighting, ample pixel resolution and focus, and the physical map roughly parallel to the image plane of the camera.

The first stage of the workflow transforms raw map images to prepare them for computational analysis. Each image must first be (roughly) photogrammetrically registered to a common coordinate system (cf. Mikhail, Bethel, & McGlone, 2001). After registration, shapes within maps are traced, their texts transcribed and the resulting data stored in file formats that are straightforward to process programmatically.

#### Image Registration and Cleaning

Before reliable measurements can be taken from a digital image, or precise digital processing performed across groups of images, it is customary to first perform *camera resectioning* (Hartley & Zisserman, 2003). That is, camera positions and orientations must be recovered (so-called extrinsic camera parameters), and idiosyncrasies in the cameras' lens and optical configurations (intrinsic camera parameters) must be calculated. Once these parameters are available, images produced by the camera can be rectified such that lens distortion is negligible and precise digital measurements are possible.

For our experiments, however, we take a straightforward and simplified approach by assuming all cameras have ideal, and therefore equivalent, intrinsic parameters. This simplifies image preprocessing, as there is no work to be done to estimate these parameters. However, some image artifacts, such as varying degrees of barrel or pincushion distortion, remain in many of our images, and fine measurements of distance and area will not be completely reliable. These kinds of distortion and artifacts tend to be somewhat common on low-quality CMOS-based devices such as cellphone cameras.

Fortunately, the exploratory nature of our work does not necessarily require the precision provided by camera resectioning. In practice, we have found that lens distortion is tolerable for the kinds of processing conducted with V&R maps.

Next, the images must be aligned through a process called *image registration* (Brown, 1992). This process indirectly recovers the camera positions and orientations (under the assumption that intrinsic parameters are accounted for). This is straightforward to do with perspective transformation tools available in photo editing software such as Adobe Photoshop and GIMP. Each image is adjusted using a perspective transformation tool until the outer rectangular boundary of the V&R mapping template is close to a prescribed canonical rectangle. Occasionally, a photograph will cut off part of the rectangular boundary of the mapping template. In this scenario, other features within the mapping template, such as the endpoints of the coordinate axes, can be used to register the image instead. In general, a minimum of four-point correspondences are needed to register an image to a reference under a perspective transformation.

Due to modest distortion that tends to intensify around the boundaries of images, it may not be possible to perfectly align the template's rectangle with the canonical rectangle. This introduces some error into the shape analysis portions of our methodology, especially with shapes located near image boundaries. If more precise imaging is desired, a flatbed scanner can be used to acquire imagery that is photogrammetrically consistent and reliable. However, flatbed scanners tend to not be as convenient to use during busy V&R mapping sessions.

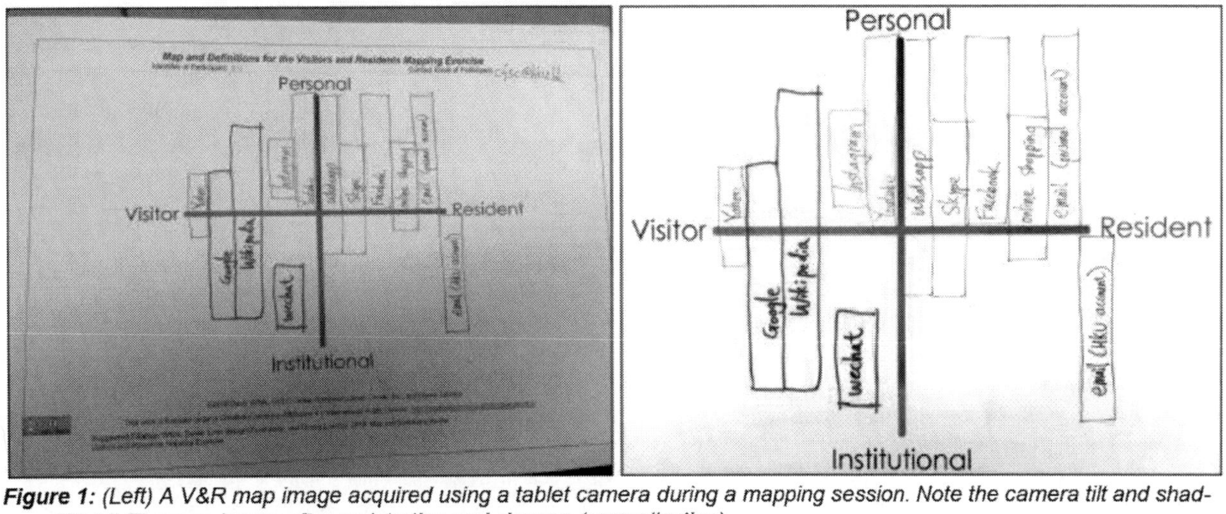


***Figure 1:*** *(Left) A V&R map image acquired using a tablet camera during a mapping session. Note the camera tilt and shadows. (Right) The map image after registration and cleanup (normalization).*

Figure 1 shows a raw map image acquired using a tablet camera before perspective adjustment is applied and the image after registration. We also apply some color contrast enhancement and remove shadows using a dodge tool, as this facilitates downstream processing. In total, we call this process *image normalization* and its result a *normalized image*.

### *Vectorization and Labeling*

When an image has been normalized, the user-drawn shapes within it must be vectorized (traced) for computational processing. Scalable Vector Graphics (SVG) is a popular, nonproprietary, W3C-standardized XML file format that can store these vectorized shapes (W3C, 2017). There are several graphics applications for working with SVG files, including Inkscape (free and open source) and Adobe Illustrator (proprietary). Additionally, each graphical element in SVG supports a description text field within each shape. We transcribe the text drawn within a shape by a user into the description field of its corresponding vectorized shape. At the end of the process, each V&R map is represented as a collection of labeled SVG shapes such as squares, ovals, polygons and polylines. We refer to these vectorized maps as *SVG maps*. Figure 2 shows a V&R map and its vectorized representation.

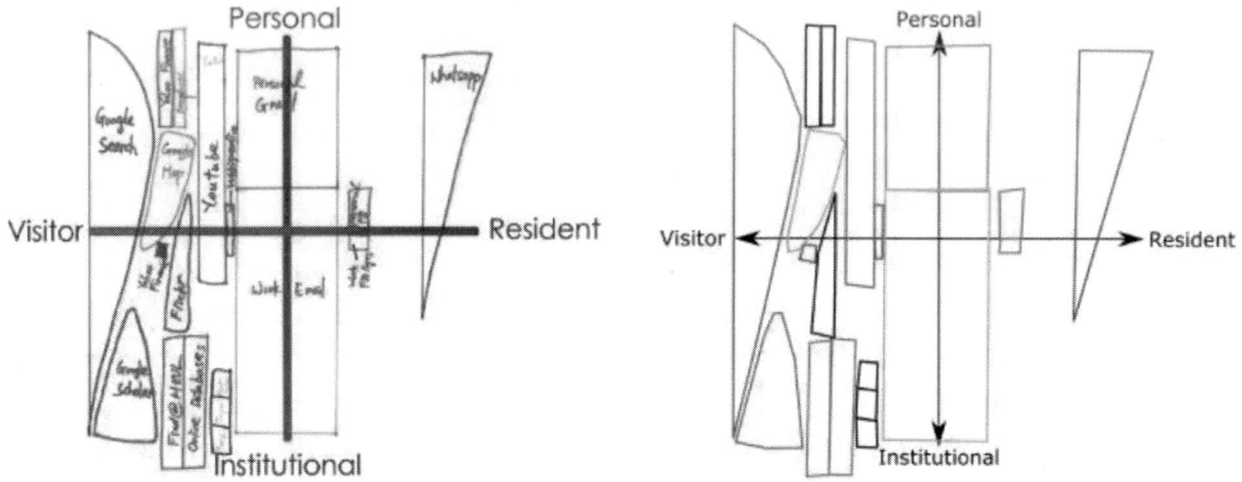


***Figure 2:*** *A normalized V&R map image (left) and its vectorized rendition (right). Each shape is represented as an SVG shape (e.g., square, ellipse or polyline) and the handwritten text is transcribed into the SVG description fields.*

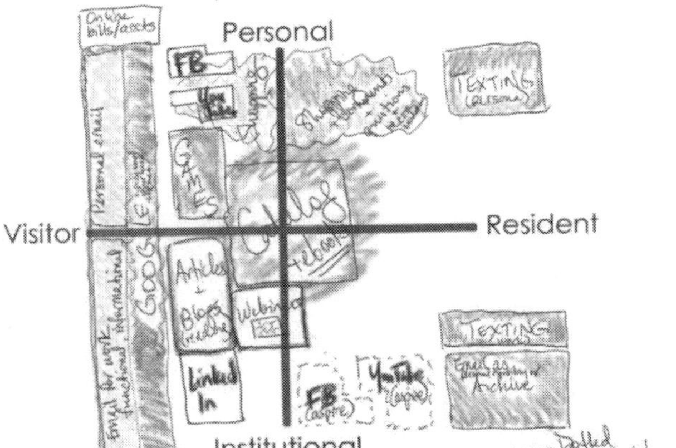


***Figure 3:*** *A map with several examples of multiple modes of engagement. Facebook, YouTube, Texting, and Email appear at multiple locations in the map.*

### ***Activity Statistics via Bag-Of-Words Models***

While each SVG map contains rich geometric data, it can be valuable to temporarily ignore the data and focus only on each map's constituent listed activities. This effectively models each map as a bag-of-words (a word multiset) – a familiar format to researchers who work in information retrieval or machine learning (Harris, 1954).

This representation can help a researcher get a sense of the kinds of activities reported within, and between, groups of maps. Traditional bag-of-words analyses can be applied to map data to reveal patterns. For example, when a single activity appears in multiple parts of a map within different shapes, its term frequency in the bag-of-words setting will be greater than one. This has an interesting interpretation in the V&R framework, because the user engages with that activity using multiple distinct modes of engagement. provides an example of a V&R map with several examples of multiple modes of engagement.

Histograms of the top 10 most frequently reported activities within maps collected from faculty, students and librarians during exercises in 2016 at the University of California, Los Angeles (UCLA, n=39) and Hong Kong University (HKU, n=74) libraries are shown in Figure 4. Each bar in the histogram is a stack of two smaller bars. The bar on the bottom is the frequency with which an activity appears as a single shape in a map, and the bar on the top represents the frequency with which that activity is drawn using multiple distinct shapes. At a glance, we can see that activities such as Google Search, Facebook and YouTube are popular at both institutions. Wikipedia makes the top 10 at UCLA, but not at HKU. And, overall, we tend to see more prevalence of multiple modes of engagement within UCLA maps than HKU maps.

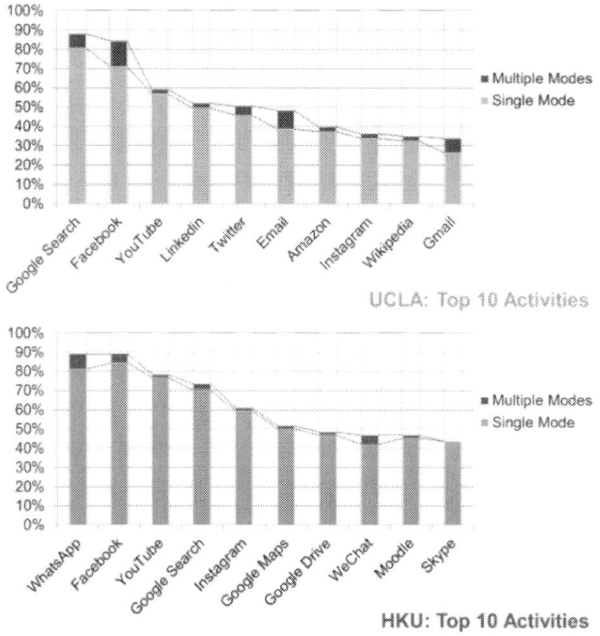


***Figure 4:*** *Top ten activities reported in maps collected during UCLA (n=39) and HKU (n=74) mapping exercises. The height of each bar is the percentage of maps containing a given activity. The caps at the tops of the bars indicate multiple modes of engagement.*

### *Identifying Distinguishing Features Within a Group of Maps*

Moving beyond summary statistics and histograms, the bag-of-words model is well-researched and offers a wide array of techniques for finding features that are effective for differentiating between two groups of data (Sivic & Zisserman, 2009). For providing contrast between two groups of maps, we choose (out of familiarity) an algorithm from bioinformatics for finding differences in gene expression between two bacterial samples called the SVM-RFE algorithm (Rakotomamonjy, 2003). Intuitively, we would like to see which activities (features) most strongly differentiate two groups, but in the case of V&R map analysis we are looking for differences in activities listed rather than genes expressed. We use a simplified SVM-RFE approach which merely considers the support vector machine (SVM) weights calculated for each term (activity) within two groups of maps (Cortes & Vapnik, 1995). Figure 5 shows the top 10 SVM weights, by magnitude, for differentiating between HLU and UCLA maps.

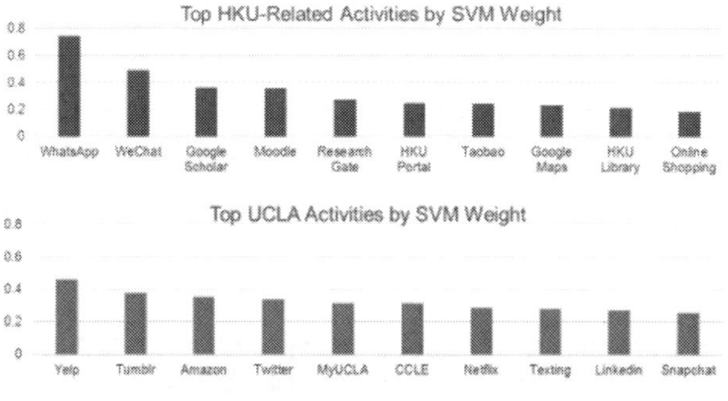


***Figure 5:*** *Top ten SVM weights and activities for differentiating between HKU maps (top) and UCLA maps (bottom).*

The bag-of-words term vector representation of V&R maps is amenable to a host of statistical and machine learning algorithms that extends beyond SVMs (Duda, Hart, & Stork, 2012). For example, we trained a fixed-depth decision tree classifier for differentiating between maps drawn by a group of 30 students and 53 librarians at UCLA (Rokach & Maimon, 2014; Safavian & Landgrebe, 1991).

The split rule at each node chooses the activity that yields the greatest reduction in Gini impurity (Breiman, Friedman, Stone, & Olshen, 1984).

Figure 6 shows a decision tree with a depth of 3. The "CCLA" activity (the Common Collaborative Learning Environment student portal) appearing in the left side of the tree easily picks out students, but interestingly, this activity was less informative than Snapchat. We computed another decision tree, this time ignoring the CCLA term. The decision tree algorithm readily recovered an alternative feature (in this case, Spotify usage) for differentiating between librarians and students based on the contents of their maps. Such an analysis can be beneficial in helping librarians learn how their own engagement with technologies may differ from that of their students.

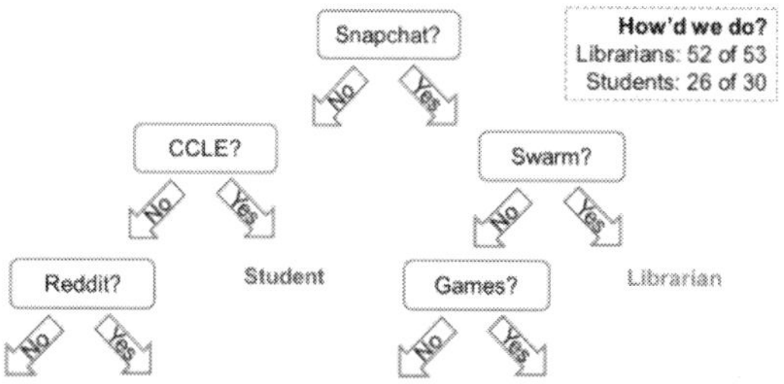


***Figure 6:*** *Fixed-depth decision tree classifiying UCLA students (n=30) and librarians (n=53).*

### *Finding Commonalities Between Groups of Maps*

Finding activities that occur frequently between two sets of maps can reveal the common ground between those two groups. Our analysis considers the geometric mean of the percentages of maps reporting each activity. For example, the top 10 activities among UCLA and HKU maps based on the geometric mean of their frequencies is given in Figure 7.

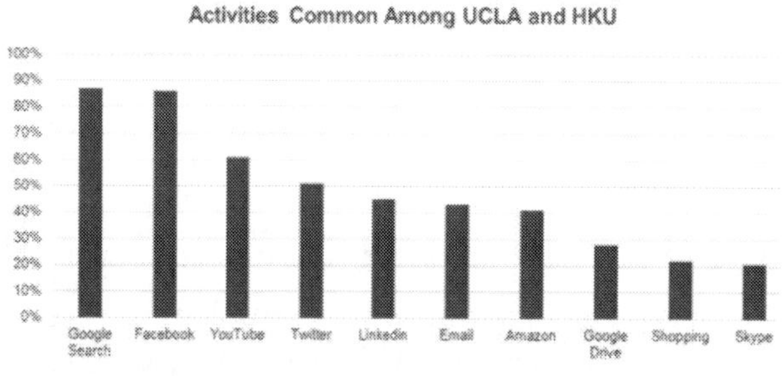


***Figure 7:*** *Top ten common activities between UCLA and HKU mapping exercise participants. The height of each bar is the geometric mean of the relative frequency of each activity within the two sets of maps.*

Figure 5: To|
ing between

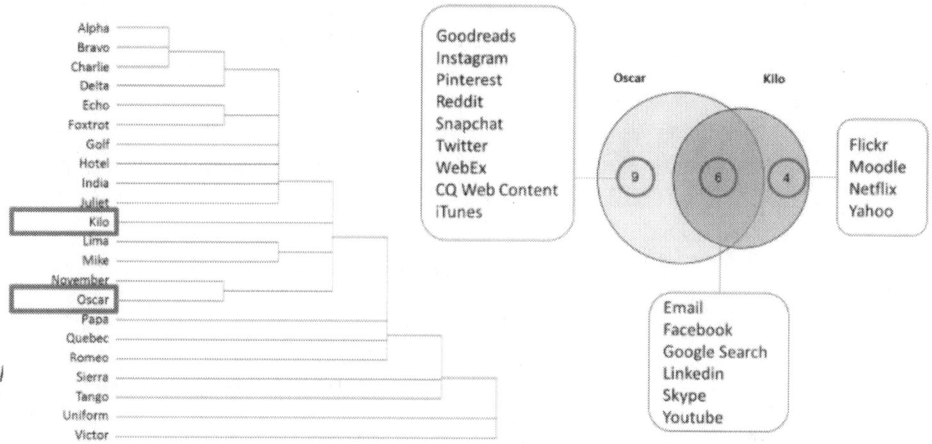


***Figure 8:*** *Dendrogram of OCLC staff according to decreasing order of their common activities*

Perhaps unsurprisingly, Google Search and Facebook occur in first and second place. This sort of analysis can be helpful when assessing the common behaviors and potential needs of multiple diverse groups of users.

### *Set-of-Words Representation and Set Similarity Measures*

Numerous set similarity and distance measures such (e.g., Hamming distance, Dice's coefficient, Tversky index, etc.) can be used to compare V&R maps if each map is represented as a set of activities rather than a multiset (Sørensen, 1948; Hamming, 1950; Tversky, 1977). These measures enable interesting possibilities for exploring similarities and differences within an entire group of participants based on reported activities.

We conducted a mapping exercise with 22 staff members working within the same organizational unit at OCLC. A term set (binary term vector) was calculated for each map, and an agglomerative clustering was derived by merging clusters in decreasing order by set intersection cardinality. See Figure 8 (staff were given NATO alphabet codenames for anonymity). A dendrogram indicates the similarities and differences between the activities reported. In this case, the dendrogram reveals that Alpha, Bravo and Charlie reported many common activities on their maps relative to the other participants. These three individuals are software developers who tend to use similar technology tools and websites in their work. A Venn diagram interface reveals the specific relationship between pairs of selected individuals' maps (Venn, 1880). Here, we show the Venn diagram of websites and technologies enumerated by users Kilo and Oscar. This sort of presentation provides a convenient means of exploring specific similarities and differences between pairs of maps.

### ***V&R Map Compositing***

Standard image files can be difficult to compare en masse without resorting to techniques such as image averaging, which has the negative side effect of reducing detail of each constituent image. However, SVG maps are ideal for creating composite images, especially composites restricted to one or more activities. Such images are a straightforward first step in collecting information about users through the geometric arrangement of shapes in their V&R maps.

Figure 9 illustrates composite images of YouTube shapes drawn by the HKU and UCLA participants. Juxtaposing these composite images reveals that HKU participants exhibited a tendency to engage with YouTube in Resident mode more often than UCLA participants. In these images, the dotted lines extending from the coordinate axes indicate parts of the V&R maps that extended beyond the bounds of the V&R map template. Interestingly, HKU participants more frequently drew shapes outside of the template, whereas UCLA participants tended to keep their shapes within the confines of the template. We do not yet have a hypothesis for this phenomenon, though it could be considered a compelling curiosity.

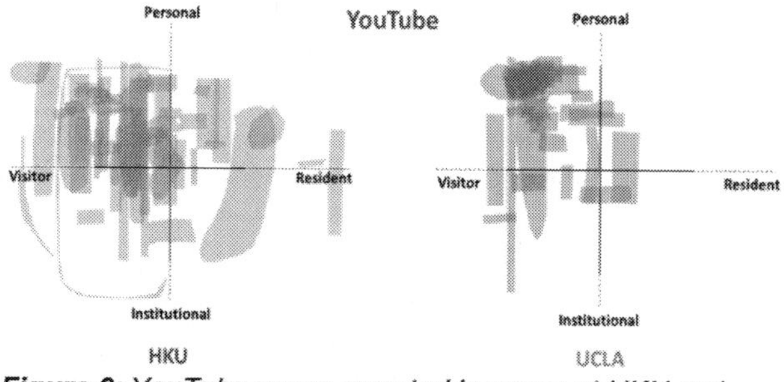


***Figure 9****: YouTube usage reported by users at HKU and UCLA. HKU users engage with YouTube as a Resident more frequently than UCLA users.*

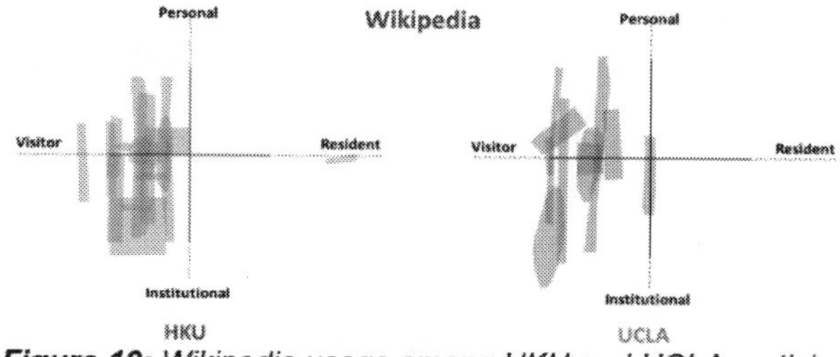


***Figure 10:*** *Wikipedia usage among HKU and UCLA participants of the V&R mapping sessions. Note the putative "Wikipedia Editor" at the extreme end of the Resident side in the HKU composite image.*

Like summary statistics, composite images can quickly reveal patterns within a given set of maps, including certain types of users (potential archetypes) that may emerge as clusters or outliers. The most notable example of this phenomenon may be the Wikipedia editor. Figure 10 shows Wikipedia usage at HKU, with a single likely Wikipedia editor inhabiting an extreme Resident area within the map.

Occasionally an unexpected pattern may arise that is coarse enough to notice through composite images alone. We explored maps created by UCLA librarians and a combined cohort of librarians from the University of Pittsburgh (Pitt) and Carnegie Mellon University (CMU). Composite images reveal that, in general, the UCLA librarians tend to report very little on the Resident side of their maps relative to the Visitor side. In contrast, the librarians at Pitt and CMU exhibit a balance between Visitor and Resident engagement. Such an observation can help library staff attain awareness about their web browsing preferences as a group and how their experiences may differ from the full spectrum of behaviors and preferences demonstrated among their users.

### Shape Analysis

#### *Shape Intersection*

Perhaps the most straightforward meaningful method for comparing two shapes is to consider their intersection area. Each shape is a set (specifically a subset of $\mathbf{R}^2$), and their intersections, unions and differences can be combined in an arbitrary set similarity measure (e.g., Jaccard distance) depending on the desired application (Jaccard, 1901).

Unfortunately, shape intersection may not always be informative. For example, if two shapes are very similar, but their overlap is small or empty due to their placement within the maps (see Figure 11), they will fail to yield a large intersection area. In our experience, this happens often, as there is much freedom for placement of shapes within each map.

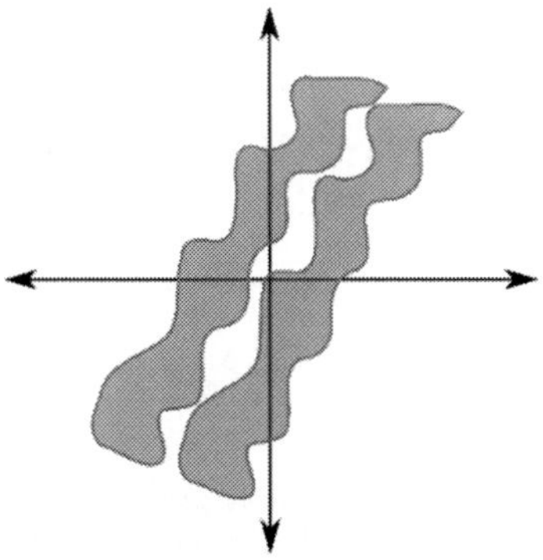

***Figure 11:*** *Shapes from two different V&R maps that appear similar, and are geometrically close, but do not intersect.*

#### *Interior Matching via the Wasserstein Metric*

We wish to ascribe a high degree of similarity to shapes whose interiors overlap while allowing slack. Non-overlapping but visually similar shapes that are adjacent or near each other should also be considered highly similar. To do this, we turn to a technique called the Wasserstein metric. This is sometimes called the Wasserstein distance or "earth mover's distance" (Rubner, Tomasi, & Guibas, 2000). The intuition behind this metric is as follows: Imagine that one shape represents a mound of dirt that is flat on top, like a plateau, and the other shape a pit with capacity identical to that of the mound. The Wasserstein metric captures the minimum amount of work required to transport all dirt within the mound into the pit. Naturally, it favors not having to move dirt (cost is low when shapes overlap), and is forgiving if shapes are nearby but do not overlap.

In practice, we calculate this metric by computing each shape's centroidal Voronoi tessellation (CVT) using Lloyd's method to partition it into $p$ small tiles of roughly equal area and calculate their centers (the so-called "generating points" or "generators" of each Voronoi cell) (Du, Faber, & Gunzburger, 1999; Lloyd, 1982). In our experiments, we use $p = 1000$. Traditionally, one would calculate the Wasserstein distance between two shapes by solving the transportation problem (also known as the assignment problem) between the two sets of Voronoi generators using the Hungarian algorithm. The cost function for a pair of Voronoi generators is their Euclidean distance. The solution to the transportation problem provides both the Wasserstein metric (the total cost of the bipartite graph matching[1] produced by the Hungarian algorithm) as well as the optimal pairwise correspondences between the two sets of Voronoi generators (the bipartite graph matching itself) (Kuhn, 1955; Munkres, 1957). Figure 12 (a-c) depicts the basic workflow.

Calculating the Wasserstein metric in this way can be used for V&R map analysis, but point correspondences may not be continuous across the shape. For example, two points which are nearby in one shape may be matched to points that are far apart from each other in the other shape. This is because the transportation problem does not enforce continuity in its matching. To mitigate this, we recursively partition a shape's Voronoi generators into two sets of equal cardinality using balanced k-means with k = 2 (Malinen & Fränti, 2014). This is repeated until the shape is divided into a tree of parts with a prescribed dyadic number of leaf parts (usually 8 or 16). To calculate the transportation cost between two Voronoi generators, we take their Euclidean distances plus the sum of the Euclidean distances between the centroids of their corresponding ancestor parts within the parts tree. Figure 12 (d) illustrates the partitioning of a shape into Voronoi cells, and the division of these cells into a nested hierarchy of parts.

[1] A *matching* of a graph G = (V, E) is a subset S of E such that no two edges in S share a common vertex.

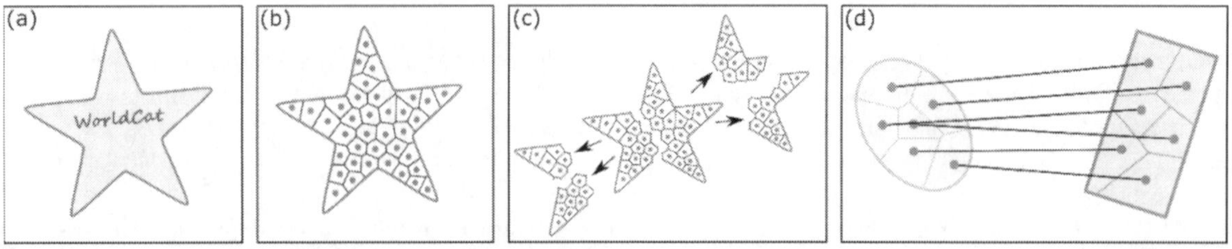


***Figure 12:*** *Basic workflow for calculating and using the Wasserstein metric to compare shapes. (a) An example shape represented as a polyline. (b) A centroidal Voronoi tessellation calculated using p = 37 generators. (c) Hierarchical decomposition of the shape using balanced k-means. (d) The minimal cost matching between two shapes. The total cost of this matching is their Wasserstein distance.*

Figure 13 gives an example of two shapes, their CVT decompositions, with correspondences shown as a color gradient.

Note that the correspondence is not guaranteed to be continuous (see, e.g., the red cells along the bottom boundary of the shape on the right), although the hierarchical shape decomposition encourages continuity by favoring matches that lie within corresponding hierarchical parts.

Finally, we remark that application of the Wasserstein metric has a probabilistic interpretation, as it was originally formulated as a metric on probability distributions (Olkin & Pulekshеim, 1982). Specifically, each shape could be considered a uniform probability distribution (in the Bayesian sense) of a user's engagement with a technology (Bernardo & Smith, 2001). This Bayesian interpretation may provide some interesting perspectives for devising methods for V&R map analysis and inference and potentially firmer theoretical grounding for analyzing and interpreting results.

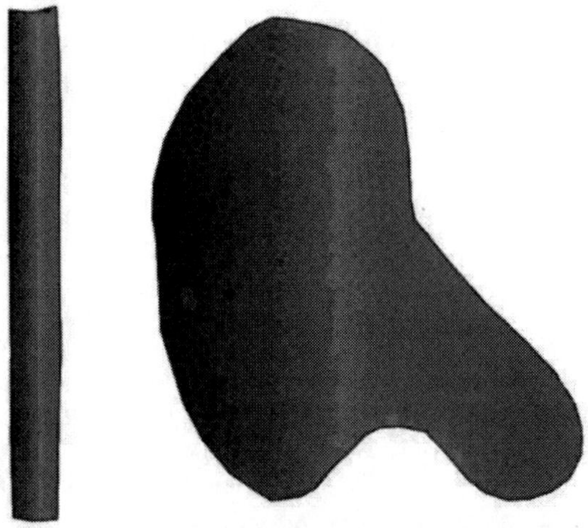

***Figure 13:*** *Optimal correspondences found between two shapes are indicated by color. Note that the Wasserstein metric is not guaranteed to be continuous.*

### *Statistical Shape Analysis*

There are many ways to compare and analyze 2D shapes. For example, shapes can be characterized as smooth curves, and techniques from differential and Riemannian geometry can both smoothly deform shapes into each other and measure the amount of "deformation energy" needed to transmogrify one into the other (Joshi, Su, Zhang, & Amor, 2016). Or, the boundary of the shape can be sampled at regular intervals, shape descriptors calculated at each sampled point and the descriptors matched using optimization algorithms (Belongie, Malik, & Puzicha, 2002). Or, the interior of shapes may be summarized using, e.g. shock graphs, medial axes, straight skeletons or Reeb graphs, and graph matching techniques used to compare them (Siddiqi, Shokoufandeh, Dickenson, & Zucker, 1998; Lee, 1982; Aichholzer & Aurenhammer, 1996; Bauer, Ge, & Wang, 2014). We encourage researchers to survey the vast literature available on statistical shape matching and consider useful applications in both their analysis of V&R maps, as well as other spatial data such as cognitive maps that is collected during research projects.

## THE DIGITAL VISITORS AND RESIDENTS MAPPING APP

The V&R mapping session can be enjoyable and educational for participants. However, conducting a mapping session requires some modest resources on behalf of coordinators and researchers (e.g., drawing implements, mapping templates, a camera and ideally a projector for presenting individual maps

***Figure 14:*** *The "stretchy scrapbooking" interface of the Digital Visitors and Residents Mapping App. Visit http://oc.lc/vrmap to create your own V&R map using a touch-enabled mobile device or computer.*

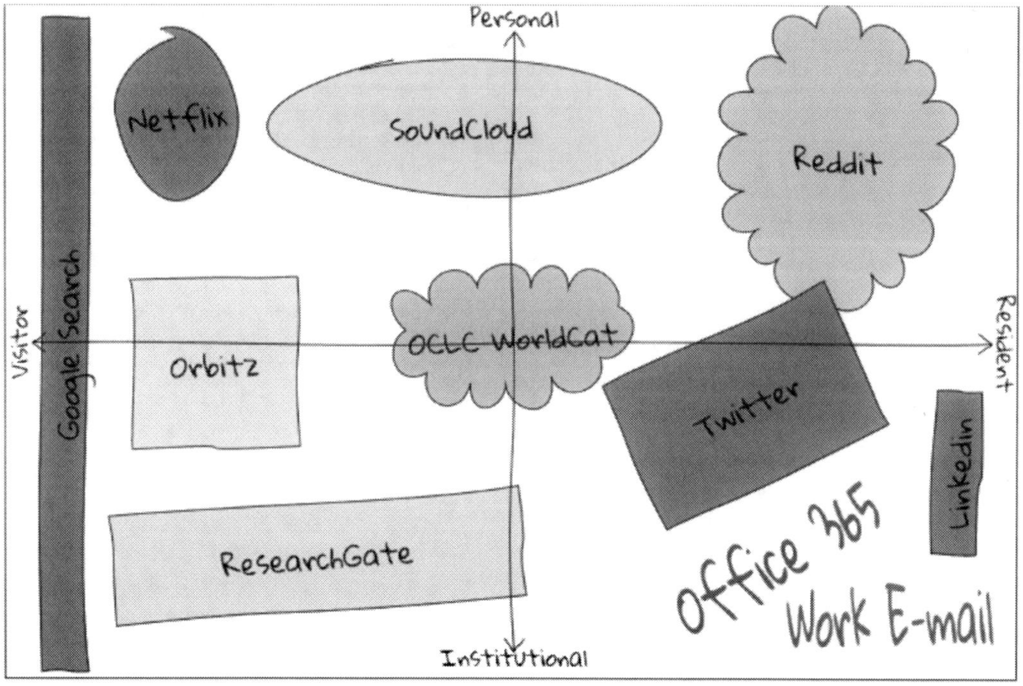


***Figure 15:*** *An example of a V&R map created using the Digital Visitors and Residents Mapping App.*

at the end). It is important to have a moderator skilled in conducting focus group and individual interviews since the moderator will ask questions about how and why the participants engage in the technologies. The moderator of the V&R mapping sessions is trained in the same way as moderators for focus group interviews are trained. The moderators of the mapping sessions review the maps with the individual participants and ask probing questions that are specific to the individuals' maps. The questions address the hows and whys of using the technologies and apps.

It also is important to have a note taker, who can document the discussions between the moderator and the participants. The notes are used to create a more detailed picture of the participants' engagement with technology by including the hows and whys in the analysis with the demographic information provided by each participant. Analyzing the maps quantitatively requires image normalization and vectorization that can be time-intensive and laborious.

Participants suggested that it would be fun to have an app for creating V&R maps on mobile devices during a mapping session. As a benefit, the data would already be digital and could be readily analyzed without any preprocessing. We developed an online web application that preserves the fun feeling of creating V&R maps on pen and paper (according to participants in our usability testing through the OCLC Usability Lab). The Digital Visitors and Residents Mapping App is available at http://oc.lc/vrmap. It is compatible with most touchscreen devices, such as tablets and phones, and can be used on laptop and desktop computers equipped with a modern web browser. Figure 14 shows the basic app interface (which we characterize as "stretchy scrapbooking"), and Figure 15 is a map created using the app.

## LIMITATIONS OF COMPUTATIONAL MAP ANALYSIS

Computational analysis of V&R maps can help researchers to extract, investigate and understand patterns and trends. However, researchers should be mindful of some limitations. Users' map drawings are subjective, and as such they cannot be considered traditional experimental quantitative measurements. We justify this by adopting a Bayesian interpretation of V&R maps, i.e., we assume that the placements of shapes reflect users' beliefs about their own behaviors. Users may also omit certain activities from their maps due to forgetfulness or intentional self-censorship. Precise spatial measurements are most likely not reliable due to photogrammetric factors and lack of precision in hand-drawn sketches. Even if such factors were corrected, differences in fine spatial measurements would be difficult to interpret as meaningful information about users over ascribing them to chance.

## CONCLUSION AND FUTURE WORK

Individuals may better understand their interactions with technology by going through the mapping exercise. But there is a wealth of information available to researchers in the form of collections of V&R maps. A collection of V&R maps readily is transformed into various data formats amenable to computational analysis. Some of these formats, such as bag-of-words or sets of activities, may be familiar to most data scientists and programmers. Working with shapes and spatial data may be less familiar, especially due to the vast literature expended on 2D shape analysis. However, we propose the use of the Wasserstein metric for comparing shapes within V&R maps. This metric intuitively captures differences in shapes as well as their positions on maps. The metric allows researchers to use a wide variety of standard techniques for processing V&R map data, including statistical analysis and machine learning.

In this exploration, we investigated the methodology for computationally analyzing maps in depth. We have collected hundreds of map images from a variety of mapping sessions and hundreds of V&R maps collected through the Digital Visitors and Residents Mapping App. In the future, we plan to investigate the data we have collected in depth using the techniques described here.


## ACKNOWLEDGMENTS

We extend our thanks to Vanessa Kitzie and anonymous reviewers for providing valuable feedback and suggestions.


## REFERENCES


Aichholzer, O., & Aurenhammer, F. (1996). Straight skeletons for general polygonal figures in the plane. In J. Y. Cai & C. K. Wong (Eds.), *International computing and combinatorics conference* (pp. 117-126). Berlin: Springer Berlin Heidelberg. doi:10.1007/3-540-61332-3_144

Bauer, U., Ge, X., & Wang, Y. (2014). Measuring distance between Reeb graphs. In *Proceedings of the thirtieth annual symposium on computational geometry* (p. 464). New York: ACM.

Belongie, S., Malik, J., & Puzicha, J. (2002). Shape matching and object recognition using shape contexts. *IEEE Transactions on Pattern Analysis and Machine Intelligence, 24*(4), 509-522. Retrieved from http://citeseerx.ist.psu.edu/viewdoc/download?doi=10.1.1.441.6897&rep=rep1&type=pdf

Bernardo, J. M., & Smith, A. F. (2001). *Bayesian theory*. New York: John Wiley & Sons.

Breiman, L., Friedman, J. H., Olshen, R. A., & Stone, C. J. (1984). *Classification and regression trees*. New York: Chapman & Hall/CRC.

Brown, L. G. (1992). A survey of image registration techniques. *ACM Computing Surveys (CSUR), 24*(4), 325-376. Retrieved from http://www.geo.uzh.ch/ microsite/rsl-documents/research/SARlab/ GMTILiterature/Ver09/PDF/Bro92.pdf

Chatman, E. A. (1987). The information world of low-skilled workers. *Library & Information Science Research, 9*(4), 265-283.

Chatman, E. A. (1992). *The information world of retired women*. New York: Greenwood Press.

Chu, H. (2015). Research methods in library and information science: A content analysis. *Library & Information Science Research, 37*(1), 36-41.

Connaway, L. S. (2016a, May 10). Mapping the role that technology plays in your life: The Visitors and Residents app. *Hangingtogether.org*. Retrieved from http://hangingtogether.org/?p=5627

Connaway, L. S. (2016b, December 6). *Visitors and Residents: A mapping exercise* [PowerPoint slides]. Retrieved from http://www.slideshare.net/LynnConnaway/visitors-and-residents-a-mapping-exercise-70216588

Connaway, L. S., & Dickey, T. J. (2010). *The digital information seeker: Report of the findings from selected OCLC, RIN, and JISC user behaviour projects*. Retrieved from http://www.jisc.ac.uk/media/documents/publications/reports/2010/digitalinformationseekerreport.pdf

Connaway, L. S., Kitzie, V., Hood, E. M., & Harvey, W. (Forthcoming). The many faces of Digital Visitors & Residents: An international compilation of online behaviors of secondary school, undergraduate, and graduate students, faculty, and researchers. With contributions from A. Benedetti, A. Canals, L. Gregori, E. O. Espinet, D. Lozano, M. Man, J. C. Morales, S. G. Ricetto, R. Melgrati, E. M. M. Rodríguez, A. Sada, P. Sidorko, P. Sirito, V. Steel, & E. Woo. Dublin, OH: OCLC Research.

Connaway, L. S., Lanclos, D., & Hood, E. M. (2013, December 6). 'I always stick with the first thing that comes up on Google…' Where people go for information, what they use, and why. *EDUCAUSE Review Online*. Retrieved from http://www.educause.edu/ero/article/i-always-stick-first-thing-comes-google-where-people-go-information-what-they-use-and-why

Connaway, L. S., & Radford, M. L. (2017). *Research methods for library and information science* (6th ed.). Westport, CT: Libraries Unlimited.

Cool, C. (2001). The concept of situation in information science. In M. E. Williams (Ed.), *Annual review of information science and technology, 35*, 5-42.

Cortes, C., & Vapnik, V. (1995). Support-vector networks. *Machine Learning, 20*(3), 273-297. Retrieved from http://image.diku.dk/imagecanon/material/cortes_vapnik95.pdf

Davies, E. R. (2004). *Machine vision: Theory, algorithms, practicalities*. San Francisco: Morgan Kaufmann Publishers.

Dervin, B. (2003). Given a context by any other name: Methodological tools for taming the unruly beast. In B. Dervin, L. Foreman-Wernet, & E. Lauterbach (Eds.), *Sense-making methodology reader: Selected writings of Brenda Dervin* (pp. 111-132). Cresskill, NJ: Hampton Press.

Dryden, I. L., & Mardia, K. V. (1998). *Statistical shape analysis*. Chichester: John Wiley & Sons. Retrieved from http://people.stat.sc.edu/dryden/book/

Du, Q., Faber, V., & Gunzburger, M. (1999). Centroidal voronoi tessellations: Applications and algorithms. *SIAM Review, 41*(4), 637-676. Retrieved from http://www.personal.psu.edu/qud2/Res/Pre/dfg99sirv.pdf

Duda, R. O., Hart, P. E., & Stork, D. G. (2012). *Pattern classification*. New York: John Wiley & Sons.

Hamming, R. W. (1950). Error detecting and error correcting codes. *Bell Labs Technical Journal, 29*(2), 147-160.

Harris, Z. S. (1954). Distributional structure. *Word, 10*(2/3), 146-162. http://dx.doi.org/10.1080/00437956.1954.11659520

Hartley, R., & Zisserman, A. (2003). *Multiple view geometry in computer vision*. Cambridge: Cambridge University Press.

Jaccard, P. (1901). Etude comparative de la distribution florale dans une portion des Alpes et du Jura. *Bulletin del la Société Vaudoise des Sciences Naturelles, 37*, 547-579.

Joshi, S. H., Su, J., Zhang, Z., & Amor, B. B. (2016). Elastic shape analysis of functions, curves and trajectories. In P. K. Turaga & A. Srivastava (Eds.), *Riemannian computing in computer vision* (pp. 211-231). Cham: Springer International Publishing Switzerland.

Kuhn, H. W. (1955). The Hungarian method for the assignment problem. *Naval Research Logistics Quarterly, 2*(1-2), 83-97. doi:10.1002/nav.3800020109

Lee, D. T. (1982). Medial axis transformation of a planar shape.

*IEEE Transactions on Pattern Analysis and Machine Intelligence, 4,* 363-369. Retrieved from https://www.cs.jhu.edu/~misha/Spring16/Lee82.pdf

Lloyd, S. (1982). Least squares quantization in PCM. *IEEE Transactions on Information Theory, 28*(2), 129-137. Retrieved from http://www-evasion.imag.fr/people /Franck.Hetroy/Teaching/ProjetsImage/2007/Bib/lloyd-1982.pdf

Loncaric, S. (1998). A survey of shape analysis techniques. *Pattern Recognition*, 31(8), 983-1001. Retrieved from http://doi.org/10.1016/S0031-2023(97)00122-2.

Luo, L., & McKinney, M. (2015). JAL in the past decade: A comprehensive analysis of academic library research. *The Journal of Academic Librarianship, 41*(2), 123-129. Retrieved from http://dx.doi.org/10.1016/j.acalib.2015.01.003

Malinen, M. I., & Fränti, P. (2014). Balanced k-means for clustering. In P. Fränti, G. Brown, M. Loog, F. Escolano, & M. Pelillo (Eds.), *Structural and syntactic pattern recognition (S+SSPR)* (pp. 32-41). Berlin: Springer Berlin Heidelberg. doi: 10.1007/978-3-662-44415-3

Mikhail, E. M., Bethel, J. S., & McGlone, J. C. (2001). *Introduction to modern photogrammetry*. New York: John Wiley & Sons.

Munkres, J. (1957). Algorithms for the assignment and transportation problems. *Journal of the Society for Industrial and Applied Mathematics, 5*(1), 32-38. Retrieved from https://www.math.ucdavis.edu/~saito/ data/emd/munkres.pdf

Olkin, I., & Pukelsheim, F. (1982). The distance between two random vectors with given dispersion matrices. *Linear Algebra and Its Applications, 48,* 257-263. Retrieved from https://doi.org/10.1016/0024-3795(82)90112-4

Pavlovic, V. I., Sharma, R., Huang, T. S. (1997). Visual interpretation of hand gestures for human-computer interaction: A review. *IEEE Transactions on Pattern Analysis and Machine Intelligence, 19*(7), 677-695. doi:10.1109/34.598226

Prabha, C., Connaway, L. S., Olszewski, L., & Jenkins, L. (2007). What is enough? Satisficing information needs. *Journal of Documentation, 63*(1), 74-89. Retrieved from http://www.oclc.org/research/publications/archive/2007/prabha-satisficing.pdf

Rakotomamonjy, A. (2003). Variable selection using SVM-based criteria. *Journal of Machine Learning Research, 3,* 1357-1370. Retrieved from http://www.jmlr.org/ papers/volume3/rakotomamonjy03a/rakotomamonjy03a.pdf

Rubner, Y., Tomasi, C., & Guibas, L. J. (2000). The earth mover's distance as a metric for image retrieval. *International Journal of Computer Vision, 40*(2), 99-121. doi:10.1023/A:1026543900054

Safavian, S. R., & Landgrebe, D. (1991). A survey of decision tree classifier methodology. *IEEE Transactions on Systems, Man, and Cybernetics, 21*(3), 660-674.

Siddiqi, K., Shokoufandeh, A., Dickenson, S. J., & Zucker, S. W. (1998). Shock graphs and shape matching. In *Proceedings of the IEEE international conference on computer vision (ICCV)* (pp. 222-229). Retrieved from http://www.cs.toronto.edu/~sven/Papers/iccv98-shocks.pdf

Sivic, J., & Zisserman, A. (2009). Efficient visual search of videos cast as text retrieval. *IEEE Transactions on Pattern Analysis and Machine Intelligence, 31*(4), 591-606. doi: 10.1109/TPAMI.2008.111

Sonnenwald, D. H. (1999). Evolving perspectives of human information behavior: Contexts, situations, social networks and information horizons. In T. Wilson & D. Allen (Eds.), *Exploring the contexts of information behavior: Proceedings of the second international conference in information needs* (pp. 176-190). London: Taylor Graham. Retrieved from http://eprints.rclis.org/7971/1/isic98%2Bpaper.pdf

Sørensen, T. (1948). A method of establishing groups of equal amplitude in plant sociology based on similarity of species and its application to analyses of the vegetation on Danish commons. *Biologiske Skrifter, 5,* 1-34.

Su, J., Kurtek, S., Klassen, E., & Srivastava, A. (2014). Statistical analysis of trajectories on riemannian manifolds: Bird migration, hurricane tracking and video surveillance. *Annals of Applied Statistics, 8*(1), 530-552. doi:10.1214/13-AOAS701

Tversky, A. (1977). Features of similarity. *Psychological Review, 84*(4), 327-352. Retrieved from http://www.ai.mit.edu/projects/dm/Tversky-features.pdf

Venn, J. (1880). I. On the diagrammatic and mechanical representation of propositions and reasonings. *Philosophical Magazine, Series 5, 10*(59), 1-18. Retrieved from http://www.cis.upenn.edu/~bhusnur4/ cit592_fall2014/venn%20diagrams.pdf

W3C. (2017). *Scalable vector graphics (SVG) 1.1.* Retrieved from https://www.w3.org/TR/SVG/

White, D. (2008, July 23). *Not 'natives' & 'immigrants' but 'visitors' & 'residents'* [Blog]. Retrieved from http://tallblog.conted.ox.ac.uk/index.php/2008/07/23/notnatives-immigrants-but-visitors-residents/

White D. S., & Le Cornu, A. (2011). Visitors and Residents: A new typology for online engagement. *First Monday, 16*(9). Retrieved from http://firstmonday.org/ojs/index.php/fm/article/view/3171/3049

Wilson, T. D. (1981). On user studies and information needs. *Journal of Documentation, 37*(1), 3-15. Retrieved from http://informationr.net/tdw/publ/papers/1981infoneeds.html

# Yet Another Method for Author Co-citation Analysis: A New Approach Based on Paragraph Similarity

**Tsung-Ming Hsiao**
*Department of Library and Information Science, National Taiwan University, Taiwan. f03126010@ntu.edu.tw*

**Kuang-hua Chen**
*Department of Library and Information Science, National Taiwan University, Taiwan. khchen@ntu.edu.tw*

## ABSTRACT

**Co-citation analysis has been widely adopted to represent the intellectual structure of a discipline. In general, all co-cited author pairs are regarded equal. With the development of computer technology and easy accessibility of machine readable full-text articles, new weighting schemes for measuring co-citation strength (CCS) have been proposed. However, in previous studies, only distance and sentence similarity are used to adjust CCS when applying co-citation analysis. In this study, we propose a new approach to measuring CCS based on paragraph similarity. Investigation was carried out to compare our approach and traditional author co-citation analysis (TACA), as well as other different parametric ACAs. Preliminary results show that TACA and distance-based ACA (DACA) share many commonalities. In contrast, similarity-based ACAs reveal the different structure from that of TACA and DACA. However, differences in resulting network structure were still found between paragraph-similarity-based ACA (PACA) and sentence-similarity-based ACA (SACA). Compared to SACA, PACA produces less number of factors and clusters and moderate size of clusters.**

## KEYWORDS

author co-citation analysis; bibliometrics; citation analysis

## INTRODUCTION

Citation analysis has been widely used to identify intellectual linkages among authors/publications by their cited/citing relationships (Davis, 2009; Eom, 2003). Both Small (1973) and Marshakove (1973) proposed that the relationship of two publications can be measured by counting the frequency with which two publications are cited together. Years later, White and Griffith (1981) proposed different analysis unit in co-citation analysis. Instead of using individual documents, White and Griffith used author name as an *oeuvre,* a body of writing by a person, as the unit of analysis. Authors who are repeatedly cited together in later documents are seen to be more similar than who are rarely or never cited together. Although there are two different types of co-citation analysis, they both answer two questions: (1) what relationships do citers create through co-citation and (2) what do these relationships tell us about the state of the field (Jarneving, 2005; Small, 1973; White & Griffith, 1981, 1982).

With the development of co-citation analysis, some issues about applying co-citation analysis raised, including threshold for co-citation clusters, normalization of CCS, name homograph and primary author restriction (Gmür, 2003; Small, 2009; Small, Sweeney, & Greenlee, 1985a, 1985b). One critical issue is how to measure CCS. Traditionally, all co-citation pairs in one article were counted equally. However, authors cite references for various reasons. Since the early 1960s, researchers have begun to classify relationships between cited and citing articles and analyzed why author cited an article (Lipetz, 1965). Yet despite the importance of citations in an article varies, it is extremely difficult, if not impossible, to measure the importance of different citations by analyzing their characteristics or functions.

Recently, with the advance of computer technology and the increase of available machine readable full-text articles, some researchers have tried to conduct co-citation analysis with data extracted from text body when conducting co-citation analysis (Boyack, Small, & Klavans, 2013; Callahan, Hockema, & Eysenbach, 2010; Eto, 2007, 2008a; Gipp & Beel, 2009; Jeong, Song, & Ding, 2014; Liu & Chen, 2011a, 2011b). The previous studies used different parameters to adjust the CCS, including the distance between two citations or sentence similarity of two citations. No matter which methods that are used to measure CCS, stronger CCS should be given when a pair of citations is cited to discuss more similar topics. Therefore, method based on the surrounding text of a citation may be a better way to adjust the CCS. However, some recent studies also noted that it is not enough to capture the concept of a citation based on fixed sized window or the sentence around a citation (Elkiss et al., 2008, Ritchie, Teufel, & Robertson, 2008).

Hence, in the spirt of exploring more nuanced measure of cited pair similarity, this study proposes to measure CCS based on paragraph similarity. The research questions are shown as follows:

**Q1**. How to use the linguistic parameters extracted from text body when conducting author co-citation analysis (ACA)?

**Q2**. What are the differences between these results of traditional ACA and various parametric ACAs?

In order to answer the first question, this study applies different methods to generate co-citation matrices and examine the

80th Annual Meeting of the Association for Information Science & Technology, Washington, DC | Oct. 27-Nov. 1, 2017

results. For the second question, two statistical analyses, factor analysis and cluster analysis will be performed to investigate the characteristics of results. Furthermore, we used social network analytical methods to help us assess the network statistics of different ACA methods and explored the characteristics of these networks.

## RELATED WORK

This section starts with a review of the development of co-citation analysis, followed by recent studies that explored different methods to improve co-citation analysis with full-text articles.

### *Co-citation analysis*

Small proposed that "co-citation is defined as the frequency with which two documents are cited together" (Small, 1973, p. 265). Small argued that the relationships between two works can be measured by the strength of co-citation which is determined by the numbers their being cited jointly in later works (Small, 1973). Marshakove noted that co-citation analysis "is the logical opposite of the method of bibliographic coupling" (Marshakove, 1973, p. 3). Combined with cluster analysis, co-citation analysis constructs a comprehensive map of certain discipline (Small et al., 1985a).

Originally, document is the only unit for analyzing in co-citation analysis. White and Griffith (1981) proposed that authors could be the unit for analyzing as well. They regarded author name as an *oeuvre* that represented a set of documents authored by a certain person. The relationship between two authors is measured by counting how many times two authors are cited jointly. Therefore, the level of aggregation in ACA is not documents but *oeuvres* (White & Griffith, 1982). McCain (1990) summarized the steps for ACA shown as follows:

1. Selection of authors
2. Retrieval of co-citation frequencies
3. Compilation of raw co-citation matrix
4. Convert to correlation matrix
5. Multivariate analysis of correlation matrix
6. Interpretation and validation

As described above, there are two different types of co-citation analysis, i.e., document co-citation analysis and ACA. Both of them are used to (1) identify groups of specific scientific specialties, (2) locate these groups with respect to each other, (3) measure the proximities between different groups, (4) and map a particular area of science (Jarneving, 2005; Small, 1973; White & Griffith, 1981). The results of co-citation analysis can help finding relevant documents and make subject retrieval possible even without knowledge of subject terms (Eto, 2012; Small, 1973; White & Griffith, 1982).

### *The method issues of co-citation analysis*

With the development of co-citation analysis, some method issues arise, including how to determine the proper threshold of cluster analysis, normalization of co-citation counts and measurement of co-citation counts (Davis, 2009; Eom, 2009; Gmür, 2003; Small, 2009). In ACA, there are some special issues, i.e., name ambiguity and primary author restriction (Small et al., 1985a; White, 2009).

The setting of threshold is a longstanding issue of co-citation analysis. Small et al. (1985a) indicated that it is very likely to aggregate too many documents when using single-link clustering algorithm with low threshold. However, because the sizes and structures of research areas are diverse, some research areas are dense and compact while others are loose and dispersed. Hence, there exists a question that "what thresholds are appropriate to set in delineating individual research areas" (Small, 2009, p. 332).

Another important issue is the normalization of co-citation counts. There are numerous normalization procedures used in co-citation analysis, including mean citation frequency, CoCit-Score, Pearson's r, Salton's cosine and Jaccard Index. Gmür (2003) analyzed the characteristics of the results based on different methods used in counting co-citation counts and argued that there are plentiful diversities between the networks with different normalization methods. Eom (2009) summarized a series of papers discussing the normalization procedure used in ACA. It was shown that when different normalization procedures were applied, the results of ACA may differ accordingly.

Because author is the measure unit in ACA, there are two specific issues about author in ACA: primary author restriction and name ambiguity. The former is due to the restriction of early ISI citation index database. Primary author restriction has been pointed out as an issue in author co-citation study (Small et al., 1985a). After 2000, a series of studies compared the pros and cons between primary author co-citation analysis and all author co-citation analysis (Eom, 2008; Persson, 2001; Schneider, Larsen, & Ingwersen, 2007; Zhao, 2006). Most studies indicated that all author co-citation analysis presented a more coherent result. Another issue is name ambiguity. In ACA, an author name is used to represent the *oeuvre* of a certain author. However, it is possible that an author has many names and vice versa. Rotenberg and Kushmerick (2011) stated some reasons that makes author name identification problematic. While there are some techniques that may be helpful, it is still hard to solve name ambiguity.

Finally, one fundamental question of citation analysis is how to measure the CCS of a citation pair. On the one hand, one assumption of citation analysis is that every citation is equal. Smith (1981) proposed that there are five assumptions underlying citation analysis and one of them is "all citations are equal." On the other hand, however, from 1960s, Garfield (1965) has noted that researchers cited references for numerous reasons. Recently, White (2009) proposed that contexts and content of citations should be analyzed to find out the implicit and explicit meanings of citations. By extracting explicit words from the context of citations, citations can be classified in numerous ways and recounted. With surrounding text of citations, researchers also can discover the implicit relationships between citing and cited articles. However, White also noted that "these forms of analysis are labor-intensive" (White, 2009, p. 1024).

### *Co-citation analysis with full-text articles available*

Traditionally, co-citation analysis measures the relationship between different works and authors in article level. The CCS of work or author pairs gains an equal weight of one whenever a pair of works or authors is cited in an article. However, with the ready accessibility of machine readable full-text articles, it is possible to count the CCS with data extracted from text body. It means that it is possible to measure the relationship in a finer granularity, e.g. section, paragraph, or sentence level.

Eto (2007) indicated that both location and citing words can be used to measure relationship between citations. In Eto's study, the relationships of co-citation were classified into two types depended on whether the references are cited in the same sentence or not. Furthermore, Eto argued that the closer the two citations are, the stronger the CCS ought to be. Therefore, the enumerated co-citation should have most close relationship (Eto, 2007, 2008b). Although Eto argued new method to measure the relationship between two cited articles and verified that the enumerated co-citation does have high similarity, Eto's researches did not propose new schemes to measure CCS by their location or citing words.

Gipp and Beel (2009) reported their new distance-based method to calculate citation proximity based on which granularity two citations are co-cited. If two citations are co-cited in fine-granularity, they have higher citation proximity and vice versa. For example, when a pair of citations is co-cited in sentence level, this pair of citation has highest citation proximity. In the contrary, if a pair of citations is co-cited in article level, it only has lowest citation proximity. The research result shows that this method can improve the results of information retrieval by providing more relative resources. In the following year, Callahan et al. (2010) proposed a novel co-citation analysis coined "contextual co-citation analysis." They used tree structure to describe an article and measure CCS by the depth of the most common nested parent node of two citations. Boyack et al. (2013) used another method to improve the accuracy of co-citation clustering based on absolute distance of two cited references. According to Boyack et al. (2013), "we find that accounting for reference proximity from full-text can increase the textual coherence (a measure of accuracy) of a co-citation cluster solution by up to 30% over the traditional approach based on bibliographic information" (p. 1759).

No matter methods based on granularity, depth of common nested parent node, or absolute distance, all these methods are based on distance between two cited references as a variable to adjust the CCS of two cited references. However, it is more reasonable to measure CCS by what two citations are about than by how far they are from each other. Recently, Jeong et al. (2014) proposed another approach coined content-based ACA to measure the CCS of a citation pair. The CCS of a citation pair is defined as the similarity of two sentences within which two references are cited. Jeong et al. claimed that their approach provides more details about the sub-disciplines than traditional ACA while showing a similar intellectual structure.

The line of research seems to suggest that a more accurate result can be gained when conducting co-citation analysis with data extracted from text body, yet there are questions that remain unsolved. First, because of complex citation context, it is problematic to use only sentence-level information to find out the characteristics of different citations. Elkiss et al. (2008) indicated that two sentences may carry exactly the same information without lexical similarity. Therefore, it is questionable to use sentence similarity as measurement of CCS. Second, it is reasonable to assume that two citations have closer relationship when they are cited closer, but it is not yet clear that which level is appropriate to be used in co-citation analysis. If we conduct co-citation analysis with too fine granularity only strong relationships will be reveal and other relationships may be neglected. An appropriate level of granularity is critical for co-citation analysis.

Hence, in this study, we follow the approach proposed by Jeong et al. (2014) that ACA can be a content-based method. However, due to the limitations of sentence similarity noted by Elkiss et al. (2008), this study uses paragraph similarity to measure CCS of a citation pair. A paragraph is usually composed of several sentences about one topic; therefore it should be a more appropriate level to reveal what a citation is cited about. If two citations are cited to discuss same topic, there should be higher paragraph similarity and higher CCS will be given to this pair of citations. In order to investigate the characteristics of the result of ACA based on paragraph similarity, we also conduct three ACA methods for comparison purpose, including traditional ACA, ACA based on distance and ACA based on sentence similarity.

## METHOD

The objective of this study is to explore ways to improve the results of traditional co-citation analysis by utilizing data extracted from full-text articles. Three different methods of ACA were used to generate co-citation matrix, including distance, sentence similarity and paragraph similarity. The results of these three methods were used to compare with the result of traditional ACA. When building CCS matrix, all authors of a citation, not only primary author, were counted in this study. The research procedure is composed of six stages:

1. data collection
2. data preprocessing
3. co-citation matrix generation
4. factor analysis
5. cluster analysis
6. network analysis

The data set used in this study is composed of all articles published in *Journal of the Association for Information Science and Technology* (JASIST) during 2006 to 2015. The full-text articles are collected from Wiley Online library in the data collection stage. There are 2,522 articles used in this research. Due to the downloaded articles are HTML documents, it is necessary to remove noises and HTML tags. When cleaning these unnecessary data, we also collected bibliographic data of a reference and the location where a reference is cited in an article. Using bibliographic data, we can conduct a traditional co-citation analysis. With more data extracted from text body, not only we can calculate the distance between two cited references in the article, but also it is possible to identify that a reference is cited in which sentence and paragraph.

Four co-citation matrices were generated based on different settings for ACA shown as follows. Hereafter, traditional ACA will be denoted as TACA. The ACA with different parameter settings are called parametric ACA in general. Three parametric ACAs are considered in this study. ACA with distance consideration is called DACA; ACA based on sentence similarity and based on paragraph similarity are called SACA and PACA, respectively.

1. Traditional method (TACA)

Traditionally, the CCS of an author pair is defined as how many articles cite two different works that created by two authors jointly (White & Griffith, 1981). In other words, CCS is measured in article level. In this study, this method is defined as the traditional method.

2. Distance method (DACA)

The method is applied by some recent studies with different weighting schemes (Boyack et al. 2013, Callahan et al, 2010, Gipp, & Beel, 2009). Depending on the distance between two citations, different CCS value is assigned to an author pair. Basically, CCS value is inversely proportional to the distance between two citations. The underlying assumption of the method is that the closer two cited references are in an article, the closer the relationship between them. In this study, the CCS between author $i$ and author $j$ is defined as follows:

$$DCCS_{ij} = \sum_x \sum_y \frac{(L_{article} - L_{x,y})}{L_{article}} / (x \times y) \qquad (1)$$

$DCCS_{ij}$ represents the *CCS* of an author pair, author $i$ and author $j$.

$x$ and $y$ represent the 1st, 2nd, …, xth/yth time that author $i$ and $j$ are cited in the article respectively.

$L_{article}$ is the length of the whole plain-text article.

$L_{x,y}$ is the length between the locations of two cited authors.

Using this formula, the farer two cited references are, the less their DCCS is. If two authors are cited in same sentence, their DCCS will be 1. On the contrary, if two authors are cited in the beginning and end of the article separately, their DCCS will be close to 0.

3. Sentence similarity method (SACA)

The sentence similarity method is proposed by Jeong et al. (2014). The CCS is given by the degree of similarity between citing sentences of two cited references. After removing stop words in these sentences and stemming remaining words, cosine similarity is used to measure the similarity of two sentences. The way to calculate CCS of an author pair is shown as follows:

$$SCCS_{ij} = \sum_x \sum_y sim(\overrightarrow{sm_x} \cdot \overrightarrow{sn_y}) / (x \times y) \qquad (2)$$

$SCCS_{ij}$ represents the *CCS* of an author pair, author $i$ and author $j$.

$x$ and $y$ represent the 1st, 2nd, …, xth/yth time that author $i$ and $j$ are cited in the article respectively.

$sm_x$ and $sn_y$ represent the sentence text of the 1st, 2nd, …, xth/yth cited reference in the article respectively.

Using this formula, the more common terms between surrounding texts of two cited references have, the larger the SCCS is. The range of SCCS of an author pair will be 0~1, i.e., no common terms and exactly identical, respectively.

4. Paragraph similarity method (PACA)

According to Elkiss et al. (2008) and Ritchie et al. (2008), it may not be enough to capture the characteristics of a citation by using the sentence information only. Therefore, in this study, we proposed using paragraph as the unit of analysis. Because it is reasonable to assume that authors will discuss one topic or some relevant topics in single paragraph, it should be proper to use words of a paragraph to represent the implicit topics the citations cited in this paragraph. That is to say, by comparing text similarity of two paragraphs, we can measure CCS based on topic similarity implicitly. The way to calculate CCS of an author pair is shown as follows:

$$PCCS_{ij} = \sum_x \sum_y sim(\overrightarrow{pm_x} \cdot \overrightarrow{pn_y}) / (x \times y) \qquad (3)$$

$PCCS_{ij}$ represents the *CCS* of an author pair, author $i$ and author $j$.

$x$ and $y$ represent the 1st, 2nd, …, xth/yth time that author $i$ and $j$ are cited in the article respectively.

$pm_x$ and $pn_y$ represent the paragraph text of the 1st, 2nd, …, xth/yth cited reference in the article respectively.

Same with previous method, after removing stop words and stemming remaining words, cosine similarity is used to measure the similarity of two texts. The formula used to calculate CCS of an author pair based on paragraph similarity is the same as equation (2) mentioned above.

After generating co-citation matrix, we use SAS statistics package to conduct factor analysis to group numerous selected authors into a much smaller set of factors to represent research fields. Following the procedures described by Eom (2003), co-citation matrix in Excel format is imported into

SAS. After reviewing similar studies, we use 1 as the threshold for eigenvalue (Eom, 2003, 2009; Jeong et al., 2014). The results of factor analysis uncover the number of factors and the total variance that factors could explain. The results of factor analysis are used as the criteria to evaluate different ACA methods. Besides, we also apply cluster analysis to find out the latent cluster structure of these ACA methods and identify the characteristics of each method. Finally, network analysis is conducted to investigate the characteristics and structure of the co-citation networks. In this study, we use Gephi, a social network analysis tool (Bastian, Heymann, & Jacomy, 2009), as a network analysis tool.

## RESULTS AND DISSCUSSION

### *Basic statistics*

The numbers of extracted authors in our dataset are 66,163 in TACA method and 63,618 in parametric ACA methods. The difference is because the data used to calculate different ACA are collected from two different methods. Data used in TACA are based on the references in the end of an article. However, due to information extracted from full-text body is necessary for parametric ACA methods, we check every reference whether this reference is cited in the full-text body or not. Therefore, in parametric ACA methods, some references are filtered out because these references are not cited in full-text body. For that reason, there is difference in author number between TACA and parametric ACA. Table 1 shows these numbers.

The top 10 author pairs of TACA and DACA are identical. The only difference is the rank order of certain author pairs. However, the author pairs of ACA based on sentence similarity are quite different. In SACA, only five of ten author pairs of TACA remain in top ten. In PACA, eight of ten author pairs of TACA remain in top ten, more than SACA. There are seven common author pairs between SACA and PACA. Table 2 shows the details.

Furthermore, we compare top 100 author pairs of different ACA methods. There are 64 of 100 author pairs in common among four different ACA methods. In the results of TACA and DACA, 94 of 100 author pairs are the same. When comparing the results of TACA and PACA, 88 author pairs are the same. However, there are only 72 identical author pairs in the results of TACA and SACA. When we compare the results of PACA and SACA, 80 author pairs are in common.

The results show that there may be two different categories of ACA. Due to the high similarity between the results of TACA and DACA, we assume that both methods are based on distance and measure CCS by how far two cited references are. The difference between two methods is how to assign the CCS to an author pair. The other two methods are based on text similarity and show a different rank order of co-cited author pairs. In the following section, we will further discuss the result of factors analysis.

### *Factor analysis*

As Table 1 shows, there are more than 60,000 authors in our data. Therefore, we choose two small sets of authors and conduct factory analysis. The criteria used to filter author is how many times an author is cited. The top 100 most cited authors are chosen to form the first author set and the top 10% most cited authors (each author is cited more than five times) are chosen as the second author set. There are 7,600 authors in the second author set. Authors in these author sets are used to construct CCS matrix. After having CCS matrix, factor analysis will be conducted accordingly.

Table 3 and 4 show the results of factor analysis. Eight factors are found in the experiment of TACA with top 100 authors and could explain 81.25% variance. The number of factors increases 1 and 2 when using DACA and PACA, but the total variance explained stands 81.11% and 80.12% respectively. Thirteen factors are found in SACA with 78.87% variance explained. The results of factor analysis for top 10% authors are very similar to those for top 100. SACA produces more factors, but TACA explain most variance.

Comparing these results with Jeong et al. (2014), our study shows that similarity-based ACAs produce much more factors, but total variance explained by SACA is a little less than TACA. This difference may be due to the different procedures used in processing full text articles, natural language processing techniques, or the composition of raw data. It needs further investigation to answer this question.In concordance with the previous studies, more factors tend to emerge when applying ACA with other data extracted from text body. Especially when using surrounding text of cited reference as a variable, it will produce many more factors. Jeong et al. (2014) argued that "this result can be interpreted as the information science domain consists of sub-disciplines and there are more factors that influence the factor structure" (p. 204). From this point of view, parametric ACAs will be helpful to find out more specific sub-disciplines. However, this does not mean that the more factors a method produces, the better the method is. In fact, it seems that SACA may produce too many factors. On the contrary, PACA produces less and a reasonable number of factors with only a little loss in explanation of variance.

### *Cluster analysis*

The top 100 most cited authors are used to construct CCS matrix based on different ACA methods in cluster analysis stage. Cluster analysis is used to investigate the latent clusters in these matrices. The semi-partial R-squared and pseudo T-squared are criteria applied to identifying clusters. Table 5 presents the number of clusters of different ACA methods.

| | Traditional ACA | Parametric ACA |
|---|---|---|
| # of Authors | 66,163 | 63,618 |
| # of Pairs | 7,758,578 | 7,122,987 |

***Table 1.*** *Comparison of the number of authors*

| Rank | TACA | DACA | SACA | PACA |
|---|---|---|---|---|
| 1 | Garfield, E. & Leydesdorff, L. (126) | Egghe, L. & Rousseau, R. (90.36) | Egghe, L. & Rousseau, R. (76.72) | Egghe, L. & Rousseau, R. (93.70) |
| 2 | Egghe, L. & Rousseau, R. (117) | Garfield, E. & Leydesdorff, L. (86.16) | Saracevic, T. & Spink, A. (61.73) | Garfield, E.& Leydesdorff, L. (87.80) |
| 3 | Leydesdorff, L. & Rousseau, R. (108) | Leydesdorff, L. & Rousseau, R. (75.47) | Jansen, B.J. & Spink, A. (61.67) | Leydesdorff, L.& Rousseau, R. (78.30) |
| 4 | Garfield, E. & Moed, H. F. (102) | Garfield, E. & Moed, H.F. (74.39) | Glänzel, W. & Schubert, A. (56.84) | Saracevic, T. & Spink, A. (75.67) |
| 5 | Glänzel, W. & Rousseau, R. (101) | Saracevic, T. & Spink, A. (72.75) | Garfield, E. & Leydesdorff, L. (55.78) | Jansen, B.J. & Spink, A. (73.29) |
| 6 | Glänzel, W. & Leydesdorff, L. (100) | Leydesdorff, L. & Small, H. (70.87) | Leydesdorff, L. & Rousseau, R. (55.67) | Leydesdorff, L. & Small, H. (75.50) |
| 7 | Saracevic, T. & Spink, A. (97) | Glänzel, W. & Rousseau, R. (70.83) | Leydesdorff, L. & Waltman, L. (51.56) | Glänzel, W. & Schubert, A. (69.04) |
| 8 | Leydesdorff, L. & Small, H. (97) | Garfield, E. & Small, H. (70.82) | Bornmann, L. & Leydesdorff, L. (51.22) | Glänzel, W. & Leydesdorff, L. (68.04) |
| 9 | Garfield, E. & Small, H. (94) | Glänzel, W. & Schubert, A. (70.70) | Bar-Ilan, J. & Thelwall, M. (48.75) | Leydesdorff, L. & Waltman, L. (67.12) |
| 10 | Glänzel, W. & Schubert, A. (93) | Glänzel, W. & Leydesdorff, L. (69.64) | Leydesdorff, L. & Rafols, I. (47.76) | Garfield, E. & Moed, H.F. (64.28) |

***Table 1**. Top 10 author pairs*

| | # of factors | Total variance explained |
|---|---|---|
| TACA | 8 | 0.8125 |
| DACA | 9 | 0.8111 |
| PACA | 10 | 0.8012 |
| SACA | 13 | 0.7887 |

***Table 3**. The results of factor analysis (top 100 authors)*

| | # of factors | Total variance explained |
|---|---|---|
| TACA | 759 | 0.8878 |
| DACA | 780 | 0.8818 |
| PACA | 797 | 0.8725 |
| SACA | 900 | 0.8547 |

***Table 4.** The results of factor analysis (top 10% authors)*

| | # of clusters | Authors of each cluster |
|---|---|---|
| TACA | 5 | 10/12/20/21/37 |
| DACA | 5 | 10/12/20/21/37 |
| PACA | 8 | 1/5/8/9/11/15/20/31 |
| SACA | 11 | 1/1/1/5/7/7/10/12/13/17/26 |

***Table 5.** Number of clusters of different ACA methods*

Both TACA and DACA have five clusters in which the components are very similar. In fact, three clusters out of the five clusters are identical, i.e., the authors in the three clusters are the same no matter TACA or DACA is conducted. In the other two clusters, there are only three authors, Waltman, L., Thelwall, M. and van Raan, A. F. J., are assigned to the different clusters when using TACA and DACA.PACA shows more different results with comparison to TACA and DACA. There are eight clusters in this result. A few clusters in TACA are spilt into small clusters while conducting PACA. Therefore, more specific sub-fields are identified based on paragraph similarity. The tendency will be much clearer with the fact that SACA produces 11 clusters. However, more than a quarter of clusters produced in SACA method are composed of only one author. It seems that SACA produces too many small clusters.

According to these results, DACA and TACA produce the similar structure when mapping structures to certain domains. Although Gipp and Beel (2009) have pointed out ACA based on distance may enhance closer relationship, the structure revealed by both TACA and DACA are very similar. On the contrary, similarity-based ACA reveal different structure of disciplines. According to the results PACA and SACA, not only number of factors but also number and size of clusters show different outcomes in comparison to the results of TACA and DACA. However, again, PACA produces reasonable number of and size of clusters in comparison to the results of SACA.

### *Network analysis*

In network analysis stage, we analyze the network composed from top 100 authors. It is necessary to apply filtering to prevent a fully connected network which increases the difficulty to map the structure of a discipline. Therefore, in this study, only those relationships with a Pearson's correlation value over 0.6 are used to construct the network map.

Table 6 shows average degree and graph density of the networks mapped by Gephi with four different co-citation matrices. The average degree means how many links a node connects. In ACA, this represents how many authors are co-cited with an author on average. The highest average degree is 25.34 in TACA and the lowest is 14.26 in SACA. This shows that the network of SACA is sparser than network of TACA. Graph density indicates the same trend. In TACA, the graph density is 0.256. However, in SACA, the graph density is only 0.144. The result also indicates that the number of high correlation relationships has substantially reduced. Compared with TACA, the result in PACA is only moderately reduced. In PACA, the average degree and graph density are 20.42 and 0.206 respectively. It supports our finding that PACA produces a reasonable result when conducting analysis in a finer analysis level. Figure 2 shows the tendency of average degree and graph density produced by four methods.

| | Average degree | Graph density |
|---|---|---|
| TACA | 25.34 | 0.256 |
| DACA | 23.78 | 0.240 |
| PACA | 20.42 | 0.206 |
| SACA | 14.26 | 0.144 |

***Table 6.*** *Average degree and graph density*

Figure 3, 4, 5 and 6 show the network diagrams produced by Gephi with co-citation matrices of different ACA methods. All nodes in these network diagrams are clustered together with the same threshold. Due to the different algorithms used by SAS and Gephi the clusters produced by Gephi were somewhat different even though the general trend is the same. The algorithm used by SAS is Ward's minimum variance method. The criterion to merge the pair of clusters in Ward's minimum variance method is to minimize the increment in total within-cluster variance after merging. The model to uncover groups in Gephi is based on modularity, a method based on the ratio of with-in/with-out partition ties. The modularity method categorizes nodes by comparing the ratio to its expected value when ties are produced at random.

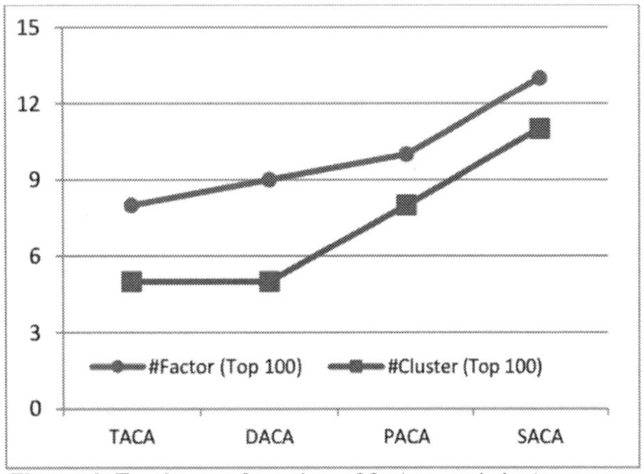


***Figure 1.*** *Tendency of number of factors and clusters*

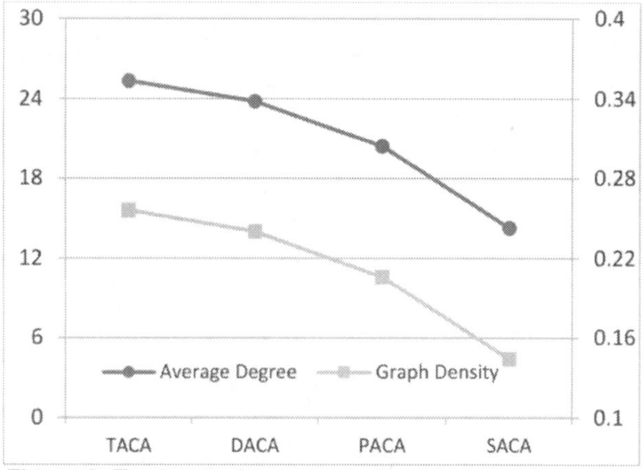


***Figure 2.*** *Tendency of average and graph density*

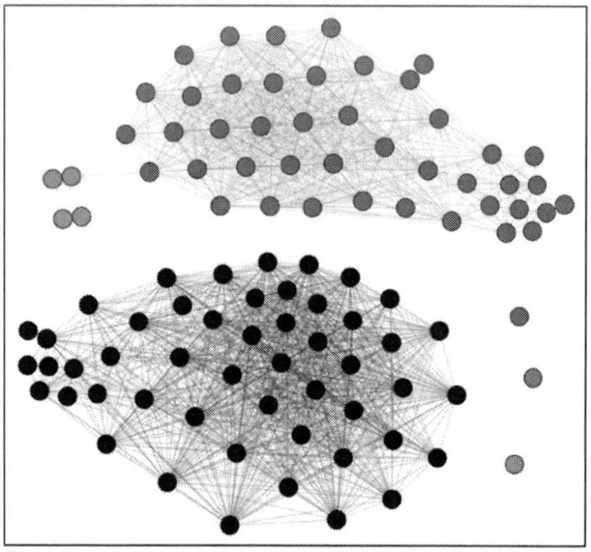

***Figure 3.*** *Network diagram of TACA*

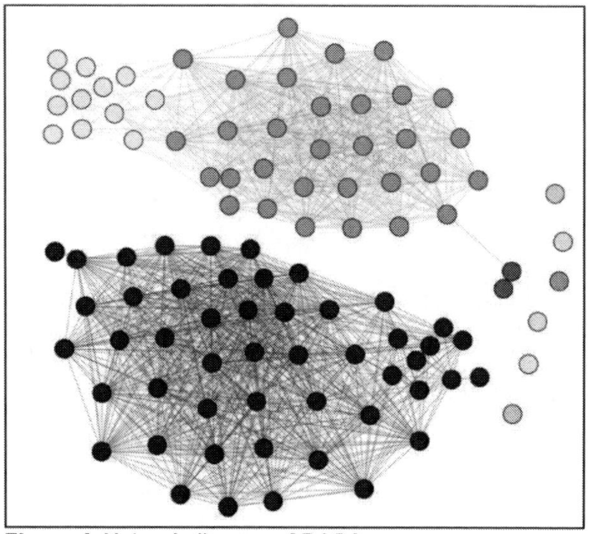

***Figure 4.*** *Network diagram of DACA*

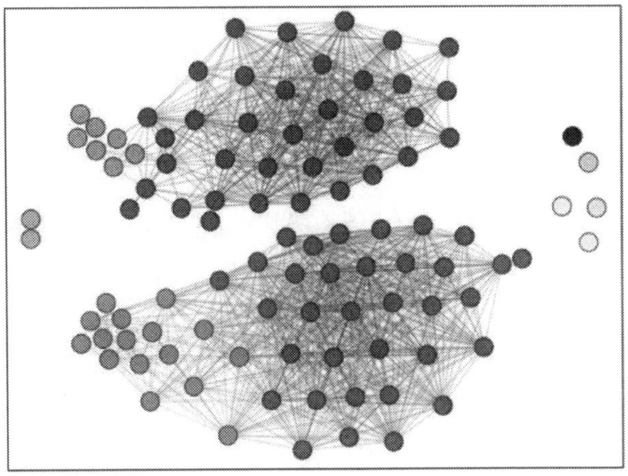

***Figure 5**. Network diagram of PACA*

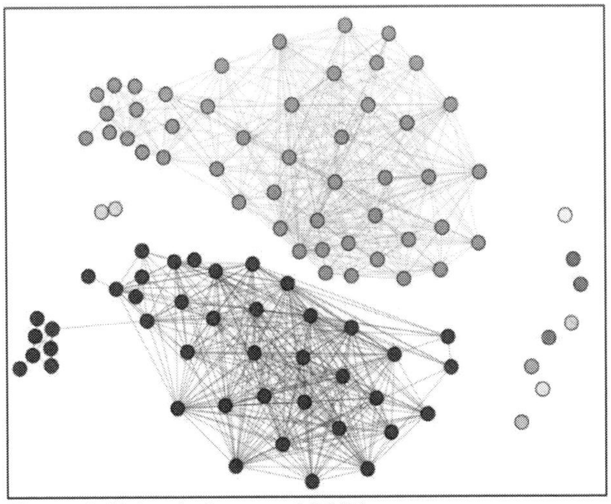

***Figure 6**. Network diagram of SACA*

Figure 3 is the network diagram of TACA. There are two large clusters, two small clusters and three isolated nodes in TACA. Figure 4 is the network diagram of DACA. DACA produces three large clusters, one small cluster and six isolated nodes. In comparison with the network diagram of TACA, there are more large clusters and isolated nodes. After examining the details of clusters, we find out that one large cluster in TACA is split into two clusters when using DACA. This indicates that DACA reveals more sub-disciplines than TACA.

Figure 5 is the network diagram of PACA. The network diagram shows five clusters and five isolated nodes. When examining the five clusters, we find out that two large clusters produced by TACA are split into four clusters in PACA. In comparison with data of DACA, one large cluster produced by DACA is split into two clusters in PACA. These findings show that PACA not only provides more sub-disciplines but also presents a different perspective to observe science fields.

Finally, Figure 6 shows the network diagram of SACA. The network is composed of five clusters and eight isolated nodes. Although the clusters and their nodes in SACA are similar to those in PACA, the number of isolated nodes in SACA is almost double the number in PACA. The results demonstrate PACA produces less isolated nodes than SACA does.

## CONCLUSION AND FUTURE WORK

This study compares the results of four different approaches, TACA, DACA, SACA and PACA, to measure CCS of an author pair. The results show that these four approaches can be separated into two categories: approach based on distance and approach based on text similarity.

TACA could be regarded as a special case of DACA. Some previous researches show that TACA could be enhanced using information extracted from text body (Boyack et al., 2013, Gipp & Beel, 2009, Eto, 2007, Eto, 2012). Our results demonstrate that the enhancement based on distance provides little extra information. As a result, the factors and clusters of TACA and DACA are very similar.

On the other hand, the results of SACA and PACA, two similarity-based methods, are very different to TACA and DACA in this study. Therefore, similarity-based ACA could cast different lights on the latent structures of research fields and provide different insights for us to understand disciplines. However, PACA and SACA still demonstrate different trends in factor analysis and cluster analysis. PACA produces reasonable number of factors and clusters and reasonable size of clusters in comparison to SACA does. As a result, PACA could be regarded as an "in-between" among other ACA methods and provide different latent structures in comparison to TACA and DACA.

Although similarity-based ACA may provide different latent structure of science, only lexical similarity is considered in this study. In the future, we try to apply techniques of natural language processing, like topic detection and discourse analysis, when conducting co-citation analysis. With techniques of natural language processing, CCS of two cited references could be measured by semantic similarity or in discourse level. Therefore, co-citation analysis could provide much more accurate structures or trend of science.

## ACKNOWLEDGMENT

Parts of this work are supported by Ministry of Science and Technology, R.O.C. (Taiwan) under the grant numbers MOST105-2410-H-002-118 and MOST105-2420-H-002-056-MY2. The authors would like to thank Professor Muh-Chyun Tang for his insightful suggestions. The authors are also grateful to anonymous reviewers for their comments and suggestions.

## REFERENCES

Bastian, M., Heymann, S., & Jacomy, M. (2009). Gephi: An open source software for exploring and manipulating networks. In *Proc 3rd Intl ICWSM Conf.*

Boyack, K. W., Small, H., & Klavans, R. (2013). Improving the accuracy of co-citation clustering using full text. *Journal of the American Society for Information Science and Technology, 64*(9), 1759-1767. https://doi.org/10.1002/asi.22896

Callahan, A., Hockema, S., & Eysenbach, G. (2010). Contextual cocitation: Augmenting cocitation analysis and its applications. *Journal of the American Society for Information Science and Technology*, *61*(6), 1130-1143.

Davis, P. M. (2009). Reward or persuasion? The battle to define the meaning of a citation. *Learned Publishing*, *22*(1), 5-11. https://doi.org/10.1087/095315108X378712

Elkiss, A., Shen, S., Fader, A., Erkan, G., States, D., & Radev, D. (2008). Blind men and elephants: What do citation summaries tell us about a research article? *Journal of the American Society for Information Science and Technology*, *59*(1), 51-62. https://doi.org/10.1002/asi.20707

Eom, S. B. (2003). *Author co-citation analysis using custom bibliographic databases: An introduction to the SAS approach*. Lewiston, N.Y: Edwin Mellen Press.

Eom, S. B. (2008). All author cocitation analysis and first author cocitation analysis: A comparative empirical investigation. *Journal of Informetrics*, *2*(1), 53-64. https://doi.org/10.1016/j.joi.2007.09.001

Eom, S. B. (2009). *Author cocitation analysis: Quantitative methods for mapping the intellectual structure of an academic discipline*. Hershey, PA: Information Science Reference.

Eto, M. (2007). Multivalued co-citation measure based on semantic distance between co-cited papers in a citing paper: A case study focused on enumeration of citations. *Library and Information Science*, (58), 49-67.

Eto, M. (2008a). A new co-citation measure based on structures of citing papers. *情報処理学会論文誌データベース（TOD）*, *49*(7), 1-15.

Eto, M. (2008b). Document retrieval method using context based co-citation relationship. *Digital Libraries*, (35), 53-60.

Eto, M. (2012). Evaluations of context-based co-citation searching. *Scientometrics*, *94*(2), 651-673. https://doi.org/10.1007/s11192-012-0756-z

Garfield, E. (1965). Can citation indexing be automated? In *Statistical association methods for mechanized documentation, symposium proceedings* (pp. 189–192). Washington: National Bureau of Standards Miscellaneous Publication.

Gipp, B., & Beel, J. (2009). Citation proximity analysis (CPA) – A new approach for identifying related work based on co-citation analysis. In *Proceedings of ISSI 2009*.

Gmür, M. (2003). Co-citation analysis and the search for invisible colleges: A methodological evaluation. *Scientometrics*, *57*(1), 27-57. https://doi.org/10.1023/A:1023619503005

Jarneving, B. (2005). A comparison of two bibliometric methods for mapping of the research front. *Scientometrics*, *65*(2), 245-263. https://doi.org/10.1007/s11192-005-0270-7

Jeong, Y. K., Song, M., & Ding, Y. (2014). Content-based author co-citation analysis. *Journal of Informetrics*, *8*(1), 197-211. https://doi.org/10.1016/j.joi.2013.12.001

Lipetz, B.-A. (1965). Improvement of the selectivity of citation indexes to science literature through inclusion of citation relationship indicators. *American Documentation*, *16*(2), 81-90. https://doi.org/10.1002/asi.5090160207

Liu, S., & Chen, C. (2011a). The effects of co-citation proximity on co-citation analysis. *Proceedings of ISSI2011-The 13th international conference on scientometrics and informetrics*, 474-484.

Liu, S., & Chen, C. (2011b). The proximity of co-citation. *Scientometrics*, *91*(2), 495-511. https://doi.org/10.1007/s11192-011-0575-7

Marshakove, I. (1973). System of document connections based on references. *Nauchno-Tekhnicheskaya Informatsiya*, *2*(6), 3-8.

McCain, K. W. (1990). Mapping authors in intellectual space: A technical overview. *Journal of the American Society for Information Science*, *41*(6), 433-443. https://doi.org/10.1002/(SICI)1097-4571(199009)41:6<433::AID-ASI11>3.0.CO;2-Q

Persson, O. (2001). All author citations versus first author citations. *Scientometrics*, *50*(2), 339-344. https://doi.org/10.1023/A:1010534009428

Ritchie, A., Teufel, S., & Robertson, S. (2008). Using terms from citations for IR: Some first results. In C. Macdonald, I. Ounis, V. Plachouras, I. Ruthven, & R. W. White (Eds.), *Advances in information retrieval* (pp.211-221). Springer Berlin Heidelberg. Retrieved from http://link.springer.com/chapter/10.1007/978-3-540-78646-7_21

Rotenberg, E., & Kushmerick, A. (2011). The author challenge: Identification of self in the scholarly literature. *Cataloging & Classification Quarterly*, *49*(6), 503-520. https://doi.org/10.1080/01639374.2011.606405

Schneider, J. W., Larsen, B., & Ingwersen, P. (2007). Comparative study between first and all-author co-citation analysis based on citation indexes generated from xml data. In D. Torres-Salinas & H. F. Moed (Eds.), *Proceedings of ISSI 2007* (pp. 696-707). Madrid, Spain: CSIC.

Small, H. (1973). Co-citation in the scientific literature: A new measure of the relationship between two documents. *Journal of the American Society for Information Science*, *24*(4), 265-269. https://doi.org/10.1002/asi.4630240406

Small, H. (2009). Critical thresholds for co-citation clusters and emergence of the giant component. *Journal of Informetrics*, *3*(4), 332-340. https://doi.org/10.1016/j.joi.2009.05.001

Small, H., Sweeney, E., & Greenlee, E. (1985a). Clustering the science citation index ® using co-citations. *Scientometrics*, *7*(3–6), 391-409. https://doi.org/10.1007/BF02017157

Small, H, Sweeney, E., & Greenlee, E. (1985b). Clustering the science citation index using co-citations. II. Mapping science. *Scientometrics*, *8*(5-6), 321-340. https://doi.org/10.1007/BF02018057

Smith, L. C. (1981). Citation analysis. *Library Trends*, *30*(1), 83-106.

White, H. D. (2009). Citation analysis. In *Encyclopedia of library and information sciences, third edition* (pp. 1012-1026). Taylor & Francis. Retrieved from http://www.tandfonline.com/doi/abs/10.1081/E-ELIS3-120043464

White, H. D., & Griffith, B. C. (1981). Author cocitation: A literature measure of intellectual structure. *Journal of the American Society for Information Science*, *32*(3), 163-171. https://doi.org/10.1002/asi.4630320302

White, H. D., & Griffith, B. C. (1982). Authors as markers of intellectual space: Co-citation in studies of science, technology and society. *Journal of Documentation*, *38*(4), 255-272. https://doi.org/10.1108/eb026731

Zhao, D. (2006). Towards all-author co-citation analysis. *Information Processing & Management*, *42*(6), 1578-1591. https://doi.org/10.1016/j.ipm.2006.03.022

# F#%@ That Noise: SoundCloud as (A-)Social Media?

**Chris Hubbles**
*Information School, University of Washington, USA. chubbles@uw.edu*

**Jin Ha Lee**
*Information School, University of Washington. jinhalee@uw.edu*

**David W. McDonald**
*Human-Centered Design & Engineering, University of Washington. dwmc@uw.edu*

## ABSTRACT

**SoundCloud is an audio uploading, streaming and sharing website. The site allows listeners to leave public comments at specific time stamps within a graphical display of an audio file as it plays and offers support for user communication through a publicly viewable reply function. We extracted user comments and conducted a qualitative content analysis in order to characterize and examine participation on the site. Commenting consisted primarily of short, positive comments toward the song or artist and use of the reply function was minimal, though some artists made use of it to communicate with listeners. We speculate that the commenting function is used less as a means toward community-building or social interaction and more for fostering or indicating shared mutual experiences. Comment design implications are also explored.**

## KEYWORDS

SoundCloud, social media, music streaming, user behavior, communication

## INTRODUCTION

Social platforms are compelling and interesting to users. Systems like Facebook, YouTube, Twitter and Pinterest attract a great deal of attention and carry much of the mindshare of the social media landscape. Attempts to build social systems for audio, however, have been marked by failure after failure across multiple platforms. Music is a prominently social vehicle in modern society – the explosion of peer-to-peer services in the late 1990s and early 2000s, for instance, was driven partly by social sharing of music files – but online platforms have struggled to support social audio functionalities. Platforms for upload and download of music files (e.g., Napster, Kazaa, Grokster, Morpheus) were perpetually hobbled by legal issues; platforms for sharing personal collections (e.g., iTunes, Windows Media Player, Google Play Music) often have proprietary restrictions that make them functionally difficult to use socially. Furthermore, they rarely have interpersonal communication tools built into them. Sites for promoting, discussing, and sharing favorite musical artists (e.g., MySpace Music, PureVolume, Facebook, Reverb Nation) seem perpetually poised to get swallowed up by the next big platform; Facebook, perhaps the site *du jour* in this arena, competes with upstarts such as BandCamp and Tumblr, which may themselves take Facebook's place in a few years, just as Facebook did to MySpace not long ago. On-demand streaming services are sometimes built with social applications in mind, and services such as Spotify and (recently defunct) Grooveshark offer some opportunity for interpersonal sharing and discovery. However, they lack the open social discussion available on a site like YouTube, which is often thought of primarily as a vehicle for video uploading, but is used as a *de facto* audio streaming and sharing tool by many of its users (Lee et al., 2017).

One website for social audio, SoundCloud, exhibits several of these elements at once: user uploading, playlist building and sharing, artist promotion, and streaming. SoundCloud also includes interpersonal communication and public discussion tools, but neither artist nor listener behavior on SoundCloud has received much study, despite the site's popularity and its unique combination of functionalities. Our study focuses on the listener side of the SoundCloud user base. We began with the research question: What does the SoundCloud comment function provide to listeners? In particular, how do SoundCloud listeners use the commenting function? Do listeners attempt to communicate with musical artists, and if so, how? Do listeners attempt to communicate with each other, and if so, how?

By addressing these questions through a qualitative study of user commenting, we seek to understand behavior in a social music system that offers novel avenues for personal expression and interaction. We collected and examined SoundCloud user comments using a modified grounded theory approach. We scraped comments from tracks on the site over the course of the entire year 2013 and developed a content codebook, qualitatively evaluating 5,608 comments using a consensus coding strategy. We found that commenting on SoundCloud tended toward short, positive comments, often forcefully and profanely stated, with sparse and light interpersonal communication, though some artists used the commenting function as a means of responding to fan outreach. Our analysis indicates that the site's timestamped commenting function – an innovative tool indicative of SoundCloud's latent capabilities as a platform for social interaction between music fans – goes largely unutilized for this purpose. Instead, user postings tend

80th Annual Meeting of the Association for Information Science & Technology, Washington, DC | Oct. 27-Nov. 1, 2017

more toward the declaratory, functioning more like broadcasts than invitations to dialogue. We postulate that this creates, in aggregate, a sense of shared mutual experience, a virtual analog of spaces that are social even when there is no interaction between attendees, such as the cinema or concert hall.

## WHAT IS SOUNDCLOUD?

SoundCloud is an audio social networking site that enables users to upload digital sound files. The files can then be played by listeners on the site, and can be embedded easily into other news sites, blogs, and social networking sites. The site was founded in Berlin in 2008, and soon became a hub for German electronic musicians to share tracks and ideas (Mac, 2013). By 2009, the site had launched internationally and was already challenging MySpace, the then-dominant platform, in the online music-sharing universe (Van Buskirk, 2009). SoundCloud grew rapidly, expanding from 10 million registered users in 2011 to 40 million by mid-2013 (Graham, 2013). As of August 2014, SoundCloud was reporting over 175 million monthly listeners (not all of whom make accounts) (Sisario, 2014), a figure the site has not since updated. Its creators aspirationally call it the "YouTube of audio," and it is used as a distribution channel by major-label musicians, popular podcasters and even U.S. government offices such as the White House (under Obama) and NASA. The site's reach is worldwide, with significant user populations in North America, Europe and Southeast Asian countries such as Indonesia, the Philippines and Vietnam (Bonanos, 2014).

Registration for accounts is free, and up to three hours of audio may be uploaded with a free account; paid accounts have larger upload limits and increased customizability options. An uploaded track on SoundCloud displays as a two-dimensional graph of the sound file's waveform, and a tracking line moves across the waveform during playback. If an uploader allows it (the default is to allow), users can leave time-stamped comments on tracks, which display publicly for a few moments, along with users' avatars, as the song is played. Users may also post replies to existing comments, offering a conduit for communication. SoundCloud also supports uploader tags that function like a folksonomy, as they are not supported by a controlled vocabulary structure (Giannetti, 2013).

## RELATED WORK

### Studies of Social Media

SoundCloud is an instance of *social multimedia,* "an online source of multimedia resources that fosters an environment of significant individual participation and that promotes community curation, discussion and re-use of content" (Tian et al., 2010, p. 28, quoting Mor Naaman). Such platforms have recently attracted much academic attention, yet SoundCloud has been the subject of little empirical study, though it is occasionally mentioned by musicians in qualitative interviews (Baym, 2012; Hoare et al., 2014).

Content analysis of user comments is a common method of analyzing social media spaces such as Slashdot (Gomez 2008), blogs (Mishne & Glance, 2006), and Twitter (Honeycutt & Herring, 2009; Dann, 2010; Naaman et al., 2010), but these sites differ starkly from SoundCloud in terms of content and purpose. User behavior on social multimedia site Tumblr has received recent study (Xu et al., 2014), but the site is known more for visual media than audio, and it farms much of its audio content out to SoundCloud and Spotify. Closer is YouTube, whose model of media uploads and user comments resembles SoundCloud's. Benevenuto et al. (2009) examined video responses to other videos on YouTube and found evidence of significant opportunistic behavior and spam-like tendencies. De Choudhury et al. (2009)'s analysis of YouTube comments found that participation increases when conversations are interesting, when familiar people are speaking, and when engaging dialogue is observed. Madden et al. (2013) carried out a classification of YouTube comments, identifying 10 top-level categories of behavior, though with little discussion of relative importance. Thelwall et al. (2012) conducted quantitative and sentiment analyses of YouTube comments, noting vigorous interaction over contentious issues such as politics and religion, and comparatively little response to positive comments in comparison to negative comments. A follow-up study by Tsou & Thelwall (2014) used a qualitative coding approach to compare user behavior on YouTube comment pages for TED talks with the TED website, though it did not address user communication. Shoham et al. (2013) qualitatively evaluated comments on a single YouTube video, finding more broadcasting of messages than interaction. Rotman et al. (2009) executed a grounded theory analysis of commenting on YouTube videos, finding that users tended to believe YouTube enabled them to hold a sense of community, even though this was at odds with the content of actual comments (which did not show evidence of fostering tight-knit groups, and which rarely hosted prolonged conversations).

We speculated that the real-time display of SoundCloud's comment system might uniquely influence commenting behavior, since commenting at specific time points within a track allows for greater referential specificity. Moreover, the continuously unfolding comment layout results in a textual interface quite different from other platforms, which may affect commenting patterns. The design implications of SoundCloud's model have not gone unnoticed; Guimaraes et al. (2012) proposed a tool for real-time display of comments on YouTube uploads, essentially adapting the SoundCloud comment structure for video, and video sites such as Viki (Russell, 2013) employ similar interfaces in practice. Empirical work is needed to understand how such design changes impact media use and users.

SoundCloud began attracting scholarly inquiry only recently. Several reports by Jourdanous (Jourdanous et al., 2014; Allington et al., 2015; Jourdanous et al., 2015) investigated SoundCloud qualitatively, through musician interviews, and quantitatively, by tracking site 'following' behavior. They noted clusters of social behavior (both via following of artists and commenting on tracks) revolving around genre scenes and local geographies. Ishizaki et al. (2015) used a speech act analysis approach to qualitatively evaluate user commenting on SoundCloud and Last.FM. The analysis indicated that most SoundCloud comments were primarily short claims about, or reactions to, songs, with relatively little interpersonal interaction. In our study, we seek to extend Ishizaki's work by using an alternate qualitative coding strategy, which will help surface more about *what* commenters are talking about, rather than the linguistic function of their statements. Furthermore, by executing a more in-depth analysis of user replies, we hope to provide additional insight into the site's conversational reach, and evaluate the tentative conclusions reached by Ishizaki on SoundCloud as a social system.

### *Studies of Music Services*

There is a substantial body of research on evaluation of online music services in the music information retrieval (MIR) domain, particularly within MIREX (Music Information Retrieval Evaluation eXchange), the annual evaluation campaign for music tools and services led by researchers at the University of Illinois. However, few studies evaluate performance, user interaction, or experience with *commercial* music services. The field of MIR is still relatively young, and has focused on testing algorithms for functions such as feature extraction, classification, and clustering, in order to assess their applicability to music data. Interest in evaluating and understanding user experiences of MIR systems has only surfaced recently, as evidenced by the MIREX User Experience Grand Challenge 2014. Scholarly evaluation of music services is also hindered by the fact that many commercial music services tend to be short-lived.

Commercial music services such as Last.fm, Apple iTunes Genius, Pandora, and Musicovery have been reviewed and used in a few studies in MIR (Kaminskas & Ricci, 2012). Previous studies that make use of user data from commercial music services tend to either extract data (e.g., tags, user questions, playlist results) and use them for quantitative experiments, or to evaluate the performance of particular system features, rather than aiming to holistically understand how the service is being used. Representative examples of the former category include Hu & Downie (2007) and Laurier (2009), both of whom used social tags to understand music mood. Examples of the latter category include Barrington (2009) and Lamere (2011), who evaluated the performance of music recommender systems, including some commercial systems like Apple's iTunes Genius and Google's Instant Mix. In these studies, systems are evaluated through an experimental setup (e.g., the subject listens to a given seed song and evaluates the playlist) or via personal observation and opinion.

There are also a few studies aimed at improving general understanding of user needs and behaviors based on data from commercial music services. Bainbridge (2003) and Lee (2010), for instance, analyze users' music-related queries from online Q&A services to understand different types of music information needs. Other studies like Lee & Waterman (2012) focus on collecting users' opinions about commercial music services to identify user requirements and desires. However, these studies are not focused on investigating users' interactions and experiences within a large-scale commercial music service, despite this being a common conduit for musical consumption in the digital age. Such a focus can uncover emergent and changing social behaviors, as well as offer insights on how to design services to support user needs effectively. Our qualitative study begins to fill this gap by exploring what kinds of user activities and interactions occur using the commenting function on a popular social music platform.

## STUDY DESIGN

### *Pilot Study*

We conducted a pilot study to explore strategies for collecting and analyzing data from SoundCloud. We settled on attempting to obtain a representative sample of popular songs, from which we would then draw user comments for analysis. SoundCloud does not provide a public ranking of its most popular tracks, but it hosts an application programming interface (API) which can be used to make a range of track-based requests. We piloted data collection and analysis by pulling tracks from SoundCloud's database through the API in February 2013 using the "hotness" parameter. This returned random tracks with high play counts that had been uploaded in the previous two weeks. We collected comments from these tracks and used them to develop initial content codes via a grounded theory approach. However, we could not use the same approach to draw a sample for the full study, because the hotness parameter was deactivated by the site in April 2013 due to backend issues.[1]

Our troubles with the hotness parameter illustrate Karpf's Rule of Online Data (Karpf, 2012). SoundCloud is prone to rapid change in the behavior of its users (both listeners and artists) as well as in site architecture and server response, and the more visible it becomes commercially, the less representative and trustworthy its data will be for empirical analysis. Nevertheless, a certain measure of messy data is necessary in order to study fast-moving new media settings such as SoundCloud, and we follow Karpf's embrace of transparency and "kludginess" in data collection and analysis, in hopes of capturing insights regarding this valuable, but volatile, online environment.

### *Data Collection*

For the full study, we wrote custom code to collect a wide sample of track, comment and user data through the SoundCloud API. We collected track metadata using the SoundCloud *search* API, which supported an unconstrained

[1] See Osman, P. Removing 'Hotness' Parameter. *SoundCloud Backstage Blog*, April 16, 2013. developers.soundcloud.com/blog/removing-hotness-param

search of tracks that were present in the system as of a specified date. In response to that request, SoundCloud returned metadata for up to 8,000 tracks that had been uploaded to the system as of the date specified in the query. Exactly how the 8,000 items were selected in response to the query was not specified by the SoundCloud documentation, but, like the hotness parameter, appears to be some function of popularity, related to the number of times the song has been played, the number of comments, the number of times it has been favorited, and how long the track has been in the system. As each track was collected, metadata from the track was stored in a database.

Comment data was collected using the SoundCloud *track* API, which provides resources associated with individual tracks. For each track in our database, we queried the track API and requested all comments available for the track. Comment metadata includes data about the individual who posted the comment, the date of the comment, and the millisecond location of the comment in the timecode of the track. We stored comment and user metadata in a database. A data collector, collecting tracks and comment data, was run repeatedly beginning in June 2013; we continued to run the collector through early 2014.

Our dataset is limited by the opacity of the SoundCloud API. For example, it is possible that a date search for tracks uploaded to SoundCloud as of a specific date could return tracks from any prior month. This is a function of how SoundCloud's servers and code decide to respond to the request. We collected 240,774 tracks, some of which had been posted as early as 2007. 4,383,874 comments had been posted to these songs by 1,800,630 unique users. 43,568 of the tracks had no comments; 63,209 had 1-9 comments; 108,071 had 10-99 comments; 27,725 had 100-999 comments; and 530 had 1,000 or more comments.

Our dataset contained data for every day of 2013 and so our analysis focused on 2013. Figure 1 is a graph of the total number of tracks uploaded per day. Uploads per day is fairly consistent at first, generally ranging between 100 and 200 tracks per day, with a slight increasing trend at the start of the year. From the middle of June through the middle of July, there was a concerted spike in the number of uploaded tracks per day. The peak day was July 21, with 7,547 tracks uploaded. For subsequent months, the number of total uploads per day again ranged between 100 and 200 tracks per day, with a slight drop-off as the year ended.

Figure 2 is a graph of the total number of comments uploaded per day. Total comments per day showed a slightly different pattern, but also peaked in July, with 27,533 comments uploaded on July 19. While the number of track uploads seems to have returned at the end of the year to values similar to the beginning of the year, total comment uploads per day ended the year at a rate of nearly 5,000 comments per day more than early in the year.

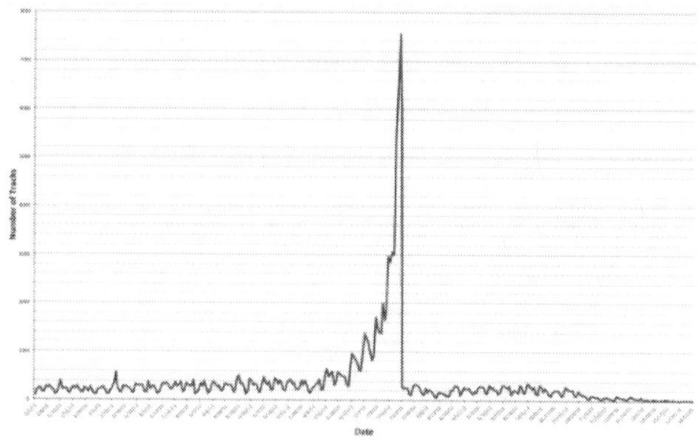

***Figure 1**. Total track uploads per day for 2013*

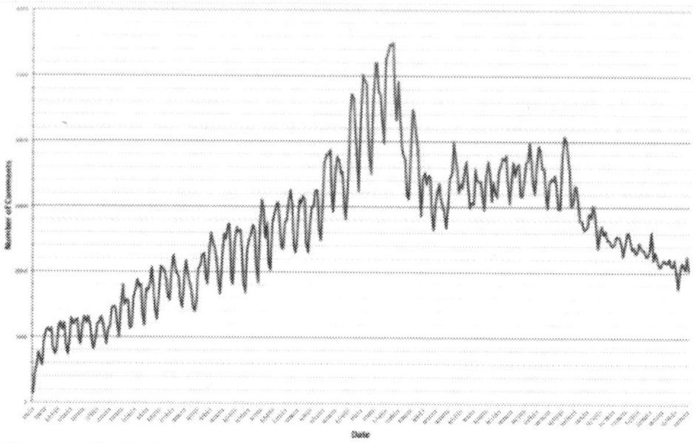

***Figure 2**. Total comment uploads per day for 2013*

### Sampling

We decided to focus our analysis on the data from 2013, which narrowed the working dataset to 134,075 tracks. We chose to sample at the *track* level, rather than the comment level, because we believed it was important to understand comments in context. Our focus for this project was on SoundCloud's *musical* content, so spoken-word tracks (podcasts, comedy, etc.) were removed from the dataset. While we found much commenting occurring on spoken-word tracks, we believe these would require a separate analysis with a *sui generis* qualitative coding scheme.

Tracks were stratified by duration into bins of less than 10 minutes (primarily single songs and song previews), 10-25 minutes (mostly extended mixes and mini-album streams), and greater than 25 minutes (typically full album streams, concert recordings and megamixes). Tracks with fewer than 10 comments were excluded from analysis due to anticipated paucity of social activity. To make coding manageable for an exploratory study, we restricted our sample to the 0-10 minute bin and to tracks with between 10 and 500 comments. Random track samples were taken from each calendar quarter, with slightly more samples taken from the third quarter because of the spike in activity.

### *Codebook Development*

A qualitative codebook was drawn up based on patterns observed in the pilot set. Each comment was manually evaluated and classed into categories. Iterative codebook refinements were made as analysis continued, following grounded theory methods (Corbin & Strauss, 2008). At least one code was assigned to each comment (including an "unintelligible" code for comments having no interpretable content), and the number of codes assigned to a comment was not limited. The codebook underwent five iterations of sample coding. The three authors independently coded comments, then met and sought unity on the meaning and boundaries of each code, as well as the need for new codes. This resulted in 39 codes at the end of piloting. Four top-level code categories were recognized:

*Mood*: whether the comment was positive, negative, or contained elements of both

*Content*: what common attributes comments shared

*Music*: essentially a subset of *Content*, but split out to cover specifically musical aspects of commenting

*Reply*: whether the comment is a reply, and what type

Our comment analysis was conducted as a *consensus code*. Each comment set was coded independently by two coders, who then met and discussed disparities until as much common ground as possible was established. One project lead was assigned to look for codes the first two may have missed or misused; this researcher then engaged the first two in dialogue once more. The third researcher also acted as a tie-breaker when the first two coders could not initially come to consensus. We hoped that the use of three coders and the consensus strategy would help mitigate problems with comment ambiguity, short length, lack of context, and variety in slang and dialect present in the sample set.

## RESULTS

### *Sample Composition*

The sample set of SoundCloud tracks consisted of 64 different songs. The number of comments for a track ranged from 10 to 443, and track length ranged from 44 seconds to 6 minutes 44 seconds. Four songs were removed from the set because they had been deleted from SoundCloud, and two songs were removed because a preponderance of their comments were not in English. This left a workable set of 58 songs with 5,608 comments, all of which were consensus coded. Because our analytic strategy was so labor-intensive, it was not feasible to process a larger percentage of our dataset. Nevertheless, our analysis evaluates the same number of tracks as Ishizaki et al. (2015) (58 songs, 24,111 comments) and employs a more thorough coding method, which should offer new insights into the conversational world of SoundCloud's listenership.

The set of songs retrieved was dominated by electronic music and hip-hop, which broadly mirrors the predominant tastes of the SoundCloud user base both historically and at current. In some cases, our codebook reflects the genre biases of our sample set. For instance, in pilot coding, comments about "the drop" (a sudden rhythmic shift, usually a slowdown, often coupled with heavy bass and a change in melodic material) were so common on electronic music tracks that we assigned the phenomenon its own code (Yadati et al., 2014). Commenting behavior likely differs in genres not well represented in our sample.[2] The type of track uploader also varied, which had the potential to affect commenting behavior. Some tracks were uploaded by the original artist, but others were uploaded by a remixer, record label, promotional company, blogger, or fan. Songs from both famous (e.g., Avicii, Busta Rhymes, Capital Cities, Black Violin) and relatively unknown artists were present in the sample; fan uploads were responsible for the presence of songs by several of the most famous artists.

### *Comment Contents*

The first three code categories (mood, content, and music) are discussed in this section. User comments are drawn from our sample set and are identified by a unique internal assignation. By far, the most common types of comments were simple statements praising the song or the artist. Examples include "Favorite song" (338113), "sick tune !!" (3772901), "fuck yeah!" (4483935), "shits hottt my gawd" (4483905) and "fuckinggggggg amazing!" (3772879). The inclusion of cursing is by no means accidental; significant portions of the user base felt it necessary to express themselves using oaths, often seemingly in a battle to outdo each other in extremity. Occasionally, commenters posted overtly sexual or scatological comments such as "EAR SEX" (1808282) or "I just ruined a good pair of underwear." (4483968), and at some points considerable cleverness came into play, just as on any men's bathroom wall (Dundes, 1965). Furthermore, the frequency with which users explained their musical loves in terms of sexual gratification and drug references, such as "perfect for a nice doob. i love it keep it up guys" (437943), reflects a persistent cultural metaphor associating the emotional states experienced during these activities. "Sex, drugs, and rock-n-roll" as a close-knit club of dionysian affairs is still alive and well, if this sample set is any indication.

Positive comments far outnumbered negative ones, confirming Jourdanous's (2015) findings; over 92% of comments were judged by our coders to be generally positive in disposition. Even on the most-criticized track in our sample, a dance remix of Nirvana's "Smells Like Teen Spirit," 38 of 71 comments were coded positively. The general lack of negative comments suggests that users tend not to comment on things they do not like, but since much listening is self-select-

[2] For a list of artists, song titles, genres, numbers of comments and reply percentages for all tracks in the sample set, please contact the first author.

ing, it may be that users are not encountering music objectionable enough to comment on, or are clicking away instead of dwelling and responding. The use of caps lock, repeated letters, excess punctuation and emoticons or ASCII art for emphasis and versatility of expression was pervasive.

Users would sometimes point to aspects of the music that drew them in or pushed them away. This could be as simple as "Dig the low climax" (706607) or "Sound quality sucks…" (1873962), and, in general, commenters were rather inarticulate about musical substance. Yet music comments could also get quite involved, with users providing detailed accounts of musical characteristics. Some users made observations about instrumentation, rhythm, vocals, stylistic peculiarities, genre designations and song structures. Because of the timed commenting function, users were able to key their responses to the exact point in the song they wished to highlight. Comments such as "that snare just punched me in the face" (967477) and "I think megatron, just jizzed himself" (5734693) (the latter left in response to an abrupt, robotic interlude in an electronic music track) illustrate how this can allow some users to speak to precise musical moments with great effect. The most common music-related codes were in the realms of genre/style, lyrics (especially direct quotations from lyrics), rhythm, production/remixing and comments about artists.

Aside from spam and self-promotional comments, most comments pertained to the song, the artist or something closely related, like genres, record labels, or similar artists. Many users divulged when, where and how many times they listened to a song. Another recurrent topic was an artist's concert appearances; some users noted instances in which they heard the artist play the track in a club or concert, or would express how they were looking forward to a future live event. Users would sometimes leave notice via comment if they had blogged about the song, posted it to a public playlist, or publicized the track in some other way, serving both promotional and informational purposes.

The different types of tracks posted could attract different types of responses. While many songs garnered comments requesting download links or inquiring about release details, these were more common on track previews, which left listeners with only part of the song to listen to. Likewise, electronic music frequently incorporates sampled recordings or interpolations of other musicians' work, and it was common to see users commenting on, or asking about, sample sources on such tracks.

We also created a code that served as a miscellaneous bin, to capture instances where comments recounted stories or personal anecdotes, experiences with the song or generally unusual commenting behavior. Some examples include, on the simpler end, "This song made my summer" (642908) or "This track makes me dance while driving!!" (4373925), and on the more profuse and profane end, "This is prolly the worst fucking song ive ever hear fuck tmills fight me you douchebag" (3843825). This reflects significant use of the commenting function to do more than merely make the simplest of telegraphic statements. There is no apparent length limit to SoundCloud comments; we encountered comments with more than 900 characters (~175 words).

### Reply Comments

Since reply functionality is built into the commenting system, we explored whether users take advantage of the reply function to communicate with one another, or with the artist or uploader of the song. For the 58 songs in the sample set, each comment was coded as a reply if it had been entered as a response to a previous comment using SoundCloud's reply function. However, a simple count of this nature would be misleading. Some users reply to their own comments; these self-replies were removed. Occasionally, users repost the same text more than once as a reply; these were not removed. Some replies appear to be spam, and others were thematically unrelated to the original comment; these also were not removed. Additionally, many tracks had large numbers of replies to the first comment left at time point 0:00, sometimes in excess of commenting elsewhere in the song. This appears to have been the result of a defect in an earlier version of the commenting function. Unless context indicated genuine response to an earlier post, these were removed as replies. Finally, non-reply comments were combed for indicators of inter-user communication. Comments that mentioned other users in the form @username were classed as replies, as were comments that included contextual indicators of reply. The contribution of manually-classed replies was very small.

For each of the 58 songs, an adjusted reply count was figured according to these rules. Twenty-two songs had no adjusted replies. While there seems to be a comment threshold over which at least one reply per track will be present, our sample set included tracks with as many as 77 comments without a single adjusted reply. Of the 5,608 comments in the sample set, 517 were found to be adjusted replies, a rate of 9.22%. However, the distribution of adjusted replies per track is strongly skewed; all but nine of the 58 tracks had adjusted reply rates under 10%, and the median percentage of a track's comments which were adjusted replies was only 2.36%. Most adjusted replies were single responses to comments, often approaching non sequitur, with no further discussion. Back-and-forth conversations are rare. There were 403 conversation threads between two or more parties in our sample set, with an average thread length of 2.21 comments per thread. Only four threads had lengths longer than four comments, though one additional conversation between a listener and an uploader was carried on across several short threads.

A small number of tracks, however, had larger numbers of replies. For all six of the tracks in our sample set with adjusted reply percentages greater than 20%, the track uploader had meticulously given responses to many – in some cases nearly all – of the comments that users had left on the track, often to express gratitude for listeners' appreciation and support. In fact, the number of replies left by uploaders in our sample set approached the number left by listeners; 231 replies were left by uploaders, while replies from listeners totalled 286. This indicates that fans sometimes used the service to reach musicians directly, and that some artists fostered that interaction via the reply function. Thirteen tracks had instances of musicians replying at least once to comments about their own music. However, we also looked for instances where listeners appeared to call out directly to the artist, to offer praise or blame, or to request something, such as more music, the identification of a sample, tour dates, changes to a song, or a link to a digital download of the track. Such comments were observed both on tracks artists uploaded to their own accounts and on tracks uploaded by labels, promoters, and blogs. They were posted to the songs of relative unknowns as well as those of stars, and few received a response. This seems to indicate that many users are speaking at artists without much expectation or hope of a reply.

## DISCUSSION

The analysis we have conducted indicates that while the SoundCloud comment function is used extensively by listeners to respond to the music they are hearing, it is comparatively rare that they use it to respond to each other. Communication between listeners using the reply function is generally uncommon, and what communication does occur through the comment function is almost as likely to be artist-to-listener as it is to be listener-to-listener.

Our findings in part corroborate Rotman's work on YouTube comments, despite the fact that SoundCloud, in theory, allows for more focused conversations around particular moments in a musical work. Rotman et al. (2009) noted, "Comments do not generally create a prolonged discussion, and most are left unanswered" (p. 44), and that "Comments... create, at best, an interaction that culminates in 2-3 exchanges, and is seldom addressed by users other than the channel-owner and the original commentator" (p. 45). This is precisely what occurs in SoundCloud, at least among genres well represented in our sample set. In further explorations of YouTube sociability via user interviews, Rotman finds public commenting to be one small piece in a larger ecosystem of channels for sustaining the felt sense of community professed by some of its users (Rotman & Preece, 2010). It may be that SoundCloud's comment design is insufficiently attractive to draw users in for conversation, and interpersonal communication is being pushed out to the site's personal messaging system or to other venues such as Facebook (with which SoundCloud integrates well). Even if SoundCloud's commenting interface carries with it the appropriate conversational affordances (Norman, 1990; Reid & Reid, 2010) to support interaction, the mere presence of community-building tools does not mean that users will take them up in that way. The multiplicity of online communication spaces may make any single tool, even a well-designed one, minimally important to users for that explicit function (Baym, 2007).

The sociability of SoundCloud comments may be hampered by real-time display design choices. Some tracks, especially short ones, have large numbers of comments such that, if all were displayed sequentially, the listener would see a blur of comments as the waveform progresses. SoundCloud now throttles the number of comments displayed to slightly less than one per second (in most browsers) where comments bunch together. The display appears to be randomized, and different comments may show if the song is replayed, though older comments do not appear to age out of display. On popular tracks, listeners may see only a small portion of comments posted to a song, which may discourage participation. Managing comment volume is a persistent challenge for streaming media services (Haimson & Tang, 2017), and changes in spatial positioning, size, and length of display may increase the likelihood of genuine response.

The initial impression given by our analysis seems to be of an environment akin to a rather asocial party; many people present, milling about, muttering to themselves, mostly ignoring each other. Yet an impressive mass of comments is being left here, hundreds in a matter of days for the site's more popular tunes. Who is their audience? Our findings lend support to Ishizaki et al. (2015)'s claim that user motivations for commenting relate more to expression than interaction. Consistent with Shoham et al. (2013), listeners may employ the comment system more as a medium for self-expressive broadcasting, directing speech at the whole world, but no one in particular. Similarly, one could conceptualize SoundCloud as a public space or platform for airing opinions about the music and attempting to influence others' experiences of it. On this view, SoundCloud's comment function acts like a town square soapbox; anyone may stand and shout, but no one is obligated to listen.

This raises a further question: Is anybody actually reading the comments? Listeners may well use SoundCloud merely as background music, hitting the play button without giving the comments a glance. SoundCloud's streaming function smoothly glides on to new tracks as the user browses, without displaying the new track's waveform or comments unless the user navigates to the new track's page. Those who leave comments are probably more likely to read comments themselves (though further empirical work would be needed to confirm this). Commenters post because they *believe* their words will be read, and so perhaps SoundCloud's comment function satisfies a more fundamental human desire to leave a mark of existence, which Gregory Benford, in homage to the ubiquitous mid-20$^{th}$-century graffito, called the "Kilroy Was Here" impulse (Benford, 1999). The comment function may serve as a sort of sanctioned graffiti (Shoham et al., 2013), a wall to be filled with whatever comes to mind, regardless of how inconsequential or ignorant.

Nevertheless, there is probably more to such commenting from the user standpoint than merely flinging notice of one's existence into the ether. The comments alert listeners that there are other people listening in a more robust way than play counts, favorite counts, or chronologically-arranged comment boxes can (as on YouTube or discussion threads). Listeners are asynchronous with respect to each other, but they see the comments synchronously as they play the song, which simulates a listening experience shared with other people. The notion of copresence, derived from Goffman (1963) and later refined in communications literature, refers to "the sense of being together with other people in a remote environment" (Zhao, 2003) and comes close to capturing this idea. Copresence has been connected to online multimedia commenting (Weisz et al., 2007), but it better describes systems that allow for synchronous interaction; a closer analog would be live-streaming services with response functions, such as Twitch (Hamilton et al., 2014) or Facebook Live and Periscope (Haimson & Tang, 2017). Nevertheless, SoundCloud does afford a felt sense of having others around who are also appreciating (or belittling) the same entertainment one is consuming. In this way, it may serve as a stand-in for shared mutual experiences, like going to hear music at a concert or seeing a film in a theater. Despite having a large number of people gathered together in one place, there is often little direct conversation between attendees at these occurrences. We do not always think of such shared experiences as *social*, perhaps because they are not principally composed of interaction events. Yet these experiences are different than they would be if one were there by oneself, creating a sense of social presence (Ducheneaut et al., 2006) which helps explain their continuance as major entertainment draws.

While listener-to-listener interaction was scarce, the one peripheral, but significant, social activity we identified was occasional artist-listener communication via commenting, enriching Jourdanous et al. (2015)'s qualitative findings about the social value of SoundCloud for artists. If SoundCloud wishes to support artist-listener commenting more fully, it could change its comment notification structure. Uploaders may elect to be notified via e-mail when users comment on their tracks, but this is buried in the settings menu and is handled at the account level, rather than at the track level. If a notification box were offered at the time of upload, and a comment management interface included at the playlist and account levels (with e.g. radio buttons for each track, in addition to a blanket all-on/all-off option), more artists might begin to employ commenting as a vehicle for making personal connections with fans.

## ISSUES AND CHALLENGES

SoundCloud's interface has not remained static. A site redesign in late 2012 shrank the playback icons and comment display boxes, which led to complaints that the site was "slighting the worth of comments as a social feature" (Hill, 2012). Some early adopters felt alienated by this change; Peter Owen, a songwriter who used SoundCloud to share audio, claimed in 2013 that "Most musicians are finding that the number of plays are up and the number of comments has fallen....Those that haven't left are starting to use the site differently. Now they're using it just as an advertising space...instead of the collaboration and creative communication that was there before" (Mac, 2013). Our sample set is composed of tracks uploaded after this redesign, so we cannot empirically evaluate Owen's claim. In August 2014, the site began incorporating audio advertising (Sisario, 2014), and in 2016 it announced plans to launch a subscription streaming service modeled after sites like Spotify (Pierce, 2016). Commenting behavior may be strongly sensitive even to very small changes in site design, underscoring the importance of studying systems over time in order to provide a fuller picture of dynamic user conduct.

The site's burgeoning popularity has also made it a magnet for stooge accounts and artificially inflated play counts; along with this has come the possibility of falsified comments posted to build a buzz around an artist (Matthew, 2013). Since exposure and high numbers, even if faked or bought, bring in real fans, there is a strong incentive here, as on many online platforms, to spam. It remains possible that portions of our data beyond what we could identify are composed of social spam.

Lastly, the public nature of our dataset has eroded over time. Portions of the data we scraped, including data that was qualitatively coded, was subsequently removed from the site, often presumably because remixed, sampled, or fan-uploaded material was flagged for copyright infringement. SoundCloud now uses automated detection tools to remove allegedly infringing tracks, and, like YouTube, has granted Universal Music Group broad, direct power to remove material at Universal's own discretion (Cushing, 2014). When tracks are removed, associated comments go down with them, meaning that future attempts to compile similar data will lack potentially valuable corpuses of user communication. As with most web content, the integrity of SoundCloud's historical record receives little consideration from its designers, making our study a glimpse into a species of technological ephemera whose intellectual content disappears far faster than the paper, wax, and tape throwaways of prior generations.

## CONCLUSION

Future work building on this study could include qualitative analysis of non-musical audio, which is a significant subset of SoundCloud's holdings (Alcorn, 2014). Our dataset indicates much commenting is occurring on these tracks, which may differ substantially from what we analyzed. Other qualitative approaches might be employed to give a more well-rounded picture of SoundCloud's conversational world; techniques such as sentiment analysis, linguistic inquiry and word count, or topic modeling could help evaluate larger and more varied genre sample sets.

Our analysis also excludes non-English music, and as we noted above, SoundCloud is truly a global platform, with users commenting in dozens of languages. Cross-cultural comparisons of SoundCloud commenting behavior may yield a much richer picture of actual user behavior than can be presented in this limited study. Characterizing the user base demographically would also be of value. Surveys, interviews, or ethnographic work would help develop a more detailed picture of why and how users comment.

## ACKNOWLEDGMENTS

Special thanks to Adrian DSa for help with SoundCloud's API, and to Alaina Bull, Rosanna Lui, Andy Magnusson, Maulik Mishra, Malavika Ravi, Bhargav Shah, Emily Spracklin, and Carolyn Tweedy for consensus coding.

## REFERENCES

Alcorn, S. (2014, Jan. 15). Why audio never goes viral. *Digg.* http://digg.com/originals/why-audio-never-goes-viral

Allington, D., Dueck, B., & Jordanous, A. (2015). Networks of value in electronic music: SoundCloud, London, and the importance of place. *Cultural Trends* 24, 211-222.

Bainbridge, D., Cunningham, S. J., & Downie, J. S. (2003). How people describe their music information needs: A grounded theory analysis of music queries. In *Proc. ISMIR 2003.*

Barrington, L., Oda, R., & Lanckriet, G. R. (2009). Smarter than genius? Human Evaluation of music recommender systems. In *Proc. ISMIR 2009,* 357-362.

Baym, N. (2007). The new shape of online community: The example of swedish independent music fandom. *First Monday* 12:8.

Baym, N. (2012). Fans or friends: Seeing social media audiences as musicians do. *Participations: Journal of Audience and Reception Studies* 9, 286-316.

Benevenuto, F., Rodrigues, T., Almeida, V., Almeida, S., & Ross, K. (2009). Video interactions in online video social networks. *ACM Trans. Multimedia Computing, Communications and Applications* 5, 1-25.

Benford, G. (1999). *Deep time: How humanity communicates across millennia.* New York: Avon.

Bonanos, P. (2014, May 15). In developing Asian markets, mobile and SoundCloud dominate listening. *Billboard.*

Corbin, J. M., & Strauss, A. (2008). *Basics of qualitative research: Techniques and procedures for developing grounded theory.* Los Angeles: Sage.

Cushing, T. (2014, Jul. 2). SoundCloud has given universal music group the ability to directly move content. *TechDirt.* http://www.techdirt.com/articles/20140702/10252827760/soundcloud-has-given-universal-music-group-ability-to-directly-remove-content.shtml

Dann, S. (2010). Twitter content classification. *First Monday* 15:12.

De Choudhury, M., Sundaram, H., John, A., & Seligmann, D.D. (2009). What makes conversations interesting: Themes, participants and consequences of conversations in online social media. In *Proc. WWW 2009,* ACM Press, 331-340.

Ducheneaut, N., Yee, N., Nickell, N., & Moore, R. (2006). "Alone together?" Exploring the social dynamics of massively multiplayer online games. In *Proc CHI 2006,* ACM Press, 407-416.

Dundes, A. (1965). Here I sit: A study of American Latrinalia. *Kroeber Anthropological Society Papers* 34, 91-105.

Giannetti, F. (2014). Digital media reviews: SoundCloud. *MLA Notes* 70, 499-503.

Goffman, E. (1963). *Behavior in public places.* New York: The Free Press.

Gómez, V., Kaltenbrunner, A., & López, V. (2008). Statistical analysis of the social network and discussion threads in slashdot. In *Proc. WWW 2008,* ACM Press, 645-654.

Graham, J. (2013, Jun. 17). Who's listening to SoundCloud? 200 million. *USA Today.*

Guimarães, R.L., Cesar, P., & Bulterman, D.C. (2012). "Let me comment on your video": Supporting personalized end-user comments within third-party online videos. In *Proc. WebMedia '12,* ACM Press, 253-260.

Haimson, O., & Tang, J. (2017). What makes live events engaging on Facebook Live, Periscope, and Snapchat. In *Proc. CHI 2017,* ACM Press, 48-60.

Hamilton, W., Garretson, O., & Kerne, A. (2014). Streaming on Twitch: Fostering participatory communities of play within live mixed media. In *Proc. CHI 2014,* ACM Press, 1315-1324.

Hill, B. (2012, Dec. 7). Editorial: The new SoundCloud Is optimized for listeners, not uploaders. *Engadget.* http://www.engadget.com/2012/12/07/editorial-soundcloud-optimized-for-listeners-not-artists/

Hoare, M., Benford, S., Jones, R., & Milic-Frayling, N. (2014). Coming in from the margins: Amateur musicians in the online age. In *Proc. CHI 2014,* ACM Press, 1295-1304.

Honeycutt, C., & Herring, S. C. (2009). Beyond microblogging: Conversation and collaboration via Twitter. In *Proc. HICSS 2009,* 1-10.

Hu, X. & Downie, J. S. (2007). Exploring mood metadata: Relationships with genre, artist and usage metadata. In *Proc. ISMIR 2007,* 67-72.

Ishizaki, H., Herring, S. C., Hattori, G., & Takishima, Y. (2015). Understanding behavior on online music distribution sites: A discourse approach. In *Proc. iConference 2015,* IDEALS.

Jourdanous, A., Allington, D., & Dueck, B. (2014). Using online networks to analyse the value of electronic music. In *Proceedings of the 5th international conference on computational creativity.*

Jourdanous, A., Allington, D., & Dueck, B. (2015). Measuring cultural value using social network analysis: A case study on valuing electronic musicians. In *Proceedings of the 6th international conference on computational creativity,* 110-117.

Kaminskas, M. & Ricci, F. (2012). Contextual music information retrieval and recommendation: State of the art and challenges. *Computer Science Review* 6, 89-119.

Karpf, D. (2012). Social science research methods in internet time. *Information, Communication, and Society* 15, 639-661.

Lamere, P. (2011). How Good Is Google's Instant Mix? http://musicmachinery.com/2011/05/14/how-good-is-googles-instant-mix/

Laurier, C., Sordo, M., Serrà, J., & Herrera, P. (2009). Music mood representations from social tags. In *Proc. ISMIR 2009,* 381-386.

Lee, J. H. (2010). Analysis of user needs and information features in natural language queries seeking music information. *Journal of the American Society for Information Science and Technology* 61, 1025-1045.

Lee, J. H., & Waterman, N. M. (2012). Understanding user requirements for music information services. In *Proc. ISMIR 2012*, 253-258.

Lee, J. H., Wishkoski, R., Aase, L., Meas, P., & Hubbles, C. (2017). Understanding users of cloud music services: Selection factors, management and access behavior, and perceptions. *Journal of the American Society for Information Science and Technology* 68, 1186-1200.

Mac, R. (2013, Apr. 26). SoundCloud manages criticism as it moves to become the YouTube of audio. *Forbes*.

Madden, A., Ruthven, I., & McMenemy, D. (2013). A classification scheme for content analyses of YouTube videos. *Journal of Documentation* 69, 693-714.

Matthew, T. (2013, Apr. 10). How to become a SoundCloud superstar, one fake fan at a time. *5 Magazine*. http://www.5chicago.com/features/april2013/ how-to-become-a-fake-soundcloud-superstar/

Mishne, G., & Glance, N. (2006). Leave a reply: An analysis of weblog comments. In *Proc. WWW 2006*, ACM Press.

Naaman, M., Boase, J., & Lai, C-H. (2010). Is it really about me? Message content in social awareness streams. In *Proc. CSCW 2010*, ACM Press, 189-192.

Norman, D. (1990). The design of everyday things. New York: Doubleday.

Pierce, D. (2016, Mar. 29). SoundCloud go: An audacious answer to Spotify that's dying to stand out. *Wired*.

Reid, F., & Reid, D. (2010). The expressive and conversational affordances of mobile messaging. *Behaviour & Information Technology, 29*, 3-22.

Rotman, D., Golbeck, J., & Preece, J. (2009). The community is where the rapport is – On sense and structure in the YouTube community. In *Proc. C&T '09*, ACM Press, 41-49.

Rotman, D., & Preece, J. (2010). The "WeTube" in YouTube – Creating an online community through video sharing. *International Journal of Web Based Communities* 6, 317-333.

Russell, J. (2013, May 9). Global video site Viki is bringing social back, as it reintroduces improved real-time commenting system. *Thenextweb*. http://thenextweb.com/media/2013/05/09/global-video-site-viki-is-bringing-back-social-rolls-out-improved-real-time-commenting-system

Shoham, M., Arora, A., & Al-Busaidi, A. (2013). Writing on the wall: An online "community" of patrons as communication network or cyber-graffiti? In *Proc. HICSS 2013*, 3951-3960.

Sisario. B. (2014, Aug. 21). Popular and free, SoundCloud is now ready for ads. *New York Times*.

Thelwall, M., Sud, P., & Vis, F. (2012). Commenting on YouTube videos: From Guatemalan rock to el big bang. *Journal of the American Society for Information Science and Technology* 63, 616-629.

Tian, Y., Srivastava, J., Huang, T., & Contractor, N. (2010). Social multimedia computing. *IEEE Computer* 43, 27-36.

Tsou, A., Thelwall, M., Mongeon, P., & Sugimoto, C. A. (2014). Community of curious souls: An analysis of commenting behavior on TED talks videos. *PLoS ONE* 9:4.

Van Buskirk, E. (2009, Jul. 6). SoundCloud threatens MySpace as music destination for Twitter era. *Wired*.

Weisz, J. D., Kiesler, S., Zhang, H., Ren, Y., Kraut, R.E., & Konstan, J.A. (2007). Watching together: Integrating text chat with video. In *Proc. CHI 2007*, ACM Press, 877-886.

Xu, J., Compton, R., Lu, T., & Allen, D. (2014). Rolling through Tumblr: Characterizing behavioral patterns of the microblogging platform. In *Proc. WebSci '14*, ACM Press, 13-22.

Yadati, K., Larson, M., Liem, C., & Hanjalic, A. (2014). Detecting drops in electronic dance music: Content based approaches to a socially significant music event. In *Proc. ISMIR 2014*, 143-148.

Zhao, S. (2003). Toward a taxonomy of copresence. *Presence: Teleoperators & Virtual Environments* 12, 445-455.

# Viewed by Too Many or Viewed Too Little: Using Information Dissemination for Audience Segmentation

**Bernard J. Jansen**
*Qatar Computing Research Institute, Qatar.*
*jjansen@acm.org*

**Jisun An**
*Qatar Computing Research Institute, Qatar.*
*jan@hbku.edu.qa;*

**Soon-Gyo Jung**
*Qatar Computing Research Institute, Qatar.*
*sjung@hbku.edu.qa*

**Haewoon Kwak**
*Qatar Computing Research Institute, Qatar.*
*hkwak@hbku.edu.qa*

**Joni Salminen**
*Qatar Computing Research Institute, Qatar.*
*jsalminen@hbku.edu.qa*

## ABSTRACT

**The identification of meaningful audience segments, such as groups of users, consumers, readers, audience, etc., has important applicability in a variety of domains, including for content publishing. In this research, we seek to develop a technique for determining both information dissemination and information discrimination of online content in order to isolate audience segments. The benefits of the technique include identification of the most impactful content for analysis. With 4,320 online videos from a major news organization, a set of audience attributes, and more than 58 million interactions from hundreds of thousands of users, we isolate the key pieces of content in terms of identifying audience segments that are both (a) least and most discriminating in terms of audience segments and (b) the least and most impactful. By empirical methods, we show that 25.3 percent of the videos are so widely disseminated (i.e., viewed by so many different segments) that they are non-discriminatory, while 29.7 percent of the videos are very discriminatory (i.e., can clearly identify one or more audience segments) but their impact is marginal, as the user base is small. Implications are that there are critical values that can be identified to isolate the set of both distinct and impactful content in a given data set of online content. We demonstrate the utility of this line of analysis by using the approach to identify critical cut-off values for dynamic persona generation.**

## KEYWORDS

Social Media Analytics, User Experience Research, Data-driven design, Data Science, User Analytics, Market Segmentation

80th Annual Meeting of the Association for Information Science & Technology, Washington, DC, VA | Oct. 27-Nov. 1, 2017



## INTRODUCTION

Understanding the audience is a critical task in many domains, from marketing to advertising to system design to publishing to website architecture. In fact, there has been substantial work in many areas in understanding audience information consumption patterns (Hendahewa & Shah, 2017; Tan, Na, & Ding, 2015), as this is often critical to success in publishing and other areas. However, understanding the audience is a misnomer, as in many situations there is not one audience but many audiences, referred to as audience segments. Identifying audience segments in many contexts is difficult, for reasons ranging from a lack of data to privacy concerns to isolating what data to use. It is the last difficulty that motivates our work. Determining what content to use to accurately distinguish audience segments can be quite challenging. Some content may be widely viewed, but so widely that it is non-discriminatory. Other content may be extremely discriminatory but the volume of views may be so small as to not be impactful. This dichotomy motivates our research, as we want to identify that content that is both discriminatory and impactful for ascertaining audience segments for future content creation.

For this research, we use the online videos from a major news organization, along with associated audience demographic attributes and views from a major social media platform, to identify the optimal values for content separation for identifying both distinct audience segments (the upper value) and impactful audience segments (the lower value). We use the concept of information dissemination, which in this context refers to the breadth of audience segments to which a piece of content has been distributed.

We lead off with a brief background section, introduce our data site and data collection, and then present our methods and results. We then show the utility of the analysis by using the information dissemination analysis for the dynamic generation of personas for audience data. We end with discussion, implications, and directions for our next stages of research.

## BACKGROUND

Audience segmentation (Mellor, 2006) is the process of dividing a group of people into homogenous subgroups, typically based on behaviors and demographics, grounded around some product, brand, advertisement, or message (Stern, 1994), with many factors affecting audience consumption (Chen et al., 2017; Fu & Sim, 2011), which are brands target audience or customers. Identification of audience segments has long been important in marketing and advertising (Smith, 1956), and it is increasingly important in the technology and content publishing areas. Identification of audience segments is typically driven towards understanding a subset of people's reactions, interactions, uses, etc., based on one or more key performance indicators (KPI), in order to achieve some goal or objective, such as increasing revenue (Ortiz-Cordova & Jansen, 2012).

For this research, we investigate the use of information dissemination (Song, Lin, Tseng, & Sun, 2005) to identify meaningful audience segments, in terms of audience size, for content from a major news corporation. Some content may be widely disseminated among many audience segments. While good in one sense, this makes this particular content less valuable in discerning distinct segments. Other information may be very useful for identifying audience segments; however, its impact may be minimal if the audience segment(s) do not represent significant percentages of the overall user base or content views.

In this research, we are interested in using specific pieces of content (Zhang, Zheng, & Tai-QuanPeng, 2017), in this case videos, in order to discern key audience segments, which can then be used for key marketing and other decisions (Jisun An, Cho, Kwak, Hassen, & Jansen, 2016), including the development of software systems. The issue is that some content can very popular, viewed by some in nearly all audience segments (Wang, Zhou, Jin, Fang, & Lee, 2017). In these cases, these pieces of content are not very useful for discerning audience segments. Conversely, there may be content that is very discriminative in that it is viewed by one or few audience segments. However, if these audience segments are small, the actual impact of the content is minimal. It is this situation that motivates our research, as personas can represent only the meaningful audience segments.

## RESEARCH OBJECTIVE

Our objective is to develop metrics for identifying online content with which an audience interacts that both identify distinct audience segments (i.e., information discrimination) and impactful audience segments (i.e., information dissemination). These two concepts are used to create upper and lower bounds, isolating the data to be used for analysis or system development.

Such metrics would be valuable in a variety of venues including web analytics analysis and design of systems for audience analysis.

As part of this research, we implement our approach in the design of a system for dynamically generating personas, which is a technique used for understanding audience segments by use of a fictitious person.

## DATA SITE AND COLLECTION

Using actual user data from AJ+, a major online media and mobile channel based in the United States, we validate our premise concerning the discriminatory value of information dissemination for audience segmentation. In the highly competitive online news industry, an understanding of audiences is notably important to both increase the consumption of digital content and also get relevant and noteworthy information to the readers that may be impacted by the news events.

### *Data Site: AJ+*

AJ+ is natively digital content platform. AJ+ was designed from the ground up to serve news in the medium of the viewer, with no redirect to a website. AJ+ is based mainly on social platforms. Therefore, the digital content is specifically designed to be viewed in the Facebook Newsfeed, YouTube Channel, or Twitter Timeline depending on the readers who are most active (i.e., interacting with online content.

### *Data Collection: AJ+ YouTube Channel*

For the data collection for the research reported here, we use the AJ+ YouTube Channel, reserving analysis for the Twitter and Facebook platforms for future work, as the technique is generalizable to any channel. The principal reason to focus on the YouTube channel is that the analytics platform gives the detailed statistics for every video, although we believe the approach transferable to other social media platforms as well. As an example of an AJ+ YouTube video, see Figure 1, noting the number of views.

***Figure 1**. Example of YouTube video from the AJ+ YouTube channel, with number of views*

Being quite robust, the YouTube analytics platform provides, for each piece of the AJ+ content collection, user profile attributes (e.g., gender, age, country location, and which site the user comes from), also at an aggregate level. We use these user and video attributes to explore if information dissemination can identify meaningful audience segments values based on video content interaction and related demographics provided by YouTube.

One can access the data in the YouTube analytics platform by using the YouTube APIs[1]. The parameters we use for this research are listed below. There are various video KPI metrics; we focus in this research only on *viewCount* (the number of views).

For our data analysis, we collected 4,320 videos uploaded on June 13, 2014 to July 27, 2016, that had more 58 million user views. We should note that the data values for the YouTube channel is private and available only to the owner of the channel (i.e., AJ+ in this case), and thus not publicly accessible.

- **Audience Attributes**
  - *ageGroup* - YouTube viewers are classified into multiple age categories (13-17 years, 18-24 years, 25-34 years, 35-44 years, 45-54 years, 55-64 years, and 65 years and older), so there are seven possible age categories for a user.
  - *gender* - YouTube viewers are classified into either male or female, so there are two possible categories.
  - *country* - YouTube uses the two-letter ISO-3166-1 country code index to classify where viewers are from, with 249 current officially assigned country codes at the time of this study.

- **Video Attributes**
  - *viewCount* – YouTube provides the number of views per video.

## METHODS

We now begin our approach for identifying the portion of the data set that is both distinct and has an impact. We first look at how widely the content is disseminated (although there may be a correlation between how widely (i.e., breadth) that a piece of content is has been viewed by members of audience segments and the number (i.e., volume) of views, this is not a necessary condition).

We define information dissemination, $I_{Dissemination}$ as:

$$I_{Dissemination} = \frac{Segments_{Information}}{Segements_{Total}}$$

where $Segments_{Information}$ is the number of audience segments that interact with a piece of content from the complete set of information items, and $Segments_{Total}$ is the number of audience segments that have interacted with ***any*** item of information from the set. We define $I_{Dissemination}$ for each piece of content in the collection.

We then examine how useful a piece of content is for identifying distinct audience segments. We define information discrimination, $I_{Discrimination}$ as:

$$\tau_L < I_{\text{Discrimination}} < \tau_U$$

where tau with a subscript L, $\tau_L$, is a predefined lower limit and tau with a subscript U, $\tau_U$, is a predefined upper limit of audience segments. Particularly, $\tau_L$ is determined by the number of content views. $\tau_U$ is determined by a percentage of the number of audience segments. Presently, $\tau_L$ and $\tau_U$ are heuristically determined (i.e., we use rules logically determined). We leave more rigorous analysis in calculating tau values for future work.

In this case, we are interested in an optimal balance between $I_{Dissemination}$ and $I_{Discrimination}$ for videos, although the approach could apply to any distributed information content for which one is interested in audience segmentation.

Videos that have a large $I_{Dissemination}$ would not be good candidates to identify unique audience segments, as these videos are available and can be watched by for many audience segments, which informs us of $\tau_U$.

Videos that have a small $I_{Dissemination}$ might not have enough impact, as measured by a metric such as *viewCount*, to make the audience segment identification worthwhile, which informs us of $\tau_L$.

With this information dissemination approach, we analyze our data set to determine appropriate $I_{Dissemination}$ and $I_{Discrimination}$, values to identify both distinct and meaningful audience segments.

## RESULTS

Given our dataset, we define an audience segment as a unique combination of (*country*, *gender*, *ageGroup*). So, with two gender groups, seven age groups, and 249 counties, we have an upper limit of 3,486 audience segments. (i.e., 2 x 7 x 249). In actuality, our data set has 2,214 audience segments, as the data has users from 190 unique countries and not all age groups for each country are represented. Thus, in the rest of this work, we use 2,214 as the baseline for maximum audience segments ($Segments_{Total}$).

We then calculate $I_{Dissemination}$ for each of the 4,320 videos in our data set toward our goal of identifying meaningful audience segments. We first determine the number of unique audience segments ($Segments_{Information}$) for each video. The average audience segment per video is 200, and the median is 136. The maximum audience segment is 1,980, and the minimum is 10. The standard deviation is 208.45.

It is interesting to note that the video with the maximum number of audience segments has an $I_{Dissemination}$ of 0.8618, meaning that more than 86% of all audience segments viewed this video. Obviously, this video would not be a discriminative candidate in our dataset.

Conversely, the video(s) with the minimum number of audience segments has an $I_{Dissemination}$ of 0.0045, meaning that 0.45% of audience segments viewed this video. So, the three

[1] https://developers.google.com/youtube/analytics/

videos with an $I_{Dissemination}$ of 0.0045 have good discriminative power. However, when we examine the *viewCounts* of each of these videos, in total, they represent 0.0012% of total views, which is not impactful. Therefore, these audience segments are not meaningful.

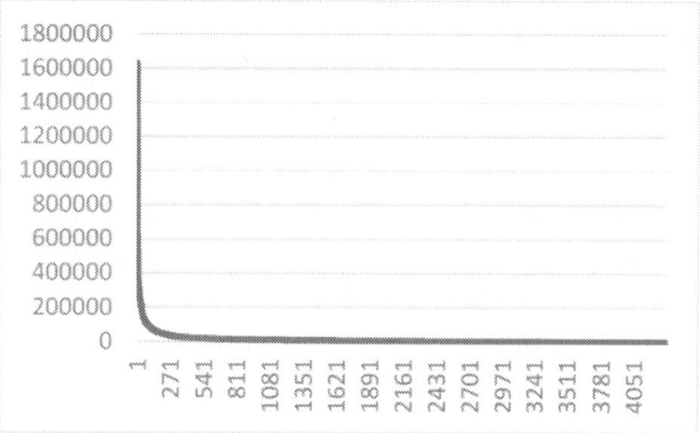


***Figure 2**. Rank (x axis) vs. frequency (y axis) of* Information$_{Dissemination}$ *for each video in the YouTube dataset*

We graph the $I_{Dissemination}$ for all videos in a rank – frequency plot as shown in Figure 2. From Figure 2, the rank – frequency plot follows a classic power law distribution, with a head consisting of a relatively small number of videos that are very popular with many audience segments. Then, there is the long tail consisting of a relatively lot of videos that are popular with a small number of audience segments. This highly skewed pattern of popularity is repeatedly reported in many services (Cha, Kwak, Rodriguez, Ahn, & Moon, 2007).

In fact, when we graph the rank-frequency of $I_{Dissemination}$ in a log-log plot, we find $I_{Dissemination}$ results in the expected power law outcome of a nearly straight line, as shown in Figure 3.

As shown in Figure 3, the log-log plot gives us a nearly straight line, with a slight negative slope, although with some curvature at the ends. A trend line (the dashed line) is a linear equation to which the data points conform quite nicely ($R^2$ = 0.9574).

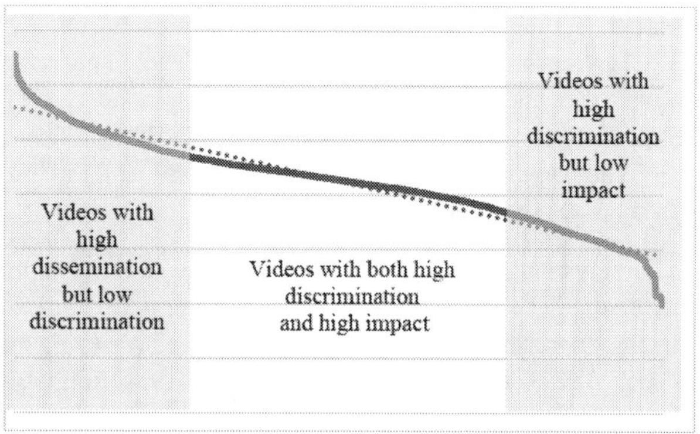


***Figure 3.** Log-log plot of rank (x axis) vs. frequency (y axis) of* Information$_{Dissemination}$ *for each video in the YouTube dataset*

In Figure 3, we have also highlighted and labeled three areas of interest. To the far left, we have the videos with high $I_{Dissemination}$, which are videos with high dissemination and therefore low discriminative power. To the far right, we have the videos with low $I_{Dissemination}$, which are videos with high discriminatory factors but which have low impact, so the audience segments are not meaningful. In our dataset, the volume of views correlates nearly perfectly with a number of audience segments. This investigation of these boundaries leads us to define both $\tau_L$ and $\tau_U$.

We first factor out videos with very high $I_{Dissemination}$, which we defined as any video with an $I_{Dissemination}$ equal to or greater than 0.50. This results in 34 videos being removed, representing 25.3 percent of total *views*. We then factor out videos with high $I_{Discrimination}$ but low impact, which we defined as any video with a *view* percentage equal to or less than 0.02 percent of total *views*. This results in 3,649 videos (84.5 percent) being removed, representing 29.7 percent of total *views*.

These results are consistent with expectations, given the power law distribution of our content collection. There are a few videos each with a large frequency of interaction, so their total frequency is quite sizeable. Conversely, there are a lot of videos that individually have few interactions, but collectively represent a sizeable portion of the content but with fewer interactions.

### Case Study of the Most Impactful Content

Our analysis to this point leaves us with a set of key content items that have reasonable values for both $I_{Dissemination}$ and $I_{Discrimination}$. Collectively, we identified 637 videos (15 percent of our original dataset) representing 45.0 percent of *views*. These 637 are the key content within the larger collection for discerning meaningful audience segments. As a case study of the applicability of our information dissemination approach for making key business decisions, we focus only on these 637 key videos. Again, we define an audience segment as a unique combination of (*country*, *gender*, *ageGroup*). Using these key videos, we now determine those that are most beneficial, identifying those videos that are particularly impactful in identifying the most unique audience segments.

Our set of 637 videos resonates with users from 170 countries. So, with two gender groups, seven age groups and 170 counties, we have an upper limit of 2,380 audience segments. (i.e., 2 x 7 x 170), assuming that all age groups are represented in each audience segment, which we want to assume in order to identify the videos with discerning impact, So, in this analysis, we use 2,214 as the baseline for maximum audience segments ($Segments_{Total}$).

| Unique Audience Segments | Videos | Percentage |
|---|---|---|
| 0 | 605 | 95.4% |
| 1 | 13 | 2.1% |
| 2 | 2 | 0.3% |
| 3 | 3 | 0.5% |
| 4 | 3 | 0.5% |
| 5 | - | - |
| 6 | 1 | 0.2% |
| 7 | 1 | 0.2% |
| 8 | 2 | 0.3% |
| 9 | 2 | 0.3% |
| 10 | - | - |
| 12 | 2 | 0.3% |
| Total | 637 | 100.0% |

***Table 1.*** *637 of the most impactful content in terms of both a large number of views and number of distinct audience segments*

We then identify the number of unique audience segments, $Segments_{Information}$, for each of our 637 videos, relative to the other videos in the set, shown in Table 1. We find that the most selective audience attribute for videos is the *country*. We identify 18 videos (2.8%) with maximum impact, meaning each audience segment for these videos is unique. However, the *view* for these videos is still somewhat low, which is an outcome of the fractal nature of power law distributions (i.e., nearly every segment of a power law distribution is, in itself, also a power distribution with head and tail.). However, we have 32 videos that specifically and meaningfully identified only one unique audience segment. Naturally, the specific number many change.

### *Discussion of Data Analysis*

Using actual user data from AJ+, an online media outlet, we validate our premise concerning the discriminatory value of information dissemination for determining audience segments for content distributed online. There are several implications for our approach. The major value is the method provides a straightforward yet effective technique for greatly simplifying a complex data set, allowing decision makers to focus on the key content aspects.

In our case, for example, we reduce the dataset by 85 percent, allowing detailed focus and analysis on the ley 15 percent of the dataset that was most impactful in terms of audience segmentation and achievement of a critical KPI.

We were able to determine the most impactful content in terms of resonating with both unique audience segments and individual users. While this is preliminary work, the research results are quite promising with potential impact for understanding how various users interact with online information (at least online videos), aiding content publishers in both producing information that users want to read and, simultaneously, getting content that certain audiences ought to read disseminated in an appealing manner to that audience segment.

Also, we note that the skewed popularity pattern, so-called *long tail*, in AJ+ is not so unique, but is prevalent in various web content services, such as YouTube, Amazon, Netflix, etc. Thus, our findings utilizing such pattern have high generalizability to identify user segments for various services for content publishing.

## IMPLEMENTATION OF FINDINGS

We demonstrate the practicality of this line of analysis via use in implementation of a working system (Jung et al., 2017). Our development objective is to develop a system for mining aggregated large scale user data from major social media platforms (e.g., YouTube) in order to identify both distinct and meaningful user segments, and then dynamically generate personas that represent these key user segments. Persona generation is a perfect application for the dissemination analysis presented above, as we need to identify both distinct and impactful audience segments in order to generate the personas.

A persona is a representation of a segment of actual users, presented as an imaginary person. The persona concept is used in IT-development, system design, and marketing. The ultimate artifact is typically a persona description embodying attributes of the user segment that the fictionalized person represents. Personas are an extension of efforts from a variety of domains for identifying, assessing, and constructing groups of people (i.e., users, customers, audience, or market segments) in order to optimize some performance metric (i.e. the speed of task or ease of use). Personas are allegedly well integrated into current design processes (Dharwada, Greenstein, Gramopadhye, & Davis, 2007; Eriksson, Artman, & Swartling, 2013; Friess, 2012; Judge, Matthews, & Whittaker, 2012; Nielsen & Hansen, 2014) for both long and short term projects (Judge et al., 2012).

To dynamically build personas, our methodology requires a multiple-step approach, consisting of:

a) identifying distinct user interaction patterns from the data, using the methodology presented above
b) associating these distinct user interaction patterns to user demographic groups,
c) categorizing meaningful user demographic groups from the data,
d) generating skeletal personas via demographic attributes, and
e) enriching the skeletal personas to create rich personas description.

We initially developed a matrix representing users' interaction with the online products. We denote by V the g×c matrix of g user groups ($G_1$, $G_2$, ..., $G_g$) and c contents ($C_1$, $C_2$ ,...,

$C_c$). The element of the matrix V, $V_{ij}$, is any value that represents the interaction of user group $G_i$ for content $C_j$. Using this matrix as the basis, we can identify first distinct user behavior patterns (which can be patterns of any set of user touch points) and then the meaningful user segments from this set of distinct user patterns.

After we have the matrix V, discovering the underlying latent factors, the user interaction patterns that will become the basis of the personas is the next step. There are numerous ways to decompose a given matrix; for this proof-of-concept, we used nonnegative matrix factorization (NMF) (Lee & Seung, 1999) (see Figure 5). Compared to a simple clustering of user groups (Jisun An, Jwak, & Jansen, 2017; J. An, Kwak, & Jansen, 2017), NMF has advantages in that it can find multiple behavioral patterns even from a single group.

The matrix decompositions work as following:

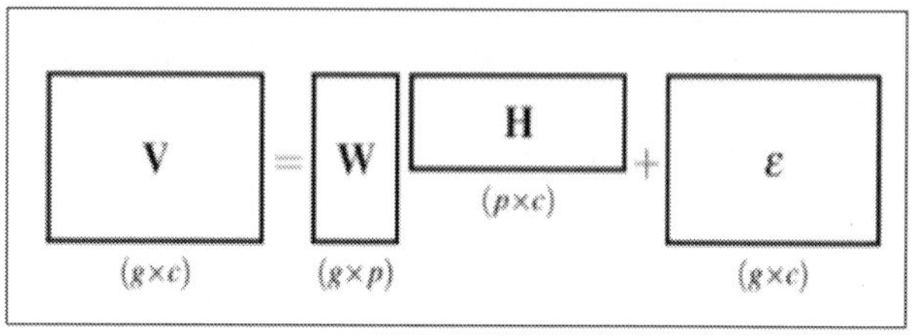


***Figure 4.*** *Matrix decomposition, which identifies distinct interaction patterns and then impactful demographic segments, which form the basis for the resulting personas*

Where **W** is a $g \times p$ matrix, **H** is a $p \times c$ matrix, and ε is an error term. Here, $p$ is the number of latent factors that we can choose. The column in **W** is a basis, and the column in **H** is an encoding that consists of coefficients that combine with each basis and represent a linear combination of the basis. So, W = (demographics x personas). **H** = (personas x contents)

However, there are two factors that must be considered prior to this, which are:

- which meta-hit content to discard, in that content which all demographics viewed is not a discriminator (i.e., nearly everyone watches the certain videos), and
- which demographic groups to discard because they are so small that they are not impactful in any meaningful manner.

In actually generating the personas, we use the method presented above to figure out the content that is too popular (i.e., viewed by too many audience segments) and the content that rarely interacted with (i.e., a very small number of views).

Once done and after application of NMF, we can then generate personas that have distinct sets of user touch points on content and that are also impactful in terms of being meaningful demographics. A set of personas for a major online news organization is shown in Figure 5.

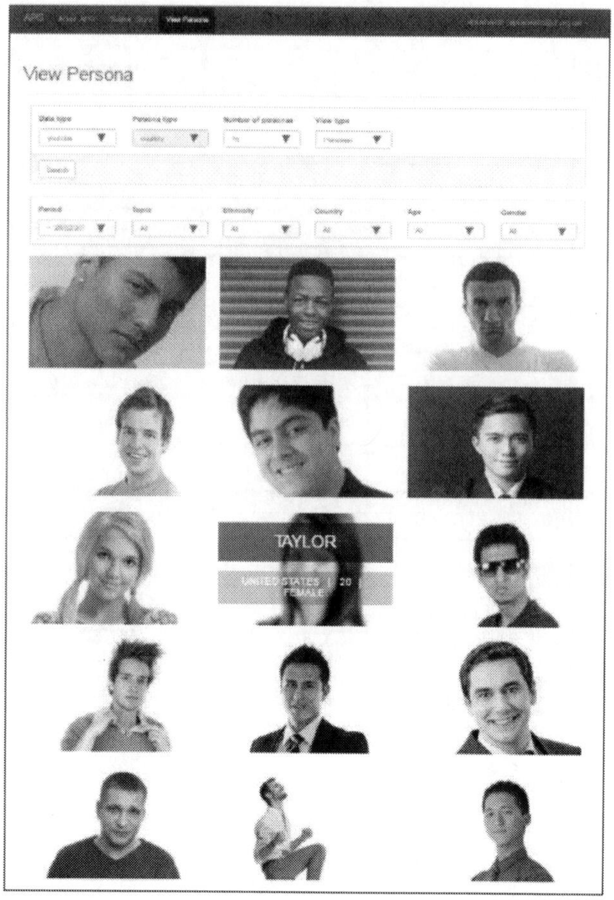


***Figure 5.*** *Set of 15 personas generated based on distinct user touch points and impactful audience demographic size. Mouse over a persona to display persona attributes.*

As shown in Figure 5, a user who wishes to see the audience segments for YouTube, can select the number of personas to generate (the system is currently set for a minimum of five and a maximum of 15). The selected number of personas is then generated. By mousing over one of the personas images, the basic persona attributes are displayed, in this case "Taylor, United States, 20, Female."

The listing of the personas, combined with the mouse overs, afford the user the ability to get an overview of the audience segments in terms of base demographic information. The user can also change content collections, change the number of personas, or apply different filtering, such as data set, topics of interest, ethnicity, country, age or gender.

Each of the images in this persona listing is clickable. Clicking on one icon generates the completed persona description, as shown in Figure 6.

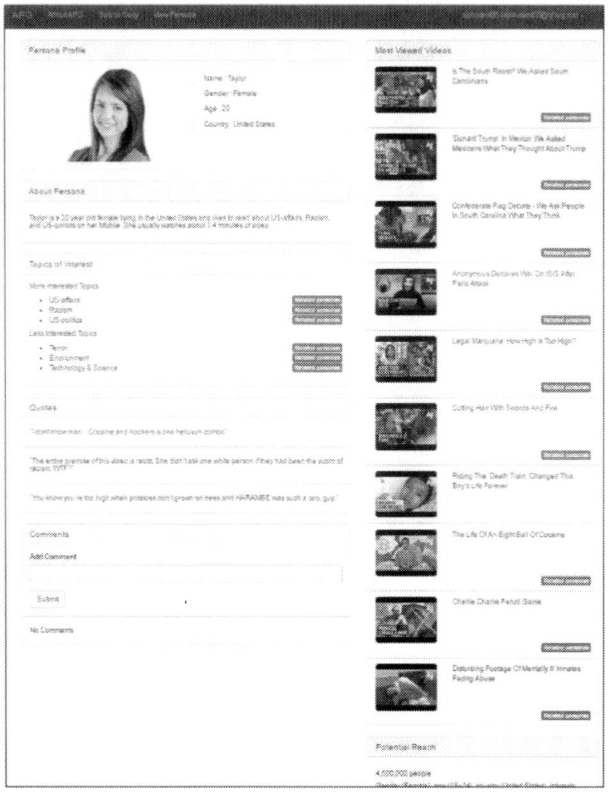

*Figure 6. Persona description with persona attributes, including distinct content viewed*

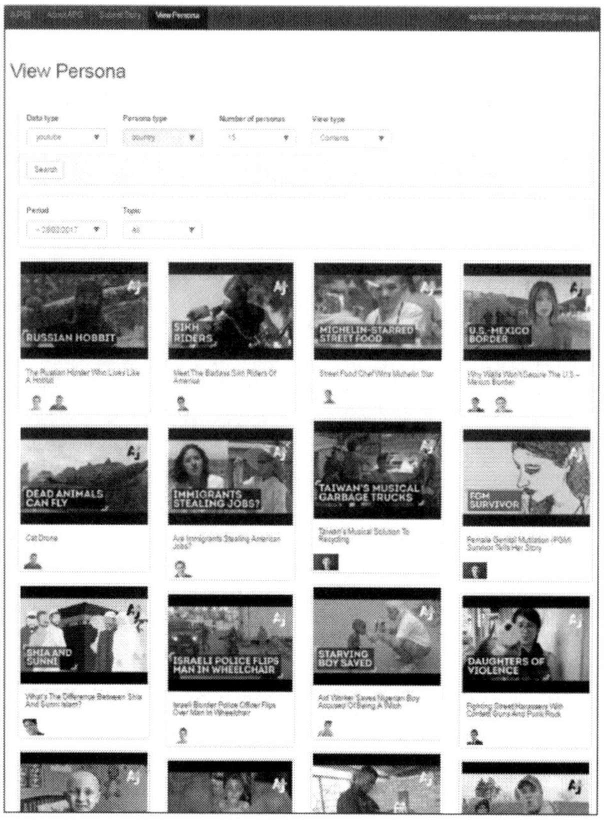


*Figure 7. Content results listing with personas for which content resonates*

Additionally, we can flip the presentation and present the content and the associated personas, as shown in Figure 7. This view, the individual content is presented and within each content image, the personas for which that content resonated.

## DISCUSSION AND IMPLICATIONS

Certainly, there is much additional work to be done, such as a more rigorous definition of determining tau (beyond straightforward heuristics) and the integration of additional KPIs to define the behavioral aspects of users. However, the strength of the research is that we use real content and real audience data from a major social media platform to investigate our concepts for identifying content that can be leveraged to categorize both distinct and impactful audience segments via content dissemination and discrimination.

Our approach, in some sense, is an adoption of the concept of tf-idf for an audience segmentation area. A word is a video, and a document is a demographic group. Following that analogy, term frequency (i.e., video views) maps to the number of views of a video by a given demographic group, and inverse document frequency maps to $Segments_{Information}$. (Thus, $I_{Dissemination}$ because $Segments_{Total}$ is constant).

Then, just as we search a document by a keyword, we can search for a demographic group via a video. The resulting demographic group is a compromise between the high contribution of the view counts and the uniqueness of preference. However, our work is unique in its application of these concepts, of both volume and distinctness, to this context.

## CONCLUSION

In this research, we show that the concepts of information dissemination and information discrimination can be used as underlying constructs for meaningful audience segmentation based on content products, when combined with specific performance metrics. Our research shows that audience segmentation can be accomplished rapidly and dynamically using large scale, real time, user data from major online social media platforms, resulting in analysis that reflects the behavior of real people.

Although specifically focusing on digital content, our approach is flexible, resilient, and can be applied in a wide range of contexts. While we limited our focus here to understanding the meaningful audience segments with current levels of information dissemination, it would be interesting to apply the approach to the long tail of audience segments to investigate possible patterns of information diffusion (Rogers, 1976), cultural differences (Salminen et al., 2017), and other social media news aspects (AL-Smadi, Jaradat, AL-Ayyoub, & Jararweh, 2017).

## ACKNOWLEDGMENTS

Our thanks to AJ+ of the Al Jazeera Media Network for their wonderful partnership for this research.

## REFERENCES


AL-Smadi, M., Jaradat, Z., AL-Ayyoub, M., & Jararweh, Y. (2017). Paraphrase identification and semantic text similarity analysis in Arabic news tweets using lexical, syntactic, and semantic. *Information Processing & Management, 53*(3), 559-750.

An, J., Cho, H. Y., Kwak, H., Hassen, M. Z., & Jansen, B. J. (2016, 29 November-2 December). *Towards Automatic Persona Generation Using SocialMedia.* Paper presented at the The Third International Symposium on SocialNetworks Analysis, Management and Security (SNAMS2016), The 4th International Conference on Future Internet of Things and Cloud, Vienna, Austria.

An, J., Jwak, H., & Jansen, B. J. (2017, 31 July-3 August). *Personas for Content Creators via Decomposed Aggregate Audience Statistics.* Paper presented at the Advances in Social Network Analysis and Mining (ASONAM 2017), Sydney, Australia.

An, J., Kwak, H., & Jansen, B. J. (2017, 4-7 January). *Automatic Generation of Personas Using YouTube Social Media Data.* . Paper presented at the Proceedings of the 50th International Conference on System Sciences (HICSS-50), Waikoloa, Hawaii.

Cha, M., Kwak, H., Rodriguez, P., Ahn, Y. Y., & Moon, S. (2007). *I tube, you tube, everybody tubes: Analyzing the world's largest user generated content video system.* Paper presented at the Proceedings of the 7th ACM SIGCOMM Conference on Internet Measurement, Chicago, IL.

Chen, L., Holsapple, C. W., Hsiao, S.-H., Ke, Z., Oh, J.-Y., & Yang, Z. (2017). Knowledge-dissemination channels: Analytics of stature evaluation. *Journal of the Association for Information Science and Technology, 68*(4), 911-930. doi:10.1002/asi.23725

Dharwada, P., Greenstein, J. S., Gramopadhye, A. K., & Davis, S. J. (2007, 1-5 October). *A Case Study on Use of Personas in Design and Development of an Audit Management System.* Paper presented at the Human Factors and Ergonomics Society Annual Meeting Proceedings, Baltimore, Maryland.

Eriksson, E., Artman, H., & Swartling, A. (2013). *The Secret Life of a Persona: When the Personal Becomes Private.* Paper presented at the Proceedings of the SIGCHI Conference on Human Factors in Computing Systems (CHI2013), Paris, France.

Friess, E. (2012). *Personas and Decision Making in the Design Process: An Ethnographic Case Study.* Paper presented at the Proceedings of the SIGCHI Conference on Human Factors in Computing Systems (CHI2012), Austin, Texas, USA.

Fu, W. W., & Sim, C. C. (2011). Aggregate bandwagon effect on online videos' viewership: Value uncertainty, popularity cues, and heuristics. *Journal of the American Society for Information Science and Technology, 62*(12), 2382-2395. doi:10.1002/asi.21641

Hendahewa, C., & Shah, C. (2017). Evaluating user search trails in exploratory search tasks. *Information Processing & Management, 53*(4), 905-922.

Judge, T., Matthews, T., & Whittaker, S. (2012). *Comparing Collaboration and Individual Personas for the Design and Evaluation of Collaboration Software.* Paper presented at the Proceedings of the SIGCHI Conference on Human Factors in Computing Systems (CHI2012), Austin, Texas, USA.

Jung, S., An, J., Kwak, H., Ahmad, M., Nielsen, L., & Jansen, B. J. (2017, 6-11 May). *Persona Generation from Aggregated Social Media Data.* Paper presented at the ACM Conference on Human Factors in Computing Systems 2017 Extended Abstracts (CHI2017), Denver, CO, USA.

Lee, D. D., & Seung, S. H. (1999). Learning the parts of objects by non-negative matrix factorization. *Nature, 401*(6755), 788-791.

Mellor, V. (2006). *Mastering audience segmentation: How to apply segmentation techniques to improve internal communication* London: Melcrum.

Nielsen, L., & Hansen, K. S. (2014). *Personas is Applicable: A Study on the Use of Personas in Denmark.* Paper presented at the Proceedings of the 32nd Annual ACM conference on Human factors in Computing Systems (CHI2014), Toronto, Ontario, Canada.

Ortiz-Cordova, A., & Jansen, B. J. (2012). Classifying web search queries in order to identify high revenue generating customers. *Journal of the American Society for Information Sciences and Technology, 63*(7), 1426-1441.

Rogers, E. M. (1976). New product adoption and diffusion. *Journal of Consumer Research, 2*(1), 290-301.

Salminen, J., Sengün, S., Kwak, H., Jansen, B. J., An, J., Jung, S.-G., . . . Harrell, F. (2017, 21-23 Aug.). *Generating Cultural Personas From Social Data: A Perspective of Middle Eastern Users.* Paper presented at the The Fourth International Symposium on Social Networks Analysis, Management and Security (SNAMS-2017). Prague, Czech Republic.

Smith, W. R. (1956). A product differentiation and market segmentation as alternative marketing strategies. *Journal of Marketing, 21*(1), 3-8.

Song, X., Lin, C.-Y., Tseng, B. L., & Sun, M.-T. ( 2005). *Modeling and predicting personal information dissemination behavior.* Paper presented at the Proceedings of the eleventh ACM SIGKDD International Conference on Knowledge Discovery in Data Mining (KDD '05), New York, NY.

Stern, B. B. (1994). A revised communication model for advertising: multiple dimensions of the source, the message, and the recipient. *Journal of Advertising, 23*(2), 5-15.

Tan, L. K.-W., Na, J.-C., & Ding, Y. (2015). Influence diffusion detection using the influence style (INFUSE) model. *Journal of the Association for Information Science and Technology, 66*(8), 1717-1733. doi:10.1002/asi.23287

Wang, C., Zhou, Z., Jin, X.-L., Fang, Y., & Lee, M. K. O. (2017). The influence of affective cues on positive emotion in predicting instant information sharing on microblogs: Gender as a moderator. *Information Processing & Management, 53*(3), 721-734.

Zhang, L., Zheng, L., & Tai-QuanPeng. (2017). Structurally embedded news consumption on mobile news applications. *Information Processing & Management, 53*(5), 1242-1253.

# ERA 2.0: The National Archives New Framework for Electronic Records Preservation


**Leslie Johnston**

*National Archives and Records Administration, USA. leslie.johnston@nara.gov*



## ABSTRACT

**The United States National Archives and Records Administration (NARA) is refactoring its Electronic Records Archive (ERA) systems used for scheduling, transferring, processing, reviewing, describing, transforming, and storing electronic records received from U.S. government agencies for permanent preservation in support of long-term public access to federal records. The project is following an Agile approach, toward the end of implementing a modular, cloud-based suite of tools and microservices to support archival functions across the electronic records lifecycle. The implementation will also upgrade digital preservation functionality extant in the current production system, and enable additional efficiencies and automation in the processing of electronic records at scale to make records available to the public more quickly.**



## KEYWORDS

electronic records, federal records, records management, National Archive, Electronic Records Archive, digital preservation, digital processing environment, digital object repository, agile software development


## THE NARA MISSION

The mission of the United States National Archives and Records Administration (NARA) is to "provide public access to Federal Government records in our custody and control. Public access to government records strengthens democracy by allowing Americans to claim their rights of citizenship, hold their government accountable, and understand their history so they can participate more effectively in their government." (NARA, 2014, p. 4) Preservation of the permanent records of the federal government in all formats (analog, born-digital, and digitized) is the critical first step to ensuring NARA can provide the public with access to these records. These records are increasingly born-digital, including documents, email, datasets, publications, websites, social media, and the contents of systems used in federal agencies to perform their vital work. To manage these records and ensure future access requires a robust, scalable, and increasingly automated processing and preservation infrastructure.


80th Annual Meeting of the Association for Information Science & Technology, Washington, DC, VA | Oct. 27-Nov. 1, 2017




## WHAT IS ERA?

An electronic records archive is, at its most basic, a suite of workflows and tools to receive born-digital electronic records, process them, and store them in a managed environment for preservation and access. The NARA Electronic Records Archives, or ERA, encompasses a set of the operations for scheduling, transferring, processing, describing, transforming, and preserving electronic records received from U.S. government agencies, as well as exporting them for inclusion in the National Archives Catalog.

It comprises multiple systems handling different types of electronic records (e.g., unclassified and classified Federal, Presidential, and Legislative), each with its own regulatory management and access controls, alongside the tools needed to support functions across the archival life cycle.

## THE CURRENT ERA SYSTEM

ERA was developed through a large-scale project in the early 2000s (Thibodeau, 2004, 2007; Weinstein, 2005), which involved business owners from across the agency who identified functional requirements. The project was scoped with a single system in mind to deliver all aspects of functionality from records scheduling by agencies through public delivery.

There were several lessons learned from that implementation (Phillips, 2012). The scale of the project (over 1400 complex functional and regulatory requirements) made it difficult to achieve in the timeframe originally envisioned, and when the system went into production in 2008 it did not include all the planned-for functionality, including subsuming other customized NARA production systems or providing the full range of necessary preservation functions. There were challenges in maintaining ongoing communication about the status of the development during the project to several hundred staff and colleagues at federal agencies with a role in the design and use of the system; this required more aggressive communication strategies than were generally employed. There was also a large-scale change management effort that was difficult to guide; it was not solely technical but also organizational, as the roles of some staff would change with the launch of the system.

The current production system successfully supports records schedule submission and approval, records transfer by agencies, a single processing workflow for federal records, and the storage and management of records. It is used by dozens of NARA staff across the country and by records managers at over two hundred federal agencies to schedule and transfer records to NARA and respond to records access requests from the public. The project successfully leveraged work from the community, including the integration of open source tools such as PRONOM,[1] DROID,[2] and JHOVE.[3] The initiative introduced the first integration of online U.S. federal government records management processes with the archival repository for electronic records. Workflows and systems were simultaneously implemented to manage and preserve Presidential records, which fall under different regulatory and access controls. A single initial manual workflow to move metadata into the National Archives Catalog was also put in place to more efficiently move records through processing to access.

Soon after going live, ERA development was put on hold to review the state of the system and plan for future work. It was determined in 2012 that the system required extensive modernization and refactoring to improve the user experience and add needed functionality.

## THE ERA 2.0 PROJECT

One of the key drivers behind ERA 2.0 is a recognition that NARA must increase the flexibility of the system to support the variable approaches required in processing and preserving a wide variety of electronic records. Specifically, ERA must be refactored – restructuring the existing body of code in a way that minimizes changes to its core business behaviors – to move away from current restrictive workflow and provide the ability to more easily integrate new software tools used for processing records into the system, while building on the foundational community work based on OAIS [4] and PREMIS,[5] and continuing the use of community-developed tools PRONOM, DROID, and JHOVE.

The high-level goal for the current project is to improve the efficiency of the records life cycle from scheduling to public access. In order to enable new levels of efficiency and automation, what ERA 2.0 cannot be now is a single system solution for all operations; instead there must be a modular suite of microservices and tools – commercial, open source, and developed in-house – that are interchangeable in response to fast-moving technology changes, new business needs, and to handle new record formats that will appear in the future. The system additionally must be interoperable with other tools and systems at NARA, exchanging metadata and data through APIs.

In 2011, the U.S. White House issued Memorandum M-12-18 (Executive Office of the President, 2011), which directed federal agencies to reform electronic records management, requiring updates to procedures agencies use to manage their records and transfer records to NARA. In 2014 NARA issued an update to its Transfer Guidance (NARA, 2014) which greatly expanded the formal list of acceptable file formats for electronic records, and restructured that guidance in a way that it can be easily updated as format use waxes and wanes. NARA is taking a modular approach in modernizing ERA in an effort to reduce overall complexity of the system and support its own guidance to agencies and ever-changing federal electronic record management requirements. This modular approach emphasizes separating the functionality of a system into independent, interchangeable modules, such that each contains everything necessary to execute only one aspect of the desired functionality. This improves system maintainability due to the separation of functional concerns in independent code modules, as well as being more reusable than a traditional monolithic design, since all (or many) of these modules may then be reused in other system implementations that support the same business functions and data types (Parnas, 1972).

In 2013 NARA began the process of meeting with business owners from across the agency to identify the gaps in functionality and identify requirements to modernize ERA. It was decided that not only would the upgraded system and its tools be more modular and interface directly with other NARA systems, but that the implementation process itself would be very different. Research shows that an Agile approach improves both the productivity of the development and the quality of the end product (Ahmed et.al, 2010; Petersen & Wohlin, 2011), so a decision was made to identify an appropriate Agile methodology for the implementation. After consideration, the project chose to follow an "Agile with Discipline" approach where more up-front requirement identification and architecture planning takes places than in many other methodologies (Ambler & Lines, 2012). A set of User Stories are documented instead of a massive list of fixed requirements, and development takes place in four-week sprints, producing working code that the staff can see and provide feedback on every month. The User Stories provide implementation guidance and acceptance criteria for the functional requirements, and each four-week sprint both closes stories and surfaces requirements for new stories. Each development iteration produces working code that is tested directly by stakeholders and users with real world records processing use cases. The process leverages work done to date, and is more transparent than in the past, and provides for a much greater level of participation from NARA staff to guide the development. The project began in fall 2014, and is being implemented in conjunction with IBM, which has a contract with NARA to manage the current ERA systems and refactor the system to add the new functionality.

---

1 https://www.nationalarchives.gov.uk/PRONOM/Default.aspx
2 https://digital-preservation.github.io/droid
3 http://jhove.openpreservation.org/
4 https://www.iso.org/standard/57284.html
5 https://www.loc.gov/standards/premis/

## HIGH-LEVEL ERA 2.0 FUNCTIONAL ARCHITECTURE

The system comprises three modules: the digital processing environment, the digital object repository, and business object management. The digital processing environment (DPE) in ERA 2.0 supports the ingest process and provides the software tools and metadata editing capabilities necessary for electronic records verification and processing functions, where tools can be swapped in and out as needs change. The initial implementation is scoped to include approximately fifteen tools, both embedded thin client as well as thick client tools accessed through Windows virtual machine "workbenches" provided for each processing archivist. Initial tools include those for format characterization, bulk file reformatting, image manipulation, common business productivity software, PII recognition, and redaction. The list currently includes over 100 proposed tools, ranging from community-based preservation tools such as DROID and Bulk Extractor to licensed commercial desktop applications, such as Adobe Photoshop and Microsoft Office. The tool management framework has already been built to allow the simple addition and substitution of tools, and to support multiple VM workbench images customized for specialized needs such as textual processing versus video or audio processing.

The long-term storage, search and retrieval capabilities for electronic records, once they have been processed and verified, in the DPE will be provided by a digital object repository (DOR) component of ERA. DOR will provide all holdings management and preservation functions, including recording of fixities, object versioning, search, auditing, and reporting. When additional processing is needed, such as bulk preservation actions or creation of new public use versions of records to meet researcher requests, files are copied into the DPE environment for the work to take place, then versioned back into the DOR. DOR maintains the audit trail for all actions performed automatically or manually in its data warehouse.

Lastly, the current on-line forms and approval workflows for the scheduling and both physical and legal transfer of government records to NARA will be provided by the business object management (BOM) component of ERA. The current system includes only a single workflow for federal records that excludes other record types; ERA 2.0 will comprise multiple workflows for Federal, Presidential, Legislative and Judicial records, digitized analog records, and donated materials, with a mechanism to easily update workflows or instantiate new workflows as requirements change.

Each module – DPE, DOR, and BOM – is an independent codebase; the goal is to implement modules that can be updated or replaced with minimal if any dependent code changes in the other aspects of the system. The implementation is a custom Java application but leverages open source tools in the stack and will, at least for unclassified records, be cloud-based. Government agencies are increasingly managing their electronic records in the cloud, and NARA would like to be able to take advantage of an interpretation of the "Data at Rest" concept (De Capitani di Vimercati et al., 2016) where records stored by agencies in the cloud do not need to be repeatedly moved to come under NARA control, be processed, or made accessible. The National Archives Catalog is already a cloud-based service (Maucione, 2013). Given the scale projections for the transfer of electronic records to NARA and the digitization of analog records, the elasticity of the cloud is a must for the review and processing of records. Processing archivists will be working entirely in the cloud, utilizing embedded tools for bulk actions such as format characterization and reformatting, and working in virtualized workbenches directly on the files in the cloud to take advantage of elastic compute capabilities.

While public access to records is enabled through the National Archives Catalog, the DOR will include advanced search functions for staff of both metadata and record content. This will support highly granular discovery requirements to review records for personally identifiable information (PII), classification status, and to find responsive records for special access or Freedom of Information Act (FOIA) requests, access requests mandated by law to support litigation or to supply access to government information that is not yet publicly available.

## WHY THE CLOUD?

NARA has chosen to aggressively leverage cloud technology in the development of ERA 2.0 for several reasons, which reflects both current research and the growing adoption of cloud for archival storage and processing at other national cultural heritage organizations, including the National Archives UK and the National Library of New Zealand (Oliver & Knight, 2015). In addition, NARA, as an executive agency of the U.S. Government, is adhering to the mandate from the White House, the CIO Council, and OMB of adopting a "Cloud First" posture with regard to new system development. (Kundra, 2010).

The requirements of cultural heritage institutions differ from private sector business users of the cloud in terms of data quantity, the required longevity of holdings, and unpredictable spikes in activity levels. But when faced with a government mandate to take advantage of cloud services, electronic records archiving and the Open Archival Information System model (ISO 14721, 2012) have been proven to not be inconsistent with cloud storage (Askhoj, Sugimoto, & Nagamori, 2011; Franks, 2015). The advantages of cloud computing are particularly compelling in the context of a national archive's mission to ingest and preserve permanently valuable content from a wide variety of sources across the government (Beagrie, Charlesworth & Miller, 2014). This content includes a wide and almost infinitely variable set of file formats, transferred in a process that is profoundly unpredictable with regard to volume and timing. Stated simply, it is often impossible for the agency to know how much content will need to be processed and when it will arrive. Thus, the well-established capability in a cloud environment to add storage and computing power for preservation functions virtually upon demand (Nguyen & Lake, 2011; Pop, Neagul, & Petcu, 2014) becomes more than just a convenience - it can be considered an essential component of the agency's ability to respond to its mission.

This flexibility is particularly valuable when considering the budgetary environment in which NARA and all government agencies operate - highly constrained and often unpredictable and inflexible. NARA must operate to maximize cost savings and economies of scale, particularly in large capital-intensive purchases. The purchase, establishment, installation, operation and maintenance of single-use, high-volume, high-throughput data centers capable of rapid and significant expansion such as that required by NARA is simply not possible in a practical sense, given NARA's need to operate with the realities of the Federal budget process.

Basing ERA 2.0 on a cloud architecture provides NARA with the inherent advantages of sharing these enormous capital outlays with a larger community, in this case the federal government. It also allows the agency to adopt a much more cost-effective pay-as-you-go, incremental approach to acquiring new storage or processing capability for digital preservation based on rapidly changing needs. As is typical in cloud environments, the addition of storage or computer processing power becomes a much more straightforward and direct question of answering "how much" rather than "how."

With the cost and institutional burden of data center operations transferred to the cloud, NARA is able to concentrate its assets more fully and efficiently on the core mission of developing and utilizing the tools and procedures needed to process and preserve the permanently valuable records of the United States. Research has shown that the underlying cloud infrastructure becomes a tool itself in fulfilling this mission of preservation and public access, rather than an impediment to its accomplishment (Han, 2015; Nguyen & Lake, 2011; Pop, Neagul, & Petcu, 2014). Cloud technology is inherently based on an information architecture that provides significant redundancy, and thus provides for one of the hallmarks of electronic preservation: that there will be several copies of each electronic record held safely in geographically dispersed areas. Also, by its very nature, a mature, proven cloud environment provides robust disaster recovery capabilities that cannot hope to be reasonably achieved within local, on-premises infrastructure.

## ADDRESSING A MAJOR GAP: DIGITAL PRESERVATION FUNCTIONS

Development of the current production ERA system was ended before anything but the most basic of digital preservation functionality was implemented. The scope of development of ERA 2.0 includes the implementation of all core digital preservation functions and the framework to greatly extend functionality to include automated preservation actions and bulk preservation actions such as reformatting.

Digital preservation is at its essence an exercise in risk management. Technological limitations to digital preservation have been broadly addressed in terms of systems, storage, and computing power, but are still pervasive in two areas: data loss and technological obsolescence, both of which involve technological, institutional, and human factors (Freitas, 2010; Kastellac, 2012).

To document the automated and human activities required to address as many risks as possible, digital preservation user stories were written against the requirements outlined in the Open Archival Information System standard (ISO 14721, 2012) and the Trustworthy Digital Repositories standard (ISO 16363, 2012), and validated against TRAC (RLG/NARA Task Force on Digital Repository Certification, 2005) and DRAMBORA (McHugh, A., et al., 2007) as proposed assessment tools.

Examples of user stories include, but are not limited to:

- As an administrator, I want to be able to monitor the digital object inventory in the DOR and maintain reports on the inventory.
- As an administrator, I want to receive regular reports on all incidents of data corruption or loss and steps taken to repair/replace corrupt or lost data.
- As an administrator, I want to receive regular reports on any events or maintenance that occur within and on the system-level operations that might impact the digital objects in the DOR (i.e. major system upgrades, electrical malfunctions, unexpected system downtime, etc.) and steps taken to repair/restore system.
- As an administrator, I want to have reports on the hardware and software and locations that are supporting the back-up functionality necessary for preservation and that the system is sufficient for the DOR services to be maintained at a low-risk of data loss.
- As an administrator, I want to ensure that not one person has write access to all copies.
- As an administrator, I want to be able to demonstrate that any/all multiple copies of digital objects are synchronized and maintain reports on a periodic basis.
- As an administrator, I want to be able to ensure that software and hardware systems are capable of maintaining and recording provenance information, and that these systems are reviewable in the future.
- As an archivist, I want to be able to demonstrate the provenance of digital objects through downloadable reports documenting their traceability from receipt and each interaction they have been subject to.
- As an archivist, I want monitoring and notification when digital objects approach obsolescence.
- As an archivist, I want to view the selection of the digital materials for deletion in order to verify and review the selection prior to deletion.
- As an archivist, I want to ingest transformations of digital object(s) stored in DOR in order to store reference and preservation copies of digital objects.

Context for digital objects has been proven to be vital both for the preservation of digital objects and the enabling of their discovery and use (Askhoj, Sugimoto, & Nagamori, 2011; Beaudoin, 2012). The preservation architecture of the system includes the capability to store extensive technical, structural, and descriptive metadata that has been defined as both necessary and effective in the digital preservation community (Caplan & Guenther, 2005; Lavoie & Gartner, 2005; Wendler, 2006). Transaction logging for life cycle actions associated with the objects are also tracked in the repository (ingest checksums, file format identification, preservation and public use versions created over time, auditing outcomes, etc.), which are maintained in a data store to support these preservation functions. Work already completed includes basic digital preservation functions: checking and assignment of fixities, format characterization, and audit reporting on format characterization and the state of the holdings.

The National Archives is reviewing and revising its digital preservation strategy, and wants to ensure that ERA 2.0 is built on a flexible framework that can support all extensions to agency and federal policies and to the file formats received.

## CONCLUSIONS

Following several months of system architecture planning and software development, NARA launched a Pilot Digital Processing Environment in 2015 with an updated workflow and a new modular processing environment with a suite of utilities and tools, as well as a Pilot Digital Object Repository for managed preservation services and storage. The pilot has been tested by over 100 NARA staff members to ensure that this next generation of ERA fits into the new federal frameworks for electronic records management and transfer to NARA. Iterative development has continuously incorporated the feedback from the testing toward a production launch currently scheduled for mid-2018. Development will continue after the initial launch, as will the development of an accompanying separate environment for classified records.

This implementation using an Agile methodology rather than a traditional Waterfall practice met the goals to increase the amount of stakeholder engagement, improve development productivity, and produce a more usable product. Waterfall does not allow for functional changes after a certain stage of the development, which can lead to large scale software projects failing to meet their objectives due to both the inflexible nature of the requirements and the scale of documentation required by the process (Ahmed et.al, 2010). NARA experienced this in its initial ERA development project. NARA has found in this project that Agile software practices can mitigate the risks of a Waterfall-style project by encouraging close stakeholder interaction with the software development teams throughout the implementation, supporting ongoing iteration on the work that has been completed to integrate any newly recognized user requirements or enhancements in a flexible way during the development phase. In this way, the product is much less likely fail by meeting needs expressed in an obsolescent set of requirements developed years earlier, and instead meets current requirements, leading to a higher level of engagement in the development process and an expected higher acceptance level when it goes into production in 2018. Users started asking to use the system for real processing in place of the current ERA over a year before the scheduled production release date.

The ultimate goal is to greatly expand the functionality of ERA to include workflows for all record types and digitized records, greatly expand the range of tools needed to process records and create public use versions, and to implement a robust preservation environment, all in a framework that makes it easier to update the system to meet as yet unknown needs.

NARA works in conjunction with agencies to determine which federal records must be permanently preserved for access by future generations. It is one of the most important responsibilities of NARA, because good records management is the backbone of open government. It makes possible transparency and accountability, the hallmarks of the agency's Open Government Initiative (NARA, 2016). The long-term success of the National Archives hinges on the ability of each federal agency to manage its records in accordance with the applicable laws, regulations, and standards, and NARA's ability to preserve those records.

NARA's main approach to providing access to records is to support "traditional" archival research using its holdings. For decades, this meant providing physical access to finding aids and records in research rooms across the country, whether in the National Archives Building in downtown Washington DC, in Presidential Libraries, or in the many other NARA facilities distributed nationwide. Today, supporting archival research means providing descriptions and, increasingly, digital content in an engaging online environment. In addition, NARA has used exhibits, workshops, and other outreach programming to highlight selected records and provide opportunities for on-site visitors to learn about their history. Increasingly, however, NARA is working to broaden its audience by providing access to curated digital content – through social media channels as well as web-based exhibits. None of NARA's access approaches can succeed without reliable access to the growing body of digitized and born-digital records in NARA's care.

In expanding the capabilities of ERA, NARA is directly supporting all the missions of the agency. Increasing the capacity for the transfer of electronic records and the efficiency and automation of records processing translates to records moving more quickly from ingest to availability through the National Archives Catalog, improving both the transparency of the workings of government and engagement of the public with the U.S. government through research into its records while also preserving the records for the future.

## REFERENCES


Ahmed, A., Ahmad, S., Ehsan, N., Mirza, E., & Sarwar, S. Z. (2010, June). Agile software development: Impact on productivity and quality. In *Management of innovation and technology (ICMIT), 2010 IEEE international conference on* (pp. 287-291).

Ambler, S. W. (2008). Has agile peaked? *Dr Dobbs Journal, 33*(6), 52-54. http://www.drdobbs.com/architecture-and-design/has-agile-peaked/207600615#

Ambler, S. & Lines, M.. Disciplined agile delivery: A practitioner's guide to agile software delivery in the enterprise. IBM Press, 2012.

Askhoj, J., Sugimoto, S., & Nagamori, M. (2011). Preserving records in the cloud. *Records Management Journal, 21*(3), 175-187.

Beaudoin, J.E. (2012). A framework for contextual metadata used in the digital preservation of cultural objects. *D-Lib Magazine* 18(11/12). Retrieved from http://www.dlib.org/dlib/november12/beaudoin/11beaudoin1.html

De Capitani di Vimercati, S., Foresti, S., & Samarati, P. Data protection in cloud scenarios. In Data privacy management, and security assurance: 10th international workshop, DPM 2015, and 4th international workshop, QASA 2015, Vienna, Austria, September 21-22, 2015, pp 3-11.

Caplan, P., & Guenther, R. S. (2005). Practical preservation: The PREMIS experience. *Library Trends, 54*(1), 111-124.

Executive Office of the President. *Presidential Memorandum -- Managing Government Records*. (November 28, 2011) https://www.whitehouse.gov/the-press-office/2011/11/28/presidential-memorandum-managing-government-records

Franks, P. C. (2015, September). Government use of cloud-based long term digital preservation as a service: An exploratory study. In *Digital heritage, 2015* (Vol. 2, pp. 371-374).

Freitas, F. (2010). Designing digital preservation solutions: A risk management-based approach. *International Journal of Digital Curation, 5*(1), 4-17.

Han, Y. (2015). Cloud storage for digital preservation: Optimal uses of Amazon S3 and Glacier. *Library Hi Tech, 33*(2), 261-271.

ISO 14721. Space data and information transfer systems. Open archival information system (OAIS), reference model. International Organization for Standardization, Geneva, Switzerland, 2012.

ISO 16363. Information transfer systems—Audit and certification of trustworthy digital repositories. International Organization for Standardization, Geneva, Switzerland, 2012.

Kastellec, M. (2012). Practical limits to the scope of digital preservation. *Information Technology and Libraries (Online), 31*(2), 63.

Kundra, V. 25 Point Implementation Plan to Reform Federal Information Technology Management. United States Office of Management and Budget, 2010.

Lavoie, B. F., & Gartner, R. (2005). *Preservation metadata*. OCLC.

Maucione, S. Putting back together US history, one bit and byte at a time. *Fedscoop*, December 15, 2013. Available at http://fedscoop.com/michael-wash-digitizing-history

A. McHugh., S. Ross, R. Ruusalepp, & H. Hofman. *The digital repository audit method based on risk assessment (DRAMBORA)*. Digital Curation Centre, 2007.

National Archives and Records Administration. *NARA Bulletin 2014-04: Revised Format Guidance for the Transfer of Permanent Electronic Records*. Available at http://www.archives.gov/records-mgmt/bulletins/2014/2014-04.html

National Archives and Records Administration. *Strategic Plan 2014-2018*. Available at https://www.archives.gov/files/about/plans-reports/strategic-plan/2014/nara-strategic-plan-2014-2018.pdf

National Archives and Records Administration. *Open Government Plan 2016-2018*. Available at https://usnationalarchives.github.io/opengovplan/

Nguyen, Q. L., & Lake, A. (2011, July). Content server system architecture for providing differentiated levels of service in a digital preservation cloud. In *Cloud computing (CLOUD), 2011 IEEE international conference on* (pp. 557-564).

Oliver, G., & Knight, S. (2015). Storage is a strategic issue: Digital preservation in the cloud. *D-Lib Magazine, 21*(3/4).

Parnas, D. L. (1972). On the criteria to be used in decomposing systems into modules. *Communications of the ACM, 15*(12), 1053-1058.

Petersen, K. and Wohlin, C. (2011), Measuring the flow in lean software development. *Software: Practice and Experience*, 41: 975–996. doi:10.1002/spe.975

Phillips, M.E.. Lessons learned from NARA's electronic records archives project. In *Archiving conference,* Copenhagen, Denmark, 2012, pp 8-12.

Pop, D., Neagul, M., & Petcu, D. (2014, September). On cloud deployment of digital preservation environments. In *Digital libraries (JCDL), 2014 IEEE/ACM joint conference on* (pp. 443-444).

RLG/NARA Task Force on Digital Repository Certification. *Audit Checklist for Certifying Digital Repositories*, 2005. Available at http://www.rlg.org/en/pdfs/rlgnara-repositorieschecklist.pdf.

Thibodeau, T. NARA's electronic records archives program. *Law Library Journal*, vol. 96, no. 4, pp. 633-642.

Thibodeau, K. The electronic records archives program at the National Archives and Records Administration. *First Monday*, vol. 12, no 7. Available at http://firstmonday.org/article/view/1922/1804

Weinstein, A. NARA enters new ERA of electronic records management. *Information Management*, vol. 39, no. 5, pp. 22-24

Wendler, R. (2006). The status of preservation metadata in the digital library community. *Digital Preservation*, 61-6

# De-Constructing the Co-Construction: Researcher Stance, the Nature of Data and Community Building in an Online Participatory Platform to Create a Knowledge Repository


**Samantha J. Kaplan**
*School of Information and Library Science, University of North Carolina, Chapel Hill, USA. sjkaplan@live.unc.edu*

**Rachel M. Carriere**
*Content Management, EBSCO Information Services. rcarriere@ebsco.com*

**Annie T. Chen**
*Dept. of Biomedical Informatics and Medical Education, School of Medicine, University of Washington, USA. atchen@uw.edu*



## ABSTRACT

**In this article, we provide a reflexive account of the design of the Body Listening Project, a participatory platform in which participants were invited to engage collectively in the building of a public repository. The Body Listening Project was an online collaborative space, with a designated "ThinkSpace," for participants and moderators to share their experiences of "body listening" and more broadly, self-management of health. The participatory platform on which the study took place was an active, evolving environment that was shaped by participants of many different backgrounds. In particular, we elaborate upon three critical aspects of our research design: researcher stance, the nature of data, and online community development. It is our hope that explicating the design decisions that were made in this study can stimulate researchers' consideration of these issues in their own projects, as well as inform the design of future research involving collaborative and participatory frameworks.**



## KEYWORDS

researcher stance, online research, research methods, research design, online community, knowledge collaboration, knowledge production


## INTRODUCTION

The nature of data and researcher stance are fundamental issues to be considered in research design. Words like *neutral*, *objective*, and *unobtrusive* are commonly used to describe good science and thus become qualities researchers try to realize. In their work, they emphasize the steps they have taken to distance themselves from the object of their study. While the idea that researchers should not allow their personal feelings to cloud their work may make sense at face value – in some settings it can undermine research. In many research traditions, one may strive for objectivity and reproducibility, but there are contexts where doing so might result in failing to appreciate the uniqueness of participants and to recognize their vulnerability, while at the same time, overlooking phenomena of scientific interest.

Previous research has observed that an increasing number of researchers are designing online discussion forums for qualitative health research, and yet there is limited literature in which researchers have documented their experiences and lessons learned to demonstrate the viability and validity of this method (Ferrante et al., 2016). In this article, we report our experiences in an effort to ameliorate this knowledge gap. We present an example of a study in which we grappled with tensions that can appear as one considers research validity, including quantitative vs. qualitative research, epistemological purism and pluralism, and rigor and creativity (Whittemore, Chase, & Mandle, 2001). We show how we dealt with these tensions as we considered three critical aspects of the research design: researcher stance, the nature of data, and community building.

The Body Listening Project was an online collaborative space for participants and researchers to reflect upon and share their experiences of body listening, and more broadly, self-management of health, particularly in the context of chronic conditions. Chronic illness management has been recognized as an important component of health care, and there is an increasing awareness that similar strategies may be effective across different types of chronic illnesses (Schulman-Green et al., 2012). Additionally, there is evidence to suggest that body awareness, defined as the ability to recognize subtle body cues, is helpful in the management of chronic conditions (Mehling et al., 2009).

This study involved a moderated discussion that occurred over a period of 10 weeks – a Guided Exploration – about themes relating to body listening, including tuning into body rhythms; movement, energy and fatigue; and pain management. The long-term goals of this project were to create a repository of knowledge that could help those wishing to learn how to listen to their bodies and improve their health management, as well as to use the content contributed to improve extant health knowledge resources. The results of this work


80th Annual Meeting of the Association for Information Science & Technology, Washington, DC, VA | Oct. 27-Nov. 1, 2017

will be reported elsewhere, but in this article, we focused on the ways that our study design contributes to methodological considerations for research involving online communities.

## RESEARCHER STANCE

Qualitative researchers clearly recognize their role in the shaping and interpretation of data. Research that does not bear the mark of its researcher does not exist. In this study, we take a constructivist perspective, in which participant and researcher are engaged together in the co-construction of meaning (Mills, Bonner, & Francis, 2006). As Holloway and Biley (2011) articulate, "The self is always present in fieldwork," (p.971) and as such, it is important to explore the concept of researcher stance. To understand possible alternatives, we now take a moment to review common positions on researcher stance.

One typology that is often mentioned is Gold's typology of field roles, which ranges from the complete participant at one extreme, to the complete observer at the other, and participant-as-observer and observer-as-participant in between (Gold, 1958). One might also think of oneself as an insider, partaking in the experience under study, or an outsider to the experience (Dwyer & Buckle, 2009). Yet another set of related terms includes the emic vs. etic distinction. In extant literature researchers have often employed the terms "emic" and "etic" in different ways (e.g. Harris, 1964; Pike, 1967). Simply put, the emic approach results from studying culture, language and meaning through an insiders' perspective, whereas an etic approach results from studying culture, language and meaning from an external view and is often cross-cultural (Olive, 2014; Xia, 2011).

Extant literature has also argued that the concepts of insider and outsider in research are not strictly dichotomous (Merriam et al., 2001). Harris (2015) exemplified this in her account of conducting research with persons with Hepatitis C and persons who used injectable drugs. Harris had personal experiences with both which she disclosed to her participants during recruitment, but in the case of heroin use, she asserted, "I also knew that my way of thinking about drug use had changed from the early days" (p. 1692). While she was more of an insider than someone who had never used injectable drugs, is she still an insider if her mentality had since changed? Dwyer and Buckle (2009) argue that, as researchers, regardless of whether we are insiders or outsiders, our own perspective is always shaped by our position as a researcher.

In this study, there were multiple ways that one could conceptualize the terms, "insider" and "outsider." Those who have a given illness often speak of the inability of others who do not have that illness to understand (Carter-Edwards, Skelly, Cagle, & Appel, 2004; Kool, van Middendorp, Boeije, & Geenen, 2009; Ussher, Kirsten, Butow, & Sandoval, 2006). Thus, in relation to the concept of illness, there were those who might be considered or would consider themselves "insiders" to the experience of living with a chronic condition. This status could be different depending on the perspective of the viewer (the individual, family, friends, or the health care system). Conversely, there are those who would then consider themselves "outsiders" to the experience of managing a chronic condition. But one might argue that this is a state that is largely defined by our perceptions, which are in turn influenced by those around us, the health care system, and the information that we receive concerning health and wellness. Factors such as technological support for health management, changing expectations toward life and quality of life, and perceptions of health and wellness can affect our interpretations of our own health. The question of whether one is healthy or not is not strictly dichotomous. This is the perspective from which this study was designed, and thus, one part of the rationale to include participants regardless of health status.

The question of who is an "insider" or "outsider" with regard to illness also has implications for the status of the researcher. The research team comprised individuals who might see themselves, and be viewed by others, differently in terms of health status. They might also have different views of themselves as researchers. Gail, for example, viewed herself primarily as a layperson assisting researchers in the study, though this distinction was not explicitly made during the study, and Gail was as engaged in research activities as much as the rest of the team.

The Body Listening Project team members, who collectively varied extensively in terms of health history; academic, industry, and other work experience; demographics including age and ethnicity; and researcher stance; worked together to shape the study content and participated in the study along with the participants. Regardless of background, there was an effort to ensure that each member of the research team was able to contribute to the research design. Lastly, it is important to consider not only our stances, but also the effects of how we were perceived. Regardless of whether or not we consider ourselves insiders, the fact that the research team on the whole may have been perceived as insiders by the participants served to boost participation and build community.

### *Conflicting Research Design Priorities*

Typically, in qualitative settings, researchers broach the insider/outsider aspect gingerly. While the overarching approach of the study was a constructivist one, this study was conceptualized to allow for variability in the stances taken by members of the research team. In many domains including the biomedical sciences, one might see researchers adopt the perspective that there is an absolute truth that one is trying to discover, and that knowledge is objective and neutral (Kuper, Reeves, & Levinson, 2008), and this perspective was present among the study team. There were also team members who behaved more as unapologetic, subjective insiders – researchers who possessed scientific expertise but used it to buttress their insider knowledge instead of silence it. While not every moderator might be so characterized, this approach guided the research design, and was expressed in the project's framing and in the materials that guided the moderators.

Researchers acting as "unapologetic, subjective insiders" meant that many of those who were also moderators made no effort to hide their own experiences or make them more relatable. This effectively set a tone throughout the course of the study that differences of opinion and experience were allowed and encouraged. Participants had tacit (and with some moderators, verbal encouragement) permission to express radical disagreement. When the moderators expressed potentially transgressive ideas, it resonated with participants that they were members of the same stakeholder group and had shared experiences, though the details of those experiences might have been different.

This was visible when Sami, a moderator, shared "I still feel conflicted about his response" in regard to a doctor dismissing a symptoms diary that a different provider had requested she keep. Others responded with similar "confessions." Rachel wrote she "gave up [tracking], which I'm embarrassed to admit because I know how beneficial it can be," and Midan said, "I think doctors just love to throw drugs at them because that's the easiest thing."

There are aspects of this study design that are consistent with the principles of action research, in which researchers and stakeholders work together towards a common goal (Greenwood & Levin, 2007). Action research focuses on "doing 'with' rather than doing 'for' stakeholders and credits local stakeholders with the richness of experience and reflective possibilities that long experience living in complex situations brings with it" (Greenwood & Levin, 2007, p. 1), and is thus inherently participatory.

This research explicitly rejects the concept of the research subject as the subject of observation. In this study, we regarded the researcher as a collaborator and a facilitator in a common endeavor – to develop a repository representing the collective product of the knowledge and experience of participants and researchers, together. Ultimately, consideration of the role of the researcher should be viewed as an endeavor to achieve rigor and internal validity, not as a heuristic on whether researchers shape their work.

Star and Griesemer's (1989) seminal paper on boundary objects acknowledged that "science requires cooperation" among "extremely diverse groups" (p. 387). In this research, we considered the researcher one of many groups cooperating to produce science, rather than the definitive viewpoint. Negotiating the boundary between researcher and participant allowed us "to bring disparate communities of practice into alignment" (Lee, 2007, p. 316).

## ON THE NATURE OF DATA

### *Data as the Product of a Living Environment*

In this study, as we have stated, we took the perspective that the researcher influences the shape of the data. Moreover, we considered the study platform a living, organic environment that grew and evolved based on the initial study design, as well as participants' and researchers' combined efforts during the Guided Exploration. The platform was a discussion forum style space built using the Wordpress platform (Figure 1). The name of the discussion space, ThinkSpace, was meant to represent the value of the activity – and the products of it – in which participants and researchers engaged in collectively, on an equal plane.

The Body Listening Project aimed to create a space where all kinds of information were welcome. Though for the most part, participants shared written information, some participants shared photos or images, as did some moderators. In addition to the topics explored through guided moderation, there was a separate section that invited participants to "Help Steer the Project." This section served as a help desk for both participants and moderators. Moderators assisted participants who felt lost or had administrative issues, and participants were asked to participate in more general knowledge collaboration tasks, such as sharing the types of information sources they used and the information management tools that they used. A weekly email newsletter also introduced the topics of each upcoming week and encouraged participants to contribute.

Study recruitment occurred through multiple recruitment mechanisms including university listservs and health-related social media venues. Some weeks benefited more from these recruitment efforts as compared to other weeks when less advertising occurred, based on engagement and posting numbers (Table 1). This, along with changing themes and participant fatigue, possibly contributed to some weeks eliciting richer feedback from participants.

| Week # | Theme | Topics | Posts |
|---|---|---|---|
| N/A | Steer the Project | 7 | 21 |
| 1 | Getting in Touch with Your Body Rhythms | 8 | 111 |
| 2 | Movement, Energy and Fatigue | 8 | 75 |
| 3 | Food and Environment | 9 | 34 |
| 4 | Pain Management | 9 | 38 |
| 5 | Mood Management | 8 | 26 |
| 6 | Sense-making and Conveying What Your Body Tells You in Health Care Contexts | 8 | 24 |
| 7 | Conveying What Your Body Tells You in Life Contexts | 9 | 24 |
| 8 | Tuning in to Your Body with Arts-Based Techniques | 9 | 30 |
| 9 | Mindfulness as a Way to Get in Touch with Your Body | 9 | 30 |
| 10 | The Body as a Vehicle for Self-Growth | 7 | 19 |

***Table 1.*** *Study schedule and engagement*

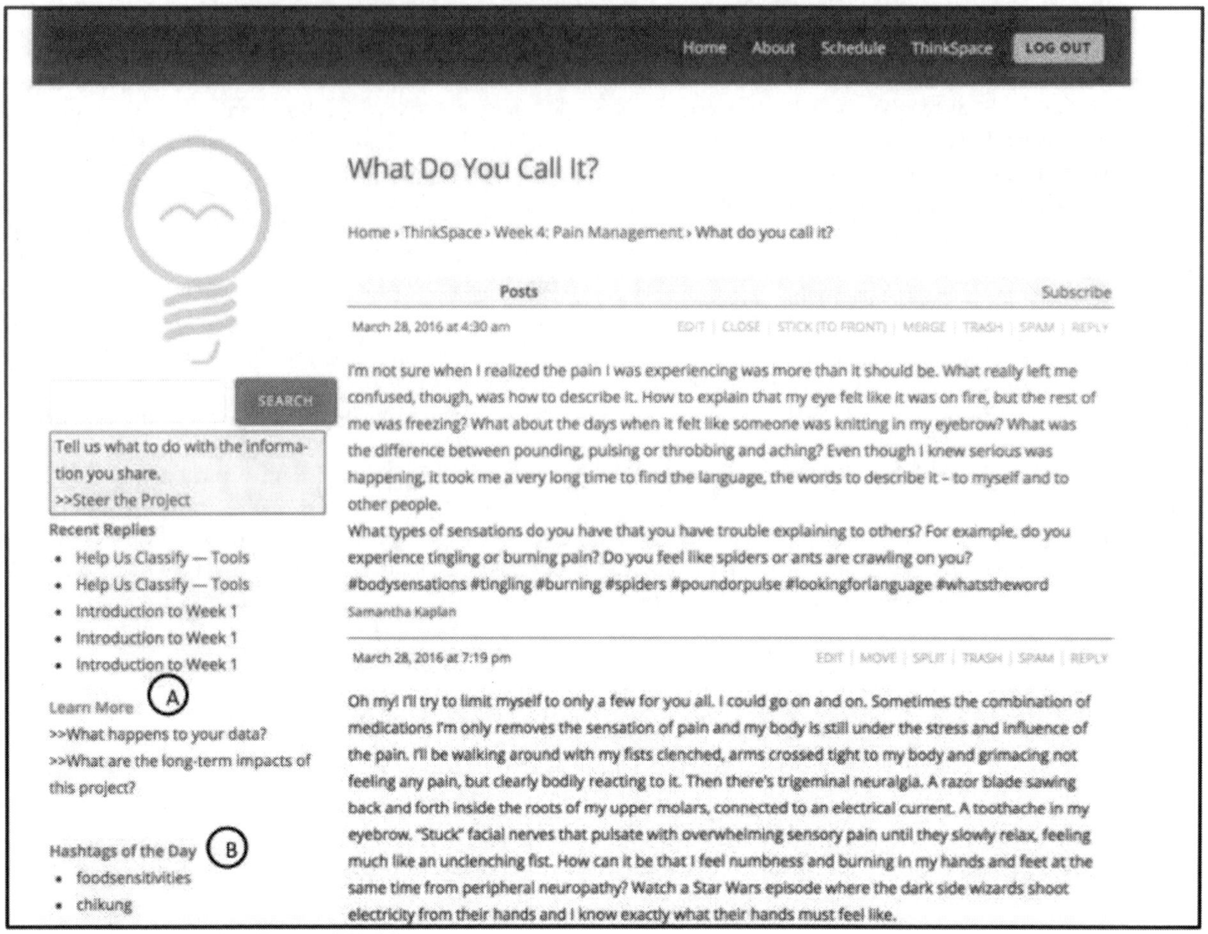

***Figure 1.*** *Body Listening Project ThinkSpace.*

In addition, the moderators played an active role in encouraging activity in the ThinkSpace. The members of the research team, and particularly the moderators, were encouraged to think about the effect that their actions would have on participants' contributions, but they also had significant latitude in style, length, content, and tone. Some moderators chose to share personal details from their lives, akin to those that they hoped would be shared by participants. Others were more restrained and crafted posts less explicitly linked to their own experiences.

Aside from the great variation between main moderation content and tone, all moderators provided supporting moderation during weeks they were not leading. This encompassed responding to participants' posts and also responding to the lead moderator's posts. With this assistance it was less likely for a particular topic to languish without response and more likely that participants' responses received timely replies (with gratitude or requests for clarification or further detail).

While moderators met weekly via conference calls, there was not a set "tone" they were told to try and achieve, nor was there a list of recommended behaviors to improve sharing by participants. However, common techniques emerged. Moderators did not delegitimize or question the validity of something shared – sometimes they asked for clarification, but always affirmed the experience and perspective of participants. In some settings, this might be perceived sycophantic or dubious, but because body listening is not well understood, and life with a chronic condition often involves recognizing the body as an information source that only the self can interpret, all information was equally valuable and no one was considered more or less of an expert than anyone else. Moderators made a conscious effort to minimize the power differential and/or distance that may be felt between moderators and participants in an online discussion space.

By embracing the uniqueness of their own experiences and asking participants for theirs, the moderators endeavored to cultivate an atmosphere of allowed difference. Moderators shared their own personal experiences, but repeatedly emphasized that these experiences and the resulting expertise were potentially unique to them and not authoritative. They did not share these simply as "prompts" but from an authentic place of true curiosity – having been touched by a phenomenon they were still ruminating over. Gail remarked, "Zepplin, yours is a really, really, interesting perspective on the pain that can come from a strenuous workout or bike ride as opposed to chronic pain." Gail continued to encourage Zepplin and shared a similar personal experience, while qualifying it with, "I'm not sure that everyone will identify or even understand this concept, but I do."

Moderators modeled this affirming behavior and others followed. In this next example, AppleStrudel emphasizes that she is providing a general reflection for others to consider, rather than a targeted comment pertaining to an individual: "You mentioned unrecognized trauma, and even if you don't remember what it is (*I'm not speaking of 'you' specifically, here maud*, but of people in general), the body remembers" (emphasis added).

This study design enabled researchers to interact with the data as it emerged and adapt to it in real-time, potentially eliciting richer data. This interaction raises questions about the permeability of the boundary between researcher and instrument, and whether it is possible to separate the researcher from their data.

A skilled interviewer considers respondents' answers, their body language, what they're *not* saying, together to craft follow-up questions in the moment or make a personal disclosure that will put a participant at ease. When an interviewer uses the latter technique, sharing from their own life in a way that resonates with a participant and encourages or empowers them, we must consider if such information should also be treated as data. In a virtual environment, this is even more important as such spaces do not allow for the passive body language that a researcher could use to speak without speaking. Encouraging glances, sustained eye contact, and other cues are largely absent from virtual, anonymous spaces, and thus people use different techniques to build rapport.

The context that elicited participants' contributions is important, and indeed, there were many situations in which content, devoid of context, may not be interpretable. Thus, in analyzing the data from the Body Listening Project, all posts – from participants and from moderators – were treated as data. All posts, regardless of author, were input into the qualitative data analysis software Dedoose, coded, and given equal consideration in data analysis. We employed a data analytic method that was based on a grounded theory approach (Charmaz, 2014).

### The Changing Landscape of Internet Research

The fluid nature of the virtual landscape necessitates careful consideration of topics such as research ethics, the elicitation and collection of data both online and offline, and the relationship between researchers and study participants.

*The Internet and its various technologies, tools, platforms, and venues have provided novel research grounds for decades, and there is no sign of stopping. What has changed is the dynamic raised between researchers and researched. Feenberg, Bakardjieva, and Goldie (2004) asked directly, 'what do the subjects get out of it anyway?' and this question continues to give us pause, as the boundaries between subjects and objects lessen more and more. (Buchanan, 2011, p. 103)*

In this study, we addressed this paradigm shift head-on, endeavoring to decrease the distance between participants and researchers by engaging participants in collaborative brainstorming and knowledge production, as well as respect and affirmation of the value of participants' contributions.

The question of how to handle data collected from the Internet is a complex one that requires close examination of contextual details such as the object of analysis, the use expectations of the site and participants, and sensitivity of the information collected (McKee & Porter, 2009). In the "What happens to your data?" section of the website's Mission statement, we aimed to be transparent about our data collection practices, informing participants about the data that would be public (the discussion posts), and the data that would remain private (the survey completed as part of the registration process). There was also a link to this statement from the ThinkSpace page (Figure 1A).

The sections of the website that explained how we dealt with data generated commentary in other spaces, both online and offline. For example, there were comments in social media platforms where we recruited, such as Facebook, warning others that the discussion forum data was public. But there were also other comments in defense of the study procedure, and additionally pointing out that the study had been reviewed by the Institutional Review Board. The study was also promoted by face-to-face support group leaders, showing that the lines between one social media platform and another, and between online and offline worlds, are no longer so distinct.

### Conflicting Research Design Priorities

The features that a site offers have a strong effect on what participants can and might do. A foundational principle of this study was to design features that would enable participants to express themselves, but also refrain from influencing participants to take a certain direction, much like a researcher might avoid asking leading questions. There were some aspects of the design that one might consider more assistive, such as the provision of clear instructions on how to contribute tags, which foregrounded their importance in the data collection process, as well as assisted those who were not familiar with tagging. This was coupled by work on the part of the moderators to remind participants to add tags whenever it seemed that there had been a lapse of tags on a given thread, and to encourage such contributions by setting an example.

We also provided a search function and a randomized Hashtags of the Day feature to encourage participants to explore and reflect upon their tag use (Figure 1B). Initially we also considered more extensive implementations of interactivity, including sophisticated search functionality and/or interactive visual representations of the content, but ultimately went with the simpler final set of features to avoid unduly influencing the production of data.

## BUILDING THE ONLINE COMMUNITY

The Internet has long been recognized as a fertile ground for research, often through the use of virtual ethnographic approaches (Hine, 2000; Sade-Beck, 2004). This study engaged a community for a different purpose, knowledge collaboration, and thus a critical part of the research design was the conceptualization of the virtual community. We discuss three critical aspects: collaborative knowledge production, sense of community, and membership.

### *Collaborative Knowledge Production*

This community was created for knowledge construction, sharing and collaboration. In recent years, there has been increased recognition of the value of patient-contributed knowledge, as well as interest in the crowdsourcing of patient expertise (Swan, 2012). Collaborative and participatory platforms are seen as a democratizing vehicle for the process of knowledge discovery (Celi, Ippolito, Montgomery, Moses, & Stone, 2014). For example, data from a health-related social networking site, PatientsLikeMe, has been used to augment existing health knowledge resources (Doing-Harris & Zeng-Treitler, 2011). However, this work has primarily focused on augmenting professional controlled vocabularies (Chen et al., 2016). Aside from encouraging patients to contribute data, we involved patients further in the process of knowledge creation by offering them a say in the subsequent organization of this data through the use of tag contributions that might be used later in indexing, and by inviting them to contribute their ideas for organizing the knowledge contributed in a form called, "Steer the Project." In so doing, we hoped to increase their agency and impart a sense of purpose. The website content and recruitment material emphasized this through phrasing such as "Come think with us," and an informational page that illustrated how the project involved participants in knowledge organization (Figure 2).

The moderators endeavored to nurture a culture of reflection and exploration, and participants picked up on this, employing tags to describe their content, including references to health information sources, and adding their own examples to Guided Exploration topics. In addition, participants and moderators took notice of each other's perspectives and built upon on one another's thoughts:

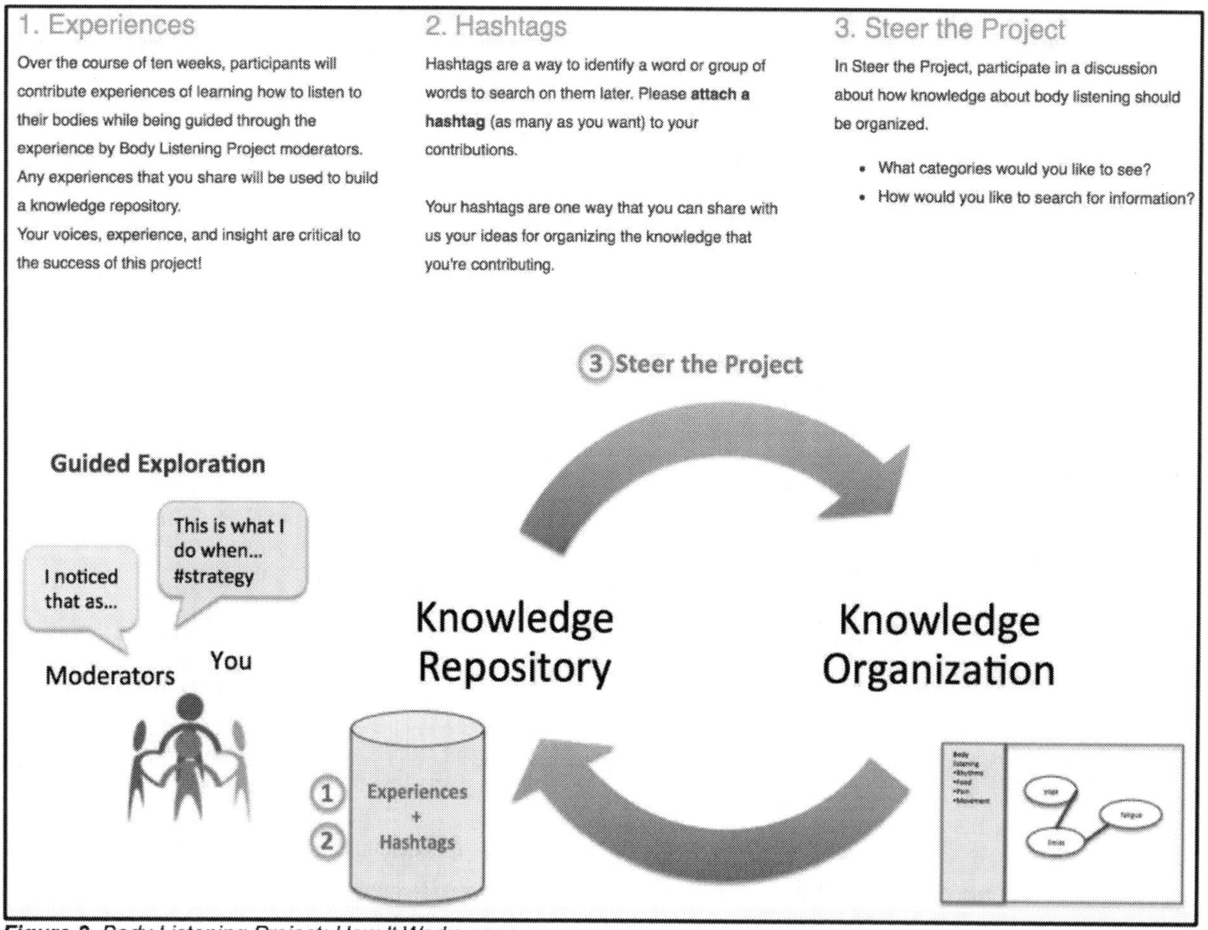


***Figure 2.*** *Body Listening Project: How It Works page.*

*I'm amazed and thoroughly impressed at how ya'll are so mindful and can recognize such body signs... The other side of the coin is... sometimes, do we think too much? – sgc1203*

Similar to findjoyagain the positive that I can see is patience and being in the moment. – Zepplin

We asked participants to engage in a difficult task: elucidating their natural and acquired abilities to attend to their bodies. Rachel ruminated, "but what I still don't know is: does the language I've chosen for describing my pain make sense to anyone else?" While this is a difficult question to answer, the responses of some community members did suggest a resonance:

*Wow!! Whoa! I feel that MyndiR you have written the holy grail synopsis of my life biorhythm!... I don't think I ever accepted my rhythm for what it is and narrowed it down like this. #totallystruckinawe #thanksfortheadvicetoplan – QnVz*

Community members were also reminded of points that they were aware of, but had forgotten: "Thanks for reminding me about the Healing Trauma CD" (findjoyagain).

It has been argued that fluidity in online communities nurtures a dynamic flow of resources such as passion, time, identity, social disembodiment of ideas, socially ambiguous identities, and temporary convergence (Faraj, Jarvenpaa, & Majchrzak, 2011). We saw the enthusiasm for this temporary convergence in the words of the participants.

### Sense of Community

Sense of community has long been a popular topic in research pertaining to both online and offline environments (Blanchard, 2007; Liu, Magjuka, Bonk, & Lee, 2007). Sense of community and participation in online support groups have been shown to be positively associated with health outcomes (van Uden-Kraan et al., 2008; Welbourne, Blanchard, & Boughton, 2009).

In order to foster a sense of community, we endeavored to create a strong sense of social presence. Social presence has been defined as "the extent to which a medium allows a user to experience others as being psychologically present" (Gefen & Straub, 2003, p. 11). The research team shared their names, photos, and aspects of their life experience relevant to the project, on the site. Other than this and their ability to create forum threads, no other distinction was made between them and participants. This is different from other online discussion studies, such as Ferrante et al. (2016), who defined moderators "as someone who would clarify postings, elicit elaboration or explanation, foster interaction, encourage reflection, keep participants on track, offer support, and enforce the rules of engagement" (p. 1854). The moderators aimed to create a community of individuals working toward a shared goal, who shared similar journeys and experiences – and endeavored to avoid power inequities which would emphasize differences.

Much qualitative work occurs face-to-face where human encounters can soften the divide between those approaches. Online however, there is not the same opportunity to exploit the advantages of a warm smile or an introductory handshake to build trust and rapport. Given the lack of shared physical space or context, and the removal from human cues (such as the audible voice of a moderator), for the perception of community, diction and tone held more import than in non-digital or semi-digital qualitative studies. Nielsen (1990) posits, "all knowledge is culture-bound, theory-bound, and/or historically specific" (p. 3) and it stands to reason that the data that produces said knowledge is as well. Cultivating a sense of community was crucial to the study's success, given how isolating living with.a chronic illness can be – as expressed by the study's participants. Boboo began a post with, "Fibromyalgia has been very isolating experience for me."

Moderators' tactic of using their own experience to show that difference was allowed and encouraged cultivated a community atmosphere that did not delegitimize or question what someone shared. Instead, participants and moderators typically affirmed someone's response and/or mentioned that it aligned with their experience(s). Even if their experiences and backgrounds were different – they were not alone. Researcher contributions implicitly and explicitly set the tone that difference was allowed and could find sanctuary in the project. One participant, byrt, wrote, "Forgive any strange language or dropped words. cfs affects language for me too, especially right now when I'm post PT and quite sleepy!" to which Gail responded, "Byrt, thank you for sharing this and I am happy that you have a system that is working for you. The tracking, the stickers (a key component!) and the feedback loop with your PT are essential to your success. BTW, everything came through loud and clear, no language issues were detected."

Moderators also nurtured the nascent community with gratitude. Marygrace validated and thanked the sharer for their contribution by writing, "I have friends who swear by their netipots, and I've been meaning to try that approach, thanks for the reminder. #netipotforallergies." The moderators were also acknowledged for their contributions: "This is very helpful to me" wrote findjoyagain, in response to Gail's post on acceptance.

We believe these interactions successfully engendered a sense of community. During the first week, QnVz wrote:

*Now knowing that I am not [alone], it makes the journey to finding answers more doable for me and I am thankful it is possible to move forward from the comatose state ☺. #littlethingseveryday*

### Membership

We have described two more abstract factors affecting community, a sense of purpose and a sense of community. We now turn to a discussion of more structural factors, including member composition, size, and activity.

The study website stated that anyone over the age of 21 who was interested in or would like to contribute to knowledge on "body listening" was eligible to participate, and we employed multiple recruitment mechanisms that were not disease-specific, including university listservs and flyers in high traffic areas such as university campuses and coffee shops. However, we also engaged in social media recruitment efforts targeting conditions of interest such as chronic pain, Fibromyalgia, Chronic Fatigue Syndrome, and Irritable Bowel Syndrome. These conditions were selected because they have unclear etiologies, share similar symptoms, and are often comorbid with one another.

On the one hand, our intention was to open up the study to all, and potentially increase the diversity of viewpoints and experiences offered on "body listening." On the other hand, we wanted to ensure that we collected an adequate amount of content on the particular conditions of interest.

There are strengths and weaknesses to this positioning. The main strengths were the potential for diverse viewpoints and for participation on the part of people that did not have conditions that we had explicitly targeted, and these goals were achieved. However, the fact that the study focused on topics that have been shown to be of interest to our target conditions might have meant that those who were not explicitly targeted did not find the Guided Exploration topics of interest, and thus did not participate.

One might wonder why it was necessary to select focal conditions at all. From a practical point of view, in any study, one must identify a population or populations from which to sample and select recruitment venues accordingly. Aside from these practical concerns, the potential for conflicting information was considered. For example, with conditions such as diabetes, patients may be accustomed to the use of medical devices for health management, and this may not be the case in other conditions. In this study, there was an effort to minimize exposure to conflicting information by selecting conditions in which people might develop similar health management strategies.

As previously illustrated, participants expressed sentiments reflecting demonstrated benefits from the information exchange. However, it is perhaps inevitable that within any community, there are members of the group who share a greater proportion of common experiences with others, and those who share less, and there may be participants who did not end up feeling as if their experiences resonated with the larger whole. Within the context of this study, the shared experience was to come from the experience of engaging in "body listening" or self-management, and thus, the differences in people's health histories most likely then accounted for their shared experience, or lack thereof.

One might think of large health-related online communities and/or social networks, where there are countless participants who may never post, and interventions with a virtual chat room feature, with a smaller number of participants that may engage in more sustained activity. This study perhaps tended towards the former, and with this, there are strengths/weaknesses. Over the course of the ten-week study, 234 participants registered to participate, and ultimately, 28 participants actually participated in a visible way by posting. Thus, similar to previous studies of online communities and discussion forums, we had a high proportion of "lurkers", who are users who visit online communities, but rarely post (Sun, Rau, & Ma, 2014).

Participants also varied in their extent of participation. Among those who posted in the ThinkSpace were individuals who were quite prolific, and many others who only posted once or twice. While this variation is common in large-scale social networks, it may be worthwhile to employ additional strategies to increase participation, including messaging new participants directly to invite them to participate. It might also help to make activities other than posting visible, including the integration of displays showing recent visitors, current page views, or rating and voting tools. These features might increase the sense of activity within the community (Malinen, 2015).

### *Conflicting Research Design Priorities*

This study raises some critical questions about the cultivation of community. First, we emphasized the creation of a knowledge resource as the ultimate goal of this community. Is this focus on knowledge construction congruent with the tendency of this type of community to provide virtual support, or does the function of support hinder the collective production of knowledge? For example, one might consider the emotional support helpful in the sense that a heightened sense of support might be accompanied by a greater desire to contribute. Alternatively, one might argue that the question of whether one feels emotionally supported is moot, since there is inherent value in a vehicle for social support, regardless of whether it leads to greater knowledge. Is it even possible to separate emotional support from informational support?

Another interesting question might be whether sustenance of participation is even an important consideration in a community such as this. Given that knowledge collaboration was the stated purpose of this study, perhaps continuity among the participants is not so important. To this, we offer a couple of points of discussion. First, if the goals of the research were to reach as broad of a span of people as possible with little regard for eliciting depth of experience of any given individual, it might be sufficient to reach out to individuals. However, in a study such as this where arguably, our aim is to engage "knowledge workers", the type of community that we should attempt to nurture is akin to communities of practice: "groups of people who share a concern, a set of problems, or a passion about a topic, and who deepen their knowledge and expertise in this area by interacting on an ongoing basis" (Wenger, McDermott, & Snyder, 2002, p.4). In such communities, satisfaction with being able to help can also affect people's intention to continue sharing (Cheung, Lee, & Lee, 2013).

Thus, we speculate here whether reaching out to and sustaining the involvement of a dedicated team in a longer-term effort of collaborative knowledge production might increase productivity. If a group of patient experts were to engage in collaborative knowledge work over time, might they become more productive due to greater familiarity with one another and with the work, as might occur with work teams? Extant literature has reported that duration of community membership is positively associated with tag contribution (Nov, Naaman, & Ye, 2010). There is perhaps also opportunity to experiment with other structures for knowledge production. For example, we might create subgroups that brainstorm together and then pool the results of their contributions, which would mix public and private components of activity for those who are not comfortable contributing publicly. Lastly, perhaps clearer indicators of progress in the building of the repository might encourage participants to contribute more and/or stay engaged longer.

## CONCLUSION

In this paper, we provided a reflexive account of the design of the Body Listening Project, a participatory platform in which participants engaged collectively in the building of a public repository. The project and participatory platform was an active, evolving environment shaped by participants of different backgrounds. In particular, we elaborated upon three critical aspects of our research design: researcher stance, the nature of data, and community development. It is our hope that explicating the design decisions that were made in this study can help researchers evaluate their own stances in other projects, as well as inform the design of future studies. In online participatory settings when we cannot share space and, perhaps, time, we can at least share authentic experiences to build trust and rapport.


## ACKNOWLEDGMENTS

The authors wish to acknowledge and express our profound gratitude to the participants of the Body Listening Project, as well as the other members of the research team.


## REFERENCES


Blanchard, A. L. (2007). Developing a sense of virtual community measure. *CyberPsychology & Behavior*, *10*(6), 827-830. https://doi.org/10.1089/cpb.2007.9946

Buchanan, E. A. (2011). Internet research ethics: Past, present, and future. In *The handbook of internet studies* (pp. 83-108). West Sussex, UK: Wiley-Blackwell.

Carter-Edwards, L., Skelly, A. H., Cagle, C. S., & Appel, S. J. (2004). "They care but don't understand": Family support of African American women with type 2 diabetes. *The Diabetes Educator*, *30*(3), 493-501. https://doi.org/10.1177/014572170403000321

Celi, L. A., Ippolito, A., Montgomery, R. A., Moses, C., & Stone, D. J. (2014). Crowdsourcing knowledge discovery and innovations in medicine. *Journal of Medical Internet Research*, *16*(9), e216. https://doi.org/10.2196/jmir.3761

Charmaz, K. (2014). *Constructing grounded theory* (2nd ed.). London ; Thousand Oaks, Calif: Sage.

Chen, A. T., Carriere, R., Kaplan, S. J., Colht, K., Morey, O. T., Flaherty, M. G., ... Price, C. (2016). Exploring collective tagging as a mechanism to elicit language about health management. In *Proceedings of the 79th ASIS&T annual meeting: Creating knowledge, enhancing lives through information & technology* (p. 104:1-104:6). Copenhagen, Denmark: American Society for Information Science.

Cheung, C. M. K., Lee, M. K. O., & Lee, Z. W. Y. (2013). Understanding the continuance intention of knowledge sharing in online communities of practice through the post-knowledge-sharing evaluation processes. *Journal of the American Society for Information Science and Technology*, *64*(7), 1357-1374. https://doi.org/10.1002/asi.22854

Doing-Harris, K. M., & Zeng-Treitler, Q. (2011). Computer-assisted update of a consumer health vocabulary through mining of social network data. *Journal of Medical Internet Research*, *13*(2). https://doi.org/10.2196/jmir.1636

Dwyer, S. C., & Buckle, J. L. (2009). The space between: on being an insider-outsider in qualitative research. *International Journal of Qualitative Methods*, *8*(1), 54-63. https://doi.org/10.1177/160940690900800105

Faraj, S., Jarvenpaa, S. L., & Majchrzak, A. (2011). Knowledge collaboration in online communities. *Organization Science*, *22*(5), 1224-1239. https://doi.org/10.1287/orsc.1100.0614

Ferrante, J. M., Friedman, A., Shaw, E. K., Howard, J., Cohen, D. J., & Shahidi, L. (2016). Lessons learned designing and using an online discussion forum for care coordinators in primary care. *Qualitative Health Research*, *26*(13), 1851-1861.

Gefen, D., & Straub, D. W. (2003). Managing user trust in B2C e-services. *E-Service Journal*, *2*(2), 7-24.

Gold, R. L. (1958). Roles in sociological field observations. *Social Forces*, *36*(3), 217-223. https://doi.org/10.2307/2573808

Greenwood, D. J., & Levin, M. (2007). *Introduction to action research: Social research for social change* (2nd ed). Thousand Oaks, Calif: Sage Publications.

Harris, M. (1964). *The nature of cultural things*. Random House.

Harris, M. (2015). "Three in the room" embodiment, disclosure, and vulnerability in qualitative research. *Qualitative Health Research*, 1049732314566324.

Hine, C. (2000). *Virtual ethnography*. SAGE.

Holloway, I., & Biley, F. C. (2011). Being a qualitative researcher. *Qualitative Health Research*, *21*(7), 968-975.

Kool, M. B., van Middendorp, H., Boeije, H. R., & Geenen, R. (2009). Understanding the lack of understanding: Invalidation from the perspective of the patient with fibromyalgia. *Arthritis & Rheumatism*, *61*(12), 1650-1656. https://doi.org/10.1002/art.24922

Kuper, A., Reeves, S., & Levinson, W. (2008). An introduction to reading and appraising qualitative research. *BMJ*, *337*, a288. https://doi.org/10.1136/bmj.a288

Lee, C. P. (2007). Boundary negotiating artifacts: Unbinding the routine of boundary objects and embracing chaos in collaborative work. *Computer Supported Cooperative Work (CSCW)*, *16*(3), 307–339.

Liu, X., Magjuka, R. J., Bonk, C. J., & Lee, S. (2007). Does sense of community matter? An examination of participants' perceptions of building learning communities in online courses. *Quarterly Review of Distance Education: Research That Guides Practice*, *8*(1), 9–24.

Malinen, S. (2015). Understanding user participation in online communities: A systematic literature review of empirical studies. *Computers in Human Behavior*, *46*, 228–238. https://doi.org/10.1016/j.chb.2015.01.004

McKee, H. A., & Porter, J. E. (2009). *The ethics of internet research: A rhetorical, case-based process*. Peter Lang.

Mehling, W. E., Gopisetty, V., Daubenmier, J., Price, C. J., Hecht, F. M., & Stewart, A. (2009). Body awareness: Construct and self-report measures. *PLoS ONE*, *4*(5), e5614. https://doi.org/10.1371/journal.pone.0005614

Merriam, S. B., Johnson-Bailey, J., Lee, M.-Y., Kee, Y., Ntseane, G., & Muhamad, M. (2001). Power and positionality: Negotiating insider/outsider status within and across cultures. *International Journal of Lifelong Education*, *20*(5), 405-416. https://doi.org/10.1080/02601370120490

Mills, J., Bonner, A., & Francis, K. (2006). The development of constructivist grounded theory. *International Journal of Qualitative Methods*, *5*(1), 25-35.

Nielsen, J. M. (1990). *Feminist research methods: Exemplary readings in the social sciences*. Westview Press.

Nov, O., Naaman, M., & Ye, C. (2010). Analysis of participation in an online photo-sharing community: A multidimensional perspective. *Journal of the American Society for Information Science and Technology*, *61*(3), 555-566. https://doi.org/10.1002/asi.21278

Olive, J. L. (2014). Reflecting on the tensions between emic and etic perspectives in life history research: Lessons learned. In *Forum qualitative sozialforschung/forum: qualitative social research* (Vol. 15). Retrieved from http://www.qualitative-research.net/index.php/fqs/article/view/2072

Pike, K. L. (1967). *Language in relation to a unified theory of the structures of human behavior*. The Hague: Mouton.

Sade-Beck, L. (2004). Internet ethnography: Online and offline. *International Journal of Qualitative Methods*, *3*(2), 45-51. https://doi.org/10.1177/160940690400300204

Schulman-Green, D., Jaser, S., Martin, F., Alonzo, A., Grey, M., McCorkle, R., … Whittemore, R. (2012). Processes of self-management in chronic illness: Self-management processes. *Journal of Nursing Scholarship*, *44*(2), 136-144. https://doi.org/10.1111/j.1547-5069.2012.01444.x

Star, S. L., & Griesemer, J. R. (1989). Institutional ecology,'translations' and boundary objects: Amateurs and professionals in Berkeley's Museum of Vertebrate Zoology, 1907-39. *Social Studies of Science*, *19*(3), 387-420.

Sun, N., Rau, P. P.-L., & Ma, L. (2014). Understanding lurkers in online communities: A literature review. *Computers in Human Behavior*, *38*, 110-117. https://doi.org/10.1016/j.chb.2014.05.022

Swan, M. (2012). Scaling crowdsourced health studies: The emergence of a new form of contract research organization. *Personalized Medicine*, *9*(2), 223-234. https://doi.org/10.2217/pme.11.97

Ussher, J., Kirsten, L., Butow, P., & Sandoval, M. (2006). What do cancer support groups provide which other supportive relationships do not? The experience of peer support groups for people with cancer. *Social Science & Medicine*, *62*(10), 2565-2576. https://doi.org/10.1016/j.socscimed.2005.10.034

van Uden-Kraan, C. F., Drossaert, C. H. C., Taal, E., Shaw, B. R., Seydel, E. R., & van de Laar, M. A. F. J. (2008). Empowering processes and outcomes of participation in online support groups for patients with breast cancer, arthritis, or fibromyalgia. *Qualitative Health Research*, *18*(3), 405-417. https://doi.org/10.1177/1049732307313429

Welbourne, J. L., Blanchard, A. L., & Boughton, M. D. (2009). Supportive communication, sense of virtual community and health outcomes in online infertility groups. In *Proceedings of the fourth international conference on communities and technologies* (pp. 31–40). ACM.

Wenger, E., McDermott, R. A., & Snyder, W. (2002). *Cultivating communities of practice: A guide to managing knowledge*. Harvard Business Press.

Whittemore, R., Chase, S. K., & Mandle, C. L. (2001). Validity in qualitative research. *Qualitative Health Research*, *11*(4), 522-537.

Xia, J. (2011). An anthropological emic-etic perspective on open access practices. *Journal of Documentation*, *67*(1), 75-94. https://doi.org/10.1108/00220411111105461

# Evaluation of Features to Predict the Usefulness of Online Reviews

**Heejun Kim**
*School of Information and Library Science, University of North Carolina, USA. heejunk@email.unc.edu*

**Jaime Arguello**
*School of Information and Library Science, University of North Carolina, USA. jarguello@unc.edu*

## ABSTRACT

**Checking online reviews before purchasing goods or using services has become increasingly common. However, it is difficult to select useful reviews, and concerns about fake reviews are growing. Many online review systems use recency and user-generated usefulness votes in order to prioritize reviews for users, but there is much room for improvement. In this work, we focus on evaluating the effectiveness of a large number of features for predicting the usefulness of online reviews, including features that have not been commonly evaluated in prior work (e.g., social network measures). Features were grouped into hierarchical categories that might represent factors impacting perceived usefulness of Yelp users. Using all features, a binary classifier achieved a high level of accuracy (0.889). Additionally, a feature ablation study found that several feature groups yielded statistically significant improvements. Interestingly, many of the features that improved performance are not the types of measures that are displayed to users in commercial online review services such as Yelp and are the measures that are rarely used to prioritize reviews for users. Our study results suggest different types of information that online review services might want to use in ranking and displaying reviews for users.**

## KEYWORDS

online review, text mining, review usefulness, review quality, fake review

## INTRODUCTION

Purchasing goods or services online is becoming as commonplace as purchasing offline. It has also become more common to consult related reviews before purchasing services such as hotels and restaurants. Making online purchase decisions is difficult, as there is a certain limit to experiencing and testing the goods or services before making an actual purchase. Therefore, online consumers read other people's reviews, predict the quality of products or services, and make final purchase decisions. Reading online reviews is the first step in most decision-making processes involving online purchasing (Levi & Mokryn, 2014).

80th Annual Meeting of the Association for Information Science & Technology, Washington, DC, VA | Oct. 27-Nov. 1, 2017



Online reviews, especially the top reviews, have a huge influence on sales. Existing studies have uncovered that online consumers are paying particular attention to reviews on the first two pages (Racherla & Friske, 2012). Clemons et al. (2006) found that the strength of the reviews in the top quartile have a positive and significant correlation with sales of microbrewery products. In other words, the influence of a few reviews is disproportionately larger than the influence of other reviews. Therefore, having positive reviews in the top is important to sellers, and placing reviews with useful information in the top is also important to online review services such as Yelp.

Concerns about fake reviews are also growing because online reviews have a huge impact on the market. An extra half-star rating for a particular online review can lead to a 19% increase in sales at restaurants (Anderson & Magruder, 2012). Due to the benefits that extra star ratings can make, many restaurateurs are tempted to leave fake reviews (Anderson & Magruder, 2012). According to the analysis by Luca and Zervas (2013), 16% of Yelp users were predicted to be fake users. Therefore, it is critical for online review services to decide the rank of reviews to show to their users, and for users to find and select relevant, useful, and credible reviews.

Online review systems are different from search engines. There are usually no search keywords from users and thus no textual similarity is used to decide the order of display. The most commonly used criteria to determine the order of online reviews are recency (Kim, Pantel, Chklovski, & Pennacchiotti, 2006) and usefulness votes from users (Racherla & Friske, 2012). The latest reviews are helpful, but there are many chances that useful reviews will be buried down under the screen. As Amazon.com prioritizes the top two most favorable and critical reviews ranked by other consumers, peer ranking of reviews has been regarded as the best method for prioritizing useful reviews (Racherla & Friske, 2012). However, it is uncertain whether these criteria are sufficient to select useful reviews.

In the peer online review, especially, it is not clear who the information provider is and what social reputation he/she has. Previous studies have used heuristics from past behaviors such as the number of total reviews (Weiss, Lurie, & MacInnis, 2008) and positive feedback from others (e.g., number of friends), but it is difficult to link those simple heuristics to the social relationship and corresponding social reputation. Although Yelp dataset has a wealth of network-related information (e.g., list of friends) indicating relationships among users, it has been uncommon to apply social network metrics to the prediction of the usefulness of Yelp reviews. Thus, we applied social network metrics as features for machine learning to examine whether the social relationship can be an indicator of the usefulness of Yelp reviews.

While most online review services and retailers rely on peer judgments (e.g., "usefulness votes") to prioritize reviews for users (Racherla & Friske, 2012), content-based informational cues are also likely to influence the perceived usefulness of a review (Forman, Ghose, & Wiesenfeld, 2008). As an example, Wilson (1983) argues that the plausibility of information can influence the degree of cognitive authority attributed to the author of the information. According to uncertainty reduction theory, the value of a review assessed by a user increases when it provides more information (Daft & Lengel, 1986). Similarly, prior studies have explored content-based features such as sentiment (Levi & Mokryn, 2014) and length of the text (Chevalier & Mayzlin, 2006; Gupta & Harris, 2010) to predict the usefulness of a review. We build on this prior work and include additional content-based features aimed to measure the informativeness of an online review.

In this paper, we focus on the task of predicting the usefulness of Yelp reviews. To this end, we explored a wide range of features, derived from the review content, author, and business. In particular, we used features based on social network metrics to capture the social relationships among users and features that can represent the informativeness of the review content. We grouped our features into multiple categories (e.g., informativeness, sentiment, readability, and reputation) forming a three-level hierarchy and analyzed each category (i.e., group of individual features) as a potential factor in predicting the usefulness of a Yelp review. A feature ablation study was conducted to determine the marginal contribution of different feature categories. Several different feature categories were found to be significantly predictive of usefulness. Our results have potential implications for the design of online review services such as Yelp. For instance, our feature ablation analysis points to important features that should be used to display and prioritize reviews for users.

## BACKGROUND AND RELATED WORK

The usefulness of online reviews is important for consumers to find practical information in daily life, for local business operators to make profits, and for information scientists to present users with relevant information in the right order. Therefore, there have been various studies relevant to this topic in different fields, but we focused on the previous studies that are related to factors affecting usefulness and predictive modeling in this survey.

According to Horgan (1987), evaluative judgment refers to expressing preference after people inspect the search results, while predictive judgment denotes the expectation of what will happen before people actually look at the search results. When considering a huge amount of information enabled by the development of information technology, the predictive judgment becomes more and more important (Rieh & Danielson, 2007). In the case of online shopping, factors that signal the product quality are more important than in offline shopping for decision making (Biswas & Biswas, 2004). It is important to know where those factors that signal product quality originate. Judgments of online reviews include information processing as well as social processing underlying word-of-mouth (WOM). Therefore, both informational as well as social cues play an important role in the dissemination and acceptance of online reviews (Forman, Ghose, & Wiesenfeld, 2008; Racherla & Friske, 2012).

Usefulness and credibility are different, but they are closely related. Petty and Cacioppo (1986) argue that only credible information is typically recognized as useful. When searching for useful information, people often make decisions based on the concepts of quality and authority (Rieh & Belkin, 2000). When predicting based on machine learning, it is imperative to understand the factors that influence the prediction and to create features that successfully operationalize them. Features on other relevant concepts such as credibility will be helpful and selectively included in this study because the research on predictive modeling for the usefulness of online reviews is not very rich. The features operationalizing factors affecting usefulness judgment in previous studies are divided into two related to source and content, and are summarized below.

The desire to be socially perceived is a powerful motivation for people to leave useful online reviews and can be an important clue to finding useful online reviews (Racherla & Friske, 2012). Bator and Cialdini (2000) find reputation to be one of the basic principles in the process of persuasion. The following source-related features have been investigated in the context of online reviews: number of friends, number of compliments (Racherla & Friske, 2012), reviewer impact score tweaking h-index (Levi & Mokryn, 2014), elite of the year (Racherla & Friske, 2012), identity disclosure (e.g., name and photo) (Fogg et al., 2001), number of reviews (Weiss, Lurie, & MacInnis, 2008), and perceived social similarity (Smith, Menon, & Sivakumar, 2005).

Social network metrics can represent actual social relationships better than the features mentioned above. Network analysis originated from sociology to find meaningful patterns in people's social networks. The Yelp dataset we used has rich network-related attributes (e.g., list of friends) that can be used for network analysis, so there have been several related studies. However, they focused on the role of social networks in customer relationship management (Mosadegh & Behboudi, 2011), personalized entity recommendation (He & Chu, 2010), and prediction of star rating a user gives to a restaurant (W. Yang, Yuan, & Zhang, 2015). Social network metrics have rarely been used to predict the usefulness of Yelp reviews, although there is a great potential in those metrics. To our knowledge, there is one study (Lu, Tsaparas, Ntoulas, & Polanyi, 2010) to exploit social network metrics (degree and PageRank) in the context of predicting review usefulness or helpfulness.

Attributes of the source of the review are often peripheral cues to select useful reviews, while attributes of the review itself are more likely to influence its usefulness. Prior work has considered the following content-based features: star ratings (Racherla & Friske, 2012; J. Yang, Kim, Amblee, & Jeong, 2012), message sidedness and extremeness (Cheung, Luo, Sia, & Chen, 2009; Schlosser, 2005), vividness and strength of the message (Sweeney, Soutar, & Mazzarol, 2008), sentiment (Levi & Mokryn, 2014; Sweeney, Soutar, & Mazzarol, 2008), amount of information (Chevalier & Mayzlin, 2006), and organization/structure of information presentation (Rieh, 2002).

Previous studies that looked at factors affecting judgments of usefulness (or helpfulness) in online reviews used Amazon reviews (Ghose & Ipeirotis, 2011; Kim, Pantel, Chklovski, & Pennacchiotti, 2006), Yelp Reviews (Levi & Mokryn, 2014; López & Farzan, 2014; Pentina, Bailey, & Zhang, 2015; Racherla & Friske, 2012), or other sources (Lu, Tsaparas, Ntoulas, & Polanyi, 2010). Of this prior work, three studies (Ghose & Ipeirotis, 2011; Kim, Pantel, Chklovski, & Pennacchiotti, 2006; Lu, Tsaparas, Ntoulas, & Polanyi, 2010) have focused on predicting the usefulness of an online review. We build on this prior work by considering a larger number of features and evaluating the predictiveness of different feature groups.

## METHODOLOGY

### Data

We utilized the dataset provided as part of Yelp Dataset Challenge ("Yelp Dataset Challenge," 2017). Yelp is the largest business listing site for service businesses. Due to the large data size, Yelp is considered as a representative online review service when considering service review part only (Racherla & Friske, 2012). The dataset contains online reviews of local businesses across four countries (US, Canada, England, and Germany) written between March 2005 and July 2016. There are 2,685,065 reviews written by 686,555 reviewers for 85,950 local businesses.

Data for review, reviewer, and business were provided as JSON objects in separate files. The last date when the online review was written is July 19th, 2016. The data includes attributes that can be used as features of machine learning by themselves and also has attributes that can be converted to features through processing, such as review texts and lists of friends. The review object has star rating, review text, date, and number of votes for "*useful*," "*funny*," and "*cool*." The business object includes basic information about local businesses such as location, star rating, review count, and service category. The user object consists of review count, average stars, number of compliments, and list of friends.

In order to develop and evaluate predictive models for usefulness, we decided to use the number of "usefulness votes" associated with each Yelp review. One important factor that can influence the number of Yelp "usefulness votes" is the review's exposure time---older reviews have a greater opportunity of accumulating "usefulness votes" than newer ones. In order to control for this potential confounding factor, we decided to sample reviews written during the limited time period: April to June 2015. By sampling reviews from this three-month time period, we aimed to control for exposure time and also selected some of the most recent reviews available in this dataset. We also excluded reviews in which the percentage of English words is less than 70%. This threshold value was set slightly low because emoticons were not counted as English.

In this work, we decided to cast the usefulness prediction task as binary classification rather than regression. Thus, it was necessary to determine how to binarize the data into "*useful*" and "*not_useful*" labels using the number of usefulness votes. The distribution of the number of usefulness votes is highly positively skewed (Table 1). The average is 0.81 and the median is 0. For the experiments, the threshold $\zeta$ was set to 2 and binary labels were generated using the following heuristic. Reviews with two or more "usefulness votes" were considered *useful* and reviews with zero "usefulness votes" were considered *not_useful*. Reviews with one "usefulness vote" were ignored in order to reduce ambiguity, for example by ignoring "usefulness votes" produced by accident or by fake users. Finally, in order to create a balanced dataset, we randomly sampled an equal number of *useful* and *not_useful* reviews. In total, our final dataset contained 42,722 reviews.

| Min | Median | Mean | Max | SD |
|---|---|---|---|---|
| 0 | 0 | 0.81 | 137 | 2.12 |

***Table 1**. Distribution of the number of usefulness votes*

### Features

Features utilized in this study are grouped into three categories at the top: content, source, and business. The content and source categories, but not business, have subcategories. For the business category, there is not enough information in the Yelp dataset to create sub-categories. Each category was designed to represent a potential factor influencing the perceived usefulness of a Yelp review. We utilized 104 features in total. The overall hierarchy of the feature categories is summarized in Table 2, and a description of each feature type is provided below. The numbers in parentheses indicate the number of features corresponding to each category.

#### Content (69)

We generated features related to content from the review by using natural language processing (NLP). WordNet-Affect (Strapparava & Valitutti, 2004) is an extension of WordNet database (Miller, 1995) and includes a subset of synsets that represent affective concepts and corresponding words. For example, *joy* is one of the positive emotional concepts, and *amusement*, *happiness*, and *cheerfulness* are its corresponding words. We counted the frequency of sentiment related words corresponding to each concept and normalized it using the total word count of the review.

| Top-level | Middle-level | Lower-level |
|---|---|---|
| Content | Informativeness | Content informativeness |
| | | Rating informativeness |
| | Sentiment | Positive sentiment |
| | | Neutral sentiment |
| | | Negative sentiment |
| | Readability | |
| Source | Reputation | Extrinsic reputation |
| | | Intrinsic reputation |
| | Geographical entropy | |
| Business | | |

***Table 2.*** *Hierarchy of feature categories*

Our emotion detection method uses a bag-of-words representation. One of the most challenging parts of sentiment analysis is negation (Wiegand, Balahur, Roth, Klakow, & Montoyo, 2010). Thus, we were also interested in modeling negated emotions. Stanford CoreNLP (Manning et al., 2014) is one of the most popular NLP tools and the accuracy of its negation detection module reaches up to 81.8% (Socher et al., 2013). When a negated word was found using Stanford CoreNLP, the concept of the corresponding emotion was reversed. For instance, if the word "*amusement*" is negated, a reversed concept called "*not_joy*" was used to update the frequency. In other words, we doubled the number of affective concepts by introducing "negated affective concepts". The Natural Language Tool Kit (NLTK) (Bird, 2006) was used for all other NLP tasks such as tokenization and removal of stopwords.

Although the informativeness of the review has a considerable effect on the usefulness evaluation, features relevant to the informativeness have not been introduced in the previous studies with the exception of simple features such as the length of a review. We created three features in the content informativeness category by examining 200 randomly selected reviews. The new features were limited to the ones that can operationalize the informativeness of the review. For instance, we found that a review is useful if the content is structured by describing pros and cons or price information is included. The detailed features that correspond to each category are described below and separated by bullets.

- Content informativeness features (4): Measures informativeness of content. We included: the count of words, whether the review is structured (e.g., pros/cons, +/-, and plus/minus), whether the review includes ratings for a specific aspect (e.g., taste, service, and amenity), and the count of price information.
- Rating informativeness features (3): Measures informativeness from ratings. There are three types of star ratings: the average of all ratings received by the business, the average of all the ratings the reviewer has made, and the average of all ratings on a specific review. The deviation among average star ratings for the business, review, and reviewer can deliver abnormality of a specific review. We included: the review's average star rating, absolute difference between the review's average star rating and the business's average star rating, and absolute difference between the review's average star rating and the reviewer's average star rating.
- Positive sentiment features (22): Measures specific positive emotion such as *joy*, *love*, and *affection* as well as aggregate positive emotion combining frequencies of all positive concepts.
- Neutral sentiment features (2): Measures specific neutral emotion of apathy as well as aggregate neutral emotion combining frequencies of all neutral concepts.
- Negative sentiment features (22): Measures specific negative emotion such as *sadness*, *shame*, and *despair* as well as aggregate negative emotion combining frequencies of all negative concepts.
- Readability features (10): Measures readability of each review. In prior work (Eysenbach, Powell, Kuss, & Sa, 2002), readability is considered as one of the major criteria in deciding quality of Web content. Due to space constraints, we refer the reader to the systematic review of readability scores available in Friedman and Goetz (2006). We included: ARI, FleschReadingEase, FleschKincaidGradeLevel, GunningFogIndex, ColemanLiauIndex, LIX, and RIX. The accuracy of spelling and the diversity of words can also affect readability although they are not part of readability scores, so we included both features as well.
- Other sentiment features (6): Some sentiment features were difficult to be classified into any of the above sentiment categories. A review may be useful when the sentiment in the review matches its star rating. For instance, a positive review with five-star rating might indicate real satisfaction of a user involving a useful review. In order to capture this type of evidence, we generated four additional features by using the cross-product between positive/negative sentiment weights and the review's star rating or the business' star rating. Polarity and subjectivity were also included by using TextBlob library[1].

### Source (32)

Features related to source (reviewer) were generated from the user profile. Simple features such as the number of compliments were extracted from the user profile and more complex features such as social network metrics based on the list of friends were created by the Pajek tool (Batagelj & Mrvar, 1998). We categorized simple features that can be extracted

[1] https://textblob.readthedocs.io/en/dev/

from the user profile and are displayed to users in Yelp as extrinsic reputation. The more complex features of social network metrics were categorized as intrinsic reputation, because it is difficult for a user to know even though it actually exists.

We created four new features in the source category. It was hypothesized that if a reviewer left a lot of reviews for local businesses in different cities within a short period of time, it could be problematic. In other words, we assumed that if the distance that a user traveled for making reviews is not rational compared to other users, the user is likely to be a fake one. We refer to this feature category as the user's *geographical entropy*.

One important factor that influences reputation-related attributes in the user profile is the difference in exposure time. Older users are more likely to receive more votes than newer users. Therefore, we normalized those features by using the period the reviewer has used Yelp.

- Extrinsic reputation (18): This category is to capture the previous activities of a user and his/her corresponding explicit reputation. We included: the number of past reviews, the number of fans, the average of star ratings the reviewer made, the total months the user used Yelp, the number of compliments from other users for a specific aspect of the reviews (e.g., profile, writing, and photo), and whether the user was selected as an elite user in 2015.
- Intrinsic reputation (10): This category is to capture the importance of a user on social networks in Yelp and the user's corresponding implicit reputation. We included: degree, betweenness, eigenvector, clustering coefficient, and closeness. These five features were calculated based on the friendship among all Yelp users without considering the time when the reviewers left the review. We reapplied the same five metrics by only considering the relationships among users who left a review between April 2015 and June 2015. As a result, 10 features were produced. Due to space constraints, we refer the reader to the book written by Borgatti et al. (2013) on more details about those social network metrics.
- Geographical entropy (4): This feature category captures the geographical distance among the businesses associated with a user's reviews. We assumed that users visited local businesses in the time order that they wrote reviews. We included: the total distance to the centroid from each local business a user visited, the total distance for a user to navigate in the time order, the sum of the distance from each local business to others, and the number of visits.

#### Business (3)

Business itself can have an effect on gaining usefulness votes. If the business is very good, there is a good chance that there will be more good reviews. When consumers have uncertainty, they use brand reputation as a signal of product quality (Erdem & Swait, 2004). We included the business's average star rating, the number of reviews on the business, and whether the business was open as of July 2016 when the Yelp dataset started being distributed to the public.

### Experimental Procedure

We trained logistic regression classifiers and tested the performance of them using the features described above in predicting the binary class of usefulness of each review in the Yelp data. Logistic regression classifier predicts dependent variable as a function of a set of independent variables. Logistic regression is appropriate for cases where we have a binary dependent variable (*useful* and *not_useful* in this study) and several binary or continuous independent variables. Logistic regression has been used successfully for similar predictive tasks and the main focus of this paper is on measuring the marginal contribution of different feature types by conducting a feature ablation study. Latest algorithms such as deep learning might be effective in terms of increasing performance. However, there are convoluted nodes in the hidden layers of deep learning that make it difficult to comprehend which factors are influential in determining the usefulness of reviews. The logistic regression classifier based on generalized linear model was implemented by using R Caret package.

We trained and evaluated models using 30-fold cross-validation. The 30-folds were randomly selected and the same 30-folds were used in all experiments. The evaluation metric is the classification accuracy, as it is most intuitive to examine the results when binary classification is done using an evenly distributed dataset. The reported accuracy is the average accuracy across 30 iterations.

While creating our data for training and testing, we used the threshold of $\zeta = 2$ in deciding whether a review is useful. Levi & Mokryn (2014) also used Yelp data, but considered a threshold of $\zeta = 5$. In other words, reviews with five or more "usefulness votes" were considered *useful* and reviews with less than five "usefulness votes" were considered *not_useful*. We also present classification results using $\zeta = 5$, but only reviews with zero "usefulness vote" were considered *not_useful*. All other reported results are based on the threshold of 2.

We conducted an extensive feature ablation study to look at the marginal contribution of these different feature groups. In the feature ablation study, the same 30-folds from the previous experiment were used for all experiments. The accuracies of each fold obtained using the full features were compared with the accuracies of the same fold obtained using reduced feature set in which features in one feature category were removed. In this way, we could examine the influence of the features of the removed category and the statistical significance of the performance. We iterated these feature ablation studies through all feature categories introduced in Table 2. For every iteration, we conducted a *paired* sample t-test in which the difference in means across a set of paired samples is tested. In our feature ablation study, the paired samples were made using 30 held-out test sets.

## RESULTS

Table 3 shows the results with two threshold values in predicting the usefulness of Yelp reviews. When the threshold was 2, the accuracy was 74.4%, and it increased to 88.9% when the threshold was changed to 5. As one might expect, by increasing the threshold, the classification task becomes easier and accuracy improves.

| Threshold (ζ) | Accuracy |
|---|---|
| 2 | 0.744 |
| 5 | 0.889 |

***Table 3.*** *Accuracy of usefulness prediction*

Results from the feature ablation study are presented in Table 4 in terms of accuracy, percent change, and p-value. The row labeled "*All*" indicates the performance of a model that uses all features. The rows labeled "*-X*" indicate the performance of a model using all features except those in feature category "*X*". Rows "*-X*" are ordered in descending order of performance drop. The letter in parentheses indicates whether the feature category "*X*" is a top-level category (t), middle-level category (m), or lower-level category (l) in our feature hierarchy. The "*Percent change*" column indicates the percent decrease (-) or increase (+) in performance compared to the model with all features. In all rows except the first row, a decrease in accuracy means that the contribution of the feature group of that row is positive. In other words, the feature group in that row has discriminative power in predicting the usefulness of reviews.

| Feature group | Accuracy | Percent change | P-value |
|---|---|---|---|
| All | 0.744 | | |
| - Cotent (t) | **0.689** | **-7.39%** | *** 3.13E-23** |
| - Source (t) | 0.695 | -6.59% | * 6.81E-22 |
| - Reputation (m) | **0.716** | **-3.76%** | *** 8.20E-12** |
| - Informativeness (m) | 0.729 | -2.02% | * 2.86E-05 |
| - Rating informativeness (l) | **0.736** | **-1.08%** | *** 1.90E-02** |
| - Intrinsic reputation (l) | 0.737 | -0.94% | * 2.51E-02 |
| - Content informativeness (l) | 0.738 | -0.81% | * 0.046 |
| - Extrinsic reputation (l) | 0.742 | -0.27% | 0.586 |
| - Business (t) | 0.743 | -0.13% | 0.686 |
| - Readability (m) | 0.743 | -0.13% | 0.696 |
| - Geographical Entropy (m) | 0.744 | -0.00% | 0.982 |
| - Sentiment (m) | 0.745 | +0.13% | 0.787 |

***Table 4.*** *Feature ablation study results*

Two-tailed tests were used and the asterisk symbol (*) in p-value column indicates a statistically significant difference at $\alpha = 0.05$ level. The results of the analysis indicate seven statistically significant differences in means of accuracies across 30 sets of paired samples. The most discriminative feature group for each level of feature category (top, middle, and lower level in Table 2) is marked in bold.

The results in Table 4 suggest several important trends. First, among the top-level feature categories, the content features were more effective and influential than the source features and business features. Both the content features and source features had statistically significant effects, but the business features did not have statistically significant effects. This result contradicts a widely used mechanism in online review services to show reviews based on reputation. This will be covered in more detail in the discussion session.

Second, among the middle-level feature categories, reputation features and informativeness features were influential and statistically significant in predicting usefulness. In contrast to the top-level feature categories, the source-based reputation features were more influential than content-based informativeness features. Interestingly, other middle-level content feature categories (readability, geographical entropy, and sentiment) were not influential and they were ranked at the bottom. In the case of the content feature category, the influences of the sub-features (except informativeness features) were small, but it had the greatest influence overall if used together. This indicates that sub-features of the content category might have a huge interaction (informativeness vs. readability or informativeness vs. sentiment).

Third, among the lower-level feature categories, rating informativeness features, intrinsic reputation features, and content informativeness features were effective and had statistically significant effects. Only the extrinsic reputation features were not influential. This result is interesting because the extrinsic reputation features are based on the previous activities representing the user's explicit reputation and are presented to users through Yelp's user interface. In the case of intrinsic reputation features, it is not available information to users since they are social network metrics calculated using the list of friends by this study. On the other hand, in the case of informativeness features, ratings informativeness features that are easily identifiable by the user and based on star ratings appear to be more influential than the content informativeness features extracted from the content itself. Interestingly, sentiment features hurt performance in accuracy.

## DISCUSSION

The results of our study show that the combination of carefully selected features and machine learning can effectively predict the usefulness of online reviews marked by users. Overall, our binary classifiers showed fairly good performance (0.744 when $\zeta = 2$, 0.889 when $\zeta = 5$). One existing study (Levi & Mokryn, 2014) conducted a similar experiment to predict useful reviews using Yelp dataset. Their study used a threshold of 5 to determine the usefulness class of the reviews and their accuracy was 0.953, which is higher than the accuracy of our model. However, the usefulness class in their study was not evenly distributed as in our study (*useful*: 50% vs. *not_useful*: 50%), but was centered on the *not_useful* class (*useful*: 6.2% vs. *not_useful*: 93.8%). With this distribution, a model that always predicts "*not useful*" would obtain an accuracy of 0.938. This indicates that the performance improvement of their study is limited. We need to note that our study considered the *not_useful* class only if the number of usefulness votes was zero, and their study considered the *not_useful* class if the number of usefulness votes was less than five. It is possible that more false negative cases in the *not_useful* class could be introduced than in their study and they might not confine the exposure time.

The good performance of our binary classifiers is most likely because we could select and create high-quality features through literature review and random inspection. We introduced new features that were not commonly used to predict the usefulness of online reviews. Among these new features, intrinsic reputation features ($p < .05$) and content informativeness features ($p < .05$) had statistically significant effects in predicting usefulness. Among the content features that were not influential, sentiment features or readability features have potential interactions with informativeness features. It is because content features had the greatest influence overall if they were used together despite their sub-categories' small effects. We believe that the negative influence of sentiment features was due to data sparseness, but this needs further examination.

There were several interesting findings in our experiment results. First, the content features were more effective and influential than the source features in the top-level feature categories, although most online review services and retailers utilize social-based information retrieval (Racherla & Friske, 2012). However, this study demonstrated that content-related factors are also critical in judging the usefulness of online reviews. In other words, the characteristics of individual reviews should be considered for retrieving useful reviews. Our study results support the Elaboration Likelihood Model (Petty & Cacioppo, 1986). The central route (assessing content logically) works more influentially than the peripheral route (using cognitive clue) does. The information retrieval only based on reputation-based features can introduce information bias because it does not go through the central route. We like reviews from people who are similar to us, but obsession with personal similarity can cause another dimension of the problem. The importance of content is also supported by the results of other sub-feature categories. The second influential feature category in the middle-level feature categories was informativeness features ($p < .001$) that included the amount of information, structured review, and price information. This is partly because informativeness is linked to usefulness and this feature category includes information needed to select a service in the local businesses. Both the rating informativeness features ($p < .05$) and the content informativeness features ($p < .05$) have statistically significant impacts on the usefulness of reviews.

Second, the extrinsic reputation features ($p = 0.586$) did not have a statistically significant impact. This finding contradicts existing research results (Bator & Cialdini, 2000; Levi & Mokryn, 2014; Racherla & Friske, 2012). On the other hand, the intrinsic reputation features based on the social network metrics did have a statistically significant impact ($p < .05$). This indicates that there are significant patterns of social networks that cannot be revealed by simple numbers included in the extrinsic reputation features such as the number of friends and the number of reviews. The results from our study partly explain the cognitive authority theory (Wilson, 1983) in that the cognitive authority varies depending on the relationship between people. The people who are deemed experts become cognitive authorities, and the authority varies depending on the relationship and sphere of interest (Wilson, 1983). The PageRank algorithm (Brin & Page, 1998) has been used by Google to identify high-quality websites. Social network metrics such as eigenvector, which takes into account the importance of friends similar to the PageRank, were used in the computational trust models (Mui, Mohtashemi, & Halberstadt, 2002). As a result of our experiments, we found that the patterns of social networks are closely related to usefulness.

Third, our experiment results have implications for how to present reviews to help users select useful reviews. In many cases, the rank in which online reviews are arranged depends on recency (Kim, Pantel, Chklovski, & Pennacchiotti, 2006) and source-based reputation (Racherla & Friske, 2012). Users often rely on very limited clues available such as title, number of votes, and number of friends. Without enough clues, users often guess rather than make informed decisions (Rieh, 2002). To support users' predictive judgment, it is necessary to develop a way that helps them find more reliable information and sources (Rieh, 2002). If online review systems could provide more clues indicating the facets of the usefulness of reviews, users could make their predictive judgments more effectively. Fallis (2004) stated that "Instead of just trying to change the people who are seeking information (by teaching them how to evaluate information), we can also try to increase the verifiability of the information they seek" (p. 17).

## CONCLUSION

The goal of this paper was to evaluate a large number of features for the purpose of predicting the usefulness of Yelp reviews. We generated features from review content, author, and business. Our results found that several features contribute significantly to performance. Interestingly, many of the features that improved performance are not the types of measures that are displayed to users on commercial websites such as Yelp and are not the measures that are commonly used to prioritize reviews for users. Our study points to several measures that could be used by online review systems to rank and display reviews for users---exposing users to content that is more often perceived to be useful.

There are a few studies in which usefulness is predicted by using the Yelp dataset and our experimental setting is different from previous studies. Therefore, complete comparisons with existing studies are difficult, but our binary classifier showed fairly high performance (close to 90%). In the feature ablation study, we found that intrinsic reputation based on social network metrics is more influential than extrinsic reputation mostly used in online review sites as mentioned in the discussion above. Content informativeness features of reviews that included the amount of information, structured review, and price information indicates that content itself is a crucial factor in judging the usefulness of Yelp review.

Despite the insights discovered, there are some limitations in this study. The effectiveness of WOM depends on characteristics of both the provider and user of information. However, the user's personal context is missing in our study. People might tend to search for the reviews that are written by someone who is similar to them. Consumers may use extreme ratings in combination with socio-demographic characteristics of the reviewer to find similar people and consequently judge the information provided by them (Lim & Chung, 2011). However, the Yelp Dataset does not include that personal-level data, so this limitation is somewhat inevitable.

Many of the features we developed could also be generated in other domains such as product reviews. Future work is needed to evaluate the generalizability of our features to other domains. Additionally, future work could also investigate the effectiveness of our features for specific service categories (possibly within Yelp).

## REFERENCES


Anderson, M., & Magruder, J. (2012). Learning from the crowd: Regression discontinuity estimates of the effects of an online review database. *The Economic Journal, 122*(563), 957-989.

Arguello, J., & Shaffer, K. (2015). Predicting speech acts in MOOC forum posts. Paper presented at the *Icwsm,* pp. 2-11.

Batagelj, V., & Mrvar, A. (1998). Pajek-program for large network analysis. *Connections, 21*(2), 47-57.

Bator, R., & Cialdini, R. (2000). The application of persuasion theory to the development of effective proenvironmental public service announcements. *Journal of Social Issues, 56*(3), 527-542.

Bird, S. (2006). NLTK: The natural language toolkit. Paper presented at the *Proceedings of the COLING/ACL on interactive presentation sessions,* pp. 69-72.

Biswas, D., & Biswas, A. (2004). The diagnostic role of signals in the context of perceived risks in online shopping: Do signals matter more on the web? *Journal of Interactive Marketing, 18*(3), 30-45.

Borgatti, S. P., Everett, M. G., & Johnson, J. C. (2013). *Analyzing social networks* SAGE Publications Limited.

Brin, S., & Page, L. (1998). Anatomy of a large-scale hypertextual web search engine. 7th intl world wide web conf.

Cheung, M. Y., Luo, C., Sia, C. L., & Chen, H. (2009). Credibility of electronic word-of-mouth: Informational and normative determinants of on-line consumer recommendations. *International Journal of Electronic Commerce, 13*(4), 9-38.

Chevalier, J. A., & Mayzlin, D. (2006). The effect of word of mouth on sales: Online book reviews. *Journal of Marketing Research, 43*(3), 345-354.

Clemons, E. K., Gao, G. G., & Hitt, L. M. (2006). When online reviews meet hyperdifferentiation: A study of the craft beer industry. *Journal of Management Information Systems, 23*(2), 149-171.

Daft, R. L., & Lengel, R. H. (1986). Organizational information requirements, media richness and structural design. *Management Science, 32*(5), 554-571.

Erdem, T., & Swait, J. (2004). Brand credibility, brand consideration, and choice. *Journal of Consumer Research, 31*(1), 191-198.

Eysenbach, G., Powell, J., Kuss, O., & Sa, E. (2002). Empirical studies assessing the quality of health information for consumers on the world wide web: A systematic review. *Jama, 287*(20), 2691-2700.

Fallis, D. (2004). On verifying the accuracy of information: Philosophical perspectives. *Library Trends, 52*(3), 463-487.

Fogg, B., Marshall, J., Kameda, T., Solomon, J., Rangnekar, A., Boyd, J., et al. (2001). Web credibility research: A method for online experiments and early study results. *CHI'01 Extended Abstracts on Human Factors in Computing Systems,* pp. 295-296.

Forman, C., Ghose, A., & Wiesenfeld, B. (2008). Examining the relationship between reviews and sales: The role of reviewer identity disclosure in electronic markets. *Information Systems Research, 19*(3), 291-313.

Friedman, D. B., & Hoffman-Goetz, L. (2006). A systematic review of readability and comprehension instruments used for print and web-based cancer information. *Health Education & Behavior, 33*(3), 352-373.

Ghose, A., & Ipeirotis, P. G. (2011). Estimating the helpfulness and economic impact of product reviews: Mining text and reviewer characteristics. *IEEE Transactions on Knowledge and Data Engineering, 23*(10), 1498-1512.

Gupta, P., & Harris, J. (2010). How e-WOM recommendations influence product consideration and quality of choice: A motivation to process information perspective. *Journal of Business Research, 63*(9), 1041-1049.

He, J., & Chu, W. W. (2010). A social network-based recommender system (SNRS). Springer.

Hogarth, R. M. (1987). Judgment and choice: The psychology of decision John Wiley & Sons.

Kim, S., Pantel, P., Chklovski, T., & Pennacchiotti, M. (2006). Automatically assessing review helpfulness. Paper presented at the *Proceedings of the 2006 conference on empirical methods in natural language processing,* pp. 423-430.

Levi, A., & Mokryn, O. (2014). The social aspect of voting for useful reviews. Paper presented at the *International conference on social computing, behavioral-cultural modeling, and prediction,* pp. 293-300.

Lim, B. C., & Chung, C. M. (2011). The impact of word-of-mouth communication on attribute evaluation. *Journal of Business Research, 64*(1), 18-23.

López, C., & Farzan, R. (2014). Analysis of local online review systems as digital word-of-mouth. Paper presented at the *Proceedings of the 23rd international conference on world wide web,* pp. 457-462.

Lu, Y., Tsaparas, P., Ntoulas, A., & Polanyi, L. (2010). Exploiting social context for review quality prediction. Paper presented at the *Proceedings of the 19th international conference on world wide web,* pp. 691-700.

Luca, M., & Zervas, G. (2013). Fake it till you make it: Reputation, competition, and Yelp review fraud. *Harvard Business School NOM Unit Working Paper,* (14-006)

Manning, C. D., Surdeanu, M., Bauer, J., Finkel, J. R., Bethard, S., & McClosky, D. (2014). The stanford corenlp natural language processing toolkit. Paper presented at the *ACL (System Demonstrations),* pp. 55-60.

Miller, G. A. (1995). WordNet: A lexical database for english. *Communications of the ACM, 38*(11), 39-41.

Mosadegh, M. J., & Behboudi, M. (2011). Using social network paradigm for developing a conceptual framework in CRM. *Australian Journal of Business and Management Research, 1*(4), 63.

Mui, L., Mohtashemi, M., & Halberstadt, A. (2002). A computational model of trust and reputation. *System Sciences, 2002. HICSS. proceedings of the 35th annual hawaii international conference On,* pp. 2431-2439.

Pentina, I., Bailey, A. A., & Zhang, L. (2015). Exploring effects of source similarity, message valence, and receiver regulatory focus on Yelp review persuasiveness and purchase intentions. *Journal of Marketing Communications,* , 1-21.

Petty, R., & Cacioppo, J. (1986). Communication and persuasion: Central and peripheral routes to attitude change. Springer.

Petty, R. E., & Cacioppo, J. T. (1986). *The elaboration likelihood model of persuasion.* Springer.

Racherla, P., & Friske, W. (2012). Perceived 'usefulness' of online consumer reviews: An exploratory investigation across three services categories. *Electronic Commerce Research and Applications, 11*(6), 548-559.

Rieh, S. Y. (2002). Judgment of information quality and cognitive authority in the web. *Journal of the American Society for Information Science and Technology, 53*(2), 145-161.

Rieh, S. Y., & Belkin, N. (2000). Interaction on the web: Scholars' judgment of information quality and cognitive authority. *Proceedings of the annual meeting-American Society for Information Science, , 37.* pp. 25-38.

Rieh, S. Y., & Danielson, D. R. (2007). Credibility: A multidisciplinary framework. *Annual Review of Information Science and Technology, 41*(1), 307-364.

Schlosser, A. E. (2005). Posting versus lurking: Communicating in a multiple audience context. *Journal of Consumer Research, 32*(2), 260-265.

Smith, D., Menon, S., & Sivakumar, K. (2005). Online peer and editorial recommendations, trust, and choice in virtual markets. *Journal of Interactive Marketing, 19*(3), 15-37.

Socher, R., Perelygin, A., Wu, J. Y., Chuang, J., Manning, C. D., Ng, A. Y., et al. (2013). Recursive deep models for semantic compositionality over a sentiment treebank. Paper presented at the *Proceedings of the conference on empirical methods in natural language processing (EMNLP), , 1631.* pp. 1642.

Strapparava, C., & Valitutti, A. (2004). WordNet affect: An affective extension of WordNet. Paper presented at the *Lrec, , 4.* pp. 1083-1086.

Sweeney, J. C., Soutar, G. N., & Mazzarol, T. (2008). Factors influencing word of mouth effectiveness: Receiver perspectives. *European Journal of Marketing, 42*(3/4), 344-364.

Weiss, A. M., Lurie, N. H., & MacInnis, D. J. (2008). Listening to strangers: Whose responses are valuable, how valuable are they, and why? *Journal of Marketing Research, 45*(4), 425-436.

Wiegand, M., Balahur, A., Roth, B., Klakow, D., & Montoyo, A. (2010). A survey on the role of negation in sentiment analysis. Paper presented at the *Proceedings of the workshop on negation and speculation in natural language processing,* pp. 60-68.

Wilson, P. (1983). Second-hand knowledge: An inquiry into cognitive authority. Greenwood Press.

Yang, J., Kim, W., Amblee, N., & Jeong, J. (2012). The heterogeneous effect of WOM on product sales: Why the effect of WOM valence is mixed? *European Journal of Marketing, 46*(11/12), 1523-1538.

Yang, W., Yuan, Y., & Zhang, N. (2015). Predicting Yelp ratings using user friendship network information. Retrieved from http://snap.stanford.edu/class/cs224w-2015/projects_2015/Predicting_Yelp_Ratings_Using_User_Friendship_Network_Information.pdf

Yelp Inc. (2017). *Yelp dataset challenge.* Retrieved Mar/21, 2017, from https://www.yelp.com/dataset_challenge/

# Affordances and Constraints in the Online Identity Work of LGBTQ+ Individuals

**Vanessa L. Kitzie**
*University of South Carolina, School of Library & Information Science, USA. vkitzie@gmail.com*

## ABSTRACT

**This research examines how social networking sites (SNS) and search engines (SE) afford and constrain practices related to the development of lesbian, gay, bisexual, transgender, and queer (LGBTQ+) identities. Semi-structured interviews were performed with 30 LGBTQ+ individuals from the United States between the ages of 18 and 38. Data analysis identified these key affordances: a) identity expression, b) connecting to similar others, c) information access, and d) information control. Key constraints are: a) identity expression, b) information control, c) curation, and d) information access. Whether SNS and SE provide affordances or constraints is influenced by how participants ascribe meaning to these technologies within their everyday lives. Therefore, SNS and SE do not yield deterministically good or bad outcomes. Instead outcomes are shaped by sociocultural context and material properties of the technologies. Findings reveal implications of everyday technology use for LGBTQ+ individuals and suggest how they can leverage affordances and mitigate constraints of SNS and SE to manage identity work.**

## KEYWORDS

social networking sites, search engines, sociomateriality, LGBTQ+

## INTRODUCTION

Consider the following scenarios. Participant Jamie, assigned at birth and socialized as female, created a social networking site (SNS) profile using male pictures to express masculinity and be recognized by others as male. Due in part to this embodied practice, Jamie now identifies as male. Another participant, Joanna, sought information about her queer identity using search engines (SE). The results pages made visible information that stigmatized this identity, tainting Joanna's search experience.

Both scenarios represent how SNS and SE afford and constrain practices related to the development of lesbian, gay, bisexual, transgender, and queer (LGBTQ+) identities.[1] SNS and SE were chosen for exploration since participants identified them as important for identity work.

## SIGNIFICANCE

Research findings enhance understanding of how LGBTQ+ individuals engage with online technologies in unanticipated, creative ways. Such understanding legitimizes these practices and highlights sociocultural issues of technology use. This research incorporates the materiality of technological artifacts with a sociocultural examination of LGBTQ+ identity work online – a key theoretical contribution. Such incorporation highlights how LGBTQ+ individuals can leverage affordances and mitigate constraints of online technologies to manage identity work, which yields design-based implications.

## LITERATURE REVIEW

Online technologies have become critical resources for LGBTQ+ identity development (Pullen & Cooper, 2010). Within online contexts, LGBTQ+ individuals establish a shared set of sensibilities (Rothbauer, 2004; Bond, Hefner & Drogos, 2008) and assist one another with identity work (O'Riordan & Phillips, 2007; Craig & McInroy, 2014). Yet their use of online technologies does not occur in a vacuum. Experiences of LGBTQ+ individuals within online contexts influence their practices in offline ones (Hillier & Harrison, 2007). Such overlap not only evokes new meanings for LGBTQ+ identities online but also reflects structural disadvantages faced offline.

Systems not designed with LGBTQ+ identities in mind evoke norms that reinforce hetero and gender normativity (Lingel & Golub, 2015; Haimson & Hoffman, 2016). Even within LGBTQ+ contexts, metanarratives of a singular LGBTQ+ experience reinforce the commodification and fetishization of certain identity characteristics, e.g., whiteness (Mitra & Gajjala, 2008; Raj, 2011). Further, individuals may pass judgment on what constitutes an authentic LGBTQ+ identity performance in an online context (Gray, 2009). Such homogenization of LGBTQ+ identities renders individuals with outside experiences as "Other," marginalizing the marginalized (Foucault, 1978).

This study builds on prior work that refutes determinist and neo-liberalist ideals of online technologies as emancipatory

80th Annual Meeting of the Association for Information Science & Technology, Washington, DC, VA | Oct. 27-Nov. 1, 2017



[1] "LGBTQ" reflects labels most used by participants. Use of the plus sign recognizes the inability of labels to capture all identity expressions (Gamson, 1995). Participants are referred to by pseudonyms and their preferred pronouns.

for marginalized groups (Cartensen, 2009), while recognizing that they afford new possibilities for identity work (Wakeford, 2000). Using the theory of sociomateriality, the study also examines how this tension is materially expressed within technological artifacts.

## THEORY

The sociomaterial lens of affordances and constraints captures interrelationships between sociocultural context (i.e., one's memberships to social groups and cultures), and material properties of technological artifacts (e.g., search box). This research envisions neither technology nor sociocultural context as determined or determining. Rather, both are engaged in a co-constitutive relationship that produces this meaning (Gillespie, Boczkowski, & Foote, 2014; Leonardi, Nardi, & Kallinikos, 2014).

Affordances represent the materially-based construction and features of technological artifacts suggesting their use, while constraints pose restrictions for how artifacts can be used (Norman, 1999; Baym, 2015). Affordances and constraints do not constitute properties of technologies nor people (Leonardi, 2012). Take the search box of an online dating site. Its construction and design suggest a certain use: entering criteria describing individuals one would like to date and pressing the "search" button to see a display of results. Such meaning is enacted by a combination of affordances (e.g., the ability to enter criteria such as radius, suggesting the importance of proximity for a potential partner) and constraints (e.g., no ability to search the full-text of an online dating profile, prioritizing physical characteristics over how personality is articulated). If this meaning of "search box" is continually enacted over time it becomes taken for granted (Suchman, 2007).

People can also realize new goals by exploiting a technology's material features (Leonardi, 2012). For instance, an online dating site's search box can be used in unintended ways, such as to identify and harass individuals with LGBTQ+ identities. These practices, in turn, influence the further shaping of the technology, e.g., the decision of popular online dating site OkCupid to let LGBTQ+ individuals hide profiles from heterosexual users.[2]

## METHOD

Thirty LGBTQ+ individuals between the ages of 18 and 38 from the US participated in this research. Participants were recruited using a mix of purposive and snowball sampling. Individuals from this age range have traits and values shaped by their interactions with online technologies (Howe & Strauss, 2009, p. 4; "Social Media Use by Age Group Over Time," 2016). Additionally, these individuals are likely to have performed identity work in their adolescence and, therefore, can recall and articulate these experiences (Savin-Williams & Diamond, 2000; Grov et al., 2006).

Although identity labels are problematic (see Gamson, 1995), participants most often described themselves as female (n=19, 64%), queer (n=18, 60%), and not cisgender (n=17, 57%) meaning that their sense of personal identity does not correspond with the sex and gender they were assigned at birth ("Cisgender," n.d.). Of those not cisgender (n=17, 57%), the majority identified as transgender (n=9, 53%). This sample captures the perspectives of those with underrepresented LGBTQ+ identities, who often are treated as outsiders by mainstream LGBTQ+ groups. Such groups instead attend to the demands of gay and, to lesser extent, lesbian, cisgender individuals (Jagose, 1996; Ward, 2000).

Participants were interviewed using a semi-structured interview protocol that employed the critical incident technique (CIT) to elicit recall of memorable, past experiences critical to a participant's identity work when using online technologies (Flanagan, 1954). CIT allowed the researcher to inductively derive information related to each concept rather than impose her own meanings and theoretical assumptions on participant accounts.

Interviews took place either face-to-face or via Skype and averaged 60 minutes. They were audio-recorded and transcribed by the researcher to maintain participant privacy. Participants also selected pseudonyms. The researcher analyzed the transcripts using emic/etic coding (Miles & Huberman, 1994), in which high-level deductive codes are applied from the theoretical approach, i.e., affordances and constraints, while emic codes are inductively derived from participant accounts and applied under each high-level etic code. The unit of analysis was practices related to identity work (e.g., identity expression). A validity check denoted an inter-coder reliability (ICR) value of 0.93 kappa, indicative of excellent agreement.

## FINDINGS – OVERVIEW OF THEMES

Tables 1 and 2 depict the etic themes of affordances and constraints, and the emic sub-themes emerging from participant accounts. "Total Sources" represent the total number of interview transcripts (out of 30), while "Total Codes" denote the number of times the code was applied.

As indicated by Table 1, the most prominent affordance sub-themes, i.e., discussed in >=50% of transcripts, are identity expression, connecting to similar others, information access, and information control. Although fewer participants mentioned information control, they discussed this theme frequently when addressed.

Per Table 2, while more participants mentioned constraints than affordances, they discussed this theme less frequently than affordances. While only the identity expression theme was discussed in >=50% of transcripts, the themes of information control and curation were discussed frequently enough to be considered key sub-themes.

[2]https://okcupid.desk.com/customer/portal/articles/2161224-privacy-controls

| Affordance Themes and Sub-themes | Total Sources | Total Codes |
|---|---|---|
| Affordances | 23 (77%) | 293 (100%) |
| Identity expression | 22 (73%) | 56 (19%) |
| Connecting to similar others | 19 (63%) | 47 (16%) |
| Information access | 16 (53%) | 39 (13%) |
| Information control | 15 (50%) | 126 (43%) |
| Curation | 7 (23%) | 12 (4%) |
| Moderation | 4 (13%) | 5 (2%) |
| Autonomy | 3 (10%) | 5 (2%) |
| Convenience | 3 (10%) | 3 (1%) |

***Table 1.*** *Affordance themes and sub-themes*

| Constraint Themes and Sub-themes | Total Sources | Total Codes |
|---|---|---|
| Constraints | 26 (87%) | 259 (100%) |
| Identity expression | 17 (57%) | 43 (17%) |
| Information control | 13 (43%) | 32 (12%) |
| Curation | 12 (40%) | 140 (54%) |
| Information access | 9 (30%) | 6 (2%) |
| Connecting to similar others | 9 (30%) | 14 (5%) |
| Moderation | 8 (27%) | 22 (8%) |
| Autonomy | 2 (7%) | 2 (1%) |
| Convenience | 0 (0%) | 0 (0%) |

***Table 2.*** *Constraint themes and sub-themes.*

Comparing the two tables, identity expression and information control represent both an affordance and constraint. This finding suggests that affordances and constraints do not solely constitute objective, material properties of technologies, but are also shaped by sociocultural context and individual agency. These key themes and sub-themes are now discussed and exemplified using participant accounts.

## FINDINGS – IN-DEPTH DISCUSSION OF THEMES

### *Affordances*

#### Identity Expression

An identity expression represents an instance where participants feel that they can convey a facet of their LGBTQ+ identities using SNS and SE. Findings from data analysis indicate that participants use SE to type in anything and receive results. This affordance is useful for individuals lacking the language to express their identities who might not be able to locate information using systems requiring articulated queries. As participant Rose states:

> *Google's great because you can type in a whole question. I put in "Are you gay if you kissed a girl?" Questions like that, [which] were specific based on my own experiences hoping something might come up that was similar.*

Since Rose did not know whether the label "gay" would be appropriate to describe her identity, she relied on a blank search box, which visually afforded the perception that she was not restricted in formulating her search query. She could literally type whatever she wanted. As a result, Rose relied on the natural language query, "Are you gay if you kissed a girl?" When the researcher asked Rose if she remembered what this query returned, she stated: "Mostly Yahoo! Answers. People putting in whole questions that usually weren't very helpful because anyone can answer them and not all people are very intelligent or nice."

This account exemplifies the imbrication of material, social, and cultural agencies. Via its simple design, Google offers the perception that participants can freely express their identities by typing whatever they want into the search box. Yet as Rose suggests, the retrieved results are not necessarily relevant; they are not envisioned by Rose to be trustworthy and might stigmatize LGBTQ+ identities. Given that Google's algorithm relies in part on a match between keywords, as well as semantic and syntactic structures,[3] Rose encounters information that shares a similar structure, but not her desired meaning.

SNS afforded participants ways to express their identities online by attaining new forms of embodied practice (Merleau-Ponty, 1962; Lloyd, 2010). Consider Jamie's recollection of catfishing, a term popularized by a documentary and current television series to describe "a person who sets up a false personal profile on a social networking site for fraudulent or deceptive purposes" ("Catfish," n.d.). When Jamie was catfishing, he identified and was recognized by others as female, but wanted to explore a male identity. He states:

[3]https://www.google.com/insidesearch/howsearchworks/algorithms.html

*[When] I was catfishing using male pictures, I would wake up and be like, "Oh yeah, that's not me. I can't go to school and act the same way as at home [when catfishing]." It was a lot of self-exploring, and finding out what [practicing a male identity] was like.*

By catfishing, Jamie could escape norms confining his physical body to an undesired, female presentation. Jamie seized on the importance others placed on pictures as indicative of one's authentic identity to represent himself as male. He could accomplish this practice given the disintermediation between online technologies and bodies. When going online, one has the potential to escape the corporeal, the literal "meatspace" ("Meatspace," n.d.). Jamie could be recognized as male and practice being male in a way not afforded in offline places, such as at home or at school, where his physical body was made visible. Thus, Jamie's account supports arguments made by cyberqueer scholars of the potential for online technologies to reshape embodied practices (Haraway, 1990; Wakeford, 2000).

### Connecting to Similar Others

Data analysis denotes that SNS and SE connect participants with others who share their LGBTQ+ identities. This finding parallels prior research on technology use for LGBTQ+ identity development (Pullen & Cooper, 2010). Consider how Mark explains his preference for the photo-sharing site, Instagram, and video-sharing site, YouTube:

*I enjoy being able to go on social media and having 400 people going through the same thing to use as resources instead of having a book that can't talk back. Having that video and visual evidence is much better. [Using] social media, I've met up [in person] with a bunch of different trans guys. You can't find that in a book. One of them is becoming my best friend. He's my resource. We can bounce stories off each other and sometimes it's like, "Oh my gosh that's happened to my body, has it happened to yours?"*

A simplistic interpretation of this account would be that Mark prefers interpersonal resources to books. Yet such an interpretation discounts the importance of features beyond the format of an object, such as practices, bodies, and spatial arrangements. Considering the intersection of these factors, SNS rely on social networks through which to channel information flow. Features like the ability to "follow" someone and recommendations of similar individuals to follow facilitate this affordance. Per Mark: "Once you follow one person, [the site] comes up with more people you can follow … that [lead] to more information." These connections can be made regardless of geographic location. SNS are not necessarily geographically bound, which circumvents some of the physical dispersion of individuals with LGBTQ+ identities and other physical barriers that might prevent them from convening in person. However, Mark does not envision his engagement with other transgender men as only occurring in an online environment. Rather, he also envisions SNS as affording him the ability to connect with those geographically co-located. This finding echoes that boundaries between online and offline are blurred and mutually reinforcing (Gray, 2009).

SNS like Instagram and YouTube also afford Mark the ability to identify those sharing similar embodied practices. Since Mark has yet to experience certain forms of embodiment, e.g., the effects of hormones, he can rely on a variety of experiences from those sharing his male, transgender identity to feel fully informed about the possibilities. Site features, such as the ability to upload evidence of one's embodied practices via videos and photos, afford Mark the ability to determine who represents a trusted source.

The importance placed on source verification leads participants to use technologies in unanticipated ways. For instance, Sierra explains why she used 4Chan, an image-based bulletin board, to explore information related to her transgender identity:

*This is so weird because I hate 4Chan, they're this misogynistic hellhole. [But] they have an LGBT board that was useful but problematic. Since everyone's posting anonymously, you could have people who aren't trans posting whatever it is they wanna say. You also have people who use tripcodes, which [are] user names with passwords so the person has an identity on the site. [It] is weird for an anonymous site. But on that board and for the trans girls, there's more people with names than anonymous.*

Sierra's account differed from the experiences of others who view 4Chan as an offensive site (see Manivannan, 2013). Despite its reputation, 4Chan was considered useful by Sierra for exploring information related to her transgender identity. Like Mark's account, 4Chan allowed individuals to post pictures that documented embodied practice; Sierra could consume these pictures and recognize herself in them. 4Chan's tripcode feature also facilitated Sierra's verification of people's identities. By using this feature coupled with photos, Sierra could determine who constituted a trustworthy source, e.g., an individual using a tripcode and posting pictures, versus an untrustworthy one, e.g., individuals posting anonymously.

Aside from the technological features of image uploading and tripcodes, who used 4Chan's LGBT board and their use of it were also socioculturally shaped. Certainly, other affordances of 4Chan can be used in the LGBT board to render it unsafe or irrelevant for Sierra, such as individuals afforded anonymity on the site posting vitriolic content to the board. However, the social group of "trans girls" engaged in a shared set of practices centered on collective conceptions of meaning and relevance for transgender identity work. For this reason, participants reported that they engaged with site features perceived to afford these practices, which became stabilized over time. Thus, the sociocultural and the material are mutually co-constitutive, rather than mutually exclusive categories.

### Information Access

Participants identified SE as affording access to information not found in formal sources. Stefan explains their preference for Google to access information authored by LGBTQ+ individuals:

I go to Google because that's where people [are] writing. People who are writing on queer stuff are queer people and you're going to have an income and access problem. You're going to find stuff on blogs, Tumblr, [and] niche sites because there's not access to publishing or research.

Unlike formal channels of production, such as a peer review system for research studies, Google does not discern what it indexes. It thus affords an individual with access to variegated information types, including information that exists outside of these formal channels. Since individuals with LGBTQ+ identities do not have access to resources, e.g., economic and social capital, which would lend visibility to the information they produce, they can rely on self-publishing this information online using blogging platforms or image and video-based sites, and disseminating access to and visibility of this information across SNS and via SE. Therefore, Stefan's account not only signifies the importance of these online technologies affording access to information but also to resources for self-publishing and sharing of information.

Access to self-publishing also facilitates up-to-date information on LGBTQ+ identities. The reason why participants appreciate current information can be explained by the value they place on embodied practices. Such practices are individualized and subject to context. What constitutes embodied practice changes over time as more individuals share these practices and social groups debate the meanings ascribed to them. Given that information produced by formal sources undergoes a publishing process, by the time the information is available, it is already irrelevant. For these reasons, participants like Autumn do not think that cultural institutions like the library are relevant to LGBTQ+ individuals:

> *The reason why I wouldn't go to a library [for information on LGBTQ+ identities] is that I'd expect to find more forward-thinking works online. I [don't] think the people who work at libraries have an inherent bias, but people publishing things can put them up online themselves. [There's no] time in-between.*

### Information Control

Participants use online technologies to manage the visibility of their LGBTQ+ identities. One of the ways this visibility can be managed is via anonymity, defined as not having to reveal identifying features, such as real names. Consider Eva's rationale for why she used the online classified advertisements website, Craigslist, rather than the online dating site, OkCupid, to meet women:

I was too afraid to put myself on OkCupid. The idea of putting my photo up terrified me. I would more comfortably look at Craigslist "Women seeking women" [advertisements] because I was so scared of revealing myself. When in reality, Craigslist is much more terrifying.

Eva perceives her anonymity as compromised by OkCupid making her picture visible. Given that Craigslist does not require pictures, Eva felt comfortable browsing without her identity being revealed. Yet the material features of Craigslist do not necessarily afford anonymity. Eva's browser might be tracking her search history, Craigslist could get hacked, or Eva might provide information, such as a phone number or email address, which can be used by others to identify her. Eva may be unaware of these potential breaches to her anonymity or she might just perceive a picture as indicative of her "true" identity. After all, she equates posting a picture with "revealing" herself.

Both Eva and Mark's accounts address a perception held by several other participants that one's "true" identity is expressed by their body. Certainty this perception is not exclusive to LGBTQ+ individuals. Shows like *Catfish* exemplify the equivalencies made between authenticity and the body. Yet given the importance of embodied practice among LGBTQ+ individuals, the body may be valued as the primary means by which individuals denote their trustworthiness. Therefore, when someone like Eva desires anonymity, she must weigh this desire with the perceived consequence of engaging with information or individuals not considered trustworthy, which is "terrifying."

Privacy represents another affordance related to information control. Privacy differs from anonymity in that the latter signifies that individuals do not have to divulge identifying features, such as pictures or real names, to access information. With privacy, individuals might divulge identifying information, but it is free from public attention. Features such as the ability to create private profiles and groups engender information sharing and exchange among LGBTQ+ insiders. For instance, Stefan regards their private account on Twitter, an online news and social networking site, as "where me and all my super queer friends hang out." The privacy afforded in online contexts can mitigate unwanted visibility to identity expressions that are stigmatized in offline contexts. As Campbell explains:

Queer shopping [is] easy to [do] online and find things that are your size. You don't have to go to a suit shop where an old man will judge you. It's hard to go to the boy's section at Target and avoid eye contact with these moms wondering what you're doing in the children's section.

Yet online and offline cannot be dichotomized into private and public, as other participants identify online technologies as constraining their privacy (see following "Constraints" section). Affordances do not only represent a natural property of a technology but also features that can be appropriated to fulfill a task or goal. This task or goal is subject to sociocultural context, geographic and spatial organization, and embodied practice. In Campbell's case, the discomfort they experienced (i.e., embodied practice) entering places that stigmatize LGBTQ+ identities (i.e., geographic and spatial organization) to shop for gendered and age-specific clothing (i.e., sociocultural context) could be alleviated by the privacy of online shopping.

### ***Constraints***

#### Identity Expression

While in some instances permitting identity expressions, SNS and SE also can reinforce strategies that compact LGBTQ+ identities into monolithic categories. Jessica describes how these categories are produced by LGBTQ+ individuals using YouTube:

> *All the YouTubers [with] their video editing, fit their whole story into five minutes. It takes a lot longer to explain parts of it. They can cut out the bad things and all the confusion that they went through. They seem a lot more confident in their identities than people I know that are offline.*

Jessica perceives the video editing features offered by YouTube as allowing individuals to condense their identities into a shared set of sensibilities, or metanarratives characterizing the "normal" LGBTQ+ experience (Pullen & Cooper, 2010). Individuals may be limited in determining how to express and share their identity expressions given that these features bolster norms suggesting a "right" way of conveying these expressions.

Individuals may also experience regulation of their identity expressions due to the visibility required to make them. Findings from data analysis indicate that participants perceive the SNS site Facebook as constraining their ability to express their LGBTQ+ identity due to the visibility these expressions are afforded. Rose explains why she avoids Facebook to express her queer identity: "[I have] family friends on Facebook. If I ever shared or posted anything that would indicate my sexuality, I would feel uncomfortable." Over time, Facebook has become perceived as a site in which one's social networks are collapsed and "the lack of spatial, social, and temporal boundaries makes it difficult to maintain distinct social contexts" (boyd, 2011, p. 249; see also Duguay, 2016). Facebook also affords such collapse by offering features such as "People You May Know"[4] and "Ticker,"[5] which lend visibility to those who might not be in one's immediate social network, but are tangentially linked, e.g., a friend of a friend. Although Facebook has features that afford individuals control over how their content is shared and to whom it is made visible these features are perceived by Rose to be: "Too complicated. It would be too much of a hassle to block certain people."

Due to this collapse in context, individuals lack control over who can use an online technology, what types of content are shared, and to whom their identity expressions are made visible. Such lack of control can prevent participants from engaging in identity expressions for fear of negative identity-based outcomes. Consider Sage's explanation for why they consider Tumblr problematic:

> I've had issues [on Tumblr] where I'd tag a post and someone I didn't know went through the tags and jumped on me for it. There's certainly an expectation that you may have social justice warriors on one hand and men's rights activists on the other and never the twain shall meet except by slinging mud at each other. There's this sense of picking through a minefield, which is very, very difficult and scary. With Tumblr, it's easy to pull conversations out and quote different parts so you'll have a million different versions of the same post going around. It's easy for people to dogpile on one person.

Sage identifies several features of Tumblr that constrain identity expression. One feature is social tagging. In some instances, such tagging can be envisioned as an affordance for locating certain discourses, such as those of social justice warriors. Yet in other instances, the tagging feature can constrain identity expression given it allows those outside of the discourse, such as men's rights activists, to also identify and access this content. Further, the synchronous nature of communications means that content is disseminated more rapidly than can be controlled by the original poster. Combined with the ability to re-post content or portions of it devoid from its initial context, Tumblr's features contribute to Sage feeling a lack of control over their ability to manage how their identity expressions are recognized, interpreted, and responded to by others.

What becomes apparent through discussion of these examples is that the roles technologies play in affording and constraining information practices are not determining. What affords and what constrains are subject to individual interpretation as well as privy to sociocultural context. Like Jamie (see the above "Affordances" section), Stefan perceived features of SNS as affording the practice of multiple identity expressions. They inhabited two identities within the same site:

> *I was two people on the same forum. And when I outed myself there was a lot of drama. Some people were like, "We're never talking to you again." I kind of got scared and completely backed off.*

Many platforms encode demands for authenticity, such as a real names policy. However, even if platforms do not encode these demands, authenticity often constitutes a normative expectation within online social groups and as a result, participants who break these norms experience negative social consequences. Some members of the group in which Stefan interacted envisioned Stefan's inhabiting more than one identity, and further, an identity that did align with the ways Stefan's body presented, as deceptive. Such expectations may have resulted from the value of embodied practice within LGBTQ+ social groups. Given that Stefan's identity expressions belied their physical body, it is possible that those who never spoke to Stefan again did so because they rendered Stefan as an untrustworthy source.

---

[4]https://www.facebook.com/help/501283333222485
[5]https://www.facebook.com/help/ticker

### Information Control

Given the importance participants placed on embodied practice, anonymity was not a desired feature of interpersonal sources. Consider Cole's preference for YouTube, as opposed to a blog, for identity work:

I could physically see myself in [butch lesbian women] on YouTube channel[s] instead of having to imagine [them]. Anybody could write anything on a blog. It could be like, a ninety-year-old super feminine gay man that's writing it. You don't know who it is behind the keyboard.

To Cole, technological features afford individuals who deceive others with anonymity to facilitate such deception. Cole provides the antithesis of a valuable information source: someone of a different generation who desires men and presents as feminine. These traits are embodied and derived from experience, again signifying their importance to participants as markers of relevancy and trustworthiness.

This example questions what constitutes an intentionally deceitful act meant to harm others. As exhibited by the accounts of Jamie and Stefan, an individual with embodied knowledge and characteristics that belie demands for authenticity are considered deceptive by others. In many instances, this deception is interpreted negatively, as exemplified by the enforcement mechanisms Stefan experienced when revealing their "true" identity. But can there be instances where such deception can elicit positive information outcomes for an individual and not harm others? Perhaps the ninety-year-old, feminine gay man Cole envisions has been questioning both their desires and gender identity and uses technological features that afford anonymity to facilitate this exploration.

Regardless of the multiplicity and fluidity of LGBTQ+ identities, participants have less tolerance for online technologies that afford such identity expressions. There exists a tension between participants desiring technologies that afford their own anonymity while viewing the anonymity of others as constraining their ability to evaluate information. Stefan recognizes this tradeoff:

I look for resources created by the voices I'm looking to represent. As opposed to cisgender, straight people. At the same time, it's not necessarily safe to disclose. I can't ask people to disclose to know whether their research is something I'm going to consider more valid.

While SNS and SE afford participants the ability to manage visibility afforded to their identities, anonymity prevents Stefan from knowing whether a source can be trusted. Expectations for LGBTQ+ visibility complicate outcomes related to identity work. Participants wish to manage disclosure of their identities but expect or at least hope that others will disclose. The tension between these conflicting expectations produces an environment where the visibility of identity expressions is both avoided and desired.

SNS and SE also constrain participant's privacy by inhibiting their ability to control what information is being shared about them within a specific context (Nissenbaum, 2004; Boyd, 2011). As Amina recounts:

*I was the executive director for an organization funded by Catholics. I gave a workshop at a gender and sexuality conference. That's public online. If you Google my name you'll find that. The watchdog of this Catholic group and conservative bloggers wrote about me and how I was this homosexual activist and took screenshots of this conference. My job found out and told me [to] not be super visible as queer because [I] represent the organization.*

In this instance, information shared about Amina online impacted her life offline by regulating how she could express her identity both within and outside of the workplace. Amina could not control what could be posted about her online and by whom. Further, her preferred identity labels were dismissed to render her identity as pathological. As Amina states, "I don't even identify as homosexual." Although Amina attended the gender and sexuality conference outside of her time working for the organization, certain features of the online technologies that made her attendance visible collapsed the contexts in which Amina could manage her various identity expressions.

By posting her name to conference program published online and indexed by Google, anyone who searched for Amina's name could view this result. After the researcher spoke with Amina, she Googled her name to see if any of the results Amina mentioned would be visible. One of the first results was a blog created by a conservative group with the exclusive purpose of trying to get Amina fired. The posts reflect what she described. Of interest is the fact that the group acquired screenshots of content Amina had "liked" and events she indicated "attending" on Facebook. Amina may not have been aware that such metadata was visible, given Facebook's complicated and consistently changing privacy policy, or she may have known that this metadata was visible, but did not consider that anyone other than her friends would be able or care to see it. SNS like Facebook and SE like Google, therefore, have features that flatten the various contexts in which participants have everyday information interactions. Flattening such contexts can lead to participants feeling devoid of the ability to engage in identity expression online and lack control over what visibility is given to these identities.

### Information Curation

Curation signifies that participants have control over what information is presented to them. Participants indicate that SE constrain their ability to curate information, since they cannot control what information is made visible. Rihanna compares Google to Facebook regarding how well each affords curation:

*I think part of the reason I have relied so much on Facebook is because other people are doing the finding. I've even tried finding stuff [on LGBTQ+ identities] I know exists using Google and haven't been able to find it.*

Rihanna's issue does not constitute an access problem, but rather a visibility one given she cannot locate known items. It is possible that Google may not have indexed these items. More likely, Google's ranking algorithm does not present the known item within the first page or two of results. Since Google constrains Rihanna's ability to locate known items, she instead uses sites like Facebook, which present information curated by a known set of intermediaries.

There exist several means by which Google's algorithm may occlude visibility of LGBTQ+ content. Since Google does not publish its algorithm, there is no way to know all the technological features that produce a rank list and how they interact to do so. Even those who design the algorithm cannot predict precisely which results will be returned for a given search query and in what order; the algorithm makes machine learning decisions that render it impossible to determine (LaFrance, 2015). Instead, one can only consider what type of content the algorithm does show and make inferences regarding its logic.

Participants infer that like other formal sources, internet technologies were not created for them. Per Joanna: "The internet is made for only white men." Since most individuals in information technology fields reflect Joanna's demographic description,[6] it stands to reason that online technologies like algorithms do not possess logics complimentary of LGBTQ+ relevancies or meanings. Rather, algorithms (re)produce sociocultural discourses, meaning that information made visible on marginalized groups communicates stigma discourses (Noble, 2013). Consider Joanna's comparison of how a "Queer Google" would differ from its current version:

> *It would be exactly what I see on Google except everything related to identity would not [be] centered around a certain kind of identity, but everyone. It would be amazing if the first results would be queer people. If you're looking up the history of Russia, have a queer person be the first search result. It would be nice if you could put a blocker onto any violent things or hate speech. That's one of the biggest challenges with data science. How do you know what's hate speech? In Queer Google, you'd put in "swim suit," and just see images of swim suits, rather than images of women wearing them.*

This account signifies how Google constrains Joanna's ability to locate desired information. She attributes such constraints to several technological features. First, SE rank results based on their popularity, determined in part by the number of clicks a result receives (Gillespie, Boczkowski, & Foot, 2014). Given popularity is determined by the *number* of people that click on a link rather than *who* clicks on it, the type of identity representations made visible reflect sociocultural discourses espoused by the majority (Noble, 2013). Participants like Sebastian are aware of this logic: "Groups [which are] very heavily underrepresented in media and mainstream culture [won't] come up on Google cause no one's talking about it in the mainstream." Instead, what results do "come up" reflect cultural strategies, such as heterocentricity, biological determinism, and stigmatized portrayals of individuals who do not conform to them.

Joanna recognizes that context is lost upon automation. What one might consider "hate speech," for instance, depends on the individual and is shaped by sociocultural context. Joanna perceives machines as further complicating this determination given that the definition of hate speech would be left to the system designers, as well as the algorithm's automated learning and subsequent decision-making. Therefore, automated curation of content found in SE constrains participant's ability to determine what content is relevant since they are unaware of the parameters shaping the algorithm's ranking decisions.

## IMPLICATIONS

Research findings denote the benefit of applying a sociomaterialist lens to how SNS and SE afford and constrain the identity work of LGBTQ+ individuals. While prior research has focused on how sociocultural context shapes their online technology use, this research also considers the materiality of online technologies, which has implications for their designers and creators. These implications center on an ethic of design within the field of Human Computer Interaction (HCI) – recognizing "stress" cases (Meyer & Wachter-Boettcher, 2016, p. 2). Stress cases are defined as technological features ostensibly created to fulfill specific functions, which yield meanings that differ from the creator's intent, impacting a small number of people. An example would be Facebook's "People You May Know" feature. While this feature may have been designed to expand the social networks of people with weak ties, it takes on a different meaning for someone like Amina, where this same feature may have been used to surveil her (see previous "Constraints" section). Stress cases exemplify that while affordances and constraints may not take on the same meanings for everyone, they do disseminate dominant sociocultural discourses.

Designing for stress cases requires identifying them, which can be difficult when designers share similar experiences, and have uniform ideas of the way things are. Incorporating a diversity of perspectives challenges these taken-for-granted assumptions of who will use a technology and how they will use it. For instance, cisgender male designers might not consider offering gender identity options beyond male or female within the online technologies they create. But put a non-binary individual on the team and this feature becomes a stress case.

Stress cases can be employed as a design ethic to address issues presented by SNS related to LGBTQ+ identities. For instance, a potential solution to the stress case of "People You

[6] https://www.eeoc.gov/eeoc/statistics/reports/hightech/

May Know," might not be getting rid of the feature, but rather giving individuals the ability to decide whether they are made visible in search results as a person someone else might know. Stress cases promote transparency. By uncovering the assumptions inherent to a technological feature, stress cases render these assumptions visible, and, in the process, give participants autonomy to decide whether and how to use a feature. Stress cases thus call attention to the intersection of sociocultural context and materiality and offer a way to appropriate them for one's own purposes.

The design of SE can also benefit from identifying stress cases. By employing a vertical rank list, SE impart visibility to a certain set of results, reflective of larger sociocultural discourses. While this ranking mechanism works well for most, it does not consider marginalized groups who find the search results to be stigmatizing. To address this stress case, SE could provide more options for individuals to curate the display of search results. Rather than present results vertically, as in a rank list, results could be presented horizontally, clustered around certain topical themes. This feature would give those who do not know the language the ability to see the discourse centered on certain search terms and select terms that are identity-affirming.

## LIMITATIONS

This research does not exist without limitations. Specifically, the participant sample is not generalizable given the low sample size and non-random sampling methods. For this reason, certain perspectives are less represented in this study, such as those of individuals identifying as male (n=6, 20%). Further, participants interviewed had access to technological devices (e.g., mobile phones) and infrastructure (e.g., broadband) from which to access SNS and SE, signifying that this research reflects an assumption of stable, consistent access, which does not reflect the realities of many marginalized groups, including LGBTQ+ ones. Given the difficulty inherent to recruiting individuals from marginalized groups and the exploratory nature of this research, future work should apply the coding scheme (see Kitzie, 2017) to other samples to determine its generalizability.

Another limitation is methodological. While semi-structured interviews elicited participant accounts related to their identity work using online technologies, another way to capture the materiality of these technologies is via participant observation. For example, Duguay (2016) studied how LGBTQ+ individuals from the UK manage context collapse using both semi-structured interviews and Facebook walkthroughs. This method adds transferability to the study design by supporting the coding scheme across two separate data sources and represents another avenue for future research.

## CONCLUSION

This research examined how online technologies, namely SNS and SE, afford and constrain the identity work of LGBTQ+ individuals. By adopting a sociomaterial approach, findings revealed the interrelationship between sociocultural context and technological artifacts in shaping the meanings participants assigned to their technology use. The coding scheme established for this study (see Kitzie, 2017) can be used in future research to describe online technology use for other marginalized groups to test the applicability of the scheme. Further, findings from this study can be used to inform design ethics and practices that support non-dominant means through which LGBTQ+ individuals engage with technology for identity work.


## ACKNOWLEDGMENTS

Special thanks to Marie Radford, Ross Todd, Gary Burnett, Melissa Aronczyk, and the anonymous ASIS&T reviewers for their thoughtful feedback and revisions.


## REFERENCES


Baym, N. K. (2015). *Personal connections in the digital age*. Hoboken, NJ: John Wiley & Sons.

Bond, B. J., Hefner, V., & Drogos, K. L. (2008). Information-seeking practices during the sexual development of lesbian, gay, and bisexual individuals: The influence and effects of "coming out" in a mediated environment. *Sexuality & Culture, 13*(1), 32–50.

boyd d. (2011) Social network sites as networked publics: Affordances, dynamics, and implications. In: Z. Papacharissi (Ed.) *A networked sself: Identity, community, and culture on social network sites* (pp. 39-58). New York, NY: Routledge.

Carstensen, T. (2009). Gender trouble in web 2.0. Gender perspectives on social network sites, wikis and weblogs. *International Journal of Gender, Science and Technology, 1*(1).

Catfish. (n.d.). In Oxford English Dictionary online. Retrieved from https://en.oxforddictionaries.com/definition/catfish

Cisgender. (n.d.). In Oxford English Dictionary online. Retrieved from https://en.oxforddictionaries.com/definition/us/cisgender

Craig, S. L., & McInroy, L. (2014). You can form a part of yourself online: The influence of new media on identity development and "coming out" for LGBTQ youth. *Journal of Gay & Lesbian Mental Health, 18*(1), 95-109.

Duguay, S. (2016). "He has a way gayer Facebook than I do": Investigating sexual identity disclosure and context collapse on a social networking site. *New Media & Society, 18*(6), 891-907.

Flanagan, J. C. (1954). The critical incident technique. *Psychological Bulletin, 51*(4), 327–58.

Foucault, M. (1978). *The history of sexuality* (R. Hurley, Trans.) (Vol. I). New York, NY: Pantheon Books.

Gamson, J. (1995). Must identity movements self-destruct? A queer dilemma. *Social Problems, 42*(3), 390–407.

Gillespie, T., Boczkowski, P. J., & Foot, K. A. (Eds.). (2014). *Media technologies: Essays on communication, materiality, and society* (1st ed.). Cambridge, MA: MIT Press.

Gray, M. L. (2009). Out in the country: Youth, media, and queer visibility in rural America. New York, NY: NYU Press.

Grov, C., Bimbi, D. S., Nanín, J. E., & Parsons, J. T. (2006). Race, ethnicity, gender, and generational factors associated with the coming-out process among gay, lesbian, and bisexual individuals. *Journal of Sex Research, 43*(2), 115-121.

Haimson, O. L., & Hoffmann, A. L. (2016). Constructing and enforcing" authentic" identity online: Facebook, real names, and non-normative identities. *First Monday, 21*(6).

Haraway, D. (1990). A cyborg manifesto: Science, technology, and socialist feminism in the late twentieth century. In L. Nicholson (Ed.), *Feminism/postmodernism* (pp. 190-233). New York, NY: Routledge.

Hillier, L., & Harrison, L. (2007). Building realities less limited than their own: Young people practising same-sex attraction on the internet. *Sexualities, 10*(1), 82–100.

Howe, N., & Strauss, W. (2000). *Millennials rising: The next great generation*. New York, NY: Vintage Books.

Jagose, A. (1996) *Queer theory: An introduction*. New York, NY: New York University Press.

Kitzie, V. (2017). Beyond behaviors, needs, and seeking: A qualitative investigation of information practices among individuals with LGBTQ+ identities (Unpublished doctoral dissertation). Rutgers University, New Brunswick, NJ.

LaFrance, A. (2015). Not even the people who write algorithms really know how they work. *The Atlantic*. Retrieved from: https://www.theatlantic.com/technology/archive/2015/09/not-even-the-people-who-write-algorithms-really-know-how-they-work/406099/

Leonardi, P. M. (2012). Car crashes without cars: Lessons about simulation technology and organizational change from automotive design. Cambridge, MA: MIT Press.

Leonardi, P. M., Nardi, B. A., & Kallinikos, J. (Eds.). (2014). *Materiality and organizing: Social interaction in a technological world* (1st ed.). Oxford, UK: Oxford University Press.

Lingel, J., & Golub, A. (2015). In face on Facebook: Brooklyn's drag community and sociotechnical practices of online communication. *Journal of Computer-Mediated Communication, 20*(5), 536-553.

Lloyd, A. (2010). Corporeality and practice theory: Exploring emerging research agendas for information literacy. *Information Research, 15*(3).

Manivannan, V. (2013). FCJ-158 Tits or GTFO: The logics of misogyny on 4chan's Random–/b. *The Fibreculture Journal, 22*, 109-129.

Meatspace. (n.d.). In Oxford English Dictionary online. Retrieved from https://en.oxforddictionaries.com/definition/meatspace

Meyer, E.A. & Wachter-Boettcher, S. (2016). *Design for real life*. New York, NY: A Book Apart.

Miles, M. B., & Huberman, A. M. (1994). *Qualitative data analysis: An expanded sourcebook*. Thousand Oaks, CA: Sage.

Mitra, R., & Gajjala, R. (2008). Queer blogging in Indian digital diasporas: A dialogic encounter. *Journal of Communication Inquiry, 32*(4), 400-423.

Merleau-Ponty, M. (1962). *Phenomenology of perception*. (C. Smith, Trans.). Abingdon, UK: Routledge & Kegan Paul.

Nissenbaum, H. (2004). Privacy as contextual integrity. *Washington Law Review, 79*, 101-139.

Noble, S. U. (2013). Google search: Hyper-visibility as a means of rendering black women and girls invisible. *InVisible Culture, 19*.

Norman, D. A. (1999). Affordance, conventions, and design. *Interactions, 6*(3), 38-43.

O'Riordan, K., & Phillips, D. J. (2007). *Queer online: Media technology & sexuality* (Vol. 40). New York, NY: Peter Lang.

Pew Research Center. (2016). Social media use by age group over time. Retrieved from http://www.pewinternet.org/data-trend/social-media/social-media-use-by-age-group/

Pullen, C., & Cooper, M. (Eds.). (2010). *LGBT identity and online new media*. Oxford: Routledge.

Raj, S. (2011). Grinding bodies: Racial and affective economies of online queer desire. *Critical Race and Whiteness Studies, 7*(2), 1-12.

Rothbauer, P.M. (2004). The internet in the reading accounts of lesbian and queer young women: Failed searches and unsanctioned reading. *Canadian Journal of Information and Library Science, 28*(4), 89-110.

Savin-Williams R.C. & Diamond L.M. (2000). Sexual identity trajectories among sexual-minority youths: Gender comparisons. *Archives of Sexual Behavior, 29*(6), 607-627.

Suchman, L.A. (2007). *Human-machine reconfigurations*. Cambridge, UK: Cambridge University Press.

Wakeford, N. (2000). Cyberqueer. In D. Bell & B. M. Kennedy (Eds.), *The cybercultures reader* (pp. 403-415). New York, NY: Routledge.

Ward, J. (2000) Queer sexism: Rethinking gay men and Masculinity In: P. Nardi (Ed.), *Gay Masculinities* (pp. 152-75). Thousand Oaks, CA: Sage.

# Questioning Science with Science: The Evolution of the Vaccine Safety Movement

**Kolina S. Koltai**
*School of Information, The University of Texas at Austin, USA. koltai@utexas.edu*

**Kenneth R. Fleischmann**
*School of Information, The University of Texas at Austin, USA. kfleisch@ischool.utexas.edu*

## ABSTRACT

**This paper sets out to understand the values that motivate vaccine safety advocates who question the safety of vaccines and oppose vaccination mandates. As is generally the case for public scientific controversies, the vaccination debate is inherently asymmetrical. The vast majority of medical researchers advocate for vaccination mandates. While a (smaller) majority of the general public also support vaccination mandates, a vocal and growing minority opposes vaccination mandates. This minority is generally dismissed by most mainstream voices in the scientific literature and the mass media as uninformed and irrational. However, efforts to sway these individuals through public health campaigns have been largely ineffective to date. To understand the factors that motivate individuals within the vaccine safety movement, we conducted interviews with 10 individuals who self-identify as vaccine safety advocates, asking them about the values and information behaviors that have shaped their skepticism of vaccines. Using thematic analysis, we identified four key themes that reoccurred across these interviews: benevolence toward children, intellectual curiosity about vaccines, skepticism toward scientific elites, and respect for the scientific method. The results of this study can help us to understand how values motivate individuals to take positions outside of the mainstream in public scientific controversies, such as climate change and genetically modified foods. Further, the findings help to demonstrate that enhanced understanding of the values that motivate vaccine safety advocates can help us to create shared dialogues that unite rather than divide factions within the vaccination debate, moving from conflict to consensus.**

## KEYWORDS

public scientific controversies, vaccination debate, vaccine hesitant, anti-vaccine, information and human values

## INTRODUCTION

A common tendency is to treat those outside of the scientific mainstream as ill-informed or irrational. In contrast, Martin (2014) argues for the need to understand and highlight the human values that animate scientific controversies. He asserts that scientists and engineers routinely act as if debates around scientific controversies such as abortion, creation science, pesticides, fluoridation, nuclear power, smoking, climate change, nanotechnology, genetically modified organisms, and vaccination are purely factual in nature, however the judgment is in itself a value judgment, but an unstated (and often unquestioned) one.

This paper focuses on one particular public scientific controversy, the vaccination debate, focusing in particular on understanding the values that motivate the beliefs of individuals who self-identify as vaccine safety advocates. The paper begins with a brief history of the vaccination debate, culminating in posing the question of what values motivate individuals to self-identify as members of the vaccine safety movement. We then describe the interview-based approach that we took to understanding these individuals' values, and the open-coding approach that we used to analyze the interview data. We report the results of the interviews, describe how they relate to the literature to date, and discuss their implications for theory and practice.

## TERMINOLOGY

Both in the literature around the vaccination debate and among people in the movement, there is inconsistency with the terminology used to describe people who are critical of vaccines. These individuals are often referred to as "anti-vaccine" or, often pejoratively, "anti-vaxxers." They may identify as "vaccine hesitant" in cases where they seek a more moderate positioning or "pro-vaccine safety" to cast their position as affirmative rather than negative (similar to the abortion debate, where the two sides label themselves as "pro-life" and "pro-choice," with few seeking to be labeled as "anti-life" or "anti-choice"). While any binary classification inherently flattens a much richer spectrum of opinion on this debate (MacDonald & SAGE Working Group on Vaccine Hesitancy, 2015), in the spirit of attempting to adhere with how our participants articulate their stance, we adopt the term *vaccine safety advocate*.

## BACKGROUND

In 2000, the Centers for Disease Control and Prevention (CDC) declared measles eliminated from the United States (Papania et al., 2014). In 2014, more than 50 years after the introduction of a vaccine for measles in 1963, 667 cases of measles from 27 states were reported to the CDC, more cases in one year than the total of a 10-year period from 2002-2011. In addition, the United States has seen a rise in cases of per-

---

80th Annual Meeting of the Association for Information Science & Technology, Washington, DC, VA | Oct. 27-Nov. 1, 2017

tussis, also known as whooping cough. There was a 15% increase in reported cases of pertussis just from 2013 to 2014 (28,639 to 32,971 cases respectively) (CDC, 2015). The recent spike of preventable diseases like measles and pertussis is a pertinent public health concern because both are highly contagious and have the potential for negative, lifelong effects. With the widespread availability, distribution and promotion of vaccines that prevent these communicable diseases, it is surprising to see an uptick in cases over the past few years.

This recent rise in vaccine-preventable communicable diseases in children has been attributed to the growing trend of parents deliberately choosing not to vaccinate their children. While there are a variety of reasons why a parent may choose to not vaccinate, the most common reason is because they do not believe that the benefits of the vaccines outweigh the risks (Funk, Kennedy, & Hefferon, 2017; Kennedy, Brown, & Gust, 2005; Olpiński, 2012). In the United States, it is mandatory that a child be vaccinated to attend private, public or parochial school. While legislation varies from state to state, most states offer a medical exemption and a personal belief/religious exemption to this requirement. While this has worked for many years, there are growing pockets/clusters of parents who are opting out of vaccinating their children.

This is a major public health concern because when there are large clusters of people who are not vaccinated, it is much easier for communicable diseases to spread. The choice to not vaccinate against those diseases potentially affects not only the health of their own children but also the health of immunocompromised children and adults, and those too young to be vaccinated. Their immune systems are either too weak or not adequately prepared to defend against measles, whooping cough or other like diseases. Through herd immunity, communities are able to keep those who are unable to be vaccinated and the immunocompromised safe from infection. Herd immunity is the concept that if a large portion of a community is vaccinated, then when someone who is not vaccinated catches a disease, the disease will have much greater difficulty spreading through the community and protect those are not vaccinated (Fine, 1993; Fu, Rosenbloom, Wang, & Nowak, 2011).

Vaccine dissent is not new. As long as there have been vaccines, there has been resistance against them. The modern-day movement has arisen largely as a result of a (since retracted) journal article published in 1998 by Andrew Wakefield that suggested a link between the MMR (measles, mumps, and rubella) vaccine and autism. Although the claim of a link between vaccines, particularly the MMR vaccine, and autism has been widely discredited, it is still one of the most commonly cited reasons of causing distrust in the MMR vaccine and other vaccines (Jones et al., 2012; Kata, 2012; MacDougall et al., 2015). Wakefield continues to advocate against the use of vaccines, and still holds a strong following among vaccine safety advocates.

Throughout the literature on the vaccination debate, values come up as an emergent theme. Values are commonly described as what is important and salient to a person in their life (Fleischmann, 2014; Friedman & Kahn, 2008; Rokeach, 1973; Schwartz, 2003). These can manifest through goals, preferences, attitudes and beliefs. There are a wide number of ways that researchers operationalize or measure values. Cheng & Fleischmann (2010) developed a meta-inventory to bridge different disciplines' understanding of values. Schwartz (1994) proposes in his work that values are universal throughout cultures and people. Martin (2014) argues in his book that there is a need to understand the relationship between human values and opinions, decisions, and behavior, particularly in relation to scientific controversies. Values are cognitively related to attitudes about topics which can influence the decisions people make about topics (Hitlin & Piliavin, 2004). Previous studies have shown that there is a relationship between values and attitudes towards controversies (Cheng, Fleischmann, Wang, Ishita, & Oard, 2012; Templeton & Fleischmann, 2011) and this arguably applies to scientific controversies as well (Fleischmann, 2003). Values prove to be a consistent predictor of how a person will feel, generate an opinion or even vote on a particular issue.

Values are relevant and key to understanding the vaccine controversy. Values have influence in public policy (Fisher, 1978; Wallace, 1963). It has been found that values guide decision and opinions on health care policy issues, particularly in cases in which people have low ambivalence about the topic and low knowledge about health care reform (Blendon et al., 1994). Values are often used as a guide for voting or decision making, particularly in cases where a person lacks information or interest in a topic (Price, 1992). Values have even been found to influence attitudes and how issues are framed regarding vaccine legislation (Dekker, 2008). Values have relevance when discussing legislative matters involving the vaccination debate and public health policies. They are also seen when discussing community level influences. There seem to be unique values salient to the vaccine safety community as observed through a content analysis of vaccine safety websites and messages (Brunson & Sobo, 2017; Mitra, Counts, & Pennebaker, 2016; Moran, Lucas, Everhart, Morgan, & Prickett, 2016; Wang, Baras, & Buttenheim, 2015). A content analysis of vaccine safety websites found that values of freedom, choice and individuality were prevalent throughout their content (Moran et al., 2016). There is also evidence to support that values play a role in forming opinions and attitudes about different organizations and institutions. Vaccine safety advocates tend to hold more negative views or attitudes and less trust in pharmaceutical companies and the government. (Funk, Kennedy, & Hefferon, 2017; Goldstein, MacDonald, Guirguis, & SAGE Working Group on Vaccine Hesitancy, 2015; Gust et al., 2005; Salmon et al., 2005; Scherer, Shaffer, Patel, & Zikmund-Fisher, 2016). For both interpersonal and individual levels, values are inherent in how a person interacts with other people & health care providers, and in how they form opinions and decide what is salient. A study of vaccine safety messages and attitudes in social media found that new converts to the vaccine safety movement converted as a result of their prior values and beliefs (Mitra et al., 2016). As such, it is evident that values play a vital role in the formation of attitudes about vaccines.

What the public thinks about scientific institutions and scientists ultimately can reflect upon what they think about scientific claims. Based upon theories about how elites influence the public's opinions, the Gateway Belief Model (GBM) has emerged. The GBM states that people's beliefs on scientific issues are heavily influenced by the beliefs of the scientific community (van der Linden, Leiserowitz, Feinberg, & Maibach, 2015b). When there is low consensus within the scientific community (or elites), there will be greater confusion or conflicting opinions about that scientific issue in the public. If there is greater consensus among the scientific community, there is less uncertainty among public opinion. This model shows some promise for application to scientific controversies such as genetically modified (GM) foods and vaccines. A study found evidence that by increasing the perception of consensus in the scientific community, it improved support of GM foods; however they found that people who had low support of GM foods prior to the start of the study were less affected by the GBM (Dixon, 2016). This model was also applied to improving opinions and support of vaccines, which did find evidence to support for the GBM, but the GBM may not work for those who already have very low vaccine support (van der Linden, Clarke, & Maibach, 2015a). While the model shows promise for the majority of the public, it may not be effective for vaccine safety advocates.

This brings up concerns about whether there should be efforts to reduce the prevalence of online information advocating for vaccine safety. As per the GBM, providing a balanced message of both positive and negative information about vaccines can increase uncertainty about the autism-vaccine link versus receiving only pro-vaccine materials (Dixon & Clarke, 2013). Following this model, the appropriate tactic would be to limit the amount of vaccine safety content available. This question brings up part of the vaccine safety community's complaints about censorship. There have been numerous incidents where vaccine safety articles are removed from sites like Huffington Post or delisted from Google's search results. This echoes Brian Martin's concerns about censorship and free speech in the vaccination debate. Martin (2015) suggests, while acknowledging the danger of giving the vaccine safety community a platform, censorship of vaccine safety material only amplifies tensions between the two sides of the debate. Besides being exposed to multiple messages causing confusion, misinformation can have long-lasting effects. Both sides in the vaccine debate hold that the main challenge is misinformation, although what they would label as misinformation varies widely. Belief echoes, which are attitudinal effects of misinformation, are incredibly difficult to change, even after the misinformation has been corrected (Thorson, 2016). Not only does misinformation have long lasting effects, trying to correct information about vaccines can have a backfiring effect and further polarize a person on this topic (Martin, 2015). A common side effect in vaccine information studies is that vaccine safety advocates, after being exposed to vaccine advocacy material, become more confident and solidified in their vaccine safety advocacy (Attwell & Freeman, 2015; Betsch & Sachse, 2013; Nyhan, Reifler, Richey, & Freed, 2014). There is some work being done on how to minimize the backfiring effect through prevention strategies, but there is still much to be done on this topic (Peter & Koch, 2016).

In addition, there is growing evidence that following a deficit model to change attitudes in scientific issues is not effective (Sturgis & Allum, 2004). The deficit model states that low knowledge on a scientific topic is what leads to low public understanding and therefore negative attitudes about scientific topics; however, this model is proving to be less and less precise in explaining attitudes on scientific topics, particularly vaccines as a person can be highly knowledgeable on a topic and still hold negative attitudes (Faasse, Chatman, & Martin, 2016; Hart & Nisbet, 2012; Sturgis & Allum, 2004). In a study analyzing comments from both sides of the vaccination debate on Facebook, vaccine safety comments were found to have more analytical thinking and provide more scientific sources when compared to vaccine advocacy comments (Faasse et al., 2016). As it stands, the models that are currently used to understand dissenting opinions on vaccines are incomplete and do not capture the entire vaccine safety movement. There are still unknowns and misconceptions about the movement.

## METHODS

This study focused on active and vocal members of the vaccine safety movement. Ten participants (eight women, two men) were recruited from an autism conference, an online forum and through snowball sampling. All participants completed an online consent form approved by the University of Texas at Austin IRB before engaging in a phone interview. Interview questions covered topics from how they came to hold their beliefs about vaccines, the sources of information they trust, their interactions with others about vaccines, and their values. Semi-structured interviews lasted on average for an hour (45 - 80 min) and were recorded to facilitate transcription. Participants were geographically distributed across the United States and had occupational roles ranging from advocating full time for vaccine safety to health care, academic research and technology. In addition, participants also had a range of higher education degrees (e.g., PhD, MA) and certifications.

We used thematic analysis (Braun & Clarke, 2006) to analyze the interview data. The first author, who conducted all 10 interviews, took detailed notes during each interview and audio recorded each interview. Based on a review of the detailed notes, the first author identified some emergent themes from the data, informed by the broader literatures on human values and the vaccination debate discussed above. The second author then independently reviewed the notes and themes, and they collaboratively developed an analytical framework for understanding and interpreting the interview data, boiled down into four key value-related themes that cut across multiple interviews and best represented the interview data.

Finally, we employed respondent validation as a means for validating our results (Torrance, 2012). Participants were given the opportunity to review a draft of this paper to provide feedback on the content of the paper and their own quotes. We used this feedback to ensure that our results accurately depicted the views of our interview participants.

## RESULTS

As a result of our thematic analysis, we identified a consistent pattern in the values and evolutionary decision-making process of our participants in their journey to becoming vaccine safety advocates. Eight of the ten participants were initially in support of or ambivalent about vaccines prior to eventually evolving to become vaccine safety advocates. This pattern of conversions was made up of four values: benevolence toward children, intellectual curiosity about vaccines, skepticism toward scientific elites, and respect for the scientific method. This section will outline each of these emergent themes.

### *Benevolence toward Children*

During the interviews, participants were asked to describe how they came to hold their attitudes and beliefs about vaccines. While not all of the participants had children of their own, several participants described incidents involving their own children, or children they were close to, having serious, negative health effects, and in the case of one participant, death, in reaction to the child receiving a vaccine. While not every parent in this study has a child (or close to a child) with a vaccine injury, the participants' concern for children (both their own and others) was consistently mentioned. To sum up the theme of what led most participants to first doubt the benevolence of vaccines, participants consistently stated a strong concern for the safety, health and wellbeing of children. This conflicts with the trope that vaccine safety advocate parents are "selfish" and "only care about their children and not others." Participants' concern for children's well-being goes beyond just their own children, but extends to all children, both in the United States and worldwide.

Participants emphasize that their viewpoints or their attitudes come from a desire to protect children. One participant stated, "So the question becomes how can we protect against diseases...the best way possible without doing collateral damage to children's bodies and children's brains." One participant stated, "I think we are screwing up a whole generation of kids and something has to change." Another participant described how she had never questioned vaccines. Her children and grandchildren were vaccinated because that is what they thought was best. Only after learning and hearing about countless stories of girls suffering from side effects from the human papillomavirus (HPV) vaccine and experiencing terrible injustices from the medical system, she shifted her opinion. When asked about her advocacy work, she said, "I know it's saving lives. I know it's saving families." In addition, many participants brought up the predictive statistic that if the autism rate keeps climbing at the same rate, by 2032, one out of two children will develop autism spectrum disorder (ASD). Another participant stated, "I want us to be having these conversations that are so vitally important to the health of our [children] and humankind." These statements reflect a deep desire for the health and the protection of children.

Often the language used by participants captures this sentiment that their concern is not out of a selfish want for their own child, but the for the protection of all children. One participant stated when asked about their values, "I very, very, very much value the Earth and the environment and I am concerned about human behavior harming our society and harming our planet. I value having a healthy future for our children." The use of "our children" in this person's interview and in others does not refer specifically to their own children, but rather to all children around the world. Another participant stated, "Our children aren't dying of vaccine preventable diseases. Healthy children aren't dying of measles." This participant and statement expressed a high level of worry and concern for the health of children everywhere. They expressed a genuine desire to help prevent children from vaccine injuries or side effects. The sentiment among all the participants emphasized that their position on vaccines was not out of an isolationist viewpoint of focusing just on their own family and needs, but on the welfare and safety of other families and children.

### *Intellectual Curiosity about Vaccines*

The next emergent theme found was that participants had a deep intellectual curiosity about vaccines. Since it is a generally accepted norm that vaccines are safe and necessary, many people feel no need to seek out additional information. However, once a person becomes interested in the topic of vaccines, a search for more information occurs. Several participants stated that, initially, they "never questioned anything about vaccines" or "always believed what they were told." As one participant stated, "I was definitely in the camp of follow in the mainstream. You always follow what the doctors tell you. Why would you ever question it? That is what science says and they know best." There is a consistent trend among most (8/10) participants: they started out from a point of acceptance or non-questioning about vaccines. While reasons vary about what started the participants down the path of vaccine information seeking (e.g. own child's reaction, testimonies of others, news stories), they were in support of vaccines by default prior to this search. Misinformation is often discussed as a main cause for parents to begin to doubt vaccines' safety, but participants argue that misinformation stems primarily from the opposite side of the debate as they were initially in support of vaccines.

Parents describe an internal questioning and curiosity about vaccines. One participant stated, "I can't necessarily trust what a doctor tells me in his office. I need to research these things for myself as a parent. And I'm you know, I knew how to research. And so I started researching." There seems to be a moment when participants do not just trust information blindly. They often talk about conducting their own efforts of researching and exploring sources beyond their healthcare provider. One participant said, "I started realizing that I wasn't getting any of the truth from mainstream sources and that route that was the single biggest change. The single biggest change was 'you are on your own with regard to finding out information because you're not going to get the truth.'" This participant felt that their information needs were not being met by the typical sources. They had to go out and go search out for more. This does not mean that these participants were searching for non-trustworthy sources. Participants emphasized that they specifically were looking that sources they could trust and critically evaluating them.

In asking about what sources of information they trust, many participants listed PubMed and other reputable scientific journals as among their main sources. "I've done a lot of research in the last...year and a half. I've read every PubMed article I could find." Participants consistently stated that they heavily rely on peer reviewed scientific journal articles about vaccines. They often stated that in their research process, they focus on scientific sources. Another example of this is that many participants stated that they read the vaccine package inserts that are written by the pharmaceutical companies that produce the vaccines. They often rely on those package inserts as a source of information about the potential side effects of vaccines. This may go against the popular notion that vaccine safety advocates do not trust any information from the pharmaceutical companies. There is a high degree of focus on relying on scientific and reputable sources. We will discuss this finding in more detail below. Despite participants saying that they trust and rely on these scientific journals and sources, all of the participants described evaluating information very critically.

When asked about their system of evaluating sources of information, they use a rather rigorous set of standards. They evaluate studies by their logic and reasoning. They critically evaluate elements like methods, the argument and the data analysis of a study. "You need to ask yourself if this makes sense." Another participant reiterated this statement. "When I started, I trusted CDC (The Centers for Disease Control and Prevention), NIH (National Institutes for Health), etc., they now come second. Peer reviewed published papers are a much better source. You need to look at who funded it. How did they do it? Placebo? Control? Does it make sense?" Many participants also mentioned being aware of financial conflicts of interest, but that will be discussed in the next section. When asked about their interactions with people when discussing vaccines, participants described enjoying intellectual conversations with other people about vaccines.

Often, when trying to share information that is critical of vaccines, participants received highly negative feedback from others. A participant described the response they received when they shared a vaccine safety post on Facebook. "Everything that came back at me from the other side was this vitriol with no facts. It was all shaming, put down, name calling, no scientific facts behind their side of the issue at all." Participants stated that most of the time people would attack them through emotional means and not through factual means. Participants wished that vaccine advocates would take the time to have a conversation with them instead of resorting to insults about them. One participant recalled a time she was able to sit down and chat with a medical student and address each one of these arguments. The participant stated that it was a calm, levelheaded, adult conversation in which they were able to talk about each of their concerns.

Another participant said "...you know what I actually really, really enjoy is an intelligent person who is for vaccination and challenges me with their understanding of what's going on because then I almost invariably have an interesting discussion and we often come out with a lot of common ground and they start to realize that the 'anti-vaccine' community isn't as crazy as they think it is because there's a lot of rational argument a lot of scientific understanding in the community." There is a concurrent theme that participants want to engage in an intellectual conversation based on their own intellectual curiosity and exploration of the topic. They want to push and continue the conversation in a scientific way.

### *Skepticism toward Scientific Elites*

When participants were asked how they evaluate sources of information, a theme that emerged is the idea of challenging scientific elites. To clarify, the use of the term *scientific elites* does not mean that the community distrusts all researchers and scientists, but instead pushes against the idea of accepting a scientific claim, entity or institution based solely on the prestige of the title.

In evaluating peer reviewed journal articles about vaccines, they often question financial conflicts of interest (FCOI). While the concept of FCOIs in research is often addressed by an acknowledgment at the end of papers, participants go beyond that. They investigate how the study was funded and if the authors have any ties that would be of concern. As one participant described their process, "I trust *Lancet*, mostly. I trust the *New England Journal of Medicine*, but the advertisers make a difference. I trust some journals, but I also know most of the research is funded by drug companies, by agriculture companies, corporations, and it's funneled through universities. So it's unbelievable, the bad research that gets out there."

Participants are conscious about considering if a pharmaceutical company is responsible for funding a study on vaccines, and if so, they consider it an FCOI. FCOIs have been an issue in the past. Cigarettes, now known to be carcinogenic, used to have scientific research backing claims of their safety. Participants have brought up this connection in their interviews. "...the thing that really can get my ire is fraud in research because that's where you lose the public trust. And I feel like there's been so much fraud in this area. I've read the studies. It's like tobacco science. I mean like they want to convince us just like they tried to convince us that smoking cigarettes was just fine and dandy for your health. They're trying to convince us through that same kinds of data manipulation and science that they used in tobacco studies. It's appalling what I've seen." Participants are very wary of work supported by CDC, the Federal Drug Administration (FDA) or other like organizations. Participants are conscious of the fallibility of these groups from previous events like drug recalls. As one participant described, "The FDA makes mistakes. All of those medicines taken off the market were first approved."

Participants are highly concerned with how the FCOI of these large organizations, both private and government, potentially affect scientific findings by these organizations. And similar to vaccines, participants did not always hold these attitudes about these organizations. "I used to be one of those people who believed the CDC had our back and the FDA had our back and they wouldn't recommend something unless...it made sense." Organizations like the CDC and the FDA are often thought to be trustworthy and a source of accurate information. The CDC is a commonly recommended source for information about disease prevention and health concerns. Participants challenge this assumption by holding skeptical views about these organizations and the research that is connected with them. This is not to say that participants think that these organizations are out to intentionally harm the public.

While certainly a few fringe people may think that the government and research organizations are out to intentionally cause harm, this is not the prevailing thought. As one participant stated, "I don't believe the government is out to kill us all. There are those conspiracy theorists out there. I mean, maybe they are, but choose not believe that. It doesn't help. You have to be open minded, but just have a little bit of brain. Does it make sense? Are there sources that corroborate it?" In a follow-up exchange that occurred during respondent validation, the participant later clarified, "So while I don't think that our government is into eugenics, I do believe they are certainly complicit in the 'crime.'" Another participant also wanted to emphasize that "this is a movement because we believe that the government is in collusion with the vaccine industry to conduct a policy of 'the greater good' in public health which is unacceptable. We want to choose what vaccines our kids get. There is a disregard for the injured by our government." There is questioning of the assumptions of the government and the scientific institutions that they support, such as the CDC, the FDA and the NIH.

Many participants brought up the desire to be able to have a conversation about vaccines. As discussed in the previous section, participants want to be able to engage with people in a productive, not insult-based, discussion about vaccine safety. They expressed great frustration that indicating the slightest concern or doubt about vaccines results in them being labeled as "anti-vaccine." As one participant lamented, "I consider myself pro-vaccine. Although I would like to say I think that some of those categories are completely misguided and that there really is no such thing as pro-vaccine/anti-vaccine but we push people who are vaccine hesitant so far into a corner that they've kind of tended to become very, sort of, you know, one sided in their thinking. And so now people embrace that as anti-vaccine but I'm not anti-vaccine. I'm pro-vaccine in the sense that I'm also pro-antibiotic." This participant compared her views about vaccines with her views about antibiotics. She often expresses concerns that antibiotics, while useful, are often misused. This view does not cause her to be marginalized in any way; however, expressing similar concerns about the safety of how vaccines are currently used causes her to be ostracized by her peers. Participants, like this one, discussed the phenomenon they experience that they were immediately called "anti-vaccine" just because they had some questions and concerns. They wonder how science can tout itself in being rooted in asking questions and pushing the boundaries of what humans know, but when people begin to ask questions or doubt vaccines, they are called "anti-science." One participant described the case of Dr. Stephanie Seneff, a senior research scientist at Massachusetts Institute of Technology (MIT). Dr. Seneff is a highly accomplished researcher who never had her work questioned until she began questioning vaccines and genetically modified organisms (GMOs). A participant described her story. "Because she suggested that vaccines are implicated they had to destroy her career as well. Even a high integrity researcher at NIH for years, and when she used the words 'vaccine might have caused this,' career destruction. And I'm seeing the same pattern with Andy Wakefield, with Dr. Mikovitz, with…researchers repeatedly where whenever they implicate vaccines the powers that be have to destroy their careers and discredit them. It's really an amazing thing and it makes me sound like a conspiracy theorist." Participants described case after case of educated, respected people whose standing in the scientific community changed drastically when they questioned vaccines. They wonder why scientists can question just about anything else except for vaccines. As a participant said, "My desire is that we can get back to scientific normalcy in this area."

### Respect for the Scientific Method

While these statements might indicate that these participants have a negative perception of science or the scientific community, they actually have a great deal of respect for science. Several of the participants come from an academic background in science. As discussed in the last section, they want to be able to question vaccines just like any other scientific issue. One participant described how, at least in the case of vaccines, science is losing its historical emphasis on questioning theories and traditional orthodoxy: "I think there's been so much just propaganda through the press, through doctors' offices, and everything else. People really are brainwashed on this. It's become a religion for people. It's like I was attacking a religion when I said what I said. And so, I feel like on the vaccine issue anyway, science has become a religion to them and it's not science so it's actually not the science. If they actually worship science they would know what I know. You see what I'm saying? Yeah I was I was told I was 'anti-science.' Are you kidding me? I'm just pro-science person I've ever met in my life. You know, I want the science. They just haven't done the studies yet…Vaccines has become just like politics and religion. Vaccines is one of the conversations we can't have. Why? Is it because this whole area of science has become a religion and no questions are allowed? To contradict it because it's heresy if you do. That's what it feels like right now and so to me that's not very scientific. That's very theological." This participant was frustrated by the "religion of science" around vaccines, the idea that scientific elites have determined that people cannot question scientific orthodoxy in any way, as in the case of organized religion, particularly vaccines. One participant described how the medical education process supports this ideology. They described how medical students are taught to accept the curriculum as-is without questioning the faculty about the content. The part of the message that seems to get lost in public perception of the vaccine safety movement is that these participants want more research into vaccines that is free of FCOI and done in a rigorous manner. They often refer to the striking lack of double blind placebo-control studies about vaccines, which are generally considered the gold standard for drug testing. While there are certainly people who may never trust another vaccine, some participants described a desire for better vaccines, or perhaps using vaccines only when they are appropriate. "I don't think that vaccines are all bad and we should throw them out and never use them again. I don't think that vaccines are all good and we should get every single one that's ever been tested, you know, suggested to us necessarily unless we think it's safe or effective and necessary. I think that vaccines have a place in public health. But in the United States are being grossly overused and inappropriately overused to the point where we are now all hurting so many children that I understand why people are vaccine hesitant to the point of not wanting to do any vaccine." This participant describes the phenomenon of over vaccination and expresses a desire for more scientific scrutiny to be focused on vaccines. There are people within this community who hold a great deal of respect for science, vaccines and the health of people. They have adopted a way of being critical of science by scientific means and reasoning. For example, there is the notion that scientists should change and adapt theories and hypotheses if they are presented with new information. As one participant described, "I'm old enough that when I went to school I was taught to question everything. That is what science was." Another participant also conveyed this same manner of thinking. "I want to say my views are not set in stone. I think that any time you have any medical intervention you should always be open minded about it and there's always room for improvement. There's always room for additional knowledge with always room for change." This quote further supports the respect that vaccine safety advocates have for science. Perhaps one of the biggest misconceptions about people who question vaccines is that they are 'anti-science.' One participant who focuses on advocacy work said, "I have a standing statement to never use anything that cannot be backed up scientifically." While vaccine safety advocates are often written off as "anti-science," the interviews reveal that, to the contrary, vaccine safety advocates articulate strong admiration for and adherence to the scientific method.

## DISCUSSION

To date, efforts to change of attitudes or behavior of vaccine safety advocates have been largely futile (Nyhan et al., 2014). Survey data indicates that the number of vaccine safety advocates is growing (Funk, Kennedy, & Hefferon, 2017). Our findings suggest that there is more to the vaccine safety movement than what current theories and models propose. We identified four emergent value-laden themes: benevolence toward children, intellectual curiosity about vaccines, skepticism toward scientific elites, and respect for the scientific method. These findings challenge what is currently understood about how people make decisions about vaccines and assumptions and stereotypes about the community. There is an assumption that the vaccine safety community is inherently anti-science and that they are selfish in caring only about their own children. These interviews indicate an evolutionary development to their beliefs that go against these assumptions. Our participants express deep care not only about their own children but also about children everywhere. Their desire to protect and improve the health of all children spurred their interest in exploring more about vaccines. This exploration and examination of vaccine information is done with a highly critical lens, particularly of scientific elites and financial conflicts of interest. Our participants expressed a high value and appreciation for science and the process of questioning and discussing scientific issues and concerns. These value laden themes seem to support previous work that indicate values play a larger role in vaccine decision making than once thought (Brunson & Sobo, 2017; Mitra et al., 2016; Moran et al., 2016; Wang et al., 2015).

The deficit model, which holds that these individuals do not have enough or accurate information about vaccines, is not supported by these findings. Participants were highly knowledgeable about vaccines, including their ingredients, legislation and scientific studies about their effectiveness and safety. Lack of information about vaccines does not seem to explain why these participants question vaccines. This suggests that this model is insufficient in understanding the movement. In addition, gaps in other models, like the GBM, highlight a deficiency in our understanding of how decisions about vaccines are made (van der Linden et al., 2015a, 2015b). While the GBM has been useful in increasing positive attitudes about vaccines this has not been effective for those who already hold some skepticism or negative attitudes about vaccines.

The results of this study support previous work highlighting the importance of values unique to the vaccine safety advocacy movement. This study improves upon previous work by providing a deeper understanding of those values through an ethnographic methodology as well as challenging assumptions about their perception of science. Research and literature about the vaccination debate have been heavily focused on content analysis of vaccine content online or through mass surveys that are distributed to an entire geographic community. This study provides a qualitative field research-based approach to understanding their decision making. The values that emerged from this study also widen our understanding about how values influence the assessment and evaluation of scientific information. In addition, there is currently no proven intervention or theory that has proven to be effective in shifting opinions, attitudes and behaviors of vaccine safety advocates. While there are a variety of theories available from the health behavior literature, they have been applied primarily to addressing improving vaccine uptake across a whole community (e.g., a geographic area, school setting), not to the specific vaccine safety community. In a review of strategies to address vaccine hesitancy, tailoring to meet the needs of the group due to the complexity of the movement is identified to be a key area for future work (Jarrett et al., 2015). Our results suggest that current communication and public opinion theories about science need to be combined with health behavior theory to develop a model that addresses the gap in previous models.

In addition, the results of this study can help us to understand how values motivate individuals to take positions outside of the mainstream in public scientific controversies, such as climate change and genetically modified foods. Further, the findings help to demonstrate that enhanced understanding of the values that motivate individuals within the vaccine safety movement can help us to create shared dialogues that unite rather than divide factions within the vaccination debate.

## LIMITATIONS AND FUTURE DIRECTIONS

There are several limitations with this study. First, there is a self-selection bias with these participants. This community tends to be cautious when participating in research studies. It can be difficult to convince people to trust that the research is not designed to mischaracterize their testimonies. The participants that agreed to be interviewed may be more familiar with research and therefore were more willing to participate. These participants may not be, and should not be considered, completely representative of the entire vaccine safety advocacy community. However, these individuals work and participate within those communities and their ideologies can be reflective of the community in some capacity. The second limitation is the sample size. This was an exploratory study. While there were only ten participants, the interviews indicate that there do seem to be values unique to the community that influence a switch from vaccine acceptance to questioning vaccines. Third, participants may be influenced by social desirability bias. The vaccine safety advocacy position is still taboo. Participants may have skewed their responses to seem more appealing or less extreme as they were aware they were being interviewed by an academic researcher. They may have had reservations still about divulging extreme opinions.

Future studies can include further exploration into the relationship values play in decision making about vaccines. Evidence from this study indicates there are unique values salient to the vaccine safety movement. Future studies can explore this concept with larger sample sizes, more embedded participant observation and deeper analysis.

## IMPLICATIONS

The theoretical implications of this study challenge what is understood about the rationale of those who question vaccines. Often, the deficit model is considered a primary way to change people's opinions about vaccines; however, this study gives evidence that the lack of positive vaccine information does not seem to be the cause of why people question vaccines. While arguably misinformation or conflicting information about vaccines can decrease a person's certainty about vaccines, it does not explain the full evolutionary change from being in support of vaccines to questioning them. This research gives indication that values play a key role in decision making in this topic and potentially other controversial scientific issues.

Practical implications of this study can inform on how to develop interventions, craft messages, and support dialogue with those who question vaccines. Themes from this study suggest that the way this community interacts with healthcare professionals and others does not foster healthy or productive discussion for either side. By understanding the reasoning and the values of vaccine safety community, recommended guidelines for healthcare professionals and health information campaigns can be developed to reach a wider audience.

This study can also inform the "fake news" debate and how people develop belief systems based upon their values (Verma, Fleischmann, & Koltai, 2017). The information that a person is willing to ingest and trust in their everyday life can have major effects on their life choices and voting behavior. By understanding how values affect how people interpret information, particularly information related to controversial topics, we can gain insights into how information shapes decision making, and how values influence the interpretation of information and how exposure to the same information may lead different people with different values to make different decisions.

## ACKNOWLEDGMENTS

The authors gratefully acknowledge funding from the Vara Martin Daniel Regents Professorship in Libraries, Archives, and Information Studies Fellowship, which provided financial support that made this research possible. The authors would also like to thank all of the participants who generously took the time to participate in this study.

## REFERENCES

Attwell, K., & Freeman, M. (2015). I Immunise: An evaluation of a values-based campaign to change attitudes and beliefs. *Vaccine, 33*, 6235-6240.

Betsch, C., & Sachse, K. (2013). Debunking vaccination myths: Strong risk negations can increase perceived vaccination risks. *Health Psychology, 23*, 146-155.

Blendon, R. J., Marttila, J., Benson, J. M., Shelter, M. C., Connolly, F. J., & Kiley, T. (1994). The beliefs and values shaping today's health reform debate. *Health Affairs, 13*, 274-284.

Braun, V., & Clarke, V. (2006). Using thematic analysis in psychology. *Qualitative Research in Psychology, 3*(2), 77-101. http://doi.org/10.1191/1478088706qp063oa

Brunson, E. K., & Sobo, E. J. (2017). Framing childhood vaccination in the United States: Getting past polarization in the public discourse. *Human Organization, 76*, 38-47.

CDC. (2015, September). Pertussis Outbreak Trends. Retrieved April 6, 2016, from http://www.cdc.gov/pertussis/outbreaks/trends.html

Cheng, A.-S., & Fleischmann, K. R. (2010). Developing a meta-inventory of human values. *Proceedings of the American Society for Information Science and Technology, 47*, 1-10.

Cheng, A.-S., Fleischmann, K. R., Wang, P., Ishita, E., & Oard, D. W. (2012). The role of innovation and wealth in the net neutrality debate: A content analysis of human values in congressional and FCC hearings. *Journal of the American Society for Information Science and Technology, 63*, 1360-1373.

Dekker, R. L. (2008). Human papillomavirus vaccine legislation in Kentucky: A policy analysis. *Policy, Politics, & Nursing Practice, 9*, 40-49.

Dixon, G. (2016). Applying the gateway belief model to genetically modified food perceptions: New insights and additional questions. *Journal of Communication, 66*, 888-908.

Dixon, G. N., & Clarke, C. E. (2013). Heightening uncertainty around certain science: Media coverage, false balance, and the autism-vaccine controversy. *Science Communication, 35*, 358-382.

Faasse, K., Chatman, C. J., & Martin, L. R. (2016). A comparison of language use in pro- and anti-vaccination comments in response to a high profile Facebook post. *Vaccine, 34*, 5808-5814.

Fine, P. E. M. (1993). Herd immunity: History, theory, practice. *Epidemiologic Reviews, 15*, 265-302.

Fisher, W. R. (1978). Toward a logic of good reasons. *Quarterly Journal of Speech, 64*, 376-384.

Fleischmann, K. R. (2003). Frog and cyberfrog are friends: Dissection simulation and animal advocacy. *Society & Animals, 11*, 123-143.

Fleischmann, K. R. (2014). *Information and human values*. San Rafael, CA: Morgan & Claypool.

Friedman, B., & Kahn, P. H., Jr. (2008). Human values, ethics, and design. In A. Sears & J. A. Jacko (Eds.), *The human-computer interaction handbook fundamentals, evolving technologies and emerging applications* (Second edition) (pp. 1241-1266). New York.

Fu, F., Rosenbloom, D. I., Wang, L., & Nowak, M. A. (2011). Imitation dynamics of vaccination behaviour on social networks. *Proceedings, Biological Sciences*, 278(1702), 42-49.

Funk, C., Kennedy, B., & Hefferon, M. (2017). *Vast majority of Americans say benefits of childhood vaccines outweigh risks*. Washington, DC: Pew Research Center.

Goldstein, S., MacDonald, N. E., Guirguis, S., & SAGE Working Group on Vaccine Hesitancy. (2015). Health communication and vaccine hesitancy. *Vaccine, 33*, 4212-4214.

Gust, D. A., Kennedy, A., Shui, I., Smith, P. J., Nowak, G., & Pickering, L. K. (2005). Parent attitudes toward immunizations and healthcare providers. *American Journal of Preventive Medicine, 29*, 105-112.

Hart, P. S., & Nisbet, E. C. (2012). Boomerang effects in science communication. *Communication Research, 39*(6), 701-723.

Hitlin, S., & Piliavin, J. A. (2004). Values: Reviving a dormant concept. *Annual Review of Sociology, 30*, 359-393.

Jarrett, C., Wilson, R., O'Leary, M., Eckersberger, E., Larson, H. J., & SAGE Working Group on Vaccine Hesitancy. (2015).

Strategies for addressing vaccine hesitancy - A systematic review. *Vaccine, 33*, 4180-4190.

Jones, A. M., Omer, S. B., Bednarczyk, R. A., Halsey, N. A., Moulton, L. H., & Salmon, D. A. (2012). Parents' source of vaccine information and impact on vaccine attitudes, beliefs, and nonmedical exemptions. *Advances in Preventive Medicine, 2012*(12), 1-8.

Kata, A. (2012). Anti-vaccine activists, web 2.0, and the postmodern paradigm - An overview of tactics and tropes used online by the anti-vaccination movement. *Vaccine, 30*, 3778-3789.

Kennedy, A. M., Brown, C. J., & Gust, D. A. (2005). Vaccine beliefs of parents who oppose compulsory vaccination. *Public Health Reports, 120*, 252-258.

MacDonald, N. E., & SAGE Working Group on Vaccine Hesitancy. (2015). Vaccine hesitancy: Definition, scope and determinants. *Vaccine, 33*, 4161-4164.

MacDougall, D. M., Halperin, B. A., MacKinnon-Cameron, D., Li, L., McNeil, S. A., Langley, J. M., & Halperin, S. A. (2015). The challenge of vaccinating adults: Attitudes and beliefs of the Canadian public and healthcare providers. *BMJ Open, 5*(9), e009062-12.

Martin, B. (2014). *The controversy manual*. Sparsnäs, Sweden: Irene Publishing.

Martin, B. (2015). Censorship and free speech in scientific controversies. *Science and Public Policy, 42*, 377-386.

Mitra, T., Counts, S., & Pennebaker, J. W. (2016). Understanding anti-vaccination attitudes in social media. In *Proceedings of the tenth international AAAI conference on web and social media*, pp. 269-278.

Moran, M. B., Lucas, M., Everhart, K., Morgan, A., & Prickett, E. (2016). What makes anti-vaccine websites persuasive? A content analysis of techniques used by anti-vaccine websites to engender anti-vaccine sentiment. *Journal of Communication in Healthcare, 9*, 151-163.

Nyhan, B., Reifler, J., Richey, S., & Freed, G. L. (2014). Effective messages in vaccine promotion: a randomized trial. *Pediatrics*, 133, e835-42.

Ołpiński, M. (2012). Anti-vaccination movement and parental refusals of immunization of children in USA. *Pediatria Polska, 87*, 381-385.

Papania, M. J., Wallace, G. S., Rota, P. A., Icenogle, J. P., Fiebelkorn, A. P., Armstrong, G. L., ... Seward, J. F. (2014). Elimination of endemic measles, rubella, and congenital rubella syndrome from the western hemisphere. *JAMA Pediatrics, 168*, 148-155.

Peter, C., & Koch, T. (2016). When debunking scientific myths fails (and when it does not): The backfire effect in the context of journalistic coverage and immediate judgments as prevention strategy. *Science Communication, 38*, 3-25.

Price, V. (1992). *Public opinion*. Newbury Park, CA: Sage.

Rokeach, M. (1973). *The nature of human values*. New York: Free Press.

Salmon, D. A., Moulton, L. H., Omer, S. B., deHart, M. P., Stokley, S., & Halsey, N. A. (2005). Factors associated with refusal of childhood vaccines among parents of school-aged children. *Archives of Pediatrics & Adolescent Medicine, 159*, 470.

Scherer, L. D., Shaffer, V. A., Patel, N., & Zikmund-Fisher, B. J. (2016). Can the vaccine adverse event reporting system be used to increase vaccine acceptance and trust? *Vaccine, 34*(21), 2424-2429. http://doi.org/10.1016/j.vaccine.2016.03.087

Schwartz, S. H. (1994). Are there universal aspects in the structure and contents of human values? *Journal of Social Issues, 50*(4), 19-45.

Schwartz, S. H. (2003). A proposal for measuring value orientations across nations. In *Questionnaire package of the European social survey* (pp. 259-319).

Sturgis, P., & Allum, N. (2004). Science in society: Re-evaluating the deficit model of public attitudes. *Public Understanding of Science, 13*, 55-74.

Templeton, T. C., & Fleischmann, K. R. (2011). The relationship between human values and attitudes toward the Park51 and nuclear power controversies. *Proceedings of the American Society for Information Science and Technology, 48*, 1-10.

Thorson, E. (2016). Belief echoes: The persistent effects of corrected misinformation. *Political Communication, 33*, 460-480.

Torrance, H. (2012). Triangulation, respondent validation, and democratic participation in mixed methods research. *Journal of Mixed Methods Research, 6*, 111-123.

van der Linden, S. L., Clarke, C. E., & Maibach, E. W. (2015a). Highlighting consensus among medical scientists increases public support for vaccines: Evidence from a randomized experiment. *BMC Public Health, 15*, 352.

van der Linden, S. L., Leiserowitz, A. A., Feinberg, G. D., & Maibach, E. W. (2015b). The scientific consensus on climate change as a gateway belief: Experimental evidence. *PloS One, 10*, e0118489.

Verma, N., Fleischmann, K. R., & Koltai, K. S. (2017). Human values and trust in scientific journals, the mainstream media, and fake news. *Proceedings of the Association for Information Science and Technology*.

Wallace, K. R. (1963). The substance of rhetoric: Good reasons. *Quarterly Journal of Speech, 49*, 239-249.

Wang, E., Baras, Y., & Buttenheim, A. M. (2015). "Everybody just wants to do what's best for their child:" Understanding how pro-vaccine parents can support a culture of vaccine hesitancy. *Vaccine, 33*, 6703-6709

# Toward an Understanding of Cross-Media Appeals for Readers' Advisory

**Jin Ha Lee**
*University of Washington, USA. jinhalee@uw.edu*

**Hyerim Cho**
*University of Washington, USA. chohr113@uw.edu*

**Travis Windleharth**
*University of Washington, USA. travisw@uw.edu*

## ABSTRACT

**Readers' advisory services in libraries have traditionally focused heavily on the recommendation of books and audiobooks, excluding wide swaths of other media in the library's collection. To provide readers' advisory across a variety of media formats, we identify and investigate common appeal factors across multiple types of media, including books, films, video games, graphic novels, and music. The project was conducted in two phases: a domain analysis and a user study. During the first phase, we reviewed existing literature and consulted with domain experts to identify 19 appeals across different media types. In the second phase, we interviewed 30 participants who actively consume two or more types of media to understand what kinds of appeals are important and relevant to them when selecting media to consume. We discuss the five most prominent appeals—mood, setting, complexity, character, and theme—in detail, followed by implications on using these cross-media appeals in readers' advisory.**

## KEYWORDS

Appeals, Cross-media appeals, Readers' Advisory services, Recommendation

## INTRODUCTION

Libraries have a long tradition of recommending materials to users via services such as readers' advisory (RA). RA has been a core library service and vital to public libraries since the 1950s (Haines, 1950). A survey of 694 public librarians conducted by Library Journal, with NoveList and the Reference & User Services Association (RUSA), also revealed that librarians consider the provision of RA as "mission-critical and an area of growth" (Thornton-Verma & Schwartz, 2014). Furthermore, more than half of respondents reported that RA will become even more important in the next three years. Given the current and growing importance of RA as a critical library service, it is imperative that we have a solid framework and guidelines for providing such services.

80th Annual Meeting of the Association for Information Science & Technology, Washington, DC, VA | Oct. 27-Nov. 1, 2017



Although RA was deemed critical by respondents to the aforementioned survey, one out of five expressed angst in providing RA. Respondents cited several reasons for such a feeling, including the inability to keep up with new books and unfamiliarity with certain genres. Moreover, 23% of respondents reported that their institution provides no training or support for such services, and thus most librarians rely on external recommendation databases such as NoveList (61%) or social networking tools like Goodreads (34%) for recommendations. These services, though useful, only support recommendations of books and audiobooks.

Two additional survey findings are especially noteworthy: only about half of respondents felt confident in advising children or young adults, and most RA work focused heavily on recommendation of books and audiobooks, excluding much of the library's media collection. One way to effectively engage younger populations in digital libraries is to incorporate and suggest materials they are already regularly consuming, such as video games, graphic novels, films, and music.

As an example, video games are rarely suggested in library advisory services, despite the explosive growth of the video game industry and increasing consumer use. Video games play an important role in attracting teens to libraries. Branston (2006) reports that 69% of teens play video games each week, and urges, "educators and librarians need to be aware of these statistics" (p. 24). It would be imprudent not to include materials with a powerful appeal to youth in library advisory services. Games can support literacy and provide tangential learning experiences (Gee, 2010), and may also serve as a potential entry point for youth to access different types of media and print formats, supporting transliteracy, "the ability to read, write and interact across a range of platforms, tools and media" (Ipri, 2010, p. 532).

The Guidelines for Media Resources in Academic Libraries[1] published in 2012 by the Association of College & Research Libraries and Guidelines for Library Services to Teens[2] distributed by RUSA arrive at the same conclusion: audio-visual materials are becoming increasingly important in teaching,

[1] http://www.ala.org/acrl/standards/mediaresources
[2] http://www.ala.org/rusa/resources/guidelines/guidelinesteens

learning, and research. Both state the importance of meeting youth where they are, developing and promoting resources, tools, and technologies youth use on a daily basis.

We seek to address these pressing challenges in RA by developing provisions for high-quality cross-media advisory services based on the idea of *appeals*— certain people being attracted to certain types of materials, regardless of format. For instance, a patron who likes to read novels with elaborate and complicated storylines may also enjoy a role-playing game with a well-established narrative component. A patron who likes experimental and non-mainstream music may also be interested in watching indie films. Fundamentally, patrons are seeking various types of experiences when they interact with library materials, and it is the aim of RA to be a useful guide. Trott and Williamson (2011) also discuss the importance of cross promotion of library materials given the wide range of connections that exist among different media objects. They highlight the fact that users' consumption of different types of library materials will allow us to draw new connections between users and collections.

To support RA in libraries, we aim to identify and investigate common appeal factors across different media types and develop ways to describe those appeals in a manner that facilitates cross-media advisory services. Search/browse features in catalogs and recommender systems based on appeal factors would help improve the quality of current RA services by allowing librarians to make suggestions with increased confidence, even when the genre or media is unfamiliar. For instance, an appeal "mood" will be easier to understand than genres of materials with which librarians are unfamiliar (e.g., 4X games, mathcore music). To advance RA services, we seek to address the following research questions:

RQ1. What are the most common appeal factors across multiple types of media?

RQ2. What features or characteristics of these common appeal factors are relevant when users describe them across multiple types of media?

## RELATED WORK

### *Appeals Defined and Discussed in Prior Literature*

Previous research on users' motivations for consuming media objects such as books (Saricks, 2005; Pearl, 2012), audiobooks (Mediatore et al., 2003), video games (Bartle, 1990; Ipri, 2010; Sherry et al., 2006), and movies (Kunkel, 2009; Tamborini & Stiff, 1987) suggest that patterns of user preferences can be reduced to a small number of fundamental categories. This idea of appeals has been discussed in multiple domains, and various authors have provided definitions and explanations. Forsyth (2010) views appeals as what users enjoy about a book, film, art work, or other works, while Saricks (2005) defines appeals as elements to which a reader relates.

Several different terms have been used to refer to appeals, including appeal characteristics/elements/factors, doorways, aesthetics, gratifications, motivations (motivators), and personality types. Each type of appeal is also often referred to by multiple terms (e.g., "mood," "tone," "feel," and "emotion" all refer to the same aesthetic concept). Literature in RA (e.g., Saricks, 2005; Pearl, 2012; Trott & Williamson, 2011) tends to use "appeals" or "doorways" more often to describe elements (especially those of fiction) such as pacing, characters, storyline, tone, mood, style, language, frame, or setting. Pearl (2012) offers a helpful explanation of appeals, claiming that what we must think about is "what it is about a book that draws us in, rather than what the book is about." She suggests *the rule of four*, which refers to four doorways: story, character, setting, and language.

Media studies (e.g., Rosengren, 1974; Malone, 1981; Sherry et al., 2006) tend to use the terms gratifications, motivations, or motivators more frequently to describe user consumption of video games or television. Among several different types of gratifications discovered, the most prominent appeal is entertainment.

In the video game domain, discourses on appeals include factors that also reflect active involvement or interactions with media. Hunicke et al. (2004) suggest the MDA (Mechanics, Dynamics, and Aesthetics) framework to describe the appeals of video games. The authors explain "aesthetics" as desirable emotional responses evoked in the player during interaction with the game. Their framework has eight core aesthetic goals, which include sensation, fantasy, narrative, challenge, fellowship, discovery, expression, and submission. Similarly, Malone (1981) explains that users consume media because of intrinsic motivations rather than extrinsic rewards.

Based on previous literature on appeals, we are defining appeals as "elements of media that draw people in by evoking certain emotional and intellectual experiences when interacting with the media." We will also consistently use "appeals" among many choices, hereinafter.

### *Need for Understanding Cross-Media Appeals*

Understanding different types of appeals and identifying which appeals matter to different users is widely recognized as critical to the success of recommendation services in libraries (Saricks, 2005). Despite a substantial body of research on the appeals associated with media, most previous research focuses on investigating appeals for a single type of media. We still lack an understanding of common appeals across different types of media. The gap also exists in commercial recommendation services (e.g., Netflix, Pandora). Users currently must rely on several different services to find what they may want to read, watch, play, or listen to next.

Additionally, no standard terminology exists to describe appeals across media (e.g., for the appeal "mood," which mood terms can we use to describe the moods evoked by interacting with different types of media?). NoveList provides controlled vocabularies for the six appeals it employs, but is limited to appeals for books. For librarians to be able to effectively use appeal factors to suggest suitable materials, it is necessary to establish controlled vocabularies for common content-based and aesthetic appeals across media.

Previous research on appeals has almost exclusively focused on one specific type of media, such as fiction, video games, or movies, and often with a narrower scope depending on the type of game (e.g., massively multiplayer online role-playing games) or movie (e.g., Horror). We still do not understand whether there are unifying cross-media appeal factors, and if they exist, how feasible it is to use them as a basis for recommendation. In previous literature (especially regarding RA), most appeals are content-based rather than aesthetic appeals describing the user's experience. Previous ideas for providing cross-media advisory seem to be centered on genre and common themes/topics (e.g., Theme: Lost - book: *Bad Twin* by Laurence Shames, DVD: *Lost: Season One*, CD: *Hurley* by Weezer or *Lost* soundtrack). Our work aims to look beyond genres or themes that are common access points in library catalogs and other recommendation services.

Several librarians have started to explore ways to provide recommendation services for audiovisual materials and compiled lists of online resources for librarians (Pitman, 2001; Nicholson, 2010; Trott & Williamson, 2011). While these provide an excellent starting point as guidelines for librarians, the appeals discussed are often based on personal opinion and experience rather than a systematic analysis of empirical user data. In our work, we attempt to identify and discuss common appeals of media from empirical user data. Insights gleaned from our work will help us better understand the different domains of cross-media and provide a deeper understanding of appeals in future attempts to increase discoverability and access for different interactive media objects.

## STUDY DESIGN AND METHODS

This project was carried out in two phases, building upon our previous research on the appeals of video games as part of a larger research effort to establish a metadata schema for video games and interactive media (Lee et al., 2016). The first phase focused on a domain analysis based on review of existing literature and consultation with domain experts. Building on results from the first phase, we conducted an empirical user study in the second phase to obtain a richer understanding of the relevance and importance of various appeals to users when they choose media to consume.

### *Phase I: Domain Analysis*

In this phase, we conducted a domain analysis as described by Hjørland (2002) as our initial approach in identifying possible cross-media appeals. The analysis consisted of surveying the literature in a domain and was complemented by a consultation with domain experts.

We started by reviewing bodies of literature related to appeal factors in multiple domains, including library and information science, psychology, marketing, and media studies. We also comprehensively identified and reviewed online resources, including websites, bibliographies, indexes, and databases that employed appeal factors or similar concepts for providing access to media objects.

Based on our analysis of these resources, we derived a combined taxonomy of 19 appeals across different media types with descriptions and references to source materials (Table 1). After that, we consulted with the advisory board established for this project, consisting of three experts in RA and multimedia organization/recommendation: Nancy Pearl, Lecturer, Librarian, and Author, University of Washington, Information School; John Vallier, Head of Distributed Media, University of Washington Libraries Media Center; and Judi Windleharth, Director of Learning Resource Center at DigiPen Institute of Technology. With these domain experts, we discussed potential values and limitations of each of the appeals with specific media, such as fiction, games, music, and film.

As this is an exploratory study, the primary goal was to identify a small number of cross-media appeals from 19 identified appeals to explore in-depth in the subsequent user study in the second phase. *Genre* was the first appeal eliminated in the selection process, as this project was explicitly designed to think beyond genre. This work intends to deconstruct genre elements that appeal to readers and articulate them. Further selection of potential cross-media appeals to explore in the next phase was based on multiple criteria such as the transferability across multiple media types, degree of subjectivity, and ability to measure and describe the appeals.

The first step of the selection process focused on filtering appeals that were difficult to transfer across multiple media types, resulting in the exclusion of certain appeals such as *Language, Pacing, Sensation, Accomplishment, Fellowship,* and *Interactivity*. For instance, *Language*, as described in the literature, typically refers to writing style in printed materials and predominantly applies to books. While a case can be made that film, games, and music also contain text, the references in the literature are highly specific to books and especially fiction; in other media formats, describing language as an appeal is typically less central.

| | Appeal | Description | Literature |
|---|---|---|---|
| Content-based | Characters (also referred to as Characterization) | People in a story with whom readers have an emotional connection | Saricks (2005); Pearl (2012) |
| | Setting (Frame, Background) | The world in which a story takes place | Saricks (2005); Trott & Williamson (2011); Pearl (2012) |
| | Language (Style) | Writing style, grammar, and word use in a piece of literature | Mooney & Roy (2000); Saricks (2005); Pearl (2012) |
| | Narrative (Story, Storyline) | Plot and events that media take the reader through | Hunicke, LeBlanc, & Zubek (2004); Saricks (2005); Pearl (2012) |
| | Pacing | How the story unfolds | Saricks (2005) |
| | Genre (Style, Format) | A style or form of content | Trott & Williamson (2011) |
| | Theme (Subject, Topic) | Main subject of the media | Saricks (2005); Trott & Williamson (2011) |
| Experiential | Accomplishment (Achievement, Completion, Reward structures, Satisfaction) | Feeling the satisfaction of acquiring and/or accomplishing something | Wigand, Borstelmann, & Boster (1985); Bartle (1990); Klimmt (2003); Yee (2006); King &Defarbo (2009); Tocci (2012) |
| | Arousal (Excitation, Stimulation, Adrenaline, Exhilaration) | Feeling excited and/or stimulated | Wigand, Borstelmann, & Boster (1985); Griffiths (1991); Vorderer, Hartmann, & Klimmt (2003); Klimmt (2003); Hunicke, LeBlanc, & Zubek (2004); Sherry et al. (2006); Abbott (2010); Greenberg et al. (2010) |
| | Sensation (Sense-pleasure, Audiovisuality, Graphics, Sound) | Appreciating the visual and/or auditory content | Klimmt (2003); Hunicke, LeBlanc, & Zubek (2004); Ermi & Mäyrä (2005); Abbott (2010) |
| | Fantasy (Imaginative fiction, Make-believe) | Immersing oneself in a fantasy world, and thus being able to do things not possible in real life | Malone (1981); Myers (1990); Hunicke, LeBlanc, & Zubek (2004); Ermi & Mäyrä (2005); Tocci (2012); Choi et al. (2013) |
| | Mood (Tone, Feel, Emotion) | Achieving a particular emotional state, and/or immersing oneself in media expressing a particular mood | Goldberg & Gorn (1987); Nell (1988); Ross & Chelton (2001); Saricks (2005); Banerjee et al. (2008); Hollands (2006); Rossi, Lee, & Clarke (2014) |
| | Challenge (Obstacle course) | Feeling the joy of overcoming obstacles or challenges | Malone (1981); Vorderer, Hartmann, & Klimmt (2003); Csikszentmihalyi (1990); Hunicke, LeBlanc, & Zubek (2004); Ermi & Mäyrä (2005) |
| | Fellowship (Social framework, Cooperation, Teamwork, Social reward) | Enjoying the company of others | Griffiths (1991); Hunicke, LeBlanc, & Zubek (2004); Jansz & Tanis (2007); Greenberg et al. (2010) |
| | Discovery (Exploration, Uncharted territory, Curiosity) | Feeling of exploring uncharted territory | Malone (1981); Bartle (1990); Myers (1990); Hunicke, LeBlanc, & Zubek (2004); Abbott (2010) |
| | Expression (Self-discovery, Ego) | Self-discovery/actualization | Hunicke, LeBlanc, & Zubek (2004); Sherry et al. (2006) |
| | Cognitive (Thinking, Knowledge, Learning) | Learning and/or thinking about something | Ermi & Mäyrä (2005); Stewart (2011) |
| | Submission (Pastime, Recreation, Abnegation) | Passing time, "turning off one's brain" and/or unwinding/relaxing | Hunicke, LeBlanc, & Zubek (2004); Schuurmaan et al. (2008) |
| | Interactivity (Interactions between user and game elements, Social interaction) | Selecting and/or modifying elements to which users are exposed | Selnow (1984); Bartle (1990); Myers (1990); Sherry et al. (2006); Tocci (2012) |

***Table 1.*** *Summary of appeal discussed in previous literature*

Similarly, *Pacing* was also specifically articulated to refer to books. *Sensation* also relates to different types of sensory experiences based on the type of media (e.g., auditory, visual, tactile), and thus is more difficult to transfer across media. *Achievement, Interactivity*, and *Fellowship* are also predominantly discussed in literature exploring video game appeals. It is also unclear how it would transfer to other media that tend to be more passively consumed without a specific set of goals by individuals. *Challenge* did emerge in discussions of other media, but most of the work detailing what *Challenge* entails also referred to the level of challenge in video games. Of the remaining appeals, some were eliminated from consideration because determining concrete terms and aspects related to these appeals proved difficult due to their subjective nature. For instance, *Discovery* and *Expression* are explained in several different manners in the literature, and their meaning and interpretation can substantially differ between individual users discussing the same media (e.g., discovering oneself, discovering new things in an environment such as a game, discovering new knowledge). *Submission* is another example where the ways people unwind and relax can be very different based on their familiarity with the media and personal taste—for instance, playing a first-person shooter game versus playing a puzzle game, or listening to classical music versus heavy metal to relax.

We ultimately decided to focus on *Mood, Cognitive,* and *Setting*, based on the results of testing the applicability of individual appeals across multiple media in a series of exercises, describing the appeals for sample media objects of different types. The advisory board members also supported the decision, considering the potential of individual appeals as cross-media appeals. The term *Cognitive* was renamed to *Complexity* to account for specific ideas about the complexity of a work in terms of intellectual content, structure, and time commitment to complete it (further discussion in Section 4.1.3).

### Phase II: User Study

With the decision to focus on *Mood, Setting,* and *Complexity* as candidates for cross-media appeals, we proceeded to collect empirical user data regarding how these appeals manifest for users across different media. We recruited 30 participants via various university mailing lists and researchers' social networks. All participants were 18 or older, and were active users of at least two different types of media objects. We conducted a semi-structured interview and asked participants about their preferred media objects and appeals for those objects to gain an improved understanding of appeals in general, as well as how users may describe appeal factors across multiple media (e.g., "I like games and books that are dark and gritty.").

The interview process was piloted with a small number of test participants in a graduate level course on multimedia metadata at the University of Washington Information School. Based on feedback, some questions were revised for clarity. Response options for collecting information regarding *Setting* were also modified. During pilot testing, we noticed that while users often talk about a wider variety of different specific settings (e.g., Western, Space), they are easily grouped into three broad categories: our world (the setting of media reflects reality, as it is now), imaginary world (usually a fantasy world, where users can enjoy imaginary settings and characters, as in *Lord of the Rings*), and alternate world (between our world and an imaginary world, keeping a mostly real setting but with a twist, such as zombie or vampire characters, as in *The Walking Dead*). The research team and test participants agreed that using three broad categories allowed for noting some meaningful distinction among settings without listing all the specific settings, which could grow to an untenable size quickly. After these revisions, we proceeded to collect user data from 30 participants.

Participants were asked to fill out a pre-interview questionnaire before coming to the session. They were asked to 1) specify which types of media they generally consume among options including books, video games, films/animations/TV shows, graphic novels/manga, music, and other; 2) provide two to three examples of the kinds of works they typically enjoy for each media type; 3) explain what they liked about the listed examples; and 4) describe common characteristics of the examples listed. This was intended to prompt users to think about how these different media objects appeal to them prior to the interview session. Three participants specified that they regularly consume two types of media, 14 specified three types of media, nine specified four types of media, and four specified five types of media.

In the interview session, we asked more specific questions regarding the importance of the three appeals (i.e., *Mood, Setting,* and *Complexity*). Regarding *Mood*, we asked if they felt there was a prominent mood among the media objects they generally like to consume. Regarding *Setting*, we asked if the media objects they like tend to be based on our world, an imaginary world, or an alternate world. Regarding *Complexity*, we asked if the media they typically like tend to have complex plots or structures, and if they have a preferred level of mental or intellectual engagement when choosing certain media. In addition, we asked how important *Mood, Setting,* and *Complexity* were in determining whether they want to engage with certain media. We also asked them to describe any appeals (other than *Mood, Setting,* and *Complexity*) that were important to them when they choose to consume more than one type of media. Responses from the pre-interview questionnaire and recordings of the interviews were open-coded. Four independent coders conducted coding, identifying all the instances where each appeal was mentioned, following a codebook of 23 appeals created through an iterative process.

## FINDINGS AND DISCUSSION

### *Overview of Appeals by Media Type*

Analyzing responses from the pre-interview questionnaire revealed that users seek media objects based on a diverse set of appeals. Several participants mentioned how the activity helped them see connections among different media objects they liked which they did not recognize before. Participant six (P6) noted:

*"Before answering the questions above, I would have said there aren't any common characteristics, but I now think there may be a few: I like problem solving and engagement...I like media that requires for me to put some work into it."* (P6)

The five most frequently cited appeals were each mentioned by over half of all respondents. They were either an important appeal among media they already consume, or something they consider when seeking new media. In order of frequency of citation, these five dominant appeals are *Mood* (24), *Theme* (23), *Setting* (21), *Complexity* (20), and *Character* (16). In addition to these five major appeals, 23 additional appeals were articulated by more than one user, resulting in a long tail of media characteristics. While less frequently cited, some (e.g., popularity, characteristics of creators such as gender) may remain important to specific stakeholders such as game publishers/developers or sub-groups of media consumers. In this paper, we focus on discussing the five most frequently mentioned appeals (which will be referred to as "primary" appeals hereinafter).

#### Mood

Overall, mood was the most commonly mentioned appeal by our participants. When the core reason for consuming media objects is to experience or appreciate feelings, we considered mood as the core appeal. It is noteworthy that, specifically for music, mood was predominantly mentioned compared to other appeals—20 out of 24 participants who mentioned mood as important said mood was particularly relevant to music. For other media types, the mood appeal seemed to be more distributed. Other than some comments regarding the complexity of music, and one participant discussing theme, participants primarily relied on mood to explain why they were drawn to certain music. This could indicate that mood is especially important in music preference, or perhaps that it is more difficult to describe other aspects of music when compared to other types of media objects. The latter may especially be true for music without any lyrical content or music in foreign languages. Calming aspects of mood (e.g., peaceful, relaxing, calm, etc.) were most frequently noted as the feeling that is sought by the participants (18 responses), followed by humorous (17) (e.g., humorous, light-hearted, etc.), exciting (14) (e.g., intense, excited, aggressive, etc.), and sad (13) (e.g., sad, melancholy, depressing, etc.). Other moods mentioned by more than five participants included: serious (12), unsettling (12), dark (8), and happy (8).

It also was apparent that the mood of music was especially relevant to tasks participants were carrying out as they were listening to music. Several mentioned that they select the type of music that helps them better focus on their work, although the type of work could vary, such as studying, writing, exercising, or manual work. The following user quote highlights the importance of mood in music when creating an atmosphere suitable for accompanying user tasks.

> *"If I need to get something done that's just kind of mindless, doing the task that's very repetitive, I'll listen to more upbeat music. If I'm reading or writing, I might listen to music that's slower, like more meditative." (P4)*

In addition to the mood of the media itself, the mood of the day was also important to participants. It indicates that a mood appeal to users may be context-dependent and tend to change depending on an individual's given situation and current feelings.

> *"I guess it has to match my feelings of the day, that day, and like...so...it could be all related to me in some sort of situations, to be appealing." (P1)*

Another interesting tendency was that some participants found it easier to note which moods they wanted to avoid, as opposed to moods they prefer and seek (e.g., "*Horror. Scary movies. I really hate that.*" (P11)). Several participants mentioned specifically that they do not enjoy a scary or frightening mood. For users, being able to avoid unappealing moods may be as important as being able to select preferred moods, and should be considered when designing recommendation systems.

#### Setting

Setting also played an important role in 21 participants' selection of media. Despite being mentioned frequently, in currently available systems and services relating to media, setting information is often difficult for users to access. For instance, video streaming services such as Netflix or Amazon video do not provide browsing options for setting, except for "fantasy." The video game website Giant Bomb allows users to search for terms which include some general (e.g., desert, underwater) and specific (e.g., Jakku, Ivalice) locations, but search or browsing can be challenging due to the large number of terms.

When participants discussed setting, they tended to view it as an appeal broadly relevant to their general media consumption, rather than specific types of media. Setting was mostly mentioned when discussing media objects with strong narrative components such as films, TV shows, books, and games, but rarely to music.

For participants who mentioned setting as a relevant appeal to them, we asked them to identify what kind of setting primarily appeals to them among three categories: our world, imagined world, and alternate world. The categorization received positive reactions from participants, as they found it helpful in broadly characterizing settings that matter to them, in addition to providing a more detailed description of setting in their own words.

**Our world**: "It's too much work to imagine that...like elves, fairies, and things like that, I want to focus more on the characters, themes, and the questions." (P3)

**Alternate world**: "Like some settings, most would be places that are in real...but like these people exist there. There are fairies there, or something like that." (P7)

**Imaginary world**: "I prefer more imaginary worlds like Game of Thrones." (P4)

Overall, imaginary world was mentioned most as a relevant setting to our participants (20), followed by alternate (14) and our world (10).

### Complexity
Aspects of media complexity were mentioned by 20 participants. Participants' comments regarding complexity clustered into three sentiments: intellectual complexity (mentioned by 12 participants), structural complexity (11 participants), and time commitment (four participants). Intellectual complexity represents cognitive challenges posed by the media, and asks a greater share of a consumer's mental focus to process and understand it. In books, this typically means elaborate and complex writing, more characters with complex relationships, denser plots, and complicated subject matter requiring higher mental engagement from the user (e.g., *"I like compelling narratives and philosophically weighty media"* (P22)). Many comments referenced the intellectual appeal of media and specifically indicated learning as a desired outcome of consuming the media (e.g., *"I really like to read books and watch documentaries where I am actually learning something"* (P17)). This ties closely to the concept of media as intellectual stimulation and as such, comments specifically referencing learning were included in the "Intellectual" component of complexity.

The second type of complexity, structural complexity, represents a clearly articulated set of characteristics that multiple users found particularly relevant. Structural complexity is defined as a significantly non-linear or multi-layered means of presenting media, such as the use of framing, non-linear timelines and flashbacks, stories within stories, and multiple alternate points of view.

> *"I really like non-linear stories, with flashbacks and a bunch of plots going on at once in different places at different times, that all start to connect later in the book." (P14)*

Lastly, time commitment, as an element of complexity, represents the time investment required to process the entirety of a media object. This aspect of complexity was important to some users because they had limited time to consume media objects in their everyday lives and thus had to make decisions as to which media objects they could afford time to consume.

> *"It's a special sort of challenge to need to invest time into working through something, like a long movie or book, there is a special kind of commitment that is often lost these days, but can be nice to get back to using that kind of focus." (P25)*

### Character
Character was mentioned as an appeal by 16 participants, and character development (i.e., how characters grow up/change throughout the story) by four participants. Except for music, all media types with a stronger narrative component tend to draw references related to this appeal. A few participants mentioned being drawn to media objects featuring characters with specific characteristics, as shown in the following sample quotes:

> *"Books for sure, almost every single book I read has a strong female lead. I didn't notice that until today, but, clearly that's something I look for." (P7)*

> *"Heroic, about likeable characters." (P9)*

Participants also mentioned preferring characters to which they can relate. One participant (P1) specifically mentioned that she avoids any type of media that does not have relatable characters. A few participants focused on describing how characters evolve and change in the narrative, rather than specific types of characters, indicating the importance of considering characters and narrative concurrently.

> *"Of course, like a lot of people, I've been binging lately on Jessica Jones, that Netflix series, and I like that because there's a lot of strong female characters and there's like an element of figuring out how she got to be the way she is, and you know you don't know everything about her in the first episode, you just get little hints. I like that. I like discovering more about the characters." (P3)*

It may be fruitful to further explore what aspects of character information (e.g., personality, occupation, gender, or appearance) users find meaningful, which would help establish a controlled vocabulary for character. Once such a controlled vocabulary is built, character information related to different media objects can be cataloged, and individual users could potentially indicate their preference for specific characteristics to improve recommendation results.

### Theme
Of the five primary appeals that emerged from the user data, theme seems to be the most well represented appeal in existing systems and frameworks via metadata elements such as themes, subjects, and topics. Some examples of themes mentioned by users include references to appreciating post-apocalyptic themes in games and comic books, or historical themes in film and books. Most respondents (23) listed one or more themes they considered useful or important in media. For instance, users made statements such as *"I like movies that explore other cultures"* (P12), or *"I really like things about space or astronomy"* (P13). In addition to comments about specific themes or motifs, several general comments about the relevance of theme were observed, such as *"I'll search for something about a topic I am interested in at that time in my life"* (P17). This suggests that certain subject matter is more important to the user at a given time, representing some manner of "content" appeal in a given context.

## IMPLICATIONS

The outcome of this study reveals three primary cross-media appeals, and when more deeply explored, these appeals were in fact relevant to media users. Users articulated these appeals by mentioning and categorizing specific moods, types of settings, and levels of complexity. This implies that a multifaceted classification of appeals, to some degree, was understandable and usable by the participants in this study. Users demonstrated that the concept has merit and can potentially be employed in future recommendation systems.

*Mood* as an appeal was consistently relevant to users across media and participants often utilized specific media to achieve a specific mood. For instance, nearly one-third of users indicated seeking and using music to help achieve a relaxing mood. This represents a strong link between a specific media type and a specific mood in the data. As another example, among video game players, a "dark" mood was mentioned significantly more often than other moods, and film users frequently articulated a preference for "serious" or "exciting" films. This seems to suggest that media users have a common use case for mood and associate it with specific media.

While the interview data in this study does not provide enough basis for statistical analysis, it is interesting to note that specific moods seem to be sought in certain media more often than others. It is also noteworthy that while book and film media sources were used and discussed roughly equally, users articulated a preference for specific moods in film more often than books. However, for literature, consumers frequently mentioned characters as an important appeal. These differences underscore the notion that, aside from general preferences and trends in these appeals, users might want to seek media for specific purposes or gratifications in some instances. Future research could reveal how common these patterns are among a larger group of users.

It may also be useful to explore whether we will still be able to identify a relatively small set of predominantly important moods for users along with a long tail of other types of moods, if more data was collected from a larger number of users. We established three broad categories to distinguish different types of *Setting*, and we may be able to identify a small number of mood clusters that can be used to categorize different media objects.

Of the three different aspects of *Complexity*, time commitment may be difficult to measure due to each user's varied speed in consuming media objects. What may be more important is how we measure and specify intellectual and structural complexity. Although one may argue that these aspects are not completely objective, there may be a way to decompose the different aspects of the narrative, which affects the overall complexity of the media object—for instance, the number of characters, the plot progression, and the number of different views/perspectives. An alternative way would be to crowdsource this information from people who have already consumed the media.

Findings from this study validate certain appeals (i.e., *Mood, Setting,* and *Complexity*), utilizing their respective subcategories and terms, providing a basis for filtering and searching in service to user retrieval of media items. These appeal terms can be applied to various media of all types, and a recommendation system could potentially track appeals aligned with media for individual users, to provide a media appeal "profile" for each user.

In addition, these appeals could aid users filtering results in recommendation systems, complementing other common access points. Adding these appeal categories as metadata in digital libraries (perhaps via a crowdsourced method, such as user tags provided in library catalogs) can also help librarians provide recommendations transcending dependence on genre and theme, and serve as a bridge to assist users in discovering new media in novel ways. This would also work across media boundaries. For instance, in the current paradigm, fans of science fiction literature often simply search for the narrative genre "science fiction" for games or graphic novels. It may turn out that the specific appeal that draws them to science fiction is intellectual complexity, or a setting in an alternate world, or an adventurous mood. Suggesting literature based on appeals matching the aforementioned criteria that are not science fiction may aid users in finding other media that fit their interests.

Finally, the emergence of a multifaceted system that describes media items could itself provide insight into how specific appeals relate to one another. For instance, this framework implies that user data in a future study could be analyzed to see if, for instance, users seeking intellectual complexity are more likely to seek out or appreciate alternate worlds.

## CHALLENGES AND LIMITATIONS

The limitation of sample size should be noted regarding our user data. While we provided the frequency of citations for different appeals, these numbers are based on a limited user base of 30 people, thus they should not be considered as representative of a larger population. Another big challenge in this study was that people often had difficulties describing the appeals of media that were important to them. What became apparent to us during the pilot interviews was that people can easily provide examples of what they like, but if they are directly asked to articulate reasons for their preference of media consumption, many could not immediately describe them. To fix this problem, we chose a method of eliciting users' responses on appeals, starting with sample items they like for each type of media. We then provided them an opportunity to think about commonalities among those items, and prompted them to explicate the reasons for their preferences.

Another issue we observed was that people often resorted to genre labels when asked to describe appeals. This is not surprising, considering that as flawed or limited as they may be, genres are probably the most familiar way for users to group and characterize the kinds of media they like. When this occurred during the interview process, we encouraged users to try to move away from simple genre descriptions by asking them to more specifically describe which aspects they liked about given genres.

Lastly, some interviewees do not consume all the media types we were investigating—they might like two or three media types, but were not interested at all in another type. Thus, our data skewed towards certain media types. We expect that this limitation could be addressed in a future study by surveying a larger number of users to further verify the findings from this study.

## CONCLUSION AND FUTURE WORK

This research aims to contribute to renovating the recommendation of digital media objects, widely recognized as a mission-critical service in libraries. There is also a growing recognition that we need to understand how to provide meaningful recommendation services incorporating audiovisual and interactive media materials. The fact that average users are format omnivores and consume a variety of different media must be reflected in recommendation services in digital libraries. In addition to improving the ability of digital libraries to provide valuable recommendation services in the age of new media, cross-media recommendations will contribute to improving the trans-literacy of library users as they are increasingly exposed to a wider variety of media. Particularly for young library users as well as seniors, robust and effective cross-media recommendation services are a promising and resonant means of introducing patrons to media forms they may not have previously considered embracing. Our study revealed the following findings:

Based on the frequency of citation, the five dominant appeals were *Mood, Theme, Setting, Complexity,* and *Character*.

*Mood* is predominantly mentioned with music, and the mood of music was especially relevant to tasks participants were carrying out as they listened to music.

*Setting* was frequently mentioned with strong narrative components, and could be organized into three broader categories: our world, imagined world, and alternate world.

Participants' comments regarding *Complexity* can be classified into three elements: intellectual complexity, structural complexity, and time commitment.

All media types with a stronger narrative component tend to draw references related to *Character*. Further exploration will be necessary to understand what aspects of character information (e.g., personality, occupation, gender, or appearance) users find most meaningful.

Some participants noted that subject matter (*Theme*) is important to them at different points in time, representing "content" appeal in certain contexts.

Based on findings obtained from the initial exploratory study, in future work we plan to conduct a survey to further evaluate the relevance of the primary appeals identified and test the applicability of the categories established for describing these appeals with a larger group of users. We also hope to more fully explore and enumerate the descriptors users employ and possibly uncover other potential cross-media appeals.

## ACKNOWLEDGMENTS

We thank our advisory board members Nancy Pearl, John Vallier, and Judi Windleharth for their help in guiding this research. We also thank Amber Kim and Matthew Phillips for their valuable contributions in coding the user data. This research was supported by the OCLC/ALISE Library & Information Science Research Grants.

## REFERENCES

Abbott, M. (2010). Fun Factor Catalog. Brainy Gamer. http://www.brainygamer.com/the_brainy_gamer/2010/08/fun-factors-catalog.html

Banerjee, S. C. et al. (2008). The Role of Gender and Sensation Seeking in Film Choice: Exploring Mood and Arousal. *Journal of Media Psychology: Theories, Methods, and Applications*, 20(3), 97–105.

Bartle, R. A. (1990). Interactive Multi-User Computer Games. http://mud.co.uk/richard/imucg.htm

Branston, C. (2006). From Game Studies to Bibliographic Gaming: Libraries Tap into the Video Game Culture. *Bulletin of the ASIST* (April/May 2006).

Choi, B., Huang, J., Jeffry, A., & Baek, Y. (2013). Development of a Scale for Fantasy State in Digital Games. *Comp. in Human Behavior*, 29(5), 1980–1986.

Csikszentmihalyi, M. (1990). *Flow: The Psychology of Optimal Experience*, 1st ed. New York: Harper & Row.

Ermi, L. & Mäyrä, F. (2005). Fundamental Components of the Gameplay Experience: Analysing Immersion. In *Proceedings of DiGRA 2005 Conference: Changing Views - Worlds in Play*, Vol. 3.

Forsyth, E. (2010). From Assassins Creed 2 to the Five Greatest Warriors: Games and Reading. *Australasian Public Lib. and Info. Services*, 23(2), 117-128.

Gee, J. P. (2010). What Video Games Have to Teach Us about Learning and Literacy, NY: Palgrave Macmillan.

Goldberg, M. E. & Gorn, G. J. (1987). Happy and Sad TV Programs: How They Affect Reactions to Commercials. *Journal of Consumer Research*, 14(3), 387–403.

Greenberg, B. S., Sherry, J., Lachlan, K., Lucas, K., & Holmstrom, A. (2010). Orientations to Video Games among Gender and Age Groups. *Simulation & Gaming*, 41(2), 238–259.

Griffiths, M. D. (1991). Amusement Machine Playing in Childhood and Adolescence: A Comparative Analysis of Video Games and Fruit Machines. *Journal of Adolescence* 14(1), 53–73.

Haines, H. E. (1950). *Living with Books: The Art of Book Selection*, 2nd ed. New York: Columbia University Press.

Hardiman, S. (2010). Library's Game to Attract Teen Patrons. Portland Press Herald (August 12, 2010). http://www.pressherald.com/2010/08/12/librarys-game-to-attract-teen-patrons_2010-08-12/

Hjørland, B. (2002). Domain Analysis in Information Science: Eleven Approaches – Traditional as Well as Innovative. *Journal of Documentation*, 58(4), 422–462.

Hollands, N. (2006). Improving the Model for Interactive Readers' Advisory Service. *Reference and User Services Quarterly*, 45(3), 205–212.

Hunicke, R., LeBlanc, M., & Zubek, R. (2004). MDA: A Formal Approach to Game Design and Game Research. http://www.aaai.org/Papers/Workshops/2004/WS-04-04/WS04-04-001.pdf

Ipri, T. (2010). Introducing Transliteracy: What Does It Mean to Academic Libraries? *College & Research Libraries News* 71(10), 532–533.

Jansz, J. & Tanis, M. (2007). Appeal of Playing Online First Person Shooter Games. *CyberPsychology & Behavior*, 10(1), 133–136.

King, D. & Delfabbro, P. (2009). Motivational Differences in Problem Video Game Play. *Journal of Cyber Therapy and Rehabilitation*, 2(2), 139-149.

Klimmt, C. (2003). Dimensions and Determinants of the Enjoyment of Playing Digital Games: A Three-Level Model. In *Level Up: Digital Games Research Conference*, M. Copier & J. Raessens (eds.), 246-257.

Kunkel, V. (2009). Instant Appeal: The 8 Primal Factors that Create Blockbuster Success. NY: AMA.

Lee, J. H., Clarke, R. I., & Rossi, S. (2016). A Qualitative Investigation of Users' Discovery, Access, and Organization of Video Games as Information Objects. *Journal of Information Science*, 42(6), 833-850.

Malone, T. W. (1981). Toward a Theory of Intrinsically Motivating Instruction. *Cognitive Science*, 4, 333-369.

Mediatore, K., Pearl, N., & Chelton, M. K. (2003). Reading with Your Ears: Readers' Advisory and Audio Books. *RUSQ*, 42(4), 318–23.

Mooney, R. J. & Roy, L. (2000). Content-Based Book Recommending Using Learning for Text Categorization. In *Proc. of the ACM Conf. on Digital Libraries*, 195–204.

Myers, D. (1990). A Q-Study of Game Player Aesthetics. *Simulation & Gaming*, 21(4), 375–396.

Nell, V. (1988). *Lost in a Book: The Psychology of Reading for Pleasure*. New Haven, CT: Yale University Press.

Nicholson, J. (2010). Viewers' Advisory. http://slideplayer.com/slide/686691

Pearl, N. (2012). Check It Out with Nancy Pearl: Finding That Next Good Book. Publishers Weekly, http://www.publishersweekly.com/pw/by-topic/columns-and-blogs/nancy-pearl/article/51109-check-it-out-with-nancy-pearl-finding-that-next-good-book.html

Pitman, R. (2001). Viewers' Advisory: Handling Audiovisual Advisory Questions. In *The Readers' Advisor's Companion*, ed. K. D. Shearer & R. Burgin, Englewood, CO: Libraries Unlimited, 229–236.

Rosengren, K. E. (1974). Uses and Gratifications: A Paradigm Outlined. In *The Uses of Mass Communications: Current Perspectives on Gratifications Research*, Sage Annual Reviews of Communication Research. Beverly Hills, CA: SAGE, 269–286.

Ross, C. S. & Chelton, M. K. (2001). Reader's Advisory: Matching Mood and Material. *Library Journal*, 126(2), 52–55.

Rossi, S., Lee, J. H., & Clarke, R. I. (2014). Mood Metadata for Video Games and Interactive Media. In *Proc. of the 2014 IEEE/ACM JCDL*, 475–476.

Saricks, J. G. (2005). Readers' Advisory Service in the Public Library, 3rd ed. Chicago: ALA.

Schuurman, D., De Moor, K., De Marez, L., & Looy, J. V. (2008). Fanboys, Competers, Escapists and Time-Killers: A Typology Based on Gamers' Motivations for Playing Video Games. In *Proc. of the 3rd Int. Conf. on Digital Interactive Media in Entertainment and Arts*, 46–50

Selnow, G. W. (1984). Playing Videogames: The Electronic Friend. *Journal of Communication*, 34(2), 148–156.

Sherry, J. L., Lucas, K., Greenberg, B. S., & Lachlan, K. (2006). Video Game Uses and Gratifications as Predictors of Use and Game Preference. In *Playing Video Games: Motives, Responses, and Consequences*, ed. P. Vorderer & J. Bryant. Mahwah, NJ: Routledge, 213–224.

Stewart, B. (2011). Personality and Play Styles: A Unified Model. Gamasutra. http://www.gamasutra.com/view/ feature/134842/personality_and_play_styles_a_.php

Tamborini, R. & Stiff, J. (1987). Predictors of Horror Film Attendance and Appeal: An Analysis of the Audience for Frightening Films. *Comm. Research*, 14(4), 415–436.

Thornton-Verma, H. & Schwartz, M. (2014). The State of Readers' Advisory. http://lj.libraryjournal.com/2014/02/ library-services/the-state-of-readers-advisory/

Tocci, J. 2012. Five Ways Games Appeal to Players. Gamasutra, http://www.gamasutra.com/view/feature/ 168807/ five_ways_games_appeal_to_players.php

Trott, B. & Williamson, T. B. (2011). Materials Matchmaking: Articulating Whole Library Advisory. *Reference & User Services Quarterly*, 50(3), 230–34.

Vorderer, P., Hartmann, T, & Klimmt, C. (2003). Explaining the Enjoyment of Playing Video Games: The Role of Competition. In *Proc. of the 2nd International Conference on Entertainment Computing*, 1–9.

Wigland, R. T., Borstelmann, S. E., & Boster, F. J. (1986). Electronic Leisure: Video Game Usage and the Communication Climate of Video Arcades. *Annals of the International Communication Association*, 9(1), 275-293.

Yee, N. (2006). The Demographics, Motivations, and Derived Experiences of Users of Massively Multi-User Online Graphical Environments. *PRESENCE: Teleoperators and Virtual Environments*, 15(3), 309–329.

# Exploring Prestigious Citations Sourced from Top Universities across Disciplines

**Feiheng Luo**
*Wee Kim Wee School of Communication and Information, Nanyang Technological University, Singapore. fhluo@ntu.edu.sg*

**Aixin Sun**
*School of Computer Science and Engineering, Nanyang Technological University, Singapore axsun@ntu.edu.sg*

**Moijsola Erdt**
*Wee Kim Wee School of Communication and Information, Nanyang Technological University, Singapore. mojisola.erdt@ntu.edu.sg*

**Aravind Sesagiri Raamkumar**
*Wee Kim Wee School of Communication and Information, Nanyang Technological University, Singapore. aravind002@ntu.edu.sg*

**Yin-Leng Theng**
*Wee Kim Wee School of Communication and Information, Nanyang Technological University, Singapore. TYLTheng@ntu.edu.sg*

## ABSTRACT

**There have been many studies on the factors influencing paper citation counts. A number of studies have focused on the citing papers, and corresponding methods were proposed to measure the prestige of citations based on the journal impact factors, the total citation counts and the PageRank algorithm values. However, there are drawbacks to these methods. In this paper, we propose a novel method to identify prestigious citations from the affiliation of the citing paper. Specifically, if the authors of the citing paper are affiliated with a prestigious university, the citing paper could be counted as a prestigious citation. As a pilot, we used the top 200 universities on the QS World University Rankings 2015 to identify the prestigious universities so that the prestigious citations, named as QS citations, were identified accordingly. Experimental results validated that QS citations have more important impact on the cited papers than other citations. Papers with QS citations have better performance across most disciplines not only in total citation counts, but also in altmetrics such as the Altmetric Attension Score and Mendeley reader counts.**

## KEYWORDS

citation analysis, university ranking, altmetrics, citation counts, QS citations

## INTRODUCTION

Citation counts have been one of the most dominant indicators in assessing the impact of articles, researchers, journals and affiliations. Many researchers have been engaged in exploring the factors which affect citation counts. On the one hand, a number of researches have concentrated on the factors related to the papers, such as the number of authors and the journal impact factor (Tahamtan et al., 2016; Aksnes, 2003; Khor & Yu, 2016; Didegah & Thelwall, 2013; Filion & Pless, 2008). These studies can be classified to two main categories. The first category of studies investigated the relationship between citation counts and the related factors (Bornmann et al., 2012; Slyder et al., 2011; Kulkarni et al., 2007; Didegah & Thelwall, 2013), while the other category predicted future citation counts using statistical regression approaches or progressively improved machine learning techniques with the related factors as input (Stegehuis, Litvak, & Waltman et al., 2015; Yu et al., 2014; Brizan et al., 2016; Chen, 2012). The findings from these studies showed that the impact of the related factors varied across disciplines. An influential factor in a particular discipline could be much less important in another discipline.

On the other hand, there were studies which focused on the citing papers instead of the cited papers (Chen et al., 2007; Ding & Cronin, 2011; Yan & Ding, 2010; Habibzadeh & Yadollahie, 2008; Bollen, Rodriquez, & Sompel, 2006). A citation can be considered as a scholarly vote, and thus these researchers held that the weight of citations should be differentiated to reflect the prestige of the citing paper (Ding & Cronin, 2011; Yan & Ding, 2010). According to Tahamtan (2016), the citation count of a paper could be influenced by its citing papers as the citing papers increase the cited paper's visibility and subsequently induce further citations. Hence, one can assume that a prestigious citation would have a more important impact on the cited paper than a less prestigious citation.

For measuring the prestige of citations, primarily three different ways have been proposed in the previous studies. However, there are drawbacks in all the three methods. The first method relies on the impact factors of the citing journals (Yan & Ding, 2010; Habibzadeh & Yadollahie, 2008). In this way, the possible flaws of journal impact factors, such as the skewed distribution across all disciplines, would be subsequently propagated. Besides, impact factors are not available for conference proceedings, while proceeding papers also play a critical role in some disciplines, such as computer science. The second method uses the citation counts of the citing

80th Annual Meeting of the Association for Information Science & Technology, Washington, DC, VA | Oct. 27-Nov. 1, 2017

paper (Ding & Cronin, 2011; Yan, Ding, & Sugimoto, 2011). One concern of this method is that the citing papers need to accumulate citations before they can become eligible as a highly cited paper and eventually become a prestigious citation. The last method constructs a paper citation network and then applies the PageRank algorithm to evaluate the papers (Chen et al., 2007; Liu et al., 2005; Yan, Ding, & Sugimoto, 2011). Potential problems in this method include computing complexity and dynamic network structure caused by newly published papers.

In this paper, we propose a novel method to identify prestigious citations. We postulate that a prestigious citation can be defined by the affiliation of the citing paper. Specifically, if the authors of the citing papers are affiliated with a prestigious affiliation, the citing papers could be counted as prestigious citations. An explicit advantage of our proposed method is that once the citing paper is published, it can be identified whether it is a prestigious citation or not. Complicated calculations are not required in our proposed method, and more importantly, our method does not suffer from the drawbacks mentioned above in the previous three methods. Furthermore, as will be shown in the following experiments, the prestigious citations identified by our method could be applied to all disciplines.

In order to evaluate our proposed method, we used the top 200 universities on the QS World University Rankings 2015[1] in our study to identify prestigious affiliations so that the prestigious citations could be identified accordingly. These prestigious citations are referred to as *QS citations* in this paper. Comparative experiments are designed to detect and analyse the relationship between QS citations and total citation counts for papers. Additionally, since altmetrics have attracted increased attention as an alternative measure of impact (Costas, Zahedi, & Wouters, 2015; Bornmann, 2015; Erdt et al., 2016), we also analysed the relationship between QS citations and the Altmetric Attention Score[2] provided by Altmetric.com[3], and the relationship between QS citations and Mendeley[4] reader counts. Therefore, the following research questions (RQs) were investigated in this study:

**RQ1**: Do papers with QS citations outperform papers without QS citations in terms of total citation counts across disciplines?

**RQ2**: Do papers with QS citations outperform papers without QS citations in terms of the Altmetric Attention Score and Mendeley reader counts across disciplines?

In the following sections, we present related work, followed by a description of the methodology applied, explaining how the data was collected and how the experiments were designed. We then present the results and conclude with a discussion and future work section.

## RELATED WORK

As mentioned in the previous section, there are two main sets of studies on the factors influencing citation counts. The first set of studies investigated the relationship between the factors and the citation counts, and in the second set, statistical or machine learning techniques were used to predict future citation counts based on the factors. A recent literature review by Tahamtan et al. (2016) summarized 28 related factors from 198 relevant papers. They classified the factors into three categories: paper related factors, journal related factors and author related factors. They found that several factors such as the journal impact factor and the number of authors could be more important than other factors in the growth of citation counts. In addition, the relationship between social media factors and citation counts have also been investigated. Erdt et al. (2016) give an overview of studies comparing altmetrics with citations, with a meta-analysis showing low to medium correlations between most altmetrics and citation counts, thereby confirming the findings in a previous meta-analysis by Bornmann (2015) investigating studies on Twitter[5], Mendeley, CiteULike[6] and blogs.

Moreover, many researchers have studied the impact of related factors in some disciplines. Slyder et al. (2011) examined the influence of seven different factors in geography and forestry disciplines, in which the seniority of author and journal impact factor have shown stronger impacts on the citation counts. In chemistry discipline, according to Bornmann et al. (2012), there were correlations between citation counts and four factors: the citation performance of the cited references, the language of the publishing journal, the chemical subfield and the reputation of the authors, but no statistically significant correlation was detected between citation counts and number of authors. As for medical research fields, Kulkarni et al. (2007) found the industry related factors, such as declared industry funding, were the most impactful factors. A study by Costas, Zahedi & Wouters (2015) found the highest presence of altmetrics in the fields of social sciences, humanities, medical and life sciences, but the relationship between citation counts and altmetrics remained weak, implying that altmetrics might measure a different aspect of impact than citations. Haustein et al. (2014) also measured low correlations between citation counts and tweets in the medical research fields. Another study by Mohammadi & Thelwall (2014) found low to medium correlations between citation counts and Mendeley reader counts across several disciplines.

[1]https://www.topuniversities.com/university-rankings/world-university-rankings/2015
[2]https://www.altmetric.com/blog/the-altmetric-score-is-now-the-altmetric-attention-score/
[3]https://www.altmetric.com
[4]https://www.mendeley.com
[5]https://twitter.com
[6]http://www.citeulike.org

Furthermore, when researchers predicted future citation counts, different sets of factors were selected based on the predictive model. In a study by Stegehuis et al. (2015), a quantile regression approach was employed with the journal impact factor and the first-year citation counts as input, to predict the long-term citation impact. Brizan et al. (2016) converted the prediction to a binary classification problem. They extracted six categories of 48 factors from the papers and then input them into the well-known classifiers such as Random Forest and SVM. Yu et al. (2014) built a predictive model based on regression analysis of 24 chosen factors.

From all these previous studies, we observe that a wide range of factors has been covered. However, only a few were concerned about the citations, i.e., the citing papers, and the prestigious citations defined by the affiliations as proposed in this paper have never been discussed. Furthermore, most of the studied factors have varied extents of impact in different disciplines. As the number of authors, while it was concluded as a stronger factor in the literature review (Tahamtan et al., 2016), it did not correlate with citation counts in chemistry (Bornmann et al., 2012).

In the prestigious citation studies, the "prestige" was quantified primarily in three different ways. Yan & Ding (2010) held that the prestige of citing journal and citation time interval should be considered, and thus designed a formula to calculate weighted citations based on the impact factors of citing journals and publication time of the citing papers. In the study by Ding & Cronin (2011), *prestige* was defined by the citation counts of citing papers. Besides, Chen et al. (2007) constructed a paper citation network, and applied the PageRank algorithm to the network. The citation prestige is intrinsically involved in the algorithm. Compared to the three methods, our proposed prestigious citations identified by the affiliations have the following advantages: easy recognition, simple calculation and applicability to all disciplines. Specifically, it can be determined whether it is a prestigious citation as soon as the citing paper is published. The method does not require complex calculation such as PageRank algorithm. In addition, it will be shown in the following experiments that the method is applicable to all disciplines.

## METHODOLOGY

The overall aim of this study was to investigate the impact of QS citations on papers across different disciplines from the dual perspectives of bibliometrics and altmetrics. In order to answer RQ1, comparisons on total citation counts were made between papers with QS citations and papers without QS citations. To answer RQ2, similar comparisons were made on the Altmetric Attention Score and the Mendeley reader counts between papers with QS citations and papers without QS citations. The following sections will describe the data used in our study, and the experiment design will be subsequently explained.

### *Data collection*

This study considered four data sources: (1) Microsoft Academic Graph (MAG) dataset (Sinha et al., 2015), (2) QS World University Rankings 2015 (QS ranking), (3) Scopus source list[7], and (4) Data collected from Altmetric.com. The MAG dataset was our main data source, from which we retrieved papers, related citing papers, authors and the affiliations of the authors. The MAG dataset version used in this paper was released on 5 February 2016. Since most of the papers contained in the MAG dataset were published before 2016, the QS ranking list for year 2015 was utilized in our study. The Scopus source list contains all research journals indexed in Scopus and classifies them into different disciplines. The Scopus source list is updated three times a year, and the version used in our study was downloaded in February 2017. As for the altmetric data, it was collected via an official API provided by Altmetric.com.

#### Data from MAG dataset

In the Scopus source list, there are 26 disciplines along with a generic entry called General (GEN), which includes multidisciplinary journals such as *Science* and *Nature*. A mapping of journal entries was made between the Scopus source list and the MAG dataset, and then according to these mapped journals, we retrieved related papers as well as their citing papers from the MAG dataset for all disciplines. Table 1 shows the numbers of mapped journals and retrieved papers for each discipline. It is to be noted that some journals were classified into multiple disciplines in the Scopus source list, and thus related journals and papers were duplicated. The papers that have never been cited were not considered in our study. Another mapping of affiliation entries was made between the QS ranking and the MAG dataset. If a university was one of the top 200 universities on the QS ranking, it was referred to as a *QS university*. Consequently, each citation can be identified as a *QS citation* or *non-QS citation*, according to the affiliation of the first author of the citing paper.

#### Data from Altmetric.com

Since Altmetric.com was founded in 2011, the papers with DOIs that were published between 2011 and 2013 were considered for collecting altmetric data. The numbers of these considered papers and related journals for each discipline are presented in Table 1. However, it would be intensely time consuming if we collected altmetric data for all 5,547,742 papers. Therefore, we made a stratified sampling based on the number of papers per discipline, and obtained a paper sample of size 100,000. The number of sampled papers for each discipline is also shown in Table 1. For example, with Agricultural and Biological Sciences (AGRI) discipline, there were 339,281 papers considered for altmetric data collection, accounting for 6.116% over 5,547,742 considered papers. The overall sample size is set as 100,000, and thus 6,116 papers were sampled for this discipline.

---

[7] https://www.elsevier.com/solutions/scopus/content

| Scopus Discipline | # of Journals | # of Papers | Papers with DOI Published between 2011 and 2013 for Altmetric Data Collection | | |
|---|---|---|---|---|---|
| | | | # of Journals | # of Papers | # of Sampled Papers (N = 100,000) |
| Agricultural and Biological Sciences (AGRI) | 1,385 | 3,712,125 | 1,114 | 339,281 | 6,116 |
| Arts and Humanities (ARTS) | 1,934 | 2,538,486 | 1,193 | 44,855 | 809 |
| Biochemistry, Genetics and Molecular Biology (BIOC) | 1,419 | 7,134,763 | 1,283 | 637,537 | 11,492 |
| Business, Management and Accounting (BUSI) | 847 | 832,677 | 763 | 90,706 | 1,635 |
| Chemical Engineering (CENG) | 633 | 4,853,863 | 538 | 344,676 | 6,213 |
| Chemistry (CHEM) | 364 | 1,636,927 | 315 | 159,620 | 2,877 |
| Computer Science (COMP) | 1,013 | 1,567,820 | 923 | 174,802 | 3,151 |
| Decision Sciences (DECI) | 244 | 389,949 | 223 | 31,775 | 573 |
| Dentistry (DENT) | 107 | 289,642 | 98 | 22,696 | 409 |
| Earth and Planetary Sciences (EART) | 673 | 1,947,342 | 579 | 153,393 | 2,765 |
| Economics, Econometrics and Finance (ECON) | 630 | 793,170 | 558 | 49,191 | 887 |
| Energy (ENER) | 190 | 698,310 | 171 | 74,084 | 1,335 |
| Engineering (ENGI) | 1,439 | 3,946,128 | 1,251 | 393,842 | 7,099 |
| Environmental Science (ENVI) | 813 | 1,825,014 | 706 | 181,120 | 3,265 |
| General (GEN) | 65 | 712,424 | 46 | 29,947 | 540 |
| Health Professions (HEAL) | 271 | 508,011 | 238 | 33,268 | 600 |
| Immunology and Microbiology (IMMU) | 381 | 1,556,296 | 334 | 143,670 | 2,590 |
| Materials Science (MATE) | 704 | 3,415,533 | 569 | 282,391 | 5,090 |
| Mathematics (MATH) | 974 | 2,308,453 | 867 | 161,686 | 2,914 |
| Medicine (MEDI) | 4,073 | 15,066,308 | 3,586 | 1,162,438 | 20,951 |
| Neuroscience (NEUR) | 390 | 1,599,651 | 367 | 141,109 | 2,544 |
| Nursing (NURS) | 355 | 723,835 | 326 | 57,921 | 1,044 |
| Pharmacology, Toxicology and Pharmaceutics (PHAR) | 453 | 1,654,308 | 396 | 125,863 | 2,269 |
| Physics and Astronomy (PHYS) | 774 | 6,040,032 | 705 | 405,952 | 7,317 |
| Psychology (PSYC) | 870 | 1,328,573 | 745 | 94,023 | 1,695 |
| Social Sciences (SOCI) | 3,608 | 4,530,485 | 2,751 | 181,282 | 3,268 |
| Veterinary (VETE) | 164 | 404,876 | 106 | 30,614 | 552 |
| Total | 24,773 | 72,015,001 | 20,751 | 5,547,742 | 100,000 |

***Table 1****. Numbers of mapped journals, retrieved papers, and sampled papers for altmetric data collection*

### *Experiments*

To address RQ1 and RQ2, a series of comparative experiments were designed. In each experiment, papers were classified into different groups so that differences could be observed and analyzed to better understand the impact of QS citations. All 72,015,001 papers were divided into two groups based on whether they had QS citations or not. A paper with at least one QS citation was referred to as a *QS-Ci paper*, otherwise it was a *non-QS-Ci paper* as it had no QS citation. Besides, it was found in the literature review that papers from highly-ranked universities had more citations (Tahamtan et al., 2016). Thus, for comparisons to *QS-Ci papers*, all papers were also classified based on affiliation, i.e., whether the affiliation entry was a QS university or not. A paper from a QS university was referred to as a *QS-Pub paper*, otherwise as a *non-QS-Pub paper*. It is to be noted that a *QS-Ci paper* is identified by its citation, while a *QS-Pub paper* is by itself. A *QS-Ci paper* is not necessarily a *QS-Pub paper* and vice versa. For a better comparison, *QS-Ci papers* were further split into groups based on whether they were from QS universities or not, hence two more groups were created: (1) *QS-Pub & QS-Ci papers*, which consisted of papers that were published by QS universities and had QS citations; (2) *non-QS-Pub & QS-Ci papers*, which consisted of papers that were published by other universities other than QS universities and had QS citations. When comparing citation performance amongst groups of papers, the median of total citation counts for each group was utilized.

We also investigated the difference in impact linked to QS citations and non-QS citations. We examined if a QS citation really had more important impact on the cited paper than a non-QS citation. If a QS citation and a non-QS citation have similar or even identical impact on the cited papers in terms of total citation counts, it should be observed that with comparable counts of QS citations and non-QS citations, the papers should have a comparable citation performance, i.e., the total citation counts for these papers should be almost the same. For instance, if Paper A has 11 QS citations and Paper B has 12 non-QS citations, it should be observed that the two papers have approximately similar total citation counts. However, if a considerable difference in total citation counts was observed, it could be inferred that QS citations and non-QS citations have distinctively different impact. Therefore, based on the number of QS citations and the number of non-QS citations, papers were classified into two groups and each group had seven count ranges: 1 to 5, 6 to10, 11 to 15, 16 to 20, 21 to 25, 26 to 30, and 30 to the maximum. For example, Paper A with 11 QS citations belongs to QS group at the range 11 to 15, while Paper B with 12 non-QS citations belongs to non-QS group at the same range 11 to 15. It is to be noted that when classifying the papers, the QS citation counts and the non-QS citation counts were considered, but when comparing citation performance between the groups, the medians of the total citation counts of the groups were considered.

Regarding altmetrics, the altmetric data we collected from Altmetric.com via the official API included not only the Altmetric Attention Score, but also Mendeley reader counts, tweet counts and others. The Altmetric Attention Score is calculated and provided by Altmetric.com for each indexed paper. It is an aggregated value, which is intended to measure the online influence of the paper based on the collected social media metrics (e.g., tweet counts, blog mentions). In our study, the Altmetric Attention Score, and Mendeley reader counts were considered in the comparison amongst the groups of *QS-Pub papers*, *non-QS-Pub papers*, *QS-Ci papers* and *non-QS-Ci papers*, since the coverage of other metrics was too low for analysis.

## RESULTS

Addressing RQ1, the citation performance of *QS-Ci papers* and *non-QS-Ci papers* are illustrated using a column chart in Figure 1. Each column in Figure 1 denotes the median of the total citation counts for the paper group and discipline. It can be observed that, across all disciplines, the *QS-Ci papers* had higher citation counts than *non-QS-Ci papers*. Specifically, the values for *QS-Ci papers* were approximately four times higher than the values for *non-QS-Ci papers*.

Citation performance of *QS-Pub papers*, *non-QS-Pub papers*, *QS-Pub & QS-Ci papers*, and *non-QS-Pub & QS-Ci papers* are illustrated in Figure 2. The columns in Figure 2 also denote the medians of total citation counts. It can be observed that for 21 out of 27 disciplines, *QS-Pub papers* had more citations than *non-QS-Pub papers*, which is in accordance with the finding in previous studies (Tahamtan et al., 2016), while there were exceptions in 6 disciplines such as Arts and Humanities (ARTS) and Decision Sciences (DECI). However, when only *QS-Ci papers* were considered, as seen in the last two columns for each discipline, *QS-Pub & QS-Ci papers* did not show stronger performance than *non-QS-Pub & QS-Ci papers*. This means if a paper received QS citations, it could have relatively higher citation counts even though it was not from a highly ranked university. Furthermore, the last two columns were higher than the first two columns across all disciplines, which means papers with higher citation counts in the first two groups were identified by QS citations.

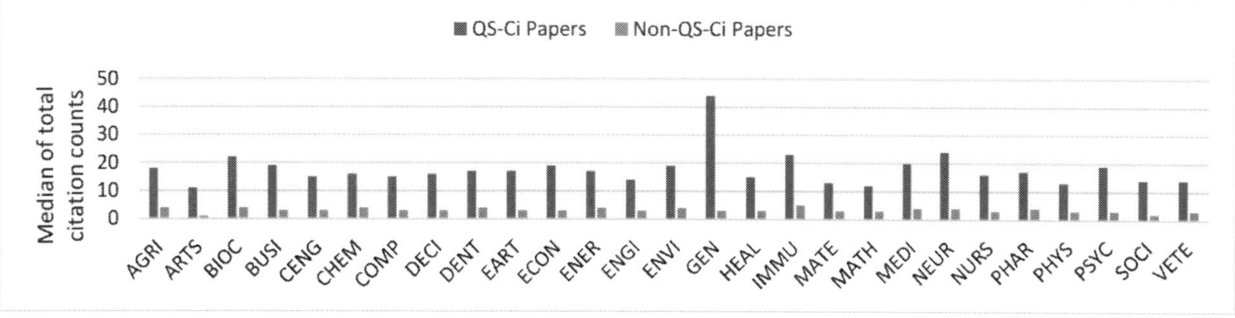


***Figure 1.*** *Citation performance of QS-Ci and non-QS-Ci papers across disciplines*

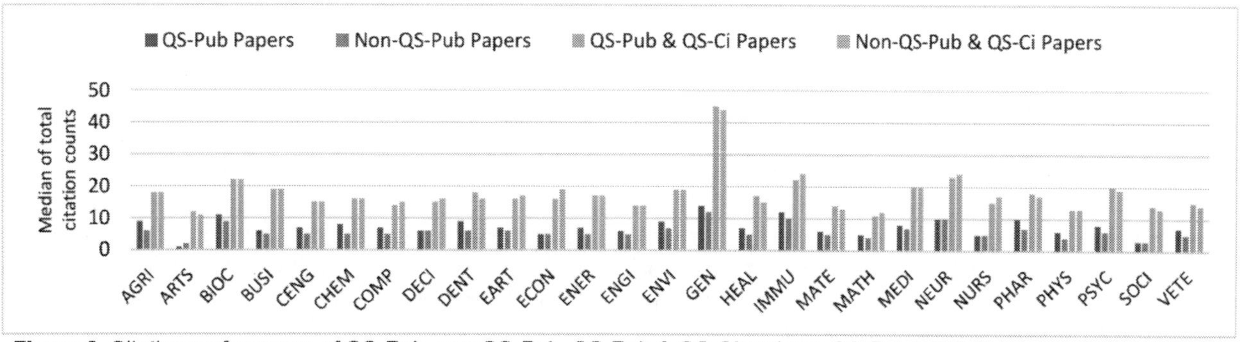


***Figure 2.*** *Citation performance of QS-Pub, non-QS-Pub, QS-Pub & QS-Ci and non-QS-Pub & QS-Ci papers*

counts was close to 100. In contrast, for papers that had 1 to

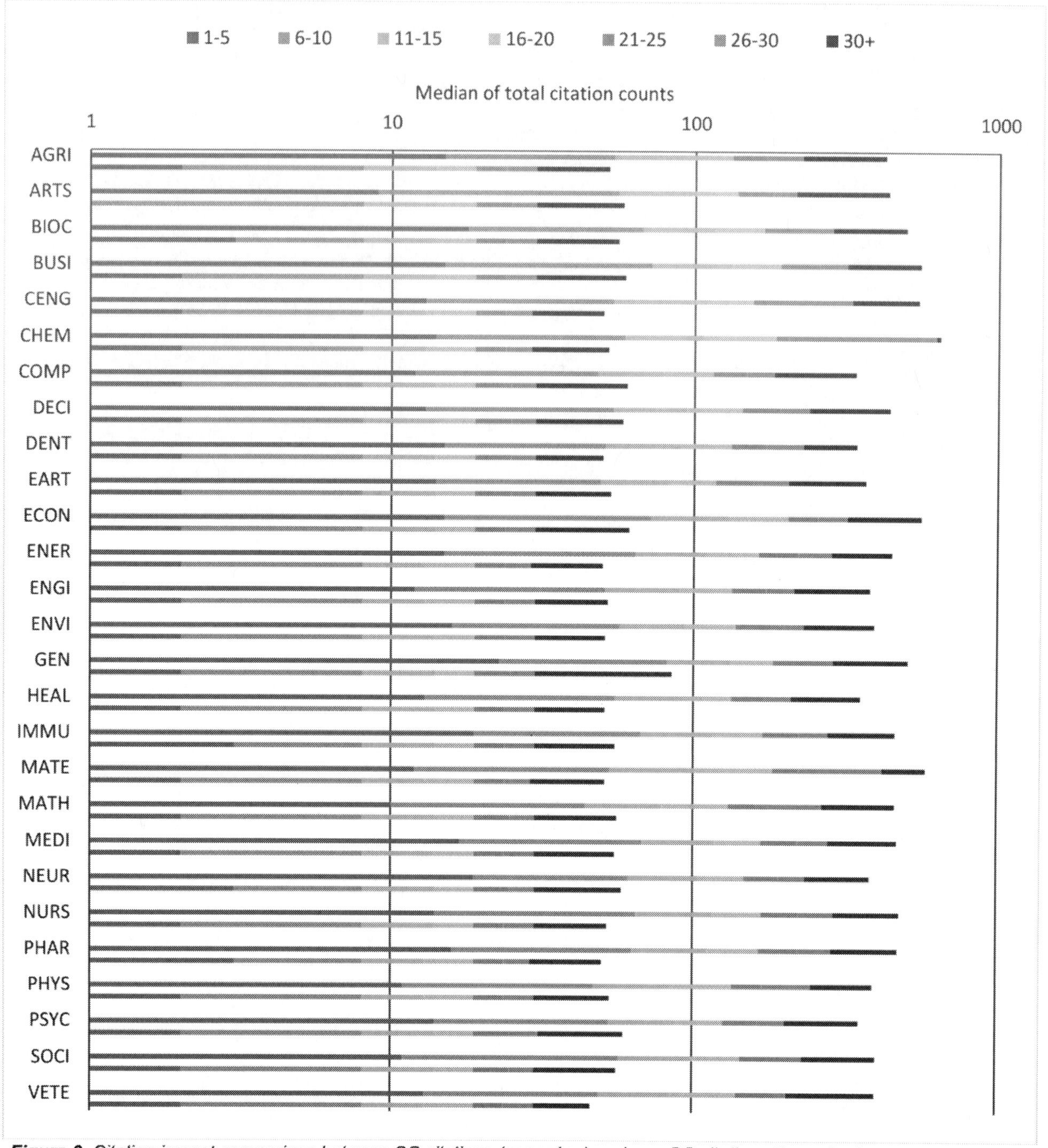


***Figure 3.*** *Citation impact comparison between QS citations (upper bar) and non-QS citations (lower bar)*

The citation impact comparison between QS citations and non-QS citations is illustrated in Figure 3. For each discipline, the upper bar indicates the median values of the total citation counts for the different groups of papers that were allocated by the QS citation counts, while the lower bar indicates the median values for papers grouped by the non-QS citation counts. Let us take Biochemistry, Genetics and Molecular Biology (BIOC) as an example. As seen in Figure 3, for papers that had 1 to 5 QS citations, the median of the total citation counts was slightly higher than 10, and for papers that had 6 to 10 QS citations, the median of the total citation 5 non-QS citations, the median of the total citation counts was lower than 10, and even for papers that had 6 to 10 non-QS citations, the median of the total citation counts was still lower than 10. Similar patterns are observed across all disciplines. Therefore, in answer to RQ1, it was detected that QS citations and non-QS citations have distinctly different impact. The QS citations were clearly associated with papers that had higher total citation counts. From the perspective of altmetrics, and in answer to RQ2, the results of comparison on the Altmetric Attention Score amongst the *QS-Ci, non-*

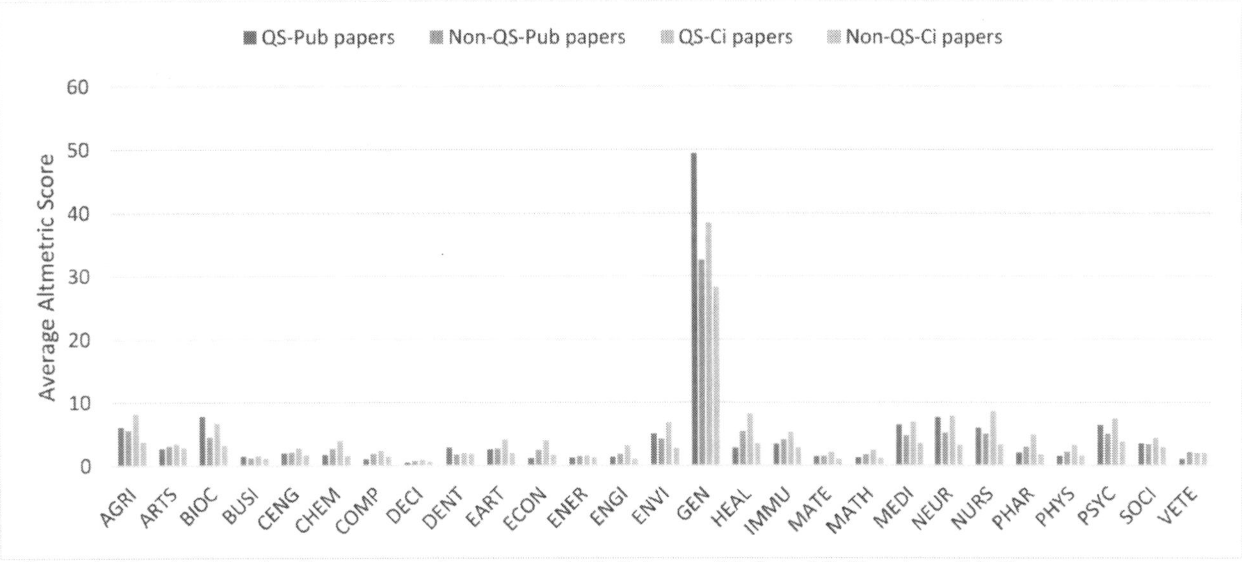


*Figure 4. Altmetric Attention Score comparison amongst QS-Pub, non-QS-Pub, QS-Ci and non-QS-Ci papers.*

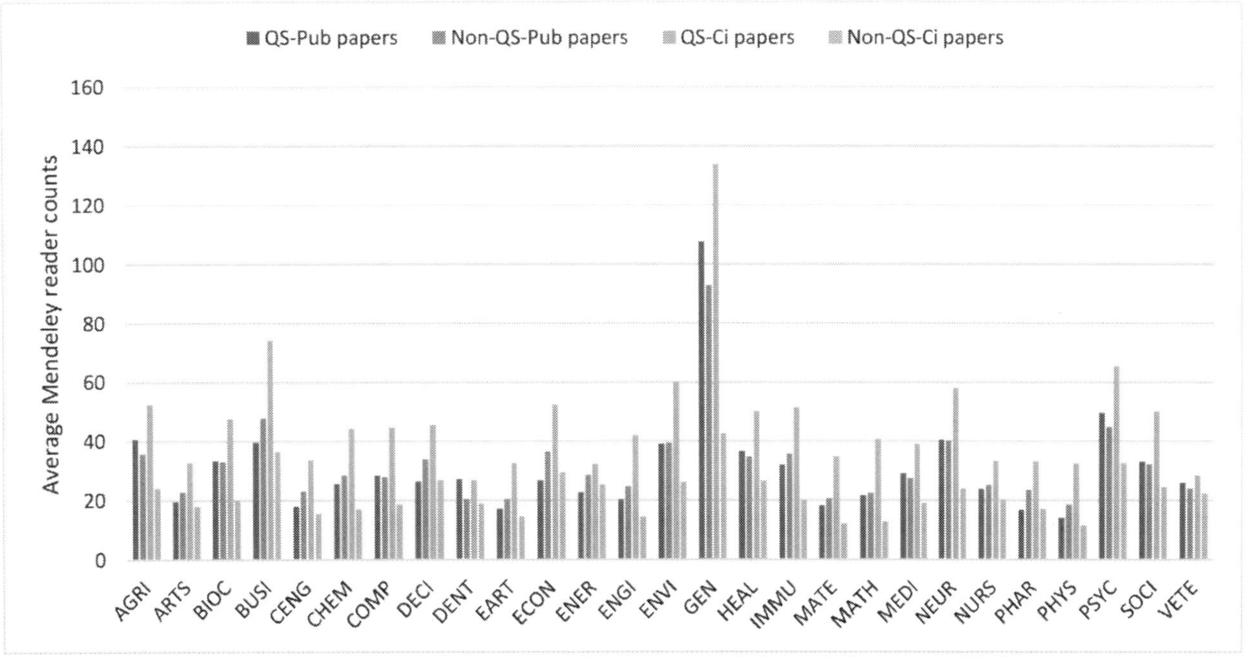


***Figure 5.** Mendeley reader counts comparison amongst QS-Pub, non-QS-Pub, QS-Ci and non-QS-Ci papers*

*QS-Ci, QS-Pub and non-QS-Pub papers* are presented in Figure 4, and the comparison results on Mendeley reader counts amongst the four groups of papers are presented in Figure 5. The columns in both Figure 4 and Figure 5 denote the average values of the groups. As shown in Figure 4, overall, the values of the Altmetric Attention Score for most disciplines were low, except for General discipline (GEN) which contains the most influential journals such as *Science* and *Nature*. When comparing the four paper groups within the same discipline, the *QS-Pub papers* in the three disciplines Biochemistry, Genetics and Molecular Biology (BIOC), Dentistry (DENT) and General Discipline (GEN) had the highest values, the *non-QS-Pub papers* in Veterinary (VETE) had the highest value, while the *QS-Ci papers* had the highest values across the remaining 23 disciplines. In addition, across all disciplines, *QS-Ci papers* had higher values than *non-QS-Ci papers*. However, this pattern cannot be observed between *QS-Pub* and *non-QS-Pub papers*.

In Figure 5, the Mendeley reader counts are displayed. Overall, the values of Mendeley reader counts are higher than the values of the Altmetric Attention Score. Similar to Figure 4, the four paper groups in General discipline (GEN) had highest values, compared to other disciplines. When comparing the four paper groups within the same discipline, *QS-Ci papers* had highest values across all disciplines, and *non-QS-Ci papers* had lowest values in most disciplines except for Decision Sciences (DECI), Economics, Econometrics and Finance (ECON), Energy (ENER) and Pharmacology, Toxicology and Pharmaceutics (PHAR). Furthermore, in both figures, almost for all disciplines, the difference between *QS-Ci* and *non-QS-Ci papers* was larger than the difference between *QS-Pub* and *non-QS-Pub papers*. Therefore, in answer to RQ2, it was illustrated that QS citations were also associated with the papers that had higher values in altmetrics.

## CONCLUSION

In this paper, we proposed to identify prestigious citations by the affiliations of the citing papers. Our claim was that citations could be considered as prestigious citations, if the authors of the citing papers are affiliated with prestigious universities. In order to evaluate our proposed method, we used the top 200 universities on the QS World University Rankings 2015 to identify the prestigious citations, named QS citations. A series of comparative experiments were designed across most disciplines. Results from the experiments in our study demonstrated that papers with QS citations had considerably higher total citation counts than papers without QS citations. Besides, findings also showed that the QS citations had distinctly different impact, compared to the non-QS citations. In fact, papers with a certain number of QS citations had higher total citation counts than papers with a comparable number of non-QS citations. While absolute numbers were used in the comparison in this paper, we will compare the impact of QS citations and non-QS citations based on percentiles in future work. Furthermore, from the perspective of altmetrics, papers with QS citations also had stronger performance in terms of the Altmetric Attention Score and Mendeley reader counts. It is to be noted that these findings were observed across all disciplines. Therefore, our proposed method identifying prestigious citations by the affiliations of the citing papers can be considered to be well validated. This approach is not only effective and efficient, but also applicable to all disciplines. While the QS ranking was employed in this paper, it is reasonable to infer that prestigious citations identified using other university ranking schemes should have similar impact. One limitation of using universities to identify prestigious citation is that some influential researchers who are affiliated with less prestigious universities or research centers might be overlooked. In future studies, we will address this issue. We also plan an in-depth investigation into the relationship between QS citations and total citation counts, with the aim of developing an effective model for predicting future citation counts of papers.

## ACKNOWLEDGMENTS

This research is supported by the National Research Foundation, Prime Minister's Office, Singapore under its Science of Research, Innovation and Enterprise programme (SRIE Award No. NRF2014-NRF-SRIE001-019).

## REFERENCES

Aksnes, W. (2003) Characteristics of highly cited papers. *Research Evaluation*, 12(3), 159-170.

Bornmann, L. (2015). Alternative metrics in scientometrics: A meta-analysis of research into three altmetrics. *Scientometrics*, *103*(3), 1123-1144.

Bornmann, L., Schier, H., Marx, W., & Daniel, H. D. (2012). What factors determine citation counts of publications in chemistry besides their quality? *Journal of Informetrics*, *6*(1), 11-18.

Brizan, D. G., Gallagher, K., Jahangir, A., & Brown, T. (2016). Predicting citation patterns: Defining and determining influence. *Scientometrics*, *108*(1), 183-200.

Chen, P., Xie, H., Maslov, S., & Redner, S. (2007). Finding scientific gems with Google's PageRank algorithm. *Journal of Informetrics*, *1*(1), 8-15.

Chen, C. (2012). Predictive effects of structural variation on citation counts. *Journal of the Association for Information Science and Technology*, *63*(3), 431-449.

Costas, R., Zahedi, Z., & Wouters, P. (2015). Do "altmetrics" correlate with citations? Extensive comparison of altmetric indicators with citations from a multidisciplinary perspective. *Journal of the Association for Information Science and Technology*, *66*(10), 2003-2019.

Didegah, F., & Thelwall, M. (2013). Determinants of research citation impact in nanoscience and nanotechnology. *Journal of the Association for Information Science and Technology*, *64*(5), 1055-1064.

Ding, Y., & Cronin, B. (2011). Popular and/or prestigious? Measures of scholarly esteem. *Information Processing and Management*, *47*(1), 80-96.

Erdt, M., Nagarajan, A., Sin, S. C. J., & Theng, Y. L. (2016). Altmetrics: An analysis of the state-of-the-art in measuring research impact on social media. *Scientometrics*, *109*(2), 1117-1166.

Filion, K. B., & Pless, I. B. (2008). Factors related to the frequency of citation of epidemiologic publications. *Epidemiologic Perspectives & Innovations*, *5*(1), 1.

Habibzadeh, F., & Yadollahie, M. (2008). Journal weighted impact factor: A proposal. *Journal of Informetrics*, *2*(2), 164-172.

Haustein, S., Peters, I., Sugimoto, C. R., Thelwall, M., & Larivière, V. (2014). Tweeting biomedicine: An analysis of tweets and citations in the biomedical literature. *Journal of the Association for Information Science and Technology*, 65(4), 656-669.

Khor, K. A., & Yu, L. G. (2016). Influence of international co-authorship on the research citation impact of young universities. *Scientometrics*, 1-16.

Kulkarni, A. V., Busse, J. W., & Shams, I. (2007). Characteristics associated with citation rate of the medical literature. *PLoS ONE*, *2*(5), 1-5.

Liu, X., Bollen, J., Nelson, M. L., & Van De Sompel, H. (2005). Co-authorship networks in the digital library research community. *Information Processing and Management*, *41*(6), 1462-1480.

Mohammadi, E., & Thelwall, M. (2014). Mendeley readership altmetrics for the social sciences and humanities: Research evaluation and knowledge flows. *Journal of the Association for Information Science and Technology*, 65(8), 1627-38.

Sinha, A., Shen, Z., Song, Y., Ma, H., Eide, D., Hsu, B. P., & Wang, K. (2015). An overview of Microsoft Academic Service (MAS) and applications. *Proceedings of the 24th international conference on world wide web*, 243-246.

Slyder, J. B., Stein, B. R., Sams, B. S., Walker, D. M., Beale, B. J., Feldhaus, J. J., & Copenheaver, C. A. (2011). Citation pattern and lifespan: A comparison of discipline, institution, and individual. *Scientometrics*, *89*(3), 955-966.

Stegehuis, C., Litvak, N., & Waltman, L. (2015). Predicting the long-term citation impact of recent publications. *Journal of Informetrics*, *9*(3), 642-657.

Tahamtan, I., Safipour Afshar, A., & Ahamdzadeh, K. (2016). Factors affecting number of citations: a comprehensive review of the literature. *Scientometrics*, *107*(3), 1195-1225.

Yan, E., & Ding, Y. (2010). Weighted citation: an indicator of an article's prestige. *Journal of the Association for Information Science and Technology*, *61*(8), 1635-1643.

Yan, E., Ding, Y., & Sugimoto, C. (2011). P-rank: an indicator measuring prestige in heterogeneous scholarly networks. *Journal of the Association for Information Science and Technology*, *62*(3), 467-477.

Yu, T., Yu, G., Li, P. Y., & Wang, L. (2014). Citation impact prediction for scientific papers using stepwise regression analysis. *Scientometrics*, 1233-1252.

# Identifying Structural Genre Conventions Across Academic Web Documents for Information Use

**Cui–Chang Ma**
*Sun Yat–sen University Library, China.*
*macch@mail.sysu.edu.cn*

**Shu–Jin Cao**
*School of Information Management, Sun Yat–sen University, China. caosj@mail.sysu.edu.cn*

## ABSTRACT

**The organization and presentation of academic documents on the web are mostly on the documental level. However, what the researchers need is always the particular information pieces of documents rather than the whole. Genre provides us with an expected form and content from both authors and readers; therefore, functional analysis of genre might be employed to decompose web documents into information units for information use. In this vein, this study aims to build the taxonomy of information units within academic web documents for information use based on structural genre theory. The genres chosen include abstract from online bibliography, research article from open access journal, entry of online encyclopedia and academic weblog post. Two sequential studies are conducted. In the first study, the taxonomy with the hierarchy of genre – component – functional unit is firstly built by identification of information units within academic web document genres, and then is validated and refined through corpus in the domain of citation analysis in Chinese. In the second study, user survey is conducted to validate the information units in the taxonomy. The results suggest that the knowledge of social convention of academic web genres in the taxonomy in domain of citation analysis in Chinese is well identified, which can inform the design of search engine to support effective and efficient web information use for academic purposes.**

## KEYWORDS

academic web document, information unit, functional unit, move analysis, genre

## INTRODUCTION

Genres are naturally occurring features of written communication and are prevalent in most large document collections. Most existing studies on digital genre have focused on the level of documents, such as journal articles (Dillon, 2004), web newspapers (Vaughan, 1999) or even academic and corporate sites (Symonenko, 2007). However, genre instances vary in granularity – an individual webpage, multiple webpages, a website or part of a webpage can all be considered as comprising a genre (Crowston & Williams, 2000; Rosso, 2008; Shepherd& Watters, 1998). Document components have their functions for use, especially for introduction, method/date, result, discussion/conclusion (mentioned as IMRD below) components of research article indicated by Vaughan and Dillon (1998). In addition, the utilization of functional units within IMRD components of research articles was also explored by Zhang (2011, 2012).

Academic web document is one kind of the indispensable reference sources for research, teaching and learning in a variety of disciplines. General or vertical search engines for scholars nowadays are qualified in collecting and organizing academic documents belonging to a variety of genres, such as research article from journal or archive, book, law case or patent. However, most of those search engines still do a poor job in identifying and aggregating information pieces from a certain part of the documents, which are often useful or interesting to searchers, rather than the whole (Bishop, 1999; Sandusky and Tenopir, 2008).

Thus, the identification and utilization of granular information units of web documents should be a potential area to explore. Instead of focusing on one genre, we consider it important to have a representative sample of genres for academic web use. Since there are similarities between some kinds of genres with similar social purposes (Connor and Mauranen, 1999), greater detail about the similarities and differences of genres would be found in the taxonomic work, which are valuable to inform the granular utilization and the automatic decomposition, organization and presentation of academic web documents.

The goal of this paper is to explore the approach of genre analysis for decomposition of a representative sample of genres of academic web documents in Chinese. Because of the variations of genres in different domains or fields, this study focuses on one specific domain – citation analysis within library and information science (mentioned as LIS below). Considering the usage rate (Cao and Li, 2014; Mou, Liu and Liang, 2013; Yang and Qiu, 2012; Ding and Yang, 2012) and the distribution survey results conducted for web genres in the field of LIS in Chinese, genres chosen in this study include abstract from online bibliography, research article from open access journal, entry of online encyclopedia and academic weblog post. Although the genre structures of research articles have been studied before in various disciplines, the identification of information units within research article is still needed, together with other genres on the web in the do-

80th Annual Meeting of the Association for Information Science & Technology, Washington, DC, VA | Oct. 27-Nov. 1, 2017

main of citation analysis, to build a unified taxonomy of information unit. Under investigation are the main bodies of texts of these genres. Research questions are as follows:

What are the genre structures of academic web documents in the domain of citation analysis in Chinese, including abstract from online bibliography, research article from open access journal, entry of online encyclopedia and academic weblog post?

What is the validity of the taxonomy of information units identified in the genre analytic approach within Chinese academic web documents for social convention?

## LITERATURE REVIEW

### *The Originality and Development of Swales' Model for Research Article*

Move analysis led by Swales (1981, 1990, 2004) aims to help non–native speakers or junior scholars to "master or control the macro level organizational structures and the micro level of linguistic features conventionally used in texts required in their disciplines and professions" (Kanoksilapatham, 2003).

According to Swales (1981), the overall communicative purpose of the genre is achieved by a series of functionally distinct moves. Each move is a section of text that performs a specific communicative function, and may contain a set of steps with which the move is realized. Swales claimed four distinct moves as used in research article introductions: Move 1–establishing a territory; Move 2–summarizing previous research; Move 3–establishing a niche; and Move 4–occupying the niche. Later, Swales (1990) modified his framework by merging the first two moves, resulting in the three move–step patterns known as the CARS model based on a move analysis of 48 articles in the hard sciences, social sciences and life and health sciences. Again, Swales (2004) revised his model while keeping the three distinct moves and added potential cycling of Move 1 and Move 2 sequences and changed the steps included in each move.

Swales' model (1981, 1990) has inspired studies of rhetorical organizational patterns in the Introduction component of research article in other disciplines (Crookes, 1986; Hopkins & Dudley–Evans, 1988; Posteguillo, 1999; Samraj, 2002), demonstrating the wide acceptability of Swales' model. Also, Swales' model has stimulated studies on various components of research articles, including analyses of the individual components of abstract (Swales, 1990; Bhatia, 2002; Samraj, 2005; Rij–Heyligers and Li, 2011), method (Bruce, 2008), result (Brett, 1994; Thompson, 1993) and discussion (Hopkins & Dudley–Evans, 1988), on a combination of components (Lewin et al., 2001) and on all four components (Kanoksilapatham, 2005; Nwogu, 1997).

Yang (2006) extended the scope of move analysis research from empirical research article to both empirical research article and non-empirical research article, naming primary research article and secondary research article. Yang (2006) found alternative components for secondary research article, including theoretical background and implications. Thus, secondary research articles consist of introduction, argumentation and conclusion components, among which the argumentation component consists of several sub–arguments. Theoretical background can be an alternative component for secondary research article.

Originally used to analyze the structural conventions for writing, move analysis provides an insight into the granular genre characteristics and enables a better understanding and utilization of document components in information science. Vaughan and Dillon (1998) utilized IMRD components to categorize a set of paragraphs in journal articles by asking expert users and coded by "why, what, how." Dillion (2004) even distinguished text typologies as why, what and how in terms of individuals' reading strategy, its relevance to their work or the amount/type of information that a text contains. Based on Swales' model and move analysis, Zhang (2011) formed the basis for developing a functional unit taxonomy that manifested types of information within components of journal article and examined its utility in journal information use.

### *Granular Characteristics Across Academic Web Document Genres*

According to social purposes, genres can be categorized as academic writing genres and persuasive genres. That there would be both similarities and differences in the moves when compared with related genres might be expected on the basis of a genre theory, which relates preferred form to shared social purpose: a good deal of overlap in functional units ought to be found where we observe similar social purposes, and less where the purposes differ. For example, Cornell (1999) found that grant proposals represented persuasive genre and had a great deal in common with the genre of the research article, especially with introduction component. They need to establish the importance of the field, show the problem or gap in the field and show how the proposed research will fill the gap. Thus, the grant proposal genre shares important elements with two related genres that have been studied in a similar way.

Also, academic weblog post shares the academic nature with research article. The content, the communities of authors and audience for both academic weblog post and research article are homologous while academic weblog post has lesser restriction on the style, structure and language used (Chen, et al, 2012; Shi and Xiao, 2009). However, despite observed similarities with related genres, weblog post seems to have its own special features that emerged from the identification of moves.

The conventionalized knowledge of linguistic and discourse features for entry of online encyclopedia has been identified and described in the contributing guidelines of online encyclopedia. However, little published research has examined the conventionalized knowledge of it. Instructions for contributing entry of online encyclopedia demonstrate the general conventions and components of this kind of genre. The entry of encyclopedia has fixed constitutions to be readable[1]. For example, the key information for 'The first law of newton' in Baidu Encyclopedia[2] includes the content, the discoverer and the condition of the law, the missing of which would lead to misunderstanding of the entry. What's more, the key information for 'Song Dynasty' includes the period, the territory, the economy and the important events of the dynasty[3].

*Studies of Genre Analysis in Chinese Documents*

Based on the theories of move analysis, most Chinese genre studies focus on the differences of components and moves of research articles between Chinese and English. Li (2010) compared the genre structures of academic book review between Chinese and English. She found that Motta-Roth (1995a, 1995b)'s studies on genre structure were suitable for move analysis for book reviews in both Chinese and English. Liu (2009) focused on the moves and steps of Conclusion component for doctoral thesis in the field of science, arts and humanities and made comparison according to fields and language.

For encyclopedia, Jiang and Jin (1982) claimed that the entry of encyclopedia in Chinese was consisted of the qualitative description (or definition), origin of the subject, historical origin, basic facts (people, things and important data about the subject), the see also (such as academic debate of different views, the authority, the exhibition and comments about the subject), figure and captions, illustrations and charts, hierarchical titles and the references.

## CONSTRUCTION OF TAXONOMY OF INFORMATION UNITS

### Method

#### Definition of Information Unit and the Granularity

The hierarchies of document genres chosen in this study are different, for example, there are two hierarchies for the abstract, entry of online encyclopedia and weblog post (component and move) while there are three hierarchies for the research article (component, move and step). So the granularities of information units are not consistent for these genres. What's more, the naming ways for the information units are different. For example, Move 2 in the Introduction component of research article is named as "establishing a niche" in Swale (1990)'s model while named as "establishing the gap present research is meant to fill" in Lewin, Fine, and Young (2001)'s model. Thus, the names of the moves or steps from the genre studies should be unified and revised to reflect the differences and relationships for the genres in the taxonomy.

We choose to build a two – hierarchies structure in this study, naming taxonomy with information units on the component and the functional unit (move or step) level. The reasons are as follows: first, users' needs for academic web documents are mostly on the granularity of paragraph rather than sentence (Agrawal, et al, 2009), so move is taken as the basic information unit in the taxonomy. Second, current studies of digital genre focus mostly on the granularities of meso (e.g., IMRD components) and micro (e.g., functional units as move and step) level, thus, the two – hierarchies structure would make possible the comparative studies with existing and even further studies

#### Identification of Information Unit

The development of information units for the genres studied drew on many sources. Firstly, related researches on structural genre of research article are principle sources for identification of components and functional units within research article and abstract of online bibliography, such as Lewin, Fine & Young (2001), Nwogu (1997), Kanoksilapatham (2005), Zhang (2011) and Yang (2006)'s studies. Secondly, writing rules and guidelines for entry of online encyclopedia. The initial drafting of the information units for entry of online encyclopedia was mainly analyzed in terms of the constitution based on the rules and guidelines for entry writing. They are quite detailed in some examples, and even include necessary components, such as specifying titles, the length of summaries and other sections. Thus, the guidelines offer a rough initial basis for exploring the rhetorical structuring of the texts in terms of likely functions involved. Thirdly, researches on move analysis for various genres. The initial drafting of the information units for academic weblog post and for entry of online encyclopedia not covered by writing rules and guidelines, are mainly rooted in move analysis of the text of sample documents.

Thus, information units within academic weblog post, entry of online encyclopedia and occasionally research article, were analyzed in terms of the rhetorical moves, the notion of which is essentially that developed by Swales (1981, 1990) with minor modifications. Essentially, a move in a text is a functional unit, used for some identifiable rhetorical purpose. Moves can vary in size, but normally contain at least one proposition. In addition, they typically exhibit some internal coherence (Mauranen, 1993). The underlying constitution – step – is taken as the interpretation of this move. The steps that are significantly important in previous research, such as review related research, clarify the definitions, are isolated as information units too. The naming way of the moves follows the form of verb + noun.

---

[1] The structure of the entry. Retrieved June 18, 2016, from Baidu Encyclopedia. http://baike.baidu.com/view/10811960. htm#sub11072681

[2] The first law of newton. Retrieved June 18, 2016, from Baidu Encyclopedia. http://baike.baidu.com/item/%E7%89%9B%E9%A1%BF%E7%AC%AC%E4%B8%80%E8%BF%90%E5%8A%A8%E5%AE%9A%E5%BE%8B?fromtitle=%E7%89%9B%E9%A1%BF%E7%AC%AC%E4%B8%80%E5%AE%9A%E5%BE%8B&fromid=316252

[3] Song Dynasty. Retrieved June 18, 2016, from Baidu Encyclopedia. http://baike.baidu.com/item/%E5%AE%8B%E6%9C%9D/2919

For the information units derived through move analysis, it is important to start from the rhetorical objectives of the texts at first. The overall goal of a genre can inform the move structures through other genres with similar purpose and offer a rough initial basis for exploring the rhetorical structure of the texts in terms of likely functions involved. Then the text must be divided up into meaningful units on the granularity of component and functional unit, essentially on the basis of linguistic clues. The identification of information units in a text depends on both function indicators and boundary indicators (Connor, 1999).

First of all, the rhetorical objectives of the genres can be determined from the communication purposes of the texts. The goal of academic weblog post is spreading academic ideas of the author. Specifically, academic weblog post is a form of persuasive writing. Their communicative purpose is to persuade readers to read the authors' ideas. Sharing a similar communicative purpose, weblog post can be likened to two promotional genres studied by Bhatia (2014), namely sales letters and job applications. They need to capture the attention of the reader, describe the idea and establish the writer's competence. In addition, academic weblog posts have a great deal in common with secondary research article proposed by Yang (2006), especially the argumentation component. They need to propose viewpoint, argue for viewpoint and make conclusion. For entry of online encyclopedia, the overall goal of knowledge communication is given through the entries. Specifically, the entry of online encyclopedia is a form of academic writhing for knowledge and has a great deal in common with secondary research article, especially for the introduction and theoretical background component. They need to provide a theory/concept and make definition.

Secondly, a fairly straightforward source for component recognition is the texts' explicit division devices, such as section boundaries indicated with numbering and/or subheadings and paragraph divisions. They are generally helpful in chunking for components, with subheadings often indicating functions as well (e.g., define the entry for entry of online encyclopedia). The identification of components within a genre is easier than the identification of moves within a component for the explicit discrete division devices indicating functions and boundaries as well.

Thirdly, linguistic clues can be utilized for both boundary and function identification of functional unit. The chunking of text on move or step level is the harder case. However, there are a number of linguistic clues that texts generally use to indicate internal boundaries, which together with more obvious boundary markers, can be utilized in analysis (for discussion, see Mauranen 1993: 224–234; see also Connor et al. 1995a: 463– 465). Boundaries can be marked with linguistic changes of various kinds, and in particular, simultaneous changes in more than one indicator. Typical boundary indicators utilized in the analysis are discourse markers (connectors and other metatextual signals: consequently, however, firstly, to sum up). For function indication, the linguistic clues are usually lexical: The disadvantage of citation analysis for evaluation of a discipline is..., the definition of citation analysis..., etc.

For all the genres, the functional units are mainly analysis by paragraph within a particular component, with one to three functional units in a paragraph. The paragraphs, with semantic continuity and belong to the same type of move, are grouped into one functional unit. Functional units are derived by sentences in the abstract genre or component. New types of component or functional unit derived would be added into the taxonomy.

### *Corpus of Sample Documents*

Collection of sample documents and identification of the information units within these documents took place during the two-month duration in May 2015.

Web documents with the Chinese keyword – citation analysis – were collected through Chinese search engine by the present researchers. Before collecting the sample documents, a genre distribution survey of web documents in the domain of citation analysis in Chinese was conducted with search engines including Baidu and Sogou. Results showed that research article, online encyclopedia, weblog post and forum are predominant genres on the web. According to the researchers' preference (Maron and Smith, 2008; Chen, 2014) and genre distribution, web documents belonging to primary and secondary research article (28), online bibliography (18), entry of online encyclopedia (13) and academic weblog post (23) genres were chosen to construct the corpus (81). The selection criteria of the sample documents are the topical relevance and authority.

### *Construct Validity and Reliability of the Coding Scheme for Information Units*

Analyses of the web documents by us individually, as a research team, as well as discussions with the entire team, produced a set of information units that seemed to describe all functional elements within the genres of web documents studied. In the development of the coding scheme of information units, we were particularly concerned about the construct validity and reliability. Following Yin (2014), construct validity refers to "establishing correct operational measures for the concepts being studied." Reliability refers to "demonstrating that the operations of a study – such as the data collection procedures can be repeated with the same results."

In order to increase construct validity by developing a sufficiently operational taxonomy of information units across different genres, we adopted the steps recommended by Yin (2014) for case study research. As principal individual researchers in the study, we reviewed each other's analysis during frequent discussions, which lead to redefinitions and reformulations of the moves or components to develop a coding scheme. In addition, at project meetings, the entire team had an opportunity to react to the progress of the work.

The reliability of the initial taxonomy of information units for coding was tested through the entire collection of 81 academic web documents by two of the researchers. Since the identification of information units would be influenced by an individual's comprehension of the text and understanding of the textual functions, inter–coder reliability procedures were performed to ensure reliability. For the 81 academic web documents, one third of documents chosen randomly according to genres were coded by a second coder (primary research article: #1, #3, #7, #9, #11, #13, #17; secondary research article: #5, #18; online bibliography: #1, #3, #5, #8, #10, #12; entry of online encyclopedia: #2, #4, #6, #8, #11; weblog post: #1, #3, #5, #10, #12, #14, #17, #20). The coders independently coded the texts and had a discussion to resolve uncertainties in their practices in applying the various codes. The inter–coder reliability was determined by Cohen's kappa value and percentage agreement. Because each genre and component varied in length and structural regularity, Cohen's kappa value and percentage agreement were measured for each component as well as for all the components and genres.

A value of .5 for kappa represents moderate agreement, above .7 represents good agreement and above .8 represents very good agreement. Kappa values ranged from 0.652 to 1.000 and percentage rates from 80% to 100%, showing a high level of agreement in identifying these functional units across genres and components.

## *Result*

In total, seven components were identified within research articles, five components were identified within online encyclopedia and four components were identified within weblog posts. On the micro level, 55 functional units were identified, including four functional units within abstracts of online bibliographies, 33 functional units within research articles (including the four functional units overlapping with abstract component of online bibliography), 11 within entry of encyclopedias and 11 within weblog posts, as Table 1 shows.

| Taxonomy of information units | | |
|---|---|---|
| Genre | Component | Functional unit |
| Research article / Bibliography | Abstract | Summarize the topic |
| | | Summarize the method |
| | | Summarize the result |
| | | Summarize the conclusion |
| Research article | Introduction | Establish a niche |
| | | Review literature |
| | | Comment on related research |
| | | Present the current study |
| | | Clarify the definition |
| | Theoretical background | Provide a theory / concept |
| | | Argue for a theoretical position |
| | | Relate theory to the proposed study |
| | Argument | Introduce the research |
| | | Introduce the background |
| | | Propose viewpoint |
| | | Argue for viewpoint |
| | Method/ Data | Introduce the background of method |
| | | Describe data |
| | | Introduce the method of analysis |
| | | Clarify the definition |
| | Result | Provide meta text |
| | | Introduce the background of result |
| | | Describe analysis conducted |
| | | Justify the method or procedure |
| | | Present the finding |
| | | Comment on finding |
| | Conclusion/ Discussion | Recapitulate current research |
| | | Provide meta text |
| | | Highlight overall outcome |
| | | Discuss outcome |
| | | Comment on outcome |
| | | Propose future research |
| Online encyclopedia | Entry abstract | Define the entry |
| | | Provide key information |
| | Entry summary | Describe the entry qualitatively |
| | | Introduce the historical origin |
| | | Introduce the basic information |
| | | Introduce the life story |
| | Knowledge points | Provide reference |
| | | Describe by knowledge points |
| | Influence for people | Introduce the achievement |
| | | Provide list of honors |
| | | Provide list of works or viewpoints |
| | | Comment on the people |
| Weblog posts | Introduction | Establish the communicative topic |
| | | Digress from the topic |
| | | Provide topic related info. |
| | | Provide topic related event |
| | Viewpoint | Propose viewpoint |
| | | Argue for viewpoint |
| | | Make conclusion |
| | Source and linking | Provide source |
| | | Provide linking |
| | Comment | Questioning and reply |
| | | Comment and reply |

***Table 1**. Preliminary taxonomy of information units across genres*

## VALIDITY OF THE TAXONOMY OF INFORMATION UNITS

### *Method*

We conducted a survey through online questionnaire to validate the conventional knowledge of taxonomy of information units from the first phase.

#### Participants

The survey span from September 6th to 22th in 2015, during which email advertisements were sent to the graduate students of the Department of Information Management in Sun Yat–sen University. The survey was conducted along with a series of other surveys and experiments to explore the relationship between information units and information use. This survey includes two sections: rating for frequency of the functional units occurring in the components and components occurring in the genres, and rating for the frequency of information search tasks they use. The result of section one is reported here. For the entire survey, each participant was compensated with 50 RMB (approximately equal to 7 dollars) for completing the online surveys, each of which took approximately 30 minutes. Referencing the number of participants in Zhang's study (Zhang, 2011, 2012), 14 participants were recruited, nine female and five male, including five doctoral students, nine master students. All of them specialized in information management and library science.

#### Instruments

From the first phase, 55 functional units were identified, including 33 functional units within research articles (including the four functional units within Abstract component of online bibliography), 11 within entry of encyclopedias and 11 within academic weblog posts. To avoid cognitive overload and inadequate understanding, a one-sentence definition was provided for each functional unit instead of a title. Each definition of a functional unit was listed as a separate item for rating.

Participants were asked to indicate how frequently they thought each functional unit typically occurred in the component and how frequently each component typically occurred in the genre on a five–point Likert scale (1 for rarely and 5 for always). They were also free to suggest information units that they thought frequently occurred within a particular genre or component other than those in the list.

### *Result*

The participants rated how frequently each listed functional unit occurred in a component. Most functional units had a standard deviation lower than 1.0, suggesting the participants' ratings were quite consistent. Among all the functional units, the mean score of "provide meta text" for research article is lower than 3.0, suggesting this functional unit occurred rarely, which is the same with Zhang's study (Zhang, 2011, 2012). So it was dropped. The mean scores of information units by components of genres are as follows:

- For the abstract component in the online bibliography, the mean score of "summarize the topic" is over 4.5, suggesting it is the most typical functional unit in abstract. The mean scores of other functional units are more than 3.5, suggesting these information units are common in the abstract component.
- For research article, the mean score of "establish a niche" in introduction component is over 4.5, suggesting it is the most typical functional unit in research article. The mean score of "clarify the definition" is less than 3.5, suggesting it rarely occurs in research articles in the domain of citation analysis in Chinese. The mean score of functional units in the theoretical background, argumentation and method/data components are all more than 3.5, suggesting that they are common constitutions in research article. The mean score of "introduce the background of result" in the result component is lower than 3.5, suggesting it is occasional occurred in research article. Other functional units in result component are common constitutions in research articles.
- For entry of online encyclopedia, the mean scores of "define the entry" and "provide key information" in entry abstract component, "describe the entry qualitatively" in entry summary component, "describe by knowledge points" in knowledge points component and "introduce the achievement" in influence for personal component are all over 4.0. The mean score for "provide reference" and "comment on the people" is 7 lower than 3.5, suggesting that these functional units are occasional occurred in entry of online encyclopedia.
- For academic weblog post, the mean scores for "introduce the topic" and "digress from the topic" in Introduction component are over 4 scores, while for "provide topic related information" and "provide topic related event" are over 3.5. The mean score for "propose viewpoint" in viewpoint component is over 4.5, for "argue for viewpoint" is over 4.0, for "make conclusion" is over 3.5. The mean score for "provide source" in source and linking component is over 4.5 while for "provide linking" is over 3.5. The mean score for "questioning and reply" in comment component is over 4.0 while for "comment and reply" is lower than 3.0. The rating of the information units for academic weblog post, implying the common constitution of which, validates the taxonomy base on the niche of conventional study for academic weblog post.

The result of frequency rated in the survey indicates the knowledge of social convention of academic web genres in the domain of citation analysis in Chinese is typically recognized in the taxonomy. For example, for Abstract component from online bibliography and research article, "summarize the topic" (4.57) and "summarize the result" (4.36) are rated as most frequently used while "summarize the conclusion" (3.64) and" summarize the method" (3.57) are rated frequently used. The high frequency rated in all of the four functional units of Abstract component indicates the social convention on Abstract component in the domain of citation analysis is consensus. For academic weblog post, "establish the communicative topic" (4.21), "digress from the topic" (4.21) and "provide topic related information" (3.71) are typical functional units in Introduction component except for "provide topic related event "(3.36), which indicates that the community in LIS still have different opinions on the convention of this functional unit.

## CONCLUSION

In this research, we developed the taxonomy of information units for genres of academic web documents, including abstract, research article from open access journal, entry of online encyclopedia and academic weblog post. Based on the results, the conclusions related to the original research questions are:

(i) Based on the theories of genre analysis and social construction of meaning (Swales 1990; Bhatia 2014; Berkenkotter & Huckin 1995), 55 functional units were identified, with 33 functional units in research article, 11 in entry of online encyclopedia and 11 in academic weblog post. There are seven components with 33 functional units in research article, four components with 12 functional units in entry of online encyclopedia, four components with 10 functional units in academic weblog post.

Since there is a solid base of research of genre structure for research article and abstract, their identification of information units are mostly based on these researches with minor revision. However, research on genre structure of weblog post and entry of online encyclopedia is rare. So we developed the taxonomy by move analysis and chunking the sample articles into information units on component and information unit level. For academic weblog post, as a form of persuasive writing, it has a great deal in common with the genres of sales letter and job application. Also, with the purpose of communication of viewpoint or knowledge, the academic weblog post and the entry of online encyclopedia share important elements with research article that have been studied in a similar way.

The construct validity in the development of the taxonomy of information units has ensured the operational definitions for the information units being studied. The validation in the user survey has further ensured that the information units identified across genres in Chinese represented the conventional knowledge of the Chinese research community well. However, as a validation method, whether the taxonomy is complete or fully representative across genres is still not covered. We have found commonalities among the 81 documents, but that is the merest glimpse of the universe of discourse. Thus, the validity of the taxonomy should be tested with greater breadth and variety of articles, blogs and encyclopedias and also outside of the highly specific domain of citation analysis studies further.

Operationally, the manually identification of information units in a text depends on both function indicators and boundary indicators as Connor (1999) proposed. These indicators can inform the automation recognition of information units in the text. Rules for components recognition can be learned from both the texts' explicit text division devices and subheadings. For functional units, linguistic clues such as connectors, metatextual signals and lexical features can be learned to build rules for automation recognition.

(ii) From the results of frequency rated in the survey, we have validated for social convention the taxonomy of information units within chosen academic web genres in the domain of citation analysis in Chinese. Specifically, "provide meta text" for research article is dropped for its mean score for frequency is lower than 3.0.

The results of functional units identified and validated for research article genre are mostly consistent with Zhang's (2012) research, suggesting that the conventional knowledge of functional units for research article genre is typical and well acknowledged by research communities. The rating scores for validity test of information units for entry of online encyclopedia and academic web blog post are mostly high, suggesting that a structural genre analysis approach to decompose a whole document text into information units is well acknowledged and understood by research communities.

Since the utilization of functional units has been proven effective and efficient in the process and outcome of journal article reading (Zhang, 2011), the utilization of the information units for academic web document genres can be further explored. Would conventional knowledge within the information units improve the search process and outcome of aggregated search? What is the relationship among different types of information units in the taxonomy? The exploration of these questions will devote not only to text reading but also to knowledge organization and presentation of aggregated search for web documents.

## ACKNOWLEDGMENTS

This paper is supported by the National Social Science Fund of China (Grant No. 14CTQ015 and Grant No. 12&ZD222) in the entire research process. We would like to thank the anonymous reviewers for their thoughtful suggestions.

## REFERENCES

Agrawal, R., Gollapudi, S., Halverson, A., & Ieong, S. (2009). Diversifying search results. In R. Baeza-Yates, P. Boldi, B. Ribeiro-Neto, & B. B. Cambazoglu (Eds.), *Proceedings of the second ACM international conference on web search and data mining* (pp. 5-14). New York: ACM Press.

Bhatia, V. K. (2002). A generic view of academic discourse. In J. Flowerdew (Ed.). *Academic discourse.* London: Longman, Pearson Education.

Bhatia, V. K. (Ed.). (2014). Analyzing genre: Language use in professional settings. Routledge.

Bishop, A.P. (1999). Document structure and digital libraries: How researchers mobilize information in journal articles. *Information Processing & Management, 35(3)*, 255-279.

Brett, P. (1994). A genre analysis of the results section of sociology articles. *English for Specific Purposes, 13(1)*, 47-59.

Bruce, I. (2008). Cognitive genre structures in methods sections of research articles: A corpus study. *Journal of English for Academic Purposes, 7(1)*, 38-54.

Cao, S., & Li, J. (2014). The analysis of researchers, utilization of web resources in the field of library and information science. *Journal of the China Society for Scientific and Technical Information, (9)*, 994-1008.

Chen, P., Zhang, M., & Huang, L., et al. (2012). Competition and cooperation between academic blogs and traditional academic journals. *Acta Editologica, 24(1)*, 19-22.

Connor, U., & Mauranen, A. (1999). Linguistic analysis of grant proposals: European Union research grants. *English for Specific Purposes, 18(1)*, 47 - 62.

Crookes, G. (1986). Towards a validated analysis of scientific text structures. *Applied Linguistics, (7)*, 57-70.

Dillon, A. (2000). Spatial semantics: How users derive shape from information space. *Journal of the American Society for Information Science, 51(6)*, 521- 528.

Dillon, A. (Ed.). (2004). *Designing usable electronic text.* Boca Raton FL: CRC press.

Ding, J., & Yang, L. (2012). Type, distribution and accessibility of web citation of Chinese library and information science journals. *Library and Information Service, 24*, 60-64.

Hopkins, A., & Dudley–evans, T. (1988). A genre-based investigation of the discussion sections in articles and dissertations. *English for Specific Purposes 7*, 113-121.

Jiang, C., & Jin, C. (1982). Contribution to the explanation of encyclopedia. *Lexicographical Studies, (3)*, 19-26.

Kanoksilapatham, B. (2005). Rhetorical structure of biochemistry research articles. *English for Specific Purposes, 24(5)*, 269-292.

Lewin, B. A., Fine, J., & Young, L. (Eds.). (2001). Expository discourse: A genre based approach to social science research texts. London: Continuum.

Li, C. X. (2010). Comparison between English and Chinese academic book reviews. Changsha: Central South University.

Li, Y.L., & Belkin, N. J. (2008). A faceted approach to conceptualizing tasks in information seeking. *Information Processing & Management, 44*, 1822-1837.

Liu, X. (2009). Generic structure of chinese phd dissertation concluding chapters: Cross-disciplinary and cross-cultural perspectives. Unpublished master thesis. Shanghai: Dong Hua University.

Mauranen, A. (1993). Contrastive ESP rhetoric: Metatext in Finnish–English economics texts. *English for Specific Purposes, 12(1)*, 3-22.

Motta-Roth, D. (1995a). Book reviews and disciplinary discourses: Defining a genre. *TESOL 29th Annual Convention & Exposition* (pp.385-385).

Motta-Roth, D. (1995b). Rhetorical features and disciplinary cultures: A genre-based study of academic book reviews in linguistics, chemistry, and economics. Unpublished doctoral dissertation. Florianopolis: Federal University of Santa Catarinal.

Mou, P., Liu, W., & Liang, S. (2013). Analysis on current web citation of library and information science. *Library Tribune, 3*, 69-73, 96.

Nwogu, K. N. (1997). The medical research paper: Structure and functions. *English for Specific Purposes, 16(2)*, 119-138.

Posteguillo, S. (1999). The schematic structure of computer science research articles. *English for Specific Purposes, 18(2)*, 139-160.

Rosso M. (2005). *Using genre to improve web search*. Unpublished doctoral dissertation. Chapel Hill: University of North Carolina at Chapel Hill.

Roussinov, D., Crowston, K., & Nilan, M., et al. (2001). Genre based navigation on the web. In E. Dennis (Ed.), *Proceedings of the 34th Hawaii international conference on system sciences* (pp. 1-10). IEEE.

Samraj B. (2002). Introductions in research articles: Variations across disciplines. *English for Specific Purposes, 21*, 1-17.

Samraj B. (2005). An exploration of a genre set: Research article abstracts and introductions in two disciplines. *English for Specific Purpose, 24(2)*, 141-156.

Sandusky, R. J., & Tenopir, C. (2008). Finding and using journal–article components: Impacts of disaggregation on teaching and research practice. *Journal of the American Society for Information Science and Technology, 59(6)*, 970-982.

Shi, Y., & Xiao, X. (2009). Link structure of academic blog and characteristics of communication analysis. *Document, Information & Knowledge, (5)*, 79-83.

Swales, J.M. (Ed.). (1981). Aspects of article introductions. *Aston ESP Research Reports No1*. Birmingham: University of Aston.

Swales, J.M. (Ed.). (1990). *Genre analysis: English in academic and research settings*. Cambridge: Cambridge University Press.

Swales, J.M. (Ed.). (2004). *Research genres: Explorations and applications*. Cambridge: Cambridge University Press.

Symonenko, S. (2007). Websites through genre lenses: Recognizing emergent regularities in websites content structure. Unpublished doctoral dissertation. Syracuse: Syracuse University.

Thompson, D. K. (1993). Arguing for experimental "facts" in science: A study of research article results sections in biochemistry. *Written Communication, 10(1)*, 106-128.

Van Rij-Heyligers, & Li, P. J. (2011). A corpus-based comparative genre analysis of research article abstracts. *Journal of Xi'an International Studies University, 1*, 11.

Vaughan, M. W. (1999). Identifying regularities in users' conceptions of information spaces: Designing for structural genre conventions and mental representations of structure for web–based newspapers. Unpublished doctoral dissertation. Indiana: Indiana University.

Vaughan, M. W., & Dillon, A. (1998). The role of genre in shaping our understanding of digital documents. *Proceedings of 61st Annual Meeting of the American Society for Information Science.* (pp. 559-566). Medford NJ: Information Today Inc.

Williams, K. C. M. (2000). Reproduced and emergent genres of communication on the world wide web. *The Information Society, 16(3)*, 201-215.

Yang, R. Y. (2006). Application of genre analysis: Structure analysis of research article in the field of Applied linguistic. *Foreign Languages and Their Teaching, (10)*, 29-34.

Yang, S., & Qiu, J. (2012). The distribution of web citation based on the Chinese and English Wikipedia. *Journal of the National Library of China, 6*, 7-19, 38.

Yin, R. K. (Ed.). (2014). *Case study research: Design and methods*. Los Angeles: Sage.

Zhang, L. (2011). *A study of functional units for information use of scholarly journal articles*. Unpublished doctoral dissertation. Vancouver: University of British Columbia.

Zhang, L.(2012). Grasping the structure of journal articles: Utilizing the functions of information units. *Journal of the Association for Information Science and Technology, 63(3)*, 469-480.

# Assessing the Implementation of Authentic, Client-Facing Student Projects in User Experience (UX) Education: Insights from Multiple Stakeholders

**Craig M. MacDonald**
*School of Information, Pratt Institute, USA. cmacdona@pratt.edu*

**Lillian Rozaklis**
*School of Pharmacy & Health Sciences, Fairleigh Dickinson University, USA. lilyr@fdu.edu*

## ABSTRACT

**User experience (UX) is often cited as one of the fastest growing occupations, creating opportunities across nearly every sector for individuals skilled in the application of user-centered design principles and methods. Many information and library schools have responded to this demand by introducing more UX coursework into their curriculum, but the proliferation of agile software development and lean product design has incentivized organizations to look for experienced individuals for UX roles, even those that are considered entry-level. As a result, aspiring information professionals face a paradoxical situation in which they are required to *have* UX experience before they can *gain* UX experience. This article provides an assessment of one institution's efforts to overcome this experience gap by offering opportunities for students to participate in three types of authentic client-facing UX projects. Through surveys of students and clients served over four academic years, we provide a set of lessons learned and recommended best practices for incorporating project-based learning opportunities into UX courses.**

## KEYWORDS

HCI, user experience, education, project-based learning

## INTRODUCTION

With digital technologies now fully integrated into most people's personal and professional lives, organizations across nearly every domain are beginning to prioritize user experience (UX) as a key competitive advantage (Rosenberg & Daniel, 2014). The UX profession is therefore often cited as one of the fastest growing and most highly paid occupations (Baldwin, 2013; Glassdoor, 2015), creating a wide array of new opportunities for individuals with knowledge, skills and abilities related to user-centered design (Onward Search, 2014). However, with those opportunities comes added pressure to keep pace with the rapid technological advancements and their associated changes to how interactive technologies are designed, evaluated and implemented (Churchill, Bowser, & Preece, 2013). In turn, employers now seek individuals with previous experience for UX roles, even for entry-level positions. Thus, students and aspiring information professionals are faced with a so-called "experience paradox" whereby they are required to *have* experience before they can *gain* experience (Gonzalez, Ghazizadeh, & Smith, 2014).

Overcoming the experience paradox poses a unique challenge for UX education. Educators are already tasked with both deepening and broadening the scope of the UX curriculum to cover an increasingly diverse set of skills and knowledge areas (Faiola, 2007). Now, educators must also seek more and better ways to integrate practical, real world projects into their courses (Fernandez, 2004; Henneman, Ballay, & Wagner, 2016).

In this paper, we describe and assess one institution's efforts to address this challenge by integrating three types of authentic client-facing projects into a graduate-level UX curriculum: course-embedded projects, course-long projects and extracurricular projects. Project experiences are examined from the perspective of student participants, client participants and the instructor, with the goal of determining the extent that client-facing projects can bridge the "experience gap" by providing students with opportunities to apply UX methods in real world contexts.

## LITERATURE REVIEW

Researchers have evaluated many different approaches to teaching user-centered design, UX and related concepts from human-computer interaction (HCI). Some examples include examining the effectiveness of using crowd feedback to inform students' iterative design process (Dow, Gerber, & Wong, 2013), assessing the benefits of teaching HCI to a novice audience using the book *Zen and the Art of Motorcycle Maintenance* (Harper, 2016) and using a studio-based approach inspired by architecture education (Reimer & Douglas, 2003). Others have explored innovative ways to introduce a sense of authenticity into UX courses. In one example, educators developed a learning activity called the "prototype walkthrough" in which students presented in-progress prototypes to the class to simulate the real world design practice of studio critiques (Hundhausen, Fairbrother, & Petre, 2012). In another, educators developed an approach called "the panda hat of doom" in which student presenters drew from a stack of cards listing various doom scenarios that could happen during a professional presentation and were forced to wear a plush panda hat as they attempted to complete the scenario (Hunsucker, Gobbo, Stallings, & Siegel,

80th Annual Meeting of the Association for Information Science & Technology, Washington, DC, VA | Oct. 27-Nov. 1, 2017

2016).

A more common approach for providing authentic experiences in the classroom is through the use of problem-based learning, which puts the process of problem solving at the center of the learning experience, or project-based learning, which emphasizes the creation of an end product or deliverable (Kokotsaki, Menzies, & Wiggins, 2016). While there have been several individual attempts to incorporate problem-based learning into UX learning contexts (Koutsabasis & Vosinakis, 2012; Nordahl & Serafin, 2008), most UX educators have adopted a project-based learning pedagogy – or, what may be more accurately called "project-led problem-based learning" (Hanney & Savin-Baden, 2013) – through client-facing projects that serve as a form of "service learning" for students (Mankoff, 2006). These service learning experiences have been shown to help students better understand the trade-offs required in real design projects (Lazar, 2011), provide students with extra motivation to deliver quality work (Lasserre, 2011; Ritter, 2014), and help students build a stronger work portfolio (Shneiderman et al., 2006). On a more practical level, the uniqueness of these projects is an effective way to prevent plagiarism (Ritter, 2014). In short, service learning experiences have shown to be an effective way of offering students authentic, real world UX experience, though it should be noted that most of these studies focused on undergraduate HCI courses in computer science programs and covered only one type of project. The current study is among the first to assess the implementation of multiple types of client-facing projects within the context of a graduate-level UX curriculum in the information/library science domain.

## METHODOLOGY

The researchers developed two questionnaires for this study: one questionnaire was developed and administered to students/alumni who had participated in a client-facing project and a separate questionnaire was developed and administered to the primary representative from each client organization who liaised with the student team. A survey research methodology was selected because it allowed the researchers to optimize data collection for the populations in the least intrusive way. It also allowed for use of the retrospective pretest technique in the students/alumni survey. For this technique, after engaging in a particular experience or intervention participants are asked to first report their *current* levels of knowledge, behavior, or interest. Next, participants are asked to report their perceived level of knowledge, behavior, or interest *prior to* the experience or intervention; this second measure is the retrospective pretest (Pratt, McGuigan, & Katzev, 2000). Compared to traditional pre/post testing, the retrospective technique is considered more convenient since there is only one data collection period, more accurate since it enables participants to reflect on their growth over time (Pohl, 1982), and more reliable since it reduces the possibility of response shift bias (Howard, 1980).

The students/alumni survey was designed to elicit information from students about their experience participating in a client-facing project. The survey prompted students/alumni to answer the same questions for each type of client-facing project for which they self-reported their participation: a course-embedded project, a course-long project, and/or an extracurricular project (more details on these project types is presented in the next section). Next, respondents were asked to rate their knowledge, skills and interest level both *after* and *before* participating in the project (the retrospective pretest). From relevant literature, the researchers identified several indicators of effective project-based learning opportunities: knowledge of core concepts (Kokotsaki et al., 2016), interest in the topic/domain (Lasserre, 2011; Shneiderman et al., 2006), confidence in applying core concepts (Helle, Tynjälä, & Olkinuora, 2006), ability to work within real-world time/resource constraints (Lazar, 2011), ability to interact with clients (Ritter, 2014), and ability to work effectively in teams (Hanney & Savin-Baden, 2013). Then, respondents rated their overall satisfaction with several aspects of the project experience, such as the amount of opportunities for self-reflection (Mankoff, 2006; Ritter, 2014), the sense of authenticity or "realness" of the experience (Webster & Mirielli, 2007), and the supportiveness of the learning environment (Warren, 1988). Next, they were asked to describe the most important thing they learned from the experience. To conclude, respondents were asked about their perceptions of the overall value of client-facing projects in their education and whether they received a job or internship based on their experience.

The client survey was designed to elicit information from the primary representative from the client organization about their experience participating in a student project. First, respondents were asked to rate whether several aspects of the students' work met expectations. Next, they assessed the level of involvement in the project and rated their overall satisfaction with the students' work. Finally, respondents were asked to explain how, if at all, their organization had benefitted from the project, whether they used or planned to use any of the students' ideas, and whether they would participate in another student project.

Both surveys were administered online using SurveyGizmo. A solicitation message was sent via email to 87 students/alumni and to 25 clients who were project participants at some point between the 2012-2013 and 2015-2016 academic years. A reminder message was sent 10 days later to anyone who had not yet responded. Messages to one student/alum and three clients could not be delivered due to invalid email addresses.

To contextualize the results, we begin by describing each project type and providing brief vignettes of recent projects. Results are discussed separately from the students/alumni and client perspectives. Finally, we discuss the projects from the instructor's perspective by offering recommended best practices for integrating client-facing projects into UX curricula.

## PROJECT TYPES

As mentioned previously, this research addresses three distinct types of client-facing projects: course-embedded projects, course-long projects, and extracurricular projects. Below, we provide sample project vignettes to further explain the nature of each project type and highlight key differences in their implementation. For additional context, all of the participating students were enrolled in Pratt Institute's graduate (masters-level) program in information/library science, where all courses are offered in a face-to-face setting at the institute's Manhattan campus.

### *Course-Embedded Project*

Course-embedded projects refer to projects that students completed to satisfy a portion of their overall course grade. Specifically, course-embedded projects took the form of an assigned usability study conducted on behalf of an outside client in which teams of 3-5 students were responsible for planning the study with respect to the client's goals and objectives, recruiting participants, moderating usability test sessions, analyzing data, and writing and submitting a formal report with major findings and recommendations for improvement. From start to finish, these projects lasted between 6 and 8 weeks. The project has been included as an assignment in a graduate-level usability course every fall and spring semester since spring 2014. In that time, 61 students have participated and delivered usability evaluation reports to 17 clients spanning the non-profit, library, museum, archive, government, financial, and start-up sectors. In spring 2016, the project was modified to add more interaction between students and clients and now includes three student-client interactions: a kick-off meeting to outline project goals and expected outcomes, a check-in at the halfway point to review progress, and a final presentation held in the final class session.

### *Project Vignette: NYC Open Data Portal*

The New York City Open Data Portal, a key aspect of the city's "Open Data for All" initiative, is a groundbreaking effort to promote government transparency and accountability by providing public access to over 1,400 data sets from over 80 city offices and agencies. In spring 2016, the School of International and Public Affairs (SIPA) at Columbia University launched a collaboration with the city to gain a better understanding of the pain points and barriers faced by non-technical users of the data portal. As part of this project, SIPA sought outside experts to evaluate the usability of the portal's interface. A group of four students from a graduate-level usability course at Pratt Institute worked with a SIPA representative to conduct a usability evaluation of the portal for their final class assignment.

From mid-March through early May 2016, the student group planned and implemented a usability study with 16 participants, including 4 in-person moderated sessions recorded with the LookBack usability software and 12 remote unmoderated sessions conducted through UserTesting.com as part of their university partnership program. The students developed and administered pre-test and post-test questionnaires and used the think aloud protocol to elicit feedback directly from participants as they attempted to use the portal to complete one task focused on finding a specific dataset and one task related to using the portal's built-in data visualization tools. Overall, students found that participants had generally positive impressions of the portal but struggled to understand the full scope of the portal and complete basic tasks. They offered four recommendations to improve the overall usability of the site for non-technical users (e.g., add stronger labels and better prompts to help non-technical users find relevant datasets). The students compiled their results and recommendations into a formal usability evaluation report, which they submitted to the SIPA representative and to the course instructor. In a change from previous semesters, students also delivered a face-to-face presentation with SIPA during the final class session. However, only the evaluation report was graded by the instructor, determining 20% of the students' overall course grade.

### *Course-Long Projects*

Course-long projects refer to projects that lasted the entire duration of a course and determined the majority of students' course grade. In this case, course-long projects were completed as part of a graduate-level course titled Projects in Information Experience Design. The primary goal of this course is to offer students practical, hands-on experience applying user-centered methods to solve a real-world problem for an outside client. Guided by the "inspiration, ideation, implementation" design thinking framework (Brown, 2008), students in this course conduct discovery research and stakeholder interviews to understand the organization's challenges, apply collaborative brainstorming to explore potential solutions, and develop a set of desirable, feasible, and viable proposals for the organization to consider. The course has been offered twice, in spring 2015 and summer 2016, and included the participation of 18 students (nine in each semester) and two cultural heritage organizations.

### Project Vignette: Intrepid Museum

The Intrepid Sea, Air & Space Museum is a non-profit educational and cultural institution located in New York City. As part of its mission to promote awareness and understanding of history, science, and service, museum leaders recently launched a multi-year project to improve the visitor experience and grow the museum's audience. As part of these efforts, the museum agreed to participate as a client in the Projects in Information Experience Design course at Pratt Institute in summer 2016.

Through bi-weekly four-hour class sessions from May-June 2016, the course instructor and nine students engaged in an intensive research and design project aimed at exploring ways to improve the museum experience specifically for international visitors. The students began by conducting stakeholder interviews with two key museum staff members, who outlined the major challenges they face in engaging with international visitors and shared relevant data and statistics from their internal program evaluation efforts. Next, the students split into groups to conduct discovery research, which included a competitive analysis of organizations both inside and outside the cultural domain; a content analysis of user reviews from TripAdvisor, Yelp, Facebook and Twitter; a wayfinding audit of museum signage; a heuristic evaluation of the museum's online ticketing interface; interviews with 19 museum visitors; and 10 hours of museum observations. After a check-in meeting with the client, the class used collaborative brainstorming and sketching exercises to iteratively develop three proposals: a color-based iconography and navigation system to provide universal wayfinding aids, interactive prototypes for a revamped web interface and new kiosk-based interface for purchasing tickets online, and recommendations for an improved visitor's guide and standardized wayfinding system. Students delivered their proposals in an on-site presentation with museum staff and the museum leadership team. Students also provided extensive documentation of their research and analysis to aid future implementation efforts. Course grades were determined by group's achievement of interim milestones (30%), the quality of the group's final presentation and deliverables (40%), a deliverable telling the story of each student's contributions to the group project (20%), and each student's participation (10%).

### *Extracurricular Projects*

Finally, extracurricular projects refer to projects that students completed outside of their regular course requirements. Since they were not connected to any individual course, extracurricular projects were designed to satisfy the needs of each individual client rather than serve specific educational objectives. As a result, projects ranged from eight to 12 weeks in duration, involved teams of three to eight students, and incorporated a variety of different design and evaluation methods, from summative and formative usability studies to user research, persona development and prototyping. Six extracurricular projects have been completed since spring 2013 involving a total of 24 students (some of whom participated in more than one project). Clients for these projects included a cultural heritage organization, a university research team, a school of continuing education, two start-up companies and a large media organization. Three of these projects were completed for a modest consulting fee while the remaining three were provided pro bono.

### *Project Vignette: The Press Play Project*

The New York City Media Lab is a university consortium dedicated to spurring innovation in research and development and strengthening relationships between industry and academia. With backing from the NYC Economic Development Corporation, one of the organization's primary roles is facilitating collaborative research projects between its corporate members and local universities. These "seed projects" enable companies to work directly with a team of faculty and students to explore an area of interest. In fall 2015, Pratt Institute was invited to partner with a major media company on the "Press Play" project, a funded project aimed at improving the experience of watching videos on the mobile web.

Featuring a team of four students led by one faculty member (the first author), the Press Play project ran for 11 weeks between October and December, 2016, and featured weekly team working sessions and conference calls with the client. The first project phase sought data on users' preferences for watching videos on mobile devices. With guidance from the faculty leader, the student team analyzed internal mobile video viewing data, conducted a one-week diary study with 7 participants, held interviews with 11 participants, administered a survey to 98 mobile video users, and analyzed six competing mobile video platforms. From these efforts, the team identified several insights about users' mobile video preferences and developed six unique personas. In the second phase, the team explored interface solutions to the identified pain points through iterative design of paper and digital mobile prototypes. The final product was a walkthrough video showcasing a new mobile web interface that featured a cleaner display of video content, more accurate and descriptive video metadata, and unique personalization options to drive user engagement with relevant content. Students delivered their final proposal in an on-site presentation to company staff and provided extensive documentation, including prototype files and all of the raw research data collected.

## RESULTS: STUDENTS/ALUMNI

The students/alumni survey received 59 usable responses out of a possible 86, resulting in a 68.6% response rate. Within this sample, 44 respondents indicated participating in a course-embedded project (44 of 61; 72.1%), 16 indicated participating in a course-long project (16 of 18; 88.9%), and 12 indicated participating in an extracurricular project (12 of 24; 50.0%). Note that these percentages do not add to 100% since some students participated in more than one type of project. While a majority (45 of 59; 76.3%) reported participating in one type of project, 13 (22.0%) reported participating in two types of projects, and one reported participating in all three types of projects. Finally, respondents indicated working with 23 of a possible 25 clients, which indicates that the response sample is representative of the target population.

Results from students/alumni survey are presented in four parts: retrospective pretest, satisfaction with project participation, lessons learned and overall perceptions.

### *Retrospective Pretest*

The retrospective pretest data was analyzed separately for each project type. Using the statistical package R, we calculated the mean before and after scores provided by the respondents for eight indicators. We then conducted a one-sided exact Wilcoxon Signed Rank Test, the non-parametric alternative to the paired samples t-test. To control the false discovery rate and account for possible dependencies, p-values were adjusted using the Benjamini-Yekutieli method. Table 1 presents results for all three project types.

| Indicator | Course-Embedded (n = 44) | | | Course-Long (n = 16) | | | Extracurricular (n = 12) | | |
|---|---|---|---|---|---|---|---|---|---|
| | *Before (mean)* | *After (mean)* | *p-value (adj)* | *Before (mean)* | *After (mean)* | *p-value (adj)* | *Before (mean)* | *After (mean)* | *p-value (adj)* |
| my knowledge of UX concepts and methods | 2.77 | 4.05 | < 0.001* | 3.50 | 4.38 | 0.017* | 3.25 | 4.42 | 0.170 |
| my ability to create quality deliverables for clients | 2.86 | 4.11 | < 0.001* | 3.38 | 4.63 | 0.008* | 3.00 | 4.25 | 0.176 |
| my ability to work in teams | 3.91 | 4.18 | 0.038* | 3.94 | 4.44 | 0.027* | 3.67 | 4.42 | 0.176 |
| my ability to interact with clients | 3.14 | 3.64 | 0.002* | 3.27 | 4.00 | 0.017* | 2.92 | 4.00 | 0.176 |
| my ability to work within time/resource constraints | 3.93 | 4.25 | 0.005* | 3.50 | 4.38 | 0.008* | 3.58 | 4.42 | 0.226 |
| my ability to manage the "messiness" of real world projects | 3.02 | 3.98 | < 0.001* | 3.50 | 4.25 | 0.027* | 3.00 | 4.00 | 0.265 |
| my interest in UX | 3.95 | 4.41 | 0.017* | 4.63 | 4.81 | 0.679 | 4.00 | 4.50 | 0.265 |
| my confidence in applying UX methods | 2.64 | 4.41 | < 0.001* | 3.69 | 4.56 | 0.008* | 2.83 | 3.83 | 0.176 |

***Table 1**. Retrospective pretest analysis for students/alumni. Each indicator was rated on a 1-5 scale where 1=Low and 5=High. P-values marked with an asterisk (*) are statistically significant.*

Overall, respondents who participated in a course-embedded project (a client-facing usability study) reported statistically significant improvements on all eight indicators: their knowledge of UX concepts/methods, their ability to create quality deliverables, their ability to work in teams, their ability to work with clients, their ability to work within time/resource constraints, their ability to manage the "messiness" of real world projects, their interest in UX, and their confidence in applying UX methods

Respondents who participated in a course-long project (a client-facing design research project) reported statistically significant improvements on seven of the eight variables, with "my interest in UX" being the only exception. In this case, the relatively high "before" score for this variable (4.63) is indicative of the fact that nearly all students participating in a course-long project had completed a UX course and were already interested in the topic.

Notably, there were no statistically significant improvements on any of the eight indicators related to respondents' participation in an extracurricular project. This lack of statistical significance seems primarily driven by the small number of respondents who reported participating in this type of project. Another important factor is that unlike the other project types – which were structured relative to course goals, adopted a similar methodology and followed roughly the same schedule – each extracurricular project was uniquely designed to meet the goals, expectations and timelines of the client. In other words, we do not interpret the lack of statistically significant results for this project category to reflect a low impact of these projects on students' knowledge, abilities, and interests; instead, it is likely a byproduct of grouping all "extracurricular projects" into a single category and treating them as equal despite their inherent differences. In the future, we will explore alternate methods for evaluating the impact of these projects on a more individualized basis.

Overall, the above results indicate that participation in client-facing projects led to positive improvements in students' UX-related knowledge, abilities and interests.

## Satisfaction with Project Participation

Next, respondents were asked to rate their agreement with six questions about specific aspects of their client-facing project experience. Table 2 provides mean scores for these six questions across the three project types.

Importantly, these scores indicate that the vast majority of students felt that their participation in a client-facing project was a positive experience, with mean scores ranging from 4.38 to 4.67 across the three project types. Other positive results are that most respondents felt that they completed the project in a supportive environment (mean range of 4.34 to 4.44) and that they felt a sense of pride and ownership of their chosen project (mean range of 4.08 to 4.38). Further, most respondents felt that the course-long projects and extracurricular projects felt sufficiently authentic (mean scores of 4.25 and 4.08, respectively). Course-embedded projects were rated slightly lower in terms of authenticity, which is to be expected given their status as a class assignment. As mentioned previously, this project was changed recently to incorporate more student-client interaction, which should boost the perceived authenticity of these projects going forward.

While the results as a whole are positive, they also indicate two potential areas for improvement: opportunities for reflection and amount of client interaction. These areas are not unrelated; one of the biggest challenges of incorporating client-

| Question | Course-Embedded (n = 44) | | Course-Long (n = 16) | | Extracurricular (n = 12) | |
|---|---|---|---|---|---|---|
| | *n* | *Mean* | *n* | *Mean* | *n* | *Mean* |
| Participating in the project was a positive experience. | 43 | 4.40 | 16 | 4.38 | 12 | 4.67 |
| I had enough opportunities for self-reflection or de-briefing. (r) | 44 | 3.66 | 16 | 3.25 | 12 | 3.00 |
| I completed the project in a supportive environment. | 44 | 4.34 | 16 | 4.44 | 12 | 4.33 |
| I felt a sense of pride/ownership of the project. | 43 | 4.30 | 16 | 4.38 | 12 | 4.08 |
| The project felt authentic/"real world." (r) | 44 | 3.89 | 16 | 4.25 | 12 | 4.08 |
| There was enough interaction with client during the project. (r) | 44 | 2.59 | 16 | 2.88 | 12 | 3.17 |

***Table 2.*** *Summary of students/alumni perceptions of their participation in each type of client-facing project. Each question was rated on a 1-5 scale where 1=Strongly Disagree and 5=Strongly Agree. Questions marked with (r) were negatively phrased on the questionnaire and have been reverse scored to aid interpretation.*

facing projects into a learning environment is devoting sufficient time to both reflecting on what is being learned and communicating with the client to ensure goals and expectations are being met, all while ensuring the actual project work gets completed. This challenge is practical as well as pedagogical in nature: how do you incorporate client interaction into a classroom setting without disrupting the learning environment? Likewise, how do you incorporate opportunities for self-reflection into a tightly managed project timeline that is driven by client demands and timelines? These are critical questions for future research in this area.

## Lessons Learned

Respondents were also asked to describe the most important thing they learned from their participation. The open-ended responses to this question were analyzed using the constant comparative method (Glaser & Strauss, 1967), which consists of reading and re-reading through textual data and iteratively grouping it until coherent themes emerge. Data were analyzed separately for each project type.

Respondents who indicated participating in a course-embedded project identified six important takeaways from their experience. First, several participants cited the simple benefit of gaining practical experience designing and implementing a usability study from start to finish. Second, participants thought the added responsibility of working with a client taught them how to balance client expectations with practical needs. Third, participants mentioned learning how to make their work more impactful by offering direct, actionable recommendations. Fourth, participants said they learned how to communicate with clients and tactfully deliver critical results in a productive and constructive manner. Fifth, participants cited the benefits of learning how to manage group dynamics and communicate more effectively with their teammates. Finally, participants identified learning specific lessons about project management and usability testing that they found valuable, such as the importance of having back-up plans, how to record user testing sessions, and how to write formal evaluation reports. As one respondent summarized:

"The project was good for putting concepts we were learning into practice - it was [also] helpful conducting proper usability tests, and understanding all the nuances that go into making them successful and effective."

Respondents who participated in a course-long project identified four major takeaways from their experience. First, participants learned how to effectively communicate with clients to discover their true needs and understand their expectations. Second, participants learned how to overcome issues of group dynamics and collaborate effectively in a team environment. Third, participants learned the importance of "satisficing" when trying to meet client needs on a tight deadline, which required balancing tradeoffs and delegating work to their teammates. Finally, participants also identified specific lessons, such as how to use and apply UX methods in a real-world setting, how to identify and overcome individual weaknesses and how to identify an organization's key stakeholders. One participant summarized these lessons as follows:

"The fact that we had so little time to work for a client really forced me to learn how to manage the 'mess' of real world circumstances…I now feel more confident that I can tackle a messy project in a short period of time, while still completing quality deliverables."

Finally, respondents who participated in an extracurricular project cited two major takeaways from their experience. First, respondents stressed the value of gaining hands-on experience working in a client-driven environment, which taught them the importance of communicating the value of their work, managing client expectations and effectively responding to client feedback. Second, respondents cited the general benefits of learning to apply UX methods and techniques in a practical setting. These lessons were best encapsulated by one participant, who stated:

"[The project] provided invaluable early exposure to the stakeholder/client relationship and to communication strategy issues within project development, concepts that are critical in a professional environment but are often hard to fully grasp in a classroom setting."

## Overall Perceptions

Finally, respondents were asked to consider the overall impact of their participation in client-facing projects as part of their education (see Table 3). Overall, respondents had positive perceptions of their project experience, with most indicating that they were able to apply what they learned in other academic or professional contexts (mean = 4.45). Furthermore, most respondents felt more prepared for employment in the UX field because of participating in a client-facing project (mean = 4.16) and that their experience made them more marketable to employers (mean = 4.25). Additionally, seven respondents said they received a job offer or secured an internship as a direct result of their participation in a client-facing UX project.

| Question | All Responses (n = 59) | |
|---|---|---|
| | *n* | *Mean* |
| I have applied what I learned from a client-facing UX project(s) in other coursework or in my professional work. | 58 | 4.45 |
| After participating in a client-facing UX project(s), I feel more prepared for employment in the UX field. | 57 | 4.16 |
| My participation in a client-facing UX project(s) has made me more marketable to employers. | 56 | 4.25 |

***Table 3**. Students/alumni overall perceptions of client-facing project experiences. Question were rated on a 1-5 scale where 1=Strongly Disagree and 5=Strongly Agree.*

Several respondents also chose to leave open-ended feedback about their overall experience. In analyzing these responses, several prominent themes emerged. The most common theme expressed by participants was the value of including their client-facing project experience to build their portfolio. Many respondents shared the sentiment that participating in a client-facing project was "one of the best parts of [their] graduate school experience," with one participant stating that "the client-facing UX project is on par with an internship, as far as making real world connections and gaining practical experience." In addition to helping students build their portfolio, respondents also noted how their project experience made them more confident in their ability to actually complete UX work in a practical environment. As one participant explained:

"Working with a client…exposes the 'messiness' of working as an actual UX designer. Knowing how a UX study works and actually completing a UX study are inherently different."

Other respondents reported that their employers valued their client-facing experience, and others noted that they had been able to successful apply the skills they learned in other projects. Not surprisingly, many respondents explicitly requested more client interaction, particularly at the conclusion of the project. For example, one respondent wanted a final debrief session with the client "to see what was learned, what worked/didn't, and talk about…key results from doing the studies: we reduced errors by X, we drove increased revenue by X, whatever the key metric for the projects." This type of interaction is obviously beneficial, but may not always be possible given the finite timelines associated with client-facing projects completed in an educational setting. Nevertheless, we are exploring strategies for increasing student-client engagement on all types of projects, with a particular focus on finding effective and scalable ways to determine the long-term impacts of student contributions.

| Expectations: | Below | Met | Exceeded |
|---|---|---|---|
| Quality of the work products or deliverables | 0<br>- | 5<br>(35.7%) | 9<br>(64.3%) |
| Depth of the work conducted | 0<br>- | 5<br>(35.7%) | 9<br>(64.3%) |
| Usefulness of ideas/solutions provided | 1<br>(7.1%) | 4<br>(28.6%) | 9<br>(64.3%) |
| Creativity of ideas/solutions provided | 0<br>- | 6<br>(46.2%) | 7<br>(53.8%) |

***Table 4**. Client expectations of student work*

| Level/Amount of: | Not Enough | Just Right | Too Much |
|---|---|---|---|
| Input on project outcomes | 3<br>(21.4%) | 11<br>(78.6%) | 0<br>- |
| Interaction with student team | 3<br>(21.4%) | 11<br>(78.6%) | 0<br>- |
| Interaction with faculty | 1<br>(7.7%) | 12<br>(92.3%) | 0<br>- |
| Time you needed to commit to the project | 1<br>(7.1%) | 13<br>(92.9%) | 0<br>- |

***Table 5**. Client assessment of their involvement*

| Satisfaction with: | Dissatisfied | Neutral | Satisfied |
|---|---|---|---|
| Professionalism of student team | 0<br>- | 0<br>- | 14<br>(100%) |
| The manner in which work products were delivered | 0<br>- | 1<br>(7.1%) | 13<br>(92.9%) |
| The appropriateness of the ideas/solutions provided | 0<br>- | 2<br>(14.3%) | 12<br>(85.7%) |

***Table 6**. Client satisfaction with student work*

## RESULTS: CLIENTS

The client survey received 14 complete responses out of a possible 23, resulting in a 63.6% response rate. Respondents included three clients (out of five valid contacts) who participated in an extracurricular project, two clients (out of two valid contacts) who participated in a course-long project and nine clients (out of 15 valid contacts) who participated in a course-embedded project. Thus, we are confident that respondents to the client survey are representative of the target population.

Results from the client survey are presented in three parts: perceptions of the client experience, impact of the students' contributions, and willingness to participate again.

### Perceptions of the Client Experience

In addition to ensuring client-facing projects are impactful and valuable for students, the continuation of these project opportunities is also dependent on the quality of the experience for clients. Three dimensions of the client experience were considered: match between student work and client expectations, clients' assessment of their involvement in the project, and client's overall satisfaction with the work students provided. Results for these three areas are presented in Tables 4, 5 and 6.

Respondents indicated that students met or exceeded their expectations in the quality of their work products or deliverables, the depth of the work they conducted, and the creativity of the ideas/solutions provided. All but one respondent indicated the usefulness of the students' ideas/solutions met or exceeded their expectations.

In terms of client involvement, the majority of respondents said the amount or level of input on project outcomes, interaction with the project team, interaction with the faculty, and time they needed to commit to the project was "just right." However, echoing student concerns, three respondents said they did not have enough input on project outcomes and three said they did not have enough interaction with the student team.

Finally, the vast majority of respondents were satisfied or very satisfied with the professionalism of the student team, the manner in which work products were delivered, and the appropriateness of the ideas/solutions provided.

Overall, these results suggest that the clients are generally satisfied with the project, though additional student-client interactions would be welcomed.

### Impact of Students' Contributions

In addition to being satisfied with the experience of being a client, it is also important to consider the ultimate impact of the students' contributions to the client organization. To that end, almost all of the client respondents (12 of 14) said their organization had either already used or had plans to use some of the ideas or solutions provided by the students. Specifically, five respondents said they had already made changes to their websites based on the students' recommendations, four respondents had concrete plans to implement the students' ideas pending leadership approval and/or additional funding, and one respondent opted to discontinue their start-up project based on the students' feedback. The remaining two respondents who said they used or planned to use students' ideas did not provide further details. Of the two respondents did not plan to use the students' ideas, one respondent indicated that the ideas were too costly to implement while the other stated that the feedback was not sufficiently actionable.

Clients were also asked to describe the benefits, if any, their organization received as a result of their participation, and four themes emerged from the responses. First, respondents mentioned the improved quality of their product or service based on implementing students' recommendations. Second, respondents indicated that the students' work helped them set strategic priorities, mainly by providing "ideas [that] hadn't occurred to anyone else before." Third, respondents cited the benefit of seeing the UX process modeled by the student team, noting the value of not just the students' ideas but also "their observations, methodology and insights." Finally, several respondents cited some general benefits from participating, such as getting tips to improve their "on-boarding" process or "confirmation of their hunch."

### Willingness to Participate Again

Finally, as perhaps the ultimate measure of satisfaction, all 14 client respondents said they would participate in a student project again.

When asked to explain why they would participate in another student project, respondents cited three primary reasons. First, respondents cited the value of their previous experience as a reason to come back, both because they found it enjoyable (e.g., two clients used the phrase "very fun for us") and because they found the students' ideas to be useful and relevant. Second, respondents cited student projects as a means to ensure they regularly conduct UX projects, observing that "UX is something we should be doing constantly to make [our organization] better." Third, respondents explained how working with students was an effective way to "get the fresh eyes on problems" and bring to the organization "skills sets we don't have."

Finally, although all respondents said they would participate in another student project, three respondents identified specific things they would change if given an opportunity to participate again: one respondent wanted the project to be more focused, one would benefit from more project updates and offers of input/feedback during the project, and another wished they had opportunities to challenge students on their observations.

## RESULTS: INSTRUCTOR

The results presented in the previous two sections indicate that the client-facing project opportunities at Pratt Institute have been useful and valuable experiences for both student and client participants. However, a third perspective is necessary to provide a complete picture of the program's long-term effectiveness and sustainability: the instructor's. To do so, we offer four insights and observations to help instructors incorporate client-facing projects into the UX curriculum. These insights extend similar lessons identified from previous studies and were derived from critical reflections and observations from the first author, who was responsible for leading and organizing all of the project opportunities described in this paper.

First, offering multiple models of client-facing project experiences is a sustainable and flexible way to provide opportunities for students to gain practical UX experience. Extracurricular projects are the closest simulation to the "agency model" of professional UX practice, but finding, organizing, and leading these types of projects is incredibly time-consuming, especially during the academic year. The results of this study show that course-embedded and course-long projects are valuable models for incorporating client-facing projects into the curriculum; in fact, these models were developed because the instructor realized that it would not be feasible to engage in extracurricular projects on a regular basis. With a variety of other project models available, instructors can be more selective about extracurricular projects and only accept them if they are a unique opportunity (i.e., a high-profile client).

Second, instructors should take the lead on recruiting clients for student projects because they have the knowledge to properly explain the value of client participation and the authority to set expectations and timelines (Lasserre, 2011; Mankoff, 2006). While client recruitment can be time-consuming, instructors can use a variety of strategies to ease the process. For example, instructors should establish relationships with local professional associations to assist with outreach to potential clients. In addition, instructors should target their outreach efforts to specific communities that may not be able to afford UX assistance and are more amenable to working with students (e.g., start-ups, cultural heritage organizations, non-profits and small businesses). Importantly, client recruitment becomes easier as more projects are completed because past client participants can serve as valuable sources of referrals and past student participants (once they graduate) can recommend that their employers serve as clients. To aid with this process, the instructor should make an effort to document and publicize completed projects either through the institution's website or the instructor's personal website (Ritter, 2014).

Third, it is critical to clearly define client expectations prior to beginning a client-facing project, regardless of format. To help with this process, the instructor should develop a client orientation protocol that sets forth the overall expectations and outcomes for a project and pre-schedules specific client-student interactions based on expected project timelines and milestones (Lazar, 2011). Following this protocol allows the instructor to confirm that a client has a real and solvable need that can be realistically met by the student project while also ensuring that clients have appropriate expectations about their involvement and the project's outcomes. As recommended by (Lazar, 2011), it is helpful to formalize this protocol through a simple contract or memorandum of understanding.

Fourth, balancing the dual roles of educator and project manager is a learned skill that is developed through experience (Ritter, 2014). Incorporating client-facing projects into the classroom necessarily changes the role of the instructor by combining educational and leadership responsibilities; what Shneiderman may consider a merging of the "sage on the stage" and "guide on the side" roles (Shneiderman, 1998). The instructor must not only define the student learning outcomes at the outset of the project and provide instruction about specific methods or tools that students will use, they must also set timelines, provide feedback on deliverables and ensure students are making sufficient progress toward project goals. Further, educators also need to scaffold projects so that students are fully prepared to succeed at each stage (Lasserre, 2011; Lazar, 2011). For course-embedded projects, it may mean scheduling the project to begin later in the course after students have gained sufficient knowledge; for course-long projects, it may mean establishing pre-requisites or other requirements to ensure students have sufficient experience prior to entering the course; for extracurricular projects, it may mean selecting students with a complementary mix of skills and experience.

## CONCLUSION AND FUTURE WORK

This paper described and assessed one institution's efforts to integrate authentic client-facing projects into a graduate-level UX curriculum using three unique project types: course-embedded projects, course-long projects, and extracurricular projects. Through analysis of survey data from 59 students/alumni and 14 clients served over the past four academic years, we found that the overwhelming majority of students/alumni and clients found their project experience to be positive and impactful. Specifically, students/alumni said their participation increased their knowledge of UX concepts, their ability to create quality deliverables and interact with clients, their ability to work within the "messiness" of real world projects, and their confidence in applying UX methods. While some students wished for more opportunities for self-reflection and more client interaction, they generally felt their project offered a valuable opportunity to put their knowledge into practice and build a strong portfolio. Likewise, a majority of clients expressed high levels of satisfaction with their involvement and with the performance and professionalism of the student team, indicated that project work met or exceeded their expectations, and said they had already used or planned to use some of the ideas or solutions provided by the students. Furthermore, all client respondents said they would participate in a student project again. We also offered four insights about implementing client-facing projects into UX courses: (1) offer multiple project models to increase flexibility and sustainability; (2) have instructors take the lead on identifying clients to leverage existing relationships and target specific communities; (3) establish a formal protocol for establishing client expectations; and (4) develop skills in project management and scaffold projects to help students succeed.

Of course, a key limitation of this study was its exclusive focus on a single program within a graduate school of library and information science located in a major urban center and with courses offered exclusively in a face-to-face format. Thus, these results may not generalize to other disciplines (e.g., design or computer science), other levels (e.g., undergraduate), other formats (e.g., online), or other locations (e.g., non-urban). Future research efforts in this area will explore the role of client-facing projects in a broader array of educational contexts, with the ultimate goal of developing a more universal set of best practices and guidelines for implementing client-facing projects in UX education programs. A secondary goal, currently in progress, is evaluating approaches for enhancing student learning through self-reflection and enhancing feelings of "authenticity" by requiring more student-client interaction.

Despite this limitation, an important takeaway from this research is that although implementing client-facing projects can be time-consuming, they offer immense value to all involved stakeholders. As shown in this paper, students had universally positive feedback about their experience and many actually wished they could participate in *more* client-facing projects. Likewise, clients praised the students for providing valuable insights they would not have gotten otherwise and all said they would participate again. Finally, organizing and leading students through client-facing projects can be challenging for the instructor, but they are also a personally and professionally fulfilling experience (Ritter, 2014). From the educational value of watching students successfully apply concepts learned in the classroom to the practical value of helping an organization improve a product or service, client-facing projects offer educators unique opportunities to both observe and contribute to the real-world impact of UX practice. With that said, although some students/alumni indicated that they received a job or internship because of their client-facing experience and others said their experience was valued by their employers, only a small fraction of the student participants were interested in pursuing full-time UX careers. While these early results are promising, further work is needed to assess whether and to what extent these types of projects can truly help students overcome the UX "experience gap" on a consistent basis and on a wider scale.

## REFERENCES


Baldwin, H. (2013). Tech hotshots: The rise of the UX expert. Retrieved September 3, 2015, from http://www.computerworld.com/article/2493971/app-development/tech-hotshots--the-rise-of-the-ux-expert.html

Brown, T. (2008, June). Design thinking. *Harvard Business Review*, 84–92.

Churchill, E. F., Bowser, A., & Preece, J. (2013). Teaching and learning human-computer interaction. *Interactions*, *20*(2), 44.

Dow, S., Gerber, E., & Wong, A. (2013). A pilot study of using crowds in the classroom. In *Proceedings of the SIGCHI conference on human factors in computing systems - CHI '13* (pp. 227-236). New York, New York, USA: ACM Press.

Faiola, A. (2007). The design enterprise: Rethinking the HCI education paradigm. *Design Issues*, *23*(3), 30-45.

Fernandez, J. D. (2004). A paradigm for community-based human computer interaction education. *Journal of Computing Sciences in Colleges*, *19*(4), 329-334.

Glaser, B. G., & Strauss, A. L. (1967). *The discovery of grounded theory: Strategies for qualitative research*. Hawthorne, NY: Aldine de Gruyter.

Glassdoor. (2015). 25 Highest Paying Jobs in Demand. Retrieved September 3, 2015, from https://www.glassdoor.com/blog/highest-paying-jobs-demand/

Gonzalez, C. A., Ghazizadeh, M., & Smith, M. (2014). Perspectives on the training of human factors students for the user experience industry. *Proceedings of the Human Factors and Ergonomics Society annual meeting*, *58*(1), 1807-1811.

Hanney, R., & Savin-Baden, M. (2013). The problem of projects: Understanding the theoretical underpinnings of project-led PBL. *London Review of Education*, *11*(1), 7-19.

Harper, S. (2016). The user experience in *Zen and the Art of Motorcycle Maintenance*. In *Proceedings of the 2016 CHI conference extended abstracts on human factors in computing systems - CHI EA '16* (pp. 317-327). New York, New York, USA: ACM Press.

Helle, L., Tynjälä, P., & Olkinuora, E. (2006). Project-based learning in post-secondary education – Theory, practice and rubber sling shots. *Higher Education*, *51*(2), 287-314.

Henneman, R. L., Ballay, L., & Wagner, L. (2016). The master's degree in HCI at 20. In *Proceedings of the 2016 CHI conference extended abstracts on human factors in computing systems - CHI EA '16* (pp. 1111-1114). New York, New York, USA: ACM Press.

Howard, G. S. (1980). Response-shift bias: A problem in evaluating interventions with pre/post self-reports. *Evaluation Review*, *4*(1), 93-106.

Hundhausen, C. D., Fairbrother, D., & Petre, M. (2012). An empirical study of the "prototype walkthrough." *ACM Transactions on Computer-Human Interaction*, *19*(4), 1-36.

Hunsucker, A. J., Gobbo, D., Stallings, M., & Siegel, M. A. (2016). The panda hat of doom. In *Proceedings of the 2016 CHI conference extended abstracts on human factors in computing systems - CHI EA '16* (pp. 647-654). New York, New York, USA: ACM Press.

Kokotsaki, D., Menzies, V., & Wiggins, A. (2016). Project-based learning: A review of the literature. *Improving Schools*.

Koutsabasis, P., & Vosinakis, S. (2012). Rethinking HCI education for design: Problem-based learning and virtual worlds at an HCI design studio. *International Journal of Human-Computer Interaction*, *28*(8), 485-499.

Lasserre, P. (2011). Service learning: An HCI experiment. In *Proceedings of the 16th western Canadian conference on computing education - WCCCE '11* (pp. 12-16). New York, New York, USA: ACM Press.

Lazar, J. (2011). Using community-based service projects to enhance undergraduate HCI education. In *Proceedings of the 2011 annual conference extended abstracts on human factors in computing systems - CHI EA '11* (p. 581). New York, New York, USA: ACM Press.

Mankoff, J. (2006). Practical service learning issues in HCI. In *CHI '06 extended abstracts on human factors in computing systems - CHI EA '06* (pp. 201-206). New York, New York, USA: ACM Press.

Nordahl, R., & Serafin, S. (2008). Using problem based learning to support transdisciplinarity in an HCI education. In *Proceedings of HCIed (HCI in education) conference*. Association for Computing Machinery.

Onward Search. (2014). UX Careers Guide. Retrieved September 3, 2015, from http://www.onwardsearch.com/career-center/ux-careers-guide/

Pohl, N. F. (1982). Using retrospective pre-ratings to counteract response-shift confounding. *The Journal of Experimental Education*, *50*(4), 211-214.

Pratt, C. C., McGuigan, W. M., & Katzev, A. R. (2000). Measuring program outcomes: Using retrospective pretest methodology. *American Journal of Evaluation*, *21*(3), 341-349.

Reimer, Y. J., & Douglas, S. A. (2003). Teaching HCI design with the studio approach. *Computer Science Education*, *13*(3), 191-205.

Ritter, F. E. (2014). Semester projects on human–computer interaction as service and outreach. In M. J. Carroll (Ed.), *Innovative practices in teaching information sciences and technology* (pp. 133-141). Cham: Springer International Publishing.

Rosenberg, D., & Daniel. (2014). Introducing the business of UX. *Interactions*, *21*(1), 74-76.

Shneiderman, B. (1998). Relate-create-donate: A teaching/learning philosophy for the cyber-generation. *Computers & Education*, *31*(1), 25-39.

Shneiderman, B., Bishop, A., Friedman, B., Lazar, J., Marsden, G., & Nass, C. (2006). Making a difference: Integrating socially relevant projects into HCI teaching. In *CHI '06 extended abstracts on human factors in computing systems - CHI EA '06* (pp. 41-44). New York, New York, USA: ACM Press.

Warren, K. (1988). The student directed classroom: A model for teaching experiential education theory. *Journal of Experiential Education*, *11*(1), 4–9.

Webster, L. D., & Mirielli, E. J. (2007). Student reflections on an academic service learning experience in a computer science classroom. In *Procedding of the 8th ACM SIG-information conference on information technology education - SIGITE '07* (p. 207). New York, New York, USA: ACM Press.

# After Serendipity Strikes: Creating Value from Encountered Information

**Stephann Makri**
*City University of London, UK. Stephann@city.ac.uk*

**Dana McKay**
*University of Melbourne. Australia. danamckay@gmail.com*

**Mina Ravem**
*Telia Norge AS, Norway. minaravem@gmaiol.com*

## ABSTRACT

**Existing research into serendipitous information encountering has focused on how people stumble upon information, rather than how they create value from the information encountered. This online diary study with follow-up interviews provides an enriched understanding of the subjective value of information encounters and the motivators, barriers and actions involved in creating value from them. We leverage our findings to generate design suggestions for digital information tools aimed at assisting in creating value from encountered information.**

## KEYWORDS

serendipity, information encountering, relevance, value

## INTRODUCTION

Information seeking (i.e., search and browse) has been the historic focus of information behavior research. Recently, however, information encountering (IE) has received increased recognition as an important mode of information acquisition. IE happens when people are looking for information on a different topic, when they are not looking for any information in particular or when they are not looking for information at all. IE can facilitate connection-making between seemingly unrelated pieces of information, spark new insights, propel people forward in new directions and surprise and delight them along the way.

Prior research on IE has focused on how people stumble upon information and how digital information tools can support this (e.g., through recommendations or information visualization). For IE to be beneficial, though, it is necessary to create value from the encountered information, by following it up and applying it in one's life or work. Therefore, stumbling upon information is not enough; the finder must also take action to maximize the potential value of the information. What taking action in this way involves remains largely unstudied.

The notion of *value* has been examined in the context of whether or not users are likely to pursue acquired information and incorporated into several models of serendipity (e.g., Foster & Ford, 2003; Makri & Blandford, 2012a; McCay-Peet & Toms, 2015). We have some idea of why encountered information is considered valuable; it can be knowledge-enhancing, impactful, timely or time-saving (Makri & Blandford, 2012a). Other aspects of value creation from encountered information, e.g., the actions, motivators and barriers involved, are less well understood; this is an area ripe for study and enhanced digital support.

We conducted an online diary study to discover how people create value from encountered information, and their related motivators and barriers. Participants took screenshots of information they encountered and shared them privately with us in the cloud. Screenshots were then used as probes in follow-up interviews. Interviews focused on whether participants had found encountered information valuable and whether they had followed it up (or intended to) and why or why not. Several motivators, barriers and actions involved in value creation emerged. These elements form an empirically grounded framework for discussing how people create value from their information encounters and how they subjectively experience that value. The primary contribution of this work is that framework and the resultant design suggestions for creating value from encountered information. In the remainder of this paper, we discuss background literature on IE, outline and justify our method, present our findings and build a framework that describes aspects of post-encounter value creation. We then discuss our findings in the context of previous work and present design implications. Finally, we draw conclusions.

## BACKGROUND

In this section, we provide a theoretical definition of IE and examine work on influencing IEs. We briefly discuss what value might mean in an IE context, then give an overview of the sparse literature on how it might be created.

### *Information Encountering*

Erdelez coined the term *information encountering*, defining it as "accidental discovery during an active search for some other information" (Erdelez, 2005). This definition has since been expanded by other researchers (e.g., Agarwal, 2015; Kefalidou & Sharples, 2016) to include information discovered when browsing or when not looking for information at

80th Annual Meeting of the Association for Information Science & Technology, Washington, DC, VA | Oct. 27-Nov. 1, 2017

all. Erdelez has referred to this broader scope as "opportunistic information discovery" (Erdelez, 2004).

The precise definition we use for information encountering aligns with the more commonly used broader scope, and is grounded in our own earlier work (Makri & Blandford, 2012a, 2012b; Makri, Blandford, Woods, Sharples, & Maxwell, 2014; Makri et al., 2015). We define an information encounter as finding useful or potentially useful information when looking for different information, not looking for any information in particular or not looking for information at all. This definition aims to capture the essence of serendipity in the context of information acquisition; in this paper we describe such serendipitous experiences as IE rather than serendipity.

Given this definition, IE sits outside many traditional information seeking models (Kuhlthau, 1991; Marchionini, 1997), though Bates' berrypicking model does allow for a shift in focus as a result of IE (Bates, 1989). IE is a component of McKenzie's (2003) model. However, while this model proposes that IE only happens during non-directed monitoring, it has also been found to occur during active information seeking (Erdelez, 2004; Makri et al., 2015). Many empirical studies note that IE, rather than being marginal, is an important mode of information acquisition (D'Antonio et al., 2012; Erdelez, 1997; Foster & Ford, 2003; Makri & Blandford, 2012a, 2012b; Makri & Warwick, 2010; McCay-Peet & Toms, 2015).

### *Influencing Information Encountering*

Several studies have sought to examine ways in which IE might be influenced on both an individual level (Heinström, 2006; Makri et al., 2014; McBirnie, 2008; McCay-Peet, Toms, & Kelloway, 2015; McCay-Peet & Toms, 2015) and an organizational level (Cunha, Clegg, & Mendonça, 2010; Napier & Quan, 2013). At an individual level, the influence of personality has been examined, but findings have varied; Heinström (Heinström, 2006) found that IEs were more likely for students who were outgoing, confident and took a strategic approach to information seeking. Findings of a recent study (McCay-Peet et al., 2015) were more modest; extroverts were more likely to report experiencing serendipity in general, but this did not extend to IE.

Some environments are notable for creating opportunities for productive IEs; especially the library shelves (Kleiner, Rädle, & Reiterer, 2013; Thudt, Hinrichs, & Carpendale, 2012). Semantic addressing is designed specifically to make it easier for information seekers to find other books that may pique their interest (Svenonius, 2000). In view of this, various digital tools have emerged to attempt to facilitate IE within the limited scope of the digital library (e.g., Kleiner et al., 2013; Pearce & Chang, 2014; Thudt et al., 2012). Although these tools have not been investigated in terms of whether and how users leverage the encountered information, McCay-Peet has shown that digital tools can influence IE (McCay-Peet et al., 2015). Her work demonstrates that tools that provide opportunities for consuming a variety of information, that facilitate connection making and that offer unexpected interactions best encourage IE. These findings are aligned with our own earlier work on serendipity generally (Makri et al., 2014). This paper investigates how tools might support not just the occurrence of IE, but also the extraction of value from them.

Some work has examined control in IE; findings here have been mixed. Foster and Ford found academic researchers' perceptions of control varied considerably; some thought encountering information was "almost deliberate randomness" while others a result of persistence and hard work (Foster & Ford, 2003). McBirnie noted a paradox in control and IE; that it is not possible to control the process, but that it is possible -- for example by being open and flexible during information acquisition -- to control the perception of it (McBirnie, 2008). This evaluation, though, rests on the process of IE ending immediately once the information is encountered. Our earlier work highlights that the process continues post encounter, and can be influenced by taking action to leverage unexpected encounters to make them valuable (Makri & Blandford, 2012a). This paper extends our work on value, looking at how value is created.

### *"Value" in the Context of Information Encountering*

Traditionally the value of a given piece of information in an information seeking context has been precision, a measure of how well the textual content of a document matches a user's query (Baeza-Yates & Ribeiro-Neto, 1999). However, this approach requires the information seeker to know and describe the information they need; something Borgman noted to be notoriously difficult (Borgman, 1996). Barry (1994) proposed a framework for user (as opposed to system) defined relevance, but this does not address value when encountering information (i.e., outside of active information search). Serendipity is, by definition, a happy accident; the value of encountered information, therefore, is what makes the accident happy. This value may be derived from the match to a non-specified, often unconscious information need or gap. As there are no user or system-determined relevance criteria to meet, users subjectively determine the value of encountered information.

### *Creating Value from Encountered Information*

Value creation has been recognized as important in both IE and serendipity in general (Cunha et al., 2010; Makri & Blandford, 2012a; Makri et al., 2014; McCay-Peet & Toms, 2015; Napier & Quan, 2013). In our empirical model of serendipity, mental projections are made as to the value of encountered information, actions are taken to exploit said value, then through an iterative process of reflection and action, value to the individual is maximized (Makri & Blandford, 2012a). These stages are termed "follow up" in another model of serendipity (McCay-Peet & Toms, 2015). Other models do not describe these actions directly but give examples of them (see Foster & Ford, 2003; McKenzie, 2003). Our study elaborates on the actions taken to extract value from IE, and the associated motivations and barriers.

Our own earlier work examined creative professionals' approaches to serendipity (Makri et al., 2014), and (incidentally) value creation, and Napier and Quan (Napier &

Quan, 2013) examined value creation from serendipity in organizations. Creative professionals maximized their chances of value creation by seizing opportunities when they arose. This involved exploring places stumbled upon and, most relevant to this study, making use of encountered information. Napier and Quan (2013) identified two evaluation strategies for identifying value from encountered information in organizations: flash and systematic. Flash evaluation is based on a rapid "gut feel" assessment; systematic evaluation is more analytical. They found organizational decisions on whether to invest time and money in pursuing serendipitous discoveries were often "entirely politically pragmatic" and made on factors such as sponsorship of an idea rather than its inherent quality. They also identified a need to take action to generate value from IE, and identified motivators and barriers in doing so for organizations (e.g., loose deadlines, space for mental planning, lack of vested interest, internal politics). This paper examines IE motivators and barriers for *individuals*.

## METHOD

We conducted an online diary study and follow-up interviews, mirroring McKenzie's approach for obtaining accounts of everyday information practices (McKenzie, 2003). We recruited a convenience sample of 14 master's students from Ravem's social network. The study was timed to coincide with their dissertation literature search, though many of the encounters they describe are social, rather than academic. We asked the students to restrict their diary entries to examples of information encounters in digital environments. Thirteen students provided entries, however one did not give enough information to generate useful interview questions. As such, our study is based on data from 12 participants (7 female, 5 male), studying on various degrees including Human-Computer Interaction, Engineering and Economics. This section describes our data collection and analysis approach, and its limitations.

### *Diary study*

IEs are "regular but rare" (McBirnie, 2008). As such, we used a four-week diary study duration to capture IEs. This timing was important because IE tends to happen when people are given enough opportunity to interact with information (Makri et al., 2015).

Diary studies can be used for feedback or "elicitation"; the latter typically includes cultural probe style prompts for images, text and other media (Carter & Mankoff, 2005). Like in a previous study of serendipity in everyday life (Sun, Sharples, & Makri, 2011) we combined feedback and elicitation. Specifically, we asked participants to:

1. Take screenshots of useful or potentially useful information they found unexpectedly. The instructions explained this might be when:
    - Looking for different information (i.e., partly or seemingly unrelated information);
    - Looking for information with no particular aim;
    - Not looking for information at all (i.e., not actively seeking information).
2. Note down (a) why they thought finding the information was **unexpected** and (b) why they thought the information was **useful** or might be **potentially useful**.

This approach was designed to maximize the opposing benefits of both simple data entry and creating a useful memory prompt without unduly burdening participants (Carter & Mankoff, 2005; Makri et al., 2015; Sun et al., 2011). We used the word *useful* (rather than valuable) because we did not want to overstate the case for value; *valuable* is defined as "having considerable importance or worth," whereas *useful* as "able to be used for a practical purpose or in several ways" (Oxford English Dictionary). Similarly, we took the same approach as previous work, (e.g., Makri & Blandford, 2012a; McCay-Peet & Toms, 2015), and did not provide examples or definitions of *information*, *useful* or *unexpected*, to avoid restricting or biasing responses.

We further simplified diary entries by using familiar technologies; our diaries comprised screenshots and notes captured in Google Docs. We provided several template diary entries, and participants shared their diaries with us. We instructed them to delete their diaries at the end of the study to preserve their privacy. Participants were encouraged to take screenshots of IEs using whatever type of device they were using at the time, and to fill out diary entries as soon as possible after their encounters, while their memories were fresh. This type of online, cloud-based diary study is new, and was lightweight and simple for both participants and researchers; we advocate its future use in information behavior studies.

### *Follow-up interview*

Following the diary study, we conducted interviews using the diary entries as prompts. We used the entries to elicit the context of IEs, the reason participants experienced the encounter as unexpected, why they thought the information was likely to be useful and their motivations for and barriers to leveraging the information. Interview questions included "what were you doing when you took that screenshot?"; "were you looking for any information in particular? If so, what?," "how was the information you found unexpected?," "was the information you found useful? If so, how? If not, why not?" and (where relevant) "what is preventing it from being useful?." We also asked probing questions to flesh out the story of each encounter, to test our assumptions and elicit more detail. Interviews were transcribed and anonymized on transcription.

The interviews were also used to triangulate findings from our diary study; the overlapping data enhances the validity of our findings (Fidel, 1993).

### *Analysis*

We used an inductive grounded method based on Grounded Theory (GT) (Corbin & Strauss, 2015) to analyze the interview data. However, unlike in GT, we analyzed it all in succession rather than feeding findings into questions for subsequent participants. The cloud-based qualitative data analysis tool Dedoose was used to support coding. Codes emerged related to dimensions of expected and actual usefulness, motivators for and barriers to value creation and actions taken to create value from encountered information. These codes gave rise to a framework that classified each IE by the value created, the motivators and barriers to value creation that were inherent in the encounter and the value-creating actions taken by participants. While the framework can be considered an empirically derived theoretical output, it is not a grounded theory because integrative coding was not deemed to be useful for our purpose of informing design.

We wrote the equivalent of a "serendipity story" for each encounter (Makri & Blandford, 2012a). Each story is a third-person account of participants' goals, the information they encountered, why they considered the encounter unexpected and the actions they took to extract value from the information. These stories are excerpted in our findings.

Our findings illustrate the fine line between information seeking and encountering; most encounters occurred during active seeking. We allow participants' judgments of *unexpected* and *useful* to stand, considering them the authority on the serendipity of their own experiences. We include all entries participants deemed both unexpected and useful (or potentially useful).

### Limitations

A limitation of this study is that information capture changes the experience from fleeting and ephemeral to concrete. According to Loizides & Buchanan (2013) the act of capturing a piece of information is an investment and therefore an explicit statement about the value of that information. Therefore, the very act of capturing IEs has the potential to influence their occurrence, frequency and perceived value. This means the volume and perceived usefulness of encounters are likely to be overrepresented here. However, their *nature* (which was what our study was interested in) *is* likely to be representative.

As four weeks is a relatively short timeframe for a longitudinal diary study, the long-term value of encountered information cannot be fully evaluated. Even so, only 7/31 diary entries described an information use that had not yet happened (see Table 1); value had already been realized in most cases.

McKenzie (McKenzie, 2003) notes that findings on academic information use may not be applicable outside academia. While our participants are fledgling academics, many of the IE examples they provided are social; as such, our findings have broader applicability than just academia.

## FINDINGS

All participants made at least one diary entry (max 5, mean 2.6, s.d. 1.78). The low number of entries is unsurprising given the rarity of IEs. In this section, we present our findings on value creation, motivators and barriers to value creation, and actions taken to create value. These findings form an emergent framework for discussing how people create value from their information encounters, and how they subjectively experience that value.

| Expectation | Reality | N° of entries | Expectation met? |
|---|---|---|---|
| Useful for a specific purpose | Useful for several specific purposes | 2 | Surpassed 😀 |
| Useful for a specific purpose | Useful for that specific purpose | 12 | Met 🙂 |
| Useful for a specific purpose | Useful for a different specific purpose | 3 | Surpassed or met 😀🙂 |
| Useful for a specific purpose | Not yet happened | 5 | Not yet met 😐 |
| Useful for a specific purpose | Not useful | 2 | Not met 🙁 |
| Useful for vague/unknown purpose | Useful for several specific purposes | 1 | Surpassed 😀 |
| Useful for vague/unknown purpose | Useful for a specific purpose | 1 | Met 🙂 |
| Useful for vague/unknown purpose | Not yet happened | 2 | Not yet met 😐 |
| Useful for vague/unknown purpose | Not useful | 3 | Not met 🙁 |

***Table 1:*** *Expectations vs. reality*

### Value of information encounters

Participants' experience of the value of their encounters can be classified according to both their *expectation* of value and the *reality*—their perception of the actual value (see Table 1). Value assessment is made subjectively by participants; this classification reflects their views. While one might see the value gained from these IEs as relatively modest, participants noted their encounters as useful because they seemingly happened with little or no effort.

Participants expected the information might either be *useful for a specific purpose* or for a *vague/unknown purpose*. In reality, they either deemed the information *useful for several specific purposes*, for the *specific purpose* they initially thought it might be useful for or for a *different specific purpose*. Sometimes they decided the information was *not useful* after all. Other times, value had not yet been created from the encounter (*not yet happened*).

#### Expectations surpassed

**Better book: useful for a specific purpose—useful for several specific purposes:** P1 was searching the library catalogue for a specific book recommended by her dissertation supervisor. Based on the publisher's description she was concerned about the book's readability. While the library did not stock her target book, an eBook with a similar title caught her eye and by reading excerpts, she decided it was a better match for her information need than her original target. The book provided a readable overview of her topic and was also useful for helping her to write her literature review *and* for designing her questionnaire-based study. She commented: *"I didn't expect it to have interviews, I expected it to be just explaining concepts. Those interviews gave me practical knowledge for* *my methodology. It was really helpful for designing my approach."* Her expectations were surpassed.

**Comic connection: useful for vague/unknown purpose—useful for several specific purposes:** P1 was "aimlessly" scrolling through her Facebook feed when she noticed a post by Joseph Gordon-Levitt. The post contained a comic strip with a distinct, familiar style of illustrated characters (Figure 1). Upon zooming, she discovered it was signed by an artist she knew, and it contained a link to his website. This pleased her: *"the useful bit is that it gave me the actual link of the artist."* While browsing his website, she discovered the artist had an online shop. This delighted her as she had previously seen his work on Tumblr and wondered how to buy it. She considered printing comic strips from the website or buying them, but did not have the spare money. P1 did not know exactly how the image would be useful when she first saw it, but after examining it in more detail and visiting the artist's website and e-shop, she found it useful for several purposes.

*Figure 1: Comic strip encountered on Facebook (P1)*

## Expectations met

**High School musical: useful for a specific purpose—useful for that specific purpose:** While P5 was browsing an events website looking for Cirque du Soleil tickets as an anniversary present for her boyfriend, she noticed Kadanza, a featured junior musical. She thought tickets would make an excellent birthday gift for her niece: *"there's a different junior musical each year. My niece liked it so much last year she bought the DVD. So that's why I thought we could go again."* Before examining the encountered information on Kadanza in detail, she found Cirque du Soleil tickets and ordered them. She then returned to the Kadanza page, read the show description, and booked tickets. When she encountered the information on Kadanza, she immediately thought it might be useful as a gift for her niece; this was indeed the case. P5's expectations of the usefulness of the encountered information were met.

**Elusive equation: useful for a specific purpose—useful for a different specific purpose:** P7 needed help solving a complex mathematical equation; although he did not expect to find a solution online, he did hope for guidance. While looking for papers and books that might help, he found a reply to a blog post asking for help on a similar equation. The reply only mentioned literature P7 had seen, but it also mentioned its author was trying to solve exactly the same equation as he was. P7 contacted the author of the reply via LinkedIn; he had not solved the equation but shared a Dropbox folder of papers with P7. P7 had previously been unable to access many of the papers in the folder and found them useful for his literature review. While P7 thought the encountered blog post might help him solve the equation, instead it helped with his literature review—a different outcome than he anticipated, but useful all the same.

**Olympic beach: useful for a vague/unknown purpose—useful for a specific purpose:** P7 noticed new barriers going down the staircases at Queen Elizabeth Olympic Park in London. This led him to wonder whether there were to be any events at the venue in the near future: *"maybe there will be a concert, maybe something interesting."* When he got home, he checked the Olympic Park website and noticed there was to be a cycling race soon. His eye was caught by a snippet of information about turning part of the park into a temporary beach. He clicked the link above the snippet to find out more and thought to himself *"it's been here for three months and I didn't notice!"* He visited the beach and enjoyed it, sending photos to friends in Italy to show them he has a beach in London. His expectations that the beach would be worth visiting were met.

## Expectations not yet met

**Passport to London: useful for a specific purpose—not yet happened**: While booking train tickets from Brussels to London on the Eurostar website, P5 noticed a carousel advertising free entry to London museums with the purchase of a train ticket. As she likes to visit museums, P5 clicked for more information and *discovered "you can go to galleries that I didn't even know existed in London. So it was pretty interesting to know."* The page mentioned a few attractions she would like to visit, but she was not sure if she would have time; she made a mental note of these attractions and booked her train tickets. The information she had encountered had the potential to be useful but this potential had not yet been realised.

**Storyboard studies: useful for a vague/unknown purpose—not yet happened:** P2 was searching for a basic overview of the HCI storyboard technique on the Web. She clicked on the Usability Body of Knowledge website, which contains an overview of many HCI topics, including storyboards. While browsing the site, she noticed a section on "published studies" on storyboards. She commented *"I was really generally looking for information on storyboards to get a basic overview. So I didn't expect it to have other public [sic] studies in there. That's why I thought it was kind of serendipitous, because I wasn't seeking out academic papers."* P2 followed the links from the website to several of the published studies and made notes on one paper in particular. She commented, *"I don't know how much I'll actually end up using it, but it was an interesting paper to read. It may feed into my literature review."* There is still potential for the encountered information to be useful, but in this case, time will tell.

## Expectations not met

**True or Hocus Pocus?: useful for a specific purpose—not useful:** P2 saw a poster advertising a movie—Hocus Pocus 2—on Facebook (Figure 2). She was excited, as she had enjoyed the first film: *"the poster popped up on my feed and I really, really liked the first movie. So immediately I was very excited when I saw that."* When she investigated further, however, she discovered it was a hoax. Later that day, her friend texted her the very same poster (as she had also encountered it online). P2 broke the news to her friend that the poster was a fake. P2 expected the encountered information to lead to her watching a sequel to a beloved movie but her expectations were not met. Interestingly, the encounter did lead to information of potential objective value—P2 told her friend the movie was not real. But her expectation of seeing a movie she would enjoy was not met.

***Figure 2:*** *The poster for a fake movie P2 wanted to see*

**False Identities: useful for a vague/unknown purpose—not useful:** P2 was "mindlessly" browsing her Twitter feed when she noticed an article by Patrick Smith, an online journalist. The post was entitled "this is why people create false identities on the internet" and included a link to a BuzzFeed article on the topic (Figure 3). A month earlier, P2 had read an interesting blog post about false identities and commented that this was one of the reasons she clicked on the link. She stated *"it wasn't anything I was looking for, but it was an article that looked like it may be interesting, without me seeking it out particularly."* She started reading the article, but soon "lost interest" and commented that this article was not as interesting as the blog post she had read a month ago. Her expectations of usefulness were not met.

*Figure 3: Article (right) P2 encountered on Twitter (left)*

### *Motivators for value creation*

We identified several motivators for creating value from IEs. These are described in Table 2 and, as in the previous section, illustrated with serendipity stories.

**More promising than initial goal:** P7 initially searched for a book on non-linear acoustics but stumbled upon an interesting paper that provided an introduction to acoustics. He decided to stop searching for the book and to make use of the encountered paper in his literature review.

| Motivator | Explanation | N° of entries |
|---|---|---|
| More promising than initial goal | Encountered information deemed to be more potentially useful than continuing to pursue the initial information goal | 2 |
| Likely to address existing goal | Encountered information deemed to potentially address an existing (but not the initial) information/life goal | 5 |
| Likely to enhance knowledge | Encountered information was deemed to potentially provide new knowledge or enhance existing knowledge | 8 |
| Likely to be useful for someone else | Encountered information deemed to be potentially useful to someone else, based on knowledge of their interests | 2 |
| Relates to existing interest | Encountered information deemed to be related to one of the participant's existing interests | 13 |
| Likely to be enjoyable | Participant expected pursuing encountered information to be fun, entertaining or otherwise enjoyable | 5 |

***Table 2:*** *Motivators for value creation*

**Likely to address existing goal:** P2 needed some new outfits. She noticed an ad for clothing store Topshop on her mobile Facebook feed because several of her friends had liked Topshop on Facebook. The ad featured a limited edition clothing line she was not previously aware of. As the link did not work on her mobile, she visited the Topshop website when she got home and looked at various products. She bought a dress from the clothing line and, when it arrived, liked it so much she ordered several other items from the same line. This addressed her existing life goal of needing new outfits (in an unexpected way).

**Likely to enhance knowledge:** P1 was searching the web for information on designing web pages for emotion and stumbled upon an article entitled "10 Cool Things that HTM Tags Can Do." She commented that in her future career as an HCI designer *"I may have to brief developers on website design, so I should know what basic HTML can do. Maybe it will be helpful to me in the future."*

**Likely to be useful for someone else:** P7 had a friend in Switzerland whose office was relocating to London. Her friend was trying to decide if she would relocate and wanted to gain an overview of the UK tax system. P7 offered to search the Web for this general information. Although she was not looking specifically to estimate the amount of tax her friend was likely to pay if she decided to relocate, she came across a UK tax calculator site. Her friend found the calculator useful for making her decision.

**Relates to existing interest:** P2 came across a news article on false identities (a topic she had previously read about) and a fake poster advertising a sequel to a movie she loved.

**Likely to be enjoyable***:* P11 came across information on a band he had heard of but nor listened to before, as it was only partly related to his musical tastes. Although he said he might not end up listening to them again, he "ended up listening to that band for the next hour."

### *Barriers to value creation*

Three barriers to value creation from encountered information emerged (Table 3). These were **insufficient time** to pursue the information, **no current use** for it and the information **not being as useful** as they first thought.

| Action | Explanation | N° of entries |
|---|---|---|
| Examine | Participant examined encountered information to determine if it was likely to be useful and how | 31 |
| Gather | Participant sought more information related to encountered information to determine if it would be useful and how | 5 |
| Contact | Participant contacted someone who could help determine if and how information would be useful | 1 |
| Buy | Participant added encountered product to online basket or wish list | 3 |
| Save | Participant saved encountered information for later review | 3 |
| Share | Participant shared encountered information | 2 |
| Bookmark | Participant bookmarked encountered information for later review or saved a desktop shortcut | 3 |
| Monitor | Participant continued to monitor encountered information source in hope of additional value creation | 4 |
| Open in new tab | Participant opened encountered information in a new browser tab for later review, continuing their original information task | 3 |
| Make mental note | Participant made a mental note to make use of the encountered information later | 4 |

***Table 3**: Barriers to value creation*

**Insufficient time** was the most common barrier to creating value from encountered information. None of the participants was working to a strict deadline, but dissertation pressures meant they had to weigh up the potential value they stood to gain from investing time in creating value from the information they encountered with the amount of time it was likely to take. Referring to an article she encountered, P1 said *"it's in my bookmarks but...I haven't used it, because I don't have free time."*

| Barrier | Explanation | N° of entries |
|---|---|---|
| Insufficient time | Participant did not feel they had sufficient time to pursue encountered information | 10 |
| No current use | Participant could not currently think of a use for the encountered information | 3 |
| Not as useful as first thought | After examining the encountered information in more detail, the participant did not think it was as useful/potentially useful as they first thought | 5 |

***Table 4:** Actions taken to create value*

**Not having a current use** for the encountered information was discussed as a barrier to value creation by several participants. While searching for information on how to automatically number his mathematical equations, P7 stumbled upon a YouTube channel with several tutorials on using Microsoft Word. He bookmarked the YouTube channel for future use, but did not need to learn anything other than auto-numbering about Word at that time.

**Information not as useful as first thought:** P4 received a Facebook invitation to the Three Peaks Challenge—a hiking event that involves climbing to the summit of three UK mountains in one weekend. She was very interested in participating, but upon checking her calendar, she realized the event clashed with an important religious festival. She said *"I thought 'oh no,' I can't divide myself into two to go to both of these things. So I just rejected the event."*

### *Actions taken to support value creation*

Participants took several actions to support value creation from the encountered information; these are outlined in Table 4. Again, we follow our descriptions with examples.

Participants **examined** information they encountered, reading text and viewing images and video. They read in varying detail from skimming to close reading. Referring to her "morning routine" of checking BBC News, P5 explained *"I don't read the entire website, I just go through the whole website reading the titles."*

In many cases, participants **gathered** additional information related to the encountered information to determine if it would actually be useful and how by searching or browsing. For example, P11 browsed the biography of a new band he encountered information on before listening to them.

P7 **contacted** someone who replied to a blog post he encountered, resulting in sharing resources. Some participants **bought** a product they encountered or added it to a wish list; e.g., P2 bought the "limited edition" dress featured in the Facebook ad she encountered (along with several other items from the same clothing line). P1 **saved** a copy of the eBook she encountered on "designing for emotions." P7 **shared** the tax calculator she encountered with her friend. Several participants **bookmarked** encountered information for later review (e.g., P13 bookmarked a wedding gift for a friend).

Some participants continued to **monitor** the source of encountered information to see if it would result in additional interesting information. For example, P5 made it part of her morning routine to browse the BBC Food website in addition to BBC news, after encountering a tapas recipe that "went down well" with her friends.

Most participants also opened the encountered information in a **new browser tab** for later review, continuing their original information task in the meantime. For example, P2 opened the paper she encountered on storyboarding in a new tab, skim reading it after she finished browsing the Usability Body of Knowledge.

Several participants made a **mental note** to make use of the encountered information later. For example, P1 encountered information about design and innovation consultancy firm IDEO when browsing a Wikipedia article on her dissertation topic of "empathetic design." She was pleased to find out from the article that IDEO were also interested in the topic, as she had considered applying for a job with them. She made a mental note to incorporate the encountered information into a cover letter when applying for a job at IDEO, which she did a few days later.

### *Bringing it all together: Expectation vs. reality, motivators, barriers and actions*

Some information encounters involved multiple motivators, barriers or actions. For other encounters, participants did not identify explicit motivating factors, barriers or actions (perhaps because some time had passed between the encounters and the follow-up interview). Across these axes, many combinations of expectation and reality can and do exist. We illustrate these complexities with an example from our interviews.

**Information intersection:** P6 was hoping to develop a collaborative information visualization tool for his dissertation, but had not yet chosen a domain to focus on. While searching online for collaborative InfoVis tools, P6 remembered he had previously taken a class with InfoVis researcher Marian Dörk. He decided to look for articles by Dörk in the hope they would provide examples of tools. He came across a paper entitled *Urban Co-Creation* by Dörk and Monteyne, on digital tool support for urban civic participation. He stated, *"Weirdly enough I found this paper which isn't really about visualization as such, but about urban planning and how urban co-creation can be supported by digital tools."* P6 did not read the paper in detail, but had the idea of adopting the domain of urban planning for his collaborative InfoVis tool.

P6's **expectation** was that the article would be *useful for the specific purpose* of informing his domain choice. In **reality,** this had *not yet happened*, as he did not have sufficient *time* (**barrier**) to read the paper in more detail. However, he took the **action** of *making a mental note* to read it thoroughly when writing his literature review as it had the potential to *enhance his knowledge* (**motivator**) and to *address his existing goal* (**motivator**) of choosing a domain to focus on.

As seen in this example, information encounters are complex and context-sensitive. Factors such as time, tools and mindset interact to determine whether, for an individual encounter, the encounterer's expectations of value will be met. What is consistent is that information encounters do not end when serendipity strikes, they are only beginning; after a happy information accident, information seekers must work to generate value from the encounter.

## DISCUSSION

In this section, we will relate our findings to previous work and discuss design implications.

### *Relation to previous work*

Previous work on serendipitous information acquisition has emphasized that the most successful information encounterers "make their own luck" (Foster & Ford, 2003; Makri et al., 2014). Our work has shown that the desire to make one's own luck is not just a precursor to serendipity; it is also a determinant of it. Not one encounter in this study was immediately valuable without any work on the part of the participant; there is work involved in generating encounters that are post-hoc deemed serendipitous (Makri & Blandford, 2012a, 2012b).

In some of the examples we give, the effort expended in pursuit of serendipity was considerable, spanning time and tools. This effort was no guarantee of success, however; many encounters generated expectations that remained unmet. Conversely, some encounters resulted in participants' expectations being exceeded. The concept of "expectation" during information acquisition has been addressed before. Kuhlthau (Kuhlthau, 1991) explains that people develop *expectations* of information as they interact with it, making predictions of potential relevance. Marchionini (1997) explains that people may not always know what precise information they need, but will have an expectation of what it might "look like"—e.g., a fact, idea, interpretation. In both of these models, people's assessment of whether their expectations are met involves making relevance judgments. McKenzie's model (McKenzie, 2003) alludes to both this more formal relevance assessment, and a less structured approach where information-seekers do not know what they will find. None of these previous models, though, account for how value is determined.

Our work identifies a similar judgement process for information encounters: sometime after encountering information, people will make a decision on whether their expectations of value are met. Consistent with a previous study (Makri & Blandford, 2012a), we found participants' assessments of the usefulness of encountered information were subjective. Even in instances where an encounter could be objectively considered to have delivered value—such as knowing the Hocus Pocus 2 poster was fake—participants' own assessments were what determined value.

The motivators, barriers and actions identified in our study are not new; all have been discussed in the context of information seeking and some in the context of information encountering. For example, information and entertainment have been discussed as intrinsically linked (Cermak, 1996), IE has been found to result in knowledge enhancement (Makri et al., 2015; Makri & Blandford, 2012a, 2012b). Time has been discussed as important in information seeking behaviour (Savolainen, 2006) and identified as a constraint to serendipity (Makri et al., 2014). Monitoring sources has been identified as an important information behaviour (Ellis, 1989; Makri, Blandford, & Cox, 2008; Meho & Tibbo, 2003) and a means of encountering information (Makri & Warwick, 2010). Gathering more information to determine usefulness is similar to the notion of "confirming" or "disputing" the encountered information (Napier & Quan, 2013). The actions we identified complement Erdelez's model, where information is "captured" after it is noticed (Erdelez, 2014). We noted several means of capturing, including saving bookmarking and mental capturing. Sharing encountered information with others who may find it useful has also been seen in previous work (D'Antonio et al., 2012; Erdelez & Rioux, 2000). While all these features have been seen previously, the novelty in our work is that we discuss them features in relation to the subjective value generated by each IE.

Finally, our study crosses a boundary in information behaviour research: many information behaviour studies are of academics (e.g., D'Antonio et al., 2012; Foster & Ford, 2003;

Sun et al., 2011). McKenzie (McKenzie, 2003) notes that academic or work-related information behaviour is likely to be notably different from social information seeking and presents a model of non-professional information seeking that is quite different from traditional models of information behaviour (e.g., Kuhlthau, 1991; Marchionini, 1997). Our work captures information encounters in both contexts, and there is not a notable difference in terms of value creation behaviour. This is a notable finding in its own right.

### Design implications

Digital information tools are beginning to offer dedicated and meaningful support for IEs (e.g., Kleiner et al., 2013; Thudt et al., 2012); however, these tools are focused on discovery not use and therefore not value creation.

Our value creation framework can be leveraged by designers of digital information tools on all four axes: the reality/expectation gap, motivators and barriers, and (most readily) actions. Tools could encourage users to ask themselves questions such as "do I (still) think this information might be useful? How so? Can I do anything to make it useful?" Such questions can nudge users to reflect on whether and how their value expectations match reality or what they need to do to leverage information.

Technology can allow users to capture, review and reflect on encountered information, thus supporting them in generating value from it. Capture for later review allows users to delay the decision of deciding to keep or discard encountered information; allowing them to annotate and highlight could further support this later review. Tools could also automatically capture features such as date and time that might offer valuable context for the encounter at a later date. Ease of capture would ameliorate the time barrier to value creation, and review could diminish barriers involved in assessment of current or future potential use. This latter barrier could be further reduced by the ability to set up an alert for review, allowing users to choose a time to keep or discard information.

Tools could augment motivators for value creation by supporting information sharing, or automatically generating a list of related content previously accessed by the same individual. They could also allow users to easily categorise encountered information according to their interests.

While it is not possible to force value from encountered information, digital tools could certainly better support value creation. Many of the features described above already exist in some tools, but bringing them together to create one-click capture, annotation and categorization would minimize the time spent away from a primary information task. The smaller the disruption to whatever users were doing when serendipity struck, the more likely they will be to justify the investment in value creation.

Such tools are most likely to be successful if they balance ease of capture with simplicity of review. Users should not be required to categorise or annotate information, but it should be easy for them to do so if desired. Design inspiration can be sought from existing web capture tools—from browser extensions (e.g., Evernote Web Clipper) to annotation tools (e.g., Microsoft OneNote, Google Keep).

## CONCLUSION

Information encountering is a richly satisfying information experience that happens unexpectedly and seemingly effortlessly. For an information encounter to be experienced as serendipitous, though, the encounterer must take action to generate value from it. (Makri & Blandford, 2012a); this paper is the first, to our knowledge, that considers in detail what happens after serendipity strikes.

Our work highlights that information encounterers' actions may be as simple as making a note, or very complex, spanning multiple information sources and tools. All efforts, though, occur within a framework of expectations and outcomes, barriers and motivators. This empirically grounded framework is the major contribution of this paper.

This framework can be leveraged not only to describe information encounters and reason about their subjective value, but also to relate information encountering to other types of information acquisition and to make design suggestions. By designing tools that more adequately support the creation of value from encountered information, we can maximize opportunities for users to make the most of their "happy information accidents." Future research might examine how best to design such tools to maximize the opportunity for value creation and to evaluate the success of these tools in this regard.


## ACKNOWLEDGMENTS

Our warmest thanks go to our participants.


## REFERENCES


Agarwal, N. K. (2015). Towards a definition of serendipity in information behaviour. *Information Research, 20*(3).

Baeza-Yates, R., & Ribeiro-Neto, B. (1999). *Modern information retrieval* (Vol. 463): ACM Press. New York.

Barry, C. L. (1994). User-defined relevance criteria: An exploratory study. *User-defined relevance criteria: An exploratory study, 45*(3), 149-159. doi:10.1002/(SICI)1097-4571(199404)45:3<149::AID-ASI5>3.0.CO;2-J

Bates, M. J. (1989). The design of browsing and berrypicking techniques for the online search interface. *Online Review, 13*(5), 407-424. doi:10.1108/eb024320

Borgman, C. L. (1996). Why are online catalogs *still* hard to use? *JASIS, 47*(7), 493-503. doi:10.1002/(SICI)1097-4571(199607)47:7<493::AID-ASI3>3.0.CO;2-P

Carter, S., & Mankoff, J. (2005). *When participants do the capturing: The role of media in diary studies*. In Proc *CHI 98*, Portland, Oregon, USA. 899-908. doi:10.1145/1054972.1055098

Cermak, G. W. (1996). An approach to mapping entertainment alternatives. *New infotainment technologies in the home: Demand-side perspectives* (pp. 115-134). NY: Routledge.

Corbin, J., & Strauss, A. (2015). *Basics of qualitative research* (4th Ed.). London: Sage.

Cunha, M. P. e., Clegg, S. R., & Mendonça, S. (2010). On serendipity and organizing. *Europe Man J, 28*(5), 319-330. doi:10.1016/j.emj.2010.07.001

D'Antonio, L., Makri, S., & Blandford, A. (2012). Coming across academic social media content serendipitously. *ASIST Proceedings, 49*(1), 1-10. doi:10.1002/meet.14504901002

Ellis, D. (1989). A behavioural model for information retrieval system design. *J Inf Sci, 15*(4-5), 237-247. doi:10.1177/016555158901500406

Erdelez, S. (1997). Information encountering: A conceptual framework for accidental information discovery. In Proc *ISIC 97*, Tampere, Finland. 412-421.

Erdelez, S. (2004). Investigation of information encountering in the controlled research environment. *IP&M, 40*(6), 1013-1025. doi:10.1016/j.ipm.2004.02.002

Erdelez, S. (2005). Information encountering. In K. E. Fisher & L. McKechnie (Eds.), *Theories of information behavior* (179-184). Medford NJ: Information Today.

Erdelez, S., & Rioux, K. (2000). Sharing information encountered for others on the web. *New Rev. Inf. Behav. Res., 1*, 219-233.

Fidel, R. (1993). Qualitative methods in information retrieval research. *Lib Inf Sci Res, 15*(3), 219-247.

Foster, A., & Ford, N. (2003). Serendipity and information seeking: An empirical study. *J. Doc, 59*(3), 321-340. doi:10.1108/00220410310472518

Heinström, J. (2006). Psychological factors behind incidental information acquisition. *Lib Inf Sci Res, 28*(4), 579-594. doi:10.1016/j.lisr.2006.03.022

Kefalidou, G., & Sharples, S. (2016). Encouraging serendipity in research: Designing technologies to support connection-making. *IJHCS, 89*, 1-23. doi: 10.1016/j.ijhcs.2016.01.003

Kleiner, E., Rädle, R., & Reiterer, H. (2013). *Blended shelf: Reality-based presentation and exploration of library collections*. In *proc.* ACM SIGCHI *13*, Paris, France. 577-582. doi:10.1145/2468356.2468458

Kuhlthau, C. C. (1991). Inside the search process: Information seeking from the user's perspective. *JASIST, 42*(5), 361-371. doi:10.1002/(SICI)1097-4571(199106)42:5<361::AID-ASI6>3.0.CO;2-#

Loizides, F., & Buchanan, G. (2013). *Towards a framework for human (manual) information retrieval*. In *proc. IRFC 13*, Limassol, Cyprus. 87-98. doi:10.1007/978-3-642-41057-4_10

Makri, S., Bhuiya, J., Carthy, J., & Owusu-Bonsu, J. (2015). Observing serendipity in digital information environments. *ASIST Proceedings, 52*(1), 1-10. doi:10.1002/pra2.2015.145052010019

Makri, S., & Blandford, A. (2012a). Coming across information serendipitously: Part 1 – A process model. *J. Doc, 68*(5), 685-704. doi:10.1108/00220411211256030

Makri, S., & Blandford, A. (2012b). Coming across information serendipitously: Part 2 - A classification framework. *J. Doc., 68*(5), 706-724. doi:10.1108/00220411211256049

Makri, S., Blandford, A., & Cox, A. L. (2008). Investigating the information-seeking behaviour of academic lawyers: From Ellis's model to design. *IP&M, 44*(2), 613-634. doi:10.1016/j.ipm.2007.05.001

Makri, S., Blandford, A., Woods, M., Sharples, S., & Maxwell, D. (2014). "Making my own luck": Serendipity strategies and how to support them in digital information environments. *JASIST, 65*(11), 2179-2194. doi:10.1002/asi.23200

Makri, S., & Warwick, C. (2010). Information for inspiration: Understanding architects' information seeking and use behaviors to inform design. *JASIST, 61*(9), 1745-1770. doi:10.1002/asi.21338

Marchionini, G. (1997). *Information seeking in electronic environments* (Vol. 9). Cambridge, UK: CUP.

McBirnie, A. (2008). Seeking serendipity: The paradox of control. *Aslib Proceedings, 60*(6), 600-618. doi:10.1108/00012530810924294

McCay-Peet, L., Toms, E. G., & Kelloway, E. K. (2015). Examination of relationships among serendipity, the environment, and individual differences. *IP&M, 51*(4), 391-412. doi:dx.doi.org/10.1016/j.ipm.2015.02.004

McCay-Peet, L., & Toms, E. G. (2015). Investigating serendipity: How it unfolds and what may influence it. *JASIST, 66*(7), 1463-1476.

McKenzie, P. J. (2003). A model of information practices in accounts of everyday-life information seeking. *J. Doc., 59*(1), 19-40. doi:10.1108/00220410310457993

Meho, L. I., & Tibbo, H. R. (2003). Modeling the information-seeking behavior of social scientists: Ellis's study revisited. *JASIST, 54*(6), 570-587. doi:10.1002/asi.10244

Napier, N. K., & Quan, H. V. (2013). Serendipity as a strategic advantage? In T. J. Wilkinson & V. R. Kannan (Eds.), *Strategic management in the 21st century* (pp. 175-199). Santa Barbara, CA: Praeger.

Oxford English Dictionary. *"valuable, adj. and n."*: Oxford University Press.

Pearce, J., & Chang, S. (2014). *Exploration without keywords: The bookfish case*. In *proc. OzCHI 2014*, Sydney, Australia. 76-79. doi:10.1145/2686612.2686639

Savolainen, R. (2006). Time as a context of information seeking. *Lib. Inf. Sci. Res., 28*(1), 110-127. doi:10.1016/j.lisr.2005.11.001

Sun, X., Sharples, S., & Makri, S. (2011). A user-centred mobile diary study approach to understanding serendipity in information research. *Information Research, 16*(3).

Svenonius, E. (2000). The Intellectual Foundation of Information Organization. Boston, MA: MIT Press.

Thudt, A., Hinrichs, U., & Carpendale, S. (2012). *The bohemian bookshelf: Supporting serendipitous book discoveries through information visualization*. In proc. ACM SIGCHI, Austin, TX. 1461-1470. doi:10.1145/2207676.2208607

# "A Process of Controlled Serendipity": An Exploratory Study of Historians' and Digital Historians' Experiences of Serendipity in Digital Environments

**Kim Martin**
*School of English and Theatre Studies, University of Guelph. kmarti20@uoguelph.ca*

**Anabel Quan-Haase**
*Faculty of Information and Media Studies, University of Western Ontario. aquan@uwo.ca*

## ABSTRACT

**We investigate historians' experiences with serendipity in both physical and digital environments through an online survey. Through a combination of qualitative and quantitative data analyses, our preliminary findings show that many digital historians select a specific digital environment because of the expectation that it may elicit a serendipitous experience. Historians also create heuristic methods of using digital tools to integrate elements of serendipity into their research practice. Four features of digital environments were identified by participants as supporting serendipity: exploration, highlighted triggers, allowed for keyword searching and connected them to other people.**

## KEYWORDS

historians, serendipity, digital environments

## INTRODUCTION

A digital environment is a platform or tool used to access and manipulate information, such as digital libraries, databases, social media and journals. However, not all disciplines have embraced these digital environments to the same extent and, even within a single discipline, scholars have made use of digital tools to different degrees. This paper takes historians as its focus, including the subsection of historians that self-identify as digital historians. Historians have become increasingly digital over the past decade, using and designing different tools to aid their own research (Fyfe, 2015; Leary, 2015). Often the designation digital historian is used to describe those history scholars who integrate various digital sources and tools into their work practice. While distinctions between historians and digital historians have been questioned, the label of digital historian is used in the context of this paper to describe those historians that self-define as *digital* in the context of our survey. To date, information scholars have tended to focus on humanities scholars as a group without paying much attention to the unique information needs and scholarly practices of historians (some exceptions include I. Anderson, 2010; W. M. Duff & Johnson, 2002; Tibbo, 2003). Historians, however, have attributes that stand out from other humanities scholars, including extensive use of the library and archives (Case, 1991; Delgadillo & Lynch, 1999), the importance of primary sources to their research (Rutner & Schonfeld, 2012) and the common experience of serendipity while researching (Anderson, 2010; Duff & Johnson, 2002; Martin & Quan-Haase, 2013). It is important to study digital historians to understand how the use of digital sources and tools is influencing the unique attributes of historical research.

The present paper examines historians' perceptions of how digital environments have affected their experiences of serendipity. Much research has looked at the role of serendipity in historical scholarship. Anderson (2010) lists serendipity as an information-seeking method used by historians in his examination of their work with primary resources. Kirsch and Rohan (2008) in the introduction to their collection *Beyond the Archives* argue that their work teaches historians to attend to the facets of their research that "seem merely intuitive, coincidental, or serendipitous" (p. 4) in order to identify areas of scholarly research. Fyfe (2015) sees the recognition of a serendipitous connection as a skill in which historians can be, and should be, trained. Despite the attention that serendipity has received in the literature on historians' scholarly practices, little is known about what specific environments are perceived as most conducive for serendipity and few attempts have been made to isolate the effect of specific features for serendipitous experiences. The present paper investigates the following two research questions:

- What digital environments are historians using to encourage serendipity in their research?
- Which features of digital environments do historians see as supporting serendipity?

## LITERATURE REVIEW: SERENDIPITY IN THE DIGITAL ENVIRONMENT

Several recent studies investigate the role of serendipity in the digital environment, and lay the groundwork for our own examination of this experience by historians. In an attempt to trigger a serendipitous encounter in a digital environment Toms and McCay-Peet (2009) set up an observational laboratory study that saw 96 participants complete three tasks using a Wikipedia-based tool developed for the study, called "Suggested Pages". Forty percent of their participants used the tool, reporting that the links they found through "Suggested Pages" were relevant to their assigned tasks, and were surprising, but some also deemed them as a distraction from the task at hand. The authors concluded that the lab setting

80th Annual Meeting of the Association for Information Science & Technology, Washington, DC, VA | Oct. 27-Nov. 1, 2017

did not replicate typical behaviour, and that there was much left to understand about how to trigger in a digital environment a serendipitous encounter with information.

Race (2012) examined the serendipitous features associated with web-scale, user-friendly discovery tools such as WorldCat and EBSCO. She noted the importance of personalizing the search process, and demonstrated that interactivity between the user and the computer system could help users better realize interconnections. The main strength in Race's article lies in her summary of web-scale discovery tools that support serendipity. Here Race managed to break down the various tenets of serendipity (browsability, hypertext links, visualization of results, etc.) and determine whether each of the aforementioned tools supports these features or not.

McCay-Peet, Toms, and Kelloway (2014) conducted a series of studies with the aim of developing robust measures of serendipity that were specifically geared to the unique context of digital environments. They identified five features of a serendipitous digital environment or SDE:

- *Trigger-rich*: The digital environment is filled with a variety of information, ideas or resources interesting and useful to the user.
- *Enables connections*: The digital environment exposes users to combinations of information, ideas or resources that make relationships between topics apparent.
- *Highlights triggers*: The digital environment actively points to or alerts users to interesting and useful information, ideas or resources using visual, auditory or tactile cues.
- *Enables exploration*: The digital environment supports the unimpeded examination of its information, ideas or resources.
- *Leads to the unexpected*: The digital environment provides fertile ground for unanticipated or surprising interactions with information, ideas or resources.

Other studies of serendipity in digital environments focus on how best to capture these experiences, which are most often collected in the form of self-reports (Makri et al., 2015). Makri et al. (2014) interviewed 14 creative professionals about their personal strategies for influencing serendipity, and then discussed the various ways in which digital environments support these personal strategies. For example, a creative professional mentioned "varying their routines" as a personal strategy. Makri et al. (2014) suggested that designers of digital environments could support serendipity by recommending material tangentially related to the users' work, or by encouraging users who have similar interests to share links to web sites. For the authors digital environments that support these personal serendipity strategies would be more beneficial to both creative professionals and general users because they support elements of serendipity rather than attempting to offer "serendipity on a plate" (Makri et al., 2014, p. 2181).

The literature review shows various approaches in which digital environments can be designed to promote serendipity. The literature so far has not focused on historians and how digital environments may be designed to aid in their scholarly work. As serendipity is central to their practice, designing digital environments with their information needs in mind could help support their work.

## METHODS

The survey was developed by building on previous findings based on interviews with historians about their scholarly practice (Martin, 2016; Martin & Quan-Haase, 2013, 2016). The online survey was chosen as a method to reach a diverse set of historians, after attempts to recruit members of this population for interviews proved challenging.

### *Sample*

A total of 142 participants started the survey, of which 90 participants provided answers to all questions ($N$=90). We did not require that participants answer all questions, as only those who could recall a specific serendipitous experience were able to answer the survey in full. Also, several of our questions were open-ended, and required more time and effort than simply clicking a button, which may have influenced question non-response (Reja, Manfreda, Hlebec, & Vehovar, 2003). As the number of respondents to each question differed due to how the survey was set up in Qualtrics, we will report the number of participants – $n$ – who provided responses to each question.

Demographics were collected at the end of the survey, and were completed by 88 participants. We had 55% women, 42% men, and 1% who identified as "other," with 2% preferring not to provide an answer. The ages of participants were well spread out, with 9% between 18-24, 33% between 25-34, 23% between 35-44, 17% between 45-54, 11% between 55-64, and 7% aged 65 or older. Most participants held PhDs (49%), while 36% held master's degrees, 9% held undergraduate degrees and 5% completed high school (1% preferred not to answer).

### *Online Survey*

Data were collected via an online survey that took about 15 minutes to complete (Martin, 2016). There were four sections to the survey: Section A: background on participants' historical research, Section B: serendipitous experiences while conducting research, Section C: serendipitous experiences while in physical and digital environments, and Section D: demographic information. Where available, we relied on previously validated measures. McCay-Peet's (2013) scales provide a "direct measure of serendipity" in digital environments and in life in general (Q19, Q21, and Q23). These helped to establish the basis for historians' experiences with serendipity and to test to what extent the digital environments they used in their research encouraged serendipity. Open-ended questions were included to allow participants to expand on their experience. These open-ended questions help triangulate findings from the questionnaires and also expand on the numeric values by adding rich data about the experiences of scholars (Makri & Blandford, 2012).

To understand what role digital tools played in participants' research the following question was included: *Would you describe yourself as a digital historian?* (Q17) to which 48% of the participants answered "Yes" ($n$=87).

Q19 asked respondents to list three types of digital environments in which they had experienced serendipity: "Please list up to 3 digital environments where you have experienced serendipity. Please be specific, for example, if this occurs on social media, please indicate the platform (e.g., Twitter)." As a follow up to this, respondents were also asked to describe what features of each of the three listed digital environments (in Q19) they thought were most conducive to serendipity. Specifically, Q21 stated, "Please describe the features (e.g., keyword searches, browsing options, interaction with others) of this specific digital environment that you find to be most conducive to the serendipitous encounter." We were also interested in the features they thought promoted serendipity across all digital environments. For this purpose, Q23 asked, "Please describe the features of a digital environment that you find to be most conducive to the serendipitous encounter."

Online surveys have the benefits of being convenient to the participant and timesaving to the researcher (Evans & Mathur, 2005; Sax, Gilmartin, & Bryant, 2003). However, there are also downsides to online surveys, such as a lack of response from non-internet users, and privacy and security issues (Evans & Mathur, 2005). As we were particularly interested in the research habits of digital historians, the use of an online survey was justified. The survey access link was distributed via social media, listservs and emails to history departments across Canada to reach a wide and diverse audience. As Twitter was popular among many historians, we also disseminated the link to the online survey using the hashtag #twitterstorians, which is followed by historians. To reduce concerns over privacy and security, Qualtrics was employed for the collection of data. Qualtrics does not rely on cloud-based data storage, as data is stored locally on a secure university server. We collected demographic information from our participants such as age, gender and academic background, and no identifying information was collected to guarantee the anonymity of respondents. We obtained ethics approval and the survey was live from February through April 2015, during which time the primary researcher did weekly checks to ensure there were no cases of intentional misuse.

### Data Analysis

As this paper reports on preliminary analysis, questionnaire responses were analyzed using descriptive statistics in R.

For Q19 (see wording above), participants could list up to three digital environments where they had experienced serendipity. Seventy-nine participants listed a total of 194 digital environments, and these were then separated into the types of digital environment that historians had previously been asked to report their comfort with in Q18. As the participants were not asked to rate these environments, they were then coded according to the same 10 digital environments as Q18, with the addition of three categories ("Databases," "Archives" and "Ancestry websites") to account for the digital environments mentioned by participants that fell outside of the original ten.

Because of the complexity of the answers to Q21 and Q23, a deductive content analysis approach was utilized. Usually this approach is recommended when "the structure of analysis is operationalized on the basis of previous knowledge and the purpose of the study is theory testing" (Elo & Kyngäs, 2007). We used the previously established categories of serendipity by McCay-Peet, et al. (2014). Their five facets of an SDE identified in the literature review above provided a starting point for the content analysis. To ensure that as many of the historians' responses as possible were included in the analysis, it was important to remain open to other categories being created if the five facets of SDEs previously identified by McCay-Peet, et al. (2014) did not account for most of their responses. In the first phase, themes or phrases were used as the unit of analysis (Berg, 2005) and each of the historians' responses to Q21 were categorized into the five facets, with many answers being divided into multiple phrases and some phrases fitting into multiple categories. There were three additional themes that emerged as prominent in the responses to Q21: "People," "Heuristic Search," and "Keyword Search." "People" and "Heuristic Search," were created as sub-categories to "Enables Connections" and "Highlights Triggers," respectively. The final coding scheme used for the analysis is shown in Table 1.

After the codes were refined and finalized, Q21 and Q23 were recoded according to the same set of categories. One additional reliability coder went through about half of the data to assess the reliability. The intercoder reliability for Q21 was Cohen's Kappa = .62. According to Landis and Koch (1977), this score is at the lower end of "substantial" agreement strength. The intercoder reliability for Q23 was higher, at Kappa = .72, at the higher end of "substantial" agreement strength. This indicates that there is room for clarification of the coding scheme we employed, to avoid any room for confusion between codes in future studies.

## FINDINGS

### Digital historians, digital environments

Respondents reported where they experienced serendipity. Figure 1 shows that serendipity was experienced more frequently in a physical library or archive than it was in digital library interfaces or while researching on the web.

We compared responses from those who had identified as digital historians with those from respondents who did not identify as digital historians. We found that those who identified as digital historians experienced serendipity more frequently in digital environments than non-digital historians. Serendipity was experienced more frequently on the web than in a library interface, but this may also be due to the frequent use of web-based search engines (Kemman, Kleppe, & Scagliola, 2013).

| CODES | DESCRIPTIONS |
|---|---|
| Trigger Rich | The digital environment is filled with a variety of information, ideas or resources interesting and useful to the user. |
| Enables Connections | The digital environment exposes users to combinations of information, ideas or resources that make relationships between topics apparent. |
| Sub-code EC - People | Where the connection is made as above, but involves people as either the providers of information or the link to information. |
| Highlights Triggers | The digital environment actively points to or alerts users to interesting and useful information, ideas, or resources using visual, auditory, or tactile cues. |
| Sub-code HT - Heuristic Search | Same as above but search is involved, showing an agency on behalf of the historian |
| Enables Exploration | The digital environment supports the unimpeded examination of its information, ideas or resources. |
| Leads to the unexpected | The digital environment provides fertile ground for unanticipated or surprising interactions with information, ideas or resources. |
| Keyword Search | Anytime the respondents include keyword search. Often with none, or very little, description. |

***Table 1.*** *Final coding scheme*

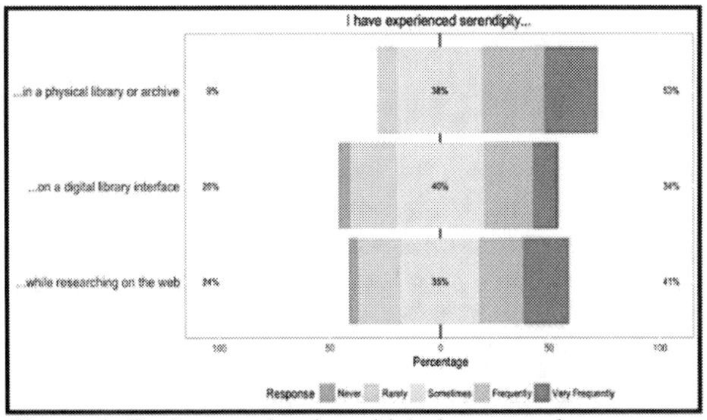


***Figure 1****. Environments where historians experience serendipity*

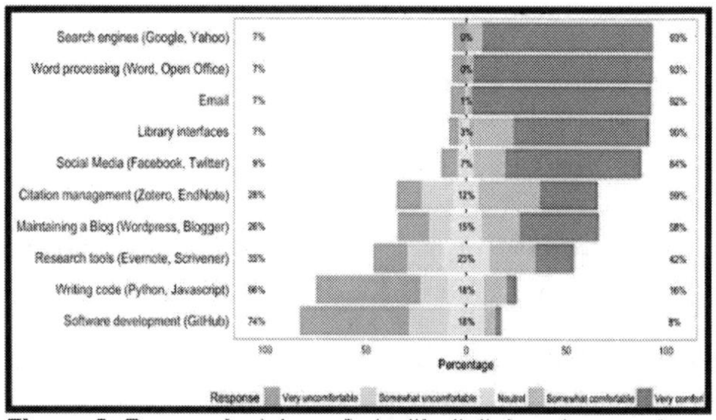


***Figure 2.*** *Respondents' comfort with digital environments*

We then listed ten different digital environments and asked the respondents to rate their comfort level with these environments on a five-point Likert-type scale ranging from "very uncomfortable" to "very comfortable" (Q18). Figure 2 shows that respondents were comfortable with digital environments that they would come across as part of their working day, such as search engines, word processing tools, email and library interfaces. As the survey was conducted online and recruitment was partially done via Twitter, it is not surprising that the participants were also comfortable with social media. Finally, the two digital environments where the participants indicated to be the least comfortable with were "Writing Code" and "Software Development Tools," where only 16% and 8% indicated to be "somewhat comfortable" or "very comfortable."

The answers to the question "*Please list up to three digital environments where you have experienced serendipity"* (Q19) resulted in a list of 194 digital environments. The answers to Q19 can be seen in Figure 3. Social media is the digital environment most commonly named by historians as a place where they experience serendipity. While the answers to the questions regarding features of digital environments (see below) support this finding, it should be noted that we used Twitter as one method of recruitment for this study, thus many of our participants are likely to feel comfortable using social media, and to use it frequently, possibly increasing their experiences of serendipity in this digital environment. "Library Interfaces," "Databases" and "Archives" are digital environments in which the historians also reported experiencing serendipity.

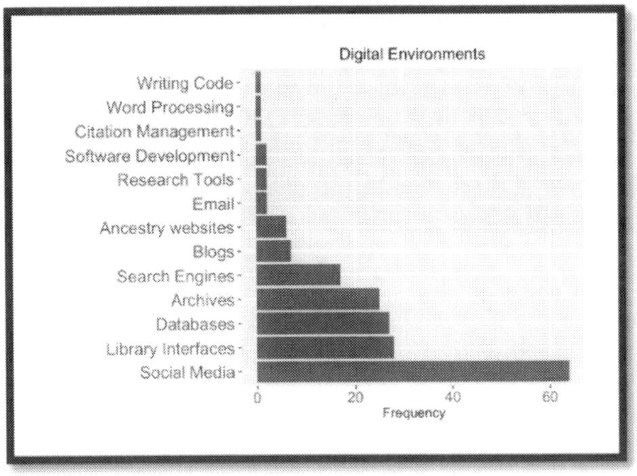


***Figure 3.*** *Digital environments where historians experience serendipity*

As we originally only included "Library Interfaces" in our list of digital environments, and later added "Databases," "Archives" and "Ancestry websites" to account for the historians' own answers about where they experience serendipity, more work is needed to explore this breakdown of digital environments and the experiences of serendipity in the digital and physical versions of each. Though the participants were largely comfortable using a variety of digital environments, including email, social media and search engines, there are some digital environments, like software tools and writing code that have not yet been integrated into the digital tools of most of these historians.

### The Frequency of Serendipitous Experiences

Encountering useful information while using digital environments was the most frequent response amongst our participants, who also tended to experience work-related serendipity slightly more often than serendipity that impacts their everyday life (see Figure 4).

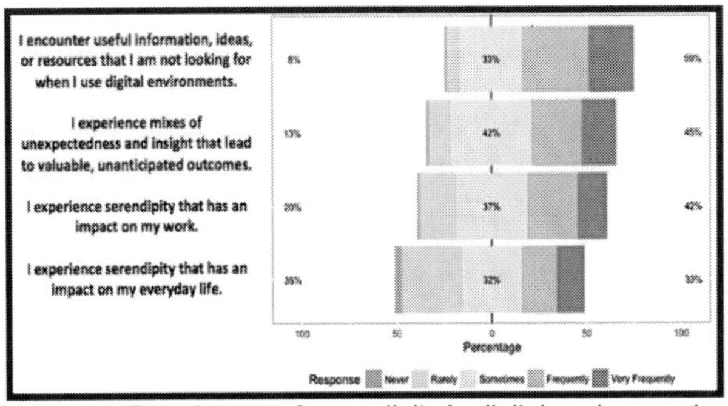


***Figure 4.*** *Experiences of serendipity in digital environments (n=80)*

A large percentage of historians selected "sometimes" as their response to these questions. It was evident from Figure 5 that digital historians experienced serendipity more frequently in digital environments than other respondents.

Again, digital historians were more likely to experience work-related serendipity when using a digital environment, than they were to experience serendipity that impacts their everyday life. To further understand our population's experiences with serendipity, we then asked them to think about their life experiences in general (Q23), not just in digital environments. As Figure 6 demonstrates, these responses were similar to the responses regarding the participants' experiences using digital environments.

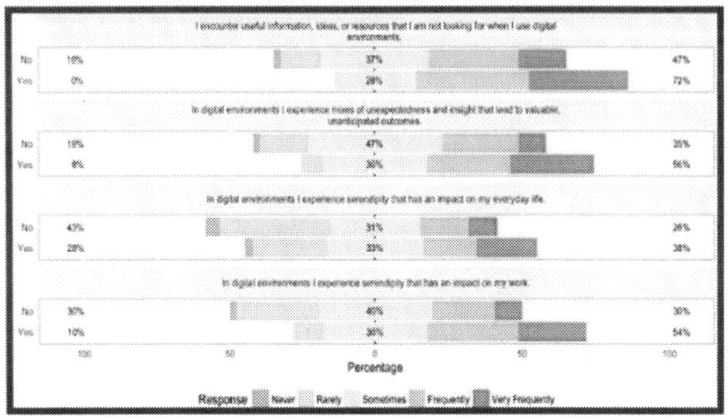


***Figure 5.*** *Experiences of serendipity in digital environments for digital/non-digital historians*

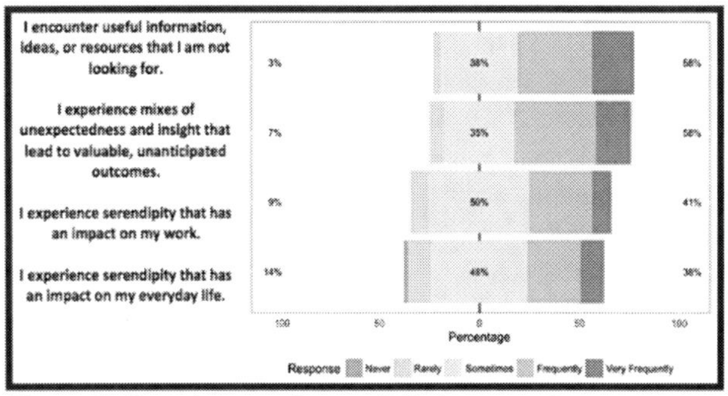


***Figure 6.*** *Experiences of serendipity in general*

However, when we broke these responses down into the "Yes" or "No" answers to Q17 (*Would you describe yourself as a digital historian?*) (Figure 7), the result was that both groups reported experiencing serendipity to a similar extent across the four questions. In fact, very few historians reported to "Never" experience serendipity, except for a small percentage that reported that this phenomenon had never impacted their everyday lives.

Overall then, despite our population reporting similar experiences with serendipity in their lives in general (online and offline), when it came to using digital environments, those who identified as digital historians were more likely to experience serendipity when working in a digital environment.

### Features That Support Serendipity

To begin answering RQ2, we coded the number of times each category was mentioned (Table 2). Each of the features was mentioned in the historians' responses to both Q21 and Q23, to varying extents. "Highlights Triggers," "Enables Exploration," "People" and "Keyword Search" were all prominent categories, though all eight categories were represented by the participants' responses, showing that serendipity was an experience that could occur in many different contexts, and that digital environments require multiple features to support serendipitous information behavior. The features are discussed individually below in detail, from the most commonly identified feature ("Enables Exploration") to the least commonly identified feature ("Trigger Rich").

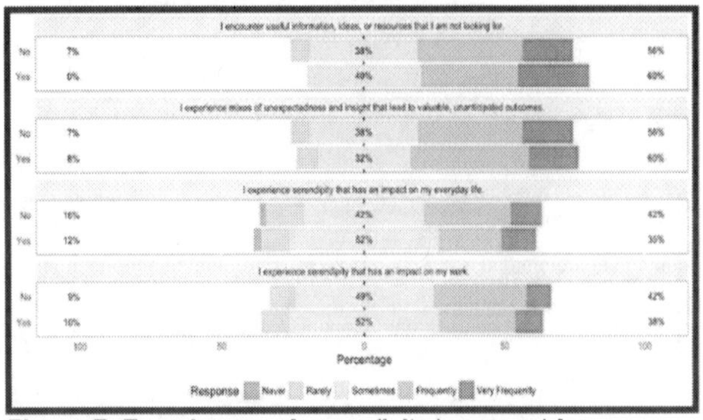


***Figure 7.*** *Experiences of serendipity in general for digital/non-digital historians*

| Features of a Digital Environment that Support Serendipity | No. of mentions in Q21 (*n*=72) | No. of mentions in Q23 (*n*=63) | Total No. of mentions |
|---|---|---|---|
| Trigger Rich | 2 | 4 | 6 |
| Enables Connections | 8 | 10 | 18 |
| Subcode EC – People | 19 | 13 | 32 |
| Highlights Triggers | 19 | 8 | 27 |
| Subcode HT - Heuristic Search | 7 | 10 | 17 |
| Enables Exploration | 19 | 20 | 39 |
| Leads to the Unexpected | 5 | 10 | 15 |
| Keyword Search | 25 | 13 | 38 |

***Table 2.*** *Features of a digital environment that support serendipity*

### Enables Exploration

Of the features that supported serendipity, there were three types that historians used to explore information. First, there were those related to browsing material on the web, either using links available on blogs, websites or in citations. Google was mentioned several times, with participants indicating they use the search results to explore and browse comparable to how they would in a physical environment, as Participant 22 pointed out:

> *"I use Google and Google books like a library interface." (P22)*

Second, historians also spoke about the relevance of linked open data and the semantic web to their research. Finally, historians indicated that exploring a full text primary source, particularly one that was previously unavailable to them, often resulted in finding new and relevant information.

### Keyword Search

As outlined in the methods section, the high number of historians who mentioned keyword search in their answers to Q21 and Q23 might have been due to our decision to mention this as an option in the wording for Q21. However, many historians expanded upon the reasons they found keyword search to lead toward serendipitous results. For example, Participant 52 reported:

> *"Keyword searches often bring up serendipitous results because they do are not confined to the usual 'silos' of archival references. They search across fonds and can bring up results from the entire archive, provided that enough is made searchable." (P52)*

Thus, it is not so much the keyword search feature that results in serendipity, but the ability of the algorithm to gather material from different places and to cast a wider net than historians might be able to on their own.

### People

Social media was reported by the historians to be the digital environment where they most commonly experienced serendipity. For these scholars, comments on blog posts, Facebook conversations, and connections to their Twitter community often led to new insights. The historians largely recognized that they self-selected this community, curating their connections, and that they had interests in common with those who they followed, particularly on Twitter. For Participant 16, this was one way in which she could exert agency over her serendipitous experiences:

> *"It's a process of controlled serendipity: I follow people I'm interested in, for example, or start on a webpage that is key to my work. From there, I go on structured explorations." (P16)*

We placed "People" as a sub-code under the heading of "Enables Connections" because historians spoke of people sharing information they could relate to, or having conversations with those in their field that inspired new ideas. Some of these phrases were also coded as "Highlights Triggers," but we felt it necessary to categorize the times that people were mentioned to demonstrate the prominence of social media amongst the historians' responses.

### Highlights Triggers

For our participants, the most common way that triggers, or alerts to interesting or useful information, were presented in digital environments was as hashtags on Twitter. Typing words this way turns them into links that allow users to click on them and see a list of current posts that include the same hashtag. Our participants noted how useful it was to be able to follow relevant hashtags, particularly around a conference they were interested in ("following conference hashtags is helpful" P25) or debates by colleagues ("hashtags that help follow debates" P36). Other ways that digital environments highlighted triggers were recommendations presented with search results and links shared by others on social media.

### *Enables Connections*

Digital environments that enable connections often presented our historians with new ways of looking at material. Word clouds and other types of visualizations enabled new associations between materials, as Participant 57 pointed out:

> *"Interfaces that allow to see connections I wouldn't have thought of, like tag clusters. This seems to somehow recreate the effect of browsing the shelves or folders in a physical archive/library." (P57)*

Another feature of digital environments that historians indicated lead them to serendipitous finds were the algorithms for keyword searches in tools such as Evernote or DEVONthink that showed you material around the term searched for, instead of just that specific term. Because these tools allow a user to collect information from the Web and collate it in one location, when historians search, they know the information is relevant to their work. The feature they found most useful was the algorithm found and presented material, which, according to Participant 54

> *"Shows you what's CLOSE to what you were looking for." (P54)*

The participants reported that this allowed them to make connections from there.

### *Heuristic Search*

Although participants reported relying on the algorithms to present information in meaningful ways, they also take it upon themselves to understand the tools they use in digital environments and learn to use them to their advantage, as Participant 64 indicated:

> *"I think that test digital tools once and once again and by different ways, you can know the tools, find how use it and, if it is possible, adapt it to your needs." (P64)*

Search tools were one method of information seeking in the digital environment that many of our participants were used to manipulating. Some mentioned constantly changing their search terms, or purposefully misspelling names and places they searched for to get a wider variety of results, and therefore having a greater chance of experiencing serendipity. Participant 13 demonstrated this:

> *"Key word searches are good, but you must be flexible with them and change the words until you get a strike. This is something like fly fishing." (P13)*

As historians do in physical libraries and archives, our participants used the digital tools available to them in ways that supported serendipity in their research.

### *Leads to the Unexpected*

The unexpected was a very common term in these historians' definitions and stories of serendipity (Martin, 2016). However, it did not feature prominently amongst the features of a digital environment that the historians felt supported serendipity. Although there were a few historians who mentioned having "illuminating, and occasionally serendipitous conversations" on Twitter that took them to unexpected places (P38), it was largely the results of a find or a conversation that lead them in a new direction, not a feature that could be relied upon. It may have been difficult for the historians to think in terms of features that "Lead to the Unexpected" as users might not recognize that the digital environment is "fertile ground for unanticipated or surprising interactions" until after they have made a serendipitous connection (McCay-Peet et al., 2014).

### *Trigger Rich*

Finally, we only found six references to digital environments that were "Trigger Rich," which were usually in passing, in phrases such as "Mostly just following hyperlinks" (P17). This does not necessarily mean that environments that include a lot of links to other material were not found to be serendipitous, because it seemed to us that these historians simply took for granted the links available on the web, and only drew attention to them when they were in useful or unexpected places, such as links to citations in online Works Cited sections of journal articles. Twitter was another place that could have been classified as being "Trigger Rich," as the information on this site is constantly changing, and links are provided here to other sources of information. However, here the historians predominantly mentioned the people they connected with through Twitter and how they followed conversations that interested them, rather than the preponderance of links available.

Overall, the five facets of serendipity in a digital environment (McCay-Peet et al., 2014) served well as a classification structure for the historians' responses to Q21 and Q23. While there was some difficulty with classifying features of digital environments under the facet "Trigger Rich," this largely stemmed from historians' immersion in the online world, and their taking pages with many links for granted. It must be noted that we used these categories as a coding scheme, which is different from how McCay-Peet et al. (2014) employed them in their studies. The authors discerned five facets of serendipity and showed their connection to serendipity in the digital environment via concentrated statistical analyses. We expand this work not by further validating the established measures, but rather by using them as a framework for guiding our understanding of serendipity in the digital environment, which also allowed us to remain open to the creation of sub-codes where necessary.

## DISCUSSION

We presented the findings of a preliminary analysis of historians' experiences with serendipity in digital environments. Our investigation of their comfort in these environments demonstrated a large range – while many participants were comfortable with digital tools that they used in their everyday lives (email, word processing and social media) there were only a small percent of the participants who reported to be comfortable writing code or using software development sites such as GitHub. Over half of the sample were comfortable using citation management tools such as Zotero or Endnote, as well as maintaining a blog.

The variety of digital environments where historians worked was highlighted throughout our investigation of serendipity. Not only did participants describe themselves selecting their digital environment based on whether they felt it supported serendipity, but they also found various ways to make digital environments they chose to use more serendipitous for their research. For many this meant learning how to change their search terms to get fewer or more results, depending on their current need. In our previous paper, we used the term "heuristic" to describe the various methods that historians used to support elements of serendipity in digital environments (Martin & Quan-Haase, 2016, p. 1016). The descriptions of the features of serendipity in the present study provide further detail about the ways historians are working to support serendipity in their digital research environments. This led us to coin the term "Heuristic Serendipity", which we define here as: *a process of information behavior in which historians use trial and error to create new, innovative methods of supporting serendipity throughout their research*. For the participants of our current study, this type of heuristic serendipity usually took place on Google or on library interfaces, both digital environments in which participants indicated to be comfortable.

Our participants often spoke of wanting search results that were "close to perfect," but not necessarily limited to a single, correct answer. To create results of this nature historians have started to manipulate their search tools and other digital environments they use for research. There are two main ways that our participants indicated doing this. First, they tried out a variety of digital tools until they found what works for them. What digital environment they use, and how advanced the features are within it will obviously be impacted by their comfort and level of technological expertise. Some historians mentioned generating visualizations, which would "somehow recreate the effect of browsing the shelves or folders in a physical archive/library" (P57), while others spoke of finding a research tool with an interface they preferred, which allowed them to keep their own personal database of research material. The second method of manipulating their search tools was to introduce flexibility into their searches, by including misspellings, wrong words and different combinations of terms. Several historians also mentioned that faceted or advanced search options allowed them to encounter things that they considered unlikely in other environments. Once they have obtained the results they were looking for, using either of the above methods of heuristic searching, the participants describe looking around this material in various ways. This form of information behavior was described much like other scholars have discussed browsing the stacks of a library (Björneborn, 2008; McKay, Smith, & Chang, 2014): searching around material, browsing through search results, etc. It is this information behavior that enables heuristic *search* to become heuristic *serendipity*. This is where historians' own ability to connect the dots between historical research materials comes into play, and their recognition of useful, enlightening or significant information can create a serendipitous experience. These skills are something that cannot be replaced by a single feature of a digital environment, which is one reason that historians are learning to control and manipulate these environments to suit their needs.

Finally, we asked our participants about the various features of digital environments that they felt supported serendipity. We found that there was a wide variety of features that historians found to support serendipitous experiences; some of them were features of the environments themselves, while others were the results of historians' heuristic serendipity. Four features were prominent: those that enabled exploration (by supporting links to other material, or having full text access available), those that highlighted triggers (such as hashtags on social media, or highlighted materials as suggestions), those that allowed for keyword search (where historians could alter their search terms fluidly) and finally, those that connected them to other people.

Dantonio et al. (2012) found that academics got the most out of Twitter when they were using it while taking a break from their research work, but our historians seemed to use the tool throughout their process, as a way of following along with conferences and engaging with other about their research. Participant 63 notes that it is the "constant flow of information" that helps support their serendipitous experiences. This use of Twitter aligns more closely with the serendipitous experiences that were reported in a study of Twitter use by digital humanities scholars (Quan-Haase, Martin, & McCay-Peet, 2015). These participants reported that the ubiquitous qualities of Twitter helped them to maintain awareness of new information in their research area. For our historians, it is not only the ubiquity of the Twitter interface, but also knowing that they exert control over its features and functions that helps to support serendipity in this particular digital environment.

## CONCLUSION

Historians themselves are operationalizing serendipity – remaining aware of the multiple ways to access information and then exerting control over their digital research environments to make serendipity possible. Just as historians of the past were trained to use libraries and archives to their fullest extent, digital historians must now be trained with the "critical awareness" that Solberg (2012) calls for; they must continue to recognize the strengths and weaknesses of the digital environment to continue to be agents in their own experiences with serendipity.

## FUTURE WORK

Future work by the authors on this topic will include further integration of McCay-Peet's (2013) serendipity questionnaire, including a factor analysis to compare to her more recent findings (McCay-Peet et al., 2014). Now that we have made a significant step in understanding how serendipity plays a role in historians' research process, future work may include studies of other disciplines. Also, as this study benefitted from the knowledge of previous LIS studies on historians, using the results of the current study as a guide for future work on the use of technology by historians would help to show how historians' comfort level with technology, and uses of digital environments changes over time.

## ACKNOWLEDGMENTS

This research was made possible by a graduate scholarship awarded to Kim Martin and an Insight Grant awarded to Quan-Haase (No. R3603A13) both from the Social Sciences and Humanities Research Council of Canada (SSHRC).

## REFERENCES

Anderson, I. (2010). Are you being served? Historians and the Search for Primary Sources. *Archivaria, 1*(58), 81-116.

Berg, B. L. (2005). *Qualitative Research Methods* (5th Edition). Boston Mass.: Pearson.

Björneborn, L. (2008). Serendipity dimensions and users' information behaviour in the physical library interface. *Information Research, 13*(4).

Case, D. O. (1991). The collection and use of information by some american historians: A study of motives and methods. *The Library Quarterly, 61*(1), 61-82.

Dantonio, L., Makri, S., & Blandford, A. (2012). Coming across academic social media content serendipitously. In *Proceedings of the American Society for Information Science and Technology*. Baltimore, MD.

Delgadillo, R., & Lynch, B. P. (1999). Future historians: Their quest for information. *College & Research Libraries, 60*(3), 245-259.

Duff, W. M., & Johnson, C. A. (2002). Accidentally found on purpose: Information-seeking behavior of historians in archives. *The Library Quarterly, 72*(4), 472-496. http://doi.org/10.2307/40039793

Elo, S., & Kyngäs, H. (2007). The qualitative content analysis process. *Journal of Advanced Nursing, 62*(1), 107-15.

Evans, J. R., & Mathur, A. (2005). The value of online surveys. *Internet Research, 15*(2), 195-219. http://doi.org/10.1108/10662240510590360

Fyfe, P. (2015). Technologies of serendipity. *Victorian Periodicals Review, 48*(2), 261-266.

Kemman, M., Kleppe, M., & Scagliola, S. (2013). Just Google it: Digital research practices of humanities scholars. *Cornell Digital Libraries*, 1-17. Retrieved from http://arxiv.org/abs/1309.2434

Kirsch, G. E., & Rohan, L. (2008). *Beyond the archives : Research as a lived process*. Carbondale: Southern Illinois University Press.

Leary, P. (2015). Response: Search and serendipity. *Victorian Periodicals Review, 48*(2), 267-273.

Makri, S., Bhuiya, J., Carthy, J., & Owusu-Bonsu, J. (2015). Observing serendipity in digital information environments. In *ASIST*. St. Louis.

Makri, S., & Blandford, A. (2012). Coming across information serendipitously – Part 1: A process model. *Journal of Documentation, 68*(5), 684-705.

Makri, S., Blandford, A., Woods, M., Sharples, S., & Maxwell, D. (2014). "Making my own luck": Serendipity strategies and how to support them in digital information environments. *Journal of the American Society for Information Science and Technology, 65*(11), 2179-2194.

Martin, K. (2016). *Creating context from curiosity: The role of serendipity in the research process of historians*. University of Western Ontario.

Martin, K., & Quan-Haase, A. (2013). Are e-books replacing print books ? Tradition, serendipity, and opportunity in the adoption and use of e-books for historical research and teaching. *Journal of the American Society for Information Science and Technology, 64*(5), 1016-1028.

Martin, K., & Quan-Haase, A. (2016). The role of agency in historians' experiences of serendipity in physical and digital information environments. *Journal of Documentation, 72*(6). http://doi.org/10.1108/JD-11-2015-0144

McCay-Peet, L. (2013). *Direct measures of serendipity*. Halifax, Nova Scotia.

McCay-Peet, L., Toms, E. G., & Kelloway, K. (2014). Development and assessment of the content validity of a scale to measure how well a digital environment facilitates serendipity. *Information Research, 19*(3).

McKay, D., Smith, W., & Chang, S. (2014). Lend me some sugar : Borrowing rates of neighbouring books as evidence for browsing. In *Digital Libraries 2014*. London.

Quan-Haase, A., Martin, K., & McCay-Peet, L. (2015). Networks of digital humanities scholars: The informational and social uses and gratifications of Twitter. *Big Data & Society, 2*(1), 1-12. http://doi.org/10.1177/2053951715589417

Race, T. M. (2012). Resource discovery tools : Supporting serendipity planning and implementing resource discovery tools in academic libraries. *DLTS Faculty Publications, Paper 22*. Retrieved from http://digitalcommons.wku.edu/dlts_fac_pub/22/

Reja, U., Manfreda, K. L., Hlebec, V., & Vehovar, V. (2003). Open-ended vs. close-ended questions in web questionnaires. *Developments in Applied Statistics, 19*, 159-177. Retrieved from http://www.websm.org/uploadi/editor/Reja_2003_open_vs_close-ended_questions.pdf

Rutner, J., & Schonfeld, R. C. (2012). *Supporting the changing research practices of historians*. New York. Retrieved from http://www.sr.ithaka.org/sites/default/files/reports/supporting-the-changing-research-practices-of-historians.pdf

Sax, L. J., Gilmartin, S. K., & Bryant, A. N. (2003). Assessing response rate and nonreponse bias in web and paper surveys. *Research in Higher Education, 44*(4), 409-432.

Tibbo, H. R. (2003). Primarily history in America: How U.S. historians search for primary materials at the dawn of the digital age. *The American Archivist, 66*(Sping/Summer), 9-50.

Toms, E. G., & McCay-Peet, L. (2009). Chance encounters in the digital library. *Lecture Notes in Computer Science, 5714*, 192-202.

# Legal Information Acquisition by the Public: The Role of Personal and Environmental Factors

**Sheila O'Hare**
*School of Library & Information Management, Emporia State University. sohare1@emporia.edu*

**Sanda Erdelez**
*School of Information Science & Learning Technologies, University of Missouri. erdelezs@missouri.edu*

## ABSTRACT

**This paper reports a portion of the results of a 2016 mixed methods study on the acquisition of legal information by members of the public. While information acquisition by health information seekers has been extensively studied, similar studies of legal consumers are almost nonexistent. Even less research has focused on incidental encounters with legal information. Based upon established models of human information behavior, and informed by numerous studies of health information acquisition by consumers, this study examined the relationship of personal, contextual, affective and environmental factors with frequency of legal information acquisition. In one phase of the study, an online survey was administered to 385 adults without formal legal training. Reported frequency of legal information searching and incidental encountering (IE) of legal information were assessed for significant relationships with personal characteristics and environmental factors. Age, income and previous experience with the legal system were associated with greater legal search frequency. Age, race and previous experience with the legal system were associated with greater frequency of legal IE. Exposure to multiple information sources and multiple mass media sources were associated with greater frequency of both legal search and IE. The study was exploratory in nature, but it serves as a first step in assessing civil legal information acquisition by American adults without specialized legal training. It also explicitly ties legal consciousness, and legal access, to information acquisition practices.**

## KEYWORDS

legal information, legal consciousness, information seeking, information searching, information encountering

## INTRODUCTION

"American society is filled with signs of legal culture," declared Ewick and Silbey (1998) in their study of differential voluntary use of the legal system entitled *The Common Place of Law: Stories from Everyday Life*. Labels, copyrights, trademarks, limitations of liabilities, warranties and other manifestations of the law are ubiquitous. However, in spite of their embeddedness in a law-saturated environment, studies reveal that Americans display a number of inconsistencies in their understandings of legal concepts and actions. Ewick and Silbey, who explored the subject through interviews with 430 people in four New Jersey counties, noted that law was experienced as irrelevant and significant, episodic and constant. A single coherent concept of "law" did not seem to exist. The authors, however, did not see these contradictions as a negative; rather, law in people's lives was a process, "an emergent feature of social relations" (p. 17), working itself out in varied and often ambiguous ways.

Ewick and Silbey situated their study within the scope of studies of "legal consciousness," or how legality is understood and experienced by ordinary citizens as they interact, avoid or refuse to interact with legal meanings and processes. The concept has its roots in "rights consciousness" (Sarat, 1977): how individuals see themselves as possessing either general or specific claims that could be asserted through public authority. Sarat, among others, cautioned that assessing legal consciousness presents difficulties. Its character is often situational, and it tends to function as an unexamined apparatus. As Nielsen (2000) concluded, "legal consciousness also refers to how people do *not* think about the law; that is to say, it is the body of assumptions people have about the law that are simply taken for granted" (p. 1059).

As a result of this difficulty, most studies of legal consciousness have been qualitative (see, e.g., Harding, 2006; Berrey, Hoffman et al., 2010); a few combine qualitative research with preexisting quantitative data (see Blackstone, Uggen et al., 2009, using data from the longitudinal Youth Development Survey in St. Paul, Minnesota). More recently, access to justice research has gathered descriptive data, particularly through state reports (see summary table in Hadfield and Heine, 2015) related to outcomes of cases brought by represented versus unrepresented litigants. The twain has yet to meet, and this is problematic (see, e.g., Leitch, 2013).

Scholars of legal consciousness do not address "legal information" per se as a concept, nor do they focus on acquisition of information in the development of legal consciousness or decision-making. (In fact, the growth in studies of information seeking by the public coincided with a decline in the influence of critical legal theory and legal consciousness.) Quantitative studies in access to justice, on the other hand, are focused on the role of the formal legal system and its availability to citizens. This is linked to information seeking, but it is narrowly focused (on, for example, legal aid turnaways) (see, e.g., Rhode, 2004; Lobel and Chapman, 2015).

80th Annual Meeting of the Association for Information Science & Technology, Washington, DC, VA | Oct. 27-Nov. 1, 2017

Recently, Chambliss, Knake and Nelson (2016) opined that "currently…we know little about the legal resource landscape – especially services for 'ordinary Americans' – and our research infrastructure is underdeveloped compared to such professions as medicine" (p. 193).

It is here that information science has a role to play. First, the rapid expansion of information technology over the last twenty years has drastically altered the information landscape. Information of all kinds is more accessible, available in a wider variety of formats, and produced and disseminated by a wider range of providers. The trend is especially evident in domains that were formerly controlled by professionals: medicine and law. Second, e-government initiatives have made legal information much more widely accessible, though barriers still exist; a similar evolution in the field of health/medicine occurred, beginning with PubMed in 1997. In the health domain, the rise of the "patient-consumer" has been widely documented; many studies focus on the accuracy of consumer health information, its effect on doctor-patient relationships, and/or consumer health information seeking, evaluation and processing, and decision-making. We lack similar knowledge about the role of information technology for the legal consumer, or any information about the relationship of information acquisition and legal consciousness. If law pervades everyday life, are people better at recognizing it today, both in terms of searching for and finding the legal information they need, and in incidental encounters with legal information?

## THEORETICAL APPROACH

Historically, studies of the relationship between non-lawyers and the legal system were framed in terms of dispute resolution and whether legal problems reached a lawyer or courthouse (Kritzer, 1990; Felstiner, Abel and Sarat, 1981). Studies of information acquisition by lawyers (e.g., Leckie, Pettigrew and Sylvain, 1996; Wilkinson, 2001) followed, but they did not lead to similar research on legal consumers. The most significant recent research on public legal information acquisition came from the large-scale (N=10,512 adults) 2009 English and Welsh Civil and Social Justice Survey (CSJS), which was prompted both by efforts in the United Kingdom to make government services electronically accessible. Researchers connected with the Legal Services Research Centre (LSRC) in London produced several analyses of the data focusing on online information, frequently noting the dearth of research on the use of the internet as an advice resource in any non-health setting in the process. Various combinations of LSRC associates produced analyses of the data; see, e.g., Denvir, Balmer and Pleasance, 2011; Denver, Balmer and Buck, 2012, 2013a; Buck, Pleasance and Balmer, 2008). Pleasance was an advisor on a National Science Foundation grant-funded project (Sandefur, 2014) that surveyed a U.S. nationwide sample on their experiences with "civil justice situations;" findings indicated that people used self-help (taking action on their own without third party assistance) in 46% of these situations.

This study adopted a more holistic approach, based on research in human information behavior (HIB). Of particular importance are theories recognizing that individuals acquire information as a part of routine activities, both through acts of searching and incidentally as a part of passive monitoring of everyday life (Savolainen, 1995; Williamson 1998). In contrast to legal professionals, lay consumers of legal information have a wider array of purposes (e.g., practical, affective) and a larger potential information sources, both formal and informal. Most notably, Savolainen's (1995, 2008) everyday life information seeking (ELIS) model has been adopted by many scholars in consumer health information seeking studies (see, e.g., Zhang, Zambrowicz et al., 2004; Genuis, 2012) and studies of opportunistic information discovery (Yadamsuren, 2010). As both legal and health issues carry the potential for significant disruption of routine activities, the integrative focus of the theory is particularly appropriate here.

Other theoretical frameworks informed this study. A three-part assessment of information seeking -- the seeker's context, the system (or means of discovery) employed, and the sources utilized -- was made explicit in models by Wilson (1981, 1999, 2005; Wilson and Walsh, 2005). This tripartite division of seeker, system and source has proven to be robust and durable. Erdelez (1999) introduced the concept of information encountering (IE), or serendipitous information discovery. She found several elements useful in understanding the experience of IE: the information user/encounterer; the environment in which the encountering occurred; the problem- or interest-based characteristics of the information encountered; and the temporal characteristics of the information need (Erdelez, 1999, 2004, 2005; see also Fisher, Landry, and Naumer, 2007; Foster and Ford, 2003). Subsequent studies have affirmed the role of opportunistic information discovery in human information behavior (see Andre, Teevan and Dumais, 2009; Miwa, Egusa et al., 2011; Williamson, Quayyum et al., 2012; Yadamsuren and Erdelez, 2010).

For this study, relevant general models of information seeking and acquisition were used to determine independent variables. Consumer health studies were particularly instructive: race/ethnicity, gender, level of education, income and age have been examined, usually in the context of the frequency of information seeking. In fact, health studies on the relationship of demographic factors and information acquisition are so numerous that only a few examples can be summarized here. A meta-analysis on health information seeking by Anker, Reinhart and Feeley (2011) found that females, those with higher levels of education, and higher-income persons were more likely to search for health information, particularly on the internet. Health information seeking was also associated with having a Caucasian racial background, a younger age or greater health literacy. See also, e.g., Cotton and Gupta, 2004 (several demographic characteristics distinguished online and offline information seekers, including age, income, and education); Fox and Duggan, 2013 (women, younger people, white adults, those who live in households earning $75,000 or more, and those with college or advanced degrees were more likely to go online to figure out a possible diagnosis).

More specifically, age was significant in studies by Hall, Bernhardt et al. (2014), Getz and Weissman (2010), Manafo and Wong (2012), Sharit, Czaja, Hernandez et al. (2012) (and, in the legal setting, Denvir, Balmer and Pleasance, 2013b). A meta-analysis by Hallyburton and Evarts (2014) looked at the gender disparity in health information seeking by males and females; studies indicate that men use the internet more than women do, but women are more likely to search for health information online, regardless of other demographic factors. Both males and females turned to the internet first for health information, and it was the information source they consulted the most frequently (see also Manierre, 2015). Studies of racial and ethnic groups conducted by Rooks, Wiltshire et al. (2012), Nguyen and Bellamy (2006), and Kim (2013), among others, identified differences in health information seeking behavior. Numerous health information studies have looked at socioeconomic factors, though hardly ever to the exclusion of other demographic characteristics (see, e.g., Kontos, Emmons et al., 2011; Bell, 2014.

Along with the customary demographic variables, personal experience has consistently been shown to be a strong predictor of subjects' perceptions (see Dirikx, Gelders and van den Bulck, 2013). Studies of procedural justice, while focused on courtroom experiences, reveal the role an individual's previous experience with the legal system plays in opinions of the law's fairness and the likelihood of gaining a just outcome. Negative experiences in court lead to a reluctance to rely on formal legal action – and possibly, by extrapolation, either increased self-help in the form of information seeking or avoidance. Perceived procedural injustice, previous experience, and race were analyzed by Longazel, Parker and Sun (2011); the authors noted that the scholarly consensus is that court users have more confidence in the system if they perceive they were treated fairly – regardless of the outcome of their cases (see Rottman, 2015; Tyler, 2003, 1984). In the health information arena, studies by Lillie-Blanton, Brodie et al. (2000), Jha, Orav et al. (2008), and Rutten, Squiers et al. (2006) examined aspects of health information seeking and previous experience.

Acquisition of information has also been tied to source type. Studies have shown that source characteristics (e.g., quality and accessibility) and information source types (e.g., relational and nonrelational sources) influence the selection of information resources (see, e.g., Fidel and Green, 2004; Zimmer, Henry and Butler, 2007). Source type is relevant in both search and IE experiences. A health study by Palsdottir (2010) looked at the use of types of information sources in health and lifestyle information acquisition – both purposefully and opportunistically – grouping them into four channels: media, health specialists, internet and interpersonal sources. She concluded that information encountering was an integral part of health information behavior. Further, those subjects who were active (frequent) purposive information-seekers were also "active" at information encountering, and "passive" (less frequent) information seekers were passive (less frequent) encounterers. See also, e.g., Arora, Hesse et al., 2007 and Zhang, 2013b.

Finally, exposure is relevant to experiences of IE, as the likelihood of "stumbling upon" current law-related issues is increased by mass media attention. Studies indicate that when called upon to respond to survey questions about the courts, members of the public will draw upon images presented in various forms of media (Rottman, 2015; Papke, 2007). Further, survey respondents have identified both fictional and non-fictional TV programming with legal themes as frequent sources of information about courts (National Center for State Courts, 1999; Annenberg Foundation, 2006). However, research in channel complementarity theory indicates that mass media channels and interpersonal channels are often strategically linked (Tian and Robinson, 2008; Dutta-Bergman, 2004; Ruppel and Rains, 2012) in purposeful search experiences as well.

## METHODOLOGY

The survey consisted of 45 multiple-choice questions. It was administered through Qualtrics (www.Qualtrics.com), a private software research company based in Provo, Utah. Qualtrics provides researchers with the option of drawing subjects for online surveys from panels. These panels are groups of individuals who have agreed to participate in a series of online surveys, **in return for** incentives in the form of points toward gift cards. While individual studies of online surveys generally found that incentives had little to no effect in increasing participation (Fricker, 2008, citing Coomly, 2000, and Kypri and Gallagher, 2003), Goritz's (2006) meta-analysis found an overall 19% increase in response rate when incentives were offered. Some particular issues identified in using panels include survey fatigue and the inability to verify screening and administration protocols (Schoenherr, Ellram and Tate, 2015). However, they have the advantage of providing participants that are less uniform than the student-based samples; Roulin (2015), in a comparison of student versus Qualtrics and Amazon Mechanical Turk panels, found that the latter subjects were older, mostly employed, almost evenly divided by gender, and more ethnically diverse.

Survey questions were adapted from the study on health and lifestyle information-seeking behavior by Palsdottir (2010). Palsdottir looked at both purposive and opportunistic information acquisition in relation to demographic characteristics and information sources used. These questions were subsequently used by Basic (2015) in a study of online health information acquisition (see also Basic and Erdelez, 2015). In the instant study, search experiences were examined through questions about the frequency of intentional legal information acquisition ("Very frequently," "frequently," "occasionally," "rarely," and "never") in the previous six months.

The survey questionnaire contained an introduction to the subject matter of the survey (both searching for and opportunistically discovering legal information) and the time period upon which subjects should base their responses (the previous six months). The limited time period was selected so that subjects would have a better recollection of their experiences, and thus more valid responses. Exclusionary factors were covered in initial questions to limit subjects to adults (over age 18) without formal legal training.

Questions in the survey used non-technical language and key terms were defined at the start. In order to make the serendipitous nature of IE apparent, the phrase "stumble[d] on information unexpectedly" was used. Since a potential validity problem exists if subjects do not have an accurate understanding of the questions, domain-specific terminology was avoided.

A concept that was defined specifically was "legal problem." Denvir, Balmer and Pleasance (2011) used "problems with a legal dimension"; as discussed previously, the definitions in their study were often imprecise. A later study by Pleasance, Balmer and Reimers (2011) focused on information seeking looked at the extent to which laypersons characterized different types of problems as being "legal." Almost 80% of problems concerning personal injury caused by another, immigration, medical negligence and divorce were characterized as legal; fewer than 40% of problems with neighbors and approximately 30% of problems concerning homelessness, children's education, and landlord-tenant issues were seen as legal. To avoid this misapprehension, a definition was developed that (1) broadly defined the scope of a "legal problem" and (2) conveyed the idea that a "legal problem" involved a situation with any potential legal ramifications, and not necessarily a lawsuit.

To draw attention to the definitions, the directive "PLEASE READ THE FOLLOWING DEFINITIONS CAREFULLY" was included in capital letters. Legal information was defined as referring to "any topic that has or potentially could have legal consequences." The definition also noted that subjects should view the definition broadly and included examples (information about legal procedures, citizen's rights, news stories, etc.). A legal problem was defined as a particular issue that might involve legal consequences. Again, examples were included that illustrated the expansive nature of the definition (e.g., personal experience in the legal system as a plaintiff or defendant, a dispute where you needed to identify your options or legal rights, curiosity about a legal topic, hearing a passing reference to a legal topic).

Survey questions were designed to elicit information about information acquisition related to the civil justice system and civil legal matters. Frequency of search ("Within the last six months, how often did you search for legal information?") and IE ("Within the last six months, how often did you unexpectedly stumble upon legal information?") were examined in terms of their relationships to the independent and control variables.

The survey was pretested in preview mode over a two-week period in March 2016 prior to its administration by Qualtrics; several questions were reworded for greater clarity. A second pilot test of the survey was administered by Qualtrics to 35 subjects during the week of May 8, 2016, after which bolding and underlining were added for emphasis and an attention filter question was inserted to deter insufficient-effort responding (IER) and to ensure validity (McGonagle, 2015; Huang, Liu et al., 2014). It was reopened in May 2016, and a total of 385 unique completed responses were collected. Fill-in-the-blank responses were reviewed and, when possible, coded.

## FINDINGS

### *Personal Characteristics*

One component of the study targeted the relationship of demographic characteristics and previous experience with the legal system on the frequency of search and IE. Six variables – age, gender, education, race, income, and previous experience with the legal system – were used to provide foundational information about the relationship of legal information acquisition and personal characteristics. The data were used in a regression analysis to determine which variables were significant predictors of search and IE.

| | Search (*n* = 257) | | IE (*n* = 228) | |
|---|---|---|---|---|
| Characteristic | *n* | % | *n* | % |
| Age | | | | |
| 18–29 | 27 | 87.1 | 23 | 74.2 |
| 30–29 | 51 | 67.1 | 46 | 60.5 |
| 40–49 | 66 | 78.6 | 57 | 67.9 |
| 50–59 | 60 | 65.9 | 53 | 58.2 |
| 60+ | 53 | 51.5 | 49 | 47.6 |
| Gender | | | | |
| Female | 157 | 64.3 | 138 | 56.6 |
| Male | 100 | 71.4 | 90 | 64.3 |
| Education | | | | |
| High school or less | 64 | 58.7 | 52 | 47.7 |
| Some college | 83 | 68.6 | 80 | 66.1 |
| College degree | 80 | 70.2 | 72 | 63.2 |
| Graduate degree | 30 | 73.2 | 24 | 58.5 |
| Race | | | | |
| White | 193 | 65.0 | 165 | 55.6 |
| Black | 31 | 66.0 | 30 | 63.8 |
| Other | 33 | 80.5 | 33 | 80.5 |
| Income | | | | |
| < $20,000 | 36 | 53.7 | 43 | 64.2 |
| $20,000 – $34,999 | 41 | 59.4 | 38 | 55.1 |
| $35,000 – $49,999 | 48 | 66.7 | 39 | 54.2 |
| $50,000 – $74,999 | 61 | 75.3 | 50 | 61.7 |
| $75,000 – $99,999 | 33 | 76.7 | 25 | 58.1 |
| $100,000+ | 27 | 79.4 | 24 | 70.6 |
| Experience with legal system | | | | |
| None | 67 | 58.8 | 51 | 44.7 |
| One occasion | 86 | 71.1 | 76 | 62.8 |
| Two occasions | 77 | 70.0 | 69 | 62.7 |
| Three to six occasions | 27 | 67.5 | 32 | 80.0 |

***Table 1.*** *Demographic characteristics of respondents conducting searches and experiencing IE*

While most of the demographic variables were straightforward, Black, Asian, Hispanic and other racial groups were combined as "nonwhite" because of their low numbers. The "previous experience" variable was based upon responses to three survey questions, which were used to create a combined score ranging from zero to six.

| Item on questionnaire | n | % |
|---|---|---|
| Consulted an attorney | 217 | 56.4 |
| Member of immediate family is a legal professional | 17 | 4.4 |
| Experience with court system in following roles | | |
| As a criminal defendant | 45 | 11.7 |
| As a party in a civil case | 50 | 13.0 |
| As a juror | 102 | 26.5 |
| As a witness or some other type of participation | 43 | 11.2 |
| None of the above | 196 | 50.9 |
| Number of experiences with legal system (*M* = 1.23, *SD* = 1.06) | | |
| 0 | 114 | 29.6 |
| 1 | 121 | 31.4 |
| 2 | 110 | 28.6 |
| 3 | 29 | 7.5 |
| 4 | 10 | 2.6 |
| 5 | 0 | 0.0 |
| 6 | 1 | 0.3 |

***Table 2**. Creation of previous experience variable*

### Regression analysis: search

A direct logistic regression analysis was performed on the frequency of search (as outcome) and six demographic predictors: age, gender, education, race, income and previous experience with the legal system. After the deletion of standardized residuals greater than two standard deviations, data from 355 respondents were available for analysis (246 who conducted a search, and 109 who did not). A test of the full model with all six predictors against a constant-only model was statistically reliable, $\chi2$ (6, 355) = 57.23, $p < .01$, indicating that the predictors, as a set, reliably distinguished between respondents who conducted a search and those who did not. Prediction was satisfactory, with 89% of those who conducted a search and 33% of those who did not conduct a search correctly predicted, for an overall success rate of 72%.

Table 3 shows regression coefficients, Wald statistics, odds ratios, and 95% confidence intervals for each of the six predictors. According to the Wald statistic, only age ($z$ = 27.29, $p < .01$), income ($z$ = 13.315, $p < .01$), and experience with the legal system ($z$ = 4.919, $p$ = .03) were found to be significant predictors after controlling for all other variables in the model. With each increase in the age variable (approximately 10 years), the likelihood of conducting a search decreased 42% (Exp($B$) = .58). With each increase in income, the likelihood of a search increased 40% (Exp($B$) = 1.40) and with each increase in experience with the legal system, the likelihood of a search increased 33% (Exp($B$) = 1.33). In other words, the lower the age, the higher the income, and the more previous experience with the legal system, the more likely the subject was to conduct a search for legal information.

### Regression analysis: IE

A direct logistic regression analysis was performed with IE as outcome and the same six demographic predictors: age, gender, education, race, income and experience with the legal system. After deleting cases with missing data ($n$ = 20) and deletion of standardized residuals greater than two standard deviations ($n$ = 6), data from 359 respondents were available for analysis: 219 who were associated with an IE experience, and 140 who were not. A test of the full model with all six predictors against a constant-only model was statistically reliable, $\chi2$ (6, 359) = 52.26, $p < .01$, indicating that the predictors, as a set, reliably distinguished between respondents who were associated with IE experience and those who were not. Prediction was satisfactory, with 83% associated with IE experience and 46% of those who were not, for an overall success rate of 69%.

| | | | | 95% CI for odds ratio | |
|---|---|---|---|---|---|
| Variable | *B* | Wald test (z-ratio) | Odds ratio Exp(*B*) | Upper | Lower |
| Age | -.540 | 27.290 | .583 | .476 | .714 |
| Gender (0 = female/1 = male) | -.153 | .335 | .858 | .510 | 1.442 |
| Education | .058 | .174 | 1.060 | .806 | 1.394 |
| Ethnicity (0=White/1=Nonwhite) | .793 | 2.303 | 2.210 | .794 | 6.157 |
| Income | .336 | 13.315 | 1.400 | 1.169 | 1.677 |
| Experience with legal system | .283 | 4.919 | 1.328 | 1.034 | 1.705 |
| (Constant) | 1.318 | 4.827 | 3.737 | | |

***Table 3**. Logistic regression analysis of search as a function of demographic variables*

Table 4 shows regression coefficients, Wald statistics, odds ratios, and 95% confidence intervals for each of the six predictors. According to the Wald statistic, only age ($z$ = 16.420, $p < .01$), race ($z$ = 6.242, $p$ = .01), and previous experience with the legal system ($z$ = 19.229, $p < .01$) were found to be significant predictors of IE after controlling for all other variables in the model. With each increase in the age variable (approximately 10 years), the likelihood of being associated with an opportunistic discovery of information decreased 32% (Exp($B$) =.68). The likelihood of a white person, compared to a nonwhite person, experiencing IE was approximately 70% (Exp($B$) = 1.704), and with each increase in experience with the legal system, the likelihood of IE experience increased 75% (Exp($B$) = 1.75). In other words, younger, nonwhite individuals with more previous experience with the legal system were associated with IE.

### Environmental Exposure

"Environmental exposure" related to information sources and mass media exposure. It was operationalized as the amount of contact with various source types. For search, these encompassed five types of contacts (personal contacts with non-legal professionals, internet searching for laws, internet searching for discussions, contacts with legal professionals, and searches for print material). For IE, eight types of contacts (search engine results, general website, social media, internet news, TV news, fictional TV programs, print material and non-lawyer personal contacts) were included. Cronbach's alpha was satisfactory for both the search sources (.71) and the IE sources (.93).

| Variable | $B$ | Wald test (z-ratio) | Odds ratio Exp($B$) | 95% CI for odds ratio | |
|---|---|---|---|---|---|
| | | | | Upper | Lower |
| Age | -.381 | 16.420 | .683 | .568 | .821 |
| Gender (0 = female/1 = male) | -.318 | 1.654 | .728 | .448 | 1.181 |
| Education | .174 | 1.828 | 1.191 | .925 | 1.533 |
| Race (0=White/1=Nonwhite) | .533 | 6.242 | 1.7041 | 1.222 | 2.589 |
| Income | -.018 | .048 | .982 | .836 | 1.154 |
| Experience with legal system | .559 | 19.229 | 1.750 | 1.363 | 2.247 |
| (Constant) | .184 | .077 | 1.202 | | |

***Table 4**. Logistic regression analysis of IE as a function of demographic variables*

Approximately 42% of searchers used the internet often to search for applicable laws. Twenty-two percent often looked for internet discussions on their legal topic. When these percentages are combined with the category of "sometime" searchers for applicable laws and legal discussions, the dominance of web sources for legal information is even more apparent (over 76% for applicable laws, 54.7% for discussions). This is consistent with health information studies, which emphasize the role of web searching as the initial and most popular research source. Legal professionals were rarely contacted, suggesting that self-help is the preferred option. Using the same combination of "often" and "sometimes," family and friends were consulted about 1/3 of the time by searchers.

| Source | Never* | Rarely | Sometimes | Often |
|---|---|---|---|---|
| Contacted family, friends | 42.2 | 25.4 | 25.4 | 7.0 |
| Searched internet for applicable laws | 10.2 | 13.3 | 34.8 | 41.8 |
| Search internet for discussions from others | 28.5 | 16.8 | 32.8 | 21.9 |
| Contacted a legal professional | 57.4 | 21.1 | 15.2 | 6.3 |
| Looked for books on the topic | 62.5 | 14.8 | 14.8 | 7.8 |
| Other | 92.6 | 2.3 | 2.0 | 3.1 |

* Percentage of respondents

***Table 5.** Sources used to conduct searches for legal information (n = 256)*

Searchers indicated that they were most frequently motivated to use certain sources based on ease of access. They identified ease of access as the most influential factor in their use of search engines (84.7%), general websites (64%), social media (55%) and advice from friends/family (45%). Trustworthiness and accuracy were identified as the main reasons for using law-specific websites like FindLaw (54.3%) and for contacting a legal professional (48.4%). Expense played a very minor role in the choice of any of the listed information sources (0-3.8%); this result was contrary to the expectation that internet sources would be preferred based on low cost.

| | $n$ | Ease of access* | Trustworthy accurate | Expense | Anonymity, privacy | Other |
|---|---|---|---|---|---|---|
| Search engine | 216 | 84.7 | 5.6 | 2.8 | 4.2 | 2.8 |
| Law-specific website | 81 | 25.9 | 54.3 | 3.7 | 3.7 | 12.3 |
| General website | 105 | 63.8 | 18.1 | 3.8 | 4.8 | 9.5 |
| Lawyer or law firm website | 60 | 33.3 | 36.7 | 1.7 | 8.3 | 20.0 |
| Contacted legal professional directly | 62 | 25.8 | 48.4 | 0.0 | 6.5 | 19.4 |
| Social media | 45 | 55.6 | 6.7 | 2.2 | 11.1 | 24.4 |
| Family, friends, or acquaintances | 107 | 44.9 | 33.6 | 1.9 | 8.4 | 11.2 |

* Percentage of respondents

***Table 6.** Reason for using source to search for legal information*

Sources of IE experiences were somewhat different. As combined, 51% of the information encounterers identified internet-based sources (search engines, general websites, social media and internet news) as "very frequent" and "frequent" sources of legal *IE*. Non-internet media was a less important source; TV programs (fictional and news) accounted for a little less than ¼ of legal IE experiences. Friends and family were less frequent sources of legal IE than search.

| | Never* | Rarely | Occasionally | Frequently | Very frequently |
|---|---|---|---|---|---|
| Search engine results | 28.5 | 36.0 | 22.4 | 7.5 | 5.7 |
| General website | 45.6 | 29.4 | 14.0 | 6.6 | 4.4 |
| Social media | 49.6 | 25.4 | 13.6 | 6.6 | 4.8 |
| Internet news | 36.4 | 27.6 | 20.6 | 8.8 | 6.6 |
| TV news | 36.8 | 30.7 | 18.4 | 9.6 | 4.4 |
| Fictional TV programs | 58.8 | 17.1 | 14.5 | 6.6 | 3.1 |
| Print material | 51.8 | 26.3 | 13.6 | 4.8 | 3.5 |
| Friends, family | 50.0 | 25.9 | 11.8 | 7.5 | 4.8 |
| Other | 92.5 | 1.8 | 1.3 | 0.9 | 3.5 |

* Percentage of respondents

***Table 7.** Sources of legal IE experiences (n = 228)*

Participants' exposure to mass media was measured based on yes or no responses to seven types of activities ("Do you engage in any of the following activities more than once or twice a month?"). Environmental exposure was also measured by the sources that subjects used to search for legal information within the past six months (Q10); again, they responded Yes or No to seven types of sources. Responses from those participants who indicated that they had conducted a search in the past 6 months (n = 257) or experienced IE over the same period (N=228) were used.

| Type of exposure | *n* | % |
|---|---|---|
| Watch fictional TV programs about lawyers or criminal investigation | 261 | 69.6 |
| Watch nonfiction TV programs about legal cases or crime investigation | 220 | 58.7 |
| Watch TV news | 329 | 87.7 |
| Read new on the web | 313 | 83.5 |
| Read newspapers in print | 212 | 56.5 |
| Read true crime books | 68 | 18.1 |
| Read fictional books about lawyers or crime investigation | 98 | 26.1 |
| Exposure to media ($M = 3.90$, $SD = 1.72$) | | |
| 0 | 10 | 2.6 |
| 1 | 22 | 5.7 |
| 2 | 50 | 13.0 |
| 3 | 73 | 19.0 |
| 4 | 87 | 22.6 |
| 5 | 80 | 20.8 |
| 6 | 29 | 7.5 |
| 7 | 34 | 8.8 |

***Table 8***. *Exposure to multiple forms of media (more than once or twice a month)*

Two *t* tests indicated that subjects who conducted searches and experienced IE reported significantly higher exposure scores. These higher scores indicated that they engaged with more forms of media, which may show greater interest in general legal information, more willingness to pursue legal information by active means, and more recognition of unintended encounters with legal information.

| | *n* | *M* | *SD* | *t* | *p* |
|---|---|---|---|---|---|
| Search | | | | | |
| Yes | 257 | 4.24 | 1.67 | | |
| No | 128 | 3.21 | 1.60 | -5.78 | < .01 |
| IE | | | | | |
| Yes | 228 | 4.17 | 1.65 | | |
| No | 157 | 3.51 | 1.73 | -3.76 | < .01 |

***Table 9***. *Exposure to multiple forms of media by search and IE*

## DISCUSSION

To summarize, relationships between search frequency and three personal characteristics (age, income and previous experience) were found. Null hypotheses could not be rejected for the other personal characteristics variables (gender, education and race). As with search, relationships between IE frequency and age and previous experience were found; however, race (nonwhite) was also positively associated with IE, and income was not (along with gender and education). In addition, a positive relationship was found between environmental exposure and frequency of search and IE.

The personal characteristics results were interesting. As noted above, previous experience has been found to be a predictor of information acquisition in health and other HIB studies. While most studies in human information behavior found that age was associated with search/IE frequency (such that younger persons are associated with more frequent information acquisition), higher income and more education are often found to be predictors as well.

Further, many of the health studies found that women searched and encountered health information more than men, and that white individuals were more likely to search and encounter health information than nonwhites. The lack of a relationship between search/encounter frequency and gender in the legal information setting may deserve more exploration. The health studies suggest that women play a larger role in the dissemination of health information than men, possibly because of the strength of their affective ties. A study of "lay information mediaries" (LIMs) by Abrahamson et al. (2008) looked at the relationship of gender and health information seeking. Of the 211 survey participants in the Abrahamson study, 77% of the LIMs identified were female, and most searched because of family members and people they were "extremely close" to (81%). Fifty-one percent undertook these searches mostly without prompting. The authors concluded that LIM behavior may be related to gender and relationship tie strength, and might be more internally than externally motivated. See also Hupfer and Detlor, 2006 (gender-related self-concept traits known as self- and other-orientation are associated with self-reported search frequency for medical and government information). These motivations may not hold in the legal setting.

As noted above, income was related to search frequency, but not to frequency of IE. Again, the health information studies may shed some light on the issues of gender, race and income. For example, Bell (2014) conducted 58 interviews of women of varied socioeconomic status (SES) on the topic of infertility; all of the lower SES subjects were Black, and all of the higher SES subjects were white. Bell found that women of lower SES used the media, especially entertainment television, as their primary source of information on infertility; women of high SES used a greater variety of sources, including friends, family, physicians, books, the internet, etc. While Bell was not interested in IE, her conclusions related to social and cultural capital have some explanatory value in that context: mass media sources are more likely than professional sources, or medical literature, to lead to "accidental" acquisition of health information. Bell's lower SES women were also less frequent searchers, lacking the time, means and research skills to do so. (See also Keeley, Wright and Condit, 2009; Shieh, Broome and Stump, 2010.) Similarly, a study by Kontos, Emmons et al. (2011) identified determinants of what the authors called "health information mavenism" (the tendency to share health information by word of mouth) among lower socioeconomic and minority subjects. A larger social network, being female and being older were factors associated with higher mavenism scores, along with being moderate consumers of general media. Untangling the relationships between gender, income and race in the health context is tricky; a more narrowly focused analysis of these factors in terms of legal information acquisition might be helpful.

The environmental exposure results aligned more closely with expectations. The dominance of the internet as the source of for both legal search and IE was confirmed by the study results, and this is consistent with health information acquisition. In terms of legal search, the implication is that most individuals will do at least some preliminary investigation related to their legal problem on their own. Sandefur (2014) found the same reliance on self-help in her study of Americans faced with civil justice situations; 46% of subjects did not seek assistance from any third party, and very few (8% of a subset selected for in-depth follow-up) involved courts or tribunals of any kind. Here, ease of access, rather than expense, was the main factor in subjects' selection of internet self-help; this was also the result in Sandefur's survey, where only 17% of subjects identified cost as a reason for not seeking formal legal assistance.

It is important to note the limitations of the study. First, convenience sampling was used, resulting in a demographic profile that was not representative of the U.S. population. The use of an online survey meant that persons without ready access to the internet were excluded. The use of subjects from a Qualtrics panel for the survey phase further limited the sample to volunteers who were motivated by point rewards for survey completion. Finally, the study makes use of self-reported data, which carries the risk that respondents will forget information, misinterpret it or answer dishonestly.

Finally, the results reported here are partial. Other components of the research examined the role of affective factors (self-efficacy, vigilance, perception of the legal system) and perceived risk. The survey results were augmented by a qualitative interview phase, which proved to have significant explanatory value. However, the demographic and environmental results provide initial foundational data for additional studies.

## CONCLUSION

The results reported here are part of a first step toward a fuller understanding of legal information acquisition – one that may eventually hold the same investigatory allure as health information behavior. The broader theoretical significance of the study lies in its relationship to legal consciousness. In this notoriously hard-to-define area, the process of acquisition of legal information may shed light on citizens' perceptions of issues and rights as "legal," relevant, or actionable. The roles of multiple information sources in legal information acquisition are worthy of additional scrutiny. Demographic characteristics, as in health studies, identify segments of the population that are receiving and recognizing legal information – or not.

Moreover, the study is directed at legal information acquisition. The term *acquisition* is used to encompass information about legal rights and remedies that is obtained by purposive search *and* opportunistically. The focus on the roles of intentional and serendipitous acquisition of legal information broadens the scope of our knowledge and provides a fuller, holistic exploration of the role of "the law" within the everyday life experience of ordinary citizens.

## REFERENCES

André, P., Teevan, J., & Dumais, S. T. (2009). From x-rays to Silly Putty via Uranus: Serendipity and its role in web search. In *CHI '09: Proceedings of the SIGCHI conference on human factors in computing systems*, 2033-2036.

Anker, A.E., Reinhart, A.M., & Feeley, T.H. (2011), Health information seeking: A review of measures and methods. *Patient Education and Counseling, 82*(3), 346-54.

Arora, N. K., Hesse, B. W., Rimer, B. K., Viswanath, K., Clayman, M. L., & Croyle, R. T. (2008). Frustrated and confused: The American public rates its cancer-related information-seeking experiences. *Journal of General Internal Medicine, 23*(3), 223-228.

Basic, J., & Erdelez, S. (2015). The role of risky behaviors and health education in college students' health information acquisition on the internet. *Proceedings of the Association for Information Science and Technology, 52*(1), 1-10.

Berrey, E., Hoffman, S. G., & Nielsen, L. B. (2010). Situated justice: Plaintiffs' and defendants' perceptions of fairness in employment discrimination cases. *Law & Society Review, 46*, 1-56.

Bell, A. V. (2014). "I think about Oprah": Social class differences in sources of health information. *Qualitative Health Research, 24*(4), 506-516.

Blackstone, A., Uggen, C., & McLaughlin, H. (2009). Legal consciousness and responses to sexual harassment. *Law & Society Review, 43*(3), 631-668.

Buck, A., Pleasence, P., & Balmer, N. J. (2008). Do citizens know how to deal with legal issues? Some empirical insights. *Journal of Social Policy, 37*(04), 661-681.

Chambliss, E., Knake, R. N., & Nelson, R. L. (2016). What we know and need to know about the state of access to justice research. *South Carolina Law Review, 67*, 193-201.

Cotten, S. R., & Gupta, S. S. (2004). Characteristics of online and offline health information seekers and factors that discriminate between them. *Social Science & Medicine*, 59(9), 1795-1806.

Denvir, C., Balmer, N. J., & Pleasence, P. (2011). Surfing the web–recreation or resource? Exploring how young people in the UK use the internet as an advice portal for problems with a legal dimension. *Interacting with Computers, 23*(1), 96-104.

Denvir, C., Balmer, N. J., & Buck, A. (2012). Informed citizens? Knowledge of rights and the resolution of civil justice problems. *Journal of Social Policy, 41*(3), 591-614.

Denvir, C., Balmer, N. J., & Pleasence, P. (2013a). When legal rights are not a reality: Do individuals know their rights and how can we tell? *Journal of Social Welfare and Family Law, 35*(1), 139-160.

Denvir, C., Balmer, N. J., & Pleasence, P. (2013b). Portal or pot hole? Exploring how older people use the 'information superhighway' for advice relating to problems with a legal dimension. *Ageing and Society, 34*(4), 670-699. doi:10.1017/S0144686X12001213

Dirikx, A., Gelders, D., & den Bulck, J. V. (2013). Adolescent perceptions of the performance and fairness of the police: Examining the impact of television exposure. *Mass Communication and Society, 16*(1), 109-132.

Dutta-Bergman, M. J. (2004). Primary sources of health information: Comparisons in the domain of health attitudes, health cognitions, and health behaviors. *Health Communication, 16*(3), 273-288.

Erdelez, S. (1999). Information encountering: It's more than just bumping into information. *Bulletin of the American Society for Information Science, 25*(3), 25-29.

Erdelez, S. (2004). Investigation of information encountering in the controlled research environment. *Information Processing and Management, 40*, 1013-1025.

Erdelez, S. (2005). Information encountering. In K. E. Fisher, S. Erdelez & L. E. F. McKechnie (Eds.), *Theories of information behavior* (pp. 179-185). Medford, NJ: Information Today, Inc.

Ewick, P., & Silbey, S.S. (1998). *The common place of law: Stories from everyday life.* Chicago, IL: University of Chicago Press.

Felstiner, W. L., Abel, R. L., & Sarat, A. (1981). The emergence and transformation of disputes: Naming, blaming, claiming... *Law and Society Review, 15*(3/4), 631-654.

Fisher, K. E., Landry, C. F., & Naumer, C. M. (2007). Social spaces, causal interactions, meaningful exchanges: 'Information ground' characteristics based on the college student experience. *Information Research, 12*(2). Retrieved from http://informationr.net/ir/12-2/paper291.html

Foster, A., & Ford, N. (2003). Serendipity and information seeking: An empirical study. *Journal of Documentation, 59*(3), 321-340.

Fox, S., & Duggan, M. (2013). Health online 2013. [Pew Internet and American Life Project Report.] Retrieved from http://www.pewinternet.org/files/old-media//Files/Reports/PIP_HealthOnline.pdf

Fricker, R. D. (2008). Sampling methods for web and e-mail surveys. In N. Fielding, R.M. Lee, & G. Blank (Eds.), *Sage handbook of online research methods* (pp. 195-216). London: Sage Publications.

Genuis, S. K. (2012). Constructing "sense" from evolving health information: A qualitative investigation of information seeking and sense making across sources. *Journal of the American Society for Information Science and Technology, 63*(8), 1553-1566.

Getz, I., & Weissman, G. (2010). An information needs profile of Israeli older adults, regarding the law and services. *Journal of Librarianship and Information Science, 42*(2), 136-146.

Hadfield, G. K., & Heine, J. (2015). Life in the law-thick world: The legal resource landscape for ordinary Americans. Preprint from S. Estreicher & J Radice (Eds.), *Beyond elite law: Access to civil justice in America* (forthcoming, Cambridge University Press, 2016).

Hall, A.K., Bernhardt, J.M., Dodd, V., & Vollrath, M.W. (2014). The digital health divide: Evaluating online health information access and use among older adults. *Health Behavior & Education, 42*(2), 202-209.

Hallyburton, A., & Evarts, L.A. (2014). Gender and online health information seeking: A five-study meta-analysis. *Journal of Consumer Health on the Internet, 18*(2), 128-142.

Harding, R. (2006). 'Dogs are "registered," people shouldn't be': Legal consciousness and lesbian and gay rights. *Social & Legal Studies, 15*(4), 511-533.

Huang, J. L., Liu, M., & Bowling, N. A. (2014). Insufficient effort responding: Examining an insidious confound in survey data. *Journal of Applied Psychology, 100*(3), 828-845.

Hupfer, M. E., & Detlor, B. (2006). Gender and web information seeking: A self-concept orientation model. *Journal of the American Society for Information Science and Technology, 57*(8), 1105-1115.

Jha, A. K., Orav, E. J., Zheng, J., & Epstein, A. M. (2008). Patients' perception of hospital care in the United States. *New England Journal of Medicine, 359*(18), 1921-1931.

Keeley, B., Wright, L., & Condit, C. M. (2009). Functions of health fatalism: Fatalistic talk as face saving, uncertainty management, stress relief and sense making. *Sociology of Health & Illness, 31*, 734–747. doi:10.1111/j.1467-9566.2009.01164.x

Kim, W. (2013). The role of social support and social networks in health information seeking behavior among Korean Americans. (Doctoral dissertation.) George Mason University.

Kontos, E. Z., Emmons, K. M., Puleo, E., & Viswanath, K. (2011). Determinants and beliefs of health information mavens among a lower-socioeconomic position and minority population. *Social Science & Medicine, 73*(1), 22-32.

Kritzer, H.M. (1990). *The justice broker: Lawyers and ordinary litigation.* New York, NY: Oxford University Press.

Kypri, K., & Gallagher, S.J. (2003). Incentives to increase participation in an internet survey of alcohol use: A controlled experiment. *Alcohol and Alcoholism, 38*(5), 437–441.

Leckie, G. J., Pettigrew, K. E., & Sylvain, C. (1996). Modeling the information seeking of professionals: A general model derived from research on engineers, health care professionals, and lawyers. *Library Quarterly, 66*(2), 161-193.

Leitch, J. A. (2013). Looking for quality: The empirical debate in access to justice research. *Windsor Yearbook of Access to Justice, 31*, 229-255.

Lillie-Blanton, M., Brodie, M., Rowland, D., Altman, D., & McIntosh, M. (2000). Race, ethnicity, and the health care system: Public perceptions and experiences. *Medical Care Research and Review, 57(*4 suppl), 218-235.

Lobel, J., & Chapman, M. (2015). Bridging the gap between unmet legal needs and an oversupply of lawyers: Creating neighborhood law offices-the Philadelphia experiment. *Virginia Journal of Social Policy & Law, 22*(1), 71-102.

Longazel, J., Parker, L., & Sun, I. (2011). Experiencing court, experiencing race: Perceived procedural injustice among court users. *Race and Justice, 1*(2), 202-227.

Manafo, E., & Wong, S. (2012). Exploring older adults' health information seeking behaviors. *Journal of Nutrition Education and Behavior, 44*(1), 85-89.

McGonagle, A. K. (2015). Participant motivation: A critical consideration. *Industrial and Organizational Psychology, 8*(02), 208-214.

Miwa, M., Egusa, Y., Saito, H., Takaku, M., Terai, H. & Kando, N. (2011). A method to capture information encountering embedded in exploratory web searches. *Information Research, 16*(3). Retrieved from http://informationr.net/ir/16-3/paper487.html

Nielsen, L. B. (2000). Situating legal conciousness: Experiences and attitudes of ordinary citizens about law and street harassment. *Law & Society Review, 34*, 1055-1090.

Palsdottir, A. (2010). The connection between purposive information seeking and information encountering. A study of Icelander's health and lifestyle information seeking. *Journal of Documentation, 66*(2), 224-244.

Papke, D. R. (2007). The impact of popular culture on American perceptions of the courts. *Indiana Law Journal, 82*, 1225-1234.

Pleasence, P., Balmer, N. J., & Reimers, S. (2011). What really drives advice seeking behaviour? Looking beyond the subject of legal disputes. *Oñati Socio-Legal Series, 1*(6).

Rhode, D. L. (2004). *Access to justice*. New York, NY: Oxford University Press.

Rooks, R. N., Wiltshire, J. C., Elder, K., BeLue, R., & Gary, L. C. (2012). Health information seeking and use outside of the medical encounter: Is it associated with race and ethnicity? *Social Science & Medicine, 74*(2), 176-184.

Rottman, D.B. (2015). Who trusts the trial courts, to what extent, and why? In B.H. Bornstein & A.J. Tomkins (Eds.), *Motivating cooperation and compliance with authority* (pp. 117-144). New York, NY: Springer.

Roulin, N. (2015). Don't throw the baby out with the bathwater: Comparing data quality of crowdsourcing, online panels, and student samples. *Industrial and Organizational Psychology, 8*(02), 190-196.

Ruppel, E. K., & Rains, S. A. (2012). Information sources and the health information-seeking process: An application and extension of channel complementarity theory. *Communication Monographs, 79*(3), 385-405.

Rutten, L. J. F., Squiers, L., & Hesse, B. (2006). Cancer-related information seeking: Hints from the 2003 Health Information National Trends Survey (HINTS*). Journal of Health Communication, 11*(Suppl. 1), 147-156.

Sandefur, R. L. (2014). Accessing justice in the contemporary USA: Findings from the community needs and services study. Chicago, IL: American Bar Foundation.

Sarat, A. (1977). Studying American legal culture: An assessment of survey evidence. *Law & Society Review, 11*, 427-487.

Savolainen, R. (1995). Everyday life information seeking: Approaching information seeking in the context of "way of life." *Library & Information Science Research, 17*(3), 259-294.

Savolainen, R. (2008). Everyday information practices: A social phenomenological perspective. Lanham, MD: Scarecrow Press.

Schoenherr, T., Ellram, L. M., & Tate, W. L. (2015). A note on the use of survey research firms to enable empirical data collection. *Journal of Business Logistics, 36*(3), 288-300.

Sharit, J., Czaja, S. J., Hernandez, M. A., Lee, C. C., & Lang, S. (2012). Assessing the usefulness of software tools for aiding meaningful access of internet health information. *Proceedings of the Human Factors and Ergonomics Society annual meeting, 56*, 130-134.

Shieh, C., Broome, M. E., & Stump, T. E. (2010). Factors associated with health information-seeking in low-income pregnant women. *Women & Health, 50*, 426–442.

Tian, Y., & Robinson, J. D. (2008). Media use and health information seeking: an empirical test of complementarity theory. *Health Communication, 23*(2), 184-190.

Tyler, T. R. (1984). The role of perceived injustice in defendants' evaluations of their courtroom experience. *Law and Society Review, 18*(1), 51-74.

Tyler, T. R. (2003). Procedural justice, legitimacy, and the effective rule of law. *Crime and Justice, 30*, 283-357.

Wilkinson, M. (2001). Information sources used by lawyers in problem-solving: An empirical exploration. *Library & Information Science Research, 23*, 257–276.

Williamson, K. (1998). Discovered by chance: The role of incidental information acquisition in an ecological model of information use. *Library & Information Science Research, 20*(1), 23-40.

Williamson, K., Qayyum, A., Hider, P., & Liu, Y.H. (2012). Young adults and everyday-life information: The role of news media. *Library & Information Science Research, 34*, 258–264.

Wilson, T.D. (1981). On user studies and information needs. *Journal of Documentation, 37*(1), 3-15.

Wilson, T.D. (1999). Models in information behaviour research. *Journal of Documentation, 55*(3), 249-270.

Wilson, T.D. (2005). Evolution in information behavior modeling: Wilson's model. In K. E. Fisher, S. Erdelez & L. McKechnie (Eds.), *Theories of information behavior* (pp. 31-36). Medford, N.J: Information Today, Inc.

Wilson, T.D., & Walsh, C. (1996). Information behavior: An interdisciplinary perspective. Sheffield, UK: University of Sheffield, Department of Information Studies. Retrieved from http://www.informationr.net/tdw/publ/infbehav/cont.html

Yadamsuren, B. (2010). Incidental exposure to online news in everyday life information seeking context: Mixed method study. (Doctoral dissertation.) University of Missouri-Columbia.

Yadamsuren, B., & Erdelez, S. (2010). Incidental exposure to online news. *Proceedings of the American Society for Information Science and Technology, 47*(1), 1-8.

Zhang, Y. (2013b). Toward a layered model of context for health information searching: An analysis of consumer-generated questions. *Journal of the American Society for Information Science and Technology, 64*(6), 1158-1172.

Zhang, D., Zambrowicz, C., Zhou, H., & Roderer, N. K. (2004). User information-seeking behavior in a medical web portal environment: A preliminary study. *Journal of the American Society for Information Science and Technology, 55*(8), 670-684.

# Investigating the Information Gaps in Refugee Integration

**Olubukola Oduntan**
*Dept. of Computer and Information Sciences, University of Strathclyde, UK. olubukola.oduntan@strath.ac.uk*

**Ian Ruthven**
*Dept. of Computer and Information Sciences, University of Strathclyde, UK. ian.ruthven@strath.ac.uk*

## ABSTRACT

**Refugee integration processes and systems are complex for refugees. They find them difficult to navigate and thus often end up disadvantaged. This paper presents the first set of findings from an ongoing information behaviour research study into refugee integration. The study explores the situational experiences of refugees and asylum seekers engaging with integration processes and systems through individual semi-structured interviews. Dervin's sense-making methodology was used to elicit the information gaps. The findings reveals refused asylum situation during integration and highlight information needs embedded in processes and systems of refugee integration. The results have implications for reducing the complexity of service provision during refugee integration. In addition, the approach expands previous studies and highlights the depth a situational investigation can bring to information behaviour studies.**

## KEYWORDS

human information behaviour, refugee integration, sense-making, situational information behaviour

## INTRODUCTION

Refugee integration is a complicated phenomenon that attempts to deal with the sociological and psychological consequences of forced displacement. It deals with the changing relationship between refugees and host societies. However, due to complex integration systems and processes, refugees often end up marginalised. The design and delivery of integration services and systems is therefore pivotal for successful integration of refugees. The aim of this research is to understand the information behaviour of refugees and identify information gaps in situations as they seek integration into the host country. This knowledge can be used to inform and enhance the design and delivery of integration provisions. In this paper, the information gaps surrounding refused asylum situation are discussed.

## LITERATURE REVIEW

Information behaviour focuses on information needs, seeking and use. It concerns the creation of information as well as the processes in service of information transfer to solve problems (Bates, 1999) and design products and services (Borko, 1968). The role of information behaviour studies in any given context is therefore to inform the design of person-centred services and systems through the identified information needs, sources and seeking behaviour. However, it could be particularly daunting with marginalised groups, especially refugees as challenges of access and disparate contextual factors for conception are encountered. This is further complicated by the differing terminologies used for these groups. As a result, the majority of information studies have centred on general migrant information behaviour whilst refugee specific ones are slowly emerging.

The identified information needs of general migrant include: social, cultural knowledge and skill-based knowledge (Fisher, Durrance, & Hinton, 2004); health insurance, emergency care, vaccinations, dental, preventive care, pregnancy, what to expect from health services, school enrolment, housing and employment (Courtright, 2005). Silvio (2006) identified academic, apprenticeship, health, employment, political and how to deal with discrimination and Shoham & Strauss (2008) identified housing, schooling, health, driving, banking, legal issues, work and language. Lingel (2011) identified information need around neighborhood, grocery shopping, local routes, libraries and hospitals. These studies also identified a broad range of information sources that included family and friends (Shoham & Strauss, 2008) and social networks such as ball parks, bike shops, day care centers, church, barber shops, hair salons and garage (Fisher et al., 2004).

However, these information needs are at an individual-level and are set within certain specific confined instances. Individual-level information needs isolate the studied from either others in a process and surrounding contextual factors of situations. For instance, Fisher et al. (2004) studied the use of library programs by the Queens Borough public library and Courtright (2005) studied health information seeking investigation of Latino newcomers to Southern Indiana in the United States. Similarly, Shoham & Strauss (2008) investigated the information needs of new immigrants' families from North America to Israel and Lingel (2011) studied new immigrants at an international center.

The refugee specific studies includes the work of Lloyd, Kennan, Thompson, & Qayyum (2013) that identified information needs around everyday living and compliance, and Lloyd (2014) that identified health information needs. The information sources identified included trusted mediators, social networks and visual sources. These studies, like the general migrants studies, were individual-level and set within confined instances: Lloyd (2014) studied African refugees and focused on health while Lloyd et al. (2013) studied newly arrived refugees. In this study, we examine contextual and

80th Annual Meeting of the Association for Information Science & Technology, Washington, DC, VA | Oct. 27-Nov. 1, 2017

individual variables including sociological processes in refugee integration for the identification of refugee information needs.

Although information needs, sources and seeking behaviour have indeed been identified, they do not address the processes and procedural dimensions involved. This may be attributed to Wilson (1981) observation of "a failure to identify with the situations within which information needs investigations are carried out." It is advocated that a holistic approach to migrant information studies be adopted, encompassing closer examination of theories and principles of social inclusion and social capital in addition to information behaviour (Caidi, Allard, & Quirke, 2010).

Information behaviour studies being person-centred need not only identify individual-level information needs. The scope of identified information needs can be broadened. A situational approach to information behaviour during refugee integration can provide fuller perspectives to help understand the relationships between contextual factors and human information behaviour in situations that can be used in the actual design of services and provision. This is because information needs identified from situations put any potential person in context.

## CONCEPTUAL BASIS

Those who are forced displaced, i.e., refugees and asylum seekers, are a challenging population to study. Their integration discussion cuts across social, political, economic, structural, socio-cultural and institutional dimensions. In this study, facts, theories and practices of refugee integration were synthesised with theories of information behaviour (Oduntan, 2017). The key topics surrounding refugee integration and information behaviour are discussed in this section. It covers integration, refugee integration systems and the concept of situational information behaviour in refugee integration.

### *Integration*

The humanitarian crisis in the world has continued to escalate. Presently, the UNHCR records over 65 million forcibly displaced persons in the world and refugee integration is now of global concern. However, the concept of integration is "individualised, contested and contextual" (Robinson, 1998). It varies by country depending on the interests, value and perspective of the people concerned, and changes over time (Castles, Korac, Vasta, & Vertovec, 2002). It involves many actors, agencies, logics and rationalities, disparate range of state policies, laws, local initiatives and societal dispositions and the interplay of these agendas (Sigona, 2005).

Integration is surrounded by discussions of whose integration is to be examined as *migrants* is a broad term consisting of many categories. The Council of Europe argued that integration deals with the changing relationship between migrants in general and host societies (Council of Europe, 1997) but the Economic Council on Exiles and Refugees (ECRE) argued that refugees have additional and distinctive needs than other types of migrants thus the integration emphasis is on refugees (ECRE, 2002).

There is a consensus that integration is not straightforward: it is a process of change that is dynamic, two-way, long term and multidimensional (ECRE, 2002). There are processes and systems in host countries to facilitate integration, but, ultimately these are unfamiliar processes, systems and cultures for the migrant especially the refugees who may not have planned their migration, suffer considerable loss, trauma and dislocation amongst others (Korac, 2003). This situation could be made worse by their experiences of navigating the processes and systems for integration in the new country.

### *Refugee Integration Systems*

Globally "refuging" is a right guided according to the UN 1951 Refugee Convention which describes a refugee as someone who "owing to a well-founded fear of being persecuted for reasons of race, religion, nationality, membership of a particular social group or political opinion, is outside the country of his nationality and is unable or owing to such fear, is unwilling to avail himself of the protection of that country." Host countries appropriate the convention as applicable in individual integration systems that are evaluated.

For instance, in the United Kingdom, refugee integration is defined as "the process that takes place when refugees are empowered to achieve their full potentials as members of British society, to contribute to the community, access public services and to become fully able to exercise the rights and responsibilities that they share with other residents in the UK" (Home Office, 2004). Integration is evaluated with an Indicator of Integration framework that includes employment, housing, education and health.

The UN convention is operated in an asylum system in which refugees arrive under different elements. The systems incorporate varied levels of access to provisions including support, benefits, work entitlements and rights to remain. Thus, refugee integration starts on arrival in the host country through the transition process.

There are primarily two categories of persons navigating the integration system. Firstly, there are asylum seekers: people who arrive into the country on their own. They have applied for protection and are awaiting decision. The asylum seekers have minimum access to provisions until granted refugee status. Secondly, there are refugees: people accepted after either asylum applications in their host countries or by selection from refugee camps or their home countries. Such persons have maximum access to provisions and support. However, irrespective of the level of access to provisions, they face the same processes and systems which are unfamiliar and new to them (Da Lomba, 2010).

Refuge seekers are expected to successfully achieve integration over time with the provided processes and systems. However, integration literatures have described the navigation of these processes and systems by the refugees as cumbersome, which has devastating consequences on emotional health, and other aspects of personal integration (Favell, 2001); (Heckmann et al., 2001); (Sigona, 2005); (Zetter, Griffiths, & Sigona, 2005).

The UNHCR reports that over 80% of refugees live below the poverty line in host countries (UNHCR, 2016). This might be related to the cumbersome processes that results in insurmountable difficult situations and the stalling of their integration journey. Thus, in the identification of information needs, there is a need to put into perspective the cumbersome processes and difficult situations during integration. This information behaviour study is approached from a situational angle. A situational perspective enables a focus on the situations in the sociological processes to elicit the information gaps-in-situations.

### *Situational Information Behaviour*

The idea of situations in information behaviour is founded on context. This approach can be traced to Dervin (1976, 1983) who proposed a complex communication-based approach for the contextual study of information needs, seeking and use. This notion of context is also supported by Wilson (1981) who stated the context of any information needs may be the people themselves or the role demands of people's work or life or the environments, including political, economic, technological amongst others within which that life or work takes place.

The power of context for information behaviour studies have been expounded through the literatures including Belkin (1980), Kuhlthau (1993) and Wilson (1997), to name a few. Context is also the feature of the progress and numerous developments achieved in this field. For instance Savolainen's Everyday Life Information Seeking (Savolainen, 1995), Sonnenwald's Information Horizon (Sonnenwald, 1999) and Fisher's Information Grounds (Pettigrew, 1999). Contexts are multi-dimensional and can be described by a variety of attributes and one of the many attributes of context is situation (Brenda Dervin, 2003). Sonnenwald (1999) expanded on situation expressing that situations may be characterised by actions or behaviours that occur over time and are connected by participants. Furthermore, that there may be a variety of situations and a flow of situations arises within any context. Cool (2001) summed situation as a focus of analysis in its own right as it has the potential for bringing together both individual cognitive-level and social-level analyses of human information behaviour. Situations are therefore sub-contextual circumstances where information gaps may be identified following from the above.

**Context ➡ Situations ➡ Information Needs**

Information needs, sources and seeking behaviour are always a by-product of any information studies as has been shown. However, focusing on the power of the situations in a context will specifically target fundamental information needs in and from situations that provides a fuller capacity for inclusion into the design of services and not only in the isolation of provision of services. This promotes further the importance of person-centred investigations and eliminates the limitation of individual-level needs. A situational information behaviour investigation is thus most appropriate in the refugee integration context. This will avoid Wilson (1981) observation of "failure to identify with the situations within which information needs arises" and heed Caidi (2010) advice of "a holistic approach to immigrant's information studies" highlighted earlier.

### *Information behaviour and refugee integration*

Refugee integration is evidently a complicated social process that takes place over time. Information behaviour follows the red thread of information in the social lives of people (Bates, 1999). Refugees find themselves in numerous situations where perhaps a flow of situations arises. In information behaviour, situations are the dynamic environments in which interpretive processes unfolds (Cool, 2001). The situations in refugee integration are a focus for information behaviour study because of the complexities they are characterised by. A couple of inherent complexities are briefly highlighted as a complete discussion of the complexities of refugee integration is not possible.

Firstly, the key word in the UN convention is "persecution" but it has no single definition. Persecutions can be for various reasons as defined by the host country and the scope of persecutions for each host country keeps expanding and evolving with time. Secondly, there are numerous routes of arrival into the host country integration systems. This is alongside the earlier highlighted categories of persons in the integration system. Refugee integration is indeed a complicated phenomenon; a situational information behaviour approach is the only chance that all the variables in the complexity will be factored into the understanding.

## RESEARCH DESIGN

The study adopts an idiographic socio-cognitive approach (Bates, 2005) informed by Dervin sense-making methodology. Sense-making uses a *situation-gap-outcome* metaphor to investigate human experiences (Dervin, 2003). The focus is on where one is coming from, what one is struggling with and where one is going. Refugees navigating the processes and systems in an unfamiliar country are in a move across time-space, they are on an integration journey and the evidence of this journey is their story (Oduntan, 2016). Information behaviour in refugee integration can therefore be accounted using the sense-making metaphor on refugee experiences. The *situation-gap-outcome* metaphor was used in the design of semi-structured interviews taking a cue from the sense-making methodology micro-moment timeline interview (Dervin, 2003). As such, participants recounted their experiences situationally and the information gaps in the situations elicited. The research received ethical approval from the University of Strathclyde ethical board.

The study population was 20 participants: 11 female participants and 9 male participants. Their age ranged between 15 and 50. Two of the participants were minors (accompanied by parents) and five were part of families with young children. Two participants arrived as minors but at the time of interviews were adults. Ten participants had elementary education and 10 graduate level. Participants had lived between one month and 15 years in the host society at the time of data collection between July and December 2016.

| Route | Number of participants |
|---|---|
| Road travel | 7 |
| Port of entry | 4 |
| In-country | 6 |
| Humanitarian/Reunion | 3 |

***Table 1.*** *Arrival routes*

The population consisted of 12 asylum seekers and 8 refugees. Participants were recruited through diversity sampling rather than snowballing, as the latter might have resulted in access to only a specific group either by age or geography. The population geography spans 14 countries including the top countries in the United Kingdom Home Office list of nationalities applying for asylum – Iran, Iraq, Pakistan, Eritrea, Afghanistan and Syria (Home Office, 2016). This wide breadth in countries enables a multi-dimensional exploration of the integration processes and systems experiences since integration is meant for all irrespective of origin.

Table 1 shows the broad range of reasons for persecution in the study population. The reasons include business, political, safety, religious, sexual and war. This highlights the many definitions that can be attributed to the persecution in the UN convention. Likewise, there is no one way of arrival into the system. Table 2 shows the routes of arrival identified in this study population.

The routes are road travel, port of entry, in-country and humanitarian/family reunion. The road travel route includes those that traveled by road through countries including those that journeyed through the Mediterranean Sea. The port of entry route includes those that travelled by air into the host

| Persecution | Number of participant |
|---|---|
| Business persecution | 3 |
| Political persecution | 2 |
| Religious persecution | 3 |
| Safety | 3 |
| Sexual persecution | 1 |
| War | 8 |

***Table 2.*** *Persecution reasons*

country and applied for asylum at the airport. The in-country routes are by those that have been in the country for other reasons and now cannot go back to their home countries for fear of persecution.

The humanitarian/family reunion route includes those that have been given protection status or visas from their home countries. There are two sides to this, either humanitarian – as a result of government going to recruit refugees in refugee camps amongst other places, or family reunion – taken by a refugee already in the host country inviting their family to join them. These arrival routes in relation to the earlier highlighted categories of persons in the integration systems implies the first 3 arrival routes in Table 2 start the integration journey as asylum seekers while those from the humanitarian/family reunion route starts as refugees.

Twenty narrative semi-structured interviews were completed. All interviews were audio recorded and transcribed by the first author. The average interview lasted 1hr 5minutes. Only two of the participants required an interpreter whilst a few others who did not require an interpreter took time in articulating responses to questions. Data was thematically analysed and coded in an iterative process based on the commonalities and diversities in experiences. This allowed a connection to be made between the individual and contextual factors, which enabled the circling out of information gaps in the experiences as they navigated the processes and systems. The emergent themes and patterns from the different experiences were sorted and labelled. Quotes as spoken directly by participants are highlighted in the findings and discussion section to support the themes. Participants requested anonymity; as a result, quotes are not identified.

## FINDINGS AND DISCUSSION

The benefit of a situational approach became immediately apparent as the contextual variables of refugee integration and their effect on information behaviour soon emerged. Asylum applications can be refused before being granted refugee status, and there are sociological provisions for it thus it is a part of the integration process. The first set of information gaps that emerged were around the refused asylum situation. In this section, the information needs and the information sources in asylum refusal situation are discussed. This first set of findings answers one of the research questions in the ongoing study: "*What are the information gaps during refugee integration*?"

### *Asylum refusal*

Asylum refusal is when an asylum application has received negative decision. There are sociological provisions associated with this decision; however, it is surrounded by restrictions and limitation. The asylum process starts with an asylum application submitted to the Home Office – the UK immigration authority. On submission of the application, the asylum seeker is provided with financial support and accommodation through service providers while waiting for decision. This is called the waiting period (in this population sample the waiting period was between 1-6 months).

The positive of the waiting period is stability for asylum applicants while waiting for the asylum decision. This matched participants' anticipation of a "safe haven."

*"When I got to this country, I was like the happiest man in the world, I was so glad. I planned for what I had to do; everything I had to do for my life like how I could go to the university, get married, get a house, have a beautiful life like everyone."*

However, upon receiving a refusal, the data suggests the abruptness with which the newfound stability comes to end is like a sudden crush on utopia. Participants all said they felt lost. They did not understand why they were not granted asylum after the journey that was made, and they did not know what to do.

*"I am still confused now about everything; I am confused about what I have to do next."*

This is because as soon as a negative asylum decision is made, the financial support might stop:

*"The money stop, I am stressed, what will I eat?"*

They might be sent out of their accommodation:

*"The letter came that I should leave the house, I wondered where I will go, where I will sleep? Again another headache problem."*

If not immediately deported after this decision, the refused asylum seeker might be required to fulfil certain conditions such as signing regularly at the Home Office.

*"Even when I was in pain that I could not walk, they forced me to come and sign or else they will stop the money."*

All refused asylum seekers associated this time with uncertainty, confusion, depression, ill health amongst others. This included the in-country applicants who may be thought of as having the advantage of being in the country already but they also do not understand the process.

Some participants expressed frustration at the reasons for their refusal. They felt like it was like the end of the world – especially the newly arrived asylum seekers.

*"After the interview one month later they refused, they say I am lying I am not from Eritrea. When they refused, they say I am not a Christian when I am even a singer in church, I got confused. I ask myself all the time who am I? So I have a court appointment, I took all my photo etc. Then the court said I am a Christian but not Eritrean. I am confused more."*

It is a time of helplessness: some refused asylum seekers, while attending the immigration authority office to sign documents, are removed to a detention center such as Dungavel – a detention center in Glasgow. They are either sent back into society or deported after one or two months. Three of the asylum seekers in this study population have been detained at Dungavel and two have been in and out of detention a number of times.

*"I went to the Home Office to report as usual then they ask me to meet the manager in the office, then I went there and they bring me to Dungavel."*

Participants that had been to Dungavel had difficulties settling back into society after detention.

*"When I was released from Dungavel, actually I slept on the street that night that state was painful, cold and hungry. I went to charities they said no, I went to police station, they said no you can't sleep here. I was trying to get somewhere to sleep and go back to Edinburgh with zero money."*

Asylum refusal is an extreme situation during integration. It is a time of erratic uncertainty. The daily financial support may stop and suddenly start again. Some participants do not know what happens next after the refusal; even though they are often given appeal options, unfortunately most do not understand it. It is a period of numerous events for which the asylum seekers are not prepared, as they have no information on how to deal with it. The information gaps in- situations were circled out from the experiences as it arose during their journey. The identified information gaps in refused asylum situation are detailed below.

### *Legal*

Although refuge seeking is humanitarian, there are legal implications in the host countries. Asylum refusal is in particular a legal issue because refused asylum seekers are allowed to appeal the asylum decision until a time when the appeal is exhausted. The legal information gaps centred on:

### *Solicitor*

The data showed participants were unclear about solicitor roles and reputation despite how crucial they were to the process. This was irrespective of the level of education. A graduate level participant said:

*"They gave me a paper to call the lawyer but they did not tell me what to call the lawyer for."*

There is no dignity in the selection of solicitors as there is no way offered to select solicitors such as by reputation.

*"They gave us a list of contacts for immigration lawyers I ask them which one is a good solicitor and they say they are all OK and can pick whichever one you like."*

For most, it is an interpreter who takes them to a legal firm. Solicitors send staff as representatives to promote their services – an employee that speaks the language of the asylum seekers.

*"When we are coming new, one boy works with a lawyer as an interpreter and any new person to red road, he comes and takes them to the lawyer, so he took me to the lawyer."*

For some, such as those in detention centers, contact with solicitors is through a drop-in while others receive a contact list by the official service providers only.

> *"The solicitor do not help you get out, they only say when you get out call me."*

There were issues of complacency, poor treatment and discrimination. All participants said the solicitors treated their cases poorly but they continued working with the solicitor for fear of the consequences. All participants who were refused asylum on their first application attributed this to the solicitor, while those successful on first application said a solicitor was not needed until asylum was refused. Either way, this can be associated to the lack of information on the roles of the solicitor and selection criteria.

> *"It took him 2 months to finish my assessment just to translate and write everything which is too long."*

Some did not know lawyers were free. In an exceptional case, one in-country participant struggled with payments to a lawyer until informed of Legal Aid – the government financial support for the costs of legal advice.

### *Appeals and Court*

The data showed dealing with appeals and the different courts processes was an area of difficulty. A few refused participants did not understand what the process entailed and the implications:

> *"Now, I like Glasgow people. But the system do not do me good. I am not killing anyone or fighting and they tell me to go to court."*

The reasons for this can be multidimensional, though might be related to their level of education but it could also be a cultural issue. There is a need for appeals and courts practices to be clear. Some did not know how to deal with the appeals. Some do not know what it is called:

> *"When they refused I got confused, so I have another court appointment, I took all my photo etc."*

The other "court appointment" is an appeal, where more evidence is required to defend the refusal. Others did not know what to do when they felt discriminated against. An in-country applicant said:

> *"I was called a liar, a criminal, my kids were told to go back to where their color origin from, when they are 18 they should come back."*

It is evident that dealing with legal processes is complicated for the refused asylum seeker and the arrival route appeared to have an impact on the experiences.

### *Housing*

The experiences showed asylum housing is surrounded by numerous issues. The UK Home Office provides accommodation through a service provider – all participants complained of the attitudes, lack of respect, approaches and poor treatment by the accommodation provider and they had no information on how to deal with it.

> *"The service providers don't treat us like humans, they treat us treat us like s**t."*

### *Content*

There were breach of privacy experiences. Half the study population were not provided information on what was allowed in the allocated flats. Participants said the service providers visited the provided accommodation in the absence of occupants to check the contents of the house especially electronic appliances. The outcomes of those visits are often traumatic: it may include the Home Office suddenly stopping support for asylum seekers possessing electronics such as television or tablets in the accommodation. For example, an asylum seeker in Glasgow was asked to go to London:

> *"Now the Home Office stop the money because I have a television and ask me to appeal it at the first hearing tribunal in London."*

### *Eviction*

There is no eviction procedure. Eight of the asylum seekers had experienced an attempt by the service provider to lock them out of the accommodation in their absence. Participants indicated not being given any notification to prepare them for the event and being unaware of how to deal with the situation.

> *"I put my key it did not go in, I was worried what do I do, then I call my solicitor then solicitor said he will contact the service provider to find what happened. The owner turned up and was introduced and he said I'm not supposed to be there that I should go to friends, I told him I had no friend, I have nowhere to go. So he knocks on the door and a man with a box of tools comes out embarrassed and I went in quick because I know once I went inside there is no way, they'll move me, they said I have 24 hours to move out and leave. Once they left you start thinking, it's so painful, so stressful don't know how to put it."*

The data suggested eviction resulted in homelessness. The refused asylum participants had no information on where to get help or how to deal with homelessness.

> *"I got a letter from the home Office that my asylum is refused. They take the flat keys from me, I was homeless for 1 month. They did not tell me anything, nothing."*

Homelessness and destitution often end up being a recurring event for the refused asylum seeker as refused asylum decision are appealed repeatedly until they are eventually granted status.

### *Allocation*

There were issues around accommodation sharing that revolved around tolerance. It is not clear how flats are shared but appeared to be between people of different nationalities and languages. Participants were not provided information on the rules of co-habitation. Quite a number of participants had difficulties agreeing with flatmates on issues of cleanliness, visitors, late nights etc.

> *"My flatmate said he is not able to clean the bathroom because he does not speak English and I said to him you do not need to speak English to clean yourself."*

This may appear domestic and not require the involvement of authorities, however the existence of co-habitation rules will not only drastically reduce disputes but most importantly will prolong the life of the asylum accommodation, as quite a number of these homes end up being demolished.

## EDUCATION

Participants had no information on what education is accessible. This particularly concerned the minors in the population. A young participant said

> *"I never knew I go to school, I stayed at home for 7 months until a day my mum took me to a meeting with the council that was when we were told I go to school."*

Although, adult refused asylum seekers are not entitled to formal education, minors are entitled to formal education until the end of high school.

The minor participants had no information on how to fulfil the education curriculum requirements. For instance, the education curriculum requires work experience as part of high school; however, immigration laws prevent the asylum seeker from any form of employment.

> *"All my friends are on work experience but I can't because I am asylum seeker so I stay at home."*

This was a major dilemma for the young participants and they expressed how much they wanted to fully complete the high school education curriculum.

### *Language*

English language classes were a major difficulty on arrival, especially for those from countries where English is not their first language. Participants had no information on how to get into language classes. It appeared there were many English language classes available however getting into an English class proved difficult. All participants lamented how long it took to get into a class. A recently arrived asylum seeker broke down in tears during the interview as she discussed her ordeal with language.

> *"The most important thing for me is the language, I can't speak any English, I can't do anything without it."*

Participants had no information on the boundaries of the roles of service providers during integration. Half the research population got into language classes by themselves after waiting for the service providers for a period of time.

### *Social*

Participants had difficulties forming bonds in society, and as a result resorted to staying indoors.

> *"I stay indoor all day because I am afraid to go out, I only go out when I have appointment with the lawyer or Home Office."*

This also included minors that did not know how to tell their schoolmates they were asylum seekers.

### *Extra-curricular*

The minors that have been refused asylum with their parents had no information on how to attend events and make friends. They did not know how to go on camping trips, beach trips and prom like other kids in school. They had no information on how to access the required attire for special events.

> *"There was this charity shop and I saw this very nice dress, it was £10 but I cannot afford it and asked them can I borrow it for 1 day and return it and they asked why do you need it and I said for prom and she said if you can't afford a dress for a party then don't think to go to the party."*

The circumstances surrounding asylum refusal are tough and it appeared that the authorities understand the implications of the actions but the goals are unclear.

> *"I go to the Home Office every Friday to sign and every time the Home Office ask me who help you."*

The measures surrounding the provision for refused asylum seekers creates destitution which could be tantamount to desperate situations. This unfortunately forces hooliganism and bears considerable psychological and physical trauma on the individuals. This was understandably evident in the behaviour of some of the participants who involuntarily turned aggressive during interviews.

> *"I feel like I am like in a prison, though I am in safety but in a big prison."*

The irony of these actions results when such persons are eventually granted status: it would seem that the society gets a now emotionally unstable person, considering how long refused asylum seekers may live in the country. The period of asylum refusal for this study population was between 11 months and 11 years.

These information needs identified from the refused asylum situation provide a two-way benefit that will mitigate refused asylum circumstances significantly for both asylum seekers and the host society. They will guide the availability of appropriate information to asylum seekers and enable the design of person-centred integration services by the host society, which will alleviate the marginalisation of refugees in the long term.

### *Information Sources*

Information sources are also outcomes of information behaviour studies. The identified information sources during refused asylum include:

### *Friends*

Friends were the most popular source of information consistent with previous research (Lingel, 2011), (Silvio, 2006), (Courtright, 2005) (Fisher et al., 2004). A participant said her friend from the English class told her she could go to a computer school. Another participant heard about volunteering from friends. For another it was a friend that told him to go to service providers for transport support to fulfil an identity request by the Home Office.

> *"We did not know these things existed but when you talk to people we get information about what is for us."*

Friends included inmates at the detention center. A participant currently in their 11th year as a refused asylum seeker said:

> *"All through this times I look for friends to talk to, some who are in the same situation or someone who can speak my language."*

### *Internet*

The internet was a common source of information in this study population.

> *"I went to the library close to the accommodation and used the computers to get information about schooling."*

Only three participants did not use the internet. This is because of their inability to speak English.

## INTERPRETERS

Interpreters emerged as a key source of information for the non-native English speakers in the study population.

> *"I trust to go with him go the lawyer because he can speak my language."*

This applied especially for getting a lawyer and local travel.

## CASEWORKERS

A caseworker is assigned by service providers to facilitate the provision of services to refugees and asylum seekers.

> *"My caseworker gave me advice, she gave me everything in a paper and showed me everything and where I can go to college."*

These sources of information are not completely surprising considering the participant were dealing with asylum refusal. Friends such as people in similar situations will be more comfortable sources of information. As one of them accurately compared

"The condition is really different between asylum seeker and refugee, if you come as a refugee lots of people help you there is benefit and support from service providers but who come as asylum seeker no one help them they start from zero."

Furthermore, the information sources could be implied to emphasize the role of social capital and its types in the integration of refugees explicated in Oduntan (2017). Bonding social capital of close family and friends in this case just friends. Bridging social capital of loose friends and workmates as seen in participants that got information from inmates at the prison. Linking social capital of people out further as in the participants that got information from case workers and interpreters.

## CONCLUSION

Refugee integration systems are indeed complicated sociological processes that refugees and asylum seekers journey through in numerous dissimilar states. The study findings pinpoints refused asylum as one of the states in refugee integration and highlights the information needs embedded in this situation. The situational information behaviour approach enabled a new kind of generalisable findings that honours diversity and individuality while at the same time addressing the human universals in refugee integration such as legal aspects, education aspects and others. The idea of situational information need extends the outreach of person-centred investigations and eliminates the isolation of individual-level needs.

The research data demonstrated the systems complexity and individual complications in refugee integration processes. Firstly, refugee integration is not straightforward. In addition to the individual factors such as the origin, the level of education, the journey and others, there are numerous reasons for persecution – the key word in the UN 1951 convention statement. Secondly, there are numerous routes of arrival into the system. These characteristics emphasise diversity as a strength for situational information behaviour studies.

The research findings show that information behaviour can be used to inform and enhance the design of integration services and provisions. The information behaviour in refused asylum situation revealed information needs across legal, accommodation, education and social dimensions. These have implications for the design of person-centred sociological provisions by the host society while providing for availability of information to asylum seekers during refugee integration. In addition, the identified information sources – friends, internet, interpreters and caseworkers, have implications for access to information and service delivery during refugee integration.

The findings also suggest the likely existence of other unexplored situations in refugee integration which can be the subject of further research locally and internationally. Refugee integration is a revolving geopolitical issue that will always be complicated, however the understandings from information behaviour investigations will reveal the emergent information needs at any given point in time strengthening the capacity of integration provisions and services.

## ACKNOWLEDGMENTS

I would like to especially thank my research participants – refugees and asylum seekers, for their openness. I am also grateful for the support of Strathclyde iSchool Research Group.

## REFERENCES

Bates, M. J. (1999). The invisible substrate of information science. *Journal of the American Society for Information Science, 1999, Vol.50(12), p.1043-50, 50*(12).

Bates, M. J. (2005). An introduction to metatheories, theories, and models. In Fisher, Karen E., Erdelez, Sanda, and McKechnie, Lynne, Eds. *Theories of information behavior*. Medford, NJ: Information Today.

Belkin, N. J. (1980). Anomalous states of knowledge as a basis for information retrieval. *Canadian Journal of Information Science, 5*, 133-143.

Borko, H. (1968). Information science: What is it? *American Documentation, 19, 3-5.*

Caidi, N., Allard, D., & Quirke, L. (2010). Information practices of immigrants. *Annual review of information science and technology, 2010, Vol.44, pp.493-531, 44.*

Castles, S., Korac, M., Vasta, E., & Vertovec, S. (2002). Integration: Mapping the field.

Cool, C. (2001). The concept of situation in information science. *Annual review of information science and technology, 35*, 5-42.

Council of Europe. (1997). Measurement and indicators of integration.

Courtright, C. (2005). Health information-seeking among Latino newcomers - An exploratory study. *Information research: An International Electronic Journal, 10*(2), 224.

Da Lomba, S. (2010). Legal status and refugee integration: A UK perspective. *Journal of Refugee Studies, 2010, Vol. 23(4), pp.415-436, 23*(4).

Dervin, B. (1976). Strategies for dealing with human information needs: Information or communication? *Journal of Broadcasting, 1976, Vol.20(3), p.323-333, 20*(3).

Dervin, B. (1983). *An overview of sense-making research: Concepts, methods and results to date.* Paper presented at the International Communication Association Annual meeting, Dallas.

Dervin, B. (2003). Given a context by any other name: Methodological tools for taming the unruly beast. In B. Dervin & L. Foreman-Wernet (Eds.), *Sense-making methodology reader:Selected writings of Brenda Dervin*. Cresskill, NJ: Hampton Press.

Dervin, B. (2003). A theoretic perspective and research approach for generating research helpful to communication practice. In B. Dervin & L. Foreman-Wernet (Eds.), *Sense-making methodology reader:Selected writings of Brenda Dervin*. Cresskill, NJ: Hampton Press.

ECRE, Economic Council on Refugees and Exile. (2002). Position on the integration of refugees in Europe.

Favell, A. (2001). Integration policy and integration research in Europe: A review and critique. In T. A. Aleinikoff & D. B. Klusmeyer (Eds.), *Citizenship today: Global perspectives and practices* (pp. 349-399). Washington, DC: Brookings Institute/ Carnegie Endowment for International Peace.

Fisher, K. E., Durrance, J. C., & Hinton, M. B. (2004). Information grounds and the use of need-based services by immigrants in Queens, New York: A context-based, outcome evaluation approach. *Journal of the American Society for Information Science and Technology, 55*(8), 754-766. doi: 10.1002/asi.20019

Heckmann, F., Lederer, H., Worbs, S., Dominique, S., Krief, P., & Peignard, E. (2001). Effectiveness of national integration strategies towards second generation migrant youth in a comparative European perspective.

Home Office, UK. (2004). *Integration matters: A national strategy for refugee integration*. http://217.35.77.12/archive/England/papers/welfare/pdfs/COI_NATI.pdf: Home Office.

Home Office, UK. (2016). *Immigration Statistics, April to June 2016*. https://www.gov.uk/government/publications/immigration-statistics-april-to-june-2016/asylum#key-facts.

Korac, M. (2003). Integration and how we facilitate it: A comparative study of the settlement experiences of refugees in Italy and the Netherlands. *Sociology-The Journal of the British Sociological Association, 2003 Feb, Vol.37(1), pp.51-68, 37*(1).

Kuhlthau, C. (1993). *Seeking meaning : A process approach to library and information services*. Greenwich CT: Ablex Publishing Company.

Lingel, J. (2011). Information tactics of immigrants in urban environments. *Information Research, December 2011, Vol.16(4), 16*(4).

Lloyd, A. (2014). Building information resilience: How do resettling refugees connect with health information in regional landscapes – implications for health literacy. *Australian Academic & Research Libraries, 45*(1), 48-66. doi: 10.1080/00048623.2014.884916

Lloyd, A., Kennan, M. A., Thompson, K. M., & Qayyum, A. (2013). Connecting with new information landscapes: Information literacy practices of refugees. *Journal of Documentation, 2013, Vol.69(1), p.121-144, 69*(1).

Oduntan, O. (Producer). (2016). Doctoral Student Research Video Competition: Information Behaviour of Refugees.

Oduntan, O. (2017). Information behavior of refugees: Viewing refugee integration through an information science lens. *Bulletin of the Association for Information Science and Technology, 43*(3), 63-69. doi: 10.1002/bul2.2017.1720430320

Pettigrew, K. E. (1999). Waiting for chiropody: Contextual results from an ethnographic study of the information behaviour among attendees at community clinics. *Information Processing and Management, 35*(6), 801-817. doi: 10.1016/S0306-4573(99)00027-8

Robinson, V. (1998). Defining and measuring successful refugee integration. *Proceedings of ECRE international conference on integration of refugees in Europe*: European Council on Refugees and Exiles.

Savolainen, R. (1995). Everyday life information seeking: Approaching information seeking in the context of " way of life." *Library and Information Science Research, 1995, Vol.17(3), pp.259-294, 17*(3).

Shoham, S., & Strauss, S. (2008). Immigrants information needs: Their role in the absorption process. *Information Research-An International Electronic Journal, 13*(4).

Sigona, N. (2005). Refugee integration(s): Policy and practice in the European Union. *Refugee Survey Quarterly, 2005, Vol.24(4), pp.115-122, 24*(4).

Silvio, D. H. (2006). The information needs and information seeking behaviour of immigrant southern Sudanese youth in the city of London, Ontario: An exploratory study. *Library Review, 55*(4), 259-266. doi: 10.1108/00242530610660807

Sonnenwald, D. H. (1999). *Evolving perspectives of human information behavior: Contexts, situations, social networks and information horizons*. Paper presented at the Exploring the Contexts of Information Behavior: Proceedings of the second international conference in information needs, seeking and use in different contexts, Sheffield England.

UNHCR, United Nations High Commissioner for Refugees. (2016). UNHCR Global Trends Report - 2015 in review. *UNHCR Global Trends Report - 2016 June*, p1-67.

Wilson, T. D. (1981). On user studies and information needs. *Journal of Documentation, 1981, Vol.37(1), pp.3-15, 37*(1).

Wilson, T. D. (1997). Information behaviour: An interdisciplinary perspective. *Information Processing and Management, 1997, Vol.33(4), pp.551-572, 33*(4).

Zetter, R., Griffiths, D., & Sigona, N. (2005). Social capital or social exclusion? The impact of asylum-seeker dispersal on UK refugee community organizations. *Community Development Journal, 2005, Vol.40(2), pp.169-181, 40*(2).

# Investigating Barriers to "Using Information" in Electronic Resources: A Study with e-Book Users

**Devendra Potnis**
*University of Tennessee at Knoxville, USA. dpotnis@utk.edu*

**Janine Pino**
*Pellissippi St. Comm. College, USA. jcpino@pstcc.edu*

**Kanchan Deosthali**
*University of Mary Washington, USA. kdeostha@umw.edu*

## ABSTRACT

**Students' ability to use information plays a key role in influencing their adoption and continued usage of e-books. This pilot study investigates the barriers to using (i.e., searching, managing, processing and applying) information in e-books experienced by 25 library and information science graduate students (LISGS) at a land-grant university in the United States. The analysis of study participants' in-depth qualitative responses using grounded theory principles reveals 60 barriers that affect their ability to use information. These barriers are related to (a) e-readers, (b) features of e-books, (c) psychological, somatic, and cognitive status of the respondents, (d) cost and (e) policies. We present the adverse effects of these barriers on the respondents' ability to search, manage, process and apply information in e-books. For instance, the psychological, somatic and cognitive statuses of respondents affect their ability to process information the most. Barriers related to e-readers and e-books have collectively the most damaging effect on the respondent's ability to search, manage, process and apply information. Due to a series of unavoidable barriers, respondents who originally intend to use e-books for utilitarian purposes end up using this electronic resource mostly for hedonistic reasons. Implications are discussed at the end.**

## KEYWORDS

use of information, barriers to using information, electronic resources, e-Books, library and information science, graduate students.

## INTRODUCTION

The use of information in e-books plays a key role in creating a number of utilitarian and hedonistic benefits, and hence, incentivizing students to adopt and continue using e-books (Cassidy, Martinez, & Shen, 2012; Walters, 2013). For instance, a gain in academic productivity serves as one of the main utilitarian benefits for the students capable of using information in e-books (Chen, 2015; Hoseth & Clure, 2012; Nicholas, Rowlands, & Jamali, 2010). Typically, such students use e-books to create work and study flexibility in their busy schedules. Students can do faster research by "fact finding" and "finding relevant information" (Johnston, Berg, Pillon, & Williams, 2015; Lee, 2015; Staiger, 2012). Students use e-books as reference books by locating specific textual and numeric data. Some students use information in e-books for hedonistic purposes like leisure reading, pleasure and fun activities (Berg, Hoffman, & Dawson, 2010; Cassidy, Martinez, & Shen, 2012; Jamali, Nicholas, & Rowlands, 2009). Hence, to understand, explain and predict the adoption of e-books, it is important to study the barriers to using information in e-books.

### Use of Information

T.D. Wilson (2000) describes the *use of information* as a combination of the physical act (e.g., highlighting sections in a text) and mental act of comparing of new information with existing knowledge for processing information to learn something new. The process of using information also involves the application of mental schemas and emotional responses within a larger socio-cultural context.

The existing literature suggests the following four broad stages of using information in e-books: searching information in the resources, managing information in the resources, processing information and applying information to complete specific tasks (Chen, 2015; Joo & Choi, 2015; Mishra, Allen, & Pearman, 2015). Searching involves formulating a query to locate information within a particular information resource (Makri, Blandford, & Cox, 2008). Meho and Tibbo (2003) define information managing as filing, archiving and organizing information collected or used in facilitating various tasks or activities. Ellis and Haugen (1997) propose distinguishing, filtering, selecting and extracting information as key components of processing information. Application of information involves matching the ability of information to create value for the user to accomplish tasks and goals like enjoyment for deriving utilitarian and hedonistic benefits respectively (Nicholas, Rowlands & Jamali, 2010).

### Research Questions

Rarely any study shows barriers to using information in e-books, and the way in which these barriers affect various physical and mental acts, and emotional responses to using information in e-books. This paper fills the gap by studying the following research questions:

80[th] Annual Meeting of the Association for Information Science & Technology, Washington, DC, VA | Oct. 27-Nov. 1, 2017

**R1**: What barriers do students experience when using (i.e., searching, managing, processing and applying) information in e-books?

**R2**: How do barriers to using information shape their e-book usage?

## RELATED RESEARCH

### *Barriers to Using Information in Electronic Resources*

Past studies show that individual factors such as cognitive and psychological state, awareness and knowledge about electronic resources, and literacy level and skills adversely affect information use by students. The following individual factors could negatively influence students' use of information found in electronic resources in libraries: low level of commitment to finding information, lack of time to search information, negative attitude toward searching information, lack of awareness about available information sources and how to search them, awareness of their friends' specific information seeking behavior, and willingness to abide by tutors' instruction (Rowley, 2016). A study with 221 undergraduate students found that bit literacy, one's ability to use information, influences the use of information most, followed by virtual community literacy and technical literacy in that order. Low perceived utility of libraries' electronic resources also shapes students' intention to use the information in those resources (Lee, 2015). However, user training could change this perception. A mixed methods study surveying undergraduate students in three rounds (pre-course, post-course, and follow-up) highlights the significance of training students for using information in electronic resources in libraries; the user training positively influences students' use of electronic resources including e-books (Chen, 2015). A study conducted with 332 undergraduate students discovered that usefulness and ease-of-use positively influence undergraduate students' use of online library resources (Joo & Choi, 2015). Lack of confidence and expertise constrain individuals' ability to use information for making decisions, especially to reduce uncertainty in various information environments (Mishra, Allen, & Pearman, 2015). Thus, individual factors associated with students' psychological and cognitive status primarily discourage them from using electronic resources and information in them.

## BARRIERS TO USING E-BOOKS BY STUDENTS

A majority of studies point out technology-related barriers (e.g., software associated with e-books, devices in the form of e-readers, etc.) to using e-books. After reviewing 92 papers, which include 75 user studies (i.e., studies conducted with students, faculty/researchers, staff, and librarians) and 17 literature reviews, Adam Girard (2014) identifies three categories of barriers: physical barriers (software and hardware), cognitive barriers, and socio-cultural barriers, which deter users, including students, from adopting e-books. According to Girard's (2014) classification, physical barriers include ability to print, ability to highlight, ability to bookmark, searchable file formats, screen size or resolution, ability to annotate, and ability to copy and paste dictionary terms. Cognitive barriers cover general perception, barriers to adoption, and barriers to learning; and finally, socio-cultural barriers are comprised of a group-thinking that equates the use of e-books to betraying paper books and cultural norms that reading print books slow down the adoption of e-books (Landoni & Hanlon, 2007).

Student-centric studies also find eyestrain (Marques de Oliveira, 2012), price (Foasberg, 2011), uncertainty in using e-books for research, lack of awareness about e-books (Wang & Bai, 2016), and the limited availability of free e-books and digital rights management as other key barriers that inhibit students' e-book adoption and usage (Eschenfelder, 2008). Lack of usability is a major factor creating barriers to using e-books for students. A study conducted with undergraduate students found that the usability of e-books influenced by learning task characteristics, technology characteristics, and individual student characteristics shape the e-book usage by study participants (Mafunda, Bere, & Swart, 2016). Viewing experience, perceived mobility, readability of e-books and text satisfaction were found to have a positive and significant association with acceptance of e-book devices by 219 students (Park, Sung & Cho, 2015). In addition, low performance expectancy, high price or unaffordability of e-books, and the habit of using print books detract undergraduate students from adopting e-books on mobile devices (Yee, Qi, Yong, Wee & Yee, 2015).

In recent years, several empirical investigations employ or identify theoretical constructs from psychology and communication to examine or confirm the factors influencing adoption of e-books by students. For instance, Cassidy, Martinez and Shen (2012) studied the differences in behavior, perception and attitude of graduate students adopting e-books for research purposes. Johnston et al. (2015) explored the ease of using e-books and their usefulness as measures of student experience in a multi-platform e-textbook pilot. Deosthali, Potnis, Elliott & Fesmire (2015) find perceived ease of using e-books, compatibility, and attitudes of 140 undergraduates influence their adoption of e-books. To study e-book adoption by undergraduates, Marques de Oliveira (2012) focused on the attitudes, perceptions and behaviors of the e-book users. Hoseth and McLure (2012) explored students' negative and positive attitude and perception toward e-books. A study conducted with undergraduate students enrolled in a large course at a Midwestern university found that perceived usefulness of e-books positively predicts e-book views, which does not necessarily reflect e-book usage, but perceived ease of use predicts e-book highlights, an indicator of using e-books (Peng, Ratan & Khan, 2015). Thus, rarely any study on e-book adoption studies the barriers to using information in e-books, which is the unique contribution of this study.

## METHODOLOGY

We designed a semi-structured survey using Drupal, a content management platform, to collect data from the potential study participants. Considering the chronic debate and subsequent variation in conceptualizing the term "e-books," highlighted in Velagić's (2014) article "The Discourse on Printed and Electronic Books," we decided to build a common understanding among the respondents for the term e-books before they take the survey. Hence, we displayed the following definition of "e-book" on the survey website: "text in digital form, a book converted into digital form, digital reading material, a book in a computer file format, or an electronic file of words and images" (Rao, 2003; Velagić, 2014). This broad definition indicates that e-books could be used for any purpose and the reading or interaction could take place on any digital platform, including personal computers, mobile phones, tablets and dedicated e-readers. However, it is important to note that all study participants reported dedicated e-readers like Kindle and Nook as their only way to read or interact with e-books, and hence, reported barriers to using these dedicated e-readers alone.

After IRB clearance, a link to the online survey was broadcast on a pre-existing email listserv for library and information science graduate students (LISGS) at a land-grant university in the United States. This survey was announced in the middle of a semester in 2015. There was no incentive to complete the survey. Students' participation was voluntary. They were assured of anonymity and confidentiality of their responses. This data collection approach gave potential respondents plenty of time to reflect on their experience of using e-books in the past. To learn about the barriers to using information in e-books, we asked respondents to share their experience of using information in e-books in detail. In particular, our open-ended questions required LISGS to tap into their memory of the *process* of learning, using, and extending e-book features for carrying out various activities. Key survey questions asked respondents to report the barriers to searching, managing, processing and applying information in e-books. Multiple stories and instances of using or not using information helped us contextualize the barriers that respondents experienced to using information in e-books. We received 25 responses with a response rate of 13.83%. We analyzed responses received from unique IP addresses alone. We did not consider multiple responses from a single student. Only the last attempt of respondents to fill in the survey was considered for data analysis.

### *Choice of Participants*

The academic disciplines of students shape their perception and ability to use e-books (Nicholas, Rowlands & Jamali, 2010). Hence, we decided to focus on students from a single discipline for this study. LISGS often receive formal training to access, evaluate and use a myriad of information resources and information within those resources. Several of them work or volunteer for libraries, which exposes them to library patrons' ability to use or not use information in e-books. In addition, LISGS are likely to explain the *process* of using information in e-books better, which is a unique feature of this study when compared to a majority of past studies involving undergraduate students.

Study participants generated rich details of the process of using information in e-books. For instance, study findings provided insight to understand: (a) the way barriers to using information shape study participants' intended purpose (utilitarian vs. hedonistic) of using e-books, (b) why they do not use e-books for quick reference, (c) how they form a negative perception toward e-books, and (d) their overall opinion and expectations from e-books.

For instance, by applying grounded theory principles, we developed open, axial, and selective codes manually to identify 60 barriers to using information in e-books, which we then clubbed into the following five clusters related to: (a) e-readers, (b) features of e-books, (c) psychological, somatic, and cognitive status of LISGS, (d) cost, and (e) policies (Strauss & Corbin, 1998). Table 1 demonstrates how we used open codes and axial codes to identify *features of e-books*, a selective code, as one of the barriers to using information in e-books. Two authors coded the barriers independently and the inter-coder reliability was around 90%.

| **Open Codes Line by line coding of sample barriers** → | **Axial Codes Clustering of barriers** |
|---|---|
| Lack of or insufficient hyperlinks to go back and forth between the main body and table of content/footnote/endnote/external web resources or switching windows back and forth on screen | Navigation and bookmarking issues related to interactive e-books |
| Too many "clicks" required to access the required content | |
| Absence or lack of user-friendly table of content | Issues related to information editing and organizational characteristics of e-books |
| Naming convention for snippets or poorly labelled files | |
| Lack of OCR or OCR sometimes does not allow searching | |
| Cannot photocopy e-book pages like print books | |
| Separation of text and relevant images/charts on diff. screen views | |
| Uneven page formatting | |
| Content format other than PDF | Issues related to formatting, and presentation of information in e-books |
| Dysfunctional content enhancements | |
| Images are not resizable in e-books | |
| Poor text quality | |
| High text density, tiny text, or small details on a particular page or view | |
| Frequent loading and reloading of pages | Access and retrieval issues |
| Slow load time for PDFs | |
| PDFs as images are not searchable | |
| Page numbers don't match up with the print version | |
| Lack of integration of e-books with other software like Evernote | |
| Lack of "search" feature | |
| Slow search time for large file size | |

***Table 1**. Selective code: features of e-books*

## FINDINGS

All of the respondents had prior experience of using e-books. Due to the distance education model of the research site, survey respondents were based out of Florida, Georgia, Kentucky, Michigan, Tennessee, Texas and Virginia. Around 50% of respondents were in the age group of 25 and 35. Around 75% of respondents (n=18) were female. Table 2 shows the adverse effect of 60 barriers on four broad stages of using information in e-books.

| # | Barriers | Four Sets of Activities For "Using Information" Adversely Affected by the Barriers | | | |
|---|---|---|---|---|---|
| | | S | M | P | A |
| | Cluster A: e-readers | | | | |
| 1 | Clunky, older generation of e-readers | | | | √ |
| 2 | Awkward to hold devices | √ | | | √ |
| 3 | Reading from backlit screens | | | √ | |
| 4 | Unintuitive or difficult to understand user interface | √ | √ | | |
| 5 | Variation in page/location depending on the device | √ | | | |
| 6 | Accessing e-books on assistive devices | | √ | | |
| 7 | Glaring screens | | | √ | √ |
| 8 | Lengthy process to operate e-readers | | | | √ |
| 9 | Difficulty in browsing/navigating | √ | √ | | √ |
| 10 | Difficult to see or access notes | | √ | | √ |
| 11 | Highlighting and making marginal notes is more complicated than print books – OCR often does not allow highlighting | | √ | √ | |
| 12 | Losing place if not bookmarked | √ | | | |
| 13 | Cannot always copy, paste, or print desired content directly from e-readers | | √ | | |
| 14 | Slow to flip from one page to another compared to print books | √ | | | |
| 15 | Cut and paste formatting is not always clean | | √ | | |
| 16 | Difficult to annotate | | | √ | |
| | CLUSTER B: FEATURES OF E-BOOKS | | | | |
| 17 | Absence or lack of user-friendly table of content | √ | | | |
| 18 | Lack of or insufficient hyperlinks to go back and forth between the main body and table of content/footnote/endnote/external web resources or switching windows back and forth on screen | √ | | | √ |
| 19 | Cannot photocopy e-book pages like print books | | √ | | |
| 20 | Naming convention for snippets or poorly labelled files | | √ | | √ |
| 21 | Separation of text and relevant images/charts on different screen views | | | √ | |
| 22 | Frequent loading and reloading of pages | √ | | √ | |
| 23 | Slow load time for PDFs | | | | √ |
| 24 | Uneven page formatting | √ | | | √ |
| 25 | High text density, tiny text, or small details on a particular page or view | | | √ | √ |
| 26 | Poor text quality | | | √ | √ |
| 27 | PDFs as images not searchable | √ | | | |
| 28 | Images are not resizable in e-books | | | | √ |
| 29 | Page numbers don't match up with the print version | √ | | | |
| 30 | Dysfunctional content enhancements | | | √ | √ |
| 31 | Content format other than PDF | √ | | | |
| 32 | Lack of OCR or OCR sometimes does not allow searching | √ | √ | | |
| 33 | Slow search time for large file size | √ | | | |
| 34 | Lack of "search" feature | √ | | | |
| 35 | Lack of integration of e-books with other software like Evernote | | √ | | √ |
| 36 | Too many "clicks" required to access the required content | | | √ | |
| | CLUSTER C1: PSYCHOLOGICAL STATUS | | | | |
| 37 | Feel unsafe to carry e-readers everywhere | | | | √ |
| 38 | Seems harder to get absorbed in the same way compared to print books | | | √ | |
| 39 | Not as fun to read for pleasure | | | √ | |
| 40 | Annoying when grabbing block quotes | | √ | | |
| 41 | Don't like to read text on screen | | | √ | |
| 42 | Feel strange to read short pages | | | √ | |
| 43 | Emotional connection or personal preference for print books | | | | √ |

| | | | | | |
|---|---|---|---|---|---|
| CLUSTER C2: SOMATIC STATUS | | | | | |
| 44 | Strain on fingers due to constant scrolling | | √ | | |
| 45 | Strain on eyes due to flowing screens | | | √ | |
| 46 | Typing errors | √ | √ | | |
| | | | | | |
| CLUSTER C3: COGNITIVE STATUS | | | | | |
| 47 | Doesn't lend itself well to visual remembering "where" the information was written vs. in a physical book for study purposes – lack of spatial memory | √ | | | |
| 48 | Gets distracted more easily by e-books; harder to focus/concentrate to remember the content; and less attention span with screens | | | √ | |
| 49 | Less understanding of the content when read from screen as opposed to read from the print page | | | √ | √ |
| 50 | Difficult to visually estimate the progress of reading – harder to determine how much you've read and how much is left | | | | √ |
| 51 | Lack of knowledge about the capabilities of a particular resource or platform | | √ | | |
| 52 | Lack of willingness to learn using e-books | | | √ | |
| | | | | | |
| CLUSTER D: COST | | | | | |
| 53 | More expensive than print books | | | | √ |
| 54 | A number of pre-requisites to use e-books (e.g., internet, e-readers, memory required to store e-books, etc.) | | | | √ |
| 55 | Inability of libraries to purchase all available catalogues | | | | √ |
| | | | | | |
| CLUSTER E: POLICY | | | | | |
| 56 | Lack of interoperability among platforms | √ | | | |
| 57 | e-books platforms without updates | | | | √ |
| 58 | Unable to download any content | | √ | | |
| 59 | Digital rights management (DRM) restrictions on the amount of content that can be copied and pasted | | √ | | |
| 60 | DRM restrictions on the amount of content that can be downloaded | | √ | | |

***Table 2.*** *Barriers to using information in e-books*

**S**: Searching Information; **M**: Managing Information; **P**: Processing Information; **A**: Applying Information

The following sub-sections describe the barriers to using information in e-books, and their adverse effects in detail.

### *A. E-readers*

A majority of respondents shared barriers to using their old Nook and Kindle e-Readers when asked about barriers to using information in e-books, which highlights the significance of e-Readers in using information in e-books. Respondents, irrespective of gender, complained that clunky, older generation e-readers are often awkward and heavy to hold and carry around, which in turn adversely affects the ability to apply information within e-books. R5, a 34-year-old male student from Tennessee, complained: "…when I use e-books that are cook books it is difficult to apply that information because I need to be able to look at a recipe but I cannot always bring my device into the kitchen with me." A majority of features of e-readers create hurdles to carry out physical activities associated with e-books. One of the most common complaints made by respondents was their inability to highlight, copy, paste, or annotate the content in e-books, which does not allow them to manage information in e-books efficiently. R15, a 34-year-old female student from Kentucky cannot highlight, copy, and paste into another document. R17, a 31-year-old female student from Texas, reported the incompatibility between software programs, which does not allow her to manage information: "Sometimes it isn't easy to copy portions of e-books over into another program if you want to take notes, as well as having an effective system to manage the notes that are taken. Some e-books won't allow the user to copy and paste the info into another program." Due to screen glare, R21, a 31-year-old female student from Tennessee, prefers reading actual paper and hardback books. She noted that other challenges experienced by patrons at her library include reading from backlit screens and accessing e-books from assistive devices. As academic institutions and publishers move away from print materials toward e-books, it becomes an imperative to make all e-books accessible.

Multiple steps involved in operating e-readers make it a lengthy process to use information in e-books. As a result, R13, a 26-year old female student from Georgia, prefers to use print books over e-books, especially when she needs a quick reference: "It still seems quicker to flip through a book in a hurry…there are just too many steps to turn on device and open up e-reader app. E-reader is uncomfortable to hold; don't have same sense of progress by looking at thickness of book, and how much is left." Thus, a majority of the criticism related to "e-readers" creates unsatisfactory usability experience for the respondents.

### *B. Features of e-books*

Visual appearance of the textual content and images also play a key role in shaping the reading experience for respondents. R24, a 45-year-old female from Tennessee said, "Pleasure is certainly muted in stories. The images in e-books are often not resizable. As a person who has trouble reading tiny print, [it] is very limiting when viewing images that include text or small details." R16 noted, "PDFs sometimes reproduce poor text quality; text density on a particular page or view."

Lending, sharing and photocopying have all been accepted as the prerogative of print book users, which is not the case with e-book readers (Marques de Oliveira, 2012). R1, a 31-year-old female from Tennessee, noted, "I have sometimes wished that I could photocopy a page of an e-book like with a physical book. I haven't found a good way to reproduce bits of an e-book for note-taking or quick reference like I could by photocopying a useful graph in a physical book'. R12 informed us about her preference for print books: 'If I'm using a book as a reference for a paper or assignment, I prefer to have a print copy of the book so I can look at its pages while working directly on the assignment (in Word or another program)."

While venting her dissatisfaction for the features of e-books, which make it challenging for the respondent to search information, R17 said, "Some e-books don't have an effective search feature and are more difficult to navigate. If you hit the wrong button--you can be taken to the end or the beginning of the book and unless you can place multiple bookmarks--your place is lost. Your page/location can be different depending on what device you access an e-book from." She also complained that e-books' varied in formatting styles, and e-readers like Kindle, Nook, etc. put the same text on different pages. As reported by past research, the lack of consistency challenges users' efforts to search and manage information in e-books (D'Ambra, Wilson, & Akter, 2013). Some e-book features also create obstacles for respondents to process information found in e-books. R18 recorded his dissatisfaction about multiple features of e-books: "most e-books are searchable, but sometimes the table of contents is not designed well and [it is] difficult to jump to a certain part. Also, some e-books don't keep page numbers that relate to the physical counterpart." R7, a 50-year-old female student from Tennessee, blames the naming convention of e-book files for not being able to search and manage information in e-books: "poorly labelled files (i.e. "I'm sure I'll remember this--I don't need to write it down" syndrome)." She added, "optical character recognition (OCR) inadequacy, online library books often don't allow cutting and pasting."

### *C. Individual Factors*

#### C1. Psychological

Anyone with an emotional attachment to paper books is likely to negatively influence the relationship between user attitude towards e-book readers and adoption of e-books (Yee et al., 2015). After being an avid reader for years, R10, a 35-year-old female from Kansas, seems to be emotionally bonded with print books; hence, she finds it difficult to use e-books. Her personal preference is to use print books over e-books anytime. Readers like her sometimes equate the use of e-books to betraying paper books (Landoni & Hanlon, 2007).

#### C2. Somatic

R10 pointed out a number of somatic barriers to using information in e-books: "Screens are physically taxing for some people--eyestrain, keyboard/mouse = wrist/elbow strain--less attention to the info." These barriers adversely affect one's ability to manage, process, and use information found in e-books. An excess of screen reading strains several respondents' eyes, which makes it challenging for them to continue reading e-books. Eyestrain has been the most frequently reported somatic barrier to using e-books by students (Marques de Oliveira, 2012).

#### C3. Cognitive

Respondents with visual memory have a hard time managing and processing information in e-books. R23, a 40-year-old male student from Tennessee said, "In a physical book, it seems easier for me to remember where things are. If I make a note on a page or attach a tab to a page in a physical book, I'm able to flip right to it when I'm looking for it. I can't do that as easily in e-books." R15 finds it harder to remember it afterwards, harder to flip back and re-read favorite parts or parts to refresh memory. R17 encounters the same issues: "If I am having difficulty processing information or fully understanding information, I like to be able to write it down and I associate e-books with mobility and not having the ability to stop and take physical notes and write." Some respondents have inherently less cognitive abilities to process digital information. R5 admitted that she has less understanding when she reads from a screen as opposed to reading from the page. Due to the lack of wider attention spans with a screen, R8 also finds it challenging to process, and hence, use information in e-books. R3, a 50-year-old male student from Michigan, finds it a little harder to concentrate with e-books. R22, a 25-year-old female from Tennessee said, "Many readers (including myself) find it much harder to focus and understand information when reading from a screen." R25, a 30-year-old female from Virginia, gave a technical explanation for her inability to process information in e-books: "Even though it is not popular to say, there is a tactile-brain connection that is missing from digital resources."

Several e-book features create cognitive barriers in terms of breaking concentration of respondents when processing and using information in e-books. R5 reported how the navigation features of e-books distract him: "I have trouble flipping back and forth between pages because I have to think about the process and not about what I am reading or looking for." R12 presented a long list of problems caused by different types of features of e-books, which make it difficult for him to search and manage information: "I find them relatively hard to browse. On my PC, I usually have to zoom in to be able to read the text of an e-book, and as a result, I have to use the scrollbar to read a full page. I also have to click between pages, loading and re-loading each page individually, which breaks concentration more than simply flipping a page. These things aren't huge problems, but such issues add up to make the experience of reading an e-book less immersive than reading print, in my experience."

### *D. Cost*

Typically, price serves as one of the greatest barriers for students to use e-readers (Foasberg, 2011). For instance, to be able to use e-books, one needs have an e-reader, a high-speed internet connection and access to an e-book collection. This combination of pre-requisites makes it harder for students to use information in e-books. R9 said, "Internet, e-book subscription charges, expensive memory to download e-books, etc. make it an expensive proposition to use e-books." R10 complained that e-books are always less expensive than print books, but one can hardly own them. In addition, the cost of using mobile data on e-readers deters respondents from using e-books on the go. Due to the unaffordability of operating e-readers on the go, respondents prefer to use information found in e-books whenever they are in public areas with free Wi-Fi, which takes away one of the main advantages of using e-books –around-the-clock availability (Staiger, 2012).

R2, R15 and R21, who access e-books made available by academic libraries, pointed out the cost of catalogues as one of the key constraints, limiting the ability of libraries to purchase e-book catalogues. Due to licensing fees and the increased cost of perpetual access to content, the total cost of e-books is typically higher than their printed counterparts (Slater, 2010). In an online journal, the content available can grow with every new issue for the duration of the library's subscription. An e-book, on the other hand, charges libraries for sustained use of the same exact content. Most of the time, a new edition of an e-book counts as a new title leading to a new set of annual payments (Walters, 2013).

### *E. Policies*

A majority of the respondents held different types of policies (e.g., organizational policies, digital rights management, etc.) accountable for not being able to manage information. R6, a 30-year-old female from Tennessee, complained that some e-books only allow a limited amount of copying, which discourages her from using e-books. R11 and R13 do not like DRM since DRM restrictions limit her ability to copy, print, or save files. R4, a 35-year-old male student from Tennessee, noted his frustration for using e-books: "Copy-paste functionality and other storage functionality is often hindered, poorly implemented, or altogether impossible within a publisher's proprietary e-book environment." R20 reported how accessing e-books through library websites limits her ability to manage information in e-books: "I don't like having to download things, and many library-provided e-books limit the amount you can download." Past research identifies additional policy barriers in the form of license terms, lease conditions and access restrictions, which are likely to affect students' use of information in e-books (Walters, 2013).

## PURPOSE OF USING INFORMATION IN E-BOOKS, PERCEPTIONS, AND EXPECTATIONS FROM E-BOOKS

As a result of experiencing a large number of barriers to searching, managing, processing, and applying information in e-books, almost all of the respondents end up using e-books for pleasure rather than completing any work-related task or professional activities. R17 informed us that she currently uses e-books more frequently for pleasure reading rather than completing homework due to the inability to take effective notes. R11, who has formed a negative perception toward e-books, thinks that e-books are a pain. However, he thinks that reading e-books for pleasure is easier, because there isn't the time constraint of "I need to get this information NOW." This clear distinction between the utility of e-books and print books suggests that e-books and print books are not competitors, confirming that the two formats are coexisting, with each answering to different purposes and learning styles (Staiger, 2012). R23 never follows and remembers information from e-books as well as she does from physical books. Hence, she uses e-readers for casual/leisure reading. The respondents' preference for using e-books for leisure is in congruence with what Foasberg (2011) discovered after surveying students at a four-year public college. He found that they use e-books primarily for leisure reading and rely on print books for their homework and other reading related activities. Respondents in this study cannot take notes in their e-books; they cannot navigate e-books in a non-linear fashion. Some of these limitations of interacting with e-books also prompt them to use e-books for leisure reading.

Typically, students do not immerse themselves in e-books. They use e-books for fact-finding and prefer bite size chunks of information (Nicholas, Rowlands, Jamali, 2010). This "use rather than read" approach undermines the intellectual value of e-books. However, R12 and several other respondents reported non-reliance on e-books for fact-finding or quick reference. R12 said, "If I need a quick reference, I'm less likely to use an e-book, as it seems like going to more trouble than a print book or smaller electronic resource (e.g., an online article)." Previous research shows that due to self-determined need, students use e-books for brief skimming rather than readings on any one title (Slater, 2010). In contrast, this study finds that due to multiple steps involved in firing up e-readers and opening them to access e-books, LISGS do not rely on e-books for skimming or quick reference. E-books do not meet the users' urgency for searching and using information. They prefer print books to e-books for quick reference, especially since it is easier to flip through any section of the book they wish using print books. Printing, searching full-text, and ease of use are the top-three features that typically influence users' opinion about e-books (Zhang & Beckman, 2011). Due to multiple barriers related to the features of e-books, several respondents use negative labels like "annoying," "frustrating," "painful," etc. when detailing their inability to use information in e-books. For instance, R24 finds it annoying when grabbing block quotes from e-books. Multiple steps required to copy and paste the e-book content creates a hurdle to manage information.

## LIMITATION

This study was conducted with a small sample of 25 LISGS. Hence, study findings do not represent the entire student population in North America. All of the respondents often referred to dedicated e-readers like Nook and Kindle, which suggest that study findings and conclusions related to e-readers might not be applicable to other forms of e-readers like computers, mobile phones, tables, iPads, etc. Unlike some studies (e.g., Wang & Bai, 2016), this study did not distinguish between academic and non-academic e-books, or publishers of e-books, and hence, it could not distinguish between the barriers to using information in different types of e-books. A majority of respondents reported reading e-books for leisure, which suggests that their responses are with reference to non-academic e-books.

## CONCLUSION AND IMPLICATIONS

This pilot study adopts a process-based, qualitative approach and taps into the experiences of LISGS to learn about the barriers to using information in e-books accessed mostly over Kindle and Nook. This study advances the existing research on e-book usage by identifying 60 barriers to searching, managing, processing, and applying information in e-books. Around 72% of barriers negatively affect only one out of four sets of activities that respondents undertake to use information. Barriers related to e-readers and features of e-books, collectively, have the most damaging effect on the respondent's ability to search, manage, process, and apply information. The inability of the respondents to carry out a set of physical activities associated with using e-books creates a mental dissatisfaction for using e-books, thereby hindering the use of information found in e-books. However, none of the respondents intend to discontinue using e-books. This finding suggests that the value created by advantages of e-books outweigh that of disadvantages. One of the key advantages frequently mentioned by respondents in this study was the "searchability" feature.

The inability of respondents to address the barriers to "using information" related to e-readers and e-books is one of the key factors restricting their use of e-books to hedonistic purposes. For instance, respondents who originally intended to use e-books for utilitarian purposes end up using this information resource mostly for hedonistic reasons like leisure reading, fun activities (e.g., guide for cooking, stitching instructions, etc.), and pleasure. As a result, none of the respondents mentioned identifying information needs, query formulation, or evaluation of information, which are some of the key steps for using information for utilitarian purposes (Ellis & Haugan, 1997; Makri, Blandford, & Cox, 2008). Unlike previous research studies, this study discovers that respondents do not use information in e-books for quick reference, in part because e-books do not meet their urgency for searching and using information (Nicholas, Rowlands, & Jamali, 2010; Slater, 2010). Multiple steps involved in operating e-readers make it a lengthy process to use e-books as a quick reference.

## THEORETICAL IMPLICATIONS

This study finds that psychological and cognitive factors mostly affect only the ability of respondents to *process* information, one of the four sets of activities undertaken by them to use information in e-books. This fact explains the low variance theoretical models with psychological and cognitive variables proposed and tested for understanding the factors influencing adoption of e-books by students (For example D'ambra, Wilson, & Akter, 2013). Since factors related to e-readers and features of e-books have the most damaging effect on the student's ability to search, manage, process, and apply information, it is necessary for future studies on e-book usage to examine the adoption of e-books from a human-computer interaction perspective instead of heavily relying on psychological and cognitive variables.

This study informs the literature on IT adoption by demonstrating the role of information use in the continued usage of IT artefacts. This study identifies 60 barriers to using information in e-books. Their overall process of using information is likely to shape the perceived usefulness of e-books, the perceived ease of using e-books, and the degree to which they can control the process of using e-books (i.e., perceived behavioural control), which are cognitive and psychological variables frequently employed by past research on IT adoption (Potnis, 2015). Hence, the future research could consider "information use" (i.e., a combination of searching, processing, managing, and applying information), a theoretical construct from the information science discipline, to better understand, explain, and predict the continued usage of IT.

## PRACTICAL IMPLICATIONS

This study finds that the psychological, somatic, and cognitive statuses of LISGS affect their ability to process information the most. Hence, to measure the success of e-book initiatives for training students, academic libraries should consider developing key performance indicators that assess the ability of students to process information in e-books. Technological barriers have the most damaging effect on all four activities that are part of using information in e-books. Hence, to improve the usability of students' interaction with e-books, device manufacturers and e-book publishers need to address the technological barriers with a high priority, which is also likely to influence the continued usage of e-books by students. Device manufacturers, publishers, and content aggregators can become more responsive to address the barriers reported in this study, by having DRM with easier access, note-taking feature improvements, enhanced hardware to make viewing the e-books easier, etc. This responsiveness is likely to enhance the continued and future student usage of e-books for utilitarian as well as hedonistic purposes.

## REFERENCES


Berg, S., K. Hoffman, & D. Dawson. (2010). Not on the same page: Undergraduates' information retrieval in electronic and print books. *Journal of Academic Librarianship,* 36 (6), 518-525.

Cassidy, E., M. Martinez, & L. Shen. (2012). Not in love, or not in the know? Graduate student and faculty use (and non-use) of e-books. *Journal of Acad. Librarianship* 38, (6), 326-332.

Chen, Y. (2015). Testing the impact of an information literacy course: Undergraduates' perceptions and use of the university's libraries' web portal. *Library and Information Science Research,* 37 (3), 263-274.

D'Ambra, J., C. Wilson, & S. Akter. (2013). Application of the task-technology fit model to structure and evaluate the adoption of e-books by academics. *JASIST,* 64 (1), 48-64.

Deosthali, K., Potnis, D., Elliott, D., & Fesmire, S. (2015). Factors influencing adoption of e-books by students. *International conference of the Association of Global Management Studies,* New York, NY, 195-205.

Ellis, D., & M. Haugan. (1997). Modelling the information-seeking patterns of engineers and research scientists in an industrial environment. *Journal of Documentation,* 53 (4), 384-403.

Eschenfelder, K. (2008). Every library's nightmare? Digital rights management, use, restrictions, and licensed scholarly digital resources. *College & Research Libraries*, 69 (3), 202-225.

Foasberg, N. (2011). Adoption of e-book readers among college students: A survey. *IT and Libraries,* 30 (3).

Girard, A. (2014). Reader's block: A systematic review of barriers to adoption, access and use in e-book user studies. *Information Research,* 19 (June).

Hoseth, A., & M. Clure. (2012). Perspectives on e-books from instructors and students in the social sciences. *Reference & User Services Quarterly, 51* (3), 278-288.

Jamali, H., D. Nicholas, & I. Rowlands. (2009). Scholarly e-books: The views of 16,000 academics. *Aslib Proceedings, 61*(1), 33-47.

Johnston, D., S. Berg, K. Pillon, & M. Williams. (2015) Ease of use and usefulness as measures of student experience in a multi-platform e-textbook pilot. *Library Hi Tech, 61*(1), 65-82.

Joo, S., & N. Choi. (2015). Factors affecting undergraduates' selection of online library resources in academic tasks: Usefulness, ease-of-use, resource quality, and differences. *Library Hi Tech, 33*(2), 272-291.

Landoni, M., G. Hanlon. (2007). E-book reading groups: Interacting with e-books in public libraries. *The Electronic Library, 25*(5), 599-612.

Lee, J. (2015). An exploratory study on adolescents' perceptions of library and their information use. *Journal of the Korean Society for LIS, 49*(3), 351-370.

Mafunda, B., A. Bere, & J. Swart. (2016). Establishing determinants of electronic books utilisation: An integration of two human computer interaction adoption frameworks. In M. Kurosu (Ed.), *HCI. Novel user experiences: 18th intl. conf., HCI International, Toronto, Canada, July 17-22, 9733.* (pp. 549-562). Springer.

Makri, S., A. Blandford, & A. Cox. (2008). Investigating the information-seeking behavior of academic lawyers. *Information Processing & Management, 44*(2), 613-634.

Marques de Oliveira, S. (2012). E-books usage by students at Andrews University: A study of attitudes, perceptions, and behaviors. *Library Management, 33*(8/9), 536-560.

Meho, L., & H. Tibbo. (2003). Modeling the information-seeking behavior of social scientists: Ellis's study revisited. *JASIST, 54*(6), 570-587.

Mishra, J., D. Allen, A. Pearman. (2015). Info. seeking, use, and decision making. *JASIST, 66*(4), 662-673.

Nicholas, D., I. Rowlands, & H. Jamali. (2010). E-book use, info. seeking behavior and its impact: Case study business and management. *Journal of Information Science, 36*(2), 263-280.

Park, E., J. Sung, & K. Cho. (2015). Reading experiences influencing the acceptance of e-book devices. *The Electronic Library, 33*(1), 120-135.

Peng, W., R. A. Ratan, & L. Khan. (2015). *Ebook uses and class performance in a college course.* Paper presented at the 48th Hawaii International Conference on System Sciences. Koloa, Hawaii.

Potnis, D. (2015). Applying information science lens for advancing critical research on IT adoption: Insights from continued usage of mobile phones by poor women in rural India. *International Journal of Technology Diffusion, 6*(1), 76-99.

Rao, S. (2003). Electronic books: A review and evaluation. *Library Hi Tech, 21*(1), 85-93.

Rowley, J. (2016). *Information Marketing.* New York: Routledge.

Slater, R. (2010). Why aren't e-books gaining more ground in academic libraries? E-book use and perceptions: A review of published literature and research. *Journal of Web Librarianship, 4*(4), 305-331.

Staiger, J. (2012). How e-books are used: A literature review of the e-book studies conducted from 2006 to 2011. *Ref. & User Services Quarterly, 51*(4), 355-365.

Strauss, A., & J. Corbin. (1998). *Basics of qualitative research: Techniques and procedures for developing grounding theory* (2nd ed.). Thousand Oaks, CA: Sage.

Walters, W. (2013). E-books in academic libraries: Challenges for sharing and use. *Journal of Librarianship and Information Science, 46*(2), 85-95.

Wang, S., & X. Bai. (2016). University students awareness, usage and attitude towards e-books: Experience from China. *Journal of Acad. Librarianship, 42* (3), 247-258.

Wilson, T. (2000). Human information behavior. *Informing Science: The International Journal of an Emerging Discipline, 3*(2), 49-56.

Yee, C., Qi, N., Yong, S., Wee, Y., & Yee, Y. (2015). Factors influencing behavioral intention to adopt mobile e-books among undergraduates: UTAUT2 framework. Universiti Tunku, Petaling Jaya.

Velagić, Z. (2014). The discourse on printed and electronic books: Analogies, oppositions, and perspectives. *Information Research, 19*(2).

Zhang, Y., & R. Beckman. (2011). E-book usage among chemists, biochemists and biologists: Findings of a survey and interviews. *Issues in Science and Technology Librarianship, 65*(8).

# Identifying the Reasons Contributing to Question Deletion in Educational Q&A

**Manasa Rath**
*School of Communication & Information (SC&I), USA.*
*manasa.rath@rutgers.edu*

**Diana Floegel**
*School of Communication & Information (SC&I), USA.*
*diana.floegel@rutgers.edu*

**Chirag Shah**
*School of Communication & Information (SC&I), USA.*
*chirags@rutgers.edu*

## ABSTRACT

Community question-answering (CQA) services are widely used by information seekers looking to ask questions and obtain accurate, personalized answers. Though general CQA sites such as Yahoo! Answers attract a diverse pool of users from many walks of life, other sites cater to a specific user pool. While identifying bad CQA content is generally important in order to improve sites' overall health and community knowledge-sharing, examining educational CQAs is particularly urgent in order to help struggling students understand why their questions fail, re-frame their inquiries in a more accurate manner based on feedback, and ultimately receive correct answers that facilitate their learning process. Otherwise, students' questions would merely be deleted, meaning they lose multiple opportunities to enrich their knowledge base. In this work, we focus on questions posted to Brainly, the largest educational CQA site, in order to first identify "bad" questions and next understand what textual (content-based) features contribute to such questions' poor quality. Using a sample of 1,000 questions–500 of which were deemed "good" and 500 of which were deemed "bad" by site moderators– we attempt to automatically classify question quality in order to label which questions would be deleted and therefore go unanswered. We then use human assessment to expand upon a typology to classify poor quality questions based on 14 textual features in order to identify why they have been marked for deletion. Finally, we propose a method to automatically identify questions' problematic textual features in order to provide feedback to students posting "bad" questions and ensure that they are given the opportunity to revise and improve their inquiries to obtain accurate answers that resolve their information needs.

## KEYWORDS

community question-answering; question deletion; quality factors; textual features; classification

80th Annual Meeting of the Association for Information Science & Technology, Washington, DC, VA | Oct. 27-Nov. 1, 2017



## INTRODUCTION

Community question-answering (CQA) sites are online platforms on which users can ask and answer questions using natural language. Such activity allows information seekers and sharers to satisfy their information needs and impart knowledge in a personalized manner, as discussed by Shah et al. (2012); Ponzanelli et al. (2014). Some CQAs such as Yahoo! Answers and Quora do not focus on specific topics or populations, but rather facilitate information exchanges between a diverse group of users with a wide range of search topics and knowledge expertise. Other sites such as Stack Overflow cater to a specific topical area such as programming. Here, we focus on a third and vital type of CQA site: those that exist for educational purposes. Such platforms present their own unique potential–and set of potential challenges–due to the students who depend on them for school assistance. In general, it is important for any CQA to contain high quality content. Posted questions should meet a high standard (e.g., be clear, appropriate, and comprehensible) in order to attract sufficient and accurate answers. Such exchanges contribute to a site's reputation, which in turn expands its user community and increases user satisfaction. Typically, platforms select human moderators to evaluate their content, and said moderators delete any questions they deem to be inappropriate, incomprehensible, or otherwise "bad." It follows that those who ask deleted questions receive neither feedback on their submission nor answers to their intended inquiry. In the context of educational CQA, this process is dangerous and counter to CQA sites' main purpose; e.g., to help users satisfy their information needs with the help of their peers as discussed in Chua and Banerjee (2013).

Educational CQA provides a number of teachable moments that should be taken advantage of to benefit individual student sites' overall communities, and sites' reputations. In this work, we strive to improve educational CQA sites by ensuring that students who post "bad" questions understand where they went wrong and how to fix it so they both obtain an answer to satisfy their original query and learn how to better phrase their information needs in the future. To meet our goal, we examined a number of questions deleted by moderators on Brainly. We selected Brainly specifically because it is the largest educational CQA, allowing middle school and high school students to ask and answer questions related to eighteen subjects (e.g., Physics, Arts, Social Studies, etc.).

Thus, data from Brainly lends us a tremendous opportunity to aid student CQA users. As with other CQAs, moderators within Brainly delete questions that contain atypical, inscrutable or otherwise inappropriate content, as researched by Correa and Sureka (2014); Xia et. al. (2016); Ponzanelli et al. (2014). In other words, questions are evaluated for their quality, and those deemed "bad" are merely deleted from the site, leaving their askers wondering where they went wrong and how they will obtain help with their information needs.

In this work, we hope to amend this process to give educational CQA users the opportunity to understand their mistakes and revise their questions for re-posting. According to Agichtein et al. (2008), "properly framed" or "good" questions receive accurate answers. Thus, our work will help student askers attract sufficient responses. Additionally, by providing feedback, we hope to improve askers' overall skills to ensure their ability to post high quality questions in the future, thus benefiting students' education process and Brainly's overall content. We begin by using Brainly moderators' evaluations as ground truth. We attempt to automatically replicate their quality assessments to first classify questions as "good" or "bad." This mere dichotomy, however, is not enough to truly assist students with their information needs in CQA. Therefore, based on a typology developed by Harper et al. (2008); Shah et al. (2012) as well as moderators' unstructured annotations, we next build a classifier using textual features that indicate what content contributes to questions' inefficiencies. By automatically detecting some specific attributes that make a question poor, we can provide helpful feedback to its initial asker. Our paper seeks to answer the following inquiries:

**RQ1:** Given a question, how well can we predict the likelihood of the question being deleted?

**RQ2:** What possible attributes contribute to a "bad" question?

The paper proceeds as follows. First, we present a literature review that discusses the background of content-based studies on CQA sites. Next, we explain our research method, which combines both human and textual assessments of the questions collected in Brainly. We follow with an explanation of the proposed prediction model along with our findings. Finally, we review the study's limitations and discuss future directions.

## LITERATURE REVIEW

Though this study presents a novel way in which to assist educational CQA users through automatic classification of question-type and textual features, previous research provides a solid foundation on which we can base our understanding of both CQA users' behaviors and CQA content. The purpose of our research is not only to identify and understand "bad" questions, but also to use question improvement as an opportunity to foster student learning. We hope that, by teaching students how to properly phrase CQA inquiries, they will be better equipped to engage in information seeking via Q&A sites in the future.

### *Question-Answering*

Because we are ultimately examining students' questioning skills, it is important to review research that examines potential reasons for information seekers' behaviors. These works deepen our understanding of why users may post improperly framed questions. Question-answering behavior is characterized by a large amount of uncertainty. Taylor (1968) explained that the information seeker at first is unable to articulate their information need (e.g., visceral need, conscious need) in its beginning stages. However, after forming a mental description of said need, the information seeker resorts to their inter-subjective interpretation and formulates a query. Consequently, the askers who are looking for information may need to specify their questions in order to obtain relevant answers.

Question-answering services can be categorized into online and face-to-face interactions that include library reference services. In fact, the role of library virtual reference services (VRS) has been compared to online Q&A sites by Shah and Kitzie (2012). As of today, many library VRS are considered expert-based services that provide better quality content than peer-based Q&A services, as discussed by Shah et al. (2012). However, publicly funded VRS tend to dwindle as explained by Henderson and Bosch (2010). Thus, though libraries continue to provide vital resources for students, the students themselves may be more likely to turn to CQA for help with their queries. It is therefore important to examine the existing content-based studies of Q&A sites, which have looked into the evaluation of question-answer pairs and answer pairs.

### *Content Quality in CQA sites*

Our work requires an understanding of overall content quality both as a concept and as a factor behind related phenomena. In order to understand the stakes behind our aim to evaluate question quality, it is important to review salient literature related to CQA content. Agichtein et al. (2008); Aritajati and Narayanan (2013) demonstrated the high correlation between question quality and answer quality. They also showed that high-quality answers improve a CQA's popularity. Li et al. (2012) developed three dimensions that examine a question's "social quality": (1) user attention, (2) answering attempts, and (3) best answer. In other words, high-quality content should attract user attention, which leads to more answering attempts that provide a "best answer" within a period of time.

Content-based Q&A sites evaluate answer quality when predicting overall information quality. Information quality itself has been studied in regard to questions and answers with different textual features (e.g., answer length, number of words, etc.) and non-textual features (e.g., information about the asker's profile, etc.). Agichtein et al. (2008) defined question quality in a CQA as "well-formedness, readability, utility, and interestingness" (p.7). There have been associated relationships found among users, questions, and answers that can estimate the question quality.

Asaduzzaman et al. (2013) explain why a question fails to be answered. According to their research, a question may fail to attract an expert answerer if it is too short, unclear, vague or hard to follow, a duplicate question, impatient, irregular or inconsiderate, too specific, or too time-consuming. Other studies have investigated question quality within CQA sites like Stack Overflow and Yahoo! Answers. Arora et al. (2015) proposed a method to improve the question quality prediction accuracy based on questions in Stack Overflow on the basis of guidelines and quality standards listed by the forum. Asaduzzaman et al. (2013) assessed questions based on how long they took to answer, and proposed an approach that would automatically detect the questions that would receive delayed responses.

Li et al. (2012) proposed mutual reinforcement-based label algorithm to detect question quality using textual features and askers' respective profiles. Ravi et al. (2014) presented a technique to automatically detect question quality with the help of topic models. The authors also extended their work to examine the effect of question quality on the dynamics of user behavior and the longevity of questions in CQA sites. Correa and Sureka (2014) proposed a way to investigate the deleted questions and reported 66% accuracy in predicting the dataset based on four feature categories: user profile, community based, content based, and stylistic features. Our research strives to build on such work to obtain higher accuracy and extend examinations into practical performance improvement. It has been observed that deleted questions contain syntactical errors, misspellings, and/or semantic errors (Correa and Sureka (2014); Xia et al. (2016); Ponzanelli et al. (2014); Arora et al. (2015)).

Our research expands upon these factors and demonstrates that it is necessary to automatically identify low quality questions to reduce moderators' workload. The automatic classification of questions into "good" and "bad" categories detects whether a question needs revision or deletion. This feature helps the user to reformulate their query once the system classifies its standing. As indicated by the literature reviewed above, allowing a user to reformulate their inquiry into a better quality question will likely result in better quality answers and more informed users. This is a stronger alternative to simply deleting a low quality question. Given the urgent and educational nature of sites such as Brainly, this concept becomes only more relevant when applied to school-related CQAs where users would benefit from constructive feedback. Thus, this research falls under the realm of question quality and investigations that explore possible reasons behind questions' inefficiencies.

As Mai (2013) explains, such explorations are paramount because, with respect to content quality, "for the quality of the information accessed, it must mean something to somebody in some context" (p.675). In other words, poor question quality begets poor overall content quality, and thus impedes a CQA's ability to function and a student's ability to learn.

## METHOD

Given that our study seeks to recognize, identify, and analyze "bad" content in an educational context, we considered a dataset from Brainly, the largest educational CQA. Based on automatic classification's potential to identify "bad" questions and present helpful feedback through textual analysis, we chose to focus on translating human assessment into automatic classification of textual features. Though this presents limitations–particularly in terms of context–that will be discussed later, it provides an excellent start into an untapped area with immense potential to improve educational CQA experience. We collected a random sample of deleted and undeleted questions from Brainly's database from the first week of January 2016. Those questions that were answered by community members were labeled as "good." Currently, Brainly moderators manually evaluate questions for quality control. When they determine, a question is "bad," they delete it in order to maintain the site's impressive collection of quality content. For the purposes of this paper, deleted questions are "bad" questions.

Two trained coders from a major U.S. university examined a total of 820 deleted questions (here considered the "bad" questions) from the first week of January 2016. After removing non-content based questions (e.g., mathematical equations), they developed a coding scheme (or typology) based off commonalities and patterns present in low quality questions. They also adopted question-type labels to assign to each "bad" inquiry. They based their work off typologies developed by Harper et al. (2008); Shah et al. (2012). Some questions were assigned to more than one category based on their content, as proposed by Tesch (2013). Throughout this process, the coders revisited the scheme to ensure consistently assigned labels and to resolve the mutual differences in their work. They began with a set of ten questions, then convened to discuss their thought processes and eliminate mutual disagreements. In the end, a total of 500 deleted questions comprised our main analysis.

Cohen's Kappa was used to calculate the inter-coder reliability (ICR) among the coders which is listed in Table 4. Questions in which the content appeared in a different language, was garbled, or contained typos demonstrated higher inter coder reliability. However, the coders had diverging opinions regarding overly broad and meaningless questions. Coders were first asked to examine questions and determine their question-type. The types developed here are based on Harper et al. (2008); Shah et al. (2012), both of whom used a dataset from Yahoo! Answers. Inquiries were sorted into five types: Opinion-Seeking, Advise-Seeking, Information-Seeking, Self-Expression, and Not-Applicable.

Table 1 provides definitions for each question type. After coding an ini-tial set of ten questions and convening to discuss differences, the coders separately examined 50 questions and established an acceptable ICR value, as noted in Table 4. Remaining questions were evenly divided between the assessors, who were instructed to first assign each question to one of the five question-types, and then further classify questions using the typology presented in Tables 2 and 3 (e.g., Too broad, Meaningless, etc.). Each question was coded "Yes" or "No" for each category. For example, if they considered a question to be "Too broad," they would mark "Yes"; if not, they would "No."

| Question Type | Definition and Example |
|---|---|
| Opinion-Seeking | An act of asking for non-factual information from others, perhaps when considering a purchase.<br>Example: Toyota Corolla or Honda Civic for mileage? |
| Advise-Seeking | When individuals seek guidance/help from others (who are assumed to have experience or knowledge) when making a decision.<br>Example: Can we use an Android charger in place of an Apple charger for an iPhone? |
| Information-Seeking | The act of actively seeking information to answer a specific query.<br>Example: How do we make an appointment with a doctor? |
| Self-Expression | The act of expressing your personality, feelings, and opinions in daily life.<br>Example: Write an essay on "A friend in need is a friend indeed." |
| Not Applicable | A question that cannot be identified as one of the categories mentioned above.<br>Example: ANDNSKJNMMdnd-klfflmkf |

***Table 1:*** *Types of Deleted Questions in Brainly using the typology provided by Shah et al. (2012).*

## OBTAINING TEXTUAL FEATURES

We considered 500 "good" and 500 "bad" questions from Brainly. For the purpose of this study, "bad" questions are those that were deleted by the moderators, whereas "good" questions are those that were not deleted by the moderators. Using our data from the first week of January 2016, we used a Python program to automatically extract the following 14 textual features:

1. Total number of words: The total words per question was calculated to determine the question's specificity.
2. Total number of characters: The total characters in each question, including special characters and white spaces, were recorded.
3. Average number of words in a sentence: The average number of words per sentence was calculated using the mean total number of words present in the question's total number of sentences.
4. Total number of sentences: This measure reflected the total number of sentences written by an asker to express their information need.
5. Total number of misspelled words: A dictionary was created using PyEnchant, a Python based spell checker, to detect the misspelled words present in each question.
6. Question beginning with an interrogative word: The presence of interrogative words – "what", "where", "when","who","whom","why","how"– at the beginning of each question was noted.
7. Question starting with a small letter: The presence of a small letter can be discovered using a pattern-matching function to locate lower-case letters present in the beginning of a question.
8. Readability scores of the question: Flesch Kincaid (Kincaid et al. (1975)) readability scores were calculated that signified the ease of reading the questions based on the number of syllables present in a word.
9. Total number of punctuation marks: The total number of punctuation used in each question was detected. Marks included: , (), ., ;, , [].
10. Question ending with a question mark: It was determined whether each question ended with a question mark (?).
11. Total number of interrogative words: The total number of interrogative words present in each question was recorded.
12. Presence of a taboo word: A pre-built dictionary was used to extract the taboo words from the questions.
13. Presence of a URL: The presence of a URL often signified the asker's need.
14. Presence of grammatical errors: The presence of grammatical errors makes a question ill-framed.

Each of these fourteen features contribute to the quality of a question according to existing research. Adamic et al. (2008); Harper et al. (2008) show that very short questions fail to receive answers. On the flip side, very lengthy questions tend to distract their potential answerers. Healy and Drewnowski (1983); Hale (2003) demonstrate the need to detect misspelled words, as a greater number of spelling errors attracts fewer answerers.

A question that begins with a small letter is assumed to have been typed in haste or carelessly constructed.

Angell and Heslop (1994) show that lower case letters tend to affect communication style between users, as a greater mental effort is required to comprehend the questions that contain them. Kincaid et al. (1975) proposed readability scores that were calculated to prove that questions requiring higher cognitive load would attract fewer potential answerers. The presence of punctuation marks implies well-constructed sentences, which are hypothesized to clarify a question's meaning and reduce potential answerers' mental efforts. On the other hand, punctuation can be problematic; the presence of multiple question marks at the end of an inquiry, for example, might confuse the potential answerer. The presence of interrogative words in a question increases the likelihood that it will be answered. The presence of taboo words–often considered "inappropriate" content–also turns potential answerers away. Gazan (2007) explained that askers may include external sources and other content-specific information in their questions in order to attract answerers who are specialists or synthesists. Grammatical errors in a question, as mentioned by Celce-Murcia (1985), affect its overall content and answerability.

Using these fourteen textual features and the question-type and category data determined by human coders, we constructed our predictive model of question quality to further our overall agenda regarding improving students' learning experiences through educational CQA.

| Category | Definition and Example |
|---|---|
| Too broad | The question is complicated and few people have the ability and/or resources necessary to provide answers, even though enough details are provided to identify the asker's intended information seeking goal.<br><br>Example: What did the first iPhone look like? |
| Meaningless | The question has content that poses more than one question (although they are related), so the answerer may be confused in interpreting the asker's intended information- seeking goal.<br><br>Example: what a sentence for a bread basket. |
| General statement | The question is in fact a general statement and not a question.<br><br>Example: Happy new years everyone. Hope yall have a great 2016!!! |
| Presence of a confusing word | The question consists of an unclear word that can puzzle the answerer.<br><br>Example: Determine the meter of this poem. Which sentence describes the metrical pattern? |
| Socially awkward content | The question is inappropriate, too personal, or consists of a social taboo word.<br><br>Example: Butts are sooooooooo biiiiiiiiiiggggggggg |
| Question written in a different language | The question is written in a different language and cannot be comprehended by the answerer.<br><br>Example: Fonction politique de Paris. |

***Table 2:*** *Typology of Deleted Questions in Brainly using Shah et al. (2012).*

## EXPERIMENTS

In order to improve users' experience with educational CQA and address multiple aspects of their learning process, we had to begin by separating "good" questions from "bad" questions. In order to do so, we checked for the presence or absence of our fourteen identified textual features and conducted three sets of experiments. In the first set of experiments, a predictive model was built to classify the set of 500 "good" and 500 "bad" questions, applying ten-cross fold validation and 80/20 training-test set split. We tried different classifiers such as J-48 Decision Trees, Logistic Regression, and Random Forest, and achieved the best accuracy with J48-Decision Trees. Each classifier's performance is reviewed in Table 5. After our initial classification using the fourteen textual features, we expanded our model based off information provided by the coders that comprised a more nuanced analysis of "bad" questions. The coders mutually discussed their coding scheme and findings. We built a predictive model based on the information discerned by the coders and the fourteen textual features using an 80/20 training-testing split for the different question-types of the second set of experiments. The accuracy values increased and are reported in Table 6.

We also report the precision and recall values in Table 7. With this expanded model, we were able to obtain a deeper understanding of each feature and how it functioned to detract from question quality.

After the coders finished assigning each of the 500 questions to the question categories, they mutually developed a way to map the textual features onto the categories. After grouping the textual features with question types, we engaged in a third set of experiments with our machine learning model. Given a question and its set of textual features, we examined how well we could predict the question-type. The ability to automatically identify both problematic features and their corresponding question-type would facilitate our ability to provide Brainly users with constructive feedback and guidelines for revision.

## FINDINGS

The findings reported below demonstrate that our model is in its beginning stages, but shows promise in terms of developing a reliable way in which to improve educational CQA and help students correct "bad" questioning behavior. The accuracy values obtained for the first set of experiments were found to be 74.5%, meaning the J48 Decision tree classifier performed reasonably well when distinguishing "good" from "bad" questions. The results found for the "bad" set of questions based on their accuracies and other key metrics like precision and recall are shown in Tables 6 and 7.

The true negatives (tn), on the other hand, are the correctly misidentified cases, while false negatives (fn) are the incorrectly misidentified cases by the classifier in the prediction model as defined in Witten et al. (2016).

Accuracy can be defined as the proportion of correct classifications (true positives and negatives) from the overall number of cases. The accuracy measure is defined by the following expression:

Accuracy = (tp+tn)/ (tp+tn+fp+fn) (1)

Precision can be defined as the proportion of correct positive classifications (true positives) from the cases that are predicted as positive. The precision measure can be defined by the expression:

Precision = (tp)/ (tp+fp) (2)

| Category | Definition and Example |
|---|---|
| Presence of too many sentences | The question consists of an excessive amount of information that may lose the answerer's attention. Example: I'm not going out to the game and the first time I get to the game and I love you so much for the next two years of my life and death of a good day for a while ago I was a little bit more like a little too much for a while ago I was a great day for a while to figure out what to do it all the way you are the same time as well as a whole lot better then the other side of my friends. |
| Presence of typos | The question consists of ill-formed phrases and typos that hamper the answerer's understanding. Example: why would the task force recmmend that turbines have on yhe animal that make this region their home |
| Missing information | The question consists of incomplete information such as options for a multiple choice inquiry. Example: Which word does not contain a reference to the male gender |
| Presence of garbled text/non-formatted text | The question consists of garbled/non-formatted text that hampers the answerer's understanding. Example: Toplamlari ve farklar eit olan iki doal saydan k katir |

***Table 3**: Typology of Deleted Questions in Brainly using Shah et al.(2012)*

| Question-type | ICR |
|---|---|
| Opinion-Seeking | 0.667 |
| Advise-Seeking | NA |
| Information-Seeking | 0.707 |
| Self-Expression | 0.725 |
| Not Applicable | 0.768 |
| Too broad | 0.624 |
| Meaningless | 0.703 |
| General statement | 0.729 |
| Presence of a confusing word | 0.790 |
| Socially awkward content | 1.000 |
| Question written in a different language | 0.852 |
| Missing information | 0.719 |
| Presence of too many sentences | 0.790 |
| Presence of typos | 0.878 |
| Presence of garbled text | 0.811 |

***Table 4:** Inter-coder Reliability (ICR) Values for the "Bad" Questions for Different Question Types.*

Recall can be defined as the proportion of correct positive classifications (true positives) from the cases that are actually positive. The recall measure can be defined by the expression:

Recall = (tp)/ (tp+fn) (3)

As explained, accuracy refers to whether questions were correctly classified as "good" or "bad." However, based on the information pertaining to specific items within our dataset, the class labels were found to be imbalanced. This means the classes were poorly represented, which we can call a "rare event." Synthetic Minority Over-Sampling Technique (SMOTE) helps to over-sample the rare event present in the data set, as described by Chawla (2005). Thus, SMOTE filter was applied on the classes for all the respective items and the key evaluation metrics were reported.

| Classifier | Accuracy |
|---|---|
| J48-Decision Trees | 74.5% |
| Logistic Regression | 73.0 % |
| Random Forest | 69.5% |

***Table 5**: The Accuracy Values for Different Classifiers Used to Classify Questions as "Good" and "Bad."*

The true positive (tp) instances are the correctly identified cases, while false positives (f p) are the incorrectly identified cases by the classifier in the prediction model. In the second set of experiments we found strong agreement between the precision and recall measures for the presence of socially awkward content, questions written in a different language, presence of too many sentences, and the presence of garbled text. The high precision values show the presence of greater true positives, meaning we can automatically classify these questions' problems. This offers relief to students who may make such errors on Brainly, as they can receive clear guidelines for question revision. On the other hand, questions showing a poor precision value (such as 0.61 for "Missing Information") require further clarification, as they may be inaccurately labeled and/or may display a number of problematic traits.

The higher accuracy values shown for advice-seeking, and presence of garbled text show that the questions were correctly classified by the coders. The results reported in Tables 6 and 7 support the literature review and show that the classifier performed decently. Our poor precision and recall values, however, highlight a shortcoming of the present study that must be addressed in future research to truly assist CQA users; namely, question quality is affected by contextual features–such as the time of day a question was posted–as well as textual features.

| Question-type | Accuracy |
|---|---|
| Opinion-Seeking | 92.26 % |
| Advise-Seeking | 89.90% |
| Information-Seeking | 68.93% |
| Self-Expression | 70.22% |
| Not Applicable | 72.00% |
| Too broad | 78.00% |
| Meaningless | 66.20% |
| General statement | 84.00% |
| Presence of confusing word | 58.50% |
| Socially awkward content | 75.80% |
| Missing information | 60.99% |
| Presence of too many sentences | 90.17% |
| Presence of typos | 67.53% |
| Presence of garbled text | 82.00% |

***Table 6**: The Accuracy Values Found for Different Quality Factors for the Questions Classified as "Bad" using Logistic Regression.*

| Question-type | Precision | Recall |
|---|---|---|
| Opinion-Seeking | 0.89 | 0.92 |
| Advise-Seeking | 0.89 | 0.89 |
| Information-Seeking | 0.68 | 0.68 |
| Self-Expression | 0.64 | 0.70 |
| Not Applicable | 0.72 | 0.72 |
| Too broad | 0.71 | 0.78 |
| Meaningless | 0.66 | 0.66 |
| General statement | 0.77 | 0.84 |
| Presence of a confusing word | 0.58 | 0.58 |
| Socially awkward content | 0.75 | 0.75 |
| Missing information | 0.61 | 0.61 |
| Presence of too many sentences | 0.90 | 0.90 |
| Presence of typos | 0.68 | 0.67 |
| Presence of garbled text | 0.80 | 0.82 |

***Table 7**: Key Evaluation Metrics to Evaluate the Prediction Model to Detect "Bad" Questions.*

In the third set of experiments, a predictive model was built by mapping the textual features and the question categories. It demonstrated high accuracy for questions with garbled text and socially awkward content, as reflected in Table 8. For example, regarding the question category "Too broad," the coders mapped the textual features like total number of words, total number of characters, average number of words in a sentence, total number of sentences, total number of misspelled words, question beginning with an interrogative word, and the readability scores. Upon building the predictive model with the mentioned textual features, we obtained 77.4% accuracy. However, we obtained even higher accuracies for the "Missing information" and "Socially awkward content" question categories, as the classifier was able to detect the higher number of correctly classified instances. However, for the question category "Presence of a confusing word," we obtained very low accuracy, and this can be attributed to human coders' variant definitions of "confusing." Thus, our current progress would assist students who made certain mistakes, but could not offer constructive feedback to all Brainly users. We also noted that for our "question written in a different language" category, we can forgo our model and easily detect such inquires using a language detection pro-gram; thus, we do not report results from that category in this study.

## DISCUSSION

Our experiments were designed to both identify "bad" questions and determine what textual features may have contributed to said inquiries' low quality in order to help educational CQA users best satisfy their information needs. Our work is unique in that it seeks to not only separate "good" questions from "bad" questions, but also expands upon the notion of "bad" to examine what specific textual features contribute to question quality. To that end, we strove to construct an automatic classifier that both identified a poor question and highlighted what contributed to its evaluation. Thus, we are no longer limited by automatic processes that classify questions as "good" or "bad"; we can now examine more microcosmic question features that indicate how an inquiry may be improved or rephrased to attract a satisfactory answer. This is particularly salient in educational CQA, as students must be made aware of their queries' shortcomings in order to learn how to better phrase questions and ultimately satisfy their information needs.

Our study's results show that we can automatically detect question quality based on textual features. To answer our RQ1, we can say that our model was able to predict question quality with about 74.5% accuracy. Thus, we are able to postulate why certain questions are considered to be "bad." Potential shortcomings defined by our classifications and typology allow us to peg problematic questions based on their contents. The possible reasons suggested by the coders and the previously devised code book by Shah et al. (2012) show that although a question may intuitively appear to contain only one issue, it can in fact have multiple problems.

Our numbers indicate that this work is in its preliminary stages. Due to its middling accuracy and the limitations discussed below, our model cannot yet stand on its own; moderators will need to assist users as they re-frame their questions. Still, preventing automatic deletion and fostering an environment that is more centered on learning from every perspective represents a significant shift. Iimportantly, such studies may also consider elements beyond the "good"/"bad" dichotomy to further investigate content quality and ultimately determine what elements comprise sufficiency. Given such a task's tall order, our idea to automatically classify such features makes a great deal of sense and saves much time and labor. Improving the level of content quality in CQAs could increase their use in online learning while simultaneously increasing the authenticity and credibility of online Q&A services.

| **Question category** | **Textual Feature** | **Accuracy** |
|---|---|---|
| Too Broad | Total no. of words<br>Total no. of Characters<br>Avg. words in a sentence<br>Total no. of sentences<br>Total no. of misspelled words<br>Ques. Beg. With an inter. word<br>Readability scores | 77.4% |
| Meaningless | Total no. of words<br>Total no. of characters<br>Avg. words in a sentence<br>Total no. of sentences<br>Total no. of misspelled words<br>Ques. beg with an inter. word<br>Total punctuation marks<br>Readability scores | 74.% |
| General Statement not a question | Ques. beg with an inter. word<br>Ques. ending with ?<br>Total no. of sentences<br>Total no. of misspelled words<br>Ques. beg with an inter. words<br>Readability scores | 67.7% |
| Presence of a confusing word | Total misspelled word<br>Ques. starting with a small letter<br>Total no. of sentences<br>Presence of a taboo word<br>Readability scores | 37.8% |
| Socially awkward content | Ques. beg. With an inter. word<br>Total no. of characters<br>Total misspelled words<br>Presence of a taboo word<br>Presence of an URL | 82.4% |
| Missing information | Ques. beg. with an inter. word<br>Readability scores<br>Grammar-related | 89.9% |
| Presence of many sentences | Total no. of sentences<br>Total no. of characters | 77.8% |
| Question category | Textual Feature | Accuracy |
| Presence of typos | Total no. of misspelled words<br>Grammar-related<br>Total no. of sentences<br>Total no. of inter. words | 67.7% |
| Presence of garbled text | Total no. of words<br>Total no. of characters<br>Avg. words in a sentence<br>Readability scores<br>Total punct.marks<br>Total no. of misspelled words<br>Total no. of sentences<br>Total no. of inter. words | 89.2% |

*Table 8. Mapping of Textual features with the*

## QUESTION CATEGORY

Our future research will involve moderators' correction and re-posting of "bad" questions to CQA platforms to see whether those resolved questions get answered, and if they do get answered, what kind of quality those answers reflect. Thus, our quantitative approach also contributes a great deal to CQA studies, as it represents another way in which to process data. Though our typology does not cover every contributor to "bad" questions, it does stem from a unique collection method that could be utilized and expanded upon in the future. Our initial definition of "bad" questions came from moderators' assessments, while our feature set came from both the literature and moderators' unstructured commentary on deleted questions. We were able to achieve higher specificity with our coders' criteria, and the resulting subset of features yielded better accuracy. Thus, although our work is in its beginning stages, it's already forming into an effective way to productively examine question content and improve students' learning experiences through CQA.

## LIMITATIONS

While our overall concept contributes to CQA literature and opens exciting possibilities for future research, the current study presents a number of limitations. We centered our model on textual features, however, the list we developed is certainly not exhaustive. Future research will need to discover and account for a larger expanse of factors. Additionally, those features we did include may not be relevant in every scenario. A question coded as too broad, for example, may not be affected by its length; a broad question may be short or long. Our features also focused specifically on question content, which does not construct a complete picture of question quality. Contextual factors also contribute to "goodness" and "badness," and should be accounted for in future work. A query posted to Brainly may, for example, be impeccably written in a language other than English; it would still be coded "bad" because it went unanswered, but its quality is not based off textual features as we define them. Essentially, more information needs to be parsed out and added in order to reach a more granular level in which we can account for a wider number of factors that contribute to low quality questions.

Our study is also limited by our small dataset. Though this research is exploratory in nature, we aim to provide an in-depth analysis of what makes a question "bad" or "poorly-framed," and may need a larger sample to do so. That way, we can achieve a more granular level of specificity and better assist users with question revisions.

Our work is also limited because we arbitrarily chose a uniform distribution of 500 "good" and 500 "bad" questions. This makes the proposed setting unrealistic, as it does not necessarily reflect the actual distribution of inappropriate questions posted to Brainly. Additionally, this generates a random baseline of 50%, which clearly shows that the accuracy of 70% does not necessarily indicate a good performance. On the basis of the question quality pyramid proposed by Correa and Sureka (2014), questions' quality can be divided into regular questions, closed questions, and deleted questions.

Our research deals only with the regular "good" and deleted "bad" questions. It does not consider the closed questions nor the questions that go unanswered regardless of their quality. In future research, we would like to investigate the difference between question quality in the regular, closed, and deleted categories. That way, we could expand our reach even further and access a wider number of students who may be struggling to help them both better frame their information needs and obtain more satisfactory answers.

## CONCLUSION

CQA presents a rich and nuanced area in which we can study and improve human information seeking behaviors. In particular, we can focus on educational CQA to make a large impact on middle school and high school students' ability to express their information needs, obtain answers to their questions, and ultimately deepen their understanding of a salient topic. In this work, we examined a dataset from Brainly, the largest educational CQA site, in order to determine whether we could automatically identify "bad" questions and determine what textual features contribute to their low quality. Our approach showed promising preliminary results that support our ability to provide Brainly users with helpful feedback. Thus, rather than merely have their questions deleted, students could be presented with the opportunity and guidance needed to improve their inquiries and subsequently receive desired information. This would improve student's overall learning process, as they would both satisfy their information needs and obtain the skills necessary to frame better questions in the future, yielding benefits for both themselves and Brainly's overall knowledge-base. In the future, we hope to expand our model to include a larger number of both textual and contextual features. Our trajectory also includes the ability to consider question categories beyond "bad" in order to better understand the elements of question quality and best assist CQA users.


## ACKNOWLEDGMENTS

The authors thank Sameera Somisetty and Dhrashti Mehta for their inputs in this work. The work reported in this paper is supported by the US Institute of Museum and Library Services (IMLS) grant LG-81-16-0025-16. We are also thankful to Brainly for providing us with the data.


## REFERENCES


Adamic, L. A., Zhang, J., Bakshy, E., and Ackerman, M. S. (2008). Knowledge sharing and yahoo answers: Everyone know something. In Proceedings of the 17th international conference on World Wide Web pages 665–674. ACM.'

Agichtein, E., Castillo, C., Donato, D., Gionis, A., and Mishne, G. (2008). Finding high-quality content in social media. In Proceedings of the 2008 international conference on web search and data mining, pages 183–194. ACM.

Angell, D. F. and Heslop, B. (1994). Elements of e-mail international conference on World Wide Web pages 665–674. ACM.'

Aritajati, C. and Narayanan, N. H. (2013). Facilitating students' collaboration and learning in a question and answer system. In Proceedings of the 2013 conference on Computer supported cooperative work companion, pages 101– 106. ACM.

Arora, P., Ganguly, D., and Jones, G. J. (2015). The good, the bad and their kins: Identifying questions with negative scores in Stackoverflow. In Proceedings of the 2015 IEEE/ACM International Conference on Advances in Social Networks Analysis and Mining, 2015, pages 1232-1239. ACM.

Asaduzzaman, M., Mashiyat, A. S., Roy, C. K., and Schnei der, K. A. (2013).Answering questions about unanswered questions of StackOverflow. 10th IEEE Working Conference on In Mining Software Repositories (MSR), 2013, , pages 97–100. IEEE.

Celce-Murcia, M. (1985). Making informed decisions about the role of grammar in language teaching. Foreign language annals, 18(4):297–301.

Chawla, N. V. (2005). Data mining for imbalanced datasets: An overview. In Data mining and knowledge discovery handbook, pages 853–867. Springer.

Chua, A. Y. and Banerjee, S. (2013). So fast so good: An analysis of answer quality and answer speed in community question-answering sites. *Journal of the American Society for Information Science and Technology*, 64(10):2058– 2068.

Correa, D. and Sureka, A. (2014). Chaff from the wheat: characterization and modeling of deleted questions on Stack Overflow. In Proceedings of the 23rd international conference on World wide web, pages 631–642. ACM.

Gazan, R. (2007). Seekers, sloths and social reference: Homework questions submitted to a question-answering community. New Review of Hypermedia and Multimedia, 13(2):239–248.

Hale, J. (2003). The information conveyed by words in sentences. Journal of Psycholinguistic Research, 32(2):101– 123.

Harper, F. M., Raban, D., Rafaeli, S., and Konstan, J. A. (2008). Predictors of answer quality in online Q&A sites. In Proceedings of the SIGCHI Conference on Human Factors in Computing Systems, pages 865–874. ACM.

Healy, A. F. and Drewnowski, A. (1983). Investigating the boundaries of reading units: Letter detection in misspelled words. Journal of Experimental. Psychology: Human Perception and Performance, 9(3):413.

Henderson, K. S. and Bosch, S. (2010). Seeking the new normal: Periodicals price survey 2010. Library Journal, 135(7):36–40.

Kincaid, J. P., Fishburne Jr, R. P., Rogers, R. L., and Chissom, B. S. (1975). Derivation of new readability formulas (automated readability index, fog count and flesch reading ease formula) for navy enlisted personnel. Technical report, DTIC Document.

Li, B., Jin, T., Lyu, M. R., King, I., and Mak, B. (2012). Analyzing and predicting question quality in community question answering services. In Proceedings of the 21st International Conference on World Wide Web, pages 775– 782. ACM.

Mai, J.-E. (2013). The quality and qualities of information. Journal of the American society for information science and technology, 64(4):675–688.

onzanelli, L., Mocci, A., Bacchelli, A., Lanza, M., and Fullerton, D. (2014). Improving low quality Stack Overflow post detection. In Software Maintenance and Evolution (ICSME), 2014 IEEE International Conference on, pages 541–544. IEEE.

Ravi, S., Pang, B., Rastogi, V., and Kumar, R. (2014). Great question! question quality in community Q&A. ICWSM, 14:426–435.

Shah, C. and Kitzie, V. (2012). Social Q&A and virtual reference - comparing apples and oranges with the help of experts and users. Journal of the American Society for Information Science and Technology, 63(10):2020–2036.

Shah, C., Radford, M. L., Connaway, L. S., Choi, E., and Kitzie, V. (2012). How much change do you get from 40? analyzing and addressing failed questions on social Q&A. Proceedings of the American Society for Information Science and Technology, 49(1):1–10.

Taylor, R. S. (1968). Question-negotiation and information seeking in libraries. College & research libraries, 29(3):178–194.

Tesch, R. (2013). Qualitative research: Analysis types and software. Routledge.

Witten, I. H., Frank, E., Hall, M. A., and Pal, C. J. (2016). Data Mining: Practical machine learning tools and techniques. Morgan Kaufmann.

Xia, X., Lo, D., Correa, D., Sureka, A., and Shihab, E. (2016). It takes two to tango: Deleted stack overflow question prediction with text and meta features. In Computer Software and Applications Conference (COMPSAC), 2016 IEEE 40th Annual, volume 1, pages 73–82. IEEE.

# An Exploration of Reasons for Query Reformulations

**Eun Youp Rha**
*School of Communication and Information, Rutgers University, USA. eunyoup.rha@rutgers.edu*

**Nicholas J. Belkin**
*School of Communication and Information, Rutgers University, USA. belkin@comminfo.rutgers.ed*

**Wei Shi**
*School of Communication and Information, Rutgers University, USA. ws307@scarletmail.rutgers.edu*

## ABSTRACT

**Query reformulation is the major method by which information seekers can communicate their information searching intentions to information retrieval systems. Despite a good deal of significant research on types of query reformulations, we still know little about why people reformulate their queries in various ways. We report on a study which elicited people's reasons for query reformulation and investigated the relationships between those reasons and types of query reformulations, and to the searchers' previous information search intentions. Based on these data, we propose a faceted classification of reasons for query reformulation; we find that the frequency of reasons for query reformulation is highly skewed to one type; we find that multiple reformulation types are used for multiple reasons; and, we both confirm and expand upon Xie's (2002) inventory of interactive search intentions. Implications of these results for further work and information retrieval system design are discussed.**

## KEYWORDS

query reformulation, query purposes, information search intentions

## INTRODUCTION

Query reformulation, the process of altering a given query to improve search performance (Jansen, Booth & Spink, 2009), has long been viewed as a key activity of information search in information retrieval (IR) systems. Understanding query reformulation has been an important and useful application for IR system designers to develop more effective search system features that support users' query manipulation (Hu, Lu & Joo, 2013). For instance, query suggestions can be implemented in search systems based on the evaluation of users' query history (Liu et al., 2010). Hence, analysis of query reformulation strategies has been helpful for identifying how to design and improve retrieval systems that assist users' search activities.

80th Annual Meeting of the Association for Information Science & Technology, Washington, DC, VA | Oct. 27-Nov. 1, 2017



Given the benefits from understanding query reformulation behavior, scholars in IR have continuously strived to articulate patterns and strategies of query reformulation applied by users. However, little attention has been paid to *why* people change their queries. Since reformulating a query is the only way for users to directly interact with a retrieval system throughout the search process and is primarily triggered by user's underlying search goals, a careful investigation into specific reasons for query reformulation may be helpful to advance understanding of search intentions. Current knowledge of patterns and strategies of query reformulation seems limited in addressing the true goals or intentions of query reformulation. Although people modify a query in a particular way, diverse underlying reasons and goals could exist in that certain reformulation activity, more than simply finding information that they need. For instance, a user might add more words to change a query, which could be primarily motivated by his or her goal of gaining more detailed information compared to the search result retrieved with the prior query, or that of learning background information about a search topic. In other words, it is hard to pinpoint user's specific reasons for query reformulation only with patterns or types of query reformulation since multiple intentions can be embedded in each reformulation activity. Therefore, in-depth analysis of query reformulation *reasons* could help identify users' search intentions more specifically than superficial categorization of reformulation types. We report here on a study designed explicitly to identify and characterize people's reasons for entering new queries during an information search session.

In order to identify users' reasons causing query reformulation, it is also necessary to understand users' previous situations since purposes or goals of query reformulation can be affected by preceding events or their cognitive status in the interactive information seeking processes. Some previous intentions may lead users to have a particular purpose in modifying a query. This could also help to understand whether specific types of query reformulations can detect important user intentions in searching. Besides, satisfaction or failure of such previous intentions could be a crucial factor influencing reasons of the next query change. This study therefore also explored the relationship between previous search intentions and reasons of subsequent query reformulation by reviewing an effect of success of such prior intentions on reformulation reasons.

Hence, the primary goals of this study are to characterize users' reasons for query reformulation in their search process when they perform search tasks, to identify relationships between query reformulation reasons and query reformulation types, and to consider the relationships between query reformulation reasons and preceding search intentions.

## RELATED WORK

### *Query Reformulation Patterns*

Since submitting query terms has been considered a fundamental interaction between users and information retrieval systems (Xie & Joo, 2010), how users choose and transition queries has been a major focus of research, particularly specific types and patterns of query reformulations. Fidel (1985) classified reformulation moves into two categories, operational moves indicating the query change within the same meaning and conceptual moves that change the meaning of query. Rieh and Xie (2006) derived patterns of multiple web query reformulations by applying a faceted approach. Three major facets, content, format and resource, were identified, to holistically characterize the process of web query reformulation. Huang and Efthimiadis (2009) studied users' reformulation strategies in web search engines, identifying certain strategies of reformulations including: add/remove words, word substitution, acronym expansion, and spelling correction, and different usefulness of reformulation types depending on user's behavior in response to an initial set of results. Teevan et al. (2007) explored users' information retrieval behavior and identified taxonomies of query reformulation such as word merge, remove words, and stemming and pluralization. Liu et al. (2010) developed five query reformulation types: generalization; specialization; word substitution; repeat; and new, according to the common terms and query length difference in two successive queries, and examined influences of task type and users' satisfaction on query reformulation. Jansen et al. (2009) also examined query reformulation patterns to develop predictive models of how users transition from one query to the next one using an n-gram modeling approach. Xie and Joo (2010) identified specific types of search tactics occurring and transitions of them in the process of web searching. Guan, Zhang and Yang (2012) focused on query change in a search session, deriving three primary groups of query changes which include theme terms, added terms and removed terms. Ghosh (2016) showed a series of reformulation strategies such as Same; Reorder; AddWords; RemoveWords; Substring; Stem; Common; NewWords. All of these works focus primarily on identifying patterns and strategies of query reformulation adopted by users for their web searching, with no attention to detailed reasons or intentions for query reformulation.

### *Reasons for Query Changes*

Early work investigating reasons for query reformulation was largely conditioned by the characteristics of exact-match information retrieval systems. Fidel (1985) identified users' three problematic situations when they reformulate a query to improve query performance: when retrieved sets were too large; when retrieved sets were too small; and when retrieved sets were off-target. Shenouda (1991) explained that the most frequent reason for query reformulation was when documents examined in a subset had been judged all irrelevant. Later work, investigating Web search, considered ranked-output retrieval. Hsieh-Yee (1998) concluded that users modified queries when too many items were retrieved and when nothing useful was retrieved. Recently, Jiang and Ni (2016) analyzed users' underlying intentions for different word changes in query reformulation. The authors focused on three particular types of word changes and specified the reasons of each case: removing a word when the word becomes less useful and when users move forward in a search session; adding a brand-new word when they see a word appearing frequently in result titles; reusing a word when they revert from a subtask to the main task or another subtask (Jiang & Ni, 2016). Although their research reveals the state-of-the-art understanding of word changes in query reformulation from the user's perspective, it is limited in that reasons were inferred from analysis of independent variables that influenced word changes, not extracted directly from users.

## METHODS

To explore the association between users' observable behaviors and cognitive goals during query reformulation, three research questions were proposed in this study:

**RQ1**. What are reasons for query reformulation?

**RQ2**. How are types of query reformulation related to users' reasons for query reformulations?

**RQ3**. How do previous interactive search intentions affect reasons of following query reformulations?

We designed an experimental study to address the research questions, which asked participants to conduct search tasks and to indicate intentions and query reformulation reasons of searches while watching a replay of their searches. We drew upon a list of possible intentions from Xie's (2002) work on interactive search intentions. The user behavior data were logged and recorded during each search session.

### *Search Intentions*

Following Xie's (2002) work, we used a subset of the interactive search intentions for participants to choose from. Participants were given the list of 20 intentions (shown in Table 1) at the beginning of a search session and they could refer back to this list throughout the task.

**Identify search information**

- Identify something to get started - For instance, find good query terms
- Identify something more to search - Explore a topic more broadly

**Learn**

- Learn domain knowledge - Learn about the topic of a search
- Learn database content - Learn the type of information/resources available at a particular website – e.g., a government database

**Find**

- Find a known item - Searching for an item that you were familiar with in advance.
- Find specific information - Finding a predetermined piece of information.
- Find items sharing a named characteristic - Finding items with something in common.
- Find items without predefined criteria. - Finding items that will be useful for a task, but which haven't been specified in advance

**Keep record**

- Keep record of a link - Saving a good item or an item to look at later

**Access an item or set of items**

- Access a specific item - Go to some item that you already know about.
- Access items with common characteristics - Go to some set of items with common characteristics.
- Access a web site/home page or similar - Relocating or going to a website

**Evaluate**

- Evaluate correctness of an item - Determine whether an item is factually correct
- Evaluate usefulness of an item - Determine whether an item is useful.
- Pick best item(s) from all the useful ones - Determine the best item among a set of items.
- Evaluate specificity of an item - Determine whether an item is specific or general enough
- Evaluate duplication of an item - Determine whether the information in one item is the same as in another or others

**Obtain**

- Obtain specific information - Finding specific information to highlight or copy
- Obtain part of the item - Finding part of an item to highlight or copy
- Obtain a whole item(s) - Finding a whole item to highlight or copy

***Table 1**. Search intentions*

### Search Tasks

For this study, we designed four motivating tasks from the field of journalism: copy editing, interview preparation, relationships and story pitch. Copy editing and interview preparation were adopted from the work of Cole, Hendahewa, Shah and Belkin (2015), and relationships and story pitch are novel to this study.

All types of task were created according to the combination of three specific facets of task: product, level and goal, as shown in Table 2. Copy editing is concerned with finding known facts, and story pitch is to find unknown facts. Interview preparation aims to find many different kinds of unknown things and relationship is finding relationships between known facts. Our task design using general facets of task (facets based on the classification of Li & Belkin, 2008, as modified by Cole, et al., 2015) should allow some measure of generalizability of results beyond a specific domain of journalism, to any motivating and search tasks sharing these facet values, and their combinations

| Task Type | Product | Level | Goal |
|---|---|---|---|
| Copy Editing | Factual | Segment | Specific |
| Story Pitch | Intellectual | Segment | Amorphous |
| Relationships | Intellectual | Document | Amorphous |
| Interview Preparation | Intellectual | Document | Amorphous |

***Table 2**. Task types*

These four task types were paired into four groups based on differences in facet values, and two different topics were used for task design: coelacanths, and methane clathrates and global warming. We tried to choose unusual topics for participants to minimize the effect of their prior knowledge on task performance. Each participant conducted two different tasks, each from one of four pairs, with different topics. Table 3 shows the four tasks for the topic "coelacanths"; the same form was used for the topic "methane clathrates and global warming." The total of 24 participants conducted 48 search tasks, which resulted in 14 searches from the pair of copy editing and interview preparation and 10 searches from the pair of story pitch and relationships.

### Procedure

The data was collected in a lab setting in a university with undergraduate journalism students who had completed at least one course in news writing. Participants each conducted two different task/topic combinations; after each search, they engaged in search annotation marking on intention types through replay of that search. After the two search tasks, they responded to an exit interview. Participants used a specially designed Firefox plugin to finish all of the tasks except the exit interview. Search activity was recorded by the plugin and annotatable video of the search by Morae[1].

Participants first filled out a demographic questionnaire and observed a tutorial video on the features of the browser interface. They were then presented the task description and responded to a questionnaire on anticipated task difficulty and task/topic familiarity. Then they were given 20 minutes to work on the first search task. Afterwards, participants reported task difficulty and performance in a post-search questionnaire. For the intention annotation task, with no time

[1] https://www.techsmith.com/morae.html

limit, participants first read a description of the search intentions (Table 1) and watched a video showing the procedures of the annotation task. They then were asked to choose intention(s) applied to each query segment (a *query segment* is all that occurs between an initial query and the subsequent query) from the intention list provided, indicating whether each intention was satisfied or not. They were also asked to explain why they changed their previous query to the next one for each query reformulation activity. The same process was repeated for each query segment. After the two searches, the session was completed with an exit interview, asking about their two search experiences. Each session took about two hours.

| |
|---|
| **Assignment 1. Copy Editing**<br>**Your Assignment**: You are a copy editor at a newspaper and you have only 20 minutes to check the accuracy of six italicized statements in the excerpt of a piece of news story below.<br>**Your Task**: Please find and save an authoritative page that either confirms or disconfirms each statement. |
| **Assignment 2. Story Pitch**<br>**Your Assignment**: You are planning to pitch a science story to your editor and need to identify interesting facts about the coelacanth ("see-la-kanth"), a fish that dates from the time of dinosaurs and was thought to be extinct.<br>**Your Task**: Find and save web pages that contain the six most interesting facts about coelacanths and/or research about their preservation. |
| **Assignment 3. Relationships**<br>**Your Assignment**: You are writing an article about coelacanths and conservation efforts. You have found an interesting article about coelacanths but in order to develop your article you need to be able to explain the relationship between key facts you have learned.<br>**Your Task:** In the following, there are five italicized passages, find an authoritative web page that explains the relationship between two of the italicized facts. |
| **Assignment 4. Interview Preparation**<br>**Your Assignment**: You are writing an article that profiles a scientist and their research work. You are preparing to interview Mark Erdmann, a marine biologist, about coelacanths and conservation programs.<br>**Your Task**: Identify and save authoritative web pages for the following: Identify two (living) people who likely can provide some personal stories about Dr. Erdmann and his work. Find the three most interesting facts about Dr. Erdmann's research. Find an interesting potential impact of Dr. Erdmann's work. |

***Table 3**. Search task descriptions*

### *Classification of Query Reformulation Types*

In order to identify types of query reformulation, we created a taxonomy of query reformulation, shown in Table 4. We modified the existing classification of query reformulation originally created by Liu et al. (2010): we used five categories from their work including Generalization, Specialization, Repeat, Word Substitution and New, and added Stem-Identical (Hollink et al., 2011) and Spelling Correction after preliminary analysis of query reformulation activities with our data.

| Reformulation | Definition/Example |
|---|---|
| Generalization | At least one term in common in two queries; second query contains fewer terms than first query<br>e.g., world economic impact on global warming on Arctic region → global warming on Arctic region |
| Specialization | At least one term in common in two queries; second query contains more terms than first query<br>e.g., impact Dr. Erdmann → impact Dr.Mark Erdmann |
| Word Substitution | At least one term in common in two queries; second query has the same length as first query, but contains some terms not in the first query<br>e.g., Igor Semiletov research → igor semiletov methane |
| Repeat | Exactly the same term(s) repeated from any previous queries within the session<br>e.g., Coelacanths (1st query)→ Coelacanths (5th query) |
| New | No common terms in two queries<br>e.g., where is madagascar → coelacanths live young |
| Spelling Correction | The second query corrects misspelling of the previous query<br>e.g., methane clarites artic economic immpact → methane clarites arctic economic impact |
| Stem Identical | Two queries with the same morphological root<br>e.g., methane km → methane kilometers |

***Table 4**. Query reformulation types*

We manually assigned a type of query reformulation between two successive queries for each search session. For this analysis, navigational queries (e.g., "google scholar," "database") were excluded. We strictly focused on the change of query length to label a reformulation type with no consideration of a sematic relationship between queries, following the rules by Liu et al. (2010).

## RESULTS

The analysis was conducted descriptively since our central aim of study is to learn why users change their queries during the search processes, which has not been well studied. Using the relatively small amount of data we collected (24 participants, 48 search sessions), our results focus on demonstrating a broad range of reasons described by users based on descriptive analysis. The total number of queries from the sessions was 434 and query reformulation activities were 383 after excluding the first query of each search session and three navigational queries.

### *A Classification of Reasons for Query Reformulation (RQ1)*

During the intention annotation task, participants were asked the question, "Please explain why you entered this new query, and what you were hoping to accomplish by doing so." They wrote in detail to indicate their rationales for reformulating the old queries and the objectives they hoped to achieve with the new queries. The answers were categorized as the "reformulation reason" for data analysis. We believe that the participants' interpretation of the elicitation was of query "reformulation," but it is possible that they could interpret it as a reason for query "formulation." We thank an anonymous reviewer for pointing this out and will consider it in future work.

In order to capture what users were actually saying about their intention by their own words and terms, the reason descriptions were analyzed using the open coding technique: reading through the reasons and assigning tentative labels to each of the descriptions as a short phrase taken from their response. Two authors read through the reformulation reasons to identify general patterns with particular attention to the three following dimensions: 1) the specific actions in which the participants engage in the new queries; 2) the features of the things on which they focus in the new queries; 3) the channels they use to search for the target things. The authors first coded all of the cases each based on these three dimensions and reviewed the coded data to ensure the reliability of the coding categories.

The open coding step revealed that the structure of verb, adjective and noun was useful to clarify users' intention of query reformulation across the dataset. As a result, we decided to set three main facets of the reason as verb, adjective and noun, and combine values from each of the facets to characterize each reason. Table 5 demonstrates examples of the initial coding labels from reason descriptions.

Since we confirmed that multiple synonyms and overlapping words existed in verb, adjective, and noun as coding labels throughout the reasons, classification categories were elaborated by selecting one representative word among several synonyms (e.g., find, look for, locate, seek → Find; verify, confirm, prove, validate → Verify; credible, authoritative, reliable → Credible, etc.) and merging some categories into a higher semantic level of category (e.g., article, scholarly article, news article → Publication). Table 6 shows how the phrases from open coding were modified to the final combination of a reformulation reason.

Finally, we relabeled three facets – verb, adjective and noun – as Process, Aspect and Entity, respectively. Table 7 demonstrates the classification scheme for query reformulation reasons.

| Reason | Open Coding |
|---|---|
| "Trying to find information that is truthful, and more specific to the subject." | Find truthful information<br>Find specific information |
| "Clarify my original search" | Clarify original search |
| "Looked up for any recent news regarding Arctic oil and gas to see if I could bolster my argument with any recent facts that were perhaps in the news." | Look for recent news<br>Bolster my argument |
| "I entered this new query because I felt I did not use the right word in my first query referring to people the scientist would have had relations with to provide the answer to the first question of the assignment." | Use right word |
| "I used a more general phrase to get more background information on the topic and hopefully find authoritative sources that supported the facts." | Get background information<br>Find authoritative sources |

***Table 5**. Open coding examples*

| Open Coding | Final Combination |
|---|---|
| Find truthful information | Find-accurate-information |
| Clarify original search | Clarify-previous-search |
| Look for recent news<br>Bolster my argument | Find- up-to-date -publication<br>Verify-specific-knowledge |
| Use right word | Correct-previous-query |
| Get background information<br>Find authoritative sources | Obtain-background-information<br>Find-credible-source |

***Table 6**. Rephrasing initial codes to reason combinations*

| Facet | Sub-facets | Values |
|---|---|---|
| Process | Mechanical | Find; Obtain; Access; Expand; Combine; Correct; Change; Narrow down; Start |
| | Interpretive | Evaluate; Verify; Focus on; Learn; Clarify; Use; Understand |
| Aspect | Depth | General; Specific; Background Basic; Detailed |
| | Time | New; Previous; Up-To-Date |
| | Quality | Interesting; Accurate; Credible; Better; Useful |
| | Quantity | Multiple; Single |
| | Relationship | Similar; Different; Relevant More |
| Entity | Content | Knowledge; Information; Topic; Definition; Fact; Domain |
| | Resource | Source; Website; Publication |
| | Search | Search result; Query; Search |

***Table 7**. A faceted classification of query reformulation reasons*

The first facet is Process, human interactive behavior that occurs in the process of searching. It is further classified into two sub-facets, Mechanical and Interpretive. Mechanical process refers to all types of straightforward procedural activities, not requiring interpretation or understanding, while Interpretive process is concerned with behavior relating to complex human mental activities. Entity is a physical or abstract thing related to searching, which has three sub-facets: Content, Resource and Search. Content is information items. Resource is things from which information can be found, and Search is things directly related to search activity, including characterizing the search as a whole. Finally, Aspect is a characteristic of an entity. It is further clustered by sub-facets, various characteristics of an entity, such as Depth, Time, Quality, Quantity and Relationship. Based on this three-dimensional structure, reasons for query reformulation were rephrased as a combination of three facets; for instance, find (Process)-specific (Aspect)-information (Entity).

### *Frequencies of Reason Facets and Combinations (RQ1)*

Our user data-driven classification scheme that consists of three facets (Process-Aspect-Entity) is used to identify a wide range of dimensions and characteristics of underlying intentions of query reformulation. Based on the scheme, we created combinations of three facets that illustrate each reason. Through this process, 445 reason combinations were derived from 383 query reformulation activities, since some of the reason descriptions generated more than one combination. We obtained frequency of the combinations to examine the existence of various user intentions in query reformulation. Also, results of reason combination analysis were compared with a set of interactive search intentions from Xie (2002) used for our intention study design, to verify any similarities or differences of users' search intentions.

We looked at distributions of the facets of Process and Entity, and the whole reason combination. First, the distribution of Process shown in Figure 1 reveals that the most frequent process occurring as a query reformulation reason is Find, followed by Verify and Obtain. Find accounts for approximately 60% of all reason data.

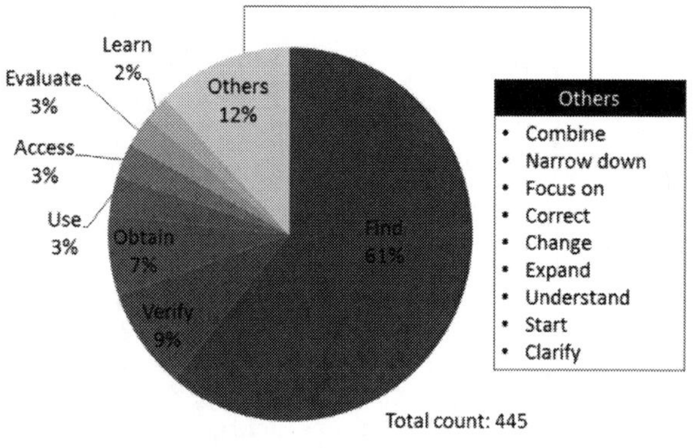


***Figure 1**. Distribution of Process*

We also examined distribution of Entity. Among three sub-facets of Entity in classification (Content, Resource, Search), Content is considerably associated with reformulation reasons as 65% of the entire reason set, compared to two other sub-facets, Resource and Search, with the proportion of 21% and 14% respectively. Across 12 different values of Entity from our classification (in Table 7), the highest frequency is found from Information, under Content, which comprises 50% of the all reason combinations. Fact and Publication follow with 9% each. This result reveals that information is (perhaps unremarkably) the most common entity cited as users' search goal for query reformulation.

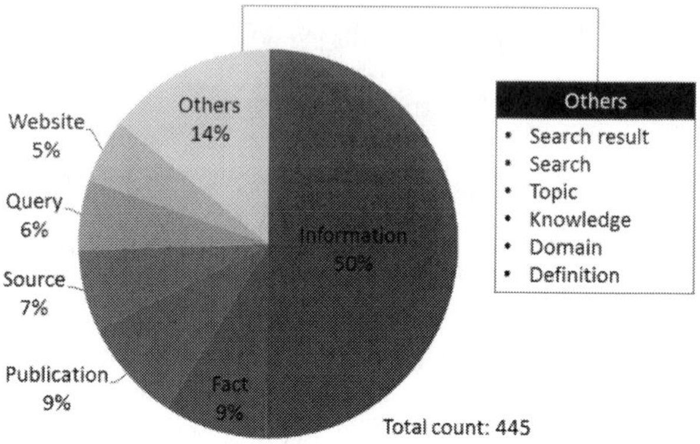


***Figure 2**. Distribution of Entity*

We also calculated frequency of the whole reason combinations (Process-Aspect-Entity). Due to the diversity of categories from each facet in our classification scheme, the large number of combination types was created, 130 in total, which include some of the combinations having a very low frequency. Figure 3 illustrates six most frequent reason combinations in our data. Find-specific-information is the most frequently stated by users as a reason for query change, counting 20% of the total reason combinations. The second most frequent one is Find-more-information, counting 7%, followed by Verify-specific-fact with 6% of the total combinations. The frequency of reason combinations clearly demonstrates that the data is skewed toward the top frequent reason, Find-specific-information, and entails a very wide range of reasons as proven by the fact that Others comprised 55% of the whole combinations with 124 different combinations, such as Find-relevant-information; Find-credible-source; Find-interesting-fact; Find-background-information, and so on.

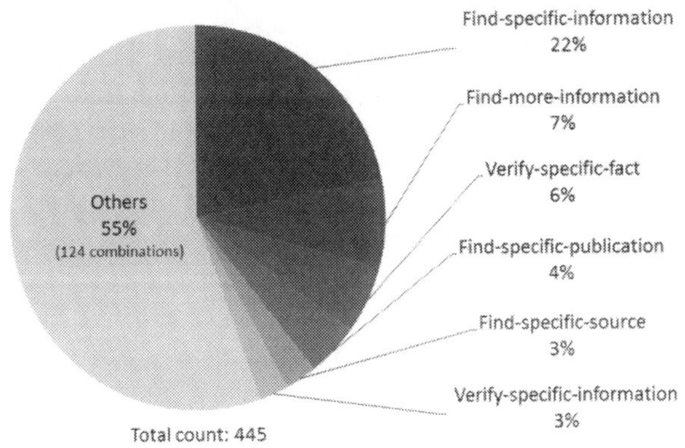


***Figure 3**. Distribution of reason combinations*

Furthermore, we compared our result of reason combinations with Xie's interactive search intentions since those two groups are comparable in terms of a structure of intentions that is comprised of a verb and a related entity.

Basically, there are common verbs describing an action related to search goals in two sets: Learn, Find, Access, Evaluate and Obtain. The difference lies in inclusion of different verbs: Identify and Locate in Xie's; and Change, Expand, Narrow down and Start in our result.

Then we compared between the whole reason combination structures and patterns of interactive intentions by Xie. Table 8 shows that some combinations were identical to the interactive intentions; such as "find specific information," "verify/evaluate specific information" and "obtain specific information." Other combinations were also comparable to the intentions in terms of a similar meaning, such as Find-more-information to "identify more to search"; Find-interesting-fact/find-different-information to "find items without pre-defined criteria"; Learn-specific-topic to "learn domain knowledge."

| Xie's Search Intention | Reason Combination |
|---|---|
| Find specific information | Find-specific-information<br>Find-specific-publication<br>Find-specific-source<br>Find-specific-website |
| Identify more to search | Find-more-information |
| Evaluate correctness | Verify-specific-fact<br>Verify-specific-information |
| Obtain specific information | Obtain-specific-information |
| Find items without pre-defined criteria | Find-interesting-fact<br>Find-different-information |
| Learn domain knowledge | Learn-specific-topic |

***Table 8.** Mapping reason combinations to Xie's (2002) interactive intentions*

However, several distinctions between our reason combinations and Xie's interactive intentions were also noted. First of all, our combinations tend to reveal more dynamic characteristics of intentions occurring during the search process. Since we suggest numerous types of Aspect in the classification, various kinds of information in which users are interested were included to the combinations, such as relevant, credible, interesting, accurate, different, and background information. This highlights that users tried to interact with a particular kind of information rather than just any information. Furthermore, our combinations imply that users kept on managing their search activity during the search process reflected by the combinations containing search-related entities, such as Correct-previous-query/search, Combine-multiple-information and Start-new-search. Such intentions were newly discovered in our study since Xie's intentions were derived from analysis of library users' information seeking processes. Also, it is worth noting that users needed to learn and understand about a topic throughout the search process via query reformulation activities, which can be understood as an expansion of Xie's intention of "learn domain knowledge." Finally, our data show that users were fairly interested in credible entities (e.g., Find-credible-information, Find-credible-source). This confirms that intentions related to issues of reliability or credibility of information or items are significant for users in information retrieval (cf. Rieh, 2002).

In sum, our analysis of RQ1 manifests various reasons for query reformulations that users have in general. Despite the small sample size, we strive to demonstrate the existence of diverse query reformulation reasons that people could have in the process of search performance

### *Relationships Between Reason Combinations and Query Reformulation Types (RQ2)*

We compared reason combinations and query reformulation types to investigate how query reformulations are associated with users' underlying reasons for query change. For this analysis, we focused on frequencies of query reformulation types in 28 different combinations only among 130 of the total, which occurred at least four times across the whole dataset. Each of these 28 combinations revealed distinctive patterns and frequencies of reformulation types. Figure 4 demonstrates six most frequent combinations and their reformulation frequency. While people having the reasons of Find-specific-information and Verify-specific-fact used Specialization most frequently, those who had Find-more information used both Specialization and Repeat most frequently. Also, when users had a reason of Find-specific-publication, most of them employed Repeat as a primary reformulation tactic. Thus, each reason combination seems to show diverse patterns and frequencies of reformulation types.

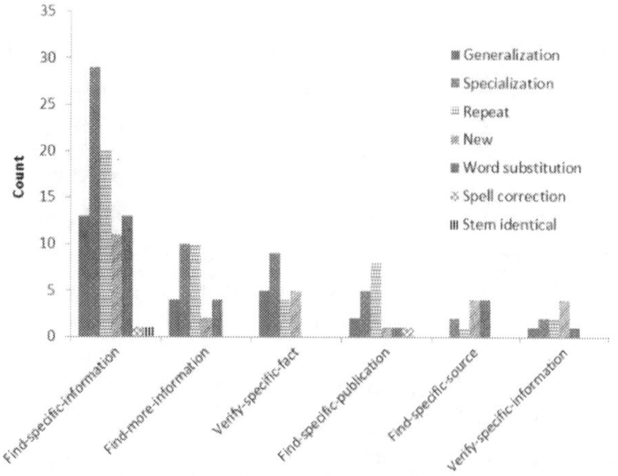


***Figure 4.*** *Frequency of query reformulation types in reason combinations*

Similarly, there are multiple reasons associated with each reformulation type. For instance, Specialization was frequently manipulated on the basis of various reasons: Find-specific-information; Verify-specific-fact; Find-interesting-fact, and so on. New frequently occurred with the reasons of Find-specific-source, Verify-specific-information, and Find-credible source. In other words, query reformulations tend to be generated by several purposes of users, not just by one particular purpose.

In addition, some of the reason combinations were closely related to their reformulation activity. That is, the reason and query reformulation behavior was well matched. For instance, the most frequent reformulation used with the reason of Find-specific-information, Verify-specific-fact, and Narrow down-previous-search/query is Specialization, which aims to specify a query by adding more words. Also, Generalization, broadening a query by reducing the word, was most frequently used by users who had intentions of Find-relevant-information and Find-new-information. On the contrary, a few combinations show unexpected relationships with their reformulation type: Start-new-search used Specialization and Repeat more than New, Obtain-specific-information triggered Generalization and Word Substitution as often as Specialization, and Correct-previous-query leads to Specialization more often than other types, especially Word substitution or Spelling Correction.

In consequence, the query reformulation reasons and reformulation types seem meaningfully related each other. However, it seems hard to elicit straightforward associations between two based on our result. Rather, it mainly tells that each type of reformulation is linked with a diversity of users' underlying goals and each goal also brings about a multiplicity of users' reformulation tactics.

### *Effect of Previous Search Intentions on Query Reformulation Reasons (RQ3)*

In order to analyze how preceding search intention leads to specific reasons of query reformulation, we compared search intentions that users had prior to query reformulation to reason combinations.

Figure 5 presents overall distribution of total intentions of users, satisfied and unsatisfied. The total number of search intentions leading to query reformulations is 1,824 including 1,575 satisfied intentions and 249 unsatisfied intentions. Participants could choose multiple intentions for each query. The most frequently selected search intention is "find specific information," followed by "obtain specific information" and "identify something more to search."

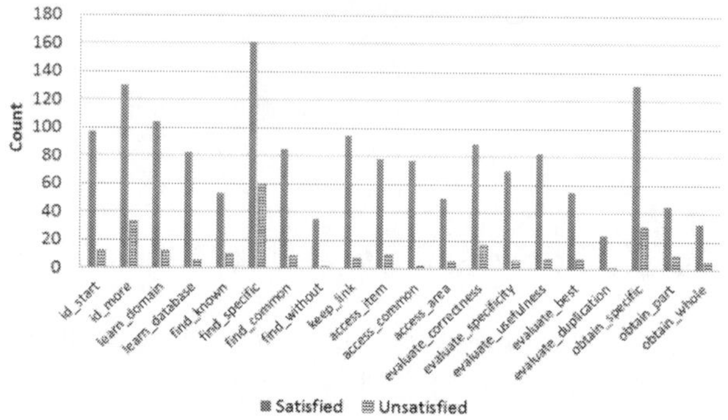


***Figure 5.*** *Frequency of search intentions*

We analyzed the most frequently described reason combination after each type of intention. Even though each of the intentions shows slightly different patterns and frequencies of following reformulation reasons, certainly, Find-specific-information is the most frequent reason after the majority of preceding search intentions, such as "identify something to get started", "identify something more to search", "learn domain knowledge", "evaluate correctness of information", "obtain specific information", and others. It reflects users altered their query mainly to find specific information regardless of their search intention prior to query change. It may be caused by the nature of our search tasks assigned to the users that is primarily concerned with finding information or facts. Besides, since frequency of reason combinations is already heavily skewed to Find-specific-information compared to other combinations, the relationship between intentions and reasons seems also skewed in the same way.

In order to explore whether intention is satisfied or not has influence on reasons of query reformulation, we investigated the most frequent reason combination after two cases, when the preceding intention was satisfied and when it was not satisfied. There were only four intentions that differ in the subsequent reformulation reason depending on intention success: "learn database content"; "find a known item"; "access a specific item"; "evaluate duplication of an item." Other intentions except these four yielded the same reason in two cases, mostly as Find-specific-information. That is, whether the previous intention is successful or not may not be a critical factor influencing users' reformulation reasons. However, it is difficult to draw a strong conclusion based on the current findings. Since we obtained intention data highly skewed to a set of satisfied intentions as Figure 5 hints, reasons after satisfied intentions and those after unsatisfied intentions are also unbalanced; reason combinations after unsatisfied intentions are much smaller than those after satisfied intentions.

## DISCUSSION

With respect to *RQ1: What are reasons for query reformulation?*, we have developed and presented a novel classification scheme of reasons for query reformulation, which could serve as the basis for further investigations of query reformulation in different contexts. Using this scheme, we've shown that there is a wide variety of reasons for query reformulation, although the frequency of occurrence of specific reasons, in our data, is highly skewed to one reason, Find-specific-information. This may be due to the type of tasks set the participants. It may also be due to the characteristics of the classification scheme, in which we opted for a large number of values in the facets, rather than grouping concepts, as this was still an exploratory exercise.

We investigated the validity of the classification scheme and its use by comparing the reasons for query reformulation to Xie's (2002) interactive search intentions. The results both confirm (or match) those intentions and also expand them in interesting ways that are probably due to the rather different contexts in which her data and ours were collected. For instance, our reason classification highlights that users' search intentions are closely related to a web search activity itself. In the process of interactive information searching, they seem to make use of their queries and search results previously experienced in improving their next search quality. That is, search intentions are not limited to accomplishing their general task or search goals, but are also relevant to managing their search performance throughout the search session. Furthermore, an increasing attention to quality of information items and sources is identified in our study. We note that people become more interested in good quality of information or sources than any types of information in their search.

With respect to *RQ2: How are types of query reformulation related to users' reasons for query reformulations?* – Our most important finding is that the same reformulation types were used for many different purposes/reasons. This has two major implications. One is that merely noting the type of reformulation will not be predictive of the person's interactive search intention in the next query segment. The other is that this demonstrates the poverty of available methods for the person to communicate with the information retrieval system. Only query reformulation seems likely to be insufficient as a means for supporting many of the different intentions identified by our results. For instance, if a person's intention is to learn about a domain, offering the ability to explore a network representation of the database could be a better support technique than offering the ability to reformulate a query through, e.g., Generalization.

However, our results do indicate the possibility of identifying clearer relationships between reformulation types and those intentions. Some query reformulation reasons in our results are frequently well matched with a particular type of reformulation (e.g., Find-specific-information and Specialization; Find-new-information and Generalization). Because, in our dataset, the frequencies of reformulation types by reason combinations are low, more data may help identify whether such relationships are reliable.

With respect to *RQ3: How do previous interactive search intentions affect reasons of following query reformulations?* – Although we investigated the relationships between previous search intentions and reasons for query reformulation, our results are inconclusive. The overwhelming frequency of just one type of reason, Find-specific-information, meant that it was related to almost all previous intentions. Also, the number of unsatisfied intentions was quite small in our dataset, so that meaningful relationships with respect to any difference in satisfaction couldn't be found. The effect of prior intention's success on following reformulation reasons should be further articulated with the larger amount of data in order to verify our tentative conclusion on the weak relationship between two. We hope that, with a planned expansion of our dataset, some of these issues might be resolved; also, having different types of motivating and search tasks could change this situation.

## CONCLUSION

The results presented and discussed in this paper are just a first step in characterizing and understanding what searchers hope to accomplish when reformulating queries during an information search session. We primarily make claims about the existence of reasons for query reformulation, not their typicality, by this exploratory exercise. We believe that the classification scheme of reasons for query reformulation is an important basis for further work on this problem, and that the results of our application of the scheme demonstrate is potential utility. Clearly, there are limits to the generalizability and interpretation of our results, given the specific context in which our data were collected, and the amount of data which we were able to analyze. However, our development of tasks using general task facets (e.g., product, goal, level) that are applicable to any task domains or settings can still illuminate the relevance of results to tasks in other domains or search systems. In the future, it will be worthwhile to create different types of task in a different field, not limited to the domain of Journalism chosen for this study, to validate or expand our tentative knowledge of query reformulation reasons gained from this work.

The number of different reasons the participants were able to express suggests that we have at least a good starting point for further research. Our results suggest that the ways in which people are allowed to interact with search engines, i.e., query reformulation and clicking, may be inadequate for supporting them in achieving the intentions implied by the reasons for query reformulation which we have identified in this study. A possible use of our results and similar work could be to develop support techniques specific to the various intentions which are not well-served by query reformulation, and thus to more effective personalization of the search experience.

## ACKNOWLEDGMENTS

This research was supported under NSF Grant III: Small: 1423239: Characterizing and Evaluating Whole Session Interactive Information Retrieval

## REFERENCES

Bowman, M., Debray, S. K., & Peterson, L. L. (1993). Reasoning about naming systems. *ACM Trans. Program. Lang. Syst.* 15, 5 (Nov. 1993), 795-825. DOI= http://doi.acm.org/10.1145/161468.16147.

Brown, L. D., Hua, H., & Gao, C. (2003). A widget framework for augmented interaction in SCAPE. In *Proceedings of the 16th annual ACM symposium on user interface software and technology* (Vancouver, Canada, November 02 - 05, 2003). UIST '03. ACM, New York, NY, 1-10. DOI= http://doi.acm.org/10.1145/964696.964697.

Cole, M.J., Hendahewa, C., Belkin, N.J. & Shah, C. (2015) User activity patterns during information search. *ACM Transactions on Information Systems*, *33*(1): Article No. 1 (39 p.)

Ding, W. & Marchionini, G. (1997). *A study on video browsing strategies*. Technical Report. University of Maryland at College Park.

Fidel, R. (1985). *Moves in online searching. Online Review, 9*(1), 61-74.

Forman, G. (2003). An extensive empirical study of feature selection metrics for text classification. *J. Mach. Learn. Res. 3* (Mar. 2003), 1289-1305.

Fröhlich, B. & Plate, J. (2000). The cubic mouse: A new device for three-dimensional input. In *Proceedings of the SIGCHI conference on human factors in computing systems* (The Hague, The Netherlands, April 01 - 06, 2000). CHI '00. ACM, New York, NY, 526-531. DOI= http://doi.acm.org/10.1145/332040.332491.

Ghosh, D. (2016). Effects of topic familiarity on query reformulation strategies. In *Proceedings of the 2016 ACM on conference on human information interaction and retrieval* (pp. 261-264). ACM.

Guan, D., Zhang, S., & Yang, H. (2013). Utilizing query change for session search. In *Proceedings of the 36th international ACM SIGIR conference on research and development in information retrieval* (pp. 453-462). ACM.

Hollink, V., Tsikrika, T., & de Vries, A. P. (2011). Semantic search log analysis: a method and a study on professional image search. *Journal of the American Society for Information Science and Technology*, *62*(4), 691-713.

Hsieh-Yee, I. (1998). Search tactics of web users in searching for texts, graphics, known items and subjects -- A search simulation study. *The Reference Librarian*, *28*(60), 61-85.

Hu, R., Lu, K., & Joo, S. (2013). Effects of topic familiarity and search skills on query reformulation behavior. *Proceedings of the American Society for Information Science and Technology*, *50*(1), 1-9.

Huang, J., & Efthimiadis, E. N. (2009,). Analyzing and evaluating query reformulation strategies in web search logs. In *Proceedings of the 18th ACM conference on information and knowledge management* (pp. 77-86). New York:

Jansen, B. J., Booth, D. L., & Spink, A. (2009). Patterns of query reformulation during Web searching. *Journal of the American Society for Information Science and Technology*, *60*(7), 1358-1371

Jiang, J., & Ni, C. (2016). What affects word changes in query reformulation during a task-based search session?. In *Proceedings of the 2016 ACM on conference on human information interaction and retrieval* (pp. 111-120). ACM.

Li, Y. & Belkin, N.J. (2008). A faceted approach to conceptualizing tasks in information seeking. *Information Processing & Management*, *44*(6): 1822-1837

Liu, C., Gwizdka, J., Liu, J., Xu, T., & Belkin, N. J. (2010). Analysis and evaluation of query reformulations in different task types. *Proceedings of the American Society for Information Science and Technology*, *47*(1), 1-9.ACM.

Rieh, S. Y. (2002). Judgment of information quality and cognitive authority in the web. *Journal of the American Society for Information Science and Technology*, *53*(2), 145-161

Rieh, S. Y., & Xie, H. (2006). Analysis of multiple query reformulations on the web: The interactive information retrieval context. *Information Processing & Management*, *42*(3), 751-768.

Sannella, M. J. (1994). *Constraint satisfaction and debugging for interactive user interfaces*. Doctoral Thesis. UMI Order Number: UMI Order No. GAX95-09398., University of Washington.

Shenouda, W. (1991). Online bibliographic searching: How end users modify their search strategy. In *Proceedings of the 53rd annual meeting of the American Society for Information Science*, 27, 111-129.

Spector, A. Z. (1989). Achieving application requirements. In *Distributed systems*, S. Mullender, Ed. ACM Press Frontier Series. ACM, New York, NY, 19-33. DOI= http://doi.acm.org/10.1145/90417.90738.

Tavel, P. (2007). *Modeling and Simulation Design*. AK Peters Ltd., Natick, MA.

Teevan, J., Adar, E., Jones, R., & Potts, M. A. (2007). Information re-retrieval: Repeat queries in Yahoo's logs. In *Proceedings of the 30th annual international ACM SIGIR conference on research and development in information retrieval* (pp. 151-158). ACM.

Xie, H. (2002). Patterns between interactive intentions and information-seeking strategies. *Information Processing and Management*, *38*(1), 55-77.

Xie, I., & Joo, S. (2010). Transitions in search tactics during the web-based search process. *Journal of the American Society for Information Science and Technology*, *61*(11), 2188-220.

Yu, Y. T. & Lau, M. F. (2006). A comparison of MC/DC, MUMCUT and several other coverage criteria for logical decisions. *J. Syst. Softw.* 79, *5*(May 2006), 577-590. DOI= http://dx.doi.org/10.1016/j.jss.2005.05.030.

# Investigating Relations of Information Seeking Outcomes to the Selection and Use of Information Sources


**Shawon Sarka**
*School of Communication & Information (SC&I), Rutgers University, USA. shawon.sarkar@rutgers.edu*

**Chirag Shah**
*School of Communication & Information (SC&I), Rutgers University, USA. chirags@rutgers.edu*

**Yiwei Wang**
*School of Communication & Information (SC&I), Rutgers University, USA. yw498@scarletmail.rutgers.edu*



## ABSTRACT

**This paper reports the findings of a study investigating the relationship between information seekers' selection and use of information sources and their perceptions of information seeking outcomes (i.e., successes and failures) in the context of information seeking barriers as well as contextual factors such as knowledge, emotions and social role. Fifty-three participants performed four simulated information-seeking tasks over a two-day period and reported their experiences and findings in an online logbook. Semi-structured interviews with 23 participants were also conducted in order to examine the issues that arose from the logbook. Data collected from the study were analyzed by applying both qualitative and quantitative methods. The findings suggest that use of impersonal sources provides a higher likelihood of successful outcomes in information seeking episodes compared to interpersonal sources. Meanwhile, interpersonal sources were found to be more effective in providing personalized information. Moreover, there were no significant associations among users' education, cognitive and emotional characteristics, and other contextual factors and successes and failures in information seeking. Lastly, constraints such as, lack of help from people, unreliable information, and time limitation seemed to influence information seeking outcomes and increase the chances of unsuccessful results.**



## KEYWORDS

information seeking, information sources, information seeking barriers, information seeking outcomes


## INTRODUCTION

Any single information-seeking episode is a complex activity that may include different information behaviors (Belkin, Cool, & Stein, 1995). Researchers have investigated information seeking behaviors from different perspectives and developed various models to analyze them. Previous studies have identified information goals, tasks, resources, seeking strategies and seeking outcomes as important aspects of an information-seeking episode. Moreover, a user's experience in information seeking and prior domain knowledge can influence how they seek information. Other contextual elements such as the situation in which the information need arises and social and cultural environment can also affect a user's information seeking episodes (Hsieh-Yee, 2001).

The quality of information seeking outcomes influences the seeker's decision to continue seeking information, reformulate strategies or abandon the search process. However, although existing models of information seeking and searching behavior explain users' approaches, judgements, and actions while attempting to satisfy their information needs (e.g., Kuhlthau, 1991), there has been relatively little research on users' perceptions of information seeking success and failure and what factors influence these interpretations. Several studies have shown that users experience many difficulties when they seek information and often fail to retrieve desired information, which cause doubts about the quality of results as well as reformulations of needs (e.g., Kuhlthau, 1993). In order to evaluate and improve users' information seeking experiences, we need to further investigate information seeking outcomes and their relationship with aspects of information seeking strategies to characterize the outcomes and identify what makes them successes or failures.

A user's selection of information sources is an important strategic action within their information seeking strategy as a whole (Xie, 2002). Having realized a scarcity of past studies regarding the relationship between information sources and seeking outcomes, the study reported here attempts to understand the outcomes of information seeking episodes by investigating the relationship between users' selection and use of information sources within an information seeking episode and users' perception of said episode's outcome. In this paper, we first present the theoretical framework of the study and then define our research question based on the literature review. Next, we report our study's methodology, analysis and results. Finally, we present our plans for future research and our conclusion.


80th Annual Meeting of the Association for Information Science & Technology, Washington, DC, VA | Oct. 27-Nov. 1, 2017

## LITERATURE REVIEW

In order to identify the relationship between information seeking outcomes and users' selection of sources, we first defined information sources and seeking outcomes. Then, we reviewed related past studies to create our theoretical framework.

### *Information Sources*

Individuals utilize all types of sources while fulfilling their information needs within a seeking episode. An information source is a repository that carries and provides knowledge (Xu & Chen, 2006). Information sources are one of the two dimensions of information seeking strategies, indicating how people plan their information seeking process, search and select information sources, and finally exit from the process (Xie, 2002; Savolainen, 2016). Sources of information can be impersonal/non-human (e.g., online sources, search engines, physical documents) or interpersonal/human (e.g., friends, colleagues) on a variety of online or offline channels (e.g., Agarwal, 2011).

There are different criteria by which users value and select information sources including users' previous experience with a source, accessibility of the source, and the format and content of the information available (e.g., Lin, Cole, & Dalkir, 2014). When selecting among information sources available to them, users sometimes look for information in such a way that require the least amount of effort in the process, regardless of the quality of the information they expect to obtain. This is accomplished by choosing the information source which has the least physical or psychological and financial cost in its use (Allen, 1977). Anderson, Glassman, McAfee, and Pinelli (2001) found that users perceived information sources that are easier to use as more accessible and choose them frequently. In addition, time constraints appear to be an influential consideration in the selection of the impersonal and interpersonal source (Wang, Sarkar & Shah, 2017).

Several studies on information source selections and preferences have found that different types of information sources are preferred in different situations, in diverse everyday life and work related contexts (e.g., Savolainen, 2008). Fisher and Naumer (2006) identified several preference criteria for information sources in their study such as, trustworthiness, contact, access or convenience, inexpensiveness, and ease of use.

### *Information Seeking Outcomes and Measuring Them*

Studying information seeking outcomes can be hard because it is often not clear exactly what constitutes a successful or failed seeking episode. Sometimes, the outcome is considered a success when a user finds the desired information, while a failure may occur when the information is not located. Other times, results may be neither successes or failures – the episode is a partial success or failure in that the process retrieves some pieces of information that do not completely fulfill users' needs. Such outcomes may occur due to a variety of reasons, both internal and external, including the selection of information sources and other socio-cognitive elements (Mansourian, 2006).

There are several qualitative and quantitative methods to measure the outcomes of the information seeking episodes such as retrieval effectiveness method (precision and recall), transaction log analysis, critical incident technique, and user satisfaction measures (Tonta, 1992). In retrieval effectiveness method, precision and recall measures are used to evaluate seeking outcomes in document retrieval systems. Precision is defined as the proportion of retrieved documents that are relevant, whereas recall is defined as the proportion of relevant documents retrieved (Blair & Maron, 1985). To examine the success or failure of a user's information seeking process, many studies have analyzed transaction logs of online catalogs that record users' interactions with the information retrieval systems (Tonta, 1992). However, these two methods have some limitations. Transaction logs and precision/recall can record the number of successes or failures (e.g., zero hits), but they cannot explain why a particular search failed or succeeded and they cannot reveal users' intentions or whether they are satisfied with the results (Larson, 1991). In the critical incident technique, researchers collect and then classify detailed incident reports and make inferences based on the observed incidents (Flanagan, 1954). Some researchers examined information seeking outcomes in light of user satisfactions. In this method, seeking outcomes are identified and analyzed based on users' own reported identification of successes and failures when they retrieve required information in an information-seeking episode (Mansourian, 2006).

### *Users' Perceptions of Information Seeking Outcomes*

A number of studies have explored user's performance and their perceptions and feelings in relation to their information seeking outcomes (i.e., successes and failures). Failure to find information within an information seeking episode has been studied a few times (e.g., Meho and Tibbo, 2003; Mansourian and Ford, 2007). Meho and Tibbo (2003) defined failure as an inability to obtain needed information or access desired sources of information, whereas Wilson (2006) classified an information seeking episode as a failure if the resulting information was not used. Huotari and Wilson (2001) investigated organizational information needs and measured the effects of failed seeking outcomes on an organization's overall success. Mansourian and Ford (2007a) found that searchers themselves attributed their failures to external factors (e.g., luck or information not being available) or internal ability and effort.

In a comprehensive study of failure and success, Mansourian (2006) explored factors that influence web searchers' perceptions and feelings towards their search failures and successes. He identified success and failure based on users' identification of success when they retrieve required information. He categorized success and failure in information seeking into six types according to users' expectancy of information on the web: *Anticipated Success, Serendipitous Success, Unexpected Success, Unexpected Failure, Unexplained Failure* and *Inevitable Failure*. In another study, Shenton (2007) found that information seeking failure is a more subjective feeling of dissatisfaction based on individuals' needs. In his study, Ankeny (1991) surveyed 600 end-users and asked them to answer three questions that affirmed that each was fully satisfied with the search result, found exactly what was needed, and was not dissatisfied in any way. Of the 600 searches in the sample, 233 met all three above criteria for complete success and 367 were less than successful, yielding an overall success rate of 38.8 percent. Moreover, users reported reasons for dissatisfaction such as, system problems, relevancy of the information retrieved and more.

Despite researchers' efforts to study information seeking sources and outcomes, existing studies have several major limitations. First, while some studies investigated information seeking failures, successful information seeking episodes or partial successes have hardly been examined. Investigating the relationship between seeking outcomes and information sources in the context of other characteristics of information seeking (e.g., users' education, and social role) are even scarcer. Second, the literature has mostly explored information seeking outcomes – particularly failures – in the Web environment. Information seeking processes do not always start on the Web, nor do they necessarily stop on the Web. In some scenarios, the Web may not even be the ideal place to look for information. Studies considering offline contexts (e.g., face-to-face communication, physical documents) should also be conducted. Third, researchers have heavily focused on users in academic or professional context (e.g., college students) who may or may not represent the general population's information seeking behavior.

To fill in the gaps in existing research, the study reported here attempts to procure a broader picture of information seeking outcomes and their relationship to individuals' selection and use of information sources in the context of other aspects of information seeking episodes with a diverse sample of participants. Therefore, this study employs a user-oriented, exploratory and mixed-method approach. The findings contribute to the general understanding of information seeking strategies, information source preferences, and especially information seeking outcomes.

Implementing information seeking outcome measure is complex because it is difficult to define the concept of outcome, which can be subjective and dependent on users' own perceptions and judgements about failures and successes in information seeking. For this study, in order to understand outcomes from participants' perspectives, we solely asked them to explain their level of successfulness in words and to provide their reasoning, and the later defined three categories emerged from their explanations.

Based on the work of Lamm, Mandl, and Koellex (2009), Mansourian (2006), and our observations of the collected data for this study, we defined three levels of seeking outcomes to categorize users' own perceptions:

> Success – an information seeking episode is considered successful *when the user finds desired information that fulfills their information needs* with the strategic action taken (e.g., searching on Google, asking a colleague).
>
> Failure – an information-seeking episode is considered a failure when the user is unable to find information that fulfills their information needs.
>
> Partial Success – an information-seeking episode is considered a partial success *when the user finds some information that fulfils part of their information need.*

## RESEARCH QUESTION

Based on the literature review, the basic research question we hope to address is:

**RQ**: What are the relationships between individuals' selection and use of information sources and their information seeking outcomes in the context of their information seeking barriers as well as factors such as knowledge, emotions and social role?

## METHOD

### *Participants*

As the study attempts to investigate users from a general population that go beyond heavy information users (e.g., academic users) and professional contexts, we recruited 53 participants from Amazon's Mechanical Turk [1] (hereafter MTurk) which provides access to a very diverse participant pool (Mason & Suri, 2012). MTurk is a crowdsourcing platform for individuals and businesses to post tasks that require human intelligence (e.g., surveys, usability testing, labeling). Registered MTurk users from all over the world can select work to finish and be compensated. It has been increasingly utilized by researchers to recruit participants for behavioral research (e.g., Evans & Chi, 2010) due to its diverse subject pool and low cost. We only recruited participants residing in the United States this time to reduce issues in English proficiency and time differences. Among the 53 participants, 26 were male and 27 were female. Their ages ranged from 19 to 65 with an average of 35.8 (SD=11); 67.9% had at least a college education. Their professional or educational backgrounds were in a wide variety of fields such as software engineering, biology, retailing, painting and firefighting. A few of them were self-employed or full-time MTurkers.

### *Task Design*

Four simulated information-seeking tasks with four different scenarios were designed and assigned to participants, all of

[1] https://www.mturk.com/mturk/welcome

which were exploratory tasks without a specific answer. Task topics were initially inspired by a qualitative survey conducted on MTurk for another study that examined individuals' failures in information seeking (see Wang & Shah, 2016). We designed the tasks based on those that participants rated as highly difficult. We also referred to Wildemuth and Freund's (2012) guideline that exploratory search tasks should provide specific context and situation while also offering flexibility in task outcomes, thus inspiring multi-stage and multi-faceted information seeking endeavors. Below are the task descriptions presented to the participants:

> **Task One (T1):** Suppose you are preparing for a debate tournament. One of the topics will be whether abortion should be legal. Find at least five arguments that support legalizing abortion and five arguments that oppose legalizing abortion.

> **Task Two (T2):** Suppose you are considering purchasing a hybrid car and want to compare the pros and cons of different manufacturers and models (e.g., Honda, Ford and Toyota). You also want your potential car to cost no more than $25,000. Please find a hybrid car model that fits your budget and requirement.

> **Task Three (T3):** Suppose you are writing a report to discuss whether cell phones are safe. Please find at least five arguments to support that cell phones are safe and five arguments to oppose it.

> **Task Four (T4):** Suppose you are looking for an affordable apartment (under $1000/month) in the city of Providence, Rhode Islands that best matches your needs. You want the apartment to be in a convenient location (e.g., close to grocery stores, restaurants). You also want to consider the neighborhood (e.g., safety). Please find at least two apartments that satisfy your requirements.

### Study Design

We designed the study in two stages. First, we provided participants with access to the tasks and an online logbook in which they were to detail their information seeking experiences. They were given up to two days to finish the tasks and logbook entries. After they submitted their logbook responses, we invited each of them to participate in a half-hour semi-structured follow-up interview. Twenty-three of them agreed to be interviewed via GoToMeeting[2]. Both stages of the study could be finished remotely (online logbook & audio call). This permitted us to recruit participants from all over the country to diversify the sample. Each participant was compensated $15 for finishing the tasks and logbook and an extra $10 for completing the interview.

The purpose of the study is to analyze and compare individuals' experiences of looking for information, not to complete the information seeking tasks. In other words, we did not expect participants to spend more than an hour on each task or thoroughly complete the task (e.g., have a car in mind to purchase). Therefore, we considered the fact that MTurk Workers only get paid if their work is accepted by Requesters, so they typically try to achieve satisfactory outcomes. Our instructions specifically emphasized that their compensation would not be affected by the information they found because we aimed to understand their experiences. They were encouraged to spend up to an hour on each task, though they could stop at any time within that hour if they found enough information or decided to give up. They did not have to finish the tasks in one sitting. If they did not finish the tasks in two days following acceptance, MTurk would automatically end their access to the tasks. The unfinished tasks would be re-opened for others to sign up.

### Logbooks

In their logs, we asked participants to provide their information seeking strategies, the difficulties they encountered (if any), their findings and whether they considered each strategy to be successful. For the study, we characterized users' information seeking strategies as a two-dimensional concept based on methods and resources (Xie, 2002). Methods refer to actions performed by users to interact with information such as scanning, browsing, etc. Resources include information, information objects and humans with whom users interact (Xie, 2002). In other words, participants described both their methods employed and sources consulted as their information seeking strategies. For each task, they were required to use at least three different strategies to look for their desired information. At least one of the three should have included interpersonal source(s) (e.g., interacting with people online or offline). In addition to the open-ended descriptive questions, they also needed to rate the accuracy, trustworthiness, relevance and adequacy of the retrieved information on a five-point Likert scale. We gave participants two days following their acceptance of the tasks on MTurk to work on the questions and write in their logbooks. Their partial responses were automatically saved by the system so they could pause at any time and start at their previous stopping point. Here is a portion of the information we asked users to record in their logbooks:

Please describe step-by-step the first strategy you adopted to look for information, including but not limited to the sources you consulted (e.g., people, websites) and the questions asked or keywords entered if it was an online search.

> What difficulties did you encounter when using this strategy?
>
> What did you find out?

---

[2] https://www.gotomeeting.com/

Do you think you succeeded in finding the information you needed with this strategy? Why?

Data collected from the logbooks does not always completely capture the dynamic nature or complexity of many situations or explain participants' perspective. Since filling in the logbook was not an iterative process and participants did not always know what elements to report, they sometimes left out informative details such as the reasons behind certain moves (e.g., why they picked some sources over the other available ones). The follow-up interviews provided us with a more complete picture about their experiences than the logbook data alone.

### *Semi-Structured Interview*

Semi-structured individual interviews were conducted to gather in depth explanations of participants' activities and to answer questions that resulted from unclear or incomplete logbook descriptions. For example, one participant complained that a Website *"was not organized enough for someone who has no knowledge on cars,"* but did not elaborate. We were able to learn about how the website was badly organized in the interview.

In the first section of the interview, we asked questions based on users' reported task experiences, and in the second section, we asked about their information seeking habits in general. Below are some sample questions we asked during the interviews:

Regarding your response to the first task about abortion, you said, *"Some sites are more opinion than facts."* Is that the reason you rate accuracy and trustworthiness pretty low?

What do you mean by facts? Could you give me an example?

Regarding your response to the third task, cellphone and safety, you did a Google search as your second strategy, and gave high ratings because *"a lot of information was from very reputable sources."* How do you define *"reputable sources"*?

## DATA ANALYSIS

Fifty-three participants submitted a total of 636 information-seeking episodes (everything occurred after they started one strategy and before they started the next strategy). Participants' choices of information sources (e.g., Websites, people), the channels in which they consulted the sources (e.g., face-to-face, phone), the barriers they faced, and the contextual factors that shaped their information seeking approaches were coded using three different coding schemes (coding process reported in following paragraphs). We used a mixed-method approach to analyze seeking outcomes. In the qualitative analysis, we classified the outcome of each information-seeking episode into success, failure or partial success based on participants' reported level of success with each strategy. We next explored the relationship between users' selected information sources and information seeking outcomes. In the quantitative analysis, we used statistical methods to analyze information sources, self-reported information seeking barriers, and the outcome of an information-seeking task. We then compared the two analyses' findings to see if the statistical analysis echoed our qualitative observation.

We used Agarwal's (2011) classification of source/channel types to categorize the sources and channels employed by participants to look for information. This classification considered three dimensions of sources/channels: 1) interpersonal-impersonal; 2) physical-electronic; 3) synchronous-asynchronous, thus enabling us to summarize all information sources being used. Six categories of sources/channels were taken into consideration including face-to-face, phone, online chatting/texting, email/online forums, online information, and physical book/manual. We modified the original classification by separating phone and online chat into two categories to achieve a finer-grained distinction.

Our initial codebook consisted of codes collected from the literature related to individuals' information seeking barriers such as time constraints, unavailability of information, unreliability of information, lack of help from people and so on (e.g., Chowdhury, Gibb, & Landoni 2011; Mansourian & Ford, 2007; Savolainen, 2015; Świgoń, 2011). We also inductively drew new codes from our data. To analyze the contextual factors that influenced seekers' activities, we modified the intervening variables in the second Wilson (1999) model of information behavior. Codes were collapsed into six main categories of contextual factors: characteristics of the sources (e.g., accessibility and credibility), demographics (e.g., age and gender), education, knowledge, experience, social environment, factors related to one's social role, as well as physiological, cognitive and emotional characteristics.

To gather data on seeking outcomes, we asked participants to provide a detailed answer to this question: *Do you think you succeeded in finding the information you needed with this strategy? Why?* We then coded their responses based on the aforementioned coding schema (Lamm et al., 2009). Each information-seeking outcome was manually classified into a success, partial success, or a failure. Participants wrote about their experiences in detail so the outcome of each seeking episode was clear and could be drawn directly from the data in most cases. For example, in the excerpt below, it was clear that the participant failed at this particular episode:

NO, I was unable to find the requested information despite looking in this manner.

Two coders first analyzed 20% of the data independently and achieved satisfactory inter-coder reliabilities for all three coding schemes (see Table 1 for the ICR for each scheme). After resolving the disagreement, each then coded half of the remaining data.

| | Sources | Barriers | Contextual Factors |
|---|---|---|---|
| Cohen's Kappa | .91 | .89 | .91 |

***Table 1**: Inter-coder reliability for each scheme*

The quantitative analysis reported here was conducted to comprehensively and empirically examine relationships between information seeking outcomes and users' selection of information sources within an information-seeking episode, as well as other contextual factors (e.g., knowledge and unreliable information) that influence users' information seeking experiences. After each episode's outcome was coded, we ran frequency analysis for all variables in order to understand the data distribution. Apart from exploring the relationship between each type of information source and information-seeking outcome, we also decided to explore the relationships between each information-seeking barrier and contextual factor with the outcome.

Next, a 2x2 contingency table was created for each pair of variables. A contingency table counts the number of observations for each combination of levels of two or more categorical variables. We conducted *Pearson's Chi-Square* tests (if the expected frequencies for the variable was larger than *5*) or *Fisher's Exact Test* (if the expected frequencies in a cell was smaller than *5*) to explore whether two variables in each pair were significantly related to each other. Since our data is categorical, using statistical methods designed for normal, quantitative outcomes (*ANOVA* or *regression*) would have yielded incorrect $p$-values due to violation of the normality and equal variance assumptions. They also would have given meaningless out-of-range predictions for some levels of the variables (Seltman, 2015). *Pearson's Chi-Squared* test is used to determine whether an association between two categorical variables (i.e., data has been counted and divided into categories) in a sample is likely to reflect a real association between these two variables in the population. The *Chi-Square* test is intended to determine how likely it is that an observed distribution is due to chance.

## FINDINGS

Our study produced 636 information seeking episodes related to our four tasks, 389 (61%) of which were successful, 93 (14.6%) of which were partially successful, and the rest (154, 24.2%) were unsuccessful or failures. In 636 information-seeking episodes, participants decided to use impersonal sources 457 (71.9%) times, and interpersonal sources 198 times (31.1%). Descriptive statistics for the whole dataset are summarized in Table 2.

| Information Sources, Barriers & Contextual factors | # of Observations | Information-Seeking Outcomes (% within the variable) | | |
|---|---|---|---|---|
| | | Success | Partial Success | Failure |
| Contextual Factors | | | | |
| Social Role & Network | 69 | 33 (47.8%) | 8 (11.6%) | 28 (40.6%) |
| Knowledge/Education | 58 | 41 (70.7%) | 10 (17.2%) | 7 (12.1%) |
| Environment | 11 | 5 45.5% | 1 9.1% | 5 45.5% |
| Emotional/Cognitive | 29 | 11 (37.9%) | 8 (27.6%) | 10 (34.5%) |
| Barriers | | | | |
| Information is not available | 78 | 20 (25.6%) | 13 (16.7%) | 45 (57.7%) |
| Unreliable Information | 100 | 32 (32%) | 20 (20%) | 48 (48%) |
| Lack of help from people | 37 | 9 (24.3%) | 4 (10.8%) | 24 (64.9%) |
| Time Constraint | 14 | 3 (21.4%) | 3 (21.4%) | 8 (57.1%) |
| Ads and Spams | 10 | 6 (60%) | 0 (0%) | 4 (40%) |
| Technical Problems | 19 | 12 (63.2%) | 4 (21.1%) | 3 (15.8%) |
| Sources | | | | |
| Websites | 402 | 283 (70.4%) | 53 (13.2%) | 66 (16.4%) |
| Search engines | 282 | 197 (69.9%) | 36 (12.8%) | 49 (17.4%) |
| Online Posts | 15 | 8 (53.3%) | 4 (26.7%) | 3 (20.0%) |
| Chatting & Texting | 30 | 10 (33.3%) | 3 (10%) | 17 (56.7%) |
| Phone | 59 | 28 (47.5%) | 9 (15.3%) | 22 (37.2%) |
| Posting on online forums | 29 | 12 (41.4%) | 1 (3.4%) | 16 (55.2%) |
| Face to Face | 55 | 23 (41.8%) | 11 (20.0%) | 21 (38.2%) |
| All Impersonal Sources | 457 | 314 (68.7%) | 63 (13.8%) | 80 (17.5%) |
| All Interpersonal Sources | 198 | 82 (41.4%) | 33 (16.7%) | 83 (41.9%) |

***Table 2:** Descriptive statistics of information-seeking episodes in relation to seeking outcomes (only the variables with more than 10 observations are reported here)*

Overall, participants chose impersonal sources more often than interpersonal sources. Among impersonal sources, participants primarily used search engines (e.g., Google, and Yahoo!) and various Websites (e.g., Wikipedia, and apartment.com) 61.7% (282 times) and 87.9% (402 times), respectively. The success rates were higher for impersonal sources (S = 68.7%, F = 17.5%) than interpersonal sources (S = 41.4%, F = 41.9%). It is also noticeable that the failure rates were higher than the success or partial success rates in cases of user reported information seeking barriers, e.g., information is not available (S = 25.6%, F = 57.7%), unreliable information (S = 32%, F = 48%), lack of help from people (S = 24.3%, F = 64.9%), and time constraint (S = 21.4%, F = 57.1%).

## Chi-Square *Test*

*Pearson's chi-square* values (assuming the variable's expected frequencies were larger than *five*; *Fisher's Exact test* was conducted otherwise) were generated to explore the relationships between all observable behaviors and seeking outcomes. We defined the null hypothesis for the test as the following.

**$H_0$:** there is no relationship between the two categorical variables.

Results of the relations for each information-seeking episode are reported in Table 3.

| Variables and Seeking Outcomes | Pearson's Chi-Square value | df | *p*-value |
|---|---|---|---|
| Social Role & Network | 11.298 | 2 | .004 |
| Knowledge/ Education | 5.134 | 2 | .077 |
| Environment | 2.494† | | .238 |
| Emotional/Cognitive | 7.571† | | .021 |
| Information is not available | 59.747 | 2 | .000 |
| Unreliable Information | 46.572 | 2 | .000 |
| Lack of help from people | 30.192† | | .000 |
| Time Constraint | 10.256† | | .004 |
| Ads and Spams | 2.148† | | .335 |
| Technical Problems | 1.221† | | .531 |
| Websites | 44.204 | 2 | .000 |
| Search engines | 17.240 | 2 | .000 |
| Online Posts | 1.877 | | .413 |
| Chatting & Texting | 15.267† | | .000 |
| Phone | 6.606 | 2 | .037 |
| Posting on online forums | 14.007† | | .001 |
| Face to Face | 9.726 | 2 | .008 |
| All Impersonal Sources | 46.071 | 2 | .000 |
| All Interpersonal Sources | 56.377 | 2 | .000 |

*†Fisher's Exact Test*

***Table 3:*** *Chi-square values (statistically significant associations with the p-value <0.05 are shown in bold)*

When the *p*-value is less than *0.05*, we can reject the null hypothesis that two variables are not related. We conclude that there is an association between the two variables. Therefore, *p*-values were compared and the statistically significant associations with the $p<0.05$ were selected as the best associations to predict information seeking outcomes. The relationships that yielded the best *p*-value only included variables related to information seeking barriers, impersonal and interpersonal sources. Only social roles and networks as contextual factors, was statistically significant in relation to seeking outcomes. There were no statistically significant relationships between any of the contextual behavioral variables such as, participants' prior domain knowledge, educational background, emotional or cognitive characteristics and seeking outcomes in simulated tasks.

The results of our quantitative analysis corroborated our qualitative analysis. In the quantitative analysis, we saw that participants decided to use impersonal sources more often (457 times out of 636) than interpersonal sources (198 times). Moreover, in 68.7% of information seeking episodes, users who selected impersonal sources reported that they succeeded in finding necessary information, whereas they reported failure in only 17.5% of episodes. Furthermore, most users who turned to search engines and online websites as sources successfully located necessary information in 70.4% and 69.9% of searches, respectively. Similarly, in our qualitative analysis, we saw that the majority of participants started seeking information with a general Google search, and then from the result page choose a website to visit. They even utilized search engines to locate other information sources they had in mind (e.g., "*I first googled Craigslist*"). Among these participants, the majority reported that they had succeeded in finding desired information while very few reported that they failed to find information online. One stated:

> *Yes, using Google and looking at their search results gave me a robust list of websites that had valuable data for me to reference.*

The unsuccessful seeking outcomes associated with interpersonal sources are a little higher than the successful seeking outcomes rate (S = 41.4%, F = 41.9%). We also observed that many participants encountered difficulties while interacting with interpersonal sources. Some participants reported that the person they choose as a source did not have the information they needed. For example, one participant said:

> *No, I did not succeed in finding info, since I didn't find any info from my wife.*

> *Sometimes, the participants could not find a human source to help with the task:*

> *No as I was not able to find someone to talk to about apartments in that area.*

The partial success rates are also higher in cases of interpersonal sources (16.7%) over impersonal sources. While interacting with human sources, many participants felt that they could not get the full picture or that they received opinions over facts. For example:

> *Yes and no, her opinions aren't always one that I follow but this one does seem to make sense to me.*
>
> *Another participant pointed out,*
>
> *Yes, a little bit. It was an opinion but it did point out a few things on both sides of the argument but heavily resting on that they are safe.*

While reporting failures, participants mentioned various types of contextual, environmental and internal barriers and problems related to information seeking strategies. One participant complained that she could not go to the library because of time constraint despite the fact that she preferred it over the Internet because *"anybody can post anything on the Internet,"* therefore, the quality is not always satisfactory. Another participant blamed unreliable information:

> *No, although I thought some were great prices and photos looked great, I don't feel comfortable using craigslist at all.*

These observations are also evident in the quantitative analysis. The information seeking failure rates are higher than the success or partial success rates in cases of user reported information seeking barriers such as, information is not available, unreliable, lack of help from people, and time constraint.

## DISCUSSION

The data analysis presents some interesting findings about the seeking outcomes. In this section, we discuss our findings in light of the proposed research question. From our mixed-method analysis, we found that there are indeed relationships between individuals' selection and use of information sources and their information seeking outcomes. Moreover, there are barriers and other contextual factors that affect both the selection and use of sources and the seeking outcomes in information seeking episodes.

From the qualitative analysis, we found that the main reason behind the higher success rate with the use of impersonal sources is their easy accessibility. Impersonal sources – especially search engines and websites – are typically available anywhere and anytime. Therefore, it is easier to find required information on the Internet. Contrastingly, interpersonal sources were not always accessible irrespective of communication media. Many participants reported that they could not find any person to talk with (especially in our two-day's time limit) and thus could not find the information that way. One participant reported,

> *The phone call was a failure. I wasn't able to speak to anyone.*

The two prominent information-seeking barriers that we unearthed in the study – *lack of help from people* and *time constraints* – were primarily associated with interpersonal sources. In addition, because the debate topics are controversial, some participants indicated their difficulties with soliciting information from friends and family (e.g., *watching [her friend's name] cry for about an hour, asking such sensitive questions to my family and friends*). The majority of participants who used interpersonal sources and experienced failures reported these two barriers in their logbooks. Therefore, it was evident that under strict time constraint, selection and use of interpersonal sources increase the chances of failure in an information-seeking episode.

One of our main reasons for recruiting participants from Amazon's MTurk was to make our population sample diverse with different ages, educations and professions. We wanted to observe whether these factors had any influence on participants' selection of sources and on information seeking success and failure. We did not find a significant relationship between contextual factors such as user demographics, knowledge and educational backgrounds, and seeking outcomes, barring the social role factor. Nevertheless, in our qualitative data, we found out that participants who had a large network of people or who held a particular social position had access to sources that provided necessary information for a successful outcome. However, such sources were usually unavailable to the general population. For example, a company CFO who participated in our study could ask employees who owned hybrid cars for information:

I analyzed the roster of employees at my company with regards to their parking applications to see which has a hybrid vehicle. Then I approached them to discuss their opinion of their vehicle and the price point they paid for the vehicle. I also asked them if they had any other information which they thought would be valuable…

Another interesting observation regarding contextual factors derived from our qualitative analysis of the data: participants' perception and definition of information sometimes influenced their perception of success and failure in their information seeking behaviors. This did not appear in the quantitative analysis because it was not statistically significant. Some participants did not consider personal opinions to be information, especially regarding the debate topic tasks, and that influenced their perception of seeking outcomes. One participant mentioned,

> *I do not think I succeeded with this strategy, because it was based off opinions and not statistics or fact as the others were. For that reason, I do not find it beneficial.*

Despite all the advantages, impersonal sources have some limitations such as providing information that is neither personalized nor trustworthy (e.g., *I am not sure on the trustworthiness of the site but everything else is good enough; it is sometimes hard to judge if the pictures and information is a true representative of what the apartment actually looks like*). Interpersonal sources, particularly participants' friends and family, were more credible in providing personalized advice, as these participants described:

> *I trust the opinions of these coworkers as I have worked with them for 3 years, and know them well enough to know their opinion is valid and beneficial.*
>
> *My friend has owned his Prius for several years. It was reasonably priced, gets great gas mileage, and he genuinely recommends it. This is just a friend but I trust him a lot.*

Interpersonal sources were especially valuable in the hybrid car task since not everyone was an expert in this area. Human sources could tailor information to fit a seeker's need:

> *I usually take that [friends' or experts' opinions] into consideration, especially from a friend ... Friends usually give me information in a condensed manner, make it easier to understand.*

For the debate topics, participants liked to collect facts rather than opinions. However, some of the "opinions" they gathered from people could be informative and helpful in completing the tasks. Although participants did not normally consider such information to be successful, we think that kind of experience could be beneficial, and thus should not be simply defined as a failure. For example:

I talked to a female friend I have who had an abortion and asked her opinion. She told me she regretted it sometimes and it was a very hard decision. She said that sometimes she thinks about what life would be like with that child.

This study has some limitations. First, our four simulated search tasks are not related to participants' daily lives, and participants were not required to complete the tasks. These may have triggered some of them to complete the tasks differently. One of our participants mentioned that in real life, if they had to purchase a car, they would have contacted the dealer and asked for a test drive, but did not do so for our task because they felt it would waste the dealer's time. In addition, this study is based on users' self-reported data. As with other self-reported data research, it is prone to some biases.

## CONCLUSION AND FUTURE RESEARCH

The purpose of this study was to examine the relationship between individual's information source preferences and the outcomes of the information seeking episodes in the context of their information seeking barriers and contextual factors. The study identified that users' information source preferences affect the outcomes of the information seeking episodes in various ways and four main conclusions can be drawn from the findings presented in the previous section.

First, this study demonstrated that users who selected and used impersonal sources had a higher probability of success, mostly because the information within impersonal sources and the sources themselves are easily accessible anytime. Second, although interpersonal sources provided better understanding of information seeking context, they did increase searchers' chances of failure in finding the information. Third, contrary to previous studies (e.g., Hsieh-Yee, 2001), our findings indicate that there are no statistically significant associations among users' educational, cognitive, and emotional characteristics that relate to users and their information seeking successes and failures. However, a few cases showed that individuals' social network affect their chances of getting help from interpersonal sources and success in finding information they needed. Lastly, there are some constraints, such as lack of help from people, unreliable information and especially time limitation, that did influence seeking outcomes and increase the chances of unsuccessful results. The source that users choose to seek information is an important consideration in making sure that they obtain the required information. Users' preferences for some information sources over others available to them along with the contextual factors and barrier are of great significance to the understanding of users' information seeking outcomes and overall information seeking behaviors. This understanding can result in the improvement of information services that better serve users' information needs and furthermore, improve the chances of successful outcomes in information seeking. In the future, we would continue to work in this line of research by further analyzing the partial successes and failures and also the task or goal characteristics in relation to seeking outcomes.

## ACKNOWLEDGEMENTS

The work reported in this paper is supported by the U.S. Institute of Museum and Library Services (IMLS) grant #LG-81-16-0025-16.

## REFERENCES

Agarwal, N. K. (2011). Information source and its relationship with the context of information seeking behavior. In *Proceedings of the 2011 iConference*, 48-55.

Allen, T.J. (1977). *Managing the flow of technology*. Cambridge, MA: MIT Press

Anderson, C. J., Glassman, M., McAfee, R., B., & Pinelli, T. (2001). An investigation of factors affecting how engineers and scientist seek information. *Journal of Engineering and Technology Management, 18(2),* 131-155.

Ankeny, M. L. (1991). Evaluating end-user services: Success or satisfaction? *Journal of Academic Librarianship, 16*(6), 352–356.

Belkin, N., Cool, C., Stein, A., & Thiel, U. (1995). Cases, scripts, and information seeking strategies: On the design of interactive information retrieval systems. *Expert Systems with Applications, 9(3),* 379-395.

Blair, D. C., & Maron, M. E. (1985). An evaluation of retrieval effectiveness for a full-text document-retrieval system. *Communications of the ACM, 28(3),* 289-299.

Chowdhuri, S., Gibb, F., & Landoni, M. (2011). Uncertainty in information seeking and retrieval: A study in an academic environment. *Information. Processing & Management, 47(2),* 157-175.

Evans, B. M., & Chi, E. H. (2010). An elaborated model of social search. *Information Processing & Management*, *46*(6), 656-678.

Fisher, K. E., & Naumer, C. M. (2006). Information grounds: Theoretical basis and empirical findings on information flow in social settings. In *New directions in human information behavior*, 93-111. Springer Netherlands.

Flanagan, J. C. (1954). The critical incident technique. *Psychological Bulletin*, *51*, 327.

Hsieh-Yee, I. (2001). Research on web search behavior. *Library & Information Science Research*, *23*(2), 167–185.

Huotari, M., & Wilson, T. D. (2001). Determining organizational information needs: The critical success factors approach. *Information Research, 6(3).*

Kuhlthau, C. C. (1991). Inside the search process: Information seeking from the user's perspective. *Journal of the American Society for information Science, 42(5),* 361.

Kuhlthau, C. C. (1993). A principle of uncertainty for information seeking. *Journal of Documentation, 49(4),* 339-355.

Larson, R. R. (1991). Between Scylla and Charybdis: Subject searching in the online catalog. *Advances in Librarianship, 15,* 175-236.

Lin, Y., Cole, C., & Dalkir, K. (2014). The relationship between perceived value and information source use during KM strategic decision-making: A study of 17 Chinese business managers. *Inform. Process. Manag. 50(1)*, 156-174.

Mansourian, Y. (2006). Information visibility on the web and conceptions of success and failure in web searching (Doctoral dissertation). University of Sheffield.

Mansourian, Y., & Ford, N. (2007). Search persistence and failure on the web: A "bounded rationality" and "satisficing" analysis. *Journal of Documentation*, *63*(5), 680–701.

Mansourian, Y., & Ford, N. (2007). Web searchers' attributions of success and failure: An empirical study. *Journal of Documentation*, *63*(5), 659–679.

Mason, W., & Suri, S. (2012). Conducting behavioral research on Amazon's Mechanical Turk. *Behavior Research Methods, 44(1),* 1–23.

Meho, L. I., & Tibbo, H. R. (2003). Modeling the information-seeking behavior of social scientists: Ellis's study revisited. *Journal of the Association for Information Science and Technology, 54(6),* 570-587.

Savolainen, R. (2008). Source preferences in the context of seeking problem-specific information. *Information Processing & Management, 44(1),* 274-293.

Savolainen, R. 2015. Cognitive barriers to information seeking. *Journal of Information Science, 41(5),* 613-623.

Savolainen, R. (2016). Information seeking and searching strategies as plans and patterns of action: A conceptual analysis. *Journal of Documentation, 72(6),* 1154-1180.

Shenton, A. K. (2007). Causes of information-seeking failure: Some insights from an English research project. *Youth Information-Seeking Behavior II: Contexts, Theories, Models and Issues.*

Seltman, H. J. (2015). *Experimental Design and Analysis, Technical Report.* Pittsburgh: Carnegie Mellon University.

Świgoń, M. (2011). Information limits: Definition, typology and types. *Aslib Proceedings, 63(4),* 364-379.

Tonta, Y. (1992). Analysis of search failures in document retrieval systems: A review. *The Public-Access Computer Systems Review, 3(1),* 4-53.

Wang, Y., Sarkar, S., & Shah, C. (2017). Investigating information seekers' selection of interpersonal and impersonal sources. In *Proceedings of the 2017 conference on human information interaction and retrieval*, 353-356.

Wang, Y., & Shah, C. (2016). Exploring support for the unconquerable barriers in information seeking. In *Proceedings of the Association for Information Science and Technology annual meeting, 53*(1).

Wildemuth, B. M., & Freund, L. (2012). Assigning search tasks designed to elicit exploratory search behaviors. In *Proceedings of the ACM symposium on human-computer interaction and information retrieval*, 4.

Wilson, T. D. 1999. Models in information behavior research. *Journal of Documentation, 55(3),* 249-270

Wilson, T. D. (2006). On user studies and information needs. *Journal of documentation, 62(6),* 658-670.

Xie, H. I. (2002). Patterns between interactive intentions and information seeking strategies. *Information Processing and Management, 38(1),* 55–77.

Xu, Y., & Chen, Z. (2006). Relevance judgment— What do information users consider beyond topicality? *Journal of the American Society for Information Science and Technology, 57(7),* 961–973.

# Computational Content Analysis of Negative Tweets for Obesity, Diet, Diabetes, and Exercise

**George Shaw, Jr.**
*School of Library and Information Science, University of South Carolina, USA. gshaw@email.sc.edu*

**Amir Karami**
*School of Library and Information Science, University of South Carolina, USA. karami@mailbox.sc.edu*

## ABSTRACT

**Social media based digital epidemiology has the potential to support faster response and deeper understanding of public health related threats. This study proposes a new framework to analyze unstructured health related textual data via Twitter users' post (tweets) to characterize the negative health sentiments and non-health related concerns in relations to the corpus of negative sentiments regarding diet, diabetes, exercise and obesity (DDEO). Through the collection of six million Tweets for one month, this study identified the prominent topics of users as it relates to the negative sentiments. Our proposed framework uses two text mining methods, sentiment analysis and topic modeling, to discover negative topics. The negative sentiments of Twitter users support the literature narratives and the many morbidity issues that are associated with DDEO and the linkage between obesity and diabetes. The framework offers a potential method to understand the publics' opinions and sentiments regarding DDEO. More importantly, this research provides new opportunities for computational social scientists, medical experts and public health professionals to collectively address DDEO-related issues.**

## KEYWORDS

diet, diabetes, exercise, obesity, text mining, social media

## INTRODUCTION

Social media has provided an additional source that enables us to view, like and disagree with opinions and experiences of those we know and those who we may not know. Social media also provides a platform to communicate information and market products, and for everyday individuals to express their sentiments (feelings) regarding multiple political, entertainment and societal issues (Mejova, Weber, & Macy, 2015; Pang & Lee, 2008).

The ability to analyze various sentiments of social media users provides candid insight to users' feelings and opinions. Social-media based digital epidemiology can support faster response and deeper understanding of public-health threats than traditional methods (Eichstaedt et al., 2015). The publicly available data on Twitter has created a new intersection of public health, health informatics and data science. Automatic systems can probabilistically infer what is happening around the world by using the data of what people are thinking and doing (Nasukawa & Yi, 2003; Wiebe et al., 2003; Zabin & Jefferies, 2008). With roughly 328[1] million active users, Twitter is seen as a reliable data source to provide real-time feedback and opportunity to understand users' concerns (Mejova, Weber, & Macy, 2015).

While there are many social phenomena that we are able to determine by users' sentiments, common health issues will be the focus of our conversation. From 1980 to 2014, obesity has doubled according to the World Health Organization (WHO). Moreover, roughly 29% of the world's population is considered overweight and over 600 million adults are considered obese. The lack of physical activity, coupled with the excess intake of energy from food, contributes to weight gain and diabetes (Hill, Wyatt, & Peters, 2012; Wing et al., 2001). While we know that some populations are more affected than others, fears have risen in that this generation may have a shorter life expectancy than their parents (Flegal, Carroll, Kit, & Ogden, 2012; Ogden, Carroll, Kit, & Flegal, 2012; Wang, Beydoun, Liang, Caballero & Kumanyika, 2008).

A change in lifestyle behaviors, such as proper diet and exercising, can drastically alleviate the obesity public health epidemic through these modifiable behaviors (Wing et al., 2001). The lack of exercising and its link to obesity increases the risk for heart disease, hypertension, diabetes, arthritis and certain cancers (Blackwell, Bass, Bishop, & Hussaini, 2012). It is estimated that by 2050, roughly 29 million Americans will be diagnosed with Type 2 diabetes; which is a substantial increase of 165% from the 11 million diagnosed with the condition in 2000. Furthermore, several studies have shown the relations that exist among diet, diabetes, exercise and obesity (DDEO) (American Diabetes Association, 2004; Barnard et al., 2009; Hartz, Rupley, Kalkhoff, & Rimm, 1983).

"Sentiment and subjectivity are quite context-sensitive, and, at a coarser granularity, quite domain dependent" (Pang & Lee, 2008, p. 21). Meaning, sentiment opinions are different

80th Annual Meeting of the Association for Information Science & Technology, Washington, DC, VA | Oct. 27-Nov. 1, 2017



[1]https://www.statista.com/statistics/282087/number-of-monthly-active-twitter-users/

across various domains and its intended use. Two exact expressions posted on two different webpages or social media platforms can elicit different meanings. Researchers must remain cognizant of this issue when doing sentiment analysis research; however, sharing millions of posts in social media, such as Twitter, provides a great opportunity to track people's health concerns.

This research proposes a framework, using two text-mining methods, to analyze health related text data via Twitter users' post (tweets). This study seeks to characterize the negative health sentiments and non-health related concerns in relations to corpora of negative sentiments regarding DDEO. Diabetes is a significant medical condition that is normally associated with overweight and obesity (Flegal, Carroll, Kit, & Ogden, 2012). Two behavioral factors that can reduce an individual's risk of being obese and consequently, developing diabetes, are proper dieting and getting the recommend daily physical activity suggested by the evidence-based Physical Activity Guidelines of America (Wing et al., 2001)[2]. Based on these studies, diet, diabetes and exercise, in addition to obesity were chosen as topics.

While the focus of the framework will be applied to unstructured Twitter data, there is potential for this framework to be used on reports and notes generated from health information systems or web-based weight management interventions with social media components. The results from this framework can also offer health professionals' additional insight to individuals' negative sentiments about exercising regularly, dieting and diabetic concerns. This study attempts to answer this question: *"What are the negative characteristics of health and non-health concerns of people with respect to DDEO?"*

## LITERATURE REVIEW

Surveys and behavioral risk factor surveillance systems such as those utilized by the CDC are commonly used methods to collect health data. However, it can take weeks or years to collect, clean, and analyze the data (Wartell, 2015). Given the dynamic nature of Twitter, it offers researchers a new method to collect relatively real-time data (Eichstaedt et al., 2015). By using data from Twitter, we are able to identify sentiments and topics using sentiment analysis and topic modeling. The automatically identified topics and corresponding opinions provide a fine-grained understanding of opinionated text data that is done through social media to identify public opinion (Rahman & Wang, 2016; Jo & Oh, 2011; Lin & He, 2009, Paul & Dredze, 2012). This study defines negative sentiments as those opinions that express a desirable state away from a neutral positioning (Yi, Nasukawa, Bunescu, & Niblack, 2003; Nasukawa & Yi, 2003).

Researchers have shown that Social Networking Site (SNS) users, particularly Twitter, are more inclined to share their health information within Twitter than they would with their doctor (Paul & Dredze, 2014). SNS such as Facebook, Twitter, and Instagram have grown in their tracking of health issues and show strong correlation between the trends in social media and the U.S. Centers for Disease Control and Prevention reports (Paul & Dredze, 2011; Paul & Dredze, 2014). The following sections will describe how Twitter has been used to track and identify non-health and health-related issues and those studies that have specifically utilized Twitter for sentiment analysis and topic modeling.

### *Twitter and Tracking Health Issues*

Twitter has been used to mirror the offline sentiments of the general public based on a content analysis; and its prediction power to determine the likely outcomes of the stock market based on mood analysis (Bollen, Mao, & Zeng, 2011; Tumasjan, Sprenger, Sandner, & Welpe, 2010). From a health perspective, Twitter has been used to address a number of issues. There have been numerous studies showing Twitter's ability to predict influenza outbreaks. In 2009, Twitter was instrumental in predicting the swine flu pandemic using n-grams historical context (Culotta, 2010; Lampos & Cristianini, 2012; Lampos, Bie, & Cristianini, 2010; Paul & Dredze, 2011).

A study by Abbar, Mejova, and Weber (2015) demonstrated that friends on Twitter normally live in close geographic context of each other and share similar demographic variables. Friends are also likely to show similar interest toward food. A similar study showed that people, who tweet about drug abuse, also have friends that are dealing with similar problems (Hanson, Cannon, Burton, & Giraud-Carrier, 2013).

Another study utilized Twitter to identify evidence regarding the influence of social media on public health and its use to communicate health information. Using #childhoodobesity to monitor private person, for profit, nonprofit, media, government, educational tweets, and network connections; the researchers found lack of government, media, and educational sources of childhood obesity (Harris, Moreland-Russell, Tabak, Ruhr, & Maier, 2014). This may suggest a limited presence of credible sources and information about childhood obesity on Twitter. In addition, the limited information regarding home or school based strategies for reducing childhood obesity show that limited information regarding these evidence-based strategies are available (Harris et al., 2014). These research studies demonstrate Twitter's ability as a tool to track, predict, and model offline behavior.

The analysis of Tweets can help allied health professionals identify users' negative sentiments as it relates to the characteristics of DDEO. This research identifies the prominent topics of users as it relates to the negative sentiments (feelings). Statements themselves may be negative and understanding prominent topics among negative sentiments (corpus of negative statements) is an alternative approach to identifying the

[2] https://health.gov/paguidelines/guidelines/summary.aspx

topics related to DDEO based solely on negative expressions (Nasukawa & Yi, 2003).

## METHODOLOGY

In conjunction with data collection, the proposed framework utilizes sentiment analysis and topic modeling (Figure 1) to identify the prominent negative expression of Twitter users by applying the topic modeling on negative sentiments.

The question of "What are the negative characteristics of health and non-health concerns of people with respect to DDEO?" will be addressed through the collection of a large number of tweets using the Twitter API (Application Program Interface).[3]

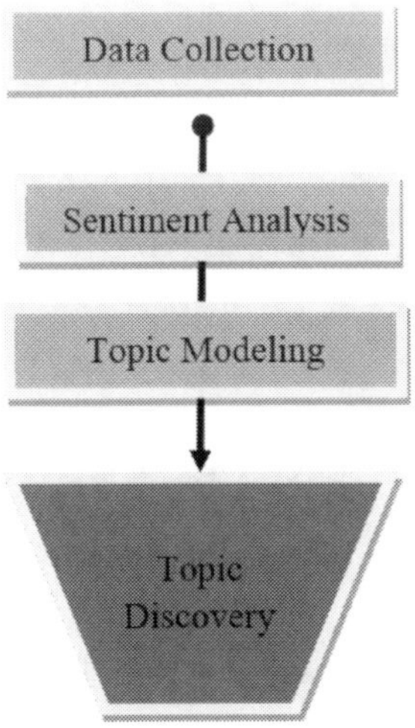


***Figure 1**: Negative analytics framework*

## DATA COLLECTION

This study collected the Twitter data using a real-time data collection method. By using this method, we are able to collect 10% of the publicly available English tweets. Previous research has analyzed a particular health topic such as influenza or mental health issues (Lampos et al., 2010; Eichstaedt et al., 2015). However, the data collected for this study will focus on the four areas key terms diet, diabetes, exercise and obesity. From these key terms, the search terms for the Twitter API were created. Eight queries were used to collect nearly 6 million tweets with 61 million tokens between June 1, 2016 and June 30, 2016 (Table 1).

As part of the data collection process, post processing of the data collected requires cleaning by removing stop words such as *and*, *of*, *the* (based on a standard list of stop words). This will allow the topic modeling toolkit used for the discovery of topics, to correctly identify the topics for analytics purposes.

| DDEO Topics | Twitter API Queries |
|---|---|
| DIABETES | #diabetes OR diabetes |
| DIET | #diet OR diet |
| EXERCISE | #exercise OR exercise |
| OBESITY | #obesity OR obesity |

***Table 1**: Queries for Twitter API*

### *Sentiment Analysis*

Sentiment analysis shows subjectivity and polarity in text data with two main approaches: learning-base and lexicon-base. Learning-based approach applies machine learning techniques to build classifiers from data. Lexicon-based approach uses a pre-defined dictionary of positive and negative words to find the frequency of positive and negative words. (Medhat, Hassan, & Korashy, 2014). In this research, we use Linguistic Inquiry and Word Count (LIWC) that is a Lexicon-based tool. This tool assisted with identifying the negative sentiments, based on the corpus of data collected. We found ~2 million negative tweets.

### *Discovery of Topics*

Topic discovery among the negative tweets to identify themes is done using topic modeling. As a commonly used method, the latent Dirichlet allocation model (LDA) was appropriate to use for this type of experiment. In addition to topic modeling abilities to cluster semantically related words, topic modeling has been used to discover relevant clinical concepts and structure in patient's health records, predict protein-protein relationships based on the literature knowledge, find patterns that exist within genetics data and image topic discovery (Arnold, El-Saden, Bui, & Taira, 2010; Blei, 2012).

LDA is based on the notion that the corpus contains topics and that each word in each document can be assigned to each of the topics with varying degree of weight per topic. In this experiment, we use LDA to identify the topics by using the corpus of negative tweets. Therefore, we utilize the results of the sentiment analysis for negative Tweets, employing topic modeling to discover the negative topics. We utilized the Mallet natural language processing program to identify topics in the negative tweets.[4]

After the data was cleaned, the model was trained to find the number of topics. To determine a proper number of topics, 80% of tweets for training and 20% of tweets for testing were used to estimate log-likelihood (Wallach, Murray, Salakhutdinov, & Mimno, 2009). Based on the log-likelihood estimation, we were able to determine that the optimum number of topics needed for training and testing was 425 topics (see Figure 2).

[3] https://dev.twitter.com/overview/documentation
[4] http://mallet.cs.umass.edu/topics.php

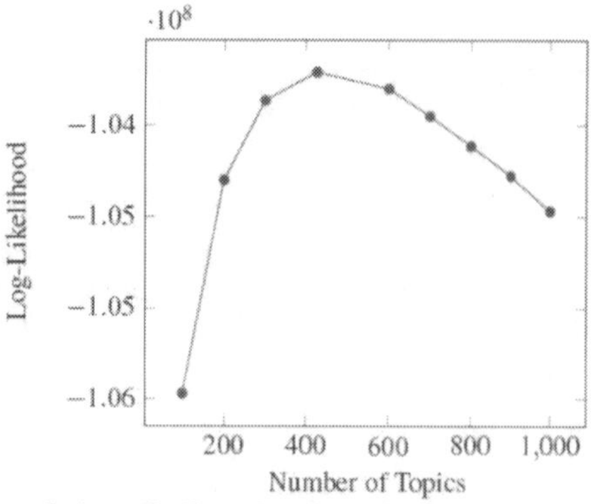

***Figure 2****: Log-likelihood topic estimation*

## RESULTS AND DISCUSSION

There were unique sub-topics discovered in addition to topics that represented the keywords of our search. The discovered topics were assigned to one of the four search terms (DDEO words) that were used for data collection. The discovered topics that had more than half of the associated words relating to the DDEO words was labeled as Diet, Diabetes, Exercise or Obesity. Table 2 shows the detected topics and sub-topics in the negative tweets. The main DDEO topic of exercise had a sub-topic of "mental health." We also see that the DDEO topics of exercise and diet are connected (Table 2).

### Obesity

"Diet, diabetes, medical, and cancer" were the four sub-topics identified from the collected Twitter data as it relates to obesity. Based on the sub-topics, there are negative feelings towards things such as *bodyweight*[5] and obtaining *weight loss tips*. There was great concern regarding the impacts of obesity with relation to diabetes. Characteristics of "diabetes" included pre-diabetic (*prediabetes*), *arthritis*, and the *stress* with managing *weight* with foods high in *glycemic* (See Figure 3[6]). Survey data shows that when individuals do not meet their individualized targets for glycemic control, blood pressure, or lipid control, they are at greater risk of diabetes (Ali et al., 2013).

| DDEO Topics | Sub-Topics |
|---|---|
| Diet | Food; Fastfood; Medications; Wellness; Alternative Diets; Religious Diets; Sweets |
| Diabetes | **Obesity**; Hypertension; Kidney; Cancer; Food; |
| Exercise | Lifestyle; Weightless; Body Image; **Diet**; Mental Health |
| Obesity | **Diet**; **Diabetes**; Medical; Cancer; Weight; Food |
| Non-Health Topics | People; Emotions; Celebrity; Government; Events |

***Table 2****: Topics and sub-topics*

There are also negative sentiments towards medical fads or conditions that promise *extreme weight loss*. *Gout* and pancreatitis (*paynecreatitis*) were listed as negative medical impacts of being obese. While there was no mentioning of specific foods, the inclusion of "diet" as a sub-topic does bring awareness to the nutritional impacts of food and obese individuals.

### Diabetes

The most significant sub-topics identified included "obesity,

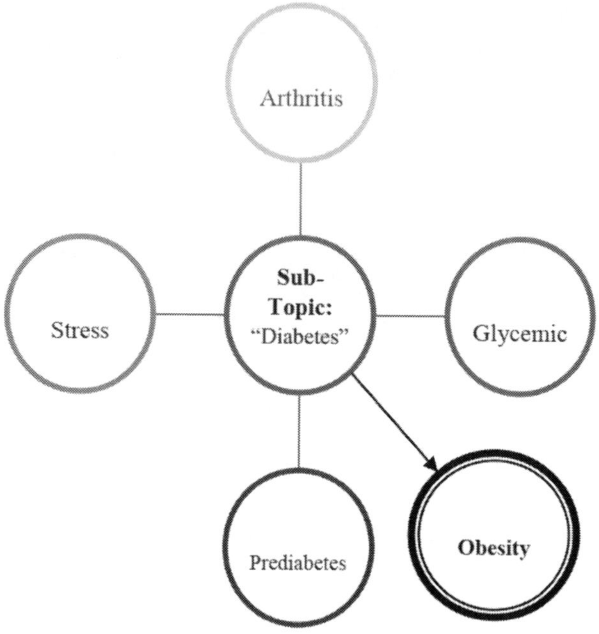

***Figure 3****: Characterizing words for sub-topic "diabetes" in relation to obesity*

hypertension, and kidney." Researchers have documented the link between obesity and diabetes (Harris et al., 2014; Harvard, n.d; Reilly & Kelly, 2011). The data reveal commonly seen results with characterizing words such as *excess fat*, difficulty *working out*, *belly fat*, and consuming excessive amounts of *sugar*. A surprising negative feeling about obesity was *genetic*. It is inconclusive, based on the sub-topics, the concern of genetics regarding obesity; but this may suggest a conversation involving the obesity pandemic that needs to be discussed. "Hypertension" (see Figure 4) was another sub-topic that yielded interesting characteristics. *Insulin* and *glucose* were concerns with regards to hypertension

A study in the 1980s, using random population sampling, identified the possible link between hypertension, obese individuals, and glucose intolerance (Modan et al., 1985). Furthermore, recent studies continue to show the link between

---

[5] To assist readers with distinguishing between sub-topics and words that characterize the sub-topics, Quotation Marks "" are used to identify sub-topics words and *Italics* style is used to represent the words that characterize sub-topics

[6] Additional characterizing words included *lipolysis*, *weight*, and *diabetesawarness* (diabetes awareness).

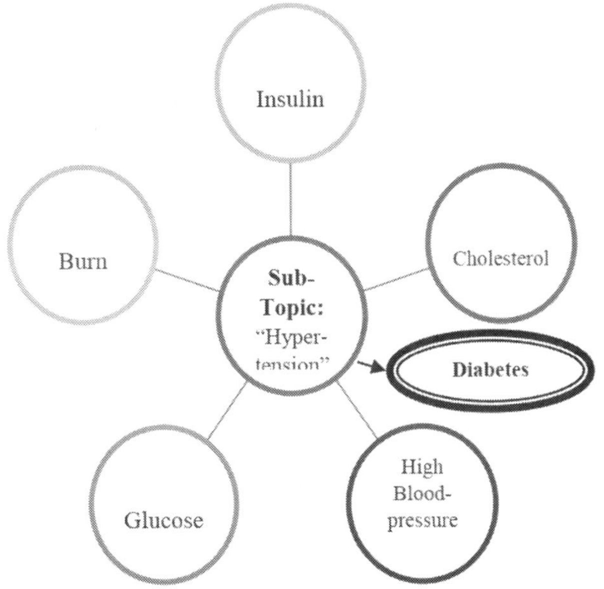


***Figure 4:*** *Characterizing words for sub-topic "hypertension" in relation to diabetes*

***Figure 5:*** *Characterizing Words for Sub-topic "Lifestyle" in relation to Exercise*

diabetes and hypertension that affirms the negative sentiments Twitter users have regarding glucose levels and insulin (DeVallance, 2015; Lukic et al., 2014; Willig et al., 2015). Continued issues with weight and high glucose levels can lead to kidney (renal) failure.

### Exercise

Much of the public understands the connection between obesity and the health risks associated with the condition; such as diabetes and heart disease. Increased TV and computer time with lack of exercise are factors that contribute to obesity (Tompson et al., 2012). "Lifestyle" was one of the significant sub-topics identified with exercise. *Biking,* sporting activities (*sports*), and *running (*see Figure 5) were characterized as negative sentiments for engaging in physical activity. However, *soreness* and *inflammation* were also identified as words that characterized a lifestyle of physical activity.

These negative sentiments (i.e. *Biking, sporting activities*, and *running)* support data from the 2006 National Health Interview Survey in that "many overweight and obese people with prediabetes and diabetes do not report behaviors conducive to weight loss or physician advice for such behaviors" (Dorsey & Songer, 2011). The inability to change lifestyles may not only be a result of not engaging in physical activity, but dealing with the inflammation and physical aches (*soreness* and *inflammation* ) that are a result of being physically active and creates barriers to a physical lifestyle.

"Mental Health" was another significant sub-topic identified with the exercise topic. Engaging in physical activity releases endorphins that trigger a positive feeling in the body, contributing to positive psychological benefits (Mead et al., 2009)[7]. However, being included as a negative sentiment, what do characterizing words such as *brain*, *Alzheimer's*, and *endorphins* imply for the sub-topic "mental health?" It is possible that individuals are concerned about their mental well-being due to the lack of exercising.

### Diet

Of the four main topics, Diet yielded the most sub-topics. Expected sub-topics based on previous studies included "food" and "wellness" (Abbar et al., 2015; Turner-McGrievy & Beets, 2015). Food tweeted by users are predictive of the national obesity and diabetes statistics (Abbar et al., 2015).

"Medications" was another sub-topic of diet that was intriguing. Considering that many fad diets advertise the use of some super pill to assist with losing weight within Twitter, a negative sentiment towards "medication" within this context is not alarming. However, *cancer* was one of the words that characterized medications. "Types of diets" was another significant sub-topic that described Diet. As seen in Figure 6, *nutrisystem*, *skinny diets*, and *vegan* are words that describe this sub-topic of diet. *Juicing* is a growing alternative diet trend that has conflicting sentiments regarding its effectiveness as a healthier option to eating fruits and vegetables (MacVean, 2015).

### Non-health Topics

Examples of the non-health related topics based on our corpus can be seen in Table 2. While the framework did not perform extremely well with detecting non-health related topics, there were some topics identified that are applicable to the DDEO related tweets. Although "Emotions" was not identi-

[7]http://www.webmd.com/depression/guide/exercise-depression#1

fied as a sub-topic of our DDEO words, some of the characterized words for "emotion" (*feeling*, *piss*, *disabled*, and *burden*) may help explain how individuals who are struggling with being psychically inactive or have diabetes feel. This, again, supports Dorsey and Songer's (2011) study and how those with prediabetes and diabetes report behaviors to their doctor or primary care physician, despite the advantages of weight loss that can be achieved through lifestyle modification (Wing et al., 2001). Understanding the affective components of obese individuals can be beneficial to addressing their dietetic, diabetic, and physical activity concerns and behaviors.

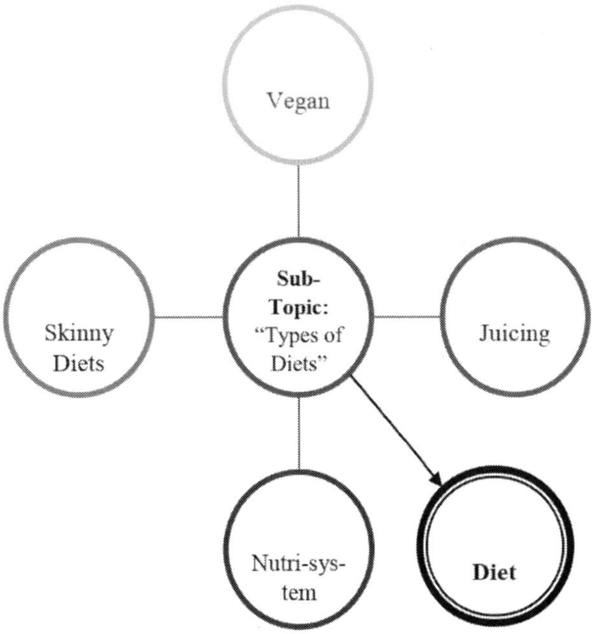


***Figure 6**: Characterizing words for sub-topic "types of diets"*

### *Analysis of DDEO Topics*

At least one DDEO related topic was represented for every topic, except Diet. There is a relationship that exists between the two topics, Diabetes and Obesity, as seen in Figure 7. Based on the characterizing words of the sub-topic "diabetes" for Obesity (ex. *prediabetes, weight glycemic, arthritis, stress*), this may suggest a negative opinion surrounding the conditions of being overweight or obese. Also, there appears to be a need for diabetes awareness (*diabetesawareness*).

Obesity included Diet as one of its sub-topics. With words such as *fatloss tips, veggie health tips*, and *fattening,* Twitter users are looking for help with their dieting efforts and weight control. Although the non-health related sub-topic of emotions was absent in Diabetes and Obesity, these emotions support the struggle and frustration that overweight and obese individuals deal with (Blackwell et al., 2012; Dorsey & Songer, 2011).

"Diet" was also a sub-topic of Exercise. The negative association of "body image" was a reason to *lose weight* and avoid being labeled a *fatty*, while dealing with the *frustration* and motivation to exercise (Dorsey & Songer, 2011). However, a caveat with this analysis is the notion of sarcasm and slang. As in many sentiment analysis studies, it is difficult to account for this complexity, as in some contextual settings, the use of the word fatty may suggest hunger and not indicative of an individual's physical or medical state, based on the meaning of the word[8].

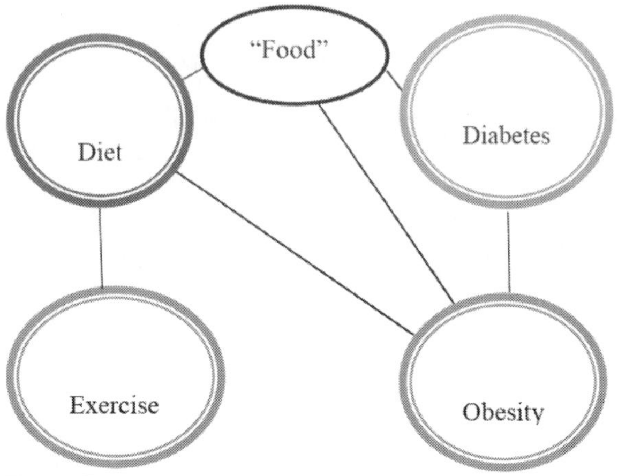


***Figure 7**: Relationship among the DDEO topics*

As previously noted, Diet did not contain any of the other DDEO topics, however, it contained a sub-topic ("food") that was also associated with Diabetes and Obesity. "Food" and "fastfood" were found in diet and the characterizing words of *fries*, *Doritos*, *McDonalds*, *beer*, show foods high in sodium, sugar, or no nutritional value. "Nutritional status is an integral component of and has vital implications on the health of individuals," (Boumtje, Huang, Lee, & Lin, 2005, p. 116). Consistently eating the proper nutritional food is important with preventing excessive spikes in your glucose levels and preventing insulin intolerance (DeVallance, 2015; Lukic et al., 2014).

The relationship of "food" among the topics also illustrates a consistent factor with the literature regarding food, exercising and maintaining a healthy weight. Exercising is important, but those efforts are negated when our eating habits remain unchanged (Marks, 2004; Oaklander, 2015). More importantly, these results provide health educators with the covertly, yet blaring alarm of proper nutrition with regards to dieting efforts to prevent obesity that are not necessarily factors of genetics, psychological well-being, or environment.

Extensive analysis of the results from our framework can elicit numerous questions and analyses; such as the brief, aforementioned analysis demonstrated (coupled with sup-

---

[8]characterized by overproduction or excessive accumulation of fat: http://www.dictionary.com/browse/fatty?s=t

porting literature). These results also provided policy makers, health professionals/educators, and dietitians with reliable, significant probabilistic results that are based on millions of user provided information. Whether through direct topic or sub-topics and their characterizing words, in our case, our framework assisted with adding an intricate narrative to the negative content regarding obesity, and latent factors that help explain these negative sentiments.

## CONCLUSION

The negative sentiments of Twitter users support the literature narrative and the many morbidity issues that are associated with obesity, diabetes, diet, and exercise. While diet was not topically associated with diabetes, exercise, and obesity, the sub-topic of "food" reveals the connection that it has with diabetes and obesity (Figure 4). Characterizing words such as *fries*, *beer*, *Doritos*, and *cookies*; are high in saturated fat, sugar, and excess calories (American Heart Association, 2017; Oaklander, 2015).

The negative sentiments in the study supports Arizona's 2012 Behavioral Risk Factor Surveillance System survey results and the Centers for Disease Control and Prevention statistics with regards to the negative impacts of not being physically active and the linkage between obesity and diabetes (Blackwell et al., 2012). This paper identifies the negative sentiments of Twitter and supports the concern that public health experts have regarding the obesity epidemic, based on literature and survey results. A majority of the public understands the connection between obesity, proper exercise, and the health impacts (Tomspon et al., 2012). In spite of the conversation and academic literature that has documented this issue, there seems to be an unclear direction with how to collectively address this problem among academic domains.

Two-thirds (67%) of adults' favor requiring chain restaurants to list calorie counts on menus, however, only 31% support limits on the size of sugary soft drinks in restaurants and convenience stores - 67% oppose this idea (Pew Research Center, 2013). "Government" was revealed as a negative non-health topic. While there is a clear understanding by the public to increase transparency and ingredients placed in foods, government restrictions on these issues are often faced with backlash.

Some form of a medical condition or concern was expressed in each of the DDEO related topics. This included characterizing words such as *cancer*, *diabetes*, *arthritis*, and *stress*. In many of these cases, the uses of drugs are prescribed to help individuals control or alleviate the medical condition. Most of the cost that is associated with treating obesity is related to the diseases that are associated with obesity and those required prescription drugs to treat the diseases or medical condition (Finkelstein, Trogdon, Cohen, & Dietz, 2009). This research study provides public health advocates with supporting evidence of the severity of obesity, particularly from a prescription drug standpoint. If this trend continues, 1 and every 6 dollars spent will be for healthcare reasons (Wang et al., 2008). Our approach to identify negative sentiments regarding obesity demonstrates the ability to discover common concerns associated with obesity and medical cost.

Instead of using a linguistic only computational analysis that is commonly seen is this type of research, we were able to identify negative public health sentiments and opinions in DDEO related tweets using sentiment analysis. The sub-topics presented, represented the vastness of issues that concerns users with regards to DDEO. Characterizing words such *lipolyis* to acupuncture (*acupunture)*, our framework was able to capture many sub-topics that would assist public health professionals. This research shows that computational scientists, medical experts, and public health professionals need to work on a united front to address issues regarding obesity.

This research has two specific limitations: time and space. The time limitation is that the data were collected during a one-month time period, June 1 – June 30 2016. We will need to extend the data collection period to address seasonal and temporal trends that impact our DDEO words used for collecting the data.


## ACKNOWLEDGMENTS

We would like to thank the information technology staff (Jill Chappell-Fail and Jeff Salter) for the technical support and School of Library and Information Science PhD committee for supporting and mentoring the doctoral student that participated in this research study.


## REFERENCES


Abbar, S., Mejova, Y., & Weber, I. (2015). You tweet what you eat: Studying food consumption through twitter. In *Proceedings of the 33rd annual ACM conference on human factors in computing systems*, (pp. 3197-3206).

Ali, M. K., Bullard, K.M., Saadine, J.B., Cowie, C. C., Imperatore, G., & Gregg, E.W. (2013). Achievement of goals in U.S. diabetes care. *New England Journal of Medicine*, *368*(17), 1613-1624.

American Diabetes Association. (2004). Physical activity/exercise and diabetes. *Diabetes care*, *27*(1), s58-s62.

American Heart Association. (2017, March 24). *Saturated fats*. Retrieved from https://healthyforgood.heart.org/Eat-smart/Articles/Saturated-Fats

Arnold, C. W., El-Saden, S. M., Bui, A. A., & Taira, R. (2010). Clinical case-based retrieval using latent topic analysis. In *AMIA annual symposium proceedings* (Vol. 2010, p. 26). American Medical Informatics Association.

Barnard, N.D., Cohen, J., Jenkins, J.A., Turner-McGrievey, G., Gloede, L., Green, A., & Ferdowsian, H. (2009). A low-fat vegan diet and a conventional diabetes diet in the treatment of type 2 diabetes: A randomized controlled 74-wk clinical trial. *The American Journal of Clinical Nutrition*.

Blei, D. M. (2012). Probabilistic topic models. *Communications of the ACM*, *55*(4), 77-84.

Blackwell, J., Bass, J., Bishop, N., & Hussaini, K. (2012). 2012 Arizona Behavior Risk Factor Surveillance System Survey.

Retrieved from http://www.azdhs.gov/documents/preparedness/public-health-statistics/behavioral-risk-factor-surveillance/annual-reports/brfss-annual-report-2012.pdf

Bollen, J., Mao, H., & Zeng, X. (2011). Twitter mood predicts the stock market. *Journal of computational science*, *2*(1), 1-8.

Boumtje, P. I., Huang, C. L., Lee, J. Y., & Lin, B. H. (2005). Dietary habits, demographics, and the development of overweight and obesity among children in the United States. *Food Policy*, *30*(2), 115-128.

Culotta, A. (2010, July). Towards detecting influenza epidemics by analyzing Twitter messages. In *Proceedings of the first workshop on social media analytics* (pp. 115-122). ACM.

DeVallance, E., Fournier, S. B., Donley, D. A., Bonner, D. E., Lee, K., Frisbee, J. C., & Chantler, P. D. (2015). Is obesity predictive of cardiovascular dysfunction independent of cardiovascular risk factors?. *International Journal of Obesity*, *39*(2), 244-253.

Dorsey, R., & Songer, T. (2011). Lifestyle behaviors and physician advice for change among overweight and obese adults with prediabetes and diabetes in the United States, 2006. *Preventing Chronic Diseases*, *8*(6), 132.

Eichstaedt, J. C., Schwartz, H. A., Kern, M. L., Park, G., Labarthe, D. R., Merchant, R. M., ... & Weeg, C. (2015). Psychological language on Twitter predicts county-level heart disease mortality. *Psychological science*, *26*(2), 159-169.

Finkelstein, E. A., Trogdon, J. G., Cohen, J. W., & Dietz, W. (2009). Annual medical spending attributable to obesity: Payer-and service-specific estimates. *Health affairs*, *28*(5), w822-w831.

Flegal, K. M., Carroll, M. D., Kit, B. K., & Ogden, C. L. (2012). Prevalence of obesity and trends in the distribution of body mass index among U.S. adults, 1999-2010. *Journal of the American Medical Association*, *307*(5), 491-497.

Hanson, C. L., Cannon, B., Burton, S., & Giraud-Carrier, C. (2013). An exploration of social circles and prescription drug abuse through Twitter. *Journal of Medical Internet Research*, *15*(9), e189.

Harris, J. K., Moreland-Russell, S., Tabak, R. G., Ruhr, L. R., & Maier, R. C. (2014). Communication about childhood obesity on Twitter. *American Journal of Public Health*, *104*(7), e62-e69.

Hartz, A. J., Rupley, D. C., Kalkhoff, R. D., & Rimm, A. A. (1983). Relationship of obesity to diabetes: Influence of obesity level and body fat distribution. *Preventive Medicine*, *12*(2), 351-357.

Harvard, School of Public Health. (n.d.). *Obesity definition*. Retrieved from https://www.hsph.harvard.edu/obesity-prevention-source/obesity-definition/

Hill, J. O., Wyatt, H. R., & Peters, J. C. (2012). Energy balance and obesity. *Circulation*, *126*(1), 126-132.

Jo, Y., & Oh, A. H. (2011, February). Aspect and sentiment unification model for online review analysis. In *Proceedings of the fourth ACM international conference on web search and data mining* (pp. 815-824). ACM.

Lampos, V., Bie, T.D., & Cristianini, N. (2010). Flu detector-tracking epidemics on Twitter. In *Joint European conference on machine learning and knowledge discovery in databases*, (pp. 599-602). Springer.

Lampos, V., & Cristianini, N. (2012). Now-casting events from the social web with statistical learning. *ACM Transactions on Intelligent Systems and Technology (TIST)*, *3*(4), 72.

Lin, C., & He, Y. (2009). Joint sentiment/topic model for sentiment analysis. In *Proceedings of the 18th ACM conference on information and knowledge management* (pp. 375-384). ACM.

Lukic, L., Lalic, N. M., Rajkovic, N., Jotic, A., Lalic, K., Milicic, T., ... & Gajovic, J. S. (2014). Hypertension in obese type 2 diabetes patients is associated with increases in insulin resistance and IL-6 cytokine levels: Potential targets for an efficient preventive intervention. *International Journal of Environmental Research and Public Health, 11*(4), 3586-3598.

MacVean, M. (2015, January 29). Juicing trend still going strong in 2015. *LA Times*. Retrieved from http://www.latimes.com/health/la-he-juice-20150131-story.html

Marks, J. B. (2004). Obesity in America: It's getting worse. *Clinical Diabetes*, *22*(1), 1-2.

Mead, G. E., Morley, W., Campbell, P., Greig, C. A., McMurdo, M., & Lawlor, D. A. (2009). Exercise for depression. *The Cochrane Library*.

Medhat, W., Hassan, A., & Korashy, H. (2014). Sentiment analysis algorithms and applications: A survey. *Ain Shams Engineering Journal, 5*(4), 1093-1113.

Mejova, Y., Weber, I., & Macy, M. W. (Eds.). (2015). Twitter: A digital socioscope. Cambridge University Press.

Modan, M., Halkin, H., Almog, S., Lusky, A., Eshkol, A., Shefi, M., ... & Fuchs, Z. (1985). Hyperinsulinemia. A link between hypertension obesity and glucose intolerance. *Journal of Clinical Investigation, 75*(3), 809.

Nasukawa, T., & Yi, J. (2003, October). Sentiment analysis: Capturing favorability using natural language processing. In *Proceedings of the 2nd international conference on knowledge capture* (pp. 70-77). ACM.

Oaklander, M. (2015, June 11). Should I eat french fries?. *Times Health*. Retrieved from http://time.com/3896083/french-fries-potato/

Ogden, C. L., Carroll, M. D., Kit, B. K., & Flegal, K. M. (2012). Prevalence of obesity and trends in body mass index among US children and adolescents, 1999-2010. *Journal of the American Medical Association*, *307*(5), 483-490.

Pang, B., & Lee, L. (2008). Opinion mining and sentiment analysis. *Foundations and Trends® in Information Retrieval, 2*(1–2), 1-135.

Paul, M. J., & Dredze, M. (2011). You are what you tweet: Analyzing Twitter for public health. *Icwsm, 20*, 265-272.

Paul, M. J., & Dredze, M. (2012). A model for mining public health topics from Twitter. *Health, 11*, 16-6.

Paul, M. J., & Dredze, M. (2014). Discovering health topics in social media using topic models. *PloS one, 9*(8), e103408.

Pew Research Center. (2013). *Public agrees on obesity's impact, not government's role.* Retrieved from http://www.people-press.org/2013/11/12/public-agrees-on-obesitys-impact-not-governments-role/

Prier, K. W., Smith, M. S., Giraud-Carrier, C., & Hanson, C. L. (2011, March). Identifying health-related topics on twitter. In *International conference on social computing, behavioral-cultural modeling, and prediction* (pp. 18-25). Springer. Berlin, Heidelberg.

Rahman, M. M., & Wang, H. (2016, April). Hidden topic sentiment model. In *Proceedings of the 25th international conference on world wide web* (pp. 155-165). International World Wide Web Conferences Steering Committee.

Reilly, J. J., & Kelly, J. (2011). Long-term impact of overweight and obesity in childhood and adolescence on morbidity and premature mortality in adulthood: Systematic review. *International Journal of Obesity, 35*(7), 891-898.

Tompson, T., Benz, J., Agiesta, J., Brewer, K. H., Bye, L., Reimer, R., & Junius, D. (2012). Obesity in the United States: Public perceptions. *The Food Industry*, 53(26), 21.

Tumasjan, A., Sprenger, T. O., Sandner, P. G., & Welpe, I. M. (2010). Predicting elections with Twitter: What 140 characters reveal about political sentiment. *ICWSM, 10*(1), 178-185.

Turner-McGrievy, G. M., & Beets, M. W. (2015). Tweet for health: Using an online social network to examine temporal trends in weight loss-related posts. *Translational Behavioral Medicine, 5*(2), 160-166.

Wallach, H.M., Murray, I., Salakhutdinov, R., & Mimno, D. (2009). Evaluation methods for topic models. In *Proceedings of the 26th annual international conference on machine learning,* (pp. 1105-1112). ACM.

Wang, Y., Beydoun, M. A., Liang, L., Caballero, B., & Kumanyika, S. K. (2008). Will all Americans become overweight or obese? Estimating the progression and cost of the U.S. obesity epidemic. *Obesity, 16*(10), 2323-2330.

Wartell, D. (2015). The geography of obesity: Predicting obesity rates in California based on access to health care. *Harvard Dataverse.* doi: 10.7910/DVN/LQ4DY6

Wiebe, J., Breck, E., Buckley, C., Cardie, C., Davis, P., Fraser, B., ... & Day, D. S. (2003, March). Recognizing and organizing opinions expressed in the world press. In *New directions in question answering* (pp. 12-19).

Willig, A. L., Westfall, A. O., Overton, E. T., Mugavero, M. J., Burkholder, G. A., Kim, D., ... & Willig, J. H. (2015). Obesity is associated with race/sex disparities in diabetes and hypertension prevalence, but not cardiovascular disease, among HIV-infected adults. *AIDS Research and Human Retroviruses, 31*(9), 898-904.

Wing, R. R., Goldstein, M. G., Acton, K. J., Birch, L. L., Jakicic, J. M., Sallis, J. F., ... & Surwit, R. S. (2001). Behavioral science research in diabetes. *Diabetes Care*, 24(1), 117-123.

Yi, J., Nasukawa, T., Bunescu, R., & Niblack, W. (2003). Sentiment analyzer: Extracting sentiments about a given topic using natural language processing techniques. In *Proceedings of the Third IEEE international conference on data mining*. IEEE

Zabin, J., & Jefferies, A. (2008). Social media monitoring and analysis: Generating consumer insights from online conversations.

# On the Citation Advantage of Tweeted Papers at the Journal Level

**Fei Shu**
*School of Information Studies, McGill University, Canada.*
*fei.shu@mail.mcgill.ca*

**Stefanie Haustein**
*École de bibliothéconomie et des sciences de l'information, Université de Montréal, Canada.*
*stefanie.haustein@umontreal.ca*

## ABSTRACT

**This study investigates the effect of diffusing scientific articles on Twitter on their citation impact. For a set of 1.3 million papers covered by the Web of Science and published in 2012, normalized citation rates are compared between tweeted and non-tweeted articles published in the same journal. The results indicate that tweeted papers, published in the same year and in the same journal received around 30% higher citation rates than papers which were not diffused on Twitter. This type of citation advantage appeared across disciplines and countries of authors, but varied in extent.**

## KEYWORDS

Twitter, citation analysis, journal, altmetrics, scientific impact

## INTRODUCTION

The concept of altmetrics, created by Priem, Taraborelli, Groth, and Neylon (2010), is proposed as an alternative to more traditional citation-based metrics. Compared to traditional bibliometrics based on citation counts, altmetrics intend to measure scholarly impact on the basis of activities on social media and other online platforms (Haustein, Larivière, Thelwall, Amyot, & Peters, 2014; Priem, 2014). Altmetrics have often been compared with traditional citation-based metrics to try to find correlations between the two (Li, Thelwall, & Giustini, 2012) in order to confirm their alternative nature (Fausto et al., 2012; Priem, 2014). Most studies show that the correlation between citations and various social media metrics is weak (Bornmann & Leydesdorff, 2013; Costas, Zahedi, & Wouters, 2015a, 2015b; Eysenbach, 2011; Fausto et al., 2012; Haustein, Costas, & Larivière, 2015; Thelwall, 2013; Thelwall, Haustein, Larivière, & Sugimoto, 2013), questioning their validities as indicators of impact. Altmetrics and social media have been claimed to democratize science and its reward system, as they potentially overcome the Matthew effect reflected in traditional citation-based metrics (Haustein, Sugimoto, & Larivière, 2015). However, low social media visibility of scientific publications from China (Wang, Fang, Li, & Guo, 2016), Iran (Maleki, 2014) and Latin America (Alperin, 2014, 2015) suggest that instead of leveling the playing field and contributing to global equality in scholarly communication, social media seem to widen the gap between countries.

Although altmetric research investigates almost all social media as tools for providing a measure of the influence of scholarly activities, Twitter has been in the centre of altmetric research because of its coverage (Thelwall et al., 2013). Compared to other social media, Twitter shows the largest signal related to scientific papers among non-academic, general audience social media platforms. About one fifth of recent publications are mentioned on Twitter, which is topped only by Mendeley among currently captured altmetrics (Haustein, Costas, et al., 2015). Although some studies have associated Twitter exposure with an overall increase in citations in medical science (Eysenbach, 2011; Thelwall et al., 2013), the direct correlations between tweets and citations have been shown to be weak (Costas et al., 2015a; de Winter, 2015; Haustein, Costas, et al., 2015).

Since the distributions of both tweets and citations are highly skewed, a large set of papers that were not tweeted or cited also makes it difficult to find a strong correlation between tweets and citations received through traditional statistical tests. Thus, in this study, we compare the citation rate between tweeted papers and non-tweeted papers published in the same year and in the same journal.

## GOALS AND OBJECTIVES

The purpose of this study is to investigate whether scientific articles diffused on Twitter do receive more citations than their non-tweeted counterparts published in the same journal in the same year. It thus investigates whether a citation advantage is associated with increased visibility on social media. More specifically, the study seeks to answer the following questions:

15. Does the overall normalized citation rate of papers shared on Twitter exceed those of non-tweeted papers published in the same journal in the same year?
16. How does the difference in citation impact of tweeted and non-tweeted papers vary across scientific disciplines?
17. How does the difference in citation impact of tweeted and non-tweeted papers vary by country of the authors?

80th Annual Meeting of the Association for Information Science & Technology, Washington, DC, VA | Oct. 27-Nov. 1, 2017

## METHODS

Publication and citation data were retrieved from the Web of Science (WoS) including the Science Citation Index Expanded (SCIE), the Social Science Citation Index (SSCI) and the Arts and Humanities Citation Index (AHCI), which annually indexes documents published in about 12,000 journals, covering all areas of research. In this study, all papers published in 2012 were retrieved (N=1,339,279). Citations to these articles were considered until the end of 2015, which allows for a citation window of three complete years. In this study, the number of citations was normalized to provide a relative citation rate.

Altmetric.com was chosen as the data source for tweet counts, as it is the most comprehensive source of social media data associated with scientific papers (Robinson-Garcia, Torres-Salinas, Zahedi, & Costas, 2014). Our local copy of Altmetric.com Twitter data includes tweets up to June 2015. Since the majority of tweets occurs within the first days after publication (Eysenbach, 2011; Shuai, Pepe, & Bollen, 2012) and are rare several years after, the selected tweet window is considered sufficient.

The digital object identifier (DOI) was used to link the bibliographic and citation data from WoS with the Twitter data from Altmetric.com. Since DOIs are not available in all publications, only publications with a DOI as recorded in WoS (N=1,131,358; 84.5%) were included in our investigation. For specific disciplinary differences of the use of DOIs refer to Haustein, Costas, & Larivière (2015).

The comparisons of citation difference of tweeted and non-tweeted papers were conducted at the journal level. In other words, this study focuses on comparing the difference of citation impact of papers with and without Twitter exposure published in the same journal and same year. This eliminates potential biases and confounding factors at the journal level. This includes the effect of disciplinary differences, open access and journal prestige, which are known to influence citation rates, as well as journal-specific social media policies, which might have an effect on a journal's visibility on Twitter. The citation advantage of tweeted papers was defined as the difference of relative citations between tweeted papers and non-tweeted papers divided by the relative citations of non-tweeted papers.

To check whether the difference in relative citation impact of tweeted and non-tweeted articles was significant, we used estimation statistics and presented the 95% confidence intervals. Pairwise comparisons of tweeted and non-tweeted articles were carried out on the level of journals, disciplines and countries of authors to address the three research questions. Specific methods and applied thresholds are described below.

### *Journal Comparison*

Various thresholds were applied at the journal level to obtain robust results and minimize the effect of outliers. As shown by Haustein, Costas, & Larivière (2015), 21.9% of papers (N=247,621) published in 2012 were diffused on Twitter; however, almost 82.2% of the 9,318 journals (N=7,655) contain at least one tweeted paper, which suggests that Twitter diffusion occurs across journals and disciplines.

Although 7,655 journals published papers with and without Twitter diffusion in 2012, more than half of these journals only contain a few tweeted papers due to the skewed distribution of tweets, which would give potentially high weight to outliers, making results less robust. To avoid the effect of outliers, different thresholds were applied, which represents a trade-off between robustness of results and sample size:

- Threshold 0: selected journals contain at least one tweeted and one non-tweeted paper; 7,589 journals, 245,225 tweeted (23.8%), 784,811 non-tweeted papers (76.2%).
- Threshold 1: selected journals contain at least 10 tweeted and 10 non-tweeted papers; 3,579 journals, 215,452 tweeted (29.2%), 521,446 non-tweeted papers (70.8%).
- Threshold 2: selected journals contain at least 20 tweeted and 20 non-tweeted papers; 2,042 journals, 183,945 tweeted (31.4%), 401,353 non-tweeted papers (68.6%).
- Threshold 3: selected journals contain at least 50 tweeted and 50 non-tweeted papers; 785 journals, 133,503 (34.7%) tweeted, 250,801 non-tweeted papers (65.3%).
- Threshold 4: selected journals contain at least 100 tweeted and 100 non-tweeted papers; 308 journals, 90,980 tweeted (36.4%), 158,905 non-tweeted papers (63.6%).

By definition, the number of journals selected for the pairwise comparison decreases with each increase in threshold. Interestingly, the higher the applied threshold, the higher the share of tweeted papers. Based on all journals with at least one tweeted and non-tweeted article, less than one quarter of papers were diffused on Twitter (Threshold 0), while the ratio increased to 36.4% for journals with at least 100 tweeted and non-tweeted papers (Threshold 4). High threshold could reduce the effect of outliers and make the results robust, but it also limited the sample size when conducting the discipline comparison and source country comparison. For example, when Threshold 2 was applied, no eligible journal was found in *Arts* and *Humanities*, and only nine journals in *Mathematics* were included. Thus, we decided to only apply Threshold 1 in the discipline comparison and source country comparison to keep an adequate sample size for each discipline or source country.

### *Discipline Comparison*

As described above, relative citation rates were used to normalize known differences in citation rates across disciplines. However, Twitter use, as well as the extent to which scientific papers are shared on Twitter is also known to differ between scientific fields. To understand the effect of disciplinary cultures on the difference of citation impact between tweeted and non-tweeted papers, journal-level pairwise comparisons applying Threshold 1 were aggregated by discipline using the 14 major disciplines of NSF journal classification system, which assigns each journal to a single discipline. The Twitter coverage per NSF discipline (see Table 1) shows that the twitter diffusion varies by discipline – 41.5% of papers in *Health* are shared in Twitter while only 4.9% of papers in *Engineering and Technology* are tweeted. This confirms findings regarding disciplinary differences reported in previous altmetrics studies (e.g., Haustein et al., 2015).

### Source Country Comparison

The countries of all authors contributing to the 1,131,358 papers were retrieved and identified based on their affiliated institutions. The comparison was made based on national affiliation of authors to investigate whether citation advantage or disadvantage between tweeted papers and non-tweeted papers differs among countries authors are affiliated with. Again, to limit the effect of disciplines, journal prestige and social media policy, the comparison was performed comparing tweeted and non-tweeted papers per country at the journal level applying Threshold 1. Since the distributions of tweeted and non-tweeted papers was also highly skewed on the level of the 204 contributing countries, we applied an additional threshold per country. This country threshold includes countries with affiliated authors contributing to at least 40 journals selected under Threshold 1 described above. This limits the set of 204 contributing countries to 15 countries analyzed.

| Discipline | Total papers | Tweeted papers | % of tweeted papers |
|---|---|---|---|
| Health | 25,144 | 10,446 | 41.5% |
| Psychology | 23,404 | 8,562 | 36.6% |
| Biomedical Research | 146,099 | 51,154 | 35.0% |
| Clinical Medicine | 284,905 | 93,962 | 33.0% |
| Social Sciences | 37,972 | 10,257 | 27.0% |
| Professional Fields | 29,103 | 7,478 | 25.7% |
| Chemistry | 119,387 | 18,958 | 15.9% |
| Biology | 71,119 | 11,154 | 15.7% |
| Earth and Space | 68,546 | 10,012 | 14.6% |
| Humanities | 12,558 | 1,600 | 12.7% |
| Physics | 108,615 | 13,458 | 12.4% |
| Arts | 1,937 | 235 | 12.1% |
| Mathematics | 39,794 | 2,343 | 5.9% |
| Engineering and Technology | 162,775 | 8,002 | 4.9% |

***Table 1**. Distribution of Twitter coverage (tweeted papers) by discipline*

## RESULTS

Among 1,131,358 papers published in 2012, 247,621 papers were tweeted while 883,737 papers were not tweeted. When the number of citations was normalized, the tweeted papers received 1.512 citations on average while the average citation rate of non-tweeted papers was only 0.898. The tweeted papers received 68.4% more citations on average than non-tweeted papers. However, Thelwall (2016) points out that the arithmetic mean is not a precise and accurate indicator for citation-based comparison since the citation data distribution is extremely skewed. In addition, as described above, journal is a confounding factor influencing both the citation and the tweets received. The comparison of the citation advantage between tweeted papers and non-tweeted papers at the journal level is necessary to eliminate possible biases from journal itself.

### Journal Comparison

When comparing the average number of citations to tweeted papers with non-tweeted papers in each journal, we found that tweeted papers received about 30% more citations on average than non-tweeted papers. As Table 2 indicates, applying higher thresholds resulted in higher ratios of journals in which tweeted papers have a citation advantage as compared to non-tweeted papers. Although the citation rate of both tweeted papers and non-tweeted papers varied when applying different thresholds, the gaps between the citation rate of tweeted papers and non-tweeted papers were all around 30%. Moreover, there was no overlap between the 95% confidence interval of average citations to tweeted papers and the 95% confidence interval of average citations to non-tweeted papers at each threshold. Thus, the differences of citation rate between tweeted papers and non-tweeted papers were statistically significant.

In addition, as Table 3 shows, among all journals having at least 10 tweeted papers and 10 non-tweeted papers in 2012 (Threshold 1), tweeted papers have a citation advantage in 2,856 journals (79.8%) while non-tweeted papers have a citation advantage in 722 journals (20.2%). The citation advantages of tweeted papers are between 20% and 50% in 30.3% of journals, while they are less than 20% in 22.5% of journals; the citation advantages of tweeted papers are between 50% and 100%, between 100% and 200%, and over 200% in 18.3%, 6.5% and 2.2% of journals, respectively. On the other hand, the citation advantages of non-tweeted papers were found to be less than 20%, between 20% and 50%, and between 50% and 100% in 14.3%, 5.1% and 0.8% of journals, respectively. Similar results were also found when Thresholds 2, 3 and 4 were applied. With the increase of the threshold, the share of journals in which tweeted papers had the citation advantage also increased. When all journals having at least 100 tweeted papers and 100 non-tweeted papers published in 2012 (Threshold 4) were investigated, we found that tweeted papers had a citation advantage in more than 90% of journals, and their citation advantages were between 20% to 50% in almost 40% of journals.

| Threshold | # of journals | Journals favor tweeted papers | Citation rate of tweeted papers (95% confidence intervals) | Citation rate of non-tweeted papers (95% confidence intervals) | Average citation advantage of tweeted papers |
|---|---|---|---|---|---|
| 1 | 3,579 | 2,856 (79.8%) | 1.246 (1.211-1.280) | 0.938 (0.916-0.959) | 32.9% |
| 2 | 2,042 | 1,704 (83.4%) | 1.306 (1.266-1.346) | 0.997 (0.970-1.024) | 31.0% |
| 3 | 785 | 706 (89.9%) | 1.426 (1.365-1.487) | 1.095 (1.051-1.140) | 30.2% |
| 4 | 308 | 287 (93.2%) | 1.526 (1.439-1.613) | 1.175 (1.111-1.240) | 29.9% |

***Table 2**. Citation rate and 95% confidence interval between tweeted papers and non-tweeted papers*

| | Threshold 1 | | Threshold 2 | | Threshold 3 | | Threshold 4 | |
|---|---|---|---|---|---|---|---|---|
| Size of citation advantage | Tweeted papers | Non-tweeted papers | Tweeted papers | Non-tweeted papers | Tweeted papers | Non-tweeted papers | Tweeted papers | Non-tweeted papers |
| < 20% | 804 (22.5%) | 512 (14.3%) | 527 (25.8%) | 289 (14.2%) | 235 (29.9%) | 75 (9.6%) | 106 (34.4%) | 19 (6.2%) |
| 20% - 50% | 1,086 (30.3%) | 183 (5.1%) | 704 (34.5%) | 43 (2.1%) | 308 (39.2%) | 4 (0.5%) | 122 (39.6%) | 2 (0.7%) |
| 50% - 100% | 654 (18.3%) | 27 (0.8%) | 347 (17.0%) | 6 (0.3%) | 127 (16.2%) | | 45 (14.6%) | |
| 100% - 200% | 232 (6.5%) | | 123 (6.0%) | | 33 (4.2%) | | 12 (3.9%) | |
| > 200% | 79 (2.2%) | | 23 (1.1%) | | 3 (0.4%) | | 2 (0.7%) | |
| **All** | **2,856 (79.8%)** | **722 (20.2%)** | **1,704 (83.4%)** | **338 (16.6%)** | **706 (89.9%)** | **79 (10.1%)** | **287 (93.2%)** | **21 (6.8%)** |

***Table 3**. Number of journals in which tweeted papers (or non-tweeted papers) have citation advantages*

| Discipline | # of journals having citation advantage of | | Citation Rate | |
|---|---|---|---|---|
| | tweeted papers | non-tweeted papers | tweeted papers | non-tweeted papers |
| Biology | 167 (78.8%) | 45 (21.2%) | 1.481 (1.347-1.616) | 1.144 (1.072-1.217) |
| Biomedical Research | 379 (84.0%) | 72 (16.0%) | 1.043 (0.963-1.124) | 0.780 (0.734-0.826) |
| Chemistry | 85 (68.5%) | 39 (31.5%) | 1.189 (1.054-1.324) | 1.024 (0.915-1.133) |
| Clinical Medicine | 1,121 (80.5%) | 268 (19.5%) | 1.059 (1.022-1.096) | 0.834 (0.806-0.861) |
| Earth and Space | 108 (78.8%) | 29 (21.2%) | 1.371 (1.193-1.549) | 1.019 0.928-1.111) |
| Engineering and Technology | 111 (71.2%) | 45 (28.8%) | 1.721 (1.470-1.972) | 1.351 (1.175-1.527) |
| Health | 174 (82.5%) | 37 (17.5%) | 1.184 (1.103-1.265) | 0.886 (0.824-0.947) |
| Humanities | 22 (81.5%) | 5 (18.5%) | 3.528 (1.986-5.070) | 1.976 (1.425-2.527) |
| Mathematics | 30 (75.0%) | 10 (25.0%) | 1.589 (1.171-2.007) | 1.097 (0.921-1.274) |
| Physics | 78 (75.7%) | 25 (24.3%) | 1.323 (1.090-1.556) | 0.880 (0.720-1.041) |
| Professional Fields | 171 (81.4%) | 39 (18.6%) | 1.515 (1.375-1.655) | 1.080 (0.985-1.176) |
| Psychology | 181 (84.2%) | 34 (15.8%) | 1.170 (1.065-1.275) | 0.880 (0.816-0.945) |
| Social Sciences | 228 (76.8%) | 69 (23.2%) | 1.601 (1.418-1.785) | 1.104 (1.007-1.202) |

***Table 4**. Citation rate and 95% confidence interval between tweeted papers and non-tweeted papers by discipline (journal level, Threshold 1)*

| Discipline | # of journals having citation advantage of | | Citation Rate | |
|---|---|---|---|---|
| | tweeted papers | non-tweeted papers | tweeted papers | non-tweeted papers |
| Biology | 167 (78.8%) | 45 (21.2%) | 1.481 (1.347-1.616) | 1.144 (1.072-1.217) |
| Biomedical Research | 379 (84.0%) | 72 (16.0%) | 1.043 (0.963-1.124) | 0.780 (0.734-0.826) |
| Chemistry | 85 (68.5%) | 39 (31.5%) | 1.189 (1.054-1.324) | 1.024 (0.915-1.133) |
| Clinical Medicine | 1,121 (80.5%) | 268 (19.5%) | 1.059 (1.022-1.096) | 0.834 (0.806-0.861) |
| Earth and Space | 108 (78.8%) | 29 (21.2%) | 1.371 (1.193-1.549) | 1.019 0.928-1.111) |
| Engineering and Technology | 111 (71.2%) | 45 (28.8%) | 1.721 (1.470-1.972) | 1.351 (1.175-1.527) |
| Health | 174 (82.5%) | 37 (17.5%) | 1.184 (1.103-1.265) | 0.886 (0.824-0.947) |
| Humanities | 22 (81.5%) | 5 (18.5%) | 3.528 (1.986-5.070) | 1.976 (1.425-2.527) |
| Mathematics | 30 (75.0%) | 10 (25.0%) | 1.589 (1.171-2.007) | 1.097 (0.921-1.274) |
| Physics | 78 (75.7%) | 25 (24.3%) | 1.323 (1.090-1.556) | 0.880 (0.720-1.041) |
| Professional Fields | 171 (81.4%) | 39 (18.6%) | 1.515 (1.375-1.655) | 1.080 (0.985-1.176) |
| Psychology | 181 (84.2%) | 34 (15.8%) | 1.170 (1.065-1.275) | 0.880 (0.816-0.945) |
| Social Sciences | 228 (76.8%) | 69 (23.2%) | 1.601 (1.418-1.785) | 1.104 (1.007-1.202) |

***Table 4**. Citation rate and 95% confidence interval between tweeted papers and non-tweeted papers by discipline (journal level, Threshold 1)*

### *Discipline Comparison*

Applying threshold 1 results based on 3,579 journals, tweeted papers received, on average, more citations than non-tweeted papers in the majority of journals in all 13 disciplines (Arts was excluded as only 4 Arts journals remained when Threshold 1 was applied). As Table 4 indicates, the percentage of journals in which tweeted papers received more citations on average than non-tweeted papers varied from 68.5% in *Chemistry* to 84.2% in *Psychology*. The relative delta of the citation impact of tweeted over non-tweeted papers ranged from between 16.1% (*Chemistry*) to 78.5% (*Humanities*) at the journal level. There was no overlap between the 95% confidence interval of average citations to tweeted papers and the 95% confidence interval of average citations to non-tweeted papers in 9 disciplines, but there were small overlaps in *Chemistry*, *Engineering and Technology*, *Humanities*, and *Mathematics*, which might be largely due to the small sample sizes that remained when Threshold 1 was applied to these four disciplines.

### *Source Country Comparison*

The 1,131,358 papers published in 2012 were contributed by authors from 204 countries. The US (317,935), China (163,635), the UK (89,756), Germany (85,846), Japan (67,215), France (59,657), Canada (52,058), Italy (48,569), Spain (45,602) and Korea (44,910) are the top 10 source countries when counting the authorship. US scholars also contributed the most tweeted papers (100,016), followed by the UK (30,748) and Germany (21,565). However, among the 15 source countries investigated, the United States has only the fourth highest ratio of tweeted papers (31.5%); 35.6% of Dutch papers, 34.3% of British papers and 32.0% of Swiss papers were tweeted.

When comparing the percentage of journals in which tweeted papers have a citation advantage, although the sample sizes varied from 41 eligible journals (Brazil) to 1,512 eligible journals (United States), we still found these ratios were all over 30% in 14 countries in addition to China, from 21.4% in China to 63.2% in Sweden. As shown in Table 5, the percentage of journals in which tweeted papers received more citations on average than non-tweeted papers varied but was all over 60%, from 68.7% in Korea to 90.5% in Sweden. There was no overlap between the 95% confidence interval of average citations to tweeted papers and the 95% confidence interval of average citations to non-tweeted papers in all countries except for Korea and Brazil, which also may be due to the small sample sizes.

Finally, we found that six of 15 countries accounted for more than 75% of journals in which tweeted papers have citation advantage and the citation advantage at paper level is significant over 35%: the United States, the UK, France, Canada, Australia, Sweden and Switzerland. Indeed, all four English-speaking countries were included in this list. This is not a surprise when considering that English is the dominant language of both scholarly communication and Twitter.

| Country | # of papers | # of journals (Threshold 1) | # of Journals having citation advantage of tweeted papers | Citation Rate | |
|---|---|---|---|---|---|
| | | | | tweeted papers | non-tweeted papers |
| US | 255,849 | 1,512 | 1,224 (81.0%) | 1.549 (1.489-1.609) | 1.136 (1.100-1.173) |
| China | 146,282 | 265 | 183 (69.1%) | 1.457 (1.311-1.604) | 1.200 (1.094-1.307) |
| UK | 60,948 | 439 | 352 (80.2%) | 1.732 (1.621-1.843) | 1.249 (1.175-1.322) |
| Germany | 58,656 | 284 | 223 (78.5%) | 1.827 (1.695-1.959) | 1.368 (1.284-1.453) |
| Japan | 55,571 | 190 | 143 (75.3%) | 1.297 (1.153-1.440) | 0.972 (0.891-1.053) |
| France | 39,040 | 167 | 137 (82.0%) | 1.875 (1.688-2.063) | 1.368 (1.264-1.472) |
| Korea | 38,473 | 83 | 57 (68.7%) | 1.437 (1.125-1.748) | 1.082 (0.903-1.260) |
| Canada | 36,451 | 149 | 128 (85.9%) | 1.811 (1.636-1.986) | 1.210 (1.108-1.313) |
| Italy | 35,216 | 134 | 100 (74.6%) | 1.774 (1.555-1.993) | 1.362 (1.188-1.537) |
| Spain | 33,367 | 109 | 80 (73.4%) | 1.635 (1.426-1.844) | 1.245 (1.126-1.363) |
| Australia | 28,854 | 125 | 97 (77.6%) | 1.692 (1.452-1.931) | 1.221 (1.096-1.346) |
| Brazil | 20,222 | 41 | 32 (78.0%) | 1.252 (0.793-1.712) | 0.817 (0.653-0.981) |
| Netherlands | 20,070 | 109 | 81 (74.3%) | 1.972 (1.696-2.247) | 1.306 (1.175-1.437) |
| Sweden | 12,794 | 42 | 38 (90.5%) | 2.015 (1.536-2.494) | 1.235 (1.050-1.420) |
| Switzerland | 12,554 | 53 | 40 (75.5%) | 2.159 (1.822-2.496) | 1.576 (1.381-1.771) |

***Table 5****. Citation rate and 95% confidence interval between tweeted papers and non-tweeted papers by source country (journal level, Threshold 1, 40+ eligible journals)*

## CONCLUSION

In this study, after investigating the tweets and citations to 1,131,358 papers published in 2012, we determined the difference in citation rate between tweeted papers and non-tweeted papers. The results of this study show that in the majority of journals tweeted papers received more citations than non-tweeted papers:

From the same journal, the same published year, tweeted papers received on average 30% more citations than non-tweeted papers.

The citation advantage of tweeted papers exists in all scientific disciplines, but the extent varies by discipline.

The citation rate of tweeted papers exceeds that of non-tweeted papers in the same journal in all analyzed countries contributing academic literature, and is most pronounced in English-speaking countries.

Although our analysis shows that in the majority of journals across disciplines and contributing countries, tweeted papers are on average cited more frequently than non-tweeted papers, we cannot infer any causation between Twitter visibility and citations received. In fact, most studies report no or low correlations between the number of tweets and citations, indicating that no direct link exists on the article level (Costas et al., 2015a; de Winter, 2015; Haustein, Costas, et al., 2015).

To understand in more detail the impact of tweets on citations to publications, the content of tweets and their relationship with the citations to publications need to be investigated.

## ACKNOWLEDGMENTS

The authors would like to thank Altmetric.com for providing access to their Twitter data. FS is supported by iFellows Doctoral Scholarship provided by Andrew W. Mellon Foundation and The Fonds de recherche du Québec - Société et culture (FRQSC).

## REFERENCE

Alperin, J. P. (2014). South America: Citation databases omit local journals. Nature, 511(7508), 155-155.

Alperin, J. P. (2015). The public impact of Latin America's approach to open access. Stanford University.

Bornmann, L., & Leydesdorff, L. (2013). The validation of (advanced) bibliometric indicators through peer assessments: A comparative study using data from InCites and F1000. Journal of Informetrics, 7(2), 286-291. doi:10.1016/j.joi.2012.12.003

Costas, R., Zahedi, Z., & Wouters, P. (2015a). Do "altmetrics" correlate with citations? Extensive comparison of altmetric indicators with citations from a multidisciplinary perspective. Journal of the Association for Information Science and Technology, 66(10), 2003-2019. doi:10.1002/asi.23309

Costas, R., Zahedi, Z., & Wouters, P. (2015b). The thematic orientation of publications mentioned on social media large-scale disciplinary comparison of social media metrics with citations. Aslib Journal of Information Management, 67(3), 260-288. doi:10.1108/Ajim-12-2014-0173

de Winter, J. C. F. (2015). The relationship between tweets, citations, and article views for PLOS ONE articles. Scientometrics, 102(2), 1773-1779.

Eysenbach, G. (2011). Can tweets predict citations? Metrics of social impact based on twitter and correlation with traditional metrics of scientific impact. Journal of Medical Internet Research, 13(4). doi:10.2196/jmir.2012

Fausto, S., Machado, F. A., Bento, L. F. J., Iamarino, A., Nahas, T. R., & Munger, D. S. (2012). Research blogging: Indexing and registering the change in science 2.0. PLoS ONE, 7(12), e50109. doi:10.1371/journal.pone.0050109

Haustein, S., Costas, R., & Larivière, V. (2015). Characterizing social media metrics of scholarly papers: The effect of document properties and collaboration patterns. PLoS ONE, 10(3), e0120495.

Haustein, S., Larivière, V., Thelwall, M., Amyot, D., & Peters, I. (2014). Tweets vs. Mendeley readers: How do these two social media metrics differ? IT-Information Technology, 56(5), 207-215.

Haustein, S., Sugimoto, C., & Larivière, V. (2015). Guest editorial: Social media in scholarly communication. Aslib Journal of Information Management, 67(3), null. doi:doi:10.1108/AJIM-03-2015-0047

Li, X., Thelwall, M., & Giustini, D. (2012). Validating online reference managers for scholarly impact measurement. Scientometrics, 91(2), 461-471.

Maleki, A. (2014). Twitter users in science tweets linking to articles: The Case of Web of Science articles with Iranian authors. Paper presented at the SIG/MET workshop, Association for Information Science and Technology Annual Meeting, Seattle, USA.

Priem, J. (2014). Altmetrics. In B. Cronin & C. R. Sugimoto (Eds.), Beyond bibliometrics: Harnessing multidimensional indicators of performance. Cambridge, MA: MIT Press.

Priem, J., Taraborelli, D., Groth, P., & Neylon, C. (2010). Altmetrics: A manifesto. Retrieved from http://altmetrics.org/manifesto/

Robinson-Garcia, N., Torres-Salinas, D., Zahedi, Z., & Costas, R. (2014). New data, new possibilities: Exploring the insides of Altmetric.com. El Profesional de la información, 23(4), 359-366.

Shuai, X., Pepe, A., & Bollen, J. (2012). How the scientific community reacts to newly submitted preprints: Article downloads, twitter mentions, and citations. PLoS ONE, 7(11), e47523. doi:10.1371/journal.pone.0047523

Thelwall, M. (2013). Assessing non-standard article impact using F1000 labels. Scientometrics, 97(2), 383-395.

Thelwall, M. (2016). The precision of the arithmetic mean, geometric mean and percentiles for citation data: An experimental simulation modelling approach. Journal of Informetrics, 10(1), 110-123. doi:http://dx.doi.org/10.1016/j.joi.2015.12.001

Thelwall, M., Haustein, S., Larivière, V., & Sugimoto, C. R. (2013). Do altmetrics work? Twitter and Ten other social web services. PLoS ONE, 8(5), e64841.

Wang, X., Fang, Z., Li, Q., & Guo, X. (2016). The poor altmetric performance of publications authored by researchers in Mainland China. Frontiers in Research Metrics and Analytics, 1(8). doi:10.3389/frma.2016.00008

# Patient Portals and Human Values

**Rachel N. Simons**
*School of Information, The University of Texas at Austin, USA. rnsimons@utexas.edu*

**Kenneth R. Fleischman**
*School of Information, The University of Texas at Austin, USA. kfleisch@ischool.utexas.edu*

**Yan Zhan**
*School of Information, The University of Texas at Austin, USA. yanz@ischool.utexas.edu*

**Jin Gao**
*School of Information, The University of Texas at Austin, USA. jin.gao@utexas.edu*

**Bo Xi**
*School of Information & School of Nursing; The University of Texas at Austin, USA. boxie@utexas.edu*

## ABSTRACT

**This paper reports quantitative and qualitative findings from a systematic literature review of user studies of patient portals. A deductive content analysis was performed using six human values identified in a prior study: privacy, confidentiality, security, trust, transparency and agency. Each of the 52 articles in the corpus included invocations of at least one of these human values, supporting their salience for understanding the user experience of patient portals. The paper concludes with a discussion of the implications of this analysis for value-sensitive design of patient portals, including indicating potential future research directions.**

## KEYWORDS

human values, value-sensitive design, values and design, user studies, electronic health records, patient portals

## INTRODUCTION

As health information and services increasingly move online, it is critical to consider the user experience of health information systems such as patient portals. Patient portals allow patients to view some information from their electronic health records (EHRs, also referred to as electronic medical records, or EMRs), check scheduled appointments and access educational resources. As patient portals have become more technologically sophisticated and as pressure from government agencies and health insurance companies has spurred adoption by health care providers, there is growing attention to the user experience of these information and communications technologies (ICTs).

Typically, user experience designers and researchers focus on user needs such as tasks and requirements. However, the design of ICTs such as patient portals must also be sensitive to users' values to ensure that users will choose to adopt patient portals, which may influence satisfaction with health care providers and improve health care outcomes. User experience designers and researchers must be aware of users' values and work to understand and support them.

We begin by introducing and defining the core concepts of human values and patient portals.

### *Human Values*

Human values can be defined as "what a person or group of people consider important in life" (Friedman, Kahn, & Borning, 2008). Values are trans-situational (Hitlin & Piliavin, 2004), insofar as they apply to many aspects of life. Human values can be used to explain sentiment, or individuals' positive and negative reactions to individuals, groups, concepts, policies, and ICTs (Fleischmann, 2014).

Human values are an important subject of research in fields ranging from advertising, anthropology, human-computer interaction (HCI), information studies, management, psychology, science and technology studies, and sociology; each of these fields has developed inventories of salient human values (reviewed in Cheng & Fleischmann, 2010). Human values are attributes of individuals shared through interpersonal interactions (predominantly at an early age) and can also be used to characterize broad differences among communities and societies (Schwartz, 1994, 2007). Human values have a significant impact on the design process, and should be considered explicitly by designers to ensure that technologies are sensitive to users' values (Fleischmann, Hui, & Wallace, 2017; Fleischmann & Wallace, 2010; Friedman & Kahn, 2008).

### *Patient Portals*

Patient portals are secure online websites that allow patients to access health information such as their medical history, current and past medications, laboratory test results, and educational materials. Advanced portals also allow patients to communicate with providers in various ways, such as contacting caregivers, requesting prescription refills, and scheduling appointments (Office of the National Coordinator, 2015). In most cases, patient portals are tethered to health care institutions' existing EHR; the health information in a patient portal is therefore typically owned and maintained by

---

80th Annual Meeting of the Association for Information Science & Technology, Washington, DC, VA | Oct. 27-Nov. 1, 2017

the managing health care organizations (Zhang, Fleischmann, Gao, & Xie, 2015).

The increasing development of patient portals is largely supported by the belief that easier access to their clinical information can better engage patients in monitoring and managing their own health (Goldzweig et al., 2013; Or & Tao, 2014). Proponents also argue that patient portals will enable health care providers to increase the quality of care and to reduce medical errors (Committee on Quality of Healthcare in America, 2001). Evidence about the positive impacts of patient portals on health outcomes has started to emerge over the past few years (Kruse, Argueta, Lopez, & Nair, 2015).

### Paper Overview

This paper presents our research into the role of human values within the design and use of patient portals; it is intended to contribute both to the current research on user studies of patient portals (by contributing a nuanced understanding of human values within design) and to the broader ongoing discussion of how ICT design can better support human values. Now that we have defined some important concepts related to our study, we next provide an overview of related research on the relationship of human values to user experience within patient portals. We then outline our methods for conducting our content analysis. Next, we describe both the quantitative and qualitative results of our examination of six specific human values (privacy, confidentiality, security, transparency, trust, and agency) within the corpus. Finally, we conclude with some overall observations about our findings and offer potential future directions for better understanding the role of human values in ICT design, particularly for patient portals.

## BACKGROUND

A growing body of literature explores the role of human values in the design and use of ICTs (Fleischmann, 2014; Friedman et al., 2008). However, the primary emphasis of research on patient portals has been on the usability of these ICTs, with very little research examining the role of human values in patient portal design and use. In this section, we review some of the most related previous research for understanding the role of human values in patient portals.

### Understanding the Role of Human Values in ICT Design

As fundamental and trans-situational aspects of our lives, human values undeniably play a critical role in the design and use of ICTs (Friedman et al., 2008). Designers, researchers, and theorists have increasingly emphasized the need to make ICTs more user-friendly (Nielsen, 1999; Preece, 2000; Rubin & Chisnell, 2008) and to remove some of the perceived "authority" of the designer as all-knowing. In order for a product to be successful, it not only needs to have good usability, but also needs to be desirable, valuable, and credible (Garrett, 2011). Friedman and Kahn (2008) differentiate usability from human values with ethical import, and argue that both usability and values are critical considerations for designers; because unusable systems that are sensitive to users' values *and* usable systems that run counter to users' values are both highly problematic, designers should consider both perspectives simultaneously when designing information systems.

Previous research has broadly examined how human values can be embedded within ICT design and influence the design process (e.g., Friedman et al., 2008), as well as how values can affect ICT adoption and use (e.g., Isomursu, Ervasti, Kinnula, & Isomursu, 2011). However, as Fleischmann, Zhang, Gao, and Xie (2015) note, it is important to consider how values impact health care ICTs.

### Human Values in the Design and Use of Patient Portals

As discussed above, the demand for patient portals has greatly increased over the past decade—primarily due to the expectation that patient portals increase patient involvement and improve patient care. However, the degree to which this promise is being achieved currently remains unclear (Goldzweig et al., 2013; Kruse et al., 2015). While providers have been quick to adopt patient portals, patients have not always followed suit (Zhang et al., 2015). Moreover, among patients who have used patient portals, many only logged into the system once and never returned, or used the portals only for viewing information, but not for more interactive functions (e.g., secure messaging) that are intended to enhance patient-provider communication (Jones, Weiner, Shah, & Stewart, 2015).

This continued underuse of patient portals is typically attributed to poor usability (Byczkowski, Munafo, & Britto, 2014). Patients' difficulties in navigating the portal systems have been widely documented (Byczkowski et al., 2014; Lyles, López, Pasick, & Sarkar, 2013). However, few studies have specifically examined human values in relation to patient portals and their interaction with system usability.

Despite the lack of systematic examination of human values concerning patient portals, some recent research has begun to shed light on the role of human values in patient portals and related ICTs. For example, Fleischmann et al. (2015) conducted an inductive thematic analysis of values discussed in the research literature reporting user studies of personal health records (PHRs), a related ICT. (PHRs are similar to EHRs, the backbone of patient portals, although PHRs are maintained by patients, while EHRs are maintained by providers.) They identified six values of ethical import as most salient within this literature: privacy, confidentiality, security, transparency, trust, and agency.

**Privacy** (Buckovich, Rippen, & Rozen, 1999; Irizarry, DeVito Dabbs, & Curran, 2015) focuses on users and their own ability to control access to their information. **Confidentiality** (Buckovich et al., 1999) focuses on the providers' legal and ethical responsibilities to protect sensitive information. **Security** (Buckovich et al., 1999; Irizarry et al., 2015) involves keeping others from accessing information without permission from either patients or providers. **Transparency** (Brin, 1998; Fleischmann & Wallace, 2005) ensures that users are able to make informed choices based on a thorough understanding of their options. **Trust** (Fukuyama, 1995) ensures that patients believe that the information provided is accurate and reliable. **Agency** (Giddens, 1984) ensures that patients feel empowered to make their own choices.

Since patient portals provide online access to extremely personal and sensitive health information, all six of these human values are salient to patient portals. However, the virtual monopoly and singular control of the patient's information within a patient portal places patients in a particularly vulnerable position, in which they have little choice (short of leaving their health care provider in favor of another) in how they use this ICT, even if their values are not always supported by the portal. Therefore, better understanding how designers, health care providers, and patients consider these values specifically in relation to patient portals is particularly timely and critical.

Moreover, patient portals represent a fundamentally new way for people to interact with their own health information and with their health care providers; the patient portal may mark potentially the largest shift thus far from interacting with health care providers via only face-to-face interaction. Although medical records (both paper and digital) have existed for some time—along with the rise of telemedicine in last few decades—the combination of so much information, communication, and practice within a singular interface is particularly unique. The system of health care that is supported by patient portals could potentially be dramatically different from the previous system in terms of health outcomes, and may mark the beginning of a fundamentally different way of practicing medicine.

Thus, patient portals are an increasingly important health ICT; user experience of patient portals (including the role of human values) has clear implications for the degree of use, success of use, satisfaction of use, and potentially even for choice of provider and for health outcomes. Accordingly, a systematic understanding of the human values invoked during the use of patient portals is urgently needed to better inform the design of more user-friendly portal systems. By analyzing a corpus of articles on patients' use of patient portals, we seek to answer several key questions in order to help us better understand how human values are discussed in these user studies:

- How frequently do the six human values of privacy, confidentiality, security, transparency, trust, and agency (Fleischmann et al., 2015) occur in these studies of patients' perceptions and use of patient portals?
- How many papers included invocations of multiple values?
- How frequently did the values co-occur?

In addition to these quantitative questions, we also conducted an in-depth qualitative analysis to find and analyze common themes concerning values across articles.

## METHODS

We performed a deductive content analysis of a corpus of articles on patients' use of patient portals. This section explains how we assembled the corpus, how we operationalized the six human values employed in our analysis, and how we coded those values within the articles.

### *Assembling the Corpus*

We performed a systematic literature search of user studies of patient portals, based on a previous search process (described in detail in Zhang et al., 2015). First, we selected nine relevant databases using the following criteria:

- Be relevant to the scope of the present review.
- Contain peer-reviewed journal articles and/or conference proceedings, with full text in English.
- Allow keyword search in the title or abstract.

The nine databases were: ACM Digital Library, PubMed/Medline, Communication & Mass Media Complete, Cumulative Index to Nursing & Allied Health Plus with Full Text, PsycINFO, Sociological Abstracts, Cochrane Library, Health Source, Nursing/Academic Edition, and Psychology & Behavioral Sciences Collection. To expand our coverage beyond these library databases, we additionally utilized Google Scholar in our searches.

We searched for the keywords "patient portal*," in the Title and/or Abstract fields within these 10 databases for papers in peer-reviewed journals and conferences; 253 unique publications were thereby identified. (Note that we did *not* search specifically for any of the six human values under analysis in this study, nor for "human values" more generally; see also the "Discussions" section of this paper.)

We then examined the titles and abstracts of these publications and excluded 72 non-empirical studies. Finally, we evaluated the remaining 181 articles based on the following criteria:

1. Only include publications of user studies of patient portals that involved patients as end users—such as studies of patients' actual use of patient portals, reports of patients' perceptions of the portals, and descriptions of patient portal design requirements.
2. Only include publications with full text, thus omitting free-standing abstracts.
3. Exclude publications that only reported aggregated statistical information about patient portals, such as the adoption rate of patient portals or the characteristics of adopters.
4. Exclude publications that only analyzed messages within patient portals.
5. Exclude publications that only reported clinicians' use of or attitudes towards patient portals.

This selection process resulted in a final corpus of 52 articles, all published between 2005 and 2015.

### *Selecting Human Values for Analysis*

As mentioned earlier, our closed-ended set of human values

for deductive content analysis is based on the results of a previous, open-ended thematic analysis of articles on PHRs (Fleischmann et al., 2015). Our study thus extends this prior research by further examining how the six values of ethical import identified within discussions of PHRs (Fleischmann et al., 2015) are discussed within usability studies on patient portals. The definitions for these six values are as follows:

**Privacy (P)**: how patients control access to their own records and personal health information

**Confidentiality (C)**: how practitioners and others restrict others' access to patient records

**Security (S)**: preventing unauthorized access to patients' records and personal health information

**Transparency (Tra):** ensuring patients understand the systems and the information provided therein

**Trust (Tru)**: ensuring patients have confidence in the systems and the information provided therein

**Agency (A):** ensuring patients feel empowered to make their own decisions about their records

### *Deductive Content Analysis*

Content analysis is an established method for identifying and examining human values embedded within ICTs, as well as for discussing users' invocations of values (Fleischmann, Oard, Cheng, Wang, & Ishita, 2009). This study followed prior content analyses of human values (e.g., Cheng, Fleischmann, Wang, Ishita, & Oard, 2012; Koepfler & Fleischmann, 2012; Rokeach, 2008). Specifically, since prior research had already identified salient values (Fleischmann et al., 2015), we conducted a deductive content analysis operationalizing these six values (Elo & Kyngäs, 2008).

First, quotes were selected from Fleischmann et al.'s (2015) prior thematic analysis of PHRs to guide us in our analysis of the six values. Then, the first two authors worked independently to identify whether or not a value was invoked within the text of a particular paper in the corpus used for this research. Values could be identified and coded from within any section of an article and a single coded invocation was considered sufficient to code that value's presence in the document as a whole; the number of invocations per document was not considered. After this independent coding, the two coders compared their findings to achieve consensus, a process that has previously been used to identify human values in text (Fleischmann et al., 2017; Fleischmann & Wallace, 2010, 2009).

## RESULTS

### *Quantitative Analysis*

We present our quantitative findings first, before delving into the results of our more in-depth qualitative analysis.

#### How frequently did any of the values occur in studies of patients' perceptions and use of patient portals?

As Table 1 illustrates, the most frequently occurring value was security (in 67% of the papers), followed by transparency (54%), agency (52%), trust (46%), privacy (46%), and confidentiality (23%).

#### How many papers included invocations of multiple values?

All 52 papers included invocations of at least one of the six values. 4 (8%) of the papers included invocations of all six values; 7 (13%) included invocations of five of the values; 9 (17%) included invocations of four of the values; 14 (27%) included invocations of three of the values; 8 (15%) included invocations of two of the values, and 10 (19%) included the invocation of only one value.

#### How frequently did the values co-occur?

The most frequent pairing was security and agency (50%), followed by transparency and agency (44%), and privacy and security (42%). Security was the most frequently co-occurring value for privacy, confidentiality, and agency, while agency was the most frequently co-occurring value for security, transparency, and trust (Table 1).

| | *P* | *C* | *S* | *Tra* | *Tru* | *A* |
|---|---|---|---|---|---|---|
| *P* | *46%* | *19%* | *42%* | *27%* | *27%* | *38%* |
| *C* | | *23%* | *21%* | *17%* | *13%* | *17%* |
| *S* | | | *67%* | *35%* | *33%* | *50%* |
| *Tra* | | | | *54%* | *27%* | *44%* |
| *Tru* | | | | | *46%* | *38%* |
| *A* | | | | | | *52%* |

*Table 1. Frequency of Values and Value Pairs*

### *Qualitative Analysis*

After identifying the presence/absence of each value within each document, we next used thematic analysis (Braun & Clarke, 2006) to analyze and classify subthemes within each of the six human values.

#### Privacy

Discussions relating to privacy invoked particular concerns of exposing or accessing personal contact information (such as email accounts and/or telephone numbers) or demographic information to various parties (including medical personnel, strangers, or family members and caregivers). Issues surrounding the recording and storing of sensitive and "detailed personal information about patients' medical, social, and family histories" (Vodicka et al., 2013, Introduction section, para. 1)—including issues specifically related to Health Insurance Portability and Accountability Act (HIPAA) compliance—were also frequently invoked and were apparently a concern of several categories of related stakeholders in the use of patient portals.

Similarly, privacy was considered to be a form of "respect for personal boundaries" (Osborn et al., 2011, p. i20) within several papers. These "personal boundaries" also extended, in some instances, to expressing related concerns involving individuals (primarily patients) accessing the patient portal in a public space, for reasons including a lack of access to a home computer. However, some stakeholders also expressed a preference for "sending psychosocial messages by portal because it affords privacy and distance" (Lin, Wittevrongel, Moore, Beaty, & Ross, 2005, Discussion section, para. 2). This example indicates some of the conflict—including internal, individual conflict—between different aspects and understandings of what "privacy" can mean within the context of patient portals.

In fact, one of the papers (Vodicka et al., 2013) points directly to this difficulty in unravelling the complex ideas associated with this particular value in both portal users' and designers' minds. The authors note that "the word 'privacy' in itself carries different meanings for different people" and that "patients may not distinguish between the privacy risks of digitizing their health records (e.g., hospital breaches of data security) and the risks of accessing those records online (e.g., forgetting to log off a public computer, printing sensitive information). As a result, self-reported concerns about privacy may reflect diverse interpretations of potential associated risks" (Vodicka et al., 2013, Limitations section, para. 2). However, this kind of self-reflection on the invocation of this value (or on any of the other five values analyzed here) was exceedingly rare amongst the documents within the corpus.

Despite the rich invocations of this value described above, several documents within the corpus only included a superficial invocation or non-specific use of the term "privacy," such as making a passing mention of "privacy" as one among many "concerns" or "barriers," without any detailed discussion of the concept or of its specific relevance to patient portals. Thus, "privacy" was perhaps used (both with self-awareness and without apparent intention) in many documents as a blanket term that included multiple concepts. This kind of "umbrella" usage of the concept may partially explain why the particular term "privacy" was found in so many of the documents touching upon this value (23 out of 24 documents that were coded to invoke this value), as well as why privacy was so often found in conjunction with other concepts (particularly security, confidentiality, and trust) within the corpus.

### Confidentiality

Confidentiality was closely linked with both privacy and security and frequently *only* co-appeared in one or two sentences with one of these two other values; confidentiality was not coded in a single document without either privacy or security (and usually both) also appearing.

Authors invoking confidentiality most frequently described using secure online messaging as a means of "communicating sensitive information (e.g., depression/anxiety symptoms, sexual dysfunction)" (Wade-Vuturo, Mayberry, & Osborn, 2013, p. 519), particularly in terms of HIPAA compliance (similarly to privacy). Several other invocations of confidentiality involved issues specifically related to the "openness" or availability of visit notes (these are notes that were generally made by the physician about a specific patient appointment, although in some cases, such notes were generated before or after the appointment by the patients themselves). One particular concern, for example, focused on the perceived conflict of confidentiality in contrast to patient autonomy around patients "sharing their visit notes with others, including other doctors" (Walker et al., 2011, p. 816).

In addition to these discussions, several articles discussed more specifically technological or design aspects of patient portals in relation to maintaining confidentiality while allowing different categories of users. These discussions included ideas such as tiered access within the portals and health information (non-family specific), as well as issues of access and information availability between family members or between patients and caregivers—particularly between parents and children or teenagers. For example, Zarcadoolas, Vaughon, Czaja, Levy, and Rockoff (2013) describe "the issue of parental access to an adolescent's online health records" as "complicated to resolve" (Results section, para. 15). Bergman, Brown, and Wilson (2008) similarly note that "there would have to be ground rules around confidentiality and disclosure of important health issues that would have to be negotiated by each family" (Results section, para. 17).

### Security

As discussed above, privacy and security were frequently invoked together, often as completely interrelated or interchangeable concepts, including in subsection headings of the document (e.g., Latulipe et al., 2015), and frequently in a somewhat superficial way. For example, Latulipe et al. (2015) describe a clear (technological design) security concern with patient portals in that "while many of the participants understood that the system was password protected, they still felt that their information would be at risk" (p. 3864). However, the authors then go on to somewhat conflate privacy and security by arguing that "this [concern] demonstrates a lack of understanding that medical records are already stored on networked computers, but shows that privacy of medical information and lack of security of online systems is a critical concern" (Latulipe et al., 2015, p. 3864). Only rarely, as with privacy, did authors acknowledge that the concept of "security" might be complex or unclearly defined for both patients and researchers (or even designers).

The more detailed discussions of security within the articles addressed several different facets of digital and information security, including: specifics of the login process for the portal and/or the authentication process; the ramifications and complications caused by shared/sharing passwords between patients and their surrogates or guardians; the importance of the login process and the necessity of having secure passwords; the (often unspecified) dangers of unauthorized individuals (including other personnel or staff involved in the patient's care or in portal design and maintenance, total strangers, or family members and past or present acquaintances) accessing personal data; "hacking" and identity theft; data encryption features (such as SSL); and the avoidance of "insecure" mediums of communication for sensitive information. Similar to many of the more detailed invocations of confidentiality, the majority of these discussions revolve around more technical aspects of the design of patient portals.

### Transparency

Although a few articles used the word "transparency" in the exact wording that we were looking for—for example, when "many participants expressed the need for full transparency of the record and worried that providers would be able to limit access to some records or portions thereof" (Dhanireddy et al., 2014, p. 727)—most documents coded for invoking "transparency" did not use the exact word itself. We identified two main themes within invocations of transparency: 1) the transparency of the ICT (the patient portal) *itself* and 2) the transparency of the *information* presented within the patient portal.

Discussions related to the transparency of the *ICT itself* were closely related to issues with accessing and understanding the portal features. Several of these invocations were directly related to classic concerns within user experience design and research, such as concerns with user interface design, and with HCI and usability issues related to fundamental access of patient-desired information. Other discussions focused on unclear expectations from either the patient or physician end of the portal (e.g., what precise actions were expected of the user, or what the user should expect from the other parties involved) and on a lack of clarity regarding specific practices or criteria of the portal, including a desire for increased "transparency of confidentiality policies in play" (McNamara et al., 2015, p. 1613). Similarly, some papers explored issues surrounding the ambiguity/lack of clear explanation for intentional or unintentional withholding or restricting of access and/or information (either by patients or medical personnel) within the patient portal.

Discussions surrounding issues of a lack of transparency in the *information* presented within the patient portal primarily involved a lack of explanation, context, or clarity in patient records and/or the patient's ability to understand and utilize this information. As Barron, Bedra, Wood, & Finkelstein (2014) describe: "The patient portal introduces a world of medical terminology, and both patients and caregivers seek help in interpreting the information contained in the electronic medical record. Readability, simplicity, and clearly explained medical concepts seem to be values underlying the comments of patients, caregivers, and IT experts" (p. 184). Thus, these researchers clearly identified transparency as a salient value in the use of patient portals.

These two main variations of transparency were frequently encountered together within the same document—and even within the same paragraph or sentence. This confluence is perhaps unsurprising: it may be difficult for a user to understand, access, and interpret the *information* found within a patient portal (or any ICT) without first being able to understand the portal *interface* itself—and vice versa.

### Trust

Invocations of "trust" and "trustworthiness" typically involved concepts of "accuracy," "reliability," "credibility," and "correctness," either in lieu of the word "trust" or in support of it. Similar to our findings related to transparency, however, we found some distinction in the corpus between the concepts of having trust in the *system* (the patient portal and how it operates) as opposed to trust in the *health information* contained and presented within the patient portal (including general disease and health information, patient records entered by the medical care centers, and patient-recorded information).

The former case (trust in the system) often involved "privacy" and "security" issues, or issues relating to the constancy and reliability of access and maintenance of the portal, including concerns that "information was not made available in the portal or the portal was not up-to-date" (Giardina, Modi, Parrish, & Singh, 2015, p. 150). Examples of the latter case (trust in the health information presented) include patients' preference for a "direct link to accurate and trustworthy health information (via search engine or hospital-based website)" (Dhanireddy et al., 2014, p. 729), or concerns such as, "'I am not quite sure who maintains the information. If someone else does it, I don't trust it 100%'" (Chou, Nagykaldi, Aspy, & Mold, 2010, p. 90).

In addition to these two main themes, authors within the corpus also discussed trust in relation to perceptions of and relationships with medical professionals involved in care; provider endorsement of the portal; general distrust of technology and/or a lack of prior access to ICTs (e.g., digital divide); unfamiliarity with the particular portal, previous negative experiences with similar technology, and perceived reputation of the agencies and sources involved in the creation and maintenance of the portal.

### Agency

When discussing the concept of agency, authors often focused on issues of empowerment, management (including self-management), engagement, autonomy, control, and active (including proactive) or collaborative involvement with the patient's health or health information. Documents often invoked several of these concepts simultaneously, for example, asserting that "if the underlying purpose of empowerment is to increase patients' autonomy, providing access to test results allows patients to exert control over their health in ways they find meaningful" (Giardina et al., 2015, p. 153) and that "participants noted that access was a means to empowerment that would allow self-management of disease and enable them to be more proactive about their health" (Dhanireddy et al., 2014, p. 728).

We also found, however, that these related concepts were often used in a somewhat shallow way, particularly concepts related to the "management" of patient health and disease and of patient engagement. This potential difficultly in adequately and accurately invoking agency was also addressed specifically by Giardina et al. (2015), who argue that "though a recent review of controlled trials found insufficient evidence to support increased empowerment, it may be an issue of how empowerment is conceptualized (i.e.; self-efficacy, control, activation). Despite patient empowerment being ubiquitous in the literature related to health information technology, there is no consensus on the definition" (p. 153). Thus, agency is identified in the literature as a salient value worthy of further study.

## DISCUSSION

Our quantitative analyses show that security, transparency, and agency occurred most frequently, with each of them found in more than half of the papers in the corpus. While trust and privacy were each invoked in nearly half of the publications, confidentiality occurred in only 23%. This low occurrence of confidentiality was a surprise, given that this value (which considers how anyone who has legitimate access to patient records also has the responsibility to fully protect patients' personal information in the portals) is strictly mandated by federal and state regulations (e.g., HIPAA and HITECH in the United States).

This low occurrence of confidentiality perhaps reflects a more technology-centric view of patient portals in the current conversations about these systems, as security often lies more explicitly at the technological level. However, confidentiality involves a subtler balance of relationships among different stakeholders and different types of information. The lack of emphasis on confidentiality in the majority of the papers may also be due to our focus on user studies by patients, instead of providers.

Interestingly, while we did not limit our searches to patient portal studies involving values (i.e., we did not use the keyword "value" or any of the six values in our searches), we still found that all publications in our final sample invoked at least one of these values. Our analysis therefore indicates that both researchers and users consider human values as part of their interactions with patient portals. Moreover, many of the articles invoked multiple values (although the direct relationship between these multiple values may sometimes be unclear), indicating that users apparently find that several values in combination are salient to their perceptions on user experiences of patient portals. Thus, researchers and designers should not necessarily examine any single value in a vacuum while considering the role of human values within patient portals.

The invocation of at least one value in each article is also a promising sign that patient portal researchers and users are already sensitive to value-related issues, although more attention on various combinations of multiple values—and particularly their interactions or design tradeoffs—is still much needed. For instance, in a small practice where two or three physicians regularly cover for each other (i.e., "share" their patients) while their colleagues are out of the office for any reason, confidentiality might be less important than security. However, in a large hospital with over 30 different units employing hundreds of providers that typically have little need to share patient information in their care of the patients, confidentiality may be as important as security.

Somewhat in contrast to the promising invocation of at least one human value in each paper, however, our qualitative analyses show that these invocations are not often clearly articulated or defined (particularly on the part of the author, but also apparently by the study participants described within the corpus). Although we did find a few richly-detailed examples of each human value, the majority of invocations were discussed by the document authors in a superficial, ambiguous, or only partially-conscious manner—particularly when it came to the seemingly more "obvious" values of privacy, confidentiality, and security. Additionally, while the exact phrases for "transparency," "trust," and "human agency" were rarely used within the documents coded to contain these values, authors were more inclined to use concrete examples and details when discussing these values—perhaps precisely because they could not fall back on a single word that they felt could be understood to convey the concept that they wished to describe. Although the topic of human values in relation to patient portal design is not the main focus of analysis in any of the articles in the corpus, we argue that a more careful inclusion and thoughtful definition of these terms would benefit future user studies of patient portals.

This lack of a clear, defined approach to understanding and addressing human values within user studies of patient portals is potentially troubling in two main ways. First, it is important to re-iterate that, as discussed earlier in the "Background" section, general concepts of "usability" widely used in these studies do not adequately cover analyses of values within ICTs by default. In fact, values and usability may even be in conflict—or multiple values may be in conflict with each other within the ICT design. Thus, only a clear focus and analysis on human values within the design can fully bring these conflicts—as well as any support or cooperation—into view.

Second, we should remember that human values, while perhaps universal or culturally uniform in certain regards, will still vary and that "similar values will play out in different ways for different users" (Friedman & Kahn, 2008, p. 1247). In terms of patient portals, this diversity may be represented by the use of these portals within several different countries (as represented within the corpus)—however, despite potential significant differences between cultural contexts and values, researchers commonly cite user studies conducted in other geographic areas. Additionally, users of patient portals cover a number of demographics, even within the same nation (including race, class, culture, language, age, gender, and education), as everyone needs access to their health information. (Although everyone may not, in fact, have equal access to patient portals and their health information, as indicated by some of the concerns described within the corpus related to an ability to securely and/or privately access a computer.)

As Ryan et al. (2016) argue, the poor adoption and return rates associated with patient portals indicate that it is "not sufficient to engage patients in the use of a portal; it is critical that patients be engaged in the early stages of implementation" (p. 848). Unfortunately, the lack of patient choice for selecting a patient portal may offer particularly little incentive for designers to be sensitive to user's values or to usability more broadly, especially compared to other ICTs. This lack of control, coupled with a perceived lack of support for their values, may in turn push patients away from using or returning to the portal to manage their health—or, alternatively, towards choosing a different health care provider. Thus, in supporting users' values, there are also indirect benefits to providers: these decisions could affect patient satisfaction with providers and can even affect positive health behavior and outcomes.

Likewise, when it comes to understanding the role of human values within the design and use of patient portals, "tools are not enough" to truly support patient health; true patient engagement "requires patient-centered partnerships between patients and health care providers" (Ryan et al., 2016, p. 848). Patient portal designers and researchers are also crucial members of these "partnerships" and should understand and support the role of human values within the user experience of patient portals. Although there are many potential ways to approach such user-centered design, we recommend Friedman et al.'s (2008) value-sensitive design approach for addressing patient vulnerability and well-being, which is necessary for successful patient portal use.

We argue, therefore, that user experience designers and researchers might take a similar approach to accounting for differences in human values as the one described by Friedman and Kahn (2008) for the HCI community; that is, by striving to find a "value adaptable," "middle ground" for understanding values within user experience that "allows for an analysis of universal moral values, as well as allowing for these values to play out differently in a particular culture at a particular point in time," and between different individuals within that culture (p. 1247). This practice could enable more explicit discussions of human values within patient portals, particularly as a related part of user experience design and research.

### *Implications and future research*

Our research provides a groundwork for understanding how user research within the area of patient portals can improve our understanding of human values. Specifically, we analyzed an existing body of publication on this topic and looked for invocations of the six human values that we deemed to be most relevant to this body of research. The findings of our study raise several important implications that can only be addressed through further research in this area. Significant questions include:

*Are there other values of ethical import (Friedman & Kahn, 2008) related to patient portal use and design?* The set of values used in our deductive content analysis is drawn from previous related work on PHRs (Fleischmann et al., 2015). Although our identification of each of the six values within this corpus indicates that these six values are salient to patient portals, further research might illuminate additional salient values.

*Does a specific value invocation reflect the authors' perceptions or those of the end users?* Due to the nature of this research, we were severely limited in our ability to access patients' discussions of their own values directly. Although we were able to analyze some direct quotations from participants within the corpus, even those quotations have been pre-filtered by the articles' authors.

Do patient portal designers and health care providers fully understand the differences—and design tradeoffs—between different values (e.g., security and confidentiality)? Because none of the articles in the corpus gave a stated focus on discussing values within patient portals, it may be somewhat unfair to judge their lack of clear discussion around the six values that we analyzed. Follow-up studies or interviews might shed more light on the perspectives of these stakeholders.

If portal designers did consider multiple values simultaneously, would the final product be more likely than otherwise to ensure them all? Our analyses suggest that noticeable percentages of—and different combinations of—values co-occur in patient portal studies. It would be interesting to examine if and how the final portal product might have achieved what designers intended to support (e.g., when designers intentionally invoke both security and confidentiality in the design).

Addressing these questions will require ongoing discussions with and among various stakeholders involved with patient portals—including user experience designers and researchers, health care providers, patients, and sometimes caregivers. These conversations may need to take a variety of forms, perhaps including in-depth interviews and focus groups, holding focused iterative and participatory design sessions, and continuing analysis of the published body of research. We hope that our analysis can act as a starting point for future study of the role of human values as an integral part of the user experience of patient portals.

## CONCLUSION

Our study findings have important implications for patient portal researchers and designers, as well as for healthcare providers. First, researchers need to pay more systematic attention to the potential effects of human values on the adoption and use of patient portals (among patients and healthcare providers alike). Second, designers should always have a good understanding of the target users' values and strive to achieve the best balance that can accommodate the values of target users, who may prioritize different values and whose prioritized values may even change over time under evolving circumstances.

Finally, in order to improve the adoption and reuse rate of patient portals among patients with diverse characteristics, healthcare providers need a good understanding of the values that a specific portal may implicitly or explicitly promote (or, alternatively, may suppress, both intentionally and unintentionally). Likewise, they must have the necessary skills and background information to assess whether or not a portal matches patients' values—or even whether or not the values embedded within the portal match their own values. Ultimately, however, the role of human values within patient portals can only be understood and supported through a more concerted effort on the part of researchers and designers. Thus, there is a need for further user studies of the role of privacy, confidentiality, security, transparency, trust, agency, and other values in the user experience of patient portals.

## ACKNOWLEDGMENTS

This research was funded by the Center for Identity at The University of Texas at Austin.

## REFERENCES

Barron, J., Bedra, M., Wood, J., & Finkelstein, J. (2014). Exploring three perspectives on feasibility of a patient portal for older adults. *Studies in Health Technology and Informatics*, *202*, 181–184.

Bergman, D. A., Brown, N. L., & Wilson, S. (2008). Teen use of a patient portal: A qualitative study of parent and teen attitudes. *Perspectives in Health Information Management*, *5*.

Braun, V., & Clarke, V. (2006). Using thematic analysis in psychology. *Qualitative Research in Psychology*, *3*(2), 77–101.

Brin, D. (1998). *The transparent society: Will technology force us to choose between privacy and freedom?* Reading, MA: Addison-Wesley.

Buckovich, S. A., Rippen, H. E., & Rozen, M. J. (1999). Driving toward guiding principles: A goal for privacy, confidentiality, and security of health information. *Journal of the American Medical Informatics Association*, *6*(2), 122–133.

Byczkowski, T. L., Munafo, J. K., & Britto, M. T. (2014). Family perceptions of the usability and value of chronic disease web-based patient portals. *Health Informatics Journal*, *20*(2), 151–162.

Cheng, A.-S., & Fleischmann, K. R. (2010). Developing a meta-inventory of human values. *Proceedings of the American Society for Information Science and Technology*, *47*(1), 1–10.

Cheng, A.-S., Fleischmann, K. R., Wang, P., Ishita, E., & Oard, D. W. (2012). The role of innovation and wealth in the net neutrality debate: A content analysis of human values in congressional and FCC hearings. *Journal of the American Society for Information Science and Technology*, *63*(7), 1360–1373.

Chou, A. F., Nagykaldi, Z., Aspy, C. B., & Mold, J. W. (2010). Promoting patient-centered preventive care using a wellness portal preliminary findings. *Journal of Primary Care & Community Health*, *1*(2), 88–92.

Committee on Quality of Healthcare in America. (2001). Crossing the quality chasm: A new health system for the 21st century. Washington, DC: National Academy Press.

Dhanireddy, S., Walker, J., Reisch, L., Oster, N., Delbanco, T., & Elmore, J. G. (2014). The urban underserved: Attitudes towards gaining full access to electronic medical records. *Health Expectations*, *17*, 724–732.

Elo, S., & Kyngäs, H. (2008). The qualitative content analysis process. *Journal of Advanced Nursing*, *62*, 107–115.

Fleischmann, K. R. (2014). *Information and human values*. San Rafael, CA: Morgan & Claypool.

Fleischmann, K. R., Hui, C., & Wallace, W. A. (2017). The societal responsibilities of computational modelers: Human values and professional codes of ethics. *Journal of the Association for Information Science and Technology*, *68*(3), 543–552.

Fleischmann, K. R., Oard, D. W., Cheng, A., Wang, P., & Ishita, E. (2009). Automatic classification of human values: Applying computational thinking to information ethics. *Proceedings of the American Society for Information Science and Technology*, *46*(1), 1–4.

Fleischmann, K. R., & Wallace, W. A. (2005). A covenant with transparency: Opening the black box of models. *Communications of the ACM*, *48*(5), 93-97.

Fleischmann, K. R., & Wallace, W. A. (2009). Ensuring transparency in computational modeling. *Communications of the ACM*, *52*(3), 131–134.

Fleischmann, K. R., & Wallace, W. (2010). Value conflicts in computational modeling. *Computer*, *43*(7), 57–63.

Fleischmann, K. R., Zhang, Y., & Xie, B. (2015). Human values and personal health records. *Proceedings of the Association for Information Science and Technology*, *52*(1), 1–4.

Friedman, B., & Kahn, P. H. (2008). Human values, ethics, and design. In A. Sears & J. A. Jacko (Eds.), *The human-computer interaction handbook: Fundamentals, evolving technologies, and emerging applications* (2nd ed, pp. 1241–1266). New York: Lawrence Erlbaum Associates.

Friedman, B., Kahn, P. H., & Borning, A. (2008). Value sensitive design and information systems. In K. E. Himma & H. T. Tavani (Eds.), *The handbook of information and computer ethics* (pp. 69–101). Hoboken, NJ: John Wiley & Sons.

Fukuyama, F. (1995). *Trust: The social virtues and the creation of prosperity*. New York: Free Press.

Garrett, J. J. (2011). *The elements of user experience: User-centered design for the Web and beyond* (2nd ed). Berkeley, CA: New Riders.

Giardina, T., Modi, V., Parrish, D., & Singh, H. (2015). The patient portal and abnormal test results: An exploratory study of patient experiences. *Patient Experience Journal*, *2*(1), 148–154.

Giddens, A. (1984). *The constitution of society: Outline of the theory of structuration*. Berkeley, CA: University of California Press.

Goldzweig, C. L., Orshansky, G., Paige, N. M., Towfigh, A. A., Haggstrom, D. A., Miake-Lye, I., … Shekelle, P. G. (2013). Electronic patient portals: Evidence on health outcomes, satisfaction, efficiency, and attitudes: A systematic review. *Annals of Internal Medicine*, *159*(10), 677.

Hitlin, S., & Piliavin, J. A. (2004). Values: Reviving a dormant concept. *Annual Review of Sociology*, *30*, 359–393.

Irizarry, T., DeVito Dabbs, A., & Curran, C. R. (2015). Patient portals and patient engagement: A state of the science review. *Journal of Medical Internet Research*, *17*(6), e148.

Isomursu, M., Ervasti, M., Kinnula, M., & Isomursu, P. (2011). Understanding human values in adopting new technology—A case study and methodological discussion. *International Journal of Human-Computer Studies*, *69*(4), 183–200.

Jones, J. B., Weiner, J. P., Shah, N. R., & Stewart, W. F. (2015). The wired patient: Patterns of electronic patient portal use among patients with cardiac disease or diabetes. *Journal of Medical Internet Research*, *17*(2), e42.

Koepfler, J. A., & Fleischmann, K. R. (2012). Studying the values of hard-to-reach populations: Content analysis of tweets by the 21st century homeless. In *Proceedings of the 2012 iConference* (pp. 48–55). New York: ACM.

Kruse, C. S., Argueta, D. A., Lopez, L., & Nair, A. (2015). Patient and provider attitudes toward the use of patient portals for the management of chronic disease: A systematic review. *Journal of Medical Internet Research*, *17*(2), e40.

Latulipe, C., Gatto, A., Nguyen, H. T., Miller, D. P., Quandt, S. A., Bertoni, A. G., … Arcury, T. A. (2015). Design considerations for patient portal adoption by low-income, older adults. In *Proceedings of the 33rd annual ACM conference on human factors in computing systems* (pp. 3859–3868). New York, NY, USA: ACM.

Lin, C.-T., Wittevrongel, L., Moore, L., Beaty, B. L., & Ross, S. E. (2005). An internet-based patient-provider communication system: Randomized controlled trial. *Journal of Medical Internet Research*, *7*(4).

Lyles, C. R., López, A., Pasick, R., & Sarkar, U. (2013). "5 mins of uncomfyness is better than dealing with cancer 4 a lifetime": An exploratory qualitative analysis of cervical and breast cancer screening dialogue on Twitter. *Journal of Cancer Education*, *28*(1), 127–133.

McNamara, M., Arnold, C., Sarma, K., Aberle, D., Garon, E., & Bui, A. A. T. (2015). Patient portal preferences: Perspectives on imaging information. *Journal of the Association for Information Science and Technology*, *66*(8), 1606–1615.

Nielsen, J. (1999). *Designing web usability: The practice of simplicity*. Berkeley, CA: New Riders.

Office of the National Coordinator. (2015). What is a patient portal? Retrieved April 9, 2017, from https://www.healthit.gov/providers-professionals/faqs/what-patient-portal

Or, C. K. L., & Tao, D. (2014). Does the use of consumer health information technology improve outcomes in the patient self-management of diabetes? A meta-analysis and narrative review of randomized controlled trials. *International Journal of Medical Informatics*, *83*(5), 320–329.

Osborn, C. Y., Rosenbloom, S. T., Stenner, S. P., Anders, S., Muse, S., Johnson, K. B., … Jackson, G. P. (2011). MyHealthAtVanderbilt: Policies and procedures governing patient portal functionality. *Journal of the American Medical Informatics Association*, *18*(Supplement 1), i18–i23.

Preece, J. (2000). *Online communities: Designing usability and supporting socialbilty*. John Wiley & Sons, Inc.

Rokeach, M. (2008). *Understanding human values*. Simon and Schuster.

Rubin, J., & Chisnell, D. (2008). *Handbook of usability testing: How to plan, design and conduct effective tests*. New York: John Wiley & Sons.

Ryan, B. L., Brown, J. B., Terry, A., Cejic, S., Stewart, M., & Thind, A. (2016). Implementing and using a patient portal: A qualitative exploration of patient and provider perspectives on engaging patients. *Journal of Innovation in Health Informatics*, *23*(2), 848.

Schwartz, S. H. (1994). Are there universal aspects in the structure and contents of human values? *Journal of Social Issues*, *50*(4), 19–45.

Schwartz, S. H. (2007). Value orientations: Measurement, antecedents and consequences across nations. *Measuring attitudes cross-nationally: Lessons from the European social survey*, 161–193.

Vodicka, E., Mejilla, R., Leveille, S. G., Ralston, J. D., Darer, J. D., Delbanco, T., … Elmore, J. G. (2013). Online access to doctors' notes: Patient concerns about privacy. *Journal of Medical Internet Research*, *15*(9).

Wade-Vuturo, A. E., Mayberry, L. S., & Osborn, C. Y. (2013). Secure messaging and diabetes management: Experiences and perspectives of patient portal users. *Journal of the American Medical Informatics Association*, *20*(3), 519–525.

Walker, J., Leveille, S. G., Ngo, L., Vodicka, E., Darer, J. D., Dhanireddy, S., … Delbanco, T. (2011). Inviting patients to read their doctors' notes: Patients and doctors look ahead. *Annals of Internal Medicine*, *155*(12), 811–819.

Zarcadoolas, C., Vaughon, W. L., Czaja, S. J., Levy, J., & Rockoff, M. L. (2013). Consumers' perceptions of patient-accessible electronic medical records. *Journal of Medical Internet Research*, *15*(8).

Zhang, Y., Fleischmann, K. R., Gao, J., & Xie, B. (2015). A systematic review of the literature on consumers' use of patient portals: Preliminary results. *Proceedings of the Association for Information Science and Technology*, *52*(1), 1–4.

# Disciplinary Assessment of Scientific Content by Higher-Order Citation Mining

**Sergej Sizov**
*Institute for Language and Information, Web Science Group, Heinrich-Heine-University, Germany. sizov@hhu.de*

**Mikel Bahn**
*Institute for Language and Information, Web Science Group, Heinrich-Heine-University, Germany. mikel.bahn@uni-duesseldorf.de*

## ABSTRACT

**Discovery of disciplinary fields, their relationships, and key contributors is an important research field of modern scientometrics. In this contribution, we study the problem of disciplinary/interdisciplinary interpretation of scientific content in the context of higher-order citation graphs. In doing so, we introduce the general approach for representing scientific publishers (conferences, journals) and their relationships by means of multi-dimensional tensor models. Consequently, tensor decomposition methods allow us to identify scientific fields in terms of key authorities, hubs and topical context expressed by keywords and/or fields of study.**

**The proposed strategy of tensor importance sampling allows for efficient and effective analysis of large-scale publication databases in state-of-the art cloud computing infrastructures. Consequently, we present results of our large-scale evaluations for the Microsoft Academic Graph dataset with various tensor modeling strategies, in direct comparison with state of the art content mining and graph mining methods common to the scientometric domain.**

**The comprehensive comparative analysis shows that tensor-based interpretations show considerable agreement with established content mining methods and graph-based authority ranking. At the same time, tensor based analysis allows for discovery of novel inter-disciplinary and trans-disciplinary fields, which are focused on subjects of investigation rather than on established methodologies and strongly connected research communities. In this sense, our approach complements existing mining methods for scientific content, and allows for novel insights into research collaboration patterns.**

## KEYWORDS

inter-disciplinarity, tensor analysis, authority ranking, research fields, PARAFAC, EigenFactor, SVD, cloud computing, scientometric analysis

## INTRODUCTION

Analysis and mining of scientific content is one of the key research fields of modern scientometrics. Established goals of investigation include comparative assessment of research performance, discovery of new research frontiers, facilitation of inter-disciplinary investigations, improvements of search/ranking/navigation within digital libraries and databases of content aggregators, and many others (Bar-Ilan, 2008). In this context, the key concepts of *disciplines* and *inter-disciplinarity* play often an essential role.

Our approach is conceptually motivated by recent discussions regarding the mentioned foundational scientific concepts. Based on a recent systematic literature review, (Aboelela, et al., 2007) recommend the definition of interdisciplinary research as follows:

"Interdisciplinary research is any study or group of studies undertaken by scholars from two or more distinct scientific disciplines. The research is based upon a conceptual model that links or integrates theoretical frameworks from those disciplines, uses study design and methodology that is not limited to any one field, and requires the use of perspectives and skills of the involved disciplines throughout multiple phases of the research process."

A closer consideration of this working definition raises several questions of interest for modern scientometric analysis. First of all, it deems reasonable to clarify what may be a model of a "*distinct scientific discipline*" in terms of its content and/or collaboration patterns. Furthermore, we are interested to understand how "*integrations*" between disciplines can be efficiently recognized and described. Finally, we are interested in deeper understanding how possible discovery methods are aligned with state of the art content and graph mining methods that are widely used in bibliometric and scientometric research.

### *Motivating example*

We exemplify our motivation by an (over-simplified) citation network shown in Figure 1. This example will be used for constructing run-through examples in the forthcoming sections.

80th Annual Meeting of the Association for Information Science & Technology, Washington, DC, VA | Oct. 27-Nov. 1, 2017

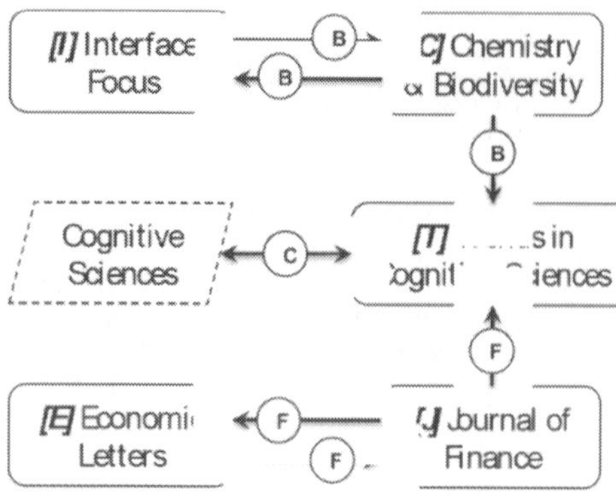


***Figure 1**: Motivating citation example*

The sample citation network contains five journals. Two of them (Interface Focus [I] and Chemistry & Biodiversity [C]) cite each other in the context of the field "Biodiversity" (B). In opposite, two further journals (Economic Letters [E] and Journal of Finance [J]) are connected to each other by citations in the context of "Finances" (F). Occasionally, both mentioned fields cite the journal "Trends in Cognitive Sciences" [T]. In turn, this journal is rather tightly connected with other sources from the field "Cognitive Sciences", but neither with "Finances" nor with "Biodiversity".

The exemplified situation allows for the following interpretation. We are given three "*scientific disciplines*" (Biodiversity, Finances, Cognitive Sciences). Occasionally, both Finances and Biodiversity employ certain user behavior models, studied by Cognitive Sciences. However, we may assume that the intensive inter-disciplinary cooperation between three fields, at all stages of the research process, appears underrepresented. This assumption can be made due to missing references in opposite directions, as well as direct connections between the fields "Finances" and "Biodiversity".

The data-driven mining and model-based description of such disciplinary contexts (like (B), (F) and (C) in our example) as well as discovery of possible collaboration opportunities between them, are in the main focus of this paper.

In our contribution, we instantiate this discussion in the context of higher-order referencing models (**tensors**) for semantically enriched citation graphs. The key advantage of the chosen approach is a seamless integration of context aspects (e.g. by keywords, fields of study) and knowledge transfer directions (e.g. by citations) in one complex model. Consequently, appropriate multi-modal component analysis (by means of tensor decomposition, in our case) allows for joint mining of disciplinary context (fields), key cited sources (authorities), and key citing facilities (hubs). Comparisons between hubs and authorities of same scientific field open up new possibilities for discovery of inter-disciplinary and trans-disciplinary collaboration opportunities.

### *Outline*

The rest of the contribution is organized as follows. First, we set our approach into the context of established scientometric methods by discussing related work. Next, we introduce the general tensor-based citation model, discuss its possible instantiations (various models for journals / conferences, keywords / fields as graph nodes), and propose an efficient approximation mechanism for large-scale tensor decompositions by means of importance sampling. Consequently, we systematically evaluate various tensor models with a large-scale publication dataset of the Microsoft Academic Graph (Sinha, et al., 2015), and discuss key observations and lessons learned.

The evaluation is complemented by systematic comparisons of tensor models with state of the art content and graph mining methods, including EigenFactor, Latent Semantic Indexing, and original disciplinary taxonomies of the Microsoft Academic Search[1] engine.

As an important result of our experimental evaluations, we observe considerable similarities between approaches regarding capturing and interpretation of scientific fields. At the same time, we recognize promising potentials of the tensor approach in discovering novel inter-disciplinary fields that are focused on *subjects of investigation* rather than on established methodical frameworks, terminologies, or tightly connected researcher communities. The discussion is complemented by multiple characteristic examples from our investigations, based on large-scale models for real data.

## RELATED WORK

The main objectives of this contribution are closely related to recent scientometric investigations on discovery of new research fronts and emerging research areas. Characteristic properties and distinguishing factors of such fronts are systematically discussed in (Upham & Small, 2010). Many approaches have been proposed for their discovery and analysis. Several methods like (Shibata, Kajikawa, Takeda, & Matsushima, 2009), (Fujita, Kajikawa, Mori, & Sakata, 2014), (Small, Boyack, & Klavans, 2014), and (Persson, 2010) address the problem by analyzing different types of weighted citation networks. In contrast, the model presented in (Guo, Weingart, & Börner, 2011) aims at combining multiple content-based and graph-based indicators of emergence. The content-centric approach can be found e.g. in (Zan, Tsim, Yeung, Chan, & Liu, 2007), which uses probabilistic latent semantic analysis for technology forecasting. The approach presented in (Daim, Shibata, Kajikawa, & Sakata, 2011) analyzes the technological uptake of scientific results by comparing research publications and patents. A milestone-based model for discovering new technologies is described in (Abercrombie, Udoeyop, & Schlicher, 2012).

[1] *http://academic.research.microsoft.com/*

The approach presented in this contribution uses tensor-based models for representing both structure and context of citation networks. Moreover, we show that results of higher-order decomposition of semantic graphs allow for discovery of both emerging inter-disciplinary fields and inter-disciplinary *potentials*, i.e. preliminary cases of *possible* emergence of new collaborations between different disciplinary perspectives around shared subjects of investigation.

From the conceptual perspective, tensor based decomposition of semantic citation networks allows for computation of topic-specific centrality / authority scores. In this sense, it is closely related to graph-based authority ranking approaches, such as EigenFactor (West, Bergstrom, & Bergstrom, 2010) or SJR (González-Pereira, Guerrero-Bote, & Moya-Anegón, 2010) and can be used as a novel indicator of scientific performance that complements the broad range of existing citation impact indicators, systematically reviewed in (Waltman, 2016) and (Alonso, Cabrerizo, Herrera-Viedma, & Herrera, 2009). At the same time, context scores can be interpreted as scientific fields or topics, analogously to probabilistic topic discovery methods for scientific content, e.g. by means of Latent Dirichlet Allocation (Griffiths & Steyvers, 2004) or Latent Semantic Analysis (Zan, Tsim, Yeung, Chan, & Liu, 2007). In this sense, it combines advantages of both context-based and structure-based mining methods.

The mining of semantic networks by tensor decomposition (Kolda & Bader, 2009) gained increasing attention over the last years. It has been used in various application scenarios, e.g. mining of Web search results (Kolda & Bader, 2006), Semantic Web graphs (Franz, Schultz, Sizov, & Staab, 2009), and many others. In the domain of scientometric analysis, this development was delayed due to limited scalability of decomposition algorithms and naturally large scale of citation networks. However, recent investigations have shown that computational problems can be efficiently solved by decomposition and parallelization of numeric iterations (Park, Jeon, Lee, & Kang, 2016) or dimensionality reduction by importance sampling (Papalexakis, Faloutsos, & Sidiropoulos, 2015). The latter approach was adopted in this contribution for efficient computations on realistic, large-scale citation networks such as Microsoft Academic Graph (Sinha, et al., 2015).

## HIGHER-ORDER CITATION MODELS

In a general setting, we consider the citation graph model $G$ as a structure $G = (V, C, E, edgeType)$, where $V$ is the set of graph vertices (e.g. journals), $E \subset V \times V$ is the set of directed graph edges (e.g. references), $C$ is the set of edge contexts (e.g. keywords or disciplines), and ***edgeType:*** $E$ ⌫$C$ is the mapping function that assigns to graph edges their context-specific semantics.

Depending of the modeling strategy for constructing $G$, the same citation data set can be interpreted in terms of different models. In the context of our problem, we primarily account for the established citation graph models $G$ according to (Small, 1997):

direct citation ($G^{DC}$),

co-citation ($G^{CC}$),

bibliographic coupling ($G^{BC}$)

as well as

field citation ($G^{FC}$)

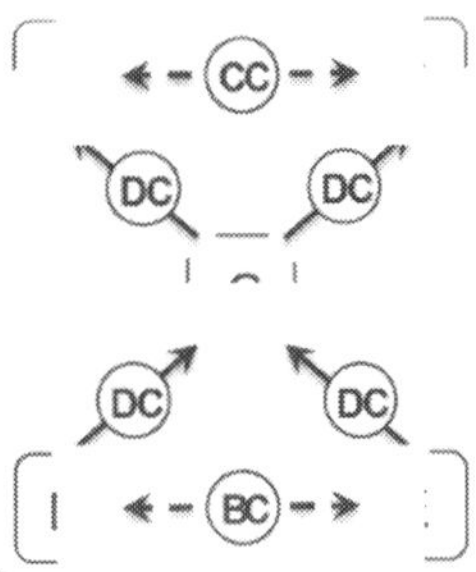

***Figure 2**: Citation graph models*

Figure 2 illustrates different strategies of edge construction. The sample graph consists of nodes $V=\{A,B,C,D,E\}$ and direct citations $E^{DC}=\{(C,A),(C,B),(D,C),(E,C)\}$. The co-citation edges $E^{CC}=\{(A,B),(B,A)\}$ represent the fact that $C$ is co-citing both sources $A$ and $B$. Analogously, the bibliographic coupling model contains edges $E^{BC}=\{(D,E),(E,D)\}$. By combining this common notion with edge contexts $C$, we define edges in $G$ as follows.

**(1)** In the direct citation model $G^{DC}$, the edge $E_k$ in the context $C_k$ between vertices $V_1$ and $V_2$ of $G^{DC}$ indicates the presence of citations of $V_2$ by $V_1$ in the context $C_k$; the edge weight is the count of such citations in the data set.

**(2)** In the co-citation model $G^{CC}$ according to (Small, 1973) vertices $V_1$ and $V_2$ are mutually connected, when their sources (e.g. publications) are simultaneously cited by a certain node $V_3$ in a certain context $C_k$.

**(3)** Analogously, in the bibliographic coupling model $G^{BC}$ (Kessler, 1963), vertices $V_1$ and $V_2$ are mutually connected if they simultaneously cite a certain shared source $V_3$. In both the cases, edge weights represent the number of co-citations or coupled citations, respectively.

**(4)** As a possible design alternative, we consider in parallel the graph model for *field citation* $G^{FC}$. In this setting, graph vertices represent research fields. In turn, edge contexts $C$ correspond to scientific sources (e.g. journals or conferences). The edge from $V_1$ to $V_2$ in a context $C_k$ represents the fact that there is a reference by a contribution from $C_k$, produced in the context $V_1$ and referencing some source produced in the context $V_2$.

Further discussion on constructing citation based graph models and their properties can be found in (Yan & Ding, 2012).

### *Tensor Model*

An alternative view on $G$ is its representation by a three-dimensional **tensor** $X$, i.e. a multi-dimensional array, where each of the slices represents the adjacency matrix of $G$ for a specific context from $C$. Figure 3 illustrates the sample tensor for the direct citation graph of our sample scenario, as introduced in Figure 1. The first adjacency matrix of $X$ models references in the context "Biodiversity" (B). An ***entry>0*** corresponds to the existence of a reference by this context, empty entries are considered as zeros. The second matrix represents references in the context "Finances" (F). For instance, the tensor expresses that the "Journal of Finance" [J] cites the journal "Trends in Cognitive Sciences" [T] in the context of the field "Finances" (F), which corresponds to

$$X(J, T, F) = X(5, 3, 2) = 1$$

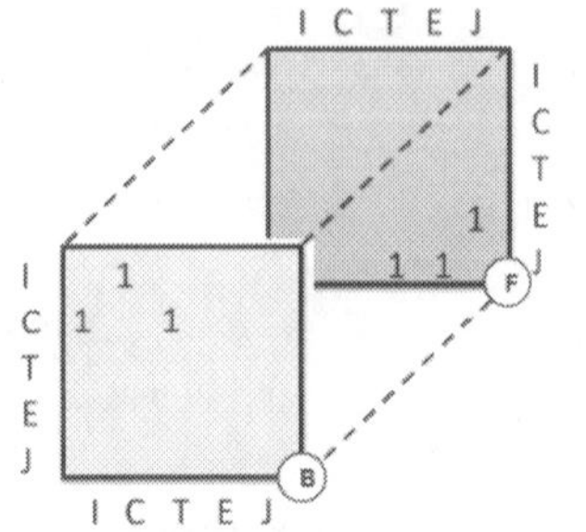


***Figure 3**: Sample direct citation tensor model*

Figure 4 shows the corresponding Co-Citation and Field Citation tensor models for our sample application scenario. We note that the adjacency matrices of the tensor for $G^{BC}$ are symmetric by design, unlike the direct citation model shown previously in Figure 3. In parallel, the $G^{FC}$ tensor model significantly differs from $G^{CC}$, $G^{BC}$ and $G^{DC}$ regarding both dimensionality and edge weights computation.

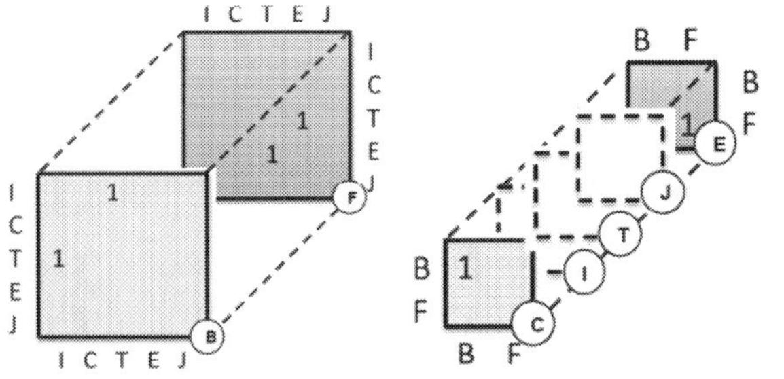


***Figure 4**: Tensors for co-citation/field citation models*

In general, the 3-mode citation tensor as a multi-dimensional array can be denoted by

$$X \in \mathbb{R}^{\,I_u \times I_v \times I_w} \tag{1}$$

where $I_u$ is the dimension of citing nodes, $I_v$ is the dimension of cited nodes, and $I_w$ is the dimension of citation context. Further details regarding formal tensor models are given by (Kolda & Bader, 2009). In order to discover disciplinary fields and their relationships from citation data, we employ the component-based decomposition methods for high-order graph models as described in the forthcoming sections.

### Tensor decomposition

From the conceptual perspective, tensor decomposition aims at finding latent factors or relations among observed data. Formally, an arbitrary tensor $X$ can be decomposed into $n$ components and represented in the form

$$X \approx \sum_{r=1}^{n} \lambda_r \cdot \mathbf{u_r} \circ \mathbf{v_r} \circ \mathbf{w_r} \tag{2}$$

i.e. as a linear combination of tensor components

$$X_r = \lambda_r \cdot \mathbf{u_r} \circ \mathbf{v_r} \circ \mathbf{w_r}, r = 1..n \tag{3}$$

with values $X_r$ *[a:b:c]* given by

$$X_r^{abc} = \lambda_r \cdot \mathbf{u_r}^a \cdot \mathbf{v_r}^b \cdot \mathbf{w_r}^c \tag{4}$$

Each component $r$ is essentially characterized in terms of its vectors $u_r$, $v_r$, and $w_r$. The common aim of the tensor decomposition is finding the best possible approximation of $X$ by means of a limited number of $n$ components, by minimizing the objective function

$$min \;\; ||X - \sum_{r=1}^{n} \lambda_r \cdot \mathbf{u_r} \cdot \mathbf{v_r} \cdot \mathbf{w_r}||_n^2 \tag{5}$$

among all possible candidate vectors $u_r$, $v_r$, and $w_r$. The most popular algorithm for fitting the components with respect to (5), also known as PARAFAC decomposition, is the Alternating Least Squares (ALS) approach (Kolda & Bader, 2009).

Figure 5 illustrates the idea of (2) by representing our sample tensor from Figure 3 as a combination of two components $X_1$ and $X_2$.

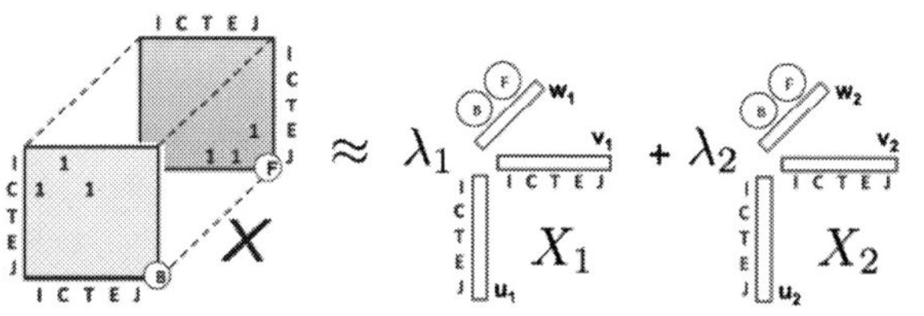


***Figure 5**: Tensor decomposition: sample idea*

The result of the decomposition allows for the following interpretation. In a given component $k$, vector $u_k$ represents *hub scores* of nodes, i.e. indicating their importance as citers. Analogously, $v_k$ contains *authority scores*, indicating the importance of nodes in being cited by others. The notion of hub and authority scores is similar to the popular HITS algorithm introduced by (Kleinberg, Kumar, Raghavan, Rajagopalan, & Tomkins, 1999) for authority ranking in two-dimensional graphs. Furthermore, the notion of authority is similar to the centrality measures for two-dimensional graphs used by EigenFactor (West, Bergstrom, & Bergstrom, 2010) and SJR (González-Pereira, Guerrero-Bote, & Moya-Anegón, 2010), both based on the idea of the well-known PageRank model (Page, Brin, Motwani, & Winograd, 1999).

At the same time, $w_k$ contains *context scores*, i.e. relevance weights for particular contexts from $C$ with regard to component $k$. In this sense, $w_k$ can be interpreted as a "topic model" of $k$-th component. This notion is conceptually similar to topic models produced by algorithms like Latent Semantic Indexing (LSI) (Deerwester, Dumais, Furnas, Landauer, &

Harshman, 1990), Probabilistic Latent Semantic Indexing (PLSI) (Hofmann, 1999) or Latent Dirichlet Allocation (LDA) (Blei, Ng, & Jordan, 2003) for two-dimensional term-document matrices.

In summary, the outcome of the tensor decomposition allows for joint interpretation of connectivity and context in the citation environment.

Figure 6 shows the outcome of PARAFAC tensor decomposition for our sample tensor model, previously introduced in Figure 3. The component vectors $u_r$, $v_r$, and $w_r$ are composed into matrices $U$, $V$, and $W$. This representation form is also known as a Kruskal tensor model (Kruskal, 1977).

$\lambda$

| $\lambda_1$ | $\lambda_2$ |
|---|---|
| 1.4142 | 1.4142 |

$U$

| | $u_1$ | $u_2$ |
|---|---|---|
| I | 0.0000 | 0.0099 |
| C | 0.0000 | 1.0000 |
| T | 0.0000 | 0.0000 |
| E | 0.0028 | 0.0000 |
| J | 1.0000 | 0.0000 |

$V$

| | $v_1$ | $v_2$ |
|---|---|---|
| I | 0.0000 | 0.7071 |
| C | 0.0000 | 0.0070 |
| T | 0.7071 | 0.7071 |
| E | 0.7071 | 0.0000 |
| J | 0.0020 | 0.0000 |

$W$

| | $w_1$ | $w_2$ |
|---|---|---|
| B | 0.0000 | 1.000 |
| F | 1.000 | 0.000 |

***Figure 6**: Sample tensor decomposition results*

For our sample scenario, by examining $W$ we recognize the presence of two clearly separated topics, with strong emphasis on Finances ($w_1$) and on Biodiversity ($w_2$). By analyzing $U$, the Journal of Finance [J] and Chemistry & Biodiversity [C] can be recognized as strongest hubs in both topics. From $V$ follows that Economic Letters [E] and Interface Focus [I] have high authority scores in respective topics.

The situation with Trends in Cognitive Sciences [T] demands closer consideration. As we can see from $U$, this journal cannot be seen as a considerable hub in both topics. At the same time, it has reasonably high scores in both vectors of $V$. This can be seen as an indication that [T] receives considerable attention from both topics $w_1$ and $w_2$, but actually belongs to a different topic / discipline. These observations are in line with our preceding empirical interpretation of the motivating example in the introduction.

### Decomposition Scalability

The computational complexity of the ALS decomposition algorithm for a $I_u \times I_v \times I_w$ tensor and $n$ components is known to be $O(nI_uI_vI_w)$ per iteration. At the same time, the iterative computation of ALS for factor matrices operates on dense data, even if the original citation data and the true latent factors are sparse, since least-squares estimates tend to be dense (Kolda & Bader, 2009), (Papalexakis, Faloutsos, & Sidiropoulos, 2015). For this reason, direct application of ALS to realistic, large-scale citation networks is computationally intractable, mainly due to main memory limitations of computation nodes.

In order to allow for processing of large-scale citation graphs on state of the art cloud computing infrastructures, we adopt suitable component approximation mechanisms. The approach is based on importance sampling from original data, parallel decomposition of multiple lower-rank sub-tensors, and subsequent consolidation of partial decomposition results (Jeon, Papalexakis, Faloutsos, Sael, & Kang, 2016). The core idea of the approach can be summarized as follows.

First of all, we assume that a large-scale tensor $X$ cannot be directly decomposed by means of ALS due to its size. As an intermediate step, we create multiple sub-tensors $X_i$, $i = 1..m$. The tensors $X_i$ are significantly smaller than $X$ by factor $s$: in each mode, they contain $I_u/s$, $I_v/s$ *and* $I_w/s$ dimensions (and corresponding values) of the original tensor, respectively. Every sub-tensor $X_i$ is characterized by the sets of dimensions $I^i$, $J^i$, $K^i$ that it directly adopts from the original tensor $X$. A certain fraction of dimensions $I_p^i$, $J_p^i$, $K_p^i$ is shared among all tensors $X_i$; the rest is chosen by importance sampling.

The approach is illustrated in Figure 7**Figure** for an original tensor $X$ and two sub-tensors $X_1$ and $X_2$. Red parts represent common dimensions of $X_1$ and $X_2$; green/blue fractions are (different) parts of $X$ by importance sampling.

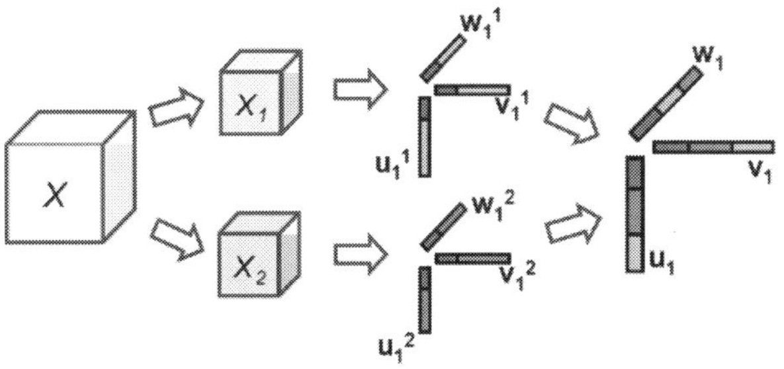


***Figure 7**: Tensor decomposition by sampling*

Consequently, sub-tensors $X_i$ are individually decomposed by means of ALS into $n$-component models. Unlike $X$, its sub-tensors $X_i$ can be efficiently processed on the nodes of state of the art cloud computing infrastructures. Consequently, the approximation of $X$ is obtained by merging partial decompositions of $X_i$. In doing so, we use shared dimensions $I_p^i$, $J_p^i$, $K_p^i$ (shown in red in Figure 7) for aligning components of partial decompositions and aggregating scores. From Figure 7 it can be seen that aggregated vectors $u$, $v$, $w$ contain values of shared dimensions (red part) and individual scores from particular decompositions (green and blue parts). Further details of the tensor merging algorithm are given in (Papalexakis, Faloutsos, & Sidiropoulos, 2015).

## EVALUATION

In order to systematically evaluate the proposed approach in a realistic setting, we performed multiple large-scale experiments with differently constructed semantic citation graphs and corresponding tensor models. Key quantities of interest include interpretability of results in terms of discovered disciplines, inter-disciplinary relations, and potentials for emerging research fields. Further aspects include method scalability as well as the influence of model parameters, such as the number of decomposition components, sampling rate or number of sub-tensors, on model outcome and its interpretation. In addition, we systematically compared tensor based results with outcome of common scientometric approaches for authority ranking and content mining.

Full evaluation results, computational scripts and software are available online for reproducibility. [2]

### Hardware

Computation of tensor decompositions was performed in a parallelized setting on a HPC infrastructure of our facility.

### Data

#### Microsoft Academic Graph

As a basis of our investigation we have used the publicly available Microsoft Academic Graph (Sinha, et al., 2015). This is a heterogeneous large scale dataset containing scientific publication records, citation relationships between publications, as well as authors, institutions, journals, conferences, fields of study, and keywords.

More specially there 120.887.833 papers that are present in the graph, 119.892.201 unique authors, 19.849 institutions, 23.568 journals, 1.275 conferences, 53.834 fields of study, and 157.052.442 keywords that indicate the link of a citation. As described in the next subsection from its inherent hierarchical and contextual information we have designing different data models in order to tackle the main objective of this paper.

#### Microsoft Academic Search Crawl

Since rankings that consider scholarly network is our subject of investigation we have additionally collected the first and second level structure of the disciplinary taxonomies of the Microsoft Academic Search[3] engine. The first level structure comprises 19 major topics such as Physics and Computer Science and the second level structure comprises 289 minor or more specialized topics such as bioinformatics or computer linguistics.

### Tensor Models

In order to compute tensor decomposition, modeling of the data has been an essential part of the work. Recall, a model can be thought of a collection of nodes and edges that builds a network of references. For instance, model "Journals Fields" that is a representation of the interconnection of all papers within each journal on the level of journals. Similar approaches were made for different variations of nodes and edges. Table 1 shows the structure of each model in the exemplary manner and with respect to the underlying graph classification.

| Overview: Strucutre and Type of Models | | |
|---|---|---|
| Model Name | Structure | Type of Graph |
| Conf Fields | conf × conf ⇒ field | direct citation |
| Conf Keywords | conf × conf ⇒ keyword | direct citation |
| Journals Fields | journal × journal ⇒ field | direct citation |
| Journals Keywords | journal × journal ⇒ keyword | direct citation |
| Merged Fields | conf+journal × conf+journal ⇒ field | direct citation |
| Merged Fields Self | conf+journal × conf+journal ⇒ field | direct citation |
| Merged Keywords | conf+journal × conf+journal ⇒ keyword | direct citation |
| Merged Keywords Self | conf+journal × conf+journal ⇒ keyword | direct citation |
| Merged Paper Fields | conf+journal × field ⇒ field | field coupling |
| Merged Paper Fields Self | conf+journal × field ⇒ field | field coupling |
| Merged Papers Keywords | conf+journal × keyword ⇒ keyword | field coupling |
| Merged Papers Keywords Self | conf+journal × keyword ⇒ keyword | field coupling |
| Journals Fields Cocite | journal × journal ⇒ field | cocite coupling |
| Journals Keywords Cocite | journal × journal ⇒ keyword | cocite coupling |
| Journals Fields Couple | journal × journal ⇒ field | bilbiographic coupling |
| Journals Keywords Couple | journal × journal ⇒ keyword | bilbiographic coupling |

***Table 1**: Overview of data models used their structure and type the underlying graph*

Furthermore, Table 1 shows a list of the evaluated models. Each row provides fundamental information of the structure of the multi-way representation of the data. In terms of that, it shows the number of non-zero elements as well as the density of the whole data tensor.

| Overview: Evaluated models | | | | |
|---|---|---|---|---|
| Models | Topics | Dimension | Non Zeros | Density |
| Conferences Fields | 19,50,289 | 593x593x2567 | 218530 | 2.4209e-04 |
| Conferences Keywords | 50 | 572x510x2919 | 202923 | 2.3830e-04 |
| Journal Fields | 19,50,289,1000 | 12670x12670x12613 | 35813437 | 1.7688e-05 |
| Journal Keywords | 50 | 116731x11151x11900 | 36362045 | 2.3475e-06 |
| Merged Fiedls | 50,289 | 13262x13262x13088 | 336857404 | 1.4634e-04 |
| Merged Fields Self | 50 | 12555x11539x13087 | 35124949 | 1.8526e-05 |
| Merged Keywords | 50 | 12489x11714x17510 | 37453773 | 1.8526e-05 |
| Merged Keywords Self | 50 | 12555x11539x13087 | 35538162 | 1.4255e-05 |
| Merged Papers Fields | 19,289,1000 | 12179x13089x13086 | 125230468 | 6.0032e-05 |
| Merged Papers Fields Self | 19,289,1000 | 12071x13089x13086 | 123576062 | 5.9769e-05 |
| Merged Papers Keywords | 19,289,1000 | 12093x17510x17507 | 127013487 | 3.4262e-05 |
| Merged Papers Keywords Self | 19,289,1000 | 11969x17510x17506 | 125401030 | 3.4180e-05 |
| Journals Fields Cocite | 19,289 | 12670x12670x12612 | 26685124 | 1.3181e-05 |
| Journals Keywords Cocite | 19,289 | 12670x12670x15219 | 20109406 | 8.2311e-06 |
| Journals Fields Couple | 19,289 | 12670x12670x12614 | 43194060 | 2.1331e-05 |
| Journals Keywords Couple | 19,289 | 12670x12670x12614 | 32395545 | 1.1321e-05 |

***Table 2**: Overview of evaluated models*

Additionally, information about the number of analyzed components is given. The number of topics 19 / 289 was chosen equivalently to the number of topics at the first and second level of the Microsoft Academic Search engine.

### Alternative Methods

As previously mentioned, the outcome of tensor decomposition is conceptually similar to the results of common scientometric methods for structure mining and content mining. Consequently, we systematically compared our results with outcomes of two representative approaches from both fields.

#### EigenFactor

The concept of eigenvector centrality is at the core of this metric. EigenFactor is a modified form of the eigenvector centrality of a given graph node (West, Jensen, Dandrea, Gordon, & Bergstrom, 2013). There are two intuitions behind the EigenFactor score: First, it indicates the percentage of the time that a hypothetically user spends on a given node within a considered graph. Second, it describes the number of votes per node that is reached if votes are passed along all nodes within the considered graph round based. (West, Bergstrom, & Bergstrom, 2010)

---

[2] *http://www.web-science.eu/research*
[3] *http://academic.research.microsoft.com/*

### Latent Semantic Analysis

Latent Semantic Analysis (LSA) is a well-known technique for extracting and inferring relations of expected contextual information (Deerwester, Dumais, Furnas, Landauer, & Harshman, 1990). In the setting of our problem, it represents data within a matrix $M$ where rows correspond to contexts and columns to journals or conferences. The matrix is decomposed by means of Singular Value Decomposition (SVD) into a product of three matrices (Manning & Schütze, 1999) in the form $M = U \times S \times V^T$. In this decomposition, column vectors of $U$ describe the discovered topics (groups of correlated contexts), $V$ describes original entities (journals, conferences) in terms of discovered topics in the new feature space, and $S$ contains scaling factors (singular values) that can be interpreted as topic importance scores.

## KEY RESULTS

This section presents findings made separately by providing illustrative examples. We outline our observation and the circumstances under which we have observed them.

### *Interdisciplinarity*

#### Structural Findings

In the context of our contribution we have identified two different types of interdisciplinarity. Figure 8 shows the structure of relevant relations identified which play a necessary role in order to observe interdisciplinarity. From left to right, the first couple represents a necessary condition on possible interdisciplinarity where a node *i1*, the dashed and skewed box, is cited by another node *a* but does not have citation into the citing field of *a*. Note that this relation is the basis for the following two forms depicted in Figure 8. Starting with the middle one, this is really the notion of existing interdisciplinarity where node *x* is citing *y* but *y* is also a representative of another field than *x*. We have found those objects by simply identifying the first form and then check for each element within such forms whether they occur as hubs and authorities within other decompositions components since in a concrete context of an experiment a form represents a relation of journals or components.

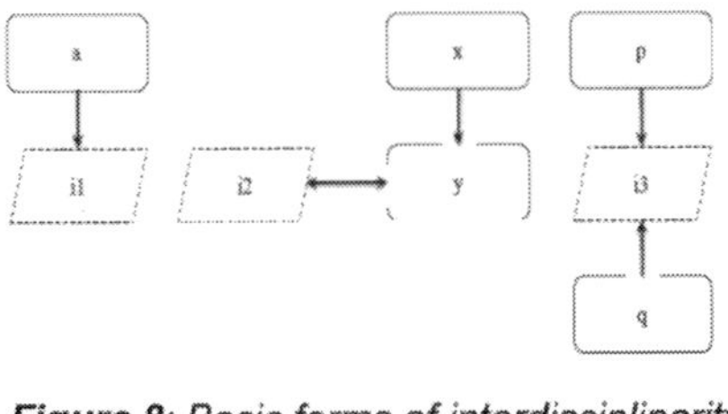


***Figure 8**: Basic forms of interdisciplinarity*

Special interest was given to the form on the far right. This is the abstract presentation of potential interdisciplinarity aligned with the working definition of interdisciplinarity. Note how this also holds for different Citation Graph Models. Imagine that nodes p and q cite a paper within a field i3 but i3 does not contribute to neither of one. Without closer consideration of i3 but knowing that p and q are different from each other we have identified a link between p and q. Further, more, allowing the cited paper i3 to be a hub and authority within any other field from the context of p and q the form on the right reveals an implicit relationship between nodes such as p and q via the field i3.

#### Interdisciplinary Findings

For detection of interdisciplinarity, finding formations as those on the left in Figure 8 was necessary. First, we have analyzed datasets depicted in Section Data for existence of such forms. For all citation models, occurrence of forms from Figure 8 is depicted in Figure 9. Without loss of generality, we focus on models calculated on the basis of 19 decomposition components. We have found that in this case results are composed out of more general themes. For the sake of interpretability, we stick to such models since such results are closer to conventional knowledge of the regarded graph structure. Figure 9 shows the percentage allocation of interdisciplinarity detected within each model.

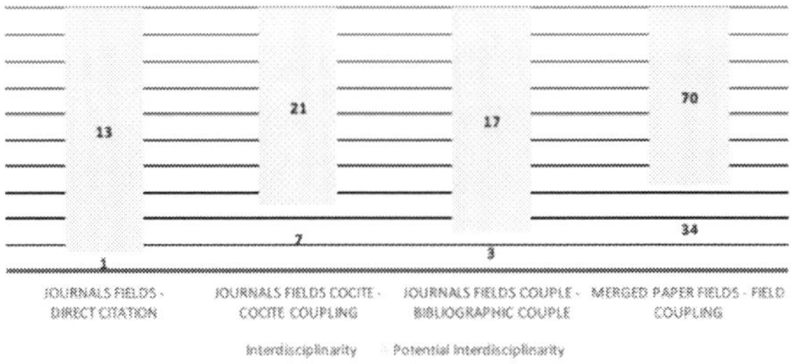


***Figure 9**: Fractions of interdisciplinarity*

According to different graph models $G^{DC}$, $G^{CC}$, $G^{BC}$, $G^{FC}$ each pillar in Figure 9 represents the allocation of interdisciplinary and potential interdisciplinary elements in direct comparison. Similar results have been observed for $G^{BC}$ and $G^{DC}$ models. Most interdisciplinarity was observed within $G^{FC}$ followed by $G^{CC}$. The green colored parts show to which degree interdisciplinary elements occur. Since an element is interdisciplinary for any natural number $t > 2$ of nodes $p$ pointing to it as it is depicted in Figure 8 on the far right, these elements were unified within one class containing such interdisciplinary elements only. In contrast to the latter class potential interdisciplinarity is depicted by the yellow colored parts. These parts represent elements that at least does occur as nodes *i1* as shown in Figure 8. Since this is not enough for having identified an element *i1* as interdisciplinary as it might be the case if it turns out that *i1* is simply a node *y* that is already a representative of an interdisciplinary field as depicted in the middle of Figure 8.

Since the power of tensor decomposition comes from the potential of selecting the best k-approximation in order to identify underlying structure Figure 10 shows the effect of raising the number of decomposition components while at the same time having one model fixed. For this purpose, model "Merged Fields" have been evaluated with 19, 50, and 289 decomposition components. Note that the colors have the same meaning as pointed out before but are just adjusted in color saturation for the sake of comprehensibility. As the figure shows, raising the number of decomposition components increases the number of interdisciplinary connections found. It could be also observed that raising the number of components leads to more elements being identified either being interdisciplinary or having the potential for being interdisciplinary.

The next step in interpretation was done qualitatively by human experts in the field of scientometrics from our team. An exemplary instance of an interdisciplinary element identified is the "Journal of Crystal Growth". First, we detected this journal within a topic in model "Journals Fields Couple" and identified it as interdisciplinary.

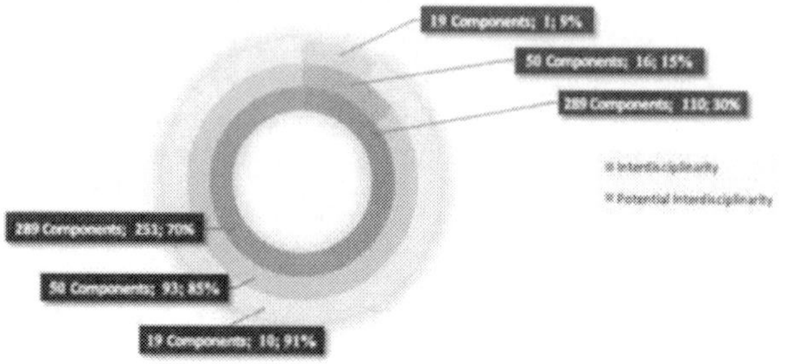


***Figure 10**: Fractions of interdisciplinarity*

This topic is described mostly by a mix of journals with respect to drying, refrigeration, and packaging technologies but thematically shifted towards the field of study that strongly focuses on issues regarding heat and mass management as shown below in Table 3.

The other topic, depicted in Table 4, where this exemplary journal occurred is a mix of journals that have a range of distinct themes: Energy Research, Solar Energy, Energy Management and Conversion, Electronic Packaging, Fire Safety Journal, Membrane and Acoustical Science. Since these are common themes a red thread is revealing. Further we have found that this journal is thematically strongly embedded within the field of energy science, especially heat and mass transfer by being hub and authority in that context that is represented by its cited sources depicted in Table 5.

| **Model: Journals Fields Couple, Topics: 19, Component: 11** | |
|---|---|
| Rank | Journals |
| 1 | International Journal of Heat and Mass Transfer |
| 2 | International Journal of Heat and Fluid Flow |
| 3 | Numerical Heat Transfer Part A-applications |
| 4 | International Journal of Refrigeration-revue Inter.. |
| 5 | Energy Conversion and Management |
| 6 | Journal of Electronic Packaging |
| 7 | Heat Transfer Engineering |
| 8 | Isij International |
| 9 | Drying Technology |
| 10 | Physics of Fluids |

***Table 3**: Model: Journal Fields Couple, top 10 hubs, Topic 1*

| **Model: Journals Fields Couple, Topics: 19, Component: 15** | |
|---|---|
| Rank | Journals |
| 1 | Journal of Heat Transfer-transactions of The Asme |
| 2 | Numerical Heat Transfer Part B-fundamentals |
| 3 | Fire Safety Journal |
| 4 | Journal of Electronic Packaging |
| 5 | International Journal of Energy Research |
| 6 | International Journal of Heat and Fluid Flow |
| 7 | Solar Energy |
| 8 | Energy Conversion and Management |
| 9 | Journal of Membrane Science |
| 10 | Journal of the Acoustical Society of America |

***Table 4**: Model: Journal Fields Couple, top10 hubs, Topic 2*

| **Model: Journals Fields Couple, Topics: 19, Component: 1** | |
|---|---|
| Rank | Journals |
| 1 | Journal of Heat Transfer-transactions of The Asme |
| 2 | Solar Energy |
| 3 | Journal of Manufacturing Science and Engineering-.. |
| 4 | International Journal of Heat and Fluid Flow |
| 5 | Numerical Heat Transfer Part A-applications |
| 6 | Numerical Heat Transfer Part B-fundamentals |
| 7 | Heat and Mass Transfer |
| 8 | Experimental Thermal and Fluid Science |
| 9 | Applied Thermal Engineering |
| 10 | Journal of Solar Energy Engineering-transactions of.. |

***Table 5**: Model: Journal Fields Couple, top 10 auth.*

Thus, the two disciplines where this journal is not actively involved by citing these fields both have in common some aspects from knowledge about heat and mass transfer. Thus, a possible conclusion is that researches publishing in the "Journal of the Acoustical Society of America" may profit from sharing knowledge with researches publishing in "Drying Technology" since they at least share some topic that is identified as research on heat and mass transfer.

### Discovered thematic structures

The application of several methods on the underlying graph revealed the thematic structures of the graph. Due to the different approaches and by variation of each method it turned out that the main topic that dominates the whole graph consists out of elements that are from the field of biology or strongly related to it. Thus particular attention has been paid to topics that have had a bigger thematic displacement such as mathematics, engineering or arts. It turned out that all applied methods have represented the main topic by placing biological top journals, conferences, and keywords at the top of their rankings.

### Tensor Decomposition – Striking Points

#### Switching the Context

First, we have observed the effect of switching the context on the same data. At the top of Table 6, the top 10 authoritative journals with the context set to keywords is shown. At the bottom of Table 6, the top 10 authoritative journals within the context of fields of study is presented. Since both journals cover the same thematic structure the additional information of the context gains insights into the relation between the detected journals but from a different point of view.

### Varying the size of suspected Components

We have observed that for small numbers of components one can see only big journals or conferences such as "Nature" or "PLOS ONE".

| Model: Journals Keywords, Topics: 50, Component: 1 | | |
|---|---|---|
| Rank | Keyword | Journals |
| 1 | ionosphere | Journal of Geophysical Research |
| 2 | seasonality | Geophysical Research Letters |
| 3 | solar wind | Journal of Atmospheric and Solar-Terrestrial Physics |
| 4 | electric field | Annales Geophysicae |
| 5 | ozone | Science |
| 6 | boundary layer | Planetary and Space Science |
| 7 | interplanetary magnetic field | Atmospheric Environment |
| 8 | quantum mechanics | Radio Science |
| 9 | magnetohydrodynamics | Nature |
| 10 | plasma physics | The Astrophysical Journal |

| Model: Journals Fields, Topics: 50, Component: 1 | | |
|---|---|---|
| Rank | Fields of Study | Journals |
| 1 | Ionosphere | Journal of Geophysical Research |
| 2 | Solar wind | Clinical Pharmacology & Therapeutics |
| 3 | Electric field | Advanced Drug Delivery Reviews |
| 4 | Remote sensing | Journal of General Virology |
| 5 | Ozone | Geophysical Research Letters |
| 6 | Boundary layer | Science |
| 7 | Global change | IEEE Transactions on Geoscience and Remote Sensing |
| 8 | Earth's magnetic field | Nature |
| 9 | Magnetohydrodynamics | Archives of Microbiology |
| 10 | Mantle | Annales Geophysicae |

*Table 6: Model: Journal Fields, top 10 authority*

On the other hand, increasing the number of components yielded result lists where journals or conferences occurred that have been not seen before in any of the lists of calculations having smaller numbers of components.

| Model: Journals Fields | |
|---|---|
| Affiliation | Journals |
| Topics: 289, Component: 1 | Journal of High Energy Physics |
| Topics: 289, Component: 15 | Journal of Chromatography A |
| Topics: 289, Component 26 | Brain Research |
| Topics: 289, Component: 43 | IEEE Transactions on Information Theory |
| Topics: 289, Component: 48 | Climate Dynamics |

| Model: Journals Fields, Topics: 19, Component: 14 | | |
|---|---|---|
| Rank | Fields of Study | Journals |
| 1 | Nature | Nature Cell Biology |
| 2 | Cell cycle | Nature |
| 3 | microRNA | Nature Reviews Molecular Cell Biology |
| 4 | Molecular biology | Proceedings of the National Academy of Sciences of the.. |
| 5 | Biochemistry | Cell |
| 6 | Ageing&Nature Structural | Molecular Biology |
| 7 | Zebrafish Information Network.. | Science |
| 8 | Phosphorylation | The EMBO Journal |
| 9 | Parasitology&Genes | Development |
| 10 | Metabolomics | British Journal of Cancer |

| Model: Journals Fields, Topics: 1000, Component: 138 | | |
|---|---|---|
| Rank | Fields of Study | Journals |
| 1 | Partial differential equation | Nature |
| 2 | Neuroscience | Nature Neuroscience |
| 3 | Nature | The EMBO Journal |
| 4 | Structural biology | Nature Chemical Biology |
| 5 | Computational biology | Trends in Pharmacological Sciences |
| 6 | Environmental science | Bulletin of the American Mathematical Society |
| 7 | Pharmacology | Mechanisms of Development |
| 8 | Cell cycle | Nature Reviews Neuroscience |
| 9 | Immunology | Siam Journal on Mathematical Analysis |
| 10 | Molecular biology | Journal of Experimental Botany |

*Table 7: Model: Journal Fields, effect due to variation of amount of components*

### *Parameters of approximation*

Application of the approximate approach introduced in Decomposition Scalability has shown that size of sampling as well as the size of such smaller tensors have had a strong effect on the results. In a nutshell our experiments have shown that increasing the sampling size led to denser results in form of factorized representation of the original data tensor. Additionally, this approach covered mostly highly connected nodes as strong players within detected decomposition components. Having smaller sample sizes led to more thematic variation. Additionally, resulting factorized representation have been sparser.

The table at the top in **Table** shows five elements having rank 1 within their decomposition component. These thematic topics obviously belong to distinct disciplines, while the table in the middle shows a typical example of a top ten list computed by the same model but with a lower number of components. These results with a smaller number of components consisted always out of big journals such as represented in the middle of **Table**. This is plausible since we suggest that a smaller amount of suspected components takes the macro structure more into account than the one with more component does which represents more granular structures. The table at the bottom in **Table** shows the same model but with 1000 topics. As expected, topics were observed that could not be detected with a smaller amount of components. Interestingly, some of these elements only emerged on this granularity level and were previously rarely up to never seen. Since they also belong to previously detected sub-structures, such patterns tended to become more present in the results. Here it was mathematics and computer science as well as social sciences are related to mathematical subjects. This sub disciplines first appeared by setting the topic number on 1000. Thus we conclude that the number of topics can be used to enable emergence of sub structures of the graph.

Also strongly related to quantitative and qualitative effects is the size of sub tensors. Regarding quantitative effects, we could observe that increasing the size will lead to higher computational costs – what obviously was to be expected. Furthermore, there have been qualitative implications in changing sub tensor size. It could be observed that the bigger the size the more of thematic sub-structures emerge while smaller sizes showed such emergence of sub-structures but mostly underpopulated. Especially and interestingly, the combination of a big sample size and bigger sized sub tensors increased the latter effect.

Also worth noting, by increasing the number of decomposition components while raising the number of sampled sub tensors we have found that the higher the number of sub tensors is the more likely thematically variations occurred. Mostly these groups increased within each topic and elements from related fields were added that have not been seen before. This strengthens our assumption that by systematically adjusting the number of components, sample size, and sub tensor size different levels of thematic/topical granularity can be made tangible.

## *A comparison: Evaluation of methodological variety*

In order to find interdisciplinarity it is important to find disciplines first. Within each method applied, we have again asked human research experts to interpret our findings. We focused on top ten lists gained from each method. From these findings, if possible, interdisciplinarity was deduced.

### EigenFactor

There is an open problem with this metric. The rankings will be dominated by strong web pages. We observed that only journals listed that are obviously popular. Since we were interested in interdisciplinarity as proposed above and no other information was given, we were not able to identify elements as such.

### LSA

We have found that identified topics were dominated by highly cited papers such as "Nature", etc. This behavior was very similar to the ranking of EigenFactor. Thus, since the discovered topics had a mono-thematic structure we could not find any interdisciplinarity applying our methods to the results of LSA. In order to enhance the perspective on latent structures that might have interdisciplinary nature we applied k-means on the data within the new feature space in order to detect cluster centroids of latent topics.

We have found that the resulting ranking is just the same as the results of SVD applied within LSA but it turns out to represent a wider variety of themes and is not that determined by well-known and popular journals. Since we encountered the same problem of mono-thematic structure as before we were not able to identify interdisciplinary elements. We suggest that this thematic bias is due to the lack of contextual differentiation. Thus the term-document matrix is overpopulated and thus yields to a rougher abstraction of latent structures which corresponds with our findings where only mono-thematic topics could be detected.

### Microsoft Academic Search

At least and in comparison to the disciplinary taxonomies of the Microsoft Academic Search engine it is important to note our graph was biased such that it was dominated by biological topics. Nevertheless, we have found elements of existing ratings but within the space that is enriched by information of context. Note that this is just the same result as it holds for EigenFactor.

## CONCLUSION AND FUTURE WORK

In this contribution, we introduced a novel approach for mining context-aware semantic citation networks by means of tensor decomposition. The approach naturally combines advantages of content-centric and structure centric mining methods and allows for joint interpretation of research fields and their key players. Moreover, our comprehensive evaluations have shown the ability of the approach for discovering both emerging research fronts and (not yet sufficiently exploited) inter-disciplinary potentials. The approach can be efficiently applied to realistic, large scale citation networks by means of parallelization of key computations and use of state of the art cloud infrastructures.

In the future, we plan to extend the presented model by further aspects of interest. For instance, the temporal structure of scientific development can be analyzed by adding the time dimension to presented model variations. Furthermore, detailed analysis of decomposition strategies should allow for better understanding of influential factors, such as sampling factor and sampling size. In turn, this should allow for improved discovery of scientific structures and fields at different levels of granularity. In addition, the presented methodology can be applied to alternative citation and collaboration models, e.g. author citation models.

## REFERENCES


Abercrombie, R. K., Udoeyop, A. W., & Schlicher, B. G. (2012). A study of scientometric methods to identify emerging technologies via modeling of milestones. *Scientometrics, 91*, 327-342.

Aboelela, S. W., Larson, E., Bakken, S., Carrasquillo, O., Formicola, A., Glied, S. A., et al. (2007). Defining interdisciplinary research: Conclusions from a critical review of the literature. *Health services research, 42*, 329-346.

Alonso, S., Cabrerizo, F. J., Herrera-Viedma, E., & Herrera, F. (2009). h-Index: A review focused in its variants, computation and standardization for different scientific fields. *Journal of Informetrics, 3*, 273-289.

Bar-Ilan, J. (2008). Informetrics at the beginning of the 21st century—A review. *Journal of informetrics, 2*, 1-52.

Blei, D. M., Ng, A. Y., & Jordan, M. I. (2003). Latent dirichlet allocation. *Journal of machine Learning research, 3*, 993-1022.

Daim, T. U., Shibata, N., Kajikawa, Y., & Sakata, I. (2011). Detecting potential technological fronts by comparing scientific papers and patents. *Foresight, 13*, 51-60.

Deerwester, S., Dumais, S. T., Furnas, G. W., Landauer, T. K., & Harshman, R. (1990). Indexing by latent semantic analysis. *Journal of the American society for information science, 41*, 391.

Franz, T., Schultz, A., Sizov, S., & Staab, S. (2009). Triplerank: Ranking semantic web data by tensor decomposition. *The Semantic Web-ISWC 2009*, 213-228.

Fujita, K., Kajikawa, Y., Mori, J., & Sakata, I. (2014). Detecting research fronts using different types of weighted citation networks. *Journal of Engineering and Technology Management, 32*, 129-146.

González-Pereira, B., Guerrero-Bote, V. P., & Moya-Anegón, F. (2010). A new approach to the metric of journals' scientific prestige: The SJR indicator. *Journal of informetrics, 4*, 379-391.

Griffiths, T. L., & Steyvers, M. (2004). Finding scientific topics. *Proceedings of the National academy of Sciences, 101*, 5228-5235.

Guo, H., Weingart, S., & Börner, K. (2011). Mixed-indicators model for identifying emerging research areas. *Scientometrics, 89*, 421-435.

Hofmann, T. (1999). Probabilistic latent semantic indexing. *Proceedings of the 22nd annual international ACM SIGIR conference on Research and development in information retrieval*, (S. 50-57).

Jeon, I., Papalexakis, E. E., Faloutsos, C., Sael, L., & Kang, U. (2016). Mining billion-scale tensors: algorithms and discoveries. *The VLDB Journal, 25*, 519-544.

Kessler, M. M. (1963). Bibliographic coupling between scientific papers. *Journal of the Association for Information Science and Technology, 14*, 10-25.

Kleinberg, J. M., Kumar, R., Raghavan, P., Rajagopalan, S., & Tomkins, A. S. (1999). The web as a graph: measurements, models, and methods. *International Computing and Combinatorics Conference*, (S. 1-17).

Kolda, T. G., & Bader, B. W. (2009). Tensor decompositions and applications. *SIAM review, 51*, 455-500.

Kolda, T., & Bader, B. (2006). The TOPHITS model for higher-order web link analysis. *Workshop on link analysis, counterterrorism and security, 7*, S. 26-29.

Kruskal, J. B. (1977). Three-way arrays: rank and uniqueness of trilinear decompositions, with application to arithmetic complexity and statistics. *Linear algebra and its applications, 18*, 95-138.

Manning, C., & Schütze, H. (1999). *Foundations of statistical natural language processing.* Cambridge: MIT press.

Page, L., Brin, S., Motwani, R., & Winograd, T. (1999). *The PageRank citation ranking: Bringing order to the web.* Tech. rep., Stanford InfoLab.

Papalexakis, E. E., Faloutsos, C., & Sidiropoulos, N. D. (2015). Par Cube: Sparse Parallelizable CANDECOMP-PARAFAC Tensor Decomposition. *ACM Transactions on Knowledge Discovery from Data (TKDD), 10*, 3.

Park, N., Jeon, B., Lee, J., & Kang, U. (2016). Bigtensor: Mining billion-scale tensor made easy. *Proceedings of the 25th ACM International on Conference on Information and Knowledge Management*, (S. 2457-2460).

Persson, O. (2010). Identifying research themes with weighted direct citation links. *Journal of Informetrics, 4*, 415-422.

Shibata, N., Kajikawa, Y., Takeda, Y., & Matsushima, K. (2009). Comparative study on methods of detecting research fronts using different types of citation. *Journal of the American Society for Information Science and Technology, 60*, 571-580.

Sinha, A., Shen, Z., Song, Y., Ma, H., Eide, D., Hsu, B.-j. P., et al. (2015). An overview of microsoft academic service (mas) and applications. *Proceedings of the 24th international conference on world wide web*, (S. 243-246).

Small, H. (1973). Co-citation in the scientific literature: A new measure of the relationship between two documents. *Journal of the Association for Information Science and Technology, 24*, 265-269.

Small, H. (1997). Update on science mapping: Creating large document spaces. *Scientometrics, 38*, 275-293.

Small, H., Boyack, K. W., & Klavans, R. (2014). Identifying emerging topics in science and technology. *Research Policy, 43*, 1450-1467.

Upham, S. P., & Small, H. (2010). Emerging research fronts in science and technology: patterns of new knowledge development. *Scientometrics, 83*, 15-38.

Waltman, L. (2016). A review of the literature on citation impact indicators. *Journal of Informetrics, 10*, 365-391.

West, J. D., Bergstrom, T. C., & Bergstrom, C. T. (2010). The Eigenfactor Metrics: A network approach to assessing scholarly journals. *College & Research Libraries, 71*, 236-244.

West, J. D., Jensen, M. C., Dandrea, R. J., Gordon, G. J., & Bergstrom, C. T. (2013). Author-level Eigenfactor metrics: Evaluating the influence of authors, institutions, and countries within the social science research network community. *Journal of the American Society for Information Science and Technology, 64*, 787-801.

Yan, E., & Ding, Y. (2012). Scholarly network similarities: How bibliographic coupling networks, citation networks, cocitation networks, topical networks, coauthorship networks, and coword networks relate to each other. *Journal of the American Society for Information Science and Technology, 63*, 1313-1326.

Zan, W., Tsim, Y. C., Yeung, W. S., Chan, K. C., & Liu, J. (2007). Probabilistic latent semantic analyses (PLSA) in bibliometric analysis for technology forecasting. *Journal of Technology Management & Innovation, 2*, 11-24.

# Is Ignorance Really Bliss?: Exploring the Interrelationships Among Information Avoidance, Health Literacy and Health Justice

**Beth St. Jean**
*College of Information Studies, University of Maryland. USA.*
*bstjean@umd.edu*

**Yuting Liao**
*College of Information Studies, University of Maryland. USA.*
*yliao598@terpmail.umd.edu*

**Gagan Jindal**
*College of Information Studies, University of Maryland. USA.*
*gjindal@terpmail.umd.edu*

## ABSTRACT

**Although many people cope with illness by seeking information, a considerable proportion of the population prefers to avoid information, aiming to maintain or increase their uncertainty in order to control their anxiety and/or maintain hope. Drawing on a large ($n$ = 3,677), nationally representative survey dataset (the U.S. National Cancer Institute's 2014 Health Information National Trends Survey (HINTS)), this paper investigates the prevalence of information avoidance (defined here as agreement with the statement, "I'd rather not know my chance of getting cancer") among the U.S. adult population and identifies associations between information avoidance and other types of demographic, information-seeking, cognitive/perceptual and social factors. The overarching aim of this research is to explore whether and how the concepts of information avoidance, health literacy and health justice are interrelated. Based on a literature review and a secondary analysis of the HINTS data set, information avoidance, limited health literacy and a lack of health justice appear to be intricately interwoven. In conclusion, suggestions are made as to how we might use these findings to interrupt the usual progression from low health literacy to poor health outcomes, thereby helping to decrease health disparities and address the lack of health justice in this country.**

## KEYWORDS

consumer health information behavior, information avoidance, health information seeking, health literacy, health justice.

## INTRODUCTION AND BACKGROUND

Health justice describes an ideal in which everyone, regardless of personal factors such as age, gender, gender identity, sexuality, race/ethnicity and income, has the same opportunities to live a long and healthy life. As Venkatapuram (2011) puts it, "Every human being has a moral entitlement to a capability to be healthy" (p. 19). However, there is a large body of evidence that shows we have not yet reached (or even approached) this ideal in the United States. For example, life expectancy has been found to positively correlate with income – 40-year-old men in the top 1% income bracket in the United States have a life expectancy 15 years greater than 40-year-old men in the bottom 1% income bracket (87.3 vs. 72.7 years). The pattern is similar for 40-year-old women— those in the highest 1% income bracket have a life expectancy 10 years greater than those in the bottom 1% income bracket (88.9 vs. 78.8 years). Such income-related gaps in terms of life expectancy actually grew between 2001 and 2014 (Chetty et al., 2016). Olshansky et al. (2012) identified analogous differences in life expectancy based on people's educational attainment and race, finding that Whites with at least 16 years of education by the time they were 25 had a life expectancy of 10.3 (for females) to 14.2 (for males) years greater than Blacks with less than 12 years of education by this age. Like Chetty et al. (2016), Olshansky et al. (2012) found that these gaps have only continued to widen over time.

One of the primary factors underlying these health inequities and the lack of health justice in the United States are disparities in health literacy, a term defined as "the degree to which individuals have the capacity to obtain, process, and understand basic health information and services needed to make appropriate health care decisions" (Ratzan & Parker, 2000). Nearly 90% of U.S. adults have a below-proficient level of health literacy (Kutner et al., 2006), and low health literacy levels are more prevalent among older, minority, immigrant, and low-income populations (NN/LM, 2014). People with low health literacy levels are less likely to get preventative health care (Bennett et al., 2009; Institute of Medicine, 2004) and are more likely to be hospitalized and to have poor health outcomes (Ad Hoc Committee on Health Literacy, 1999; Baker et al., 2002; Baker et al., 2007; IOM, 2004; Schillinger et al., 2002). The central role of low health literacy in contributing to health disparities is underscored by the finding that it is a stronger predictor of one's health than one's age, race, educational attainment, employment status, and income (Weiss, 2007).

80th Annual Meeting of the Association for Information Science & Technology, Washington, DC, VA | Oct. 27-Nov. 1, 2017

Health literacy is a multi-faceted construct that encompasses not only reading ability and health-related knowledge (IOM, 2004), but also many different types of skills, including critical thinking and communication skills (Ormshaw et al., 2013); numeracy and visual literacy (NN/LM, 2014); and media and computer literacy (Norman & Skinner, 2006). However, to be truly health literate, an individual also needs to have the motivation and self-efficacy to put these skills to use (Nutbeam, 1996). A health literate individual is one who is motivated and able to, as well as confident in his/her ability to, seek, access, and evaluate health-related information; set goals related to his/her health; make sound health-related decisions; and act on these decisions in working toward maintaining and/or improving his/her health.

Although many people cope with a potential or actual illness by engaging in information seeking and acquisition (Ankem, 2006a; Clark, 2005; Hack et al., 1994; Mills & Davidson, 2002; Wong et al., 2000), some people may, at times and in certain situations, prefer to avoid information, aiming to maintain or increase their level of uncertainty (Brashers et al., 2000; Case et al., 2005). Information avoidance can help people to control their anxiety (Pifalo et al., 1997) and/or to retain some hope (Brashers et al., 2000). Information avoidance can result from, and result in, low health literacy; however, the associations between these two factors remain largely unexplored (Strekalova, 2014).

Many studies of the information behavior of patients with life-threatening illnesses (e.g., Baker, 1998; Clark, 2005; Hack et al., 1994; Miller, 1995; Wong et al., 2000) have identified a subpopulation of patients who would rather avoid information about their health condition. Hack et al. (1994) found that more than half of his participants (women who had breast cancer) preferred to be told the best possible diagnosis instead of the most likely outcome. Wong et al. (2000) similarly found that one-fourth of their participants (men who had prostate cancer) preferred to be told the best possible outcome rather than the most likely outcome.

Several studies (e.g., Ankem, 2006b; Clark, 2005; Degner & Sloan, 1992; Eheman et al., 2009; Hack et al., 1994; Mills & Davidson, 2002) have identified two different groups of patients: (1) patients who prefer to gather as much information as possible about their health condition and to participate actively in making decisions related to their treatment and (2) patients who would rather not seek and understand information, instead preferring to rely on their doctors' expertise. These two groups have been postulated to arise based on disparities in patients' gender (Butow et al., 1997; Degner & Sloan, 1992; Eheman et al., 2009), age (Degner & Sloan, 1992; Eheman et al., 2009; Mills & Davidson, 2002), socioeconomic class (Clark, 2005), educational attainment (Degner & Sloan, 1992; Eheman et al., 2009; Hack et al., 1994), occupation (Eheman et al., 2009), marital status (Eheman et al., 2009), and/or health status (Butow et al., 1997; Degner & Sloan, 1992; Eheman et al., 2009).

Information avoidance, along with the resulting lack of information about a health condition that one has or is at risk for developing, can have significant consequences for one's health trajectory and outcomes. Avoiding health-related information has been linked with negative outcomes, such as patients being offered less information by their physicians (Brashers et al., 2002), being unable to fully participate in treatment-related decision-making (Degner et al., 1997; Hack et al., 1994), and being treated paternalistically by their physicians and ultimately feeling less satisfied with their health decisions (Clark, 2005).

This paper draws on a large, nationally-representative survey data set (the National Cancer Institute's Health Information National Trends Survey (HINTS) (NCI, 2015a)), to investigate two research questions: (1) How prevalent is information avoidance (as measured by a survey question that asked respondents to rate how much they agree or disagree with the statement, "I'd rather not know my chance of getting cancer") among the U.S. adult population? and (2) What types of demographic, information-seeking, cognitive/perceptual, and social factors are associated with information avoidance? The overarching goal of this analysis is to identify potential interrelationships among the concepts of information avoidance, health literacy, and health justice.

## METHODS

### *Recruitment and Data Collection*

NCI has been conducting HINTS since 2003 to learn about U.S. adults' cancer-related perceptions and knowledge, their health behaviors, and their information access, needs, seeking, and use. HINTS is a nationally representative survey that NCI administers every few years to civilian, non-institutionalized adults in the United States (NCI, 2015a).

This paper makes use of the publicly available HINTS 4 Cycle 4 SPSS data set (NCI, 2015b), for which data was collected from August through November of 2014. The sampling frame was the entirety of a Marketing Systems Group database which includes all occupied residential addresses in the U.S ($n$ = 139,955,764). Addresses from this database were categorized into three strata: (1) Areas with high minority population concentrations ($n$ = 34,994,266); (2) Areas with low minority population concentrations ($n$ = 103,796,143); and (3) Addresses located in Central Appalachia counties ($n$ = 1,165,355). An equal-probability sample of 14,000 addresses was then drawn from across these three strata, oversampling addresses from the high-minority stratum (25% of the sampling frame; 63% of the actual sample), under-sampling addresses from the low-minority stratum (74.2% of the sampling frame; 35.6% of the final sample), and sampling addresses in Central Appalachia counties proportionate to size (0.8% of both the sampling frame and the final sample). (Westat, 2015)

A cover letter and a paper questionnaire were mailed to the final sample of 14,000 addresses (13,996 after de-duplication), along with a $2 incentive. A Spanish-language version of the questionnaire was included in mailings to households in linguistically isolated areas (i.e., areas with relatively greater proportions of households in which everyone over the age of 14 speaks some language other than English and does not speak English very well) and to households associated with a potentially Hispanic last name. Spanish-language questionnaires were also sent to anyone who called to request one ($n$ = 13). One week after the initial questionnaires were mailed out, a thank you/reminder postcard was sent to all households. Three weeks later, and again after another month, another follow-up cover letter and the original questionnaire were sent to non-responding households. (Westat, 2015)

In order to ensure a random sample, one adult was sampled from each household using the Next Birthday Method – the cover letter instructed the reader to ask the adult in their household with the next birthday to fill out the survey. A total of 3,677 questionnaires were returned, for a final response rate of 34.4%; however, response rates varied across the strata (high-minority: 25.9%; Central Appalachia: 34.6%; low-minority: 37.2%). (Westat, 2015)

### Data Analysis

The HINTS 4 Cycle 4 SPSS data set and accompanying documentation (NCI, 2015b) were downloaded into IBM SPSS Statistics (version 22) for analysis. Analysis focused on participants' responses to question M3 ("How much do you agree or disagree with this statement: 'I'd rather not know my chance of getting cancer'?"), both independently and in connection with their responses to other survey questions. Blank responses and those reported incorrectly were not included in this analysis. To test associations between pairs of variables, cross-tabs were calculated and Chi-square tests of independence were conducted. Yates' Correction for Continuity was applied to all 2 x 2 tables to avoid inflated estimates of the chi-square statistic. Effect sizes are reported using phi (Φ) coefficients (for 2 x 2 tables) and Cramer's $V$ (for larger tables).

### Participants

The set of respondents was quite diverse. Table 1 shows the distributions of respondents for key demographic variables.

## FINDINGS

In this section, we first report participants' responses to the main question of interest (M3) for this analysis, and then explore some of the statistically significant relationships between participants' responses to this particular question and their responses to other questions on the HINTS survey. A total of 3,541 (96.3%) respondents indicated their agreement/disagreement with the statement: "I'd rather not know my chance of getting cancer." Figure 1 shows that although the majority ($n$ = 2,432; 68.7%) either somewhat or strongly disagreed with this statement, a considerable proportion (nearly one-third) of respondents either strongly agreed ($n$ = 375; 10.6%) or somewhat agreed ($n$ = 734; 20.7%) that they would rather not know their chance of getting cancer. In the remaining subsections below, patterns between respondents' answers to this question (M3) and their answers to demographic- and other information-related questions on the survey are reported.

### Demographic Patterns

Many statistically significant differences were found in participants' responses to question M3 based on reported demographic characteristics, including age, educational attainment, household income, occupational status, and health insurance coverage. However, chi-square tests of independence showed no statistically significant association between gender and responses to M3 [$\chi^2$ (1, $n$ = 3608) = 1.79, $p$ = .18] and between race/ethnicity and responses to question M3 [$\chi^2$ (4, $n$ = 3273) = 7.76, $p$ = .10].

| Factor | Distribution of Survey Respondents |
|---|---|
| Gender | Male: 1,424 (39.5%)<br>Female: 2,184 (60.5%)<br>Total: 3,608 (100.0%) |
| Age | Range: 18 – 98<br>Average (SD): 51.9 (21.17) |
| Race/ Ethnicity | Non-Hispanic White: 1,960 (59.9%)<br>Hispanic: 540 (16.5%)<br>Non-Hispanic Black or African-American: 534 (16.3%)<br>Other: 239 (7.3%)<br>Total: 3,273 (100.0%) |
| Educational Attainment | Less than 8 years: 90 (2.6%)<br>8 to 11 years: 218 (6.2%)<br>High school or 12 years: 670 (19.0%)<br>Post-high school training other than college (vocational or tech.): 284 (8.1%)<br>Some college: 806 (22.9%)<br>College graduate: 889 (25.2%)<br>Postgraduate schooling: 569 (16.1%)<br>Total: 3,526 (100.0%) |
| Annual Household Income | Less than $20,000: 774 (23.6%)<br>$20,000 to $35,000: 489 (14.9%)<br>$35,000 to $50,000: 482 (14.7%)<br>$50,000 to $75,000: 550 (16.8%)<br>$75,000+: 979 (29.9%)<br>Total: 3,274 (100.0%) |
| Occupational Status | Employed: 1,763 (51.2%)<br>Retired: 956 (27.7%)<br>Disabled: 262 (7.6%)<br>Homemakers: 200 (5.8%)<br>Unemployed: 191 (5.5%)<br>Students: 74 (2.1%)<br>Total: 3,446 (100.0%) |

***Table 1**. Demographics of survey respondents.*

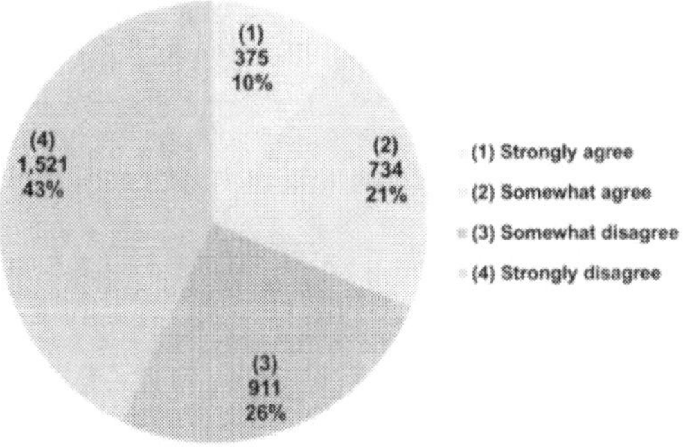


***Figure 1****. How much do you agree/disagree that "I'd rather not know my chance of getting cancer"?*

### Age

With regard to age, older respondents (aged 50+) were the most likely to agree that they would rather not know their chance of getting cancer. Participants between the ages of 35 and 49, on the other hand, were the most likely to disagree with this statement. Figure 2 shows the percent of respondents who agreed with this statement, by age group. A chi-square test of independence showed that there was a statistically significant association between age and agreement/disagreement with this statement [$\chi^2$ (4, $n$ = 3495) = 14.96, $p$ = .005, Cramer's $V$ = .065].

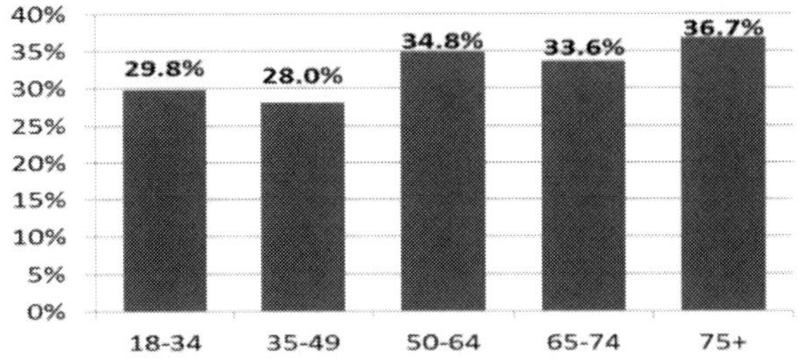


***Figure 2****. Percent agreement (M3) by age group*

### Educational Attainment

Respondents with lower educational attainment levels were much more likely to agree that they would rather not know their chance of getting cancer. Figure 3 shows this relationship. A chi-square test of independence identified a statistically significant association between educational attainment and agreement/disagreement with this statement [$\chi^2$ (6, $n$ = 3526) = 73.41, $p$ = .000, Cramer's $V$ = .144].

### Household Income

Similarly, respondents with lower household incomes were much more likely to agree with the statement, "I'd rather not know my chance of getting cancer." Figure 4 shows this relationship. This association between household income and responses to question M3 was statistically significant [$\chi^2$ (4, $n$ = 3274) = 45.47, $p$ = .000, Cramer's $V$ = .118]. A somewhat related variable— whether anyone in the respondent's family owns a working cell phone— yielded similar findings. Respondents whose families did not own a working cell phone were more likely to agree that they would rather not know their chance of getting cancer. A chi-square test of independence showed statistical significance [$\chi^2$ (1, $n$ = 3520) = 24.95, $p$ = .000, $\Phi$ = -.085].

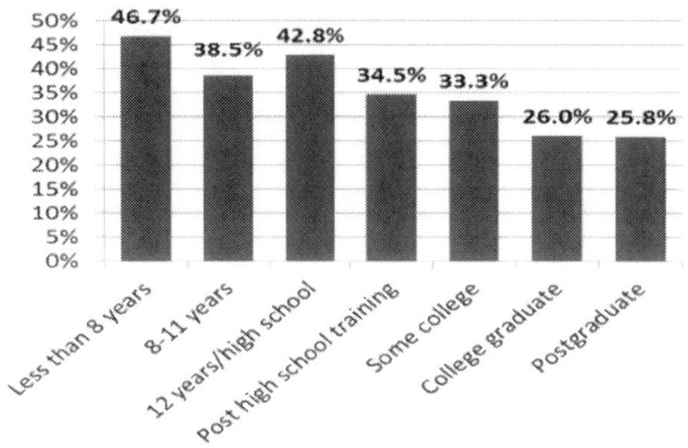


***Figure 3****. Percent agreement (M3) by education*

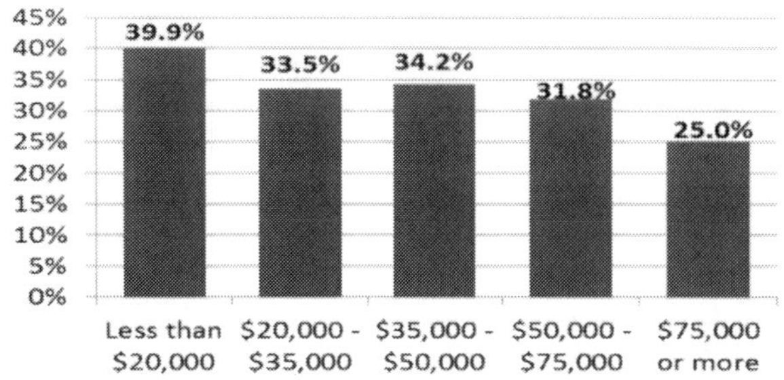


***Figure 4****. Percent agreement (M3) by household income*

### Occupational Status

With regard to occupational status, agreement that one would rather not know one's chance of getting cancer was more common among respondents who were unemployed (40%), disabled (35%), or retired (35%) than among those who were employed (31%), homemakers (30%), or students (26%). This association between occupational status and respondents' agreement/disagreement with this statement was found to be statistically significant [$\chi^2$ (5, $n$ = 3446) = 11.21, $p$ = .047, Cramer's $V$ = .057].

### Health Insurance Coverage

Respondents who reported that they do not have any kind of health care coverage (whether health insurance, a prepaid plan such as an HMO, or a government plan such as Medicare) were more likely than other respondents to agree that they would rather not know their chance of getting cancer. A chi-square test of independence indicated that this association was statistically significant [$\chi^2$ (1, $n$ = 3615) = 12.68, $p$ = .000, $\Phi$ = -.060].

### *Internet Access and Use*

Respondents who reported they never "go online to access the Internet or World Wide Web or to send and receive e-mail" (NIH, 2014) were more likely than other respondents to agree they would rather not know their chance of getting cancer [$\chi^2$ (1, $n$ = 3629) = 52.83, $p$ = .000, $\Phi$ = -.121]. Similarly, respondents who reported that they do not access the Internet using broadband, such as DSL, cable, or FiOS, were also more likely than other respondents to agree with this statement [$\chi^2$ (1, $n$ = 2731) = 6.17, $p$ = .013, $\Phi$ = -.048].

Respondents who reported that they had not used the Internet to look for information about cancer for themselves during the past 12 months were much more likely than those who had to agree with that they would rather not know their chance of getting cancer. A chi-square test of independence indicated this association was statistically significant [$\chi^2$ (1, $n$ = 2753) = 13.06, $p$ = .000, Φ = -.070].

Respondents who reported that they did not have a tablet, smartphone, or a basic cell phone were more likely than other respondents to agree that they would rather not know their chance of getting cancer and this difference was statistically significant [$\chi^2$ (1, $n$ = 3546) = 28.74, $p$ = .000, Φ = .091] Respondents who reported that they have only a basic cell phone were also more likely to agree with this statement [$\chi^2$ (1, $n$ = 3546) = 11.24, $p$ = .001, Φ = .057].

Respondents who reported they do not have health-related apps on their tablet or smartphone were more likely than those who do to agree they would rather not know their chance of getting cancer. Furthermore, respondents who said they did not know whether they have health-related apps on their tablet or smartphone were much more likely than both those who reported having or not having such apps to agree with this statement. Just 27% of respondents with health apps agreed they would rather not know their chance of getting cancer. This figure rose to 31% of those who did not have health apps and to 40% of those who did not know whether they had health apps. These differences were statistically significant [$\chi^2$ (2, $n$ = 2403) = 8.84, $p$ = .012, Cramer's $V$ = .061].

### Health Information Seeking

Respondents who reported they had never looked for information about health or medical topics from any source were much more likely than those who had to agree with the statement "I'd rather not know my chance of getting cancer." While 30% of those who had looked for health information agreed with this statement, nearly 45% of those who had not looked for health information indicated their agreement. This difference was statistically significant [$\chi^2$ (1, $n$ = 3644) = 43.17, $p$ = .000, Φ = -.110]. Similarly, respondents who reported they had never looked for information about cancer from any source were more likely than other respondents to agree with this statement. This difference was also statistically significant [$\chi^2$ (1, $n$ = 2969) = 20.85, $p$ = .000, Φ = -.085].

### Health Information Seeking Barriers

Of the respondents who had ever looked for information about cancer from any source (54.3%), those who reported encountering difficulties the last time they searched for cancer information were more likely to agree that they would rather not know their chance of getting cancer. Just over one-third (35.3%) of them agreed with the statement "It took a lot of effort to get the information you needed." These respondents were more likely than others to also agree that they would rather not know their chance of getting cancer. This difference was statistically significant [$\chi^2$ (3, $n$ = 1551) = 12.99, $p$ = .005, Cramer's $V$ = .092].

Twenty-nine percent of respondents strongly or somewhat agreed with the statement "You felt frustrated during your search for the information." These respondents were more likely than those who disagreed with this statement to also agree that they would rather not know their chance of getting cancer. This difference was statistically significant [$\chi^2$ (3, $n$ = 1533) = 9.84, $p$ = .020, Cramer's $V$ = .080].

Just over thirty percent (30.4%) of the respondents strongly or somewhat agreed with the statement, "The information you found was hard to understand." These respondents were more likely than those who strongly or somewhat disagreed with this statement to agree that they would rather not know their chance of getting cancer. This difference was statistically significant [$\chi^2$ (3, $n$ = 1540) = 11.03, $p$ = .012, Cramer's $V$ = .085].

More than half (50.3%) of the respondents strongly or somewhat agreed with the statement "You were concerned about the quality of the information." These respondents were more likely than those who strongly or somewhat disagreed with this statement to agree that they would rather not know their chance of getting cancer. This difference was also statistically significant [$\chi^2$ (3, $n$ = 1547) = 8.32, $p$ = .040, Cramer's $V$ = .073].

Respondents who strongly or somewhat agreed that "There are so many different recommendations about preventing cancer, it's hard to know which ones to follow" were more likely to agree that they would rather not know their chance of getting cancer. While just 20% of the respondents who strongly disagreed with this statement agreed that they would rather not know their chance of getting cancer, more than 40% of those who strongly agreed with this statement did so. These differences were statistically significant [$\chi^2$ (3, $n$ = 3539) = 78.88, $p$ = .000, Cramer's $V$ = .149].

### Trust toward Health Information Sources

One survey question asked respondents to rate how much they would trust information about cancer from various sources, using a 4-point scale: (1) A lot; (2) Some; (3) A little; and (4) Not at all. Table 2 summarizes respondents' mean trust toward each source, ranging from greatest trust toward cancer information from a doctor ($M$ = 1.38) to least trust toward cancer information from the radio ($M$ = 2.97).

Respondents who expressed no trust at all in cancer information from a doctor, the Internet, government health agencies, and charitable organizations were more likely than other respondents to agree they would rather not know their chance of getting cancer. See Figure 5. All of these differences were statistically significant [Doctor: $\chi^2$ (3, $n$ = 3581) = 31.80, p = .000, Cramer's $V$ = .094; Internet: $\chi^2$ (3, $n$ = 3360) = 36.69, p = .000, Cramer's $V$ = .104; Government health agencies: $\chi^2$ (3, $n$ = 3396) = 44.43, p = .000, Cramer's $V$ = .114; Charitable organizations: $\chi^2$ (3, $n$ = 3348) = 33.20, p = .000, Cramer's $V$ = .100].

| A7. In general, how much would you trust information about cancer from ___________? | | | |
|---|---|---|---|
| **Information source:** | ***n*** | ***M*** | ***SD*** |
| A doctor | 3,581 | 1.38 | .653 |
| Government health agencies | 3,396 | 2.05 | .877 |
| Internet | 3,360 | 2.15 | .821 |
| Family or friends | 3,394 | 2.40 | .753 |
| Charitable organizations | 3,348 | 2.43 | .872 |
| Newspapers or magazines | 3,371 | 2.64 | .793 |
| Television | 3,371 | 2.72 | .832 |
| Religious organizations/leaders | 3,381 | 2.89 | .915 |
| Radio | 3,332 | 2.97 | .810 |

***Table 2**. Mean trust ratings toward cancer info. sources*

### *Self-Efficacy*

Respondents with lower health- and information-related self-efficacy were more likely to agree they would rather not know their chance of getting cancer. While 52% of the respondents who said they were not confident at all about their ability to take good care of their health agreed with this statement, while just 32% of respondents who were completely or very confident in their ability to take good care of their health did so. These differences were statistically significant [$\chi^2$ (4, $n$ = 3568) = 11.56, $p$ = .021, Cramer's $V$ = .057]. Similarly, respondents somewhat, a little, or not confident at all that they could get advice or information about cancer if they needed it were more likely than those completely or very confident to agree they would rather not know their chance of getting cancer. While 51% of respondents who were not confident at all agreed they would rather not know their chance of getting cancer, just 31% of respondents who felt completely or very confident did so. These differences were statistically significant [$\chi^2$ (4, n =3603) = 29.84, $p$ = .000, Cramer's $V$ = .091].

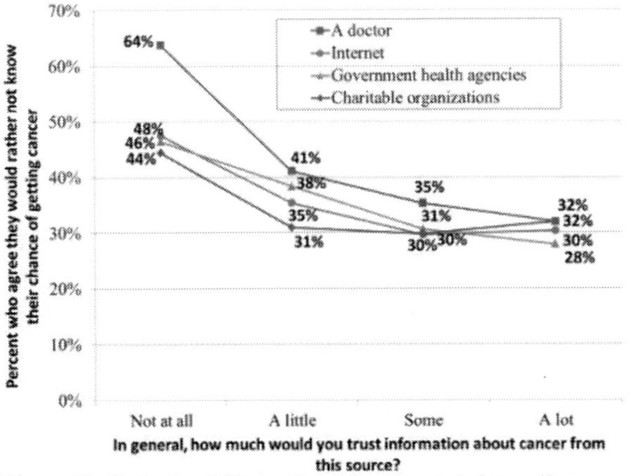


***Figure 5**. Question M3 vs. Trust in cancer information.*

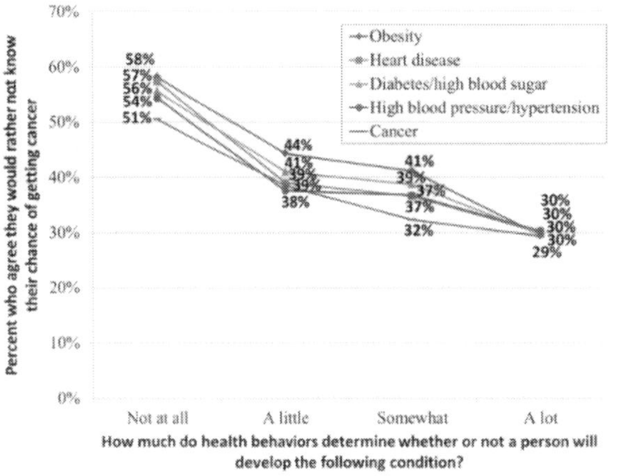


***Figure 6**. Question M3 vs. Belief that health behaviors determine whether one will develop a condition.*

Respondents with lower expectations regarding one's ability to prevent disease through their health behaviors were also more likely to prefer not to know their chance of getting cancer. Those who felt that health behaviors (such as diet, exercise, or smoking) play little or no role in determining whether someone will develop diabetes/high blood sugar (D), obesity (O), heart disease (HD), high blood pressure/hypertension (HBP), or cancer (C) were statistically significantly more likely to agree they would rather not know their chance of getting cancer [D: $\chi^2$ (3, n =3516) = 51.35, $p$ = .000, Cramer's $V$ = .121; O: $\chi^2$ (3, n =3502) = 80.00, $p$ = .000, Cramer's $V$ = .142; HD: $\chi^2$ (3, n =3502) = 43.57, $p$ = .000, Cramer's $V$ = .112; HBP: $\chi^2$ (3, n =3516) = 34.25, $p$ = .000, Cramer's $V$ = .099; C: $\chi^2$ (3, n =3502) = 44.39, $p$ = .000, Cramer's $V$ = .113]. See Figure 6. Interestingly, results were similar regarding the perceived role of genetics – respondents who felt genetics plays little or no role in the development of these conditions were also statistically significantly more likely to agree they would rather not know their chance of getting cancer [D: $\chi^2$ (3, n =3526) = 16.47, $p$ = .001, Cramer's $V$ = .068; O: $\chi^2$ (3, n =3495) = 14.62, $p$ = .002, Cramer's $V$ = .065; HD: $\chi^2$ (3, n =3507) = 23.84, $p$ = .000, Cramer's $V$ = .082; HBP: $\chi^2$ (3, n =3513) = 14.79, $p$ = .002, Cramer's $V$ = .065; C: $\chi^2$ (3, n =3510) = 23.56, $p$ = .000, Cramer's $V$ = .082].

Respondents who agreed that "body weight is something basic about a person that they can't change very much" were more likely to agree they would rather not know their chance of getting cancer. While 49% of the respondents who agreed with this statement also agreed they would rather not know their chance of getting cancer, just 29% of those who disagreed with this statement agreed they would rather not know their chance of getting cancer. These differences were statistically significant [$\chi^2$ (3, $n$ = 3613) = 121.19, $p$ = .000, Cramer's $V$ = .183]. Respondents who agreed that "smoking behavior is something basic about a person that they can't change very much" were more likely to prefer not knowing their chance of getting cancer [$\chi^2$ (3, $n$ = 3581) = 110.86, $p$ = .000, Cramer's $V$ = .176].

Respondents who thought that quitting smoking would not help to reduce the harmful effects of smoking were more likely to agree that they would rather not know their chance of getting cancer. While 31% of those who thought that quitting would help a lot agreed that they would rather not know their chance of getting cancer, 55% of those who thought that quitting would not help at all agreed with this statement. These differences were statistically significant [$\chi^2$ (3, $n$ = 3599) = 41.21, $p$ = .000, Cramer's $V$ = .107]. Respondents who strongly or somewhat agreed that "It seems like everything causes cancer" were more likely to agree they would rather not know their chance of getting cancer [$\chi^2$ (3, $n$ = 3542) = 48.61, $p$ = .000, Cramer's $V$ = .117]. Similarly, respondents who strongly or somewhat agreed that "There's not much you can do to lower your chances of getting cancer" were more likely to agree they would rather not know their chance of getting cancer [$\chi^2$ (3, $n$ = 3528) = 127.23, $p$ = .000, Cramer's $V$ = .190].

### Health Behaviors

Respondents who less frequently used menu information (when available) regarding calories in deciding what to order [$\chi^2$ (4, $n$ = 3640) = 36.55, $p$ = .000, Cramer's $V$ = .100] and those who smoked every day [$\chi^2$ (2, $n$ = 1459) = 19.15, $p$ = .000, Cramer's $V$ = .115] were statistically significantly more likely to agree that they would rather not know their chance of getting cancer.

### Perceived Cancer Incidence and Susceptibility

Respondents who agreed that cancer is more common in adults than heart disease were more likely to agree that they would rather not know their chance of getting cancer. While 44% of the respondents who strongly agreed that cancer is more common than heart disease agreed that they would rather not know their chance of getting cancer, just 26% of those who strongly disagreed that cancer is more common than heart disease did so. These differences were statistically significant [$\chi^2$ (3, n =3476) = 55.77, $p$ = .000, Cramer's $V$ = .127]

Respondents who perceived themselves as unlikely to get cancer were more likely than others to agree they would rather not know their chance of getting cancer. While 43% of respondents who said they were unlikely to get cancer in their lifetime agreed that they would rather not know their chance of getting cancer, just 24% of respondents who said they were very likely to get cancer in their lifetime did so. These differences were statistically significant [$\chi^2$ (4, n =3511) = 24.35, $p$ = .000, Cramer's $V$ = .083].

Respondents who were less worried about getting cancer were more likely to agree that they would rather not know their chance of getting cancer. More than 40% of those who were not at all worried agreed that they would rather not know their chance of getting cancer, while just 29% of those who were extremely worried agreed with this statement. These differences were statistically significant [$\chi^2$ (4, n =3563) = 53.29, $p$ = .000, Cramer's $V$ = .122]

### Perceived Social Support

Respondents who reported that they do not have anyone they can count on to provide them with emotional support when they need it and who reported that they do not have friends or family members they talk to about their health were more likely to agree that they would rather not know their chance of getting cancer. These differences were statistically significant [Someone to count on for emotional support: $\chi^2$ (1, $n$ = 3552) = 11.50, $p$ = .001, $\Phi$ = -.058; Friends/family members to talk to about their health: $\chi^2$ (1, $n$ = 3555) = 18.09, $p$ = .000, $\Phi$ = -.072].

Respondents who indicated that they do not have a particular doctor, nurse, or other health professional (other than a psychiatrist or other mental health professional) that they see most often were more likely than other respondents to agree that they would rather not know their chance of getting cancer. This difference was statistically significant [$\chi^2$ (1, $n$ = 3608) = 23.66, $p$ = .000, $\Phi$ = -.082].

### Preferred Role in Cancer Treatment Decision-Making

Given the hypothetical situation in which they have been diagnosed with cancer with a moderate chance of survival and several treatment options, respondents who selected either "I prefer to make the decision with little or no input from my doctor" or "I prefer to leave all decisions about my treatment to my doctor" were more likely than respondents selecting one of the three more collaborative options ["I prefer to make the decision after seriously considering my doctor's opinion"; "I prefer that my doctor and I share responsibility for the decision together"; "I prefer my doctor to make the decision after seriously considering my opinion"] to agree that they would rather not know their chance of getting cancer [$\chi^2$ (4, $n$ = 3517) = 40.59, $p$ = .000, Cramer's $V$ = .107]. This same pattern held when respondents were presented with the hypothetical situation in which they have been diagnosed with cancer with a *low* chance of survival and *limited* treatment options [$\chi^2$ (4, $n$ = 3541) = 46.38, $p$ = .000, Cramer's $V$ = .114]. With regard to both of these scenarios, it was the respondents who selected "I prefer to make the decision with little or no input from my doctor" that were the most likely to agree that they would rather not know their chance of getting cancer.

## DISCUSSION

### Summary of Findings

Based on this analysis, we find that nearly one-third of the respondents would rather not know their chance of getting cancer. The respondents who agreed with this statement tended to be older (particularly those aged 75 and up); be less well-educated; have lower household incomes; be unemployed, disabled, or retired; and to not have health care coverage. They were also more likely to report that they never "go online to access the Internet or World Wide Web or to send and receive e-mail"; they do not access the Internet using broadband (such as DSL, cable, or FiOS); they do not own a tablet, smartphone, or a basic cell phone; they do not have health-related apps on their tablet or smartphone (if they do own one); and they have not used the Internet during the past 12 months to look for information about cancer for themselves.

Respondents who would rather not know their chance of getting cancer were also more likely to report that they have never looked for information about health or medical topics from any source and that they have never looked for information about cancer, in particular, from any source. They also tended to report encountering greater difficulties the last time they searched for information about cancer, as they were much more likely to agree that: (1) "It took a lot of effort to get the information you needed"; (2) "You felt frustrated during your search for the information"; (3) "The information you found was hard to understand"; and (4) "You were concerned about the quality of the information." They were also more likely to agree that "There are so many different recommendations about preventing cancer, it's hard to know which ones to follow."

There were also statistically significant differences with regard to the level of trust that respondents felt toward various sources of cancer information. Although doctors, government health agencies, and the Internet were the three most trusted sources on average across all respondents, those who agreed that they would rather not know their chance of getting cancer indicated less trust than other respondents toward these sources.

Based on a number of different variables, respondents who agreed they would rather not know their chance of getting cancer tended to have lower health- and information-related self-efficacy. They were less confident about their ability to take good care of their health and less confident that they could get advice or information about cancer if they needed it. Furthermore, they were more likely to believe that both health behaviors, such as diet exercise, or smoking, play little or no role in determining whether someone will develop diabetes/high blood sugar, obesity, heart disease, high blood pressure/hypertension, or cancer. Respondents who agreed they would rather not know their chance of getting cancer were also more likely to agree that both body weight and smoking behavior are "something basic about a person that they can't change very much." Furthermore, they were more likely to think that quitting smoking would not help to reduce the harmful effects of smoking and to agree that "It seems like everything causes cancer" and that "There's not much you can do to lower your chances of getting cancer." Regarding their actual health behaviors, this group of respondents less frequently used menu information on calories (when available) in deciding what to order and were more likely to smoke every day.

The respondents who agreed that they would rather not know their chance of getting cancer tended to simultaneously have a more elevated sense of the incidence of cancer, a reduced sense of their own susceptibility to developing this disease, and a lower level of worry about getting cancer. Relatedly, they were more likely to agree that cancer is more common in adults than heart disease and to say it was unlikely they would get cancer in their lifetime and that they were not at all worried about getting cancer.

Another set of variables that were found to be associated with not wanting to know one's chance of getting cancer were those pertaining to perceived social support, whether relating to informal or formal connections. Respondents who preferred not to know their chance of getting cancer were more likely than other respondents to report that they do not have anyone they can count on to provide them with emotional support when they need it and that they do not have friends or family members they talk to about their health. These respondents were also less likely than other respondents to say that they have a particular doctor, nurse, or other health professional (other than a psychiatrist or other mental health professional) that they see most often.

When given two hypothetical situations— one in which respondents have been diagnosed with cancer with a moderate chance of survival and several treatment options and another in which respondents have been diagnosed with cancer with a low chance of survival and limited treatment options— respondents who preferred not to know their chance of getting cancer were more likely than other respondents to prefer either the most active role ("I prefer to make the decisions with little or no input from my doctor") or, to a lesser degree, the most passive role ("I prefer to leave all decisions about my treatment to my doctor) with regard to making decisions relating to cancer treatment. They were less likely than other respondents to select one of the three more collaborative options: "I prefer to make the decision after seriously considering my doctor's opinion"; "I prefer that my doctor and I share responsibility for the decision together"; and "I prefer my doctor to make the decision after seriously considering my opinion".

### *Implications*

The findings from this analysis confirm that there are interrelationships among information avoidance, health literacy, and health justice. Information avoidance is not an uncommon phenomenon among U.S. adults; however, it is significantly more common among the very people who tend to be negatively impacted by the lack of health justice in this country and who tend to have low levels of health literacy: older people (NN/LM, 2014), people with lower household incomes (Chetty et al., 2016; NN/LM, 2014), and people with lower educational attainment levels (Olshansky et al., 2012). Novel findings from this analysis further link information avoidance with the related states of being unemployed, disabled, or retired and lacking health care coverage. This study also revealed a connection between information avoidance and both non-use of the Internet and encountering difficulties in searching for information about cancer. Additionally, information avoidance was found to be linked with lower trust in some sources of cancer information (including doctors, government health agencies, and the Internet), lower self-efficacy, a higher perception of the incidence of cancer but a lower sense of one's own personal susceptibility to it, and less perceived social support. Information avoidance was also found to be most common among the respondents who preferred a less collaborative role in cancer treatment-related decision-making.

Many of the variables that this analysis has found to be associated with information avoidance pose possible avenues through which we might interrupt the connections between low health literacy, poor health outcomes, and, ultimately, health disparities (as established in, for example, Ad Hoc Committee on Health Literacy, 1999, IOM, 2004, Schillinger et al., 2002, Weiss, 2007). While demographic variables are often impossible (or quite difficult) to change, we can work to ensure that everyone has healthcare coverage, Internet access, and the health and information literacy skills needed to reduce the barriers they may encounter when seeking health information. Furthermore, we can help to increase people's health-related self-efficacy and provide them with an accurate picture of both the incidence of cancer and their personal susceptibility to it. We can also make strides toward ensuring that people have the social support they need and a particular health professional in whom they can place their trust and whom they are able to see and rely upon when they need health care. We can also educate people about the potential benefits of taking a more collaborative role in treatment-related decision-making, enabling them to benefit from their doctor's expertise and experience while also being able to make an informed decision as to the treatment they believe will be the best option for them as an individual.

In addition to new educational strategies directed toward patients, addressing the structural and institutional barriers that limit individuals with specific demographic characteristics from effectively managing their own care will also be a critical component in addressing health disparities. For example, Betancourt et al. (2003) found that patients belonging to racial/ethnic minority groups encountered several sociocultural barriers to care, including organizational (e.g., non-diverse health care workforce), structural (e.g., language barriers, long wait times for appointments) and clinical barriers (e.g., discriminatory treatment by health care providers). Organizational solutions altering clinical workforce composition, clinical workflows and current processes of care will require significant shifts in hiring and in the existing modes of healthcare delivery; however, such alterations are necessary to optimize the quality and efficacy of the health care that all individuals receive. Healthcare entities must begin to take additional responsibility for determining sociocultural barriers that can prevent patients from actively engaging in their own care and provide them with the resources necessary to overcome these barriers. These resources could include materials or instructions that are educationally, culturally, and linguistically more appropriate for specific demographic groups, more clearly written instructions or health care plans, and additional time and touch points with healthcare providers and/or paraprofessionals as needed. Each individual will have a different set of needs and limitations associated with their unique constellation of demographic variables, so a one-size-fits-all approach will likely be only minimally effective. Organizational entities must allocate additional resources for these individuals routed directly through existing processes of clinical care. By taking a dual approach involving both providing instrumental support to patients in terms of information access, education, and social support and taking steps to address the sociocultural barriers that these individuals encounter in striving to get their healthcare needs met, we can make tremendous progress toward reducing health disparities.

### Limitations and Future Research

This research has several limitations. First, the data itself is limited to U.S. residents and is subject to sampling bias, as the people who responded to the survey may differ in some systematic way from those who did not (for example, people who are healthier or who do not smoke may have been more willing to respond to a survey that relates to their health). It is also possibly subject to social desirability bias (for example, respondents may have reported that they do not smoke even though they do, as smoking is viewed by many as socially undesirable), although the fact that the respondents completed the survey forms in the privacy of their own homes should help to ameliorate this potential bias. Second, the data is also limited in that we can only work with the questions that were asked and the way in which the questions and response options were worded and ordered may have influenced respondents' answers. Third, our data analysis process is also limited. This was an initial exploration of the bivariate relationships between respondents' answers to question M3 and their answers to demographic, information-seeking-related, and other types of questions on the survey. Some of the demographic variables included in this analysis, such as household income and educational attainment levels, are highly correlated with one another.

Future research will aim to use this data set to build multivariate models of information avoidance, identifying the combination of variables that seem to coalesce in contributing to the lack of health justice in the United States. By applying conditional process modelling, we can uncover the boundary conditions under which one factor influences other. For example, we can investigate whether respondents' levels of trust in cancer information from various sources influences their tendency to feel fatalistic (e.g., agree that "There's not much you can do to lower your chances of getting cancer" and feel that quitting smoking will not help at all in reducing smoking's harmful effects). Findings from these types of analyses can help public health and information professionals to design more cost-effective interventions that can help to minimize health information avoidance in potentially problematic situations and to tailor their communications more precisely to particular audiences. In addition to further quantitative research, qualitative methods will be used to directly engage with patients to learn more about the types of situations in which they tend to avoid health information, the specific reasons why they do so, and both the positive and negative consequences that can result from health information avoidance. This more in-depth and explanatory data will help to further shed light on the interrelationships among information avoidance, health literacy, and health justice.

## CONCLUSION

This exploratory analysis of the NCI HINTS survey data has revealed some important associations between information avoidance and other types of demographic (e.g., older age, lower educational attainment, and lower household income); information-seeking (e.g., lower likelihood of health-related information seeking and Internet use; greater likelihood of encountering difficulties when looking for cancer-related information; less trust in cancer information from a doctor, the Internet, government health agencies, and charitable organizations); cognitive/perceptual (e.g., lower health- and information-related self-efficacy; increased perceptions of cancer incidence; decreased perceptions of one's susceptibility to cancer); and social factors (e.g., perception that one doesn't have anyone to count on for emotional support; not having a particular health care provider that they see most often; preferring to make cancer treatment-related decisions with little or no input from their doctor).

By specifically targeting some of these more malleable associated variables and by working to eliminate the sociocultural barriers that can impede people from actively engaging in their own health care, we may be able to interrupt the progression from low health literacy to poor health outcomes that frequently unfolds. Ensuring that everyone has better access to health information and health care, adequate information and health literacy skills, optimal levels of health-related self-efficacy and social support, and the opportunity for a sustained, trustworthy, and collaborative doctor-patient relationship can help to lead to higher health literacy levels, a lower incidence of health disparities, and a much-needed improvement in the state of health justice in this country.

## REFERENCES


Ad Hoc Committee on Health Literacy for the Council on Scientific Affairs, American Medical Association. (1999). Health literacy: Report of the Council on Scientific Affairs. *Journal of the American Medical Association, 281*(6), 552-557.

Ankem, K. (2006a). Use of information sources by cancer patients: Results of a systematic review of the research literature. *Information Research, 11*(3), paper 254.

Ankem, K. (2006b). Factors influencing information needs among cancer patients: A meta-analysis. *Library & Information Science Research, 28*(1), 7-23.

Baker, D. W., Gazmararian, J. A., Williams, M. V., Scott, T., Parker, R. M., Green, D., Ren, J., Peel, J. (2002). Functional health literacy and the risk of hospital admission among Medicare managed care enrollees. *American Journal of Public Health, 92*(8), 1278-1283.

Baker, D. W., Wolf, M. S., Feinglass, J., Thompson, J. A., Gazmararian, J. A., & Huang, J. (2007). Health literacy and mortality among elderly persons. *Archives of Internal Medicine, 167*(14), 1503-1509.

Baker, L. M. (1998). Sense making in multiple sclerosis: The information needs of people during an acute exacerbation. *Qualitative Health Research, 8*(1), 106-20.

Bennett, I. M., Chen, J., Soroui, J. S., & White, S. (2009). The contribution of health literacy to disparities in self-rated health status and preventive health behaviors in older adults. *Annals of Family Medicine, 7*(3), 204-211.

Betancourt, J. R., Green, A. R., Emilio Carrillo, J., & Ananeh-Firempong II, O. (2003). Defining cultural competence: A practical framework for addressing racial/ethnic disparities in health and health care. *Public Health Reports, 118*(4), 293-302.

Brashers, D. E., Goldsmith, D. J., & Hsieh, E. (2002). Information seeking and avoiding in health contexts. *Human Communication Research, 28*(2), 258-271.

Brashers, D. E., Neidig, J. L., Haas, S. M., Dobbs, L. K., Cardillo, L. W., & Russell, J. A. (2000). Communication in the management of uncertainty: The case of persons living with HIV or AIDS. *Communication Monographs, 67*(1), 63-84.

Butow, P. N., Maclean, M., Dunn, S. M., Tattersall, M. H. N., & Boyer, M. J. (1997). The dynamics of change: Cancer patients' preferences for information, involvement and support. *Annals of Oncology, 8*(9), 857-863.

Case, D. O., Andrews, J. E., Johnson, J. D., & Allard, S. L. (2005). Avoiding versus seeking: The relationship of information seeking to avoidance, blunting, coping, dissonance, and related concepts. *Journal of the Medical Library Association, 93*(3), 353-362.

Chetty, R., Stepner, M., Abraham, S., Lin, S., Scuderi, B., Turner, N., Bergeron, A., & Cutler, D. (2016). The association between income and life expectancy in the United States, 2001-2014. *Journal of the American Medical Association, 315*(16), 1750-1766.

Clark, J. (2005). Constructing expertise: Inequality and the consequences of information-seeking by breast cancer patients. *Illness, Crisis & Loss, 13*(2), 169-185.

Degner, L. F., & Sloan, J. A. (1992). Decision making during serious illness: What role do patients really want to play? *Journal of Clinical Epidemiology, 45*(9), 941-50.

Degner, L. F., Kristjanson, L. J., Bowman, D., Sloan, J. A., Carriere, K. C., O'Neil, J., Bilodeau, B., Watson, P., & Mueller, B. (1997). Information needs and decisional preferences in women with breast cancer. *JAMA, 277*(18), 1485-1492.

Eheman, C. R., Berkowitz, Z., Lee, J., Mohile, S., Purnell, J., Rodriguez, E. M., et al. (2009). Information-seeking styles among cancer patients before and after treatment by demographics and use of information sources. *Journal of Health Communication, 14*(5), 487-502.

Hack, T. F., Degner, L. F., & Dyck, D. G. (1994). Relationship between preferences for decisional control and illness information among women with breast cancer: A quantitative and qualitative analysis. *Social Science & Medicine, 39*(2), 279-289.

Institute of Medicine (IOM). (2004). *Health literacy: A prescription to end confusion*. Washington, DC: The National Academies Press.

Kutner, M., Greenberg, E., Jin, Y., & Paulsen C. (2006). *The health literacy of America's adults: Results from the 2003 National Assessment of Adult Literacy* (NCES 2006–483). Washington, DC: U.S. Department of Education, National Center for Education Statistics.

Miller, S. M. (1995). Monitoring versus blunting styles of coping with cancer influence the information patients want and need about their disease. *Cancer, 76*(2), 167-77.

Mills, M. A. & Davidson, R. (2002). Cancer patients' sources of information: Use and quality issues. *Psycho-Oncology, 11*(5), 371-378.

NCI (National Cancer Institute) (2015a, June). *Analytics Recommendations for HINTS 4 – Cycle 4 Data.* Retrieved March 14, 2017, from https://hints.cancer.gov/dataset/HINTS_4_Cycle_4_SPSS.zip

NCI (National Cancer Institute). (2015b, June.). *HINTS 4 Cycle 4 Public Use Dataset* (SPSS data and supporting documents). Retrieved March 14, 2017, from https://hints.cancer.gov/dataset/HINTS_4_Cycle_4_SPSS.zip

National Institutes of Health (NIH), U.S. Department of Health and Human Services. (2014). *HINTS 4 Cycle 4 English-version Annotated Form.* Retrieved March 16, 2017, from https://hints.cancer.gov/docs/Instruments/HINTS_4_Cycle_4_English_Annotated_Form.pdf

National Network of Libraries of Medicine (NN/LM). (2014, Aug 5). *Health literacy.* Available: http://nnlm.gov/outreach/consumer/hlthlit.html

Norman, C. D. & Skinner, H. A. (2006). eHealth Literacy: Essential skills for consumer health in a networked world. *Journal of Medical Internet Research, 8*(2), e9.

Nutbeam, D. (1996). Health outcomes and health promotion – Defining success in health promotion. *Health Promotion Journal of Australia, 6*(2), 58-60.

Olshansky, S. J., Antonucci, T., Berkman, L., Binstock, R. H., Boersch-Supan, A., Cacioppo, J. T., Carnes, B. A., Carstensen, L. L., Fried, L. P., Goldman, D. P., Jackson, J., Kohli, M., Rother, J., Zhen, Y., & Rowe, J. (2012). Differences in life expectancy due to race and educational differences are widening and may not catch up. *Health Affairs, 31*(8), 1803-1813.

Ormshaw, M. J., Paakkari, L. T., & Kannas, L. K. (2013). Measuring child and adolescent health literacy: A systematic review of literature. *Health Education, 113*(5), 433-455.

Pifalo, V., Hollander, S., Henderson, C. L., DeSalvo, P., & Gill, G. P. (1997). The impact of consumer health information provided by libraries: The Delaware experience. *Bulletin of the Medical Library Association, 85*(1), 16-22.

Ratzan, S. C. & Parker, R. M. (2000). Introduction. In C. R. Selden, M. Zorn, S. C. Ratzan, & R. M. Parker (Eds.), *National Library of Medicine Current Bibliographies in Medicine: Health Literacy.* NLM Pub. No. CBM 2000-1. Bethesda, MD: National Institutes of Health, U.S. Department of Health and Human Services.

Schillinger, D., Grumach, K., Piette, J., Wang, F., Osmond, D., Daher, C., Palacios, J., Diaz Sullivan, G., & Bindman, A. B. (2002). Association of health literacy with diabetes outcomes. *Journal of the American Medical Association, 288*(4), 475-482.

Strekalova, Y. A. (2014). Seekers and avoiders: Using health information orientation to explore audience segmentation. *Journal of Communication in Healthcare, 7*(3), 228-237.

Venkatapuram, S. (2011). *Health justice: An argument from the capabilities approach.* Malden, MA: Polity Press.

Weiss, B. D. (2007). *Health literacy and patient safety: Help patients understand* (2nd ed.). American Medical Association Foundation and American Medical Association. Retrieved May 10, 2016, from http://med.fsu.edu/userFiles/file/ahec_health_clinicians_manual.pdf

Westat. (2015, Feb.). *Health Information National Trends Survey 4 (HINTS 4): Cycle 4 Methodology Report.* Retrieved March 14, 2017, from https://hints.cancer.gov/docs/Instruments/HINTS_4_Cycle_4_Methodology_Report_Final.pdf

Wong, F., Stewart, D. E., Dancey, J., Meana, M., McAndrews, M. P., Bunston, T., & Cheung, A. M. (2000). Men with prostate cancer: Influence of psychological factors on informational needs and decision making. *Journal of Psychosomatic Research, 49*(1), 13-19.

# Does It Matter Which Search Engine Is Used? A User Study Using Post-Task Relevance Judgments

**Sebastian Sünkler**
*Hamburg University of Applied Sciences, Germany.*
*sebastian.suenkler@haw-hamburg.de*

**Dirk Lewandowski**
*Hamburg University of Applied Sciences, Germany.*
*dirk.lewandowski@haw-hamburg.de*

## ABSTRACT

**The objective of this research was to find out how the two search engines, Google and Bing, perform when users work freely on pre-defined tasks, and judge the relevance of the results immediately after finishing their search session. In a user study, 64 participants conducted two search tasks each, and then judged the results on the following: (1) the quality of the results they selected in their search sessions, (2) the quality of the results they were presented with in their search sessions (but which they did not click on), (3) the quality of the results from the competing search engine for their queries (which they did not see in their search session). We found that users heavily relied on Google, that Google produced more relevant results than Bing, that users were well able to select relevant results from the results lists and that users judged the relevance of results lower when they regarded a task as difficult and did not find the correct information.**

## KEYWORDS

search engines, evaluation, results quality, interactive information retrieval, task-based user studies, retrieval effectiveness, Google, Bing

## INTRODUCTION

Search engines are an important means for finding information on the web, and because of the web's importance to knowledge acquisition, they are also an important means to what users get to know online. Users predominantly use Google, especially in the European countries, where Google has a market share of well over 90% (comScore, 2013). This raises the – admittedly not new – question whether Google is really better than its competitors in providing the user with relevant results. While the question is old, we still lack methods for realistically and reliably comparing search engines in a natural setting. In this paper, we propose a method and present a user study aimed at allowing for such comparisons.

The objective of our research was to find out how the two search engines, Google and Bing, perform when users work freely on pre-defined tasks (i.e., formulating their own queries and determining the length of their search sessions), and judge the relevance of the results immediately after finishing their search session. Approaches taken so far either focus on comparing the results of search engines using jurors who are not aware of where each result comes from (for an overview, see Lewandowski, 2015), on comparing search engines' results ranking to users' rankings of the same results (Bar-Ilan, Keenoy, Yaari, & Levene, 2007), or on measuring task success or user satisfaction in user studies where users use either the one or the other search engine (cf. White, 2016, p. 328ff.).

In this paper, we describe a method and an empirical study extending user-centered approaches by adding system-oriented tests to the model, and also by developing software support for efficiently conducting such studies. We conducted a lab-based user study with 64 participants. All search queries used in the users' sessions were sent to Google and Bing to collect the top ten results to the queries. Participants were given all of the collected results and asked to judge their relevance. So, users were able to judge (1) the relevance of the results for their own queries, (2) the results for all queries within their session, and (3) results coming from a search engine they had not used.

## LITERATURE REVIEW

### *Users' satisfaction with search engine results*

When users are asked, the majority states that they are satisfied with the results quality of search engines (Purcell, Brenner, & Raine, 2012), and "91% of search engine users say they always or most of the time find the information they are seeking when they use search engines" (Purcell et al., 2012, p. 3). A search engine's ranking of results is even considered as a criterion for credibility (Westerwick, 2013). Furthermore, users usually do not reflect on the relevance calculations made by search engine algorithms and the resulting results ordering (Tremel, 2010). Users most often choose only from the first results page, and they prefer the first few results listed (Joachims et al., 2007). Petrescu (2014) reports that more than two-thirds of all clicks go to the first five positions, and the result ranked first alone accounts for 31% of all clicks. In a large-scale study analyzing millions of queries from the Yahoo search engine, Goel at al. (2010) found that only 10,000 different websites account for approx. 80% of clicks on the search engine results pages (SERPs). Users are generally satisfied with the first few results, even when the results positions are mixed, and therefore, less relevant results are shown on the first position(s) (Keane, O'Brien, & Smyth, 2008; Pan et al., 2007). Users generally prefer Google's results to those from other search engines. This may

---

80th Annual Meeting of the Association for Information Science & Technology, Washington, DC, VA | Oct. 27-Nov. 1, 2017

have to do with quality issues, but studies also found that branding plays an important role (Jansen, Zhang, & Schultz, 2009). This raises the question whether the perceived superiority of Google can be confirmed when comparing this search engine's results to the ones from its competitors. There is a vast body of research on comparing commercial search engine results (for overviews, see Lewandowski, 2008, 2015). Most recently, Lewandowski (2015), in a large-scale retrieval effectiveness study, found that while Google outperforms Bing on navigational queries, Google's results for informational queries are, on average, only slightly more relevant than Bing's. He conjectured that a user would not recognize these small differences when using these two search engines. Schaer, Mayr, Sünkler, & Lewandowski (2016) compared top-ranked results with so-called "long tail" results, i.e., results shown on lower results positions. They found that the top results are judged as only slightly more relevant than the long tail results and concluded that the long tail provides a rich resource, as it provides the user with *different*, although still relevant results.

### *Measuring retrieval effectiveness*

Retrieval effectiveness studies rely on the design of "classic" Cranfield-style information retrieval tests and in cases of investigating web search engines adjust these methods (Gordon & Pathak, 1999; Griesbaum, 2004; Hawking, Craswell, Bailey, & Griffiths, 2001). In general, such tests consist of the following steps: A sample of search queries will be sent to the information systems under investigation, then the returned results will be collected, their ranking position randomized and the source anonymized to avoid learning and branding effects. After that, jurors judge the relevance of the results. Then, the results will be allocated again to the search engines and analyzed by using established evaluation metrics like recall and precision. This approach is sometimes considered as being too narrow, as it does not focus on the users' side of the search. However, conducting retrieval effectiveness studies in such a controlled environment still has its merits (Voorhees, 2009), although most researchers agree that these Cranfield-style tests should be replenished by user-focused studies. While Cranfield-style studies are usually conducted to compare the relevance of the results from different information retrieval systems, in the context of web search, the approach has also been used for questions going beyond that. For instance, researchers considered the relevance of sponsored results versus organic results (Jansen, 2007) and the commercial intent of results providers (Lewandowski, 2011). Information retrieval evaluation has seen a turn from system-centered towards user-centered evaluation (Kelly, 2009). It has become clear that while Cranfield-style studies (still) have their benefits, focusing on the user perspective (and process-oriented metrics, see White (2016), p. 309ff.) adds significantly to improving information retrieval systems. We also argue that focusing not only on the results to a single query but all the results seen by a user in a search session would greatly add to our understanding of concepts such as search engine bias and the influence of commercial search engines on what information users actually consume. User-centered studies are often criticized for the low number of users investigated, for the choice of participants (often undergraduate students), and for their lack of control of effects that search engines' branding and interfaces might have. From this short review of the two paradigms of information retrieval evaluation, it becomes clear that there is a need for combining the two approaches, or at least taking elements from the two approaches to building new evaluation frameworks combining "the best of the two worlds."

## FRAMEWORK TO EXTEND USER-BASED STUDIES

For our approach, we first analyzed given frameworks and models (Belkin, Cole, & Liu, 2009; Borlund, 2003). Based on that analysis we aimed to create a simple and flexible framework to extend user tests by explicit relevance judgments. Our aim was a model where users judge results they have actually seen in the test, as well as other search results, shortly after they worked on a task. Overall, our method is separated into nine parts, some of which are decisions researches have to make when designing a test (cf. Gordon & Pathak, 1999; Hawking et al., 2001; Tague-Sutcliffe, 1992), and therefore, these parts are independent of any software implementation: (1) Selection of search engines to investigate. To collect natural user interactions, users should be able to select a search engine of their choice to solve tasks. It should be possible to define a set of search engines (not necessarily used by the users when working on their tasks) for relevance judgments, to support a comparison between search systems. (2) Definition of user groups. (3) Definition of test timeframe and test environment (making it possible to conduct long-time studies in natural environments or lab studies). (4) Design of questionnaires (allowing users to, e.g., rate difficulty, outcome, effort, and learning success of tasks). (5) Design of simulated search tasks. (6) Definition of scales and questions about the search results (e.g., binary decisions, Likert-scales). (7) Collecting interaction data, taking into account the search engine(s) used, results clicked, and the search queries used. (8) Build result sets based on search engines used, search queries, clicked results and additional search results from other search engines, which have not necessarily been used by the actual user in the study. (9) Analyze user interactions and results judgments.

In theory, all of these parts can be used in studies without using special software. Parts 1 to 6 are independent of any software, as these are the parts where researchers have to make these decisions for the experimental set-up. Parts 7 and 8, however, cannot be practically conducted without software support: Researchers would need to collect all logging data to create the results sets they want to have judged by users. For example, they would need to send the search queries to the search engines themselves and save the results locally. This would make it impossible to let participants judge the results shortly after they finished the task.

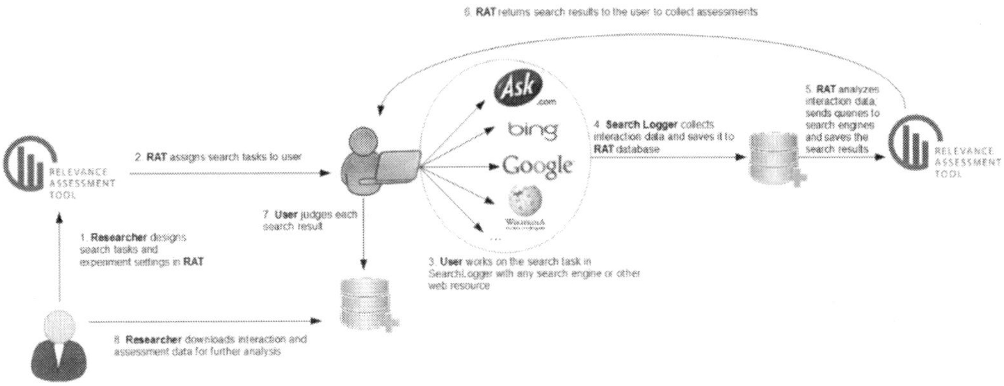


***Figure 1**. Process of the model in practice*

Figure 1 shows the simple process and the resulting possibilities when our framework is implemented in software. Users work on search tasks using a search engine or other web resource of their choice while all interactions are logged in the background. When they finish the task, the logged data get analyzed. These data contain timestamps stating when a user started and finished a task, all search queries used, clicks on search results and the web pages opened. The software also has an option to gather data using questionnaires before starting a task, and after finishing it. This makes it is possible to add demographic data and statements to the tasks or anything else researchers may want to know from their users. After analyzing the log data, search queries are extracted from the log data and sent to the search engines under investigation. The returned search results are saved through screen scraping (up to a defined maximum of results, e.g., the top ten results for each query). All other websites used by the participant will be added to the returned results to create the result set the user has to judge later. To avoid bias or branding effects, the user will not see the source of the given website she has to assess (i.e., the name of the search engine that produced the result).

In summary, this new approach of combining a task-based user study with a system-oriented retrieval effectiveness study has the following advantages: (1) The participant can formulate her own queries, and therefore, realistic search queries are used. (2) Relevance judgments are made by the same person that formulated the queries. This is based on the assumption that the person who formulated the query statement is best able to judge on the results to that query. (3) We can directly compare the results from the search engine a participant actually used to the results from any competing search engine.

## SOFTWARE DEVELOPMENT

We developed software to use our method in practice. As said in the introduction, one obstacle to conducting user-centered retrieval effectiveness studies is the lack of software tools supporting such studies. There are some tools available to evaluate search systems (for an overview, see Sünkler, 2013), but they are limited in different ways. Most of them lack supporting tests with web search engines or they just allow for using their Application Programming Interfaces (APIs). However, search results from APIs differ from the results seen by a search engine user (Mayr & Tosques, 2005). Furthermore, only a few commercial web search engines provide an API. Most importantly, Google does not. Further disadvantages of existing tools are that they either only focus on a specific use case (Tawileh, Griesbaum, & Mandl, 2010) or were even developed for and used in a single project only (Fox, Karnawat, Mydland, Dumais, & White, 2005; Machill, Neuberger, Schweiger, & Wirth, 2004; Pan et al., 2007). More sustainable tools already available either focus on rather fragmented tasks (like the Digital Methods Tools), on crawling for web data analysis (like SocSciBot and Webometric Analyst), or on study designs based on test collections (like the Lemur Toolkit and Revelation)[1]. Our aim, therefore, was to build software to use with search engines that are actually used by Internet users on an everyday basis. The Relevance Assessment Tool (RAT) is a software toolkit that allows researchers to conduct large-scale studies based on results from (commercial) search engines and other information retrieval systems (Lewandowski & Sünkler, 2013)[2]. It consists of modules for (1) designing studies, (2) collecting data from search systems, (3) collecting judgments on the results, (4) downloading/analyzing the results. A starting point to developing RAT was the fact that retrieval effectiveness studies usually require a lot of manual work in designing the test, collecting search results, finding jurors and collecting their assessments, and in analyzing the test results, as well. RAT addresses all these issues and aims to offer help in making retrieval studies more efficient and effective. While RAT allows for efficiently conducting retrieval effectiveness tests, it does not support any user interactions with the search engines to be analyzed. The Search Logger (Singer, Norbisrath,

[1] See https://wiki.digitalmethods.net/Dmi/ToolDatabase, http://socscibot.wlv.ac.uk, http://lexiurl.wlv.ac.uk, https://www.lemurproject.org/lemur.php, and http://ielab.github.io/relevation/, respectively.

[2] While the software toolkit is not available for download, we invite researchers to contact us if they are interested in using RAT for their research.

Vainikko, Kikkas, & Lewandowski, 2011) is a tool developed to log user interactions in a Web browser. While there are several such tools available (Capra, 2010; Jansen, 2006), the Search Logger was our choice, as it provides options to design search tasks and logging features to collect interaction data related to the designed search tasks but also came from developers with whom we had already worked. The Search Logger allows for designing search tasks as well as pre- and post-task questionnaires. It is a Firefox Browser Add-on that offers a simple interface for letting users start search tasks. Interaction data are collected in the background as a user uses search engines and browses websites. Actions from that data which are important for our software are: user starts a new task, user finishes a task, used search engines in a task, used search queries in a task, opened tabs, clicked links (for details on the data the Search Logger can collect, see Singer et al., 2011, p. 753). While the Search Logger allows for collecting interaction data conveniently, its output is only raw data. Therefore, software based on the Search Logger first has to analyze the log output and extract data from it for further investigation. The basic idea of the software designed for extending system-orientated tests by user interactions is described in our framework above. For this purpose, we built an application that analyses the Search Logger output, extracts queries and search engines used from it, and feeds the resulting data into the Relevance Assessment Tool.

## RESEARCH QUESTIONS

As said in the introduction, the objective of our study was to find out how the two search engines Google and Bing perform when users work freely on pre-defined tasks and judge the relevance of the results immediately afterwards. This resulted in the following research questions:

**RQ1**: To what extent do users use different search engines when working on search tasks given by the experimenter?

**RQ2**: Do users judge results they actually selected when performing their tasks as more relevant than results not selected during the task?

**RQ3**: Would users be equally satisfied with the results of another search engine; i.e., would Google users be equally satisfied with results from Bing?

**RQ4**: Would users judge search results as more relevant if they themselves judged the retrieved information as correct to solve the task?

**RQ5**: Do the two search engines perform differently when considering simple vs. complex tasks?

While the first four research questions relate to users' behavior when searching for information, the last two research questions relate to comparing the results quality of the two dominant commercial search engines.

## METHODS

### Choice of search engines

We selected the two search engines Bing and Google, as these are the two major commercial search engines. Given the predominant use of Google in Germany (the country where we conducted our research), it is interesting to consider its major, though concerning usage far behind, competitor Bing. Does this search engine produce results at least comparable to Google's?

### Tasks and participants

We recruited a convenience sample of 64 participants. We aimed at creating a sample that consisted of adolescents and adults of all ages and an even gender distribution. The average age was 37.2 years (SD=12.29). 31 participants were female and 33 male. With such a sample, we hope to get better insight into actual searching behavior, even though we may face problems with statistical significance (Singer, Norbisrath, & Lewandowski, 2012). Each user was given two tasks, one simple and one complex. Each user worked on different tasks, and a total 60 different search tasks were used, evenly divided between simple and complex. For creating the search tasks, we used tasks from a previous study (Singer, Norbisrath, et al., 2012), as well as tasks we derived from questionnaires given to students in our department. Following Singer, Norbisrath, & Lewandowski (2013), we define simple tasks as lookup tasks that can be satisfied with just one document. Examples we used included searches for birthdates and birthplaces of scientists, news facts, historical facts, facts about television and movies and geographical information. Complex tasks are tasks in which a user has to collect information about a topic from multiple documents and has to use more than one query to successfully complete the task. Examples we used included the collection of information for leisure activities, essential information for a specific purchase, and different recreational opportunities at a certain location. For a more detailed discussion on simple and complex tasks, as used in this study, see Singer, Danilov, & Norbisrath (2012). We also used pre- and post-task questionnaires. We showed the participants the task and asked them to judge its difficulty, and whether they felt able to find the correct information related to the stated information need, as well. After they had finished the task, we asked them the same questions again, this time relating to their actual performance.

### Data Collection

Data were collected in our lab in Hamburg, Germany. While users were allowed as much time as they needed to complete their tasks, we planned 30 minutes for each participant, which turned out to be more than sufficient. While users were allowed to use any search engine (or other search tool) they knew, all participants solely relied on the Google search engine. Participants first addressed the simple tasks and then judged the relevance of the results shown in that session before completing the complex tasks. Again, they judged the results after completing the task. Users were allowed to use their own queries. This leads to a more realistic setting, even though we are aware that the wording of the task descriptions may have influenced the way participants formulated queries. The users acted in interactive query sessions. They were able to refine their search queries to adjust the given search results to solve the tasks. We also asked users for assessing the difficulty of the given tasks and whether they found the correct information to solve the task. The corresponding questions were, "The search task was easy to solve (yes/no)", and, "I found the correct information (yes/no)", respectively. For their simple task, seven participants said it was not easy to solve it, and ten participants said that for their complex task. Overall, seven participants thought they did not find the correct information (three simple tasks, four complex tasks).

### Collecting session data

Participants started their search sessions by opening the Search Logger plugin in Firefox. First, they saw the simple task and answered the pre-task questionnaire for it. The participants were asked to assess the difficulty level, to estimate the time for the task and whether they would be able to find the correct information to solve the search task. Then, they were free to choose whatever tool(s) they wanted, search engine or not, to solve the task. They were allowed to spend as much time as they liked on the task, and when they were finished, they had to fill in the post-task questionnaire. They were again asked about the difficulty level, their actual time effort, the number of search queries, and whether they thought they found the correct information to solve the task. Session data collected by the Search Logger was then automatically loaded into the Relevance Assessment Tool. Processing the data there took a few minutes; therefore, participants had a short break before judging the results. After judging the results, the participants opened the Search Logger again to work on the complex task. The process was similar to the work on simple tasks. The users answered the same pre-task questionnaire, used a search engine or other tool(s) of their choice, and then answered the post-task questionnaire. Then, they judged the collected search results from their search session.

### Collecting relevance judgments

From the logged session data, the following were extracted: Search queries, search engine used, and results selected on the SERPs. The Relevance Assessment Tool then automatically queried the search engine the participants had used (which was Google in all cases) and collected the first ten results for each query. The same queries were sent to Bing, as well, and the results were collected accordingly. For practical reasons, we had to limit the maximum number of queries sent to each search engine to three. We assumed that it would not be reasonable to give participants more than 60 results (3 queries × 10 results × 2 search engines) to judge. The collected documents were presented to the participants in a random order. Results from both Google and Bing were mixed, and participants did not know the source of a particular result or whether they had selected that result during the first part of the study. Duplicates (i.e., URLs returned by both search engines) were filtered out, and a participant only had to judge them once. Participants were then asked to judge the relevance of each result. We asked users to judge each result first on a binary scale (relevant or not) and then on a 5-point Likert scale[3].

Due to limitations caused by actual user behavior during the test and technical difficulties we were not able to use all collected session data to create the result sets for judgments. Some participants simply used the descriptions on the SERPs to solve tasks; others relied on Wikipedia to find the required information, and therefore, did not use a search engine at all. In total, participants assessed 1,156 results from Google and 1,132 from Bing, from a total of 101 search tasks.

## RESULTS

### *Click distribution on SERPs*

First, we looked at the distribution of clicks on the Google SERPs (Fig. 2). The graph shows that participants heavily relied on the results order presented by the search engine. These findings are in agreement with previous studies (e.g., Goel et al., 2010; Pan et al., 2007). However, we have to keep in mind that in seven cases, participants only used the information on the SERPs or used other web resources like Wikipedia to solve the task, and therefore, these tasks did not result in any clicks on the SERPs.

### *Results precision (all results)*

One aim of our study was to compare the participants' preferred search engine (Google) with its major competitor, Bing. To answer RQ3, we investigated the differences in users' satisfaction with the retrieved results. We plotted precision graphs for all results from both search engines (Fig. 3).

We can see that Google results are, on average, judged better on all results positions. However, the differences between Google and Bing are small. This finding is again in agreement with previous studies (e.g., Lewandowski, 2015). Calculating standard precision measures for measuring retrieval performance does not show significant differences in retrieval effectiveness of the two search engines in most cases, except for MAP@5 (see Table 1).

[3] Labels of the scale were: 1 = completely irrelevant, 2 = irrelevant , 3 = relevant, 4 = highly relevant, 5 = completely relevant. We used the same scale as in Lewandowski (2015).

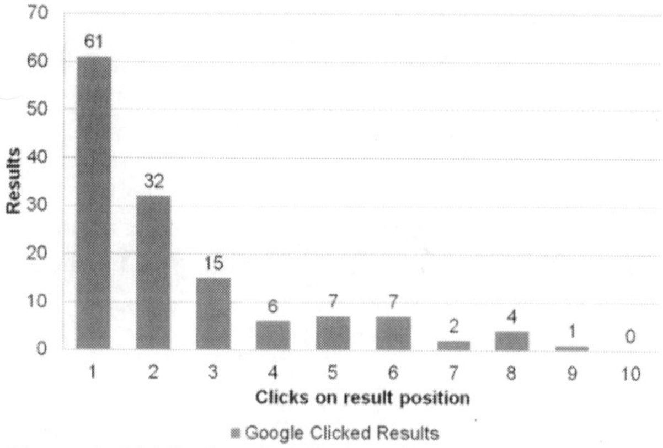


*Figure 2. Distribution of clicked results on result positions in Google*

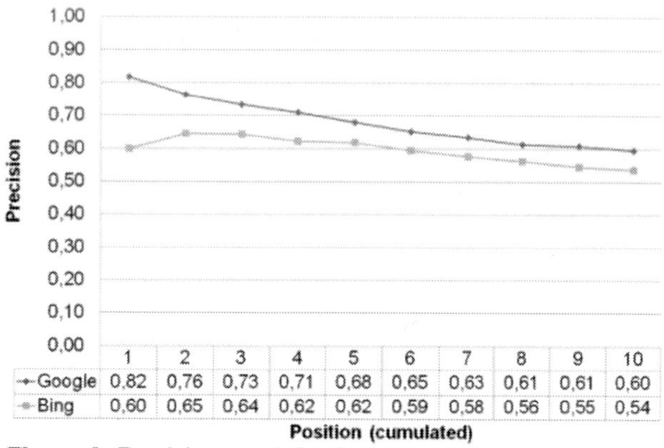


*Figure 3. Precision graph for Google and Bing results*

When looking at the more differentiated scale judgments (Fig. 4), we can see that Google outperforms Bing. Especially noteworthy are the results judged as "completely irrelevant," which account for approximately 36% of all Bing results.

### *Results precision (clicked results)*

We measured the precision of *clicked results* to investigate RQ2 and to find out if users judge selected results as being more relevant than results not selected during the tasks. As all users chose Google for their tasks, we only have click data for that search engine. The precision graph in Fig. 5 shows that regardless of results position, the precision of the clicked results falls at approximately 0.8, which is higher than the precision for all results, even those positioned first (see Fig. 3). This means that users are well able to judge the relevance of the results presented when selecting results based on descriptions (snippets) on the SERPs. The ratio of relevant results to relevant snippets is in agreement with results from a study by Lewandowski (2008) that compared users' judgments of the relevance of results descriptions with their judgments of the actual results.

Looking at the distribution of scale judgments (Fig. 6), we can see that users are well able to select results that they later (when they see the result instead of the snippet only) judge as highly relevant. 36% of the results selected are judged as completely relevant, and taken together, results judged as highly relevant or completely relevant account for approximately 58% of all selected results.

| | P@5 | P@1 0 | MAP @5 | MAP @10 | NDC G@5 | NDC G@1 0 |
|---|---|---|---|---|---|---|
| Google | 0.68 | 0.60 | 0.85 | 0.79 | 0.81 | 0.90 |
| Bing | 0.62 | 0.54 | 0.74 | 0.72 | 0.78 | 0.88 |

*Table 1. Retrieval results for Google and Bing using a two-tailed Student's t-test (α <= 0.05) results on time P@5 (p=0.256), P@10 (p=0.259), MAP@5 (p=0.035), MAP@10 (p=0.098), NDCG@5 (p=0.244) and NDCG@10 (p=0.181)*

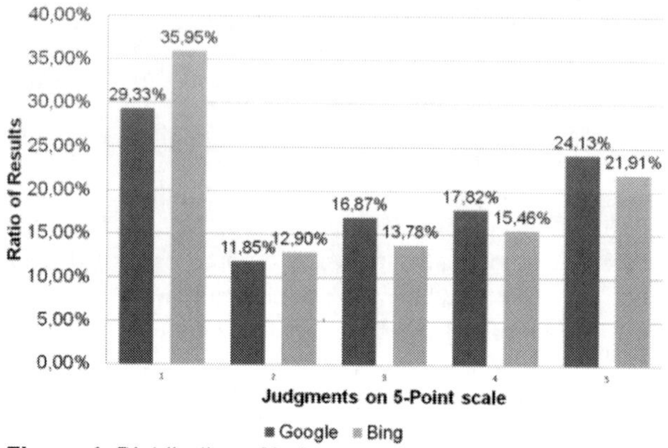


*Figure 4. Distribution of judgments on the 5-point scale*

When looking at the total number of clicks on each result position and their relevance as judged on the 5-point scale, we can see that results for the first positions are not only clicked more often but are also considered more relevant. It should be noted that even though participants were not able to see the results position, remembering documents seen during the first part of the study might have had an influence on the judgments.

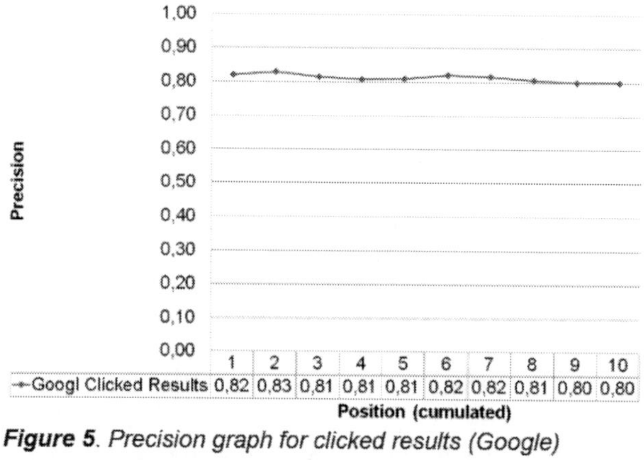


*Figure 5. Precision graph for clicked results (Google)*

Taken together, we can see that the relevance ranking (as expressed through results position and users' selections) and selection decisions based on results descriptions go hand in hand and lead to users getting relevant results to their searches.

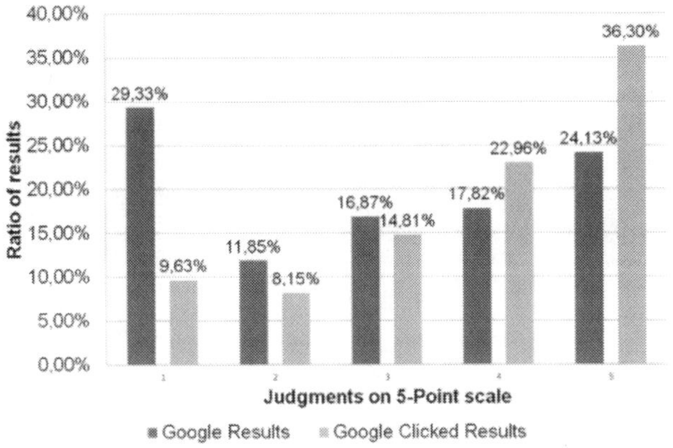


***Figure 6**. Distribution of judgments for clicked results*

### Results precision (task difficulty, task success)

Another aim of our study was to investigate how relevance judgments correlated with task difficulty and task success. We asked participants to assess the difficulty of a task and their success on it after they had finished it. First of all, we calculated the average precision for all search results for Google and Bing using the binary judgments. We found an average precision of 0.57 for Google and 0.50 for Bing. Most participants said they had found the correct information and judged a task as not being difficult. Even if we see differences in precision scores between both search engines, and also in comparison to the general average precision of both search engines, we cannot state any significant correlation between task difficulty and relevance judgments or task success and relevance judgments due to the low amount of assessed search results.

We also analyzed the judgments on the 5-point-scale. We found no significant differences between successful tasks and unsuccessful tasks. The same applies to 5-point scale judgments for difficult and not difficult tasks, except of results rated as completely irrelevant (1 point on the scale). In Google, participants rated 30% of the results as completely irrelevant, compared to 36% on Bing. Compared to all given judgments on the scale (see Fig. 4), participants tended to judge results lower when they rated a task as difficult.

### Overlap between search engines

To calculate the overlap of search results from Google and Bing we followed the method used by Spink and Jansen (Spink, Jansen, Blakely, & Koshman, 2006). First, we removed all query duplicates. This resulted in 119 search queries from 50 simple and 51 complex tasks, leading to 1,888 unduplicated search results. 1,545 results (81.8%) were unique to one search engine, 343 (18.2%) were shared by both search engines. 777 results were unique to Bing, 768 results unique to Google. This finding shows that even when the two search engines are comparable regarding relevance, a user may still benefit from using the other search engine to get different results.

### Simple vs. complex search tasks

Next, we investigate the influence of task complexity (RQ5). Table 3 shows the number of clicked results on the SERPs for simple and complex tasks. The data show that participants clicked on significantly more results for the complex tasks. However, the number of results selected is quite low. In some cases, it was possible to find an answer already on the SERP, so no results selection was needed. This explains the minimum numbers in Table 3.

| | | N | Min | Max | Mean | Std. Deviation |
|---|---|---|---|---|---|---|
| Time effort | Simple task | 64 | 6 | 1085 | 157.13 | 154.73 |
| | Complex task | 64 | 37 | 774 | 195.13 | 112.45 |
| Search queries | Simple task | 64 | 0 | 8 | 1.53 | 1.31 |
| | Complex task | 64 | 1 | 5 | 1.59 | 0.94 |
| Clicked results | Simple task | 64 | 0 | 5 | 1.48 | 0.96 |
| | Complex task | 64 | 0 | 7 | 1.81 | 1.37 |

***Table 3**. Statistics on tasks complexity using a two-tailed Student's t-test ($\alpha <= 0.05$) on time effort ($p=0.114$), search queries ($p=0.757$) and clicked results ($p=0.119$)*

Details about average time needed to complete the tasks and the average number of search queries used are also shown in Table 3. Surprisingly, there are no significant differences between the number of queries needed for the simple and the complex tasks. However, there is a significant difference between the median times needed to complete these two task types. While other studies found task time and queries per task to be good measures for distinguishing between simple and complex tasks (Singer, Norbisrath, et al., 2012), our data may be explained by user characteristics. Furthermore, since our users worked first on the simple tasks and then on the complex ones, it may well be that they put more effort into the first task and therefore spent more time and queries on them.

## DISCUSSION

As users often solely rely on a single search engine, user studies comparing different search engines are flawed because users are aware of the search engines that are used. Therefore, branding effects may play a larger role than the actual differences in results quality. Furthermore, when users are accustomed to a certain user interface, they may face problems with other interfaces and therefore judge the quality of these search engines as being lower. The method presented in this paper addresses this problem by letting users choose the search engine of their preference and then comparing datasets from that search engine to the results from another one.

In our study, users solely relied on using Google. Although users were free to use any search tool they liked, none of our 64 participants decided to use any alternative (RQ1). However, we can only speculate on the reasons for this, the most obvious one being that users are so used to Google that they did not think of any alternatives. This is also illustrated by Google's overwhelming market share in Germany.

Regarding RQ2, we see that results actually selected are judged better than the results not selected. From this, we can see that users are well able to make their decisions about relevant results based on results positions and descriptions, meaning that the snippets are helpful and users can use them to their benefit. This leads us to question the exclusive use of precision-based measures in search engine results evaluations. It may even be questionable to use the whole results set in retrieval effectiveness studies. While it is surely important to know how many results are irrelevant when a larger number of results needs to be examined (at least on the SERPs), some irrelevant results may not be too problematic when Web searchers tend to select only one or a few results that just need to be "good enough."

Regarding RQ3, we found that the results from Google were judged as being more relevant than those from Bing, but the differences are not too big (and for most measures applied not significant). This is in line with findings from previous studies (Lewandowski, 2015) and suggests that it is not superior quality that explains users' heavy reliance on Google, but other factors probably play a role, as well. This leads to the conclusion that while Bing also produces a large ratio of relevant results, there is no motivation for users to switch to Bing as their standard search engine. This would only be the case if Bing produced results of an appreciable better quality. However, users may have good reasons for using Bing as an *additional* search engine. This is illustrated by the low overlap between the results from the two search engines.

Regarding RQ4 and RQ5, we tried to investigate if task success and task difficulty have influences on the relevance judgments of the participants in the study. We found differences in binary judgments, as well as in graded judgments on the 5-point scale. Users tended to judge results lower when they were not able to find the correct answer and when they rated a search task as difficult. However, we cannot assume a statistically significant correlation between task success and relevance judgments or task difficulty and relevance judgments because, probably due to the low amount of collected search results.

## CONCLUSION

In this study, 64 participants each worked on two tasks, using whatever search tool they liked, and formulating their own queries. Their log data was automatically analyzed immediately after task completion, and results from the search engine used for solving the tasks (which in all cases was Google) and from a competing search engine (Bing) were automatically collected. All collected results were given to the same user who conducted the search for judging their relevance. With this approach, we were able to compare the results quality of the two search engines, controlling for brand effects and interface issues.

Maybe the most important finding of this study is that while participants judged Google's results as slightly more relevant than Bing's, the differences are not too big. Only considering results quality, we can assume that users would also be satisfied with using Bing, as we assume that they would not recognize the small differences. Furthermore, we found that the overlap between the results from the two search engines is low. Therefore, users would benefit from using Bing (or other search engines) as an addition to Google, as they would get a different picture to their information need.

Our research has several limitations. Results could have been influenced by choice of participants, although we took great care of having a varied sample regarding age and gender. More severely, our choice of tasks might have affected the results, i.e., the search engines could have performed differently when using different tasks (cf. Lewandowski, 2008). However, to avoid this effect, we used a large variety of tasks, distributed randomly over users.

On the software side, the contribution of this paper is a new framework for interactive information retrieval evaluation, focusing on Web search, combining a task-based user study with a system-oriented retrieval effectiveness study. Our research offers a framework for studying actual users' behavior in correlation with relevance judgments more deeply than before. The major advantage to this approach is that it allows studies with users formulating their own queries, going through whole search sessions, and then judging the relevance of their own results. Furthermore, we can use the Relevance Assessment Tool to collect results from search engines that users did not use and inject these results into the set of documents the participants are given to judge.

While our research was designed as a lab study, the software could also be used in any setting where participants use a Firefox browser. All the user needs to do is select the "Firefox to go" installation option provided by the tool.

In future research, we plan to conduct further studies using the framework presented in this paper. A limitation of our study was that while our new approach was presented, we were not able to systematically compare it with conventional retrieval effectiveness studies. A first step for future work would be to set up two such studies and then compare whether our approach leads to more meaningful results. Another step would be conducting studies with bigger samples to investigate correlations between user-based metrics and relevance judgments. Conceivably, such studies could be accomplished as long-term studies in "natural" environments.

## REFERENCES


Bar-Ilan, J., Keenoy, K., Yaari, E., & Levene, M. (2007). User rankings of search engine results. *Journal of the American Society for Information Science and Technology*, *58*(9), 1254–1266.

Behnert, C., & Lewandowski, D. (2017). A framework for designing retrieval effectiveness studies of library information systems using human relevance assessments. *Journal of Documentation*, *73*(3), 509-527. http://doi.org/10.1108/JD-08-2016-0099

Belkin, N., Cole, M., & Liu, J. (2009). A model for evaluation of interactive information retrieval. In *Proceedings of the SIGIR 2009 workshop on the future of IR evaluation* (pp. 7–8).

Borlund, P. (2003). The IIR evaluation model: A framework for evaluation of interactive information retrieval systems. *Information Research*, *8*(3). Retrieved from http://informationr.net/ir/8-3/paper152.html

Capra, R. (2010). HCI browser: A tool for studying web search behavior. In *ASIST 2010* (pp. 1–2).

comScore. (2013). *Europe digital future in focus: Key insights from 2012 and what they mean for the coming year. Report*. Retrieved from http://www.comscore.com/layout/set/popup/Request/Presentations/2013/2013_Europe_Digital_Future_in_Focus_Report_PDF_Request?req=slides&pre=2013+Europe+Digital+Future+in+Focus

Fox, S., Karnawat, K., Mydland, M., Dumais, S., & White, T. (2005). Evaluating implicit measures to improve web search. *ACM Transactions on Information Systems*, *23*(2), 147–168. http://doi.org/10.1145/1059981.1059982

Goel, S., Broder, A., Gabrilovich, E., & Pang, B. (2010). Anatomy of the long tail: Ordinary people with extraordinary tastes. In *Proceedings of the third ACM international conference on web search and data mining* (pp. 201–210). ACM.

Gordon, M., & Pathak, P. (1999). Finding information on the World Wide Web: The retrieval effectiveness of search engines. *Information Processing & Management*, *35*(2), 141–180.

Griesbaum, J. (2004). Evaluation of three German search engines: Altavista.de, Google.de and Lycos.de. *Information Research*, *9*(4). Retrieved from http://informationr.net/ir/9-4/paper189.html

Hawking, D., Craswell, N., Bailey, P., & Griffiths, K. (2001). Measuring search engine quality. *Information Retrieval*, *4*(1), 33–59.

Jansen, B. J. (2006). The wrapper: An open source application for logging user–system interactions during searching studies. In *Logging traces of web activity: The mechanics of data collection workshop at WWW 2006* (pp. 1–4).

Jansen, B. J. (2007). The comparative effectiveness of sponsored and nonsponsored links for Web e-commerce queries. *ACM Transactions on the Web*, *1*(1), article 3.

Jansen, B. J., Zhang, M., & Schultz, C. D. (2009). Brand and its effect on user perception of search engine performance. *Journal of the American Society for Information Science and Technology*, *60*(8), 1572–1595.

Joachims, T., Granka, L., Pan, B., Hembrooke, H., Radlinski, F., & Gay, G. (2007). Evaluating the accuracy of implicit feedback from clicks and query reformulations in web search. *ACM Transactions on Information Systems*, *25*(2), article 7. http://doi.org/10.1145/1229179.1229181

Keane, M. T., O'Brien, M., & Smyth, B. (2008). Are people biased in their use of search engines? *Communications of the ACM*, *51*(2), 49–52.

Kelly, D. (2009). Methods for evaluating interactive information retrieval systems with users. *Foundations and Trends in Information Retrieval*, *3*(1—2), 1–224. http://doi.org/10.1561/1500000012

Lewandowski, D. (2008). The retrieval effectiveness of web search engines: Considering results descriptions. *Journal of Documentation*, *64*(6), 915–937.

Lewandowski, D. (2011). The influence of commercial intent of search results on their perceived relevance. In *Proceedings of the 2011 iConference* (pp. 452–458). ACM. http://doi.org/10.1145/1940761.1940823

Lewandowski, D. (2012). A framework for evaluating the retrieval effectiveness of search engines. In C. Jouis (Ed.), *Next generation search engines: Advanced models for information retrieval* (pp. 456–479). Hershey, PA: IGI Global.

Lewandowski, D. (2015). Evaluating the retrieval effectiveness of web search engines using a representative query sample. *Journal of the Association for Information Science and Technology*, *66*(9), 1763–1775. http://doi.org/10.1002/asi.23304

Lewandowski, D., & Sünkler, S. (2013). Designing search engine retrieval effectiveness tests with RAT. *Information Services & Use*, *33*(1), 53–59.

Machill, M., Neuberger, C., Schweiger, W., & Wirth, W. (2004). Navigating the internet: A study of German-language search engines. *European Journal of Communication*, *19*(3), 321–347.

Mayr, P., & Tosques, F. (2005). Google web APIs - An instrument for webometric analyses? In P. Ingwersen & B. Larsen (Eds.), Proceedings of the 10th international conference of the International Society for Scientometrics and Informetrics (ISSI 2005). Stockholm (Sweden) (pp. 677–678).

Pan, B., Hembrooke, H., Joachims, T., Lorigo, L., Gay, G., & Granka, L. (2007). In Google we trust: Users' decisions on rank, position, and relevance. *Journal of Computer-Mediated Communication*, *12*(3), 801–823.

Petrescu, P. (2014). Google organic click-through rates in 2014 - Moz. Retrieved April 25, 2016, from https://moz.com/blog/google-organic-click-through-rates-in-2014

Purcell, K., Brenner, J., & Raine, L. (2012). *Search engine use 2012. Search*. Washington, DC. Retrieved from http://pewinternet.org/~/media/Files/Reports/2012/PIP_Search_Engine_Use_2012.pdf

Schaer, P., Mayr, P., Sünkler, S., & Lewandowski, D. (2016). How relevant is the long tail? A relevance assessment study on million short. In N. Fuhr, P. Quaresma, T. Gonçalves, B. Larsen, K. Balog, C. Macdonald, … N. Ferro (Eds.), *CLEF 2016* (Vol. 9822, pp. 227–233). Cham: Springer International Publishing. http://doi.org/10.1007/978-3-319-44564-9_20

Singer, G., Danilov, D., & Norbisrath, U. (2012). Complex search: Aggregation, discovery, and synthesis. *Proceedings of the Estonian Academy of Sciences*, *61*(2), 89–106. http://doi.org/10.3176/proc.2012.2.02

Singer, G., Norbisrath, U., & Lewandowski, D. (2012). Ordinary search engine users assessing difficulty, effort, and outcome for simple and complex search tasks. In *Proceedings of the fourth information interaction in context symposium* (pp. 110–119). New York: ACM.

Singer, G., Norbisrath, U., & Lewandowski, D. (2013). Ordinary search engine users carrying out complex search tasks. *Journal of Information Science*, *39*(3), 346–358.

Singer, G., Norbisrath, U., Vainikko, E., Kikkas, H., & Lewandowski, D. (2011). Search Logger: Analysing exploratory search tasks. In *SAC2011. Proceedings of the 2011 ACM symposium on applied computing* (pp. 751–756). New York: ACM.

Spink, A., Jansen, B. J., Blakely, C., & Koshman, S. (2006). A study of results overlap and uniqueness among major web search engines. *Information Processing & Management*, *42*(5), 1379–1391.

Sünkler, S. (2013). Software-Tools für die Evaluierung von Suchmaschinen. In D. Lewandowski (Ed.), *Handbuch Internet-Suchmaschinen 3: Suchmaschinen zwischen Technik und Gesellschaft* (pp. 223–252). Heidelberg: Akademische Verlagsgesellschaft Aka.

Tague-Sutcliffe, J. (1992). The pragmatics of information retrieval experimentation, revisited. *Information Processing & Management*, *28*(4), 467–490.

Tawileh, W., Griesbaum, J., & Mandl, T. (2010). Evaluation of five web search engines in Arabic language. In M. Atzmüller, D. Benz, A. Hotho, & G. Stumme (Eds.), *Proceedings of LWA2010* (pp. 1–8). Kassel, Germany. Retrieved from http://www.kde.cs.uni-kassel.de/conf/lwa10/papers/ir1.pdf

Tremel, A. (2010). *Suchen, finden–glauben?: Die Rolle der Glaubwürdigkeit von Suchergebnissen bei der Nutzung von Suchmaschinen.* Ludwig-Maximilians-Universität München. Retrieved from http://edoc.ub.uni-muenchen.de/12418/

Voorhees, E. M. (2009). I come not to bury Cranfield, but to praise it. In *Proceedings of the workshop on human-computer interaction and retrieval* (pp. 13–16). http://doi.org/10.1080/2158379X.2013.849369

Westerwick, A. (2013). Effects of sponsorship, web site design, and Google ranking on the credibility of online information. *Journal of Computer-Mediated Communication*, *18*(2), 80–97. http://doi.org/10.1111/jcc4.12006

White, R. (2016). *Interactions with search systems*. New York: Cambridge University Press.

# Developing Young Children's Technology-based Communication Skills Using iPads and Creation Apps: An Action Study

**Monika Tavernier**
*German Swiss International School & The University of Hong Kong, Hong Kong. Mtavernier@learning.gsis.edu.hk*

**Xiao Hu**
*The University of Hong Kong, Hong Kong. xiaoxhu@hku.hk*

## ABSTRACT

**Today's young children are exposed to new information technology and communication practices from early on, but the usage activities they engage in may not help fulfilling their needs in developing technology-based communication skills. This article presents preliminary findings of an action study with eight children of four to five years old in using one creation app, SeeSaw, to create artifacts to express themselves in ways that suit their personal abilities. A sequence of 11 teacher-initiated activities guided the children towards the development of age appropriate technology-based communication skills (TBCS). Digital artifacts produced by the children and videos of learning sessions were collected and analyzed using a thematic content analysis approach. The findings reveal that four- to five-year-old children acquire TBCS quickly and progressively. They are also able to use their developing TBCS effectively to communicate their experiences, knowledge and ideas using a variety of audio and visual elements. This study contributes to the literature of new learning opportunities in this information environment, with a focus on the user group of young children which has been understudied in information science.**

## KEYWORDS

early childhood education, technology, communication skills, iPad, applications, digital content creation

## INTRODUCTION

In the information society today, wide ranges of mobile technologies are used in everyday life. They are ubiquitous, and even kindergarten children have some sense of their operation and purpose. For more than two decades, scholars, governments, schools, and teachers have been exploring how different technologies such as desktop computers and digital cameras can be best used for educational purposes. It was found that behavior shaping gamified learning software can be helpful in learning certain predetermined learning contents such as phonetics or numbers (Plowman & Stephen, 2005; Clements, 2002). Currently, the focus of interest lays on mobile technologies such as tablet (Parmar, 2014; Falloon, 2013). Tablets are perceived to be more appropriate for young children. Their touch gesture operation and multi-functionality are perceived as major advantages (Falloon, 2013b). Additionally, creation apps allow user to easily create and share digital content and progress from content consumers to producers. Open-ended creation applications allow flexible implementation and inspire teachers to explore new uses of these technologies in kindergarten. Hence, the combination of these factors and creation apps may enhance and transform teaching and learning in similar ways as aforementioned behavior shaping gamified learning software. However, little has been known about the learning effect that digital content creation has on young children.

Since the creation of content (e.g. drawings or stories) is a form of communication (Bragg, 2011; Pezzica, Pinto, Bigozzi, & Vezzani, 2015), this study investigates how a creation app, SeeSaw, can support the development of communication skills. In the context of this study, the meaning of communication skills is a combination of the definition of communication and communication competences. Communication describes the effective sharing of thoughts, questions, and ideas to a target audience (Kivunja, 2015). Communication competence refers to the ability to effectively use oral, written, and non-verbal communication skills to inform, instruct, motivate, persuade, and share ideas (Dilley, Fishlock, & Plucker, 2015). Therefore, this study uses a working definition of communication skills that suggests: *Technology-based communication skills (TBCS) are one's ability to effectively use different means of digital communication (in this case photo, drawing, audio recording, text) to externalize and share some form of information, ideas, or experiences with others.*

This work contributes to the emerging field of new learning opportunities enabled by ubiquitous digital technologies. In particular, this study focuses on digital creation activities for facilitating learning of young children. It follows the lead of studies conducted in primary schools that observed positive effects creation apps had on students' learning and motivation (Goodwin, 2012), and pushes forward the research frontier to kindergarten level. Based on this background this study sets out to answer the following two research questions:

80th Annual Meeting of the Association for Information Science & Technology, Washington, DC, VA | Oct. 27-Nov. 1, 2017

1. How can teachers support four to five years old children's development of technology-based communication skills?
2. How do four to five years old children use technology-based communication skills?

## LITERATURE REVIEW

Young children use a wide range of communication tools (Kinnunen & Einarsdottir, 2013) including drawings, storytelling, dance, role play (Rinaldi, 2001). Drawings have a special place within children's communication repertoire. They can serve as a means to illustrate their inside perspectives (Braggs, 2011), reflect distinctive features of represented experiences (Bruner, 1964), and voice their understandings of the world (Hardy, 1977). Children create meaning as they clarify things for themselves during the drawing process (Kinnunen & Einarsdottir, 2013). Therefore, using drawings or artifacts as a way to communicate is important when we consider young children's communication skills.

With the rapid changes of technology, and the growing acceptance and use of mobile technologies, it is possible to consider mobile technologies as a new tool in our cultural toolbox (Wohlwend, 2010). They have become a new form of communication that shapes the way we use language. People communicate using text, voice messages, emojis and a range of abbreviations called texting language. Although, young children may not have their own device or engage in using texting language, they can participate in today's technology communication to some extent (Chiong & Shuler, 2010). It is argued that allowing young children to use mobile technologies to communicate relates to learning to use a cultural-specific tool and the related skills (Wohlwend, 2010).

To date most studies on young children's use of tablets remained explorative and contributed to the shaping of implementation ideas and identifying the emerging educational potentials that these technologies may have for young children. The implications of these studies were limited to the practical classification of applications (Goodwin, 2012; Falloon, 2013b; The Michael Cohen Group and USDOE, 2011), application type related higher and lower order thinking processes (Goodwin, 2012; Falloon, 2013b), documentations of children's ability to operate tablets and applications (Couse & Chen, 2010; Falloon,2013; The Michael Cohen Group and USDOE, 2011), and the efficacy of behavior shaping application on predetermined learning outcomes (Yelland & Gilbert, 2012; Goodwin, 2012; Falloon, 2013, Beschorner et al., 2013; Parmar, 2014). While there have been other studies on young children's use of tablets and apps, no studies focused on the use of creation apps. The rich history of computer-assisted learning showed a particular interest in behavioral shaping activities that enhance children's learning of language and arithmetic skills (Kelly & Schorger, 2001; Clements, 2002). Few studies (Couse & Chen, 2010; Einarsdottir, 2005; Hertzog & Klein, 2005), however, exposed young children to digital creation and open-ended activities. The review of these studies revealed that further investigations are needed on young children's digital content creation activities and their implications on learning and teaching, especially in the areas of knowledge and skills acquisition, pedagogy practices, and long-term implementation effects. To fill the gaps, this study focuses on young children's use of creation apps and technology-based communication skills (TBCS).

## METHODOLOGY

This article is based on one action study that is anchored in the constructivist paradigm (Guba & Lincoln, 1994), adopts the action research approach, and aims to construct theories from the emerging understandings. It is part of an ongoing explanatory study for the same goals, which employs qualitative data collection methods, including: 1) observations (observation records and videos), 2) digital artifacts, and 3) participant feedback. The digital artifacts and observation records were prioritized in this article for the analysis of young children's TBCS.

### *Sampling Frame*

The purposive sample involved one group of children attending an international kindergarten in Hong Kong that follows with the international baccalaureate primary years program. The sample group includes eight children ranging from four to five years. All twenty children in the class were invited to join the study, however, only the parents of eight children provided full consent for their children to participate. The sample represents children that have a middle class socioeconomic background which allows them to attend a private, non-subsidized international kindergarten. These children are not technology savvy, but are likely to be exposed to mobile devices in the out-of-school and in-school environments. However, their independent and purposeful engagement with these devices may vary widely.

### *Ethical Considerations*

In addition to attaining the school principals, teachers', and parents' consent, the children's informal consent was considered. All activities were voluntary, children decided by themselves if they wanted to join the activity. The digital camera was always visible to the children to make sure that they are aware that they are being filmed. Therefore, their decision to join an iPad activity was deemed as their personal and temporary consent (Stephen, McPake, Plowman and Berch-Heyman, 2008). Young children are a special group of participants. Due to their young age, they are particularly vulnerable and can be easily influenced and manipulated by more experienced others, such as their teachers, and may be emotionally affected by a change of location and people around them (Hill, 2005). So, all activities took place within their zone of comfort: their classroom, surrounded by the things they knew and the people they trusted. To keep the distraction of the class routines to a minimum, all iPad activities took place during free play times. As a result, the children's participation varied and was based on their own decision. The children's voluntary participation in the iPad activities ensured that the children felt comfortable during the activities and allowed them to leave when they felt they were done.

### *Study Design*

Eleven pedagogical activities were designed in this study to help the children familiarize with the device, application, learning procedure, and related behaviors. The 'Apple Classroom of Tomorrow' (ACOT; Dwyer, Ringstaff, Haymore, & Sandholtz, 1994), as presented in Table 1, was adopted as the framework of designing these activities.

| Stage | Observable Actions |
|---|---|
| Entry | Learning of the basics of the technology & app |
| Adoption | Use technology to support traditional information sharing |
| Adaption | Integrate technology into existing class activities |
| Appropriation | Develop new cooperative, project-based teaching and learning |
| Invention | Discover new uses of technology for teaching and learning |

Note: Highlighted stages are those involved in this study.

***Table 1**. ACOT – Stages of teacher's technology integration*

The eleven activities are detailed in Table 2, including descriptions of the activities and the stage of technology integration (see ACOT, table 1) the activity is related to. Each activity followed a similar repertoire:

1. children gathered in a circle around the teaching adult.
2. The adult presented the activity.
3. The adult demonstrated the activity, involving the children in the description of the sequence of action and purpose of each action.
4. The children received one iPad for every two children and engaged in the activity.
5. The adult monitored and supported the activities.

At all times, a guiding topic was provided (e.g., take a photo of the environment and find shapes) to frame the children's activities. Further, a selection of functions (photo, video, audio, drawing) was suggested to inspire the children's artifact creation. Activity 2, 5, 11 were conducted by the teacher while the rest by the researcher. This ratio was not preplanned and depended on the teacher's availability on the day of observation. During all activities, the children decided how they made use of the functions and developed the content of their artifacts by themselves.

| # | Activity Description |
|---|---|
| | Stage: Entry |
| 1 | Introduce a friend: Take a photo of your partner and add a voice recording to introduce the partner |
| 2 | Share your day's activity: Take a photo of an artifact of your activity (e.g., a Christmas crafts). Add a voice recording that tells us 1. what you made; 2. How you made it; and What it is for? |
| 3 | Toy Tracing: Choose a toy, take a photo of the toy, draw around the toy, and add a voice recording that explains what toy this is and why you chose it. |
| | Stage: Adaption |
| 4 | Count and trace: Select one set of small objects and a number. Take a photo of the objects, draw around as many objects as the number you selected. |
| 5 | Comment: Look at the images we shared with you. Use the comment function to share what you see and what it makes you think of. |
| 6 | Kids Teach 1: Introduce the iPad and app to your partner. Show him/her how to add a new artifact, take a photo, draw on it and add a voice recording. |
| 7 | Kids Teach 2: Introduce the iPad and app to your partner. Show him/her how to add a new artifact, take a photo, draw on it and add a voice recording. |
| 8 | Comment, Like, Listen: 8.1. Review your peers' work. Use heart to show that you like it, add a voice comment to ask a question about his/her work. 8.2. Look at the shared image, listen to the voice recording. Answer the spoken task using either the commenting function. |
| | Stage: Appropriations |
| 9 | Shape Constructions: Look at the photos of shape constructions. Choose the one you like. Take a photo add a recording about what you think it is. Then use the shapes and create your own constructions. Take a photo and explain what you created. |
| 10 | 2D Shapes: Take a photo of our environment at school. Look for 2D shapes in the photo. Draw to highlight the shapes that you found and document explain your findings. |
| 11 | Numicons: Use the Numicon jigsaw and create tens. Take a photo of your jigsaw combinations and share your findings. You may use the drawing and voice recording function. |

***Table 2**. Overview of activities*

The planned learning outcomes focused on developing children's ability to digital artifacts using photos, drawings, speech or text or combinations of such that

- embed the children's accurate, complete, and believable views/knowledge/ideas about a given topic (intrinsic quality);
- are relevant to the topic, useful for the child's reflection of own skills and knowledge, and include an appropriate in the amount of embedded information/knowledge/ideas/views (contextual quality);
- are unique, can be read and understood by others (representational quality).

The children are not specifically taught how to achieve high levels of intrinsic, contextual, and representational quality. Personalized feedback, prompts and the option to review and listen back to their artifacts to develop children's self-efficacy to increase the IQ of their artifacts. The data set included the digital artifacts, videos of the activity.

### *Data Collection and Analysis*

The data set included the digital artifacts, videos of the activity sessions, and the researcher's notes including activity plans and reflections, teacher's written and verbal feedback and children's verbal feedback. The researcher joined the class once a week to either observe a teacher lead an activity or lead an activity herself. Each activity lasted about 25 minutes, including the non-screen time (e.g. activity introduction and demonstration) and actual screen time. The activities were video recorded from the moment the teacher started the activity until the last student finished it. By the time of writing this, eleven iPad activities were conducted, producing 107 digital artifacts and about 300 minutes of video recordings. The artifacts, videos and transcripts of both were analyzed for this paper, as they provide direct evidence for the children's TBCS.

### *Data Analysis*

All data was reviewed and analyzed following a thematic content analysis approach. The coding scheme for the artifacts (see figure 1) was based on Cameron and Dickfos (Elevator Pitch Assessment, EPA; 2014) and McCabe and Bliss' (Narrative Assessment Profile, NPA; 2003) work on narrative and communication skills. These were deemed suitable, because their work focused on the verbal narrative abilities and content of children's narrations. The data embedded in the artifacts consists mainly of these two elements. Using similar criteria to evaluate the verbal and visual content helped to compare the two (e.g. information quality and topic maintenance; see Figure 1).

To monitor and evaluate the children's developing TBCS, each element was scored following a scale of four:

0 – no audio or respectively visuals included in an artifact,

1 – audio or visual element were of low quality.

2 – audio or visual elements are of appropriate quality.

3 – audio or visual elements are of excellent.

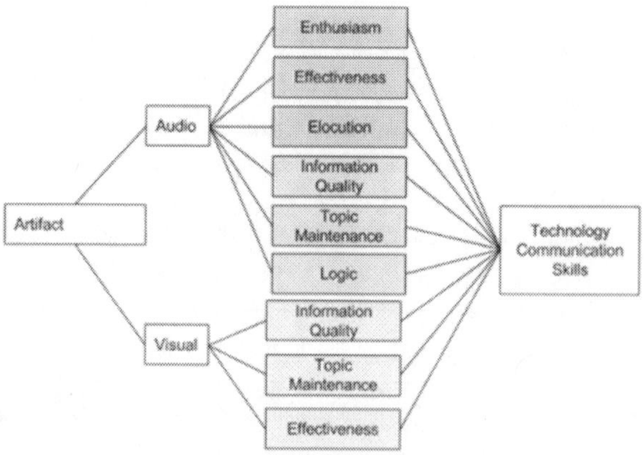


***Figure 1**. Coding scheme*

While enthusiasm, effectiveness and elocution of the verbal audio elements were evaluated independently, IQ and topic maintenance of the audio and visual elements were scored regarding the given activity topic (see Table 2). The non-convergence triangulation (Patton, 2002) of the audio and visual elements lead to the evaluation of the children's TBCS: one's ability to make effective use of the different means of digital communication tools to externalize and share some form of information idea, or experience with others (Gerald's, 2015; Kivunja, 2015; Dilley, Fishlock, & Plucker, 2015).

| Interaction | Definition |
|---|---|
| Demon-strating | Showing (Physical and oral) how to do something. |
| Enjoying | Showing pleasure (movement, smile, etc.) in features |
| Explaining | Explaining (oral) illustrations |
| Instructing | Tell the children what they shall do in general or with a certain tool (oral and gesture) |
| Managing | Intervening in turn-taking, arranging pairs, manage iPads |
| Monitoring | Observing students (gestural) |
| Prompting | Making suggestions (oral) |
| Feedback | Giving encouragement, smiling at child, praising |
| Supporting | Offering help when needed and providing emotional support (physical, oral, gestural) |

***Table 3**. Guided interactions*

The video data was used to analyze the interactions between the adult, the children and the creative app. Preliminary findings were based on Plowman and Stephen's (2007) 'Guided

Interactions' (see Table 3), which encompasses all interactions between teacher, child and technology. It classifies the interactions into direct and indirect interactions. For this study, direct interactions such as physical actions, oral and facial expressions, and gestures are most important. Both enable teachers to facilitate the purposeful use of technology and support children's learning through engagement with technology. Every two minutes the adult's interactions with the children were summarized in one descriptive word that aimed to capture the overall purpose of adult's interactions during every two minutes.

The coding process was done by two coders, the researcher and an independent coder with five years of teaching experiences in early childhood settings and a Master degree in education. The inter-code reliability was 63% percent. The areas that needed refinement in the codes included the definition and use of 'supporting' and the identification of a code that captures interactions that help children understand the task and the use of the app functions. Currently, such actions are embedded within demonstrating, explaining and prompting. A second round of coding is planned for the future and should lead to an improved inter-coder reliability.

## FINDINGS AND DISCUSSION

The quantified findings are presented in two graphs that show the triangulated average development of all children's verbal TBCS (evident in their speech) and their verbal content (evident in their understandable outcomes of recorded speech, see Figure 2), and their visual TBCS (evident in the drawings and photos; see Figure 3).

### *Overview of TBCS*

The children's verbal, verbal content and visual TBCS appear to develop simultaneously and in similar ways. The main difference are the activities when the score reaches 0, which means there is no evidence. Activity 4 and 7 did not require a voice recording and as such the average score reaches 0. Similarly, activity 5 and 8 asked the children to verbally comment and as a result the children did not include visuals in their digital creations.

While the evident TBCS are similar during the entry and adoption stage, they differ during the appropriation stage. The verbal TBCS scores slightly decrease after activity 8, while the visual TBCS score slightly increase.

The video data showed that the first activity was supported by two adults and included a lot of scaffolding in form of demonstration, modeling, and guidance, therefore the average scores are high. After this activity, the adults' scaffolding changed, in response to the children's developing skills. This allowed the children room to explore with application's functions, experiment with them and develop their own TBCS and practices.

After the entry stage, the children were competent app users and the adults' scaffolding of operation skills were not necessary. Therefore, the children created their verbal components of their work independently. The adults monitored the children' activity and interfered rarely in the creation of their verbal content, leading to the decrease of the verbal content TBCS after the adaption stage.

The average scores of the visual TBCS are slightly higher during the entry stage. However, compared to the verbal TBCS they decrease more during the adoption stage and thereafter increase steadily. Compared to their ability of maintaining a given topic with their visuals, the IQ and effectiveness of their visuals are slightly less strong. The video data showed again that the adult's scaffolding influenced this development. Once the children achieved a good amount of technical competence to create visuals, the adult's scaffolding decreased allowing them the freedom to apply their skills by themselves, refine their competencies through hands-on experiences and develop visual TBCS. Thus, the monitoring of the visuals' creation was less direct and lead to the decrease of the IQ and effectiveness.

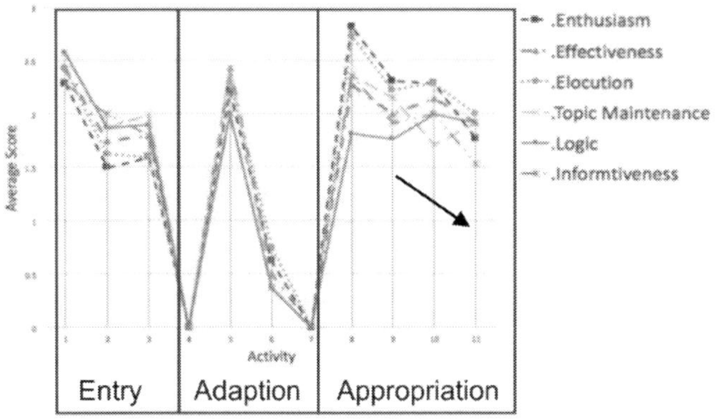


***Figure 2**. Average audio TBCS*

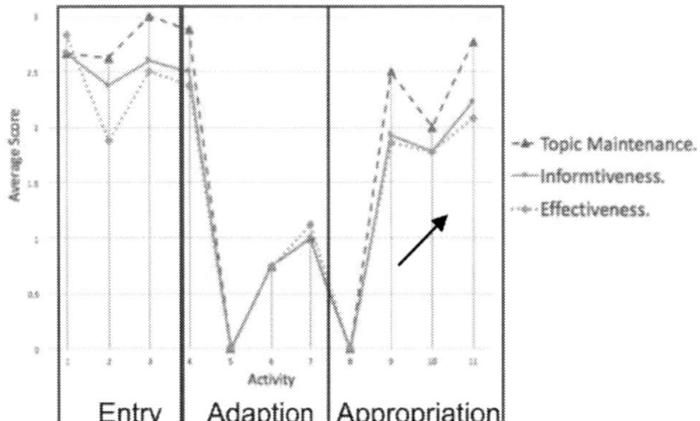


***Figure 3**. Average visual content TBCS*

### *Audio TBCS*

The analysis of the verbal TBCS allow three main observations. Firstly, after the first activity there is a drop of evident verbal speech TBCS. Secondly, after the second activity, the evident and measurable verbal speech TBCS increase until activity 8. Thirdly, after the average scores of all but one (logic) verbal TBCS decrease after activity 8, the scores remain around the 'appropriate level (score 2).

During activity one the teacher and researcher supported the children by modeling and gently guiding them to the desired behaviors. This included encouraging them to 'listening back' to their recordings and the recommendation to redo them, if they could not be heard or understood well. Therefore, the audio outcomes were highly influenced by the active involvement of the adults in the creation process.

The justification of this lays in the novelty of the activity and the aim to help children familiarize with the device and app, while accommodating their different levels of iPad operation skills. It was known that some children had pre-study iPad experience, but these experiences mostly related to games and coloring activities. Therefore, it was important to give the children plenty of support and ensure that they would experience positive feelings (e.g. competency, joy, personal achievement) towards the in-class iPad activities. The provided support and encouragement reduced the risk of frustration due to lacking iPad and app competencies. Further, the listening back and reviewing of their work helped them experience positive feelings such as pride about the first digitally create multimedia artifacts. These first experience paved the way for all the following activities in terms of motivation and usage repertories.

The analysis of the adults' interactions with the children showed the changing interactions. Table 4 shows the observable changes of interaction types across the activities. This overview needs more refinement in the future to include all the adults' interactions when they occur, instead of using a summarized code to capture all interactions that occurred within every two minutes. Also, supporting interactions often took place throughout any activity and they were found to overlap with others such as explaining. So, the definition of supporting needs revision and was therefore excluded of the current analysis. However, the current two-minute approach allowed the comparison of interactions between the activities.

The most obvious changes happened after activity 4. The adults were more likely to engage in modeling and explaining interaction in the first four activities. After that they were more able to provide feedback and prompt children's thinking and actions. Helping the children with their increasing technology operation competencies required less time after activity four. This allowed the adult to change the scaffolding activities from using individualized modeling and explaining to using prompting and feedback to gently influence the direction of the children's actions.

Interestingly, instructing and demonstrating are evident in nearly all activities. This is due to the activity design that always started with some form of task description. The video transcripts showed that this included either very clear instructions or a demonstration of an activity. Both served as a point of reference for the children's own activities.

| Activity | Instructing | Demonstrating | Modeling | Explaining | Monitoring | Managing | Prompting | Feedback | Supporting |
|---|---|---|---|---|---|---|---|---|---|
| 1 | 1 | 2 | 4 | 0 | 0 | 1 | 0 | 0 | 0 |
| 2 | 2 | 3 | 3 | 0 | 0 | 0 | 2 | 0 | 0 |
| 3 | 1 | 1 | 0 | 3 | 1 | 1 | 3 | 0 | 0 |
| 4 | 0 | 1 | 3 | 2 | 1 | 3 | 0 | 0 | 0 |
| 5 | 0 | 1 | 2 | 0 | 1 | 3 | 2 | 1 | 0 |
| 6 | 1 | 4 | 0 | 0 | 0 | 0 | 4 | 1 | 0 |
| 7 | 1 | 0 | 0 | 0 | 3 | 1 | 4 | 1 | 0 |
| 8 | 1 | 3 | 0 | 2 | 2 | 1 | 1 | 0 | 0 |
| 9 | 1 | 2 | 0 | 1 | 0 | 2 | 4 | 0 | 0 |
| 10 | 1 | 1 | 0 | 0 | 0 | 2 | 5 | 1 | 0 |
| 11 | 1 | 2 | 0 | 0 | 0 | 2 | 4 | 1 | 0 |

***Table 4.*** *Observed guided interactions per activity*

Depending on the task and the children's understanding of it, more or fewer demonstrations were necessary. If children asked questions such as "What do I do now?", "What do I do next?", or "How do I ...?", the adults often responded with demonstrations instead or prompts to let the children solve their problem independently afterwards. The adult's intense involvement at the beginning of the study balanced the children's excitement, risk of perceived failure, and the elements that affect one's self-determination to learn: perceived autonomy, competence, and relatedness (Ryan & Deci, 2000). Deci and Ryan (2000) argued that stimulating feelings of *competence*, *autonomy* and *relatedness* can enhance intrinsic motivation. These three keywords relate are very subjective and depend on the individual person:

- Autonomy described the ability to control the course of the activity),
- Relatedness described the ability to relate to social contact during the activity, and
- Competence described the ability to effectively manage the challenges of the activity.

Activity one asked the children to take a photo of their partner and introduce the partner. They were asked to, at least, mention their partner's name. The transcripts show how similar the children's audio elements were (see Table 5). The video transcripts showed that the children replicated the adult's examples and demonstrations, changing only the name of their partner. Only child 2 added additional content.

| Child | Transcript |
|---|---|
| Child 1 | This is my friend (name). |
| Child 2 | This is (name), but she is a little bit of my friend. |
| Child 3 | This is (name). |
| Child 4 | This is (name) |

***Table 5**. Extracts of artifacts in activity 1*

Activity two was conducted by the teacher, while both the teacher and the researcher assisted the children. Their involvement was less outcome oriented and more guiding (see Table 6, child 3). Instead of suggesting the children what to say, they prompted the children using questions. The children's answers were based on their own ways of answering these questions and their confidence in completing the activity with less adult involvement. Activity two asked the children to take a photo of an artifact of the craft they completed on that day, and add a voice recording that provides information about what it is, how they created it, and what it is for (see Table 6).

| Child | Transcript |
|---|---|
| Child 2 | You know, I made a Christmas tree with Fiona's group. Mine is nine layers tall. |
| Child 5 | I made a reindeer. |
| Child 3 | I made a star. (pause) Look. You see the photo of my star. Researcher: Yes. How did you make your star? Anton: With clay. Researcher: With clay? Anton: Yes, it is made of clay (pause), sprinkles and glue. Researcher: Sprinkles and glue? Anton: Where is my star now? Researcher: Are you done with talking? Because then you should click on the red button. Here, the red button. |
| Child 4 | (Inaudible) .... and the sprinkle on it |

***Table 6**. Extracts of activity 2*

By activity five the children's speech elements and content quality increased. This activity asked the children to look at two pictures, choose one and add an audio comment that explains what they think they see and what the picture makes them think of. The teacher modeled the activity and involved the children by asking them what they thought the image of a cartoon brain meant. She gathered the children's feedback, enriched it with her own example of an activity that 'makes the brain grow' and recorded it. The teacher modelled the following voice recording:

"I am looking at a picture of a brain. I know that a brain grows. To make brains grow we have to do things that challenge us and try and try and try again. I know what I have done to help my brain grow. I learn to dive. It was hard the first time I then I tried and tried and tried until I got better at it."

Since this type of task was new, the children referred to her example and were less likely to share their own, unbiased thoughts about the image (see Table 7). The comparison of the transcripts of activity five and nine show the differences of content between activities that included more (activity 5) and less (activity 9) detailed model to follow (see Table 7).

Among the audio recordings of activity 9, only child 3's seems to differ and spontaneously turn into a short story (see highlighted extract of table 7). His recording indicated the beginning of a new way of using the application and finding their own ways to effectively use the different functions to express their views, knowledge and ideas.

| Child | Transcript activity 5 | Transcript activity 9 |
|---|---|---|
| Child 1 | Your brain will only grow when you do something new. Like when I first started, I went on my bike first and then I thought it was (...) and then I tried and tried and tried and then it became very, very, very, very easy. The end. | No recording included |
| Child 2 | My brain. When you do something hard. A challenge is hard. You only try something hard and if you do it many times then you will find it easy. | I made a, a thing, a, I think it is also a alien rocket. |
| Child 3 | I will .... You go in the water you go like this and I go like when I was swimming there forever time I go. I need to press .. (Child 4 says: Name press the green one.) | This is a firetruck and a fire truck can take the fire, because they are super cool and their ... can nenanenanena, and the fire had been taked out |
| Child 4 | My brain can grow. My brain can grow bigger, and bigger, bigger, bigger, bigger. | I like it because it's got two squares in it, Its got the shape. Because it is very, very, very, ... lovely. |

***Table 7**. Extracts from activity 5 and activity 9*

The diversity of the verbal elements of activity nine was deemed a sign of their growing confidence and ability to make use to the device and app to communicate through digital creations. At this point the children were less focused on the basic operation of the device and app and paid more attention to their creations. Simultaneously, the adults further reduced their level of scaffolding.

After activity eight the children's audio TBCS decreases. It is noteworthy that the evaluation of the verbal content was related to the task. So, it is possible that the scores for the topic maintenance and IQ are low, because the content related only very little to the actual task.

Activity eight was another activity that asked the children to select an image and add an audio comment that shares what they see and what it makes them think. The children were undecided about what to say, so the researcher modeled one comment and as a result the children followed her example (see table 8). She guided the child 5 and child 6 through the image (see figure 4) and help them identify all the animals. Then she modelled a sample comment: "I saw a bee, ant, and a butterfly".

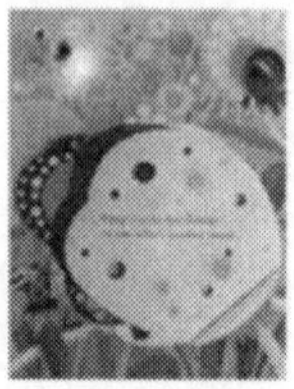

***Figure 4**. Task 8 image 1*

Similarly, to activity five, this activity was the first of this kind, because it embedded a task embedded within a digital artifact. Therefore, the researcher helped children a number of times, by starting the sentence with "I see" and then letting the children start the voice recording afterwards, affecting the children's audio TBCS significantly (see table 9).

| Child | Transcript |
|---|---|
| Child 1 | I can see lots of ladybirds, and a butterfly, and lots of bumblebees and a flowers and flowers and a heart picture. |
| Child 5 | I see some, a butterfly, two flies and a bee and a ladybird, and a fly, and an ant |
| Child 6 | I saw little bees. |
| Child 4 | I see a ladybird, and two ants, and one bee, and then a caterpillar, and then another, another, what |

***Table 8**. Extracts from activity 8*

The teacher and researcher had different approaches to the activities. The researcher allowed the children more freedom and engaged less in modeling activities after the activity introduction, therefore the artifacts created during her activities left more room for the children's own experimentation and agency. The comparison of the verbal elements of activity nine and ten (both led by the researcher) shows the effect that less modeling activities had on the children's work (see Table 8 & 9). After the activity demonstration, the children went to create their artifacts independently without further modeling. While Child 7 used the opportunity to talk about her class and her feelings towards the class (her photo showed the door to her classroom with a class photo), children 3 and 5 related their audio elements closely to the demonstrated example, and child 4 described his actions rather than the shapes as asked for (see highlighted extract of Table 8). As it can be seen, what they said is what they wanted to say, instead of what the adult had planned the children would say.

| Child | Transcript |
|---|---|
| Child 7 | I like this. I love my class and I love the number. My school... Hello, Bye Bye |
| Child 5 | Um, I found a rectangle and a square, and a rectangle. Um, a circle and .... I am finished. I am finished. |
| Child 3 | This is a circle on our playground, because playground you can play in it. And we have a square, and I don't know. I already ... |
| Child 4 | My name is (name). And I take the picture and I love that picture so much. I delete it (the drawing on it) again and then two times and then this now is very clean. |

***Table 9**. Extracts from activity 10*

### *Visual TBCS*

The development of the children's visual TBCS is slightly different, possibly due to the different nature of audio and visual elements (e.g. creating a visual element is less intimidating than creating a voice recording, hearing oneself), the task design, and the repeating pattern of the task structure. Although each activity occurred only once (see Table 2), they all followed the same sequence of actions (see study design).

The visual elements mostly related closely to the activity topic, and thus the scores on topic maintenance remained were higher (Figure 3), but the IQ and effectiveness of these TBCS varied. The visual artifacts (see sets of visuals in Figures 5 to 9) show that if the task asked to take a photo of a partner (activity 1), a shape construction (activity 10) or a Numicon (activity 11), the children followed this part of the activity closely. Therefore, the topic maintenance ranged between 2.5 and 3.

During activity 1 the teacher and researcher were very involved in the creation process, which resulted in task appropriate visual TBCS (see Figure 6). The photos still differed because the adults did not impose a certain design on the children, but required that the partner was clearly visible on the photo. If that was not the case they were asked to try again. This specific requirement also explains that the relatively high scores for activity one.

*By child 6 by child 2 by child 3*

***Figure 5**. Activity 1 visuals*

Activity three introduced the children to the drawing function and asked them to choose a toy, take a photo, draw around and outline their toy, and add a voice recording that explains why they chose this toy (see Figure 6). The video data showed that the children took these photos by themselves and the researcher provided support with the operational skills rather than the photo composition. Furthermore, after this activity, the children did not ask for help with photo taking. Therefore, all visual TBCS in subsequent activities were based on the children's thinking and actions only.

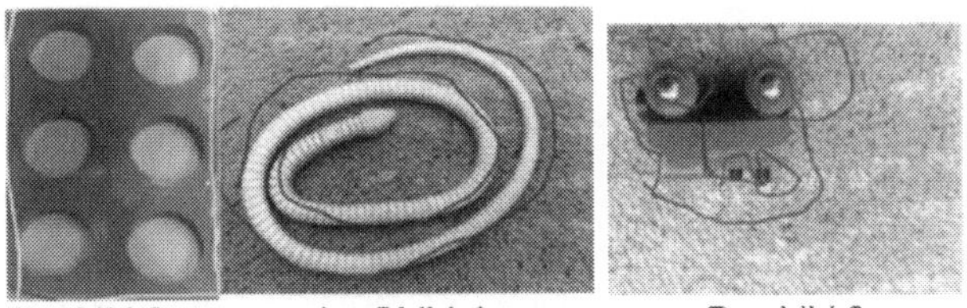

*By child 6* *by Child 4* *By child 3*

***Figure 6**. Activity 3 visuals*

The set of images in figure 7 selection shows resulting diversity in the range of IQ and efficacy. The drawings on top of the photo of child 5's shape construction leave the audience wonder what this could be. Also, child 2 seems to have drawn some vehicle on top of her photo, but the link between the drawing and the shape construction is not clear.

*By child 5* *by Child 2* *by Child 7*

***Figure 7**. Visual artifacts of activity*

Child 7, on the other hand, enhanced the elements of her shape construction. Although the meaning of the shape construction is unclear, the drawing and the photo clearly relate to another. It appears that child 5 was not sure what she should draw, child 2 had some idea in mind, and child 7 enhanced and highlighted the elements of her construction which helped informing the viewer about what she might have considered beautiful in her shape.

Activity eleven was less open-ended compared activity nine. The children were asked to manipulate Numicons to create a total of ten units (visible as circles). They were asked to find as many Numicon combinations as possible to make the sum of ten, take a photo of the combinations and share their findings. Using the audio and drawing was optional. Figure 8 illustrates some of the artifacts from which we can see the children's range of visual TBCS and their ability to use these skills.

Child 5 took a photo that includes only the Numicon combination, highlighted the 10 individual circles and the total of ten. Child 7 took a photo of a number of Numicons and used the drawing function to highlight the Numicon combination that he wanted to share. The photo of child 2 presents a number of things, including an unrelated bag. While she chose not to highlight the Numicon combination directly, she does lead the viewer towards the Numicon by writing the equation on top of the photo.

*By child 5* *by child 7* *by child 2*

***Figure 8**. Visual artifacts of activity 11*

### *Development of TBCS*

The children's development of TBCS and the use of the device and the creation app follow similar stages as the teacher's technology integration (see Table 1). It appears that the children's development, as present in activity one to three, covers the entry stage and the learning of the basic functionalities. The artifacts of activities four to eight related to the adaption of their skills to follow the activity framework imposed by the leading adult. All the following activities could be related to the appropriation stage where the children were using the different functions to communicate in the way that suited them personally the most. In this stage, they appropriated the modeled TBCS to suit their own preferences and purposes.

The experience from this study suggests that four to five years old children can acquire TBCS when they are given a combination of teacher- and child-led learning activities that provide them with a guiding activity framework while, simultaneously, enough freedom to experiment and redefine their developing skills. The children were situated in a supportive non-fail environment that allowed them to create their digital content using the digital communication tools as they deemed appropriate. This led to digital artifacts with audio and visual elements that might not align closely to the task (e.g. Figure 8, child 2). However, in most of these cases the children were able to convey a clear message (e.g. Table 8, child 4). The provided freedom and gradual decrease of scaffolding, based on the individual's skill development and need, allowed room for self-initiative and agency. The more competent the children were, the more likely they were to create unique audio or visual elements of their artifacts. Based on the elements of the self-determination theory (Ryan & Deci, 2000), the designed activities have been shown as a good recipe to ensuring a smooth and gradual development of TBCS within four to five years old children. The produced artifacts were based on activities that encouraged the children to share their ideas, thoughts, and knowledge using the available digital communication tools in ways that suited them best. The artifacts of child 4 (see Table 8), child 3 (see Table 9), and child 2 (Figure 5 and 8) show that these tools have the potential to engage young children in a range of creative communication activities such as storytelling.

## CONCLUSION

The children's development of TBCS and the use of the device and the creation app follow similar stages as the teacher's technology integration (see Table 1). It appears that the children's development, as present in activity one to three, covers the entry stage and the learning of the basic functionalities. The artifacts of activities four to eight related to the adaption of their skills to follow the activity framework imposed by the leading adult. All the following activities could be related to the appropriation stage where the children were using the different functions to communicate in the way that suited them personally the most. In this stage, they appropriated the modeled TBCS to suit their own preferences and purposes.

The experience from this study suggests that four to five years old children can acquire TBCS when they are given a combination of teacher- and child-led learning activities that provide them with a guiding activity framework while, simultaneously, enough freedom to experiment and redefine their developing skills. The children were situated in a supportive non-fail environment that allowed them to create their digital content using the digital communication tools as they deemed appropriate. This led to digital artifacts with audio and visual elements that might not align closely to the task (e.g. Figure 8, child 2). However, in most of these cases the children were able to convey a clear message (e.g. Table 9, child 4). The provided freedom and gradual decrease of scaffolding, based on the individual's skill development and need, allowed room for self-initiative and agency. The more competent the children were, the more likely they were to create unique audio or visual elements of their artifacts. Based on the elements of the self-determination theory (Ryan & Deci, 2000), the designed activities have been shown as a good recipe to ensuring a smooth and gradual development of TBCS within four to five years old children. The produced artifacts were based on activities that encouraged the children to share their ideas, thoughts, and knowledge using the available digital communication tools in ways that suited them best. The artifacts of child 4 (see Table 7), child 3 (see Table 9), and child 2 (Figure 5 and 8) show that these tools have the potential to engage young children in a range of creative communication activities such as storytelling.

## REFERENCES


Beschorner, B., & Hutchison, A. (2013). iPads as a literacy teaching tool in early childhood. *Online Submission*, *1*, 16-24.

Bragg, S. (2011) "'Now it's up to us to interpret it": Youth voice and visual methods in creative learning and research. In *Researching creative learning: Methods and issues*, ed. P. Thomson, and J. Sefton-Green (88-103), London and New York: Routledge

Bruner, J. S., & Potter, M. C. (1964). Interference in visual recognition. *Science*, *144*(3617), 424-425.

Cameron, C., & Dickfos, J. (2014). 'Lights, camera, action!' Video technology and students' perceptions of oral communication in accounting education. *Accounting Education*, *23*(2), 135-154.

Chiong, C., & Shuler, C. (2010). Learning: Is there an app for that. *Investigations of young children's usage and learning with mobile devices and apps. New York.*

Clements, D. H. (2002). Computers in early childhood mathematics. *Contemporary issues in early childhood*, *3*(2), 160-181.

Cohen, M., Hadley, M., & Frank, M. (2011). *Young children, apps & iPad.* Research report prepared for US Department of Education Ready to Learn program, 2011. http://mcgrc.com/wp-content/uploads/2012/06/ipad-study-cover-page-report-mcg-info_new-online.pdf accessed on February 17, 2014.

Couse, L.J. & Chen, D.W. (2010) A tablet computer for young children? Exploring its viability. *Early Childhood Education Journal of Research on Technology in Education.* Vol. 43 (1) p75-98.

Dilley, A., Fishlock, J., & Plucker, J.A. (2015) What we know about communication. Part of the 4Cs Research Series. P21 Partnership for 21st Century Learning.

Dwyer, DC., Ringstaff, C, Haymore, J., & Sandholtz, P. D. (1994). Apple classrooms of tomorrow. *Educational Leadership* 51, no. 7 (1994): 4-10.

Falloon, G. (2013). Young students using iPads: App design and content influences on their learning pathways. *Computers & Education.* 68, 505-521

Falloon, G. (2013b). Creating content: Building literacy skills in year 1 students using open format apps. *Computers in New Zealand Schools*, *25*(1–3), 77-95.

Goodwin, K. (2012). Use of tablet technology in the classroom. *NSW Department of Education and Communities.*

Guba, E. G., & Lincoln, Y. S. (1994). Competing paradigms in qualitative research. *Handbook of qualitative research*, *2*(163-194), 105.

Hertzog, N. & Klein, M. (2005). Beyond gaming: A technology explosion in early childhood classrooms. *Gifted Child Today*, *28*(3), 24.

Hardy, B. (1977). Narrative as a primary act of mind. *The cool web: The pattern of children's reading*, 12-23.

Hill, M. (2005). Ethical considerations in researching children's experiences. *Researching children's experience*, 61-86.

Kelly, K. L., & Schorger, J. R. (2001). "Let's play 'puters": Expressive language use at the computer center. *Information Technology in Childhood Education Annual*, *2001*(1), 125-138.

Kivunja, C. (2015). Exploring the pedagogical meaning and implications of the 4Cs "Super Skills" for the 21st century through Bruner's 5E lenses of knowledge construction to improve pedagogies of the new learning paradigm. *Creative Education*, *6*(02), 224.

Kinnunen, S., & Einarsdottir, J. (2013). Feeling, wondering, sharing and constructing life: Aesthetic experience and life changes in young children's drawing stories. *International Journal of Early Childhood*, *45*(3), 359-385.

McCabe, A., & Bliss, L. S. (2003). *Patterns of narrative discourse: A multicultural, life span approach.* Allyn & Bacon.

Parmar, N. (2014). *New learning pedagogy: A study in determining an appropriate pedagogy and pedagogical strategies to support phonetic awareness, whilst using new technology with young children* (Doctoral dissertation). Bournemouth Univ.

Pezzica, S., Pinto, G., Bigozzi, L., & Vezzani, C. (2016). Where is my attention? Children's metaknowledge expressed through drawings. *Educational Psychology*, *36*(4), 616-637.

Plowman, L., & Stephen, C. (2005). Children, play, and computers in pre-school education. *British Journal of Educational Technology*, *36*(2), 145-157.

Plowman, L., & Stephen, C. (2007). Guided interaction in pre-school settings. *Journal of Computer Assisted Learning*, *23*(1), 14-26.

Ryan, R. M., & Deci, E. L. (2000). Self-determination theory and the facilitation of intrinsic motivation, social development, and well-being. *American Psychologist*, *55*(1), 68.

Stephen, S., J. McPake, L. Plowman, and S. Berch-Heyman (2008) Learning from the children. Exploring preschool children's encounters with ICT at home. *Journal of Early Childhood Research* *6*(2), 99–11.

Wohlwend, K. 2010. A is for avatar: Young children in literacy 2.0 worlds and literacy 1.0 schools. *Language Arts* *88*(2), 144–152.

Yelland, N. & Gilbert, C. (2012). iPlay, iLearn, iGrow. London: IBM Paper. http://www.ipadsforeducation.vic.edu.au/userfiles/files/IBM%20Report%20iPlay,%20iLearn%20%26%20iGrow.pdf accessed on Jan 14, 2014

# Human Values and Trust in Scientific Journals, the Mainstream Media and Fake News

**Nitin Verma**
*School of Information, University of Texas at Austin, USA.*
*nitin.verma@utexas.edu*

**Kolina S. Koltai**
*School of Information, University of Texas at Austin.*
*koltai@utexas.edu*

**Kenneth R. Fleischmann**
*School of Information, University of Texas at Austin, USA.*
*kfleisch@ischool.utexas.edu*

## ABSTRACT

**What factors influence trust in online information? Americans increasingly get information from social media, public distrust in the mainstream media is growing and "fake news" is an important new phenomenon. This paper examines the factors that influence trust in scientific claims posted via social media, including the use of hyperlinks and readers' values. The paper describes a crowdsourcing-based experimental design using Amazon's Mechanical Turk platform. The core of the experiment was a set of 10 scientific findings reported in open-access, peer-reviewed scientific journals, which were in turn linked to in articles in both the mainstream media and "fake news" sites. Data analysis involved exploration of relationships between trust and the presence or absence of hyperlinks, and between trust and human values using nonparametric statistical methods. In terms of the influence of hyperlinks on trust, inclusion of hyperlinks to scientific journals, mainstream media articles, and even hidden URLs led to higher trust than hyperlinks to "fake news" sites or posts without hyperlinks ($p < 0.001$). Participants who clicked on hyperlinks to scientific articles placed higher trust in the claims than those who did not ($p < 0.001$). In terms of the influence of values on trust, values had the most impact in cases where individuals saw, but decided not to click on, hyperlinks; this finding seems to indicate that in the absence of firsthand examination of the hyperlinked sites, participants tend to rely more heavily on their values to determine their trust in a scientific claim. These findings indicate that both the presence and absence of hyperlinks and the values of the reader both significantly impact trust judgments.**

## KEYWORDS

human values, trust, online communication, social media, science communication, science journalism

## INTRODUCTION

In the 2016 U.S. presidential election, "fake news" stories outperformed mainstream media content on Facebook (Silverman, 2016). The prominent role of fake news on social media is alarming as about 14% of Americans identified social media as their "most important" source of election news (Allcott & Gentzkow, 2017). Berghel (2017) argues that a lack of emphasis on critical analysis in our educational system ill equips the general population to make informed judgments about what to trust. This raises the question whether such massive circulation effectively renders all information subjective (Hope, Hunter, & McLeod, 2015), ushering in a post-truth era (Harsin, 2015). At the same time, public trust toward institutions, particularly the mainstream media, has steadily declined (Smith & Son, 2013). According to Pew Research Center (Funk & Kennedy, 2016), while 76% of the public had either "a great deal" or "a fair amount" of confidence in scientists to act in the common good, only 38% shared that sentiment about the mainstream media.

Human values play an important role in influencing behavior, attitudes and sentiment (Fleischmann, 2014). Values can also predict attitudes toward opinion pieces about controversies (Templeton & Fleischmann, 2011). Price (1992) asserts that individuals rely on values, schemas, and group identifications to help guide their attitudes toward complex issues. This situation is particularly relevant in the social media era in which multiple sources of information compete for user attention and put pressure on users' capacity to vet all of the information that they consume.

The goal of our study was to examine the factors that influence trust in information, including how individuals with different life priorities, or human values, make different trust judgments toward information from scientific journals, the mainstream media and fake news. We set out to answer three main research questions. First, does the presence or absence of hyperlinks influence trust? Second, does the type of hyperlink used influence trust? Third, do the values of the reader influence trust? To answer these questions, we used an experimental design employing crowdsourcing, modeling how a Twitter user might review their timeline.

In this paper, we present results from our exploratory study of the relationships among hyperlinks, human values, and

80th Annual Meeting of the Association for Information Science & Technology, Washington, DC, VA | Oct. 27-Nov. 1, 2017

trust in different media sources. In the following section, we discuss prior research on values and trust in online content. In the methods section, we describe the design of our study, including how we collected and analyzed the data. In the subsequent sections, we present our findings and discuss implications, limitations, and future research directions, followed by the conclusion of the paper.

## BACKGROUND

Online social networks flatten hierarchies for publishing and information sharing, allowing anyone with an account to create, access, and distribute content. As a result, content gets published and shared without editorial oversight by subject-matter experts (Shao, Ciampaglia, Flammini, & Menczer, 2016). Traditionally, information originating from the mainstream media has been perceived to be more credible owing to the expectation that the organizations apply rigor and fact-checking before publishing (Flanagin & Metzger, 2007). On social media, fake news articles get shared alongside peer-reviewed scientific articles and fact-checked mainstream media articles. The many "economies of attention" thus generated within social networks compete for user attention and result in distinctive patterns of information production and user participation (Bessi, Scala, Rossi, Zhang, & Quattrociocchi, 2014). To understand the implications on trust in the different types of information sources, it is important to understand both the elements of trust in information (Kelton, Fleischmann, & Wallace, 2008) and users' motivations for using social media (Oh & Syn, 2015). Rieh (2014) compared users' evaluations of the trustworthiness of traditional media content and user generated content, finding that traditional media content was judged more trustworthy for health and news information.

Devos et al.'s (2002) work on trust towards institutions offers fertile grounds to argue that human values play a substantive role in formation of belief or knowledge about, and therefore trust towards, institutions. They found that values that emphasize stability, protection and preservation of tradition positively affect trust towards institutions, whereas values that emphasize independent thought affect such trust negatively (Devos et al., 2002). Whereas that study dealt with a broad set of institutions such as the healthcare system, the media, the law enforcement system, and political and religious institutions, our study focuses specifically on online media and how they report science news. It has also been argued that values, too, are influenced by media, and that people embed their values in both information and technology (Fleischmann, 2014). Existing research from a wide range of fields has produced multiple value inventories (reviewed in Cheng & Fleischmann, 2010); the most widely used value inventory is the Schwartz (1994) Value Inventory (SVI).

Gil & Artz (2007) offer a detailed set of criteria that people apply (consciously or subconsciously) to establish trust in online information. Their criteria include topic, context and criticality, popularity, authority, direct experience, recommendation, related resources, provenance, user expertise, bias, incentive, limited resources, agreement, specificity, likelihood, age, appearance, deception and recency. Subramaniam et al. (2015) add top-level domains, finding that users were generally more likely to trust .org sites than .com or .gov sites. Our study seeks to further build upon this research, examining in detail the influence of the presence of hyperlinks, the linked information itself, and the values of the reader on trust in online information.

## METHODS

As mentioned in the introduction, we designed this exploratory study to look for relationships between values and trust in different types of information sources. At the outset, we wanted to create a study that closely approximated the information environment of our participants. This led us to two important design considerations: (i) the experiment had to be conducted with participants who had at least basic computer literacy and who were likely to be regular consumers of information online; and (ii) the core portion of the study instrument, where the participants interacted with articles, had to mimic a contemporary social media platform. Both of these design considerations led us to employ online crowdsourcing, as this approach allowed us access to an appropriate study population and the technical ability to set up a realistic Twitter timeline.

In the following subsections, we describe in detail our crowdsourcing platform, the process of building our corpus of scientific news claims, the design of our instrument, our data collection, our data cleaning, and our data analysis.

## CROWDSOURCING PLATFORM

We used Amazon's Mechanical Turk (MTurk) as our crowdsourcing platform. We chose MTurk because comparative studies have found that MTurk performed favorably relative to alternatives such as university subject pools and posts on internet message boards in terms of accuracy of results and demographic diversity (e.g., Behrend, Sharek, Meade, & Wiebe, 2011; Hauser & Schwarz, 2016; Paolacci & Chandler, 2014). Specifically, MTurk has previously been applied to studies of trust in online information (e.g., Golbeck & Fleischmann, 2010) and the relationship between human values and attitudes toward news media texts (e.g., Templeton & Fleischmann, 2011). MTurk works by allowing "requesters" to design human intelligence tasks (HITs) and distributing them to "workers" on the platform. Workers then complete the HITs and receive monetary compensation from requesters.

## SELECTION OF SCIENTIFIC NEWS CLAIMS

At the core of our HIT design was a corpus of scientific claims with corresponding scientific, mainstream media and fake news articles. The corpus was rigorously built through a process that involved multiple criteria. At the core of each post was a scientific claim that had to be published in a peer-reviewed academic journal and had to be openly accessible so that participants could read (or at least connect to and skim) the article for themselves. Thus, we selected only open-access scientific articles. We limited the selection of peer-reviewed academic journals to those indexed in ISI Web of Science's Science Citation Index (SCI) Journal Citation Reports (JCR). We excluded articles that were corrected or retracted. As such, the set of open-access scientific articles were from high-quality venues and did not have any cloud of suspicion surrounding their publication.

In addition, each open-access scientific article had to be linked to by both a mainstream media outlet and a fake news site. We operationalized mainstream media using the list developed by Silverman (2016), referenced in Berghel (2017) and DiFranzo and Gloria-Garcia (2017); additionally, the selected sites were also independently identified by Flaxman, Goel, and Rao (2016) as among the 20 most popular news outlets. Specifically, the seven mainstream media outlets used in our corpus were *CBS News*, *CNN*, *Fox News*, *The Huffington Post*, *LA Times*, *USA Today*, and *The Washington Post*. The mainstream media article had to include a direct hyperlink to the open-access scientific article. The mainstream media articles also had to be native to the mainstream media outlets, rather than originating from another news service. The mainstream media articles had to be primarily textual in nature, in parallel with the open-access scientific articles, although some also had accompanying video clips. The mainstream media articles also had to appear on sites that were open-access without viewing restrictions. For example, we intentionally excluded *The New York Times* because it has a partial paywall that restricts the number of views per month for non-subscribers.

We operationalized fake news sites using a list from Fake News Watch (2016), previously employed by Shao, Ciampaglia, Flammini, and Menczer (2016). Specifically, two fake news sites used in our scientific claim corpus were InfoWars and Natural News. As in the case of the mainstream media articles, the fake news articles had to include direct hyperlinks to the open-access scientific articles, had to be native to the fake news site rather than originating from another source and had to be primarily textual in nature. This criterion was the primary reason why only two fake news sites were used; there is a great degree of cross-referencing among fake news sites, and several other fake news sites listed in the clickbait list from Fake News Watch are merely content aggregation sites, which do not produce their own original content.

The end result was a corpus of 10 scientific claims, listed in Table 1. Each claim originated from an open-access scientific article, which was directly hyperlinked-to by a mainstream media article and a fake news article. The carefully controlled development of this corpus makes it ideal for implementing in a HIT such as the one described in this paper.

### HIT DESIGN

We designed our HIT using the TurkSuite Template Generator created by Alper (2014). The HIT comprised a series of 10 "screens" – the first three carried the informed consent form and instructions to complete the HIT, and the rest presented the various experimental and survey components of the study. In addition to collecting user-provided form data such as text input, Likert ratings, and drop-down selections, we recorded the amount of time a participant spent on each screen and whether or not they clicked on hyperlinks included in the HIT. We were sensitive to concerns of frequent exploitation of workers on MTurk (Irani, 2016), so we based our compensation on our estimated completion time – given our estimate of 20 minutes to complete the HIT, we offered $2.50 as compensation, equating to a pay rate above the Federal minimum wage. Fortunately, our results bore out that the average completion time was approximately 20 minutes, so, as such, we managed to comply with ethical compensation for our participants (Pittman & Sheehan, 2016). We also paid all

| No. | Post Text |
|---|---|
| 1 | Gene editing tested for the first time in humans |
| 2 | Dolphins use specific whistles to call each other by a "name" |
| 3 | Children today now more prone to whooping cough because of weaker vaccine |
| 4 | Study found that GM Corn consumption by rats leads to organ damage |
| 5 | Some fast food packaging contains cancer-causing chemicals |
| 6 | Banning large sodas may lead to higher soda consumption |
| 7 | Human activity may lead to extinction of majority of primate species |
| 8 | Study links gut bacteria with chronic fatigue syndrome |
| 9 | Injecting mice brains with human fetal brain cells makes lab mice "smarter" |
| 10 | Ancient continental crust discovered in Indian Ocean under the island of Mauritius |

***Table 1**. Scientific claims used in posts*

workers who completed the HIT, whether or not we used their data in our final analysis, to reward their effort.

The core of our study was to ask participants to read a set of 10 posts as if they appeared in their social media news feed. Each of the10 posts was made up of two components. The first component was one of 10 scientific claims derived from the corpus described in the previous section. We attempted to keep the scientific claims easy to understand yet faithful to the original scientific article. To achieve this, the three authors each independently evaluated each set of articles (scientific, mainstream media and fake news) and independently proposed text for the scientific claim. The three authors then reviewed the independently generated text and reached consensus on the most appropriate text to use. We intentionally kept the scientific claims brief (8-12 words in length) to mimic social media content.

The second component of each post was a hyperlink. We created five experimental conditions using the hyperlink component as an independent variable. The first experimental condition involved not including any hyperlink. Each of the next three experimental conditions included a full hyperlink (i.e., the anchor text containing the full URL) to an open-access scientific article, a mainstream media article, or a fake news article. The fifth experimental condition used URLs shortened using Google's URL shortening service (Google, n.d.) to create hidden URLs (i.e., shortened URLs with the same generic base domain name). We refer to these different conditions as "post types" throughout the remainder of this article.

The aforementioned components informed the design of the emulated social media "newsfeed" component of the HIT. We decided to present our posts as tweets appearing on a typical Twitter user timeline. We mimicked the Twitter user timeline by emulating the HTML structure of individual tweets as rendered in a desktop web browser. In order to avoid potential confounds we did not emulate tweet features such as the number of replies, retweets, or likes since these could act as confounding cues for credibility. For similar reasons, we used generic handles (such as "Twitter User 1") and a neutral profile image (the Twitter new user "egg" avatar) to avoid any framing effects.

We displayed the emulated Twitter timeline on two screens: once by itself, and on the following screen with a 5-point Likert trust rating scale ranging from "Trust Completely" to "Don't Trust At All" against each individual post. We did this to separate the process of reading the posts, and of providing trust ratings. We intended this delay between the two phases to discourage workers from inattentively clicking on the radio buttons for ratings in order to complete the HIT quickly. Before displaying the first of these screens, we displayed a sample tweet screen to workers so as to familiarize them with what elements they would see on the emulated newsfeeds. We included the sample tweet screen to tell the users how to interact with the hyperlinks if they wished to. The posts appeared in identical order on both timeline screens. We recorded hyperlink clicking behavior (i.e., whether or not, and which, hyperlinks a worker clicked) independently for both timeline screens. Our need to record this clicking behavior was also one of the reasons for us to include the sample tweet screen described above. Due to limitations on tracking mouse clicks using Javascript, we advised workers to use only the left mouse click to open a hyperlink. At the same time, we provided them assurance that left-clicking the hyperlink would open the linked page in a new browser tab and would not interfere with the completion of their HIT.

One of our research objectives was to study whether human values influence people's trust in online news and their motivation to investigate hyperlinked resources in social media posts. To collect data on the values of our participants, we employed a gender-neutral version of the 21 item Portrait Values Questionnaire (PVQ) (Schwartz, 2003), adapted from the European Social Survey (ESS) (Schwartz, 2007). In the PVQ, each of the 21 statements provides a short personality "portrait," and participants indicate the extent to which the portrait describes their own personality. We used a 5-point Likert scale extending from "Absolutely Like Me" to "Not Like Me At All" for the participants to indicate the degree to which they believed each portrait described them. All 21 portraits were presented on the same screen, with the 5-point Likert scale appearing to the right of each item. Each participant was presented with the set of 21 portraits in a randomized order to mitigate any bias stemming from ordering or pattern effects. The 21 portraits correspond with Schwartz's ten value types (*power, achievement, hedonism, stimulation, self-direction, universalism, benevolence, tradition, conformity* and *security*), the complete middle-level of the Schwartz (1994) Value Inventory (SVI). We will discuss the process of calculating results from the level of 21 portraits to the level of ten value types in more detail below.

## DATA COLLECTION

We created 100 HITs, each intended to be completed by a unique worker. We randomized the distribution of posts across the 100 HITs in such a way that each HIT had exactly two posts of a type, and that all five types were represented in each HIT for a total of 10 posts per HIT. We also ensured that all the 10 posts in a HIT were unique, implying that each HIT would carry 1 out of 5 versions per news story. We implemented the randomization and the subsequent apportioning of posts using a Python script.

As previously mentioned, we collected most of the data using the form elements in our HIT, but we also instrumented our HIT with Javascript to record the time workers spent on each screen, and which hyperlinks they clicked on.

## DATA CLEANING

The 100 HITs were completed within approximately three hours of publication, which speaks both to the rapidity of data collection using MTurk and as an indication that our payment rate was deemed fair (at least relative to other HITs) by MTurk workers. We carefully reviewed all HITs for criteria such as uniqueness (we discarded one repeat HIT from a participant who completed the HIT twice), completeness (we discarded eight HITs for being incomplete), correct answer to a dummy question (used as a validation step), and inconsistent answers to repeat questions (also used as a validation step; we discarded six HITs based upon this criterion), and inconsistent answers to questions about clicking on hyperlinks. For the last of the aforementioned criteria, we tallied worker responses to the following two assertions: "I carefully reviewed the linked articles" and "The content of the linked page influenced my trust in the post," with their actual clicking behavior. We found 16 people who had shown a general level of agreement with these assertions but had not clicked on *any* hyperlink. We defined "general level of agreement" as a "Strongly Agree" or the level just below and adjacent to it on the 5-point Likert scale. We reasoned that those who had not clicked on any hyperlink but reported that they had reviewed the content of the linked articles were contradicting themselves, and therefore their other responses could not be relied upon. The resulting dataset included complete and valid data from 69 unique participants.

## DATA ANALYSIS

To facilitate analysis, the 5-point Likert scale corresponding to each portrait was converted to an ordinal scale ranging from -2 ("Not Like Me At All") to 2 ("Absolutely Like Me"). Then, for each of the 69 records, we converted the responses to the 21 PVQ portraits down to 10 values types using Schwartz's (2007) mapping of portraits to values types. Following Schwartz, while nine of the value types were measured using two portraits, one (universalism) was measured using three portraits. Schwartz justifies this additional acuity to measure universalism by citing that it is "the most complex value construct" (Schwartz, 2003). Following the calculation of the value type scores based upon Schwartz, we classified each participant as being "high" or "low" in terms of identification with a particular value. We defined "high" as a score higher than the median score for the value, and "low" as a score lower than or equal to the median score for that value.

Similarly, we converted the 5-point Likert scale for trust ratings into an ordinal scale ranging from -2 ("Don't Trust At All") to 2 ("Trust Completely"). Also, for this analysis, we combined the two independent sets of measurements of hyperlink clicking behavior into a third set: one binary value for each of the ten posts, indicating whether the hyperlink (if present) was clicked on or not. We achieved this by registering a particular hyperlink as clicked if it was clicked on in either of the two screens it was displayed on. If a hyperlink was not clicked on *either* screen, it was registered as not clicked. For each HIT, the number of hyperlinks clicked on was in the range 0 to 8 (since exactly two posts in each HIT were without any hyperlinks).

We used nonparametric methods to evaluate significance, as they carry fewer assumptions and are safer in cases where $N$ is low (Gibbons & Chakraborti, 1991). We used Mann-Whitney U (alternatively, the Wilcoxon rank-sum test), the nonparametric equivalent to an unpaired t-test, and Kruskal-Wallis H, the nonparametric equivalent to ANOVA. Since the study was exploratory, all statistical tests were run two-tailed. We evaluated significance at the levels of $p < 0.05$, 0.01, and 0.001. To be conservative and reduce the chance of a Type I error, we focus most heavily on findings which were very highly significant, at the level of $p < 0.001$, as these significance levels were far less likely to occur randomly.

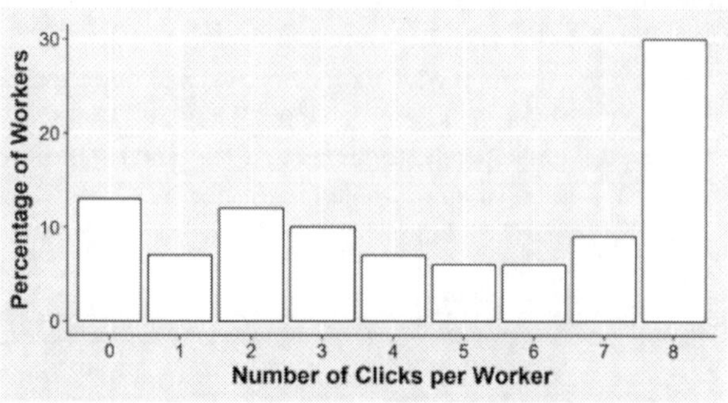


***Figure 1**. Distribution of the number of hyperlinks clicked by participants*

## RESULTS

For this paper, we focused on the relationships among hyperlink clicking behavior, trust ratings, and human values across the five types of posts. We will begin with results related to hyperlink clicking behavior, and then move on to trust ratings, and then to human values.

## HYPERLINK CLICKING BEHAVIOR

One preliminary finding across all participants ($N = 69$) was that the distribution of number of clicks per user ($M = 4.58$) had a relatively wide dispersion ($SD = 3.01$). As the bar graph in Figure 1 shows, 21 participants (30%) clicked on all eight hyperlinks in their HIT, while 9 participants (13%) did not click on any of the hyperlinks; the remaining 39 participants (57%) clicked on some but not all of the hyperlinks. Interestingly, Mann-Whitney U tests did not reveal any significant relationships between any of the ten values and the number of clicks per participant.

## TRUST RATINGS BETWEEN POST TYPES

A Kruskal-Wallis H test for trust ratings across all five post types revealed a highly significant ($p < 0.001$) difference in trust ratings across post types. As the boxplots in Figure 2 show, trust ratings improved with the presence of hyperlinks. We then did Mann-Whitney U tests to compare each post type with every other post type. Based on the results, we can safely group the types into two groups, whereby trust in posts containing hyperlinks to scientific journals, mainstream media, and hidden URLs was higher than trust in fake news or posts without hyperlinks ($p < 0.001$ for all six pairwise comparisons). No significant differences were found in pairwise comparisons among the first three types, and hyperlinks to fake news earned more trust than posts without hyperlinks ($p < 0.05$).

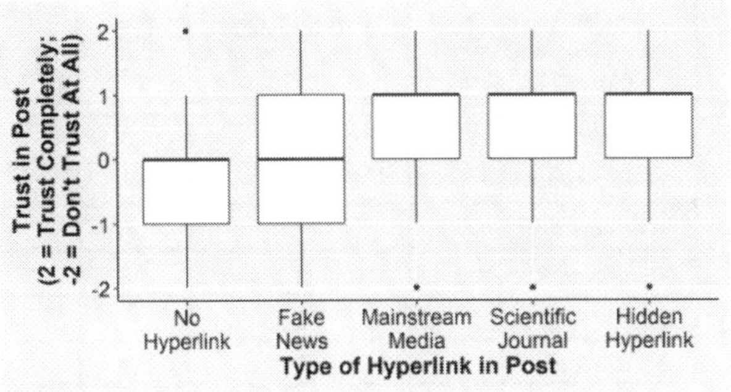


***Figure 2**. Boxplots of trust ratings across all five post types*

## TRUST RATINGS AND HYPERLINK CLICKING BEHAVIOR (WITHIN POST TYPES)

Next, for the four post types that contained hyperlinks, we compared the trust ratings between individuals who did or did not click on the hyperlink to determine the effects of hyperlink clicking behavior. We found that clicking on a hyperlink significantly increased trust for posts with hyperlinks to fake news ($p < 0.05$), scientific journals ($p < 0.001$), and hidden URLs ($p < 0.001$). The boxplots for all four post types containing hyperlinks are shown in Figure 3. Plots on the left in each pair show the trust rating distribution when hyperlinks were not clicked, and those on the right show the distribution when hyperlinks were clicked.

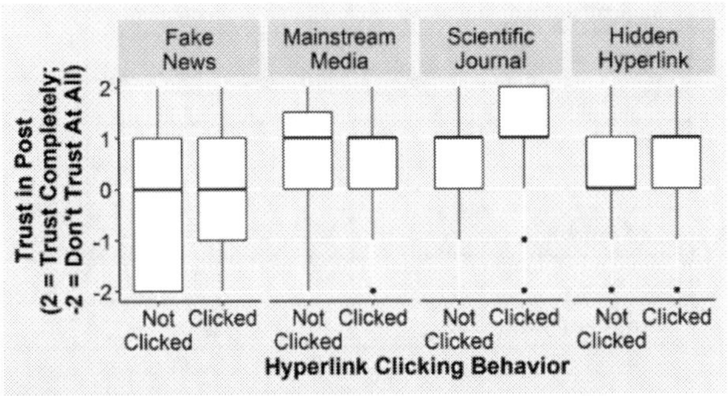


***Figure 3**. Trust ratings within each post type with clicking behavior*

## TRUST RATINGS ACROSS POST TYPES (HYPERLINK NOT CLICKED)

For the case where the participant did not click on the hyperlink (Figure 4), Kruskal-Wallis H across all five post types) revealed a significant ($p < 0.001$) relationship between trust ratings and post type. To discern which post types were most significantly different, we ran ten Mann-Whitney U tests across pairs of post types. As shown in Figure 4, participants expressed significantly lower trust in posts without hyperlinks in comparison to posts with hyperlinks to mainstream media, scientific journals, or even hidden URLs ($p < 0.001$). Similarly, participants had significantly lower trust in posts with fake news hyperlinks than in posts with hyperlinks to mainstream media or scientific journals ($p < 0.001$).

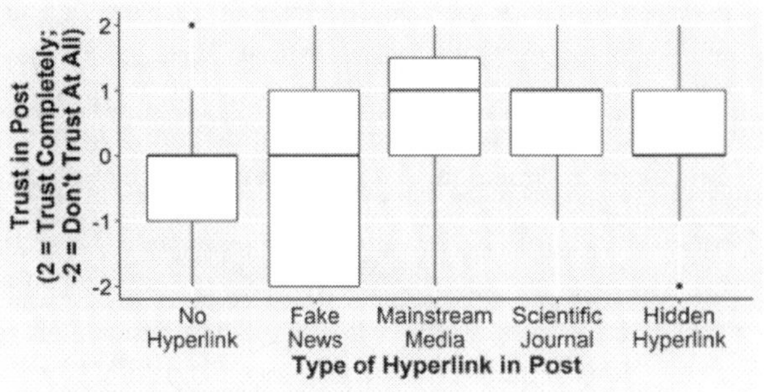


***Figure 4**. Trust ratings across post types (hyperlinks not clicked)*

## TRUST RATINGS ACROSS POST TYPES (HYPERLINK CLICKED)

For the case where the participant clicked the hyperlink, Kruskal-Wallis H across all four post types containing hyperlinks revealed a highly significant ($p < 0.001$) relationship between trust ratings and post type. To discern which of the post types were significantly different, we ran pairwise Mann-Whitney U tests. As shown in Figure 5, participants had significantly lower trust in posts with fake news hyperlinks than in posts with hyperlinks to scientific journals ($p < 0.001$) or hidden URLs ($p < 0.001$).

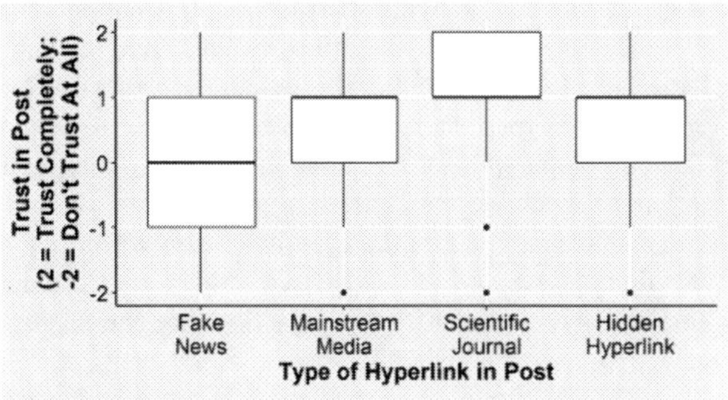


***Figure 5**. Trust ratings across post types (hyperlinks clicked)*

## TRUST RATINGS AND VALUES

As explained previously, we reduced each worker's value scores for all ten SVI (Schwartz, 1994) values into a categorical variable with two levels: *high* (score above the median for that value) and *low* (score less than, or equal to, the median score). This categorization allows us to make assertions about what a person values (i.e., a "high" score), or does not value (i.e., a "low" score). We initially performed pairwise comparisons between the "high" and "low" for each of the ten values for each of the five post types. We found some statistically significant relationships, although none reached the level of $p < 0.001$. Given the differences that we had found between cases where individuals had clicked or had not clicked on a particular hyperlink, we performed more fine-grained comparisons, separating out the cases where the hyperlink was clicked or not clicked. We found more differences within the not clicked data than within the clicked data. Two of these differences were significant at the level of $p <$

0.001: highly valuing *stimulation* increased trust, while highly valuing *achievement* decreased trust. Considering the four conditions with hyperlinks which appear on both sides of the table, we identified a total of 15 significant differences; 13 of these differences were found in the not clicked condition (Table 2), while only two were found in the clicked condition (Table 3).

## DISCUSSION

Overall, the results of our study demonstrate some interesting relationships among hyperlinks, trust, and human values. Specifically, we found that most participants clicked some, but not all, of the hyperlinks, illustrating that they made conscious choice about which hyperlinks to click. Participants demonstrated greater trust in posts that contained hyperlinks to scientific articles, mainstream media, and hidden URLs than to posts with no hyperlinks or hyperlinks to fake news, illustrating that participants were generally more willing to trust these more reputable sources despite the growing concerns about the influence of sharing of fake news via social media (Silverman, 2016). Trust was greater for scientific articles, hidden URLs, and fake news in cases where individuals clicked on hyperlinks; the first two results are unsurprising, particularly considering that they led to the same content; the latter result is interesting insofar as the content of the fake news appears to have outperformed the perceptions of the URL. However, due to the study design, it is not possible to tease out whether the greater trust resulted from reading the hyperlinked article or rather if it was greater trust that led to clicking the hyperlink in the first place, as these results indicate correlation rather than causation. Finally, values seemed to have a much more significant effect in cases where individuals did not click on the hyperlinks than when they did; this finding seems to add to the list of criteria for trust identified by Gil & Artz (2007), along the lines of Subramaniam et al. (2015) except going into attributes of the reader as well as the URL. This finding is particularly interesting and provides an opportunity for further research into how that trust in limited information such as URLs is mediated by the values of the reader.

## LIMITATIONS

During the execution and analysis phases of our study, we identified limitations along the following themes:

Although we used a consensus based framing of the text of each post, the posts themselves dealt with only science-related topics. While this was a design choice to facilitate a focused exploration, the obvious limitation is that we cannot generalize our results for online posts outside the domain of science reporting.

Because we designed a "naturalistic" study (by selecting actual scientific news items) as against creating totally fictitious news items ourselves, there may be confounds (e.g., the lengths of the hyperlinked articles, writing styles, differing page layouts and ads) that could also affect trust.

| Values ↓ | No Hyperlink | Fake News | Mainstream Media | Scientific Journal | Hidden Hyperlink |
|---|---|---|---|---|---|
| *Hedonism* | | | | | |
| *Stimulation* | | | | + | + + + |
| *Self-direction* | | | | + | |
| *Universalism* | | - - | + + | + | |
| *Benevolence* | | - - | | | |
| *Conformity* | | + | | | |
| *Tradition* | + + | | | - | |
| *Security* | | | | | |
| *Power* | | | - | | |
| *Achievement* | | | - - - | - | - |

+: trust *increases* as importance of value *increases*
-: trust *decreases* as importance of value *increases*
+++/- - -: $p < 0.001$; ++/--: $p < 0.01$; +/-: $p < 0.05$

***Table 2**. Relationship between trust ratings and importance of values (hyperlinks not clicked)*

| Values ↓ | Fake News | Mainstream Media | Scientific Journal | Hidden Hyperlink |
|---|---|---|---|---|
| *Hedonism* | | | | |
| *Stimulation* | | | | |
| *Self-direction* | | | | |
| *Universalism* | | | | |
| *Benevolence* | | | | |
| *Conformity* | | - | | |
| *Tradition* | + | | | |
| *Security* | | | | |
| *Power* | | | | |
| *Achievement* | | | | |

+: trust *increases* as importance of value *increases*
-: trust *decreases* as importance of value *increases*
+++/- - -: $p < 0.001$; ++/--: $p < 0.01$; +/-: $p < 0.05$

***Table 3**. Relationship between trust ratings and importance of values (hyperlinks clicked)*

Our sample size is relatively small ($N = 69$), and thus it is possible that we obtained false negative findings because we did not have sufficient power based on the number of participants used. Given that we used very conservative non-parametric analyses, it is far less likely that we had false positive results, so as such, a larger N would possibly reveal additional significant findings, but is less likely to invalidate any of the significant findings from this study, particularly those at the level of $p < 0.001$.

Ours was a "laboratory" experiment, conducted in a simulated environment where there is an existing "marketplace" of workers with predetermined skill sets, rather than an observational field study of users' exploration of and trust in news content within their own social media accounts.

Our experimental design does not allow us to infer causality in the decision to click or not click on a hyperlink; for example, when comparing individuals who clicked or did not click on a given hyperlink, the differences could be explained by participants learning from clicking and changing their degree of trust as a result, or by participants with more (or less) initial trust based on the hyperlink feeling more (or less) inclined to click on a hyperlink. Potentially, we could ask users to look at a URL first, measure trust, ask them to visit the website, and measure trust again; this type of study would be best performed in a usability lab setting.

## FUTURE RESEARCH

One future direction would be to replicate the current study with a larger *N*, which is our next planned step. The study design could also be applied to domains beyond science, such as politics or health information. During the process of developing the corpus of posts we observed that fake news sites appeared to include hyperlinks to open-access scientific articles more often than their mainstream media outlet counterparts; systematic examination of this phenomenon was beyond the scope of this project but would make interesting further research. We also believe that seeking more incisive inputs from participants about the heuristics they deploy in establishing trust online would provide further nuance to our findings, such as being able to determine causality in the relationships we have discovered. Future efforts should also seek to minimize dependence on participant-reported data about whether, and to what extent, they examined the hyperlinked articles. One way to do this would be to conduct follow-up studies in a controlled environment such as a usability lab. Motivated by our findings pertaining to the influence exerted by values on people's trust judgment, the role played by the type of media outlet in persuading people, and the body of literature on trust, we encourage others to conduct similar studies, and therefore add to the research on trust in online information.

## CONCLUSION

The dramatic rise in the volume of content posted online threatens to render most information "subjectively true" (Hope et al., 2015), and seems to be creating "truth markets" (Harsin, 2015) that make the task of establishing trust very demanding. While the Web, in facilitating the creation of this content, has created an egalitarian society when it comes to information access and diffusion, much of this content gets published without any editorial or journalistic oversight. In addition, the sheer volume and speed of this information puts pressure on people's limited attentional resources when they are confronted with the task of making a trust judgment. Given this complex situation, there is a need to understand the factors that influence trust in information exchanged via social media.

To develop that understanding, our study explored the role of hyperlinks and human values in trust in information exchanged via social media. Some of our findings were in line with our expectations. For example, we had expected that the presence or absence of a hyperlink in a post would influence trust in that post. We found that in comparison to the condition where there is no hyperlink, each post in which there was some type of hyperlink (fake news, mainstream, scientific journal, or even a hyperlink to a hidden URL) had a significantly *higher* trust level.

In addition, we found that the different types of hyperlinks elicited significantly different levels of trust, with trust in posts with hyperlinks to scientific journal, mainstream media, and hidden URLs higher than in posts with fake news hyperlinks or no hyperlinks. We discovered that clicking or not clicking (and thus, presumably, inspecting or not inspecting the contents of) a hyperlink significantly affected trust ratings only for posts carrying hyperlinks to scientific journals and hidden URLs, and to a marginally significant extent for posts with fake news hyperlinks. Specifically, posts with these three types of hyperlinks fared better in trust ratings when the corresponding hyperlinks were clicked on. We cannot assume with absolute certainty that mere clicking or opening of a hyperlink implies assessment of the contents of the linked page. Viewing scientific journal or fake news articles was correlated with higher trust ratings relative to choosing not to view them. Perhaps, for the case of scientific journals, this is because participants were not previously familiar with the outlets, but were impressed by the format and formality of the journal web pages. Further, for fake news articles, participants may have been influenced positively by seeing hyperlinks to the scientific journals (see footnote 5), or it is also possible that individuals who immediately had low trust in the fake news sites based upon the hyperlinked URLs chose not to click on them; determining the reason would be an interesting opportunity for future research. Fourth, among posts in which the embedded hyperlinks were clicked, we found that fake news was less trusted than the other outlets.

For values, the two most significant relationships involved the values of *achievement* and *stimulation*. First, when participants were shown but chose not to click the hyperlink to a mainstream media article, individuals who highly valued *achievement* were less likely to trust mainstream media articles than those who put less value on *achievement*. Schwartz (2007) defines *achievement* as "personal success through demonstrating competence according to social standards" (p. 174), so it seems reasonable to conclude that individuals who highly value *achievement* are more likely to care about social standards of excellence (and therefore seek to distinguish themselves from others), and are thus less inclined to trust mainstream media sources that are adopted by the masses. Second, when the participants were shown but chose not to click on the hyperlink to a hidden URL, individuals who highly valued *stimulation* were more likely to trust the article pointed to by the hidden URL than those who put less value on *stimulation*. Schwartz (2007) defines *stimulation* as "excitement, novelty, and challenge in life" (p. 174), so it seems reasonable to conclude that individuals who highly value *stimulation* are more likely to take risks, such as blindly trusting a hyperlink with a hidden URL. Overall, the results for participants who did not click the hyperlink were more influenced by values than those who did click the hyperlink; one possible explanation is that when shown a hyperlink, in the absence of more information, individuals make gut trust decisions based upon their values; however, when individuals explore the linked content, they have other factors that they can use to inform their trust judgments.

Thus, this study provides preliminary insights about the role that human values play in influencing trust in different media outlets. We believe that further research is called for to better understand how human values shape trust in online content.

## ACKNOWLEDGEMENTS

The authors wish to acknowledge funding from a Special Research Grant from the Office of the Vice President for Research of the University of Texas at Austin, as well as the anonymous crowdworkers who participated in this study.

## REFERENCES

Allcott, H., & Gentzkow, M. (2017). Social media and fake news in the 2016 election. *Journal of Economic Perspectives*, *31*, 211-236.

Alper, M. (2014). TurkSuite Template Generator. Retrieved April 23, 2017, from http://mturk.mit.edu/template.php

Behrend, T. S., Sharek, D. J., Meade, A. W., & Wiebe, E. N. (2011). The viability of crowdsourcing for survey research. *Behavior Research Methods*, *43*, 800-813.

Berghel, H. (2017). Lies, damn lies, and fake news. *Computer*, *50*(2), 80-85.

Bessi, A., Scala, A., Rossi, L., Zhang, Q., & Quattrociocchi, W. (2014). The economy of attention in the age of (mis)information. *Journal of Trust Management*, *1*, 12.

Cheng, A.-S., & Fleischmann, K. R. (2010). Developing a meta-inventory of human values. *Proceedings of the American Society for Information Science and Technology*, *47*, 1-10.

Devos, T., Spini, D., & Schwartz, S. H. (2002). Conflicts among human values and trust in institutions. *British Journal of Social Psychology*, *41*(4), 481-494.

DiFranzo, D., & Gloria-Garcia, K. (2017). Filter bubbles and fake news. *XRDS*, *23*(3), 32-35.

Fake News Watch. (2016, January 18). Retrieved April 23, 2017, from http://fakenewswatch.com/

Flanagin, A. J., & Metzger, M. J. (2007). The role of site features, user attributes, and information verification behaviors on the perceived credibility of web-based information. *New Media & Society*, *9*, 319-342.

Flaxman, S., Goel, S., & Rao, J. M. (2016). Filter bubbles, echo chambers, and online news consumption. *Public Opinion Quarterly*, *80*, 298-320.

Fleischmann, K. R. (2014). *Information and human values*. San Rafael, CA: Morgan & Claypool.

Funk, C., & Kennedy, B. (2016). *The politics of climate*. Pew Research Center.

Gibbons, J. D., & Chakraborti, S. (1991). Comparison of the Mann-Whitney, Student's t, and alternate t tests for means of normal distributions. *The Journal of Experimental Education*, *59*, 258-267.

Gil, Y., & Artz, D. (2007). Towards content trust of web resources. *Web Semantics: Science, Services and Agents on the World Wide Web*, *5*(4), 227-239.

Golbeck, J., & Fleischmann, K. R. (2010). Trust in social Q&A: The impact of text and photo cues of expertise. *Proceedings of the American Society for Information Science and Technology*, *47*, 1-10.

Google. (n.d.). Google URL shortener. Retrieved April 23, 2017, from https://goo.gl/

Harsin, J. (2015). Regimes of posttruth, postpolitics, and attention economies. *Communication, Culture & Critique*, *8*(2), 327-333.

Hauser, D. J., & Schwarz, N. (2016). Attentive Turkers: MTurk participants perform better on online attention checks than do subject pool participants. *Behavior Research Methods*, *48*(1), 400-407.

Hope, A., Hunter, R., & McLeod, J. (2015). Climate change and social media: Trust, literacy, legitimacy and subjectivity. Presented at the Global Sustainability Institute Research Conference 2015, Cambridge, UK. Retrieved from http://nrl.northumbria.ac.uk/21360/

Irani, L. (2016). The hidden faces of automation. *XRDS*, *23*(2), 34-37.

Kelton, K., Fleischmann, K. R., & Wallace, W. A. (2008). Trust in digital information. *Journal of the American Society for Information Science and Technology*, *59*, 363-374.

Oh, S., & Syn, S. Y. (2015). Motivations for sharing information and social support in social media: A comparative analysis of Facebook, Twitter, Delicious, YouTube, and Flickr. *Journal of the Association for Information Science and Technology*, *66*, 2045-2060.

Paolacci, G., & Chandler, J. (2014). Inside the Turk: Understanding Mechanical Turk as a participant pool. *Current Directions in Psychological Science*, *23*, 184-188.

Pittman, M., & Sheehan, K. (2016). Amazon's Mechanical Turk a digital sweatshop? Transparency and accountability in crowdsourced online research. *Journal of Media Ethics*, *31*(4), 260-262.

Price, V. (1992). *Public opinion*. Newbury Park, CA: Sage.

Rieh, S. Y. (2014). Credibility assessment of online information in context. *Journal of Information Science Theory and Practice*, *2*(3), 6-17.

Schwartz, S. H. (1994). Are there universal aspects in the structure and contents of human values? *Journal of Social Issues*, *50*(4), 19-45.

Schwartz, S. H. (2003). A proposal for measuring value orientations across nations. *Questionnaire Package of the European Social Survey*, 259-290.

Schwartz, S. H. (2007). Value orientations: Measurement, antecedents and consequences across nations. In R. Jowell, C. Roberts, R. Fitzgerald, & G. Eva (Eds.), *Measuring attitudes cross-nationally: Lessons from the European Social Survey* (pp. 169-203). London: Sage.

Shao, C., Ciampaglia, G. L., Flammini, A., & Menczer, F. (2016). Hoaxy: A platform for tracking online misinformation. In *Proceedings of the 25th international conference companion on world wide web* (pp. 745-750). Republic and Canton of Geneva, Switzerland: International World Wide Web Conferences Steering Committee. https://doi.org/10.1145/2872518.2890098

Silverman, C. (2016, November 16). This analysis shows how viral fake election news stories outperformed real news on Facebook. Retrieved April 21, 2017, from https://www.buzzfeed.com/craigsilverman/viral-fake-election-news-outperformed-real-news-on-facebook

Smith, T. W., & Son, J. (2013). General Social Survey 2012 final report: Trends in public attitudes about confidence in institutions. NORC at the University of Chicago.

Subramaniam, M., St. Jean, B., Taylor, N. G., Kodama, C., Follman, R., & Casciotti, D. (2015). Bit by bit: Using design-based research to improve the health literacy of adolescents. *JMIR Research Protocols*, *4*(2), e62.

Templeton, T. C., & Fleischmann, K. R. (2011). The relationship between human values and attitudes toward the Park51 and nuclear power controversies. *Proceedings of the American Society for Information Science and Technology*, *48*, 1-10.

# Search Successes and Failures in Query Segments and Search Tasks: A Field Study


**Yiwei Wang**
*School of Communication & Information (SC&I), Rutgers University, USA. yw498@scarletmail.rutgers.edu,*

**Soumik Mandal**
*School of Communication & Information (SC&I), Rutgers University, USA. sm1828@scarletmail.rutgers.edu,*

**Jiqun Liu**
*School of Communication & Information (SC&I), Rutgers University, USA. jl2033@scarletmail.rutgers.edu,*

**Chirag Shah**
*School of Communication & Information (SC&I), Rutgers University, USA. chirags@rutgers.edu*



## ABSTRACT

**Searching for information could be difficult or problematic in situations where searchers possess inadequate knowledge and/or vague information needs, often leading to unsuccessful outcomes. Existing studies on search outcomes (successes and failures) have lacked a detailed analysis at query (expression of information need) level from a searcher's perspective and the connection between queries and their corresponding search tasks. In the work reported here, we adopt a mixed-method approach to both explore how and why searchers succeeded or failed to fulfill their information need with each query and to link these query level outcomes to searchers' overall task goal realization. Twenty-six participants finished two search tasks in three days in naturalistic settings and reported their experiences in online diaries. The log data containing their actions in nearly 200 query segments, their diary responses and post-task semi-structured interviews inspire both in-depth discussion on search experiences and interesting comparison between successful and unsuccessful searchers. While quantitative analysis depicts the overall relationships between behavioral variables and search outcomes at both query and task levels, qualitative analysis reveals why those relationships took place. In general, searchers who viewed more pages and spent more time in each query segment were more likely to succeed. We also report reasons behind these phenomena.**



## KEYWORDS

search failures, query analysis, search tasks, field study, mixed methods


## INTRODUCTION

Despite user-friendly modern search engines, information seeking failures are not uncommon in today's web environment. Existing research on information seeking and search failures has explored reasons for failing in both library and web contexts and reported the relations between users' search behaviors and search outcomes (e.g., Evans & Chi, 2010; Kress, Del Bosque, & Ipri, 2011), as well as searchers' perception of information seeking failures and successes (Mansourian, Ford, Weber, & Madden, 2008). However, the literature has primarily focused on outcomes at a task level (if a person has successfully finished a search task) without offering sufficient insights into the connections between searchers' query level behavior and results, and the final task goal realization.

To overcome this limitation, we should start with analyzing a search session at a query level by considering the outcome of each query from a searcher's perspective (i.e., if a searcher has successfully found desired information). Then, query level outcomes could be linked to a searcher's task goal realization in the context of the barriers they face during a session and how they conquer (or fail to conquer) these barriers. In this work, 26 participants finished two search tasks in naturalistic settings in a three-day span and detailed their experiences in an online diary. Their diary responses, follow-up interviews, and log data gathering all their actions generated exciting findings about search behaviors and outcomes. A mixed-method approach was adopted to examine the successes and failures of each query segment in search sessions and to draw connections between search behaviors and searchers' query intention fulfillment. Relationships between various search barriers, query level outcomes, and task level outcomes were also explored. Naturalistic settings are arguably more likely to reflect individuals' natural search behavior than experimental settings. To the best of our knowledge, this is the first mixed-method work investigating search successes and failures in naturalistic settings at both a query and a task level.

## LITERATURE REVIEW

Early studies of search failures on a query level heavily focused on library catalogs and bibliographical databases. The definition for "search failure" was different across studies; most defined it as a search that returned zero hits (e.g., Peters, 1989; McCray & Tse, 2003), while others defined it as failing to retrieve at least one useful result (e.g., Drabenstott & Weller, 1996). Although researchers from the former studies admitted the limitation of the zero-hit approach, they were not able to assess the outcome of the searches that returned at least one result due to various reasons (e.g., relying on trans-


80th Annual Meeting of the Association for Information Science & Technology, Washington, DC, VA | Oct. 27-Nov. 1, 2017

action log only). Reasons for failing included query formulation issues (e.g., spelling, vocabulary), difficulties in navigating online catalogs, and low user perseverance. The introduction of web search engines exacerbated some problems with library and database searching because searchers brought their web searching habits to library searching. For example, Kress et al. (2011) discovered in their study of known-item search that users expected to parse the library system with any pieces of information from a citation (as they would via search engines), but some terms were not indexed in the library system. Rosman, Mayer, and Krampen (2016) suggested that database interfaces are usually more complex than search engine interfaces, so even students with high search knowledge could get poor results due to their insufficient practical experience with database features (e.g., using specific terms in some fields).

Some barriers that occur in library system or database searching – such as spelling and syntactical errors – are unlikely to be problematic in modern search engines because of auto correction and completion features. Li, Schijvenaars, and de Rijke (2017) observed that frequent zero-hit problems are a unique phenomenon in academic database search, and they happened much less frequently on web search engines. However, even skilled searchers still encounter searching failures on the web, particularly in informational search (acquiring information assumed to be present on the web, as defined by Broder, 2002) (Aula, Khan, & Guan, 2010; Evans & Chi, 2010). Early research on web searching compared search behaviors between experts and novices and suggested that search expertise played an important role in search performance (Jenkins, Corritore, & Wiedenbeck, 2003). Expert searchers performed tasks faster and more accurately than novice searchers (Lazonder, Biemans, & Wopereis, 2000). Studies have defined expert and novice in different ways, usually measuring a searcher's weekly usage on the web or their years of experience.

As the internet became increasingly embedded in individuals' everyday lives, researchers started to make connections between behavioral strategies and search outcomes rather than solely focus on the comparison between experts and novices. Aula et al. (2010) observed that searchers used more question queries and spent more time on search result pages (SERPs) when having difficulties with closed information tasks. Evans and Chi (2010) reported that informational searches accounted for 86.7% of failed searches and people turned to friends for help when facing difficulties. Bateman, Teevan, & White (2012) argued that many searchers do not know how to search effectively due to an absence of system feedback regarding how search behavior can be improved. Mansourian et al. (2008) categorized search successes and failures by emphasizing searchers' perception of whether the search engines indexed the information. When searchers believed that the information existed on the web but failed to retrieve it, they blamed their own inabilities.

To evaluate a search's outcome (success or failure), it is important to understand the searcher's intention behind that search. Xie (2002) proposed a classification of interactive intentions to construct patterns of users' information seeking intentions and the strategies they adopt. Her findings were used to design systems that support various types of interactions. To the best of our knowledge, only Rha, Mitsui, Belkin, and Shah (2016) draw on the outcome of a query based on a searcher's intention. Their work primarily focused on participant's query reformulation following satisfied or unsatisfied intentions, rather than how intentions were satisfied or unsatisfied. The majority of the intentions resulted in the same query reformulation type in both satisfied and unsatisfied cases.

To summarize, existing studies have provided meaningful explanations of reasons for search successes and failures, and how search task outcomes have been reflected in search behaviors like query length. However, most studies on web search outcomes have investigated searchers' successes and failures on task level without giving fine-grained consideration of how queries were connected with each other and how each query contributed to a searcher's final task outcome. To accomplish a search goal, a person may engage in a sequence of search activities, each of which has a sub-goal (intention) contributing to the general search goal (Xie, 2002). These sub-goals are expressed as queries in case of online searching using search engines. A searcher's sub-goals constantly change as they obtain new information while the end goal may remain the same (Bates, 1989), making a query an appropriate unit of analysis to track a person's behavioral and cognitive changes over the course of a search session. Query level analysis examining searchers' intention fulfillment and the connections between queries and their task outcomes may offer us an unprecedented amount of richness and specificity regarding a searcher's experience. Here we build on previous research and examine query level outcomes and connect them to final search task outcomes to offer specific insights on how searchers reach their final results. Specifically, we propose the following research questions:

**RQ1:** *What are the relationships between search behaviors (e.g., query length, query segment time) and search outcomes (i.e., success or failure) at query level?*

**RQ2:** *What information seeking barriers are connected to a searcher's task level outcome?*

**RQ3:** *How are query level outcomes connected to their corresponding task outcome?*

## METHOD

This section provides details of the primary method – a field study – used to address the research questions.

### Data Collection

#### Participants

Twenty-six undergraduate students at a major research university participated in this study. Recruitment calls were sent through various university email lists and Facebook groups. Participants represented all areas of study and grade levels. Age ranged from 18 to 24 years, with an average age of 20.4. 62% were females and 80% were native English speakers. Since we used a Chrome browser plugin to collect log data, we limited the recruitment to Chrome browser users because switching browsers may affect individuals' regular search behavior. Each participant was compensated $40 in cash after finishing the entire study.

### Tasks
In the field study, each participant was asked to finish two simulated search tasks, both of which were factual tasks following Li and Belkin's (2008) classification (i.e., a task locating facts or data in information systems). We also considered the *goal* facet when designing and selecting the tasks. Task One (T1) has a specific goal, while Task Two (T2) provides an amorphous goal. The two tasks are:

**T1 (Factual Specific)**: *You saw a clip of a TV movie on a bus and want to watch the full movie. You don't know the name of the movie. You only saw that the heroine is an amateur sleuth who owns a bakery. In the clip you were watching, she was worried about her competitor stealing her business. You really like the actor who plays the heroine's friend, a dentist. Find out the name of that actor.*

**T2 (Factual Amorphous)**: *Suppose you are an employee at a U.S. non-profit organization. You are trying to decide whether to contribute money to your employer-offered 403(b) retirement plan or to a personal IRA (Individual Retirement Account). Find resources that could help you decide which is best for your needs.*

We designed T1 ourselves and selected T2 from TREC 2014. The inclusion of both tasks was inspired by a previous survey exploring individuals' failures in information seeking (see Wang & Shah, 2016). Tasks that involve locating a specific item with incomplete information or making decisions between two products/services/plans present extreme challenges. The primary difference between the two tasks lies in their end goals. While T1 only has one correct answer, T2 has an open-ended goal that depends on individuals' interpretation of the factual information retrieved and their personal situations. We specifically designed T1 so that participants needed to use the vague information provided to locate a specific name in a limited amount of sources. T1 is arguably more difficult than other factual tasks in which most keywords needed for locating the information were already provided in the task descriptions (e.g., where is Bollywood located).

### Pilot test
Pilot tests with five participants were conducted prior to the main study to verify if 1) the system containing the tasks was functioning well, 2) the tasks and questionnaires were understandable, and 3) T1 was vague enough for searching but also specific enough to match the single answer.

### Task flow, log data, and diaries
All participants signed up for the study through a link provided in the recruitment message. A confirmation email was sent to each participant containing the study procedure, a link to install a Chrome browser plug-in, and a unique username and password combination to log in to our system. Although the two tasks were not supposed to take more than one hour, we hoped to capture participants' natural search behavior by giving as little constraint as possible. Therefore, they were given three days to complete the two tasks at any location with the device of their choice. They did not have to finish the tasks in one sitting. If they chose to leave and logout in the middle, they would be brought back to their stopping place when they logged in again. They could choose any search engine for their tasks, though all but one used Google.

Participants first finished a demographic questionnaire asking about their age, gender, area of study, and English proficiency. This was followed by instructions for T1 and a pre-search questionnaire in which participants rated their understanding of the task, topical knowledge, etc. on a seven-point Likert scale. Next, participants were instructed to start searching and to detail their search process and outcome in an online diary. For the search process, they were asked to write about their search steps, reasons behind their search strategies, what they found out, and any barriers they might have encountered. In addition to the open-ended questions, a list of 16 search barriers were selected from Chowdhury, Gibb, and Landoni's (2014) list of information seeking problems to allow participants to select anything they faced during the session. Then participants proceeded to complete a post-search questionnaire that included the same set of questions as the pre-search questionnaire, except that the ratings they provided were based on their actual search experience. For the last question, they rated their success and explained their reasoning. T2 followed with the same set-up.

All user actions (e.g., queries, pages viewed) were automatically saved in a remote server by the Chrome browser plugin. Query length (number of words in each query), pages per query (number of pages viewed in each query segment), average page dwell time in each query segment, and query segment time (amount of time spent on each query segment) were calculated for data analysis.

### Follow-up Interviews
We arranged a brief semi-structured follow-up interview with each person to further inquire about their experience with the search tasks. Interviews are not to be analyzed alone, but to serve as a complement to the diary and log data. A researcher reviewed the participant's actions and diary responses before their interview and brought up any unclear or incomplete information during the interview. Questions raised were primarily about queries, search strategies, and difficulties in finishing the tasks (e.g., *Was this query related to your task? What did you intend to do with this query? Why did you feel the information was scattered?*) For example, one participant wrote in her diary that "*there might be other websites that*

*help to solve this problem of finding movies where you don't know the name*" without clarifying what those websites were and if and how she used those websites. We learned what she meant through the interview. We did not tell participants the correct answer to T1 to avoid potential contamination.

## Data Analysis

The log data contained 3,055 pages and 452 queries including pages and queries unrelated to our study because participants sometimes digressed from their tasks. We manually cleaned the log by removing all unrelated pages and queries. It was not difficult to extract unrelated entries since the search topics were specific. Only very occasionally, we were not able to tell whether a query related to a task. Such incongruities were often discussed during the interviews and could thus be confirmed with interview transcripts. Identical consecutive queries were treated as one query segment. We then used the dwell time of all the study-related pages to derive the query segment time for each query segment. This only included the time participants actually spent on task-related pages. We took a mixed-method approach in analyzing the search outcome. In the qualitative analysis, we categorized each query segment and task answer into success or failure (coding process reported later) and explored how and why a query or a task succeeded or failed by analyzing query content, diaries and interviews. In the quantitative analysis, we conducted statistical tests using observable variables (e.g., query length), self-reported search barriers, and the outcome of a query or a task. After, we compared the findings between two analyses to see if the statistical analysis mirrors our observation.

### *Query level analysis*

Each query segment (i.e., everything that occurred between one query and the next) was manually classified into a success or a failure. We considered a query segment successful *if a participant successfully located desired information with that query*. This desired information was not necessarily the final answer to a task, but could be any information that helped them finish the task, as perceived by them. As long as their need was fulfilled, the query was coded as a success regardless of whether it eventually solved the task. Some participants wrote about their experiences in great detail so the outcome of each query was clear and could be drawn directly from the diaries. For example, in the excerpt below, it was clear that this participant failed at the first and second query segment and found desired information with the third attempt:

> *I searched "tv movie heroine owns bakery". After scanning the results* ***I realized this would not give me an answer [F]*** *... I then changed my search to "bakery owner and dentist".* ***Realizing this was not specific enough [F]****, I changed it to "bakery owner and dentist tv movie". Then, I found "Murder She Baked: A Chocolate Chip Cookie Mystery" ...* ***Upon review, I decided Murder She Baked was the movie talked about. [S]***

However, that was not always the case. In order to code if a participant was successful with a query, we sometimes needed to know what they intended to do with that query; namely, their query intention. We manually derived the intention behind each query segment based on its query content and corresponding diary response and interview transcript. Then we coded the result of each query based on its content, intention, corresponding diary responses, and interview transcripts. Derived query intention types were inductively drawn from the data. Unlike previous studies on search intentions, we focus not on participants' intentions, but on their outcomes. Intentions were used for judging the success of a query only when participants did not explicitly specify if they were successful with that query. To derive their query outcomes, we extracted the information/sources participants located from their diaries and matched those to their intentions. For example, one participant issued a query "*Murder, She Baked: A Chocolate Chip Cookie Mystery actor*," meaning she was looking for an actor in the movie. Her diary indicated that she only found out the title of the movie. This query was coded as a failure because her result did not match her initial intention. Intention categories and examples are provided in Table 1.

| Derived Intentions | Examples and Quotes |
|---|---|
| Find if a question has been asked by others | [Query was the entire task description] - "There was a possibility that someone else had searched the same thing." |
| Narrow down the topic | amateur sleuth owning a bakery movie - "Shortlisted movies where the heroine is an amateur sleuth owning a bakery." |
| Find information contributing to the final answer | personal IRA – "learn about 403b plans first, then about personal IRAs." |
| Find the final answer | murder she baked dentist – "looked up the actor's name" |
| Verify the information retrieved | IRA or 403(b) – "to make sure that my search results were consisted with each other" |
| Learn topical knowledge | sleuth – "wanted to know what that word meant" |

***Table 1****. Derived query intentions and examples*

After coding the outcome of each query segment, we conducted one-way ANOVA to explore if the values of each observable behavior (i.e., query length, pages per query, average page dwell time, and query segment time) were significantly different between successful queries and failed queries. Normality assumption was tested using Shapiro-Wilk test and homogeneity of variance was tested using Levene's Test. Normality assumption was violated for all dependent variables, and homogeneity of variance was violated for query segment time and pages per query. Although ANOVA has proved to be robust under the condition of non-normality, the accuracy of F can be affected when group sizes are not equal (Wilcox, 2005), which was the case here (we had more successful queries). Robust ANOVA was run using Wilcox's t1way function based on 20% trimmed means in R for each variable. Next, each observable behavior was added to a logistic regression model one at a time as an independent variable to predict query outcome. Multicollinearity and the linearity of the logit were tested to make sure the models would not be biased. Akaike information criterion (AIC) of each model was compared to select the best predictive model of query outcomes. These statistical tests were conducted for the whole dataset and separate tests for each task's subset. Query content, diaries, and interviews were also analyzed to explain how and why participants succeeded or failed with a query, though the reasons may or may not be reflected in observable behaviors.

### *Task Level Analysis*

Each task answer was evaluated and categorized into a success or a failure. Evaluation for the task level result was very straightforward. T1 had one answer so there was not any ambiguity in judging participants' answers. T2 was considered as a success if a participant was able to find factual information about two retirement plans to help them differentiate between the plans and make a rough decision, considering the task description (e.g., non-profit organization) and the participant's current situation (e.g., marital status). Next, participants' descriptive search barriers were coded using Chowdhury et al.'s (2014) typology to investigate how and why those barriers occurred and if they led to task failures.

Since our dataset is relatively small on task level (52 responses, 26 of each task type), we decided to mainly explore the relationship between each search barrier and the task outcome. A 2x2 contingency table was generated for each pair of variables. Pearson's Chi-squared test was conducted if the expected frequencies in each cell were larger than 5; otherwise, Fisher's exact test was conducted. We also calculated the query failure rate (the proportion of failed query out of all queries), average time per query, and total query segment time per task and used ANOVA to explore if they were connected to task outcomes.

## RESULTS

### *Query Level Results (RQ1)*

The log data yielded 199 query segments related to our study tasks, 109 of which were successful while the rest were unsuccessful. Participants spent 86.17s (roughly a minute and a half) on each query segment in average (SD=146.95) with an average query length of 7.13 words (SD=7.55). Overall, participants issued shorter queries, viewed more pages per query, spent more time on each query segment, and spent more time on each page in successful query segments than in failed query segments. Descriptive statistics for the whole dataset and for each task (i.e., T1 and T2) are summarized in Table 2.

| | Success Mean (SD) | Failure Mean (SD) |
|---|---|---|
| Query Length (words) | 6.18 (5.53) | 8.28 (9.34) |
| Pages per Query (number of pages) | 2.04 (2.09) | 1.28 (1.81) |
| Query segment time (seconds) | 109.12 (154.23) | 58.36 (133.20) |
| Average Page Dwell Time (seconds) | 69.47 (132.45) | 49.13 (128.69) |
| T1 – Query Length | 6.13 (3.54) | 9.01 (10.36) |
| T1 – Pages per Query | 2.06 (2.06) | 1.31 (1.92) |
| T1 – Query segment time | 72.14 (107.03) | 37.55 (67.71) |
| T1 – Average Page Time | 33.93 (65.03) | 27.10 (50.54) |
| T2 – Query Length | 6.26 (7.49) | 5.53 (2.14) |
| T2 – Pages per Query | 1.98 (2.19) | 1.16 (1.34) |
| T2 – Query segment time | 159.76 (191.77) | 136.16 (248.60) |
| T2 – Average Page Time | 118.14 (179.12) | 131.42 (250.76) |

***Table 2**. Descriptive statistics for query segments*

When considering all query segments, ANOVA tests showed that participants tended to view more pages in successful query segments than in failed query segments ($F(1, 102.85)=9.12$, $p=.003$), and the time they spent on each query segment was usually longer in successful queries than in failed ones ($F(1, 81.84)=7.69$, $p=.007$). Participants also issued shorter queries ($F(1, 112.34)=2.49$, $p=.12$) and spent more time on each page ($F(1, 109.81)=3.43$, $p=.07$) in successful query segments, though these were statistically insignificant. When considering each task individually, the results of T1 mirrored the results of the whole dataset, showing that pages per query ($F(1, 57.58)=6.64$, $p=.01$) and query segment time ($F(1, 60.02)=4.46$, $p=.04$) were significantly higher in successful query segments than in failed ones. Query length ($F(1, 74.83)=0.58$, $p=.45$) and average page dwell time ($F(1, 75.08)=0.77$, $p=.38$) were also different across two classes, but not significant. For T2, none of the behavioral variables was significantly different between two classes:

> Query length: $F(1, 38.24)=2.36$, $p=.13$;
> Query segment time: $F(1, 36.07)=1.65$, $p=.21$;
> Pages per query: $F(1, 35.30)=2.23$, $p=.14$;
> Average page dwell time: $F(1, 22.01)=0.03$, $p=.84$.

Four logistic regression models were generated first using the whole dataset to explore the association between observable behaviors and query outcomes. Four behavioral variables were added to the model one at a time as independent variables. AIC values were compared and the model with the lowest AIC (indicating the lowest information lost) was selected as the best model to predict query outcome. In this case, it was the model with all independent variables. We only report results of this model in Table 3 for brevity.

| | Coefficient (Standard Error) | Pr(>\|z\|) |
|---|---|---|
| Query Length | -0.06 (0.02) | **.03** |
| Pages per Query | 0.08 (0.10) | .40 |
| Query segment time | 0.01 (0.01) | **.02** |
| Average Page Dwell Time | -0.01 (0.01) | **.04** |

***Table 3**. Logistic regression for whole dataset (best model) (Note: Cells in bold highlight the significant coefficients.)*

When logistic regressions were conducted using query segments for T1, the model that yielded the best AIC value only included pages per query and query length as independent variables; both of their estimated coefficients were statistically significant. None of the models created for T2 demonstrated significant effects of independent variables, indicating that there was no statistically significant relationship between any of the behavioral variables and query outcomes in the factual amorphous task. Results of each task's best model are reported in Table 4.

| | | Coefficient (Standard Error) | Pr(>\|z\|) |
|---|---|---|---|
| T1 | Query Length | -0.10 (0.05) | **.02** |
| | Pages per Query | 0.25 (0.10) | **.01** |
| T2 | Pages per Query | 0.27 (0.19) | .15 |

***Table 4**. Logistic Regression for T1 and T2 (best models).*

Quantitative results correspond to our observations in the qualitative analysis, which was conducted before the statistical tests. For T1, participants who viewed more pages in a query segment were more likely to succeed for a reason. The movie described in T1 was not famous and only a few sources discussed it. Meanwhile, information about detective movies and fictions with similar storylines was all over the web. A webpage about this specific movie may not be ranked on the top of a search engine result page (SERP) so participants went through trial and error before landing on the right direction. For instance, one participant indicated his difficulty in finding the right link:

There were many wrong sources that had the same keywords that were in the task. For example, when I searched for the amateur detective I found out that there was a series for just detectives. So there were many results that did not make sense.

Many participants pointed out that the "the search topic had results from a book and a movie," their search "came up with the wrong movie," and they "had to read about the movie on several different websites to get a definite answer." Another difficult factor was that not every relevant webpage contained the answer: the actor who plays the dentist. Going through multiple results on a SERP may deviate from some people's common behavior (e.g., only clicked on the first link), so a few participants claimed to lose patience when the information did not appear at the top of the results page (e.g., I also was starting to lack patience because I'm so used to just finding information in a couple seconds.)

When some participants could not find the information by visiting one or two sites, they assumed that the query was bad. Though they frequently changed their queries, the results returned might be similar and still required them to click on multiple links. Participants who succeeded with a query frequently mentioned that they found the information *"after going through many links."* This was reflected in the statistics that participants who rapidly entered more than ten queries failed almost every time. In contrast, when participants only issued a couple of queries but spent more time on each one, they were more likely to find the information. Below (Table 5) is an interesting comparison between two participants. While P16 used a list of queries but failed at most of them, P22 located the right answer with only two queries. The content of several of P16's queries were not very different from P22's; however, the second user spent a few minutes in each query segment while the first one spent less than a minute.

| P16 | |
|---|---|
| movie where heroine is an amateur sleuth who owns a bakery | F |
| strawberry shortcake murder movie | F |
| heroine | S |
| a chocolate chip cookie mystery | F |
| the heroine is an amateur sleuth who owns a bakery and is worried about her competitor stealing... | F |
| movie where the heroine is an amateur sleuth who owns a bakery and is worried about her competitor stealing the bakery | F |
| movie where the heroine's friend is a dentist | F |
| compromising position | F |
| compromising position imdb | F |
| ... | |
| **P22** | |
| amateur sleuth who owns bakery movie | S |
| murder she baked dentist | S |

***Table 5**. Query segment comparison between two participants. S=Success, F=Failure.*

This finding also applies to T2, for which participants who spent more time on a query segment were more likely to have good outcomes, though this was not statistically significant. The topic of retirement plans does not usually fall into students' area of expertise. The majority of the participants rated themselves as not knowledgeable in this topic. They often struggled to find information *"in clear enough language."* Thus, it could take them a few links to reach to a site that can be understood, as reported by this participant:

*Since 403(b) and IRA are each a very broad category, it was very difficult to find clear and concise webpages that contained the information that I needed in a summary type way ... I tried to avoid any sites that looked above my knowledge in this field, or else I would be completely confused.*

Some participants gave up before they could locate something in plain English, and thus failed. Interestingly, although participants visited multiple links, they might primarily rely on one or two resources written in a language understandable to lay people (e.g., *I admit using only one link to make my decision isn't great but the fact that it was in plain English was appealing.*) Also, because of the nature of the topic, advertisements and spams were likely to show up and it was hard for a non-expert to sort out credible information sources (e.g., *There were a lot of results that wanted to advertise financial services in my search results. This made finding credible sources difficult.*)

Query length seemed to be influential in T1, probably because the difficulty with specifying a query triggered a big diversity in query lengths. Compared to the 2-5 words mean query length reported in previous studies (e.g., Jiang, He, & Allan, 2014), average query lengths in T1 were considerably higher, particularly in the failed cases (9.01 words). Participants often entered long queries that included all important keywords in the task description (e.g., "*amateur sleuth who owns a bakery her competitor stealing her business movie*"). Some even copied the entire task description into search box. Such long queries were very unlikely to deliver satisfactory results. Two main types of participants used lengthy queries. The first type started with long queries but switched to shorter ones after experiencing trouble. For example:

- [movie that heroine is an amateur sleuth who owns a bakery ... You really like the actor who plays the heroine's friend, a dentist]
- [movie that heroine is an amateur sleuth who owns a bakery … that includes a dentist]
- [TV movie that heroine is an amateur sleuth who owns a bakery]

Another type of participants started with relatively shorter queries but started to throw every clue in after failing to find the answer:

- [movie where heroine is an amateur sleuth who owns a bakery]
- [strawberry shortcake murder movie]
- [a chocolate chip cookie mystery]
- [the heroine is an amateur sleuth who owns a bakery and is worried about her competitor stealing…]
- [movie where the heroine is an amateur sleuth who owns a bakery and is worried about her competitor…]

It is worth noting that this participant once entered the movie title as a query, which would have returned the page with the right information. However, he only spent a few seconds clicking on one page and gave up. Subsequent longer queries were not helpful. This again corresponds to our finding that some failures are not necessarily due to the query itself or the results returned, but participants' lack of persistence in the process. Their chances of getting the answer decreased as they kept adding random words into a query. Participants willing to look at more pages and spend more time on each query had better luck. The participant above jumped between long and short queries, but failed with most of them. This echoes Aula et al. (2010), who found that struggling users tended to refine queries in an unsystematic way. One of our participants even entered *"how to search in google"* out of frustration to learn search skills. Several participants issued long sentence-like queries because they wanted to see if other people have also had the same question (e.g., *there was a possibility that someone else had searched the same thing.)*

The length of a query somewhat depends on a participant's habits and expectations. Some participants preferred to add everything in one query and were often disappointed by the results (e.g., *I always gear towards looking up the entire task first...I was not getting regular websites or words in English text*). A few of them indicated that they aimed to find the final answer by one query and realized the impossibility (e.g., *I realized that probably it (the movie) wasn't popular enough that would be right there; I was hoping I would find something that just gives me the pros and cons, give me everything in one ... then it wasn't as specific*). There were also participants who searched one step at a time with relatively shorter queries. Although it took them a few tries to obtain sufficient information, they generally had a smooth experience at each stage, as this participant described:

*I didn't know what the 403 retirement plan was so I looked that up first. Once I knew at least a bit about that and saw its advantages and disadvantages, I looked up the personal IRA to see if its advantages were better or if it had worse disadvantages. Once I knew more about the IRA, I decided to look up what other people thought about the debate. So, I searched "403(b) retirement plan vs. personal IRA".*

### Task Level Results (RQ2 & RQ3)

There were 21 task failures and 31 successes. Eleven participants successfully completed one task, ten succeeded in both, and the other five failed in both. Pearson's Chi-square tests or Fisher's exact tests for each participant-reported search barrier and task outcome are reported in Table 6. Only barriers reported for more than eight times were selected for the tests.

There was a significant association between "unaware of information sources" and the task outcome. Only two participants who had this barrier eventually succeeded. When they selected this barrier, they usually referred to their uncertainty in selecting sources for T2, and this was also associated with a lack of knowledge:

*I am not knowledgeable in retirement planning so I had no idea as to what resources to approach in doing this task. And because I am not well versed in personal finance, I did now know what words to use to search.*

| Barriers | Frequencies | Test Results |
|---|---|---|
| Too many irrelevant results | 16 | $\chi^2(1) = 3.37$, p=.06 |
| Lack of topical knowledge | 14 | $\chi^2(1) = .05$, p=.83 |
| Lack of patience | 12 | $\chi^2(1) = .60$, p=.44 |
| Unconfident about finding information | 12 | $\chi^2(1) = .01$, p=.92 |
| Unaware of information sources | 9 | Fisher's exact test, **p=.02** |
| Too much information | 9 | Fisher's exact test, p=.53 |

***Table 6**. Relations between barriers and task results*

Most barriers were not significantly associated with task outcomes, meaning that barriers did not necessarily result in unfavorable results overall. For example, some participants perceived the tasks to be very difficult and felt unconfident going into the task: "*I was unconfident that I would be able to find anything because it was so vague...*" But their confidence increased while searching: "*I gained confidence in my searches as I found more information about the movie and fit the information together.*" Despite that "*too much information was unnecessarily annoying*" and participants sometimes were "*not able to fully understand the information,*" they were not prevented from getting useful information if they invested enough effort. Participants who have gone through the following type of systematic thinking usually succeeded in their tasks:

I realized after reading that in order to decide, I needed to substitute something for a couple of the 'X's I had in the situation. For example, being married and my income greatly affects the outcome ... Once I considered it again with these factors and took the advice of the article, it was only logical that I come to the conclusion to select the 403(b) retirement plan. The possibility of my employer matching me in contribution definitely tipped it too. The main strategies I used were clarifying what I didn't know, learning and analyzing the advantages/disadvantages of the plans, considering the opinion of a credible source, considering how my living situation affects everything, and combining all of that.

The query failure rates in successful tasks were not significantly different from the failure rates in failed tasks as presented by ANOVA ($F(1, 23.2) = 0.61$, $p=.44$). Nevertheless, successful tasks did have a lower average query failure rate (29%) than failed ones (39%). Total query segment time was significantly longer in successful cases than in failed cases ($F(1, 29.51) = 19.39$, $p < .001$) and average time per query in successful cases was also longer, though not statistically significant ($F(1, 29.82) = 2.08$, $p=.16$). Having some query failures was not always an indicator of task failure. A few participants remained very persistent despite their difficulties in the middle. One participant had 11 query segments and went through quite a few wrong sources before finally locating the answer to T1. He did not give up when wrong movies were retrieved and successfully finished the task. Patience and search persistence were repeatedly shown to be important in this study.

## DISCUSSION

The data analysis presents intriguing findings that explain how and why searchers succeeded or failed at both query level and task level. In this section, we synthesize our results through revisiting proposed research questions.

**RQ1:** *What are the relationships between search behaviors and search outcomes at query level?*

Participants demonstrated two general types of starting strategy: finding everything with one attempt or dividing a task into steps. These two strategies manifested in starting with a long query containing every clue provided or starting with short queries and adding one clue at a time, respectively. Neither option was absolutely better than the other. While some participants pointed out that short queries might return many unrelated sources, long queries might not give any related sources. Participants who used very long queries often either shortened them (e.g., *I first searched the entire task that was told with deleting words that were unnecessary. I then decided to be as simple as possible*), or gave up.

Despite how they planned and started their search, no one could finish the task with one query. Whether they could succeed largely depended on their subsequent steps, and shorter queries offered no guarantee of success. Since our tasks involved a movie that is not widely discussed on the web (T1) and a topic on which many college students have limited knowledge (T2), searchers could not use their usual method of instantly obtaining an answer using the first SERP's top results (e.g., *I just basically looked at top links*). Therefore, participants who went through more links in a query segment performed better than those who quickly reformulated queries. As we discussed in the last section, some of those failed queries were not worded very differently from successful ones. However, searchers' habit of assuming a query was useless after spending only a few seconds with its results led to failures. Ironically, quickly abandoning a query segment did not necessarily save time because of the time spent issuing subsequent queries.

This is one of our most substantive findings: that user perseverance still matters even in today's web environment where finding information is assumed to be easy and fast. This has a practical implication for system design. As researchers are trying hard to improve system performance and query recommendation, it may also be helpful to assist searchers in changing search behavior. On one hand, we do not wish to let searchers go through a long and frustrating process and want to reduce their effort in searching. On the other hand, search engines fall short in returning results about unpopular topics and capturing searchers' prior knowledge. Therefore, patience and persistence are still useful when having trouble locating information. We do not intend to suggest that searchers should stick to a query no matter what results are returned. For example, domain experts may be able to tell whether a query is promising from a SERP. Our findings may only be suitable in explaining searching behavior when participants are not familiar with a topic or have vague information at hand.

All four behavioral variables (i.e., query segment time, query length, pages per query, average page dwell time) were different across two classes; however, only the differences of pages per query and query segment time in T1 were significant. This is not entirely surprising because T2 is an open-ended task with fewer details, and thus participants' behaviors did not widely vary, particularly in query lengths. Many of their queries for T2 included the names of two retirement plans with an operator in the middle. The regression model showed that query length and pages per query in T1 were closely related to the search outcome at query level. This corroborates our qualitative finding that issuing shorter queries and viewing more pages led to better query outcomes in T1.

**RQ2:** *What information seeking barriers are connected to a searcher's task level outcome?*

Overall, most information seeking barriers reported by participants were not significantly associated with their task outcomes. Encountering barriers did not mean failing, or vice versa. "Unaware of information sources" is significantly related to a task outcome. However, participants might not draw this barrier from their experience, but from their reflection afterwards. In other words, they might perceive that they were not aware of some sources because they did not find an answer.

Interestingly, some participants had great difficulties during the search (e.g., *I have very limited knowledge on this topic, in fact my only knowledge came from doing research for this study*) but successfully finished the task, while other participants who did not report any difficulties failed. A few participants expressed great confidence in their diary but did not ultimately supply a satisfactory answer (e.g., *the information between sources seemed to overlap and mostly be saying the same thing, so I am fairly confident that it is correct*). We also noticed a mismatch between participants' perceptions of task outcomes and their real task outcomes. In some cases, they were certain that they found the right answer when their answer was incorrect. A few participants utilized several queries to verify the information retrieved even after they found the correct name (e.g., *I triple checked that everything matched the description, dotting my Is and crossing my Ts at every opportunity*). The majority of participants did not talk about verifying their answers.

**RQ3:** *How are query level outcomes connected to their corresponding task outcome?*

We did not find a significant relationship between query failure rates and task outcomes, despite failure rates in failed cases being higher on average. Similar to the relationship between barriers and task outcomes, having temporary failures did not prevent participants from succeeding. Task outcomes were not simply the summation of query outcomes and successful searchers could also struggle when working on the tasks. In some cases, it was the last query that supplied the right answer and led to an overall success. Having more successes than failures in the middle of a task did not guarantee a good outcome.

That being said, we believe that it is necessary to reduce query failures to enhance search efficiency and experience and to reduce user frustration during a search. For example, we learned from some participants that each task could be completed by entering as little as two queries. However, a few participants went through several query failures before retrieving the right information. Although both types of participants had an overall success, the former apparently had a more enjoyable experience. Combining analyses at both query and task levels not only looks at searchers' task outcomes, but also reveals the details that could offer practical implications for interface or search intervention design. On system side, search engines may take the level of easiness of information into consideration in document ranking. One of the most frequent search barriers faced by the participants was the insufficiency of knowledge. As indicated by some participants, information in "plain English" that could be comprehended by lay people was desirable when they did not possess enough topical knowledge. On user side, interventions may be needed to inform users about effective search strategies. Bateman et al. (2012) made an attempt to change searchers' behavior by allowing them to reflect on their previous actions and compare those with others' behavior. Their results present a promising future for the direction of changing people's search behaviors.

This study has several limitations. First, we noticed that later participants had more successes in T1 than earlier participants (e.g., better outcomes in first several queries). It might be possible that Google improved search performance as more and more users searched within the same topic, especially since this movie was not well-known before. This is an uncontrollable inherent limitation of our study. Second, simulated search tasks were not related to participants' daily lives and they were not required to finish the tasks, which might trigger some of them to give up quickly. Third, we define success and failure rather arbitrarily without considering possible serendipity in the middle. It could be possible that participants found out something useful with a query even though that information did not fulfill their initial intention.

Serendipity was not observed in diaries or interviews this time so we could not surmise if it really took place. The definition of success and failure should be open to refinement in future research.

## CONCLUSION AND FUTURE RESEARCH

We reported here our findings from a field study on the relationships between individuals' search behaviors and search outcomes on both query and task level. Our main findings based on a mixed-method analysis are briefly summarized as follows. First, it was found that searchers who stayed longer in a query segment and viewed more pages had a higher chance to succeed, primarily because the information could not be easily located on the top of the first SERP. Second, although shorter queries were not found to be necessarily better, they did increase searchers' chances to find the answer in general. Third, encountering difficulties and failures in the middle of a search session was not always deemed to be a bad sign. Searchers' persistence and proper adjustment of strategy led to their successes. Finally, the results indicate that there is still room to improve search engines to assist searchers with vague search goals or little prior knowledge to locate information, and it may be helpful to shape searchers' behavior in addition to enhancing system performance. Our next step would be continuing this line of research by further classifying failure types, exploring user's behavior patterns and search outcomes in open-ended intellectual search tasks, and studying the underlying relationships between query level behavior and the usefulness of the entire interaction process in a search session.

## ACKNOWLEDGEMENT

The work reported here is supported by the Institute of Museum and Library Services (IMLS) grant no. LG-81-16-0025-16. We would like to thank Matthew Mitsui for developing the study system.

## REFERENCES

Aula, A., Khan, R. M., & Guan, Z. (2010). How does search behaviour change as search becomes more difficult? In *Proceedings of the 28th SIGCHI conference on human factors in computing systems*, 35-44.

Bateman, S., Teevan, J., & White, R. W. (2012). The search dashboard: How reflection and comparison impact search behavior. In *Proceedings of the SIGCHI conference on human factors in computing systems*, 1785-1794.

Bates, M. J. (1989). The design of browsing and berrypicking techniques for the online search interface. *Online review*, 13(5), 407-424.

Broder, A. (2002). A taxonomy of web search. In *ACM SIGIR forum, 36*(2), 3-10.

Chowdhury, S., Gibb, F., & Landoni, M. (2014). A model of uncertainty and its relation to information seeking and retrieval. *Journal of Documentation, 70*(4), 575-604.

Drabenstott, K. M., & Weller, M.S. (1996). Failure analysis of subject searches in a test of a new design for subject access to online catalogs. *JASIST, 47*(7), 519-537.

Evans, B. M., & Chi, E. H. (2010). An elaborated model of social search. *Information Processing and Management (IP&M), 46*(6), 656-678.

Jenkins, C., Corritore, C. L., & Wiedenbeck, S. (2003). Patterns of information seeking on the web: A qualitative study of domain expertise and web expertise. *IT & Society, 1*(3), 64-89.

Jiang, J., He, D., & Allan, J. (2014). Searching, browsing, and clicking in a search session: Changes in user behavior by task and over time. In *Proceedings of the 37th international ACM SIGIR conference on research & development in information retrieval*, 607-616.

Kress, N., Del Bosque, D., & Ipri, T. (2011). User failure to find known library items. *New Library World, 112*(3/4), 150-170.

Lazonder, A. W., Biemans, H. J., & Wopereis, I. G. (2000). Differences between novice and experienced users in searching information on the world wide web. *Journal of Association for Information Science and Technology (JASIST), 51*(6), 576-581.

Li, Y., & Belkin, N. J. (2008). A faceted approach to conceptualizing tasks in information seeking. *Information Processing & Management, 44*(6), 1822-1837.

Li, X., Schijvenaars, B. J. A., & de Rijke, M. (2017). Investigating queries and search failures in academic search. *Information Processing & Management, 53*(3), 666-683.

Mansourian, Y., Ford, N., Weber, S., & Madden, A. (2008). An integrative model of "information visibility" and "information seeking" on the web. *Electronic Library and Information Systems, 42*(4), 402-417.

McCray, A. T., & Tse, T. (2003). Understanding search failures in consumer health information systems. In *AMIA,* 430-434.

Rha, E. Y., Mitsui, M., Belkin, N. J., & Shah, C. (2016). Exploring the relationships between search intentions and query reformulations. In *Proceedings of the Association for Information Science and Technology, 53*(1).

Rosman, T., Mayer, A. K. & Krampen, G. (2016). On the pitfalls of bibliographic database searching: Comparing successful and less successful users. *Behaviour & Information Technology, 35*(2), 106-17.

Peters, T. A. (1989). When smart people fail: An analysis of the transaction log of an online public access catalog. *The Journal of Academic Librarianship, 15*(5), 267-273.

Xie, H. (2002). Patterns between interactive intentions and information-seeking strategies. *Information Processing and Management, 38*(1), 55-77.

Wang, Y., & Shah, C. (2016). Exploring support for the unconquerable barriers in information seeking. In *Proceedings of the Association for Information Science and Technology annual meeting, 53*(1).

Wilcox, R. R. (2005). Introduction to robust estimation and hypothesis testing (2nd ed.). Burlington, MA: Elsevier.

# Assessing Technologies for Information Sharing in International Research Teams: Developing an Intercultural Heuristic Evaluation Tool

**Wesley S. Ward**
*Institute for Land, Water and Society, Charles Sturt University, Australia. wward@csu.edu.au*

**Lisa M. Given**
*Faculty of Health, Arts and Design, Swinburne University of Technology, Australia. lgiven@swin.edu.au*

## ABSTRACT

**Collaborative research teams working in developing countries rely on information and computer technologies (ICTs), both hardware and software, to overcome barriers to information sharing including, language, distance, time, economic development and politics. However, studies have shown impediments to information sharing between team members from different cultures, nations and institutions. This paper reports on a study in which a model was developed to highlight the most important barriers for communication and information sharing in international research teams, which was the basis for the development of a heuristic evaluation tool. The communication model was created using the results of 30 semi-structured interviews with agricultural scientists working in international research teams based in Australia and Lao People's Democratic Republic. Interview data outline a number of barriers and facilitators for team communication, which informed the development of eight intercultural heuristics. These were combined with Jakob Nielsen's general usability heuristics to form the intercultural heuristic evaluation tool, or I-CHET. The tool was then tested in a pilot study to assess the utility and usability of two ICTs used by international research teams: email and Skype. The initial assessment using I-CHET showed that while email theoretically lacked the richness of cues seen in Skype, email better complied with the needs of international research groups for sharing information and communicating in multicultural teams dispersed over language, cultural and geographic divides.**

## KEYWORDS

heuristic evaluation, information behavior, research collaboration, communication technologies, intercultural communication, scholarly communication

## INTRODUCTION

Agricultural research in many developing countries is implemented by collaborative teams comprising local and international scientists (Ynalvez & Shrum, 2011). These teams rely on effective communication to build sound professional relationships and deliver successful outcomes (Jirotka, Lee, & Olson, 2013), exemplifying how people from different cultures, experiences and disciplines forge connections with each other. However, research team members are often dispersed across national, institutional, economic, geographic, temporal and cultural boundaries and often must rely on information and computer technologies (ICTs), such as computers and mobile phones, for technologically mediated communication (TMC) (Fulk, Monge, & Hollingshead, 2005; Sonnenwald, 2007). Various ICTs are selected by team members to facilitate collaborative work, but little research assesses the effectiveness of these ICTs to support scientific communication among diverse international teams.

This paper reports the development and initial testing of a heuristic evaluation tool designed to assess ICTs used by international research teams in Australia and the Lao People's Democratic Republic (PDR) in South-East Asia. The tool's evaluative heuristics were developed from empirical results of an intercultural communication model that emerged from a study showing that cultural boundaries presented major barriers to effective communication within the research teams (see Ward (2016) for a full discussion of the research findings). This paper explores how communication boundaries can be addressed through the application of intercultural heuristics to best estimate the effectiveness of ICTs used by international research teams.

## LITERATURE REVIEW

### *Communication barriers*

Agricultural research projects in developing countries are often implemented by teams comprising scientists from international research and/or donor agencies working alongside local scientists from developed countries; these local scientists may work for national government agencies or universities from the developing country (Shrum, 1997). Teams typically include members with different knowledge, skills, and access to information sources or other resources required for scientific collaboration (Katz & Martin, 1997). Gibson and Grubb (2005) recognized that to be a successful team, team members from various countries and institutions must communicate with each other effectively.

Communication barriers impede information sharing and other forms of interaction between team members. Extensive research has identified individual barriers between team

80th Annual Meeting of the Association for Information Science & Technology, Washington, DC, VA | Oct. 27-Nov. 1, 2017

members and subgroups, including: time differences (Olson & Olson, 2000); geographic and institutional dispersal (Huang & Ocker, 2006; Olson, Bos, & Zimmerman, 2008; Polzer, Crisp, Jarvenpaa, & Kim, 2006); use of English as the common team language (Hwang, 2013; Voss, Albert, & Ferring, 2014); cultural differences (Kealey, Protheroe, MacDonald, & Vulpe, 2006); differences in economic development (Velho & Velho, 1996); and, diplomatic challenges (Windsor, 2011). In many cases of international collaboration, especially those focused on economically developed countries, these types of barriers may be addressed using TMC (Sonnenwald, 2007), while email has been used between scientific collaborators from developed and developing countries in Asia, Africa and South America (Duque, Miller, Barriga, Shrum, & Henríquez, 2012; Duque et al., 2005; Ynalvez & Shrum, 2008). Research by Gervedink Nijhuis, Voogt, and Pieters (2012) is one of few studies to investigate communication barriers for a research and development team operating in a developing country, Ghana.

### Selecting ICTs

ICTs have been recommended as vital tools for overcoming communication barriers in scientific collaboration in developed countries (e.g., Maglaughlin & Sonnenwald, 2005) and in Asia (Ballantyne, Maru, & Poncari, 2010; Singh, 2006), and some recommendations have made using a number of theories that address the selection of ICTs for use in international research. However, few studies have addressed the usefulness of ICTs for overcoming barriers between members of scientific team from both economically developed and developing countries.

In their explication of behavioral complexity theory, Shachaf and Hara (2007) recognized that globally dispersed business teams selected ICTs for TMC through the lens of six communication barriers that fall into three broad categories: physical (temporal and geographic distance); social (language, culture); and, macro-societal (economic development, political differences). Behavioral complexity theory also presumes that more than one ICT can be used for a given task or context (Shachaf & Hara, 2007). This is a more natural, holistic approach to ICT selection in international research teams than that proposed in the simpler yet more widely cited theories of media richness (Daft & Lengel, 1986), unified theory acceptance and use of technology (Venkatesh & Davis, 2000), or media synchronicity (Dennis, Fuller, & Valacich, 2008), which can fill particular needs of groups as proposed in media niche theory (Dimmick & Rothenbuhler, 1984).

Behavioral complexity theory is derived from fault line theory for geographically dispersed workers (Lau & Murnighan, 1998) to explain how fault lines or barriers can impede communication between members of a work group. The theory was refined by Huang and Ocker (2006) to explain communication barriers for dispersed IT work groups. As a more realistic, holistic approach than proposed by previous theories, behavioral complexity theory was used in the research reported in this paper as an analytic lens to explore the usefulness of tools for communicating between members of international research teams.

### Evaluating ICTs

Qualitative and quantitative testing methods, including heuristic evaluation, have been used since the 1980s by academics and information technology practitioners to analyze and identify both usability and utility problems in computer programs during and after development (Nielsen, 1994a). Usability evaluation examines how well people can use an ICT's functions, while utility assessment explores whether the technology offers the functions users need (Johannessen & Hornbæk, 2014).

Heuristic evaluation, first described in Nielsen and Molich (1990), uses ten general problem domains, or 'heuristics,' to detect usability problems in software using expert and/or novice evaluators (Nielsen, 1994b). Heuristic evaluation has been used extensively to evaluate ICTs in various contexts in developing countries, including studies of commercial websites (Chen & Macredie, 2005; Hasan, Morris, & Probets, 2012), databases (Azadi, Eskrootchi, Jamshidi Orak, & Mohaghegh, 2014), and mobile phones (Po, Howard, Vetere, & Skov, 2004) in Asia. However, heuristic evaluation has also been criticized for producing inaccurate attributions to particular problem domains (Hvannberg, Law, & Lérusdóttir, 2007), being unsuitable for use in non-Western cultures (Haddad, McGrenere, & Jacova, 2014; Hasan et al., 2012), and for producing differing opinions between evaluators from different cultures regarding perceived usability of some ICTs (Frandsen-Thorlacius, Hornbæk, Hertzum, & Clemmensen, 2009),.

In addition, some authors have questioned who can effectively use heuristic evaluation for assessing programs and products. Mack and Nielsen (1994) recognized that users who were non-experts in heuristic evaluation could offer fresh perspectives on program use compared to evaluation experts. Furthermore, Fu, Salvendy, and Turley (2002) believed while heuristic evaluation experts could simulate the novice user's mental model for a program's usability and utility, user experts offered different and equally valuable perspectives on ICTs due to the differing mental models they used. This concern was addressed in the study reported in this paper.

In response to these criticisms, Nielsen's general heuristics have been modified or supplemented by some researchers to account for multicultural contexts and to assess ICT utility. For example, Clemmensen (2011) modified Nielsen's heuristics and developed additional schema for use by evaluators from Denmark, India and China. Similarly, Chen and Macredie (2005) modified Nielsen's heuristics to assess online shopping websites, while Hasan et al. (2012) developed extra heuristics for evaluating commercial websites in Asia. These modified heuristics demonstrate that organizational and multicultural contexts need to be accounted for when applying heuristic evaluation to ICTs used in different circumstances. These types of specific heuristics can help to evaluate the utility of the ICT, questioning whether the ICT has the function the user needs to accomplish tasks within a multicultural context (Johannessen & Hornbæk, 2014). However, these studies have not specifically addressed the needs of agricultural research teams working in developing nations. This paper presents results that address this gap in the research literature by exploring the specific needs of international research teams working in both developed and developing countries, simultaneously.

## RESEARCH DESIGN

This study specifically identified the barriers and facilitators to the free sharing of information between agricultural research scientists working as members of international research teams in Lao PDR, including the effectiveness of the ICTs team members used. The study consisted of two iterative phases to address these research objectives; this section outlines the research design that was used in both phases of the project.

### *Phase 1: Using qualitative interview results to develop the I-CHET tool for intercultural heuristics*

Many issues can impinge on team communication through various social, cultural, organizational, economic and political lenses. For this reason, the study used an exploratory, qualitative approach to examine the unique contexts shaping communication between Australian and Lao research teams. The study was designed using a constructivist grounded theory methodology (Charmaz, 2014). The emergent theory that was developed around team communication was, therefore grounded, in actual experiences and how and why they occur, akin to the processes advocated by Walsh and Downe (2006).

This phase of the project involved one-hour, face-to-face, semi-structured interviews (in English) with 25 agricultural research and project managers and scientists residing in Australia and Lao PDR. Five additional interviewees were conducted with key informants in the Australian Centre for International Agricultural Research (ACIAR) in Canberra, ACT. This agency oversees international agricultural research projects between Australia and other countries. The ACIAR interviews were conducted first so that participants could recommend potential researchers to approach, based on interviewees' knowledge of research team members working between Australian and Lao PDR. This snowballing technique resulted in the recruitment of seven interviewees residing in regional Australia and 18 interviewees in Lao PDR; the latter group included twelve Lao researchers and six expatriates, who were international scientists residing and working in Lao PDR alongside their Lao research counterparts. The 30 researcher interviewees were employed by international and national agencies, universities and non-governmental organizations as research scientists and managers or as communication specialists. All interviewees held masters or PhD degrees, and were aged from their 20s to 60s. There were four females and 26 males, which is typical of the gender breakdown in the agricultural sciences.

The interview transcripts and field notes compiled during the interviews were analyzed using the constructivist grounded theory methodology detailed in Charmaz (2014). Interviews and field notes were coded and categories and themes developed, based on the rich experiences provided by the interviewees as well as a prior literature search. For example, interview data under the theme of *language as a barrier between native and non-native English speakers* were further allocated under the categories *recognizes English language as a barrier*, *addresses language barriers between non-native and native speakers*, and *native English speakers learn local language*. The themes and categories were refined into a communication model, similar to the model development approach used in Preece, Abras, and Maloney-Krichmar (2004). The communication model formed the basis for developing intercultural heuristics for the intercultural heuristic evaluation tool, or I-CHET, which is discussed in the following (results) section.

### *Phase 2: Assessing ICTs using the intercultural heuristics in I-CHET*

Once the I-CHET was developed, heuristic evaluation was applied to assess nine ICTs used by the interviewees. Johannessen and Hornbæk (2014) recognized heuristic evaluation as a low-cost method of finding and assessing usability problems in ICTs by heuristic evaluation experts and expert users. Eight intercultural heuristics were developed from the barriers identified in the communication model, which enabled ICTs to be assessed for their utility. The ICTs assessed in the pilot were listed by the interviewees as those used for technologically mediated communication between members of their international research teams. The evaluation results of two of the most commonly used ICTs – i.e., email and the videoconferencing program Skype – are reported in this paper.

The pilot test was carried out by the first author, who was experienced user with nearly 30 years working in geographically dispersed teams, often across political, economic and cultural borders. During the pilot test, each ICT was assessed twice, as proposed by Nielsen (1995). The goal of the first review of the ICT was to get a feel for its interface and its functionality. A second, more detailed evaluation of various parts of the interface addressed specific compliance questions for each heuristic. By using a template in Microsoft Excel, each question was ticked "yes" or "no" regarding compliance, with positive or negative comments and examples presented for most compliance questions, particularly to indicate the severity of non-compliance. A "no" tick was scored as 1, a "yes" scored 0, and an ambivalent result indicated by a tick each in "yes" and "no" scored 0.5. Compliance scores for each heuristic were then summed across specific compliance questions for each heuristic to achieve a Total Compliance score.

The I-CHET tool was also assessed for clarity and precision during the pilot assessment. For example, some specific compliance questions did not clearly define the features being assessed. These problems were clearly evident within the first two (of nine) ICTs evaluated, and these questions were amended on the I-CHET tool. The new questions were then re-applied to the ICTs being evaluated. The results presented in the next section reference the two most commonly used ICTs (email and Skype), to demonstrate the usefulness of the I-CHET tool for intercultural heuristic assessment.

## RESULTS

### *Phase 1: Developing I-CHET*

The interview analysis shows seven barriers to effective communication between team members, as well as three personal moderators and three structural moderators, which are issues that could enhance or detract from effective communication. These are listed in Table 1. The barriers mirror communication fault lines outlined in Lau and Murnighan (1998) and incorporated into behavioral complexity theory (Shachaf & Hara, 2007). The moderators are additional to that theory and represent a key new finding from the present study.

| Communication barriers | Personal moderators |
|---|---|
| English language | Cultural intelligence |
| Geographic distance | Postgraduate education |
| Temporal distance | Personal attributes |
| Cultural differences | **Structural moderators** |
| Economic power | Institutional context |
| Online infrastructure | Inter-organizational context |
| Political differences | International context |

***Table 1**. Communication barriers and moderators identified for the communication model for the international agricultural research teams*

### *Deriving 'international heuristics'*

Initially, nine barriers and moderators were selected from Table 1 to be recombined into seven intercultural heuristics. The barriers *online infrastructure* and *economic power* were combined into the intercultural heuristic *ready to use* to avoid inter-heuristic interaction during evaluations; this was necessary as the study showed a high correlation between national human development (which includes economic development) and network readiness to use the internet in a national network. In addition, the moderator *cultural intelligence* was included with moderator *personal attributes* into the intercultural heuristic *personal attributes* to more comprehensively evaluate the utility of an ICT by individual users for intercultural TMC.

Four moderators listed in the communication model were not used in the intercultural heuristics. *Institutional context*, *inter-organizational context* and *international context* were excluded as the content communicated through ICTs that explicates an organization's context have been shown to be unrelated to any ICT features (see Sulaiman Sulaiman, Hall, Kalaivani, Dorai, and Reddy (2012), and Ward and Spennemann (2000)). Therefore, evaluating content was outside the purpose of this evaluation. The moderator *postgraduate education* was also excluded, as it is the content communicated through ICTs that help form and maintain professional relations (Ynalvez & Shrum, 2008) rather than the features of the ICTs that encourage professional and personal relations. Finally, after a trial application of the intercultural heuristics to an ICT, the intercultural heuristic *cultural differences*, was separated into *specific cultural cues* and *conversation and group support* to better reflect heuristics based on cues for individual and team support respectively.

### *Operationalizing the intercultural heuristics*

A draft set of general conformance and specific compliance questions was developed for each heuristic. These were derived from previous studies, both historic, landmark works, as well as more recent examples of cultural differences. For example, Walther and Tidwell's (1995) early study of non-verbal cues in TMC was included with recent work on the different use of emoticons as non-verbal cues in TMC by users from Asian and Western cultures (e.g., Derks, Bos, & Grumbkow, 2007; Kato, Kato, & Akahori, 2007; Park, Baek, & Cha, 2014). Finally, between three and six specific compliance questions were developed for each heuristic to guide the evaluation of each ICT.

After a trial application, heuristic labels, conformance questions, and specific compliance questions were reviewed and refined. One conformance and three to six specific compliance questions for each intercultural heuristic were developed for each intercultural heuristic, similar to those developed for general heuristics by Lavery, Cockton, and Atkinson (1996). Table 2 provides the final list of intercultural heuristics and general compliance questions resulting from this review. For example, the conformance question for the intercultural heuristic *Interpersonal relations* asked if non-verbal and paralanguage cues (e.g., an image of a facial expression; a sound) could be transmitted between dispersed team members using an ICT. Specific compliance questions then explored the addition of hierarchical positions to messages, the transmission of non-verbal cues through message structure, the use of emoticons in messages, and the message timing as a non-verbal cue.

### *Developing I-CHET*

Overall, eight intercultural heuristics were developed from the interview data, which were then combined with Nielsen's 10 general heuristics (Nielsen, 1995). This provided a robust set of intercultural heuristics to sit alongside the standard usability heuristics that are applied by Nielsen and other researchers. The result was the final I-CHET heuristic model, which was tested in this study. The general and intercultural heuristics that form the I-CHET are listed in Table 3.

| Intercultural heuristics | Conformance questions |
|---|---|
| Language used | Are some features available to understand content, both for |

| | |
|---|---|
| | native and non-native speakers of English? |
| Geographic / temporal distance | Can team members use system features to overcome geographic and time barriers to communicate with each other? |
| Interpersonal relations | Can non-verbal and paralanguage cues be transmitted between dispersed team members? |
| Specific cultural cues | Are appropriate system features available for users from different cultures regarding non-verbal cues? |
| Conversation and group support | Are appropriate system features available for users from different cultures that support the initiation and maintenance of conversations and subgroups? |
| Communication style | Are appropriate system features available for individual users to express cultural empathy or enact turn-taking skills during ICT-enabled conversations? |
| Readiness to use | Can the system work within the online infrastructure and economic contexts available in partner countries? |
| Legal adaptability | Can the system adapt to suit cross-national legal frameworks? |

***Table 2**. Intercultural heuristics and conformance questions used for heuristic evaluation of ICTs for international research teams*

| General Heuristics | Intercultural Heuristics |
|---|---|
| Visibility of system status | Language used |
| Match between system and real world | Geographic/temporal distance |
| User control and freedom | Interpersonal relations |
| Consistency and standards | Specific cultural cues |
| Error prevention | Conversation and group support |
| Recognition rather than recall | Communication style |
| Flexibility and efficiency of use | Readiness to use |
| Aesthetic and minimalist design | Legal adaptability |
| Help users recognize, diagnose and recover from errors | |
| Help and documentation | |

***Table 3**. General and intercultural heuristics used in the intercultural heuristic evaluation tool (I-CHET).*

One strength of I-CHET is that it combines the evaluation of an ICT's usability and utility. It assesses the ICT as a product while also assessing its possible uses. Assessing utility addresses a major criticism of Nielsen's general heuristics by a number of researchers, most recently by Johannessen and Hornbæk (2014). As I-CHET analyses the use of individual ICTs by people from different cultures and for various purposes, it provides a platform for comparing ICTs across cultures. As suggested by Po et al. (2004), including 'real world' contexts in ICT assessment also reduces the incidence of falsely identified problems, or 'false positives,' which can save time and resources in the system design (or redesign) process.

### *Results – Phase 2: Evaluating I-CHET*

The I-CHET tool was pilot tested with two ICTs listed and described by Lao, Australian and expatriate interviewees in Phase 1 of the project: 1) Microsoft Outlook (email program); and, 2) Skype (video-conferencing program).

Table 4 shows the tallied scores for each ICT across I-CHET's general and intercultural heuristics. These scores indicate the usability and utility of each ICT.

| General Heuristics | Skype | Email |
|---|---|---|
| HE01. Visibility of system status | 1 | 1.5 |
| HE02. Match between system and real world | 3 | 0.5 |
| HE03. User control and freedom | 2 | 0 |
| HE04. Consistency and standards | 0 | 0 |
| HE05. Error prevention | 1 | 0 |
| HE06. Recognition rather than recall | 0.5 | 0 |
| HE07. Flexibility and efficiency of use | 1 | 0.5 |
| HE08. Aesthetic and minimalist design | 2 | 1 |
| HE09. Help users recognize, diagnose and recover from errors | 0.5 | 1.5 |
| HE10. Help and documentation | 1.5 | 0.5 |
| Intercultural Heuristics | Skype | Email |
| HE11. Language used | 2.5 | 1 |
| HE12. Geographic/temporal distance | 2.5 | 0 |
| HE13. Interpersonal relations | 0.5 | 0.5 |
| HE14. Specific cultural cues | 4 | 0.5 |
| HE15. Conversation and group support | 1.5 | 1.5 |
| HE16. Communication style | 1 | 1.5 |
| HE17. Readiness to use | 2 | 0.5 |
| HE18. Legal adaptability | 1.5 | 0 |

***Table 4**. Tallied non-compliance scores for general and intercultural heuristics used in I-CHET to evaluate one text and one video-based ICT*

### *Using languages other than English*

Analysis of interview data indicated the ability of an ICT to incorporate languages other than English would be an important feature for TMC between team members. The I-CHET analysis showed, however, that such support was not forthcoming in Skype's interface, and that such support was available in email but was buried deeply in the navigation hierarchy of the program. This was indicated by the higher non-conformance score for the intercultural heuristic *Language used* (HE11) for Skype and email. In addition, neither program had direct or easy access to translation programs or keyboard layouts for the Thai alphabet (used by Lao researchers). This limits the utility of both programs for TMC between native and non-native English speakers.

Interestingly, recent studies show mixed findings into the importance of alternative languages in the use of various ICTs. Setlock and Fussell (2011) found fluency in English had little influence in the use of audio- or video-conferencing ICTs by Chinese students, regardless of whether they spoke Mandarin or English to each other. However, Hautasaari, Yamashita, and Gao (2014) observed that the English language fluency of Japanese students significantly influenced their understanding of negative emotions conveyed by native English speakers in text based TMC. Therefore, the need for language support could depend on the communication task and the level of non-verbal cues required for effective TMC between team members, and the non-verbal cues transmitted via the ICT.

### *Improving User Assistance*

The I-CHET analysis showed more problems were apparent for Skype compared to email in the general heuristics for *error prevention* (HE05) and *help and documentation* (HE10), while more problems were apparent for email compared to Skype in *helping users recognize, diagnose and recover from errors* (HE09).

Qualitative analysis showed this non-conformance was related to the dominance of English in the assistance and documentation provided to users, which could be problematic for non-native speakers of English and/or for users who are inexperienced with an ICT. I-CHET analysis of Skype noted the user of two-way interactive Help forums, which may be better suited to providing assistance to more inexperienced users from developing countries; this feature is also supported by research by Swarts (2015).

### *Variable suitability for different cultures*

I-CHET analysis of *Specific cultural cues* (HE14) indicated a higher non-compliance score for Skype, and moderate non-compliance scores regarding *Conversation and group support* (HE15) for both Skype and email. Analysis showed problems regarding inability to customize interfaces or messages by non-native English users. However, Skype did allow use of emoticons from non-Western sources by Asian users, which is a growing preference as noted by Park et al. (2014).

I-CHET analysis also highlighted an overall bias towards Western design standards in the general heuristics, which reduced its ability to assess an ICT's usability in intercultural situations. For example, Cyr, Head, and Larios (2010) and Thatcher (2010) noted Asian preferences for bright colors, changing fonts and animated information in program interfaces. However, general heuristic *Aesthetic and minimalist design* (HE08) scores interfaces with such colors, fonts or animations as problems, compared to simpler interfaces. Therefore, HE08 may not be a useful criterion by which an ICT designed for non-Western users should be judged.

## CONCLUSION, IMPLICATIONS, LIMITATIONS

This study showed that a communication model indicating barriers to information sharing between members of international research teams could be operationalized into a set of intercultural heuristics for inclusion in a heuristic evaluation tool. ICT evaluation using I-CHET can demonstrate that commonly used ICTs show considerable variability in their utility for international research teams which have members from different language and cultural groups. Furthermore, a pilot test of I-CHET showed that while email theoretically lacked the richness of visual cues seen in Skype, email better complied with the needs of international research groups for sharing information and communication in multicultural teams across language and cultural barriers.

The development of I-CHET demonstrates a new use for heuristic evaluation in assessing both the usability and utility of existing and new ICTs for use in dispersed international research groups with members from various cultural and language groups. I-CHET considers limitations to communication and ICTs from the viewpoints of team members from both developed and developing countries and accounts for their personal, cultural and institutional differences in information sharing. With this in mind, the tool could also be adapted for use in development sectors such as health, education and community development, as well as for global business teams where members are from economically developed and newly industrialized or developing nations with access to a range of ICTs.

As this was an exploratory study, findings outlined in this paper are limited by the development of the communication model using interviewees only located in Lao PDR and Australia. Verifying the model using national groups from other developed and developing countries would add to the robustness of the model, and so the I-CHET which is derived from the model. In addition, using only one evaluator facilitated the iterative refinement of the I-CHET during the pilot testing process. However, single evaluation leaves results open to the *evaluator effect* explicated by Hertzum and Jacobsen (2003), whereby evaluators are seen to detect "markedly different sets of usability problems when they evaluate a system" and also "seem to differ substantially in their rating of the severity of the detected problems" (p. 184). This limitation indicates the need for verification of I-CHET by at least two other expert users, particularly in Lao PDR.

## ACKNOWLEDGMENTS

The authors wish to acknowledge the particular assistance of the Australian Centre for International Agricultural Research and the National Agriculture and Forestry Research Institute in Lao PDR for enabling and encouraging interviews for this research in both countries.

## REFERENCES

Azadi, T., Eskrootchi, R., Jamshidi Orak, R., & Mohaghegh, N. (2014). Usability evaluation of the web pages of the Islamic world science citation center (ISC), Islamic Countries SCI database. *International Journal of Information Science & Management, 12*(1), 11-22.

Ballantyne, P., Maru, A., & Poncari, E. M. (2010). Information and communication technologies - opportunities to mobilize agricultural science for development. *Crop Science, 50*, S63-69.

Charmaz, K. (2014). *Constructing grounded theory* (2 ed.). London: SAGE.

Chen, S. Y., & Macredie, R. D. (2005). The assessment of usability of electronic shopping: A heuristic evaluation. *International Journal of Information Management, 25*(6), 516-532. doi:10.1016/j.ijinfomgt.2005.08.008

Clemmensen, T. (2011). Templates for cross-cultural and culturally specific usability testing: Results from field studies and ethnographic interviewing in three countries. *International Journal of Human-Computer Interaction, 27*(7), 634-669. doi:10.1080/10447318.2011.555303

Cyr, D., Head, M., & Larios, H. (2010). Colour appeal in website design within and across cultures: A multi-method evaluation. *International Journal of Human-Computer Studies, 68*(1–2), 1-21. doi:10.1016/j.ijhcs.2009.08.005

Daft, R. L., & Lengel, R. H. (1986). Organizational information requirements, media richness and structural design. *Management Science, 32*(5), 554-571.

Dennis, A. R., Fuller, R. M., & Valacich, J. S. (2008). Media, tasks and communication processes: A theory of media synchronicity. *MIS Quarterly, 32*(3), 575-600.

Derks, D., Bos, A. E. R., & Grumbkow, J. v. (2007). Emoticons and social interaction on the internet: The importance of social context. *Computers in Human Behavior, 23*(1), 842-849. doi:10.1016/j.chb.2004.11.013

Dimmick, J., & Rothenbuhler, E. (1984). The theory of the niche: Quantifying competition among media industries. *Journal of Communication, 34*(1), 103-119. doi:10.1111/j.1460-2466.1984.tb02988.x

Duque, R., Miller, B. P., Barriga, O., Shrum, W., & Henríquez, G. (2012). Is internet use associated with reporting fewer problems in collaboration?: Evidence from the scientific community in Chile. *Science Communication, 34*(5), 642-678. doi:10.1177/1075547011432364

Duque, R., Ynalvez, M., Sooryamoorthy, R., Mbatia, P., Dzorgbo, D.-B. S., & Shrum, W. (2005). Collaboration paradox: Scientific productivity, the internet, and problems of research in developing areas. *Social Studies of Science, 35*(5), 755-785. doi:10.1177/0306312705053048

Frandsen-Thorlacius, O., Hornbæk, K., Hertzum, M., & Clemmensen, T. (2009). *Non-universal usability? A survey of how usability is understood by Chinese and Danish users*. Paper presented at the CHI 2009: Proceedings of the 2009 SIGCHI Conference on Human Factors in Computing Systems, Boston, MA, USA. http://dl.acm.org.ezproxy.csu.edu.au/citation.cfm?id=1518701&CFID=559344942&CFTOKEN=10346572

Fu, L., Salvendy, G., & Turley, L. (2002). Effectiveness of user testing and heuristic evaluation as a function of performance classification. *Behaviour & Information Technology, 21*(2), 137-143. doi:10.1080/02699050110113688

Fulk, J., Monge, P., & Hollingshead, A. (2005). Knowledge resource sharing in dispersed multinational teams: Three theoretical lenses. In D. L. Shapiro, M. A. V. Glinow, & J. Cheng (Eds.), *Managing Multinational Teams: Global Perspectives* (pp. 155-188). Burlington, Canada: Emerald Group Publishing.

Gervedink Nijhuis, C. J., Voogt, J. M., & Pieters, J. M. (2012). The cultural complexity of international collaboration: Conditions for sustainable curriculum development in Ghana. *International Journal of Intercultural Relations, 36*(5), 647-658. doi:10.1016/j.ijintrel.2012.02.003

Gibson, C. B., & Grubb, A. R. (2005). Turning the tide in multinational teams. In D. L. Shappiro, M. A. V. Glinow, & J. Chen (Eds.), *Managing Multinational Teams: Global Perspectives* (Vol. 18, pp. 69-95): Elsevier.

Haddad, S., McGrenere, J., & Jacova, C. (2014). *Interface design for older adults with varying cultural attitudes toward uncertainty*. Paper presented at the CHI 2014: Proceedings of the SIGCHI Conference on Human Factors in Computing Systems, Toronto, Canada. http://delivery.acm.org.ezproxy.csu.edu.au/10.1145/2560000/2557124/p1913-haddad.pdf?ip=137.166.68.70&id=2557124&acc=ACTIVE%20SERVICE&key=65D80644F295BC0D%2EC3714298A2589389%2E4D4702B0C3E38B35%2E4D4702B0C3E38B35&CFID=565733483&CFTOKEN=75004869&__acm__=1410867836_b898d4461da66488a20ac3417a15d3dc

Hasan, L., Morris, A., & Probets, S. (2012). A comparison of usability evaluation methods for evaluating e-commerce websites. *Behaviour & Information Technology, 31*(7), 707-737. doi:10.1080/0144929x.2011.596996

Hautasaari, A., Yamashita, N., & Gao, G. (2014). *"Maybe it was a joke" - Emotion detection in text-only communication by non-native English speakers*. Paper presented at the CHI 2014: Proceedings of the SIGCHI Conference on Human Factors in Computing Systems, Ontario, Canada. http://delivery.acm.org.ezproxy.csu.edu.au/10.1145/2560000/2557215/p3715-hautasaari.pdf?ip=137.166.68.70&id=2557215&acc=ACTIVE%20SERVICE&key=65D80644F295BC0D%2EC3714298-A2589389%2E4D4702B0C3E38B35%2E4D4702B0C3E38B35&CFID=565733483&CFTOKEN=75004869&__acm__=1410869122_-66233e8e1a62960d8dfe1e22191161f6

Hertzum, M., & Jacobsen, N. E. (2003). The evaluator effect: A chilling fact about usability evaluation methods. *International Journal of Human–Computer Interaction, 15*(1), 183-204. doi:10.1207/S15327590IJHC1501_14

Huang, H., & Ocker, R. (2006). *Preliminary insights into the in-group/out-group effect in partially distributed teams: An analysis of participant reflections*. Paper presented at the SIGMIS CPR '06: Proceedings of the 2006 ACM SIGMIS CPR conference on computer personnel research. http://dl.acm.org.ezproxy.csu.edu.au/citation.cfm?id=1125170.1125232&coll=DL&dl=ACM&CFID=436372096&CFTOKEN=78887611

Hvannberg, E. T., Law, E. L.-C., & Lérusdóttir, M. K. (2007). Heuristic evaluation: Comparing ways of finding and reporting usability problems. *Interacting with Computers, 19*(2), 225-240. doi:10.1016/j.intcom.2006.10.001

Hwang, K. (2013). Effects of the language barrier on processes and performance of international scientific collaboration, collaborators' participation, organizational integrity, and interorganizational relationships. *Science Communication, 35*(1), 3-31. doi:10.1177/1075547012437442

Jirotka, M., Lee, C. P., & Olson, G. M. (2013). Supporting scientific collaboration: Methods, tools and concepts. *Computer Supported Cooperative Work, 22*(4-6), 667-715. doi:10.1007/s10606-012-9184-0

Johannessen, G. H. J., & Hornbæk, K. (2014). Must evaluation methods be about usability? Devising and assessing the utility inspection method. *Behaviour & Information Technology, 33*(2), 194-205. doi:10.1080/0144929X.2012.751708

Kato, Y., Kato, S., & Akahori, K. (2007). Effects of emotional cues transmitted in e-mail communication on the emotions experienced by senders and receivers. *Computers in Human Behavior, 23*(4), 1894-1905. doi:10.1016/j.chb.2005.11.005

Katz, J., & Martin, B. R. (1997). What is research collaboration? *Research Policy, 26*(1), 1-18. doi:10.1016/S0048-7333(96)00917-1

Kealey, D. J., Protheroe, D. R., MacDonald, D., & Vulpe, T. (2006). International projects: Some lessons on avoiding failure and maximizing success. *Performance Improvement, 45*(3), 38-46. doi:10.1002/pfi.2006.4930450309

Lau, D. C., & Murnighan, J. K. (1998). Demographic diversity and faultlines: The compositional dynamics of organizational groups. *Academy of Management Review, 23*(2), 325-340. doi:10.5465/AMR.1998.533229

Lavery, D., Cockton, G., & Atkinson, M. (1996). *Heuristic evaluation: Usability evaluation materials*. Retrieved from Glasgow, UK: http://www.dcs.gla.ac.uk/asp/materials/

Mack, R. L., & Nielsen, J. (1994). Executive summary. In J. Nielsen & R. L. Mack (Eds.), *Usability inspection methods* (pp. 1-24). New York: John Wiley & Sons.

Maglaughlin, K. L., & Sonnenwald, D. H. (2005). *Factors that impact interdisciplinary natural science research collaboration in academia*. Paper presented at the 2005 Conference of the International Society for Scientometrics and Informetrics.

Nielsen, J. (1994a). Heuristic evaluation. In J. Nielsen & R. L. Mack (Eds.), *Usability inspection methods* (pp. 25-62). New York: John Wiley & Sons.

Nielsen, J. (1994b). *Usability inspection methods*. Paper presented at the Computer Human Interface 1994 of the ACM. http://www.idemployee.id.tue.nl/g.w.m.rauterberg/lecturenotes/0H420/Nielsen[1994].pdf

Nielsen, J. (1995). How to conduct a heursitic evaluation. Retrieved from http://www.nngroup.com/articles/how-to-conduct-a-heuristic-evaluation/

Nielsen, J., & Molich, R. (1990). *Heuristic evaluation of user interfaces*. Paper presented at the Computer User Interface Conference 1990 for the ACM. http://mestrado-watinha.googlecode.com/svn/trunk/hci/monografia/artigosUtilizados/revisao/p249-nielsenAvaHeu.pdf

Olson, G. M., Bos, N., & Zimmerman, A. (Eds.). (2008). *Scientific collaboration on the internet*. Cambridge, MA, USA: MIT Press.

Olson, G. M., & Olson, J. S. (2000). Distance matters. *Human-Computer Interaction, 15*(2/3), 139-178.

Park, J., Baek, Y. M., & Cha, M. (2014). Cross-cultural comparison of nonverbal cues in emoticons on Twitter: Evidence from big data analysis. *Journal of Communication, 64*(2), 333-354. doi:10.1111/jcom.12086

Po, S., Howard, S., Vetere, F., & Skov, M. B. (2004). *Heuristic evaluation and mobile usability: Bridging the realism gap*. Paper presented at the Proceedings of Mobile HCI 2004, Glasgow, Scotland.

Polzer, J. T., Crisp, C. B., Jarvenpaa, S. L., & Kim, J. W. (2006). Extending the faultline model to geographically dispersed teams: How colocated subgroups can impair group functioning. *Academy of Management Journal, 49*(4), 679-692. doi:10.5465/AMJ.2006.22083024

Preece, J., Abras, C., & Maloney-Krichmar, D. (2004). Designing and evaluating online communities: Research speaks to emerging practice. *International Journal of Web Based Communities, 1*(1), 2-18.

Setlock, L. D., & Fussell, S. R. (2011). *Culture or fluency? Unpacking interactions between culture and communication medium*. Paper presented at the CHI 2011: Proceedings of the SIGCHI Conference on Human Factors in Computing Systems, Vancouver, BC, Canada. http://delivery.acm.org.ezproxy.csu.edu.au/10.1145/1980000/1979112/p1137-setlock.pdf?ip=137.166.68.70&id=1979112&acc=ACTIVE%20SERVICE&key=65D80644F295BC0D%2EC3714298A2589389%2E4D4702B0C3E38B35%2E4D4702B0C3E38B35&CFID=423755074&CFTOKEN=21289156&__acm__=1410413021_-70e455f6ad01676e0a6b9e0c3656453d

Shachaf, P., & Hara, N. (2007). Behavioral complexity theory of media selection: A proposed theory for global virtual teams. *Journal of Information Science, 33*(1), 63-75. doi:10.1177/0165551506068145

Shrum, W. (1997). View from afar: "Visible" productivity of scientists in the developing world. *Scientometrics, 40*(2), 215-235. doi:10.1007/bf02457438

Singh, S. (2006). *Selected success stories in agricultural information systems*. Retrieved from Bangkok, Thailand: http://www.apaari.org

Sonnenwald, D. H. (2007). Scientific collaboration. *Annual Review of Information Science and Technology, 41*(1), 643-681. doi:10.1002/aris.2007.1440410121

Sulaiman, V. R., Hall, A., Kalaivani, N. J., Dorai, K., & Reddy, T. S. V. (2012). Necessary, but not sufficient: Critiquing the role of information and communication technology in putting knowledge into use. *Journal of Agricultural Education & Extension, 18*(4), 331-346. doi:10.1080/1389224X.2012.691782

Swarts, J. (2015). Help is in the helping: An evaluation of help documentation in a networked age. *Technical Communication Quarterly, 24*(2), 164-187. doi:10.1080/10572252.2015.1001298

Thatcher, B. L. (2010). Understanding digital literacy across cultures. In R. Spilka (Ed.), *Digital literacy for technical communication: 21st century theory and practice* (pp. 169-198). Hoboken: Taylor and Francis. Retrieved from http://reader.eblib.com.ezproxy.csu.edu.au/(S(silbzqbthec0e0kikugud4qn))/Reader.aspx?p=465575-&o=476&u=Y5mr7RVP4Lc%3d&t=1453613772&h=36694F812C694B95300DB646853275FC6C8B93C9&s=41480254&ut=1443&pg=186&r=img&c=-1&pat=n&cms=-1&sd=2.

Velho, L., & Velho, P. (1996). Scientific collaboration of advanced/developing countries in biological sciences: The case of the Maraca Rain Forest project. *Cadernos de Ciência & Tecnologia, 13*(1), 9-20.

Voss, J., Albert, I., & Ferring, D. (2014). Language use and value orientations in multinational work teams in Luxembourg: Conflict or harmony? *International Journal of Intercultural Relations*(0). doi:10.1016/j.ijintrel.2014.04.006

Walsh, D., & Downe, S. (2006). Appraising the quality of qualitative research. *Midwifery, 22*, 108–119. doi:10.1016/j.midw.2005.05.004

Walther, J. B., & Tidwell, L. C. (1995). Nonverbal cues in computer-mediated communication, and the effect of chronemics on relational communication. *Journal of Organizational Computing, 5*(4). doi:10.1080/10919399509540258

Ward, W. (2016). *Exploring in-person and technologically-mediated communication within international agricultural research teams.* (PhD). Charles Sturt University, Waga Wagga, NSW, Australia. Retrieved from http://trove.nla.gov.au/version/235880785

Ward, W., & Spennemann, D. (2000). Meeting local needs? Case study of a communication project in the Pacific Islands. *Public Administration and Development, 20*, 185-195.

Windsor, P. A. (2011). Perspectives on Australian animal health aid projects in South-East Asia. *Transboundary and Emerging Diseases, 58*, 375-386. doi:10.1111/j.1865-1682.2011.01216.x

Ynalvez, M., & Shrum, W. (2008). International graduate training, digital inequality and professional network structure: An ego-centric social network analysis of knowledge producers at the "Global South". *Scientometrics, 76*(2), 343-368. doi:10.1007/s11192-007-1936-0

Ynalvez, M., & Shrum, W. M. (2011). Professional networks, scientific collaboration, and publication productivity in resource-constrained research institutions in a developing country. *Research Policy, 40*(2), 204-216. doi:10.1016/j.respol.2010.10.004

# Two Views of the Data Documentation Initiative: Stakeholders, Collaboration and Metadata Standards Creation

**Rachel D. Williams**
*School of Library and Information Science, Simmons College, USA. willir@simmons.edu*

**Kristin R. Eschenfelder**
*School of Library and Information Science, University of Wisconsin-Madison, USA. eschenfelder@wisc.edu*

**Kalpana Shankar**
*School of Information and Communication Studies, University College Dublin, Ireland. kalpana.shankar@ucd.ie*

## ABSTRACT

**This paper uses boundary work theory (Gieryn, 1983, among others) to analyze the differences in organizational participation in the creation and maintenance of the Data Documentation Initiative (DDI) standard. The Data Documentation Initiative is a global consensus standard created to describe social science research data. Specifically, the paper addresses how two key social science data archives (SSDA) – the Interuniversity Consortium of Political and Social Research (ICPSR) and the United Kingdom Data Archive (UKDA) – mobilized their differences as resources to create DDI. This paper describes the collaborative activities of the two organizations. It also analyzes how those differences in collaboration resulted in boundary or "juncture" activities and the role those activities played in organizational maintenance. Our study compares how one organization, ICPSR, engaged in translating and aligning activities related to the development of the standard, while the other data archive, UKDA, engaged in decentering activities. The paper uses this case of standards work to reflect on the role of boundaries as resources for organizational resilience over the long-term.**

## KEYWORDS

data archives, standards development, organizational collaboration, Data Documentation Initiative (DDI), boundary work

## INTRODUCTION

Standards for data formatting and exchange are essential components of networked systems. They also represent an instantiation of values, needs and practices of particular stakeholders (with the exclusion of others) (Bowker and Star 2000). As Williams et al. (2004) write, "the standardisation process ...represents an attempt to align interests, business practices and expectations of an array of people" (p. 3). Therefore, standardization is not only about providing workable solutions, but most importantly, it refers to articulating and aligning expectations and interests. The more institutions and actors are involved, the greater the articulation, bridging, and management challenge. Thus standards development, particularly in scientific/research infrastructure work, is typically an interorganizational effort that can take significant resources and years, if not decades, to complete. Furthermore, the successful adoption and diffusion of information standards has widespread effects on the evolution of scholarly disciplines, related professions, and the institutions involved in their development.

This paper describes the interorganizational collaboration that has gone into the development and maintenance of social science metadata standards, specifically the Data Documentation Initiative (DDI). The DDI standard is a free metadata standard used to document a variety of social science research data. The first version of the DDI was made available in 2000, after five years of collaborative efforts to create, beta test and revise the standard (Miller and Vardigan, 2005). The present analysis considers how the stakeholders involved in the DDI development connected with one another in a long-term standards development project. Although these stakeholders worked together to create the DDI metadata standard, they also established and maintained their own specific orientations toward both the project and the boundaries between institutions. This collaborative work has made an impact on the field, in that it supported the creation and successful implementation of a metadata standard still in use by a variety of institutions.

Our paper describes how the DDI was collaboratively created and enacted between two SSDA in two different countries. These two archives are the Interuniversity Consortium for Social and Political Research at the University of Michigan (ICPSR) in the United States and the UK Data Archive in Essex UK (UKDA – now part of the larger UK Data Service). We draw upon theories of boundary work and boundary spanning to orient this history of DDI as a story of managing difference and mobilizing those differences as sociotechnical resources. We analyze the distinct collaborative actions of ICPSR and UKDA in relation to the DDI development over

80th Annual Meeting of the Association for Information Science & Technology, Washington, DC, VA | Oct. 27-Nov. 1, 2017

the long term and conclude with reflections on the role of boundary work in understanding organizational resilience in data infrastructures.

## STANDARDS WORK AS COLLABORATIVE WORK

Star and Griesemer (1989) and Lampland and Star (2009) describe standards as boundary objects. As such, they bring people from different worlds together, even though these people may have different interpretations of the object because the meanings and uses of that standard are specific to communities of practice. Standards development work often serves as points of connection by enabling the development of user communities, permitting the interconnection of technical systems across groups and institutions, and fostering distributed work (Millerand et al., 2013; Bertot et al., 2014). Standards serve as supports for what Millerand and Bowker (2009) term the coordination of different social worlds. Scientific data collections, and the standards that surround them, are sites of collaborative activity involving diverse and shifting groups of people (Cragin and Shankar, 2006), many of whom become quite committed to the complex organizational networks that result (Busch, 2011).

Creating and then maintaining consensus standards is challenging. Past infrastructure studies have pointed to long term challenges of balancing the competing goals of stakeholders, keeping participants motivated, and ensuring useful participation and implementation across temporal, geographical, and organizational scales, even as institutions change and grow (Ribes and Finholt, 2009; Monteiro, Pollock, Hanseth, and Williams, 2013).

Standards span boundaries. In the organizational collaboration literature, boundaries are conceptualized as points of connection (Faraj and Yan, 2009) that make it easier to reassemble resources and activities following a disruption (for example, acute crises or general disruptions to services). This may occur as a form of boundary spanning, where actors are able to reach outside the organization to create connections that afford access to additional resources, information, or tools. These are the 'intermediary artifacts and end products' Lee (2005) describes. At other times, people in organizations act as brokers who build bridges between different worlds, in this case, different organizations (Akkerman and Baker, 2011). Brokering also involves "facilitating transactions and the flow of knowledge" (Pawlowski, Robey, and Raven, 2000).

From this view, boundaries are not merely things to "get around" but can be actively deployed to achieve goals. One can create flexible connections that allow for this efficient reassembling or redesign of the "system". Gieryn (1983) first coined the term "boundary work" to describe the activities groups engage in to manage sites of difference. The term has had extensive utility in understanding sociotechnical labor, particularly in interorganizational collaboration which involves "discovering, making, testing, developing, and arguing over practices and how to instantiate those practices into intermediary artifacts and end products" (Lee, 2005).

In their discussion of organizational boundary work, Quick and Feldman (2014) identified three boundary-crossing strategies: translating across differences, aligning among differences, and decentering differences. They describe "translating across differences" as an activity that deemphasizes expertise and focuses on the inclusion of multiple perspectives "to create a new, shared domain" (p. 677). Aligning among differences involves acknowledging differences and finding connections across them. This aligning practice allows organizations to maintain their distinctions while pursuing new and shared interests. Finally, decentering differences relies on avoiding the boundaries that make barriers or distinctions meaningful.

Using administrative and organizational documents from the two SSDA involved in the development of DDI, we examine the history of DDI as a standards development project with the following question in mind:

- What kinds of boundary work do ICPSR and UKDA perform in the development of DDI and with what objectives in mind?

## METHODS

### *Data Collection and Analysis*

The Interuniversity Consortium for Social and Political Research at the University of Michigan (ICPSR) and the UK Data Archive in Essex UK (UKDA – now part of the larger UK Data Service) were both involved in the DDI project. With institutional permission, the authors gathered administrative documents from these archives as part of a larger project on organizational longevity in the SSDA field. We were granted access to this archival material provided agreed to limit our interest to "history" and not recent or current activities. For this reason, we limited our documentary analysis to 2002. We chose 2002 as an artificial if reasonable 'historical' cut off; preliminary documentary and literature analysis suggested that 2001/2002 heralded a new set of standards and technologies (the web in particular) that would easily provide another rich set of studies.

To explore specific organizational issues related to UKDA's and ICPSR's involvement in the DDI project, the authors looked at a series of 15 documents that included annual reports, memos, articles, and historical timelines related specifically to the DDI standard. The authors conducted an inductive analysis and focused on paragraphs in longer documents or whole documents for shorter memos/notes as the units of analysis for our qualitative coding. Coding of institutional documents and interviews included exploration of each archive's role in the DDI project. The researchers began by coding the archival documents for instances of organizational collaboration around technology interests and/or concerns. With this initial step in the coding, it became apparent that the DDI standard development was an important technology project to both SSDA. From there, the authors searched for and coded historical and professional articles related to the creation of the DDI standard to garner perspectives external to the organizations' archival documents. Two members of the research team coded all documents.

## SETTING THE STAGE: SOCIAL SCIENCE DATA ARCHIVES AND THE EMERGING NEED FOR A NEW DATA STANDARD

SSDA are exemplars of long-lived information infrastructures, some existing since the 1920s. SSDAs are information infrastructures focused on curating and managing data generated from surveys, national census data sets, longitudinal research projects, government agencies, and similar (mostly) quantitative data (Bisco, 1996; Green and Gutmann, 2007). Recently, they have recently also been acquiring qualitative data (Corti, 2011). SSDA reside at the nexus of multiple types of institutions and intersect with other information infrastructures. These include research communities, universities, standards bodies, professional societies, and others (Mayernik, 2016; Jackson, et al., 2007, among others).

The 1960s and 1970s saw the establishment of over a dozen SSDA services and SSDA related professional associations. These services and associations were created to coordinate quantitative data collection, to promote data sharing, and to educate students and scholars about quantitative and machine processing analysis methods (White, 1977). In the United States, data archives such as the Interuniversity Consortium for Political and Social Research (ICPSR) started acquiring machine-readable election and polling data for researchers in the 1960s (Eulau, 1989; House, et al., 2004; Scheuch, 2003). In the UK, the UK Data Archive (UKDA) was established in 1967 to encourage sharing of government social science survey data on punch cards (United Kingdom Data Archives, 2017).

Computerization in the 1980s and the growth of early computer networks in the 1990s held the promise of facilitating the SSDA mission of promoting sharing and reuse of social science data and study documentation. The drive to coordinate the collection and use of social science data across institutions, however, required more accessible and machine-readable data and study documentation. Researchers needed metadata and structured document rules for codebooks because they wanted to more easily exchange research data. Efficient sharing of data required that the producers of data and users of data agree on format issues. Further, researchers wanted to use data on desktop computers and easily transfer data into statistical software packages without additional "setup" work (DDI "About," 2003). In short, with the ability to describe data and document it on the computer networks came a need to create a standard that connected the user community to the data producers, and to connect both to statistical software vendors. In the wake of these concerns and challenges, the DDI Initiative was born (DDI "About," 2003).

ICPSR took a leadership role. In 1993, before the creation of the DDI working group, ICPSR acknowledged that its own organization needed a new standard that complied with existing and emerging technology. Its internal standard, OSIRIS, a "set of mainframe-based computer programs for data management and analysis" was imminently obsolete (ICPSR, 2017) thanks to the impending arrival of the Standard Generalized Markup Language (SGML) and later, eXtensible Markup Language (XML). With the introduction of these two new tools, ICPSR needed a new standard. Although staff members had begun working internally on a new standard, they recognized that other data archives would similarly need to revamp their documentation standards to accommodate emerging technologies. Subsequently, members of ICPSR sought collaborators and developed a working group in 1993 to discuss the issue (which we describe in the next section).

By 1995, UKDA became very interested in the outcome of the working group, as it shared concerns about the variety of formats for electronic documentation. Like other organizations at the time, UKDA was interested in developing standards that allowed data to be shareable and interoperable in the face of technological change. However, while ICPSR played a pivotal role in the collaboration that led to the DDI Alliance, UKDA played a more ancillary role.

It is important to understand the extensive level of coordination work involved in creating the DDI standard shared by data users, SSDA and software vendors. The standard created rules for codebook structures, elements that could be contained in codebooks, and the details of the characters contained in elements (e.g., field length). The rules had to be specific enough to promote uniformity, but flexible enough to allow for local variance. Further, they had to sufficiently address a variety of user needs to be adopted widely and hold influence as a standard. Finally, they had to adjust to changes in the underlying technologies (e.g., the shift from SGML based document type definitions to XML) that supported the new standard.

## ANALYSIS: COLLABORATION AND BOUNDARY WORK IN THE DEVELOPMENT OF DDI

This analysis adopts Quick and Feldman's (2014) framework for understanding boundary work as resource mobilization rather than as a function for creating and enforcing barriers between organizations. The following analysis considers several specific moves and activities in which the two SSDA translated across differences, aligned among differences, and decentered differences.

### TRANSLATING ACROSS DIFFERENCES

In this section, the analysis is centered on ICPSR's leadership of the DDI Initiative using the concept of "translating across differences." This practice involves deemphasizing expertise and creating a new, shared domain for collaboration between organizations or groups. Rather than focusing only on the voice of the leader or expert, translating across differences can create connection points that encourage giving equal weight to multiple perspectives (Quick and Feldman, 2014).

To this end, in 1993 ICPSR formed a working group committed to the development of the DDI standard, a metadata standard for describing social science research data. This working group, or committee, came to be known as the DDI Alliance. ICPSR led the effort that included SSDA from around the world that were interested in developing an interoperable standard for describing and documenting social science data. ICPSR reached out to several organizations that arguably had different priorities, values, clientele, and services including the Danish Data Archives, the Consortium on European Social Science Data Archives (CESSDA), and the International Association for Social Science Information Services (IASSIST). One of ICPSR's goals in the creation of the working group was to minimize reliance on individual leadership and expertise and instead enhance the collaborative capabilities inherent across partner institutions. ICPSR had already been working on a standard internally but saw the value in creating a standard that was widely adopted and ready for use in a short amount of time. As such, council members of ICPSR pointed out the importance of seeking collaborations that involved "people who care deeply about codebooks" (ICPSR, 1994). The challenge of the working group was to develop a new standard that both met the diverse needs of the organizations involved and allowed each individual organization the flexibility it needed.

The DDI Alliance was structured such that organizations could maintain their disparate interests while having the opportunity to translate across differences, or "negotiate to discover and act on" on their shared interest in standards development (Quick and Feldman, 2014). Not everyone on the committee was expected to make the same contributions, have the same goals or levels of expertise, or even the same interest in the development of the standard. ICPSR provided the initial idea, formed the committee, and provided some funding to the group to initiate the development of the standard.

By 1995, this collaborative effort produced results, when the members of the Alliance met and developed a draft list of codebook elements. The codebook was further refined, and a more formal draft created, by individuals affiliated with ICPSR and the University of Michigan Library. The revised draft was reviewed and revised by the Alliance the following year, in 1997. The University of California Berkeley Data Archives implemented the DDI standards in

1998 (DDI "Introduction," 1999). By involving different members of the Alliance at different times, and relying on their interest and expertise to guide involvement in the development of DDI, the Alliance's flexible participation rules created a space that allowed for multiple perspectives.

Finding points of connection between different organizations that embraced multiple perspectives was an essential strategy in creating a space for collaboration on standards development. This strategy ultimately led to broader support for and implementation of the DDI standard.

As pointed out by the DDI committee in 1999, it was important to have a variety of stakeholders involved in "the social science research enterprise" ("DDI "Introduction," 1999). This group of stakeholders emphasized what the DDI Alliance referred to as "broad consultation concerning content and scope of the emerging standard" which was viewed as "crucial to the ultimate widespread acceptance of the standard" (1999). By creating connections between multiple organizations, ICPSR facilitated an interorganizational work project that solved its own internal problem with OSIRIS, while also strengthening the larger social science data research community (Quick and Feldman, 2014).

Beyond functioning as connectors between organizations, ICPSR's actions in promoting and managing the DDI standard can be seen as acts of "constructive coping." As Maaninen-Olsson and Mahring (2009) explain, project oriented boundary activities can aid in "constructive coping" via one of two ways. First, constructive coping may include either closing off project boundaries to retain momentum in executing project tasks. Constructive coping may also include opening up or spanning boundaries to outside "requests, knowledge, expertise and resources" (p. 8). And as Faraj and Yan (2009) underscore, boundary spanning is imperative in teamwork, where spanning their own frontiers can help groups acquire critical resources that may not otherwise be accessible.

ICPSR began by introducing the idea of and coordinating membership in the DDI Alliance. Although participants were interested in the project for a variety of reasons, ICPSR could find enough overlap in the interests of the participating organizations to develop the standard as something all the collaborating organizations would want to use. By enrolling several organizations involved in the development of the standard early in the process, ICPSR could encourage investment on the part of those organizations, which helped demonstrate the value of involvement in the Alliance's work.

## ALIGNING AMONG DIFFERENCES

This section contrasts ICPSR's early involvement with creation of DDI with the initially tenuous relationship of UKDA and the DDI Alliance using the idea of recognizing and maintaining differences rather than attempting to resolve them. At the time of the creation of the DDI Alliance, Rasmussen's (1994) survey noted there was an expectation among SSDA for the development of a standardized codebook that could meet the diverse needs of organizations implementing that standard. Meeting the needs of multiple organizations involved aligning the goals and needs of the participating organizations so that they could see the value of collaborating on the development of the standard. Asking what data archives wanted from a new standard to do was important in getting institutions invested in the developing DDI standard. The DDI committee focused not just on developing the standard, but on situating it as a widely employable standard with richer content and a tool that produces a single document with a wide array of uses (Miller and Vardigan, 2005).

UKDA's focus on interorganizational work was rooted initially in negotiating and maintaining the distinction between its organization's documentation work and that of the DDI Alliance.

As Quick and Feldman (2014) assert, in collaborative work it is sometimes useful to recognize and maintain differences rather than attempt to resolve them. This approach can help avoid competing groups from wasting time and resources in that competition. UKDA adopted this approach by maintaining its interest in other documentation projects and practices in Europe, while also following the progress of the DDI Alliance. In 1995, UKDA held an expert seminar for SSDA and invited the director of ICPSR to join the seminar. Discussions about the relationship between American and European data communities were a focus of the seminar, but afterward UKDA still did not become actively involved with the DDI committee. UKDA demarcated its own interests from those of the DDI Alliance. Arguably, these actions were designed to distinguish UKDA and also legitimize it (Quick and Feldman, 2014).

As we describe below, while UKDA initially distanced itself from the DDI committee, with the introduction of the NESSTAR project came an opportunity for UKDA to connect its needs to the development of the standard.

## DECENTERING DIFFERENCES

This section describes UKDA's more tenuous involvement with the DDI Alliance using the concept of "decentering differences," or relying on avoiding the boundaries that make barriers or distinctions meaningful. In its annual reports, UKDA explained that it was keen to improve documentation and was working toward consolidating electronic technical documentation. While UKDA's documentation goals were similar to those of the DDI committee, UKDA initially avoided joining the collaborative effort. The annual reports indicate that while UKDA maintained interest in the project, it was unwilling to commit extensive time and resources to the working group.

UKDA recognized the importance of collaboration to create a standard that met the criteria for its own organizational needs and strategized accordingly. UKDA relied on NESSTAR, a project implemented in 1996 as a collaboration between UKDA, the Norwegian Social Science Data Services, and the Danish Data Archive. The goal of the NESSTAR project was to develop generic tools that made it easier to "locate multiple data sources across national boundaries, browse detailed information about these data, tabulate and visualize data, and disseminate data and documentation in forms suitable for immediate use" (UKDA Annual Report 1998-1999). Thus, the NESSTAR project had similar needs as those driving the developing DDI standard, and therefore they adopted the DDI standard. NESSTAR then became a point of connection between UKDA and DDI--a means by which the UKDA had and could continue to be invested in the development of the DDI standard.

In 1999, the DDI Alliance cited NESSTAR as an example of a project that implemented the DDI standard, describing DDI as central to the ability of NESSTAR to meet its objectives. But as described by UKDA, DDI was one of several technologies that helped the NESSTAR project both incorporate the latest technologies and maintain expertise as technology continued to change (UKDA Annual Report, 1998-1999).

As Miller and Vardigan (2005) explain, organizations "need proof of productivity gains or improvements in the quality of products or services to demonstrate that the investments are worthwhile" (n.p.). The NESSTAR project proved to be just that proof for the development of the DDI standard. It provided an opportunity to see how the DDI standard could be implemented. As a result of the success of NESSTAR, "the standard gained a wider and more general acceptance" (Miller and Vardigan, 2005, n.p.). However, Miller and Vardigan conclude by saying that while NESSTAR was a great example of how implementing DDI can be successful, NESSTAR could not have been built without the use of a metadata standard like DDI.

UKDA saw the relationship between its project and the DDI committee as less symbiotic than Miller and Vardiagn described it. An organizational report from UKDA states that the archive had a *leading* role in the DDI committee. From the perspective of actors in UKDA, adopting the standard for its NESSTAR project in 1998 meant that UKDA was playing a critical part in the widespread use of the standard. UKDA was, in essence, shaping how and to what extent the standard would be implemented by other organizations. Both the DDI committee and UKDA perceived their investment in standards development as essential for the SSDA community. They used each other as examples of the kinds of technical expertise and user services possible with the adoption of the DDI standard, although their perspectives on their respective roles differed. Both the DDI committee and UKDA benefited from this partnership and had lasting effects on the DDI project. This was possible because UKDA and the DDI committee decentered differences, or minimized the importance of the distinctions between the committee and the archive.

## DISCUSSION

**Boundary Work and Organizational Collaboration** At different points throughout the creation of the DDI standard, UKDA and ICPSR relied on different kinds of boundary work activities. These involved one of Quick and Feldman's three strategies: translating across differences, aligning among differences, and decentering differences.

During the early development of the DDI standard, ICPSR focused on translating across differences. This strategy was centered on de-emphasizing expertise and finding people who cared about standards development to participate on the committee. ICPSR viewed this translating activity as a way to create a standard that could be used by a variety of organizations and for multiple purposes. It was also a strategy designed to include multiple perspectives, thereby garnering maximum support for the development and growth of the standard.

Although ICPSR and UKDA took on different roles in the committee that developed the DDI standard, both organizations viewed this interorganizational project as valuable. At various points, both archives acknowledged the differences among SSDA and sought connections across those differences. This aligning among differences activity resulted in the ability for collaborators to maintain their distinct interests while pursuing the shared work of standards development. ICPSR used its involvement as the organizer of the DDI working committee to help push its needs for a standard that would meet current and emerging technology needs. Leaders in ICPSR viewed the collaborative endeavor as an opportunity to reach outside its organization to create the DDI standard more quickly and efficiently, and with wider support and adoption. UKDA, by contrast, became involved with the DDI Alliance at a time that allowed it to further its goal of demonstrating its value to stakeholders. Through involvement with NESSTAR and the beta testing phase of the DDI project, UKDA was able to situate itself as promoting the development of the DDI standard with minimal risk.

Finally, UKDA decentered differences by using NESSTAR as a means by which to become a leader in the DDI standards project. NESSTAR introduced an opportunity for decentering differences by providing a way for UKDA to become involved in the development and application of the DDI standard without having the "differences among their identities or interests become central to their interactions" (Star and Griesemer, 1989, p. 407).

## ORGANIZATIONAL RESILIENCE VIA STANDARDS DEVELOPMENT

Over the longer term, the development of DDI allowed ICPSR and UKDA to become more efficiently embedded in the work of social science in their respective countries and elsewhere. ICPSR emerged as a leader in the archives community who supported the development of high quality, interoperable standards. UKDA emerged as an organization that led the way in implementing the adoption of emerging technologies. These institutions became essential resources to several generations of social science scholars and policy makers as repositories for longitudinal and administrative data. By pooling their resources around the development of DDI, they were able to maintain and increase their value to their user communities and to the SSDA community. These activities created goodwill among stakeholders (Faraj and Yan, 2009) and enabled stakeholders to address issues more effectively (Quick and Feldman, 2014).

Further, the kind of interorganizational networks that were developed and sustained over the course of DDI development contribute to the organizational resilience of the constituent SSDA. By organizational resilience, we refer to the interrelated adjustments that are ongoing to keep an organization in a state of what might be called "dynamic equilibrium" in the face of continuous opportunity and change (Bhamra, Dani, and Burnard, 2011). Quick and Feldman (2014) argue that these forms of boundary work enacted to create connections require and result in flexibility in organizations. These efforts result in what the authors term "efficient resilience," or the ability to use multiple resources and paths to achieve success and the capability to reassemble resources and activities in ways that enable systems to continue to work despite adversity and disruption (p. 681). In that vein, Wildavsky (1988) argues that boundary work can result in an organization's ability to "do better through adversity" (p. 2).

When boundaries can be conceptualized as points of connection (Faraj and Yan, 2009), they support resilience by making it easier to reassemble resources and activities following a disruption (for example, acute crises or general disruptions to services). In this case, the boundary work around the collaborative effort to develop DDI allowed both organizations and other SSDA to cope with changing technologies and "do better" through the adversities that can come about because of difficulties adapting to emerging technologies. Thus, the implementation of DDI arguably allowed SSDA to improve services by developing a range of detailed materials that provided advice and guidance on standards for creating data documentation, streamlined working practices, demonstrate value and save money.

## CONCLUSION

This study contributes to a growing body of literature and practice on long-term maintenance of data infrastructures, a theme that several researchers have drawn attention to in recent years (Ribes and Finholt, 2009; Lee and Paine, 2015; Jackson, Gillespie, and Payette, 2014; Centivany, 2016). Over time, data infrastructures and similar institutions adapt business models, create and maintain networks of relationships, and continually redefine their value to depositors, users, and funders (Shankar and Eschenfelder, 2015; Bietz, Baumer, and Lee, 2010). Organizations often provide shared research infrastructures through collaboration, sometimes through direct interaction and sometimes through larger networks of field-level and professional organizations (Eschenfelder and Shankar, 2017).

These kinds of analyses rely on consideration of standard organizational artifacts as well as other kinds of administrative documents that are not always used in such studies, including memoranda, institutional budgets, and contracts. These documents illustrate work that happens between and among institutions and the examination of activities that go beyond the daily work of routines, meetings, and other quotidian activities that often dominate even studies of the "long term" (Karasti, Millerand, and Baker, 2010; Stoll, Edwards, and Mynatt, 2010). Such organizational and temporal scales can account for slower paced, but interlinked cooperative activities that might stretch out over years.

Studies of interorganizational work such as we have begun in this paper fit into the capacious but uncomfortable space between "chaos and routine" (Lee, 2005). Our analysis of ICPSR's and UKDA's collaborative work around standards development is important in demonstrating how enacting boundary work to create junctures can be an important way in which organizations seek to cope with change, access, shape, and implement new technology, and become embedded institutions within their field.

As public and private expenditures on research infrastructures continue to proliferate, understanding why some such infrastructures become foundational for the work of entire scholarly disciplines for half a century while others become digital tumbleweeds is paramount. To this end, we would also argue for more studies of longevity and organizational resilience and how the going concerns of CSCW - the study of routines, plans, articulation work, devices, and artifacts - factor into design for what Lee and Paine (2015) deem "planned permanence".

### ACKNOWLEDGMENTS

The authors would like to acknowledge the Alfred P. Sloan Foundation, the Irish Research Council, the Wisconsin Alumni Research Foundation, the SLIS Sarah M. Pritchard Faculty Support Fund, and the ASIS&T SIG/History and Foundations of Information Science Fund for their support for this project. We would also like to thank Allison Langham for her help developing the codebook and coding primary documents.

### REFERENCES

Akkerman, S. F., & Bakker, A. (2011). Boundary crossing and boundary objects. *Review of Educational Research, 81*(2), 132-169.

Bhamra R, Dani S., and Burnard K. (2011). Resilience: The concept, a literature review and future directions. *International Journal of Production Research, 49*(18), 5375-5393.

Bertot, J. C., Butler, B. S., and Travis, D. M. (2014). Local big data: The role of libraries in building community data infrastructures, In *Proceedings of the 15th annual international conference on digital government research*, 17-23.

Bietz, M.J., Baumer, E.P.S. and Lee, C.P. (2010). Synergizing in cyberinfrastructure development. *Computer Supported Cooperative Work, 19*, 245.

Bisco R. L. (1996). Social science data archives: A review of developments, *American Political Science Review, 60*(1), 93-109.

Bowker, G. C., & Star, S. L. (2000). *Sorting things out: Classification and its consequences.* Cambridge, MA: The MIT Press.

Busch, L. (2011). *Standards: Recipe for reality.* Cambridge, MA: The MIT Press.

Centivany, A. (2016). Policy as embedded generativity: A case study of the emergence and evolution of HathiTrust. In *Proceedings of the 19th ACM conference on computer-supported cooperative work & social computing*, 926-940.

Corti, L (2011). The European landscape of qualitative social research archives: Methodological and practical issues. *Forum Qualitative Social Research: Sozialforschung, 12*(3), 11.

Cragin, M., and Shankar, K. (2006): Scientific data collections and distributed collective practice. *Computer Supported Cooperative Work* (CSCW), *15*(2), 185-204.

Data Documentation Initiative (1999): Retrieved Feb 9, 2017 from http://web.archive.org/web/19991007104409/http://www. icpsr.umich.edu/DDI/intro.html

Data Documentation Initiative (1999): *Introduction.* Retrieved Feb 9, 2017 from http://web.archive.org/web/19991007104409/ http://www. icpsr.umich.edu/DDI/intro.html

Data Documentation Initiative (2003): *About the organization.* Retrieved Feb 9, 2017 from

https://web.archive.org/web/20030418065421/http://www.icpsr.umich.edu/ DDI/ORG/index.html

Eulau H. (Ed.) (1989). Crossroads of social science: The ICPSR 25th anniversary volume. New York: Agathon Press.

Eschenfelder, K.R.; Shankar, K. (2017). Infrastructuring social science data archives: The role of field level organizations. Workshop on e-infrastructure for collaboration in the social sciences and the humanities at the computer supported cooperative work conference, Portland, OR.

Faraj, S., and Yan, A. (2009). Boundary work in knowledge teams. *Journal of Applied Psychology, 94*(3), 604.

Green, A. G., and Gutmann, M. P. (2007). Building partnerships among social science researchers, institution-based repositories and domain specific data archives. *OCLC Systems & Services: International digital library perspectives, 23*(1), 35-53.

Hanseth, O., Monteiro, E., Hatling, M. (1996). Developing information infrastructure: The tension between standardization and flexibility, *Science, Technology, & Human Values, 21*(4), 407-426.

House, J.S. (ed.) (2004). A telescope on society: Survey research and social science at the University of Michigan and beyond. Ann Arbor, MI: University of Michigan Press.

ICPSR (2017). ICPSR: The founding and early years. Retrieved Febuary 9, 2017 from http://www.icpsr.umich.edu/icpsrweb/-content/membership/history/early-years.html

Jackson, S. J., Gillespie, T., & Payette, S. (2014). The policy knot: Re-integrating policy, practice and design in CSCW studies of social computing. In *Proceedings of the 17th ACM conference on computer supported cooperative work & social computing*, 588-602.

Jackson, S. J., Edwards, P. N., Bowker, G. C., and Knobel, C. P. (2007). Understanding infrastructure: History, heuristics and cyberinfrastructure policy. *First Monday*, 12(6).

Kantur, D., and İşeri-Say, A. (2012). Organizational resilience: A conceptual integrative framework. *Journal of Management & Organization*, 18(6), 762-773.

Karasti, H., Baker, K. S., and Millerand, F. (2010). Infrastructure time: Long-term matters in collaborative development. *Computer Supported Cooperative Work (CSCW)*, 19(3-4), 377-415.

Lampland, M. and Star, S.L. (Eds) (2009). Standards and their stories: How quantifying, classifying, and formalizing practices shape everyday life. Cornell, NY: Cornell University Press.

Lee, C.P. (2005). Between chaos and routine: Boundary negotiating artifacts in collaboration, *ECSCW*, 387-406.

Lee, C.P., and Paine, D. (2015). From the matrix to a model of coordinated action (MoCA): A conceptual framework of and for CSCW. In *Proceedings of the 18th ACM conference on computer supported cooperative work & social computing*, 179-194.

Maaninen-Olsson, E., and Mahring, M. (2009). Balancing boundaries: Everyday boundary work in information technology project management. In *System sciences*, 2009. *HICSS'09. 42nd Hawaii international conference on systems sciences*, 1-10.

Mayernik, Matthew S. (2016). Research data and metadata curation as institutional issues. *Journal of the Association for Information Science and Technology*, *67*(4), 973-993.

Miller, K., & Vardigan, M. (2005). How initiative benefits the research community-the data documentation initiative. In *First international conference on e-social science, Manchester, UK.*

Millerand, F. and Bowker, G.C. (2009). Metadata standards: Trajectories and enactment in the life of an ontology. In S.L. Star and M. Lampland (Eds.) *Standards and their stories: How quantifying, classifying, and formalizing practices shape everyday life.* Cornell, NY: Cornell University Press.

Millerand, F., Ribes, D., Baker, K.S. and Bowker, G.C. (2013). Making an issue out of a standard: Storytelling practices in a scientific community. *Science, Technology, & Human Values*, 38, 7-43.

Monteiro, E., Pollock, N., Hanseth, O., and Williams, R. (2013). From artefacts to infrastructures. *Computer Supported Cooperative Work: CSCW: An International Journal*, *22*(4), 575-607.

Pawlowski, S. D., Robey, D., & Raven, A. (2000). Supporting shared information systems: boundary objects, communities, and brokering. In *Proceedings of the twenty first international conference on information systems, Association for Information Systems*, 329-338.

Quick, K. S., and Feldman, M. S. (2014). Boundaries as junctures: Collaborative boundary work for building efficient resilience. *Journal of Public Administration Research and Theory*, 24(3), 673-695.

Rasmussen, K. (1994). Documentation--what we have and what we want: Report of an enquete of data archives and their staff, *IASSIST Quarterly*, 19(1), 22-35.

Ribes, D., and Finholt, T. A. (2009). The long now of technology infrastructure: Articulating tensions in development. *Journal of the Association for Information Systems*, *10*(5), 375–398.

Scheuch E.K. (2003). History and visions in the development of data services for the social sciences. *International Social Science Journal*, 55(177), 385-399.

Shankar, K., and Eschenfelder, K. R. (2015). Sustaining data archives over time: Lessons from the organizational studies literature. *New Review of Information Networking*, *20*(1-2), 248-254.

Star, Susan Leigh, and James R. Griesemer. (1989). Institutional ecology, "translations" and boundary objects: Amateurs and professionals in Berkeley's Museum of Vertebrate Zoology, 1907–39. *Social Studies of Science*, *19*, 387–420.

Stoll, J., Edwards, W. K., and Mynatt, E. D. (2010, February). Interorganizational coordination and awareness in a nonprofit ecosystem. In *Proceedings of the 2010 ACM conference on computer supported cooperative work*, 51-60.

UKDA (2017). About the Archive. Retrieved February 9, 2017 from http://www.data-archive.ac.uk/about/archive.

UKDA Annual Report 1998-1999, Retrieved February 9, 2017 from http://web.archive.org/web/19991007104409/http://www.icpsr.umich.edu/DDI/intro.html.

White, H.D. (Ed.) (1977). Reader in machine-readable *social data*. Englewood, CO: Information Handling Services.

Wildavsky, Aaron B. (1988). *Searching for safety*. New Brunswick, NJ: Transaction.

Williams, R., Bunduchi, R., Gerst, M., Graham, I., Pollock, N., Procter, R., & Voss, A. (2004, August).

Understanding the evolution of standards: Alignment and reconfiguration in standards development and implementation arenas. In *Proceedings of the 4S & EASST Conference*, 225-239.

# Role of Communication in Data Reuse

**Ayoung Yoon**
*Indiana University Purdue University Indianapolis (IUPUI), USA. ayyoon@iupui.edu*

## ABSTRACT

**In acknowledging the potentials of existing data, researchers' interests in sharing and reusing data have recently emerged. However, sharing and reusing data is not a simple one-step process for researchers. Because data reusers build their work on other researchers' findings, the process of data reuse involves various interactions and communications with other relevant parties. Exploring the nature of communications around data is thus important to fully understand data reuse practices and to support smoother processes of data reuse. This study investigates communications occurring around data during data reusers' experiences through qualitative interview studies involving this group. This study's results show that the communications with different stakeholders mainly support data reuse in three areas: searching, learning, and problem solving. The findings provide valuable insights into the domain of scholarly communication, data reuse, and data services.**

## KEYWORDS

data reuse, scholarly communication

## INTRODUCTION

As data form the basis of scientific research, the importance of data and their roles in research has already been well recognized. Researchers conceive of the value of data as a way to address specific knowledge gaps, and valuable data help researchers answer their questions and/or test hypotheses (Akmon, 2014). In acknowledging the potentials of existing data, researchers' interests in sharing and reusing data have emerged. Existing research data can be used to not only validate current results but also to generate new findings built on the work of others (Birnholtz & Bietz, 2003; Borgman, 2011). Existing data can be reanalyzed or combined with new data to verify published results or to arrive at new conclusions (Committee on Ensuring the Utility and Integrity of Research Data in a Digital Age, 2009). Revolutions in the practices of science, known as data-intensive research or eScience, also support the need for sharing and reusing data (Kunze et al., 2011), as eScience promises discoveries and benefits that are not possible with more traditional methodologies.

However, sharing and reusing data is not a simple one-step process for researchers. Several studies have pointed out the difficulty of locating data for reuse, and understanding data is often a time-consuming process for data reusers, which sometimes lead to a failure in data reuse (e.g., Yoon, 2016a, 2017). Birnholtz and Bietz (2003) suggest that data are not simple carriers of meanings, and "converting raw data into scientific and social meaning is an active, context dependent process" (p. 341). Some studies have indicated the fundamental challenges of data reuse, showing the contextual nature of data from examinations of data reuse practices (e.g., Berg & Goorman, 1999; Zimmerman, 2007). Data reuse is not simply a transfer of numbers or images; it also entails the transfer of knowledge that is locally embedded during data creation. Additionally, documentation, which is one channel that is used to transfer contextual information about data, is often insufficient, which can make data reuse difficult (e.g., Fienberg, Martin, & Straf, 1985; McCall & Appelbaum, 1991; Niu & Hedstrom, 2008). Perhaps due to these challenges, the data reuse process is often not only an internal knowledge process for data reusers but also involves external communications and interactions with other researchers.

A dataset becomes an integral part of scholarly communication in data reuse, which is "a social process, in which scholars share ideas, data, resources, methodologies, innovations, and discoveries with their peers and with the public" (Martin, 2014, p. 53). Because data reusers build their work on other researchers' findings, the process of data reuse involves these interactions and communications with other relevant parties. Most commonly, previous research has found that data reusers contact data producers (the original investigators of the project in which the data for reuse were created) with questions (Niu, 2009; Yoon, 2016a, 2017). Sometimes mentors have been involved in locating and understanding data (Kriesberg, Frank, Faniel, & Yakel, 2013; Rolland & Lee, 2013).

These interactions and communications have been only sparsely examined in previous data reuse literature, as they naturally appeared as part of discussions about data reuse practices, but they have not been a major focus of past research. Understanding the nature of communications around data is important to fully understand data reuse practices and to support smoother processes of data reuse. This study investigates communications occurring around data during data reusers' experiences. The specific questions asked in this study are as follows:

- Who (what types of communities or individuals) is involved in communications with data reusers during their data reuse experiences?
- Why and how are data reusers interacting with those individuals or communities?

80th Annual Meeting of the Association for Information Science & Technology, Washington, DC, VA | Oct. 27-Nov. 1, 2017

This study's findings provide valuable insights into the domain of scholarly communication and data reuse. Reusing data requires researchers' deep understanding of these data, and the process involves engaging in the different types of communications and interactions with relevant parties. By disclosing the nature of communications for reuse, this study offers insights into how to ease communications among researchers and how to support their reuse experiences.

## LITERATURE REVIEW

Because data reuse practices are influenced by different disciplinary cultures and the processes for creating various types of data, the majority of this research has investigated data reuse practices and reusers' behaviors within specific disciplines, including cancer epidemiology research (Rolland & Lee, 2013), ecology (Borgman, Wallis, & Enyedy, 2007; Zimmerman, 2003), biological science (Chin & Lansing, 2004), environmental science (Van House, Butler, & Schiff, 1998), astronomy (Sands, Borgman, Wynholds, & Traweek, 2012), and earthquake engineering (Faniel & Jacobsen, 2010). Data reuse practices can be distinctive, depending on the types of data being reused, and some research has focused on certain types of data for reuse, such as quantitative (Faniel, Kriesberg, & Yakel, 2016) or qualitative data (e.g., Broom, Cheshire, & Emmison, 2009; Moore, 2007; Yoon, 2014). Several researchers have also conducted multidisciplinary studies, for instance, Birnholtz and Bietz's (2003) research on earthquakes, HIV/AIDS, and space physics, as well as Faniel, Barrera-Gomez, Kriesberg, and Yakel's (2013) investigation of quantitative social science, archaeology, and zoology, through the Dissemination Information Packages for Information Reuse (DIPIR) project from the University of Michigan and OCLC Research.

In addition to these efforts to understand data reuse practices in various disciplines, recent research has also investigated the criteria for data reuse from reusers' perspectives. Chin and Lansing (2004) present general data properties that are important to make data reusable, while Huang, Stvilia, and Jörgensen (2012) and Yoon (2016b) specifically address data quality dimensions. Faniel and Jacobsen (2010) discuss data reusability and point out relevancy, understandability, and trustworthiness as criteria. Adopting a theory of trust, Yoon's (2017) study also demonstrates users' criteria for judging the trustworthiness of data.

While different disciplines have various cultures and practices relating to data, existing research presents some common challenges in data reuse across disciplines. The major challenge is transferring information regarding the contexts of data. Many researchers have pointed out the contextual nature of data, as data are originally created for a specific purpose, with a local context embedded in them. To be reused beyond their original purpose, data are moved from the local sphere to the broader world (e.g., for interdisciplinary research), creating distance from their original context (Zimmerman, 2008). This distance poses problems when reusers try to understand how data were originally used (Cragin & Shankar, 2006; Faniel & Zimmerman, 2011; Jirotka et al., 2005; Zimmerman, 2008). Additionally, researchers often argue about the difficulty of deciding what contextual information is important for reusers beyond the original research purpose (Birnholtz & Bietz, 2003; Carlson & Anderson, 2007; Markus, 2001). Each reuser also has different technical skills and tacit knowledge about understanding data from other researchers and fields, which creates another layer of difficulty in understanding (Faniel & Zimmerman, 2011).

While documentation – which can include codebooks, related bibliographies, data-collection instruments, and metadata for resource discovery – is one channel for transferring contextual information to data reusers (Niu & Hedstrom, 2008), a number of researchers have also reported problems and challenges with it (Borgman, 2007; Corti, 2005; Fienberg et al., 1985; McCall & Appelbaum, 1991; Niu & Hedstrom, 2008; Zimmerman, 2003). Similar to the challenges of transferring contextual information embedded in data, documentation can be inherently insufficient because of the nature of tacit knowledge and communication reduction (Niu, 2009). People sometimes know things implicitly, and it is inevitable to miss information; not everything can be transferred (Carlson & Anderson, 2007; Niu, 2009; Niu & Hedstrom, 2008). On the other hand, documentation can be simply poor, as data producers might not want to prepare documentation well because of their lack of motivation or inadequate skills to do so (Baker & Yarmey, 2009).

Previous research findings also suggest active communications and interactions around data among various scholarly communities during the data reuse process. Besides the interactions with data producers, Zimmerman's (2007) study indicates that primary methods of locating data for reuse include human interactions and communications from other scientists. Similarly, Sands and colleagues (2012) report informal or formal methods of communication involved in astronomers' data reuse processes. Communications regarding data appear important in transferring knowledge beyond locating the data. Niu (2009) points out interactive conversation as an important channel for transferring knowledge when data reuse is not supported by adequate documentation. Both Rolland and Lee (2013) and Kriesberg et al. (2013) discuss mentors' roles in data reuse, helping novice researchers understand data. While these studies imply rich communication and interaction occurring around data for reuse, such communication has not been a main focus of previous literature. Concentrating on the nature of communication around data and investigating it further would advance the understanding of data reuse practices and find better methods of supporting data reuse.

## METHOD

This study employed a qualitative research method and conducted in-depth semi-structured interviews with quantitative data reusers in the fields of public health and social work. These two disciplines have a culture of data reuse and share similar characteristics, such as a professional orientation in research. Some datasets were also used by researchers in both disciplines, which helped in recruiting a homogeneous sample. The study participants were identified from searching major scholarly databases, such as EBSCOhost, SAGE Journals, ProQuest Social Science, and ERIC, using the keywords "secondary data" and "secondary analysis."

In total, 299 data reusers were identified from the search. An email invitation for an interview was sent to the potential participants. A total of 38 data reusers responded and were interviewed. Given the diverse geographic distribution of the study participants, all interviews were conducted by phone. The duration of the interviews ranged from 40 to 95 minutes, with an average of 60 minutes.

All interviews followed a predeveloped protocol. Non-directive, open-ended questions were asked about the participants' reuse experiences, as well as any interaction and communication they had during such experiences. They were encouraged to draw multiple experiences from their past if relevant, as their experiences using one dataset were often related to their past experiences or experiences in using other datasets. The interviews were recorded, fully transcribed, and analyzed using a qualitative data analysis tool, NVivo 10 for Mac.

The participants were researchers in various positions, consisting of six PhD students, one postdoctoral fellow, 12 assistant professors, nine associate and full professors, and nine research scientists. More women (25) participated in the study than men (13), with ages ranging from 20s to 70s. They had a minimum of two years to a maximum of 45 years of experience as researchers in their disciplines, averaging about 15 years. Their years of experience in research data (both secondary and primary) also varied and were not always the same as their years of experience in their disciplines. Some participants had changed disciplines during their careers or worked with data only later in their research training. Their years of data experience in research ranged from two to 40, averaging about 16 years. With the exception of two participants, all researchers in this study had used more than three different datasets as secondary data for their research.

## FINDINGS

The participants' data reuse experiences did not involve a linear process. Generally, their experiences consisted of the following multiple steps: discovering and searching for potential data for their research, selecting the data they wished to use, understanding the data through thorough examination, conducting analyses, and writing manuscripts. During this data reuse process, the participants communicated and interacted with different individuals and communities for various purposes.

### *Searching for new data and new opportunities*

The data discovery and search process was an important first step in data reuse, but locating data was not always easy for the participants. A couple noted, "It's not like there is a unified library catalog for entire datasets" (IP17), and "It would be nice if there were more opportunities to find out what data is available. I know some people that will not necessarily post their data" (IS09). While the participants searched the published literature to see what data were produced and reused by other researchers, checked major data resources from government agencies, such as the Centers for Disease Control or the National Institutes of Health, as well as looked in other data repositories, they also actively interacted with other scholarly communities to learn what data existed or to search for new data.

Interestingly, several participants reported having a "data talk" as part of their casual conversation with other researchers around them even when they were not in the process of actively searching for new data for their research. IS01 said, "It's just part of your research life; you hang out with your buddies, basically, after you work, coffee hour, lunch time, like that, and you talk about research [...] and data." This casual data talk with other researchers could initiate a new project that would reuse existing data. IP05 said that this casual data talk led to collaboration with other colleagues as they "share[d] a lot of ideas about data pretty frequently [...] and found a shared interest." The participants were interested in new ideas and opportunities that data could bring into their research. "I'm always willing to learn about [what] kind of data is available that I don't know about. I usually ask my colleagues about what their research is and what data they are using" (IS04).

When the participants more actively searched data for their research, they commonly reached out to different communities around them. Some participants reported being connected with the networks of their mentors or advisors. In addition to the participants' common practice to reuse data from their advisors' projects, several participants talked about their experience in being introduced to data created by a member of their advisor's network. The advisor's network served not only as a connection to the established network(s) in the field but also as a gateway to discover and obtain permission to reuse data. IP11 reused data produced by the "friend of my advisor, who was the director of [name] center" and recalled that "[the director] was willing to share her data with me" because of the relationship between the advisor and the director. For IP11, obtaining permission to reuse this data was "rather easy" compared to the case of "a total stranger, especially a student or a junior [researcher] asking to use your data." Similarly, IS13 used his advisor's network—a large one of past advisees, the advisor's colleagues, and the latter's own colleagues—to locate data for reuse. As a junior researcher, IS13 found this network a significant resource for identifying interesting data that he could reuse and for facilitating his collaborations with senior researchers. IS13 explained that his advisor's network was a community where people "just [hung out] together out of mutual scholarly interest and then interpersonal friendship." The community members helped one another, and data reuse among them was more open "even if I didn't know them personally" because of the scholarly lineage. "I always think of it as a family [...]. I say to the people who are full professors and got their PhDs in the 70s, I'm like, 'So, I'm your littlest brother' [...] in terms of the family lineage" (IS13).

The participants also communicated with their own scholarly social networks and particularly noted these networks' impact on discovering new data for their research. IP09 mentioned conferences as venues to network with other researchers and to gather new information about data. IS08 also shared a successful experience of actively searching for a particular dataset of interest through networking at a conference and a committee meeting:

> *So, we actually didn't have any data related to the research questions that I was most interested in. And so, it was incumbent upon me to find somebody who was collecting data about this population [of interest] and to try and work with them in order to get my foot in the door, as someone who could become, hopefully, an expert in this area. So [...], I went to conferences and networked that way. I also got on a planning committee for a specialty conference in my area of interest, and through that, I was able to meet a number of researchers interested in my [topic] [... and] had access to data in my area. [...] [T]hrough that process, [i]f you make the right and the best connections, I was able to actually find quite a few people willing to work on data with me. At least two people came forward and said, 'Hey. You know, I think I might have what you're looking for in my dataset.'*

Similar to the participants' experiences with their mentors' networks, being in the same network helped the data producers feel safe and willing to share data with the participants, which made data discovery and reuse easier for them. Although previous literature pointed out researchers' reluctance to share their data for various reasons, the participants found that locating data and contacting the data producers through their networks often lowered the barriers to data sharing. IS09 talked about his group's experience in gaining access (through networking) to "some mildly restricted data" from a data producer who was not very open about sharing her data. IS09 said, "People are like, '[...] I own my data. And you've got to give me a real[ly] good reason to allow me to [let you use it ...].'" IS09 came to know the data producers from one of his network colleagues and believed that the reason for his being able to use data "that couldn't be networked [reused ...] ha[d] to do with his social network."

### *Learning through communication*

For many participants, communications and interactions around data with different individuals and communities comprised the process of learning data for reuse. IS11 argued for the importance of interactions and communications around data during the reuse process:

> *So [...] do these interactions do anything for me? Using secondary data is [...] not just [gaining] access to it but [doing so ...] as if you know it well. [...] [I]t's like moving to a new neighborhood. If you don't make friends in [the] neighborhood, your life is gonna be more difficult because you need to be able to talk to somebody and [ask], 'Can you recommend a good plumber?' [...] Talking to other people can make the experience easier because they increase your learning of the dataset more quickly. You can get to the real work. [...] When you use secondary data, it's like a two-step process. The first thing you need to do is get to know the data or get to know the neighborhood, right? Then you can get down to real living. Or in this case, doing the actual research, right? So, in that sense, I think being able to talk to people who use the data or have used the data, or official representatives who make the data available, that's very helpful in basically getting you to the real living things more quickly.*

Learning and acquiring a deep understanding of data were important in data reuse, and other participants' experiences in communicating with different groups of people supported IS11's opinions on the importance of learning about data through various methods.

#### Learning through mentoring

Several participants recalled their experiences in being mentored during data reuse in their earlier careers as researchers, which occurred particularly when they acquired data through their advisors and their advisors' networks. Due to the existing mentor–mentee relationship, it was natural for both participants and data producers (their advisors or members of their advisors' networks) to have teaching–learning sessions about data in the participants' processes of examining and understanding data. IP11's regular meetings with the producer of the data he was using, his advisor, and his advisor's friend covered basic information and his questions about the data, issues he encountered during his analysis, and discussions for problem solving. IP02 enjoyed meeting with her mentor and the data producer, who was also a member of the mentor's network. According to IP02, it was extremely helpful because "it provide[d] a level of collaboration and mentoring that you [wouldn't] see when you just [got] a dataset." IS13 also pointed out the importance of this aspect, saying that he had "not just access to the data but more importantly, access to people. [...] [I]t's very easy for me to go and talk to the [data producers] and ask what they're thinking about, [...] what's acceptable to [them], what should be done, what shouldn't be done." This close interaction with data producers and mentoring regarding data were not always possible for the participants when they acquired and used data without personal connections.

### Learning from data producers

Perhaps the most important communication around data reuse is with the data producers, who were the principal investigators of the original studies (or their equivalent). Many participants emphasized the significance of gaining access to the data producers. They expressed their preference for communicating with the data producers because sometimes, the data did not come with thorough and sufficient documentation, and speaking with the data producers would enhance the participants' understanding during the process of using and analyzing the data. The participants believed that direct communication with data producers would provide a behind-the-scenes examination of the study (IS08) and illuminate "potential problems, issues, or simply questions" (IP02). IP04 explained the greatest benefit of having access to data producers: "They know what the challenges [associated with data] are and how to get around those challenges." Those challenges are often difficult to fully explain and document; the participants mentioned that additional help might not be possible without direct interaction with data producers. Interaction with the data producers was also essential for the participants when they found errors or inconsistencies in the data as only the data producers could explain what those were.

### Problem solving and peer learning

Active communications with different communities occurred during the participants' processes of understanding data and their efforts to deal with any questions or issues with the data. For some participants, such contact involved an alternative way to handle data when they could not interact with data producers; others valued communicating with various communities regardless of their communications with data producers.

*Scholarly community.* As the participants were already members of larger scholarly communities, such as online forums, workshops, and conferences, they relied on these communities to solve data-related problems. These scholarly communities tended to be those that the participants already belonged to and engaged with regularly. Because these communities were not specifically formed around the use of certain data but coalesced around similar research topics and interests, the participants reported the frequent information exchange about data reuse. IP05 said, "It's pretty common in my field to go online and look for forums or discussion boards about [a] particular topic, which can be a data topic." IP08's community, a forum for members of research centers, was also "very active," with "a lot of talk about data in general."

Because these communities were not formed specifically around the use of certain data or data types, finding solutions or answers to data problems might not be guaranteed, and the chance of having data experts in such communities might be lower than in a data-driven community. However, IP08 also discussed getting help from a forum that was related to her research. The forum was "pretty active," and the members "share[d] a lot of things about research, ask[ed] each other questions, [and] answer[ed] the questions" (IP08). Data-related questions and discussions were just among the common themes in the forum. Because they already "talk[ed] about what they were using in terms of secondary analysis of existing data," it was not a "weird thing to do if I [brought] in a data question" (IP08). Interestingly, the participants did not simply communicate with these communities about searching for and discovering new data. Rather, they posed questions about the data they had found, raised issues about using these, and tried to obtain comments from the communities' members.

*Data reuser groups.* The participants often reached out to other data reusers. Data reuser groups were good sources of information when the participants knew what data they wanted to work with or were already working on a specific dataset. The different ways to contact other reusers included a listserv for specific data, data workshops at conferences, webinars, and user group meetings.

As data producers sometimes held workshops and webinars, attending those sessions was one valuable way to find other reusers. The workshops were also helpful in interacting with data producers. As IS04 said, "Not just the original investigators, the project manager, and [the] data manager but [also] the faculty members who worked directly with the data" attended the workshops. Similarly, on the listserv regarding the data that IP03 used, there was "a mix of university faculty, [...] university researchers, and federal researchers." Those data reusers were not necessarily researchers in the same fields or disciplines as those of the participants but shared similar interests in the data. Neither IS04 nor IP03 recognized all of the people in the workshops or the listserv and had no established relationship with them; nonetheless, they expressed appreciation for the other data reusers' help and the experiences that the latter shared with them. IP03 said, "It was [the] more experienced researchers who answered the most [...] questions," which she found "super helpful" because "they'd know how to [solve the issue and] [...] understand why [I had it]." For the same reason, IS04 noted "knowing other people who were closely working with the data," and "talking among ourselves" gave us "confidence" about solving the issue.

*Local research community.* The participants already belonged to their local research communities through research meetings, laboratory meetings, and even casual conversations with their colleagues at their universities or research institutions. Local research communities were often the most accessible, reliable, trustworthy, and easiest sources for discussing any research-relevant topic, including data reuse. Thus, the participants used these communities for problem solving. IP04 attended a weekly team meeting where the group members discussed their research progress, shared research ideas, and presented their challenges with the data. Although the group meetings were not specifically about the data that IP04 was using, IP04 said, "We'[d] discuss [the data]; we'[d] bring [these] to the group and see what the group ha[d] to say because everyone ha[d] a different experience and expertise about things." The participants also showed respect for those who were members of local research communities. For IP04, the "collaborative effort to solve issues" was helpful when the members needed advice on dealing with errors and when one member had already worked on the data. By the same token, IP14 tried to find "people around me who were more familiar, who could help me with understanding the data and the whole process." IS06 felt "very lucky to have [a peer's] expertise on the dataset while I [was] working on it" when she was unable to obtain assistance from the data producers or others. IS14 said, "[My colleague] has worked [on] the data quite a bit. He has a lot of insider knowledge, which is very helpful. And he knows a few people who've worked [on] the dataset as well." Some participants' colleagues also introduced them to someone who could help. IS13's colleague said, "Oh, I have a friend who knows a bunch about it" and initiated an informal e-mail exchange.

### Working with data professionals

Not all participants had extensive experiences in working with data professionals, but some discussed their experiences in communicating with statisticians and data repository staff during their data reuse processes. The participants who approached statisticians or statistical programmers during their data reuse experiences argued for the need for and the importance of statistical consultations in data reuse. IP07 said, "We talked with the statistician if we had a problem or commiserated," and the statistician could let them know "if the problem [was] really me or the data." When it was "more like a programming issue of why my merge[d dataset] wasn't working," the participant was able to get help from the statisticians. When the issue was "really about the actual data, like if the variable didn't seem to be reflecting what it was supposed to be" (IP13), the participant directly approached the data producers or others.

The participants also interacted with the staff at data repositories for help with questions if they had acquired the data from those repositories. Those participants initially contacted the repositories rather than the data producers. Although the participants perceived the repositories as "neutral" places, often as "warehouse[s]" (IS09), and thought of the data producers as primarily responsible for any issues with the data, the participants still expressed appreciation for the repositories' help with their questions. IS09 contacted one data repository when he found that some of his results did not make sense. The repository staff first responded, "We're not really sure," which made IS09 think of the repository as just a warehouse. However, the staff later offered to examine the data and helped him solve the problem.

IS09: The people who [were] warehousing it were totally different people. And those people could sometimes be more helpful because they felt like that was their job. It's like, I was not talking to the PI but was [instead] talking to people [who] had [...] energy and expertise about the data.

### *Limitations of communication around data*

Despite many participants reporting the importance of communicating with different individuals and communities about data reuse, several participants also mentioned some challenges and limitations of these communications. One was the challenge of being junior researchers, causing some participants to feel the barriers to becoming part of an established network to obtain data. IS09 said, "My problem is, being junior, I don't have a great social network. I'm not strongly affiliated with a lab or [a] large research outfit." IS09 was aware that certain data were shared among researchers but not with him because sharing was done through networks, and "people don't know me, and [in] a lot of the cases, I don't even know what [other researchers have] got." IS09 recognized the opportunities that networks could bring him, but without an established network, it was difficult to gain access to other existing networks and discover what data would be available.

Another difficulty involved communication and interaction with data producers, which was not always successful. A few participants experienced difficulty in receiving responses. Sometimes it took too long for them to do so, or they received only "partial answers," which they found "very frustrating" (IS09). IP12 found the interaction "tricky, as it [would] just depend [on] get[ting] the right person who ha[d] the knowledge [of the questions]," particularly when working on a large amount of institutional data. Usually the institutional data provided a contact person, who might or might not have been directly involved in the data collection or the original analysis. Although the participants believed that the contact person would be an expert on the data and the right person to speak to, the negative experiences made IP12 wonder whether "all the staff [members] were really busy or they [might] not exactly know."

## DISCUSSION

This study has examined the role of communication during the data reuse process, as well as the nature of the communication. This study's findings reveal various individuals and communities engaging in data reuse to ease the process. Communication is not always necessary for all data reusers. Several participants experienced working on data without any external communication because the dataset was well documented, well prepared, and easily understandable. However, this was not consistently reported by the participants, as they worked on multiple datasets from different data producers with varying conditions for reuse.

This study's results show that the communications with different stakeholders mainly support data reuse in three areas: searching, learning, and problem solving. While data reusers usually have their own strategies and practices for finding and understanding data and figure out any issue encountered during the process of reusing data, communications with various parties provide often complementary and sometimes the only means of successfully reusing data and overcoming challenges associated with reuse.

Data discovery and search is the most important first step in data reuse, but difficulties in finding data for reuse are among the well-known challenges. As reported by the participants, datasets are stored in various locations without any unified catalog or search system. Additionally, existing research on data sharing points out various factors that inhibit data producers' sharing behaviors (e.g., Cragin, Palmer, Carlson, & Witt, 2010; Tenopir et al., 2011), meaning that not all data are shared. Using scholarly lineage or scholarly networks is an effective alternative way to learn about new data that are not publicly available or deposited in repositories, and having in-person or casual conversations often lowers the barriers to data access. The participants reported being connected to an established community as a huge benefit in terms of learning about data and obtaining permission to reuse the data. On the contrary, not being part of this established community can be a disadvantage for other participants, usually junior faculty members, by not gaining access to data. Due to the person-to-person data exchange or frequent sharing, building relationships among scholarly communities and having formal or informal data talks are significant for data searching and access.

Communications with others also add a level of collaboration and learning. Data reuse was not always solo work for the participants, who learned more about the data from others' experiences. As IS11 argued, communication with others might be the core component of data reuse because in that process, researchers would work with unfamiliar data that they did not create. The participants had to rely on the given information about the data through different mechanisms, which were not always thorough or sufficient. As much of existing research has already pointed out, understanding data is not always easy because of their contextual nature (e.g., Berg & Goorman, 1999; Bishop, 1999; Sandusky & Tenopir, 2007; Stewart, 1996; Zimmerman, 2007). External communications and interactions with other researchers, mentors, and data producers play an important role in sufficiently transferring embedded knowledge in the data.

Finally and most importantly, communications around data are central in problem solving, which help researchers overcome challenges and difficulties in reusing data. The participants experienced different challenges and difficulties in the various phases of data reuse, from data discovery and search, understanding data, and seeking answers to questions, to solving issues and problems that emerged during data reuse. Interacting with different individuals and communities and sharing information with one another were common ways for the participants to solve the problems they encountered. This finding suggests that effective communications can be the key to support successful data reuse. Existing research has argued that the lack of support in data reuse is one of the critical components of failed reuse (Yoon, 2016a). Communications with peers, data professionals, and relevant research communities are ways to provide support for problem solving, which can even turn unsuccessful data reuse experiences to successful ones.

While active communications around data produce rich conversations and collaborations among scholars, they also reveal the need to provide more formal support for data reuse. Communication with others was often the only way to overcome the challenges of data reuse—in this study, searching, learning, and problem solving—because data reusers did not know where else to get help. IS02 said that she was just "wandering around to see who [would] know this." Sometimes, early in their careers, data reusers found it even difficult to engage in data talk without an established network. While academic libraries have initiated efforts to support scholars' data work, their data services usually aid in scholars' data sharing by providing data management and documentation guidelines; not many offer services relevant to data reuse (Yoon & Schultz, 2017). Active support for scholars' communications around data would be necessary, such as developing a tool to foster effective communications among scholars and their information sharing for data reuse.

## CONCLUSION

As the findings demonstrated, data talk was an aspect of scholarly conversation for the participants. It was natural for them to use or rely on existing scholarly communities and connections for their data reuse. Even if contacting such communities might not always guarantee answers to the participants' questions regarding the data or help with their data reuse experiences when those communities were not specifically built around data, the participants naturally discussed data issues and found the communities helpful. New communities also formed around the data, such as data reuser groups, which could support reusers' experiences more effectively.

As shown by previous studies, data reuse is not a simple process for researchers. Finding and understanding data require certain efforts on the part of data reusers. This study suggests that communications with and among other researchers and/or data reusers play an important role in searching, learning, and problem solving during the data reuse process. Considering the roles and the importance of communications occurring around data, ways to support these communications among scholars should be investigated further.

## REFERENCES


Akmon, D. R. (2014). The role of conceptions of value in data practices: A multi-case study of three small teams of ecological scientists. (Doctoral dissertation). Retrieved from http://deepblue.lib.umich.edu/handle/2027.42/107162

Baker, K. S., & Yarmey, L. (2009). Data stewardship: Environmental data curation and a web-of-repositories. International Journal of Digital Curation, 4(2), 12-27. doi:10.2218/ijdc.v4i2.90

Birnholtz, J. P., & Bietz, M. (2003). Data at work: Supporting sharing in science and engineering. In Proceedings of the ACM conference on supporting group work (pp. 339-348). Sanibel Island, FL. New York, NY: ACM.

Berg, M., & Goorman, E. (1999). The contextual nature of medical information. International Journal of Medical Informatics, 56(51-6), 51-60. doi:10.1016/S1386-5056(99)00041-6

Borgman, C. L. (2007). Scholarship in the digital age: Information, infrastructure, and the internet. Boston, MA: MIT Press.

Borgman, C. L. (2011). The conundrum of sharing research data. Retrieved from SSRN eLibrary: http://papers.ssrn.com/sol3/papers.cfm?abstract_id=1869155

Borgman, C. L., Wallis, J. C., & Enyedy, N. (2007). Little science confronts the data deluge: Habitat ecology, embedded sensor networks, and digital libraries. International Journal on Digital Libraries, 7(1-2), 17–30. doi:10.1007/s00799-007-0022-9

Broom, A., Cheshire, L., & Emmison, M. (2009). Qualitative researchers' understandings of their practice and the implications for data archiving and sharing. Sociology, 43(6), 1163-1180. http://doi.org/10.1177/0038038509345704

Carlson, S., & Anderson, B. (2007). What are data? The many kinds of data and their implications for data re-use. Journal of Computer-Mediated Communication, 12(2). 635-651.

Chin, G., & Lansing, C. S. (2004). Capturing and supporting contexts for scientific data sharing via the biological sciences collaboratory. In Proceedings of CSCW'04, ACM conference on computer supported cooperative work (pp. 409-418). Chicago, IL: ACM.

Committee on Ensuring the Utility and Integrity of Research Data in a Digital Age. (2009). Ensuring the integrity, accessibility, and stewardship of research data in the digital age. Retrieved from National Academy of Sciences: http://www.nap.edu/catalog.php?record_id=12615#toc

Corti, L. (2005). Qualitative archiving and data sharing: Extending the reach and impact of qualitative data. IASSIST Quarterly, 2005(Fall), 8-13.

Cragin, M. H., Palmer, C. L., Carlson, J. R., & Witt, M. (2010). Data sharing, small science and institutional repositories. Philosophical Transactions of the Royal Society A: Mathematical, Physical and Engineering Sciences, 368(1926), 4023-4038.

Cragin, M. H., & Shankar, K. (2006). Scientific data collections and distributed collective practice. Computer Supported Cooperative Work, 15(2-3), 185–204. http://doi.org/10.1007/s10606-006-9018-z

Faniel, I. M., Barrera-Gomez, J., Kriesberg, A., & Yakel, E. (2013). A comparative study of data reuse among quantitative social scientists and archaeologists. iConference 2013 Proceedings (pp. 797-800). .doi: 10.9776/13391

Faniel, I. M., & Jacobsen, T. E. (2010). Reusing scientific data: How earthquake engineering researchers assess the reusability of colleagues' data. Computer Supported Cooperative Work, 19(3-4), 355–375. http://doi.org/10.1007/s10606-010-9117-8

Faniel, I. M., Kriesberg, A., & Yakel, E. (2016). Social scientists' satisfaction with data reuse. Journal of the Association for Information Science and Technology, 67(6), 1404-1416 doi: 10.1002/asi.23480

Faniel, I. M., & Zimmerman, A. (2011). Beyond the data deluge: A research agenda for large-scale data sharing and reuse. International Journal of Digital Curation, 6(1), 58-69. doi:10.2218/ijdc.v6i1.172

Fienberg, S., Martin, M., & Straf, M. (1985). Sharing research data. Retrieved from National Research Council: http://www.nap.edu/openbook.php?isbn=030903499X

Huang, H., Stvilia, B., & Jörgensen, C. (2012). Curation roles and perceived priorities for data quality dimensions and skills in genome curation work. Proceedings of the American Society for Information Science and Technology, 49(1), 1-3. http://doi.org/10.1002/meet.14504901312

Jirotka, M., Procter, R., Hartswood, M., Slack, R., Simpson, A., Coopmans, C., … Voss, A. (2005). Collaboration and trust in healthcare innovation: The eDiaMoND case study. Computer Supported Cooperative Work, 14, 369-398.

Kriesberg, A., Frank, A., Faniel, I. M., & Yakel, E. (2013). The role of data reuse in the apprenticeship process. In Proceedings of the Association of Information Science and Technology, 50(1), 1-10. Montréal, QC. doi: 10.1002/meet.14505001051

Kunze, J., Cruse, P., Hu, R., Abrams, S., Hastings, K., Mitchell, C., & Schiff, L. R. (2011). eScholarship: Practices, trends, and recommendations in technical appendix usage for selected data-intensive disciplines. Retrieved from http://escholarship.org/uc/item/9jw4964t

Markus, M. L. (2001). Toward a theory of knowledge reuse: Types of knowledge reuse situations and factors in reuse success. Journal of Management Information Systems, 18, 57-93.

Martin, V. (2014). Demystifying eResearch: A primer for librarians. Santa Barbara, CA: ABC-CLIO.

McCall, R. B., & Appelbaum, M. I. (1991). Some issues of conducting secondary analyses. Developmental Psychology, 27(6), 911-917. http://doi.org/10.1037/0012-1649.27.6.911

Moore, N. (2007). (Re)using qualitative data. Sociological Research Online, 12(3).

Niu, J. (2009). Overcoming inadequate documentation. In Proceedings of the Annual Meeting of the American Society for Information Science & Technology. Vancouver, BC.

Niu, J., & Hedstrom, M. (2008). Documentation evaluation model for social science data. In Proceedings of the Annual Meeting of the American Society for Information Science & Technology, 45(1), 11-11. Columbus, OH. doi: 10.1002/meet.2008.1450450223

Rolland, B., & Lee, C. P. (2013). Beyond trust and reliability: Reusing data in collaborative cancer epidemiology research. In Proceedings of the 2013 conference on computer-supported cooperative work (pp. 435-444). New York: ACM. Retrieved from http://doi.org/10.1145/2441776.2441826

Sands, A., Borgman, C. L., Wynholds, L., & Traweek, S. (2012). Follow the data: How astronomers use and reuse data. Proceedings of the American Society for Information Science and Technology, 49(1), 1-3. http://doi.org/10.1002/meet.14504901341

Tenopir, C., Allard, S., Douglass, K., Aydinoglu, A. U., Wu, L., Read, E., … (2011). Data sharing by scientists: Practices and perceptions. Plos One, 6(6). Retrieved from http://journals.plos.org/plosone/article?id=10.1371/journal.pone.0021101

Van House, N. A., Butler, M. H., & Schiff, L. R. (1998). Cooperative knowledge work and practices of trust: Sharing environmental planning data sets. In Proceedings of the ACM conference on computer-supported cooperative work (pp. 335-343). Seattle, WA.

Yoon, A. (2014). Making a square fit into a circle: Researchers' experiences reusing qualitative data. In Proceedings of the Association of Information Science and Technology, 51(1), 1-4. Seattle, WA. doi: 10.1002/meet.2014.14505101140

Yoon, A. (2016a). Red flags in data: Learning from failed data reuse experiences. In Proceedings of the 79th Association for Information Science and Technology Annual Meeting, 53(1), 1-6. Copenhagen, Denmark. doi: 10.1002/pra2.2016.14505301126

Yoon, A. (2016b). Visible evidence of invisible quality dimensions and the role of data management. In Proceedings of iConference 2016. Philadelphia, PA.

Yoon, A. (2017). Data reusers' trust development. Journal of Association for Information Science and Technology, 64(8), 946–956. doi: 10.1002/asi.23730

Yoon, A., & Schultz, T. (2017). Research data management services in academic libraries in the US: A content analysis of libraries' websites. College & Research Libraries [pre-print is available at: http://crl.acrl.org/index.php/crl/article/view/16620/0].

Zimmerman, A. S. (2008). New knowledge from old data: The role of standards in the sharing and reuse of ecological data. Science, Technology & Human Values, 33(5), 631-652. http://doi.org/10.1177/0162243907306704

Zimmerman, A. S. (2007). Not by metadata alone: The use of diverse forms of knowledge to locate data for reuse. International Journal on Digital Libraries, 7(1-2), 5-16. doi:10.1007/s00799-007-0015-8

Zimmerman, A. S. (2003). Data sharing and secondary use of scientific data: Experiences of ecologists (Doctoral dissertation). Retrieved from http://search.proquest.com.libproxy.lib.unc.edu/docview/287907131/abstract?accountid=14244

# Using Social Media in Formal Learning: Investigating Learning Strategies and Satisfaction

**Quan Zhou**
*Wee Kim Wee School of Communication and Information, Nanyang Technological University, Singapore.*
*zhou0245@e.ntu.edu.sg*

**Sei-Ching Joanna Sin**
*Wee Kim Wee School of Communication and Information, Nanyang Technological University, Singapore.*
*joanna.sin@ntu.edu.sg*

**Chei Sian Lee**
*Wee Kim Wee School of Communication and Information, Nanyang Technological University, Singapore.*
*leecs@ntu.edu.sg*

## ABSTRACT

**Social media have been widely adopted by digital natives for learning purposes due to the wealth of educational resources afforded by these platforms. As such, educational researchers and practitioners have been advocating the integration of social media in formal learning. While a majority of research has highlighted the benefits of using social media in formal education, still lacking is research that examines students' learning behaviors and experience with social media. From the perspective of self-regulated learning, we investigate students' learning strategies in social media, as well as the relationship between using these strategies and students' learning satisfaction. Drawing on a survey of 270 undergraduate and graduate students, we found that in the formal learning context, students employed four types of self-regulated learning strategies (i.e., goal setting, environment structuring, performance control and self-evaluation) to achieve effective learning with social media. Among the four strategies, goal setting was most commonly used. Further, a regression analysis revealed that all four types of self-regulated learning strategies were significantly related to students' learning satisfaction with social media, while goal setting was the most prominent strategy. This article concludes by presenting limitations as well as implications for research and practice.**

## KEYWORDS

social media, formal learning, learning strategies, self-regulated learning, learning satisfaction

## INTRODUCTION

Social media have contributed to an information society in which people can get access to knowledge and establish connections with others around the world efficiently (Kind & Evans, 2015). In particular, social media, which refers to a group of internet-based applications that allow users to create, edit, evaluate and/or connect to content or to other creators of content (Kaplan & Haenlein, 2010), have been widely adopted by young adults for work, play and school. The latest report on social media usage from the Pew Research Center (Greenwood, Perrin, & Duggan, 2016) has indicated that 68% of all American adults (accounting for those who do not use the internet at all) are Facebook users, while 28% use Instagram, 26% use Pinterest, 25% use LinkedIn and 21% use Twitter. Along with the popularity, educational researchers and practitioners have been advocating the integration of these social media in formal educational practice. A survey ($N$ = 8,016) conducted by Moran, Seaman and Tinti-Kane (2011) showed that the use of social media by faculty for formal teaching is on the rise. It was reported that 44.1% of faculty respondents in higher education use social media in their teaching. Recent research also suggests that students are more likely to accept the integration of social media, such as Facebook, Twitter and YouTube, in formal learning contexts (Matzat & Vrieling, 2015).

Underlying the popularity of using social media in formal learning is the fact that teachers and students have recognized the benefits of social media for learning, such as boosting interaction and collaboration, accessibility of learning resources beyond the classroom, and the development of online communities consisting of users with common learning interests and experiences (Hamid, Waycott, Kurnia, & Chang, 2015). It has also been argued that social media can be efficient and effective in lifelong learning by enabling people to keep up-to-date with new knowledge (Kind & Evans, 2015). In sum, a wealth of research has paid attention on how social media could add values to support formal learning (e.g., Ahn, 2011; García-Peñalvo, Greenhow & Lewin, 2016; Song & Lee, 2014).

In spite of the benefits, success in social media learning heavily relies on a student's ability to autonomously and actively engage in the learning process (Wang, Shannon, & Ross, 2013). Different from traditional face-to-face teaching and learning in classrooms, social media empower students with more autonomy and control over their learning (Greenhow & Lewin, 2016). Regarding a learning context with high autonomy, educational scholars (e.g., Dabbagh & Kitsantas, 2012; Garrison, 2003; Schunk & Zimmerman, 2012) have high-

80th Annual Meeting of the Association for Information Science & Technology, Washington, DC, VA | Oct. 27-Nov. 1, 2017

lighted that it is necessary for students to use learning strategies to regulate their learning, thus maintaining active engagement in learning and attaining desirable learning outcomes. Hence, examining the learning strategies adopted by learners in their learning process with social media is an important endeavor.

Prior research has reported that students employ learning strategies to foster active engagement in academic learning, which could lead to higher levels of achievement. For example, some self-regulated students set goals for their study, while others persist at a difficult task or block out distractions to enable them to perform better (Pintrich & de Groot, 1990). Some studies also reported that students used strategies such as organizing, coding and rehearsing information related learning tasks, monitoring performance, managing time effectively, and seeking help when needed (Barnard et al., 2010; Pintrich & de Groot, 1990; Zimmerman & Pons, 1986). It has also been demonstrated that using learning strategies, such as goal setting, environment structuring and help seeking, could influence students' satisfaction with learning (e.g., Kuo, Walker, Schroder, & Belland, 2014; Puzziferro, 2008). However, in terms of using social media, in spite of its popularity and potential benefits to support formal learning, there has been very limited work done on students' learning behaviors and experience in the social media context.

Only few studies have specifically examined students' learning strategies related to social media use. For example, Dabbagh and Kitsantas (2012) discussed how technological affordances of different social media tools (e.g., blogs, wikis, video sharing sites, social networking sites) allow users to help strategize their learning effectively. Specifically, social media afford personal information management, social interaction and collaboration, and information aggregation. Kitsantas (2013) also suggested that students' engagement in learning strategies, such as goal setting, time management and self-evaluation, could be supported by blogs and wikis, whereas social networking sites could enhance learning strategies such as seeking help and self-evaluation. However, these studies only discussed the pedagogical affordances of social media to scaffold students' use of learning strategies for formal learning. Still lacking is an understanding of the strategies students actually employ when they use social media for formal learning in school, as well as how using these strategies is related to student's learning satisfaction with social media.

Due to their accessibility and availability, social media have been deemed as promising methods to foster lifelong learning (Kind & Evans, 2015). It is thus necessary to prepare students to be capable of actively engaging in social media learning with appropriate learning strategies so that they can gain satisfactory outcomes from the learning. In this vein, the present research is timely as we seek to uncover the types of learning strategies employed by students when using social media in formal learning. In addition, we will also investigate how using these strategies can be related to students' learning satisfaction with social media. In sum, this study aims to explore the following overarching research questions: *What are the learning strategies that students use to regulate their learning in social media, and what are the relationships between the strategies adopted and learning satisfaction?*

## LITERATURE REVIEW

### *Using Social Media in Formal Learning*

In a formal learning setting, the learning experience is supported by an educational institution (Manca & Ranieri, 2016). Courses are generally designed by a specified group of instructors and delivered to students in a very structured way. Students are engaged in a systematic approach to acknowledge the specific content or material. With the advancement of information and communication technologies, formal teaching and learning has evolved. In higher education, learning management systems (LMS) (e.g., Blackboard, WebCT, Moodle applications, etc.) are widely used as technology-enhanced learning environments (Dabbagh & Kitsantas, 2012). These learning technologies enable teachers to deliver course materials efficiently and students to carry out individual or collaborative academic tasks effectively (Guo, Lu, Li, & Li, 2011). However, some researchers have questioned that these traditional institution-based LMS have mainly focused on institutional needs and content delivery, but do not support self-directed learning and continuing education (Dabbagh & Kitsantas, 2012).

Since social media are increasingly popular among young adults, scholars have advocated that the adoption of social media would allow educational institutions to overcome the limitations of the current LMS (Kind & Evans, 2015; Siemens & Weller, 2011). Examples of popular social media range from media-sharing tools such as YouTube and Flickr to social networking sites such as Facebook, Ning and LinkedIn. Others include social bookmarking tools (e.g., Delicious), collaborative knowledge development tools (e.g., Wikipedia) and creative tools such as blogs (e.g., WordPress and Blogger) and microblogs (e.g., Twitter). A key feature of these tools is the interactive nature, where information is shared either synchronously and/or asynchronously through chats, comments, videos and other interactions (Au, Lam, & Chan, 2015). Specifically, some scholars are of the viewpoint that young adults are likely to reap the benefits of social media since they are already familiar and experienced with these platforms in their everyday lives (e.g., Kind & Evans, 2015; Siemens & Weller, 2011).

Indeed, research has suggested that both educators and students would benefit from integrating everyday use of social media in formal learning contexts (Greenhow, Robelia, and Hughes 2009; Manca & Ranieri, 2016). For example, some studies have suggested the following benefits: YouTube could provide students with more video illustrations to enhance students' understanding of course materials in and out of classrooms (Lee & Lehto, 2012) and empower students to take charge of the learning process (Lee et al., 2015); and wikis could increase student engagement and collaboration to produce better work (Franklin & Thankachan, 2013).

Different from traditional face-to-face learning in classrooms, learning in social media allows students to take charge of their learning in terms of time and space. This means that effective learning in social media heavily relies on a student's ability to autonomously and actively engage in the learning process. Students who are not able to manage the autonomy in a learning context will be more likely to get distracted and remove themselves from the experience, resulting in dissatisfaction with the learning experience and unwillingness to participate in an autonomous learning environment like social media (Dabbagh & Kitsantas, 2012). It is therefore particularly important for students to have the ability to use learning strategies to regulate their effort, time and motivation in their learning with social media (Greenhow & Lewin, 2016).

Despite the popularity and benefits of using social media in formal learning, there has not been extensive assessment related to students' learning behaviors and experience with these new technologies in formal learning contexts (Dabbagh & Kitsantas, 2012; Garrison, 2003; Schunk & Zimmerman, 2012). When individuals move beyond structured formal learning environments, taking advantage of various social media for learning purposes can be part of lifelong learning (Kind & Evans, 2015). To prepare students as lifelong learners in the social media age, it is timely and necessary to investigate the learning strategies students use to manage their learning with social media and how using these strategies relate to their satisfactory learning experience.

### Self-Regulated Learning Strategies

To examine the strategies for managing learning in social media, we draw on the notion of self-regulated learning. Self-regulated learning (SRL) is "*an active, constructive process whereby* learners set goals for their learning and then attempt to monitor, regulate, and control their cognition, motivation, and behavior, guided and constrained by their goals and the contextual features in the environment" (Pintrich, 2000, p. 453). There are four assumptions underlying SRL (Zimmerman, 2008; Pintrich, 2000). First, learners are active and constructive participants in the learning process. Second, learners have potential control over their learning process. Third, there is a goal, criterion or standard for the learning task that can guide regulatory processes. Fourth, using SRL strategies is a mediator between personal and contextual characteristics and actual learning achievements.

Based on these assumptions, Zimmerman (1986, 1989) conceptualized SRL in academic learning in three cyclical phases: forethought, performance control and self-reflection processes. First, forethought refers to the skilled and strategic processes that precede and set the stage for performance in learning. The forethought phase consists of learning strategies that typically occur prior to the actual learning process. Capable students prepare for their learning tasks by understanding their learning objectives and blocking out distractions in the learning environment, which enable them to perform better (Pintrich & de Groot, 1990). Hence, learning strategies such as goal setting and environment structuring are related to the forethought phase (Barnard et al., 2009; Wolters, Pintrich, & Karabenick, Moore, & Lippman, 2005).

In the second phase, the performance control phase, students engage in the learning process towards his or her goals. Specifically, to maintain active engagement in learning, students monitor their learning progress and use selected strategies to perform learning tasks. Learning strategies such as time management, task strategies and help seeking are associated with the performance control phase (Barnard et al., 2009; Wolters, Pintrich, Karabenick, Moore, & Lippman, 2005).

In the third and final phase, the self-reflection phase, individuals react and respond to their self-regulated efforts in the learning process by evaluating the outcomes of their performance. Feedback from prior performance is used to make adjustments during current efforts. SRL strategies such as self-evaluation are associated with the self-reflection phase (Barnard et al., 2010). Further, these self-evaluative judgments can affect future course of actions related to the forethought phase. In this light, self-regulated learners engage in a cyclic feedback loop until they successfully achieve their learning goals.

From the perspective of SRL, learning strategies refer to the deliberate actions that people employ in the learning process to maintain active engagement in learning and achieve learning goals (Zimmerman & Pons, 1986; Zimmerman, 2008). The SRL strategies can influence learning process through aiding cognition, controlling effort and time, and directing motoric execution (Pressley & Wolloshyn, 1995). It is suggested that SRL learning strategies can affect learning outcomes by assisting learners to acquire and retain knowledge in a structured and methodological way (Zimmerman, 1989). Earlier studies in the traditional academic context conducted by Zimmerman and his colleagues have revealed consistent positive relationship between the use of SRL strategies and academic achievements (e.g., Zimmerman & Pons, 1986; Zimmerman, 1989). In the online course learning context, prior research also revealed that students' use of learning strategies not only influences their academic achievement (Broadbent & Poon, 2015), but also predicts their satisfactory learning experience and continuous intention to enroll in future online courses (Artino, 2007). In this vein, SRL strategies, in terms of goal setting, environment structuring, time management, help seeking, task strategies, and self-evaluation are found to be salient. To attain successful learning outcomes, students should adopt and maintain active engagement in the learning process (Barnard et al., 2010; Barnard et al., 2009). Taken together, appropriate use of SRL strategies is essential to foster active engagement in learning and result in higher levels of achievement (Zimmerman & Martinez-Pons, 1988).

While it is possible that the SRL strategies identified in prior online learning research can theoretically be applied to the context of learning with social media, to our knowledge, no prior paper has examined the prevalence of these strategies in the social media learning context. Therefore, the first aim of the present study is to investigate whether the SRL strategies uncovered in prior research, in terms of goal setting, environment structuring, time management, help seeking, task strategies and self-evaluation, are used by students in social media to support formal learning. The first research question (RQ) is:

**RQ 1:** From the perspective of self-regulated learning, what are the learning strategies that students employ when they are using social media in formal learning?

### *Learning Satisfaction*

Learning satisfaction refers to a positive affective outcome resulting from an evaluation of a learning experience (Elliott & Healy, 2001). When students take online course learning programs, satisfaction is an important indicator of the success of the programs (Biner et al., 1997; Liao & Hsieh, 2011). In particular, student satisfaction is associated with perceived usefulness of online learning systems, perceived course quality, knowledge retention and academic achievement in online courses (Ali & Ahmad, 2011). Liaw (2008) also found a positive relationship between satisfaction and the behavioral intention to continuous use of an e-learning system. This satisfaction-intention association reflects that the higher a user's satisfaction with an information system, the more likely the user will intend to use the system. Therefore, learning satisfaction is a critical indicator to evaluate the effectiveness of using certain technologies for learning (Piccoli, Ahmad, & Ives, 2001).

When students use social media to support formal learning, the extent to which they engage in SRL strategies may exert influence on their learning satisfaction in social media. For example, as suggested by goal learning theories, by using the SRL strategies of goal setting, students invest personal meanings with the goals. When students make progress towards the goal, they will feel fulfilled and satisfied (Pintrich, 2000). In addition, through structuring a distraction-less learning environment, students can be more focused on learning, thus gaining more enjoyment from the learning process (Wu, 2015). Moreover, when using effective task strategies, such as notes-taking and highlighting, the acquisition of knowledge and skills can be facilitated. This cognitive achievement can also bring satisfaction to the learner (Paechter, Maier, & Macher, 2010). Some studies suggest that time management is important in the learning process as it is related to procrastination and anxiety (Michinov, Brunot, Le Bohec, Juhel, & Delaval, 2011). Further, help seeking via various forms of social interactions (e.g., learner-learner and learner-instructor) has been recognized as an important factor in promoting student satisfaction within online course learning environments (Kuo et al., 2014). Through help seeking, learners can also gain encouragement from other users on social media to alleviate their anxiety caused by problems (Cheng, Liang, & Tsai, 2013). Lastly, perceived learning satisfaction with social media can be deemed as a result of self-evaluation of the learning experience.

Although students' use of SRL strategies may explain the satisfaction that students gain from learning with social media, it is still an open question whether and how using these learning strategies relates to students' satisfactory learning experience. Moreover, earlier studies had not examined different learning strategies simultaneously. It is thus unclear which learning strategies have stronger association with learning satisfaction. Therefore, the second aim of this study is to investigate the effects of using these learning strategies on learning satisfaction. Hence, the following research question is proposed:

**RQ 2:** What are the relationships between the self-regulated learning strategies and students' learning satisfaction with social media?

## METHOD

### *Sample and Data Collection*

This study employed a cross-sectional survey research design, involving collecting quantifiable data from a group of people at a particular time (Creswell, 2013). A survey instrument was developed and the snowball sampling technique was adopted in our data collection (Biernacki & Waldorf, 1981). This sampling method was appropriate in the current study as the target respondents were students who have experience of using social media for coursework in university, which is a typical formal learning context.

Data was collected via a mixed-mode survey, in which both online and paper-based surveys were administered. The use of a mixed-mode data collection has been used in many past studies to increase response rate (Bradley & Sankar, 2003). Social media types and examples covered in our survey include social networking sites (e.g., Facebook, LinkedIn, Academia.edu), microblogging (e.g., Twitter, Weibo), multimedia sharing (e.g., YouTube, Instagram, SlideShare), wikis (e.g., Wikipedia), social bookmarking (e.g., Delicious), virtual communities (e.g., Quora, Reddit, GitHub), video teleconferencing (e.g., Skype), text chat (e.g., WhatsApp, LINE, WeChat), and web-based (cloud-computing) office tools (e.g., Google Doc, Calendar sharing). Responses to all social media learning-related questions were based on respondents' personal experience in the most recent course in university for which they used at least one social media for study. Here, it should be noted that this study did not narrow the focus to a specific social media tool or a particular course subject for two reasons. First, with easy access to various social media tool, research has suggested that students tend to harness multiple social media to construct a social media learning environment for their formal learning (Dabbagh & Kitsantas, 2012). Second, this study contends that it is more meaningful to investigate student's use of social media to support formal learning broadly versus narrowly by a particular subject, as social media can be used for learning in various subjects (Greenhow & Lewin, 2016).

In sum, this study obtained valid responses from 270 undergraduate and graduate students from a large university in Singapore, of which 115 were male students and 155 were female students. Their age ranged from 18 to 35 ($M$ = 21.6, $SD$ = 2.23). Among the participants, there were 6.7% ($n$ = 18) working for a degree lower than bachelor's (e.g., polytechnic), 48.9% ($n$ = 132) for bachelor's, 30% ($n$ = 81) for master's, and 14.4% ($n$ = 39) for doctorate degree. About 66.3% ($n$ = 179) had an educational background in computer science/IT, engineering, or arts, humanities, social sciences, while the rest of participants (33.7%, $n$ = 91) were from business, medicine, education and others.

### *Measures*

#### Learning Strategies

Learning strategies from the SRL perspective were drawn from the Online Self-regulated Learning Questionnaire (OSLQ; Barnard et al., 2009), which consists of six subscale constructs including goal setting, environment structuring, task strategies, time management, help seeking, and self-evaluation. The reliability and validity of the OSLQ has been tested in Barnard et al. (2009) and it was used in past studies to compare students' SRL strategies use in blended and fully online courses (Barnard et al., 2009) and to help establish profiles of SRL (Barnard et al., 2010). In this study, all items in OSLQ were adapted to suit the social media context. A total of 24 question items were used to assess the degree to which students employed SRL strategies in social media in formal by asking questions on how students used social media for a course they were taking for credits. Following the original instrument, the five-point Likert-like scale, ranging from "Strongly disagree" to "Strongly agree," was used for these questions. Higher scores on this scale indicate a higher level of using SRL strategies. This study further used principal component analysis to extract meaningful groupings of SRL strategies that students use when learning in social media (refer to the section *Principal Component Analysis* for details).

#### Learning satisfaction with social media

Learning satisfaction with social media refers to a positive affective learning outcome that results from the evaluation of a learning experience. The six items measuring this construct were drawn from previous online learning studies (Hong et al., 2016; Piccoli et al., 2001) and then modified to suit the context of present study. Respondents were asked to indicate how satisfied they were with the learning experience in which they used social media for a recent course in school. These items were measured by a 5-point Likert-like scale ranging from 1 (strongly disagree) to 5 (strongly agree). A principal component analysis using Varimax rotation was executed on the six items. All items were loaded together as one variable, named "Learning satisfaction with social media" ($M$ = 3.77, $SD$ = .67, Cronbach $\alpha$ = 0.79). Table 1 shows that the range of factor loadings of learning satisfaction with social media is from 0.65 to 0.76, which meets the criterion for acceptable convergent validity.

## DATA ANALYSIS AND RESULTS

Data from the survey shed light on the types of SRL strategies students employ when using social media to support formal learning. In addition, our results also provide insights on the relationships between the SRL strategies employed and students' learning satisfaction.

| Construct and Items | Factor Loadings | *M* | *SD* | *α* |
|---|---|---|---|---|
| **Learning satisfaction with social media** | | **3.77** | **0.67** | **0.79** |
| I enjoyed my use of social media for this course/training. | .76 | 3.86 | 0.96 | |
| Overall, social media has met my learning expectations. | .72 | 3.64 | 0.99 | |
| I am satisfied with my learning experience of using social media. | .69 | 3.57 | 0.99 | |
| By using social media for this course/training, I have solved the learning problems I had. | .68 | 3.80 | 0.95 | |
| By using social media for this course/training, I have acquired knowledge and skills I need. | .66 | 3.85 | 0.89 | |
| The learning experience in social media stimulated my desire to learn. | .64 | 3.93 | 0.99 | |
| Variance explained (%) | 48.27 | | | |
| Eigenvalue | 2.90 | | | |

***Table 1****. Measurement and principle component factor analysis of learning satisfaction* (n = *270)*

### *Principal Component Analysis*

To address RQ 1, we conducted a principal component analysis to identify the potential groupings of these learning strategies question items (Table 2). Principal component analysis with Promax rotation was run iteratively to identify the potential groupings of question items of SRL strategies. Following recommended practices in item selection, items with high cross-loadings to multiple constructs were dropped to ensure

| Factors and Items | Factor Loadings | | | | *M* | *SD* | α |
|---|---|---|---|---|---|---|---|
| | 1 | 2 | 3 | 4 | | | |
| **1. Performance control** | | | | | **3.64** | **0.84** | **.90** |
| I used social media to work on extra problems of my course/training to master the content. | **0.89** | -0.06 | -0.10 | -0.07 | 3.70 | 1.00 | |
| I read aloud the learning materials in social media to fight against distractions. | **0.85** | -0.19 | 0.01 | -0.12 | 3.57 | 1.20 | |
| I prepared my questions and thoughts when joining in an online discussion. | **0.82** | -0.07 | -0.02 | 0.00 | 3.66 | 1.09 | |
| I tried to take more thorough notes when I was learning in social media because notes are even more important for learning in social media than in face-to-face learning. | **0.72** | -0.01 | 0.04 | 0.10 | 3.59 | 1.16 | |
| I connected with or follow someone who I thought knowledgeable in social media so that I could consult with him or her when I need help. | **0.69** | 0.05 | 0.10 | 0.04 | 3.66 | 1.03 | |
| I allocated extra studying time for my learning in social media because I knew it would be time-demanding. | **0.67** | 0.10 | 0.04 | 0.09 | 3.64 | 1.16 | |
| I shared my study problems in social media so that I could figure out what I was struggling with and how to solve my problems. | **0.65** | 0.12 | 0.07 | 0.03 | 3.63 | 1.04 | |
| Although the time to use social media for my learning was flexible, I still tried to distribute my studying time evenly across days. | **0.64** | 0.22 | -0.07 | 0.07 | 3.68 | 1.12 | |
| **2. Environment structuring** | | | | | **3.79** | **0.91** | **.84** |
| I would find a comfortable place to study. | -0.16 | **0.89** | -0.06 | 0.07 | 3.83 | 1.10 | |
| I chose a time with few distractions. | -0.11 | **0.88** | 0.02 | 0.05 | 3.80 | 1.07 | |
| I knew where I could study most efficiently. | 0.15 | **0.79** | -0.04 | -0.09 | 3.71 | 0.99 | |
| I chose a place where I could avoid too much distraction. | 0.10 | **0.78** | 0.08 | -0.12 | 3.82 | 1.23 | |
| **3. Goal setting** | | | | | **3.82** | **0.92** | **.88** |
| I set standards for my learning in social media. | -0.02 | 0.04 | **0.95** | -0.07 | 3.92 | 0.96 | |
| I didn't compromise the quality of my learning because it was in social media. | 0.03 | -0.09 | **0.90** | 0.02 | 3.71 | 1.15 | |
| I set goals to help me manage study time when learning in social media. | -0.01 | 0.05 | **0.84** | 0.06 | 3.83 | 0.97 | |
| **4. Self-evaluation** | | | | | **3.79** | **0.92** | **.83** |
| I asked myself a lot of questions when learning about the materials in social media. | -0.09 | 0.03 | 0.07 | **0.88** | 3.79 | 0.99 | |
| I compared with peer learners to find out the difference between my learning in social media and theirs. | 0.06 | 0.02 | -0.10 | **0.88** | 3.88 | 1.04 | |
| I summarized what I have learned in social media to examine my understanding. | 0.04 | -0.10 | 0.04 | **0.83** | 3.69 | 1.17 | |
| Variance explained (%) | 41.41 | 10.90 | 9.47 | 6.33 | | | |
| Eigenvalue | 7.45 | 1.96 | 1.70 | 1.14 | | | |

***Table 2**. Measurement and principal component analysis of SRL strategies (n = 270)*

Sharma, 2003). After that, four factors of SRL strategies emerged from the remaining 18 items, with eigenvalues greater than 1.00 explaining a total of 68.11% of the variance. The items of three SRL strategies – specifically, task strategies, time management and help seeking – were loaded together. This indicates that on the basis of users' evaluations, these three SRL strategies were highly interrelated in the context of using social media in formal learning. Indeed, in Zimmerman's (2000) conceptualization of SRL as three phases, task strategies, time management and help seeking were categorized into the phase of performance control. That is, when people engage in actual task learning, they control their learning performance by using effective learning strategies, managing time effectively and get social assistance (Zimmerman, 1989).

Hence, in subsequent analyses, task strategies, time management and help seeking were combined as one variable and labeled as *performance control*, which describes the strategies that people enact during the actual learning process to regulate their performance. Taken together, four factors emerged from principal component analysis: goal setting, environment structuring, performance control and self-evaluation. The factor loadings of SRL strategies range from 0.64 to 0.95 (Table 2), which meets the criterion for acceptable convergent validity. The groupings of the remaining 18 items to the respective 4 factors from the final run of the principal component analysis are shown in Table 2 and discussed as follows.

### Performance control

Performance control (Factor 1) describes the strategies that people enact during the actual learning process to regulate their learning performance, including task strategies, time management and help seeking. In particular, task strategies include actions that learners undertake to acquire knowledge such as rehearsing, elaborating and organizing information. Time management refers to strategies that assist learners to manage their time effectively. Help seeking refers to people's behavior of identifying and calling upon social resources for assistance. On the basis of users' evaluations, these three SRL strategies are highly interrelated, which can be combined to manifest strategies that people use to control their performance in the process of actual learning (Barnard et al., 2010). In this vein, eight items were used to assess people's use of performance control strategies. The mean was 3.64 ($SD$ = 0.84, Cronbach's $\alpha = .90$).

### Environment structuring

Environment structuring (Factor 2) reflected items measuring students' efforts to reduce distractions in their environment and to arrange their surroundings to make completing a task without interruption. There were four items to measure environment structuring and it has a mean value of 3.79 ($SD$ = 0.91, Cronbach's $\alpha = .84$).

### Goal setting

Goal setting (Factor 3) is measured by strategies that reflect people's learning behaviors of making decisions on specific objective of learning. Three items were utilized to measure the use of goal setting strategies. The mean was 3.82 ($SD$ = 0.92, Cronbach's $\alpha = .88$).

### Self-evaluation

Self-evaluation (Factor 4) refers to comparing outcomes of performance with a standard or a goal. When students evaluate their learning in social media, they monitor their progress towards goal attainment. That is, they make evaluative judgments about their learning performance to ensure that learning goals can be accomplished. This construct was measured with three items and had a mean value of 3.79 ($SD$ = 0.92, Cronbach's $\alpha = .83$).

| Independent variables | Dependent variable – Learning satisfaction | |
|---|---|---|
| | Standardized Beta | t-values |
| Goal setting | .33*** | 6.423 |
| Environment structuring | .23*** | 4.865 |
| Performance control | .17** | 3.329 |
| Self-evaluation | .24*** | 4.809 |
| Total Adjusted $R^2$ (%) | .56*** | |

*Note.* * $p < .05$, ** $p < .01$, *** $p < .001$

***Table 3.*** *Summary of simultaneous multiple regression analysis (n = 270)*

In sum, the results of principal component analysis in Table 2 revealed that when students use social media for formal learning, they engage in SRL strategies in terms of goal setting, environment structuring, performance control and self-evaluation. The results also showed that goal setting was most likely to be used ($M$ = 3.82) by students, followed by environment structuring ($M$ = 3.79), self-evaluation ($M$ = 3.79), and performance control ($M$ = 3.64). Thus, the RQ 1 was addressed.

## *Regression Analysis*

Following the principal component analysis, a simultaneous multiple regression was conducted to address RQ 2. In particular, learning satisfaction with social media was the dependent variable and four types of SRL strategies were the independent variables. Statistical significance for all tests was set at a .05 level.

The multiple regression results in Table 3 showed that the model accounted for 56% of the variance. Regarding the relationships between SRL strategies and learning satisfaction with social media, statistically significant positive relationships were found for all four types of SRL strategies (goal setting, $p < .001$; environment structuring, $p < .001$; performance control, $p < .01$; self-evaluation, $p < .001$). Among the four SRL strategies, goal setting ($\beta$ = .33) was the most influential predictors of learning satisfaction, followed by SRL strategies of self-evaluation ($\beta$ = .24), environment structuring ($\beta$ = .23), and performance control ($\beta$ = .17).

## DISCUSSION

The first aim of the present study is to uncover what SRL strategies are used by students when they are learning with social media in formal learning contexts and to what extent they use these strategies. Past online learning research identified six dominant learning strategies: goal setting, environment structuring, task strategies, time management, help seeking and self-evaluation. However, in this study we found four learning strategies students used when they were learning in social media. These four strategies are goal setting, environment structuring, performance control and time management. In particular, goal setting refers to the learning strategies of making decisions on the specific objective of learning in social media. Environment structuring describes students' efforts to arrange their surroundings to make completing a task more likely to occur without interruptions when learning with social media. Performance control refers to learning strategies in the process of performing learning tasks in social media, including task strategies that are purposive actions directed at acquiring knowledge (Zimmerman, 1989), time management strategies that assist learners to manage their time effectively (Dabbagh & Kitsantas, 2012), and help seeking strategies that the learner identifies and calls upon social resources for assistance with specific learning tasks (Zimmerman, 2008). Self-evaluation refers to comparing outcomes of performance with a standard or a goal (Zimmerman, 2000). Among the four types of SRL strategies (i.e., goal setting, environment structuring, performance control, and self-evaluation), goal setting was used most commonly by students in our study. The act of setting a goal will make learners to be more aware of the effort, time and resources needed to reach the goal (Pintrich, 2000). The information gained will help to guide learners and navigate the learning process more effectively. In addition, with various social media available, the learning goal will also serve as a guidance regarding what resources and social media platforms to harness.

The second aim of this study is to investigate how these SRL strategies relate to students' learning satisfaction with social media. This was addressed using a regression analysis. The results suggest that all four SRL strategies significantly predict learning satisfaction in social media. This is consistent with prior research which indicated the effect of using learning strategies on students' learning satisfaction with online course learning (e.g., Artino, 2007; Kuo, Walker, Schroder, & Belland, 2014). Previous studies on online course learning have suggested that the more the students are satisfied with their online learning experiences, the more they are motivated to engage in continuous online learning, which in turn can lead to better academic achievements (Johnson, Hornik, & Salas, 2008; Lee & Lee, 2008). In this light, it is crucial to understand students' learning satisfaction with social media, which may exert influence on people's overall evaluation of their learning effectiveness and continuous motivation to use social media for formal learning. Regarding this, the findings of this study provide evidence that learning strategies in social media can play important roles in students' learning satisfaction.

Goal setting was found to be the most influential predictor of learning satisfaction, followed by environment structuring, self-evaluation and performance control. Not surprising, it has been confirmed by Tabuenca, Kalz, Drachsler, and Specht (2015) that learners who set goals were more likely to feel satisfied with their learning. This study revealed that the association between goal setting and learning satisfaction also existed saliently in the social media learning context. It is possible that by setting goals, people are more likely to be satisfied when goals are achieved in the learning process as they are likely to experience a sense of achievement. We will also like to explain that the respondents in this study were from a top university in Asia. As such, these students are likely to be goal-oriented and high achievers (Stoynoff, 1997). Hence, their learning satisfaction is positively linked with goal setting and accomplishment.

Self-evaluation emerged as the second highest predictor of students' learning satisfaction with social media. That is, learning satisfaction can be derived from the action of evaluating what one has done. It is possible that when learning in social media, students evaluate their learning through comparison with other online learners (Greenhow & Lewin, 2016). While general research on social comparison in social media has largely focused on its negative effects on students, such as on their self-esteem and well-being (e.g., Kalpidou, Costin, & Morris, 2011), the findings of this study suggest that social comparison afforded by social media can have positive effects on students learning in social media. It is posited that social comparison may serve as a motivating force driving students to improve academically and achieve better results (Wan, Compeau, & Haggerty, 2012). Further studies are needed to investigate this proposition.

In addition, this study found that environment structuring was also a significant antecedent of satisfactory learning experience in social media. This is consistent with a previous study by Wu (2015), which suggested that students would get distracted and less satisfied if there were too many distractions in the learning environment. Specifically, prior research has cautioned that social media platforms can sometimes become a massive collection of garbage and not contribute to the learning process (Lee et al., 2015). Specifically, students may get distracted by other non-learning related materials and hence managing distractions can be a huge challenge for students who are learning on these platforms. Lastly, in terms of performance control strategies, our findings suggest that the more performance control strategies (i.e., task strategies, time management and help seeking) students use, the more likely they will perceive satisfaction of acquiring knowledge and solving problems. This is consistent with prior online learning research (e.g., Kuo et al., 2014; Kuong, 2015; Michinov et al., 2011), which suggests that the more control and effort students engage in managing their learning process (e.g., in terms of updating problem-solving skills, time management and seeking help from peers and/or experts), the more confident they are in accomplishing their task well and timely, which can lead to satisfaction with their learning experience.

## CONCLUSION

This study has identified new findings on students' learning behaviors with social media in the formal learning context. As the study has found statistically significant positive relations between the use of SRL strategies and learning satisfaction, further studies can be conducted to explore these relationships in more details. The current study has some limitations that future studies may address. First, this study did not differentiate the different contexts of learning (e.g., mandatory vs. voluntary use) when students were using social media. It is possible that the strategies employed by the students may differ across contexts. Future work needs to explore the different contexts of learning. Next, our respondents were students who were based in Singapore. This could limit the generalizability of the study findings as outcomes could differ with respondents from other cultures or countries.

Despite these limitations, this study contributes to a better understanding of learning strategies used by students to maintain active engagement when learning with social media from the SRL perspective. To the best of our knowledge, no other studies have examined how students self-regulate their learning in social media learning contexts. Drawing from the self-regulated learning perspective, the following conclusions can be derived. First, students employed four types of SRL strategies when they used social media in formal learning contexts: goal setting, environment structuring, performance control and self-evaluation. Second, the SRL strategy that was most likely employed was goal setting, followed by environment structuring, self-evaluation and performance control. Third, using all four SRL strategies can contribute to learning satisfaction with social media. In particular, students' learning satisfaction is more associated with using goal setting strategy, followed by self-evaluation, environment structuring and performance control.

From a practical standpoint, the findings of this study suggest that in addition to students' technical skills and competencies of using social media for learning, their ability to regulate their learning in a technological context is also an important factor of their learning experience. From a research perspective, this study has taken an important first step to expand our knowledge on students' learning behaviors and experience in the social media learning context. Ultimately, the results from this study can be utilized by policymakers, teachers and other stakeholders to facilitate better technology usage for formal teaching and learning across different educational levels.

## REFERENCES


Ahn, J. (2011), The effect of social network sites on adolescents' social and academic development: Current theories and controversies. *Journal of the American Society for Information Science and Technology, 62,* 1435-1445.

Ali, A. & Ahmad, I. (2011). Key factors for determining students' satisfaction in distance learning courses: A study of Allama Iqbal Open University. *Contemporary Educational Technology, 2*(2), 118-134.

Artino, A. R. (2007). Online military training using a social cognitive view of motivation and self-regulation to understand students' satisfaction, perceived learning, and choice. *The Quarterly Review of Distance Education, 8,* 191-202.

Au, M., Lam, J., & Chan, R. (2015). Social media education: Barriers and critical issues. In *Technology in education. Transforming educational practices with technology communications in computer and information science* (pp. 199-205). Berlin: Springer.

Barnard, L., Lan, W. Y., & Paton, V. O. (2010). Profiles in self-regulated learning in the online learning environment. *International Review of Research in Open and Distance Learning, 11,* 61-80.

Barnard, L., Lan, W. Y., To, Y. M., Paton, V. O., & Lai, S.-L. (2009). Measuring self-regulation in online and blended learning environments. *The Internet and Higher Education, 12,* 1-6.

Bradley, R. V., & Sankar, C. S. (2003). Outcomes assessment: Electronic surveys versus paper-based surveys. *Proceedings from the Southeastern Section of the American Society for Engineering Education, Macon, GA,* 1-11.

Broadbent, J., & Poon, W. L. (2015). Self-regulated learning strategies & academic achievement in online higher education learning environments: A systematic review. *The Internet and Higher Education, 27,* 1-13.

Cheng, K.-H., Liang, J.-C., & Tsai, C.-C. (2013). University students' online academic help seeking: The role of self-regulation and information commitments. *The Internet and Higher Education, 16,* 70-77.

Dabbagh, N., & Kitsantas, A. (2012). Personal learning environments, social media, and self-regulated learning: A natural formula for connecting formal and informal learning. *Internet and Higher Education, 15,* 3-8.

Garrison, D. R., & Cleveland-Innes, M. (2005). Facilitating cognitive presence in online learning: Interaction is not enough. *American Journal of Distance Education, 19*(3), 133-148.

Guo, Z., Lu, X., Li, Y. and Li, Y. (2011). A framework of students' reasons for using CMC media in learning contexts: A structural approach. *Journal of the American Society for Information Science and Technology, 62,* 2182-2200.

Greenhow, C., & Lewin, C. (2016). Social media and education: Reconceptualizing the boundaries of formal and informal learning. *Learning, Media and Technology, 41*(1), 6-30.

Greenwood, G., Perrin, A., & Duggan, M. (2016). Social media update 2016. Retrieved from http://www.pewinternet.org/2016/11/11/social-media-update-2016/

Hamid, S., Waycott, J., Kurnia, S., & Chang, S. (2015). Understanding students' perceptions on the benefits of online social networking use for teaching and learning. *The Internet and Higher Education*, *26*, 1-9.

Johnson, R. D., Hornik, S., & Salas, E. (2008). An empirical examination of factors contributing to the creation of successful e-learning environments. *International Journal of Human Computer Studies*, *66*(5), 356-369.

Kalpidou, M., Costin, D., & Morris, J. (2011). The relationship between Facebook and the well-being of undergraduate college students. *Cyberpsychology, Behavior and Social Networking*, *14*(4), 183-189.

Kaplan, A. M., & Haenlein, M. (2010). Users of the world, unite! The challenges and opportunities of social media. *Business Horizons*, *53*, 59-68.

Kind, T., & Evans, Y. (2015). Social media for lifelong learning. *International Review of Psychiatry (Abingdon, England)*, *27*, 124-32.

Kuo, Y.-C., Walker, A. E., Schroder, K. E. E., & Belland, B. R. (2014). Interaction, internet self-efficacy, and self-regulated learning as predictors of student satisfaction in online education courses. *The Internet and Higher Education*, *20*, 35-50.

Kuong, H. C. (2015). Enhancing online learning experience: From learners' perspective. *Procedia - Social and Behavioral Sciences*, *191*, 1002-1005.

Liaw, S.-S. (2008). Investigating students' perceived satisfaction, behavioral intention, and effectiveness of e-learning: A case study of the Blackboard system. *Computers & Education*, *51*(2), 864-873.

Lee, C. S., Osop, H., Kelni, G., & Goh, D. H.-L. (2015). Investigating the use of YouTube as a self-directed learning platform. In B. R. Allen, J. Hunter, & L. M. Zeng (Eds.), *Digital libraries: Providing quality information: 17th international conference on Asia-Pacific digital libraries, ICADL 2015, Seoul, Korea, December 9-12, 2015. Proceedings.* (pp. 308-310). Cham: Springer International Publishing.

Lee, J.-K., & Lee, W.-K. (2008). The relationship of e-learner's self-regulatory efficacy and perception of e-learning environmental quality. *Computers in Human Behavior*, *24*(1), 32-47.

Lee, D. Y., & Lehto, M. R. (2013). User acceptance of YouTube for procedural learning: An extension of the technology acceptance model. *Computers and Education*, *61*(1), 193-208.

Manca, S., & Ranieri, M. (2016). Is Facebook still a suitable technology-enhanced learning environment? An updated critical review of the literature from 2012 to 2015. *Journal of Computer Assisted Learning*, *32*(6), 503-528.

Moran, M., Seaman, J., & Tinti-Kane, H. (2011). *Teaching, learning, and sharing: How today's higher education faculty use social media.* Boston, MA: Pearson Learning Solutions and Babson Survey Research Group.

Michinov, N., Brunot, S., Le Bohec, O., Juhel, J., & Delaval, M. (2011). Procrastination, participation, and performance in online learning environments. *Computers and Education*, *56*, 243-252.

Netemeyer, R., Bearden, W., & Sharma, S. (2003). *Scaling procedures.* London: Sage.

Paechter, M., Maier, B., & Macher, D. (2010). Students' expectations of, and experiences in e-learning: Their relation to learning achievements and course satisfaction. *Computers & Education*, *54*(1), 222-229.

Piccoli, G., Ahmad, R., & Ives, B. (2001). Web-based virtual learning and a research framework environments: A preliminary assessment of effectiveness in basic IT skills training. *MIS Quarterly*, *25*(4), 401-426.

Pintrich, P. (2000). The role of goal orientation in self-regulated learning. In M. Boekaerts, P. Pintrich, & M. Zeidner (Eds.), *Handbook of self-regulation* (pp. 452-502). San Diego, CA: Academic Press.

Pintrich, P. R., & de Groot, E. V. (1990). Motivational and self-regulated learning components of classroom academic performance. *Journal of Educational Psychology*, *82*(1), 33-40.

Puzziferro, M. (2008). Online technologies self-efficacy and self-regulated learning as predictors of final grade and satisfaction in college-level online courses. *American Journal of Distance Education*, *22*(2), 72-89.

Schunk, D. H., & Zimmerman, B. J. (2012). *Motivation and self-regulated learning: Theory, research, and applications*. NY: Routledge.

Song, D., & Lee, J. (2014). Has web 2.0 revitalized informal learning? The relationship between web 2.0 and informal learning. *Journal of Computer Assisted Learning*, *30*(6), 511-533.

Stoynoff, S. (1997). Factors associated with international students' academic achievement. *Journal of Instructional Psychology*, *24*(1), 56.

Tabuenca, B., Kalz, M., Drachsler, H., & Specht, M. (2015). Time will tell: The role of mobile learning analytics in self-regulated learning. *Computers & Education*, *89*, 53-74.

Wan, Z., Compeau, D., & Haggerty, N. (2012). The effects of self-regulated learning processes on E-learning outcomes in organizational settings. *Journal of Management Information Systems*, *29*, 307-340.

Whipp, J. L., & Chiarelli, S. (2004). Self-regulation in a web-based course: A case study. *Educational Technology Research and Development*, *52*(4), 5-21.

Winters, F. I., Greene, J. A., & Costich, C. M. (2008). Self-regulation of learning within computer-based learning environments: A critical analysis. *Educational Psychology Review*, *20*(4), 429-444.

Wolters, C. A, Pintrich, P. R., and Karabenick, S. A. (2005). Assessing academic self-regulated learning. In L. H. Lippman & K. A. Moore (Eds.), *What Do Children Need to Flourish? Conceptualizing and measuring indicators of positive development* (pp. 251-270). New York: Springer.

Wu, J.-Y. (2015). University students' motivated attention and use of regulation strategies on social media. *Computers & Education*, *89*, 75-90.

Zimmerman, B. J. (1989). A social cognitive view of self-regulated academic learning. *Journal of Educational Psychology*, *81*, 329-339.

Zimmerman, B. J. (2000). Attaining self-regulation: A Social Cognitive Perspective. In M. Boekaerts, P. R. Pintrich, & M. Zeidner (Eds.), *Handbook of self-regulation* (pp. 13-39). San Diego: Academic Press.

Zimmerman, B. J., & Pons, M. M. (1986). Development of a structured interview for assessing student use of self-regulated learning strategies. *American Educational Research Journal, 23*(4), 614-628.

Zimmerman, B. J. (2008). Investigating self-regulation and motivation: Historical background, methodological developments, and future prospects. *American Educational Research Journal, 45*, 166-183.

# Information Seeking Among Latinos in the Midwestern United States

**Denice Adkins**
*School of Information Science & Learning Technologies, University of Missouri. USA. adkinsde@missouri.edu*

**Heather Moulaison Sandy**
*iSchool at the University of Missouri, USA. moulaisonhe@missouri.edu*

## ABSTRACT

**This paper is the first to present a study of information behavior of Latinos in the Midwestern U.S. It begins addressing gaps in knowledge about Latinos, particularly immigrants, and their information seeking and use of the mobile, social web in rural areas of the U.S. Midwest. Interviews were conducted in 2016 and 2017 with 20 Midwestern Latinos -- 15 immigrants to the United States and five native-born. We find that interviewees use many well-known social media platforms such as Facebook and YouTube as well as online resources to meet their information needs. Many prefer to consult trusted sources, making social media access desirable. Midwestern Latinos have adopted a number of the same information seeking practices as other immigrants and marginalized peoples, which may be different from practices of dominant populations in rural areas. Given their preferences, Latinos we interviewed will be best served by access to trusted information in the languages they speak, often presented orally such as in video format. For this, a reliable internet connection and internet-enabled device are key.**

## KEYWORDS

information seeking and use, social media engagement, Midwestern Latinos, immigrants, information behavior

## INTRODUCTION

In concert with the theme of this conference, this paper addresses Midwestern United States (U.S.) Latinos' use of social media as part of their everyday information seeking activities. In the United States, the Latino population tends to be less wealthy and less educated than the general population (U.S. Census Bureau, 2015), with a large percentage being immigrants who are speakers of non-English languages, including Spanish, but also indigenous languages (Semple, 2014).

A good deal of research has been carried out on information seeking and technology use among members of the Latino community (e.g., Clayman, Manganello, Viswanath, Hesse, & Arora, 2010; Elder, Ayala, Parra-Medina, & Talavera, 2009; Luevano-Molina, 2001; Tripp & Herr-Stevenson, 2009; Vyas, Landry, Schnider, Rojas, & Wood, 2012). These studies tend to focus on Latinos in populous areas of the United States, generally where large percentages of the entire population are Latinos. Little is known, however, about the smaller communities of Latinos in less-populous areas of the United States such as the Midwestern states; we believe the experiences of Midwestern states' Latinos have the potential to be unique and thus merit investigation.

### *Latinos in the Midwestern United States*

This paper articulates the results of a study of Latinos living in the U.S. Midwest. The term *Latino* is a designation of geographic origin of one's immediate family, indicating individuals of any race whose family identifies as coming from Mexico, Central or South America or the Caribbean. Due to complex colonial practices, many Latinos may be *Hispanic*, or speakers of Spanish. Also linked to the question of colonialism in the Americas is the question of race. Latinos may include individuals who identify as any number of races including Caucasian, black, indigenous or Asian. The current research project focuses on Latinos, irrespective of language or race. We acknowledge that all U.S.-based Latinos will likely find themselves increasingly marginalized given the current political climate in the United States (Adkins, Moulaison Sandy, & Derpic, 2017). The *Midwest* is the grouping of primarily agricultural and low-population density states located in the center of the United States [1]

### *Research question*

To investigate Latinos' information seeking behavior, we address the following research question:

What can we learn about information behavior (especially as mediated by web-based mobile technology) of Latinos in the U.S. Midwest?

## LITERATURE REVIEW

This brief review of the literature investigates immigrant and Latino information seeking behaviors and the use of technology for information seeking.

80th Annual Meeting of the Association for Information Science & Technology, Washington, DC, VA | Oct. 27-Nov. 1, 2017



[1] See U.S. Census Regions and Divisions map: https://www2.census.gov/geo/pdfs/maps-data/maps/reference/us_regdiv.pdf

### *Immigrant and Latino information use and preferences*

In recent years, a great deal of work in information seeking and use among immigrants has been published in the library and information science (LIS) literature, including the many papers cited by Caidi, Allard, and Quirke in their review (2010). More recent work includes research on information behaviors of specific ethnic groups (e.g., Sirikul & Dorner, 2016), immigrants to specific countries (e.g., Machet & Govender, 2012), immigrants during the border-crossing process (e.g., Newell, Gomez, & Guajardo, 2016), and immigrants in specific occupations (e.g., Sibal & Foo, 2016). Immigrants likely have information-seeking practices that are not aligned with mainstream ones. Upon arrival, their social networks in their receiving communities are often limited. "Although immigrants may have difficulty accessing information sources within their new countries, they may have access to transnational network ties not available to non-immigrants" (Caidi, Allard, & Quirke, 2010, p. 509).

Roughly one-third (U.S. Census Bureau, 2015) to half (Brown & Lopez, 2015) of Latinos in the United States are estimated to be foreign-born immigrants. Information preferences of Latinos, especially immigrants, can differ from preferences of mainstream groups. For example, written sources may not correspond with the ways that Latino information users prefer to consume their information (Brown & Lopez, 2015). This echoes previous findings (Ayala & Ayala, 1994; Haro, 1979; Luevano-Molina, 2001) in which Latinos reported that in libraries they sought Spanish-speaking staff, and more culturally-relevant materials such as Spanish-language materials including videos and music.

### *The digital divide, smartphones, and social media*

Mobile phones are the "dominant mode of interpersonal communications" (Newell et al., 2016, p. 188) for transnational migrants. The increased penetration of mobile phones has extended internet access to marginalized populations (Hudson, 2010). National surveys in the United States suggest that Latinos are more likely to use their smartphones for internet access than to use broadband connections (Lopez, Gonzalez-Barrera, & Patton, 2013). A large percentage of Hispanic adults (71%) owns a smartphone; the Pew Research Center also reports that 17% of Hispanic adults who own a smartphone do not have broadband at home, with 13% being smartphone dependent (Smith & Page, 2015). Pew's Hispanic sample for the smartphone usage study was "predominantly native born and English speaking" (p. 48). That sample, then, may not necessarily reflect the immigrant experience, especially in rural areas with limited broadband penetration.

For U.S. respondents overall, information seeking through social networking sites is most commonly done through Facebook, followed by media-sharing services such as YouTube (Kim & Sei-Ching, 2014, p. 7). Counts and Fisher (2009) looked at a mobile social networking community as an "always-on information ground that bridged geographic separation" (p. 106). A survey of almost 400 Latino teenagers, for example, found that 97% had social media accounts (Vyas et al., 2012). The Pew Research Center finds that, overall, 65% of Hispanics use social media, and that 58% of all individuals in rural areas use social media (Perrin, 2015).

## METHOD

This study is primarily qualitative and exploratory in nature. In it, local community gatekeepers were identified with the assistance of the Cambio Center (www.cambio.missouri.edu/), and gatekeepers served to identify community informants and to facilitate interviews. Interviews were semi-structured, to allow conversational flow and exploration of topics the interviewees found most meaningful about their interactions with technology and social media. Interview notes were transcribed shortly after the interview, and if the interview was conducted in Spanish, notes were made in English. The constant comparative method (Glaser & Strauss, 1967) was used throughout the course of the interviews to assess findings continually and to explore the personal element of Latinos' mobile and social media technology use for information seeking purposes. In total, we interviewed 20 community informants.

## RESULTS

Interviews were carried out throughout towns and rural areas in the Midwestern states of Illinois, Iowa and Missouri in late 2016 and early 2017, with 20 participants ranging in age from 13 to 55. Five men and 15 women were interviewed, 15 of whom were immigrants to the United States and five of whom were native born.

All but one respondent mentioned using social media platforms and other web-based technologies as part of everyday information seeking and use. The most common social media platform mentioned was Facebook, with all 15 immigrants using it, and overall, a total of 95% (n=19) of participants using it. WhatsApp and Instagram were next most common and were used by 40% of participants, with Snapchat, Pandora and YouTube being used by 30%. Twitter and Pinterest were the least used social media platforms, with only 10% of participants mentioning either. Other websites and resources were mentioned by participants as well, often for carrying out specific tasks. Table 1 contains the full list of web- and app-based resources mentioned by participants, broken out by participants' immigration status.

Notable in these conversations was the way mobile devices were used by immigrant populations. Many immigrant respondents indicated that they preferred people as sources of information over information obtained through the internet or their smartphones. When seeking information, they used their mobile phones primarily to call other people such as parents or siblings. Social networks like Facebook and WhatsApp were used primarily to stay in touch with family and friends in their home countries and seldom used specifically for information-seeking.

| Social media and web technologies | Immigrants N=15 | Native Born N=5 | Total |
|---|---|---|---|
| Facebook | 15 | 4 | 19 |
| WhatsApp | 7 | 1 | 8 |
| Instagram | 7 | 1 | 8 |
| Snapchat | 5 | 1 | 6 |
| Pandora | 4 | 2 | 6 |
| YouTube | 4 | 2 | 6 |
| Twitter | 2 | 0 | 2 |
| Netflix | 2 | 0 | 2 |
| Pinterest | 1 | 1 | 2 |
| Spotify | 1 | 1 | 2 |
| Tango | 1 | 1 | 2 |
| Weather Channel | 2 | 0 | 2 |
| Translation | 2 | 0 | 2 |
| Ebay | 1 | 0 | 1 |
| Amazon | 1 | 0 | 1 |
| Dictionary | 1 | 0 | 1 |
| Language learning | 1 | 0 | 1 |
| Health | 1 | 0 | 1 |
| School | 1 | 0 | 1 |

*Table 1. Social media apps used, by immigration status*

A few immigrants used social media apps and their mobile devices to help them navigate American institutions. This included accessing translation and dictionary apps used when writing letters to schools or doctors, as well as the use of one school-based communications system to monitor children's school performance. Other interviewees reported receiving email or text messages from their children's schools. Several participants indicated using YouTube as a source of how-to information, from how to make certain recipes to how to repair small engines. This reinforces the strong desire for audiovisual materials as opposed to text-based materials noted by Brown & Lopez (2015).

Additional information came to light during the course of the interviews, including topics of interest to Midwestern Latinos (e.g., medical information, schooling, and politics), information grounds supporting in-person interactions (e.g., churches, Latin American grocery stores), and the lack of public library use by the group overall (Adkins et al., 2017).

## DISCUSSION AND CONCLUSION

The interviews focused largely on Latino immigrants in rural areas and towns of three Midwestern states, a demographic that has not been explored before in the LIS literature and one for which an understanding of use of social media will support information professionals in these geographic areas. This qualitative interview data supplements and extends survey data available through the Pew Research Center and others. Responses reported here potentially begin to explore the differences between rural and town-based Latinos (especially immigrants) in low-population areas versus Latinos in high-population areas, which is more commonly studied in the literature (e.g., Clayman et al., 2010; Elder et al., 2009, etc.).

We discovered that Midwestern Latinos are, as expected, using social media including Facebook and YouTube (Kim & Sei-Ching, 2014). We suspect that immigrants use mobile, social web-based applications to bridge geographical distances (Counts & Fisher, 2009), potentially for linguistic and emotional as much as network-based reasons. Rurally located Latinos have adopted many of the same information seeking practices as other immigrants and marginalized peoples, which may be different from practices of dominant populations in rural areas. Future research will compare the information needs of rural, Midwestern Latinos with the information needs of urban Latinos.

Given their preferences, rural Midwestern Latinos we interviewed will be best served by access to trusted information in the language they speak, often presented orally such as in video format. For this, a reliable internet connection and internet-enabled device are key.

## ACKNOWLEDGEMENTS

This research was sponsored in part through a grant from OCLC/ALISE.

## REFERENCES

Adkins, D., Moulaison Sandy, H., & Derpic, J. (2017). Information sources of Latin American immigrants in the rural Midwest in the Trump era. *Library Quarterly, 87*(3), 243-256

Ayala, R., & Ayala, M. S. (1994). Report card on public library services to the Latino community: Final report. N.p.: REFORMA.

Brown, A., & Lopez, M. H. (2015). Public libraries and Hispanics. Pew Research Center. Retrieved from http://www.pewhispanic.org/2015/03/17/public-libraries-and-hispanics/

Caidi, N., Allard, D., & Quirke, L. (2010). Information practices of immigrants. *Annual Review of Information Science and Technology, 44*(1), 491-531.

Clayman, M. L., Manganello, J. A., Viswanath, K., Hesse, B. W., & Arora, N. K. (2010). Providing health messages to Hispanics/Latinos: Understanding the importance of language, trust in health information sources, and media use. *Journal of Health Communication, 15*(sup3), 252-263.

Counts, S., & Fisher, K. E. (2010). Mobile social networking as information ground: A case study. *Library & Information Science Research, 32*(2), 98-115.

Elder, J. P., Ayala, G. X., Parra-Medina, D., & Talavera, G. A. (2009). Health communication in the Latino community: Issues and approaches. *Annual Review of Public Health, 30*, 227-231.

Glaser, B. G., & Strauss, A. L. (1967). The discovery of grounded theory: Strategies for qualitative research. Chicago, IL: Aldine.

Haro, R. P. (1970). How Mexican Americans view libraries. *Wilson Library Bulletin, 44*(7), 736-742.

Hudson, A. (2010). Measuring the impact of cultural diversity on desired mobile reference services. *Reference Services Review, 38*(2), 299-308. doi: 10.1108/00907321011045052

Kim, K-S., & Sei-Ching, J. S. (2014). Social media as information sources: Use and evaluation of information from social media, 2013 OCLC Research Grant Award. OCLC Research. Retrieved from http://www.oclc.org/content/dam/research/grants/reports/2013/kim2013.pdf

Lopez, M. H., Gonzalez-Barrera, A., & Patten, E. (2013). Closing the digital divide: Latinos and technology adoption. Retrieved from http://www.pewhispanic.org/2013/03/07/closing-the-digital-divide-latinos-and-technology-adoption/

Luevano-Molina, S. (2001). Mexican/Latino immigrants and the Santa Ana Public Library: An urban ethnography. In Luevano-Molina, S. (ed.), *Immigrant politics and the public library* (pp. 43-63). Westport, CT: Greenwood Press.

Machet, M., & Govender, K. S. (2012). Information behavior of recent Chinese immigrants in Auckland, New Zealand. *South African Journal of Libraries & Information Science, 78*(1), 25-33.

Neuman, S. B., & Celano, D. (2006). The knowledge gap: Implications of leveling the playing field for low-income and middle-income children. *Reading Research Quarterly, 41*(2), 176-201.

Newell, B. C., Gomez, R., & Guajardo, V. E. (2016). Information seeking, technology use, and vulnerability among migrants at the United States-Mexico border. *Information Society, 32*(3), 176-191.

Pendell, K. D., & Bowman, M. S. (2012). Usability study of a library's mobile website: An example from Portland State University. *Information Technology & Libraries, 31*(2), 45-62.

Perrin, A. (2015). Social media usage: 2005-2015. Pew Research Center. Retrieved from http://www.pewinternet.org/2015/10/08/social-networking-usage-2005-2015/.

Pew Research Center. (2015, March 17-April 12). Libraries and Technology Use [dataset]. Retrieved from http://www.pewinternet.org/datasets/april-2015-libraries-and-technology-use/#

Semple, K. (2014, July 10). Immigrants who speak indigenous languages encounter isolation. *New York Times*. Retrieved from https://www.nytimes.com/2014/07/11/nyregion/immigrants-who-speak-indigenous-mexican-languages-encounter-isolation.html?_r=0.

Sibal, H. T., & Foo, S. (2016). A study on the information seeking behavior of Singapore-based Filipino domestic workers. *Information Development, 32*(5), 1570-1584.

Sirikul, P., & Dorner, D. (2016). Thai immigrants' information seeking behaviour and perception of the public library's role during the settlement process. *Library Review, 65*(8/9), 535-548. doi: 10.1108/LR-01-2016-0008

Smith, A., & Page, D. (2015). U.S. smartphone use in 2015. Pew Research Center. Retrieved from http://www.pewinternet.org/2015/04/01/us-smartphone-use-in-2015/

Tripp, L. M., & Herr-Stevenson, R. (2009). Making access meaningful: Latino young people using digital media at home and at school. *Journal of Computer-Mediated Communications, 14,* 1190-1207.

U.S. Census Bureau. (2012, last update). U.S. Census Bureau guidance on the presentation and comparison of race and Hispanic origin data. Retrieved from https://www.census.gov/population/hispanic/about/comparison.html

U.S. Census Bureau. (2015). 2011-2015 American Community Survey 5-Year Estimates, American FactFinder. Retrieved from https://factfinder.census.gov

Vyas, A. N., Landry, M., Schnider, M., Rojas, A. M., & Wood, S. F. (2012). Public health interventions: Reaching Latino adolescents via short message service and social media. *Journal of Medical Internet Research, 14*(4), e99.

# The Effects of BeNetWise Program on Youth Media Literacy: A Mixed Methods Research

**Kevin P.C. Cheng**
*The University of Hong Kong, Hong Kong. kevin51@hku.hk*

**Chun Kit Leung**
*The University of Hong Kong, Hong Kong. leungkit@connect.hku.hk*

**Joanne C.Y. Mok**
*The University of Hong Kong, Hong Kong. jomok@hku.hk*

**Jesus Alfonso D. Datu**
*The University of Hong Kong, Hong Kong. jaddatu@hku.hk*

**Jana Patricia M. Valdez**
*The University of Hong Kong, Hong Kong. janapatriciavaldez@yahoo.com*

**Hong Huang**
*University of South Florida, USA. honghuang@usf.edu*

**Kris Unsworth**
*Stockton University, USA. unsworthk@gmail.com*

**Andy Chan**
*Hong Kong Federation of Youth Groups, Hong Kong. andy.chan@hkfyg.org.hk*

**Cecilia Ng**
*Hong Kong Federation of Youth Groups, Hong Kong. cecilia.ng@hkfyg.org.hk*

**Samuel Kai Wah Chu**
*The University of Hong Kong, Hong Kong. samchu@hku.hk*

## ABSTRACT

**Existing literature has demonstrated that cultivating media literacy skills may optimize various indicators of student success. However, limited research has been conducted to examine how media literacy programs can improve effective consumption and production of media contents. The present research addresses these gaps through providing preliminary evidence about the effectiveness of BeNetWise, which is a two-year project launched in Hong Kong to educate youth on proper attitude and behavior in the cyberworld. This study was based on a sample of 196 secondary school students who participated in the media literacy intervention. The Chinese version of the New Media Literacy Scale was used to assess functional consumption, critical consumption, functional prosumption and critical prosumption. The results indicated that students who were exposed to this program significantly improved on functional consumption, critical consumption and critical prosumption. Findings point to the advantageous impacts of the BeNetWise project on the adaptive consumption and production of various media contents.**

## KEYWORDS

BeNetWise, consumption, media literacy, prosumption

## INTRODUCTION

Although the rapid growth of media content (e.g., blogs and wikis) has been perceived as having advantageous impacts on personal, social, educational and even work-related functioning (Chu, Chan & Tiwari, 2012; Chu, Zhang, Chen, Chan, Lee, Zou, Lau *in press*), the possible hazards of using media points to the significance of educating youth on its proper use. Studies have offered potential evidence about the practical benefits of developing media literacy in various contexts. For instance, Hobbs and Frost (2003) have demonstrated that students who attend a media literacy curriculum improve their capacity to pinpoint objectives, target audience and conveyed perspectives in a specific form of media. Chu, Lau, Chu, Lee and Chan (2016) have also found that Hong Kong primary school students could differentiate true and false information from various sources of media.

However, previous literature has pinpointed three major issues in the media literacy education research. First, little research has explicitly assessed the impact of media literacy curriculum on students' academic achievement and non-academic outcomes like attitude towards the use of different types of media (Hobbs & Frost, 2003). Second, researchers have faced challenges in accurately measuring media literacy skills (Primack, Gold, Switzer, Hobbs, Land & Fine, 2006). Third, very few studies have adopted a quantitative research approach to examine the effects of media literacy education (Hobbs & Frost, 2003) which may provide limited insights regarding the impact of such curricula on relevant student outcomes.

The motivation of media literacy education lies in the point that we, as educators, are obliged to strengthen students' competencies in using and even producing various types of media. Among various media literacy education programs in Hong Kong, BeNetWise is a two-year project launched by The Hong Kong Federation of Youth Groups and aims to educate youths on proper attitude and behavior in the cyberworld. Hence, it is crucial to examine the effectiveness of the program. In this study, quantitative and qualitative research designs were used to provide comprehensive insights on how this program influenced the media literacy skills of high school students.

80th Annual Meeting of the Association for Information Science & Technology, Washington, DC | Oct. 27-Nov. 1, 2017

### *The BeNetWise Program*

The National Association for Media Literacy Education (NAMLE) defines *media literacy* as the "ability to access, analyze, evaluate, create, and act using all forms of communication" (2012, p.1). The BeNetWise program has, to a large extent, been based on the principles of the NAMLE model of media literacy curriculum. This program consists of lessons, class activities and interactive hyrkshops. The underlying concept of the curriculum points to understanding and decoding of new media literacy. Teachers also share knowledge about internet behavior, self-protection, interaction, respectability, etc. as part of the core concepts of the curriculum to students.

### *Theoretical Framework*

This research adopts the four-factor model of new media literacy (Chen, Wu & Wang, 2011; Koc & Barut, 2016). The model posits that there are four dimensions of media literacy: functional consumption, critical consumption, functional prosumption and critical prosumption. The term *prosumption* characterizes the concept of production by consumers (Toffler, 1980). Their functions are shown in Figure 1. Chen et al. (2011) has pointed out that critical prosumption is the most optimal category of media literacy skill in the 21st century.

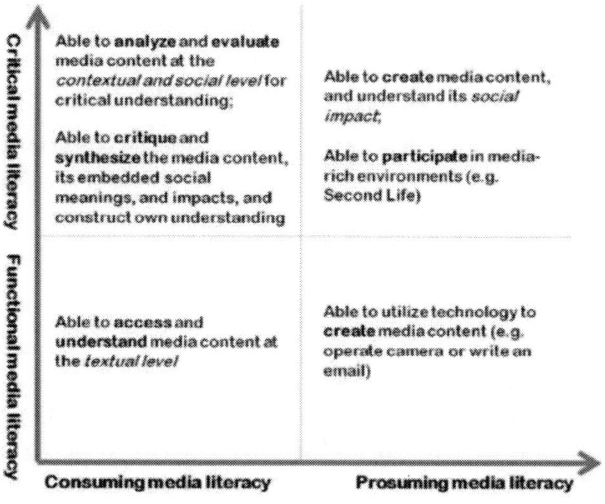


***Figure 1.*** *Conceptual representation of media literacy skills (Chen et al., 2011)*

## METHODS

### *Quantitative Phase*

#### Participants

Participating in the survey were 196 Hong Kong Chinese secondary school students aged 12 to 13 (102 and 94 students from Secondary One and Two respectively). The sample comprised 70 girls and 117 boys. Nine students did not identify with one of the two genders or missed this question. The consent forms were distributed to the participants and their parents.

#### Instrument

The Chinese version of the 31-item New Media Literacy Scale (Koc & Barut, 2016) was used to assess the participants' degree of functional consumption, critical consumption, functional prosumption and critical prosumption. Items were rated on a 5-point Likert scale (1 = Strongly disagree; 5 = Strongly agree). The participants' responses were collected at pretest period (Time 1) and post-test period (Time 2).

#### Data Analysis

Confirmatory factor analysis (CFA) was conducted using the 23rd version of the Analysis of Moment Structures (AMOS) in the pretest and post-test datasets to provide evidence about the validity of the hypothesized four-factor model of media literacy. A measurement or structural model is considered valid if the following guidelines were met (Schermelleh-Engel, Moosbrugger & Müller, 2003): a) non-significant chi-square statistics; b) Comparative Fit Index (CFI), Goodness of Fit Index (GFI), Tucker Lewis Index (TLI) should be greater than .90; and c) Root Mean Square Error of Approximation (RMSEA) should be less than .08. Then, the Cronbach's alpha reliability coefficients of the four subscales (i.e., functional consumption, critical consumption, functional prosumption and critical prosumption) were calculated. Additionally, dependent sample-tests were carried out to examine whether the mean scores on the four dimensions of media literacy differed before and after the implementation of the media literacy program. Finally, d values were computed to provide a concrete index of effect size in the present study.

### *Qualitative Phase*

#### Participants

Students were recruited in two different local secondary schools. They were separated into nine different groups. Each of the groups consisted of three to six students. These students were then invited to participate in a post-curriculum interview, sharing their learning experiences within the program. Interviews with the students were recorded and transcribed.

#### Instrument

Interview guide questions were developed to identify pattern of responses that characterized the students' learning experiences and to pinpoint potential areas of improvement for the BeNetWise program. Six different questions, including "please describe within the program the most successful aspect, the least useful aspect and any missing components" (for details of the questions, refer to the first author), were developed.

#### Data Analysis

Group interview sessions were recorded and transcribed. The transcribed data were imported to NVivo version 11 to identify the pattern of codes that reflected the four media literacy dimensions. In analyzing the qualitative data, we referred to the analytic strategies of Miles and Huberman (1994) and Chen et al. (2011) in categorizing the participants' responses. Two coders (the first and second authors of this paper) performed coding of the participants' responses. The raters' coding consistency was examined to determine whether the codes were reliable.

## RESULTS

### *Quantitative Phase*

#### Preliminary Analyses

Findings of CFA at pre-test ($\chi^2$=107.36, $p<.001$, CFI=.97, GFI=.92, TLI=.96, and RMSEA=.08; confidence Interval or CI 90% = .059 – .100) and post-test ($\chi^2$=70.93, $p<.05$, CFI=.99, GFI=.94, TLI=.99, and RMSEA=.05; CI 90% = .021 – .073) showed that the scores of the four major dimensions at the two time points were valid. The Cronbach's alpha coefficients of the four subscales at the two time points were high (from .86 to .96).

#### Effects of the BeNetWise Program on Media Literacy

The descriptive findings (means, standard deviations and sample sizes before and after the participants were exposed to the media literacy program) are shown in Table 1. Paired t-test and d-test values are also reported in the said table.

| Outcome | Pretest | | Post-test | | 95% CI for Mean Difference | r | t | d |
|---|---|---|---|---|---|---|---|---|
| | M | SD | M | SD | | | | |
| Functional Consumption | 3.53 | .67 | 3.72 | .89 | -0.30, -0.07 | .44* | -3.07** | 0.22 |
| Critical Consumption | 3.52 | .66 | 3.73 | .87 | -0.16, 0.02 | .47* | -3.52*** | 0.25 |
| Functional Prosumption | 3.83 | .87 | 3.78 | .79 | -0.09, 0.19 | .32* | .73 | 0.05 |
| Critical Prosumption | 3.32 | .71 | 3.65 | .82 | 0.55, 0.83 | .28* | -4.97*** | 0.36 |

*** p < .001, ** p < .01, N = 196, df = 195

*Table 1. Descriptive statistics and t-test results*

Results of the paired-samples t-test showed that, except for functional prosumption, the means for functional consumption, critical consumption and critical prosumption after undergoing the BeNetWise program was significantly higher than the mean before joining the program. In terms of the effect size, the d values demonstrated that about 5% to 36% of the changes in media literacy dimensions were caused by the media literacy program. These values may be interpreted as small effect sizes according to the criteria of Cohen (1988).

### *Qualitative Phase*

A total of 217 relevant phrases/sentences were coded. Assessment of the inter-rater reliability based on the coding scheme resulted in 90.90% to 94.88% inter-rater agreement. Table 2 summarizes the frequency of coded responses. Critical media literacy is the most frequently cited code (46.55%). Responses in this category indicate that students were carefully reviewing and analyzing media contents before posting them and were aware of possible risks of certain media contents. A considerable percentage of the participants' responses fell under the category of prosuming media literacy (35.48%). Examples of responses include identification and specification of authentic ideas, as well as the proper use of online language.

The four aspects of the media literacy were also analyzed based on the two continuums (see previous sections). Another 104 responses were coded. Table 3 describes the results on the number of responses and the corresponding percentages for the four coding scheme categories. There were 73 responses (70.1%) that fell under the critical prosumption category, followed by the critical consumption category (21.5%). These findings imply that students are capable of creating media content, understanding its social impact, and participating in media-rich environments.

| Types of Media Literacy behaviours | References (Total = 217) | Percentage in total | Sample coded content |
|---|---|---|---|
| Consuming Media Literacy | 26 | 11.98% | 1) School A, form 1, class H – Student 28<br>"I know that we can't always click on all website. Some website are promoting erroneous information<br><br>2) School A, form 1 class F – Student 18<br>"We must be very careful about browsing" |
| Functional Media Literacy | 13 | 5.99% | 1) School A, form 1, class F – Student 20<br>"We can talk to everyone around the globe instantly without barriers."<br><br>2) School A, form 2, class F – Student 1<br>"We learn how to communicate and search for information online." |
| Critical Media Literacy | 101 | 46.55% | 1) School A, form 1, class H – Student 29<br>"I will check clearly about the registration procedures and the terms they entailed, as well as the long term treatment of information form these media platform."<br><br>2) School A, form 2, class F – Student 2<br>"Make us realize that we should never criticize without full understanding of the issue" |
| Prosuming Media Literacy | 77 | 35.48% | 1) School A, form 1, class H – Student 25<br>"In terms of language skills, how to specify and identify your own ideas and generate decent/non-misleading opinions."<br><br>2) School A, form 2, class E – Student 26<br>"I should not do anything related to the defamation of others online" |

***Table 2**. Sample coded content*

| | | |
|---|---|---|
| Critical media literacy | 22 (21.5%) | 73 (70.1%) |
| Functional media literacy | 5 (4.7%) | 4 (3.7%) |
| Total: 104 | Consuming media literacy | Prosuming media literacy |

***Table 3**. Frequency and percentage of the codes*

## DISCUSSION

### *The Four-Factor Model of Media Literacy*

The research demonstrated that the scores from the four-factor model of media literacy were valid and reliable in a sample of Hong Kong secondary school students. The current research points to the significance of using psychometrically sound assessment tools to effectively measure media literacy competencies among student populations.

### *The Effects of BeNetWise Program*

The research showed that students significantly improved on functional consumption, critical consumption and critical prosumption. Even the findings of qualitative phase seemed to indicate that the participants' responses characterized high levels of critical consumption and prosumption media literacy. Our findings corroborated previous investigations which demonstrated that media literacy could yield desirable impact among student populations (Arke & Primack, 2009; Hobbs & Frost, 2003).

### *The Practical Value of Critical Consumption and Prosumption*

The rapid pace of technological advancements has offered enormous opportunities to get access to information in the cyberworld. Although the continuous development in the production and dissemination of knowledge may hold several beneficial impacts (e.g., better learning prospects and faster dissemination of information in the school setting), existing literature has also shown that the use of technology may have detrimental effects on students' academic and psychological functioning (Walsh, Fielder, Carey & Carey, 2013). Therefore, it is crucial for schools to develop a concrete platform to enhance students' adaptive use and production of media contents. The learner-centered media education approach is potentially valuable to cultivate better critical thinking skills among students (Chu, 2010). The adoption of an inquiry-based approach in teaching effective strategies to consume and produce media contents is recommended (Chu, 2010).

## CONCLUSION

This research examined the effectiveness of the BeNetWise program. The findings emphasize the significance of developing sound pedagogies for improving students' media literacy production and consumption. The research also suggests that a comprehensive approach towards understanding media literacy entails a careful assessment of how students are consuming and producing media contents. However, our research has limitations. For instance, as we used a self-report questionnaire to measure how the BeNetWise impacts on media literacy, it may be desirable to use alternative approaches in assessing students' media literacy competencies. Indeed, more research is needed to investigate the impacts of media literacy interventions on students' academic and non-academic outcomes.

## REFERENCES


Arke, E.T., & Primack, B.A. (2009). Quantifying media literacy: Development, reliability, and validity of a new measure. *Educational Media International 46*(1), 53-65.

Chen, D.-T., Wu, J., & Wang, Y.-M. (2011). Unpacking new media literacy. *Journal on Systemics, Cybernetics and Informatics 9*(2), 84-88.

Chu, D. (2010) A pedagogy of inquiry- toward student-centered media education. *New Horizons in Education 58*(3), 44-57.

Chu, S.K.W., Chan, C.K.K., & Tiwari, A.F.Y. (2012). Using blogs to support learning during internship. *Computers & Education 58*(3), 989-1000.

Chu, S.K.W., Lau, W.W.F., Chu, D.S.C., Lee, C.W.Y., & Chan, L.L.H. (2016). Media awareness among Hong Kong primary school students. *Journal of Librarianship and Information Science 48*(1), 90-104.

Chu, S.K.W., Zhang, Y., Chen, K., Chan, C.K., Lee, C.W.Y., Zou, E., & Lau, W. (in press). The effectiveness of wikis for project-based learning in different disciplines in higher education. *The Internet and Higher Education.*

Cohen, J. (1988). *Statistical power analysis for the behavioral sciences* (2nd ed.). Hillsdale, NJ: Lawrence Earlbaum Associates.

Hobbs, R., & Frost, R. (2003). Measuring the acquisition of media-literacy skills. *Reading Research Quarterly 38*(3), 330-355.

Koc, M., & Barut, E. (2016). Development and validation of New Media Literacy Scale (NMLS) for university students. *Computers in Human Behavior 63*, 834-843.

Miles, M., & Huberman, A.M. (1994). *Qualitative Data Analysis.* Thousand Oaks, CA: Sage Publications.

National Association for Media Literacy Education (NAMLE) (2012) Media Literacy Defined. Retrieved March 10, 2017 from http://namle.net/publications/media-literacy-definitions/.

Primack, B.A., Gold, M.A., Switzer, G.E., Hobbs, R., Land, S.R., & Fine, M.J. (2006). Development and validation of a smoking media literacy scale. *Archives of Pediatric & Adolescent Medicine 160*, 369–374.

Schermelleh-Engel, K., Moosbrugger, H., & Müller, H. (2003). Evaluating the fit of structural equation models. Methods of Psychological Research Online 8, 23–74.

Toffler, A. (1980). *The Third Wave.* New York: Morrow.

Walsh, J.L., Fielder, R.L., Carey, K.B., & Carey, M.P. (2013). Female college students' media use and academic outcomes: Results from a longitudinal cohort study. *Emerging Adulthood 1*(3), 219-232.

# Evaluating Metadata Schema for Murals and Stone Cave Temples: Towards Digitizing Cultural Heritage

**Xiao Hu**
*The University of Hong Kong, Hong Kong. xiaoxhu@hku.hk*

**Jeremy Ng**
*The University of Hong Kong, Hong Kong. jeremyng@hku.hk*

**Shengping Xia**
*Dunhuang Research Academy, China. dhxiashengp@hotmail.com*

**Yonnie King Yiu Fu**
*The University of Hong Kong, Hong Kong. ykyfu@connect.hku.hk*

## ABSTRACT

**Despite efforts and attempts on preserving cultural heritages around the world, few studies have been conducted on metadata schema of murals and stone cave temples which are often high value heritages dating from ancient times. The literature is also scarce in user-centered evaluation of metadata schema of this kind. This study therefore aims to offer insights on developing and evaluating a drafted metadata schema for digitizing and preserving historic murals and stone cave temples. In-depth interviews were conducted with 15 scholars and professionals whose work was related to murals and stone cave temples. A coding framework was designed to analyze the interview transcripts. Initial findings show that users' seeking behaviors for cultural heritage information corroborated with their perceived importance of specific metadata elements. The coding schema developed in this study can serve as a framework for follow-up evaluations of metadata schemas of this kind, contributing to the ongoing development of cultural heritage metadata.**

## KEYWORDS

metadata, cultural heritage, murals, stone cave temples, user-centered evaluation

## INTRODUCTION

Culture heritages are important records of human activities in history, providing irreplaceable evidence across diverse and various disciplines including archaeology, history, anthropology, information science, linguistics, and religious studies. As some culture heritages are non-movable, people who need to study these heritages have to travel. More importantly, these heritages may experience damage due to natural and/or man-made causes. Digitalizing cultural heritages for documentation and preservation is considered a viable solution to this problem (Garoufallou et al., 2008). When numerous digital resources are produced, metadata of cultural heritage information become crucial for organizing and accessing these resources.

China is renowned for its rich historic and cultural background; however, digitization of non-movable cultural heritages in China is still at an initial stage. Murals and stone cave temples are two of the seven major categories of non-movable cultural heritages identified in China[1]. For instance, Mogao Cave near Dunhuang, China is a representative site with hundreds of stone cave temples decorated with numerous murals, constructed during a period of about 1,000 years starting from 366 C.E. (Hu et al., 2017).

Despite the efforts spent on digital preservation of cultural heritages around the world, there is no metadata schema developed specifically for murals and stone cave temples. In addition, there is very little literature that evaluates metadata schema of cultural heritages in a user-centered approach through which improvements on the schema can be made and sustained. In order to bridge this gap, this study aims to evaluate metadata schemas for the purpose of digitalizing and preserving cultural heritages, in particular murals and stone cave temples. A draft metadata schema[2 2] was developed based on a series of existing standards for other types of cultural heritages such as ancient books. By evaluating the metadata schema, we aim to identify potential problems and make suggestions for further improvement. Considering the unprecedented scholarly and historic values of murals and stone cave temples, as the first step towards thorough and systematic evaluations of the metadata schema, this study focuses on scholarly and professional users whose jobs are related to cultural heritage, particularly murals and stone cave temples. The scholar group includes researchers and professors in related disciplines such as art history, Buddhism, architecture, etc. Professionals referred to participants who had jobs related to cultural heritage such as teachers, artists, and library or museum staff. Specifically, this study focuses on the following research questions:

80th Annual Meeting of the Association for Information Science & Technology, Washington, DC | Oct. 27-Nov. 1, 2017



[1] According to "Cultural relics protection law of the people's Republic of China," the other five categories of non-movable cultural heritage are archeological sites, ancient architecture, ancient tombs, large stone carvings, and historical sites.
[2] Definition of core elements are available at: goo.gl/OMuSme

**RQ1**: How do scholarly and professional users seek and use information on murals and stone cave temple resources?

**RQ2**: Which elements are important and useful to scholarly and professional users in the drafted metadata schema for murals and stone cave temples?

**RQ3**: Are there any issues or problems on the metadata elements pointed out by scholarly and professional users?

The questions set out to 1) understand the practices of how scholarly and professional users access and use resources of murals and stone cave temples, which could inform their evaluation of the metadata schema, 2) to identify elements of the metadata schema that may or may not be perceived important or useful by users, and 3) to identify issues or problems with elements of the metadata schema, thereby making suggestions on modifications of the elements.

## RELATED WORKS

There are significant challenges to creating metadata for cultural heritage information. Cultural items that are born digital such as video games have already faced difficulties in the creation of metadata (Lee et al., 2013) and digitized cultural heritages will anticipate more challenges. For instance, digital representations of physical artefacts require considerable technical information (e.g., parameters related to creation, storage, and manipulation) in the metadata in order to maintain and preserve these cultural objects (Patel et al., 2005).

Many cultural institutions and national bodies have attempted to develop standards to address the wide-ranging metadata requirements of the cultural heritage sector. Well known standards include:

The CIDOC Conceptual Reference Model (CRM)[3]: intended to cover all concepts relevant to museum documentation. It is used to clarify the documentation process, and to ensure no loss of semantic content when integrating heterogeneous cultural heritage data sources.

EDM[4]: Europeana is a digital collection of European cultural heritages. The Europeana Data Model (EDM) aims at being an integration medium for collecting, connecting and enriching all the elements included on the descriptions provided by Europeana content providers.

SPECTRUM[5], a standard originally for documentation of UK museum collections, is coordinated by the Museum Documentation Association (MDA). It comprises procedures for documenting objects and the processes that they undergo. It also identifies and describes the information that needs to be maintained to support those procedures. The intention is that the standard should contain all those functions that are common to most museums.

VRA Core[6]: consists of a single element set that can be applied to create records to describe works of visual culture as well as the images that document them.

In addition to the above, there are also a number of national standards existing such as ICCD form (Italy)[7] and the UK Historic Environment Data Standard (MIDAS Heritage[8]). Regardless of the complexity or the modernity of metadata schemas, they are often created based on resources in hand and existing standards, without taking into account the perspectives of end-users. There is currently a lack of a standardized metadata schema for murals and stone cave temples. More significantly, a user-centered evaluation of this metadata schema is required for its improvements. This study thus attempts to bridge some of these gaps.

## METHOD

To answer the research questions, this study adopted a qualitative approach where semi-structured individual interviews were conducted with scholarly and professional users. Interviews are considered a suitable method for this study as there is little literature on this topic and thus a lack of framework for quantitative approaches. The codebook developed from this study can provide a framework to enable follow-up studies to conduct surveys as well as user experiments.

For users in the researcher/scholar group, it is important but difficult to identify and recruit experts in related domains (e.g., architecture, art history), and thus snowball sampling was adopted (Berg el al., 2004). The group pf professionals was recruited with a combination of convenience and snowball sampling, in that we started from professionals in our networks who then referred their colleagues to participate in this study.

Each interview was structured into three parts. The first part sought to collect information seeking behaviors of the interviewees relating to mural and stone cave temples. Interviewees were expected to answer the questions based on their past experiences in seeking related information. In the second part, interviewees were asked to brainstorm suggestions for improving access to mural and stone cave temple information. This part aimed to collect users' viewpoints of how

---

[3] http://www.cidoc-crm.org/

[4] http://pro.europeana.eu/page/edm-documentation

[5] http://collectionstrust.org.uk/spectrum/

[6] https://www.loc.gov/standards/vracore/

[7] http://www.iccd.beniculturali.it/

[8] http://heritage-standards.org.uk/midas-heritage/

such information could be organized in a more user-friendly way. It is noteworthy, that in this stage, the drafted metadata scheme was still hidden to the interviewees. In the third part, the core elements in the draft metadata schema were introduced to the interviewees. They were asked to comment on the importance and usefulness of every core element of the metadata schema. The interviews were conducted in 2016, with each session lasting for about one hour. The participants voluntarily joined the interviews with no remuneration provided.

## RESULTS

Fifteen participants joined this study, with five scholars and ten professionals. There were 303 excerpts extracted from the interview transcripts and 85 excerpts (28%) were double coded. Cohen's kappa coefficient values ranged from 0.78 to 0.92 across the interview questions, indicating an overall substantial to excellent level of agreement between coders (McHugh, 2012).

### *Current practices of information seeking*

In terms of the methods in seeking information of murals and stone cave temples, websites/databases (12) and search engines (nine times) together accounted for around two-thirds of the total count of 33 responses. The rest included one-fourth of total (eight) opting for using library catalogues, leaving the minority using personal contacts (two), visiting targeted museums and exhibitions (one), or bookstores (one). These results showed that electronic resources were used by most scholarly and professional users in looking for information related to murals and stone cave temples, predetermining users' potential in benefitting from digitizing cultural heritage information as well as metadata schemas well designed for digital information.

Job-related (7) and personal interests (4) were the major purposes of seeking cultural heritage information, whereas research (3) and teaching purposes (2) were also mentioned. The types of cultural heritage information being sought included visualized materials (e.g., images, videos) (4), the historical or cultural background (2), and travelling information (1).

When asked about how information of mural and stone cave temples can be organized in a more user-friendly way, half of the responses included that resources should be available online (4) and well cataloged (1). Search function (1) was also mentioned as a desirable way in facilitating access to such information. High quality metadata are therefore a potential requirement from users' perspectives.

### *Codebook and opinions on metadata elements*

A grounded theory approach (Strauss and Corbin, 1994) was adopted to develop a codebook from the data through an iterative coding process. Table 1 presents the codes on users' perceived importance and usefulness of elements in the metadata schema.

Among the excerpts containing interviewees' views on individual metadata elements in the schema, 67 are on importance, 49 on functions, and 12 on issues of the elements.

| Categories | Codes | Definition |
|---|---|---|
| Importance | Necessary | Element is important and must exist for identifying the heritage. |
| | Informative | Element is useful in learning more about the heritage but not necessary. |
| | Not interested | Interviewee is not interested in learning this information but does not mind having it. |
| | Redundant | Element overlaps with other elements. |
| Functions (searching; browsing; organizing) | Useful | Element can be used in searching / browsing / organizing resources related to the heritage. |
| | Not useful | Element is not useful in searching / browsing / organizing related resources. |
| | Not useful personally | Element is not useful for oneself due to lack of knowledge or other reasons, but might be useful for others. |
| Issues | Confusing terminology | Element definition is unclear or hard to understand. |
| | Lack of cataloging standards | Element is problematic because there are no standard rules to catalogue this element. |

***Table 1.*** *Codebook for each metadata element*

Table 2 presents the distributions of codes on importance of the elements. Nearly three quarter of the excerpts (73.1%) are coded as "Necessary" or "Informative," indicating that most elements are considered important. "Title," "Current Location" and "Description" of a mural or a stone cave temple can be viewed as the most important elements among all, closely followed by "Related Knowledge" and "Materials." Some participants indicated "Not interested" on some elements but others regarded them as "Necessary" and/or "Informative." Seven elements are regarded as "Redundant" for at least once, which will be discussed further in relation to issues of the elements.

Metadata elements that were considered to be useful in supporting searching included "Classification," "Creation" and "Current Condition." In contrast, metadata elements "Materials," "Techniques," "Measurements," "Damage" and "Environment" were viewed as not useful or not useful personally for searching. Participants expressed that these elements might be too technically detailed and thus perhaps only experts highly specialized in these aspects could come up with meaningful search terms.

For browsing, "Current Condition" was also one of the most useful elements, along with "Title" and "Current Location," "Inscriptions/Marks," "Object/Work Type,", "Grade," "Measurements" and "Related Knowledge." Unlike searching, participants thought technical details in "Measurement" (e.g., size, area) were useful for choosing specific murals and stone cave temples for further studies. Not surprisingly,

"Identifier" is mentioned as useful for the purpose of organizing related information. Interviewees commented that this element could be much more useful for administrators of digital collections than themselves.

In terms of issues with the elements, interviewees thought some elements were confusing. In particular, they mentioned it was difficult to distinguish "Object/Work Type" and "Type," also "Context" and "Coverage." Other elements that need clearer definitions and further refinement include "Description," "Inscriptions/Marks," "Damage" and "Related Visual Documentation." "Grade" and "Creation" were also concerned by the participants on the possible difficulty in cataloging them in a standardized manner.

| Element | Necessary | Informative | Not interested | Redundant | Total |
|---|---|---|---|---|---|
| Classification | 1 | | | | 3 |
| Title | 5 | | | | 5 |
| Identifier | | 1 | 1 | | 2 |
| Current Location | 4 | 1 | | | 5 |
| Creation | 2 | | 1 | | 3 |
| Materials | 3 | 1 | 1 | | 5 |
| Techniques | 1 | 1 | | | 2 |
| Measurements | 1 | 2 | | | 3 |
| Description | 3 | 2 | | 1 | 6 |
| Inscriptions/Marks | 1 | | | | 1 |
| Object / Work Type | 1 | | | 1 | 2 |
| Context | 1 | 1 | | 2 | 4 |
| Grade | 1 | 1 | | | 2 |
| Current Condition | 1 | | 2 | | 3 |
| Environment | 1 | | | 1 | 2 |
| Damage | 1 | 1 | 1 | 1 | 4 |
| Right | 1 | | | | 1 |
| Related Works | 1 | | | | 1 |
| Related Visual Documentation | 2 | | 1 | | 3 |
| Related Knowledge | 3 | 1 | | | 4 |
| Coverage | 1 | | 1 | 1 | 3 |
| Disposal History | 1 | | 1 | | 2 |
| Type | 1 | | 1 | 1 | 3 |
| Total | 37 | 12 | 10 | 8 | 67 |

***Table 2.*** *Coded comments on element importance*

## DISCUSSION AND CONCLUDING REMARKS

Users' perceived importance or usefulness of specific elements in the metadata schema corroborated with their information seeking practices which were job-oriented and mainly relied on online channels. "Title," "Current Location" and "Current Conditions" were regarded as highly important elements in supporting searching and browsing, while "Identifier" was deemed as useful for organizing information on murals and stone cave temples. In addition, librarians in the professional group deemed "Title" as necessary, attributable to their needs of titles for cataloging information and managing collections. "Related Knowledge" is also an important element in that it can facilitate the indexing and searching of not only the cultural heritage itself but also knowledge related to it (e.g., related historic events, jargon). These were valued by users in both groups as research and teaching materials as well as learning resources to help further ones' understanding of a mural or a stone cave temple.

This study also reveals issues on definition clarity of some elements and confusions among similar or overlapping elements. Based on these findings, the following modifications are suggested to refine the schema: 1) "Object/Work Type" should be renamed to "Subject," to improve clarity; 2) "Type" should be eliminated as it overlaps with "Object/Work Type"; 3) "Coverage" should be removed as it is often confused with "Context" and its meaning is not straightforward; and 4) "Damage" could be specified as "Damage Cause," as the extent of damage can be included in "Current Condition."

Due to the complexity of the cultural heritage resources, there could be more elements, sub-elements and quantifiers added in the future. Application profiles would continue being developed to inform local practice. It is also essential for the schema to offer greatest flexibility for customization to users from multiple disciplines with different information needs. Future studies will continue refining and evaluating the drafted metadata schema. Feedback from the general public will be elicited by interviews and questionnaires. Findings of this series of investigation can contribute to the ongoing development of cultural heritage metadata and the improved access of non-movable cultural heritage resources.

## ACKNOWLEDGEMENTS

This study is partially supported by Key Technologies Research and Development Program of China, for the project titled "Metadata Standard for Cultural Relics Digital Preservation," project No.: 2014BAK07B02.

## REFERENCES

Berg, B. L., Lune, H., & Lune, H. (2004). *Qualitative research methods for the social sciences* (Vol. 5). Boston, MA: Pearson.

Garoufallou, E., Siatri, R., & Balatsoukas, P. (2008). Virtual maps–virtual worlds: Testing the usability of a Greek virtual cultural map. *Journal of the American Society for Information Science and Technology, 59*(4), 591-601.

Hu, X., Ho, E. M. Y., & C. Qiao (2017). Digitizing Dunhuang cultural heritage: A user evaluation of Mogao Cave Panorama Digital Library, *iConference*, Wuhan, China.

Lee, J. H., Tennis, J. T., Clarke, R. I., & Carpenter, M. (2013). Developing a video game metadata schema for the Seattle Interactive Media Museum. *International Journal on Digital Libraries, 13*(2), 105-117.

McHugh, Mary L. (2012) Interrater reliability: The kappa statistic. *Biochem Med (Zagreb), 22*(3), 276-282.

Patel, M., White, M., Mourkoussis, N., Walczak, K., Wojciechowski, R., & Chmielewski, J. (2005). Metadata requirements for digital museum environments. *International Journal on Digital Libraries, 5*(3), 179-192. doi:10.1007/s00799-004-0104-x.

# Public Services or Private Gains: Motives Behind Participation on a Mobile Crowdsourcing Application in a Smart City

**Chei Sian Lee**
*Wee Kim Wee School of Communication and Information, Nanyang Technological University, Singapore.*
*leecs@ntu.edu.sg*

**Sei-Ching Joanna Sin**
*Wee Kim Wee School of Communication and Information, Nanyang Technological University, Singapore.*
*joanna.sin@ntu.edu.sg*

**Dion Hoe-Lian Goh**
*Wee Kim Wee School of Communication and Information, Nanyang Technological University, Singapore.*
*ashlgoh@ntu.edu.sg*

**Yin Leng Theng**
*Wee Kim Wee School of Communication and Information, Nanyang Technological University, Singapore.*
*yltheng@ntu.edu.sg*

**Hamzah Osop**
*Wee Kim Wee School of Communication and Information, Nanyang Technological University, Singapore.*
*hamzah@ntu.edu.sg*

## ABSTRACT

The increased use of crowdsourcing to support smart city initiatives has been reported in the literature. However, a gap remains in understanding the needs motivating crowdsourcing participation in smart city projects. Integrating perspectives from self-determination theory and public service motivation, this study investigates the motives driving the use of a mobile crowdsourcing platform prototype known as My Smart Mobile City app (i.e., MSMC) that aims to help smart cities manage public engagement with their residents. Data was collected from 100 participants. Factor analysis was conducted and results indicate that the motives driving the use of MSMC fell into three categories: affective, norm-based and rational. Results and implications of our work are discussed.

## KEYWORDS

crowdsourcing, motivation, smart city, self-determination theory, public service motivation

## INTRODUCTION

The increased use of crowdsourcing platforms to support smart city initiatives has been reported in the literature (e.g., Schuurman Baccarne, De Marez & Mechant, 2012). Fundamentally, crowdsourcing harnesses diverse groups of online users to address specific problems (Doan, Ramakrishnan & Halevy, 2011) and through the process, enables information to be shared efficiently with different stakeholders. Hence, information from such platforms has the potential to provide accurate and continuous updates regarding how a society is evolving, which can be used by city stakeholders (i.e., governments, designers and businesses) to manage and design public spaces. In this regard, crowdsourcing plays important roles to empower city residents as such platforms allow residents to have a say in how their city is designed and managed.

Thus, understanding the needs motivating residents to participate in crowdsourcing is important in smart city projects. However, such motivation studies are still limited. To fill this gap, this study aims to identify the motives behind participation on a mobile crowdsourcing platform in the context of a smart city. First, we draw from the theoretical lens of self-determination theory (SDT) to understand individuals' needs as SDT suggests that individuals tend to be driven by a need to grow and gain fulfilment. Next, we investigate the categories of motives to meet these needs by integrating perspectives from SDT with public service motivation (PSM). PSM links personal action with public interest (Perry & Wise 1990).

## RELATED WORK

### *Crowdsourcing in a Smart City*

Crowdsourcing refers to the use of internet platforms to collect innovative ideas, answers or solutions from the crowd, which is a diverse group of individuals (Howe, 2006; Surowiecki 2004). An example is OpenStreetMap (www.openstreetmap.org) which allows people with basic geographic skills and an affinity for digital mapping to collaboratively contribute to a free map of the world (Haklay, 2010). Additionally, the untapped knowledge of city residents can be utilized via crowdsourcing to support city planning (Brabham, 2012). Furthermore, to motivate participation, some studies highlighted the use of gaming mechanics to encourage quality participation (e.g., Goh, Lee & Low, 2012). Finally, with the proliferation of mobile devices, crowdsourcing apps for the smartphone are used to harness

80th Annual Meeting of the Association for Information Science & Technology, Washington, DC, VA | Oct. 27-Nov. 1, 2017

the power of the mobile crowd to share information or improve a service (e.g., Jones, Layard, Speed & Lorne, 2015).

### *Understanding Motivating Factors*

To understand why residents in a smart city will be motivated to participate in a mobile crowdsourcing app we first draw from the lens of self-determination theory (SDT) to identify the fundamental needs that human beings desire to satisfy and fulfil (Deci & Ryan, 1985). According to SDT, the autonomy need refers to the extent to which an individual perceives a sense of freedom when performing an activity, while the competence need is regarded as the extent to which an individual perceives the feelings of effectiveness while dealing with challenges (Deci & Ryan, 2000). The relatedness need is the extent to which an individual perceives the feelings of being connected to others in an activity (Deci & Ryan, 2000; Goh, Pe-Than & Lee, 2017). These are the fundamental needs that humans beings desire to satisfy and fulfil.

Next, we investigate the motives from the perspective of public service motivation (PSM). PSM provides the explanations on why individuals have a desire to serve the public and link their personal actions with the overall public interest (Knoke & Wright-Isak, 1982; Perry & Wise, 1990). This perspective is relevant because participation on the crowdsourcing platform can be viewed as a form of public engagement. In order to ensure consistent and high-quality participation (Sharma, 2010), the crowd's motivation must align with the long-term objective of the crowdsourcing initiative (Eagle, 2009). Therefore, crowdsourcing platforms need to consider possible motivational mechanisms that will appeal to a large group of users. As such, we explore the different types of motives in fulling the needs identified in SDT. Three categories of motives based on PSM are rational, norm-based, and affective (Knoke & Wright-Isak, 1982). Rational motives involve reasons grounded in individual utility maximisation while norm-based motives are based on feelings of altruism and affective motives are grounded in emotional responses to various social contexts (Knoke & Wright-Isak, 1982).

## INTRODUCING MY SMART MOBILE CITY APP (MSMC)

The crowdsourcing prototype we developed is called My Smart Mobile City (MSMC) (refer to Figure 1). The aim of the application is to create a social network of online users (i.e., residents) who are empowered to share information, voice a concern or seek help in a public domain. The roles that users can participate in MSMC:

- *Contributors*. Contributors (i.e., residents, businesses or city officials) can submit a request for any city-related information. Contributors are the active participants in MSMC.
- *Evaluators*. Evaluators are the participants that evaluate the content in MSMC. Specifically, evaluators review and rate responses and questions provided by the contributors.
- *Consumers*. Consumers are the participants who consume the content in MSMC. They are the passive participants in MSMC who browse and seek content in MSMC.

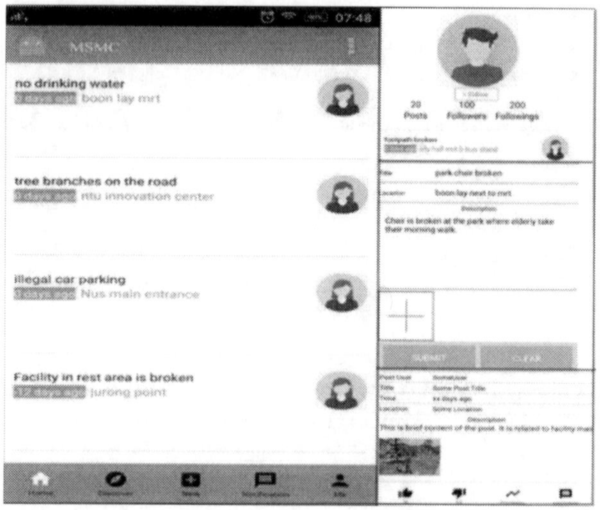


*Clockwise: A) List of user posts (sorted by time), B) Social Networking/Gamification Features, C) Creating a new post and D) Details of a user post*
***Figure1.** Different screenshots of MSMC*

Factor Analysis (n=100)

| | Factors | | |
|---|---|---|---|
| | 1 | 2 | 3 |
| Active Motives ($\lambda$=93625, $\sigma^2$=48.127) | | | |
| What would motivate you to use the application? | | | |
| Because I am concerned about others | .634 | .185 | -.013 |
| Because it is fun. | .676 | .278 | .249 |
| Because it helps me pass time. | .682 | .097 | .210 |
| Because it helps me combat boredom. | .714 | .212 | .271 |
| To keep in touch with people. | .782 | .178 | .330 |
| Because I need to interact with people | .707 | .336 | .340 |
| Going forward, will you use this app? | | | |
| To be connected to other people who have same opinions/interests. | .591 | .435 | .381 |
| Rational Motives ($\lambda$ =1.663, $\sigma^2$ =8.315) | | | |
| What would motivate you to use application? | | | |
| Because it helps me gain status. | .398 | .765 | -.058 |
| Because it helps me fell important. | .392 | .788 | .037 |
| Because it allows me to be part of a community. | .343 | .602 | .394 |
| Going forward, will you use this app? | | | |
| To get social support | .275 | .688 | .291 |
| To share content if I am rewarded financially. | -.194 | .632 | .465 |
| To share content if given recognition (i.e loyalty points) | .121 | .700 | .401 |
| Norm-based Motives ($\lambda$ =1.456, $\sigma^2$ =7.282) | | | |
| What would motivate you to use application? | | | |
| Because it is more convenient than sharing and getting information elsewhere. | .432 | .236 | .621 |
| Because it provides access to up-to-date information related to public spaces | .184 | .146 | .779 |
| Going forward, will you use this app? | | | |
| To share content related to a public space in Singapore | .301 | .265 | .633 |
| To retrieve content related to a public space in Singapore | .244 | .137 | .820 |
| To be connected to government. | .254 | .465 | .523 |

*$\lambda$: eigenvalues, $\sigma^2$: variance*
***Table1.** Factor Analysis Results*

MSMC is developed using Java for Android systems. More details about MSMC may be found in (Lee, Anand, Han, Kong & Goh, 2016).

## METHODOLOGY

### *Participants and Data Collection Procedures*

A total of 100 participants (65 males and 35 females) with an average age of 25.1 were recruited in a large university in Singapore to participate in the study. More than half of the participants were aged between 21 to 29 years old. Around 29.3% of the participants surveyed indicated they obtained information regarding public spaces in Singapore mainly from their personal social networks.

Each participant attended a 10-minute briefing and a short practice session with a member of the research team. Once the participants familiarized themselves with the app, four scenarios were presented to them. The participants were asked to create, browse and rate content for all the scenarios. Upon completion of the given tasks, an online questionnaire (described next) was administered. Participants were given an incentive of S$5 for their effort.

### *Measures*

The questions assessing the motivations for participation on MSMC were drawn from prior studies on SDT as well as prior research on motivations (e.g., Brabham, 2012; Lee et al., 2010; Pe-Than et al., 2016). The questions were adapted and modified for use in this study. A total of 20 questions were developed to assess the different motives categories and they were measured using a 5-point Likert scale with a range of 1 (Strongly disagree) to 5 (Strongly agree).

## ANALYSES AND RESULTS

The entire set of 20 motivational items was analyzed by a principal component factor analysis using Varimax rotation. Two items were dropped due to high cross factor loadings and the remaining 18 items fell into three factors. A minimum loading of 0.4 was chosen here as cutoff criteria (Comrey, 1973; Nunnally, 1978). The items belonging to each factor are summarized in Table 1. Three factors emerged with eigenvalues greater than 1.00 explaining a total of 63.72 percent of the variance. We also assessed the reliability of the factors by calculating the Cronbach's alpha values for each factor. The Cronbach's alpha values for the three factors were in the range of 0.85 to 0.89, exhibiting acceptable values.

The results from our factor analysis can be explained using the three categories of motives related to PSM (i.e., affective, rational, and norm-based (Knoke & Wright-Isak, 1982). These motives are associated with the underlying needs in SDT, which are autonomy, competence, and relatedness (Gagné, 2009). Our results indicate that the first factor comprised of having fun, concern for others, and the need to keep connected or interact with others. This is the most important factor as it accounts for more than 48 percent of the variance and the Cronbach $\alpha$ is 0.89. We labelled the first factor as "affective motives" which reflects the desire to identify with a group and form affective bonds with them. The affective motives are associated with the relatedness need underlying the SDT framework.

Our second factor items such as to gain status or feel important, to get social support or financial rewards. As such, we labelled it as "rational motives". Specifically, rational motives are based on the pursuit of self-interest and pertain to the needs to gain acceptance as well as be effective and competent. Rational motives are related to meeting needs of autonomy and competence needs in SDT. The second factor accounts for more than 8 percent of the variance and the Cronbach $\alpha$ is 0.87.

The third factor included sharing and retrieving city-related content and linking up with the different government agencies. We labelled the third factor as "norm-based motives". The third factor accounts for more than 7 percent of the variance and the Cronbach $\alpha$ is 0.85. Norm-based motives explain the motives to conform to social norms. Here, MSMC creates the opportunity to contribute to social norms through a collaborative effort. Strong autonomy needs to operate within MSMC, as defined by SDT, are likely to play important roles in the development of norm-based motives.

## DISCUSSION AND CONCLUSION

Our results reveal three primary motive categories – affective, rational and norm-based. A significant finding is uncovering the most important motivational category –affective motives (i.e., show concern for others and to interact with others). This indicates that crowdsourcing platforms should include design features (e.g., chatting, social networking) that encourage social connection and promote a sense of community among city residents. In addition, we found that norm-based motives are related to content contributing and seeking behaviours in MSMC to meet the everyday information needs of the residents. The third category of motives is rational and such motives are present in individuals who believe that their personal interests coincide with those of the larger community (Mann, 2006). Here, participants were of the viewpoint that using apps like MSMC would either enhance their status in the community or helped to gain financial rewards in the form of accumulated credits.

This study has important contributions. In terms of practical contributions, our study uncovers the motives behind crowdsourcing as a form of public engagement in a smart city. The findings from this research could aid governments and city officials in developing their crowdsourcing platforms to improve quality and effectiveness of engaging with citizens and residents. From a research standpoint, this study confirms the relevance of integrating SDT and Knoke and Wright-Isak's (1982) motivational categories on PSM to shed light on users' participation on a mobile crowdsourcing platform to support public engagement in a smart city. Specifically, future work should consider delving into public service motivation to understand needs of the public and people when it comes to smart city projects.

There are some limitations in our work. First, the findings were obtained from one application. Thus, caution must be taken when interpreting our results. Second, our participants were mostly recruited in the university and the majority of our participants were between 21 to 29 years old. We acknowledge this reduce the generalizability of the findings. Replication of this study with participants from more diverse age groups would be beneficial to validate the present findings. Despite these shortcomings, the present study contributes to a better understanding of the use of a mobile crowdsourcing app in a smart city context.


## ACKNOWLEDGMENTS

This work was supported by NTU MOE/Tier 1 grant RG149/15. The authors would like to thank Vishwaraj Anand, Feng Han, Xiaoyu Kong and Jody Wong for providing research assistance.


## REFERENCES


Brabham, D. C. (2012). Motivations for participation in a crowdsourcing application to improve public engagement in transit planning. *Journal of Applied Communication Research, 40*(3), 307-328. doi:10.1080/00909882.2012.693940

Comrey, A. L. (1973). *A first course in factor analysis*. New York, NY: Academic Press.

Deci, E. L. & Ryan, R. M. (1985). *Intrinsic motivation and self-determination in human behavior*. New York and London: Plenum.

Deci, E. L. & Ryan, R. M. (2000). The "what" and "why" of goal pursuits: Human needs and the self-determination of behavior. *Psychological Inquiry, 11*(4), 227-268. doi:10.1207/S15327965PLI1104_01

Doan, A., Ramakrishnan, R. & Halevy, A. Y. (2011). Crowdsourcing systems on the world-wide web. *Commun. ACM, 54*(4), 86-96. doi:10.1145/1924421.1924442

Eagle, N. (2009). Mobile crowdsourcing. In N. Aykin (Ed.), Internationalization, design and global development: Third international conference, IDGD 2009, held as part of HCI international 2009, San Diego, CA, USA, July 19-24, 2009, proceedings (pp. 447-456). Berlin, Heidelberg: Springer Berlin Heidelberg.

Gagné, M. (2009). A model of knowledge-sharing motivation. *Human Resource Management, 48*(4), 571-589. doi:10.1002/hrm.20298

Goh, D.H., Lee, C.S., & Low, G.H. (2012). I played games as there was nothing else to do: Understanding motivations for using mobile content sharing games. *Online Inform Review*. 36(6), 784-806.

Goh, D. H.-L., Pe-Than, E. P. P. & Lee, C. S. (2017). Perceptions of virtual reward systems in crowdsourcing games. *Computers in Human Behavior, 70*, 365-374. doi:http://doi.org/10.1016/j.chb.2017.01.006

Haklay, M. (2010). How good is volunteered geographical information? A comparative study of OpenStreetMap and ordnance survey datasets. *Environment and Planning B: Planning and Design, 37*(4), 682-703. doi:10.1068/b35097

Howe, J. (2006). The rise of crowdsourcing. Retrieved from https://www.wired.com/2006/06/crowds/

Jones, P., Layard, A., Speed, C. & Lorne, C. (2015). MapLocal: Use of smartphones for crowdsourced planning. *Planning Practice & Research, 30*(3), 322-336. doi:10.1080/02697459.2015.1052940

Knoke, D. & Wright-Isak, C. (1982). Individual motives and organizational incentive systems. *Research in the Sociology of Organizations, 1*(2), 209-254.

Lee, C. S., Anand, V., Han, F., Kong, X. & Goh, D. H.-L. (2016). Investigating the use of a mobile crowdsourcing application for public engagement in a smart city. In A. Morishima, A. Rauber, & C. L. Liew (Eds.), *Digital libraries: Knowledge, information, and data in an open access society: 18th international conference on Asia-Pacific digital libraries, ICADL 2016, Tsukuba, Japan, December 7-9, 2016, proceedings* (pp. 98-103). Cham: Springer International Publishing.

Lee, C. S., Goh, D. H.-L., Chua, A. Y. K. & Ang, R. P. (2010). Indagator: Investigating perceived gratifications of an application that blends mobile content sharing with gameplay. *Journal of the American Society for Information Science and Technology, 61*(6), 1244-1257. doi:10.1002/asi.21305

Mann, G. A. (2006). A motive to serve: Public service motivation in human resource management and the role of PSM in the nonprofit sector. *Public Personnel Management, 35*(1).

Nunnally, J. C. (1978). *Psychometric theory (2nd ed.)*. McGraw-Hill: New York, NY.

Perry, J. L. & Wise, L.R. (1990). The motivational bases of public service. *Public Administration Review 50*(3), 367-373. doi: 10.2307/976618.

Pe-Than, E. P. P., Goh, D. H.-L. & Lee, C. S. (2016). Personality, motivations, and information quality: A comparative study across games for human computation. *Proceedings of the Association for Information Science and Technology, 53*(1), 1-10. doi:10.1002/pra2.2016.14505301049.

Schuurman, D., Baccarne, B., De Marez, L. & Mechant, P. (2012). Smart ideas for smart cities: Investigating crowdsourcing for generating and selecting ideas for ICT innovation in a city context. *Journal of Theoretical and Applied Electronic Commerce Research, 7*(3), 49-62.

Sharma, A. (2010). Crowdsourcing critical success factor model: Strategies to harness the collective intelligence of the crowd. *London School of Economics (LSE), London*.

Surowiecki , J. (2004). The wisdom of crowds: Why the many are smarter than the few and how collective wisdom shapes business, economies, societies and nations: Doubleday: New York.

# Document Representation and Clustering Models for Bilingual Documents Clustering

**Shutian Ma**
*Department of Information Management, Nanjing University of Science and Technology, China.*
*mashutian0608@hotmail.com*

**Chengzhi Zhang**[†]
*Department of Information Management, Nanjing University of Science and Technology, China*
*zhangcz@njust.edu.cn*

## ABSTRACT

**Currently, the internet has created many documents in languages other than English. People face challenges when seeking and using information; for example, non-native English-speaking students tend to have problems when utilizing libraries in North American universities. To help people efficiently organize information, bilingual documents clustering has advantages for practical utilization, it can divide documents into groups with the same topic and there is no need for a training dataset. Document representation and clustering models are two important parts in clustering. This paper compares four popular representation methods, vector space model (VSM), latent semantic indexing (LSI), latent Dirichlet allocation (LDA) and doc2vec (D2V), together with four different types of clustering algorithms, K-means++, BIRCH, DBSCAN and affinity propagation (AP) to identify appropriate combinations for bilingual documents clustering. Parallel corpus and comparable corpus are all used for the bilingual datasets. Experimental results show that, clustering performance varies when combining different representation methods with clustering algorithms. It's important to make good choice of models for better documents organization.**

## KEYWORDS

bilingual documents clustering, document representation, clustering algorithm, text mining, digital library

## INTRODUCTION

Currently, lots of people find and share information in two or even more languages. In order to cater to the needs of users, digital libraries will provide multilingual information openly. However, problems often come out when using such portals. Some studies report on challenges that non-native English-speaking students face in North American universities. English proficiency is one of the main factors that affect their use of the library and information (Sin, 2015). To efficiently organize multilingual information, techniques are proposed, like multilingual documents clustering, thesauri automatic construction, cross-lingual information retrieval and so on. Among them, multilingual documents clustering aims to cluster documents in different languages into groups under the same sub-topic. Compared with classification, another typical method for documents management, clustering doesn't need annotated corpus and is more feasible to apply in practical scenarios.

There are two main parts in documents clustering: document representation methods and clustering algorithms. Efforts can be made in these two steps to improve performance. We have compared four popular representation methods for bilingual documents clustering to find the best one (Ma et al., 2016). Although conclusions are made, there are two downsides: firstly, only one clustering algorithm was applied; if the algorithm changes, performance might change as well. Secondly, data size of previous comparable corpus is too small, and its true labels are unknown which might lead to inaccurate evaluation. In this paper, to make a more standard comparison, four different types of clustering algorithms and a larger comparable corpus with labels are used.

## RELATED WORK

Documents clustering was initially focused on the strategies to group unstructured text data. Due to increased amount of multilingual information, new challenge for clustering is to overcome language diversity. Current approaches can be divided into two broad categories: first one is transforming documents from source language into target language with help of machine translation or external semantic resources; second one is transforming documents into a language-independent representation mode.

Above all, most existing methods can't effectively build semantic correspondence across multilingual documents via language-independent features, while machine translation are more often used. Therefore, how to choose document representation model is a fundamental problem to solve. The most widely used one is vector space model (VSM), which can project texts into vector space (Salton et al., 1975). However, semantic relations are neglected in VSM due to independence between dimensions, researchers are putting forward more improved methods. Latent semantic indexing (LSI) uses matrix algebra technique to represent documents with fewer dimensions and can model sematic relations between words, like synonymy (Papadimitriou et al., 1998). In 2003, latent Dirichlet allocation (LDA) was proposed (Blei et al., 2003) which can recognize latent topics of documents and use topic probability distribution to represent texts. So far, deep learning models have also been applied in data representations. Le and Mikolov (2014) built doc2vec to train distributed vector representation of texts in variable-length.

---

80th Annual Meeting of the Association for Information Science & Technology, Washington, DC, VA | Oct. 27-Nov. 1, 2017



[†]Corresponding Author

Except representation models, clustering algorithm is also a key factor. Present algorithms can be broadly classified into: partitioning clustering, hierarchical clustering, density-based, grid-based, model-based clustering algorithms and so on. Partitioning clustering needs to set up cluster numbers ahead and get the best results when error value of target function is at the minimum, and common algorithms are K-means, K-means++ (Arthur & Vassilvitskii, 2007), K-medoids, etc. Hierarchical algorithms build nested clusters by merging or splitting them successively until results satisfy evaluation function and the predefined cluster number, such as BIRCH (Zhang et al., 1996), Rock, Chameleon, etc. Density-based methods explore data space at a high-level of granularity and post-process them to put together dense regions into an arbitrary shape, typical one is DBSCAN (Ester et al., 1996). In 2007, Frey and Dueck (2007) proposed a noted algorithm called affinity propagation (AP) which works based on similarity between pairs of all data points.

Though document representation and clustering models have been explored for many years, there has been very little work in comprehensive comparisons between them. In this paper, we want to find out the suitable combinations of representation and clustering models for bilingual documents clustering.

## METHODOLOGY

Framework of bilingual documents clustering is divided into three steps which are shown in Figure 1 and 2 respectively.

In this experiment, documents in source languages are all translated into monolingual one which are in target language. In Figure 1, $\{T_1, T_2, \cdots, T_i, .., T_n\}$ and $\{S_1, S_2, \cdots, S_i, \dots, S_n\}$ represent documents sets which are translations to each other in target language $T$ and source language $S$, $n$ is the number of documents. After machine translation, document $S_i$ is converted to document $T_i'$, $\{T_1', T_2', \cdots, T_i', \dots, T_n'\}$ represents documents set in language $T$. Then, original and translated corpus are combined. For parallel corpus, we combine document $T_i$ and translated document $T_i'$ into one document, then we obtain $T_iT_i'$. The same combinations are done for the other pairs of original and translated documents, new corpus is organized like $\{T_1T_1', T_2T_2', \cdots, T_iT_i', \dots, T_nT_n'\}$. This new documents set is then used for clustering. For comparable corpus, we combine the original $\{T_1, T_2, \cdots, T_i, \cdots, T_a\}$ and translated $\{T_1', T_2', \cdots, T_j', \dots, T_b'\}$ into a new set. It's organized like$\{T_1, T_2, \cdots, T_i, \cdots, T_a, T_1', T_2', \cdots,, T_j', \dots, T_b'\}$, which is also the input for clustering.

After transformation from original corpus to new combined corpus, the remaining steps of these two frameworks are all the same. Corpus is represented by four representation methods and clustered via four clustering algorithms. When representing documents, VSM is tested at: 500, 1000,···, 29500, 30000 dimensions, with 500 as interval, and the other models are all tested at: 10, 20, ···, 190, 200 dimensions, with 10 as interval. Parameters in clustering are set differently to find the best performance of each algorithm.

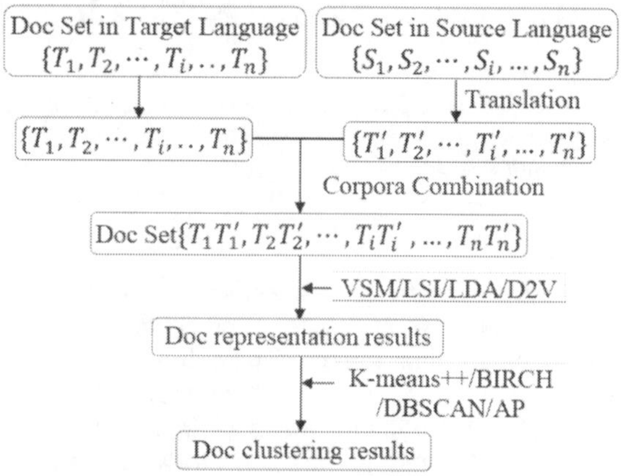


***Figure 1.*** *Clustering framework of parallel corpus*

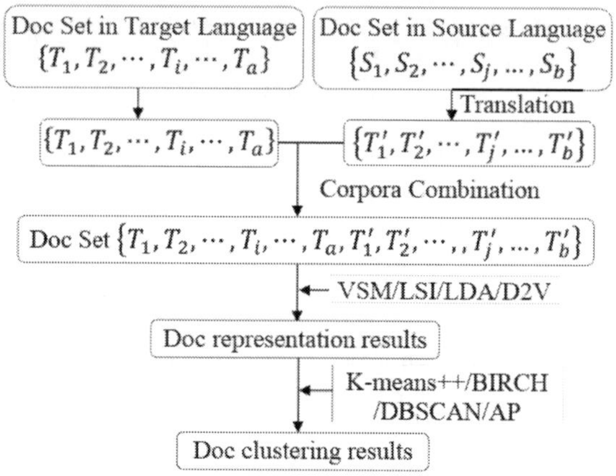


***Figure 2.*** *Clustering framework of comparable corpus*

## EXPERIMENT AND RESULTS ANALYSIS

### *Experimental Dataset*

Generally, there are two typical kinds of cross-language resources, parallel corpus and comparable corpus. Parallel corpus contains documents in two languages which are translations to each other. Comparable corpus contains documents in two languages but covering the same or similar topic. We used these two corpora in this experiment.

#### Parallel corpus

We collected parallel corpus from a technology blog called Engadget, downloading 4,904 pairs of blogs (between 2006 and 2013) from Chinese[1] and English[2] versions of website. Here, we make use of the title, full text of blog and category of each blog and there are 20 categories in all.

#### Comparable corpus

Comparable corpus is chosen from CLTC (Xia et al., 2012) which is a newly developed Chinese-English cross-lingual

[1] Available at http://cn.engadget.com/
[2] Available at http://www.engadget.com/

topic corpus, covering 150 topics of Chinese and English articles. We extracted 25 topics of 9, 394 documents in English and 9, 435 documents in Chinese.

### *Evaluation Metrics*

V-measure is the harmonic mean between homogeneity and completeness which are two important aspects of clustering. Rosenberg and Hirschberg (2007) defined these two indexes for cluster assignment. A higher V-measure score means better clustering results. Formulation is shown as follows:

$$V = 2 \times \frac{(homogeneity \times Completeness)}{(homogeneity + Completeness)}$$

### *Experimental Results Analysis*

In this section, we compare performances based on V-measure. Figure 3 and 4 illustrate clustering results when using K-means++, BIRCH, DBSCAN and AP. Texts are represented by LSI (blue star), LDA (red triangle) and D2V (green circle). VSM method is using disparate words for representations, therefore its dimension setting is different with the other methods. Figure 5 illustrates clustering results when using VSM. Algorithms are K-means++ (yellow), DBSCAN (red), BIRCH (green) and AP (black).

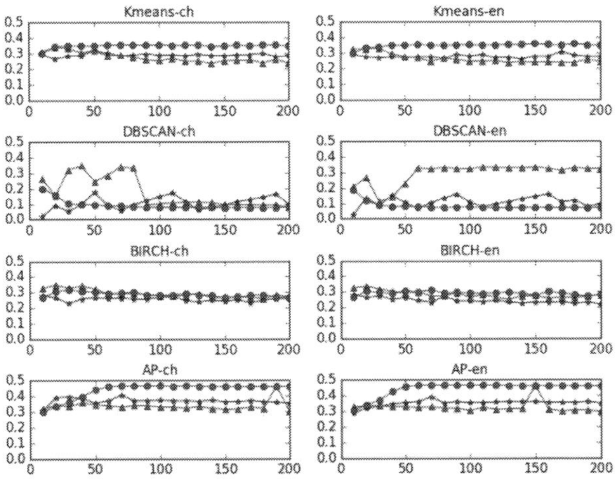


*Note: ch is combined Chinese corpus, en is combined English corpus.*
***Figure 3**. V-measure of parallel corpus clustering*

From tendencies of lines, we can find that when using different algorithms, representation methods will perform differently when increasing dimension. When clustering parallel corpus, for VSM, there are large differences in V-measure of K-means++, BIRCH, DBSCAN and AP. Its combination with AP outperforms than others, and result in the best clustering result on English corpus. V-measure values of LSI have fluctuations and values of D2V tend to have a key turning point and then lead to smooth. Referring to LDA, it shows unexceptionable performance at some dimensions, although has decrease trend in some cases. Taking the best clustering result into consideration, when doing parallel corpus clustering, LDA sets up a stable performance in most tasks. Besides, D2V also function well except using the DBSCAN algorithm. Differences between clustering algorithms are obvious to find according to their performance. Affinity propagation behaves best in this task with combinations of all representation methods while DBSCAN performs the worst.

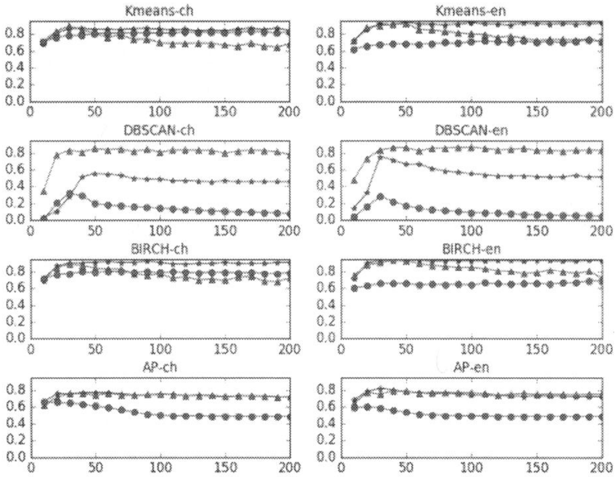


*Note: ch is combined Chinese corpus, en is combined English corpus.*
***Figure 4**. V-measure of comparable corpus clustering*

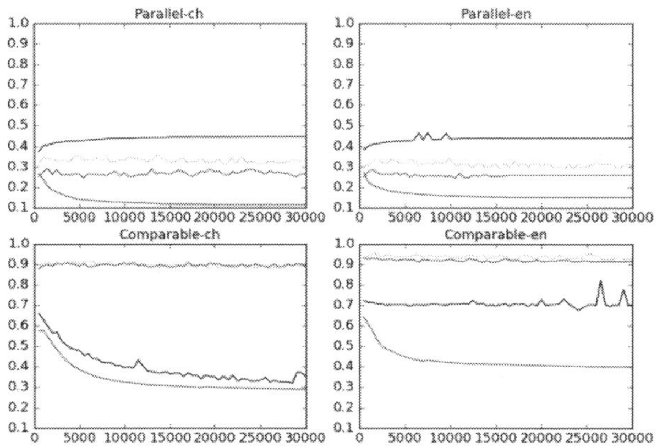


*Note: ch is combined Chinese corpus, en is combined English corpus.*
***Figure 5**. V-measure of corpus represented by VSM*

When clustering comparable corpus, results are little different from parallel one. For VSM, it can achieve best performance when combining with K-means++ and BIRCH. V-measure values of LSI and LDA all have a key turning point which will then lead to smooth. And the key points are often the highest value of V-measure. Referring to D2V, it shows unexceptionable bad performance. Taking the best clustering result into consideration, LDA still performs more stable. Referring to clustering algorithms, K-means++ and BIRCH behave better in this task while DBSCAN still performs the worst.

## DISCUSSION

Several conclusions can be made according to experimental results. For each method, when clustering parallel corpus, classical VSM shows better performance than LSI. Previous study (Xu et al., 2015) has also found that measurement method of terms based VSM is better than LSI. When clustering comparable corpus, VSM performs better than LDA and D2V, but it will cost a lot of time for clustering too. Performance of LSI is different between parallel corpus and comparable corpus, therefore it will be affected by datasets, which is the same conclusion with previous work (Ma et al., 2016). We also found that when topic number is proper, LDA will have terrific performance. D2V tends to behave better for parallel corpus. For each clustering algorithm, DBSCAN method is not proper for such a task, while AP and K-means++ will be better options. Rangrej et al. (2011) found that AP clusters better than K-means in short text data. When clustering long texts in this experiment, AP outperforms K-means++ as well. Besides, when labels are unknown, it will be more suitable to use AP algorithms, since it does not have to choose initial centers.

Furthermore, parameter settings will affect clustering quality. There are two sets of parameters here, first is representation dimensions. Findings show that when dimension is big enough, performance will not get improved and may even get worse. So, increasing dimensions will not certainly bring improvement. This can explain that why many studies are attempting to investigate proper parameters in representation models (Kiela & Clark, 2014). The second is parameters in algorithms. Here, K-means++ and BIRCH perform much better than AP and DBSCAN, one of the reasons might be the known cluster number settings. And quality of labels will also affect measurements. Additionally, languages of each corpus don't distinguish models from each other.

## CONCLUSION

In this paper, document representation and clustering models are compared in bilingual corpora clustering. We found that representation methods should be chosen based on corpus characteristics to find proper dimension numbers. Besides, clustering algorithm should also be combined carefully to have better performance. Since our study is a preliminary investigation, more work is needed. For example, evaluation metrics and clustering strategies on translating steps are also important in such tasks.

## ACKNOWLEDGMENTS

This work is supported by Major Projects of National Social Science Fund (No. 16ZAD224), Fujian Provincial Key Laboratory of Information Processing and Intelligent Control (Minjiang University) (No. MJUKF201704) and Qing Lan Project.

## REFERENCES

Arthur, D., & Vassilvitskii, S. (2007). K-means++: The advantages of careful seeding. *Proceedings of the Proceedings of the eighteenth annual ACM-SIAM symposium on discrete algorithms* (pp. 1027-1035).

Blei, D. M., Ng, A. Y., & Jordan, M. I. (2003). Latent Dirichlet allocation. *The Journal of Machine Learning Research, 3*, 993-1022.

Ester, M., Kriegel, H.-P., Sander, J., & Xu, X. (1996). A density-based algorithm for discovering clusters in large spatial databases with noise. *Proceedings of the Kdd* (pp. 226-231).

Frey, B. J., & Dueck, D. (2007). Clustering by passing messages between data points. *Science, 315*(5814), 972-976.

Kiela, D., & Clark, S. (2014). A systematic study of semantic vector space model parameters. *Proceedings of the 2nd workshop on continuous vector space models and their compositionality (CVSC) at EACL* (pp. 21-30).

Le, Q. V., & Mikolov, T. (2014). Distributed representations of sentences and documents. *arXiv preprint arXiv:1405.4053*.

Ma, S., Zhang, C., & He, D. (2016). Document representation methods for clustering bilingual documents. *Proceedings of the Association for Information Science and Technology, 53*(1), 1-10.

Papadimitriou, C. H., Tamaki, H., Raghavan, P., & Vempala, S. (1998). Latent semantic indexing: A probabilistic analysis. *Proceedings of the 7th ACM SIGACT-SIGMOD-SIGART symposium on principles of database systems* (pp. 159-168).

Rangrej, A., Kulkarni, S., & Tendulkar, A. V. (2011). Comparative study of clustering techniques for short text documents. *Proceedings of the 20th international conference companion on world wide web* (pp. 111-112).

Rosenberg, A., & Hirschberg, J. (2007). V-measure: A conditional entropy-based external cluster evaluation measure. *Proceedings of the EMNLP-CoNLL* (pp. 410-420).

Salton, G., Wong, A., & Yang, C.-S. (1975). A vector space model for automatic indexing. *Communications of the ACM, 18*(11), 613-620.

Sin, S.-C. J. (2015). Demographic differences in international students' information source uses and everyday information seeking challenges. *The Journal of Academic Librarianship, 41*(4), 466-474.

Xia, Y., Tang, G., Jin, P., & Yang, X. (2012). CLTC: A Chinese-English cross-lingual topic corpus. *Proceedings of the LREC* (pp. 532-537).

Xu, H., Zeng, W., Gui, J., Qu, P., Zhu, X., & Wang, L. (2015, 15-17 Aug. 2015). Exploring similarity between academic paper and patent based on latent semantic analysis and vector space model. *Proceedings of the 2015 12th International conference on fuzzy systems and knowledge discovery (FSKD)* (pp. 801-805).

Zhang, T., Ramakrishnan, R., & Livny, M. (1996). BIRCH: An efficient data clustering method for very large databases. *Proceedings of the ACM SIGMOD Record* (pp. 103-114).

# Electronic Commerce and Consumption: Semiotic Scenario and Information Architecture in Online Stores

**Maria Aparecida Moura**
*Information Science School, UFMG, Brazil.*
*mamoura@ufmg.br*

**Cássia Adriana Gomes**
*Information Science School, UFMG, Brazil.*
*cassiaglayds@gmail.com*

## ABSTRACT

**This work discusses changes in consumption patterns with the spread of electronic commerce, which started to demand new informational competences in commercial relations. We highlight the concepts of semiotic scenario and information architecture, analyzing the implications of such concepts in the structure of websites dedicated to electronic commerce. In addition, we describe a system for informational organization of the Brazilian e-stores, analyzing the interactions between the e-customer with the website's information architecture, along with the subjacent semiotic scenario to the business model.**

## KEYWORDS

electronic commerce, electronic consumption, information architecture, semiotic scenario

## INTRODUCTION

The consumption patterns for Brazilian citizens have transformed visibly in the last few years, with increased sophistication in taste and the incorporation of new criteria for finalizing purchases.

Electronic consumption and emergent sociability have brought a process of decision-making oriented by testimonials from other customers in websites and virtual interaction channels. Thus, the strategies and the stimuli for registering a subject's opinion have widened, along with his/her strategies for qualifying a product or service.

Electronic commerce may be considered as all transactions between an organization and a third party, electronically mediated. It is not restricted to the real purchase and dealing of products, but it also includes all activities occurring before the sale and after it (Chaffey, 2006).

The advent of collaborative web made it possible to reduce the several intermediary stages in access to information and consumption in digital environments. In such environments, we can verify the superposition of social actors when effectively creating multiple roles, carried out through autonomous informational identities, enabled by the intensification of informational flows and the diminishing reduction of contemporaneous sociability when it comes to electronic interfaces.

80th Annual Meeting of the Association for Information Science & Technology, Washington, DC, VA | Oct. 27-Nov. 1, 2017



New alignments enabled by these digital environments have created the perfect scenario to experience the identity based on the information achieved via a description provided by the social subject in context of interaction or by tracing the characteristics that evidence informational trajectories performed by him/her in cyberspace. Digital platforms and their tools of benefit made it possible to optimize new business models, including sociability and business in the same context.

The juxtaposition provoked by the articulation of informational, technical, technological and market elements eventually engenders a civilization of desire performed through proximity among customers, products and services. In that case, when watching a catwalk show, for instance, the subject may go online and purchase the items being exhibited or just-in-time recommend the product for his/her network of online friends. It is possible, yet, to compare editions, prices, to purchase and download the book mentioned by a lecturer in a conference, through mobile applications available in mobile phones. We can note, then, that in contemporaneity, the cultural experience of production, circulation and usage of information and products in strongly affected by the mobility and latency of such instantaneously available devices, subject to modelling as infotainment products, or *net-a-porter* consumption ones.

Considering such changes in sociocultural patterns for national consumption, we sought, in this study, to analyze from the semiotic and informational perspective the informational architecture in Brazilian websites dedicated to electronic commerce of goods and services. The implementation of electronic commerce, its availability as a value service added to networking and georeferenced monitoring of user profiles online has provided several alterations in our ways of consuming in the current era. One of those main changes is, without a doubt, the transformation of massive consumption in niche consumption. In that modality of service, though the distribution of products occurs in networks, the current appeal lies towards the individualization of experience for consumption.

Along those lines, new forms of commercial product and services distribution were formed from the following adjoining forces: democratization of production tools and the distribution and approximation between offer and demand. That phenomenon was named *long tail*,

> ...which is nothing more than infinite choice. Abundant and cheap distribution means wide, accessible and unlimited choice – which, on its own end, means that the public tends to spread as diversely as its range of choices. Considering the

perspective of dominating media and entertainment industry, this situation is similar to a battle between the dominant mass communication media and the Internet. However, the problem is that, when people shift their attention towards online vehicles, they do not just migrate from one to the other, but they also spread among innumerable offers. Infinite choice equals maximum fragmentation (Anderson, 2006, p. 179).

A fundamental dimension for niche consumption to work is the media, which, in this context, works mapping niches, broadcasting benefits of segmentation and support for personalization of consumption experience.

## ELECTRONIC CONSUMPTION, INFORMATION ARCHITECTURE AND SEMIOTIC SCENARIO

Information architecture is the art and science of organizing information with the purpose of making it manageable and possible to locate, in addition to being useful to their purposes since the level of infrastructure to the user interface (Bailey, 2002; Banerjee and Downey, 2010).

Information architecture involves data architecture, managing metadata and knowledge. Making information architecture effective as a product or guidance service is oriented around the following stages: preparation and organization of information through structuring and composing a repository, enriching content; access to information via research and recovery of information and its possibilities of recovery. These stages aim at making that information available and possible to localize and navigate.

Banerjee and Downey (2010) propose a checklist of the four main areas to be considered on the structuring of an architecture of informational product or service. They are organization and access to information, governance and usage experience.

When organizing information, it is necessary to take into account data modelling, composition strategies and metadata structuring, along with the classification of information through controlled vocabulary, thesaurus, taxonomies or incorporating terms or tags in usage by service users.

In the stage concerning access to information, it is necessary to think search technology as available or desirable to model the scope of research (web, mobile applications or desktop structures), types of researches to be enabled, navigation design, measures for evaluating usage and security models for access to information. Governance is related to the maintenance and monitoring of the constant changes operated within information architecture. Finally, user experience deals with user research and the usage feasibility of the elements used within information architecture in which one must comprehend the categories of users or personas, tasks to be executed, understanding definitions of information flows and wireframes, along with usage tests and the evaluation of the general architectural structure from the user perspective.

In the specific case of electronic commerce, thought must reach beyond information architecture, for a perspective of meaning production to be implemented so the customer may perceive the informational structure as a product display of desirable services from the consumption's point of view. In this perspective, electronic stores seek to provide a consumption experience through electronic semiotic scenarios, in which signification processes are carried out.

The semiotics is a philosophical discipline that intends to explain and interpret the knowledge. For this, the semiotics analyzes the facts of a perspective simultaneously phenomenological and ontological. Like this, a narrowing in the relationships between semiotics and science of the information became, in the last years, perceptible and desirable. The semiotics has for objective the exam of the manners of constitution of all of the possible languages, in other words, it has for objective the exam of the manners of constitution of whole and any process like a phenomenon of meaning production and of sense.

According to Stockinger (1999) the semiotic description of a document or documentary corpus should consider the following elements: the institutional context, the interest or need to produce or interpret to respond to a lack or fulfill a purpose, the arbitration of the production and interpretation process, the ability to produce or interpret a document, the performance adopted in a concrete situation to produce, to interpret and use of a document.

In this work, the websites to the online stores were analyzed from a semiotic perspective. The commercial environment was analyzed as semiotic scenario.

The semiotic scenario is the representation of a generic structure or model, controlled for specification or modelling of an information product that shapes concrete versions or realizations. It aims at guaranteeing semiotic recognition and legitimation of documents in space and time (typologies + conceptual specification). The semiotic scenario is subjacent to traditional electronic documents, in products of dynamic information. They possess a structural composition that includes representations and the semiotic project, along with a functional composition that presupposes demonstration of a reading pact and the formalization of the semiotic project (Stockinger, 1999).

Considering these new agencies, the market of goods and services models, through information architecture, semiotic scenarios adequate to signification processes and the consumption of goods and services of interaction with technological devices.

In the face of this alteration in contemporary forms of carrying out consumption and the picture of consumption in Brazil, we sought, in this study, to understand the sociocultural elements that compose these new patterns of consumption. The study aimed at understanding the movement of ordinary subjects and the new agencies in products, goods and services consumption patterns via information architecture in electronic stores.

## ANALYSIS OF BRAZILIAN WEBSITES OF ELECTRONIC COMMERCE

This study aimed at characterizing electronic commerce and describing the tools used by companies in their virtual establishments in Brazil. In that process, we aimed at identifying and analyzing transformations that took place in conception and consumption patterns, as well as analyzing, from the informational and semiotic perspectives, information architecture of these websites dedicated to the electronic commerce of goods and services.

In the stage of characterization of information architecture and project analysis in these websites dedicated to the Brazilian electronic commerce, a form was elaborated to describe the websites, aiming at characterizing and supporting the information architecture analysis and the implemented semiotic project. In order to do so, the instrument for information collection covered the following topics: identification data; commercial characterization; information architecture; legal aspects and safety of purchase; usability; communicational approach, interface and sociability.

In the next phase, 23 modalities of commercial transactions performed electronically in the country were selected, among which online food stores were contemplated, along with airlines, department stores, telephone and banking services, etc. For each modality, three websites of national stores were analyzed, totalling 69 websites.

## FINDINGS AND DISCUSSION

The Brazilian electronic commerce is currently undergoing a period of exponential growth and regulation in the field, thus activating sensibly the semiotic scenario and information architecture of the websites dedicated to that commercial modality.

In our analysis, it was possible to identify a model of information architecture present in every website. In that sense, the elements related to organization, access, governance and information quality are reflected in website interfaces to ensure customers the seriousness and pertinence of commercial transactions carried out.

Concerning the semiotic scenario, it was possible to identify that the symbolic aspects (icon, index and symbol) are structured in website interface based on the commercialized product or service. We noticed a strong movement of signification devices aiming at providing the customer a synesthetic experience of purchase really close to that in current contexts.

In the model below, it is possible to identify the articulation between the semiotic scenario and information architecture in favor of everywhere consumption.

The model highlights the possibility that the client may personalize the interface and act as a salesperson/owner of a virtual store. In that sense, the client's social network is mobilized around the enterprise and he/she receives commission on businesses carried out in the personalized store.

Concerning information organization, several of the analyzed electronic commerce websites are structured via catalogues (25%) and segmentation of products (22%), both elements present in physical stores. The so-called "tag cloud" is noted as a new development by electronic stores.

As a way of customer support, we highlight the following options: system of search by product and FAQs. We noticed that in some websites the most frequent questions are related to the utilization of the product or service offered.

Concerning the security and purchase management, we verified that all the analyzed websites worked on transmitting to the customer the idea of a safe environment of information exchange, one of the main elements that should compose information architecture. The safety may be transmitted to the customer via information architecture: through website consistency, digital certificates, enabling clear information with easy access to customer support in the solution of doubts and problems.

Another aspect covered by our study refers to the forms of communication with the customer. Research has revealed a strong bond of electronic commerce websites with social networks (32%), through which they communicate with customers, broadcast their brand and incentive shopping. That can be justified by the fact that through social networks companies may monitor services, user perception of their product's quality, better understanding clients' needs, opinions and preferences.

Sharing experiences may influence shopping decisions and, consequently, a company's value. Shopping experience testimonials was already part of customer's practices before stores migrated to the online environment; however, the Internet certainly multiplied this sharing.

With the advent of social networks, customers gained a more active role as market intermediates. As customers engage in conversation with other customers and other companies, they may significantly influence a company's value, especially because their opinions may affect other customers and provide different insights for the company in matters of development and improvement of commercialized products (Souza, 2012).

Regarding information organization in the analyzed websites, we can highlight that data collection aimed at researching is very complex, due to the disposition of interface information and the taxonomy used by electronic stores, more oriented towards final customers in situation of actually purchasing items.

## CONCLUSION

The analysis of semiotic scenario and information architecture, present in those websites dedicated to electronic commerce in Brazil, enabled us to understand informational, technological, economic and legal advancements in that commercial modality in the country.

Exaggerating customer experience personalization and the superposition of fruition-dedicated environments along with communication and consumption in the same device have evidenced the need for interdisciplinary studies, both for establishing this business model and for understanding cultural and ethical unfolding results.

In cultural terms, the change in consumption patterns in the country is already perceptible, with the expansion of electronic consumption leading customers to easily access international products, enabling a wider taste range, an amplification of aesthetic sense and an alteration of technological demands.

The interoperation between mass communication media and mobile technologies also altered synchronic rituals of going out shopping to the extent that, due to new semiotic scenarios and information architecture available in the form of virtual stores, all moments are potential shopping ones.

Finally, it was possible to perceive that there is a consistent attempt at reducing perception of the social and economic differences of electronic commerce. In virtual stores' semiotic scenarios, there is an attempt to directly connect customers to products or services displayed in "non-places" where information, people and goods are exchanged. In such spaces, the modulator of an identity is the desire to consume.

## ACKNOWLEDGEMENTS

We thank the National Council for Scientific and Technological Development (CNPq) and the *Foundation for Support* of *Research* of the State of *Minas Gerais*, Brazil (*FAPEMIG*) for their support during the development of this work.

## REFERENCES

Anderson, Chris (2009). A cauda longa: do mercado de massa ao mercado de nicho. São Paulo: Editora Campus.

Chaffey, D., (2006). E-business and e-commerce management: Strategy, implementation and practice. London: Pearson Education.

Bailey, Samantha, (2002). Do you need a taxonomy strategy? Inside Knowledge, volume 5, issue 5, at http://www.ikmagazine.com/xq/asp/sid.0/articleid.E4F31EEC-FB65-413A-A24B-13AA6ACDD12D/eTitle.Do_you_need_a_taxonomy_strategy_A_primer_on_information_architecture_and_taxonomy_development/qx/display.htm, accessed 12 February 2015.

Brasil, 2013. Decreto nº 7.962 de 15 de março de 2013. Regulamenta a Lei no 8.078, de 11 de setembro de 1990, para dispor sobre a contratação no comércio eletrônico, at http://www.planalto.gov.br/ccivil_03/_Ato2011-2014/2013/Decreto/D7962.htm, accessed 7 January 2017.

Downey, Laura and Banerjee, Sumit, (2010). Building an information architecture checklist. Journal of Information Architecture, volume 2, number 2, pp. 25-42, at http://journalofia.org/volume2/issue2/03-downey/, accessed 14 January 2017.

Magazine Luiza at http://www.magazineluiza.com.br/, accessed 14 January 2017.

Souza, Bruno Brito Pereira de, (2012) Antecedentes e dimensões do engajamento dos usuários de redes sociais: um estudo com o facebook. Orientadora: Marlusa Gosling. 2012. 233 pp. Tese (Doutorado em Mercadologia e Administração Estratégica) – Faculdade de Ciências Econômicas, Universidade Federal de Minas Gerais, Belo Horizonte.

Stockinger, Peter (1999). Les nouveaux produits d' information: conception et sémiotique du document. Paris: Hermes.

# Passive Information Behaviors While Grocery Shopping

**Melissa G. Ocepek**
*University of Illinois, USA. mgocepek@illinois.edu*

## ABSTRACT

**Information behavior addresses how individuals use information throughout the various contexts of their daily lives. Previous research in the field has explored passive information behaviors, but not addressed them in the quotidian aspects of life, such as grocery shopping. The current work fills this gap by addressing passive information behaviors throughout the grocery shopping process providing useful insights into how individuals interact with information in a new domain. Data was gathered through two empirical studies using qualitative methods emphasizing the lived experience of primary grocery shoppers. Findings show that information encountering, browsing and monitoring are prevalent in the grocery store and during the planning of a shopping trip demonstrating the information richness of grocery shopping.**

## KEYWORDS

information behavior, everyday information behavior, passive information behavior, browsing, encountering

## INTRODUCTION

Research into the information behaviors of individuals has largely focused on active information seeking in workplaces and educational environments (Case & Given, 2016). As studies increasingly explore a wider variety of information domains, our understanding of information grows. Whereas previously information behavior scholars focused solely on active seeking of task-based information seeking, contemporary scholars have taken a more holistic approach to how individuals interact with information.

The present work aims to continue extending everyday information behavior research further into domains of the quotidian by addressing the information environment of grocery shopping and specifically detailing passive information behaviors. Based on two empirical studies, this paper will highlight the information richness of the quotidian aspects of everyday life.

## BACKGROUND

### *The Everyday*

Information behavior scholars have expanded their research domain beyond the libraries and laboratories where their research began and into the everyday parts of life (Case & Given, 2016). Much of the everyday information behavior research began with studying non-work contexts of individuals (Savolainen, 1995). Studies have addressed serious hobbyists (Hartel, 2011) and the everyday life of health information seeking (McKenzie, 2003), but few studies have highlighted the quotidian world that most of us experience as our everyday (Julien & Michels, 2004). This gap means that information professionals are not as well equipped to help individuals with information needs relating to the quotidian parts of their life.

The theoretical concept of the everyday was established by Lefebvre (2008) and Schütz (Schütz & Luckman, 1973). Schütz, a phenomenologist and social scientist, believed that "the world of the everyday life is consequently man's fundamental and paramount reality" (p. 3) and that before we can understand scientific thought we must first understand how individuals see the world around them. Before entering the classroom or workplace, we learn to interact with information in spaces like the grocery store.

Grocery shopping was selected to explore the information-rich, everyday world because it is a task in which most U.S. households participate on a weekly basis (Hartman Group, 2016). It has not previously been studied by information behavior scholars, even though grocery shopping is a process consisting of an amalgam of important concepts in information behavior, such as seeking, browsing, decision making and information overload.

### *Passive Information Behaviors*

The information behavior field originated as information seeking behavior research, where most of the field focused on active, purposive information behaviors (Case & Given, 2016). Erdelez (1999) has argued against the catch-all term "information-seeking behavior" for all types of information acquisition saying, "the label is a misnomer because passive and opportunistic information acquisition such as some types of browsing, environmental scanning or information encountering more resembles 'gathering' than 'hunting' - the active pursuit suggested in the term seeking" (p. 25). In this section, the passive information behaviors of encountering, monitoring and browsing are described.

Encountering is a passive type of information behavior defined as "the accidental or serendipitous exposure to information that turns out to be relevant to a preexisting information need, or which sparks curiosity about an emerging topic of interest" (Case & Given, 2016, p. 369). Unlike browsing, where a participant may be scanning the store looking for a sale, encountering occurs while a person's attention is on something else entirely and a switch in attention occurs. This process causes a background problem to become the person's focus (Erdelez, 2004).

---

80th Annual Meeting of the Association for Information Science & Technology, Washington, DC, VA | Oct. 27-Nov. 1, 2017

Monitoring is a passive information behavior described by Savolainen (1995) "as a lifelong activity focused on the care of everyday matters" in which individuals keep up with a topic but do not actively seek information about it (p. 272). Monitoring occurs when people watch the news or read sale flyers regularly.

Finally, browsing is one of the oldest concepts of unplanned or passive information behaviors (Case & Given, 2016). It "is an examination of unknown items of potential interest by scanning or moving through an information space in order to judge the utility of the items, to learn about something of interest in the item, or to satisfy curiosity about something" (Chang, 2009, p. 73). It is also a recreational activity such as when someone goes window-shopping. The term has been used to describe a variety of information behaviors from aimless scanning to more focused searching. In this discussion, browsing will refer to the passive act of scanning without a clear goal or an expectation of discovering new information (Case & Given, 2016).

## METHODS

To learn more about the information behaviors of grocery shoppers, I conducted two empirical studies that addressed two different aspects of grocery shopping: creativity and nurturing. Both studies used an interpretive research design using semi-structured interviews focused on the lived experience of the participants (Smith, 1987) with similar methods to other studies on consumer behavior (Carrigan & Szmigin, 2006; Thompson, 1996).

### *Creative Shopper Study*

The creative shopper study addressed the creative process and motivations of grocery shopping. The study consisted of an interview and a shopping observation using the think-aloud technique (O'Brien et al. 2014). The sample design was purposive with a focus on individuals with a love for food, cooking or grocery shopping. The final sample consisted of 18 individuals who were interviewed and 17 of the 18 participated in the shopping observation. All participants received at $10 grocery store gift card at the beginning of the interview and observation portion of the study. All of the creative shopper participants live in a rural and suburban area of the U.S. Midwest near a large research university. The sample consists of 14 women and four men.

### *Nurturer Shopper Study*

The nurturer shopper study addressed the role of food provider and its impact on grocery shopping and decisions made about feeding one's family. The study's interviews were designed to explore a shopper's self-identity, moral obligations and the social norms that influence grocery shopping. The sample design focused on finding participants who had recently (in the last 12 months) gone through a change in their household. Six participants had recently been married, six had recently had a first child, and six had someone recently move out of their home. The final sample of 18 participants consisted of 10 women and eight men. All of the participants lived in a large metropolitan city in the U.S. Southwest. The participants received a $20 gift card to a local grocery chain at the beginning of their interviews.

### *Data Collection and Analysis*

All of the interviews and observations were audio recorded and notes were taken with the participants' consent. In total, both studies produced 2,173 minutes of recorded audio.

Data analysis was conducted in an iterative process using triangulation to find meaning from multiple perspectives. A codebook was created using information behavior research literature for preset codes while allowing for emergent coding based on themes that developed through iterative coding. Higher-level concepts were created and grouped by shared properties (Corbin & Strauss, 2008).

## FINDINGS AND DISCUSSION

Passive information behaviors are ever present in the grocery store. Between my two studies, I identified 209 occurrences of information encountering, monitoring and browsing. Table 1 presents the frequency of all three information behaviors in both studies. Although the interviews in both studies provided fewer descriptions of passive information behaviors, all but two participants described at least one passive information behavior.

| Information Behaviors | All Shoppers | Creative Shoppers | Nurturer Shoppers |
|---|---|---|---|
| Encountering | 83 | 71 | 12 |
| Monitoring | 82 | 49 | 33 |
| Browsing | 44 | 41 | 3 |
| Total | 209 | 161 | 48 |

***Table 1.*** *Frequency of passive information behavior occurrences*

### *Encountering*

In both of my empirical studies, participants described times when they encountered information related to some aspect of their grocery shopping. Encountering occurred in several different forms including encountering new items, reminders and news stories that all affected their shopping.

Encountering a new item often occurs while a grocery shopper is looking for another product in the grocery store and sees a new product or a new variety of a familiar product. Grocery stores typically use end caps or displays to highlight new products and draw shoppers to them. Samples are also used in many grocery stores to entice shoppers to try something new. For example, during one shopping observation a participant was asked by a store employee to try some black bean guacamole and after tasting the sample the participant said, "*[this] is something I would buy for the house. It's cool that they had it there.*" This participant, like many others, described enjoying both the sample and the experience of encountering a new product.

Participants also described encountering items in the store that acted as reminders of things they needed to buy, sale items and promotions and a new location for a product they were unable to find previously. Encountering also occurred outside the grocery store; several participants encountered grocery shopping information from a news story or article.

The present work provides insights into how consumers encounter information both in and out of the store that affects their shopping behavior. Encountering was found to occur throughout the grocery shopping process as well as while some participants were involved in other activities such as reading the news. Grocery shopping illuminates the variety of information encountering because food is such an ever-present part of many peoples' lives.

### *Monitoring*

Unlike the other passive information behaviors explored in this work, monitoring was observed more outside of the grocery store than in. Many participants described keeping up with sale prices and promotions, recipes and nutritional information while at home or described comparing the prices or product selections between different stores.

Several participants read store sale flyers at home or clipped virtual coupons on store apps or websites. One participant explained part of her weekly shopping routine, *"I do go online to the store's website, and see if they have special offers, and sometimes in the mail I get these papers of the stores."*

Getting a good deal was a strong motivator for participants, both in terms of monitoring sale prices at home and in-store, as well as keeping track of different prices between stores. One participant described her own process of price comparison in this way.

Participant: I don't keep a price book. I know some people do that, but I pay a lot of attention to prices. When the price of butter goes up and I'm used to paying $2.25 for it at a certain place and it goes up there, I will pay attention to how much it is at other locations. I always keep a mental book for it.

Several participants monitored prices by keeping a running tally of prices in their head as they grocery shop at different stores; a few even described checking prices on products they were not buying just to keep their mental price books up to date.

Shoppers also described monitoring other types of food information. Recipe monitoring was the most common type of monitoring after sale prices. Participants in both studies described keeping up with new recipes in newspapers, magazines and through social media. In addition to recipes, participants also described keeping up with information about the nutrition, ethical implications, ingredients and the point of origin of the products they purchase.

The variety of information that participants described monitoring shows the diversity of concerns shoppers have when making purchase decisions. Although grocery shopping is a mundane chore for many, the amount and variety of information monitoring my participants described shows that it can also be very complicated. Grocery shopping provides a new way to look at monitoring because it is a routine activity that involves information that consistently changes. Grocery stores change prices, sales, seasonal items, as well as adapting to wider food trends. For many participants, food was a very important "everyday matter" (Savolainen, 1995) where health, politics, family and tradition all meet.

### *Browsing*

Browsing occurred mostly in the grocery store as shoppers look through a specific department for which bag of chips to purchase. For example, one participant told me that sometimes she browses the coffee and tea department of the grocery store even when she is not buying anything. She said, *"Sometimes, I just look, I don't buy anything. I just look at what I could buy and what I might buy in the future [...]to know what stores have which kind of tea, which flavor, stuff like that."*

Participants in both studies described browsing in the grocery store and its multiple purposes. Another participant described browsing as a way to learn about food. When I asked him if there are any places he looks for information about food, he said, *"Not particularly. I would say probably just more the general browsing would be the way to learn about that stuff."* The browsing that both participants describe is functional in that it provides them with additional information relating to their grocery shopping.

Browsing was also mentioned by participants in general terms when describing their approach to grocery shopping. For example, several participants described browsing in relation to their positive feelings toward grocery shopping. One participant said, *"I like looking at all the different stuff on the shelves [...] I feel like they do a good job in grocery stores of presenting food in a way that makes it look appealing, [...] it looks comforting."* Browsing is an aspect of grocery shopping that he enjoys whether he learns new information or not.

Browsing is the information behavior that grocery stores and other retail environments are designed for (Figueroa, 2014). It allows shoppers to take in a lot of information and gives an opportunity to explore the grocery store and discover new things. The present work adds to the browsing research literature by addressing an everyday retail activity with an information behavior lens.

## CONCLUSION

Food is an aspect of life that impacts a grocery shopper's wallet and health, as well as the sustainability of the local and global ecosystem. Grocery shopping is more than just a weekly chore; it is a complicated information activity where shoppers struggle to make the best decisions for their families. Grocery shopping is a task that our culture largely assumes adults know how to do, but my participants described concerns and confusion that could be remedied with better information.

Future work should expand on the present work with larger sample sizes and address other types of grocery shoppers. Additionally, exploration into passive information behaviors should continue to address the quotidian aspects of everyday life to further explore complexity of information in under-studied domains.

Passive information behaviors help scholars to understand how individuals interact with information outside of the task specific "hunting" that Erdelez (1999) argued was only part of the variety of behaviors that should be the focus of information behavior research. By addressing passive information behaviors in the quotidian parts of everyday life, this work demonstrates the complicated and information-rich nature of the everyday world while also furthering our understanding of passive information behaviors. Deeper understanding of how individuals passively interact with information can help information professionals provide better information to individuals trying to make the good decisions in their everyday life.

## ACKNOWLEDGMENTS

This research project was supported by the Institute of Museum and Library Services grant RE-02-12-0009-12, awarded to researchers at the University of Texas at Austin, School of Information.

## REFERENCES

Carrigan, M., & Szmigin, I. (2006). "Mothers of invention": Maternal empowerment and convenience consumption. *European Journal of Marketing*, *40*(9/10), 1122-1142.

Case, D. O., & Given L. M. (2016). Looking for information: A survey of research on information seeking, needs, and behavior (4th ed.). Bigley, UK: Emerald Group Publishing.

Chang, S. J. L. (2009). Chang's browsing. In K. E. Fisher, S. Erdelez, & L. E. F. McKechnie (Eds.), *Theories of information behavior* (pp. 69-74). Medford, NJ: Information Today Inc.

Corbin, J., & Strauss A. (2008). *Basics of qualitative research* (3rd ed.). Los Angeles, CA: Sage Publications, Inc.

Erdelez, S. (1999). Information encountering: It's more than just bumping into information. *Bulletin of the American Society for Information Science and Technology*, *25*(3), 26-29.

Erdelez, S. (2004). Investigation of information encountering in the controlled research environment. *Information Processing & Management*, *40*(6), 1013-1025.

Figueroa, H. (2014). Grocery store design. In P. B. Thompson & D. M. Kaplan (Eds.), *Encyclopedia of food and agricultural ethics* (pp. 1141-1147). Dordrecht: Springer Science + Business Media.

Hartel, J. (2011). Information in the hobby of gourmet cooking–four contexts. In Aspray, W., & Hayes, B. M. (Eds.), *Everyday information: The evolution of information seeking in america* (pp. 217-248). Cambridge: MIT Press.

Julien, H., & Michels, D. (2004). Intra-individual information behaviour in daily life. *Information Processing & Management*, *40*(3), 547-562.

Lefebvre, H. (2008). *Critique of everyday life* (Vol. 1) (2nd ed.). (J. Moore, Trans.). London: Verso.

McKenzie, P. J. (2003). A model of information practices in accounts of everyday-life information seeking. *Journal of Documentation*, *59*(1), 19-40.

O'Brien, M. C., McConnon, A., Hollywood, L. E., Cuskelly, G. J., Barnett, J., Raats, M., & Dean, M. (2014). Let's talk about health: Shoppers' discourse regarding health while food shopping. *Public Health Nutrition*, 1-10.

Savolainen, R. (1995). Everyday life information seeking: Approaching information seeking in the context of "way of life." *Library & Information Science Research*, *17*(3), 259-294.

Schütz, A., & Luckman, T. (1973). *The structures of the life-world.* (R. M. Zaner & H. T. Englehadt, Jr., Trans.). Evanston, IL: Northwestern University Press.

Smith, D. E. (1987). *The everyday world as problematic: A feminist sociology*. Boston: Northeastern University Press.

Hartman Group. (2016). *U.S. grocery shopping trends, 2016.* Bellevue, WA: The Hartman Group, Inc.

Thompson, C. J. (1996). Caring consumers: Gendered consumption meanings and the juggling lifestyle. *Journal of consumer research*, *22*(4), 388-407.

# Web Search Selection Criteria of Foreign-Language Searchers

**Victor K. Ondego**
*University of Maryland Baltimore Campus, USA.*
*victor.ondego@gmail.com*

**Anita Komlodi**
*University of Maryland Baltimore Campus, USA.*
*komlodi@umbc.edu*

## ABSTRACT

**Searchers today are often faced with searching in a language that is not their native language. Searching in a foreign language will necessarily differ from searching in a native language. In this paper we examine one step of the foreign-language searching process: selection decisions about web search results. We report the results of an analysis of participant statements about why a certain web result was selected by 15 Hungarian and 15 Chinese native language speakers who searched in English. Our results confirm selection criteria from the literature and identify new selection criteria that foreign-language searchers pay attention to when selecting search results.**

## KEYWORDS

Relevance, web credibility, information retrieval, foreign-language web search, information seeking.

## INTRODUCTION

Web users around the globe often search for information in a language that is not their native language. During this process they have different factors that they consider while deciding whether some information source or content is relevant to their search. In this paper, we are extending our previous work (Young, 2016) to examine dimensions of relevance used by foreign-language searchers when selecting information from search results.

## BACKGROUND

Research on relevance has looked at result selection decisions made by searchers of online databases, and later web search engines. In our analysis, we utilized the criteria below because they often appeared in the literature and we also added other criteria reported by our participants.

### *Author/Credentials/Source*

We saw significant overlap between relevance criteria selected by field experts between 1959 and 1976, and by end users or information seekers between approximately 1977 and 1997. This included credentials, reputation, trust, expertise (Nilan, Peek, & Snyder, 1988), and source and authority/credentials/reputation (Tombros et al., 2005, Crystal & Greenberg, 2006; Schamber, 1991; Barry and Schamber, 1998; Mizzaro, 1997). We define this as criteria with specific emphasis on not only where the presented information is originating from, but the kind of background or reputation that the users afford that particular author or source.

### *Content/Topic*

We saw some significant overlap in content/topic and depth/scope (Tombros et al., 2005, Crystal & Greenberg, 2006; Schamber, 1991; Barry and Schamber, 1998; Mizzaro, 1997). We define this as a scrutiny of what the information is actually about and not only where it is originating from.

Our extensive literature review leads us to the conclusion that there has not been an effort to look closely at relevance criteria from the perspective of information seekers who were not native English speakers, but were searching in English.

### *Making Decisions in a Foreign Language*

In psychology literature, studies have investigated the issue of making decisions and judgments among bilinguals in both language contexts (Keysar, Hayakawa and An, 2012; Chen, Patrick & Nan, 2014; Geipel, Constantinos & Luca, 2015).

There are notable differences in decision making and judgment based on the language context due to factors such as a reduced activation of moral and social norms (Geipel, Constantinos & Luca, 2015), biases that are inherently part of the cultural aspects and values (Chen, Patrick & Nan, 2014), reduced heuristic biases when faced with an emotionally laden problem in a foreign language, and the disappearing of the "framing effect" (a cognitive bias in which choice or decision making behavior can be influenced by varying the salience of positive or negative aspects of the given choices (Whitney, 2008)) when presented with choices in a foreign language (Keysar, Hayakawa and An, 2012).

Due to similarities in decision-making circumstances, these findings may have an impact on how users select documents in web searches. Thus, the goal of this exploratory study is to identify relevance criteria used by non-English speakers in English language searching to select search results.

## METHODOLOGY

Qualitative methods were selected for this study in order to better understand not the just patterns of behavior but also the motivations and reasons for the search behavior. The analysis

80th Annual Meeting of the Association for Information Science & Technology, Washington, DC, VA | Oct. 27-Nov. 1, 2017

carried out for this paper is part of a larger study of foreign-language web search behavior. Data for this study was collected through the use of a diary instrument capturing searches. Fifteen native Hungarian and fifteen native Chinese web users searching in English were asked to make 15 diary entries each, describing their web search behavior over a period of time. Most students completed the diaries in three to five weeks. The Hungarian participants were Hungarian native-speaking students in Budapest, Hungary, while the Chinese students were native Chinese-speaking international students in the US. These two groups thus differed in their status. The Chinese students were relatively recent arrivals in the US. The longest time spent in the US by a Chinese participant was three years, the average was one year.

The researchers met with the participants, explained the goals of the research and shared the editable diary form (In MS Word format), a template which they edited to record online searches when they searched in English. They were instructed on how to take screenshots and insert them into the template. The diaries captured the topic of the search, the source (search engine versus direct website access), the keywords used, any changes made to the original query, and one selected result from the search that they used to answer their original question, and the reason why that site was selected. They were instructed to record searches carried out in English and select the result they felt best answered their question.

There were two criteria that qualified our participants (mostly students) for the purposes of our study. First, they all spoke English at a conversational level (a requirement for their studies), and secondly, they regularly searched in English. Participants filled out a questionnaire asking about their cultural background, computer, and searching expertise. They were also asked to list five topics they regularly searched in English and in their native language.

The participants were asked to capture those searches that naturally occurred in English, and to utilize any search engine of their choosing. We aimed to capture natural behavior as much as possible. They were each then interviewed twice by the researchers to complement and clarify some of the observations captured within the diaries, with the first interview after the first 7-8 diary entries were made, and the second interview after the last entries were entered. The initial meeting and interviews were conducted in university laboratories in Hungary and the US.

The diary entries were recorded in Hungarian and Chinese. The answers to the question: "Which result did you select and why?" were translated to English and analyzed in this study. For the purposes of our analysis for this paper, the responses were categorized. Some of these categories were predefined based on literature; others were added from our data. As a starting point, we coded the data under the user criteria that exhibited the most overlap across past research: author/credentials/source and content/topic.

We focused on the category of relevance at a granular level. We scrutinized the users' quotes categorized under relevance and reclassified them into user criteria specifically under relevance judgments. An occurrence is defined here as one mention of the criterion by participants. Each participant could mention multiple criteria for any one search. We then calculated percentages as a direct proportion to the whole. The whole in this particular case was the sum of all criteria occurrences. Our findings are described in the following results section.

## RESULTS

The focus of this phase of our research was identifying a set of relevance criteria used by non-native English speakers. Our focus was not on looking at differences between our Chinese and Hungarian participants or native-language and foreign-language searchers. For these reasons, we report our results from an aggregated perspective (Table 1), followed with a more detailed perspective (Table 2).

| Relevance types | # Occurences | %Occurences |
|---|---|---|
| Content/topic | 189 | 54.47% |
| Author/credentials/ source | 109 | 31.41% |
| format | 43 | 12.39% |
| rating/review | 2 | 0.58% |
| comprehensiveness | 2 | 0.58% |
| others' confirmation | 2 | 0.58% |
| total | 347 | 100% |

***Table 1**: Relevance criteria number and percentage of occurrences*

We started our analysis with criteria derived from the literature (Content/Topic, Author/Credentials/Source) and later added criteria from our data (Format, Past experience, Rating/Review, Amount, and Others: confirmation). Our Chinese student participants were relatively recent arrivals to the US, with an average time spent within the country of about one year. This may have impacted their behavior and potentially made it somewhat different from Chinese students living in their native country. It would be difficult to assess the level of cultural familiarity and acclimatization that the Chinese students would have acquired at an individual level, and consequently, to know how that acculturation would have affected their information seeking behavior and decision-making. Our results show that foreign-language searchers in our study mostly utilized the following criteria: content/topic, author/credentials/source and format. Based on past research, we can see some overlap across the different categories identified as relevant most of the time by our participants, such as content/topic and authority/credentials/source (Tombros et al., 2005, Crystal & Greenberg, 2006; Schamber, 1991; Barry and Schamber, 1998; Mizzaro, 1997). Next we will describe how our participants used these criteria in selecting web search results.

| Relevance types | Occurences | | | | |
|---|---|---|---|---|---|
| | Chinese | | Hungarian | | Total % |
| | # | % | # | % | |
| Content/Topic | 120 | 59.11% | 69 | 47.92% | 54.47% |
| Author/Credentials /Source | 64 | 31.53% | 45 | 31.25% | 31.41% |
| Format | 18 | 8.87% | 25 | 17.36% | 12.39% |
| Rating/Review | 1 | 0.49% | 1 | 0.69% | 0.58% |
| Amount/ Comprehensivenes | 0 | 0.00% | 2 | 1.39% | 0.58% |
| Others: confirmation | 0 | 0.00% | 2 | 1.39% | 0.58% |
| Total | 203 | 100% | 144 | 100% | 100.00% |

***Table 2:*** *Relevance criteria number and percentage of occurrences, broken down by participant blocks*

### *Content/Topic*

It is assumed that every selection in our result set was primarily based on topical relevance. That is, it is not likely that the website would have been selected if it was not topically matching the searcher's information need. In topical relevance, both the queries entered by the participants and the information objects returned by the information retrieval system can be identified as being about the same specific topic or subject (Saracevic 2007). As observed, "I chose the 4th result as here the URL described exactly what I needed." As illustrated in Table 2, relevance based on content/topic is prevalent across both sets of participants. Content/topic was the most frequently occurring criterion at 54.47%. As shown in our data, for any of the other criteria to be present, the search result selected has to most likely be topically relevant as well. The remaining 45% or so, we would argue, expect that the results returned by Google in response to their search, are automatically relevant and thus did not mention content/topic as a criterion.

### *Author/Credentials/Source*

The second most frequently mentioned criterion was author/credentials/source at 31.41%. Source refers to where the document is perceived to be coming from, such as editors, organizations involved in the creation of or affiliated with the document, as well as where the document publication appeared (Crystal & Greenberg, 2006). As one participant put it, "I chose the first non-advertisement result as it was Microsoft Office site and I thought there will be a general template." Participants selected information from specific sources as they deemed the sources concerned as either reputable or familiar. In the case of the participant described here, for example, the name Microsoft was well known to them and seemingly reputable as a brand. Other factors that are also associated with the author/credentials or where the content is being generated from (source) such as institutional affiliation, geographical location and genre were taken into consideration by our participants as they gleaned this information from the associated URLs.

Websites that were associated with institutions that were not considered well known by our participants did not seem to garner the trust of our participants as credible or relevant. Similar observations were made for websites that had URLs implying that they were located at different places geographically. Well known institutions websites such as the European Council seemed to solicit better trust from some of our participants as stated: "This is the official website of the European Council. Basically, it is the most credible source it is even more credible than academic papers". Websites that implied companies that were geographically closer seemed to solicit better trust from some of our participants as observed here: "I open the fifth result but I didn't pay attention that it transfers me to an Australian website. I didn't want to trust in it because it's far away despite the fact that it's an online shop. I think it's far away if '.au' would mean Austria I said fine but I didn't check this site deeply. The 9th result was a '.nz' domain name and I think there are more credibly sites. [...] I prefer sites with '.com' domain name."

We define websites belonging to one genre as ones characterized by similarities based on their perceived origins as displayed by their domain names. Websites with domain names ending in similar letters would be perceived as having similar credibility (e.g. .gov sites). An example of participants making their decisions based on the genre of domain names as stated by them include: "I chose the first one on the list because it is a .gov website" Some of the participants relied on familiarity and previous encounters, criteria we called past experience (with a specific author or source). We decided to combine the past experience criterion with author/credentials/source for our aggregated analysis. One participant talked about their choice as follows: "I opened the first link as the first three result were Wikipedia, which I previously had good experiences with."

### *Format*

Format identifies the style by which the document or information within the document is presented. This could be in the form of a video or a map and so on. Our participants considered and utilized format as a relevance criterion 12.39% of the time during their result selection process. Some participants, for example, picked the documents that looked like tutorials as illustrated here, "I opened the 2nd link as it seemed a tutorial." For participant interested in tutorials, mentioned above, video formats turned out to be the selection of choice. A video seemed like it gave the participant the idea that it would be easier to follow the visuals as opposed to text on a tutorial presented as a document, for example.

### *Other Criteria*

Some other criteria used by the information seekers included rating/review (recommendations made by other users) at 0.58%, amount (more information providing a comprehensive view of the topic) at 0.58% and Others: confirmation (presence of other websites providing similar or supporting information), also at 0.58%.

### *Forums*

Our participants' opinions were somewhat divided when it came to forums as a source of the information they were searching for. Nine participants stated that they considered forums as not completely credible sources of information, and talked about not paying much attention to information that was displayed there. As one participant put it: "I consider the genre of the website. I mean if it's a forum or a blog, I don't spend time on these."

## DISCUSSION

The main contribution of our research is the identification of the most important selection criteria used by foreign-language searchers while searching in English online. The topic/content criterion was expected to be important (Tombros et al., 2005, Crystal & Greenberg, 2006; Schamber, 1991; Barry and Schamber, 1998; Mizzaro, 1997), and this was confirmed in our data. There have also been studies of native language speakers where author/credentials/source was significant selection criteria (Nilan, Peek, & Snyder, 1988, Tombros et al., 2005, Crystal & Greenberg, 2006; Schamber, 1991; Barry and Schamber, 1998). This may be an even more important category for foreign-language searchers, as they may not be familiar with the cultural contexts surrounding the language, and the information landscape (Young, 2016) of the source documents. They may thereby rely more on the sources/authors they recognize, perhaps due to having encountered or even utilized the sources/authors in the past or recognizing their name or brand as an official authority in regard to the topic of their search.

The format was also a factor that the web searchers applied when making relevance-based decisions, but to a much lesser degree than topical relevance and author/credentials/source. The format of the information, which includes the style (PDF, video, etc.) in which the information is presented, accounted for 12.39% of the total selections by the participants. Some of the other remaining criteria accounted for less than 1% of the total selections by our group of web searchers.

## CONCLUSION

Our results identified the three most important selection criteria used by foreign-language searchers: topic/content, author/credentials/source, and format. This foundational work will allow us to more systematically compare native and foreign language searchers web search selection criteria and how they make these decisions. A more formal study would afford us the chance to better investigate not only the criteria mentioned within the literature, but also perhaps unique criteria that we may encounter from our own data.

## ACKNOWLEDGEMENTS

We thank all the volunteers, Sanda Erdelez, publications support, staff, and authors. This research was supported by Google Faculty Research Award #2012_R1_667

## REFERENCES

Barry, C. L., & Schamber, L. (1998). Users' criteria for relevance evaluation: a cross-situational comparison. Information processing & management, 34(2), 219236.

Chen, N., Rau, P. P. L., & Yao, N. T. (2014, September). The influence of Chinese-Western Bilingualism on Rationality in Decision Making Behavior. In Proceedings of the Human Factors and Ergonomics Society Annual Meeting (Vol. 58, No. 1, pp. 375-379). Sage CA: Los Angeles, CA: SAGE Publications.

Crystal, A., & Greenberg, J. (2006). Relevance criteria identified by health information users during Web searches. Journal of the American Society for Information Science and Technology, 57(10), 1368-1382.

Geipel, J., Hadjichristidis, C., & Surian, L. (2015). How foreign language shapes moral judgment. Journal of Experimental Social Psychology, 59, 8-17.

Keysar, B., Hayakawa, S. L., & An, S. G. (2012). The foreign-language effect thinking in a foreign tongue reduces decision biases. Psychological science, 23(6), 661-668.

Mizzaro, S. (1997). Relevance: The whole history. JASIS, 48(9), 810-832.

Nilan, M. S., Peek, R. P., & Snyder, H. W. (1988, October). A methodology for tapping user evaluation behaviors: An exploration of users' strategy, source and information evaluating. In Proceedings of the 51st Annual Meeting of the American Society for Information Science (Vol. 25, No. 152-159).

Saracevic, T. (2007). Relevance: A review of the literature and a framework for thinking on the notion in information science. Part III: Behavior and effects of relevance. Journal of the American Society for information Science and Technology, 58(13), 2126-2144.

Schamber, L. (1991). Users' Criteria for Evaluation in a Multimedia Environment. In Proceedings of the ASIST Annual Meeting (Vol. 28, pp. 126-33).

Tombros, A., Ruthven, I., & Jose, J. M. (2005). How users assess web pages for information seeking. JASIST, 56(4), 327-344.

Whitney, P., Rinehart, C. A., & Hinson, J. M. (2008). Framing effects under cognitive load: The role of working memory in risky decisions. Psychonomic Bulletin & Review, 15(6), 1179-1184.

Young, A. L., Komlodi, A., Rózsa, G., & Chu, P. (2016). Evaluating the credibility of English web sources as a foreign-language searcher. Proc. ASIST, 53(1), 1-9

# The Topical Interconnections Within the Realm of Information Behavior Research

**Rong Tang**
*School of Library and Information Science Simmons College, USA. rong.tang@simmons.edu*

**Chaoqun Ni**
*School of Library and Information Science, University of Iowa, USA. chaoqun-ni@uiowa.edu*

## ABSTRACT

**In response to the lack of clarity concerning both the conceptual boundaries of information behavior (IB) and the interrelationship between IB and multiple related topics, this study attempts to establish an intellectual profile of IB scholarship by examining publications of IB and 13 other related topics. Results show a similar growth pattern of IB publications and authors over past 45 years. Multidimensional scaling analysis (MDA) based on top frequent terms of the 14 topics revealed a configuration of three clusters and one individual entity (information ecology). IB is found to cluster with topics of seek, need, use, practice, and experience. As the very first study investigating the underlying conceptual connection between IB and 13 other related topics, results of the study help to outline the intellectual affinity of various concepts used in IB related research, add further insights into identifying points of convergence and departure as well as scholarship configuration within the realm of information research.**

## KEYWORDS

information behavior concepts, interrelationships between IB and other areas, points of convergence and departure, topic analysis, bibliometric analysis

## INTRODUCTION AND PROBLEM STATEMENT

In the scholarly discourse concerning information science research, the concept of "information behavior" (also known as IB) has been used as a general umbrella term that "captures a broad range of information related phenomena" (Fisher, Durrance, & Hinton, 2004, p. 754). As noted by Wildemuth and Case (2005), "investigations of those who seek and use information have been an important aspect of information science since its beginnings" (p. 35). Despite significant advancements in the development of IB theories and models, as well as rich empirical insights gained from research work over the years, researchers have found it tremendously challenging to identify, specify, and/or present a meaningful boundary for the concept of "information behavior." In his recent book entitled *Introduction to Information Behavior*, Ford (2015) warned of the danger of "under- or over-specifying" the IB field (p. 10). "With such an expansion in conceptions of what information behaviour covers," he argued, "it is all the more important precisely to define the boundaries of the field, and to negotiate its relationship with other established fields which may appear to overlap" (p.16). As observed by Savolainen (2007, 2008), however, the discourse of information behavior has been mostly postulative and unreflective, which has left the concept somewhat hollow and elusive. This has, in turn, produced fuzzy and fragmentary empirical investigations as scholars struggle to utilize a framework that may or may not be appropriate to study the phenomena in question (Savolainen, 2007).

As the corpus of information behavior research continues to grow and expand without a consensus on the conceptual delimiters of the notion itself, one approach to defining IB is to provide a comprehensive list of its component elements, since "it is difficult to think of an activity which is *not* [emphasis is original] some form of information behaviour" (Ford, 2015, p. 16). In 2015, Ford proposed that information behavior is "engaging in any or all of" the activities of information need, interaction, evaluation, use, and organization (p. 23). Ford (2015) hoped that his definition would provide a map to the complex maze of IB. However, several researchers have offered another prospective: IB as a process encompassing a cycle or sequence of information activities that include "information needs, seeking, searching, retrieval, and use as a whole" (Savolainen, 2007, p. 127). A number of researchers have employed frameworks such as "information activities" (Thivant, 2005) or "information journey" (Du, 2014). While Thivant's (2005) information activities diagram outlined the relationship between information need and infor further connected information use with both information management and information production. In Du's (2014) research paper, those information activities form a path beginning with information need and progressing to information seeking, information judgments, information use, and finally information sharing and collaboration. She considers these as the routes of an information journey.

Despite these efforts to clarify the meaning of "information behavior," the fact remains that IB, as an umbrella term, refers to a variety of research endeavors relating to information need, information seeking, information searching, information retrieval, information context, information use, information management, information sharing, information practice, and information ecology. What exactly constitutes the intellectual structure of IB scholarship? How do these pockets of research link to, or influence, one another? Using publication data to

80th Annual Meeting of the Association for Information Science & Technology, Washington, DC, VA | Oct. 27-Nov. 1, 2017

explore the interconnection of 14 areas of IB-related research, the present research study hopes to reveal the cognitive underpinning of IB and its associated realms of research.

## RESEARCH QUESTIONS

This research study seeks to answer following research questions:

**RQ1**: What is the overall growth pattern of IB research in terms of its publication quantity?

**RQ2**: What are the most frequently covered IB topical areas?

**RQ3**: What are the interconnectedness and differential boundaries among IB and 13 other information research topics?

## METHOD

### *Dataset and Procedure*

Data utilized in this study were retrieved from the Web of Science Core Collection by conducting the following topical search query: "information behaviour" OR "information behavior." Double quotes were used to retrieve documents that contained either the British or American spelling of this topic. The search was performed in February 2016 and returned 814 documents (Non-English results were excluded as WoS is English dominant and the few non-English documents retrieved would not accurately represent research in those languages). Thirteen other topics were then searched in the similar manner. Table 1 lists the 14 topics and various publication attributes, including number of publications, unique authors, citations, venues, and WoS Subject Categories (SC).

Of the 14 topics, "information retrieval" held the highest number of publications, unique authors, citations and venues, but "information needs" had the highest number of subject categories. "Information ecology" had the lowest number of publications, unique authors, citations, venues and subject categories. The number of publications and other attributes of "Information behavior/our" is in the middle range among the 14 topics.

| Topics | Pubs | AU | Cites | Venues | SCs |
|---|---|---|---|---|---|
| behavior | 814 | 1216 | 3314 | 262 | 62 |
| context | 167 | 439 | 659 | 160 | 48 |
| discovery | 375 | 946 | 1029 | 321 | 48 |
| ecology | 80 | 143 | 199 | 74 | 25 |
| experience | 152 | 339 | 631 | 128 | 65 |
| interaction | 363 | 850 | 2327 | 304 | 67 |
| management | 9260 | 19270 | 14221 | 4888 | 141 |
| Need | 7212 | 17951 | 19067 | 3361 | 142 |
| Practice | 336 | 662 | 1996 | 196 | 56 |
| retrieval | 19726 | 27107 | 41851 | 6361 | 133 |
| Search | 497 | 1042 | 2684 | 359 | 63 |
| Seek | 4983 | 10028 | 23192 | 1616 | 117 |
| Share | 7012 | 14458 | 16051 | 4036 | 135 |
| Use | 1114 | 2696 | 6369 | 655 | 110 |

***Table 1****. Publication patterns of 14 ib related topics*

## RESULTS

### *Overview of Information Behavior Research Output*

#### Documents

The final dataset consisted of 814 documents. It should be noted that journal articles (66.71%) are the dominant publication genre for IB, followed by conference proceedings papers (23.41%). The publication dates range from 1970 to 2014. According to our data, IB research steadily increased after 2002 and peaked in 2014. Overall, it is interesting that the number of publications per year has not yet exceeded 100. As a frame of reference, the number of publications on "information need" has exceeded 100 publications per year since 1995, "information seeking" exceeded 100 publications in 1999, and "information retrieval" exceeded 100 publications in 1999 and 1,000 per year between 2005 to 2014. These 814 IB publications were cited by a total of 6,825 other resources, making their average citation rate 8.38.

#### Authorship

Between 1970 and 2015, 1,216 authors produced publications on information behavior. Before 2004, the number of unique authors who published each year was less than 35. The number of unique authors increased greatly between 2004 and 2008, from 50 in 2004 to 138 in 2008. In 2009 and 2010, the number of authors dropped to 67 and 88, respectively. In 2011, the number of unique authors (n=154) almost doubledwhen compared to 2010. In 2014, there were a staggering 208 unique authors. Overall, the data reveal that significant growths in the IB author community occurred after 2004. Despite some fluctuations, these growths exhibited an obvious upward trend.

#### Topics of IB Research

This paper examines topics of IB research by looking at the relative frequency of terms and phrases. Further topic analysis was performed based on title and abstract words of IB documents. Relative word/phrase frequency revealed top 20 terms in IB publications (See Table 2). Terms with a relative frequency of over 25%, besides *information, behavior,* and *information behavior,* include *use, seek, need, base, information seek, design, library, social, model,* and *user.* Topic analysis produced five topics: (1) *Health Information,* (2) *Student, Information Literacy,* and *Library,* (3) *Social Context, Information Practice,* and *Use,* (4) *User, System Design,* and *Information Retrieval,* and (5) *Information Searching, Tasks,* and *Information Seeking* (See Table 3).

| Term | Freq | Term | Freq |
|---|---|---|---|
| information | 96.8% | social | 26.4% |
| Behavior | 90.4% | model | 26.2% |
| information behavior | 85.0% | user | 25.5% |
| Use | 62.7% | focus | 24.6% |
| Seek | 34.0% | context | 23.0% |
| Need | 32.8% | process | 21.8% |
| Base | 32.5% | interview | 21.0% |
| information seek | 31.2% | support | 19.6% |
| Design | 29.1% | system | 18.6% |
| Library | 26.7% | group | 18.3% |

***Table 2****. Top 20 IB terms by relative frequency*

| Topic | Terms and Phrases |
|---|---|
| health information | Health information; health_information_behavior; health_information_seek; use; sample; internet; family_member; patient; source; health_care; |
| student; information literacy; library | student; information_literacy; university; librarian; library; academic; skill; learning; school; project; use; practical |
| social context; information practice & use | information_behavior; social; context; model; practice; use; concept; theory; individual; process; focus; theoretical; framework; perspective |
| user; system design; information retrieval | user; system; design; information_retrieval_system; search; user_information; digital_library; search_engine; information_retrieval; user_group; library; system_design |
| information search; tasks; information seeking | information_search_process; search; task; behavior; student; information_seek |

***Table 3****. Topics for IB research publications*

## Topical Relationship with IB-Related Terms

Analysis of the interrelationship of 14 topics was performed by selecting words and phrases that appear in at least 10% of the total documents of each area. The proximity between two topical areas was measured by the number of shared terms and phrases between them. We then mapped the distance among these areas using multidimensional scaling (MDS). As shown in Figure 1, three clusters and one individual entity – *ecology* outlines intellectual affinities of 14 areas of research. The color code of the MDS map reflects the result of these areas using hierarchical clustering. The BEHAVIOR cluster is the biggest one, containing *seek, need, use, practice,* and *experience*, in addition to *behavior*. The CONTEXT cluster is the second richest cluster, containing *management, share,* and *interaction*, in addition to *context*. The RETRIEVAL cluster includes *retrieval, search* and *discovery*. The fact that ECOLOGY stands on its own, might suggest that information ecology publications have yet to establish a conceptual or rhetoric linkage with other IB related areas.

Within the BEHAVIOR cluster, we further examined the frequent terms used by publications of the six topics. This paper uses a network to present detailed connections among these six topics, by illustrating actual terms/phrases that connect each two topics. The network diagram (Figure 2) is a 2-mode network: blue denotes the six areas within the IB cluster while orange the terms. *Behavior* publications have strong relationships with *need, seek, use, experience,* and *practice*articles through terms such as "information." In addition to "information," terms such as "personal" and "social" connect *behavior* with *practice*. "Knowledge," "process," "use," and "share" link *behavior* with *experience*. *Need* is associated with *behavior* thorough bridging terms such as "user," "base," and "system," whereas *seek* interconnects with *behavior* through the term "search." *Use* solely relies on "information," "behavior" and "use" to connect with *behavior* publications, while "Health" connects with *seek* with *practice*.

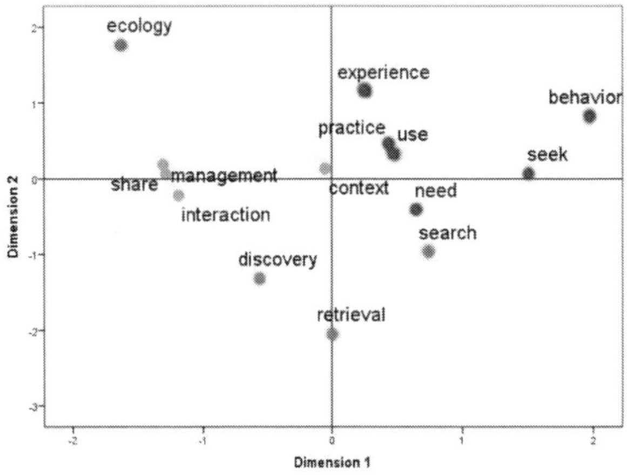


***Figure 1****. Clustering of publications in 14 IB-related areas*

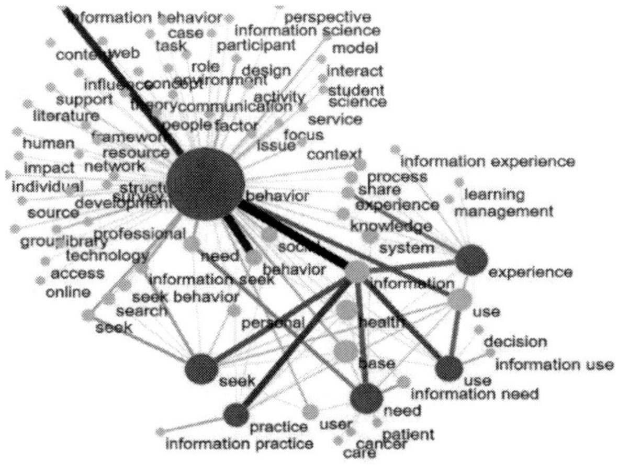


***Figure 3****. Terms linking areas within the IB cluster*

## DISCUSSION AND CONCLUSION

By looking into IB publication history, author communities, and topical areas, as well as the clustering configuration of 14 topical areas, we were able to achieve greater understanding of the scholarly realm of IB research. The growth of IB publications occurred in 2004, 2007, and peaked in 2014. With the publication of Case's first edition of *Looking for Information* in 2002, *Theories of Information Behavior* (Fisher, Erdelez, & McKechnie, 2005), and Nahl and Bilal's (2008) *Information and Emotion*, in addition to a series of IB articles by Wilson and others, a growth after 2004 was expected. The growth pattern of the number of authors is very similar to the number of publications. The top 20 words/phrases of IB publications and the five topical areas revealed through LDA to some extent accentuated IB intellectual structure. It would be interesting to study whether LDA results change over time and what new topics have emerged in the recent five years.

Results of MDS cluster configuration help to answer the research question regarding the interconnection between IB and 13 other research subjects. With the BEHAVIOR cluster differentiated from the CONTEXT and RETRIEVAL clusters, as well as from the ECOLOGY stand-alone entity, we are able for the first time to present the core and parallel domainsof IB. While Wilson (1981, 1999) and others define information behavior as encompassing seeking, searching, and using, results of this study put *search* and *context* outside the central area of IB. It does confirm that *seek, need,* and *use* are closely connected to IB. Most elements in RETRIEVAL and CONTEXT clusters are understandably related, however, *management* was found to reside within the cluster of CONTEXT, even though one might assume a strong linkage between *management* and *ecology*.

The analysis of terms that bridge two topics within the BEHAVIOR cluster was helpful as bridging terms, excluding the self-concept, could signal points of intellectual convergence. For instance, "user" and "system" are shared between *behavior* and *need*; "search" and "social" link IB with *seek*; and "personal" and "social" connect *behavior* and *practice*.

As the very first study investigating the underlying intellectual connection between IB and 13 other topics, results of the MDS clustering serve as a first step towards obtaining a closer understanding of the IB domain. Identifying bridging terms between two topics, as well as unique terms attached to a single topic, present great promise to uncover points of convergence and departure between various topics. Such investigations might enable the disambiguation of IB as an umbrella term, and outline the conceptual affinity within the general domain of information research.

## ACKNOWLEDGMENTS

We wish to thank Steven Gentry, the graduate student assistant for Dr. Rong Tang, for his assistance in data collection and his edits of earlier version of this paper.

## REFERENCES

Case, D. O. (2002). Looking for information: A survey of research on information seeking, needs and behavior. London, United Kingdom: Elsevier Science and Technology Books.

Du, J. T. (2014). The information journey of marketing professionals: Incorporating work task-driven information seeking, information judgments, information use, and information sharing. Journal of the Association for Information Science and Technology, 65(9), 1850-1869.

Fisher, K.E., Durrance, J. C., & Hinton, M. B. (2004). Information grounds and the use of need-based services by immigrants in Queens, New York: A context-based, outcome evaluation approach. Journal of the American Society for Information Science and Technology, 55(8), 754-766.

Fisher, K. E., Erdelez, S., &McKechnie, E. F. (Eds.). (2005). Theories of information behavior. Medford, NJ: Information Today.

Ford, N. (2015). Introduction to information behaviour. London, UK: Facet Publishing

Nahl, D., & Bilal, D. (2007). Information and emotion: The emergent affective paradigm in information behaviour Research and Theory. Medford, NJ: Information Today.

Pettigrew, K. E., Fidel, R. and Bruce, H. (2001. Conceptual frameworks in information behavior. Annual review of information science and technology, 35(1), 43-78.

Savolainen, R. (2007). Information behavior and information practice: Reviewing the "umbrella concepts" of information-seeking studies. Library Quarterly, 77(2), 109-132.

Savolainen, R. (2008). Everyday information practices: A social phenomenological perspective. Lanham, MD: The Scarecrow.

Thivant, E. (2005). Information seeking and use behavior of economists and business analysts. Information Research, 10(4). http://www.informationr.net/ir/10-4/paper234.html

Wildemuth, B.M., & Case, D.O. (2010). Early information behavior research. Bulletin of the American Society for Information Science and Technology, 33(3), 35-38.

Wilson, T. D. (1981). On user studies and information needs. Journal of Documentation, 37(1), 3–15.

Wilson, T. D. (1999). Models in information behaviour research. Journal of Documentation, 55(3), 249–270.

Wilson, T. D. (2000). Human information behavior. Informing Science, 3(2), 49–56.

# Factors Influencing Faculty Attitudes Towards Open Access Institutional Repositories

**Ahmet Meti Tmava**
*College of Information, University of North Texas, USA.*
*Ahmet.Tmava@unt.edu*

**Shawne D. Miksa**
*College of Information, University of North Texas, USA.*
*Shawne.Miksa@unt.edu*

## ABSTRACT

**Open access institutional repositories (OA IR) have increased in popularity in last decade. However, research shows they remain thinly populated in large part due to faculty reluctance to participate. The focus of previous research has been on external factor (social or technological context) and there is a lack of understanding of the internal factors and the psychology of the reluctance. This study investigated the factors affecting faculty participation in IRs and examined the extent to which these factors influenced faculty willingness to participate in IRs by drawing upon the theory of planned behavior and the model of factors affecting faculty self-archiving.**

## KEYWORDS

open access, institutional repositories, scholarly communications, digital repositories, scholarly publishing

## INTRODUCTION

Open access institutional repositories (OA IRs) are electronic systems that capture, preserve and provide access to the scholarly digital work of an institution. The birth of OA IR is significant within the context of scholarly communication. Academic libraries play an important role in facilitating the scholarly communication process and transforming the scholarly publication process. IRs reform scholarly communication by stimulating innovation in a disaggregated publishing structure. In addition, IRs provide long-term sustainable storage, preservation and open access to resources. IRs also serve as tangible indicators of an institution's productivity, and thereby increasing an institution's visibility, prestige and value. However, this is a value that has to be communicated to faculty and researchers as they are an integral part that can make-or-break an IR. Although open access idea has been around for over two decades' research shows that majority of faculty members still consider publishing in open access repositories as detrimental to their academic career, potentially posing a threat to earning tenure or risking their chances at obtaining research grants. The purpose of this research is to shed light on faculty attitudes towards OA publishing as a positive change in the scholarly communication system.

80th Annual Meeting of the Association for Information Science & Technology, Washington, DC, VA | Oct. 27-Nov. 1, 2017



## RATIONAL FOR CURRENT STUDY

Despite all of the benefits described by the proponents of OA, a large number of IRs remain thinly populated. There are a multitude of factors (both internal and external) that will have significant impact on faculty participation. One of the most important issues that needs to be considered is the faculty attitudes and behavior towards IRs. Johnson (2002) writes that the problem of resistance from faculty members is more one of indifference than active resistance. Furthermore, Quinn (2010) argues that faculty resistance can manifest itself at both the cognitive and affective, or behavioral, level. This study sought to analyze the relationship between faculty perception of IRs (active and passive resistance), and their willingness (intent) to deposit their work into an IR.

## LITERATURE REVIEW

A number of qualitative studies investigated incentives and concerns that affect faculty members in depositing their scholarly work in OA IR (Foster, and Gibbons, 2005; Kim 2010; Watson, 2007). Other studies used quantitative approaches and assessed deposit data directly from repositories (Covey, 2009; Xia, 2008). Many of these studies have investigated the motivating and hindering factors using different forms of surveys that were focused on external factors, which were either social or technological in context. However, scholars tend to be motivated not only by social and contextual factors but by their psychological judgment (i.e., perceptions) as well (Heterick, 2002).

### *Factors influencing faculty participation in IR*

The literature review reveals numerous reasons that prompt faculty to not participate in IR. The main factors identified by Kim (2010) that affect faculty participation in OA repositories are: copyright concerns, lack of time, fear of plagiarism, self-archiving culture and/or peer pressure, and reward system (tenure and promotion). Findings from other studies (Davis & Connolly, 2007) confirm technical barriers, fear of plagiarism, as well as a lack of understating the purpose of IRs, and a fear that publishing in IRs may taint their work. Laughtin-Dunker (2014), several faculty members perceived publishing in IRs as "low quality," "weaker," "easy to publish in," "probably not scholarly," "less prestige" and "less quality control than traditional journal" (p. 9). Another hindering factor identified by Creaser et al (2010) was lack of knowledge on how to deposit materials into an IR. All these factors that affect faculty participation in OA publishing were extracted from the previous studies, defined and transformed into research variables.

## THEORETICAL FRAMEWORK

The goal of this research was to investigate the relationship between attitudes and intention to deposit. Thus it was necessary to take a more holistic approach that maps out the relationships among beliefs, attitudes, subjective norms, behavioral controls, intentions, and behavior. This relationship is best described and documented by the theory of planned behavior (TPB).

### *Rational for the Theory of Planned Behavior*

TPB considers beliefs as the fundamental blocks of attitude, representing the information an individual has about specific behavior and the attributes of this behavior (Ajzen, 1991). TPB has frequently been shown to be the best predictor of behavioral intention. According to TPB, people act in accordance with their intentions and perceptions of control over behavior, while intentions in turn are influenced by attitudes toward the behavior, subjective norms, and perceptions of behavior control (p. 43). The major assumption behind this theory is that human beings are rational and make systematic decisions based on available information. The TPB developed by Ajzen provided a useful framework to examine more closely the factors affecting faculty intention to participate in OA IRs.

### *Rational for the Model Affecting Faculty Self-Archiving*

The most prominent model that identifies main factors that affect faculty members' self-archiving behavior was developed by Kim (2010). This model was developed based on the empirical study conducted in 17 universities, with 684 faculty members. Thus, the current research has incorporated the factors identified in the model of factors affecting faculty self-archiving.

#### Model of factors affecting faculty self-archiving

Kim (2010) investigated factors that motivate or impede faculty participation in self-archiving behavior. In this study the self-archiving behavior was considered to be any type of placement of research work in various types of archiving venues, such as a personal webpage, departmental/university webpage, disciplinary repository and IR. The analysis from survey responses of 684 professors and 41 telephone interviews revealed five groups of factors that affect faculty self-archiving behavior.

#### Current Research Framework

The TPB has been adapted for investigating faculty attitudes towards participation in OA IR. The theory postulates that a person's (faculty) intention of depositing his or her scholarly work into a repository is determined by three categories of factors: attitude towards participation in OA IRs, social influence of participation in OA IRs, and perceived control of participation in OA IRs.

The attitude towards participation in OA IRs follows closely the definition from the theory of planned behavior. Attitude is defined as faculty member's positive or negative perception towards using an OA IR for disseminating their scholarly works. Also, according to TPB social influence refers to the faculty member's perception that most peers, colleagues and department heads think they should, or should not, use OA IRs for disseminating their scholarly work. The first component is a direct influence on behavioral intentions while the second is considered to have an indirect influence. The perceived control behavior refers to faculty members' perception of their ability to use OA IRs for disseminating their scholarly work. Based on the framework developed from the TPB, intention to use OA IRs is a dependent variable, which will be measured through self-reporting, while independent variables comprise attitude, social influence, and perceived control.

## METHODS

This study employs correlational research method. The assumed correlational relationship between the predictor variables and outcome variables in this study is as follows. Faculty who score high in factors affecting faculty attitudes towards IRs (perceived barriers) are less likely to deposit than those who score low. On the other hand, the higher the scores on motivating factors (i.e., perceived academic reward) the more likely they are to deposit (positive relationship).

(1) The predictor (independent) variables were: perceived copyright concerns (PCC), plagiarism concerns (PPI), difficulty with submission (PDS), low quality venues (PLQV), additional time needed (PATN), altruism (ALT), academic reward (AREW), academic culture (ACUL), discoverability, access and readership (DAR), self-efficacy (SE) and controllability (CO). The identified outcome (dependent) variable was faculty intention to participate in IR (INTE)

### *Survey Population and Participants*

The target population for this study was all faculty members at the University of North Texas (UNT) who teach undergraduate and graduate students. At the time of survey administration Fall 2016, and according to UNT faculty fact sheet, there were a total of 1,158 faculty members.

### *Data Collection*

Data was collected through anonymous, web-based, confidential questionnaires administered through the online tool Qualtrics. All faculty members at UNT (1158) were invited to participate in the survey via e-mail. A total number of 172 surveys were partially completed (14.8% responses rate), and 138 were fully completed for a total completion rate of 80%.

### *Factor Analysis*

The current research was primarily interested in identifying the underling constructs from the data collected and assessing the extent to which these constructs represent the original variables derived from a priory theory. Thus, principal component analysis (PCA) was chosen to extract the latent constructs. According to Kieffer (1999) PCA uses the total variance of each variable in examining the shared variances between variables. The number of factors to retain was 11, and was initially determined based on the a priori theory. Following closely the procedure described by Velicer and Jackson

(1990), the current study used Eigenvalue and Velicer's minimum average partial (MAP) test to confirm the number of factors to extract, determined by *a priori* theory. All three criteria indicated the extraction of eleven factors. Most items showed simple structure and had adequate communality values (.4 or higher).

### *Principal Component Analysis*

Following recommendations by Field (2009), an EFA was conducted using PCA factor extraction method and oblique oblimin rotation technique. In summary, the eleven factors together explained about 76.5% of variance (see Table 1). Factor 1 (ALT) accounted for 24.8% of the variance, which were attributed to the four highest loadings for this factor. Factor 2 (PPI) accounted for 11% of the variance that included four items with the highest loadings on this factor. Factor 3 (PDS) accounted for 8.5% of the variance that included three items with the highest loadings. Two other variables were found to merge into this factor with significant loadings (SE3 with .706 and CO3 with.804) pertaining to faculty self-confidence. Factor 4 (influence by ACUL) accounted for 6.2% of the variance. Two items loaded the highest on this factor pertaining to the influence by colleagues. Factor 5 explained 5.6% of the variance. Four items loaded the highest on this factor indicating the influence of academic reward. Factor 6 explained about 4.6% of the variance. Four items loaded the highest on this factor, indicating the perception of IRs as low-quality publishing venues. Factor 7 accounted for about 3.9%, four items loaded on this factor, indicating the perception of faculty for PATN. Factor 8 accounted for 3.7% of the variance. Four items loaded on this factor indicating PCC. Factor 9 explained about 3.1% of the variance. Two items loaded on this factor indicating the influence of self-efficacy. Factor 10 accounted for about 2.5% of the variance. Six items had significant loadings on this factor, four items indicated the discoverability and ease of access, and two items with lower loadings indicated academic reward. The name of this factor changed to discoverability access and readership (DAR) because the highest loadings of the four items on this factor reflected the influence of discoverability and ease of access, and two items reflect the influence of readership. Lastly, factor 11, accounted for about 2.4% of the variance. Only two items loaded on this factor, indicating the influence of controllability.

### Assessment for subscales

Prior to running a regression analysis, the internal reliability coefficients were assessed for the 11 hypothesized subscales of the factors affecting faculty attitudes towards OA IRs. All of the subscales had adequate internal reliability coefficients (See Table 1).

| Variables | Factor order | % of variance accounted for | Cronbach's Alpha |
|---|---|---|---|
| ALT | 1 | 24.8 | 0.878 |
| PPI | 2 | 10.9 | 0.943 |
| PDS | 3 | 8.5 | 0.849 |
| ACUL | 4 | 6.2 | 0.863 |
| AREW | 5 | 5.6 | 0.835 |
| PLQV | 6 | 4.6 | 0.876 |
| PATN | 7 | 3.9 | 0.841 |
| PCC | 8 | 3.7 | 0.731 |
| SE | 9 | 3.3 | 0.789 |
| DAR | 10 | 2.5 | 0.906 |
| CO | 11 | 2.3 | 0.628 |

***Table 1**. Percentage of variance and internal reliability for factors affecting faculty attitudes towards OA IR*

## LOGISTIC REGRESSION ANALYSIS

The binary logistic regression (LR) was utilized to predict the extent of the likelihood 'odds ratio' of faculty intent to participate in OA IRs as a dependent variable, which was affected by the eleven factors extracted as independent variables. Once the factors (components) were identified individual scores were created to incorporate factor information as a part of predictive analysis – factor scores. The analyses of normality, independence of error and multi-collinearity did not find serious violations any of the assumptions for LR.

### *Results for multiple logistic regression*

A binary LR method was conducted to predict faculty intent to participate in OA IRs (Yes vs. No). The Goodness-of-fit with all predictors in the model showed a very good fit for all the predictors, they explained 84.4% of the variance ($R^2$) in the change in the dependent variable (intention to participate in OA IR).

| Predictors | B | SE | Wald | df | Sig. | Exp (B) |
|---|---|---|---|---|---|---|
| ALT | -.92 | 0.38 | 5.73 | 1 | .017 | 0.399 * |
| DAR | 1.04 | 0.45 | 5.25 | 1 | .022 | 2.824 * |
| PDSE | -1.89 | 0.57 | 10.97 | 1 | .001 | .150*** |
| COLE | .32 | 0.35 | .84 | 1 | .359 | 1.378 |
| AREW | .26 | 0.39 | .44 | 1 | .505 | 1.3 |
| PATN | .52 | 0.38 | 1.88 | 1 | .170 | 1.68 |
| PLQV | -1.09 | 0.43 | 6.52 | 1 | .011 | .335** |
| PCC | .49 | 0.37 | 1.78 | 1 | .181 | 1.63 |
| SE | .11 | 0.35 | .09 | 1 | .755 | 1.115 |
| PPI | .19 | 0.34 | .31 | 1 | .575 | 1.213 |
| CO | -.19 | 0.42 | .21 | 1 | .647 | 0.825 |

***Table 2**. Summary of multiple logistic regression predicting faculty intention to participate in IR*

Table 2 shows logistic regression results, and 95% confidence intervals for odds ratios for each of the 11 main predictors. A test with all predictors against a constant-only model was statistically significant, $X^2$ (11) = 76.88, $p < .001$, Nagelkerke $R^2 = .716$. Overall factors were significant with the value of $p<0.05$. Four out of the eleven independent variables were significant ($p<.05$) in influencing the intention of faculty to participate in OA IR. Examination of individual predictors revealed that PDS was a significant predictor of faculty intent to participate in OA IRs (Odds ratio .150, p =.001), indicating that the odds of faculty that perceive the submission process as difficult decreased by a factor of .150 for each unit increase in PDS. The PLQV also showed that the faculty intent to participate decreased by a factor .335 for a unit increase in faculty perception of IR as a low quality publishing venues. On the other hand, DAR reflected an increase in the likelihood of faculty intent to participate. For a unit increase in this predictor the odds ratio of faculty intent to participate was increased by 2.82, $p<.05$. The altruism predictor also proved significant with the odds ratio of .399, $p < .05$, indicating that for a unit increase in altruism, there was a decrease in likelihood of faculty intent to participate. The remaining predictors were not statistically significant; they exceeded the $p < .05$.

## CONCLUSION

The overall faculty intention to participate in an OA IR was slightly more than half (53%). This fairly small and unique pool of faculty respondents allows for only preliminary results of the factors that affect faculty. Difficulty with submission process was an important factor that hider faculty participation in OA IR. Also, faculty perception of OA IR as low quality publishing venues has not changed from previous studies and still proved to be a significant factor. In addition, faculty did seem to recognize the importance of OA IR in disseminating their work to a wider audience, which in turn can increase their readership. Lastly, like previous findings faculty did seem to agree with the principles of OA in theory, but they were not as willing to participate in OA IRs.

## IMPLICATIONS

Current study extends the vision shared by OA proponents of utilizing the advancement of information and communication technologies (ICT) in transforming scholarly communication. Furthermore, two decades after the OA declarations the perception of scholars regarding OA scholarly publishing remains rather unchanged. This study is an attempt to gain a better understanding of why this is the case by engaging in research that enables us to understand faculty as the major stakeholders in scholarly publishing.

## LIMITATIONS

Current study investigated the attitudes of faculty toward OA IR within a large public university in Texas although there is a variation of OA IR. The term *open access* is poorly understood by faculty in general and often misunderstood. Depending on the person's background and/or point of view, context and time frame the term *open* has a different meaning. Thus, one of the major issues with open access is the ambiguity of the term *open* that often leads to misinterpretations and should be taken into account.

## REFERENCES


Ajzen, I. (1991). The theory of planned behavior. *Organizational Behavior and Human Decision Processes*, *50*, 179–211.

Covey, D.T. (2009). Self-archiving journal articles: A case study of faculty practice and missed opportunity. *Portal: Libraries and the Academy*, 9(2), 223–251.

Creaser, C., Frey, J., Greenwood, H., Oppenheim, C. Probets S., Spezi, V., & White, S. (2010). Authors' awareness and attitude toward open access repositories. *New Review of Academic Librarianship, 16*(1), 145-161.

Crow, R. (2002). The case for institutional repositories: A SPARC position paper. Retrieved from http://www.sparc.arl.org/sites/default/files/media_files/instrepo.pdf

Davis, P. M., & Connolly, M. J. L. (2007). Institutional repositories: Evaluating the reasons for non-use of Cornell University's installation of DSpace. *D-Lib Magazine*, *13*(3/4). doi: 10.1045/march2007-davis

Field, A. P. (2009). Discovering statistics using SPSS: (and sex and drugs and rock 'n' roll). Los Angeles. Thousand Oaks, Calif.: SAGE Publications.

Foster, N. F. & Gibbons, S. (2005). Understanding faculty to improve content recruitment for institutional repositories. *D-Lib Magazine*, *11*(1). Retrieved from http://www.dlib.org/dlib/january05/foster/01foster.html

Heterick, B. (2002). Faculty attitudes toward electronic resources. *Educause Review*, *37*(4), 10.

Johnson, R. K. (2002). Institutional repositories: Partnering with faculty to enhance scholarly communication. *D-Lib Magazine*, *8*(11).

Kim, J. (2010). Faculty self-archiving: Motivations and barriers. *Journal of the American Society for Information Science and Technology*, *61*(9), 1909–1922. doi: 10.1002/asi.21336.

Kieffer, K. (1999). An introductory primer on the appropriate use of exploratory and confirmatory factor analysis. *Research in the Schools*, *2*, 75-92.

Laughtin-Dunker, K. (2014). Assessing the scholarly communication attitudes and practices of faculty: Lessons from a "failed" survey. *Journal of Librarianship and Scholarly Communication* 2(3) http://dx.doi.org/10.7710/2162-3309.1164

Quinn, B. (2010). Reducing psychological resistance to digital repositories. *Information Technology & Libraries*, *29*(2), 67-75

Velicer, W. F. (1976). Determining the number of components from the matrix of partial correlations. *Psychometrika, 41*, 321-327.

Watson, S. (2007). Authors' attitudes to, and awareness and use of, a university institutional repository. *Serial, 20*(3), 225-230.

Xia, J. (2007). Assessment of self-archiving in institutional repositories: Across disciplines. *Journal of Academic Librarianship, 33*(6), 647-654.

# Detecting Dietary Preference of Social Media Users in China via Sentiment Analysis

**Qingqing Zhou**
*Department of Information Management, Nanjing University of Science and Technology & Fujian Provincial Key Laboratory of Information Processing and Intelligent Control (Minjiang University), China. Breeze7zhou@163.com*

**Chengzhi Zhang**[†]
*Department of Information Management, Nanjing University of Science and Technology & Fujian Provincial Key Laboratory of Information Processing and Intelligent Control (Minjiang University), China.zhangcz@njust.edu.cn*

## ABSTRACT

**Dietary preferences are linked to all aspects of the human culture. Currently, researches on dietary preferences are mainly based on questionnaires, etc., which are mature and feasible. However, high cost, small scale and long timeframes are difficult to avoid. With the rapid development of social media, massive dietary reviews are shared in social media. Therefore, researches on users' dietary preferences by mining data from social media may overcome the disadvantages of traditional methods. In this paper, we use microblogs from weibo.com (one of the most popular social media platforms in China) to detect dietary preferences of social media users in China via sentiment analysis. Specifically, we compared four different aspect extraction methods and chose an optimal one to obtain aspects about dietary preferences. Secondly, sentiment polarities of the aspects and dishes are identified by sentiment classification. Empirical analysis on 3,975,800 microblogs presents that social media users in China are not satisfied with the overall status quo of dietary. In addition, experimental results show that semantic information is useful in extracting dietary aspects.**

## KEYWORDS

dietary preference, opinion mining, sentiment classification, social media, user generated content

## INTRODUCTION

Traditionally, researchers investigate dietary preferences with online questionnaires, observation methods and face-to-face interviews. However, these data collection methods are costly and time consuming. Hereby, an emerging trend is large scope survey with data from social media. In 2015, Digital, Social & Mobile Worldwide (http://wearesocial.net/blog/2015/01/digital-social-mobile-worldwide-2015/) shows that the number of active social media users in China has reached 629 million. These social media users' data contain massive dietary preferences and behaviors. Therefore, we can conduct users' dietary mining based on online user-generated contents (UGC). In this paper, we use large numbers of UGC as the experimental data and take sentiment analysis as research tools, which can make up for the deficiency of traditional methods about sample and size and reduce periods of data acquisition and analysis.

In this paper, we examine microblogs in Sina Weibo (http://weibo.com/) as experimental data and process them via fine-grained sentiment analysis, so as to detect dietary preferences of social media users in China. Our analysis framework includes extracting aspects about dietary, and identifying sentiment polarities (positive or negative) of aspects and dishes. Empirical analysis on 3,975,800 microblogs presents that users are not satisfied with the overall status quo of dietary, and they have higher levels of demands. Atmosphere and appearance are important aspects for users. In addition, experimental results show that semantic information is important in identifying users' preference aspects.

## LITERATURE REVIEW

### *User' dietary preference mining*

Traditional users' dietary preferences are mainly based on questionnaire methods. Jaeger et al. (2017) conducted an investigation with consumers in the United States and China, and found that emoji may have potential as a method for direct measurement of emotional associations to foods and beverages. In order to save cost of traditional research methods, researchers have used social media data to mine dietary preferences. Vidal et al. (2015) used Twitter data as a source to analyze "what people say when they tweet about different eating situations," and they found that Twitter data merited inclusion in the researcher's toolbox, but that it was no panacea. Vidal et al. (2016) analyzed the use of emoticon and emoji in tweets for food-related emotional expression, and the result showed that emoticon and emoji could represent an opportunity for development of non-verbal subjective methods to measure food-related emotions.

### *Sentiment analysis*

Sentiment analysis identifies opinions or preferences involved in user-generated contents, which contains various granularities: document level (Tang, 2015), sentence level (Täckström & McDonald, 2011), aspect level (Liu, 2012) etc. This paper focuses on aspect-level sentiment analysis.

---

80th Annual Meeting of the Association for Information Science & Technology, Washington, DC, VA | Oct. 27-Nov. 1, 2017



[†] Corresponding author. +86-84315963

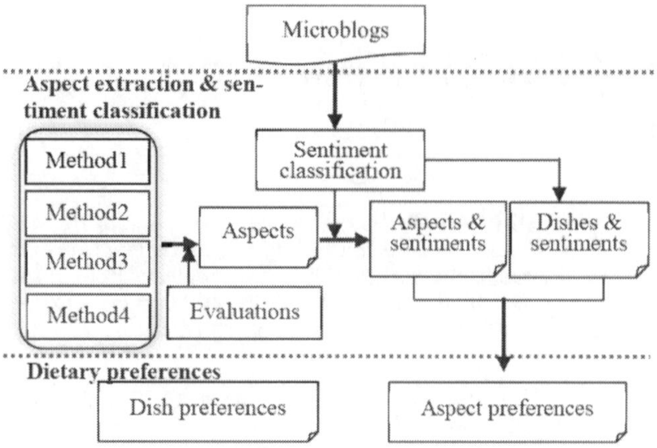


*Figure 1. Framework of detecting dietary preference*

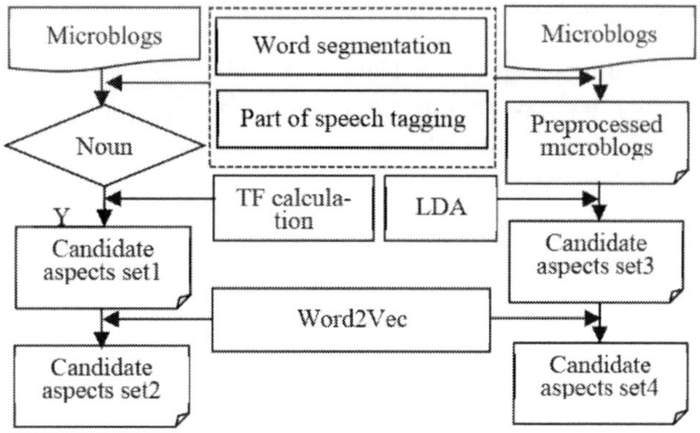


*Figure 2. Aspect extractions*

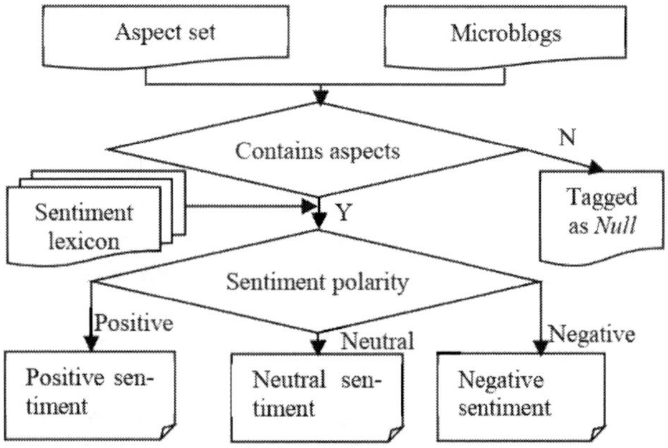


*Figure 3. Aspect sentiment classifications*

Aspect-level sentiment analysis consists of two sub-tasks: aspect extraction and aspect sentiment classification. Yan et al. (2015) integrated an extended PageRank algorithm, synonym expansion, and implicit feature inference to extract product features automatically. Yousefpour et al. (2017) proposed an ordinal-based method to integrate feature sets and feature vectors to extract aspects. Aspect sentiment classification has also become a hot topic. Hoogervorst et al. (2016) incorporated structural information of reviews by employing Rhetorical Structure Theory to conduct aspect-based sentiment classification.Giatsoglou et al. (2017) adopted a machine learning approach with which textual documents were represented by vectors and were used for training a polarity classification model, so as to detect out of textual snippets with people's opinions in different languages.

In summary, questionnaire survey is the main method of preference analysis. To overcome the shortcoming of traditional survey, some researches take online data to analyze dietary-related behavior. Meanwhile, technologies of sentiment analysis are becoming more and more mature. Hence, in this paper, we take microblogs as the experimental data to mine users' dietary preferences via sentiment analysis.

## METHODS

### Framework

This paper aims to analyze dietary preference of social media users based on microblogs. The framework (Figure 1) includes three key technologies: aspects extraction, aspect sentiment classification and dishes sentiment classification. Finally, we obtain users' dietary preferences, including dish preferences and aspects preferences.

### Key technologies

#### Aspect extraction

People have different dietary preferences such as *taste*, *price*, etc. In order to extract aspects, we compared four extraction methods (Figure 2). Regarding method 1, a Chinese word segmentation tool is used for word segmentation and part-of-speech tagging. Then, nouns with higher term frequency (TF) values are extracted for candidate aspect set 1. For method 2, the candidate aspect set is expanded from candidate aspect set 1 using a deep learning method, including two main steps: word embedding and word similarity calculation. Word embedding aims to represent words to feature vectors (Hinton, 1984). In this paper, skip-gram model in Word2Vec is used to conduct word embedding, and Cosine distances are used to calculate word similarity. Finally, five most similar words are selected to expand the aspect set. Candidate aspect set of method 3 is obtained via LDA, and candidate aspect set 4 is expanded from candidate aspect set 3 using the method same as method 2.

#### Aspect sentiment classification

In order to identify sentiment polarities of aspects, an unsupervised learning method is used (Figure 3). Specifically, (1) we match the aspect set and microblog contents to identify whether a microblog contains aspects or not; then (2) a sentiment lexicon is used to identify sentiment polarities of aspects in each microblog. In detail, we combine HowNet (http://www.keenage.com/) and NTUSD (http://www.datatang.com/data/44317/) as the sentiment lexicon, and then sentiment polarities of aspects are identified by sentiment word nearest to the aspects. Finally, (3) we obtain sentiment polarities of aspects.

#### Dish sentiment classification

Dish sentiment classification is similar to aspect sentiment classification. Specifically, (1) we check microblogs with the dish lexicon to identify whether a microblog contains a dish name or not; then (2) we match a sentiment lexicon and microblogs to identify sentiment polarities of the dishes in each microblog; (3) repeat the above two steps and determine sentiment polarities of all dishes.

## RESULTS

### Experimental data acquisition

This paper aims to detect social media users' dietary preferences. Hence, we take 25,675 dish names from meishijie (http://www.meishij.net/) as queries to retrieve related microblogs in Sina Weibo. The corpora contain the user ID, nickname, microblogs contents, launch dates, and users' regions (which are identified from users' registration information). Finally, we obtained 3,975,800 microblogs.

### Aspect extraction and Sentiment classification

Performance evaluation of aspect extraction

We use four methods to extract aspects, and parts of results are shown in Table 1. It can be seen from Table 1 that performance of method 2 is superior to the other three methods. Therefore, we take candidate aspect set 2 by method 2 as the final aspect set. In addition, performance of method 4 is better than method 3, which means that Word2Vec is useful in extracting aspects. In other words, semantic information is important for aspects extrication.

### Performance evaluation of sentiment classification

Performance evaluation metrics

We use the following metrics to evaluate sentiment classification performance: macro-average precision, macro-average recall, and $F_1$ value (Salton & McGill, 1986). These metrics can be calculated using following equations.

Macro-average precision: $$\text{MacroPre} = \frac{\sum_{i=1}^{3} P_i}{3} \quad (1)$$

Macro-average recall: $$\text{MacroRec} = \frac{\sum_{i=1}^{3} R_i}{3} \quad (2)$$

$F_1$ value: $$F_1 = \frac{2 * \text{MacroPre} * \text{MacroRec}}{\text{MacroPre} + \text{MacroRec}} \quad (3)$$

where, $P_i$ means precision of class $i$, $R_i$ is recall of class $i$.

| Methods | Taste | Distance |
|---|---|---|
| Method 1 | 味道(taste), 口味(taste), 口感(texture) | 地址(address), 距离(distance), 行程(route) |
| Method 2 | 味道(*taste*), 口感(*texture*), 口味(*taste*), 味儿(*taste*), 味(*taste*) | 距离(distance), 车程(drive distance), 路程(distance), 耗时(duration), 历时(duration) |
| Method 3 | 口味( taste) | |
| Method 4 | 味道(taste), 口感(texture), 口味(taste), 味儿(taste), 味(taste) | |

***Table 1**. Parts of aspects extracted by four methods (Note: Results of aspect extraction are the aspect set in Chinese. English words in brackets only denote corresponding English meanings of these aspects respectively.)*

| Results | MacroPre | MacroRec | $F_1$ | Accuracy |
|---|---|---|---|---|
| Aspect results | 0.7146 | 0.7638 | 0.7384 | 0.9078 |
| Dish results | 0.7349 | 0.7987 | 0.7655 | 0.7862 |

***Table 2**. Evaluation results of sentiment classification*

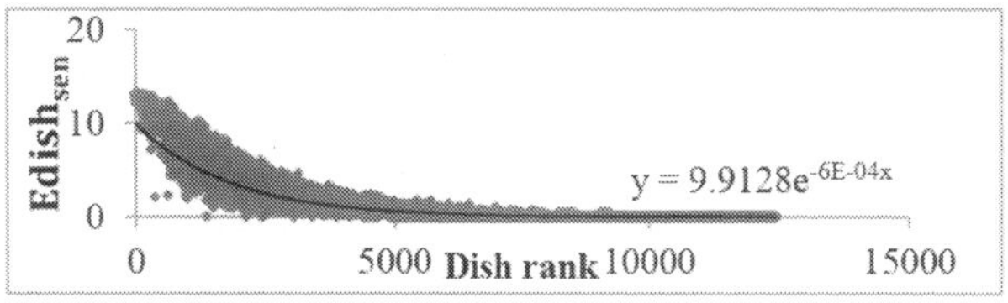


***Figure 4**. $Edish_{sen}$ of dishes*

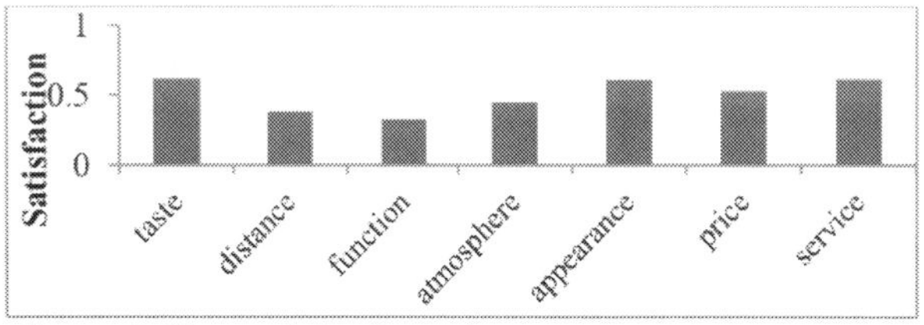


***Figure 5**. User satisfactions of aspects*

### Performance evaluation of sentiment classification

We use 5000 labeled microblogs as a test corpus to evaluate the sentiment classification performance. Results of the performance evaluation are shown in Table 2 (where aspect sentiment classification is based on aspects extracted by method 2). Accuracy of aspect sentiment classification is higher than 0.9, and all metrics of dish sentiment classification are about 0.75. Hence, we can conclude that the performances of sentiment classification are reliable. Therefore, we use our methods to conduct sentiment classification on the 3,975,800 microblogs.

### Dietary preferences analysis of social media users in China

Dish preference analysis

In order to compare users' attitudes about different dishes, we calculated users' satisfactions of 12,451 dishes in each region and use the entropy value to measure the differences among dishes, which can be calculated using equation 4:

$$Edish_{sen} = -\sum_{i=1}^{N_{sen}} \left(\frac{Reg_i^{sen}}{\sum_{i=1}^{N_{sen}} Reg_i^{sen}} * log \frac{Reg_i^{sen}}{\sum_{i=1}^{N_{sen}} Reg_i^{sen}}\right) \quad (4)$$

where $Reg_i^{sen}$ can be calculated via equation 5:

$$Reg_i^{sen} = Reg_i^{pos} / Reg_i^{fre} \quad (5)$$

Where $Reg_i^{sen}$ means satisfaction of a dish in the $i$th region, $Reg_i^{pos}$ denotes the number of positive microblogs of a dish in the $i$th region, $Reg_i^{fre}$ means microblogs number of a dish in the $i$th region, and $N_{sen}$ denotes the number of regions. Here, it equals 36.

We ranked the dishes by the frequencies and represented the $Edish_{sen}$ of all 12,451 dishes in Figure 4. We can see that a frequently mentioned dish tend to get higher $Edish_{sen}$ value.

Hence, we can conclude that hot dishes have less regional differences, while uncommon dishes have obvious regional restrictions.

### Aspect analysis

According to performance evaluation of aspect extraction described above, we obtained aspects of dietary by method 2. The aspects include *taste, distance, function, atmosphere, appearance, price* and *service*. Figure 5 shows the

| Aspect | taste | distance | function | atmosphere |
|---|---|---|---|---|
| Correlations | 0.190** | 0.155** | 0.135** | 0.222** |
| Aspect | appearance | price | service | |
| Correlations | 0.125** | 0.059** | 0.068** | |

*Note: **. Correlation is significant at the 0.01 level (2-tailed).*
***Table 3**. Correlation analysis of aspect preferences*

users' satisfaction of each aspect. We can see that Chinese users are most satisfied with *taste*, while the most unsatisfied aspect is *function*. In addition, users' satisfactions on the three most satisfied aspects are only about 0.6. Hereby, user satisfactions of aspects need to be improved.

In order to analyze effects of aspects on users' dietary preferences, we conducted a correlation analysis between aspect sentiments and dish sentiments. Specifically, we first obtained sentiment polarity of each aspect in each microblog. Then we identified sentiment polarities of dishes in those microblogs. Finally, we conducted a correlation analysis between aspects and dishes to get the Pearson correlation coefficients (Table 3). Table 3 shows that all aspects have significant positive correlations with dish sentiments. *Atmosphere* has the highest coefficient, while coefficients of *price* are the lowest. In other words, if restaurateurs want to improve users' satisfactions, they should pay more attention to upgrading dining atmosphere.

From the analysis above, we can conclude that, currently, social media users in China are not content with status quo of dietary. They pay attention to atmosphere of restaurants, more than just comparing tastes of dishes, which indicates that Chinese users are gradually taking dietary as a kind of enjoyment of life. Restaurateurs should not only enhance taste of dishes, but also pay more attention to dining atmosphere.

## DISCUSSION AND CONCLUSION

In this paper, we mined dietary preferences of social media users in China based on fine-grained sentiment analysis. We compared four aspect extraction methods and performance evaluation results revealed that the combination of a frequent noun method and a deep learning method has the optimal performance. Important conclusions can be drawn from empirical analysis on 3,975,800 microblogs; among them is that social media users in China have high levels of dietary demands, and atmosphere and appearances become important evaluating factors. In addition, semantic information is important in aspects extrication.

There are obvious advantages to detecting users' dietary preferences via fine-grained sentiment analysis. First, we use sentiment analysis to analyze online data, which has low time cost for data collection and results acquisition. Second, we have larger data size, which can get more samples. This paper has collected 8,748,195 microblogs about 25,675 dishes from 3,980,659 users. With the development of social media, users are getting accustomed to sharing opinions online. Massive UGC provide a solid basis for mining users' dietary preference. Meanwhile, technologies for sentiment analysis are mature and easy to operate, which can strengthen the dietary preference analysis. However, our method is limited in scope of application. Due to the protection of users' privacy, it is difficult to obtain users' personal information, such as age, occupation, etc. The other disadvantage is fake information. How best to filter fake microblogs is a challenging question for future research.


## ACKNOWLEDGMENTS

This work is supported by Major Projects of National Social Science Fund (No. 16ZAD224), Fujian Provincial Key Laboratory of Information Processing and Intelligent Control (Minjiang University) (No. MJUKF201704) and Qing Lan Project.


## REFERENCES


Giatsoglou, M., Vozalis, M. G., Diamantaras, K., Vakali, A., Sarigiannidis, G., & Chatzisavvas, K. C. (2017). Sentiment analysis leveraging emotions and word embeddings. *Expert Systems with Applications, 69*, 214-224.

Hinton, G. E. (1984). *Distributed representations*. MIT Press.

Hoogervorst, R., Essink, E., Jansen, W., Helder, M. V. D., Schouten, K., Frasincar, F., & Taboada, M. (2016). Aspect-based sentiment analysis on the web using rhetorical structure theory. *Proceedings of the Web Engineering*, 317-334.

Jaeger, S. R., Vidal, L., Kam, K., & Ares, G. (2017). Can emoji be used as a direct method to measure emotional associations to food names? Preliminary investigations with consumers in USA and China. *Food Quality and Preference, 56*, 38-48.

Liu, B. (2012). Sentiment analysis and opinion mining. *Synthesis Lectures on Human Language Technologies, 5*(1), 1-167.

Salton, G., & McGill, M. J. (1986). *Introduction to modern information retrieval*.

Täckström, O., & McDonald, R. (2011). Semi-supervised latent variable models for sentence-level sentiment analysis. *Proceedings of the ACL*, 569-574.

Tang, D. (2015). Sentiment-specific representation learning for document-level sentiment analysis. *Proceedings of the 8th ACM international conference on web search and data mining*, 447-452.

Vidal, L., Ares, G., & Jaeger, S. R. (2016). Use of emoticon and emoji in tweets for food-related emotional expression. *Food Quality and Preference, 49*, 119-128.

Vidal, L., Ares, G., Machín, L., & Jaeger, S. R. (2015). Using Twitter data for food-related consumer research: A case study on "what people say when tweeting about different eating situations." *Food Quality & Preference, 45*, 58-69.

Yan, Z., Xing, M., Zhang, D., & Ma, B. (2015). EXPRS: An extended pagerank method for product feature extraction from online consumer reviews. *Information & Management, 52*(7), 850-858.

Yousefpour, A., Ibrahim, R., & Hamed, H. N. A. (2017). Ordinal-based and frequency-based integration of feature selection methods for sentiment analysis. *Expert Systems with Applications*, 80-93.

# Information Literacy in an Era of Information Uncertainty

**Noa Aharony**
*Bar-Ilan University, Israel. Noa.Aharony@biu.ac.il*

**Kendra Albright**
*Kent State University, USA. kalbrig7@kent.edu*

**Louise Limberg**
*University of Borås, Sweden. louise.limberg@hb.se*

**Ina Fourie**
*University of Pretoria, South Africa. ina.fourie@up.ac.za*

**Heidi Julien**
*University at Buffalo, USA. heidijul@buffalo.edu*

**Jenny Bronstein**
*Bar-Ilan University, Israel. Jenny.Bronstein@biu.ac.il*

## ABSTRACT

**Recently, in the election that took place in the United States, we have heard a lot about "fake news" and its influence. The discourse regarding "fake news" and "alternative facts" points to the importance of information literacy, a set of skills that enables people to seek, evaluate and use information in an effective way. The objective of this panel is to bring together experts from different countries to discuss how they perceive the future of information literacy (IL). The question that arises is will IL be the sole focus of librarians, information professionals and educators, or will it be regarded as a lifelong learning skill that affects different aspects of our everyday life such as health, workplace and even culture? The session will begin with a short overview of the recent literature on this issue, followed by the panellists' findings and examples of research projects, as well as their insights about new approaches in the area of IL. The panel will conclude with an engaging discussion with the audience to identify future trends in IL.**

## KEYWORDS

information literacy, library and information science, conceptual change, health, workplace, migrants

## INTRODUCTION

The term *information literacy* (IL) has developed since its inception in 1974 when Paul Zurkowski, who was the first to use the phrase *information literacy,* suggested that information-literate people know how to use information resources in their workplace (Aharony, 2010). Librarians have been the primary profession to deal with the topic of IL. The American Library Association (ALA) (1989) and the Association of College and Research Libraries (ACRL) (2000) have stressed the importance of IL as a set of essential skills for society in general and in particular for students in higher education.

80th Annual Meeting of the Association for Information Science & Technology, Washington, DC, VA | Oct. 27-Nov. 1, 2017



In 2016 the ACRL presented a new Framework for Information Literacy for higher education which replaced the previous ACRL Standards (2000). This Framework is based on a cluster of interconnected core concepts, with flexible options for implementation, rather than on a set of standards or learning outcomes. The Framework is organized into six frames, each consisting of a concept central to information literacy, a set of knowledge practices and a set of dispositions. These are the six frames: authority is constructed and contextual; information creation as a process; information has value; research as inquiry; scholarship as conversation; and searching as strategic exploration. This Framework highlights the concept of metaliteracy that suggests a new vision of IL as an overarching set of abilities, where students are consumers and creators of information who can take part in collaborative spaces. Metaliteracy demands behavioral, affective, cognitive and metacognitive engagement with the information ecosystem.

Hence, it has become evident that the process of becoming information literate is no longer as simple as mastering a set of skills in order to access, disseminate or present information. Lloyd (2011) suggests that becoming an information literate person requires developing an understanding of what forms information in a particular setting; considering the discourses that impact activities related to the creation, dissemination and operationalization of information; and understanding how information is enabled or constrained through the social activities rooted within the special environment. This approach along with the new ACRL Framework (2016) leads to a new consideration that perhaps IL is no longer the sole focus of librarians, information professionals and educators and that the attitudes and perspectives towards IL should be changed.

## PANEL ORGANIZATION

This panel brings together researchers to present an overview of IL in a dynamic environment. Each panelist will contribute a unique perspective, based on her own disciplinary background, theoretical orientation and programs of research. The session will begin with an overview of the key issues: 1) conceptual understandings, 2) fresh perspectives, 3) IL in health care, 4) IL in workplaces and 5) IL among migrants.

The panel will conclude with an engaging discussion with the audience to identify future trends and fruitful areas for research and collaboration. These are among the initial questions we will offer to stimulate the discussion: 1) Do you agree with at least one of the perspectives that was presented in the panel? 2) What other directions do you assume IL will turn to?

We will structure the proposed panel session in the following manner.

- Introduction - The moderator (Prof. Noa Aharony) briefly introduces the aim and structure of the panel, followed by the introduction of panelists (5 minutes).
- Prof. Louise Limberg will present the issue of conceptual understandings of IL (10 minutes).
- Prof. Heidi Julien will present a provocative, different perspective on IL (10 minutes).
- Prof. Kendra Albright will present the issue of IL in the context of health care (10 minutes).
- Prof. Ina Fourie will present the issue of IL in the context of workplaces (10 minutes).
- Dr. Jenny Bronstein will present the issue of IL in the context of immigrants (10 minutes).
- All panelists will express their perspectives concerning the future of IL.
- Free discussions with audience members who can share their personal or scientific experience with IL or their expectations or concerns regarding the future of IL (10 minutes).
- Wrap-up. The moderator summarizes the outcomes of the panel discussions (5 minutes).

#### CONCEPTUAL UNDERSTANDINGS OF IL

Prof. Limberg will present examples of changing conceptual understandings of IL over the last decades with a point of departure in the view of IL as a set of skills concerning searching, seeking and evaluating information for various purposes and applicable across contexts, according to core documents (e.g., ACRL, 2000; CILIP, 2013). These basic ideas were coined in the field of academic librarianship. During the last decade, however, conceptions of IL have taken different shapes mainly since IL became the object of serious theoretical research with the purpose of exploring the concept of IL, rather than trying to indicate most information users as being deficient in IL, and demonstrating the expertise of librarians in the domain. Changes concerned broadening the context of IL studies from education environments to wider fields, such as work life, everyday life, health, etc. (Examples are provided in this panel.) This led to new aspects of IL being identified (e.g., Huvila, 2011; Lloyd, 2006; Lundh & Dolatkhah, 2016; Sundin & Carlsson, 2016). Theoretical approaches, e.g., phenomenography, sociocultural perspectives, practice theories and related frameworks contributed more in-depth understandings, implying IL as embracing a range of features beyond the classical qualities (Limberg, Sundin & Talja, 2012; Pilerot, 2016). Continued theory development is an essential objective for IL research. One challenge for continued work in the area is the relationship between research and practice. There is a need for active efforts on this issue. Theory-based research and continued digitization of media in society, such as user generated media without any editorial check or control before publication, indicate the need for new ways of critical scrutiny of various genres of publications. This, in turn, will require continued research in the area of IL with relevance for various aspects of life, including citizenship and society.

#### A PROVOCATIVE, DIFFERENT PERSPECTIVE ON IL

Prof. Heidi Julien will play devil's advocate, proposing that librarians should refocus their attention away from IL instruction. Prof. Julien will argue that librarians should minimize their IL instruction efforts for a range of reasons: most people assume they have sufficient IL skills to achieve their modest informational goals; librarians are not viewed (outside of librarianship) as central to the IL agenda; and the most appropriate context for developing IL skills is the K-12 education system, where school librarians have a decreasing role.

The first issue is a pressing one. There is clear evidence that many people are unable to evaluate online information (Stanford History Education Group, 2016), and that people regularly overestimate their own skill levels (Gross & Latham, 2012). The second issue is that despite librarians' claim on IL as a primary professional responsibility, those outside of the field do not share that perception. Libraries are widely viewed as outdated in the age of the internet, and librarians continue to be discounted as low-level employees with little to no professional expertise. These perceptions are evident in schools, where school librarians often do not receive professional respect or the opportunity to fulfil the responsibilities for which they are prepared. Similar perceptions are evident among postsecondary students who rely on open web searches rather than library databases for academic purposes and among the general public which fails to support public libraries sufficiently. The final issue is that because IL skills are so central to success, development of that skill set should truly rest with K-12 teachers, who currently have responsibility for developing other fundamental skill sets. Giving teachers the training and mandate to address IL would prioritize this essential set of skills.

#### IL IN HEALTH CARE

Prof. Albright will talk about IL and health care. According to the National Assessment of Adult Literacy (U.S. Department of Education, 2006), only 12% of adults have what they consider to be "proficient health literacy." This suggests that nearly 90% of American adults may not have health literacy skills that are sufficient enough to manage their own health care, including disease prevention. Another 14% are considered to have health literacy skills that are below basic, of which 42% may not have health insurance and are more likely to describe their health as poor. Low health information literacy can lead to poor health outcomes including "more frequent hospitalization and less use of prevention services" (ODPHP, https://health.gov/communication/-literacy/quickguide/factsbasic.htm). On the other hand, increased knowledge of health conditions and treatment options can lead to better decision making which impacts health outcomes. From an LIS standpoint, there needs to be a way to make complex health information available in a format that best meets the needs of either the local community being served and/or for individual consumption. Information professionals can transform information into a format that is usable and suits the needs of the target population. The result should be an information "product" that can be utilized more easily by the users.

## WORKPLACE IL

Prof. Fourie will talk about IL within the context of workplaces. Workplace IL requires a deepened conceptualization and contextualization to address the complexities of workplaces. Workplace IL needs to be part of lifelong learning (Webber & Johnston, 2013). It must prepare working adults to deal with the numerous challenges of the 21st century: mastery of digital literacies, workplace readiness and employability, multiculturalism, collaboration, big data, cyber security, social responsibility and community involvement (Crawford & Irving, 2009).

Discussion will be focused on:

- Conceptualisation of workplace information literacy
- Limited availability and use of models and theories developed from workplace information literacy research.

## IL: MIGRANT WORKERS' PATH TO SOCIAL INCLUSION

Dr. Bronstein will present IL within the context of migrants. Migration to a new country results in a disruption to the immigrants' existing knowledge bases and in an inability to recognize information needs and access information sources related to basic needs such as housing, employment, education and health (Baron, Neils & Gomez, 2014). The literature related to migrants' integration into new societies indicates that the IL skills that allow people to understand how information is situated and made accessible is a primary driver for successful participation in society (Hicks & Lloyd, 2016). Following the social interactionist perspective that conceptualizes IL as common to and situated in all environments, IL is viewed as a sociocultural practice transcending mere possession of a set of skills to a complex understanding of the social modalities (Lloyd, Lipu, & Kennan, 2010). This view regards IL as a learning process situated in social interactions that provides the learner with the opportunity for information sharing for the conception of new knowledge (Hoyer, 2011). That is, people become information literate through multiple information behaviours and practices within their social environments (Khoir, Du, & Koronios, 2015).

## THE PANEL MEMBERS

**Prof. Noa Aharony**, moderator, is an associate professor and the head of the Information Science Department at Bar-Ilan University (Israel). Prof. Aharony has taught the course of IL for undergraduate and graduate students for about 15 years. Prof. Aharony is the author of numerous articles and presentations on IL. Recently, she has contributed a section to the ACRL paper: *Global Information Literacy Perspectives*.

**Prof. Louise Limberg**, panelist, is a senior professor of library and information science (LIS) at the Swedish School of Library and Information Science, University of Borås, Sweden. Her research interests concern the interaction between information seeking and use, and learning, linked to issues of IL. Dr. Limberg's early work was pioneering in the area of IL and she continues to work in wide international networks focusing on IL research, including close collaboration within the Nordic countries as well as Australia.

**Prof. Heidi Julien**, panelist, is professor and chair of the Department of Library & Information Studies at the University at Buffalo. Her research and teaching interests focus on IL and information behavior. She is the author of numerous articles and presentations on IL, including several keynote addresses. She authored the article "Digital Literacy" in the *Encyclopaedia of Information Science and Technology*.

**Prof. Kendra Albright**, panelist, is professor and director of the School of Library and Information Science at Kent State University. Dr. Albright's primary research focuses on the use of information and communication to solve human problems, particularly in the areas of HIV/AIDS and domestic violence. She currently serves as editor-in-chief for *Libri: International Journal of Libraries and Information Studies*.

**Prof. Ina Fourie**, panelist, is a full professor in the Department of Information Science, University of Pretoria (South Africa). She supervises masters' and doctoral studies in information literacy (including workplace information literacy, advanced research information literacy, online training in information literacy), the digital divide, etc. She is co-author of *Navigating Information Literacy: Your Information Society Survival Toolkit* (published by Pearson, 5th edition, 2017; available as an enhanced e-book) and collaborated on a UNESCO-funded project to teach information literacy skills to teachers from rural environments.

**Dr. Jenny Bronstein**, panelist, is senior lecturer in the Information Science Department at Bar-Ilan University, Ramat-Gan, Israel. Her interests focus on information behaviour and different perspectives of IL in academia over the years. Presently, she is investigating the role that IL plays in the process of social inclusion of migrant workers based on the notion that IL is viewed as a learning process situated in social interactions and common to and situated in all environments.

## EXPECTED OUTCOMES

By the end of the panel discussions, panelists and audience members will share the basic understanding of IL in a changing evolving environment and try to outline new conceptualizations of the concept.

## REFERENCES


ACRL. (2000). *Information Literacy Competency Standards for Higher Education*. Chicago, IL. Retrieved from http://www.ala.org/acrl/sites/ala.org.acrl/files/content/standards/standards.pdf

ACRL. (2016). *Framework for Information Literacy for Higher Education*. Chicago, IL. Retrieved from http://www.ala.org/acrl/sites/ala.org.acrl/files/content/issues/infolit/Framework_ILHE.pdf

Aharony, N. (2010). Information literacy in the professional literature: An exploratory analysis. *Aslib Proceedings 62,* (3), 261-282.

ALA. (1989) *Presidential committee on information literacy: Final report*. Retrieved from http://www.ala.org/acrl/publications/whitepapers/presidential

Baron, L. F., Neils, M., & Gomez, R. (2014). Crossing new borders: Computers, mobile phones, transportation, and English language among Hispanic day laborers in Seattle, Washington. *Journal of the Association for Information Science and Technology, 65*(1), 98-108. CILIP. (2013). *Information literacy – Definition*. Retrieved from http://www.cilip.org.uk/cilip/advocacy-campaigns-awards/advocacy-campaigns/information-literacy/information-literacy

Crawford, J., & Irving, C. 2009. Information literacy in the workplace: A qualitative exploratory study. *Journal of Librarianship & Information Science, 41*(1), 29-38.

Gross, M., & Latham, D. (2012). What's skill got to do with it?: Information literacy skills and self-views of ability among first-year college students. *Journal of the American Society for Information Science & Technology, 63*(3), 574-583.

Hicks, A., & Lloyd, A. (2016). It takes a community to build a framework: Information literacy within intercultural settings. *Journal of Information Science, 42*(3), 334-343.

Hoyer, J. (2011). Information is social: Information literacy in context. *Reference Services Review, 39*(1), 10-23.

Huvila, I. (2011). The complete information literacy? Unforgetting creation and organization of information. *Journal of Librarianship and Information Science*, *43*(4), 237-245.

Khoir, S., Du, J.T., & Koronios, A. (2015). Everyday information behavior of Asian immigrants in South Australia: A mixed-methods exploration. *Information Research, 20*(3), paper 687. Retrieved from http://InformationR.net/ir/20-3/paper687.html

Limberg, L., Sundin, O., & Talja, S. (2012). Three theoretical perspectives on information literacy. *Human IT: Journal for Information Technology Studies as a Human Science, 11*(2), 95-130.

Lundh, A., & Dolatkhah, M. (2016). Reading as dialogical document work: Possibilities for library and information science. *Journal of Documentation*, *72*(1), 127-139.

Lloyd, A. (2006). Information literacy landscapes. *Journal of Documentation, 62*(5), 570-583.

Lloyd, A. (2011). Trapped between a rock and a hard place: What counts as information literacy in the workplace and how is it conceptualized? *Library Trends*, *60* (2), 277-296.

Lloyd, A., Lipu, S., & Kennan, M.A. (2010). On becoming citizens: Examining social inclusion from an information perspective. *Australian Academic & Research Libraries, 41*(1), 42-53.

Office of Disease Prevention and Health Promotion (ODPHP) (n.d.). *Quick Guide to Health Literacy*. Retrieved from https://health.gov/communication/literacy/quickguide/factsbasic.htm.

Pilerot, O. (2016). A practice-based exploration of the enactment of information literacy among PhD students in an interdisciplinary research field. *Journal of Documentation*, *72*(3), 414-434.

Stanford History Education Group (2016). *Evaluating Information: The Cornerstone of Civic Online Reasoning*. Executive Summary. Retrieved from https://sheg.stanford.edu/upload/V3LessonPlans/Executive%20Summary%2011.21.16.pdf

Sundin, O., & Carlsson, H. (2016). Outsourcing trust to the information infrastructure in schools. How search engines order knowledge in education practices. *Journal of Documentation*, *72*(6), 990-1007.

U.S. Department of Education. (2006). Retrieved from https://nces.ed.gov/naal/

Webber, S., & Johnston, B. (2013). Transforming information literacy for higher education in the 21st century: A lifelong approach. In Hepworth, M. & Walton, G. Bingley (Eds.), *Developing people's information capabilities: Fostering information literacy in educational workplace and community contexts*. UK: Emerald, pp. 27-30.

# Tribute to Eugene Garfield

**Judit Bar-Ilan**
*Bar-Ilan University, Israel. Judit.Bar-Ilan@biu.ac.il*

**Howard D. White**
*Drexel University, USA. whitehd@drexel.edu*

**Katherine W. McCain**
*Drexel University, USA. mccainkw@drexel.edu*

**Dietmar Wolfram**
*University of Wisconsin-Milwaukee, USA. dwolfram@uwm.edu*

**Henry Small**
*SciTech Strategies, Inc., USA. hsmall@mapofscience.com*

**Paul Wouters**
*CWTS, Leiden University, Netherlands. p.f.wouters@cwts.leidenuniv.nl*

## ABSTRACT

**This panel pays tribute to Dr. Eugene Garfield, one of the "fathers" of bibliometrics, former president of ASIS (1999-2000) and the founder of the ISI citation databases. Dr. Garfield passed away on February 25, 2017. In this panel, we will highlight his contributions to information science. The panelists are all well-known researchers who have known and worked with r. Garfield. Each panelist will highlight an aspect of Dr. Garfield's contributions that has transformed science and scholarship and how, in turn, their own work has been influenced by his contributions. The panel will be moderated by Judit Bar-Ilan and Dietmar Wolfram.**

## KEYWORDS

Eugene Garfield, tribute, citation databases, invited panel

## INTRODUCTION

Scholarly communication is the lifeblood of knowledge creation and dissemination. Over the centuries, practices for scholarly communication have evolved. The exponential growth of scientific literature since the 17th century (Price, 1986) has made effective methods for documenting and accessing recorded discourse essential. The design and study of these methods have played a key role in the development of what would become information science in the 20th century. The evolution of indexing and abstracting services into today's bibliographic databases provides the foundation for much of the research that is undertaken in information science.

The concept of a citation is simple, but powerful. The recognition of earlier research on which knowledge is built is a cornerstone of this communication. Today's citation databases have made it possible for bibliometrics and scholarly communications researchers to explore the intricate web of relationships that exists among authors, publications, journals and domains. Although citation-based research evaluation metrics have not been without their critics (e.g., Gingras, 2016; MacRoberts & MacRoberts, 1989), the global community of scholars owes a debt of gratitude to Dr. Eugene Garfield for his pioneering efforts in the development of the Science Citation Index and its successors.

Dr. Garfield was well known to the ASIST community for many decades, having received the Award of Merit in 1975 and having served as president of the association in 1999-2000. His influence on the field of information science is evident in his many publications and publications devoted to his contributions such as *The Web of Knowledge: A Festschrift in Honor of Eugene Garfield* (Cronin & Atkins, 2000).

With Dr. Garfield's passing, we have lost a true pioneer in information science.

## PANEL ORGANIZATION

The impact of Dr. Garfield's vision and work cannot be overstated. This panel pays tribute to Dr. Eugene Garfield, one of the "fathers" of bibliometrics and the founder of the ISI citation databases. Dr. Garfield passed away on February 25, 2017. Our prestigious speakers will present reflections on Dr. Garfield's life and contributions to information science and scholarship, more broadly. Each presenter had the good fortune to have known Dr. Garfield over many years.

The panel will conclude with a discussion with the audience on how Dr. Garfield's initiatives and work have changed information science.

## TRI-CITATION ANALYSIS – KATHERINE MCCAIN

I will be discussing an extension of White's "citation image" assessment of a scholar's research visibility and position in citation networks, applying a contextual constraint to co-citation counts for authors also frequently co-cited with Garfield. This "tri-citation analysis" (or contextual author co-ci-

80th Annual Meeting of the Association for Information Science & Technology, Washington, DC, VA | Oct. 27-Nov. 1, 2017

tation analysis) approach is used to explore Garfield's influence in the interrelated areas of bibliometrics, scientometrics, scholarly communication and sociology of science over three successive decades (1978 to 2007) of citations to Garfield's *oeuvre*. Changes in research topics and key cited authors can be observed and the most important of Garfield's publications in these topic areas can be identified.

### THE SCIENCE CITATION INDEX – HENRY SMALL

The topic of this presentation will be "What Gene Garfield's citation index for science could have been and may yet become." The exchange of letters between Gene Garfield and Joshua Lederberg in 1959 was decisive in the development of what became the Science Citation Index (SCI). These letters show that Gene had a broad range of ideas on what the citation index could be, both in terms of its organization and the nature of the data captured. In particular, he had many ideas on how the citing context or citing passage could be utilized and its value in indexing the cited material. These ideas were based on earlier work he had done at the Welch Medical Library.

With the availability of an increasing volume of scientific literature accessible in machine-readable form and formatted in XML, it now becomes possible to revisit some of Gene's early, more radical ideas. We will attempt to envision what a young Gene Garfield would have designed had he lived in a 21st century, web-centric and AI enabled world.

### GARFIELD IN PENNANT DIAGRAMS – HOWARD WHITE

My talk is called "Garfield in Pennant Diagrams." Given (1) a seed author, (2) the names and co-citation counts of other authors co-cited with the seed and (3) a total citation count for each author, one can create a pennant diagram. This is a two-dimensional plot in which the two kinds of counts, suitably transformed, align on the two dimensions, and the co-cited authors' names form a roughly pennant-like shape with the seed author at the tip. Remarkably, these simple diagrams consistently reveal certain facts about the seed's social and intellectual position with respect to the other authors. Over the past decade I have done a number of pennants with different information scientists as seeds. Eugene Garfield figures in most of them, and I will use them as examples to discuss him and other authors in relation to specific seeds. All the speakers on the panel also appear in one or more of the pennants, and this may add to the human interest of the account.

### RETHINKING GARFIELD'S IDEAS – PAUL WOUTERS

The consequence of Garfield's invention of the Science Citation Index was the development of a completely new "meta-language" about science and scholarship. Garfield was intent on innovation. Inspired by John Desmond Bernal's thinking about fundamentally transforming science, he developed with Joshua Lederberg more ideas than they could realize. Yet, the radical redefinition of the concept of scientific quality that has come about was expected by neither. Citations have inserted themselves in the fabric of science more deeply and in more complex ways than could be foreseen in the world of the 1950s. Since then, comparable information structures and tools based on them, such as search engines, have developed in a range of other sectors of society (health care, logistics, markets, etc.). Information about information plays an increasing role in structuring our lives. As a result, it no longer seems to make much sense to maintain the good old modernist distinction between "representation" and "world" or between "word" and "object." If pragmatism is indeed replacing modernism, we need to rethink what knowledge creation and circulation mean for the world of the near future, since the very idea of science has mostly been built on modernist foundations. In this rethinking, some of Garfield's early ideas may get a new life both practically and in terms of fundamental concepts.

### PANEL MEMBERS IN ALPHABETICAL ORDER

**Judit Bar-Ilan**, moderator, is professor at the Department of Information Science of Bar-Ilan University in Israel. Her areas of interest include informetrics, information retrieval, Internet research, information behavior and usability. Additional details are available at http://is.biu.ac.il/en/judit/.

**Katherine W. McCain** is professor emerita in the Department of Information Science, College of Computing & Informatics, Drexel University. She received her PhD in information studies from Drexel in 1985 and never left. Her post-retirement research interests focus on the context and content of acknowledgment patterns in model organism literature – a topic area related to citation content analysis, but much less tractable.

**Henry Small** is currently a senior scientist (and senior citizen) at SciTech Strategies, Inc. He was director of research and chief scientist at ISI (now Clarivate Analytics) and a close associate of Gene Garfield for nearly 40 years. His research interest continues to be citation analysis in tandem with full text.

**Howard D. White,** who took his PhD in library and information science at UC Berkeley, is a professor emeritus in Drexel University's College of Computing and Informatics. His more recent work draws on both bibliometrics and information retrieval, and he has sought to integrate ideas from both with ideas from relevance theory, a major subfield of linguistic pragmatics.

**Dietmar Wolfram,** moderator, is professor at the School of Information Studies at the University of Wisconsin-Milwaukee. He received his PhD in library and information science from the University of Western Ontario. His research interests include informetrics, information retrieval, the intersection between these two areas, scholarly communication and user studies.

**Paul Wouters** is professor of scientometrics at Leiden University and director of CWTS (http://www.cwts.nl/). He met Garfield while writing his doctoral thesis about the creation of the Science Citation Index and its influence on scholarly behavior and research evaluation and policy. He is particularly interested in how the notion of scientific quality keeps developing as part of the historical development of science and scholarship.


## ACKNOWLEDGMENTS

This panel is sponsored by ASIST SIG/MET and by Clarivate Analytics. We thank Clarivate Analytics for its generous support of this panel.


## REFERENCES


Cronin, B., & Atkins, H. B. (Eds.). (2000). The web of knowledge: A Festschrift in honor of Eugene Garfield. Medford, NJ: Information Today, Inc.

de Solla Price, D. J., (1986). Little science, big science... and beyond. New York: Columbia University Press.

Gingras, Y. (2016). Bibliometrics and research evaluation: Uses and abuses. Cambridge, MA: MIT Press, 2016.

MacRoberts, M. H., & MacRoberts, B. R. (1989). Problems of citation analysis: A critical review. Journal of the American Society for Information Science, 40(5), 342-349.

# Global Human Trafficking Seen Through the Lens of Semantics and Text Analytics

**Denise A. D. Bedford**
*Georgetown University, USA. db233@georgetown.edu*

**Jyldyz Bekbalaeva**
*American University of Central Asia, Kyrgyzstan. bekbalaeva_j@auca.kg*

**Kyle M. Ballard**
*U.S. Department of State, USA. BallardKM@state.gov*

**Thomas J. Hernandez**
*Granicus, USA. tjh47@georgetown.edu*

### ABSTRACT

**Human trafficking is understood as a modern-day form of slavery. It involves the recruitment, transportation, transfer, harboring, or receipt of persons by improper means (such as force, abduction, fraud, or coercion) for an improper purpose including forced labor or sexual exploitation. Human trafficking is global, is found in every country, affects all genders, and persons of all ages. While pervasive, it is also invisible. Quantitative and qualitative research methods into human trafficking have significant challenges. This program presents collegial collaborative research by the U.S. Department of State and Georgetown University into the use of text analytics and semantic analysis methods to map trafficking, to identify trafficking hubs around the world, and to expose human trafficking.**

### KEYWORDS

human trafficking, semantic profiles, text analytics, information dissemination

### INTRODUCTION

The United Nations (2007) defines ***human trafficking*** as the recruitment, transportation, transfer, harboring or receipt of persons by improper means (such as force, abduction, fraud or coercion) for an improper purpose including forced labor or sexual exploitation. The U.S. government defines human trafficking as (1) sex trafficking in which a commercial sex act is induced by force, fraud or coercion or in which the person induced to perform such act has not attained 18 years of age; and (2) the recruitment, harboring, transportation, provision or obtaining of a person for labor or services, through the use of force, fraud or coercion for the purpose of subjection to involuntary servitude, peonage, debt bondage or slavery. In summary, human trafficking is a modern day human slave trade which is found in and is a threat to every nation in the world (U.S. Department of State, 2013). It speaks to the core of human rights abuse, and it has legal, social, economic, health and cultural consequences. We know that it destroys families, is associated with organized crimes, is a huge threat to the development of human capital and generally leads to or is fueled by economic corruption.

Human trafficking is fueled by economic gain for the trades and has lifelong negative economic impacts to those people who are commodities in the trade (Wheaton Schauer and Galli, 2010; Mahmoud and Trebesch, 2010; Jakobsson and Kotsadam; 2013; Belser, 2005). Where economic incentives do not exist, e.g., where there are not alternatives for economic gain and prosperity for individuals, trafficking will not thrive. Human trafficking will thrive where cultures tolerate different status and rights for individuals. Where social classes are traditionally defined and social mobility is challenging, it will be hard to move out of the lower and impoverished classes (Zimmerman, Hossein and Watts, 2011; Alvarez and Alesai, 2012; Lobasz, 2009; Goodale and Merry, 2007). Where the legal system does not punish human traffickers, there will be little recourse for those who are trafficked (Shelley and Lee, 2007; Ruggiero, 1997; Gallagher, 2010; Goodale and Merry, 2007; Srikantaiah, 2007; Wilson and Dalton, 2008). And, by definition, because the work performed by trafficked peoples is often illegal, they are often not viewed sympathetically by the host country population. Rather than seen as victims, the victims are often seen or portrayed as criminals. We can look to the media's treatment of human trafficking in the United States to understand the predicament of the victims (Srikantiah, 2007).

Human trafficking involves all genders and people of all ages (Rafferty, 2008), from young children through young adults to mature adults (Feingold, 2005; Kempadoo, Sanghera and Pattanaik, 2015; Rao and Presenti, 2012). If we look hard enough, we will see human trafficking in every country around the globe. There are, though, hubs for human trafficking just as there were stations along the Underground Railroad. Health problems are among the most prevalent and pervasive but least well recognized impacts of human trafficking (Oberdorster et al., 2005; Tsutsumi et al., 2008; Gushulak and MacPherson, 2000; Kinney, 2006). Trafficked persons are often not in a position to seek medical or health care. In sum, this is a very broad and deep challenge.

In addition to the challenges noted above, research into human trafficking is challenging (Laczko and Gozdziak, 2005; Tyldum and Brunovskis, 2005; Gozdziak, 2011). Typically,

80th Annual Meeting of the Association for Information Science & Technology, Washington, DC, VA | Oct. 27-Nov. 1, 2017

the trafficked population is invisible to the society they serve. While we can use quantitative methods to try to track the traffic, it will by definition be an underrepresentation of the actual traffic. In order to conduct qualitative research into the effects of human trafficking on individuals, we must have access to those individuals. For many reasons, individuals may be unwilling to work with researchers – for fear of reprisals, exposure or physical violence (Oram et al., 2012). We have challenges to both quantitative and quality research.

The U.S. Department of State and Georgetown University's Communication, Culture and Technology program established a collegial collaboration in 2015 to begin to address these challenges. Text analytics methods (e.g., stochastic methods) were applied to structured and semi-structured data. A global map of a human trafficking network was produced for review by subject matter experts. This collaboration produced a visualization of human traffic flows and nubs which is easily understood by the average citizen.

In addition, students in a semantic analysis methods course in 2016 investigated the dimensions of human trafficking and collaboratively constructed a profile for semantic analysis. Semantic analysis profiles begin with an understanding of the language of the subject domain (e.g., linguistic register) and the knowledge structures (e.g., noun phrases). These methods – in contrast to text analytics – make use of natural language processing engines, extensive rule development and rigorous validation from human subject matter experts. The profile is a complex, multidimensional model that represents the way we talk and think about human trafficking, its causes and its impacts. The profile was developed working with a wide range of types of documents and has been applied to the State Department's annual trafficking in persons reports. The panel will share the results of the application of the semantic profile to publicly available sources. The results will be demonstrated in English and perhaps in other languages depending on the progress made by the research teams at the time of the meeting. While English is an important language, the profile must also be available in Italian, Russian, Spanish and Asian languages to ensure it aligns with trafficking hubs around the world.

The intent of both the text analytics and the semantic analysis work is to develop tools and methods that can help us discover, disclose and raise awareness of human trafficking. The extent of the traffic in 2017 is too great for individual investigators to track. The causes and consequences are too broad for subjective human detection. In essence, this work looks at how we can better make the invisible trade in human slavery visible, and raise awareness on a global level.

## FORMAT

Panelists will each provide a summary of their contribution to the research. Presentations will be short and will be followed by open dialog with the audience participants. SIG/III members will be particularly important participants in the discussion. In addition, discussion of the two distinct analytical methods – text analytics and semantic analysis methods – will be encouraged. The format is designed to encourage other researchers to join to collegial collaboration.

## BENEFITS

There are several levels of benefits from this program. The first level of benefit is to the community of individuals engaged in fighting human trafficking. Research is a challenge in this area, and the expectation is that these methods, carefully crafted and rigorously tested, may offer some support. The next level of benefit will be to ASIST members through outreach to the development and social justice communities in the MD-DC-VA region. ASIST has been open to taking up critical community research topics and controversial topics in recent years, which is enhancing the image of the association. SIG/KM and SIG/III collaborated on program development and research in the past, and this program offers us an opportunity to revive that collaboration. Finally, we believe that because this is a very challenging area of research it will generate a rich discussion about appropriate applications for text analytics and semantic analysis methods.

## CO-SPONSORS

This program proposal is jointly sponsored by SIG/KM and SIG/III.

## PROMOTION

The panel will be promoted to SIG/KM and SIG/III members, to the federal knowledge management community, to the local chapters of AIIM, SIM and SLA, and to the Knowledge Leaders Forum and SIKM. In addition, we will promote the program to local international development organizations (e.g., World Bank Group, IADB and United Nations), federal agencies such as DHS, FBI and Department of State and to non-profit and non-governmental organizations with offices in the MD-DC-VA area. We will also promote the program to European KM associations and the International Association for Knowledge Management.

## PANELISTS

**Dr. Jyldyz Bekbalaeva** is director of the library at American University of Central Asia, where she manages library services and resources. She is currently a Fulbright Scholar at Georgetown University, working in collaboration with Dr. Bedford. Prior to joining the university in 2015, Jyldyz worked as the information specialist at the U.S. Embassy in Bishkek, where she managed countrywide library assistance programs. In the early 2000s, Dr. Bekbalaeva worked with Dr. Bedford on the World Bank Thesaurus, supporting the creation of the Russian language version. She is a member of the executive board of the Library and Information Consortium of Kyrgyzstan. She holds an MSLIS from the University of Illinois and a PhD in linguistics from Kyrgyz National University. Dr. Bekbalaeva will speak to the country perspective and the challenge of raising awareness of the dimensions of human trafficking.

**Dr. Denise Bedford** is adjunct faculty at Georgetown University and Schulich School of Business at York University, a visiting scholar at Coventry University, and distinguished practitioner, U.S. Department of State. Previously, she was senior information officer, World Bank, and Goodyear Professor of Knowledge Management, Kent State University. Denise earned a PhD from the University of California at Berkeley, a master of arts and a bachelor of arts from the University of Michigan and a master of science from Western Michigan University. Dr. Bedford's research interests include semantic analysis, linguistic registers, knowledge structures and the role of language in knowledge sharing and translation. Dr. Bedford will speak to on-going research focused on semantic profiles for human trafficking. She and Dr. Bekbalaeva will demonstrate a fully built out profile and discuss the efforts involved in constructing the profile

**Kyle M. Ballard** is senior coordinator, Office to Monitor and Combat Trafficking in Persons, U.S. Department of State, Washington, DC. Previously, he was strategic planner, Defense Security Cooperation Agency, Office of Secretary of Defense, and supervisory foreign affairs officer, Bureau of Democracy, Human Rights and Labor, Department of State. He holds degrees in diplomacy and world affairs from Occidental College, computational social science from George Mason University, and international policy studies from Middlebury Institute of International Studies at Monterey. Mr. Ballard will speak to the international challenge of human trafficking and some of the Department of State's recent efforts to use text analytics to map the global traffic.

**Thomas J. Hernandez** is owner of Granicus, provider of cloud-based solutions for communications, citizen engagement and digital services to public sector organizations. Previously Mr. Hernandez was senior program assistant for Eurasia at the National Democratic Institute and project assistant in the Civil Society Partnership Program at the Eurasia Foundation. Mr. Hernandez is a graduate of the Georgetown CCT program where his research focused on the acquisition and use of information and communication technologies in civic and public sector. Mr. Hernandez will speak to communication mechanisms for promoting what we are learning through semantic and text analytics.

## REFERENCES


Alvarez, M. B., & Alessi, E. J. (2012). Human trafficking is more than sex trafficking and prostitution: Implications for social work. *Affilia, 27*(2), 142-152.

Belser, P. (2005). Forced labour and human trafficking: Estimating the profits.

Feingold, D. A. (2005). Human trafficking. *Foreign Policy*, 26-32.

Gallagher, A. T. (2010). *The international law of human trafficking*. Cambridge University Press.

Goodale, M., & Merry, S. E. (Eds.). (2007). *The practice of human rights: Tracking law between the global and the local*. Cambridge University Press.

Gozdiak, E. M. (2011). *Data and research on human trafficking: Bibliography of research-based literature*. DIANE Publishing.

Gushulak, B. D., & MacPherson, D. W. (2000). Health issues associated with the smuggling and trafficking of migrants. *Journal of Immigrant Health, 2*(2), 67-78.

Jakobsson, N., & Kotsadam, A. (2013). The law and economics of international sex slavery: Prostitution laws and trafficking for sexual exploitation. *European Journal of Law and Economics, 35*(1), 87-107.

Kempadoo, K., Sanghera, J., & Pattanaik, B. (2015). *Trafficking and prostitution reconsidered: New perspectives on migration, sex work, and human rights*. Routledge.

Kinney, E. C. (2006). Appropriations for the abolitionists: Undermining effects of the US mandatory anti-prostitution pledge in the fight against human trafficking and HIV/AIDS. *Browser Download This Paper*.

Laczko, F., & Gozdziak, E. M. (Eds.). (2005). *Data and research on human trafficking: A global survey*. SAGE Publications.

Lobasz, J. K. (2009). Beyond border security: Feminist approaches to human trafficking. *Security Studies, 18*(2), 319-344.

Mahmoud, T. O., & Trebesch, C. (2010). The economics of human trafficking and labour migration: Micro-evidence from Eastern Europe. *Journal of Comparative Economics, 38*(2), 173-188.

Oberdorster, G., Maynard, A., Donaldson, K., Castranova, V., Fitzpatrick, J., Ausman, K., ... & Olin, S. (2005). Principles for characterizing the potential human health effects from exposure to nanomaterials: Elements of a screening strategy. *Particle and Fibre Toxicology, 2*(1), 8.

Oram, S., Stöckl, H., Busza, J., Howard, L. M., & Zimmerman, C. (2012). Prevalence and risk of violence and the physical, mental, and sexual health problems associated with human trafficking: Systematic review. *PLoS Med, 9*(5), e1001224.

Rafferty, Y. (2008). The impact of trafficking on children: Psychological and social policy perspectives. *Child Development Perspectives, 2*(1), 13-18.

Rao, S., & Presenti, C. (2012). Understanding human trafficking origin: A cross-country empirical analysis. *Feminist Economics, 18*(2), 231-263.

Ruggiero, V. (1997). Trafficking in human beings: Slaves in contemporary Europe. *International Journal of the Sociology of Law, 25*(3), 231-244.

Shelley, L., & Lee, M. (2007). Human trafficking as a form of transnational crime. *Human Trafficking*, 116-137.

Srikantiah, J. (2007). Perfect victims and real survivors: The iconic victim in domestic human trafficking law. *Immigr. & Nat'lity L. Rev., 28*, 741.

Tsutsumi, A., Izutsu, T., Poudyal, A. K., Kato, S., & Marui, E. (2008). Mental health of female survivors of human trafficking in Nepal. *Social Science & Medicine, 66*(8), 1841-1847.

Tyldum, G., & Brunovskis, A. (2005). Describing the unobserved: Methodological challenges in empirical studies on human trafficking. *International Migration*, *43*(1-2), 17-34.

United Nations (2007). UN Protocol to Prevent, Suppress, and Punish Trafficking in Persons, Especially Women and Children, summary Web Page. Retrieved from http://www.unodc.org/unodc.en/treaties/CTOC/index.html

United States Department of State (2013). Trafficking in Persons Report. Retrieved from https://www.state.gov/j/tip/rls/tiprpt/2013/index.htm

Wheaton, E. M., Schauer, E. J., & Galli, T. V. (2010). Economics of human trafficking. *International Migration*, *48*(4), 114-141.

Wilson, J. M., & Dalton, E. (2008). Human trafficking in the heartland: Variation in law enforcement awareness and response. *Journal of Contemporary Criminal Justice*, *24*(3), 296-313.

Zimmerman, C., Hossain, M., & Watts, C. (2011). Human trafficking and health: A conceptual model to inform policy, intervention and research. *Social Science & Medicine*, *73*(2), 327-335.

# Knowledge Translation in Health Sciences

**Denise A. D. Bedford**
*Georgetown University, USA. db233@georgetown.edu*

**Jeanine Turner**
*Georgetown University, USA. Jeanine.Turner@georgetown.edu*

**Theresa Norton**
*Jhpiego/Johns Hopkins University, USA. Theresa.Norton@jhpiego.org*

**Liz Sabatiuk**
*National Campaign to Prevent Teen and Unplanned Pregnancy, USA. ees89@georgetown.edu*

**Homira G. Nassery**
*World Bank, USA. HNassery@worldbank.org*

## ABSTRACT

**Knowledge Translation (KT) is a term used by healthcare professionals and practitioners to represent a process of ensuring that what is learned in research is applied in the field. Knowledge Translation includes all stages in the research and research uptake life cycle. In the knowledge management field, the concept of Knowledge Translation is characterized as knowledge transfer, knowledge exchange, knowledge sharing and knowledge use. This panel brings together these two perspectives around a common application area – delivery of health services to a multicultural community by international development organizations. The goal of the program is to build a shared view of the concept, and to expand our understanding of the challenges and opportunities of "doing" knowledge translation in a complex environment.**

## KEYWORDS

Knowledge translation, Evidence-based practice, Research uptake, Knowledge transfer

## INTRODUCTION

Knowledge Translation (KT) is a term increasingly used by healthcare professionals and practitioners to represent a process of ensuring that what is learned in research is applied in the field – the use of research in practice. Knowledge Translation is a complex and multidimensional concept that rests on a rich research foundation and years of practical applications in the real world. There are two contexts in which we might hear the term knowledge translation. The general concept - knowledge translation - may be equated with knowledge exchange, knowledge transfer, expert-novice learning, and knowledge sharing (Jacobson Butterill & Goering 2003), the technical term "Knowledge Translation" is supported by models, methods, measurements and well established influence factors (Graham & Tetroe, 2007; Johnson, 2005; Sudsawad, 2007) The technical term was first coined by the Canadian Institutes of Health Research in 1998 (Cegala Coleman & Turner, 1998). Since then it has been adapted by the University of Toronto Faculty of Medicine (2004) and the World Health Organization (2005). Knowledge Translation is defined by CIHR as "the exchange, synthesis and ethically-sound application of knowledge – within a complex system of interactions among searchers and users – to accelerate the capture of the benefits of research for Canadians through improved health, more effective services and products, and a strengthened health care system." (Kiefer et al, 2005, p. 2). Other Knowledge Translation models include Ottawa Model of Research Use (OMRU) (Logan and Graham, 1998), the Knowledge-to-Action Process Framework (Graham et al, 2006), the Promoting Action on Research Implementation in Health Services Framework (PARIHS (Kitson Harvey and McCormack, 1998), the Coordinated Implementation Model (Lomas, 1993), and the Stetler Model of Research Utilization (Stetler & Marram, 1976; Stetler, 1994, Sterler, 2004).

Knowledge Translation involves multidirectional communications, is interactive, presumes on-going relationships among all of those involved, presumes communication among different "knowledge enabled" individuals, reflects both the research knowledge itself but is interpreted to the relevant context, is a nonlinear process, focuses on knowledge generated through research, and takes as an end-game a positive health outcome for the patient. It starts with the identification of research questions, includes all phases of "doing research", recording research results, identification and use of research knowledge, making decisions and taking action based on research, and finally feeding back the results of the application and outcomes back into the research process.

Knowledge Translation can be applied to any field of science and technology where complex knowledge is produced and consumed by individuals with varying levels of understanding. From some perspectives, it resembles the discourse in many fields focused on research uptake. Knowledge Translation and its evidence-based practice approach, are core to health sciences and services deliver and outcomes in the international development community. In evidence-base practice, practitioners must take into consideration research evidence, clinical expertise, and the patient's unique values and circumstances (Straus, Richardson, Glasziou and Haynes, 2005). This synthesis and interpretation is critical to the delivery of health knowledge in cultures which are different

---

80th Annual Meeting of the Association for Information Science & Technology, Washington, DC, VA | Oct. 27-Nov. 1, 2017

from where the research originated, where trust is often a factor in acceptance and adoption, and where provider-patient communication must bridge an expert-novice gap. While the value of Knowledge Translation has been recognized in the international development community for more than 20 years now, it is equally valuable in health services delivery in underserved and low-income communities in the United States and Canada.

The term – knowledge translation – is not a term generally found in the literature of Knowledge Sciences and Knowledge Management. The same underlying concepts, though, are treated under four closely related terms, including knowledge transfer, knowledge exchange, knowledge sharing, and knowledge use. A cursory review of the top ranked journals in the field - *Journal of Knowledge Management, Journal of Information and Knowledge Management, VINE Journal of Information and Knowledge Systems, Electronic Journal of Knowledge Management* – reveals a large number of scholarly articles focused on these four concepts. The gap is not simply one of semantics but of communication, shared research and shared experiences between these two disciplines. This panel is a small attempt to bridge these gaps.

The goal of this panel is to begin a discourse around common interests of the health sciences and the knowledge management communities around the concept of Knowledge Translation. This will benefit the KM community by lending greater rigor to the still-emerging concepts of knowledge transfer, knowledge exchange, and expert-novice learning. This collaborative work will lend value to the health sciences by introducing rigorous linguistic methods and semantic analysis of knowledge structures coming out of the knowledge management field.

The panelists will speak to practical challenges and successes they have encountered with the exchange, synthesis and application of knowledge in health sciences. Theresa Norton, Johns Hopkins University, will speak to the experiences of Jhpiego (http:www.jhpiego.org) working on issues of reproductive health, family planning, women's and newborn health around the world. Liz Sabatiuk, Georgetown University CCT graduate and Senior Manager of Digital Media at The National Campaign, will speak to language issues in managing and preparing content for use in different international settings. Dr. Jeanine Turner, Associate Professor, Georgetown University, will share her research into doctor-patient and doctor-doctor communications in low income areas of Washington DC. Dr. Denise Bedford, CCT Adjunct Faculty, will speak to the linguistic analysis of health Knowledge Translation, including the development of machine-based semantic representations of Bales (Bales, 1950), Korsch (Korsch Gozzi & Francism 1968), Patel (Patel Evans & Kaufman, 1989), Roter (Roter & Hall, 1989) and Stiles (Stiles et al, 1979) models. While these models and characteristics of effective doctor patient communication are well grounded and extensively tested, their use may be subject to the interpretation or perspectives of coders. The application of semantic analysis methods introduces rigor and consistency to the research.

## FORMAT

The format is a facilitated discussion among panelists and audience. Each panelist will offer a short presentation of their experiences, with particular focus on challenges and opportunities for future collaborative work. The short presentation will be followed by open discussion with audience members who will be encouraged to share their experiences, and propose future collaborative work. The moderator will track suggestions from both panelists and participants and ensure that the topics are shared following the program.

## BENEFITS

The panel will produce benefits to several communities. First, benefits will accrue to the Health sciences community through the expansion of the discourse and a strengthened network of professionals working on similar topics within the ASIST community. We also expect a renewed dialog and knowledge exchange to occur to individuals working in this area within the MD-VA-DC geographical area. In addition, benefits will accrue to the knowledge management community from the exposure of real world applications of traditional methods and tools. There is also an opportunity to synthesize reference models developed in two distinct domains. We also expect benefits to accrue to both communities from exposure to new 21st century semantic technologies and their application to communication models developed in the mid- to late-20th century. Benefits should also accrue to ASIST through extended involvement of non-ASIST members in the ASIST conference. We would also expect benefits to accrue to ASIST PVC through the promotion of a potentially important focus area to the MD-DC-VA community.

## COSPONSORS

This program proposal is jointly sponsored by SIGKM and SIG HLTH.

## PROMOTION

The panel will be promoted to SIGKM and SIGHLTH members, to the Federal Knowledge Management Community, the local chapters of AIIM, SIM, SLA, as well as to the Knowledge Leaders Forum, and SIKM. In addition, we will promote the program to local international development organizations (e.g., World Bank Group, IADB, United Nations) and health- and gender-focused non-profit and non-governmental organizations with offices in the MD-DC-VA area. We will also promote the program to European KM associations and the International Association for Knowledge Management.

## PANELISTS

**Theresa Norton** is Knowledge Management Director, Jhpiego (a non-profit affiliate of Johns Hopkins University). In her current role, she leads the creation and implementation of Jhpiego's KM Strategy, manages Jhpiego's SharePoint global deployment to support Jhpiego's Intranet for knowledge sharing and collaboration among staff in more than 30 countries, oversees cataloging, indexing and Jhpiego enterprise master taxonomy. Theresa holds an M.B.A. from the University of Baltimore, and a B.A. in Anthropology from Towson University. Her research interests focus on the role of knowledge intermediaries in helping global health stakeholders translate research findings into improved health policy and practice. Ms. Norton will introduce the topic of knowledge translation and share experiences, challenges and opportunities in knowledge translation in a global community.

**Liz Sabatiuk** is Senior Manager of Digital Media at the The National Campaign to Prevent Teen and Unplanned Pregnancy. In her current position, she supports the Bedsider program (Bedsider.org). Bedsider is an online birth control support network for women 18-29. It is a private non-profit organization whose goal is to help women find the method of birth control that's right for them and learn how to use it consistently and effectively. In her current role, Ms. Sabatiuk is responsible for planning, producing, editing, and curating content for Bedsider.org and related properties including Bedsider Providers and Bedsider en Español. Ms. Sabatiuk's daily work is an example of knowledge translation of culturally sensitive topics for a multicultural community.

**Dr. Jeanine Turner** is Associate Professor, Georgetown University Communication, Culture and Technology (CCT). Dr. Turner holds a B.A. and M.A. in Communications from the University of Dayton, and a PhD in Communications from the Ohio State University. Professor Turner's recent publications include: "Computer-based Telecommunication Among an Illness-Related Community: System Design, Service Delivery and Early Use," published in *Health Communication*; "The Ohio Telemedicine System for Prison Inmates," published in *Telemedicine Journal*; "Economic Advantage of Telemedicine in a Corrections Environment," published in *Telemedicine and Telehealth Networks*; "Telemedicine: An Alternative Method of Prison Inmate Care," published in *Administrative Radiology Journal*; and "Organizational Telecompetence: Creating the Virtual Organization," published in *Telemedicine: Practicing in the Information Age*. Dr. Turner will share insights from on-going research on doctor-doctor and doctor-patient communication.

**Dr. Denise Bedford** is Adjunct Faculty at Georgetown University and Schulich School of Business York University, a Visiting Scholar at Coventry University, and Distinguished Practitioner, U.S. Department of State. Previously, she was Senior Information Officer, World Bank, and Goodyear Professor of Knowledge Management, Kent State University. Denise earned a PhD from the University of California at Berkeley, a Master of Arts and a Bachelor of Arts from the University of Michigan, and a Master of Science from Western Michigan University. Dr. Bedford's research interests include semantic analysis, linguistic registers, knowledge structures and the role of language in knowledge sharing and translation. Dr. Bedford will speak to on-going research in analyzing the language of doctor-patient communication.

**Homira G. Nassery** is currently Knowledge and Learning Coordinator and Public Health Specialist, The World Bank. Homira has devoted her career to working on public health issues in post-conflict countries, most recently in Afghanistan where she worked in all regions of the country as a consultant for NGOs, the United Nations, NATO and USAID. At the World Bank, she served as Gender Specialists and Monitoring and Evaluation Coordinator for the Alternative Livelihoods Project South (ALP/S) based in Lashkargah, Helmand. Her background is primarily social development, with 13 years of working as a registered respiratory therapist in emergency rooms and critical care units prior to joining the World Bank.

## REFERENCES


Bales, R. F. 1950. Interaction Process Analysis. Cambridge, Mass.: AddisonWesley

Canadian Institutes of Health Research (2005). About knowledge translation. Accessed http://www.cihr-irsc.gc.ca/e/29418.html

Cegala, D. J., Coleman, M. T., & Turner, J. W. (1998). The development and partial assessment of the medical communication competence scale. *Health communication*, *10*(3), 261-288.

Graham, I. D., & Tetroe, J. (2007). CIHR research: How to translate health research knowledge into effective healthcare action. *Healthcare Quarterly*, *10*(3).

Graham, I. D., Logan, J., Harrison, M. B., Straus, S. E., Tetroe, J., Caswell, W., & Robinson, N. (2006). Lost in knowledge translation: time for a map?. *Journal of continuing education in the health professions*, *26*(1), 13-24.

Jacobson, N., Butterill, D., & Goering, P. (2003). Development of a framework for knowledge translation: understanding user context. *Journal of health services research & policy*, *8*(2), 94-99.

Johnson, L. S. (2005). From knowledge transfer to knowledge translation: Applying research to practice. *Occupational Therapy Now*, *7*(4), 11.

Kiefer, L., Frank, J., Di Ruggiero, E., Dobbins, M., Manuel, D., Gully, P. R., & Mowat, D. (2005). Fostering evidence-based decision-making in Canada: examining the need for a Canadian population and public health evidence centre and research network. *Canadian Journal of Public Health/Revue Canadienne de Sante'e Publique*, *96*(3), I1-I19.

Kitson, A., Harvey, G., & McCormack, B. (1998). Enabling the implementation of evidence based practice: a conceptual framework. *Quality in Health care*, *7*(3), 149-158.

Knowledge Translation Program. Faculty of Medicine, University of Toronto (2004). About knowledge translation. Definition.

Korsch, B. M., Gozzi, E. K., & Francis, V. (1968). Gaps in doctor-patient communication. *Pediatrics*, *42*(5), 855-871.

Logan, J. O., & Graham, I. D. (1998). Toward a comprehensive interdisciplinary model of health care research use. *Science communication*, *20*(2), 227-246.

Lomas, J. (1993). Retailing research: increasing the role of evidence in clinical services for childbirth. *The Milbank Quarterly*, 439-475.

Patel, V. L., Evans, D. A., & Kaufman, D. R. (1989). Cognitive framework for doctor-patient interaction. *Cognitive science in medicine: Biomedical modeling*, 253-308.

Robinson, J. D., & Turner, J. (2003). Impersonal, interpersonal, and hyperpersonal social support: Cancer and older adults. *Health communication*, *15*(2), 227-234.

Roter, D. L., & Hall, J. A. (1989). Studies of doctor-patient interaction. *Annual review of public health*, *10*(1), 163-180.

Stetler, C. B. (1994). Refinement of the Stetler/Marram model for application of research findings to practice. *Nursing Outlook*, *42*(1), 15-25.

Stetler, C. B. (2001). Updating the Stetler model of research utilization to facilitate evidence-based practice. *Nursing Outlook*, *49*(6), 272-279.

Stetler, C. B., & Marram, G. (1976). Evaluating research findings for applicability in practice. *Nursing outlook*, *24*(9), 559-563.

Stiles, W. B., Putnam, S. M., Wolf, M. H., & James, S. A. (1979). Interaction exchange structure and patient satisfaction with medical interviews. *Medical Care*, *17*(6), 667-681.

Straus, S. E., Richardson, W. S., Glasziou, P., & Haynes, R. B. (2005). Evidence-based medicine: how to practice and teach EBM.

Sudsawad, P. (2007). Knowledge translation: Introduction to models, strategies, and measures. *Austin, TX: Southwest Educational Development Laboratory, National Center for the Dissemination of Disability Research*.

World Health Organization (2005). Bridging the "Know-Do" gap: Meeting on knowledge translation in global health. Accessed http://www.who.int/kms/WHO_EIP_KMS_2006_2.pdf

# What Research and Theory Inspires IA/UX, and How Can this Change Behavior and Help Make a Political and Humanitarian Difference?


**Joseph Busch**
*Taxonomy Strategies/Semantic Staffing, USA. jbusch@taxonomystrategies.com*

**Dave Cooksey**
*Saturdave, USA. dave@saturdave.com*

**Jeff Pass**
*Booz Allen Hamilton, USA. pass_jeffrey@bah.com*

**Ren Pope**
*Industrial Medium, USA. rlpope3@yahoo.com*

**Stacy Surla**
*ICF International, USA. stacy@greenfx.net*

**Thomas Vander Wal**
*thomas@vanderwal.net*

**Lisa Welchman**
*me@lisawelchman.com*

**Dan Willis**
*U.S. Digital Service, The White House, USA. dan@dswillis.com*



## ABSTRACT

**This session is a moderated panel discussion among senior IA/UX practitioners from the greater Washington, DC area. Its goal is to challenge and inspire the ASIST research community. Among themes the panel will discuss are: 1) how research and theory inspires client project work – what types of research is needed, and what would be considered accessible and practical research; and 2) how IA/UX (including content strategy, taxonomy, governance, etc.) can change behavior, and help make a political and humanitarian difference.**



## KEYWORDS

information architecture, user experience, applied research, ethics, invited panel


## BACKGROUND

Since the IA Summit was first convened by ASIST in Boston in 2001, there's been an ongoing discussion about applying information science and human computer interaction (HCI) to information architecture and user experience design. Just as within ASIST the IA community has engaged in a discussion about research versus practice. Peter Morville (2004) posted a bibliography of information architecture research grouping the work into four broad categories –

- Information Seeking Behavior,
- Structure and Organization (e.g., depth vs. breadth),
- Navigation, and
- Search

Karl Fast (2006) cautioned that IA research should not be done "by and for academics." Resmini & Instone (2010) suggested that "there is no such thing as IA research by itself: there is HCI, IS or LIS research that IAs care about." Ironically, Resmini (2009-2013) was the Editor-in-Chief of the *Journal of Information Architecture* during its five-year existence.

Rosenfeld & Morville (2d ed., 2002) include a chapter on ethical considerations of information architecture in their foundational book *Information Architecture for the World Wide Web* first published in 1998. The ethical issues include:

- Intellectual access,
- Labelling,
- Categories and classification,
- Granularity,
- Physical access, and
- Persistence

Simply put, there are consequences of website design, how information is communicated, and whether it is found or obscured. This can have a great impact on what individuals believe, how they make decisions, and how they act.

The discussion about an IA research agenda, ethics and politics continues today with this panel of practitioners, who are also thought leaders and educators.

## REFERENCES


Fast, K. (2006). "The Confluence of Research and Practice in Information Architecture". *Bulletin of the American Society for Information Science and Technology* 32:5 (p. 27). http://onlinelibrary.wiley.com/doi/10.1002/ bult.2006-.1720320510/full. Last checked September 3, 2017.

Morville, P. (2004). "Information Architecture Research". Semantic Studios blogpost. http://semanticstudios.com/information_architecture_research/. Last checked September 3, 2017.



80th Annual Meeting of the Association for Information Science & Technology, Washington, DC, VA | Oct. 27-Nov. 1, 2017

Resmini, A. & Instone, K. (2010). "Research and Practice in IA". *Bulletin of the American Society for Information Science and Technology* 36:6 (pp. 19-23). http://onlinelibrary.wiley.com/doi/-10.1002/bult.2010.1720360607/epdf. Last checked September 3, 2017.

Resmini, A. Editor-in-Chief. (2009-2013). *Journal of Information Architecture*. Vol 1-5. http://journalofia.org/. Last checked September 3, 2017.

Rosenfeld, L. & Morville, P. (2002). *Information Architecture for the World Wide Web*. 2d edition. (pp. 311-314). Sebastopol, CA: O'Reilly, 2002.

# Incorporating Values Sensitive Design into Crowdsourcing Methodologies for Knowledge Collaboration

**Annie T. Chen**
*Department of Biomedical Informatics and Medical Education, University of Washington, USA.*
*atchen@uw.edu*

**Samantha J. Kaplan**
*School of Information and Library Science, University of North Carolina, Chapel Hill, USA.*
*sjkaplan@live.unc.edu*

**Pamella Lach**
*Library and Information Access, San Diego State University, USA. plach@sdsu.edu*

**Lu Xiao**
*School of Information Studies, Syracuse University, USA.*
*lxiao04@syr.edu*

## ABSTRACT

**In recent years, we have seen a dramatic increase in crowdsourcing approaches to solve problems and engage in other types of knowledge work in many domains, including genetics, health, cultural heritage, digital preservation and design. Crowdsourcing initiatives offer many potential benefits, including engaging individuals of diverse backgrounds in collaborative meaning-making and production. And yet, the potential challenges and dangers, such as issues related to quality and false confidence, can hardly escape our attention. This panel will explore how human-centered approaches to crowdsourcing can help minimize its challenges. In particular, this panel will ask how we implement crowdsourcing methods, what our outcomes should be, and how we should go about developing and defining our outcomes in relationship to the workers. The first half of the session will be devoted to an introduction to crowdsourcing initiatives and associated critical issues. Each presentation will drill progressively deeper into the mechanisms and implications of crowdsourcing. In the second half of the session, we invite session attendees to engage with us in a collaborative activity employing techniques from the value sensitive design approach to design crowdsourcing initiatives that are sensitive to the communities with whom we engage and thereby endeavor to realize humanistic goals. It is our hope that the panel session will result in new collaborations and spark the development of more thoughtful, reflexive and productive crowdsourcing activities.**

## KEYWORDS

crowdsourcing, knowledge collaboration, value sensitive design

80th Annual Meeting of the Association for Information Science & Technology, Washington, DC, VA | Oct. 27-Nov. 1, 2017



## INTRODUCTION

In recent years, we have seen a dramatic increase in crowdsourcing approaches to solve problems and engage in other types of knowledge work in many domains, including genetics, health, cultural heritage, digital preservation and design. Due to the internet, a set of distributed actors can be drawn together to tackle large challenges (Dodge & Kitchin, 2013). Crowdsourcing expertise can enable people of diverse backgrounds to work together and facilitate the discovery of new knowledge (Celi, Ippolito, Montgomery, Moses & Stone, 2014). Additionally, it has been argued that folksonomies, the product of collaborative tagging, can facilitate collective interpretation and meaning production (Mai, 2011). Social media might also be leveraged in order to build platforms that reach out to multiple communities to integrate the perspectives of diverse and hard-to-reach populations into strategy and public policy (Hildebrand, Ahumada, & Watson, 2013). Similarly, Moxley (2008) argues that commons-based peer-to-peer technologies can nurture a climate in which there is respect for diversity and independent thinking.

On the other hand, there are also many potential dangers of crowdsourcing, including finding enough knowledgeable and loyal workers, maintaining a reasonable level of quality, homogeneity, and a general lack of representation (Brabham, 2008; Hack et al., 2011; Oomen & Aroyo, 2011). Just as the conclusions drawn from a study would not necessarily apply to a population other than the one from which the study sample was drawn, so too one must ask when one speaks of the "wisdom of the crowd," which crowd? Does one community possess enough expertise and authority to "speak" for another? Moreover, social influence and false confidence can also "undermine the wisdom of the crowd" (Lorenz, Rauhut, Schweitzer, & Helbing, 2011).

Another dimension to consider is whether and how crowdsourcing methods have changed traditional conceptualizations of knowledge production. Regardless of the method chosen, there are issues that one might encounter in the execution of that method, and crowdsourcing is no exception. Design decisions such as the use of explicit coordination, in which editors plan the activity through communication, as opposed to implicit coordination, in which a subset of editors set direction by doing the majority of the work, can have a significant influence on the nature and quality of the work (Kittur & Kraut, 2008). It is critical to take potential workers into account when designing crowdsourcing tasks, as design decisions impact the ways in which user communities engage in a crowdsourcing project.

If we are to employ crowdsourcing methods, then how do we implement those methods? Moreover, what should our outcomes be, and how should we go about developing and defining our outcomes? And can potential user communities shape our outcomes in different ways? Our proposed panel session seeks to explore and work through these questions.

The panel will be divided into two parts. In the first half, panelists will deliver a series of short presentations intended to engage the members of the audience in reflection on the values that they consider most important in crowdsourcing. In the second half, panelists and session attendees will form groups and engage in a design activity based on value sensitive design methods to develop a crowdsourcing design.

The panelists are diverse in terms of background, and they are actively engaged in research in a variety of disciplines, including information science, medicine and the digital humanities. We also bring experience with and interest in different types of crowdsourcing, including classification and co-curation and knowledge co-construction. We look forward to and invite everyone to attend and contribute, regardless of whether crowdsourcing is a passing interest or an area of deep expertise.

## SESSION AGENDA

Each panelist will present a short presentation on a specific topic relating to the human aspects of crowdsourcing for knowledge collaboration.

**Annie Chen** will begin by presenting a short introduction to crowdsourcing approaches for knowledge collaboration. This introduction will include examples of crowdsourcing initiatives in different disciplines, relevant definitions and typologies, an overview of critical questions and tensions, and then delve into crowdsourcing methods and their potential implications on data quality.

**Samantha Kaplan** will then discuss the trade-offs implicit in crowdsourcing approaches and the dangers they pose for researchers, the crowd, the crowd's platform and the public. This segment will review several known examples of engagement that did not produce the anticipated or desired outcome, such as Reddit's false identification of Sunil Tripathi as the Boston Marathon bomber. Other examples include when 4chan united to award a Taylor Swift concert to a school for the deaf or the numerous challenges of letting people vote to name a new animal at the zoo. Through these examples we will consider how a misalignment of values contributes to the negative outcomes and what this could mean for researchers using crowd-sourcing tools.

Following this more high-level discussion, we will provide specific examples of crowdsourcing projects to concretize some of the particular challenges in knowledge collaboration.

**Pamella Lach** will introduce "Tagging for Justice," a project that she and Annie Chen are planning. This project explores the possibilities and limitations of employing crowdsourced folksonomic tagging to enhance digital archival collections of social movement histories. Using digital objects from San Diego State University's Lambda Archives Digital Collection, our experiment will study the extent to which user tagging democratizes knowledge organization, reflects individual biases and challenges or reifies expert/hegemonic frameworks and perspectives. The Lambda Archives of San Diego includes photos relating to annual Pride activities, Gay Liberation Front protests of the 1970s and various ephemera from over the years, and it is "one of the best-maintained collections of LGBT history in the country" (http://www.lambdaarchives.us/about.htm).

The goal of this experiment is to see if we can produce metadata that is sensitive to issues related to sexuality and gender identity and thereby capture elements of the digital archive that are not yet categorized or described. We are currently exploring different design approaches for the study based on diverse user communities in order to determine whether it is possible to use folksonomic tags to capture more fluid aspects of these historical events, such as shifting gender identities. In designing this project, we are asking whether crowdsourcing could enable new stories to emerge between the gaps of the digital objects and their metadata.

Following this initial exploration of the potential influences of collaborative tagging, **Lu Xiao** will take us deeper into the mental space of workers engaged in crowdsourcing, sharing her experience with online crowdsourcing experiments (e.g., Xiao, 2014). The main interest in these experiments is to explore whether and how one's awareness of the other workers' rationales affect the quality of the crowdsourced work. In the creative task, a worker's rationale is his/her justification of why the idea the worker proposed is a good idea. Through three experiments, Xiao shows that sharing good quality rationales from the previous workers improves the average quality of the crowdsourcing task. In addition, when good quality rationales are available in evaluating the generated ideas, the workers' evaluations are more agreeable to each other. But when poor quality rationales are provided in the evaluation task, the workers' evaluations are more disagreeable. Xiao is currently conducting a crowdsourcing experiment to explore the applicability of these observations in a different type of crowdsourcing task – a task in which workers need to write the description for a given image.

## GENERATIVE DESIGN ACTIVITY

The introductory set of presentations will start session attendees thinking about the promises, perils and mechanisms by which crowdsourcing might be undertaken. As such, engaging in human-centered and values-sensitive design practices can potentially lead to crowdsourcing designs that realize the potential of those involved and is congruent with humanistic goals. Thus, in the second half of the panel session, we will employ techniques from a participatory design approach called value sensitive design to engage in collaborative design of crowdsourcing initiatives. Value sensitive design is an approach that proactively considers human values throughout the process of technology design (Davis & Nathan, 2013). The phenomenon of crowdsourcing has brought many critical questions of values to the fore, such as power, representation and quality, and thus, the integration of a values-sensitive approach may lead to crowdsourcing approaches that are more purposefully geared to intended workers, and thereby might be better positioned to meet user-centered project objectives.

Following the initial panel discussion, the panelists and session attendees will form groups and engage in a crowdsourcing design activity using value sensitive design methods. We will employ envisioning cards and value scenarios to design a crowdsourcing platform for citizen science. Envisioning cards are intended to provide opportunities for values-oriented reflection, iteration and course correction throughout the design, implementation and evaluation of information tools (Friedman & Hendry, 2012). Each card features an image that is meant to evoke that card's particular theme and highlights one of four envisioning criteria (stakeholders, time, values or pervasiveness), a card theme and an activity. We will employ the envisioning cards to stimulate our thinking concerning how we might design a crowdsourcing platform to address those needs. The panelists will bring creative materials (large pieces of paper and markers) for session attendees to participate in design activities.

Value scenarios extend traditional scenario-based design (SBD) approaches, using narrative descriptions of individuals interacting with technologies to guide the design process (Nathan, Klasnja & Friedman, 2007). However, in contrast to traditional SBD approaches, value scenarios are more likely to focus on indirect stakeholders, pervasive and long-term technology use and systemic effects. Doing so facilitates an exploration of both positive and negative effects and unintended consequences of technologies.

Following the design activity, session participants will reconvene as a larger group and share their designs. In addition, the design products will be digitized and placed on a public site for future reference, with the consent of the creators.

## SCHEDULE

1. Introduction and overview of crowdsourcing for knowledge work (5 minutes)
2. Issues and concerns (10 minutes)
3. Tagging for justice (10 minutes)
4. Rationale sharing and crowdsourcing quality presentation (10 minutes)
5. Introduction to the crowdsourcing design activity (5 minutes)
6. Crowdsourcing design activity using value sensitive design methods (30 minutes)
7. Discussion and reflection on the design activity (20 minutes)

## PRESENTERS

**Dr. Annie T. Chen**, moderator, is assistant professor in the Department of Biomedical Informatics and Medical Education at the University of Washington School of Medicine. Her research interests include chronic illness information behaviors, health-related social media use and research methods. She is particularly interested in long-term health knowledge acquisition and formation, leveraging patient expertise to augment knowledge resources, and the ways in which interface and visualization design can shape people's interpretations of information. She is also currently involved in crowdsourcing initiatives in multiple domains, including chronic disease self-management, genetics and the digital humanities. At the University of Washington School of Medicine, she teaches graduate-level courses in consumer health informatics, biomedical informatics and human-centered design, and she mentors students in research on health information behavior, health information quality and social media text mining and visualization.

**Samantha J. Kaplan** is a third-year doctoral student in the School of Information and Library Science at the University of North Carolina at Chapel Hill. She is interested in how individuals encounter and label misinformation, particularly at the intersection between health and everyday life contexts. She is currently working on her dissertation, a case study of the information practices of a parent who has not vaccinated her child. Before beginning her PhD, she completed a master's in library and information science at the University of South Carolina. She also worked as an indexer of digital databases on topics including, but not limited, to transportation, LGBT studies, psychology and counseling, colonial Australia and New Zealand, consumer electronics and education.

**Pamella Lach** is the digital humanities librarian at San Diego State University. Her work explores how new and emerging technologies transform humanistic scholarship and pedagogy. Her areas of interest include data visualization, information retrieval, user experience design and digital pedagogy. She is currently studying how folksonomy, or user-generated social tagging, can enhance and disrupt traditional authority-driven classification schemas. She previously served as the head of the Center for Faculty Initiatives and Engagement at the University of Kansas Libraries. Prior to that she was the associate director of the Digital Innovation Lab at the University of North Carolina at Chapel Hill. She has a PhD in U.S. cultural history with an emphasis on gender and film history from UNC and a MS in information science from UNC's School of Information and Library Science.

**Lu Xiao** is associate professor in the School of Information Studies at Syracuse University. Her main research interests are related to understanding and supporting people's reasoning behavior through socio-technical interventions. She applies various research methods in her studies from interviews, questionnaires, lab experiments to user interface design, participatory design and computational techniques with natural language processing and machine learning. Dr. Xiao currently studies internet users' online reasoning behavior, the effects of sharing the users' reasoning in crowdsourcing context and explores ways for automatic detection of reasoning traces (e.g., rationales and persuasion acts). She has also been collaborating with oral historians to support the researchers' process of reasoning through the interview collections and conducting qualitative analysis of the interview data through computational and visualization techniques.

## REFERENCES


Brabham, D. C. (2008). Crowdsourcing as a model for problem solving: An introduction and cases. *Convergence: The International Journal of Research into New Media Technologies, 14*(1), 75-90. https://doi.org/10.1177/1354856507084420

Celi, L. A., Ippolito, A., Montgomery, R. A., Moses, C., & Stone, D. J. (2014). Crowdsourcing knowledge discovery and innovations in medicine. *Journal of Medical Internet Research, 16*(9), e216. https://doi.org/10.2196/jmir.3761

Davis, J., & Nathan, L. P. (2013). Value sensitive design: Applications, adaptations, and critiques. In J. van den Hoven, P. E. Vermaas, & I. van de Poel (Eds.), *Handbook of Ethics, Values, and Technological Design* (pp. 1-26). Dordrecht: Springer Netherlands. Retrieved from http://link.springer.com/10.1007/978-94-007-6994-6_3-1

Dodge, M., & Kitchin, R. (2013). Crowdsourced cartography: Mapping experience and knowledge. *Environment and Planning A, 45*(1), 19-36. https://doi.org/10.1068/a44484

Friedman, B., & Hendry, D. (2012). The envisioning cards: A toolkit for catalyzing humanistic and technical imaginations. In *Proceedings of the SIGCHI conference on human factors in computing systems* (pp. 1145-1148). ACM. Retrieved from http://dl.acm.org/citation.cfm?id=2208562

Hack, M. D., Rassokhin, D. N., Buyck, C., Seierstad, M., Skalkin, A., ten Holte, P., … Agrafiotis, D. K. (2011). Library enhancement through the wisdom of crowds. *Journal of Chemical Information and Modeling, 51*(12), 3275-3286. https://doi.org/10.1021/ci200446y

Hildebrand, M., Ahumada, C., & Watson, S. (2013). CrowdOutAIDS: Crowdsourcing youth perspectives for action. *Reproductive Health Matters, 21*(41), 57-68. https://doi.org/10.1016/S0968-8080(13)41687-7

Kittur, A., & Kraut, R. E. (2008). Harnessing the wisdom of crowds in wikipedia: Quality through coordination. In *Proceedings of the 2008 ACM conference on Computer supported cooperative work* (pp. 37-46). ACM. Retrieved from http://dl.acm.org/citation.cfm?id=1460572

Lorenz, J., Rauhut, H., Schweitzer, F., & Helbing, D. (2011). How social influence can undermine the wisdom of crowd effect. *Proceedings of the National Academy of Sciences, 108*(22), 9020-9025. https://doi.org/10.1073/pnas.1008636108

Mai, J.-E. (2011). Folksonomies and the new order: Authority in the digital disorder. *Knowledge Organization, 38*(2), 114-122.

Moxley, J. (2008). Datagogies, writing spaces, and the age of peer production. *Computers and Composition, 25*(2), 182-202. https://doi.org/10.1016/j.compcom.2007.12.003

Nathan, L. P., Klasnja, P. V., & Friedman, B. (2007). Value scenarios: A technique for envisioning systemic effects of new technologies. In *CHI'07 extended abstracts on Human factors in computing systems* (pp. 2585-2590). ACM. Retrieved from http://dl.acm.org/citation.cfm?id=1241046

Oomen, J., & Aroyo, L. (2011). Crowdsourcing in the cultural heritage domain: Opportunities and challenges. In *Proceedings of the 5th International Conference on Communities and Technologies* (pp. 138-149). ACM. Retrieved from http://dl.acm.org/citation.cfm?id=2103373

Xiao, L. (2014). Effects of rationale awareness in online ideation crowdsourcing tasks. *Journal of the American Society for Information Science and Technology*, 65, 1707-1720. doi: 10.1002/asi.23079

# How International Is Your LIS/IS Program in the Global Higher Education Era?


**Hsin-liang Chen**
*University of Massachusetts, USA. hsinliang.chen@umb.edu*

**Tatjana Aparac-Jelušić**
*University of Osijek, Croatia. taparac@unizd.hr*

**Ina Fourie**
*University of Pretoria, South Africa. ina.fourie@up.ac.za*

**Sandra Hirsh**
*San Jose State University, USA. sandy.hirsh@sjsu.edu*

**Ruhua Huang**
*WuHan University, China. rhhuang@whu.edu.c*



## ABSTRACT

**Internationalization is a critical issue in LIS/IS education and the LIS/IS profession. This panel assembles educators from various continents to discover their experiences and to address the following issues:**
**International students should comprise what percentage of a student body in order to adequately represent the spectrum of disciplines that are critical to contemporary LIS/IS schools?**
**International faculty members should comprise what percentage of a faculty in order to adequately represent the spectrum of disciplines that are critical to contemporary LIS/IS schools?**
**How international must a curriculum be in order to adequately prepare graduates for the challenges of the rapidly changing information environment of the future?**
**How do our panelists build beneficial partnerships with international professional stakeholders?**
**How do our panelists ensure the quality of LIS education from an international perspective?**


## INTRODUCTION

Higher education institutions worldwide have embraced the globalization movement because of such factors as the rapid transformation of population growth, social changes, advanced technology, national economic growth and the shifting of regional politics (Altbach & Knight, 2007; Gibb, Haskins & Robertson, 2012; Knight, 2011; de Wit, 2011). For example, 29 European countries signed the Bologna Accord in 1999 to ensure their comparability on academic standards and the quality of higher education (Keeling, 2006). A recent report noted 48 members of the Bologna Process (EHEA, 2017). Other examples of this trend are international university associations such as the Association of Pacific Rim Universities, the Association of African Universities and Universitas 21. Generally, the primary purposes of these associations are to promote research collaboration and to advance student-exchange programs among member universities. These efforts were highlighted by Gibb, Haskins and Robertson (2012), who advocated using an entrepreneurial mode for shaping change in organizational and governance structures of higher education institutions.

In the library and information science (LIS) field, scholars and educators have been examining the development of LIS programs from an international perspective (Abdullahi and Kajberg, 2004; Mehra and Bishoh, 2007; Subramaniam and Jaeger, 2010, Johnson, 2013). Regarding the development of LIS professionals, Eisenberg and Fullerton (2012) emphasized the importance of cross-cultural experiences in forming the incoming generation of information professionals. Moran and Marchionini (2012) led the *Information Professionals 2050* forum to develop strategies for educating the next generation of information professionals. At the *International Quality Assessment of LIS Education Programs event*, a satellite meeting held in 2016 by the International Federation of Library Associations (IFLA), scholars and educators addressed academic quality issues from an international perspective.

Internationalization is a critical issue in LIS/IS education and the LIS/IS profession. This panel assembles educators from various continents to discover their experiences and to address the following issues:

- International students should comprise what percentage of a student body in order to adequately represent the spectrum of disciplines that are critical to contemporary LIS/IS schools?
- International faculty members should comprise what percentage of a faculty in order to adequately represent the spectrum of disciplines that are critical to contemporary LIS/IS schools?
- How international must a curriculum be in order to adequately prepare graduates for the challenges of the rapidly changing information environment of the future?
- How do our panelists build beneficial partnerships with international professional stakeholders?


80th Annual Meeting of the Association for Information Science & Technology, Washington, DC, VA | Oct. 27-Nov. 1, 2017

- How do our panelists ensure the quality of LIS education from an international perspective?

## INTEGRATION OF INTERNATIONAL PERSPECTIVES IN SOUTH AFRICAN LIS/IS PROGRAMS – INA FOURIE

South African LIS/IS programs differ in whether they emphasize library science, information science, information management, knowledge management, records management, archival science or combinations of these. Although not guided by formal institutional requirements of accountability of internationalization or an equivalent of the Bologna Agreement, all strive for international recognition and competitive programs. International conference attendance and publication, serving on program committees and on journal editorial advisory boards, as well as engaging in international research collaboration and memorandums of agreement (UK, USA, Germany, Finland, etc.), are essential. These apply to requirements for national and international institutional rating and individual national/international research rating. The latter is managed by the National Research Foundation.

All are required to ensure that content, didactic practices, the use of technology and the online/virtual delivery of programs are internationally competitive. All programs are available in English, and all draw students from African countries and to various extents from other continents – especially on master's and doctoral levels. Hybrid and blended learning practices are widely promoted. Inter-disciplinary collaboration (Scheepers, De Boer, Bothma & Du Toit, 2011), sporadic assessment of curriculum content (Ocholla, 2001; Ocholla & Ocholla, 2014) and comparative studies (Raju & Arsenault, 2007) contribute to reflection on the quality of programs.

LIS/IS programs in South Africa also face considerable pressure for the Africanization of programmes, local relevance, addressing indigenous knowledge and knowledge systems (Botha, 2007; Dube, 2012; Ngulube, Dube & Mhlongo, 2015; Raju, 2015). The cultural diversity to be accommodated is reflected in the 11 South African official languages.

The Department of Information Science (University of Pretoria) is the largest department in the country and serves as example for discussion. It falls under the Faculty of Engineering, the Building Environment and Information Technology and is part of the School of Information Technology including the departments of Informatics and Computer Science. The initiative for internationalization is reflected in the following:

**Programs**: The department offers three-degree programmes ranging from undergraduate through to doctoral studies: information science (including content related to library science, knowledge management and competitive intelligence), publishing studies and multimedia. It offers a master's degree in information technology specializing in library and information science and participates in a general master's degree in information technology and one in big data science. Theses and dissertations are examined internationally.

**International collaboration on funded post-graduate programs:** Since 2011 the department offers a master's degree in information technology which was fully funded by a Carnegie Corporation of New York grant until 2016. This was specifically aimed at students from Africa and was offered with input from universities in Africa and the United States. It included extended site visits to Uganda, South Africa and the United States, visits to academic libraries and teaching input from partner institutions. From 2017 it is offered as a fully self-funded, technologically enabled distance program.

## INTEGRATION OF INTERNATIONAL PERSPECTIVES IN AN AMERICAN LIS/IS PROGRAM – SANDRA HIRSH

The SJSU School of Information (iSchool) provides online graduate education to more than 1800 students across 47 states in the United States and 18 countries; faculty members hail from across the United States as well as Canada, the United Kingdom and New Zealand. SJSU iSchool is committed to incorporating a global perspective throughout every level of its education process – through its curriculum, programs, learning outcomes, partnerships, research and outreach (Hirsh, et. al., 2015).

**Curriculum:** Some SJSU iSchool courses are fully focused on international perspectives, such as international and comparative librarianship, intercultural communication, Virtually Abroad: Global Projects, and globalization and information. SJSU iSchool also partners with SJSU World Languages Department to create custom language and culture courses for iSchool online students in Spanish, French and Mandarin (Ford et al., 2017). As of Fall 2016, more than 40 iSchool courses have at least one international assignment.

**Programs:** One unique international program at SJSU iSchool is the San José Gateway PhD Program, which launched in 2008 as a collaboration between the SJSU iSchool and Queensland University of Technology (QUT) in Australia. This program provides the opportunity for doctoral students, who currently live in the United States, Canada, Suadi Arabia, Jamaica and Qatar to undertake a primarily online PhD program with research experts from around the world (Partridge et al., 2016).

**Learning outcomes**: One of the required core competencies that graduate students must demonstrate in their culminating experience through an ePortfolio is how "...information professionals can contribute to the cultural, economic, educational and social well-being of our global communities."

**Partnerships:** SJSU iSchool has established many global relationships in Asia, Africa and Europe. For example, SJSU iSchool partners with global organizations like Librarians Without Borders. SJSU iSchool has also participated in collaborative initiatives with partners in countries such as Vietnam, Asia and Pakistan (Hirsh, et. al., 2015).

**Research**: SJSU iSchool created a virtual Center for Information Research and Innovation (CIRI), which showcases the school's faculty and student research and innovative projects aimed at generating exemplary new practices to benefit a global audience. CIRI is governed by an International Advisory Board.

**Outreach**: SJSU iSchool co-founded a fully online free global conference in 2011 called the Library 2.0 virtual conference series. Library 2.0 virtual conferences help build a global community among information professionals and global conversations around the future of libraries.

For the long term, SJSU iSchool is committed to growing its globalization efforts by continually identifying new course offerings, internships, programs and collaborations that offer both faculty and students continued exposure to global learning experiences.

### INTEGRATION OF INTERNATIONAL PERSPECTIVES IN EUROPEAN LIS/IS PROGRAMS – TATJANA APARAC-JELUŠIĆ

There are three departments of information sciences in Croatia, the oldest one at the University of Zagreb (from 1976) and two others established at the University of Osijek (in 2003) and University of Zadar (in 2008). All three departments have cooperated with LIS/IS schools mainly from Europe and the United States. European cooperation is based on European Union (EU) funded mobility and research projects (Erasmus plus, Horizon 2020, for instance) and cooperation with U.S. partners was assured through Fulbright programs.

**International students and visiting scholars:** From the perspective of a small country, it is hard to attract international students. Albeit the percentage of international students is low, there is an upward tendency: more students have been showing interest, mainly for graduate and postgraduate programs. It is healthy to have international faculty members involved in teaching and research. Our experience shows that students enjoy visiting professors (some of them include N. Belkin, C. Borgman, M. Dahlstrom, A. Gilliland, C. Kulthau, T. Saracevic, R. Todd and T. Weech). It is hard to estimate what percentage they should comprise, but certainly one course per semester should be welcomed. In Croatian experience, students benefit from visiting professors and students from abroad (mostly through LIDA conference and ASIST/European chapter cooperation). Students also expose themselves to different cultural and language circumstances by establishing their own networks, collaborating on research proposals and projects for conferences and journals, traveling abroad and acting as hosts to colleagues.

**International collaboration:** EINFOSE (*European Information Science Education: encouraging mobility and learning outcomes harmonization*) is funded through European program Erasmus plus. Partners from universities in eight European countries (based in Barcelona, Boras, Graz, Hildesheim, Ljubljana, Osijek, Pisa and Ankara) have worked to investigate differences in entry requirements and learning outcomes with a goal to propose some new approaches. There are a number of differences that cause barriers between higher education institutions (HEIs) that offer MA programs in LIS/IS. It is expected that the agreement upon a basic core content that will prepare students for enrolment at graduate level should make the recognition process easier. Furthermore, it will also enable students to specialize in certain topics (such as digital humanities, scholarly communication and big data, economy of information, sociology of media, etc.) at a particular HEI that has experts on these or other relevant topics. The partners envision that some of the existing barriers can be eliminated through several modes of teaching and learning in the digital environment, such as summer schools, tutorials for teachers from partner institutions, intellectual outputs that sufficiently prepare students to start a particular MA program in IS, etc. EINFOSe project seeks to reach agreement between partners upon the basic principles, entry requirements and recognition of certain number of credits to be transferable between partners' institutions.

### INTEGRATION OF INTERNATIONAL PERSPECTIVES IN A CHINESE LIS/IS PROGRAM – RUHUA HUANG

The School of Information Management (SIM) at Wuhan University in China is the earliest, largest and strongest teaching and research institution in the field of library and information management in China. China was the first developing country to become a member of the iSchools and iCaucus in 2009. The International Collaborative Academy of Library and Information Science, Wuhan University was established in 2008 and has three foreign teachers (two American, one Canadian). Each year, more than 30 overseas scholars are invited to SIM; through these interactions, both university-level faculty exchanges and grass root level exchanges and cooperation have continued to grow and flourish. The following are among examples of how an international focus is addressed in the SIM:

**Programs/ Curriculum:** SIM has set up exchange programs for faculty members and students with international first-class LIS schools. Every year, about 30 experts from Hong Kong, Macau, Taiwan and other countries around the world are invited to SIM to offer courses and deliver academic lectures.

**Learning outcomes**: As an institution supported by the Ministry of Education of China, SIM has an important responsibility to serve all students and guarantee fair and equal access to higher education. SIM has established cultural diversity goals to increase the quantity of international students.

**Partnerships:** In the last five years, SIM has invited approximately 30 famous foreign experts each year to visit the school to give academic reports or to teach. iConference 2017 was co-hosted by SIM and Sungkyunkwan University Library & Information Science and Data Science Department. The event was held in Wuhan, China and was the first time the iConference was held in the Asia-Pacific region.

**Research**: As a member of the International Federation of Library Associations and Institutions (IFLA), SIM faculty members are actively involved in a variety of international organizations. Each year, it has approximately 30 faculty members acting as directors, vice-chairman, vice-editor and members. Approximately 35 faculty members act as associate senior editor and reviewer, including for the top 10 journals in the LIS field.

**Outreach**: To implement the university's strategy of globalized student education, our school continues to develop cooperative relationships with prestigious universities, research institutions and enterprises around the world, cooperate with scholarship programs and send students overseas for degree programs, student exchanges, short-term exchanges, summer internships and international conferences. SIM has signed 3+2 cooperation agreements with several international universities.

## CONCLUSION

The four LIS/IS schools from four different continents present unique strategies to support their educational missions in the globalization era. Various actions have been taken to create innovative curriculum, to enhance student learning experience, to support faculty research, to strengthen international partnership and to ensure the quality of LIS/IS education in a global environment. However, LIS/IS programs are still facing several key challenges: local relevance addressing indigenous knowledge and knowledge systems; continuing assessment on new learning and research demands; international LIS/IS program accreditation. Currently, IFLA is conducting an international survey regarding LIS program accreditation standards and process. More interaction and discussion are needed for LIS/IS programs worldwide to address those important issues collaboratively.

## REFERENCES


Abdullahi, I., & Kajberg, L. (2004). A study of international issues in library and information science education: Survey of LIS schools in Europe, the USA and Canada. *New Library World, 105*(9/10), 345-356.

Altbach, P. G., & Knight, J. (2007). The internationalization of higher education: Motivations and realities. *Journal of Studies in International Education, 11*(3-4), 290-305.

Eisenberg, M. B., & Fullerton, S. P. (2012). ED and INFO 2052: Oh, the places you'll go! Information Professionals 2050: Educational Possibilities and Pathways, 2.

EHEA, The European Higher Education Area. (2017). Members. Retrieved January 9, 2017 from http://www.ehea.info/pid34250/members.html

Dlamini, P. & Mbatha, B. 2005. A report on the 3rd ProLISSA / DISSAnet Conference, 28-29 October, Pretoria: General contribution. *South African Journal of Libraries and Information Science, 71*: 201-204.

Ford, C., Faires, D., Hirsh, S., and Carranza, N. (2017). The significance of language study in library and information science: A comparison of two programs in the United States and Honduras. *Journal of Education for Library and Information Science*, 58(2), to be published.

Gibb, A., Haskins, G., & Robertson, I. (2012). Leading the entrepreneurial university: Meeting the entrepreneurial development needs of higher education institutions. In *Universities in change* (pp. 9-45). New York, NY: Springer.

Hirsh, S., Faires, D., Holschuh Simmons, M., Christensen, P., Sellar, M., Stenström, C., Hagar, C., Bernier, A., Alman, S., & Fisher, J. (2015). International perspectives in LIS education: Global education, research & collaboration at the SJSU School of Information. *Journal of Education for Library and Information Science*, 56(*Supplement 1*), S27-S46.

IFLA, International Federation of Library Associations (2016). Retrieved January 9, 2017 from http://www.ifla.org/node/10578

Johnson, I. M. (2013). The impact on education for librarianship and information studies of the Bologna process and related European Commission programmes and some outstanding issues in Europe and beyond. *Education for Information, 30*(1, 2), 63-92.

Keeling, R. (2006). The Bologna Process and the Lisbon Research Agenda: The European Commission's expanding role in higher education discourse. *European Journal of Education, 41*(2), 203-223.

Knight, J. (2011). Education hubs: A fad, a brand, an innovation? *Journal of Studies in International Education, 15*(3), 221-240.

Mehra, B., & Bishop, A. P. (2007). Cross-cultural perspectives of international doctoral students: Two-way learning in library and information science education. *International Journal of Progressive Education, 3*(1), 44-64.

Moran, B. B., & Marchionini, G. J. (2012). Information professionals 2050. *Information Services and Use, 32*(3-4), 95-100.

Ngulube, P., Dube, L. & Mhlongo, M. 2015. Towards a cartography of indigenous knowledge systems in library and information science training and education in Anglophone eastern and sourthern Africa. *Indilinga African Journal of Indigenous Knowledge Systems, 14*: 145-168.

Ocholla, D.N. 2001. Curriculum response to a changing national and international environment: Theoretical and methodological paradigms on review and revision. *Education for Information, 19*(2): 143-167.

Ocholla, L. & Ocholla, D. 2014. Cataloguing and classification education (CCE) and training in library and information science/studies departments in South Africa. *South African Journal of Libraries and Information Science*: 1-7.

Partridge, H., Bruce, C., Edwards, S., Gasson, S., Hirsh, S., Stenstrom, C. & Haycock, K. (2016). Trans-Pacific doctoral success – A collaborative cohort model. *Proceedings of the 12th Biennial Quality in Postgraduate Research (QPR) Conference: Society, Economy & Communities: 21st Century Innovations in Doctoral Education*, 125-131.

Raju, J. 2015. LIS education in the digital age for an African agenda. *Library Trends, 64*(1): 161-177.

Raju, J. & Arsenault, C. 2007. First-level LIS education and training: A comparison between South Africa and Canada. *Education for Information, 25*(3/4): 179-193.

Scheepers, M.D., De Boer, A-L., Bothma, T.J.D. & Du Toit, P.H. 2011. A mental model for successful inter-discipinary collaboration in curriculum innovation for information literacy. *South African Journal of Libraries and Information Science*, 75-84.

Sewdass, N. 2004. A study of an international development project in library and information science in South Africa. *Education for Information*, *21*(1):13-22/

Subramaniam, M. M., & Jaeger, P. T. (2010). Modeling inclusive practice?: Attracting diverse faculty and future faculty to the information workforce. *Library Trends, 59*(1), 109-127.

de Wit, J. H. (2011). Globalization and internationalisation of higher education. *RUSC, 8*(2), 241-247.

Wormell, I. 1998. Establishment of a LIS research and education network in the Republic of South Africa: A project with roots in the FID/ET committee work. *Education for Information*, *16*(3): 253-254.

# Digital Literacy in the Era of Fake News: Key Roles for Information Professionals

**Lynn Silipigni Connaway**
*OCLC Research, USA. connawal@oclc.org*

**Heidi Julien**
*SUNY, Buffalo, USA. heidijul@buffalo.edu*

**Michael Seadle**
*Humboldt- Universität zu Berlin, Germany. Seadle@hu-berlin.de*

**Alex Kasprak**
*Staff Science Writer, Snopes.com, USA. alex@snopes.com*

## ABSTRACT

**Fake news has itself become a prominent news topic in recent years. This ASIST President's Invited Panel will focus on the need for and roles filled by information professionals in preparing the public to become more critical consumers of information products and services, as well as discuss research around the development of tools and algorithmic solutions that filter, detect and flag fake stories.**

**Noted educators, researchers and practicing professionals will discuss how and in which contexts information professionals can provide needed literacy education. Following the invited panelists' presentations and a time for group discussion and questions, attendees will form discussion groups, address questions and document their discussions. The small group members will share their discussion topics with all session attendees. The notes from the discussions will be documented and used to develop a continued discussion of the topic at a session at the ALISE 2018 meeting.**

## KEYWORDS

fake news, information literacy, internet rumor site, science news, communication strategies, algorithmic filters, President's invited panel

## PANEL DESCRIPTION

The proliferation of seemingly credible news stories and information sources that turn out to be inaccurate, at best, or completely fabricated, at worst, has left the public to wonder which information sources to trust. Information and digital literacy have become important skills for consumers of information products in today's society. The information sources to which people have access shape their understanding of the world and inform their decision making in their daily lives and how they participate in and give voice to their communities. The ability for readers to critically evaluate the merits of information sources, whether in print, electronic form or other media formats, is vital for an informed democracy. Research has indicated that millennials and post-millennials, although quite at ease with information technology, also struggle with the evaluation of online sources (Connaway, Lanclos & Hood, 2013; Connaway, White, Lanclos & Le Cornu, 2013; Stanford History Education Group, 2016). Where and how do people achieve levels of information and digital literacy that allow them to navigate the perils of questionable information sources and identify the hallmarks of validity and veracity? This ASIS&T President's Invited Panel presentation will explore the myriad challenges (societal, institutional, social, behavioral and cognitive) to providing that support.

Information professionals, including librarians, archivists, journalists and information architects, can play key roles in helping the public to become informed consumers of information products and services. These professionals are ideally situated to educate and provide tools and strategies to the audiences they serve so individuals feel confident with how they select, evaluate and use information resources. But in order to help others achieve digital and information literacy, information professionals themselves must be effectively educated.

Information authority also has been profoundly destabilized in recent years, providing significant potential for information professionals to guide information consumers and creators. Dr. Julien's contribution to the panel will focus on ways in which clients can be supported to sharpen their interpretive competencies, develop their critical thinking skills and stay afloat on a sea of information (fake or otherwise).

Dr. Seadle will discuss a grayscale measure for fake news (Seadle, 2016). Fake news and fake science are subject to the same measures that we use for research integrity violations. There is rarely a simple black and white distinction between true and false news reports, but rather a broad range of grayscale options that blend some degree of truth with claims that may be less well grounded in fact. In a post-Foucault world, it is clear that facts themselves are cultural artifacts. A group that hates a particular politician may accept any slander as a

80th Annual Meeting of the Association for Information Science & Technology, Washington, DC, VA | Oct. 27-Nov. 1, 2017

fact because it seems plausible. A measure of both fake science and fake news is the degree to which they rely on "facts" that do not meet the standards of evidence of the international scholarly community. While these standards include their own (scholarly) cultural bias, they provide a broad measure for sorting and counting facts. The degree of truth or fakeness can then be measured by the density of facts that fail reasonable scholarly tests of evidence. This presentation will include specific examples with measurements for sorting and counting facts.

As a science specialist at an internet rumor site, Alex Kasprak often writes about sensationalized scientific claims, the misuse of science to make political or social points and the occasional alien conspiracy theory – a slightly different niche of the internet than the most common fake news stories his colleagues are fighting on a daily basis. He will speak to the ways in which science fake news differs from other fake news, highlight communication strategies employed in the creation of both science and political viral stories, and provide strategies for identifying inaccurate or false science online.

This planned session is the first part of a two-part panel that examines the important issues laid out in this paper. The conference planners of the 2017 ASIS&T Annual Meeting and the 2018 ALISE Annual Meeting, in cooperation with the iSchools consortium, will present the second panel to continue the discussion at the ALISE meeting to be held in Denver, Colorado, in early February 2018.

Following brief presentations by invited panelists, the moderator and speakers will encourage a dynamic exchange with audience members, who will form discussion groups to address questions that will be discussed with all audience members.

Among the possible questions are these examples:

- What role/s can information professionals play in helping the public to become better informed consumers of information?
- Are we educating information professionals to play a role in helping the public to become better informed consumers of information?
- If so, what exemplars should be considered? If not, what types of teaching and learning for information professionals should be implemented?
- How will the outcomes of these educational offerings be measured in terms of effectiveness?
- What types of research and dissemination of research would provide a means for the library and information science (LIS) discipline to become leaders in the global initiative to help the public become better informed consumers of information?
- How are we, as LIS educators, researchers and professionals, able to utilize the various tools and algorithmic solutions that detect and flag fake stories in preparing other information professionals to help the public to become better informed consumers of information?

The notes from the discussions will be documented and used as the catalyst for the continued exploration of this topic at a panel organized for the ALISE 2018 meeting.

The ALISE session will continue the dialogue by integrating the discussion topics from the 2017 ASIS&T panel in a debate of how LIS schools/iSchools can best prepare students in their various programs to take on information and digital literacy roles after graduation. Panelists will represent relevant education programs in LIS and allied fields.

## REFERENCES


Connaway, L. S., Lanclos, D. M., & Hood, E. M. (2013, December 6). "I always stick with the first thing that comes up on Google…" Where people go for information, what they use, and why. *EDUCAUSE Review Online*. Retrieved from http://er.educause.edu/articles/2013/12/i-always-stick- with-the-first-thing-that-comes-up-on-google---where- people-go-for-information-what-they-use-and-why

Connaway, L. S., White, D., Lanclos, D., & Le Cornu, A. (2013). Visitors and residents: What motivates engagement with the digital information environment?

*Information Research, 18*(1). Retrieved from http://informationr.net/ir/18-1/infres181.html

Seadle, M. (2016). Quantifying research integrity. *Synthesis Lectures on* Information *Concepts, Retrieval, and Services, 8*(5) 1-141. doi:10.2200/S00743ED1V01Y 201611ICR053

Stanford History Education Group. (2016). *Evaluating information: The* cornerstone *of civic online reasoning*. Retrieved from https://sheg.stanford.edu/upload/ V3LessonPlans/Executive%20Summary%2011.21.16.pdf

# Digital Liaisons Virtual Uncommons: Connecting Information and People in Order to Enhance Lives via Digital Librarianship


**Chris Cunningham**
*University of Southern Mississippi, USA. christopher.a.cunningham@usm.edu*

**Virginia Dressler**
*Kent State University, USA. vdressle@kent.edu*

**Ekatarina Grguric**
*McGill University Library, Canada. ekatarina.grguric@mcgill.ca*

**Alyson Gamble**
*Simmons College, USA. gamblea@simmons.edu*

**Nushrat Khan**
*North Carolina State University, USA. njkhan@ncsu.edu*



## ABSTRACT

**Digital librarianship is a rich space in which new practitioners often find their feet on the job, picking up needed skill sets and adapting to new technologies on the fly. Creating a space for peer information sharing and mentorship is particularly important for this community. Virtual chat sessions and unconferences are two innovative ways to connect established practitioners with less experienced students and professionals in supportive, collaborative environments. By combining these two formats, it is possible to create a more inclusive space for mentorship and peer information sharing. We propose hosting a virtual uncommons that transcends geographical locations and other physical barriers. The digital liaisons virtual uncommons (DLVU) will feature leaders in digital libraries who will act in a mentoring capacity by responding to questions posed by new information professionals throughout a series of virtual chat sessions and an in-person unconference session. In the DLVU, students and early career professionals will be able to connect with peers and mentors in the field of digital librarianship. The virtual uncommons will be a space for informal mentoring and serendipitous networking. This session will be composed of a series of Twitter chats under the hashtag #SIGDLchats and a reflective panel structured as an attendee driven unconference in which panelists serve as moderators.**



## KEYWORDS

digital libraries, modern librarianship, future of digital librarianship, LIS4Good, digital collections, early-career professionals, mentorship, graduate students, students, student research


## INTRODUCTION

This year's conference theme, Diversity of Engagement: Connecting People and Information in the Physical and Virtual Worlds, offers SIG/DL the opportunity to propose a digital liaisons virtual uncommons focusing on enabling the skills of modern librarians to better support the communities we serve. Digital liaisons has historically been delivered as a combination of poster and panel session highlighting innovative research in digital libraries and has been recognized as a format that supports student involvement. Last year, due to the difficulty for North American students or early career professionals to attend the first ASIS&T Annual Meeting in Europe, and the clear implicit need of international mentorship and idea-sharing, we presented digital liaisons as a virtual uncommons: a Twitter chat and networking opportunity to foster conversations about ways in which digital libraries enhance lives and the future of the profession followed by a reflective panel session at the Annual Meeting. The panel session was an unstructured session, similar to an unconference, and acted as a supplement to the Twitter chat. The combination of virtual and in-person elements provided a mechanism for participation regardless of location. This year, building on the success of DVLU in 2016, we have expanded the scope of our Twitter chats from one session to multiple regularly occurring sessions.

Beginning in April 2017, SIG/DL started hosting a monthly Twitter chat session devoted to issues in digital libraries (see Figure 1). This panel will continue the discussions started through the 2016 DVLU session, as well as build on the chats that we have hosted since. In the past, digital liaisons has successfully fulfilled three goals. First, the panel provided students with an opportunity to present their research at a national conference, thereby serving as a form of outreach for new professionals who desire to take part in the information science research community. Second, the panel provided a venue for presenters to exchange ideas with peers and experienced colleagues, as well as for the more experienced members to learn from presenters' fresh perspectives and recent


80[th] Annual Meeting of the Association for Information Science & Technology, Washington, DC, VA | Oct. 27-Nov. 1, 2017

involvement in LIS programs. This included ideas such as how one defines being a digital librarian, skill sets involved, common issues both positive and negative that practitioners encounter and common support structures, such as professional organizations such as ASIS&T. Third, the digital liaisons panel increased student participation and recruitment of both individual members and student chapters. In 2017, SIG/DL was able to capitalize on the location of the ASIS&T Annual Meeting in order to engage more of the European Chapter students and encourage them to participate. In addition, SIG/DL specifically reached out to a number of practitioners within the EU in order to gain from their expertise as well as introduce them to ASIS&T and SIG/DL.

The 2017 DVLU builds on this past impact and will continue to provide opportunities for students to be involved in conversations about the future of our field and grow an active membership for ASIS&T. The conversational approach within the Twitter chats will provide a venue for early-career practitioners to connect with more seasoned mentors while lowering barriers to participation. This year, we will further develop the structure of the panel to support an applied discussion and further delve into a deeper conversation about the changing nature of digital librarianship.

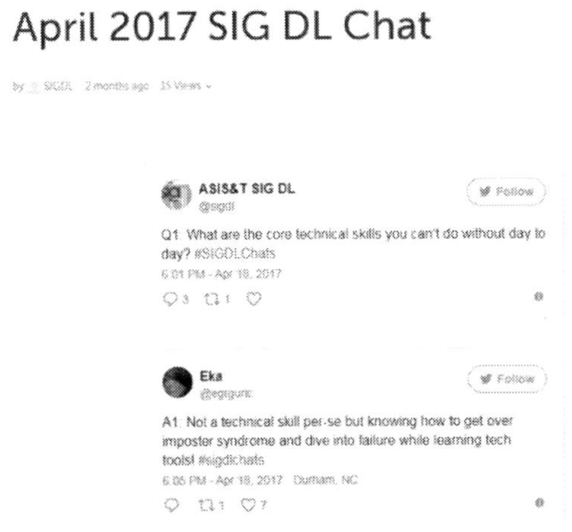


***Figure 1**. Example of April virtual uncommons chat from Storify*

## TOPIC

In adherence to the 2017 Annual Meeting theme, this year's panel will focus on the diverse ways in which people from different backgrounds, cultures and disciplines forge connections with each other, discover and use information, and engage with technology. The open-ended theme will allow participants to engage with a broad range of topics and interests related to knowledge creation and life enhancement. Subtopics may include citizen science, community projects, crowd-sourced metadata, digital humanities, non-text digital libraries, open access and new publishing models, open source software, information ethics, social network analysis, the skill set of the modern librarian, the future of digital libraries, the responsibilities of knowledge creation and the impact of the creation of digital libraries on communities. Exploring digital librarianship through the lens of professional responsibility and community involvement allows participants a great deal of latitude in the subjects covered. The broad range of focuses that may develop for the session listed here are meant to be illustrative, not inclusive.

## STRUCTURE AND FORMAT

The digital liaisons panel will be a multi-part, interactive session in which students and early-stage professionals have an opportunity to communicate directly with peers and mentors. The virtual uncommons will take the form of consecutive Twitter chats that connect established digital librarians as well as students and new professionals. A collection of library professionals focused in digital librarianship were invited to frame the theme in the beginning of the Twitter chat to help synthesize conversation over the course of the conference. Participants will engage candidly with the presenters' offerings, giving them an opportunity to learn from and network with seasoned professionals. In turn, attendees will benefit from learning about current interests and directions of students and early-career researchers. At the conclusion of the Twitter chats, participants will be encouraged to reach out to their peers directly with additional questions. Unfortunately, one constraint of this method will be the loss of participants from countries that restrict access to Twitter or whose internet access is limited.

There will be ample time for discussion among all participants, including audience members, both physical and virtual. Following the conclusion of the conference, the presenters will compile and electronically present the unconference outcomes through a Storify and a Google Drive folder for further dissemination. At the conclusion of the unconference, participants will participate in a summative evaluation via a Google Form. The results of this survey and a summary of the Twitter chat will be compiled and presented at the digital liaisons panel session during the Annual Meeting. This session will be structured as a collaborative working meeting structured like an unconference and intended to overcome divisions in the field of digital librarianship resulting from jargon. Outcomes of this working session are expected to include a document identifying what the work of a digital librarian is, what digital library initiatives look like and what the terminology surrounding this work really means in a glossary format.

## RECRUITMENT

After the panel is approved, SIG/DL will begin promotion in June. SIG/DL has begun the use of Twitter chats through an aggressive promotion campaign using a variety of media channels, including LIS programs and other relevant professional listservs, as well as social media outlets and personal invitations. SIG/DL members will also contact ASIS&T student chapters and LIS program faculty teaching pertinent coursework.

Submissions to the digital liaisons panel have grown every year over the five years the session has been held at the Annual Meeting, and we anticipate another strong pool of participants, including students as well as working professionals.

### TIMELINE

Twitter chats will be held monthly from April 2017 through October 2017 on a flexible time schedule. We will collect the findings from the various chats and present the findings at the Annual Meeting, highlighting how digital librarians exemplify the ability to connect people and information regardless of physical location. Expansive hours for the chats will allow for participation across global time zones. Social media, such as Twitter, uniquely allows us to account for scheduling issues as well as the ability to archive discussions for future reference.

### VIRTUAL UNCOMMONS MODERATORS/CONCLUSION

Moderation duties were allocated to all of the 2016-2017 SIG/DL executive officers, allowing for a longer duration of the Twitter chat as well as fresh perspectives being added to the discussion. Further, the viewpoints and perspectives of the executive officers provide a wide variety from many different types of digital librarians, including United States members as well as those from outside North America.

# Navigating the Next Step: An Interactive Panel for Doctoral Students

**Liz Hartnett**
*School of Library & Information Science, University of South Carolina, USA. ejhart@mailbox.sc.edu*

***Hassan Zamir***
*School of Library & Information Science, University of South Carolina, USA. zamir@email.sc.edu*

**Rajesh Singh**
*Division of Library and Information Science, St. John's University, USA. singhr1@stjohns.edu*

## ABSTRACT

**The proposed session builds on the successes of interactive doctoral student panels sponsored by SIG/ED at earlier ASIS&T Annual Meetings. This year's panel features faculty in various stages of their academic careers. The panelists are prepared to address audience questions on topics of concern to doctoral students, such as the traditional academic job market, alternative career paths including post-doctoral opportunities, the development of personal research agendas and the challenges of online instruction.**

**The panel discussion will focus on the academic job market and how applicants can present themselves in the best light depending upon the type of position sought. By interacting with the panelists, doctoral students will gain valuable insights on finishing their dissertations, weighing postdoctoral opportunities and preparing for their first academic positions. This session will also provide an anonymous mechanism for doctoral students and new faculty to ask questions without feeling inhibited or intimidated. The panel may be of greatest benefit to those doctoral students nearing the end of their doctoral programs, but will also be useful to new doctoral students and new assistant professors.**

## KEYWORDS

doctoral students, faculty, academic jobs, academe

## INTRODUCTION

The completion of the doctoral dissertation is the culmination of a long journey for doctoral students, but for most it is also a time to enter into another challenging undertaking: entering the highly competitive academic job market. A deeper understanding of the nature and expectations of academic positions and the application process will help doctoral students prepare for this pursuit.

80th Annual Meeting of the Association for Information Science & Technology, Washington, DC, VA | Oct. 27-Nov. 1, 2017



Depending on the institution, library and information science faculty members are expected to demonstrate excellence in three areas – research, teaching and service. There are differences in the amount of emphasis placed upon each of these areas at different schools, and knowledge of these can inform a more successful job search. For example, institutions with an emphasis on teaching require a heavier class load than do those that focus on research and publishing. Furthermore, faculty at any institution are expected to participate in academic life through service, both at their school and in the greater academic community. Being aware of these expectations and what they mean for new faculty is an important part of preparing for an academic job search.

Making the transition from graduate school to an academic position can be very challenging. Entering academia can be a complex and very competitive process. Individual experiences vary, and some doctoral students have had greater exposure to conducting and reporting on research, while others may have gained considerable teaching experience during their programs. Service opportunities abound, but it's essential to be strategic in determining where best to focus one's efforts. Success in academia requires the ability to balance the demands of all three areas: teaching, research and service.

This panel will provide doctoral students valuable insights into critical issues such as dissertation completion, tailoring their applications, crafting teaching and research statements, considering post-doctoral opportunities and knowing what to expect when starting new faculty positions and working towards tenure. The panel's interactive nature will facilitate the smooth exchange of ideas, viewpoints and perspectives among doctoral students and panelists.

## FORMAT

The event will take place during a single ASIS&T paper session time slot. If possible, the panel will be assembled in a u-shape at the front of the room, allowing for better interaction among the panelists. The students will be seated in concentric u-shapes mirroring the panel. The informality of the room set-up is intended to induce conversation between the panelists and the attendees. A SIG/ED officer will tweet the questions and answers for the benefit of those students who are unable to attend the panel session.

Questions for the panelists will be solicited prior to the conference on the ASIS&T student listserv, and attendees will transmit their questions electronically to the designated SIG/ED officers, program coordinators Rajesh Singh and Liz Hartnett, who will transmit questions electronically to the panel moderator, Naresh Agrawal. Index cards will also be available for students to convey their questions for the panelists, if they do not wish to use electronic media. Whether submitted electronically or by index card, the anonymity of the questions' source will be maintained to promote the free exchange of ideas and perspectives.

At the start of the session, panel moderator **Naresh Agarwal** will ask the panelists to give a brief introduction including their names, current positions and institutional affiliations, relevant highlights of their past experience, and the qualities they believe are most important for success in academia. Thereafter, the moderator will ask panel members the questions transmitted by the SIG/ED officer. When there are 10 minutes left in the session, each of the panelists will be asked to provide a summary of the quality indicators they look for in an applicant; then the panel moderator will ask each panelist to offer one final piece of advice for the attendees that was not covered previously during the discussion.

## BENEFITS

This event will provide an opportunity for informal interaction between doctoral students and experienced faculty. The panel includes faculty members who are at all stages of their academic careers. Through the discussion, doctoral students will gain understanding of how academic careers progress and of the value of ASIS&T membership in creating and maintaining a professional network. Participation in this discussion offers doctoral students connection, not only with established faculty, but with other doctoral students as well. Although this panel is primarily for doctoral students nearing completion of their PhDs, the discussion may also be useful to current faculty who are planning a transition from one institution to another.

## PROMOTION

This panel will be heavily promoted using ASIS&T listservs, the SIG/ED website and SIG/ED social media accounts, including Facebook and Twitter. Furthermore, a list of all student members will be requested from the ASIS&T executive staff, and the students will be emailed individually with an invitation to participate in the event by submitting their questions and attending the panel. The panel will also be listed in the conference program.

## PANELISTS

The panelists represent all stages of an academic career, six different institutions and diverse academic experiences. Furthermore, some of the panelists also possess either educational or work experience in countries other than the United States.

Naresh Agarwal, moderator, is associate professor at the School of Library and Information Science at Simmons College, Boston. He earned his PhD from the National University of Singapore (NUS) Department of Information Systems, School of Computing. His teaching areas are technology/web development, evaluation, knowledge management and theories of information science and technology. Naresh's research area is information behavior and knowledge management – the way people look for information and the contextual factors that impact their choice of information sources. He seeks to understand and synthesize the apparent contradictions in this phenomenon and tries to reconcile multiple perspectives. His publications span these areas. He is currently writing a book on context in information behavior. Prior to entering the doctoral program at NUS, Naresh worked for six years in technology roles in the voice-over-IP, bio-informatics and digital cinema industries. You can learn more about him at http://web.simmons.edu/~agarwal.

Naresh has held various leadership positions at ASIS&T. He is currently the chair of the membership committee and conference co-chair of the 80th Annual Meeting of ASIS&T. Naresh has been the director of Chapter Assembly and a board member, and chair of SIGs. In 2012, he was awarded the James M. Cretsos Leadership Award. As moderator and panelist, Naresh provides the perspective and unique experience of an international student background coupled with a successful professional career.

**Dr. Keren Dali** is assistant professor at the School of Library & Information Studies, University of Alberta, Canada. Her primary research interests are in diversity and marginalized communities, relationships between LIS and social work, the inclusion of people with disabilities in work places, policy-related implications for inclusion in academia, LIS education with the focus on creativity, accreditation and humanistic pedagogies, and reading behaviors as an adaptation strategy. With a background in social work and LIS and graduate teaching experience in both Canada and the United States, Dr. Dali will start her master of social work degree in the fall of 2017 in order to enhance her interdisciplinary teaching and research. A specific goal is to develop large-scale, international, grant-funded projects spanning several fields of practice, education and scholarship. She holds the inaugural Outstanding Instructor Award from the Faculty of Information, University of Toronto; the inaugural ALISE/Connie Van Fleet Award for Research Excellence in Public Library Services to Adults; and the Outstanding Reviewer distinction and the Highly Commended Paper distinction from the Emerald Literati Network Awards for Excellence. Her work has been funded by grants from the Social Sciences & Humanities Research Council of Canada (SSHRC) and the American Library Association, among others. With 15 years of intensive publication and research experience, Dr. Dali serves as an editorial board member of *Library Quarterly* and *Journal of Education in Library & Information Science* (*JELIS*); an international advisory board member for *Journal of Librari-*

*anship & Information Science (JoLIS)*; and an associate editor of *International Journal of Information, Diversity & Inclusion*. She's been chairing and co-chairing the Education & Professional Advancement Committee (EPAC) for ASIS&T since 2015, while also consistently reviewing submissions for ASIS&T conferences and participating in the adjudication of awards outside of EPAC.

**Sanda Erdelez** is a professor at University of Missouri iSchool (School of Information Science and Learning Technologies) where she is also the founding director of the MU Information Experience Laboratory (IE Lab) and most recently chair of the Library and Information Science Program. She received her LL.B. and LL.M degrees from University of Osijek Law School (Croatia) and PhD in information transfer from Syracuse University. She was also a faculty member at University of Osijek and University of Texas at Austin. Dr. Erdelez is a former Fulbright Scholar and recipient of the Texas Excellence Teaching Award and the ALISE Pratt-Severn Faculty Innovation Award. Her research interests include human information behavior, human-computer interaction and usability evaluation in online environments. She has been internationally recognized for her pioneering research in the areas of information encountering and opportunistic discovery of information. Her research has received funding from both corporate and government sources including Dell Inc., SBC Communication, Texas State Government and NSF. She has been an active member of ASIS&T since 1987 and has served in numerous leadership roles including chair of Special Interest Group/Information Seeking and Use (SIG/USE) and member of the ASIS&T Board of Directors. In 2015, Dr. Erdelez received the Outstanding Contribution to Information Behavior Research Award from SIG/USE and also became member of the SIG/USE Academy of Fellows.

In terms of contribution to the panel, as an academic with an international background Dr. Erdelez can speak about experiences in going through all the stages of visa processing for academic employment in the United States and about managing family life with two children through this process.

Darin Freeburg is assistant professor in the School of Library and Information Science at the University of South Carolina, where he has been for three years. His research focuses on applications of knowledge management in religious, community and library contexts to help them achieve stated goals and objectives. Part of this includes the development of a new knowledge lens for information literacy, which focuses on creation, relationship, ambiguity and integration of information. A related interest is barriers to information reception that go beyond ability, including beliefs and organizational narcissism. He teaches courses in knowledge management, information literacy and communication transfer.

**Barabara Kwasnik** is a full professor at the School of Information Studies at Syracuse University. She currently serves as associate dean for academic affairs. She also teaches in the areas of organization of information, theory of classification and information science. She is especially interested in how classifications intersect with everyday human endeavor; for example, how they are translated from one culture or application to another. The purpose is to help support increasingly diverse contexts. Previous research (with Kevin Crowston) includes investigating whether genre information can help in searching, personal information management and browsing. Barbara brings the perspective of a successful career of balanced research, teaching and service to the panel.

**Howard Rosenbaum** is professor of information science in the Department of Information and Library Science in the School of Informatics and Computing at Indiana University, where he has been on the faculty since 1993. He is director of the master of information science program in the Department of Information and Library Science. Rosenbaum studies social informatics, social impacts of algorithms and online communities; has published in a variety of information science journals; and presented at ASIS&T, iConferences and elsewhere. He has recently published two books, "Social Informatics: Past, Present, and Future" with Pnina Fichman and "Social Infomatics Evolving" with Fichman and Madelyn SanFilippo.

Rosenbaum teaches digital entrepreneurship, information systems design, intellectual freedom and other classes. He has been recognized often for excellence in teaching and for the innovative use of technology in education, receiving the 2011 Thomson Reuters Outstanding Information Science Teacher Award from ASIS&T, the 2005 Frederic Bachman Lieber Memorial Award for Teaching Excellence from Indiana University, a 2003 statewide MIRA Award for Technological Innovation in Education from Techpoint, the 2002 Indiana Partnership for Statewide Education Award for Innovation in Teaching with Technology, and in 2000 was named one of the first SBC Fellows at Indiana University.

# Health Information Behavior Research with Marginalized Populations

**Blake Hawkins**
*University of British Columbia, Canada.*
*blake.hawkins@alumni.ubc.ca*

**Amelia Gibson**
*University of North Carolina, USA.*
*angibson@email.unc.edu*

**Kaitlin Costello**
*Rutgers University, USA. k.costello@rutgers.edu*

**Devon Greyson**
*Children's Hospital Research Institute, USA.*
*dgreyson@bcchr.ubc.ca*

**Tiffany Veinot**
*University of Michigan, USA. tveinot@umich.edu*

## ABSTRACT

**As part of an increasingly vibrant area of research, information behavior scholars have shown that traditionally marginalized populations (e.g., older adults, LGBTQ people, people of color, low-income people and people with chronic diseases or disabilities) may have distinct health information needs and information behaviors. These differences may arise from unique patterns in marginalized groups' life experiences, health risks and burdens, social networks and available resources, as well as dynamics of social marginalization and exclusionary service design. This subfield of information studies challenges established notions of health information-seeking behaviours to further develop theories and models, as well as propose new models for information services and technologies. The unique characteristics of marginalized populations have necessitated the development of novel research approaches and methods, as well as interdisciplinary collaborations and community-based partnerships. This panel invites audience members to think critically about what it means to engage marginalized populations in research and the methods and approaches needed to do so in a health context. It will also allow participants to broaden their understanding about the health information-seeking behaviors of marginalized populations. Panelists will introduce and contextualize marginalized populations' health information-seeking behaviours and explore potential or existing connections between themes from a variety of disciplines. Following a brief introduction and presentations from five panelists (who are themselves exploring marginalized populations' health information-seeking behaviours), there will be an open discussion session with the audience in a World Café format.**

## KEYWORDS

health information behaviors; marginalized populations; community engagement

80th Annual Meeting of the Association for Information Science & Technology, Washington, DC, VA | Oct. 27-Nov. 1, 2017



## INTRODUCTION

This panel focuses on the panelists' health information behavior research among different marginalized populations. We focus on marginalized populations for three reasons:

1. In recent years, the health sciences and medical practitioners have placed increasing importance on patient empowerment, individualized and contextualized care, and informed medical decision-making. All of these trends are predicated on by successful health information seeking.
2. Marginalized patient populations experience greater barriers to empowerment and medical decision-making.
3. Research in health information behavior is often disease-oriented, not population-oriented.

The panelists will discuss their health information behavior research with a wide variety of marginalized populations, including men who have sex with men, LGBTQ youth, young parents, parents of trans and gender creative youth, vaccine-hesitant parents, low-income families managing chronic illness, parents of individuals with Down syndrome and Autism Spectrum disorder, young Black women, adults on dialysis and women with chronic pain.

## BACKGROUND

Traditionally, research in health information behavior focuses on information seeking, often among groups of people who share a specific diagnosis (Lambert & Loiselle, 2007). This work emphasizes the motivations for and outcomes of information seeking behavior in health. These studies indicate that the motivations for seeking out health information are multifaceted and change over time; they include making choices about treatments, determining whether to modify a health-related behavior, learning what questions to ask the doctor, feeling in control of an illness, coping with the emotional impact of chronic disease, constructing a positive identity and satisfying curiosity (Barbarin, Klasnja & Veinot, 2016). Participants in these studies have a preference for getting health information from healthcare providers, but they typically consult multiple sources when they are experiencing health information needs. Source selection is impacted by factors related to the source, to the patient, the relationship between patients and sources, characteristics of the information need and social norms (Zhang, 2014). Health information seeking is linked to positive and negative health outcomes, including sense making, decision making, uncertainty management, confusion, avoidance and fear (Johnson & Case, 2012). Often, factors related to the patient (e.g., capacity for understanding health information, demographic characteristics) or to the information (e.g., quality of health information, presentation or format of information) are the focus of studies in this domain. We argue that conducting research with marginalized populations allows for a more comprehensive picture of the causes, conditions and consequences of health information behavior. Focusing on marginalized populations highlights central issues in information behavior that are otherwise overlooked, including the social costs of information seeking, information access and the ways in which social structures enable, enhance or prevent information behaviors within and among communities.

We position our understanding of marginalized populations using a conceptual framework of access to health care, considering approachability of healthcare resources, acceptability of seeking out and availing one's self of healthcare resources, availability and accessibility of health care, affordability of care and appropriate fit between the services offered and the populations who will access those services (Levesque, Harris & Russell, 2013). This dynamic perspective on access allows us to better define marginalization not as a static quality that can be easily quantified (e.g., "income below 200% of the poverty level"), but as interwoven processes that relate both to individual characteristics (e.g., income level, social capital) and to the characteristics of healthcare services (e.g., their location and cost). We include both individuals with chronic diagnoses who must manage their illnesses over the course of their lifetimes and individuals who experience population-specific health information needs.

## PANEL AGENDA

The purpose of this panel is to (1) examine issues surrounding health information behavior research with marginalized populations and (2) consider the intersection of multiple disciplines in health information behavior research (e.g., public health). We will address the following topics:

- Why is health information behavior research with marginalized populations necessary?
- What are some useful methods for this research?
- How can researchers build relationships with marginalized populations?
- When and how should other disciplinary approaches be incorporated into this work?

The organization of our panel is as follows:

1. A brief introduction to marginalized populations and health information behavior research will be presented by the panel moderator, Blake Hawkins (5 minutes).
2. Five examples of health information behavior research with marginalized populations will be presented by the panelists Blake Hawkins, Amelia Gibson, Kaitlin Costello, Tiffany Veinot and Devon Greyson (50 minutes).
3. Brief closing remarks and additional discussion of marginalized populations research will be presented by Blake Hawkins (5 minutes).
4. World Café discussions in small groups, with each panelist acting as a facilitator for discussions about the topics discussed in panel, giving participants the opportunity to share perspectives and discuss future research (Carson, 2011) (30 minutes).

To structure the World Café discussions, the following questions will be used as a starting point:

1. How do you work with marginalized populations in your research?
2. How can we address some of the challenges of working with marginalized populations?
3. Are there additional approaches to consider when studying marginalized populations? What kinds of methods have you used, either successfully or unsuccessfully?
4. How do researchers move beyond deficit-based frameworks when working with marginalized populations?

## PANEL DISCUSSIONS

### *Building Relationships with Participants*

Blake Hawkins, MLIS, moderator/panelist, is a doctoral student from the University of British Columbia iSchool and School of Population and Public Health interested in community-based research with LGBTQ youth and sex workers. Over the last four years he has had a variety of opportunities to collaborate with community groups in different capacities (as a researcher and community engagement roles with academia). As an academic and community member, he has completed research on information behavior, online interactions, knowledge mobilization and public policy impact on accessing health services. As a panelist he will discuss some of his master's research on LGBTQ health information-seeking behaviours. This work involved a year of building partnerships and engaging with the community to understand their needs and what would be appropriate for a research project. He will briefly reflect on his experiences building relationships with community partners – this includes the power dynamics, managing expectations and some myths both researchers and community partners may have about these relationships. Additionally, Blake will discuss the importance of being aware about the community context (e.g., location) and how this may impact the engagement process with community partners. In the case of his research project, Blake had to deal with some gendered obstacles when recruiting young gay, bisexual and other men who have sex with men due to the legacy of masculinity in the community. By sharing his academic and professional experiences, in the context of this one project, he hopes to emphasize the importance of context with information researchers who are interested in building partnerships and complete research with marginalized populations.

Amelia Gibson, PhD, is an assistant professor at the University of North Carolina at Chapel Hill where she studies health information behavior and local communities and places as information systems. Her current work focuses on information poverty and how intersections of identity, place, space and social and economic power/privilege influence information access and information behavior. She will discuss her work in information poverty, information access and geographies of health-related information seeking among parents of people with disabilities and young Black women, as examined in two projects - Healthy Girls Know and the Disability LINES project. Healthy Girls Know is a youth participatory action study that engages a pilot cohort of 6 Black teen girls (ages 12-15). The Disability LINES project examines the information needs and information worlds of parents of individuals with Down syndrome and Autism Spectrum Disorder. The project encompassed two studies – an interview study that examined health information access and behavior among 41 parents of individuals with developmental disabilities and a survey (n=935) of the information needs and information source choices of parents of individuals with Autism Spectrum Disorders (ASD) in the state of North Carolina. Together, the two studies informed an expanded understanding of information poverty as experienced by parents and caretakers who rely on medical data and research (available on the internet), as well as local procedural and institutional knowledge.

### *Methods and Approaches*

Kaitlin Costello will discuss some of the methodological challenges in health information behavior research with marginalized populations by presenting the methods from her current study. This study employs a qualitative approach to interactive information retrieval research and employs home visits, semi-structured interviews and retrospective think-alouds to uncover the causes and consequences of online health information seeking in the context of chronic pain. Although many studies evaluate how people use the internet to interact with information, most of the research in this area cannot be generalized to adults diagnosed with chronic diseases for several reasons: interactive information retrieval studies have not typically targeted health information needs; the studies are primarily conducted with college-aged students, who interact with the internet differently than older adults diagnosed with chronic illnesses; and the studies usually impose search tasks on participants rather than allowing them to search for information that meets their own information needs. Previous research, which has been largely concerned with interactions during information seeking, also generally does not examine information use, a central component of information behavior. The current study aims to understand how real patients diagnosed with chronic conditions search the internet for health information, what information they are interested in finding, how they understand and evaluate that information and how it is used after the search sessions are concluded. Costello is an assistant professor at the School of Communication and Information at Rutgers, the State University of New Jersey. She studies health information behavior with a focus on how patients diagnosed with chronic conditions use social websites, such as Twitter, Facebook, online support groups and other social websites, to communicate with other patients about their health. She has conducted multiple qualitative studies in this domain, interacting directly with participants with various health information needs and often diagnosed with chronic health conditions.

Tiffany Veinot, MLS, PhD, is an associate professor at the Schools of Information and Public Health at the University of Michigan. Veinot will argue that health information behavior research with marginalized populations should incorporate study of the networks, families and communities in which individuals are embedded. To do so, she contends that information behavior researchers should "make the 'meso' visible" in their research. The "meso" level of society includes small scale collectivities that fall between the micro level of individuals and the macro level of nation states, including entities such as families and communities. Research conducted at a meso level of analysis permits identification of emergent informational phenomena that are not reducible to individual behavior, such as differential patterns of access to information and connections between collective information behavior. Furthermore, multilevel analyses can permit rigorous modeling of the relationships between individuals and their meso-level contexts. This talk describes methods used in a longitudinal study of the information activities and networks of low-income families in which at least one member has a chronic illness. In this study, the family was taken as the central unit of analysis, and individual participants were sampled by family group. This mixed methods study involved five contacts with 25 families (with two-six members each) over two years. The study used two family-centered interviewing methods: 1) individual interviews conducted using a whole family methodology; and 2) family group interviews, which adapt the focus group method for people who know one another. Individual surveys, including family network items, were completed at each contact, and a home tour was conducted once. All data analyses were conducted at both the individual and group levels. The value of these methods will be illustrated with examples of analyses of both individual and group-level information phenomena.

### *Incorporating Multidisciplinarity*

Devon Greyson, PhD MLIS, is a postdoctoral research fellow at the British Columbia Children's Hospital Research Institute and the University of British Columbia Department of Pediatrics and instructor of women's and gender studies at Capilano University. Greyson's research focuses on health-related information practices of youth and parents and on the ethics and effectiveness of health information interventions. Greyson's work includes ethnographic research with young parents and vaccine hesitant populations; health services and policy survey research with parents of trans and gender creative youth, healthcare providers and the general population; and normative-empirical analyses of population health information interventions with a particular eye to the distributive justice implications for marginalized populations. On this panel, Greyson will discuss adapting dimensions of healthcare access to apply to health information access, as well as the strategy of conducting interdisciplinary research in order to flexibly and appropriately give back to participant populations by co-creating research outputs that matter to their communities.


### ACKNOWLEDGEMENTS

Blake Hawkins' project was supported by small grants from the University of British Columbia and the LOUD (LGBTQ Vancouver) Business Association. He also wishes to acknowledge the LGBTQ youth who participated in the fieldwork he discussed as a panelist.

Kaitlin Costello would like to thank Rutgers School of Communication and Information for providing funding for participant incentives for this research.

Amelia Gibson's research was funded by the University of North Carolina at Chapel Hill through a Junior Faculty Development Award and the Kilgour Research Award. Recruiting for the survey research presented in this panel was supported by the Carolina Institute for Developmental Disabilities Research Participant Registry, which is funded by NICHD U54HD079124.

Tiffany Veinot's research was made possible by funding from the Institute of Museum and Library Services (Grant # RE-04-10-0038-10). All views, findings and conclusions expressed in this article are hers and do not necessarily represent those of the funder.

Devon Greyson is supported by fellowships from the Michael Smith Foundation for Health Research and the Canadian Immunization Research Network. Projects discussed on this panel received funding from the Canadian Institutes of Health Research, British Columbia Immunization Committee and Canadian Immunization Research Network.


### REFERENCES


Barbarin, A. M., Klasnja, P., & Veinot, T. C. (2016). Good or bad, ups and downs, and getting better: Use of personal health data for temporal reflection in chronic illness. *International Journal of Medical Informatics*, *94*, 237–245.

Carson, L. (2011). Designing a public conversation using the World Café method. *Social Alternatives, 30*(1), 10-14

Johnson, J. D., & Case, D. O. (2012). *Health information seeking*. Peter Lang Publishing.

Lambert, S. D., & Loiselle, C. G. (2007). Health information seeking behavior. *Qualitative Health Research*, *17*(8), 1006–1019.

Levesque, J.-F., Harris, M. F., & Russell, G. (2013). Patient-centred access to health care: Conceptualising access at the interface of health systems and populations. *International Journal for Equity in Health*, 12, 18. https://doi.org/10.1186/1475-9276-12-18

Zhang, Y. (2014). Beyond quality and accessibility: Source selection in consumer health information searching. *Journal of the Association for Information Science and Technology*, *65*(5), 911–927. https://doi.org/10.1002/asi.23023

# Teaching Information Science and Technology to the World? Practices, Challenges and Visions

**Xiao Hu**
*Faculty of Education, University of Hong Kong, China. xiaohu@hku.hk*

**Allen H. Renear**
*School of Information Sciences, University of Illinois, USA. renear@illinois.edu*

**Bei Yu**
*School of Information Studies, Syracuse University, USA. byu@syr.edu*

**Toni Carbo**
*School of Information Sciences, University of Pittsburgh, USA. tcarbo@mail.sis.pitt.edu*

**Sue Alman**
*School of Information, San Jose State University, USA. alman.sjsu@gmail.com*

## ABSTRACT

**Information science and technology (IST) has made unprecedented impacts on society. Teaching IST should by no means be limited within the boundary of the discipline. Based on their experiences in teaching IST in various levels, speakers in this panel will reflect the past, share current practices and envision the future of teaching IST to the world. Collectively we aim to stimulate further discussions on increasing the impact of the field through education.**

## KEYWORDS

impact, information science and technology, interdisciplinary, international, education

## INTRODUCTION

In this information age, information science and technology (IST) stands as a prominent interdisciplinary field in academia and in society. Nonetheless, the impacts of an academic and professional field to other fields and to the world can be exerted, to a large extent, through education (Nicholescu, 2005). In terms of teaching and learning, higher education has been devoting efforts and resources to cultivate and inspire future information professionals, through various programs in various levels.

However, due to the highly interdisciplinary nature of this field, teaching IST-related knowledge, theories, practices, applications and contributions should not and has never been limited to students and learners within the field. Instead, it should also be university-wide, academia-wide, community-wide and ultimately world-wide. Furthermore, introducing, promoting and connecting our field with other fields exerts positive internal and external influence. Insiders in our field can take these education-infused opportunities to gain more exposure among all disciplines and to establish our identity in the bigger landscape of sciences as well as the entire society. In light of the theme of this Annual Meeting, connecting and engaging people from diverse backgrounds with information and technology, this panel aims to explore and stimulate discussions on various issues related to teaching IST to a broad and diverse audience in this information environment. As this Annual Meeting celebrates the 80th anniversary of ASIS&T, it is high time to reflect on what we learned from past experience in teaching IST beyond our own profession and look into the future on how we can improve.

Initial attempts and efforts toward the goal of connecting IST with people in all fields, all countries and all walks of life could generally be categorized into the following modes with progressively increasing scale of impact.

## JOINT PROGRAMS

A step toward connecting IST with other fields is to create joint or inter-faculty programs drawing professional expertise from one or more fields besides IST. For instance, the master of science in bioinformatics at the University of Illinois at Urbana-Champaign is a collaborative endeavor between the top ranking iSchool in Illinois and the departments of animal sciences, computer science, corp sciences and the Illinois Informatics Institute on the same campus. Through this joint program students from various backgrounds can systematically learn fundamental theories and research methods in developing information management systems in biological applications. More recently, the iSchool in Syracuse collaborates with Syracuse University's Whitman School of Management, in offering a master of science program in applied data science. Aiming for educating people in applying data science to solve problems for organizations, this program provides learning opportunities on information and data management which would not normally be available outside the iSchools.

## GENERAL EDUCATION

Another opportunity to strengthen the teaching of IST to students in other fields is to offer general education courses that

80th Annual Meeting of the Association for Information Science & Technology, Washington, DC, VA | Oct. 27-Nov. 1, 2017

are open to all undergraduate students across a university. General education courses aim at helping students broaden their horizons and gain perspectives from different disciplines other than their own majors. For instance, the University of Hong Kong, one of the top universities in Asia, offers *Common Core Curriculum* that requires undergraduate students to select six common core courses from all four predeigned Areas of Inquiry (AoI). A new common core course offering proposed for 2017-2020 is on digital preservation of cultural heritage which is an example of teaching IST concepts and skills to a broader audience within a university.

### MASSIVE OPEN ONLINE COURSES

Massive open online courses (MOOCs) are a type of course allowing open access and unlimited online participation from all over of the world. Delivery of MOOCs is an ideal channel for IST education to learners in all disciplines, nations and sectors of society. One of the relevant significant contributions is the MOOC organized by the iSchool in San Jose State University, titled *The Emerging Future: Technology Issues and Trends*, which attracted more than 1,700 global participants of a variety of fields (Alman & Jumba, 2017).

### COMBINED MODE

The above modes are by no means separated from one another. They can be combined in real use. For example, when data science gained its popularity in this decade, every school at Syracuse University planned to launch its own program on data science. Professor Jeff Stanton from the iSchool first developed an introductory level MOOC on applied data science[1], followed by the launch of a lightweight, five-course Certificate of Advanced Study (CAS) program in data science. The CAS program attracted many students from different schools on campus and eventually led to the collaboration between the iSchool with other schools on campus to jointly launch the master's program in applied data science.

Notwithstanding the significance of the different teaching modes that aim to expand the efforts on increasing the impact of our field, there still exist numerous fundamental issues worth attention of information scientists and educators. This panel brings together international educators and scholars in the IST field to lead and stimulate a discussion on (but not limited to) the following proposed questions:

- What have we learned from past experience?
- What are the effective strategies and practices in teaching IST beyond boundaries?
- What kinds of topics in the field of IST are among the most relevant to the fast-changing information society?
- What are the challenges in teaching IST to the world?

The panel discussion will include short presentations from the panelists in a lightning talk model with 10 to 15 minutes for each speaker. The experience, opinions and insights brought by the panelists who are in different stages of their careers will hopefully stimulate discussions with the audience. With rich experience in moderating numerous panels in her professional life and being an outstanding IST educator herself, Professor Toni Carbo will moderate this panel session to ensure an effective discussion on this very important topic and fruitful experience of the audience.

### PANELISTS

#### *Xiao Hu, assistant professor, University of Hong Kong*

What we have learned from the past?

Past critiques have pointed out that LIS faculties might not be proactive in reaching out of their disciplines and were suggested to be more confident and engaged in playing the transformational roles in an information literate university (Johnston & Webber, 2004). Attempts were then made to bring LIS to a wider audience, both on the undergraduate and postgraduate levels. General education courses focusing on information management skills were shown to benefit undergraduate students (Garg & Garg, 2007).

For augmenting public awareness of the IST field, MOOCs were recommended for their unprecedented scale of impacts. Wilson and Gruzd (2014) argued that MOOCs could help attract previously disinterested students as prospective information professionals and showcase various interdisciplinary IST topics to the public, such as social computing, information visualization, computer supported collaborative work, etc. However, few existing MOOCs in LIS seemed to have generated interest beyond the profession (Pujar & Bansode, 2014). The trend started to change recently. Based on very successful practices, Alman and Jumba (2017) offer a systematic reflection on how to optimize MOOCs from an LIS perspective.

What kinds of topics are most relevant?

Information is inseparable from everyone's life nowadays, and thus topics close to people's daily lives would be in great demand. Digital collections or digital libraries is among these topics. With the amount of digital information growing in exponential rates, organizations and individuals seek to learn the principles, skills and tools to organize their digital assets and make them easily accessible. This is the essential spirit of the digital collection course and its variations that are commonly taught in IST programs.

With proper repurposing and possible connections to specific application domains, digital collection courses can be developed into courses that fit a range of objectives. For instance, one common core course to be offered at the University of Hong Kong (HKU) for the purpose of general education is titled *Digitizing Cultural Heritage in Greater China*. The course is in fact a repurpose of a digital library course regularly taught in the information management program in HKU. While the course is situated in the domain of cultural heritage to meet the curricular goal of enhancing students' interests and intellectual ability in understanding China from past to

[1] https://www.class-central.com/mooc/1806/open-education-by-blackboard-applied-data-science-an-introduction

present[2], the principles of information organization, access and use as well as techniques of building digital collections are core knowledge and skills of IST. Other examples include undergraduate elective courses on *Digitizing Everyday Life*, where students built digital collections to manage their personal assets such as makeups or aircraft models.

#### What are the challenges?

A broad audience beyond the IST field may not necessarily share our professional interests, and thus one challenge of teaching IST to the world is to make connections to the audience's experiences and lives. Another issue is to strike a balance between the breadth and depth of the content. While the learning should be substantial, useful and intellectually challenging, we need to avoid overwhelming the audience. That said, the biggest challenge in teaching IST to students with diverse backgrounds seems to be the (unnecessary) fear of unfamiliar body of knowledge, be it programming or ontology. This makes it an important task of educators to cultivate a mindset of "Yes, I can."

### *Bei Yu, associate professor, Syracuse University*

#### Lessons learned from the past educational experience

Traditionally IST education focused on information literacy and research methods to train students to become effective navigators of library services. IST has moved into a broader definition of information literacy as people are interacting with the internet and all kinds of information resources. Our goal becomes to train students and the public to become nuanced consumers who can utilize broad information resources and live comfortably in digital culture.

#### Suggested topics

In addition to data science that has been part of the university-wide interdisciplinary curriculum, there are at least two topics in the IST field that are highly relevant in this information industry and society. The first is information literacy. With the heated discussion on fake news and misinformation recently, people come to realize that the information literacy level of the public is far from adequate. Researchers and practitioners in science and media communications have begun work on training materials for science advocacy and media literacy. For example, AAAS just launched an advocacy toolkit to call for members to "tell your story; connect and collaborate; make an impact."[3] *New York Times* developed a learning network with lesson plans to teach the public on media literacy.[4] Although our field of IST is the best fit for teaching information literacy, our efforts and expertise have been less known to the public. In this session, I will introduce current research on misinformation and lead discussion on how IST can lead the effort for curbing the spread of misinformation.

The second topic is advocacy for user engagement in the development of new frontiers, such as data science and the internet-of-things, which seems a natural continuation of the discussion at the iConference workshop on data science held earlier this year (Greenberg et al., 2017). The focus on users is commonly recognized as a unique perspective of IST education, and it touches virtually everyone in today's information environment where people interact with algorithms and robots in everyday life. This trend will be even more prominent in the future. These topics can easily fit into a university-level general education course or as a general topic for public forums.

#### Challenges

One of the biggest challenges in teaching IST seems to be the definition of *IST*. How do we define ourselves when teaching learners in other disciplines? A discussion on this with the panelists and panel audience will be beneficial to all of us in this field and especially those who plan to teach IST to a broader audience.

### *Sue Alman, lecturer, San Jose State University*

#### MOOCs & MicroMasters: Professional credentialing and interdisciplinary models

Searching for new and effective teaching and learning strategies that keep pace with the changing demographics of students and working adults has led to new models such as MOOCs and MicroMasters. The original MOOC framework has changed in the relatively short time it has been in existence. In addition to MOOCs there are SOOCs (small open online courses), COOCs (corporate open online courses), SPOCs (small private open courses) and more. Early in 2017 EdX introduced another online concept of the MicroMaster. These teaching models can be used to reach a wide variety of global audiences.

The Online Learning Consortium and Quality Matters are two organizations that provide online course standards to ensure sound pedagogy, and many institutions like the San Jose State University (SJSU) iSchool use those standards and provide faculty development workshops focusing on best practices. The iSchool offers all programs online including two (2) master's degrees, specialized certificates, post-master's certificates, PhD and MOOCs and the Library 2.0 professional development online conferences. The current discussion is focused on the types of education that are valued by employers and members of the information professions. MOOCs and MicroMasters initiatives provide educators from multiple disciplines with opportunities to collaborate with one another. Currently the SJSU iSchool has a partnership with the School of Business for cybersecurity education, and additional collaboratives are being negotiated.

---

[2] https://commoncore.hku.hk/china-culture-state-and-society/

[3] https://www.forceforscience.org/toolkit?utm_source=membercentral&utm_medium=email&utm_campaign=Membercentral-12396&et_rid=299010080&et_cid=1297321

[4] https://learning.blogs.nytimes.com/2004/03/12/media-literacy/

Two main challenges face higher education:

1. The technological infrastructure used for online educational programs provides excellent resources for faculty and student engagement; however, developing a financial model is a challenge.
    a. Are traditional tuition models realistic?
    b. How will online courses be supported for development and delivery? Will participants and/or their employers be willing to pay for these educational experiences?
2. What types of credentials are valued in the profession?
    a. Accredited masters
    b. Certificates issued from academic institutions
    c. Certificates or badges issued by academic institutions or for-profit organizations
    d. Post-master's degrees or certificates

This session will provide an overview of MOOCs, the good practices summarized from highly successful cases (Alman & Jumba, 2017) and MicroMasters models, and questions will be raised about the types of possible credentials and partnerships that impact teaching information science and technology globally.

#### *Allen H. Renear, professor and dean, University of Illinois at Urbana-Champaign*

We now know that a sound curriculum delivered with care and skill can provide all learners with both a deep understanding of the most important ideas in information science and technology and with the skills that will be immediately valuable in the workplace. The former provides key insights and a foundation for future learning, the latter secures a robust embedded understanding as well as the practical capabilities that ensure momentum at the outset. The mechanisms and modalities of information science education are many, and that is as it should be: there are many circumstances to be accommodated. And we must accommodate them – this is the education needed not only for the 21st century workplace, but for 21st century citizenship. In this panel, I will further reflect on our experience in developing the joint program in data science as well as a MOOC to be offered on Coursera, with regard to effective practices, challenges and other relevant issues.

### MODERATOR

#### *Toni Carbo, professor emerita and former dean, University of Pittsburgh*

Professor Carbo is a highly experienced educator in IST, dedicated member and past president of ASIS&T and ALISE and a long-time strong advocate for increasing diversity. She serves as the ASIS&T representative to the AAAS Science and Human Rights Coalition and is a fellow of AAAS and of SLA. She is also a member of the ASIS&T 80th Anniversary Celebration Taskforce, chaired the 50th Anniversary Conference Committee and co-chaired the 75th Anniversary Celebration Committee. She serves on the Brown University Library Advisory Council.

An expert in information ethics and information policy, Prof. Carbo has directed and been involved in several international research projects related to the use of scientific and technical information and has been involved in the development of information policies in the United States and Europe. She has chaired and/or participated in the planning and implementation of numerous international conferences and workshops.

### EXPECTED OUTCOMES

The panelists from different institutions in different parts of the world will present their reflections, visions, strategies and best practices on teaching information science across the boundaries of disciplines, countries and social roles. The short presentations are expected to stimulate discussions among the audience on how best to increase the impact of IST through teaching. The discussed points will be shared with the ASIS&T community. We hope that the panel will encourage further attempts and collaborations in and beyond our field to meet the challenges and to magnify the impact of IST to the world.

### ACKNOWLEDGMENTS

We would like to deliver our gratitude to SIG/ED and SIG/III for their support to this panel proposal.

### REFERENCES

Alman, S. & Jumba, J. (2017). MOOCs Now: Everything You Need to Know to Design, Set Up and Run a Massive Open Online Course, Libraries Unlimited.

Garg, D., & Garg, A. K. (2007). General education courses at the university of Botswana: Application of the theory of reasoned action in measuring course outcomes. The Journal of General Education, 56(3), 252-277.

Greenberg, J. et al. (2017). Information Science to Data Science: New Directions for iSchools, Workshop in iConference, March 22, 2017, Wuhan, China, Retrieved from http://cci.drexel.edu/mrc/news/2016-12-iconference2017/

Johnston, B., & Webber, S. (2004). The role of LIS faculty in the information literate university: Taking over the academy? New Library World, 105(1/2), 12-20.

Nicolescu, B. (2005). Towards transdisciplinary education. TD: The Journal for Transdisciplinary Research in Southern Africa, 1(1), 5-15.

Pujar, S. M., & Bansode, S. Y. (2014). MOOCs and LIS education: A massive opportunity or challenge. Annals of Library and Information Studies (ALIS), 61(1), 74-78.

Wilson, L., & Gruzd, A. (2014). MOOCs – international information and education phenomenon? Bulletin of the American Society for Information Science and Technology, 40(5), 35-40.

# Archaeological Perspectives in Information Science

**Isto Huvila**
*Department of ALM, Uppsala University, Sweden. isto.huvila@abm.uu.se*

***Marija Dalbello***
*School of Communication and Information, Rutgers University, USA. dalbello@rutgers.edu*

**Michael Olsson**
*University of Technology Sydney, Australia. Email: michael.olsson@uts.edu.au*

***Costis Dallas***
*Faculty of Information, University of Toronto, Canada. costis.dallas@utoronto.ca*

***Ixchel M. Faniel***
*OCLC Research, USA. fanieli@oclc.org*

**ABSTRACT**

**Archaeology is a domain that has intersections with information science and technology research both as an empirical domain of investigation and as a perspective to inquire into how people interact with information. The aim of this panel is to highlight this interdisciplinary nexus of diverse engagements and to explicate how archaeology has informed and could inform information science research and practice in the future, and how empirical information science research on archaeological practices has enhanced our understanding of both archaeological work and human information behavior and practices in general.**

**KEYWORDS**

archaeology, information science, information practices, archives

**INTRODUCTION**

Information science has often been described as an interdisciplinary domain. It brings together a diversity of insights from widely different disciplines to create new knowledge and enhance theoretical and practical understanding about how information influences our lives. This panel digs deeper into an intriguing interdisciplinary nexus of engagements between information science and archaeology to highlight 1) how archaeology, archaeological methods and archaeological metaphors have informed and could inform information science research and practice in the future, 2) how empirical information science research on archaeological practices has enhanced our understanding of both archaeological work and human information behavior and practices in general and 3) what implications these areas of research have had and could have on the advancement of research and practice in the information science and technology domains. The panelists represent information science researchers who have conducted empirical research on archaeological information practices and knowledge production and have used archaeologically inspired methods and theory in their work.

The relevance of discussing the links between information science and archaeology relates to the increasing societal significance of the cultural heritage domain around the globe, especially in Europe, where it has been one of the key areas of cooperation for a long time. More recently, the link between information science and archaeology has become more significant, given the integration of a rapidly increasing migrant population. In addition, a better understanding of archaeological information work has become critical for managing and exploiting the escalating amounts of archaeological data from current and prior archaeological excavations around the world. From a theoretical and practical perspective, archaeology also is a good example of a cross-disciplinary domain of information use and methodology that engages diverse fields from the humanities to the natural sciences and serves as an interesting showcase of the problems, challenges and opportunities related to inter- and multi-disciplinary domains of information practices. Finally, archaeology has functioned as a powerful metaphor for critical research in information science and technology.

**ARCHAEOLOGY IN AND FOR INFORMATION SCIENCE**

Information science and technology research have worked in tandem with archaeology research for several decades. Despite the sporadic rate of the references back and forth, the literature shows a depth and breadth of topics. Archaeology-related and archaeological information science research can be roughly divided to three areas: 1) information management-, organization- and retrieval- oriented studies, 2) research on archaeological information practices and 3) archaeological and archaeology-inspired research on information science topics. Moreover, several studies span these lines of research which indicates how archaeology has interested information science and technology researchers and vice versa.

The focus of management-, organization- and retrieval- oriented research has been on the development of theories, methods and practices of archaeological information work. Much of this work has been informed only indirectly by information science but there are some exceptions with links to

80th Annual Meeting of the Association for Information Science & Technology, Washington, DC, VA | Oct. 27-Nov. 1, 2017

knowledge organization, information management and digital libraries research (e.g., Huvila, 2006; Tudhope et al., 2011; Vlachidis & Tudhope, 2015; Dallas, 2016b).

The second line of research focuses on information behavior and practices of archaeologists, including studies about archaeological documents, documentation and the sociotechnical aspects of archaeological knowledge production. Studies range from archaeologists' information behavior (e.g., Huvila, 2006), studies of sociotechnical practices in archaeology (e.g., Khazraee, 2013), pervasive digital curation practices in archaeological fieldwork (Dallas, 2015), grey literature (e.g., Seymour, 2009), images (Beaudoin, 2014) and research data (e.g., Faniel et al., 2013; Faniel & Yakel, 2017) to information and knowledge management practices (e.g., Huvila, 2016a,b) and materiality, especially bodily aspects of archaeological information practices (Olsson, 2016).

In contrast, the third line of research has used archaeology as a method or approach for studying diverse information science topics. Dalbello-Lovric (1999) adopted an archaeological approach in her study of bibliographies and Radford et al., (2012) used Foucault's archaeology of knowledge to investigate the deaccessioning of library collections. Mak (2014) also used it to investigate the practices related to digitization. Although Foucault's archaeology of knowledge may seem relatively popular, Dewey's (2016) findings suggest that the approach has been used less than expected. It also is surprising that media archaeology (Parikka, 2012), a popular approach in media and communication studies has been used rarely in information science and technology research.

## LAYOUT OF THE PANEL

The moderator begins the panel with a 10-minute overview of archaeological and archaeology-related research in information science. Next, each of the four panelists gives a five-minute lightning talk describing how they have used archaeology as a perspective or a topic of empirical research with a focus on theoretical and empirical insights and implications of working with archaeology as a branch of professional, scholarly activity or as a perspective in the context of the information science research.

After the lightning talks, each panelist takes three minutes to react to their colleagues' presentations, highlighting commonalities and differences in approaches, followed by one-minute future-looking reflections on how to push the current state-of-the-art in their areas of study. During the final 30 minutes, the moderator facilitates a discussion with the audience to reflect on archeology's usefulness as a perspective and topic of empirical research in information science and technology. The panel closes with an invitation and a short round of proposals for future engagements with archaeology both within and beyond information science from the panelists and the audience, including a call for contributions to a forthcoming special issue on the topic of the panel.

The presentations combine two parallel approaches to engage with archaeology in the context of information science research. All presentations explicate practices that are archaeological within the domain of archaeology (Huvila, Olsson, Faniel, Dallas) and simultaneously or alternatively in other contexts such as archives, libraries and museums (Dalbello, Dallas, Huvila, Faniel). At the same time, all presentations highlight empirical and conceptual insights from archaeology-related research pertaining to topics such as embodiment and materiality, trust, sharing and boundaries, information behavior and practices, records and evidence. The presenters will each make a connection of their work to implications to information science pedagogy (teaching and curriculum development).

## PANELISTS AND THEIR CONTRIBUTIONS

### *Isto Huvila, Uppsala University*

Isto Huvila presents empirical findings of his research on the documentation of archaeology and archaeological work and the making of archaeological knowledge. The presentation draws both on his earlier and ongoing empirical research on archaeological information work and information management in archaeology. Huvila shows how his empirical research has provided multiple practical and theoretical insights into information work and management research beyond archaeology, including insights into such theoretical concepts as boundary objects, trust and anonymity, and how an empirical archaeological perspective can be useful in explicating information practices in other contexts such as libraries, archives and museums.

Professor Isto Huvila holds the chair in library and information science at the Department of ALM (Archival Studies, Library and Information Science and Museums and Cultural Heritage Studies) at Uppsala University in Sweden and is adjunct professor (docent) in information management at Åbo Akademi University in Turku, Finland. Archaeology has been a long-lasting context of his research that ranges from information and knowledge management, information work, knowledge organization and documentation to social and participatory information practices.

### *Michael Olsson, University of Technology Sydney*

Michael Olsson describes his study of the information practices of archaeologists in the field based on ethnographic fieldwork at two excavation sites with archaeologists from the University of the Highlands and Island son Orkney, Scotland. The findings demonstrate the centrality of embodied information practices, such as haptic analysis (McGregor, 1999) for archaeologists' sense-making. It suggests that archaeologists learned these embodied practices experientially via a kind of apprenticeship, as described by Lave & Wenger (1991). The study's findings therefore raise important questions for the field of information practices/behavior research, where embodied information practices have until now received relatively little attention.

Michael Olsson is a senior lecturer in information & knowledge management in the School of Communication, University of Technology Sydney. He is active in the field of information behavior/practices research with particular interest in embodied and affective information practices. He has also written extensively about a range of conceptual and methodological approaches including practice theory, Foucauldian and critical discourse analysis and Sense-Making.

### *Ixchel M. Faniel, OCLC Research*

Ixchel Faniel draws from her research that started with studies examining data reuse practices that were meant to inform the preservation of data's meaning through documentation and curation practices that support reuse. She discusses how findings from her reuse studies not only evolved her perspective to studying key practices throughout the data lifecycle, but also grew her understanding of human information behavior and practices.

Ixchel Faniel is a research scientist at OCLC. Current work includes examining how academics manage, share and reuse research data and librarians' experiences designing and delivering supportive research data management programs. Her research has been funded by the National Science Foundation, Institute of Museum and Library Services and National Endowment for the Humanities.

### *Costis Dallas, University of Toronto*

Costis Dallas is interested in probing the material-semiotic dimensions of the archaeological record and its entanglement with archaeological work as an epistemic "contact zone" between archaeology and information studies. In this panel, he first introduces relationships such as archaeological vs. archival record, provenience vs. provenance, archaeological (post-depositional) context vs. archival bond, archaeological documentation vs. archival representation, archaeological typology vs. classification in information science, object agency vs. digital materiality and archaeological curation vs. digital curation. Second, drawing from earlier information behavior and digital curation models, he introduces a formal conceptualization of archaeological work as cultural-historical information activity which may adequately articulate actual (descriptive) with normative (methods laden) dimensions, as well as human archaeological agency with artefact-tool mediation.

Costis Dallas is associate professor and director of the collaborative programs at the Faculty of Information, University of Toronto and research fellow of the digital curation unit, "Athena" Research Centre, Greece. His current research focuses on the theory of digital curation of thing cultures, on archaeological and heritage practices in the pervasive digital environment, and on identity and memory work in social network site interactions around tangible cultural heritage.

### *Marija Dalbello, Rutgers, the State University of New Jersey*

Archeology is a science of the positive in that it traces and studies what had a physical presence. The relevance of archeological perspectives for information science are in the positivist space – of how mute evidence of texts and artifacts, embedded in the material documentary cultures and material traces, can be interpreted structurally and read as patterned production in time-space, as a formation and in-formation. I first outline the interpretation of presence that focuses on traces through the lens of digital humanities, bibliographic archaeology and media archaeological perspective. All of these carry relevance for the readings of patterned production as evidence, structurally and contextually situating these interpretations in relation to situated contexts of production, use and reuse conforming to a functionalist-structuralist model. I argue that physical presence can provide a launching point for a critical archeological reading of traces in the negative space of presence by surfacing the absence in archeological readings of physical presence and evidence, against the grain. Interventions that focus on the missing picture and the expressions of absence in an information archeological sense highlight the incomplete presence of texts and objects from a critical perspective. I will attach this argument to examples from the context of archivist activism and exemplify how insertions into the past can provide the interpretations in the present and are similarly archaeological in approach.

Marija Dalbello is an associate professor of information science in the School of Communication and Information, Rutgers University. Her teaching and publications focus on the history of knowledge and history of the book.

## ACKNOWLEDGEMENTS

A part of this work has been based upon work from COST Action ARKWORK, supported by COST (European Cooperation in Science and Technology). Faniel acknowledges support from IMLS for the DIPIR project (LG-06-10-0140-10) and NEH for the SLO-data project (PR-234235). Huvila's work has been supported by the Swedish Research Council Grant 340-2012-5751.

## REFERENCES

Beaudoin, J. E. (2014). A framework of image use among archaeologists, architects, art historians and artists. *Journal of Documentation, 70*(1), 119–147.

Börjesson, L. (2016). Beyond information policy: Conflicting documentation ideals in extra-academic knowledge making practices. *Journal of Documentation, 72*(4), 674 – 695.

Dalbello, M. (2013). Digitality, epistolarity and reconstituted letter archives. *Information Research 18*(3).

Dalbello, M. (2011). A genealogy of digital humanities. *Journal of Documentation 67*(3), 480-506.

Dalbello-Lovric, M. (1999). The case for bibliographical archeology. *Analytical & Enumerative Bibliography*, *10*(1), 1–20.

Dallas, C. (2015). Curating archaeological knowledge in the digital continuum: From practice to infrastructure. *Open Archaeology*, *1*(1), 176–207.

Dallas, C. (2016a). Digital curation beyond the "wild frontier": A pragmatic approach. *Archival Science*, *16*(4), 421–457.

Dallas, C. (2016b). Jean-Claude Gardin on archaeological data, representation and knowledge: Implications for digital archaeology. *Journal of Archaeological Method and Theory*, *23*(1), 305–330.

Dewey, S. H. (2016). (Non-)use of Foucault's Archaeology of Knowledge and Order of Things in LIS journal literature, 1990-2015. *Journal of Documentation*, *72*(3), 454–489.

Faniel, I., Kansa, E., Whitcher Kansa, S., Barrera-Gomez, J., & Yakel, E. (2013). The challenges of digging data: A study of context in archaeological data reuse. *Proceedings of the Joint Conference on Digital Libraries (JCDL)*, 295-304.

Faniel, Ixchel M. and Yakel, Elizabeth (2017). Practices do not make perfect: Disciplinary data sharing and reuse practices and their implications for repository data curation. In *Curating Research Data, Volume One: Practical Strategies for Your Digital Repository* (pp. 103–126). Chicago, Illinois: Association of College and Research Libraries.

Huhtamo, E. & J. Parikka, eds. (2011). *Media archaeology: Approaches, applications, and implications*. University of California Press.

Huvila, I. (2006). *The ecology of information work – A case study of bridging archaeological work and virtual reality based knowledge organisation*. Diss. Åbo Akademi University.

Huvila, I. (2016a). Awkwardness of becoming a boundary object: Mangle and materialities of reports, documentation data and the archaeological work. *The Information Society*, *32*(4), 280–297.

Huvila, I. (2016b). 'if we just knew who should do it,' or the social organization of the archiving of archaeology in Sweden. *Information Research*, *21*(2).

Khazraee, E. (2013). Information recording in archaeological practice: A socio-technical perspective. In *iConference 2013, February 12-15, 2013 Fort Worth, TX.*

Lave, J. and Wenger, E. *Situated learning*. Cambridge: Cambridge University Press, 1991.

Mak, B. (2014). Archaeology of a digitization. *JASIST*, *65*(8), 1515–1526.

MacGregor, G. Making sense of the past in the present: A sensory analysis of carved stone balls. *World Archaeology 1999, 31*(2): 258–271.

Olsson, M. (2016). Making sense of the past: The embodied information practices of field archaeologists. *Journal of Information Science*, *42*(3), 410–419.

Parikka, J. (2012). *What is media archaeology?* Cambridge: Polity.

Radford, G. P., Radford, M. L., & Lingel, J. (2012). Alternative libraries as discursive formations: Reclaiming the voice of the deaccessioned book. *Journal of Documentation*, *68*(2), 254–267.

Seymour, D. J. (2009). Introduction: International perspectives on the archaeological grey literature. *Grey Journal*, *5*(2), 64–66.

Tudhope, D., Binding, C., Jeffrey, S., May, K., & Vlachidis, A. (2011). A STELLAR role for knowledge organization systems in digital archaeology. *Bulletin of American Society for Information Science and Technology*, *37*(4), 15–18.

Vlachidis, A., & Tudhope, D. (2015). A knowledge-based approach to information extraction for semantic interoperability in the archaeology domain. *JASIST*, *67*(5), 1138–1152.

# Engaging at the Margins: Theoretical and Philosophical Approaches to Social Justice

**Vanessa L. Kitzie**
*School of Library & Information Science, University of South Carolina, USA. vkitzie@gmail.com*

**Marie L. Radford**
*School of Communication & Information, Rutgers University, USA. mradford@rutgers.edu*

**Gary P. Radford**
*Department of Communication Studies Fairleigh Dickinson University, USA. gradford@fdu.edu*

**John M. Budd**
*School of Information Science & Learning Technologies, University of Missouri, USA. buddj@missouri.edu*

## ABSTRACT

**This interactive panel demonstrates how critical, interdisciplinary theoretical and philosophical approaches outside the field of library and information science (LIS) can foster new ways of thinking about the concept of social justice. The panel consists of four researchers whose scholarship connects to these approaches. The following areas will be discussed: extending the philosophy of justice-as-fairness using the work of Amartya Sen, employing Umberto Eco's theoretical approach of semiotics to critique contemporary LIS practices and ideologies and adopting an information practices approach to highlight the importance of sociocultural context, embodiment and unsanctioned resources among those with lesbian, gay, bisexual, transgender and queer (LGBTQ+) identities.**

**The panel will consist of a brief introduction followed by panelist presentations and time for questions and answers from the audience. To build on the potential implications for research and practice, panelists will engage the audience in a paired activity to discuss a set of relevant questions. This activity informs a full audience discussion that concludes the panel. Attendees will leave the panel with an understanding of the current issues related to applying social justice-centric approaches within LIS that can be implemented into future research and practice.**

## KEYWORDS

theory, semiotics, philosophy, marginalized populations

## INTRODUCTION

Media attention and current events have increased expectations for libraries to provide services for individuals and issues at the margins (Mehra & Braquet, 2014). Despite the moral and ethical mandates inherent to the library and information science (LIS) field, the field lacks internal theoretical development to address these expectations (Mehra, Rioux, & Albright, 2009). This panel addresses this issue and the conference theme, diversity of engagement, by connecting outside, interdisciplinary philosophies, methods and results to research and practice that foster critical approaches to social justice within the LIS field.

Panelists build on a social justice framework that embraces ambiguity and subjectivity inherent to the critical approaches discussed. The work of Amartya Sen can steer the LIS field toward adopting foundational concepts of social justice more encompassing than those currently adopted (e.g., not envisioning justice as a binary). Umberto Eco's theoretical approach of semiotics uncovers what is left unsaid in the library, ostensibly a place that offers equitable access to information, by contending that the library hides certain information. An information practices approach can further uncover how the library, as well as other information systems and institutions, can further marginalize a specific group of LGBTQ+ individuals based on what information these systems and institutions render visible versus what information they hide.

Various facets were chosen not only for the panel but also to engender built-in audience participation and guided reflection. Such integration will help provide ideas and thoughts for each attendee's specific LIS context and how they can take action to adopt a critical, social justice approach in their own environment.

Implications for development of systems and services are also discussed.

## PANEL FORMAT

This interactive panel will feature four researchers who engage in research that connects to social justice approaches and issues within LIS. The panel will have the following parts: introduction (three minutes), panelist presentations (40 minutes, 10 minutes/panelist), questions and answers (20 minutes, five minutes/panelist), paired audience activity – in pairs the audience will discuss a set of questions posed by panel (seven minutes) and full audience discussion of questions (20 minutes).

80th Annual Meeting of the Association for Information Science & Technology, Washington, DC, VA | Oct. 27-Nov. 1, 2017

## SESSION INTRODUCTION

Vanessa Kitzie, moderator, will briefly introduce each panelist and key issues to be overviewed during the session. She will pose a set of overarching questions that will be used in the cumulating activity involving paired and large group discussions. Audience members will be asked to consider these questions when listening to the panelist presentations and during the discussion. These are the questions:

What are the advantages of critical approaches, such as those taken in this panel as lenses to view LIS contexts and situations? How about disadvantages?

What new questions are possible when critical approaches are taken in LIS to examine different contexts and situations?

The panel recognizes that there are inherent ambiguity and subjectivity in the critical approaches discussed. How do members of the audience grapple with these aspects of critical approaches in your own work?

What are the implications of a social justice-centric approach for LIS research and practice?

What are the implications of this approach for systems design?

## PANELIST PRESENTATIONS

Each panelist will give a 10-minute presentation. These four presentations cover three topical areas that proceed in order of scope – from metatheory to theory to practice.

### JOHN BUDD – AMARTYA SEN ON JUSTICE AND INCLUSIVENESS

As has been stated, the matters of social justice and diversity can be approached from a variety of theoretical and practical standpoints. One of these – more theoretical, but still practical – draws from the work of Amartya Sen, especially his *The Idea of Justice* (2009). Sen (2009) admits that it is very difficult to speak about justice, but adds that it is imperative to formulate a sound theory that embraces an optimal justice for all inclusiveness. At the heart of the theory is "bringing reason into play in the diagnosis of justice and injustice" (Sen, 2009, p. 5). While the social contract approach has both a long history and many followers, there is good cause to transcend the received view and to develop a more complete and encompassing approach to generating a theory of justice.

Sen (2009) offers comparisons of extant viewpoints on theories of justice that embrace the social positioning of players and the effects of the loci of those positions. There is not space here to relate the entirety of his comparisons, but his analysis of two theorists must be discussed. The two positions (which will not come as a surprise) are those of John Rawls (1971) and Adam Smith (1976). Finding shortcomings with Rawls' idea of the "veil of ignorance," Sen turns to Smith's conceptions of a broader justice.

Sen (2009) concentrates on "open impartiality" as a procedure according to which judgments from within the central group are invoked, to avoid parochial bias (p. 123). One of the things that he finds attractive about Smith's thought is the inclusion of dialectics as a means for questioning commonly held beliefs. Those beliefs can be questioned internally and externally to arrive at the most open stance regarding the positions of individuals, thus ensuring the broadest forms of justice for all. It should be noted that Sen does not completely disagree with Rawls; much of Rawls notion of fairness applies, but Smith adopts a different concept of impartiality, which is in keeping with a sweeping social justice. The stance of open impartiality, it must also be noted, does not silence internal voices, but adds external ones that can make room for multiple points of view, rendering a genuine social justice more possible.

Also integral to Sen's (2009) theory is "illumination of positionality" through reasoning (pp. 157-61). Each principal in any consideration occupies a position that must be considered, as rationality is applied by all who are involved in making decisions. To illustrate his point, he adds mention of the biblical question of who constitutes one's neighbor. That is one of the major discussion points for the proposed presentation of Sen's (2009) theory of justice. It will be a point of focus of the conference panel.

### GARY P. RADFORD & MARIE L. RADFORD – SEMIOTICS

This presentation explores the use of Eco's (1976) semiotics as a theoretical framework to critique LIS research and practice, especially in relation to populations at the margins, including youth, ethnic minorities, LGBTQ+ individuals, the impoverished, etc. First, Gary Radford will overview the semiotics approach. Semiotics explores the nature and interpretation of signs, "*everything* that, on the grounds of a previously established social convention, can be taken as standing for something else" (Eco, 1976, p. 16). Radford (2003) further notes that "For the modern academic discipline of semiotics, anything in a culture can be considered as a sign: a text, an image, a building…These signs are read and a meaning imputed to them. Interpretation allows us to make sense of the objects we encounter" (p. 3).

Following Gary's overview, Marie Radford will detail how Eco's scholarship informs the LIS field. In regarding the library/library practice as problematics that can be semiotically analyzed, Eco (2006) discusses "fanciful models of the library" as well as the "certain and uncertain purposes of a library" (p. 8), arguing that libraries exist to "create a collection" and to organize books and scrolls so that they are not merely "lying around" (p. 8). However, there may also be a less obvious, and perhaps nefarious, purpose. Eco contends: "I believe that libraries came into being whose purpose was *not* to encourage reading, but to hide, to conceal books" (p. 8). He has also characterized the library as a fortress and a labyrinth (Eco, 1983). Library professionals can also be viewed as forbidding gatekeepers who are continually shushing and reprimanding users, simultaneously existing to be guides to the collection, and guardians against its misuse (Radford & Radford, 2001, 1997; Radford, Radford, &

Alpert, 2015). For Eco, libraries exist to "discover books whose existence we never suspected, only to discover that they are of extreme importance to us" (p. 10). However, library collections, having become quite extensive with an increasing number of formats and systems, and having become more complex, can be labyrinthine and difficult to navigate. Commenting on Eco's writings, Winter (1994) asserts that "finding a place for something is also finding a place where it can become hidden" (p. 122). This presentation explores the nature of professional practice that enables some, perhaps critically important, resources, access and technology, to have become hidden and perhaps forbidden. It also examines how semiotics can reveal how library spaces, signs, services, policies and procedures privilege some users (mainstream) over others (those at the margins) and how some objects become seen (available) or hidden (out of reach).

### VANESSA KITZIE – INFORMATION PRACTICES OF LGBTQ+ INDIVIDUALS

This presentation overviews dissertation research examining the information practices of LGBTQ+ individuals (Kitzie, 2017). Information practices represent an emerging umbrella concept within LIS (Savolainen, 2007). Practices differ from behaviors in that the former captures the constitutive relationship among individuals, information and sociocultural context. However, the boundaries between information behaviors and practices are contested (Wilson, 2008). Addressing this relationship is essential to understanding marginalized groups from the social justice agenda of equity, given it highlights contexts of injustice and unfairness (Mehra, Rioux & Albright, 2009). For LGBTQ+ individuals, such injustice and unfairness manifest in contexts that disrupt or deny the legitimacy of their existences. Such context shapes the information practices of LGBTQ+ individuals, who identify a litany of important practices beyond needs, seeking and use when performing identity work.

This presentation also builds on a social justice agenda of equity by critiquing mainstream LIS conceptions of access relative to marginalized groups. It refutes the idea that information is a given, or an objective reflection of reality, as well as the related transmission model of information (Shannon & Weaver, 1943) where, given that information reflects reality, its transmission always leads to a successful outcome. This transmission model is reflected in discussions of information access, e.g., some digital divide studies, which contend that simply providing someone with access to information will fulfill their related information need (Dervin, 1999, p. 740-741). On the contrary, research findings denote that access to information does not deterministically lead to positive outcomes among LGBTQ+ individuals. Instead, the information they can access and that is made visible reflects dominant sociocultural narratives that refute the legitimacy of their identities. Institutions such as libraries that render certain information as hidden or invisible therefore are considered irrelevant by this group (Kitzie, 2017; see also Rothbauer, 2010). This presentation does not make the implicit assumption that "there is one right way to produce knowledge" (Dervin, 1999, p. 732), but rather asserts the importance of investigating what practices are useful "under some conditions and methodologically mandates research to unearth these conditions" (Dervin, 1999, p. 732).

### PAIRED ACTIVITY

Returning to the set of five overarching questions that was introduced at the start of the panel, the audience will break into pairs to discuss one or two of these questions. They will be asked to both reflect on panelist presentations and to identify extant gaps in LIS approaches to social justice.

### FULL AUDIENCE DISCUSSION

The panel concludes with a full audience discussion of the five overarching questions, inviting audience pairs to share thoughts. During this discussion, panelists will comment on the emerging conversation, seeking to identify broad themes, possible research agendas and synergies, and collaborations to be established beyond the conference.

### PANELISTS

Panelists encompass a diversity of research and practice experience with topics with both direct and indirect implications for LIS-specific approaches to social justice. Brief biographies of each panel member are provided below.

**John M. Budd** is a professor emeritus in the School of Information Science and Learning Technologies of the University of Missouri. He has studied the place of social justice and ethics in the informational world.

**Vanessa L. Kitzie** is an assistant professor in the School of Library and Information Science of the University of South Carolina. She studies the information practices of marginalized groups and the implications of research findings for LIS research and practice.

**Gary P. Radford** is professor and chair of the Department of Communication Studies at Fairleigh Dickinson University, Madison, New Jersey. He studies communication theory, communication philosophy, semiotics, Eco and Foucault.

**Marie L. Radford** is a professor in the Department of Library and Information Science at Rutgers, the State University of New Jersey, School of Communication and Information. She studies interpersonal communication, qualitative methods, application of postmodern and cultural studies approaches to LIS research.

### CONCLUSION

This panel reviews current theoretical and philosophical approaches to social justice within LIS to engage issues at the margins. Via presentations and a question-answer portion, panelists build on a social justice framework for LIS that embraces lived experience, sociocultural context and power dynamics. Audience members are asked to consider a set of five overarching questions meant to advance critical perspectives relating to social justice-centric approaches to LIS. Using the presentations as a starting point, the audience will engage in both paired and full group discussion, giving them a chance to both respond to panelist presentations and push the conversation into new areas for research and practice. Audience members will leave the panel with an understanding of the current issues related to bridging social justice theoretical and research approaches with LIS that can be implemented into future research and practice.

## REFERENCES


Eco. U. (1983). *The name of the rose.* (William Weaver, Trans.). New York, NY: Harcourt Brace Jovanovich.

Eco, U. (1976). *A theory of semiotics.* Bloomington, IN: Indiana University Press.

Dervin, B. (1999). On studying information seeking methodologically: The implications of connecting metatheory to method. *Information Processing & Management, 35*(6), 727–750.

Kitzie, V. (2017). *Beyond behaviors, needs, and seeking: A qualitative investigation of information practices among individuals with LGBTQ+ identities.* (Unpublished doctoral dissertation). Rutgers University, New Brunswick, NJ.

Mehra, B., Rioux, K.S., & Albright, K.S. (2009). Social justice in library and information science. In M.J. Bates & M.N. Maack (Eds.) *Encyclopedia of library and information sciences* (3rd ed.) (pp. 4820-4836). Boca Raton, FL: CRC Press.

Mehra, B. & Braquet, D. (2014). Marriage between participatory leadership and action research to advocate benefits equality for lesbian, gay, bisexual, and transgendered people. In B.L. Eden & J.C. Fagan (Eds.). *Leadership in academic libraries today: Connecting theory to practice.* Lanham, MD: Rowman & Littlefield.

Radford, G. P. (2003). On Eco. Belmont, CA: Wadsworth.

Radford, G. P. & Radford, M. L. (2001). Libraries, librarians, and the discourse of fear. *The Library Quarterly 71*(3), 299-329.

Radford, G. P., Radford, M. L., & Alpert, M. (2015). Slavoj Žižek, Rex Libris and the traumatic real: Representations of the library and the librarian in a modern comic book series. *Journal of Documentation. 71*(6), 1265-1288.

Radford, M. L. & Radford, G. P. (1997). Power, knowledge, and fear: Feminism, Foucault and the stereotype of the female librarian. *The Library Quarterly 67*(3), 250-266.

Rawls, J. (1971). *A theory of justice.* Cambridge, MA: Harvard University Press.

Rothbauer, P. (2010). Locating the library as place among lesbian, gay, bisexual, and queer patrons. In J.E. Buschman & G.J. Leckie (Eds.) *The Library as Place: History, Community, and Culture* (pp. 101-116).

Savolainen, R. (2007). Information behavior and information practice: Reviewing the "umbrella concepts" of information-seeking studies. *The Library Quarterly, 77*(2), 109–132.

Sen, A. (2009). *The idea of justice.* Cambridge, MA; Belknap Press of Harvard University Press.

Shannon, C. E., & Weaver, W. (1949). *The mathematical theory of communication.* Urbana, IL: University of Illinois Press.

Smith, A. (1976). *The theory of moral sentiments.* Oxford: Clarendon Press.

Wilson, T.D. (2008). Review of: Savolainen, Reijo Everyday information practices: A social phenomenological perspective. Lanham, MD: Scarecrow Press, 2008. *Information Research, 14*(1), review no. R327. Retrieved from: http://informationr.net/ir/reviews/revs327.html

Winter, Michael F. (1994). Umberto Eco on libraries: A discussion of "De Bibliotheca." *The Library Quarterly, 64*(2), 117-129.

# Evolving Traditions: From 'Documentation' to 'Information Science & Technology'

**Kathryn La Barre**
*School of Information Sciences, University of Illinois at Urbana-Champaign, USA. klabarre@illinois.edu*

**Colin Burke**
*History Department, University of Maryland Baltimore County, USA*

**Fidelia Ibekwe-SanJuan**
*School of Journalism and Communication, Aix-Marseille Université, France. fidelia.ibekwe-sanjuan@univ-amu.fr*

**Robert D. Montoya**
*Information and Library Science, Indiana University Bloomington, USA. montoya@indiana.edu*

## ABSTRACT

**This invited panel session will engage the audience through presentation and discussion of the work of three scholars representing a broad trajectory of career accomplishments. The work of these three individuals has been selected in order to showcase the breadth, depth, and richness of Information History in celebration of the 80th anniversary of the Association for Information Science and Technology.**

## KEYWORDS

ASIS&T 80th anniversary panel, invited panel

## INTRODUCTION

This invited panel session will engage the audience through presentation and discussion of the work of three scholars representing a broad trajectory of career accomplishments. The work of these three individuals has been selected in order to showcase the breadth, depth, and richness of Information History in celebration of the 80th anniversary of the Association for Information Science and Technology.

## MODERATOR

The panel will be moderated by Kathryn La Barre, an Associate Professor at the School of Information Sciences, University of Illinois at Urbana-Champaign, the Chair of the 80th Anniversary Advisory Group, and ASIS&T Director-at-Large.

## PANELISTS

The following are the speakers and the abstracts of their talks.

### *Colin Burke*

Colin Burke is Associate Professor Emeritus, History, University of Maryland Baltimore County. The title of his presentation is, "It isn't easy being green".

With a deep research trajectory in the history of American non-profit organization and the history of America's intelligence agencies including the books: Information and Intrigue (2014) and Information and Secrecy: Vannevar Bush, Ultra, and the Other Memex (1994), Colin Burke has also recently completed American Information Wars, a monograph on post-WWII developments, including early systems of the CIA, and technologies for intelligence. This talk will examine the career of James Perry, as an example of the challenges faced by information scientists during the 1940s and 1950s.

### *Fidelia Ibekwe-SanJuan*

Fidelia Ibekwe-SanJuan is Professor, School of Journalism and Communication, Aix-Marseille Université, France. She will present on, "In search of connections: The European origins of LIS."

As the recipient of the ASIST History Research Award in 2016, Fidelia is working on a book about the European origins of IS as a follow-up to a book she previously published in French in 2012 entitled "Information Science: origins, theories and paradigms (La science de l'Information: Origines, théories et paradigmes, Hermès-Lavoisier, 261 pages). She has been conducting interviews with IS scholars in Croatia, Denmark and Spain in order to determine who their modern IS pioneers were and their contribution towards the emergence of IS as higher education field of teaching and inquiry. She'll share her preliminary findings of this research with a focus on the interconnections and influences of these European pioneers on one another.

### *Robert D. Montoya*

Robert D. Montoya is Assistant Professor, Information and Library Science, Indiana University Bloomington. He will present on, "Tracing Changes: Evolving Knowledge in Biodiversity Classifications."

Montoya's recently defended dissertation, "Contingent Consensus: Documentary Control in Biodiversity Classifications," focuses on knowledge organization and its intersections with biodiversity studies, philosophy of information, documentation, and science and technology studies. In this research, he examines how control functions within the biodiversity environment, defined as it is by conceptual and documentary contingency, and how scientists negotiate the tensions that arise between competing classification structures. The presentation will illustrate how global biodiversity

80th Annual Meeting of the Association for Information Science & Technology, Washington, DC, VA | Oct. 27-Nov. 1, 2017

knowledge systems have ingrained epistemological commitments that arise from consensus-based social structures, and how such systems trace changes to these commitments as they evolve over time. This research, currently being turned into a book, contextualizes the importance of creating more inclusive, diverse, and ethical knowledge organizing structures both within and without the field of biodiversity.

# Seeking Balance: Professional Development Needs of Tenured Information Science Faculty

**Irene Lopatovska**
*School of Information, Pratt Institute, USA. ilopatov@pratt.edu*

**Martina Dragija Ivanović,**
*Department of Information Sciences, University of Zadar, Croatia. mdragija@unizd.hr*

**Heather O'Brien**
*School of Library, Archival & Information Studies, University of British Columbia, Canada. h.obrien@ubc.ca*

**Heidi Julien**
*Department of Library and Information Studies, University at Buffalo, USA. heidijul@buffalo.edu*

**Abebe Rorissa**
*Department of Information Science, University at Albany, USA. arorissa@albany.edu*

## ABSTRACT

**There is minimal, mainly anecdotal, evidence of discourse about the professional development of information science (IS) academics. In an effort to initiate discussion on professional development and encourage information sharing among IS faculty and administrators, we organized a panel at the 2016 Annual Meeting of ASIS&T (Lopatovska et al., 2016). The panel brought attention to the professional development resources and strategies available to mid-career faculty and uncovered the need to continue the discussion. This proposed interactive panel aims to identify tenured IS faculty members' needs related to their scholarly, teaching and service pursuits, explore professional wellbeing and work climate, share best practices and brainstorm potential solutions for some of the identified issues. The issues and solutions uncovered during the panel discussion will be shared with the broader community with the hope that recommendations can be adopted and acted upon by individuals, academic institutions and professional associations. The panel will be of interest to faculty, doctoral students and academic administrators.**

## KEYWORDS

professional development, faculty development, academic career development, information science, library and information science education

## INTRODUCTION

Academia in general, and departments and schools of information science (IS) in particular, face an ever-changing climate of multidisciplinarity, increasing diversity of students and their needs and changes in service demands and institutional cultures (Nicholls, 2014). Not all institutions of higher education offer specialized services to assist faculty to cope with these changes or to advance their research, teaching and service agendas while maintaining their wellbeing.

Although much emphasis has been placed on the career development and mentorship of pre-tenure faculty, senior (i.e., tenured) faculty also require support. A literature review by Russell (2010) found that increased administrative tasks, workplace inequities, lack of collegiality, poor departmental leadership, workload issues and lack of autonomy, recognition and resources to carry out research pursuits are all sources of dissatisfaction amongst senior faculty. These factors generate workplace dissatisfaction and stress that are harmful to individual wellbeing; this stress may be perpetuated by the publish or perish culture of academia.

Vera, Salanova and Martín (2010) found that faculty who performed primarily management tasks experienced more incidence of burnout and job dissatisfaction and had lower workplace engagement than those who spent more time on research. Although Vera et al. (2010) did not distinguish between tenured and non-tenured faculty, others have found that faculty tend to spend more time on administrative duties post-tenure (Russell, 2010). Yet, faculty burnout affects more than just individual faculty members.

Faculty performance issues related to stress are often tolerated by the academic culture. These dysfunctional attributes, if gone unchecked, and not discussed with the stress victim, can easily become chronic and negatively impact other faculty, staff, students, and program quality (Minter, 2009, p. 1).

Thus, the health of IS programs and their future growth and sustainability are predicated on the balanced of meaningful research, teaching and service contributions of the professoriate.

We found only one recent study on the needs of IS faculty. Hahn and Lester (2012) surveyed library and information science (LIS) and iSchool faculty in the United States and Canada and identified significant gaps in the availability and quality of faculty mentorship programs. The study partici-

80th Annual Meeting of the Association for Information Science & Technology, Washington, DC, VA | Oct. 27-Nov. 1, 2017

pants identified a number of important areas for their professional development, including teaching and learning, work-life balance and grant writing and the conduct of research. They also indicated a preference for receiving professional development training in-person (e.g. workshops at conference venues) over digital web-based options. Their study did not extensively explore the availability of resources to address the main areas of professional development, but it recommended a more active role of professional organizations in developing guidelines and workshops for improving professional development options for IS faculty.

In an effort to identify the need for conversations among IS academics about issues related to professional development, we organized a panel at the 2016 ASIS&T Annual Meeting (Lopatovska et al., 2016). While the panel's aim was to discuss issues of particular interest to mid-career faculty, it attracted participants from all academic ranks and facilitated exchange of information related to career planning, work-life balance, importance of professional networks, strategies for coping with work expectations, management of service demands, the need to reinvent personal research agendas and other related topics. The panel participants expressed interest in continuing the conversation about their professional development needs and solutions during future ASIS&T Annual Meetings.

The goals of the proposed panel include raising awareness of current issues and concerns of tenured IS faculty, identifying resources that are available and/or used to address some of these concerns and brainstorming additional tools and strategies that can be developed to address professional needs of IS academics. The expected outcomes include a set of common professional development issues and coping strategies that will be shared with the IS community through the *Bulletin of ASIS&T* or publications of other sister professional associations. This could be used by organizations such as ASIS&T and Association for Library and Information Science Education (ALISE) to explore mentorship and professional development opportunities, and the means through which to fulfill these needs.

## PANEL AGENDA

The panel aims to explore and facilitate conversations around tenured IS faculty's main concerns and professional development solutions related to their research, teaching, service, general work environment and wellbeing. Each panelist will lead a discussion on one of the panel's themes: research, teaching, service and work environment/ wellbeing.

The structure of the 90-minute panel will include an introduction, identification of the audience's main professional development needs and discussion of existing and potential solutions to address these needs.

At the beginning of the session, the panelists will introduce themselves and outline the main discussion themes to the audience [10 minutes].

Next, participants will organize into small discussion groups and will be tasked with identifying issues/questions related to their experiences in the areas of research, teaching, service, general work environment and wellbeing. The issues will be captured on paper and posted to the wall. The color of the paper or ink (red, yellow and green) will indicate the importance of the identified issues in participants' professional lives. The panelists will walk around the room to facilitate the discussions and keep the groups on task [20 minutes].

After the groups finalize discussions of their professional experiences and concerns, the panel organizers will present preliminary thematic analysis of the content of participants' notes, ask the audience to share similar experiences and describe professional development resources they already use or can develop to address their professional needs. For example, a participant(s) might identify high number of or demanding service activities as being detrimental to their research and teaching. The panelists will share their experiences of balancing the three main areas of an academic's role and ask the audience members to share their coping strategies. Examples of additional issues may include healthy work environments and tips for dealing with micro-aggressions, stress and burnout, balancing short- and long-term professional goals (e.g., the "quantification imperative" of publishing (Vostal, 2015), finding professional identity in an increasingly multidisciplinary environment, fostering support for mentoring, developing matrices to measure service contributions, balancing work and personal life and promoting professional development resources within professional organizations (e.g. ASIS&T) [60 minutes].

The panelists will record the main discussion themes and disseminate their findings to the ASIS&T community through the *Bulletin* or other publications.

Participants or audience members will also be invited to continue the discussion on Twitter using the hashtags #WorkLifeBalanceASIS&T2017].

## EXPECTED OUTCOMES

The panel aims to generate a discussion of the current needs in professional development of IS faculty and share tools and strategies for addressing these issues. Understanding the needs of IS faculty is the first step in developing support for their professional growth and job satisfaction, which in turn translates into productive research, empowered students and meaningful service contributions.

The panel will be relevant to ASIS&T as a professional organization because it may inform creation of new services for members in terms of professional development, such as guidelines for publishing and peer-review process, mentorship database or matching service, webinars and a professional development column in the *Bulletin*. Identified concerns and means of addressing them might be particularly relevant in light of ASIS&T's stake in the LIS program accreditation process.

## PANELISTS

Each panelist brings a unique perspective on the issues in professional development based on her/his personal and professional experiences, seniority and institutional affiliation.

**Martina Dragija Ivanović** is an assistant professor and vice dean at the University of Zadar, Department of Information Sciences. She obtained her PhD in information science from Zadar University, Croatia. She is a co-director for the biennial international conference, Libraries in the Digital Age (LIDA), which has been organized since 2000 by Rutgers University (U.S.), Zadar University and Osijek University (Croatia). She is working with the European Network for Work Information (ENWI) group on investigations of workplace information. Her teaching and research interests include evaluation of information services, research methods and, in particular, qualitative methods and the role of public and university libraries in information society.

**Heidi Julien** is professor and chair at the Department of Library and Information Studies in the Graduate School of Education, University at Buffalo. Her research focuses on information behavior and digital literacy. She is president-elect of the Association for Library and Information Science Education. She served as president of the Canadian Association for Information Science and as chair of the ASIS&T Special Interest Group/Information Seeking and Use (SIG/USE). She also serves on the Permanent Committee for ISIC: the information behaviour conference.

**Abebe Rorissa** is an associate professor in the Department of Information Science, University at Albany. Prior to his current position, he worked in four countries as a lecturer and systems librarian for 17 years. He has consulted for academic institutions, national governments and international organizations, including the United Nations. His research interests include multimedia information organization and retrieval, scaling of users' information needs/perceptions and use/acceptance/adoption and impact of information and communication technologies. Dr. Rorissa is a member-at-large on the ASIS&T Board of Directors.

## ORGANIZERS

Irene Lopatovska is associate professor at the Pratt Institute School of Information, where she has worked in various positions for 10 years. Dr. Lopatovska graduated from Rutgers University in 2009 with a PhD in information science and her research interests include the role of emotion in the information interaction context, human information behavior and research methods. She is currently a Student Chapter Representative at ASIS&T.

Heather O'Brien is associate professor at the School of Library, Archival and Information Studies, University of British Columbia, Vancouver, Canada. She earned her PhD at Dalhousie University in Halifax, Canada in 2008. Dr. O'Brien's research focuses on user engagement with digital information environments, specifically the conceptual nature of engagement and its evaluation. She is currently a member-at-large for the ASIS&T Board of Directors and chair of Special Interest Group/Information Seeking and Use (SIG//USE).

## REFERENCES


Baldwin, R. G., Lunceford, C. J., & Vanderlinden, K. E. (2005). Faculty in the middle years: Illuminating an overlooked phase of academic life. *Review of Higher Education, 29*(1), 97-106.

Hahn, T. B. & Lester, J. (2012). *Journal of Education for Library and Information Science, 53*(2), 82-97

Lopatovska, I., Byström, K., Given, L. M., O'Brien, H. & Rorissa, A. (2016). Life after tenure: Professional development strategies for mid-career faculty. *The Annual Meeting of the Association for Information Science and Technology*, October 14-18, 2016, Copenhagen, Denmark.

Minter, R.L. (2009). Faculty burnout. *Contemporary Issues in Education Research, 2*(2), 10 pp.

Nicholls, G., (2014) *Professional Development in Higher Education: New Dimensions and Directions*. Routledge. Retrieved from https://books.google.com/books?hl=en&lr=&id=CdjgAwAAQBAJ&oi=fnd&pg=PP1&dq=professional+development+of+academics&ots=quuAx2RKpP&sig=FrOI-VmFa1YhlQO39BWA4gm6_MGA#v=onepage&q=professional%20development%20of%20academics&f=false

Pontis, S., Blandford, A., Greifeneder, E., Attalla, H. and Neal, D. (2017), Keeping up to date: An academic researcher's information journey. *Journal of the Association for Information Science and Technology. 68*, 22–35.

Russell, B.C. (2010). Stress in senior academic careers. *New Directions for Higher Education, 151*, 61-70.

Vera, M., Salanova, M., & Martín, B. (2010). University faculty and work-related well-being: The importance of the triple work profile. *Electronic Journal of Research in Educational Psychology, 8*(2), 581-602.

Vostal, V. (2015) Speed kills, speed thrills: Constraining and enabling accelerations in academic work-life. *Globalisation, Societies and Education, 13*(3), 295-314.

# Making a Case for Open Research: Implications for Reproducibility and Transparency

**Heather Moulaison Sandy**
*iSchool, University of Missouri, USA.*
*moulaisonhe@missouri.edu*

**Erik Mitchell**
*University Libraries, University of California, Berkeley, USA.*
*emitchell@berkeley.edu*

**Edward M. Corrado***
*Dudley Knox Library Naval Postgraduate School, USA.*
*ecorrado@ecorrado.us*
**participating in his personal capacity*

**John Budd**
*School of Information Science & Learning Technologies, University of Missouri, USA. buddj@missoui.edu*

**Jevin D. West**
*Information School, University of Washington, USA.*
*jevinw@uw.edu*

**Jenny Bossaller**
*iSchool, University of Missouri, USA.*
*bossallerj@missouri.edu*

**Amy VanScoy**
*Dept. of Library & Information Studies, University at Buffalo, USA. vanscoy@buffalo.edu*

## ABSTRACT

**Scientific work is time-consuming and expensive. However, after data has been collected and reports have been written, science becomes an information problem. There are thousands of journals and funding agencies across specialized disciplines with different requirements for data transparency. Science-focused domains substantiate research findings through defined research methods and data analysis techniques, and emerging practices around data storage and code publishing now allow other scientists to see exactly how researchers come to their conclusions. These new practices not only increase transparency of the scientific process, they also enable replication and derivative research. Despite these emerging practices, the work of research transparency does not always easily enable reproducibility.**

**At face value, the requirements (e.g., America COMPETES Act; G8 Open Data Charter, etc.) for data sharing seem straightforward: a scientist receives funding and therefore is required to share her data with other scientists. However, the physical sciences and social sciences produce different kinds of data that are more or less easily stored. Additionally, in some cases, researchers can (and should) put restrictions on who can view their data, because of ethical concerns.**

**This panel will begin with current reasons for and methods of sharing data, including national and global initiatives, then will move into problems with open data, sharing data and reproducibility in both quantitative and qualitative research.**

80th Annual Meeting of the Association for Information Science & Technology, Washington, DC, VA | Oct. 27-Nov. 1, 2017



## KEYWORDS

reproducibility, open data, open research, qualitative research datasets, retractions, current data practices in LIS

## INTRODUCTION

Reproducibility is an integral part of the scientific method, a method that relies on openness and exchange to advance knowledge and to connect people and information. With the recent push to open data (Joseph, 2016; Ramjoué, 2016; Williamson, Kennan, Johanson, & Weckert, 2016) as well as concerns about the validity of published, statistically significant research findings (Ioannidis, 2005), the need for transparency and a resulting concern about reproducibility are of increasing interest in the scholarly community. Reproducibility can be defined as "the calculation of quantitative scientific results by independent scientists using the original datasets and methods" (Stodden, Leisch, & Peng, 2014, p. vii).

Reproducibility is related to the notion of replication, where conditions for observing findings are sought (Open Science Collaboration, 2015; Schmidt, 2009). Although sometimes used interchangeably in the literature, reproducibility applies to the use (or re-use) of data to recreate findings, and replication applies to the broader testing of hypothesis and potentially the recreation of entire studies – where a methodology is followed, and datasets and subsequent findings are reproduced as part of the exercise. In empirical studies, the researcher is only as strong as the research that is produced and shared for peer validation. In accordance with the scientific method as first codified by the Royal Society in England in the 17th century, "Scientific claims should not gain credence because of the status or authority of their originator but by the replicability of their supporting evidence" (Open Science Collaboration, 2015, p. 6251). Yet, carrying out replications is not common, especially in the social sciences (Schmidt, 2009), and can even be grounds for rejection (Cronin, 2012), potentially making reproducibility through the re-evaluation of datasets even more essential.

To support open research, access to the underlying data is paramount, yet data is not always made available. Although there are other ways to share data, open data is perhaps the most straightforward. Borgman (2012) identifies four rationales for sharing data: reproducibility, serving the public interest, asking new research questions and advancing research. There are, however, some barriers, both real and imagined, to making data openly available. Some researchers have legitimate concerns that discourage, or perhaps prevent them, from sharing data, including privacy concerns.

Researchers need to make decisions about their data management plans when they embark on research, rather than figuring out where and how they will store their data after they have completed their research. It should be included in the institutional review board (IRB) application if the research uses human subjects. If the researchers do not use human subjects, but rather use online data (such as tweets or other social media, etc.), they will usually bypass the IRB. However, the researchers should examine the terms of service and privacy policies to determine if they can ethically use the data for research and if they can later store and share the data; they should also carry out a review of other privacy regulations if the data is collected online (e.g., regarding scraping data, terms of service, etc.) The Menlo Report (Dittrich & Kenneally, 2012) covers some of these ethical conundrums. Diesner & Chin (2015, 2016) explore both laws and ethics of scraping and storing publicly available data.

Openness to data and code is not an all or nothing binary proposition; openness may be more accurately looked at as a sliding scale (Schopfel et al., 2014). There are different levels of openness. Nichols and Twidale (2017) described potential metrics for openness of data and code based on various factors. Such openness can help shore up transparency, promoting high quality and accurate scholarship that will not need to be retracted due to errors relative to the data. Data clearly show that few authors who cite retracted papers acknowledge the retraction. Since most citing authors treat retracted work as though it were valid, replication becomes especially problematic. In some instances, reliance upon work that has shown to be flawed could result in compromised efforts to reproduce findings. The endeavor of benchtop science may be put at risk by work that is erroneous or, worse, the result of misconduct.

Access to data is not the only barrier to reproducibility and transparency of scholarly research. Access to custom software code is often required. This may be especially true when working with large datasets. Because of the volume of data and the nature of the discipline, code plays an important role in the scientific communication, transparency and reusability of astronomical research (Shamir, 2017). The unavailability or lack of on-going maintenance of software programs is "detrimental to long-term research and reproducibility" (Astropy Collaboration, 2013). Many researchers advocate for code to be available as open source software.

The topic of reproducibility and replication of research has been discussed in a wide number of fields. It has also received attention by the general media, such as recent coverage by National Public Radio of the U.S. National Academy of Sciences report, "Fostering Integrity in Research," released April 11, 2017 (Harris. 2017). Detrimental research practices can undermine findings and inhibit the ability of other labs to reproduce studies or can lead other researchers to follow dead ends, wasting the time of many researchers, and "and time is an irreplaceable resource" (Harris, 2017, para 12) according to C. K Gunsalus, a member of the committee that wrote the report.

## PROBLEMS RELATED TO OPENNESS AND TRANSPARENCY

A number of problems can be identified concerning the need for transparency and openness in research products. For example, workflows for qualitative data archiving can be neglected or misunderstood or simply not adequately codified. Reproducibility and transparency in fields such as data science can present unique problems. Additionally, research can go bad in a number of ways, leading to false claims published in the literature. Studies have shown that although works have been retracted, they are still being citied even a year after the retraction has been issued (Budd, Abritis, & Coble, 2016). Unknown or unacknowledged retractions can waste valuable time of researchers. Finally, current practice in code and data publishing and availability in LIS can be analyzed based on research published in top-tier LIS journals to ascertain the extent to which researchers are following best practices to promote transparency.

## PANEL PRESENTATIONS

This panel includes a wide range of perspectives and approaches to open scholarship. Heather Moulaison Sandy, Erik Mitchell, Edward Corrado, John Budd, Jevin West, Jenny Bossaller and Amy VanScoy each come to the topic with a different approach and with a different background related to open scholarship.

**Heather Moulaison Sandy** will serve as the moderator of the session and will situate the panel through an overarching presentation of the relevant literature.

**Jevin West** will focus on reproducibility in the realm of data science. He will provide examples of what can go wrong without accessible data and software and what can be done to correct this. He will also discuss projects and guidelines in his lab (DataLab) that address issues of reproducibility.

**Jenny Bossaller** and **Amy VanScoy** will discuss the reproducibility and ethical concerns related to sharing of qualitative data. Qualitative data often is meaningless taken out of context, yet the limits of sharing due to its sensitive nature potentially undermine the worthiness of qualitative studies to funding agencies.

**John Budd** will discuss implications of retractions for replicability and reproducibility. Retractions can waste researchers' time, especially if the retraction is not acknowledged. Researchers' time is very valuable, and the time and effort spent working with retracted content could be spent on legitimate work.

**Erik Mitchell** and **Edward Corrado** will present results from a study with **Heather Moulaison Sandy** on research data management practices of LIS researchers. This study is based on a survey of authors in leading LIS journals about the availability of datasets, and if applicable, software code. The study also examines how data and code is published in LIS and why researchers choose to make their data available. Additionally, Mitchell and Corrado will discuss some of the barriers to sharing code and publishing data relating to LIS research.

These panelists therefore represent diverse interests in the information science, data science, and library science fields.

The panelists will collaborate to define themes that work across their research and, as part of the reserved discussion time, will interact with the audience as well as other panelists. The goal of the interactive section of the panel will be to connect threads of research and lines of inquiry. The intended outcome of the panel and audience discussion is to spark new ideas and deeper thinking about research and practice in research transparency.

## BIOGRAPHICAL INFORMATION FOR PANELISTS

**Jenny Bossaller, PhD**, is associate professor at the University of Missouri's iSchool. Her research interests include public libraries and access to information, information policy and ethics. She earned a master's degree and PhD from the University of Missouri.

**John Budd, PhD**, is professor emeritus at the University of Missouri's School of Information Science and Learning Technologies. He is the author of 13 books and more than 100 journal articles. He can also be found with his cat, Bitsy.

**Edward M. Corrado** is associate university librarian at the Naval Postgraduate School (NPS). He is a librarian, administrator, academic and information technology expert. His research interests include digital preservation, cloud computing, open source software and open data. Previously, he was the associate dean of library technology planning and policy at University of Alabama and the director of library technology at Binghamton University. He has a master of library service from Rutgers University and a bachelor of arts in mathematics from Caldwell University.

**Dr. Erik Mitchell**, PhD, is associate university librarian at the University of California, Berkeley. In addition to studying information technology adoption and use in libraries, Erik examines metadata issues and professional development in library and information science. Before joining the University of California, Berkeley, Erik served as an assistant professor at the University of Maryland. Erik is a columnist for Technical Services Quarterly has published and presented on library IT, metadata use and pedagogical approaches. He holds a PhD in information and library science from the University of North Carolina at Chapel Hill, a master's degree in library science from the University of South Carolina and a bachelor of arts in literature from Lenoir-Rhyne College.

**Heather Moulaison Sandy, PhD,** is associate professor at the University of Missouri's iSchool. Dr. Moulaison Sandy's teaching and research interests include organization of information (including cataloging, metadata) and emerging technologies in libraries. Dr. Moulaison Sandy earned her PhD at Rutgers's School of Communication and Information, an MSLIS at the University of Illinois, Urbana-Champaign GSLIS and an MA in French from UIUC.

**Amy VanScoy, PhD**, is assistant professor in the Department of Library & Information Studies at the University at Buffalo. Her work explores professional thinking and its influence on practice, particularly in the area of information services. VanScoy holds a PhD in information and library science from the University of North Carolina at Chapel Hill.

**Jevin West** is assistant professor at the Information School at the University of Washington and co-director of the DataLab (https://datalab.ischool.uw.edu/). Broadly, he works in the area of data science and data reasoning. He has developed education programs at UW for undergraduates, master's and PhD students. His most recent course with Carl Bergstrom, Calling BS in the Age of Big Data (http://callingbullshit.org/), has received international attention. Jevin's core research centers around the Science of Science. He co-founded the Eigenfactor Project (http://www.eigenfactor.org/) with the aim of reading the literature at the scale of millions of publications (1) to identify the origin of ideas and discipline, (2) investigate social biases in science, (3) understand publishing and funding decisions and (4) build better search interfaces for better navigating the literature. More details on his research and teaching can be found at: jevinwest.org.

## REFERENCES

Astropy Collaboration. (2013). Astropy: A community Python package for astronomy, *A&A, 558*, A33. doi: 10.1051/0004-6361/201322068

Borgman, C. (2012). The conundrum of sharing research data. *Journal of the American Society for Information Science and Technology, 63*(6): 1059-1078. doi: 10.1002/asi.22634

Budd, J., Abritis, A., & Coble, Z. (2016). An investigation of retracted articles in the biomedical literature. *Proceedings of the Association for Information Science and Technology, 53*, 1-9.

Corrado, E. (2005). The importance of open access, open source, and open standards for libraries. *Issues in Science and Technology Librarianship, 42*. doi: 10.5062/F42F7KD8

Cronin, B. (2012). The resilience of rejected manuscripts. *Journal of the American Society for Information Science & Technology, 63*(10), 1903-1904. doi:10.1002/asi.22794

Diesner J, & Chin, C. (2016). Seeing the forest for the trees: Considering applicable types of regulation for the responsible collection and analysis of human centered data. *Human-Centered Data Science (HCDS) Workshop at 19th ACM Conference on Computer-Supported Cooperative Work and Social Computing (CSCW 2016)*, San Francisco, CA. Retrieved from https://cscw2016hcds.files.wordpress.com/2015/10/diesner_hcds2016.pdf.

Diesner, J., & Chin, C. (2016). Gratis, libre, or something else? Regulations and misassumptions related to working with publicly available text data, *ETHI-CA² Workshop (ETHics In Corpus Collection, Annotation & Application), 10th Language Resources and Evaluation Conference (LREC)*, Portoroz, Slovenia.

Dittrich, D., & Kenneally, E. (2012, August). *The Menlo Report: Ethical principles guiding information and communication technology research,* Tech. rep., U.S. Department of Homeland Security.

Harris, R. (2017, April 11). Top scientists revamp standards to foster integrity in research. *Morning Edition: NPR.* Retrieved from http://www.npr.org/sections/health-shots/2017/04/11/523406710/top-scientists-revamp-standards-to-foster-integrity-in-research

Ioannidis, J. P. A. (2005). Why most published research findings are false. *PLoS Medicine, 2*(8), e124. doi: 10.1371/journal.pmed.0020124

Joseph, H. (2016). The evolving U.S. policy environment for open research data. *Information Services & Use, 36*, 45-48. doi: 10.3233/ISU-160806

Nichols, D. M., & Twidale, M. B. (2017). Metrics for openness. *Journal of the American Society for Information Science and Technology, 68*(4) 1048-1060. doi: 10.1002/asi.23741

Open Science Collaboration. (2015). Estimating the reproducibility of psychological science. *Science, 349*(6251), aac4716–1–aac4716–8. doi: 10.1126/science.aac4716

Raymond, E. S. (1999). *The cathedral and the bazaar.* O'Reilly Media. p. 30.

Ramjoué, C. (2016). Towards open science: The vision of the European Commission. *Information Services & Use, 35*(3), 167-170.

Schopfel, J., Chaudiron, S., Jacquemin, B., Prost, H., Severo, M., Thiault, F. (2014). Open access to research data in electronic theses and dissertations: An overview. *Library Hi Tech, 32*(4), 612-627. doi: 10.1108/LHT-06-2014-0058

Shamir, L., (2017). Reproducibility and reusability of scientific software, Special Session, "Perspectives in Research Software: Education, Funding, Reproducibility, Citation, and Impact" 229th American Astronomical Society Meeting, 321.03. Dallas, TX.

Stodden, V., Leisch, F., & Peng, R. D. (2014). *Implementing reproducible research.* Boca Raton: CRC Press.

Williamson, K., Kennan, M. A., Johanson, G., & Weckert, J. (2016). Data sharing for the advancement of science: Overcoming barriers for citizen scientists. *Journal of the Association for Information Science and Technology, 67*(10), 2392–2403. doi: 10.1002/asi.23564

Worldbank. (2016). Open data essentials. Retrieved April 15, 2017 from http://opendatatoolkit.worldbank.org/en/essentials.html

# Addressing Barriers to Engaging with Marginalized Communities: Advancing Research on Information, Communication and Technologies for Development (ICTD)

**Devendra Potnis**
*University of Tennessee at Knoxville, USA. dpotnis@utk.edu*

**Denice Adkins**
*University of Missouri, USA. adkinsde@missouri.edu*

**Nicole Cooke**
*University of Illinois at Urbana-Champaign, USA. nacooke@illinois.edu*

**Rakesh Babu**
*University of Wisconsin Milwaukee, USA. babu@uwm.edu*

### ABSTRACT

**Researchers' inability to address challenges related to planning, collecting or interpreting data collected from marginalized communities is one of the main reasons for the failure of projects using information, communication and technologies for the development (ICTD) of marginalized communities. This panel consists of information science experts who have conducted research with marginalized communities like women earning less than a dollar a day in slums in India, farmers, Latino community in the Midwest, racial minorities and visually impaired population. Panelists will share various challenges that they encountered while planning, collecting and interpreting data collected from marginalized communities; they will also provide guidance, advice, lessons learned and tips for addressing the challenges encountered during data collection with marginalized communities in the developing and developed world. This panel will inform information science researchers, who work at the intersection of information technologies and social justice, for better engaging with marginalized communities.**

### KEYWORDS

marginalized communities, data collection, challenges, solutions, ICTD research

### INTRODUCTION

Most projects using information, communication and technologies for the development (ICTD) of marginalized communities fail to meet their goals (Avgerou & Walsham, 2000; Bailur, 2007; Heeks, 2002). One of the main reasons for the failure of ICTD projects is the aggregate of issues associated with data collection among marginalized communities (Mamba & Isabirye, 2014; Potnis, 2015; Qureshi, 2008). Due to the inability of researchers to address data collection challenges, a majority of ICTD projects fail to sustain (i.e., remain continuously operational), scale (i.e., spread, enhanced, scoped and enlarged heterogeneous networks of technology, people, processes and institutional contexts) or benefit marginalized communities without undesired outcomes (Heeks, 2002; Krishna & Walsham, 2005).

The purpose of this panel is to understand and explain key barriers to engaging with marginalized communities. Information science experts on this panel will also share their experiences in addressing barriers to collecting data from marginalized communities like visually impaired population, financially marginalized women earning less than a dollar a day in India, farmers, racial minorities in the United States, and a Latino community in the Midwest. Panelists will provide actionable solutions by sharing their advice, lessons learned, guidance and tips for addressing barriers to planning and collecting data from marginalized communities when conducting various information science research inquiries. This panel will also be useful for seeking IRB clearance for field research with marginalized communities.

### PANEL STYLE

This panel will last for 60 minutes. We will use PechaKucha model where each of the four panelists will have about 10 minutes to present. The last 20 minutes will be reserved for an open discussion.

This panel will cover topics including but not limited to

- Dynamic inter-relationship among contextual factors (e.g., policy, environmental conditions, culture, etc.), research methods, researchers and local assistants in ICTD field research
- Solutions to failures in ICTD research: reflection and analysis; what went wrong? Why?
- Managing scope, time, cost, quality, human resources, communication and risks related to ICTD projects
- Issues related to data security, privacy, ethics, copyrights and intellectual property

### DEVENDRA POTNIS, UNIVERSITY OF TENNESSEE AT KNOXVILLE

Dr. Potnis has eight years of experience collecting data from marginalized communities in India. In the past, he actively participated in nine ICTD projects focusing on the (a) barri-

80th Annual Meeting of the Association for Information Science & Technology, Washington, DC, VA | Oct. 27-Nov. 1, 2017

ers to the adoption of mobile phones by female slum-dwellers, (b) adoption and continued usage of mobile phones by women earning less than dollar a day, (c) over-indebtedness of microfinance borrowers, (d) factors influencing the adoption of IBM's spoken web service by farmers, (e) success and failure of mobile banking initiatives that do not require the ownership of mobile phones by clients in remote rural areas and (f) factors essential for the catalytic innovation in microfinance, which helps microfinance institutions scale rapidly to serve millions of unbanked poor in developing countries. He and his teammates encountered and addressed a number of data collection challenges at various stages of the above ICTD projects.

Based on this past experience and existing ICTD research, he identifies the following six actors associated with the challenges, barriers and issues facing ICTD projects: outside researchers, marginalized communities, local assistants, information and communication technologies (ICTs), contextual factors and research methods. He plans to present the interrelationship among these six actors (see Figure 1 – Please zoom in to view the figure). Dr. Potnis plans to share some of the following challenges.

### *1. Researchers*

Adapting to local culture and understanding the needs and customs of marginalized communities are the most frequent challenges faced by researchers who are often considered outsiders by most marginalized communities (Blom, Chipchase & Lehikoinen, 2005; Walsham & Sahay, 2006). Visible differences between marginalized communities and researchers, and researchers' assumptions, preconceptions and limitations, including the inability to understand local concerns, needs and realities, could create hurdles to collecting data from marginalized communities (Krauss & Turpin, 2013).

### *2. Marginalized Communities*

Psychological, physical, cultural, lack of trust for technology solutions and research teams and several other issues associated with marginalized communities negatively affect their interest and ability to participate in field research (Potnis, 2014). Sometimes community and political leaders pressure potential participants not to cooperate with outside researchers to demonstrate their loyalty toward the community (Hewett, Erulkar & Mensch, 2004). Marginalized communities living in remote areas pose logistical and technical problems making data collection cumbersome (Elahi, 2008).

### *3. Local Assistants*

Violation of project protocol and data collection policies by local assistants affects the quality of data collected. Lack of lucrative incentives, sudden disappearance from research sites, lack of technical expertise, etc. are a few other issues associated with local assistants, which negatively affect the process of planning and collecting data (Potnis, 2016).

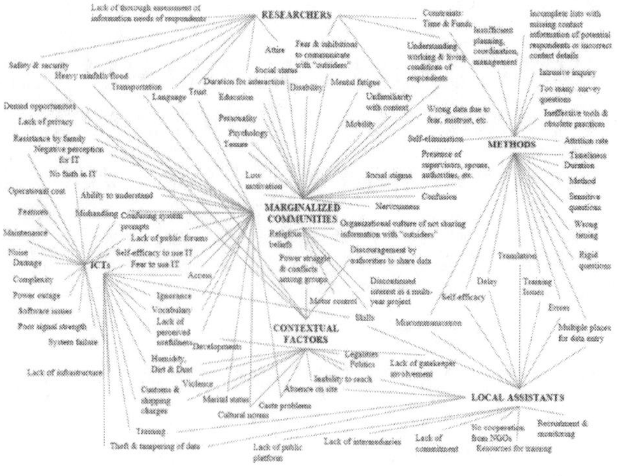


***Figure 1.*** *Visualizing ICTD Data Collection Challenges (Source: Adapted from Potnis, 2016 – Zoom in for details)*

### *4. ICTs*

Technical issues like power outages and interruptions (Anokwa, Smyth, Ramachandran, Sherwani, Schwartzman, Luk & DeRenzi, 2009; Brewer, Demmer, Ho, Honicky, Pal, Plauche & Surana, 2006), noisy communication channels, etc., create hardware and software problems and delay or interrupt the execution of ICTD projects (Potnis, 2015).

### *5. Contextual Factors*

Bureaucratic systems, government policies, organizational norms, intermittent political interference, a lack of supporting policies crafted by organizations or governments and deeply ingrained unfair local practices and processes shape data collection initiatives research design for worse or delay the implementation of ICTD projects (Krishna & Walsham, 2005; Potnis, 2016).

### *6. Methods*

Research methods involving lengthy data collection instruments, research protocols violating the privacy of study participants, untimely data collection (e.g., drought, riots, etc.), etc., could create challenges for data collection.

## DENICE ADKINS, UNIVERSITY OF MISSOURI

My work with the Midwestern Latino community focuses on how members of that community use mobile phones and social media to gain information. This research will result in the development of personae to assist in sharing information with this group. Here I address the challenges of gathering information from a marginalized community and in using this information to change communication practices.

To collect information for this research project, I interviewed Latinos in several Midwestern states. Though this did not involve any major challenges, it involved multiple smaller challenges that might dissuade more in-depth or unfunded research.

**Distance and language are challenging**. The communities I studied were rural, without airports or other means of transportation. I drove long distances to speak to small numbers of people. Most of the people I interviewed spoke Spanish. However, some immigrants from Latin American communities speak neither Spanish nor English, but indigenous languages such as K'iche'. These people, who were inaccessible to me, may have different stories than the people I spoke with.

**Immigration status was a challenge.** My interviews were conducted just after the 2016 election season, in a period of uncertainty about immigration laws. Some people were uncomfortable sharing information.

**Gatekeeping may have limited my population**. Local gatekeepers connected me with people who were convenient, but perhaps not with the full variety of people in the community.

Utilizing the results has also been challenging, due to cultural differences in communication between recent immigrants and the host community.

**What we want to tell them is not what they need to know**. University extension and other departments were interested in learning how better to provide information to Latino communities. However, the topics being communicated to Latin American immigrants often did not reflect their needs, because they were based on funded grants and not authentic community information needs.

**The way we want to communicate is not how they receive**. Some colleagues implied that they thought that translating materials into Spanish and posting them on the right social media accounts was enough to reach the immigrant community. However, there was limited awareness of cultural context or communicative preferences of the population.

**There's no one-size-fits-all solution**. It is not realistic to generate one persona to accommodate all Latinos, nor is it realistic to generate enough personae to accommodate every type of Latino. Complexity, though, reduces the likelihood that the personae will be used appropriately.

### NICOLE COOKE, UNIVERSITY OF ILLINOIS AT URBANA-CHAMPAIGN

When focusing on marginalized populations in the research process, extra care should be taken to protect participants and their experiences. Research should not lead to further marginalization, discomfort or vulnerability; rather, research should amplify silenced and underrepresented voices and be a benefit to those entrusting researchers with their stories. This also applies when conducting this research online and through ICTD technologies. Given the often-sensitive nature of the experiences of those from marginalized communities, violations of privacy and exploitation are possible, albeit unintentional, outcomes of collecting data via ICTD tools.

In my experience as a researcher, particularly as a member of a marginalized population, I am acutely aware of interacting with such participants. Research in this realm is ultimately rewarding and valuable, but it is not without challenges or barriers. In my short talk, I will talk about my experiences as a primarily qualitative researcher that studies issues of diversity and social justice in library and information science graduate programs and within the larger profession (Cooke, 2017, 2014). Specifically, I will mention issues of participant recruitment; developing trust and rapport with participants and balancing the maintenance of this trust through technological means; and balancing data collection needs against a lack of technology skills, distrust of technology and/or reluctance of participants who do not want to provide information via ICTDs. I will also discuss my preference for synchronous communication as an aid in interpreting collected data.

### RAKESH BABU, UNIVERSITY OF WISCONSIN - MILWAUKEE

My research focuses on empowering people with vision impairment in the information society using ICTs. Specifically, it investigates the enabling role of accessible, usable, and useful ICTs for the attainment of educational, vocational, social and personal objectives by people who are blind or visually impaired. The long-term goal is to develop design guidelines, organizational policies and training programs that bridge the gulf between this marginalized community and mainstream society and technology.

Since this is a highly under-researched area, the projects I have conducted thus far have primarily been exploratory in nature with a goal to create the necessary knowledge base of the needs, abilities, challenges, preferences and strategies of this atypical ICT user population. These projects typically involve field research or case studies employing think-aloud observations and interview techniques to collect data, and verbal protocol analysis technique to analyze this data. Conducting these research projects has been quite challenging compared to research with mainstream ICT users. I have experienced challenges at every phase of these projects, starting from the planning phase to reporting the results. Challenges in project planning are primarily related to research funding, sample and site selection, technology procurement, optimal study duration and participant compensation, project staffing, etc. In data collection, challenges are primarily concerned with recruiting, transporting and motivating participants, accidentally losing data, participant fatigue and frustration, dealing with technology updates, training participants to continually verbalize loud enough without pausing the screen-reader speech, etc. In data analysis, challenges have typically come from transcribing, interpreting participant actions, identifying and applying relevant theories, deriving statistical generalizability, etc. Challenges in reporting results have primarily come from positioning the findings in an existing conversation within the discipline, defending qualitative methods and small sample size, finding high quality publication outlets, satisfying novice, disinterested or overly-critical reviewers.

As a part of this panel, I will elaborate on these challenges, how I have overcome some of these, which of these still remain challenging and what might fellow researchers learn from my experience.

## REFERENCES


Anokwa, Y., Smyth, T., Ramachandran, D., Sherwani, J., Schwartzman, Y., Luk, R., & DeRenzi, B. (2009). Stories from the field: Reflections on HCI4D experiences. *Information Technologies and International Development 5*(4), 101-115.

Avgerou, C., & Walsham, G. (Eds.). (2000). *Information technology in context: Implementing systems in the developing world.* Aldershot, UK: Ashgate.

Bailur, S. (2007). The complexities of community participation in ICT Frontiers. *International Conference on Social Implications of Computers in Developing Countries* (pp. 1-17), London School of Economics.

Blom, J., Chipchase, J., & Lehikoinen, J. (2005). Contextual and cultural challenges for user mobility research. *Communications of the ACM 48*(7), 37-41.

Brewer, E., Demmer, M., Ho, M., Honicky, R., Pal, J., Plauche, M., & Surana, S. (2006). The challenges of technology research for developing regions. *IEEE Pervasive Computing 5*(2), 15-23.

Cooke, N. A. (2017). The GSLS Carnegie Scholars: Guests in someone else's house. *Libraries: Culture, History, and Society 1*(1), 46-71.

Cooke, N. A. (2014). The Spectrum Doctoral Fellowship Program: Enhancing the LIS Professoriate. *InterActions: UCLA Journal of Education and Information.* Retrieved from http://escholarship.org/uc/gseis_interactions

Elahi, A. (2008). Challenges of data collection in developing nations – the Pakistani experience as a way forward. *Statistical Journal of the IAOS 25*, 11-17.

Heeks, R. (2002). Information systems and developing countries: Failure, success, and local improvisations. *The Information Society 18*(2), 101-112.

Hewett, P., Erulkar, A., & Mensch, B. (2004). The feasibility of computer-assisted survey interviewing in Africa: Experience from two rural districts in Kenya. *Social Science Computer Review 22*(3), 319-334.

Krauss, K., & Turpin, M. (2013). The emancipation of the researcher as part of information and communication technology for development work in deep rural South Africa. *The Electronic Journal of Information Systems in Developing Nations 59*(2), 1-21.

Krishna, S., & Walsham, G. (2005). Implementing public information systems in developing countries: Learning from a success story. *Information Technology for Development 11*(2), 123-140.

Mamba, M., & Isabirye, N. (2014). A framework to guide development through ICTs in rural areas in South Africa. *Information Technology for Development 20*, 211-217.

Potnis, D. (2016) Managing seven dimensions of ICT4D projects to address project challenges. In Rahman, H. (Ed.), *Human development and interaction in the age of ubiquitous technology.* (pp. 227-249). Hershey: IGI-Global Publications.

Potnis, D. (2015). Addressing data collection challenges in ICT for development projects. *International Journal of ICT and Human Development 7*(3), 36-55.

Potnis, D. (2014). Managing gender-related challenges in ICT4D research. *The Electronic Journal of Information Systems in Developing Countries 65*(2), 1-26.

Qureshi, S. (2008). Assessing the effects of information and communication technologies on development. *Information Technology for Development 14*(4), 259-261.

Walsham, G., & Sahay, S. (2006). Research on information systems in developing nations: Current landscape and future prospects. *Information Technology for Development 12*(1), 7-24.

# Learnsourcing: Is it Working or Failing, and Where to Go from Here?

**Manasa Rath**
*School of Communication and Information, Rutgers University, USA. manasa.rath@rutgers.edu*

**Oleksandr Zakharchuk**
*Brainly, Inc., USA. oleksandr.zakharchuk@brainly.com*

**Chirag Shah**
*School of Communication and Information, Rutgers University, USA. chirags@rutgers.edu*

**Sanghee Oh**
*Department of Library and Information Science, Chungnam National Univ, South Korea. sanghee.oh@cnu.ac.kr*

**Rich Gazan**
*Department of Information and Computer Sciences, University of Hawaii at Manoa, USA. gazan@hawaii.edu*

**Mega Subramaniam**
*College of Information Studies, University of Maryland College Park, USA. msubram@umd.edu*

## ABSTRACT

**Online learning has taken great leaps forward with the emergence of Web 2.0 and has paved the path for learning technologies that can be conveniently accessed by users provided they are connected to the Internet. One of the most profitable learning techniques, "Learning from the crowd," or augmenting "collective intelligence," has attracted the attention of several learners who seek information in terms of knowledge access. This provides an admirable environment for learning with peers rather than learning alone. However, having access to these online learning technologies does not simply give the users the chance to optimize learning. In addition, researchers have expressed ethical concerns related to issues like accessibility, quality, authenticity, and reliability of content. Taking into consideration the pluses and minuses of "crowdsourced learning," each of the panelists in this program will shed light on how to use the "wisdom of crowds" or "collective intelligence" to better articulate the process of learning in context of such ethical issues. Each of the panelists comes from a different field of expertise (Information Science, Library Science, e-Learning, Learning Analytics, and Education). This diversity of experience will be reflected in the different perspectives presented in the area of crowdsourcing in education. The session will conclude with the panelists' presentation of significant comments that would emerge in the discussion.**

## KEYWORDS

crowdsourcing; education; learning; Q&A sites; crowd collaboration

80th Annual Meeting of the Association for Information Science & Technology, Washington, DC, VA | Oct. 27-Nov. 1, 2017



## INTRODUCTION

Existing Internet technologies provide unique learning opportunities for users online. These learning opportunities include "learning as a group" or "learning individually." The learning tools that support "learning as a group" have strengthened the novel concept of harnessing the "wisdom of crowds" or "collective intelligence." Wisdom of crowds refers to situations in which people in a group think as a whole. Another phenomenon called "crowdsourcing" has also grabbed attention in the recent years for collaboration in learning as explained by Malone et al. (2009). Howe (2006) defined crowdsourcing as "the act of a company or institution taking a function once performed by employees and outsourcing it to an undefined (and generally large) network of people in the form of an open call. This can take the form of peer-production (when the job is performed collaboratively), but is also often undertaken by the sole individual" (p.94). Schenk and Guittard (2011) defined "crowdsourcing" as "the compound contraction of the word crowd and outsourcing" (p.94). Surowiecki (2004), and Sawhney and Nambisan (2007), defined "crowd" as "the large set of individuals" (p.94). So, essentially a crowdsourced environment portrays a practice from where we obtain information from a large number of people, say for example Q&A sites with the help of Internet technologies.

Research in the area of crowdsourcing shows that an increasing proportion of formal education is being mediated by technology. For example, coursework offered in an academic environment may be in the form of videos and other interactive tools to provide better experiences among learners as discussed by Beaven et al. (2014). This phenomenon relates to the socio-cognitive theory proposed by Bandura (1977) that points out how a relevant part of a human behavior is shaped by observing, imitating, and modeling others' behaviors. This theory represents a bridge between behaviorist and cognitive learning theories as it accounts for the roles of attention, memory, and motivation in human functions. Crowdsourcing in the educational domain gained momentum alongside the massive online open course ware "MOOC." MOOC that relies on Information Technology (IT)-mediated approaches is open to the public as a whole, tuition-free in most cases, and enmeshed in formal learning, thus drawing upon large enrollments as discussed by Dalsgaard (2006); Sinclair et al. (2015); Glassman et al. (2015); Li and Mitros (2015); Mitros (2015). Schenk and Guittard (2011) founded a corpus of literature for studying crowdsourcing and related practises. Schenk and Guittard (2011) pointed out the different benefits of crowdsourcing that include cost, quality, network externalities, agency issues and motivations, and incentives. The authors also articulated the disadvantages, and pitfalls of crowdsourcing that include transaction and knowledge appropriability, lack of contributors, and request definition. With the emergence of community question-answering sites like StackOverflow, Chegg, and Brainly, it is expected that students will benefit from group knowledge creation as discussed by Anderson et al. (2012). However, crowdsourcing for learning has also raised ethical concerns that must be considered. These two perspectives create tension. For example, Harris and Srinivasan (2012) argued that students make use of the crowdsourced knowledge to complete their assignments. This puts forward the larger question of how crowdsourced learning differs from traditional learning in an online environment. It is also important to determine whether peer mentoring in a crowdsourced environment demonstrates better results than one-to-one learning. Finally, we must determine whether "crowdsourcing" or "social learning" help students effectively learn from many individuals rather than a few.

The panel thus, proposes the term "Learnsourcing", which would surround the area of "Learning" in a crowd-sourced environment. The panel will address the inquiries that in-clude: Has traditional education taken a back seat in the presence of online learning or has learning become diversified in different knowledge environments? Has crowdsourced knowledge cropped up as an avatar of traditional learning in a virtual classroom where learners learn from many individuals rather than from a few? How has learning changed from the physical world to the virtual world? Such inquiries rightly fit with this year's ASIS&T Annual Meeting "Diversity of Engagement: Connecting People and Information in the Physical and Virtual Worlds." With this panel, we wish to unearth the answers to these questions. Moreover, we hope to obtain a nuanced understanding of crowdsourced learning in different levels of education (i.e., K-12, undergraduate, and graduate levels) with the presence of our panelists from diverse research backgrounds.

## PANEL STRUCTURE

### *Panel Discussion*

The panel will discuss the following topics: Each panelist will briefly introduce themselves and the way their research has informed the crowdsourced learning and social learning approaches. Then, they will address one of the discussion questions outlined below. The four main discussion questions are as follows:

1. How do you as a researcher perceive the presence of "crowdsourced learning" over "peer mentoring"?
2. How would "crowdsourcing in education" play a role for students at different learning levels?
3. What are the different ethical and logistic concerns that are expected to emerge from "crowdsourced learning"?
4. How do you as a researcher situate "crowdsourced learning" in the future of learning environments?

### *Small Group Discussion*

Following the panel discussion, the attendees will break out into small groups of three or four and the panelists will serve as facilitators. Each group of attendees will be asked to confer on the main discussion questions among themselves. The additional questions that can be considered during these group-sessions may include:

1. How often do we make use of crowdsourced learning over traditional learning?
2. Given a choice, which form of learning - crowdsourced or traditional - would you choose if you were to play a role as a researcher, undergraduate student, or K-12 student?
3. What would you be mindful of while choosing "crowdsourced learning" over "traditional learning" if asked to choose one of the two?

## SESSION WRAP-UP

The panel will conclude with the moderator wrapping up the session by presenting final comments about the discussion. In addition, the panel attendees will be invited to ask questions to the panelists in the question-answering period.

## PANELISTS AND TOPICS

### *Manasa Rath, Moderator*

Manasa Rath is a PhD student at School of Communication & Information (SC&I) at Rutgers University. Her research interests lie in studying information seeking behavior, on-line behavior analysis and social media. She examines online Q&A sites related to STEM education to gather meaningful insights.

### *Chirag Shah, Panelist*

Chirag Shah is an Associate Professor in both the School of Communication & Information (SC&I) and the Department of Computer Science at Rutgers University. His research interests include information seeking/retrieval in individual, social, and collaborative contexts. He directs the InfoSeeking Lab at Rutgers where he investigates issues related to information seeking, interactive information retrieval, and social media, supported by grants from National Science Foundation (NSF), Institute of Museum and Library Services (IMLS), Google, and Yahoo! In addition to numerous articles on information seeking, crowdsourcing, and social media, he has published a book on Collaborative Information Seeking (see Shah (2012)) and Social Information Seeking (see Shah (2017).

Shah will discuss how students are increasingly using social and crowdsourcing services to fulfill their information needs spanning homework problems to disciplinary curiosity. He will draw on his work with collaborative and social information seeking in education contexts (specifically, undergraduate education) to describe what we know and what we still do not understand about students' information behaviors that include online peer-based and social services, and the issues of quality, control, and social constructive learning.

#### *Rich Gazan, Panelist*

Rich Gazan is Associate Professor and Chair of the University of Hawaii Library & Information Science Program. His research interests include how people integrate information from diverse sources in professional environments such as interdisciplinary scientific collaborations, and in informal environments such as online social Q&A communities. He was recently a Visiting Researcher at the NASA Astrobiology Institute at Ames Research Center studying metrics of interdisciplinary science, and served as Chair of the Interdisciplinary PhD Program in Communication & Information Sciences, which spans four units and three colleges across the University of Hawaii.

Gazan will discuss the development of a crowdsourced graduate program based on the X-Informatics model, where students take a small socio-technical core designed for students from any background, to learn and compare what counts as knowledge across a subset of disciplines relevant to their interests, and how information is created, sought and shared within them. Gazan will also discuss how students would apply these skills in gateway courses from a variety of relevant units to build a customized, crowdsourced degree program in areas such as sustainability informatics, culinary informatics, and so on.

#### *Oleksandr Zakharchuk, Panelist*

Oleksandr Zakharchuk is a machine learning consultant at Brainly, an online social learning Q&A platform. He has a background in creating personalized recommender systems and conducting machine learning courses at Google, as well as creating deep learning systems for text analysis. Za-kharchuk also provides solutions to startups using artificial intelligence methods.

In this panel, Zakharchuk will give an industry perspective to crowdsourced learning, question-answering, and learning analytics.

#### *Sanghee Oh, Panelist*

Dr. Sanghee Oh is an Assistant Professor in the Department of Library and Information Science, Chungnam National University, South Korea. Prior to joining the faculty in March 2017, she served as an Assistant Professor in the School of Information, Florida State University, from 2010 to 2017. Oh obtained her PhD in Information & Library Science from the University of North Carolina at Chapel Hill, and her Master of Library and Information Science from the University of California at Los Angeles. Her areas of research interest are health informatics, social informatics, user-centered information system design and development, and digital libraries. She has studied people's motivations and usages of social media/social Q&A in seeking and sharing information about health as well as other topics. She has taught courses in health informatics, human information behaviors, information architecture, databases management, and digital libraries.

In this panel, Oh will discuss about the K-12 students and their online behavior in Q&A sites.

#### *Mega Subramaniam, Panelist*

Mega Subramaniam, PhD is an Associate Professor at the College of Information Studies (iSchool) at the University of Maryland. She is the Associate Director for the Information Policy and Access Center (iPAC) at the University of Maryland and serves as the co-editor of School Library Research Journal. Her research focuses on enhancing the role of school and public libraries in fostering the mastery of information and new media literacy that are essential to STEM learning among underserved young people. Mega is the lead PI for the IMLS-funded Graduate Certificate of Professional Studies in Youth Experience (YX), co-leads two IMLS-funded projects, ConnectedLib and Safe Data Safe Families, and recently received a grant from Google for Libraries Ready to Code Phase 2 project - all intended to bring research and practice together to enhance the skills of in-service and pre-service librarians. To learn more about her research and teaching interests, please visit https://terpconnect.umd.edu/ mmsubram/.

Subramanian will discuss the role of "crowdsourcing" in education with respect to youth learners and the role of school librarians in this regard.

### CONCLUSION

This panel will engage with the important perspectives, challenges, and future of crowdsourcing in education. It will also discuss how various disciplines like Information Science, Library Science, and Education play a role in this groundbreaking learning strategy that's emergence will involve direct engagement from researchers regarding how inherent issues can be addressed and how the overall process can transform the education field.

### ACKNOWLEDGEMENT

The work reported in this proposal is supported by the US Institute of Museum and Library Services (IMLS) grant LG-81-16-0025-16.

### REFERENCES

Anderson, A., Huttenlocher, D., Kleinberg, J., and Leskovec, J. (2012). Discovering value from community activity on focused question answering sites: a case study of stack overflow. In Proceedings of the 18th ACM SIGKDD international conference on Knowledge discovery and data mining, pages 850–858. ACM.

Bandura, A. (1977). Self-efficacy: toward a unifying theory of behavioral change. Psychological review, 84(2):191.

Beaven, T., Hauck, M., Comas-Quinn, A., Lewis, T., and de los Arcos, B. (2014). MOOCS: Striking the right balance between facilitation and self-determination. *Journal of Online Learning and Teaching*, 10(1):31.

Dalsgaard, C. (2006). Social software: E-learning beyond learning management systems. *European Journal of Open, Distance and E-Learning*, 9(2).

Glassman, E. L., Terman, C. J., and Miller, R. C. (2015). Learnersourcing in an engineering class at scale. In Pro-ceedings of the Second (2015) ACM Conference on Learning@ Scale, pages 363–366. ACM.

Harris, C. G. and Srinivasan, P. (2012). With a little help from the crowd: Receiving unauthorized academic assis-tance through online labor markets. In Privacy, Security, Risk and Trust (PASSAT), 2012 International Conference on and 2012 International Conference on Social Computing (SocialCom), pages 904–909. IEEE.

Howe, J. (2006). The rise of crowdsourcing. Wired magazine, 14(6):1–4.

Li,S-W.D. and Mitros, P. (2015). Learnersourced recommendations for remediation. In Advanced Learning Technologies (ICALT), 2015 IEEE 15th International Conference on, pages 411–412. IEEE.

Malone, T. W., Laubacher, R., and Dellarocas, C. (2009). Harnessing crowds: Mapping the genome of collective intelligence.

Mitros, P. (2015). Learnersourcing of complex assessments. In Proceedings of the Second (2015) ACM Conference on Learning@ Scale, pages 317–320. ACM.

Sawhney, M. and Nambisan, S. (2007). The global brain: Your roadmap for innovating faster and smarter in a networked world. Pearson Prentice Hall.

Schenk, E. and Guittard, C. (2011). Towards a characterization of crowdsourcing practices. *Journal of Innovation Economics & Management*, (1):93–107.

Shah, C. (2012). Collaborative information seeking: The art and science of making the whole greater than the sum of all, volume 34. Springer Science & Business Media.

Shah, C. (2017). Social information seeking: Leveraging the Wisdom of the Crowd, volume 38. Springer Science & Business Media.

Sinclair, J., Boyatt, R., Rocks, C., and Joy, M. (2015). Massive open online courses: A review of usage and evaluation. International *Journal of Learning Technology*, 10(1):71–93.

Surowiecki, J. (2004). The wisdom of crowds: Why the many are smarter than the few and how collective wisdom shapes business. Economies, Societies and Nations, 296.

# Organizational and Institutional Work in Data Infrastructures

**Kalpana Shankar**
*School of Information and Communication Studies, University College Dublin, Ireland. Kalpana.shankar@ucd.ie*

**Kristin Eschenfelder**
*School of Library and Information, University of Wisconsin, Madison, USA. Eschenfelder@wisc.edu*

**ABSTRACT**

**The long-term sustainability of data archives and other research information infrastructures is a growing concern as stakeholders seek to ensure that resources invested in infrastructure development endure beyond the original project funding period. For this reason, data infrastructure research has gone beyond the technical work of data management, standardization and digital preservation. There is also a growing body of research that looks at the organizational practices and structures of data repositories and infrastructures for the long term and how they shape and reflect technologies, policies, stakeholder needs and priorities, professions and business models.**

**We intend to use this panel to engage the audience in an ongoing conversation about organizational studies, sustainability planning and infrastructure. Panel members will present their research on these topics in different case sites and explore how governance, policies and organizational structures and practices are involved in the maintenance and repair of data infrastructures. We want to know more from the audience about how they are examining policies, business models, governance structures and artifacts in other sites; gaps and needs in research and practice; and next steps for researchers. Some questions of interest: How do repositories define success? How do they make their case for long-term funding and institutional homes? What scalar issues will arise in the context of even bigger data sources? How do data projects end? We will engage each other and the audience in discussing these questions and concerns.**

**KEYWORDS**

data archives, cyberinfrastructures, organizational studies

**PRESENTATION 1:**
**Data archive sustainability:**
Science policy and/or business model planning?

**Authors**: Kristin Eschenfelder, University of Wisconsin-Madison, School of Library and Information Science, and Kalpana Shankar, University College Dublin, School of Information and Communication Studies

There are a number of competing narratives and assumptions that underpin discussions of data archives and their longevity. In this presentation, we focus on exploring two: science policy and management. The first set argues that data archive sustainability is an issue of national or global science policy. From this perspective, the activity of data archiving is an activity that national governments or national science organizations may choose to emphasize (and fund) in order to pursue national (or in the case of the EU, regional) science goals. A second set of arguments represents data archive sustainability as a business model problem. From this perspective, the activity of data archiving is an activity that ought to cover its own costs and ideally leave sufficient revenue for self-funding of innovation. Sources of revenue are likely diverse and may include, but are likely not limited to, public science funding. We will examine the assumptions that are made in these approaches to data sustainability to understand how these narratives shape data institutions and infrastructures. We review several prominent data archive business model initiatives and reports from over the past decade from U.S., European and global projects. For each we describe the major funders of the projects and the stakeholders who took part in them and the purported target audience(s) of project outputs. We will consider how the origins of the project (funders, stakeholders) shape them, their outputs and their representation of data archiving vis-à-vis the science policy and management arguments for developing business models for sustainability. We will also consider governance, the relative importance of stakeholders, accountability, proving value to the user community and science advancements.

**PRESENTATION 2:**
**Same Data, Differing Objectives:**
What happened when research libraries took on a large scientific dataset

**Authors**: Peter T. Darch, School of Information Sciences, University of Illinois at Urbana-Champaign; Ashley E. Sands, information studies, UCLA; Christine L. Borgman, information studies, UCLA; Sharon Traweek, gender studies and history, UCLA; Milena S. Golshan, information studies, UCLA

The Sloan Digital Sky Survey (SDSS) is a major astronomy project that has generated massive datasets for use by researchers. SDSS faced the critical challenge of ensuring long-

80th Annual Meeting of the Association for Information Science & Technology, Washington, DC, VA | Oct. 27-Nov. 1, 2017

term accessibility of the data generated during its first two phases (SDSS I/II) beyond the end of these phases' periods of funding. We report on a qualitative case study of how SDSS leaders addressed this challenge. These leaders partnered with two university libraries to sustain long-term access to SDSS I/II data. At 160TB of data, the data transfer process between SDSS and these libraries was the largest ever attempted.

Deep differences emerged between the perspectives of library team members and of SDSS leaders about the main legacy of the data transfer process. In recent years, university libraries have faced enormous financial and institutional pressure to demonstrate and enhance their relevance to researchers. In this context, the libraries involved in the SDSS data transfer process regarded the infrastructure they were building to curate and serve SDSS I/II data as the main legacy of this transfer process. They hoped this infrastructure would serve as the foundation of data curation services that could be offered to a wide range of scientific projects and domains, beyond astronomy. By contrast, SDSS leaders expected the continued accessibility of SDSS I/II data to be the main legacy of the data transfer process.

These differing perspectives on the legacy of the data transfer process contributed to misunderstandings between SDSS leadership and the library teams as the transfer process unfolded. We consider how these misunderstandings complicated this data transfer process and whether and how SDSS leaders and library team members overcame them. We conclude with recommendations and implications for policy, infrastructure and institutions for the curation of scientific datasets.

### PRESENTATION 3:
### Place-Based Field Site Infrastructuring:
Data work at launch and termination

**Author**: Karen Baker, School of Information Sciences, University of Illinois at Urbana-Champaign

The configuration of place-based data infrastructure for two long-term environmental sites is presented. For projects studying a designated biome at a well-defined geographic location, the growth of digital infrastructure often involves layered partnerships and shared practices. Central to the field-based natural sciences is the notion of place and, in recent decades, collective data work. Emergent digital data practices are creating shared information spaces that contribute to the integrative activities of a shared place. A multi-case, longitudinal ethnography illustrates the process of infrastructuring at two stages of development, one project beginning collective data work and one closing down the data system of a 32-year project with embedded data management.

### PRESENTATION 4:
### Sustainability Under Construction:
The DataONE experience

**Author**: Suzie Allard, University of Tennessee-Knoxville, School of Information Sciences/Center for Information & Communication Studies

The DataONE cyberinfrastructure supports enhanced search and discovery of Earth and environmental data and enables new science and knowledge creation by providing access to data across multiple member repositories around the world. DataONE had a unique organizational design when it was funded by the National Science Foundation as one of the initial DataNet partners and it has been evolving over the past decade. Discussion will focus on how sustainability has been addressed from inception including the role of community engagement, business models and change management. Lessons learned that might provide insight for other projects will be shared.

### PRESENTATION 5:
### Rubbing Shoulders:
Data Sharing Approaches in Scientific Data Repositories

**Authors**: Steve Sawyer, School of Information Sciences, Syracuse University, and Sarika Sharma, School of Information Sciences, Syracuse University

This presentation focuses on the governance of shared data, contrasting network-based and repository-based approaches to data infrastructures. In network-based approaches, the sharing is done via networks of scholars who have learned of each other (often through the good work of scientists who work to create and sustain the network) and agree to certain data standards, sharing conventions and other issues with use. In the more common repository-based approaches to data infrastructures, the ascension and curation of data are standardized, and interactions among participants are more ephemeral. In action, any form of data infrastructure has to do some of both, making these comparisons useful as to the scale and scope of such approaches and for the trade-offs these demand.

### PANELIST BIOGRAPHIES

**Suzie Allard** is a professor in the School of Information Sciences and CCI associate dean for research and director of the Center for Information and Communication Studies at the University of Tennessee at Knoxville. Her research interests focus on how scientists and engineers use and communicate information. She is a co-investigator and member of the leadership team for DataONE, an NSF- funded cyberinfrastructure for environmental science information. Allard is the principal investigator on other projects related to science data. She was a founding member and past-chair of the American Society for Information Science and Technology's (ASIS&T) Special Interest Group/Digital Libraries. Previously, Dr. Allard provided consulting services to the television and motion picture industries as a vice president of Research Frontiers Corporation.

**Christine L. Borgman** is professor and Presidential Chair in Information Studies at UCLA. From September 2012 through June 2013 she was an Oliver Smithies Visiting Fellow and Lecturer at Balliol College, University of Oxford, where she is also affiliated with the Oxford Internet Institute and the Oxford eResearch Centre. Prof. Borgman is the author of more than 200 publications in information studies, computer science and communication. Her monographs, *Scholarship in the Digital Age: Information, Infrastructure, and the Internet* (MIT Press, 2007) and *From Gutenberg to the Global Information Infrastructure: Access to Information in a Networked World* (MIT Press, 2000), each won the Best Information Science Book of the Year award from the American Society for Information Science and Technology. She conducts data practices research with funding from the National Science Foundation, Sloan Foundation and Microsoft Research. Current collaborations include Monitoring, Modeling, and Memory, Data Conservancy, and *The Transformation of Knowledge, Culture, and Practice in Data-Driven Science*, and Empowering Long Tail Research. She is a member of the Board of Directors of the Electronic Privacy Information Center, c o-chair of the CODATA Task Group Data Citation Standards and Practices, a fellow of the American Association for the Advancement of Science and previously served on the U.S. National Academies' Board on Research Data and Information and the U.S. National CODATA. In 2011, Prof. Borgman received both the Paul Evan Peters Award from the Coalition for Networked Information, Association for Research Libraries and EDUCAUSE, and the Research in Information Science Award from the American Society for Information Science and Technology.

**Peter Darch** is an assistant professor in the School of Information Sciences at the University of Illinois at Urbana-Champaign. Prior to joining the iSchool at Illinois, Darch worked as a postdoctoral researcher in the UCLA Department of Information Studies and Center for Knowledge Infrastructures, with which he continues to collaborate on studies of the building, running and effects of information infrastructures that support scientific collaboration. His dissertation for the DPhil in computer science from the University of Oxford (2012) addressed how scientists and software engineers in online citizen science projects manage members of the public to process and generate large datasets. This doctorate followed an MA in the history and philosophy of science and medicine (Durham University, 2006) and an MMath in mathematics from the University of Oxford (2004). He is particularly interested in the profound changes in the organization and conduct of contemporary scientific research that result from the interaction of technologies that afford collection of increasing quantities and types of scientific data with broader sociotechnical factors. To study these changes, he conducts longitudinal ethnographic studies of large, multidisciplinary scientific projects, applying theoretical approaches from science and technology studies to examine relationships between contexts in which these collaborations are embedded, information infrastructures and scientists' day-to-day data practices.

**Kristin R. Eschenfelder** is a professor at the School of Library and Information Studies at the University of Wisconsin-Madison. Her research interests focus on access and use regimes – or the complex, multi-level networks of laws, customs, technologies and expectations that shape what information we can access in our daily lives and what we can make of it. Her recent work examines development of and changes to access and use regimes for digital scholarly works including electronic publications (journals, books, citation databases), digital cultural materials (such as museum, archival or anthropological works) and datasets. Her past work explored web-based government information and policy and management issues inherent in digital production of government information and records. She has also published in the areas of public libraries and financial literacy.

**Milena Golshan** is the UCLA Center for Knowledge Infrastructures' data scientist and project manager. She organizes and mines the trove of data which the UCLA Center's teams have collected since 2002 and facilitates the process of exploiting these resources for longitudinal and comparative research. Milena holds MLIS degrees from UCLA and Sofia University St. Kliment Ohridski in Bulgaria. She is especially interested in open data, digital archiving and data analysis, management and curation. Milena's experience includes academic research support, qualitative data analysis, content management, information architecture and electronic networking for environmental protection.

**Ashley Sands** is a doctoral candidate in information studies at UCLA. Joining us from the field of archaeology, she brings nearly a decade of experience working with scientific data. Sands is in the process of conducting her dissertation research, which examines astronomy data management practices to reveal the expertise and infrastructure most appropriate for maximizing the utility of scientific data. Research methods include semi-structured interviews, participant observation and document analysis. Ashley's research interests include scholarly communication, scientific data practices and data management workforces.

**Sarika Sharma** is currently a PhD student at Syracuse University's School of Information Sciences. Born and raised outside of Chicago, Illinois, she holds a master's degree in library and information science from the University of Pittsburgh and a bachelor's degree from University of Wisconsin-Madison in zoology and South Asian studies. Sarika is interested in large-scale, long-term technology investments in the form of information infrastructures within organizations. She is currently investigating the coordination and governance of infrastructure efforts that aim to preserve, store and provide access to data within scientific communities. Her dissertation work is supported by the NSF-CHS. She is currently a research assistant on the NSF-VOSS grant with co-principal investigators Dr. Steve Sawyer and Dr. Carsten Osterlund. Using the sociomateriality lens, the research aims to understand how academic researchers use documents in their distributed, virtual collaborations.

**Professor Steve Sawyer**, School of Information Studies, Syracuse University, conducts research in the social informatics tradition with particular attention to the ways in which people organize to work together and use information and communication technologies. He leads courses that focus student's attention to the design, development and implementation of information systems, managing projects and systems, and to the roles of information and communication technologies relative to organizational and social change.

**Kalpana Shankar** is professor of information and communication studies and head of school at University College Dublin's School of Information and Communication Studies. Her research examines how data practices and systems reflect and reify the larger society, culture and institutions where they are enacted. Her current research projects focus on the sustainability and longevity of data archives and Irish attitudes towards climate change. Past projects include open data in Ireland and aging and technology for the home.

**Professor Sharon Traweek**, gender studies and history, UCLA, is the author of *Beamtimes and Lifetimes: The World of High Energy Physicists* (Harvard, 1988), which is used in courses worldwide as an exemplar of how to conduct ethnographic research on knowledge-making practices among scientists. Her many years of studying data practices in high-energy physics is essential expertise for the project's studies of astronomy and astrophysics.

# From Sensors to Sense-Making: Opportunities and Challenges for Information Science


**Vivek K. Singh**
*School of Communication & Information, Rutgers University, USA. v.singh@rutgers.edu*

**Hideo Joho**
*Faculty of Library, Information and Media Science, University of Tsukuba, Japan. hideo@slis.tsukuba.ac.jp*

**Chirag Shah**
*School of Communication & Information, Rutgers University, USA. chirags@rutgers.edu*

**Cathal Gurrin**
*School of Computing, Dublin City University, Ireland. cgurrin@computing.dcu.ie*

**Jacek Gwizdka**
*School of Information, University of Texas at Austin, USA. asist2017@gwizdka.com*



## ABSTRACT

**With the growth in sensing devices, data logging capabilities and multi-sensory presentation interfaces, it has been argued that the future of documents is "multisensory, pervasive, and immersive," and building an agenda around these themes is critical for future information science research. Hence, in this panel, we bring together an international group of researchers actively engaged in research at the intersection of sensors and information science. The panel will discuss the new research opportunities and challenges afforded by the use of different kinds of sensors (e.g., fitness trackers, phones, cameras, fMRIs) for information science research. The panel aims to raise awareness and catalyze a strong research activity on sensor-enriched information science, which is expected to have multiple implications for human information behavior, health informatics, neuro-information science, data science, social informatics and computational social science.**



## KEYWORDS

sensors, information practices, social informatics, computational social science, neuro-information science, multi-method research, lifelogging, wearable devices, mobile computing, data analytics


## PANEL OVERVIEW AND MOTIVATION

Understanding humans as they interact with information and with each other is one of the fundamental goals of information science research. This is important in multiple contexts such as human information behavior, health informatics, neuro-information science, data science, social informatics and computational social science. With the growth in sensing devices, data logging capabilities and multi-sensory presentation interfaces, it has been argued that the future of documents is "multisensory, pervasive, and immersive," and building an agenda around these themes is critical for future information science research (Robinson, L., 2015).

These growth trends in sensors and devices afford multiple opportunities for enhancing research in information science. For instance, while self-report methods such as diary methods, surveys and ethnography have been widely applied in prior research to understand human behavior, these methods tend to require significant manual effort and are cost, time and labor intensive. Automated logging approaches like phone logs, search logs, Fitbit logs can now be harnessed to understand and shape human behavior (Shmueli, Singh, Lepri & Pentland, 2014; Choi, Shah & Singh, 2016).

In fact, multiple information science researchers have embraced and begun to utilize a multitude of sensors (e.g., fitness trackers, eye-trackers, smart phones, emotion sensors) to understand human beings as they interact with information and each other. For example, Choi, Shah & Singh (2016) have utilized mobile phone-based location tracking to study the interconnections between exploration in online search and physical geo-exploration. Nagaoka, Furuhashi, Ninei & Joho (2016) have utilized lifelogging methods to understand the lifestyle and academic activities of undergraduate students in Japan. Mostafa and Gwizdka (2016) have argued a case for using neuro-physiological measures obtained from EEG, eye-tracking or fMRI for understanding information behavior. Gwizdka (2014) showed relationship between eye-tracking measures and text relevance for question answering tasks and static texts and for information search on the web (Gwizdka & Zhang, 2015).

Further, Joho, Gurrin & Hopfgartner (2016) have been leading multiple workshops at iConference and ASIS&T meetings to bring together researchers engaged in research at the intersection of lifelogging and information science.

Given the growing interest in this area, we propose to bring together an international group of researchers actively engaged in research at the intersection of sensors and information science. The panel aims to engage with the audience


80th Annual Meeting of the Association for Information Science & Technology, Washington, DC, VA | Oct. 27-Nov. 1, 2017

to identify the possibilities and challenges in this emerging area, including its impact on information science research and education. This would include the opportunities for research, potential pitfalls like "big-data hubris" (Lazer et al., 2014) and the identification of multiple information science relevant areas that are likely to be impacted by these trends.

## OPPORTUNITIES

Some of the opportunities for sensor-enriched information science lie in improving and abetting:

***Objectivity***: The measurements of human behavior can benefit from complementing current sources of data with emerging sensor-based data sources. For example, evidence from brain imaging data while interacting with documents can be taken as being objective and not subject to biases (e.g., subjectivity bias and reporting bias).

***Scale***: New sensors can help transform the scale at which different studies are conducted. For example, capturing physical and social interactions using phones and other devices used by billions of individuals on a daily basis could yield newer insights for social informatics and computational social science.

***"In the wild" observations***: An ability to study users in their natural settings is an important design goal for information science studies. Sensors worn and carried by users in their everyday life (e.g., phones, fitness trackers, cameras) now allow for understanding their behavior in natural settings. For example, different life-logging applications are allowing researchers to create detailed accounts of the academic activities and lifestyles of students in everyday settings.

***Measurement of unobservable (or difficult to observe) variables***: Traditional methods of eliciting user response are not conducive to measure some of the important user response variables (e.g., mental load, beliefs, emotions). Newer approaches like the fMRI can allow for verification of hypothesized links between these variables and observable behavior (e.g., information source selection, choice of search tactic, stopping search) by mapping them on brain areas and their activation.

***Complementarity of information channels***: Understanding human behavior is often a complex process. Complementing the information coming from different channels, some focusing on the cognitive and experiential aspects, while others focusing on the behavioral aspects (e.g., via a combination of surveys, interviews, lifelogs, fMRI and phone logs) could provide a more holistic view of the underlying processes and hence move the field forward.

## CHALLENGES

There remain multiple challenges in the process:

***Cost***: The hardware, software, training and support cost for many of these devices and sensors can be a bottleneck in their widespread adoption by the community. While some of these sensors cost less than $100 each (wristbands), others run into several millions of dollars (fMRI machines). We will discuss such challenges as well as opportunities to leverage cross-departmental collaborations to counter some of these challenges.

***Awareness***: Many of these sensors are being utilized in new information science relevant contexts for the first time. Hence, there is a need to create broader awareness on the opportunities (and challenges) associated with their use. This includes raising awareness in the broader research community as well as the broader set of stakeholders including practitioners, publishers and funding agencies. Raising this awareness is one of the key aims of this panel.

***Expertise***: Utilizing some of these sensors and dealing with the emerging data may require some newer skills (e.g., connecting with APIs, multimodal data analytics) that go beyond traditional information science curriculums. Hence, planning for newer curriculum and developing expertise in these areas are an important challenge and an opportunity.

***Privacy and ethics***: While understanding human behavior is helpful in multiple scientific and business contexts, such advantages need to be balanced with the ethical and privacy needs of the society.

***"Big data hubris"***: An important challenge is to avoid the trap of assuming that more data is necessarily a good thing. Multiple recent research efforts have identified the problems with overfitting the data or simply employing the wrong type of data to tackle the problem encountered. Hence, identifying the right processes for deciding on when to use which channel of information is an important challenge.

## POTENTIAL APPLICATION AREAS

The emerging sensors and the corresponding data can impact multiple research areas of interest to the information science research community.

***Human information behavior***: New sensors could allow for better understanding of cognitive, affective, experiential and neurological basis for multiple information interaction behaviors. For example, new sensors could allow for the creation of multi-dimensional model of information relevance for humans.

***Computational social science***: New sensors can support multi-method logging and mining of human social interactions (e.g., in meetings, classrooms, libraries and everyday settings). This could allow researchers to gain an in-depth understanding of the social behaviors and processes that make humans productive, happy and healthy.

***Human-centered data science***: Information science research has often been sandwiched between the low level statistical analysis of unidimensional data and high-level concepts like affects, intentions and behaviors studied in the social sciences. Hence, there is an important need to bridge the gap to build tools and techniques that transform low-level sensor signals into information science relevant building blocks (e.g., intentions) and support seamless data analysis over it.

***Health informatics***: Sensors enable new opportunities for understanding and inferring health and well-being of individuals, its social interconnections and its implications on information behavior. For example, long-term changes in gaze patterns could yield predictive clues for Alzheimer's disease. Multiple such applications in the broader umbrella of health informatics could benefits from such sensor data.

## PANEL STRUCTURE

1. Introduction to the topic: 10 minutes, by the moderator
2. Presentations by the panelists on work they have completed, current projects and their opinions on applications of neuroimaging to information science: each 10 minutes
3. Discussion among the panelists based on questions posed to them by the moderator, both in advance of the panel and based on the presentations, with contributions/questions from the audience: (30 minutes)
4. Summary discussion from the panel, led by the moderator: 10 minutes.

## PANELISTS AND THEIR CONTRIBUTIONS

**Dr. Vivek K. Singh** is assistant professor in the School of Communication and Information at Rutgers University. Before joining Rutgers, he was a post-doctoral researcher the MIT Media Lab.

Dr. Singh's work focuses on sensing, understanding and shaping human behavior in a data-driven manner. Recently, he has been leading the Rutgers Wellbeing Study, where phone-based data (call, SMS, GPS logs) are being utilized to understand the health, well-being, trust and privacy attitudes of students on campus. His broader work in the area of computational social science has been published in leading scientific venues (e.g., *Science*) and has received significant media coverage (e.g., *BBC, New York Times, Wall Street Journal*).

Dr. Singh will moderate the discussion and also provide a brief overview of his work in using phone and fitness sensors for understanding human behavior.

**Chirag Shah** is associate professor in both the School of Communication & Information (SC&I) and the Department of Computer Science at Rutgers University. His research interests include information seeking/retrieval in individual, social and collaborative contexts. He investigates ways to collect and analyze passive data from personal sensors to model and predict information-seeking behaviors. He directs the InfoSeeking Lab at Rutgers where he investigates issues related to information seeking, interactive information retrieval and social media, supported by grants from National Science Foundation (NSF), Institute of Museum and Library Services (IMLS), Google and Yahoo!

Dr. Shah will present his experience with using fitness trackers, affective sensors and phones for studying the (1) interconnections between affect and information search and (2) studying the interconnections between geo-exploration and information exploration.

**Jacek Gwizdka** is assistant professor and Information eXperience Lab co-director at School of Information at University of Texas, Austin. He studies human information interaction and retrieval and applies cognitive psychology and neurophysiological methods to understand information searchers and improve search experience. He is particularly interested in creating models that describe and predict cognitive and affective phenomena in human information interaction. Recent projects investigate search as a learning process and employ eye-tracking and EEG in assessment of reading, mind-wandering and in inferring information relevance. Dr. Gwizdka has been affiliated with University of Toronto, Rutgers University and University of Texas at Austin. He conducted research at industrial labs (Xerox PARC, FXPAL, HP Labs). Dr. Gwizdka has co-organized successful related workshops and panels at international conferences, including CHIIR (NeuroIIR'2017); SIGIR (NeuroIR'2015, SaL'2016); IIiX (SaL'2014), ASIS&T (2016, 2013). Dr. Gwizdka has been using eye-tracking in his research since 2008 and fMRI/EEG since 2010. More on Dr. Gwizdka's research can be found at http://gwizdka.com/research

Dr. Gwizdka will present his experience with using eye-tracking, EEG and fMRI in exploring the possibility of detecting cognitive activity related to relevance judgments.

**Hideo Joho** is an associate professor in Research Center for Knowledge Communities, Faculty of Library, Information and Media Science, University of Tsukuba, Japan. Dr. Joho is also a visiting scholar at National Institute of Informatics (Japan) and RMIT (Australia).

Dr. Joho is interested in cognitive and affective interaction between users and search systems, involving behavioural analyses, user modelling and user studies.

Dr. Joho will be sharing his views from computational approaches based on his experiences in both laboratory-based user studies and recently performed long-term fieldwork of lifelogging exercise with undergraduate students.

**Cathal Gurrin** is a senior lecturer at the School of Computing, at Dublin City University, a visiting researcher at the University of Tromso and a principal investigator at the Insight Centre for Data Analytics.

Dr. Gurrin is a renowned lifelogger and leading lifelog researcher (Gurrin, et al., 2014). He and his colleagues have developed a number of lifelog data collection and analysis systems over the last decade.

Dr. Gurrin will show some of the systems developed by his team to demonstrate the real examples of lifelog data collected by various wearable devices. Dr. Gurrin will also present the research dataset for lifelogging research, which was recently constructed in the context of the NTCIR Lifelog task. Finally, Dr. Gurrin will discuss both opportunities and limitations of lifelogging technologies, as well as their future directions.

## REFERENCES


Choi, D., Shah, C., & Singh, V. (2016, September). Probing the interconnections between geo-exploration and information exploration behavior. In *Proceedings of the 2016 ACM International Joint Conference on Pervasive and Ubiquitous Computing* (pp. 1170-1175). ACM.

Nagaoka, N., Furuhashi, Y., Minei, N., & Joho, H. (2016). Lessons learned from 8 months of lifelogging. *Information Retrieval and Learning with Lifelogging Devices, 13.*

Robinson, L. (2015). Multisensory, pervasive, immersive: Towards a new generation of documents. *Journal of the Association for Information Science and Technology*, *66*(8), 1734-1737.

Mostafa, J., & Gwizdka, J. (2016, March). Deepening the role of the user: Neuro-physiological evidence as a basis for studying and improving search. In *Proceedings of the 2016 ACM on Conference on Human Information Interaction and Retrieval* (pp. 63-70). ACM.

Gwizdka, J. (2014, August). Characterizing relevance with eye-tracking measures. In *Proceedings of the 5th Information Interaction in Context Symposium* (pp. 58-67). ACM.Gwizdka, J., & Zhang, Y. (2015, August). Differences in eye-tracking measures between visits and revisits to relevant and irrelevant web pages. In *Proceedings of the 38th International ACM SIGIR Conference on Research and Development in Information Retrieval* (pp. 811-814). ACM.

Joho, H., Gurrin, C., & Hopfgartner, F. (2017). Second workshop on interaction and engagement on information research and learning with lifelogging devices. In *Proceedings of the iConference.*

Lazer, D., Kennedy, R., King, G., & Vespignani, A. (2014). The parable of Google Flu: Traps in big data analysis. *Science, 343*(6176), 1203-1205.

Shmueli, E., Singh, V. K., Lepri, B., & Pentland, A. (2014). Sensing, understanding, and shaping social behavior. *IEEE Transactions on Computational Social Systems*, *1*(1), 22-34.

# Wearable Devices: Information Privacy, Policy and User Behavior

**Natalie Greene Taylor**
*University of South Florida, USA. ngtaylor@usf.edu*

**Loni Hagen**
*University of South Florida, USA. lonihagen@usf.edu*

**Ersin Dincelli**
*University at Albany, SUNY, USA. edincelli@albany.edu*

**Kristene Unsworth**
*Stockton University, USA. Kristene.Unsworth@stockton.edu*

### ABSTRACT

**As wearable devices continue to rise in popularity and become more embedded in our lives, there is a growing need for better information privacy policies protecting users' privacy and education raising users' awareness for such privacy-invasive technologies. This panel is an exploration of the interplay between privacy policies and user behavior. The panel will address (1) current privacy policies for wearable devices, (2) how users' perceptions of privacy affects their responses to these policies and use of wearable devices and (3) the potential gaps in users' understanding of how their personal information from such devices is collected, transmitted and stored for undefined future use. Panelists will discuss these concepts from the perspectives of law, psychology, information systems and digital literacy. This panel is intended to be interactive and will encourage the audience to discuss their own understandings of information privacy in the context of wearable devices. The panel aims to contribute in developing information science-specific approaches to wearable device privacy policy and education and in making suggestions for future research.**

### KEYWORDS

wearable devices, quantified self, digital literacy, information privacy, security, policy, user behavior

### INTRODUCTION

Use of wearable devices, defined herein as technology that is stored in some way on the body, is increasing. Devices range from watches to bracelets to glasses and to attachable pods (e.g., the Fitbit). One global mobile communication analyst firm, CSI Insight, suggests that over 400 million wearable devices will be sold worldwide in 2020 (CSI Insight, 2016). With this swift rate of adoption, however, there is a danger that policymakers and information professionals will fail to protect consumers from the inherent privacy risks these devices pose, such as location data shared through use of GPS-enabled fitness trackers or the misuse by insurers of health data recorded by such devices (Kellogg, 2016; Raij, Ghosh, Kumar, & Srivastava, 2011).

Prior research suggests that users are not careful when it comes to their data on mobile devices and cites the potential risks for sensitive health data to be used for marketing and insurance purposes (Anderson and Olmstead, 2017; Cha, 2015). A recent report from the Center for Digital Democracy at American University suggests that legislation on and current corporate practices with wearable devices need to fundamentally change to accommodate the way that users operate in a big data era (Montgomery, Chester and Kopp, 2016). This triangulation of issues – a lack of user understanding on how to protect their privacy, the collection of increasingly sensitive data by these devices and a slowly adapting policy environment – suggests an urgent need for researchers to address how users interpret privacy and how the information science field can better educate users.

This panel will examine these issues, including how users understand privacy policies, the interrelationship of privacy and security and its impacts on user behavior, the psychological components of privacy and wearable devices, and the specific issues that arise when youth are the users of this technology. Panelists will discuss these concepts from the perspectives of law (e.g., what constitutes a legal privacy right), psychology (e.g., a user's mindset surrounding privacy and how this affects behavior), information systems (e.g., how wearable devices can collect information and/or protect user privacy) and digital literacy (e.g., the education that may be needed to inform users regarding how the devices work, what the companies collect and how users can protect their data).

In the first discussion, Dincelli will discuss users' decision-making processes regarding information disclosure through wearable device use. He will review the benefit structure of use and privacy calculus associated with the information disclosure behavior on such devices. Dr. Hagen will review new risks arising from the use of wearable devices in relation to trends in the use of big data. She will then discuss problems involving the important privacy principle of "informed consent and control," especially by reflecting on the typically inadequate level of users' knowledge regarding the technological capabilities of wearable devices. Finally, Dr. Taylor will review current research on young people, wearable devices and privacy. Dr. Bashir will serve as a discussant and Dr. Unsworth will moderate the discussion.

80th Annual Meeting of the Association for Information Science & Technology, Washington, DC, VA | Oct. 27-Nov. 1, 2017

Ultimately, this panel aims to develop an understanding of information science-specific approaches to privacy and wearables to inform policymakers, user education and future research. Attendees will have a better understanding of the role of the library and information science community in informing policy and educating users with regards to privacy and wearable devices.

## PROMOTION

This panel will be promoted through ASIS&T SIG/IEP Listservs, Facebook pages and Twitter accounts.

## PANEL SECTIONS

### *Self-disclosure on Wearable Devices – Ersin Dincelli*

Individuals are likely to be driven by different values and motives compared to similar privacy-invasive technologies for their cognitive assessment of wearable device use and subsequent information disclosure. According to the privacy calculus model, individuals engage in self-disclosure by comparing perceived risks and benefits associated with disclosure (Dinev & Hart, 2006). However, individuals do not necessarily process all the relevant information to carry out a rational risk-benefit assessment and emphasize the criteria they perceive as salient at the time the decisions need to be made (Petronio, 2002). In the context of wearable devices, the decision to disclose personal information could be affected by (1) social benefits (e.g., social approval by peers), (2) hedonic benefits (e.g., enjoyment) and/or (3) utilitarian benefits (e.g., accessibility to health-related information). Weight of each benefit may vary depending on users' experiences with the technology as well as the perceived privacy risks (Dincelli & Zhou, 2017). This section of the panel will review the privacy calculus model and various psychographic factors that affect users' decision-making processes in the context of wearable devices.

### *Overcoming the Privacy Challenges of Wearable Devices – Loni Hagen*

As technological innovations become increasingly dependent on personal information, privacy concerns become heightened. These concerns often focus on the extent to which users have control over access to personal information collected and used. Recent adoption of wearable devices brings new questions: What should we do about technologies that enable transmission of personal information in the background, often without a clear perception of the user? Dr. Hagen will review new risks arising from the use of wearable devices in relation to trends in the use of big data. She will then discuss problems involving the important privacy principle of "informed consent and control," especially by reflecting on the typically inadequate level of users' knowledge regarding the technological capabilities of wearable devices. She will conclude the presentation by suggesting possible approaches to address the raised issues through computational technologies and digital literacy education.

### *Youth, Privacy, and Wearable Devices – Natalie Greene Taylor*

There are few available studies on young people's engagement with wearable devices. While this may be a result of a lack of use (one recent study found that fewer than 5% of surveyed teens use wearable devices for health) (Wartella, Rideout, Montague, Beaudoin-Ryan & Lauricella, 2016), the growing market for such devices suggests that general use will increase (CSI Insight, 2016). Given this overall trend in technology consumption, more research into young people's interactions with wearable devices is needed. This section of the panel will discuss emerging trends in wearable devices for youth and the implications of the use of these devices on their privacy. Existing studies on young people's privacy behaviors with mobile devices and how this behavior may translate to wearable devices will also be discussed. Finally, literature on young people's digital literacy regarding privacy will be covered, as well as possible ways to improve privacy education.

## THE PANELISTS

**Ersin Dincelli** is a doctoral candidate and an adjunct professor in the Department of Informatics at the University at Albany, State University of New York (SUNY). He works as a senior research analyst at the New York State Center for Information Forensics and Assurance (CIFA), focusing on multiple research projects including investigating cultural and socio-psychological impacts on information security and privacy behavior, cognitive biases and phishing, cybersecurity education and self-organization in the context of complex traffic systems. He received his MBA. with a specialization in information technology management from the University at Albany, SUNY and his BA in economics from Uludag University in Turkey. His primary research interests include individual behavior in the context of information security and privacy, privacy-invasive technologies, cybersecurity education and cross-cultural issues in information systems.

**Loni Hagen** is assistant professor at the School of Information at the University of South Florida. She received degrees in law, information studies (specializing in information law), advertising and public relations, and she earned her PhD in information science from University at Albany, SUNY. She has worked diverse government administrative positions over 10 years including time as an e-government specialist at the headquarters of the Korean National Police Agency. Her current research interests are in use of computational techniques including human language technologies for policy decision making in the domains of e-participation, privacy, cybersecurity and health emergency communication. She created a new track named "Cybersecurity and Government" in the Digital Government Conference 2017 and serves as a track chair.

**Natalie Greene Taylor** is assistant professor at the University of South Florida. She has a bachelor's degree in political science and received both her master of library science and her PhD in information studies from the University of Maryland. Her research broadly focuses on young people's access to information. More specifically, she studies youth information behavior, information intermediaries and information policy as it affects youth information access. Taylor also serves as an associate editor of *Library Quarterly* and has co-authored two books, *Digital Literacy and Digital Inclusion: Information Policy and the Public Library* and *Libraries, Human Rights, and Social Justice: Enabling Access and Promoting Inclusion*.

**Kristene Unsworth**, moderator, is visiting assistant professor in computer science and information systems at Stockton University. She has a bachelor's degree in comparative history and German, and MLIS and PhD degrees in information science, all from the University of Washington. Her research interests and teaching expertise are in the areas of ethics, information policy, government information and the sociotechnical aspects of information interaction. She has conducted research on the use of social categorization in national security policy in historical, international and contemporary contexts. Current projects include an NSF-funded project *Ethics of Algorithms* which examines the values individuals and teams have when designing algorithms that are used in data mining.

## REFERENCES


Anderson, M., & Olmstead K. (2017). Many smartphone owners don't take steps to secure their devices. Pew Research Center. Retrieved April 28 from www.pewresearch.org/fact-tank/2017/03/15/many-smartphone-owners-dont-take-steps-to-secure-their-devices/

Cha, A.E. (2015, May 9). The revolution will be digitized. *Washington Post*. Retrieved April 25 from www.washingtonpost.com/sf/national/2015/05/09/the-revolution-will-be-digitized/?utm_term=.e6f335c12869

CSI Insight. (2016). Wearables momentum continues. Retrieved April 30 from www.ccsinsight.com/press/ company-news/2516-wearables-momentum-continues

Dincelli, E., & Zhou, X. (2017). Examining self-disclosure on wearable devices: The roles of benefit structure and privacy calculus. *Proceedings of 23rd Americas Conference on Information Systems 2017*. Boston, MA.

Dinev, T., & Hart, P. (2006). An extended privacy calculus model for e-commerce transactions. *Information Systems Research 17*(1), 61-80.

Kellogg, S. (2016). Every breath you take: Data privacy and your wearable fitness device. *J. Mo. B.*, *72*, 6-76.

Montgomery, K.C., Chester, J., & Kopp, K. (2016). Health wearable devices in the big data era: Ensuring privacy security, and consumer protection. *Center for Digital Democracy, American University*. Retrieved April 9 from www.democraticmedia.org/sites/default/files/field/ public/2016/aucdd_wearablesreport_final121516.pdf

Petronio, S. 2002. *Boundaries of privacy*. Albany, NY: State University of New York Press.

Raij, A., Ghosh, A., Kumar, S., & Srivastava, M. (2011, May). Privacy risks emerging from the adoption of innocuous wearable sensors in the mobile environment. In *Proceedings of the SIGCHI Conference on Human Factors in Computing Systems* (pp. 11-20). Vancouver, BC, Canada.

Wartella, E., Rideout, V., Montague, H., Beaudoin-Ryan, L., & Lauricella, A. (2016). Teens, health and technology: A national survey. *Media and Communication*, *4*(3).

# In Between Data Sharing and Reuse: Shareability, Availability and Reusability in Diverse Contexts

**Ayoung Yoon**
*Indiana University Purdue University Indianapolis, USA.*
*ayyoon@iupui.edu*

**Wei Jeng**
*National Taiwan University, Taiwan. wjeng@ntu.edu.tw*

**Renata Curty**
*Universidade Estadual de Londrina, Brazil.*
*renatacurty@uel.br*

**Angela Murillo**
*Indiana University Purdue University Indianapolis, USA.*
*apmurill@iu.ed*

## ABSTRACT

**Although data availability cannot be considered the sole predictor of effective reuse, because only accessible and well-managed data can make reuse possible, data reuse is contingent on the availability of data. It is critical to understand the nature of shareability, availability and reusability, and their synergy and relationships, to further understand the dynamics of data reuse practices in multiple environments and contexts.**

**This panel aims to closely examine aspects related to data shareability, availability and reusability, based on the assumption that each condition poses a cumulative effect on each other and impacts the efficiency and efficacy of the research data reuse process. The panelists will present their findings and perspectives regarding data availability, between academic and non-academic; data shareability and data reusability, social sciences and earth science, researchers' and journal publishers' perspectives. Presentations will be followed by an interactive session taking the team-based approach, with the expectation to engage participants in discussion and experience-sharing, and to contribute in terms of practice and research with the current knowledge and applications.**

## KEYWORDS

research data, data availability, data reuse, data sharing, reusability, data curation

## INTRODUCTION

The potential for data reuse to impact scientific research and help solve many social problems is increasingly recognized. Research data reuse can only be accomplished through data sharing and availability (Hey, Tansely & Tolle, 2009) and has immediate and long-term benefits to discovery and innovation, including the ability to extract additional value from data, ask new questions of existing data, reexamine existing scientific theories and models, and to enable reproducible research (Borgman, 2012). On this note, Fabic, Choi, & Bird (2012) demonstrate how increased availability and proliferated data stimulate peer- reviewed research as well as evidence-based policy and program development.

There is little discussion about how data producers and reusers handling data shareability, availability and reusability outside of the context of higher education institutions, research centers and laboratories. The availability of data, the ability and motivation to share data and reuse data has increased significantly with the proliferation of data repositories and infrastructures dedicated to house data for further reuse. It is thus critical to understand their synergy and relationships, to further understand the dynamics of data practices in multiple environments and contexts.

This panel aims to closely examine aspects related to research data shareability, availability and reusability, based on the assumption that each condition poses a cumulative effect on each other and impacts on the efficiency and efficacy of the data reuse process – the desired outcome of data sharing endeavors.

## RESEARCH DATA SHAREABILITY, AVAILABILITY AND REUSABILITY

Even though data availability cannot be considered the sole predictor of effective reuse, because only accessible and well-managed data can make reuse possible, data reuse is contingent on the availability of data. In other words, ample and improved data availability acts as a key precondition for ultimate reuse. It is important to pinpoint, though, that not all data are shareable and, therefore, cannot be easily made available. The degree of shareability is established taking into account legal, ethical and technical aspects with regard to the nature of data. For example, sharing data involving vulnerable populations – such as minors, survivors of domestic violence or subordinates in the workplace – without proper de-identification or anonymization may face negative consequences if identities are disclosed (Kaiser, 2009).

Rarely studies on data reuse formally define the term *data availability* or unfold its attributes. Data availability can be understood as the state or property of data being handy

80th Annual Meeting of the Association for Information Science & Technology, Washington, DC, VA | Oct. 27-Nov. 1, 2017

and ready for use. However, *availability* and *accessibility* cannot be used interchangeably. Different aspects of data have to be considered to make data available and ultimately accessible. Borrowing from the definition in the context of information technology and management (Techopedia, n.d.), we understand data availability as the process of ensuring that data are available to end-users in a timely fashion, to the degree that the data are readily and continuously usable by the necessary management procedures, infrastructure, technologies and policies.

Along these lines, data availability involves different aspects to consider, and the data cannot be reliably available by individuals in a long term (Vines et al., 2010). Different stakeholders, such as regulatory parties, funding agencies, journal editors and repository managers, have shown their concerns on the data's public availability (e.g., Alsheikh-Ali, Qureshi, Al-Mallah & Ioannidis, 2011; Guttmacher, Nabel & Collins, 2009; Godlee, 2009; Sommer, 2010). This shows that various factors and conditions influence data availability, not just researchers' attitudes on data sharing. Other influential factors include ethical and legal concerns, federal regulations, journal policies, management procedures and access restrictions of proprietary data.

While data availability is a prerequisite for potential reuse and a condition which can be controlled by data providers, data reusability, that is, the degree to which data are capable of being reused in a given context and to fit a given purpose (Faniel & Jacobsen, 2010; Curty, 2015), involves an evaluation process from the reuser perspective. Not only should data conform to some quality attributes in order to be considered reusable, but it also must fit a purpose of interest. Thus, reusability can be only appraised from the potential reuser perspective, who will juxtapose best judgment about the attributes of the available data to their reuse intention/purpose.

## PANELIST AND TOPICS

### *Topic 1: Data availability for community data reusers*

**Ayoung Yoon** is an assistant professor at the School of Informatics and Computing at Indiana University Indianapolis (IUPUI). She is also a RDA/US Data Share fellow for 2016-2017. Her research areas include data curation, data sharing/reuse and open data practices. She is particularly interested in constructing effective cyberinfrastructure for data sharing and reuse through proper curation and preservation practices. Currently she is conducting several research projects focusing on communities' needs of data sharing, reuse and curation.

Her presentation in this panel will focus on the issue of data availability for community data reusers. The potential for data to help address current societal problems (e.g., education, health, economic development, environment) is significant not only at the federal and state levels but also in smaller communities, neighborhoods and individual lives. While the proposition for this potential is that data are and will be shared with and reused by and for communities at different levels, many data are not systematically or routinely shared for reuse with communities, particularly data collected by university and research institutes. From her recent research project that investigated community members' data practices in a small city in the Midwest, she will discuss the challenges associated with community members' data reuse focusing on data availability issues with their strategies to access and utilize data for their community development. Because community members' data needs and reuse practices are different from scientists, her findings will broaden the scope of discussion on data availability.

### *Topic 2: Before making data available: Handling data involving vulnerable populations*

**Wei Jeng** is assistant professor at the Department of Library and Information Science, National Taiwan University. She completed her PhD studies at the School of Information Sciences (iSchool), University of Pittsburgh. Her dissertation study investigates social scientists' data-sharing practices, especially those dealing with qualitative data (Jeng, 2017).

Given the increasing need for academic communities to manage an enormous amount of data, her long-term research goal is to provide insights for improving research infrastructure for scholars in all disciplines, particularly the social sciences, humanities and related scholarly communities.

In this panel, Jeng will share her research findings and perspectives on two aspects:

***The tension between data shareability and confidentiality concerns regarding qualitative data***. Jeng will report her findings regarding a group of social scientists' qualitative data-sharing practices, especially for those who handle sensitive data or un-shareable data.

***The best practices for managing research data involving vulnerable populations***. Jeng will share her proposed strategies for handling research data with minors, using a research project she has worked as an example. The research project explores teens' data awareness and involves interview and observation data with young people between the ages of 6 and 17 (Bowler, Acker, Jeng & Chi, 2017).

### *Topic 3: Data reusability for earth and environmental science data reusers*

**Angela P. Murillo** is a visiting assistant professor at the School of Informatics and Computing at Indiana University Indianapolis (IUPUI). Her dissertation research investigated facilitators and inhibitors of data sharing and data reuse in the context of earth and environmental sciences and newly developing infrastructures. Additionally, she has completed research in scientific data management, metadata for data science and science data curation. Her research areas include scientific data management, scientific data cyberinfrastructure and reuse and sharing.

In this panel, Murillo will present findings from a qualitative study, which identified facilitators and inhibitors of data reuse among earth and environmental scientists. This study addresses these questions: how do scientists determine data reusability and what information inhibits or facilitates data reusability. Murillo will discuss what information scientists need about the data to determine reusability, as well as what inhibits and/or facilitates data reusability. Murillo will describe how scientists evaluate data to determine reusability. Finally, she will provide guidance on best practices for ensuring reusability of shared data.

### *Topic 4: Amplifying data availability through enhanced publications*

**Renata Curty** is an assistant professor in the Information Science Department at the State University of Londrina (Universidade Estadual de Londrina), in Southern Brazil. Her research relates to scholarly communication, data curation and research data reuse. Her current research project focuses on how technological affordances influence and shape data reuse intentions and behaviors among scientists.

In this panel Curty will present findings of an ongoing study on enhanced publications and their role on effective data reuse. She will start by introducing different approaches to make research data systematically available and accessible to a broader audience, taking into account different levels of ties research data may have with the original research and its outputs, as well as with related research. Then, she will discuss how each of these approaches is expected to facilitate, more or less, one or more data reuse purposes (i.e., aggregation, integration, meta-analysis, replication, repurposing and synthesis). Later, the presentation will focus on preliminary results of an analysis of enhanced scientific journals, in quest of answering the following questions: What technological affordances and policy strategies enhanced journals usually adopt in order to make data available? What are the common challenges and limitations such journals face in order to promote data availability?

## Expected Contributions

The panel aims to bring different perspectives on research data shareability, availability and reusability, also taking into account multiple data sharing-reuse contexts, within and beyond the traditional scientific fields (i.e., universities and other research institutions). The topics covered by the panelists will include accessibility, ethics and policy, technology and discipline practices. The panel also expects attendees to speak about the experiences and challenges of handling the availability of their own data or the data they have reused. Our contributions will be two-fold. In terms of research, we aim to contribute to conceptualizing terms that are still poorly defined in the literature (i.e., data shareability, availability and reusability), which will bring a richer and more diverse discussion to the current data sharing and reuse research. In terms of practice, we expect this panel to be valuable to librarians, policymakers, open data advocates and data repository stakeholders to reflect on community data reusers, scientific data reusers, vulnerable populations and infrastructure and policy requirements. This will serve as a foundation to build more sustainable data infrastructures and facilitate data openness.

## Panel's Structure

The structure of the proposed panel is as follows:

### *Introduction (5 minutes)*

Introduce the panel theme, core definitions, purposes and objectives of the panel.

### *Presentations (30 minutes)*

The panelists (Yoon, Jeng, Murillo, and Curty) will present their individual research projects and empirical findings.

### *Q&A session (10 minutes)*

We will host an open Q&A session about panel presentations and discussion.

### *Interactive Session (40 minutes)*

The interactive session will be moderated by Curty and follow the team-based learning approach, which consists of a three-step cycle: 1) preparation, 2) readiness assurance testing and 3) application-focused exercise.

***Preparation***. The first step will be covered by presenters, where panelists will briefly introduce or recap the aspects related to data shareability, availability and reusability.

***Readiness assurance testing***. This stage will be approached in two parts. First, a set of questions based on real-life and controversial situations will be handed to each participant. These questions will be based on key themes and core concepts covered in the presentations. Second, participants will be grouped to discuss the questions and their answers, with the goal to collectively agree upon the best answer.

***Application-focused exercise***. In the third and final stage, the moderator will go through each of the questions and discuss them. Then, participants will propose, in groups, possible strategies and alternatives for solving or handling situations regarding data shareability, availability and reusability. The ultimate goal of this interactive session is to promote individual metacognition, as well as stimulate discussion, and engage participants on experience sharing about controversial topics and real-life situations practitioners and researchers may encounter on a daily basis.

### *Wrap-Up (5 minutes)*

Debriefing and wrapping up the topic with all attendees.

## REFERENCES


Alsheikh-Ali, A. A., Qureshi, W., Al-Mallah, M. H., & Ioannidis, J. P. (2011). Public availability of published research data in high-impact journals. *PloS one, 6*(9), e24357.

Borgman, C. L. (2012). The conundrum of sharing research data. *Journal of the American Society for Information Science and Technology, 63*(6), 1059–1078.

Bowler, L., Acker, A., Jeng, W., & Chi, Y. (2017). "It lives all around us": Aspects of data literacy in teen's lives. In the *Proceedings of ASIS&T 2017 Annual Meeting.*

Curty, R. G. (2015). Beyond "data thrifting": An investigation of factors influencing research data. Unpublished doctoral dissertation. Syracuse University. Retrieved from http://surface.syr.edu/cgi/ viewcontent.cgi?article=1266&context=etd

Fabic, M. S., Choi, Y., & Bird, S. (2012). A systematic review of demographic and health surveys: Data availability and utilization for research. *Bulletin of the World Health Organization, 90*(8), 604–612.

Faniel, I. M. & Jacobsen, T. E. (2010). Reusing scientific data: How earthquake engineering researchers assess the reusability of colleagues' data. *Computer Supported Cooperative Work, 19*(3), 355-375.

Godlee F. (2009) We want raw data, now. *BMJ* 339: b5405.F.

Guttmacher, A. E., Nabel, E. G., & Collins, F. S. (2009). Why data-sharing policies matter. *PNAS 106*(40) 16894.

Hey, A. J. G., Tansley, S. & Tolle, K. M. (2009). Redmond, WA: Microsoft Research.

Jeng, W. (2017). Qualitative data sharing practices in social sciences. Unpublished doctoral dissertation. University of Pittsburgh. Retrieved from http://d- scholarship.pitt.edu/id/eprint/31728

Kaiser, K. (2009). Protecting respondent confidentiality in qualitative research. *Qualitative Health Research, 19*(11), 1632-1641.

Sommer, J (2010) The delay in sharing research data is costing lives. *Nat Med* 16: 744.J.

Techopedia. (n.d.) Data Availability. Retrieved from https://www.techopedia.com/definition/14678/data- availability

Vines, T. H., Albert, A. Y. K., Andrew, R. L., Débarre, F., Bock, D. G., Franklin, M. T., … Rennison, D. J. (2014). The availability of research data declines rapidly with article age. *Current Biology, 24*(1), 94–97.

# Standards and Best Practices Related to the Publication, Exchange and Usage of Open Data


**Marcia Lei Zeng**
*Kent State University, USA. mzeng@kent.edu*

**Marjorie Hlava**
*Access Innovations, USA. mhlava@accessinn.com*

**Jane Greenberg**
*Drexel University, USA. jg3243@drexel.edu*

**Mark Needleman**
*ASIS&T Standards Committee Co-chair, USA.*
*needleman_mark@yahoo.com*



## ABSTRACT

**The panel aims to update ASIS&T members and information professionals about important standards, specifications and best practice guidelines that have been developed or initiated by the international standards institutions and communities in dealing with open data. The openness and flexibility of the web have created both new opportunities and new challenges for data publishers and data consumers, such as how to represent, describe and make data available (by publishers) in a way that it will be easily found, understood, used and re-used (by consumers). The panelists will introduce related standards, bring insight to the adoption and implementation of new standards, comment on success and progress in the realm of certain areas such as research data, data on the web (in terms of publishing, annotation and use), metadata in for special domains (such as electronic health records, space debris and genealogical archives) and look at the raising questions and issues. Using the chart from the 2017-01 W3C recommendations, Data on the Web Best Practices, as context for the panel's presentations, the benchmarks to be used by the panel include the comprehension, processability, discoverability, reuse possibility and effectiveness, trust, linkability, accessibility and interoperability.**



## KEYWORDS

data standards, data best practices, research data, metadata, data on the web, data publishing, data reuse, open data, data consuming


## PANELISTS AND PRESENTATIONS

Short biographies and presentation descriptions are listed below. The presenters have played important roles in the area of standards for data and information for many years and are serving at various standards committees at community, national and international institutions.

## PRESENTATIONS

The openness and flexibility of the web have created both new opportunities and new challenges for data publishers and data consumers, such as how to represent, describe and make data available (by publishers) in a way that it will be easily found, understood, used and re-used (by consumers). Many of us perform dual roles as data publisher and data consumer, witnessing the increased attention to data sharing, re-use, re-purposing and reproducible computation research. Yet challenges can be found in any part of the open data ecosystem, including metadata, data licenses, data provenance, data quality, data versioning, data identification, data formats, data vocabularies, data access and APIs, data preservation, feedback, data enrichment and data republication. Added to the mix is the larger context of big data and data science, where scientific data can serve as an important resource.

The panel aims to update ASIS&T members and information professionals about important standards, specifications and best practice guidelines that have been developed or initiated by the international standards institution ISO, the World Wide Web Consortium (W3C), communities such as the Research Data Alliance (RDA), the International Image Interoperability Framework (IIIF) Consortium (IIIF-C), the Semantic Interoperability Community (SEMIC) and more.

In addition to introducing standards and best practices, the panelists will bring insight to the adoption and implementation of new standards, comment on success and progress in the realm of certain areas, such as research data, data on the web (in terms of publishing, annotation and use), metadata in for special domains (such as electronic health records, space debris and genealogical archives), while also raising questions and issues, including working with data sharing in not-always-open environments. The panel plans to generate discussion vital to assessing effective developments and implementations of standards.

The panel uses the following chart from the 2017-01 W3C recommendations, Data on the Web Best Practices, as context for the areas we would like to address; here a resource may be a whole dataset or a specific item of a given dataset. The benchmarks to be used by the panel include comprehension, processability, discoverability, reuse possibility and effectiveness, trust, linkability, accessibility and interoperability, mainly based on the benefits introduced in the W3C Recommendations.


80th Annual Meeting of the Association for Information Science & Technology, Washington, DC, VA | Oct. 27-Nov. 1, 2017

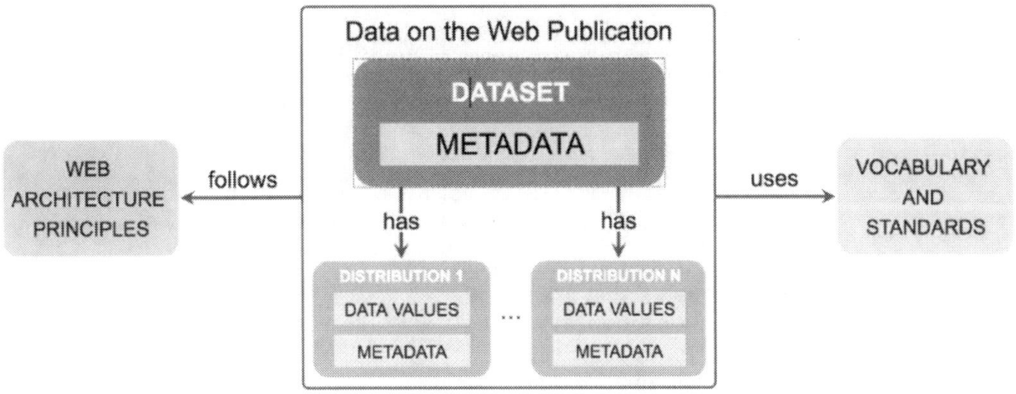


***Figure 1**. The context considered in the Best Practices proposed for publication and usage of Data on the Web. Source: Data on the Web Best Practices, W3C Recommendation 31 January 2017. https://www.w3.org/TR/dwbp/*

## PANELISTS

Short biographies below are arranged in order of presentation.

**Mark Needleman** is the co-chair of the ASIS&T standards committee. He has worked for the University of California's MELVYL project, library automation vendors Data Research Associates (DRA) and Sirsi Corporation and the Florida Center for Library Automation. He has been involved in several standards organizations such as NISO (National Information Standards Organization), ANSI (American National Standards Institute), ISO (International Standards Organization), the W3C (Worldwide Web Consortium), the Unicode Consortium and the IETF (Internet Engineering Taskforce). Among other things, he has been involved with the development of the Z39.50 protocol, the ISO ILL protocol, NCIP (NISO Circulation Interchange Protocol), the NISO OpenURL Standard and the W3C XML Query Language.

**Jane Greenberg** is the Alice B. Kroeger Professor and director of the Metadata Research Center (MRC) at the College of Computing & Informatics, Drexel University. Her research activities focus on metadata, knowledge organization/semantics, Linked Data, and data science. She serves on the advisory board for the Dublin Core Metadata Initiative (DCMI) and the steering committee for the NSF Northeast Big Data Innovation Hub (NEBDIH). She is the PI for the HIVE (Helping Interdisciplinary Vocabulary Engineering) Linked Data initiative, a PI for the NEBDIH "A Licensing Model and Ecosystem for Data Sharing" initiative and a co-PI for the NSF I/UCRC Center for Visualization and Decision Informatics (CVDI). She has been involved in metadata activities of the Research Data Alliance (RDA) and number of national and global metadata activities addressing scientific research data.

**Marcia L. Zeng** is a professor in the School of Information at Kent State University. Her major research interests include knowledge organization structures and systems (KOS), linked data, metadata and markup languages, database quality control, multilingual and multicultural information processing and digital humanities. Her research projects have received funding from the NSF, IMLS, OCLC, Fulbright and other foundations. She has chaired and served on standards committees and working groups for IFLA, SLA, ASIS&T, NISO and ISO. She served as a working group member of the ISO 25964 Thesauri and Interoperability with Other Vocabularies. She was an invited expert of the W3C Linked Library Data Incubator Group and the Asset Description Metadata Schema (ADMS) of the European Union. Currently she is serving as an executive board member of the International Society for Knowledge Organization (ISKO).

**Marjorie Hlava** is president, chairman and founder of Access Innovations, Inc. She is past president of both NFAIS and ASIS&T and the recipient of the ASIS&T 1996 Watson Davis Award and the ASIS&T 2014 Award of Merit. She is the author of multiple books and over 200 articles, including her newest publication, The Taxobook, a three-volume collection on the history and implementation of taxonomies. She holds two U.S. patents encompassing 21 patent claims. Her research areas include furthering the productivity of content creation and the governance layer for information access through automated indexing, thesaurus development, taxonomy creation, natural language processing, machine translations and machine- aided indexing. She is a popular speaker on topics involving information organization, semantic enrichment and taxonomy and thesaurus creation.

## REFERENCES

Data on the Web Best Practices, W3C Recommendation 31 January 2017. https://www.w3.org/TR/dwbp/

International Image Interoperability Framework (IIIF) community, http://iiif.io/community/

Research Data Alliance (RDA), https://www.rd-alliance.org/node

Semantic Interoperability Community (SEMIC), https://joinup.ec.europa.eu/community/semic/description

# Using Virtual Reality to Counter Extremism

**Waseem Afzal**
*School of Information Studies, Charles Sturt University, Australia. wafzal@csu.edu.au*

**Andrew Hagan**
*School of Communication and Creative Industries, Charles Sturt University, Australia. ahagan@csu.edu.au*

## ABSTRACT

**Extremism presents a significant danger to safe and healthy environment of communities. In recent times, some extremist groups are treacherously using informational content to influence public perception. More seriously, these groups are targeting youth using religiously significant terms described with distorted interpretations. The discourse of these groups presents a romanticized view of destruction, trivializes loss of life and breeds hatred to anyone adhering to a different set of values. These extremist groups pose three important risks to communities: (1) influencing public perception and gaining silent sympathizers, (2) creating a sense of us versus them which then leads to discord and identity conflicts and (3) radicalizing and/or recruiting youth. This research presents a digital prototype developed in a 3D-environment, based on research concerning informational and affective properties of extremists' content, with an objective to educate youth against extremism.**

## KEYWORDS

information, information behavior, virtual reality, extremism

## INTRODUCTION

Extremism is not a new phenomenon; individuals and groups with extremist leanings have always been present. What is new and different in our times is the ubiquity of information networks, digital devices and social media affordances that amplify the affective, emotional and behavioral implications of any informational message. Realizing the presence of this leverage, extremist groups have started using these networks and associated affordances to advance their totalitarian designs. More recently, these networks have been used by extremist groups to influence public perception and to recruit foreign fighters. This research presents a digital prototype involving a scenario where a recruiter from an extremist organization identifies a vulnerable teen and tries to instill in this teen feelings of identity conflict and to create a belief centered around an "us versus them" dichotomy. This prototype will inform counter-extremism efforts engaging youth by using virtual reality.

## METHODOLOGY

The research problem in this study was addressed by developing a scenario using role playing. Role playing has been extensively used in organisation research to understand attitudes, behavior and basic psychological processes such as perception, cognition and judgment (Greenberg & Eskew, 1993). To develop this scenario, content of an extremist group (ISIS) was analysed. The content analysis was done to (1) identify themes in the data and (2) assess qualitative properties of information. Qualitative properties (e.g., balanced, accurate, consistent) of the selected information were assessed based on the works of Knight and Burn (2005) and Lee et al. (2002).

To start with, the current issue of Dabiq - ISIS's Magazine (issue number 13) and three of its news bulletins (March 7-March 9, 2016) were analysed. This data was content analysed to identify major themes and important terms. The terms were identified based on theological/religious and emotional/affective dimensions (see table 1 for examples). Furthermore, some terms were identified based on their function to describe an event, qualify an action and usually also including an affective component. Work of Ortony, Clore and Foss (1987) was used to identify terms with affective and emotional connotations.

The identified terms were then used to develop a script for the scenario where one character acted as a recruiter and the other character responded as a teen who somehow got in touch with the first character. The teen in this scenario was depicted as someone who is lost and struggling in life. The recruiter is someone who takes notice of vulnerable teens and attempts to create internal conflict in teens' psyche by inciting us versus them mentality.

For 3D visualization following six steps were followed:

- Concept/script development with actors
- Full-body motion and facial performance capture
- Translation of motion into digital characters
- Live and post-production animation work on virtual performances
- Rendered animation in sync with original audio
- Playback to multiple formats

| Terms | Theological / Religious | Emotional / Affective |
|---|---|---|
| 1 | Shahaada | Terrorizing |
| 2 | Murtaddin | Shamelessly |
| 3 | Mushrikin | Desperate |
| 4 | Hijrah | Love |
| 5 | Ummah | Mock |

***Table 1.** Examples of identified terms*

80th Annual Meeting of the Association for Information Science & Technology, Washington, DC | Oct. 27-Nov. 1, 2017

During modelling, professional photogrammetry software was trialled to develop a technique of digitising real people from high-resolution still and video imagery. Rapid development in the creation of 3D avatars was achieved from hand-held video footage using a GoPro Hero 5 Black.

The decision was made to move away from a photorealistic depiction of an existing person and design a generalised 3D-model without focusing on any particular ethnicity. Issues regarding the representation of marginalized groups led to the development of an interchangeable character framework to minimise the potential for stereotypes (Shaw, 2010). This requires the custom creation of original geometry or generating meshes from pre-existing baseline models.

***Figure 1**. Motion capture session with actors with real-time preview on projector*

Motion capture sessions were recorded with two actors and offered a real-time preview of their movements (Figure 1). The live data was mapped to full-body skeletons (Figure 2) in Autodesk Motion-Builder and provided ample evidence of a working pre-visualisation pipeline. Faceware Technologies Inc. (Faceware Technologies, n.d) provided the most accurate and consistent results for detailed facial capture. The Live client and AutoTrack features were trialled but proved unreliable due to extreme poses and/or changed lighting conditions. The decision was made to render digital characters in post-production in preference to live performance (Figure 3).

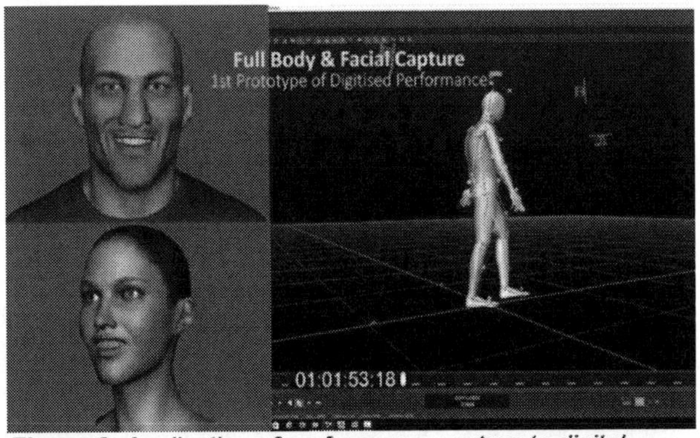


***Figure 2**. Application of performance capture to digital characters*

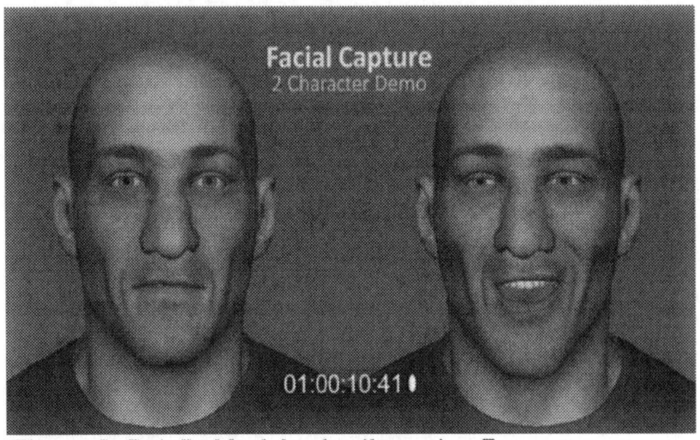


***Figure 3**. Detailed facial animation using Faceware Technologies*

## CONCLUSION

This research identified some terms used by extremist groups and used role playing to propose a digital prototype in 3D environment. This prototype will be further enhanced using different scenarios and used in educating youth against extremism.


## FUNDING

This research was funded by a grant from the Faculty of Arts and Education Compacts Funding-Charles Sturt University, Australia.

## ACKNOWLEDGEMENTS

We want to thank Dominique Sweeney and Robert Lewis for their acting in the scenario.


## REFERENCES


Faceware Technologies. Available at http://facewaretech.com/

Greenberg, J., & Eskew, D. E. (1993). The role of role playing in organizational research. Journal of Management, 19(2), 221-241.

Knight, S-A., & Burn, J. (2005). Developing a framework for assessing information quality on the World Wide Web. Information Science Journal, 8, 160-172.

Lee, Y. W., Strong, D. M., Kahn, B. K., & Wang, R. Y. (2002). AIMQ: A methodology for information quality assessment. Information & Management, 40, 133-146.

Ortony, A., Clore, G. L., & Foss, M. A. (1987). The psychological foundations of affective lexicon. Journal of Personality and Social Psychology, 53, 751-766.

Shaw, A. (2010). Toward an ethic of representation: Ethics and the representation of marginalized groups in videogames. In K. Schrier & D. Gibson (Eds.), Designing Games for Ethics: Models, Techniques and Frameworks (pp. 159-176).

# Information Behavior in the Technology Transfer Process

**Grant Allard**
*Policy Studies Program, Clemson University. USA: gallard@clemson.edu*

**Suzie Allard**
*School of Information Sciences, University of Tennessee, USA. sallard@utk.edu*

## ABSTRACT

**Technology transfer is a vital part of knowledge creation. It is the "process of transferring scientific findings from one organization to another for the purpose of further development and commercialization" (AUTM, 2016). Technology transfer enhances society by allowing universities and national laboratories to contribute to economic development. This visual presentation presents a brief history of information science's study of technology transfer and introduces the Technology Transfer Information Intermediary (T2I2) Model. The T2I2 provides a framework for identifying and understanding information behavior related to technology transfer. The poster also includes a mechanism to dialog with the researchers.**

## KEYWORDS

information behavior, technology transfer, information ethics, user-centered systems

## INTRODUCTION

In the United States, universities and federal national laboratories each create new knowledge and cutting-edge technologies. One desired outcome from these activities is to commercialize the value of the knowledge and technology created at these institutions. *Technology transfer*, a term which is often used interchangeably with technology or research commercialization, is the "process of transferring scientific findings from one organization to another for the purpose of further development and commercialization" (AUTM, 2016). Technology transfer allows universities and national labs to contribute to regional and local economic development, in addition to improving the human condition (Bozeman, 2000; Council, 2011; Matkin, 1997; NSF, 2016). In the technology transfer process, a research organization exchanges the right to information and the right to use the knowledge or technology to a licensee, who will, in return, pay for the information and develop a commercial use for the technology. This exchange is an important arena for further investigation by information scientists. Information science has a history of studying technology transfer dating back to the 1980s, when technology transfer typically referred to the process of diffusing innovations across national borders, in the corpus of information science literature (Backer, 1993; Dosa, 1985; Eres, 1981; Frame & Baum, 1978; Mendelsohn, 1992; Veith, 1980). Our work acknowledges this rich foundation, but it is based on the construct of technology transfer as it has been referenced since the early 2000s, which is more focused on the process of commercializing research.

## IS AND TECHNOLOGY TRANSFER

Information science's rigorous methodology that tracks and links flows of information through bibliographic analysis, and the theoretical models describing the diffusion of innovation, have provided a vital framework for technology transfer study. Information science scholars have approached technology transfer – in the research commercialization frame – from four perspectives. First, a small subset of information science scholars have investigated the ethical implications of how scholars use information in university technology transfer (Carbo & Smith, 2008; Froehlich, 1991). Second, information science scholars have investigated technology transfer using bibliometric analyses to explore the relationship between publishing research and patenting the knowledge and technology from that research (Bornmann, 2017; Desouza, 2008; Leydesdorff, 2004; Leydesdorff & Rafols, 2011; Orduna-Malea, Thelwall, & Kousha, 2017; Su, 2012). Third, information science scholars have also investigated how innovation diffuses across national boundaries using geospatial analyses (Leydesdorff & Ahrweiler, 2014; Leydesdorff & Bornmann, 2012; Su, 2012). This vein of literature includes a focus on university-industry linkages using the "triple helix model" of innovation (Choi, Yang, & Park, 2015; Swar & Khan, 2013; Ye, Yu & Leydesdorff, 2013). Fourth, researchers examined how collaborations between scholars from different disciplines impact the outcomes of funded research (Jaffe & Rassenfosse, 2017; Orduna-Malea et al., 2017).

## T2I2: INFORMATION BEHAVIOR AND TECH TRANSFER

We believe these four approaches provide the foundation for a fifth area of study which explores the information behavior of inventors, licensees and technology transfer professionals during the technology transfer process. We are developing the Technology Transfer Information Intermediary (T2I2) Model to provide a framework for identifying and understanding these behaviors and the relationship to the information lifecycle, the data lifecycle (Allard, 2012) and policy. The T2I2 model provides the ability to integrate the information/data/policy perspectives in order to better address three substantial technology transfer challenges expressed with the following research questions. First, how can the technology transfer process be designed to overcome the institutional structure that creates information asymmetry during the exchange of information between research organizations and licensees (Kodama, 2008; Yusuf, 2008)? Second, how can we

80th Annual Meeting of the Association for Information Science & Technology, Washington, DC | Oct. 27-Nov. 1, 2017

address the ethical and moral questions related to professional roles of the people involved in technology transfer? These include issues related to conflict of interest (Bastedo, 2009; Hasselmo, 2002; Matkin, 1997), the ability of technology to be used for both good and bad purposes (Dubov, 2014; Miller & Selgelid, 2007) and the process of turning information into property (Allard, 2016). Third, what are the information flows within university technology transfer? Currently these are not well researched and there is a figurative "black box" obscuring how information is transferred and used.

In addition to the information science foundation noted above, the T2I2 Model is informed by role morality theory (Wueste, 1994). Role morality theory is a framework for analyzing and resolving ethical challenges that arise due to conflict of interest and information asymmetry, frequently found in technology transfer transactions. A role morality is a set of duties and responsibilities that one accepts to uphold the integrity of the institution (Wueste, 1994). This framework guides how people create, use and share information when there are competing moral claims of equal gravity during a conflict of interest or transaction.

## CONCLUSION

Utilizing the T2I2 Model to investigate the information behavior of people involved in the technology transfer process adds a useful dimension to technology transfer scholarship. Currently there is an understanding of what is legal, but there is a gap in understanding the information behavior of technology transfer actors and an understanding of the ethics associated with it (Hayter & Rooksby, 2016).

The T2I2 model provides a framework for expanding the study of the technology transfer process. Results of T2I2 model-based studies can provide a basis to inform the information behaviors of practitioners. They may also inform national research policy to help researchers and policymakers work better together on translating basic and applied research into an economic impact. By providing explicit understanding of the roles and interactions of different actors in the technology transfer process, the T2I2 model could (1) help higher-education policymakers improve the innovation ecosystem so researchers can more effectively create new knowledge and technology that improves our world and (2) help higher-education policymakers make policies that facilitate the career development of researchers. Overall, the focus is on understanding the process of technology transfer in order to provide a more efficient and effective process, which has important economic and national defense implications.

## WHAT YOU WILL SEE; WHAT WE ASK OF YOU!

Our visual presentation is anchored by a poster that provides a timeline presentation of technology transfer research, highlights the critical research questions and introduces the T2I2 model. The poster includes a means to dialog with us by providing comments and feedback using media both on-site and through social media.

## REFERENCES


Allard, G.A. (2016). The four ethical principles of university technology transfer. Under review.

Allard, S. (2012). The data life cycle & information professionals. Third Annual ASIST Research Data Access and Preservation Summit. New Orleans, LA. 21 March 2012.

AUTM (Association of University Technology Managers). (2016). About technology transfer. Retrieved June 14, 2017 from http://www.autm.net/autm-info/about-tech-transfer/about-technology-transfer/

Backer, T.E. (1993). Information alchemy: Transforming information through knowledge utilization. *Journal of the American Society for Information Science 44*(4), 217-221. doi:10.1002/(SICI)1097-4571(199305)44:4<217::AID-ASI9>3.0.CO;2-D

Bastedo, M.N. (2009). Conflicts, commitments, and cliques in the university: Moral seducation as a threat to trustee independence. *American Educational Research Journal 46*(2), 354-386.

Bornmann, L. (2017). Is collaboration among scientists related to the citation impact of papers because their quality increases with collaboration? An analysis based on data from F1000Prime and normalized citation scores. *Journal of the Association for Information Science and Technology 68*(4), 1036-1047. doi:10.1002/asi.23728

Bozeman, B. (2000). Technology transfer and public policy: A review of research and theory. *Research Policy 29*, 627-655.

Carbo, T., & Smith, M.M. (2008). Global information ethics: Intercultural perspectives on past and future research. *Journal of the American Society for Information Science and Technology 59*(7), 1111-1123. doi:10.1002/asi.20851

Choi, S., Yang, J.S., & Park, H.W. (2015). The triple helix and international collaboration in science. *Journal of the Association for Information Science and Technology 66*(1), 201-212. doi:10.1002/asi.23165

Council, N.R. (2011). *Managing university intellectual property in the public interest*. Washington, D.C.: The National Academy Press.

Desouza, K.C. (2008). Advancing knowledge and the knowledge economy. *Journal of the American Society for Information Science and Technology 59*(2), 331-333. doi:10.1002/asi.20741

Dosa, M.L. (1985). Information transfer as technical assistance for development. *Journal of the American Society for Information Science 36*(3), 146-152. doi:10.1002/asi.4630360304

Dubov, A. (2014). The concept of dual-use research. *Medicine, Health Care, and Philosophy 17*, 447-457.

Eres, B.K. (1981). Transfer of information technology to less developed countries: A systems approach. *Journal of the American Society for Information Science 32*(2), 97-102. doi:10.1002/asi.4630320204

Frame, J.D., & Baum, J.J. (1978). Cross-national information flows in basic research: Examples taken from physics. *Journal of the American Society for Information Science 29*(5), 247-252. doi:10.1002/asi.4630290507

Froehlich, T.J. (1991). Ethical considerations in technology transfer. *Library Trends 40*(2), 275-302.

Hasselmo, N. (2002). Individual and institutional conflict of interest: Policy review by research universities in the U.S. *Science and Engineering Ethic 8*, 421-427.

Hayter, C.S., & Rooksby, J.H. (2016). A legal perspective on university technology transfer. *Journal of Technology Transfer 41*, 270-289.

Jaffe, A.B., & Rassenfosse, G.D. (2017). Patent citation data in social science research: Overview and best practices. *Journal of the Association for Information Science and Technology 68*(6), 1360-1374. doi:10.1002/asi.23731

Kodama, T. (2008). The role of intermediation and absorptive capacity in facilitating university-industry linkages – An empirical study of TAMA in Japan. *Research Policy 37*, 1224-1240.

Leydesdorff, L. (2004). The university–industry knowledge relationship: Analyzing patents and the science base of technologies. *Journal of the American Society for Information Science and Technology 55*(11), 991-1001. doi:10.1002/asi.20045

Leydesdorff, L., & Ahrweiler, P. (2014). In search of a network theory of innovations: Relations, positions, and perspectives. *Journal of the Association for Information Science and Technology 65*(11), 2359-2374. doi:10.1002/asi.23127

Leydesdorff, L., & Bornmann, L. (2012). Mapping (USPTO) patent data using overlays to Google Maps. *Journal of the American Society for Information Science and Technology 63*(7), 1442-1458.

Leydesdorff, L., & Rafols, I. (2011). Local emergence and global diffusion of research technologies: An exploration of patterns of network formation. *Journal of the American Society for Information Science and Technology 62*(5), 846-860. doi:10.1002/asi.21509

Matkin, G.W. (1997). University technology transfer and the problems of conflict of interest. In Y.S. Lee (Ed.), *Technology transfer and public policy*. Westport, CT: Quorum Books.

Mendelsohn, L.D. (1992). Technology transfer policy: Its role as a scientific and technical information policy and its impact on technological growth. *Journal of the American Society for Information Science 43*(1), 80-89.

Miller, S., & Selgelid, M.J. (2007). Ethical and philosophical consideration of the dual-use dilemma in the biological sciences. *Science and Engineering Ethics 13*, 523-580.

NSF (National Science Foudation). (2016). Academic technology transfer and commercialization of university research. Retrieved June 5, 2017 from https://www.research.gov/research-portal/appmanager/base/desktop?_nfpb=true&_pageLabel=research_node_display&_nodePath=/researchGov/Generic/PublicAffairs/CommercializationofResearchResults.html

Orduna-Malea, E., Thelwall, M., & Kousha, K. (2017). Web citations in patents: Evidence of technological impact? *Journal of the Association for Information Science and Technology*. doi:10.1002/asi.23821

Su, H.N. (2012). Visualization of global science and technology policy research structure. *Journal of the American Society for Information Science and Technology 63*(2), 242-255. doi:10.1002/asi.21520

Swar, B., & Khan, G.F. (2013). An analysis of the information technology outsourcing domain: A social network and triple helix approach. *Journal of the American Society for Information Science and Technology 64*(11), 2366-2378. doi:10.1002/asi.22918

Veith, R.H. (1980). Informatics and transborder data flow: The question of social impact. *Journal of the American Society for Information Science 31*(2), 105-110. doi:10.1002/asi.4630310207

Wueste, D.E. (1994). Role moralities and the problem of conflicting obligations. In D.E. Wueste (Ed.), *Professional ethics and social responsibility* (pp. 103-120). Lanham, MD: Rowman & Littlefield.

Ye, F.Y., Yu, S.S., & Leydesdorff, L. (2013). The triple helix of university-industry-government relations at the country level and its dynamic evolution under the pressures of globalization. *Journal of the American Society for Information Science and Technology 64*(11), 2317-2325. doi:10.1002/asi.22931

Yusuf, S. (2008). Intermediating knowledge exchange between universities and businesses. *Research Policy 37*, 1167-1174.

# Data Play: Participatory Visualisation to Make Sense of Data

**Theresa Dirndorfer Anderson**
*University of Technology Sydney, Australia.*
*Theresa.Anderson@uts.edu.au*

**Kelly Tall**
*University of Technology Sydney, Australia.*
*Kelly.E.Tall@student.uts.edu.au*

**Simon Knight**
*Connected Intelligence Centre, University of Technology Sydney, Australia. Simon.Knight@uts.edu.au*

## ABSTRACT

**This visual presentation invites conference participants to use data play to tap into the creative capacity of visual ideation for individual and collaborative learning about (their) data. The authors discuss the application of a hand-drawn self-visualisation approach to data understanding to draw attention to the space of representational possibilities, the power of representation interactions and the performativity of information representation. The visual presentation takes an interactive and emergent approach to exploring tactile, visual modes of self-expression, sense-making and communication, inviting conference participants to dabble and doodle and think visually about the conference. Over time, the visual artefact will be transformed by and through this community input. Through this collective visual practice, we heed Lupi's call to bring data to life as we make sense of our data traces.**

## KEYWORDS

information visualisation, data practice, creativity

## INTRODUCTION – THE POWER OF THE VISUAL

Exploratory approaches to visualisations of ideas, text and data are increasingly recognised for their role in knowledge production and organisation, particularly with large sets of qualitative and quantitative data (Sadokierski & Sweetapple, 2014). Casual, rough planning and design activities intertwining text, image and drawing help explain ideas and make sense out of complexity, social variance and uncertainty (Anderson, 2013; Francois, 2013). Selvin and Buckingham Shum (2014) explore how highly evocative representations can become touchstones of meaning they refer to as knowledge artistry. Harnessing the power of this mapping dialogue in environments that bring together people, data and technology is a necessary literacy for 21st century work (Okada et al., 2014).

Award-winning information designer Georgia Lupi goes further, calling for a paradigm shift in the way we represent data and information visually. As part of her call for data humanism she urges us to design better ways to connect data to knowledge, behaviours and people:

The ways we relate to data are evolving more rapidly than we realize, and our minds and bodies are naturally adapting to this new hybrid reality built of both physical and informational structures. And visual design – with its power to instantly reach out to places in our subconscious without the mediation of language, and with its inherent ability to convey large amounts of structured and unstructured information across cultures – is going to be even more central to this silent but inevitable revolution (Lupi, 2016, p77).

Drawing with data, she argues, can help us connect more meaningfully with representations of our (data)selves and the world around us.

Can hand-drawn representations help us make sense of our own data? How does the process both represent and shape the behaviours represented in the data? Can we create more informed data publics and increase their analytics literacy through playful interaction/performance? This visual presentation will provoke thinking about such questions, inviting conference participants to use data play to tap into the creative capacity of visual ideation for individual and collaborative learning about (their) data.

## PARTICIPATORY DATA CULTURES

Self-tracking is a growing phenomenon arising from the increased ubiquity of activity trackers and smart devices with in-built sensors that make it easier to continuously and automatically collect data about our movements, moods and fitness (Crawford et al., 2015). These data practices gave rise to a global community of self-trackers, such as the Quantified Self Meetups, where members share their self-tracking experiences and explorations with data tools and hacks (Chamberlain et al., 2015).

As these data tools become more readily available and ubiquitous, they become part of the everyday life of communities who can now not only produce rich stories and visualisations but share them with audiences on a global scale. Enabling collective sense-making thus becomes a necessary feature of such communities.

80th Annual Meeting of the Association for Information Science & Technology, Washington, DC | Oct. 27-Nov. 1, 2017

## INFORMED DATA PUBLICS

At the same time, some have voiced concerns about a loss of agency in our emerging relationships with data-generating devices:

> ...as algorithms are increasingly being designed to anticipate users and make predictions about their future behaviours, users are now reshaping their practices to suit the algorithms they depend on. This constructs 'calculated publics,' the algorithmic presentation of a public that shapes its sense of itself (Williamson, 2015).

There is a growing cry to "turn data around" and design data systems that take into account the well-being of people from whom the data is taken in the first place. Thorp (2016), for instance, makes a compelling case for creating "real, functioning data publics" by bringing data into public, shared spaces.

Human-centred data practices focus on algorithmic accountability, data transparency and AI ethics. Contrary to the idea we are in an era of rational decision-making where "data speaks for itself," the contention is that data is ascribed meaning only when given a voice by people who play increasingly critical roles in the transformation of data into informing insight.

## PLAYING WITH DATA

As part of her own push for data humanism, Lupi – together with Posavec – devised an analogue drawing project, dear data (www.dear-data.com), in which the two visual designers sent hand-drawn personal-data postcards to each other (Lupi & Posavec, 2016). Each week they both drew by hand a representation of some pre-defined (and shared) data theme. Their process would involve, in parallel, collecting data about the chosen topic (but not necessarily the same types of data), only creating the visualization at the end of the week (and again, these differ). So, inevitably, the collection and visualisation of the data itself has a performative quality, impacting on the very behavior being observed.

Inspired by this hand-drawn data activity, we have been piloting a personal-data-visualization approach with our own students and colleagues. Our approach takes a micro-level perspective on making sense of ones-own data traces and processes of data visualization.

## VISUAL PARTICIPATION: PRODUCT(ION) AS PROCESS

Building on our own prototyping and performativity of information representations, this visual presentation takes an interactive and emergent approach to exploring tactile, visual modes of self-expression, sense-making and communication, inviting conference participants to dabble, doodle and think visually as we collect and interpret data about the conference and the ASIST community. Over time, the visual artefact will be transformed by and through the community input. Through this collective visual practice, we heed Lupi's call to bring data to life to "... find new languages, and explore how to convey knowledge and inspire feelings simultaneously with data" (Lupi, 2016, p84).

## REFERENCES


Anderson,T.D. (2013). The 4Ps of innovation culture: Conceptions of creatively engaging with information. Information Research, 18(3) paper C28.

Chamberlain, A., Poole, E., Munson, S., Danis, C. & Churchill, E. (2015). Moving beyond e-Health & the quantified self: The role of CSCW in collaboration, community & practice for technologically supported proactive health & wellbeing. In Proceedings of 18th ACM Conference Companion on Computer Supported Cooperative Work & Social Computing 273-276.

Crawford, K., Lingel, J., & Karppi, T. (2015). Our metrics, ourselves: A hundred years of self-tracking from the weight scale to the wrist wearable device. European Journal of Cultural Studies, 18, 4-5, 479-496

François, A., (2013). SketchyTruth: Somewhere in between the good news and the bad news lies the truth. DCA, UTS Faculty of Arts & Social Sciences. Available https://opus.lib.uts.edu.au/bitstream/10453/21865/5/02Whole.pdf.

Lupi, G. (2016). Data humanism: The revolutionary future of data visualization. PrintMag, 70(Fall), 76-85.

Lupi, G. and Posavec, S. (2016). Dear data: The story of a friendship in fifty-two postcards. Penguin.

Okada, A., Buckingham Shum, S., Sherborne, T., (2014). Knowledge cartography: Software tools and mapping techniques, 2nd Edition, Springer.

Sadokierski, Z.A. & Sweetapple, K, (2014). Drawing out: How designers analyse written texts in visual ways. In Rodgers, P. & Yee, J. (eds), Routledge Companion to Design Research, Routledge, UK.

Selvin, A., & Buckingham Shum, S., (2014). Constructing knowledge art: An experiential perspective on crafting participatory representations. Morgan Claypool.

Thomas, S., et al. (2007). Transliteracy: Crossing divides. First Monday, 12(12), Available at http://firstmonday.org/ojs/index.php/fm/article/view/2060/1908.

Thorp, J. (2016). Turning data around. OCR Journal #2. Office for Creative Research, Brooklyn, NY.

Williamson, B. (2015). Coding/learning: Software and digital data in education. Organizing algorithms in digital education. B. Williamson, ed. University of Stirling.

# Visual Research Methods with Children and Youth: Opportunities & Challenges


**Sarah Barriage**
*Rutgers University, USA. sarah.barriage@rutgers.edu*

**Xiaofeng Li**
*Rutgers University, USA. xiaofeng.li@rutgers.edu*

**Irene Lopatovska**
*School of Information, Pratt Institute, USA. ilopatov@pratt.edu*

**Cass Mabbott**
*University of Illinois at Urbana-Champaign, USA. mmabbot2@illinois.edu*



## ABSTRACT

**Visual research methods involve the incorporation of visual material such as photographs, artwork and video into the research process. This approach to research is particularly well suited for use with children and youth as it complements verbal and written data collection methods, which some children and youth may find challenging. This video presentation includes a brief overview of three specific types of visual research methods used in recent library and information science research studies with children and youth. An overview of each visual research method is provided, as well as a discussion of the advantages and challenges associated with each method. The video includes examples of the types of research questions for which the surveyed visual research methods might be best suited, as well as associated ethical issues.**



## KEYWORDS

information practices, research with children and youth, visual literacy, visual research methods


## INTRODUCTION

Researchers working with children and youth across disciplines have articulated the value of incorporating visual research methods in their work. Visual research methods can involve photographs, artwork, videos or other graphical representations generated by the participants or the researcher, or pre-existing visual materials such as well-known paintings or images from the media (Rose, 2016).

Thomson (2008) asserts that "images communicate in different ways than words" (p. 11). Visual research methods can enable participation from children and youth who are not able or comfortable with providing written and/or verbal responses (Kaplan, 2008). The use of visual methods in research with children and youth may also elicit different responses than research methods that depend on verbal or written language (Leitch, 2008; Noyes, 2008; Thomson, 2008) and allow for the "surfacing of... unknown unknowns" (Noyes, 2008, p. 141). In other words, topics pertinent to research that the adult researchers may not have previously considered may emerge through the use of visual methods.

Researchers who have made use of visual research methods have asserted that children and youth often find these methods to be engaging (Christensen & James, 2008; Leitch, 2008) and enjoyable (Einarsdottir, 2005; Thomson, 2008) and may have the potential to increase children's participation (Christensen & James, 2008). Some researchers have also noted the potential for these methods to be empowering for the participants due to the active role they take on in the research process (Julien, Given & Opryshko, 2013).

In this video, we discuss both participant-generated visual materials and the use of visual materials as elicitation devices. Participant-generated visual materials such as photography or artwork place primary focus on the children's perspectives, allowing the researcher to see phenomena from the children's viewpoint (Einarsdottir, 2005). The use of visual materials as elicitation devices in interview or focus group settings give children a "clear, tangible prompt" to discuss with interviewers (Clark-Ibanez, 2008) and with peers (Julien et al., 2013), enabling the discussion of abstract concepts. In this way, visual research methods can "mediate communication between children and adults" (Leitch, 2008, p. 48).

## PROPOSED VIDEO PRESENTATION OVERVIEW

A five-minute video, created using iMovie, features voiceover descriptions of three recent research studies, examples of the visual materials used in each study and other engaging visual elements. Presenters will be on hand to engage in discussion with conference attendees about the use of visual research methods in studies with children and youth. The video is organized as follows:

### *Introduction (45 seconds)*

A brief overview of visual research methods and their use in research with children and youth is provided.

### *PixStori: A Mobile Photography App (1 minute)*

PixStori is a mobile app developed by researchers at the University of Buffalo; it combines user-generated still photography with audio recordings. This app is being used in Sarah Barriage's dissertation research investigating the ways in


80th Annual Meeting of the Association for Information Science & Technology, Washington, DC | Oct. 27-Nov. 1, 2017

which young children engage with information in their everyday lives. The children are asked to use PixStori to take photographs related to their individual interests and information activities and to then record an audio message explaining what is in the photograph. After creating a PixStori, the image and accompanying audio message are shared with the researcher by uploading to a designated web portal. This method enables the children to remotely and asynchronously share aspects of their everyday lives with the researcher. The children and the researcher then discuss the PixStoris together at a later date, using the PixStoris as elicitation devices. Examples of PixStoris created by the children in this research project are shared in this video presentation, highlighting their potential for use in research in library and information science. Additionally, challenges faced in implementing this research method are discussed.

### *Video Re-Enactment (1 minute)*

In Xiaofeng Li's ongoing doctoral study that examines young people's information practices and collaborations in informal learning environments, including an after-school technology club in a school library makerspace and a public library makerspace, the visual method of video recorded re-enactment (Pink & Mackley, 2014) is included in addition to participant observations and semi-structured interviews. The method of asking young people to re-enact what they normally do while the researcher records it on the video camera offers a new way to capture young people's "in situ encounters with the material, affective, personal and political elements of everyday as lived and experienced" (Pink & Mackley, 2014, p. 146). With this method, the young people in this study are able to show how they usually go around the makerspace, work with the technologies and materials and identify resources with which they routinely interact. Meanwhile, the researcher asks contextual inquiries to elicit why they do certain things, such as questions of what about the selected technologies attract them, why they prefer using certain resources in problem solving and how they feel while they make something. Strengths and weakness of this method are shared in the video presentation.

### *Visual Literacy Instruction (1 minute)*

Irene Lopatovska discusses her recent research that examines methods for developing visual literacy skills in young children. Visual literacy (VL) is usually defined as an ability to interpret and create visual messages and is considered an integral part of overall literacy (Eckhoff, 2010; Edwards & Willis, 2000). In order to advance VL education for young children, Dr. Lopatovska conducted a multi-phase study that a) examined young children's readiness to receive VL instruction and b) tested methods of engaging young children in VL instruction. The study used visual materials to generate individual and group discussions, gauge children's understanding of VL elements and to determine successful strategies for VL instruction. The study engaged participants in hands-on activities that required them to create visual content based on the discussed concepts. The study found that visual materials, including artworks, book illustrations and photographs, generated interest and creative interpretations and served as an excellent medium for instruction and data collection. Details of the study and lessons learned are shared.

### *Conclusion (1 minute 15 seconds)*

This video presentation concludes with a discussion of the ways in which these three different visual research methods are suited for different types of research questions and the types of ethical considerations that arise when these methods are employed.

## REFERENCES


Christensen, P., & James, A. (2008). Introduction: Researching children and childhood cultures of communication. In P. Christensen & A. James (Eds.), *Research with children: Perspectives and practices* (2nd ed., pp. 1-9). New York, NY: Routledge.

Clark-Ibanez, M. (2008). Gender and "being bad": Inner-city students' photographs. In P. Thomson (Ed.), *Doing visual research with children and young people* (pp. 95-113). New York, NY: Routledge.

Eckhoff, A. (2010). Young children - using games to explore visual art with young children. *National Association for the Education of Young Children*. Retrieved from http://www.nxtbook.com/nxtbooks/ naeyc/youngchildren_201001/index.php?startid=17#/20

Edwards, C. P., & Willis, L. M. (2000). Integrating visual and verbal literacies in the early childhood classroom. *Early Childhood Education Journal, 27(4)*, 259-265.

Einarsdottir, J. (2005). Playschool in pictures: Children's photographs as a research method. *Early Child Development & Care, 175*, 523-542.

Julien, H., Given, L. M., & Opryshko, A. (2013). Photovoice: A promising method for studies of individuals' information practices. *Library and Information Science Research, 35*(4), 257–263. http://doi.org/10.1016/j.lisr.2013.04.004

Leitch, R. (2008). Creatively researching children's narratives through images and drawing. In P. Thomson (Ed.), *Doing visual research with children and young people* (pp. 37-58). New York, NY: Routledge.

Noyes, A. (2008). Using video diaries to investigate learner trajectories: Researching the 'unknown unknowns'. In P. Thomson (Ed.), *Doing visual research with children and young people* (pp. 132-145). New York, NY: Routledge.

Pink, S., & Mackley, K. (2014). Re-enactment methodologies for everyday life research: Art therapy insights for video ethnography. *Visual Studies, 29*(2), 146-154. http://doi.org/10.1080/1472586X.2014.887266

Rose, G. (2016). Visual methodologies: An introduction to researching with visual materials (4th ed.). Los Angeles, CA: Sage.

Thomson, P. (2008). Children and young people: Voices in visual research. In P. Thomson (Ed.), *Doing visual research with children and young people* (pp. 1-19). New York, NY: Routledge.

# An Open Health Data Engagement Ecosystem Model: Are Facilitators the Key to Open Data Success?

**Grace M. Begany**
*State University of New York (SUNY) at Cobleskill and University at Albany, USA. BeganyGM@cobleskill.edu*

**Erika G. Martin**
*Rockefeller Institute of Government and University at Albany (SUNY), USA. emartin@albany.edu*

## ABSTRACT

**Over the last decade, a rapidly growing open data movement has resulted in government agencies quickly publishing a large volume of data, and the data's subsequent use among a variety of open data consumers. Understanding the activities, actors, technologies and factors enabling open data publication and use has been the subject of discussion among academic researchers and practitioners. However, research is limited, with few empirical studies on open data collecting primary research data from the health domain. To address this gap, we conducted 53 semi-structured key informant interviews with participants in the open health data ecosystem in a variety of roles. Interview data were analyzed using a grounded theory approach to identify common themes and develop insights into the objectives, activities and desired outcomes of the open health data ecosystem. We found that data facilitators – data advocates, typically external to government agencies – are critical to this process by facilitating open data awareness and successful use. We applied activity theory to examine the facilitator theme and develop a preliminary model of the open health data ecosystem, including the roles, responsibilities and activities of different participants and the role of these facilitators. Our findings suggest that consumers' successful engagement with open health data is fostered by, and perhaps dependent upon, facilitators' activities. These empirically based insights into the structure and workings of the open health data engagement ecosystem can inform jurisdictions' development of open health data engagement strategies thereby improving the success of their open health data initiatives.**

## INTRODUCTION AND BACKGROUND

There are many perceived benefits of open health data, including improved health literacy, data-driven changes in health care and empowering health consumers (Martin and Begany, 2016). However, there is limited understanding of who the consumers of open data are or how open data are used (Susha, Grönlund and Janssen, 2015; Zuiderwijk, Janssen and Dwivedi, 2015), particularly in the health domain (Hossain, Dwivedi, and Rana, 2016). Gaining a deeper understanding of the open health data ecosystem is crucial to the success of open health data initiatives, as data are only valuable if they are used. These insights can aid government agencies who are seeking to provide appropriate opportunities for consumers to engage with open health data and thereby improve the value of these data.

Some foundational studies investigate open data ecosystems and data use. For example, a key study by Zuiderwijk, Janssen and Davis (2014) reviews the essential elements of open data ecosystems, finding that ecosystems comprise applications, tools and portals. Their work is based on a literature review about open data ecosystems and a scenario about open data publication and use. Additionally, the use of open data is examined via a case study approach by Ruijer, Grimmelikhuijsen and Meijer (2017). The researchers use activity theory to develop a heuristic model based on analysis of democratic processes to understand the influence of these processes on open data use. The model provides insight into the relationship between open data and citizens' and governments' activities in three types of democratic processes – monitorial, deliberative and participatory. These studies provide valuable insights about the open data ecosystem in general; however, they do not focus on the distinct domain of health.

## THEORETICAL FRAMEWORK

We use the activity theory framework (Engeström, 1987) as a lens to examine the complex ecosystem of open health data. Specifically, we use the elements "Subject," "Object/Objective," "Tools," "Rules," "Division of Labor," "Community" and "Outcome" to provide structure to our analysis of our interview data and interpretation of results.

Activity theory is an approach used in psychology, other social sciences and, increasingly in human-computer interaction (Rogers, Sharp & Preece, 2011; Kaptelinin & Nardi, 2009; Kaptelinin & Nardi, 2012). Researchers argue that activity theory is a strong framework for better understanding and developing conceptual models of ill-defined domains and activities (Karanasios et al., 2013). This makes it a promising and suitable lens through which to examine and describe the emerging domain of open health data and consumers' engagement with these crucial resources, particularly given (1) the general lack of theoretical frameworks in open data research (Charalabidis, Alexopoulos & Loukis, 2015; Susha, Grönlund & Janssen, 2015; Zuiderwijk, Helbig, Gil-Garcia & Janssen, 2014; Zuiderwijk, Janssen & Dwivedi, 2015) and (2)

80th Annual Meeting of the Association for Information Science & Technology, Washington, DC | Oct. 27-Nov. 1, 2017

the limited empirically based studies on the use of open data, especially in the health domain (Hossain, Dwivedi and Rana, 2016). We aim to address these research gaps in open data use, engagement of open data consumers and structure of open data ecosystems. As our case, we focus on the specialized domain of health, given that the most extensive use of open data is within the health community (Hossain, Dwivedi and Rana, 2016) and resources for study are extensive.

## RESEARCH OBJECTIVES

We use the lens of activity theory and a rich qualitative interview dataset to understand the structure and workings of the open health data ecosystem, particularly with respect to consumers' engagement with open health data.

## RESEARCH DESIGN AND METHODOLOGY

We conducted qualitative semi-structured key informant interviews with practitioners and policymakers at the New York State Department of Health, U.S. Department of Health and Human Services, other New York agencies, non-governmental organizations and individuals from other jurisdictions that were early innovators in releasing open health data. Participants were recruited via purposive and snowball sampling, aiming for diversity in (a) professional roles (executive leadership, program directors, data owners, open data staff, legal affairs, independent contractors, entrepreneurs) and (b) areas of expertise (leadership, project management, public health, information technology, open data).

Interview questions elicited key informants' perspectives on a variety of topics related to the open health data ecosystem, including (1) the members of the ecosystem and their roles and responsibilities, (2) the goals and desired outcomes of open health data initiatives, (3) activities related to ecosystem members' interaction with open health data and tools used to mediate their activities, (4) interactions between members of the ecosystem and the community within which they are situated and (5) barriers, challenges and tensions in the ecosystem. Interview transcripts were analyzed using a grounded theory methodological approach to systematically discover and report themes in the qualitative interview data (Charmaz, 2014; Corbin, 2007; Maxwell, 2005). The participant sample evolved until no new topics or viewpoints emerged and resulted in a final sample of 53 participants and 43 interviews.

## RESULTS

### *Elements of an Open Health Data Engagement Ecosystem*

Table 1 will summarize the open health data ecosystem, using the activity theory framework. This encompasses the primary activity, objective and outcome; key actors and community members; their relative roles, responsibilities and activities; the relevant tools; and important rules. Collectively, these elements define the health-related open data ecosystem and the ways in which participants engage with open data.

### *Open Data "Facilitators"*

A key theme in the interviews is the importance of "facilitation." In addition to the creators-producers and consumers of open health data, key informants described a third group of open data "facilitators," who are committed to the philosophy and promise of open data and strive to foster the development of the open data movement by bringing together and coordinating key players and providing strategy and implementation support for open data initiatives. This support frequently focuses on improving consumer engagement. These facilitators are commonly third-party consultants, volunteers and non-governmental organizations who are involved in the open data movement. Additionally, some open data portal vendors and other open data-related business entities also serve in a facilitator role.

So-called "health data ambassadors" are a unique category of facilitator specific to the health domain and seemingly limited to the state of California. The health data ambassadors, part of an initiative supported by the California Health Care Foundation, are independent contractors and serve to make California's open health data portal more useful to the local communities. The work of these facilitators involves ongoing coordination and meetings with state officials to identify high impact opportunities. A key activity they engage in to accomplish their goals is holding roundtables with representatives of the local health community, including non-profit organizations, county public health departments, as well as local and state government representatives. Such roundtables have resulted in ideas for tools to engage consumers with open health data and partnerships with local contractors to realize the ideas (e.g., web-based interactive map applications). Additional activities coordinated by the health data ambassadors to facilitate successful open health data initiatives and consumer engagement include brown bag series, "city camps" (lightning talk sessions), hackathons and recurring hack nights.

### *Activity in an Open Health Data Engagement Ecosystem*

All of these elements come together to form a system of activity, which will be shown in Figure 1. When the open health data ecosystem is fully functional, the data released by the data creators-producers are used by a diverse set of data consumers, who each have unique interests, skills and intended use. The interactions between the data creators-producers and data consumers largely occur through open data engagement points. The open data facilitators interact directly with all three elements, thereby facilitating increased engagement with open health data.

## CONCLUSION

Our findings reveal a complex interplay between large varieties of actors in the open health data ecosystem surrounding consumers' engagement with open health data. While the facilitator theme was frequently mentioned by key informants – and it has not yet been described by other open data studies – persons and/or organizations that can serve in a facilitator role and devote the necessary time to effectively coordinate activities may be a crucial factor in the success of open health data initiatives.

## STUDY CONTRIBUTIONS

This study offers empirically based insights into the structure and workings of the open health data ecosystem, based on a comprehensive, rich set of primary qualitative data. These insights can inform jurisdictions' development of open health data engagement strategies and potentially aid in the success of their open health data initiatives.

## STUDY LIMITATIONS

Participant selection only included early innovators in the open health data ecosystem, and individuals with optimistic views of open data are over-represented. There may be potential researcher bias, although this was minimized by having two reviewers conducting interviews and analyzing transcripts. As we deliberately focused on the open health data ecosystem, findings may not be generalizable to other open data topic domains. The preliminary framework does not yet include activity theory's concepts of "contradictions," "transformations" and "tensions"; these will be explored in future analysis along with a deeper investigation of all ecosystem elements.


## ACKNOWLEDGEMENTS

This work was supported by the Robert Wood Johnson Foundation's Public Health Services & Systems Research Program (Grant ID#71597 to E.G.M. and Guthrie S. Birkhead). Additional support for interview transcriptions was provided by a University at Albany Graduate Student Association's Research Grant Award and a United University Professionals (UUP) Individual Development Award from the SUNY Cobleskill UUP chapter.


## REFERENCES


Charalabidis, Y., Alexopoulos, C., & Loukis, E. (2016). A taxonomy of open government data research areas and topics. Journal of Organizational Computing and Electronic Commerce, 26(1-2), 41-63.

Charmaz K. (2014). Constructing grounded theory (2nd Ed.). Thousand Oaks, CA: SAGE Publications, Inc.

Corbin J, Strauss A. (2007). Basics of qualitative research (3rd Ed.). Thousand Oaks, CA: SAGE Publications, Inc.

Engeström, Y. (1987). Learning by expanding: An activity theoretical approach to developmental research. Orienta-Konsultit: Helsinki, Finland.

Hossain, M.A., Dwivedi, Y.K. & Rana, N.P. (2016). State-of-the-art in open data research: Insights from existing literature and a research agenda. Journal of Organizational Computing and Electronic Commerce, 26(1-2), 14-40.

Kaptelinin, V. & Nardi, B. (2009). Acting with technology: Activity theory and interaction design. Cambridge, MA: MIT Press.

Kaptelinin, V. & Nardi, B. (2012). Activity theory in HCI: Fundamentals and reflections. San Rafael, CA: Morgan & Claypool.

Karanasios, S., Allen, D., Norman, A.W.T., Thakker, D.A., Lau, L. & Dimitrova, V. (2013). Making sense of digital traces: An activity theory driven ontological approach. Journal of the Association for Information Science and Technology, 64(12), 2452-2467.

Martin, E. G., & Begany, G. M. (2017). Opening government health data to the public: Benefits, challenges, and lessons learned from early innovators. Journal of the American Medical Informatics Association, 24(2), 345-351.

Maxwell JA. (2005). Qualitative research design: An interactive approach (2nd Ed.). Thousand Oaks, CA: Sage Publications, Inc.

Rogers, Y., Sharp, H., & Preece, J. (2011). Interaction design: Beyond human-computer interaction. West Sussex, United Kingdom: John Wiley & Sons Ltd.

Ruijer, E., Grimmelikhuijsen, S., & Meijer, A. (2017). Open data for democracy: Developing a theoretical framework for open data use. Government Information Quarterly, 34(1), 45-52.

Susha, I., Grönlund, A. & Janssen, M. (2015). Organizational measures to stimulate user engagement with open data. Transforming Government: People, Process and Policy, 9(2), 181-206.

Zuiderwijk, A., Helbig, N., Gil-Garcia, J.R., & Janssen, M. (2014). Special issue on innovation through open data – a review of the state-of-the-art and an emerging research agenda: Guest editors' introduction. Journal of Theoretical and Applied Electronic Commerce Research, 9(2), I-XIII.

Zuiderwijk, A., Janssen, M. & Davis, C. (2014). Innovation with open data: Essential elements of open data ecosystems. Information Polity, 19, 17-33.

Zuiderwijk, A., Janssen, M., & Dwivedi, Y.K. (2015). Acceptance and use predictors of open data technologies: Drawing upon the unified theory of acceptance and use of technology. Government Information Quarterly, 32, 429-440.

# Uncertainties and Information Behaviors of Alcohol and Other Drug (AOD) Counselors

**William A. Bejarano**
*Rutgers University, USA. bejarano@rutgers.edu*

## ABSTRACT

**The purpose of this study is to assess the uncertainty-driven problem-solving model posited by Wilson (1999) as applied to the information behaviors of alcohol and other drug (AOD) counselors in their daily work practices. With the Wilson model serving as a framework, a series of semi-structured interviews was developed and the data analyzed to uncover the uncertainties of each of the interrelated domains of the profession, as well as the subsequent information behaviors that serve to address those uncertainties. Results show a strong match between the Wilson model and the empirical data in most functions of the job. That is, most information behaviors in the various job functions tend to stem from some uncertainty.**

## KEYWORDS

addiction, counselors, health, information behaviors, uncertainty

## INTRODUCTION

The job of an AOD counselor is largely centered on managing uncertainty regarding, among other things, the optimal match of a client's situation and particular needs to a specific type of treatment. In order to address these uncertainties, these counselors engage in a number of information behaviors. To date, there have been no studies explicitly speaking to these information behaviors or to the specific uncertainties that give rise to them. The present study aims to focus on the information behaviors of AOD counselors from the perspective of the counselors themselves by taking into account their contextual, day-to-day work functions and behaviors. This study is a contrast to previous work on the profession that focused on the way that the job ought to be done.

## BACKGROUND

In order to ground this study in sound theory, Wilson's (1999) problem-solving model served as the framework, as it was developed specifically in the context of professional practice. The idea behind this model is that information is generally used to serve practical needs, which often arise from various levels of uncertainty. These needs occur over the four iterated stages of problem identification, problem definition, problem resolution and solution statement, each of which is informed by uncertainty resolutions (i.e., information).

80th Annual Meeting of the Association for Information Science & Technology, Washington, DC | Oct. 27-Nov. 1, 2017



The fragmented needs of an AOD counselor can be organized per Kulewich (1990) into 12 essential functions, as well as Taleff and Swisher's (1997) seven additional functions for master's level counselors. This particular study is organized around the eight higher-level domain headings under which these sets of functions are grouped (Bryant & Delerme, 2011), as seen below.

## METHOD

To determine the fit between the problem-solving model and the information behaviors of counselors, the author conducted five semi-structured interviews totaling approximately four hours. The sample was acquired via snowball technique, and interview subjects ranged widely. Subjects included two private practice therapists with less than five years experience in their practice, a licensed clinical social worker with 10 years experience at a therapeutic community, a counselor in her 14th year at a nonprofit intensive outpatient facility and a director of a counseling program with four decades experience at a large public university. All counselors were female, with a master's level education or higher, and all work in the northeastern region of the United States.

The interview protocol was designed to ask about the general life needs, and not necessarily the information needs, of the participants in order to elicit context and deduce the information behaviors from the explanations of the events. Interviews were transcribed, sorted into domain categories, then cross tabulated with the Cool and Belkin (2002) faceted classification of information behaviors (i.e., create, disseminate, organize, preserve, access, evaluate, comprehend, modify, use), based on the method provided by Huvila and Widén-Wulff (2006).

## RESULTS

The visual presentation is organized around the eight domains of the AOD counselor, with sub-categories listed underneath each domain for specific functions, if applicable. The uncertainties most prevalent in the data are then listed, followed by the information behaviors that commonly take place within each function to address those uncertainties, accompanied by some relevant quotes from the interview subjects to support these findings. Here follows a brief overview of these findings.

The **Clinical Evaluation** domain, which includes the functions of screening, assessment, intake and orientation, primarily deals with the uncertainties of the client's specific needs and whether or not the client is eligible for treatment at this level of care. The information behaviors that emerge to address these uncertainties are the broad use of survey instruments and assessment tools, such as the patient placement criteria (Mee-Lee, 2001), evaluation of the entirety of a client's situation and creation of a profile of the client that will be updated and assessed periodically. Further, modification of an intake form, along with further access to information about the client, are essential to this early stage of the process.

The general uncertainty that is being addressed in the **Treatment Planning** domain is an understanding of the client's goals, first and foremost, before any strategy is discussed to reach them. To address this uncertainty, there is a wide use of goal-planning heuristics or problem lists as well as psychotherapy treatments. There is also the creation and dissemination of educational material, as well as access to and modification of scholarly literature.

The main uncertainty in the domain called **Referral to Treatment** is to where exactly the client should be referred, based not just on what level of care he or she needs, but also what level facility the client is willing to attend, whether the quality of the facility is adequate and whether the client has any particular insurance or payment limitations. The typical information behavior exhibited to address this issue is accessing a list of potential facilities and evaluating those facilities for quality, match and cost.

The **Service Coordination** domain is designed to address the uncertainty of areas beyond the expertise of the counselor. This is essentially a communication-level domain, where the main activity is the creation and dissemination of information to other professionals or access of information from other professionals or the central facility.

Somewhat ironically, as the job title of those interviewed is "counselor," the **Counseling** domain is the one that seemed to be the hardest to define. Put simply, this domain is the treatment plan being put into action. The main information behavior in this domain, then, is the use of therapy techniques, scholarly literature and training. Because the situation determines the action, it seems that this is the most situated of all of the domains, and that proper training and a sharp instinct are more important than the ability to merely understand and apply specific methods competently.

In order to effectively build efficacy on the part of the client, the **Education** domain consists of the counselor attempting to figure out the information clients lack in their process of staying sober and then matching a technique that can best fill those gaps. Some behavioral practices include the creation and dissemination of educational material and handouts to clients, as well as aiding them in comprehending the material. To be clear, the counselors are not implying that substance misuse is an issue that is solely related to information need, but they agree that education plays a significant role in treatment.

**Documentation** does not exist as an isolated function, but it was useful to ask direct questions about this process in order to understand it more clearly. Through the creation, evaluation and dissemination of notes, often structured in a formalized way, the individual or group can better understand the client's position on a weekly basis.

The uncertainties that arise in the domain of **Professional and Ethical Responsibilities** are related to which policies apply to the counselors in their various roles and how exactly these policies affect their day-to-day operations, which are addressed by the access to and comprehension of the policies.

The advanced domain of **Understanding and Applying Research** is unique in that it is not driven by any specific urgency or uncertainty and may indeed transcend Wilson's model, falling more into Schutz and Luckmann's (1973) "theoretical attitude," stemming less from practical need.

## CONCLUSION

Wilson's problem-solving model serves as a useful fit in assessing the reality of the counseling process, in that each information behavior exhibited in the data, with the exception of the research domain, could be understood as a deliberate act to reduce specific uncertainties. By making this connection clearer and more explicit, this model can help in thinking through the different dimensions of these information behaviors. This study offers uncertainty resolution as a new lens through which the profession of AOD counseling can be viewed. This was a pilot study and was deliberately wide-ranging. Follow-up studies might be better served by focusing in on fewer of these functions in greater depth. Studying these functions using the problem-solving model keeps the focus on the actions of counselors as they are situated in their day-to-day practice and can help shed further light on areas for improved services and/or for systems that can be designed with these specific practical needs in mind.

## REFERENCES

Bryant, K., & Delerme, A. (2011). 12 core functions/8 domains of substance abuse counseling. [Powerpoint slides]. Retrieved from http://www.mli-inc.org/pacct/resources1011/12%20CORE%20FUNCTIONS%208%20DOMAINS%202011.pdf

Cool, C. & Belkin, N. J. (2002). A classification of interactions with information. In H. Bruce, R. Fidel, P. Ingwersen & P. Vakkari (Eds.) Emerging frameworks and methods. Proceedings of the fourth international conference on conceptions of library and information science (CoLIS4) (pp. 1-15). Greenwood Village, CO: Libraries Unlimited.

Huvila, I., & Widén-Wulff, G. (2006). Perspectives to the classification of information interactions: The Cool and Belkin faceted classification scheme under scrutiny. In Proceedings of the 1st international conference on information interaction in context (pp. 144-152). ACM.

Kulewicz, S. F. (1990). The twelve core functions of a counselor. Counselor Publications.

Mee-Lee, D. (Ed.) (2001). ASAM Patient placement criteria for the treatment of substance-related disorders (2nd rev. ed.). Chevy Chase, MD: American Society of Addiction Medicine.

Schutz, A. & Luckmann, T. (1973). The structures of the life world. Evanston, IL: Northwestern University Press.

Taleff, M. J., & Swisher, J. D. (1997). The seven core functions of a master's degree level alcohol and other drug counselor. Journal of Alcohol and Drug Education, 42(3), 1.

Wilson, T. D. (1999). Models in information behavior research. Journal of Documentation, 55(3), 249-270.

# EINFOSE Project: Stimulating Diversity of Students and Teachers' Engagement in the European Higher Education Area

**Boris Bosancic**
*Faculty of Humanities and Social Sciences, University of Osijek, Croatia. bbosancic@ffos.hr*

**Boris Badurina**
*Faculty of Humanities and Social Sciences, University of Osijek, Croatia. badurina@ffos.hr*

**Sanjica Faletar Tanackovic**
*Faculty of Humanities and Social Sciences, University of Osijek, Croatia. sfaletar@ffos.hr*

**Thomas Mandl**
*Stiftung Universität Hildesheim, Germany. mandl@uni-hildesheim.de*

## ABSTRACT

**The poster aims to present the findings of the study related to the EU research project EINFOSE – European Information Science Education: Encouraging Mobility and Learning Outcomes Harmonization. The project's main goal is to investigate how to remove barriers to students' enrolment in LIS/IS graduate programs across Europe and at the same time introduce diverse social, cultural and technological experience. The first phase of the longitudinal study conducted in June 2017 explored the motivation and expectations of students enrolling in the EINFOSE European Summer School in Information Sciences (ESSIS). In the final report, the results will attempt to align the expectations of students from different areas with the ESSIS program and thus contribute to the main EINFOSE project goal.**

## KEYWORDS

EINFOSE project, EU higher education, harmonization, internationalization, diversity, mobility

## INTRODUCTION

The topics of harmonization, mobility, internationalization and modernization of library and information science (LIS)/information science (IS) education have been discussed around the globe for over 20 years. Several attempts have been made, in this effort, to strengthen the cooperation between North America and Europe (cf Abdullahi and Kajberg, 2004; Abdullahi, Kajberg and Virkus, 2007). In Europe, the European Association for Library and Information Education and Research (EUCLID) has been very active in promoting internationalization and joint curriculum development by organizing several events (seminars, conferences) in Italy, Greece and Germany at the beginning of 2000s. Eventually, the joint efforts of EUCLID and Royal School of LIS (RSLIS), Denmark, resulted in an EU funded project (2004-2005) culminating in the final conference on LIS curriculum development, held in Copenhagen, Denmark, in 2005 (cf Kajberg and Lörring, 2005; Kajberg, 2007). Initiatives from both sides of the Atlantic Ocean resulted in various activities dedicated to higher education (HE) in the LIS/IS field. For example, the European Union has launched initiatives such as *Rethinking Education, European Higher Education in the World* and *Opening Up HE* (cf Johnson, 2013; Virkus, 2015), while in the United States, the conference on the future of the information profession was organized at Chapel Hill in 2012 (Marchionini and Moran, 2012). In the European context such efforts imply that modernization of HE should contribute to the Europe 2020 goals by boosting EU competitiveness and growth through better skilled workforce, more employment, growth of students and teachers mobility and more active role of HE in the society (cf European Commission, 2013; Aparac-Jelušić, 2016).

The EINFOSE is the first EU project on LIS/IS university education in European higher institutions (EHI) to be funded after the joint EUCLID and RSLIS project on curriculum development in 2005. In this project, funded under Erasmus+ Key Action 2 - Strategic Partnerships for Higher Education for the period 2016-2018, partnering institutions from eight European countries (Barcelona, Spain; Böras, Sweden; Graz, Austria; Hildesheim, Germany; Ljubljana, Slovenia; Pisa, Italy; and Ankara, Turkey) have been working together to develop educational guidelines and recommendations for LIS/IS education. One of the project's goals is to investigate ways and means of lowering barriers to the students' enrolment at graduate programs in LIS/IS and introducing various social, cultural and technological experiences in IS education across Europe. In order to investigate how different entry requirements observed in partnering institutions could be harmonized and students with different educational backgrounds allowed to enroll in graduate programs in LIS/IS, the project aims to produce five main intellectual outputs (IO): online teaching and communication platform; online educational resources (OER) to be used during and after European summer schools in IS (ESSIS), evaluation and didactic frameworks, and policy recommendations. Teachers and students from all partnering universities/countries will participate in ESSIS. During the summer school (to be held in August 2017 in Germany) students will listen to four courses. A one-month online pre-assignments and two months of online communication following the ESSIS are obligatory for all participating students.

80th Annual Meeting of the Association for Information Science & Technology, Washington, DC | Oct. 27-Nov. 1, 2017

## STUDY

In the poster authors will present only a portion of results obtained in the first phase (conducted in 2017) of the longitudinal study (which will be conducted prior to and after ESSIS in 2017 and 2018) focusing on the students participating in the summer school.

## RESEARCH QUESTIONS (RQ):

What is the background of students attending ESSIS 2017? What is their motivation to participate in ESSIS 2017? What are their expectations from ESSIS 2017? How are they satisfied with ESSIS 2017?

## METHODOLOGY

The 2017 study will be conducted in two parts, with the help of qualitative methods. First, in the period June 1-14, 2017 students who have applied to participate in ESSIS (N=20) were asked to fill out the online questionnaire via EINFOSE platform. The survey consisted of 13 questions (11 open-ended and two closed). The first group of questions, referring to the RQ1, focused on the students' background (age, gender, education, mobility experience etc.). The second group of questions investigated students' motivation to enroll into EINFOSE summer school program (RQ2) and the third group of questions looked into their expectations from ESSIS (RQ3). So far, this data has been analyzed and will be presented in this proposal. In September 2017, following the closure of ESSIS, onsite and Skype interviews with students will be conducted to find out about their satisfaction with ESSIS (RQ4). These interviews will be recorded and presented as video clips complementing the poster.

## RESULTS AND DISCUSSION

Out of total of 20 students participating in ESSIS, only 15 responded. Although it was initially planned to attract only students from outside LIS/IS fields, seven respondents come from the undergraduate LIS/IS study, and only eight students have undergraduate education other than LIS/IS (e.g., civil engineering, administration, language study and digital humanities). Interestingly, four hold BA degrees in management-related studies. Also, it was interesting to see that only five respondents have spent some time abroad during their BA studies. However, at the same time the large majority of students (N=12) would like to study outside their home countries. Also, it was interesting to find out that most respondents (seven out of eight) who have undergraduate education other than LIS/IS have already been introduced to the field of LIS/IS in some way (read some literature, took some elective courses, etc.).

When asked about their motivation to participate in ESSIS, majority of students (N=13) described that they plan to enroll into the LIS/IS graduate program of study. Four respondents also listed social and cultural benefits of participating in such an event. When asked about topics/problems within the field of information sciences in which they are particularly interested they evenly listed computer-related (AI, data mining, information retrieval, digital library) and LIS topics (library, information and knowledge management, information organization, reference services, bibliometrics). When asked about their expectations from participation in ESSIS, the respondents listed both benefits of sharing the educational experience with international students (N=4) and getting better insight into and knowledge about LIS/IS field (N=12). Finally, all respondents agreed that participation at ESSIS will facilitate their graduate study in LIS/IS, if they choose to follow that educational path.

## CONCLUDING REMARKS

The study has responded to all research questions. Overall, it is expected that the results will be very useful for academics teaching at ESSIS because they will provide them with background information about their students and their motivation for and expectations of ESSIS. Thus, the content of the courses can be selected and adapted in advance. The results of the second phase of the (qualitative) study (interviews regarding their satisfaction with the summer school), which will be conducted in September 2017, will surely provide additional valuable information which will help the evaluation of the program and indicate possible areas of improvement. All this will be used in redesigning the summer school program which will have positive impact on the students' understanding of LIS/IS area and which will adequately introduce them to basic concepts and problems in LIS/IS.

## ACKNOWLEDGMENTS

Authors would like to thank Professor Tatjana Aparac-Jelušić, the EINFOSE project coordinator, for her kind support and encouragement.

## REFERENCES

Abdullahi, I., & Kajberg, L. (2004). A study of international issues in library and information science education: survey of LIS schools in Europe, the USA and Canada. New Library World, 105, 345-356.

Abdullahi, I., Kajberg, L., & Virkus, S. (2007). Internationalization of LIS education in Europe and North America. New Library World, 108(1/2), 7-24.

Aparac-Jelušić, T. (2016). Obrazovanje za digitalne knjižnice: pogled iz Europe (Education for digital libraries: European perspective). Libellarium, 9(2), Retrieved June 17, 2017 from http://libellarium.org/index.php/libellarium/article/view/289/427

European Commission (2013). Opening up education: Innovative teaching and learning for all through new technologies and open educational resources. Brussels, 25.9.2013. Retrieved June 17, 2017 from http://eur-lex.europa.eu/legal-content/EN/TXT/PDF/?uri=CELEX:52013DC0654&from=EN

Johnson, I. (2013). The impact on education for librarianship and information studies of the Bologna process and related European Commission programmes – and some outstanding issues in Europe and beyond. Education for Information 30, 63–92.

Kajberg L. & Lorring L. (eds.) (2005). European curriculum reflections on library and information science education. Copenhagen: The Royal School of Library and Information Science, Denmark. Retrieved June 17, 2017 from http://euclid-lis.eu/wp-content/uploads/2014/02/european-curriculum-reflections.pdf

Kajberg, Leif. (2007). The European LIS curriculum project: An overview. Journal of Education for Library and Information Science, 48(2) 68-81.

Marchionini, G. & Moran, B. (eds.) (2012). Information professionals 2050: Educational possibilities and pathways. North Carolina: School of Information and Library Science of University of North Carolina at Chapel Hill. Retrieved June 17, 2017 from http://sils.unc.edu/sites/default/files/news/Information-Professionals-2050.pdf

Virkus, S. (2015). Change and innovation in European library and information science education. BiD: textos universitaris de biblioteconomia i documentació, 35. Retrieved June 17, 2017 from http://bid.ub.edu/en/35/virkus.htm

# Collaborative Syllabus Design for Studying Information Work

**Sarah A. Buchanan**
*University of Missouri, USA. buchanans@missouri.edu*

**Julia Bullard**
*The University of Texas at Austin, USA.*
*julia.a.bullard@gmail.com*

**William Aspray**
*University of Colorado Boulder, USA.*
*william.aspray@colorado.edu*

**Diane Bailey**
*The University of Texas at Austin, USA.*
*debailey@ischool.utexas.edu*

**Lecia Barker**
*University of Colorado Boulder, USA.*
*lecia.barker@colorado.edu*

**Daniel Carter**
*The University of Texas at Austin, USA.*
*carter.daniel.w@gmail.com*

**Tanya Clement**
*The University of Texas at Austin, USA.*
*tclement@ischool.utexas.edu*

**Nicholas Gottschlich**
*The University of Texas at Austin, USA.*
*nickgott@utexas.edu*

**James Howison**
*The University of Texas at Austin, USA.*
*jhowison@ischool.utexas.edu*

**Stephen McLaughlin**
*The University of Texas at Austin, USA.*
*stephen.mclaughlin@utexas.edu*

**Melissa Ocepek**
*University of Illinois at Urbana-Champaign, USA.*
*mgocepek@illinois.edu*

**Daniel Sholler**
*The University of Texas at Austin, USA.*
*sholler.daniel@gmail.com*

**Ciaran B. Trace**
*The University of Texas at Austin, USA.*
*cbtrace@austin.utexas.edu*

## ABSTRACT

**Recognizing that current curricula address but a sliver of the wide range of careers pursued by information studies graduates, a team worked collaboratively to design a syllabus for a graduate course dedicated to exploring the societal frames and characteristics of information work. Ultimately comprising 10 modules, the syllabus centers students' awareness of an expanded occupational landscape and evaluation of policies and labor structures impacting information workers. Created over the course of a semester, the syllabus complements an earlier set of empirical studies that revealed areas in which information educators might focus future teaching efforts. This paper articulates the role for iterative and collaborative processes in curriculum development and doctoral study around information work – a research arena requiring macroscopic and future-oriented thinking. We present the topical and pedagogical organization of the new syllabus and suggest paths forward for integrating its key concepts at other graduate and undergraduate levels of information studies coursework.**

80th Annual Meeting of the Association for Information Science & Technology, Washington, DC | Oct. 27-Nov. 1, 2017



## KEYWORDS

information work, graduate education, workplace technology, curriculum development, research skills

## INTRODUCTION

Students graduating from information studies programs, broadly understood, increasingly do not limit their target careers to the traditional information professions. A study of information schools found that while school leaders have latitude in what topics are addressed throughout the graduate curricula, consistently these schools prepare students not just to navigate through but to exercise leadership and management "in tomorrow's information infrastructure, which they fully intend to help create" (Seadle & Greifeneder, 2007). Through coursework, especially at the master's level, educators prepare students in such programs to actively shape the systematic ways by which humans interact with information on a daily basis. Educators and researchers recognize the need to prepare students to assume expanded responsibilities around the tasks of information creation, organization, preservation, presentation and retrieval – activities which today lend themselves to careers as data analysts, content managers and information architects. Research by Maceli & Burke (2016) finds that newer information practitioners share technology skill sets focused on the end-user side of tools and must know how to apply advanced technical skills. Information scholars implore us to engage with our new professional diaspora (Marcum, 1997; Thomas, von Dran, & Sawyer, 2006) and attend to the concerns of practitioners working across the field. Tracking graduates' careers not only allows leaders to assess program readiness (Wu, He, Jiang, Dong & Vo, 2011) but also and more importantly to refine curricula in response to changing workplace expectations. Information faculty must address emerging areas of information work, new occupational trends and research skills development in order to prepare graduate students to lead fulfilling careers.

Concurrently, we see widespread recognition on the part of community leaders that one strategy to address complex phenomena involving people and technology is to create a collaborative syllabus. Sharing the process of creating learning resources with many contributors can produce an unexpectedly rich resource and, in the process, grow community interest (Hudd, 2003). For example, when individuals began tweeting links to scholarly resources with the hashtag #CharlestonSyllabus, librarians stepped in to organize the materials and preserve them for public access; a resulting list of resources is currently hosted on WorldCat.org (OCLC, 2017; Williams, Williams, & Blain, 2016). Focusing on the domain of information work, we argue that while some existing information studies curricula bisect occupational trends, on the whole instructors lack a concise syllabus with which to prepare students for today's information career spectrum. We set out to develop master's-level curricula on information work focused on practitioners' knowledge, skill sets and areas of concern. In forming the Information Work Research Group (IWRG), the first in the information field, faculty and doctoral students together pursued interests in comprehending the work that information graduates are likely to perform.

## SYLLABUS DEVELOPMENT

The IWRG carried out its research and pedagogical goals through doctoral-level coursework, advising and reading groups over an initial four-year period. In the new courses, doctoral students in the IWRG conducted empirical studies and produced short videos with librarians, archivists, data scientists, records managers, social media professionals and digital humanists (e.g., Carter & Sholler, 2016; Simons, Ocepek & Barker, 2016). Reading group meetings held twice per month with a dozen+ student and faculty members introduced significant literature on permutations of information work in corporate organizations, scientific enterprise and everyday leisure and information behavior activities. The group dedicated its efforts in the spring semester 2016 to building a syllabus for a graduate course on information work for an information school.

The group members' prior empirical research experiences enabled rapid progress through an initial agenda-setting stage and towards group consensus. Each member of the IWRG first proposed five topics (phrases) and a clarifying sentence, appropriate for a week-long module for the stated course syllabus. We then discussed the aggregated topics as a group, synthesized them as appropriate and prioritized those to be included as core modules for the course. The collaborative process established 10 topics:

- definitions, statistics, information society
- occupation trends, race, class and gender data
- work
- digital artifacts
- law and policy
- effects of information technology in the workplace
- space and time altered: the case of virtual teams
- labor
- education and training
- information work for and against the state, industry and individuals

Using the above working list (presented here in final form), the group director assigned one or two group members to each topic. The assignments permitted each contributor to then draft a set of course materials for her module. Upon compilation, the collected materials constituted a first draft of the syllabus, and at the subsequent meeting we engaged in small group iterative design, refining each set. Some breakout groups trimmed readings and simplified lecture themes while others brainstormed in-class exercises and shifted perspectival scope. Our synoptic goal for three emergent components of the course modules – learning objectives, readings and exercises – centered students' familiarization with key concepts, definitions, research patterns and resources examining information work in society. Emphasis is placed on analyzing impact, forming critical response and evaluating policies and outcomes for workers and organizations.

The learning objectives address specific contemporary work issues in historical, social, technological and political contexts; secondarily, they inculcate familiarity with research skills necessary for evaluating policies and predicting their outcomes for workers and organizations. Though we open the course with two introductory modules exploring general concepts and trends, including the intersection of race, class and gender with occupation, we integrate these topics in all modules in addition to giving them their own space. The required and supplementary module readings for the syllabus draw heavily from information studies, human-computer interaction, organizational science and those intersections, positioning foundational scholars alongside late-breaking scholarship on emerging technologies and professions.

Exercises in the information work course ask students to apply predictive tools, map processes, make arguments with data and synthesize knowledge about current work expectations and labor conditions. To structure the components as a whole, group members reviewed, revised and produced a final version. The group director wrote an opening paragraph and supervised formatting of the syllabus. The syllabus consists of a 10-week module-based master's-level outline of a graduate course on information work, with enough supplementary materials provided for readers who might teach an advanced undergraduate seminar or a doctoral seminar.

## FUTURE WORK AND DIRECTIONS

Over the development period of the collaborative syllabus, the effort shifted in both coverage and scope, but we find that the collaborative process instrumentally facilitated high-quality synthesis of broad and complex topics. First, the shift in coverage is most prominently seen in two particular topics; one (data work) which began as "management" of various kinds and another (information work for and against) which evolved from (in hindsight) duplicative attention to issues of communication through coordination. Second, we found that our approach to teaching each topic prioritized small-group discussion and generative idea-sharing at the possible expense of particular skills development. Given the nature of the topical content we selected, we structured module outcomes around students' ability to articulate the most important challenges and resources pertinent to an area of inquiry, rather than on their ability to work through a particular information technology (e.g., building an O*NET report is an intermediate step toward a written end product).

The effort was positively shaped at every juncture by peer review conducted across the research group. The peer review interactions were at first carried out at the large scale of a whole-group meeting but by the second half of the semester had evolved into individual two-way feedback between members. Continual sharing and revising of the module drafts improved each lesson component and ensured that each module could stand on its own and function within a graduate course.

The next steps for our work are to circulate this syllabus to information studies faculty to generate feedback and to iteratively develop additional, suggested modules. We also plan to implement the syllabus at an information school and, in specific contexts, adapt module components for both undergraduate and doctoral coursework. Such courses will retain the overall rationale that study of contemporary information work will proactively introduce students to the breadth of information careers as well as the ways in which technology might continue to change the future of work.

## ACKNOWLEDGMENTS

We gratefully acknowledge the U.S. Institute of Museum and Library Services (IMLS) for supporting this work under grant RE-02-12-0009-12, awarded to researchers at The University of Texas at Austin School of Information.

## REFERENCES

Carter, D. & Sholler, D. (2016). Data science on the ground: Hype, criticism, and everyday work. Journal of the Association for Information Science and Technology 67(10): 2309-2319. doi:10.1002/asi.23563

Hudd, S.S. (2003, Apr.). Syllabus under construction: Involving students in the creation of class assignments. Teaching Sociology 31(2): 195-202.

Maceli, M. & Burke, J.J. (2016). Technology skills in the workplace: Information professionals' current use and future aspirations. Information Technology and Libraries 35(4): 35-62. doi:10.6017/ital.v35i4.9540

Marcum, D. (1997, Mar.). Digital libraries: For whom? For what? The Journal of Academic Librarianship 23(2): 81- 84. doi:10.1016/S0099-1333(97)90002-1

OCLC Online Computer Library Center. (2017). "African American Intellectual History Society: Share history's most difficult lessons to improve the future." Retrieved from http://www.oclc.org/en/member- stories/charlestonsyllabus.html

Seadle, M. & Greifeneder, E. (2007). Envisioning an iSchool curriculum. Information Research 12(4), paper colise02. Retrieved from http://www.informationr.net/ir/12-4/colis/colise02.html

Simons, R.N., Ocepek, M.G., & Barker, L.J. (2016, Winter). Teaching tweeting: Recommendations for teaching social media work in LIS and MSIS programs. Journal of Education for Library and Information Science 57(1): 21-30. doi:10.12783/issn.2328- 2967/57/1/2

Thomas, J., von Dran, R., & Sawyer, S. (2006, April/May). The I-Conference and the transformation ahead. Bulletin of the American Society for Information Science and Technology 34(4): 16-18.

doi:10.1002/bult.2006.1720320407

Williams, C., Williams, K.E., & Blain, K.N. (Eds.). (2016). Charleston Syllabus: Readings on race, racism, and racial violence. Athens: University of Georgia Press.

Wu, D., He, D., Jiang, J., Dong, W., & Vo, K.T. (2011).

The state of iSchools: An analysis of academic research and graduate education. Journal of Information Science 38(1), 15-36. doi:10.1177/0165551511426247

# Diversity by Design: From Concept to Action

**Nadia Caidi**
*Faculty of Information, University of Toronto, Canada.*
*nadia.caidi@utoronto.ca*

**Keren Dali**
*SLIS, University of Alberta, Canada.* *kdali@ualberta.ca*

## ABSTRACT

**Last year, in a guest editorial for the *Library Quarterly* (LQ) we proposed the concept of diversity by design (DbD) and posited it as a concept relevant to workplace environments, community engagements and graduate LIS education. We invited LQ readers "to contemplate whether this concept ma[de] sense to them and, if yes, how it work[ed] in their respective" situations [1: 88]. We brought to light "the multiplicity of contexts that give diversity meaning and life in our complex field" [ibid] and demonstrated that it was integral, rather than superfluous, to our field and way of being. Finally, we gave examples of how "discounting or underappreciating" diversity "may have a disintegrating effect on our practice, scholarship, and education" [ibid]. This poster will introduce the concept of DbD; provide examples of several case studies which show the difference between "diversity as a bonus" and "diversity by design"; and include feedback and insight from the DbD grant-funded international symposium in Toronto, Canada, in September 2017.**

## KEYWORDS

guides, instructions, author's kit, conference publications

## INTRODUCTION

Last year, in a guest editorial for the *Library Quarterly* (*LQ*) we proposed the concept of diversity by design (DbD) and posited it as a concept relevant to workplace environments, community engagements and graduate LIS education. We invited LQ readers "to contemplate whether this concept ma[de] sense to them and, if yes, how it work[ed] in their respective" situations [1: 88]. We brought "to light the multiplicity of contexts that give diversity meaning and life in our complex field" [ibid] and demonstrated that it was integral, rather than superfluous, to our field and way of being. Finally, we presented examples of how "discounting or underappreciating" diversity "may have a disintegrating effect on our practice, scholarship, and education" [ibid]. The concept was developed in response to an uneasy question: why, despite our best efforts, is the state of diversity not getting better significantly or quickly enough in both educational and professional environments? This poster will have the following sections corresponding to the sections in this proposal.

80th Annual Meeting of the Association for Information Science & Technology, Washington, DC | Oct. 27-Nov. 1, 2017



## WHAT IS DBD?

Diversity by design promotes the idea of diversity as "integral and structural," not a "mere add-on" [1: 89]. It is the kind of diversity that is "there by design, not by chance," that is "part of the foundation, part of the core" [ibid]. We support curricula, workplace organizations, decision-making processes and academic research that integrate ideas of diversity from the start instead of throwing them in for reasons of trendiness and popularity. A diversity by design approach also entails looking underneath the surface and starting an uncomfortable (at times) conversation within our circles, our conferences, our boardrooms about the personal, social, familial, historical, community-wide causes of diversity tensions [2]. By so doing, libraries (and archives and museums) can become sites of potential disruption, but this approach is essential if we are serious about being truly inclusive of other ways of knowing, learning and being, and making space for these in our practices, processes, values and payrolls.

## INTERPRETING DIVERSITY IN LIS

1. Diverse information practices and research agendas; diverse resources
2. Diverse roles performed by information professionals
3. Engagement of diverse communities
4. Diversity considerations in preservation and digitization
5. Diversity in the professional workforce, academic faculty and students
6. Diversity as intellectual freedom
7. Diversity as an economic imperative and a competitive advantage

## ELEMENTS OF DBD IN EDUCATIONAL SETTINGS

1. Instructors' awareness of the need to integrate diversity considerations in every course design
2. Support from the faculty administration on building diversity into the overall curriculum
3. Students willing to engage with diversity in all its manifestations irrespective of their own background
4. Partnerships with diverse community groups
5. Diversity integration into technological learning platforms and educational resources
6. The diversity mind-set

## DIVERSITY MINDSET

1. Diversity "is a reality of life, not a problem to solve" [1: 91]
2. Diversity "is everybody's business"; "depending on the context, we are all diverse" [ibid]

3. "Diversity is not an option or an add-on: it is integral" [ibid]
4. The "diversity debate should proceed from concern for specific groups to concern for the health and function of the diverse society as a whole" [ibid]
5. Seeing "the multiple contexts and expressions of diversity in our professional and academic settings" [ibid]

## THE DBD SYMPOSIUM IN TORONTO, ON, CANADA

Since last year, we have developed this concept further. Currently in the making is the international DbD symposium that brings together representatives from the LIS and artistic communities, the general public and the government. The symposium is set to generate an honest and uncomfortable conversation about the lack and oversimplification of diversity discussion in various contexts. The symposium will try to overcome the tokenistic approach, geared toward increasing diversity numbers, and expand the definition of diversity beyond the demographic and personal characteristics traditionally associated with diversity. The outcome of symposium engagement will be integrated into the poster as well in the form of attendees' comments; feedback received through social media; photographs and other visual material; and snapshots from the symposium website and the ensuing living document that will archive the symposium content.

## CASE STUDIES

### Building Diversity into the Core Curriculum

This case study will show examples of how to diversify the content of core and elective courses that are not exclusively or directly related to diversity.

### Building Diversity into Technology Design

This case study will show the benefits of integrating diversity into technological design from the start as opposed to after-the-fact modifications.

### Building Diversity into the Hiring and Interview Process

This case study will point out several things that disadvantage diverse candidates in hiring and job interviewing and make suggestions for changed practices that welcome diversity.

### Building Diversity into Information Science Practices

This case study will provide several examples of how to think of diversity from the start (rather than after the fact) in designing community engagement initiatives and developing resources in libraries, governmental organizations and information agencies.

### Allowing Ourselves to Change

This case study will point out how the institutional location of information professionals and their engagement at the intersection of knowledge and culture can and should foster a climate for constructive conversations on difficult but crucial social issues (e.g., racism, etc.) along with the willingness to alter our practices, collections, intellectual tools and worldviews.

## REFERENCES


Caidi, N. & Dali, K. (2015). Can we talk?... *New Library World, 116* (11/12): 748-80.

Dali, K. & Caidi, N. (2017). Diversity by design. *The Library Quarterly, 87*(2), 88-98.

Hastings, S. K. (2015). If diversity is a natural state... *Library Quarterly, 85*(2): 133-38.

Jaeger, P.T. (2015). Disability, human rights, and social justice: The ongoing struggle for online accessibility and equality. *First Monday, 20*(9). Retrieved from: http://firstmonday.org/article/view/6164/4898

Overall, P. M. (2009). Cultural competence...*Library Quarterly, 79*(2): 175-204.

Subramaniam, M. & Jaeger, P.T. (2010). Modeling inclusive practice? *Library Trends 59* (1): 109-127.

# Design and Implementation of Domain Knowledge Service Platform Based on Spring Framework

**Qimei Chen**
*National Science Library, Chinese Academy of Sciences & University of Chinese Academy of Sciences, China. chenqm@mail.las.ac.cn*

**Hongbo Shi**
*National Science Library, Chinese Academy of Sciences, China. shihb@mail.las.ac.cn*

## ABSTRACT

**With so many places to look for information and the uncertainty surrounding the credibility of many free web resources, researchers' demand for knowledge services continues to grow under the e-science environment. Academic libraries facing the challenge of determining which information will be value-added when integrated with current collections makes it necessary to build an incorporate knowledge platform that integrates knowledge, skills, tools and services of certain professional field. This paper describes the technical solution of domain knowledge service platform based on Spring Framework, including resource organization, platform design and development. The practical application of domain knowledge service platform is shown in catalytic domain.**

## KEYWORDS

domain knowledge, integrated retrieval, knowledge service

## INTRODUCTION

Any research on scientific and technological innovation is inseparable from the support of science and technology information resources. Scientific users have increasing needs for integrated information retrieval, knowledge management and knowledge services under the e-science environment. This makes it necessary to build a knowledge service platform to integrate knowledge, technology, tools, services of certain domain, to embed information services into users' research process, innovate services and support the scientific and technological innovation.

Research on the construction of domain knowledge service platform has made significant progress in the world. Various types of systems or software tools are used, such as the Spring Framework technology. The Spring Framework is a Java platform that provides comprehensive infrastructure support for developing Java applications. This paper describes the technical solution of domain knowledge service platform based on Spring Framework, including resource organization and platform design and development. Current construction and application situation in catalytic domain is introduced in this paper.

80th Annual Meeting of the Association for Information Science & Technology, Washington, DC | Oct. 27-Nov. 1, 2017



## METHODOLOGY

### *Resource Organization*

Resource organization is the base of building knowledge service system. In our study, resource types include journals, dissertations, proceedings, books, specialized courses, academic reports, scientific data, patents, standards, industrial product, scientists, etc. Based on the DCMES (Dublin Core metadata element set) and JATS (Journal Article Tag Suite), the domain information resources are standardized. In addition, we had added some special resource types, such as industrial product-related fields.

### *Platform Architecture and Function*

The domain knowledge service platform is a scientific information platform for professional researchers and an integrated information system which is the organic integration of library services, users' information seeking behavior and the web service environment.

This paper presents the 4-layer architecture of domain knowledge retrieval services platform, which includes resource collections management layer, knowledge organization layer, indexing layer and application layer (Figure 1).

- The resource collections management layer is responsible for resource organization, clearly defines the resources elements of domain knowledge service platform, carries out the collection and procession of the resources and builds the domain knowledge base using metadata.
- The knowledge organization layer is used to organize materials for the purpose of retrieval and to manage a collection. It as a bridge between the user's information need and the material in the collection. With it, the user should be able to identify an object of interest without prior knowledge of its existence. Whether through browsing or direct searching, whether through themes on a webpage or a site search engine, the knowledge organization system guides the user through a discovery process.
- The indexing layer indexes the metadata of various sources and the relationships between metadata, providing users with fast, simple, easy-to-use resource discovery and access services.
- The application layer provides users with integrated retrieval, resource browsing, relationship display, website navigation, full text download, open interface, visual presentation, mobile services, etc.

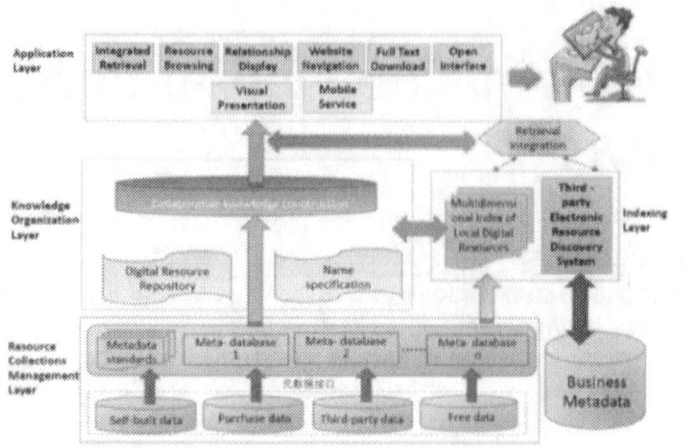


*Figure 1. Overall architecture of the domain knowledge service platform*

### *Platform Development*

The platform is based on J2EE connector architecture. The Spring Framework is used to be the base software, which provides many mature solutions, such as Spring MVC and Spring DATA module (Spring).

For the data organization, we reference the PMC FTP article package (PMC). The physical documents are identified by Globally Unique Identifier standard (UUID).

In order to reveal data resources efficiently and simply, the Solr indexing is built for multiple or single indexes. The users can retrieve the information they want through the indexing.

## PRACTICAL APPLICATION IN CATALYTIC DOMAIN

Catalysis is the chemical reaction brought about by a catalyst (Wikipedia). The importance of catalysis for the world's economic and sustainable growth cannot be overemphasized (ACS). We selected catalysis as the target domain and built the catalytic domain knowledge service platform (Figure 2). It's a one-stop retrieval system which affords users various kinds of catalysis resources, such as historical materials, famous scientists, specialized courses, e-books, research papers, patents, industrial products, reports and so on. The platform has four main functional modules.

- Knowledge service functions mainly provide the core services of domain knowledge service platform, including domain knowledge navigation, knowledge retrieval and acquisition, domain knowledge association, knowledge management and other functional components.
- The domain knowledge organization and management tools mainly achieve content construction of domain knowledge service platform, maintenance of metadata, as well as the processing and transformation of resource materials to database.
- Data service interface mainly achieves the scalability and extensibility of domain knowledge service platform, supporting data exchange between the platform and third-party systems or services.
- The system's basic functions, such as system management, user and privilege management and statistics, support the system's normal operation.

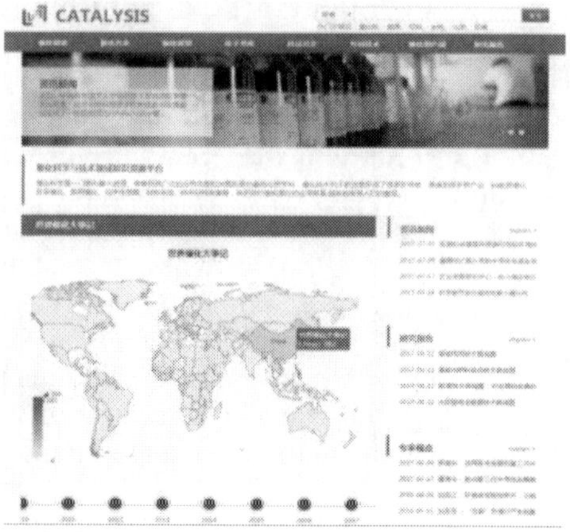


*Figure 2. Catalytic domain knowledge service platform*

## CONCLUSION

There is a general trend of building knowledge service platform. Meanwhile, with the development of big data and the changing scholarly communication process, there is a need to constantly explore new technology to provide better knowledge services.

## ABOUT VISUAL PRESENTATIONS

The visual presentation will guide the audience to experience multiple application scenarios from integrated data processing to retrieval services by poster presentation.

## REFERENCES

Wikipedia. Catalysis. Retrieved from https://en.wikipedia.org/wiki/Catalysis.

ACS (American Chemical Society). Catalysis – A key technology for sustainable development. Retrieved from http://catl.sites.acs.org/.

Spring. Retrieved from https://spring.io/.

PMC Open Access Subset. FTP Service. Retrieved from https://www.ncbi.nlm.nih.gov/pmc/tools/ftp/.

UUID (Globally Unique Identifier). Class UUID. Retrieved from http://docs.oracle.com/javase/8/docs/api/java/util/UUID.html.

# How Do Medical Researchers Use Open Health Data? A Case Study on Data Reuse Behavior of Using NHIRD in Taiwan

**Wei-Chung Cheng**
*Graduate Institute of Library and Information Studies, National Taiwan Normal University, Taiwan.*
*weichung1222@gmail.com*

**Ming-Hsin Phoebe Chiu**
*Graduate Institute of Library and Information Studies, National Taiwan Normal University, Taiwan.*
*phoebechiu@ntnu.edu.tw*

## ABSTRACT

**Data reuse is an emerging academic practice in information sciences studies, and there are diverse studies focusing on this topic. The concept of open health data is becoming a main stream in government administration, academic fields and business/industry. In this study, we analyzed 36 medical journal articles that used data from National Health Insurance Research Database through qualitative method to illustrate open health data reuse behavior in the medical field. The results indicated five stages of data reuse procedure: data re-appropriating, data recreating, data re-segmenting, data reconstructing and data revalidating. This paper demonstrates not only medical researchers' data reuse behavior with a practical perspective, but also how they transform quantitative data to valuable clinical discoveries. Moreover, the implications suggest different functionalities for an ideal open health data platform to support researchers' data reuse behavior in each research stage.**

## KEYWORDS

data reuse, research behavior, open health data, big data

## FORMAT OF PRESENTATION

This paper would be presented via poster.

## BACKGROUND AND RELATED STUDIES

The open data practice has been emerged for some time, not only in academic field and business/industry, but also in government administration. Following former president Obama's "Memorandum on Transparency and Open Government" and HITECT Act in 2009, how government could provide efficient health-related open data benefiting the healthcare industry and improve people's health and wellbeing became a priority issue (Martin, Helbig, & Birkhead, 2015; Stark, 2010). As in research and academics, the importance and research potential of using open health data and the platform are drawing attention. Martin, Helbig and Birkhead (2015) concluded that open health data could provide opportunities, such as improving public health practice and fueling innovation, to facilitate research. They also discussed how open health data platform fulfills users' multiple needs with different functionalities. Some researches illustrated the benefits of open health data for improving public health care and medical technology advancement (Kostkova et al., 2016; Bullinger, Rass, Adamczyk, Moeslein & Sohn, 2012; Demski, Garde & Hildebrand, 2016). The others focused on developing platforms for promoting uses of open health data, such as addressing issues about building trustworthy system of reusing health data (Geissbuhler et al., 2013) and improving the design of open health data platforms through various techniques (Tilahun, Kauppinen, Kessler & Fritz, 2014; Almeida et al., 2015).

With the movement in open health data and the practice of data reuse, this study aims to investigate how medical researchers reuse and interact with previously collected health-related open data. We chose the medical researchers of published peer-reviewed journal articles who had experiences of using the National Health Insurance Research Database (NHIRD), the largest and most complete open health database in Taiwan, as our research subjects. National Health Insurance system in Taiwan is well-known for its nationwide, mandatory-enrollment and single-payer features. This system was created in 1995 and managed by National Health Insurance Administration (NHIA); nearly 99% of Taiwanese population (around 23 million residents) and 97% of hospitals and clinics are enrolled. For advancing medical research and practice through those evidence-based datasets, National Health Research Institute was appointed by the NHIA to establish National Health Insurance Research Database (NHIRD) in 2000. NHIRD is free for both academic and non-academic purposes, but datasets are available upon request and permission from NHRI (National Health Research Institute, 2016). Our objective was to identify features of the stages that medical researchers were involved in when working with the datasets from NHIRD and to establish a data reuse workflow through a qualitative analysis approach.

## STUDY DESIGN AND METHODS

### *Data collection*

To focus of the study, we selected "cancer" and "oncology" – pertaining to the main cause of death in Taiwan in 2016

80th Annual Meeting of the Association for Information Science & Technology, Washington, DC | Oct. 27-Nov. 1, 2017

(Ministry of Health and Welfare, 2017) – as the keywords for database search, and we collected only the medical journal articles published in 2016. Thirty-six articles were retrieved and considered as the analysis subjects.

### *Data Analysis*

This study employed a qualitative content analysis method to analyze the behavioral features of these researchers when using NHIRD datasets. First, we observed the "Methods" section of all 36 articles and extracted the characteristics related to the stages of how data was used. Second, the characteristics were categorized to build a structural process which could explain the researchers' data reuse practices. Two coders with research expertise in health and medical informatics were recruited to verify the coding schemes. We randomly assigned 11 articles to the coders and had them analyze the "Methods" sections based on the coding schemes. Inter-coder reliability rate achieved 95%.

## PRELIMINARY FINDINGS

The findings revealed five main stages in the NHIRD data reuse process, and each stage includes subsets of detailed activities (see Table 1):

| **Stage1** | **Data re-appropriating** |
|---|---|
| Behavioral components | Examples |
| Determining research topic | …aimed to investigate the association of long-term use of different antihypertensive agents with incident breast cancer. |
| Determining research approach | …in this nationwide population-based case-control study. |
| Applying for Institutional Review Board | This study was approved by the Institutional Review Board of China Medical University. |
| Applying for datasets | ...were selected from the Catastrophic Illnesses Patient Database (CIPD) … |
| **Stage 2** | **Data recreating** |
| Behavioral components | Examples |
| Identifying study population | We identified all cancer patients who were added to the registry of catastrophic illness dataset from 1996 to 2010. |
| Filtering study population with inclusion criteria | We identified an HD cohort of patients with newly diagnosed, end-stage renal disease. |
| Filtering study population with exclusion criteria | Patients with any other cancer (ICD-9-CM codes 140–208) diagnosed before the index date were excluded. |
| **Stage 3** | **Data re-segmenting** |
| Behavioral components | Examples |
| Determining the period of datasets | … who made a claim between January 2003 and December 2006. |
| Determining the index date of observing study population | The index date for each case was the date of diagnosis of gastric cancer. |
| Determining the follow-up period of observing study population | … censored because of loss to follow-up, death, withdrawal from insurance, or the end of follow-up on 12/31/2011. |
| Stage 4 | Data reconstructing |
| Behavioral components | Examples |
| Determining statistical variables | …variables such as age, occupation, comorbidities of abortion… |
| Analyzing data linkage | Data linkage, processing, and computation were performed using Microsoft Structured Query Language Server 2008… |
| Adopting statistical model | We used Chi-squared tests to explore differences… |
| Utilizing statistical software | The SAS statistical package (SAS Institute) was used for statistical analyses. |
| **Stage 5** | **Data revalidating** |
| Behavioral components | Examples |
| Validating statistic results | We used a two-sided p value of 0.05 to determine significance in this study. |
| Cross-validating datasets | …selected from the CIPD. Control subjects were identified from the LHID 2000. |

***Table 1.*** *Stages of medical researchers' behaviors*

## CONCLUSIONS

This study shows that medical researchers typically go through five stages of data reuse process. Through these stages, we gain a clear picture of how the medical researchers transform quantitative data, which are provided by government and usually in forms of numerical registration files and original claim, to significant clinical discoveries. This process not only demonstrates how researchers use large scale datasets to reproduce valuable scientific findings with collecting, filtering and validating datasets, which represents the concept of what big data could achieve, but also shows the academic productivity of government datasets. On the other hand, we notice a convergence of open data and big data in the government, of which the scholars may take more advantage and the public may be served better. In addition, we also realize that the values and meanings of open health data aren't unleashed well without understanding the data reuse process. The preliminary findings imply that an ideal open health data platform could be developed with different functionalities according to each reuse stage: employ semantic technologies or ontology structure to make data discoverable (stage 1), provide data filtering and profiling functions (stage 2) and provide data remix, mashup and integration functions to support data recreating and re-segmenting (stage 3 and 4). Furthermore, the platform may recommend appropriate statistic models, variables, tools and validating methods for different kinds of data (stage 4 and 5) through analyzing previously used methods. In addition to providing featured functionalities that benefit medical researchers' workflow, the stages may be elaborated to a module for better using big data with detailed functionally design in the future. For instance, establishing data warehouse to provide well-structured datasets in initial stages; applying data fusion and data integration techniques in the middle of the stages to support data analysis work; and using data mining techniques to help users find associations between datasets and extract meaningful patterns in rear-end stages (Manyika et al., 2011).

Above all, our findings indicate a pattern of reusing government-released open health data of medical professionals. Also, it can be considered as a basis for building a platform for using open health data, even big data, more efficiently. Future research direction may focus on obtaining more detailed behavioral characteristics by interviewing researchers, which is the limitation of this study, and investigating the interfaces and functionalities of the data platform that facilitates data use and reuse under real circumstances. Finally, we specifically suggest constructing a health open data reuse model that incorporates workflow with resources needed and used in each stage to provide a full coverage of open data reuse in the medical research.

## REFERENCES


Almeida, J. S., Hajagos, J., Crnosija, I., Kurc, T., Saltz, M., & Saltz, J. (2015). OpenHealth platform for interactive contextualization of population health open data. *AMIA Annual Symposium Proceedings 2015*, 297-305.

Bullinger, A. C., Rass, M., Adamczyk, S., Moeslein, K. M., & Sohn, S. (2012). Open innovation in health care: Analysis of an open health platform. *Health Policy 105(2),* 165-175.

Demski, H., Garde, S., & Hildebrand, C. (2016). Open data models for smart health interconnected applications: The example of openEHR. *BMC Medical Informatics and Decision Making 16(1)*, 137-146.

Geissbuhler, A., Safran, C., Buchan, I., Bellazzi, R., Labkoff, S., Eilenberg, K., . . . De Moor, G. (2013). Trustworthy reuse of health data: A transnational perspective. *International Journal of Medicine Informatics 82(1)*, 1-9.

Kostkova, P., Brewer, H., de Lusignan, S., Fottrell, E., Goldacre, B., Hart, G., . . . Tooke, J. (2016). Who owns the data? Open data for healthcare. *Frontiers in Public Health 4*, 7.

Manyika, J., Chui, M., Brown, B., Bughin, J., Dobbs, R., Roxburgh, C., & Byers, A. H. (2011). Big data: The next frontier for innovation, competition, and productivity. Retrieved from http://www.mckinsey.com/business-functions/digital-mckinsey/our-insights/big-data-the-next-frontier-for-innovation.

Martin, E. G., Helbig, N., & Birkhead, G. S. (2015). Opening health data: What do researchers want? Early experiences with New York's open health data platform. *Journal of Public Health Management and Practice 21(5)*, E1-7.

Ministry of Health and Welfare (2017). 2015 Main causes of death analysis in Taiwan. Retrieved June 5, 2017 from http://dep.mohw.gov.tw/DOS/lp-1777-113.html

National Health Research Institute (2016). National Health Insurance Research Database. Retrieved June 7, 2017 from https://nhird.nhri.org.tw/

Stark, P. (2010). Congressional intent for the HITECH act. *The American Journal of Managed Care 16(12)*, SP24-8

Tilahun, B., Kauppinen, T., Kessler, C., & Fritz, F. (2014). Design and development of a linked open data-based health information representation and visualization system: Potentials and preliminary evaluation. *JMIR medical informatics 2(2)*, 1-13.

# Examining Information Search Behaviors in Small Physical Space: An Escape Room Study

**Dongho Choi**
*School of Communication & Information (SC&I), Rutgers University, USA. dongho.j.choi@rutgers.edu*

**JiHo An**
*School of Communication & Information (SC&I), Rutgers University, USA. jiho.an@rutgers.edu*

**Chirag Shah**
*School of Communication & Information (SC&I), Rutgers University, USA. chirags@rutgers.edu*

**Vivek Singh**
*School of Communication & Information (SC&I), Rutgers University, USA. vivek.k.singh@rutgers.edu*

## ABSTRACT

**In this experimental study for understanding individuals' searching behavior in different environments, we investigated activities that involved looking for information in a limited physical space. 31 participants were asked to navigate an escape room installed in our lab and their behavior was recorded by a wearable camera. Annotated activities were analyzed by information behavior models developed by Kuhlthau (1991) and Ellis (1989). While the two models are associated with different aspects of information search behavior, dichotomous behavior - such as depth-first vs. breadth-first approaches - were observed between participants.**

## KEYWORDS

Search Behavior, Information Seeking Model, Physical Space, Experimental Study

## INTRODUCTION

In our daily lives, we interact with different environments to search for information that is presented in diverse formats such as books, papers, Web documents, etc. Several models were suggested to describe the general behavior of information seeking. Kuhlthau (1991) proposed information search process (ISP), viewing information seeking as a process of construction, which consists of six stages: *initiation, selection, exploration, formulation, collection,* and *presentation*. Focusing more keenly on information retrieval, Ellis (1989) found different types of activity labeled *starting, chaining, browsing, differentiating, monitoring*, and *extracting*.

The aim of this study is to investigate information search behaviors performed in physical space in order to identify behavioral patterns. Here, an escape room game was designed and carried out to observe participants' physical activities in a small, limited space. Collected and annotated behavioral data was analyzed using the ISP model (Kuhlthau, 1991) and Ellis's model (Ellis, 1989) to address the following research question:

What kinds of physical activities regarding information seeking are observed in a physical search task?

## METHOD AND ANALYSIS FRAMEWORK

We recruited undergraduate students of Rutgers University through open calls via various email lists and social networking sites. Participants were each compensated $100 in cash upon completion of the study. A total of 31 students participated in the fall semester of 2016.

An experimental game, *escape room*, was designed and carried out in a single room at the lab. The game utilized three types of information sources: twenty books, eight movie posters, and five research posters. Each book and poster is considered as a distinct *information patch* (Pirolli and Card, 1995) that a user may explore to consume the "fruits" of information. Each participant was asked to play the game, exploring and searching for certain clues in the space to complete a series of tasks in twenty minutes. For instance, to solve the first problem, a participant needed to locate the answer in a specific book. Once they successfully used the correct answer to open a lock, the next question was provided from the unlocked box.

Participants' physical activities in the game were captured by a wearable video recorder that's data was analyzed by two trained coders. While the recorder could not capture users' exact eye movements, it was enough to judge their cognitive statuses and behavioral intentions during the experiment. There was missing data from two participants, so we analyzed the behavioral data of 29 participants using ISP and Ellis's model as points of comparison. While ISP explicates the search tasks related to the stages that participants attempt to pass in order to move forward, Ellis's model focuses on searching activities' different characteristics.

## RESULTS

We mapped and grouped the observed behavior with the two models and Figure 1 describes the result. Activities annotated with regard to the escape room such as *approaching books or posters, scanning books, reading a book*, etc., are presented in the middle. Areas of interest captured by the recorder are also presented in the figure.

---

80th Annual Meeting of the Association for Information Science & Technology, Washington, DC, VA | Oct. 27-Nov. 1, 2017

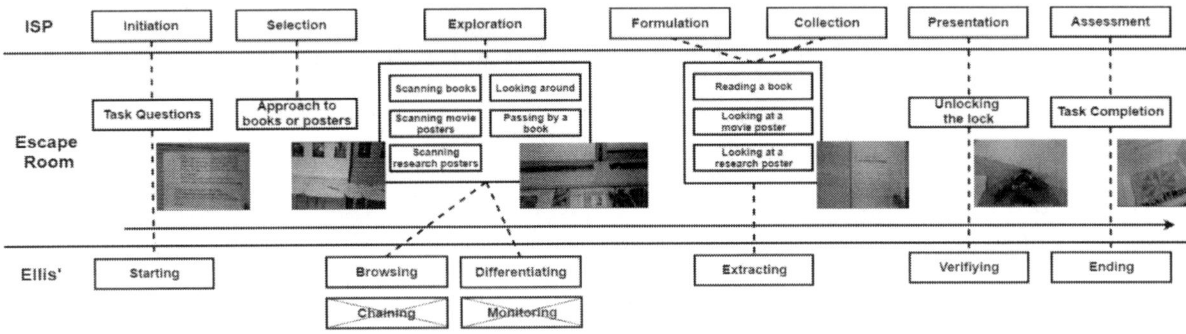


***Figure 1.*** *Relations between ISP and Ellis's model and observed physical activities during escape room*

When it comes to the ISP model, with some variances in frequency and duration time, escape room activities were mapped on each stage in the model, showing most participants followed the process. For instance, the selection stage was related to approaching to places where books, movie or research posters were located. Actions such as scanning books and looking around in the room were considered parallel to the *exploration* stage, as users were attempting to investigate information about the given topic.

Some escape room activities were categorized either into the *formulation* stage or the *collection* stage depending on whether the user gathered the correct answer or information. *Formulation* stage refers to a status in which the user forms a focused perspective and gains confidence. *Collection* stage implies the user gathers information pertinent to the focused perspective. In this regard, for instance, if the user could not obtain an answer while reading a book they know to be pertinent to finding the clue, their reading behavior remains in the *formulation* stage.

In Ellis's model, the *extracting* action was associated with *reading a book and poster*. In the context of escape room behavior, several activities could be considered both *browsing* and *differentiating*. However, *chaining* and *monitoring* were not observed in escape room behavior, indicating the context of Ellis's model might not be applicable to physical search in limited time and space.

A dichotomous behavior pattern was observed in the *selection* and the *exploration* stages when users initially approached to the information patches. Klöckner et al. (2004) defined depth-first vs. breadth-first processing of search result lists in Web search, and we observed a similar pattern (see Table 1). Approximately 62% to 69% of participants utilized the depth-first approach when exploring *books, movie posters*, and *research posters*. They visited and explored the information patches without scanning or skimming other patches. On the other hand, the remainder scanned and skimmed more patches before selecting the patch they visited. This finding shed lights on the relationship between physical search and Web search behavior, which will be examined in future research.

| Task | Book | Movie | Research |
|---|---|---|---|
| Depth-first | 18 (62.1%) | 20 (69.0%) | 18 (62.1%) |
| Breadth-first | 11 (37.9%) | 9 (31.0%) | 11 (37.9%) |

***Table 1****. Search behavior observed in escape room.*

## CONCLUSION

In this study, information search behavior in a small physical space was observed and analyzed using the ISP model and Ellis's model. The results demonstrated activities associated with the models as well dichotomous information exploration behavioral patterns. The study is significant in that its discovered behavior patterns can guide research into search patterns in other contexts such as broader or different physical spaces. Future research includes a study regarding the dichotomous behaviors between physical space and online environments to understand the relationships between searching behavior in different contexts.

## ACKNOWLEDGMENTS

The work is supported by the Google Research Award received by Dr. Chirag Shah and Dr. Vivek Singh.

## REFERENCES

Ellis, D. (1989). A behavioural approach to information retrieval system design. *Journal of documentation*, 45(3), 171-212.

Klöckner, K., Wirschum, N., & Jameson, A. (2004, April). Depth- and breadth-first processing of search result lists. In *CHI'04 extended abstracts on Human factors in computing systems* (pp. 1539-1539). ACM.

Kuhlthau, C. C. (1991). Inside the search process: Information seeking from the user's perspective. *Journal of the American Society for information Science*, 42(5), 361.

Pirolli, P., & Card, S. (1995, May). Information foraging in information access environments. *In Proceedings of the SIGCHI conference on Human factors in computing systems* (pp. 51-58). ACM Press/Addison-Wesley Publishing Co.

# Stress, adaptation, growth: International students' approaches to scholarly research and academic integrity

**Amanda B. Click**
*American University, Bender Library, USA.aclick@american.edu*

## ABSTRACT

**International students often face unique challenges in adapting to higher education in the United States, and may benefit from specialized academic support. This paper and the accompanying poster outline the findings of a qualitative study exploring international graduate students' adaptation processes as evidenced by their information seeking and use activities. The study was informed by Kim's cross-cultural adaptation theory. Semi-structured interviews developed using critical incident technique were conducted with 30 international graduate students enrolled at three North Carolina universities. Participants described a variety of difficulties related to information seeking including finding and understanding resources, and explained how they addressed these challenges. They generally recognized the significance of American academic integrity standards, acknowledging the importance of proper citation and understanding faculty expectations. This paper explores the study findings through the lens of Kim's stress-adaptation-growth dynamic. Findings have practical implications for librarians, and other faculty and staff who provide support and training to international students in the United States.**

## KEYWORDS

international students, cross-cultural adaptation, research process, academic integrity, information seeking

## INTRODUCTION

During the 2015-2016 academic year, the number of international students enrolled in the U.S. surpassed one million for the first time (Institute of International Education, 2016). Many of these students face adapting to a new system of higher education. They may struggle with conducting the high-level research needed to complete their graduate work, as well as adhering to potentially unfamiliar academic integrity standards. International students make significant contributions to American higher education, providing global perspectives in the classroom (Trice, 2003) that help prepare students for intercultural work environments (Pandit, 2013). It is important that colleges and universities provide appropriate assistance for these students, and librarians can play a major role by offering specialized support and services. The study provides information to assist with these efforts by exploring the following research questions:

RQ1: How do international graduate students studying in the United States conduct their academic research and writing?

RQ2: How do international graduate students studying in the United States perceive, engage with, and negotiate issues of academic integrity?

This paper and the accompanying poster will share study findings related specifically to the cross-cultural adaptation process and its connection to information seeking and use.

### *International Students and the Academic Library*

The library and information science literature about international students tends to be descriptive instead of research-based (Click, Wiley, & Houlihan, 2017). The research that does exist indicates that these students need help with the research process as a whole (Chen & Van Ullen, 2011; Han, 2012; Mehra & Bilal, 2006). They tend to begin their research on Google (Chen & Brown, 2012; Morrissey & Given, 2006, Sin, 2015), but also use library resources (Liao, Finn & Lu, 2007; Hughes, 2013). In addition, they may not understand exactly how to adhere to academic integrity guidelines (Chen & Brown, 2012; Liu & Winn, 2009; Morrissey & Given, 2006), and struggle with paraphrasing in particular (Chen & Van Ullen, 2011; Gunnarsson, Kulesza, & Pettersson, 2014; Han, 2012). Previously, no study has used cross-cultural adaptation theory to explore the research processes of international students, and the ways that the adaptation process is present in information seeking and use. Nor has critical incident technique been used to study this population in the context of specific, graduate-level assignments and the information and research processes used to complete them.

### *Cross-cultural Adaptation Theory*

Kim (2001) defines cross-cultural adaptation as "the dynamic process by which individuals, upon relocating to new, unfamiliar, or changed cultural environments, establish (or reestablish) and maintain relatively stable, reciprocal, and functional relationships with this environment" (p. 31). The theory asserts that a human being is an open system, and will "struggle to regain an internal equilibrium in the face of adversarial environmental conditions" (Kim, 2009, p. 244). This human desire to reach a stable relationship with the host

80th Annual Meeting of the Association for Information Science & Technology, Washington, DC | Oct. 27-Nov. 1, 2017

environment supports the theory's stress-adaptation-growth process model (Figure 1), which informed data analysis in this study. Instances of the stress-adaptation-growth dynamic were identified in the participants' descriptions of information seeking and use.

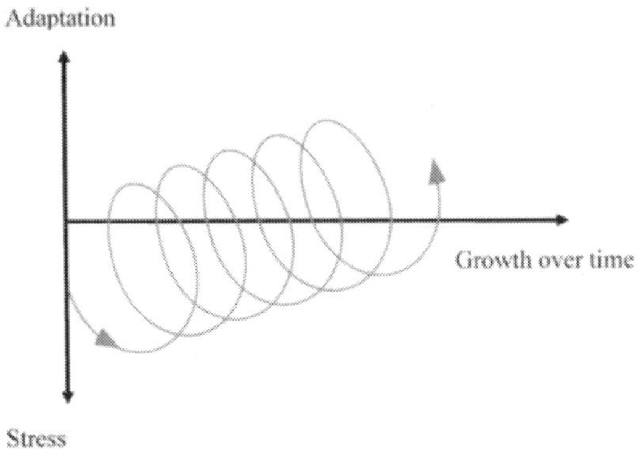


***Figure 1**. The stress - adaptation - growth dynamic, adapted from Kim (2001, p. 57)*

## METHOD

This qualitative, constructivist study was designed using critical incident technique (CIT). CIT, pioneered by Flanagan (1954), is "a research process that invites respondents to identify events (incidents) they deem significant (critical) for a particular purpose" (Kain, 2007, p. 135). There are five steps in CIT research: 1. ascertaining the general aims, 2. establishing plans and specifications, 3. collecting the data, 4. analyzing the data, and 5. interpreting and reporting the data. Steps 3 and 4 usually take place concurrently. Thirty semi-structured interviews were conducted with international graduate students at three North Carolina universities. During the interviews, participants described completing a class assignment that required research – the critical incident - and discussed their perceptions of academic integrity in the American context. Participants hailed from a variety of countries, and all were studying in the U.S. for the first time and spoke English as an additional language. Approximately half of the participants were Chinese or Indian. International students are a heterogeneous group, and this study seeks to identify themes that are specific to this particular sample population and not necessarily generalizable.

## FINDINGS

The cross-cultural adaptation theory's stress-adaptation-growth dynamic was evident in participants' descriptions of their experiences with scholarly research and academic integrity. Participants described challenges they faced (stressors) and the ways that they managed these challenges (adaptations). Growth was more difficult to identity; Kim (2009) calls it "subtle and often imperceptible" (p. 245).

### *The Research Process*

Marisa, from Russia, described the stress of trying to do academic research: "I was even crying because I wasn't able to find something that I needed." She adapted by learning techniques from her American classmates. Once she better understood how to find the information she needed, her perspective changed: "But the most fun part I think was, you know, as soon as I got some skills, like how to do research, I really enjoyed it." Professors were an important source of information as well. Rita, a Chinese student, struggled with reconciling the variety of opinions and perspectives she discovered in her research. She spoke with her professor, who advised her to pick one position and work from that angle. This guidance helped Rita understand research expectations and move forward with her assignment.

Many participants expressed an appreciation of learning new things, demonstrating growth as a scholar. Santi, from Colombia, explained: "I liked what I learned when I started reading all these journal articles and see what people are doing, and it was actually a lot of things that I didn't know."

The literature indicates that international students may need support for each step of the research process, and not only with finding appropriate resources, for example (Mehra & Bilal, 2006; Chen & Van Ullen, 2011; Han, 2012). The experiences of the participants in this study support this notion. Their research stressors ranged from identifying a topic to presenting findings.

### *Perceptions of Academic Integrity*

After a classmate borrowed and subsequently copied his work, Victor, an Indian student, learned that his previous view on academic integrity was not acceptable in U.S. higher education: "But now, at least with this incident, I realized that there is a way in which you can help [your classmates], and that's the way I should adopt. Giving someone your work is not the best way to help." Mary, from China, worried about inadvertently committing an academic integrity infraction, particularly plagiarism. She learned to use tools, including Google Scholar and the Citations & Bibliography tab in Microsoft Word: "For reference things I feel like Google Scholar is really easy to use. [I just enter] the paper's title or book's name into Google Scholar and it will just jump out of a box and you just paste." When she first arrived in the U.S., Sally, from India, did not understand her professors' academic integrity expectations so she asked for clarification on every assignment until she understood: "What is academic integrity going to be like in this course? Can I Google stuff or should I do everything by myself? Can I ask my friends?'

The literature tends to argue that international students do not understand the concept of "Western" academic integrity (Chen & Brown, 2012; Liu & Winn, 2009; Morrissey & Given, 2006; Shi, 2006). The participants in this study, however, generally demonstrated an understanding of the concept and a willingness to develop new behaviors and skills in order to meet expectations.

## CONCLUSION

Study participants faced stressors and demonstrated adaptive behaviors. Their perspectives changed and became more complex. These findings show that information seeking and use for scholarly purposes plays a role in cross-cultural adaptation. Thus, research and general academic support for this population may be even more important than it seems. Academic librarians are already committed to helping students develop research and information literacy skills. Learning these skills may contribute not only to academic success, but also to the cross-cultural adaptation process overall.

## REFERENCES


Chen, Y. H., & Van Ullen, M. K. (2011). Helping international students succeed academically through research process and plagiarism workshops. *College & Research Libraries, 72*(3), 209-235. http://doi.org/10.5860/crl-117rl

Chen, Y., & Brown, C. (2012). Ensuring Chinese engineering graduate students' academic success: A study at the University of Oklahoma. *Science & Technology Libraries, 31*(3), 320-341. http://doi.org/10.1080/0194262x.2012.705144

Click, A. B., Wiley, C. W., & Houlihan, M. (2017). The internationalization of the academic library: A systematic review of 25 years of literature on international students. *College & Research Libraries, 78*(3), 328-358. http://doi.org/10.5860/crl.v78i3.16591

Flanagan, J. C. (1954). The critical incident technique. *Psychological Bulletin, 51*(4), 327-358. http://doi.org/10.1037/h0061470

Gunnarsson, J., Kulesza, W. J., & Pettersson, A. (2014). Teaching international students how to avoid plagiarism: Librarians and faculty in collaboration. *The Journal of Academic Librarianship, 40*(3), 413-417. https://doi.org/10.1016/j.acalib.2014.04.006

Han, J. (2012). Information literacy challenges for Chinese PhD students in Australia: A biographical study. *Journal of Information Literacy, 6*(1), 3-17. http://doi.org/10.11645/6.1.1603

Hughes, H. (2013). International students using online information resources to learn: Complex experience and learning needs. *Journal of Further and Higher Education, 37*(1), 126-146. http://doi.org/10.1080/0309877X.2011.644778

Institute of International Education. (2016). *Open Doors report on international education exchange*. Retrieved from https://www.iie.org/Research-and-Insights/Open-Doors/Open-Doors-2016-Media-Information

Kain, D. L. (2007). Critical incident technique. In S. G. Rogelburg (Ed.), *Encyclopedia of industrial and organizational psychology* (pp. 135-137). Thousand Oaks, CA: SAGE Publications. http://doi.org/10.4135/9781412952651.n55

Kim, Y. Y. (2001). *Becoming intercultural: An integrative theory of communication and cross-cultural adaptation*. Thousand Oaks, CA: SAGE Publications.

Kim, Y. Y. (2009). Cross-cultural adaptation theory. In S. W. Littlejohn & K. A. Foss (Eds.), *Encyclopedia of communication theory* (pp. 244-248). Thousand Oaks, CA: SAGE Publications.

Liao, Y., Finn, M., & Lu, J. (2007). Information-seeking behavior of international graduate students vs. American graduate students: A user study at Virginia Tech 2005. *College & Research Libraries, 68*(1), 5-25. http://doi.org/10.5860/crl.68.1.5

Liu, G., & Winn, D. (2009). Chinese graduate students and the Canadian academic library: A user study at the University of Windsor. *The Journal of Academic Librarianship, 35*(6), 565-573. https://doi.org/10.1016/j.acalib.2009.08.001

Mehra, B., & Bilal, D. (2007). International students' perceptions of their information seeking strategies. In *Proceedings of the 2007 Canadian Association for Information Science* (pp. 1-14). Retrieved from http://www.cais-acsi.ca/ojs/index.php/cais/issue/archive

Morrissey, R., & Given, L. (2006). International students and the academic library: A case study. *Canadian Journal of Information and Library Science, 30*(3/4), 221-239.

Pandit, K. (2013). International students and diversity: Challenges and opportunities for campus internationalization. In H. C. Alberts & H. D. Hazen (Eds.), *International students and scholars in the United States: Coming from abroad* (pp. 131-141). New York, NY: Palgrave Macmillan.

Shi, L. (2006). Cultural backgrounds and textual appropriation. *Language Awareness, 15*(4), 264-282. https://doi.org/10.2167/la406.0

Sin, S. C. J. (2015). Demographic differences in international students' information source uses and everyday information seeking challenges. *The Journal of Academic Librarianship, 41*(4), 466-474. http://doi.org/10.1016/j.acalib.2015.04.003

Trice, A. G. (2003). Faculty perceptions of graduate international students: The benefits and challenges. *Journal of Studies in International Education, 7*(4), 379-403. http://doi.org/10.1177/1028315303257120

# Human Dimensions of Peer Review in Information Science

**Keren Dali**
*University of Alberta, Canada. kdali@ualberta.ca*

**Lilith Lee**
*University of Alberta, Canada. yinwaili@ualberta.ca*

**Paul T. Jaeger**
*University of Maryland College Park, USA. pjaeger@umd.edu*

## ABSTRACT

**While peer review is a popular research subject in academia, including information science, most sources focus on the mechanics, benefits and shortcomings of the process. In departure from this trend, this poster will address the human dimension of peer review and its role as a community building instrument and a locus of relationship formation. The poster will look at how "negligent and unscrupulous reviewing can detrimentally affect" "a sense of community" (Dali & Jaeger, n.d.) and support this argument through a new analytical framework based on humanistic pedagogy. It will address the role of peer review in the changed information science landscape; present a positive outlook on peer review "as a privilege and an unmatched academic opportunity"; "examine in detail the elements of helpful and unhelpful reviews"; and provide "advice to authors on how to respond to reviews, especially the unhelpful ones" (Dali & Jaeger, n.d.). The poster should appeal not only to junior faculty and PhD students, but also to practitioners who aspire to publish and experienced authors involved in scholarly communication and grant reviewing.**

## KEYWORDS

peer review, academic community, relationship building, impact of negative reviewing, authors, editors

## INTRODUCTION

In a relatively small information science community, both scholarly and professional, peer review presents a centripetal force and a focus of dialog and engagement. Peer review "is ubiquitous, permeat[es] every facet of our activities [and] applies not only to scholarly and professional publications but also to job/performance evaluations, instructor evaluations (in courses, workshops, etc.), evaluations of student work, and grant proposals, to name just a few" (Dali & Jaeger, n.d.). As such, it can be considered "a space whereby relationships are built and nurtured and the exchange of valuable experience and succession planning take place" (Dali & Jaeger, n.d.). Peer review is important in the context of both mentorship and collaboration, which has determined the poster focus on "the human dimension rather than the logistics of the process" (Dali & Jaeger, n.d.). Specifically, this poster "demonstrates how negligent and unscrupulous reviewing can detrimentally affect [interpersonal professional] relationships and a sense of community." It then presents an analytical framework which derives from the tenets of humanistic pedagogy by Carl and Natalie Rogers. From the practical standpoint, this poster also stands

to help researchers in LIS navigate the review and editorial processes, both as an author and a reviewer, evaluate the quality of reviews they receive and write, formulate responses to reviews, and defend their work when warranted (Dali & Jaeger, n.d.).

Having surveyed several major trends in LIS journal publishing, the poster will also foster an uplifting and positive image of peer review as "a gracious educational opportunity and a privilege that should not be extended to those who take it lightly or abuse it" (Dali & Jaeger, n.d.).

This poster presents selected highlights of the larger conceptual paper, not yet published. We have chosen the aspects of our discussion which lend themselves to successful visual presentation in order to share our work with a wider audience in a succinct and accessible way. The following sections correspond to the sections that will be integrated into the poster.

## RECONSIDERING THE RHETORIC OF PEER REVIEW: A GIFT, A PRIVILEGE AND A REASON FOR GRATITUDE

Instead of looking at peer review as "an extremely important work" and "an ever-so-important duty that we carr[y] out" at the expense of our research, teaching and personal time, we reposition peer review as "an invitation for an intellectual conversation" and "a gift that we neither asked for nor dreamed of but that came to us nonetheless by virtue of our hard work, academic stature and expertise." The poster will promote this positive image of peer review that "allows us to have a sneak peek into the budding academic production" and to be "privy to thoughts and ideas that no one except the author may yet be privy to" (Dali & Jaeger, n.d.). For reviewers who can relate to this perception of peer review, adopting humanistic attitudes in reviewing would be a natural choice. These attitudes comprise the analytical framework described in the next section.

80th Annual Meeting of the Association for Information Science & Technology, Washington, DC | Oct. 27-Nov. 1, 2017

## ROLE OF REVIEWERS IN SCHOLARLY COMMUNITY BUILDING: AN ANALYTICAL FRAMEWORK

Our framework consists of the five parameters, which liberally derive from the humanistic pedagogical principles developed by Carl Rogers (1959, 1969, 1989, 1995) and Natalie Rogers (Corey 2009):

- Empathy: when reviewers and editors walk in the author's shoes
- Unconditional positive regard: the ability of reviewers to focus on and criticize ideas, not the author personally
- Realness of reviewers: the ability of reviewers to respect the authors' autonomy instead of playing the role of judges (and remain true to their own research nature)
- Psychological freedom (CR): authors' freedom to choose intellectual directions
- Psychological safety (CR): authors' freedom to experiment with no fear of ridicule and ad hominem
- Opportunity for stimulating and challenging experiences

This framework gives us a lens to scrutinize the peer review process as a community building instrument in the context of scholarly publishing.

## ELEMENTS OF HELPFUL REVIEWS

- Evidence that the paper has been read and considered in its entirety
- Evidence of the reviewer's supportive and collegial attitude toward the author
- Signs of gratitude for a chance to have an early look into scholarship in the making
- Relevant and clear comments
- Evidence of interest in what the author has to say rather than in pursuing the reviewer's own agenda
- Suggestions of alternative publication routes if the paper is rejected
- Evidence of the reviewer's expertise and subject knowledge

## ELEMENTS OF UNHELPFUL REVIEWS

- Signs that the manuscript has been skimmed or scanned rather than carefully read
- The imposition of the reviewer's preferences on the paper under consideration
- Unsubstantiated criticism
- A stylistic "straight jacket"
- Disallowing for varying scholarship formats and a narrow definition of scholarship
- The non-expert opinion
- Meanness
- Tardiness

## RESPONDING TO REVIEWS

Experienced and novice authors alike are frequently unprepared "to deal – emotionally and intellectually – with the effects of reviews, be they fair, highly critical reviews resulting in major revision or rejection, or unscrupulous and painful reviews" (Dali & Jaeger, n.d.). To help authors cope, the following suggestions are offered.

- How to thank reviewers, including the unkind ones
- Separating the "mandatory" from the "desired" revisions – standing your ground
- Understanding what *rejection* means and acting accordingly
- Raising respectful objections to unsubstantiated and hurtful reviews
- Writing a response to reviewers and a letter to editors
- Withdrawing your paper and placing it elsewhere

## ADDITIONAL FORMAT DETAILS

Selected concepts will be represented through attractive lists, charts and original pictures and drawings to illustrate ideas and to convey feelings and interactive aspects.

## REFERENCES


Corey, Gerald. (2009). *Theory and practice of counselling and psychotherapy*. 8th ed. Belmont: Thomson/Brooks/Cole.

Dali, K. & Jaeger, P. Beyond scholarly publishing: Peer review in library & information science as a community staple. (forthcoming in *The Library Quarterly*)

Rogers, Carl R. (1959). Significant learning [...]. *Educational Leadership, 16*(4): 232–242.

Rogers, Carl R. (1969). *Freedom to learn [...]*. Columbus, OH: Charles E. Merrill.

Rogers, Carl R. (1989). *The interpersonal relationship in the facilitation of learning*. New York: Houghton Mifflin.

Rogers, Carl R. (1995). *On becoming a person*. Boston, MA: Houghton Mifflin.

# Information World Mapping to Explicate the Information-Care Relationship in Dementia Care

**Nicole Dalmer**
*Faculty of Information and Media Studies, The University of Western Ontario, Canada. ndalmer@uwo.ca*

## ABSTRACT

**Information world mapping is a helpful data elicitation technique to make visible the hidden work of finding, using and making sense of information. This methods-based paper explores the utility of a mapping exercise both within an institutional ethnographic study and in eliciting informants' understandings and descriptions of their care-related information work. Eleven family caregivers of community-dwelling older adults living with dementia drew maps of their information worlds. Each map depicts a unique combination of information resources (people, agencies, texts and websites) accessed, relationships that shape the information work in addition to key locations frequented to access information. Given the difficulty in delineating the boundaries of information, the mapping exercise served as a helpful tool for caregivers to make visible the intricacies of their information work, including the barriers encountered and inventive strategies created to access, use and translate information needed to guide and support their care work.**

## KEYWORDS

dementia, family caregivers, information work, institutional ethnography, information worlds

Introduction

As the proportion of older adults will more than double in the next 20 years (Statistics Canada, 2010), the aging of Canada's population necessitates innovative supports from familial, societal and governmental institutions. The federal government's endorsement of aging in place (the ability to live at home for as long as possible) combined with a shifting away from institutionalization and decreasing availability of government-funded home care programs is increasingly transferring responsibilities and demands for unpaid care work onto families. Of particular interest for this study are the implications of aging in place for people living with dementia, the most significant cause of disability among Canadians over the age of 65, affecting nearly 747,000 Canadians, a number expected to double by 2031 (Alzheimer Society of Canada, 2012).

80th Annual Meeting of the Association for Information Science & Technology, Washington, DC | Oct. 27-Nov. 1, 2017



The information work that informs and guides care is one invisible and unrecognized form of work done by family caregivers. The provision of, access to and ability to navigate and use information enables family caregivers to be involved in the care and wellbeing of aging family members. With access to an increasing wealth of health and care-related information, increasing responsibility is being passed "to individuals, with their effectiveness determined by their ability to gather, then intelligently act on, health information" (Johnson & Case, 2012, p. 5). This expectation that family caregivers will do information work is confounded, however, by a significant number of studies "indicating that extensive unmet caregiver information needs persist" (Washington, Meadows, Elliott & Koopman, 2011, p. 39).

The act of searching for information on behalf of another (such as a family caregiver searching for or on behalf of an older adult) represents an especially under-articulated and complex form of work as "the information-seeking work involved in taking responsibility for one's ... family members' health involves much more than simply looking for and locating data relevant to a specific condition ... it means sifting through, interpreting and dealing with the implications of the information one finds" (Harris, 2009, p. 78). Barnes and Henwood (2015) critique the "informatization of care," a trend in which information may marginalize or replace care. These authors draw attention to the distinction between informing to care and informing with care; the latter indicative that information is neither separate nor outside care, but is instead inextricably linked to care (p. 159).

Corbin and Strauss (1985) first described *information work* as a form of work done by people living with chronic illness. Within library and information science (LIS), Hogan and Palmer (2005) and Souden (2008) have taken up the concept, both characterizing information-related activities as part of the work of managing one's own chronic illness. This present study aims to advance the conceptualization of information work by focusing on the additional work of searching on behalf of or because of another. In alignment with Corbin and Strauss (1985), I assert that care work "has an information component and presumes some degree of information processing whether the work is manual labor or highly abstract decision making" (Huvila, 2009, p. 3). Characterizing caregivers' information practices as work brings attention to the time, effort, resources, etc. that are often made invisible in literature and policy, owing to the construction of caregiving as a gendered concept of social and familial responsibility.

## FRAMEWORK OF INQUIRY

Originating in the 1970s by Canadian sociologist Dorothy E. Smith, institutional ethnography (IE) is a method of inquiry that maps how the everyday world of people's experiences are "put together by relations that extend vastly beyond the everyday" (Smith, 2005, p. 1). While rooting itself in individuals' knowledge and the actualities of their everyday experiences, this method of inquiry simultaneously acknowledges that these every day, local experiences are permeated and coordinated by relations, decisions and institutions that are outside of and may be invisible to those living in their local environments. Mapping and making known these relations that extend beyond the local and the everyday is the crux of institutional ethnography. While notably implemented in education, nursing and other professional and service-oriented fields, as Stooke and McKenzie (2009) observe, institutional ethnography is not yet "widely taken up by library and information science researchers" (p. 660).

## STUDY DESCRIPTION

Eleven family caregivers of community-dwelling older adults living with dementia were interviewed about their information-related care work. Caregivers ranged in age from 58 to 73 years of age and represented a variety of relationships to the care recipient: wife, husband and daughter. The older adults living with dementia receiving care ranged in age from 67 to 87 years of age and had diagnoses of Alzheimer's disease, early-onset Alzheimer's, Parkinson's-disease dementia, mixed dementia and Frontotemporal dementia. For the interview process, work, and more specifically, work knowledges focused the interview conversation, with the intention to ground interviews in the accounts of caregivers' everyday activities. To complement the caregivers' reported experiences, in response to the mapping metaphor that runs throughout the IE method of inquiry, informants were asked to map out the information work they described in the earlier interview. Caregivers were given a large degree of control over the design and interpretation of their information worlds. In addition to items, places and relationships that might shape or guide their information work, informants were encouraged to include social context, including what they might do with information once it was found.

This mapping activity is based on the concept of Sonnenwald's information horizons (1999) and builds on subsequent mapping exercises outlined by Greyson, O'Brien and Shoveller (2017), and Freund, Hawkins and Saewyc (2016). An information horizon is created within a context and a situation and is determined individually and socially in which any number of information resources may be contained. While caregivers' information work may occur in a broader, more generalizable context or situation than that prescribed by Sonnenwald, this concept served as a useful framework for understanding caregivers' experiences of their information work. Informants were asked to talk out loud as they created their unique world (Sonnenwald, 1999). Prompting questions included asking informants why they drew their map in a certain order or why items mentioned in the interview did not appear on the map (or conversely, what items appeared on the map that were not discussed throughout the interview). Following the completion of a pilot study, a template information world was created so that informants could choose to work from a blank paper or from the template, which made the mapping exercise less onerous.

## RESULTS

***Figure 1.*** *Catherine's information world*

As exemplified in Figure 1, each map depicts the caregiver's unique interpretations of their work, representing the information resources (family members, health care professionals, agencies, texts, tools and websites) they accessed within their care context. In addition to mapping information sites and resources, caregivers included relationship dynamics, quotes and self-care activities, indicating how information more broadly intersects with and may both support and complicate their care work. A majority of caregivers were eager to participate in this exercise and the mapping exercise served as a memory aid, eliciting a discussion of a number of information activities not mentioned in the interview. As the informants completed the mapping exercise, they noted that they were both surprised and validated by the work they had done. The mapping exercise made visible to them the amount and the different types of work that they have performed throughout their caregiving trajectory. While each world was distinct, commonalities observed between the information worlds included the degree to which relationships shaped and modulated the amount and the type of information shared. Informants also drew how their own background, education and personality traits have come to shape their information work.

## CONCLUSIONS

Good care is often positioned as a natural by-product of the widespread availability of good information. As the information world maps reveal, however, information work is not separate or outside of care, but is instead inextricably linked to care work and involves mobilizing and negotiating different types of information depending on the situation, the timing, the contexts or the different individuals involved.

The use of institutional ethnography to approach the information world mapping exercise privileges the everyday work of family caregivers of community-dwelling older adults living with dementia. IE also attunes the analysis of each map to the work, and more specifically, the information-related care work that is often invisible, permitting a more holistic view of the role of information as caregivers navigate spaces, agencies, resources, tools and other individuals throughout their everyday lives.

As the concept of information work is still in flux, the mapping exercises suggest some amendments to consider as a means to continue to make the work of finding, using, sharing and managing information more visible; building a concept of information work that goes beyond purposive, conscious and intended actions, but instead allows for the incorporation of information avoidance as work, that acknowledges the complex work of searching on behalf of or for another, the work of information storage and management, and the affective or emotional components of information activities that may be relationally influenced. If we allow for more nuanced understandings of the complexities of information practices, we may be able to move from informing to treat to informing to care.

## ACKNOWLEDGMENTS

I am humbled by and indebted to those informants who so openly and willingly shared their experiences. This research is supported by the Social Sciences and Humanities Research Council of Canada.

## REFERENCES

Alzheimer Society of Canada. (2012). *A new way of looking at the impact of dementia*. Retrieved from http://www.alzheimer.ca/~/media/Files/national/Media-releases/asc_factsheet_new_data_09272012_en.pdf

Barnes, M., Henwood, F., & Smith, N. (2016). Information and care: A relational approach. *Dementia, 15*(4), 510-525.

Corbin, J., & Strauss, A. (1985). Managing chronic illness at home: Three lines of work. *Qualitative Sociology, 8*(3), 224-247.

Freund, L., Hawkins, B., & Saewyc, E. (2016). Reflections on the use of participatory mapping to study everyday health information seeking by LGBTQ youth. *Proceedings of the American Society for Information Science and Technology, 53*(1).

Greyson, D., O'Brien, H., & Shoveller, J. (2017). Information world mapping: A participatory arts-based elicitation method for information behavior interviews. *Library & Information Science Research, 39*(2), 149-157.

Harris, R. (2009). Cyber-burdens: Emerging imperatives in women's unpaid care work. In E. Balka, E. Green & F. Henwood (Eds.), *Gender, health and information technology in context* (pp. 72-87). New York: Palgrave Macmillan.

Hogan, T. P., & Palmer, C. L. (2005). "Information work" and chronic illness: Interpreting results from a nationwide survey of people living with HIV/AIDS. *Proceedings of the American Society for Information Science and Technology, 42*(1).

Huvila, I. (2009). Ecological framework of information interactions and information infrastructures. *Journal of Information Science, 35*(6), 695-708.

Johnson, J. D., & Case, D. O. (2012). *Health information seeking*. New York: Peter Lang.

Smith, D. E. (2005). *Institutional ethnography: A sociology for people*. Lanham, MD: Altamira Press.

Sonnenwald, D. H. (1999). Evolving perspectives of human information behavior: Contexts, situations, social networks and information horizons. In T. Wilson & D. Allen (Eds.), *Exploring the contexts of information behaviour* (pp. 176-190). London: Taylor Graham.

Souden, M. (2008). Information work in the chronic illness experience. *Proceedings of the American Society for Information Science and Technology, 45*(1), 1-6.

Star, S. L. (1991). The sociology of the invisible: The primacy of work in the writings of Anselm Strauss. In D. Maines (Ed.), *Social organization and social process: Essays in honor of Anselm Strauss* (pp. 265-283). Hawthorne, NY: Aldine de Gruyter.

Stooke, R., & McKenzie, P. J. (2009). Leisure and work in library and community programs for very young children. *Library Trends, 57*(4), 657-675.

Washington, K. T., Meadows, S. E., Elliott, S. G., & Koopman, R. J. (2011). Information needs of informal caregivers of older adults with chronic health conditions. *Patient Education and Counseling, 83*(1), 37-44.

# Connecting People with Their Communities Through Proximity-Based Digital Storytelling

**Brian Detlor**
*McMaster University, Canada. detlorb@mcmaster.ca*

**Claudia Crippa**
*McMaster University, Canada. crippaclaudia91@gmail.com*

**Fariba Nosrati**
*McMaster University, Canada. nosratif@mcmaster.ca*

## ABSTRACT

**This visual presentation describes the results of a library-led initiative involving the use of iBeacon proximity-based technologies to connect people with their communities. The two libraries involved in this initiative developed and tested an app that pushed community-based digital stories to users' smartphones and tablets when users were physically near a historic or cultural object (e.g., statue, landmark) about which the digital story was based. Using proximity-based technologies to deliver stories about cultural and historic objects of interest to a community was thought to be a novel and engaging way to rally emotional connection and pride in one's own community. To test this hypothesis, as well as the viability of using iBeacon technology as a storytelling delivery mechanism, a pilot study was conducted with 50 participants from the general public at the two libraries involved in the initiative. Participants used the app to browse and read stories pertaining to a prominent park in the city. Posters with pictures of historic or cultural objects within the park were installed throughout each library. Each poster was enabled with iBeacon technology so that digital stories about the historic or cultural object displayed on the poster were automatically pushed to participants' smart devices as participants became near. To collect data on users' experiences and satisfaction with the app and the digital stories, on-the-spot interviews were conducted with participants after they finished visiting the posters and reading the digital stories. Interview data were analyzed using content data analysis techniques. A Likert-scaled questionnaire was also administered; this data was analyzed using factor analysis and hierarchical regression. Results suggest that proximity-based digital storytelling is a viable approach to connect people with their communities, especially if the stories provide people with relevant, timely, location-based community information that stirs a positive emotional response.**

## KEYWORDS

digital storytelling, proximity-based technologies, libraries, community

80th Annual Meeting of the Association for Information Science & Technology, Washington, DC | Oct. 27-Nov. 1, 2017



## INTRODUCTION

This visual presentation investigates the use of iBeacon proximity-based technologies as an opportunity to foster community connection. Proximity-based technology systems allow users to receive information automatically when they are close to a physical spot. Using Bluetooth Low Energy, iBeacons provide users with high-quality, time-sensitive information based on a user's close physical locale (iBeacon Insider, 2017). Information from an iBeacon is automatically pushed to a user's mobile phone or tablet when users are in close physical proximity.

Specifically, this presentation describes an iBeacon project led by two libraries in a medium-sized city in Canada. The pilot was launched to test the use of proximity-based digital storytelling as a means of connecting people with their communities. The pilot involved the setup of iBeacons that disseminated stories pertaining to a prominent park in the heart of the city. Posters advertising the park were installed in both libraries to entice citizens to download and experience a custom-made app on their smartphones and tablets. Each poster installed in the libraries pertained to a collection of stories about a particular object located in the park (e.g., a fountain, a statue). If users installed the app on their smartphones or tablets and enabled Bluetooth, then their mobile devices would "wake up" when the users were physically close to one of the posters (i.e., the app would automatically receive stories about the image on the poster).

The high-level research question guiding this study is: What is the viability of using proximity-based digital storytelling as a mechanism to provide information to people in a way that enhances their connection with the community in which they live, work or play?

## CONCEPTUAL FRAMEWORK

To set the boundaries around this investigation, a conceptual framework was constructed based on two theoretical models: i) the Information Systems Success Model (Delone & McLean, 2003; 1992; Petter et al., 2008); and ii) the Model of Effective Use of Information Systems (Burton-Jones & Grange, 2013).

## METHODOLOGY

The study comprised both qualitative and quantitative research methods. The qualitative portion involved one-on-one interviews with 50 participants from the general public who used the iBeacon app to experience the digital stories developed about the city's prominent downtown park. These interviews were conducted "on-the-spot" – that is, immediately after the participants were finished using the iBeacon app in the library. Interview questions asked participants to reflect on their experience using the iBeacon app and the impact the iBeacon app had in terms of their perceptions of, emotional attachment to and interest in the city. The interviews were digitally recorded and transcribed. From there, interview transcripts were analysed using content data analysis techniques advocated by Strauss & Corbin (Corbin & Strauss, 2014; Myers, 2013) to identify categories and relationships between those categories. DeDoose text analysis software was used to help conduct this analysis.

The quantitative portion involved these same 50 participants completing a short paper-based questionnaire immediately after the participants were finished using the iBeacon app in the library. The survey quantitatively polled user perceptions of the app's systems quality, information quality, as well as user satisfaction and net benefits. Likert-scale questions polled user perceptions on a 7-point scale. Factor analysis and hierarchical regression techniques were conducted on this dataset to verify and test the relationships between the categories identified in the qualitative phase of the study.

The study's conceptual framework informed the design of both the interview and survey instruments, as well as the analysis of the data.

Participants comprised a diverse and representative sample.

## FINDINGS

Findings indicate that proximity-based digital storytelling can play an important role in strengthening the connection between people and their communities by providing relevant, timely and location-based community information when needed. Importantly, this connection is heightened if the stories are of interest to the readers and if the stories elicit a strong, positive emotional attachment.

The comments made by participants in their interviews were very positive. People loved the digital stories and the iBeacon app. Many of the participants wanted to see more stories. Several participants asked when the stories would be available for everyone to see and experience. A good percentage of the participants took the time to read all the stories. Some participants were emotional reading the stories. All participants said they learned something new about the city and that the app was very informative. Most participants were satisfied with the app's system quality (90%). Some participants mentioned the app helped revive their own personal stories and memories of the city. Overall, most mentioned that by experiencing the stories in the iBeacon app that they gained benefit (89%).

Specifically, analysis of the interview and survey data showed that i) information quality and system quality are important to participants; ii) middle-aged and older participants were more satisfied with the app and digital stories than younger participants; and iii) participants experience a layered impact of benefits from using the iBeacon app. The primary (1st order) benefit was the impact of digital storytelling. That is, community cultural heritage stories captured people's attention, engaged their emotions, fostered personal connections and refreshed personal memories about the community. The secondary (2nd order) benefit was improved impressions about the community. That is, the 1st order impact led to a secondary benefit of creating positive perceptions about the community and increasing people's personal appreciation and emotional attachment towards the community.

## ACKNOWLEDGMENTS

This research is kindly supported by a Partnership Development Grant from the Social Sciences and Humanities Research Council of Canada.

## REFERENCES

Burton-Jones, A., & Grange, C. (2012). From use to effective use: A representation theory perspective. *Information Systems Research, 24*(3), 632-658.

Corbin, J., & Strauss, A. (2014). *Basics of qualitative research: Techniques and procedures for developing grounded theory.* Sage Publications. Los Angeles, USA.

Delone, W. H., & McLean, E. R. (2003). The DeLone and McLean model of information systems success: A ten-year update. *Journal of Management Information Systems, 19*(4), 9-30.

DeLone, W. H., & McLean, E. R. (1992). Information systems success: The quest for the dependent variable. *Information Systems Research, 3*(1), 60-95.

iBeacon Insider (2017). Retrieved May 18, 2017 from http://www.ibeacon.com.

Myers, M. D. (2013). *Qualitative research in business and management.* Sage. London, UK.

Petter, S., DeLone, W., & McLean, E. (2008). Measuring information systems success: Models, dimensions, measures, and interrelationships. *European Journal of Information Systems, 17*(3), 236-263.

# Blogging as Recovery: The Use of Blogs by Survivors of Military Sexual Trauma

**Brian Dobreski**
*School of Information Studies, Syracuse University, USA.*
*bjdobres@syr.edu*

**Bryan Semaan**
*School of Information Studies, Syracuse University, USA.*
*bsemaan@syr.edu*

## ABSTRACT

**Military sexual trauma (MST) is a significant concern in the United States military and poses distinct challenges to survivors in seeking traditional means of support. While research has shown blogs to be an effective means of working through crises and seeking support, little work has focused on MST survivors and their use of blogs. In this study, we drew on Herman's stages of recovery in an analysis of 659 posts from five blogs written by MST survivors to understand their blogging behavior. We found that bloggers frequently use their blogs to perform what may be thought of as traditional recovery work. In particular, MST survivors blogged as a means of reconstructing their personal narratives and identities, as well as reaching out and reconnecting with others. In contrast, recovery work focused on establishing safety was underrepresented. Overall, findings suggest blogs to be a useful tool in recovering from sexual trauma and warrant further examination of other online spaces for recovery.**

## KEYWORDS

military sexual trauma, blogging, recovery

## INTRODUCTION

Being diagnosed with a disease, getting a divorce, experiencing job loss: all of these events are forms of life disruption (Massimi, Dimond, & Le Dantec, 2012). When a person experiences a life disruption, this often leads to a transition phase; a process of adjustment through which people learn to re-negotiate key aspects of their lives, such as relationships, roles and routines (Bridge, 2004). This adjustment work – or, what we will refer to as the recovery process – can be further complicated by the type of disruption experienced.

In this study, we focus on a particular type of life disruption – military sexual trauma (MST) – which refers to sexual assault, harassment or stalking that occurs to a victim while in military service (Surís & Lind, 2008). MST is a significant issue within the United States military, particularly for service women (Semaan, Britton, & Dosono, 2017). While both men and women are affected, women are 20 times more likely to experience MST (Surís & Lind, 2008). Recent data suggest that 20%–30% of women have experienced sexual assault or attempted sexual assault during the course of their military service (Campbell & Raja, 2005). In the aftermath of MST and as veterans re-integrate into civil society, regardless of gender, the recovery process can be difficult as survivors of MST may be reluctant to come forward or seek formal support, fearing professional or social retaliation or further harm (Patterson, Greeson, & Campbell, 2009).

In this work, we employ a qualitative study of the blog activities engaged in by MST survivors during the veteran re-integration process. While previous scholarship reveals that veterans leverage online spaces (e.g., private Facebook groups) to manage the re-integration process (Semaan, Britton & Dosono, 2016), little is known about the role of blogs during the MST recovery process, and this research aims to address this gap. We draw on Herman's (1997) stages of recovery as a lens to make sense of these blogging activities. Results reveal specific aspects of the recovery process that are enacted through blogging.

## RELATED WORK

The process through which individuals recover from personal crises, such as psychological trauma, have been conceptualized by Herman (1997) as taking place across three stages: establishing safety, reconstructing their story and restoring connections with others.

The first stage, establishing safety, entails survivors establishing safety in their own bodies or environments; for example, addressing immediate threats such as homelessness or problems with alcohol. The second stage, reconstructing their story, is focused on reconstructing traumatic events and their meanings. An example would be articulating the series of events surrounding an assault. The third and final stage, restoring connections with others, includes reaching out and connecting with others, as well as taking on new engagements with the world; for example, publicly advocating for female veterans.

The affordances of blogs, which enable people to both write about their experiences as well as connect with others through social features, such as linking and commenting, can enable MST survivors to engage in recovery work. Blogging has long been recognized as a useful means of self-expression and social support. Articulating opinions, expressing emotions and forming and maintaining communities have been cited as some of the major motivations behind blogging (Nardi et al., 2004). Blogging can offer a safe outlet for individuals experiencing crises or trauma to discuss their experiences and socially connect with others (Al-Ani, Mark, & Semaan, 2010).

80th Annual Meeting of the Association for Information Science & Technology, Washington, DC | Oct. 27-Nov. 1, 2017

## METHODS

This study is part of a larger, ongoing project to understand the uses of online spaces in the recovery process. The present study was limited to personal blogs, written by one or two individuals, and not sponsored by or featured as part of a larger website. Blogs written by either female or male authors who reported experiencing MST while in service were considered. We identified relevant blogs through keyword searching online, as well as snowball sampling via links between blogs. A total of five blogs representing six authors were identified, with one blog being shared by two of the authors. Bloggers included four female and two male. The blogs covered time spans of between one and 10 years, with post counts ranging from 35 to 510. All blogs indicated addressing personal MST experiences as a primary purpose.

A combination of inductive and deductive approaches was used in coding blog data. First, blogs were analyzed at the post level for the apparent purpose or function of the post; only the main text of the posts was analyzed, with comments not considered at this time. After an initial set of codes was developed, two researchers worked to align these codes within the Herman recovery framework. Codes were grouped into Stages 1, 2, 3, or no stage. Using the newly formed codebook, two coders analyzed posts from all blogs, assigning a broader stage code as well as a 1-2 specific subcodes. For the present study, only the broader stage codes are considered. Two coders reached 78% agreement in assigning stage codes to the posts.

A total of 659 posts were coded, constituting a random subsample of all posts gathered from all five blogs. Any posts that had been coded as more than one stage were classed with the latest stage for this analysis. This resulted in a total of four Stage 1 posts, 333 Stage 2 posts, 286 Stage 3 posts and 36 posts with no stage.

## RESULTS: BLOGGING AS RECOVERY

Our data shows that the use of blogs supported MST recovery across the stages of Herman's model, particularly Stages 2 and 3.

Only four posts in the current sample were coded as Stage 1. These posts focused explicitly on current, perceived threats to personal safety or strong expressed desires to seek isolation. For example, P1 wrote a post explaining recent experiences with homelessness and his current frustrations with attempting to find a stable living environment.

Slightly more than half of the posts coded in the sample were identified as Stage 2 (333 out of 659). Many Stage 2 posts were focused on personal narrative construction; both stories of specific traumatic events and generally contextualizing stories were included here. P5 has devoted many posts to reconstructing his life story, explaining his storytelling in one such post: "parts of me are stuck there [in the past] and are trying to repair the damage…". Beyond narrative construction, other Stage 2 posts focused on identity construction and working through emotions.

The 286 posts considered to be Stage 3 focused on advocating for others, promoting awareness of specific issues and offering advice or support to others. Though MST is a major topic of Stage 3 posts, other topics ranging from medical cannabis to LGBT rights were also confronted. P2, who co-wrote a blog with P6, often used her posts to reach out and provide support to other survivors of any sexual trauma: "I try to use this blog to encourage others, so that we all know that we are going through much of the same things…"

Finally, 36 posts were coded as exhibiting no stage. These posts did not refer to any specific recovery work, but included things like holiday messages and brief personal updates.

## DISCUSSION

Herman presents a model of recovery that is not strictly linear, though as recovery progresses, activities from later stages are more expected than those from earlier stages. Analysis of the MST blogs revealed posts focused mostly on activities from the later stages. Though Stage 1 activities and concerns were present, they were the focus of only a handful of posts. There are several explanations for the absence of Stage 1 work: it is possible that traditional blogging is not conducive to addressing these kinds of personal safety issues or that much of the work of this stage must be completed before survivors could undertake blogging.

The majority of posts were found to reflect work from Stage 2 and Stage 3. MST bloggers devoted significant amounts of their posts to telling and retelling their stories, often in vivid detail. Herman's second stage predicts the importance of this kind of narrative work, and blogs provided a controlled space for survivors to establish their stories. Blogs also provided a number of affordances for third stage work. All bloggers used their blogs often as a platform to raise awareness of MST and other issues, as well as to reach out to readers with specific advice or calls to action. All of these activities are important in the final stage of recovery, in which survivors seek ways reconnect and reengage with the world.

A number of posts fell outside of the Herman framework and were unable to be coded with a stage. The relatively small amount of these posts suggests that the MST bloggers were very focused around the original intent of these blogs. Still, their presence is significant and may reflect a further progression of the recovery process. The nature of these posts reflects many of the motivations recognized in general blogging, including offering updates on day to day things (Nardi et al., 2004). These posts show that MST bloggers at times use their blogs for more mundane purposes outside of recovery work.

## CONCLUSION

We analyzed 659 posts from five blogs written by MST survivors. In examining the intended purpose or focus for each post, we applied Herman's stages of recovery as a framework. Results found a general fit with this framework, particularly around Stage 2 (reconstructing stories) and Stage 3 (reconnecting), though Stage 1 work (establishing safety) appears relatively underrepresented. This suggests that MST bloggers utilize their blogs for specific aspects of their recovery. Further work is warranted to understand how and why these individuals engage in blog work and how Stage 1 work could be better supported through blogging, as well as the use and affordances of other online spaces in recovery from sexual trauma.

## ACKNOWLEDGMENTS

This research was funded by NSF award No. IIS-1657429. Any opinions, findings and conclusions, or recommendations expressed in this material are those of the authors and do not necessarily reflect the views of the NSF.

## REFERENCES

Al-Ani, B., Mark, G., & Semaan, B. (2010). Blogging in a region of conflict: Supporting transition to recovery. In *Proceedings of the SIGCHI Conference on human factors in computing systems* (pp. 1069-1078). New York: ACM.

Bridges, W. (2004). *Transitions: Making sense of life's changes*. Cambridge, Mass.: Da Capo Press.

Campbell, R., & Raja, S. (2005). The sexual assault and secondary victimization of female veterans: Help-seeking experiences with military and civilian social systems. *Psychology of Women Quarterly, 29*(1), 97-106.

Herman, J. L. (1997). Trauma and recovery: The aftermath of violence--from domestic abuse to political terror. New York: Basic Books.

Massimi, M., Dimond, J. P., & Le Dantec, C. A. (2012). Finding a new normal: The role of technology in life disruptions. In *Proceedings of the ACM: 2012 conference on computer supported cooperative work* (pp. 719–728). New York: ACM.

Nardi, B. A., Schiano, D. J., Gumbrecht, M., & Swartz, L. (2004). Why we blog. *Communications of the ACM, 47*(12), 41-46.

Patterson, D., Greeson, M., & Campbell, R. (2009). Understanding rape survivors' decisions not to seek help from formal social systems. *Health & Social Work, 34*(2), 127-136.

Semaan, B., Britton, L. M., & Dosono, B. (2017). Military masculinity and the travails of transitioning: Disclosure in social media. In *Proceedings of the 2017 ACM Conference on computer supported cooperative work and social computing* (pp. 387-403). New York: ACM.

Semaan, B. C., Britton, L. M., & Dosono, B. (2016). Transition Resilience with ICTs:'Identity Awareness' in Veteran Re-Integration. In *Proceedings of the 2016 CHI Conference on human factors in computing systems* (pp. 2882-2894). New York: ACM.

Surís, A., & Lind, L. (2008). Military sexual trauma: A review of prevalence and associated health consequences in veterans. *Trauma, Violence, & Abuse, 9*(4), 250-269.

# Film Content Analysis on FIAF Cataloguing Rules and CEN Metadata Standards

**Rubén Domínguez-Delgado**
*University of Seville, Spain. rdd@us.es*

**María-Ángeles López Hernández**
*University of Seville, Spain. alhernan@us.es*

## ABSTRACT

**Cataloguing manuals published by the International Federation of Film Archives (FIAF) and the film metadata standards EN 15744 and EN 15907 have proven to be really useful for film archives in the process of film cataloguing. However, beyond the technical or formal aspects of films contemplated on these rules, there are some important aspects about the film content analysis which have not been taken into consideration.**

**We are showing with examples and analyzing all the references to the important task of content analysis on the historical evolution of these standards for film archives, discussing about the possibilities of adoption of more film content fields on them, what would suppose better possibilities of retrieval of film information by the users of film archives, adapting to their needs and to the new era.**

## KEYWORDS

film librarianship, film archives, film content analysis, film cataloguing, metadata, retrieval of film information

## INTRODUCTION

Most theorists in archival and library and information sciences agree about the importance of content analysis in information systems for convenient retrieval of information by users. The UNESCO *Recommendation for the Safeguarding and Preservation of Moving Images* asked moving-image archives to provide the best access possible to their collections by users (UNESCO, 1980, 158).

However, two recently published studies showed that current film content analysis in film archives, unlike moving images content analysis in TV archives, has alarming shortcomings, and it is characterized by a heterogeneity of criteria and models and by the absence of a systematic and general application of specific content analysis methodologies that allow for the selective retrieval of moving images by users (Domínguez-Delgado & López-Hernández, 2016a and 2016b).

## OBJECTIVES AND METHODOLOGY

Wondering about these deficiencies in film archives and knowing of the scientific hole about this topic, we decided to do this research, focused on the attention that the main international institutions which are the reference point in cataloguing for film archives have historically paid to film content analysis on the standards they produce. These institutions are the International Federation of Film Archives (FIAF) and the European Committee for Standardization (CEN).

We have selected and review the most important standards edited by these two model institutions: 1979 FIAF *Film cataloguing*, 1980 FIAF *Handbook for film archives*, 1991 *FIAF Cataloguing Rules for Film Archives*, 2016 *FIAF Moving Image Cataloguing Manual*, as well as the two *Cinematographic Work Standards* (CWS) published by CEN: *EN 15744* (2009) and *EN 15907* (2010).

On them, we have paid attention to the cataloguing fields and recommendations linked to the film contents, leaving formal or technical aspects aside. Our main goal is to find out the depth of the moving image content analysis on these rules, discussing about how it affects the current possibilities of retrieval of information by users.

## RESULTS

On 1979 Film Cataloguing, it was recommended that, just for the case of non-fiction films, "the content of each scene should be descripted, including times and places where actions take place". Besides, contents should be divided "in different categories, using descriptors which can be selected from a formal thesaurus" (FIAF, 1979, p. 51). However, FIAF left in each archive´s hands the application or not of these recommendations, depending on their collections, needs, goals and resources.

On 1980 *A Handbook for film archives*, it was included on it the same recommendation about content description for non-fiction films than on 1979 rules. Besides, there were new recommendations, such as the inclusion, just for the case of newsreels and magazines, of "*one descriptor per sequence*", as well as the next indications: "*the content description should be always, as a goal, a style which can be achieved*" or "*the film should be watched to make sure the description is precise, better than the accumulation of subjective information from secondary resources*" (FIAF, 1980, p. 49).

Besides, it was recommended to include the *thematic classification* and, inside this area, the *film genre* and the *classification of the film content*, according to Dewey Decimal Classification. It was also recommended a *controlled vocabulary* if film archives want to index the topics of films (FIAF, 1989, p.55).

80th Annual Meeting of the Association for Information Science & Technology, Washington, DC | Oct. 27-Nov. 1, 2017

On 1991 *FIAF Cataloguing Rules for Film Archives* there was not any content field on the first six *obligatory* cataloguing areas. Only on the *optional "Notes area"*, there were some references to film content to be followed by film archives *"depending on their resources"*: the field *Nature, scope or artistic form of the item* (FIAF, 1991, p. 107) – the relevant film genre –, the field *Contents* and the field *Summary*. On *Contents*, it could be included *"a list of contents of each segment which composes a film consisting on different parts, like newsreels"* (FIAF, 1991, p. 125).

The Summary which could be given by archivists "should be an accurate and objective description of the film's actual content, based on a viewing of the item". Despite its optionality, FIAF considered it important since it "is designed to assist the user in pre-selecting moving image materials for viewing, thus helping him/her to eliminate unwanted materials and to concentrate upon those items most useful for his/her purposes". It was also indicated that the summary should include "an introduction outlining the plot, subject, or nature of the moving image, preferably including genre(s), time period(s), and location(s) of the events depicted, if appropriate". Additionally, it was pointed that "if known, indicate the presence and nature of stock footage or excerpts from other moving image materials which are used" (FIAF, 1991, p. 126).

On the 2016 FIAF Moving Image Cataloguing Manual, FIAF has already recognized that "the archival moving image field has changed dramatically in recent years, with technological advances revolutionizing cataloguing, preservation, and access practices" (2016, p. 1). However, although the content description fields on these rules are not already inside optional Notes but inside two specific spaces – Content Description and Subject/Genre/Form terms –, it is just recommended these indications on the first of them:

> *"Write a concise, objective, non-critical summary of the content of the moving image Work and/or Variant. Content descriptions can be synopses, brief TV guide-like one sentence description, shotlists, etc. There can be more than one type of content description in the record (...) If acceptable summaries are already available in secondary sources, cataloguers may use these, instead of taking the time to prepare summaries of their own (...) A content description may also be a shotlist or listing of the contents of an aggregate Work/Variant." (FIAF, 2016, p. 126).*

Besides, "the content description can be based on a viewing of the work – not necessarily, as recommended on 1980 FIAF standards and as theorists advise –, accompanying documentation, or secondary sources, but the source should be clearly noted". Finally, it is pointed that just for unedited works – not for non-fiction films, as recommended on 1979 standards and on the FIAF 2013 working draft previous to the current cataloguing rules (FIAF, 2013, p. 33) –, and "where time and resources permit, each scene should be summarized". However, it is at least pointed that "if there are shots of particular significance or interest – of, for example, prominent people or places – these should be recorded – example on Figure 1. Otherwise a general description of scenes and sequences will suffice" (2016, p. 127).

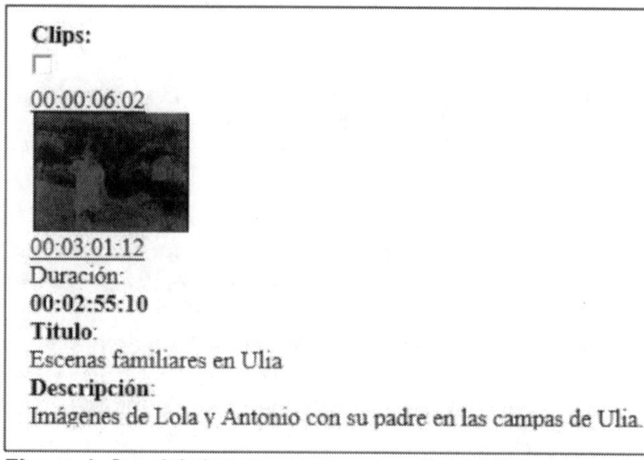


***Figure 1.*** *Special shots´ content description at Filmoteca Vasca (Spain).*

On the other hand, on the field *Subject/Genre/Form terms*, it is recommended:

> *"Provide access to the Work by means of subjects (or subject identifiers) that describe the content of the Work (i.e., what the Work is about) – but places, times or names of people or entities are not considered to be recorded, as recommended by theorists in the field of moving image librarianship (Caldera Serrano and Sánchez Jiménez, 2009) –. Use an existing data value standard such as Library of Congress Subject Headings (LCSH). Alternatively, or additionally, use standards such as Universal Decimal Classification (UDC), Dewey Decimal Classification (DDC) – the only one recommended on the previous 1991 FIAF rules –, or equivalent (...) In addition, access to the Work can be provided by means of genre(s) and/or form(s) (or identifiers) of which the Work is an example" (FIAF, 2016, p. 44).*

About metadata standards for cinematographic works (CWS) published by CEN, the first one, *EN 15744* (2009), only paid attention to film content on the field *Genre* (Flores Riesco, 2009, p. 31), recommending on it the use of descriptors taken from a controlled vocabulary. Surprisingly, this standard does not have into consideration even the general summary nor any kind of indexing.

Finally, on the standard *EN 15907* (2010) there are four references linked to film content analysis. Inside the space *Elements*, there are two content fields: *content description* and *subject fields*, being indicated about the last ones that "*controlled and uncontrolled terms may be used together, but not within a single set of subject terms*" (CEN, 2010). Inside *Common element types*, we find the fields "*region*", for places, and "*timespan*", for times represented in films.

Although it seems that there is a greater concern about film content description on the last CEN metadata standards than on the one in 2009, as well as on the last FIAF cataloguing manual, since they consider places and times in the description of film content – no other standard did it –, there is a large lack of information or examples about each one of these four fields.

Due to these deficiencies on film metadata and cataloguing standards, some film archives have created some initiatives to improve the possibilities of access to film collections by their users, like the project *I-Media-Cities* (IMediaCities.eu, 2016-2019).

## CONCLUSIONS

In spite of the considerable work of FIAF and CEN during last years, if they do not pay more attention to film content on their recommendations for film archives, asking them to analyze much more deeply and systematically the content of films to let their users a selective and exhaustive retrieval of film information, according to the new digital and technological era, as many TV archives already did, users, researchers and citizens in general can lose their interest for this important patrimony as a resource of information and film archives could lose their visibility and useful for Society and Governments. In fact, it seems to be already happening in many countries like Spain, whose main national archive´s budget has been reduced the 60% between 2010 and 2014 (Domínguez-Delgado and López-Hernández, 2016c, p. 14).

## ACKNOWLEDGMENTS

This research has been financed by the VI Plan Propio de Investigación de la Universidad de Sevilla.

## REFERENCES

Bowser, E. & Kuiper, J (1980). *A Handbook for Film Archives*. Bruselas: FIAF.

Caldera-Serrano, J. & Sánchez-Jiménez, R. "Recuperación de Secuencias de Información Audiovisual con Rdf y Smil". In *El Profesional de la Información*, vol. 18, n. 3, 2009, pp. 291-299.

European Committee of Standardization (CEN) (2010). "EN 15907. Film identification –Enhancing interoperability of metadata – Element sets and structures". In *Filmstandards.org*. Retrieved May 15, 2017 from http://filmstandards.org/fsc/index.php/EN_15907

Domínguez-Delgado, R. & López-Hernández, M.A. (2016a). "Film content analysis at six major Spanish film libraries". In *El Profesional de la Información*, v. 25, n. 5, pp. 787-794. eISSN: 1699-2407.

Domínguez-Delgado, R. & López-Hernández, M.A. (2016b). "The Retrieval of Moving Images at Spanish Film Archives: The Oversight of Content Analysis". In ***Proceedings of the Association for Information Science and Technology***, volumen 53, issue 1, 2016, pp. 1-4. Online ISSN 2373-9231.

Domínguez-Delgado, R. & López-Hernández, M.A. (2016c). "Film Librarianship: historical contextual framework". In *Documentación de las Ciencias de la Información*, 39, pp. 13-49.

Imediacities.eu (2016-2019). *I-Media-Cities*. Retrieved June 2, 2017 from https://imediacities.eu/

International Federation of Film Archives (FIAF) (1979). In *Film Cataloguing*. New York: Burt Franklin & Co., 1979.

International Federation of Film Archives (FIAF) (1991). *FIAF Cataloguing Rules for Film Archives*. München, London, New York, Paris: KG Saur.

International Federation of Film Archives (FIAF) (2013). *Working draft of the FIAF Moving Image Cataloguing Manual*, February. Retrieved May 9, 2017 from http://www.filmstandards.org/fiaf/wiki/doku.php

International Federation of Film Archives (FIAF) (2016). *FIAF Moving Image Cataloguing Manual*. FIAF.

Flores Riesco, C. (2011). *Metadatos para Documentos Audiovisuales. La Normalización en Europa*. Master Thesis directed by Carmen Caro Castro. Salamanca: University of Salamanca.

Unesco (1980). "Recommendation for the Safeguarding and Preservation of Moving Images", *Records of the General Conference, 21st session, Belgrade, 23 September to 28 October*, Vol. 1, Resolutions, pp. 156-161.

# Image Indexing Through Hashtags in Instagram

**Isabelle Dorsch**
*Dept. of Information Science, Heinrich Heine University, Germany. isabelle.dorsch@hhu.de*

**Wolfgang G. Stock**
*Dept. of Information Science, Heinrich Heine University, Germany. stock@phil.hhu.de*

**Franziska Zimmer**
*Dept. of Information Science, Heinrich Heine University, Germany. franziska.zimmer@hhu.de*

## ABSTRACT

**Image indexing and knowledge representation on Instagram are organized by folksonomy-oriented hashtags. What kinds of hashtags do Instagram users apply for different picture categories? We distinguish between food, pets, selfies, friends, activity, art, fashion, quotes (captioned photos), landscape and architecture as image categories, as well as content-related (ofness, aboutness, iconology), emotiveness, isness, performativeness, fakeness, "Insta"-tags and sentences as hashtag categories. Are there any differences in relative frequencies of hashtags in the image categories? What hashtag categories dominate users' indexing activities? Given an image category, what is the distribution of hashtag categories? Given a hashtag category, what is the distribution of image categories? We analyzed 1,000 pictures on Instagram with all-in-all 14,649 hashtags deploying content analysis.**

## KEYWORDS

image indexing, Instagram, knowledge organization, folksonomy, hashtag, picture, user behavior, tagging behavior

## INTRODUCTION

Besides indexing through controlled concepts (Stock & Stock, 2013), folksonomies (Peters, 2009) obtain a huge impact on indexing especially on social media. Folksonomies allow for the free allocation of keywords, called "tags" or "hashtags," by everyone. In Instagram, a mobile social networking application for sharing photos and videos, image indexing is realized through hashtags, e.g., #Loersfeld, #Castle and #Kerpen in Figure 1. The creator of a post has the possibility to add a description text and up to 30 distinct hashtags.

How do Instagram users tag their pictures? Our model of tagging behavior on Instagram is depicted in Figure 2.

Based upon this theoretical model, our research questions (RQs) are:

***Figure 1.*** *Tagged image on Instagram*

**(RQ1)** Are there any differences in relative frequencies of hashtags in the image categories?

**(RQ2)** Given an image category, what is the distribution of hashtag categories?

**(RQ3)** Given a hashtag category, what is the distribution of image categories?

***Figure 2.*** *Theoretical model of users' tagging behavior on Instagram*

80th Annual Meeting of the Association for Information Science & Technology, Washington, DC | Oct. 27-Nov. 1, 2017

## METHODS

To analyze the tagging behavior of Instagram users, a content analysis (Krippendorff, 2014) of image postings was conducted. Applying a codebook, two coders independently categorized 1,000 pictures and 14,649 hashtags each. There were ten image categories (food, pets, selfies, friends, activity, art, fashion, quotes, landscape and architecture). Here, we follow predominantly Hu et al. (2014). Additionally, we worked with seven hashtag categories. Content-related tags contain *ofness* and *aboutness* (Shatford, 1986) which in turn are based on Panofsky's levels of meaning in art (Panofsky, 1955). Besides the known keyword categories *emotiveness* (emotional hashtags as #sad) (Knautz, 2012), *isness* (describing properties of the post as #photo) (Ingwersen, 2002), *performativeness* (requests of actions as #like4like) (Peters & Stock, 2007), *complete sentences* (#Ifeelgood), the hashtag categories fakeness (tags with no relation to the image) and *"Insta"-tags* (e.g., #instagood) were exclusively designed for this study. The data collection took place between November 2016 and January 2017.

## RESULTS

**RQ1.** The average number of hashtags per image post on Instagram varies from nearly 11 to about 19 hashtags with an average of 15 hashtags. The person-related categories *selfie* (⌀ 10.9 tags per picture) and *friends* (⌀ 11.7 tags per picture) received the lowest average values. *Pet* (⌀ 18.6 tags), *fashion* (⌀ 17.6 tags) and *landscape* (⌀ 16.8 tags) are the categories with the highest average hashtag count.

**RQ2.** With 60.20%, the majority of all hashtags were classified into the category *content-related*, followed by *isness* with 14.87%, *"Insta"-tags* (7.32%) and *performativeness* (7.20%). Only a minority of hashtags was classified into the categories *emotiveness* (about 4.38%) and *sentences* (0.99%). 5.03% of all tags are *fake* keywords.

**RQ3.** The highest value of relative frequency of *content-related tags* is in the category *activity* (74.29%), the lowest is *selfie* (51.05%). Most emotions are shown in *friends* (8.74%) and *pets* (8.02%), least of all in *art* (1.05%). *Landscape* images call at most for actions, as 10.75% of all landscape-tags are performative. High values for "Insta"-tags in the category *pet* (20.24%) and *fakeness* in *quotes* (11.80%) are striking.

All in all, after a chi-square test of independence, there is a statistically significant association between hashtag categories and image categories on Instagram.

| | Content-related | Emotiveness | Fakeness | "Insta"-Tags | Isness | Performativeness | Sentences | % |
|---|---|---|---|---|---|---|---|---|
| #activity | 74.29 | 4.35 | 3.75 | 1.72 | 9.90 | 5.25 | 0.75 | 100.00 |
| #architecture | 63.20 | 2.54 | 2.54 | 6.67 | 15.41 | 9.35 | 0.28 | 100.00 |
| #art | 68.54 | 1.05 | 5.62 | 4.19 | 14.68 | 5.69 | 0.22 | 100.00 |
| #fashion | 59.51 | 3.52 | 7.38 | 5.91 | 16.70 | 6.02 | 0.97 | 100.00 |
| #food | 51.34 | 1.81 | 6.71 | 6.31 | 25.84 | 7.11 | 0.87 | 100.00 |
| #friends | 57.75 | 8.74 | 3.94 | 7.88 | 14.40 | 6.17 | 1.11 | 100.00 |
| #landscape | 61.68 | 3.98 | 1.66 | 5.47 | 16.16 | 10.75 | 0.30 | 100.00 |
| #pet | 53.93 | 8.02 | 3.82 | 20.24 | 7.59 | 4.31 | 2.10 | 100.00 |
| #quote | 61.67 | 5.16 | 11.80 | 3.46 | 7.33 | 8.75 | 1.83 | 100.00 |
| #selfie | 51.05 | 4.57 | 2.38 | 7.96 | 23.70 | 9.06 | 1.28 | 100.00 |
| Total | 60.20 | 4.38 | 5.03 | 7.32 | 14.87 | 7.20 | 0.99 | 100.00 |

***Table 1.** Relative frequency of hashtag categories by picture categories (N = 1,000 posts; 100 posts per picture category)*

## REFERENCES


Hu, Y., Manikonda, L., & Kambhampati, S. (2014). What we Instagram: A first analysis of Instagram photo content and user types. In *Proceedings of the 8th International Conference on weblogs and social media, ICWSM 2014* (pp. 595-598). Palo Alto, California: AAAI Press.

Ingwersen, P. (2002). Cognitive perspectives of document representation. In H. Bruce, et al. (Eds.), *Emerging Frameworks and Methods: CoLIS 4* (pp. 285-300). Greenwood Village, CO: Libraries Unlimited.

Knautz, K. (2012). Emotion felt and depicted: Consequences for multimedia retrieval. In D. R. Neal (Ed.), *Indexing and retrieval of non-text information* (pp. 343-375). Berlin, Boston, MA: De Gruyter Saur.

Krippendorff, K. (2004). *Content analysis: An introduction to its methodology* (2nd ed.). Thousand Oaks, CA: Sage.

Panofsky, E. (1955). *Meaning in the visual arts*. Garden City, NY: Doubleday Anchor Books.

Peters, I. (2009). Folksonomies: Indexing and retrieval in web 2.0. Berlin: De Gruyter Saur.

Peters, I., & Stock, W. G. (2007). Folksonomy and information retrieval. In Joining research and practice: Social computing and information science. Proceedings of the 70th ASIS&T Annual Meeting (pp. 1510-1542).

Shatford, S. (1986). Analyzing the subject of a picture: A theoretical approach. *Cataloging & Classification Quarterly, 6*(3), 39-62.

Stock, W. G., & Stock, M. (2013). *Handbook of Information Science*. Berlin, Boston, MA: De Gruyter Saur.

# Adapting Digital Collection Interface for Special Collections and Archives Collections and Improving Workflow

**Virginia Dressler**
*Kent State University, USA. vdressle@kent.edu*

## ABSTRACT

**This paper will address a recent project at Kent State University to adapt the interface of Special Collections and Archives Digital Collections to better reflect textual archival content. As our project team discovered, some of these changes also improved ingestion workflows and the quality of the optical character recognition as a result. Automated processes of creating PDF files and updating related finding aid pages will also be discussed. The visual presentation during the 2017 ASIST Annual Meeting will provide visitors the opportunity to view the digital collections and interact directly with the project through the live library website as outlined in this paper. The project to date is based on open source technologies, and our team actively works to share code back to the respective community.**

## KEYWORDS

digital collections, interface improvements, workflow

## INTRODUCTION

In September 2016, Kent State University received a Digital Dissemination of Archival Collections grant from the National Historical Publications and Records Commission (NHPRC) to digitize roughly 72,500 pages of the May 4 Collection. The selection of items for the grant is comprised of 32 archival subcollections of the larger May 4 collection and reflects a wide variety of primarily textual content. Before the award of this grant, the digital archive focused mainly on audio and visual image content, so the challenge of adding a large number of multiple paged textual items provided a reason to assess the interface to better display the particular archival the folder structure and organization. With the assistance of a library developer, we believe we have adapted the open source Omeka-based system to better address internal workflows as well as improve the user interface.

## BACKGROUND

At the start of the project, the head of Special Collections and Archives and the Digital Projects Librarian met with a library developer to address new workflows resulting from a larger-scale digital initiative. After some discussion, the library developer made many suggestions to better improve the workflow processes during post-production and ingestion. Our team also discussed the need to add an image viewer that could better reflect the folder level archival arrangement of mixed media content.

Before that point in time, text items to be ingested into a digital collection were scanned as image files (raw tiff files of each page) and then combined into a single PDF file as the access copy. The high-res images were then saved to an offline server, while the PDF file is ingested into the appropriate digital collection. On the recommendations from the library developer, adaptations were made to the system to move raw image files directly into Omeka. This first change has eliminated the need to load files into two different locations, saving valuable time for our staff.

Once the image files are ingested, the library developer implemented a new way to run the optical character recognition (OCR) on images. Previously, the text recognition tool in Adobe Acrobat Pro was used, but the open source Tesseract provided a way to improve the quality and accuracy of the OCR and also removes the processing time spent by digital projects staff and students through the automation process.

The next enhancement covered will address the respective special collections finding aid webpages and how to easily link to the newly created digital object. The items in the grant project are from various archival collections in the May 4 Collection. Each ingested item contains a URL to the respective, existing finding aid within the metadata record. Once the item is published, a logic was applied to update the related folder description on the Drupal based website housing the finding aids, using the Finding Aids Auto-Link.

And moving to the public facing side of the project, the interface was adapted with the Mirador image viewer to provide a way for users to view and interact with the individual pages (image files) without the need to download a file. Viewers can scroll through the images, using a number of different tools in Mirador to zoom, scroll and directly interact with the archival content.

80th Annual Meeting of the Association for Information Science & Technology, Washington, DC | Oct. 27-Nov. 1, 2017

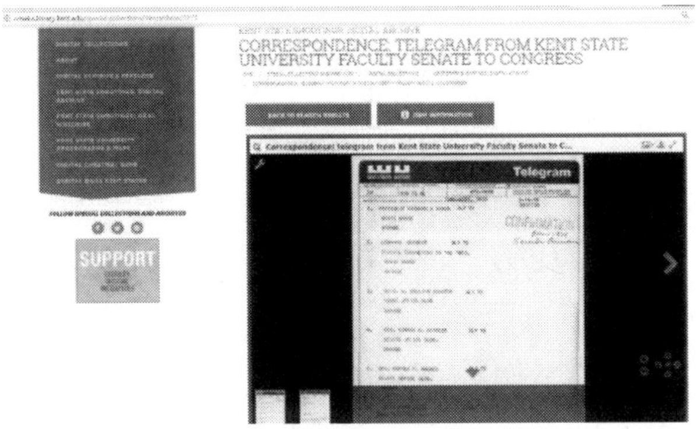


*Figure 1*. *Screenshot of Mirador image viewer. Item #3773, http://omeka.library.kent.edu/special-collections/items/show/3773*

Lastly, we did want to provide a download option for users in addition to the Mirador image viewer. The PDFCreate Omeka Plugin was developed to create a PDF upon publication of the item in Omeka. This piece combines all the images into one PDF for download, as the previous version had included.

## CONCLUSION

Our project has successfully reduced post-production processing time by more than half and greatly improved the accuracy of OCR by eliminating the need to upload content to two locations and by automating PDF creation and OCR processes. Also, the addition of Mirador image viewer has been implemented to better reflect the archival arrangement. Our team will continue to seek out methods to better enhance digital collections, particularly for special collections and archival content. A live presentation of the website and related processes will be provided during the visual presentation at the conference to allow attendees to directly interact with the finished project, through the use of a laptop to demonstrate the work described in this paper.

## ACKNOWLEDGMENTS

The work to date on this project was funded by the Digital Dissemination of Archival Collections grant (RD-10196) from NHPRC, and our project team (Haley Antell, Virginia Dressler and Cara Gilgenbach) would like to thank the National Historical Publications and Records Commission office for the support of the project. In addition, the core project team, Joe Corall, Jeph Remley, Cindy Kristof and Lae'l Hughes-Watkins, should also be acknowledged in the work done to date on the adaptations of the Omeka instance as well as addressing copyright concerns as well as the outreach and marketing of the project.

## REFERENCES

Drupal.org (2017, February 12). Drupal key contributed modules. Retrieved June 14, 2017 from https://www.drupal.org/project/key

Drupal.org (2017, June 1). Drupal linkchecker module. Retrieved June 1, 2017 from https://www.drupal.org/project/linkchecker

George Mason University. (2017, January 30). Omeka.org; Retrieved June 14, 2017 from http://omeka.org/

George Mason University (2014, June 25). Omeka `add_file_display_callback` Documentation. Retrieved June 14, 2017 from http://omeka.readthedocs.io/en/latest/Reference/libraries/globals/add_file_display_callback.html

George Mason University (2013, January 28). Omeka `after_save_item` Documentation. Retreived June 14, 2017 from http://omeka.readthedocs.io/en/latest/Reference/hooks/after_save_%3Cmodel%3E.html

George Mason University (2011, October 10). Omeka MVC pattern. Retrieved June 14, 2017 from https://omeka.org/codex/MVC_Pattern_and_URL_Paths_in_Omeka

International Image Interoperability Framework (2017, April 14). IIF presentation API manifest specification. Retrieved June 14, 2017 from http://iiif.io/api/presentation/2.0/#manifest

Kent State University Libraries (2017, February 16). Finding aid auto-link (GitHub); Retrieved June 14, 2017 from https://github.com/kent-state-university-libraries/finding-aids-auto-link

Kent State University Libraries, (2017, April 14). PDFCreate Omeka plugin (GitHub.) Retrieved June 14, 2017 from https://github.com/kent-state-university-libraries/PDFCreate

Loris IIIF Image Server. (2017, April 3) GitHub, Inc.; Retrieved June 14, 2017 from https://github.com/loris-imageserver/loris

Mirador Omeka Plugin (GitHub) (2017, March 2). Retrieved June Apr 14 from https://github.com/kent-state-university-libraries/Mirador

Project Mirador.org (2017, April 13). Mirador IIIF image viewer. Retrieved June 13, 2017 from http://projectmirador.org

University Libraries, Kent State University (2017). Special collections and archives finding aids. Retrieved June 20, 2017 from http://www.library.kent.edu/special-collections-and-archives/browse-collections

# The Value of User Feedback: Parent's Comments to Online Health and Well-being Information Providers


**Reem El Sherif**
*McGill University, Department of Family Medicine, Canada. Reem.elsherif@mail.mcgill.ca*

**Pascale Roy**
*Naître et grandir, Lucie and André Chagnon Foundation, Canada. p.roy@naitreetgrandir.com*

**David Li Tang**
*McGill University, Department of Family Medicine, Canada. david.l.tang@mail.mcgill.ca*

**Geneviève Doray**
*Naître et grandir, Lucie and André Chagnon Foundation, Canada. g.doray@naitreetgrandir.com*

**Marilyne Dubois**
*Naître et grandir, Lucie and André Chagnon Foundation, Canada. m.dubois@naitreetgrandir.com*

**Paula Bush**
*McGill University, Department of Family Medicine, Canada. paula.bush@mail.mcgill.ca*

**François Lagarde**
*Naître et grandir, Lucie and André Chagnon Foundation, Canada. lagardef@fondationchagnon.org*

**Pierre Pluye**
*McGill University, Department of Family Medicine, Canada. pierre.pluye@mcgill.ca*



## ABSTRACT

Health informatics research usually deals with quantitative feedback from information users. Little is known about how information users' qualitative feedback can be used by information providers. The Naître et grandir website (N&G) provides parents with health and well-being information during pregnancy and until their children are eight years old. In this study, researchers worked with N&G information providers to implement the Information Assessment Method (IAM) for assessing and improving parenting information. Feedback comments were collected from participants who visited the N&G website during the study period and who completed an IAM questionnaire. A coding manual for the analysis of participants' comments was created and developed by the researchers in partnership with information providers. This coding manual was used to create an online knowledge management system to facilitate all future coding of comments. This system allows website editors to receive feedback from their readers daily, allowing them to act on it more rapidly and, therefore, shortening the feedback to action time. This online system can be adapted by other websites' editors to collect information users' comments and improve their online resources.



## KEYWORDS

information assessment, online consumer health information, parenting information


## INTRODUCTION

Naître et grandir' website (N&G) provides parents with support in bringing up their children, from the time they are conceived until they are eight years old. In addition to the website, its modes of dissemination include a personalized electronic weekly newsletter (based on child's age) and a magazine. N&G offers free and trustworthy information, independent of industry funding. N&G is funded by the Lucie and André Chagnon Foundation, a philanthropic organization that seeks to contribute to the prevention of poverty through the creation of conditions and environments that are favorable to educational success of children, specifically from socially vulnerable families and communities. Since 2014, McGill University and N&G have worked in partnership to implement the Information Assessment Method (IAM) for assessing and improving the pages of parenting information. Developed at McGill, the IAM allows people to rate the situational relevance, cognitive/affective impact and use of specific information content (e.g., an N&G webpage), and ensuing health/well-being outcomes (Pluye et al., 2015).

The coding manual was developed in a previous study and includes codes pertaining to the IAM questionnaire and the N&G information, as well as codes for testimonials and reasons for visiting the website (El Sherif et al., 2015). Due to the participatory coding process, the needs of the researchers and the information providers were met, which provided a reliable, valuable and pertinent coding manual (El Sherif et al., 2015). This coding manual was used in the creation of an online knowledge management system (hereafter *system*) to facilitate the coding of website user feedback comments (hereafter *comments*). We implemented a similar system with the Canadian Pharmacists' Association to collect professionals' feedback on medical information for the last five years (Tang, Bouthillier, Pluye, Grad & Repchinsky, 2015). Prior to the development of this system, editors would not have immediate access to their readers' written feedback and would, thus, not be able to react as quickly to revise their information content. Our objective is to describe the value of such system for editors to improve informational content.


80th Annual Meeting of the Association for Information Science & Technology, Washington, DC | Oct. 27-Nov. 1, 2017

## METHODS

### Approach

We followed an organizational participatory research approach which blends action research and organizational learning to undertake research with organization members and improve practice (Waterman, Tillen, Dickson & De Koning, 2001). In this study, N&G and McGill partners participated in all stages of the research process, from developing research questions, collecting and analyzing data to interpreting and disseminating results.

### Data Source

Included comments were provided by N&G readers who completed at least one IAM questionnaire (described later) for a specific N&G webpage and coded by an N&G editor. Readers were from the province of Quebec (Canada). They accessed the N&G webpages directly or through the weekly N&G newsletter to which they were subscribed. Readers who accessed the N&G webpages directly were anonymous. Readers who accessed the webpages through the newsletter were assigned member IDs and could, therefore, be counted.

### Data collection

The IAM questionnaire includes five questions on relevance, impact, use and health/well-being outcomes of information and one open-ended question gathering comments: Do you have any other comments or suggestions? The latter allowed participants to provide feedback about the questionnaire and about N&G information such as testimonials. Comments were collected between November 16, 2015 (the implementation of the online system) and June 16, 2017.

### Data analysis

Two N&G editors coded all comments via a system that allowed them to read and code the comments online, as well as make notes. Main code categories were 1) evaluation of the IAM questionnaire, 2) evaluation of the N&G information and 3) other comments. The system also allows the editors to update the status of the N&G webpage that was rated to one of four options: new comment, being corrected, corrected or no correction necessary.

## RESULTS

Since the implementation of the system, 826 feedback comments on 366 unique N&G webpages were received and coded by two N&G editors. Of those comments, 93 were provided by 88 readers who accessed the webpage through the newsletter, and 733 comments were provided by an unknown number of readers who accessed the webpages directly. This feedback allowed editors to revise N&G webpages when needed. As a result of this review, 307 N&G webpages needed no correction; 26 were corrected and 13 were being corrected. Twenty pages received new comments that were not yet addressed by the editors.

## DISCUSSION

Results suggest that coding readers' comments with a knowledge management system can be a valuable process for web editors. The IAM stimulates reflection (reflective learning) and encourages people to write their thoughts (comment). Prior to the implementation of this system, editors worked alone to retrieve, analyze and code comments, an inherently slower process to respond to users and to revise webpage content. This system is more organized and allows editors to have instant access to comments, analyze them in a more measured deliberate manner and revise informational content accordingly.

Unlike recent work on computer-assisted content analysis or coding, this system allows editors to do the coding themselves using their expertise. Web editors working with such systems may be seen as cyborgs (Haraway, 1994). It has been claimed that we are all cyborgs: we are humans who are actively and constantly using computer systems and evolving into new beings (Stone, 1996). This merging of human (expert editors who can analyze the comments and revise informational content) and machine (an online system that facilitates knowledge management) allows editors to better perform their daily tasks more efficiently.

## CONCLUSION

An online information dissemination-assessment-feedback-improvement system can be adapted by other websites' editors to handle information users' comments, and improve their online resources.

## REFERENCES


El Sherif, R., Roy, P., Tang, D. L., Pluye, P., Bush, P., Doray, G., & Lagarde, F. (2015). Toward an information management system for handling parenting information users' comments. *Proceedings of the Association for Information Science and Technology, 52*(1), 1-3.

Haraway, D. (1994). A Manifesto for cyborgs: Science, technology, and socialist feminism in 1980s. In Steven Seidman (ed.) The postmodern turn. *New Perspectives on Social Theory*, 82-118.

Pluye, P., Sherif, R. E., Bartlett, G., Granikov, V., Grad, R. M., Doray, G., . . . Bouthillier, F. (2015). Perceived outcomes of online parenting information according to self-selected participants from a population of website users. *Proceedings of the Association for Information Science and Technology, 52*(1), 1-3.

Stone, A. R. (1996). *The war of desire and technology at the close of the mechanical age*: MIT Press.

Tang, D. L., Bouthillier, F., Pluye, P., Grad, R., & Repchinsky, C. (2015). The value of user feedback: Healthcare professionals' comments to the health information provider. *Journal of the Association for Information Science and Technology, 66*(2), 377-391.

Waterman, H., Tillen, D., Dickson, R., & De Koning, K. (2001). Action research: A systematic review and guidance for assessment. *Health Technology Assessment (Winchester, England), 5*(23), iii.

# Collective Action Framing Episodes: A Methodological Tool to Make Sense of Case Studies

**Fatima K. Espinoza Vasquez**
*School of Information Science, University of Kentucky, USA. fatima.espinozavasquez@uky.edu*

## ABSTRACT

**This visual presentation introduces Collective Action Framing Episodes (CAFEs), a method that addresses the need for a relational approach to study groups, society and ICTs. This method also speaks to the need for a visual tool to make sense of theories, constructs and data, build narratives and construct theories. This tool is based on social movement theories like the Contentious Politics Model by McAdam, D. et al., (1996) and on Benford and Snow's (2000) framing processes theory. The presentation first shows an animated illustration of the theoretical framework coming together in a multi-level unit of analysis. Then it shows a visualization of the research design process including identifying the episode components, coding, building a timeline, building a narrative and constructing theory.**

## KEYWORDS

methods, collective action, framing, ICTs, multi-level analysis, social movements, visualization, case study

## INTRODUCTION AND PROBLEM STATEMENT

This interactive visual presentation addresses two needs. The first one is a theoretical one. As we recognize the importance of considering the rich diversity of ICTs, groups and contexts, researchers stress the need for relational approaches. They suggest going beyond exploring ICT use, role or scope; to study instead, the relation between ICTs, groups and society (Orlikowski 1992). The Zapatista movement's structure, circumstances and access to ICTs is different to that of the Black Lives Matter movement. Yet, we still need to have insight into their complexity to produce theories that explain those relations.

The second need is a methodological one. Relational approaches require methodologies that give us nuanced insight into sociotechnical dynamics. Moreover, advocates for the inclusion of underrepresented perspectives emphasize the importance of context-heavy approaches like case studies (Gillham, 2000; Simons, 2009; Yin, 2013). Thus, ICT researchers are increasingly employing them. The *Journal of the Association for Information Science and Technology* published at least four case studies in 2016. Case studies require threading a complex story using several constructs and diverse data sources. Thus, the need of a methodological framework to help researchers: operationalize and make sense of several constructs, structure data collection and analysis, create a relational compelling narrative and build theory.

Thus, we propose a sociotechnical relational approach to study groups and their interaction with ICTs and their environment. Our framework takes into consideration people's diverse understandings of their world, ICTs, organizations and practices. It proposes the use of a multi-level unit of analysis drawn from social movement and frame theories. It brings together context, organizational structures and understandings. These three levels are operationalized through a multi-construct unit of analysis composed of five constructs: episodes, practices, events, frames and ICTs, which are analyzed simultaneously over a timeline. We call it Collective Action Framing Episode (CAFE).

Representing meaning visually and creating graphic narratives help make sense of complex phenomena (Snyder et. al., 2016), visualizations are a great way to represent concepts during data collection (Snyder, 2014). We argue that visualizations can be helpful throughout the whole research process, from design to theory construction. The CAFE method relies on concept maps and relational timelines to help the researcher grasp theoretical frameworks, make sense of constructs, understand relations, draw insights, tell a story and construct theory.

This visual presentation will introduce the CAFE method through an interactive animation. Participants will see the evolution and connection of concepts to theories, practices to frames, frames to events and themes and patterns to the narrative.

## THEORETICAL FRAMEWORK

Our method is grounded in the work of social movement scholars. We use the contentious politics model by McAdam, D. et al., (1996), which is a useful tool to guide relational research because it assumes a dynamic relationship between group structures and processes. It is also based on Benford and Snow's (2000) framing processes theory, which states that group actors' motivations, identities and actions are shaped by their socially constructed shared understandings.

## METHOD

We propose observing three levels of analysis simultaneously in specific sequentially connected time intervals called Collective Action Framing Episodes (CAFEs). This multi-level unit of analysis allows identifying the relationship between the organization, its context, their shared understandings and

80th Annual Meeting of the Association for Information Science & Technology, Washington, DC | Oct. 27-Nov. 1, 2017

ICTs. Moreover, it allows crafting a relational narrative that threads those elements together.

### *Step 1: Identifying CAFEs*

We define CAFEs as periods of time bounded by relevant events, where actors create frames to guide movement's actions. CAFEs can happen simultaneously or consecutively, they can also be recycled or reused. CAFEs are composed by five constructs:

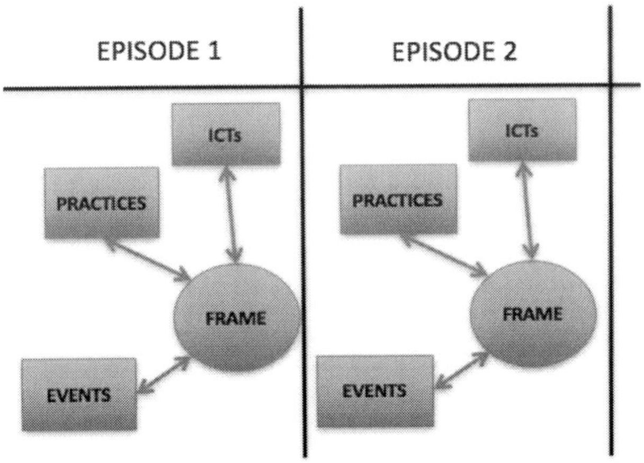


***Figure 1.*** *Constructs in CAFEs*

**Frames** are the result of collective action framing, a practice by social movements to build shared understandings to guide social movement action (Benford & Snow, 2000). Collective action framing is a purposeful practice to help constrain and guide movements' evolution. It is collectively negotiated by members of the movement.

**ICTs** are any communication device, application and services associated with the organization. They may include radio, television, cellular phones, computer and network hardware and software, satellite systems, media outlets video conferencing, social media, etc.

**Practice***s* are activities carried out by movement actors with the intention to support or propose movement goals.

**Events** are occurrences in the environment that pertain to the organization.

**Episodes** are sequentially connected events and practices that occur over time and have a beginning and an end. Drawn from Miles & Huberman (1994; 2013), episodes bound data that extend over periods of time, condensing it into manageable units. They allow capturing the characteristics of the settings, events, processes, practices and ICTs in smaller manageable units.

### *Step 2: Coding and Classifying Data into a Timeline*

The next step is to code and classify CAFEs. Frames, events, practices and ICTs are coded by date, type, characteristic and source to help establish how they relate to each other.

| TYPE OF EVENT=> | TYPE A | TYPE B | TYPE C | TYPE A | TYPE C |
|---|---|---|---|---|---|
| EVENT=> | De-scrpt. Event A | De-scrpt. Event B | De-scrpt. Event C | De-scrpt. Event D | De-scrpt. Event E |
| DATE => | DATE 1 | DATE 2 | DATE 3 | DATE 4 | DATE 7 |
| CAFE 1 | CAFE 2 | | | | |
| CAFE 2 | | CAFE 2 | | | |
| CAFE 3 | | | | CAFE 3 | |

***Table 1.*** *Visualization of CAFEs in a timeline*

### *Step 3: Building the Story*

Once we identify and code events, frames, practices and ICTs, we build a timeline depicting CAFEs. The timeline helps identify the relations between the constructs and build a narrative. The timeline is meant to highlight how groups interact with their environment, ICTs and allies, and how frames either respond to events, anticipate them or provoke them. The timeline also helps make sense of the data and narrate findings chronologically while highlighting the relations among frames, ICTs, events and practices throughout each episode.

## CONCLUSIONS

The CAFE method addresses the theoretical need for a relational approach in the ICT field. It allows connecting micro-level social processes and meso-level structures in an inhospitable macro-level.

We argue, that though it is based on social movement theories, this framework is transferable to other types of groups because it facilitates exploring how groups interact with their context, connect with each other, discover and use ICTs. Tracking collective action framing allows the analyst to attend closely to the resourceful and improvisational agency shown by organizational actors when confronted with systemic constraints. Tracking CAFEs allows the analyst to examine the meaning-making strategies used by organizations to persuade, inform the world, rally membership and sustain its momentum.

Implementing CAFEs as a framework also addresses methodological challenges of case studies by (1) making sense of complex theory and phenomena through visualizations, (2) analyzing large amounts of qualitative data through episodes and (3) building a relational narrative through a timeline.

## REFERENCES


Benford, R. D., & Snow, D. A. (2000). Framing processes and social movements: An overview and assessment. *Annual Review of Sociology, 26*, 611-639.

Gillham, B. (2000). *Case study research methods*. Bloomsbury Publishing.

Snyder, J., Baumer, E. P., Voida, S., Adams, P., Halpern, M., Choudhury, T., & Gay, G. (2014). Making things visible: Opportunities and tensions in visual approaches for design research and practice. *Human–Computer Interaction*, *29*(5-6), 451-486.

Snyder, J. (2014). Visual representation of information as communicative practice. *Journal of the Association for Information Science and Technology*, *65*(11), 2233-2247.

McAdam, D., McCarthy, J. D., & Zald, M. N. (1996). Comparative perspectives on social movements: Political opportunities, mobilizing structures, and cultural framings. Cambridge University Press.

Miles, M. B., & Huberman, A. M. (1994). Qualitative data analysis: A sourcebook. *Beverly Hills: Sage Publications.*

Miles, M. B., Huberman, A. M., & Saldana, J. (2013). *Qualitative data analysis*. Sage.

Orlikowski, W. J. (1992). The duality of technology: Rethinking the concept of technology in organizations. *Organization science*, *3*(3), 398-427.

Simons, H. (2009). *Case study research in practice*. SAGE Publications.

Yin, R. K. (2013). *Case study research: Design and methods*. Sage Publications.

# A Pilot Study of the Information Behaviors of Web Designers

T. Zachary Frazier
*University of South Carolina, USA. Frazie26@email.sc.edu*

## ABSTRACT

**Despite their large contribution to the ability of individuals to access information, little is known about how those who build websites professionally interact with information in that context. As part of a research pilot study, several individuals involved in the professional design of websites were interviewed. The interviews used a semi-structured instrument that had a sketching activity integrated within it. Preliminary results indicate a heavy reliance on visual information and social information seeking are reported.**

## INTRODUCTION

Information science has had an historical relationship with the design of information systems as well as an interest in those who work in and create those systems. Yet despite the prominent role the World Wide Web (web) plays as a platform for information systems and channel of access to them, those who design web-based systems have largely been unstudied by scholars, including those interested in information science (Kennedy, 2012). In the few studies where information science has looked at those who design the web, it has focused on their experiences of information literacy and the "proper" use of information (Abdi, 2014). This approach does not fully speak to understanding the experience of designers as actors. It ignores both the strategic implications of their experience, as well as subtle heuristics embedded in their practice of web design. Web design is here taken to mean the visual and interactive design of websites. In order to address the lack of understanding of the practices of individuals involved in the professional design of websites (web designers), a pilot research project was conducted as part of a larger more formalized study. This poster looks at the human information behavior of these designers by asking, how is knowledge constructed and utilized in the professional design of websites?

This pilot helps to define further areas of exploration and provides a preliminary understanding about these individuals' information behavior. This work can begin to be used to inform the design of information systems through its illumination of context (Dervin, 2003). In addition to its potential value for information systems for aiding the work of web designers, there is a need to understand the work involved in making information systems as a foundation for any information literacy program. Such an understanding is frequently viewed as key in other forms of literacy, most notably media literacy (Keller & Share, 2007). An enriched understanding of the production of websites is important to the application, understanding and pedagogy of information science. This study provides a preliminary and exploratory contribution to our understanding of web designers' activities.

## BACKGROUND

Fidel and Pejtresen (2004) defined *information systems* as any systems, intellectual or computerized, that facilitate and support human-information interaction. Such systems, they argued, clearly benefit from an understanding of human-information interaction. For this study *websites* are defined as documents and/or systems built using HTML. Websites are clearly an example of a computerized information system. Websites are built for a variety of reasons, from personal expression (blogs) to ecommerce (Amazon.com) to information retrieval (a library's discovery layer). The work of those who build the systems and their own human computer interaction is of interest because their interaction with information affects the way in which they build these systems. Cross and Dorst (2001) argue that creative activity, and in particular design, are built on analogic reasoning. Rather than being inspirational, they argue that design is the product of unique combinations. Thus, the interaction with information and information systems as part of web designers' labor will be reflected in the work created as product.

The diversity of work and shifted contexts noted by Damarin (2004) have not solidified much in the intervening years. As a result, most published work in the area of internet research is split into two categories: Technical examination of the infrastructure of the internet or end users (Ankerson, 2010, Brügger, 2010). For those interested in understanding the production of the web, these worker's experiences are an important, but relatively unexplored topic. From an information science perspective, this means focusing on the ways that those involved in the endeavor experience, search for and use information as part of their work.

## METHODOLOGY

As an exploratory study, qualitative methodologies were chosen as a framework for investigation. It was designed following the standards of qualitative inquiry outlined by Glesne (2010), Maxwell (2014), Siedmen (1991) and others. It is understood that the experience of individuals is the result of social constructs, processed by their individual cognitive appa-

80th Annual Meeting of the Association for Information Science & Technology, Washington, DC | Oct. 27-Nov. 1, 2017

ratuses, in line with Gibson's embodied cognition (as expressed by Hinton, 2015). As a result, each individual's perception and experience will be different, but understanding might be built by overlapping those experiences and observing commonalities and differences.

In order to understand the cognitive process of web designers, a semi-structured interview was built by adapting questions from Laing and Masoodian (2015). In addition, a drawing activity was included as part of the interview to provide a vehicle for alternative ways of expressing their experience and to facilitate a dialog about their experience of their practice. Each interview took between 40 minutes to an hour. Interviews were transcribed by the principal researcher and then imported into NVivo software for coding. Open coding was used with an emergent coding scheme. After initial descriptive codes were assigned, the codes were then grouped into themes, and these themes were situated and developed through an information behavior paradigm.

Because the interview is retrospective and general, it is assumed that it captures accurate descriptions of practices or generalities of behavior rather than specific behaviors in unique contexts. Where individual examples are given, that narrative is filtered through the general lens of this ontological perspective.

A categorical sample was used for the pilot. Individuals were sought who had the title of web designer or who were involved in web design as a primary professional context. A total of four individuals have been interviewed as part of this pilot. Each had a variety of work experience and educational background. The gender of participants is reflective of the industry data (A List Apart, 2011). Experience in design specific roles varied from 10+ years to as little as three years, though all had extensive experience in web work.

Due to the small size of the professional web services community in Columbia, the researcher knew the participants personally. Additionally, the researcher had worked with three of the participants in a limited capacity. While this complicates the validity of the pilot's results, it has a small effect on the pilot investigation and the construction instruments to answer the question posed by the research.

## FINDINGS

All of those interviewed indicated that they spend a significant portion of the time attempting to understand client needs. This was both to generate requirements for the product and frequently to understand how to translate the clients need into an information system that was aesthetically pleasing, as well as easy to use. Nearly all of the respondents mentioned user testing and the importance of the user to the work that they do. This was understood to require a formalized user experience testing process. However, it seemed that budget constraints often prevent their inclusion. One participant described user tests as completely changing their process, destroying all their previous assumptions of form, functionality and aesthetics. The use of Google image search and design specific databases of visual information was seen as a major resource by those interviewed. One participant described browsing thousands of stock images to find the exact one. Nearly all said that when they ran into an issue they frequently turned to "the Google." Websites such as The Noun Project were mentioned as tools for discovery of source material and inspiration.

The process of using information and knowledge for translation was frequently mentioned. While this occurred in its typical context of explicating project requirements, it also occurred in a manner that has commonalities with literacy discourses and the translation of meaning from one language into another. For those interviewed, the mediation between client and object frequently was a zone of troubled translation. This translation element has been noted before by Beaudoin (2014). While it was a small section of their results, these preliminary interviews suggest that in design related fields such communicative uses may play a larger role.

## CONCLUSION

The experience of conducting and analyzing results shows that more work is still needed to begin to build an understanding of information's role in the design process. However, it seems that knowledge is constructed to understand the requirements of the design challenge, as well as verify the resulting designs. Along the way a variety of information is used (though primarily visual in nature) to both solve the design problem and explain and justify that solution to clients. Because this research is a pilot study with a small sample size, the ability to generalize from the findings is limited. The preliminary results however show that the instrument and questions generated information that is useful to better understand the utilization and construction of knowledge in this context and the usefulness of information practices as a way to undergird that understanding.

## REFERENCES


Abdi, E. S. (2014). *Web professionals: How do they experience information literacy?* (Thesis). Queensland University of Technology. Retrieved from http://eprints.qut.edu.au/78982/

ALA Staff (2012). Findings from the Survey, 2011. Retrieved November 2, 2016, from http://alistapart.com/article/survey2011

Ankerson, M. S. (2010). Web industries, economic, aesthetics: Mapping the look of the web in the dot-com era. In N. Brügger (Ed.), *Web history* (First printing edition, pp. 173-194). New York: Peter Lang Inc., International Academic Publishers.

Beaudoin, J. E. (2014). A framework of image use among archaeologists, architects, art historians and artists. *Journal of Documentation*, *70*(1), 119-147.

Brügger, N. (2010). Web history, an emerging field of study. In N. Brügger (Ed.), *Web history* (First printing edition, pp. 1-28). New York: Peter Lang Inc., International Academic Publishers.

Christ, W. G., & Potter, W. J. (1998). Media literacy, media education, and the academy. *Journal of Communication*, *48*(1), 5-15. https://doi.org/10.1111/j.1460-2466.1998.tb02733.x

Damarin, A. K. (2004). *Fit, flexibility, and connection: Organizing employment in emerging web labor markets, New York City, 1993-2003* (Ph.D.). Columbia University, United States, New York. Retrieved from http://search.proquest.com.pallas2.tcl.sc.edu/pqdtft/docview/305208172/abstract?accountid=13965

Dervin, B. (2003). Human studies and user studies: A call for methodological inter-disciplinarity. *Information Research, 9*(1), 9-1.

Dorst, K., & Cross, N. (2001). Creativity in the design process: Co-evolution of problem-solution. *Design Studies, 22*(5), 425-437. https://doi.org/10.1016/S0142-694X(01)00009-6

Fidel, R., & Pejtersen, A. M. (2004). From information behaviour research to the design of information systems: The Cognitive Work Analysis Framework. *Information Research, 10*(1). Retrieved from http://www.informationr.net/ir/10-1/paper210.html

Gill, R. (2007). Technobohemians, or the new cybertariat?: New media work on Amsterdam a decade after the web: Report. Institute of Network Cultures.

Glesne, C. (2015). *Becoming qualitative researchers: An introduction* (5th edition). Boston: Pearson.

Hinton, A. (2014). Understanding context: Environment, language, and information architecture (1st edition). Sebastopol, CA: O'Reilly Media.

Kellner, D., & Share, J. (2007). Critical media literacy, democracy, and the reconstruction of education. In D. Macedo & S. R. Steinberg (Eds.), *Media literacy: A reader* (pp. 3-23). New York: Peter Lang Publishing Inc. Retrieved from https://cxarchive.gseis.ucla.edu/xchange/critical-uses-of-media-and-technology/xpress/critical-media-literacy-democracy-and-the-reconstruction-of-education

Kennedy, H. (2011). *Network: Ethics and values in web design* (2012 edition). New York: Palgrave Macmillan.

Laing, S., & Masoodian, M. (2015). A study of the role of visual information in supporting ideation in graphic design. *Journal of the Association for Information Science and Technology, 66*(6), 1199-1211. https://doi.org/10.1002/asi.23231

Maxwell, J. A. (2013). *Qualitative research design: An interactive approach* (3rd edition). Thousand Oaks, Calif: SAGE Publications, Inc.

Seidman, I. E. (1991). Interviewing as qualitative research: A guide for researchers in education and the social sciences. New York: Teachers College Press.

# Using Podcasts as Texts in the Study of Human Information Behavior

**T. Zachary Frazier**
*University of South Carolina, USA. Frazie26@email.sc.edu*

## ABSTRACT

Despite the relatively scant attention paid to individuals involved in the professional design of websites, or web design, there is a large body of literature by and for practitioners. This study examines podcasts for the ubiquitous nature of the medium and frequency of occurrence in the literature. Podcasts themselves are a little used type of text available to researchers, and this study illuminates the possibilities of their use.

## INTRODUCTION

Ecommerce accounts for $8 trillion dollars in trade globally each year (Rausas et al., 2011), yet we understand relatively little about those who make the World Wide Web. Despite a substantial body of literature produced by those working in the professional design of websites (web design), little scholarly attention has been paid to them as a subject for research (Kennedy, 2012). Podcasts represent a possible source for those interested in understanding web design and the activities of web designers. According to studies by Gill (2007) and Kennedy (2010), podcasts are a source frequently used by web workers (including web designers) to maintain an awareness of industry trends and keep their skills current. This study asks: Are there examples of information behavior present in podcasts of interest to web designers? If they do exist, what behaviors are evidenced? What are the possible uses of podcasts to scholars of information science?

## BACKGROUND

*Podcasts* are defined as audio files available to download via the internet and syndicated via a Real Simple Syndication (RSS) feed (Radcliffe & Mack, 2007). Using this definition, podcasts first appeared at or around RSS's formalized appearance in 2002. Since then, podcasts have undergone two phases of ascendency. There is contemporary revival in the popularity of podcasting occurring as of the writing of this paper, spurred by the pulp culture success of the podcast, *Serial*. Podcasts have typically been discussed in literature lumped in with web 2.0 technologies, education or branding. However, they have been pointed to as a specific type of text separate from other social forms of web 2.0 technologies in studies of web designers as a way of acquiring and sharing information on professional practices and developments in the industry (Gill, 2007).

| Podcast Name | Discourse Structure |
|---|---|
| Boag World | Panel of agency principals and senior designers |
| The Style Guides Podcast | Interviews with individual designers and developers about their work |
| Responsive Web Design | Interviews with members of different project teams about their projects and process |

***Table 1**. Podcast formats*

The study of human-information interaction, or human information behavior, is fundamentally interdisciplinary (Borko, 1968; Wilson, 1997). The specific phenomena investigated under the human information behavior label can be described as information encountering (Erdeldez, 2000), information organization, information avoidance, information sharing and information needs, seeking and use or INSU (Fisher & Julian, 2009). Some specific frameworks may not be represented; however this typology is generally encompassing. For example, in his book, *Everyday Information Practices* (2008), Savolainen constructs and distributes information practices over three general areas: information source, information use and information sharing, effectively placing practices as a constructivist parallel to INSU (Savolainen, 2009).

## METHODOLOGY

Three podcasts of different formats (see Table 1) were selected based on their high ranking on several lists of podcasts for web designers. Podcasts with the highest mentions and list rankings were selected and, of those with transcripts, were selected based on their placement in the compiled rankings. Transcription was an important criterion for selection because it represents the accessibility of the texts to designers across ability and language contexts and denotes a certain focus on the quality of the podcast. Finally, transcription is a signal that there is the intent to preserve and keep the podcasts available and hosted online, and that resources are available to do so.

80th Annual Meeting of the Association for Information Science & Technology, Washington, DC | Oct. 27-Nov. 1, 2017

| Podcast | Information seeking | Information Use | Information Need | Information Organization | Information Avoidance | Information Sharing |
|---|---|---|---|---|---|---|
| Boag world | + | + | + | / | + | + |
| The Style Guides Podcast | + | + | + | + | / | + |
| Responsive Web Design | + | + | + | + | - | + |
| Legend | + = High Presence in podcast discourse | | /= Medium Presence e | | - = Low Presence | 0 = No presence |

***Table 2**. Information behavior present in podcasts*

For each podcast, the five most recent transcripts published before January 1st, 2017 were downloaded. These podcasts were loaded into NVivo software and coded using grounded theory. Each transcript was read, and texts reflective of information behavior were assigned descriptive codes which were then grouped into the six facets of information behavior identified previously.

## FINDINGS

The discourse contained in the podcasts contained evidence of information behaviors in the context of web design. Many of the information behaviors were clearly occurring within the context of the podcasts as discourses. The podcasts had the potential to serve as documents containing evidence of information behavior and also as explicit examples of information sharing, seeking, encountering and in some cases avoidance.

For researchers of information behavior, these podcasts have use as textual source. From the perspective of qualitative research, such texts can be used as documental elements of studies, serving as a triangulation point to increase quality and validity in research. For those interested in mixed and quantitative studies, podcasts and transcripts can easily be put into software for processing and mining in much the same way as other documents. Podcasts represent a chance to study the practices of populations from a distance in discursive forms that a researcher's direct presence might prohibit.

Table 2 illustrates the relative presence of each concept within the podcasts studied. Each has a rich description of many information behaviors. The presence of information behavior is particularly high, likely because design is a communicative profession. Additionally, Laing & Masoodian (2015) note that designers frequently have to share and promote their design process as a way of proving economic value. Such sharing behavior is also likely a product of a medium that inherently involves broadcasting and documenting the interviewer, interviewees or panel members' ideas and thoughts via the internet as recorded sound.

## CONCLUSION

Podcasts, while frequently studied as part of web 2.0 pedagogy, remain underused as documents for the study of individual experiences. As this study demonstrates, podcasts can be a rich text to use in the study of human information behavior. Future works should incorporate such documents into their research design as either primary text of analysis or as a way of creating additional contexts of understanding to increase validity. Directly related to the subject of these podcasts, further study should be undertaken to understand how reflective of experience of web designers these texts truly are.

## REFERENCES


Borko, H. (1968). Information science: What is it? *American Documentation, 19*(1), 3-5.

Erdelez, S. (2000). Towards understanding information encountering on the web. *Proceedings of the ASIS Annual Meeting, 37*, 363-71.

Fisher, K. E., & Julien, H. (2009). Information behavior. *Annual Review of Information Science and Technology, 43*(1), 1-73. https://doi.org/10.1002/aris.2009.1440430114

Gill, R. (2007). Technobohemians or the new cybertariat?: New media work on Amsterdam a decade after the web: Report. Institute of Network Cultures.

Kennedy, H. (2010). The successful self-regulation of web designers. *Ephemera: Theory & Politics in Organization, 10*(3), 374-389.

Kennedy, H. (2011). *Net work: Ethics and values in web design* (2012 edition). New York: Palgrave Macmillan.

Laing, S., & Masoodian, M. (2015). A study of the role of visual information in supporting ideation in graphic.

# A Knowledge Lens for Innovation: Seeing the Ambiguity, Conversations and Barriers in Social Systems

**Darin Freeburg**
*University of South Carolina, USA. darinf@mailbox.sc.edu*

## ABSTRACT

This poster introduces the knowledge lens, a way of seeing more clearly the opportunities for knowledge creation within social systems. It includes three groupings and six elements. The groupings bring into focus the complexity of organizational life, the power of conversation in knowledge creation and barriers to the integration of information and the application of knowledge. The poster outlines the foci of the knowledge lens, along with several new insights gained by viewing social systems through this lens. It suggests that information professionals are best equipped to use the lens, articulating a new place for information professionals within organizations and other social systems.

## KEYWORDS

knowledge lens, innovation, imprecision, conversation, information barriers

## OVERVIEW

This poster outlines a new approach to viewing social systems that reveals the value of ambiguity and imprecision, the importance of conversation and the impact of barriers to information and knowing. The elements within these groups control for aberrations in the image of social systems due to a fuzzy view of human potential and agency, an illusion of perfection, a distorted view of power, excessive homogeneity and barriers that limit the power of an organization's information and knowledge. The knowledge lens both carves out a new role within organizations and suggests that information professionals are uniquely positioned to fill this need. Yet, this will happen only in-so-far as LIS curriculum adapts to prepare the new information professional, and organizations recognize the unique capabilities of information professionals.

## SEEING COMPLEXITY

The complexity group brings into focus the complex and adaptive nature of human systems, which are self-emergent and unpredictable (McElroy, 2002; Stacey, 1996). Leaders first notice the role of human agency within this system and the richness of self-emergent solutions. This agency allows for the expression of imagination and creativity, and it allows for collective action (Davidson, 2010). Equipped with this focus, leaders recognize the potential of tapping into the system, rather than trying to control it in order to maintain a sense of predictability.

80th Annual Meeting of the Association for Information Science & Technology, Washington, DC | Oct. 27-Nov. 1, 2017



Leaders next notice the lack of predictability within an open system in constant flux, one that never reaches a static state of equilibrium (von Bertalanffy, 1968). Within the discomfort this brings is the innovative power of the system to change and abruptly adapt to external changes. Leaders notice that the various continuous improvement models touted as best practice in business and education attempt to ignore this unpredictability and increase efficiency at such a rate that creativity is stifled. As an example, an organization may gradually increase their efficiency in building stone towers without ever stopping to ask if they should actually be building stone towers. Allowing for unpredictable disruption frees the system up to adapt and innovate.

## PRACTICING COMPLEXITY

With this new complexity focus, leaders are able to see new behaviors that encourage knowledge creation. These come from Stacey's (1996) three control parameters for complex adaptive systems – rate of information flow, diversity and richness of connectivity. These are viewed through the knowledge lens as faucets that can be turned down or up to increase stability or instability, respectively. Instead of forcing desired behavior, leaders can turn up the information flow faucet to create a more optimal environment for innovation. For instance, educators can bring in more targeted information about the backgrounds of their students to facilitate innovative pedagogical decision. Leaders can turn up the diversity and connection faucets to guide creative abrasion that brings diverse thought processes, experiences and expertise together in a guided effort to escape the "comfortable clone syndrome" (Leonard & Straus, 1997).

## SEEING CONVERSATION

The conversation group brings into focus the power of conversation to pool unique information to create innovative knowledge solutions. Leaders see that conversation is the foundation for productive inquiry (PI), a concept from John Dewey outlined by Cook and Brown (1999) as "a problem, a question, a provocative insight . . . [that] aims to produce an answer, solution or resolution" (p. 62). Innovation does not occur through the mere build-up of information; rather, it occurs as a result of asking questions that catalyze the search for answers. The value of conversation is clear. Poor policies continue to be implemented, often, as a result of poor communication that lacks honest and open questioning (Argyris, 1977). It was only through conversation that Xerox technicians developed non-canonical solutions for printer problems that went beyond the established and formal solutions in existing manuals (Brown & Duguid, 1991).

## PRACTICING CONVERSATION

With this new conversation focus, leaders are able to see ways to encourage conversation. They do so with an awareness that good instruction – and innovation – brings a conversation from Pask's (1975) L0 language that is simple and highly directional to L1 language that is specialized and characteristic of someone highly knowledgeable in an area (Lankes, 2011). This is best accomplished as individuals are encouraged to contribute and pool their unique L1's as they converse. Not only does the contribution of unique information in a conversation increase the quality of decisions (Larson et al., 1998), but it also helps others in the conversation make contextual connections between a new L1 and their own L1. For instance, consider a group conversation about a recent political election and voter turnout. Individual A – a lawyer – recounts the implications of the National Voter Registration Act on making it easier to register at the same time you get your license. Individual B – an economist – recounts reasons why lower income Americans tend to vote less. Individual C – a machinist – notes the role of the local steel union in getting out the vote. Each individual uses specialized language, but they do so in the context of a shared conversation that they all relate to. This makes it easier to make sense and learn this specialized language, as it is connected to a shared conversational area in which each individual can ask follow-up questions. After the conversation, the entire group now has its own new L1 vocabulary that can be used to develop non-canonical knowledge.

## SEEING BARRIERS

Information is never an end in itself; rather, it can serve as a means to the true end of actionable knowing. The barrier group first brings into focus the inability for many to integrate information into their minds as knowledge. Information cannot impact behavior unless it first gets combined in one's head and related purposively to what is already known through past experiences, expertise, etc. Yet this is often blocked by beliefs (Batson, 1975), lack of attention, organizational narcissism (Stein, 2003) and social norms (Chatman, 1999). But even if information *is* integrated as knowledge, this knowledge often does not impact behavior in any meaningful way. If knowledge is a "tool at the service of knowing" (Cook & Brown, 1999, p. 61), it too often sits on the shelf.

## PRACTICING BARRIER REMOVAL

With this new view of barriers, leaders are able to see ways to increase the ability of information and knowledge to lead to action and – as a result – the creation of new knowledge and information. The knowledge lens suggests that leaders engage individuals in self-reflection to bring beliefs, mental models and social norms surrounding information behavior to the surface where their relevancy can be questioned (Senge, 1990).

Leaders can overcome the barriers of acting on knowledge by addressing the variables identified by Ajzen's (1985) theory of planned behavior as influencing intentions to attempt a certain behavior. This includes increasing the perceived advantages and likely success of the behavior, showing them that individuals they admire think they should attempt the behavior and increasing perceptions of self-efficacy that they have control over the variables surrounding the successful completion of the behavior.

## WHO?

Information professionals both serve in these leadership roles and advance the objectives of knowledge creation with other leaders in the system. This builds on momentum in a shifting view of the roles of information professionals. Lankes (2011) argued that the facilitation of knowledge creation is essential to the mission of new librarianship. Bedford, Donley & Lensenmayer (2015) called for a shift in librarianship away from collections and toward knowledge assets: "The primary value of a library in the knowledge society will shift from the library's resource collections to librarians' intellectual capital assets" (p. 83). Yet, these are calls for a change in librarianship. Although revolutionary, they are done within a well-established profession. This poster is a call for a new profession – a new information professional situated primarily outside of the library. This will occur as LIS curriculum adapts to meet the changing needs of social systems – namely, organizations – and as organizations realize these needs and the capabilities of information professionals to meet them. It is suggested that the innovators of tomorrow will come not from schools of business, but from schools of information that teach and practice the knowledge lens.

## CONCLUSION

The knowledge lens can be used by leaders of any social system. It provides the foci, insights and practices that leaders can use to guide their systems toward innovation. It draws on decades of literature from a wide variety of disciplines and provides researchers with several areas of continued investigation into the nature and function of innovation. The poster itself is a nod to the power of design to spark knowledge creation and is expected to create several collaborations in theoretical and applied research.

## REFERENCES

Argyris, C. (1977, Sept.-Oct.). Double loop learning in organizations. *Harvard Business Review*.

Ajzen, I. (1985). From intentions to actions: A theory of planned behavior. In J. Kuhl & J. Beckmann (eds), *Action control: From cognition to behavior*. Berlin: Springer, pp. 11-39

Batson, C.D. (1975). Rational processing or rationalization? The effect of disconfirming information on a stated religious belief. *Journal of Personality and Social Psychology, 32*(1), 176-184.

Bedford, D.A., Donley, J. K., & Lensenmayer, N. (2015). The role of librarians in a knowledge society: Valuing our intellectual capital assets. In A. Woodsworth & W.D. Penniman (eds.), *Current issues in libraries, information science and related fields (Advances in Librarianship, Volume 39)*, pp. 81-113.

Brown, J.S. & Duguid, P. (1991). Organizational learning and communities of practice: Toward a unified view of working learning and innovation. *Organization Science, 2*(1), 40-57.

Chatman, E. (1999). A theory of life in the round. *Journal of the American Society for Information Science, 50*(3), 207-217.

Cook, S.D.N. & Brown, J.S. (1999). Bridging epistemologies: The generative dance between organizational knowledge and organizational knowing. *Organization Science, 10*(4), 381-400.

Davidson, D.J. (2010). The applicability of the concept of resilience to social systems: Some sources of optimism and nagging doubts. *Society & Natural Resources, 23*(12), 1135-1149.

Lankes, D. (2011). *The atlas of new librarianship*. Cambridge, Mass: The MIT Press.

Larson, J.R., Christensen, C., Franz, T.M., & Abbott, A.S. (1998). Diagnosing groups: The pooling, management, and impact of shared and unshared case information in team-based medical decision making. *Journal of Personality and Social Psychology, 75*(1), 93-108.

Leonard, D. & Straus, S. (1997, July-August). Putting your company's whole brain to work. *Harvard Business Review*.

McElroy, M.W. (2002). The new knowledge management. *Knowledge and Innovation: Journal of the KMCI, 1*(1), 43-67.

Pask, G. (1975). Conversation, cognition and learning: A cybernetic theory and methodology. Amsterdam: Elsevier.

Senge, P.M. The fifth discipline: The art & practice of the learning organization. New York, NY: Doubleday/Currency.

Stacey, R. (1996). *Complexity and creativity in organizations*. San Francisco, CA: Berrett-Koehler Publishers.

Stein, M. (2003). Unbounded irrationality: Risk and organizational narcissism at long term capital management. *Human Relations, 56*(5), 523-540.

Von Bertalanffy, L. (1968). *General system theory: Foundations, development, applications*. New York, NY: George Braziller.

# A Tentative Evaluation Framework for Digital Archaeological Data Sites

**Mark Antony Freeman**
*University of Tennessee, Knoxville, USA. mfreem12@utk.edu*

**Xiaohua Zhu**
*University of Tennessee, Knoxville, USA. xzhu12@utk.edu*

## ABSTRACT

**In this poster presentation, we describe a tentative evaluation framework for digital archaeological data sites and a test of this framework using 148 Virginia archaeological websites. Archaeological data dissemination situates in the overlapping demands of openness, scholarship and outreach. This analysis suggests that, while there are some exemplary websites, much of the archaeological record remains publicly inaccessible. These websites did provide many supporting characteristics for public outreach, but concerns about preservation, data "openness" and limited datasets remain.**

## KEYWORDS

open data, open science, archaeological data, scholarly communication, public outreach, digital curation

## INTRODUCTION

One of the important trends in scholarly communication, perhaps partially driven by the government open data initiative and the open science movement, is publishing research data. This trend is not limited to "sciences" but virtually all disciplines, including humanities. With the increasing availability of research data comes the question of evaluation. This poster proposes a tentative framework for evaluating websites that publish archaeological data in digital formats: looking at scholarly communication; how well the data meets the criteria of openness; and how useful it is to broader publics. The framework has the potential to be modified and used for evaluating research data publication in other domains and disciplines.

Archaeology is an interesting discipline to investigate in the context of open data and open science because data publication has always been integral to the practice of archaeology. The 19th-century English archaeologist Augustus Henry Lane-Fox Pitt-Rivers noticed, "publication provided an objective record," and yet he also said that his voluminous excavation volumes were "not intended for casual readers" (Richards, 2004). Digital technologies have allowed archaeologists to capture more information from archaeological sites and preserve these culture records and products for both researchers and the public. This information includes digitizing what had been paper records (field notes and artifact catalogs); increased photography from digital images, supplemented by video data; digital spatial data; and laboratory data including databases, images and telemetry. For the purpose of this study, archaeological data was defined as site reports, field data, artifact data, spatial data and data visualization and models.

## RESEARCH DESIGN

In this study, we used an inductive approach to develop the evaluation framework. It started from a specific discipline, archaeology. Based on the characteristics and expectations of research data presentation in the discipline, we identified a conceptual framework including three basic aspects for research data in archaeology: scholarly publishing, open data and public outreach. From an analysis of literature on the three concepts, we developed a set of evaluation criteria for digital archaeology data, using a sample of websites that include digital archaeological data to test the framework.

## CONCEPTUAL FRAMEWORK

This study is situated in concepts from the open data movement, scholarly publishing and public outreach. Scholarly access and public outreach are closely intertwined with open data concepts, but each maintains some distinctions in focus. For scholars, making data available can mean more citations, the ability for new research and collaborations, the reuse of data and the validation of results. The presentation of these data supports the practice of archaeology, differentiating it from pot hunting. For the public, there may be economic benefits – archaeological sites feature in development and tourism decisions – and the possibility for citizen science, as well as the need for public trust since archaeological data are often created with public funds. There is some justification in saying that even if the public never looks at archaeological data, they should know that the data are available. Preserving data, often excavated at considerable cost, and making them accessible, thus serves many constituents. Although it is unlikely that any one website can meet the needs of multiple publics, this study is an attempt to see what data are accessible, and how data dissemination is balancing these characteristics of openness, scholarship, and outreach.

For each concept in the conceptual framework, a set of criteria was developed to measure whether the website satisfies the requirement of publishing research data in that aspect (Table 1).

80th Annual Meeting of the Association for Information Science & Technology, Washington, DC | Oct. 27-Nov. 1, 2017

| Metrics | Criteria |
|---|---|
| Scholarly publishing | Citation |
| | Licensing |
| | Permanent URIs |
| | Permanence/Archiving |
| | Contact Information |
| Open Data | Type (based on 5-star open data rating) |
| | Access |
| | Accessibility |
| | Thesaurus/Data dictionary |
| Public Outreach | Site Summaries |
| | Blog |
| | Social Media |
| | Contextual Information |
| | Media |
| | Community Outreach |
| | Educational Content |

***Table 1.*** *Evaluation criteria by category*

## DATA COLLECTION AND ANALYSIS

The study used an exhaustive sample of 148 archaeology websites from the State of Virginia. We limited the scope to archaeological data that originated from archaeological excavations conducted in Virginia, a heavily studied area providing a variety of projects and websites, and supported by a pre-existing study of archaeological collections.

Based on the evaluation framework (Table 1), data were collected and recorded in a codebook, on one browser, over a one-month period. Since the data often existed within a broader website, a navigation structure was constructed to look for archaeological content. Characteristics that were not present within this structure were not recorded. Data were cleaned and normalized according to allowable values with descriptive statistics generated using Excel. Results were tabulated within each of the conceptual areas. The analysis allowed quantification of how websites satisfy the requirements of openness and exhibit characteristics in support of scholarly publishing and public outreach.

## PRELIMINARY RESULTS

Of the 148 websites examined, 109 were identified as having no archaeological webpages; 39 contained archaeological webpages; only 26 websites included defined archaeological data. The characteristics of public outreach were identified for those 39 websites with archaeological webpages. One or more of the characteristics of public outreach were found in all of these sites. Appropriately for the archaeology, contextual information was provided by nearly 80% of the websites. Blogs and other social media were used by about half of the websites.

Open data and scholarly communication aspects were identified for the 26 websites with archaeological data. Just over half of these websites shared data textually, usually in the form of site reports through a linked PDF document, but also as simple html pages. Only 11 websites had re-usable data. Six of these websites included a data dictionary, providing database field information and detailing how the fields were used, allowing for better interpretation and greater interoperability. When assessing these websites with the five-star open data rating system developed by Berners-Lee (2006), 11 websites reach level 3.

Regarding scholarly communication, we only found limited instances of explicit use statements, or licenses, at 19.2%. Citation information was provided on only seven sites (26.9%). About 61.5% or 16 sites provided easy access to contact information, which was defined as a link or email address to a person connected with the digital or physical collections (rather than a generic webmaster email). There was no use of URIs and no statements on archiving data were found on any of the websites.

## CONCLUSION

The analysis of the Virginia archaeological websites shows an overall lack of access to reusable archaeological data failing both the public and other scholars. This absence means a lack of access to a potential set of valuable cultural heritage data and a lack of visibility for how archaeological scholarship informs our understanding of the past. This quantitative content analysis of websites provides a benchmark to available data from archaeological projects in Virginia and an insight into what data are unavailable. Archaeology is representative of many research communities that are increasingly looking for comparative datasets for research needs and developing a desire for public engagement and data sharing. While there are many criteria judging openness, this conceptual framework allowed for potentially more nuanced evaluation criteria. The instrument proposed in this research has the potential to be re-used or modified for analyzing open data websites in other disciplines, especially humanities.

## REFERENCES


Berners-Lee, T. (2006). Linked data. Retrieved from https://www.w3.org/DesignIssues/LinkedData.html

Richards, J. (2004). Online archives. *Internet Archaeology, 15*. Retrieved from http://intarch.ac.uk/journal/issue15 /7/jr1.html

# Emergent Trends in Research to Increase Participation of Underrepresented Populations in Cancer Clinical Trials: A Qualitative Analysis of the HSRProj Database

**Lynette Hammond Gerido**
*Florida State University, USA. lhg16@my.fsu.edu*

**Zhe He**
*Florida State University, USA. zhe@fsu.edu*

**Michelle M. Kazmer**
*Florida State University, USA. mkazmer@fsu.edu*

**Marcia A. Mardis**
*Florida State University, USA. marcia.mardis@cci.fsu.edu*

## ABSTRACT

**Over the years studies have been conducted to identify barriers to participation in clinical trials. Many researchers strive to discover evidence-based approaches for increasing participation of underrepresented groups to improve the generalizability of the study findings and to decrease health disparities. The Health Services Research Projects in Progress (HSRProj) database has over 800 studies related to cancer clinical trials. This study will analyze the data from the HSRProj database to identify trends in research related to increasing the participation of underrepresented groups in cancer clinical trials. For each study in this sample the researchers will identify the target population and research objectives to explore trends, identify potential gaps and highlight opportunities to support efforts to make research accessible to everyone involved in the health care decision-making process. The researcher will develop a classification system based on the stated research goals of each study and compare with public policies aligned with increasing participation of underrepresented groups in clinical trials.**

## KEYWORDS

health, disparities, informatics, qualitative, cancer, clinical trials

## INTRODUCTION

In 1993, the National Institutes of Health (NIH) Revitalization Act was signed into law. This act identified a need to include women and minority groups in all NIH-funded clinical research (Heller et al., 2014). Since that time many researchers have strove to discover evidence-based approaches for increasing participation in clinical trials by underrepresented groups. Clinical trials are viewed as the gold standard of evidence about efficacy and safety of cancer prevention, early detection and treatment interventions. Increasing underserved racial and ethnic populations in clinical research is especially important because cancer health disparities disproportionately impact these groups (Wallington et al., 2016). Also including underrepresented groups in cancer clinical trials improves the generalizability of the study findings.

In general, enrollment in cancer trials is low for all patient groups. Studies have shown the overall recruitment rate for National Cancer Institute-sponsored trials to be less than 2% of all newly diagnosed cancer patients (Byrne et al., 2013). Racial and ethnic minorities, women and the elderly were less likely to enroll in cooperative group cancer trials than were whites, men and younger patients, respectively (Murthy et al., 2004). The reporting and analysis of data based on minorities in clinical trials remain inadequate. Less than 2% of the National Cancer Institute's clinical trials focus on any racial/minority population as their primary emphasis (Chen et al., 2014).

Health Services Research Projects in Progress (HSRProj) is a publicly available database provided by the National Library of Medicine. This study will mine the HSRProj database to answer the following research questions:

- Which underrepresented populations are being served by research to increase participation in cancer clinical trials?
- When the research goal is to increase participation of underrepresented groups in clinical trials, is it primary, secondary or tertiary?
- What is the trend in research over the years since the National Institutes of Health (NIH) Revitalization Act of 1993?

## METHOD

A sample of studies will be acquired by querying the HSRProj database using *cancer*, *clinical trial* and *participation* as keywords. The results will be exported from the HSRProj database. Each study in the sample will be imported into Nvivo as cases. The study abstracts will be coded to identify underrepresented groups and to classify participation research goals. After coding is complete, trends related to the study start date and corresponding public policies will be assessed.

### *Data Collection*

Data collection is an inductive approach using open coding and constant comparison techniques as described in health services research by Bradley, Curry & Devers (2007). The

80th Annual Meeting of the Association for Information Science & Technology, Washington, DC | Oct. 27-Nov. 1, 2017

researcher will review the study abstracts line by line and as an underrepresented group becomes apparent, it will be assigned a code by highlighting words or phrases that indicate conceptually the alignment with a group historically underrepresented in cancer clinical trials. As the researchers review more abstracts the codes may be refined to better describe the underrepresented groups. For example, an underrepresented group may be the elderly. Some studies may indicate an age of 65 or older whereas others may refer to the elderly as senior citizens. The researchers will compare the text segments to other segments that have been previously assigned the same code and will decide whether they reflect the same concept. Using the constant comparison method (Glaser and Strauss 1967), the researchers will refine existing codes and identify new codes.

The approach to classifying the research goals will be more deductive than inductive. The researcher has devised a classification scheme to organize the studies based on the extent to which increasing participation in cancer clinical trials is fundamental to the study. The researcher will code a research goal as primary when it directly indicates increasing participation as a major goal or outcome of the research. A secondary classification indirectly approaches participation by identifying factors that influence or describe future interventions and communications strategies. Finally, the researcher will code noncommittal goals describing possible positive outcomes as tertiary.

### *Qualitative Analysis*

The researcher will identify themes that emerge as recurrent and unifying ideas. Themes are expected to evolve from coding as taxonomy and may also be observed as relationships between concepts. For example, there may be an association between the frequency of a specific underrepresented group and the likelihood a study will have increasing participation as a primary goal.

The researcher will conduct qualitative analysis using a secondary data source, the National Institute of Health's (NIH's) Research Portfolio Online Reporting Tool (RePORT), to discover if similar trends are observed. Additionally, the researcher will comparatively analyze the coded concepts with the enactment of public policies like the NIH Revitalization Act of 1993 to identify potential trends in related research to increase participation.

## PRELIMINARY FINDINGS

The researcher's initial coding for underrepresented groups has revealed the emergence of five groups: African-American/Black (27), Rural (16), Hispanic (11), Latino/a (10) and Women (8). Further refinement may merge groups or cause others to splinter into distinct groups.

The researcher identified the following text segments, excerpted directly from the study abstracts, as examples of a research goal classified at each level:

**Primary** – "to increase recruitment and retention of racial/ethnic minorities into therapeutic clinical trials"

**Secondary** – "to describe the factors that black cancer patients consider important in their decision to participate and remain in research"

**Tertiary** – "to attract and educate potential study participants, especially minorities, about participation in cancer clinical research"

## PRESENTATION FORMAT

The visual presentation will be a poster. The researcher will provide a brief oral presentation and will respond to questions afterwards.

## REFERENCES

Bradley, E. H., Curry, L. A., & Devers, K. J. (2007). Qualitative data analysis for health services research: Developing taxonomy, themes, and theory. *Health Services Research, 42*(4), 1758-1772.

Byrne, M. M., Tannenbaum, S. L., Glück, S., Hurley, J., & Antoni, M. (2014). Participation in cancer clinical trials: Why are patients not participating? *Medical Decision Making, 34*(1), 116-126.

Chen, M. S., Lara, P. N., Dang, J. H., Paterniti, D. A., & Kelly, K. (2014). Twenty years post-NIH Revitalization Act: Enhancing minority participation in clinical trials (EMPaCT): Laying the groundwork for improving minority clinical trial accrual. *Cancer, 120*(S7), 1091-1096.

Heller, C., Balls-Berry, J. E., Nery, J. D., Erwin, P. J., Littleton, D., Kim, M., & Kuo, W. P. (2014). Strategies addressing barriers to clinical trial enrollment of underrepresented populations: A systematic review. *Contemporary Clinical Trials, 39*(2), 169-182.

Murthy, V. H., Krumholz, H. M., & Gross, C. P. (2004). Participation in cancer clinical trials: Race-, sex-, and age-based disparities. *JAMA, 291*(22), 2720-2726.

Wallington, S. F., C. Dash, V. B. Sheppard, T. D. Goode, B. A. Oppong, E. E. Dodson, R. N. Hamilton, and L. L. Adams-Campbell (2016). Enrolling minority and underserved populations in cancer clinical research. *American Journal of Preventive Medicine, 50*(1), 111

# Using Cognitive Dissonance Theory to Understand Privacy Behavior

**Isha Ghosh**
*Rutgers University, USA. isha.ghosh@rutgers.edu*

**Vivek Singh**
*Rutgers University, USA. vivek.k.singh@rutgers.edu*

## ABSTRACT

**While individuals are keen to take advantage of the rewards (e.g., discounts) associated with using location-based apps on smartphones, they also express concern over location information being disclosed. This imbalance between expressed attitudes and demonstrated behavior has been termed the "privacy paradox." Current literature examines this phenomenon based on users' interactions with e-commerce systems; however, given the sensitive nature of location information generated from smartphones, gaining an understanding of this phenomenon as it is demonstrated in daily smartphone usage is important. Based on information gathered from qualitative interviews, we find that evaluation of benefits associated with disclosure do not play as strong a role in motivating disclosure as has previously been suggested. Instead we find that using a behavior-based approach rather than an investigation of attitudes governing disclosure provides newer insights and a more granular understanding of the privacy paradox. This nuanced understanding can be used to design apps more suited to user privacy needs as well as have implications for further research concerning this phenomenon.**

## KEYWORDS

privacy, location-based information, cognitive dissonance theory, smartphones

## INTRODUCTION

Evidence from news and research sources indicates that individuals are willing to trade their personal information for relatively small rewards (Spiekermann, Grossklags & Brendt, 2001, Acquisti & Gross, 2006, Acquisti & Grossklags, 2005). On the other hand, surveys of internet users' attitudes show a growing concern over privacy of their data (Pew Research Center, 2014). This dichotomy of information privacy attitude and actual behavior has been coined the "privacy paradox" (Barnes, 2006, Norberg, Horne & Horne, 2007).

The literature on this phenomenon currently centers on trust, privacy calculus or risk-benefit calculation from the perspective of transactions in e-commerce websites (Utz & Kramer 2009, Spiekermann et al., 2001). While these studies examine an important aspect of online information disclosure, we argue that selective willingness to disclose personal information in daily interactions is not limited to commercial transactions. It can occur in the day-to-day usage of smartphone-based apps that gather location information. Given the ubiquity of smartphones, location-based information is constantly generated either from GPS signals or apps that gather and transmit this information. The sensitive nature of this information opens the door to potential threats that range from an adversary's ability to localize an individual to profiling and identifying them based on the places they visit.

Cognitive dissonance theory (CDT) discusses the "cognitive justifications individuals' use to explain an irrational behavior" (Festinger, 1979). It does not connect attitudes to behavior; rather it attempts to understand how individuals justify behavior. This paper argues that rather than attempting to identify the gap between attitude and behavior, it would be beneficial to understand the process of rationalization for such seemingly erratic behavior. We posit that individuals' often have a pro-privacy attitude; therefore, rather than attempting to increase awareness of privacy, the discussion around privacy paradox should focus on individual justifications for disclosure as explained by CDT.

We apply this theory to understand the strategies employed by individuals to justify their decisions when using location-based services on their mobile phones. Based on information gathered from 14 semi-structured interviews, this paper attempts to answer the following research question: What strategies do individuals use to rationalize location-based information disclosure over smartphones?

## DISCUSSION

Participants were recruited via email and social media near a large institution in northeast United States and invited to answer a question regarding their phone usage. They had previously participated in a study where their location data had been collected for 10 weeks for understanding the interconnections between their mobility traces and personal wellbeing. They were paid $100 for the 10-week study and additional $20 for the follow up interviews.

During these interviews we asked participants: What types of information would you be more likely to give out (in a smartphone interaction)? Participants stated that they were most protective about sharing their physical home or work address. One participant (K1) stated that "I would not give my current home address to even my family members unless they had a reason for asking, and even then, I would ask a lot of questions before giving them my address." This implies

80th Annual Meeting of the Association for Information Science & Technology, Washington, DC | Oct. 27-Nov. 1, 2017

that location information is guarded carefully by individuals' and shared only among trusted members (if that). However, when asked about using location-sharing apps on the phone K1 stated "I'm not exactly against it, because companies track data all the time." These statements clearly show a disconnect between their long-held beliefs about protecting location information and the behavior of installing apps that make this information available.

In order to understand the cognitive process behind this decision, we asked participants what factors they take into consideration when installing location-based services. Nine out of 14 participants mentioned checking the information that the app was collecting before installing it. This implies that participants were seeking an external justification that would help resolve the dissonance between their desire to protect their location privacy and their need to use location-based apps.

Participants also discussed the ubiquity of information tracking devices in today's world as reasoning for installing discount-based apps. When asked about concerns over location information being tracked through apps a participant stated, "the app is not the only way I'm being tracked...there is enough data for them to know everything about me if they want, so it's not like by not installing the app I'm preventing something (being tracked)." The free-choice paradigm (Brehm, 1956) of the CDT discusses behavior exhibited when the two alternatives are similar. As the participant stated, individuals are aware of their information being tracked and, therefore, perceive the consequences of using or not using apps as similar. Hence, they attribute greater benefits to the chosen alternative than to the non-chosen alternative in order to avoid dissonance. In response to the same question participant R1 states "I usually clean out my phone pretty frequently so I know not too much information is being collected about me." In these cases, the perception of control over information being shared increases the desirability of installing the app and thus helps individuals to act upon their chosen alternative.

The induced compliance paradigm (Festinger & Carlsmith, 1959) of the CDT discusses the phenomenon of individuals' using a perception of high benefits as an external justification for exhibiting behavior contrary to their long-term attitude. In the case of location-based apps, an app that provides discounts based on location information would encourage individuals to share their location information even though this is contrary to their privacy attitudes. Participant G1 mentioned "For now, the discount is a big factor for me because I'm a student ... like if I'm broke I may install an app that gives me coupons but I'll probably uninstall it once I'm fine." This statement implies that individuals are aware of the risk involved in sharing location-based information and install and uninstall apps as needed in order to avoid experiencing dissonance between their privacy attitudes and behaviors. Participant T1 states "if my insurance is using my data to track my driving skills and lower or raise my premium accordingly that's fine because it's my data and being used to provide me a service, but they should not use that data to make money from some other means which i don't know about." In this case the collection of location-based information through an insurance agency is rationalized by the justification that the data is being used to provide services to the same individual. This behavior fits in with the induced compliance paradigm of the CDT where insurance benefits act as an external motivation to reduce dissonance.

## CONCLUSION

In this paper, we present an understanding of the privacy paradox phenomenon based on the CDT. As seen in previous research (Keith, Babb, Furner, Abdulla, 2010; Acquisti & Grossklags, 2005), the motivations guiding information sharing over smartphone apps are diverse and individualistic in nature. Different people attribute dissimilar values to different types of information and perceptions of cost and benefits associated with information disclosure vary from person to person. In such a scenario, an analysis of intentions to disclose may yield only a superficial understanding of actual disclosure behavior. However, a study of demonstrated disclosure behavior may lead to an understanding of how and what types of information individuals are willing to disclose. While the privacy paradox has been studied from the perspective of risk and trust (Norberg et al., 2007) and the mismatch between attitudes and behaviors (Acquisti & Gross, 2006), this paper discusses the use of the CDT as a newer direction of research to gain an understanding of this phenomenon. Given the growing popularity of phone- based apps, research needs to understand behavioral cues that guide disclosure over this medium. This paper provides an initial insight into this cognitive decision-making process and motivates the need for future work to investigate privacy paradox from a behavioral science perspective.

## REFERENCES


Acquisti, A. and Gross, R. Imagined communities: Awareness, information sharing, and privacy on the Facebook. In *Privacy enhancing technologies*, pp. 36-58. Springer, 2006.

Acquisti, A and Grossklags, J. Privacy and rationality in individual decision making. *IEEE Security & Privacy*, 2:24-30, 2005.

Barnes, S. B. (2006). A privacy paradox: Social networking in the United States. *First Monday*, 11(9).

Brehm, J. W. (1956). "Postdecision changes in the desirability of alternatives." *Journal of Abnormal and Social Psychology*, 52 (3): 384-89.

Festinger, J. J. (1957). *Cognitive dissonance theory*.

Festinger, L., and J. Carlsmith. (1959). Cognitive consequences of forced compliance." *Journal of Abnormal Psychology*, 58 (2): 203-10.

Freudiger, J., Shokri, R., & Hubaux, J. P. (2011, February). Evaluating the privacy risk of location-based services. In *International conference on financial cryptography and data security* (pp. 31-46).

Keith, M.J., Babb, J.S., Furner, C.P., Abdulla, A., 2010. Privacy assurance and network effects in the adoption of location-based services: An iphone experiment. In *Proceedings of the international conference on information systems* (ICIS '10), St. Louis, MO, pp. 237.

Madden, M., (2014) Public perceptions of privacy and security in the post-Snowden era. *Pew Research Center*. http://www.pewinternet.org/2014/11/12/public-privacy-perceptions/

Norberg, P.A., Horne, D.R., Horne, D.A., 2007. The privacy paradox: Personal information disclosure intentions versus behaviors. *The Journal of Consumer Affairs* 41, 100–126

Smith, A., (2017). Record shares of Americans now own smartphones, have home broadband. *Pew Research Center*. http://www.pewresearch.org/fact-tank/2017/01/12/evolution-of-technology/

Spiekermann, S., Grossklags, J. and Berendt, B. E-privacy in 2nd generation e-commerce: Privacy preferences versus actual behavior. In *Proceedings of the 3rd ACM conference on electronic commerce*, pages 38–47. ACM, 2001.

Utz, S., & Krämer, N. C. (2009). The privacy paradox on social network sites revisited: The role of individual characteristics and group norms. *Cyberpsychology: Journal of Psychosocial Research on Cyberspace*, 3(2).

# Information Seeking in Learning-oriented Search

**Souvick Ghosh**
*Rutgers University, USA. souvick.ghosh@rutgers.edu*

**Chirag Shah**
*Rutgers University, USA. chirags@rutgers.edu*

## ABSTRACT

**In this paper, we describe the different search behaviors exhibited by participants while performing learning-oriented search tasks. The search tasks have been designed to represent the cognitive levels of learning hierarchically. We investigate how the searcher's behavior and perceived learning outcomes vary with increasing levels of cognitive complexity. In this study, we analyze the search log data of the participants, self-reports, questionnaires and interviews both descriptively and statistically. Our results suggest that the perceived topic knowledge of the participants, perceived interest and difficulty assessments increase with increasing levels of the task. We use this study to discuss the preliminary results and highlight the limitations and future directions of this study.**

## KEYWORDS

searching, learning, searching as learning, information behavior

## INTRODUCTION

In recent years, searching as learning has emerged as a popular area of research in library and information science (LIS) (Rieh, Collins-Thompson, Hansen, & Lee, 2016; Hansen & Rieh, 2016). This area of study concentrates on how searching can be understood within the broader context of learning. Information scientists have explored various aspects of learning which occurs during online and offline search activities. Information search, retrieval, processing and assimilation with our existing knowledge structures can be considered as a learning process. However, the link between searching and learning has often been implied rather than being articulated or studied explicitly (Hansen & Rieh, 2016). The constructivist paradigm conceptualizes searching as a collection of search activities – which may occur online or offline – and involves accessing, retrieving, processing and presenting information to achieve some task goal (Vakkari, 2016). Similarly, learning involves the creation of new knowledge or modification and alteration of existing knowledge. Therefore, the framework of searching is an appropriate framework for our study, as this notion theorizes that the aim of searching is supporting investigative or learning activities (Vakkari, 2016; Marchionini, 2006).

In our paper, we investigate the research question: What is the relationship between individual search behavior and perceived learning processes and outcomes?

## BACKGROUND

According to Wilson (2000), human information behavior may involve different types of information seeking, various channels for information sharing and numerous modes of communication. Information seeking is a specific type of human information behavior, which is more active than passive, and occurs when an individual encounters a problematic situation (or realizes an inadequacy in the knowledge) and tries to remedy it by collecting relevant information. Dervin (1992), for example, proposes the sense-making model, which views the information seeking behavior as an endeavor to mitigate a knowledge gap. Information seeking can also be thought of as a series of evolving search tasks (Bates, 1989) which may involve some strategic and fortuitous information encounters (Foster and Ford, 2003). In this study, we examine how people engage in information seeking behavior, investigating especially how they seek knowledge, learn new concepts and resolve the gap in their knowledge.

In our study, we explore the relationship between searching and learning behaviors as exhibited in various stages of the search process, depending on the levels of cognitive complexity according to Anderson and Krathwohl's revised taxonomy of learning domain (Anderson and Krathwohl, 2001; Krathwohl, 2002). The revised taxonomy of learning – an extension of the original taxonomy suggested by Bloom (1956) – conceptualizes learning into six categories: remember, understand, apply, analyze, evaluate and create (Krathwohl, 2002). While few studies have explored how the cognitive dimensions of learning could be connected to the information search process (Jansen, Booth and Smith 2009; Collins-Thompson, Rieh, Haynes & Syed, 2016), we attempt to explicitly connect the cognitive dimensions of learning to search behaviors through learning-oriented search tasks.

We investigate whether certain search behavioral types and measures (e.g., queries, query length, URLs visited, dwell time, etc.) appear to show certain patterns for each learning-oriented task level.

## METHOD

A total of four university undergraduate students (except freshmen) were recruited for this study, the distribution being three seniors and one sophomore, and two male and two female. The participants self-reported that they conduct more than ten information searches daily on the web. The average

80th Annual Meeting of the Association for Information Science & Technology, Washington, DC | Oct. 27-Nov. 1, 2017

level of search expertise as reported by the participants was 4.25 on a 5-point Likert scale (where 1=Novice, 5=Expert). The study was conducted for two weeks, during which the participants were asked to perform four learning-oriented search tasks (each belonging to different levels of cognitive complexity). The topic of all the four tasks was cyberbullying. The participants were instructed to maintain an online record of the sources which they consulted for the task. The search log (along with timestamps) was also captured automatically using the Chrome plug-in Coagmento. This includes search queries, websites that the participants visited and dwell time on each page. Before and after completing each task, we asked the participants to fill out the pre- and post-task questionnaires to further probe their perceived search processes and learning experience. The participants were asked to write a comprehensive report at the end of the final task.

The task questions were designed according to the revised taxonomy of learning. We followed an approach similar to the search task development work by Wu et al. (2012) and Kelly et al. (2015). In our task design, we have combined the two basic levels of cognitive processes – remember and understand – into one, included apply, analyze and evaluate and removed the final level, create. All four tasks were related to the same topic, cyberbullying.

For our task-related questions, we utilized task measures (questionnaires) on task complexity and difficulty, topic familiarity and interests, perceived help of prior knowledge and knowledge gained, as these are potentially indicative of learning processes and outcomes (Collins-Thompson et al., 2016). At the end of the study, the participants were asked to come for a brief in-person semi-structure interview, where they were asked a few questions about their overall experiences. We also asked more specific questions on their perceived learning process and task-related experiences.

## DISCUSSION

For quantitative analysis, we used one-way between subjects ANOVA with posthoc analysis using Tukey HSD.

With respect to our research question, we relied on the participants' pre- and post-task questionnaire responses to identify potential patterns that may be exhibited in their perceived search and learning processes and outcomes. Post-task topic knowledge showed a significant increase over pre-task topic-knowledge for all of the four tasks.

As the task complexity increased, the participants reported an increase in topic interest after the task. This finding was also supported by our qualitative data. Three out of four participants mentioned that the final task (Evaluate) was the most interesting task. The participants also mentioned the Apply task as one of the most interesting tasks. These two tasks, according to the participants, were interesting because they were personally relatable and applicable. Even when we asked them in general about their overall learning experiences and what surprised them during the entire study, participants also recalled and mentioned these two tasks. For the Evaluate task, for example, one participant said,

I think from this I learned way more than I did in any assembly during high school, or anything like that. I think the most productive part was, like I said, learning about the ways to mitigate it. This isn't tackled the right way. Yeah like you can talk to your counsel about it, but that may not [give you] all the help you need. It's a shame that a lot of people don't know about these things... I learned a lot.

Another participant similarly mentioned when he was asked about the most surprising aspect of the entire process:

I guess I remember on the last task I think the prompt was what are some methods that people use today to deter cyber bullying in schools and universities...I thought the lack of substantial answers for that was surprising a lot of it was very general and non-helpful stuff...'just delete the app' or you 'just turn off the monitor' and things of that nature.

The results also indicate that with increasing complexity of the task, the participants found the task more difficult.

## CONCLUSION

In this study, we aim to contribute in the area of searching as learning. We explore the information seeking behavior of people and how it can be related to the various complexity levels associated with learning. This study will also offer insights on how some aspects of searching can be related to the various aspects of learning and cognitive processes. As there are a limited number of studies that attempted to connect searching and learning explicitly, our work will be an attempt to integrate various aspects of searching and learning. In future, we aim to continue this study with a larger group of participants, and task questions not limited to a single topic.

## FORMAT OF THE PRESENTATION

The presentation will be in the form of a poster which will highlight the details of the study and the key findings.


## ACKNOWLEDGEMENT

The work reported here is supported by the Institute of Museum and Library Services (IMLS) grant no. LG-81-16-0025-16. We would also like to thank SeoYoon Sung, Matthew Mitsui and Manasa Rath, all of whom made significant contributions to this user study.


## REFERENCES


Anderson, L. W., & Krathwohl, D. (Eds.). (2001). A taxonomy for learning, teaching, and assessing: A revision of Bloom's taxonomy of educational objectives. New York: Longman.

Bates, M. J. (1989). The design of browsing and berrypicking techniques for the online search interface. *Online Review*, *13*(5), 407-424.

Bloom, B. *Taxonomy of educational objectives*. New York: McKay, 1956.

Collins-Thompson, K., Rieh, S. Y., Haynes, C. C. & Syed, R. (2016). Assessing learning outcomes in web search : A comparison of tasks and query strategies. *Proceedings of the 2016 ACM on Conference on human information interaction and retrieval - CHIIR '16*, 163-172.

Dervin, B. (1992). From the mind's eye of the user: The sense-making qualitative-quantitative methodology. *Qualitative Research in Information Management, 9*, 61-84.

Foster, A., & Ford, N. (2003). Serendipity and information seeking: An empirical study. *Journal of Documentation, 59*(3), 321-340.

Hansen, P., & Rieh. S. Y. (2016). Recent advances on searching as learning: An introduction to the special evaluating exploratory web search for individuals and teams. *Journal of Information Science*, 67(6).

Jansen, B. J., Booth, D., & Smith, B. (2009). Using the taxonomy of cognitive learning to model online searching. *Information Processing and Management, 45*(6), 643–663.

Kelly, D., Arguello, J., Edwards, A., & Wu, W. (2015). Development and evaluation of search tasks for IIR experiments using a cognitive complexity framework. *Proceedings of the 2015 international conference on the theory of information retrieval*, 101-110.

Krathwohl, D. R. (2002). A taxonomy for learning, teaching, and assessing: A revision of Bloom's taxonomy of educational objectives (Abridged Edition). *Theory into Practice, 41*(4), 212-218.

Marchionini, G. (2006). Exploratory search: From finding to understanding. *Communications of the ACM, 49*(4), 41-46.

Rieh, S. Y., Collins-Thompson, K., Hansen, P. & Lee, H. J. (2016). Towards searching as a learning process: A review of current perspectives and future directions. *Journal of Information Science, 42*(1), 19-34.

Vakkari, P. (2016). Searching as learning: A systematization based on literature. *Journal of Information Science*, 42(1), 7-18.

Wilson, T. D. (2000). Human information behavior. *Informing Science, 3*(2), 49-56.

Wu, W., Kelly, D., Edwards, A., & Arguello, J. (2012). Grannies, tanning beds, tattoos and NASCAR: Evaluation of search tasks with varying levels of cognitive complexity. *Proceedings of the 4th information interaction in context symposium*, 254-257.

# User-Engaged App Development: Building Better Apps for the Vineyard

**Lisa M. Given**
*Swinburne University of Technology, Australia.*
*lgiven@swin.edu.au*

**Wade Kelly**
*Swinburne University of Technology, Australia.*
*wkelly@swin.edu.au*

**Alain Deloire**
*Montpellier SupAgro, France. alain.deloire@supagro.fr*

**Philip Paschke**
*Swinburne University of Technology, Australia.*
*ppaschke@swin.edu.au*

## ABSTRACT

Wine scientists and industry organisations are increasingly creating mobile web applications (apps) to support vineyard management and monitoring. While such tools are intended to improve wine industry practices, embedding user testing and user experience design in app development has not been implemented. User-focused design is essential for determining the need for new apps, for assessing the effectiveness of existing tools and to optimize usability. This poster presents the results from an exploratory, interdisciplinary study drawing on information science theory and best practices to examine vineyard managers' and grape growers' experiences with two apps: Fit Vine and VitiCanopy. This study used hands-on exploration of users' experiences with the apps in the vineyards to assess the usefulness of these tools from the users' perspective. Results include the need for consistent intuitive navigation, which is necessary to address a range of users' technological literacy levels; the need for help features to be integrated into the primary interface, which guides the users' experience; and, tools that provide added value to the work practices of users in vineyards in order to influence decision making. The results underscore the importance of involving wine industry members throughout the app- building process.

### *KEYWORDS*

mobile, app, user experience, information behavior

## INTRODUCTION

Mobile web application (app) development has seen tremendous growth in the wine industry, with apps designed for various purposes and to work on multiple devices. While such tools are intended to improve wine industry practices, there has been insufficient testing to understand the effectiveness of apps from a user-focused perspective. This poster presents results of an exploratory user experience study of two apps (FitVine and VitiCanopy) that are freely available to industry members. Fit Vine is an app designed to help users assess the health (i.e., fitness) of vines prior to planting and includes video how-to for cutting vines to assess plant health. The app leads users through a series of questions to guide vine assessment. VitiCanopy is designed to help users assess the grapevine canopy by taking photos of the vine canopy so that leaf area index can be calculated. Data are then output in Excel format for analysis.

The study design was interdisciplinary, drawing on expertise from both viticulture-oenology (for example, Lehmann, Reiche & Schiefer, 2012; Ohmart, 2008; Santiago-Brown, Metcalfe, Jerram & Collins, 2014; Walcroft, Taylor & others, 2013) and information science. Information science is well positioned to inform this research area as various usability testing methodologies and user-centred design best practices for web-enabled technologies have been developed and applied in a variety of situations and industries (for example, Houtkamp, La Rivière, de Groot, Janssen & de Jong, 2016; Starasts, 2015). By better understanding how wine industry members use apps and by identifying users' information needs, wine industry app developers can be more responsive to members' needs.

## RESEARCH QUESTIONS

The following research questions were addressed:

A. What technologies (including mobile apps) do industry members use in their work?

B. What are users' experiences of Fit Vine & VitiCanopy as examples of apps designed to support industry members' needs?

   a) How easy are these apps to navigate?

   b) How do users respond to the overall look and feel of the apps?

   c) Do users have accessibility or usability concerns?

   d) How can these apps enhance work practices?

## RESEARCH DESIGN

Qualitative focus group interviews and in-the-vineyard tests were conducted with 25 grape growers and vineyard managers to explore the strengths and weaknesses of each app's content and design from an end-user perspective. The focus groups provided a forum for an exploratory discussion of participants' information gathering and sharing practices related to research innovations and technology use. A hands-on ex-

80th Annual Meeting of the Association for Information Science & Technology, Washington, DC | Oct. 27-Nov. 1, 2017

ploration of user experience, conducted with focus group participants in the vineyard, highlighted the strengths and weaknesses of app content and design by testing the apps in a real-world situation. The rationale for testing apps in the vineyard was to ensure that the experience was as close to real-world use as possible. Data were gathered on ease of navigation, overall look and feel of app design, accessibility issues, the apps' ability to enhance work practices and other relevant topics.

## KEY FINDINGS

Overall, the results demonstrate significant disconnects between user needs and app designs, particularly where existing (non-app) tools provide comparable practice outcomes. As one participant noted:

> "This particular app might come into use [for] showing where…uniformity is breaking down in the vineyard. [But this app is] a big clumsy method of doing it because there's already other stuff out there to do it that's better."

Participants highlighted that in many cases the apps were providing solutions to non-existent problems. In order to invest the time and resources in a new technology, the payoff had to be significant; participants noted that this was payoff was not evident with Fit Vine and VitiCanopy. One participant reflected:

> "I think the older you get, the bigger the payback has to be to make the effort to pick up that new technology…I mean, rather than using an app, you should use shoes. Go and walk [in the vineyard] and use your eyes."

The results identify design changes needed to support usability of these apps (e.g., relabeling features, embedding instructions). The study also reinforces the need to apply user experience best practices and usability testing in app development. As one participant illustrated:

> "having the instructions on a different page from the page you are trying to write on [is important]. So, all of a sudden, you've gone through the instructions, 'oh right, I've got to that point, now I've got to go back to the instructions,' read some more, then go back to the thing… It's not user friendly."

The findings also highlight broader issues around access to internet infrastructure needed to support real-time app use. Focus groups participants stressed that internet access in vineyards was unreliable or unavailable entirely. For widespread industry adoption of mobile technologies, lack of internet access must be taken into account.

User experience research must be part of prototype app design with ongoing assessment during design and post-launch phases. By engaging users throughout the development process, app developers can enhance users' experience and encourage adoption of appropriate tools.

## CONCLUSION

The development process must begin from a value-added proposition. It is therefore prudent that development teams start with the end user by doing a thorough needs assessment to identify the problem that an app might address. Users are quick to abandon an app if they do not perceive added value to their work. This speaks to a larger issue: the general disconnect between wine scientists and those in industry. Developers must consider how they might best position themselves to bridge this divide. To that end, user-focused design and testing are critical to the process.

## VISUAL PRESENTATION FORMAT

The presentation format is a mixed media approach. A printed poster will provide the results with screenshots of app features. In addition, iPads will be available for attendees to demo the Fit Vine and VitiCanopy apps for themselves. Study results will be presented as a printed poster along with a handout summarizing the project's key findings. A poster is an appropriate medium as it provides adequate space to provide visual examples of both the research context (i.e., the vineyard) and screenshots. The hands-on component will give conference attendees tangible insight into the research findings.


## ACKNOWLEDGMENTS

The team thanks Wine Australia for funding this research.


## REFERENCES


Houtkamp, J., La Rivière, I., de Groot, H., Janssen, S. & de Jong, A. (2016). From research data to web-based policy tools: User-centered design techniques in the development of the AgMIP impacts explorer. *International Congress on Environmental Modelling and Software, France July 2016.*

Lehmann, R. J., Reiche, R., & Schiefer, G. (2012). Future internet and the agri-food sector: State-of-the-art in literature and research. *Computers and Electronics in Agriculture*, 89, 158-174.

Ohmart, C. (2008). Innovative outreach increases adoption of sustainable winegrowing practices in Lodi region. *California Agriculture*, 62(4), 142-147.

Santiago-Brown, I., Metcalfe, A., Jerram, C., & Collins, C. (2014). Transnational comparison of sustainability assessment programs for viticulture and a case-study on programs' engagement processes. *Sustainability*, 6(4), 2031-2066.

Starasts, A. (2015). Unearthing farmers' information seeking contexts and challenges in digital, local and industry environments? *Library & Information Science Research*, 37(2), 156-163.

Walcroft, J., Taylor, A., & others. (2013). Listening to end-users improves access and usability for climate change website. *Extension Farming Systems Journal*, 9(1), 28.

# NEURONE: oNlinE inqUiRy experimentatiON systEm

**Roberto González-Ibáñez**
*Departamento de Ingeniería Informática, Universidad de Santiago de Chile, Chile. roberto.gonzalez.i@usach.cl*

**Daniel Gacitúa**
*Departamento de Ingeniería Informática, Universidad de Santiago de Chile, Chile. daniel.gacitua@usach.cl*

**Eero Sormunen**
*Faculty of Communication Sciences, University of Tampere, Finland. eero.sormunen@uta.fi*

**Carita Kiili**
*Department of Education, University of Oslo, Norway. c.p.s.kiili@iped.uio.no*

## ABSTRACT

In this poster we introduce NEURONE, an open source web-based system for assessing online inquiry competences (OIC). NEURONE is a fully customizable solution that can be adapted to different research conditions through eight modules and a set of tools. To date, NEURONE has been successfully used to implement, deploy and run an online assessment contextualized in a pretest-posttest study design, in which nearly 1400 sessions were conducted with 350 elementary school students in their early adolescence.

## KEYWORDS

online inquiry competences, information literacy, assessment, tests, elementary schools

## INTRODUCTION

Information literacy (IL), the competences of searching, evaluating and using information sources, is a traditional research theme in library and information science. In today's web-dominated information environment, the assessment of online inquiry competences (OIC) as part of IL is an open and hot research problem.

Library associations have developed standards for IL competences (e.g., American Library Association, 2000). Competency standards explicate the goals for IL instruction and the criteria for the assessment of learning outcomes. In this sense, a key challenge is how to design and implement valid and reliable tests that can be applied effectively to assess OIC.

To address the above challenge, we have created NEURONE (oNlinE inqUiRy experimentatiON systEm), an open source system to implement and conduct tests focused on assessing OIC. The following sections of this poster focus on describing background aspects, NEURONE architecture, a brief discussion of its success and some considerations for the actual visual presentation session.

## BACKGROUND

Usually online research takes place when readers engage in complex processes of inquiry and problem solving. We refer to this broader task as online inquiry. In online inquiry, a person seeks answers to questions and uses the internet to learn from sources retrieved (Leu et. al., 2015). Interestingly, studies on exploratory search and searching as learning (Rieh et al., 2014) focus on similar phenomena.

Different approaches have been devised to test IL. In particular, fixed-choice tests, performance assessments and rubrics are well-documented alternatives to assess OIC (Oakleaf, 2008). Each of these approaches supposes pros and cons. For instance, fixed-choice tests are efficient to use, but they fail in measuring higher-level thinking skills. Conversely, performance-based assessments may be good at capturing higher-level thinking skills, but they tend to be expensive to implement.

Some attempts have been made to create technology to aid the assessment of OIC. For instance, the international test PISA includes a component to capture data about students' capacity to select and evaluate information (OECD, 2015). Others have built tools such as Meta-Analyzer to serve specific research needs (Tseng et al., 2009). These kinds of systems provide tools to assess both the end products and the process of online inquiry.

The approach introduced in this poster is based on this kind of system; however, it expands the views to OICs, and it is presented as an open source solution for researchers and educators.

## NEURONE

Contextualized in an international research project, which focuses on building a deeper understanding of students' OIC and developing an instructional model to enhance OIC learning in primary education (iFuCo project), we designed NEURONE, a web-based solution to implement OIC performance assessments (www.neurone.info).

NEURONE is an all-in-one distributed solution to implement and conduct OIC tests. The system comprises eight components (modules and set of tools): (1) a search engine that operates on a user-defined corpus of webpages, and which appearance mimics that of well-known search engines; (2) tools for information gathering, which enable subjects to bookmark webpages and collect snippets from them for later usage; (3) a customizable form to let subjects express their critical evaluations of information sources; (4) synthesis tools in

80th Annual Meeting of the Association for Information Science & Technology, Washington, DC | Oct. 27-Nov. 1, 2017

which subjects can revisit information gathered and write syntheses relying on multiple sources; (5) a powerful logger of users' search behaviors, which enable researchers and assessors to take a closer look to online inquiry as a process; (6) a module to automatically control session flow according to a test protocol; (7) a module to build customized forms that can be used to create surveys contextualized within the test; and (8) a general user interface that operates as a common container of all modules and tools. NEURONE's conceptual architecture is depicted in Figure 1.

Besides the above components, NEURONE has several features that make it a powerful system. First of all, it follows internationalization standards (i18n); as a result, its user interface labels can be easily translated into different languages. Second, despite the kind of functionalities supported by NEURONE, the system does not require browser extensions to work. For example, the logger component can automatically collect data such as keystrokes, mouse actions (i.e., clicks, scrolls and movements), queries, pages visited, time spent in pages and click through behavior, to name a few. However, to operate properly, it requires a browser that supports ECMAScript 6. Third, at the communication level, NEURONE supports both WebSockets and AJAX, thus it is flexible depending on the network conditions where tests will be conducted. Fourth, the flow administration component lets researchers express a test as a set of stages (e.g., search, information gathering, critical evaluation) in a particular order and under specific constraints (e.g. time, relevant documents required, etc.).

NEURONE was implemented with state-of-the-art technology for web development, namely, Node.js, Meteor, MongoDB, Apache Solr, AngularJS and Docker, to name a few. With the hope that others can use and extend NEURONE, we release it as an open source solution. Therefore, researchers can use it as is or they can change the source code to meet their particular needs. To ease both processes, fully detailed documentation (in English) is provided for both researchers and system administrators.

## SUCCESS CASE

NEURONE has been successfully used in the context of the iFuCo project. To date, nearly 1400 sessions have been conducted in Finland with approximately 350 elementary school students (between 11 and 12 years old) performing four tasks in the context of a pretest-posttest study design. As a result, approximately 11 million records were collected (surveys, search logs, synthesis responses, critical evaluation, etc.).

Preliminary results of OIC assessments and the design of an evaluation framework have been published elsewhere (Sormunen et al., 2017). Moreover, data is now being used to build prediction and classification models of students' search performance using behavioral data.

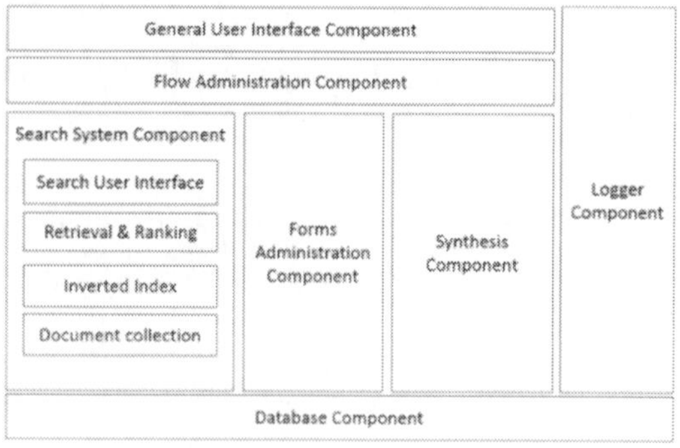


**Figure 1**. NEURONE's conceptual architecture

## NEXT STEPS

NEURONE and its documentation will be available to download through a dedicated website and an online Git repository. Moreover, additional user interface components are being developed to ease the process of setting up a new study (e.g., loading and indexing of a corpus of documents, changing tasks descriptions, changing language, customizing session flow). Furthermore, with the aim of replicating our success case in a different cultural context, NEURONE will be used during the second half of 2017 in a study in Chile with nearly 500 elementary school students.

## FORMAT OF THE PRESENTATION

During the visual presentation at ASIST 2017, a live demonstration of NEURONE will be performed. Audience will be able to use an instance of NEURONE and take a look at the kind of data captured by NEURONE. Moreover, examples of data analysis and preliminary results of the success case will be discussed with the audience.

## ACKNOWLEDGMENTS

The study was part of the iFuCo project funded by the Academy of Finland (grant's no. 294186) and the National Commission for Scientific and Technological Research (CONICYT) in Chile (grant's AKA/EDU-03).

## REFERENCES

American Library Association. (2000). Information literacy competency standards for higher education. Chicago, IL.

Leu, D. J., Forzani, E., Rhoads, C., Maykel, C., Kennedy, C. & Timbrell, N. (2015). The new literacies of online research and comprehension: Rethinking the reading achievement gap. *Reading Research Quarterly*, 50(1), 37-59. Oakleaf, 2008.

Oakleaf, M. (2009). Using rubrics to assess information literacy: An examination of methodology and interrater reliability. *Journal of the American Society for Information Science and Technology*, 60(5), 969-983.

OECD (2015). Using log-file data to understand what drives performance in PISA (case study), PISA. OECD Publishing, Paris, DOI: 10.1787/9789264239555-10-en

Rieh, S. Y., Gwizdka, J., Freund, L. & Collins-Thompson, K. (2014). Searching as learning: Novel measures for information interaction research. *Proceedings of the American Society for Information Science and Technology*, 51(1), 1-4.

Sormunen, E., González-Ibáñez, R., Kiili, C., Leppänen, P.H.T., Mikkilä-Erdmann, M., Erdmann, N. & Escobar-Macaya, M. (2017). A performance-based test for assessing students' online inquiry competences in schools. Submitted to the European Conference on Information Literacy (ECIL), 18-21 September 2017, Saint-Malo, France. 10 pages.

Tseng, J. C., Hwang, G. J., Tsai, P. S., & Tsai, C. C. (2009). Meta-analyzer: A web-based learning environment for analyzing student information searching behaviors. *International Journal of Innovative Computing, Information and Control*, 5(3), 567-579.

# Health Information Assessment by Vaccine Hesitant Parents

**Devon Greyson**
*Vaccine Evaluation Center, BC Children's Hospital Research Institute, Department of Pediatrics, University of British Columbia, Canada. dgreyson@bcchr.ubc.ca*

**Julie A. Bettinger**
*Vaccine Evaluation Center, BC Children's Hospital Research Institute, Department of Pediatrics, University of British Columbia, Canada. jbettinger@bcchr.ubc.ca*

## ABSTRACT

**Vaccines are widely considered to be one of the greatest successes of public health, but vaccine hesitancy has been internationally recognized as a health threat. Efforts to use information to increase vaccine acceptance have largely been unsuccessful, highlighting the need to better understand the information practices, values and experiences of hesitant populations. This constructivist grounded theory study explored health information experiences of 23 mothers in the Greater Vancouver region of Canada who had changed their minds about vaccines, in order to understand the ways information may have influenced their vaccination beliefs and practices. While health information sources were similar across the study population, assessment of vaccine-related information varied a great deal. In particular, mothers reported difficulty triangulating and assessing information during periods of affective stress, such as following their first birth or around a child's illness. Helping mothers triangulate information among trusted sources may help build vaccine confidence.**

## KEYWORDS

information assessment, information triangulation, health information, parents, vaccination

## INTRODUCTION

Vaccines are widely considered to be one of the greatest successes of public health (Koppaka, 2011). However, vaccine hesitancy, defined as "reluctance, delayed acceptance, or refusal of some or all vaccines despite the availability of vaccination services" (MacDonald & SAGE Working Group on Vaccine Hesitancy, 2015), poses a significant challenge to global immunization efforts (UNICEF Canada, 2013). Although a small percentage (~2-5%) of parents in wealthy, Westernized countries may hold strong anti-vaccination convictions, many others exist somewhere on the hesitancy spectrum (Leask, 2011) and may be amenable to changing their vaccination beliefs and practices over time. However, we do not yet understand how these changes occur.

Attempts to provide information to decrease vaccine hesitancy and have thus far been met with little success. Interventions designed to increase acceptance, including face-to-face education (Kaufman et al., 2013), provision of scientifically accurate information about vaccine safety (Nyhan, Reifler, Richey, & Freed, 2014) and individually tailored education for hesitant parents (Gowda, Schaffer, Kopec, Markel & Dempsey, 2013) have failed to significantly increase vaccine acceptance and uptake. Some of this research has even found that providing evidence-based information and correction of myths about vaccine risks actually served to increase rather than ameliorate hesitancy and fear regarding vaccines. This failure of information interventions to increase vaccine acceptance highlights a need to better understand the information practices, values and experiences of vaccine hesitant populations.

Although health information interventions have been deployed in attempts to address vaccine hesitancy, information science has only recently engaged with this topic and has largely focused on online information seeking and sharing. Regarding vaccine-related information behaviour, Bossaller (2014) analyzed online comments about vaccination, exploring attributions of authority and finding that personal experience was trusted more than many authoritative (expert) sources in often-hostile online environments. Hara and Sanfilippo's (2016) content analysis of online communities' discussions of the MMR vaccine found that knowledge frameworks and norms of an online community influenced the authority ascribed to different types of information. Narayan and Preljevic (2017) studied 12 online narratives of individuals who switched from anti-vaccine to pro-vaccine beliefs, finding that online information seeking was associated with anti-vaccine views and seeking from authoritative sources (e.g., a health care professional) with revising such views. In one of the few studies to collect primary data directly from participants, Kim and Real (2016) surveyed healthcare workers, finding an association between information seeking and influenza vaccine uptake, challenging some perceptions of those who seek out vaccine information as more hesitant than non-seekers. The current study delves further into primary data collection with vaccine hesitant individuals, in order to understand their vaccine-related information behaviour.

## STUDY OBJECTIVES

This study investigated the experiences of mothers who changed their minds about vaccination, in order to explore the role of information in these changes.

80th Annual Meeting of the Association for Information Science & Technology, Washington, DC | Oct. 27-Nov. 1, 2017

## METHODS

In this constructivist grounded theory study (Charmaz, 2007), mothers in the Greater Vancouver region of Canada, whose attitudes toward vaccination had changed since their school-aged (6-12 years) children were born, were recruited via primary schools, home learner groups and Facebook advertisements. Data was collected via semi-structured individual interviews that included critical incident technique (Urquhart et al., 2003) and information world mapping (Greyson, O'Brien & Shoveller, 2017). Interviews were transcribed, member-checked and analyzed using constant comparison. This poster focuses on information assessment, which emerged as a major theme.

## RESULTS

We interviewed 23 mothers who had at least one child aged 6-12 years and were currently or previously hesitant regarding routine childhood vaccinations. Nine had become less vaccine hesitant over time, nine more hesitant, and five had experienced multiple changes in vaccine attitudes. Eight participants had one child, 11 had two, and four had three children. Thirteen participants identified as having European heritage, eight as Asian, and two with other backgrounds. All had some postsecondary education, and the majority had at least a bachelor's degree.

Health information sources cited by study participants whose hesitancy had decreased did not substantially differ from those mentioned by those whose hesitancy had increased. Common sources included a nurse hotline, books, brochures, friends, health care providers, websites (specific sites or search engine results), teachers and daycare providers and their own parents or elders. Some felt that other mothers were an important source, while others described avoiding or blunting information from peers. Information assessment arose as a major theme, and some participants recalled assessment as having been particularly difficult in times of vulnerability, such as in the postpartum period or when dealing with a child's illness.

## ASSESSMENT: SOURCE AUTHORITY AND CREDIBILITY

Study participants had developed various heuristics for assessing health information. Source authoritativeness and credibility were important, but were not constructed in a universal manner. For example, several mothers ascribed high authority to academic medicine in the western tradition. One mother in this group who stated, "I'm always skeptical about what I find online," explained that she would read research, assessing source authority by asking:

Where is it coming from? Is it coming from the Lancet, is it coming from the *New England Journal of Medicine* [... or] is it some no-name brand journal [no one's] ever heard about, you know?

Formal authority based on credentials (e.g., medical degree, university affiliation) did not automatically make a source credible to all mothers, however. Some expressed distrust of government or medical bodies, often coupled with concern about pharmaceutical industry funding and source conflict-of-interest. Others felt that while medical credentials allowed one to ascribe a degree of authority, they were not sufficient to make a source fully credible. Personal attributes – either ones that allowed a mother to relate to an information provider (e.g., another parent, shared values) or characteristics that established the source as successful (e.g., thinness, wealth) – also served to construct credibility in the eyes of participants. One mother, for example, explained, "I feel the healthcare professional should be healthy themselves," in order for their advice to be credible.

## TRIANGULATION OF VACCINE INFORMATION

It has been noted elsewhere that parents may seek to triangulate information among sources in order to aid assessment of contested health information (Greyson, 2015). Participants in this study did engage in triangulation of health information including vaccine-related information, consulting multiple sources for a variety of purposes (including to prepare for medical appointments), to obtain a second authoritative opinion to confirm or dispute a first, to seek more authoritative answers to a question of importance, to verify or interpret information obtained from an authoritative source, and, in times of distress, to collect as much information from as many sources as possible.

One mother, who had initially been concerned about vaccines causing autism based on media reports, described a satisfying information triangulation process in which sources to which she ascribed authority and felt were credible created a consensus that allowed her to disregard the sources that were causing her worry and fear:

I was very concerned about it when my daughter was born, and I had the *Doctor Sears Baby Book*, [which suggested] an optional schedule for your vaccines and stuff [...and] I was like, "Is it right for me to do this?" and so I felt really kind of stressed about that. Then, because I was stressed about it I did a lot of research. I went and like read like proper journals and stuff like that and when I did that I felt a lot better about it and so my daughter's all vaccinated.

For participants, triangulation experiences that felt "successful" resulted in a confident conclusion regarding the answer to their vaccination question. Such experiences were often associated with decreases in vaccine hesitancy in this population. Feelings of unsuccessful triangulation – in which comparing sources led to greater confusion rather than building a consensus – were more likely to be expressed by mothers whose hesitancy had increased or had changed several times.

## DISCUSSION

Mothers whose vaccine hesitancy had decreased tended to ascribe authority to healthcare providers whom they found credible and valued consistent and verifiable vaccine safety and effectiveness information that was possible to triangulate among trusted sources. Those whose hesitancy had increased reported experiencing a lack of clear and reliable information, particularly following a health event such as autoimmune diagnosis or adverse event following immunization. Affective stress such as that experienced in times of medical vulnerability appeared to be associated with difficulty triangulating and assessing health information.

While these findings are preliminary, and the data is limited by being retrospectively self-reported, they do suggest ways to improve the use of information to increase vaccine confidence among this and similar populations. Information interventions aiming at influencing vaccine attitudes and uptake are frequently tested apart from participants' everyday contexts, with little or no follow up regarding what participants do with, for example, pro-vaccine information provided to their social media feeds. It may be that assisting mothers in effectively triangulating such information among sources they find authoritative and credible would enhance the effectiveness of such efforts. Further implementation science research along these lines is recommended.

## CONCLUSION

Vaccine hesitancy poses a public health challenge that risks being dismissed as information-insensitive. However, findings of this study suggest that information may be highly influential in changing mothers' minds about childhood vaccinations, when understood in the context of mothers' own life experiences, information assessment heuristics, affective state and triangulation practices.

## ACKNOWLEDGMENTS

This study was funded by the British Columbia Immunization Committee.

## REFERENCES

Bossaller, J. S. (2014). Evidence, not authority. *Reference & User Services Quarterly*, *53*(3), 232-241. doi:10.5860/rusq.53n3.232

Charmaz, K. (2007). *Constructing grounded theory: A practical guide through qualitative analysis*. Thousand Oaks, CA: Sage Publications.

Gowda, C., Schaffer, S. E., Kopec, K., Markel, A., & Dempsey, A. F. (2013). A pilot study on the effects of individually tailored education for MMR vaccine-hesitant parents on MMR vaccination intention. *Human Vaccines & Immunotherapeutics*, *9*(2), 437-445.

Greyson, D. (2015). Health information triangulation: A complex and agentic practice among young parents. *Proceedings of the Association for Information Science and Technology*, *52*(1), 1-3. doi:10.1002/pra2.2015.1450520100132

Greyson, D., O'Brien, H., & Shoveller, J. (2017). Information world mapping: A participatory arts-based elicitation method for information behavior interviews. *Library & Information Science Research*, *39*(2), 149-157. doi:10.1016/j.lisr.2017.03.003

Hara, N., & Sanfilippo, M. R. (2016). Co-constructing controversy: Content analysis of collaborative knowledge negotiation in online communities. *Information, Communication & Society; London*, *19*(11), 1587-1604. doi:http://dx.doi.org/10.1080/1369118X.2016.1142595

Kaufman, J., Synnot, A., Ryan, R., Hill, S., Horey, D., Willis, N., … Robinson, P. (2013). Face to face interventions for informing or educating parents about early childhood vaccination. *Cochrane Database of Systematic Reviews*, *2013*(5), CD010038. doi: 10.1002/14651858.CD010038.pub2

Kim, S., & Real, K. (2016). A profile of inactive information seekers on influenza prevention: A survey of health care workers in Central Kentucky. *Health Information & Libraries Journal*, *33*(3), 222-238. doi:10.1111/hir.12132

Koppaka, R. (2011). Ten great public health achievements --- United States, 2001--2010. *Morbidity and Mortality Weekly Report*, *60*(11), 619-623.

Leask, J. (2011). Target the fence-sitters. *Nature*, *473*(7348), 443-445. doi:10.1038/473443a

MacDonald, N. E., & SAGE Working Group on Vaccine Hesitancy. (2015). Vaccine hesitancy: Definition, scope and determinants. *Vaccine*, *33*(34), 4161-4164. doi:10.1016/j.vaccine.2015.04.036

Narayan, B., & Preljevic, M. (2017). An information behaviour approach to conspiracy theories: Listening in on voices from within the vaccination debate. *Information Research; Sheffield*, *22*(1), 1.

Nyhan, B., Reifler, J., Richey, S., & Freed, G. L. (2014). Effective messages in vaccine promotion: A randomized trial. *Pediatrics*, *133*(4), e835-e842. doi:10.1542/peds.2013-2365

UNICEF Canada. (2013). *Stuck in the middle. Child well-being in rich countries: A comparative overview.* (No. Canadian Report Card 11.) (pp. 1-16). UNICEF. Retrieved from unicef.ca/IRC11

Urquhart, C., Light, A., Thomas, R., Barker, A., Yeoman, A., Cooper, J., … Spink, S. (2003). Critical incident technique and explicitation interviewing in studies of information behavior. *Library & Information Science Research*, *25*(1), 63-88. doi:10.1016/S0740-8188(02)0016

# Information Needs, Seeking and Assessment of Parents of Gender Creative Children and Transgender Youth

**Devon Greyson**
*Department of Pediatrics, University of British Columbia, Canada. dgreyson@bcchr.ubc.ca*

**Elizabeth Saewyc**
*School of Nursing, University of British Columbia, Canada. elizabeth.saewyc@ubc.ca*

**Beth Clark**
*Interdisciplinary Studies Graduate Program, University of British Columbia, Canada. beth.clark@alumni.ubc.ca*

## ABSTRACT

Strong family support has been identified as key to mitigating negative health outcomes for gender creative children and transgender youth (GCCTY). While a variety of information resources exist for parents/caregivers of GCCTY, we have limited knowledge of which are most useful and why. This poster reports on preliminary analysis of an anonymous online survey of 103 parents/caregivers of GCCTY, ages 4-23, in the United States and Canada. The most commonly sought topics of information were general support for gender creative children, trans youth and their parents; however, a substantial minority also sought specific information related to medical or social transition and over 10% sought faith-based information. The most useful sources tended to be those that both met information needs and filled affective needs such as normalizing and affirming the experiences and information needs of seekers.

## KEYWORDS

information seeking, information assessment, information use, parents, transgender, children, youth

## INTRODUCTION

Many gender creative children and transgender youth (GCCTY) encounter societal stigma, family rejection and barriers to supportive care – challenges that can lead to depression, anxiety, self-harm, suicidality, social isolation and substance use (Edwards-Leeper & Spack, 2012; Khatchadourian, Amed & Metzger, 2014; Ryan, Russell, Huebner, Diaz & Sanchez, 2010). Recent research provides evidence that strong family support is key in promoting positive health outcomes for this population (Simons, Schrager, Clark, Belzer & Olson, 2013; Travers et al., 2012; Veale et al., 2015). Most GCCTY have cisgender (non-transgender) parents who may have little or no prior knowledge about transgender or gender creative experiences and resources. A growing array of information resources – ranging from autobiographies to healthcare websites – are available to parents/caregivers (see, for example, Ehrensaft, 2016; "Parents and Caregivers," n.d.; Whittington, 2015). However, it is not clear which information resources parents/caregivers find most helpful as they seek to support the GCCTY in their care.

Previous information behaviour research related to LGBT youth well-being has found that stigma remains a substantial barrier to seeking and obtaining useful information. However, this work has focused primarily on information seeking of youth themselves (Curry, 2005; Magee, Bigelow, Dehaan & Mustanski, 2012), or occasionally that of healthcare providers (Fikar & Keith, 2004), rather than lay caregivers such as parents. Understanding the information behaviour of parents/caregivers of GCCTY can help inform creation of targeted, effective and acceptable information resources and services for this population. Two related bodies of literature may help inform this investigation: 1) Studies of the health information behaviour of lay information mediaries, who seek information on behalf or because of others, often as part of caregiving practices (e.g., Abrahamson & Fisher, 2007; Abrahamson, Fisher, Turner, Durrance & Turner, 2008); and 2) Research focused on the information behaviour and practices of parents (e.g., Fisher & Landry, 2007; McKenzie, 2006; Papen, 2013). Based on these bodies of prior work, it is understood that contextual, cognitive and affective factors all influence information seeking and sharing by caregivers, and that information literacy, social location and information source trust play a role in assessment and use of health information.

## OBJECTIVE

The purpose of this investigation is to better understand the information behavior of parents/caregivers of GCCTY in order to inform development of accessible and useful information resources and services.

## METHODS

An anonymous online survey was conducted in English in August to November 2016. Parents and caregivers (age 18+) of GCCTY (≤ age 25) in the United States or Canada were recruited through postings to social media groups and e-mail invitations sent to organizations that support parents/caregivers of GCCTY. Preliminary analysis includes descriptive statistics of quantitative data and qualitative descriptive content analysis of free-text responses.

80th Annual Meeting of the Association for Information Science & Technology, Washington, DC | Oct. 27-Nov. 1, 2017

## RESULTS

### Population

One hundred and three parents/caregivers completed the survey to an extent sufficient to be included in the analysis. Their children ranged from 4 to 23 years old (mean 12.1; median 13). The majority (*n*=59) of their GCCTY identified as trans, with 12 gender creative, 12 non-binary and 20 otherwise identified. Sixty-four percent of respondents hailed from the United States (from 21 states), and 36% were Canadian (7 provinces). Parent/caregiver ages ranged from 29 to "70+" years of age (mean 44.9; median 46).

### Information Needs and Seeking

*We asked respondents to select which topics, from a list created by staff of a transgender health information service, had been a subject of their information seeking in the past year (Figure 1). The most common responses included general parenting and support for themselves and their children, along with information on healthcare providers for their children. Over half of all respondents sought information regarding school and social transition and nearly half on hormone therapy (for adolescent children and young adults) and child gender identity development. Substantial minorities also sought information about puberty blockers (for preadolescent children) and surgery (for young adults), and approximately 1 in 10 parents sought faith-related information.*

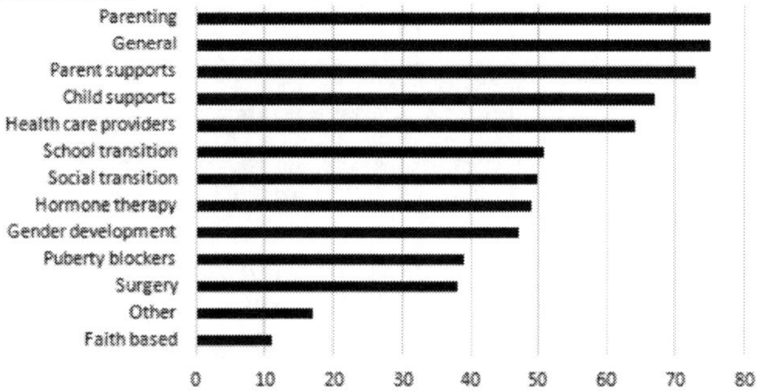


***Figure 1.*** *Topics of information seeking in the past year*

When selecting from a list of information source types, respondents demonstrated clear preferences (Figure 2). Nearly all respondents had used Google or other search engines to seek information. Slightly over half had consulted health professionals, online groups, books and people they knew for information. Substantially fewer parents had consulted videos, and hardly any consulted social Q&A websites or librarians.

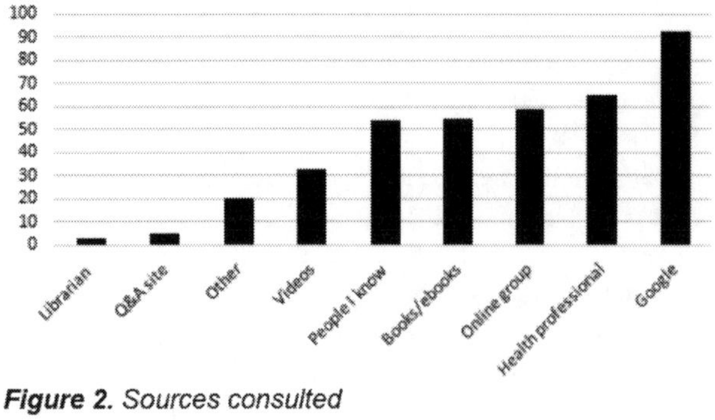


***Figure 2.*** *Sources consulted*

### Information Assessment and Values

In order to understand how parents/caregivers of GCCTY valued and assessed information, we asked them to supply their three most useful information resources. Table 1 summarizes these resources by format. We then asked why those resources were useful and conducted a thematic analysis of the responses. Some resources were perceived to be useful because they directly satisfied the seeker's information need. However, satisfying affective needs such as a desire to be validated, affirmed, welcomed and for one's experience to be normalized, emerged as important aspects of information that contributed to a parent/caregiver's assessment of that information/source as useful. As one parent stated, "My questions were answered and I realized I wasn't alone."

| Resource Type | # of Responses |
|---|---|
| Trans websites/blogs | 48 |
| Face-to-face | 44 |
| Online groups | 39 |
| Books | 39 |
| Legal/advocacy organizations | 6 |
| Research/journal articles | 6 |
| Conferences | 5 |
| Other | 24 |

***Table 1.*** *Most useful resources, by category*

While satisfying cognitive needs for information and providing affective support were dominant themes related to information utility, certain other attributes were also associated with parent/caregiver assessment of an information resource as useful. For example, source credibility was important to many. Such credibility could be ascribed either due to formal expert authorship (e.g., a medical professional) or via authorship by someone with lived expertise (e.g., another parent of a GCCTY or a trans adult). Additionally, being easily shareable with others, containing links/references and being written in accessible language were all attributes that increased the utility of information resources for some parents/caregivers.

## DISCUSSION

Preliminary analysis suggests that information services aiming to support parents/caregivers of GCCTY should be mindful of the affective needs that are frequently coupled with cognitive information needs. Ideal resources may not only provide clear and accessible information that fills needs, but also be from a credible source and offer privacy and appropriate reassurances to those seeking normalization and affirmation. Some parents/caregivers may need faith-based information, a topic that should not be overlooked.

This study addresses a gap in the literature surrounding information behavior of, and appropriate information resources to support, parents/caregivers of GCCTY. Due to lack of documentation about the population as a whole, we are unable to state with confidence how representative or generalizable these results are. Given the nature of the online survey, one might assume pro-internet bias; however, this potential bias did not extend to use of online Q&A sites, perhaps due to the age of participants or the sensitive nature of the information they sought.

Data analysis is ongoing, and will include exploration of the influence of demographic factors on parent/caregiver information behaviour and comparison with existing studies of lay information mediaries and parent information behaviours. Findings are being shared with parents/caregivers of GCCTY, as well as with organizations and practitioners focused on the health and well-being of GCCTY. By understanding the information needs, seeking patterns and assessment criteria, we can begin to refine information resources and services to meet parent/caregiver cognitive and affective information needs, ultimately enabling them to better support their children.

## ACKNOWLEDGMENTS

The authors would like to thank the parents/caregivers who participated and the organizations that shared this survey with their members.

## REFERENCES

Abrahamson, J. A., & Fisher, K. E. (2007). "What's past is prologue": Towards a general model of lay information mediary behaviour. In *Proceedings of the sixth international conference on conceptions of library and information science* (Vol. 12 no 4). Borås, Sweden: Information Research. Retrieved from http://www.informationr.net/ir/12-4/colis/colis15.html

Abrahamson, J. A., Fisher, K. E., Turner, A. G., Durrance, J. C., & Turner, T. C. (2008). Lay information mediary behavior uncovered: Exploring how nonprofessionals seek health information for themselves and others online. *Journal of the Medical Library Association: JMLA*, *96*(4), 310–323. doi:10.3163/1536-5050.96.4.006

Curry, A. (2005). If I ask, will they answer? Evaluating public library reference service to gay and lesbian youth. *Reference & User Services Quarterly*, *45*(1), 65-75.

Edwards-Leeper, L., & Spack, N. P. (2012). Psychological evaluation and medical treatment of transgender youth in an interdisciplinary "Gender Management Service" (GeMS) in a major pediatric center. *Journal of Homosexuality*, *59*(3), 321-336. doi:10.1080/00918369.2012.653302

Ehrensaft, D. (2016). *The gender creative child: Pathways for nurturing and supporting children who live outside gender boxes*. New York, NY: The Experiment.

Fikar, C. R., & Keith, L. (2004). Information needs of gay, lesbian, bisexual, and transgendered health care professionals: Results of an internet survey. *Journal of the Medical Library Association (JMLA)*, *92*(1), 56-65.

Fisher, K. E., & Landry, C. F. (2007). Understanding the information behavior of stay-at-home mothers through affect. In D. Nahl & D. Bilal (Eds.), *Information and emotion: The emergent affective paradigm in information behavior research and theory* (pp. 211-234). Medford, NJ: Information Today, Inc.

Khatchadourian, K., Amed, S., & Metzger, D. L. (2014). Clinical management of youth with gender dysphoria in Vancouver. *The Journal of Pediatrics*, *164*(4), 906-911. doi:10.1016/j.jpeds.2013.10.068

Magee, J. C., Bigelow, L., Dehaan, S., & Mustanski, B. S. (2012). Sexual health information seeking online: A mixed-methods study among lesbian, gay, bisexual, and transgender young people. *Health Education & Behavior: The Official Publication of the Society for Public Health Education*, *39*(3), 276-289. doi:10.1177/1090198111401384

McKenzie, P. J. (2006). The seeking of baby-feeding information by Canadian women pregnant with twins. *Midwifery*, *22*(3), 218-227. doi:10.1016/j.midw.2005.03.006

Papen, U. (2013). Conceptualising information literacy as social practice: A study of pregnant women's information practices. *Information Research*, *18*(2). Retrieved from http://informationr.net/ir/18-2/paper580.html#.Ub0_YNicGSo

Parents and Caregivers. (n.d.). Retrieved July 4, 2016, from http://transhealth.phsa.ca/support/families/parents-and-caregivers

Ryan, C., Russell, S. T., Huebner, D., Diaz, R. & Sanchez, J. (2010). Family acceptance in adolescence and the health of LGBT young adults. *Journal of Child and Adolescent Psychiatric Nursing*, *23*(4), 205-213. doi:10.1111/j.1744-6171.2010.00246.x

Simons, L., Schrager, S. M., Clark, L. F., Belzer, M. & Olson, J. (2013). Parental support and mental health among transgender adolescents. *Journal of Adolescent Health*, *53*(6), 791–793. doi:10.1016/j.jadohealth.2013.07.019

Travers, R., Bauer, G. R., Pyne, J., Bradley, K., Gale, L. & Papadimitriou, M. (2012). *Impacts of strong parental support for trans youth*. Toronto, ON: TransPULSE. Retrieved from http://transpulseproject.ca/wp-content/uploads/2012/10/Impacts-of-Strong-Parental-Support-for-Trans-Youth-vFINAL.pdf

Veale, J., Saewyc, E., Frohard-Dourlent, H., Dobson, S. & Clark, B. (2015). *Being safe, being me: Results of the Canadian trans youth health survey*. University of British Columbia. Retrieved from http://www.saravyc.ubc.ca/2015/05/05/being-safe-being-me-results-of-the-canadian-trans-youth-health-survey/

Whittington, H. (2015). *Raising Ryland: Our story of parenting a transgender child with no strings attached*. New York, NY: Harper Collins.

# Factors Affecting Psychologists' Adoption of an Open Data Badge

**Lindsey M. Harper**
*University of Kentucky, USA. lindsey.harper@uky.edu*

**Youngseek Kim**
*University of Kentucky, USA. youngseek.kim@uky.edu*

## ABSTRACT

**The purpose of this research is to investigate the individual, normative and resource factors affecting psychologists' adoption of an open data badge. The theory of planned behavior is employed as the theoretical framework to explain how these factors impact behavioral intention to adopt an open data badge. A national survey (n=341) of psychologists found that perceived benefits, norms of data sharing and attitude towards an open data badge had a significant positive relationship with attitude toward the open data badge, whereas perceived risk had a significant negative relationship. Perceived effort had a negative relationship to behavioral intention to adopt the open data badge, but had no relationship to attitude formation surrounding the open data badge adoption. The availability of a data repository and pressure from an open science journal did not have a significant relationship to behavioral intentions to adopt an open data badge. The implications for psychologists from a practical and theoretical perspective, and future directions for improving psychologists' data sharing behaviors are discussed.**

## KEYWORDS

data sharing, open data badge, psychologist, theory of planned behavior, social psychology, individual motivation

## INTRODUCTION

In 2014, an open data badge was promoted within the discipline of psychology as part of an initiative to create more open and transparent research among scholars in the field. The American Psychological Association journal, *Psychological Science*, adopted a badge incentive program to acknowledge researchers' willingness to share open data and materials after a manuscript was set to be published. To earn these badges, researchers must share data and/or materials digitally in an open access repository. Those who comply receive a badge for sharing raw data, materials from the study or both. The corresponding badges go at the top of the corresponding author's published manuscript. In the *Psychological Science* journal six months preceding the introduction of badges, an average of 2.5% of articles contained open data (range: 1.5%-4.0%). After the badge system was introduced, open data sharing practices increased significantly to 22.8% (range: 12.8%-39.4%) after January 1, 2014 (Kidwell et al., 2016).

The objective of the present study is to investigate the individual, normative and resource factors influencing psychologists' adoption of an open data badge through using a theoretical model based on Fishbein and Azjen's (1975) TPB (theory of planned behavior). By examining these factors under this theoretical framework, researchers can gain a better understanding of the areas that predict data sharing behaviors among psychologists.

## LITERATURE REVIEW

There are several factors that influence researchers' data sharing behaviors. There are individual factors, which include perceived benefits, risks and effort (Tenopir et al., 2011). There are also resource factors, which include the availability of an open data repository and journal requirements (Witt, 2008). Additionally, norms of data sharing can influence social scientists' decisions to engage in data sharing behaviors (Freese, 2007).

Data sharing behaviors among psychologists have remained relatively stable over time, but are still low considering the APA's ethical code to share data when requested. Wolins (1962) wrote to 37 authors of major APA journals inquiring about their data from a published manuscript, and nine authors provided data, leaving a data sharing rate of 24.3%. Similarly, Craig and Reese (1973) wrote to 53 authors of APA journal articles and received 20 responses, leaving a data sharing rate of 37.7%. Additionally, Wichets, Borsboom, Kats and Molenaar (2006) wrote to 141 authors of APA journal articles and received 38 responses, leaving a data sharing rate of 27.0%.

## THEORETICAL FRAMEWORK

This research utilizes the TPB to understand psychologists' behavioral intentions to adopt an open data badge. The TPB is a widely known social psychological theory and was developed as a means to explain various aspects of human behavior across different situations (Fishbein & Ajzen, 1975). This theory comprises attitudinal beliefs, subjective norms and perceived behavioral control factors. These factors influence behavioral intention, and that intention determines whether an actual behavior will be performed. In this particular study, the TPB can explain psychologists' intentions to adopt an open data badge.

---

80th Annual Meeting of the Association for Information Science & Technology, Washington, DC | Oct. 27-Nov. 1, 2017

## RESEARCH MODEL AND HYPOTHESES DEVELOPMENT

The following research model provides an overall map of psychologists' adoption of an open data badge. The model is designed to facilitate an understanding of individual, normative and resource factors influencing the decision to adopt the open data badge. The TPB provides insight into how the attitudinal beliefs (e.g., perceived benefit, risk and effort) influence a psychologist's attitude toward an open data badge. Perceived benefit, risk and effort refer to the degree to which a psychologist believes that sharing data could provide academic rewards, negative outcomes and difficulties in terms of time and energy. The TPB also provides insight into how subjective norms and perceived behavioral control (i.e., resource) factors impact a psychologist's decision to adopt an open data badge. Figure 1 shows the research model.

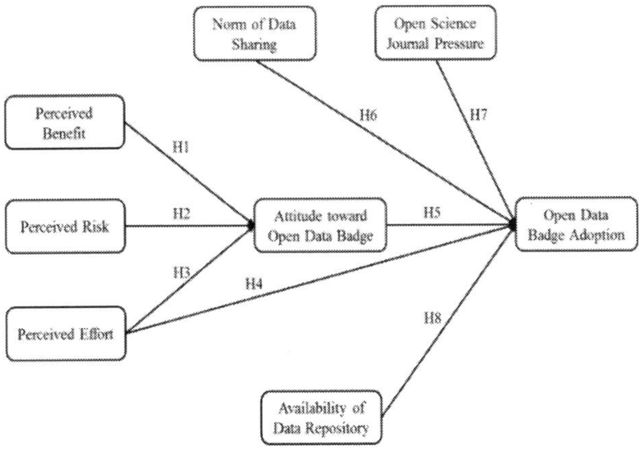


*Figure 1. Research model for psychologists' adoption of open data badge*

## RESEARCH METHOD

This study empirically evaluated the psychologists' open data badge adoption model and related hypotheses with survey data collected. The target population of this study mainly includes psychologists in U.S. research institutions. This research utilized the Community of Scientists (CoS) Scholar Database for its sampling frame. The survey was initially distributed to 2,919 potential participants through Qualtrics in November 2016, and it was closed for data collection on February 2017. A total of 341 responses from only psychologists were used for the final data analysis.

## DATA ANALYSIS AND RESULTS

This study used a structural equation modeling (SEM) approach to evaluate the hypothesized relationships in the psychologists' open data badge adoption model. A measurement model was evaluated to examine the reliability and validity of measurement items for each research construct, and then a structural model was assessed to investigate the hypothesized relationships among the research constructs by using partial least square method. Figure 2 presents the results of the structural model evaluation.

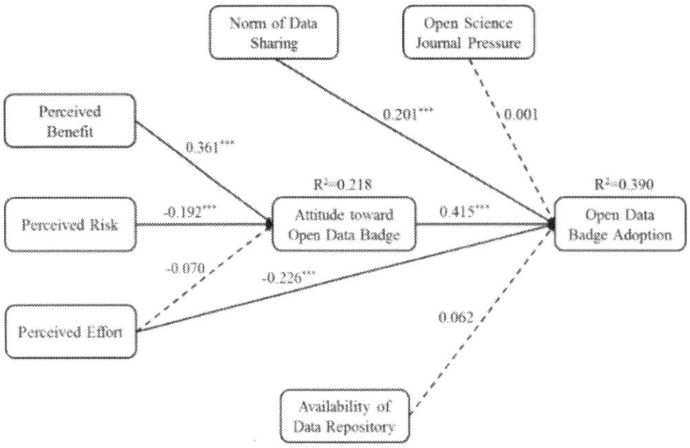


*Figure 2. Hypothesis testing results based on social scientists' data sharing behavior model*

## DISCUSSION AND CONCLUSION

As results, in regard to attitude formation toward an open data badge, perceived benefit and risk had significant positive and negative impacts respectively. Then, psychologists' attitudes toward an open data badge had a significant positive impact toward their behavioral intention to adopt an open data badge. Perceived effort did have a significant negative direct impact toward behavioral intention to adopt an open data badge. By emphasizing the perceived benefits and reducing the perceived risks, scholars can expect to see more favorable attitudes toward open data badge adoption. Also, psychologists' intentions to adopt an open data badge can be encouraged by reducing the effort expectancy involved in data sharing.

The results of this study also indicate that norms of data sharing positively influence psychologists' behavioral intentions to adopt the open data badge. Through fostering more open communication within the research community about scientific data sharing, psychologists can begin working more collectively to make strides toward more transparent research within the profession. They will eventually develop a strong norm of data sharing in their research community. By normalizing conversations about data sharing, we can expect to see higher involvement with data sharing practices. Due to the often sensitive nature of psychologists' research, ensuring additional confidentiality and privacy of participant information ought to be secured. Academic libraries that offer data services ought to consider the ways to reduce effort expectancy of researchers to de-identify, organize and manage data. In addition, libraries can provide data sharing education for psychology researchers to better understand the positive benefits of data sharing and to resolve any misunderstandings about the negative outcomes of data sharing.

## REFERENCES


Craig, J. R., & Reese, S. C. (1973). Psychology in action – retention of raw data – problem revisited. *American Psychologist, 28*(8), 723.

Fishbein, M., & Ajzen, I. (1975). *Belief, attitude, intention, and behavior*. Reading, MA: Addison-Wesley.

Freese, J. (2007). Replication standards for quantitative social science why not sociology? *Sociological Methods & Research, 36*(2), 153-172.

Kidwell, M. C., Lazarević, L. B., Baranski, E., Hardicke, T. E., Piechowski, S., Falkenberg, L. S., Kennett, C., Slowik, A., Sonnleitner, C., Hess-Holden, C., Errington, T. M., Fiedler, S. & Nosek, B. A. (2016). Badges to acknowledge open practices: A simple, low-cost, effective method for increasing transparency. *PLoS Biol, 14*(5), e1002456.

Tenopir, C., Allard, S., Douglass, D., Aydinoglue, A. U., Wu, L., Read, E. & Frame, M. (2011). Data sharing by scientists: Practices and perceptions. *PLoS ONE, 6*(6).

Wicherts, J. M., Borsboom, D., Kats, J., & Molenaar, D. (2006). The poor availability of psychological research data for reanalysis. *American Psychologist, 61*(7), 726-728.

Witt, M. (2008). Institutional repositories and research data curation in a distributed environment. *Library Trends, 57*(2), 191-201.

Wolins, L. (1962). Responsibility for raw data. *American Psychologist, 17*(9), 657-658.

# Does Quality Matter? Health Information Behaviors of LGBTQ Youth in Prince George, Canada

**Blake Hawkins**
*University of British Columbia, Canada. Blake.hawkins@alumni.ubc.ca*

## ABSTRACT

**A large proportion of lesbian, gay, bisexual, trans and queer (LGBTQ) health information behavior scholarship emphasizes sexual health topics. This project, however, concerned LGBTQ youth information behaviors on everyday health topics. We asked youth to map where they prefer to go for health information and when in those places, how they find health information. The most commonly discussed topic by participants was either how to find or what is quality information. Interestingly, participants had varying opinions on what is associated with both how to find or what is quality information. This paper describes the opinions of the youth on the significance and characteristics of quality information.**

## KEYWORDS

health information, sexuality, information behaviors

## INTRODUCTION

Little is known of the health information behaviors of LGBTQ youth and where they prefer to go for this type of information (Mehar & Braquet, 2006). This is problematic as LGBTQ youth have unique health needs due to their sexuality and they face constraints and are challenged when seeking information in different spaces (DeHaan et al., 2013; Veinot et al, 2013). Current scholarship on LGBTQ youth health information seeking is targeted primarily at gay, bisexual and men who have sex with men (GBMSM) and focuses on sexually transmitted illness or HIV health literacy. A disproportionate emphasis on HIV/AIDS information behaviors among GBMSM resulted from the worldwide epidemic that affected these men during the 1980s to the early 2000s. Previous research examined information about GBMSM and where men with or trying to prevent HIV/AIDS could access the proper information (Siegel & Raveis, 1997).

Youth health information behavior literature does not accurately relate to most LGBTQ youth needs. There has been a recent proliferation of so-called "hook-up apps" and cyberspaces for LGBTQ people. These applications provide the opportunity for types of interactions that were previously far less accessible. In 2016, for example, an 18-year-old GBTQ man can easily use a popular hook-up app to find a sexual partner (Hawkins & Watson, 2017). There is also the opportunity to use cyberspaces to build social networks and have unmoderated discussions without health professionals about different health topics (e.g., dieting, relationships and mental or sexual health). The potential of taking unsubstantiated and inaccurate information is a cause for concern as this might result in unhealthy outcomes (Hawkins & Watson, 2017).

The purpose of this paper is to briefly describe LGBTQ youth opinions on how to find information and to assess its quality. Based on responses from participants, there are a multitude of contributing factors.

## LGBTQ YOUTH AND INFORMATION BEHAVIORS

There has recently been a growing body of research concerning LGBTQ youth information behaviours either online or offline. This scholarship has described the characteristics of the information and online behaviors of LGBTQ youth social networks, how sexual identity influences information behaviors (including health information). However, there has also been criticism in some scholarship regarding the emphasis on urban queer youth and their information behaviors.

In danah boyd's work on online networks, *It's Complicated*, she briefly discusses that LGBTQ youth need to use secondary identities online when seeking information or interacting with others in virtual communities. boyd proposed that these behaviors are caused by the stigma faced by many LGBTQ youth in their everyday lives due to their sexual orientation. She also stated that LGBTQ youth do not always have the privilege of heterosexual youth to use their online presence as a continuation of their everyday life. boyd's representation of LGBTQ youth, however, can be rather one-dimensional and requires further investigation regarding their online interactions when seeking information.

Mehra & Braquet (2006) research has highlighted the role of libraries in the coming-out process of LGBTQ youth. They describe libraries as having the potential for being safe spaces with necessary information during the coming-out experience. At the time of the article, youth found it challenging to find information and spaces that would have helpful LGBTQ information. This need for information driven by youth needs is also highlighted in Agosto (2011). Agosto advocates for a reimagining of youth and their information behaviors as there is a connected individual context driving the process

An additional factor contributing to LGBTQ youth health information behavior is social cost. Veinot et al. (2013) study

80th Annual Meeting of the Association for Information Science & Technology, Washington, DC | Oct. 27-Nov. 1, 2017

on African American young men who have sex with men describes the social costs when visiting LGBTQ HIV information centres. This study demonstrates that there is an anticipated social cost contributing to how and where LGBTQ youth visit for information.

This study and other LGBTQ studies on health information behaviors demonstrate a geographical bias for urban study locations. Gray (2009) has criticized that there is too much of an emphasis on urban queer research across disciplines. Furthermore, Gray argues that there is a misconception of rural and non-metropolitan queer populations that needs to be better understood. This study is one example of de-emphasizing urban populations as it is based in a smaller Canadian city, Prince George, with 65,000 people.

## STUDY DESIGN

This study took place in Prince George, British Columbia at the University of Northern British Columbia. The student-led Northern Pride Centre acted as a community partner on the project. The Northern Pride Centre provided a safe space to host the research activities and an opportunity to recruit participants who use the space. The overall study was focused on the everyday health information seeking behaviours of LGBTQ youth and this paper will report on findings related to the notion of social cost.

Data was collected through participatory maps and focus groups held in January 2016 with groups of two and three LGBTQ youth (n=11). The mapping method provided the opportunity for the youth to critically consider how they seek health information and the characteristics of the places they visited (see Freund et al., 2016 for further detail). Following the participatory mapping activity, focus groups were held in which the youth discussed their health information seeking behaviours in further detail.

Transcripts of the five participatory mapping activities and focus groups were analyzed through an inductive coding process that identified major themes related to the two guiding research questions for the project. A codebook was prepared and the lead researcher carried out several iterations of coding. The six themes were 1) places that left a negative impression for the participants; 2) convenience; 3) social costs; 4) comfort; 5) queer friendly spaces; 6) quality of information. These were interpreted through several lenses: theories of everyday health information seeking and critical emotional, sexual and cyberspace geographies.

## RESULTS

### *Information for Us by Us*

Participants had varying opinions about content and quality of information, based on factors such as relevancy and the source of the information. For instance, some youth were uncritical when a local lesbian health nurse gave them information as a fellow queer/lesbian/bisexual woman and a health professional. However, other participants were skeptical of most sources of information and wanted secondary information to back up any claims that were made by a healthcare professional.

The youth were not willing to use heterosexual sexual health materials and preferred health information with an LGBTQ perspective Only in certain situations would they consider it acceptable for information not to be targeted at LGBTQ populations. Having access to LGBTQ health knowledge was important for both practical and contextual reasons, as their lived experiences differed from heterosexual youth.

### *Enacting Online Health Information*

Participants expressed that when they went online they were also concerned about the quality of the content. Only two or three participants of the 11 did not express being critical about the content from online sources. These few claimed that they did not cross-reference the information or question the quality or relevance. Essentially, they assumed the information was good based on the source, such as WebMD; however, the majority of the youth were more cognizant and critical about online sources. When on different websites they want to double check the information before they implement it as part of their everyday health practices. Solely including information because it was found online was not good enough for the youth.

"I personally, depending on what the subject is, I like using the websites that I am normally on because I can normally tell if somebody's being like factual or not... And that's a forum. Also, I'll read websites that have medical advice that has been reviewed by doctors. Mhmm. I find that to be good, but of course if anything is ever bad that's the only uhh prelude to actually going to the doctors. Umm, and you? I'd probably get I give highest credit to something like uhh BC health guide or something like that. I might go to forums for something I can't find or something that I want to. Discuss? Corroborate. Yeah like a discussion. Yeah."

Participants wanted to know that they were making sound decisions when selecting medical information. They generally were not as interested in finding one source to make the decisions. Instead they wanted to view multiple sources and corroborate the best solutions.

### Discussion

The variability in how the participants decided on quality information demonstrates that there is still much to be explored about how youth, whether LGBTQ or not, choose information. Likely the fact that these participants were LGBTQ youth also influenced how engaged they were with different sources of information. Most LGBTQ youth have to teach themselves or go online to learn about health issues associated with their sexuality due to the non-existence at most North American high schools (Hawkins & Watson, 2016).

Youth cared about who was giving them their everyday health information. The participants wanted to have someone who was either LGBTQ or an ally to the community that could provide relevant information. This perspective makes sense as channels of information influence how one engages and uses information, along with the age and relevancy of information being shared (Johnson & Case, 2012). If a healthcare provider is not informed about the everyday challenges and stigma many LGBTQ face and has outdated perspectives/information, why would the youth trust them as sources of information?

The participants emphasized the importance of feeling safe while they were seeking information in different places. During the focus groups, participants described a multitude of situations where they anticipated stigmatization based on their information needs as LGBTQ youth. These narratives produced emotional connection for youth in different Prince George places. Stories shared involved experiences or awareness about homophobic hospital staff or feeling social costs to seek information on their own in different places with computer or wi-fi access.

## CONCLUSION

Responses from the project participants demonstrate that a variety of factors contribute to the everyday health information seeking behaviour of LGBTQ youth in Prince George. Previous to this study, the limited scholarship on LGBTQ health information seeking, nearly always concerned sexual health information seeking and emphasized young bisexual, gay and MSM populations. However, this project described the everyday health information seeking behaviours of non-urban LGBTQ youth and characteristics of places preferred for this information.

The study demonstrates that LGBTQ youth have to consider many factors on their own when finding health information. There is also more to be understood about their information behaviors than solely sexual health. As LGBTQ youth become a more visible population information studies can continue to understand how they find information relevant to them and assess its quality.

## REFERENCES


Agosto, Denise. (2011). Young adults' information behavior: What we know so far and where we need to go from here. Retrieved from http://www.yalsa.ala.org/jrlya/2011/11/young-adults%E2%80%99-information-behavior-what-we-know-so-far-and-where-we-need-to-go-from-here/ on June 1, 2017

DeHaan, Samantha, Laura E. Kuper, Joshua C. Magee, Lou Bigelow and Brian S. Mustanski. (2013). The interplay between online and offline explorations of identity, relationships, and sex: A mixed-methods study with LGBT youth. *Journal of Sex Research* 50 (5): 421–34. doi:10.1080/00224499.2012.661489.

Freund, Luanne., Hawkins, Blake., & Saewyc, Elizabeth. (2016). Reflections on the use of participatory mapping to study everyday health information seeking by LGBTQ youth. *Proceedings from the 2016 American Society for Information Science and Technology Meeting*

Gray, Mary. (2009). Out in the country: Youth, media, and queer visibility in rural America. New York: New York University Press

Gray, Nicola J., Jonathan D. Klein, Peter R. Noyce, Tracy S. Sesselberg and Judith A. Cantrill. (2005). Health information-seeking behaviour in adolescence: The place of the internet. *Social Science & Medicine (1982)* 60 (7): 1467-78. doi:10.1016/j.socscimed.2004.08.010.

Greyson, Devon L., and Joy L. Johnson. (2016). The role of information in health behavior: A scoping study and discussion of major public health models. *Journal of the Association for Information Science and Technology* 67 (12): 2831-41. doi:10.1002/asi.23392.

Hawkins, Blake, and Ryan J. Watson. (2017). LGBT cyberspaces: A need for a holistic investigation. *Children's Geographies* 15 (1): 122-28. doi:10.1080/14733285.2016.1216877.

Johnson, J. David, and Donald O. Case. (2012). *Health information seeking*. First printing edition. New York: Peter Lang Inc., International Academic Publishers.

Mehra, Bharat., & Braquet, Donna. (2006). A "queer" manifesto of interventions for libraries to "come out" of the closet! A study of "queer" youth experiences during the coming out process. *Library and Information Science Research*.16(1)

Siegel, Karolynn., & Raveis, Victoria. (1997). Perceptions of access to HIV-related information, care, and services among infected minority men. *Qualitative Health Research*, 7, 9-30.

Veinot, Tiffany Christine, Chrysta Cathleen Meadowbrooke, Jimena Loveluck, Andrew Hickok, and Jose Artruro Bauermeister. (2013). How 'community' matters for how people interact with information: Mixed methods study of young men who have sex with other men." *Journal of Medical Internet Research* 15 (2): e33. doi:10.2196/jmir.2370.

# Seeking Ways to Our Transgender Bodies, by Ourselves: Rationalizing Transgender-Specific Health Information Behaviors

**Blake Hawkins**
*University of British Columbia, Canada.*
*Blake.hawkins@alumni.ubc.ca*

**Jack Giesking**
*Trinity College, USA. jack.gieseking@trincoll.edu*

## ABSTRACT

**Transgender people have typically been pooled in studies on lesbian, gay, bisexual, transgender and queer (LGBTQ) health information behavior. We, however, argue that transgender people have unique health needs and context that differ from LGBQ people. To demonstrate our argument, we are using the transitioning process from male-to-female or female-to-male as a case study. We are using data currently being analyzed from Tumblr to demonstrate how their process of seeking health information differs from LGBQ and highlights why information science needs to better understand this population and their information needs.**

## KEYWORDS

health information behavior, transgender health, transitioning, social media, sexuality & information behaviors

## INTRODUCTION

Scholars in information studies are beginning to conceptualize the ways in which gender and sexuality impact health information-seeking behaviors. These studies address a wide range of issues, including the affordance of safe spaces to interact with health professionals, rates of human immunodeficiency virus (HIV) and sexually transmitted infection (STI), cancer prevention and information sharing, and mental health discrepancies (Scheim et al., 2015). It is clear that gender and sexuality can influence where one will seek or avoid health information (Hawkins, 2017). Do these advancements in health information behavior scholarship on sex and gender properly represent the challenges faced by the transgender population and gender non-conforming (GNC) people? In most of this scholarship, transgender and GNC populations are integrated with lesbian, gay, bisexual and queer people, typically in a homogenous manner. The scholarship from public health (Bauer et al., 2012; Scheim et al., 2015) has demonstrated with population-based data that transgender and GNC people have unique context for health needs. One of the most prevalent topics is identifying trained healthcare professionals who understand health issues for transgender people during the transitioning period. As the process for transitioning is not a straightforward or monolithic process, there is a need for scholarship to recognize their information needs, health information seeking behaviors, resources and health information best practices.

In this paper, we argue that health information literature needs to improve representation of the transgender and GNC population's information behaviors. We summarize an example of transgender online health information behaviors by transgender youth utilizing the photo blogging and social network site Tumblr. This study highlights some of the information behaviors of transgender youth exploring and needing health information on transitioning from male-to-female (MTF) or female-to-male (FTM). This paper is based on recent empirical health research that called for the development of transgender-specific health interventions designed to meet the unique needs of this marginalized group and questions how that will materialize. Transgender-specific and GNC social determinants of health include racism, transphobia, cultural competence and training support for healthcare professionals, and a lack of safe spaces in healthcare settings (e.g., waiting rooms with other patients) (Hawkins and Watson 2017; Veale et al., 2015). We believe that mirroring this call for lesbian, gay, bisexual, transgender, queer/questioning (LGBTQ) and gender-oriented health information behavior, researchers will discover an opportunity to develop new research trends within this health information behavior sub-discipline.

## HEALTH INFORMATION-SEEKING BEHAVIORS

Health information-seeking behaviors traditionally lack a homogenous definition as they are used distinctly in multiple disciplines without interdisciplinary concern and hence bear assumed simplicity (Lambert and Loiselle, 2007). Health information seeking is in fact a complex process influenced by many factors, such as motivation and channels of information, and should not be reduced to the simple act of "looking" for information (Lambert and Loiselle, 2007; Johnson and Case, 2012). Much of the literature demonstrates that health information seeking is primarily an active process whereby people search for information based on their medical condition(s) (Case 2012; Greyson and Johnson 2016; Harris and Wathen 2011; Lambert and Loiselle 2007). However, other scholars recognize that health information seeking can be enacted in different forms based on their specific needs, such as exercise, parenting and other less important forms of

80th Annual Meeting of the Association for Information Science & Technology, Washington, DC | Oct. 27-Nov. 1, 2017

information (Johnson and Case 2012). Monitoring health literature for issues like new parenting or transitioning are on-going and do not stop after one particular issue is resolved (McKenzie, 2006)

Multiple social determinants of health influence the information-seeking process, including the medical condition, level of education, place, internet access, age and sexuality (Harris and Wathen, 2011; Johnson and Case, 2012; Lambert and Loiselle, 2007; Greyson and Johnson, 2016; Veinot et al., 2013). Previous research has demonstrated that youth are critical when locating health information (Greyson, in press). In the case of LGBTQ youth, they are cognizant of their information source and where they can go for different types of information (Hawkins, 2017). LGBTQ youth may have online networks and social support (nurses, parents, friends or others) that they trust to provide information (Hawkins, Morris, Nguyen et al., 2017). This is in contrast to previous literature that describes youth as uncritical and passive in regard to their health information-seeking behaviors (Grey, 2005).

Another contributing factor on health information-seeking is an individual's ability to construct his or her own information channels, which is a complex process. Channels are where one goes to find information when an one rarely trusts a single person or information source. For instance, having people share their opinions or experiences on a transgender or GNC health topic may result in a better understanding of the issue (Johnson & Case, 2012). For example, transgender youth may only reach out to friends and non-family adults for information, while middle-age and elderly transgender adults are less likely to seek medical care in an emergency because of the pathologization of their gender in past years (DeHaan et al., 2013; Veinot et al., 2013). If transgender youth seek health information from family, they might ask broader questions since they might not be "out" as transgender to family members (Veale et al., 2015).

Although there is a growing body of literature concerning LGBTQ population's health information seeking, there are severe limitations to the construction and framing of this work (Hawkins, 2017). The majority of the current studies are only relatable to gay, bisexual and men who have sex with men sexual health information-seeking behaviors. Despite its importance, the majority of the literature on LGBTQ health information is related to a specific health topic within a sub-population that does not properly include transgender and GNC populations. For example, transgender populations in different geographical regions negotiate specific transphobic laws and local assumptions from healthcare providers and other medical professionals that share or regulate access to health information (Doan, 2007).

## THE CASE OF TRANSGENDER YOUTH ON TUMBLR

In the author's research on transgender youth use of Tumblr, Hawkins found patterns in medical knowledge exchange which indicate that informal and pseudo-anonymous online networks are a key source of health information. Tumblr is a photo-blogging site where users follow one another and like or re-blog another's images and comments on their own curated pages. Tumblr is particularly popular with transgender youth who find the site useful to not only develop their own identities, but exchange knowledge and develop community (Fink and Miller, 2014). Using a Python script, the authors examined over two years of posts that utilized the #ftm and #mtf hashtags on Tumblr. As of this writing, the Python script examined over 700,000 discussions. As Tumblr users are usually anonymous, the photos shared usually reveal them to be teen youths. Earlier social network analysis of this data suggests that young transgender populations primarily use the site as a channel to gather and share knowledge and experiences about their transition. In a subset of six months of #ftm data, a significant key trend in their posts is to note temporal elements such as "days," "years" or "months" until or since transitioning, whether that be self-identifying as transgender populations or GNC, taking hormone therapy or surgery to complete their gender transition. A visual analysis of photos shared also highlights pre- and post-surgery or hormone experiences, such as images after surgery or congratulatory photos that mark one, two, three or six months or a year on testosterone.

Health information behaviors shape transgender experience on Tumblr as health-sharing information is a focus of the group's experience. The hashtags #testosterone ranks 8th and #topsurgery ranks 16th in the number of hashtags used by FTM youth on Tumblr to mark their #ftm posts. Young transgender populations are eager to offer thoughts and feedback on their doctors, and the doctors themselves become hashtags (ex. #drgarramone, #drcrane, etc.) so that young people can critique the work of and find doctors for their own surgeries. These knowledge exchanges become a networked history of visual and textual reflections leading up to and following these gender transition surgeries. Similarly, communications studies scholar Laura Horak (2014) found that young populations use YouTube in a similar fashion in sharing and seeking health information. The LGBTQ health information behaviors discipline is only beginning to map the various and vast wealth of medical information within or across platforms. The project of querying online spaces such as social media platforms, operating systems and data itself is on-going (Keeling, 2014).

## TRANSGENDER HEALTH: WHAT CAN WE LEARN FROM WHERE WE ARE

Health information behavior literature on LGBTQ people, within the last 10-15 years, has substantial growth in scholarship and topic areas for discussion. However, many of the studies that include transgender and GNC populations are combined with other sexual minority populations. These studies do not reflect the important experiences of trans-specific information needs and are primarily based in North America. This body of scholarly research could benefit from transgender population projects focused on youth or adults pre- and post-transition, differences between races and FTM and MTF transitions (Scheim et al., 2016). As we reflect on the state of transgender and GNC populations seeking and sharing health information on Tumblr or other social media platforms, we see that these channels have a helpful role in their everyday life. These social networks provide a safe space to share and learn from others during the pre- and post-operative periods of FTM and MTF transition. At the same time, transgender health information is found at random and by word-of-mouth (or hashtag), rather than from a trusted source.

The current published literature from information studies could build on public health, media studies and other health disciplines to create a variety of opportunities for future scholarship and projects on transgender information behaviors on health or other topics. Within this community, there are high rates of enacted and anticipated stigma that significantly deter their ability to feel safe. The issue of feeling safe provides an opportunity to explore the social costs (i.e., the potential risk either enacted or anticipated) of finding information (Hawkins, 2017; Veinot et al., 2013). Additional research into the social determinants of health can be explored in the discipline like finding information (person-to-person, social networks and/or social workers) about housing, food insecurity or accessing trans-friendly health organizations (Bauer et al., 2012). An additional topic includes the cultural competencies of libraries and staff in the development of safe spaces for transgender people.

Much remains to be done to shape and support the lives of transgender individuals and their health information behaviors. Transgender populations face a variety of social determinants that can be connected to their information seeking behaviors and/or needs due to their identity. The Tumblr project is an example that demonstrates this need for focused scholarship. Producing research specific to the needs of transgender populations distinct from but related to lesbian, gay, and bisexual populations affords insights beyond social media is an important next step.

## REFERENCES


Bauer, G., Travers, R., Scanlon, K., & Coleman. T. (2012). High heterogeneity of hiv-related sexual risk among transgender people in Ontario, Canada: A province-wide respondent-driven sampling survey. *BMC Public Health 12* (April): 292.

Case, D. (2012). Looking for information: A survey of research on information seeking, needs and behavior. (3rd edition) Bingley, UK: Emerald Group.

DeHaan, S., Kuper, L., Magee, J., Bigelow, L & Mustanski, B. (2013). The interplay between online and offline explorations of identity, relationships, and sex: A mixed-methods study with LGBT youth. *Journal of Sex Research 50* (5): 421-34.

Fink, M., & Miller, Q. (2014). Trans media moments Tumblr, 2011-2013. *Television & New Media.*

Greyson, D., & Johnson, J. (2016). The role of information in health behavior: A scoping study and discussion of major public health models. *JASIST.*

Greyson, D. (in press). Health information practices of young parents. *Journal of Documentation.*

Harris, R, & Wathen, N. (2011). If my mother was alive I'd probably have called her. *Reference & User Services Quarterly 47* (1): 67-79.

Hawkins, B. (2017). Affect, social cost and place in everyday health information seeking of LGBTQ youth in Prince George, BC. *Proceedings of CAIS*

Hawkins, B., & Watson, R. (2017). LGBT cyberspaces: A need for a holistic investigation. *Children's Geographies 15* (1): 122-28.

Horak, L. (2014). Trans on YouTube intimacy, visibility, temporality. *TSQ: Transgender Studies Quarterly 1* (4): 572-85.

Johnson, D., & Case. D. (2012). Health information seeking. First printing edition. New York: Peter Lang.

Keeling, K. (2014). Queer OS. *Cinema Journal 53* (2).

Lambert, S., & Loiselle, C. (2007). Health information seeking behavior. *Qualitative Health Research.*

McKenzie, P. (2006). The seeking of baby-feeding information by Canadian women pregnant with twins. *Midwifery*, Vol. 22 No. 3, pp. 218-227.

Scheim, A., Bauer, G & Travers, R. (2015). HIV-related Sexual risk among transgender men who are gay, bisexual, or have sex with men." *Journal of Acquired Immune Deficiency Syndromes*,

Veale, J., H. Frohard-Dourlent, S. Dobson, B. Clark, and Canadian Trans Youth Health Survey Research Group. (2015). Being safe, being me: Results of the Canadian trans youth health survey. Vancouver, BC, Canada: Stigma and Resilience Among Vulnerable Youth Centre

Veinot, T., Chrysta, C., Meadowbrooke, C Loveluck, J., Hickok, A & Bauermeister, J. (2013). How "community" matters for how people interact with information: Mixed methods study of young men who have sex with other men. *JMIR*

# Case Studies on Open Innovation in Libraries

**Maria Henkel**
*Heinrich Heine University Düsseldorf, Germany.*
*Maria.Henkel@hhu.de*

**Aylin Ilhan**
*Heinrich Heine University Düsseldorf, Germany.*
*Aylin.Ilhan@hhu.de*

**Agnes Mainka**
*Heinrich Heine University Düsseldorf, Germany.*
*Agnes.Mainka@hhu.de*

**Wolfgang G. Stock**
*Heinrich Heine University Düsseldorf, Germany.*
*Stock@phil.hhu.de*

## ABSTRACT

**Open innovation (sometimes also called design thinking, user participation or co-creation) means the participation of an institution's stakeholders (customers, suppliers, competitors, etc.) in its innovation processes. Concerning libraries, open innovation integrates the views of users (as customers), software houses or design companies (as suppliers) as well as other libraries (as competitors) into the development strategy of a library. Innovation processes include information inflows (application of external knowledge in the innovating library) and information outflows (dissemination of internal knowledge for reuse in other institutions). Innovations happen on a large scale (for instance, planning new library buildings) as well as on a small scale (e.g., modifying an existing library service). The poster will present the open innovation framework, methods used, results of a questionnaire and will introduce paradigmatic case studies of open innovation in libraries. In addition, we will use the poster to invite conference attendees to share their own experiences and opinions.**

## KEYWORDS

open innovation, design thinking, library, case study

## INTRODUCTION

Open innovation considers both importing external ideas into an institution's knowledge and innovation processes as well as exporting its experiences to others. Chesbrough was the first to introduce open innovation into research. One of his most important findings is "equal importance given to external knowledge, in comparison to internal knowledge" (Chesbrough, 2006, p. 11). Open innovation means the participation of an institution's multiple stakeholders (customers, suppliers, competitors, etc.) in its innovation planning as well as the dissemination of internal ideas to others. The majority of open innovation approaches can be identified in large high-tech and – later – in other companies in different industries; however, there are some projects in government and public administration as well (Feller, Finnegan & Nilsson, 2011). The use of open innovation can deploy pathways outside an institution's current businesses and evoke new products or even new markets (Chesbrough, 2006).

There are two important aspects in open innovation projects, namely the stakeholder (especially user) involvement and the creation of a supporting eco-system. "The users are in the spotlight: an invention becomes an innovation only if users become a part of the value creation process. … Creating a well-functioning eco-system that allows co-creation becomes essential for Open Innovation. In this eco-system stakeholders are collaborating along and across industry and sector-specific value chains to co-create solutions to socio-economic and business challenges" (European Commission, 2016, p. 16). As a basic principle, "open" is a quasi-synonym for "user-centric," whereby "users" are both actual users as well as potential users, including former, possibly dissatisfied users.

A perfect example for public sector innovation and a user-centric institution that benefits from open innovation is the library (Scupola & Zanfei, 2016). It already was an ever changing and evolving institution in the past, which now, more than ever, has "to keep pace with the needs of a modern information society" (Jantz, 2012, p. 3). Concerning libraries, open innovation integrates the views of users and non-users (as actual and potential customers), publishing houses, information services, software houses, design companies, etc. (as suppliers) as well as other libraries or further institutions (as competitors) into the development strategy of a library. Library knowledge and innovation processes include information inflows (application of external knowledge in the innovating library) and information outflows (dissemination of internal knowledge for reuse in other institutions). Innovation happens both on a large scale (for instance, planning new library buildings) as well as on a small scale (e.g., slightly modifying an existing library service). Of course, open innovation is applicable to all kinds of innovation, including library services (services of the physical as well of the digital library and those which are needed in the present or future knowledge society), new library organizational processes and new infrastructures.

Open innovation in libraries is also known as co-creation or the "participatory library." Sometimes, processes of open innovation are called "design-thinking" (Bech-Petersen, Mærkedahl, & Krogbæk, 2016). The governance is always distributed; library staff, users and other stakeholders work together as co-producers of innovative processes.

80th Annual Meeting of the Association for Information Science & Technology, Washington, DC | Oct. 27-Nov. 1, 2017

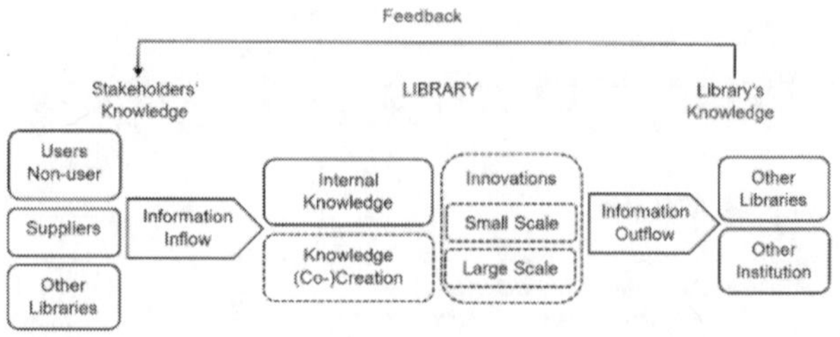


***Figure 1.** Theoretical model of open innovation in libraries*

Since the advent of open innovation in research dates back more than a decade and first (however, very rare) projects in libraries started shortly after this, it is about time to study the success (or failure) of such projects. Our model of open innovation in libraries is depicted in Figure 1. Based on this theoretical model, we have three research questions (RQs):

**RQ1** If a library applies open innovation, what are its sources, means and tools of information inflow?

**RQ2** What concrete innovations do result from the open innovation process?

**RQ3** If a library successfully applied open innovation, what are the addressees of information outflows in order to reuse the innovation?

## METHODS

Besides literature review and content analysis of libraries' websites, our method is strongly related to case study research (Eisenhardt, 1989). While analyzing literature and websites we were able to identify six libraries (Table 1), which reported on experienced open innovation projects.

| Case | Country | Library Type |
|---|---|---|
| Chicago Public Library | USA | Public |
| Dokk1, Aarhus | Denmark | Public |
| Helsinki Public Library | Finland | Public |
| National Library Board | Singapore | National & Public |
| Roskilde Univ. Library | Denmark | Academic |
| ZBW, Kiel | Germany | Special |

***Table 1.** Case studies of open innovation in libraries*

In order to gather empirical data on open innovation projects in libraries, we created a questionnaire with 14 questions and sent it to all our case study libraries. Published literature on our case completed our analyses.

## SUMMARY OF RESULTS (SHORT VERSION)

Currently, libraries are adapting the idea and allow information inflows from diverse stakeholders. We can confirm that an information inflow may result in small as well as in large-scale innovations in the investigated libraries. Small-scale innovations refer to additional services that have been introduced through co-creation activities. In contrast, large-scale innovations evolve a change in the library, like the definition of a library as public space for the community. In the investigated libraries, new products have been developed together with users, suppliers, other libraries and companies. The main challenge is to share these best practices with other libraries.

## FORMAT AND EXPERIENCE

Results of the survey and literature review will be presented in the form of a poster. Additionally, we would like to invite conference attendees to share their own experiences and opinions by adding sticky notes to the poster. This way, a dialogue will be possible among attendees visiting our poster at different times (markers and materials will be provided by us). These contributions will be summarized and presented later on in a blog post on the ASIS&T European Chapter website.

## REFERENCES


Bech-Petersen, S., Mærkedahl, L., & Krogbæk, M. (2016). Dokk1: Co-creation and design thinking in libraries. *Proceedings of the 14th participatory design conference: Short papers, interactive exhibitions, workshops - Volume 2*, 92-93 https://doi.org/10.1145/2948076.2948109

Chesbrough, H. (2006). Open innovation: A new paradigm for understanding industrial innovation. In H. W. Chesbrough, W. Vanhavebeke, & J. West (Eds), *Open innovation. Researching a new paradigm* (pp. 1-12). Oxford, UK: Oxford University Press.

Eisenhardt, K. M. (1989). Building theories from case study research. *Academy of Management Review, 14*(4), 532-550.

European Commission. (2016). *Open innovation, open science, open to the world. A vision for Europe*. Luxembourg, LUX.

Feller, J., Finnegan, P. & Nilsson, O. (2011). Open innovation and public administration: Transformational typologies and business model impacts. *European Journal of Information Systems, 20*, 358-374.

Jantz, R. C. (2012). Innovation in academic libraries: An analysis of university librarians' perspectives. *Library & Information Science Research, 34*(1), 3-12.

Scupola, A., & Zanfei, A. (2016). Governance and innovation in public sector services: The case of the digital library. *Government Information Quarterly, 33*(2), 237-249.

# Linking Scholarly Literature to Research Data and Software - Lessons Learned in Astronomy

**Edwin A. Henneken**
*Smithsonian Astrophysical Observatory, USA. ehenneken@cfa.harvard.edu*

## ABSTRACT

Publishing articles in scholarly journals is essential to furthering science. However, it is only one stage in the research cycle; one of the later stages, actually. After formulating a research goal, typically one or more proposals are written. When accepted, data is gathered, processed and compared to existing data and literature. Software plays an essential role in the data processing and comparison process. Often, before articles are published, papers and posters are presented at conferences. In short, there is a plethora of "products" associated with the entire research lifecycle. An essential ingredient in this cycle is the ability to find literature and associated products that were used to create it. Reproducibility of and the ability to add to existing results should be the norm, not the exception, for robust scientific research. Discoverability of data products and software needs an infrastructure and a culture. Astronomy has a long tradition of sharing data, but there is still a lot of work to do. Having this infrastructure will not only support discoverability, it will also enable measurement of impact and proper attribution. Both elements will help in getting funding for future research, which completes the cycle.

## KEYWORDS

research data, research software, discovery, research impact, data and software citation, digital libraries

## INTRODUCTION

Being able to read the literature and access to the data and/or software discussed or used in the paper with just one click is obviously of great convenience for the end-user, in addition to providing evidence in support of the scientific arguments in the paper and the reproducibility of its results. Integration and indexing of this kind of associated information in a digital library, used by the research community, greatly enhances the discovery process. This is exactly what the NASA/Smithsonian Astrophysics Data System (ADS; Henneken et al., 2012) has been doing for the astronomy community for many years. Besides benefits to the research community, there are also benefits of this integration to the data archives, software repositories and projects providing their data to ADS. First of all, by having a bibliography integrated in the ADS database, it becomes trivial to retrieve metrics associated with it and thus evaluate the scientific impact of its datasets as well as using bibliographic-based analytics to gain insights on how the data or software is used in current research. Also, the act of linking literature with data products by itself has been shown to have impact. Studies by Henneken & Accomazzi (2012) and Dorch et al. (2015) have shown a "data sharing advantage" for papers which have links to data products, resulting in higher citation counts. Similarly, data re-use increases upon the publication of papers studying them (Winkelman et al., 2006), leading to an increase in archival research (White et al., 2009). In other words, well-linked data is more heavily used, and well-linked publications are more heavily cited, a win-win scenario and the primary reason to have well-described, well-curated data products indexed in the ADS or any other digital library for that matter. The linking of software to scholarly literature is still in its infancy (Allen et al., 2015; Muench et al., 2017).

## CREATION STAGE

In order for data preservation to work, people need to be convinced to invest effort in depositing their data products and software in repositories like Dataverse, Zenodo, TheAstroData, the Astrophysics Source Code Library (ASCL) and Github. Many of these repositories assign persistent, unique identifiers (PDIDs) to support access. The PDID is often a DOI. Assigning a PDID helps discoverability and citability of the products (attribution). Astronomy has a long tradition of sharing data. For example, in 1972 the Centre de Donées Astronomiques de Strasbourg (CDS) was established to collect and distribute astronomical information. Publishers of major astronomy journals have shown willingness to innovate and participate in community initiatives (see e.g., the Policy Statement on Software of the American Astronomical Society, 2016). If a publisher requires data products used in publications to be available in a persistent manner, authors will find a way to meet them. A big challenge is attempting to unlock or even revive data that is not carefully indexed or stored. Attempts are made to unlock this so-called "dark data" (Heidorn, 2008; Akers, 2013; Gallaher et al., 2015).

## USE AND DISCOVERY STAGE

The research community uses the PDID to access the data products/software and carry out related research. This community also generates new publications using the PDID to reference the dataset or software. The ADS harvests and merges bibliographic data from multiple sources (arXiv, CrossRef, publishers, astronomy archives, ASCL, Zenodo). It also enriches metadata via text-mining of the full text sources (extract references, acknowledgments, keywords, plots and images). Furthermore, it generates and maintains citation and usage networks, and cross-correlates content.

---

80th Annual Meeting of the Association for Information Science & Technology, Washington, DC | Oct. 27-Nov. 1, 2017

The ADS collects and maintains external links to publishers and archives (SIMBAD, VizieR, NED, MAST, ESO, etc.) and incorporates bibliographies from institutes and archives. Important datasets are often described in data papers, but can also be available as electronic catalogs, e.g., from VizieR (the most complete library of published astronomical catalogues and data tables, with links to about 33,000 records in the ADS). Once in the ADS, they become easily discoverable, citable. Proposals contain early descriptions of current and ongoing science activities. They provide a direct link to existing or planned observations. In total, the ADS has about 337,000 links to online data.

## IMPACT MEASUREMENT STAGE

Formalizing data/software citation supports giving credit where credit is due, enhances discoverability of data products and facilitates the compilation of metrics for data products (usage or citation based). These metrics are critical for evaluating an instrument, project, mission or grant, because they are a measure for productivity and impact. It takes community effort for data (and software) citation to work properly. Only with well-defined standards will data citation become as transparent as it is for publications. The Force11 community has formulated a set of "Data Citation Principles" (Smith et al., 2016). These principles are supposed to encourage a good practice of data citation and, as a result, create a data and software citation culture. Measures for the impact of data products will only be meaningful when such a culture is in place. The metrics service of the ADS is an example of how impact measures are generated for the community. In addition to proper attribution of credit, being able to measure use of data and software can also be of vital importance to a project or mission: continued funding is often justified through use of data.

## REWARD AND REUSE STAGE

Funding and research groups review publication and dataset metrics. These metrics can influence the future funding of a researcher, project or instrument. In addition, having these metrics will help in providing scholarly credit and attribution to everybody who contributes to acquiring and creating the data (or software). Studies have found that publications linked to data products receive higher citation rates, which, besides helping with the visibility of the data, is an additional incentive for authors to make their data public in a persistent way and to link to it in their publications. Only when there is a seamless network of repositories, publishers and discovery services, with transparent access to the creators of data and software, can a culture grow where data products are just a different type of publication (see e.g., Force11 declaration of data citation principles).

## ACKNOWLEDGEMENTS

This work has been supported by the NASA Astrophysics Data System project, funded by NASA grant NNX16AC86A.

## REFERENCES

AAS Editorial Board (2016). Policy statement on software. http://journals.aas.org/policy/software.html

Akers, K. G. (2013), Looking out for the little guy: Small data curation. *Bulletin of the Association for Information Science and Technology 39*, 58-59. doi:10.1002/bult.2013.1720390317.

Allen, A., Berriman, G.B., DuPrie, K., Mink, J., Nemiroff, R., Robitaille, T., Shamir, L., Shortridge, K., Taylor, M., Teuben, P. and Wallin, J. (2015). Improving software citation and credit. eprint arXiv:1512.07919

Data citation synthesis group: Joint declaration of data citation principles. Martone M. (ed.) San Diego CA: FORCE11; 2014 [https://www.force11.org/group/joint-declaration-data-citation-principles-final]

Dorch, S. B. F., Drachen, T. M. & Ellegaard, O. (2015). The data sharing advantage in astrophysics. arXiv e-prints. arXiv:1511.02512

Gallaher, David, G. Garrett Campbell, Walter Meier, John Moses and Dennis Wingo (2015). The process of bringing dark data to light: The rescue of the early nimbus satellite data. *GeoResJ 6*, 124-34. doi:10.1016/j.grj.2015.02.013.

Goodman, A., Pepe, A., Blocker, A.W., Borgman, C.L., Cranmer, K., Crosas, M., Di Stefano, R., Gil, Y., Groth, P., Hedstrom, M., Hogg, D.W., Kashyap, V., Mahabal, A., Siemiginowska, A., and Slavkovic, A. (2014). Ten simple rules for the care and feeding of scientific data. *PLoS Computational Biology 10*(4), e1003542. doi:10.1371/journal.pcbi.1003542

Heidorn, P. Bryan (2008). Shedding light on the dark data in the long tail of science. *Library Trends 57*(2), 280-299. doi:10.1353/lib.0.0036

Henneken, E. A., & Accomazzi, A. (2012). Linking to data - Effect on citation rates in astronomy. ASP Conference Series, 461, 763-766. arXiv:1111.3618

Henneken, E.A., Kurtz, M.J. & Accomazzi, A. (2012): The ADS in the information age - Impact on discovery. organizations, people and strategies in astronomy Vol. 1, Edited by Andre Heck, Venngeist, Duttlenheim, 253-263

Kohler, S. (2015). AAS publishing news: Astronomical software citation workshop. AAS Nova Highlights, 24 Jul 2015 (http://aasnova.org/2015/07/24/aas-publishing-news-astronomical-software-citation-workshop/)

Mooney, H. & Newton M. (2012). The anatomy of a data citation: Discovery, reuse and credit. *Journal of Librarianship and Scholarly Communication 1*(1), eP1035. doi:10.7710/2162-3309.1035

Muench, A., Accomazzi, A., & Holm Nielsen, L. (2017). Asclepias: Enabling software citation & discovery workflows. Zenodo. doi:10.5281/zenodo.803474

Smith, A.M., Katz D.S., Niemeyer K.E., FORCE11 Software Citation Working Group (2016): Software Citation Principles. *PeerJ Computer Science* 2:e86. doi:10.7717/peerj-cs.86

White, R.L., Accomazzi, A., Berriman, G.B., Fabbiano, G., Madore, B.F., Mazzarella, J.M., Rots, A., Smale, A.P., Storrie-Lombardi, L., and Winkelman, S. (2009). The high impact of astronomical data archives. In *astro2010: astronomy and astrophysics decadal survey*, no. 64. (http://www8.nationalacademies.org/astro2010/DetailFileDisplay.aspx?id=423)

Winkelman, S., Rots, A., Duffy, A., Blecksmith, S., & Jerius, D. (2006). Where do the data go? An analysis of chandra data dissemination. ASP Conference Series, 351, 93-96.

# “Not What I Thought!” Information Seeking Behaviors of International Students During the Application for Graduate Study in the USA

**Li-Min Huang**
*School of Information Sciences, University of Tennessee, USA. lhuang23@vols.utk.edu*

**Dania Bilal**
*School of Information Sciences, University of Tennessee, USA. dania@utk.edu*

## ABSTRACT

**A recent study revealed that international students' reading comprehension scores on the Test of English as a Foreign Language (TOEFL) equates to 12th-grade reading comprehension level (Taylor, 2017). In evaluating the admission materials at selected flagship universities in the United States, Taylor (2017) found that the reading comprehension level ranges from 15th-grade to 19th-grade level. The readability of these materials can be challenging to international graduate students. Though a large body of literature exists about international graduate students in the United States, scant work has explored international doctoral students' information seeking behaviors and experiences while applying for doctoral study. We report the results of a study that explored the behaviors and experiences of 14 international doctoral students studying at a flagship university in the United States. Using in-depth interviews, we found that the students used two types of resources, experiential (EXR) and authorized (AUR), and began looking for information by exploring the former. We identified three common themes of their information seeking behaviors and problems they experienced in using official websites. The findings have implications for improving the design of websites to support international students' information seeking and needs.**

## KEYWORDS

international students, information seeking behavior, graduate education, doctoral students, application process

## INTRODUCTION

The number of international students in the United States grew drastically from 475,168 in 2001 to 907,251 in 2015 (United Nations Educational, Scientific and Cultural Organization, 2016).

Applying for a graduate program involves various tasks, including finding appropriate programs to one's area of study, examining admissions requirements and preparing the required application materials. Unlike their U.S. counterparts, international students are required to take an English language proficiency test in order to qualify for admission to a graduate program.

A recent study revealed that international students' reading comprehension scores on the Test of English as a Foreign Language (TOEFL) equate to 12th-grade reading comprehension level (Taylor, 2017). In a recent study, Taylor (2017) found that the reading comprehension level of admission materials on academic websites ranges from 15th-grade to 19th-grade level, thus, creating issues for international students' understanding of instructions while applying to graduate programs in the United States. This problem, combined with differences in educational systems and varied cultural experiences, makes the students' application process for admission to a graduate program in the United States not only challenging, but also complex (Carson, 2008; Chen, 2007) and frustrating (Alpaslan & Yalvac, 2017).

Most literature concerning international students in the United States has focused on cultural adjustment and acculturation (Akhtar & Kröner-Herwig, 2015; Bartram, 2008; Oh, Butler & Lee, 2014), language barrier (Liao, Finn & Lu, 2007; Zhao & Mawhinney, 2015), library use (Amsberry, 2008; Curry & Copeman, 2005; Howze & Moore, 2003; Mehra & Bilal, 2007; Yi, 2007), as well as motivation for pursuing advanced study (Chen, 2007; Sahasrabudhe, 2007; Szelényi, 2006; Tanyildiz, 2008). However, little is known about international graduate students' information seeking behaviors and experiences while applying to graduate programs in the United States. This study begins to fill this gap with the goal of suggesting design improvements for making academic websites and other resources supportive of international students' information seeking and needs.

## RELATED WORK

Studies have found that international students' decisions to study abroad involve a combination of searching academic resources, seeking advice from authority people such as professors (Amsberry; 2008; Chen, 2007; Szelényi, 2006), using the internet and search engines (Chung & Yoon, 2017; Oh, et al., 2004), and social networking sites such as Facebook (Sin & Kim, 2013). A recent study found that international students' information needs are diverse and that they seek information from human-mediated sources and web search engines (Chung & Yoon, 2017). Studies also show that international students face many challenges while in the US, including but not limited to academic and social isolation (Erichsen & Bolliger, 2011), acculturation (Ramachandran, 2011; Rose-Redwood, 2010) and English language difficulties

80th Annual Meeting of the Association for Information Science & Technology, Washington, DC | Oct. 27-Nov. 1, 2017

(Mehra & Bilal, 2007). Many international students experience a high level of anxiety and depression in the early stages of study in the United States (Alpaslan & Yalvac, 2017).

In summary, we lack understanding of international graduate students' information seeking behaviors and experiences while applying for graduate study in the United States, especially doctoral programs.

## RESEARCH QUESTION

This study addressed the following question: What are international doctoral students' information seeking behaviors and experiences while applying for graduate study in the United States?

## METHOD

We developed a questionnaire to collect background data from the participants (gender, age, years in doctoral program, country of origin and area of study) and an interview instrument with eight questions. We pilot-tested the two instruments with doctoral students and used during the interview. We recruited 14 first- and second-year doctoral students from across campus at a flagship university in the United States through personal social networks (e.g., Facebook, emails). We also employed snowballing and word-of-mouth techniques. The instrument consisted of demographic items. The sample population consisted of eight males and six females, aged from 27 to 41. Interview time ranged from 45 to 85 minutes. We audio-recorded and transcribed the interviews, and coded and analyzed the data using a grounded theory approach entailing open, axial and selective coding (Corbin & Strauss, 1990).

## MAJOR FINDINGS

The participants' information needs emerged from a knowledge gap pertaining to finding relevant graduate doctoral programs in the United States in specific areas of study. To select a program, the participants indicated application requirements and deadlines, as well as criteria such as social expectations, personal preferences and financial conditions (Figure 1). They used both experiential resources (EXR) and authorized resources (AUR). As shown in Figure 1, EXR consist of personal networks (e.g., peers, senior friends and advisors) and social media (e.g., discussion forums, blogs and online communities). AUR include both unofficial/commercial sites (e.g., program ranking sites, Google, and Google Scholar) and official sites (e.g., government, institutions and universities).

## INFORMATION SEEKING BEHAVIORS

We identified three main themes from the analyzed data:

1) Use EXR at the start, such as asking friends who had applied for graduate programs. This is exemplified by Patty who noted: "I remember one of my friends had applied for PhD programs in the U.S., and she mentioned some materials of application, so I asked her when I started to apply."

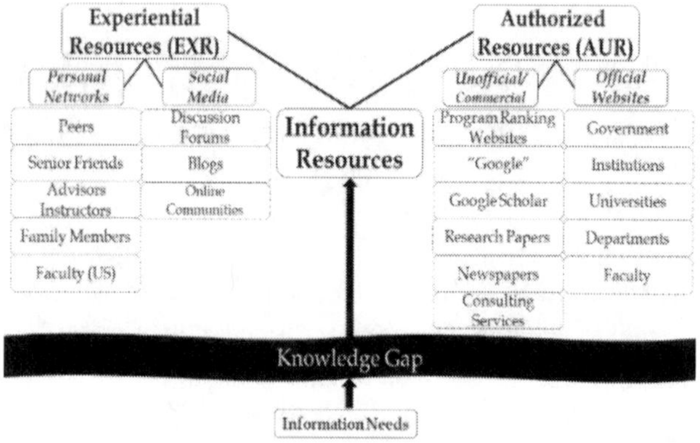


***Figure 1**. Information needs and resources*

2) Shift from EXR (or "story") and transfer what is learned from it to searching AUR (or "reality.") This shift is illustrated by Anna's comments: *"You basically see your friends in college doing that, and you get basic knowledge for what they are going through, but when you trying to be exact, there are many online forums that people who are at the same stage as you have...If you do not know about certain stuff, you can simply go through the website, and search the question."*

3) Problems finding information. This theme is typified by these comments: *"...some links are not available anymore but they still put them on the website" ...[I had] to finish application process in 10 minutes, if there is no active in 10 minutes your process will be expired. Because I lost my progress during the application, but they did not provide auto save"...The website affects my impression for the program. ...I gave up applying for one program because I could not find the requirements and I felt so mad."*

## DISCUSSION

This study revealed that international doctoral students resorted to EXR at the start of their application to doctoral programs in the United States and shifted to AUR to look for relevant programs. The main problems the students experienced in using official websites are attributed to poor usability. Their suggestions for improving them include 1) provide one-stop shopping sites, 2) keep information updated, 3) improve the functionality and content of the sites and 4) provide options for international usage.

We developed a preliminary representation of the information resources the student used based on their information needs. In future work, we will develop a model of their information seeking behaviors and combine it with the information resources they use.

## CONCLUSIONS

The preliminary findings of this study have increased our understanding of international doctoral students' information seeking behaviors and experiences in using resources to apply for graduate study in the United States. They also unveiled students' suggestions for improving the usability of academic websites, especially those pertaining to admissions to graduate programs. These findings should augment the research in human information behavior and should lead to guidelines in developing effective websites for use by international students.

## REFERENCES


Akhtar, M., & Kröner-Herwig, B. (2015). Acculturative stress among international students in context of socio-demographic variables and coping styles. *Current psychology, 34*(4), 803.

Alpaslan, M. M., & Yalvac, B. (2017). Exploring the anxiety state of the science majoring international graduate students with conditional acceptance in the United States. *International Journal of Research in Education and Science, 3*(2), 614-623.

Amsberry, D. (2008). Talking the talk: Library classroom communication and international students. *Journal of Academic Librarianship, 34*(4), 354-357.

Bartram, B. (2008). Supporting international students in higher education: Constructions, cultures and clashes. *Teaching in Higher Education, 13*(6), 657-668.

Carson, B. M. (2008). Research on the experiences of international graduate students: A selective literature review. *DLPS Faculty Publications*. Paper 62. Retrieved from: http://digitalcommons.wku.edu/dlps_fac_pub/62

Chen, L. H. (2007). East-Asian students' choice of Canadian graduate schools. *International Journal of Educational Advancement, 7*(4), 271-306.

Chung, E., & Yoon, J. (2017). International students' information needs and seeking behaviours throughout the settlement stages. *Libri, 67*(2), 119-128.

Corbin, J. M., & Strauss, A. (1990). Grounded theory research: Procedures, canons, and evaluative criteria. *Qualitative Sociology, 13*(1), 3-21.

Curry, A., & Copeman, D. (2005). Reference service to international students: A field stimulation research study. *The Journal of Academic Librarianship, 31*(5), 409-420.

Erichsen, E. A., & Bolliger, D. U. (2011). Towards understanding international graduate student isolation in traditional and online environments. *Educational Technology Research and Development, 59*(3), 309-326.

Howze, P. C., & Moore, D. M. (2003). Measuring international students' understanding of concepts related to the use of library-based technology. *Research Strategies, 19*(1), 57-74.

Liao, Y., Finn, M., & Lu, J. (2007). Information-seeking behavior of international graduate students vs. American graduate students: A user study at Virginia Tech 2005. *College & Research Libraries, 68*(1), 5-25.

Mehra, B., & Bilal, D. (2007). International students' perceptions of their information seeking strategies. *Proceedings of the 2007 Canadian Association for Information Science (CAIS/ACSI' 37)*, 10-12.

Oh, C. Y., Butler, B. S., & Lee, M. (2014). Information behavior of international students settling in an unfamiliar geo-spatial environment. *Proceedings of the American Society for Information Science and Technology, 51*(1), 1-11.

Ramachandran, N. T. (2011). Enhancing international students' experiences: An imperative agenda for universities in the UK. *Journal of Research in International Education, 10*(2), 201-220.

Rose-Redwood, C. R. (2010). The challenge of fostering cross-cultural interactions: A case study of international graduate students' perceptions of diversity initiatives. *College Student Journal, 44*(2).

Sahasrabudhe, U. (2007). *International Student Mobility: A Perspective of Graduate Engineering Students from India.* [Master's Thesis.] Long Beach, CA: California State University.

Sin, S. C. J., & Kim, K. S. (2013). International students' everyday life information seeking: The informational value of social networking sites. *Library & Information Science Research, 35*(2), 107-116.

Szelényi, K. (2006). Students without borders? Migratory decision-making among international graduate students in the U.S. *Knowledge, Technology & Policy, 19*(3), 64-86.

Tanyildiz, Z. E. (2008). The Effects of Networks on U.S. Institution Selection by Foreign Doctoral Students in Science and Engineering. [Ph.D. Dissertation.] Atlanta: Georgia Institute of Technology.

Taylor, Z. W. (2017). Speaking in tongues: Can international graduate students read international graduate admissions materials? *International Journal of Higher Education, 6*(3), 99.

United Nations Educational, Scientific and Cultural Organization (2016). Inbound internationally mobile students by continent of origin. [Data file]. Retrieved from http://data.uis.unesco.org/

Yi, Z. (2007). International student perceptions of information needs and use. *Journal of Academic Librarianship, 33*(6), 666-673.

Zhao, J. C., & Mawhinney, T. (2015). Comparison of native Chinese-speaking and native English-speaking engineering students' information literacy challenges. *Journal of Academic Librarianship, 41*(6), 712-724

# Open Access Citation Advantage? A Local Study at a Large Research University

**David E. Hubbard**
*Texas A&M University Libraries, USA. hubbardd@library.tamu.edu*

## ABSTRACT

**This study examines the open access citation advantage of gold open access (OA) journal articles published at a large U.S. research university. Most studies that examine the open access citation advantage focus on specific journals, disciplines, countries or global output. Local citation patterns may differ from these larger patterns. Since many OA advocates mention the open access citation advantage when promoting OA journal publishing on university campuses, an understanding of local patterns is crucial. This study reports on a method and compares average citation counts for subscription and gold OA journal articles using Web of Science. Gold OA physics journals showed a definite open access citation advantage, whereas other disciplines showed no difference or no open access citation advantage.**

## KEYWORDS

bibliometrics, open access, scholarly publishing

## INTRODUCTION

Advocates of open access (OA) journal publishing often mention the open access citation advantage, which refers to higher citation counts due to greater accessibility. At many universities, the open access citation advantage is mentioned to promote publishing in OA journals. There are a number of studies that support the open access citation advantage (e.g., Archambault et al., 2014; Norris et al., 2008; Xu et al., 2011), though results vary by discipline and is complicated by various types of OA publishing: gold, green and hybrid. The aforementioned studies typically examine journals, disciplines, countries or global output; however, what occurs globally may not be the case locally at a given university. Since many universities are promoting OA, advocates need to have a better understanding of local publishing since those may differ.

## BACKGROUND

Texas A&M University (TAMU) was founded in 1876. It is a member of the Association of American Universities and a designed land-grant, sea-grant and space-grant university. The 3,500 faculty are organized into 19 colleges/schools and serve over 60,000 students. Beginning in Fall 2013, the university has provided funding for article processing charges to publish in gold OA journals and has fully or partially funded over 150 articles since 2013. When TAMU researchers publish in OA journals, most are generally in high-impact venues based on Journal Citation Reports quartiles (Dabrowski, Hartnett & Hubbard, 2017).

## METHODS

The number of journal articles published at TAMU for 2014-2016, both subscription and gold OA, was determined using Web of Science. A subject analysis of the OA journals and articles published at TAMU was then conducted at the journal level using WorldCat to assign Library of Congress (LC) classes. Citation counts for OA and subscription journals were determined for the subject areas that represented the largest amount of OA publishing at TAMU. The average citations per article for 2014-2016 journal articles were determined using Web of Science for the research areas corresponding to the major LC classes. Average citation counts were compared using the Mann-Whitney U test.

## RESULTS/DISCUSSION

The number of journal articles published at TAMU is shown in Table 1. The number and percentage of gold OA journal articles published at TAMU has increased over the three-year period, though some of that increase might be attributable to Web of Science indexing more OA journals. The researchers at TAMU have published 1,582 articles in 357 OA journals. Figure 1 shows the LC classes of OA journals where TAMU researchers published two or more articles from 2014-2016. Figure 2 shows the number of OA articles, based on the journal LC class published in those journals. Limiting to two or more articles resulted in 150 journals and 1,375 articles, which represents 42% of OA journals and 89% of the OA articles. The LC classes for journals (Figure 1) and articles (Figure 2) have a similar pattern. The LC class Q (Science) is by far the largest for both journals and articles, followed by R (Medicine), T (Technology) and S (Agriculture).

| Year | Total Articles | OA Articles | % OA Articles |
|---|---|---|---|
| 2014 | 4,518 | 450 | 10.0 |
| 2015 | 4,741 | 526 | 11.1 |
| 2016 | 5,256 | 606 | 11.5 |
| SOURCE: Web of Science Core Collection | | | |

***Table 1.*** *OA publishing at TAMU, 2014-2016*

80th Annual Meeting of the Association for Information Science & Technology, Washington, DC | Oct. 27-Nov. 1, 2017

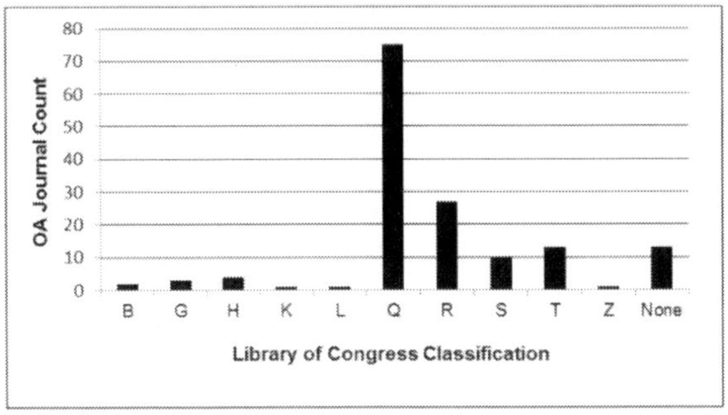


***Figure 1.*** *TAMU OA journal publishing by LC classification*

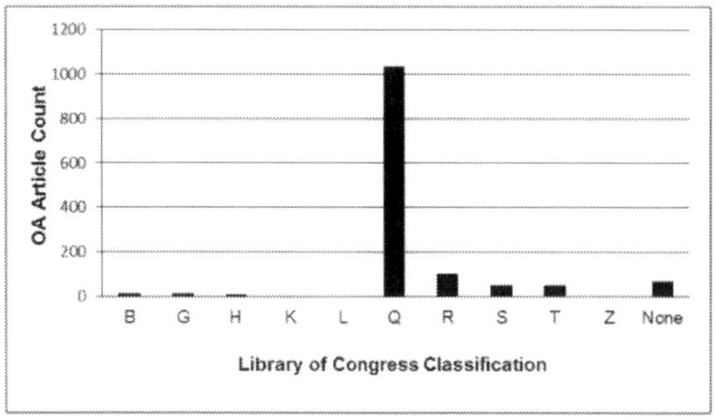


***Figure 2.*** *TAMU OA article publishing by LC classification*

| Research Areas[1] | Subscription Articles | Citation (Sub) Mean | Count Median | OA Articles | Citation (OA) Mean | Count Median | p-value (α = 0.05) |
|---|---|---|---|---|---|---|---|
| Agriculture | 495 | 3 | 1 | 37 | 4 | 2 | 0.6474 |
| Biological Sciences[2] | 2,420 | 5 | 2 | 393 | 6 | 2 | 0.9110 |
| Chemistry | 1,139 | 9 | 4 | 21 | 2 | 1 | 0.0002 |
| Engineering | 2,130 | 4 | 2 | 32 | 2 | 1 | 0.0229 |
| Medicine[2] | 2,164 | 5 | 2 | 270 | 5 | 2 | 0.9766 |
| Physics | 1,241 | 8 | 3 | 295 | 12 | 5 | < 0.0001 |
| Sci. Tech. Other Topics | 522 | 13 | 4 | 448 | 5 | 3 | < 0.0001 |

SOURCE: Web of Science Core Collection

[1] Research Areas defined by Web of Science unless otherwise noted.
[2] Biological Sciences and Medicine composed of multiple Research Areas.

***Table 2.*** *Cumulative average citations per article for TAMU articles, 2014-2016*

The 75 journals associated with the Qs are primarily in general science (Q), biological sciences (e.g., QH, QP, QR), and physics (QC). Given that OA article publishing at TAMU is primarily in agriculture, medicine and the sciences, a comparison of average citation counts per article was conducted for those subject areas using "Research Areas" as defined in Web of Science. The results are reported in Table 2. Of the seven research areas examined, only physics displayed an open access citation advantage. The fact that no statistically significant differences were observed for three of the research areas indicates that OA and subscription journals are at least equal in terms of average citation counts for those that TAMU published during that period. While not an open access citation advantage, it illustrates that gold OA and subscription citation averages are at least comparable in those three research areas. This is a useful insight that the university can use to promote OA journal publishing. One limitation of this study is the large unequal sample sizes of some research areas that may lower the power of the analysis.

## CONCLUSION

This study identified several research areas where gold OA articles published at TAMU were cited at least the same average number of times, and in one instance more (i.e., physics), compared to subscription journals. Two research areas, chemistry and engineering, showed lower average citation counts. These insights can assist in customizing messaging to promote OA publishing to researchers on a university campus.

### References

Archambault, E., Amyot, D., Deschamps, P., Nicol, A., Provencher, F., Rebout, L., & Roberge, G. (2014). *Proportion of open access papers published in peer- reviewed journals at the european and world levels: 1996-2013*. Science-Metrix: Montreal. Available from: http://science-metrix.com

Dabrowski, A., Hartnett, E., & Hubbard, D. (2017). The past, present, and future of Texas A&M University's open access fund. In *ER&L 2017 Conference*. Austin, TX. Available from http://sched.co/8waG

Norris, M., Oppenheim, C., & Rowland, F. (2008). The citation advantage of open-access articles. *Journal of the American Society for Information Science and Technology*, 59(12), 1963-1972.

Xu, L., Liu, J., & Fang, Q. (2011, February). Analysis on open access citation advantage: An empirical study based on Oxford open journals. In *Proceedings of the 2011 iConference*. Seattle, WA. Available from: http://portal.acm.org/citation.cfm?id=1940819

# Toward Automating Detection of Human Values in the Nuclear Power Debate

**Emi Ishita**
*Kyushu University, Japan. Ishita.emi.982@m.kyushu-u.ac.jp*

**Toru Oga**
*Kyushu University, Japan. toga@law.kyushu-u.ac.jp*

**An-Shou Cheng**
*National Sun Yat-sen University, Taiwan. ascheng@mail.nsysu.edu.tw*

**Kenneth R. Fleischmann**
*The University of Texas at Austin, USA. kfleisch@ischool.utexas.edu*

**Takayama Yasuhiro**
*National Institute of Technology, Tokuyama College, Japan. takayama@tokuyama.ac.jp*

**Douglas W. Oard**
*University of Maryland, USA. oard@umd.edu*

**Yoichi Tomiura**
*Kyushu University, Japan. tom@inf.kyushu-u.ac.jp*

## ABSTRACT

**This paper describes the creation of a corpus of newspaper articles about the Fukushima nuclear disaster, a coding frame for content analysis of human values expressed or reflected in that corpus and preliminary results for automation of the content analysis. Understanding the human values that motivate sentiment towards an idea can help to characterize the basis for that sentiment, and this work is a first step toward applying that approach to positions on controversial events reported in the news.**

## KEYWORDS

human values, test collection, automated content analysis

## INTRODUCTION

Newspaper articles provide a lens for viewing prominent events within their social, political, economic and cultural contexts. For controversial issues, journalists typically seek to report on a range of perspectives, along with information about the basis for those perspectives. Our goal is to study how human values can help to explain positions that people take on controversial topics (Fleischmann, 2014), and thus we are interested in coding news stories with the human values that they reflect. Because the scale of modern news media content exceeds what any person could code by hand, we are also interested in exploring the potential for automating this process using supervised machine learning.

Our approach is inspired by our earlier work (Takayama et al., 2014), in which we developed a latent value model (LVM) to automatically code a small set of human values in sentences from about 100 statements prepared for legislative and regulatory bodies in the Net Neutrality debate in the United States. The automatically coded human values were then compared with manually assigned human value labels (Cheng et al., 2012) to compute classification accuracy measures such as precision and recall, finding that the LVM classifier (which operates on both single words and pairs of words) was more accurate than several widely used classifiers for this task. Our work differs from that earlier work in several ways: (1) we focus on third-person news reporting rather than first-person prepared statements, (2) we code entire articles rather than individual sentences and (3) we code for a broader range of human values.

In the remainder of this paper, we introduce our annotated news article corpus, we report some initial experiment results using our LVM classifier, and we look ahead to the next steps in our work-in-progress.

## NEWS ARTICLE CORPUS

Our focus is on the debate over the future of nuclear power in Japan that resulted from the Fukushima Daiichi nuclear reactor disaster on March 11, 2011. The Great East Japan Earthquake that occurred on that date damaged the reactor, leading to an immediate evacuation, and ultimately leading to the temporary shutdown of every nuclear power generation facility in the country. This was a classic example of what Taleb (2007) has called a "black swan" – an unanticipated event with the power to change perceptions regarding what is possible. The controversial decision to shut down all 54 of Japan's nuclear reactors, which had previously supplied 30% of the nation's power, had substantial consequences both for economic activity and for the activities of daily life in this highly industrialized society. The subsequent decision to restart some of those reactors, and the government's ultimate decision to continue to rely on nuclear power for energy (in contrast, for example, to the contemporaneous German decision to permanently end nuclear power generation), has proven even more contentious.

The time scale over which these controversies unfolded calls for the development of a new test collection. For our initial work, we have therefore collected 13,821 news articles in

80th Annual Meeting of the Association for Information Science & Technology, Washington, DC | Oct. 27-Nov. 1, 2017

| Value | 2011 | 2012 | 2013 | P | R | K |
|---|---|---|---|---|---|---|
| Human welfare | 237 | 255 | 203 | 0.38 | 0.72 | 0.27 |
| Importance | 176 | 185 | 172 | 0.27 | 0.63 | 0.08 |
| Effectiveness | 128 | 86 | 87 | 0.15 | 0.62 | 0.09 |
| Power | 95 | 86 | 112 | 0.15 | 0.63 | 0.10 |
| Personal welfare | 63 | 74 | 91 | 0.13 | 0.68 | 0.09 |
| Nature | 67 | 52 | 95 | 0.12 | 0.67 | 0.28 |
| Other | 61 | 45 | 75 | 0.07 | 0.49 | 0.11 |
| Law and order | 49 | 71 | 47 | 0.08 | 0.55 | 0.34 |
| Wealth | 55 | 50 | 43 | 0.09 | 0.73 | 0.27 |
| Innovation | 31 | 35 | 61 | 0.07 | 0.67 | 0.26 |
| Independence | 24 | 31 | 24 | 0.05 | 0.70 | 0.13 |

***Table 1.*** *Article counts; LVM precision & recall; kappa*

Japanese from the Japanese daily newspaper CD Mainichi Shimbun (Mainichi Newspaper Annual Full-Text Data Base) between 2011 and 2013. We selected the articles using the query "[原発 (nuclear power plant) OR 原子力 (nuclear power)] AND [福島 (Fukushima)]" in the heading or body of the article. This resulted in 6,629 articles from 2011; 4,036 articles from 2012; and 3,156 articles from 2013. We then randomly selected 700 articles from each year for manual coding, resulting in the 2,100 manually coded articles that we used with 10-fold cross-validation for training and testing in these experiments.

## CODING FRAME AND CODING

Trained coders assigned six types of labels to each of the 2,100 articles. For four of those types (type, phase, source and attitude), the coders assigned a label to each article. Any number of labels could be assigned for the media and values types. In this paper, we focus on the values labels. Our values coding frame includes 11 human values (see Table 1). One author, a social scientist, initially built the values coding frame to analyze the contemporaneous discussion of nuclear power policy in Taiwan using a collection of articles from a Taiwanese newspaper. We first prepared a coding manual and then hired and trained coders. The coders examined the headline and body of each story and assigned values labels. Two coders independently coded each article. Inter-coder agreement scores computed using Cohen's (1960) kappa (K) are shown in Table 1.

## PRELIMINARY EXPERIMENTS

We conducted experiments with two types of classifiers (LVM and SVM$^{light}$ support vector machines with several kernel functions). In both cases, we first used the standard Juman package to perform tokenization and morphological analysis for Japanese and then selected noun, verb, adjective, nominal prefix and suffix and numerative parts of speech as the term space for our classifiers. Articles included headlines (average of 12.7 terms) and bodies (average of 271.3 terms). Table 1 shows our best overall results for precision and recall, which were obtained using LVM. For example, for human welfare, LVM achieved a precision of 0.38 and a recall of 0.72, whereas our best SVM (linear kernel) achieved a precision of 0.54 and a recall of 0.23. We note that LVM consistently yields higher recall than precision, whereas for SVM the opposite is true. These results are comparable to those reported in Takayama et al. (2014) for the value honor, the one category in those experiments that had a comparable number (317) of positive training examples.

## NEXT STEPS

These results will serve as a baseline for comparing future improvements. Our next step must be to refine our coding process to improve inter-coder agreement; in other work, we have found that asking annotators to focus on the lead paragraph of a news story can help to improve consistency. Next, we will try semi-supervised classification techniques that can benefit from the large number of unlabeled articles, and with joint models that can assign multiple types of labels simultaneously. It is important to consider how best to tune the tradeoff between precision and recall to optimally support social science research at web scale, which can guide future work with committees of diverse classifiers to achieve that balance. Ultimately, we hope to unify our test collection with a collection on the same topic developed in Taiwan for Chinese-language news; a first step toward creation of a multilingual collection for studying the nuclear power debate. Throughout this process, we will share our coding manual and coding results publicly so that others can replicate our work and extend it in novel ways.

## ACKNOWLEDGMENTS

This work was supported by JSPS KAKENHI Grant Number JP25280118.

## REFERENCES

Cheng, A.-S., Fleischmann, K. R., Wang, P., Ishita, E., & Oard, D. W. (2012). The role of innovation and wealth in the net neutrality debate: A content analysis of human values in Congressional and FCC hearings. *JASIS&T*, *63*, 1360-1373.

Cohen, J. (1960). A coefficient of agreement for nominal scales. *Educational and Psychological Measurements*, *20*, 37-46.

Fleischmann, K. R. (2014). *Information and Human Values*. San Rafael, CA: Morgan & Claypool.

Takayama, Y., Tomiura, Y., Ishita, E., Oard, D. W., Fleischmann, K. R., & Cheng, A.-S. (2014). A word-scale probabilistic latent variable model for detecting human values. *CIKM*, 1489-1498. Shanghai.

Taleb, N. (2007). The black swan: The impact of the highly improbable. New York: Random House.

# Exploiting Graph-based Data to Realize New Functionalities for Scholar-built Worksets

**Jacob Jett**
*University of Illinois at Urbana-Champaign, School of Information Sciences, Center for Informatics Research in Science & Scholarship, USA. jjett2@illinois.edu*

**Timothy W. Cole**
*University of Illinois at Urbana-Champaign, School of Information Sciences, Center for Informatics Research in Science & Scholarship, USA. t-cole3@illinois.edu*

**J. Stephen Downie**
*University of Illinois at Urbana-Champaign, School of Information Sciences, Center for Informatics Research in Science & Scholarship, USA. jdownie@illinois.edu*

## ABSTRACT

**In this poster, we describe how the HathiTrust Research Center (HTRC) is developing a graph-based approach to representing scholar-built worksets in the HTRC's research workflows. The use of named graphs to express relationships among worksets, workset items (volumes and pages) and relevant external resources and to manage ownership, version control and access to worksets aligns well with HTRC's non-consumptive research architecture. In addition to managing scholars' research collections, HTRC workset graphs also provide a means to link individual workset items to descriptive metadata and allows scholars to annotate their worksets and the items in them.**

## KEYWORDS

RDF, graphs, HathiTrust Research Center, worksets, research collections, annotation, HathitTrust Digital Library

## CONTEXT

The HathiTrust Digital Library (HTDL) is a large-scale digital library that aggregates digitized content from many sources. Its corpus spans over 15.5 million volumes and 5.4 billion scanned pages of digitized content. Textual representations of scanned pages are generated using optical character recognition (OCR). The HathiTrust Research Center (HTRC) is a multi-institution partnership between Indiana University and the University of Illinois at Urbana-Champaign engaged in developing an architecture through which scholars can make use of the HTDL's corpus for their research.

Because only about 38% of the collection (~5.8 million volumes) are in the public domain, the HTRC has developed a non-consumptive research paradigm (Murdock et al., 2015), wherein, scholars use metadata queries to gather together research objects (OCR'd texts and scanned pages) of interest and computational algorithms to derive features and similar statistical information. The HTRC workset is a central feature in this workflow, playing the role of a scholar's workbench research collection.

## HTRC Workset

The HTRC workset data model (see Figure 1 on next page) is designed to capture both the contents of the research collection (in the form of links that the HTRC's data API can exploit) and metadata that can help other scholars assess the fitness of a scholar's workset for reuse in their own research (Jett et al., 2015, 2016), while providing an easily shared storage solution that scales easily and presents the end user with many choices for dissemination of workset information. While the worksets are designed so that scholars can easily share them with one another, the HTRC's secure environment also affords scholars the choice to keep their worksets private.

The choice to keep their research collections private will be made possible in two ways:

1. Each workset is stored in its own distinct named graph which is bound to its creator through the HTRC's user authentication infrastructure, and
2. An access control property has been added to the workset data model which specifically records a flag which the HTRC architecture uses to determine under what conditions the workset's graph should be disseminated in the form of a workset descriptive RDF document (usually in JSON+LD format). This property is illustrated in Figure 1 as the metadata entity "Accessbility Permissions."

Storing each workset as a separate named graph affords the HTRC's infrastructure and its users additional benefits:

- Users may annotate both worksets and (in the context of the workset) items gathered into them (illustrated in Figure 1 as "Volumes"). Among other things this allows users to rank the things in their worksets and provide explanatory context for why something is part of the workset.
- Item-level metadata are maintained in a separate, global graph, avoiding duplication of item-level metadata while still allowing it to be efficiently included within graphs describing worksets.

80th Annual Meeting of the Association for Information Science & Technology, Washington, DC | Oct. 27-Nov. 1, 2017

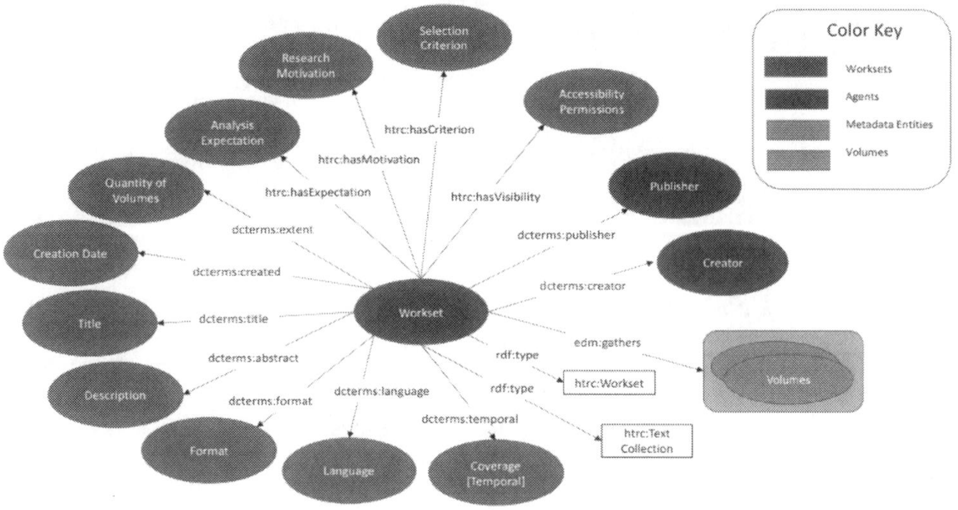


***Figure 1:*** *HTRC workset data model*

## GRAPH ARCHITECTURE

The HTRC's graph architecture maintains three classes of graphs: workset graphs, annotation graphs and a default, global graph (for item-level metadata and relationships to external contexts). Figure 1 showcases the general structure of a workset graph (a workset, the items gathered into it and some metadata that describes it). Actual instances of worksets are named graphs, and since many of the workset properties are optional, can be quite succinct – sometimes forming little more than a list of items, a workset title, the name of the user who gathered it and the number of items in it.

Annotation graphs are also named graphs unique to individual HTRC users. (In the final system as envisioned, scholarly users will be able to annotate both workset and item-level information.) This allows their visibility to be tailored to suit user preferences both with regards to which annotations a scholarly annotator wants to share with other scholars and which annotations a scholarly researcher wants to see displayed with their research objects.

Finally, a global graph of items is maintained. The primary usage of this graph is to store links between particular items and existing item-level metadata (e.g., as derived from library MARC cataloging records). It also maintains links between items and the corpuses they are part of (e.g., the HTDL corpus, the HTRC's corpus of public domain works, the HTRC Extracted Features dataset (Capitanu et al., 2016), and links to contextual resources, author and subject authorities, related Wikipedia/DBPedia resources, related digital editions, etc. In addition to these links, some string metadata are recorded (item title, author, copyright date, copyright status) which can be serialized along with the workset's metadata to provide users with a useful selection of facts in a single serialized record.

## FUTURE WORK

Our future work will consist of iterating the various graph models and their architecture to better integrate them with the HTRC's other metadata resources (e.g., HTDL Bib API, HTRC Data API, SOLR indexes, etc.).

## ACKNOWLEDGMENTS

This work is made possible through a generous grant from the Andrew W. Mellon Foundation; however, the observations, conclusions and opinions expressed are those of the authors and not necessarily shared by the sponsor.

## REFERENCES


Capitanu, B., Underwood, T., Organisciak, P., Cole, T., Sarol, M. J. & Downie, J. S. (2016). *The HathiTrust Research Center extracted feature dataset* (1.0) [Dataset]. HathiTrust Research Center. DOI: http://dx.doi.org/10.13012/J8X63JT3

Jett, J., Maden, C., Fallaw, C., Senseney, M., & Downie, J. S. (2015). Conceptualizing worksets for non-consumptive research. Poster presented at *iConference 2015* (24-27 March 2015, Newport Beach, CA). Accessible via http://hdl.handle.net/2142/73695

Jett, J., Cole, T. W., Maden, C., & Downie, J. S. (2016). The HathiTrust Research Center workset ontology: A descriptive framework for non-consumptive research collections. *Journal of Open Humanities Data 2*, p e1. DOI: http://doi.org/10.5334/johd.3

Murdock, J., Zeng, J., & McDonald, R. H. (2015). Topic exploration with the HTRC Data Capsule for non-consumptive research. Paper presented at the *15th ACM/IEEE joint conference on digital libraries (JCDL '15)*. DOI: https://doi.org/10.1145/2756406.2756929

# Content Analysis of Facebook Posts in Public Libraries Based on Textual Analysis

**Soohyung Joo**
*University of Kentucky, USA. soohyung.joo@uky.edu*

**Kun Lu**
*University of Oklahoma, USA. kunlu@ou.edu*

## ABSTRACT

**This poster presents preliminary findings from a textual analysis of social media posts created by public libraries. We collected a text corpus, consisting of 3,622 Facebook posts containing more than seven words from 151 public libraries. We conducted a term frequency analysis and latent dirichlet allocation (LDA) topic modeling to explore the content of Facebook posts. The results revealed that terms related to library programming and library event announcements appeared frequently. The LDA topic modeling identified 25 topics underlying the corpus. We observed various topics were posted on public library Facebook Pages while library programming and event related topics were most common.**

## KEYWORDS

social media, public libraries, textual analysis, LDA topic models

## INTRODUCTION

Social media became one of the popular marketing channels in public libraries to efficiently reach out library user communities online. Researchers have investigated the content of social media created by public libraries to understand the nature of social media use in the library context. For example, Alkindi and Al-Surqi (2013) identified the content types of public library social media, such as general news, new books and recommendations of books/materials, among others. Shiri and Rathi (2013) also defined a list of categories of social media messages in public libraries, such as acknowledge, advisory services, announcement and event. Chen et al. (2014) explored in what ways interactions occur in public library Facebook pages and identified different interaction types such as knowledge sharing, information dissemination and communication. Madge and Coşerea (2014) found that social media are used as a marketing tool for announcement of services and cultural and educational activities in public libraries. Social media have served as an emerging online marketing tool, and the understanding of social media content is important to come up with effective strategies to better communicate with diverse patron groups online in public libraries. This study intends to examine the content of Facebook posts uploaded by public libraries based on LDA topic modeling.

80th Annual Meeting of the Association for Information Science & Technology, Washington, DC | Oct. 27-Nov. 1, 2017



## METHODS

In total, 4,637 highlighted posts were collected from Facebook pages of randomly selected 151 public libraries between July and October 2015. Among them, we extracted 3,622 posts that included more than seven words for textual analysis. Posts having only images or video clips without any text or too short messages, which were inappropriate for textual analysis, were excluded from the analysis.

For analysis, we preprocessed all observed text through tokenization, stopword elimination and stemming. A list of English stopwords provided by R[tm] package was applied (https://cran.r-project.org/web/packages/tm/tm.pdf), and Porter Stemmer was adopted for stemming. After that, we conducted a term frequency analysis as well as LDA topic modeling. LDA topic modeling is an unsupervised machine learning technique to discover prevailing themes underlying a large text corpus (Blei, 2012; Munzert et al., 2014).

## RESULTS

First, we counted frequencies for the observed terms. In total, 61,909 tokens were observed for 8,540 unique terms after stopwords removal and stemming. Figure 1 presents most frequently observed 20 stemmed terms. Not surprisingly, *librari*, *book* and *read* were the three most common terms observed from the corpus. Library programming related terms were ranked highly, such as *program* and *join*. In addition, several highly ranked terms were related to event announcements, for example, *today*, *time* and *fun*. We can infer that terms relevant to months or dates, such as *juli*, *septemb* or *saturday*, would be also associated with library programming or event announcements.

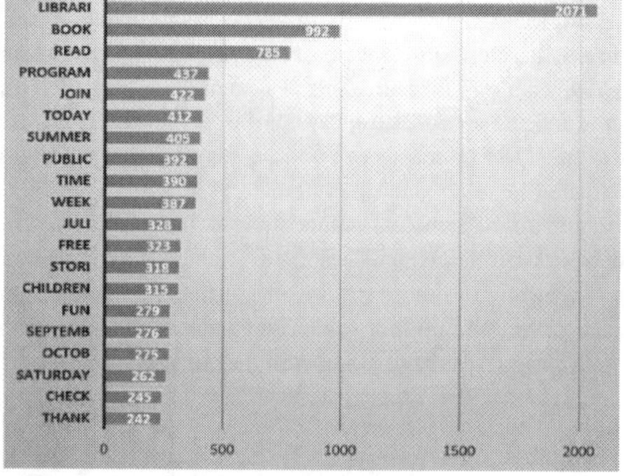


***Figure 1.*** *Most frequent stemmed terms*

LDA topic modeling uncovered 25 topics underlying the corpus of public library Facebook posts. We found that programming related topics are prevalent across the corpus. For example, topics 4, 7, 8, 9 and 24 are directly or indirectly relevant to programming offered by the libraries. Also, we can interpret that a considerable portion of the posts were associated with announcements of library events, e.g., Topics 2, 5, 10, 11, 16, 18 and 23. As the data were collected in summer, summer reading programing was extracted as one of the topics. Interestingly, the results imply a seasonal influence on social media activities. For example, topic 9 specifically represents summer reading programing while topics 10 and 15 are related to fall season and Halloween. We also observed that several topics are concerned with children and young adults. Additionally, we found that some topics are about library materials, such as books, library collections, e-books and digital items.

| | | | | |
|---|---|---|---|---|
| **Topic 1** 8.12% Books | **Topic 2** 5.50% Today's event | **Topic 3** 4.39% Branch libraries | **Topic 4** 6.79% Story time | **Topic 5** 4.47% Author event |
| **Topic 6** 3.76% Children | **Topic 7** 5.08% Program registration | **Topic 8** 4.36% Library programs | **Topic 9** 7.15% Summer reading program | **Topic 10** 4.36% Kids/ Halloween |
| **Topic 11** 4.06% Event (fun) | **Topic 12** 3.37% Library registration | **Topic 13** 3.89% Open hours | **Topic 14** 2.84% Library collection | **Topic 15** 3.09% Fall (images) |
| **Topic 16** 3.70% Event (music) | **Topic 17** 2.87% Library clubs | **Topic 18** 2.62% Library events (reminders) | **Topic 19** 2.29% School year start | **Topic 20** 4.03% ebook and digital items |
| **Topic 21** 2.49% Community events/news | **Topic 22** 2.26% Thank you messages | **Topic 23** 3.31% Movie nights | **Topic 24** 3.01% Teens program | **Topic 25** 2.15% Sign in library cards |

***Figure 2**. LDA topic modeling result (k=25)*

## DISCUSSION AND CONCLUSION

This proposal is to share some preliminary findings from the ongoing project, which applies a textual analysis technique to understand the nature of social media content in public libraries. This is one of the first attempts to apply LDA topic modeling to analyzing the content of public library Facebook posts. The frequency analysis and LDA topic modeling revealed prevailing topics and subjects in Facebook content contributed by public libraries. We found that topics related to library programming and event announcements were most frequently posted in public libraries' Facebook pages. In addition to programming and event announcement, diverse topics emerged from the corpus, ranging from books and library materials, library registration, acknowledgement messages, school year start, open hours, library clubs and to others.

Next, we plan to identify which types of topics would receive more user engagement. In the dataset, we also collected the amounts of "likes," "shares" and "comments" that each post received. Under the assumption that those "likes," "shares" and "comments" represent user engagement, we will statistically examine which topic type would draw more user engagement with posts. The findings from the planned study will produce implications for effective social media content strategies in public libraries.

## REFERENCES


AlKindi, S. S., & Al-Suqri, M. N. (2013). Social networking sites as marketing and outreach tools of library and information services. *Global Journal of Human-Social Science Research*, 13(2).

Blei, D. M. (2012). Probabilistic topic models. *Communications of the ACM*, 55(4), 77-84.

Chen, D. Y. T., Chu, S. K. W., & Xu, S. Q. (2012). How do libraries use social networking sites to interact with users? In *Proceedings of ASIS&T 2012*, October 28-31, 2012, Baltimore, MD, USA.

Shiri, A., & Rathi, D. (2013). Twitter content categorisation: A public library perspective. *Journal of Information & Knowledge Management, 12*(04), 1350035.

Madge, O. L., & Coserea, L. (2014). The Facebook challenge for public libraries in Romania. *Studii de Biblioteconomie și Știința Informării,* 18, 89-93.

Munzert, S., Rubba, C., Meißner, P., & Nyhuis, D. (2014). *Automated data collection with R: A practical guide to web scraping and text mining.* Somerset: John Wiley & Sons

# Are We Having Fun Yet? Exploring Definitions of Fun for STEAM Learning

**Castle U. Kim**
*Florida State University, USA. udk16@my.fsu.edu*

**Marcia A. Mardis**
*Florida State University, USA. mmardis@fsu.edu*

## ABSTRACT

**In this visual presentation, I present a video that illustrates preliminary findings of a study of definitions of the word fun in the context of STEAM (science, technology, engineering, arts and mathematics) learning. I begin by illustrating fun's importance, lack of clear definitions, warrant for common understanding is important for among researchers and educators who develop and assess STEAM learning activities. I demonstrate preliminary results of the study of fun definitions and conclude with implications for further research.**

## KEYWORDS

fun, STEAM, learning

## INTRODUCTION

In many respects, fun determines what we do in our free time, how we focus and what we like to learn. Integrating fun into different organizational processes has been correlated with positive outcomes in work engagement and task performance (Fluegge, 2008); enjoyable learning in museums (Lin, Fernandez & Gregor, 2010); and designing educational games (McCabe & Wise, 2009). Creating and identifying fun is a high interest topic in any human interaction studies. The term's unclear definition begs the question, especially in the education and STEAM fields: What is fun?

### *Problem and Significance*

Education needs fun to make learning meaningful, but unclear conceptualizations are making the concept subjective and hard to discern. A clear scholarly definition of *fun* is hard to find. Two major factors that have contributed into the lack of definition are 1) the paradoxical relationship between fun and academic research and 2) fun as a boundary object.

### *Fun paradox*

Without a doubt fun is an interesting topic, but there has been little research on the topic. The lack of studies may be because fun is linked to entertainment, not to fine arts (McKee, 2016). From the late 18th century, cultural elites introduced the idea of dividing the cultural resources into arts and entertainment. Arts became associated with the philosophical tradition of aesthetics. Fun is regarded as entertainment, an area in which something that was not a researchable problem, scholars noted (McKee, 2016).

### *Fun as a boundary object*

Fun is a boundary object in that the term and concept are used and interpreted differently by each researcher based on context; it is also different for each individual, being interpretive flexible (Leigh Star, 2010). Depending on the person, fun can mean simple pleasure, escape from reality or breaking the rules (McKee, 2016).

### *Fun Conceptions of Outside Education*

In *Spongebob Squarepants,* a cartoon on the Nickelodeon television channel, the Spongebob character sings "F is for friends who do stuff together! U is for you and me! N is for anywhere and anytime at all down here in the deep blue sea!" Spongebob's definition explains, but does not define, fun; similarly, many researchers conceptualize but do not commit to a specific definition of *fun*.

In studies in which researchers have attempted to define *fun*, it is said to be the result of the combination of determinant of enjoyment, control of the content, care for the content and the suspension of disbelief (Rogers, Carpentier & Barnard, 2016). Plester, Cooper-Thomas & Winquist (2015) posited that organic fun, managed fun and task fun exist within a work environment (2015). In entertainment studies, fun is "pleasure without purpose" (McKee, 2016). Other researchers have categorized five types of fun: sociability, contentment, achievement, sensual and ecstatic (McManus & Furnham, 2010).

### *Fun Approaches to STEAM Learning*

Within the STEAM field, researchers have noted high interest in studying fun and the need to focus studies on positive motivators instead of the negative stressors present in learning experiences (Monk, Hassenzahl, Blythe & Reed, 2002). Education researchers have emphasized the need for and the constructive application of fun in learning (Buckingham, 2013). However, the education researchers have no consensus definition. Scholars have identified elements of fun learning circumstances, such as behavioral, emotional and cognitive engagement (Zinn, 2008). Fun has also been described as freely chosen, stimulating emotional fulfillment and spontaneously emerging from the situation (Fine & Corte, 2017). For other STEAM researchers, fun seems not to be from external stimulus (Romano, 2009).

80th Annual Meeting of the Association for Information Science & Technology, Washington, DC | Oct. 27-Nov. 1, 2017

### Purpose and Question

To better study learning engagement, fun needs to be understood and defined. The purpose this presentation is to introduce preliminary research that systematically explores and compares definitions of fun within learning research to begin distilling a common definition. The study's central research question is *How have STEAM scholars defined fun in a learning context*?

## METHOD

### Data Collection

Study data will be collected by searching the terms *fun*, *learning* and *STEAM* in Florida State University Libraries' OneSearch academic search tool. Peer-reviewed journal articles in the education discipline will be analyzed. OneSearch is a federated search tool that allows access to a local library catalog along with millions of scholarly e-resources; while not guaranteed to be exhaustive, OneSearch is widely used by colleges and universities in the United States and its results provide a strong starting point for subsequent research and replication by other researchers.

### Data Analysis

For the first step, the collected data will be divided into two groups based on whether they define fun inductively or deductively. Inductive definitions arise when article authors have stated their definitions of *fun* and analyzed their data based on that definition. Deductive definitions are ones in which article authors conceptualize fun through descriptions that do not directly include the word *fun*; in these instances, the researchers analyze the article content to determine whether the operational definition is similar to inductively derived definitions or provides new ideas.

After the data were divided, the inductive definitions of fun were used to create categories. These categories guided the analysis of the deductive articles. Finally, the researchers compiled the similarities and differences that are communicated in the video presentation.

### Discussion and Conclusion

This two-step analysis will allow us to begin to understand categories of fun definitions and better understand how STEAM scholars have conceptualized fun. Findings of this study will be presented in a short, engaging video modeled on the YouTube *Nerdist* channel. In the video, the host uses graphics, text, video, audio and humor to clearly explain the study and its findings.

By studying how STEAM scholars define *fun*, we will better understand what it is. From this study future research will include further expanding the analyzed literature by citation snowballing to develop a fun codebook to be used in other fun related research and fun educational media resources for kids.

## REFERENCES


Buckingham, D. (2013). Beyond technology: Children's learning in the age of digital culture. John Wiley & Sons.

Fine, G. A., & Corte, U. (2017). Group pleasures: Collaborative commitments, shared narrative, and the sociology of fun. *Sociological Theory, 35*(1), 64-86.

Fluegge, E. R. (2008). Who put the fun in functional? Fun at work and its effects on job performance (Doctoral dissertation, University of Florida).

Leigh Star, S. (2010). This is not a boundary object: Reflections on the origin of a concept. *Science, Technology, & Human Values, 35*(5), 601-617.

Lin, A. C., Fernandez, W., & Gregor, S. (2010). *Designing for enjoyment and informal learning: A study in a museum context.* Retrieved June 1, 2017 from http://works.bepress.com/walter_fernandez/9/.

McCabe, J., & Wise, S. (2009). It's all fun and games until someone learns something: Assessing the learning outcomes of two educational games. *Evidence Based Library and Information Practice, 4*(4), 6-23.

McKee, A. (2016). FUN! What entertainment tells us about living a good life. London, England: Palgrave

McManus, I. C., & Furnham, A. (2010). "Fun, fun, fun": Types of fun, attitudes to fun, and their relation to personality and biographical factors. *Psychology, 1*(03), 159.

Monk, A., Hassenzahl, M., Blythe, M., & Reed, D. (2002, April). Funology: Designing enjoyment. In *CHI'02 extended abstracts on human factors in computing systems* (pp. 924-925). ACM.

Plester, B., Cooper-Thomas, H., & Winquist, J. (2015). The fun paradox. *Employee Relations, 37*(3), 380-398.

Rogers, R., Carpentier, F. R. D., & Barnard, L. (2016). Media enjoyment as a function of control over characters. *Entertainment Computing, 12*, 29-39.

Romano, T. (2009). EJ in focus: Defining fun and seeking flow in English language arts. *The English Journal, 98*(6), 30-37.

Zinn, W. O. R. (2008). Making fun of school, or why does learning have to be such a drag?: Six key elements for motivating learning. *International Journal of Learning, 15*(8), 153-160.

# Perceived Usefulness of Social Media Features/Elements: Effects of Coping Style, Purpose and System

**Kyung-Sun Kim**
*University of Wisconsin-Madison, USA. kskim@slis.wisc.edu*

**Sei-Ching Joanna Sin**
*Nanyang Technological University, Singapore. joanna.sin@ntu.edu.sg*

## ABSTRACT

**Drawing from coping and uses and gratifications theories, the study investigates how individuals' coping style, purposes and features/elements of social media interact and influence the perceived usefulness of social media elements. Over 1,000 undergraduate students in the United States participated in the study. Data are collected through an online survey. Findings and implications are discussed.**

## KEYWORDS

problem-solving style, social media, uses & gratification, system features

## INTRODUCTION

While the main purpose of using social media is known to be socialization, people seem to use different social media platforms to meet various information needs (Head & Eisenberg, 2009; Kim & Sin, 2016; Pew Research Center, 2016). Researchers have sought to identify the factors that contribute to individual differences in social media use. Prior studies have shed light on factors such as users' demographics (e.g., Kim, Sin & Tsai, 2014; Kimbrough, Guadagno, Muscanell & Dill, 2013), personalities (e.g., Blackwell, Leaman, Tramposch, Osborne & Liss, 2017; Correa, Hinsley & de Zúñiga, 2010), motivations (e.g., Lee & Ma, 2012; Oh & Syn, 2015) and system design features (e.g., McCay-Peet & Quan-Haase, 2016; Schlesinger et al., 2017). While many focused on different types of platforms (e.g., social networking sites, microblogs) or specific sites (e.g., Facebook, Twitter), little effort has been made to examine social media at a more granular level, such as particular features of social media (e.g., social feedback features such as number of likes) that individuals find useful. Rarer still are studies that investigate potential interaction effects between different classes of explanatory factors, specifically individual characteristics (e.g., coping style), context/gratification purposes and system features. Users' coping styles, for example, are a promising factor in understanding their information behavior. Problem-focused individuals tend to devise different strategies depending on the problem itself. Emotion-focused individuals, on the other hand, do not pay as much attention to problems at hand but to their own emotions or feelings.

80th Annual Meeting of the Association for Information Science & Technology, Washington, DC | Oct. 27-Nov. 1, 2017



Based on the information seeking in context paradigm (Vakkari, Savolainen & Dervin, 1997) with a focus on interactionism (Kim & Allen, 2002), and also drawing from the coping theory (Lazarus & Folkman, 1984) and the uses and gratifications (U&G) theory (Katz et al, 1974), the current study attempts to address the aforementioned research gap. The granular analysis and the investigation of interaction will contribute to deeper understandings of the information behavior on social media and inform further design and development of social media.

## RESEARCH QUESTIONS

What are the effects of (a) coping style, (b) gratification purposes and (c) features/elements of social media on the perceived usefulness of the element (PUE)? How do they interact with one another?

## METHODS

Data were collected through an online survey. The questionnaire included questions on problem solving coping style (from Problem-Solving Inventory (Heppner, 1988)); purposes (information seeking, personal identity, social integration and entertainment from the U&G literature); and elements of social media (7 elements developed from literature reviews and focus group interviews). PUE was measured on a Likert-like scale of 1 to 5, with 5 being the most useful.

Over 1,000 undergraduate students of a public university in the United States participated in the study. Data analysis methods included a correspondence analysis (CA) to visualize the relationships among the three factors, as well as a mixed ANOVA to address the research questions.

## RESULTS

The CA plot shows the relationships among the three factors (Fig. 1). It can be seen, for example, that there is a closer relation between element *physical characteristics of post* (e.g., quality & quantity of image/audio, length of article) and the *entertainment* purpose.

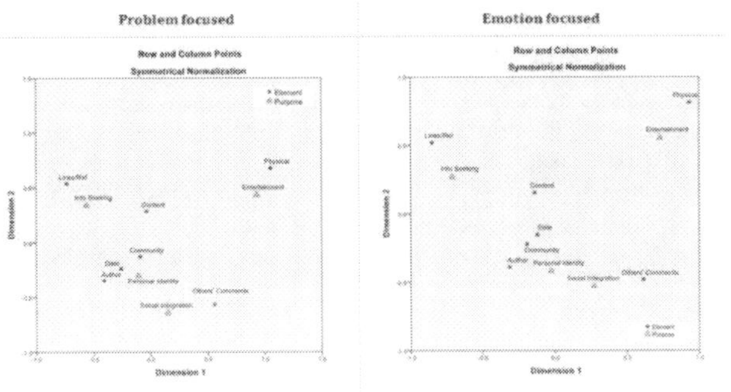


***Figure 1.** Correspondence analysis result*

Mixed ANOVA results show significant main effects for purpose ($p < .001$) and elements ($p < .001$) on PUE. Coping style's main effect was not significant. On the two significant factors, information seeking has the highest estimated marginal means of PUE ($EMM_{PUE} = 3.88$) among the four purposes, whereas among the seven elements, others' comments/reactions/tags has the highest ($EMM_{PUE} = 3.66$) – i.e., perceived as highly useful. The mixed ANOVA revealed two significant interaction effects: (a) between coping style and purpose ($p < .05$), and (b) between element and purpose ($p < .001$). Emotion- focused individuals tend to have higher $EMM_{PUE}$ than problem-focused ones, except for the information-seeking purpose. In relation to the interaction between element and purpose, elements rated high for the information-seeking tend to be rated low for the entertainment, and vice versa (Fig. 2).

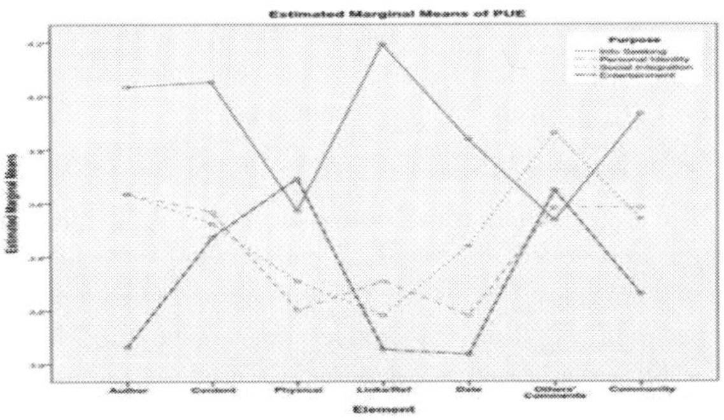

***Figure 2.** Gratification purposes and perceived usefulness of social media elements*

## DISCUSSION

The study reveals significant main and interaction effects on the usefulness of different social media elements. The significant interaction between purposes and elements suggest that users are discerning the elements they prefer when using social media for different purposes. The difference is most evident in the information-seeking vs. the entertainment situation. The practical implication is that social media designers may need to consider offering purpose-based personalization, such as placing certain elements in more prominent positions based on purposes. Another implication is that if no interaction effects had been examined, the study would have missed the nuanced findings on how the influence of coping/problem-solving style manifests in conjunction with the purpose of use. The theoretical and methodological implication of this study is that it is valuable and important to plan for extensive research designs to directly measure and test potential interactions among the user, the context and the system.

## References


Blackwell, D., Leaman, C., Tramposch, R., Osborne, C., & Liss, M. (2017). Extraversion, neuroticism, attachment style and fear of missing out as predictors of social media use and addiction. *Personality and Individual Differences, 116*, 69-72.

Correa, T., Hinsley, A. W., & de Zúñiga, H. G. (2010). Who interacts on the web? The intersection of users' personality and social media use. *Computers in Human Behavior, 26*(2), 247-253.

Head, A. J., & Eisenberg, M. (2009). Lessons learned: How college students seek information in the digital age. Retrieved from http://bit.ly/2t1yfOz

Katz, E.B., Blumler, J.G., & Gurevitch, M. (1974). Utilization of mass communication by the individual. In: Blumler, J.G. & Katz, E.B. (eds.) *The use of mass communication*. (pp. 19-32). Beverly Hills, CA: Sage.

Kim, K.-S., & Allen, B. (2002). Cognitive and task influences on web searching behavior. *Journal of the American Society for Information Science & Technology, 53*(2), 109-119.

Kim, K.-S., & Sin, S.-C. J. (2016). Use and evaluation of information from social media in the academic context: Analysis of gap between students and librarians. *Journal of Academic Librarianship, 42*(1), 74-82.

Kim, K.-S., Sin, S.-C. J., & Tsai, T.-I. (2014). Individual differences in social media use for information seeking. *Journal of Academic Librarianship, 40*(2), 171-178.

Kimbrough, A. M., Guadagno, R. E., Muscanell, N. L., & Dill, J. (2013). Gender differences in mediated communication: Women connect more than do men. *Computers in Human Behavior, 29*(3), 896-900.

Lazarus, R. S., & Folkman, S. (1984). *Stress, appraisal and coping*. New York: Springer.

Lee, C. S., & Ma, L. (2012). News sharing in social media: The effect of gratifications and prior experience. *Computers in Human Behavior, 28*(2), 331–339.

McCay-Peet, L., & Quan-Haase, A. (2016). *The influence of features and demographics on the perception of twitter as a serendipitous environment*. Paper presented at the 27th ACM Conference on Hypertext and Social Media, Halifax, Nova Scotia, Canada.

Oh, S., & Syn, S. Y. (2015). Motivations for sharing information and social support in social media: A comparative analysis of Facebook, Twitter, Delicious, YouTube, and flickr. *Journal of the Association for Information Science and Technology, 66*(10), 2045-2060.

Pew Research Center. (2016). Social media update 2016, from http://www.pewinternet.org/2016/11/11/social- media-update-2016/

Schlesinger, A., Chandrasekharan, E., Masden, C. A., Bruckman, A. S., Edwards, W. K., & Grinter, R. E. (2017). *Situated anonymity: Impacts of anonymity, ephemerality, and hyper-locality on social media*. Paper presented at the 2017 CHI Conference on Human Factors in Computing Systems, Denver, Colorado, USA.

Vakkari, P., Savolainen, R., & Dervin, B. (1997). *Information seeking in context*. London: Taylor Graham.

# Explicating the Trends of Information Literacy Studies in the Higher Education Context: A Pilot Study

**Sung Un Kim**
*Catholic University of America, USA.kimi@cua.edu*

**Yong Gu Lee**
*Keimyung University, South Korea. yonggulee@kmu.ac.kr*

## ABSTRACT

**This study aims to explicate the trends of information literacy studies in the higher education context. As a pilot study of a larger study, 1,711 articles published from January 1988 to May 2017 were selected and analyzed in terms of publication year, themes, published journals and authorship. Analysis of publications by year demonstrates four distinct periods of information literacy research with different publication patterns: development period (1988-2001), 1st proliferation period (2002-2008), maintenance (or stand-still) period (2009-2012) and 2nd proliferation period (2013-2017). Results on themes, published journals and authorship of the sample articles show not only the general patterns but also their possible association with the four periods of information literacy research. This study contributes to providing a holistic picture of information literacy research particularly in higher education.**

## KEYWORDS

information literacy, higher education, research trends

## INTRODUCTION AND BACKGROUND

As the instructional role of librarians came to be considered more important, topics about information literacy have gained more attention from researchers and practitioners. A significant amount of information literacy studies have been conducted in the higher education context due to the primary role of academic librarians in supporting research by students and faculty members. There have been efforts to systematically analyze studies about information literacy (i.e., Pinto, Cordon & Gómez Díaz, 2010); however, few have focused on the higher education context.

## PURPOSE OF THE STUDY

This study aims to explicate the trends of information literacy studies in the higher education context and to examine factors that may be associated with major patterns of publication. As a pilot study of a larger study, this article tested the data collection and analysis methods with one selected database and presented preliminary findings.

## METHODS

### *Data collection*

To collect articles to be analyzed, we selected the *Library, Information Science & Technology Abstracts* (*LISTA*) database which is one of the representative databases in the library and information science field. The following search string was applied to the title and abstract fields: "information literac*" AND ("high* education*" OR "academ* librar*" OR "research librar*" OR "college*" OR "universit*" OR "undergraduate*" OR "graduate*" OR "post-secondar*" OR "young people" OR "facult*" OR "master's" OR "doctoral" OR "ph.d."). Search results were limited to academic journals (publication type), articles (document type) and English (language). The basic metadata of the 2,008 retrieved articles were downloaded in an Excel file. We manually reviewed the titles, abstracts, journal titles and lengths of the articles to confirm whether each article met selection criteria (e.g., topic relevance, document type and language). The full-text was checked when needed. In the screening process, we eliminated 297 articles (14.79%); 193 articles were not academic papers, 73 articles were not about higher education, 22 articles were not about information literacy, 3 articles were not written in English and 6 articles were duplicates. As a result, 1,711 articles were included for analysis.

## DATA ANALYSIS

For data analysis, publication year, journal title and author information were extracted from the metadata of the 1,711 sample articles. The number of authors per article was identified and variations of author names were controlled by checking middle names, spelling errors and inversions of first names and last names. For term frequency, noun terms were extracted from the titles and abstracts using Natural Language Toolkit (NLTK). For each meaningful noun term, the number of articles which include the term in their titles or/and abstracts was counted.

## FINDINGS

The sample included 1,711 articles published from January 1988 to May 2017.

### *Publication by year*

As shown in Figure 1, the number of articles about information literacy in higher education has increased since the topic was first published in 1988. The following distinct periods were identified:

80th Annual Meeting of the Association for Information Science & Technology, Washington, DC | Oct. 27-Nov. 1, 2017

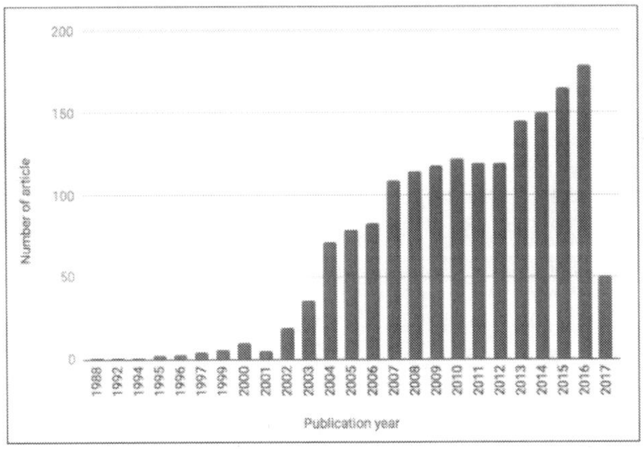


***Figure 1.*** *Number of articles by year*

- Development period (1988-2001) in which studies initiated and steadily developed
- 1st proliferation period (2002-2008) in which the number of publications rapidly grew
- Maintenance (or stand-still) period (2009-2012) in which the number of publications stood still
- 2nd proliferation period (2013-2017) in which the number of publications swiftly increased

### *Themes*

To examine the popular themes of articles and the impacts of evolving themes on the publication patterns, term frequencies in titles and abstracts were calculated. Throughout the four identified periods, *instruction* and *skill* were the two most highly ranked terms. The evolving terms during the 1st proliferation period were *course*, *learning*, *program*, *experience* and *need*. Even though the maintenance period shared the same seven top ranked terms with the 1st proliferation period, *process* and *project* were observed as evolving terms during the maintenance period. During the 2nd proliferation period, terms *development*, *need* and *assessment* moved to higher ranks compared to the maintenance period.

### *Journal distribution*

Although the 1,711 articles were published in 200 different journals, about 40% of them (n= 674) were distributed through top 10 journals. The journals in which most articles were published are *Journal of Academic Librarianship* (n=106, 6.20%), followed by *Reference Services Review* (n=103, 6.02%), *College & Undergraduate Libraries* (n=79, 4.62%), *Communications in Information Literacy* (n=71, 4.15%), *Journal of Information Literacy* (n=67, 3.92%), *Evidence Based Library & Information Practice* (n=64, 3.74%), *Journal of Library Administration* (n=51, 2.98%), *College & Research Libraries* (n=50, 2.92%), *Public Services Quarterly* (n=43, 2.51%), and *Journal of Library & Information* (n=40, 2.34%). Among these top 10 journals, six journals started during the development period, while four journals were initiated during the 1st proliferation period. The number of journals with more than one published article per each period is as follows: 19 journals during the development period, 124 journals during the 1st proliferation period, 110 journals during the maintenance period, and 122 journals during the 2nd proliferation period.

### *Authorship*

Among 1,711 articles, 768 articles (44.89%) were written by a single author, while 943 articles (55.11%) were written by co-authors. A majority of co-authored articles were written by two authors (n=610) or three authors (n=210). As shown in Figure 2, co-authored articles have been published significantly more often than single-authored articles since 2010. The significantly decreased number of single-authored articles from 2010 to 2012 may be associated with the stand-still status of publication during the maintenance period.

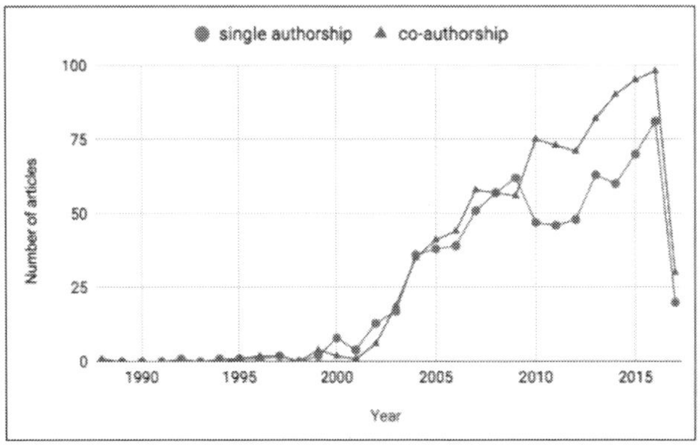


***Figure 2.*** *Authorship of articles*

Among 2,647 authors identified from the sample articles, only 362 authors (13.68%) contributed to more than one article. That is, a majority of the identified authors (86.32%) published one article.

## DISCUSSION AND CONCLUSION

This pilot study revealed the four periods of information literacy research in higher education and explored factors that might be associated with the observed publication patterns. In our poster presentation, we plan to explain the current study and also discuss with audience other applicable research methods and factors to be considered, which will be helpful for a larger study with samples from multiple databases and further analysis.

### Reference

Pinto, M., Cordon, J. A., & Gómez Díaz, R. (2010). Thirty years of information literacy (1977-2007): A terminological, conceptual and statistical analysis. *Journal of Librarianship and Information Science, 42*(1), 3-19.

# Mobile Device Use to Access Information on Well-being

**Cynthia Kumah**
*School of Information Studies, McGill University, Canada.*
*cynthia.kumah@mail.mcgill.ca*

**Jamshid Beheshti**
*School of Information Studies, McGill University, Canada.*
*jamshid.beheshti@mcgill.ca*

**Joan C. Bartlett**
*School of Information Studies, McGill University.*
*joan.bartlett@mcgill.ca*

## ABSTRACT

**The focus of this study is to identify and describe the use of mobile devices for supporting and maintaining well-being among millennials. Data collection involved semi-structured interviews of 18 undergraduate students (aged 18-24). They primarily defined their personal well-being in terms of physical health, mental health and spirituality. They used their mobile devices extensively in support of well-being, including searching for information (both text and multi-media), establishing and maintaining social connections, tracking routines (e.g., nutrition, sleep) and setting and pursuing fitness goals. Our initial findings demonstrate how mobile devices are used in support of an everyday life task such as maintaining personal well-being.**

## KEYWORDS

mobile technology, mobile information behavior, well-being

## INTRODUCTION

Mobile technology has profoundly changed the everyday-life information behavior of millennials. They are heavy users of mobiles, with 98% of 18-24 year olds owning a smartphone (Nielsen, 2016), and they are so dependent on these devices that on an average day they interact more with their smartphones than they do with other human beings (Hill, 2016). While smartphones are used for a variety of purposes, including texting and voice/video calls, access to the internet and social networks is dominant (89% and 75% respectively) (Anderson, 2015).

Yet in spite of the ubiquitous use of mobile devices, little is known about what is done with the information obtained and how mobile devices and apps are applied to supporting everyday-life tasks, particularly for well-being.

This research is part of a larger, multi-year study into the information behavior and meta-literacy of millennials (defined as those born after 1980) in the context of personal well-being. Well-being is a holistic concept, involving elements such as health, finance and social connections, among others. It is timely issue for millennials, as they are in the process of defining themselves as adults, facing for themselves factors affecting their own well-being and determining how to manage these issues on their own.

## OBJECTIVES

The overall goal of this research is to understand the role of mobile technology in accessing information on well-being. The research questions for this phase were: 1. How do millennials define their personal well-being? 2. What information do they seek to support well-being? 3. How are mobile applications used in support of personal well-being?

## LITERATURE REVIEW

Research into mobile information behavior research found that intent centered on informational needs, personal information management needs and geographical needs (Church & Smyth, 2009). Social interaction also influenced mobile information behavior (Absar, O'Brien & Webster, 2014). Other research has focused on the impact of mobile computing on library services (Peterson & Low, 2011) Findings show that since mobile devices have the capability to transform library services, libraries were advised to investigate ways to take advantage of the technology. In addition, students were interested in using their mobile devices for academic purposes (e.g., Cummings, Merrill & Borrelli, 2010). A study by Karnowski & Jandura (2014) identified three main situations within which mobile communication occurs such as at home, en route and among peers; the unexpected findings of their study was the use of mobile devices to go online while at home where a PC or a laptop was available. This suggests a gradual shift to mobile devices for information search. However, not much research has been done on mobile device usage in achieving well-being. Conceptually, this study is grounded in Wilson's (1997) model of information behavior, as it considers not only information need, seeking and use, but also the various intervening factors that influence decisions to seek or use information.

## METHODS

Participants in this first phase of the study were 18 (12 female, six male) undergraduate students, aged 18-24. We used semi-structured interviews to explore mobile information behavior in the context of well-being. Participants answered questions about how they defined their personal well-being, how they achieve or maintain it and the kind of information they search for. They also discussed how mobile devices are used to find information, when and how devices are used and what type of applications (apps) they use to help achieve or

80th Annual Meeting of the Association for Information Science & Technology, Washington, DC | Oct. 27-Nov. 1, 2017

maintain their well-being. Interviews were audio-recorded and transcribed; we used emergent coding to identify themes from the data.

## RESULTS

Millennials consider a wide range of factors to be involved in their well-being; physical health, mental health and spirituality/faith were the three elements most discussed by participants. Physical health included things such as fitness, nutrition and sleeping well. Mental health involved managing stress, pursuing non-academic interests and maintaining a state of contentment. It also involved cultivating positive social relationships. Prayer and meditation were considered important for spirituality.

The most common search topics included recipes, restaurants, maps, healthy living and fitness. Some preferred textual information, while others preferred video formats (e.g., YouTube) where they could watch and listen.

Searching on mobile devices was mostly done immediately, as soon as a need for information arose. Sometimes searching might be delayed due to the intensity of the topic. Participant 2 said: "*I search for things on my phone when I know that I don't have to do extensive typing so I can get quick answer. If I know that I have to do a lot of typing; I type super slow . . . I use my computer*". When searching on mobile devices, participants reported viewing a few pages, depending on which search engine they are using, "*. . . depends where I am searching - if scrolling there is no way to know, if Google 2 or 3 pages*" (P4).

In addition to searching, participants reported a variety of other uses of their mobile devices in support of their well-being. Physical well-being apps typically related to fitness and nutrition including tracking activities such as running, monitoring nutrition and monitoring their sleep cycle. Psychological well-being was supported by scheduling activities using calendar (thus avoiding stress), playing games, streaming videos, watching TV and reading on devices. Social well-being was supported through staying connected with family and friends through texting, live chatting, video chatting; social media apps were used to stay connected to one's social network or to acquire and disseminate information, "*I think Facebook and messengers, also the app I use to listen to music, email, I also play some games when I'm bored. I try to use the fitness app every day, also sometimes I read e-books*" (P7). Spiritual well-being involved meditation, reading religious materials, speaking to people from the same religious group.

## CONCLUSIONS

The results of our research show that millennials consider the elements of physical health, mental health and spirituality as important aspects of their personal well-being. They report a range of activities used to maintain and support their well-being, with a corresponding set of information needs. They use their mobile devices extensively, both to search for information and to use specific apps in support of their well-being.


## ACKNOWLEDGMENTS

This research is funded by SSHRC (Social Science and Humanities Research Council – Canada) Insight Grant 435-2016-1326 to the third author. We would like to thank the anonymous interview participants for their valuable contributions. We would also like to acknowledge Anna Couch for assisting in recruiting participants for the study.


## REFERENCES


Absar, R., O'Brien, H., & Webster, E. T. (2014). Exploring social context in mobile information behavior. Proceedings of the American Society for Information Science and Technology, 51(1), 1-10.

Anderson, M. (2015, April 1). 6 facts about Americans and their smartphones. Retrieved from http://www.pewresearch.org/fact-tank/2015/04/01/6-facts-about-americans-and-their-smartphones/

Church, K., & Smyth, B. (2009). Understanding the intent behind mobile information needs. Proceedings of the 14th international conference on intelligent user interfaces (pp. 247-256).

Cummings, J., Merrill, A., & Borrelli, S. (2010). The use of handheld mobile devices: Their impact and implications for library service. Library Hi Tech, 28 (1), 22-40.

Hill, C. (2016, June 21). Millennials engage with their smartphones more than they do actual humans. Retrieved from http://www.marketwatch.com/story/millennials-engage-with-their-smartphones-more-than-they-do-actual-humans-2016-06-21

Karnowski, V., & Jandura, O. (2014). When lifestyle becomes behavior: A closer look at the situational context of mobile communication. Telematics and Informatics, 31(2), 184-193. doi:10.1016/j.tele.2013.11.001

Nielsen. (2016, November 15). Millennials are top smartphone users. Retrieved from http://www.nielsen.com/us/en/insights/news/2016/millennials-are-top-smartphone-users.html

Paterson, L., & Low, B. (2011). Student attitudes towards mobile library services for smartphones. Library Hi Tech, 29(3), 412-423. doi:10.1108/07378831111174387

Reis, S., Church, K., & Oliver, N. (2012). Rethinking mobile search: Towards casual, shared, social mobile search experience. Proceedings of the Searching 4 Fun Workshop, Barcelona, Spain, April 1, 2012.

Wilson, T. (1997). Information behaviour: An interdisciplinary perspective. Information Processing & Management, 33(4), 551-572.

Yarmey, K. (2011). Student information literacy in the mobile environment. Educause Quarterly, 34(1). doi:10.1201/b19843-7.

# Skills for Research Data Management – Developing RDM Courses at the University of Oslo

**Live Kvale**
*University of Oslo, Norway. live.kvale@hioa.no*

**Elin Stangeland**
*Oslo and Akershus University College of Applied Sciences, Norway. elin.stangeland@ub.uio.no*

## ABSTRACT

**How can the library contribute to developing research data services by focusing on training? This poster presents experiences and best practices with organizing research data management (RDM) training through the University of Oslo Library. The work is based on recommendations from the report "The Data Explosion – A Great Challenge and a Big Opportunity" that mapped existing data practices at the University of Oslo (UiO) (Working group storing and sharing of research data UiO, 2015). Based on these recommendations, a division of labor among the research support services at the university was decided upon and the university library (UL) was tasked with developing courses and training for better data practices. By establishing contact with existing initiatives, inviting in experts and holding meetings for library staff to create ownership and interest in the subject the library now has a portfolio of courses in data practices and data management that is constantly expanding.**

## KEYWORDS

research data management, digital skills, RDM skills

## INTRODUCTION

The amount of digital data currently produced in research, combined with incentives for open science, is challenging researchers to share their research data. Requirements for data management plans are introduced through Horizon 2020 the EU Framework Program for Research and Innovation (European Commission, 2016). Journals and disciplinary research environments are making clearer requirements for research data. Simultaneously, the Research Council of Norway published a policy for open research data (Forskningsrådet, 2014) and is funding a program for building infrastructure for making research data available. These are all examples of new external requirements the researchers meet. There is however a digital divide in how research is conducted, often referred to as the fourth paradigm (Hey, Tansley & Tolle, 2009, p. xx). Today's researchers are expected to use digital tools in their research. In order to be able to share digital data, researchers also need to have digital expertise and skills to create shareable data; version control is one of several aspects in data intensive research essential for data sharing. Courses and workshops aim to make researchers familiar with the possibilities of digital tools and how they can take control of their data by planning how, what and if they want to share at an early stage. The requirements for data sharing do not only affect researchers, but also people in surrounding positions. As a result, our course portfolio also targets master students, research support services and librarians.

The skills development program for RDM at UiO has been part of a larger RDM project. In 2015 a report (Working group storing and sharing of research data UiO, 2015) based on a broad study of available solutions and problem areas regarding RDM among all institutes at the university was published. Current service provision was reviewed and recommendations for policy, technical services and training were made. A cross-departmental RDM group was established to follow up the recommendations from the report with members from the university center for information technology (USIT), department of academic administration (AA) and university library (UL). Key activities for the RDM group included conducting scoping work for storage of active data with an aim to implement improved services for the university's researchers, managed by USIT; development of a skills development program for stakeholders within the institution, covering researchers, students, research support staff and colleagues within the library, managed by the UL; establishment if a website providing university staff and students information regarding RDM and current university services available to them, managed by AA. In addition to the work listed above the team is also following up on the recommendation for policy and focusing on outreach and dialog trough presentations and collaborations at a national level.

## THE UIO RDM-SKILLS DEVELOPMENT PROGRAM

For the skills development program, the university library is building a portfolio of training modules addressing the various university stakeholders. We are covering quite a few groups in order to ensure that skills improve across the organization. Ensuring familiarity with concepts and requirements is crucial in order for the information flow to function. Correcting misunderstandings before they occur through training and creating one point of contact for all questions regarding RDM within the university follows up recommendations made by the report (Working group storing and sharing of research data UiO, 2015). The aim is to facilitate a culture change regarding how data is viewed, used and shared. The

80th Annual Meeting of the Association for Information Science & Technology, Washington, DC | Oct. 27-Nov. 1, 2017

training modules are tailored to the needs of the particular groups, and designed for re-use.

### Researchers and PhDs

Researchers and PhD students need good digital skills in order to manage their data well. For the purpose of the project, we therefore collaborate and expand on existing UiO initiatives providing software carpentry and data carpentry training sessions for researchers. The aim of software carpentry is to help scientists and engineers work more efficiently, as described by Wilson (2014): "Setting aside the minority who do high-performance computing, the time it takes the desktop majority of scientists to produce a new result is frequently dominated by how long it takes to write, test, debug, install and maintain software." Carpentry workshops are facilitated by UL staff, with instructors primarily from the research community. Alongside the carpentry modules[1], we are adding training in RDM aspects, based on the DC101 course[2] provided by the Digital Curation Centre. Colleagues in the UL will continue providing these over time, and we are working on adapting the content of the course to the carpentry methodology with its focus on few lectures and many hands-on exercises making the researchers hands-on familiar with available tools and platforms.

Further portfolio expansions are constantly under discussion and limited only by own capacity. Author carpentry and other modules taught last year at the 2016 CODATA-RDA School of Research Data Science[3] are some options for expansion. Requests from the digital humanities have however made this community a priority as we see that the courses provided through software carpentry in many cases are too advanced or not tailored for the needs of digital humanists and are seen to be more suitable for the sciences. As a response to this a data carpentry course for digital humanities is under development and will be ready for piloting in 2018.

For researchers who in addition to conducting research also manage projects funded by either the Norwegian Research Council or the EU, an introduction to administrative aspects relating to application writing and data management plans (DMPs) is offered on demand.

### Research Support Staff

Research support staff are offered courses on data management plans from an administrative perspective. These courses focus specifically on the H2020 requirements and DMP-online[4] as a tool for writing a data management plan using the embedded H2020 guidelines. Further, the participants are given an introduction to metadata and an overview of RDM services and resources available to researchers at UiO.

### Master Students

For UiO master students we have developed a tailored course loosely based on the DataOne education modules[5]. In collaboration with colleagues at the university library, these are adapted to align with disciplines. There will be three pilots targeting master students within medicine, geology and anthropology. The plan is to evaluate and expand the courses in 2018, based on the experiences obtained from the pilots.

### Librarians

Library staff have been offered library carpentry courses, and these have been extremely popular and we are happy to see that librarians are eager to develop new skills and learn to use digital tools to improve their daily workflow. Alongside the carpentry workshop, further meetings are arranged for all library staff. These introduce RDM and national repository services in order for the library staff to have some familiarity, knowledge and ownership to the subject. These meetings have also formed the basis for selecting pilots for the master courses, where interest from the subject specialist in the library has been one criterion.

### Sharing with the Community

The courses are open to researchers, research support staff and librarians outside of our organization. Having these courses open is one way of sharing and inspiring others to adapt or develop similar training. In particular, software carpentry being a bottom-up initiative depends on local researchers initiating and organizing courses. Training for administrative staff can also easily be transferred to other institutions; we hope that by inviting colleagues to our own courses we can facilitate an environment for collaboration on RDM training. Material developed or adapted for the courses are shared, and members of the project team are both presenting experiences at national meetings and conferences and attending meetings on other institutions on request.

### Raising Awareness Through Events

Both in 2016 and 2017 we have organized events over multiple days focusing on research data skills. In March 2016, we held Carpentry Week[6], including an open science mini-seminar and a number of carpentry workshops. In February 2017, UiO was a Research Bazaar[7] venue, as the first one in Europe. Seminars, stands, workshops and a satellite event of the Women in Data Science (WiDS) conference[8] were on the program. The Research Bazaar is a worldwide festival promoting the digital literacy emerging at the center of modern research. Both Carpentry Week and Research Bazaar bring people together and raise awareness towards the challenges and potential researchers face with new tools and require-

---

[1] http://www.uio.no/carpentry
[2] http://www.dcc.ac.uk/training/train-the-trainer/dc-101-training-materials
[3] http://indico.ictp.it/event/7658/other-view?view=ictptimetable
[4] https://dmponline.dcc.ac.uk/
[5] https://www.dataone.org/education-modules
[6] https://www.ub.uio.no/english/courses-events/events/ureal/2016/160314carpentryweek.html
[7] https://2017.resbaz.com/
[8] http://www.widsconference.org/

ments. By inviting speakers and collaborating with others interested in data management our network is expanding. We believe that events like these make UiO activities more visible and help raising awareness to a larger part of the research community than the workshop attendees.

### Seminars

In addition to the workshops and courses, a seminar has been central in both events organized. For the 2016 Carpentry Week, policymakers and central people in software carpentry were invited to speak. For the Research Bazaar in 2017 the seminar focused on digital tools, and colleagues responsible for various data storage and repository solutions were among the invited presenters. Both years the presentations were filmed and made available on YouTube[9].

### Next Steps

Piloting and testing has until now been the focus. There is, however, a need to establish more permanent frames for the skills for RDM course portfolio. Many of the courses are held on a voluntary basis; proper rewarding of volunteers and recruitment of new ones is one challenge. As of now, the courses are not giving credits; whether it is a goal to have credit giving courses that are more formally implemented in the course/credit system at the university is one important discussion. In addition, to formalize and take the training program to a next step, developing new courses based on requests and needs is a constant process. We are expecting new guidelines for RDM to be introduced within the coming year both at the institutional level and from the Research Council of Norway. This will be a challenge for us, as the course organizers will have to be one step ahead of the development of policy and requirements for research data in order to keep the courses relevant for the UiO research community.

### Conclusion

Adapting and learning new skills is crucial for the modern researcher. Today we use tools that were not available 10 years ago, and 10 years from now researchers are likely to use tools and techniques that we have not yet thought of. These changes can be called new paradigms as they represent new ways of thinking and directly affect how research is conducted. Independent of what label and what paradigm the different researchers commit to, being able to make informed decisions and reflect around this development is crucial. There are many misconceptions about data sharing and open data. By providing courses, for researchers, students and research support services we hope to contribute to improved knowledge about data sharing. Measuring the effects of training and potentially improved knowledge is hard, but both the feedback and the attendance to the courses we run at UiO encourage us to continue on this track. We believe that the university library is a knowledge hub in a knowledge institution and that we have an important role to play in organizing and facilitating courses that focus on the generic skills for researchers.

## ACKNOWLEDGMENTS

Our work builds on collaboration. Thanks to the rest of the RDM group – Margaret Fotland, Kristin Flagstad and Gard Thommassen and the software carpentry initiative at UiO with Lex Nederbragt as the primus motor.

## REFERENCES

European Commission. (2016, August 25). H2020 Programme - Guidelines on Open Access to Scientific Publications and Research Data in Horizon 2020. European Commission.

Forskningsrådet. (2014). Tilgjengeliggjøring av forskningsdata - policy for Norges Forskningsråd. Norges forskningsråd.

Hey, T., Tansley, S., & Tolle, K. (Eds.). (2009). *The fourth paradigm: Data-intensive scientific discovery* (1st edition). Redmond, Washington: Microsoft Research.

Wilson G. Software carpentry: Lessons learned [version 1; referees: 3 approved]. F1000Research 2014, 3:62 (doi: 10.12688/f1000research.3-62.v1)

Working group storing and sharing of research data UiO. (2015). The data explosion – a major challenge, and a great opportunity! Oslo: University of Oslo. http://www.uio.no/english/for-employees/support/research/research-data/engelskversjonrapport.pdf.

[9] http://tinyurl.com/yctr5ftq

# The Ethics of Contemporary Readers' Advisory

**Emily Lawrence**
*School of Information Sciences, University of Illinois, Urbana-Champaign, USA. elawrnc2@illinois.edu*

## ABSTRACT

**Readers' advisory (RA) is a library service dedicated to suggesting leisure reading materials to patrons. Through a critical examination of popular RA textbooks, this poster (1) identifies core moral principles underpinning RA and (2) demonstrates that contemporary RA follows (what I am calling) a *pure preference satisfaction model* wherein readers' advisors aim to satisfy patrons' preferences without judging or altering them. On the common view, RA functions as a kind of nonjudgmental "matchmaking service," pairing leisure readers with books they are likely to enjoy. While such an approach to RA is politically commendable in some respects, this poster will show that it places overly rigid restrictions on efforts to undermine social inequality through the promotion of diverse books.**

## KEYWORDS

readers' advisory, professional ethics, social justice, diverse books, neutrality

## INTRODUCTION

Identifying fundamental moral principles is a crucial first step in any project that aims to engage in a considered ethical analysis of readers' advisory (RA), the service dedicated to recommending leisure reading to library patrons. To that end, this poster adopts a principle-based approach to the ethics of contemporary RA. It does so in service of essential groundclearing: in order to engage in a moral analysis of the service, we must first get clear on RA's self-proclaimed goals and constraints.

This propaedeutic project is necessary because contemporary RA has so rarely been the object of sustained normative inquiry. One might object that even if this is the case, any number of accomplished thinkers in LIS have written extensively about the philosophy of librarianship more generally (see e.g., Foskett, 1962; Hauptman, 1976, 2002; Gorman, 2000; Preer, 2008). However, the library ethics literature largely privileges the informational function of the public library, focusing on moral considerations relevant to information access and dissemination while omitting any substantive discussion of the library's leisure function. In other words, much of the state-of-the-art in library ethics has effectively adopted what Chelton (1999, 42) calls an "exclusionary rhetoric of information." RA – as a service concerned primarily with promoting aesthetic reading – does not fit neatly into the prevailing moral discourse. This is not to say that RA shares none of the profession's overarching moral commitments, but rather that one ought to not presume some perfect degree of overlap at the outset. To do so would be, potentially, to obfuscate sites of tension within librarianship.

Thus, rather than endeavoring to locate RA's moral principles in the existing library ethics literature, I turn to the work of influential RA scholars and practitioners. More specifically, I examine several publications that have been used as textbooks in RA courses for MLS students. These include the flagship *Genreflecting* series (1982-2013), Saricks's (2005) *Readers' Advisory Service in the Public Library*, Shearer & Burgin's (2001) *The Readers' Advisor's Companion,* and Ross, McKechnie & Rothbauer's (2006) *Reading Matters.* These textbooks enculturate students into the RA community of practice. This makes them an ideal place to look for foundational principles, many of which will have moral purport.

In this proposal, I explain the moral methods that guide the identification of RA's ethical framework. I continue on to give a brief account of that framework, which includes three core principles that foreground the value of autonomy, egalitarianism and reading. I go on to argue that, taken together, these principles give rise to two significant theoretical corollaries: a secondary principle of neutrality and a pure preference satisfaction model for recommendation. I conclude by illustrating how RA (as it is currently theorized) places overly rigid restrictions on efforts to undermine social inequality through the promotion of diverse books.

## METHODS

This poster is a work of library ethics. Library ethics is itself a species of *practical ethics*, a term generally referring to the contextual application of moral theories – be they deontological, consequentialist, virtue-based or pluralist – to particular practical domains. Ethicists working in this area ask what is right or good in some specific situation and marshal tools from normative ethics to develop an answer. (Here, I mean "right or good" in a specifically moral sense, rather than a prudential, aesthetic or juridical one.)

A principle-based approach to practical ethics is one in which we appeal to some specific principle or principles in order to determine the correct course of action. Principle-based approaches are quite varied, though they must minimally "hold that general moral action guides are central to moral reasoning" (Childress 2007, 17). In the following section, I flesh out a framework of three ethical principles (i.e., moral action guides) underpinning contemporary RA. As the poster itself

80th Annual Meeting of the Association for Information Science & Technology, Washington, DC | Oct. 27-Nov. 1, 2017

will show, RA textbook authors appeal to these principles both directly and indirectly.

## PRINCIPLE-BASED FRAMEWORK

The following three-principle framework guides the practice of contemporary RA.

### *1. Respect for Autonomy*

Respect for autonomy is "a norm of respecting decision-making capacities of autonomous persons" (Beauchamp & Childress 2001). In the narrower RA context, it is a norm of *respecting the patrons' right to self-determination vis-à-vis their reading*. This entails opposition to paternalism, or "interference with a person's liberty of action justified by reasons referring exclusively to the welfare...of the person being coerced" (Dworkin 1972, 65). Whereas earlier approaches to leisure reading in the library aimed to set patrons on a rigorous course of self-improvement (Kimball 2006, 16), contemporary RA is fiercely anti-paternalist in its defense of the patron's right to determine their own reading interests and purposes.

### *2. A Commitment to Egalitarianism*

Although egalitarian doctrines can take a number of different forms, they "tend to rest on a background idea that all human persons are equal in fundamental worth or moral status" (Arneson 2013). At its most general, egalitarianism typically refers to some principle of equality between persons. In contemporary RA, that principle encompasses *a group of norms for treating all readers as equals and guarding against the undue influence of culturally elite tastes*. It can be roughly characterized as an anti-elitist commitment to the idea that all readers and their tastes are "equal in fundamental worth."

### *3. "Reading is Good"*

Contemporary RA takes as one of its central tenets that reading is good. Put another way, *reading – as an activity – has some non-trivial value,* although there is not universal agreement on the precise nature of that value. It may have intrinsic and/or extrinsic value, where "the distinction [is] between things which have their value in themselves and things which derive their value from some other source," respectively (Korsgaard 1983, 170). What is clear is that scholars and practitioners of RA think that reading has some value that makes it worthy of active promotion.

## THEORETICAL COROLLARIES

Taken together, the three principles outlined in the previous section generate (at least) two important theoretical corollaries: a pure preference satisfaction model for RA and a neutrality constraint. I offer fuller accounts of each below.

### *Pure Preference Satisfaction Model*

The three-principle framework gives rise to a particular model of recommendation. I have termed this the pure preference satisfaction model (PPSM) as it calls on readers' advisors to satisfy patrons' existing reading preferences without judging or altering them.

The PPSM is a direct manifestation of the three moral principles outlined in the previous section. Because we ought to treat readers as autonomous individuals with tastes that are beyond reproach, and because we have an ethical duty to promote the good (in this case, the act of reading), readers' advisors must aim to recommend to a reader only those books the advisor has good reason to believe will satisfy the reader's current preferences. Readers' advisors cannot seek to change the character of those preferences (that is, to elevate the reader's tastes) as this would violate both the autonomy and egalitarianism principles. Moreover, recommendation efforts should be geared towards promoting reading as an activity rather than particular (or particular sorts of) books.

### *Neutrality Constraint*

Together, principles (1) and (2) give rise to a secondary principle of neutrality – or, put another way, a liberal neutrality constraint for RA. Just as it is often argued that the democratic state should "remain neutral with respect to reasonable conceptions of the good life" (Husak 2000, 97), the present-day readers' advisor, by virtue of other commitments, *must remain neutral with respect to diverse conceptions of the aesthetic good*. This entails treating all reading tastes with equal respect.

## SOCIAL JUSTICE CRITIQUE

In this poster, I aim to show that, given its ethics, contemporary RA can endorse only the most mild-mannered of diversity initiatives: those that yoke the promotion of diverse books (i.e., those that feature characters from historically underrepresented populations) to patron demand. RA cannot (in a normative sense) consistently support recommendation criteria designed to, for example, increase readers' empathic capacity or improve cultural competence when the reader has not herself independently adopted these criteria. To do so would be to violate principles one and two of RA's moral framework. Thus, RA cannot endorse recommendation practices that seek to raise patrons' consciousness, except in instances where patrons are explicitly in search of such consciousness-raising experiences. I hold that this limits the political potential of RA and potentially brings the service-as-theorized into conflict with our professed commitments to social responsibility and the public good (see ALA 2004).

## CONCLUSION

Through the identification of RA's ethical framework and its significant theoretical corollaries, this poster will provide a jumping-off point for varied normative critiques of contemporary RA service. This work also represents the early part of a larger project arguing that, in light of critiques like the one above, a pure preference satisfaction model is neither workable nor desirable. Ultimately, I hold that a more promising recommendation model would seek not just to promote reading simpliciter but reading for democratic citizenship.

## ACKNOWLEDGMENTS

The author would like to thank two anonymous reviewers for their feedback on an earlier draft of this proposal.

## REFERENCES


American Library Association. (2004). Core values of librarianship. Retrieved August 8, 2017 from http://www.ala.org/advocacy/intfreedom/corevalues.

Arneson, R. (2013). Egalitarianism. In E. Zalta (Ed.), *The Stanford encyclopedia of philosophy*. Retrieved June 22, 2017 from https://plato.stanford.edu/archives/sum2013/entries/egalitarianism.

Beauchamp, T., & Childress, J. (2001). *Principles of biomedical ethics.* Oxford: Oxford University Press.

Chelton, M. (1999.) What we know and don't know about reading, readers, and readers' advisory services. *Public Libraries 38*(1), 42-47.

Childress, J. (2007). Methods in bioethics. In B. Steinbock (Ed.), *The Oxford handbook of bioethics* (pp. 15-45). Oxford: Oxford University Press.

Dworkin, G. (1972). Paternalism. *The Monist 56,* 64-84.

Foskett, D. (1962). The creed of a librarian: No politics, no religion, no morals. London: Library Association.

Gorman, M. (2000). *Our enduring values: Librarianship in the 21st century.* Chicago: American Library Association.

Hauptman, R. (1976.) Professionalism or culpability: An experiment in ethics. *Wilson Library Bulletin 50*(8), 626-627.

—. (2002). *Ethics and librarianship.* Jefferson, NC: McFarland & Company, Inc.

Husak, D. (2000). Liberal neutrality, autonomy, and drug prohibitions. *Philosophy & Public Affairs 29*(1), 43-80.

Kimball, M. (2006). A brief history of readers' advisory. In D. Herald (Ed.), *Genreflecting* (pp. 15-24). Westport: Libraries Unlimited.

Korsgaard, C. (1983). Two distinctions in goodness. *Philosophical Review 92*(2), 169-195.

Preer, J. (2008.) *Library ethics.* Westport, CT: Libraries Unlimited.

Ross, C., McKechnie, L., & Rothbauer, P. (2006). Reading matters: What the research reveals about reading, libraries, and community. Westport: Libraries Unlimited.

Saricks, J. (2005). Readers' advisory service in the public library: Third edition. Chicago: ALA.

Shearer, K. & Burgin, R. (2001). *The readers' advisor's companion.* Englewood: Libraries Unlimited.

# Practices of Metadata Use in Research Information Management Systems

**Dong Joon Lee**
*Texas A&M University USA. djlee@tamu.edu*

**Besiki Stvilia**
*Florida State University, USA. bstvilia@fsu.edu*

**Shuheng Wu**
*Queens College, The City University of New York, USA. Shuheng.Wu@qc.cuny.edu*

## ABSTRACT

**This poster reports on a study that examines the practices of metadata use in a research information management (RIM) system ResearchGate. Understanding these practices can help institutional repositories to better align their RIM metadata models with researchers' needs and priorities. The study identified three categories of RIM system users. The study's preliminary findings suggest that community members are more willing to share their personal information and provide full-texts of their works on ResearchGate compared to readers and personal record managers.**

## KEYWORDS

research information management, metadata, ResearchGate, institutional repositories

## INTRODUCTION

Many institutions actively develop and implement their local research information management (RIM) systems for various purposes. RIM systems support various stakeholder groups, including researchers, funders, university administrators, librarians and aggregators (Smith-Yoshimura et al., 2014; Wu, Stvilia & Lee, 2016). Each of these groups can use RIM metadata for different purposes and assign different levels of importance in different activities. Thus, to facilitate research identity data use and to engage researchers in its curation, it is important to identify the stakeholders' value structures and priorities for different research identity data elements and align RIM data structures and quality assurance activities with those priorities. The purpose of this study was to examine researchers' practices of using metadata elements in RIM systems. The findings can be used to develop a value model of RIM metadata elements (Stvilia & Gasser, 2008), which can help institutional repositories to better align their RIM metadata models with researchers' needs and priorities.

## METHODOLOGY

This poster reports on part of a larger study, which examined researchers' use of and engagement with RIM systems. The study's design included 15 qualitative semi-structured interviews and a survey completed by 412 researchers representing 80 universities in the United States classified as high research universities in the Carnegie Classification of Institutions of Higher Education. Detailed reports of findings from the interviews and survey can be found elsewhere (Wu, Stvilia & Lee, 2017). The findings of this poster were based on a content analysis on metadata elements of ResearchGate and an empirical analysis where the authors analyzed the use of metadata elements in the ResearchGate profiles of 126 researchers (see Figure 1), sampled from the survey participants. Based on their participation levels in ResearchGate, the sample consists of 26 readers, 50 personal record managers and 50 community members. One of the authors manually examined ResearchGate to assemble an aggregate set of metadata elements provided there. This study addressed the following research questions: (1) What metadata elements does ResearchGate provide to support researchers' activities? (2) What metadata elements do researchers use in their ResearchGate profiles?

## FINDINGS

The analysis of ResearchGate's metadata elements produced an aggregated set of user-editable metadata elements typified by nine different categories representing researchers' academic-related activities (see Figure 3). To answer the second research question, the authors examined 126 researchers' ResearchGate profiles from the sample. Figure 2-A presents the frequencies of uses of metadata categories in the sample. Most researchers' ResearchGate profiles used at least one element from the categories of *person*, *publication* and *research subject*. Since almost all researchers' profiles used metadata elements from the *person, publication* and *research subject* categories, the authors next investigated the use of individual elements within these categories. Figure 2-B summarizes the uses of specific metadata elements from the *person* category. More than 90% of the community members' profiles included *first name*, *last name*, *affiliation*, *department*, *photo* and *position*. This indicates that they are more willing to share their personal information than readers and personal record managers. All of the elements from the *publication* category were highly used except that *file* was occasionally used by readers (see Figure 2-C). This indicates that compared to readers, community members and personal record managers are more willing to provide full texts of their works (downloadable files) on ResearchGate. Similarly,

---

80th Annual Meeting of the Association for Information Science & Technology, Washington, DC | Oct. 27-Nov. 1, 2017

community members are more likely to share their disciplines, research topics, and skills and expertise on ResearchGate (see Figure 2-D).

| Participation Levels | Freq. |
|---|---|
| **Readers.** They may or may not have a profile in a RIM system, but do not maintain the profile if they have one and do not interact with other members of the system or contribute to the system. | 26 |
| **Personal Record Managers.** They maintain their profiles in a RIM system, but do not contribute to the system beyond that and do not interact with other members of that system directly or indirectly. | 50 |
| **Community Members.** They not only maintain their own profiles, but also are willing to engage in curating the research information of other members by endorsing them for skills, or share their knowledge and information via messages, emails, or Q&A forums. | 50 |

***Figure 1.*** *Distribution of the sample by participation level*

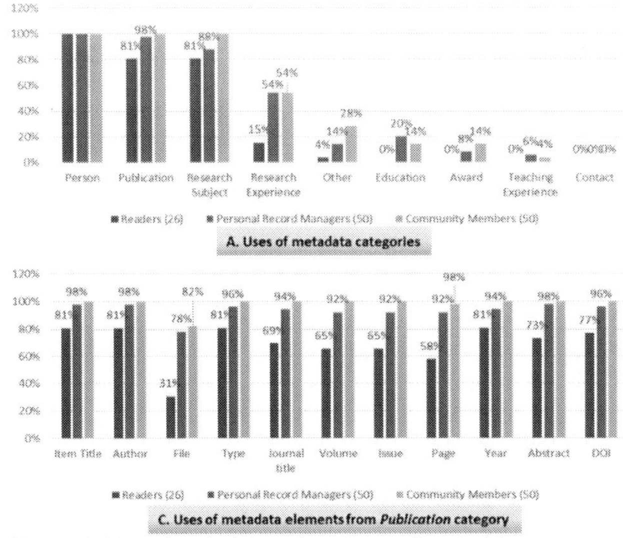


***Figure 2.*** *Use of metadata categories and metadata elements from different categories*

| Categories | Metadata Elements |
|---|---|
| **Person** | First name, Middle name, Last name, Alternative first name, Alternative middle name, Alternative last name, Degree, Institution, Department, Position, Time period, Gender, Email address, Profile photo, Time zone, About |
| **Publication** | Publication title, Author, File, Type (i.e., book, chapter, code, conference paper, method, patent, poster, proposal, technical report, thesis, working paper), Journal referee, Volume, Issue, Page, Day, Month, Year, Topic, Abstract, DOI, Publisher, Editor, Edition, ISBN, Chapter, Book title, Description, Language(s), Repository link, License, Ref. Number, Ordinal, Grant number, Report number, Supervisor, Degree, Version number, State |
| **Research subject** | Topic, Skills & Expertise, Discipline |
| **Research experience** | Position, Institution, Department, Research group, Time period, Location, Description |
| **Teaching experience** | Position, Institution, Department, Time period, Location, Description |
| **Education** | Institution, Field of study, Degree, Time period, Location |
| **Award** | Type (i.e., award, grant, scholarship), Title, Start date, End date, Amount, Funding agency, Grant reference, Principal investigator, Research institution, Co-investigator, Secondary institution |
| **Contact** | Location, Website, Phone, Mobile, Fax, Twitter, Skype, Instant messenger, Birthday, |
| **Other** | Language(s), Scientific society, Journal referee, Other interest, ORCID |

***Figure 3.*** *User-editable metadata categories and elements used in ResearchGate*

## CONCLUSION AND FUTURE RESEARCH

This poster presents researchers' use of metadata elements in a RIM system. The findings can be used to develop a value model of metadata elements for RIM. Future research will conduct interviews with researchers to learn about their motivations for using specific metadata elements in RIM systems and their perceived values of those elements.

## ACKNOWLEDGMENTS

This research is supported by an OCLC/ALISE Library and Information Research Grant for 2016 and a National Leadership Grant from the IMLS of the U.S. Government (grant # LG-73-16-0006-16).

## REFERENCES

Smith-Yoshimura, K., Altman, M., Conlon, M., Cristán, A. L., Dawson, L., Dunham, J., ... Woutersen, S. (2014). Registering researchers in authority files. Dublin, Ohio: OCLC Research.

Stvilia, B., Gasser, L. (2008). Value based metadata quality assessment. *Library & Information Science Research, 30*(1), 67-74.

Wu, S., Stvilia, B., & **Lee, D. J.** (2016). Exploring researchers' participation in online research identity management systems. In *Proceedings of the ASIS&T*. Copenhagen, Denmark, 53(1), 1-6.

Wu, S., Stvilia, B., & **Lee, D. J.** (2017). Readers, personal record managers, and community members: An exploratory study of researchers' participation in online research information management systems. *Journal of Library Metadata, 17*(2), 1-34.

# The Informatics Lifecourse: Studying the Experiences of Older Adults Learning Technology in Senior Centers

**Noah Lenstra**
*Department of Library and Information Studies, University of North Carolina at Greensboro, USA. njlenstr@uncg.edu*

## ABSTRACT

**The Pew Research Center (2017) estimates that nearly 75% of Americans aged 65 and older self-identify as needing help from another person to learn to use new digital technology. Past research suggests that technology training programs in senior centers and other community-based institutions can provide crucial supplements to the technology help older adults find within their networks of family and friends (e.g., Gardner, Kambill & Netherland, 2012; Hardill, 2014; McKee & Blair, 2006; Xie & Jaeger, 2008). Nonetheless, few studies have examined how or why technology support services in these institutions facilitate the process of learning technology among older adults. This poster presents the findings from an ethnographic, year-long study of the experiences of older adults endeavoring to learn technology in three senior centers in a medium-sized Midwestern American urban area. The overall finding from this investigation is that digital learning proceeds through what this study calls the *informatics lifecourse*: how a person learns technology throughout the stages of his or her life.**

## KEYWORDS

older adults, digital literacy, community informatics

## INTRODUCTION

Generally funded by municipal governments, senior centers emerged in local communities throughout the United States after World War II (Beisgen & Kraitchman, 2003). The National Council on Aging (2015) estimates that one million older adults participate daily in the 11,000 senior centers currently open in the United States. This number is only about two percent of the 46 million older adults aged 65 and older currently living in the United States (U.S. Census Bureau, 2016). Nonetheless, for many older adults, senior centers operate as "the one community institution that our independent elderly can identify as theirs" (Beisgen & Kraitchman, 2003). Recent research has shown that alongside other community-based institutions (e.g., public libraries), senior centers provide safe, supportive spaces for older adults seeking to learn technology (Gardner, Kamber & Netherland, 2012; McKee & Blair, 2006).

This poster presentation presents findings from a year-long ethnographic study of older adults seeking and sometimes succeeding to learn digital technologies in three senior centers located in a medium-sized Midwestern American urban area. Using stories from participants, pictures and models of the spaces, and of learning interactions that took place within them, this poster will explain some of the challenges and opportunities associated with studying the experiences of older adults learning technology in community centers. In addition, the poster presents a new concept articulated in this study, the *informatics lifecourse*. Referring to how a person learns technology throughout the stages of his or her life, this concept advances our understanding of the learning of digital literacy among older adults and in general.

## METHODS AND LIMITATIONS

To analyze the experiences of older adults learning technology in senior centers, this study utilized a case study approach to ethnography. Since Suchman's (1987) canonical work on situated action, scholars have found that in-depth and up-close analyses of how people use technology in naturalistic social settings reveal important information about how technology is incorporated into work and life. Discoveries made with this method are not possible to arrive at through other methods (Blomberg & Karasti 2013).

During a one-year period (September 2014 to August 2015), the researcher studied three senior centers in a medium-sized urban area in the Midwestern United States. The specific methods used were participant observation (i.e., ethnographic fieldwork) in technology support sessions with older adults who in the course of their daily lives participate regularly in these spaces. In addition, the researcher completed semi-structured interviews with 54 of these "regulars" to learn more about their experiences learning technology over time.

The methods used in this study were chosen to document and analyze the complex and diverse experiences of older adults learning technology. The position of the researcher within these institutions impacted what data could be gathered. To gain entry into these community-based institutions, the researcher joined and helped support technology support services offered, depending on the institution, since between 1997 and 2014. The older adults who participated in this study thus perceived the researcher to be a service provider. As such, some of the older adults that participated in this study may have adapted their actions because they sought my services. It is possible that if the researcher occupied a different role within these institutions (such as a seeker of services or a neutral external party), different data would be collected. These limitations were in part circumvented by supplement-

80th Annual Meeting of the Association for Information Science & Technology, Washington, DC | Oct. 27-Nov. 1, 2017

ing ethnographic fieldwork with interviews, in which participants were invited to reflect on and discuss their technology learning practices over time. More research is needed to understand how the experiences of the older adults learning technology in these senior centers compares to the experiences of other older adults, including those who are less connected to community-based institutions.

## FINDINGS

This study found that older adults who participate in technology support services in senior centers are determined and creative learners who with support integrate technology into the diverse rhythms of their lives. This reality can best be understood as what this study calls an *informatics lifecourse* (Figure 1). The informatics lifecourse is a portmanteau concept that combines the concept of the informatics moment (Williams, 2012) with the concept of the lifecourse (Hutchison, 2014). The informatics moment is "when a person seeks help in using some digital technology that is new to him or her" (Williams, 2012, p. 47). The lifecourse is "how historical time, social location, and culture affect the individual experience of each life stage" (Hutchison, 2014, p. 11). The informatics lifecourse is populated by many informatics moments, episodes of seeking, getting and offering help. The accumulation of these moments affect how individuals learn technology.

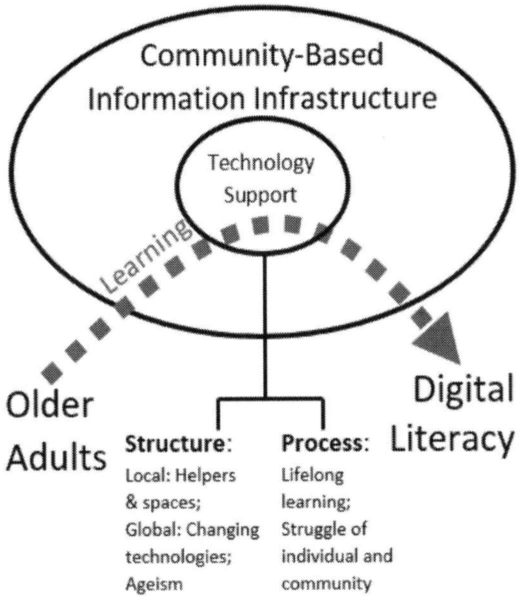


**Figure 1.** The informatics lifecourse

Many informatics moments take place throughout life because digital literacy requires learning a changing array of technologies and digital applications. In the pre-digital age one could learn to read and write, that is, practice literacy, and then continue to read and write many years after having initially learned these procedures. In the digital age, however, literacy requires learning technology over time. For example, an individual who learns Windows 3 in the workplace in the 1990s and then stops using technology upon retiring may then find that using a smartphone in the 2010s is quite challenging. Even those older adults who do not stop using technology for a period of time cope with the challenges associated with learning new digital technologies as they emerge.

This model of the informatics lifecourse is explained through the story of one woman's experiences learning technology in her senior center, as well as in other informatics moments. Hester (a pseudonym) is an 89-year-old African American who has lived her entire life in the local community. Hester started using digital technology in the 1960s, when she was employed as a stenographer in a courthouse. There she used a mainframe computer to input data on court cases. She received computer training from faculty at a local university.

In the 1980s, and in particular when she retired in 1986, Hester struggled to maintain her digital literacy skills. She said that in the 1960s she "learned how to wire a mother board! ....But I lost track of [computers] when they switched from mainframes to PCs. I quit using all of that when I retired." During the stage of her life in which she was working full-time, Hester relied on her employers to provide her with the training she needed to practice digital literacy. After Hester retired, she lost that technology support. As a result, Hester stopped using technology for more than a decade. This break in her digital practices relates to a break in her access to support services.

Hester started using technology again in the late 1990s, when she decided to purchase a digital camera so that she could take pictures at her granddaughter's wedding. She purchased the camera because a family member told her that she could take more pictures with the digital camera than she could on a conventional roll of film. She did not, however, find the support she felt she needed in order to learn how to use her digital camera within her family. Hester said "I got it [the digital camera] just to take pictures and I wanted to take pictures of my granddaughter's wedding. But I could not figure out how to use it [laughs]: What to do with the pictures after I took them!"

To address this learning need, Hester decided to seek support from her senior center. Hester joined a senior center shortly after she retired because the senior center was rooted in her local community. Many of Hester's now retired friends participated in the senior center. Furthermore, her mother was a leader in the senior center in the 1970s. This space, which already had played an important role in her life, began to also play a role in her digital learning practices:

"I got some help from some university students [who volunteered in a computer class] here at the senior center. I figured out I better buy a computer so I had some place to put my pictures. [Laughs] I just didn't realize you needed a computer if you used a digital camera. [Laughs] They never tell you what all you need, and it seems like you always need something else. So, anyhow, I bought a desktop, with XP, in 2000, 2001, something like that. I can't remember exactly when. I still have that computer. It is at home. I still use it. But it is getting old."

Although Hester found some support in her senior center, it was not enough to enable her to do everything she wanted to do with technology. The volunteers Hester turned to for support were not always present at the senior center, and as a result Hester could not always find the support she wanted. After Hester started using her desktop computer (and later her laptop) to manage her digital photographs, she did not continue to learn how to do more things with these devices, despite desiring to do so. I asked Hester to "tell me about what you have been doing with technology since" learning how to transfer the photos from her digital camera to her computer. She responded:

> "Not much. I was using my desktop a little bit, now and then, but less and less as time went on. The university students stopped coming to the senior center, I can't remember when, but sometime. And then without them here to ask questions, I guess I just used the computer less and less. Oh, I got on it from time to time. And I take pictures now and then with my digital camera .... It always changes."

Nevertheless, Hester is not a passive user of technology support services created for her. When computer classes were discontinued at the senior center because of a lack of volunteers to staff them, Hester (and others at the senior center) requested over and over again that someone help them with technology. This persistence prompted the staff of the senior center to actively seek more volunteers for its computer classes.

## DISCUSSION AND CONCLUSION

Although this study was limited to a very small geographically-based community and a small number of institutions and individuals within it, this study reveals important dimensions of the experiences of at least some of the older adults learning technology. Studying the experiences of older adults learning technology in senior centers reveals at least some of the estimated 75% of Americans aged 65 and older seeking help with technology (Pew Research Center, 2017) are creative and persistent learners of technology. Finding ways to support older adults in their learning practices can be facilitated by finding ways to support the community-based institutions to which many are deeply tied, such as senior centers, but also institutions like churches and public libraries (Hardill, 2014; Xie & Jaeger, 2008).

## REFERENCES


Beisgen, B., & Kraitchman, M. (2003). *Senior centers: Opportunities for successful aging*. New York: Springer.

Blomberg, J., & Karasti, H. (2013). Reflections on 25 years of ethnography in CSCW. *Computer Supported Cooperative Work (CSCW)*, 22(4-6), 373-423.

Gardner, P. J., Kamber, T., & Netherland, J. (2012). "Getting turned on": Using ICT training to promote active aging in New York. *The Journal of Community Informatics*, 8(1).

Hardill, I. (2014) The intergenerational help desk: Encouraging ICT use in older adults in England. In R. Vanderbeck & N. Worth (Eds.), *Intergenerational space* (pp. 273-285). London: Routledge.

Hutchison, E.D. (2014). Dimensions of human behavior: The changing life course. 5th ed. Los Angeles: Sage.

McKee, H., & Blair, K. (2006). Older adults and community-based technological literacy programs: Barriers & benefits to learning. *Community Literacy Journal*, 1(2), 13-39.

National Council on Aging. (2015). *Senior centers: Fact sheet*. Arlington, VA: National Council on Aging. https://www.ncoa.org/wp-content/uploads/FactSheet_SeniorCenters.pdf.

Suchman, L. A. (1987). Plans and situated actions: The problem of human-machine communication. Cambridge, UK: Cambridge University Press.

Pew Research Center. (2017) *Tech Adoption Climbs Among Older Adults*. http://pewrsr.ch/2pWRh2J.

Xie, B., & Jaeger, P. T. (2008). Computer training programs for older adults at the public library. *Public Libraries*, 47(5), 42-49.

U.S. Census Bureau. (2016). Annual estimates of the resident population for selected age groups. Washington, DC: U.S. Census.

# Measuring the Impact of R packages

**Kai Li**
*Drexel University, USA. kl696@drexel.edu*

**Shenmeng Xu**
*School of Information and Library Science, University of North Carolina at Chapel Hill, USA. shenmeng@email.unc.edu*

## ABSTRACT

**In this poster, we describe a framework to measure the impact of R packages from an altmetrics perspective. This framework includes search statistics on Google, the number of downloads on CRAN (the official R package repository), the number of posts on Stack Overflow and the count of papers on the Public Library of Science (PLoS) journals mentioning or citing the packages. These measures are normalized into monthly units. Six visualization packages were selected to test the method. Results are presented and discussed, particularly in light of the levels of engagement represented by these measures. The next steps of this project are also explained at the end of this poster proposal.**

## KEYWORDS

altmetrics, R packages, scientometrics, open software

## INTRODUCTION

This poster reports our preliminary exploration of potential measures to value research software. Scientific software is an becoming increasingly important research object in information science studies. Among these studies, one notable line of research is the scientific impact of software objects (Li, Yan & Feng, 2017; Pan, Yan, Wang & Hua, 2015).

The concept of altmetrics includes a group of metrics based on usage data and social media events related to scientific works. Given the broadness of such measures, they represent highly diverse meanings, from different stages of the research lifecycle (Fenner, 2014) to the various levels of engagement of information consumers (Haustein, Bowman & Costas, 2015; Lin & Fenner, 2013).

A project named Depsy (http://depsy.org/) applies the altmetrics approach to software packages in the environments of R and Python (Chawla, 2016). It integrates their download counts, citation counts, positions in the dependency network and number of reuses by other software projects, to present a more comprehensive picture of how software packages are involved in related activities.

However, one element that is missing from Depsy is the time scale of these measurements, which is important for the understanding of how the interests in and usage of each package have been changing over time. To address this gap, we conducted a study on how the measurements of R packages had been changing during the past few years. We selected visualization packages in the R ecosystem because of the popularities of R and visualization tools in both academia and industry. In the ecosystem of R, a package is a "fundamental unit of sharable code" (Wickham, 2015, p. 3) that serves as an extension of the core functionalities of the software. This poster proposal presents a brief description of the methods and preliminary results of this project, as well as how these results shed light on the next steps of the project.

## FORMAT OF PRESENTATION

Our preliminary exploration will be displayed in a poster with visualizations of our data. An interactive version of the visualization in the form of a webpage will be prepared to make it more convenient for the audience to compare different packages and data sources and to play with the data by themselves.

## RESEARCH METHOD

We selected three core packages and three non-core packages from the "Graphic Displays & Dynamic Graphics & Graphic Devices & Visualization" view of CRAN (https://cran.r-project.org/web/views/Graphics.html), the official package repository of R. The most popular packages in this category were chosen based on the authors' knowledge. Among these packages (shown in Table 1), ggplot2, lattice and plotrix are designed for general visualization tasks; igraph is designed to plot network graphs; ade4 is an ecological analysis package with visualization functionalities; RColorBrewer is a color palette tool that can be used with other visualization packages.

| Package name | Date when the package was added to CRAN |
|---|---|
| ade4 | 2002-12 |
| ggplot2 | 2007-06 |
| igraph | 2006-03 |
| lattice | 2001-05 |
| plotrix | 2004-08 |
| RColorBrewer | 2002-10 |

***Table 1.*** *Description of R packages*

We investigated all possible data sources to study the altmetrics traces of R packages, based on the following three standards: 1) the data source must be able to represent at least one specific aspect of software-related activities, 2) the measurement must be chronicled and 3) the data must be freely

80th Annual Meeting of the Association for Information Science & Technology, Washington, DC | Oct. 27-Nov. 1, 2017

available. Based on these criteria, the following four measurements were determined, as presented in Table 2. They were normalized into monthly units for each of the packages listed in Table 1. Graphs were created to compare how these packages perform differently across time on each measurement.

| Data source | Description of the measurement | How the data was collected |
|---|---|---|
| Google Trends | An index of the relative popularity of a searching term on Google (value between 0-100) | Manual searches were conducted on the web page of Google Trends (https://trends.google.com/trends/) by querying "package name + R" |
| CRAN | The download counts of each package from the CRAN repository | Data were collected using the "dlstats" package of R (Yu, 2016) using the name of each package |
| Stack Overflow | Number of posts about each package on Stack Overflow | Data were collected using the "stackr" package of R (Robinson, n.d.) using the tag of each package |
| Public Library of Science (PLoS) | Number of papers in PLoS journals that mention or cite each package | Data were collected using the "rplos" package of R (Chamberlain, Boettinger, & Ram, 2016) by using the title of the official citation format of each package |

*Table 2. Description of data sources and collection methods*

## RESULTS

This section presents the preliminary results of our analyses. As is shown in Figure 1 to Figure 4, ggplot2 is the most popular package in all four measures. igraph is popular in Google Search, Stack Overflow and PLoS, even though it is not as popular as RColorBrewer in terms of the number of downloads on CRAN. On the other end of the spectrum, even though they have been downloaded substantially, ade4, plotrix and RColorBrewer have hardly had a noticeable impact on the other three measurements. Most of the measurements have been increasing during the past decade. Although only the relative popularity index of Google Search can be collected, the other three measurements are found to have highly variant scales, which broadly correspond to the different levels of engagement.

## DISCUSSION

This project extends Depsy's efforts of understanding software impact using altmetrics measurements by adding a timeline dimension to the measurements. Our exploration of the three new measurements (Google search statistics, Stack Overflow discussions and PLoS citations) are proven to reflect our knowledge about these packages, thus demonstrating their potential be used to show interests in and usage of the packages.

As shown in the Results section, ggplot2 is the most popular package across the board, while ade4, plotrix and RColorBrewer have significantly less meaningful traces in all the measurements except for the number of downloads. Even though the sample size is small, there seem to be different patterns of packages and measures that interact with each other, which are worth exploring in the future.

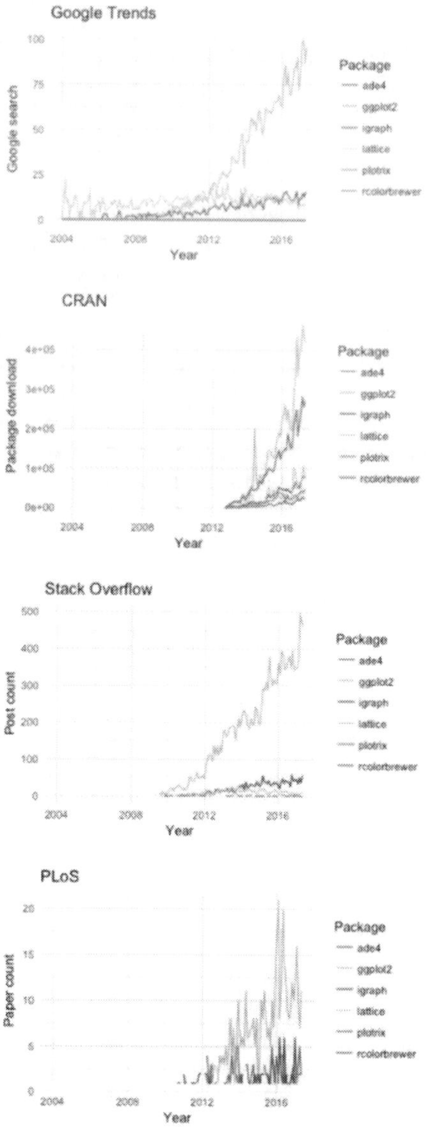


***Figure 1-4.*** *Popularity of the selected R packages on Google Trends, CRAN, Stack Overflow, and PLoS*

One significant perspective to understand the measurements is the various levels of engagement indicated by them. For example, the popularity of Google search represents the most general interests; the CRAN downloads number indicates actual uses, directly or indirectly, of the package by all users; the number of posts on Stack Overflow represents interests in the packages most possibly from the users; and the number of citations in PLoS journals represents the packages' scientific impact in certain knowledge domains. To use this framework to interpret the impact of a larger set of R packages will be one of the foci of our future work.

## REFERENCES


Chamberlain, S., Boettiger, C., & Ram, K. (2016). rplos: Interface to the search 'API' for 'PLoS' journals. R package version 0.6.4. https://CRAN.R-project.org/package=rplos

Chawla, D. S. (2016). The unsung heroes of scientific software. *Nature, 529*(7584), 115-116.

Fenner, M. (2014). Altmetrics and other novel measures for scientific impact. In *Opening science* (pp. 179-189). Springer. Retrieved from http://link.springer.com/chapter/10.1007/978-3-319-00026-8_12

Haustein, S., Bowman, T. D., & Costas, R. (2015). Interpreting" altmetrics": Viewing acts on social media through the lens of citation and social theories. arXiv preprint arXiv:1502.05701.

Li, K., Yan, E., & Feng, Y. (2017). How is R cited in research outputs? Structure, impacts, and citation standard. Manuscript submitted for publication.

Lin, J., & Fenner, M. (2013). Altmetrics in evolution: Defining and redefining the ontology of article-level metrics. *Information Standards Quarterly, 25*(2), 20.

Pan, X., Yan, E., Wang, Q., & Hua, W. (2015). Assessing the impact of software on science: A bootstrapped learning of software entities in full-text papers. *Journal of Informetrics, 9*(4), 860–871.

Piwowar, H. & Priem, J. (2016). Depsy: Valuing the software that powers science. Retrieved June 1, 2017, from https://github.com/Impactstory/depsy-research/blob/master/introducing_depsy.md#literature-reuse.

Robinson, D. (n.d.). stackr: Client for the Stack Exchange API. R package version 0.0.0.9000. http://github.com/dgrtwo/stackr

Yu, G. (2016). dlstats: Download Stats of R Packages. R package version 0.0.9. https://CRAN.R-project.org/package=dlstats

# Fake vs. Real Health Information in Social Media in China

**Yuelin Li**
*Business School, Nankai University, China.*
*yuelinli@nankai.edu.cn*

**Shanshan Wang**
*Business School, Nankai University, China.*
*1120170913@mail.nankai.edu.cn*

**Xiu Zhang**
*Business School, Nankai University, China.*
*1120160841@mail.nankai.edu.cn*

## ABSTRACT

**The purpose of this study is to examine the features of fake health information in social media in China and to develop a list of the features of fake information that can be used as a tool to help users identify fake health information in social media. The study collects 428 pieces of health information from WeChat, a dominant social media in China. Then the information is categorized into real or fake health information based on the judgment of rumor websites and health experts. Open coding is performed based on a framework that helps identify low quality information online. Chi-square tests are adopted to identify significant features of fake information. The results indicate that gender and occupation affect users' dissemination of fake health information. Based on the analysis, the study develops a list that includes the salient features of fake health information. This list can help users to identify fake health information and improve their health literacy. In addition, it can inform health information systems to automatically filter fake information and improve health information quality online.**

## KEYWORDS

health information, fake and real health information, features of fake information, information quality

## INTRODUCTION

The internet is an open cyberspace, and online information quality has been a concern. Anyone who has certain skills in computer can upload self-created content to the web, which is not accredited by any experts or authoritative agencies. For some general information, that may be not a problem. However, for health information, which is critical to people's life, this is very dangerous. Some tragedies happened because of misleading health information online (Cornish& Moraes, 2015). In addition, previous studies also indicate that the quality of health information online is low, and it is necessary to evaluate information credibility on the internet (Eysenbach, Powell & Kuss, 2002; Metzger, 2007; Zhang, Sun & Xie, 2015). Some criteria have been proposed to assist users to assess information quality online, such as accuracy, authority, objectivity, currency and coverage or scope (Metzger, 2007). Checklist approaches have been widely used to train users or help users (Metzger, 2007). However, such approaches are time consuming and cumbersome. Users are usually unwilling to evaluate information quality diligently by using those approaches (Metzger, 2007). New approaches are called for to help users identify low quality information, including discrimination of fake and real health information.

Nowadays, WeChat has been a powerful and mostly used social media in China, but information quality remains a big concern in such a platform. The current study attempts to examine the dissemination of fake health information and identify its salient features to foster development of a tool to help users identify such kind of health information in social media. Specifically, these are the research questions:

**Q1**: How are real and fake health information elements disseminated in social media?

**Q2**: What are salient features of fake health information in social media?

## RESEARCH METHODS

This study recruited 19 WeChat users and collected health information from their "WeChat Discovery" between August 2014 and August 2016. In total 482 pieces of health information were collected.

We first categorized the information as real or fake information by three rounds of identification. In the first round, we used rumor websites, for example, Shanghai Rumor (http://piyao.jfdaily.com/), to see whether the information has been identified as a rumor. If yes, the information was categorized into fake information; if not, we kept it for the second round of identification. In the second round, we recruited two health experts (one is a doctor; the other is a PhD in pharmacy) to recognize real or fake information that could not be judged in the first-round of identification. If the two experts arrived at agreement on a piece of information as real or fake one, we categorize the information according to their opinion. If they cannot, the information will be identified in the third round. For this round, we recruited another health expert (a medical big data specialist) to make judgment. The judgment result of the third expert will be taken into account. Following this process, we categorized all of the information into real or fake health information for further analysis.

80th Annual Meeting of the Association for Information Science & Technology, Washington, DC | Oct. 27-Nov. 1, 2017

To analyze the data, we adopted the CARS List (Harris, 2015), which includes the dimensions of low quality information, including lack of credibility, lack of accuracy, lack of reasonableness and lack of support. The criteria corresponding to each dimension are included in the list.

| Dimensions | Feature | Fake | Real | $\chi^2$ |
|---|---|---|---|---|
| Lack of credibility | Exaggerate/absolute tone | 157 | 27 | 95.78** |
| | Induced text | 98 | 24 | 35.51** |
| | Agitated propaganda and promotion | 81 | 18 | 30.70** |
| | Claiming unique and confidential information | 62 | 11 | 26.91** |
| | Business promotion | 25 | 14 | 0.81 |
| | Negative information | 17 | 1 | 10.56** |
| Lack of accuracy | Problematic punctuation | 84 | 20 | 29.95** |
| | Inappropriate space | 37 | 13 | 6.39** |
| | Typo | 33 | 2 | 21.14** |
| | Grammatical errors | 20 | 1 | 12.94** |
| | Unfair opinions | 20 | 1 | 12.94** |
| | Incomplete content | 18 | 1 | 11.35** |
| Lack of reasonableness | Overblown importance | 93 | 12 | 53.78** |
| | Uncontrolled tone | 88 | 10 | 53.20** |
| | Excessive declaration | 38 | 2 | 25.39** |
| | Unmatched title and text | 31 | 6 | 11.52** |
| Lack of support | No source | 79 | 8 | 48.81** |
| | Lack source file | 66 | 1 | 54.10** |
| | Under the guise of authority | 20 | 1 | 12.94** |

**: $p<.01$

***Table 1**. Distribution and features of fake and real health information*

Based on this framework, we analyzed the sample by open coding. Two rounds of coding were performed. We created a coding scheme based on the framework in the first round. Then, in the second round, two coders recoded the sample again based on the scheme and refined the results.

After identifying the features, we preformed chi-square tests to examine the frequency of the features between real and fake health information. In this way, we can identify significant features of fake health information.

## RESULTS

### Distribution of Real and Fake Health Information

Among 428 pieces of information, 206 (43%) are real and 276 (57%) are fake. Most of health information is not true. We examined the distribution of real and fake information in WeChat. In terms of gender, females disseminated more health information than males. However, 80% of the information disseminated by males was fake, while only 55% of information disseminated by females was fake. In addition, peasants disseminated higher percentage of fake health information than retired and employed people. There is no big difference in real and fake information dissemination in terms of age and educational level.

### Features of Fake Health Information

To identify salient features of fake health information, we calculated the number of pieces of fake and real health information with respect to each feature and tested whether the frequency is significant by chi-square tests. If it is significant, then we recognized the feature is a salient feature of fake health information. Table 1 shows the dimensions, feature, number of pieces of fake and real information and chi-square tests.

We further organized the features in a list and added typical statements extracted from fake health information to develop a tool for helping users to recognize fake health information in social media. The list involves features and typical text or statements of fake health information, which can also help develop a mechanism for automatically filtering fake information from social media.

## REFERENCES


Cornish, L. S., & Moraes, C. (2015). The impact of consumer confusion on nutrition literacy and subsequent dietary behavior. *Psychology & Marketing*, 32(5), 558-574.

Eysenbach, G., Powell, J. Kuss, O., & Sa, ER. (2002). Empirical studies assessing the quality of health information for consumers on the world wide web: A systematic review. *Journal of the American Medical Association*, 287(20), 2691-2700.

Harris, R. (2015). Evaluating internet research sources. Retrieved February 28, 2017 from http://www.virtualsalt.com/evalu8it.htm

Metzger, M. J. (2007). Making sense of credibility on the web: Models for evaluating online information and recommendations for future research. *Journal of the Association for Information Science and Technology*, 58(13), 2078-2091.

Zhang, Y., Sun, Y., & Xie, B. (2015). Quality of health information for consumers on the web: A systematic review of indicators, criteria, tools, and evaluation results. *Journal of the Association for Information Science and Technology*, 66(10), 2071—2084.

# Techniques of Visual Knowledge Construction in the Practices of Analog Videotape Digitization

**Zack Lischer-Katz**
*University of Oklahoma Libraries, USA. zlkatz@ou.edu*

## ABSTRACT

**This presentation describes findings from qualitative-interpretive research conducted on media preservationists carrying out small-scale digitization projects involving the digital reformatting of analog videotape. Eight preservationists working in media preservation labs were interviewed and observed carrying out digitization projects in their work sites. Adopting a social constructionist perspective and employing concepts from Reiner Keller's sociology of knowledge approach to discourse (SKAD), the research data were analyzed to gain insight into processes of knowledge construction. The object of knowledge found to be central to participants' practices of knowledge construction was the invisible video signal, a continuously varying electrical signal that necessitates techniques and technologies of visualization and observation. This research identified six epistemic techniques, arrays of sensory-cognitive micropractices that participants enact in order to construct knowledge about, act upon the video signal and produce legitimate digital copies of analog originals: applying calibrated vision; patterned looking; matching and comparing visual representations of signals; historicizing the tape; investigating the nature of errors; and constructing copies. This research offers new understanding of visual knowledge construction in workplace contexts and emphasizes the importance of studying the interpretive aspects of digitization practices.**

## KEYWORDS

knowledge construction, video preservation, digitization, moving image archives

## INTRODUCTION

Digitization has become a common technique in information institutions for preserving and making available analog originals. Yet, the transition from analog to digital representation systems is increasingly understood to be shaped by cultural and epistemological assumptions. For instance, Bonnie Mak (2014) uses the case of *Early English Books Online* (EEBO) database to show how practices of copying embed traces of the human agents involved in the translation of information between media formats. Conway (2013) has shown how techniques of mass digitization embed new errors, traces of the digitizers, in the resulting digital copies. Researchers in information studies are increasingly concerned with the nature of archival records as products of cultural and historical processes (e.g., Yakel, 2001; Gracy, 2007; Acker, 2013). It has been acknowledged in media studies that visual technologies and the cultural practices that develop around their use shape how we can know the world and embed the epistemological assumptions of particular historical and cultural contexts (Crary, 1990; Winston, 1996).

The work of digital reformatting of complex visual documents, in this case analog video recordings in small-scale, high-quality "artisanal" production, provides a well- suited context for examining the ways in which epistemological assumptions about the nature of information are embedded in digital copies through the workplace practices of preservation professionals.

This presentation describes findings from a subset of research data produced from the author's qualitative-interpretive dissertation that studied media preservationists carrying out small-scale digitization projects involving the digital reformatting of analog videotape.

## MAIN RESEARCH OBJECTIVE

The main research objective of this research was to understand the epistemic techniques and processes of knowledge construction of media preservationists engaged in the work of artisanal digital reformatting, specifically analog video digitization.

## THEORETICAL FRAMEWORK

This research adopts a social constructionist perspective and employs concepts from Reiner Keller's (2013) sociology of knowledge approach to discourse (SKAD). Keller elaborates on Foucault's (1970; 1972) concept of *dispositif*, defining it as the material configuration of human agents, tools and discourses "that are the basis for the production of a specific discourse and/or for the production of a discourse's power effects, its interventions into the world" (pp. 52-53). Dispositifs are objects through which discourses gain material reality, in the form of such things as architecture, technological artifacts, classification systems, regulations, etc. This conceptualization supports the integrated analysis of discursive and material practices associated with the technical work of digitizing analog video tape.

80th Annual Meeting of the Association for Information Science & Technology, Washington, DC | Oct. 27-Nov. 1, 2017

## METHODOLOGY

For this research, sites of "artisanal digital reformatting" were selected based on the following criteria:

- The digital reformatting of analog video recordings is currently being carried out.
- The mode of digital reformatting is highly skilled and of low output.
- Institutions committed to preserving the informational and aesthetic values of visual documents (based on their public mission statements).

Data were collected for this project as part of the author's dissertation research between October 2015 and December 2016 from 13 media preservationists (eight digitizers, four administrators, one quality control specialist) recruited from six preservation labs. Data were generated in the form of discourses and observations of material practices by conducting semi-structured interviews, video-recorded observations and think-aloud sessions, and review sessions in which participants reflected on the video-recordings of their workplace practices. For this presentation, a subset of data was analyzed, focusing solely on the eight digitizers studied in this research and their digitization work.

Table 1 provides information on participants' backgrounds, positions and the institutions that they work in. Data were analyzed using qualitative-interpretive methods, including discourse analysis and interpretive phenomenological analysis (Smith, et al., 2009). Interviews, observations and review sessions were transcribed and then coded using qualitative analysis software, MaxQDA.

## FINDINGS

Through an analysis of participants' statements and work place activities, I found that a central part of digitizers' work involves forming knowledge about the invisible and often indeterminate video signal. Unlike photochemical-based imaging technologies (such as film), the visual information the medium carries cannot be verified with the unaided human eye. Digitizers must incorporate knowledge gained through objective and subjective techniques of visualization, incorporating historical knowledge of tape formats and production histories with their own visual skills of analysis, and coordinating their hands and eyes to adjust signals and evaluate the results, re-constructing the original recording (for which the "original" is only ever partially known). This is best understood as an interpretive practice of visual translation, rather than a purely objective transfer of signals from one media format to another.

The following epistemic techniques were identified as common patterns of acquiring knowledge in participants' digitization work.

### Applying Calibrated Vision

Participants discuss "learning to see" and "developing an eye," calibrating their vision through a combination of work experience, published visual examples and advice from co-workers in order to detect typical errors in the video signal

| ID | Location | Institution Type | Job Title | Iden-tity |
|---|---|---|---|---|
| P1_L1 | Northeast | Conservation dept. of a large art museum | Assistant Media Conservator | Media Conserva-tor |
| P1_L2 | West Coast | Small community video production and preservation center | Preservationist | Video Preserva-tionist |
| P2_L2 | West Coast | Small community video production and preservation center | Preservation Project Man-ager | Preserva-tionist |
| P3_L2 | West Coast | Small community video production and preservation center | Preservation Technician | Moving Image Archivist |
| P1_L3 | Midwest | Small video and media art distrib-uter and archive | Digitization Specialist | "Doesn't think about it." |
| P1_L6 | Northeast | Audiovisual preservation lab at the academic library of a large research univer-sity | Collections Analysis Assistant | Archivist |
| P3_L6 | Northeast | Audiovisual preservation lab at the academic library of a large research univer-sity | Lab Manager | Audio Engineer |
| P1_L7 | Midwest | Small community media and video art archive | Video Techni-cian | Video Ar-chivist / AV Archi-vist |

*Table 1. Characteristics of digitizers*

and evaluate the quality of the overall image: "When I see something that I'm not real familiar with, learn more about it. *It's developing your eye* [*emphasis added, zlk*], [...] like well what really matters here and what should I stress out about or not?" (P3_L6).

### Patterned Looking

Part of the training of the eye is to develop patterns of looking, moving the eye across the image and the scopes in a structured pattern in order to compare the image on cathode ray tube (CRT) monitors and the video scopes that visualize the components of the video signal at different points in the workflow. Participants move their eyes between these devices, looking for errors or differences among different points of observation in the "signal chain" (the sequence of interconnected equipment).

### Matching and Comparing Visual Representations of Signals

Digitizers compare the visual representations produced by the video monitors (for displaying the video image) and the video scopes (for visualizing the analog video signal) at different points and work to match them to each other in order to bridge the analog and digital realms of visual representation. This can be carried out to confirm certain aspects of the system: "I would use the scopes, the reason why we have both analog and digital scopes is to make sure that they are both basically saying the same thing, or something very similar" (P1_L1).

### *Historicizing the Tape*

*Historicizing the tape* refers to the ways in which digitizers integrate knowledge about the history of a particular videotape format and the historical context in which the particular videotape was recorded in order to adjust their expectations about the visual quality of the videotape and their sensitivity to errors: "If you know your video formats, and your video history, and the way people were dubbing [i.e., copying, *zlk*], dubbing tapes in the 70s or the 80s. That's all kind of useful knowledge for, uh, ascertaining if errors that you're encountering are native to the recording" (P3_L2).

### *Investigating the Nature of Errors*

Participants often referred to the video signal as something inscrutable because it could never be directly observed, in contrast to motion picture film, which can be viewed frame by frame on a light box: "I can't describe it but you can definitely get this kind of feeling when something is 'native,' so to speak. When something [i.e., an error, *zlk*] is resolvable, and something isn't resolvable" (P1_L2).

### *Constructing Copies*

Participants construct copies by enacting the following micropractices: detecting, identifying, diagnosing, correcting and documenting errors. This enables them to produce knowledge claims about the nature of errors and to document the choices they make in constructing digital copies. Investigating the source of an error integrates historical knowledge developed about the tape formats and the particular ways in which each can produce different types of errors; distinctions between analog and digital errors; and whether errors are inherent or introduced by the signal chain or human error: "Well, I mean it's... the nature of this work, there is no original. There's the myth of the original. There's no original." (P1_L1).

## CONCLUSION

Findings suggest that due to the indeterminate nature of the analog video medium, digitizers must perceive and rationalize their work in order to resolve uncertainty about whether a visual error detected is part of the original video signal or is due to the decisions they have made in their technical work. To form knowledge in their task, digitizers must deploy an array of epistemic techniques. Working with analog video signals and making decisions about how they will appear as digitally encoded files is best characterized as an interpretive act of visual translation, rather than merely a transfer of signals that can be resolved through objective measurements and blackboxed (Latour, 1999) equipment. This calls into question mainstream assumptions often held by information institutions that the information content of an analog original can be detached unproblematically from its medium. This research contributes to theoretical discussions in information studies on the nature of preservation and archival practice in the digital age and extends research on how knowledge is constructed in workplace practices involving complex configurations of visual forms of information (e.g., Goodwin, 1995; Daipha, 2015).

## REFERENCES


Acker, A. (2013). How cells become records: Standardization and infrastructure in tissue culture. *Archival Science*, DOI 10.1007/s10502-013-9213-x

Conway, P. (2013). Preserving imperfection: Assessing the incidence of digital imaging error in HathiTrust. *Digital Technology & Culture, 42*(1), 17-30.

Crary, J. (1992). Techniques of the observer: On vision and modernity in the nineteenth century. Cambridge, MA: MIT Press.

Daipha, P. (2015). Masters of uncertainty: Weather forecasters and the quest for ground truth. University of Chicago Press.

Foucault, M. (1970). The order of things: An archaeology of the human sciences. New York: Pantheon Books.

Foucault, M. (1972). *The archaeology of knowledge*. London: Routledge.

Goodwin, C. (1995). Seeing in depth. *Social Studies of Science, 25*(2), 237-274.

Gracy, K. F. (2007b). Film preservation: Competing definitions of value, use, and practice. Chicago: Society of American Archivists.

Keller, R. (2013). Doing discourse research: An introduction for social scientists. London: Sage Publications.

Latour, B. (1999). *Pandora's hope: Essays on the reality of science studies*. Cambridge MA: Harvard University Press.

Mak, B. (2014). Archaeology of a digitization. Journal of the Association for Information Science and Technology, 65(8), 1515-1526.

Smith, J. A., Flowers, P., & Larkin, M. (2009). *Interpretive phenomenological analysis: Theory, method and research*. Los Angeles: Sage.

Winston, B. (1996). Technologies of seeing: Photography, cinematography and television. London: British Film Institute

Yakel, E. (1997). Recordkeeping in radiology: The relationships between activities and records in radiological processes (Doctoral dissertation).

# What Information Professionals Need to Know: Job Ads Analysis

**Irene Lopatovska**
*School of Information, Pratt Institute, USA.*
*ilopatov@pratt.edu*

**Hilary Baribeau**
*School of Information, Pratt Institute, USA.*
*hbaribea@pratt.edu*

## ABSTRACT
**A large number of ASIS&T members are involved in their academic programs' development, accreditation and assessment of academic degrees' offerings in relation to the professional market needs. The paper presents information about secondary sources of evidence regarding the library and information science professional market and argues that job advertisements offer rich data on desirable professional competencies and students' aspirations.**

## KEYWORDS
library and information science education, core competencies, curriculum development, iSchools, ALA accreditation

## INTRODUCTION
Information science programs are continuously involved in assessing their performance and offerings against job market demands and required professional competencies (COA, 2015). Such competencies could be gauged through the collection and analysis of primary source data, such as employers' surveys conducted by a program, or secondary sources of evidence, or data, collected, analyzed and/or presented by external sources. This paper reviews several types of secondary evidence that enables master of science library and information science (MSLIS) programs to gauge the market needs and desirable competencies for their students. This paper focuses on the job advertisements (ads) as a rich source of data on professional competencies and presents an example of the findings derived from the job ads analysis. The paper argues that job ad data provides valuable information about students' professional interests, complements other primary and secondary sources on professional competencies and is relevant to LIS and non-LIS programs.

## RELEVANT LITERATURE
The paper reviews four categories of sources on the state of the information professions' job market and competencies, including a) scholarly literature/white papers; b) statements from professional organizations; c) employer data collected by professional organizations and d) reports of the job ads analysis. Due to the paper length requirements, a small set of illustrative examples for each category is reviewed below.

### *Scholarly Literature*
The white papers produced by John Bertot and his colleagues illustrate the value of such reports in understanding the job market and professional competencies for MSLIS degree holders. In a paper produced for the American Library Association (ALA), Bertot and Sarin (2016) analyze and report on the unique values of the librarian profession, which include privacy, equity, inclusion, open government, civic engagement, human rights, intellectual freedom and democratic ideals. Among the unique competencies, the authors list the ability to understand the information needs of users, deliver instruction and programming and to facilitate openness and access to technologies and digital content. In a paper commissioned by the University of Maryland's iSchool, Bertot, Sarin and Percell (2015) outline the desirable competencies of a school's graduates, including the ability to be collaborative problem-solvers, creative, socially innovative and adaptable to changing professional needs and environments. The desirable hard skills mentioned by the authors include data-related competencies, digital technology skills, ability to make informed policy decisions and fundraising.

### *Statements from Professional Organizations*
The statements of professional associations outline expectations for all graduates of LIS programs. For example, in 2015 ALA's Committee on Accreditation (COA) released updated standards for accreditation which, among other things, highlight the need for increased emphasis on technology and communication skills in light of a "rapidly changing field" (ALA, 2015). The emphasis on the continued development of technology skills is also mentioned in the Association of College and Research Libraries in their 2016 report on the top trends in academic libraries (ACRL, 2016).

### *Employer Data from Professional Organizations*
Some professional associations routinely conduct student and employer surveys in order to gauge professional skills and competencies that are deemed important in the information field. Informative examples of the data sources from professional association include ALA Student Survey and Employer Survey Overview (ALA, 2016), ALA Task Force on the Context of Future Accreditation Online Forums Analysis Report (ALA, 2016 Dec.); ACRL Survey to employers (ACRL, 2016). Some of the most frequently mentioned competencies in these sources include leadership and management, technology, soft-skills and communication, research and practical experience.

80th Annual Meeting of the Association for Information Science & Technology, Washington, DC | Oct. 27-Nov. 1, 2017

### *Job Ads Analysis*

Analysis of the job ads is one commonly used method for assessing professional competencies (Nonthcumjane, 2011; Sproles & Ratiedge, 2004; White, 1999; Younger, 2005). A 2015 study conducted by San Juan State University examined over 400 ads for LIS professions and noted that technology, communication and collaborative skills were most common across both academic and corporate positions (ACRL, 2016). Maceli (2015) analyzed job ads in order to identify professionally required technology skills and found that web design and development, metadata and digital collection management were among the most frequently mentioned skills, along with specific programming languages and databases. In a 2013 job ads survey, Harper (2013), analyzed 326 job ads and found that management skills, instruction skills and the ability to adopt emerging technologies were most valued by employers. While the author acknowledges the limitations of job ads as expository documents, he states the value of these surveys in observing the trends on the job market.

## METHODS

The data reported here were collected over a course of eight semesters from Fall 2012 to Spring 2016 by the MSLIS students as part of a required course assignment. The aim of the assignment was to enhance students' understanding of the professional job market. The assignment required students to search for and document information about jobs they would apply for after graduation. In addition to addressing the course learning objectives, the analyzed job ads data were used in the program's curriculum development and assessment projects.

After each semester, the job ad data logged by students were aggregated and, after duplicates' removal, automatically coded into five main categories: job title, hiring institution, hard skills, soft skills and education requirements. The coding schema was informed by prior research (Han & Hswe, 2009; Younger, 2005; Nonthcumjane, 2011; Kousha & Abdoli, 2008; Lai, 2005; Sproles & Ratiedge, 2004; and Choi & Rasmussen, 2006). Frequencies of terms and their percentages in the semesters' totals were calculated and compared over the course of the eight semesters surveyed.

## FINDINGS

The presented findings are based on the analysis of 2450 unique job ads. The three most frequently occurring terms in each of the five main categories were tallied for each semester. These top terms and the ranges of their frequencies in surveyed semesters are presented below.

*Job Title:* The three most frequent terms in the job titles included "archivist," "librarian" and "assistant." This indicates distinct and continued interest in the traditional LIS positions.

*Hiring Institutions:* The coding schema included eight types of hiring institutions, including academic, corporation, museum, public, cultural heritage, government, medical and unknown. Job ads associated with academic institutions were most frequently logged by students, though these frequencies declined sharply in the semesters between 2015 and 2016. Corporations were the second highest hiring institution among the job ads. Corporations included a potentially wider range of institutions than the other categories and included law firms, technology companies and for-profit institutions, which could have contributed to its high frequency. Between Spring 2015 and Spring 2016, we observed a sharp increase in job ads from public institutions, including public libraries, indicating students' continuous, if not heightened, interest in public service. Job ads from medical institutions were consistently the least selected by students.

*Hard Skills:* The four most frequently mentioned hard skills included the terms "digital," "standard" and "EAD." These terms indicate that many of the jobs chosen by students required digital, or computer, skills, and a knowledge of professional standards and protocols. The high frequency of the EAD, a standard archiving protocol, correlated with the high frequency of archivist" job titles. Programming skills and web development, while comprising many narrower terms within the survey, yielded the fewest results despite "digital" being a high use term.

*Soft Skills:* Within the category of soft skills, the terms "communication," "service" and "management" yielded the highest results consistently throughout the eight semesters. While the job ads are primarily for LIS positions, these soft skills are applicable to all professions and are indicative of a trend towards working collaboratively with others.

*Education:* When searching for levels of education in the job ads, "masters" appeared most frequently across all eight semesters surveyed closely followed by the term "equivalent." Across all surveyed semesters, a little over 50% of master degree requirements mentioned ALA- accredited program. "Bachelors" was consistently the least frequent term.

Overall, the frequencies of terms did not fluctuate dramatically throughout the years surveyed, indicating not only consistent interests of the students, but also consistent job requirements across various hiring institutions for hard skills, soft skills and education. The data illustrates a strong desire from employers for applicants with strong collaborative skills and digital fluency.

## CONCLUSION

While the study findings complement general sources on professional competencies and reflect career interests of a particular student body, they may not objectively reflect the needs of the profession. Future work will compare the students' career interests, as reflected in the ads they identify, to the full spectrum of professional ads. Any disconnect between student career aspirations and the needs of the profession would signal the need to help students plan their careers as well as to help programs evaluate their curricula.

Our review of the sources on professional competencies indicate the dominance of LIS-relevant sources, which can be expected in light of the field's longevity and the accreditation requirements for the MSLIS programs. In a climate of growing multidisciplinary trends and the iSchool movement, we identified an opportunity for ASIS&T, the iCaucus (iSchools, 2014) and other not-exclusively LIS-focused organizations to develop their own sources of evidence on the competencies of information professionals. In the meantime, LIS and non-LIS programs should consider the job ads data as a valuable proxy for the state of the job market, professional demands and students' interests.

## ACKNOWLEDGMENTS

We would like to thank Aimee Slater, Carlos Acevedo, Marlee Walters and Rachel Smiley for the valuable contributions to the project. We are grateful to our anonymous reviewers for their helpful suggestions.

## REFERENCES

American Library Association (ALA) (2016, Dec.). Online forums analysis report. Task Force on Context for Future Accreditation. Chicago, IL: ALA. Retrieved from http://www.ala.org/aboutala/sites/ala.org.aboutala/files/content/governance/ebd5_9_TFonFutureContextofAccred.pdf

American Library Association (ALA) (2016). 2016 student survey and employer survey. Task Force on Context for Future Accreditation. Chicago, IL: ALA.

ACRL (2016). ACRL input to the ALA task force on the future context for future accreditation. Chicago, IL: ALA. Retrieved from http://connect.ala.org/files/ACRL%20AC16%20LC%20Packet_4.pdf

ACRL Research Planning and Review Committee. (2016). 2016 top trends in academic libraries: A review of the trends and issues affecting academic libraries in higher education. *College & Research Libraries News*, *77*(6): 274-81. http://crln.acrl.org/content/77/6/274.

Choi, Y. & Rasmussen, E. (2006, September). What is needed to educate future digital librarians? *D-Lib Magazine*. Retrieved from: http://www.dlib.org/dlib/september06/choi/09choi.html.

Committee on Accreditation of the American Library Association (COA). (2015). Standards for accreditation of master's programs in library and information studies. *American Library Association:* Chicago, IL.

Han, M. & Hswe, P. (2009). The evolving role of the metadata librarian. *LRTS, 54*(3), 129-141.

Harper, R. (2013). Knowledge management through the lens of library and information science: A study of job advertisements. *Library Trends*, *61*(3), 703-734.

iSchools Organization (2014). iSchools Charter. Retrieved from http://ischools.org/about/charter/

Kousha, K. & Abdoli, M. (2008, Aug). Subject analysis of online syllabi in library and information science: Do academic LIS programs match with job requirements? *World Library and Information Congress: 74th IFLA general conference and council*, Quebec, Canada, 2008. Hague, Netherlands: IFLA.

Lai, L. (2005). Educating knowledge professionals in library and information science schools. *Journal of Educating Media & Library Science, 42*(3), 347-362.

Maceli, M. (2015). What technology skills do developers need? A text analysis of job listings in library and information science (LIS) from jobs.code4lib.org. *Information Technology and Libraries*, *34*(3), 8-21.

Nonthcumjane, P. (2011, Aug.). Key skills and competencies of a new generation of LIS professionals. *World Library and Information Congress: 77th IFLA general conference and assembly*, San Juan, Puerto Rico, 2011. Hague, Netherlands: IFLA.

Sproles, C. & Ratiedge, D. (2004). An analysis of entry-level librarian ads published in American libraries, 1982-2002. *Electronic Journal of Academic and Special Librarianship, 5*(2-3).

White, G.W. (1999). Academic subject specialist positions in the United States: A content analysis of announcements from 1990 through 1998. *Journal of Academic Librarianship*, 25(5), 372-382.

Younger, P. (2005). An analysis of skills and qualities required by LIS employers 2004-2005. *Library and Information Research, 29*(92), 32-51.

# Does Collaboration Bring High-impact Studies? A Preliminary Study

**Chao Lu**
*School of Economics and Management, Nanjing University of Science and Technology, China & School of Informatics and Computing, Indiana University, USA. luchaonjust@gmail.com*

**Yi Bu**
*School of Informatics and Computing, Indiana University, USA. buyi@iu.edu*

**Chenwei Zhang***
*School of Informatics and Computing, Indiana University, USA. Zhang334@iu.edu*
**Corresponding Author*

**Ying Ding**
*School of Informatics and Computing, Indiana University, USA. dingying@indiana.edu*

**Vetle I. Torvik**
*School of Information Sciences, University of Illinois, USA. vtorvik@illinois.edu*

**Chengzhi Zhang**
*School of Economics and Management, Nanjing University of Science and Technology, China. zhangcz@njust.edu.cn*

## ABSTRACT
**Team formation becomes important when scientific collaborations become common and important to scholars. This study initially tries to understand how research team size may influence the impact of a study measured by number of citations. Thus, publications in the biology domain are specifically investigated by correlation analysis between team size and scientific impact. The weak correlation suggests that larger team size can positively increase the impact of scientific publications on average; however, it cannot literally bring more highly cited articles.**

## KEYWORDS
scientific collaboration, scientific impact, team size

## INTRODUCTION
Nowadays, scientific collaborations become common and important to scholars, especially when its positive effects have been well investigated among researchers (Wuchty, Jones, & Uzzi, 2007). This preliminary study is to discover whether larger team size can bring more high-impact studies in order to better understand scientific success for scholars.

## METHODOLOGY
To investigate the relationship between team size and scientific impact, we follow the road map as shown in Figure 1.

## DATA
Structured full text data of roughly 170,000 scientific articles are collected from *PLoS* journals. To keep the consistence and prevent potential biases caused by different subjects, we simply select the articles in biology (49,350) as our final dataset. Then their authors' information is extracted, including authors' first and last names and their rankings on the author list.

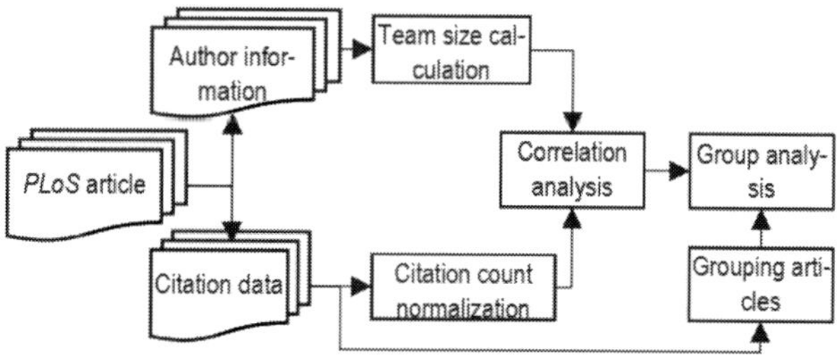


***Figure 1.*** *Road map of this study*

Using the APIs (https://github.com/PLOS?page=1) developed by *PLoS*, we access the citation count of each paper in *PLoS*. The citation data for these 49,350 articles are obtained from February 3-6, 2016, a very short time period, so that we can reduce the possible limitations in citation data caused by different harvest timelines.

## METHOD
With these data, we calculate some variables to measure the team size and scientific impact. First, we use the number of authors in the author list to measure the team size of each study shown as follows:

$$TS = N_{authors} \quad (1)$$

Then, we calculate the normalized citation count by month to mitigate the negative effects of paper age difference:

$$NCC = \frac{Citation\ count}{Month(Harvest\ date - Publish\ date)} \quad (2)$$

The function month() is to calculate the paper's age in month.

### *Correlation Analysis*
We also conduct a correlation analysis among variables. The Kolmogorov-Smirnov (KS) tests suggest that both variables are not normally distributed ($p$<0.001), so the Spearman test

80th Annual Meeting of the Association for Information Science & Technology, Washington, DC | Oct. 27-Nov. 1, 2017

is adopted to discover the potential relationships.

### *Article Group Assignment*

To better understand the relationship between team size and scientific impact, we also divide the articles into three groups according to their NCC ranking: 493 high-impact articles (top 1%), 4,935 medium-impact articles (9%), and 43,922 low-impact articles according the Bradford distribution (Leimkuhler, 1967)

## PRELIMINARY RESULTS

Table 1 shows the result of correlation analysis, where the team size shows a weak positive correlation with the normalized citation count (NCC). That is to say, as the size of a team grows, the impact of a study is relatively higher – more citations can be received. To further discover the relationship between them, we plot the average NCC grouped by the team size in 22 intervals (Figure 2).

| | Team size | NCC |
|---|---|---|
| Team size | 1.000 | |
| NCC | .156**(.000) | 1.000 |

** Correlation is significant at the 0.01 level (2-tailed); and p-values are given in parentheses.

***Table 1.*** *Results of correlation analyses*

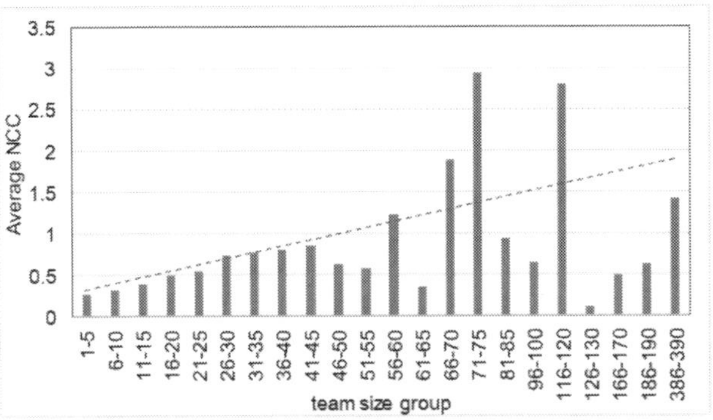


**Figure 2.** Average NCC grouped by team size

From Figure 2 we can see that in biology researches when the team size is smaller than 45, the average NCC is more strongly correlated with team size; when the team size is larger than 45 the samples become sparse, which cause more random distributions in Figure 2 (see in Figure 3-A). To discover the potential reasons, we further divide the articles into three categories. We find that the reduction of low-impact research (Figure 3-B) may explain the positive effect of team size on the scientific impact of a study and that larger teams can help reduce the percentage of low-impact studies instead of producing more high-impact ones.

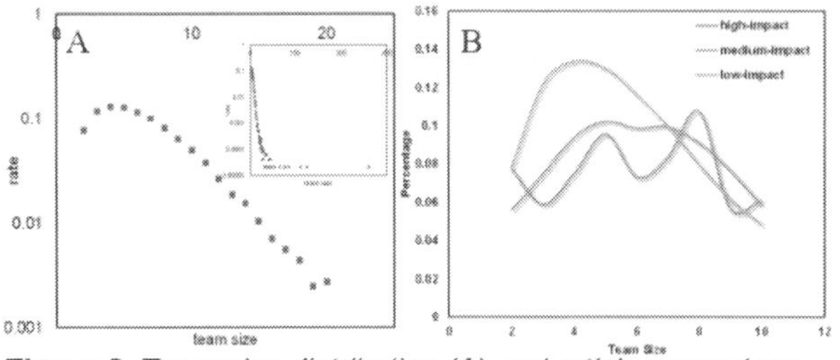


***Figure 3.*** *Team size distribution (A) and article percentage by group (B)*

## CONCLUSION

This preliminary study tries to understand whether increasing team size will affect the impact of a scientific paper. Research teams in biology are investigated to examine the relationship between team size and scientific impact. The Spearman correlation tests suggest that the increasing team size can boost the impact of a study. We suggest that less low-impact studies in larger teams can explain why their average scientific performances are much higher than those in smaller teams on average.

This study also retains some limitations. For example, this dataset only comprises publications in biology; we believe that more domains should be taken into consideration. Additionally, the distribution within smaller slides can be examined to fully understand the effect of team size on the impact of scientific publications.


## ACKNOWLEDGEMENT

This work is supported by Major Projects of National Social Science Fund (No. 16ZAD224), Fujian Provincial Key Laboratory of Information Processing and Intelligent Control (Minjiang University) (No. MJUKF201704) and Qing Lan Project, and CSC scholarship (File NO. 201606840093).


## REFERENCES


Leimkuhler, F. F. (1967). The Bradford distribution. *Journal of Documentation, 23*(3), 197-207.

Wuchty, S., Jones, B. F., & Uzzi, B. (2007). The increasing dominance of teams in production of knowledge. *Science, 316*(5827), 1036-1039.

# Textual Analysis and the History of Scholarly Communication

**Shawn Martin**
*Department of Information and Library Science, Indiana University, USA. shjmarti@indiana.edu*

## ABSTRACT

**This paper uses topic modeling and statistical analysis of keywords within early American scientific journals in order to better understand the professionalization of American science in the late 19th century. The *Journal of the American Chemical Society* was one of the first professional scientific journals developed in the United States and analyzing its content may help to understand the professional concerns of 19th century American scientists. How did these early scientists view their profession? What did chemists see as the most important scientific issues of their time? By using computational and statistical analysis of the first 40 years (1879-1922) of the journal, it becomes clear that the professionalization of chemistry took roughly 20 years and had much to do with external factors affecting science in the United States.**

## KEYWORDS

scholarly communication, topic modeling, textual analysis, history of science, American Chemical Society

## INTRODUCTION

Andrew Abbott (1991) has argued that professions develop through a series of stages and that journals are an essential part of the professionalization process of "popularizing and legitimating the profession's knowledge" (p. 364). The field of scholarly communication has often focused on analysis of journals (Borgman, Furner & Cronin, 2002). Can computational and statistical methods be used to better understand the professionalization processes that Abbott discusses? Moreover, can textual analysis of journals help to understand the social processes underlying scholarly communication? The answer to both of these questions is "yes."

Using a historical example of one of the earliest American scholarly communication systems, it is possible to better understand how the scholarly communication system (at least within a particular discipline) formed during the late 19th century. The American Chemical Society, one of the earliest professional scientific associations in the United States, formed in 1876 and began publishing its journal in 1879. Nonetheless, it was not until the 1890s that issues of professional identity became prominent. More importantly, these issues of professional identity reflect broader social issues within the scientific community during the late 19th century and reflect some of Abbott's ideas on professionalization.

## METHOD

This multi-method paper utilizes a combination of several approaches. A dataset of optical character recognition (OCR) text from all of the issues of the *Journal of the American Chemical Society* (JACS) between 1879 (the first year it was published) and 1922 (the last year in the public domain), downloaded primarily from the Hathi-Trust repository (https://www.hathitrust.org/), was created. This produced a dataset of 22,042,335 words sorted by year. After producing the dataset and doing some basic cleanup, topic modeling utilizing Mallet (http://mallet.cs.umass.edu/index.php) was performed. Topic modeling through programs like Mallet analyzes words utilizing a latent Dirichlet allocation (LDA) model. LDA determines the statistical likelihood that individual words are related to each other, thus providing researchers with a "distant reading" method for analyzing large amounts of text (Moretti, 2013).

After performing the LDA topic modeling and creating a topic list of 20 topics for each year of JACS between 1879 and 1922, a historical analysis using Browne and Weeks (1952) history of the American Chemical Society was employed to sort the data; this volume is still the most comprehensive account of the history of the American Chemical Society for the early period (1879-1922) of the society. Browne and Weeks' history also contains a history of JACS and an analysis of the kinds of topics contained within the journal. Topics produced by Mallet were sorted into expected topics, or topics that were mentioned in Browne and Weeks, and unexpected topics, or topics that were not discussed within Browne and Weeks' discussion of JACS.

After the initial analysis to determine whether there were any major differences between these two groups (expected and unexpected) topics, a second dataset of unique words from the unexpected topics was created; this dataset (n=74) represented unique words from several subgroups of unexpected topics including topics about the business of the society, topics about methodology and other miscellaneous issues. A word frequency analysis was run on these words to determine the number of times these words appeared for every year between 1870 and 1922. Finally, a dependent sample t-test was run on these word counts to determine whether there was a significant difference between the mean of the word frequencies.

80th Annual Meeting of the Association for Information Science & Technology, Washington, DC | Oct. 27-Nov. 1, 2017

## FINDINGS

The initial comparison between unexpected and expected topics showed that unexpected topics were consistently a small number of topics in any given year (less than 20% of all topics). Nonetheless, the unexpected topics doubled during the tenure of one particular editor in the years 1890- 1892, from 10% to 20% of topics, and that increase stayed consistent until the end of the dataset in 1922. This raises the question of whether this seemingly significant change in unexpected topics is actually suggesting an important variation in the content of the journal or is simply an artifact of the LDA topic modeling.

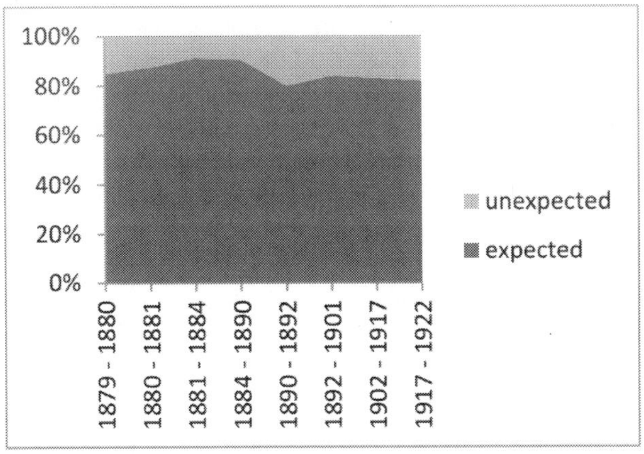


***Figure 1**. Distribution of unexpected and expected topics grouped by editorial years*

To determine whether the change in topics during this period was indeed significant, a smaller dataset of keywords found in these topics was constructed to see if there was a significant difference in the word frequencies before 1890 and after 1892. To control for the vast increase in the size of the journal (especially at end of the dataset) the word frequencies were created for 11-year periods pre-increase (1879-1890) and post-increase. (1891-1902). A dependent sample t-test showed that the mean (pre-1892) was 501.9 with a standard deviation of 592.1 and the mean (post-1892) was 1584.5 with a standard deviation of 1622.5. The t-critical value (73) for this test was 1.6 and the t-calculated was 7.6 with an effect size of 0.89. Therefore, the frequency of words is not simply an artifact of topic modeling; rather there is a statistically significant difference between the pre-increase and post-increase groups.

## CONCLUSION

Overall, this data suggests that Abbott's theories about professionalization are consistent within the field of chemistry. Professionalization moves through several stages and after about 11 years of publishing, JACS begins to discuss issues of professional identity more substantially. Furthermore, as Borgman (2000) has suggested, scholarly communication helps researchers understand both the structure and process of scholarship. According to Borgman, structure refers to the ways in which researchers communicate and process refers to "why" these researchers communicate in certain ways.

More research needs to be done to better understand why chemists were discussing issues of professionalization post-1892. Yet, this analysis of word frequencies helps to isolate a particular point in time when these changes occur. Furthermore, the theories of Andrew Abbott and a more detailed analysis of the history of the American Chemical Society may help to determine how the process of scholarly communication developed in chemistry. Since chemistry was the first professional scientific society in the United States, the method used in this study may also be applied to other scientific societies in order to determine whether the process of scholarly communication is similar in other fields and whether the professionalization of knowledge follows similar patterns throughout the scholarly communication system.

## REFERENCES


Abbott, A. (1991). The order of professionalization, an empirical analysis, *Work and Occupations*. *18*(4), 355-384.

Borgman, C. L. (2000). Digital libraries and the continuum of scholarly communication, *Journal of Documentation*. *56*(4), 412-430.

Borgman, C. L., Furner, J., & Cronin, B. (2002). Scholarly communication and bibliometrics. *Annual Review of Information Science and Technology*. 36, 3-72.

Browne, C. A. and Weeks, M. E. (1952). *A history of the American Chemical Society: Seventy-five eventful years*. Easton, PA: Mack Printing Company.

Moretti, F. (2013). *Distant reading*. London: Verso.

# Types of Research Data Management Services: An International Perspective

**Krystyna K. Matusiak**
*Department of Research Methods & Information Science, University of Denver, USA. krystyna.matusiak@du.edu*

**Frank A. Sposito**
*The Sié Chéou-Kang Center for International Security and Diplomacy, University of Denver, USA. frank.sposito@du.edu*

## ABSTRACT

**Research data management (RDM) services are increasingly offered by university libraries and data centers worldwide to support researchers in meeting funders' requirements for data management planning and to promote access to open research data. RDM remains an emergent service area and, as it continues to evolve, a dizzying array of program designs and strategies have been explored and refined to meet new technological challenges and user needs. This poster presents findings from an international study that investigated various organizational models for RDM services delivered at selected academic libraries and research centers in Australia, Europe and North America. While most RDM services examined in the study were provided by academic libraries, the research also revealed examples of embedded curation services and identified new organizational strategies, including distributed networks of RDM expertise and multi-purpose research data centers.**

## KEYWORDS

research data management, academic libraries, research data service centers, embedded services

## INTRODUCTION

Research data management (RDM) services developed at universities and other research institutions in response to demands from funding agencies and as part of the global Open Access movement. National funding agencies in several countries now require researchers to prepare data management plans (DMPs) and to provide open access to data and scholarly publications (Australian National Data Service, n.d.; European Research Council, 2017; National Science Foundation, n.d.; Research Councils UK, 2015). University libraries and research centers worldwide provide a range of data management services to support researchers in meeting the funders' requirements and in managing data at different points of the research cycle.

A number of studies have examined the roles of librarians and types of services provided in university libraries in support of RDM (Akers et al., 2014, Antell et al., 2014; Cox & Pinfield, 2014; Tenopir et al., 2015). Many researchers see RDM services as an extension of traditional academic library roles in outreach and training. However, alternative approaches have emerged in recent case studies, including studio models (Guss, 2016) and services directly embedded in research projects (Hudson-Vitale, 2016). Mohr, Johnston and Lindsay (2016) discuss collaboration among research data stakeholders and emphasize that universities "need a well-connected, distributed way to support data management" (p. 51). Most research on models and types of RDM services, however, has focused on U.S. and UK institutions. More recently, Tenopir et al. (2017) conducted a survey of research data services in European academic libraries. The study indicates that more European libraries currently offer consultative than technical services, but also manage infrastructure for data storage and collaborate with other units on campus.

This study is part of a research project undertaken by the Library Theory and Research (LTR) of the International Federation of Library Associations (IFLA). The primary objective of the project was to identify the roles and responsibilities of data curators in both international and interdisciplinary contexts. The design of the study and preliminary findings were reported at the 2016 LIDA conference (Tammaro et al., 2016). The initial study was expanded by in-depth interviews with data librarians and research data managers in several European countries.

## METHODS

The study was designed using mixed-method approach and included two phases of data collection and analysis. The first phase focused on quantitative content analysis of job announcements for data curators and RDM librarians. In the second phase, semi-structured interviews were conducted with professionals working as data librarians, data curators or research data managers. Interviews were supplemented by questionnaires and documentary evidence, including reports, RDM online tutorials and organizational websites. This poster reports the results from the second phase of the study.

The goal of interviews was to gain insight into the practice of research data management and look at the services from the perspective of the professionals working in the field. Participants were recruited from academic libraries, research centers and research data service centers in Australia, Canada, a number of European countries and the United States (see Table 1 for countries represented in the sample). Convenience

80th Annual Meeting of the Association for Information Science & Technology, Washington, DC | Oct. 27-Nov. 1, 2017

and snowball sampling were used in the recruitment. Interviews were conducted with participants at 24 international sites between March 2016 and February 2017. Twenty-six professionals actually participated in the study (two interviews included a team of two people). A site represents a unit of analysis.

| Country | No. of Sites |
|---|---|
| Australia | 3 |
| Austria | 1 |
| Canada | 3 |
| Germany | 2 |
| Netherlands | 2 |
| Sweden | 2 |
| Switzerland | 1 |
| United Kingdom | 5 |
| United States | 5 |
| **Total** | **24** |

***Table 1****. Countries represented in the interview sample*

## RESULTS

The types of RDM services identified in this study encompass both consultative and technical services. The concept of the research data lifecycle plays a central role in organizing and structuring services. RDM services are primarily located in academic libraries as part of research and consultation services or digital scholarship units. Three sites in the sample represent campus-wide data services centers and two embedded models. One site was located in the research center and one in the data archive. Table 2 provides a summary of the sites' locations.

| Location | No. of Sites |
|---|---|
| University library | 17 |
| Campus-wide research data service center | 3 |
| University department - embedded service | 2 |
| Data archive | 1 |
| Research center | 1 |
| **Total** | **24** |

***Table 2****. RDM service location*

### *RDM Services at University Libraries*

University libraries represent the largest group in the sample but the type of services, the stage of its development and the level of support for researchers varies greatly among the sites. In the early stage of RDM development, academic libraries usually focus on needs assessment, outreach, training and open access advocacy. They primarily provide consultative services on developing DMPs, metadata and data curation practices. Academic institutions with limited infrastructure for storing and sharing data recommend self-deposits of datasets in disciplinary or general open access repositories, such as figshare. Librarians offer advice on selecting a repository but are not involved in quality review or technical aspects of data management.

Building an instance of a local data repository and/or using national data archive, providing consultative as well as technical services, developing an institutional data policy and collaborating across the university with research support units were identified as salient characteristics of more advanced level RDM services at academic libraries. Support services include not only assistance with DMPs and metadata, but also with data citation, archiving and sharing. Librarians assist researchers with technical aspects of depositing data in repositories. In some cases, librarians perform quality checks and verify metadata, file formats and documentation.

### *Distributed Networks*

Another important characteristic of advanced RDM services at university libraries identified in this study is collaboration with other units and offices on campus. This approach is a prominent feature of European RDM services. Almost every participant in Europe who was interviewed for this study was involved in a university-wide network of research data experts. This observation supports the findings of the survey, which found 90.7% European libraries participating in collaborative initiatives within their institutions (Tenopir et al., 2017). The participants in this study reported participating in distributed networks, often with formal structures, which consisted of professionals with expertise in RDM, IT, copyright, research ethics and scholarly communication. Academic librarians often serve as coordinators and refer researchers to the relevant pockets of expertise in the network. Distributed networks also represent efforts in community building around improving data management practices and opening data.

### *Embedded Services*

Academic librarians assist researchers at the beginning of the data cycle, and in some cases at the end of the cycle with data deposit, but have almost no direct involvement with research projects. This limitation is addressed by embedding research data managers in research projects at university departments. Two instances of embedded RDM service were identified in this study. The first was project-based where a librarian was placed temporarily in the university department. The second case represents a more systematic approach and is part of expanding RDM services and reaching researchers in the midst of their work. In this model, librarians referred to as "data stewards" are embedded in the faculty-led research projects and research labs throughout the university. They provide support not only at the beginning and end of the research cycle, but also share expertise and advice on best data management practices throughout the research projects.

### *Research Data Service Centers*

Campus-wide research data service centers represent a new model that reflects an evolution of services and recognition that a more comprehensive suite of skills and expertise is necessary to support data management. Three cases were identified in the sample – one in the United States and two in Europe. Both European data service centers have evolved from RDM services originally located at academic libraries. These new interdisciplinary initiatives involve cross-campus collaboration and cooperation of several units, including university library, IT department, legal services and office for research. Research data service centers tend to be multi-purpose and provide university research communities not only with the expertise, tools and infrastructure necessary to manage research data but also offer support for other forms scholarly activities, including grants and publications. In addition to RDM services, the centers offer legal and ethical advice in regard to conducting research and releasing data, consultation on funding, publishing, citation metrics, copyright and open access. This interdisciplinary approach not only brings expertise from multiple areas but also increases the visibility of service and allows for building relationships with researchers.

## CONCLUSION

Effective one-size-fits-all models of academic library service delivery are rare, and this is especially evident in the variety of approaches to providing RDM services across institutional and international contexts. The model of academic libraries serving as centers of RDM services is the most prevalent in practice, but it also presents challenges with building relationships and sharing expertise. The emerging models of embedding services or building campus-wide centers are primarily present in Europe. European services are also characterized by a higher degree of collaboration with other units on campus. This study provides a perspective on the types of RDM services offered in several countries, but is limited in generalizability by a qualitative nature of data and a relatively small number of sites.

## REFERENCES


Akers, K. G., Sferdean, F. C., Nicholls, N. H., & Green, J. A. (2014). Building support for research data management: Biographies of eight research universities. *International Journal of Digital Curation 9*(2), 171-191.

Antell, K., Bales Foote, J., Turner, J., & Shults, B. (2014). Dealing with data: Science librarians' participation in data management at Association of Research Libraries institutions. *College & Research Libraries 75*(4), 557-574.

Australian National Data Service (ANDS) (n.d.). Open data. Retrieved June 15, 2017 from http://www.ands.org.au/working-with-data/articulating-the-value-of-open-data/open-data.

Cox, A. M., & Pinfield, S. (2014). Research data management and libraries: Current activities and future priorities. *Journal of Librarianship & Information Science* 46(4), 299-316.

European Research Council (ERC). (2017). Guidelines on the implementation of Open Access to scientific publications and research data in projects supported by the European Research Council under Horizon 2020. Retrieved June 15, 2017 from https://erc.europa.eu/sites/default/files/document/file/ERC%20Open%20Access%20guidelines-Version%201.1._10.04.2017.pdf

Guss, S. (2016). A studio model for academic data services. In K. Thompson and L. Kellam (Eds.), *Databrarianship: The academic data librarian in theory and practice*, (pp.9-24). Chicago: Association of College and Research Libraries.

Hudson-Vitale, C. (2016). Embedded options: A common framework. In K. Thompson and L. Kellam (Eds.), *Databrarianship: The academic data librarian in theory and practice*, (pp.25-34). Chicago: Association of College and Research Libraries.

Mohr, A. H., Johnston, L. R., & Lindsay, T. A. (2016). The data management village: Collaboration among research support providers in the large academic environment. In K. Thompson and L. Kellam (Eds.), *Databrarianship: The academic data librarian in theory and practice*, (pp.51-66). Chicago: Association of College and Research Libraries.

National Science Foundation. (NSF) (n.d.). Dissemination and sharing of research results. Retrieved June 15, 2017 from https://www.nsf.gov/bfa/dias/policy/dmp.jsp.

Research Councils UK. (RCUK). (2015). Guidance on best practice in the management of research data. Retrieved June 15, 2017 from http://www.rcuk.ac.uk/documents/documents/rcukcommonprinciplesondatapolicy-pdf/.

Tammaro, A. M., Matusiak, K.K., Sposito, F. A., Pervan, A., & Casarosa, V. (2016). Understanding roles and responsibilities of data curators: An international perspective. *Libellarium* 9 (2), 39-47.

Tenopir, C., Hughes, D., Allard, S., Frame, M., Birch, B., Baird, L., & Lundeen, A. (2015). Research data services in academic libraries: Data intensive roles for the future? *Journal of eScience Librarianship 4*(2), 1–21.

Tenopir, C., Talja, S., Horstmann, W., Late, E., Hughes, D., Pollock, D. & Allard, S. (2017). Research data services in European academic research libraries. *Liber Quarterly 27*(1), 23-44.

# Unintended and Shadow Practices of Decision Support System Dashboards in Higher Education Institutions

**Chase McCoy**
*Department of Information and Library Science, Indiana University Bloomington, USA. chamccoy@indiana.edu*

**Howard Rosenbaum**
*Indiana University Bloomington, Department of Information and Library Science, USA. hrosenba@indiana.edu*

## ABSTRACT

**Decision support system data dashboards (DSS-DD) are starting to be developed for higher education decision-making. However, there is little research concerning their impact and use. To understand the decision-making practices of DSS-DD users, this poster presents preliminary findings of a study of these systems in a large U.S. Midwestern higher education institution. We draw on the socio-technical interaction network analytic strategy and sociomateriality to examine expected and actual user decision-making practices when using these dashboards. We find that while there are expected practices, users engage in unintended and shadow socio-technical decision-making practices.**

## KEYWORDS

decision support systems, dashboards, sociotechnical, sociomateriality

## INTRODUCTION

The diverse forms of institutional data being generated and warehoused, predictive analytics and data visualization software are enabling decision-makers in higher education institutions (HEI) to integrate institutional data into their decision-making practices (Swing & Ross, 2016). To support and improve data-informed decision-making, institutions have been implementing decision support systems (DSS) to enhance strategic decision-making at institutional, program and learner levels within HEI (Daniel, 2014). These systems present information through data visualization dashboards, which display aggregated assessment information based on key performance indicators and metrics. Attention needs to be given to the sociotechnical contexts of these systems to understand the reflexive relationships through which technologies shape the contexts in which they are embedded and are shaped through use.

The poster presents preliminary findings from a case study of DSS-DD implementation and use in a large U.S. Midwestern university using a framework grounded in sociotechnical interaction networks (STIN) (Kling, McKim, & Kling, 2003) and sociomateriality (Orlikowski, 2010). This framework is being used to examine the expected decision-making practices of dashboard users from the perspective of the designers and other stakeholders and the actual practices that emerge as users interact with the dashboards. We identify the sociotechnical practices of users to suggest that 1) these systems often ignore the institutional contexts they are meant to inform and 2) as users interact with these systems they develop unintended and shadow decision-making practices.

## THEORETICAL FRAMEWORK

The framework in this study uses the STIN strategy to situate DSS-DD in the broader socio-political context of HEI, while sociomateriality draws attention to decision-makers' everyday sociotechnical practices. First, the STIN strategy (Kling et al., 2003) is used to analyze the macro-network from the stakeholders' and designers' perspectives by mapping the users and dashboards within an institutionally bound sociotechnical network. The strategy maps the network through heuristics that identify the systems' key stakeholders and users, incentive structures and resource flows, excluded actors, undesired socio-technical interactions, existing technologies and system design decisions. We then use the strategy to determine the expected decision-making practices of users.

Second, sociomateriality, a theoretically grounded approach from the information systems literature, is used to examine how actions and relations between the social and the technical are constituted in practice (Orlikowski, 2010). In this approach, people and technologies are not considered separate and distinct and the relationships and interactions between them should be the focal point of interest (Orlikowski & Scott, 2015). This part of the framework identifies actual decision-making practices of users as they engage with DSS-DD. These practices are then situated within the expected sociotechnical network identified in step one to examine how users reconfigure the network, which in turn shapes their decision-making practices.

## METHOD AND BACKGROUND

The case study focuses on enterprise DSS-DD at a large U.S. Midwestern university designed to support the decision-making practices of deans, department chairs and other campus administrators. The dashboards present real-time data and standardized reports based on key institutional metrics for assessing the financial and academic health of the university's academic units, for improving the use of institutional resources and for optimizing efficiency.

80th Annual Meeting of the Association for Information Science & Technology, Washington, DC | Oct. 27-Nov. 1, 2017

Semi-structured interviews were conducted with four designers and stakeholders and six users from four different academic units. One observation was conducted of a training session on the use of the dashboards involving one of the stakeholders and nine users. We assessed the sociotechnical structure of the DSS-DD through internal documents provided by one of the stakeholders.

## FINDINGS

The results in this section are preliminary and will be further expanded in the poster through figures.

### *DSS-DD STIN and Expected Practices*

Using the STIN strategy, we identified the relationships between the social and the technical for the DSS-DD from the perspective of the designers and project leads. The relationships, the design decisions and the undesired interactions and decision-making practices were analyzed to determine the expected practices of dashboard users.

Expected user DSS-DD practices include assessing trends in course enrollment, faculty teaching load and financial health and expenditures; modifying current data reporting practices that rely on spreadsheets and departmental systems; developing consistent standards for external reporting; allowing decision-makers direct access to the dashboards; and informing the designers of errors in the data.

### *User Practices*

As users engaged with the dashboards, their decision-making practices were influenced by their local sociotechnical networks. Users engaged in and incorporated undesired interactions into their decision-making practices. Additionally, actors excluded from the network by the designers and project leads influenced user practices.

Users reported that although the DSS-DD were designed to engender specific decision-making practices, the cost of users either rejecting the dashboards or using them to supplement their current practices outweighed the benefit of relying on the dashboards. This led to them to develop unintended and shadow practices, such as the development and use of shadow databases and reporting systems, and infrequent and mediated access to institutional data.

## DISCUSSION AND CONCLUSION

Results show that STIN and sociomateriality are useful to explain the disjunction between the expected and actual user data-informed decision-making practices. STIN helps to understand the expected user decision-making practices and situates these within the sociotechnical context of the dashboards, and sociomateriality addresses the actual practices that emerge through users' interactions with the dashboards, particularly the unintended, shadow decision-making practices, which were influenced by their existing socio-technical network.

The designers' and project leads expected users to engage in specific decision-making practices. For example, the dashboards were meant to be in a state of perpetual beta, refined through user feedback. In the event that data in the dashboards were incorrect, users were expected to inform the designers of the errors so that the errors in the dashboards could be corrected. However, when users encountered what they believed to be inaccurate data they chose instead to continue with their current reporting practices. As one user explained, he trusted his own reporting practices since the dashboards did not accurately reflect how money was allocated in his unit.

Furthermore, other actors excluded by the designers and project leads had significant impact on the users' practices. The users expressed concern about sharing the dashboards with the other decision-makers in their unit, such as faculty and staff, since traditionally these people had not had that level of access to institutional data. They were concerned about the political implications of transparent data access. This is an example of the importance of considering how the social in the users' sociotechnical network shapes the users' actual decision-making practices.

The poster will further address the decision-making practices that emerge as users engage with the DSS-DD and the influence that the users' local socio-technical network has on these emergent practices.

## REFERENCES


Daniel, B. (2015). Big data and analytics in higher education: Opportunities and challenges. *British Journal of Educational Technology*, *46*(5), 904-920.

Kling, R., McKim, G., & King, A. (2003). A bit more to it: Scholarly communication forums as socio-technical interaction networks. *Journal of the American Society for Information Science and Technology*, *54*(1), 47-67.

Orlikowski, W. J. (2010). The sociomateriality of organisational life: Considering technology in management research. *Cambridge Journal of Economics*, *34*(1), 125-141.

Orlikowski, W. J., & Scott, S. V. (2015). Exploring material-discursive practices. *Journal of Management Studies*, *52*(5), 697-705.

Swing, R. L., and Ross, L. E. (2016). Statement of Aspirational Practice for Institutional Research. Association for Institutional Research, Tallahassee, Florida. Retrieved from http://www.airweb.org/aspirationalstatement

# Rural Public Library Assets: A Multi-Classification Study

**Karen A. Miller**
*School of Library & Information Science, University of South Carolina, USA. millerk8@email.sc.edu*

## ABSTRACT

**Rural public libraries hold economic, cultural and social capital assets in trust for their communities. This study combines public data provided by the Institute of Museum and Library Services, the United States Department of Agriculture and the United States Department of Health and Human Services to (1) conduct a multi-classification study of rural public library assets to reveal differences in asset structures, (2) explore the implications of those differences on rural public library agency in the context of community development initiatives, (3) investigate differences in rural public library asset structures over time and (4) comment on sustainability issues surrounding those asset structures. Initial results indicate that even the smallest, most remote rural public libraries are positioned to ignite the creation of new community assets while connecting their communities to external revenue sources.**

## KEYWORDS

rural libraries, asset-based community development, data mining, supervised classification

## INTRODUCTION

There are over 4,100 rural public libraries scattered throughout all regions of the United States. Those libraries serve as few as 10, to as many as 250,000 residents. Approximately 40% of those libraries are located more than 25 miles from an urban area, while 12% are so close to urban areas and urban clusters that some may lose their rural status after the 2020 census. The majority of rural libraries are governed by municipalities, but all governance structures recognized by the Institute of Library & Museum Services (IMLS) are represented. Regardless of their size, location or governance structure, all rural libraries hold assets in trust for their communities' benefit (Alemanne, Mandel & McClure, 2011, pp. 26–26; Hildreth & Sullivan, 2015, pp. 650–651; Moxley & Abbas, 2016, pp. 311–312; Whitacre & Rhinesmith, 2015, p. 165; 47 U.S.C. § 1305(b)(3)(A)). When mobilizing its assets in community development initiatives, even a small, remote rural public library can improve the quality of life, fuel solutions to community issues, ignite the creation of new local assets and act as a bridge between the community and outside resources (Kretzmann & McKnight, 1993, pp. 191–205).

80[th] Annual Meeting of the Association for Information Science & Technology, Washington, DC | Oct. 27-Nov. 1, 2017



## RESEARCH PROBLEM AND RESEARCH QUESTIONS

Rural public libraries hold economic, cultural and social capital assets in trust for their communities. However, with the exception of broadband availability (Alemanne, Mandel & McClure, 2011; Bertot, Real, Lee, McDermott & Jaeger, 2014; Whitacre & Rhinesmith, 2015), there are few studies of rural public library asset structures or studies reflecting changes in asset structures over time. To help fill those gaps, this study combines public data provided by the Institute of Museum and Library Services (IMLS) Public Library Survey, the United States Department of Agriculture Rural Atlas (USDA) and the United States Department of Health and Human Services Area Health Resources File to (1) conduct a multi-classification of rural public library assets to reveal differences in asset structures, (2) explore the implications of those differences on rural public library agency in the context of community development initiatives, (3) investigate differences in rural public library asset structures over time and (4) comment on sustainability issues surrounding those asset structures.

Specifically, this research seeks to answer the following questions:

**Q1:** What are the differences in the asset holdings of rural public libraries when classified by (1) locale (distance from urbanized areas and urban clusters), (2) legal basis (governance structure), (3) service area population size and (4) geographic region; and what are the implications of those differences on rural public library community development agency?

**Q2:** How have those asset differences changed over time, and what are the implications of those changes for rural public library asset sustainability?

## METHODOLOGY

Guided by the economic, cultural and capital asset theories of Pierre Bourdieu (1985), rural public library asset variables were constructed on a per capita basis from the 2012, 2013 and 2014 IMLS Public Library Survey files and combined with select variables from the corresponding USDA and health services datasets. Due to the leptokurtic distributions of the IMLS variables and variable outliers, nonparametric statistical methodologies were adopted for this study, including median absolute deviation (MAD) calculations which corrected for differences in variable scales and identified outliers. Using the MAD-transformed 2014 dataset for supervised classifier training, WEKA (see http://www.cs.waikato.ac.nz/ml/weka/) random forest and J48 algorithms were tested to identify the most accurate predictors of the four classes identified in research question one. The best classifier predictors were evaluated using the kappa statistic and the receiver operating characteristic (ROC) area, then validated against the 2013 and 2012 test sets. Further analyses to explain the best classifier results were conducted using Excel, R and Tableau software.

## RESULTS

The most accurate classifier of rural public libraries was service area size. An 84% accuracy rate resulted from per capita outlets, hours, staff, inventory and terminals, as well as legal basis and locale predictors. A 97% to 99% accuracy rate was achieved for service areas under 1,000 persons. That unusually high accuracy rate is explained by the clustering of per capita outliers around the smallest, most remote rural libraries. Compared to larger service area sub-classes, the smallest libraries report the highest levels of median per capita state, federal and other revenue – revenue that would otherwise be unavailable to the community.

The region classifier achieved 81% accuracy using library variables (service area size, legal basis and locale); demographic variables (percentage of foreign-born and non-diploma holding residents, female households, households owning a home and veterans); and the number of primary care physicians. Non-profit, Native American, school district and library district governance structures cluster around certain regions, but the high accuracy of the region classifier is attributed to factors such as the high levels of foreign-born residents in the far west region and the high percentage of residents without a diploma in the southeast region. Such regional differences have implications for library collections and programming.

The best locale (distance from urban areas and clusters) classifier had a 66% accuracy rate, and the best legal basis classifier had a 64% accuracy rate (although municipal libraries, representing the majority of all rural libraries were classified accurately 90% of the time). The lower overall accuracy rates are explained by the presence of many small differences in library asset structures within the two classes. For example, the most remote rural libraries have generally higher median per capita numbers of computers than libraries nearer urban areas and clusters.

There were only small differences in classifier accuracy among the 2014, 2013 and 2012 datasets. For example, the service area size classifier accuracy differed by only .79% between 2012 and 2014. The small differences in classifier accuracy over time indicate (1) the predictors, trained on the 2014 dataset, did not over-fit the data and (2) in answer to research question two, rural library asset structures remained fairly constant between 2012 and 2014.

## CONCLUSION

As evidenced by per capita revenue outliers, the smallest rural libraries connect their communities to external economic capital. The negligible changes in service area classification accuracy between 2012 and 2014 indicate that the smallest rural libraries sustained their economic contributions during the period.

The analysis will be expanded to include the 2015 and 2016 periods when the IMLS releases those datasets later this year. Work will then continue to explore the implications of rural public library asset difference on community development agency and to suggest public policy directions for strengthening and sustaining rural public library assets.

## REFERENCES


Alemanne, N. D., Mandel, L. H., & McClure, C. R. (2011). Chapter 3: The rural public library as leader in community broadband services. *Library Technology Reports, 47*(6), 19-28.

Bertot, J. C., Real, B., Lee, J., McDermott, A. J., & Jaeger, P. T. (2015, October 1). *2014 digital inclusion survey: Survey findings and results*. Retrieved from http://digitalinclusion.umd.edu/sites/default/files/uploads/2014DigitalInclusionSurveyFinalRelease.pdf

Bourdieu, P. (1985). The forms of capital. In J. Richardson (Ed.), *Handbook of theory and research for the sociology of education* (pp. 241-258). New York, NY: Greenwood Press.

Hildreth, S., & Sullivan, M. (2015). Rising to the challenge: Re-envisioning public libraries. *Journal of Library Administration, 55*, 647-657.

Kretzmann, J. P., & McKnight, J. L. (1993). Building communities from the inside out: A path toward finding and mobilizing a community's assets. Skokie, IL: ACTA Publications.

Moxley, D. P., & Abbas, J. M. (2016). Envisioning libraries as collaborative community anchors for social service provision to vulnerable populations. *Practice: Social Work in Action, 28*, 311-330.

Whitacre, B., & Rhinesmith, C. (2015). Public libraries and residential broadband adoption: Do more computers lead to higher rates? *Government Information Quarterly*, 32, 164-171.

# Quantifying the Evolution of Citation Cascades

**Chao Min**
*School of Information Management, Nanjing University, China. chaomin@iu.edu*

**Ying Ding**
*School of Informatics and Computing, Indiana University, USA. dingying@indiana.edu*

**Jianjun Sun**
*School of Information Management, Nanjing University, China. sjj@nju.edu.cn*

## ABSTRACT

**Citation is an important measurement in science which provides valuable clues to the historical development and trend forecast of science. However, the evolution of citation structure remains poorly understood despite long-period and frequent use of citation counts for assessment purposes within scientific community. We observe citation structure from a cascade perspective and construct a large and long-range citation graph based on real data. Two metrics are used to quantify the structural virality and cascade size. Preliminary results show that (1) age plays an important role for the evolution of citation cascades; (2) average depth tends to be influenced by both lifespan and the whole volume of scientific literature and grows much slower than cascade size; (3) there exists a stable positive relationship between average depth and cascade size, and it seems that an ultimate status exists where most papers eventually have large values for both metrics.**

## KEYWORDS

citation cascade, citation structure, citation growth

## INTRODUCTION

Citation data are frequently used in measuring scientific impact. However, most citation indicators are based on citation counts (Hirsch, 2005; Garfield, 2006; Fersht, 2009), leaving the great value of citation dynamic process largely unexplored. Recently, we (Min, Ding & Li et al., 2017) used a classic marketing model (Bass, 1969) to characterize the diffusion process of citations and found some patterns in the spread of scientific ideas. As an extension of our prior work, this study tries to explore how structural virality (Goel, Anderson & Hofman et al., 2015) of citation cascade grows to provide better understanding of citation dynamics.

*Citation cascade* is not a familiar term, although as far as we know, it was first mentioned in literature (Mazloumian, Eom & Helbing et al., 2011). We use this term to refer to a citation tree (which is also a directed acyclic graph, DAG) initiated by a root paper (see for example Figure 1).

What is more common to us is the notion of information cascade that has been extensively studied. Information cascade is a primary mechanism by which information contents reach the audience within a social system, such as online platforms like Facebook, Twitter, Instagram, etc. Take Twitter as an example; the original post can become a large cascade by being retweeted by a large number of Twitter users. Correspondingly, a paper can also initiate a citation cascade in which the original paper is cited by following papers, and following papers are cited by their successors, and so on. See Figure 1 for a real example.

Diving into the structure of citations, we aim in this study to explore the structural virality of citation process in order to see how citation cascades evolve and how citation grows with time. Specifically, we will focus on the following research questions:

- How can one observe and quantify the structure properties of citation cascades?
- How are structural indicators distributed for papers of the same and different age?
- How do structural indicator distributions evolve over long range of time?
- What is the relationship between structural virality and cascade size?

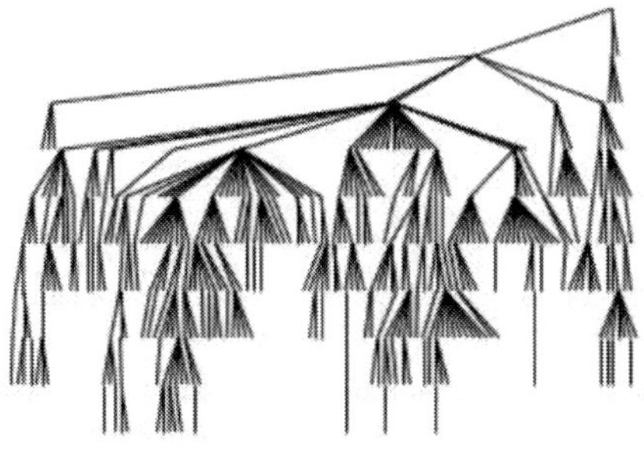


***Figure 1**. A citation cascade initiated by paper 10.1103/PhysRevE.57.2081*

80th Annual Meeting of the Association for Information Science & Technology, Washington, DC | Oct. 27-Nov. 1, 2017

## DATA AND METHOD

The American Physical Society (APS) corpus contains articles from the journal *Physical Review* and dates back to 1893. This corpus comprises two datasets: 1) metadata of over 450,000 articles; 2) more than 6 million citation pairs within *Physical Review*.

We found some errors exist in the citation pairs dataset, e.g., a paper cited another paper published long after its own publication. This could lead to severe errors in the calculation of the average depth of cascades (Equation 1). Therefore, we cleaned the dataset by retaining those citation pairs in which both the citing paper and cited paper have publication year information and the former is no earlier than the latter. Among the original 6,040,030 citation pairs, 46,282 erroneous pairs were found and 5,993,748 pairs were remained.

$$\text{Average depth} = \frac{1}{|T|-1}\sum_{v\in T, v\neq r} d(v, r), \quad (1)$$

where $T$ is a citation cascade initiated by paper $r$, $d(i, j)$ is the distance between vertices $i$ and $j$.

A directed acyclic graph was constructed based on the cleaned citation pairs, in which an edge meant that the start vertex was cited by the target vertex. We chose four samples from the dataset (papers published in 1960, 1980, 2000 and 2005, respectively) for comparison and calculated the average depth and the number of successors for the citation tree initiated by each of these papers.

| Year | 1960 | 1980 | 2000 | 2005 |
|---|---|---|---|---|
| # papers | 1,528 | 4,134 | 13,459 | 16,282 |

***Table 1.*** *Sample papers and volumes*

## PRELIMINARY RESULTS

### *Distributions of Two Structure Metrics*

If there is a competition among papers to gain more successors (papers who cite them, papers who cite who cite them, etc.), it should be fair for papers to start at the same scratch line (same publication time). Even so, the performance is diverse for these papers, let alone those with different publication time.

The 2005 papers show both a long tail and a long head in terms of cascade size distribution. This indicates that most of these papers have relatively small cascade sizes, but the interval of larger cascade sizes is very wide even though the density of each point is low. The distribution curve shows a steep monotone decreasing trend.

The 2000 papers also exhibit a monotone decreasing curve for cascade size distribution, but less steep. The cascade sizes are generally larger than those of the 2005 papers and the difference among papers is smaller.

The situation reverses in 1980, where papers with large cascade sizes become mainstream. As cascade size increases, the proportion of papers goes through a long-range growth, reaching its peak at a quite large cascade size.

For papers published in 1960, cascade sizes exhibit further growth. The situation seems almost opposite with papers in 2005: most papers have quite large cascade sizes and only a few have small sizes.

The four cascade size distributions in Figure 2 clearly show how cascade size grows as papers get older. As the 1960 case suggests, most papers eventually grow into large cascades, but there is still a small proportion with much smaller cascade sizes than the vast majority.

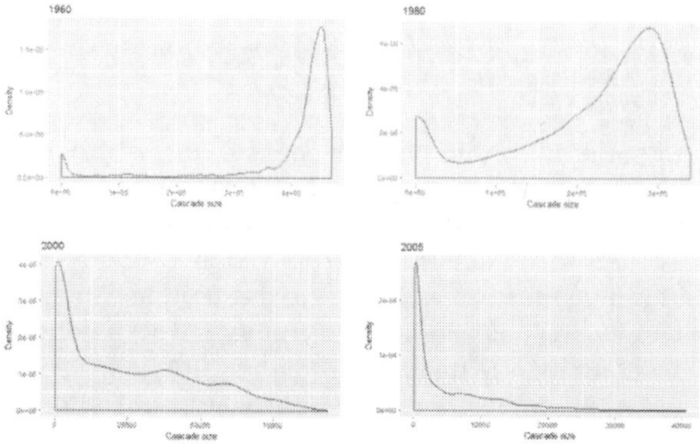


***Figure 2.*** *Distributions of cascade size over four samples*

As is shown in Figure 3, the average depths of papers in different ages have approximate intervals. Time seems to have a non-linear impact on average depth. The 1980 papers have relatively long average depths compared to 1960 papers. This may be due to the fact that APS corpus keeps growing with time. But the average depths of the 2000 papers are in general shorter than those of the 1980 papers, with the reason lying in that the 2000 papers still have large potential to grow in terms of cascade sizes. Again this pattern is repeated and the reason is confirmed by the observation that the 2005 papers have even shorter average depths than the 2000 papers.

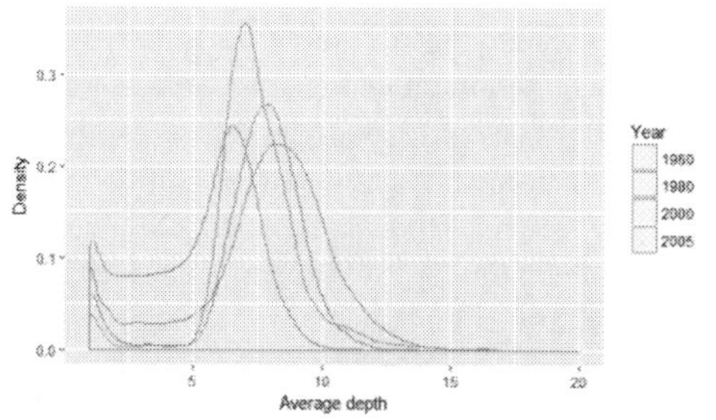


***Figure 3.*** *Distributions of average depth over four samples*

### *Virality vs. Popularity*

We drew scatter plots for average depth and cascade size on log-log scale to see their relationship. Figure 4 suggests that their relationship remains surprisingly clear and stable for papers from all groups. Most points (papers) are distributed within a ring-like contour, where average depth increases with cascade size and begins to decrease after reaching a plateau. Interestingly, although the shape of scatter plots remains very similar, the density of points exhibits significant temporal patterns. As age grows, papers tend to concentrate on the right side of the ring-like contour, leaving a migration route in time domain. Therefore, two facts are revealed by Figure 4. Firstly, the overall relationship between average depth and cascade size settles in a relatively stable range, which is not time-varying. Secondly, it seems that most papers will eventually reach a status where both average depth and cascade size are very large.

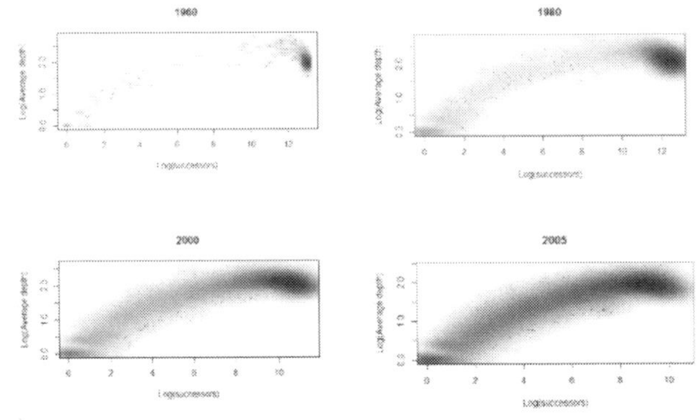


***Figure 4.*** *The relationship between cascade size and average depth*

## CONCLUSION AND NEXT STEPS

This poster gives preliminary results on a large and long-range citation graph of how citation structure evolves with time. By analogy to information cascades, we use citation cascades to observe the growth of citation structure. For a citation cascade initiated by a root paper, we take advantage of total number of successive citing papers to measure its cascade size and average depth of all successors to the root paper to measure its structural virality.

It turns out that age has a significant impact on the citation structure of a paper. Different groups of papers from different ages exhibit distinct distributions for citation size. The range of average depth, however, remains relatively changeless. And the distribution of average depth tends to be influenced by both lifespan and the whole volume of scientific literature. There exists a stable positive relationship between average depth and cascade size, and it seems that an ultimate status exists where most papers eventually have large values for both metrics.

As very little is known to us about both temporal and structural dynamics of citation process, the preliminary results of this poster have implications in respect of scientific evaluation. Cascade size and structural virality show potential in quantifying properties of citation cascades. The huge differences in patterns of cascade size distributions indicate the length of citation window chosen to assess scientific outputs might have great impact on evaluation results. The relative stable relationship between cascade size and structural virality needs further quantitative examination. In next steps of this research, we would like to investigate how citation cascades evolution can be utilized to benefit the practice of using citation data for scientific evaluation.

## ACKNOWLEDGMENTS

This research was supported by the National Natural Science Foundation of China (NSFC Nos. 71273125), Major Bidding Program of National Social Science Foundation of China (Nos. 16ZDA224) and the China Scholarship Council.

## REFERENCES

Bass, F. M. (1969). A new product growth for model consumer durables. *Management Science, 15*(5), 215-227.

Fersht, A. (2009). The most influential journals: *Impact Factor* and *Eigenfactor*. *Proceedings of the National Academy of Sciences*, 106(17), 6883-6884.

Garfield, E. (2006). The history and meaning of the journal impact factor. *JAMA, 295*(1), 90-93.

Goel, S., Anderson, A., Hofman, J., & Watts, D. J. (2015). The structural virality of online diffusion. *Management Science, 62*(1), 180-196.

Hirsch, J. E. (2005). An index to quantify an individual's scientific research output. *Proceedings of the National academy of Sciences*, 16569-16572.

Mazloumian, A., Eom, Y. H., Helbing, D., Lozano, S., & Fortunato, S. (2011). How citation boosts promote scientific paradigm shifts and Nobel prizes. *PloS One, 6*(5), e18975.

Min, C., Ding, Y., Li, J., Pei, L., & Sun, J. (2017). Innovation or imitation: The diffusion of citations. Under review.

# Too Much Information: Video Conferencing for Professional Communication

**Sarah Beth Nelson**
*University of North Carolina, USA. sbnelson@live.unc.edu*

**Mohammad Hossein Jarrahi**
*University of North Carolina, USA. jarrahi@email.unc.edu*

## ABSTRACT

**This study examines how video conferencing is living up to its potential as a substitute for face-to-face communication among remote professionals. We interviewed mobile knowledge workers to better understand how video conferencing is used in professional settings. The laws of media provided our theoretical framework. We found that video conferencing enhances the face; retrieves gesture and setting; obsolesces telephone and face-to-face communication, although imperfectly; and reverses into facelessness when sights and sounds from the background become distracting. The telephone may become more obsolete when problems like low bandwidth are resolved. Professionals would benefit from conferencing on devices on which their faces appear larger, and distracting background is less visible. Novel, in this work, are the consequences of video conferencing working too well.**

## KEYWORDS

video conference, medium theory, mobile knowledge workers

## INTRODUCTION

Video conferencing is the closest form of mediated communication to speaking in person. Speakers hear one another's voices, see one another's bodies and are both present for the conversation at the same time. As they often need to connect with colleagues and clients remotely, mobile knowledge workers (MKWs) can help us understand how video conferencing is used for professional communications.

With these thoughts in mind we ask

> How is video conference living up to its potential as a substitute for face-to-face communication among remote professionals?

## LITERATURE

### *Related Work*

Others have addressed the perceived benefits of speaking face-to-face through video conference (Nelson, Jarrahi and Thomson, 2017), video conference as a tool for collaboration (Nilsen, 2011), the difficulty of building relationships through video conference (Mülfelder et al., 1999) and struggles with video conferencing over low bandwidth. In our research, we hope to build on previous findings, and also address issues such as the possible consequences of video conference doing what it does too well.

### *Theoretical Framework*

Medium theory predicts that every medium

- enhances "some aspect of a situation" or extends a "sense or configuration of senses" (McLuhan & McLuhan, 1988, p. 227)
- retrieves "something long obsolete" and presses it "back into service, revivified" (McLuhan & McLuhan, 1988, p. 228)
- obsolesces an existing medium, "rendering a former situation impotent by displacement" (McLuhan & McLuhan, 1988, p. 227)
- reverses into its opposite: "It is the peak of form, as it were, by overload" (McLuhan & McLuhan, 1988, p. 228)

The laws of media are particularly useful for dissecting video conferencing. They help put it into the context of other media and examine its relationship with the senses.

## METHOD

We conducted in-depth interviews with 37 mobile knowledge workers, mostly from North Carolina's Research Triangle. Twelve participants agreed to participate in additional data collection and submitted twice-daily diaries on their technology use for 7-10 days. In their interviews and diary entries, MKWs frequently discussed their many means for communicating with colleagues and clients.

## FINDINGS

Our findings are grouped by the McLuhans' (1988) laws of media, describing what video conferencing enhances, retrieves, obsolesces and reverses into. We also discuss an aspect of video conferencing that falls outside the laws of media.

### *Enhances*

Video conferencing enhances the face, allowing individuals to look at one another while not in the same location. Repeatedly our participants mentioned using video conference specifically to talk to people who were "remote" (P9). The fact that they could see each other's faces was also important. P9 told us, "I like the ability to see people face to face."

80th Annual Meeting of the Association for Information Science & Technology, Washington, DC | Oct. 27-Nov. 1, 2017

### *Retrieves*

Video conferencing retrieves gesture. P7 said "it's different when it's over the phone and they can't see you versus in person." Facial expressions and gestures can contribute to communication when the body is visible.

Video conference also retrieves relevance of setting, something not present for phone conversations. The importance of location is seen in our participants' attention to it. P9 Skypes from home because "you can't really do that as well from a coffee shop." P19 reserves a conference room for Skype meetings.

### *Obsolesces*

Some of our participants mentioned video conferencing replacing phone meetings. P4's company is beginning to "incorporate video into our meetings, which, historically, has not happened."

However, this obsolescence is imperfect. P3 complains that "Skype is just not reliable enough and other services are too expensive." P5 has had problems getting Skype and Google Hangouts to work due to a poor internet connection.

Video conference also obsolesces the need for meeting in person. P9 does coaching by video conference, a professional activity that has traditionally occurred face to face.

### *Reverses*

When overextended, video conferencing reverses into facelessness. Other audio and visual elements become so important they distract from the speaker. P2's dog likes to get on her lap. She said, "most people think it's kind of funny" but "there are some clients that I would definitely not" allow to see the dog. P4 objected to his company moving to video meetings: "That means I gotta actually shower and shave, right when I get up at 4 in the morning." Other details of the setting, like clothing and pets, are projected along with the speaker's face and they are distracting.

### *Engaged with the Medium*

A comment came up in our interviews regarding video conferencing that does not fit neatly into the laws of media, but is deeply connected with the use of this medium. P6 complained that people "are typically not looking at you while they're talking to you." He said, "They're looking at their screen, or they're looking at my picture, but they're not looking at the camera. So they're looking away. It's disconcerting" (P6). Individuals in a video conference engage with the medium rather than the person they are speaking with.

## DISCUSSION

Speaking on the telephone was previously the next best thing to speaking in person. It is surprising that video conference, with the added visual has not more thoroughly displaced the phone. Perhaps when conferencing platforms work more reliably and/or internet connectivity is improved to better support video conferencing we will see it gain more dominance. It is also possible that the digital age is better able to support various communication technologies, such that multiple media remain viable even though they could easily be in competition with one another.

The fact that, often, more than just the speaker's face is projected has serious implications for using video conference in a professional context. P7 opts to use his computer rather than his phone for video conferencing because he likes to have "the bigger screen with the nicer camera." But perhaps there is something to be said for using FaceTime through a smartphone, where the speaker's face fills the screen and video quality isn't pristine. An excellent view of the speaker's clothes, hair and background are distracting.

Finally, Carr (2011) argues that people engage with the medium of the internet rather than the content. We don't fully read the articles we click on. This makes sense in light of McLuhan's (2003) claims that content is an illusion (p. 19). Missing from these discussions are human beings other than the listener/reader/consumer. Communication requires at least two people and these discussions of medium, content and engagement consider only one person. Leaving out the other person, it is easy to overlook the possibility of engaging with a human. Speakers in a video conference engage with the medium, the projected face, rather than the other person they are speaking with. How people interact with actual human beings while using communication technologies is worth further consideration.

## REFERENCES


Carr, N. (2011). The shallows: What the internet is doing to our brains. New York: W. W. Norton & Company.

Leverette, M. (2003). Towards an ecology of understanding: Semiotics, medium theory, and the uses of meaning. *Image and Narrative*, *3*(2). Retrieved from http://www.imageandnarrative.be/inarchive/mediumtheory/marcleverette.htm

McLuhan, M. (2003). *Understanding media: The extensions of man*. (W. T. Gordon, Ed.). Corte Madera, CA: Gingko Press.

McLuhan, M., & McLuhan, E. (1988). *Laws of media: The new science*. Toronto: University of Toronto Press.

Mülfelder, M., Klein, U., Simon, S., & Luczak, H. (1999). Teams without trust? Investigations in the influence of video-mediated communication on the origin of trust among cooperating persons. *Behaviour & Information Technology*, *18*(5), 349-360.

Nelson, S. B., Jarrahi, M. H., & Thomson, L. (2017). Mobility of knowledge work and affordances of digital technologies. *International Journal of Information Management*, *37*(2), 54-62. https://doi.org/10.1016/j.ijinfomgt.2016.11.008

Nilsen, L. L. (2011). Collaboration and learning in medical teams by using video conference. *Behaviour & Information Technology*, *30*(4), 507-515.

# Context, Visibility and Control: Contesting the Objectivity of Visual (Video) Records of Police-Citizen Interactions

**Bryce Clayton Newell**
*School of Information Science, University of Kentucky, USA. brycenewell@uky.edu*

## ABSTRACT

**This poster presents some initial findings from a mixed-methods study of police officer attitudes and concerns about bystander (citizen) video and the officers' own use of body-worn cameras (BWCs) within two municipal police agencies in the United States. Utilizing a data analysis methodology based in grounded theory, I argue that officers' concerns stem from their perceived inability to control context (both of what is recorded and/or disseminated, as well as the physical situations in which the recordings are made) and unwanted visibility. These concerns are heightened by the fact that officers are working in an environment filled with increasing calls to "release the tapes" (and thus to hold officers accountable for misconduct), especially because these calls are often based on assumptions about the "objectivity" of these visual records of police-civilian interactions that run counter to many officers' opinions that the video evidence lacks vital contextual information.**

## KEYWORDS

policing, body-worn cameras, surveillance, video, visibility

## INTRODUCTION

Police departments in the United States – and elsewhere – have been outfitting their officers with body-worn cameras (BWCs) for a number of years, partly in response to a host of image management problems generated by the rise of bystander (citizen) video and the recent surge in media attention to police-involved violence. Unlike with many police surveillance technologies, widespread adoption of body-worn cameras has been supported by national civil liberties organizations as a means to protect communities from police misconduct – or at least to document aberrant police behavior. Thus, the media, the police and civil society have constructed an image of body cameras as something different from typical police surveillance technology – as something more desirable and empowering of democratic civilian oversight of the police. These narratives are often based on assumptions that BWC footage can provide more objective evidence of police-civilian interactions (like that captured by bystander video).

There is a growing body of (mostly quantitative) research into the effects of BWC deployment and (mostly non-empirical) research on the role and implications of bystander video or organized "copwatching" (Farmer & Sun, 2016), but there is little qualitative social research examining how police officers understand and perceive the impact of bystander video or the use of BWCs on their work (for important exceptions see, e.g., Farmer & Sun, 2016; Koen, 2016; Sandhu, 2017; Sandhu, 2016; Sandhu & Haggerty, 2017; Tanner & Meyer, 2015; Timan, 2013). The present research builds on these earlier studies while also focusing on police officer perceptions of both phenomena, with the aim of providing a better understanding of how officers perceive and react to working on camera (theirs or someone else's), especially where the presence of a camera has the potential to increase the visibility of an individual officers' everyday work to a broad audience.

80th Annual Meeting of the Association for Information Science & Technology, Washington, DC | Oct. 27-Nov. 1, 2017



## METHODS

I present initial findings from an analysis of data collected through fieldwork (interviews, observation, ride-alongs) with, and surveys of, police officers in two municipal police agencies in the Pacific Northwest (United States). I conducted surveys in fall 2014, May/June 2015 and June 2016, respectively, and engaged in qualitative fieldwork during the same timeframe. Besides the surveys, the project also encompassed 40 ride-alongs with 29 different officers, ranging in duration from a few hours to entire 10-hour-and-40-minute shifts, as well as numerous informal discussions with other officers and department administrators. The three survey questionnaires, designed primarily to inform the qualitative investigation and, as appropriate, validate whether certain themes drawn from the qualitative work were more generalizable across the two departments, resulted in 148, 133 and 126 valid responses, respectively, across both departments. On all three surveys, officers were asked qualitative and quantitative questions designed to elicit their attitudes and concerns about the use of BWCs, bystanders recording them while they work and the dissemination of these recordings online.

## INITIAL FINDINGS

Through multiple rounds of coding, clear themes emerged from both the interviews and qualitative survey-response data. Officers are generally concerned about a loss of control, both of the immediate physical interaction and incident response (for example, in cases of bystanders recording and getting too close or interjecting themselves into a crime scene or police-citizen contact) and of the framing and disclosure of the subsequent recordings of the incident. The first concern is connected to fears about safety and the ability to do their jobs (by restricting interference, obstruction or distraction), while the second is about visibility, tied up in ambiguities about the motivations of the recording bystanders, the loss or misrepresentation of context and the potential for heightened visibility through online dissemination. The first of these concerns is predominately present in responses to questions about bystander video (although some officers also feel that the presence of their own BWC may also lessen the amount of discretion they are able to exert during a contact), while the second concern is connected more broadly to both bystander video and BWCs.

As I operationalize it here, the *loss of context* means at least two different things to officers. First, it means the recordings will not capture the full subjective experience of the officers, and thus the audience will view the video without understanding how the officers subjectively perceived the situation and why the officers chose to make the decisions they did. Second, it means the recording is limited in its ability to capture or show the entire sequence of events that led to the incidents (or interaction/use of force, etc.) of interest, because of limited visibility (on the recording), limited audio capture, distortion due to the cameras' point of view or limited coverage from the beginning of an incident until the conclusion due to practical or intentional reasons (e.g., the bystander or officer did not initiate the recording until after the incident had started, either intentionally or not).

## CONCLUSION

Police officers have historically been the most visible face of the criminal justice system. However, in the past, they were generally visible only through direct interactions with citizens – and within the view of nearby onlookers. However, this primary visibility has gradually given way to myriad additional forms of secondary visibility (Goldsmith, 2010), including from bystander video and the mandated public disclosure of officers' BWC footage under access to information laws. The rapid growth and expansion of secondary visibility of police officers has had significant ramifications for police accountability and transparency, but it also implicates a host of other concerns, both for officers and other individuals caught on camera. These concerns, especially those about disclosure and online dissemination of bystander video or BWC footage, are amplified by the officers' perception that many in the press and in their communities (and possibly in their own departmental leadership) want broad access to this footage in order to hold officers accountable for (even small or innocent) mistakes. Additionally, popular cries to "release the tapes" are not always about providing full (or at least more) information or context about an incident. Rather, these calls have at least three primary purposes: to gather evidence in order to "prove" the claimants preferred interpretation of events, vindicate their pre-existing concerns and interests and/or prosecute the police officers involved; to provide a more complete and accurate picture of the events and conduct at issue, also as a form of evidence, in order for the truth to come out and for justice to be done (no matter which side has its story bolstered); and the calls for greater transparency reflect a general call for less government secrecy and more popular and democratic oversight of government action, and are not always about procuring evidence.

## ACKNOWLEDGMENTS

Thanks to Mike Katell and Chris Heaney for assistance with data collection and to all who facilitated access to both departments. Portions of this research were funded by the University of Washington (Information School) and under a grant from the Netherlands Organisation for Scientific Research (NWO) (project number 453-14-004).

## REFERENCES

Farmer, A.K., & Sun, I.Y. (2016). Citizen journalism and police legitimacy: Does recording the police make a difference? In M. Deflem (Ed.), *The politics of policing: Between force and legitimacy* (pp. 239-256). Bingley, UK: Emerald Group Publishing Limited.

Goldsmith, A.J. (2010). Policing's new visibility. *British Journal of Criminology*, 50, 914-934.

Koen, M. (2016). On-set with body-worn cameras in a police organization: Structures, practices, and technological frames (Unpublished doctoral dissertation). George Mason University, Fairfax, VA.

Sandhu, A. (2017). 'I'm glad that was on camera': A case study of police officers' perceptions of cameras. *Policing and Society*. Advance online publication. doi: 10.1080/10439463.2017.1285917.

Sandhu, A. (2016). Camera-friendly policing: How the police respond to cameras and photographers. *Surveillance & Society, 14*(1), 78-89.

Sandhu, A., & Haggerty, K.D. (2017). Policing on camera. *Theoretical Criminology, 21*(1), 78–95.

Tanner, S., & Meyer, M. (2015). Police work and new 'security devices': A tale from the beat. *Security Dialogue, 46*(4), 384-400.

Timan, T. (2013). Changing landscapes of surveillance: Emerging technologies and participatory surveillance in Dutch nightscapes (Unpublished doctoral dissertation). University of Twente, Enschede, The Netherlands.

# Is Informal Data Citation for Data Sharing and Re-Use More Common than Formal Data Citation?

**Hyoungjoo Park**
*SOIS, U. Wisconsin-Milwaukee, USA. park32@uwm.edu*

**Dietmar Wolfram**
*SOIS, U. Wisconsin-Milwaukee, USA. dwolfram@uwm.edu*

**Sukjin You**
*SOIS, U. Wisconsin-Milwaukee, USA. yous@uwm.edu*

## ABSTRACT

**Data citation to reflect instances of data sharing and re-use is becoming more common, although it is not yet widely adopted. We investigate how common formal and informal data citation are in bioscience/biomedical research. We found that informal data citation (i.e., acknowledgments embedded in publications outside of formal references) is far more common than formal citations. Informal citations go unrecorded, and therefore authors of datasets largely do not receive credit for having informed or influenced the research of others.**

## KEYWORDS

data citation, data sharing & re-use, scholarly communication

## INTRODUCTION

This poster presentation reports on research data citation practices. Data sharing (where authors make their datasets or other products such as tissue cultures available to other researchers) and data re-use (where authors rely on these shared products for their research) are becoming more common, prompted by data sharing requirements from major funding agencies such as the National Science Foundation (NSF) and National Institutes of Health (NIH). Data citation is intended to give due credit to data sharers for their contributions. Are data citation practices reflected in the research literature through informal or formal data citations? Previous studies report that data citation is far from common (Robinson-García, Jiménez-Contreras & Torres-Salinas, 2016), although more citations or mentions in other articles are received with shared or preserved research data (Piwowar, 2011). This study focuses on the informal data citation in bioscience/biomedical disciplines.

## METHODOLOGY

Some 3,725 DOIs from the Genetics and Heredity Subject Category from the Clarivate Analytics' Data Citation Index (DCI) were collected. Of 3,725 DOIs, only 313 DOIs matched the PubMed Central IDs using the ID converter API from NIH (https://www.ncbi.nlm.nih.gov/pmc/tools/id-converter-api). The 313 full-text documents with PMC IDs were extracted in NXML format from the 2016 PMC snapshot dataset that the Clinical Decision Support Track provided (http://www.trec-cds.org/2016.html). Text without tags was extracted from each NXML document. Note that other API-accessible sources for metadata and full text, such as Google Scholar, would block multiple requests, so it could not be used as a source. Python was used for text processing.

Selected terms and phrases were used from the downloaded files as indicators to detect informal data citation by referring to terminology identified in an earlier study (Park and Wolfram, 2017): *commercial*, *Corp.*, *database*, *Database*, *donated*, *gift*, *.gov*, *Inc.*, *indebted*, *laboratories*. Text (250 characters) appearing before/after the terms were extracted to provide context for the term usage. A total of 4759 instances of these indicators were identified within the downloaded articles.

The researchers manually coded the instances to judge whether the terms were used for data sharing or re-use. Cross-checking was done among three coders for consensus. A coding scheme was created to analyze data usage (DS – data sharing, DR – data re-use, /R – repeatedly described for already cited data, O – Other) and location in the document (M – main text, A – acknowledgements, S – supplementary information, R – references, F – funding and AB – abstract). There were 931 instances of confirmed informal data sharing and re-use and only 170 formal instances.

## FINDINGS

Figure 1 summarizes the terms and phrases used in data sharing and re-use. Commonly used indicating terms and phrases for data sharing and re-use are *database*, *obtained from*, *.gov*, *publicly available*, *accession*, *Suppl*, *commercial* and *repository*.

Table 1 summarizes the frequency of data sharing and re-use and their location in the articles. Of the 313 articles examined, 212 (67.7%) contained at least one example of data sharing or re-use. The percentage of data re-use (48.7%) was much higher than the data sharing (21.3%). Some researchers collected their data from different sources, modified it by using their own data then made their modified data also available. Researchers advertised and shared their data multiple times. Some data re-use represented collected sources from a number of data sources and then were referred to multiple times in the given article.

80th Annual Meeting of the Association for Information Science & Technology, Washington, DC | Oct. 27-Nov. 1, 2017

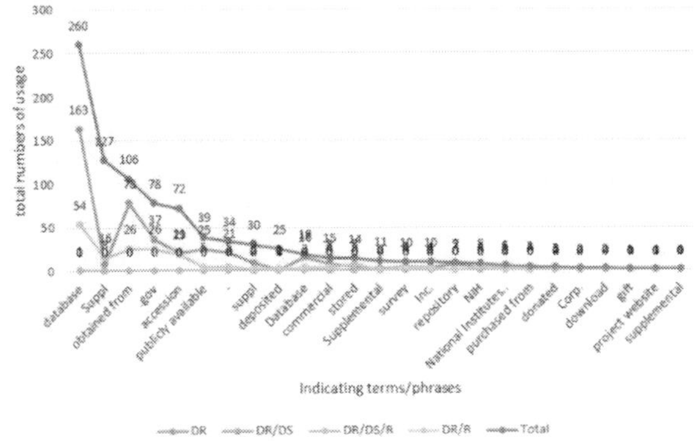


***Figure 1.*** *Terms and phrases used for data sharing and re-use on data citation*

Table 1 also demonstrates that instances of data sharing and re-use are most common in the main text of the articles (70.5 %), followed by the supplementary information and acknowledgment sections, respectively, with far fewer examples in the footnotes and references sections of the publications. In the references section, formal citation was far from common (15.3%), with only 168 examples captured. This means that data sharers or re-users do not receive due credit in scholarly communication and are largely not documented in formal citation databases such as Clarivate Analytics' Data Citation Index. However, if researchers share their data, they may not need to acknowledge this formally.

| Locat. | DR | DS | DR/R | DS/R | Oth. | Tot. |
|---|---|---|---|---|---|---|
| A | 15 | 5 | 16 | 3 | 0 | 39 |
| AB | 19 | 11 | 2 | 1 | 0 | 33 |
| F | 2 | 4 | 0 | 4 | 0 | 10 |
| M | 408 | 133 | 163 | 55 | 12 | 771 |
| R | 62 | 10 | 91 | 7 | 0 | 170 |
| S | 7 | 47 | 7 | 17 | 0 | 78 |
| Total | 513 | 210 | 279 | 87 | 12 | 1,101 |

***Table 1.*** *Location & practices for data sharing & re-use*

## DISCUSSION AND CONCLUSIONS

This study reveals that data sharing and re-use are prevalent in published articles as a community practice in the bioscience/biomedical fields, but not as formal data citations. One reason can be the relatively early data sharing requirements of NIH, one of the major funding agencies in the biosciences/biomedical fields. Compared to NIH's early requirement in 2003, other major funding agencies such as NSF mandated its data management plan relatively late, which dates back to 2011. More recently mandated years may result in a relatively low percentage of data sharing and re-use practice. The other reason may be due to the gaps in researchers' perceptions that data re-use may not meet the requirements of trust judgment and validity of data (Yoon, 2017).

Informal data citation is common in biosciences/biomedical fields. The low incidence of formal data citation corresponds to the previous findings (Robinson-García, Jiménez-Contreras & Torres-Salinas, 2016; Park & Wolfram, 2017). This means that data sharers do not receive due credit in scholarly communication for the re-use of their data. Researchers are more inclined to share their research data when they receive credit (Borgman, 2012), and formal citation or acknowledgment is important for data sharers (Tenopir et al., 2011), meaning formal bibliographic citation is the essential reward for data sharers in scholarly communication.

The primary limitation of the current study is the focus on a sample of articles from bioscience/biomedical fields in PubMed. This prevents us from generalizing our findings to other disciplines. The main contribution of this study is our examination of the actual practices of data sharing and re-use on data citation, which is largely informal. This provides direct insight into the lack of a current reward system (i.e., formal citations) for data sharers and re-users.

## REFERENCES

Borgman, C. L. (2012). Why are the attribution and citation of scientific data important? In P. F. Uhlir (Ed.), For attribution: Developing scientific data attribution and citation practices and standards: Summary of an international workshop. (pp. 1-10). Washington, D.C.: National Academies Press.

Park, H., & Wolfram, D. (2017). An examination of research data sharing and re-use: Implications for data citation practice. *Scientometrics*, 111(1), 443-461.

Piwowar, H. A. (2011). Who shares? Who doesn't? Factors associated with openly archiving raw research data. *PLoS ONE*, *6*(7), e18657.

Robinson-García, N., Jiménez-Contreras, E. & Torres-Salinas, D. (2016). Analyzing data citation practices using the Data Citation Index. *Journal of the Association for Information Science and Technology*, *67*(12), 2964-2975.

Tenopir, C., Allard, S., Douglass, K., Aydingoglu, A. U., Wu, L., Read, E, Frame, M. (2011). Data sharing by scientists: Practices and perceptions. *PLoS ONE*, *6*(6), e21101.

Yoon, A. (2017). Data reusers' trust development. Journal of the Association for Information Science and Technology, 68(4), 946-956.

# Designing a Leadership-based Inquiry into Community Digital Literacy Initiatives

**Kirstin C. Phelps**
*School of Information Sciences, University of Illinois at Urbana-Champaign, USA. kphelps@illinois.edu*

## ABSTRACT
**Digital literacy is an increasing area of focus for communities, due to its potential positive impact toward social and economic development goals. Given the unique information needs and potentially burdensome financial, human and infrastructure requirements, the implementation of such initiatives often involves a variety of community stakeholders. However, such collaborations are often fraught with difficulty and seldom result in long-term sustainability or success. This poster presents a mixed- methods research design exploring the implementation of digital literacy initiatives within a specific community context. The main conceptual foundations will be highlighted, including the use of a leadership framework to evaluate the presence or absence of essential social roles within the group. It will be argued that a leadership framework contributes important understanding to the organization and organizing processes present in multi-stakeholder community collaborations. Furthermore, research designs which expand focus beyond single individuals, single entities or formal partnerships are needed to support positive engagement with technology within communities.**

## KEYWORDS
digital literacy, leadership, mixed methods, social network analysis, community engagement

## INTRODUCTION
The information economy has catalyzed interest in ways to develop literacies to help individuals be successful in an increasingly technology-reliant daily life. These desired literacies encompass the skills and abilities seen as essential for "active participation in lifelong learning through the processes of both consuming and creating messages" (Hobbs, 2010, p. 18). Digital literacy, the literacy most associated with computers, technology and the internet, has garnered interest most notably within the educational sector as schools align preparation with changing workforce needs. However, the rise of the information economy and changing work roles have expanded concerns about digital literacy development beyond the educational realm to encompass a variety of community sectors.

80th Annual Meeting of the Association for Information Science & Technology, Washington, DC | Oct. 27-Nov. 1, 2017



At a community level, concerns about digital inclusion and workforce preparation have resulted in an emphasis on digital literacy development among citizens as a way to foster community social and economic development. The ongoing interest in urban innovation zones, technology incubators, makerspaces and smart cities can all be considered from the perspective of community-based initiatives attempting to develop the capacity of local citizens for positive outcomes. These initiatives can be considered social innovations, or "a process by which relevant stakeholders jointly develop solutions to wicked problems that none of them can solve on their own" (de Moor, 2015, p.1). Contrary to traditional notions of innovation which focus on competitive advantages, social innovations are grassroots efforts that focus on community members' efforts to create solutions to local challenges (Gurstein, 2013). However, the collaboration processes required of community members focused on addressing wicked problems do not spontaneously emerge (de Moor, 2013). Instead, they reflect the relationships among individuals and organizations who are embedded within rich, complex social contexts.

To better support the implementation, success and sustainability of community-based social innovation initiatives, such as digital literacy programs, we must first understand more about the processes of collaboration and organizing which occurs among a variety of stakeholders. To this end, this poster provides a conceptual framework and subsequent research design currently being implemented for the author's doctoral dissertation research. The conceptual framework borrows from the field of leadership studies to explore different social roles involved in digital literacy programming initiatives and provides a novel lens from which to explore digital literacy programming.

## A COLLECTIVE LEADERSHIP FRAMEWORK FOR DIGITAL LITERACY INITIATIVES
Interest in new approaches to leadership has been precipitated by the insufficiency of traditional, top-down approaches to manage the complexity and rate of change facing many organizations. The rise of knowledge work, the mass diffusion of information communication technologies (ICTs) and the shifting demands of the competitive marketplace have resulted in the use of flatter, more team-based work structures, i.e., collective leadership designs (Avolio, Walumbwa & Weber, 2009; Kocolowski, 2010; Dinh, Lord, Gardner, Meuser, Linden & Hu, 2014; Pearce & Wassenaar, 2015). Such leadership strategies are gaining prominence because they extend the role of leadership beyond a single individual and encourage the participation of all members in group processes. In

these frameworks, leadership is often defined in terms of social roles – recurring sets of behaviors taken within a group context (Zigurs & Kozar, 1994), rather than as a formal position.

The conceptual framework for collective leadership that will be presented in this poster is based upon a long tradition of defining leadership as a set of complex roles (Hollander, 1985) which was recently synthesized into four main sets of behaviors (Carson, 2006). These roles (Table 1) comprise the collective leadership framework utilized in the study, put forth by Contractor and colleagues (2012).

In comparison to traditional (i.e., vertical) leadership designs, collective (i.e., horizontal) leadership approaches have been found to better predict positive group outcomes as individuals are free to apply their knowledge and skill when and where needed (Fausing, Joensson, Lewandowski & Bigh, 2015; Pearce & Wassenaar, 2015). As will be explored within the poster, a collective leadership framework is particularly relevant to the case of community-based digital literacy initiatives. Such initiatives often involve specific information needs and demand a variety of human, financial and infrastructure resources. These resource parameters require collaboration among a variety of stakeholders. Therefore, better understanding of the ways in which individuals enact different leadership roles – varying from internal group coordination to boundary-spanning liaison, among others – and how such roles can be identified, supported and studied is an increasing necessity for positive programming outcomes.

| Role | Description |
|---|---|
| Navigator | *Establishes purpose, and direction* |
| Engineer | *Organizes the group and structures tasks* |
| Social Integrator | *Develops and maintains cohesiveness* |
| Liaison | *Develops and maintains useful external relationships* |

***Table 1****. Collective leadership roles*

## RESEARCH DESIGN

The poster will focus on the collective leadership conceptual framework and research design: a case-based, sequential mixed-methods approach. The chosen approach responds to calls for contextually situated explorations of leadership (Bolden, 2011) and the use of varied methods to address issues of emergence and dynamism within complex systems (Aiken & Hanges, 2012).

The case developed for this dissertation is a community-based, interorganizational group (IOG) formed among extension personnel, local community organizations and individuals working on digital literacy initiatives. Utilizing local informants, the research design utilizes an initial stage qualitative stage comprising semi-structured interviews with identified stakeholders in various sectors of the community working on digital literacy in efforts to understand the information needs, major challenges and successes of ongoing initiatives. The second phase includes a survey with social network components, which will evaluate the leadership roles present within the group and the various relationships among stakeholders. Finally, a final qualitative stage is proposed to interview individuals identified by peers as enacting the leadership roles to better understand the dynamics and information behaviors of each role.

## CONCLUSION

The research design and conceptual framework explored in this poster aim to help inform research exploring the intersection of technology and communities, particularly technology-based initiatives that involve a variety of stakeholders. The proposed design helps capture the nuance of context around the organization and organizing processes of collaboration around the topic of digital literacy within a specific case site. Furthermore, the poster argues that the inclusion of a leadership lens provides a novel, and valuable, perspective through which to analyze community stakeholder participation for programmatic success.

## REFERENCES


Aiken, J. R., & Hanges, P. J. (2012). Research methodology for studying dynamic multiteam systems: Application of complexity science. In Zaccaro, S., Marks, M., Church, L. (Eds.) *Multiteam systems: An organization form for dynamic and complex environments*. New York, NY: Routledge.

Avolio, B. J., Walumbwa, F. O., & Weber, T. J. (2009). Leadership: Current theories, research, and future directions. *Annual review of psychology, 60*, 421-449.

Bolden, R. (2011). Distributed leadership in organizations: A review of theory and research. *International Journal of Management Reviews, 13*(3), 251-269.

Carson, J. (2006). Internal team leadership: An examination of leadership roles, role structure, and member outcomes. (Doctoral dissertation). Retrieved from Digital Repository at the University of Maryland. http://hdl.handle.net/1903/3895

Contractor, N. S., DeChurch, L. A., Carson, J., Carter, D. R., & Keegan, B. (2012). The topology of collective leadership. *The Leadership Quarterly, 23*(6), 994-1011.

de Moor, A. (2013). Creativity meets rationale: Collaboration patterns for social innovation. In John M. Carroll (Ed.) *Creativity and rationale: Enhancing human experience by design* (pp. 377-404). London: Springer.

de Moor, A. (2015). Knowledge weaving for social innovation: Laying the first strand. *Proceedings of the 12th Prato community informatics research network conference*, November 9 – 11, 2015, Prato, Italy.

Dinh, J. E., Lord, R. G., Gardner, W. L., Meuser, J. D., Liden, R. C., & Hu, J. (2014). Leadership theory and research in the new millennium: Current theoretical trends and changing perspectives. *The Leadership Quarterly, 25*(1), 36-62.

Fausing, M. S., Joensson, T. S., Lewandowski, J., & Bligh, M. (2015). Antecedents of shared leadership: Empowering leadership and interdependence. *Leadership & Organization Development Journal, 36*(3), 271-291.

Gurstein, M. (2013) Community innovation and community informatics. *The Journal of Community Informatics, 9*(3). Retrieved from http://www.cijournal.net/index.php/ciej/article/view/1038/1022

Hobbs, R. (2010). Digital and media literacy: A plan of action. A white paper on the digital and media. literacy recommendations of the Knight Commission on the information needs of communities in a democracy. Retrieved August 4, 2016 from http://www.atalm.org/sites/default/files/Digital_and_Media_Literacy_A_Plan_of_Action.pdf

Hollander, E. P. (1985). Leadership and power. In G. Lindzey, & E. Aronson (Eds.), *Handbook of social psychology* (pp. 485-538). (3rd ed.). New York: Random House.

Kocolowski, M. D. (2010). Shared leadership: Is it time for a change. *Emerging Leadership Journeys, 3*(1), 22-32.

Pearce, C.L. & Wassenaar, C. L. (2015). Shared leadership in practice: When does it work best? *Academy of Management Perspectives, 29*(3), 13-14.

Zigurs, I., & Kozar, K. A. (1994). An exploratory study of roles in computer-supported groups. *MIS Quarterly, 18*(3), 277-297.

# Machine Learning for Name Type Classification in Library Metadata

**Mark Edward Phillips**
*University of North Texas, USA. mark.phillips@unt.edu*

**Jiangping Chen**
*University of North Texas, USA. Jiangping.Chen@unt.edu*

## ABSTRACT

**This poster reports on the effectiveness of machine learning approaches to classify common names in library metadata records using the Library of Congress Name Authority File. Features extracted from this dataset were used to train and evaluate classification algorithms including decision tree, naïve Bayes, random forest and support vector machine implemented in Weka, an open-source machine learning platform. The best performing classifiers were also tested on a collection of 30,000 names extracted from the UNT Digital Library This poster presents the feature sets, their testing results and the information gains of extracted features. The study demonstrated that machine learning could effectively classify names as persons or corporations.**

## KEYWORDS

name type classification, digital library metadata, name classification

## INTRODUCTION

Library metadata describes resources and objects using standards and schemes for encoding and representation. Metadata schemes may use different fields for storing and representing name information, e.g., machine-readable cataloging (MARC) designates "creator" field usage by name type (personal, corporate or meeting) and main or added entries (Library of Congress Network Development and MARC Standards Office, 2016). The Metadata Object Description Schema (MODS) has a repeatable name element with an attribute of "type" to denote personal, corporate or event names (Library of Congress, 2012). The Dublin Core Metadata Element Set has "creator" and "contributor" fields but cannot store types (Dublin Core Metadata Initiative, 2012). Schema.org is a vocabulary used on the web to describe resources shared or embedded online and acts as a standardized vocabulary; it defines two classes for person and organization names (Schema.org, n.d.).

Absence of name types is a known barrier to information retrieval. First, knowing the type can facilitate high precision information retrieval, e.g., to help a user retrieve documents mentioning a given name (Paik, Liddy & Yu 1996). Second, it can help natural language processing systems disambiguate names. Last, a digital library could organize names in browsable lists by type for users.

80th Annual Meeting of the Association for Information Science & Technology, Washington, DC | Oct. 27-Nov. 1, 2017



## RELATED WORK

Literature is sparse regarding name type classification and often pairs named entity recognition (NER) with named entity classification (NEC). NER is the identification of boundaries within a text where named entities occur, and NEC is the task of identifying the type of named entity. Both supervised (Heng & Grishman, 2006) and unsupervised (Collins & Singer, 1999) approaches have been used for NER and NEC tasks. Name ethnicity classification, a related area, focuses entirely on classifying personal names by ethnicity or region (Mateos, 2007).

A commercially-available tool called NameSifter (IBM, n.d) "examines a name and attempts to tell you what kind of entity (person, organization, something else) that the name represents."

Type classification on name strings is not easily identified within literature on machine learning, digital libraries or library metadata.

## METHODS

This study investigated the application of machine-learning technologies to the automatic classification of name strings as personal or corporate names, based on three research questions: 1) Can we teach a model to automatically classify names? 2) Which machine learning approach works best? 3) Which features are most useful in classifying names?

### *Dataset*

This research used the Library of Congress Name Authority File (LC-NAF) from the LC Linked Data Service (Library of Congress, n.d). It is a large (n=7,861,721) set of public data containing both personal (6,361,899, 81%) and corporate (1,499,822, 19%) names and is representative of bibliographic metadata. Long-standing practices and standards dictate the formatting of names, e.g., inverting the order of the surname and given names (Last, First).

### *Feature Selection*

We identified features of name strings that could help classify them and relevant dictionaries for common names and abbreviations. In total 27 features were tested and used in the building of classification models.

## RESULTS

### *Performance of ML Classifiers*

We experimented with classifiers implemented in Weka, a machine-learning platform, including decision tree (DT), naïve Bayes (NB), random forest (RF), and support vector machines (SVM), trained on the identified features. We tuned model hyper-parameters in 10-fold cross-validation experiments (Train+) and tested the models against 10,000 names in a test set (Test) from the dataset. A total of 31 classifiers were compared in this research. The best performing classifiers were also tested against a set of 30,000 names extracted from the UNT Digital Library (https://digital.library.unt.edu) as an external "real world" test dataset.

The three best performing classifiers using the selected features were the J48 decision tree classifier (an open source Java implementation of the C4.5 algorithm), random forest (RF) and a logistic model tree (LMT) classifier (see Table 1).

## DISCUSSION AND CONCLUSION

### *Significance of the Study*

This study was the first exploring the LC-NAF dataset for automatic name type classification on real-world metadata values. Our study showed that it was possible to teach high-performance models to classify name strings, and that some features (e.g., commas and comma placement) play an important role.

### *Conclusion*

We addressed the classification of names as personal or corporate by experimenting with 27 features and training 31 classifiers and showed that it is possible to automatically classify library name strings as personal and corporate names. Our study identified three classifiers with high precision, recall, accuracy, f1-measure and ROC area. Future work will explore machine learn ing to identify and classify named entities in library records spanning multiple elements.

| Classifier | Precision | Recall | F1-Measure | Accuracy | ROC Area |
|---|---|---|---|---|---|
| Train+ (10-fold CV) | | | | | |
| J48 | 0.990 | 0.990 | 0.990 | 99.04 | 0.991 |
| RF | 0.990 | 0.990 | 0.990 | 99.04 | 0.997 |
| LMT | 0.992 | 0.992 | 0.992 | 99.21 | 0.999 |
| LC-NAF Test | | | | | |
| J48 | 0.992 | 0.992 | 0.992 | 99.18 | 0.992 |
| RF | 0.993 | 0.993 | 0.993 | 99.28 | 0.998 |
| LMT | 0.993 | 0.993 | 0.993 | 99.31 | 0.999 |
| UNT DL Test | | | | | |
| J48 | 0.985 | 0.985 | 0.985 | 98.54 | 0.985 |
| RF | 0.989 | 0.989 | 0.989 | 98.87 | 0.987 |
| LMT | 0.989 | 0.989 | 0.989 | 98.91 | 0.991 |

***Table 1**. Best performing classifiers on Train+ and test datasets*

## REFERENCES


Dublin Core Metadata Initiative. (2012). *Dublin Core Metadata Element Set, Version 1.1.* Retrieved from http://dublincore.org/documents/dces/

Heng, J., & Grishman, R. (2006). Analysis and repair of name tagger errors. Proceedings of joint conference of the International Committee on Computational Linguistics and the Association for Computational Linguistics 420-427.

IBM (n.d). *NameSiftr. InfoSphere Global Name Management 5.0.0.* Retrieved from https://www.ibm.com/support/knowledge-center/SSEV5M_5.0.0/com.ibm.iis.gnm.api.doc/topics/gnr_ns_api_intro-description.html

Library of Congress (2012). *Dublin Core Metadata Element set mapping to MODS version 3.* Retrieved from http://www.loc.gov/standards/mods/dcsimple-mods.html

Library of Congress (n.d). *LC linked data service.* Retrieved from http://id.loc.gov/download/

Library of Congress. Network Development and MARC Standards Office. (2016). *MARC 21 format for bibliographic data.* Retrieved from http://www.loc.gov/marc/bibliographic/

Mateos, P. 2007. A review of name-based ethnicity classification methods and their potential in population studies. *Population Space and Place.*

Paik, W., Liddy, E. D., Yu, E., & McKenna, M. (1996). Categorizing and standardizing proper nouns for information retrieval. *Corpus Processing for Lexical Acquisition* p. 61-73

Schema.org (n.d.). Full hierarchy. http://schema.org/docs/full.htm

# Overcoming the Digital Divide? Low Education Low Income Parents Are Equally Likely to Report Benefits Associated with Online Parenting Information

**Pierre Pluye**
*Department of Family Medicine, McGill University, Canada.*
*Pierre.pluye@mcgill.ca*

**Reem El Sherif**
*Department of Family Medicine, McGill University, Canada.*
*Reem.elsherif@mail.mcgill.ca*

**Gillian Bartlett**
*Department of Family Medicine, McGill University, Canada.*
*gillian.bartlett@mcgill.ca*

**Vera Granikov**
*Department of Family Medicine, McGill University, Canada.*
*veragranikov@gmail.com*

**Roland M Grad**
*Department of Family Medicine, McGill University, Canada.*
*Roland.grad@mcgill.ca*

**Geneviève Doray**
*Naître et grandir | Fondation Lucie et André Chagnon, Canada. g.doray@naitreetgrandir.com*

**François Lagarde**
*Fondation Lucie et André Chagnon, Canada.*
*lagardef@fondationchagnon.org*

**Christine Loignon**
*University of Sherbrooke, Department of Family Medicine, 150 Charles Lemoyne, Longueil, QC, Canada.*
*christine.loignon@usherbrooke.ca*

**France Bouthillier**
*School of Information Studies, McGill University, Canada.*
*france.bouthillier@mcgill.ca*

## ABSTRACT

**Seeking consumer health and wellbeing information online is increasingly common. However, little is known about how people are using information targeted to a specific audience, and what happens as a result of this use. We partnered with *Naitre & grandir* (N&G), a magazine, website and newsletter offering trustworthy parenting information on child growth, development and health/wellbeing. This study was designed to uncover the outcomes of using online parenting information. We used the theory-driven Information Assessment Method (IAM) to study parental perception regarding outcomes of specific N&G webpages. We asked this research question: Is there a difference between parents with a low level of education and income vs. other parents? Over an 18-month study period, 1886 participants submitted 2532 IAM ratings that suggested N&G information was valuable in terms of situational relevance (97.2%), positive cognitive impact (99.7%), intention to use (97.9%) and expectation of benefits for child health and wellbeing (69.6%). Results suggested parents with a low level of education and income were less likely to expect that N&G information can improve their child's health and wellbeing. However, there were no differences regarding parental worries, problem prevention, problem management, information exchange (e.g., with professionals) and confidence in decision-making associated with information use. Results suggest trustworthy online parenting information for all persons, including parents with a low literacy level, can contribute to overcome the digital divide. To our knowledge, this is the first study to assess outcomes of emailed parenting information from a parental viewpoint. In future research, we will describe health and wellbeing outcomes illustrated through stories collected from parents.**

## KEYWORDS

information use, information outcomes, information assessment, online consumer health information, parenting information

## INTRODUCTION

Numerous research studies, governments and international organizations consider parenting the most important factor associated with childhood and teenage development, education, health and wellbeing (and the main predictor of problems in adulthood and the next generation). However, preventive services are rare, and the most disadvantaged parents may receive little help before problems occur. Online parenting information may help 24/7. However, parents with a low combined level of income and education can be discouraged by information they find difficult to understand, whereas, those with higher levels of income and education may benefit more from information. Our goal was to document perceived outcomes of online parenting information for two reasons: only a few studies have focused on information use and subsequent outcomes (Case & O'Connor, 2016), and the literature on parental competency suggests parents with a low

80th Annual Meeting of the Association for Information Science & Technology, Washington, DC | Oct. 27-Nov. 1, 2017

combined level of income and education are less likely to perceive positive outcomes of online parenting information. Thus, our research question was as follows: Regarding expected/perceived health/wellbeing outcomes of online parenting information, is there a difference between parents with a low combined level of income and education compared to other parents (parents with a higher level of income or education)?

The *Naître et grandir* (N&G) website provides parents with support in bringing up their children, from the time they are conceived until they are eight years old. In addition to the website, its modes of dissemination include a personalized electronic weekly newsletter and a magazine. N&G is free, independent of industry funding and offers trustworthy online parenting information with text, audio and video material for all persons, including parents with a low literacy level. N&G is funded by the Lucie and André Chagnon Foundation, a philanthropic organization that seeks to contribute to the prevention of poverty through the creation of conditions and environments favourable to the educational success of children, specifically from socially vulnerable families and communities. Since 2014, McGill University and N&G have worked in partnership to implement the Information Assessment Method (IAM) for assessing and improving the N&G website and newsletter. Using a brief questionnaire, the IAM allows people to rate the situational relevance, cognitive/affective impact and use of specific information content (e.g., a N&G web page), and any ensuing health/wellbeing outcomes (www.mcgill.ca/iam). We recently reviewed the literature and found no similar questionnaire. Specifically, the IAM documents how information is valuable from the user viewpoint. It is derived from the acquisition-cognition-application theory assessing the value of information and information services (Saracevic & Kantor, 1997): people find information (acquisition), understand it (cognition) and possibly use it (application).

## METHODS

Participants: Parents can register to receive a weekly newsletter containing links to N&G webpages personalized according to the ages of their children. Respondents were Quebec residents who viewed N&G webpages through weekly newsletters and completed at least one IAM questionnaire during the study period (December 1, 2015 - May 31, 2017). Among them, participants identified themselves as parents of children from newborn thorough 8 years old.

Instrument: The IAM questionnaire was content validated with N&G users (parents) and an expert panel (Bujold et al., 2016; Pluye et al., 2013 and 2014). Participants were asked to complete a demographic questionnaire.

Data Source: Participants were assigned anonymous individual IDs. IAM ratings and demographic data were collected by N&G, anonymized and transferred to the research team.

Statistical Analysis: With respect to descriptive statistics, categorical variables were summarized with counts and percentages. Then, a Pearson's chi-squared test was used to determine whether the differences between two groups of participants were statistically significant: the group "low" (combining a low level of income and a low level of education) vs. the group "higher" (a higher level of education or a higher level of income). Test results were deemed statistically significant when p-values (p) were less than 0.01. All tests were conducted using SAS v9.4. In line with the Quebec poverty line, a low level of income was defined as an annual family income less than $40,000. A low level of education was defined as a high school diploma or no diploma (high school not completed).

## RESULTS

Over the 18-month study period, 1886 persons submitted 2532 IAM ratings on 637 unique N&G webpages. IAM ratings showed that N&G webpages were relevant and had a positive cognitive impact 97.2% and 99.7% of the time, respectively. An intention to use N&G information and expectations of ensuing health/wellbeing outcomes were reported in 97.9% and 69.6% of the time, respectively.

Regarding our research question, 1416 participants submitted 1796 ratings (on average 1.3 ratings per person; range 1-10) on 559 N&G webpages (on average 3.2 ratings per page; range 1-22): 38 ratings were completed by 31 participants of the "low" group, and 1758 by 1385 participants of the "higher" group. There were no statistically significant differences between responses of participants of the two groups (low vs. higher) regarding expected health/wellbeing outcomes associated with N&G information such as parental worries, problem prevention, problem management, information exchange (e.g., with professionals) and confidence in decision-making.

## DISCUSSION

Our results suggest online information designed for all persons (including persons with a low literacy level) might contribute to overcoming the digital divide. Typically, the literature suggests information provides more benefit to wealthy people with high education. In contrast, our results suggest there is no difference between parents with a combined low level of education and low annual family income vs. other parents regarding perceived (self-reported) expectations of health and wellbeing outcomes associated to information use.

Our descriptive results face a limitation as they are based on a convenience sample of motivated parents (self-selection bias). This limitation led to an over-estimation of perceived positive outcomes (social desirability bias). However, the social desirability bias may equally influence ratings of participants from the "low" and "higher" groups and not affect results of statistical tests. Finally, the "low" group small sample size suggests the need to improve the IAM questionnaire for parents with a low literacy level (using photo voice or photo novel).

## CONCLUSION

Our results uncover perceived outcomes of online parenting information. They support the IAM as a novel method for assessing and improving online consumer information, which can be of interest for other information providers. These results suggest questions for future research such as "To what extent are social network and individual resources (such as health literacy) associated with these outcomes?" and "How does the use of parenting information translate into experienced outcomes?" To address these questions and overcome the limitations of the present study, we will conduct a mixed-methods study (funded by the Canadian Institutes of Health Research).

## ACKNOWLEDGMENTS

Pluye holds an award from the Fond de recherche en santé du Québec (FRQS). This study has been supported by the Fondation Lucie & André Chagnon.

## REFERENCES

Bujold M, El Sherif R, Bush PL, Johnson-Lafleur J, Doray G, Pluye P. (2016). Ecological content validation of the Information Assessment Method for parents (IAM4parents). ACM Digital Health Conference, Montreal, Canada.

Case, D. O. and O'Connor, L. G. (2016), What's the use? Measuring the frequency of studies of information outcomes. *JASIST, 67*: 649-661.

Pluye, P., Grad, R. M., Repchinsky, C., Jovaisas, B., Johnson-Lafleur, J., Carrier, M. E., . . . Bartlett, G. (2013). Four levels of outcomes of information seeking: A mixed methods study in primary health care. *JASIST, 64*(1), 108-125.

Pluye, P., Granikov, V., Bartlett, G., Grad, R. M., Tang, D. L., Johnson-Lafleur, J., . . . Stephenson, R. (2014). Development and content validation of the Information Assessment Method for patients and consumers. *JMIR research protocols, 3*(1), e7.

Saracevic, T., & Kantor, P. B. (1997). Studying the value of library and information services. Part I. Establishing a theoretical framework. *JASIST, 48*(6), 527-542.

# Development and Testing of a Model of Interactive Innovation Adoption in Health Care

**Danielle Pollock**
*College of Communication and Information, University of Tennessee, USA. dpolloc2@vols.utk.edu*

## ABSTRACT

**Understanding the factors that lead groups of professionals in healthcare organizations to adopt or reject new innovations for communication and information sharing is vital for those seeking to support the information needs of these communities. This poster presents a new model for the study of the diverse factors that impact interactive innovation adoption in research-intensive healthcare environments. It further details a method for testing the model by examining the adoption of two different interactive innovations by physicians in training at an academic medical center, one innovation developed for virtual communication between providers and the other developed to improve face-to-face communication in the physical world. Preliminary results from the first phase of the study, including barriers to adoption identified by the study participants, will be also displayed.**

## KEYWORDS

diffusion of innovations, interactive innovations, health care

## INTRODUCTION

The role of interactive innovations or new practices and technologies designed to enable multidirectional communication flow between members of a social system (Markus, 1987) in health care is a vital one; use of such innovations can improve the communication of medical information and, ultimately, patient outcomes (Steinhubl & Topol, 2015). However, introducing interactive innovations without a full understanding of the actual information needs and social practices of the actors within a health organization carries the risk that innovations will either not be accepted by intended users or that use will have disruptive consequences for communication instead (Berg, Aarts & van der Lei, 2003).

Much research utilizing Rogers' (2003) diffusion of innovation theory has focused on the perceived characteristics of innovations or the characteristics of individual adopters as drivers of or barriers to adoption. However, many of these characteristics – such as an innovation's perceived compatibility with existing needs and values or an individual adopter's level of influence within a social system – are highly context dependent.

The utility of interactive innovations is also dependent on how many members of a community are using the innovation and whether it is being used to create and share information of value (Katz & Shapiro, 1985). These network externalities and the reciprocal interdependence of earlier and later adopters further complicate the traditional contagion model used in many diffusion studies.

In healthcare environments, information and communication practices are shaped by factors including disciplinary norms and values, the need to support diverse groups of professionals, the specialized nature of information, highly time sensitive workflows, security concerns and the impact of changing information practices on the quality of patient care (see de Grood et al., 2016; Greenhalgh et al., 2005; Greiver et al., 2001). This research began with the intended goal of developing tools to allow information professionals and organization leaders within research-intensive healthcare environments to discover and leverage information about their own communities in order to predict adoption behaviors before developing or introducing an innovation.

## DEVELOPMENT OF THE MODEL

The study began with a review of the literature on diffusion and adoption of innovations meeting Markus' (1987) definition of interactive media by researchers and organizations specializing in the scientific, technical and medical research areas recognized by the National Academies, National Science Foundation (NSF) and National Institutes of Health (NIH) (National Academies 2007; NIH, n.d.; NSF, 2015). Four broad categories of factors related to interactive innovation adoption by these users were identified. A simplified version of the model is presented below.

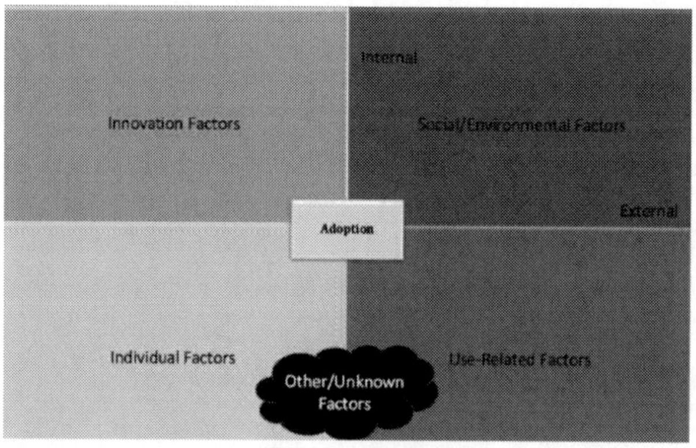


***Figure 1.** The Pollock Model of Interaction Innovation Adoption (PMIIA)*

The Pollock Model of Interactive Innovation Adoption (PMIIA) considers the following factors:

80th Annual Meeting of the Association for Information Science & Technology, Washington, DC | Oct. 27-Nov. 1, 2017

**Innovation factors** directly related to the innovation itself, such as its design, features and perceived usability.

**Individual factors** related to individual potential adopters within a social system, including demographic characteristics, experience with similar innovations and personal innovativeness.

**Social and environmental factors** related to the context in which innovation adoption takes place, including norms and values, work practices, policies and organizational culture. While many of these factors are internal to the environment under study, external factors, such as the communication norms of a discipline or regulations imposed by a larger governing body, may also impact adoption.

**Use-related factors** related to the specific use of an innovation in context, including the ability to adapt the innovation to task, the visibility of use and whether such use is voluntary.

All of the factors may overlap and all have the potential to influence adoption. The dark cloud at the bottom of the image represents potential unknown factors that are not currently part of the model but may be uncovered in the course of the research.

## METHODS

Research to test the model and determine the actual impact of the identified factors on the adoption of interactive innovations is being conducted at an academic medical center, looking at the adoption behaviors of the over 230 medical residents and fellows at the graduate school of medicine. Two interactive innovations were recently introduced to the environment, one to enhance the virtual communication of medical information and one to improve face-to-face communication during changes of shift or handoffs. Studying both of these innovations allows for the ability to compare and contrast the impact of specific innovation features on adoption.

**PerfectServe**, or PerfectServe Synchrony, is a secure communication and call management platform, compliant with U.S. Health Insurance Portability and Accountability Act (HIPAA) information privacy rules (PerfectServe, n.d.). The mobile application allows users to send secure, text and voice messages as well as photos or videos.

**I-PASS** is an innovative communication process, a verbal mnemonic, meant to standardize two-way communication during transitions in patient care (Starmer et al, 2012). Using the I-PASS process, a physician going off shift will communicate critical patient information, which is then synthesized and repeated by the receiver, allowing for questions and clarifications as needed.

## RESEARCH PHASES

The research uses a three-phase, mixed method approach to gather data on actual adoption patterns, as well as how users think and talk about the innovations and the role the innovations play in the work and social life of the organization. **Phase 1** involves semi-structured interviewers with individual residents and fellows (n=7) to gather initial qualitative data on uses and perceptions of each innovation. Data from this phase will inform development of the Phase 2 survey instrument. **Phase 2** involves an electronically administered survey of the entire population to determine the actual adoption of each innovation as well as the specific factors most strongly correlated with adoption. In **Phase 3,** follow-up interviews will be conducted with participants to obtain further information about patterns found in the data in the first two phases.

## CONCLUSION

Early results from Phase 1 show that perceptions of each innovation are mixed, and innovation, social and environmental, and use-related factors are identified as barriers to adoption. For PerfectServe, identified barriers include usability issues, lack of WiFi coverage, the application's dependence on personal cell phones and issues related to uneven diffusion of the innovation and lack of norms surrounding its use. For I-PASS, which is at an earlier stage of diffusion, identified barriers include lack of knowledge of the innovation, perceptions that it is incompatible with current work practices and user satisfaction with existing, locally developed procedures for handoffs. Additional results will be displayed on the full poster.

Healthcare organizations are complex, and the full impact of introducing interactive innovations to them is likely to be equally complex. This mixed method approach allows for research into the impact of previously identified factors related to interactive innovation adoption, as well as for a fuller understanding of factors that might be specific to the particular organization and the impact of each innovation on its social and information sharing practices.

## REFERENCES


Berg, M., Aarts, J., & van der Lei, J. (2003). ICT in health care: Sociotechnical approaches. *Methods Archive, 42*, 297-301.

de Grood, C., Raissi, A., Kwon, Y., & Santana, M. J. (2016). Adoption of e-health technology by physicians: A scoping review. *Journal of Multidisciplinary Healthcare, 9*, 335-344. doi:10.2147/JMDH.S103881

Greenhalgh, T., Robert, G., Bate, P., Macfarlane, F., & Kyriakidou, O. (2005). *Diffusion of innovations in health service organisations: A systematic literature review*. Malden, MA: Blackwell Publishing Ltd.

Greiver, M., Barnsley, J., Glazier, R. H., Moineddin, R. & Harvey, B. J. (2011). Implementation of electronic medical records: A theory-informed qualitative study. *Canadian Family Physician, 57*(e390-e397).

Katz, M., & Shapiro, C. (1985). Network externalities, competition, and compatibility. *The American Economic Review, 75*, 424-440.

Markus, M. L. (1987). Toward a "critical mass" theory of interactive media: Universal access, interdependence and diffusion. *Communication Research, 14*, 491-511. doi:10.1177/009365087014005003

National Academies Committee on Prospering in the Global Economy of the 21st Century. (2007). *Rising above the gathering storm: Energizing and employing America for a brighter economic future*. Washington, DC: National Academies Press.

National Institutes of Health (n.d.) List of NIH Institutes, Centers, and Offices. Retrieved from https://www.nih.gov/institutes-nih/list-nih-institutes-centers-offices

National Science Foundation. (2015, August). Graduate Research Fellowship Program (GRFP). Retrieved from http://www.nsf.gov/pubs/2015/nsf15597/nsf15597.htm

PerfectServe. (n.d.). Features and benefits. Retrieved from http://www.perfectserve.com/features-and-benefits/

Rogers, E. M. (2005). *Diffusion of innovations* (5th ed.) New York, NY: Free Press.

Starmer, A. J., Spector, N. D., Srivastava, R., Allen, A. D., Landrigan, C. P., & Sectish, T. C. (2012). I-PASS, a mnemonic to standardize verbal handoffs. *Pediatrics, 129*(201-204). doi:10.1542/peds.2011-2966

Steinhubl, S. R., & Topol, E. J. (2015). Moving from digitalization to digitization in cardiovascular care: Why is it important, and what could it mean for patients and providers? *Journal of the American College of Cardiology*, *66*, 1489-1496. doi:90/10.1016/j.jacc.2015.08.006

# Information Networks for Bridging Information Divide in Isolated Communities of Farmers in Rural India

**Devendra Potnis**
*University of Tennessee at Knoxville, USA. dpotnis@utk.edu*

**Gaurav Mishra**
*Nirma University, India. gmishra@nirmauni.ac.in*

**InduShobha Chengalur-Smith**
*University at Albany (SUNY), USA. shobha@albany.edu*

## ABSTRACT

**This study analyzes the process adopted by information poor communities of farmers from five remote villages in Gujarat, India, which use IBM's Spoken Web for building an information network (INet). Spoken Web enables information poor communities to create and access VoiceSites over their mobile phones. After analyzing in-depth phone interviews with 31 farmers using grounded theory principles, we propose a four-stage model of seeding, building, growing and scaling an INet among information poor communities of farmers in rural India. We conclude that (a) gatekeepers of farmer communities, (b) communities of practice, (c) collaborative information behavior (CIB) among the farmers and (d) benefits of using INet play a key role in seeding, building, growing and scaling stage respectively. Thus, the INet reduces information divide among isolated farmer communities by allowing them to seek, produce and share information in their native language at any time of the day without requiring them to invest in any new technology or travel.**

## KEYWORDS

information divide, information poverty, farmers, information network, spoken web, rural India

## INTRODUCTION

This study proposes information networks (INets) enabled by IBM's Spoken Web as a solution to reduce information divide in information poor communities of farmers in rural parts of developing countries. We define *information network* as a social network of individuals who seek, process, use and share information communicated by its members, enabled by information and communication technologies (ICTs).

## INFORMATION DIVIDE IN ISOLATED COMMUNITIES OF FARMERS

Farmers in rural India mainly rely on informal communication channels, such as neighbors and fellow farmers, for information. These traditional practices of sharing information keep knowledge local and limited to a specific community (Jha et al., 2016). There have been efforts to create regional repositories of indigenous knowledge and grassroots innovations using the internet (Cecchini and Shah, 2002), but digital illiteracy and lack of infrastructure for high-speed internet make it challenging to provide services using ICTs to rural areas, creating an information divide in isolated communities of farmers.

80th Annual Meeting of the Association for Information Science & Technology, Washington, DC | Oct. 27-Nov. 1, 2017



## IBM'S SPOKEN WEB: A TECHNOLOGY PLATFORM FOR INETS

To bridge the information divide in information poor communities in developing nations, IBM introduced the Spoken Web, a voice-based equivalent of the World Wide Web. Instead of websites, the system relies on VoiceSites, voice-based applications in the local language that are created by the users and hosted by the telecommunication infrastructure. Phone numbers play the role of web addresses and when other users access these voice sites they can hear the uploaded content, rather than reading the information. This spoken network of information connects VoiceSites using Hyper Speech Transfer Protocol and can be accessed through any phone. The phone does not require any extra software and provides a voice-based mechanism for local content creation that can be used by anyone, as it is based on a familiar technology of mobile phones. One application of Spoken Web was an interactive information service called Anubhav Khedut ni Vani (AKV service) that was customized for farmers in rural India in their local language. By calling a toll-free number, farmers could learn about market prices, weather forecasts, etc. Around 3,000 farmers from 140 villages, who registered for this free service, could use voice navigation to record their questions or hear questions posed by others (and answers recorded) or share their experiences.

## RESEARCH GOAL

The goal of our research was to identify the key steps involved in developing INets for information poor communities in isolated parts of developing countries.

## RELEVANT WORK

### *Information Divide Reinforcing Information Poverty*

Digital skills related to finding and assessing information are crucial for information literacy and those who do not possess such skills are informationally disadvantaged (van Dijk, 2005) or information poor. Topics related to "information rich and poor" (Arunachalam, 1999) and "information haves and have nots" have been extensively explored and analyzed in order to empower information poor communities in developing countries. For instance, Chatman's theory of information poverty (1996) shows that social and cultural norms influence behavior in ways that can adversely affect access to information and contribute to information poverty. Subsequent research finds that linguistic minorities (Chu, 1999), gatekeepers (Barzilai-Nahon, 2008), social stigma, communication channels, etc., affect the information rich and poor status of communities. However, few of these studies have traced the process of bridging the information poverty using information generated within the community using ICTs. An information divide is the disparity between information demanded and what is available and affordable in a timely and appropriate format. One of the most significant information divides identified in rural India was for farmers (Blattman et al., 2003) since farmers in rural areas lack timely access to data on crop prices, weather conditions, credit facilities and market opportunities.

### *Mobile Phone: A Solution to Bridge Information Divide*

Due to the relatively low learning curve, affordability and ease of availability, information poor communities prefer to use mobile phones rather than the internet. Mobile phones play a key role in the dissemination of information to isolated communities of farmers. There is a rich body of literature illustrating the use of mobile phones for agricultural information dissemination among farmers in developing countries (Potnis, 2015).

### *Issues in Bridging Information Divide Using Mobiles*

Farmers' attitudes, capacity to collect information and ability to take advantage of the opportunities offered by ICTs influence their ability to benefit from the information communicated over ICTs (Howland et al., 2015). Progressive farmers in Sri Lanka often contact and benefit from subject matter experts in government-sponsored research centers using their mobile phones (Dissanayeke & Wanigasundera, 2013). However, due to a lack of nationwide voice-based mobile information sharing service, that knowledge is not disseminated among poor farmers. Moreover, access to information is not a sufficient condition to use it for making better-informed decisions (Potnis, 2015). For instance, Esoko uses a simple text messaging system to provide current local market prices and weather forecasts with news for farmers across Africa (HowWeMadeItInAfrica, 2015). However, due to a lack of any voice-based interactions between farmers and any local experts or human mediators, illiterate and semi-literate farmers find it difficult to trust, and hence, use this agricultural and market information for making decisions. The digital literacy of rural farmers in India is limited (Jha et al., 2016), and information sharing and dissemination activities by the social network of farmers over mobile phones is a critical step for informed decision-making. Patel et al. (2012) found that farmers followed up on information significantly more often when the farming-related advice was shared by a peer, rather than a scientist. Hence, this study advocates for peer-based agricultural information dissemination, where farmers can tap into and benefit from the experiential knowledge of fellow farmers and experts in the farming community over their mobile phones.

## METHODS

With the help of IBM Headquarters, India, we identified gatekeepers who gave us mobile phone numbers of 31 users living in five different villages from Banaskantha, Rajkot and Surendranagar districts in Gujarat, who they thought would be likely to participate in the study. We conducted in-depth phone interviews in the native language of farmers, with the help of two Gujarati students. After cleaning and translating the corpus of interview transcripts from Gujarati to English, we applied grounded theory principles (Strauss and Corbin, 1998) to code data. During line-by-line coding, we identified open codes, such as *I have a good knowledge of castor crops, so I answered many questions related to castor*, etc., which helped us develop the axial code of experiential knowledge sharing. Based on two more axial codes (i.e., qwillingness to help others and quality of information), we linked the phenomena that emerged to propose "Growth of the INet through CIB of Farmers" as the selective code (see Table 1).

| Open Coding | Axial Coding |
|---|---|
| If someone asks for help to learn the system, or for me to ask the question instead of them, then I help them | Willingness to help others |
| Some of my farmer friends asked me to ask questions on their behalf, so I helped them, but after some time they also learnt to use the service and started using it | |
| I have a good knowledge of castor crops, so I answered many questions related to castor | Experiential knowledge sharing |
| Shivabhai is an expert at taking care of animals…So through this service the whole village could benefit from his knowledge | |
| Sometimes someone records Bollywood songs or foul language. Mavjibhai deletes all such recordings from the service. | Quality control of information |
| Sometimes somebody records a wrong question or uses foul language. Mavjibhai and Amitbhai deleted that recording | |

***Table 1.*** *Growth of the INet through CIB of farmers*

## FINDINGS

Based on our data analysis, we propose a four-stage model and 11 mechanisms enabling all the stages (see Figure 1).

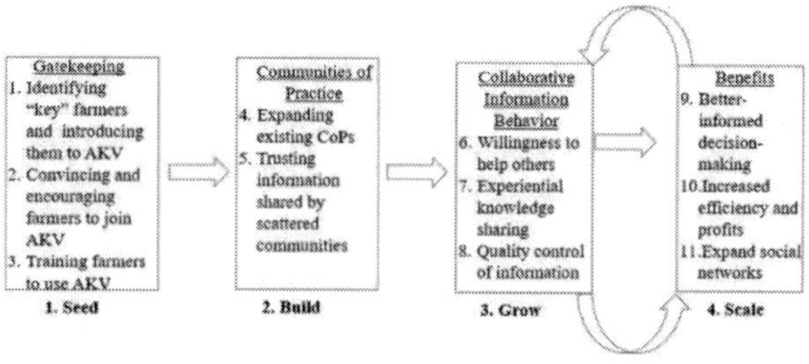


***Figure 1.*** *Stages for Reducing Information Divide among Isolated Communities of Farmers (Zoom in for details)*

### *Stage 1. Seeding of INet by Gatekeepers*

Gatekeepers like Mavjibhai introduced AKV service to few influential farmers in small communities of farmers in different villages. These farmers, in return, convinced and encouraged other farmers to join AKV. Gatekeepers also trained the majority of farmers in using the AKV service.

### *Stage 2. Building INet with Communities of Practice*

Pre-existing practices of sharing information among communities created trust among isolated communities of farmers and helped them build the INet. The pre-existing practices included group discussions on farming issues, travel to urban knowledge hubs, passive reception of broadcast information via radios and televisions and seeking personal advice from experienced farmers.

### *Stage 3. INet Growth Enabled by CIB*

All different kinds of people were part of the service; so, [farmers] got extra information like issues related to animal husbandry, etc. Teams were formed to answer farmer queries. The utility of the INet was a function of the high frequency of interactions and the amount of information sought and shared by its members. Several respondents cited the gatekeepers' services in deleting incomplete or irrelevant questions from the knowledge base, maintaining the quality of information on the INet.

### *Stage 4. Scaling of INet Enabled by Benefits*

The INet created (a) primary benefits in the form of better-informed decision-making and increased efficiency and profits and (b) secondary benefits like an expanding professional network, which rapidly scaled the INet.

## CONCLUSION

The AKV service helped farmers overcome the challenges of using mobile phones to reduce the information divide by allowing them to seek, produce and share information in their native language at any time of the day without requiring them to invest in any new technology or travelling anywhere. The INet allowed farmers to preserve and create knowledge through CIB. Improving the flow of locally relevant information in the form of experiential knowledge enhanced efficiencies in farming practices and profits, which eventually scaled the INet among isolated communities of farmers in rural India.

## REFERENCES


Arunachalam, S. (1999). Information and knowledge in the age of e-Communication: A developing country perspective. *Journal of Info. Science, 25*(6), 465-476.

Barzilai-Nahon, K. (2008). Toward a theory of network gatekeeping: A framework for exploring information control. *JASIST, 59*(3), 1493-1512.

Blattman, C., Jensen, R., & Roman, R. (2003). Assessing the need & potential of community n/w for dev. in rural India. *The Info. Society, 19*(5), 349-364.

Cecchini, S. & Shah, T. (2002) ICTs as a tool for empowerment, In empowerment and poverty reduction: A sourcebook. World Bank, Washington, D.C.

Chatman, E. A. (1996). The impoverished life-world of outsiders. *JASIST, 47*, 193-206.

Chu, C. (1999). Literacy practices of linguistic minorities: Sociolinguistic issues and implications for literacy services. *Library Quarterly, 69*, 339-359.

Dissanayeke, U. & Wanigasundera, W. (2013). Mobile-based info. comm. interactions among major agricultural stakeholders: Sri Lankan experience, *The Elec. Journal of Info. Syst. in Developing Countries*.

Howland, F., Muñoz, L. A., Staiger, S., Cock, J., & Alvarez, S. (2015). Data sharing and use of ICTs in agriculture: Working with farmer groups in Colombia. *Knowledge Mgmt. for Development, 11*, 44-63.

HowWeMadeItInAfrica (2015, July 1) How Esoko bridges the information gap faced by farmers in Africa.

Jha, S., Pinsonneault, A., and Dubé, L. (2016). The evolution of an ICT platform-enabled ecosystem for poverty alleviation: The case of eKutir. *MIS Quarterly, 40,* 431-445.

Patel, N., Chittamuru, D., Jain, A., Dave, P., & Parikh, T. S. (2010, April). Avaaj Otalo: A field study of an interactive voice forum for small farmers in rural India. In *Proceedings of the 28th International Conference on Human Factors in Computing Systems* (pp. 733–742).

Potnis, D. (2015). Beyond access to information: Understanding the use of info. by poor female mobile users in rural India. *The Info. Society, 31*(1), 83-93.

van Dijk, J. (2005). *The deepening divide: Inequality in the info. society*, Thousand Oaks, California: Sage.

# A Large-Scale Data-Driven Analysis of Censorship of Hebrew Manuscripts in Italy

**Gila Prebor**
*Bar-Ilan University, Israel. Gila.Prebor@biu.ac.il*

**Yitzchak Miller**
*Bar-Ilan University, Israel. Isaac.Miller@biu.ac.il*

**Maayan Zhitomirsky-Geffet**
*Bar-Ilan University, Israel. Ramat-Gan, Israel*
*Maayan.Zhitomirsky-Geffet@biu.ac.il*

## ABSTRACT

**In this study, we present the first large-scale quantitative analysis of the full corpus of censored historical Hebrew manuscripts that survived through the centuries. A new multi-dimensional data-driven approach was applied to explore the influence of censorship on the creation of new manuscripts by Hebrew writers in Italy during the 16th- 18th centuries. Our findings demonstrate that there was a substantial decrease in creation of new manuscripts in the periods of high censorship activity.**

## KEYWORDS

Hebrew manuscripts, censorship, digital humanities

## INTRODUCTION

This study aims to investigate the historical phenomenon of censorship of Hebrew manuscripts in Italy during the 16th-18th centuries. This is the first large-scale quantitative analysis of the historical manuscript data. Thus far, all the studies on the censorship of Jewish manuscripts and books during this period were done in a qualitative and specific manner, for example, a study of a specific censor or specific work. The first comprehensive study on the subject that was done more than a century ago was done on a relatively small amount of censored manuscripts (Popper, 1899).

In the context of the Counter-Reformation, during the 16th-18th centuries, the Catholic Church closely supervised written and printed literature. Papal bulls were issued against proscribed books, and indices were drawn up containing lists of prohibited books, which also included Hebrew books (Prebor, 2003, Raz-Krakotzkin 2007). Jewish lobbying of the Pope and Church leaders to ease directives regarding confiscation of books led to the operation of an external censorship. One of the concessions won by Italian Jews was the introduction of censorship of manuscripts and printed books possessed by the Jewish public, as an alternative to confiscation and wholesale destruction of virtually all the books they possessed (Baruchson-Arbib & Prebor, 2007). To carry out the expurgation, the Church put censors at the disposal of the communities, most of them apostates and experts in the Hebrew language, and the communities undertook to pay their fees. The owners of Hebrew books were required in the name of the Inquisition to hand them over to the censors, who kept them in the local office. The books collected were examined by the censors, who destroyed the forbidden books and punished those who kept them. The books of a controversial nature were expurgated and returned to their owners with the approval of the censor. When the expurgation of the book was completed, the censor wrote a short approval note in Latin or in Italian, sometimes also in Hebrew, or in Italian and Hebrew. Proof of the activity of the various censors can be found in a large number of manuscripts and printed works which have survived until the present day and in which ink erasures, emendations, signs of removed pages and the signature of the censor can be observed.

We found about 5000 censored manuscripts in the catalogue of the Department of Manuscripts and Institute of Microfilmed Hebrew Manuscripts in the National Library of Israel (http://web.nli.org.il) which represent the largest collection of Hebrew manuscripts metadata. The availability of a relatively large censorship database on one hand and the ability to apply to it modern analysis and visualization techniques, on the other hand, lead us to discover new insights into the censorship activity over the years and thus better appreciate its impact on the Hebrew printing, and its different manifestations.

## RESEARCH OBJECTIVES

Based on the computational analysis of the evidence of censored manuscripts presented in the catalogue, this study aims to offer a large-scale statistical exploratory analysis of the activity of the censorship of Hebrew manuscripts in Italy during the 16th-18th centuries. In particular, we focused on the temporal analysis of censorship activity and influence on the Jewish writers' activity.

## METHODS

In the first stage, the corpus of manuscripts underwent a process of data cleaning and normalization. This process includes the decomposition of catalogue fields with mixed information (people names, dates and places, as well free-text) into its defined constituents, the treatment of a variety of date formats occurred in the catalogue (e.g., specific Hebrew or Gregorian dates, ranges of years, centuries) and the treatment of names of places (which appear in different languages and

80th Annual Meeting of the Association for Information Science & Technology, Washington, DC | Oct. 27-Nov. 1, 2017

without the names of the countries) using existing authority files and ontologies such as VIAF (https://viaf.org/) and Geonames (http://www.geonames.org/). As part of this normalization process we also obtained the coordinates of all the mentioned places.

In order to create a dedicated censored manuscript corpus, we automatically scanned the general manuscript corpus of 154,160 manuscript records, looking for those manuscripts that had the word stem *censor* anywhere in the respective records (we checked this both in English and in Hebrew). In almost all the cases, a proper censor stem was found in a dedicated MARC field, leaving for manual inspection (and filtering out when appropriate) those cases where some *censor* word variation was found as a free text. The resulted corpus contains 2,485 censored manuscripts of which we retained 2,426 manuscripts that all had been censored in Italy in the period of 1500-1775.

As part of this process, we developed semi-automatic methods to complete missing data based on aggregation and consolidation of existing data; e.g., we could infer the year of censorship activity according to the name of the censor and sometimes also the place of the censorship.

Next, we performed a systematic quantitative analysis of the manuscript corpus. In addition to the descriptive statistical analysis of the censored manuscript corpus we propose a new multi-dimensional methodology for large-scale quantitative analysis of the historical manuscript data. The dependent variables in this study were the number of censorship actions, the number of censored manuscripts, the number of manuscripts that were created and the number of censors involved in censorship activities. The analysis of these variables was carried out according to the following dimensions representing independent variables of the study: 1) the time of the manuscript creation; 2) the time of the manuscript censorship. Additional dimensions might be added in future research, such as the subject of the manuscript, the geographic place of the manuscript creation, the geographic place of the manuscript censorship and the geographic place of the manuscript today.

## RESULTS AND DISCUSSION

### Descriptive Statistics

The censored manuscript corpus records 3,936 cases of censorship in Italy (1500-1775) through 3,870 unique censorship actions (CAs) applied to 2,426 manuscripts (see Table 1)[1]. In many cases manuscripts were censored more than once as shown in the table.

| number of CAs on a single manuscript | how many such manuscripts | total number of CAs |
|---|---|---|
| 1 | 1,432 | 1,432 |
| 2 | 665 | 1,330 |
| 3 | 238 | 714 |
| 4 | 67 | 268 |
| 5 | 20 | 100 |
| 6 | 2 | 12 |
| 7 | 2 | 14 |
| Total | 2,426 | 3,870 |

***Table 1.*** *Number of censor actions per manuscript*

### Temporal Analysis of the Censorship Activity

We first looked at the years where the censorship actually took place. To this end, out of the 3,870 CAs, we analyzed the 2,910 dated CAs and created a histogram of that data (see Figure 1). The immediate observation is that although the recorded range of manuscript censorship in Italy is 222 years long (1554-1775), the majority of the censorship actions took place during a shorter period. The distribution of CAs along the study period supports the historical knowledge we have about censorship activity in Italy.

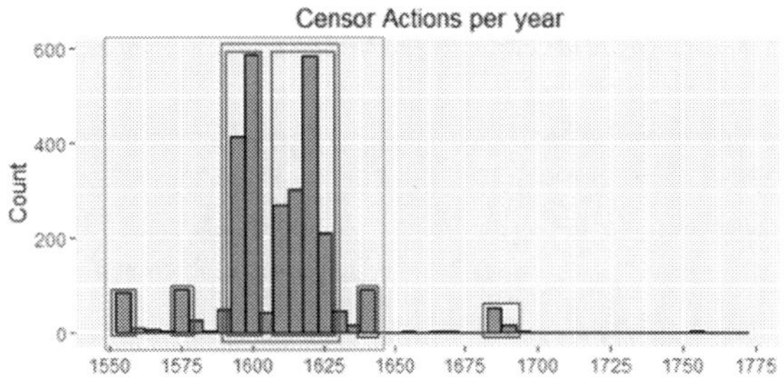


***Figure 1.*** *Number of dated (1550-1775) censor actions per year*

As can be observed from Figure 1, the first narrower period corresponds to the years 1589-1602 (with 36% of the total dated CAs). This reflects the big campaign of expurgation by a censorship committee in Mantua in 1595-1597 Baruchson-Arbib & Prebor, 2007). The second narrower period of 1607-1629 (with 49.2% of the total dated CAs), corresponds to the activity of two censors: Camillo Jagel and Giovanni Domenico Carretto. Camillo Jagel was active from 1611-1629, especially between 1619-1621, and Giovanni Domenico Carretto served as a censor in 1607-1628 (Popper, 1899, 101-2).

Next, we wanted to correlate the censorship activity in Italy of our research range (1550-1775) to the manuscripts that were actually held and/or created by the Jewish community of that time. To this end, we only used 12,917 manuscripts from all the Jewish world that have a specific year of creation date in the catalogue and were written before 1775 (see Figure 2).

[1]The actual number of censored manuscripts is more than 5,000 but in some cases several manuscripts were censored together as a single unit, thus having 2,426 (grouped) manuscripts.

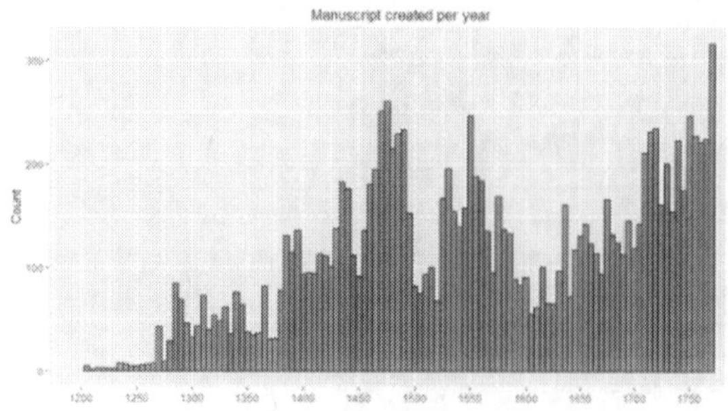


***Figure 2.*** *Number of newly created manuscripts (between 1200 and 1775)*

An immediate conclusion from the histogram examination is that the creation of manuscripts as reflected by the accurately dated manuscript collection is not evenly spread across the years. There is a more or less gradual increase in manuscript creation rate from 1200 towards 1475. Then, there are two main periods with rather sharp decline in the creation rate of new Hebrew manuscripts: between 1475 and 1525 and between 1550 and the beginning of the 17th century. In order to check for possible correlation between the different periods of high and low manuscript creation rates and the periods of censorship activities, we plotted both the manuscript creation histogram and the censorship activity histogram on the same time axis (see Figure 3).

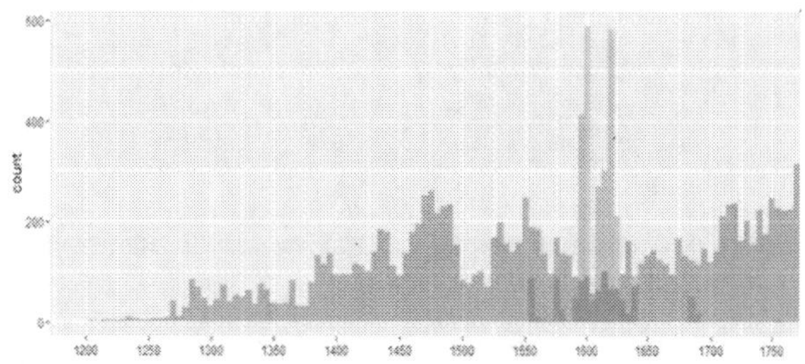

***Figure 3.*** *Number of newly created manuscripts (1200-1775) (blue bars) and censorship actions (1550-1775) (red bars)*

From Figure 3 it can be noticed that the first manuscript creation declining period that starts around 1475 is not correlated to censorship activity as this started 75 years later. This decline is attributable to the invention of the printing press (1450). However, the second manuscript creation declining period starts in 1550 which is when substantial censorship activity starts. Another decline in manuscript creation rate occurs after 1575 which is a single year of substantial censorship activity. All in all, during the period of high censorship activity (the 41-year period between 1589 and 1629), manuscript creation level was relatively lower compared to all other times in 1375-1775 time range. In addition, we obtained a strong negative Pearson correlation of $r=-0.49$ ($p<0.001$) between the amount of created manuscripts and the occurrences of censorship actions in 10-year intervals in the period of 1500-1700 which also supports our hypothesis that Jewish writers' activity was negatively influenced by the censorship activity.

In summary, our analysis showed quantitative evidence that suggests that there was an influence of the censorship activity on the Jewish writer activity in Italy.

## REFERENCES

Baruchson-Arbib, S., & Prebor, G. (2007). Sefer Ha- Ziquq: The book's use and its influence on Hebrew printing. Bibliofilia: rivista di storia del libro e di bibliografia, 109(1), 3-31.

Popper, W. (1899). The censorship of Hebrew books. Knickerbocker Press.

Prebor, G. (2003)"Sepher ha-ziqquq" by Domenico Yerushalmi (1555-1621) and its influence on Hebrew printing, Bar-Ilan University

Raz-Krakotzkin, A. (2007). The censor, the editor, and the text: The Catholic Church and the shaping of the Jewish canon in the sixteenth century. University of Pennsylvania Press.

# Investigating the Efficacy of Sentence Filtering in Predicting Analysts' Ratings Following a 10-K Filing

**Jonathan Pulliza**
*School of Communication and Information (SC&I), Rutgers University, USA. jonathan.pulliza@rutgers.edu*

## ABSTRACT

**This project proposes utilizing the textual features of only the new sentences of financial filings to predict the analyst rating following that filing. Instead of treating each document as independent, this examines the efficacy of limiting models to be trained only on sentences that do not appear in the previous filing. This approach greatly reduces the amount of text processed by a model, in the hope of counteracting overfitting, as well as controlling for boilerplate language from one document to the next, which is not expected to be informative for analysts' decision making. At the same time, this approach does not assume that information is only contained in certain sections or that the document adheres to a strict structure, as all text including any tables and footnotes are analyzed. The average amount of new sentences as a percentage of total sentences of the sample industry during the 2011–2015 period is approximately 50%, while the best performing model performs similarly well when trained on the full versus filtered documents of three years when predicting the analyst rating of the two subsequent years.**

## KEYWORDS

text mining, Python, SEC 10-K, financial analysts, machine learning

## INTRODUCTION

Financial analysts are expected to develop recommendations based on a variety of information sources, and their information behavior has been analyzed by multiple studies as early as Kuhlthau (1997). A major source of information for comparing one organization against another is the U.S Securities and Exchange Commission (SEC) Form 10-K, an annual report of financial performance from publicly traded firms that contains audited financial statements, explanatory text and required discussions around material risk and opportunity that the firm faces as a part of business operations. The SEC requires any filings adhere to the Plain English Rule, a guidance that requires communications to the public to provide the "information investors need to make informed decisions…at a level the audience can understand" (United States, 1998, p. 5).

As an extension of the SEC requirement that firms provide informative filings, this project will focus only on the potentially new information captured in new sentences in each filing. New for the purposes of this study means that the sentence does not appear in the previous filing, removing not just what is commonly referred to as "boilerplate" information as addressed by Pozen (2008). This project proposes that a sentence is informative only if it has not already been seen by the reader, so presenting sentences to an expert such as a financial analyst that have already existed in previous filings has no impact on the information outcome (i.e., stock recommendation) and therefore is not informative. For the purposes of machine learning, a model that requires less text but performs at the same level is viewed as higher quality, as it is less vulnerable to overfitting and requires less computational resources. At the same time, this approach draws from any and all text within the document, including tables and footnotes, avoiding any assumptions concerning the location of potentially valuable text across documents. Filtering for new sentences could offer these advantages while better fitting how analysts are expected to read and understand these documents.

## RELATED WORKS

The SEC 10-K has served as a rich text resource for researchers to examine and understand trends in firm performance as well as investor decision making. Loughran and McDonald (2014) remark that there is an increased interest in using the textual components of these filings with the advancement in text parsing technology and the development of the SEC's Electronic Data Gathering, Analysis and Retrieval (EDGAR) database. Early research involved readability, especially with the use of measures developed by Flesch (1948) or the Fog Index by Gunning (1952). Lawrence (2013) finds that firms with lower Fog Index scores, which are expected to be more readable, are more likely to be invested in by retail investors, which could mean investors are drawn to certain textual features in documents that then affect their decision making. Li (2010) uses a naïve Bayes classifier to track the informativeness of management disclosures as they change over time, using a manually labeled set of 30,000 sentences to train the classifier to label the tone of over 140,000 filings. Other uses of the textual features in the SEC 10-K include creating measure of industry competiveness (Li, Lundholm and Minnis (2013)) and monitoring the change in management tone through the use of negative or positive words specific to the financial domain (Feldman, Govindaraj, Livnat and Segal (2010), Davis and Tama-Sweet (2012)). Many of these studies choose to focus on specific subsections of the 10-K document, including Brown and Tucker (2011) who use the Man-

80th Annual Meeting of the Association for Information Science & Technology, Washington, DC | Oct. 27-Nov. 1, 2017

agement Discussion and Analysis (MD&A) section to measure the quality of the firm's narrative disclosure. This approach reduces the amount of text processed, but assumes the desired content is confined to certain sections. Loughran and McDonald (2013) point to examples where firms explicitly state that the content usually contained in the MD&A was incorporated throughout other sections, thus they recommend utilizing the entire document for any analysis.

Qiu, Srinivasan and Hu (2014)'s goal is to utilize the textual features of 10-K filings to predict the change in company performance from one year to the next. In order to approximate the real-life experience of users, they build models based on one time period to forecast the future performance of that particular firm in the following year, aiming to predict earnings per share (EPS) and size-adjusted cumulative return (SAR). Their work is an extension of previous incremental studies they performed in this pursuit, and many of their design choices such as utilizing support vector machines (SVM) comes from those previous efforts. They compare the forecast estimates and ratings of analysts against their models and find that their models outperform analysts' estimates, which may be a function of an underlying bias in the way analysts form their recommendations adding to "speculations about analysts' information resources and possible bias in their prediction" (Qiu et al., 2014, p. 411).

## DATA COLLECTION

This study collects the SEC 10-K filings from 2011 through 2015, with 2010 serving as a base year to establish the new sentences in 2011. All of the firms come from the manufacturing industry, the same as Qiu et al. (2014). The analysts' ratings can be accessed from the Center for Research in Security Prices (CRSP) database as provided by the Wharton Research Data Service (https://wrds-web.wharton.upenn.edu/wrds/), and only firms for which analyst ratings are available are used. This project will only have two categories, "Buy" or "Not Buy," due to very little of the companies being classified as "Sell" in this sample industry during this time period. This may be a sign of some type of bias in either this sample or analyst recommendations, but for the purposes of this project "Buy" or "Not Buy" is an operational class distinguishment that would still have value for an investor, the analysts' target audience. The SEC 10-K filings are available on the SEC EDGAR website, where the HTML and text file versions of each document are available. The files were collected using the Python package SECEdgar (https://pypi.python.org/pypi/SECEdgar), which uses the ticker and respective CIK codes to download a particular type of document from the SEC EDGAR database and save the text files into respective directories.

These filings are parsed into sentences using the Python packages Beautiful Soup (https://www.crummy.com/software/BeautifulSoup/) for parsing through XML and TextBlob (https://textblob.readthedocs.io/en/dev/) for parsing sentences. All numbers are removed using regular expressions, as two sentences with the same terms in the same order but with different numbers should be considered the same sentence. The assumption is that any substantive difference in performance from one year to another should be explained in words and not solely rely on reported numbers, as explanatory text is a mandatory feature of informative financial documents. Each sentence is then recombined into a new document that is fed into the models. The financial domain has its own particularities when it comes to semantics, as found in Loughran and McDonald (2011), so for the purpose of this project similarity of two sentences is strictly related to terms. The breakdown of the number of filings, recommendations and total versus new sentences can be viewed in Table 1.

| | 2011 | 2012 | 2013 | 2014 | 2015 |
|---|---|---|---|---|---|
| **10-Ks** | 398 | 408 | 418 | 423 | 429 |
| **% BUY** | 61% | 61% | 59% | 59% | 60% |
| **Sentences** | 963,711 | 641,020 | 664,485 | 690,397 | 709,195 |
| **% New** | 66% | 47% | 44% | 43% | 41% |

***Table 1.*** *Data collection summary*

## METHOD

This project aims to compare the performance of models trained on either the full document or just the new sentences to predict whether the majority of analysts recommend buying a stock or not following the filing of a SEC 10-K. The models will be evaluated by their precision in respect to the "Buy" class since it is expected that the "Buy" class would be of most interest to investors. The filings from the years 2011-2013 are used for training, and the filings from 2014-2015 are used for testing. Following the work of Qiu et al. (2014), the filings are fed into a SVM classifier with a linear kernel using the scikit-learn library (http://scikit-learn.org). Unigrams and bigrams are utilized with a document frequency between 25% and 75%, as this was the highest performing in terms of average precision to the BUY class during training. For evaluation purposes, a 90/10 stratified dummy model is utilized to serve as a baseline for comparison, which 90% of the time classifies as the majority class and the other 10% for the other class.

## RESULTS

As shown in Table 2, the classifiers trained on the full 10-K documents versus only the new sentences performed approximately the same in respect to precision and F-1 scores to the BUY class and outperformed the baseline dummy stratified classifier. The F-1 scores of the two models is also similar performance with the full document classifier having a very slight edge.

| | Precision | F-1 |
|---|---|---|
| **Dummy Stratified (90/10)** | 0.591 | 0.599 |
| **Full Document, Linear SVM** | 0.692 | 0.756 |
| **Filtered Document, Linear SVM** | 0.686 | 0.741 |

***Table 2.*** *Testing results summary, BUY class*

## CONCLUSION

Utilizing only the new sentences in an annual filing performs similarly well compared to using the entire document in predicting analyst recommendations, but requires a considerably lower amount of text input. Filtering sentences takes advantage of the interdependence of documents in this collection, explicitly binding the collection together to yield potentially informative content instead of assuming the value of certain sections, even including tables and footnotes. This may be an appropriate approach when examining other collections of annual filings, especially if they lack a strict adherence structure or follow different conventions such as international reporting or other firm communications.

## REFERENCES


Brown, S. V., & Tucker, J. W. (2011). Large-sample evidence on firms' year-over-year MD&A modifications. *Journal of Accounting Research*, *49*(2), 309–346. http://doi.org/10.1111/j.1475-679X.2010.00396.x

Davis, A. K., & Tama-Sweet, I. (2012). Managers' use of language across alternative disclosure outlets: Earnings press releases versus MD&A*. *Contemporary Accounting Research*, *29*(3), 804–837. http://doi.org/10.1111/j.1911-3846.2011.01125.x

Feldman, R., Govindaraj, S., Livnat, J., & Segal, B. (2010). Management's tone change, post earnings announcement drift and accruals. *Review of Accounting Studies*, *15*, 915–953. http://doi.org/10.1007/s11142-009-9111-x

Flesch, R. (1948). A new readability yardstick. *The Journal of Applied Psychology*, *32*(3), 221–233. http://doi.org/10.1037/h0057532

Gunning, R. (1952). *The technique of clear writing*. McGraw-Hill, New York.

Kuhlthau, C. C. (1997). The influence of uncertainty on the information seeking behavior of a securities analyst. In *Proceedings of an international conference on information seeking in context* (pp. 268–274). London, UK, UK: Taylor Graham Publishing. Retrieved from http://dl.acm.org/citation.cfm?id=267190.267206

Lawrence, A. (2013). Individual investors and financial disclosure. *Journal of Accounting and Economics*, *56*(1), 130–147. http://doi.org/10.1016/j.jacceco.2013.05.001

Li, F. (2010). The information content of forward-looking statements in corporate filings – A naive Bayesian machine learning approach. *Journal of Accounting Research*, *48*(5), 1049–1102.

Li, F., Lundholm, R., & Minnis, M. (2013). A measure of competition based on 10-K filings. *Journal of Accounting Research*, *51*(2), no-no. http://doi.org/10.1111/j.1475-679X.2012.00472.x

Loughran, T., & McDonald, B. (2011). When is a liability not a liability ? Textual analysis , dictionaries , and 10-Ks. *The Journal of Finance*, *LXVI*(1), 35–65.

Loughran, T., & McDonald, B. (2014). Measuring readability in financial disclosures. *The Journal of Finance*, *69*(4), 1643–1671. http://doi.org/10.1111/jofi.12162

Loughran, T., & McDonald, B. (2013). Regulation and financial disclosure: The impact of plain English. *Journal of Regulatory Economics*, *45*(1), 94–113. http://doi.org/10.1007/s11149-013-9236-5

Pozen, R. (2008). *Final Report of the Advisory Committee on Improvements to Financial Reporting to the United States Securities and Exchange Commission*.

Qiu, X. Y., Srinivasan, P., & Hu, Y. (2014). Supervised learning models to predict firm performance with annual reports: An empirical study. *Journal of the Association for Information Science and Technology*, *65*(2), 400–413.

United States. (1998). *A plain English handbook : How to create clear SEC disclosure documents*. Washington, DC.

# The Tension Between Caring Surveillance and Controlling Surveillance in the Public Library

**Elaine Robinson**
*Computer and Information Sciences, University of Strathclyde, Scotland, UK. elaine.robinson@strath.ac.uk*

**David McMenemy**
*Computer and Information Sciences, University of Strathclyde, Scotland, UK. d.mcmenemy@strath.ac.uk*

## ABSTRACT

**This visual presentation will take the format of a poster, displaying the preliminary results of a study into acceptable use policies (AUPs) in UK public libraries. This study seeks to understand how surveillance is used in the public library and if surveillance is used in a caring or controlling way. This research used discourse analysis to analyse the content of 200 acceptable use policies in the UK. Results indicate that libraries use both caring and controlling surveillance, with more instances of controlling surveillance being found, and that there appears to be tension between the usage of caring and controlling surveillance in public libraries in the UK.**

## KEYWORDS

surveillance, privacy, public libraries, discourse analysis, acceptable use policy

## INTRODUCTION

Surveillance, especially automated surveillance, has become an integral part of our lives. Although there are concerns over individual privacy and the potentially nefarious uses of surveillance, it is also used to enhance and streamline our lives on a daily basis. These different sides of surveillance have prompted David Lyon (1994) to suggest that surveillance has a dual nature; one side is used for protection, in a "caring" way, whilst the other side is used to regulate behaviour, in a "controlling" way. This understanding allows for surveillance to be analysed more fully, allowing different scenarios to be viewed in different ways and not be understood only in a despotic, Orwellian sense (Monahan, 2011). In a library context this is a clear duality: care could be interpreted as how we best help patrons access the internet as well as protect the interests of the wider community, versus control being how our procedures limit access for legal and regulatory purposes.

Both the American Library Association (ALA) and the Chartered Institute for Library and Information Professionals (CILIP) regard privacy and freedom of expression and access as fundamental aspects of the library service (ALA, 2008; CILIP, 2013). However, as a public institution, the public library has a responsibility to both the individual and the community (Trushina, 2004). Surveillance in public libraries is performed both physically and virtually. Spacey et al. (2013) found that in the UK along with filtering software and acceptable use policies (AUPs), internet access is also managed by physical monitoring by staff, along with the collection of internet use data and monitoring software. Desktops may also be viewed remotely using shadowing software.

## THE AUP

The AUP is one of the public library's main access management tools. It is an important document for both managing access (Palgi, 1996) and as an interface document between the user and library (McMenemy, 2014). It is important for the AUP to be accessible to the user. How the AUP is worded gives insight into how the library presents itself to the user. The AUP is also under-researched within the discipline (Gallagher et al. 2015; McMenemy, 2014).

## METHODS

This research employed discourse analysis to investigate the content of AUPs across the UK. In the UK, each Public Library Authority (PLA) uses an AUP, with 206 PLAs overall (CILIP, 2015). 200 AUPs were obtained from the possible 206. Discourse analysis was chosen to analyse the AUPs (Fairclough, 2001). Themes, monitoring care and monitoring control were used in coding the AUPs, informed by the literature review.

## FINDINGS

Text was coded as monitoring care if surveillance was being carried out by staff or the council for reasons of protecting the public. For example:

- Library staff have the right and ability to monitor users' computer usage if they have cause for concern.
- ... interception of personal and private communications will not normally take place unless grounds exist to show evidence of some crime or other unlawful or unauthorised use.

Of the 200 AUPs analysed, 31 AUPs featured the monitoring care node, with 36 references to monitoring care overall.

Text was coded as monitoring control if surveillance was being used in a way that was being coercive or as to regulate behaviour. For example:

80th Annual Meeting of the Association for Information Science & Technology, Washington, DC | Oct. 27-Nov. 1, 2017

- In the event that it is suspected that a user is breaking the terms and conditions of this acceptable use policy the Council reserves the right to carry out further investigation … If the breach of the AUP also suggests the commission of an offence, the information gathered will be handed over to the relevant authorities.
- A log of internet sites visited is kept. This will be examined to monitor sites visited if misuse is suspected. We reserve the right to check your computer's log without informing you.

Of the 200 AUPs analysed, 116 featured the monitoring control node, with 138 references overall. Monitoring is carried out both electronically and by staff, and this was mentioned in a number of the AUPs:

- Local authorities reserve the right to monitor and log all types of network activity including e-mail. Monitoring of computer usage may be performed electronically or manually.
- You should be aware that council security systems are capable of recording all transactions, website visits and emails made on library computers.

## DISCUSSION

In the AUPs analysed, there is clearly tension between being able to connect patrons to the information they are seeking and making sure that the community is being protected. Several of the AUPs note that the reason for restricting activities through filtering or via a misuse policy is for the community. The library is a space for users of all different age groups, and some of those working at the PC section will be children. It is an open environment and many of the AUPs note this. However, there are ethical implications of potentially blocking material that is perfectly legal, when attempting to block unsuitable material. Is protection of the community a justifiable reason for monitoring patrons?

A library may use surveillance to protect users of the library, but an AUP that frames monitoring in a way that looks to be controlling in nature risks alienating the patron or diminishing their trust.

For a lot of the public library services it is clearly about balancing the needs and personal freedoms of the individual with the interests and safety of the community as a whole. Several of the AUPs mention that they do not wish to prohibit access, as long as the sites are not troublesome to other users; again, the library must serve the needs of everyone who uses it, whilst keeping in mind the individual's intellectual and creative freedoms.

## ACKNOWLEDGEMENTS

The authors would like to thank the Economic and Social Research Council (ESRC) for funding this research.

## REFERENCES

ALA (2008). Code of ethics of the American Library Association. Retrieved October 20, 2016 from http://www.ala.org/advocacy/proethics/codeofethics/

CILIP (2013). Ethical principles. Retrieved October 20, 2016 from http://www.cilip.org.uk/cilip/about/ethics/

Fairclough, N. (2001). The discourse of New Labour: Critical discourse analysis. In M. Wetherell (Ed.), *Discourse as data: A guide for analysis.* (pp. 229-266). London: Sage.

Gallagher, C. et al. (2015). Management of acceptable use of computing facilities in the public library: Avoiding a panoptic gaze? *Journal of Documentation, 71*(3), 572-590

Lyon, D. (1994). *The electronic eye: The rise of surveillance society.* Minneapolis: University of Minnesota Press.

McMenemy, D. (2014). Towards a public library standard for acceptable use of computing facilities. IFLA world library and information congress. 80th IFLA general conference and assembly, 2014-08-16 - 2014-08-22.

Monahan, T. (2011). Surveillance as cultural practice. *The Sociological Quarterly, 52*(4), 495-508

Palgi, R.D. (1996). Rules of the road: Why you need an Acceptable Use Policy. *School Library Journal, 42*(8), 32-33.

Spacey, R. et al. (2013). Regulating internet access and content in UK public libraries: Findings from the MAIPLE project. *Journal of Librarianship and Information Science, 47*(1), 71-84.

# Building Identity in Online Environments: An Information Science Perspective

**Frances VC Ryan**
*Edinburgh Napier University, Scotland. f.ryan@napier.ac.uk*

**Hazel Hall**
*Edinburgh Napier University, Scotland. h.hall@napier.ac.uk*

**Peter Cruickshank**
*Edinburgh Napier University, Scotland. p.cruickshank@napier.ac.uk*

**Alistair Lawson**
*Edinburgh Napier University, Scotland. a.lawson@napier.ac.uk*

## ABSTRACT

**The research presented in this poster is concerned with the ways in which people use information to build identities for themselves online with reference to the themes of personal reputation management. To date these two themes have been under-explored together in the research literature, both in general and from an information science perspective. The poster content shares findings related to three areas of identity building: (1) the creation and use of online personas and identities; (2) the use of anonymity and pseudonyms through information sharing – or concealment – practices; and (3) the blurring or merging together of participants' private and professional selves. This study used participant diaries and in-depth, semi-structured interviews with 45 UK-based participants. The main finding presented here is that individuals present elements of their online persona or personality using online information, but that they do not do so with the intention of building identity. The findings explored in this presentation are contextualised with reference to identity building in the more formal setting of academic reputation management, i.e., through the use of citations.**

## KEYWORDS

citation practices, everyday life information seeking, identity, information behaviour and use, online identity, social media, social networking, reputation

## INTRODUCTION

This poster concerns an aspect of information behaviour and use related to social media with regards to the creation of online identity. The presentation derives from a larger doctoral study that investigates how online information is used in the management and evaluation of personal reputations. It follows the tradition of research into everyday life information seeking (ELIS) (Savolainen, 1995). The findings shared here relate to a research question as applied to the theme of reputation management: How do individuals use information to build identities for themselves online?

80th Annual Meeting of the Association for Information Science & Technology, Washington, DC | Oct. 27-Nov. 1, 2017



## LITERATURE REVIEW

The interdisciplinary nature of the research themes of identity and personal reputation management means that much of the relevant academic literature is dispersed across a number of subject domains. These include, for example computing, employment research, human computer interaction, human resources management, information systems, marketing, media and communication studies, physical and mental health, and sociology (Ryan, Cruickshank, Hall & Lawson, 2015).

There is a large body of research on the role that information plays in the management and evaluation of the academic reputations in general, i.e., that on citation practices (Cronin, 1985; White, 2001). Some of these practices relate to identity building, such as using information for self-promotion and self-censorship. While citation practices do not represent an everyday life information seeking activity, it is possible to match aspects of identity building using citations with human online behaviours and activities that social media users undertake in less formal settings.

## RESEARCH DESIGN

This study used qualitative methods with the use of participant diaries and in-depth, semi-structured interviews. A full account of the research design and its appropriateness to this kind of study was published in 2016 (Ryan et al., 2016). It involved 45 UK-based participants, and data collection took place between October 2015 and January 2016. Participants kept diaries for a week in which they logged everyday information sharing practices on social media that they regarded as having impacts on individual reputations, including questions related to identity. Participants then took part in semi-structured interviews of about one hour in length. Interviews were based on themes from the literature review (Ryan et al., 2015), with diary entries used as additional prompts.

## FINDINGS

Three key themes related to information and identity building and reputation management emerged from the analysis of the data, as outlined below.

**The creation and use of online personas:** The act of using information to build online identity is largely based on participants' offline identities and personalities, and participants' social media use generally acts as extensions of their everyday lives. They also hint at their "real world selves."

However, participants in this study did not consider the act of building an identity online as building identity. Instead, they discussed the idea of building or showcasing different personas or personalities.

**The use of anonymity and pseudonyms:** Twenty-one of the 45 participants in this study use anonymous accounts or pseudonyms for at least some of their online interactions. With four exceptions, these naming conventions are not deployed to mask offline identities (anonymous accounts), and even then, the four participants using anonymous accounts have shared their real identities with at least one person they know in an offline environment.

Of the 18 who use pseudonyms (including one who uses both a pseudonym and an anonymous account), the pseudonyms are associated with the participants' real identities. This association takes place either directly or indirectly through bio descriptions, links to other online content managed by the participant or through the information content itself. Further, pseudonyms are generally deployed as a "username" or as variation of the participants' "real name."

**The blurring of selves:** The levels of blurring that happen between individuals' private and professional lives can impact if and how different personas are created or showcased through the use of online information. However, most of the participants in this study do not feel that they are intentionally building their identities through the management of this blurring. Rather, they manage how they share information based on how they perceive different platforms should be used or on the information they believe interests their audience.

Similar to managing the blurring between private and professional information is the idea of managing the blurring between online and offline environments. From an identity standpoint, this can be witnessed in how people represent themselves in one environment or the other. All of the participants in this study feel that their online and offline environments blur together to some extent and that they are portraying themselves as one person most of the time.

## CONCLUSION

There are some strong alignments between the findings from this research and that of prior research. For example, this research supports the literature related to self-censorship and the regulation of online information sharing practices (Hagger-Johnson, Egan & Stillwell, 2011), the blurring between private and professional personas based on platform use (Ollier-Malaterre, Rothbard, & Berg 2013) and the presentation of personas for different audiences (Goffman, 1959). However, there are also some weaker alignments between these findings and the literature, such as the use of anonymity to experiment with identity (Bullingham & Vasconcelos, 2013) and the deliberate concealment of personal information in online profiles (Lingel & boyd, 2013).

A new theme emerging from this work suggests that the use of information for building identity is not an intentional act. Instead, the findings suggest that individuals are not creating an online identity but are managing who they share parts of their offline identity with.

The full doctoral study will investigate this theme in more detail, including the relationship between building online identities, showcasing aspects of personas and the building and maintenance of personal reputation. This work is expected to be completed in 2017.

## ACKNOWLEDGMENTS

The authors acknowledge the participants in the study.

## REFERENCES

Bullingham, L., & Vasconcelos, A. C. (2013). "The presentation of self in the online world": Goffman and the study of online identities. *Journal of Information Science*, *39*(1), 101-112.

Cronin, B. (1985). *The citation process: The role and significance of citations in scientific communication*. London: Taylor Graham.

Goffman, E. (1959). *The presentation of self in everyday life*. Garden City, N.Y.: Doubleday.

Hagger-Johnson, G., Egan, V., & Stillwell, D. (2011). Are social networking profiles reliable indicators of sensational interests? *Journal of Research in Personality*, *45*(1), 71-76.

Lingel, J., & boyd, d. (2013). "Keep it secret, keep it safe": Information poverty, information norms, and stigma. *Journal of the American Society for Information Science and Technology*, *64*(5), 981-991.

Ollier-Malaterre, A., Rothbard, N. P., & Berg, J. M. (2013). When worlds collide in cyberspace: How boundary work in online social networks impacts professional relationships. *Academy of Management Review*, *38*(4), 645-669.

Ryan, F., Cruickshank, P., Hall, H., & Lawson, A. (2015). Assessing the available and accessible evidence: How personal reputations are determined and managed online. In *Information: Interactions and impact (i3) 2015, Robert Gordon University, Aberdeen, Scotland.*

Ryan, F., Cruickshank, P., Hall, H., & Lawson, A. (2016). Personal online reputation: The development of an approach to investigate how personal reputation is evaluated and managed in online environments. In *2nd International Data Information and Information Management Conference (IDIMC)* (pp. 98-108). Loughborough: LISU.

Savolainen, R. (1995). Everyday life information seeking: Approaching information seeking in the context of "way of life." *Library & Information Science Research*, *17*, 259-294.

White, H. D. (2001). Authors as citers over time. *Journal of the American Society for Information Science and Technology*, *52*(2), 87-108.

# Using Visual Analytics to Combat Cyberbullying in New Jersey Schools

**Lindy Ryan**
*Rutgers Discovery Informatics Institute, Rutgers University, USA. lindy.ryan@rutgers.edu*

**Sierra Gratale**
*Rutgers Discovery Informatics Institute, Rutgers University, USA. sierra.gratale@rutgers.edu*

## ABSTRACT

**The rising and rapid adoption of social media has affected numerous digital behavior changes over the past several years, particularly among adolescent users. Among these, cyberbullying has become an increasingly disruptive and dangerous problem, with effects ranging from increased online aggression to psychological distress and negative effects on academic performance. This study explores the impact of school-level environmental factors such as demographics and unique student populations on cyberbullying behaviors. Specifically, this study utilized a survey and visual analytics to examine cyberbullying among 882 middle and high-school students (380 boys and 502 girls) in two New Jersey districts. Findings revealed that broad cyberbullying statistics might not be applicable at individual school level behaviors. Specifically, boys may experience more cyberbullying than girls, victimization may occur predictively in peak grades and both genders may underreport, especially in higher grades.**

## KEYWORDS

data visualization, visual analytics, cyberbullying

## INTRODUCTION

Over the past several years, cyberbullying has become a major concern, especially when correlated with two worrisome consequences. First, rates of adolescent depression and suicide ideation have increased, with many studies linking these to cyberbullying experiences (Shpiegel, Klomek & Apter, 2015). Second, peer interactions during adolescence affect a large influence on identity formation, and victims of cyberbullying may suffer long-term sociological and psychological consequences that extend beyond adolescence and into adulthood (Notar, Padgett & Roden, 2013; Albin, 2012). This makes cyberbullying intervention not only an educational initiative, but as Albin (2012) declared in his plea for cyberbullying legislation, a societal imperative. However, while research on cyberbullying is plentiful, Gan et al. (2014) note there exists a paucity of recent data exploring if the incidence of cyberbullying has changed. Discussion of how school ecosystems and unique student populations may affect cyberbullying and how assessing these might aid educators to better combat cyberbullying, is lacking.

In this study, we examined two school districts of vastly different demographics to investigate the prevalence of cyberbullying within individual school ecosystems. Our goal was to find both unique and repeatable patterns of victimization and student experiences to guide school administrators in developing customized, intervention strategies. We used visual analytics and data storytelling to increase the literacy of results and to provide a visual mechanism to communicate findings. Our presentation will explore the patterns and trends discovered and their application within each district and broader New Jersey

## METHODS

Data were collected through an anonymized survey from a sample of 882 junior-high and high-school students attending South Brunswick Public Schools (SBPS) and New Brunswick Public Schools (NBPS) (433 and 540, respectively) during the 2016-2017 school year. Both districts are located in Middlesex County, New Jersey, a diverse and multicultural area with a population of approximately 836,000.

## INSTRUMENTS

We used survey instrument Qualtrics to collect responses. We designed our survey to include 35 questions with a variety of yes/no, multi-select, single select and Likert scale answer options to increase the variety of analytics and visualizations for representing and communicating results. Questions were developed based on assessments of similar surveys (like the Quintessential Instructional Archive and DitchTheLabel.org), literature reviews and discussions with school administration. The survey sought to gauge students' comprehension, awareness and participation in cyberbullying activities, both as victims and perpetrators, and capture sentiment regarding how schools should fight back against cyberbullying. Examples of questions included comprehension questions ("Cyberbullying is") and behavior questions ("Have you ever been cyberbullied/cyberbullied another student?"). Additional questions focused on social media usage and student opinions on efforts necessary to combat cyberbullying.

80th Annual Meeting of the Association for Information Science & Technology, Washington, DC | Oct. 27-Nov. 1, 2017

## PROCEDURE

To protect student privacy, school administrators distributed an opt-in permission form to parents and guardians and maintained signed forms. Students completed the survey during school hours using school equipment.

## DEMOGRAPHIC INFORMATION

We collected information regarding the students' gender, race, grade level and sexual orientation.

## DATA ANALYSIS

Data was exported from Qualtrics into Excel and prepared for analysis in Alteryx. A sample of data was checked for accuracy. The data were analyzed using Tableau.

## RESULTS

### *Demographics*

Of the students who completed the survey, 57% identified as female and 43% as male. Approximately 47% of students were Hispanic/Latino; 28% Asian/Pacific Islander; 12% White; 6% African American; and 7% other. Notably, both schools have significant racial contributions: SBPS is 60% Asian/Pacific Islander; NBPS is 94% Hispanic/Latino.

### *Cyberbullying Victimization*

Much of the available data on cyberbullying typically asserts that females are the most likely victims and perpetrators of cyberbullying. However, our study found that boys self-reported having experienced cyberbullying more than females: 17.5% of boys compared to 14.4% of girls at NBPS and 8.9% compared to 6.3% at SBPS.

### *Experience Peaks by Grades*

In both districts, we recognized grades where cyberbullying behaviors peaked. These were early middle (6-7) and early high school grades (9). In total, these represented over 58% of all cyberbullying activity in NBPS and over 53% in SBPS. This finding suggests there may be particularly pivotal grades related to bullying behavior.

### *Underreporting of Incidents*

We found that students of both genders radically underreport cyberbullying experiences. This underreporting becomes increasingly severe as students age (Figure 1). In NBPS, female students were as likely to report cyberbullying as not; however, about 61% of males did not report. In SBPS, students of both genders significantly underreported: 58% of females and 65% of males. Additionally, as students age, underreporting increases: both districts displayed a steep decline in cyberbullying reporting beginning in grade 10. This reflects a finding by Gan et al. (2014): a majority of students who are bullied do not share about the experience.

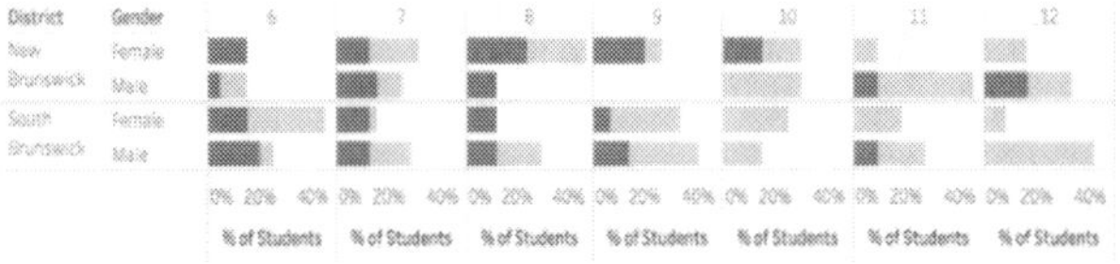


***Figure 1.*** *Underreporting problem increases with age.*

## CONCLUSION

Cyberbullying is prevalent among middle and high school students with observable patterns that may assist school administrators in developing intervention curricula, particularly in peak grades where known gaps exist. Although the specific results of the study may be difficult to apply to other schools, we believe with localized assessment educators will be able to apply similarly specific findings their schools. Additionally, students are willing to provide input on how schools should engage (Figure 2). Further research should focus on developing models with a broader application and curriculum development.

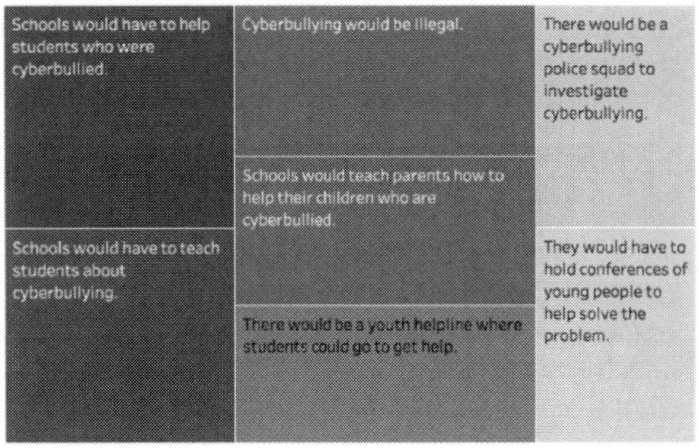


***Figure 2.*** *Students contribute thoughts on how schools should intervene against cyberbullying.*

## ACKNOWLEDGMENTS

We would like to thank NBPS and SBPS for their support.

## REFERENCES

Albin, K. A. (2012). Bullies in a wired world. The impact of cyberspace victimization on adolescent mental health and the need for cyberbullying legislation in Ohio. *Journal of Law and Health, 25*(1), 153-188.

Gan, S, S., Zhong, C., Das, S., Gan, J. S., Willis, S. & Tully, E. (2014). The prevalence of bullying and cyberbullying in high school: A 2011 study. *International Journal of Adolescent Med Health, 26*(1), 27-31.

Notar, C, E., Padgett, S. & Roden, J. (2013). Cyberbullying: Resources for intervention and prevention. *Universal Journal of Educational Research, 1*(3), 133-145.

Shpiegel, Y., Klomek, A. B. & Apter, A. (2015). Bullying, cyberbullying, depression and suicide ideation among youth: Comparing online to paper-and-pencil questionnaires. *International Journal of Child Adolescent Health, 8*(1), 161-167.

# How Recordkeeping Ensures Trust in Digital Archives

**Robert J. Sandusky**
*University of Illinois at Chicago, USA. sandusky@uic.edu*

## ABSTRACT

**Imagine a researcher in 2067 examining objects in a digital archive that were deposited in the early 21st century. How can the researcher be assured that those digital materials – whether born-digital or digital surrogates of analog materials – have not been accidentally or maliciously altered sometime during the intervening decades? Ten archival workers – archivists, metadata specialists, digitization managers and preservation technologists – were interviewed about how contemporary recordkeeping practices ensure the authenticity of born-digital files and digital surrogates for future users of the archive. This poster presents preliminary results about how archives are adapting to emergent needs for processing digital materials at scale, ensuring that workflows capture entities, activities and agents (provenance information), and ensuring that current systems support migration of provenance information to successor systems.**

## KEYWORDS

archives, records management, provenance, digital preservation, digitization, recordkeeping

## INTRODUCTION

Archivists and the other information professionals who support them (i.e., metadata specialists, digitizers, technologists and digital preservation specialists – collectively, archival workers) are challenged by rapid changes in record creation practices and underlying technology. Archivists and records managers are facing a deluge of incoming born-digital materials in a wide variety of formats for which traditional pencil and paper practices are not entirely suitable. Information professionals managing digitization initiatives are creating large collections of digital surrogates of analog artifacts at a time when standards and practices for digital libraries, digital collections and digital preservation are still evolving.

This study uses qualitative methods to understand the recordkeeping practices in use throughout the archival lifecycle and across a range of materials including analog, born-digital and digital surrogates. The fundamental question is whether the information kept during acquisition, accession, appraisal, arrangement, description, digitization and digital preservation of materials by archivists, their colleagues and their systems is sufficient to answer questions – that might be raised years or decades later – about the authenticity and trustworthiness of the collections and artifacts in their archive.

80th Annual Meeting of the Association for Information Science & Technology, Washington, DC | Oct. 27-Nov. 1, 2017



In archival science, "the principle of provenance requires records and archives to be managed in a way that secures and preserves knowledge of their origins and the circumstances of their creation" (Yeo, 2013, p. 218). Archival science provides a set of standard practices, including deeds of gift, collections files and finding aids, that help ensure trust and context for archival records (Millar, 2010). Archivists and their colleagues have extended and adapted these practices to cover born-digital records in the larger context of handcrafted arrangement and description (Dooley, 2015). However, the tools to process born-digital records at scale are not available (see Baron & Borden (2016) for a discussion of processing e-mail from U.S. presidential administrations). Additionally, the work done to digitize analog materials, utilizing more of a library science based item-by-item processing paradigm, has been criticized by archivists as depriving individual digital objects of critical context (Cocciolo, 2016; Yeo, 2013). In response to these challenges, provenance, particularly machine-actionable representations of provenance information, has been the subject of increasing interest from multiple disciplines ranging from archival science to computer science, law and library and information science (Lemieux et al., 2016).

This poster presents preliminary results from an interview study about how archives are adapting to emergent needs for processing digital materials at scale, ensuring that workflows capture entities, activities and agents (provenance information) (PROV-DM, 2015), and ensuring that current systems support migration of provenance information to successor systems.

## METHODS

Fifteen archival workers from institutions in multiple countries participated in semi-structured interviews conducted either face-to-face or via Skype. The interviews were recorded and then transcribed using an automatic transcription tool. The investigator manually corrected the generated transcripts and analyzed them using NVivo 11.4, employing grounded theory techniques to identify concepts and phenomena (Strauss & Corbin, 1990).

Participants were identified by the investigator through personal professional contacts, recommendation of earlier participants and by knowledge of published and unpublished writings. Participants were sought who play different roles in the management of archival materials and material types, from a variety of countries and institution types. In some cases, multiple participants from the same institution were interviewed.

The participants interviewed so far perform roles including archivist (3), digital preservation expert / technologist (4), metadata specialist (1) and digitization manager (2). One participant moved from being an archivist in a previous institution to a technologist in the latest institution. At this point, one participant works outside of the United States. Work contexts vary as well, with participants working in or with collecting archives in public libraries (2), private collecting archives (2), state/national archives (1), university libraries (3) and within university systems (2).

## FINDINGS AND IMPLICATIONS

Archivists continue to rely on office documents and/or archival management systems to support workflows for acquisition, appraisal, arrangement, description, creation of finding aids, creation of metadata to support digitization. These are among the findings:

- Archival management systems are not universal.
- Use of forensic tools for supporting acquisition of born-digital materials is not universal.
- Collections (or information) files, deeds of gift and donor correspondence form the bulk of the provenance chain for archivists.
- Capture and retention of comprehensive provenance information for digital materials is not widespread.

Digital preservation systems (DPS) and digital asset management systems (DAMS) are increasingly common, but typically managed by technologists, not archivists.

- Archivists take on technologist roles or technologists acquire working knowledge of archives over time; no participants performed both roles simultaneously.
- Archival management systems lack integration with the DAMS/DPS in institutions with both.
- DPS are often PREMIS-aware (PREMIS, 2008) to support future system migrations and capture information about entities, activities and actors, thus contributing to the provenance chain.
- Unification of analog and digital archiving workflows remains elusive, and thus challenges remain:
- Larger institutions with specialists in two or more of these areas – traditional archiving, born-digital processing and digitization – are ahead of other institutions in managing digital materials end-to-end.
- Handoffs between systems often utilize spreadsheets and data export/data augmentation/data import sequences.
- There is no single, comprehensive view of all information in the provenance chain.

Interviews with archival workers are continuing. The analysis will also continue with goals of (1) additional publications and (2) the dissemination of surveys to larger numbers of archival workers performing different roles.

## REFERENCES


Baron, J.R., & Borden, B.B. (2016). Opening up dark digital archives through the use of analytics to identify sensitive content. In *2016 IEEE international conference on big data (big data)* (pp. 3224-3229). https://doi.org/10.1109/BigData.2016.7840978

Cocciolo, A. (2016). When archivists and digital asset managers collide: Tensions and ways forward. *The American Archivist, 79*(1), 121-136. https://doi.org/10.17723/0360-9081.79.1.121

Dooley, J. (2015). The archival advantage: Integrating archival expertise into management of born-digital library materials. Retrieved from http://www.oclc.org/research/publications/2015/oclcresearch-archival-advantage-2015.html

Lemieux, V.L., & imProvenance Group. (2016). Provenance: Past, present and future in interdisciplinary and multidisciplinary perspective. SpringerLink, 3-45. https://doi.org/10.1007/978-3-319-40226-0_1

Millar, L. (2010). *Archives: principles and practices*. New York: Neal-Schuman Publishers.

PREMIS Editorial Committee (2008). Data dictionary for preservation metadata: PREMIS version 2.0. Retrieved May 13, 2016, from http://www.loc.gov/standards/premis/v2/premis-2-0.pdf.

PROV-DM: The PROV data model. (2015). Draft May 1, 2015. Retrieved May 13, 2016, from https://www.w3.org/TR/prov-dm/

Strauss, A.L. & Corbin, J.M. (1990). *Basics of qualitative research: Grounded theory procedures and techniques*. Newbury Park, CA: Sage Publications.

Yeo, G. (2013). Trust and context in cyberspace. *Archives and Records, 34*(2), 214-234. https://doi.org/10.1080/23257962.2013.825207

# Assessment of Intellectual Capital of Library and Information Professionals

**Jayne Sappington**
*Texas Tech University Libraries, USA.*
*Jayne.sappington@ttu.edu*

**Denise A.D. Bedford**
*Georgetown University, USA. db233@georgetown.edu*

## ABSTRACT

**Information professionals have traditionally connected people and information resources; however, that role is changing as we move into the knowledge economy. Visioning exercises and thought papers on the future of the profession continue to focus on the resources we manage – moving from paper to digital resources and from physical to digital distribution channels. These visions, though, are short sighted and do not take into account the shift from an industrial and a financial economy to a knowledge economy. In a knowledge economy, individuals with information science skills will play expanded roles beyond the library walls. While intellectual capital and knowledge assets are well understood in the economics and knowledge sciences fields, they are not widely recognized in other domains. This visual presentation reports on the results of Phase 1 of a broader research project to gauge information professionals' awareness of and investment in their own intellectual capital assets. Phase 1 focused on one area of practice – information professionals in academic research libraries – and leveraged a national survey. The survey focused on eight recognized areas of intellectual capital and existing sources of learning and investment. Phase 2 shifts the research focus to narrative descriptions of the use of intellectual capital in the working environment. In Phase 2 individual librarians focus on one of the eight types of intellectual capital and record their experiences using those assets in an electronic journal. Phase 3 will focus on the view of intellectual capital assets from the organizational perspective, i.e., an organization's stock of intellectual capital and the way in which it spends and invests in that capital.**

## KEYWORDS

knowledge economy, intellectual capital, information professionals, human capital, national survey

## INTRODUCTION

The success of any organization, city, community or individual in the 21st century knowledge economy will depend on how intellectual capital assets are invested and grown (Amidon, 2012; Bontis, 2001; Bontis, 2002; Bonfour & Edvinsson, 2005). In the knowledge economy, intellectual capital is the primary asset for investment – it is equivalent to money in the financial economy, to equipment and resources in the industrial economy and to land in the agricultural economy (Bonfour & Edvinsson, 2005; Edvinsson, 2002; Skyrme & Amidon, 1998; Stewart, 1991; Stewart, 1997; Sveiby, 2002; Teece, 2000). Intellectual capital is often misunderstood as including only highly educated individuals or highly skilled work. In fact, though, intellectual capital includes a broad range of assets which support the generation of ideas, the growth of knowledge and the exchange and sharing of knowledge. Andriessen (2004b) and Amidon, Formica and Mercier-Laurent (2005) define intellectual capital to include (1) human capital – comprising tacit knowledge, skills and attitude; (2) structural capital – comprising explicit knowledge, procedural knowledge and culture; and (3) relational capital – comprising networks and reputation.

Information professionals should recognize the importance of investing in and growing their intellectual capital assets (Bedford, Donley and Lensenmayer, 2014). The challenge for the profession, though, is that these assets are often valued less than the information resources housed and stored in library collections. Individuals with the intellectual capital assets of information professionals will play increasingly important roles in the everyday life of a knowledge society – beyond the walls of the library, beyond their traditional roles of managing physical resources.

This visual presentation reports on Phases 1 and 2 of a three-phase research project focused on the intellectual capital assets of information professionals. Phase 1 involved a national survey of academic research librarians with the goal of understanding the level of awareness of existing assets and identifying opportunities for new investment and growth. The survey also focused on the value of traditional and non-traditional learning and professional development channels. The results of the national survey suggest that it is feasible to assess the intellectual capital of a targeted population through a national survey. The researchers believe that much of the success was due to the design of the instrument and the explanations and examples it provided for each type of intellectual capital asset and to the support that was afforded to the research by the Association of Research Libraries. The survey questions included extensive lists of examples. Detailed results for each of the eight types are presented in the visual presentation.

General results for human capital were insightful and encouraging. The most highly rated tacit knowledge assets included analytical thinking, big picture and systems thinking, intellectual curiosity and creativity, problem solving, strategic

---

80th Annual Meeting of the Association for Information Science & Technology, Washington, DC | Oct. 27-Nov. 1, 2017

thinking, understanding of ethics and emotional maturity. The strongest response to skills was in the area of analytical and critical thinking skills, followed by people skills and instructional and teaching skills. In general, the assessment of structural capital highlighted opportunities for improvement, particularly in the areas of explicit knowledge and procedural knowledge. Respondents suggested there were opportunities to engage in more explicit knowledge creation. This finding also pertains to the nature of the professional education and the heavy emphasis on practice rather than publishing and research. *Procedural knowledge* was defined as how people do tasks in their jobs and what rules and standards must be met. When assessing their cultural capital, respondents believe they are perceived as ethical, trustworthy individuals – attributes that attract others to work with them. General results for reputational capital were noteworthy but mixed. The reputation is the most visible indicator of intellectual capital and respondents saw themselves as fair, team members and a source of knowledge. Professionals may not engage in all types of networks, though, due to the nature of their work and the importance of maintaining a neutral and professional image. This was born out in the results of the relational capital which showed weakness when it came to political and spiritual relationships. While respondents were largely satisfied with existing learning sources, there are opportunities for new instructional methods and delivery channels. There is an opportunity to rethink and redesign professional education to cover all eight types of intellectual capital. It is also clear that younger professionals are eager to join this discussion.

Phase 1 demonstrated the feasibility of openly assessing the intellectual capital assets of the information profession. The researchers intend to extend the research to other areas of practice within the information profession, including public libraries, college libraries, school libraries and special libraries (e.g., libraries in businesses, museums, archives, government departments and agencies, research institutes, etc.). Over the longer term, the researchers expect to extend the research to other professions, including engineers, health professionals, performing artists, business professionals and teachers. As the research continues and expands, we hope to both raise awareness of intellectual capital assets and to identify areas which may benefit from further attention and development in education and learning.

Phase 2 shifts the focus from a broad professional assessment to individual professional's intellectual capital assets and their experience using them in the everyday working environment. In Phase 2 individual professionals select one type of intellectual capital asset and record their experience for one week in an electronic journal. Phase 2 is currently in proof of concept testing. The narrative journal entries will be objectively analyzed using semantic analysis profiles representing intellectual capital asset types, the extensional and intentional nature of the language used, as well as profiles that highlight opportunities for new learning. Phase 3 of the research will focus on the organizational perspective – the library or organization's view of the level and value of the intellectual capital assets of its people. Phase 3 aims to begin to rebalance our valuation of the number of resources on our shelves with the knowledge of our information professionals.

## REFERENCES


Amidon, D.M. (2012). KM coming of age: A kaleidoscope of innovation opportunity. In E. Serventi *Innovation and transformation through knowledge management – Research report,* (pp. 1-17). London, UK: Ark Group.

Amidon, D.M., Formica, P., & Mercier-Laurent, E. (Eds.). (2005). *Knowledge economics: Emerging principles, practices and policies.* Tartu, Estonia: Tartu University Press.

Andriessen, D. (2004a). IC valuation and measurement: Classifying the state of the art. *Journal of Intellectual Capital,* 5(2), 230-242.

Andriessen, D. (2004b). Making sense of intellectual capital: Designing a method for the valuation of intangibles, London, UK: Routledge.

Bedford, D.A.D. & Donley, J. & Lensenmayer, N. (2014). The role of librarians in a knowledge society: Valuing our intellectual capital assets. *Advances in librarianship: Current issues in libraries, information science and related fields.*

Bontis, N. (2001). Assessing knowledge assets: A review of the models used to measure intellectual capital. *International Journal of Management Reviews, 3*(1), 41-60.

Bontis, N. (2002). National intellectual capital index: Intellectual capital development in the Arab Region. New York, NY: United Nations.

Bounfour, A. & Edvinsson, L. (2005). *Intellectual capital for communities: Nations, regions and cities.* Boston, MA: Butterworth-Heinemann.

Edvinsson, L. (2002). The new knowledge economics. *Business Strategy Review, 13*(3), 72-76.

Skyrme, D.J. & Amidon, D.M. (1998). New measures of success. *Journal of Business Strategy, 19*(1), 20-24.doi:10.1108/eb039905

Stewart, T.A. (1997). Intellectual capital: The new wealth of organizations. New York, NY: Doubleday

# The Role of Diversity in a Video Game Design Program

**Rachel N. Simons**
*School of Information, University of Texas at Austin, USA.*
*rnsimons@utexas.edu*

**Kenneth R. Fleischmann**
*School of Information, University of Texas at Austin, USA.*
*kfleisch@ischool.utexas.edu*

## ABSTRACT

**Video game design is an emerging educational area, related to yet distinct from programs in information technology and game studies. This pilot study aimed to explore the role of diversity in video game design education. Data collection included interviews with two instructors and three students. This poster presents two themes: 1) why diversity is important to game design education and 2) how to address diversity in game design education. The results of this pilot study indicate the need for additional research on the role of diversity in video game design education and practice.**

## KEYWORDS

diversity, inclusion, broadening participation, video games, game design, information technology education

## INTRODUCTION

Video game players and designers have called for increased diversity within game content, as a lack of diversity and representation may limit game audiences and gamer identification with games/characters, make diverse individuals and groups invisible or even perpetuate negative stereotypes (Williams et al., 2009). Individuals from underrepresented and marginalized groups may strongly identify as gamers but frequently cannot envision themselves as game creators – and, accordingly, avoid pursuing higher education and employment within game design-related fields without some active intervention (DiSalvo et al., 2013). Diversity in games and diversity in game design work are, in some ways, mutually self-constituting: more diverse teams create more diverse games, which in turn encourages more diverse participation in the workforce. As post-secondary education increasingly becomes a common requirement for video game design work, these programs have significant potential to play a vital mediating role in this content-creator cycle. Therefore, it is critical to consider the role of diversity within post-secondary game design programs and how best to achieve diversity within the game design workforce.

## BACKGROUND

While the topic of diversity has generated growing interest within game studies programs involving cultural studies of games and game play (e.g., Zagal and Bruckman, 2007), this interest has not yet translated to much exploration of diversity within video game design programs, which are fundamentally different from game studies programs in focus and career endpoint. Other studies have employed game design as a means to broaden participation in the information technology (IT) workforce (e.g., DiSalvo et al., 2013), but virtually none of these studies of the use of game design to foster diversity have focused on game design as a career path. To address the need for additional research on diversity in video game design education programs, we ask, "How is diversity understood and addressed within a video game design program?"

## METHODS

Our field site was the Game and Mobile Media Applications (GAMMA) undergraduate certificate program at the University of Texas at Austin. We conducted semi-structured, open-ended interviews with two faculty members and three students; all participants were given the option to receive credit for their contributions to the study or to remain anonymous. We began by interviewing the team lead, Dr. Paul Toprac. Next, following the team lead's recommendation, we interviewed one additional instructor, Dr. Sarah Abraham. Despite our numerous recruitment efforts and assistance from the two instructors, we were only able to recruit three students to volunteer to participate: Scott Munro and two anonymous participants. As such, our findings are not necessarily representative of the general student body within the program, but rather likely reflect students with particular interest in this topic.

During each interview, we took notes and made audio recordings. We thematically analyzed the notes and transcribed portions of the interviews relevant to the themes that emerged. Prior to publication, we sent this paper to all participants to ask for feedback in order to validate our analysis of the interview data and to allow our participants to reaffirm their preference for credit or anonymity.

## RESULTS

This poster focuses on two significant themes that emerged from our interview data related to diversity in game design: why diversity is important to game design education and how to address diversity in game design education.

80th Annual Meeting of the Association for Information Science & Technology, Washington, DC | Oct. 27-Nov. 1, 2017

### *Why Diversity Is Important to Game Design Education*

When asked, "How important do you feel it is that educational programs support students from diverse backgrounds, identities, perspectives and experiences," participants unanimously affirmed the importance of diversity in game design education. For example, Munro remarked, "it's very good to get out of your bubble and part of that is meeting people of diverse backgrounds," specifying that this was especially important "in games design and media…where we're trying to be very creative."

Participants also drew a link between a lack of diverse game creators and a lack of diversity in games. Immediately after asserting that diversity in education was "really important," a student expressed concern that, "In…the game industry…we're just seeing the same thing over and over again…we're not tapping into…most of the population…It's ridiculous!" Similarly, Abraham linked the importance of diverse workforce participation to increasing game diversity, saying, "I think that we're actually seeing a lot more of that diversity finally coming out." Abraham also noted an increase in the number of game designers who are female, LGBTQ, members of underrepresented ethnic groups or individuals with disabilities, and explains that they are "creating games that…share their view of the world." Participants thus often discussed the significance of increasing participation in the field as a way to increase diversity within games.

### *How to Address Diversity in Game Design Education*

Participants described a few specific ways of identifying and supporting diversity within education. When asked about their experiences with diversity in the program, participants frequently expressed the opinion that exposure to diversity was not only inherently positive, but was one of the best ways to increase diversity in both the workforce and in the content of games. For example, a student explained that education is "one of the best [ways to] help people meet people who are not like-minded." Additionally, participants emphasized that having diverse individuals and perspectives together in the educational program was very important: "I think the best way would just be to have diversity in the classroom and the way you're learning." Munro felt that regular classroom interactions were particularly important for modeling and showcasing diversity, saying, "Just by giving everybody the opportunity to show their work…demonstrat[es] the different kinds of people who are working on that work." In this case, having regular presentations of game projects in front of the entire class allowed students to make their diverse identities and perspectives explicitly visible to their peers, as future members of the game design workforce.

However, participants also emphasized that, while diversity in the classroom should continue to be encouraged, a diverse classroom does not necessarily accurately model the workforce that students will be entering. Toprac remarked, "compared to the professional environment, I have a feeling that we are being very inclusive" and indicated that, ironically, a diverse educational experience does not necessarily prepare students for the workforce: "I had a female student who went on to work at a very large, high-tech company…and she was surprised by the change in culture from here to the company…She could feel it immediately. They were…dismissive because she was female." Despite this disparity between the classroom and the workplace, participants indicated that diversity should be a goal for educational programs. As Abraham explained, "The unfortunate reality is that the games industry is fairly NOT diverse, so in a sense we're trying…to help make it more diverse…There's [a] balance between preparing them for the harsh reality and discourag[ing] them off the path."

## DISCUSSION

Participants re-affirmed the need for diversity in game design, similar to previous research on IT education and workforce diversity. Additionally, participants saw a clear path between including diverse individuals and perspectives in game design and increasing the amount of diversity within games – with diversity in games therefore seen as a positive, worthwhile goal for individuals entering into the field. These reciprocal associations between content and creators, and between representation and participation, also support the ongoing arguments for increased diversity in IT.

## FUTURE RESEARCH

It is important to note that these results are very preliminary as they reflect data collection from a small number of individuals affiliated with one game design program. Future directions include interviewing additional stakeholders such as alumni and employers; including a broader range of educational institutions, such as community colleges and minority-serving institutions; and conducting longitudinal studies of students' experiences at various stages within their programs. Our results indicate that game design education should not be studied within a vacuum. Accordingly, future research should also examine how diversity is understood and addressed within the daily work life of video game design professionals. Such research could then, in turn, be used to inform educational programs.

## REFERENCES


DiSalvo, B., Guzdial, M., Meadows, C., Perry, K., McKlin, T. & Bruckman, A. (2013). Workifying games: Successfully engaging African American gamers with computer science. In *Proceedings of SIGCSE* (317–322).

Williams, D., Martins, N., Consalvo, M., & Ivory, J. D. (2009). The virtual census: Representations of gender, race and age in video games. *New Media & Society, 11*, 815–834.

Zagal, J. P., & Bruckman, A. S. (2007). From gamers to scholars: Challenges of teaching game studies. In *Proceedings of DiGRA, 4*, 575–582.

# What Makes a Research Article Newsworthy?

**Harish Varma Siravuri**
*Northern Illinois University, USA. hsiravuri@niu.edu*

**Hamed Alhoori**
*Northern Illinois University, USA. alhoori@niu.edu*

## ABSTRACT

**There has been tremendous growth in the amount of scientific literature being published every year. Yet, very little of it receives press coverage. Mentions by news outlets often establish the relevance the research has to society in general. In the present study, we focus on better understanding the factors that contribute to a research article's newsworthiness. We have built three classifiers to predict the likelihood of a research article receiving online press coverage, based on features that quantify the attention it has received on various online platforms. The random forest classifier performed best with an accuracy rate of 0.92.**

## KEYWORDS

altmetrics, newsworthy research

## INTRODUCTION

Research findings are often the subject of news headlines. This is especially true when the topic is of interest to the public or when the findings have a perceptible impact on society. Based on an assessment of the findings as exciting or as particularly relevant to the readers, science journalists present stories about research they think their readers are likely to find interesting. And with the rise of fact-checking journalism (Graves & Glaisyer, 2012), it is generally assumed by the audience that the validity of the findings are confirmed prior to being presented by the news outlets. Consequently, the validity and the relevance of the research are reinforced when mentioned by news outlets. Identifying the factors that go into deciding whether a research article is newsworthy would enable researchers to better position their work to draw attention. To understand what makes a research article newsworthy, we conducted a study to determine whether a relationship exists between the attention an article receives on social media platforms and the attention it receives in news outlets as a basis for predicting the likelihood of newsworthiness.

## RELATED WORK

Fitzpatrick (1999) considered factors that might have an impact on why certain research articles are considered newsworthy whereas others are not considered to be so. These factors include the prestige of the journal, prepublication publicity and the relevance of the findings to a given audience. Badenschier and Wormer (2012) analyzed the process through which scientific issues are selected for coverage. They concluded that using factors developed for traditional subjects like politics and culture to determine if a story is newsworthy could be misleading and that a certain adaptation was necessary. Rensberger (1978) identified and analyzed three factors that go into making science news: the number of people affected, the trustworthiness of the work and the fascination value. In earlier studies, researchers criticized inaccurate coverage of published scientific papers (Schwartz, Woloshin & Welch, 1999), overstatement of results (Lebow, 1999) and sensationalism (Myers, 1996). Allan (2009) identified factual inaccuracies in news reports and how important it is to understand factors that made stories newsworthy in the first place.

## DATA COLLECTION

The data used in the present study were provided by altmetric.com. The database dump consisted of data from more than five million articles, which we divided into two categories based on the class label: news. The first category consisted of research articles mentioned in at least one news item, and the second category comprised research articles that had not received any news coverage. We randomly selected 50,000 research articles from each category and extracted information regarding how much attention each research article had received on social media. The outcome was a dataset of 100,000 articles without a class imbalance.

## FEATURE SELECTION

The dataset included a large set of variables pertinent to online attention. Initially, we tried using all the available features. Later, we filtered out certain features based on their sparsity and lack of relevance. The fields that described activity on Pinterest and StackOverflow and the field describing citations in policy were very sparse and could not have contributed much to a research article's newsworthiness. As it was discontinued in March 2013, Connotea was irrelevant to research articles published after that year. We relied on the number of mentions on Twitter, Wikipedia, Google+, Weibo, Facebook, videos, blogs and peer reviews.

## METHODS

To predict how likely a scholarly publication is to attract news coverage, we built three classification models: a support vector machine (SVM) model using a radial basis function (RBF) kernel, a random forest (RF) model with 100 decision trees and a multinomial naïve Bayes (MNB) model. We trained the models using a training set consisting of 80% of the original data. The remaining 20% of the data were used as a test set to evaluate the models. We built all three models using 10-fold cross-validation. We also calculated the weight for each feature to determine its relative importance in the

80th Annual Meeting of the Association for Information Science & Technology, Washington, DC, VA | Oct. 27-Nov. 1, 2017

decision-making process. SVM, however, could not be subjected to the same treatment because of the use of the RBF kernel, and feature weights can be calculated only for linear kernels.

## RESULTS

The classification models performed well, with the random forest classifier delivering the highest accuracy rate of 0.924. The accuracy, precision and recall values and the F-1 scores of each of the models are presented in Table 1. The receiver operating characteristic (ROC) curves and the area under the ROC curves are shown in Figure 1.

| | MNB | RF | SVM |
|---|---|---|---|
| **Accuracy** | 0.782 | 0.924 | 0.888 |
| **Precision** | 0.302 | 0.796 | 0.806 |
| **Recall** | 0.365 | 0.658 | 0.326 |
| **F1-Measure** | 0.331 | 0.720 | 0.465 |

***Table 1**. Accuracy, precision, recall and F1 scores*

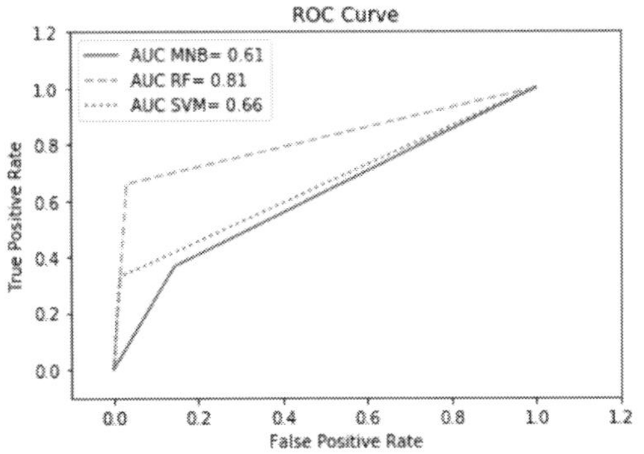


***Figure1**. ROC curves for each classification model*

The five most significant features in respect to the RF and the relative importance of each in respect to the MNB classifier are shown in Table 2. Counts on Mendeley proved to be most significant to the RF model whereas the video feature proved to be the least significant. The opposite was true in case of the MNB model.

| Feature | Random Forest | MNB |
|---|---|---|
| Mendeley | 0.168083 | 0.5792 |
| Facebook | 0.151553 | 2.8116 |
| Twitter | 0.147885 | 1.3097 |
| Blogs | 0.106562 | 4.0367 |
| Google+ | 0.093940 | 3.5126 |

***Table 2**. Relative significance of features*

## CONCLUSIONS AND FUTURE WORK

In this study, we used features that describe the attention research articles receive online to build classification models that predict whether an article is likely to receive news coverage. The RF model delivered good results that imply the existence of a relationship between the attention a research article received online and the likelihood of it receiving news coverage. The results are in agreement with the growing opinion that the newsworthiness of research is increasingly being determined by the readers who post content about it online. In future research, we plan to improve the classification models and build regression models to predict the number of mentions a research article is likely to receive from news outlets.

## REFERENCES


Allan, S. (2009). Making science newsworthy: Exploring the conventions of science journalism. *Investigating science communication in the information age: implications for public engagement and popular media*, (January), 149–165.

Badenschier, F., & Wormer, H. (2012). Issue selection in science journalism: Towards a special theory of news values for science news? (Vol. 28, pp. 59–85).

Fitzpatrick, S. M. (1999). What makes science newsworthy? *The Scientist*, *13*(23), 11–13.

Graves, L., & Glaisyer, T. (2012). The Fact-checking universe in spring 2012. *New America*.

Lebow, M. A. (1999). The pill and the press: Reporting risk. *Obstetrics and Gynecology*, *93*(3), 453–456.

Myers, M. G. (1996). "Drug may have caused huge number of deaths": Lessons learned during an encounter with the fifth estate. *CMAJ: Canadian Medical Association Journal*, *155*(6), 772.

Rensberger, B. (n.d.). What makes science news?

Schwartz, L. M., M. D., Woloshin, S., M. D. & Welch, H. G. (1999). Misunderstandings about the effects of race and sex on physicians' referrals for cardiac catheterization. *The New England Journal of Medicine*, *341*(4), 279–283.

# Illuminating Human-Rare Historic Book Interaction

**Diane H. Sonnenwald**
*University College Dublin, Ireland.*
*Diane.Sonnenwald@ucd.ie*

**Jason McElligott**
*Marsh's Library, Ireland.*
*Jason.McElligott@marshlibrary.ie*

## ABSTRACT

**This presentation showcases research that is investigating human-rare historic book interaction in order to develop a theoretical framework that takes into account the materiality of rare books and will form a foundation for technology requirements that will allow individuals to more fully experience rare historic books through the use of virtual or augmented reality technology.**

## KEYWORDS

human information behavior, rare historic books

## INTRODUCTION

Rare historic books and manuscripts provide unique insights into historic events, as well as everyday life, art, literature and culture across time and geographic locations. It is important to allow individuals access to rare books so they can experience their craftsmanship and learn from them, expanding their appreciation and understanding of the past, and with this knowledge expand their participation in contemporary society. Many people are fascinated by rare historic books and manuscripts. For example, *The Book of Kells*, created around 800 AD, is consistently the fifth most popular fee-paying attraction in Ireland with over 500,000 visitors per year (Failte Ireland, 2015).

However, except for a very few select scholars and dignitaries, individuals are not allowed to handle rare historic books – or their replicas – in libraries, museums and archives due to the fear of potential damage caused by handling. Even the literature discussing how rare historic books should be handled focuses on constraining touch (e.g., Galbraith & Smith, 2012).

Thus, individuals can only interact with rare historic books and manuscripts visually, viewing replicas or actual books through secured glass display cases and/or viewing digital versions on display screens.

Although e-book, virtual and mixed reality book technology has endeavored to increase and improve access to, and engagement with, rare historic books, these efforts have been primarily driven by available technology and less so by user needs or through an understanding of how rare historic books work. Digital access and engagement has been primarily based on a simplified, static view of user knowledge, with a primary focus on visual presentations. Human information behavior research has primarily focused on socio-cognitive strategies with respect to seeking and interacting with contemporary information resources. Increasingly researchers are acknowledging the importance of materiality and the engagement of multiple senses, especially with respect to books (e.g., Trogu, 2015). Cranny-Francis (2011) suggests that touch has meaning with respect to connection, engagement, contiguity, differentiation and positioning. Our research acknowledges the importance of materiality while building on, and ideally bridging, e-book and human information behavior research.

## RESEARCH GOAL

Our goal is to develop a theoretical framework of human-rare book interaction that illuminates how individuals interact with rare historic books and the importance of that interaction for individuals and society. The framework will provide a foundation for design requirements for emerging virtual reality technology that allows individuals to more fully experience rare historic books, including how the pages, covers and bindings of rare historic books feel, sound and smell. We envision new virtual reality (VR) rare book systems that provide integrated visual, haptic, auditory, olfactory and cognitive access. The theoretical framework may also provide insights regarding new features for rare historic book exhibits.

## RESEARCH METHOD

To the best of our knowledge there is no prior research that investigates how individuals interact with rare historic books. Thus, our research employs a mixed method empirical approach. The initial study population is young adults, a population group that typically has no contact, or very limited contact, with rare books. How will young adults interact with an actual rare book? Will their interaction with a rare book be meaningful and valued by them, and if so, how?

A focus group study design was selected. This allowed each study participant to individually interact with a rare historic book and reflect on that interaction. The primary rare book used was Rabbi Isaac Ben Judah's (d.1508) *Commentary on the Torah*; the Torah is a sacred Jewish text which consists of the first five books of the Old Testament. This book was published in Venice in 1584. This book, written in Hebrew, is significant because of the unusual way it has been bound.

The text is bound within wooden boards, and these wooden boards have a series of intricate geometric and floral patterns. The heavy boards transform this text into a weighty physical object (2.25 kg/5 lbs.). The markings on the binding are not perfectly symmetrical; the lines and patterns often do not

80th Annual Meeting of the Association for Information Science & Technology, Washington, DC | Oct. 27-Nov. 1, 2017

meet exactly where the artist intended them to meet. The decoration of the book was finished with two brass alloy clasps decorated with a crude vernacular design scraped into the metal.

The focus group participants handled the book multiple times. The first time the book and its latches were closed. The participants were free to interact with the closed book however they preferred, and each had two opportunities to handle the closed book. Next the book was opened. Due to insurance and conservation restrictions, the book was opened by a professional archivist and its spine well supported on pillows. Each participant had two opportunities to touch and turn pages in the book in whatever manner they preferred. After this the book was closed but its latches connecting its front and back covers were open. Each participant had the opportunity to interact with the latches, including opening and closing them. Participants were encouraged to talk aloud, sharing what they were thinking about as they interacted with the book. Their interactions were video-recorded using two digital cameras, capturing the interaction from two perspectives.

After interacting with the rare book the participants were given access to a laptop and asked to blog about their experiences interacting with the rare book. The blogs included three open-ended prompts regarding what the interaction experience meant to them.

Two focus group sessions have been held, each lasting approximately 2.5 hours. Fifteen young adults, ages 18-21, participated in the focus group sessions held in Dublin, Ireland. All were undergraduate students in the social sciences and they had only experienced rare books through movies and TV or digital images. The audio portion of the video recording was transcribed, and the blog data was saved in text files.

The transcribed audio and blog text data was analyzed using open and axial coding. Open coding included multiple, detailed readings of the data to identify major themes emerging from the data. Axial coding involved additional careful readings of the data to identify and verify all text relevant to the codes that emerged during open coding. As axial coding was completed, topic memos that synthesize themes and relationships among codes were created. Further details can be found in Sonnenwald & McEllgiott, 2017.

## RESULTS

Participants interacted with the book in multiple ways, including smelling the book when it was closed and open; tracing the patterns on the book's front and back covers with a finger; rubbing fingers along the book's spine and its different edges; tapping on the book's covers; moving the book up and down as if to better experience its weight; listening to sounds made when single and multiple pages in the book were turned; pressing down on book pages; rubbing fingers or entire palm over pages in the book; listening to the book's clasp when it was opened or closed.

A preliminary human-rare book interaction framework emerged from the analysis of the audio and blog data. As illustrated in Figure 1, participants expressed appreciation of, and curiosity about, the book's design and technology. They also expressed curiosity about individuals who designed and used the book and their practices as well as general social practices connected with the book across time. As one participant reported: "*The opening of the book was my favorite moment...I smelt the mustiness...the smell is exciting and promising...Interacting with a used/old/rare book is more than just being able to read it, it is feeling and touching and smelling the book's history and imagining the journey that the book has taken and that it has taken others on.*"

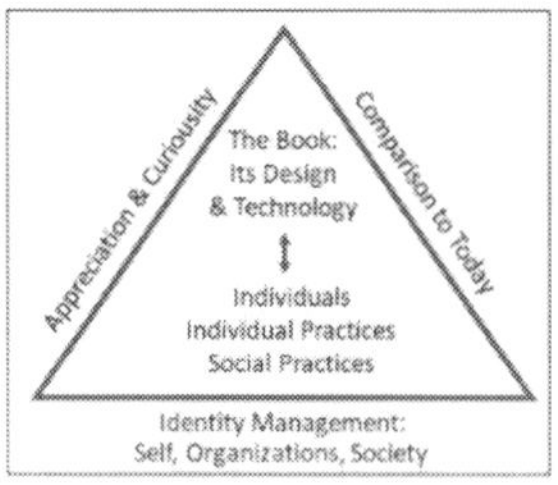

**Figure 1. A preliminary human-rare book interaction framework**

Interaction with the book further engendered comparisons with, and evaluation of, contemporary book design and technology. It also engendered comparative reflections regarding individuals who design and use contemporary books and their practices, as well as social practices around contemporary books.

Reflections focusing on identity management also emerged from interaction with the rare book. Participants reflected on their own identity, e.g., sounds produced while interacting with the book provoked personal memories and reflections. They also reflected on the identity of organizations associated with rare books and society and its values with respect to rare books. For example, several saw interaction as an issue of social equality: "*More than the privileged should be able to [interact with rare books.]*"

Design recommendations for a virtual reality system that would allow individuals to more fully experience rare historic books that emerged from our data analysis include additional types of material to augment book presentations and metadata to facilitate search; requirements for new types of fine-grained haptic feedback and audio; and, olfaction requirements.

## ACKNOWLEDGMENTS

This research received funding from the HW Wilson Foundation and the SIG/USE Elfreda A. Chatman Award. Our thanks to Adam Girard for assistance with data collection, and to the reviewers.

## REFERENCES

Cranny-Francis, A. (2011). Semefulness: A social semiotics of touch, *Social Semiotics, 21*, 463-481.

Failte Ireland. (2015). Nation's top visitor attractions revealed. http://www.failteireland.ie/Utility/News-Library/Nation's-Top-Visitor-Attractions-Revealed.aspx

Galbraith, S. & Smith, G. (2012). *Rare book librarianship*. Oxford: Libraries Unlimited.

Sonnenwald, D.H., & McElligott, J. (2017). Investigating human-rare book interaction among young adults. *ID&A, 32*, 129-146.

Trogu, P. (2015). The image of the book. *DesignIssues, 31*.

# A Transdisciplinary Team Approach to Scoping Reviews: Mapping the Polypharmacy Literature

**Jennifer Staley**
*University Hospitals Rainbow Babies and Children's Hospital, USA. jennifer.staley@uhhospitals.org*

**Jennifer Waldron**
*University Hospitals Rainbow Babies and Children's Hospital, USA. jennifer.waldron@uhhospitals.org*

**Negar Golchin**
*University of Washington, School of Pharmacy, Seattle, WA, USA. ngolchin@uw.edu*

**Alexis Horace**
*University of Louisiana at Monroe School of Pharmacy, USA. horace@ulm.edu*

**Hannah Johnson**
*Case Western Reserve University, USA. hkj9@case.edu*

**Shari Bolen**
*Case Western Reserve University & MetroHealth Medical Center, USA. sdb73@case.edu*

**Neal Dawson**
*Case Western Reserve University & MetroHealth Medical Center, USA. ndawson@metrohealth.org*

**Lawrence Kleinman**
*University Hospitals Rainbow Babies and Children's Hospital, USA. Lawrence.Kleinman@UHhospitals.org*

**Paul M. Bakaki**
*Case Western Reserve University, USA. pmb18@case.edu*

## ABSTRACT

**Pediatric polypharmacy, the practice of administering or taking multiple medications among children, is known to be a source of both benefits and harms. Yet, despite the importance of understanding its effects, research to date has been inconsistent in the way polypharmacy in children is defined and measured. This makes measuring prevalence and outcomes across different patient groups and clinical specialties challenging. This poster will introduce the work of a transdisciplinary scoping review team that is mapping the relevant literature to produce a standardized definition of pediatric polypharmacy. The findings, which will be informed by applied library and information science (LIS), will benefit research and clinical practice in pharmacy, medicine, pediatrics, neurology and other fields.**

## KEYWORDS

scoping reviews, embedded librarianship, transdisciplinary research, polypharmacy, pediatrics

## PROJECT BACKGROUND

Variation in the definition of pediatric polypharmacy lessens the capacity of future research to generate comprehensive knowledge regarding its extent in various patient populations and its outcomes across different clinical settings. To address this problem, we began a transdisciplinary pediatric polypharmacy scoping review (PPSR) project intended to bring together the disparate terms and measures used in the literature into one standardized definition. In planning the project, it was determined that a systematic review, which would emphasize a more focused approach and the grading of evidence quality to provide specific recommendations for practice (Grant & Booth, 2009), would not be optimal. Instead, the project was planned according to scoping review methods, an approach to analyzing a broad topic that includes mapping major research findings, defining key concepts or identifying gaps in available knowledge (Arksey & O'Malley, 2005; Colquhoun et al., 2014).

Due to the applicability of the PPSR study findings to multiple clinical practice areas and methodological requirements for skills in searching and managing literature for which LIS experience is recommended (Rethlefsen, Farrell, Osterhaus Trzasko & Brigham, 2015), the project's lead members sought to recruit a team with broad disciplinary backgrounds and to conduct the research as a transdisciplinary project. To this end, the PPSR team is made up of members from diverse disciplinary backgrounds, including medicine, epidemiology, quantitative sciences, pharmacy, pediatrics, LIS, evidence synthesis, health policy and public health. Stakeholders, a group who serve as advisors (Arksey & O'Malley, 2005), also represent the fields of pediatric neurology, pharmacoepidemiology, psychiatry and nursing.

## A TRANSDISCIPLINARY TEAM PROJECT APPROACH

The term *transdisciplinary* is used with variation, but can be thought of as a holistic approach to collaboration, wherein team members from different disciplines share their own expertise and acquire new skills, with the result reflecting expanded insights not easily assigned to a particular discipline (Choi & Pak, 2006).

To maximize the benefit of such a diverse team in the PPSR project, early efforts were made to understand one another

80th Annual Meeting of the Association for Information Science & Technology, Washington, DC | Oct. 27-Nov. 1, 2017

through the use of a questionnaire. Seminal papers and writing exercises were also distributed to clarify the study agenda. Additionally, frequent meetings, an open and iterative process for developing study inclusion and data extraction criteria, and pairing people together during the screening and data extraction phases allowed team members to actively influence the direction of the project and be involved in each step of the process.

## THE PPSR STUDY

Scoping reviews are defined in part by their comprehensive and replicable search queries involving multiple bibliographic databases. To locate studies for the PPSR review, controlled vocabulary and keyword terms for the concepts of polypharmacy and children were searched in Ovid Medline, PubMed, EMBASE, CINAHL, Ovid PsycINFO, Cochrane CENTRAL, ProQuest Dissertations & Theses A&I, and the Web of Science Core Collection. Search queries were discussed among several team members for appropriateness, and a set of key articles was developed to test the search for comprehensiveness.

A total of 7,905 articles were identified in these searches, with 3,811 unique items after de-duplication. Results were sent to *EPPI-Reviewer 4* (EPPI-Centre, 2010), a web-based software platform that organizes studies and holds extracted data. Studies that defined or assessed polypharmacy in children as an aim, outcome, predictor or covariate were included. Each article was reviewed for inclusion by two team members, with challenging studies resolved by consensus. Data extraction was performed by one team member and reviewed by a second and included a total of 301 articles. A database search update and additional hand search of bibliographies is currently ongoing as of this writing (July 2017).

The results of a pilot study conducted in late-2016 showed the most commonly occurring terms were *polytherapy*, *polypharmacy*, *multiple medications*, *concomitant medication*, and *combination therapy*, defined as either the use of 2 or more, 3 or more, or 5 or more concurrent medications in pediatric patients. Updates to these results will be presented in the final poster.

## DISCUSSION

The transdisciplinary approach has provided several benefits to the project. First, there is an advantage in having available many team members to review the large number of articles that result from scoping searches (Daudt, van Mossel & Scott, 2013). Additionally, a large group permits assigning dual reviewers for study inclusion and data extraction work, which has been helpful given the ambiguity inherent in reviewing articles with varied designs and purposes (Levac, Colquhoun & O'Brien, 2010). Six of the listed authors, in collaboration with four research assistants, were involved in reviewing studies and extracting data. The transdisciplinary approach has also provided a rich source of expertise, which has strengthened the process of study design and understanding the literature. For example, of the group of listed authors, pharmacists have been available to help create drug class categories for data extraction, a pediatrician to advise on study populations, a librarian to design and run the searches, an epidemiologist for questions on study design and statistics, and an evidence synthesis expert to guide the project. Working closely in an open manner has also provided a means for individual growth and development of new skills among group members.

Challenges inherent in this approach include the need to integrate varying viewpoints from people with diverse professional and research backgrounds. Deliberate efforts to encourage communication are recommended. For our team, the use of web-based software, *(EPPI-Reviewer)* that supports collaboration has also been helpful.

## REFERENCES


Arksey, H., & O'Malley, L. (2005). Scoping studies: Towards a methodological framework. *International Journal of Social Research Methodology, 8*(1), 19-32.

Choi, B., & Pak, A. (2006). Multidisciplinarity, interdisciplinarity, and transdisciplinarity in health research, services, education and policy: 1. definitions, objectives, and evidence of effectiveness. *Clinical and Investigative Medicine, 29*(6), 351-364.

Colquhoun, H. L., Levac, D., O'Brien, K. K., Straus, S., Tricco, A. C., Perrier, L., . . . Moher, D. (2014). Scoping reviews: Time for clarity in definition, methods, and reporting. *Journal of Clinical Epidemiology, 67*(12), 1291-1294.

Daudt, H. M. L., van Mossel, C. & Scott, S. J. (2013). Enhancing the scoping study methodology: A large, inter-professional team's experience with Arksey and O'Malley's framework. *BMC Medical Research Methodology, 13*, 48.

EPPI-Centre. (2010). *EPPI-reviewer*. University of London, UCL Institute of Education, Social Science Research, United Kingdom.

Grant, M. J., & Booth, A. (2009). A typology of reviews: An analysis of 14 review types and associated methodologies. *Health Information & Libraries Journal, 26*(2), 91-108.

Levac, D., Colquhoun, H., & O'Brien, K. K. (2010). Scoping studies: Advancing the methodology. *Implementation Science: IS, 5*(1), 69.

Rethlefsen, M. L., Farrell, A. M., Osterhaus Trzasko, L. C., & Brigham, T. J. (2015). Librarian co-authors correlated with higher quality reported search strategies in general internal medicine systematic reviews. *Journal of Clinical Epidemiology, 68*(6), 617-626.

# College Students' Personal Information Management: From a Perspective of Information Horizon Theory


**Sue Yeon Syn**
*The Catholic University of America, USA. syn@cua.edu*

**Sujin Kim**
*University of Kentucky, USA. sujinkim@uky.edu*

**Donghee Sinn**
*University at Albany State University of New York, USA. dsinn@albany.edu*



## ABSTRACT

**This exploratory study examined college students' personal information management behaviors in three contexts from a perspective of information horizon theory. Findings suggest that students show different density and activeness in information behaviors in different context. Academic context was most active for all activities while health was the least.**



## KEYWORDS

personal information management (PIM), information behaviors, college students, information horizon theory


## INTRODUCTION

Personal information management (PIM) refers to the activities individuals perform to collect, organize, search, use and share personal information needed to satisfy individual's daily tasks and roles. Despite the burgeoning use of PIM tools, little is known to understand a holistic spectrum of PIM contexts and activities. Sonnenwald (1999)'s information horizon (IH) theory explains human information behaviors with three elements: context, situation and social networks that can be applied to PIM setting. In this theory, information behaviors happen within a specific situation that requires actions within a context. Information horizon is a space with various information resources, which are cognitively and socially determined by individuals. From this perspective, our study adopted IH theory and applied to PIM settings among college students to observe information behaviors in three distinct situations and contexts.

## BACKGROUND

The information horizon theory suggests that within a context and situation there is "information horizon" where individuals act. The information horizon is viewed as "densely populated solution spaces" (Sonnenwald, 1999) where individuals find information sources based on their experiences and social networks. Previous studies use this theoretical framework to describe information behaviors within a specific context: information behaviors of lower socioeconomic students (Sonnenwald, 2001), archaeologists (Huvila, 2009) with analytic information horizon maps, internet users for self-development (Savolainen & Kari, 2004) and college students in academic contexts (Tsai, 2010; Tsai, 2012; Tsai & Kim, 2013).

In college settings, academic works are closely related to college students' daily life and their success in life (Mizrachi & Bates, 2013). While it is important for life, college students do not seek out assistance with maintaining their personal health records until an illness occurs (Park, 2006). College students, although known as digital natives using various technology for their information needs, show different information behaviors for different purposes, such as preferring paper-based materials when learning (Mizrachi & Bates, 2013).

In terms of PIM activities, college students preserve and manage their records based on their views of importance and potential future use and document type (Krtalić, Marčetić, & Mičunović, 2016). Previous studies identified fundamental PIM activities as organization, finding and keeping (Lush, 2014).

## STUDY DESIGN

An online survey was employed to collect information about college students' typical PIM activities (information behavior) in three distinct contexts: academic, health and personal history. To empirically test IH theory, we provide a specific situation for each context that students usually encounter: (1) writing a term paper, (2) visiting a new doctor in their college town and (3) switching to a new smartphone. We intend to see different types/activeness of information behaviors in each information horizon of context. The information activities the survey addressed are collect (preserve, identify, select, discard), organize (categorize, arrange, label) and use (own, find, share). The information sources asked to cover academic context include course syllabus, textbooks, lecture materials, class notes and instructor's communication; for health context, immunization, family medical history, emergency contact, surgery records, medication and health education materials; and for personal history context, digital photos, video clips, text messages, email messages, reading content, music content and app data.

The survey was distributed in two universities, one private and one state university, between March and May 2017


80[th] Annual Meeting of the Association for Information Science & Technology, Washington, DC | Oct. 27-Nov. 1, 2017

through listservs. Due to the restrictions, the universities have for protecting students from getting too many survey request emails, the survey was distributed by universities' research offices to selected listservs to which students subscribe which resulted in lack of control and management in data collection process. A total of 233 responses were collected and 159 responses of the collected are used for analysis based on its level of completeness. The participants were mostly female (83, 65.35%) and 21.27 years old on average. Their academic status was equally distributed: 32 1st year students (25.00%), 27 2nd year (21.09%), 36 3rd year (28.13%), 30 4th year (23.44%), and three 5th or more years (2.34%). Participants' majors widely varied including philosophy, psychology, theology, journalism, business, chemistry, biology, engineering, etc.

## FINDINGS

One-way ANOVA test showed that there are significant differences among all three contexts (academic, health and personal history) for each activities group: for collection activities, $F(2, 81)=13.710$, $p<0.001$; for organization activities, $F(2, 81)=55.642$, $p<0.001$; and for use activities, $F(2, 81)=58.640$, $p<0.001$. There are also significant differences among information activities (collection, organization and use) for each context: for academic context, $F(2, 81)=4.591$, $p=0.013$; for health context, $F(2, 81)=4.272$, $p=0.017$; and for personal history context, $F(2, 81)=7.141$, $p=0.001$.

| PIM Activities | Academic Situation | Health Situation | Personal History Situation | Total |
|---|---|---|---|---|
| Collection | 3.84 | 3.03 | 3.55 | 3.47 |
| Organization | 3.70 | 2.76 | 3.45 | 3.30 |
| Use | 4.00 | 3.12 | 3.88 | 3.67 |
| Total | 3.85 | 2.97 | 3.63 | |

***Table 1.*** *Mean ratings of PIM activities for three types of personal records*

According to a Turkey post hoc test, participants significantly highly intent to collect information in academic (M=3.84, $p<0.001$) and personal history contexts (M=3.55, $p<0.001$) than health context (M=3.03). This tendency shows similarly for the use activities: higher in academic (M=4.00, $p<0.001$) and personal history contexts (M=3.88, $p<0.001$) than in health context (M=3.12). There are statistically significances in organization activities among three contexts, meaning that there are significant differences in participants' intention to organize academic (M=3.70) and health resources (M=2.76) ($p<0.001$); academic (M=3.70) and personal history resources (M=3.45) ($p=0.022$); and health (M=2.76) and personal history resources (M=3.45) ($p<0.001$).

When comparing each activities group in each context, participants are statistically significantly interested in using academic resources (M=4.00, $p=0.009$) than organizing them (M=3.70), and using health resources (M=3.12, $p=0.17$) than organizing them (M=2.76). For personal history, participants statistically significantly highly intend to use the resources (M=3.88, $p=0.019$ and $p=0.002$ respectively) than to collect (M=3.55) and organize them (M=3.45). See Table 1 for details.

## DISCUSSION AND CONCLUSION

Our finding suggests that college students' PIM activities tend to be most active in the academic situation, followed by the personal history and the health situations. In terms of specific activities, they are mostly active with using resources, followed by collecting and organizing activities.

Most interestingly, participants are least engaged in all types of PIM activities for the health situation. This may be relevant with previous findings reporting college students and young adults are not active in searching and collecting health-related information (Vader, 2011) while they were most actively engaged in information activities for the academic situation. It may be closely related to college students' daily activities and goals (Mizrachi & Bates, 2013).

As in IH theory, our findings demonstrate that the density of information sources and the activeness of users' information behaviors may depend on contexts and situations. This study provided a situation in the contexts of academic, health and personal history which resulted to have significant differences in PIM activities. Some situation and context induce more active information behaviors than others. This can mean additional elements should be considered, such as urgency, interests, proximity and accessibility of information needs to explain PIM practices in IH framework.

The survey participants are keen to use information resources in all three contexts than other activities. As previous information behavior studies suggest, collecting and organizing information are directly related to the effectiveness of information use. Therefore, information professionals could help college students to be aware of the importance of information organization and to better manage their personal records for effective use.

## ACKNOWLEDGMENTS

This study was sponsored by University of Kentucky faculty research fund.

## REFERENCES

Huvila, I. (2009). Analytical information horizon maps. *Library and Information Science Research, 31*(1), 18-28.

Krtalić, M., Marčetić, H., & Mičunović, M. (2016). Personal digital information archiving among students of social sciences and humanities. *Information Research, 21*(2), paper 716.

Lush, A. (2014). Fundamental personal information management activities – Organisation, finding, and keeping: A literature review. *The Australian Library Journal, 63*(1), 45-51.

Mizrach, D. & Bates, M. (2013). Undergraduates' personal academic information management and the consideration of time and task-urgency. *Journal of the American Society for Information Science and Technology, 64*(8), 1590-1607.

Park, M.J., Paul Mulye, T., Adams, S.H., Brindis, C.D., Irwin, C.E. Jr. (2006). The health status of young adults in the United States. *Journal of Adolescent Health*. 39(3), 305-17.

Sonnenwald, D. H. (1999). Evolving perspectives of human information behaviour: Contexts, situations, social networks and information horizons. In T. Wilson, & D. Allen (Eds.), *Exploring the contexts of information behaviour* (pp. 176-190). Cambridge, UK: Taylor and Graham.

Sonnenwald, D. H., Wildemuth, B. S., & Harmon, G. L. (2001). A research method to investigate information seeking using the concept of information horizons: An example from a study of lower socio-economic students' information seeking behavior. *The New Review of Information Behavior Research, 2*, 65-86.

Savolainen, R., & Kari, J. (2004). Placing the internet in information source horizons. A study of information seeking by internet users in the context of self-development. *Library & Information Science Research, 26*(4), 415-433.

Vader, A.M., Walters, S.T., Roudsari, B., Nguyen, N. (2011). Where do college students get health information? Believability and use of health information sources. *Health Promotion Practice*, 12(5), 713-22.

# "In my humble opinion…": Serious YouTubers' Self-Presentations, Roles, and Authority

**Leslie Thomson**
*University of North Carolina at Chapel Hill, USA. lethomso@ad.unc.edu*

## ABSTRACT

**This visual presentation outlines preliminary findings from a research study that focuses on the information creating activities and the informal information provider role occupied by serious YouTubers. These individuals regularly upload video content to a personal channel on the website YouTube, of which they produce most, if not all, themselves. As many serious YouTubers have gained substantial online followings, questions about the place of this increasingly influential demographic in the broader world can be raised. Through an examination of the self-presentation discourse used in the monographs of four serious beauty and lifestyle YouTubers, some implications and future research avenues are given. This visual presentation will take the form of a poster and accompanying set of public YouTube videos that will be played from a laptop, with captions, on loop.**

## KEYWORDS

everyday life information practices, human information behaviour, information providing, information sharing, YouTube

## INTRODUCTION

This visual presentation outlines preliminary findings from a research study that focuses on the information creating activities and the informal information provider role occupied by serious YouTubers – specifically, serious beauty and lifestyle YouTubers. Here, "serious YouTubers" are defined as individuals who regularly upload video content to personal channels on the hosting website YouTube, most or all of which they self-produce; who relay information, advice and entertainment around a handful of focal topics to which they have special draw; and who address public audiences of viewers that they directly rally and attempt to cultivate as sub-communities. Thus, serious YouTubers are distinguished from their casual counterparts who but dabble in video-making, whose uploads may be clipped or copied, and who make little, if any, effort to maintain an audience. Because serious YouTubers must invest time, skills and resources in order to generate videos on a consistent basis, most monetize their channels, earning partial or full incomes from on-site advertisements and sponsorships.

80th Annual Meeting of the Association for Information Science & Technology, Washington, DC | Oct. 27-Nov. 1, 2017



YouTubers' videos run the gamut of imaginable topics, sitting under such broad categories as Science & Education, Music, Comedy and How-To & DIY. Beauty and lifestyle videos in particular deal with cosmetics, hair, fashion, fitness, food and day-to-day living, among other topics, and take the form of, for example, tutorials, hauls or routines. Beauty and lifestyle content on YouTube may be hastily cast off as too frivolous for information and library science (or ILS) researchers to consider, yet viewership in this area is astounding: as of April 2015, more than 1.8 million YouTuber-produced videos about beauty alone existed and had been watched over 45.3 billion times (Pixability, 2015). Furthermore, for 13-18 year olds, YouTubers in general are named as the most influential celebrities (Ault, 2014), while those in the beauty and lifestyle area are perceived as more authentic and reliable than the specialists working in retail stores (MacDonald et al., 2016; Pixability, 2014).

Beauty and lifestyle content has a long history behind it, but its commercialization truly took off during the latter half of the 20th-century with the emergence of several celebrity experts ready to guide people's images – Nigella Lawson, Martha Stewart and Steven Sabados being some examples (Bell & Hollows, 2006; Lewis, 2010). However (initially at least), beauty and lifestyle YouTubers were explicitly *not* celebrities or experts; they made videos as ordinary citizens with hobby interests, taking advantage of the technologies available to them. Most claim to have been without any expectation of success and certainly to not have foreseen a potential career path in what they were doing, referring to it as "almost by accident" (Burr, 2015, p. 269), "part of this parallel universe" (Phan, 2014, p. 15) and "not the job I ever imagined having" (p. viii). The most popular have even taken up side ventures that range from cosmetics lines to spokesperson roles, yet as Bolin (2014) points out, all seem to still be "'beauty junkies,' […] genuinely interested, […] often with an abashed caveat that they are not trained professionals."

Somewhat paradoxically, serious beauty and lifestyle YouTubers' non-expert positions vest them with authority, and it is this authority upon which they depend for continued views, brand partnerships and wages in their newly carved-out field. On the one hand, they are simply "native speakers of the language of teen girls" (Jeffries, 2011, p. 64) with "relatable, down-to-earth […] personalities and intimate one-to-one styles" (Pixability, 2014, p. 16). Absent an occupation, education or reputation that would lead to attributions of (cognitive) authority in conventional spheres, they are instead cultural authorities who use "'I'm one of you' modes of address" (Lewis, 2010, p. 585) and charismatic authorities who

| Identity | Illustrative Excerpt(s) |
|---|---|
| non-expert | *"I had zero qualifications when it came to the beauty and fashion world,* but I made that my angle. *I made it clear from the start that I had absolutely no idea what I was doing"* (Lalonde, 2016, p. 92). |
| friend | "I had grown quite a big audience by this point and I think *they felt like they were really getting to know me, almost like you get to know a friend*" (Burr, 2015, p. 269). |
| sister | "I'm going to write this chapter *as if I am talking to a little sister*" (Pentland, 2015, p. 205) "My [creative] process was simple. *If I had a big sister, what would I want from her?*" (Phan, 2014, p. 15). |
| teacher | *"I take my position as a teacher seriously"* (Phan, 2014, p. 224). |
| tastemaker | *"People are interested in your opinions and love to ask questions"* (Burr, 2015, p. 274). |
| persona | "I *don't give every little Louise-y thing out* on [social media]" (Pentland, 2015, p. 162). "I really lay it out there for everyone to see, [...but] that's *a different kind of vulnerability,* [...] *more polished*" (Lalonde, 2016, p. 32). |
| expert | *"Be an expert. [...] My fans see me as their go-to girl* for tips, tricks, and trends" (Burr, 2015, p. 273). |
| business | "People consider me a beauty expert, but *first and foremost, I consider myself a businessperson*" (Phan, 2014, p. 188). |
| brand | "Upload content that you think other people will want to share, because *you need [that] for your brand to grow*" (Burr, 2015, p. 272). |
| celebrity | "Sometimes *when people who watch my videos meet me, they fluster* and panic, and *I always remind them that we're standing on the same level and are exactly the same..* [...] *Celebrities* want what you want" (Pentland, 2015, p. 51). |

***Table 1**. Survey of identities*

have trusted personalities (Wilson, 1983). On the other hand, serious beauty and lifestyle YouTubers must simultaneously present themselves as "knowing what they are talking about" (Wilson, 1983), as having an innate "selection know-how," in order to be listened to at all (Jeffries, 2011, p. 64). Emulating the speaking styles of traditional experts, they nonetheless retain markers of ordinariness (Tolson, 2010); casual sets and amateur production quality, for example, are common.

A discursive approach (Talja & McKenzie, 2007) is taken in order to begin addressing the questions of how serious beauty and lifestyle YouTubers present themselves in one form of media (monographs) and with what implications.

## METHODS

A discursive approach, broadly conceived, is concerned with language-in-use or the ways in which language is used to accomplish real-world actions (Talja & McKenzie, 2007, p. 98). Especially pertinent here, one effect of language is "producing both the objects of which [it] speaks and the speaking subjects" themselves, aligning them with certain identities (Talja, 1999, p. 470). Multiplicity and contradictions within self-identifications (explicit or implicit) are expected, but by examining such inconsistencies, individuals' orienting concerns and assumptions are understood.

To address the questions of how serious beauty and lifestyle YouTubers present themselves and with what implications, four monographs written by serious beauty and lifestyle YouTubers were selected for constant comparative analysis (marked with * in the references). These were chosen from a comprehensive list of English-language serious beauty and lifestyle YouTuber-authored books, of which there exist seven as of June 2017. Constant comparative analysis involves the iterative generation of codes, categories and constructs that explain lived phenomena (Charmaz, 2014) and is used in grounded theory studies. The preliminary findings here are part of a larger grounded theory project; they are tentative and do not yet claim saturation or attempt a theoretical model, but instead survey the range of identities that serious beauty and lifestyle YouTubers present in their monographs, raising some implications of these.

Each of the four monographs selected details a personal journey of one's childhood passions becoming a job and includes chapters about such topics as beauty, fashion, hair, food and travel.

## PRELIMINARY FINDINGS

A range of media are enlisted in serious beauty and lifestyle YouTubers' self-presentations, books just one tool of many. Below, Table 1 lists some of the positions from which serious beauty and lifestyle YouTubers speak in their monographs.

However, the monographs analyzed here suggest that, while they claim a host of positions at different times – from close friends and relatives to savvy opinion leaders, natural-born businesspeople and brands – serious beauty and lifestyle YouTubers rarely do so straightforwardly; statements tend to be tempered, not absolute. For example, Tanya Burr (2015) mentions that, "While I'm passionate about clothes, *I don't consider myself a fashion expert*, but [...] I feel like *I'm learning more and more and hope to share some of [that]*" (p. 125). Similarly, Louise Pentland (2015) writes of skincare that, "*I'm no expert, but after spending five years writing a beauty blog, I've started collecting a good few tidbits*" (p. 15). Despite adopting non-expert fronts, these YouTubers still make clear that they have information to give. Table 1 quotations from Burr (2015), who speaks of having a large audience but nonetheless seeming a close friend, and Pentland (2015), who notes being her followers' equal but a celebrity as well, further underscore the complexity of the roles that serious beauty and lifestyle YouTubers assume.

Estée Lalonde (2016) raises this issue in her book, writing, "I've really struggled with the idea that I could be a strong woman and also make a living from talking about make-up all day. [... As] my audience became more invested in what was going on, I realized that I have to be accountable for the messages I'm sending and how I want to be portrayed. [...] I wanted my work to reflect that I was more than just a materialistic human (as much as I love lipstick)" (p. 100). She mentions feeling "like a fraud" (p. 92), while Michelle Phan (2014) discusses the "identity crisis" (p. 21) that early days of her as-yet-unknown career in a just-forming field spurred.

## CONCLUSION

YouTubers – not brands – are the most visible demographic in YouTube's beauty and lifestyle content area, responsible for over 95.4 percent of its channels (Pixability, 2015, p. 12)[1]. Their visibility and the attention they garner make them worthy of study ipso facto, but also raise questions about their place within people's everyday information source repertoires.

By "sharing my experiences" (Pentland, 2015, p. 8) and "talking about things that I personally loved" (Lalonde, 2016, p. 92), serious beauty and lifestyle YouTubers become "a true 'sister' to millions" at the same time as they become "a global brand" (both quotations appear in inside-cover reviews of Phan's monograph, p. v). Marketers refer to "informational reference group influence," an internalization of another's opinions that is especially likely to occur when subject knowledge and lack of personal motive are perceived (de Valck et al., 2009). The extent to which serious beauty and lifestyle YouTubers serve as informational references for viewers, wittingly or not, may be an avenue for future consideration.

Further, prototypical beauty and lifestyle YouTubers are white, under age 25 and middle- to upper-middle class with expendable incomes (Jeffries, 2011; Mau, 2014) and the time and skills to produce original content that results in views. Future research may critically consider the diversity within the messages they present or within the identities that they showcase as possible for their audiences.

On top of this, AnneMaree Lloyd (2007) points out that ways of speaking facilitate entry into communities of practice, which in turn "shape the development of [one's] professional identity" (p. 197). In their nascent field, serious YouTubers' words have enormous power to simultaneously shape their practice. Discursive analysis of their work, especially when it is well-known and setting standards of typicality, can surface unstated, limiting ideas and encourage reflexivity. Analysis of monographs is a first step; comparing data from YouTube videos would be an obvious next step for this project.

## REFERENCES


Ault, S. (2014, August 5). Survey: YouTube stars more popular than mainstream celebs among U.S. teens. *Variety*. Retrieved from http://variety.com/2014/digital/ news/survey-youtube-stars-more-popular-than- mainstream-celebs-among-u-s-teens-1201275245/.

Bell, D., & Hollows, J. (Eds.). (2006). Historicizing lifestyle: Mediating taste, consumption and identity from the 1900s to 1970s. Brookfield, VT: Ashgate Publishing.

Bolin, A. (2014). My imaginary friends: The beauty YouTuber economy. *Hairpin*. Retrieved from http://thehairpin.com/2014/06/my-imaginary-friends-the-beauty-youtuber-economy.

*Burr, T. (2015). *Love, Tanya*. London, UK: Penguin Books.

Charmaz, K. (2014). *Constructing grounded theory* (2nd ed.). London, UK: SAGE Publications.

de Valck, K., van Bruggen, G. H. & Wierenga, B. (1999). Virtual communities: A marketing perspective. *Decision Support Systems, 47*, 185-203.

Jeffries, L. (2011). The revolution will be soooo cute: YouTube "hauls" and the voice of young female consumers. *Studies in Popular Culture, 33*(2), 59-75.

*Lalonde, E. (2016). *Bloom*. Toronto, ON: Penguin Books.

Lewis, T. (2010). Branding, celebritization and the lifestyle expert. *Cultural Studies*, *24*(4), 580-598.

Lloyd, A (2007). Learning to put out the red stuff: Becoming information literate through discursive practice. *Library Quarterly, 77*(2), 181-198.

MacDonald, L. I., Medina, I. G., & González Romo, Z. F. (2016). A study of the impact of social networking communities on the consumption of beauty luxury products. In F. Mosca, & R. Gallo (Eds.), *Global marketing strategies for the promotion of luxury goods* (pp. 193-218). Hershey, PA: IGI Global.

Mau, D. (2014). How the fastest-rising beauty vloggers found YouTube success. *Fashionista*. http://fashionista.com/2014/01/beauty-vloggers.

*Pentland, L. (2015). *Life with a sprinkle of glitter*. London, UK: Simon & Schuster.

*Phan, M. (2014). Make up: Your life guide to beauty, style, and success—online and off. New York: Random House.

Pixability. (2014). Beauty on YouTube. Report by Pixability, Inc. Retrieved from http://www.pixability.com/industry-studies/page/2/.

Pixability. (2015). Beauty on YouTube. Report by Pixability, Inc. Retrieved from http://www.pixability.com/industry-studies/.

Talja, S. (1999). Analyzing qualitative interview data: The discourse analytic method. *Library & Information Science Research, 21*(4), 459-477.

Talja, S., & McKenzie, P. J. (2007). Editors' introduction: Special issue on discursive approaches to information seeking in context. *The Library Quarterly, 77*(2), 97-108.

Tolson, A. (2010). A new authenticity? Communicative practices on YouTube. *Critical Discourse Studies*, *7*(4), 277-289.

Wilson, P. (1983). Second-hand knowledge: An inquiry into cognitive authority. Westport, CT: Greenwood Press.


[1] This percentage includes "verified" individually run channels that YouTube has officially certified as belonging to a creator only. The actual number is likely much higher.

# The Data Sharing Practices and Challenges in Uganda

**Isaac Tomusange**
*Muteesa Royal University, Uganda. itomusange@mru.ac.ug*

**Norman Mukasa**
*Muteesa Royal University, Uganda. mukasan@mru.ac.ug*

**Ayoung Yoon**
*Indiana University Indianapolis (IUPUI), USA. ayyoon@iupui.edu*

## ABSTRACT

**With the rapid development and increased use of information and communication technology (ICT), the demand for data sharing and reuse is growing even in developing countries. This study aims to contribute to the recently emerging discussions on data sharing in developing countries with a focus on the case of Uganda. The goal of this study is to uncover the current practices of and efforts for data sharing in the public sector in Uganda and to understand the relevant stakeholders' perceptions of data sharing and reuse practices/services.**

## KEYWORDS

data sharing, developing countries

## INTRODUCTION

With the rapid development and increased use of information and communication technology (ICT), the demand for data sharing and reuse is growing even in developing countries. In the context of developing countries, data sharing offers numerous benefits, as the costs and challenges of data reuse and sharing seem to outweigh those of the initial collection of data. Many have argued that there is a need for data sharing for sustainable development (Rajabifard et al., 2006). Moreover, considering the potential of using data in policy design, disaster planning and economic development, government leaders in many developing countries have acknowledged that open data can increase cooperation among government agencies, improve citizen engagement, stimulate innovation, create jobs and attract foreign investment. However, data sharing also presents considerable challenges in developing countries where resources are often scarce, sustainability is questionable and capacities need to be developed (Harrison, 2014). For these reasons, researchers are concerned about how developing countries can secure the full benefits of open data by overcoming the barriers that block the greater impact of data sharing (Davies & Perini, 2016).

This study aims to contribute to the recently emerging discussions on data sharing in developing countries with a focus on the case of Uganda. The goal of this study is to uncover the current practices of and efforts for data sharing in the public sector in Uganda and to understand the relevant stakeholders' perceptions of data sharing and reuse practices/services. While the issue of data sharing in developing countries has gained recent attention, few research studies have examined data sharing and reuse practices in the context of Uganda despite the recent growth of digital data. This study will provide insights for understanding the data practices and challenges of developing countries by addressing the interesting and dynamic case of Uganda. The poster will present this study's preliminary findings from 20 interviews with four public institutions that have a major impact on data sharing and reuse in Uganda.

## DATA SHARING IN UGANDA CONTEXT

In Uganda, the development of ICT and the internet has provided an access platform for data sharing and reuse among interested stakeholders (e.g., scholarly researchers, business executives, political leaders, developers and security agencies). While policies for data sharing and reuse have not yet been fully defined, Uganda reformed its ICT policy in 1996 to enable government deregulation of the country's telecommunication sector, which led to the development of a platform for effective information sharing and reuse (Ssewanyana & Busler, 2007). Government agencies have tried to create data platforms for intra- and inter-exchanges so that data can be available for public consumption. For instance, in 2014, the Ministry of Internal Affairs mandated compulsory registration for all Ugandans over the age of 16; this created the first nationwide web of information on the country's citizens (Waiswa & Okello-Obura, 2014). Additionally, semi-autonomous bodies of government, such as the Uganda Revenue Authority and the Kampala City Council authority, provide a significant amount of data for others' use (Mitchinson, 2003).

However, the data sharing and reuse culture in Uganda has not been fully developed due to numerous barriers that inhibit these practices. For instance, the National Development Plan noted that the key binding constraints inhibiting the performance of the national statistics sector were limited use and appreciation of statistics for policy design and formulation (Katusiimeh & Kangave, 2015). Similarly, the village health team's situational analysis revealed that only 9% of the health-related data from communities was used for health planning (UNICEF, 2009). Sanyu (2014) also reported that local governments have at least 70% of the data they need for planning purposes, but that information was lying idle.

80th Annual Meeting of the Association for Information Science & Technology, Washington, DC | Oct. 27-Nov. 1, 2017

In order to better support data sharing and reuse by overcoming these barriers, this study aims to uncover the current practices of and efforts for data sharing in the public sector in Uganda and to investigate the relevant stakeholders' perspectives on the challenges and barriers to creating an open data culture. The project team is currently conducting an interview study with the following four institutions that have a major impact on data sharing and reuse:

Uganda Bureau of Statistics (UBoS) makes official statistics available free of charge to anyone who can reuse the data.

Uganda Communications Commission (UCC) under the Ministry of ICT and National Guidance is the government regulatory body that is in charge of protecting the interests and rights of consumers in the communication sector using an effective regulatory and licensing regime.

The Ministry of Internal Affairs handles the vast majority of personal information about Ugandan citizens due to its massive national identity registration and passport registration project.

Kampala Capital City Authority (KCCA) represents Ugandan capital's local government body and handles crosscutting functions, such as revenue collection, waste management, security, public space management, transport and advertising among others.

The study participants include data mangers in each of these four organizations and professionals whose work is relevant to sharing and reusing data (e.g., administrators and mangers in charge of operations, client security and privacy or public relations). A total of 20 interviews will be conducted (five per each organization) by September 2017. All the interviews will be audio recorded, and the data will be fully transcribed and analyzed using NVivo, qualitative data analysis software. The data will be analyzed following pre-developed high-level codes from the interview questions. However, the project team will inductively analyze the data to identify any emerging themes under the pre-developed codes.

The findings from the interviews will provide the project team with information about the lifecycle of data in each organization, the management practices used to support data sharing and reuse and the participants' perspectives on the factors that either facilitate or inhibit data sharing and reuse. The preliminary findings from the interviews will be presented in this poster.

## REFERENCES


Davies, T., & Perini, F. (2016). Researching the emerging impacts of open data: Revisiting the ODDC conceptual framework. *The Journal of Community Informatics*, *12*(2).

Harrison, T. M. (2014, June). Open data and information sharing in developing nations. In *Proceedings of the 15th Annual International Conference on Digital Government Research* (pp. 311-313). ACM.

Katusiimeh, M. W., & Kangave, J. (2015). Politics and organizational capacities of selected key fiscal and social institutions in Uganda (No. 2015-12). UNRISD Working Paper.

Mitchinson, R. (2003). Devolution in Uganda: An experiment in local service delivery. *Public Administration and Development*, 23(3), 241-248.

Sanyu, P. (2014, June 30). Promote the use of data to fight poverty. Newvision.

Ssewanyana, J., & Busler, M. (2007). Adoption and usage of ICT in developing countries: Case of Ugandan firms. *International Journal of Education and Development using ICT*, 3(3).

Rajabifard, A., Binns, A., Masser, I., & Williamson, I. (2006). The role of sub-national government and the private sector in future spatial data infrastructures. *International Journal of Geographical Information Science*, *20*(7), 727-741.

United Nations International Children's Emergency Fund (UNICEF) (2009). Situational analysis on VHTs in Uganda.

Waiswa, R., & Okello-Obura, C. (2014). To what extent have ICTs contributed to e-Governance in Uganda? *Library Philosophy and Practice*, 0_1

# Data Ecosystem in Self-Tracking Health and Wellness Apps


**Ciaran B. Trace**
*School of Information, The University of Texas at Austin, USA. cbtrace@austin.utexas.edu*

**Daiki Yonemaru**
*School of Information, The University of Texas at Austin, USA. daikiyonemaru@utexas.edu*

**Katherine Cruz**
*School of Information, The University of Texas at Austin, USA. katherinecruz@utexas.edu*

**Yan Zhang**
*School of Information, The University of Texas at Austin, USA. yanz@ischool.utexas.edu*



## ABSTRACT

**To understand information behavior associated with self-tracking and to facilitate exploration of various issues associated with quantified-self data, such as data quality and data sharing, to name a few, we logged the data in self-tracking health and wellness apps. Specifically, we selected 10 of the most popular health and wellness self-tracking apps for both iOS and Android platforms, used these apps for a period of time, and logged data input into, generated by and exported out of the apps. The data were then grouped into categories and mapped to form a data ecosystem that can be queried to reveal latent research opportunities.**



## KEYWORDS

quantified-self, personal informatics, self-tracking, data


## INTRODUCTION

Quantified self is an activity in which individuals engage in tracking any kind of biological, physical, psychological, behavioral or environmental information (Swan, 2013). The Pew Research Center reported that 69% of U.S. adults track at least one health indicator such as their weight, diet, exercise routine or symptom. Among them, 21% use some form of technology to track (Fox & Duggan, 2013), including wearable devices and self-tracking apps.

Current research chiefly focuses on users' motivations for adopting self-tracking technologies (mostly for activity tracking and food journaling), behaviors of using these technologies (e.g., usage patterns and lapses), barriers encountered and efforts to enhance the design of such technologies (e.g., data input and data visualization) (Choe, Lee, Lee, Pratt & Kientz, 2014; Li, Dey & Forlizzi, 2010; Rapp & Cena, 2016; Rooksby, Rost, Morrison & Chalmers, 2014). A common facet of studies of self-tracking activities is that they are mostly based on users' self-reported use of self-tracking technologies (using survey, interview or diary methods). They provide rich descriptions of this human information behavior and reveal many research opportunities, but at the same time, the fact that these studies are founded on existing use behaviors may constrain our purview of potential research opportunities. To broaden our view, this work-in-progress views self-tracking activities from the lens of data. By tracking data that forms the inputs and outputs for self-tracking technologies, we map out a data ecosystem to reveal potential research opportunities. We present two cases to illustrate the function of this data ecosystem.


80th Annual Meeting of the Association for Information Science & Technology, Washington, DC | Oct. 27-Nov. 1, 2017




## METHODS

We chose to focus on health and fitness apps because they are the most widely adopted self-tracking technologies.

### *App Selection*

Based on data from the Apple iTunes and the Android app stores, the most popular apps in the health and fitness category were identified. The number of reviews and app rankings determined app popularity. Four major sub-categories emerged: diet and weight loss, physical activities, women's health and sleep. To get a comprehensive and a balanced view of data in these apps, we selected two to three apps from each subcategory for review (see Table 1).

| Subject category | Apps |
|---|---|
| Diet and weight loss | MyFitnessPal, Weight Watchers, Lose It! |
| Physical activities | MapMyRun, Runkeeper, and Nike+ Run Club |
| Women's health | Period Tracker, Period tracker – my calendar |
| Sleep | Sleep Cycle alarm clock, sleep Bot |

***Table 1.** Selected apps for review*

### *App Review*

Apps were reviewed from a comparative perspective and with the aim of describing the dynamic ecosystem surrounding the inputs and outputs from the apps. Four reviewers each reviewed all apps in one subject category. For apps that offered free and paid versions, free versions were examined, but data points in paid versions were recorded when previews were available. Coding lasted from March 4th to May 5th, 2017. At weekly meetings, reviewers compared and contrasted their codes, consolidated similarities and resolved discrepancies to create a cohesive coding schema. As an outcome of the analysis the data was grouped into categories and mapped to form a data ecosystem (see Table 2).

| Facets | Sub-categories |
|---|---|
| Primary Data - Enrollment & Profile Data | Name, address, password, payment information, age, gender, bio, photo, guarantee of user suitability, activity and health information, goals and objectives, time to goal |
| Primary Data - Passive Data Captured | Mobile device data, transactional data, location data, social media data, personal data, contacts data, files/media/photos on device storage |
| Primary Data - Active Data Tracked | Food, water consumption, meals, recipes, activity/steps, exercise, weight, intimacy, period, sleep, freeform data, goals and objectives |
| Primary Data - Active Data Tracked - Source | Manual input (words, numbers, import of images from smartphone storage)<br>Automatically generated (barcode scan, image recognition, online search/database lookup, geo locator, smartphone sensors)<br>Manual followed by automatic (lookup of previously stored information) |
| Secondary Data - Output to User – Reminders & Automatic Feedback | Daily/weekly goal, performance over time, automatic reminders, automatic/targeted feedback |
| Secondary Data – Output to User - Visualization | From select primary data<br>Format (e.g. line chart, bar graph)<br>Frequency (e.g. daily, weekly)<br>Delivery mechanism - in app; associated online portal; data reporting app partners/app aggregators |
| Data Sharing | Select primary and secondary data<br>Engagement - self/user; social network (social media friends, email contacts); online community (app members) |
| Data Community | Within app/app adjacent (online blog, online social platform, app social media, app groups, app challenges, app newsfeed/wall, app push notifications from friends)<br>External to app (call from personal coach, 24/7 chat advice, meeting finder) |
| Data Exchange/Synchronization | Import (from external applications)<br>Export (to external applications) |

***Table 2.*** *Ecosystem of data in QS health and wellness apps*

## DISCUSSION

While not exhaustive, the ecosystem provides a paramount view of data (inputs and outputs) included in quantified-self health and wellness apps. The ecosystem includes primary data, which consists of data input by the user at the time of enrollment, data that is continuously and passively captured by the system, and data that is actively tracked and collected by the user through manual and/or automatic means. Secondary data is output to the user in the form of reminders and automatic feedback and in the form of visualizations suitable for analysis. Certain data can also be shared through the ecosystem as it moves in and out of the app, various generic social networks and online and offline app communities.

Such a data-centric view facilitates the identification of research opportunities. Here we provide two cases. The first case is *data quality*. As outlined, the data ecosystem posits that when studying data quality researchers need to consider not only data input into the system by the user and by user-system collaborations, but also data automatically generated by the system. This rich view of data invites investigations beyond simply data accuracy (as inputted and captured by both humans and technologies) to the ways in which information is presented in the system (e.g., how accurate the visualizations are in representing people's state of health) and the ways in which the system's motivations and philosophies, reflected in both algorithms and interface design choices, impact the data presented to the user (e.g., what weight goals are considered as healthy goals).

The second case is that of *data sharing*. As outlined, the data ecosystem posits that when studying data sharing researchers need to factor in the technological constraints apps place on the type and format of the data that can be shared; the interest and ability of users to have a say and to understand the type and format of the data that can be shared; and the manner and conditions in which data moves from the user's control to a population internal or external to the app. The data ecosystem also highlights the network of physical and online social networks and communities that exist within, alongside and external to the app and which can make the activity of self-tracking a social one. This rich view of data invites investigations into how technical and social platforms, and associated human norms and customs around data, support or constrain sharing within the quantified-self community.

## ACKNOWLEDGMENTS

This research was funded by a University of Texas at Austin, School of Information, Governor Bill Daniel Fellowship.

## REFERENCES

Choe, E. K., Lee, N. B., Lee, B., Pratt, W. & Kientz, J. A. (2014). Understanding quantified-selfers' practices in collecting and exploring personal data. In *Proceedings of the 32nd annual ACM conference on human factors in computing systems* (pp. 1143-1152). New York, NY, USA: ACM. https://doi.org/10.1145/2556288.2557372

Fox, S., & Duggan, M. (2013, January 28). Tracking for health. Retrieved April 14, 2016, from http://www.pewinternet.org/2013/01/28/tracking-for-health/

Li, I., Dey, A., & Forlizzi, J. (2010). A Stage-based model of personal informatics systems. In *Proceedings of the SIGCHI conference on human factors in computing systems* (pp. 557-566). New York, NY, USA: ACM. https://doi.org/10.1145/1753326.1753409

Rapp, A., & Cena, F. (2016). Personal informatics for everyday life: How users without prior self-tracking experience engage with personal data. *International Journal of Human-Computer Studies*, *94*, 1-17. https://doi.org/10.1016/j.ijhcs.2016.05.006

Rooksby, J., Rost, M., Morrison, A. & Chalmers, M. C. (2014). Personal tracking as lived informatics. In *Proceedings of the 32nd annual ACM conference on human factors in computing systems* (pp. 1163-1172). New York, NY, USA: ACM. https://doi.org/10.1145/2556288.2557039

Swan, M. (2013). The quantified self: Fundamental disruption in big data science and biological discovery. *Big Data*, *1*(2), 85-99. https://doi.org/10.1089/big.2012.0002

# The State-of-the-Art of Open Peer Review: Early Adopters

**Peiling Wang**
*University of Tennessee, USA. peilingw@utk.edu*

**Iman Tahamtan**
*University of Tennessee, USA. Tahamtan@vols.utk.edu*

## ABSTRACT

**This study examined 155 open peer review (OPR) journals. Open peer review is an emerging phenomenon that can be characterized by two factors: transparency and openness. Transparency requires that the referee and the author are known to each other during the process; openness requires that referees' review reports are publicly accessible in the same way as the articles. The current practices of OPR by the open access (OA) journals vary in levels of transparency and openness. The purpose of the study is to understand the state-of-the-art of OPR in publishing scientific research. The preliminary results show that the majority of the OPR journals are in the field of medicine and related. Identity of authors and reviewers may be revealed at different stages of the peer review process. As early as the time when a manuscript is submitted, the author can choose to have the manuscript under blind review or open review. For open review submissions, the reviewer must sign the report but can decline to review it. The review history, including comments, all versions of the manuscript, plus author's rebuttals, may be published alongside of the paper. The peer review process may be totally transparent and open without an editor in charge.**

## KEYWORDS

open peer review, scientific publishing, peer review, post-publication peer review, open access

## INTRODUCTION

A 2016 survey of what scientists wished to change about how science worked received 270 responses. Of the seven biggest problems in current science practice, the top four were 1) academia has a huge money problem; 2) too many studies are poorly designed; 3) replicating results is crucial and rare; and 4) peer review is broken (Belluz, Plumer, & Resnick, 2016).

A growing interest exists among scientific communities to accelerate and improve the processes of peer review. Peer review should and can be more open and transparent (Soergel, Adam, & Andrew, 2013). To innovate blind peer review models, the notion of open peer review (OPR) is evolving. Ford (2013) examined the characteristics of the OPR journals; she discussed the benefits and challenges of OPR.

One of the earliest OPR models developed by the *Atmospheric Chemistry and Physics*, opens for comments from the scientific community after the submission of the manuscript for a given period; the peer reviews are completed by the editor selected referees (Pöschl, 2012).

The most transparent peer review model opens the entire review process, during which both reviewers and authors are known to each other, and the identity attached review reports are immediately published alongside the paper as well as the authors' responses. A paper needs to pass a quality threshold for being indexed (Wang, Rath, Deike & Wu, 2016).

Another model that was not currently classified by DOAJ as OPR preserves the traditional single-blind peer review process, but the reviewers are encouraged to sign their reports and the authors are encouraged to publish the review history alongside the article if it is accepted for publishing (Wang, You, Rath & Wolfram, 2016).

## METHOD

Searches of the Directory of Open Access Journals (DOAJ at doaj.org DOAJ) were conducted on June 15, 2017. Using the filter "open peer review," 111 OPR journals were identified. Additional 58 OPR journals were further identified by following relevant literature and inquiring the editorial policies on these journals' websites as well as examining the published articles. For example, *PeerJ*, *eLife* and the set of journals named as "*Frontiers in* ..." (http://home.frontiersin.org/). It was found that 14 of the 111 journals should be excluded from analysis: some of these journals do not practice open peer review, others are blogs without rigorous peer reviews beyond readers' comments. The final dataset includes 155 OPR journals.

The collected dataset includes editorial policy and process, main subject area and article processing charge. The preliminary analysis focused on how the identities of authors and reviewers were handled, if the review reports were made public, who decided to publish the peer review history and whether the rebuttals were published as a part of the review history.

## PRELIMINARY RESULTS

As Figure 1 shows, the majority of the 155 OPR are in medicine and related fields; only a small percentage are in education, humanities and social science as grouped into *others*.

80th Annual Meeting of the Association for Information Science & Technology, Washington, DC | Oct. 27-Nov. 1, 2017

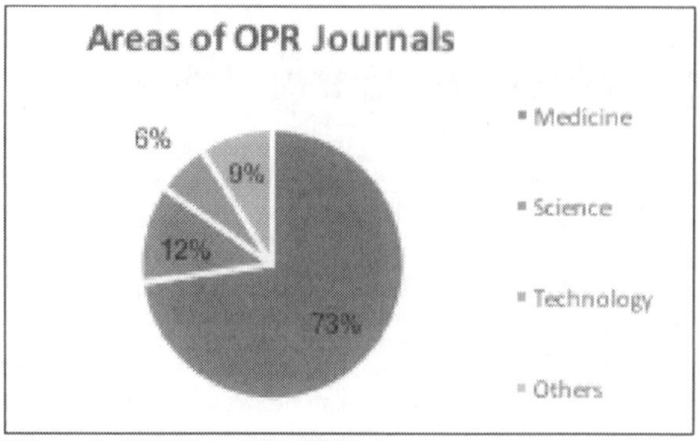


***Figure 1**. OPR journals distribution*

Of the 155 OPR journals, 92.26% require reviewers to be identified or sign their reports, 5.16% make it optional for the reviewer to reveal identity and 2.58% adopt a strategy that involves both the author and the reviewer. This strategy is that at the submission, the author will choose either double blind review or OPR review. The referee has a choice whether to agree or decline to review the submission under OPR. For an OPR manuscript, the referee will know the identity of the author and the review report will also have the identity of the referee. In the published OPR articles, referees are named but the original review reports may not be published (e.g., *eLife* and *Papers in Physics*).

Although the majority of the OPR journals remove the blindness of peer review during the process, only 52.26% of these journals publish original review reports alongside the paper. Three journals (1.94%) publish only some of the review results. *PeerJ* allows the author to decide if the review history will be made publicly accessible. Editors of *Papers in Physics* invite the referees who have made significant contribution to the paper to write a commentary that will be published with its own DOI and linked to the paper. Therefore, not all papers have a commentary. *eLife* publishes the editor's letters including integrated review comments. The letters acknowledge referees with names but without linking names with comments.

How do OPR journals handle the author's responses or rebuttals? The collected data show that 44.52% OPR journals publish rebuttals as part of the review history alongside the paper, 3.87% OPR journals indicate "upon request" and the rest of OPR journals do not publish rebuttals.

## DISCUSSION AND CONCLUSIONS

The pioneers in redesigning scientific peer review are moving from the blind process to a more transparent process using different strategies between transitional and revolutionary. The transitional models vary in levels of transparency and openness. The democratic decision process typically involves both authors and reviewers. The revolutionary models on the other hand make the process totally transparent and open. Some of the OPR journals straddle between the two approaches so that both double-blind and total open peer reviews coexist.

In the era of open science, open research, open data, etc., OPR can be seen as a much-needed renovation or modernization of the century-old peer review for scientific publishing. A variety of policies and procedures have been adopted to implement OPR. The focus of OPR is to remove blindness yet to ensure objectivity. The notion of OPR is still elusive and lacks an agreed-upon conceptualization or recognized best practices. Surrounding OPR, many new terms are being coined to identify specific elements of the OPR. Post-publication peer review (PPPR) or posteriori peer review is in contrast to the traditional pre-publication peer review. Peer review by endorsement (PRE) allows authors to invite qualified peers to evaluate their articles published in PPPR journals. Open public review (OPuR) in priori or concurrent peer review, which is not the same as open public comments, is participation by the scientific community within a defined period, moderated by editors.

The results suggest that journals in medicine and related fields are the early adopters. It is clear that systematic research is needed to better understand the future of OPR.

## REFERENCES


Belluz, J., Plumer, B., & Resnick, B. (2016). The 7 biggest problems facing science, according to 270 scientists. *Vox* http://www.vox.com/2016/7/14/12016710/science-challeges-research-funding-peer- review-process

Ford, E. (2013). Defining and characterizing open peer review: A review of the literature. *Journal of Scholarly Publishing* 44(4), 311-326.

Pöschl, U. (2012). Multi-stage open peer review: Scientific evaluation integrating the strengths of traditional peer review with the virtues of transparency and self-regulation. *Frontiers in Computational Neuroscience* 6, 33.

Soergel, D., Adam, S., & Andrew, M. (2013). Open scholarship and peer review: A time for experimentation. The *Proceedings of the 30th international conference on machine learning*, Atlanta, Georgia, USA.

Wang, P., Rath, M., Deike, M., & Wu, Q. (2016). Open peer review: An innovation in scientific publishing. Runner up of the Most Interesting Preliminary Results Paper The *iConference 2016* (Philadelphia, PA, March 20-23). https://www.ideals.illinois.edu/bitstream/handle/2142/89432/Wang315.pdf

Wang, P., You, S., Rath, M., & Wolfram, D. (2016). Open peer review in scientific publishing: A web mining study of PeerJ authors and reviewers. *Journal of Data and Information Science*, 1(4).

# Teen Nerdfighters: An Exploration of Engagement in a Complex Fan Community

**Amanda Waugh**
*University of Maryland, College Park. USA. awaugh@umd.edu*

## ABSTRACT

**This poster will examine teen Nerdfighters across a variety of social media platforms. Using both survey and interview data, this poster will draw maps of engagement to reflect on teen Nerdfighters' selection practices and flows between social media platforms.**

## KEYWORDS

fandoms, online communities. social media, information behavior, Nerdfighteria

## INTRODUCTION

It is a trope to say that teens are deeply engaged online, and yet we know that to be true in many ways. Recent data from Pew shows in the general population of teens, 92% are online daily, with 80% being connected several times a day or "almost constantly" (Lenhart, 2015). However, examining the complexity of teen engagement online is itself complex. This poster is an exploratory examination of teen engagement across platforms in one fan community, Nerdfighteria, and represents a single aspect of a larger research study.

## BACKGROUND AND RESEARCH QUESTION

Nerdfighters are fans of John and Hank Green, known as the Vlogbrothers. The Vlogbrothers have 3,000,000 subscribers to their primary YouTube channel. John Green is the author of several New York Times best-selling young adult literature novels, including *The Fault in Our Stars*. Nerdfighters watch the YouTube videos, but also follow the mantra to "decrease world suck" by explicitly engaging in acts of charity and kindness. They also follow the motto "Don't forget to be awesome," a reminder to be the best they can be regardless of societal expectations. It is unclear exactly how many Nerdfighters there are or how many are teens (defined here as ages 13-17). However in the 2015 Nerdfighter Census, approximately 43% of the over 100,000 respondents identified as between the ages of 13 and 18 (Green, 2015). Suffice it to say, there are a lot of teen Nerdfighters.

Nerdfighteria sprawls across the internet in almost every corner. In addition to YouTube, there are Nerdfighters on Facebook, Twitter, tumblr, forums, wikis, Discord, Twitch and so on. Some are created by the Green brothers, but many are created by fans. The sprawl of this community goes far beyond focusing on fandom – there are craft groups, homework help channels, Nerdfighter-Hamilton conversation groups, Google hangouts for gamers and so on. Though teens come to the Nerdfighter community as fans, the teens are staying and engaging in a wide range of social and informational practices. Despite the large size and wide ranging platforms, there is very little research in this community from any angle (Kligler-Vilenchik, 2013).

Teen engagement in Nerdfighteria moves way beyond the fandom to encompass a wide range of social and information seeking practices that have little to nothing to do with the object of their fandom. They might start a conversation on a fan forum, move to a Google hangout and then create a Google doc to share a short story collaboratively written by community members of all ages and across the globe. However, throughout this exchange, they often do not mention the object of their fandom. Their movement between social media platforms is fluid and ever changing, frequently subverting the focus of both the community and the platform.

The larger research project examines the information practices of teen Nerdfighters from several angles; however, this poster will focus on the social media selection practices. When you have such a wide variety of platforms with which to engage your fandom and your information needs, how do you choose which to engage with and navigate between? Therefore, the research question addressed here is: *How do teens engage in a fan community across social media platforms?*

## PRIOR RESEARCH

Prior research into fandoms tends to either focus on adult fans, or while examining teens, tends to examine their engagement in fanfiction. Teen fandom scholarship tends to focus on the creation of fanfiction or other fanworks (Campbell et al., 2015; Fiesler, Morrison, Shapiro & Bruckman, 2017). Scholarship on teens in online communities tends to fall into camps of those that focus on the likelihood of disaster in the form of cyberbullying, inappropriate content, internet addiction or stranger-danger (Leung & Lee, 2012; S. Livingstone, 2008; Sonia Livingstone & Brake, 2010; Youn & Hall, 2008), or the researchers paint a rosy picture of teens creating and engaging with content across the globe (boyd, 2014; Ito et al., 2010; Jenkins, 2006). Reality, however, is more nuanced. Additionally, research into teens online tends to focus on a single platform, such as Twitter, Facebook or tumblr (Asghar, 2015; Chang, Tang, Inagaki & Liu, 2014; Hillman, Procyk & Neustaedter, 2014; Vraga, Thorson, Kligler-Vilenchik & Gee, 2015). In reality, however, teens engage across a variety of social media platforms and move fluidly between them.

80th Annual Meeting of the Association for Information Science & Technology, Washington, DC | Oct. 27-Nov. 1, 2017

Simply studying the interactions of teens on a single platform gives a very narrow glimpse into their complicated and rich lives. This study aims to address these gaps by examining how teens select and move between Nerdfighter social media platforms.

## METHODS

This study was conducted using a qualitative case study framework, collecting data using survey, observation, interview and diary techniques, and analyzing data using grounded theory techniques. Data collection included a survey of 241 teen Nerdfighters conducted between November 2016 and March 2017, an examination of public teen forums and interviews with 24 teens done between 2015 and 2017. Survey participants were found by posting information about the study on Twitter and in Nerdfighter forums and groups. Interview subjects were identified by 1) inviting survey participants, 2) snowball sampling from prior participants, teen-oriented librarians and 3) posting study information on Nerdfighter forums, groups, Twitter hashtags. This study was approved by the University of Maryland Institutional Review Board.

## FINDINGS

The findings illustrate the complex layers of interactions. The survey revealed a group of teens who are constantly connected online. 99.5% are online either several times a day or almost constantly, a number that is higher than the Pew results (Lenhart, 2015). Additionally, the survey emphasized the fast-moving evolution of community engagement and social media platforms. While almost all were engaged on the traditional social media platforms (Twitter, Facebook, YouTube, tumblr, Reddit, forums, etc.) in one form or another, many referenced other media, some of which did not have a strong Nerdfighter community at the time of survey development, but did as of May 2017. One example of this is a new Discord channel. Normally used for online gaming, the Nerdfighters opened a Discord channel to manage and discuss a Nerdfighter internet scavenger hunt; however, the Discord channel rapidly evolved to include sub-channels focused on numerous other topics including literature, politics, sports and homework help.

The poster will highlight the survey findings above, as well as specific participants to illustrate a complex pattern of engagement driven by the norms and ethos of the larger community, the affordances of the specific platform and the level of engagement of the specific participant (Figure 1). All teens mentioned the norms and ethos of the community as a reason for their engagement. The experience of engaging with a wide variety of people, both teen and adult, from all over the world without fear of being flamed or otherwise called out for an opinion, life experience or gender status, was a primary motivator for engagement. These teens attributed this to the values of Nerdfighteria, including a belief in discourse and a love of learning. According to a female participant, "I'm really happy that the community likes learning, because I've always loved learning and I thought like, 'Oh, my god. I'm a kid that likes to learn. Oh, then I must be the only one.' Seeing that a whole community watches people, just to learn, it's really cool because of that."

Other teen Nerdfighters exhibited different patterns with varying levels of complexity. For example, some teens were deeply engaged in one platform, such as Reddit or a specific Facebook subgroup, but only lightly involved in others. Some teens, while strongly identifying as Nerdfighters, chose to observe a single platform, typically the YouTube channel and comments, and/or Twitter.

## CONCLUSION

2) Teen engagement in this fan community is multifaceted and driven by a combination of the affordances of the platform, the experiences of the teen (attending a con, making a social connection) and the norms of the community (valuing learning and supportiveness). These findings are limited by the unique nature of the community and the relatively small number of interview participants. Future research should examine how the ethos and values of other fan communities impact the engagement of teens.

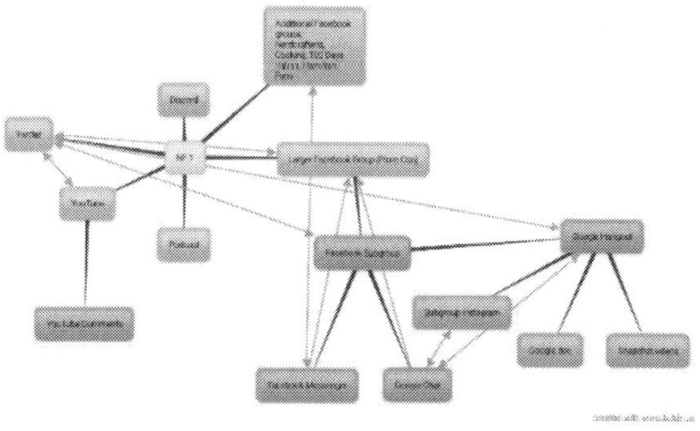

***Figure 1.*** *The engagement patterns of one teen female Nerdfighter*

## REFERENCES


Asghar, H. M. (2015). Measuring information seeking through Facebook: Scale development and initial evidence of information seeking in Facebook scale (ISFS). *Computers in Human Behavior, 52*, 259-270. https://doi.org/10.1016/j.chb.2015.06.005

boyd, danah. (2014). *It's complicated: The social lives of networked teens*. New Haven: Yale University Press.

Campbell, J. A., Aragon, C., Davis, K., Evans, S., Evans, A. & Randall, D. P. (2015). Thousands of positive reviews: Distributed mentoring in online fan communities. *arXiv Preprint arXiv:1510.01425*.

Chang, Y., Tang, L., Inagaki, Y. & Liu, Y. (2014). What is Tumblr: A statistical overview and comparison. *SIGKDD Explor. Newsl., 16*(1), 21-29. https://doi.org/10.1145/2674026.2674030

Fiesler, C., Morrison, S., Shapiro, R. B. & Bruckman, A. S. (2017). Growing their own: Legitimate peripheral participation for computational learning in an online fandom community (pp. 1375–1386). ACM Press. https://doi.org/10.1145/2998181.2998210

Green, H. (2015). *Nerdfighteria census 2015 analysis!* Retrieved from https://youtu.be/Bvb6GcGCqIg?list=PLvqC_ud-2lVo-BinQ2Qorb8L_JRmKBrTlR

Hillman, S., Procyk, J., & Neustaedter, C. (2014). Tumblr fandoms, community & culture. In *Proceedings of the Companion Publication of the 17th ACM Conference on Computer Supported Cooperative Work & Social Computing* (pp. 285–288). New York, NY, USA: ACM. https://doi.org/10.1145/2556420.2557634

Ito, M., Baumer, S., Bittani, M., boyd, danah, Cody, R., Herr-Stephenson, B., … Tripp, L. (2010). *Hanging out, messing around, and geeking out*. Cambridge, MA: The MIT Press.

Jenkins, H. (2006). *Confronting the challenges of participatory culture: Media education for the 21st century*. MacArthur Foundation. Retrieved from http://digitallearning.macfound.org/atf/cf/{7E45C7E0-A3E0-4B89-AC9C-E807E1B0AE4E}/JENKINS_WHITE_PAPER.PDF

Kligler-Vilenchik, N. (2013). *"Decreasing world suck": Fan communities, mechanisms of translation, and participatory politics* (White Paper) (p. 81). Annenberg School for Communications and Journalism. Retrieved from http://www.slideshare.net/amandafo/decreasing-world-suck-working-paper-mapp-june-25-2013?qid=a39ddc8f-86fa-4432-a2ba-5690efec4a7a&v=default&b=&from_search=2

Lenhart, A. (2015). *Teens, social media and technology overview 2015* (White Paper). Pew Research Center. Retrieved from http://www.pewinternet.org/files/2015/04/PI_TeensandTech_Update2015_0409151.pdf

Leung, L., & Lee, P. S. N. (2012). The influences of information literacy, internet addiction and parenting styles on internet risks. *New Media & Society*, *14*(1), 117–136. https://doi.org/10.1177/1461444811410406

Livingstone, S. (2008). Taking risky opportunities in youthful content creation: Teenagers' use of social networking sites for intimacy, privacy and self-expression. *New Media & Society*, *10*(3), 393-411. https://doi.org/10.1177/1461444808089415

Livingstone, S., & Brake, D. R. (2010). On the rapid rise of social networking sites: New findings and policy implications. *Children & Society*, *24*(1), 75-83. https://doi.org/10.1111/j.1099-0860.2009.00243.x

Vraga, E. K., Thorson, K., Kligler-Vilenchik, N., & Gee, E. (2015). How individual sensitivities to disagreement shape youth political expression on Facebook. *Computers in Human Behavior*, *45*, 281-289. https://doi.org/10.1016/j.chb.2014.12.025

Youn, S., & Hall, K. (2008). Gender and online privacy among teens: Risk perception, privacy concerns, and protection behaviors. *CyberPsychology & Behavior*, *11*(6), 763-765. https://doi.org/10.1089/cpb.2007.0240

# Integrating User Feedback with Open Data Quality Models

**Nicholas Weber**
*University of Washington, USA. nmweber@uw.edu*

**An Yan**
*University of Washington, USA. yanan15@uw.edu*

## ABSTRACT

**User feedback is critical to improving the quality of open data. However, most open data publishers gather only anecdotal evidence about user experiences. This unstructured and informal commentary is, consequently, difficult to translate into actionable steps towards improving data quality. Drawing on user comments collected from Data.Gov - an open data portal providing access to thousands of datasets published by city, state, and federal government agencies in the USA – we inductively develop a classification of reported data quality issues. This poster presents preliminary findings from applying this coding scheme to all issues that users filed on Data.gov in 2015 and 2016. We suggest that our classification scheme can help open data publishers collect structured, actionable information to improve data quality.**

## KEYWORDS

Open data, data quality, civic technology.

## INTRODUCTION

Over the last decade open data initiatives have demonstrably increased access to public sector information (Davies, 2010); are shown to correlate strongly with more efficient and impactful basic science research (Piwowar and Vision, 2013); and, can act as a driver of private sector innovation in critical areas of our economy such as healthcare and renewable energy (Chan, 2013). Yet, many previous studies have shown that open data remains difficult for lay users to discover (Martin et al., 2013), access (Janssen et al., 2012), and use (Braunschweig et al, 2012). Some barriers to the meaningful use of open data include poor metadata quality (Neumaier et al. 2016), insufficient provenance information (Umbirch et al. 2015), and poorly organized data portals that are supposed to match data producers with data consumers (Thorsby et al., 2017). Collectively, these barriers have been described as a function of the overall quality of open data (Saez-Martin, Rosario, & Perez, 2016).

The goal of our on-going research is to better understand how to communicate a relative notion like 'quality' to potential open data users. We believe that by avoiding rigid definitions of quality, and instead focusing on descriptive features of a dataset, we can enable users to make better judgements about a dataset's fitness for use. The preliminary work described in this poster is focused on creating an empirically informed model of user feedback, focused specifically on users of data.gov. Formally stated our research questions ask: What data quality 'issues' do users report to data.gov? How can this unstructured user feedback be generically classified in order make data quality actionable for data publishers?

## RESEARCH DESIGN

Users of data.gov can provide feedback about their use of a dataset in a number of ways - through email, social media (e.g. Twitter), or directly on the data.gov website. The latter option includes a button prominently placed at the top of each dataset that reads "Report Data Issue". Users selecting this option are given the ability to create a free text description of the issue, and publish the issue to data.gov for public viewing.

### *Data*

Using the RVest package (Wickham, 2015) for R we scraped all data issues that were published to data.gov from January 01, 2015 - December 31, 2016 (n = 956). For each issue, we collected the date the issue was reported, the status of the issue (open or closed), and a user's free-text response to the "issue" prompt.

### *Inductive Coding*

Our research team met and discussed themes that were reported in the free text of 20 randomly selected user issues. We then developed an initial coding scheme to classify each issue. Next, we selected a subset of issues from the scraped data (n = 50), and separately coded each issue with this initial coding scheme. We compared the applied codes for each issue, and revised our coding scheme to account for differences in our application of one particular code over another. A new subset was selected (n = 50) and again coded separately. For the second round of coding we calculated a Kappa score (Carletta, 1996) to measure inter-coder reliability, achieving an agreement score of 0.93. We again simplified our coding scheme to account for differences in the application of codes, selected a third subset (n=100), and separately coded each issue. For the third round, we achieved a kappa score of 0.94 - giving us confidence in the final coding scheme (presented in Table 1). Finally, we divided and separately coded the remaining issues (n= 856). The results presented below include only those issues coded during our third and final round of coding.

## RESULTS

Users of data.gov reported issues in three broad categories – Data availability, Data Quality, and Documentation. Data availability accounted for 81% (n=610) of all issues reported,

80th Annual Meeting of the Association for Information Science & Technology, Washington, DC | Oct. 27-Nov. 1, 2017

followed by unclear (as in the report was not specific enough to code) (n=136), data quality (n=73), and documentation (n=26) issues. As shown in Figure 1, of the 610 reported data availability issues, over half were a result of a broken link / 404 error (n=327).

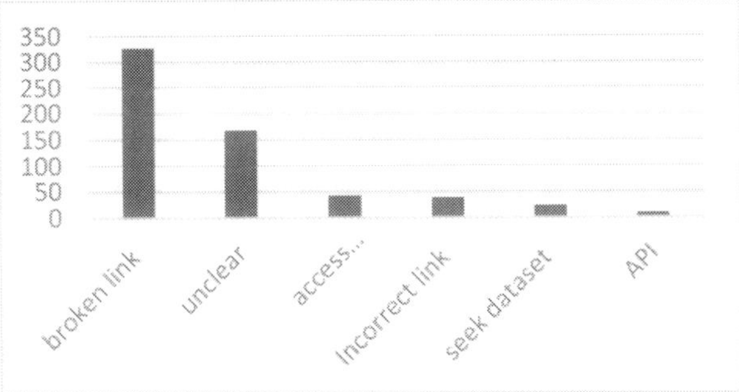


***Figure 1**. Distribution of reported data availability issues.*

Data quality and documentation issues were reported less frequently. As shown in Figure 2, data quality issues were distributed somewhat evenly over around incorrect (n=25), obsolescent (n=13) and formatting problems (n=11).

## DISCUSSION AND FUTURE WORK

The answer to our first research question is evident in the classification scheme that we inductively developed through coding user reported data issues; Users report problems with the availability, quality, and documentation of open data hosted by data.gov. Results from applying these codes show that a majority of the issues reported by users of data.gov are concerned with data availability, and in particular broken links for data that should be accessible via the data.gov portal. This finding is unsurprising given that data.gov is designed to act, in part, as a content aggregator that harvests metadata from other open data portals, and provides a unified metadata standard and search mechanism. However, a significant number (n=168) of data availability reports were simply too vague or general for us to classify. For example, on June 11, 2015 a user's free text reports "Nothing happens when I click the download link" – it's unclear from a report like this whether a resource has moved, a link has been deleted, or the user simply has lost internet connection and their browser is not properly resolving the link.

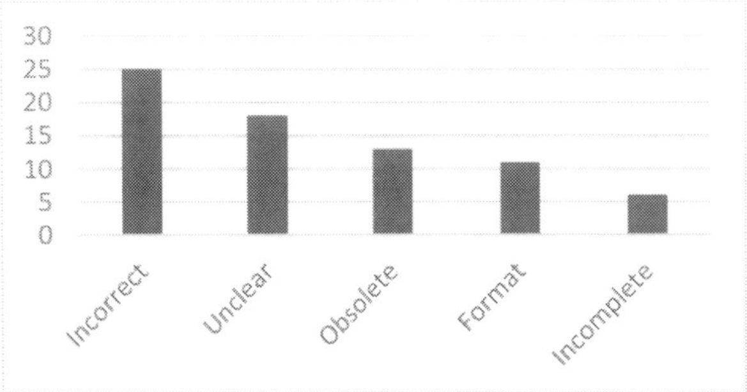


***Figure 2.** Distribution of reported Data quality issues*

In total, almost half of all reported issues (n=323) were too vague or incomplete for us to classify. The answer to our second research question thus indicates a need to give users better direction in reporting data issues. In particular, a simple menu of choices – such as the classification scheme provided here - would likely help users more accurately report the problems that they face in using open data.

| Code | Refinement | Definition |
|---|---|---|
| Data Availability | | Issue reports a problem with the accessibility of data. |
| | broken link | 404 or broken link is reported |
| | access forbidden | 403 or lack of credentials is reported |
| | Incorrect link | The link provided resolves to a dataset or resource that is different from the one described |
| | API | A user reports an error with the data.gov API, or the failure of a wget method |
| | Seeking dataset | The user is requesting a dataset be made available |
| | Unclear | User has reported an issue with accessing a dataset, but it is unclear if the problem is on behalf of data.gov or a user error. |
| Data Quality | | Issues report a problem with using available data |
| | obsolescence | The dataset is outdated, or has not been updated |
| | incomplete | The dataset is missing values |
| | incorrect | The dataset has errors, or the file is corrupt in some way |
| | format | The user reports an issue with the file format that the data are served |
| Documentation | | Issues report a problem with the existing documentation for a dataset |
| | metadata | The user reports missing, incorrect, or incomplete metadata for a dataset |
| | contact information | The user reports missing, incorrect, or incomplete contact information for a dataset |
| Others or Unclear | | Issue reports a problem that is out of scope for data.gov (e.g. irrelevant complaint about government secrecy) |

***Table 1**: Coding Scheme used to classify data issues.*

Contrary to our assumption, most users are not filing issues about the quality of the data they consume, but instead problems they encounter while trying to access data. This may be a result of the ease in filing an issue at the point of access (e.g. being denied access, one simply needs to click the "Report Data Issue" button). It may be too much to expect that a data consumer downloads a dataset, explores in some way, discovers an error, and then returns to the data.gov site to report the issue.

We therefore believe data quality issues may be reported in other locations – through email, social media, or on public forums, such as StackExchange, which has recently launched a dedicated question and answer site for developers and researchers interested in open data (https://opendata.stackexchange.com/). In future work, we plan to also harvest user issues reported on these platforms, and apply the coding scheme developed in this preliminary work.

## ACKNOLWEDGEMENTS

This work is supported by IMLS grant no. 40-16-0015-16 Data and project software can be found at:
https://github.com/OpenDataLiteracy/feedback

## REFERENCES

Braunschweig, K., Eberius, J., Thiele, M., & Lehner, W. (2012). The state of open data. WWW2012, Lyon, France: ACM.

Carletta, J. (1996). Assessing agreement on classification tasks: the kappa statistic. Computational linguistics, 22(2), 249-254.

Chen, Y., Wen, C.-Y., Chen, H.-P., Lin, Y.-H., & Sum, H.-C. (2011). Metrics for Metadata Quality Assurance and Their Implications for Digital Libraries. In ICADL (Vol. 7008, pp. 138–147). Springer.

Davies, T. (2010). Open data, democracy and public sector reform. A Look at Open Government Data Use from Data.Gov.Uk. (Dissertation)

Janssen, M., Charalabidis, Y., & Zuiderwijk, A. (2012). Benefits, adoption barriers and myths of open data and open government. Information systems management, 29(4), 258-268.

Martin, S., Foulonneau, M., Turki, S., & Ihadjadene, M. (2013, June). Open data: Barriers, risks and opportunities. In Proceedings of the 13th European Conference on eGovernment: ECEG (pp. 301-309).

Sáez Martín, A., Rosario, A. H. D., & Pérez, M. D. C. C. (2016). An international analysis of the quality of open government data portals. *Social Science Computer Review*, *34*(3), 298-311.

Neumaier, S., Umbrich, J., & Polleres, A. (2016). Automated quality assessment of metadata across open data portals. Journal of Data and Information Quality (JDIQ), 8(1), 2.

Piwowar, H. A., & Vision, T. J. (2013). Data reuse and the open data citation advantage. PeerJ, 1, e175.

Thorsby, J., Stowers, G. N., Wolslegel, K., & Tumbuan, E. (2016). Understanding the content and features of open data portals in American cities. Government Information Quarterly.

Wickham, H. (2015). rvest: Easily Harvest (Scrape) Web Pages. R package version 0.3. 1.

Umbrich, J., Neumaier, S., & Polleres, A. (2015, March). Towards assessing the quality evolution of open data portals. In Proceedings of ODQ2015: Open Data Quality: from Theory to Practice Workshop, Munich, Germany.

# Video Productions at Saint Joseph Hospital, A Teaching Hospital in Denver, Colorado

**Karen Wells**
*Saint Joseph Hospital, USA. karen.wells@sclhs.net*

**Eric Neail**
*Saint Joseph Hospital, USA. eric.neail@sclhs.net*

**Tim Rockwood**
*Saint Joseph Hospital, USA. tim.rockwood@sclhs.net*

## ABSTRACT

**In this video production, we describe our new video productions service recently added to our multi-media services team (MMS), which is part of our Libraries and Knowledge Services Department. Saint Joseph Hospital is a 400-bed teaching hospital in Denver, Colorado. We have a large medical residency program in internal medicine, obstetrics & gynecology, family practice and surgery. We have many robust research and training needs, in nursing as well, including magnet maintenance, clinical ladders, and nursing research fellows.**

## KEYWORDS

hospitals, libraries, multi-media services, video productions, video streaming

## INTRODUCTION

"SIG/VIS's mission is to promote the exchange, development, communication and dissemination of information and research related to visual and graphic information among ASIS&T members and to the larger community of practitioners and scholars."

We describe how the addition of in-house video productions aided our hospital in many ways, and encouraged the use of our MMS staff as readily available video production specialists. Outsourced video productions formerly incurred high costs to our hospital; therefore, we sought to produce quality videos onsite, hoping to realize significant cost savings. As we developed our program, we not only replaced many outsourced videos, we also increased our visibility and credibility through partnering with many different departments, creating training videos, fun and novel videos, embedding videos into power point presentations and online newsletters, creating oral historical videos and biographies, and even helping our senior administrative personnel through creative and informative organizationally minded videos. We used video streaming to allow our heavily time-conscious staff to view videos on their own time frame.

80th Annual Meeting of the Association for Information Science & Technology, Washington, DC | Oct. 27-Nov. 1, 2017



## THE CONTENT

- Video production services grew and developed to serve our residents, interns, students, staff (physicians, nurses and allied health), patients and our administrators.
- Staff, equipment and software are detailed. Two years of data reports on total productions, audience views by hospital department, views to partial or complete finish, frequency of video use by device and a composite picture of all video viewed on Vimeo, HealthStream or on MP4s on laptops. The use of individualized vs. group or formal instructional recommendation was a determinant of video viewing frequency.
- HealthStream was heavily used for formal instruction in education, for both medicine and nursing, compared to Vimeo, which was more informally used for transient video viewings outside of graduate medical education.
- Successful outcomes from this new service include effective learning modalities achieved through video instruction; development of partnerships with other hospital departments, resulting in higher visibility of the department; increase in demand for services over time; cost savings from internal production as compared to outsourcing; improved staff and student accessibility to instructions via streaming videos on demand; and the limited, although beneficial, access to video on mobile devices.
- Challenges include budget constraints; project management; marketing; discoverability of produced and archived videos; purchase of copyrighted materials used in production; incapability of sharing videos external to the hospital; and no open access to videos due to HIPAA compliance and other hospital policies.
- Future plans include the assessment of videos to determine further retention and possibility of future usage; disposition of one-time use videos; increasing in-hospital staff video discoverability to archived videos with possible long term or multipurpose use; and investigation of MARCIVE cataloging of videos via OCLC WMS or other venue. Given that recent data shows mobile video now comprises about 54% of video views worldwide, we also will seek a deeper investigation of mobile access to videos, working toward more digital maturity within our hospital.

## THE FORMAT

The video is presented in MP4 format which will be viewable to attendees through Vimeo.

## CONCLUSION

Education, both medicine and nursing, heavily used video productions in their programs.

Many departments desired to script videos for production as MMS popularity increased within the hospital.

The audience for and utility of video includes the entire staff of the hospital, as well as the patients and administrators.

There are significant cost savings to inhouse productions.

Data shows increases in worldwide video viewing and our hospitals' utilization patterns yielded an increased request for internal video production over time.

Partnering with other departments increases the visibility and interoperability of the MMS and is likely to yield more projects.

More investigations are needed to allow full digital maturity in the future in hospital settings.


## ACKNOWLEDGMENTS

Saint Joseph Hospital, 1375 E. 19th Avenue, Denver CO 80216.



Karen Wells, Ed.M., MS, LIS, manager, Libraries and Knowledge Services, (303) 812-3628, Karen.Wells@sclhs.net

Tim Rockwood, BS, data analyses and media services coordinator, (303) 812-2923, Tim.Rockwood@sclhs.net

Eric Neail, BS, video production and media services av specialist, (303) 812-2934, Eric.Neail@sclhs.net


## REFERENCES


Digital video platforms are drawing ever-increasing numbers of viewers. YouTube is the No.1 digital video platform in most countries. (2017) E-Marketer.com. Retrieved June 22, 2017, from www.emarketer.com/Article/Digital-Video-Platforms-Drawing-Ever-Increasing-Numbers-of-Viewers/1014297

Fontane, W. M. (2017) Video tutorials revisited: The relationship between their use and library assessment quiz scores. *College and Undergraduate Libraries*, *24*(1), 90-102.

Loechner, J. (2016) *Video-on-demand in demand*. Mediapost.com. Retrieved June 20, 2017, from mediapost.com/publications/article/282495/video-on-demand-in-demand.html

Mayer, R. E. (1997) Multimedia learning: Are we asking the right questions? *Educational Psychologist*, *32*(1):1-19.

Mayer, R. E. (2005) Introduction to multimedia learning. In R. E. Mayer (Ed.), *The Cambridge handbook of multimedia learning* (pp. 1-6) New York: Cambridge University Press.

Multi-Media Services, Saint Joseph Hospital. (2017) *Undercover Boss*. Retrieved June 20, 2017 from https://vimeo.com/205284998

Nielsen. (2016) *Video on demand: How worldwide video habits are evolving amid an evolving landscape*. Retrieved June 20, 2017, from www.neilsen.com/us/en/insights/reports/2016/video-on-demand.html

Owens J. *Video production handbook*. (2017) New York, New York: Routledge.

Pavio, A. (1969) Mental imagery in associative learning and memory. *Psychological Review*, *76*(3), 241-263.

# How Do Chinese Researchers Use Research Information Management Systems?: An Exploratory Study

**Shuheng Wu**
*Queens College, City University of New York, USA. Shuheng.Wu@qc.cuny.edu*

**Dong Joon Lee**
*Texas A&M University, USA. djlee@tamu.edu*

**Besiki Stvilia**
*Florida State University, USA. bstvilia@fsu.edu*

## ABSTRACT

**This poster presents how Chinese researchers use research information management (RIM) systems (e.g., ResearchGate, Google Scholar). Findings include a typology of activities in which Chinese researchers engage in RIM systems. The findings indicate that obtaining English papers and connecting with scholars from other countries motivate Chinese researchers to use specific RIM systems, while the language barrier and the Great Firewall of China discourage them to use or engage in those systems.**

## KEYWORDS

research information management, Chinese researchers, ResearchGate, ScholarMate, ORCID, Baidu Academic

## INTRODUCTION

*Research information management (RIM) systems* can be defined as systems that aggregate, curate and utilize the scholarly output of researchers (OCLC Research, 2017). There are different RIM systems from libraries, universities and content aggregators such as ResearchGate, Google Scholar, VIVO and ORCID. With the popularity of RIM systems, researchers began to study the altmetrics derived from RIM systems and their user characteristics (e.g., seniority, academic status, nationality). Thelwall and Kousha (2015) identified the extent to which various countries listed their publications in ResearchGate, with the United States having the most and China the least. A previous study had examined how researchers in the United States use and engage in RIM systems (Wu, Stvilia & Lee, 2017). However, the reason behind the low use of specific RIM systems (e.g., ResearchGate) by Chinese scholars, which RIM systems they use and how they use those systems remain unexplored. This study explores how researchers from Chinese institutions use RIM systems. Findings can better the design of RIM services and the mechanism for recruiting and engaging Chinese researchers to provide and maintain their research information. This study addresses the following research questions:

1. Which online RIM systems do researchers from Chinese institutions use?
2. How do researchers from Chinese institutions use online RIM systems?

## RESEARCH DESIGN

This study defines the research population as researchers from Chinese research institutions who have at least one peer-reviewed research publication. The authors conducted qualitative semi-structured interviews with 10 participants in eight disciplines from seven research institutions, including one full professor, two associate professors, two assistant professors, two lecturers, two postdoctoral fellows and one doctoral student. All interviews were audio recorded, transcribed and coded with NVivo 11. Two of the authors independently coded all the interviews using a coding scheme developed in a previous study (Wu et al., 2017). After comparing, discussing and resolving differences in their coding, they formed a new coding scheme with emergent codes and recoded all interviews.

## FINDINGS

### Online RIM Systems Used by Chinese Researchers

This study identified seven online RIM systems frequently used by Chinese researchers, including Academia.edu, Baidu Academic, Bing Academic, Google Scholar, ORCID, ResearchGate and ScholarMate. Five participants indicated that they started using certain RIM systems because of recommendations from colleagues, friends and advisors. For example, one participant described how he started to use ResearchGate:

> *My advisor told me that if I wanted to be an international scholar, I should do some social networking, register for some online systems, and share my publications...I followed his suggestion and began to use ResearchGate.*

Two participants were required to use ScholarMate by a funding agency (National Natural Science Foundation of China), and four were required to use ORCID by some journals. Five participants specified that they did not use, or seldom used, Google Scholar because of the Great Firewall of China. Nine participants have a profile in ResearchGate, four in Baidu Academic, four in ORCID, three in Google Scholar, two in Academia.edu and two in ScholarMate.

80th Annual Meeting of the Association for Information Science & Technology, Washington, DC | Oct. 27-Nov. 1, 2017

### *Activities and Motivations*

This study identified 10 activities (see Table 1) in which Chinese researchers engaged in using RIM systems. All 10 participants indicated that they used RIM systems to find relevant literature or patents. Some participants used different RIM systems to find papers in different languages or from different regions. Four participants mentioned that they used Google Scholar and/or ResearchGate to obtain English papers, while two found that Baidu Academic was better for finding Chinese papers. One participant specified that she used Google Scholar to find Chinese papers published outside of Mainland China:

> Sometimes I use Chinese keywords to search related papers. I found Baidu Academic could only search publications within China, but Google Scholar could include publications from Hong Kong and Taiwan.

Two participants used RIM systems to find conference information. A previous similar study (Wu et al., 2017) did not identify this use of RIM systems by U.S. researchers. Only one participant used RIM systems to document manuscripts and manage her reference lists. However, another participant pointed out his desire to incorporate into ResearchGate the bibliographic management service as provided by EndNote. Several participants mentioned that they used ResearchGate or Academia.edu to identify researchers from other countries and to build a social network with them. Six participants used RIM systems to disseminate their research, such as promoting their papers and making them accessible. One of them even translated some of her Chinese papers into English and uploaded them to Academia.edu. By doing so she received a special issue invitation:

> A scholar invited me to submit a paper to a special issue because she read some of my papers on Academia.edu. Later I contributed an English paper to that special issue.

Seven participants indicated that they curated their research information in RIM systems, such as uploading papers and updating research interests. One participant explained that she did not maintain her ResearchGate profile because of the language barrier:

> It's very important to update your profile very often...but because it [ResearchGate] is an English tool, I feel not so comfortable to use it. Language is a barrier for me...

The findings indicate that the motivations most frequently mentioned by participants to explain their lack of use of or participation in some RIM systems were the language barrier and the Great Firewall of China. RIM systems may consider automatically harvesting both Chinese and English publications for Chinese researchers and providing them with translation service to address the language barrier.

## CONCLUSION

This poster presents the activities in which Chinese researchers engage in RIM systems. More interviews will be conducted with researchers from other institutions and disciplines to gain different perspectives.

| Activities | Actions | Available functionalities |
|---|---|---|
| Find relevant literature and patents | Search | Search engine; author profile; follow papers/researchers; citing & cited papers |
| | Determine | Author and publication profiles |
| | Select | Citation count; author impact scores; publication venue impact scores |
| | Obtain | Download a paper; request a paper from author(s) |
| Identify conferences | Search | Conference papers |
| Document manuscripts | Document sources | Citation generator |
| | Verify sources | Author profile |
| Identify researchers | Identify collaborators, foreign researchers | Citing & cited papers; author profiles; follow researchers; ResearchGate reads statistics |
| Disseminate research | Make papers accessible | Upload papers |
| | Promote papers | Recommend papers; recommend researchers |
| Interact with peers | Ask and answer questions | Q&A service |
| | Send and receive private messages | Messaging service |
| Monitor the literature | Follow known researchers | Receive updates on known researchers |
| | Follow papers | Receive updates on papers |
| | Discover new papers | Recommend papers; citing & cited papers |
| | Discover new researchers | Recommend researchers; citing & cited papers |
| Evaluate | Evaluate papers | Citation count; number of reads; manuscript status |
| | Evaluate researchers | Author profile; impact scores |
| Curate | Archive papers | Upload papers |
| | Add/modify metadata for papers | Add tags; claim papers; disavow papers; add citation information |
| | Add/modify metadata for researchers | Maintain profile; merge profiles; endorse for expertise; remove suggested co-authors |
| Look for jobs | Search | Recommended job postings |

***Table 1.*** *Activities and RIM system functionalities*

## REFERENCES


Thelwall, M., & Kousha, K. (2015). ResearchGate: Disseminating, communicating, and measuring scholarship? *Journal of the Association for Information Science & Technology, 66*(5), 876-889.

OCLC Research. (2017). *An increasing role for libraries in research information management*. Retrieved from http://www.oclc.org/research/themes/research-collections/rim.html

Wu, S., Stvilia, B., & Lee, D. J. (2017). Readers, personal record managers, and community members: An exploratory study of researchers' participation in online research information management systems. *Journal of Library Metadata, 17*(2), 1-34.

# Music Literature Indexing: A Comparison Between Users' Free-text Queries and Controlled Vocabularies

**Shuheng Wu**
*Queens College, The City University of New York, USA. Shuheng.Wu@qc.cuny.edu*

**Yun Fan**
*RILM International Center, USA. yfan@rilm.org*

## ABSTRACT

**Subject indexing of music literature is known to be difficult because of language barriers and the vocabulary problem. Prior research has validated the necessity of indexing documents based on users' search queries. This study examined the characteristics of users' free-text queries created in a music literature database (RILM) and compared those queries with the controlled vocabularies used by the database. This poster presents a typology of 11 categories of user-created search terms identified in RILM. The findings indicate that the controlled vocabularies used by RILM align well with the user search terms. Based on the findings, suggestions are offered to enhance and improve the controlled vocabularies for music literature indexing.**

## KEYWORDS

music literature indexing, RILM, user queries, controlled vocabularies, search-log analysis

## INTRODUCTION

Subject indexing of music literature is known to be difficult mostly due to language barriers and the vocabulary problem – the problem of people using different words or languages to search the same concepts or information objects (Myers, 1995). The titles of musical works may be known in multiple languages and spellings, and the best-known one may not be the original one. The numbering systems for musical works of the established western composers, such as opus numbers and catalogue numbers, can be complicated and sometimes confusing for novices. For example, Beethoven's third symphony is widely known by its nickname "Heroica," while its Library of Congress (LC) uniform title is "Symphonies, no. 3, op. 55, E♭ major." Musical terminology varies in different communities, cultures and countries. Because of language barriers and the vocabulary problem, catalogers, indexers and scholars have not yet agreed upon how to index music literature (Kelly, 2010). Controlled vocabularies have long been used in libraries and bibliographic databases to address the vocabulary problem between the user and information systems. However, there are problems in using controlled vocabularies to index documents. Controlled vocabularies are rigid in their structure and may not be familiar to users. Compared to user queries, controlled vocabularies are often slow to adopt and reflect the most current terminology in a particular domain. Monitoring user queries is an effective and inexpensive means of identifying new terminology and highly technical terms that can be integrated into controlled vocabularies (Nowick & Mering, 2003). Prior research has validated the necessity and functionality of indexing documents based on users' information needs and their search queries (Soergel, 1974).

This study examined the characteristics of users' free-text queries created in a music literature database, and compared those queries to the controlled vocabularies used by the database to identify any gaps in the controlled vocabularies and how to enhance them to better serve the user and indexer. Findings can inform the design of music-related controlled vocabularies and provide insight into approaches to music literature indexing and retrieval. This study addressed the following research questions:

1. What are the categories of users' free-text queries in music literature databases?
2. How do users' free-text queries created in music literature databases differ from the controlled vocabularies used by the databases?

## STUDY DESIGN

This study selected one of the world's largest music literature databases, RILM Abstracts of Music Literature (hereafter referred to as RILM), to collect and analyze users' search queries and compared them to the controlled vocabularies used by RILM. RILM's subject experts provide each publication with a set of index strings. Each index string (e.g., "Froberger, Johann Jacob--performance practice--keyboard music--notation") begins with a headword and is followed by narrower terms specifying different aspects of the headword. All the headwords and most of the narrower terms are selected from RILM's thesaurus and authority files (including personal names, institution names, geographic names and musical work titles). The search-log data was collected from 7,924 user queries submitted to RILM in December 2015. A random sample of 367 queries was drawn from this dataset to conduct content analysis. The sample size was determined using the technique introduced by Powell and Connaway (2004). The unit of analysis is each user search query. An initial coding scheme was developed based on the literature (Nowick & Mering, 2003; White, 2013) consisting of eight categories of queries and three types of mapping to RILM's index terms (i.e., perfect match, partial match and no match). Two authors independently coded 367 queries based on the

---

80th Annual Meeting of the Association for Information Science & Technology, Washington, DC | Oct. 27-Nov. 1, 2017

initial coding scheme. After comparing, discussing and resolving differences in their coding, they formed a new coding scheme with three more categories of queries and then used it to recode all the queries. Despite subtle differences, they found no significant discrepancies in their coding and resolved the few minor discrepancies through further discussion to obtain agreement.

## FINDINGS

Of all 367 queries in the sample, 28 were omitted from the data analysis, including one invalid query and 27 queries created by directly using the bibliographic metadata (e.g., author, identifier) and RILM's index strings. Therefore, this dataset contains 339 valid user-created queries: 178 (52.51%) are single-word (e.g., "apartheid," "zydeco") or single-concept queries (e.g., "music festivals," "murky bass"), while 161 (41.49%) are multi-concept queries (e.g., "army and ww2"). The multi-concept queries were further separated into 350 separate search terms. In total, this dataset contains 528 separate user-created search terms, each of which was categorized and compared to RILM's index terms to determine its degree of matching.

## CATEGORIES OF USER-CREATED QUERIES

Of all 528 separate user-created search terms in the dataset, 193 (36.55%) are personal names, 151 (28.60%) are topical terms, 132 (25.00%) are work titles, 16 (3.03%) are geographic names, 13 (2.46%) are instruments, nine (1.70%) are corporate body names, seven (1.33%) are chronological terms, three (0.57%) are document types, two (0.38%) are identifiers, one (0.19%) is format and one (0.19%) is language. RILM's thesaurus contains four types of headword (main index terms) used as the first-level index term of each index string: personal names, geographic names, topical terms and instruments. Work title is the third most frequently occurring category of search terms in the user-created queries, but works titles are not used in RILM as a type of headword. RILM could consider instating musical work titles, especially those that are well known and those without known composers, as a type of headword.

## COMPARISON TO CONTROLLED VOCABULARIES

Of all 528 separate user-created search terms in the dataset, 42 are field searches for particular titles, authors, identifiers and languages. They were excluded from the comparison with RILM's index terms. Of all 486 user-created search terms that were compared to RILM's index terms, 166 (34.16%) perfectly matched RILM's index terms, 169 (34.77%) partially matched and 151 (31.07%) did not match. This indicates that RILM's index terms align well with users' search terms. It is apparent that RILM's index terms included in the bibliographic records are useful to searchers. Of 169 partial-matching user-created search terms, 104 (61.54%) are personal names, 31 (18.34%) are work titles, 23 (13.61%) are topical terms, four (2.37%) are chronological terms, three (1.78%) are corporate body names, three (1.78%) are instruments and one (0.59%) is a geographic name. Most of the partial-matching user-created search terms are work titles and personal names. This is mainly due to the use of partial names (e.g., missing first name, middle name and birth year) and partial titles (e.g., missing opus number) as search terms and the complexity of RILM's authorized forms of names and titles. RILM could consider incorporating into its system such functionalities as name and title suggestion and disambiguation (e.g., using Wikipedia's disambiguation pages and the LC Authority Files) to reduce users' cognitive load. Topical terms are the third most frequently occurring partial-matching user-created search terms. The reasons for partial-matching topical terms varied, including the use of singular form, broader terms, narrower terms, synonymous terms, abbreviations, phrases in different word order and variant spellings. RILM could consider several suggestions: using spell-checker and stemming; adding abbreviations, acronyms, broader, narrower and synonymous terms to RILM's thesaurus; linking terms with hierarchical and associative relationships; including more cross-references in the thesaurus; and providing users with access to the thesaurus. Of 151 non-matching user-created search terms, six are new or popular topical terms, which can be added to RILM's thesaurus; and seven are terms in a different language. RILM could consider developing multilingual thesaurus to better serve users in different countries and index literature in different languages.

## CONCLUSION AND FUTURE RESEARCH

This poster presents the categories of users' free-text queries created in a music literature database and the mapping between those queries to the controlled vocabularies used by the database. Future research will conduct interviews with database users to learn about their information needs, and how they create and revise queries.

## REFERENCES


Kelly, E. (2010). Music indexing and retrieval: Current problems. *The Indexer, 28*(4), 163-166.

Myers, J. A. (1995). Music: Characteristics for indexing and cataloguing. *The Indexer, 19*(4), 269-274.

Nowick, E. A., & Mering, M. (2003). Comparisons between internet users' free-text queries and controlled vocabularies: A case study in water quality. *Technical Services Quarterly, 21*(2), 15-32.

Powell, R. R., & Connaway, L. S. (2004). *Basic research methods for librarians* (4th ed.). Westport, CT: Libraries Unlimited.

Soergel, D. (1974). *Indexing languages and thesauri: Construction and maintenance*. Los Angeles, CA: Wiley.

White, H. (2013). Examining scientific vocabulary: Mapping controlled vocabularies with free text keywords. *Cataloging & Classification Quarterly, 51*(6), 655-674.

# AnnotationOne: A Global Annotation System

**Shenmeng Xu**
*School of Information and Library Science University of North Carolina at Chapel Hill, USA. shenmeng@email.unc.edu*

**Bradley M. Hemminger**
*School of Information and Library Science University of North Carolina at Chapel Hill, USA. bmh@ils.unc.edu*

## ABSTRACT

**Our study presents a web-based annotation tool, AnnotationOne, developed to facilitate the easier creation and global sharing of annotations. Our aim is to create conversations around scholarly content benefitting everyone and forging new connections between scholars. Using this tool, users can read and make globally accessible annotations shared with a large scale of users. User studies were conducted to investigate the utility of this universal annotations system. Subjects completed tasks including making annotations, initial reading with annotations and re-reading with annotations on our prototype system. Both observations and interviews were conducted to explore whether and how this annotation tool would be beneficial for scholarly communication. Moreover, we also collected subjects' suggestions to improve this tool's usability.**

## KEYWORDS

scholarly communication, annotation, electronic reading, digital library

## INTRODUCTION

In academic settings, one challenge in electronic reading and sense-making is to make annotations in specific parts of articles. Unlike the traditional print-based annotation approach which normally can be completed with a pen, making digital annotations relies on the utility of certain functionalities of certain tools in electronic devices. Taking notes in a separate document while reading digitally can somewhat complement the reading with a basic tool, but it loses information that annotations contain – the location of the corresponding text of the notes.

Some limitations exist in current widely used reading tools. For instance, in Adobe Reader one of the most commonly used annotation tools, annotations are made in sticky notes-like boxes. These sticky notes are made everywhere on a document, as opposed to being displayed in one single annotation panel. To avoid them blocking the main text, the sticky notes are oftentimes folded, making it highly inconvenient to browse the content of all the annotations without having to click on them one by one. It would be even more inconvenient when the amount of annotations is large. Another limitation is the cumbersomeness when switching between the highlighting and the annotation functionalities. The collaboration feature is also an important consideration in reading and annotation tools, especially in academic activities where sharing is critical to the dissemination of knowledge. Adobe Acrobat, which requires a fee-based license, allows the sharing of article documents with annotations but is only limited to relatively smaller groups of users as opposed to the public.

In this visual presentation proposal, firstly we introduce the construction and current functionalities of AnnotationOne. A brief description of the design of multiple rounds of user studies is provided. Due to limited space, our literature review will be available in our follow-up publication. We will present our preliminary results at the conference. The annotation functionality has existed in electronic reading for a long time, but its usage in academic settings is underexplored. Our study hopes to fill in this niche and potentially initialize more discussions on this topic.

## FORMAT OF PRESENTATION

Our presentation will include two parts: a printed poster and a laptop with a live display of AnnotationOne. An enlarged static screenshot of our tool will be displayed on the poster. Study design details and our preliminary results will be presented. Meanwhile, we will welcome the audience to interact with our tool on our laptop – to browse existing annotations, to make their own annotations and to play with settings of the tool, etc. On the poster, a link (TinyURL) and a QR code to an example article on AnnotationOne will be provided so that the audience can play with our tool on their own laptops after the poster session. We will also be collecting their opinions on potential improvement that can help enhance its usability.

## ANNOTATIONONE INTERFACE

As is shown in Fig. 1, the annotation tool interface mainly consists of two panes. The left pane displays the text of the article, and the right pane is the annotation area. Annotated text is highlighted with either different shades of yellow (other users') or light blue (the current user's). Both the text and the corresponding annotations become highlighted in pink when either of them is hovered on, allowing users to match the annotations with the corresponding text.

In this tool, we conceptualize highlighting and annotating in one functionality. A *highlight* is a span of highlighted text and an empty highlight; an *annotation* includes a span of highlighted text and an annotation with actual text.

80th Annual Meeting of the Association for Information Science & Technology, Washington, DC | Oct. 27-Nov. 1, 2017

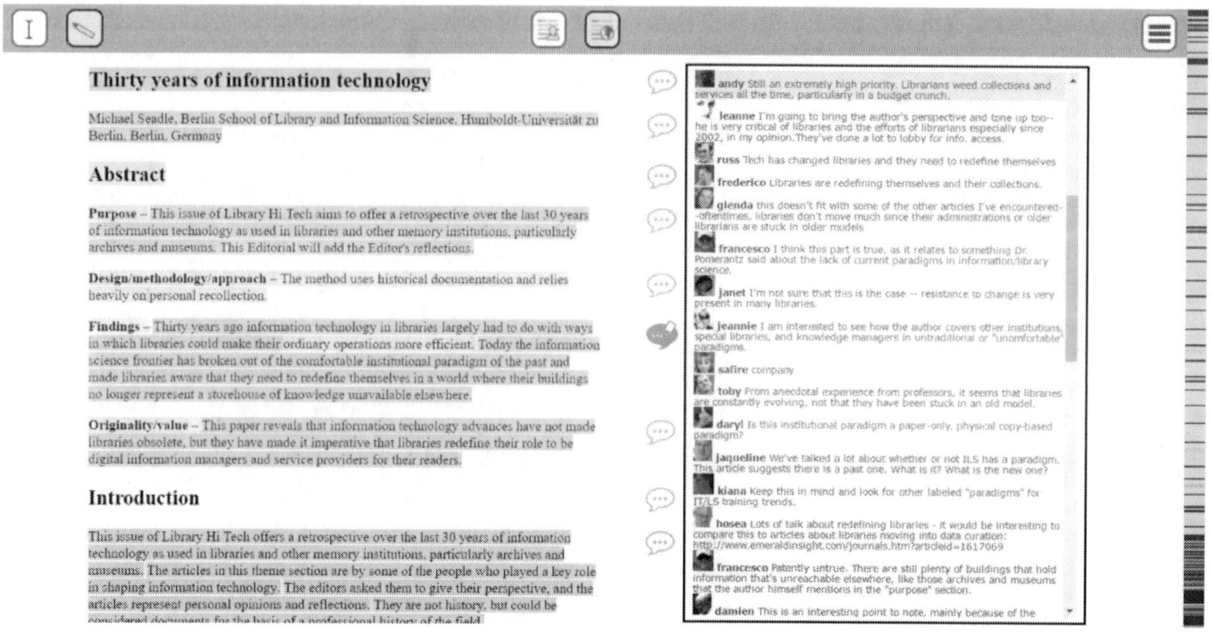


***Figure 1.*** *Screenshot of AnnotationOne interface*

The two buttons on the upper left corner allow users to switch the functionality of the mouse between a selector and an annotator. In the selector mode, the cursor functions as a normal one; in the annotator mode, text selected by the cursor is automatically annotated on. The two buttons in the middle of the upper menu allow users to turn on or off the highlights from other users. In the "show mine only" mode, only blue highlights are shown; in the "show all highlights" mode, both blue and yellow highlights are shown.

Other settings can be accessed in the "hamburger" button in the upper right corner. Statistics of annotations and users can be viewed. Annotations can be displayed in "Icons," "Snippets" or "Full." Empty annotations can be hidden. Moreover, a heat map index bar can display the density of annotations, thus assisting users in article navigation.

An example article can be accessed at http://secure-dusk-1121.herokuapp.com/version9/a2?db=annotationplaypen&user=andy.

## STUDY DESIGN

In Phase I of our study, 28 doctoral and master students were recruited from School of Information and Library Science at UNC-Chapel Hill. They were asked to play different personas and make annotations using different marking styles and note-taking styles on six articles.

In Phase II, the same participants read two articles in their own personas and were interviewed. They each read a new article (initial reading) and an old article on which they had made annotations (re-reading).

Phase III is intertwined with tool improving, testing and more user studies with more participants.

Phase IV is the final round of user studies. We recruited 27 new participants. Each of them completed two initial reading tasks and was interviewed.

## DISCUSSION

With large scale of annotations, AnnotationOne has the potential to accelerate academic reading, sense-making and scholarly communication. If properly filtered and displayed, the annotations can assist in both initial reading and re-reading of articles. AnnotationOne might help in classroom discussions, collaborative research project, online courses, reading groups, peer review, class assignments, personal research and other types of discussions among trusted people. Moreover, it could potentially generate helpful data for altmetrics as well.

One main challenge of the tool design is dealing with the large scale of annotations. It is necessary to work out a more sensible way of ordering the annotation list. Filters and ranking systems might provide complementary assistance in improving the readability of the annotations. Moreover, the functionality of searching across annotations is critical for locating the content of users' interest.

Credential and authority of users in academic reading are a big concern, especially in an environment of information overload. The inability to provide such information would hinder the utility of such an academic annotation system.

## ACKNOWLEDGEMENTS

AnnotationOne has been refined over years. We would like to acknowledge the work of previous research assistants (Jason Priem, Michael Head, Sreenivas Reddy and Zhenwei Wang) who have contributed to the development of this tool.

# Analyzing Patterns of Contribution to User-generated Tag Hierarchies Based on Core User Types


**Yuyu Yang**
*Department of Information Management, Peking University, China. yangyuyu@pku.edu.cn*

**Pengyi Zhang**
*Department of Information Management, Peking University, China. pengyi@pku.edu.cn*



## ABSTRACT

**Widely applied social tagging systems with semantic relations created by users have not been fully explored. This study aims to explore user types and their contribution during construction of the tag hierarchy of Zhihu.com, a social Q&A website in China. We conducted log analysis on 284,018 log records crawled from the website, conducted statistical analysis, social network and temporal analysis. Results show that there are four user types based on user editing preference: concept creator, concept reviser, relation editor and extensive contributor. Results suggest that there are plenty of differences between the four types, including the amount of contribution, the influence on collaboration and the temporal pattern. It was learned that relation editors play a most important role during the construction and extensive contributors contributed most on average. Besides, concept creators' activity level decreased from the beginning and concept revisers have a relatively stable activity pattern. These findings shed light on user contribution patterns during the collaborative construction of tag hierarchies.**



## KEYWORDS

social tagging, tagging behavior, tag hierarchies, Zhihu.com


## INTRODUCTION

As a powerful tool to organize information, social tagging is widely applied in many Web 2.0 applications. The collaboratively created folksonomy often lack semantic relations compared with controlled vocabulary. Plenty of methods have been put forward aiming to build semantic relations between tags, including both automatic and manual approaches, for example, using algorithms to calculate the similarity between tags to support hierarchical navigation (Heymann & Garcia-Molina, 2006; Zhou & King, 2009) and involving users in the process by asking users to provide a pair of tags "tag1-tag2" where tag1 is a label for a resource and tag2 is a broader term of tag1 (Kiu & Tsui, 2011). Crowd-sourcing the pairwise hierarchical relationship of tags to users and combining automatic and human efforts to create a taxonomy from tags (Wang, Sattar Chaudhry & Khoo, 2008) seem to be an effective approach. However, prior research on user participation in social taxonomy construction has been conducted mostly in experiment systems with limited number of users and tags. There has been little research on how users participated in generating tag hierarchies in widely used platforms.

Previous research has examined tagging behavior of flat folksonomies extensively. Golbeck, Koepfler and Emmerling (2011) found that there are significant differences in the number, order and type of tags assigned by users based on their past experience with an image, the type of image being tagged and other image features. Lin and Chen (2012) identified four user types during the construction: intermediary, secondary follower, dominator and outsider. Špiranec & Ivanjko (2013) found that users with more knowledge and expertise could create tags of higher quality than novice users. However, little research has been done to understand how users contribute to generation of tag hierarchies.

This research aims to understand users' contribution pattern during the construction of tags and their semantic relations based on their editing preferences on Zhihu.com. Zhihu.com is a popular social Q&A (SQA) website in China attracting nearly 50 million users. In addition to tagging questions, users also edit hierarchical relations between tags (topics). The tag hierarchy plays an important role in searching and navigating the questions. These relationship edits were recorded as tag (topic) editing logs.

Our research questions are listed below:

- What are the user types based on their editing preference?
- What characteristics of these types?
- What are the temporal patterns of their contribution?

## METHODS

### *Data Collection*

We used a Web crawler to collect tag hierarchy's editing records on Zhihu.com. The editing log dates from December, 2012 to October, 2015. The whole dataset contains 284,018 log records of 60,175 topics contributed by 29,985 users. Figure 1 shows some example log records.

| #LogID | Username | Action | Relationship | Term 1 | Term 2 | Date | Time |
|---|---|---|---|---|---|---|---|
| 10813029 | 陈** | Add | Narrower Term | Mobile Internet | Mobile OS | 2013-07-23 | 23:09:28 |
| 35273205 | 张** | Add | Broader Term | Mobile Internet | TMT | 2014-04-04 | 23:45:00 |
| 43135084 | 黄** | Delete | Narrower Term | Mobile Internet | weChat | 2014-06-04 | 11:01:12 |

***Figure 1**. Example log records*

The topic logs record nine types of edits, which we categorized into concept edits and relation edits.


80th Annual Meeting of the Association for Information Science & Technology, Washington, DC | Oct. 27-Nov. 1, 2017

A total of 29,985 users participated in tag hierarchy construction. Users' editing frequencies follow a power-law distribution ($R^2$=0.947), indicating that a small part of users edited most part of the tag hierarchies. Considering that the vast majority of users contributed very little to the hierarchical relationships, we selected the top 1,397 users as "core users" for analysis whose editing frequencies counts for more than 80% of all edits cumulatively.

## DATA ANALYSIS

### User Types

We selected top 1,397 core users to analyze their editing preferences and calculated the percent of each editing type including creating a concept, revising a concept, editing synonym relation and editing hierarchical relation (see Table 1). Based on the processed data, we conducted user cluster through the two-step cluster methods with SPSS.

| | | |
|---|---|---|
| Concept edits | Creating a concept | Creating topic |
| | Revising a concept | Editing topic description<br>Editing topic name<br>Editing topic picture |
| Relationship edits | Editing synonym relation | Adding topic alias<br>Removing topic alias |
| | Editing hierarchical relation | Adding parent topic<br>Removing parent topic<br>Editing weak relationship |

***Table 1.*** *Editing types*

### Collaboration Network

We constructed collaboration network based on co-editing relationships among users. In this undirected network, users are represented as vertices, and an arc exists between two users if they edit the same topic. We chose several measures to understand users' importance in the collaboration network: (1) degree – the number of neighbors of a vertex; (2) betweenness centrality – the extent to which a vertex lies on paths between other vertices; (3) eigenvector centrality, which describes the importance of a vertex's neighbors (De Nooy, Mrvar & Batagelj, 2011).

### Temporal patterns

To explore temporal patterns of each user type, including number of members and contributions, we aggregated log records by month and plotted the amount of contributions by month as an area chart.

## RESULTS

### User Types

Clustering results suggest 4 types of users:

1. Concept creator (CC): creating concepts
2. Concept reviser (CR): revising concepts
3. **Relation editor (RE):** editing hierarchical relations
4. **Extensive contributor (EC):** no inclination to any particular type of edits

Table 2 shows the number of users and edits of each type. Among them, there are more relation editors while extensive contributors contributed most edits on average.

| | CC | CR | RE | EC |
|---|---|---|---|---|
| # of users | 364 | 342 | 530 | 159 |
| (%) | 26.1% | 24.6% | 38.0% | 11.4% |
| # of edits | 19,678 | 18,336 | 193,563 | 62,078 |
| (%) | 8.3% | 7.3% | 60.3% | 24.1% |
| Average # of edits per user | 52.1 | 48.7 | 259.7 | 345.6 |

***Table 2.*** *Number of users and edits of each type*

K-Wallis test shows that there are significant differences between these four user types on editing frequencies, the number of editing topics and activity duration (see Table 3).

| Mean (rank) | # of edits | # of topics | Duration |
|---|---|---|---|
| CC | 579.25 (4) | 738.16 (2) | 823.49 (1) |
| CR | 651.60 (3) | 553.81 (4) | 736.73 (2) |
| RE | 805.46 (1) | 799.47 (1) | 615.65 (3) |
| EC | 716.14 (2) | 583.25 (3) | 601.91 (4) |
| Chi-Square | 74.212** | 94.023** | 69.699** |

***Table 3.*** *Differences between user types (**p<0.01)*

Relation editors contribute most edits and more distinct topics. Concept creators contribute less to the taxonomy than the other three types, but have the longest activity duration.

Although these 1,397 core users' contributions account for more than 80 percent of all edits, they only created 45% of the topics. The other 55% of the topics were created by other users.

### User Collaboration

The whole networks contain 1397 vertices and have average degrees of 157 (see Table 4).

| Feature | Value |
|---|---|
| Vertices (Users) | 1397 |
| Arcs (Collaboration) | 109789 |
| Density | 0.112 |
| Average degree | 156.8 |
| Diameter | 3 |
| Average Path Length | 1.9 |
| Cluster Coefficient | 0.739 |

***Table 4.*** *SNA features of collaboration network*

Topologic analysis indicates that this network has only one component, constituted by central members and other members. Central members play an important role in this network.

Analysis shows that editing frequencies are highly correlated with betweeness centrality (coefficient = 0.86, sig. < 0.01), demonstrating that the more a user contributed the higher the possibility that the user takes an important role in this network.

Results of K-Wallis test suggest there are significant diffrences between the four user types in network characteristics (Table 5). Relation editors have the highest degrees of betweeness centrality and eigencentrality, which demonstrates that they play an important role in the collaboration network, followed by extensive contributors, concept revisers, and concept creators.

| Mean (rank) | Degree | Betweeness centrality | Eigenvector centrality |
|---|---|---|---|
| CC | 470.06(4) | 451.51(4) | 471.34(4) |
| CR | 621.77(3) | 638.98(3) | 622.66(3) |
| RE | 898.97(1) | 900.67(1) | 898.90(1) |
| EC | 718.77(2) | 718.43(2) | 714.14(2) |
| Chi-Square | 260.78** | 277.798** | 258.927** |

***Table 5**. Differences between user types (**p<0.01)*

### *Temporal Patterns*

Figure 2 shows the percentage of users (a) and edits (b) contributed by each type.

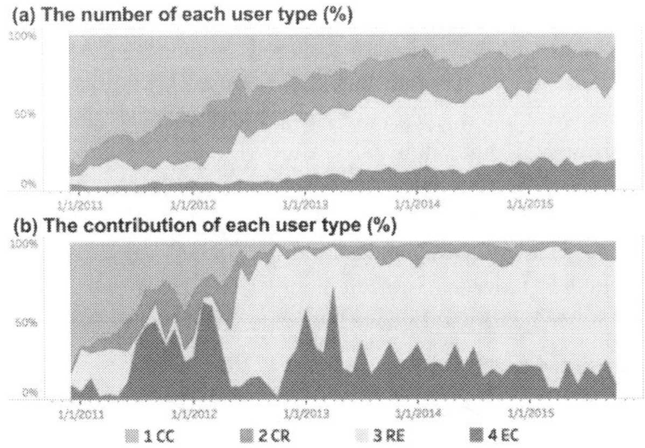


***Figure 2**. Temporal patterns of each user type*

At the beginning, concept creators take up the majority of all members and contribute most to the taxonomy. As time goes by, both the number of concept creators and their contribution decrease, while relation editors increase, contributing more to the taxonomy. The fluctuation of concept revisers is relatively stable both on the number of members and their contribution. Extensive contributors gradually increase from the beginning and their contribution fluctuates.

## CONCLUSION AND DISCUSSION

In this poster, we present four user types and their contribution patterns during the construction of tag hierarchies:

- **Concept creators** have the longest activity duration but they are least well connected in the collaboration network. They are quite active at the beginning but their activity level decreases gradually.
- **Concept revisers** are better connected than concept creators but contribute least number of edits on average. Their activity is relatively stable over time.
- **Relation editors** contribute most to the taxonomy and are best connected in the collaboration network. Their activity level was low at the beginning but became much higher over time.
- **Extensive contributors** contribute the highest edits on average. They are also well connected in collaboration network.

Our poster reports an initial attempt to explore user types and user contribution during the construction of Zhihu's tag hierarchy. The results are valuable to system designers and community servers to achieve deeper understanding of their contributors and guide them to construct tag hierarchies of higher quality. Further research could verify whether these user types exist in other similar platforms such as Quora's ontology or Wikipedia's classification.

## REFERENCES


De Nooy, W., Mrvar, A. & Batagelj, V. (2011). *Exploratory social network analysis with Pajek* (Vol. 27): Cambridge University Press.

Golbeck, J., Koepfler, J. & Emmerling, B. (2011). An experimental study of social tagging behavior and image content. *Journal of the American Society for Information Science and Technology, 62*, 1750-1760.

Heymann, P., & Garcia-Molina, H. (2006). *Collaborative creation of communal hierarchical taxonomies in social tagging systems.* Stanford InfoLab

Kiu, C.-C., & Tsui, E. (2011). TaxoFolk: A hybrid taxonomy–folksonomy structure for knowledge classification and navigation. *Expert Systems with Applications, 38*, 6049-6058.

Lin, C.-S., & Chen, Y.-F. (2012). Examining social tagging behaviour and the construction of an online folksonomy from the perspectives of cultural capital and social capital. *Journal of Information Science, 38*, 540-557.

Špiranec, S., & Ivanjko, T. (2013). Experts vs. novices tagging behavior: An exploratory analysis. *Procedia-Social and Behavioral Sciences, 73*, 456-459.

Wang, Z., Sattar Chaudhry, A. & Khoo, C. S. G. (2008). Using classification schemes and thesauri to build an organizational taxonomy for organizing content and aiding navigation. *Journal of Documentation, 64*, 842-876.

Zhou, T. C., & King, I. (2009). Automobile, car and BMW: Horizontal and hierarchical approach in social tagging systems. *Proceedings of the 2nd ACM workshop on social web search and mining*, 25-32.

# Towards Understanding Consumers' Quality Evaluation of Online Health Information: A Case Study

**Zequn Ye**
*University of Texas at Austin, USA. zequn@utexas.edu*

**Jacek Gwizdka**
*University of Texas at Austin, USA. asist2017@gwizdka.com*

**Carla Teixeira Lopes**
*Universidade do Porto, Portugal. lairesun05@utexas.edu, ctl@fe.up.pt*

**Yan Zhang**
*University of Texas at Austin, USA. yanz@ischool.utexas.edu*

## ABSTRACT

**We present a case study of quality evaluation of online health information. Two participants were selected from a health information search (HIS) study, in which we are investigating consumers' evaluation of the quality of online health information. The selected cases offered a rare example of two almost exactly opposite eye-movement patterns on the same webpage. To better understand the differences in these patterns, we investigated participants' cognitive evaluation processes by examining their textual explanations collected in post-task questionnaires and verbal explanations collected in the retrospective think-aloud (RTA) sessions. We discuss how eHealth literacy and personality scores may be related to the behavioral differences. The findings of this case study inform the formulation of hypotheses for full data analysis of the HIS study, as well as future research addressing behavior patterns and factors affecting consumers' quality evaluation of online health information.**

## KEYWORDS

eye-movement, quality evaluation, health information, eHealth literacy, personality

## INTRODUCTION

The internet has become the most used, and often the first, go-to information source for ordinary health consumers (Marrie et al., 2013). The quality of online health information presents as a major concern for all stakeholders involved in the online health information ecosystem. Evaluating information quality remains to a major challenge for consumers (Feufel & Stahl, 2012). Much research has been done to examine this topic. It was found that individual factors, such as age, education levels and health literacy, influence health information evaluation behavior (Lam & Lam, 2012; Liao & Fu, 2014). However, little is known about how consumers evaluate online health information quality and what exactly the challenges are.

In the online environment, hundreds of interface and content elements (e.g., author, dates and copyright) could serve as quality indicators (Zhang, Sun & Xie, 2015). To enhance the current understanding of consumers' quality evaluation behavior, we adopted a mixed method approach, using eye-tracking and retrospective interviews to examine what interface elements are being used for quality evaluation and whether individual differences, primarily eHealth literacy and personality, influence the behavior.

## METHODS

We recruited 12 participants (we plan to recruit 48 in total). The study was conducted in a lab with a PC and an eye-tracking device. Participants first filled out demographic, personality and e-health literacy questionnaires. They then performed a practice task to ensure that everyone understands the study process. Then, each participant was presented with five predefined health information search tasks (orders were randomized). For each task, we preselected three webpages. Participants were asked to examine the three pages and determine whether they would recommend the pages to their family or friends. A retrospective think-aloud (RTA) session was performed after the completion of all the five tasks.

In this paper, we present data from two participants, because of their drastically different eye-movement patterns on one webpage. They were scanning and reading the page for the following scenario:

> *Imagine that one of your friends is struggling with whether to have her teenage son receive an influenza vaccine. So you conducted an online search, these three webpages are among the pages that show up in the search results. After browsing each page, you will determine whether you want to share this page to your friend.*

---

80th Annual Meeting of the Association for Information Science & Technology, Washington, DC | Oct. 27-Nov. 1, 2017

## RESULTS

The gaze plots of the two participants show almost exactly opposite (i.e., not overlapping) eye-movement patterns (Figure 1). Gaze plots display the position, order and (roughly) time spent fixating at locations on a stimulus. P1's gaze plots roughly resemble an *F*, which corresponds to the F-shaped pattern in viewing text-based web content (Nielsen, 2006), and most of the fixations are on the main content area, where their sequence indicates focused reading of topical information (Gwizdka, 2014). By contrast, P2's gaze plots show an atypical pattern with fixations scattered at the top, right side and bottom areas, and only a few of them located in the main content area.

***Figure 1**. Gaze plots of P1 (left) and P2 (right)*

Task performance of the two participants (including choice made on this page, time on task, time on page, count of links clicked on) and their background information (including eHEALS and TIPI scores) are shown in Table 1. P1's eHEALS score is substantially lower than P2. P1 spent significantly longer time (both time on task and time on page) than P2.

| | | P1 | P2 |
|---|---|---|---|
| Choice (share or not) | | No | No |
| Time on Task | | 176s | 41s |
| Time on Page | | 85s | 38s |
| Click on links | | To homepage | N/A |
| eHEALS Score | | 21 | 36 |
| TIPI | Extraversion | 1.0 | 5.5 |
| | Agreeableness | 4.0 | 6.5 |
| | Conscientiousness | 2.5 | 7.0 |
| | Emotional Stability | 4.5 | 3.5 |
| | Openness to Experiences | 6.0 | 7.0 |

***Table 1**. Task performances, eHEALS and TIPI scores*

Table 2 shows examples of web elements mentioned by the two participants in the RTA interviews and their short comment on these elements.

## SUMMARY

The differences in eye-movement patterns can be attributed to many factors, such as one's demographic factors, familiarity with and interest in the task topic, as well as health literacy. Nevertheless, the preliminary observations based on currently collected data allow us to formulate working hypotheses. Here are a few plausible examples:

| | Page Element | Comment |
|---|---|---|
| P1 | A cartoon | Not serious |
| | Social media widget | Not relevant |
| P2 | Title and logo image | Don't know what it is |
| | Layout and design | Doubting a lot |
| | Related posts | Very fear based |
| | Donate sign | A big no |

***Table 2**. Example of phrases from RTA interviews*

Compared with higher eHealth literacy, people with lower eHealth literacy tend to:

**H1a:** spend more time on quality evaluation;

**H1b:** rely more on relevance than on quality indicators.

In evaluating health-related webpage quality:

**H2a:** People with lower eHealth literacy tend to rely more on the main content of a webpage than on quality indicators;

**H2b**: People with higher eHealth literacy are able to take advantage of quality indicators.

We will begin testing these hypotheses after collecting data from more participants.

## REFERENCES


Feufel MA. & Stahl SF. (2012). What do web-use skill differences imply for online health information searches? *J Med Internet Res*, *14*(3): e87.

Gwizdka, J. (2014). Characterizing relevance with eye-tracking measures. *Proceedings of IIiX'2014* (pp. 58-67). New York, NY, USA: ACM.

Nielsen, J. (2006). F-shaped pattern for reading web content. Retrieved May 25th, 2017 from https://www.nngroup.com/articles/f-shaped-pattern-reading-web-content/

Lam, M. K., & Lam, L. T. (2012). Health information-seeking behavior on the internet and health literacy among older Australians. *Electronic Journal of Health Informatics*, *7*(2), 15.

Liao, Q. V., & Fu, W. T. (2014). Age differences in credibility judgments of online health information. ACM ToCHI, *21*(1), 2:1-2:23.

Marrie, R. A., Salter, A. R., Tyry, T., Fox, R. J. & Cutter, G. R. (2013). Preferred sources of health information in persons with multiple sclerosis: Degree of trust and information sought. *Journal of Medical Internet Research*, *15*(4), e67. http://doi.org/10.2196/jmir.2466

Zhang, Y., Sun, Y. & Xie, B. (2015), Quality of health information for consumers on the web: A systematic review of indicators, criteria, tools, and evaluation results. *JASIST*, *66*: 2071–2084

# Exploring Text Classification of Social Support in Online Health Communities for People Who are D/deaf and Hard of Hearing

**Biyang Yu**
*Florida State University, USA. by13b@my.fsu.edu*

**Zhe He**
*Florida State University, USA. zhe.he@cci.fsu.edu*

**Lynette Gerido**
*Florida State University, USA. lhg16@my.fsu.edu*

## ABSTRACT

**Due to the social oppressions from the mainstream society, social support becomes fundamental for people who are D/deaf and hard of hearing (D/hh) to exchange information within their own community. We aim to examine the support content of messages and how support processes become established by exploring the interactions within a D/hh discussion forum, AllDeaf.com, which is one of the leading online communities for D/hh. In this pilot study, we first employed content analysis to code discussion posts using the Social Support Behavior Code. Two authors collaboratively coded a random sample of 25 threads and 632 posts. Informational support was observed as the most frequently exchanged type of social support for people who are D/hh. Then we identified social support features used for future text classification task. Our preliminary qualitative findings indicated that the linguistic and lexical features have the potential to support automated feature identification and social support classification typology with text mining techniques**

## KEYWORDS

social support, online health community, disability, people who are D/deaf and hard of hearing

## INTRODUCTION

As a platform to provide health care services, to discuss health and treatment related issues, experiences and problems and to provide mutual support, online health communities become one of the main sources for people who are looking for information and peer support. A Pew study reported that around 18% of internet users have looked online for peer support (Fox, 2011). For disabled people, especially those who are D/deaf and hard of hearing (D/hh), online communities serve as a critical venue to temporally suppress discrimination and promote social interactions (Guo, Bricout & Huang, 2005), which offsets their lack of and dissatisfaction with communication in the real life (Cummings, Sproull & Kiesler, 2002). Here, the terms *Deaf* or *deaf* and *hard of hearing* refer to people who are culturally Deaf (i.e., use sign language and affiliate to Deaf culture), audiologically deaf and hard of hearing, respectively. Within hearing culture, the ideology that deafness is a disability is so engrained that many D/hh people are marginalized and oppressed as a cultural group (Carter and Mireles, 2016). Many D/hh tend to feel more comfortable sharing information and support within their own online communities, rather than communities of the general public (Valentine, Skelton & Levy, 2006). Therefore, to better adapt to their unique health information needs and behaviors, it is important to understand the characteristics of social support within the D/hh online health communities.

This pilot study aims to examine the support content of messages on an online D/hh health community through qualitative content analysis. As text mining has the potential to automatically identify the patterns and classify posts on large amounts of content in online communities, we further explored the extraction of linguistic/lexical features of social support typology for text classification.

### *Research Questions*

Specifically, this pilot study aims to answer following two questions:

1. How are different types of social support distributed within online health communities for D/hh people?
2. What are the quantifiable linguistic/lexical features of social support in online health communities for D/hh people?

## METHOD

### *Social Support Behavior Code*

The theoretical framework we utilized to investigate the typology of social support is Social Support Behavior Code (SSBC), which identifies two broad categories, five types of support-intended communication behaviors and 23 subcategories (Cutrona & Suhr, 1992).

Those five support types include: *information support*, which refers to providing advice, information or experiences of an issue or problem or ways to deal with that problem; *network support,* which builds the sense of community or interpersonal relationship; *emotional support,* referring to expressing

80th Annual Meeting of the Association for Information Science & Technology, Washington, DC | Oct. 27-Nov. 1, 2017

love, empathy or concerns, etc., to comfort members in certain situations; *esteem support*, which expresses respect or confidence assurance in individuals' abilities to deal with problems; and *tangible assistance*, which offers goods or services directly to community members or participate some activities to support other members.

All five types of social support were grouped into one of two categories: action-facilitating support or nurturant support, the former fosters behavior to mitigate a stressor (including informational and tangible support), and the latter provides emotional comforts (including emotional, esteem and network support).

Previous studies utilized qualitative content analysis to code a limited number of posts in various communities (Coulson, Buchanan & Aubeeluck, 2007). In this study, we tested the feasibility of using text classification techniques to identify the social support typology for posts. Towards this goal, the first step is to identify possible quantifiable features related to social support typology, including lexical features, linguistic features, topic model features, etc. We aggregated the same kinds of features appropriately to reduce the sparseness of the feature space.

### Data Collection

We collected data from AllDeaf (http://www.alldeaf.com/), which is one of the globally leading online communities for D/hh people who can communicate in English. This community has 22 forums in which people can communicate about a wide range of everyday life concerns related to deafness, such as sign language, assistive technologies and health. The majority of the health-related issues are discussed in the forum, *Lifestyle, Health, Fitness & Food*. After manually deleting the threads that are unrelated to health (e.g., food recipe), we were left with 1,639 threads and 31,006 posts from that forum, which includes health discussions from 2005 to 2016. In this pilot study, we randomly chose 25 threads and 632 posts that are related to health.

### Data Processing and Analysis

Two authors coded the social support typology on the utterance level for each post separately, according to 23 subcategories suggested by SSBC. The authors assigned one or more codes to utterances within each post when applicable. NVivo 11.0 was used for the qualitative content analysis. The kappa coefficiency of inter-coder reliability was 0.71, indicating substantial agreement. The conflicts among the coders were resolved after the discussions.

After mapping the social support types to the utterances in each post, we extracted the linguistic and lexical features in those utterances that were unique to the mapped social support type. For example, referral is one subcategory under informational support, which means referring the recipient to some external source of information. We observed when information is shared referring a community member to another information source, not surprisingly, a URL is often included in a post. In this case "Is a URL?" is a feature of information referral. In this pilot study, we used the major classification methods, such as support vector machine, to test the feasibility of using these features for text classification.

## PRELIMINARY FINDING

Some form of social support was exchanged in every post in our sample. Within the sample, we found 493 utterances related to action-facilitating support (informational support 485, tangible assistance 8), whereas nurturant support were only found in 120 utterances (network support 13, esteem support 42 and emotional support 65). We extracted 107 quantifiable features in 23 subcategories. We also annotated individual posts that were found to have more nuanced language. Because the social support types were unequally distributed among our sample, the majority features were related to subcategories of informational support. In the visual presentation, we will report the social support distribution in our sample, our extracted features, as well as the preliminary results of text classification for two main categories of social support.

## FORMAT AND CONTENT

In the visual presentation, we will report our study in a poster format. In the poster, we will specify the introduction, research questions, method and preliminary findings of our study. Two authors will give a 3-5 minute oral presentations to the audience, and answer possible questions afterwards.

## REFERENCES


Carter, M. J., & Mireles, D. C. (2016). Deaf identity and depression. *New Directions in Identity Theory and Research*, 509-538.

Coulson, N. S., Buchanan, H., & Aubeeluck, A. (2007). Social support in cyberspace: A content analysis of communication within a Huntington's disease online support group. *Patient Education and Counseling*, *68*(2), 173-178. https://doi.org/10.1016/j.pec.2007.06.002

Cummings, J. N., Sproull, L. & Kiesler, S. B. (2002). Beyond hearing: Where the real-world and online support meet. *Group Dynamics: Theory, Research, and Practice*, *6*(1), 78-88. https://doi.org/10.1037/1089-2699.6.1.78

Cutrona, C. E., & Suhr, J. A. (1992). Controllability of stressful events and satisfaction with spouse support behaviors. *Communication Research*, *19*(2), 154-174. https://doi.org/10.1177/009365092019002002

Fox, S. (2011, February 28). Peer-to-peer health. Retrieved March 13, 2016, from http://www.pewinternet.org/2011/02/28/peer-to-peer-health/

Guo, B., Bricout, J. C., & Huang, J. (2005). A common open space or a digital divide? A social model perspective on the online disability community in China. *Disability & Society*, *20*(1), 49-66. https://doi.org/10.1080/0968759042000283638

Valentine, G., Skelton, T. & Levy, P. (2006). *The role of the internet in d/deaf people's inclusion in the information society*. Retrieved from http://www.geog.leeds.ac.uk/projects/deaf-web/FullDeaf%20report.

# Quality Assurance and Evaluation of Change for Patent Metadata

**Oksana L. Zavalina**
*University of North Texas, USA. Oksana.Zavalina@unt.edu*

**Hannah S. Tarver**
*University of North Texas, USA. Hannah.Tarver@unt.edu*

**Mark Phillips**
*University of North Texas, USA. Mark.Phillips@unt.edu*

## ABSTRACT

**The quality of metadata greatly impacts access to information resources, affecting both precision and recall of the search results. Metadata quality assurance is especially important for unique materials that are not widely available outside of the specialized digital repositories that provide access to them. One example of such unique and valuable materials is digitized historical patents. This paper describes a case study of the metadata management for a digital collection of U.S. patents issued in the 19th-early 20th centuries, discusses the results of the evaluation of metadata change intended to support the metadata quality assurance for this collection and presents plans for further research. We expect the study to make a contribution to understanding of metadata management and metadata quality assurance and the role of metadata change in these processes.**

## KEYWORDS

metadata quality, patent metadata, metadata change, metadata evaluation

## INTRODUCTION

Metadata quality assurance requires making changes to metadata to improve its quality, which is most often identified through completeness, consistency and accuracy criteria (e.g., Barton, Currier & Hay, 2003; Bruce & Hillmann, 2004; Park & Tosaka, 2010). Metadata change is the evolving area of empirical research. Several studies with the focus on metadata change analysis and categorization focused either on MARC library metadata or on non-MARC metadata in digital collections of a wide scope. The case study presented below attempts to fill the gap by focusing on a specialized collection that relies on non-MARC metadata.

Although the historical patents issued by the U.S. Patent Office are full-text searchable through Google Patents, the accessibility is limited due to lack of descriptive metadata. The Texas Patents (TP) collection maintained by the Portal to Texas History (hereafter Portal) contains official patents issued to the state residents and provides descriptive metadata to facilitate access to TP collection that are of interest to researchers within and outside the state. Currently this collection consists of over 13,700 patents and covers the period of 1840 through the 1920s.

The metadata scheme used for all collections in the Portal is a UNT Libraries (UNTL) metadata based on the qualified version of Dublin Core. The UNTL metadata scheme includes 21 metadata elements, with 20 descriptive metadata elements, which represent the information object, and 1 administrative metadata element which describes the metadata record. The UNTL metadata records are created using the online form that is part of the password-protected metadata editing interface: the descriptive metadata fields are manually populated by human metadata editors, and the administrative metadata (record editor, date stamp, etc.) is automatically captured by the system. The standard Dublin Core and METS metadata records are obtained automatically through machine transformation of UNTL records and are made available for harvesting via OAI-PMH through the Portal website.

In a situation when there is no funding specifically allocated for enhancing the metadata for these important information objects – historical patents – the Portal has for a large part relied on a kind of a crowd-sourcing approach where a variety of non-paid and not professionally trained contributors create metadata records. To support this crowd-sourcing of metadata record creation, the detailed collection-specific guidelines, complete with examples, have been developed to complement the general metadata guidelines and are regularly updated.

The uniform nature of this collection has made it an ideal way to introduce metadata to various audiences. For example, it has been used as a testing collection both for new employees of the Portal and for anyone interested in volunteering to gain metadata creation experience. The collection has also been used for a number of workshops and events intended to explain metadata creation and showcase the processes and digital library system of the state repository.

Over 400 different metadata creators and editors of varying skill levels have worked on metadata records since the first TP collection set was uploaded in 2011. The largest group (over 300) is comprised of students. For almost four years the Portal has partnered with instructors of metadata courses offered by the University of North Texas. In one of the major exercises in the introductory metadata course, students have

80th Annual Meeting of the Association for Information Science & Technology, Washington, DC | Oct. 27-Nov. 1, 2017

been creating approximately 150 metadata records per semester for the patents in this collection over the period of 11 semesters. In the process of creating patent metadata records, students learn the basics of metadata, develop understanding of patents as information objects and gain familiarity with detailed collection-specific metadata creation guidelines – prepared by the Portal staff – which students have to follow in creating fairly complete metadata records for the patents. The TP collection is also used as a target in the advanced metadata course for a metadata equality exercise in which students conduct a comparative metadata evaluation in two digital collections.

Due to the exploratory nature of the introductory course exercise which involves patent metadata creation, the consistency and accuracy of student-created records are rarely evaluated. The assumption is that beginning metadata creators – students or volunteers – study the guidelines before record creation and refer to them during record creation. However, metadata evaluation conducted by the advanced metadata course students discovers that the quality of metadata in this collection is highly variable. This might be the indication that metadata editors are not necessarily consulting the guidelines in the process of metadata creation and suggests the need for considering embedding interactive guidelines into the metadata creation form as opposed to or in addition to storing the guidelines document separately.

Unlike many other digital repositories, the Portal to Texas History employs the metadata versioning. While the end users can only see the latest version of a metadata record representing an information object, each version of each metadata record is stored and available for analysis by metadata managers. Each addition of a new version of a metadata record indicates a metadata change event.

The recent analysis of metadata change undertaken by Portal metadata managers and researchers is intended to support the metadata quality assurance in the TP collection. The analysis sought to identify the level of metadata change (in terms of the frequency of metadata change events) in metadata records and metadata fields, as well as the distribution of metadata change events among metadata editors. Our investigation also sought answers to the following questions: what are the characteristics of the changes between pairs of records (e.g., 1st and 2nd versions of the record, 2nd and 3rd versions, etc.) in each of the metadata change events; and did the data values change in a metadata field between the versions.

We collected all versions of the 13,025 unique metadata records that the TP collection included as of May 4, 2017. Eighty-six percent of these metadata records are visible to the end-users and the remaining 14% are hidden so that only the metadata editors registered in the TP collection editing system can see them. The hidden records are usually those that have not been completed yet. Each digitized patent is loaded with the initial hidden metadata record consisting of several pre-populated fields that share the same data values across the collection (e.g., *format*, *collection*, etc.).

A total of 31,068 metadata change events were identified. The number of editing events ranged widely between one and 92 per metadata record, with the mean of 2.39, mode of 2 and standard deviation of 1.88. Most of the 415 metadata editors edited between one and 15 metadata records, with the mode of 8 (this was the number of edited records for 98 editors). The editors with the small total numbers of edited records represent metadata course students and volunteers. On the other side of the spectrum, several persons edited between 145 and 7,546 metadata records. These editors represent metadata managers responsible for the collection and hourly workers employed to contribute records to the collection.

Many metadata change events included making changes to high numbers of metadata fields in a record: 7 (3,350 events), 8 (2,446) or 9 (6,284). These mostly represent the first metadata editing event for the pre-populated initial records. At the same time, in the largest proportion – over one-third (10,850) – of metadata change events, a single descriptive metadata field was changed in the record. This pattern is typical for 2nd and subsequent metadata change events. In most cases when a single metadata field was changed during a metadata change event, this field was either a *publisher* field (5,024 metadata change events) or a *contributor* field (2,203 metadata change events).

Ten descriptive metadata fields were rarely if ever altered during the metadata change events. The remaining 10 metadata fields were changed often (in at least 20% of all metadata editing events). These include in the descending order *contributor*, *description*, *creator*, *title*, *date*, *subject*, *coverage*, *identifier*, *note*, and *publisher*. *Subject* is the only one of the pre-populated fields that is often changed during the metadata editing. The same descriptive fields but in somewhat different order were changed in the highest proportion (over 50%) of unique metadata records: *title*, *creator*, *contributor*, *date*, *description*, *coverage*, *subject*, *identifier*, *note*, and *contributor*.

The next stage of our analysis includes the comparative analysis of each pair of consecutive versions of the same metadata records to identify the categories and subcategories of metadata change, such as addition, deletion, various kinds of other modifications, etc.

## REFERENCES


Barton, J., Currier, S., & Hey, J.M.N. (2003). Building quality assurance into metadata creation: An analysis based on the learning objects and e-prints communities of practice. In *DC-2003: Proceedings of the International DCMI metadata conference and workshop*. [United States]

Bruce, T.R., & Hillmann, D.I. (2004). The continuum of metadata quality: Defining, expressing, exploiting. In Hillman, D. and Westbrook, L. (Eds.), *Metadata in practice*. Chicago: American Library Association, pp. 238-256.

Park, J. & Tosaka, Y. (2010). Metadata quality control in digital repositories and collections: Criteria, semantics, and mechanisms. *Cataloging & Classification Quarterly, 48* (8), 96-715.

# Machine Reading for Relationships Between Autism Research and the Media

**Yujia Zhai**
*School of Management Tianjin Normal University, China.*
*zhaiyujiachn@gmail.com*

**Xiaoyu Wang**
*School of Business Nankai University, China.*
*wxyu1989@126.com*

**Fang Wang**
*School of Business Nankai University, China.*
*wangfangnk@nankai.edu.cn*

**Ying Ding**
*School of Informatics and Computing, Indiana University, USA. dingying@indiana.edu*

## ABSTRACT

**Autism represents a broad group of developmental disorders characterized by impaired social interactions. It has attracted widespread concern in academia and media. The reported causes of autism have an enormous impact on the people' s opinion about autistic patients and various treatments from scientific literature and media news. In this study, we use open information extraction (OIE), a machine reading technique, to automatically extract causal relationships from autism researches and news reports. We explored the differences between the scientific literature and news about the reported etiologies with respect to autism. As a result, we find that scientific papers clearly emphasize physical and biological factors, while the media emphasizes social factors as the perceived cause of autism.**

## KEYWORDS

autism, newspaper, scientific literature, open information extraction

## INTRODUCTION

Over the past decades, the field of autism spectrum disorders (ASDs) has been expanding and the volume of relevant scientific publications has been growing exponentially (LoVullo & Matson, 2009). Autism is a severe developmental disability involving impairments in social interaction – such as being aware of other people' s feelings – and verbal and nonverbal communication (Corsini & Ozaki, 1994). Indeed, the mutual relationship and influence between scientific research and media coverage could be complicated and consequential. For instance, Phillips, Kanter, Bednarczyk and Tastad (1991) found that coverage of medical research in the *New York Times* significantly boosted the visibility of academic research, which later received much higher attention from the scientific community. When new research papers about autism are published, however, media reports about this new knowledge rarely line up with the initial point and facts from the original paper. And the distortion or error in the reports is likely to produce serious social effects. Parrott et al. (2004) pointed out that the coverage of illness causality in news may greatly affect one' s knowledge of and his/her response to the disease. This project aims to determine the disparities between potential causes of autism as reported by scientific papers vs news articles.

## METHODOLOGY

### *Data*

We use the search query "autism or autistic or ASD" to get related news articles from LexisNexis and scientific publications from PubMed. Considering the influence of the news media, we choose four major online news platform which are *Washington Post*, *New York Times*, *USA Today* and *The Guardian*. We download all the full text of the news articles and the metadata of the research articles including the title, abstract, authors and keywords, etc. There are a total of 11,101 news articles from 1977 to 2015 and 19,879 research papers from 1962 to 2015. To concentrate on news discussing autism, we first remove the articles with some unrelated types such as Special Report, Series, Schedule and Review. Secondly, news with the title containing one of words from the list {book; review; bestseller; calendar; tv; television} are eliminated as well. After this, we get 6504 newspaper articles. Finally, we use NLTK's recommended sentence tokenizer to split the full text of news articles and the abstract of research papers into sentences and extract those containing word "autism" or "autistic". The result dataset constructed with 14305 sentences from news and 35397 sentences from scientific articles.

### *Open Information Extraction*

Open information extraction (OIE) is an alternative method of information extraction. An OIE system extracts a greater diversity of tuples consisting of argument phrases from the input sentence and a phrase from the sentence that expresses a relation between the arguments, in the format (Entity1; Relation; Entity2). The method is based on detecting and analyzing noun phrases (for entities) and verb-centric phrases (for relations). The extracting process is done without a pre-specified set of relations and with no domain-specific knowledge engineering.

- In this paper, we adopt the Stanford open information extraction (https://nlp.stanford.edu/software/openie.html) to extract the relation tuples (Angeli, Premkumar & Manning, 2015). We wrote a text mining program that

80th Annual Meeting of the Association for Information Science & Technology, Washington, DC | Oct. 27-Nov. 1, 2017

scanned through all the autism-related tuples. To extract the causes reported in the news and research, we designed a three-step method for recursive extraction.

- Firstly, we use this program to identify the tuples containing "autism," "autistic" or "ASD" with the relation word "cause" from the data have been filtered. As a result, we receive a set of tuples in the form of ("autism/autistic/ASD," relation: "cause," "X"), in which X represents the other entity in the tuples.
- Then, we put the other entity X from the former step and "autism" together into the query. It helps us to extract all the relation words that may represent the causal relationship.
- Next, we use the new relation words with "autism" to scan the open IE results. If there is no additional information added, then we stop. If we find more relation words or entities, then we go back to step 1.

Finally, we sorted all extractions by their frequencies. The top five most frequently mentioned causes of autism in both the scientific papers and news articles are coded into unified forms and ranked in five-year periods from 1975 onward. It should be noted that the causal relation we extracted does not mean that the article must have expressed a causal relationship which may also be a negative or denied relationship.

## PRELIMINARY RESULTS

Figure 1 shows the top five causes of autism reported in news and research papers in a five-year period since 1975. The blue lines indicate the yearly number of articles for each media. We can clearly see that in earlier scientific research, scientists have begun to infer and continue to argue that brain and nerve problems may be the cause of autism. And news reports have always stressed that the family environment might have a serious impact on autistic children. Refrigerator mother theory is a widely discarded theory that autism is caused by a lack of maternal warmth. When Leo Kanner first identified autism in 1943, he noted the lack of warmth among the parents of autistic children (Kanner, 1943).

The scientific papers clearly emphasize physical and biological factors, while the media emphasizes social factors as the perceived cause of autism. There is a clear divergence from the findings of the research papers. Interestingly enough, the mention of topics in the media all center around one social-related finding by the research papers every five years. The diffusion of this information in the media produces even more assumptions that differ from the research papers' findings.

Another interesting finding is the unequal concern about vaccine between news and scientific research. The autism-vaccine controversy can be dated back to the publication of a well-publicized study authored by Wakefield in *Lancet* in 1998 (Wakefield et al., 1998). However, the study was later discredited and an overwhelming body of research evidence has negated the link between autism and vaccine usage (Taylor et al., 1999). Although the research work by Wakefield has long been proved to be wrong, we can see that scientists made a significant effort to prove that the vaccine will not lead to autism in the next 20 years. The number of vaccine study is much bigger than the genes and nerves. This phenomenon is due to the rising number of reports about "vaccine cause autism" has led to many serious social problems and scientists are eager to defend the role of the vaccine.

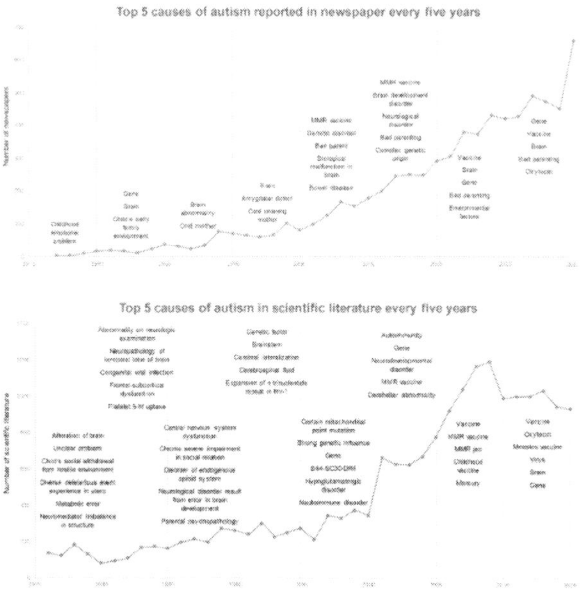


***Figure 1.*** *Top causes of autism in newspaper and scientific literature*

Obviously, the description of the autism causes is more specific in the scientific literature, but vaguer in news. There are many potential reasons leading to the differences. First of all, this is due to the different social roles played by research work and news. News has the role of science dissemination and is required to be easily understood by the readers; however, scientific literature is for innovation diffusion which promotes the development of science and technologies. Second, the audience of these two media is different. Most of the readers of the scientific literature are scientists, so the writing and description type are more rigorous. On the other hand, most of the news audience are public citizens who lack specific background knowledge and are not familiar with the specific biological terms. To better convey information, news does not often indicate which specific gene (e.g. B44-SC30_DR4) will lead to autism.

## CONCLUSION

We use open IE to extract causal relation triples from the autism news and research articles and build a relation network based on the extractions. The findings are informative: firstly, the scientific papers clearly emphasize physical and biological factors, while the media emphasizes social factors as the perceived cause of autism; secondly, scientific research has paid more attention to confirm the relationship between vaccine and autism in recent years because of the rising number of vaccine news; lastly, the description of the causes in two media is much divergent. While the cause of autism is still unknown and this research project continues, the disparities between the media and the research papers can be more clearly explained. In the future, we will continue this research for deeper understanding of the causal relations reported in the autism news and research. The remaining questions will focus on the led-lag relationship between autism news and scientific research and explore the dynamic impact with each other.

## REFERENCES


Angeli, G., Premkumar, M. J., & Manning, C. D. (2015, July). Leveraging linguistic structure for open domain information extraction. In *Proceedings of the 53rd Annual Meeting of the Association for Computational Linguistics (ACL 2015)*. from https://pdfs.semanticscholar.org/da23/bbd292aa5518d092841d7acd8bee2694b0ad.pdf

Corsini, R. J., & Ozaki, B. D. (1994). *Encyclopedia of psychology* (Vol. 1). New York: Wiley. Retrieved from http://www.elainehatfield.com/ch53.pdf

Kanner, L., & others. (1943). Autistic disturbances of affective contact. Retrieved from http://mail.neurodiversity.com/library_kanner_1943.pdf

LoVullo, S. V., & Matson, J. L. (2009). Comorbid psychopathology in adults with autism spectrum disorders and intellectual disabilities. *Research in Developmental Disabilities, 30*(6), 1288-1296.

Parrott, R., Silk, K., Weiner, J., Condit, C., Harris, T. & Bernhardt, J. (2004). Deriving lay models of uncertainty about genes' role in illness causation to guide communication about human genetics. *Journal of Communication, 54*(1), 105-122.

Phillips, D. P., Kanter, E. J., Bednarczyk, B. & Tastad, P. L. (1991). Importance of the lay press in the transmission of medical knowledge to the scientific community.

Taylor, B., Miller, E., Farrington, Cp., Petropoulos, M.-C., Favot-Mayaud, I., Li, J., & Waight, P. A. (1999). Autism and measles, mumps, and rubella vaccine: No epidemiological evidence for a causal association. *The Lancet*, 353(9169), 2026-2029.

Sabra, A., Bellanti, J. A. & Colón, A. R. (1998). Ileal-lymphoid-nodular hyperplasia, non-specific colitis, and pervasive developmental disorder in children. *The Lancet, 352*(9123), 234-235.

# Research Collaboration Prediction and Recommendation Based on Network Embedding in Co-authorship Networks

**Jinzhu Zhang**
*Department of Information Management, Nanjing University of Science and Technology, China. zhangjinzhu@njust.edu.cn*

### ABSTRACT

**In large-scale datasets, the researchers' multiple features need to be learned automatically instead of manually defined and enumerated, to improve the efficiency and effect of research collaboration prediction and recommendation. This paper applies the network embedding method to learn the context of each researcher by which the semantic similarities among researchers are calculated. Firstly, the co-authorship network is built in a large-scale dataset where research collaborations are denoted by co-authorships. Then the researchers' semantic contexts in the network are learned by the network embedding method based on deep learning, and each researcher's dense, low-dimensional vector is formed. Finally, the semantic similarities among researchers are calculated through vector similarity indices and quantitatively compared by link prediction. Experiments in the field of library and information science (LIS) verify that the method can improve the accuracy and effectiveness of research collaboration prediction and recommendation.**

### KEYWORDS

research collaboration, network embedding, co-authorship network, link prediction, deep learning

### INTRODUCTION

At present, the solutions of scientific problems are increasingly dependent on the integration of multiple disciplines. On the other hand, the researchers' interests are becoming more specialized and professional. This suggests more and more scientific research should be accomplished by collaborations rather than by individuals (Austin, Hair & Fullerton, 2012; Zhang, 2017). Research collaboration is a key mechanism for knowledge diffusion within research communities (Heinze & Kuhlmann, 2008), utilizing the expertise from multiple domains and producing high quality research outputs(Guns & Rousseau, 2014; Yan & Guns, 2014).

To facilitate research collaboration, studies have explored several different approaches, among which co-authorship prediction and recommendation is one important line of work. These studies have applied, improved and combined several similarity indicators in co-authorship networks (Zhang, Xu, Zhu & Zhou, 2015), author-paper bipartite networks, author-keyword networks and heterogeneous bibliographic networks (Zhang, 2017), for research collaboration prediction and recommendation. These similarity indicators can be classified into three categories, i.e., node-dependent, path-dependent and random walk, and compared in multiple domains to find the best indicator (Lü & Zhou, 2010; Zhao, et al., 2015). However, these studies experimented with small datasets and most of the datasets only contain top * authors with high frequency by manual filtering, Moreover, in these studies, the authors' multiple features were manually defined, and to enable big data analytics, these features need to be learned automatically.

This paper addresses the issue of automatically learning authors' features in large-scale co-authorship networks by the network embedding and forming a research collaboration prediction indicator. Firstly, the context of each researcher is learned using the network embedding. Then the semantic similarity indicators among researchers for research collaboration prediction and recommendation is formed by these contexts and evaluated by link prediction.

### DATA AND METHOD

This paper applies the network embedding method for research collaboration prediction and recommendation. Firstly, the co-authorship network is built with a large-scale dataset where research collaborations are indicated by co-authorships. Then the researchers' contexts in the network are learned by the network embedding method based on deep learning, and each researcher's dense, low-dimensional vector is formed. Finally, the semantic similarities among researchers are calculated through the vector similarity indices and quantitatively compared by link prediction.

#### *Data description*

We collected a research dataset in Thomson Reuters' Web of Science under the subject category of library and information science (LIS) from 2005 to 2009. We eliminate the authors with "[anonymous]" and merged authors with the same full name. Thus, there are 9,381 authors retained and the details are shown in Table 1, where isolated authors mean the authors with no co-authorship in this dataset. The training set and testing set of co-authorship is divided by 10-fold cross validation described in section "Predictor evaluation based on link prediction."

80th Annual Meeting of the Association for Information Science & Technology, Washington, DC | Oct. 27-Nov. 1, 2017

| All Authors | Isolated Authors | All Co-authorships | Co-authorships in Training Set | Co-authorships in Testing Set |
|---|---|---|---|---|
| 9381 | 710 | 16940 | 15246 | 1694 |

*Table 1. Description of the co-authorship network*

### Vector representation of researchers based on network embedding

Network embedding comes from word2vec (Goldberg & Levy, 2014). Word2vec is one of the word embedding methods that reconstructs linguistic contexts of each word with the input of sequence of words. Corresponding to this, each author's context can be reconstructed with the input of sequence of authors by random walking in a co-authorship network. Deepwalk (Perozzi, Al-Rfou & Skiena, 2014), one of the network embedding methods, comes from this idea. This paper applies LINE (Tang, et al., 2015) for network embedding which captures additional structural information of authors, i.e., the nodes' common neighbors. Then the semantic context of authors can be accurately captured by LINE in the co-authorship network and each researcher can be represented by a low-dimensional vector.

### Semantic similarity calculation based on vector similarity indices

The semantic similarity among researchers forms the predictor for research collaboration prediction. It can be calculated by multiple vector similarity indices. This paper selects cosine similarity index for semantic similarity computation.

### Predictor evaluation based on link prediction

Link prediction method is used for quantitatively evaluating the effectiveness of indicators. This paper uses 10-cross validation where 90% of data as the training set and 10% as the testing set and every testing dataset is totally different (Davis, Lichtenwalter & Chawla, 2011). We choose precision@k as evaluation indicator for predictor evaluation.

## RESULTS

### Vector representation of researchers based on network embedding

We use network embedding method LINE for learning the semantic contexts of each researcher. Parts of the researchers' vectors are visualized in Figure 1 using the tool provided by tensorflow (http://projector.tensorflow.org).

### Precision of predictors for research collaboration prediction and recommendation

We select CN (common neighbors) for comparison as the computation complexity is low. The precision is shown in Table 2, where top 100 means the top 100 predicted collaborations sorted by similarities computed by LINE or CN. The result shows that LINE performs better than CN in the most of times, which means network embedding method can capture more semantic information.

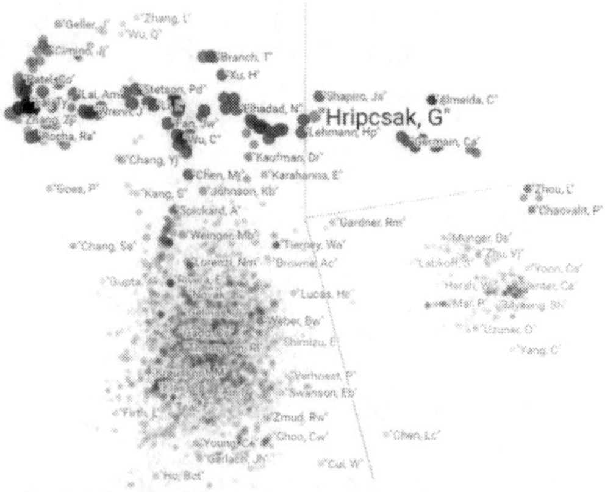


*Figure 1. Visualization of researchers' vectors*

| Indicator | Top 100 | Top 200 | Top 300 | Top 400 | Top 500 |
|---|---|---|---|---|---|
| LINE | 0.97 | 0.93 | 0.89 | 0.85 | 0.81 |
| CN | 1 | 0.91 | 0.82 | 0.78 | 0.73 |

*Table 2. Precision of indicators of research collaboration prediction and recommendation*

## CONCLUSION

This paper applies the network embedding method in co-authorship network for research collaboration prediction and recommendation which performs better than CN using precision@N as N grows large. In the next step, we would like to apply other network embedding methods for comparison, which can capture more semantic information. In addition, we would propose an improved network embedding method specifically for research collaboration prediction in co-authorship networks.


## ACKNOWLEDGMENTS

This work is supported by the National Natural Science Foundation of China (Grant No. 71503125) and the MOE (Ministry of Education of China) Project of Humanities and Social Sciences (Grant No. 14YJC870025).


## REFERENCES


Austin, M. A., Hair, M. S. & Fullerton, S. M. (2012). Research guidelines in the era of large-scale collaborations: An analysis of genome-wide association study consortia. *American Journal of Epidemiology, 175*, 962-969.

Davis, D., Lichtenwalter, R. & Chawla, N. V. (2011). Multi-relational link prediction in heterogeneous information networks. In *Advances in social networks analysis and mining (ASONAM)* (pp. 281-288): IEEE.

Goldberg, Y., & Levy, O. (2014). Word2vec explained: Deriving mikolov et al.'s negative-sampling word-embedding method. arXiv preprint arXiv:1402.3722.

Guns, R., & Rousseau, R. (2014). Recommending research collaborations using link prediction and random forest classifiers. *Scientometrics, 101*, 1461-1473.

Heinze, T., & Kuhlmann, S. (2008). Across institutional boundaries? Research collaboration in German public sector nanoscience. *Research Policy, 37*, 888-899.

Lü, L., & Zhou, T. (2010). Link prediction in complex networks: A survey. *Physica A: Statistical Mechanics and its Applications, 390*, 1150-1170.

Perozzi, B., Al-Rfou, R. & Skiena, S. (2014). Deepwalk: Online learning of social representations. In *Proceedings of the 20th ACM SIGKDD international conference on knowledge discovery and data mining* (pp. 701-710): ACM.

Tang, J., Qu, M., Wang, M., Zhang, M., Yan, J. & Mei, Q. (2015). Line: Large-scale information network embedding. In *Proceedings of the 24th international conference on world wide web* (pp. 1067-1077): ACM.

Yan, E., & Guns, R. (2014). Predicting and recommending collaborations: An author-, institution-, and country-level analysis. *Journal of Informetrics, 8*, 295-309.

Zhang, J. (2017). Uncovering mechanisms of co-authorship evolution by multirelations-based link prediction. *Information Processing & Management, 53,* 42-51.

Zhang, Q., Xu, X., Zhu, Y., & Zhou, T. (2015). Measuring multiple evolution mechanisms of complex networks. *Scientific Reports, 5,* 10350.

Zhao, J., Miao, L., Yang, J., Fang, H., Zhang, Q., Nie, M., Holme, P. & Zhou, T. (2015). Prediction of links and weights in networks by reliable routes. *Scientific Reports, 5*, 12261.

# Decision-making in Libraries: E-book Product Selection Practices in U.S. Academic Libraries

**Mei Zhang**
*The Information School, University of Wisconsin-Madison, USA. mzhang48@wisc.edu*

## ABSTRACT

**This research studies the e-book product selection practices in academic libraries by conducting one-on-one interviews of 20 selection librarians from 19 different institutions. Findings show that price and content are the two prevalent selection criteria used by my participants, and the factors affecting librarians' identification of selection criteria can be categorized as internal factors and external factors. I then examine the processes librarians use to select e-book products and find several steps that are commonly used by my participants. Further, I discuss the strategies libraries and e-book providers use to obtain powers over each other in the current e-book market.**

## KEYWORDS

e-books, academic libraries, selection, decision-making process, power strategies

## INTRODUCTION

Over the past several years, the increasing popularity of e-books for reading has resulted in their increased prevalence in academic libraries. Despite desires to maintain and expand e-book collections, academic libraries have limited purchasing power, due to the flat or even declined budgets, and the increasing prices of library e-books. Consequently, academic libraries have to make selection decisions to build their e-book collections within their budgets.

Although library scholars and professionals have long studied the selection models for printed books, it is unclear to what degree these models work for the selection of e-books, because e-books are not just the digital version of printed books: digital technologies introduce additional attributes into e-books, and many of them are not addressed in prior selection models for printed books.

Most literature on library e-book selection practices are empirical studies emphasizing local situations; therefore, they do not fully explain the "how" and "why" questions regarding e-book selection criteria and selection processes (Goedeken & Lawson, 2015; Levine-Clark, 2014). The absence of a theoretical basis in most literature encourages me to explore the potential theories that can be used to explain and even predict the factors that affect academic librarians' decision-making processes when purchasing e-book products. This study will be presented in a poster format.

## RESEARCH QUESTIONS

My study investigates the high-level question about academic libraries' selection practices of e-book products. It only studies the selection on product level, which means it does not investigate individual e-book selection. This study examines the following more specific questions.

**RQ 1**: What criteria do academic librarians employ to select e-book products?

**RQ 2**: What factors affect librarians' identification of selection criteria?

**RQ 3**: What are the selection processes for academic librarians to make e-book purchasing decisions?

## METHODS

This study used interview because interview allows researchers to figure out what is "in and out someone's mind" (Patton, 2002, p. 341), and it is particularly useful to obtain librarians' perspectives and reflections on their decision-making process.

### *Categories of Participating Libraries*

I used three characteristics of libraries to develop the categories used for sampling. First, I decided to focus on the medicine and humanities areas because they contrast in terms of the nature of e-book products, the type of e-book providers and users' e-book adoption stages. Second, I included both small and large libraries. Third, I included both individual libraries and library consortia in this study.

### *Sample Size*

I interviewed 20 librarians from 19 libraries or library consortia, as demonstrated in Table 1. Note that for one large participating library, I interviewed two librarians: one in humanities and one in medicines; for the other libraries, I interviewed one librarian in the relevant discipline.

| | Subject area<br>Size | Humanities | Medicine |
|---|---|---|---|
| Individual libraries | Large | 4 | 3 |
| | Small | 4 | 4 |
| Consortia | | 4 | |

***Table 1:** Number and types of participating libraries*

80th Annual Meeting of the Association for Information Science & Technology, Washington, DC | Oct. 27-Nov. 1, 2017

### *Sampling Strategies and Data Collection*

This study used snowball sampling and purposive sampling to identify the participants. Each librarian participated in a one-on-one interview that lasted, on average, about one hour, either face-to-face or by phone. I provided a $10 Amazon gift card to each interviewee, and two of them declined this offer. All interviews, except one, were audio recorded. Also, I used visual elicitation in the interview to help the participants articulate their selection process.

### *Data analysis*

I conducted verbatim transcriptions of all recorded interviews, which, along with the interview notes for the one that was not audio recorded, were then imported into Nvivo for analysis.

## RESULTS

### *Selection Criteria*

As demonstrated in Figure 1, participants mentioned 18 different criteria for them to select e-book products. I put them into two categories: criteria for purchasing a new product and criteria for retention decision. Participants' discussions of selection criteria mainly focus on the purchase decision of a new product, which includes a wider range of selection criteria. For the retention decision, the major criterion, along with price, is the actual usage of the product. The distinction arises because librarians are able to obtain data about the actual usage of their current collection, whereas the major factor used in making decision of a new product is projected usage, even though it could come from a trial.

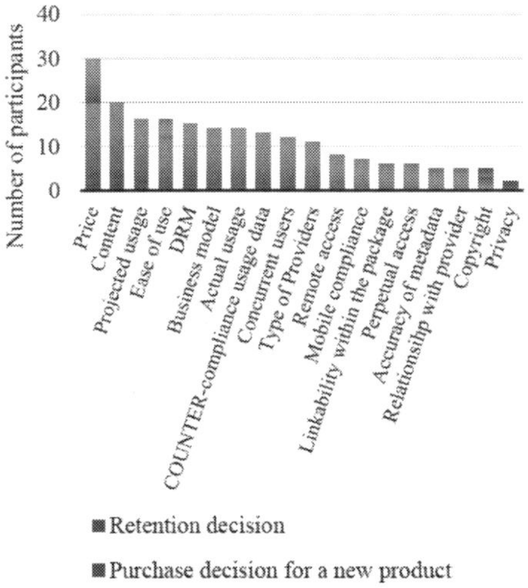


***Figure 1.*** *E-book product selection criteria mentioned by participants*

Among all these criteria, price and content criteria have been mentioned by all participants, while among the less common criteria, copyright criterion most comes from participants in medicine field.

### *Factors Affecting Selection Criteria*

This study examined how librarians form their selection criteria, and I divide the affecting factors into two groups: internal factors and external factors. The internal factors include written documents, librarians' previous selection experience, users' experience with e-journal/e-books and librarians' perceptions of current e-book market; while the external factors include other libraries' experience of e-book selection and collaboration with e-book providers.

### *Decision-making Process*

Despite that the processes provided by my participants vary, I found several steps have been mentioned by many participants. They include the following:

1. Identify candidates: Participants have mentioned a step earlier in their decision-making processes for them to identify potential e-book product candidates for further evaluation.
2. Deal breakers: Many participants mentioned the concept of "deal breaker," which refers to a condition that librarians request to be present in the e-book product, and librarians would not consider an e-book product without this condition.
3. Trial: Requesting trial for a potential product candidate is often an important step in the decision-making process described by my participants. Several participants also addressed that the usage data revealed in a trial does not equal the actual usage.
4. Involvement of other stakeholders: Participants stated that some other persons, in addition to the librarians that are directly involved with the e-book selection, participated in their decision-making processes, mainly through providing information needed for making the decisions, like campus IT department or licensing librarians.

## DISCUSSIONS: POWER RELATIONS BETWEEN LIBRARIES AND E-BOOK PROVIDERS

My findings reveal that price is one of the most important selection criteria used by all my participants; however, it is not an easy task to determine what should be a good price for a certain e-book product. Some cultural scholars suggest, instead of examining the causal relationships between price and multiple variables, exploring the power relations among stakeholder can help better understand their price, because power "shapes the scope, intensity and outcome of all negotiations" (Christophers, 2010, p. 204). Here I examine the strategies libraries and e-book
providers use to gain power over each other.

I argue that academic libraries mainly rely on the following strategies to gain power over the e-book providers: (1) consortial purchasing: library consortia often have more power over the providers than the individual members could, so consortia are often able to obtain more acceptable prices; (2) experimentation: many librarians treat their current e-book subscription as an experiment for them to better understand different variables associated with e-book products. Thus, many libraries prefer subscription model over purchase model, avoiding being locked into a certain provider, especially in an immature e-book market; (3) alternative acquisition channels: librarians try to explore some options to obtain e-books, like title-by-title purchases, or they investigate other products that contain same or similar e-book titles. This strategy reduces libraries' reliance on particular providers.

E-book providers try to gain more power over the libraries through the following two ways:

1. Consolidation among providers: acquisition or merger among providers reduces the number of providers and then the e-book products available for libraries, so it enhances providers' power over libraries. As revealed in this study, many participants complained that they did not have many options when making purchase decision;
2. Uniqueness of the content: each individual e-book title contained in an e-book product is unique in terms of content, which cannot be replaced by other similar titles. For instance, a library needs the e-books from certain authors based on users' request; therefore, it is unlikely for libraries to select e-books written by different authors, even if they are on the same topics. As a result, libraries can only choose from a few or even the only one e-book product that contains the exact titles.

## REFERENCES

Christophers, B. (2010). Envisioning media power: On capital and geographies of television. Lanham: Lexington Books.

Goedeken, E. A., & Lawson, K. (2015). The past, present, and future of demand-driven acquisitions in academic libraries. *College & Research Libraries, 76*(2), 205-221.

Levine-Clark, M. (2014). Ebooks in academic libraries. In B. Albitz, C. Avery, & D. Zabel (Eds.), *Rethinking collection development and management* (pp. 187-198). Santa Barbara, California: Libraries Unlimited.

Patton, M.Q. (2002). Qualitative research and evaluation methods. Thousand Oaks, CA: Sage.

# Decomposing the Twitter Data Stream in Healthcare: An Information Theory Perspective

**Yuan Zhang**
University of North Texas, USA. yz0209@unt.edu

**Hsia-Ching Chang**
*University of North Texas, USA. Hsia-Ching.Chang@unt.edu*

## ABSTRACT

**Recent research using Twitter as an information communication channel has shown how event organizers convey and disseminate their agendas across industries and disciplines. However, little research has been carried out on the user's choice of information components when composing a tweet through the lens of information theory. This research employs a comparative case study to examine how medical-terminology hashtags and corresponding lay-language hashtags have been used to help to communicate healthcare messages on the Twitter platform. The main result of this case study revealed patterns that both retweeting behavior and the use of a variety of components to construct a tweet contribute to higher entropy values which imply that these are more informative ways to communicate healthcare messages.**

## KEYWORDS

Twitter, tweets, hashtag, information theory, healthcare

## INTRODUCTION

Composing a tweet on the Twitter platform involves a choice of combining different components, such as photos, video clips, the @username "mention" function, hashtags, hyperlinks and up to 140 characters of text. An orchestrated presentation of various information components usually improves the usability, effectiveness and perceived quality of a campaign message. The focus of information theory (Shannon, 1948) is not on the meaning of the message but on the structure of the message. Entropy, the essence of information theory, provides researchers with a measurement to examine the variety of combinations of the different content components that form tweets. Through the lens of information theory, this study focuses on understanding healthcare communication on Twitter by examining the structure of messages in a sample of tweets associated with healthcare-related hashtags.

## RELATED WORKS

Developed by Shannon (1948), entropy in information theory was defined as the amount of information which was calculated by the logarithm of the effective number of microstates of a closed system or the effective number of possible values of a random variable. Primarily adopted in engineering and computer science (Miller, 1953; Hayes, 1993; Kinsner, 2004), information theory has also been applied to linguistic studies. With the prevalence of social media, research interests have shifted to linguistic studies of the Twitter platform using information theory. Neubig and Duh (2013) examined information content per character in a tweet. Ghosh, Surachawala and Lerman (2011) introduced an entropy-based approach to characterizing the dynamics of retweeting behavior. To the best of our knowledge, no study has used the lens of information theory to investigate the tweet composition of different components (text, hashtag, hyperlink, image, etc.) from which users can choose and construct their tweets.

## METHODOLOGY

This study applies information theory to compare the use of medical-terminology hashtags and lay-language healthcare related hashtags, namely #glucose versus #bloodsugar and #hypertension versus #bloodpressure, with a comparison of their statistical structures regarding the choice of components to compose a tweet.

### *Research Design: Using a Case Study Method to Compare the Components of Tweets in Hashtag Trails*

Using entropy as a measurement, this study analyzes two pairs of healthcare hashtag trails with a focus on six main components used in the tweets. The six components are (1) image(s), (2) text with semantic meaning, (3) hashtag(s), (4) @username(s), (5) hyperlink, and (6) unused space.

### *Data Collection and Analysis with Entropy Calculation*

Data for the comparisons of two cases, namely #glucose versus #bloodsugar and the one with #hypertension versus #bloodpressure, were collected by the software application NodeXL professional version. Table 1 shows the summary of data preparation for two groups of paired hashtag-trails. Inspired by the work of Kearns and O'Connor (2004), this study draws on their approach of calculating "form complexity" in moving image documents. Therefore, this study not only examines the complexity of the "statistical structure" (Shannon, 1948) in a hashtag trail but also extends Shannon's original entropy equation to a multi-dimensional matrix by integrating six different content components from their own coding scheme. Table 1 illustrates each coding scheme and the matrix for calculating entropy for each component and for each tweet.

80th Annual Meeting of the Association for Information Science & Technology, Washington, DC | Oct. 27-Nov. 1, 2017

| | Case 1 | | Case 2 | |
|---|---|---|---|---|
| | #glucose | #bloodsugar | #hypertension | #bloodpressure |
| Data Collection Date | 02-23-2017 | | 02-12-2017 | |
| Total Tweets Collected | 190 | 165 | 250 | 250 |
| Time Frame for Comparison | 02-13-2017 to 02-22-2017 | | 02-11-2017 to 02-12-2017 | |
| Number of Tweets in Each Trail | 96 | 95 | 61 | 96 |
| Percentage of Tweets with Image(s) | 42% | 47% | 15% | 63% |
| Tweet(s) Contain Both Compared Hashtags | 2 | | 1 | |

***Table 1.*** *Summary of data collection process and data preparation*

## DATA VISUALIZATIONS

This study uses radar graph and scatter graph as data visualizations. These graphs visualize the complexity of the structure and the characteristics of each individual tweet in the trail. The calculated results of the entropic values of six components were organized into six vectors on a radar graph by their own weighted average proportion in hashtag trail. Figure 1 illustrates the paired-up radar graphs for #glucose versus #bloodsugar and #hypertension versus #bloodpressure. The shapes of the first pair almost overlapped because these two trails had similar structure, indicating these two hashtags were interchangeable in usage because users made similar choice among these components when constructing the tweets.

The size of #hypertension graph is much smaller than the one of #bloodpressure and the shapes of this pair were also different. This finding, contrasted to the almost identical graphs of case 1, might be explained by the fact that the semantic meaning of hypertension is not exactly the same as that of blood pressure. Hypertension in English means high blood pressure and its opposite word is hypotension, low blood pressure. This study didn't include #hypotension because it was not a popular hashtag and there were less than 10 tweets with this hashtag collected in February 2017, causing insufficiency in data for further investigation.

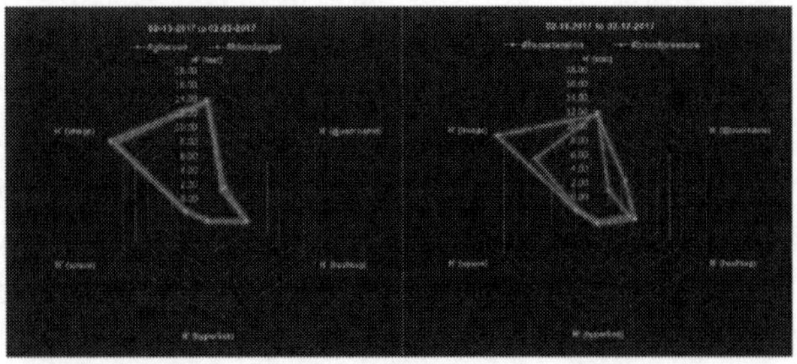

***Figure 1.*** *Paired radar graphs of case 1 and case 2*

Time factor was absent in Shannon's original entropy equation. However, each tweet has its own tweeting timestamp. Figure 2 illustrates the distribution of tweets in each trail plotted with its synthetic entropic value in the investigated time frame. The difference of density in each graph discloses various intensity of activities in each trail.

Figure 3 reveals the pattern that either being retweeted or applying a variety of components (especially image) when constructing a tweet contributes to relative medium to high synthetic entropic value because retweeting function has a direct consequence on the structure of the original tweet: increase in complexity of structure in contrast to that of the original tweet. Being retweeted leads to a higher synthetic entropic value given all other conditions remain the same.

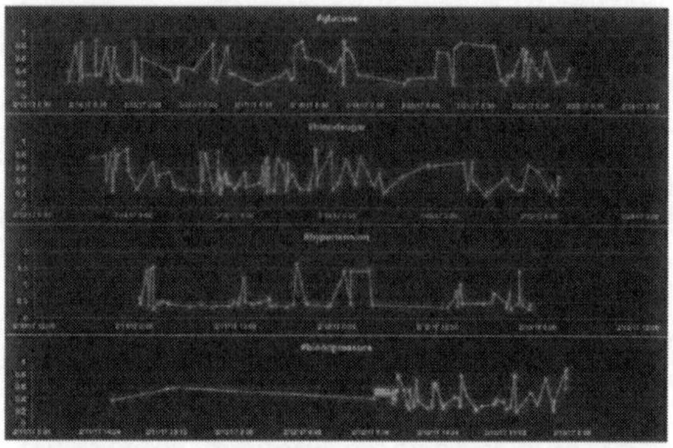

***Figure 2.*** *Scatter graphs of four investigated hashtag tweet-trails*

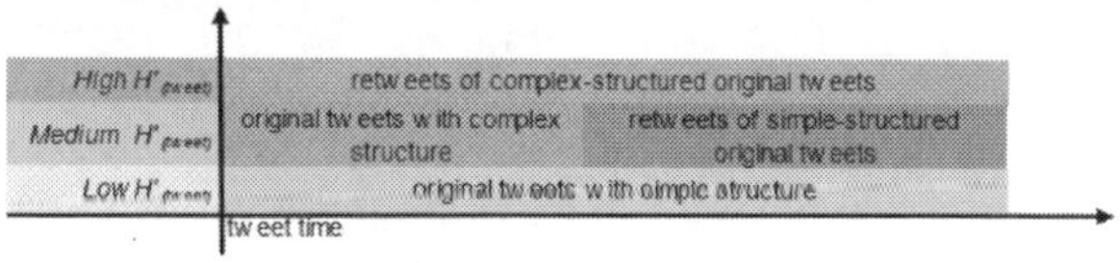


***Figure 3.*** *Distribution of individual tweet by its synthetic entropic value*

## CONCLUSION

This study is the first to apply information theory to evaluate tweet composition by accounting for the granularity of a tweet. Another contribution of this study is the novel application of data visualization methods to depict the measurement results. Both radar graph and scatter plot illustrate the complexity of structural components in the Twitter data stream, providing insight into tweet composition styles in the context of health communication.

## REFERENCES


Ghosh, R., Surachawala, T. & Lerman, K. (2011). Entropy-based classification of' 'retweeting' activity on Twitter. The 5th SNA-KDD Workshop (SNA-KDD'11) on Social Network Mining and Analysis, San Diego, CA.

Hayes, R. M. (1993). Measurement of information. *Information Processing & Management*, *29*(1), 1-11.

Kearns, J., & O'Connor, B. (2004). Dancing with entropy: Form attributes, children, and representation. *Journal of Documentation*, *60*(2), 144-163.

Kinsner, W. (2004). Is entropy suitable to characterize data and signals for cognitive informatics? *International Journal of Cognitive Informatics and Natural Intelligence*, *1*(2), 34-57.

Miller, G. A. (1953). What is information measurement? *American Psychologist*, *8*(1), 3.

Neubig, G., & Duh, K. (2013). How much is said in a tweet? A multilingual, information-theoretic perspective. In *AAAI Spring Symposium: Analyzing Microtext.*

Shannon, C. E. (1948). A mathematical theory of communication. *Bell System Technical Journal, 27(3), 379-423.*

# Who Bridged the "Valley of Death" Between Basic Research and Clinical Research? In the Case of Immune-Checkpoints CTLA-4 and PD-1 Based on Inter-Citation Network

**Qiuju Zhou**
*School of Informatics & Computing, Indiana University, USA & Institutes of Science and Development, Chinese Academy of Sciences, China. qiuzhou@indiana.edu*

**Guilin Meng**
*School of Informatics & Computing, Indiana University, USA & Shanghai Tenth People's Hospital, School of Medicine, Tongji University, China. guilmeng@iu.edu*

**Ying Ding**
*School of Informatics & Computing, Indiana University, USA & School of Information Management, Wuhan University, China. dingying@indiana.edu*

## ABSTRACT

**We explored who wrote the milestone articles in the innovation processes of immune-checkpoints CTLA-4 and PD-1. In order to map the processes, a literature inter-citation network analysis was made through HistCite and Pajek. We found knowledge flow through citations between topics (clusters), transverse knowledge diffusion between topics at the same basic research level and knowledge translation from basic research to clinical research. Betweenness Centrality showed a good performance in selecting key nodes of knowledge flow.**

## KEYWORDS

drug discovery, knowledge flow, betweenness centrality

## INTRODUCTION

Most basic research cannot cross the "valley of death" (Butler, 2008); only a few of them translate into clinical research successfully. The first generation immune-checkpoints Cytotoxic T- lymphocyte-associated antigen 4 (CTLA-4) and programmed cell death protein 1(PD-1), are among those who have crossed the "valley of death." The anti-CTLA-4 drug Ipilimumab and the anti-PD-1 drugs Nivolumab and Pembrolizumab have received approval by FDA in 2011 and 2014. The rapid-fire clinical successes from blocking CTLA-4 and PD-1 have revolutionized cancer therapy. In this domain of immune checkpoints, how do scientists cross the "valley of death" to bridge the gap between basic research and clinical research? Who and how are the "bench to bedside" linked?

To answer these questions, bibliographic and citation data of CTLA-4 and PD-1 from Web of Science was used to construct a highly cited paper inter-citation network. Modularity algorithm was used to identify scientific communities. Betweenness centrality was used to detect the key articles in the process of knowledge flow (diffusion or translation). It is hoped that this investigation will provide a reference for newcomers to understand this field and the strategic investment of the government and pharmaceutical institutions.

## METHODS AND DATA

### *Data*

Paper searching of CTLA4 and PD-1 and corresponding drugs (Ipilimumab, Pembrolizumab, Nivolumab, and Atezolizumab) that have approval by FDA was made in the Web of Science (WoS) before April 2017. Timespan = All years; Indexes = SCI-EXPANDED, SSCI, A&HCI, CPCI-S, CPCI-SSH). Two document types (article and review) were involved. Records were refined by keeping them in medical science. We got 13,054 records in WoS.

### *Methods*

The 13,054 results of WoS were inputted into HistCite (Garfield, 2009) to select the most cited papers and construct paper inter-citations network, identifying important scientific breakthroughs. Pajek was used to visualize and analyze the network.

### *Modularity*

We chose one of the modularity algorithm Louvain methods, a Pajek plug-in, to identify clusters. We colored clusters with different colors. For each cluster, the nodes are sorted by the publication year of articles from the earliest to the most recent. The historiography based on inter-citation network is shown in Fig1.

### *Betweenness centrality*

We used betweenness centrality to find out the key articles, which key articles were connected to different clusters or which key articles were important in the process of knowledge translation (diffusion, flow) between clusters. The size of the nodes represents betweenness centrality of each article.

80th Annual Meeting of the Association for Information Science & Technology, Washington, DC | Oct. 27-Nov. 1, 2017

### *Evaluation*

For a concise historical description of the events, we selected several highly cited reviews in this field, which describe the major scientific developments. The paper inter-citation networks were extensively analyzed and compared and demonstrated at a high degree of coincidence between accounts of events in scientists' reviews and the citation relationship between these milestone events.

## RESULTS

### *Identify milestone articles and their self-organized structure based on the inter-citation network*

The 90 most-cited papers (including 76 articles and 14 reviews) were chosen by HistCite.

These 14 highly cited reviews are used to evaluate the performance of our methodology. These core articles which were selected by our methodology perfectly matched these articles in domain scientists' reviews. The comparison of personal reviews with traces in the literature demonstrates the simple fact that bibliographic history is recapitulated rather well by the collective bibliographic memory of the scholars who have contributed to the literature, both at the macro and micro level of analysis

The visualization and clustering of this network revealed the basic research and clinical research of CTLA-4 and PD-1, self-organized into 3 clusters. The basic research of CTLA-4 and PD-1 are two separate clusters, while the clinical research of the two immune-checkpoints converged into one cluster. This reflects the trend of this clinical research: combination of the two different immune-checkpoints can get a higher efficiency.

### *Knowledge flow (diffusion and translation) between clusters*

With the direction of citation between clusters, we were able to find the direction of knowledge flow. Knowledge flow between clusters can be distinguished as two types: transverse knowledge diffusion between different topics of basic research and vertical knowledge translation.

### *Betweenness as an indicator to identify the key articles in knowledge flow between clusters*

In Cluster 1, the nodes of '171 Walunas TL, 1994', '408 Tivol EA, 1995' and '421 Waterhouse P, 1995' have high betweenness. They elucidated the mechanism of CTLA-4 inhibition and laid the theoretical foundation for the later research. These studies not only play an important role in the basic research of CTLA-4, but also have important implications for the study of the function of PD-1 in Cluster 2.

In Cluster 2, '1389 Dong HD, 1999', '1651 Freeman GJ, 2000' and '1771 Latchman Y, 2001' discovered that PD-L1 and PD-L2 are the two ligands for PD-1. These articles cited the articles from CTLA-4, and cited by the clinical research articles of PD-1. So, these articles are the 'broker' between Cluster 2 and Cluster 3. '2226 Dong HD, 2002', '4466 Butte MJ, 2007'. It is these basic research studies that are cited by clinical studies in Cluster 3, so knowledge is thus translated into clinical studies through these articles. In Cluster 3, '6599 Hodi FS, 2010', '8370 Brahmer JR, 2012', '8369 Topalian SL, 2012' and '9690 Wolckok JD, 2013' have the highest betweenness in Cluster 3. The role of these articles is the knowledge receiver from basic research of Cluster 1 and Cluster 2, and knowledge exporter to other subsequent clinical research. Therefore, these papers are important bridges linking basic research and clinical research, and play an important role in the process of knowledge translation.

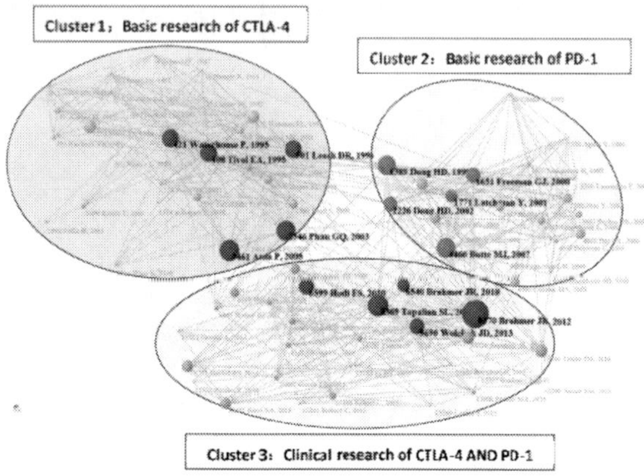


***Figure 1.*** *Historiography of 76 most-cited articles of CTLA4 and PD-1*

## CONCLUSION

Our findings demonstrate that scientometric analysis of literatures and citation data from approximately 10,000 articles can capture important research studies and key scientists in the developing history of immune-checkpoint therapy by selecting the highly cited paper inter-citation network. Seventy-six highly cited articles are all the important research that has influenced the development of immune-checkpoint therapy.

The indicator betweenness centrality shows good performance in selecting those nodes that play important roles in the processes of knowledge flow.

## REFERENCES


Butler, D. (2008). Translational research crossing the valley of death. *Nature*, 453: 840-842.

Freeman, LC. (1977). A set of measures of centrality based upon betweenness. *Sociometry*. 40: 35-41.

Garfield E. (2009). From the science of science to scientometrics: Visualizing the history of science with HistCite software. *Journal of Informetrics*, 3: 173-179.

# Systematic Investigation of Sex Disparity in Multidisciplinary Institutions – A Case Study of U.S. iSchools

**Zhiya Zuo**
*University of Iowa, USA. zhiya-zuo@uiowa.edu*

**Kang Zhao**
*University of Iowa, USA. kang-zhao@uiowa.edu*

## ABSTRACT

**In this poster, we present a systematic investigation of sex disparity in 27 information schools located in the United States. Combining hand-curated complete faculty data and automatically collected publication profiles, we portrait the landscape of sex disparity in three dimensions: (i) rank; (ii) educational backgrounds; (iii) research topics. We found that 63% of the tenured faculty members are male, although there is slightly more female (54%) among junior faculty. Across nine disciplinary categories of PhD programs, male was primarily trained in computing, while female was more evenly distributed across computing, information and library sciences. Further, male and female have significant differences in research topics extracted from their publication profiles. It is, however, worth noting that distribution of research topics becomes more homogeneous among junior faculty members. Overall, all the evidence implies a significant sex disparity in information schools and calls for immediate attention on related policies for mitigation.**

## KEYWORDS

sex disparity, educational backgrounds, research topics, information schools

## INTRODUCTION

The role of sex in the scientific community has been a sophisticated problem. During the past two decades, there have been numerous studies on sex disparity. Academic departments are appropriate units for inspections of sex disparity, where hiring and collaboration activities can be, to a great extent, affected by gender distributions (Gaughan & Bozeman, 2016). While many efforts have examined this issue in STEM fields, little research has been done in multidisciplinary academic departments.

Focusing on information schools (iSchools), this study is based on the dataset collected by (Zuo, Zhao & Eichmann, 2017). This hand-curated dataset collected in 2014 includes the complete collection of 681 full time core faculty members in 27 iSchools in the United States, along with their sex, educational backgrounds, research papers and seniority.

## RESULTS

A first glimpse on the sex distribution of the whole information school shows a moderately unbalanced distribution ($\chi^2$ test, $P < 10^{-4}$), where 396 (58%) out of 681 faculty members are male. After controlling for rank, the inequality becomes more non-trivial, where 63% of tenured faculty members were male [Fisher's Exact Test (FET), $P < 10^{-4}$]. While there are slightly more female junior faculty than their male counterparts, the number of male senior faculty is 1.7 times more than female senior faculty. This confirms the leaky pipeline phenomena (Shen, 2013) in the U.S. iSchool community, although there is critical mass of women scientists entering at the beginning (Etzkowitz, Kemelgor, Neuschatz, Uzzi & Alonzo, 1994). Such non-trivial difference in faculty rank across genders greatly influences the way administrative power is disseminated in departments (Gaughan & Bozeman, 2016), cascading the inequality in resource allocation and shapes collaborative culture that may be unfavorable for female researchers.

Divergent educational backgrounds also exist between male and female faculty members (FET, $P < 10^{-4}$). Researchers trained in the field of computing are clearly dominated by male, whereas female are more evenly distributed across computing, information and library. Such propensity persists considering seniority within the same gender group though the overall difference is not as significant ($\chi^2\ test, P_{female} > 0.01, P_{male} > 0.05$), along with the significant differences between male and female ($\chi^2\ test, P_{senior}, P_{junior} < 10^{-4}$).

Educational backgrounds are coarse approximations of research topics. Specifically, these arbitrary classifications of scientific disciplines are inaccurate in reflecting what people have really been doing, at least for multidisciplinary institutions such as iSchools (Zuo et al., 2017). To more precisely capture research topics, we apply latent Dirichlet allocation (LDA) (Blei, Ng & Jordan, 2003) on a corpus of the titles and abstracts of iSchool faculty members' publications. The number of topics is set to 20.

Topics extracted are IT and communication; computing infrastructure; digital library and library science; temporal/spatial dynamics; data mining and machine learning; robotics and cognitive systems; information privacy and policy; health informatics; computer-supported cooperative work; material/others; experiments and surveys; bioinformatics; programming language; information retrieval; social media analysis; information seeking; user interface and experience; education and learning technology; algorithms; computer networks and cybersecurity.

80[th] Annual Meeting of the Association for Information Science & Technology, Washington, DC | Oct. 27-Nov. 1, 2017

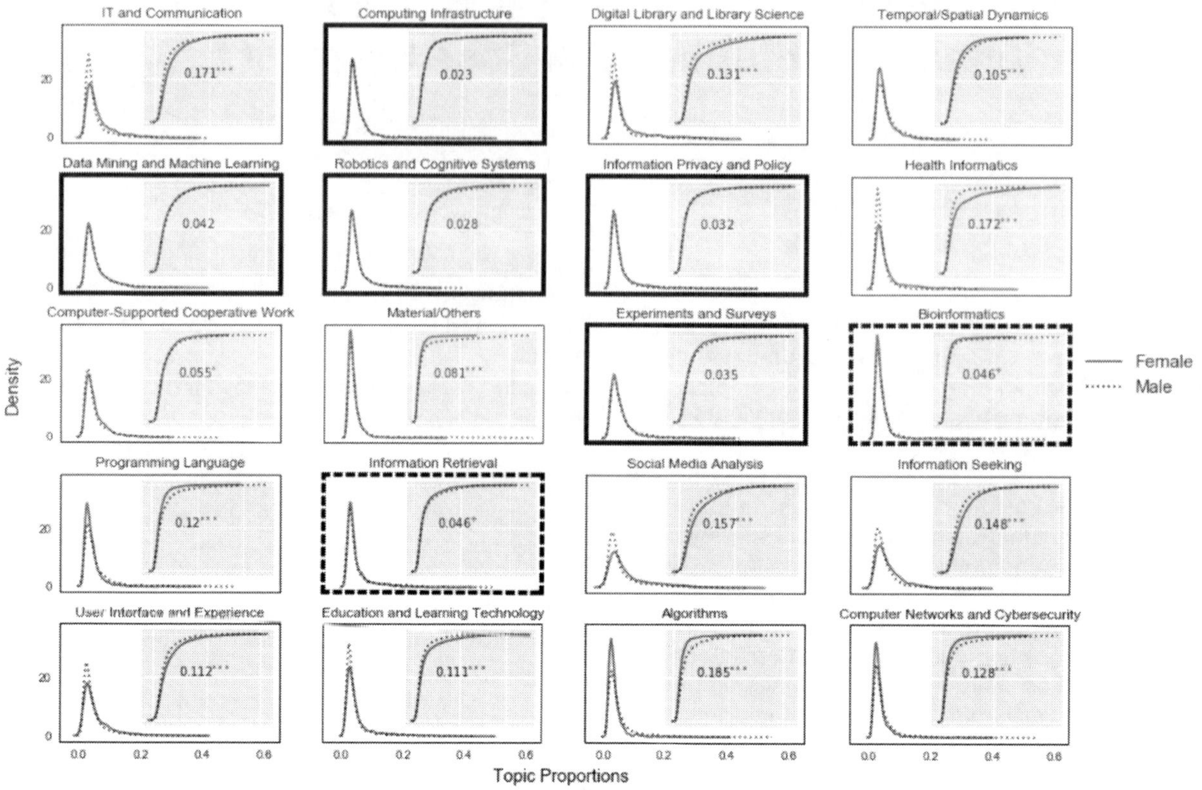


***Figure 1.*** *Density distributions of junior female and male faculty members. The KS test statistics* $\mathbf{D}$ *are shown with significance levels. Note:* $p < 0.1$: $+$; $p < 0.05$: $*$; $p < 0.01$: $**$; $p < 0.001$: $***$. *The borders of each subplot corresponds to the significance level (dashed:* $0.1 > p > 0.05$*; bold:* $p > 0.1$*). Inset figures are cumulative distributions*

We then group documents together for both genders and obtain a distribution of topic proportions for each of the 20 topics. There are significant differences between women and men researchers across 19 out of 20 topics [Kolmogorov–Smirnov (KS) Test, all $p < 0.001$], where only the topic on information retrieval is slightly nonsignificant with $0.05 < p < 0.1$. When we only examine junior faculty members (**Error! Reference source not found.**), significant differences no longer exist for topics including computing infrastructure, data mining and machine learning, robotics and cognitive systems, information privacy and policy, experiments and surveys, bioinformatics, and information retrieval (KS Test, $p > 0.05$).

## DISCUSSION

Unlike traditional academic departments which are designed for homogeneous environments, iSchools recruit researchers from diverse areas. Significant disparities, in faculty rank, educational backgrounds and research topics, present a very first image of systematic difference between female and male faculty members in these multidisciplinary institutions. While there is evidence of less difference in some research topics, the results call for attention to potential policies in moderating the current status of sex imbalance in iSchools.

## REFERENCES


Blei, D. M., Ng, A. Y. & Jordan, M. I. (2003). Latent Dirichlet allocation. *Journal of Machine Learning Research*, *1*(4-5), 993-1022. https://doi.org/10.1162/jmlr.2003.3.4-5.993

Etzkowitz, H., Kemelgor, C., Neuschatz, M., Uzzi, B. & Alonzo, J. (1994). The paradox of critical mass for women in science. *Science*, *266*(5182).

Gaughan, M., & Bozeman, B. (2016). Using the prisms of gender and rank to interpret research collaboration power dynamics. *Social Studies of Science*, *46*(4), 536-558. https://doi.org/10.1177/0306312716652249

Shen, H. (2013). Inequality quantified: Mind the gender gap. *Nature*, *495*(7439), 22-24. https://doi.org/10.1038/495022a

Zuo, Z., Zhao, K., & Eichmann, D. (2017). The state and evolution of U.S. iSchools -- from talent acquisitions to research outcome. *Journal of the Association for Information Science and Technology*, *68*(5), 1266-1277. https://doi.org/10.1002/asi.23751